Y0-CVP-631

The Mentally Disabled and the Law

The Mentally Disabled and the Law

SAMUEL JAN BRAKEL, JOHN PARRY, AND BARBARA A. WEINER

Third Edition

American Bar Foundation

750 North Lake Shore Drive, Chicago, Illinois 60611

Publication of this work by the American Bar Foundation signifies that the work is regarded as valuable and responsible. The analyses, conclusions, and opinons expressed are those of the authors and not those of the American Bar Foundation or its officers and directors.

Library of Congress Catalog Card Number: 85-71886

ISBN 0-910059-05-5

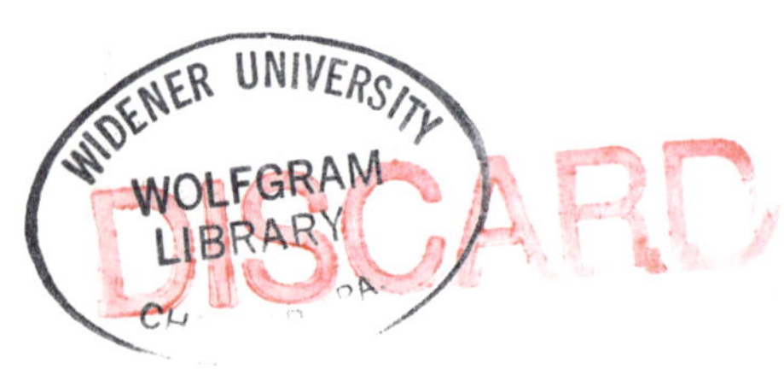

American Bar Foundation

Summary of Contents

Contents

Chapter 6

Treatment Rights

by Barbara A. Weiner

Chapter 7

Incompetency, Guardianship, and Restoration

by John Parry

Chapter 10

Provider-Patient Relations: Confidentiality and Liability

by Barbara A. Weiner

Chapter 11

Rights and Entitlements in the Community

by John Parry

Chapter 12

Mental Disability and the Criminal Law

by Barbara A. Weiner

List of Tables

Preface

While retaining the basic format of the 1961 and 1971 editions, this third edition of *The Mentally Disabled and the Law* is in other respects a major departure from the previous publications. Because of the near-revolutionary dimensions of change in the mental health law during the past decade, we have redone the text almost entirely. The chapters retained from the old editions have been either substantially or completely rewritten. Two subjects—sterilization and sexual psychopathy—which were previously dealt with in separate chapters, have been integrated into the chapters on family law (domestic relations) and criminal law, respectively. Three entirely new chapters have been added—on treatment rights, the provider-patient relationship, and the rights of mentally disabled persons in the community. Whereas the previous editions concentrated primarily on the mentally ill, the new edition devotes considerable space to the greatly expanded laws and rights relating to mentally retarded and other developmentally disabled persons. This new focus is reflected not only throughout the text but also in the statutory compilations. Sixteen new tables, supplementing the revised and updated preexisting 41, have been created to encompass this important development in the law.

In contrast to the earlier editions, which were jointly authored by researchers of the American Bar Foundation staff, the present edition is the product of one staff member, project director Samuel Jan Brakel, and two coauthors from outside the Foundation—John Parry, director of the American Bar Association's Commission on the Mentally Disabled, in Washington, D.C., and editor of the *Mental and Physical Disability Law Reporter*, and Barbara Weiner, executive director of the Isaac Ray Center, a unit of the Department of Psychiatry of the Rush-Presbyterian-St. Luke's Medical Center, in Chicago. While each of the present authors has had a substantial hand in the production of all the chapters, we have decided to indicate individual authorship on a chapter-by-chapter basis, chiefly for two reasons. First, despite significant editorial and substantive assistance from coauthors, each author deserves primary credit and assumes primary responsibility for the chapters appearing under his or her name. Second, there are some differences in style, tone, and underlying philosophy among the three of us which we felt were best left untouched, particularly since each chapter is essentially a self-contained unit. A book such as this need not be written by committee, as it were, or read as such. We have worked toward agreement on basic content. More would be lost than gained if we had decided to strive for total homogeneity and edited out all traces of individual viewpoint or style.

Despite the major reworking done in this edition, it remains appropriate to acknowledge the contributions of the editors of the previous editions—Frank Lindman, Don McIntyre, and Ron Rock—and all others associated with these earlier efforts. They created the original format and organization, set the standards of scholarship, and generally established *The Mentally Disabled and the Law* as one of the most useful and widely used reference works in the field. The contents of the present edition are, of course, the responsibility of the present authors, and the views expressed are, as always, ours alone and not those of the Foundation, its officers and directors, or any others associated with its production. Our hope is that with this edition—however expanded and revised—we have preserved the best in the tradition exemplified by the prior editions.

Acknowledgments

SAMUEL JAN BRAKEL

Many persons here at the American Bar Foundation — some working solely on this project, others with general responsibilities — have played important parts in the production of this book. Research assistants Susan Donnelly, Sheri Engelken, Joel Rice, and Laura Schnell made a major contribution to the revision and updating of the statutory tables and the construction of new ones. Significant contributions to these tasks were also made by Bill Brown, Lori Klauber, and Judith Weissman. My biggest debt in this respect, however, is to assistants Pat Finegan and Roy Reynolds, who worked on the project for almost its entire duration and who, in addition to laboring on the tables, played a major role in helping with the background research and in checking the final accuracy of both the text and its numerous footnotes.

The editorial staff of the Foundation, under the direction of Bette Sikes, deserves credit well above the usual for preparing this long and very complex manuscript for publication. Sandy Mathai supervised the various steps toward the final styling and checking of the 57 statutory tables. As general production editor, she also deserves the primary credit for having brought the whole project through every production stage to its completion. Jean Hirsch, Karen Malik, and Denny Wallace did the enormous amount of citation checking necessary with great diligence and dedication to accuracy, while Lucille Alaka and Kenner Swain-Harmon did an expert proofreading job on the text and notes. All members of the editorial staff worked on the proofing of the statutory tables. Louise Kaegi merits special recognition as the head editor of this edition. She not only edited all of the text — a very heavy assignment in its own right — but also worked with the others mentioned to pull the entire work together into final shape. No author could ask for more than she did. Elaine Hill, who has done other quality artwork for the Foundation, designed the book's jacket and cover.

A major acknowledgment is also in order for the persons on the Foundation staff who did the mechanical work, which in this case it would be particularly wrong to underestimate. Eddie Maria Clark typed several drafts of each of the 12 chapters with the skill, speed, and accuracy that is routine for her but not many others. Janet Atkins provided the finishing touches. Joanne Watson, with the assistance of Pat Ballentine, was responsible for the very demanding job of typesetting all the statutory tables as well as the text and notes. Completing it required, among other things, an unusual reserve of stamina and persistence.

Spencer Kimball, past executive director of the Foundation, and Jack Heinz, the present director, provided the support that comes with their position. For me, this consisted by and large of being left to plod along on my own — a type of support that is easily undervalued. Beyond that, they were instrumental in obtaining the initial financial support for the project and several budget increases along the way. As in the case of most Foundation research, the bulk of this financial support came from the American Bar Endowment — something that deserves special mention in a project of this scope and length.

The final word goes, as it must, to coauthors Parry and Weiner. They have stuck with the long and arduous task of producing this new edition from close to the beginning of the project to its very end. They have helped me with my work as I hope I have helped them with theirs. A book of this scope cannot be done by one person — certainly not within the time allowed for it. Their contributions are therefore indispensable in the literal sense. They deserve not only my deep gratitude but also that of the American Bar Foundation, under whose imprimatur the work appears.

JOHN PARRY

In addition to the individuals and organizations already referred to by Jan Brakel, all of whom deserve my recognition and gratitude, there are others without whose assistance and support my contributions to the book would have been impossible.

I begin with my coauthors—Jan Brakel and Barbara Weiner. Admittedly, it was sometimes difficult to visualize how three individuals with different perspectives and orientations would work together to produce an integrated review of the entire field of mental disability law; I know now that without Jan's and Barbara's strong viewpoints and critical faculties, each of my chapters would be far less than they are.

I must also acknowledge a significant debt to the *Mental and Physical Disability Law Reporter* (previously the *Mental Disability Law Reporter*), especially colleagues past and present, for providing me with an invaluable analytic base upon which I often began, and sometimes finished, each of the topics I covered. It takes five unique individuals to make the *MPDLR* function, and the tasks involved go well beyond gathering and presenting technical information. During the past three years the cast of characters has included the current staff—Della Byrd, Jeanne Dooley, David Rapoport, and Wandra Spruell—and two former staffers who have gone on to pursue other professional interests—Ann Britton and Dean Trackman.

Similarly, I owe a debt of gratitude to the American Bar Association's Commission on the Mentally Disabled for the research it has published in the field, including our reporter (*MPDLR*), as well as for the information in its files. Of special note are McNeill Smith and Bruce Ennis, each of whom served as chairman of the commission.

I would be remiss if I did not also thank the American Bar Association, not only for employing me in a position that helped to develop my expertise in this field but also for encouraging me to do this book.

John Taylor, Michael Gugerty, Larry Bird, and Leonard Tao deserve special thanks for gathering information, writing memos, and checking citations, without which my time on this project would have been considerably longer. As good law students, they also raised important issues that I had failed to address properly and offered ideas that are woven into the fabric of the chapters I contributed.

Finally, I would like to thank my parents, siblings, and friends for providing the environment that made it possible for me to devote to the completion of this volume so much of the time I wanted to spend with them.

BARBARA A. WEINER

Beyond those at the Foundation already mentioned, there are a number of people whom I would like to single out for assisting me in completing my portion of this book. Primarily, I would like to thank my husband, Howard Eglit, for his support and encouragement as well as his editorial assistance. Robert Wettstein, M.D., was an invaluable resource whose encyclopedic memory and thought-provoking discussions helped me broaden my knowledge and become more sensitive to the position of the treatment provider. My coauthors, Jan Brakel and John Parry, carefully reviewed each chapter at each stage of writing and provided valuable criticism, comments, and suggestions, for which I am very grateful. Thanks are owed to those who provided the necessary technical assistance, which was critical to the completion of this work: April Howard for legal research, and Janice Blaney, Carole Goosby, Janice Hogan, Alease Negron, and Verna Nickerson for the typing. The members of the Isaac Ray Center staff deserve thanks for their support and encouragement of my efforts and their understanding when my writing took time away from my activities at the center. Finally, I would like to acknowledge the continual encouragement of my parents, Abe and Betty Weiner.

About the Authors

Samuel Jan Brakel is the co-editor (with Ronald S. Rock) of the 1971 edition of *The Mentally Disabled and the Law*. He has also written articles on various aspects of the mental health law and he has published the results of research projects on prison law and administration, delivery of legal services to low-income clients, and American Indian law and institutions. He is a graduate of Davidson College (N.C.) and received his law degree from the University of Chicago. He has been with the Foundation since 1969.

John Parry has served as the Director of the American Bar Association's Commission on the Mentally Disabled since 1980 and the Editor of the Commission's *Mental and Physical Disability Law Reporter* since 1979. In those capacities, he has written or edited many articles on mental and physical disability law, managed several federally funded research projects, prepared amicus curiae briefs, and participated on national task forces studying mental disability law or related matters. He formerly served as the Executive Director of the Maryland Advocacy Unit for the Developmentally Disabled. He is a graduate of Lake Forest College (Ill.) and received his law degree from Washington University in St. Louis.

Barbara A. Weiner is Administrator and Counsel at the Isaac Ray Center, Inc., Section on Psychiatry and Law, Rush-Presbyterian-St. Lukes Medical Center in Chicago. She is also Assistant Professor at Rush Medical College and Adjunct Professor at IIT-Chicago Kent College of Law. Formerly an attorney for the Illinois Department of Mental Health, she has published many articles on mental health law. She received her undergraduate degree from the University of Maryland and her law degree from DePaul University.

Samuel Jan Brakel

Introduction

I. GENERAL BACKGROUND

One of the most difficult issues in law is how to deal with persons who exhibit various forms of mental disability.[1] Traditionally, the problem has been framed as one of determining when and to what extent the law should restrict the rights of these persons. Actions by the state within this framework tend to fall into these important categories: (1) restrictions on the rights and privileges of mentally disabled persons in the conduct of their personal and business affairs, (2) involuntary institutionalization procedures for those who pose a danger to or who are not wanted in the community, (3) restrictions on the rights and privileges of those who are institutionalized, and (4) accountability and dispositional determinations about mentally disabled persons charged with crime. The law, however, also has a more positive function. The affirmative features of the laws dealing with the mentally disabled have received particular emphasis during the past two decades. Much of the focus of state action today is on (5) assuring proper care and treatment of mentally disabled persons, (6) providing such care in the community, where appropriate, (7) protecting the rights of those who still need to be institutionalized, and (8) reserving the right to make decisions regarding care, treatment, and personal affairs, including the right to be left alone, to the disabled persons themselves, where possible.

Once a comparatively small but theoretically important field familiar only to a few select practitioners and scholars, mental disability law is today a substantial legal industry employing increasing numbers of "experts"—some of them in the business full time—to implement, interpret, reform, refine, elaborate, and overhaul an intricate and burgeoning mass of statutory, case, and regulatory law that aims to guide the workings of the mental disability systems in the 50 states, the District of Columbia, and limited federally regulated settings. When not practicing in the courts or operating on the legislative lawmaking level, lawyers and lawyers-to-be as well as increasing numbers of mental health professionals have written commentaries on the laws relating to mental disability. Each year, at least a half-dozen books and a whole spate of journal articles of varying breadth, interest, and utility are published in the field.

Apart from its complexity and ubiquity, mental disability law assumes major significance when viewed in terms of the large number of people and the important economic interests it affects. In 1955, a year before the project that led to the first edition of this book was approved, official reports counted a total of 1,675,352 psychiatric "care episodes" nationally.[2] Overwhelmingly these episodes were in the nature of inpatient services provided largely in public mental institutions (though sometimes in private mental hospitals, general hospital

1. The term *mental disability* is used throughout this volume in a generic sense to denote any kind of mental health or developmental disability problem that subjects the person so afflicted to laws regulating his social, civil, and personal rights. Mental illness, mental retardation and related developmental disabilities, alcoholism, and drug addiction are included in this generic term. Another point about terminology is that this volume generally uses the pronoun "he" in a gender-neutral sense in referring to patients, mental health service providers and lawyers—this despite the fact that almost half the patients in all inpatient mental facilities are female (the proportion of female patients in state and county institutions is lower), that there are many women in mental health services, and that the number of women lawyers is increasing rapidly. The alternatives, we felt, were just too awkward or ungrammatical.

2. These statistics and most of the others in this paragraph are taken from Goldman, Adams, & Taube, Deinstitutionalization: The Data Demythologized, 34 Hosp. & Community Psychiatry 129, 131 table 1 (1983). This very helpful compilation and analysis obviates the need to search and cite the various annual statistical reports put out by the Division of Biometry and Epidemiology of the National Institute of Mental Health. The 1980-81 figures are estimates supplied directly by the NIMH to the American Bar Foundation in response to our request. Special thanks go to Tom Lalley and Ron Manderscheid for helping to bring the statistical information as up to date as possible.

units, and veterans facilities), while a comparatively small component (some 23-24%) comprised outpatient services delivered at hospitals or at smaller clinics. This total amounted to a rate of 1,028 patient episodes per 100,000, or some 1% of the general population. By 1981, the latest year for which estimates are available, the total patient episodes had jumped to 6,294,000, a rate of 2,767 per 100,000, or almost 3% of the general population. Considerable shifts in distribution are hidden, however, within the changing totals. Proportionately, there has been a dramatic movement away from care and treatment in the large public institutions (where the laws of commitment and discharge have most direct relevance) to the provision of outpatient services in community mental health centers and other smaller local facilities, clinics, and "homes." As many as 72% of the total care episodes in 1981 were "outpatient." Private mental facilities and the psychiatric units of general hospitals also provide a greater amount of care today than in 1955, both proportionately and in the absolute. The provision of service in public institutions over the past two decades has been marked by the substitution of short-term care and treatment for the long confinements that characterized the 1950s. The shorter stays, however, have created the need for increased numbers of readmissions while also making room for more new admissions. Even while the in-residence totals for public institutions have dwindled, the number of admissions per year has increased rapidly.[3] Thus, the number of persons who come in contact with the mental health and disability systems and who are touched by the laws controlling civil institutionalization remains significant indeed.

When persons who receive institutional psychiatric care as a result of criminal behavior are counted in addition to the civil episodes, the importance of the laws relating to mental disability becomes clearer yet. The total numbers are not great. A survey conducted in 1978[4] reported some 20,000 admissions of "mentally disordered offenders" to public institutions, about one-third of which (6,420) were defendants found incompetent to stand trial, 1,625 were persons adjudged not guilty by reason of insanity, 1,203 were committed as mentally disordered sex offenders, and the rest were mentally disabled prisoners transferred to mental health units.[5] But in terms of the conspicuousness of such "episodes", fostered by often sensational news media coverage, and their weight in the strategic decisions of criminal defense lawyers and prosecutors (plea choices, plea bargains, requests for pretrial mental examinations, choice of post-conviction remedies) the numbers loom disproportionately large.

The financial burdens imposed on the community by providing for mentally disabled persons and by the economic losses resulting from such disabilities are of staggering proportions. Recent estimates (1975, 1981) of annual expenditures just for maintaining institutional facilities have been in the area of $4.5 billion.[6] "Treatment related costs" have been placed at more than $15 billion,[7] a figure that has increased tenfold since 1955. The total societal costs, derived from adding to these direct costs such factors as unemployability, lost productivity, lost production, criminal justice system costs, and accidents (particularly motor vehicle accidents resulting from alcohol abuse) have been reported to be in the range of $85 billion annually.[8] Whether or not one chooses to accept such figures or their derivation — and the case for their underestimation and underinclusiveness is as easily made as the contrary argument that they are overdone — no one can deny the enormity of the economic burden that mental disability imposes on our society.

The law deals with a wide variety of problems arising from mental disabilities, including the determination in the first instance of whether certain persons are mentally disabled; their institutionalization and discharge; their care and treatment, rights, and status while institutionalized; their maintenance, treatment, and entitlements in the community; the personal and property rights of all mentally disabled persons; their domestic relations rights; their relationship with psychiatrists, physicians, and other service providers; and the relation of the mentally disabled to the criminal law. Among the primary concerns of the law should be safeguarding the rights of mentally disabled persons who are caught up in the mental health and disability service systems or in the criminal justice system and, in the event of their recovery or rehabilitation, restoring such persons to society in

3. At the end of 1955, there were 558,922 resident patients in the nation's public mental facilities; at the end of 1977, there were only 159,523. The number of admissions in 1955, however, was only 178,003, while in 1977 the total "additions" (a slightly more comprehensive construct than the "admissions" recorded in the 1950s and 1960s, though roughly comparable to them) came to 414,703. Goldman, Adams, & Taube, *supra* note 2, at 132 table 2. Only in the most recent years has there been a leveling off in the rate of increase in admissions, with 1980-81 actually showing a slight decline. (Information supplied directly by NIMH; see note 2 *supra*.)

4. Steadman, Monahan, Hartstone, Davis, & Robbins, Mentally Disordered Offenders: A National Survey of Patients and Facilities, 6 Law & Hum. Behav. 31 (1982).

5. *Id.* at 33 and table 1.

6. The 1975 figure, cited by Goldman, Adams, & Taube, *supra* note 2, at 134 table 3, is $4.3 billion. The 1981 estimate supplied directly by NIMH is $4.5 billion.

7. See Office of Program Planning and Coordination, Alcohol, Drug Abuse, and Mental Health Administration, Public Health Service, U.S. Dep't of Health and Human Services, The Alcohol, Drug Abuse, and Mental Health National Data Book 95 table 41 (Jan. 1980).

8. *Id.; see also* at 96-99 and tables 42-44.

a way that minimizes any possible stigma. At the same time, the law should recognize that reasonable restrictions may need to be placed on certain mentally disabled persons to protect their interests and to insure public safety. Finally — and a point that assumes greater significance as the law increases in mass and complexity at the urgings of advocates for various interest groups — the law must be founded on a realistic basis: it must be workable, capable of being implemented by psychiatric and legal practitioners and other professionals in the field, and productive of dispositional results that are in the best interests of those it presumes to protect, the mentally disabled persons themselves.

II. DEVELOPMENT OF THE PROJECT—THE OLD EDITIONS

The American Bar Association has a long history of concern with the laws relating to the mentally disabled. For example, the Section of Real Property, Probate and Trust Law, because of its interest in incompetency and guardianship, has consistently dealt with problems of mental disability.[9] Similarly, the Section of Criminal Law has been active in this field because of its concern with criminal irresponsibility or "insanity."[10] The Section of Judicial Administration has also manifested an interest in this subject through its Committee on Procedure in Civil Mental Health Matters.

In 1943 the ABA Board of Governors authorized the appointment of an exploratory committee to survey the administrative and judicial procedures relating to mental disability in order to determine whether the ABA as a whole had sufficient present concern and understanding in this field to become active in it.[11] This committee in 1944 recommended to the board of governors that a special committee be created to advise the ABA whether the then-existing laws adequately safeguarded the rights of the mentally disabled and if they did not, to submit drafts of appropriate legislation.[12]

Appointed on the exploratory committee's recommendation, the Special Committee on the Rights of the Mentally Ill reported at the 1945 Annual Meeting of the House of Delegates that before it could discharge its duty it would have to examine existing laws to ascertain their actual effect on the rights of the mentally disabled. The report pointed out, however, that such a study would be possible only if funds were available (either from the ABA or from some foundation) to hire a research staff.[13] No action on this recommendation was taken by the House of Delegates. In succeeding years the special committee reiterated to the House of Delegates the need for a thoroughgoing study by a permanent research staff.[14]

At the 1954 annual meeting of the House of Delegates a resolution was adopted referring the proposed study to the American Bar Foundation,[15] which had been established two years earlier at the instance of the ABA. Realizing the complexity of the problem presented to it, the Foundation decided to undertake first a preliminary study of the existing statutes in a limited number of states — California, Illinois, Michigan, New York, and Pennsylvania were ultimately selected[16] — and of the Draft Act Governing Hospitalization of the Mentally Ill.[17] From an examination of the data collected, it was evident that in order to present an accurate and comprehensive report of the law in its application to the mentally disabled a more elaborate study would be necessary. Accordingly, an expanded plan for the project was approved early in 1956 by the Board of Directors of the American Bar Foundation.

As outlined in the expanded plan, the purpose of the project was to analyze, classify, and describe pertinent statutes and important court decisions affecting the rights of the mentally disabled. Treatises and other written literature in the field were to be reviewed to obtain the benefit of all prior research on this subject.

The first step in the study was the preparation of charts showing the provisions of the Draft Act and the statutes of all the (then) 48 states and the District of Columbia. Next, all available literature in this area of the law was reviewed. Major court decisions, treatises, law review and bar journal articles, and similar materials were carefully studied to ascertain the status of the law as written. From this study and the information derived

9. Illustrative of the interest and work of this section is an address by Judge McAvinchey, "The Not-Quite-Incompetent Incompetent," to the ABA Section of Real Property, Probate and Trust Law, Aug. 28, 1956, *in* 1956 A.B.A. Sec. Real. Prop., Prob. & Tr. L. Proc. (pt. 1) at 18. See also American Bar Association Section of Real Property, Probate and Trust Law: Index to Publications of the Section, 1934-1961.

10. See, e.g., Report of the Committee on Medico-Legal Problems (to be presented at the Annual Meeting (1935)), A.B.A. Sec. Crim. L. Proc. 1932-41, at 18; Report of the Committee on Criminal Procedure (to be presented at the Annual Meeting (1938)), A.B.A. Sec. Crim. L. Proc. 1932-41, at 20.

11. 68 A.B.A. Rep. 183 (1943).

12. 69 A.B.A. Rep. 143, 221 (1944).

13. 70 A.B.A. Rep. 338 (1945).

14. 72 A.B.A. Rep. 289 (1947); 73 A.B.A. Rep. 297 (1948); 77 A.B.A. Rep. 318 (1952); 79 A.B.A. Rep. 399 (1954).

15. 79 A.B.A. Rep. 151 (1954).

16. American Bar Foundation, Hospitalization and Treatment of Mental Cases: A Comparative Study of Five Selected State Laws and the Draft Act of the Federal Security Agency (Memorandum prepared by N.N. Kittrie, Feb. 1955) (mimeographed).

17. National Institute of Mental Health, Federal Security Agency, A Draft Act Governing Hospitalization of the Mentally Ill (Public Health Service Pub. No. 51, 1952) [hereinafter cited as Draft Act]. This act was prepared to serve not as a uniform code but rather as a guide to the states for the revision of their own statutes. The Draft Act appeared as an appendix to the earlier editions of this report.

from the tables, the text of the 1961 report[18] was prepared. The preparation of the second edition in 1971[19] and the present revision have followed a substantially similar pattern.

The 1961 report, a study of written law and other literature, was the first phase of a broad inquiry into the law as it relates to the rights of the mentally disabled. Mindful that the application of the law in day-to-day practice is fully as important as the provisions of the written law, the American Bar Association and the American Bar Foundation next felt that a good analysis and presentation of many of the problems in this area could be made only after considerable empirical research, including field studies and conferences with physicians and psychiatrists active in the system. Only through observation of the processes and procedures actually used by the persons responsible for the administration of the laws, supplemented by interviews and other inquiries, could a fair and accurate determination be made of the extent to which the rights of mentally disabled persons are protected. Only with an understanding of the problems and inadequacies of the law in action could improvements be made where needed.

Thus it was contemplated that as a sequel to the 1961 report a field study was necessary. In 1958 an American Bar Foundation Special Committee on Procedure in Hospitalization and Discharge of the Mentally Ill was appointed to plan and finance the field study project.

The field study was carried out and reported in two separate but related projects: Hospitalization and Discharge of the Mentally Ill,[20] a study of civil hospitalization practices in seven states, and Mental Disability and the Criminal Law,[21] a corresponding study of the relationship between mental illness and the administration of criminal justice in five states and the District of Columbia. Both studies underscored many of the difficulties originally cited in the 1961 report. More importantly, they established the need for a "process" view of the institutionalization and release of the mentally disabled and the system's treatment of the mentally disabled person accused of a crime. That is, in order to gauge the impact of law on the mentally disabled, one must understand the interaction of the various procedures, practices, resources, and attitudes at all points of the law's contact with the mentally disabled and take into account quantitative as well as qualitative dimensions of the problem.

18. F.T. Lindman & D.M. McIntyre, The Mentally Disabled and the Law (1961).

19. S.J. Brakel & R.S. Rock, The Mentally Disabled and the Law (rev. ed. 1971).

20. R.S. Rock with M.A. Jacobson & R. Janopaul, Hospitalization and Discharge of the Mentally Ill (1968).

21. A.R. Matthews, Mental Disability and the Criminal Law: A Field Study (1970).

III. THE NEW EDITION

The value of the first two editions of the report has been demonstrated by the numerous citations to them in articles, monographs, and court cases. In this edition, the same basic format has been maintained, but significant alterations have been necessary to accommodate important developments in law, policy, and medical science in the past decade. For one, there has been a marked increase in concern with the needs, problems, and rights of two special groups within the mentally disabled population—developmentally disabled persons and juveniles with mental disabilities. Many states have enacted special provisions—separate statutory schemes in some cases—covering the commitment, institutional rights, and discharge of these groups. While the old editions made only occasional passing reference to these special groups, focusing almost exclusively on the laws relating to mentally ill adults, the new edition gives them considerably more detailed attention. As the law's concern with the developmentally disabled and juveniles with mental problems ranges across the spectrum of mental health issues, the present edition's treatment of the laws relating to these groups has been integrated throughout the book. It has required the production of new tables and textual additions to the various chapters but no new chapters to deal exclusively with those populations.

A wholly new chapter has been added to cover the "arrival" of the deinstitutionalization/community treatment concept during the decade of the 1970s, with attendant changes in institutional population characteristics and the growth of statutory provisions and case law asserting the various rights and entitlements of mentally disabled persons who are able to remain in the community or who are cared for in community-based settings. The dominant role of federal law and funding in this area made integration of this material into the existing organizational format particularly impractical. Another subject area that has required the construction of a new, separate chapter is the patient-provider relationship, which includes many intricate legal questions about confidentiality, consent, the duty to protect both the patient and the public, provider liability, and related issues that were only barely emerging a decade ago. Conversely, the decline in importance of certain other subject areas has argued for a reduced emphasis. Thus, the issue of eugenic sterilization no longer warrants its own chapter but is dealt with along with other issues centering on procreative choice in the chapter on family laws. Similarly, the decline in general acceptance and use of the sexual psychopathy laws has made feasible a brief treatment of the subject in the chapter on mental disability and the criminal law, where before it had been given extensive discussion in a separate chapter.

Developments in the civil commitment law during the past 10 to 15 years have been in the nature of a turning away from the medical model and toward a reassertion of judicial scrutiny in most phases of the commitment/discharge process. This has meant an expansion of due process rights for patients and prospective patients to a point where the rights to notice, preliminary hearings, full hearings, independent medical examinations, counsel (even "adversary counsel"), and the application of more stringent rules of evidence and standards of proof have become guaranteed at most junctures. In addition, the substantive standards for commitment have been tightened and more carefully defined. Proof of dangerousness—and all the uncertainty surrounding the making of such assessments or predictions—has become a necessary predicate for civil commitment in many states. At the same time policies and standards concerning release have been liberalized. Furthermore, the growth of the concept of "least restrictive" treatment has had powerful impact on actual decision making under these new standards. The concept embraces not only the decision whether to commit but also where and on what legal status (the last factor contributing to the continuing increase in voluntary admissions as opposed to involuntary commitment). It also has a bearing on time and mode of discharge. Even the growing policy of "mainstreaming" developmentally disabled persons—and its attendant promise of "equal" housing, education, and employment opportunities—has often been articulated in terms of the principle of providing care in the "least restrictive" setting. Tracing the legislative and litigational highlights of these developments has necessitated a major rewriting and restructuring of the civil commitment and discharge chapters of the previous editions.[22]

Important developments affecting mentally disabled persons once they are in institutions center on the right to treatment ("habilitation" in the context of services for the developmentally disabled), which was just emerging in the late 1960s, and the more novel and perhaps more controversial "right" to refuse treatment. These concepts have been invoked in large numbers of mental health cases in support of a large variety of claims—against commitment, in favor of release, for placement in or transfer to one institution rather than another, for treatment by one mode rather than another, and so forth. They are connected to the least restrictive treatment concept and in their most far-reaching interpretation have required the development of detailed treatment plans geared and limited to the particular needs of each individual patient entering a mental facility. Many state statutes have now incorporated these new treatment "rights" in some form. Their salience has warranted devoting a separate chapter to them, particularly given the many other detailed developments in the area of institutionalized persons' rights—the trend toward requiring increased procedural regularity and rigor in administrative decision making, equal treatment and equal protection of patients who are distinguished only by legal status, and the application of stringent consent and review procedures where major treatment decisions must be made.

Major developments in the area of incompetency/guardianship include on the one hand the much more limited and discrete application of these concepts: institutionalization is no longer equated with civil incompetency, and the law today recognizes that mentally disabled persons who need the help of a guardian on some matters do not necessarily need it on others. On the other hand, the provision of public guardians for persons who before would have remained unaided has occupied both courts and legislatures in recent times, and the authority of the guardian has in some jurisdictions been expanded to include the power to commit his ward. Related developments in the laws governing the personal and property rights of mentally disabled persons are characterized by a new deference to these persons' own decision-making capacities. The modern statutes and cases emphasize the desirability of deferring to the informed judgment or consent of mentally disabled persons faced with decisions in these areas, whenever possible, and of resorting to substituted decisions by the legal representatives of such persons only when doing so is dictated by the particular and compelling circumstances of the case, as revealed by a procedurally proper inquiry.

In domestic relations law, the rights of both mentally disabled parents and children have been strengthened vis-à-vis those of the state and its agents. Stricter substantive criteria and procedural requirements must be met today before basic parental rights may be abrogated, and the rights of children have been reinforced by the law's deference to their best interests and to their own wishes where age and competency permit. Overinclusive prohibitions against the marriage of mentally disabled persons have been struck down, and laws, policies, and programs designed to keep them from producing offspring are on the wane. At the same time, the law

22. The utility of the old text and tables is further diminished by the fact that in the past few years evidence has begun to appear of a retrenchment or backlash to the legal developments of the 1970s.

has accorded increased protection to the right to avoid conception and birth. Also, while the state today must meet a heavier burden of proof and persuasion than before if it seeks to terminate parental rights, there have been simultaneous legislative developments (including the provision of financial inducements) that promote the adoption of children who are subject to, or who come from homes characterized by, mental instability, disability, or general neglect. The natural tension between these opposing objectives of the law has contributed to considerable litigation in these areas.

In the area of criminal law as it relates to the mentally disabled, there have been fundamental developments as well. The insanity defense has been and continues to be reformulated in many jurisdictions. More drastic alterations in the concept of criminal irresponsibility have been proposed or approved in other states, with some adopting new compromise verdict options (guilty but mentally ill) and a few jurisdictions falling back on older solutions (diminished responsibility concepts as a complement or an alternative to the traditional insanity defense). Calls for total abolition of the defense have been more frequent and louder than in previous decades. There has been much emphasis on improving dispositional decisions and procedures, as distinct from the instrumental tests and standards. As is often the case, however, the reforms have sprung from apparently opposing societal concerns: on the one hand the concern that mentally disabled offenders are left to languish in institutions for durations that exceed their treatment needs or the punishment that could have been handed out under the criminal law and on the other hand the fear that dangerous individuals will obtain premature release or avoid confinement altogether as a result of their mental disturbance. Important changes in the formulation, reach, and use of the concept of incompetency to stand trial have also been effected. Much of the reform effort has gone into devising tests or check lists that seek to improve the accuracy and objectivity of competency determinations by matching clinical observations to legal standards. At the same time, the trend to limit the potential adverse effect of an incompetency finding for the defendant has continued: the law today prescribes limits in terms of the time an incompetent may be confined, and the push persists to allow a limited set of legal issues to be litigated despite the defendant's incompentency.

It has been possible to trace these developments in the law relating to incompetency/guardianship, domestic relations, and criminal behavior within the existing organization and format of the book. But it has required a wholesale rewriting of the chapters dealing with these subject areas.

Finally, the new edition provides in the chapter on historical trends a brief discussion of the nature of mental disability from a contemporary perspective. This discussion emphasizes that the identification of someone as mentally disabled is a multidimensional judgment, having social, economic, and political aspects as well as the legal and medical components on which the book concentrates. Changes in society's treatment of mentally disabled persons cannot be understood without an awareness of this reality. Over the years, medical definitions of various forms of mental disability are reformulated. Judgments about the organic or environmental roots of any given impairment or dysfunction are modified. New treatment methods are developed or an altered reliance is placed on existing modes. These developments in medical knowledge affect the law's response — the legislature's or the court's determination of what is the most fitting legal framework (1) for helping the mentally disabled and protecting their persons and their rights both in dependent and more self-sufficient situations and (2) for protecting society. But this medical/legal dialogue fails to explain all. To comprehend, for example, why today many mentally disabled persons are in nursing homes, in community treatment centers, or in group homes located in residential areas where before they would have been in the state mental hospitals, one must also know politics and economics and have a sense of the intangibles that contribute to shifts in society's tolerance of the varying functioning capacities and behavioral characteristics of mentally disabled persons in its midst.

The scope and magnitude of the developments in the mental disability field over the past decade have created a number of dilemmas for this updating and revision effort. Though this edition is considerably larger than the previous ones, space remains finite. The virtual explosion in case law, statutory law, and legal and psychiatric commentary has necessitated a more selective coverage than the comprehensive approach that was feasible for the earlier editions. In general, we have attempted to continue to give relatively full coverage to the statutes and the major cases. But the legal and medical literature — which is voluminous to the point of being redundant in some areas — has been given less emphasis. Coverage of model legislation and proposals, exemplified previously by elaborate tabulation and discussion of the Draft Act, has been reduced to a minimum, in part because many of these models have today found their way into the law. While the text is generally informed by each author's individual acquaintance with empirical reality and the empirical literature, the primary focus remains on the laws that are on the books, and there has been no systematic attempt to describe all the variances that may accompany their practical implementation. At one point we contemplated enriching this edition with a presentation and analysis of the administrative regulations that control much of the day-to-day institutional functioning in the states, but this effort had to be abandoned in view of the volume and detail of such regulations and the realization of how large a task it would be just to give reasonable coverage to the traditional legal material. In a complex and ever developing field such as mental disability law, such trade-offs are unavoidable.

Our work on this new volume has been helped greatly by the existence of the *Mental Disability Law Reporter* (recently renamed the *Mental and Physical Disability Law Reporter* to reflect an expanded coverage consonant with the trend in the law to join its concerns with both groups and to prescribe similar rights and protections for each). This bimonthly compendium of legal developments and materials, whose opening issue was published in 1976, has become an essential tool for all those—scholars and practitioners alike—seeking to keep abreast of the rapid legal changes in this field. The *Reporter* is a creation of the American Bar Association Commission on the Mentally Disabled, an interdisciplinary committee established in 1973, whose activities over the years demonstrate as well as any other efforts or resolutions the Association's continuing commitment toward improving the laws relating to mentally disabled persons.

The final purpose in offering an encyclopedic treatment of this area of law is to encourage simplification. By bringing together what has been tried, tested, proposed, or rejected in each of the various jurisdictions, we hope to promote a consensus concerning that essence of the law that has proved to be both theoretically sound and practicable. Ultimately, the need is not for the further proliferation of intrusive rules, ungovernable standards, and futile procedures or for more special interest pleadings and polemic commentary on behalf of these but for a measured reduction in such advocacy. The need today is to consolidate the "revolution" that has occurred in the mental health law over the past decade and to select and preserve its best features.

IV. THE TABLES

Aside from providing important source material for the text, the tables appearing throughout this report are also a valuable adjunct to it. First, being limited to statutory provisions, the tables offer a visual comparison of the ways in which the rights of mentally disabled persons have been dealt with by the legislatures of the 50 states and the District of Columbia. A second function of the tables is to provide an easily accessible reference for locating specific statutory provisions that relate to the many detailed aspects of the law concerning the mentally disabled. Many of these provisions are difficult to find through statutory indexes.

These two objectives were accomplished by preparing separate tables for the various areas of the law affecting mentally disabled persons. In some instances it was necessary to divide what might be considered a single subject into a number of subcategories. For example, "Involuntary Institutionalization" was divided into 18 principal subcategories, with 18 corresponding tables to portray the appropriate statutory provisions. A list of all the tables appears on pages xvii–xviii.

Except for the tables that simply list statutory definitions, each table is subdivided into vertical columns whose headings designate (by the use of key words or phrases) the particular statutory provisions charted. The states and the District of Columbia are listed in the initial vertical left-hand column as part of the citation of the particular statute or code used in the research. The statute or code so cited governs the various titles and sections charted horizontally unless another statute or code is cited for the particular section involved.

A list of footnotes follows each table. Statutory provisions that do not precisely fit into the table or column heading under which they are charted have been footnoted; additional comments and explanations may also be found in the footnotes. The reader should be cautioned that in some instances it may be misleading to peruse the tables without taking into account the footnotes. It is especially important to refer to the footnotes in the extreme left-hand column for qualifications that may govern the entire charting of the state or jurisdiction involved.

The fact that statutory provisions on certain subjects are absent from the tables should not be interpreted as an indication that no law exists on the subject: case law may exist and in many instances be adequate. Furthermore, it must be pointed out that statutory ambiguities have been resolved primarily by reference to the statutory language and (with a few major exceptions) without an attempt to research cases on the point.

To the extent that legislation is a continuing process, the statutes of the various states are continually subject to change. There is sometimes a lag between the legislative sessions and the general distribution of the statutory materials needed to ascertain what changes, if any, have been made. To meet this situation, a cutoff date of October 1982 was set for most of the work on the tables. All the statutory citations are at least current to that date. Several tables covering particularly fast-changing and important areas of law have been updated through the end of the year 1983 and a few through the summer of 1984.

While the mental health and disabilities codes and various more specifically directed statutes contain the states' basic law governing the treatment of mentally disabled persons, it would be inappropriate in consulting the statutory tables to ignore the supplementary role of the common law and constitutional law. In addition, institutional practices are often controlled by administrative regulations when not left to unchecked institutional discretion. The text of the book tries to convey this reality in a number of places, and a sound approach to the tables must include a recognition of the operational limits of the statutory law.

V. CONCLUSIONS AND RECOMMENDATIONS

Prior editions of this book closed each chapter with a set of conclusions and recommendations. We have chosen not to replicate this format in this edition. Evaluative comments have been made and questions have been raised throughout the discussion in each chapter. To add a final section of judgmental or exhortative material seems excessive. More than that, the philosophical complexity of the concepts, the legal complexity of their working procedures, and the uncertainty regarding the costs and benefits of the procedures when implemented in any individual case should make us leery of the didactic approach. While it is true that on the whole mentally disabled persons receive better care, training, and treatment today than in previous decades, that today's institutions are better, and that community facilities are more numerous and accessible, the precise role of legal reform—as opposed to larger forces and factors—in contributing to these improvements is uncertain.

Samuel Jan Brakel

CHAPTER 1

*Historical Trends**

I. EARLY DEVELOPMENTS

In ancient times the laws that governed mentally disabled persons came in the form of tribal taboos and customs.[1] Until the Golden Age of Greece, the prevailing explanation for mental disabilities was that the person so afflicted was possessed by demons. Predicated on the theory that such maladies were a result of supernatural powers imposing punishment, the prophylaxis and cure depended entirely on magic. Exorcising the demon from the mentally disabled person was the chief method of treatment. There were a variety of bizarre, and in some instances inhuman, ways to accomplish this. Brutal physical tortures were used, such as crushing the victim's body or removing sections of a disabled person's skull to drive out, or let out, the evil spirit.

In the highly developed civilization of ancient Egypt, mentally disabled persons were taken to the temples, where the priest-physicans used incantations, threats, and such physical remedies as herbs and oils to restore their patients. In Greece during the fourth century B.C., great strides were made to dispel the previous theory that mental disabilities were supernaturally induced. Hippocrates (460-370 B.C.), the father of medicine, and the Greek physicians and philosophers who followed him recognized mental disabilities as natural phenomena and attempted to classify them. They suggested that the mentally disabled be confined in the wholesome atmosphere of a comfortable, sanitary, well-lighted place. Similar advances were made during the Roman era, and gradually mental disability came to be regarded as primarily a medical problem rather than a religious one.

One of the earliest legal references to the mentally disabled is contained in the Twelve Tables of Rome, which were promulgated in 449 B.C.

There it was provided:

> Si furiosus escit, agnatum gentiliumque in eo pecuniaque ejus potestas esto . . . est ei custos non escit [if a person is a fool, let this person and his goods be under the protection of his family or his paternal relatives, if he is not under the care of anyone].[2]

The term *furiosus* undoubtedly meant any mentally disabled person. Later texts, dating from the time of Cicero in the first century B.C., limited the term to those who had moments of lucidity. However, it is unlikely that the early law recognized such comparatively subtle distinctions. The Twelve Tables referred to a person who did not act in the normal manner. Control of the person and goods of the furiosus did not depend on a judicial decree or formal pronouncement of a magistrate but rather arose directly by reason of the condition of the furiosus. The fact that he did not act like other people was sufficient for his relatives to assume control of his person and goods.

It is interesting to note that this law affected only the head of a family, for it applied only if the mentally disabled person was not under anyone's care. In ancient Roman law, sons and daughters of any age were under the power (*potestas*) of the head of the family and could not hold property. It was therefore unnecessary to appoint an administrator for their affairs, and their personal care was a matter for the head of the family to decide.

Later, when Roman law was fully developed, the magistrate designated a guardian (*curator*).[3] The person who exercised potestas over a mentally disabled

*The present author's contribution to this chapter, with the exception of minor revisions in § I, Early Developments, taken from the previous editions, is limited to § II, Contemporary Perspectives.

1. For an enlightening account and analysis of the care of the mentally ill in primitive societies, see Biggs, The Guilty Mind: Psychiatry and the Law of Homicide 3-34 (1955); Deutsch, The Mentally Ill in America: A History of Their Care and Treatment from Colonial Times 1-12 (2d ed. 1949).

2. Bruns, Fontes Juris Romani Antiqui 23-24 (Editio alterata aucta amendata, 1871).

3. Code Just. 5.70.6; Inst. Just. 1.23.3. Under Justinian a proceeding was held before the *curator* was named; the cited passage in the Inst. Just. states that the curator will be named "ex inquisitione."

person usually nominated by testament a guardian to serve in his place in case he should die before the disabled person, and this wish was followed by the magistrate. If the testament contained no nomination, the magistrate was free to choose whomever he pleased. Ordinarily he named as guardian a close relative of the person who needed care.

Roman law was troubled with problems that seem current. What was the legal status of a mentally disabled person during his lucid moments? Was he still under the protection of a guardian? If not, was it necessary to name a new guardian each time the illness returned? And what was the status of a testament made by him during his lucid moments? These questions were answered during the reign of Justinian in the sixth century, when it was decided that the guardianship was merely suspended during the person's lucid moments and that it again became operative as soon as the illness returned.[4] In addition, it was held that testaments made during the lucid moments were valid.[5]

Problems arose as well in the field of contract and tort law. The Romans held that mentally disabled persons were unable to form the consent necessary to make a valid contract and that, therefore, they were incapable of entering into a contract.[6] Similarly, they were not legally capable of agreeing to the marriage contract. Roman law also held that mentally disabled persons were legally incapable of obligating themselves by delictual acts such as theft, for the offender could not form the intent to take the property of another.

Under fully developed Roman law, the ward lost all legal capacity. He could not, of course, make a testament, nor could his guardian do it for him. The guardian, in earlier Roman law, had full and complete power over the goods of the ward. He could buy, sell, and exchange the ward's property. Later this complete power was limited so that the guardian acted solely as the administrator of the ward's patrimony. He could not sell or transfer the real property of the ward, nor could he make a gift in his name or liberate his slaves.[7]

When guardianship terminated, through either the ward's recovery or his death, the guardian had to account either to the former ward or to his heirs. This was one method of encouraging honest stewardship.[8]

4. Code Just. 5.70.6.

5. Code Just. 6.22.9; Inst. Just. 2.12.1. However, since a *furiosus* is *non compos mentis*, he may not be used as witness to a will; if he should have temporary remission, he might serve during that period. Inst. Just. 2.10.6; Dig. Just. 28.1.20.4.

6. Inst. Just. 3.20.8: "The *furiosus* is unable to transact business, for he does not understand what he does."

7. Dig. Just. 40.1.13.

8. The former ward or his heirs could commence an action *negotiorum gestorum utilis* against the guardian.

After the decay of the Western Empire during the fifth century, the *lex barbarorum*, or the law of the Germanic tribes, was applied in Western Europe, while Roman law continued to be followed in the Eastern Empire. The Visigothic Code,[9] which was followed in Spain and France, declared that "[a]ll persons who are insane from infancy, or indeed from any age whatever, and remain so without intermission, cannot testify, or enter into a contract, and, if they should do so, it would have no validity. But such as have lucid intervals, shall not be prohibited from transacting business during those periods."[10]

During the Middle Ages, mental disabilities were again considered the product of possession by demons, and exorcism was revived as the accepted method of treament. This time it was accompanied by ceremonies more elaborate and antidotes more torturous than those used by the ancients.[11] The laws that were promulgated continued to reflect concern for the property of the disabled, with little legal attention given to his person.

In England, sometime between 1255 and 1290, the statute *De Praerogativa Regis* was enacted.[12] This law divided mentally disabled persons into two classes, the idiot and the lunatic, the former being a person who "hath no understanding from his nativity" and the latter "a person who had understanding, but . . . hath lost the use of his reason." The king was granted the custody of the lands of "natural fools" (idiots); after providing the "fool" with necessaries, the king could retain the profits from the land. After the "fool's" death the land was to be returned to the "right heirs." The land of those who happened to "fail of their wit" (lunatics) was held by the king and all of the profits therefrom applied to the maintenance of the mentally ill persons and their households. Any excess was returned to such persons "when they c[a]me to right mind."[13] Guardianship over the property of the "idiot" was profitable for the guardian; on the other hand, managing the property of a "lunatic" was a duty, and no profit could be made from it.

In *Beverley's* case,[14] decided in the early seventeenth century, Lord Coke expounded the law of insanity as it

9. This code, drafted between A.D. 466 and 485, was edited in Latin and was greatly influenced by Roman law. It served as the basic legislation of the Visigoths for nearly 200 years until it was replaced by a code edited by order of King Receswind.

10. Visigothic Code Just. 2.5.10 *in* Scott, The Visigothic Code Just. 67 (1910).

11. Shryock, The Beginnings: From Colonial Days to the Foundation of the American Psychiatric Association, *in* One Hundred Years of American Psychiatry 4 (J.K. Hall, G. Zilboorg, & H.A. Bunker eds. 1944).

12. 17 Edw. 1, c. 9; 1 Holdsworth, A History of English Law 473 (7th ed. 1956); 2 F. Pollock & F.W. Maitland, The History of English Law 464 (2d ed. 1911).

13. 17 Edw. 1, c. 9.

14. 4 Co. 123b, 76 Eng. Rep. 1118 (K.B. 1603).

had developed in England. Because of its importance, the opinion is worthy of close examination.

Lord Coke first explained that every act performed by a *non compos mentis* inevitably concerned his life, his lands, or his goods. The law of England provided that every act done by such a person in a court of record should bind him and his heirs forever while acts done *in pais* (without legal proceedings) should bind him for life and in some cases forever. However, the law of England was that the non compos mentis should not lose his life for having committed murder or felony.

The reason for this distinction is clear: the penalties inflicted on the felon were extremely severe, "so that by punishing a few, fear might come to many." However, as Lord Coke pointed out, "the punishment of a man who is deprived of reason and understanding cannot be an example to others." Lord Coke added that the non compos mentis was not able to form the felonious intent that was the very heart of the crime and that therefore he was not guilty of murder or felony, although he could be subject to conviction for high treason if the circumstances warranted.

Lord Coke listed four types of persons included in the generic term non compos mentis. They were:

1. The idiot or natural fool
2. He who was of good and sound memory, and by the visitation of God has lost it
3. Lunatics, those who are sometimes lucid and sometimes non compos mentis, and
4. Those who by their own acts deprive themselves of reason, as the drunkard.

These distinctions had certain important legal consequences. For example, an idiot was required to appear in court in person, while one who had become non compos mentis was represented by a guardian if he was under age and by an attorney if he had reached his majority. The lunatic was responsible for acts done by him during his lucid moments, while those acts performed during his nonlucid moments were of the same effect as those performed by an idiot. Lord Coke concluded this phase of his analysis with the observation that those who voluntarily deprived themselves of their reason, such as the drunkard, should not be heard to claim insanity as a defense in a civil or criminal action. Indeed, he argued that it would constitute an aggravation of the offense.

He then made an interesting comparison between the civil and the common law as these laws sought to protect the idiot and his inheritance. He noted that all acts perfomed by a non compos mentis without the accord of his tutor were void in the civil law. The lack of a similar requirement in common law was cited as a defect in the common law system. He pointed out that the law of England did in fact provide a tutor in the form of the king. As we have seen, under the statute *De Praerogativa Regis,* the person and goods of the idiot were in the custody of the king. Any transfer of property made by the idiot could be voided by action of the king, and the king could terminate any action against an idiot "brought on any bond or writing that he has made" by sending a *supersedeas* to the court where the suit had been commenced. The king could even void gifts or transfers made by the idiot before he was adjudged incompetent. However, if the idiot died before being adjudged incompetent, no formal inquiry as to his competency could be held, and transfer made by the idiot during his lifetime could not be attacked.

One who became non compos mentis, as distinguished from the person who was born an idiot, was also protected by the king. The king was accountable to the lunatic when the latter had lucid moments. Transfers attempted by the lunatic during his nonlucid moments were subject to attack in the same manner as were those made by idiots.

It is clear from *Beverley's* case that English law by the seventeenth century had established many methods to protect the property of the mentally disabled. Similarly, in criminal matters, the law had recognized that the mentally disabled could not form a criminal intent and, therefore, were not guilty of felonies and murders. Lord Coke also related that the king was given custody of the person of the afflicted individual as well as his lands. It would appear, however, that this protection of the person consisted of caring for his needs out of the proceeds from the lands. There is no indication that this care constituted a drain on the king's treasury. Nonetheless, it is interesting to note this relatively early concern for the person of one who was mentally disabled.

The method of determining an individual's mental status is worthy of attention. When a person was thought to be an idiot, the chancellor, upon petition, issued a writ *de idiota inquirendo*, which was tried by a jury of 12 men. The writ and the procedure employed in the case of lunacy were similar in nature to the writ de idiota inquirendo, and juries, simply to avoid heavy exactions by the king, often found for lunacy where idiocy would have been a more accurate finding.[15]

If an incompetent were determined by the jury to be a lunatic, the chancellor committed him to the care of some friend, who received an allowance with which to care for him. The incompetent's heir was generally made the manager of the estate, although, according to Blackstone, "to prevent sinister practices" he was not given the custody of the incompetent. For the custody of

15. 1 W. Blackstone, Commentaries 303-7 (9th ed. 1783).

the estate the heir was responsible to the court of chancery, to the recovered lunatic, or to his administrator.[16] The practices of persons charged with the custody of an incompetent and his property gradually developed into a set of customs, rules, and standards for the proper management of a lunatic's property.

During the period between the attack of lunacy and the determination by the jury, the incompetent was cared for by his nearest relatives. It may be that the impecunious non compos mentis could not enjoy the privilege of having his sanity determined by a jury, for Blackstone states that one applied to the royal authority for lasting confinement "when the disorder is grown permanent, and the circumstances of the party will bear such additional expense."[17]

The distinction is significant and may serve to explain much of the later development of detention procedures. If one held property, he was able to pay the expenses incurred in the inquiry as to his sanity. Likewise, such an inquiry was necessary to assure the proper administration of the applicant's affairs, while the proceeds from his holdings would pay the cost of administration and provide for his maintenance. On the other hand, those who were not persons of wealth did not require an administrator for their affairs, and there was no method of compensating the nearest relative for their support.

In colonial America the prospect of supporting an indigent incompetent was not a pleasant one, especially during the early years. The colonies were sparsely populated, and they lacked communal facilities—not only those for the care of the mentally disabled but others such as fire departments, public schools, and even prisons. The family, as the primary social unit, was expected to care for its own. Communal facilities slowly developed to care for those who had neither family nor friends to turn to for support. The position of mentally disabled persons with neither means nor family was desperate. Unable to secure employment, they often joined or formed transient bands, drifting from town to town.

Each such itinerant group was treated as a monolithic mass; there was no attempt to analyze its components. A "drifter" was a "drifter" and nothing more. Whether he was mentally or physically disabled or simply lazy made no difference to the townspeople, who feared they would have to support him. For these reasons the mentally disabled, during the colonial period, were often subjected to the same treatment as the itinerant poor. In the strongly puritanical atmosphere of the time, which equated work and industry with the moral life, it was inevitable that the laws should be aimed at compelling man to labor rather than at providing for his needs. In the case of the mentally disabled, these measures led to such grotesque incidents as whipping the hapless. The victims of society wandered aimlessly about the countryside, undergoing ridicule from village children and idlers and eking out an existence by begging.[18]

Early instances of community action seem to have been motivated by a desire to aid the impoverished family in caring for its charge rather than by any desire to aid directly the victim of a mental disability. For example, in Pennsylvania, the Upland court records of 1676 show that a certain Jan Vorelissen of Amesland complained to the court that his son Erik was "bereft of his naturall Senses and is turned quyt madd" and that he, the father, was a poor man and unable to maintain his son. It was therefore ordered that three or four persons be hired "to build a little block-house at Amesland for to put in the said madman."[19] A similar instance occurred in Braintree, Massachusetts, in 1689, where the inhabitants voted that a certain Samuel Speere should construct a small building to contain his sister and also that he should provide for her. The town further voted to pay the expenses incurred by Speere in maintaining his sister.[20] Likewise, instances may be found where the community made maintenance payments to persons not related to but in charge of indigent mentally disabled. This development does not appear to have involved any judicial procedure. Rather, it is quite likely that the members of the community, having a mentally deranged person in the neighborhood who perhaps plagued them by constant begging, decided it would be better for one person, reimbursed by the community, to provide for the needs of that individual.

Of course, if the mentally disabled person was violent, forcible restraint was necessary and recourse was had to the sheriff or constable to detain him. In some instances the town itself requested the police authority to take such measures. In 1676, Massachusetts enacted a statute ordering the selectmen of towns having dangerously distracted persons to take care of them, "that they do not

16. *Id.*

17. *Id.* at 305.

18. Deutsch, *supra* note 1, at 25. The situation was not much better in England. Shakespeare, writing of a somewhat earlier period, described one of his characters in this fashion:

> Poor Tom, that eats the swimming frogs, the toads, the tadpole, the wall newt and the water newt, that in the fury of his heart, when the foul fiend rages, eats cow dung, fox sallets, swallows the old rat and the ditch dog, drinks the green mantle of the slimy pool; who is shipt from tything to tything, and stocked, punished and imprisoned.

[King Lear, act 3, scene 4].

19. Deutsch, *supra* note 1, at 42.

20. *Id.*

damify others."[21] The negative wording of this statute indicates that the sole purpose of the community's action was to restrain the violent. Here again, as in the earlier instances, the laws reflected the state of medical knowledge and the level of community development. Medical knowledge provided no method of treatment, and quite naturally the community could do no more than protect itself. This Massachusetts statute provided the legal basis for the forcible restraint of the violent.

Though research on this period has uncovered no cases of anyone's requesting his release from forcible detention, it is quite probable that such detention could have been justified on the theory that the community had the right to defend itself collectively against one who would cause it harm. As has been seen, Lord Coke declared it law that a non compos mentis could not be guilty of murder or a felony because he could not form the requisite felonious intent. Lord Coke added, however, that a non compos mentis could be guilty of high treason, which was a crime against the community.[22] Furthermore, the community had the right to defend itself against acts of violence committed by the non compos mentis.

In these early cases, if the derangement and violence were apparent and, more pertinently, the mentally disabled person was without family, there probably was no objection raised about commitment. When a member of a small community acted strangely and constituted a threat to the peace, he was placed in custody. The subtleties of psychiatric diagnosis were for a later day.

The problem of proper commitment procedures did not arise until institutions for the detention and treatment of the mentally disabled had developed and their doors had been opened to less obvious cases of mental disability. Formerly, throwing a potential murderer into prison under the guise of restraining his violent tendencies probably raised no debate; today, restraining a meek and harmless mentally disabled person does raise the problem.

The establishment of hospitals to which the mentally disabled could be sent for treatment developed in the eighteenth century. In response to a petition drawn by Benjamin Franklin, the Pennsylvania Assembly in May 1751 authorized the establishment of the first general hospital to receive and cure the mentally ill as well as the sick poor. In 1773, Virginia erected at Williamsburg the first hospital devoted exclusively to the mentally disabled. It remained the only one of its kind in the country until 1824, when the Eastern Lunatic Asylum was established in Lexington, Kentucky.[23]

As noted earlier, detention by relatives was mentioned by Blackstone as being a common measure at the onset of lunacy. In 1774, Parliament enacted a statute to regulate "private madhouses."[24] Though limited specifically to England, Wales, and the town of Berwick upon Tweed, it is a significant statute, for it demonstrates the concern reflected in more populous regions for the condition of the mentally disabled. It provided that the Royal College of Physicians elect five of its Fellows to grant licenses to operate houses for the reception of lunatics in the larger cities. These commissioners were to visit and inspect at least once every year the licensed houses and those detained therein. Any person could apply to the commissioners for information about the place of detention of a particular person. The secretary of the commissioners was to be informed of each new inmate within three days of his admission, "except such pauper lunatics as shall happen to be sent there by parish officers." Such notice of arrival had to contain the name and place of abode of the person by whose direction the lunatic was sent to the house and also the name and place of abode of the physician, surgeon, "or apothecary by whose advice such direction was given." Any keeper of such a house who admitted a purported lunatic "without having an order, in writing, under the hand and seal of some physician, surgeon, or apothecary, that such a person is proper to be received into such house or place as a lunatic . . . shall . . . pay the sum of one hundred pounds."

In other areas of England, justices of the peace, accompanied by a physician, were authorized to license the houses and conduct visitations. After specifically exempting public hospitals from its provisions, this act concluded with this highly significant paragraph:

> And whereas it is not intended by this act to give the keepers of any house or houses, so to be licensed as aforesaid, or any other person concerned in confining any of his Majesty's subjects therein, any new justification from their being able to prove that the person so confined having been sent there by such direction and advice as are required by this act; be it therefore declared and enacted, That in all proceedings that shall be had under his Majesty's writ of *Habeas Corpus*, and in all indictments, informations, and actions, that shall be preferred and brought against any person or persons, for confining or ill-treating any of his Majesty's subjects, in any of the said houses, the parties complained of shall be

21. 5 Records of the Governor and Company of the Massachusetts Bay in New England 80 (1854).

22. Beverley's Case, 4 Co. 123b, 124b, 76 Eng. Rep. 1118, 1121 (K.B. 1603).

23. Deutsch, *supra* note 1, at 59, 71.

24. An Act for Regulating Madhouses, 1774, 14 Geo. 3, c. 49.

> obliged to justify their proceedings according to the course of the common law, in the same manner as if this act had not been made.[25]

It is clear from these words that habeas corpus was viewed in the common law as an appropriate method for attacking the legality of detention in an asylum. The writ of habeas corpus was highly valued in the colonies, and it was considered an integral part of the rights of Englishmen.[26] The nonviolent poor could be imprisoned under the poor laws; the nonviolent and perhaps even the violent rich were cared for privately. Probably only the violent poor were detained in the early asylums, for they constituted a threat to the community. The thorny problems arose with the commitment of the nonviolent. The statute of George III referred to a commitment procedure that depended on certification by one "physician, surgeon or apothecary." Similarly, certification by one physician was all that was required for commitment to the Pennsylvania hospital.[27]

The gradually emerging responsibility of the community, supplementary to the immediate obligation of the family, for restraining violent persons is well illustrated by a New York statute enacted February 9, 1788,[28] which notes that "there are sometimes persons, who by lunacy or otherwise are furiously madd, or are so far disordered in their senses that they may be dangerous to be permitted to go abroad." The statute then authorizes two or more justices to direct constables, by warrant, to apprehend and keep safely locked up the furiously mad and the dangerous. (If the justices found it necessary, these persons could be chained.) This section of the statute concludes with the injunction that it should be interpreted to restrain or abridge the power of the chancellor as it pertains to lunatics "or to restrain or prevent any friend or relation or [*sic*] such lunatic from taking them under their own care and protection." Here there can be no doubt that the legislators considered the asylums to be primarily for the care of those violent persons who could not be cared for privately. This attitude is all the more understandable when one recalls that the purpose of commitment was detention and not therapy.

While commitment of the non compos mentis was sometimes accomplished on certification of only one physician, or on a warrant issued by only two justices of the peace, there are records of the procedural safeguards employed to preserve the property rights of the non compos mentis. In New York, getting someone declared non compos mentis for the purpose of having his affairs administered followed in general the procedure outlined by Blackstone: an individual requested a writ de lunatico inquirendo from the chancellor.[29] The chancellor, on the issuance of the writ, empowered a jury to inquire into the mental condition of the respondent. If the jury were persuaded that the respondent was incompetent, the chancellor appointed a guardian; the chancellor could also request the respondent to appear before him for examination. Adequate notice to the respondent was necessary. Similarly, an early Louisiana case, under the civil law system, declared that one could not be deprived of his right to administer his own affairs on ex parte evidence and that he should be cited and have the opportunity to cross-examine as in any other suit.[30] The different rules applying to legal representation for idiots and lunatics that were discussed by Lord Coke in *Beverley's* case appeared in this country in 1830, when it was held that a person adjudged a lunatic might have leave to attack the finding of incompetency through an attorney, although an idiot must appear in person.[31]

The common law right of habeas corpus was available to test the detention of a "mentally disabled" person. It was the device used in the *Oakes* case. In 1845 a habeas corpus action was instituted on behalf of one Josiah Oakes,[32] who sought his release from the McLean Asylum in Massachusetts on the ground that he had been illegally committed by his family. The court acknowledged that the United States Constitution prohibited the detention of anyone against his will, unless he be deprived of his liberty by judgment of his peers or the law of the land. The court also acknowledged that private institutions for the insane had been in use and sanctioned by the courts. The court went on to state:

> The right to restrain an insane person of his liberty is found in that great law of humanity, which makes it necessary to confine those whose going at large would be dangerous to themselves or others. . . . And the necessity which creates the law, creates the limitation of the law. The question must then arise in each particular case, whether a patient's own safety, or that of others, requires that he should be restrained for a certain time, and whether restraint is necessary for his restoration, or will be conducive thereto. The restraint can continue as long as the necessity continues. This is the limitation, and the proper limitation.[33]

25. *Id* at § 31.
26. The colonists' struggle to secure the right of habeas corpus in the colonies is well described in R.L. Perry & J.C. Cooper, Sources of Our Liberties 194-95 (1959). In some instances, the writ continued to be issued as a common law remedy in the colonies despite the Privy Council's veto of colonial legislation that would have statutorily guaranteed this right to the colonists.
27. Deutsch, *supra* note 1, at 62.
28. 1788 N.Y. Laws ch. 31.
29. *In re* Barker, 2 Johns. Ch. 232 (N.Y. 1816); Blackstone, *supra* note 15, at 305.
30. Stafford v. Stafford, 1 Mart. 551 (La. Sup. Ct. 1823).
31. *In re* Covenhoven, 1 N.J. Eq. 19 (Ch. 1830).
32. Matter of Josiah Oakes, 8 Law Rep. 123 (Mass. 1845).
33. *Id*. at 125.

The significance of this decision is readily apparent: it establishes guideposts to be used in determining the propriety of detention. The old standard of "detention of the violent" has gradually become outmoded. Oakes was not a violent person; he was detained on the allegation that he suffered from hallucinations and displayed unsoundness of mind in conducting his business affairs. The charge grew out of the fact that Oakes, an elderly and ordinarily prudent man, became engaged to a young woman of unsavory character a few days after the death of his wife. The commitment of marginal cases required the courts to render more precise the common law rules as to detention. Reflecting advances in medical science as well as the change in society's view of mental disability, the court contemplated detention for therapeutic purposes as well as for the more obvious reason of defending society against its deranged members.

In 1849 a case was tried in Philadelphia which demonstrated that concern need also be shown for the protection of hospital officials acting in good faith. A man named Hinchman instituted a civil suit for wrongful detention against his mother, sister, cousins, the physicians of the asylum, and the physician who signed the certificate. He recovered a large sum of money. Dr. Isaac Ray, in reporting the case,[34] stated that the evidence showed beyond a doubt that Hinchman was violently and dangerously insane.

Aid for the mentally disabled rapidly ceased to be the concern of an isolated few; partisans of improvement in psychiatric care organized to work more effectively. In 1844 the American Psychiatric Association was founded in Philadelphia by 13 hospital superintendents.[35] By pooling their experience and knowledge in the relatively new field of psychiatry, they were able to make prodigious strides in understanding and treating the mentally disabled. Two of the original members of this group deserve special mention. Benjamin Rush, the father of American psychiatry, was the leader of his period in putting the observation and treatment of mental disability on a scientific basis. Isaac Ray, who possessed a keen insight into the medical aspects of "insanity," published an authoritative exposition of the intricate relationship between law and psychiatry.[36]

While law was progressing by means of judicial decision, and medical science by means of the work of such men as Rush and Ray, other voices were heard calling for changes. Two women were especially responsible for improvement: Mrs. E.P.W. Packard, who was interested in reforming commitment procedures, and Dorothea Lynde Dix, who stressed the inadequacy of treatment facilities.

Mrs. Packard had been committed to the Illinois State Hospital in 1860 on her husband's petition. Under the commitment statute in force at that time in Illinois, married women and infants could be involuntarily committed on the request of the husband or a guardian without the evidentiary standard applicable in cases involving others.[37]

After her release three years later, Mrs. Packard began a campaign for new commitment legislation. Specifically, she urged that a person not be committed as insane solely on the basis of the opinions he might express and that commitment should be based only on irregular conduct that indicates that the individual is so lost to reason as to render him an unaccountable moral agent. In her frequent lectures, as well as in the popular books that she wrote,[38] Mrs. Packard vividly portrayed the horror of being wrongfully placed in a mental institution. Largely through her efforts, Illinois enacted the so-called personal liberty bill, which required a jury trial to determine whether the respondent in the action should be committed to a mental institution.

The influence of Dorothea Lynde Dix was felt by lawmakers and social reformers even more keenly than that of Mrs. Packard. This Massachusetts schoolteacher, who later became Superintendent of Nurses for the Union forces during the Civil War, was so appalled at the lack of adequate facilities for the mentally disabled that she spent the last 50 years of her life crusading for improved hospital conditions. Thirty-two mental hospitals in this country and abroad were founded as a result of her efforts, and at least 20 states responded to her appeals by establishing and enlarging mental hospitals. No other individual did more in the nineteenth century to advance the idea of communal responsibility for the welfare of the mentally disabled.[39]

34. I. Ray, A Treatise on the Medical Jurisprudence of Insanity 411 (5th ed. 1871).

35. At its founding it was called the Association of Medical Superintendents of American Institutions for the Insane. For 28 years beginning in 1893 the organization was named the American Medico-Psychological Association. In 1921 it assumed its present title, the American Psychiatric Association.

36. Ray's most important work, *A Treatise on the Medical Jurisprudence of Insanity, supra* note 34, was the first systematic treatise on this topic to appear in the English language. Six editions were published in this country as well as one in England; at the time of his death, a seventh was under way. The book was often cited by appellate courts both in this country and abroad.

37. "Married women and infants, who, in the judgment of the medical superintendent are evidently insane or distracted, may be received and detained in the hospital at the request of the husband, . . . or [the] guardian of the infants without the evidence of insanity or distraction required in other cases." Ill. Laws 1851 § 10, at 98.

38. E.g., E.P.W. Packard, Modern Persecution, or Insane Asylums Unveiled, as Demonstrated by the Report of the Investigating Committee of the Legislature of Illinois (reprint ed. 1973 in one vol. of the 1875 ed. 2 vols.) (Mental Illness and Social Policy: The American Experience (G.N. Grob ed.)).

39. The greatest single project by Dorothea Lynde Dix was lobbying for the passage of a federal act granting 12,225,000 acres of government land to

Widespread, popularly supported movements such as these often culminated in the enactment of new commitment laws or the revision of old statutes. The new legislation enacted during the latter part of the nineteenth century constitutes the basic legislative patterns currently in force.

The development of the law as it affects the rights of the mentally disabled has been dependent on many factors. Three of the most important are: (1) the state of medical knowledge of the cause, care, and proper treatment of the mentally disabled, (2) the degree to which the politically organized community has acknowledged its responsibility for the care and treatment of its disabled citizens, and (3) the legal profession's awareness of the social realities of mental disability, including the role of relatives or close friends in safeguarding the rights and interests of mentally disabled persons, as well as the potential for occasional abuse of this role. There has been much progress in each of these areas, particularly in the last two decades. But the complexity and the magnitude of the problems experienced or posed by mentally disabled persons in our society leave no room for complacency.

II. CONTEMPORARY PERSPECTIVES

A. Introduction

One of the main reasons the laws relating to mental disability continue to reflect considerable uncertainty in direction, scope, and objective is the continuing ambiguity of the concept of mental disability itself. History or experience has not produced a generally accepted definition of mental disorder or of its opposite, mental health.[40] Nor is such a definition likely to be forthcoming in the foreseeable future. Certain types of mental disability, particularly those that are manifest at birth or in early infancy and that present themselves in the form of conspicuous and persistent symptoms, may be susceptible of relatively ready and consistent diagnosis, if not an equally consistent treatment response on the part of psychiatric or developmental practitioners, legal functionaries, relatives, neighbors, or others who by profession or personal relationship share a concern for mentally disabled persons. Many other mental disorders, which have symptoms that develop later in life, are episodic, or can be suppressed with some success through medication, personal resolve, or situational improvements, are far less tractable. Notwithstanding considerable advances in medical knowledge, social commitment, and legal sophistication, the goal of accurately identifying and defining these latter disorders continues to elude theorists and practitioners alike.

B. Organic Mental Disabilities

While less abrupt and made with less confidence than in earlier years (or compared with lay perceptions), a basic diagnostic division persists between mental disabilities that are primarily organic (biological) in nature and origin and those predominantly rooted in or triggered by environmental factors, whose only *known* etiologies are functional or psychological.[41] The former tend to pose fewer diagnostic problems than the latter. Some—for example, the severer forms of mental retardation[42]—are usually present at birth, detectable then

---

various states for use in providing for the mentally disabled. The act was passed by both houses of Congress in 1854 but vetoed by President Franklin Pierce. Deutsch, *supra* note 1, at 179.

40. In its introduction, the American Psychiatric Association's latest Diagnostic and Statistical Manual of Mental Disorders (DSM-III) (3d ed. 1980) [hereinafter cited as DSM-III], at 5-6 acknowledges that:

> Although this manual provides a classification of mental disorders, there is no satisfactory definition that specifies precise boundaries for the concept "mental disorder" (also true for such concepts as physical disorder and mental and physical health). Nevertheless, it is useful to present concepts that have influenced the decision to include certain conditions in DSM-III as mental disorders and to exclude others.

41. To an extent, the designation of mental disorders as biological or psychological depends on whether the organic "causes" are *known* rather than on whether they may or may not exist. Furthermore, a nonorganic classification does not mean that the disorder is independent of the organic brain process. *All* psychological processes—normal as well as abnormal—depend on brain functioning and the physical/chemical activity of the brain cells. The entire mind/body dichotomy is more in the nature of popular (perhaps intuitively useful) fiction than scientific fact. Much the same can be said of the "nature versus nurture" distinction, the lines of which are becoming increasingly blurred in the light of new findings and theories suggesting genetic predisposition toward, or inherited metabolic or neurological "errors" in, the development of disorders previously relegated to the psychological sphere. Popular conceptions of cause and effect appear correspondingly tenuous when applied toward the identification and understanding of mental disorders.

42. The DSM-III, *supra* note 40, at 39-40, replicates the standard division of mental retardation into four subclasses reflecting relative degrees of intellectual impairment as measured by standard intelligence quotient tests:

Subtypes of Mental Retardation	IQ Levels
Mild	50-70
Moderate	35-49
Severe	20-34
Profound	Below 20

> **371.0 (x) Mild Mental Retardation**
>
> Mild Mental Retardation is roughly equivalent to the educational category "educable." This group makes up the largest segment of those with the disorder—about 80%. Individuals with this level of Mental Retardation can develop social and communication skills during the preschool period (ages 0-5), have minimal impairment in sensorimotor areas, and often are not distinguishable from normal children until a later age. By their late teens they can learn academic skills up to approximately the sixth-grade level; and during the adult years, they can usually achieve social and vocational skills adequate for minimum self-support but may need guidance and assistance when under unusual social or economic stress.
>
> **318.0 (x) Moderate Mental Retardation**
>
> Moderate Mental Retardation is roughly equivalent to the educational category of "trainable." This group makes up 12% of the entire population of individuals with Mental Retardation. Those with this level of Mental Retardation during the preschool period can talk or learn to communicate, but they have only poor awareness of social conventions. They may profit from vocational training and can take care of themselves with moderate supervision. During the school-age period, they can profit from training in social and occupational skills, but are

or in early infancy, and traceable to specific organic causes and/or associated with identifiable physical deficiencies. Others — including lesser degrees of mental retardation and other milder "developmental disabilities" — may not be detected until the early school years or even until adolescence, may have no known specific biological cause, and may be identified primarily by the symptom of substandard "adaptive functioning." Nonetheless, these impairments (like severe mental retardation) are measurable by sociological ("intelligence") tests of reasonable reliability,[43] and their organic causes — including genetic factors and environmentally caused biological factors such as brain damage resulting from trauma or malnutrition — are accepted as at least contributory to the disability. Yet other biologically rooted disabilities, such as the various "organic brain disorders" or "organic brain syndromes," may be characterized by more sudden onset or by development relatively late in life, including impairments such as degenerative dementia which are often associated with old age.

The main problem these organic disabilities pose is not diagnosis or identification but how to respond. What can or should be done about persons who suffer from such impairments, what is the nature and extent of societal responsibility for them, and what habilitation or rehabilitation model is most appropriate? What role should the law play in facilitating treatment, training, and protection of such persons or in promoting their varying potentials for functioning independently? The modern history of society's approach to the mentally retarded reveals the range of answers given to these questions and of the shifts in public as well as professional attitudes toward the disabled.

Following a brief period of humanitarian concern, sparked by the work of the French psychiatrist Jean-Marc Gaspard Itard at the beginning of the nineteenth century, the societal response to the problem of mental retardation took on an increasingly negative, even destructive character.[44] Mentally retarded persons came to be seen primarily as a menace, in terms of both the effects of their presence in the community and the threat they were thought to pose to the "purity of the race." Based on an overestimation of their criminal propensities and their reproductive tendencies, an almost exclusive emphasis came to be placed on the policy of isolating the retarded from the community so as to keep them from harming others and on measures that would prevent them from further "polluting" the race with defective offspring.[45]

Remnants of this isolation/containment approach survive today, but they have in significant respects been replaced by approaches that are more benign. These new response models are not without their own drawbacks, however. They include the approach toward the retarded as objects of pity, as suffering individuals who must be protected and nurtured; the perception of them as eternal children who must be kept happy; and the notion that they are sick and therefore in need of medical treatment and hospitalization.[46] Writers have commented on the destructive paternalism inherent in these approaches, which robs mentally retarded persons of the respect and dignity they deserve as full human beings and of the education and training opportunities that many of them can benefit from.[47]

Recognition of the receptivity of many mentally retarded persons to education and training has formed the basis for the most recent response model, the developmental approach. First articulated in the 1960s,[48] this approach has during the 1970s made tremendous inroads into the traditional methods of dealing with mental retardation. It views custodial care in large institutions as inappropriate for the majority of retarded persons, who instead should be cared for in the community or family setting. The emphasis of this approach is on teaching and training the retarded to allow them to achieve their full developmental potential. The opera-

---

unlikely to progress beyond the second-grade level in academic subjects. They may learn to travel alone in familiar places. During their adult years they may be able to contribute to their own support by performing unskilled or semiskilled work under close supervision in sheltered workshops. They need supervision and guidance when under mild social or economic stress.

318.1 (x) Severe Mental Retardation

This group makes up 7% of individuals with Mental Retardation. During the preschool period there is evidence of poor motor development and minimal speech, and they develop little or no communicative speech. During the school-age period, they may learn to talk and can be trained in elementary hygiene skills. They are generally unable to profit from vocational training. During their adult years they may be able to perform simple work tasks under close supervision.

318.2 (x) Profound Mental Retardation

This group constitutes less than 1% of individuals with Mental Retardation. During the preschool period these children display minimal capacity for sensorimotor functioning. A highly structured environment, with constant aid and supervision, is required. During the school-age period, some further motor development may occur and the children may respond to minimal or limited training in self-care. Some speech and further motor development may take place during the adult years, and very limited self-care may be possible, in a highly structured environment with constant aid and supervision.

43. See note 42 *supra*. There has been much criticism of the alleged cultural bias in these intelligence tests.

44. See Mason, Menolascino, & Galvin, Mental Health: The Right to Treatment for Mentally Retarded Citizens: An Evolving Legal and Scientific Interface, 10 Creighton L. Rev. 124, 127 (1976).

45. See Roos, Basic Facts About Mental Retardation, *in* 1 Legal Rights of the Mentally Handicapped 17 (Criminal Law and Urban Problems Course Handbook, No. 57) (B.J. Ennis, P.R. Friedman, & B. Gitlin eds. 1973).

46. Roos, *supra* note 45, at 21-22.

47. *Id.* at 22.

48. The work most often associated with the articulation of this approach is W. Wolfensberger, B. Nirje, S. Olshansky, R. Perske, & P. Roos, The Principle of Normalization in Human Services (1972).

tive words are "normalization" and "mainstreaming," the goals of which are to permit achievement of a maximum level of independence and self-sufficiency for individuals who otherwise would be left in perpetual bondage to their undeveloped living skills. Part of the promise of this approach is that the economic costs involved in providing such training and education services, which are heavy indeed, will be substantially offset by the savings that are anticipated to result from the elimination of expensive institutional care and by the contributions the beneficiaries of these programs are expected to make to society. While perhaps not quite the panacea that its advocates would have it be, the "communalization"/ "deinstitutionalization" approach shows evidence of having indeed improved the lot of many mentally retarded individuals.

C. Mental Illness, or the Psychological Disabilities

Mental illness — in all its variegated forms and shifting diagnostic labels and its close though continually changing association with various types of social deviancy, substance dependency, or "alternative" lifestyles — poses difficulties in developing a proper societal response which are even greater than those that must be confronted in dealing with developmental disabilities.[49] In the absence of clear or presently known organic bases for the "illness" (true of most, though not all, mental illness categories), the capacity to formulate objective and reliable diagnostic, prognostic, and treatment models is greatly reduced.[50] Developing evidence of the relevance of biochemical variables — neurological or metabolic — in the identification of some of the major mental illnesses imparts only marginally greater certainty given the continuing lack of firm knowledge of the causal role or the contributive weight of any one of these variables in the totality of genetic indicators and interactive environmental forces.[51] The uncertainties as to cause or origin are compounded by the fact that some mental illnesses have an element of the self-induced or the self-willed.[52] Some mental illness behavior — particularly among the institutionalized — is clearly "learned" behavior.[53] Other symptoms are readily feigned and not easily distinguished from the "true" products of pathology.[54] In yet other instances, the symptoms of illness are situational responses that, while perhaps difficult to view as proper or normal, may nonetheless be essentially reparative rather than disintegrative — that is, they may be steps toward restoration and adjustment.[55] These complexities accentuate the difficulty of providing adequate answers to questions about treatment and treatability, about the efficacy of psychiatric theory and practice, and about the proper role and authority of mental health professionals in both clinical and forensic situations. They also raise fundamental questions about the law's role in compelling treatment, in assessing an alleged mentally ill person's capacity to handle his civil and domestic affairs, and — in cases involving criminal behavior — in determining the offender's capacity to participate in the trial and his legal responsibility for the offense charged.

1. Propriety of the Medical Model

Some commentators reject altogether the appropriateness of the medical model, the health-disease conception of psychological disorders and emotional problems. One of the main exponents of this rejectionist position is Thomas Szasz, a psychiatrist.[56] In his view there

49. Formulating the proper response to persons who suffer from both mental retardation and mental illness — a large group — is perhaps most problematic of all, particularly now that the laws in most states mandate separate treatment of the developmentally disabled and the mentally ill. See Carter v. State, 611 S.W.2d 165 (Tex. Civ. App. 1981); *In re* Steinhiser, 424 A.2d 1006 (Pa. Commw. Ct. 1981).

50. The uncertainties inherent in psychiatric diagnosis and treatment were well articulated by the United States Supreme Court in the recent case of Addington v. Texas, 441 U.S. 418, 430 (1979):

> The subtleties and nuances of psychiatric diagnosis render certainties virtually beyond reach in most situations. . . . Psychiatric diagnosis . . . is to a large extent based on medical "impressions" drawn from subjective analysis and filtered through the experience of the diagnostician. This process often makes it very difficult for the expert physician to offer definite conclusions about any particular patient.

The point is made more flippantly in the well-known popular cynicism describing psychotherapy as an undefined technique applied to unspecified cases with unpredictable results.

51. See generally A.M. Freedman, H.I. Kaplan, & H.S. Kaplan, Comprehensive Textbook of Psychiatry (1967); particularly, H. Weiner on the etiology of schizophrenia (at 603). Also, R.L. Spitzer & D.F. Klein, Critical Issues in Psychiatric Diagnosis (1978), esp. Fink, EEG Response Strategies in Psychiatric Diagnosis, at 253, and R.W. Cowdry & F.K. Goodwin, Amine Neurotransmitter Studies and Psychiatric Illness: Toward More Meaningful Diagnosis Concepts, at 281.

52. This would be particularly true of the substance dependencies, but the idea that mental illness behavior has "voluntary" aspects extends to many other psychological disorders and symptoms.

53. The pressure to behave as a "mental *patient*" is explored in E. Goffman, Asylums: Essays on the Social Situation of Mental Patients and Other Inmates (1961). There are other aspects to learned mental illness behavior in and outside institutions which suggest the existence of a behavioral subculture influencing the "presentations" of persons with mental or emotional problems. Such adaptive or maladaptive behavior is not confined to mental patients. Persons with chronic physical disabilities or diseases, whether hospitalized or not, also exhibit adaptive or compensatory behavior patterns.

54. See Rosenhan, On Being Sane in Insane Places, Science, Jan. 19, 1973, at 250. The article reports on an experiment showing the willingness of psychiatrists to admit to their hospitals persons with feigned symptoms of mental illness, which is used as evidence of the inability of psychiatrists to make a proper determination of the presence or absence of such illness. The motivation to feign mental illness (apart from trying to impugn psychiatry) arises in serious criminal cases where the consequences of standing trial and being convicted are judged by the defendant (or his lawyer) to be worse than those resulting from a finding of incompetency to stand trial or not-guilty-by-reason-of-insanity.

55. See, e.g., R.D. Laing, The Politics of Experience (1967).

56. See, e.g., T.S. Szasz, The Myth of Mental Illness: Foundations of a Theory of Personal Conduct (rev. ed. 1974); *id.*, Ideology and Insanity: Essays on the Psychiatric Dehumanization of Man (1970).

really is no such thing as mental illness. The designation of mental or emotional problems as "disease" is said to be only a metaphor, convenient and authority conferring for those whose profession it is to practice various interventions in the lives of persons who have such problems but bereft of literal meaning and, worse, potentially damaging to those to whom the disease label is applied. According to Szasz, "mentally ill" persons are merely persons who have problems in living (more conspicuous perhaps than run-of-the-mill difficulties or maladjustments but different only in that respect), who are out of step, who are deviant, or who make us feel uncomfortable. Szasz does not deny that these persons may need or want help, nor does he reject the notion that psychotherapy, responsibly practiced and cognizant of its limits, can be helpful. Rather, what he is arguing against is coercive psychiatry, particularly coerced institutional psychiatry—that is, involuntary commitment. We ought not presume to help or treat against their will persons who do not acknowledge that they have problems in living, those who do not recognize that they need treatment, or those who do not want help. The designation of these problems in living as illness, in Szasz's view, serves only to aggrandize the psychiatrist and to give him the coercive power over "patients" that is commonly accorded to medical practitioners who deal with physical illness. Indeed, it confers *more* power than that possessed by regular physicians, for whereas persons with physical ailments generally know of their afflictions, the person who is mentally ill can be assumed to lack the capacity to recognize his mental ailments and to make his own decisions.

Szasz's position is an extreme one, and while widely known, it is not widely shared. Except as a challenge to the complacencies in rhetoric and practice that sometimes threaten to discredit conventional psychiatry, it is not a useful perspective. Whether the rhetoric of disease is applied or not, the personal problems remain as does the need to deal with them with considerable resources and all the wisdom at society's disposal. The question of society's right to engage in interventions in the lives of persons who may not want them is not unique to the mental health field and must ultimately be addressed regardless of whether one accepts or rejects the mental illness metaphor.

2. Mixed Models, Multiple Criteria, and the Role of Psychiatry and Law

Most people who have regular professional contact with the "mentally ill" or who have personally experienced the mental disintegration of a close friend or relative appreciate the reality of psychopathology as a process qualitatively distinct from ordinary attempts to cope with the problems of life. Such an appreciation does not imply a consensus on what mental illness "is" or on what the role of psychiatry and law might be in dealing with persons who exhibit psychopathological behavior patterns, but it does form the basis for formulating and refining psycholegal strategies aimed at saving such persons from the neglect or harm that was their lot in more primitive times, to which an unrelenting application of the modern rejectionist position might return us.

The decision to act on behalf of mentally ill persons does not require abandoning an appreciation of the fundamental ambiguity of the mental illness concept.[57] Even physical illness and health are relative concepts, dependent on changing norms and measurements. Are we measuring constant, enduring dysfunctions or momentary ones? A strong man with a bad cold is healthy according to the former criterion; sick by the latter.[58] In the context of identifying mental dysfunctions, this relativism is certainly (if not simply) more pronounced. There are multiple models and criteria that can be applied to the diagnostic enterprise, but the reference to some normative standard cannot be avoided. Whether the approach is statistical/general or clinical/individual, the designation of someone as mentally ill or healthy presupposes some adaptive norm. Under the former, it may be social or cultural expectation. Under the latter, mental health or illness may be measured against a whole host of more personal criteria: living up to one's functioning potential, the dominance of conscious over

57. The problems inherent in identifying and defining mental illness have been pointed out in many writings from a variety of perspectives. In addition to the major psychiatric treatises (*supra* note 51) and the more sociologically oriented work of Goffman, Laing, and Szasz (*supra* notes 53, 55, and 56, respectively), Jonas Robitscher's The Powers of Psychiatry (1980) offers a wide-ranging and insightful critique of psychiatry's claims to objectivity and authority. A selective list of earlier relevant studies includes: Albee, Emerging Concepts of Mental Illness and Models of Treatment: The Psychological Point of View, 125 Am. J. Psychiatry 870 (1969); Goldberg, Simple Models or Simple Processes? Some Research on Clinical Judgments, 23 Am. Psychologist 483 (1968); Katz, Cole, & Lowery, Studies of the Diagnostic Process: The Influence of Symptom Perception, Past Experience, and Ethnic Background on Diagnostic Decisions, 125 Am. J. Psychiatry 937 (1969); Livermore, Malmquist, & Meehl, On the Justifications for Civil Commitment, 117 U. Pa. L. Rev. 75 (1968); Sarbin, The Scientific Status of the Mental Illness Metaphor, *in* Changing Perspectives in Mental Illness 9 (S. Plog & R. Edgerton ed. 1969); Scheff, The Societal Reaction to Deviance: Ascriptive Elements in the Psychiatric Screening of Mental Patients in a Midwestern State, 11 Soc. Probs. 401 (1964); Scher, Expertise and the Post Hoc Judgment of Insanity or the Antegnostician and the Law, 57 Nw. U.L. Rev. 9 (1962-63); Soskin, Bias in Postdiction from Projective Tests, 49 J. Abnormal & Soc. Psychiatry 69 (1954); Zubin, Classification of Behavioral Disorders, 18 Ann. Rev. Psychology 375 (1967).

58. The illustration is found in Ruth Macklin's Mental Health and Mental Illness: Some Problems of Definition and Concept Formation, *in* Biomedical Ethics and the Law 123, 127 (J.M. Humber & R.F. Almeder eds. 1976), and is credited to M. Jahoda, Current Concepts of Positive Mental Health (1958). Macklin's article is a very useful summary of the varying and sometimes conflicting theories of mental illness and serves as the basis for some of the other points made in the above paragraph.

unconscious motivation for one's actions, the presence or absence of stress or pain in one's chosen lifestyle or living decisions, the ability to handle conflict "maturely," the presence or absence of symptoms of maladaptation, and various other standards of greater or lesser circularity and subjectivity. Is mental health simply the absence of mental illness or disease? Or is it more productive, as some theorists have suggested,[59] to view mental health and mental illness as noncorrelative concepts, as functional states represented by distinct continua rather than different points on the same continuum? Does that mean mental health and illness are mutually exclusive, or is everyone in a state of less than full mental health and no one wholly ill?

The organized psychiatric profession does not pretend to have dispositive answers to these questions, and many individual psychiatrists conduct their practice in full awareness of the conflicts and ambiguities inherent in the various theories about the nature of mental illness. Progress in diagnostic theory and clinical practice is not thereby foreclosed. The American Psychiatric Association recently produced the third edition of its *Diagnostic and Statistical Manual of Mental Disorders* (DSM-III),[60] giving ample recognition to the continuing uncertainties that are part of such an effort. The editors of the document emphasize the objective of maximizing its usefulness to clinicians of various theoretical orientations practicing in a variety of clinical settings. They acknowledge the element of compromise and trial and error in settling on a broad-ranging classification scheme. Finally, the need for continual revision and refinement of the document is made explicit in its characterization by the editors as "only one still frame in the ongoing process of attempting to better understand mental disorders."[61]

Similarly, much of the tremendous progress in the chemical treatment of mental illnesses—the so-called psychopharmacological revolution (see chapters 2 and 5 for details on this development)—has occurred despite major gaps in understanding the precise remedial processes: why the treatment works, what works, what is at work. Beyond the basic knowledge that certain mental disorders are associated with certain chemical imbalances in the affected persons and that certain drugs work toward restoring a balance, there still lies a vast unknown. And much of what is accomplished with drug treatment—including the development of new drugs or the specification of type and dosage by illness—continues to be based on ad hoc clinical experience and experimentation.

As psychiatry must proceed in the face of continuing uncertainties about the nature of mental disorder with theoretical refinement and clinical application of what is known, so must the law. The law cannot afford to wait for the attainment of a scientific certainty that may not be achievable in the first place, nor can it abandon its concern with society's treatment of mentally disabled persons based on an extreme, one-dimensional position that rejects the prevailing conceptions regarding the nature of mental illness. Formulating proper identification, classification, and response models for the widely varying types and degrees of mental disability is a continuing and multidimensional enterprise for both law and psychiatry. It is based not merely on clinical experience but also on political factors, on shifts in funding and other resource allocations, financial recovery or insurability of treatment services provided, humanitarian concerns, and even definitions of professional self-interest and authority.[62] There is nothing sinister about this. An appreciation of these realities will enable psychiatrists, lawyers, public officials, and laymen to get on with the task of helping persons whose mental problems put them in need of help and to proceed with realistic expectations and a healthy skepticism of professional or ideological excesses that serve only to divert from this task.

59. See Macklin, *supra* note 58, citing Jahoda.

60. *Supra* note 40. The DSM-III, published in 1980, was preceded by the DSM-II of 1968 and the DSM-I of 1952. Notwithstanding the contribution made by the DSM-III toward the diagnosis and understanding of mental disorders, the APA's effort remains open to serious criticism on a variety of fronts. Robitscher, *supra* note 57, spends much of his ammunition on the decision to exclude homosexuality from the range of mental disorders, if only because it exposes the lack of objectivity of the profession's earlier decision to have it included. At 175 he writes:

> Critics of psychiatry have argued . . . that since diseases can be created and eliminated by a vote of APA trustees, if a condition that had almost [*sic*] been considered pathological by almost all psychiatrists can by the stroke of the pen be made unpathological, then the underpinning of psychiatric classification had become dangerously loose.

And at 182:

> The two new principles of designating disease that the [APA] task force has imparted to psychiatry—that absence of guilt or feeling of conflict can determine that no illness is present, as does general social approval of a condition—justify the deletion of homosexuality, but they destroy the pretension that the nomenclature is objective.

A scathing critique of the APA's earlier classification scheme was delivered by Livermore, Malmquist, & Meehl, *supra* note 57, at 80 (notes omitted):

> One need only glance at the diagnostic manual of the American Psychiatric Association to learn what an elastic concept mental illness is. It ranges from the massive functional inhibition characteristic of one form of catatonic schizophrenia to those seemingly slight aberrancies associated with an unstable personality, but which are so close to conduct in which we all engage as to define the entire continuum involved. . . . And, because of the unavoidably ambiguous generalities in which the American Psychiatric Association describes its diagnostic categories, the diagnostician has the ability to shoehorn into the mentally diseased class almost any person he wishes, for whatever reason, to put there.

61. DSM-III, *supra* note 40, at 12.

62. See generally Robitscher, *supra* note 57, on the influence of political and other nonclinical factors in the formulation of a classification of mental disorders.

Samuel Jan Brakel

CHAPTER 2 *Involuntary Institutionalization*

I. INTRODUCTION

To the extent that institutionalization[1] is a legal controversy, involuntary commitment is for obvious reasons the crux of it. In its pure form, involuntary commitment presupposes a conflict between the interest of the state in institutionalizing an individual who is seen to require it and the individual who does not recognize this need. That the reality of "involuntary" commitment often deviates from this pure model should come as no suprise. Nor should it negate the legal preeminence of the involuntary process. Involuntary commitment has in many states today been supplanted by voluntary admission as the main route by which individuals enter mental institutions.[2] But the main legal battles—whether theoretical or practical, in the courts or in the legislative halls—are still waged over the involuntary process.

Procedures governing the involuntary institutionalization of persons with mental disabilities are almost entirely statutory,[3] though in recent years much of the impetus behind legislative refinement and reform of the commitment laws has come from the courts.[4] Abandoning what had been in effect a hands-off policy toward institutions and institutionalization laws, during the 1970s state and federal courts in an increasing number of jurisdictions became embroiled in litigation over commitment laws and the conditions in institutions to which individuals were being committed. Whole sections of state mental health codes were struck down as unconsti-

1. The previous editions of this book used the word *hospitalization,* but since this term refers primarily to treatment and confinement of mentally ill persons in mental hospitals, the broader term *institutionalization* is used to include commitment of populations such as developmentally disabled and retarded persons to "schools," "homes," "habilitation centers," and so on. The word *commitment* itself is disfavored in some circles as having criminal connotations, but it is used here because its substitutes are hardly more satisfactory. Finally, advocates for "the disabled" prefer to speak of "disabled persons," "mentally ill persons," "developmentally disabled persons," and so on for the reason that these designations are more personal and less demeaning. Because the symbol of these terminological preferences is of some importance, this edition generally accedes to them, using older terms only when use of the new terms (because of too much repetition, for example) would be awkward.

2. Nationally, in 1949, only some 10% of all admissions to state and county mental institutions were voluntary, the rest involuntary. By 1961, voluntary admissions had risen to 24%. In 1972, almost half (48.6%) of the admissions were on a voluntary basis, while the most recent provisional figures (unpublished computer printouts from the National Institute of Mental Health, Division of Biometry and Epidemiology, Survey and Reports Branch, dated 3 May 1983), documenting a 45.1% voluntary admission rate, seem to indicate a slight reversal in the trend. See ch. 3, Voluntary Admission, *infra* for full discussion and citations.

3. At common law the restraint of an insane person without legal process was justified as an exercise of the sovereign's police power, but the use of such restraint was limited to situations involving imminent danger to persons or property in the community. Christiansen v. Weston, 36 Ariz. 200, 284 P. 149 (1930); Bisgaard v. Duvall, 169 Iowa 711, 151 N.W. 1051 (1915); Look v. Dean, 108 Mass. 116 (1871); Keleher v. Putnam, 60 N.H. 30 (1880). Such arrangements left much to be desired. Individuals who exercised this right to restrain assumed the burden of proving the imminent necessity of restraint in the event that civil damage suits were filed against them. Crawford v. Brown, 321 Ill. 305, 151 N.E. 911 (1926); Maxwell v. Maxwell, 189 Iowa 7, 177 N.W. 541 (1920); Boesch v. Kick, 97 N.J.L. 92, 116 A. 796 (1922); Annot., 45 A.L.R. 1464 (1926); Annot., 10 A.L.R. 488 (1921). The common-law rule was codified shortly after the colonial period. For example, in 1788 the state of New York enacted a law permitting "any two or more justices of the peace to cause [persons furiously mad who would be dangerous to go abroad] to be apprehended and kept safely locked up in some secure place." 1788 N.Y. Laws ch. 31. The effective protection of the personal rights of the mentally ill, however, was to require additional legislation recognizing that confinement of such persons was incidental to and necessary for proper medical treatment. 1842 N.Y. Laws ch. 135, §§ 18-23.

4. Among the most important is a federal court case from the Eastern District of Wisconsin, Lessard v. Schmidt, 349 F. Supp. 1078 (E.D. Wis. 1972), *vacated and remanded on other grounds,* 414 U.S. 473 (1974). Also: Wyatt v. Stickney, 344 F. Supp. 373 (M.D. Ala. 1972) *aff'd sub nom.* Wyatt v. Aderholt, 503 F.2d 1305 (5th Cir. 1974); Lynch v. Baxley, 386 F. Supp. 378 (M.D. Ala. 1974); Suzuki v. Yuen, 617 F.2d 173 (9th Cir. 1980); Stamus v. Leonhardt, 414 F. Supp. 439 (S.D. Iowa 1976); Welsch v. Likins, 373 F. Supp. 487 (D. Minn. 1974); Dixon v. Weinberger, 405 F. Supp. 974 (D.D.C. 1975). The role of the United States Supreme Court has been a cautious one, reserved to sanctioning legal reform on comparatively narrow issues (Donaldson v. O'Connor, 422 U.S. 563 (1975); Addington v. Texas, 441 U.S. 418 (1979); Humphrey v. Cady, 405 U.S. 504 (1972); Jackson v. Indiana, 406 U.S. 715 (1972); Baxstrom v. Herold, 383 U.S. 107 (1966)), as opposed to the sweeping changes decreed in the foregoing lower federal court cases, or even as a brake on litigation-fostered reforms viewed as too radical or far reaching (Parham v. J.R., 442 U.S. 584 (1979); Pennhurst State School & Hosp. v. Halderman, 451 U.S. 1 (1981)).

tutional—sometimes repeatedly—and treatment facilities were ordered to upgrade general conditions and operations or in some instances to begin a phased process of depopulation, when not ordered to close outright.[5]

This chapter discusses the common patterns as well as the variations in the commitment laws of the 50 states and the District of Columbia, with a particular emphasis on the changes since publication of the last edition of this book 13 years ago. While the previous editions focused mainly on the laws relating to commitment of the mentally ill, this edition also gives significant attention to laws affecting a second group, the developmentally disabled or mentally deficient, and to laws affecting one subgroup of both, minors, for whom the commitment process shows significant differences both on paper and in practice. Commitment of alcoholics and drug addicts still receives only comparatively cursory treatment, with the basic statutory references contained in summary tables 2.3 and 2.10 at the end of this chapter.

II. HISTORICAL BACKGROUND

It is hard to trace the history of commitment legislation without repeating the development of legislation on mental disability as a whole, already sketched in some detail in chapter 1. The background offered here will thus be limited to facilitating an understanding of the present institutionalization laws in a somewhat larger context.

During the colonial period there were no statutes concerned with the commitment of mentally disabled persons. The violent and dangerously insane were handled under the authority of the sovereign's police powers.[6] At the time the first asylums[7] for the mentally ill were established, in the middle of the eighteenth century, and for about 100 years thereafter, the "commitment" of patients to these hospitals was effected with surprising ease and informality.[8] The request of a friend or relative—or perhaps even an enemy—to a member of the hospital staff for an order of admission would often suffice. The staff member might then hastily scribble a few words on a scrap of paper, and sign his name, and the procedure would be completed.[9]

The relative success of the humanitarian movement to secure decent care and treatment for the mentally ill in the third quarter of the nineteenth century served to emphasize the inadequacy of the existing commitment laws.[10] Crusades by Mrs. E.P.W. Packard, Dorothea Dix, and others spurred the enactment of commitment laws that specified the use of judicial procedures designed to guard against wrongful commitments.[11] The success of these earlier crusades is reflected in the almost single-minded concern with the possibility of wrongful commitment which characterized the legislative approach to the problems of the mentally ill up until two or three decades ago.

Since then, legal developments have come fast and in some instances have been so short-lived and of such a back-and-forth quality that it is hard to see where the proverbial pendulum is presently positioned. Are we in an era of reform or of backlash? What is the thrust of reform? Backlash against what? Following the preoccupation with wrongful commitment, legislative concern broadened to the questions of treatment and rehabilitation of mentally disabled persons and on how best to obtain effective medical care, custody, and training with the least obstacles to the caretakers and minimal trauma for the patients. Many of the state laws began to incorporate measures advocated by the medical profession, such as institutionalization by medical certification, on administrative authority, or through a guardian; the use of emergency procedures or other short-term or observational commitments dispensing with full judicial process; and the relaxation of traditional legal safeguards (for example, notice and presence at the hearing) even in judicial proceedings if it could be shown that observing them would be injurious to the prospective patient. Accompanying these substantive changes were also efforts to modernize the legal terminology of mental disability and make it less offensive.[12]

5. In Halderman v. Pennhurst State School & Hosp., 446 F. Supp. 1295 (E.D. Pa. 1977), e.g., the plaintiffs urged that the Pennhurst institution be closed; and the court, finding that large institutions such as Pennhurst could not provide adequate care, ordered the closing contingent on the prompt development of alternative community facilities. See also New York State Ass'n for Retarded Children, Inc. v. Carey, 393 F. Supp. 715 (E.D.N.Y. 1975); Evans v. Washington, 459 F. Supp. 483 (D.D.C. 1978); Wuori v. Zitnay, Civ. No. 75-80-SD, 2 MDLR 729 (D. Me. July 14, 1978); Wyatt v. Stickney, 344 F. Supp. 373 (M.D. Ala. 1972), *aff'd sub nom.* Wyatt v. Aderholt, 503 F.2d 1305 (5th Cir. 1974); Lessard v. Schmidt, 349 F. Supp. 1078 (E.D. Wis. 1972), *vacated and remanded on other grounds,* 414 U.S. 473 (1974); Welsch v. Likins, 373 F. Supp. 487 (D. Minn. 1974). Judicial interventions of comparable scope and depth have become commonplace in other institutional settings, e.g., prisons, as well. For some of the cases, the literature, and the legal theory, see Brakel, Special Masters in Institutional Litigation, 1979 A.B.F. Res. J. 543.

6. A. Deutsch, The Mentally Ill in America: A History of Their Care and Treatment from Colonial Times 419–20 (2d ed. 1949).

7. The term *hospital* was not in general use until after 1900. Until that time the terms *asylum, lunatic asylum,* or *insane asylum* were used. Council of State Governments, The Mental Health Programs of the Forty-Eight States 23 (1950).

8. Deutsch, *supra* note 6, at 62, 420.

9. *Id.* at 62.

10. Curran, Hospitalization of the Mentally Ill, 31 N.C.L. Rev. 274 (1952-53).

11. *Id.* at 276.

12. See notes 1 and 7 *supra.*

Not all of these legal changes were viewed with equal favor by all observers. The propriety, and indeed the constitutionality, of some of the newer commitment procedures were challenged almost from the start. The deference to medical judgment at both the commitment and the discharge stages was viewed by some as inappropriate in a process that could be viewed as social or legal as much as medical. And it was not long before the unchallenged preeminence of medical judgment *between* the entrance and the departure points— that is, within the institutions— came under attack. Early concerns over the most drastic of medical interventions into the personality, such as psychosurgery and electroshock treatment, ultimately grew to the supposition of a legal right to refuse all unwanted treatment. At the same time, but from the opposite perspective, came the push to recognize a legal right *to* treatment as the *sine qua non* for allowing the state to commit the individual against his will. Also coming under attack was the concept of indeterminate confinement, to be replaced by commitment for shorter, finite periods or at the least tempered by the requirement of periodic judicial or administrative review. The relaxation of due process protections in commitment procedures was met by a counter thrust to assert many or all of the safeguards applicable to criminal trials. And the criteria for commitment were drastically tightened in most states, reflecting renewed concern over inappropriate institutionalization and the view that commitment should be visited only on the most unfortunate, most helpless, or most dangerous few. Indeed, in some circles— medical as well as legal— the institutions themselves, typically large and geographically isolated, were viewed as at best anachronisms to be abandoned in favor of smaller, community-oriented treatment centers located in the community— and the sooner the better.

These counter trends probably reached their culmination in the mid-1970s.[13] Since that time, a good measure of legal concern has shifted to other newer areas. There is even sporadic evidence of a trend to counter the counter trends.[14] More tellingly, the amount of legal activity— both litigation and legislation— appears of late to have undergone a general leveling off, marking the beginnings of what may well turn into a steep decline in legal activity in the mental disability field, as we enter an era of decreasing social outlays generally and, in particular, drastic cutbacks in the support for legal resources to push new legal rights or protections for the disabled or the poor or to affirm old ones. In the next few sections we highlight some of the legal terrain over which the battles have been waged, and then go on to consider present-day procedures and provisions.

A. The State's Power to Commit

While the history of commitment laws and practices is long, this has not put the concept beyond debate or controversy. The abolition of involuntary institutionalization is advocated today in the relatively measured tones of respected authors writing for matchingly respectable publications as well as in strident statements in pamphlets put out by radical fringe groups.[15] The *Platform*

13. There has been an exponential growth in mental disability litigation over the past decade and matching increases in legislative activity. A lawyer's aide publication such as the *Mental and Physical Disability Law Reporter* (previously the *Mental Disability Law Reporter)* published by the American Bar Association regularly fills 100-200 pages of short summaries and commentary on new legal activity for each of its bimonthly issues. One need not necessarily share the view expressed in an early MDLR edition (2 MDLR 167 (1977)) that such a proliferation of law is an unmitigated good.

14. For a general discussion of fluctuation in the mental health laws see Appelbaum, Civil Commitment: Is the Pendulum Changing Direction?, 33 Hosp. & Community Psychiatry 703 (1982). Recent legislative changes in the state of Washington offer a prime example of the ever-changing trends and their practical effects. (Durham & Pierce, Beyond Deinstitutionalization: A Commitment Law in Evolution, 33 Hosp. & Community Psychiatry 216 (1982)). Washington's "modern" commitment statute, first enacted in 1959, allowed for commitment of a person if he was

> found to be suffering from psychosis or other disease impairing his mental health, and the symptoms of such disease are of a suicidal, homicidal or incendiary nature, or of such nature which would render such person dangerous to his own life or to the lives or property of others. . . .

(Wash. Rev. Code § 71.23.010 (Supp. 1972)). In a change consistent with the national trend at the time, Washington in 1973 revised its laws to accord greater protection to proposed mental patients. The Involuntary Treatment Act of 1973 limited commitment to a person who "as a result of a mental disorder presents a likelihood of serious harm to others or himself or is gravely disabled" (Wash. Rev. Code § 72.23.010 (Supp. 1982)). The act defined likelihood of serious harm to self as a tendency to suicide or self-mutilation. And behavior that caused harm or substantial risk of harm or that would place others in reasonable fear of harm was made the statutory ground for a conclusion of likelihood of serious harm to others. "Gravely disabled" was defined as being in danger of physical harm because of an inability to provide for one's own essential needs. Experience with the law, as reported by the investigators, soon showed that the new criteria neglected important segments of the mentally disabled population. Psychiatric ghettoes grew up in large cities, and many mentally disabled persons ended up in jails and prisons. Citizens' action groups composed largely of relatives of the mentally disabled pressured the state to provide care for these people. In 1979 Washington once again revised the Involuntary Treatment Act to include persons dangerous to property and to expand the scope of the "gravely disabled" criterion. Under the latest law, Washington is said to be able to reach more of those who really need treatment. However, the change threatens to result in the reemergence of an old problem— the overcrowding of the state's inpatient facilities.

15. Advocates for abolishing involuntary commitment base their position on a variety of rationales, ranging from the belief that there is really no such thing as mental illness, to the position that mental disability cannot be reliably diagnosed or treated, and to the view that existing facilities to which mentally disabled persons are committed are the last places where treatment or care is forthcoming. A corresponding variety of legal, constitutional, and moral arguments are used to bolster these positions. Chambers, Alternatives to Civil Commitment of the Mentally Ill: Practical Guides and Constitutional Imperatives, 70 Mich. L. Rev. 1107 (1972); B. Ennis, Prisoners of Psychiatry (1972); Ennis & Litwack, Psychiatry and the Presumption of Expertise: Flipping Coins in the Courtroom, 62 Calif. L. Rev. 693 (1974); Ferleger & Boyd, Anti-Institutionalization: The Promise of the *Pennhurst* Case, 31 Stan. L. Rev. 717 (1979); E. Goffman, Asylums: Essays on the Social Situation of Mental Patients and Other Inmates (1961); Hardisty, Mental Illness: A

Statement of the American Association for the Abolition of Involuntary Mental Hospitalization, Inc., issued in 1970, indicts the entire process as "resting on the use of state-supported force and fraud." At the same time, involuntary commitment has been defended with comparable vigor as not only benign but also necessary for those who, because of mental incompetence, fail to seek out the medical attention they need. Some of the legal doctrine supporting the state's power to commit is old, but new facts and new perspectives keep the issue open.

1. Parens Patriae *and the Police Power*

The state's power to commit individuals rests on the inherent attributes of sovereignty[16] and may be traced to two separate aspects of sovereign authority. One is the *parens patriae* (literally: father of the country) power that allows, and perhaps obligates, the sovereign to act for the protection of those who for reasons of mental disability, physical disability, old age, or unsupervised minority are unable to protect or care for themselves.[17] In exercising this protective authority over its "wards," the state may—where the ward's judgment is opposed, unavailing, or unreasonable—substitute its own best judgment. This power to decide on behalf of or even against the expressed wishes of the individual is premised on his incapacity to make sound decisions. The individual's decisional incompetency is thus the "threshold requirement"[18] for the state to invoke its parens patriae authority—a competent individual's refusal to seek treatment is "strictly a private concern and . . . beyond reach of *all* governmental power."[19] A second stricture on the power is that it be exercised in the best interests of the individual or—more circuitously—in accordance with what he would have decided had he been competent in his judgments. A balance must be struck among the basic liberty interest of the ward, his expressed wishes, and the level of care and treatment the state is able to provide through its institutions, counting also the considerable deprivations that may be part of the institutional treatment regimen.

The other doctrinal rationale for the state's authority to commit is in its inherent *police power*. While broad and extending to concern with the welfare of individuals (or their health, safety, and morals[20]—thus paralleling the parens patriae power), the essence of the police power is its authority to act in furtherance of the general welfare and the public safety. Rather than protect individuals from themselves or others, the police power tends to be invoked on behalf of society or societal interests *against* the individual. The police power is the power to isolate or confine the unfortunate, the undesirable, the contagious, the despicable, the noisome, or the dangerous (particularly the last group) for the benefit of the rest of us.

The so-called threshold requirement for invocation of the state's police power in the case of a mentally disabled individual who has not committed a crime is that individual's diminished capacity to conform his conduct to the requirements of the law or to the limits of social tolerance and his inability to appreciate the deterrent force of the law.[21] Otherwise there would be little legal basis for such preventive intervention, tenuous as the grounds are to act on the mere potential for dangerousness. Whether the potential for dangerous behavior is suffi-

---

Legal Fiction, 48 Wash. L. Rev. 735 (1973); R.D. Laing, The Politics of Experience (1967); Matteson, Involuntary Civil Commitment: The Inadequacy of Existing Procedural and Substantive Protections, 28 U.C.L.A. L. Rev. 906 (1981); K.S. Miller, Managing Madness: The Case Against Civil Commitment (1976); Morse, A Preference for Liberty: The Case Against Involuntary Commitment of the Mentally Disordered, 70 Calif. L. Rev. 54 (1982); Rosenhan, On Being Sane in Insane Places, 13 Santa Clara Law. 379 (1973); T.J. Scheff, Being Mentally Ill: A Sociological Theory (1966); *id.*, Medical Dominance: Psychoactive Drugs and Mental Health Policy, 19 Am. Behav. Scientist 299 (1976); T.S. Szasz, Law, Liberty, and Psychiatry: An Inquiry into the Social Uses of Mental Health Practices (1963); *id.*, The Manufacture of Madness: A Comparative Study of the Inquisition and the Mental Health Movement (1970); and *id.*, The Myth of Mental Illess: Foundations of a Theory of Personal Conduct (rev. ed. 1974).

16. In Anglo-Saxon law, the origins of this concept can be traced to the thirteenth century, when the statute *De Praerogativa Regis* was enacted. 17 Edw. 1, c. 9; 1 W. Holdsworth, A History of English Law 473 (7th ed. 1956); 2 F. Pollock & F.W. Maitland, The History of English Law 464 (2d ed. 1911).

17. See Hawaii v. Standard Oil Co., 405 U.S. 251, 257 (1972) (citing 3 W. Blackstone, Commentaries 47; Beverley's Case, 4 Co. 123b, 76 Eng. Rep. 1118 (K.B. 1603)). Two early American cases frequently cited in reference to the origins of the parens patriae power in this country are *In re* Barker, 2 Johns. Ch. 232 (N.Y. 1816), and Matter of Josiah Oakes, 8 Law Rep. 122 (Mass. 1845).

18. Developments in the Law: Civil Commitment of the Mentally Ill, 87 Harv. L. Rev. 1190, 1212 (1974) [hereinafter cited as Developments in the Law—Civil Commitment]. A.A. Stone, in his Mental Health and Law: A System in Transition (1975), lists the mentally disabled person's capacity to make the treatment decision as one of the five central criteria in the medical commitment model he proposes. Whether the law requires that the individual's incapacity must extend to the specific issue of his ability to make a decision relative to treatment is unclear. The recent trend in the state statutes is toward requiring such a specific finding before commitment may be ordered, but most states do not as yet premise commitment on it. The case law on the subject is uncertain. Lessard v. Schmidt, 349 F. Supp. 1078, 1094 (E.D. Wis. 1972), *vacated and remanded on other grounds*, 414 U.S. 473 (1974); *In re* Ballay, 482 F.2d 648, 659-60 (D.C. Cir. 1973); Winters v. Miller, 446 F.2d 65 (2d Cir.), *cert. denied*, 404 U.S. 985 (1971).

19. *In re* President & Directors of Georgetown College, Inc., 331 F.2d 1010, 1016 (D.C. Cir. 1964) (emphasis added).

20. E.g., Jacobson v. Massachusetts, 197 U.S. 11 (1905)—vaccination; Paris Adult Theatre I v. Slaton, 413 U.S. 49 (1973)—obscene materials; Everhardt v. City of New Orleans, 253 La. 285, 217 So. 2d 400 (1968), *appeal dismissed for want of jurisdiction*, 395 U.S. 212 (1969)—compulsory motorcycle helmets; *In re* President & Directors of Georgetown College, Inc., 331 F.2d 1010 (D.C. Cir. 1964)—blood transfusion over religious objection of Jehovah's Witness. See generally Developments in the Law—Civil Commitment, *supra* note 18, at 1222-25.

21. See Developments in the Law—Civil Commitments, *supra* note 18, at 1222-25. Minnesota *ex rel.* Pearson v. Probate Court, 309 U.S. 270 (1940).

cient to justify commitment is a question that involves weighing the magnitude of the harm that might occur against the probability that it will.[22] While perhaps not an essential prerequisite to commitment under the police power, the "treatability" of the condition that gives rise to the potential for harmful behavior provides added justification for the state's intervention.[23]

Legal controversy surrounds both the theory and the implementation of these sovereign powers. Invocation of the parens patriae power to commit a mentally disabled person can be criticized as presuming too much—that is, not only that the disabled person needs care or treatment but also that he has no ability, indeed no overriding right, to make the decision as to treatment himself.[24] Moreover, the judgment on whether the substituted decision to commit is in the disabled individual's best interest is not made easier by the persisting, if gradually closing, gaps in the medical knowledge that informs the treatment of mentally disabled persons[25] and the deficiencies in many of the public institutions where such treatment or care is sought to be provided. Indeed, it is largely in response to an awareness of these deficiencies that some of the newer legal rights and doctrines have been developed to protect the individual from the excesses of the state's benevolence.[26]

Questions concerning the police power are no less troublesome. Several are of constitutional stature, calling into play the due process and equal protection principles of the Fifth and Fourteenth Amendments and the prohibition against cruel and unusual punishment found in the Eighth. Preventive detention of those who *may* commit harm goes against the very foundation of Anglo-American criminal law and has been justified only for discretely defined populations (for example, in the context of the decision on bail, those charged with serious crime who on the additional overt evidence of repeated prior criminal conduct have demonstrated themselves to be among the poorest of risks for release into the community).[27] Studies of mentally disabled persons, though not uncontroverted, have tried to show that as a group they are no more dangerous than the general population[28] and, moreover, that identifying those few who are likely to do harm is a task to which the medical profession is demonstrably not equal.[29] Finally, laws that single out the mentally disabled as special targets of the state's police power have been attacked on grounds of vagueness (What is mental disability? Who is disabled?)[30] as well as for "punishing" individuals for a condition, an illness—a practice that has been held unconstitutional in a variety of contexts.[31]

22. Cross v. Harris, 418 F.2d 1095 (D.C. Cir. 1969); Millard v. Harris, 406 F.2d 964 (D.C. Cir. 1968); Sas v. Maryland, 295 F. Supp. 389 (D. Md. 1969) *aff'd sub nom.* Tippet v. Maryland, 436 F.2d 1153 (4th Cir. 1971); Director of Patuxent Inst. Daniels, 243 Md. 16, 221 A.2d 397, *cert. denied*, 385 U.S. 940 (1966). See also Dershowitz, Psychiatry in the Legal Process: A Knife That Cuts Both Ways, 4 Trial 29, 30 (1968), and Developments in the Law—Civil Commitment, *supra* note 18, at 1236-37.

23. Goldstein & Katz, Dangerousness and Mental Illness, Some Observations on the Decision to Release Persons Acquitted by Reason of Insanity, 70 Yale L. J. 225, 237 (1960); Developments in the Law—Civil Commitment, *supra* note 18, at 1231-32. See also Suggested Statute on Civil Commitment, 2 MDLR 128 (1977).

24. See note 18 *supra*.

25. The advances in medical technology also bring new risks for the patient. The long-term use of psychotropic drugs may produce side effects that in the worst of cases are severely disabling and irreversible. Evidence of these effects has played a major part in the growing recognition of the patient's right to *refuse* treatment. See Rogers v. Okin, 478 F. Supp. 1342 (D. Mass. 1979), *modified*, 634 F.2d 650 (1st Cir. 1980), *cert. granted*, 101 S. Ct. 1972 (1981), and Rennie v. Klein, 462 F. Supp. 1131 (D. N.J. 1978), *modified and remanded*, 653 F.2d 836 (3d Cir. 1981).

26. Among these are stricter substantive criteria for commitment, more procedural protections, recognition of the "rights" to treatment and to refuse it, legally mandated inquiries into the availability of treatment and the prospective patient's amenability to it, patient-specific treatment plans, and the search for the least restrictive form of treatment. Deinstitutionalization and preference for treatment in the community are general policies that are congruent with these new legal rights and requisites. The pages ahead provide some discussion of each of these developments.

27. See Foote, Comments on Preventive Detention, 23 J. Legal Educ. 48 (1970); Dershowitz, The Law of Dangerousness: Some Fictions About Predictions, 23 J. Legal Educ. 24 (1970). Also Dash v. Mitchell, 356 F. Supp. 1292 (D.D.C. 1972).

28. See Developments in the Law—Civil Commitment, *supra* note 18, at 1230, citing Steadman & Keveles, The Community Adjustment and Criminal Activity of the Baxstrom Patients: 1966-1970, 129 Am. J. Psychiatry 304 (1972); Chambers, *supra* note 15. More recent studies are: Steadman & Cocozza, Careers of the Criminally Insane: Excessive Social Control of Deviance (1974); Thornberry & Jacoby, The Criminally Insane: A Community Follow-up of Mentally Ill Offenders (1979). But see Brakel, Sampling the Mental Health Law Literature: Three Recent Books, 1981 A.B.F. Res. J. 535; Sosowsky, Crime and Violence Among Mental Patients Reconsidered in View of the New Legal Relationship Between the State and the Mentally Ill, 135 Am. J. Psychiatry 33 (1978); Zitrin, Hardesty, Burdock, & Dressman, Crime and Violence Among Mental Patients, 133 Am. J. Psychiatry 142 (1976).

29. See Dershowitz, *supra* note 22; Diamond, The Psychiatric Prediction of Dangerousness, 123 U. Pa. L. Rev. 439 (1975); Ennis & Litwack, *supra* note 15; Giovannoni & Gurel, Socially Disruptive Behavior of Ex-Mental Patients, 17 Archives Gen. Psychiatry 146 (1967); Rappeport & Lassen, Dangerousness—Arrest Rate Comparisons of Discharged Patients and the General Population, 121 Am. J. Psychiatry 776 (1965); Rubin, Prediction of Dangerousness in Mentally Ill Criminals, 27 Archives Gen. Psychiatry 397 (1972); Schreiber, Indeterminate Therapeutic Incarceration of Dangerous Criminals: Perspectives and Problems, 56 Va. L. Rev. 602 (1970); and the Steadman & Cocozza and Thornberry & Jacoby studies cited *supra* note 28.

30. Cf. Papachristou v. City of Jacksonville, 405 U.S. 156 (1972)—"disorderly persons" too vague; Fleuti v. Rosenberg, 302 F.2d 652 (9th Cir. 1969)—"psychopathic personality" too vague for purposes of deportation proceedings. But Minnesota *ex rel.* Pearson v. Probate Court, 309 U.S. 270 (1940), sustained a statute on confinement of sexual psychopaths.

31. E.g., Robinson v. California, 370 U.S. 660 (1962), holds that a person cannot be punished for being a narcotic addict. But Powell v. Texas, 392 U.S. 514 (1968), distinguished criminal proceedings against a person for the act of drinking from punishment for status of alcoholism. See also Comment, Right to Treatment for the Civilly Committed: A New Eighth Amendment Basis, 45 U. Chi. L. Rev. 731 (1978), arguing that confinement without treatment amounts to punishment for the status of being mentally ill and as such violates the prohibition against cruel and unusual punishment.

2. New Limitations on the State's Power to Commit

The perception that the parens patriae and police powers often overreached the goal of treating and protecting those mentally disabled persons who needed treatment or protection, or who needed to be isolated to protect others, led to a tightening of the criteria for identifying the "committable"[32] and to a proliferation of procedural "safeguards" that had to be observed in the commitment process.[33] By narrowing the targeted population and granting the individual an array of "defenses" against the state's commitment initiatives, only those who absolutely needed it would be institutionalized. Toward the same end came the development of new legal doctrine on which the exercise of the state's power would in effect be contingent: the extension to committed patients of a right to receive treatment in the institution (including requirements for an inquiry into the availability of treatment for the particular patient, his amenability to treatment, and the development of an individualized "service" plan) and, paradoxically, also a right to refuse treatment. A final contingency check on the state's commitment power came in the requirement that the state find the least restrictive treatment setting for those it elected to institutionalize.

We will get back to these new "rights" and requirements later in this chapter and in subsequent chapters on patients' rights. For now, we point out certain countervailing realities and arguments that may take some of the blush of progress off these latest efforts to circumscribe the state's power to commit.

3. Comments on the New Limitations

(a) The new commitment criteria □□ While designed to guard against needless commitment and the accompanying indignities, the "reform" of narrowing the commitment criteria to a point where today in 25 states only "dangerous" persons may be involuntarily institutionalized may produce at least four distinct negative effects. Some of these are already evident; on others, clear evidence is not yet in. The effects range from intensely practical—what happens to people?—to more philosophical—what about the integrity of the law? Most mentally disabled persons, like most others, are not "dangerous." Many do need professional treatment. But one quite common feature of their condition is their failure to recognize this need, or their inability to articulate or assert it in a way that would satisfy present legal standards. Many others may not be "gravely disabled" mentally, but they may through a combination of physical disability, poverty, social outcast status, or old age (and the unavailability of suitable noninstitutional alternatives) nonetheless be in need of the kind of care or shelter provided in mental institutions.[34] One apparent result of the tightened commitment standards is that persons who need to be institutionalized or at least sheltered are not. They are dying with their legal rights on.[35]

Another effect already being realized is increased use of the criminal justice process against mentally disabled persons who formerly would have been dealt with through civil channels.[36] Mentally disabled persons cause great stress and friction within their families and immediate communities; at some point they "act out" in a way that exceeds the tolerance of those around them, and then *something* must be done and *someone* must intervene. In too many instances today it is the police, or the prosecutor, who must intervene. Often enough, there is no need to fabricate legal grounds: some disorderly conduct, assault, or nuisance-type law will have been violated, at least technically. It is not difficult to pressure the marginal offender, once in jail, into signing a "voluntary" admission form for the mental institution. Or incompetency to stand trial may be invoked, or other

32. See this chapter § III, Who is Subject to Involuntary Institutionalization, *infra,* particularly as regards the rise to dominance of "dangerousness" in the commitment criteria.

33. The rights to notice, hearings ("probable cause" and full), and the assistance of counsel have been strengthened in most states. Other procedural "reforms" include extension of the privilege against self-incrimination, strict standards of proof and more of the burden on the state, the application of standard evidentiary rules in civil commitment proceedings, and the right to independent psychiatric examination. Details will be discussed in the sections ahead.

34. See A.D. Brooks, Law, Psychiatry, and the Mental Health System 719-25 (1974, 1980 Supp.), for the transcript of the Illinois case of Alice Kahn (fictional name). The discussion following this case (at 725) quotes Dr. Dale Cameron, superintendent of St. Elizabeths Hospital in Washington, D.C., as saying that "[o]nly 50% of the patients . . . hospitalized required hospitalization in a mental institution" and that particularly "for many older patients, the primary need was found to be for physical rather than psychiatric care" (quoting from Hearings Before the Subcommittee on St. Elizabeths Hospital of the House Comm. on Education and Labor, 88th Cong., 1st Sess., at 23-24 (1963)). See also Roth, Mental Health Commitment: The State of the Debate, 1980, 31 Hosp. & Community Psychiatry 385, 390 (1980); Bassuk & Gerson, Deinstitutionalization and Mental Health Services, 238 Sci. Am. 46 (1978).

35. This observation, slightly paraphrased, was first made by Darold Treffert. See Treffert, The Practical Limits of Patients' Rights *in* Diagnosis and Debate 227 (R.J. Bonnie ed. 1977). Stone, *supra* note 18, at 43, speaks of the"freedom to suffer outside an institution." See also note 14 *supra* on the Washington experience.

36. See Abramson, The Criminalization of Mentally Disordered-Behavior: Possible Side-Effect of a New Mental Health Law, 23 Hosp.Community Psychiatry 101 (1972); Bonovitz & Guy, Impact of Restrictive Civil Commitment Procedures on a Prison Psychiatric Service, 136 Am. J. Psychiatry 1045 (1979); Dickey, Incompetency and the Nondangerous Mentally Ill Client, 16 Crim. L. Bull. 22 (1980); Melick, Steadman, & Cocozza, The Medicalization of Criminal Behavior Among Mental Patients, 20 J. Health & Soc. Behav. 228 (1979); K.S. Miller, The Criminal Justice and Mental Health Systems: Conflict and Collusion (1980); Monahan,The Psychiatrization of Criminal Behavior: A Reply, 24 Hosp. & Community Psychiatry 105(1973); and Whitmer, From Hospitals to Jails: The Fate of California's Deinstitutionalized Mentally Ill, 50 Am. J. Orthopsychiatry 65 (1980).

less formal, sometimes extralegal, steps may be taken to reach the end result of admission to a mental facility. But is this preferable to civil commitment? Do the mentally disabled benefit? What does it do for the law enforcement system?

The resort to extralegal procedures, the need to stretch the law to achieve mental commitment that before could have been accomplished in more straightforward fashion, is one of the undesirable side effects of the new criteria.[37] As commitment laws become more unrealistic in the eyes of practitioners, there is increasing pressure to subvert in subtle and not so subtle ways both the commitment laws themselves and their alternatives, the criminal processes. While the purposeful evasion of legal "technicalities" that obstruct "legitimate" goals is nothing new, there is a price to be paid. Disrespect for the law is not new either, but we should be wary of fostering it.

Finally, the problem with the narrowed commitment standards is that they take away what is legally and perhaps morally the most compelling justification for state intervention in the lives of individuals—the benevolent, parens patriae motive to assist those who need it.[38] The paradox is that by winding ever tighter the legal circumscriptions around the power to commit, the legalists are confining its reach to a population, the dangerously mentally disabled, which is least distinguishable from the criminal population and to whom the application of preventive measures (detention) is legally most suspect.

(b) The new "due process" □□ The proliferation of procedural safeguards[39] surrounding the commitment process also has its disadvantages. Rather than discussing the precise reach or relevance of the rules of evidence, probable cause concepts, burden or standard of proof, the right against self-incrimination, jury, counsel, or what not, this discussion examines these protections as a whole in light of the way the commitment process works. The erection of these legal safeguards is based on at least two basic assumptions about "involuntary" commitment: (1) that without the safeguards people who do not belong in mental institutions will be railroaded there and (2) that involuntary commitment is a real contest between parties with opposite interests—the party who applies for institutionalization (the state, the institution, or the family) versus the individual who does not want to be institutionalized. It is the wholesale unreality of these assumptions that threatens to make their implements, the procedural safeguards, inapposite or worse. And once the procedures are enacted, their effects are difficult to avoid: the prospect of being able to apply them with proper selectivity only to those relatively few cases in which they are useful is dim, and the price of such selectivity, as mentioned, is high.

The real nature of the commitment process has been more accurately described by scholars such as Ralph Slovenko, who reports that "[a]pproximately two-thirds of [involuntarily] committed patients are passive, stuporous, or uncommunicative, or in perfect agreement with the physician's recommendation. The others protest initially, but after a few days of hospitalization they have a change of mind."[40] The real problem with institutionalization, according to Slovenko, is not the railroading of unwilling individuals but almost the op-

37. As a backlash against this experience, a few states, such as Washington, after operating only a few years with strict criteria have gone back to looser standards. See Durham & Pierce, *supra* note 14. The liberalization of the Washington law includes new provisions for revocation of conditional release and for permitting the spouse to testify against the person for whom commitment is sought. Also, Haupt & Ehrlich, The Impact of a New State Commitment Law on Psychiatric Patient Careers, 31 Hosp. & Community Psychiatry 745 (1980); Hiday, Reformed Commitment Procedures: An Empirical Study in the Courtroom, 11 Law & Soc'y Rev. 651 (1977); Luckey & Berman, Effects of a New Commitment Law on Involuntary Admissions and Service Utilization Patterns, 3 Law & Hum. Behav. 149 (1979).

38. Stone, *supra* note 18, sees the benevolent, parens patriae doctrine as the only legitimate theory for civil commitment. Those more skeptical of the doctrine remind us, in Lionel Trilling's words in *The Liberal Imagination*, that "we must be aware of the dangers which lie in our most generous wishes. Some paradox of our nature leads us, when once we have made our fellow men the objects of our enlightened interest, to go on to make them the objects of our pity, then of our wisdom, ultimately of our coercion." Lionel Trilling, The Liberal Imagination: Essays on Literature and Society 221 (1951). And in the words of John Stuart Mill in On Liberty,

> The only freedom which deserves the name, is that of pursuing our own good in our own way, so long as we do not attempt to deprive others of theirs, or impede their efforts to obtain it. Each is the proper guardian of his own health, whether bodily, or mental and spiritual. Mankind are greater gainers by suffering each to live as seems good to themselves, than by compelling each to live as seems good to the rest.

(*Quoted in* Note, The Due Process of Community Treatment of the Mentally Ill: A Case Study, 59 Tex. L. Rev. 1481 (1981)).

39. That the state's power must be invoked in a way that meets both substantive and procedural due process requirements is basic constitutional law. But precisely what these requirements are depends on what particular action is contemplated and what the situation demands (Morrissey v. Brewer, 408 U.S. 471 (1971)). The case of Mathews v. Eldridge, 424 U.S. 319, 335 (1975), involving termination of social security benefits, outlined three basic factors that must be considered in determining what due process requires: (1) the private interest that will be affected by the official action, (2) the risk of an erroneous deprivation of such interest through the procedures used, and the probable value, if any, of additional or substitute procedural safeguards, and (3) the government's interest, including the function involved and the fiscal and administrative burdens that the additional or substitute requirements would entail. The Mathews case is routinely cited in connection with due process in civil commitment, but where these three basic principles lead in the latter context remains wide open. See also Goldberg v. Kelly, 397 U.S. 254 (1969).

40. R. Slovenko, Psychiatry and Law 205 (1973). There are also patients, however, who come willingly (i.e., voluntarily) to the hospital first but then after a week or two when the worst of their anxiety has passed (though they may still be "ill" and in need of treatment) decide they want out. In a recent medical journal, such patients were described as an identifiable group of "revolving door type" patients who have slipped into a form of sociopathy that makes them unable to deal either with the freedom of life outside the hospital or with the dependency within it (Geller, The "Revolving Door": A Trap or A Life Style? 33 Hosp. & Community Psychiatry 388 (1982)).

posite. In 1971, for example, although around four million Americans received treatment for mental illness in state hospitals, general hospitals, outpatient clinics, and private offices, another two million were turned away because of the lack of treatment personnel to handle them.[41] From this perspective, the legalization and criminalization of civil commitment are an exercise in irrelevance at best. The procedure is dysfunctional—overprotective and overly technical when observed, a block to achieving generally desired results in some cases, mere wasteful and empty ritual in others. But most often, of course, it is simply not followed. Slovenko notes that commitment statutes are ignored for essentially two reasons: "they are overly complicated, and they are for the most part unnecessary."[42]

Psychiatrists have bemoaned their plight of being part of a "belegaled" profession. They have a case, and they are not alone in our belegaled society. Slovenko has written derisively of the "junk pile theory" of law:[43] among all the legal garbage that exists to address mental health problems there must be something of use or value. The same intricate legal structure surrounding commitment that is hailed by legal reformers as crowning testimony to the law's concern for the unprotected appears to the psychiatric practitioner and others as an unwieldy, obstructionist mass of procedural "junk" that only inhibits the effort to protect.

(c) The new treatment rights □□ Considerable emotion and energy have been spent in the debate over whether the right to treatment of a patient in a mental institution is a constitutional right or not, with the present weight of opinion being that, independent of other fundamental rights, it does not have such stature.[44] The United States Supreme Court has not recognized the existence of a general right of this sort, though it recently came close to doing so in a case involving a retarded person's more limited right to receive training that would rehabilitate him to the point where he could exercise his constitutional right to liberty.[45] Whatever its present constitutional status, the notion of a patient's right to treatment has grown from early tentative articulation in a few cases and legal journals in the 1960s[46] to a concept widely recognized today as fundamental by courts and state legislatures alike.[47] A large majority of states have specific statutory language that guarantees not only a general right to treatment but often also an "individualized" right, put in terms of the admitting hospital's obligation to formulate an "individualized treatment

41. Slovenko, *supra* note 40, at 222. See also Brooks, *supra* note 34, at 133 (1980 Supplement) to the effect that 25% of the referrals from community mental health centers to Atlanta Regional Hospital are rejected by the hospital's admission staff.

42. Slovenko, *supra* note 40, at 221. See also Stone, *supra* note 18, on the tremendous waste of resources involved in duplicating dysfunctional criminal procedures in civil commitment cases, particularly given the "failure" of the criminal process in dealing with its own targeted population. *Id.* at 59.

43. *Id.*

44. Rone v. Fireman, 473 F. Supp. 92, 119 (N.D. Ohio 1979), states that there is "no constitutional right to treatment existing by itself, separate and independent of the constitutional right to liberty." According to the court's logic, only those *involuntarily* committed for treatment have a right to "minimally adequate treatment." Those committed to protect themselves have only the right to such protection. And those committed to protect others need not be provided with treatment. How well this logic holds up in the real world is unclear. Do we even know who is committed for what particular purpose, by which of several distinct criteria? Some federal district and appellate courts have held that a constitutionally derived right to treatment does exist: Welsch v. Likins, 550 F.2d 1122 (8th Cir. 1977); Eckerhart v. Hensley, 475 F. Supp. 908 (W.D. Mo. 1979).

45. The Court held that the "respondent's liberty interests require the State to provide minimally adequate or reasonable training to ensure safety and freedom from undue restraint." Youngberg v. Romeo, 457 U.S. 307, 319 (1982). Also, Addington v. Texas, 441 U.S. 418 (1979), and Donaldson v. O'Connor, 422 U.S. 563 (1975), are sometimes cited as indirect support. However, Chief Justice Burger, in his concurring opinion in Donaldson, explicitly rejects the notion of a constitutional right to treatment, (see note 49 *infra*).

46. Morton Birnbaum may be said to be the "father" of the right to treatment idea: Birnbaum, The Right to Treatment, 46 A.B.A.J. 499 (1960); *id.*, Some Comments on "The Right to Treatment," 13 Archives Gen. Psychiatry 34 (1965). The first legal case recognizing the right was Rouse v. Cameron, 373 F.2d 451 (D.C. Cir. 1966). Judge Bazelon, the author of the *Rouse* opinion, based recognition of the right on statutory grounds (D.C. Code Ann. § 21-562 (1967), which states that a patient shall "be entitled to medical and psychiatric care and treatment"). The next most important right to treatment case is Wyatt v. Stickney, 325 F. Supp. 781 (M.D. Ala. 1971), 344 F. Supp. 373 (M.D. Ala. 1972), basing the right on constitutional grounds and extending its reach beyond the individual patient to provide a rationale for treatment standards to be applied to all hospital operations and all its patients.

47. Nason v. Superintendent of Bridgewater State Hosp., 353 Mass. 604, 233 N.E.2d 908 (1968); Application of D.D. 118, N.J. Super. 1, 285 A.2d 283 (App. Div. 1971); Whitree v. State, 56 Misc. 2d 693, 290 N.Y.S.2d 486 (Ct. Cl. 1968); Welsch v. Likins, 373 F. Supp. 487 (D. Minn. 1974). Cf. Jackson v. Indiana, 406 U.S. 715 (1972): person committed as incompetent to stand trial can be held only so long as continued commitment is justified by progress toward competency (through treatment?).

From language implying a general right to treatment such as in the old D.C. Code, *supra* note 46, relied on in Rouse v. Cameron, 373 F.2d 451 (D.C. Cir. 1966), the mental health statutes have moved to explicitly requiring specific treatment plans. Ill. Ann. Stat. ch. 91½, § 3-209 (Smith-Hurd Supp. 1981-82), for example, provides: "Within three days of admission. . . a treatment plan shall be prepared for each recipient of service and entered into his or her record. The plan shall include an assessment of the recipient's treatment needs, a description of the services recommended for treatment, the goals of each type of element of service, an anticipated timetable for the accomplishment of the goals, and a designation of the qualified professional responsible for the implementation of the plan."

Some of the by now extensive literature on the right to treatment includes: A Symposium: The Right to Treatment, 57 Geo. L. J. 673 (1969), with articles by Judge David L. Bazelon, Dale Cameron, Thomas S. Szasz, Morton Birnbaum, Charles R. Halpern, and Nicholas N. Kittrie, among others; and three articles in 36 U. Chi. L. Rev. 742, 755, 784 (1969): Bazelon's Implementing the Right to Treatment, Jay Katz's The Right to Treatment—An Enchanting Legal Fiction?, and Grant H. Morris's "Criminality" and the Right to Treatment. See also Twerski, Treating the Untreatable—A Critique of the Proposed Pennsylvania Right to Treatment Law, 9 Duquesne L. Rev. 220 (1970); Notes and Comments: Civil Restraint, Mental Illness, and the Right to Treatment, 77 Yale L. J. 87 (1967); Note, The Nascent Right to Treatment, 53 Va. L. Rev. 1134 (1967); and Comment, Due Process for All—Constitutional Standards for Involuntary Civil Commitment and Release, 34 U. Chi. L. Rev. 633 (1967).

plan" for each incoming patient.[48] The right to treatment is a basic concomitant of involuntary institutionalization: without it, much of the justification for state intervention in the lives of mentally disabled persons disappears.[49]

The patient's right to treatment while institutionalized is also important as a legal tool for working to improve the institutions. It is a good concept with which to fight the medical neglect in many of our large public facilities and to try to force individualized attention on patients whose problems in the aggregate often overwhelm an overburdened and undertrained staff. The statistic that the average public mental hospital patient receives the attention of a psychiatrist less than three minutes per day shows that there is ample room for improvement in the quality and quantity of treatment provided.[50] The problems with the right to treatment have come with the later development of what at least in the eyes of many institutional psychiatrists appear to be excessively interventionist and utopian (if not radical antipsychiatric) ideas and the proliferation of mental health lawyers and advocates anxious to derive a whole host of new and far-reaching legal assertions and remedies from it. And the right to treatment has been tarnished in juxtaposition to the newer right to refuse it,[51] leaving the psychiatrist in a "damned if he doesn't and damned if he does" position that threatens to paralyze institutional functioning, at immeasurable cost, of course, to the supposed beneficiaries of the right—the patients.

Wyatt v. Stickney,[52] a case in the federal court from Alabama, was the first in a series of cases litigated during the 1970s that took the right to treatment (or habilitation, the word applied to the retarded populations) as the basis for deep judicial intervention in the day-to-day administration of mental institutions and for the prescription of detailed operating procedures and standards.[53] Parallel to similar developments in other institutional contexts,[54] *Wyatt* and its progeny in the mental disability field[55] used findings of "noncompliance" with standards of treatment (set by the courts in the first place) to keep the litigation open for years and to place institutions and sometimes entire state mental health service systems in receivership. Special masters, monitors, or human rights committees were appointed to implement court-devised remedies to cure shortcomings in areas of relatively small significance such as patients' clothing and belongings, larger and more important matters such as room space, record keeping, staffing, and medical treatment, on up to the broadest of issues such as the total allocation of state funds to mental health and developmental services, the design of state admission and discharge criteria, and the reach of the least restrictive treatment concept—the last including orders for the state to phase out admissions to particular institutions and to embark on a general deinstitutionalization policy that would gradually (and sometimes not so gradually) abolish treatment in large facilities in favor of providing it in smaller community centers.

These interventions have generated serious questions about the role and capacity of the courts.[56] What must also be asked is what their impact has been on patients. The effect of judicially sponsored deinstitutionalization, a particular point of concern, is addressed in the next section.

(d) Less restrictive alternatives and the deinstitutionalization movement □□ The idea that patients should be treated in the setting that is least restrictive of their liberties has grown over the past decade into one of the key legal concepts in the mental disability field. It has been incorporated in the mental disability statutes of a large majority of states,[57] and it has been asserted in numerous court cases, at times in support of demands to revolutionize the entire structure of mental disability

48. For further details, see ch. 6, Treatment Rights, including table 6.1, *infra*.

49. It is difficult to justify assertion of the state's parens patriae power to help and care for the disabled when the implementation of this power is limited to confining them in institutions where no treatment is provided. See Stone, *supra* note 18, at 19, 43, 49. Of course there is still the police power rationale under which commitment for the protection of *others* is the rule. And it can be pointed out that voluntary patients have a lesser claim to treatment rights than involuntary patients. (See Rone v. Fireman, 473 F. Supp. 92 (N.D. Ohio 1979), discussed *supra* note 44). Chief Justice Burger has rejected what he called the quid pro quo argument for a right to treatment. He argued that providing treatment does not compensate an individual for deprivation of his constitutional right to liberty. The state must rely on its police power or parens patriae authority to justify deprivation of liberty, and in exercising these, it incurs no constitutional obligation to treat those whom it institutionalizes. (Donaldson v. O'Connor, 422 U.S. 563 (1975)).

50. Special Article Series: Civil Commitment, 2 MDLR 82 n.68 (1977).

51. See Rennie v. Klein, 462 F. Supp. 1131 (D.N.J. 1978), *modified and remanded*, 653 F.2d 836 (3d Cir. 1981); Rogers v. Okin, 478 F. Supp. 1342 (D. Mass. 1979), *modified*, 634 F.2d 650 (1st Cir. 1980); Mills v. Rogers, 457 U.S. 291 (1982).

52. Wyatt v. Stickney, 325 F. Supp. 781 (M.D. Ala. 1971), 344 F. Supp. 373 (M.D. Ala. 1972), *aff'd sub nom.* Wyatt v. Aderholt, 503 F.2d 1305 (5th Cir. 1974). See Conference Report, Wyatt v. Stickney: Retrospect and Prospect, 32 Hosp. & Community Psychiatry 123 (1981).

53. More recent examples of such intervention are: R.A.J. v. Miller, No. C-A-3-74-394-H (N.D. Tex., April 22, 1982), *summarized in* 6 MDLR 373 (1982); Association for Retarded Citizens of North Dakota v. Olson, 561 F. Supp. 95 (D.N.D. 1982); and Deckard v. Cerro Gordo County, No. 1-C81-3014, 6 MDLR 374 (N.D. Iowa, Sept. 8, 1982).

54. See Brakel, *supra* note 5; Turner, Establishing the Rule of Law in Prisons: A Manual for Prisoners' Rights Litigation, 23 Stan. L. Rev. 473 (1971); Note, Receivership as a Remedy in Civil Rights Cases, 24 Rutgers L. Rev. 115 (1969); Comment, The Environmental Court Proposal: Requiem, Analysis, and Counterproposal, 123 U. Pa. L. Rev. 676 (1975); Chayes, The Role of the Judge in Public Law Litigation, 89 Harv. L. Rev. 1281 (1976); D. L. Horowitz, The Courts and Social Policy (1970).

55. See cases cited in notes 4 & 5 *supra*.

56. See Brakel, *supra* note 5, at 562-63.

57. See tables 2.6 and 2.8, col. 8.

services.[58] Its origin is in a school teacher's case from Arkansas that reached the U.S. Supreme Court in 1959. *Shelton v. Tucker*[59] invalidated an Arkansas law requiring public school teachers, as a condition for employment, to disclose annually all the organizations to which they belonged or regularly contributed. The Court held that while the state had a legitimate interest in inquiring into the fitness and competency of its teachers, the requirement to disclose all affiliations was unconstitutionally broad and intrusive. The Court stated that there were "*less drastic means* for achieving the same basic purpose."[60] This doctrine was first transposed to the mental disability field (where its most common wording is "least restrictive alternative" — prototypically the alternative to institutionalization in a state mental facility) in *Lake v. Cameron*,[61] a 1966 case from the District of Columbia Circuit Court. It was reiterated three years later in another D.C. Circuit Court case, *Covington v. Harris*,[62] attained a peak of sorts during the mid- to late-1970s both in terms of the number of cases in which the doctrine was asserted and in the reach of its implications,[63] and came only a year or two ago to what by some interpretations is the end of its conceptual line in the United States Supreme Court's decision of *Pennhurst State School and Hospital v. Halderman*,[64] holding that whatever the value of the least restrictive institutionalization concept, Congress had not intended to force the states to implement it.[65]

The doctrine of least restrictive alternative has been applied to a number of settings or choices. In *In re Farrow*,[66] it was used in the sense of least restrictive legal status for admission. The court invalidated an order for involuntary commitment because there was no showing that the patient would not be willing to go the less restrictive route of voluntary admission.[67] It has been applied to the type of treatment, particularly medication, given to patients within the mental institution.[68] The theory here is that the patient is entitled to the treatment that is least intrusive of his personality or personal integrity. In other words, if the patient can be helped if not cured by psychotherapy, then there is no cause to resort to electroconvulsive treatment or psychosurgery. If there is helpful medication that does not cause temporary discomfort or permanent harm, then that should be used over drugs that do produce undesirable side effects for the patient. This, of course, is a gross oversimplification of the issue — it is rarely a matter of choosing between two equally viable treatment alternatives, one of which is excessively intrusive or harmful while the other is safe. More realistically, the problem for the doctor will be to weigh the efficacy but potential hazards of one form of treatment against no hope or the sharply reduced prospect of treatment success of the other. Or it is a matter of carefully controlling medication dosages in a setting where qualified supervisors are scarce, or one of slowly reducing a patient's dependency on medication without letting him slip back into psychosis. One of the more interesting ways in which the issue of alternative treatments has been framed was in *Guardianship of Roe*,[69] where the choice was presented to the patient as one between outpatient treatment while on a regimen of compulsory medication or, if no medication, involuntary institutionalization.[70]

Placement decisions made either at the judicial or administrative level typically call into play the least restrictive alternative concept, to the extent that a choice exists between or among institutions with varying levels of security, patient freedom, or geographic isolation. The

58. The least restrictive alternative concept is relied on heavily in cases such as Pennhurst State School & Hosp. v. Halderman, 451 U.S. 1 (1981), Halderman v. Pennhurst State School & Hosp., 446 F. Supp. 1295 (E.D. Pa. 1977), 612 F.2d 84 (1979), in which the plaintiffs among other things argued that institutionalization in large state institutions was per se unlawful and unconstitutional, the only effective remedy to which was a policy of community care.

59. 364 U.S. 479 (1960).

60. *Id.* at 488 (emphasis added). See also Southeastern Community College v. Davis, 442 U.S. 397 (1979).

61. 364 F.2d 657 (D.C. Cir. 1966).

62. 419 F.2d 617 (D.C. Cir. 1969).

63. See cases in notes 4 and 5 *supra* and a more recent decision, Kentucky Ass'n for Retarded Citizens v. Conn, 510 F. Supp. 1233 (W.D. Ky. 1980), upheld in Sixth Circuit, No. 80-3560, 6 MDLR 387 (6th Cir. Apr. 6, 1982).

64. 451 U.S. 1 (1981).

65. The full impact of the Court's decision in Pennhurst remains unclear. Some deinstitutionalization proponents take solace in what they view as the limited nature of the holding, emphasizing that the Court merely outlined the limits of the federal Developmentally Disabled Assistance and Bill of Rights Act, essentially a financial assistance program for the states, in terms of this legislation's power to force the states to embark on a wholesale deinstitutionalization policy. The decision, they say, in no way alters the states' own obligation to initiate such a policy and to develop community treatment alternatives with all deliberate speed. Reinstatement by the lower courts of major parts of the original *Pennhurst* order since the Supreme Court's ruling provide support for this view (see note 178 *infra* and accompanying discussion in text). On the other hand, it is difficult to dismiss the significance of the Supreme Court's unequivocal holding (451 U.S. 1, 2) that the federal law (let alone any implicit constitutional principle) "does not create in favor of the mentally retarded any substantive rights to 'appropriate treatment' in the 'least restrictive environment.'"

66. 255 S.E.2d 777 (N.C. Ct. App. 1979).

67. Along related lines, some state statutes today require that a prospective patient be informed of the voluntary admission alternative before involuntary proceedings can be begun. [Colo. Rev. Stat. § 27-10-107(1)(b) (1973)].

68. Rogers v. Okin, 478 F. Supp. 1342 (D. Mass. 1979), *modified*, 634 F.2d 650 (1st Cir. 1980); Mills v. Rogers, 457 U.S. 291 (1982); Rennie v. Klein, 462 F. Supp. 1131 (D.N.J. 1978), *modified and remanded*, 653 F.2d 836 (3d Cir. 1981).

69. 421 N.E.2d 40 (Mass. 1981).

70. See Ransohoff, Zachary, Gaynor, & Hargreaves, Measuring Restrictiveness of Psychiatric Care, 33 Hosp. & Community Psychiatry 361 (1982); Bachrach, Is the Least Restrictive Environment Always the Best? Sociological and Semantic Implications, 31 Hosp. & Community Psychiatry 97 (1980).

case of *Eubanks v. Clarke*[71] shows that the patient is entitled to certain procedural protections when the choice is made for him. The court in *Eubanks* held that due process entitles an involuntarily committed patient to a hearing before it is permissible to transfer him to a substantially more restrictive hospital.[72] But the most common use of the least restrictive alternative concept has been as a doctrinal argument in support of deinstitutionalization—outpatient treatment or placement in community centers instead of commitment to the large institutions.

The perception that deinstitutionalization too often amounts to a choice between institutional treatment and no treatment at all has prompted a backlash against that use of the least restrictive alternative concept.[73] There is considerable evidence today that the deinstitutionalization movement has not lived up to its promises and that the ideal of community treatment has resulted in the abandonment of many mentally disabled persons to virtually unsupervised, unprotected lives in flophouses located in dangerous or delapidated areas or even in "psychiatric ghettoes" that have sprung up in some of our larger cities. In rural areas, community treatment centers exist only in relatively few, widely spaced communities, provide limited services, and are often as wanting in the trained staff to patient ratio as the most criticized of large institutions.[74] As a result we are now beginning to see litigation where the right to treatment is being asserted in the opposite direction. In cases such as *Boarding Home Advocacy Team v. O'Bannon*[75] and *In re Borgogna,*[76] patients have challenged unwanted *de*institutionalization. In *Kruelle v. Biggs,*[77] the parents of a retarded child obtained a court order for full-time residential care where the state wanted to provide only a day program. Older cases,[78] seeking to assert the right to treatment in community facilities, can now be seen as early portents of the community treatment concept's shortcomings rather than as promises of a new treatment era. And perhaps behind the "congressional intent" rationale of the U.S. Supreme Court's decision in *Pennhurst*, disavowing that the federal statute creates a mandate for the states to deinstitutionalize their mentally disabled populations,[79] lurks the justices' view that deinstitutionalization as implemented has not matched the hopes of the concept's proponents.[80] The irony of the original least restrictive alternative case, *Lake v. Cameron,*[81] was that there turned out to be no alternative, and the patient, having been accorded an empty right, remained hospitalized for the remaining five years of her life. It is far from clear that the fate of a patient like Mrs. Lake would today be different, or if different, whether that would be to her benefit.

B. Substitute Decisions, Third-Party Commitments, and the Inaptness of the Voluntary-Involuntary Dichotomy

Discussion of the state's power to commit mentally disabled persons conveys the impression that it is the state that wants to commit. The word *commitment*—

71. Eubanks v. Clarke, 434 F. Supp. 1022 (E.D. Pa. 1977). Gerhard Mueller, of New York University's Criminal Law Education and Research Center, has proposed that no convicted person should be sentenced to prison without a hearing in which the burden of proof is on the prosecution to show that imprisonment is necessary (Slovenko, *supra* note 40, at 227 n.17).

72. This requirement is statutory today in Pennsylvania [Pa. Stat. Ann. tit. 50, § 7306(c) (Purdon Supp. 1983)] as well as in a few other states.

73. In medical circles there has been opposition from the start to the concept of least restrictive alternative as a legal inquiry. Brooks, *supra* note 34, at 733 reports that the American Psychiatric Association in 1967 went officially on record as opposed to lawyers or judges exploring treatment options: "all possibilities for securing adequate treatment should be explored. . . . Such exploration is the proper function of the family physician, the social agency, and the patient's family, and *not* of the court or the hospital" (emphasis added). For the APA's full statement, see Council of the American Psychiatric Association, Official Action: Position Statement on the Adequacy of Treatment, 123 Am. J. Psychiatry 1458 (1967).

74. Regarding the unfulfilled promise of deinstitutionalization, see Slovenko, The Past and Present of the Right to Treatment: A Slogan Gone Astray, 9 J. Psychiatry & L. 263 (1981). Among other indications, Slovenko cites the statistic that 13% of those discharged from state mental hospitals in New York were dead within two months. See also Winslow, Changing Trends in CMHCs: Keys to Survival in the Eighties, 33 Hosp. & Community Psychiatry 273 (1982), for a critique of the deinstitutionalization movement and for citations to some of the medical literature on this issue. Also, the third issue of the 1981 *Journal of Social Issues* is devoted to the topic with several articles and citations to studies attempting to measure the effects (the negative ones are emphasized) of deinstitutionalization. Also Langsley, The Community Mental Health Center: Does It Treat Patients?, 31 Hosp. & Community Psychiatry 815 (1980); Talbott, Deinstitutionalization: Avoiding the Disasters of the Past, 30 Hosp. & Community Psychiatry 621 (1979). It has been said that deinstitutionalization has been more successful for developmentally disabled persons than for the mentally ill. This may be because the problems of developmentally disabled persons—inadequate living and job skills—lend themselves better to remedial services provided in the community and to the remedial atmosphere of the community setting than the psychological adjustment problems of mentally ill persons. Because of this perception and other factors, advocates for the developmentally disabled have been more vigorous and more successful in assuring the establishment of community service alternatives than those lobbying on behalf of the mentally ill. See especially ch. 11, Rights and Entitlements in the Community, *infra*.

75. Boarding Home Advocacy Team v. O'Bannon, No. 81-2872 (3d Cir. filed Dec. 15, 1981).

76. 175 Cal. Rptr. 588 (Cal. Ct. App. 1981).

77. 489 F. Supp. 169 (D. Del. 1980).

78. E.g., Dixon v. Weinberger, 405 F. Supp. 974 (D.D.C. 1975).

79. Pennhurst State School & Hosp. v. Halderman, 451 U.S. 1 (1981).

80. See literature cited in note 74 *supra* and the APA position in note 73 *supra*. Similarly, Judge David Bazelon, a leader in revising mental health laws, has come to wonder whether the "benevolent purpose of deinstitutionalization will not itself be perverted into a justification for excessive neglect. Are back alleys any better than back wards?" (Bazelon, Institutionalization, Deinstitutionalization and the Adversary Process, 75 Colum. L. Rev. 897, 908 (1975), *cited in* Shah, Legal and Mental Health Systems Interactions: Major Developments and Research Needs, 4 Int'l J. L. & Psychiatry 219, 229 (1981)). See also J.A. Talbott The Death of the Asylum: A Critical Study of State Hospital Management, Services, and Care (1978).

81. 364 F.2d 657 (D.C. Cir. 1966).

even without but especially with the adjective *involuntary* preceding it—implies state force exerted against the will of the individual. Neither impression accurately reflects the reality of the commitment process—of who initiates it, whose interests are served, or what roles are played by whom. In the vast majority of involuntary *and* voluntary cases, it is the family or relatives who move toward, pressure for, or insist on commitment. If state law enforcement personnel are involved, it is as often as not at the request of the family or relatives, who are incapable or fearful of proceeding on their own. In many instances where it orders commitment, the state's judicial machinery merely formalizes and sanctions a decision arrived at by the family and the family doctor. In admitting a mentally disabled person to one of its institutions, the state often does no more than facilitate the provision of wanted treatment that is difficult or too costly to obtain otherwise. With respect to the commitment process, the patient himself, as mentioned,[82] may be confused or indifferent, generally agitated, unable to understand its necessity, or simply unable to comprehend. The phenomenon of a freely derived, fully conscious, voluntary decision to enter a mental facility (particularly a public facility) is as rare as knowing, overt resistance to involuntary commitment. In short, the voluntary-involuntary dichotomy of mental institutionalization, the traditional roles that are assigned to the participants in this dichotomized process, and many of the laws and procedures enacted to regulate it suffer from their irrelevance to most practical situations.

To bring the laws more in line with reality, some legislation has reinforced as a central principle the sanctioning or formalizing of substituted judgment, and the facilitation of treatment, for an individual who himself is incapable of deciding to obtain it. Today these "nonprotested admission" laws tend to be limited in application to special situations or special subgroups within the mentally disabled population. Also, they have been under unrelenting attack from those of the legalist persuasion who, until the recent U.S. Supreme Court decision in *Parham v. J. R.*,[83] seemed to have all but won the battle to "proceduralize" these laws to oblivion.

Commitment laws applicable to minors who are mentally disabled and to adults who have been found incompetent are exceptional in their deference to the judgment of caretakers—the parents for minors, and guardians for incompetent adults.[84] These laws dispense with many of the processes and procedures that are felt to be needed to save other mentally disabled persons from being wrongly committed—so much so that they are often classified as "voluntary" admission laws (a practice not followed in this text). The caretakers' judgment is treated as a substitute for the mentally disabled person's—what the latter, if capable, would have decided to be in his best interest. Thus up until recently the typical state statute on the commitment of minors simply provided that a minor may be admitted to a mental facility on application of the parent and approval of the facility director.[85] For adults, the California legislature in 1967 enacted the Lanterman-Petris-Short Act.[86] While on the one hand this law provided for detailed procedural protections and frequent legal review for the episodic patient, it offered on the other hand a new expedited alternative for the chronically disabled and the gravely ill, vesting the primary commitment authority in a conservator with the emphasis on finding proper institutional placement. A conservator appointed for such a "gravely disabled" person would be empowered to make a variety of decisions for his ward, including the decision to "volunteer" him for institutionalization. The purpose of this alternative approach was to focus the inquiry on the care and treatment needs of the severely disabled person, giving wide discretion to the individual appointed to look after his interests and not burdening the commitment decision with legal requirements extraneous to this purpose.[87]

Third-party commitment of minors without the procedural protections applied to other commitments has been held by several state and federal courts to be in violation of the minors' due process rights. Where these decisions have not outlawed the procedure altogether, they have prescribed stringent pre- and post-commitment procedures to minimize the chances and effects of wrongful institutionalization, including probable cause hearings to justify the initial detention, full hearings on the need for treatment shortly after admission, written notice, representation by counsel, and personal presence including the right to confront and cross-examine witnesses—virtually all the safeguards of regular judi-

82. See R. Slovenko, *supra* note 40 and accompanying text.

83. 442 U.S. 584 (1979).

84. The District of Columbia is one of the few jurisdictions that today provide for third-party-initiated nonprotested admission of any person (D.C. Code Ann. § 21-513 (1981)).

85. See this chapter § III D, Children and Minors with Mental Disabilities, *infra*.

86. Cal. Welf. & Inst. Code § 5000 (West Supp. 1981).

87. This result, at least partially achieved, has come in for severe criticism, for reasons including that it subverts the law's true objective of better protecting the gravely disabled. See Mitchell, The Objects of Our Wisdom and Our Coercion: Involuntary Guardianship for Incompetents, 52 S. Cal. L. Rev. 1405 (1979); Morris, Conservatorship for the "Gravely Disabled": California's Nondeclaration of Nonindependence, 15 San Diego L. Rev. 201 (1978); C.A.B. Warren, The Court of Last Resort: Mental Illness and the Law (1982); and *id.*, Involuntary Commitment for Mental Disorder: The Application of California's Lanterman-Petris-Short Act, 11 Law & Soc'y Rev. 629 (1977).

cial commitment.[88] The main cases against the California scheme of commitment by conservator under relaxed procedural requirements are *Estate of Roulet*[89] and *Doe v. Gallinot*,[90] holding that the individual's need for a conservator must be based on proof beyond a reasonable doubt that the individual is gravely disabled, that he is entitled to a jury trial and a unanimous verdict on the issue, and that when committed under these provisions he must yet be given a state-initiated probable cause hearing within 72 hours. The result of burdening the third-party commitment option for gravely disabled persons with these criminal process standards is, of course, to render it as "dysfunctional" as the reformers found traditional judicial commitment to be.

Bartley v. Kremens,[91] a case from Pennsylvania and one of the leading due-process-for-minors decisions, was ultimately consolidated (under the name *Secretary of Public Welfare v. Institutionalized Juveniles*)[92] with the Georgia case of *Parham v. J. R.*[93] on appeal to the United States Supreme Court. There, most of the procedural requirements were trimmed back again. The Supreme Court held that "voluntary" admission of minors on parental application with the final decision made by a neutral medical fact-finder, who could be a doctor at the admitting facility, was constitutionally adequate. Since the children's rights were sufficiently protected, particularly with periodic medical review mandated by the statutes, little would be gained in the Court's view by requiring an adversary judicial hearing. Despite this holding, the movement to limit substituted decision making persists, as reflected in recent lower federal and state court holdings that prescribe standards exceeding the *Parham* mandate[94] and in the continuing statutory trend to lower the age at which minors may themselves apply for voluntary admission and at which third-party "voluntary" commitments remain permissible.[95] Advocates involved in further litigation and legislation would do well to remind themselves of the complex nature of the commitment decision—the shared as well as the divergent interests, the difficulty of discerning and articulating what is in the mentally disabled person's best interests, and the risks attendant upon the decision not to treat or institutionalize as well as those that accompany institutionalization. And they would be well advised to see beyond mere labels ("voluntary," "involuntary"), legal slogans masquerading as relevant principle ("due process," "equal protection"), or adversarial perspectives (the hospital versus the patient, the parent versus the child) that fail to reflect the true relationships among the parties and only hinder the prospect of arriving at workable solutions to real problems.

III. WHO IS SUBJECT TO INVOLUNTARY INSTITUTIONALIZATION?

We have described the origins of the state's power to detain and institutionalize mentally disabled persons and depicted periodic attempts to limit or expand that power as a battle between the legalists and the more medically oriented in which one side might have the upper hand for a spell only to lose it and then, in a futile version of the social dialectic, gain it back again without ever reaching the desired synthesis.[96] And we have made passing reference to changes in the scope of the commitment laws—the identification and definition of who may be committed. The commitment "criteria" vary according to the type of legal procedure used, that is, judicial, administrative, or medical; its purpose, that is, emergency, observational, or extended; and the type of disability involved, that is, mental illness, mental deficiency (or as the more modern, broader term has it, developmental disability), and alcoholism or drug addiction. In this section, we analyze the standards for extended commitment through the courts, focusing on the statutory criteria (see tables 2.6 and 2.8) but with some attention to a growing body of case law.

A. Mentally Ill Persons

A court may order institutionalization of an individual only if it finds that he meets the criteria set out in the commitment statute. In addition to descriptions of personal condition,[97] these criteria today include a requirement that can be described as systemic, namely that institutionalization be the "least restrictive" mode of treatment available or some similarly worded proviso.[98] The personal criteria can be grouped under three headings,

88. See this chapter § III D, Children and Minors with Mental Disabilities, *infra*, and cases such as Bartley v. Kremens, 402 F. Supp. 1039 (E.D. Pa. 1975).

89. 590 P.2d 1, 152 Cal. Rptr. 425 (1979).

90. 486 F. Supp. 983 (C.D.. Cal. 1979).

91. 402 F. Supp. 1039 (E.D. Pa. 1975). Before its joinder with *Parham*, the case had been before the United States Supreme Court once previously, as Kremens v. Bartley, 431 U.S. 119 (1977), at which time it was remanded so that the class of plaintiffs could be properly redrawn.

92. 442 U.S. 640 (1979).

93. 442 U.S. 584 (1979).

94. *In re* S.C., 421 A.2d 853 (Pa. Super. Ct. 1980); Doe v. Doe, 385 N.E.2d 995 (Mass. 1979); Johnson v. Solomon, 484 F. Supp. 278 (D. Md. 1979); D.C. v. Surles, No. 78-91, 4 MDLR 169 (D. Vt. Dec. 21, 1979). And in Lippmann v. Johnson, 429 N.E.2d 167 (Ohio Ct. App. 1980) a young man found incompetent and "voluntarily" admitted by his mother/guardian was found to have the right to seek release.

95. E.g., 14 years or over, Vt. Stat. Ann. tit. 18, § 7503 (Supp. 1981).

96. See note 14 *supra*.

97. See table 2.6, cols. 4, 5, & 6. These criteria must appear in the petition to commit as allegations to be proved in court.

98. See table 2.6, cols. 7 & 8.

elements of which are found in the statutes of virtually every state: that the individual be (1) dangerous to himself or others, (2) unable to provide for his basic needs, and (3) mentally ill.

The state statutes vary according to which of the three main personal criteria are included and whether they are formulated as alternatives, making each one alone a sufficient ground for commitment, or whether two or three together must be found. Mental illness is the base condition in most states, the common denominator that together with one or both of the other personal criteria warrants hospitalization. That is, the dangerousness or inability to care for the self must be *the result* of mental illness. This is no departure from the way the statutes have read for years. The problem is that "mental illness" is often defined circularly as being the condition for which there is a need for treatment or as the equivalent of one or more of the other commitment criteria.[99] The most significant change in the judicial commitment criteria over the past decade has been the rise of "dangerous" to most prominent. It is found today in the provisions of all but one (New Jersey) of the states that have judicial commitment, whereas in 1970 almost half did not include it.[100] Where dangerousness is a necessary condition for commitment, as it is in some 25 states, it raises the aforementioned question of whether the statutes are too tightly drawn to reach those who need institutionalization and to keep the integrity of the law reasonably intact.[101] In other states, where dangerousness is only an alternative to one or two other primary grounds for commitment, this is less of a problem. "Dangerous to self or others" is the prevailing formulation. The relevant California provision narrows the criterion to dangerous to others only, which makes sense if for no other reason than that danger to self is too readily interpreted as the equivalent of criteria such as inability to care for oneself.[102] Arkansas, in a very direct formulation, provides that the individual must be homicidal or suicidal.[103] Several other states stipulate that there must be a recent overt act to indicate dangerousness.[104] At least one state statute, Tennessee's,[105] speaks in terms of the "*likelihood*" that the individual will cause "serious harm," which is a prospective rather than present or retrospective finding.[106] Finally, several states include danger *to property* as a basis for hospitalization, a controversial and much litigated provision.[107]

"Unable to provide for basic needs" in many states today replaces the previously common formulation of "in need of treatment," which one surmises has been perceived as begging the commitment question too much. "Need of treatment" survives in only a few states and then not as a bare conclusion but with additional language that gives it content. In the provisions of the Arizona statute,[108] for example, a person may be alleged to be in need of treatment only "*because* he is, as a result of a mental disorder, a danger to self or others or gravely disabled." That last term, "gravely disabled," has gained considerable popularity in recent years and appears today in the judicial commitment statutes of at least nine states,[109] but always as an alternative or a complementary criterion to other commitment grounds, not as the sole ground. A finding of grave disability is the prerequisite in California's scheme of commitment by conservator, but it is not found in the state's judicial commitment law.[110]

The systemic conditions logically are phrased only as complementary to the personal ones. In other words, the court may order hospitalization only if it finds the person dangerous and/or disabled *and* if that is the least drastic form of treatment available. "Least restrictive" or "least drastic" alternative is the usual wording, but there are some wrinkles. Arizona, for instance, provides that there be "no available or appropriate alternatives to

99. See table 2.1.

100. In 1970, nine states did not have judicial commitment procedures. Today only four states (Maryland, Nebraska, New York, and South Dakota) still shy away from court-ordered commitment, operating instead on the "medical model" for commitment. Thus in New York, judicial review is possible only after the patient is hospitalized, at which point he, a friend, or a relative may at any time make a written request for a court hearing to seek release. See table 2.6.

101. See discussion this chapter § II A 3(a), The New Commitment Criteria, *supra*.

102. Cal. Welf. & Inst. Code § 5304 (West Supp. 1981).

103. Ark. Stat. Ann. § 59-1409 (Supp. 1981).

104. Ala. Code § 22-52-10(a)(3) (1975 & Supp. 1981); Ga. Code Ann. § 88-501(v)(1) (1979 & Supp. 1980); Neb. Rev. Stat. § 83-1009 (1976); Pa. Stat. Ann. tit. 50, § 7301(b)(2)(ii), (iii) (Purdon Supp. 1980); Wis. Stat. Ann. § 51.20(1)(a) (West Supp. 1981); and Wyo. Stat. § 25-3-112(k) (1977).

105. Tenn. Code Ann. § 33-604(d)(2) (Supp. 1981).

106. Predicting future dangerousness, as compared with assessing past or present dangerousness, is of course especially problematic. The American Psychiatric Association officially opposes psychiatric involvement in such predictions because of the lack of a medical or scientific basis and their general unreliability (Estelle v. Smith, 451 U.S. 454 (1981) (APA amicus brief)). See also Cocozza & Steadman, The Failure of Psychiatric Predictions of Dangerousness: Clear and Convincing Evidence, 29 Rutgers L. Rev. 1084 (1976); Monahan & Wexler, A Definite Maybe: Proof and Probability in Civil Commitment, 2 Law & Hum. Behav. 37 (1978). Simon & Cockerham, Civil Commitment, Burden of Proof, and Dangerous Acts: A Comparison of the Perspectives of Judges and Psychiatrists, 5 J. Psychiatry & L. 571 (1977). See also the literature cited in notes 27, 28, & 29 *supra*.

107. E.g., Suzuki v. Yuen, 617 F.2d 173 (9th Cir. 1980).

108. Ariz. Rev. Stat. Ann. § 36-533(A)(1) (Supp. 1983-84) (italics added).

109. Alaska Stat. § 47.30.735(c) (Supp. 1981); Ariz. Rev. Stat. Ann. § 36-540(A) (Supp. 1981); Ark. Stat. Ann. § 59-1409 (Supp. 1981); Colo. Rev. Stat. § 27-10-109(1)(a) (1973); Conn. Gen. Stat. Ann. § 17-178(c) (West Supp. 1981); Idaho Code § 66-329(k)(2) (Supp. 1981); Ind. Code Ann. § 16-14-9.1-10(d)(1) (Burns Supp. 1981); La. Rev. Stat. Ann. § 28:55(E) (West Supp. 1981); Nev. Rev. Stat. § 433A.310(1)(b) (1981); and Wash. Rev. Code Ann. § 71.05.280(4) (1975 & Supp. 1981).

110. Cal. Welf. & Inst. Code §§ 5304, 5350, 5358 (West 1972 & Supp. 1983).

court-ordered treatment."[111] The Maine statute provides not only that hospitalization be the "best available means for treatment" but also that the court approve the treatment plan designed for the patient by the hospital.[112] Several other state statutes provide more generally that treatment in the hospital be "adequate and appropriate."[113] And five states specify that judicial commitment (for relatively extended time) can be ordered only if preceded by short-term or observational treatment.[114]

Much of the inspiration for legislative change in the judicial commitment criteria has come from cases litigated in the federal and state courts, where a good part of the debate was first waged. For the requirement to find dangerousness as a necessary predicate for involuntary civil commitment of a person, the impetus has come from the highest level—the United States Supreme Court. While it has never held dangerousness to be an indispensable basis for civil commitment, the Court has used language in a couple of cases that provides indirect support. In *Humphrey v. Cady*,[115] a sex offender case from Wisconsin, the Court seemed to draw an analogy between confinement under the state's Sex Crimes Act and civil commitment and then, in words cited repeatedly since, implied approval of the requirement that such confinement be based on the "judgment that [the individual's] potential for doing harm, to himself or others, is great enough to justify such a massive curtailment of liberty."[116] *Donaldson v. O'Connor*[117] did involve civil commitment, but the dangerousness language used by the Court was stated in the negative and primarily in response to the claim of a right to treatment: "a State cannot constitutionally confine without more a nondangerous individual who is capable of surviving safely in freedom by himself or with the help of willing and responsible family members or friends."[118]

More substantial support has come from a number of landmark cases decided in the lower federal courts. *Lessard v. Schmidt*,[119] perhaps the most influential case of the 1970s in the number of issues it addressed and the scope of its holdings, posited as a prerequisite for civil commitment under the Wisconsin law the finding of "an extreme likelihood that if the person is not confined he will do immediate harm to himself or others."[120] *Colyar v. Third Judicial District Court for Salt Lake County*,[121] a case on the constitutionality of Utah's civil commitment law, went at least as far when it found inadequate the statutory reference to dangerousness as a ground for commitment *alternative* to need of care or treatment. A finding of dangerousness was a *necessary* element, according to the court. *Suzuki v. Yuen*,[122] a leading case on Hawaii's civil commitment statute, amended once already in response to earlier litigation[123] to require a showing of dangerousness "to self or others or to property," struck down the statute again because it failed to require that the danger be imminent and substantial and that it be shown by a recent overt act.[124]

111. Ariz. Rev. Stat. Ann. § 36-540(A) (Supp. 1983-84). This language appears to go to authority behind commitment. In § 36-533(A)(2), (3), which deals with what the petition must allege, the requirement is that there be no other "treatment alternatives which are appropriate or available" and that "the patient is unwilling to accept or incapable of accepting treatment voluntarily."

112. Me. Rev. Stat. Ann. tit. 34, § 2334(5)(A)(3) (1978). Some two-thirds of the states today have provisions making reference to individualized treatment plans, but they are usually located in sections of the codes dealing with treatment rights or patients' rights generally and they are not, like Maine's, part of the commitment scheme/criteria that require prior approval by the court. These treatment plan provisions, by assigning specific responsibility to the treatment staff, seek to assure that the patient, once hospitalized, receives adequate and specific medical attention. The provisions constitute an acknowledgment of the fact that patients come to the institutions with different problems and needs. In some states, the patient or his representative is entitled to participate in formulating the plan, and in this sense—consonant with their location in the codes—the planning provisions are linked to the least restrictive treatment concept and the patient's right to refuse (certain kinds of) treatment. (See ch. 6, Treatment Rights, and table 6.1 *infra* for more details on the individualized treatment concept.)

113. Mich Comp. Laws Ann. § 330.1470 (1980); Utah Code Ann. § 64-7-36(10)(e) (Supp. 1981); and Vt. Stat. Ann. tit. 18, § 7617(e) (Supp. 1981). La. Rev. Stat. Ann. § 28:55(E) (West Supp. 1981) requires "commitment to a designated treatment facility which is medically suitable."

114. Cal. Welf. & Inst. Code §§ 5150, 5213 & 5250 (West 1972); Mo. Code Ann. §§ 632.330(1), 632.305, 632.335 & 632.340 (1981); N.M. Stat. Ann. § 43-1-10, 11, 12 (1979); Tex. Rev. Civ. Stat. Ann. art. 5547-40 (Vernon 1958 & Supp. 1981); and Wash. Rev. Code Ann. § 71.05.280 (Supp. 1981).

115. 405 U.S. 504 (1972).

116. *Id.* at 509.

117. 422 U.S. 563 (1975).

118. *Id.* at 576.

119. Lessard v. Schmidt, 349 F. Supp. 1078 (E.D. Wis. 1972), *vacated and remanded on other grounds*, 414 U.S. 473 (1974).

120. *Id.* at 1093. In *In re* Seefeld, No. 454-225, 2 MDLR 363 (Wis. Cir. Ct. Milwaukee Co. Oct. 31, 1977—a sequel to Lessard—the Wisconsin statute enacted in response to that case (Wis. Stat. § 51.20(1)(a)(3)) was held unconstitutional. The *Seefeld* court found the failure of the new statute to include a clear dangerousness formulation to be in violation of a "gravely disabled" person's (i.e., a candidate for commitment) right to substantive due process. The statute's language referring to "very substantial risk of physical impairment or injury" did not, in the court's view, measure up to Lessard's requirement that the individual's dangerousness be proved beyond a reasonable doubt. Addington v. Texas, 441 U.S. 418 (1979) may in turn unsettle the *Seefeld* holding.

121. Colyar v. Third Judicial District Court for Salt Lake County, 469 F. Supp. 424 (D. Utah 1979). In *Ex parte* Webb, 625 S.W.2d 372 (Tex. Civ. App. 1981), the court held that proof of dangerousness was required by the wording of Texas's statute that a person could be committed "for his own welfare and protection or the protection of others." *Id.* at 372.

122. 617 F.2d 173 (9th Cir. 1980).

123. Suzuki v. Quisenberry, 411 F. Supp. 113 (D. Hawaii 1976).

124. Suzuki v. Yuen, 617 F.2d 173 (9th Cir. 1980). The court did not hold squarely that dangerousness to property was by itself an insufficient ground for civil commitment. It held rather that just as the dangerousness to persons criterion was inadequate for its failure to specify that the threat must be serious and immediate, so the property portion of the formulation fell short by allowing commitment for damage to *any* property regardless of its value or significance.

The issue of whether an "overt act" is required to demonstrate dangerousness is generally unsettled and complex. The *Lessard* case, heavily relied on in the *Suzuki* cases, found such a requirement to be constitutionally mandated.[125] But a number of state courts and at least one other federal court have disagreed.[126] One big question is: What constitutes an overt act? Will an overt *threat* to do harm suffice?[127] What about overt behavior that *invites* retaliatory harm from others?[128] What — to take the facts from yet another case — about a person whose overt *delusions* may predispose him to harm someone in misguided *self-defense*?[129] Also, how recent must the act (or evidence) be? One case has held that a sex offense committed as far as five years back was recent enough because the individual had been confined ever since and hence had had no opportunity to repeat such behavior or show that he could resist the impulse to repeat it.[130] Or, since the overt act requirement is essentially a procedural issue, a standard of proof, how does or should it relate to evidentiary requirements found in other parts of the commitment statute or addressed to different issues? In a jurisdiction where dangerousness or the grounds for commitment generally must be proved beyond a reasonable doubt, is an overt act requirement merely redundant? Is it, on the other hand, inconsistent in a state where the standard is a lesser "clear and convincing proof" or a mere "preponderance of the evidence?"[131] And what is the relationship between past harmful behavior and present or future dangerousness? If the relationship is one of "common sense," is there justification for medical testimony to prove dangerousness? If there is no scientifically established connection (either statistical or medical), do we still need "experts" to prove the point?[132]

Litigation and scholarly debate over these questions will certainly continue. We can merely raise the questions here. The precise effects, personal or systemic, of making dangerousness a necessary part of the proof that an individual is subject to commitment remain unknown,[133] and whether evidence of harm to *property* or the propensity to do it falls within the statutory or court-interpreted meaning of the term remains unresolved.[134] Questions also persist about the other two major criteria, mental illness and inability to provide for one's basic needs. Whether these terms in themselves have adequate content remains an open issue, with some cases holding that they are self-explanatory or that adequate meaning can be read into them upon application[135] and others concluding that they are unconstitutionally vague and uncertain.[136] In a very basic sense, these

125. Lessard v. Schmidt, 349 F. Supp. 1078 (E.D. Wis. 1972), *vacated and remanded on other grounds*, 414 U.S. 473 (1974).

126. See *In re* Janovitz, 82 Ill. App. 3d 916, 403 N.E.2d 583 (1980); *In re* Hernandez, 264 S.E.2d 780 (N.C. Ct. App. 1980); *In re* Gatson, 593 P.2d 423 (Kan. Ct. App. 1979); and United States *ex rel* Mathew v. Nelson, 461 F. Supp. 707 (N.D. Ill. 1978).

127. *In re* F. B., 615 P.2d 867 (Mont. 1980) holds that a threat suffices. Language in the Suzuki cases seems to support this view (see Suzuki v. Yuen, 617 F.2d 173, 178 (9th Cir. 1980), quoting a lower (district) court holding, 438 F. Supp. 1106, 1110 (D. Hawaii 1977), that speaks of "danger as evidenced by a recent overt act, attempt or threat.") The court found in *In re* Guffey, 283 S.E.2d 534 (N.C. Ct. App. 1981), that dangerousness must be based on a recent incident involving an attempt or threat of serious harm and a reasonable possibility of a reoccurrence of such an incident.

128. *In re* Frick, 271 S.E.2d 84 (N.C. Ct. App. 1980), took the worldly view that taking money for prostitution and then not performing the expected service may be sufficiently risky to warrant commitment.

129. Hatcher v. Wachtel, 269 S.E.2d 849 (W.Va. 1980) found such persecution delusions sufficient.

130. State v. Blythman, 302 N.W.2d 666 (Neb. 1981). There was also corroborative present testimony that the patient's condition was unchanged from that which supported the initial commitment.

131. Since the United States Supreme Court's decision in Addington v. Texas, 441 U.S. 418 (1979), holding that a "clear and convincing" standard is required to prove that a person proposed for commitment is mentally ill and in need of hospitalization, this standard of proof has been accepted for most other issues and criteria surrounding commitment. See Harris v. State 615 S.W.2d 330 (Tex. Civ. App. 1981), for a consideration of the standard of proof in relation to dangerousness, a recent overt act, and the proper jury instruction.

132. Lost among all the scientific and not-so-scientific argumentation about dangerousness and the talk about "false positives" and the like is the fact that what to do with potentially dangerous persons amounts to a political question. For example, studies such as Kozol, Boucher, & Garafalo, The Diagnosis and Treatment of Dangerousness, 18 Crime & Delinq. 371, 393 (1972), and Thornberry & Jacoby, *supra* note 28, seem to assume that the debate is over when a demonstration is made (never mind its validity, for the moment) that "only" 35% or 25% of a population committed for its potential to do harm actually winds up doing serious harm within a defined period when released into the community. However, the "community" is likely as a matter of politics to disagree with the researchers' assumption that it must forego detention of the 35% or 25% true positives in deference to the liberty interests of the "innocent" 65% or 75% (who, of course, are innocent only in the context of laws that say we must close our eyes to *past* records and indicators of dangerous behavior). See Brakel, *supra* note 28. See also the other literature on dangerousness cited in notes 28, 29, and 105, *supra*. Recall also the APA's official position against "expert" involvement in predictions of dangerousness in note 106 *supra*. A book such as the present one, which aims to give a broad overview of the law, cannot treat the dangerousness issue with all the depth and sophistication it deserves. Suffice it to say that both the empirical data and the legal theory have frequently been handled far too simplistically, as if a person's dangerousness were an objectifiable, one-dimensional fact that can be either proved or disproved, with self-evident dispositional consequences.

133. Fhagen v. Miller, 29 N.Y.2d 348, 278 N.E.2d 615, 328 N.Y.S.2d 393, *cert. denied*, 409 U.S. 845 (1972). The court held that one "afflicted with mental disease," as defined in New York mental hygiene law, does not have to be violent or dangerous in order to be confined for a short period of time prior to notice and a hearing, asserting that "the protection of society" requires the preservation of public order and public health as well as the prevention of serious crimes of violence.

134. Some state statutes include danger to property as a basis for involuntary hospitalization, for instance Washington (Wash. Rev. Code Ann. § 71.05.020(3) (Supp. 1982)) and Hawaii (Hawaii Rev. Stat. §§ 334-1, 334-60 (1976)). Hawaii's statute, however, has been ruled unconstitutional (Suzuki v. Yuen, 617 F.2d 173 (9th Cir. 1980)). See also Director of Patuxent Inst. v. Daniels, 243 Md. 16, 221 A.2d 397, *cert. denied*, 385 U.S. 940 (1966).

135. E.g., People v. Taylor, 618 P.2d 1127 (Colo. 1980). For a more thorough discussion of assessment of predictions of dangerousness see Shah, *supra* note 80, at 235.

136. Goldy v. Beal, 429 F. Supp. 640 (D.C. Pa. 1976).

criteria are no less troublesome than the dangerousness standard: the medical knowledge necessary to define precisely and to clearly identify mental illness is lacking, the sociological expertise or consensus for determining who needs treatment or who cannot provide for himself remains conspicuously absent, and the law's capacity to address the issues, to the extent that it is founded on inadequate socio-medical knowledge (and must resort to essentially political judgment for want of scientific fact) will continue to be suspect. Finally, the effects of a recent statutory trend that involuntary commitments must be premised on the additional finding that the individual is incapable of making rational or responsible decisions regarding his treatment[137] remain to be gauged. Perhaps more important than the effect on the commitment process will be the impact of this criterion on the patient's rights while he is in the hospital—particularly his "right" to refuse treatment.[138]

B. Developmentally Disabled or Mentally Retarded Persons

The statutes dealing with commitment of the developmentally disabled have been marked by two diverging trends over the past 10 to 15 years. On the one hand, separate legislation, or at least expanded statutory treatment, has been developed expressly for such persons, who earlier had been lumped in with the mentally ill either expressly or by implication. On the other hand, a movement has developed to abolish involuntary commitment of developmentally disabled or retarded persons altogether. Today, at least ten states that used to have special commitment provisions for these groups no longer have them, most having been specifically repealed within the past five years,[139] and two or three other states never enacted such legislation.[140] Also, the legal battle to deinstitutionalize the mentally disabled population and to provide treatment at home or in the community, fought mostly in the courts, has been particularly intense with reference to retarded persons.[141]

The case for separate and distinct legislative treatment of developmentally disabled persons is that the disability is distinct from that which afflicts mentally ill persons and, of course, from the conditions of people who are alcoholic or drug addicted. Developmental disabilities may stem from genetic defects passed on at conception, they may result from prenatal disease or injury afflicting the mother or from self-abuse on her part, they may come from trauma suffered at birth, or they may result from injury, disease, or malnutrition during early childhood. The disabilities are present, if not always detected, early in life.[142] And the conditions are irreversible or incurable,[143] though developmentally disabled persons are often teachable in some if not all of the basic living skills. They can be "habilitated." However, there are also arguments against distinct legal treatment. One is that a large proportion of developmentally disabled or retarded persons have emotional and mental disabilities that accompany, or result from, their developmental disability. The other is that the distinct legal treatment is often not distinct enough, that there is considerable duplication of or overlap with the provisions that cover the mentally ill, and that where there are differences, the reason for them is neither explained in the codes nor apparent on the face of the provisions. In some cases the legislative concern seems to have been less with substantive reform than with making sure that the law follows the latest trend or fad.[144]

137. Utah Code Ann. 64-7-36(10)(c) (1979 Supp.). Similar language appears in the statutes of Alaska, Delaware, Iowa, Kansas, South Carolina, and Wyoming. Michigan's law speaks of the individual's inability to understand the need for treatment. (See table 2.6.)

138. See A.E. & R.R. v. Mitchell, No. C-78-466, 5 MDLR 154 (D. Utah June 16, 1980), which holds that the finding of incapacity to make a decision as to treatment that is part of the commitment determination extends beyond commitment and means that the patient is also not competent to refuse treatment while in the hospital. Cf., Rogers v. Okin, 478 F. Supp. 1342 (D. Mass. 1979), *modified*, 634 F.2d 650 (1st Cir. 1980), *cert. granted*, 101 S. Ct. 1972 (1981), and Rennie v. Klein, 462 F. Supp. 1131 (D.N.J. 1978), *modified and remanded*, 653 F.2d 836 (3d Cir. 1981).

139. Alaska, Indiana, Massachusetts, Missouri, Nebraska, New Hampshire, New Jersey, North Dakota, Oklahoma, and Tennessee.

140. Kansas and Washington. Arizona has enacted a statute providing for commitment of retarded *juveniles* only. Ariz. Rev. Stat. Ann. § 8-242 (Supp. 1981).

141. Evans v. Washington, 459 F. Supp. 483 (D.D.C. 1978); New York State Ass'n for Retarded Children, Inc. v. Carey, 393 F. Supp. 715 (E.D. N.Y. 1975); Welsch v. Likins, 373 F. Supp. 487 (D. Minn. 1974); Kentucky Ass'n for Retarded Citizens v. Conn, 510 F. Supp. 1233 (W.D. Ky. 1980); Pennhurst State School & Hosp. v. Halderman, 451 U.S. 1 (1981).

142. See ch. 1, Historical Trends, *supra* for a more detailed discussion of the nature and classification of the various forms of mental impairment.

143. A newspaper article not too long ago reported that researchers had "cloned a gene that can prevent the genetic defect that causes Lesch-Nyhan Syndrome, a severe type of mental retardation, that may lead to a treatment." Chicago Sun-Times, Apr. 23, 1982, at 36, cols. 1-4. The jump from the report of this development to the hope for a cure for this and other forms of retardation is, however, a long one.

144. The new Illinois Code, e.g., is in several respects quite puzzling. Chapter III on Admission, Transfer and Discharge Procedures for the Mentally Ill (Ill. Ann. Stat. ch. 91½, §§ 3-100 to 3-1003 (Smith-Hurd Supp. 1981)) is essentially paralleled by chapter IV on Admission, Transfer and Discharge Procedures for the Developmentally Disabled (91½, §§ 4-100 to 4-709). But while on the one hand one may wonder at the need for this duplication, the question arises on the other hand why the parallelism breaks down at various junctures. For example, in the respective sections on Discharge and Transfer (ch. 91½, § 4-100 versus ch. 91½, § 4-709), only the mentally ill section contains provisions for restoration to competency. This difference probably exists because developmental disabilities are permanent and incurable. A more curious aspect concerns the procedures for voluntary admission. For mentally ill persons, the Code provides in distinct sections for their informal (§ 3-300) and formal voluntary admission (§ 3-400 for adults, § 3-502 for minors). For developmentally disabled persons, however, there are no equivalent provisions. A roughly analogous section may be the one labeled Administrative and Temporary Admission of the Developmentally

In those 39 states that do have separate commitment laws for the developmentally disabled, what features distinguish them from provisions for the mentally ill? One is the type of legal commitment procedures available: there is less emphasis on judicial procedures, both in the statutes on the books and in the use that is made of them. Eight states today do not provide for judicial commitment of the developmentally disabled at all (compared with only four for the mentally ill),[145] relying instead on medical certification (five states) or administrative procedures (three).[146] Two states limit the judicial role to certification as opposed to a traditional hearing, and one, Alabama, provides for commitment by medical certification upon a judicial order.[147] A number of states have judicial commitment as an alternative to medical or administrative institutionalization of the retarded.[148] While the most recent statistics still show a high percentage of involuntary commitments among the mentally retarded (about half),[149] many of these are only technically so; a quite common commitment route is the third-party or non-protested admission route, where the parents or guardian of the individual—often a minor—seek admission for the ward. In that context the traditional picture of the state's railroading the unwilling patient is most inapposite. With the parents or guardian in the position of pleading for placement, the primary problem is being turned away because of lack of facilities, lack of programs (education, habilitation), or lack of state money to help defray the costs of the ward's care. If administrative or medical authorities are involved, it is as joint decision makers with the petitioners, with certification as the legal formality. Judicial involvement, when it occurs, tends to be ministerial and in a good proportion of cases to be reserved for approving retention of the patient in the institution when he reaches majority.[150]

Statutory definitions of retardation or developmental disability, which identify the population that is subject to the commitment procedures, have undergone major change over the past decade. Indeed, the term *developmental disability* was barely known in 1970. Today about half the states employ that category for purposes of indicating the reach of their special commitment laws.[151] Typically the term is defined to include disability that is attributable to mental retardation, cerebral palsy, epilepsy, and autism,[152] but legally and practically the first of these, mental retardation, has by far the largest significance. The remaining state statutes are focused specifically on mentally retarded (or, equivalently, mentally deficient) persons. The definitions are often worded in terms of the subaverage intellectual functioning of this group, and they tend to be somewhat less circular than the statutory definitions of mental illness.[153]

The commitment criteria for developmentally disabled and retarded persons—the conditions the committing authority must find before it can order institutionalization—are quite similar to those in the statutes covering the mentally ill. They are susceptible of being grouped under the same headings. Still, there are some noteworthy differences.[154] Dangerousness appears to be

---

Disabled (§ 4-300), but why the scheme is not closer to the provisions for the mentally ill is unclear. Also baffling is why this one section combines "administrative" and "temporary" admission, when the former word describes *who* decides to admit while the latter indicates the *purpose* and *length* of institutionalization. Moreover, the section providing for admission of the mentally ill begins positively with "[a]ny person desiring admission . . . may be admitted upon his request without making formal application therefor" (§ 3-300), but the section on admission of the developmentally disabled begins with "no person may be administratively admitted . . . unless an adequate diagnostic evaluation of his current condition has been conducted" (§ 4-300). One can only speculate about the reason for opening up with such a resounding negative plus evaluative safeguards in the one case but not in the other. And there are many other unexplained differences in terminology, organization, and content between sections that in other areas offer verbatim repetition.

145. See note 100 *supra*.

146. See table 2.8. This table covers all available procedures for commitment of developmentally disabled persons, whereas table 2.6 deals only with judicial commitment of the mentally ill.

147. See table 2.8. Ala. Code § 22-52-55 (1975).

148. See table 2.8.

149. Statistics collected by the National Institute of Mental Health show 54.2% of the admissions of retarded persons to state and county mental facilities were involuntary (Division of Biometry and Epidemiology, National Institute of Mental Health, Statistical Note 105, Legal Status of Inpatient Admissions to State and County Mental Hospitals, United States 1972, at 13 table 3b (1974).

150. Legal reformers have not been content to leave things this way. There has been a concerted movement against third-party commitments of retarded adults accomplished without a full judicial hearing and other due process protections. E.g., *In re* Hop, 623 P.2d 282, 171 Cal. Rptr. 721 (1981); D.C. v. Surles, No. 78-91, 4 MDLR 169 (D. Vt. Dec. 21, 1979). Similar developments regarding the commitment of retarded minors are described in this chapter § III D, Children and Minors with Mental Disabilities, *infra*.

151. See table 2.2. Although California lacks a definition of "mentally retarded," its statute for commitment of the mentally retarded was upheld (Money v. Krall, 128 Cal. App. 3d 378, 180 Cal. Rptr. 376 (1982)).

152. See table 2.2. The federal Developmentally Disabled Assistance and Bill of Rights Act, 42 U.S.C. 6000, 6001(7) (1983) gives the following elaborate definition of developmental disability:

> (7) The term "developmental disability" means a severe, chronic disability of a person which—
> (A) is attributable to a mental or physical impairment or combination of mental and physical impairments;
> (B) is manifested before the person attains age twenty-two;
> (C) is likely to continue indefinitely;
> (D) results in substantial functional limitations in three or more of the following areas of major life activity: (i) self-care, (ii) receptive and expressive language, (iii) learning, (iv) mobility, (v) self-direction, (vi) capacity for independent living, and (vii) economic self-sufficiency; and
> (E) reflects the person's need for a combination and sequence of special, interdisciplinary, or generic care, treatment, or other services which are of lifelong or extended duration and are individually planned and coordinated.

153. See table 2.2. Cf. table 2.1.

154. See generally table 2.8.

a slightly less prominent criterion than it is in the mental illness statutes.[155] And differences in phraseology crop up with respect to the other criteria.[156] The District of Columbia Code,[157] in order to preclude institutionalization of persons with only slight disability, specifies that the person proposed for commitment be "at least moderately mentally retarded." The Florida statute[158] provides that for a mentally retarded person to be committable it must be shown that he "lacks basic survival and self-care skills." A single blanket criterion found in the Delaware Code[159] avers that further "presence in the community would be detrimental to the retarded person himself or to the community" and the same provision stated more positively in the Iowa Code[160] provides that commitment be "conducive to the welfare of such person and of the community."

The systemic criteria in the developmentally disabled statutes are also closely analogous to those for the mentally ill. The laws of about half the states explicitly require a finding that commitment to an institution be the "least restrictive" or "least drastic" disposition.[161] Some states, for example Alabama,[162] premise commitment on a showing that the parents or guardian of the disabled person have failed or have been unable to provide care at home. A good many other statutes, however, focus on the opposite (and for the developmentally disabled and retarded, particularly appropriate) concern that there be "adequate and appropriate" facilities to which to commit.[163] Such provisions bring home the reality, which deserves much greater emphasis with respect to mentally ill persons as well, that the objective of the entire commitment process is after all to try to find appropriate treatment for the disabled person, adversarial rhetoric to the contrary notwithstanding. A number of states—Florida is one[164]—seek to assure that the retarded person be no more restricted than necessary in terms of legal status, providing that to be committable it must be shown that he "lacks sufficient capacity to give express and informed consent to a voluntary application for services."

In other respects, the commitment laws covering developmentally disabled and retarded persons tend to be somewhat less detailed than those covering mentally ill persons.[165] Whatever the role of adversary process—conceptual or practical—in the commitment of these persons, the statutes are often silent on adversarial implements. Even when they fit the general commitment scheme, specifications regarding hearings, the place to conduct them, provisions on the presence of the patient, the right to a jury, the standard of proof required, and so on are sometimes not stated. One area for which there is often greater specificity than in the mental illness statutes is the place to which the retarded individual will be committed. Many statutes refer by name to the appropriate institutions, homes, centers, schools, or colonies.

The case law reflects the main points of controversy surrounding commitment procedures for the developmentally disabled and retarded. There are three recurring themes that also dominate legal activity on behalf of the mentally ill, though not necessarily with the same relative emphasis: (1) litigation regarding the adequacy of the commitment criteria or definitions, (2) cases pressing for an increased legalization of the commitment procedures, and (3) cases arguing the deinstitutionalization of developmentally disabled and retarded persons, which have been extended to their logical conclusion in legislation *abolishing* their commitment or at least their involuntary commitment to large and largely custodial institutions, in favor of schemes that emphasize consensual placement in community facilities where their "development potential" is maximized through active training and education programs.

As in the case of the mental illness statutes, the courts appear to be divided on whether some of the key definitions and phrases found in the developmental disabilities statutes provide a sufficiently clear and concise basis for commitment. In *Kinner v. Florida*,[166] for example, the district court invalidated the involuntary commitment of a "retarded" person "in need of treatment and rehabilitation" because it found these criteria[167] lacking in substantive due process. The court compared the provisions unfavorably with the more rigorous and precise language in Florida's law covering commitment of the mentally ill, which required that the person be found "likely to injure himself or others" or "in need of care or treatment and lack[ing] sufficient capacity to make a responsible application on his own behalf."[168] On the other hand, a case such as *State ex rel Vandenberg*[169]

155. Table 2.8, cols. 4, 5, & 6.
156. *Id.*
157. D.C. Code Ann. § 6-1924(b)(1, 2) (1981).
158. Fla. Stat. Ann. § 393.11(1)(c)(1) (West Supp. 1981).
159. Del. Code Ann. tit. 16, § 5522(a) (1974).
160. Iowa Code Ann. § 222.17(2) (West 1969).
161. See table 2.8, cols. 7 & 8.
162. Ala. Code § 22-52-55(a) (1975).
163. Table 2.8, cols. 7 & 8.
164. Fla. Stat. Ann. § 393.11(1)(c)(1) (Supp. 1981).
165. See generally table 2.8.
166. 382 So. 2d 756 (Fla. Dist. Ct. App. 1980).
167. Fla. Stat. Ann. § 393.11 (West 1977).
168. 382 So. 2d at 759 citing the 1979 version of Fla. Stat. Ann. § 394.467(1).
169. 617 P.2d 675 (Or. Ct. App. 1980). Cf. People v. Reliford, 65 Ill. App. 3d 177, 382 N.E.2d 72 (1978), holding that commitment *cannot* be based solely on a finding of mental retardation. A "need of treatment" must also be shown (by "clear and convincing" evidence).

sustained a statute permitting commitment of a person found to be "mentally deficient," despite the fact that the statute left the term undefined. The Oregon court felt that the law was not improperly vague, in large part because mental deficiency (unlike mental illness) could be established through scientific tests, because the initial finding was made by the examining medical institution, and because the proceedings were governed by elaborate due process standards.

Many of the cases regarding increased legalization of commitment procedures involve retarded children. For example, *Parham v. J. R.*,[170] the United States Supreme Court case that (as discussed earlier) seems to have drawn the constitutional limits to this quest by holding that adversary hearings and some of the safeguards that go with them were not constitutionally required, concerned the institutionalization of children. That fact raises special considerations. For example, varying factors, such as the age of the child, the competence and good-will of the parents, whether the parents have custody of the child at all, or whether the child is a ward of the state, have been argued to have a bearing on how rigorous the committing procedures should be.[171] At least on the surface, such differentiation would not be or would be less applicable to the process of committing adults who are retarded.[172] It is not surprising therefore that litigation involving adults has raised, and at least in some cases has succeeded[173] in obtaining, even more rigid due process requisites than those claimed for minors. Whether *Parham* draws the limits in situations involving adults, too, is an open question.

During the decade of the 1970s, arguments for deinstitutionalizing developmentally disabled and retarded persons were rewarded with striking results in the courts. *Evans v. Washington*,[174] for example, led to a court order to terminate admissions to one of the District of Columbia's existing facilities for the mentally retarded and to force the city to create "community living arrangements." A case that went on for years in New York under varying names[175] came to similar results: a moratorium on admissions to Willowbrook, one of that state's main facilities for retarded persons, and an order requiring sharp reductions in its population over a six-year period, plus the correllate that the state provide community treatment alternatives. And in Minnesota, the case of *Welsch v. Likins*[176] ended (more than six years after its initiation) in a consent decree that included, among other remedies, the extraordinarily specific stipulation that the state reduce its institutional population of retarded from the current (in 1980) 2,650 to 1,850 by 1987. *Pennhurst State School and Hospital v. Halderman*,[177] however, in which the United States Supreme Court held that the federal Developmentally Disabled Assistance and Bill of Rights Act does *not* require the states to embark on a policy of deinstitutionalization, signals, if not a full retreat from, certainly a decisive setback to the position staked out by the proponents of community care and up to then endorsed by the courts.[178]

In 1978, mentally retarded persons and persons with organic brain syndromes comprised 26.4% of the resident population in state and county mental institutions throughout the United States, but new admissions accounted for only 7.7% of the total.[179] While these fig-

170. 442 U.S. 584 (1979).

171. See Special Article Series, 3 MDLR 73 (1979), setting out the American Psychiatric Association's position on procedures for admitting minors. The APA contends that procedures should vary with such factors as (a) the age of the child, (b) the expected duration of institutionalization, (c) whether the child is cared for by the parents or is a ward of the state, (d) whether the parents have been found neglectful or abusive, and (e) whether the institution is accredited. The least amount of "due process" (e.g., no preadmission judicial hearings) would be required in the most "favorable" of cases—young child, cared for by responsible parents who intend to commit child for short duration to a reputable facility. The level of legal protections would increase in the presence of less favorable factors.

172. However, factors of length of institutionalization and reputation of the institution should count for adults as well. And the situation of adults too may vary according to whether they are wards of the state or still under the care of parents, a relative, or a guardian.

173. *In re* Hop, 623 P.2d 282, 171 Cal. Rptr. 721 (1981). The court held that the "voluntary" placement of a developmentally disabled woman in a state hospital at the request of her mother without either a judicial determination regarding her disability or a knowing and intelligent request for admission was violative of due process and that she was entitled to a prompt hearing, including the right to a jury trial on demand, the application of the standard of proof beyond a reasonable doubt, and the appointment of counsel.

174. 459 F. Supp. 483 (D.D.C. 1978).

175. New York State Ass'n for Retarded Children, Inc. v. Carey, 393 F. Supp. 715 (E.D.N.Y. 1975) is the last sputter in this litigation in which Governor Rockefeller was the originally listed defendant.

176. Welsch v. Likins, 373 F. Supp. 487 (D. Minn. 1974); Welsch v. Noot, No. 4-72 Civ. 451, 5 MDLR 155 (D. Minn. Sept. 15, 1980).

177. 451 U.S. 1 (1981).

178. *Pennhurst* may have been foreshadowed by Kentucky Ass'n for Retarded Citizens v. Conn, 510 F. Supp. 1233 (W.D. Ky. 1980), in which the district court refused to uphold the plaintiff's argument that the state's decision to create a small, new inpatient facility for the retarded, isolated from the "mainstream," went against a congressional objective favoring community care implied in the federal Developmental Disabilities Act. On the other hand, since the United States Supreme Court's holding in *Pennhurst*, the Court of Appeals for the Third Circuit has reinstated the major parts of its original order, basing it this time on state law. The order requires state and county officials to provide "habilitation" for mentally retarded persons in the least restrictive setting, including services in the community, and based on individual assessments of need. It does not require the closing of the Pennhurst institution but does uphold the appointment of a master to implement the original order and the state's liability for the latter's payment. Halderman v. Pennhurst State School & Hosp., 673 F.2d 647 (3d Cir. 1982). See notes 64 & 65 *supra* and accompanying discussion in text.

179. Survey and Reports Branch, Division of Biometry and Epidemiology, National Institute of Mental Health, Additions and Resident Patients at End of Year in State and County Mental Hospitals by Age and Diagnosis, by State, United States 1978, at 2 (Sept. 1981).

ures appear to affirm the impact of the deinstitutionalization movement, the low admission rates can also be accounted for to a significant extent by the high turnover among the other two major patient groups—the mentally ill and alcoholics. The shorter stays and many new admissions and re-admissions of these groups of patients have the effect of dwarfing the admission figures for the more long-term developmentally disabled population.

C. Persons Addicted to Drugs or Alcohol

We will only briefly cover the laws dealing with drug-addicted or alcoholic persons. In isolated form, these afflictions are rather clearly distinguishable from other mental or developmental disabilities, and indeed it is debatable whether they fall in the class of mental or developmental problems at all.[180] Some would argue that the self-inflicted and self-indulgent qualities of the dependencies place them outside the developmental or mental disability category. On the other hand, many mental disabilities also have an element of self-induced affliction.[181] Moreover, prolonged and sustained dependency on alcohol or drugs can create mental states and symptoms that are difficult to distinguish from neurotic or psychotic states. Or—perhaps this is the more compelling point—there exists a subpopulation in which various disabilities, dependencies, and even "criminality" (assuming that is a state) often exist side by side in various forms and combinations. Arguably, even economic and cultural factors are part of the equation. Finally, persons suffering from alcohol problems, and to a lesser extent drug addicts, are often treated in mental institutions, though in different wards than the psychotic and neurotic patients.

In the earlier editions of this book, epileptics were for the purposes of discussion grouped with the drug dependent and alcoholic. Since then, changes in the laws have made it more logical to put them (as we have done) with the mentally retarded and developmentally disabled, definitions of the latter often expressly including epileptics. More important than this classification artifice is the reality that today persons whose sole difficulty is an occasional epileptic seizure are no longer subjected to involuntary commitment. The commitment laws are applied only to those whose epilepsy goes together with other organic or with psychiatric disabilities.

About two-thirds (32) of the states have special statutes for the commitment of alcoholic persons.[182] Slightly fewer (29) have procedures for institutionalizing persons addicted to drugs. These are civil commitment statutes. A minority of states—9 in the case of alcoholics, 16 for drug addicts—also have separate statutes providing for the mental health processing of chemical substance addicts who have been charged with or convicted of a crime. These are listed in table 2.10 but will not be further discussed. As regards the regular civil provisions, in about 8 states the same procedures cover commitment of both alcoholics and drug addicts. In two states, Hawaii[183] and Iowa,[184] the statutory definition of the population subject to commitment refers to "substance abusers," which includes drug addicts, alcoholics, and those dependent on any chemical substance. It should not be supposed that states without special provisions lack the power to commit persons with drug or alcohol dependency or that they do in fact refrain from institutionalizing such persons. The traditional interpretation of the mentally ill commitment laws is that they are broad enough to cover these groups. A number of states, such as Alabama, Arizona, Idaho, and Oregon,[185] have statutory definitions of persons who are alcohol or drug dependent but no separate procedures for their commitment.

The statutory definitions of an alcoholic or drug-addicted person have undergone considerable modernization over the past 10 to 15 years, with substantial similarity in the language used in many states. Even among more varying formulations, one can often find at least the traces of a common "standard" definition. The description of an alcoholic in the Colorado law[186] contains most of the standard elements: "a person who habitually lacks self-control as to the use of alcoholic beverages or uses alcoholic beverages to the extent that his health is substantially impaired or endangered or his social or economic function is substantially disrupted." The reference to habit or chronicity of abuse is common to all formulations. The laws of a few states add or substitute language that emphasizes the threat of the individual's condition *to others*. In the Texas statute,[187] for exam-

180. See the discussion in ch. 1, Historical Trends, *supra* regarding the fluidity of the mental health/mental illness dichotomy and the various forms of social deviance (or life-style choices) that have been included within and excluded from the realm of mental disease. In *In re* Marquardt, 100 Ill. App. 3d 741, 427 N.E.2d 411 (1981), the court held that drug dependency in itself does not constitute a mental illness requiring commitment.

181. The term *hysteria*, which dominated the psychiatric lexicon in that discipline's early years, continues to this day to have ambivalent connotations of both the uncontrollable and the merely (or even deliberately) uncontrolled. The perception that much of the symptomology of mental illness is stylized, culture bound, or "learned" behavior (particularly the type presented in mental institutions) has similar implications.

182. See tables 2.3 and 2.10, which are the basis for this and other general statements in the preceding paragraph.

183. Hawaii Rev. Stat. §§ 334-60(b)(A), 334-1 (1976).

184. Iowa Code Ann. § 125.2(1) and § 125.2(5) (West Supp. 1979).

185. Cf. table 2.3 with 2.10.

186. Colo. Rev. Stat. § 25-1-302(1) (Supp. 1980). The statutes of at least 17 states replicate this language verbatim or with very minor variations.

187. Texas Rev. Civ. Stat. Ann. art. 5561c(3)(c) (Vernon 1958) (emphasis added).

ple, an alcoholic is someone who among other things "endangers *public* morals, health, safety or welfare." In Nevada,[188] the perceived danger is to the "health, safety or welfare of [the alcoholic] himself or any other person or group of persons."

The definitions of committable drug addicts show more diversity.[189] A few are phrased like the provisions covering alcoholics, substituting "narcotic drug" or "chemical substance" for "alcoholic beverages." Several states—Massachusetts[190] is one—expressly exclude users of alcohol or tobacco from the definition of the drug addicted, but others are silent on this point. As mentioned, a state such as Hawaii employs one statutory definition for all "substance abuse." A person suffering from it is described as one who "uses narcotic, stimulant, depressant, or hallucinogenic drugs or alcohol to an extent which interferes with his personal, social, family, or economic life."[191] The definitions in many states are quite lengthy, touching on the nature of the substance, the fact that its use is illegal or strictly circumscribed, the level and length of dependency, its psychic and behavioral effects, and the threat posed by the user to the community.

Table 2.10 at the end of this chapter cites the section numbers of the state statutes providing for the commitment of alcoholics and drug addicts, for the benefit of readers interested in learning further statutory details, patterns, and points of divergence. Suffice it to say here that the practical task of dealing with the individual and public problems resulting from chemical addiction defy the most careful and comprehensive legislative efforts. The commitment of those comparatively few who seek treatment or for whom treatment is sought and who meet the legislatively prescribed standards can never be more than a very partial solution, even if we assume that the treatment provided is uniformly effective. The problems of "substance abuse" go deep culturally, and they are massive. Estimates on the number of "alcoholics" or "problem drinkers" in the country have recently been put at some 13 million, including among them over 3 million teenagers between 14 and 17 years of age.[192] Not only is drug abuse a common phenomenon, but its growth over the past decade and a half in the numbers of persons affected and the way it pervades the social and economic strata has been described as frightening.[193] And we are dealing not just with the diminished or wasted lives of abusers but also with the devastating effects for nonusers—the general social and economic costs, including family disruption and its consequences, decreased worker productivity, automobile accidents, crime, and so on. Estimates of these total costs run into the tens of billions,[194] so large and susceptible to so many possible additions or subtractions as to be virtually meaningless.

Nationally, in 1980-81, "alcohol disorders"—cases in which the primary diagnosis is alcoholism—accounted for 22% of the admissions to public (state and county) mental institutions, 9% of those to private mental hospitals, and 8% of those to general hospitals with psychiatric units.[195] Combined, the proportion is 13%, some 136,000 out of the total of slightly more than one million mentally disordered persons admitted to the nation's inpatient facilities.[196] One can only guess the number of cases is in which alcoholism figures as a secondary or contributing factor toward institutionalization, though it is sure to be comparably high if not higher. The total number of persons with alcohol disorders admitted to public mental institutions in 1981 was 71,864, while the number of resident alcoholic patients stood at 6,708,[197] a comparatively low figure only because the comparatively short periods of hospitalization for alcoholics (11 days was the median in 1975)[198] keep the in-residence totals from accumulating higher.

In 1952, drug addicts constituted less than 1% of all

188. Nev. Rev. Stat. 458.010 (1979).

189. See table 2.3.

190. Mass. Ann. Laws ch. 123, § 38 (1981).

191. Hawaii Rev. Stat. § 334-1 (1976).

192. See Office of Program Planning and Coordination, Alcohol, Drug Abuse, and Mental Health Administration, Public Health Service, U.S. Dep't of Health and Human Services, Alcohol, Drug Abuse, and Mental Health National Data Book 15 (Jan. 1980) [hereinafter cited as National Data Book]. Terms such as "alcoholism" or "problem drinking" are of course open to definitions of varying breadth.

193. For an article that briefly summarizes some of the recent, dire statistics and some of the ideas on what can be done to reduce them, see Beck, We Can Stem Drug Abuse, 68 A.B.A. J. 691 (1982). See also notes 199-207 and accompanying text *infra* for the latest official estimates on the incidence of drug addiction.

194. The government National Data Book, *supra* note 192, at 95, reports the total economic costs of drug abuse to be some $10.5 billion, of which about 1 billion are dollars spent on treatment programs. By comparison, the total costs of mental illness are given as $31 billion, with $14 billion in treatment costs; for alcohol abuse, the total figure is $43 billion and "only" $860 million spent on its treatment. A more recent newspaper article reported the estimate of an insurance representative that the economic cost to the United States of drunk driving alone totalled more than $24 billion per year. (Chicago Sun-Times, May 3, 1982, at 22, cols. 1 & 2).

195. These figures were supplied directly to the American Bar Foundation by the National Institute of Mental Health. Older statistics (1975) show the proportions to be 28%, 8%, and 7%, respectively. See National Data Book, *supra* note 192, at 56 table 22, Patient Diagnoses in Selected Mental Health Facilities, 1975.

196. *Id.* with extrapolations. For 1975, the figures were 15%, some 150,000 out of one million-plus.

197. *Id.* These figures are significantly down from 1975, when there were 107,866 admissions and 11,480 residents.

198. *Id.* at 64 table 28, Median Length of Stay for Admissions to State and County Mental Hospitals by Primary Diagnosis, 1975. The median for all disabilities is 26 days; it is 41 days for patients who suffer from schizophrenia, 39 days for mental retardation, 68 days for persons with organic brain syndromes, and 15 days for drug disorders.

first admissions to state mental institutions[199] and 0.1% of the resident population.[200] By 1967 these figures had more than doubled, to 2.1%[201] and 0.4%,[202] respectively. The most recent figures (which comprise readmissions as well as first-time entries for 1981) are 5.0% and 2.0%[203]—that is, 19,370 admissions for "drug disorders" and 1,879 in residence. These numbers pale in the light of the full incidence of drug abuse in this country. In 1965, the United States Bureau of Narcotics reported over 57,000 known active addicts.[204] Today, with broader definitions and more "liberal" diagnosis to match increased abuse, the figures are staggering: the National Institute of Mental Health reports estimates of half a million heroin addicts alone;[205] 10 million Americans are reported to have "tried" cocaine; 42 million have tried marijuana, with 16 million identified as "current users," among whom many of the heaviest users are adolescents of high school age.[206] In addition, there are untold numbers of adults and teenagers who abuse barbiturates and other sedatives, tranquilizers, amphetamines and other stimulants, and hallucinogenic drugs.[207]

While it is clear that the imposition of criminal sanctions to suppress drug traffic, rather than civil hospitalization of users, continues to be society's primary response to drug addiction, considerable movement toward treatment is discernible.[208] Eighteen years ago Congress passed the Narcotic Addict Rehabilitation Act of 1966, which provides for civil hospitalization of narcotic addicts.[209] An eligible addict or his relative may apply for up to six months' inpatient treatment followed by a three-year period of follow-up outpatient care. Support for the latter program came to be placed under the Community Mental Health Centers Act. Authorized federal appropriations for the rehabilitation of narcotic addicts and alcoholics were $15 million for 1969 and $25 million for 1970.[210] In 1973, the amount had risen to $366 million.[211] More recent figures on the federal contribution, or those reflecting state and local and private support, are not available. However large today's outlays, few would argue that society is winning the battle against substance abuse, much less that it has been won.

D. Children and Minors with Mental Disabilities

Laws relating to the commitment of minors have already been given reference in passing. Here we give them more concentrated treatment. We focus particularly on an array of special "voluntary" commitment provisions, since involuntary commitment of minors, even in the relatively few states that provide for it, is conceptually no different from adult commitment. Table 2.11 charts both types of provisions, with the "Court Hearing" columns indicating whether for any particular state the procedure leans toward the involuntary or voluntary model.

As late as the mid-1970s three-quarters of the states had special statutory provisions whereunder parents could commit their children to mental institutions without a court hearing or any lesser form of judicial oversight.[212] Often these provisions were found in the code sections on voluntary admission, and they have been generally conceptualized as part of the states' voluntary admission schemes. In recent years, however, patients' rights advocates have been engaged in a concerted effort to pierce this veil of voluntariness, as they perceive it, and to expose the "true" nature of the child commitment laws. Being essentially involuntary procedures, these laws, they have argued, should at the very least be fitted with the same safeguards and protections that circumscribe adult commitment.[213] Without needing to support the advocates' remedy, it is possible to agree

199. U.S. Public Health Service, Public Health Service Pub. No. 483, Patients in Mental Institutions (pt. II) 26 table 8.

200. *Id.* at 50 table 17. Partial information from 183 of 204 state hospitals showed 826 first admissions for drug addiction in 1952. However, only 249 drug addicts were listed among the resident patients in these hospitals at the end of that year.

201. National Institute of Mental Health, U.S. Public Health Service, Patients in State and County Mental Hospitals 1967, at 21 (1969).

202. *Id.* at 54.

203. Statistics supplied directly by NIMH. See National Data Book, *supra* note 192, at 56, table 22 for the older—generally somewhat lower—figures.

204. U.S. Bureau of Narcotics, Traffic in Opium and Other Dangerous Drugs 17 (1966).

205. See National Data Book, *supra* note 192, at 16-17.

206. *Id.* The percentage of high school seniors reporting *daily use* of marijuana was 6% in 1975, up to 11% in 1978.

207. *Id.*

208. See W.B. Eldridge, Narcotics and the Law: A Critique of the American Experiment in Drug Control (2d ed. 1967).

209. 42 U.S.C. §§ 3401-41 (1970).

210. S. Rep. No. 1454, 90th Cong., 2d Sess. 9, *reprinted in* 1968 U.S. Code Cong. & Ad. News 4007, 4017 (legislative history of Pub. L. No. 90-574).

211. This figure includes funds allocated under The Comprehensive Drug Abuse Prevention & Control Act of 1970, Pub. L. No. 91-513, 1970 U.S. Code Cong. & Ad. News (84 Stat.) 1236; The Comprehensive Alcohol Abuse and Alcoholism Prevention, Treatment, and Rehabilitation Act of 1970, Pub. L. No. 91-616, 1970 U.S. Code Cong. & Ad. News (84 Stat.) 1848; The Drug Abuse Office and Treatment Act of 1972, Pub. L. No. 92-255, 1972 U.S. Code Cong. & Ad. News (86 Stat.) 65.

212. It is significant that under these laws, discharge too is at the behest of the parents or the institution. The child so committed has no standing to petition for his release until he reaches majority. See Ellis, Volunteering Children: Parental Commitment of Minors to Mental Institutions, 62 Calif. L. Rev. 840 (1974); Shoenberger, "Voluntary" Commitment of Mentally Ill or Retarded Children: Child Abuse by the Supreme Court, 7 U. Dayton L. Rev. 1, at 1 (1981); Comment, "Voluntary" Admission of Children to Mental Hospitals: A Conflict of Interest Between Parent and Child, 36 Md. L. Rev. (1976). But see Melville v. Sabbatino, 30 Conn. Supp. 320 (Super. Ct. 1973), and *In re* Lee, No. 68 (JD) 1326 (Cook County Cir. Ct. Juv. Div. Ill., Feb. 29 and Aug. 24, 1972), for the contrary view.

213. See, e.g., Mass. Gen. Laws ch. 201, § 6, 6A, 14 (1981), and Doe v. Doe, 385 N.E.2d 995 (Mass. 1979).

with their underlying conception that the statutes permitting parents to commit their children are something other than voluntary admission laws. Whatever the wisdom of these statutes and no matter how blurred in practice the line that runs between "voluntary" and "involuntary" institutionalizations, it seems best to save the concept of voluntary admission for procedures in which the disabled person himself is the petitioner or applicant for, or the moving party in, getting into the institution.[214]

Consistent with the dialectic quality that characterizes the history of the laws relating to mental disability, the statutes permitting parents to "volunteer" their children for commitment—now again under attack—are of recent origin. The majority of them were enacted in the late 1950s and the 1960s as part of the wider movement favoring voluntary admission to mental institutions. Under these "parental commitment" provisions—Illinois's old statute is typical[215]—the admission of a minor is achieved by the simple process of a petition or application executed by the parents and approved by an admitting physician or the director of the admitting facility. There are no requirements for notice to the child, no formal hearing on his condition or need of treatment need be held, no court approval of the decision to admit is required, and none of the other legal formalities—counsel, witnesses, precise commitment criteria, specifically assigned standards, or burdens of proof—need come into play. The process is intended to be entirely nonadversarial; there is nothing to be "proved."The age limit at which parental commitment is the rule and prior to which young persons cannot legally admit themselves has varied from state to state, with 16 being the "model" provision[216] and 21 (the standard age of majority for most legal purposes) constituting the outer limit. Much of the "reform" is directed toward at least lowering this outer limit, with many reformers arguing that for purposes of commitment even minors younger than 16 should have a voice.[217]

214. The artificiality of the legal distinction between "voluntary" and "involuntary" commitments is well illustrated in *In re* Green, 417 A.2d 708 (Pa. Super. Ct. 1980), in which the court found insufficient grounds for the *involuntary* commitment of a six-year-old, given that the commitment criterion of inability to provide for the necessities of life was obviously inapplicable to a child so young, while dangerousness was not adequately proved by an episode of self-harm that occurred more than 30 days before the court hearing. The court's solution—surely defensible on practical or humanitarian grounds but conceptually almost a joke—was to authorize the child's "voluntary" commitment.

215. Ill. Ann. Stat. ch. 91½, § 5-1 (Smith-Hurd 1966).

216. See Ellis, *supra* note 212, citing the National Institute of Mental Health's Draft Act Governing Hospitalization of the Mentally Ill, promulgated in 1951.

217. Ellis, *supra* note 212, at 878-81. The Pennsylvania statute (Pa. Stat. Ann. tit. 50, § 7201 (Purdon 1978 Supp.), which came under constitutional attack in Bartley v. Kremens, 402 F. Supp. 1039 (E.D. Pa. 1975), Secretary of Pub. Welfare v. Institutionalized Juveniles, 442 U.S. 640 (1979), for example, drew the line at age 14.

While there is no direct evidence relating the enactment of the child commitment laws to increases in the number of young persons in mental institutions, there exist general data—from individual states as well as national aggregates[218]—showing sharp increases in the percentage of institutionalized patients under 21 that do hint at such a relationship. Whether the trend, if it is real, is to be applauded depends of course on one's evaluation of the need for these commitments—an assessment not easily made in the general. The same goes for whether to applaud the "voluntary" child commitment laws themselves.

There are two rationales behind the laws: (1) the pro-family rationale, which defers to parental judgment as the most immediate, intimate, and thus the best judgment and to parental authority as the way to keep the family intact; (2) the therapeutic rationale, which holds that it is best not to make adversarial contests out of delicate commitment decisions. The second of these applies to commitment proceedings for adults too and is discussed at various points elsewhere in the text. The first deserves examination here.

While it is obvious that parents can observe the behavior of their children and evaluate their needs from a vantage point that cannot be matched by an outsider, there are circumstances of mental pathology in families that cut against extending the customary deference to parental judgment on how to deal with the problems of a child. Not infrequently, the child's mental or emotional difficulties reflect more general instability within the family, one or several of whose members may share similar difficulties.[219] The very least this suggests is that an effective treatment approach cannot be confined to the child alone. Occasionally, the child is made the scapegoat for conflicts, disabilities, or emotional deficiencies of the parents or siblings.[220] While a child so singled out may be best off removed from the family, there is no cause for the removal to be to a mental facility. And some parents who volunteer a child for commitment may be motivated more by their need to be relieved of the burdens of caring than by the treatment needs or prospects of the disabled child. In such situations, temporary respite placement may be preferable to extended commitment.[221]

The situations just described, particularly if they are common, call into question the wisdom of laws that permit parents to commit their children with few or no

218. Ellis, *supra* note 212, at 845.

219. See Lidz, Fleck, & Cornellison, Schizophrenia and the Family 131 (1965), *cited in* Ellis, *supra* note 212, at 852 n. 63.

220. See Vogel & Bell, The Emotionally Disturbed Child as the Family Scapegoat, *in* A Modern Introduction to the Family 412-27 (N.W. Bell & E.F. Vogel rev. ed. 1968), *cited in* Ellis, *supra* note 212, at 860 n.115.

221. E.g., Ind. Code Ann. § 16-13-20-1, 3 (Burns Supp. 1982).

checks. Proponents of the laws answer that a sufficient check is provided by the interposition of the medical judgment of the admitting physician or director of the facility to which the application is made. They argue that if it is not the child who is ill or needs help, but others in the family who do, then no doctor or medical administrator (other than the isolated fraud or crook) will assent to commitment of the child. Besides professional medical judgment[222] against it, they see few ulterior incentives to decisions that would overpopulate the facilities with unnecessary cases. Opponents of the laws, on the other hand, are wont to be less charitable of medical judgment and will cite studies describing the psychiatric tendency to overdiagnose, the perfunctory examinations, the inexactitude of both diagnostic classification schemes and the actual diagnoses, and the conflicting role of the doctor confronted with a parental application for the admission of a child (whose agent is he, the parents' or the child's?).[223] They will even search for financial incentives that may drive physicians or administrators to maximize admissions. In sum, it comes down to the relative amount of confidence the two sides have in medical versus legal judgment—the usual bottom line. Those of the legal faith will see the prevailing child commitment laws as deficient, and the remedy they prescribe is an application of legal safeguards and the interposition of judicial judgment to protect the interests of the child which may, according to this view, otherwise be violated by the misjudgments of parents and physicians.

There are legal precedents that support a high degree of parental authority and family autonomy and privacy as well as cases that sketch out the limits of these values. Two school cases decided by the U.S. Supreme Court, one (*Pierce v. Society of Sisters*)[224] dating from 1925 and the other (*Wisconsin v. Yoder* (1972))[225] more recent, are frequently cited for the profamily position. In *Pierce*, the Court upheld the prerogative of parents to keep children between the ages of 8 and 16 out of the public schools against the state's statutory mandate to the contrary. In *Yoder*, the teenage children of Amish families were ruled to be exempt from the state's compulsory school education laws. There is an equally strong line of cases, however, to the effect that under certain circumstances the substantive rights of children take precedence over the wishes of their parents or guardians: *Prince v. Massachusetts*,[226] applying the child labor laws against the guardian of a nine-year-old child who encouraged the child to sell religious magazines; *Planned Parenthood of Central Missouri v. Danforth*,[227] endorsing the right of minors, if sufficiently mature, to procure an abortion without parental consent; *People ex rel. Wallace v. Labrenz*,[228] holding that the state may provide needed medical treatment to the child over the parent's religious objections; *Halderman v. Pennhurst State School and Hospital*,[229] permitting the placement of a retarded child in a community setting over objections of the parents; and others. And cases such as *In re Gault*[230] and *In re Winship*[231] establish major procedural rights for children to guard against the possibility of unwarranted abrogation of their substantive rights in legal proceedings.

In the context of the child commitment laws themselves, the profamily point of view suffered major reverses in the mid- and late-1970s. Court cases in California, Colorado, Georgia, Pennsylvania, Tennessee, and the District of Columbia struck down as unconstitutional provisions permitting parents and guardians to effect "voluntary" commitment of children without exacting procedural protections.[232] Several legislatures—notably those of Massachusetts and Illinois—tightened the child commitment provisions without specific judicial prompting.[233] And in Connecticut, the case of *Melville v. Sabbatino*[234] construed the relevant statute to at least grant minors the right to seek and obtain release subsequent to parental commitment. The trend stopped (or perhaps only halted) with the U.S. Supreme Court's decision in *Parham v. J. R.*,[235] reasserting the adequacy of

222. Other expert judgment—e.g., that of the social service caseworker—may also come into play, particularly in cases involving children with developmental disabilities.

223. There exists an extensive "antipsychiatric" literature in which these points are made repeatedly. Some leading contributors to this literature are Bruce Ennis, Alan Dershowitz, and James Ellis (lawyers); Erwin Goffman (a sociologist); Thomas Scheff (a social psychologist); and Thomas Szasz, David Rosenhan, and Ronald Laing (psychiatrists themselves). See note 15 *supra*.

224. 268 U.S. 510 (1925).

225. 406 U.S. 205 (1972).

226. 321 U.S. 158 (1944).

227. 428 U.S. 52 (1976).

228. 4ll Ill. 618, 104 N.E.2d 769 (1952), *cert. denied,* 344 U.S. 824 (1952).

229. 533 F. Supp. 661 (E.D. Pa. 1982).

230. 387 U.S. 1 (1967): right in juvenile delinquency proceedings to notice, counsel, confrontation, and cross-examination of witnesses, and to remain silent.

231. 397 U.S. 358 (1970): standard of proof to be "beyond reasonable doubt" in juvenile proceedings.

232. See *In re* Roger S., Crim. 19558, 2 MDLR 7 (Cal. July 18, 1977); K.W. v. Kort, No. C-2030, Div. D., 3 MDLR 90 (Dist. Ct. Pueblo Co., Colo., Feb. 8, 1979); Saville v. Treadway 404 F. Supp. 430 (M.D. Tenn. 1974); Poe v. Califano, Civ. Act. No. 74-1800, 3 MDLR 10 (D.D.C. Sept. 25, 1978); Bartley v. Kremens, 402 F. Supp. 1039 (E.D. Pa. 1975); J. L. v. Parham, 412 F. Supp. 112 (M.D. Ga. 1976).

233. Mass. Gen. Laws ch. 201, §§ 6, 6A, 14; see Doe v. Doe, 385 N.E.2d 995 (Mass. 1979). Ill. Ann. Stat. ch. 91½, §§ 3-500 through 3-511 (Smith Hurd Supp. 1980); see *In re* Lee, from Ellis, *supra* note 212, at 849 n.43.

234. 30 Conn. Supp. 320 (Super. Ct. 1973). *In re* Lee, from Ellis *supra* note 212.

235. 442 U.S. 584 (1979); and Secretary of Pub. Welfare v. Institutionalized Juveniles, 442 U.S. 640 (1979).

parental judgment to "voluntarily" commit a mentally disabled child when complemented by a concurring medical decision and further safeguarded by periodic review.[236] For the moment, the rush to interpose legal procedure and judgment has been slowed.

As a result of the litigation and legislation of the latter part of the 1970s, however, the present state of the statutory law on the commitment of children is different from what it was in the early part of the decade. For one thing, the distinction between voluntary and involuntary procedures has become even more blurred than before with the addition to the "voluntary" parental commitment statutes in a substantial number of states of provisions requiring the consent of the child[237] and/or mandating a court hearing if he protests.[238] New statutes providing for an *automatic* court hearing,[239] regardless of the child's consent or his protest, are essentially duplicative of the involuntary commitment model for adults (though as with adults, if there is no objection from the child or his representative there is no "issue," there are no adversaries, and the court's function will be limited to ensuring the proper observance of procedures). On the other hand, with the explicit provision in an increasing number of third-party commitment statutes that after a certain age—ranging from 12 to 18—the minor may no longer be hospitalized on the petition of his parent or guardian alone[240] and that he may voluntarily admit himself,[241] some statutes have moved closer to the true voluntary model (though of course the mere passage of age limits cannot guarantee uncoerced decision making in a setting where substitute judgments may, because of the principal's mental incompetence, remain a necessity). The classic hybrid statutes authorizing the "voluntary" commitment of all minors below the standard age of majority solely on application of the parent or guardian and the approval of the hospital have dwindled to about half their former number.[242] In the other half, this scheme has been modified by the age, consent, protest, and hearing provisions just mentioned.

The discharge provisions have not escaped change either. About one-third of the statutes today grant the minor or someone on his behalf standing to request release.[243] In some cases these provisions require notice to the original petitioners, the parents or guardian. In most, the request must be honored unless the hospital director moves to retain the patient by initiating involuntary commitment procedures,[244] a proviso that also applies when it is the parents or guardians who seek the child's discharge.[245]

More discrete reforms in the child commitment laws pushed by organizations such as the American Psychiatric Association have not made much headway in the legislatures.[246] The APA's central point has been that the procedure should vary with the child's situation: Is he in custody of his parents or is he a ward of the state? Are the parents capable, responsible, and loving or is there evidence of harm and neglect? Who is the moving party in seeking commitment? The parents? A guardian? A social worker? Some other agent of the state? What is the type and reputation of the institution to which commitment is sought? For how long? Due process and other procedural safeguards would be minimized under the more "favorable" circumstances; maximized under the least favorable. Perhaps this type of scheme has been viewed as too complicated. Or maybe it is not clear which circumstances "favor" what procedures.

IV. NUMBERS OF PERSONS IN MENTAL INSTITUTIONS: LAW, POLICY, AND MEDICATION

Even a limited analysis of the statutes and statistics relevant to the handling of mentally disabled persons indicates that institutionalization has functioned as a multipurpose remedy. It has served not only to prevent breaches of the peace and harm to persons or property but also to provide for the treatment and rehabilitation of the mentally disabled, to relieve the family of responsibility for the care of a disabled member, and to provide a refuge for those people within the society—the destitute aged, the mentally deficient, and the maladjusted who are unwelcome in any social group or environment. The relative weight attached to each of these purposes in the larger pattern of involuntary commitment has not always remained the same. It fluctuates with social and technological changes and the law's response to these.

Persons most affected by state laws regulating commitment, discharge, and institutional conditions are those committed or proposed for commitment to public (state and county) mental facilities. These people are

236. *Parham v. J. R.*: "Voluntary" Commitment of Minors to Mental Institutions, 6 Am. J.L. & Medicine 125 (1980); Note, Institutionalization of Juveniles: What Process Is Due?, 59 Neb. L. Rev. 190 (1980).

237. See table 2.11, col. 4. Florida, Mississippi, New Mexico, New York, Pennsylvania, Texas, Vermont, Washington, and West Virginia.

238. Table 2.11, col. 8—Colorado, Connecticut, District of Columbia, Illinois, Iowa, Michigan, South Dakota, and Wisconsin.

239. Table 2.11, col. 7—Alabama, Alaska, Colorado, Connecticut, New Mexico, Washington, and in Georgia minors may be hospitalized in the course of any juvenile court hearing.

240. Table 2.11, ages specified in cols. 2 & 3.

241. Table 2.11, col. 15.

242. See generally table 2.11.

243. See table *id.*, col. 11.

244. Table 2.11, cols. 11 & 12.

245. See table 2.11, col. 11.

246. See note 171 *supra*.

hardly a perfect sample of the general population, the lower economic strata being significantly overrepresented.[247] Nor do their numbers indicate anywhere near the full incidence of mental disability or its treatment within the general population. Residence and admission figures for private mental facilities, specially targeted institutions (veterans mental hospitals), and the psychiatric wards of public and private general hospitals—taken together—are easily once again as large as the state and county hospital numbers.[248] And the number of mental treatment "episodes" in outpatient or day-treatment programs—over two million in 1975[249]—further serves to put in perspective the public hospital facts. However, decisions regarding the treatment of these other populations in other settings are mainly private decisions; little or no law is involved, or they are regulated by special provisions that are beyond the concern of this book.

As the public commitment laws most affect the populations in state and county inpatient facilities, so—with the caveat that nonlegal factors are also at work—the changes in these populations are indicative of the effects of the laws. The statistical changes are nothing less than startling.[250] In 1956 the number of patients in public mental institutions was 551,390. By 1969, the residential census had dropped to 369,969. With no letup in the trend, the latest (1978) statistics show only 153,544 in residence at the public institutions on an average day (one estimate for 1980 places the number at 132,000)—low enough to make us wonder about the significance of the commitment laws altogether. The admission statistics, showing a sharply different pattern, confirm the laws' continuing salience, however. In the year 1956 the total number of admissions to the state and county facilities was 185,597; in 1969, twice as many, 374,771, were admitted; and in 1971, the admission figure was 402,472 (since 1971 there has been a levelling off and even some decrease in admissions, with the report for 1980 showing slightly over 390,000). Thus while the residential population is dramatically down from its high point in the 1950s, the shorter stays of patients in the institutions permit (as well as cause) far higher admissions, with the result that the commitment laws continue to affect large numbers of persons.

One of the expected effects of the lower residential totals would be relief of the overcrowding that plagued public mental facilities in previous decades. And indeed, many of the institutions today stand empty or half empty. The expected benefits on treatment have, however, only partially materialized. The number of fully licensed psychiatrists willing to work in public facilities remains well below the need for them. The reductions in patient populations are in some jurisdictions being matched by reductions in staff, and patients today may be equally as concentrated as before, albeit in fewer facilities or wards. As a result, a serious if somewhat altered staff shortage and overcrowding problem persists.[251]

On another level, however, there has been a revolution in the treatment of mentally disabled, especially mentally ill, persons—a "psychopharmacological" revolution.[252] In the past 20 years, psychotropic drugs have come to play an increasingly important role in the treatment of mental illness, to where they are now regarded as a necessary component of any comprehensive treatment program and are used extensively in state hospitals in the treatment of virtually all psychiatric conditions.[253] By inhibiting the more serious manifestations or symptoms of mental illness, these drugs have permitted a dramatically decreased reliance on intrusive and controversial treatment modes such as electroshock therapy and psychosurgery, that were formerly used extensively for hospitalized patients. But equally important has been the effect of the new medications on the need for

247. DeRisi & Vega, The Impact of Deinstitutionalization on California's State Hospital Population, 34 Hosp. & Community Psychiatry 140 (1983), *citing* Report to the President's Commission on Mental Health and Duval & Fowler, Los Angeles County Mental Health Patients in Camarillo and Metropolitan State Hospitals: Results of the 1981 Survey, Los Angeles, California, Los Angeles County Department of Mental Health (Nov. 1981).

248. See Division of Biometry and Epidemiology, National Institute of Mental Health, Statistical Note 157, Changes in Numbers of Additions to Mental Health Facilities, By Modality, U.S. 1971, 1975, and 1977 (Sept. 1981).

249. *Id.*

250. Goldman, Adams, & Taube, Deinstitutionalization: The Data Demythologized, 34 Hosp. & Community Psychiatry 129, 132. Their data were obtained from National Institute of Mental Health publications. The most recent estimates supplied by NIMH seem to indicate a slowing of the various population changes, if not a general stabilization, with the residential population in state and county mental institutions bottomed out at around 130,000-140,000 and yearly admissions and discontinuations holding at a figure somewhat below 400,000 (370,000-390,000).

251. The shortage of licensed psychiatrists is ubiquitous, but the adequacy of support staff varies widely. For example, in 1978 Michigan's state mental health facilities had 15,507 employees to care for 10,507 residents and patients. (Michigan Dep't of Mental Health Office of Public Information, Patients and Residents in State Facilities, Number of Employees 1955 to 1981 (Jan. 29, 1982)). That same year North Carolina had only half the number of employees (5,329) caring for 18,749 patients. (Research and Planning Services Division of State Budget and Management, North Carolina State Government Statistical Abstract (4th ed. 1979)). The states that have achieved staff/patient ratios of better than one to one, (e.g., Illinois, Ohio, and Michigan), have done so primarily by deinstitutionalization. However, a leveling-off point seems to be reached after which further decreases in patient populations will result in diminished legislative appropriations and staff reductions.

252. Even though it deals with the narrower question of competency to stand trial, Winnick's Psychotropic Medication and Competence to Stand Trial, 1977 A.B.F. Res. J. 769, nonetheless provides a good general summary of this treatment revolution. Another helpful article is Comment, Madness and Medicine: The Forcible Administration of Psychotropic Drugs, 1980 Wis. L. Rev. 497.

253. Winnick, *supra* note 252, at 771-72.

persons to be hospitalized at all and on the length of hospitalizations. Persons who formerly required commitment may now be given "maintenance dosages" of drugs that allow them to continue to function in the community relatively free of psychotic symptoms. Periodic outpatient services may be all they require. Others, once committed, may now be discharged much sooner than before and "maintained" in similar fashion.[254] The effects of this treatment revolution on the movement of mentally disabled persons to and from public institutions is at least as great as any legal change has been. Indeed, to a significant extent the legal reforms have followed the medical advances, prescribing institutional and institutionalization limits that would have been unthinkable in a medically more primitive era.

The treatment of mentally disabled persons is also affected by general policy that operates in conjunction with, sometimes also independently of, medical and legal change such as administrative policy, social policy, and funding policy, the last enabling the first two to be pursued. The movement toward emptying the large institutions and to push treatment in the community, for example, has been pursued as an end in itself. And it has been the federal funding under the Community Mental Health Centers Act[255] that has given significant impetus to the states to promote the community treatment concept, irrespective of the medical resources, the state of the psychiatric art, or the legal mandates in their particular jurisdiction. It is one of the main reasons for the failure of the community treatment concept to live up to its promise.[256]

Similarly, there has been a concerted effort to reduce the role of mental facilities in caring for the old and senile and to place this population in nursing homes, not from any sudden breakthrough in medical insight that this could be done or legal reform stating that it must be but because finally the money was provided to implement a policy whose wisdom had long been accepted.[257] One of the motives behind this transfer of elderly patients was to open up the mental facilities to younger persons whose problems in living were more predominantly psychiatric in nature. And there has been some success in this regard, on the statistical evidence.[258] At the same time, many older patients whose primary need is help in taking physical care of themselves remain institutionalized in mental facilities, while many young people—a whole "generation" of mentally disabled persons in their early twenties who need but do not obtain institutional care[259]—go untreated.

Finally, the provision of personal benefits from public sources and even private money has played a part in whether and where mentally disabled persons would be treated. The coverage of psychiatric care through the Medicare and Medicaid programs and through insurance plans—employment related and employer subsidized as well as personal—has affected how much psychiatric services are used and where they are sought.[260] Earlier programs, if they provided benefits for mental care at all, tended to be confined to inpatient services.

254. There are less rosy aspects, of course. The overreliance on drugs, particularly in public institutions or when given to institutionalized persons whose disabilities are "developmental," for reasons of "management" (administration) of patients rather than for treatment reasons (medical) has been widely noted. The term *chemical restraint* has been applied to suggest that medication is open to the same uses and abuses that were formerly alleged with respect to mechanical restraints. There is the problem of the drugs' side effects, often serious when heavy doses are administered over the long term and sometimes irreversible (tardive dyskinesia). And there is the reality that many patients, whom it was possible to discharge because of medication administered, fail to "maintain" themselves outside (fail to visit the outpatient clinic to obtain or otherwise take the medication) and as a result need to be rehospitalized, sometimes again and again.

255. Pub. L. No. 88-164, tit. 2, §§ 200-207, Oct. 31, 1963.

256. See literature cited in note 74 *supra*. For some earlier critical appraisals see, e.g., R.M. Glasscote, J.N. Sussex, E. Cumming, & L.H. Smith, The Community Mental Health Center: An Interim Appraisal (1969); M.F. Shore & F.V. Mannino, Mental Health and the Community: Problems, Programs and Strategies (1969); S.E. Golann, Coordinate Index Reference Guide to Community Mental Health (1969) (a bibliography); Rosen, Wiener, Hench, Willner, & Bahn, A Nationwide Survey of Outpatient Psychiatric Clinic Functions, Intake Policies and Practices, 122 Am. J. Psychiatry 908 (1966).

257. From 1939 to 1978, the number of nursing homes grew from 1,200 to 18,722, and the number of beds available grew from 25,000 to 1.3 million. (Stotsky & Stotsky, Nursing Homes: Improving a Flawed Community Facility, 34 Hosp. & Community Psychiatry 238 (1983).) This growth is attributable primarily to funding provided by the Kerr-Mills Act of 1960 and by Medicare and Medicaid funds established in 1965 by Pub. L. No. 89-97 (*id.* at 240). Nursing homes are regulated and licensed in 30 states to ensure that they meet acceptable standards for care and the protection of patient rights. (American Bar Association, Commission on Legal Problems of the Elderly & Commission on the Mentally Disabled, Board and Care Report: An Analysis of State Laws and Programs Serving Elderly Persons and Disabled Adults, A Report to the Dep't of Health and Human Services Under Grant #90 DJ 001/01 (n.d.).) Even so, many nursing homes today are overcrowded, forcing elderly persons to remain in mental hospitals at costs that well exceed the costs of nursing home care. (Sullivan, Crisis Reported in Mental Care of Aged in Cities, N.Y. Times, Nov. 1, 1982).

258. The proportion of persons under age 35 among patients in residence at state and county mental hospitals has increased from 16% in 1965 to 27% in 1975 (National Data Book, *supra* note 192, at 55). Recent newspaper reports commenting on an as-yet-to-be-released survey by the National Institute of Mental Health detail an even starker picture. Citing that an estimated 42% of the new admissions to public mental facilities are of patients in the 18-to-34 age groups, the *Boston Globe* (July 25, 1983, at 6, cols. 1-3) reported that these young patients, "many of them confused relics of the drug culture of the 1960's and 70's, [have] started refilling the nation's mental hospitals . . . threaten[ing] to reverse more than a quarter-century of steady decline in state mental hospital populations."

259. Pepper, Kirshner, & Ryglewicz, The Young Adult Chronic Patient: Overview of a Population, 32 Hosp. & Community Psychiatry 463 (1981). But see note 258 *supra* to the effect that this younger generation is finding its way into the hospitals in increasing numbers.

260. See ch. 11, Rights and Entitlements in the Community, § VII, Financing Community Living, *infra*.

But in the past decade many programs have added coverage for outpatient care.[261]

Against the background of these other forces, the impact of legal change is difficult to measure or even to discern. The effects of the smaller refinements, the subtler distinctions, will be particularly elusive, if not illusory. When not overwhelmed by these larger forces, the subtleties of the law are often obliterated by the coarseness of the legal system itself. In the routine, essentially noncontested commitment case, the judge wanting to do right by the parties — the prospective patient, the family, the policeman, and so forth — will have every reason to take a flexible approach to interpreting such criteria as "inability to care for basic needs," "need of treatment," "mental illness," or "incapacity to make a responsible decision as to treatment." Are any of these first three criteria separable and distinct in the first place, each capable of being defined and understood without reference to the others? And is it really possible to distinguish incompetent decisions from unwise ones, as the legislatures intended?[262] In the unusual contested case, it is more likely that an effort will be made to follow the letter of these laws. Should the decision be up to a jury, however, then we are back to the situation where the legal "technicalities" easily get lost. Even with respect to the "dangerousness" criterion, major practical effects from its new prominence in the statutes can hardly be assumed. While the term is strongly connotative, the connotations are highly subjective. What constitutes evidence of dangerousness is, as argued earlier, both legally and intuitively unclear. The threat? The overt act? How recent? Danger to what (property or persons?) or whom (self or others?)? A commitment standard of "dangerousness" without more is essentially vague[263] and can become as broad as the ingenuity of the person who must apply it allows.[264] If that decision maker is not convinced of the need for change in the types of people subject to commitment, then there is unlikely to be change. If he is, then there will be, but for reasons over and above the fact that the law dictates it.

The effects of changes in procedure — for example, requirements of notice, "due process" hearings, and the like where previously such formality was not mandated — will be no easier to detect and to separate from trends caused by other changes than are the effects of changes in substantive law. While it is logical to assume that procedures that "protect" the prospective patient will, along with tighter substantive criteria, result in fewer commitments, the strength of this effect will depend on a number of additional assumptions. Foremost among these is the assumption that participants in the commitment process will observe the procedural requisites. As noted, the incentives and resources to do so are frequently lacking.[265] In the past, even where persons proposed for commitment had lawyers, the lawyers frequently did not see it as their role to challenge the petition or to invoke the procedural protections in the traditional adversarial manner.[266] However, in the past decade a new breed of lawyer has appeared on the scene who takes his orientation and often his funding from more aggressive "client rights" sources where full, adversarial advocacy is *de rigueur* and the broader best-interest-of-the-client approach is rejected.[267] While the money for many of these legal aid programs is today being cut back, this generation of advocates has already left its mark. The only question is how deep and long lasting it is.[268]

The dramatic changes that have occurred in the past two decades in the number of patients residing in state and county mental hospitals and the equally major changes, though oppositely directed, in the number of admissions result from major shifts in law and policy and from advances in medical technology. Trying to sort out which of these factors accounts for what population effects, however, soon leads to a dead end, as law, policy, and medical knowledge in this area are inseparably in-

261. In 1973, Medicaid paid for 12.8% of all psychiatric outpatient services, Medicare covered 2.2%, other government funds 7.5%, Blue Cross 5.2%, and commercial insurance 3.9%. About one quarter, 23.7%, of outpatient treatment services were provided free of charge, meaning the states absorbed the costs, and 44.5% was paid for by the patients personally or by their relatives. (These figures exclude services provided by CMHCs.) Still, outpatient care is not as well covered as inpatient care. In only 1 out of 10 cases in 1975 was insurance the principal payment source for outpatient care, compared with 4 out of 10 for inpatients. (National Institute of Mental Health, Series CN No. 2, Characteristics of Admissions to Selected Mental Health Facilities, 1975: An Annotated Book of Charts and Tables 67-69 (DHHS Publication No. (ADM) 81-1005, 1981).

262. These are old questions. See M.S. Guttmacher & H. Weihofen, Psychiatry and the Law 290 (1952); Kadish, A Case Study in the Signification of Procedural Due Process — Institutionalizing the Mentally Ill, 9 Western Pol. Q., 93, 94 (1956).

263. A. Dershowitz, *supra* note 22.

264. R.S. Rock with M.A. Jacobson & R.M. Janopaul, Hospitalization and Discharge of the Mentally Ill 132-39 (1968).

265. See Slovenko, *supra* note 40, and text accompanying note 40.

266. See, e.g., Cohen, The Function of the Attorney and the Commitment of the Mentally Ill, 44 Tex. L. Rev. 424 (1966); Andalman & Chambers, Effective Counsel for Persons Facing Civil Commitment: A Survey, a Polemic, and a Proposal, 45 Miss. L. J. 43 (1974).

267. See Brakel, Legal Aid in Mental Hospitals, 1981 A.B.F. Res. J. 21; *id.*, The Role of the Lawyer in the Mental Health Field, 1977 A.B.F. Res. J. 467. At first, private sources, e.g., the American Bar Association directly and as a funnel for contributions from various other foundations, played the major role in supporting the new mental health lawyers and programs. Later, the government became involved through the Legal Services Corporation (legal services for the poor) and through legislation such as the Developmental Disabilities Act (Pub. L. No. 94-103, U.S.C.A. tit. 42, § 6000), which required states to establish patient "protection and advocacy programs" that in many instances resulted in the strengthening of already existing legal-aid type programs for the mentally ill initiated by the states.

268. A general characteristic of these programs has been their emphasis on institutional rights through reform litigation and legislative lobbying. Comparatively few resources have been devoted to routine commitments and the day-to-day civil problems of patients.

tertwined and jointly contributive to such progress in the treatment of mentally disabled persons as has occurred during this time.

V. TYPES OF LEGAL PROCEDURES FOR ACHIEVING INVOLUNTARY INSTITUTIONALIZATION

Past editions of this book have wrestled at perhaps inordinate length with the problem of how to classify the various approaches to involuntary commitment among the various states and generally also within any single jurisdiction. Although other conceptualizations are possible, a scheme that proceeds along the lines of the following three basic characteristics seems most useful and fitting: (1) the purpose and length of the institutionalization, (2) the primary authority designated under the statute to decide whether the person shall be institutionalized, and (3) the degree of compulsion.

On the first of these—purpose and length—the statutes generally fall into three classes: (a) emergency detention statutes, (b) observational commitment procedures, and (c) procedures for extended custody and treatment. In terms of authority to decide, there are: (a) commitment by medical certification, (b) administrative institutionalization, and (c) judicial commitment. And classified by degree of compulsion, the statutory procedures can be divided between (a) voluntary admission and (b) involuntary commitment.

Each state has a multiplicity of statutory procedures for committing mentally disabled persons. All 50 states and the District of Columbia have separate voluntary provisions and involuntary provisions. Alabama is unique in that it has no voluntary procedures for admitting the mentally ill; all other jurisdictions have them.[269] Minnesota has only "informal" admission procedures for the mentally ill and retarded—a voluntary process that involves less paperwork and leaves the patient freer to come and go than does traditional voluntary admission.[270] Minnesota does provide for regular voluntary admission of drug-dependent individuals.[271] Maine has only informal admission for the mentally ill,[272] but formal voluntary procedures obtain for retarded persons.[273] As recently as a decade ago, a good number of states provided for commitment on authority of at least two and sometimes all three of the decision-making branches—judicial, medical, and administrative.[274] Today, however, the judicial route predominates as the sole means of effecting extended commitment. Institutionalization of the mentally ill on administrative authority is decidedly out of vogue, with 7 of the 10 states that had such provisions in 1970 having repealed them and only 3 states retaining them.[275] Administrative admission for the developmentally disabled is more common.[276] Typically, this form of admission applies only to persons who do not object to institutionalization. When they do protest, a judicial hearing is required. Extended commitment on medical authority alone is also an idea whose time has passed.[277] It remains more common for short-term emergency commitments,[278] where because of the pressure of time the judicial role, if there is one at all provided for in the statute, tends to be confined to endorsing the medical determination or reviewing the credentials of the physicians—a ministerial act rather than a consideration of the merits.

While sound enough for a conceptual analysis of the commitment statutes, the above schema does not and cannot cover with equal fit the way the statutes work in practice. As already discussed, the voluntary-involuntary distinction is in application quite blurred. Compulsion varies by degrees or (to mix metaphors) on a spectrum where most commitment decisions fall into a middle gray area while the more distinct extremes of either fully voluntary admission or unwilled, formally resisted commitment are rarely seen. In that sense, the distinction is arbitrary no matter where it is drawn. As indicated earlier, it has been drawn in this volume along the lines of personal initiative. Any admission process that provides for the patient to admit himself is voluntary. All other procedures, that is, where the designated applicant or petitioner is someone other than the proposed patient, are not voluntary.

A similar blurring of the lines is perceptible with reference to the purpose and authority to commit spelled out in the statutes. Extended commitment is in practice quite often preceded by one or both of the other types—emergency detention and observational commitment.[279] Indeed, the statutes of a few states today man-

269. See table 3.1 for this statement and those immediately following. The Alabama Code does make reference to the possibility of voluntary admission for mentally retarded persons [Ala. Code §§ 22-52-52, 53 (1975)], but the actual admission procedure (§ 22-52-51) is in the nature of a third-party nonprotested procedure.

270. Minn. Stat. Ann. § 253A.03(1) (West 1982).

271. Minn. Stat. Ann. § 253A.03(2) (West 1982). There have been some slight modifications in the state's informal voluntary admission scheme since. See Minn. Stat. Ann. § 253B.04 (West 1982).

272. Me. Rev. Stat. Ann. tit. 34, § 2290 (1964).

273. *Id.* at § 2657.

274. See tables 2.6, 2.7, 2.8, 2.9, 2.12, 2.13, & 2.14.

275. The remaining states are Nebraska, South Dakota, and West Virginia, see tables 2.12 & 2.13.

276. See tables 2.8 & 2.9.

277. See table 2.14.

278. See table 2.4.

279. There is also court-ordered prehearing detention strictly for purposes of conducting the psychiatric exam. See table 2.6, col. 11. In many jurisdictions, the emergency procedure, with its relative lack of procedural safeguards, has become the primary means of involuntary institutionalization. Brooks, *supra* note 34.

date observational commitment first.[280] In addition, most states in the past 10 to 15 years have radically shortened their extended commitment periods. Indeterminate commitment provisions—prevalent before that time—are today all but gone.[281] And when the longest possible extended treatment is 30 days, as it is for example in Arkansas, the state with the shortest maximum,[282] the line between it and institutionalization for emergency purposes (which can be as long as 20 days in New Jersey)[283] or for observation becomes faint indeed. Furthermore, while commitment for the longer term tends to be by judicial process and emergency and observational detention are generally on medical or administrative certification, the latter often require some form of judicial approval which, though short of a full consideration of the merits, may complicate identification of the final authority for the commitment. In sum, commitment in the real world is much more of a continuum, or better, a process of interrelated steps, that belies the separate articulation of the various statutory procedures and the clean distinctions made for purposes of conceptual analysis.

A. Emergency Detention

Emergency hospitalization or detention is a temporary measure for the speedy processing of emergency situations. Unlike the other forms of hospitalization that undertake to provide relatively complete measures for the personal treatment, care, and safety of the mentally ill, emergency procedures have only limited short-range goals.[284] They deal with the suppression and prevention of conduct likely to create a "clear and present danger" to persons or property. Under common law, any official or private person has the right to detain a dangerous mentally ill person.[285] All but three states—Alabama, Arkansas, and Mississippi—today have special statutory provisions for the emergency detention of the mentally ill.[286] (The number of jurisdictions without such procedures stood at ten as recently as a decade ago.)

The absence of special provisions may create a number of difficult problems: (1) it puts the unduly heavy burden of proving urgency on the detaining officer if the detention is later challenged as illegal; (2) some law enforcement officers may hesitate to take an action that, because it is not specifically authorized, they regard as unlawful;[287] (3) in some instances such detentions may be limited to dangerous persons who are found at large, thus no mentally ill person could be taken into custody from a private home without a warrant;[288] (4) detention is usually limited to those who are violent, and it is uncertain whether it is available in cases where an ill person may be dangerous without exhibiting signs of violence; and (5) mentally ill persons detained under the general police powers are often kept in jail. Hospital authorities are strongly opposed to the practice of jail detention as well as to the transportation of patients in police conveyances.

In all 48 jurisdictions with statutes for emergency detention, some formal application is required to initiate the action. Persons authorized by the statutes to file such an application may include any ordinary or reputable citizen (or any two such persons), friends or relatives, and often law enforcement personnel, physicians, or health officers. In a number of states the class of applicants is limited to public officials and professionals.[289]

Although the function of detaining a person with emergency psychiatric problems is usually delegated to the police or other administrative officers, judicial approval of the action sometimes remains a prerequisite.[290] Such judicial certification may be required especially where the applicant for the detention is not the public or law enforcement official charged with the duty to detain but an ordinary citizen.[291] The power of approval is in some states (e.g., North Carolina)[292] vested in the magistrate or county clerk. In a few other states, the police may serve as the certifying agent.[293] But by far the most common certification route is the medical one.[294] Considerable variation exists among the states, however, regarding which particular medical authorities or how many must approve the application before emergency admission is authorized. The power is not limited to psychiatrists. Many statutes permit certifi-

280. See table 2.6, col. 8.

281. Conn. Gen. Stat. Ann. § 17-178(c) (West Supp. 1981); D.C. Code Ann. § 21-545(b) (1981); Ind. Code Ann. § 16-14-9.1-10(d) (Burns 1983 & Supp. 1983); Iowa Code Ann. § 229.14(2) (West Supp. 1980); Kan. Stat. Ann. § 59-2917 (Supp. 1981); La. Rev. Stat. Ann. § 28:55 (West 1975 & Supp. 1981); N.J. Rev. Stat. § 30:4 (1981); Okla. Stat. Ann. tit. 43A, § 54.11(E) (West Supp. 1981); S.C. Code Ann. § 44-17-580, 820 (Law Co-op Supp. 1981); Tenn. Code Ann. § 33-604, 609 (1977 & Supp. 1981), Tex. Rev. Civ. Stat. Ann. art. 5547-52 (Vernon 1958); and Wyo. Stat. § 25-10-110, -116 (1981). West Virginia calls the period of institutionalization indeterminate, but provides that it shall expire in 2 years. W.Va. Code §§ 27-5-4(k)(1), (4) (1980 & Supp. 1981).

282. See table 2.7.

283. See table 2.4. See also Logan v. Arafeh, 346 F. Supp. 1265 (D. Conn. 1972), *aff'd sub nom.* Briggs v. Arafeh, 411 U.S. 911 (1973); Lewis v. Ottaviano, Civ. Ad. No. 76-0422-H (S.D. W.Va. March 1, 1977), 2 MDLR 26.

284. Ross, Hospitalizing the Mentally Ill—Emergency and Temporary Commitments, *in* Current Trends in State Legislation 1955-1956, at 468 n.38 (1957).

285. *Id.* at 486.

286. See table 2.4.

287. Guttmacher & Weihofen, *supra* note 262, at 290.

288. Jillson v. Caprio, 181 F.2d 523 (D.C. Cir. 1950).

289. See table 2.4, cols. 1-4.

290. Table 2.4, cols. 5-7.

291. E.g., Colorado and Connecticut.

292. N.C. Gen. Stat. § 122-58.18 (Supp. 1981).

293. E.g., Neb. Rev. Stat. § 83-1021 (Supp. 1981).

294. See table 2.4, cols. 5-7, for this plus next several statements.

cation by a general physician, sometimes two, sometimes one plus a psychiatrist, a psychologist, or an unspecified mental health worker. Medical certification alone is a sufficient basis for emergency detention in most of the medical certification states, but a few, such as Indiana,[295] require judicial endorsement. In a couple of states, the law specifies that the medical approval be based on a *recent* examination of the patient. In Minnesota, the requirement is a liberal 15 days,[296] while in one select part of Wisconsin, the metropolitan area of Milwaukee County, where medical personnel is presumably easily accessible, it is a tight 24 hours.[297]

Analogous to the procedure for long-term (usually judicial) hospitalization, an application for emergency admission must allege and a certified petition must show that the individual proposed for admission is in one or several statutorily enumerated mental conditions that necessitate the action. These conditions/criteria are in some respects similar to the long-term standards, but they are not identical. The most conspicuous, though perhaps obvious, difference is that the emergency provisions list no "systemic" criteria along the lines that confinement shall be the "least restrictive alternative" applied in the least restrictive setting.[298] To the extent that the emergency process contemplates only a short holding action with little or no intent to treat, this omission in the statutes is self-explanatory. On the other hand, there are all degrees of emergency situations, and the persons involved in them present a wide range of dangers and disabilities that possibly could lend themselves to more varied and discrete handling. But about the only statutory variation is in "place of detention"—jail or hospital—and that is stated as a general requirement or guideline as opposed to an individual determination of what is best for the particular person sought to be detained.

The jail used to be a permissible place for detention in most states, but in the past decade or two, more and more states have limited or foreclosed this option in favor of placement in a mental health facility.[299] Typical provisions, if they allow jailing at all, now read that it can be only in case of "actual" emergency (Iowa),[300] or if there is "no other suitable place" (Colorado).[301] More stringent time limits have been imposed in other states, such as New Mexico,[302] which permits detention in jail for no longer than 24 hours when detention in a medical environment without a hearing is possible for up to 7 days.

The "personal" admission criteria in the emergency statutes are most usefully grouped (as in table 2.4) under the headings of dangerousness and inability to provide for basic physical needs.[303] Mental illness is less often explicitly referred to in the emergency provisions than in those authorizing long-term commitment, but it is by implication the predicate for detention under the former as well. Also, the emergency criteria emphasize physical deprivation as the reason for intervention, whereas the longer-term statutes, having psychiatric treatment as the primary goal, speak more in terms of mental disability and deprivation. "Gravely disabled"—a term that can mean either physical or psychiatric disability, or both—crops up in the emergency provisions of seven states, almost as frequently as in the long-term commitment statutes. In the emergency statutes the role of dangerousness as a predicate for admission is as pronounced as it is in the regular commitment laws, if not more so. Every state statute has dangerousness at least as an alternative criterion for emergency admission, and in a good many it is a necessary and by itself sufficient ground. This is not illogical in a procedure whose purpose is immediate intervention and detention. There are fewer references to "overt acts" than in the long-term statutes, though in practice an emergency situation will frequently mean just that.[304]

The criteria for emergency admission in New York used to vary in accordance with the official responsible for the disabled person's detention. The director of a hospital was authorized to receive a person if he posed a "substantial risk of physical harm" to himself or others. A peace officer could take action if the person presented a "likelihood of serious harm to self or others." The court, to authorize admission, had to find that the admittee was "mentally ill" and "disorderly." And directors of community services programs had to show "mental illness," need of "immediate care," and the likelihood of serious harm in order to act.[305] Today the New York law has been simplified to where each of these offi-

295. Ind. Code Ann. § 16-14-9.1-7 (Burns 1983).

296. Minn. Stat. Ann. § 253A.04(1) (West 1982).

297. Wis. Stat. Ann. § 51.15(4)(b) (West Supp. 1981).

298. The law in Kentucky used to be an exception in that it required the medical certificate to assert that the detained person will "reasonably benefit from treatment, and that hospitalization is the least restrictive mode of treatment." (Ky. Rev. Stat. § 202A-040 (1977)). This provision, however, was repealed in 1982.

299. See generally table 2.4 cols. 10–12.

300. Iowa Code Ann. § 229.11(3) (West Supp. 1980).

301. Colo. Rev. Stat. § 27-10-105(1.1) (1982).

302. N.M. Stat. Ann. § 43-1-10(c), 11 (1979).

303. See generally table 2.4, cols. 8 & 9.

304. In Gross v. Pomerleau, 465 F. Supp. 1167 (D. Md. 1979), the court invalidated police emergency detention practices based on a police department memorandum that was "overly vague and violative of constitutional due process standards" in that it failed to spell out the statutory emergency admission criteria. The court even added an "overt act" requirement, though the Maryland provisions of that time did not.

305. See Brooks, *supra* note 34, at 766–67. The relevant provisions were, respectively, §§ 31.39, 31.41, 31.43, and 31.45 of the N.Y. Mental Hyg. Law (McKinney 1972).

cials is empowered to act when the single criterion of "likelihood of serious harm to himself or others" is met.[306]

As an emergency measure, detention of the mentally disabled is justified only until the proper legal steps for institutionalization can be taken or until the emergency passes. The statutes therefore set specific limits on the length of detention,[307] ranging today from 24 hours in states such as Arizona, Georgia, and Michigan[308] on up to 20 days in New Jersey,[309] with 3 to 5 days the most common range. Nevada's limit is 2 work days.[310] The statutory schemes of some states have gradations according to whether there has been a medical examination: in Wyoming, for example, a person may be detained 15 hours without an examination and another 36 hours after examination and certification.[311] The permissible detention periods today are shorter than they were a decade ago, when 20- and 30-day periods were not uncommon and Ohio operated with a 60-day maximum. The important emergency admission court case of *Logan v. Arafeh*[312] sustained the constitutionality of Connecticut's statute, which, among other things provided for a 45-day limit. The court in *Logan* said that 45 days was not so unreasonably long as to amount to a denial of due process,[313] but surely such lengths of time between initial detention and formal processing are rarely necessary, and the statutory movement toward stricter time limits is sound.

Before expiration of the maximum permissible period of detention, the detained person must be given a hearing to determine whether continued institutionalization is needed. The procedures and criteria for this determination are those of regular long-term commitment, or conceivably those of observational commitment if that is what the petitioner sees as advisable. Presumably, even persuasion toward voluntary admission would be proper in certain cases. If the grounds for further institutionalization are not met, or if a hearing is not held in time, the detained person must be released.

Early emergency admission statutes permitted long-term (indeterminate) institutionalization on the basis of the medical certification alone, putting the burden of request for a full hearing for release on the detained person or someone who could petition on his behalf. A Missouri statute of this type was held unconstitutional in the case of *State ex rel. Fuller v. Mallinax*,[314] which has been instrumental in the general demise of these provisions.

More recently, the emergency statutes have been under attack for a different set of alleged procedural deficiencies. The argument is that the statutes' general absence of notice requirements, preliminary hearing provision and specifications for judicial review make them constitutionally inadequate. The push for preliminary "probable cause" hearings even where full hearings are required by statute within a brief period of time has been at the center of the reformers' agenda. The courts have ruled on this issue, with some major cases such as *Logan v. Arafeh*[315] and *Fhagen v. Miller*[316] holding that such procedures are not needed or do not make sense in the context of emergency provisions but a few other cases concluding the opposite.[317]

One of the major medical arguments in support of quick and easy emergency admission is that the earlier the intervention is made the better the chances are for cure. "[P]rompt therapy is good therapy" goes the popular phrase.[318] This view has not gone unchallenged, however. One writer has argued that "[t]here is just as much evidence that most acute psychological and emotional upsets are self-terminating."[319] Another argument might be that treatment is rarely provided during the early detention period. A final criticism of the emergency admission procedures is that in practice they have in many jurisdictions become the quick and easy way to commit the bulk of the mentally disabled, without regard to whether there are emergency circumstances or not.[320] Certification or endorsement of the ap-

306. The current provisions, in the order of note 305, *supra*, are §§ 9.39, 9.41, 9.43, and 9.45 (N.Y. Mental Hyg. Law (McKinney 1978)).

307. See generally table 2.4, col. 13.

308. Ariz. Rev. Stat. Ann. § 36-527(A) (Supp. 1981); Ga. Code Ann. § 88-504.4 (1979); and Mich. Comp. Laws Ann. § 330.1429(1) (Supp. 1981).

309. N.J. Stat. Ann. § 30:4-38 (West 1981), upheld in Coll v. Hyland, 411 F. Supp. 905 (D.N.J. 1976).

310. Nev. Rev. Stat. § 433A.150(2) (1981).

311. Wyo. Stat. § 25-10-109(b) (Supp. 1983).

312. 346 F. Supp. 1265 (D. Conn. 1972), *aff'd sub nom.* Briggs v. Arafeh, 411 U.S. 911 (1973). See also Lewis v. Ottaviano, Civ. Act. No. 76-0422-H, 2 MDLR 26 (S.D. W.Va. Mar. 1, 1977), upholding West Virginia's then 20-day limit. But see *In re* Tedesco, 421 N.E.2d 726 (Ind. Ct. App. 1981), holding that 14-day prehearing detention without probable cause violates due process.

313. Logan v. Arafeh, 346 F. Supp. 1265 (D. Conn. 1972), *aff'd sub nom.* Briggs v. Arafeh, 411 U.S. 911 (1973).

314. 364 Mo. 858, 269 S.W.2d 72 (1954).

315. 346 F. Supp. 1265 (D. Conn. 1972), *aff'd sub nom.* Briggs v. Arafeh, 411 U.S. 911 (1973).

316. 29 N.Y.2d 348, 278 N.E.2d 615 (1972). To the same effect, see L.R.C. v. Klein, 400 A.2d 496 (N.J. Super. Ct. App. Div. 1979).

317. *In re* Pasbrig, No. 22305, 3 MDLR 182 (Cir. Ct. in Probate, Milwaukee Co., Wis. Dec. 19, 1978); *In re* Barnard, 455 F.2d 1370 (D.C. Cir. 1971); State *ex rel.* Doe v. Sister Mary Madonna, 295 N.W.2d 356, (Minn. 1980).

318. See Brooks, *supra* note 34, at 778, quoting from New York Bar Association Committee, Mental Illness, Due Process, and the Criminal Defendant 22 (1968).

319. T.J. Scheff, Being Mentally Ill 151 (1966), *cited in* Brooks, *supra* note 34, at 778.

320. See Brooks plus cites, *supra* note 34, at 777. But cf. (contra) Brakel & South, Diversion from the Criminal Process in the Rural Community: Final Report of the ABF Project on Rural Criminal Justice, 7 Am. Crim. L.Q. 122 (1969), *reprinted as* American Bar Foundation Research Contribution 1969, No. 6, which found that the emergency procedure in rural Illinois was underused because police were reluctant to sign petitions, to take responsibility, and because medical certification was difficult to obtain.

plication in practice takes the form of authorizing *retention* of a person who is already in the institution, which in turn sets the stage for proceedings to assure his *continued institutionalization*[321]—ends that are presumably easier to accomplish than direct long-term commitment. The validity or weight of these criticisms is debatable. They go to show, however, that despite the general acceptance of emergency provisions as sound and essential parts of a total commitment scheme, they are not without their detractors.

B. Observational Institutionalization

Observational institutionalization is "commitment for a specified period of time to permit adequate observation of the case, with the diagnosis being accompanied by at least limited treatment."[322] The use of this procedure in the United States dates back only some 35 years, but similar practices have been used extensively in other countries, for example England, for much longer.[323] At the end of the observational period, either the patient must be discharged or procedures must be instituted to renew his commitment.

Although slightly fewer than half the states have commitment procedures designated as observational, functionally today almost every state has one or several procedures that may operate to provide a period of inpatient observation prior to the final decision on the need for institutionalization. Emergency admission, just discussed, is one such functionally interchangeable procedure, particularly in states where the permissible holding period is long—longer than it might be for observational detention in many other states.[324] The use of emergency procedures is in theory limited to situations where the requirements of alternative modes of institutionalization cannot be met without undue risk to the person or the community. But they are often used to establish at least a preliminary diagnosis and to determine what further steps, if any, should be taken.[325]

Similarly, most of the "long-term" institutionalization procedures, to be discussed below, authorize (under certain circumstances) interim detention of the person proposed for commitment between the filing of the petition and the final hearing on the matter. When this authority is coupled with the power of the court to order a mental examination, the result is in effect preliminary observational hospitalization. In addition, a large number of states today provide for phased commitment even in their formal, extended-term procedures, beginning with a relatively short term (six months is common) after which there must at a minimum be a reexamination of the patient, if not a recertification or rehearing, if he is to be retained for a subsequent longer term.[326] Lastly, a number of states[327] today in their long-term commitment statutes mandate that the final determination of the need for extended institutionalization be preceded by a period of observation. Statutes with this requirement may be only formally different from those that prescribe a phased commitment scheme.

There is some difficulty then in distinguishing "true" or "independent" observational commitment from other commitment routes that may be functionally similar. One way is to go by the express labels in the statutes. By that measure there are 22 states today that have observational procedures.

The application for observational commitment can usually be made by any person or citizen,[328] but in a small minority of jurisdictions—for example, Missouri, Tennessee, and Pennsylvania[329]—it is limited to physicians or hospital personnel. There is some variation in the statutes in terms of who approves the petition and authorizes the commitment.[330] Most jurisdictions require court approval, but the nature of judicial involvement varies, and it is exclusive in some states but alternative to medical or administrative certification in others. Alabama and Tennessee provide that the judicial authorization be based on a "probable cause" hearing.[331] The West Virginia statute just speaks in terms of a hearing.[332] The remaining statutes lack even that specification, and absent empirical information, one would not know whether the court's function is in the nature of endorsement of the medical/administrative certification or more like a true review of the merits of ordering observational commitment in the particular case at hand.

In only two states, Pennsylvania and New Mexico,[333] does medical certification alone (without court approval of some form) appear to be sufficient to commit. New

321. Brooks plus studies cited *supra* note 34, at 777-78.

322. Illinois Legislative Council, Mental Hospitalization Admissions and Discharges 17 (Jan. 1956).

323. Ross, *supra* note 284, at 409-70; Royal Commission on the Law Relating to Mental Illness and Mental Deficiency 1954-57, Report, CMND No. 169, at 81 (1957).

324. See table 2.5, col. 8, *infra* and compare with table 2.6 col. 13.

325. See Rock, Jacobson, & Janopaul, *supra* note 264, at 137. See also the studies cited in note 267 *supra*.

326. See generally tables 2.7 & 2.9 *infra*.

327. See tables 2.6 & 2.7 on mandatory observational hospitalization prior to long-term hospitalization.

328. See table 2.5, cols. 1, 2, & 3.

329. *Id.* Mo. Ann. Stat. § 632.330 (Vernon Supp. 1983); Pa. Stat. Ann. tit. 50, § 7303(a) (Purdon 1979 & Supp. 1980); Tenn. Code Ann. § 33-603(b) (Supp. 1980).

330. See table 2.5, cols. 4 & 5.

331. Ala. Code § 22-52-8 (1977) and Tenn. Code Ann. § 33-603(b) (Supp. 1980).

332. W.Va. Code § 27-5-4(k) (1980 & Supp. 1983).

333. Pa. Stat. Ann. tit. 50, § 7303 (Purdon 1979 & Supp. 1980) and N.M. Stat. Ann. § 43-1-10 (1979).

Mexico actually has two separate procedures for observational institutionalization, in the second of which the medical certification must be approved by the district attorney.[334] Alaska provides that the medical evidence be reviewed by the head of the admitting hospital *or* by the court.[335] And in Louisiana, uniquely, the coroner must perform an independent examination within 72 hours if the medical admission for observation is to remain valid.[336] The remaining statutory variation centers on whether one or two physician's certificates suffice, with the majority requiring just one.[337] Administrative authorization is limited to a few states whose statutes make reference to special "screening agencies" or the "county board of health" as empowered to assist the court in approving the petition.[338]

The maximum length of time for which persons may be committed for purposes of observation varies from a low of 48 hours in Alaska[339] to 6 months in West Virginia.[340] Three states permit observation for 72 hours,[341] while three near the other extreme provide for 90-day periods.[342] The short 2- or 3-day maximums are shorter than many emergency detention maximums,[343] and doubts may be raised whether they provide adequate time for thorough examination and observation, particularly in public institutions. Perhaps the objective of the legislation is to *force* immediate and intensive review of the patient's condition. The 90-day or half-year periods, on the other hand, may be longer than necessary for observation, particularly in light of the decreasing length of extended-term commitments[344] and the practical reality that patients of all mental disabilities and undistinguished by type of admission spend on the average only 3 to 4 weeks in public mental facilities at any one stretch.[345]

At the end of the observational period either the patient must be released or an application for extended institutionalization must be filed by the proper authority—that is, generally, the court or the hospital.[346] In most states, a full hearing is required to make the determination of whether further institutionalization is warranted, but in a couple of states, Iowa and Mississippi, which base the initial observational commitment order on a full judicial hearing (rather than mere certification), continued institutionalization may be predicated on the medical report alone.[347] The patient's option to continue treatment on a *voluntary* basis is spelled out explicitly in the Kansas law.[348]

Previously hailed as enhancing the validity and reliability of the "final" commitment decision, observational procedures today seem of lesser moment than they were a decade or so ago. With so-called extended commitment increasingly broken up into discrete and relatively short periods marked by mandatory medical or judicial review regarding the need for continued treatment, this aspect of preliminary observational commitment is becoming redundant. A period of observation still serves to produce better informed medical judgments, but the same goal may be achieved through court-ordered examination and observation as part of the regular commitment process, or even through improved use of emergency detention spans. As for the greater authority that is accorded to medical judgment both at the outset and in the aftermath of observational institutionalization, the weight of legal opinion (whether valid or not) is to be skeptical of it, and the trend in observational procedures as in other commitment phases is to increasingly circumscribe medical judgment with provisions for at least judicial certification if not full review. One hesitates to call the observational commitment procedures obsolete, particularly in the absence of information on how frequently they are in fact used, but the point may have been reached where one will more readily cite the concept for the way it has transformed other procedures than for how it operates as a separate and independent form of institutionalization.

C. Extended Commitment Procedures

Extended institutionalization is accomplished by procedures of considerable formality, as compared with emergency or observational commitment routes that take short cuts justified by the exigencies of the situation and the relative brevity of the confinement. Being most formal, the extended-term procedures are most often judicial. Extended commitment is in some states also possible on administrative or medical authority, and in a very few *only* on these bases. The general trend, how-

334. N.M. Stat. Ann. § 43-1-11(E) (1979).

335. Alaska Stat. §§ 47.30.020 & 47.30.030 (1962).

336. La. Rev. Stat. Ann. § 28:53(G) (West Supp. 1981).

337. See generally table 2.5, cols. 4 & 5.

338. *Id.*

339. Alaska Stat. § 47.30.040(b) (1962). See generally table 2.5, col. 8.

340. W.Va. Code § 27-5-4(k)(1).

341. Ariz. Rev. Stat. Ann. § 36-530(B) (Supp. 1981); Cal. Welf. & Inst. Code § 5206 (West 1972); Colo. Rev. Stat. § 27-10-106(7) (1982).

342. Ind. Code Ann. § 16-14-9.1-9(g) (Burns Supp. 1982); Kan. Stat. Ann. § 59-2918 (1976); Tex. Rev. Civ. Stat. Ann. art. 5547-38(b) (Vernon Supp. 1981).

343. Cf. table 2.4, col. 13.

344. See table 2.7, col. 17.

345. See National Data Book, *supra* note 192, at 64.

346. Table 2.5, cols. 9, 10, 11, 12, & 13. There are some exceptions. It is up to the coroner in Louisiana and to the Mental Health Board in South Dakota.

347. Iowa Code Ann. § 229.14 (West Supp. 1980) and Miss. Code Ann. § 41-21-81 (1981). In Mississippi a court hearing is held only when the patient disagrees with the medical recommendation and requests one.

348. Kan. Stat. Ann. § 59-2918 (1976).

ever, is away from these alternate procedures and toward solidifying judicial commitment as the dominant, if not only, mode of extended institutionalization.

For the reasons above, extended-term judicial commitment procedures will be reviewed in considerable detail, including a close examination of the "due process requirements" and other accouterments to the commitment process which have been pushed as essential patients' rights in the voluminous case law and commentary that the past decade or two have produced. Some of these "rights" may be as applicable to shorter term or nonjudicial procedures, but they are most appropriately treated in connection with the commitment process as it is conducted formally in the courts.

1. Judicial Commitment

A procedure has not been classified as judicial unless a judge (or judicial official) or jury has discretion to determine, on the merits, whether institutionalization is required by the applicable statutory provision. The mere fact that a judge must sign a commitment order or make a perfunctory examination of the commitment papers has not been considered sufficient to classify the procedure as judicial. Similarly, a requirement that a judge or magistrate must be a member of the administrative tribunal that determines the need for institutionalization does not warrant classifying the procedure as judicial.

Hospitalization procedures were extremely informal until a century ago. The growing evidence of abuses led at that time to the adoption of more formal procedures. The emphasis then and in subsequent legislation has tended to fall on the formalities and technicalities of due process, including notice, hearing, right to counsel, and a trial by jury. Although these safeguards were primarily for the protection of the patient, they have also served to protect the institutional officers and others concerned with the custody of the mentally disabled against potential charges of improper hospitalization.[349]

A reaction to what came to be perceived as excessive legalization of the commitment process led in the 1950s and '60s to a resurgence of less technical, nonjudicial procedures. The previous edition of this book (1971) indicated 33 jurisdictions in which some form of nonjudicial process—that is, medical or administrative—could be used to achieve long-term institutionalization; in 9 states such nonjudicial procedures were the only available method. Today, however, the judicial mode has regained favor, particularly respecting commitment of the mentally ill: only four states still abjure the judicial model altogether, and the number of states in which extended commitment of mentally ill persons on medical or administrative authority alone is possible has decreased to 12.[350] The state of the law regarding commitment of developmentally disabled and retarded persons is only marginally different. Judicial commitment is almost equally predominant, with provisions for medical and administrative admission confined to less than one-third of the states.[351] The most notable aspect of the state statutes covering the developmentally disabled is the relatively large number—9—that provide for a judicial hearing *only* if the patient protests the less formal form of admission.[352] Such provisions whereby the right to challenge the medical judgment must be affirmatively exercised are commendable in that they respond to the realities surrounding the question to commit better than statutes requiring automatic judicial involvement, and a persuasive argument can be made that the laws relating to commitment of mentally ill persons would profit from development in the same direction.

While judicial commitment procedures for both mentally ill and retarded populations in the various states show increasing uniformity, consistent with the general trend toward legal homogenization, significant differences on particular features persist. These will be set out in the sections that follow. To keep the discussion within managable bounds, we focus mainly on the laws that apply to the mentally ill; but the reader may want to turn to tables 2.8 and 2.9 to check for distinct statutory treatment of the developmentally disabled.

(a) Initiation of proceedings

(1) Application□□An application to the court for the institutionalization of an alleged mentally disabled person must be made and sworn to by the persons authorized by the statute to initiate such actions. About half the states permit any (responsible, adult) person or citizen to sign such applications, while in the other half the right to file is limited to one or more of the following groups: spouses, relatives, friends, guardians, public officials, physicians, hospital superintendents, or other mental health personnel.[353] An example of the form of such an application is reproduced in figure 1. The question of who may apply has not engendered very much controversy: there are more compelling issues in the mental health field. There have been a few court cases, however, one of the more informative of which is *In re Bray*.[354] The case illuminates the nature of the commit-

349. See Deutsch *supra* note 6, at 423.

350. See tables 2.6, 2.13, & 2.14.
351. See tables 2.8 & 2.9.
352. See table 2.9, col. 2.
353. See table 2.6, cols. 1 & 2.
354. Cir. Ct. No. 78-802-572 AV, 3 MDLR 33 (Wayne Co. Cir. Ct. Sept. 12, 1978).

Fig. 1. Sample application to the court for institutionalization

Approved by the Michigan State Court Administrator
and the Department of Mental Health

JDC CODE: PET

STATE OF MICHIGAN PROBATE COURT COUNTY OF	PETITION/APPLICATION FOR HOSPITALIZATION	FILE NO.

In the matter of ____________________

1. I, ____________ (Name), an adult, make this petition/application as ____________ (Relative, neighbor, peace officer, etc.)
2. The alleged mentally ill person who is the subject of this petition was born ____________, has social security number ____________, is a resident of ____________ County and can presently be found at: ____________ (Complete address)
3. The subject of this petition is mentally ill, and:
   a. as a result of that mental illness can reasonably be expected within the near future to intentionally or unintentionally seriously physically injure self or another person, and has engaged in an act or acts or made significant threats that are substantially supportive of this expectation;

   and/or

   b. as a result of that mental illness is unable to attend to those personal basic physical needs such as food, clothing, or shelter that must be attended to in order to avoid serious harm to self in the near future, and has demonstrated that by failing to attend to those basic physical needs;

   and/or

   c. his/her judgment is so impaired that (s)he is unable to understand the need for treatment and his/her continued behavior as the result of this mental illness can reasonably be expected, on the basis of competent medical opinion, to result in significant physical harm to self or others.
4. This conclusion is based upon:
   a. My personal observation of the person doing the following acts and saying the following things:

____

____

____

____

____

____

____

____________________; and/or

(PLEASE SEE OTHER SIDE)

Do not write below - For court use only

PETITION/APPLICATION FOR HOSPITALIZATION, Form No. PCM201, Revised 3/81

MCL 330.1417; MSA 14.800(471), MCL 330.1434; MSA 14.800(434) PCR 742

b. Conduct and statements I have been informed that others have seen or heard:

____

____

____

By: ____
Witness name Complete address Telephone no.

____

____

____

By: ____
Witness name Complete address Telephone no.

5. Persons interested in these proceedings are:

NAME	RELATIONSHIP	ADDRESS	TELEPHONE
	Spouse		
	Guardian		

6. The subject of this petition/application ☐ is / ☐ is not a Veteran

7. I therefore request that the subject of this petition be determined by the Court to be a person requiring treatment and that until the hearing the individual be hospitalized.

I declare under penalty of contempt of court that this petition has been examined by me and that its contents are true to the best of my information, knowledge and belief.

____________________ Date

____________________ Signature

____________________ Attorney name Bar no.

____________________ Address

____________________ Address

____________________ City, state, zip

____________________ City, state, zip Telephone no.

____________ Home telephone no. ____________ Work telephone no.

This petition is accompanied by
☐ Certificate of Physician.
☐ Certificate of Psychiatrist.
☐ Petition for examination.

FOR HOSPITAL USE ONLY: This application for admission was filed with the hospital on ________ (Date) at ______ (Time) m.

____________________ Signature of hospital representative

ment process and the function of the petition by holding that where both the petitioner and the respondent agree to a withdrawal of the petition, the court has no option but to dismiss the case. It has no authority to proceed on its own.[355]

(2) *Supporting medical evidence at the time of application*□□Already discussed in detail in the sections on "Who is Subject to Institutionalization" have been the various mental states and related conditions that must be alleged in a petition for institutionalization and that must be proved to the court in order to justify an order for commitment. We can thus move on to the medical evidence the statutes require to support the allegations in the petition. Again, these provisions are of comparatively minor importance in that they have not generated much legal controversy. They do hint at some important Fifth Amendment questions (the applicability and scope of the "right" to remain silent) and the reach of the doctor-patient confidentiality privilege, but these issues do not really come into play until later, fuller medical examinations are ordered and their use in the court hearing is considered.[356]

Some 33 states (up from 21 a decade ago) provide that the application be accompanied by medical evidence of one variety or another.[357] The variations concern the form it must come in, who and how many must give it, and whether it is required or optional. The statutes speak of "affidavits," "certificates," or simply "recommendations" that must be sworn, signed, or made by one (usually) or two physicians and/or a psychiatrist, psychologist, a mental health board, or some similar designee. Fifteen states consider an uncertified petition valid if it is alleged that the proposed patient refused to submit to an examination.[358] In a few states, such as Virginia,[359] there must be certification of "probable cause" that the person mentioned in the petition is an appropriate candidate for institutionalization.

An example of a medical certification form usable for supporting the initial application appears in figure 2.

While scrutiny of the petition and supporting medical evidence may at times be lax, and the potential for collusion between the family and the family doctor can never be entirely eliminated, these formal requirements should nonetheless go a long way toward dampening fears of groundless applications. Coupled with data from field studies indicating a general reluctance on the part of nonrelatives to become involved in commitment proceedings even when they are authorized to do so[360] and the additional safeguards that the statutes provide for in subsequent stages of the commitment process, the procedural framework suggests that today needless institutionalization is among the least of the problems confronting the mentally disabled.

(b) Prehearing detention and medical examination on court order

Supplementary to whatever medical certification may be required to support the application, the vast majority of states give the court discretion (and some mandate it) to order special prehearing detention and medical examination.[361] While part of the extended-term judicial commitment process, the exercise of this power results, as was noted, in what are essentially brief observational commitments. The arguments in favor of this use of judicial power hold too: while the initial application may be supported by medical certification that is sufficient to screen out the frivolous or malicious petitions, there is room and need for more intensive and elaborate medical scrutiny of the person before a formal decision to commit him is made. The preliminary examination may also serve to minimize the "battle of the experts" later at the hearing.[362]

The detention/examination period is intended to be brief, with several of the states that specify the time (Alaska, Arizona)[363] limiting it to 48 hours. In Alaska also the court must find "probable cause" to support the detention. In states such as West Virginia,[364] the period during which the prospective patient is detained and examined runs until a probable cause hearing is held and can then be extended until the full hearing, if probable

355. *In re* Kossow, 393 A.2d 97 (D.C. 1978), is similarly informative, holding that a private party is permitted to continue a civil commitment suit (begun through administrative channels) to the decisive, judicial stage. Because civil commitment is different in nature and purpose from criminal proceedings, there is no requirement to involve a public agency such as the prosecutor's office.

356. See this chapter § V C 1(b), Prehearing Detention and Medical Examination on Court Order, *infra* next section on court-ordered medical examinations.

357. Table 2.6, cols. 9 & 10.

358. D.C., Hawaii, Idaho, Illinois, Kansas, Michigan, Minnesota, Nevada, Ohio, South Carolina, Tennessee, Utah, Vermont, West Virginia, and Wyoming. See table 2.6 n.5 for citations.

359. Va. Code §§ 37.1-67.1 (Supp. 1981).

360. See Rock, Jacobson, & Janopaul, *supra* note 264, at 86. On the other hand, the allegation is sometimes made that the medical supporting evidence is too easy to come by, as general practitioners or family doctors without experience or expertise in mental health problems and after only perfunctory examinations readily sign the necessary certificates.

361. Table 2.6, col. 11.

362. Doubts have been raised, however, whether the procedure really assures that considered, independent medical judgment is exercised. See Kutner, The Illusion of Due Process in Commitment Proceedings, 57 Nw. U. L. Rev. 383 (1962); Rock, Jacobson, & Janopaul, *supra* note 264, at 181; and Scheff, The Societal Reaction to Deviance: Ascriptive Elements in the Psychiatric Screening of Mental Patients in a Midwestern State, 11 Soc. Probs. 401, 407 (1964).

363. Alaska Stat. § 47.30.700(a) (Supp. 1981); Ariz. Rev. Stat. Ann. § 36.521(D) (Supp. 1981).

364. W.Va. Code § 27-5-2(b)(4) (Supp. 1983).

Fig. 2. Sample medical certification form

County ________

QUALIFIED PHYSICIAN EXAMINATION AND EVALUATION
TO DETERMINE NECESSITY FOR INVOLUNTARY COMMITMENT
TO A FACILITY OF THE N.C. DIVISION OF MENTAL HEALTH, MENTAL RETARDATION AND SUBSTANCE ABUSE SERVICES

File #________
File #________

(Pursuant to G.S. 122-58.4/G.S. 122-58.6)

NAME OF RESPONDENT: AGE BIRTHDATE SEX RACE M.S.

ADDRESS (Street, Apt., Route, Box Number, City, State & ZIP) County

Telephone

NEXT OF KIN/RESPONSIBLE PERSON: Relationship

ADDRESS: Telephone

PETITIONER: Relationship

ADDRESS: Telephone

I, the undersigned physician, licensed to practice in North Carolina, examined said person on ______________, 19__, at ______ o'clock ____m. in ________________ and made the following findings of: ☐ mental illness, ☐ inebriacy, or ☐ mental retardation with behavior disorder (FINDINGS MUST BE DESCRIBED):

And further, I made the following findings of danger to self or others (FINDINGS MUST BE DESCRIBED):

Abnormal Physicial Condition:

Current Medications (medical & psychiatric):

As a result of my examination, it is my opinion that the respondent:

☐ is ☐ is not mentally ill.
☐ is ☐ is not inebriate.
☐ is ☐ is not dangerous to self or others.
☐ is ☐ is not mentally retarded with a behavior disorder and dangerous to others because of the behavior disorder.

Tentative Diagnosis:

______________________ M.D.
Qualified Physician - Signature

______________________ M.D.
Qualified Physician - Printed

Recommendations for Disposition:
☐ Release (Preliminary Evaluation)
☐ Release pending District Court Hearing (Facility)
☐ Involuntarily Hospitalized
☐ Other (specify)________________

____
Address or Facility

City____________ State____________
Telephone Number ______________

QUALIFIED PHYSICIAN EXAMINATION AND EVALUATION TO DETERMINE NECESSITY FOR INVOLUNTARY COMMITMENT TO A FACILITY OF THE N.C. DIVISION OF MENTAL HEALTH, MENTAL RETARDATION AND SUBSTANCE ABUSE SERVICES

(Pursuant to G.S. 122-58.4/G.S. 122-58.6)

NOTE: *This is a legal document which will be placed in a court file to which there is public access. In addition, the respondent may be released by the court if this form is not completed accurately.*

EXAMINATION: Specific description of *your* findings based on *your* examination of the respondent may be used as evidence in judicial proceedings. (History of prior mental hospitalizations cannot be used as sole evidence for involuntary commitment.)

DISPOSITION: Release may be recommended by the initial qualified physician when requirements for involuntary commitment are not met.

Release pending district court hearing may be recommended by the facility qualified physician when requirements for involuntary commitment are not met.

Outpatient commitment to the mental health center after a period of inpatient stabilization may be recommended by specification following the block marked "Other."

STATUTORY DEFINITIONS:

The words "mental illness" shall mean: (1) when applied to an adult, an illness which so lessens the capacity of the person to use self-control, judgment, and discretion in the conduct of his affairs and social relations as to make it necessary or advisable for him to be under treatment, care, supervision, guidance or control. The words "mentally ill" shall mean an adult person with a mental illness; or (2) when applied to a minor shall mean a mental condition, other than mental retardation alone, which so lessens or impairs the youth's capacity either to develop or exercise age appropriate or age adequate self-control, judgment, or initiative in the conduct of his activities and social relationships as to make it necessary or advisable for him to be under treatment, care, supervision, guidance or control. G.S. 122-36(d).

The word "inebriate" shall mean a person habitually so addicted to alcoholic drinks or narcotic drugs or other habit-forming drugs as to have lost the power of self-control and that for his own welfare or the welfare of others is a proper subject for restraint, care and treatment. G.S. 122-36(c).

The words "mentally retarded" shall mean a person who is not mentally ill but whose mental development is so retarded that he has not acquired enough self-control, judgment and discretion to manage himself and his affairs, and for whose own welfare or that of others, supervision, guidance, care or control is necessary or advisable. G.S. 122-36(e).

"Behavior disorder" when used in this Article shall mean a pattern of maladaptive behavior that is recognizable by adolescence or earlier and is characterized by gross outbursts of rage or physical aggression against other persons or property. G.S. 122-58.2(4).

COPIES: Evaluation prior to admission to treatment facility—original and 3 copies to law enforcement officer. NOTE: If it cannot be reasonably anticipated that the clerk will receive the copies within 48 hours of the time that it was signed, the physician shall also communicate his findings to the clerk by telephone. G.S. 122-58.4(d)

Evaluation in treament facility:
Original—Clerk of Superior Court of sending county;
Copy—Clerk of Court of county in which facility is located;
Copy—Medical record;
Copy—Special Counsel;
Other copies that may be specified.

cause is found. A few states—Alabama[365] is an example—premise prehearing detention on a threat of immediate harm, indicating that it is aimed more at protecting the public than learning about the individual's mental state. Several state statutes refer to the fact that at this stage in the proceedings the person may already be in a mental facility for evaluation and treatment.[366] Some 20 of the state statutes[367] make explicit the important and, one could argue, only logical option that the case be dismissed if the medical evaluation warrants it. Finally, there is the familiar variation in the statutes as to precisely how many and what type of medical or mental health personnel shall conduct the examination.[368]

An example of a prehearing detention and examination order form is reproduced in figure 3.

The proposed patient's rights during the examination and in use of the results at the formal hearing are matters that have recently received considerable attention in the courts. Four basic issues are at stake: (1) the applicability of the privilege against self-incrimination, (2) the scope of the principle of doctor-patient confidentiality, (3) the assertion of a right to an independent examination, and (4) the assertion of a right to counsel at the examination.

The self-incrimination question arises both at the examination (is the examinee permitted to refrain from answering questions and cooperating with the doctor, and should he be advised of such a right?) and at the court hearing (to what extent may the results of the medical examination and observation be used to support involuntary commitment?). The law is unsettled on both points. On one side are cases such as *Lessard v. Schmidt,*[369] which hold the privilege against self-incrimination to be an essential element of due process in civil commitment. At the least this implies that an individual may not be committed on the basis of evidence gathered at the psychiatric examination if he had no knowledge of his right to refuse to cooperate with the psychiatrist.[370] The minimal requirement according to these cases (enacted as statutory law in some states today)[371] is that the examinee be given a *Miranda*-type[372] warning[373] to the effect that he has a right to remain silent during the examination and that statements he makes can be used against him at the commitment hearing. Other courts[374] and commentators[375] have found the application of the police interrogation safeguards to be wholly out of line with the nature and purpose of the commitment process. They stress the civil essence and benevolent intent of the proceedings and question how the court can be expected to make an informed decision when deprived of essential information regarding the individual's condition, particularly when the standard of proof is high and the commitment criteria are narrow. An early District of Columbia case[376] suggested that even in the case of a criminal defendant the mental examination is more in the nature of taking physical evidence (permitted under *Schmerber v. California,*[377] which involved a blood test) than an interrogation and that therefore the examination itself is permissible and evidence of general mental condition admissible, except for statements made on the issue of guilt. Whether this point of view would still find support today is debatable.[378]

The doctor-patient confidentiality issue as it arises in legal and quasi-legal proceedings is closely tied to the privilege against self-incrimination. The law seems to be fairly clear that the doctor-patient privilege is not an absolute bar to the introduction of medical evidence in civil commitment proceedings.[379] But there are some interesting legal twists and turns to this general proposition. One case suggests that the privilege does apply to *statements* made by the patient to the physician but

365. Ala. Code § 22-52-7(b) (Supp. 1981).

366. Cal. Welf. & Inst. Code § 5303 (West 1972); Colo. Rev. Stat. Ann. § 27-10-109(1) (1973); Me. Rev. Stat. Ann. tit. 34, § 2333 (Supp. 1981); and N.M. Stat. Ann. § 43-1-11(A) (1979); Tex. Rev. Civ. Stat. Ann. § 5547-47 (Vernon & Supp. 1981).

367. See table 2.6, col. 12.

368. Table 2.6, col. 11.

369. 349 F. Supp. 1078 (E.D. Wis. 1972); *vacated and remanded on other grounds,* 421 U.S. 957 (1975). See also Suzuki v. Quisenberry, 411 F. Supp. 1113 (D. Hawaii 1976), Lynch v. Baxley, 651 F.2d 387 (5th Cir. 1981); Tyars v. Finner, 518 F. Supp. 502 (C.D. Cal. 1981). See also McNeil v. Director, Patuxent Inst., 407 U.S. 245 (1972).

370. Chacko v. State, 630 S.W.2d 842 (Tex. Ct. App. 1982); People v. Collins, 102 Ill. App. 3d 138, 429 N.E.2d 531 (Ill. App. Ct. 1981). This idea can be carried pretty far, as in the case of Cramer v. Shay, 94 Cal. App. 3d 242, 156 Cal. Rptr. 303 (1979), where a mentally retarded adult confessed to relatives and police to having set several fires. Arson proceedings were not pursued, but instead civil commitment was sought. The appeals court held that the admissions were not "free and voluntary" and hence could not be used as the basis for commitment.

371. E.g., Ill. Rev. Stat. ch. 91½, § 3-208 (Supp. 1983); People v. Rizer, 87 Ill. App. 3d 795, 409 N.E.2d 383 (1980).

372. Miranda v. Arizona, 384 U.S. 4367 (1966).

373. See also *In re* Gault, 387 U.S. 1 (1967).

374. State *ex rel.* Hawks v. Lazaro, 202 S.E.2d 109 (W.Va. 1974); Tippett v. Maryland, 436 F.2d 1153 (4th Cir. 1971), *cert. dismissed as improvidently granted sub nom.* Murel v. Baltimore City Criminal Court, 407 U.S. 355 (1972); Mathews v. Oregon, 46 Or. App. 757, *cert. denied,* 49 U.S.L.W. 3743 (U.S. Apr. 6, 1981).

375. See Developments in the Law—Civil Commitment, *supra* note 18, at 1309.

376. Battle v. Cameron, 260 F. Supp. 804 (D.D.C. 1966).

377. 384 U.S. 757 (1966).

378. Cf. Estelle v. Smith, 451 U.S. 454 (1981): criminal defendant who does not initiate psychiatric evaluation or seek to introduce psychiatric testimony may not be compelled to answer to psychiatrist at capital sentencing proceeding.

379. E.g., *In re* Field, 412 A.2d 1032 (N.H. 1980); Jones v. State, 610 S.W.2d 535 (Tex. Civ. App. 1980); French v. Blackburn, 428 F. Supp. 1351 (M.D.N.C. 1977); McGuffin v. State, 571 S.W.2d 56 (Tex. Civ. App. 1978); State v. Cole, 295 N.W.2d 29 (Iowa 1980)—criminal case. But see C.V. v. Texas, 616 S.W.2d 441 (Tex. Civ. App. 1981), contra.

Fig. 3 Prehearing detention and examination order form

Approved by the Michigan State Court Administrator
and the Department of Mental Health

JDC CODE: PET

STATE OF MICHIGAN
PROBATE COURT
COUNTY OF

PETITION AND ORDER
FOR EXAMINATION

FILE NO.

In the matter of ______________________________

1. I represent that I executed the attached petition/application and:
   - ☐ there is attached a certificate, and I request that the court order the individual to be examined by a psychiatrist.
   - ☐ no certificate is attached and no examination could be secured, although reasonable effort was made, because:
     - ☐ subject of the petition refused to be examined.
     - ☐ other reasons: ______________________________

2. I request that the court order the individual to be examined.

I declare, under penalty of contempt of court, that this petition has been examined by me and that its contents are true to the best of my information, knowledge and belief.

______________________ Date

______________________ Signature

ORDER

THE COURT FINDS THAT:

1. The application/petition is reasonable and is in full compliance with section 424 of the Mental Health Code.

2. A reasonable effort was made to secure an examination.

3. ☐ The individual will not comply with an order of examination.

IT IS ORDERED that:

4. The individual be examined at ______________________________

5. ☐ A peace officer take the individual into protective custody and transport him/her immediately to the indicated place of examination provided that the individual be presented for examination by ______________ (Date), which is within 10 days of the date of execution on the petition/application.

______________________ Date

______________________ Probate Judge

Do not write below this line - For courts use only

PETITION AND ORDER FOR EXAMINATION, Form No. PCM 209

Revised 3/81 MCL 330.1428; MSA 14.800(428)

would not apply to the latter's observations and conclusions.[380] Another case, rejecting the contention that the privilege bars the medical examiner's testimony in *involuntary* commitment proceedings, tenders the legal logic but medical paradox that if the patient were *voluntarily* admitted the voluntary nature of the relationship would preclude the doctor's giving derivative testimony in favor of subsequent involuntary institutionalization.[381] If nothing else, these cases hint at the possibility of professional conflict, and they convey a sense of unease at the shifting role and responsibility of physicians who at one point provide consensual treatment and in the next instance find themselves in the position of petitioning and testifying for their patient's unconsented commitment.[382]

The right to an *independent* psychiatric examination is reasonably well established in the case law[383] and by statute in some jurisdictions,[384] but questions remain about the reach of this entitlement in terms of the patient's right to choose, who pays for the "independent" psychiatrist, and where the latter's primary allegiance lies (with the court or the patient?).[385] Whether the examinee may have counsel present at the examination is unclear: some courts hold that because the opportunity for cross-examination exists at the hearing there is no such right or need,[386] and others, on the argument that the patient is entitled to an *independent* psychiatric examination precisely because presence of counsel at the examination "is not a sufficient safeguard," at least imply that there is such a right.[387]

(c) Notice of proceedings and opportunity to be heard

Whether the person who is alleged to be mentally disabled should receive notice and appear at the proceedings instituted for his commitment has been the subject of heated controversy. Psychiatrists have long decried the traumatic effect of personal notice on a person who is mentally ill.[388] Legal papers are said to produce only anxiety and confusion in a sick mind. This stand has received the support of some leading legal writers who suggest that "where the person is mentally incapable of understanding the nature of the proceedings or preparing therefor, or is so deranged that notice would do him harm, the purpose of protecting his interest can be more effectively accomplished in some other way than by serving him with legal papers."[389] One method suggested to lessen the potential traumatic effect of formal legal notice would involve having a doctor or some other competent member of a hospital staff visit the patient for the purpose of explaining the nature of the papers.[390] Another solution is substitute notice to the alleged mentally ill person's relatives or friends. The humanitarian desire to eliminate or curtail the use of notice in such cases raises certain questions, however. It may be, for example, that the experience of receiving notice would prove no more traumatic for the patient than the experience of suddenly finding himself detained in a mental institution.

The contention that notice is ineffective or harmful has also been challenged as prejudging the individual's mental condition before the hearing.[391] In addition, some commentators have asserted flatly—more as a conclusion than an argument—that notice and the opportunity to be heard are constitutional requirements.[392] In this view, notice to the disabled person's nearest relative or friend would be acceptable only if it came *in addition* to personal notice, as a way of promoting the possibility that the proceedings would be made known and explained to him sympathetically rather than to protect him from the knowledge. As to form, mere written notice may not suffice, given the possibility that the alleged mentally disabled person's ability to understand may be impaired.[393] That, of course, is also a matter of prejudgment.

In the state legislatures, the arguments favoring full notice to the proposed patient have carried the day. Whereas mandatory notice was provided for in only 26

380. Pennsylvania *ex rel.* Platt v. Platt, 404 A.2d 410 (Pa. Super. Ct. 1979).

381. *In re* Winstead, No. 9388, 4 MDLR 96 (Ohio Ct. App. 9th Dist. Jan. 9, 1980).

382. See *In re* Farrow, 255 S.E.2d 777 (N.C. Ct. App. 1979), which refuses to find fault with such a sequence.

383. *In re* Gannon, 123 N.J. Super. 104, 301 A.2d 493 (Somerset Co. Ct. 1973); People *ex rel.* Anonymous No. 1 v. LaBurt, 17 N.Y.2d 738, 270 N.Y.S.2d 206, 217 N.E.2d 31 (1966); Dixon v. Attorney General, 325 F. Supp. 966 (M.D. Pa. 1971); De Marcos v. Overholser, 78 U.S. App. D.C. 131, 137 F.2d 698 (D.C. Cir. 1943); Proctor v. Harris, 413 F.2d 383 (D.C. Cir. 1969).

384. E.g., Ohio Rev. Code Ann. § 5122.05 (Baldwin Cum. Sup. 1978); Wash. Rev. Code § 71.05.300 (Supp. 1981).

385. See Proctor v. Harris, 413 F.2d 383 (D.C. Cir. 1969): independent psychiatrist to assist the court rather than the patient. Brelje v. Pates, 426 N.E.2d 275 (Ill. App. Ct. 1981): right to independent psychiatrist not violated by appointment of state-employed doctor serving as court's witness; state not obligated to fund patient's wish to shop around for another "independent" psychiatrist.

386. *In re* Field, 412 A.2d 1032 (N.H. 1980).

387. *In re* Gannon, 123 N.J. Super. 104, 301 A.2d 493, 494 (Somerset Co. Ct. 1973).

388. Group for the Advancement of Psychiatry, Commitment Procedures 2 (Rep. No. 4, April 1948).

389. Guttmacher & Weihofen, *supra* note 262, at 295. For more recent commentary, see Davidson, Mental Hospitals and the Civil Liberties Dilemma, 51 Mental Hygiene 371 (1967). Cf. Wexler, Scoville & contributors, Special Project: The Administration of Psychiatric Justice: Theory and Practice in Arizona, 13 Ariz. L. Rev. 1 (1971).

390. Guttmacher & Weihofen, *supra* note 262, at 296.

391. *In re* Wellman, 3 Kan. App. 100, 45 P. 726 (1896).

392. American Bar Association, Report of the Special Committee on the Rights of the Mentally Ill, 72 A.B.A. Rep. 289, 295 (1947).

393. People v. Breese, 34 Ill.2d 61, 213 N.E.2d 500 (1966); People v. Couvion, 33 Ill.2d 408, 211 N.E.2d 746 (1965).

states a decade ago, today it is a universal requirement.[394] The large majority of states also require notice to persons other than the mentally disabled individual—guardians, relatives, spouses, attorneys, "all interested persons," and so on—but this is in addition to personal notice rather than as a substitute. The possibility that the proposed patient may need to be protected from the shock of receiving threatening legal papers is dealt with today as in the following provision from the Vermont law: "If the court has reason to believe that notice to the proposed patient will be likely to cause injury to the proposed patient or others, it shall direct the proposed patient's counsel to give the proposed patient oral notice prior to written notice under circumstances most likely to reduce the likelihood of injury."[395]

The value of notice, of course, is affected by the amount of time it leaves the individual concerned or his attorney to prepare for the hearing. Most statutes therefore specify the permissible length of time, the range being between two and eight days.[396] Several states operating on the same principle but with somewhat lesser specificity, have provisions that require notice to be given "within a reasonable time" (Wisconsin[397]) or "promptly" (Missouri[398]), or that speak generally of "reasonable notice" (Connecticut,[399] Louisiana[400]).

There has not been much litigation on the notice question. Among the many reasons for finding the Wisconsin commitment law constitutionally inadequate, the landmark case of *Lessard v. Schmidt*[401] also held that the provision for discretionary notice was insufficient and that notice to the prospective patient should be mandatory. More attention has gone to the conduct of the hearing itself, including whether the prospective patient is entitled to be present. The arguments pro and con are similar to those on the issue of whether there should be personal notice, with most cases (including *Lessard*)[402] deciding in favor of personal presence. The United States Supreme Court case of *Illinois v. Allen*[403] sets down standards for the right of defendants to be present at criminal trials, concluding that this right may be forfeited only when the defendant's conduct is so disruptive as to make it impossible for the proceedings to continue. Some commentators have argued that this standard be applied to civil commitment proceedings as well,[404] but this extension of the logic of criminal trials may be too simplistic. The statutory law is mixed. Most states provide for mandatory presence as such or at least when the patient asks to be there.[405] Presumably, the patient can always waive this right—a possibility that is made explicit in some of the "mandatory" provisions. Twelve states provide for the patient to be present at the hearing unless this is harmful from a medical or psychiatric perspective.[406] In Missouri, the right of personal presence obtains unless the patient is disruptive or *physically* unable to attend.[407] The case of *Bell v. Wayne County General Hospital*[408] stands for the proposition that if the patient's presence at the courthouse is difficult or dangerous, then the judge may move the hearing to the hospital or some other more convenient place, including conceivably the proposed patient's home.[409] This judicial discretion as to the place to conduct the hearing is expressly acknowledged in the statutes of a good number of states.[410]

Considerable litigation has focused on how soon after the initial petition or from the moment of first detention a hearing must be held and what the nature of this hearing should be. The trend in the case law today is to require "probable cause" hearings at the earliest moment in order to determine the justification for further detention and the need for a full hearing on the issue of commitment.[411] These cases posit a bewildering variety of times at or from which this preliminary hearing must be held, what action or event triggers the right to have one, and at what precise juncture it fits in the overall commitment schemes already characterized by brief, determinate periods of institutionalization and punctuated by various requirements of medical, administrative, or judicial review or recertification. Taken together with the patient's right to file a habeas corpus petition any

394. Table 2.6, cols. 14, 15, 16, & 17.
395. Vt. Stat. Ann. tit. 18, § 7613(c) (Supp 1981).
396. Table 2.6, col. 18.
397. Wis. Stat. Ann. § 51.20(2) (West Supp. 1980).
398. Mo. Ann. Stat. § 632.335(1) (Vernon Supp. 1980).
399. Conn. Gen. Stat. Ann. § 17-178(a) (West Supp. 1981).
400. La. Rev. Stat. Ann. 28:54(C) (West Supp. 1981).
401. 349 F. Supp. 1078 (E.D. Wis. 1972), *vacated and remanded on other grounds*, 421 U.S. 957 (1975).
402. Lessard v. Schmidt, 413 F. Supp. 1318 (E.D. Wis. 1976); Stamus v. Leonhardt, 414 F. Supp. 439 (S.D. Iowa 1976); Doremus v. Farrell, 407 F. Supp. 509 (D. Neb. 1975); Suzuki v. Quisenberry, 411 F. Supp. 1113 (D. Hawaii 1976); Kendall v. True, 391 F. Supp. 413 (W.D. Ky. 1975); Evans v. Paderick, 443 F. Supp. 583 (E.D. Va. 1977).
403. 397 U.S. 337 (1970).
404. See 2 MDLR 99 (1977).
405. Table 2.7, cols. 6, 7, & 8.
406. *Id.*
407. Mo. Ann. Stat. § 632.335.3 (Vernon Supp. 1980).
408. 384 F. Supp. 1085 (E.D. Mich. 1974).
409. Also *In re* Watson, 91 Cal. App. 3d 455, 154 Cal. Rptr. 151 (1979).
410. Table 2.7, cols. 4 & 5.
411. Lessard v. Schmidt, 413 F. Supp. 1318 (E.D. Wis. 1976); Lynch v. Baxley, 651 F.2d 387 (5th Cir. 1981); *In re* Barnard, 455 F.2d 1370 (D.C. Cir. 1971); Stamus v. Leonhardt, 414 F. Supp. 439 (S.D. Iowa 1976); Suzuki v. Quisenberry, 411 F. Supp. 1113 (D. Hawaii 1976); Doremus v. Farrell, 407 F. Supp. 509 (D. Neb. 1975); Bell v. Wayne County Gen. Hosp., 456 F.2d 1062 (6th Cir. 1972). Contra: Logan v. Arafeh, 346 F. Supp. 1265 (D. Conn. 1972); Fhagen v. Miller, 317 N.Y. S.2d 128 (N.Y. Sup. Ct. 1970); Coll v. Hyland, 411 F. Supp. 905 (D.N.J. 1976).

time and the growth of various agencies whose mission is to notify the patient of all manner of legal rights and rites or to assist him in obtaining them,[412] the new right to an early probable cause hearing leaves the patient quite thoroughly protected, some might say overly so.

(d) Due process and other rights at the full hearing

The full judicial hearing, which in a few jurisdictions may include or be preceded by a special fact-finding procedure conducted by a referee, master, or mental health commission,[413] must of course be run in a proper and fair manner, maximizing the chances that all relevant facts will be brought to light and that the "right" result will be reached. "Due process" must be observed, as lawyers would put it. The question is (other than the requirement of the hearing itself) what does "due process" entail in the civil commitment context?

There is no full agreement on the answer, though in the last decade in particular there has been a strong and concerted push to hold applicable to civil commitment proceedings most, if not all, protections available to a defendant at a criminal trial. There are landmark United States Supreme Court cases on the order of *Humphrey v. Cady*,[414] *Specht v. Patterson*,[415] *In re Gault*,[416] and *Morrissey v. Brewer*[417] that have been argued to mandate this by analogy. Some lower federal court cases[418] have spelled out in specific detail the procedural requisites in civil commitment proceedings and these decisions in turn have brought the statutory commitment law of some states[419] very close to the criminal procedure model. But an undercurrent of resistance to this criminalization of civil commitment persists, and cases such as *Coll v. Hyland* reject the notion that "wooden application of criminal law safeguards"[420] is appropriate. Such an approach may lend, as the *Hyland* court said, "a comforting sense of order to the legal mind," but it also "tends to brush aside considerations of concern for [the mentally disabled person]."[421] Adversary, criminal procedure is not the optimum model, and uncertainty about specific rights and requisites in civil commitment proceedings remains. We turn to these one by one.

(*1*) *The rules of evidence* □□The right to confront "adverse" witnesses is one of the essential aspects of a fair hearing. Since such confrontation is not always possible or desirable, however, there exists a body of evidentiary rules that spell out limited circumstances under which exceptions to the right to direct confrontation may be made. The civil commitment process has been said to be of such a nature that it calls for yet wider exceptions to (or where they state the boundaries of the permissible, less than full application of) these "rules of evidence" that guide the admissibility of testimony in general court proceedings. By and large, the practices have conformed to this relaxed view, as psychiatric testimony in civil commitment proceedings is reported to be replete with (normally inadmissible) hearsay, based as it is on written accounts of the proposed patient's family history, his prior criminal or psychiatric record, ward notes on his institutional behavior in case he is already in an institution or was previously, and so on.[422] The agenda of the reformers has been to curb these practices and to affirm strict applicability of the rules of evidence in civil commitment proceedings.

The courts over the past decade have generally sustained this reformist position, with several of the leading cases in the civil commitment field holding, *inter alia*, that the rules of evidence are without qualification applicable to commitment proceedings.[423] The reality cannot be disposed of that simply, however. There exist special situations that cannot be handled well through crude, blanket rules. For example, legitimate concern has been expressed about the inordinate and still growing amounts of time that doctors and other mental health workers today must spend in court. One way of combatting this trend has been to extend the applicability of the "business records" exception to the hearsay rule to hospital records.[424] Under this exception,

412. See this chapter § V C 1(d) (4), Right to Legal Counsel, including discussion of nonlegal advocacy services.

413. Table 2.7, col. 3.

414. 405 U.S. 504, 509 (1972). The case concerned a Wisconsin sex offender statute but is regularly cited in civil commtment litigation for its "massive curtailment of liberty" language and the due process implications of this.

415. 386 U.S. 605 (1967): Colorado post-conviction sex offender statute. The Court, quoting Gerchman v. Maroney, 355 F.2d 302, 312 (3d Cir. 1966), held that proceedings under this law must accord the "full panoply of the relevant protections which due process guarantees in state criminal proceedings."

416. 387 U.S. 1 (1967): criminal trial type safeguards applicable to juvenile delinquency proceedings.

417. 408 U.S. 471 (1972): the basic, but not necessarily all, safeguards of criminal proceedings held applicable in parole revocation cases.

418. E.g., Lessard v. Schmidt, 413 F. Supp. 1318 (E.D. Wis. 1976); Suzuki v. Quisenberry, 411 F. Supp. 1113 (D. Hawaii 1976); *In re* Ballay, 482 F.2d 648 (D.C. Cir. 1973).

419. E.g., the laws in Wisconsin, Hawaii, and the District of Columbia. But the commitment statutes of many other states have moved equally close to the criminal process model without explicit judicial prompting.

420. Coll v. Hyland, 411 F. Supp. 905 (D.N.J. 1976).

421. *Id.*

422. See Brooks, *supra* note 34, at 806–7.

423. Lessard v. Schmidt, 413 F. Supp. 1318 (E.D. Wis. 1976); Lynch v. Baxley, 651 F.2d 387 (5th Cir. 1981); Doremus v. Farrell, 407 F. Supp. 509 (D. Neb. 1975); Suzuki v. Quisenberry, 411 F. Supp. 1113 (D. Hawaii 1976); Commonwealth *ex rel.* Finken v. Roop, 339 A.2d 764 (Pa. Super. Ct. 1975), *cert. denied*, 424 U.S. 960 (1976); State *ex rel.* Hawks v. Lazaro, 202 S.E.2d 109 (W.Va. 1974).

424. Unif. R. Evid. 63(13) (1953). See People v. Germich, 431 N.E.2d 1092 (Ill. App. Ct. 1981).

facts found in the hospital records are admissible in court if relevant and material, and the hospital "business" is spared excessive disruption as not every doctor, nurse, or social worker making entries into the record is hauled into court to give personal testimony. But of course there are limits and exceptions to that exception: for example, (1) when the proposed patient challenges the accuracy of facts contained in the hospital record and introduced in commitment proceedings, then he has been held to be entitled to live testimony,[425] or (2) when a staff doctor testifies in support of continued hospitalization that the patient had been cited *in the hospital records* for dangerous behavior prior to his commitment, then the business records exception does not apply and admitting the testimony violates the hearsay rule.[426] In sum, there remain any number of intricate questions regarding the scope of the right to confrontation in commitment proceedings to which the answers are frequently uncertain.[427]

(2) *Standard of proof*□□To convict a person of a crime, the fact that he committed, or participated in, the criminal act must be proved to the court beyond a reasonable doubt. For a spell in the early 1970s there was a trend to extend the applicability of this standard of proof to commitment proceedings. Under this standard, the petitioning party must show beyond a reasonable doubt that the patient proposed for commitment meets the statutory description of committable persons —dangerousness, grave disability, need of treatment, inability to care for self, mental illness or deficiency, or whatever. Taking their cue from cases such as *In re Winship*,[428] extending the reasonable doubt standard to juvenile delinquency proceedings, federal courts in *Lessard v. Schmidt*,[429] *In re Ballay*,[430] and the like reasoned that respondents in civil commitment proceedings were entitled to no less. Developments in this direction came to an abrupt halt, however, with the United States Supreme Court decision in *Addington v. Texas*[431] holding that "clear and convincing" proof is sufficient for civil commitment.

The standard of proof question has been subjected in various writings[432] to a complicated calculus weighing the potential social costs of erroneous decisions to the state and to the individual. Presumably, if the costs between the two are equal, then a preponderance of the evidence standard—requiring only a 50%-plus probability—is justifiable, but if the heavier costs are on the individual, then the state must be allocated a higher burden of proof, and so on. The analysis is only made more complicated in civil commitment by the need to figure into the cost/burden calculus such factors as the reason for the commitment (parens patriae or police power?), the place (maximum security institution, open ward, or halfway house?), the legal criteria (dangerousness, need of treatment, etc.?), the medical diagnosis/prognosis, and other variables that tend to undermine the value and validity of neat analytic schemes. The Court in *Addington*[433] avoided this analytical bog and, proceeding on simpler, intuitive grounds, adopted the "clear and convincing" proof standard as a sensible compromise between the too burdensome "beyond reasonable doubt" and insufficient "preponderance" standards.

The present state of the law in the various jurisdictions shows the effects of the *Addington* holding. The statutes of 31 states[434] today specify the clear and convincing standard for proving the need to commit, including 5 states that insert an additional word (clear, *cogent*, and convincing;[435] clear, *unequivocal*, and convincing[436]) that could on paper be interpreted to call for a slightly higher standard but in practice is probably without effect. A more rigorous standard is in any event permissible, as *Addington* prescribes only a minimum. Three states that have not, at least yet, adjusted the stat-

425. *In re* Barnard, 455 F.2d 1370 (D.C. Cir. 1971). This holding was in the context of a preliminary, "probable cause" hearing, in which the rules of evidence may be more relaxed than in the final hearing.

426. *In re* I.R., No. A-3820-79, 5 MDLR 182 (N.J. Super. Ct. App. Div. Feb. 26, 1981).

427. For treatment of some related issues, see Rolfe v. Psychiatric Sec. Review Bd., 633 P.2d 846 (Or. Ct. App. 1981): board responsible for discharge decisions found to have erroneously relied on the *opinions* of two of its expert members (a holding that seems to lead to the untenable proposition that either such boards should keep experts off or, alternatively, the expert members must somehow refrain from using their expertise). Pennsylvania *ex rel.* Platt v. Platt, 404 A.2d 410 (Pa. Super. Ct. 1979): interspousal immunity doctrine held not to apply in civil commitment proceedings, as husband's testimony on wife's mental condition is allowed in. State v. Hudson, 425 A.2d 255 (N.H. 1981), and *In re* Haskins, 304 N.W.2d 125 (Wis. Ct. App. 1980): use of evidence for which individual had been convicted as criminal sex offender in subsequent proceeding for civil commitment is not double jeopardy, as the nature of this latter process is not to determine guilt or innocence.

428. 397 U.S. 358 (1970). See also *In re* Gault, 387 U.S. 1 (1967); *Ex parte* Perry, 137 N.J.Eq. 161, 43 A.2d 885 (1945).

429. 413 F. Supp. 1318 (E.D. Wis. 1976).

430. 482 F.2d 648 (D.C. Cir. 1973).

431. 441 U.S. 418 (1979).

432. See Simon & Cockerham, *supra* note 106; Monahan & Wexler, *supra* note 106; Developments in the Law—Civil Commitment, *supra* note 18, at 1295–1303. *In re* Winship, 397 U.S. 358 (1970).

433. 441 U.S. 418 (1979). To think in terms of proof beyond reasonable doubt in relation to fuzzy concepts such as mental illness and need of treatment seems unreasonable. Chief Justice Burger, author of the *Addington* opinion, said that "the reasonable doubt standard is inappropriate in civil commitment proceedings because, given the uncertainties of psychiatric diagnosis, it may impose a burden the state cannot meet and thereby erect an unreasonable barrier to needed medical treatment." *Id.* at 418.

434. Table 2.7, col. 11.

435. N.C. Gen. Stat. § 122-58.7(i) (1981); Wash. Rev. Code Ann. § 71.05.310 (Supp. 1981); W.Va. Code § 27-5-4(j)(3) (Supp. 1981).

436. Ala. Code § 22-52-10(a) (Supp. 1981); Tenn. Code Ann. § 33-604(d) (Supp. 1981).

utory standard after *Addington* are Hawaii[437] and Rhode Island,[438] where beyond a reasonable doubt is still on the books, and Mississippi,[439] where the preponderance of the evidence rule is still on the books. In Montana,[440] the statute calls for proof beyond a reasonable doubt of the physical facts alleged in support of the need to commit, but the clear and convincing standard applies to the other (the mental) issues. The remaining states have no statutory provisions on the subject; the case law of some mandates the prevailing clear and convincing standard,[441] but in others—those with no post-*Addington* cases on the issue and even some where the issue has since been litigated—the reasonable doubt burden still obtains.[442]

(3) Jury trial □□ The basic purposes of a jury are (1) to interpose "the people" between the state and the individual and thus prevent the state's power from being exercised to oppress the individual or to treat him in an arbitrary manner, and (2) to introduce lay judgment and community values into legal decision making—that is, to prevent excessively "legalistic" decisions.

The use of a jury in civil commitment proceedings has been criticized by both medical and legal commentators.[443] However, since the decision to commit is neither exclusively medical nor legal, the emphasis on social consensus that the jury represents, in contrast to strict reliance on medical diagnosis or legal doctrine, is not necessarily misplaced.

Statutorily, the right to a jury trial in civil commitment cases is guaranteed in 15 states[444]—that is, a jury is mandatory if the proposed patient asks for one. No state today mandates a jury in all hospitalization proceedings, without regard to a request by the respondent. In two jurisdictions, the appointment of a jury is within the discretion of the court.[445] The Alabama law specifically provides that commitment hearings shall be held *without* a jury.[446] In the remaining states, there is no statutory law on the subject and the right depends on case law precedent, which in the general is uncertain.

The uncertainty of the law in jurisdictions with no statutory directive stems from the fact that only the federal constitutional right to a jury in *criminal* proceedings guaranteed by the Sixth Amendment, not the Seventh Amendment counterpart for civil cases, has been held to apply to the states through the due process clause of the Fourteenth Amendment.[447] Some state constitutions, however, appear to guarantee a right to a jury in civil cases, which would include commitment proceedings.[448] In other jurisdictions, the common law has been read to assure the right in this context.[449] But any argument that the federal law imposes an across-the-board requirement of this kind on the states appears to founder on the 1971 United States Supreme Court case of *Mc Keiver v. Pennsylvania*,[450] which held that a jury trial is not constitutionally mandated in juvenile delinquency proceedings.

Individual experience in the various states illuminates some subissues. The reach of the right to a jury trial is limited, for example, in Illinois through a statutory provision that says: "If the court is not satisfied with the verdict of the jury finding the respondent subject to involuntary admission, it may set aside such verdict and order the respondent discharged or it may order another hearing."[451] The jury's decision presumably is not subject to being set aside when it finds the proposed patient *not* committable. A Michigan case[452] has held that the state's statutory law entitling a prospective patient to a jury trial in commitment proceedings means he also has this right in hearings to determine *continued* institu-

437. Hawaii Rev. Stat. § 334-60(b)(4)(I) (Supp. 1981).

438. R.I. Gen Laws § 40.1-5-8(10) (1977).

439. Miss. Code Ann. § 41-21-75 (1981).

440. Mont. Code Ann. § 53-21-126 (1981).

441. E.g., *In re* Holmes, 422 A.2d 969 (D.C. 1980); Reigosa v. State, 362 So. 2d 714 (Fla. Dist. Ct. App. 1978).

442. Superintendent of Worcester State Hosp. v. Hagberg, 372 N.E.2d 242 (Mass. 1978); Lausche v. Commissioner, 302 Minn. 65, 225 N.W.2d 366 (1974), *cert. denied*, 420 U.S. 993 (1975); *In re* J.W., 44 N.J. Super. 216, 130 A.2d 64, *cert. denied*, 132 A.2d 558 (1957). Doe v. Gallinot, 486 F. Supp. 983 (C.D. Cal. 1979), indicates that California's main procedure for civil commitment continues to require the standard of proof for criminal conviction even in the post-*Addington* era. Also *In re* Doe, 440 A.2d 712 (R.I. 1982).

443. See Curran, *supra* note 10, at 283.

444. Table 2.7, cols. 9 & 10.

445. *Id.*

446. Ala. Code § 22-52-9(4) (Supp. 1981). Ohio also used to prohibit juries in civil commitments (Ohio Rev. Code Ann. § 5122.15 (Baldwin 1964)), but this is no longer the law.

447. Duncan v. Louisiana, 391 U.S. 145 (1968).

448. State *ex rel.* Kennedy v. District Court, 121 Mont. 320, 194 P.2d 256 (1948); United States Fidel. & Guar. Co. v. Spring Brook Farm Dairy, Inc., 135 Conn. 294, 64 A.2d 39 (1949); Swanson v. Boschen, 143 Conn. 159, 120 A.2d 546 (1956).

449. Shumway v. Shumway, 2 Vt. 339 (1829); *In re* McLaughlin, 87 N.J. Eq. 138, 102 A. 439 (1917); White v. White, 108 Tex. 570, 196 S.W. 508 (1917); Warker v. Warker, 106 N.J. Eq. 499, 151 A. 274 (1930).

450. 403 U.S. 528 (1971). The due process requirements in juvenile proceedings have been a favorite analogy for the advocates of strict due process in civil commitment. *In re* Gault, 387 U.S. 1 (1967), and *In re* Winship, 397 U.S. 358 (1970), are the leading cases. Since in Addington v. Texas, 441 U.S. 418 (1979), the Supreme Court refused to extend the beyond a reasonable doubt standard of proof to the civil commitment context, when *Winship* had held this standard to apply in juvenile cases, the *McKeiver* holding that the right to a jury does not apply to juvenile cases would seem to doom the argument for a mandatory right in commitment cases. See Markey v. Wachtel, 264 S.E.2d 437 (W.Va. 1979); French v. Blackburn, 428 F. Supp. 1351 (M.D.N.C. 1977), *aff'd*, 443 U.S. 901 (1979). Advocates who would pursue the issue despite McKeiver can find support in cases such as Lynch v. Baxley, 386 F. Supp. 378 (M.D. Ala. 1974); Gomez v. Miller, 337 F. Supp. 386 (S.D.N.Y. 1971); Humphrey v. Cady, 405 U.S. 504 (1972); Lessard v. Schmidt, 413 F. Supp. 1318 (E.D. Wis. 1976); and Quesnell v. State, 83 Wash. 2d 222, 517 P.2d 568 (1968).

451. Ill. Ann. Stat. ch. 91½, § 3-809 (Smith-Hurd Supp. 1980).

452. *In re* Wagstaff, 287 N.W.2d 339 (Mich. Ct. App. 1979).

tionalization. In California, the statutory right to a jury has been held to apply to the initial guardianship proceeding,[453] which under the Lanterman-Petris-Short Act can lead to commitment on the guardian's authority. But there exists no such right at the rehearing,[454] as these guardianships expire automatically after one year.

(4) Right to legal counsel[455] □□ The right of a proposed patient to legal representation in civil commitment proceedings is today beyond question. In 1970, this was provided for by statute in 42 jurisdictions. Today, 50 of the 51 jurisdictions have statutes to this effect.[456] The only exception is New York, where there is a "Mental Health Information Service,"[457] an arm of the state's supreme court, with extensive investigative and advice-giving functions intended to benefit the (proposed) patient as well as the court and with a general mandate to protect the rights of patients. More significantly, almost all jurisdictions today provide for mandatory appointment of counsel when the proposed patient is unrepresented (typically, as some statutes specify, because of indigency).[458] A sizable number of states provide that the appointment can be waived, if it is done "knowingly," "intelligently," "voluntarily," "with understanding," or "in writing."[459] In California, the appointment is not made unless requested by the proposed patient.[460] Only Indiana and Maryland today lack provisions of this nature.[461] In 1970, half the states did not have them.

For counsel to be able to function effectively, his appointment must come in time so that he can prepare, and there must be laws providing for his compensation. Most states today have specific statutory provisions on these issues, with the time measured either from the initial petition or detention or, prospectively, to the upcoming hearing,[462] and the compensation question dealt with according to whether the court, the county, or the state (occasionally, the reference is simply to the "public defender") pays when the patient is indigent.[463]

To the extent that commitment is effected not only through legal proceedings but through formal judicial hearings, the notion of providing for legal counsel seems sensible enough. Arguably, there is room for legal representation even in proceedings that are less formal and less legally oriented. While it is easy to overstate the hazards against which counsel may have to guard in the commitment process, occasionally they are real. Sometimes there *are* scheming relatives in the background. Sometimes a disposition less restrictive than institutionalization *is* appropriate. And occasionally the medical judgment that goes to support commitment *is* lax or incompetent. The questions of who pays for the institutionalization and what effect this may have on the decision to commit are also of the kind that deserve a lawyer's scrutiny. And the potential deprivation of the committed person's personal and civil rights remains a concern even today when the laws are written to prelude automatic loss of these rights as a consequence of commitment.[464]

Just as the statutory law has come a long way toward the view that the presence of counsel is essential in civil commitment, so the case law has over the years pushed in this direction. The landmark decisions come from the United States Supreme Court in the context of criminal proceedings. *Powell v. Alabama*[465] established the requirement to appoint counsel where the defendant faced a potential capital sentence. *Gideon v. Wainwright*[466] implied and *Argersinger v. Hamlin*[467] finally expressed that counsel must be provided in all cases where loss of liberty—imprisonment—was threatened. *In re Gault*[468] established the right to counsel in juvenile delinquency proceedings. And the interest-balancing formula of *Mathews v. Eldridge*[469] together with the "massive curtailment of liberty" language of *Humphrey v. Cady*[470] have provided powerful ammunition for litigants arguing the mandatory appointment of counsel in civil commitment cases. An unqualified right to counsel in the commitment setting has been recognized for some time in some of the lower federal courts.[471]

453. Estate of Roulet, 590 P.2d 1, 152 Cal. Rptr. 425 (1979).

454. Baber v. San Bernardino Super. Ct., 170 Cal. Rptr. 353 (Ct. App. 1980).

455. See ch. 11, Rights and Entitlements in the Community, § VIII, Legal Representation and Advocacy Services, *infra*.

456. See table 2.15, cols. 1 & 5. The discussion in the text focuses mainly on provisions for the mentally ill. Separate provisions—to the extent that they exist—for developmentally disabled persons are charted next to the provisions covering the mentally ill in the same table (2.15). Special provisions regarding legal representation for alcoholics and drug addicts are in table 2.16.

457. N.Y. Mental Hyg. Law § 29.09 (McKinney 1978). While initially created as an information agency with a heavy social service component, the MHIS over the years has become more and more oriented toward legal advocacy. See generally M. Goldstein, Mental Health Legal Advocacy: A Handbook on Psychiatric Hospitalization (Mental Health Information Service, 1st Dep't, N.Y. App. Div. 1982).

458. Table 2.15, cols. 2 & 6.

459. *Id.*

460. Cal. Welf. & Inst. Code § 5276 (West & Supp. 1980).

461. Table 2.15, cols. 2 & 6.

462. Table 2.15, cols. 4 & 8.

463. Table 2.15, cols. 3 & 7.

464. See chs. 8, Decision-Making Rights over Persons and Property, and 9, Family Laws, *infra* regarding the consequences of institutionalization for the patient's personal and property rights.

465. 287 U.S. 45 (1932).

466. 372 U.S. 335 (1962).

467. 407 U.S. 25 (1972).

468. 387 U.S. 1 (1967).

469. 424 U.S. 319 (1975).

470. 405 U.S. 504, 509 (1972).

471. Heryford v. Parker, 396 F.2d 393 (10th Cir. 1968); Lessard v. Schmidt, 349 F. Supp. 1078 (E.D. Wis. 1972), *vacated and remanded on*

The United States Congress has also done its share toward assuring legal representation in civil commitment. In fact, a couple of pertinent pieces of federal legislation are quite far reaching and controversial. One is the "protection and advocacy" systems section of the Developmentally Disabled Assistance and Bill of Rights Act of 1975,[472] providing $3 million to be allocated among the states to help them set up or strengthen client advocacy programs for developmentally disabled persons. The law does not call for all the advocacy to be done by lawyers, but it does require a legal service component, and the heavy lawyer involvement that characterized the original programs will undoubtedly remain a salient feature. Given the dwindling political and financial support these days for any legal services programs, the objectives of the protection and advocacy programs for the developmentally disabled seem further out of reach than when the legislation was first conceived.

The other major venture by the Congress in this area has been the passage as part of the Civil Rights of Institutionalized Persons Act[473] of a provision that grants authority to the federal Justice Department, the United States Attorney General, to legally intervene on behalf of mentally disabled persons when it finds a pattern of abuse in state institutions. Whatever the practical effects of this provision (and they will probably be small), conceptually it represents a substantial inroad into the federalist structure, and its constitutional propriety has been seriously questioned in at least one federal court decision.[474]

More to the point today than questions about the right to counsel in civil commitment cases are the questions about counsel's *role*. What is proper lawyering, what is effective in this context? The main debate is about whether counsel should stay with the traditional advocacy, adversarial approach in representing the proposed patient or whether he should move toward a more mediatory, best-interest-of-the-client role. But there are also questions about competent representation focusing on the usual interrelated factors of access, fees, and preparedness.

A common statistic presented by supporters of counsel, and particularly adversary counsel, in commitment proceedings is that significantly fewer persons so represented are committed.[475] The trouble with this argument by statistic is that it jumps from the unsupported assumption that the fewer commitments there are the better it is to the conclusion that combative lawyers who keep their clients out of institutions (and away from treatment) are playing the proper role. While the prevailing law, wisdom, and professional ethic[476] today remain more moderate, a number of courts[477] seem to have accepted the above argument and the radical view that a person who is subjected to commitment proceedings is entitled to an attorney whose role is to present the case in opposition to the petitioners for commitment, irrespective of the client's treatment needs, if not his articulated desires.

While the function of legal counsel, however carried out, is most obvious at the hearing stage, there are court cases mandating earlier appointment—"at the earliest

---

other grounds, 421 U.S. 957 (1975). See also People v. Stanley, 17 N.Y.2d 256, 217 N.E.2d 636, 270 N.Y.S.2d 573 (1966), and Thorn v. Superior Ct. of San Diego County, 1 Cal. 3d 666, 464 P.2d 56, Cal. Rptr. 600 (1970). In Vitek v. Jones, 445 U.S. 480 (1980), four of the justices felt that counsel should be provided in cases where the state seeks to transfer indigent mentally ill prisoners to mental health facilities.

472. 42 U.S.C. § 6064 (1981).

473. *Id.* § 1997c.

474. In United States v. Solomon, 419 F. Supp. 358 (D. Md. 1977), the court dismissed an action by the Attorney General to intervene on behalf of the mentally retarded in Maryland. The decision was intended to restrain the executive branch from exceeding its power, particularly in relation to Congress. It was based in part on specific evidence that Congress intended for the executive branch not to engage in such actions. The Civil Rights of Institutionalized Persons Act, on the other hand, demonstrates a clear congressional intent that the executive branch seek to enforce the civil rights of mental patients in appropriate situations. As regards predictions of the act's impact, the first and only case so far was brought recently in Davis v. Henderson, 535 F. Supp. 407 (M.D. La. 1982). See 6 MDLR 237. The official policy of the Justice Department in implementing the act is to make sure that institutions protect the safety of patients and guarantee their freedom from unnecessary restraint. The policy does not include inquiry into whether the facilities provide adequate "psychiatric care, psychological treatment or individualized therapeutic effort designed to enhance capacity, capability and competence" (William Bradford Reynolds, Justice Department Civil Rights Chief, Justice Dep't internal memo, June 24, 1982). This express policy is based on an interpretation of the recent Supreme Court decision in Youngberg v. Romeo, 457 U.S. 307 (1982). The interpretation has not gone without criticism. (See Thornton, New Policy on Mental Patient Rights Upsets Lawyers, Health, Community, Wash. Post, Sept. 29, 1982).

475. See, e.g., Developments in the Law—Civil Commitment, *supra* note 18, at 1285, citing Gupta, New York's Mental Health Information Service: An Experiment in Due Process, 25 Rutgers L. Rev. 405 (1971).

476. See Brooks, *supra* note 34, at 107-11 (1980 Supp.), particularly the discussion (at 111-12) of the ethical opinion of Michigan's Committee on Professional and Judicial Ethics (CI-184). Cf. also Model Codes of Professional Responsibility Canon 5, EC 5-1 with Canon 7, EC7-7 (1980).

477. Lessard v. Schmidt, 349 F. Supp. 1078 (E.D. Wis. 1972), *vacated and remanded on other grounds*, 414 U.S. 473 (1974); Suzuki v. Quisenberry, 411 F. Supp. 1113 (D. Hawaii 1976); Lynch v. Baxley, 386 F. Supp. 378 (M.D. Ala. 1974); Bell v. Wayne County General Hospital, 384 F. Supp. 1085 (E.D. Mich. 1974); Quesnell v. State, 83 Wash. 2d 222, 517 P.2d 568 (1968). See also State *ex rel.* Memmel v. Mundy, 249 N.W.2d 573 (Wis. 1977). Earlier cases leaned more toward the "best interest" model: Prochaska v. Brinegar, 102 N.W.2d 870 (Iowa 1960); *In re* Basso, 299 F.2d 933 (D.C. Cir. 1962). There is also an extensive literature today on the role of counsel in the mental health field: see Brakel, *supra* note 267, which deals with the lawyer's post-commitment role but cites at 34-35 n.6 some of the studies relative to commitment proceedings. A few state statutes, in response to recent court decisions, spell out that the appointment of counsel means adversary counsel (Tenn. Code Ann. § 34-12-106 (1980)) or an advocate (Iowa Code § 229.19 (1979)) rather than a guardian ad litem, but they go no further in defining the advocacy role.

stage,"[478] "at all significant stages,"[479] and so forth. In this connection, tricky questions of access may arise (for example, on what basis, under what circumsances, and when may the lawyer visit persons who are already institutionalized?),[480] and even the lawyer's standing to bring suit on behalf of mentally disabled patients whose desire for or capacity to consent to representation is unclear is sometimes raised as an issue.[481] Finally, separate from interpretation of state statutory law on lawyers' compensation (which generates its own litigation),[482] the question of who may collect attorneys' fees in individual cases brought under special federal Civil Rights provisions occasionally comes to the fore.[483] In short, while there may be a working consensus today on the right to counsel in the civil commitment context, many questions about the implementation of this right and about counsel's role remain open.

(5) *Waiving procedural rights* □□Under ordinary circumstances, the various rights discussed in the preceding sections can be waived by their intended beneficiary. The only requirement is that the waiver be made knowingly, intelligently, and voluntarily.[484] In the case of persons proposed for commitment the question arises whether in general the requirement can be met and thus whether a valid waiver can be obtained.

To conclude that all persons proposed for institutionalization are incapable of making a valid decision not to exercise their rights presumes too much, namely, (1) that they are proper candidates for institutionalization — the issue still to be decided — and (2) that they are legally incompetent — something that may not be so even if they are proper subjects for commitment. Instead the focus should be particularized: When is a proposed patient incompetent to make a valid waiver? What shows that he is? Can someone who represents his interests waive his rights for him? How? And under what circumstances?

There is some case law that touches on these questions. In *Doremus v. Farrell*,[485] the district court concluded that before an alleged mentally disabled person could waive counsel, there would have to be an inquiry to determine the former's general competency. This could be an onerous requirement if interpreted as mandating a formal, separate hearing. Still further go cases like *Dooling v. Overholser*,[486] holding that there can never be a valid waiver of counsel in jurisdictions where a statutory right to counsel exists, and *Lynch v. Baxley*,[487] concluding that the waiver must be made *by* counsel with the informed consent of the client and the approval of the court, which may in effect amount to a denial of the client's right to waive. An interesting compromise was struck in *In re Tuntland*,[488] where the court allowed the client to decline the services of a court-appointed attorney but then ordered the attorney to continue to serve as the client's advisor.

There remains then some uncharted territory in the area of the alleged mentally disabled person's power to waive important legal rights. The paradox of the issue lies in the fact that many of the patients' rights advocates who would generally presume the autonomy and competency of their clientele are drawn in the opposite direction when it comes to the capacity to waive, and whereas these advocates have traditionally pushed for competency inquiries limited to the *specific* choice or function faced by the client, their interest in the instance of a client who *waives* a specific right with apparent understanding is in exposing evidence of *general* incapacity.

(e) Place of treatment

With the emergence of the least restrictive alternative concept in commitment, statutory provisions specifying the place of treatment have acquired new significance. The provisions used to focus primarily on the choice available to the court between hospitalizing the patient in a private hospital or in a public facility. A few statutes made reference to the possibility of placement in the home of a relative. Today, provisions of this last type or, more broadly, those stipulating the general alternative of outpatient treatment have gained wide prominence.

478. *In re* Fisher, 313 N.E.2d 851 (Ohio 1974).
479. Lynch v. Baxley, 386 F. Supp. 378 (M.D. Ala. 1974).
480. See DeVito v. Murphy, No. 79 CH 2369, 3 MDLR 247 (Ill. Cook Co. Cir. Ct. May 1, 1979); Cypen v. Burton, No. 80-6183-Civ-ALH, 4 MDLR 417 (S.D. Fla. July 25, 1980); State v. Elson, 60 Wis. 2d 54, 208 N.W.2d 363 (1973).
481. Goldstein v. Coughlin, 83 F.R.D. 613 (1979); Developmental Disability Advocacy Center, Inc. v. Melton, 521 F. Supp. 365 (D.N.H. 1981).
482. See New York State Ass'n for Retarded Children, Inc. v. Carey, 631 F.2d 162 (2d Cir. 1980); Seibert v. Wayne County Probate Court, No. 79-921-758 CZ, 4 MDLR 34C (Mich. Wayne Co. Cir. Ct. June 24, 1980); and Brewster v. Dukakis, No. 76-4423-F, 6 MDLR 318 (D. Mass. July 16, 1982).
483. "In any action in which the United States joins as intervenor under this section, the court may allow the prevailing party, other than the United States, a reasonable attorney's fee against the United States as part of the costs." 42 U.S.C. 1997d (1981). Vecchione v. Wohlgemuth, 377 F. Supp. 1361 (E.D. Pa. 1974), and 481 F.Supp. 776 (E.D. Pa. 1979); Hughes v. Rowe, 449 U.S. 5 (1980); Hanrahan v. Hampton, 446 U.S. 754, (1980); Vasquez v. Fleming, 617 F.2d 334 (1980).
484. Johnson v. Zerbst, 304 U.S. 458 (1938). Similar requirements regarding waiver appear in some of the state statutes providing for the rights to a hearing, to a jury trial, and to counsel. See generally tables 2.7 and 2.9 and 2.15 and 2.16.
485. 407 F. Supp. 509 (D. Neb. 1975).
486. 243 F.2d 825 (D.C. Cir. 1957).
487. 386 F. Supp. 378 (M.D. Ala. 1974). See also Chacko v. State, 630 S.W.2d 842 (Tex. Ct. App. 1982), and People v. Collins, 102 Ill. App. 3d 138, 429 N.E.2d 531 (1981).
488. 71 Ill. App. 3d 523, 390 N.E.2d 11 (1979). Also *In re* Hop, 623 P.2d 282, 171 Cal. Rptr. 721 (1981).

The vast majority of states today specifically allude to the power of the court to order outpatient or nonresidential treatment instead of institutionalization, some actually using the "least restrictive" language in doing so.[489]

(f) Period of institutionalization: initial maximums, review, and extension procedures

One of the most important changes that has occurred in the commitment laws has been the virtual demise of indeterminate commitment provisions that prevailed in all but a handful of states as recently as 1970. Today, in all except nine states, institutionalization can be ordered for definite periods only—6 months is typical—after which there must be a new hearing if continued commitment is sought.[490] The recommitment periods are usually finite as well, sometimes equivalent to the initial length, frequently longer by a factor of 1½ or 2.[491] The nine states that still permit indeterminate or indefinite institutionalization do so only in a limited sense. Seven make explicit provision for medical or judicial review after or within one year.[492] In Texas, the law is that indefinite commitment is possible only after 60 days of observation.[493] And in West Virginia, although the statute speaks of indeterminate commitment, the power is in fact finite in that the commitment order expires after two years.[494]

The recommitment requirements generally mirror those of the initial proceedings: there must be a new petition, a new mental examination, and a new hearing. Today these requirements are statutory, but their existence owes much to earlier court rulings of what periodic review provisions—a conceptually alternate approach to limiting the power to commit—meant in practice. In *Fasulo v. Arafeh*,[495] for example, the court ruled that all persons involuntarily committed in Connecticut were entitled to state-initiated periodic judicial review in the form of a recommitment hearing replete with the safeguards of the initial proceeding and with the burden of proof regarding the need for recommitment on the state. Review requirements of this type are in effect the same as provisions that limit commitment to defined periods.

In some jurisdictions there is ambiguity as to whether the recommitment criteria are the same as the initial commitment criteria. The statutory language describing the recommitment process may not always match that of the initial process. In at least one case (from Michigan[496]), however, the court has held that the criteria should be identical even where not explicitly so in the statute. It ruled that the state's statutory recommitment standard, a person who "*continues* to require treatment," meant the same as the initial commitment standard, one "requiring treatment," and thus included the refinement of that standard, "dangerous to self or others as a result of mental illness."

The demise of indeterminate commitments by way of extension or review requirements is an important development. Among other things, it should serve to further diffuse lingering concerns with the specter of wrongful initial commitments.[497] On the negative side, there is the possibility that these procedures—particularly if following too closely—will be too burdensome or at least will be seen to be so. The potential results of that perception are several: (1) noncompliance, (2) minimal, pro forma but in effect meaningless compliance, or (3) a mental health system in a state of breakdown where the entire medical staff, already overextended, is continually required to divert time and resources away from treating patients in the futile effort to keep up with the legal requirements.

2. Nonjudicial Commitment: Administrative and Medical Procedures

Extended commitment on nonjudicial authority—via certification by a doctor or an administrative board—is (at least for the moment) a fading phenomenon. Our discussion of these procedures therefore will be brief. In 1970, 31 jurisdictions provided for medical certification as at least one way to effect institutionalization of mentally disabled persons. Today, only 8 states and the District of Columbia retain these procedures.[498] Administrative commitment for extended term was possible in 10 states in 1970 but today in only 3.[499]

The main rationales behind the laws providing for commitment on medical or administrative authority (the administrative bodies empowered to decide typically include, if they do not consist solely of, medical staff) are (1) deference to medical judgment and (2) simplification of the commitment process. In an era where medical judgment is considered less sacrosanct than it

489. Table 2.7, cols. 15 & 16.
490. Table 2.7, col. 17.
491. Table 2.7, cols. 18 & 19.
492. Table 2.7, col. 17.
493. Tex. Rev. Civ. Stat. Ann. §§ 5547-40, 52 (Vernon Supp. 1981).
494. W.Va. Code §§ 27-5-4(k)(1), 27-5-4(k)(4) (Supp. 1980).
495. 378 A.2d 553 (Conn. 1977). Also: Suzuki v. Quisenberry, 411 F. Supp. 1113 (D. Hawaii 1976); State *ex rel.* Hawks v. Lazaro, 202 S.E.2d 109 (W. Va. 1974); Nelson v. Sandritter, 351 F.2d 284 (9th Cir. 1965).
496. People *ex rel.* Book v. Hooker, No. 77-2533, 2 MDLR 575 (Mich. Ct. App. May 22, 1978).
497. The importance of periodic review provisions as a safeguard against needless retention in mental institutions was recently emphasized by the United States Supreme Court in Jones v. United States, 103 S. Ct. 3043 (1983), an insanity acquittal case.
498. See table 2.14.
499. Nebraska, South Dakota, and West Virginia. See table 2.12.

might have been in the past and where the courts, rightly or wrongly, are looked upon as remedial agents for all, including the most intricate or far-fetched problems, these rationales no longer appear so compelling.

The primary feature of medical certification procedures is that the decision to commit rests with the examining doctors. A requirement that the certificate be endorsed by the court used to be part of the law in some states, but these provisions have disappeared. In any event, the judicial function in these states was ministerial, to verify the integrity of the signatures and the qualifications of the certifiers, *not* to review the merits of the case, the need for or desirability of institutionalization. Seven of the 10 states retaining medical commitment procedures today require that the certificate and the recommendation to commit expressed therein be approved by the admitting facility.[500]

Variation exists among the states with respect to whether one or two physicians are required to sign, with four of the ten states mandating two.[501] Beyond that, the details of the procedure are unexceptional. The admission criteria, the mental condition and the need for treatment that must be alleged, are substantially similar to those for judicial commitment. The maximum periods of institutionalization permissible are on the average shorter than when institutionalization is by judicial order, three months being the most common time.

The composition of the administrative boards in the mere three states that retain administrative commitment procedures is one of the features deserving mention even in a very abbreviated discussion of the procedure. In Nebraska,[502] the decision makers are a lawyer and two mental health professionals or lay persons with a demonstrated interest in mental health issues; in South Dakota,[503] they are two county residents and a lawyer or judge; and in West Virginia[504] the "board" consists of the mental hygiene commissioner. Legally, commitment by administrative process is sound; the separation of powers doctrine does not require commitment decisions to be solely within the domain of the courts,[505] though traditionally it has been vested there, and the law mandates only that the administrative process be circumscribed by sufficient safeguards to insure that "due process" is not violated.[506] In most other respects, the efficacy of the process, judging from what has happened in the state legislatures, seems these days to be open to large doubts.

VI. LIABILITY FOR THE COSTS OF INSTITUTIONALIZATION

The costs of treatment and custodial care of patients in public institutions are substantial, and like all medical costs they have increased rapidly over the years. In 1967, the "daily maintenance expenditures per resident patient" in public mental institutions was $8.84,[507] or some $3,325 annually. By 1976, it had risen to $43.55 per day.[508] The latest estimate—for 1982—puts the daily maintenance cost at some $85 per patient,[509] or $31,025 per patient per year. High as these figures are, they are by no means exorbitant from a comparative perspective. Care and treatment in private psychiatric hospitals stood at $96 per day already back in 1974 ($36,140 annually), and general hospitals in 1979 charged $215 per day (or $78,475 per year).[510] Even community care—touted in part as an economic bargain relative to treatment in the large institutions—comes far from cheap. Indeed, delivery of the full array of inpatient services in community mental health centers in 1979 cost as much as $177 per day,[511] or $64,605 if it were provided on a 365-day basis—more than twice the cost of treatment in the state mental hospitals in 1982. Given the high per patient costs in these various treatment settings, it is natural that the law should set out who is responsible for paying them under what circumstances.

The first source for payment of the costs of institutionalization is of course the patient himself. All states today have provisions affirming the financial responsibility of the patient (or his estate), whether he entered the institution on a voluntary basis or whether he was involuntarily committed.[512] Such provisions are not entirely beyond controversy. To charge voluntary patients seems

500. Table 2.14, col. 6.

501. Table 2.14, col. 5.

502. Neb. Rev. Stat. § 83-1018 (1981). See Doremus v. Farrell, 407 F. Supp. 509 (D. Neb. 1975), upholding the constitutionality of the administrative process *per se* but requiring a restructuring, and redefinition of the function, of the administrative board.

503. S.D. Codified Laws Ann. § 27A-7-1 (Supp. 1980).

504. W.Va. Code § 27-5-4(i) (1980).

505. Doremus v. Farrell, 407 F. Supp. 509 (D. Neb. 1975). Constitutionality of Nonjudicial Confinement, 3 Stan. L. Rev. 109 (1950-51).

506. Nebbia v. New York, 291 U.S. 502 (1934); Yick Wo v. Hopkins, 118 U.S. 356 (1886); Doremus v. Farrell, 407 F. Supp. 509 (D. Neb. 1975).

507. Division of Biometry and Epidemiology, National Institute of Mental Health, Statistical Note 153, Provisional Patient Movement and Selective Administrative Data, State and County Mental Hospitals, Inpatient Services by State: United States 1976, at 6 table C (Aug. 1979).

508. *Id.*

509. Rubin, Cost Measurement and Cost Data in Mental Health Settings, 33 Hosp. & Community Psychiatry 750, 751 (1982).

510. *Id.* at 751 table 1. The years 1974 and 1979 are used because no more recent figures are available.

511. *Id.*

512. See tables 2.17 & 2.18, cols. 1 & 2. The sole qualification to this statement is that Alabama, because it has no voluntary admission statute, has naturally enough no provision for the financial responsibility of voluntary patients.

fair enough. But the involuntary patient presents a slightly different situation. An argument could be made that he is more akin to the involuntarily confined prisoner,[513] who is not charged (though maintenance and support payments may in some jurisdictions be deducted from monies earned in prison work). A possible acknowledgment of this point may have been contained in the 1970 Arizona law that charged involuntary patients only if their treatment was provided—conceivably at the patient's or his representatives' choice—in institutions *other* than the state hospital.[514] However, this distinction no longer survives in the current Arizona law, and legally the financial obligation of even the involuntary patient is today beyond question.

The real questions concern how to collect on this liability or, in case the patient does not have the means to pay in part or in total (as is common particularly among patients who wind up in public institutions), from whom to collect it. The statutes are explicit in treating the latter issue. All but three states—New Mexico, North Carolina, and Oregon—provide for financial liability of the family when the patient himself cannot pay.[515] Again, the laws generally make no distinction between voluntary or involuntary patients, the only apparent exception being Arizona, which has kept the provision that the family is liable only for private care (*not* for that which is given in public facilities),[516] after dropping the distinction with reference to the patient's *personal* liability. The family—as enumerated in some statutes, not in others—includes as a rule the spouse, parents, and adult children.[517] The limitations, if any are spelled out, are on the order of parental liability terminating when the patient reaches majority.[518] This is a fairly new development, as the laws in 1970 and before generally did not provide for such extinction of parental liability.[519] Also, in order to preclude a very long-term liability that could be catastrophic to the parents' or relatives' morale, if not their actual financial state, a few jurisdictions provide for an absolute termination date after 10 or 15 years of financial support.[520]

After the patient's relatives, the sole remaining source, practically speaking and the one specified in the statutes, is the government—the county, the state, or the federal government via some special program. Tables 2.17 and 2.18 chart the division of responsibility between the first two, the county or the state, with a clear majority of jurisdictions making it a state rather than local obligation.[521] Since in the typical case the state or county in effect pays in the first instance by providing the budget for the costs of running the facility in which the care or custody is provided, the issue of final financial responsibility arises generally in the context of the state's having exhausted attempts to get reimbursement from those who have the prior obligation. There is some interesting case law on these questions of how and from whom to collect.

First of all, some courts have held that relatives are liable for the costs of a patient's institutionalization only if or to the extent that they have been specifically notified of their liability by the institution or by the state.[522] Perhaps more than the wording of the statutes, the particular fact situations in these cases compel this result. In one of the cases,[523] the court was faced with a situation where the state proceeded against the husband's estate for reimbursement of the wife's treatment expenses despite giving no indication of its intent to do so during the 48 years that the wife was institutionalized while the husband was alive. The court went so far as to read into the state statute the need for a formal reimbursement contract. Such limits on the financial obligation of relatives are difficult to square with the statutes of other states[524] that speak of joint and several (i.e.,

513. This argument was posed, e.g., and rejected in *In re* Guardianship of Klisurich, 296 N.W.2d 742 (Wis. Sup. Ct. 1980), and in *In re* Guardianship of Nelson, 296 N.W.2d 736 (Wis. 1980). But when hospitalization results out of criminal proceedings—e.g., an accused found incompetent to stand trial—the patient is not liable according to Boldt v. Wisconsin, 297 N.W.2d 29 (Wis. Ct. App. 1980). State *ex rel.* Mental Health Comm'r v. Guardianship of Wiseman, 393 N.E.2d 235 (Ind. Ct. App. 1979), goes contra, however, holding that a patient first committed as incompetent to stand trial and later civilly committed is liable for the *entire* period of institutionalization. See also Hospital Servs., Inc. v. Dumas, 297 N.W.2d 320 (N.D. 1980), on the liability of a person arrested for drunk and disorderly conduct and commited by the county judge for temporary treatment.

514. Ariz. Rev. Stat. Ann. § 36-510 (1970).

515. Tables 2.17 & 2.18, cols. 1 & 2. Technically, the family's responsibility may be coincident with the patient's. See Arkansas statute quoted in note 517, *infra*.

516. Ariz. Rev. Stat. Ann. § 36-545.03 (1970).

517. Tables 2.17 & 2.18, cols. 3 & 4. In some states, the language is quite broad. The Arkansas statute (Ark. Stat. Ann. § 59-1421 (Cum. Supp. 1983)), for example, reads: "Every person who is legally liable for the support of a patient admitted to a State Mental Health Facility or hospital pursuant to this Act . . . shall be liable jointly and severally with the estate of the patient for the charges made by the State Mental Health Facility or hospital for the hospitalization and treatment of such patient, regardless of whether such person was a part [party] to or consented to the commitment or admission of the patient . . . and regardless of the extent of the estate of the patient."

518. *Id.*

519. See, e.g., Lansing v. Commonwealth Dep't. of Pub. Welfare, 410 A.2d 982 (Pa. Commw. Ct. 1980).

520. Colo. Rev. Stat. § 27-12-103(2) (1982); N.H. Rev. Stat. Ann. § 126-A:52 (II) (Supp. 1983); Ohio Rev. Code Ann. §§ 5121.04(b)(6), 5121.06(D) (Baldwin 1982). Pennsylvania limits the *spouse's* obligation to the first 120 days of care. Pa. Stat. Ann. tit. 50, § 4502 (Purdon Supp. 1983-84).

521. Tables 2.17 & 2.18, cols. 5-8.

522. Estate of Hinds v. State, 394 N.E.2d 943 (Ind. Ct. App. 1979); *reh'g denied and remanded*, 390 N.E.2d 172 (Ind. Ct. App. 1979); South Carolina Dep't of Mental Health v. Turbeville, 257 S.E.2d 493 (S.C. 1979).

523. South Carolina Dep't of Mental Health v. Turbeville, 257 S.E.2d 493 (S.C. 1979). The statute was S.C. Code Ann. §§ 44-23-1120 through 1140 (1976).

524. E.g., Ark. Stat. Ann. § 59-1421 (Supp. 1983).

automatic) liability or with court holdings that allow the state to "deem" (take into account, assume availability of) the income of the spouse in assessing the *patient's* liability[525] or that affirm the *spouse's* liability without proof of lack of assets on the patient's part.[526]

There are also situations in which the liability of the patient himself as well as the relatives is in doubt. A recent Wisconsin case[527] held that persons illegally committed are not liable for the costs of care. The case involved an entire class of patients committed under a Wisconsin statute that had been ruled procedurally defective.[528] In an earlier New York case,[529] the court upheld the parents' refusal to pay for their retarded child's institutional care in the light of unrebutted evidence that this care was grossly inadequate. Where personal liability survives, a question may arise about third-party payment. A recent New Jersey decision[530] held that no Medicare coverage was available in a case where an old patient who had previously been receiving treatment was now receiving merely custodial care, pending placement in a nursing home. Sometimes the third-party payment obligation depends on who furnishes the medical care, and large legal battles have been fought over whether mental health services delivered by nonpsychiatrists—by unsupervised psychologists or other mental health workers without medical degrees—are covered by various private or governmental insurance plans.[531]

Finally, there is a question about which assets of the patient can be requisitioned to pay off the liability for care and treatment, and by what procedure. Social Security benefits, which constitute one of the main sources of income if not the sole source for many patients in public institutions, are a prime target. At the same time, because of the importance of these benefits to the recipient, the law protects them from the claim of ordinary business creditors and immunizes them from the legal processess—execution, levy, attachment, and so forth by which debts may otherwise be satisfied.[532] This does not mean that social security payments may not be applied toward the costs of care—one court has stated that such "maintenance and support" are precisely what the benefits are guarded for[533]—but the claimant, the state, or the institution must go through special procedures aimed to assure that special protections are accorded to this vulnerable class of debtors.[534]

525. Schweiker v. Gray Panthers, 453 U.S. 34 (1981).

526. *In re* Estate of Decker, 422 N.Y.S.2d 293 (Ulster Co. Sur. Ct. 1979).

527. Jankowski v. Milwaukee County, No. 79-1896, 6 MDLR 29 (Wis. Sup. Ct., Nov. 3, 1981).

528. State *ex rel.* Memmel v. Mundy, No. 441-417, 1 MDLR 183 (Wis. Cir. Ct., Milwaukee Co. Aug. 18, 1976).

529. New York Dep't of Mental Hygiene v. Schneps, Nos. 203/204 (App. Term, 1st Dep't, May 1978).

530. Monmouth Medical Center v. Harris, No. 78-3139, 4 MDLR 26 (D.N.J., May 16, 1980), *aff'd on appeal,* No. 80-2138, 5 MDLR 144 (3d Cir. Apr., 1, 1981).

531. E.g., Blue Cross of Virginia v. Virginia, No. 800056, 4 MDLR 418 (Va. Sup. Ct. Aug. 28, 1980); Virginia Academy of Clinical Psychologists v. Blue Shield, 501 F. Supp. 1232 (E.D. Va. 1980), *cert. denied,* 49 U.S.L.W. 3617 (U.S. Feb. 23, 1981); Blue Shield of Virginia v. McCready, 102 S. Ct. 2540 (1982).

532. 42 U.S.C. § 407.

533. Florida Dep't of Health & Rehabilitative Servs. v. Davis, 616 F.2d 828 (5th Cir. 1980).

534. Vecchione v. Wohlgemuth, 377 F. Supp. 1361 (E.D. Pa. 1974), holding that the state may not appropriate without a hearing the social security checks of competent patients to satisfy the costs of institutionalization. As a result, the state had to return $9.1 million. See also Michigan Dep't of Treasury v. Ivy, 416 U.S.L.W. 2205 (Mich. Oct. 6, 1977).

TABLE 2.1 STATUTORY DEFINITIONS OF MENTALLY ILL PERSONS

STATE AND CITATION	STATUTORY PROVISIONS
ALA. Code (1975 & Supp. 1980)	No definition.
ALAS. Stat. (1980 & Supp. 1981) 47.30.915 (12)	"'Mental illness' means an organic, mental, or emotional impairment that has substantial adverse effects on an individual's ability to exercise conscious control of his actions or ability to perceive reality or to reason or understand; mental retardation, epilepsy, drug addiction, and alcoholism do not per se constitute mental illness, although persons suffering from these conditions may also be suffering from mental illness."
ARIZ. Rev. Stat. Ann. (1974 & Supp. 1981) 36-501.17	"'Mental disorder' means a substantial disorder of the person's emotional processes, thought, cognition or memory. Mental disorder is distinguished from: (a) Conditions which are primarily those of drug abuse, alcoholism or mental retardation, except that persons with these conditions may also suffer from a mental disorder. (b) The declining mental abilities that directly accompany impending death. (c) Character and personality disorders characterized by lifelong and deeply ingrained anti-social behavior patterns, including sexual behaviors which are abnormal and prohibited by statute unless the behavior results from a mental disorder."
ARK. Stat. Ann. (1971)	No definition.
CAL. Welf & Inst. Code (West 1972 & Supp. 1980) 5008(h)	"'Gravely disabled'" means (1) a condition in which a person, as a result of a mental disorder, is unable to provide for his basic personal needs for food, clothing, or shelter. 'Gravely disabled' means a condition in which a person, as a result of impairment by chronic alcoholism, is unable to provide for his basic personal needs for food, clothing, or shelter. The term 'gravely disabled' does not include mentally retarded persons by reason of being mentally retarded alone."
COLO. Rev. Stat. (1973) 27-10-102(7)	"'Mentally ill person' means a person who is of such mental condition that he is in need of medical supervision, treatment, care, or restraint."
CONN. Gen. Stat. Ann. (West 1975 & Supp. 1980) 17-176	"'Mentally ill person' means any person who has a mental or emotional condition which has substantial adverse effects on his or her ability to function and who requires care and treatment, and specifically excludes a person whose psychiatric disorder is drug dependence . . . or alcoholism."
DEL. Code Ann. (1974 & Supp. 1980) 16, § 5001(1)	"'Mentally ill person' means a person suffering from a mental disease or condition which requires such person to be observed and treated at a mental hospital for his own welfare and which either (i) renders such person unable to make responsibile decisions with respect to his hospitalization, or (ii) poses a real and present threat, based upon manifest indications, that such person is likely to commit or suffer serious harm to himself or others or to property if not given immediate hospital care and treatment."
D.C. Code Ann. (1973 & Supp. 1981) 21-501	"'Mental illness' means a psychosis or other disease which substantially impairs the mental health of a person."
FLA. Stat. Ann. (West 1973 & Supp. 1981) 394.455(3)	"'Mentally ill' means having a mental, emotional, or behavioral disorder which substantially impairs the person's mental health."
GA. Code Ann. (1979 & Supp. 1981) 88-501(a)	"'Mentally ill' shall mean having a disorder of thought or mood which significiantly impairs judgment, behavior, capacity to recognize reality, or ability to cope with the ordinary demands of life."

TABLE 2.1 STATUTORY DEFINITIONS OF MENTALLY ILL PERSONS—continued

STATE AND CITATION	STATUTORY PROVISIONS
HAWAII Rev. Stat. (1976 & Supp. 1981) 334-1	"'Mentally ill person' means a person having psychiatric disorder or other disease which substantially impairs his mental health and necessitates treatment or supervision."
IDAHO Code (1980 & Supp. 1981) 66-317(m)	"'Mentally ill' shall mean a person, who as a result of a substantial disorder of thought, mood, perception, orientation, or memory, which grossly impairs judgment, behavior, capacity to recognize and adapt to reality, requires care and treatment at a facility."
ILL. Ann. Stat. (Smith-Hurd 1966 & Supp. 1981) 91½, §1-119	"'Person subject to involuntary admission' or 'subject to involuntary admission' means: (1) A person who is mentally ill and who because of his illness is reasonably expected to inflict serious physical harm upon himself or another in the near future; or (2) A person who is mentally ill and who because of his illness is unable to provide for his basic physical needs so as to guard himself from serious harm."
IND. Code Ann. (Burns 1973) 16-14-1-1(1)	"A 'mentally ill person' means an individual who has a psychiatric disorder which substantially impairs his mental health, and because of such psychiatric disorder, for the welfare of such individual or for the welfare of others in the community in which such individual resides, requires care, treatment, training or detention. A psychiatric disorder means any mental illness or disease which shall include but shall not be limited to any mental deficiency, epilepsy, alcoholism, or addiction to narcotic or dangerous drugs."
IOWA Code Ann. (West 1969 & Supp. 1980) 229.1	"(1) 'Mental illness' means every type of mental disease or mental disorder except that it does not refer to mental retardation. "(2) 'Seriously mentally impaired' or 'serious mental impairment' describes the condition of a person who is afflicted with mental illness and because of that illness lacks sufficient judgment to make responsible decisions with respect to his or her hospitalization or treatment, and who: (a) Is likely to physically injure himself or herself or others if allowed to remain at liberty without treatment; or (b) Is likely to inflict serious emotional injury on members of his or her family or others who lack reasonable opportunity to avoid contact with the afflicted person if the afflicted person is allowed to remain at liberty without treatment."
KAN. Stat. Ann. (1976 & Supp. 1981) 59-2902(1)	"The term 'mentally ill person' shall mean any person who is mentally impaired to the extent that such person is in need of treatment and who is dangerous to himself or herself or others and (a) who lacks sufficient understanding or capacity to make responsible decisions with respect to his or her need for treatment, or (b) who refuses to seek treatment [religious exception]. Proof of a person's failure to meet his or her basic physical needs, to the extent that such failure threatens such person's life, shall be deemed as proof that such person is dangerous to himself or herself."
KY. Rev. Stat. (Michie 1977) 202A.010(7)	"'Mentally ill person' means a person with substantially impaired capacity to use self-control, judgment or discretion in the conduct of his affairs and social relations, associated with maladaptive behavior or recognized emotional symptions where impaired capacity, maladaptive behavior or emotional symptoms can be related to physiological, psychological and/or social factors."
LA. Rev. Stat. Ann. (West 1975 & Supp. 1981) 28:2(14)	"'Mentally ill person' means any person with a psychiatric disorder which has substantial adverse effects on his ability to function and who requires care and treatment. It does not refer to a person suffering solely from mental retardation, epilepsy, alcoholism, or drug abuse."

TABLE 2.1 STATUTORY DEFINITIONS OF MENTALLY ILL PERSONS—continued

STATE AND CITATION	STATUTORY PROVISIONS
ME. Rev. Stat. Ann. (1978) 34, §2251(5)	"'Mentally ill individual' means an individual having a psychiatric or other disease which substantially impairs his mental health. For the purposes of this chapter, the term 'mentally ill individual' does not include mentally retarded or sociopathic individuals, but does include individuals suffering from the effects of the use of drugs, narcotics, hallucinogens or intoxicants, including alcohol."
MD. Ann. Code (1979) 59, §3(g)	"'Mental illness' means any mental disorder which so substantially impairs the mental or emotional functioning of any individual as to make it necessary or advisable for the welfare of the person so suffering or for the safety of the persons or property of others that the mentally ill person receive care and treatment. The term shall replace the words 'insane,' 'insanity,' 'lunacy,' 'mentally sick,' 'mental disease,' 'unsound mind' and similar words as they appear in the statutes of the State of Maryland."
MASS. Ann. Laws (Michie/Law. Co-op. 1980) 4, §7(15)	"'Insane person' and 'lunatic' shall include every idiot, non-compos lunatic and insane and distracted person."
MICH. Comp. Laws Ann. (1981) 330.1400a	"'Mental illness' means a substantial disorder of thought or mood which significantly impairs judgment, behavior, capacity to recognize reality, or ability to cope with the ordinary demands of life."
MINN. Stat. Ann. (West 1971) 253A.02(3)	"'Mentally ill person' means any person diagnosed as having a psychiatric or other disorder which substantially impairs his mental health and as being in need of treatment or supervision."
MISS. Code Ann. (1972) 41-21-61(c)	"'Person in need of mental treatment,' . . . means any person afflicted with mental illness if that person, as a result of such mental illness, is reasonably expected at the time the determination is being made or within a reasonable time thereafter to intentionally or unintentionally physically injure himself or other persons, or is unable to care for himself so as to guard himself from physical injury, or to provide for his own physical needs."
MO. Ann. Stat. (Vernon 1979) 630.005(19)	"'Mental illness' a state of impaired mental processes, which impairment results in a distortion of a person's capacity to recognize reality due to hallucinations, delusions, faulty perceptions or alterations of mood, and interferes with an individual's ability to reason, understand, or exercise conscious control over his actions. The term 'mental illness' does not include the following conditions unless they are accompanied by a mental illness as otherwise defined in this subdivision: (a) Mental retardation, developmental disability or narcolepsy; (b) Simple intoxication caused by substances such as alcohol or drugs; (c) Dependence upon or addiction to any substances such as alcohol or drugs; (d) Any other disorders such as senility, which are not of an actively psychotic nature."
MONT. Code Ann. (1981) 53-21-102	"(5) 'Mental disorder' means any organic, mental, or emotional impairment which has substantial adverse effects on an individual's cognitive or volitional functions. "(14) 'Seriously mentally ill' means suffering from a mental disorder which has resulted in self-inflicted injury or injury to others or the imminent threat thereof or which has deprived the person afflicted of the ability to protect his life or health. For this purpose, injury means physical injury. No person may be involuntarily committed to a mental health facility or detained for evaluation and treatment because he is an epileptic, mentally deficient, mentally retarded, senile, or suffering from a mental disorder unless the condition causes him to be seriously mentally ill within the meaning of this part."

TABLE 2.1 STATUTORY DEFINITIONS OF MENTALLY ILL PERSONS—continued

STATE AND CITATION	STATUTORY PROVISIONS
NEB. Rev. Stat. (1976 & Supp. 1981) 83-1009	"Mentally ill dangerous person shall mean any mentally ill person or alcoholic person who presents: (1) A substantial risk of serious harm to another person or persons within the near future, as manifested by evidence of recent violent acts or threats of violence or by placing others in reasonable fear of such harm; or (2) A substantial risk of serious harm to himself within the near future, as manifested by evidence of recent attempts at, or threats of, suicide or serious bodily harm, or evidence of inability to provide for his basic human needs, including food, clothing, shelter, essential medical care, or personal safety."
NEV. Rev. Stat. (1979) 433.164	"'Mental illness' means any mental disfunction leading to impaired ability to maintain oneself and function effectively in one's life situation without external support."
N.H. Rev. Stat. Ann. (1977) 135-B:2(XI)	"'Mental illness' means a substantial impairment of emotional processes, or of the ability to exercise conscious control of one's actions, or of the ability to perceive reality or to reason, which impairment is manifested by instances of extremely abnormal behavior or extremely faulty perceptions; it does not include impairment primarily caused by: (a) epilepsy; (b) mental retardation; (c) continuous or noncontinuous periods of intoxification caused by substances such as alcohol or drugs; (d) dependence upon or addiction to any substance such as alcohol or drugs."
N.J. Stat. Ann. (West 1981) 30:4-23	"'Mental illness' shall mean mental disease to such an extent that a person so afflicted requires care and treatment for his own welfare, or the welfare of others, or of the community."
N.M. Stat. Ann. (1979) 43-1-3(N)	"'Mental disorder' means the substantial disorder of the person's emotional processes, thought or cognition which grossly impairs judgment, behavior or capacity to recognize reality."
N.Y. Mental Hyg. Law (McKinney 1978) 1.03(20)	"'Mental illness' means an affliction with a mental disease or mental condition which is manifested by a disorder or disturbance in behavior, feeling, thinking, or judgement to such an extent that the person afflicted requires care, treatment and rehabilitation."
N.C. Gen. Stat. (1981) 122-36(d)	"(i) The words 'mental illness' shall mean: When applied to an adult, an illness which so lessens the capacity of the person to use self-control, judgement, and discretion in the conduct of his affairs and social relations as to make it necessary or advisable for him to be under treatment, care, supervision, guidance or control. The words 'mentally ill' shall mean an adult person with a mental illness; or (ii) When applied to a minor shall mean a mental condition, other than mental retardation alone, which so lessens or impairs the youth's capacity either to develop or exercise age appropriate or age adequate self-control, judgement, or initiative in the conduct of his activities and social relationships as to make it necessary or advisable for him to be under treatment, care, supervision, guidance or control."
N.D. Cent. Code (1978 & Supp. 1981) 25-01.1-01 25-03.1-02(10)	"'Mentally ill individual' means an individual having a psychiatric or other disease which substantially impairs his mental health." "'Mentally ill person' means an individual with an organic, mental, or emotional disorder which substantially impairs the capacity to use self-control, judgment, and discretion in the conduct of personal affairs and social relations. 'Mentally ill person' does not include a mentally retarded or mentally deficient person of significantly subaverage general intellectual functioning which originates during the developmental period and is associated with impairment in adaptive behavior. Drug addiction and alcoholism do not per se constitute mental illness, although persons suffering from these conditions may also be suffering from mental illness."

TABLE 2.1 STATUTORY DEFINITIONS OF MENTALLY ILL PERSONS—continued

STATE AND CITATION	STATUTORY PROVISIONS
OHIO Rev. Code Ann. (Baldwin 1981) 5122.01(a)	"'Mental illness' means a substantial disorder of thought, mood, perception, orientation, or memory that grossly impairs judgement, behavior, capacity to recognize reality, or ability to meet the ordinary demands of life."
OKLA. Stat. Ann. (West 1979 & Supp. 1981) 43A, §3(C)	"'Mentally ill person' means a person afflicted with a substantial disorder of thought, mood, perception, psychological orientation or memory that significantly impairs judgment, behavior, capacity to recognize reality or ability to meet the ordinary demands of life."
OR. Rev. Stat. (1979) 426.005(2)	"'Mentally ill person' means a person who, because of a mental disorder, is either: (a) Dangerous to himself or others; or (b) Unable to provide for his basic personal needs and is not receiving such care as is necessary for his health or safety."
PA. Stat. Ann. (Purdon 1969 & Supp. 1981) 50, §7301(a)	"A person is severely mentally disabled when, as a result of mental illness, his capacity to exercise self-control, judgement and discretion in the conduct of his affairs and social relations or to care for his own personal needs is so lessened that he poses a clear and present danger of harm to others or himself."
R.I. Gen. Laws (1977) 43-3-7	"The words 'insane person' shall be construed to include every idiot, person of unsound mind, lunatic and distracted person."
S.C. Code Ann. (Law. Co-op. 1976) 44-23-10(1)	"'Mentally ill person' means a person afflicted with a mental disease to such an extent that, for his own welfare or the welfare of others or of the community, he requires care, treatment or hospitalization."
S.D. Codified Laws Ann. (1976) 27A-1-1	"The term 'mentally ill' as used in this title includes any person whose mental condition is such that his behavior establishes one or more of the following: (1) He lacks sufficient understanding or capacity to make responsible decisions concerning his person so as to interfere grossly with his capacity to meet the ordinary demands of life; or (2) He is a danger to himself or others. The term 'mentally ill' does not include mentally retarded persons by reasons of such retardation alone."
TENN. Code Ann. (Supp. 1981) 33-302(f)	"Mentally ill individual—an individual who suffers from a psychiatric disorder, alcoholism, or drug dependence, but excluding an individual whose only mental disability is mental retardation."
TEX. Rev. Civ. Stat. Ann. (Vernon 1958 & Supp. 1981) 5547-4(k)	"'Mentally ill person' means a person whose mental health is substantially impaired."
UTAH Code Ann. (1978 & Supp. 1981) 64-7-28(1)	"'Mental illness' means a psychiatric disorder as defined by the current Diagnostic and Statistical Manual of Mental Disorders which substantially impairs a person's mental, emotional, behavioral, or related functioning."

TABLE 2.1 STATUTORY DEFINITIONS OF MENTALLY ILL PERSONS—continued

STATE AND CITATION	STATUTORY PROVISIONS
VT. Stat. Ann. (1968 & Supp. 1981) 18, §7101(14)	"'Mental illness' means a substantial disorder of thought, mood, perception, orientation, or memory, any of which grossly impairs judgment, behavior, capacity to recognize reality, or ability to meet the ordinary demands of life, but shall not include mental retardation."
VA. Code (1976 & Supp. 1981) 37.1-1(15)	"'Mentally ill' means any person afflicted with mental disease to such an extent that for his own welfare or the welfare of others, he requires care and treatment; provided, that, for the purposes of Chapter 2 (§37.1-63 et seq.) of this title, the term 'mentally ill' shall be deemed to include any person who is a drug addict or alcoholic."
WASH. Rev. Code Ann. (1975 & Supp. 1981) 71.05.020(2)	"'Mental disorder' means any organic mental or emotional impairment which has substantial adverse effects on an individual's cognitive or volitional functions."
W.VA. Code (1980) 27-1-2	"'Mental illness' means a manifestation in a person of significantly impaired capacity to maintain acceptable levels of functioning in the areas of intellect, emotion and physical well-being."
WIS. Stat. Ann. (West 1957 & Supp. 1981) 51.01	"(13a) 'Mental illness' means mental disease to such extent that a person so afflicted requires care and treatment for his or her own welfare, or the welfare of others, or of the community. "(13b) 'Mental illness,' for purposes of involuntary commitment, means a substantial disorder of thought, mood, perception, orientation, or memory which grossly impairs judgment, behavior, capacity to recognize reality, or ability to meet the ordinary demands of life, but does not include alcoholism."
WYO. Stat. (1977) 25-3-101(a)(i)	"'Mentally ill individual'—An individual having a psychiatric or other disease which substantially impairs his mental health."
(1982) 25-10-101(a)(viii)	"'Mentally ill person' means a person who presents an imminent threat of physical harm to himself or others as a result of a physical, emotional, mental or behavioral disorder which grossly impairs his ability to function socially, vocationally or interpersonally and who needs treatment and who cannot comprehend the need for or purposes of treatment and with respect to whom the potential risks and benefits are such that a reasonable person would consent to treatment."

TABLE 2.2 STATUTORY DEFINITIONS OF DEVELOPMENTALLY DISABLED PERSONS

STATE AND CITATION	STATUTORY PROVISIONS
ALA. Code (1975)	None.
ALAS. Stat. (1979) 47.80.900(7)	"'Person with a developmental disability' means a person having a disability which (A) is attributable to (i) mental retardation, cerebral palsy, epilepsy, or autism; (ii) any other condition found to be closely related to mental retardation because the condition results in impairment of general intellectual functioning or adaptive behavior similar to impairment resulting from mental retardation; or (iii) dyslexia resulting from a disability described in (i) or (ii) of this subparagraph; and (B) constitutes a substantial handicap to the person's ability to function normally in society."
ARIZ. Rev. Stat. Ann. (Supp. 1981) 36-551	"(10) 'Developmental disability' or 'developmentally disabled' or 'developmental disabilities' means a severe, chronic disability which: (a) Is attributable to mental retardation, cerebral palsy, epilepsy or autism. (b) Is manifest before age eighteen. (c) Is likely to continue indefinitely. (d) Results in substantial functional limitations in three or more of the following areas of major life activity: (i) Self-care. (ii) Receptive and expressive language. (iii) Learning. (iv) Mobility. (v) Self-direction. (vi) Capacity for independent living. (vii) Economic self-sufficiency. (e) Reflects the need for a combination and sequence of individually planned or coordinated special, interdisciplinary or generic care, treatment or other services which are of lifelong or extended duration." "(20) 'Mental retardation' or 'mentally retarded' or 'retarded' means a condition involving subaverage general intellectual functioning existing concurrently with deficits in adaptive behavior manifested before age eighteen."
ARK. Stat. Ann. (Supp. 1981) 59-1301(1)	"'Developmentally disabled adult' means an adult having a disability attributable to mental retardation, cerebral palsy, epilepsy, or other neurological condition related to mental retardation or requiring treatment similar to that required for mentally retarded individuals, which has continued or can be expected to continue indefinitely, and substantially prevents the individual from adequately providing for his own care and protection."
(1971) 59-1002	"'Retarded' or 'mentally retarded' or 'retarded child' or 'retarded children' means (i) a person or persons with a mental deficit requiring him to have special evaluation, treatment, care, education, training, supervision or control in his home or community, or in a state institution for the mentally retarded; or (ii) a functionally retarded person who may not exhibit an intellectual deficit on standard psychological tests, but who, because of other handicaps, functions as a retarded person. Not included is a person whose primary problem is mental illness, emotional disturbance, physical handicap or sensory defect."

TABLE 2.2 STATUTORY DEFINITIONS OF DEVELOPMENTALLY DISABLED PERSONS—continued

STATE AND CITATION	STATUTORY PROVISIONS
CAL. Welf & Inst. Code (West 1972) 65000	"'Mentally retarded persons' means those persons, not psychotic, who are so mentally retarded from infancy or before reaching maturity that they are incapable of managing themselves and their affairs independently, with ordinary prudence, or of being taught to do so, and who require supervision, control, and care, for their own welfare, or for the welfare of others, or for the welfare of the community."
COLO. Rev. Stat. (Supp. 1981) 27-10.5-135(2)	"Whenever the terms 'idiot,' 'feebleminded person,' 'mental defective,' 'weak-minded person,' and 'mentally deficient person' are used in the laws of the state of Colorado, they shall be deemed to mean and be included with the term 'developmentally disabled person,' as defined in section 27-10.5-102(4)."
27-10.5-102(4)(a)	"'Developmental disability' means a disability attributable to mental retardation, cerebral palsy, epilepsy, autism, or a neurological impairment, which may have originated during the first eighteen years of life, which can be expected to continue indefinitely, and which constitutes a substantial handicap. The term 'developmental disability' as applied to section 27-10.5-133 includes, but is not limited to, a disability of a person who has a permanent physical handicap for which substantial supervision and training are required."
27-10.5-102(8)	"'Mentally retarded person' means a person whose intellectual functions have been deficient since birth or whose intellectual development has been arrested or impaired by disease or physical injury to such an extent that he lacks sufficient control, judgment, and discretion to manage his property or affairs or who, by reason of this deficiency and for his own welfare or the welfare or safety of others, requires protection, supervision, guidance, training, control, or care."
CONN. Gen. Stat. Ann. (West 1975)	None.
DEL. Code Ann. (1974)	None.
D.C. Code Ann. (1981) 6-1902	"(19) 'Mentally retarded' means a significantly subaverage general intellectual level determined in accordance with standard measurements as recorded in the Manual of Terminology and Classification in Mental Retardation, 1973, American Association on Mental Deficiency, existing concurrently with impairment in adaptive behavior, which originates during the development period. "(2) 'At least moderately retarded' means a person who is found, following a comprehensive evaluation, to be impaired in adaptive behavior to a moderate, severe or profound degree and functioning at the moderate, severe or profound intellectual level in accordance with standard measurements as recorded in the Manual of Terminology and Classification in Mental Retardation, 1973, American Association on Mental Deficiency."
FLA. Stat. Ann. (West Supp. 1981) 393.063	"(6) 'Developmental disability' means a disorder or syndrome which is attributable to retardation, cerebral palsy, autism or epilepsy and which constitutes a substantial handicap that can reasonably be expected to continue indefinitely." "(23) 'Retardation' means significantly subaverage general intellectual functioning existing concurrently with deficits in adaptive behavior and manifested during the period from conception to age 18. "'Significantly subaverage general intellectual functioning,' for the purpose of this definition, means performance which is two or more standard deviations from the mean score on a standardized intelligence test. . . . "'Adaptive behavior,'. . . means the effectiveness or degree with which an individual meets the standards of personal independence and social responsibility expected of his age, cultural group, and community."

TABLE 2.2 STATUTORY DEFINITIONS OF DEVELOPMENTALLY DISABLED PERSONS—continued

STATE AND CITATION	STATUTORY PROVISIONS
GA. Code Ann. (1979 & Supp. 1980) 88-2502	"(a) 'Mental retardation' means a state of significantly subaverage general intellectual functioning existing concurrently with deficits in adaptive behavior which originates in the developmental period. "(r) 'Mentally retarded person' means a person having a significantly subaverage general intellectual functioning existing concurrently with deficits in adaptive behavior which originates in the developmental period."
HAWAII Rev. Stat. (Supp. 1981) 333E-2	"'[D]evelopmental disabilities' means a severe, chronic disability of a person which: (1) Is attributable to a mental or physical impairment or combination of mental and physical impairments; (2) Is manifested before the person attains age twenty-two; (3) Is likely to continue indefinitely; (4) Results in substantial functional limitations in three or more of the following areas of major life activity; self-care, receptive and expressive language, learning, mobility, self-direction, capacity for independent living, and economic sufficiency; and (5) Reflects the person's need for a combination and sequence of special interdisciplinary, or generic care, treatment, or other services which are of lifelong or extended duration and are individually planned and coordinated."
(1976) 333-25	"'Mentally retarded persons,' as referred to in section 333-24 are persons: (1) Who are afflicted with: (A) A deficiency of general mental development associated with chronic brain syndrome, or (B) A deficiency of intelligence arising after birth, due to infection, trauma, or other disease process, or (2) Who are afflicted with general intellectual subnormality not due to known organic factors."
IDAHO Code (1980)	None.
ILL. Ann. Stat. (Smith-Hurd Supp. 1981) 91½, §1-106	"'Developmental disability' means a disability which is attributable to: (a) mental retardation, cerebral palsy, epilepsy or autism; or to (b) any other condition which results in impairment similar to that caused by mental retardation and which requires services similar to those required by mentally retarded persons. Such disability must originate before the age of 18 years, be expected to continue indefinitely, and constitute a substantial handicap."
91½, §1-116	"'Mental retardation' means signifcantly subaverage general intellectual functioning which exists concurrently with impairment in adaptive behavior and which originates before the age of 18 years."

TABLE 2.2 STATUTORY DEFINITIONS OF DEVELOPMENTALLY DISABLED PERSONS—continued

STATE AND CITATION	STATUTORY PROVISIONS
IND. Code Ann. (Burns Supp. 1982) 16-13-1-3(4)	"'Developmental disability' means a disability of a person which: (A) is attributable to mental retardation, cerebral palsy, epilepsy, or autism; or is attributable to any other condition found to be closely related to mental retardation because this condition results in similar impairment of general intellectual functioning or adaptive behavior, or requires similar treatment and services; or is attributable to dyslexia resulting from a disability described in this clause; (B) originates before the person is 18; and (C) has continued or is expected to continue indefinitely and constitutes a substantial handicap to the person's ability to function normally in society."
16-13-18-1(c)	"'Epilepsy' means a disorder characterized by recurrent episodes during which there are variable alterations in cerebral activity manifested by unawareness, confusion, convulsions, or coma."
IOWA Code Ann. (West Supp. 1981) 222.2(5)	"'Mental retardation' or 'mentally retarded' means a term or terms to describe children and adults who as a result of inadequately developed intelligence are significantly impaired in ability to learn or to adapt to the demands of society."
KAN. Stat. Ann. (1976 & Supp. 1980)	None.
KY. Rev. Stat. Ann. (Michie 1977) 202B.010(1)	"'Mentally retarded person' means a person with significantly subaverage general intellectual functioning existing concurrently with deficits in adaptive behavior and manifested during the developmental period."
LA. Rev. Stat. Ann. (West Supp. 1981) 28:381(17)	"'Mental retardation' means mental development that is significantly subaverage in general intellectual functioning and which exists concurrently with deficiencies in adaptive behavior and is manifested in the developmental years."
ME. Rev. Stat. Ann. (1978) 34, §2602(4)	"'Mental retardation' means a condition of significantly subaverage intellectual functioning manifested during a person's developmental period, existing concurrently with demonstrated deficits in adaptive behavior."
34, §2616(1)	"'Incapacitated person' means any person who is impaired by reason of mental retardation to the extent that he lacks sufficient understanding or capacity to make, communicate or implement responsible decisions concerning his person or property."
MD. Ann. Code (1980) 59A, §3(1)	"'Mental retardation' means significant subaverage general intellectual functioning which originates during the developmental period or which is caused by trauma resulting in a mental incapacity in which there is a demonstrated need for care and treatment to the same extent as that required if originated during the developmental period, and is associated with an impairment in adaptive behavior."
MASS. Ann. Laws (Michie/Law. Co-op. 1981) 123, §1	"'Mentally retarded person,' a person who, as a result of inadequately developed or impaired intelligence, as determined by clinical authorities as described in the regulations of the department is substantially limited in his ability to learn or adapt, as judged by established standards available for the evaluation of a person's ability to function in the community."

TABLE 2.2 STATUTORY DEFINITIONS OF DEVELOPMENTALLY DISABLED PERSONS—continued

STATE AND CITATION	STATUTORY PROVISIONS
MICH. Comp. Laws Ann. (1980) 330.1500	"(h) 'Developmental disability' means an impairment of general intellectual functioning or adaptive behavior which meets the following criteria: (i) It originated before the person became 18 years of age. (ii) It has continued since its origination or can be expected to continue indefinitely. (iii) It constitutes a substantial burden to the impaired person's ability to perform normally in society. (iv) It is attributable to 1 or more of the following: (A) Mental retardation, cerebral palsy, epilepsy, or autism. (B) Any other condition found to be closely related to mental retardation because it produces a similar impairment or requires treatment and services similar to those required for a person who is mentally retarded. (C) Dyslexia resulting from a condition described in subparagraph (A) or (B). "(g) 'Mentally retarded' means significantlly subaverage general intellectual functioning which originates during the developmental period and is associated with impairment in adaptive behavior."
MINN. Stat. Ann. (West Supp. 1981) 253A.02(5)	"'Mentally deficient person' means any person who has been diagnosed as having significantly subaverage intellectual functioning existing concurrently with demonstrated deficits in adaptive behavior who is in need of treatment or supervision.
252A.02(2)	"'Mentally retarded person' refers to any person who has been diagnosed as having significantly subaverage intellectual functioning existing concurrently with demonstrated deficits in adaptive behavior such as to require supervision and protection for his welfare or the public welfare."
MISS. Code Ann. (1981) 41-19-101	"The term 'feeble-minded' shall apply to any and all persons with such a degree of mental inferiority from birth, or from infancy or early childhood, that they are unable to care for themselves, to profit by ordinary public school instruction, . . . to manage themselves and their affairs with ordinary prudence, and consequently constitute menaces to the happiness or safety of themselves or of other persons in the community, and require care, supervision and control either for their own protection or for the protection of others."
MO. Ann. Stat. (Vernon Supp. 1981) 630.005	"(18) 'Mental disorder,' any organic, mental or emotional impairment which has substantial adverse effects on a person's cognitive, volitional or emotional function and which constitutes a substantial impairment in a person's ability to participate in activities of normal living. "(20) 'Mental retardation' significantly subaverage general intellectual functioning which: (a) Originates before age eighteen; and (b) Is associated with a significant impairment in adaptive behavior. "(8) 'Developmental disability' a disability (a) Which is attributable to mental retardation, cerebral palsy, autism, epilepsy, a learning disability related to a brain dysfunction or to a condition or conditions found by comprehensive evaluation to be closely related to mental retardation, or to require habilitation similar to that required for mentally retarded persons; (b) Which originated before age 18; and (c) Which can be expected to continue indefinitely."
MONT. Code Ann. (1981) 53-20-102	"(4) 'Developmentally disabled' means suffering from disabilities attributable to mental retardation, cerebral palsy, epilepsy, autism, or any other neurologically handicapping condition closely related to mental retardation and requiring treatment similar to that required by mentally retarded individuals, which condition has continued or can be expected to continue indefinitely and constitutes a substantial handicap of such individuals. "(12) 'Serious developmentally disabled' means developmentally disabled due to developmental or physical disability or a combination of both, rendering a person unable to function in a community-based setting and which has resulted in self-inflicted injury or injury to others or the imminent threat thereof or which has deprived the person afflicted of the ability to protect his life or health."
NEB. Rev. Stat. (1976). 83-381(1)	"Mentally retarded person shall mean any person of subaverage general intellectual functioning which is associated with a significant impairment in adaptive behavior."

TABLE 2.2 STATUTORY DEFINITIONS OF DEVELOPMENTALLY DISABLED PERSONS—continued

STATE AND CITATION	STATUTORY PROVISIONS
NEV. Rev. Stat. (1981) 433.174	"'Mental retardation' means significantly subaverage general intellectual functioning existing concurrently with deficits in adaptive behavior and manifested during the developmental period."
N.H. Rev. Stat. Ann. (1978) 171-A:2(XIV)	"'Mental retardation' means significantly subaverage general intellectual functioning existing concurrently with deficits in adaptive behavior, and manifested during the developmental period. A mentally retarded person may be considered mentally ill provided that no mentally retarded person shall be considered mentally ill solely by virtue of his mental retardation.
171-A:2(V)	"'Developmental impairment' means a disability which is attributable to: (a) mental retardation, cerebral palsy, epilepsy, autism or a specific learning disability; or (b) any other condition of an individual found to be closely related to mental retardation as it refers to general intellectual functioning or impairment in adaptive behavior or to require treatment similar to that required for mentally retarded individuals which disability: (1) originates before such individual attains age 18, (2) which has continued or can be expected to continue indefinitely, and (3) which constitutes a severe handicap to such individual's ability to function normally in society."
N.J. Stat. Ann. (West 1981) 30:4-23	"'Mental deficiency' shall mean that state of mental retardation in which the reduction of social competence is so marked that persistent social dependency requiring guardianship of the person shall have been demonstrated or be anticipated. "'Mental retardation' shall mean a state of significant subnormal intellectual development with reduction of social competence in a minor or adult person; this state of subnormal intellectual development shall have existed prior to adolescence and is expected to be of life duration."
30:6D-3(a)	"'Developmental disability' means a disability of a person which: (1) is attributable to: (a) mental retardation, cerebral palsy, epilepsy or autism; (b) any other condition found to be closely related to mental retardation because such condition results in impairment of general intellectual functioning or adaptive behavior similar to impairment resulting from mental retardation or which requires treatment and services similar to those required for mental retardation; or (c) dyslexia resulting from a disability described in subparagraphs (a) and (b); (2) originates before such person attains age 18; (3) has continued or can be expected to continue indefinitely; and (4) constitutes a substantial handicap to such person's ability to function normally in society."
N.M. Stat. Ann. (1979) 43-1-3	"'Developmental disability' means a disability of a person which is attributable to mental retardation, cerebral palsy, autism or neurological dysfunction which requires treatment or habilitation similar to that provided to persons with mental retardation."
N.Y. Mental Hyg. Law (McKinney 1978) 1.03	"(21) 'Mental retardation' means subaverage intellectual functioning which originates during the developmental period and is associated with impairment in adaptive behavior. "(22) 'Developmental disability' means a disability of a person which: (a) (1) is attributable to mental retardation, cerebral palsy, epilepsy, neurological impairment or autism; (2) is attributable to any other condition of a person found to be closely related to mental retardation because such condition results in similar impairment of general intellectual functioning or adaptive behavior to that of mentally retarded persons or requires treatment and services similar to those required for such persons; or (3) is attributable to dyslexia resulting from a disability described in subparagraph (1) or (2) of this paragraph; (b) originates before such person attains age eighteen; (c) has continued or can be expected to continue indefinitely; and (d) constitutes a substantial handicap to such person's ability to function normally in a society."

TABLE 2.2 STATUTORY DEFINITIONS OF DEVELOPMENTALLY DISABLED PERSONS—continued

STATE AND CITATION	STATUTORY PROVISIONS
N.C. Gen. Stat. (1981) 122-36(e)	"The words 'mentally retarded' refer to a person who has significantly subaverage general intellectual functioning existing concurrently with deficits in adaptive behavior and manifested during his developmental period."
N.D. Cent. Code (1978 & Supp. 1981) 25-01-01(2)	"'Mentally deficient person' means any person, minor or adult other than a mentally ill person, who is so mentally defective as to be incapable of managing himself and his affairs and to require supervision, control, and care for his own or the public welfare."
OHIO Rev. Code Ann. (Baldwin 1980 & Supp. 1981) 5123.01(K)	"'Mentally retarded person' means a person having significantly subaverage general intellectual functioning existing concurrently with deficiencies in adaptive behavior, manifested during the developmental period."
OKLA. Stat. (West Supp. 1981) 43A, §3(f)	"'Mentally deficient person' means a person afflicted with mental defectiveness from birth or from an early age to such an extent that he is incapable of managing himself and his affairs, who, for his own welfare or the welfare of others or of the community, requires supervision, control or care and who is not mentally ill or of unsound mind to such an extent as to require his certification to a facility for the mentally ill."
OR. Rev. Stat. (1981) 427.005(10)	"'Mental retardation' means significantly subaverage general intellectual functioning existing concurrently with deficits in adaptive behavior and manifested during the developmental period. . . . Mental retardation is synonymous with mental deficiency."
PA. Stat. Ann. (Purdon 1969) 50, §4102	"'Mental retardation' means subaverage general intellectual functioning which originates during the developmental period and is associated with impairment of one or more of the following: (1) maturation, (2) learning and (3) social adjustment."
R.I. Gen. Laws (Supp. 1981) 40.1-1-8.1	"The term 'developmental disability' means a severe, chronic disability of a person which —(A) is attributable to a mental or physical impairment or combination of mental and physical impairments; (B) is manifested before the person attains age twenty-two (22); (C) is likely to continue indefinitely; (D) results in substantial functional limitations in three (3) or more of the following areas of major life activity: (i) self-care, (ii) receptive and expressive language, (iii) learning, (iv) mobility, (v) self-direction, (vi) capacity for independent living, and (vii) economic self-sufficiency; and (E) reflects the person's need for a combination and sequence of special, interdisciplinary, or generic care, treatment, or other services which are of life-long or extended duration and are individually planned and coordinated."
40.1-22-3(5)	"'Mentally retarded person' shall mean a person with significant sub-average general intellectual functioning (two (2) standard deviations below the normal) existing concurrently with deficits in adaptive behavior and manifested during the development period."
S.C. Code Ann. (Law. Co-op. 1976) 44-21-30(4)	"'Mentally retarded person' means any person, other than a mentally ill person primarily in need of mental health services, whose intellectual deficit and adaptive level of behavior require for his benefit, or that of the public, special training, education, supervision, treatment, care or control in his home or community, or in a service facility or program under the control and management of the Department."
S.D. Codified Laws Ann. (1976) 27B-1-1	"The term 'mentally retarded' as used in this title shall include any person with significant subaverage general intellectual functioning and deficits in adaptive behavior."
27B-1-3	"(1) 'Developmental disability,' a disability attributed to mental retardation, cerebral palsy, epilepsy, or other neurological impairment designated by the board of social services, which originates during the developmental period or originates as a result of injury occurring any time during the life of an individual, which can be expected to continue indefinitely, which constitutes a substantial handicap, and which requires services similar to those provided to mentally retarded persons. "(2) 'Developmentally disabled person,' any person who suffers from a developmental disability."

TABLE 2.2 STATUTORY DEFINITIONS OF DEVELOPMENTALLY DISABLED PERSONS—continued

STATE AND CITATION	STATUTORY PROVISIONS
TENN. Code Ann. (Supp. 1981) 33-302(g)	"Mentally retarded individual or mentally deficient individual—an individual who has significantly subaverage general intellectual functioning existing concurrently with deficits in adaptive behavior, and manifested during the developmental period."
TEX. Rev. Civ. Stat. Ann. (Vernon Supp. 1981) 5547-201, §1.02(6)	"'Mentally retarded person' means any person other than a mentally disordered person, whose mental deficit requires him to have special training, education, supervision, treatment, care or control in his home or community, or in a state school for the mentally retarded."
5547-300(B), §3(5)	"Mental retardation means significantly subaverage general intellectual functioning existing concurrently with deficits in adaptive behavior and originating during the developmental period."
UTAH Code Ann. (1978) 64-8-13	"For the purposes of this act, mental retardation shall mean sub-average general intellectual functioning which originates during the developmental period and is associated with impairment in adaptive behavior. A mentally retarded person shall mean a person in whom there has been found, by comprehensive evaluation, a condition of mental retardation of such a nature and degree as to constitute a substantial, continuing prospective, educational, vocational, and social handicap."
VT. Stat. Ann. (Supp. 1981) 18, §7101(12)	"'Mentally retarded individual' means an individual who has significantly subaverage general intellectual functioning existing concurrently with deficits in adaptive behavior."
18, §8821(5)	["Mentally retarded person"]
VA. Code (1976 & Supp. 1981) 37.1-1(3)	"'Mental retardation' means substantial subaverage general intellectual functioning which originates during the developmental period and is associated with impairment in adaptive behavior."
WASH. Rev. Code Ann. (Supp. 1982) 72.33.020(1)	"'Mental handicap' is a state of limited development in consequence of which the individual affected is mentally incapable of assuming those responsibilities expected of the socially adequate person such as self-direction, self-support and social participation."
(1975) 71.20.015	"Persons 'developmentally disabled' as used in this amendatory act are those persons having a 'developmental disability' as defined in Public Law 91-517 [42 U.S.C.A. 2692(l), 42 U.S.C.A. §2691(l)] as now or hereafter amended." Subsequent history: §2691 repealed. Pub. L. 94-103, tit. III, §302(c), Oct. 4, 1975 89 Stat. 507. Subject matter now covered in §6001(7).*
W. VA. Code (1980) 27-1-3	"'Mental retardation' means significantly subaverage intellectual functioning which manifests itself in a person during his developmental period and which is characterized by his inadequancy in adaptive behavior."

*The definition in 42 U.S.C.A. §6001(7) (West Supp. 1981) is as follows: "The term 'developmental disability' means a severe, chronic disability of a person which—(a) is attributable to a mental or physical impairment or combination of mental and physical impairments; (b) is manifested before the person attains age twenty-two; (c) is likely to continue indefinitely; (d) results in substantial functional limitations in three or more of the following areas of major life activity: (i) self-care, (ii) receptive and expressive language, (iii) learning, (iv) mobility, (v) self-direction, (vi) capacity for independent living, and (vii) economic self-sufficiency; and (e) reflects the person's need for a combination and sequence of special, interdisciplinary, or generic care, treatment, or other services which are of lifelong or extended duration and are individually planned and coordinated."

TABLE 2.2 STATUTORY DEFINITIONS OF DEVELOPMENTALLY DISABLED PERSONS—continued

STATE AND CITATION	STATUTORY PROVISIONS
WIS. Stat. Ann. (West Supp. 1981) 51.01(5)	"(a) 'Developmental disability' means a disability attributable to mental retardation, cerebral palsy, epilepsy, autism, or another neurological condition closely related to mental retardation or requiring treatment similar to that required for mental retardation, which has continued or can be expected to continue indefinitely and constitutes a substantial handicap to the afflicted individual. 'Developmental disability' does not include senility which is primarily caused by the process of aging or the infirmities of aging. "(b) 'Developmental disability,' for purposes of involuntary commitment, does not include cerebral palsy or epilepsy."
WYO. Stat. (Supp. 1982) 9-6-642(a)	"(vii) 'Mentally retarded' means significantly subaverage general intellectual functioning existing concurrently with deficits in adaptive behavior and manifested during the developmental period. "(viii) Adaptive behavior means the effectiveness or degree with which the individual meets the standards of personal independence and social responsibility expected of his age and cultural group."

TABLE 2.3 STATUTORY DEFINITIONS OF ALCOHOLICS AND DRUG ADDICTS

STATE AND CITATION	STATUTORY PROVISIONS
ALA. Code (Supp. 1981) 27-20A-1(1)	"Alcoholism. A chronic disorder or illness in which the individual is unable, for psychological or physical reasons, or both, to refrain from the frequent consumption of alcohol in quantities sufficient to produce intoxication and, ultimately, injury to health and effective functioning."
ALAS. Stat. (1979 & Supp. 1981) 47.37.270(1)	"'Alcoholic' means a person who habitually lacks self-control in using alcoholic beverages, or uses alcoholic beverages to the extent that his health is substantially impaired or endangered, or his social or economic function is substantially disrupted."
47.30.500(2)	"'Alcoholism' means a condition related to alcohol and concerns a physical compulsion which exists, coupled with a mental obsession."
ARIZ. Rev. Stat. Ann. (1974) 36-2021.1	"'Alcoholic' means a person who habitually lacks self-control with respect to the use of alcoholic beverages or who uses alcoholic beverages to the extent that his health is substantially impaired or endangered or his social or economic functions are substantially disrupted."
ARK. Stat. Ann. (1971) 59-902	"The term 'narcotic addict' means any person who without bona fide medical need therefor, habitually uses any habit-forming narcotic drug . . . so as to endanger the public morals, health, safety or welfare, or who is so far addicted to the use of such habit-forming narcotic drugs as to have lost the power of self-control with reference to his addiction."
CAL. Welf. & Inst. Code (West 1972) 3009	"A 'narcotic addict,' as used in this division refers to any person, adult or minor, who is addicted to the unlawful use of any narcotic as defined in Division 10 of the Health and Safety Code, except marijuana."
COLO. Rev. Stat. (1973 & Supp. 1981) 25-1-302(1)	"'Alcoholic' means a person who habitually lacks self-control as to the use of alcoholic beverages or uses alcoholic beverages to the extent that his health is substantially impaired or endangered or his social or economic function is substantially disrupted."
CONN. Gen. Stat. (West 1975 & Supp. 1981) 17-155l(1)	"'Alcoholic' means a person who habitually or periodically lacks self-control as to the use of alcoholic beverages, or who habitually or periodically uses alcoholic beverages to the extent that his health is substantially impaired or endangered or his social or economic function is substantially disrupted."
(West 1977) 19-443(19)	"'Drug-dependent person' means any person who has developed a state of psychic or physical dependence, or both, upon a controlled substance following administration of that substance upon a repeated periodic or continuous basis. No person shall be classified as drug dependent who is dependent (A) upon a morphine-type substance as an incident to current medical treatment of a demonstrable physical disorder other than drug dependence, or (B) upon amphetamine-type, ataractic, barbiturate-type, hallucinogenic or other stimulant and depressant substances as an incident to current medical treatment of a demonstrable physical or psychological disorder, or both, other than drug dependence."
DEL. Code Ann. (Supp. 1980) 16, § 2203(1)	"'Alcoholic' means any person who chronically, habitually or periodically uses alcoholic beverages to the extent that they injure his health or substantially interfere with his social or economic health."
D.C. Code Ann. (1981) 24-522(1)	"The term 'chronic alcoholic' means any person who chronically and habitually uses alcoholic beverages to the extent that (A) they injure his health or interfere with his social or economic functioning, or (B) he has lost the power of self-control with respect to the use of such beverages."

TABLE 2.3 STATUTORY DEFINITIONS OF ALCOHOLICS AND DRUG ADDICTS--continued

STATE AND CITATION	STATUTORY PROVISIONS
D.C. Code Ann. (1981) 24-602(a)	"The term 'drug user' means any person, including a person under eighteen years of age, . . . who uses any habit-forming narcotic drugs so as to endanger the public morals, health, safety, or welfare, or who is so far addicted to the use of such habit-forming narcotic drugs as to have lost the power of self-control with reference to his addiction."
FLA. Stat. Ann. (West Supp. 1981) 396-032(5)	"'Alcoholic' means any person who chronically and habitually uses alcoholic beverages to the extent that it injures his health or substantially interferes with his social or economic functioning, or to the extent that he has lost the power of self-control with respect to the use of such beverages."
397-021(2)	"'Drug Dependent' means a person who is dependent upon, or by reason of repeated use is in imminent danger of becoming dependent upon, any substance controlled under chapter 893."
GA. Code Ann. (1979 & Supp. 1980) 88-401	"(a) 'Alcoholic' means a person who habitually lacks self-control as to the use of alcoholic beverages, or uses alcoholic beverages to the extent that his health is substantially impaired or endangered or his social or economic function is substantially disrupted. "(c) 'Drug dependent individual' or 'drug abuser' means a person who habitually lacks self-control as to use of opium, heroin, morphine, or any derivative or synthetic drug of that group, barbiturates, other sedatives, tranquilizers, amphetamines, lysergic acid diethylamide or other hallucinogens or any drug, dangerous drug, depressant, or stimulant drug or narcotic as defined in Chapters 79A-7, 79A-9, or 79A-10 of the Georgia Code; or who uses such drugs to the extent that his health is substantially impaired or endangered or his social or economic function is substantially disrupted: provided, however, that no person shall be deemed a drug dependent individual or abuser solely by virtue of his taking, according to directions, any drugs pursuant to a lawful prescription, issued by a physician in the course of professional treatment for legitimate medical purposes."
HAWAII Rev. Stat. (1976) 334-1	"'Person suffering from substance abuse' means a person who uses narcotic, stimulant, depressant, or hallucinogenic drugs or alcohol to an extent which interferes with his personal, social, family, or economic life."
IDAHO Code (1977) 39-302(3)	"'Alcoholic' means a person who habitually lacks self-control with respect to the use of alcoholic beverages, or uses alcoholic beverages to the extent that his health is substantially impaired or endangered, or his social or economic functions are substantially disrupted."
ILL. Ann. Stat. (Smith-Hurd Supp. 1980) 91½, § 120.3-3	"'Addict' means any person who habitually uses any drug, chemical, substance or dangerous drug other than alcohol so as to endanger the public morals, health, safety or welfare or who is so far addicted to the use of a dangerous drug or controlled substance other than alcohol as to have lost the power of self control with reference to his addiction."
91½, § 502.a	"'Alcoholic' means a person who suffers from an illness characterized by preoccupation with alcohol which is typically associated with physical disability and impaired emotional, occupational or social adjustments as direct consequence of loss of control over consumption of alcohol demonstrated by persistent and excessive use of alcohol, such as to lead usually to intoxication if drinking is begun; by chronicity; by progression; and by tendency toward relapse."

TABLE 2.3 STATUTORY DEFINITIONS OF ALCOHOLICS AND DRUG ADDICTS—continued

STATE AND CITATION	STATUTORY PROVISIONS
IND. Code Ann. (Burns Supp. 1982) 16-13-6.1-2	"'Alcohol abuser' means an individual who has had repeated episodes of intoxication or drinking which impair his health or interfere with his effectiveness on the job, at home, in the community, or in operating a motor vehicle. "'Alcoholic' means any individual who chronically and habitually uses alcoholic beverages to the extent that he loses the power of self control with respect to the use of alcoholic beverages, to the extent that he becomes a menace to the public morals, health, safety, or welfare of the members of society in general. "'Drug abuser' means an individual who has developed a psychological or physical dependence on the effects of drugs or harmful substances, or who abuses the use of drugs or harmful substances so that he or society is harmed."
IOWA Code Ann. (West Supp. 1981) 125.2	"(5) 'Substance abuser' means a person who habitually lacks self-control as to the use of chemical substances or uses chemical substances to the extent that his or her health is substantially impaired or endangered or that his or her social or economic function is substantially disrupted. "(1) 'Chemical dependency' means an addiction or dependency, either physical or psychological, on a chemical substance. Persons who take medically prescribed drugs shall not be considered chemically dependent if the drug is medically prescribed and the intake is proportionate to the medical need. "(3) 'Chemical substance' means alcohol, wine, spirits and beer as defined in Chapter 123 and drugs so defined in section 203A.2, subsection 3, which when used improperly could result in chemical dependency."
KAN. Stat. Ann. (Supp. 1981) 65-4003(1)	"'Alcoholic' means a person who habitually lacks self-control as to the use of alcoholic beverages, or uses alcoholic beverages to the extent that such person's health is substantially impaired or endangered or such person's social or economic function is substantially disrupted."
KY. Rev. Stat. Ann. (Michie 1977 & Supp. 1980) 222.011	"(2) 'Alcoholic' means a person suffering from alcoholism. "(3) 'Alcoholism' means a medically diagnosable disease characterized by chronic, habitual or periodic consumption of alcoholic beverages resulting in (a) the substantial interference with an individual's social or economic functions in the community, or (b) the loss of powers of self-control with respect to the use of such beverages. "(7) 'Drug addict' means any person whose use of an addictive substance has produced a condition which requires ingestion or injection of the addictive substance, or both, as a means of preventing withdrawal symptoms and of maintaining the individual's state of function. "(8) 'Drug dependent person' or 'drug abuser' means any person who compulsively and habitually uses drugs to the extent that they injure his health and interfere with his social and economic functioning."
LA. Rev. Stat. Ann. (West Supp. 1981) 28:2(25)	"'Substance abuse' means the condition of a person who uses narcotic, stimulant, depressant, soporific, tranquilizing, or hallucinogenic drugs or alcohol to the extent that it renders the person dangerous to himself or others or renders the person gravely disabled."
ME. Rev. Stat. Ann. (1980) 22, § 1362(1) & § 7103	"(3) 'Alcoholic' means a person who habitually lacks self-control as to the use of alcoholic beverages, or uses alcoholic beverages to the extent that his health is substantially impaired or endangered or his social or economic function is substantially disrupted. "(11) 'Drug addict' means a drug dependent person who, due to the use of a dependency related drug has developed such a tolerance thereto that abrupt termination of the use thereof would produce withdrawal symptoms. "(12) 'Drug dependent person' means any person who is unable to function effectively and whose inability to do so causes or results from the use of a dependency related drug."

TABLE 2.3 STATUTORY DEFINITIONS OF ALCOHOLICS AND DRUG ADDICTS—continued

STATE AND CITATION	STATUTORY PROVISIONS
MD. Health Gen. Code Ann. (1982) 8-101	"(c) Chronic alcoholic. 'Chronic alcoholic' means an individual who chronically and habitually drinks alcoholic beverages so much that: (1) It injures the health of the individual; (2) It substantially interferes with the social or economic functioning of the individual; or (3) The individual cannot control the drinking."
9-101	"(e) Drug abuse. (1) 'Drug abuse' means: (i) Misuse or unlawful use of a drug; (ii) Drug dependence; or (iii) Drug addiction. (2) 'Drug abuse' does not include taking a drug according to a lawful prescription that is issued, in the course of professional treatment, for a legitimate medical purpose. "(f) Drug abuser. 'Drug abuser' means an individual who: (1) Has a drug dependence or drug addiction; (2) Because of repeated use of a drug, is in imminent danger of having a drug dependence; or (3) Shows the symptoms of drug abuse. "(g) Drug addict. 'Drug addict' means an individual who: (1) Has a drug addiction; (2) Because of repeated use of a drug, is in imminent danger of having a drug addiction; or (3) Shows the symptoms of drug addiction. "(h) Drug addiction. (1) 'Drug addiction' means a physical and psychological dependence on a drug. (2) 'Drug addiction' does not include taking a drug according to a lawful prescription that is issued, in the course of professional treatment, for a legitimate medical purpose. "(i) Drug dependence. 'Drug dependence' means a psychological need for a drug."
MASS. Ann. Laws (Michie/ Law. Co-op. 1981) 123, § 35	"For the purpose of this section 'alcoholic' shall mean a person who chronically or habitually consumes alcoholic beverages to the extent that (1) such use substantially injures his health or substantially interferes with his social or economic functioning, or (2) he has lost the power of self-control over the use of such beverages."
MICH. Comp. Laws Ann. (1980) 333.6107(3)	"'Substance abuse' means the taking of alcohol or other drugs at dosages that place an individual's social, economic, psychological, and physical welfare in potential hazard or to the extent that an individual loses the power of self-control as a result of the use of alcohol or drugs, or while habitually under the influence of alcohol or drugs, endangers public health, morals, safety, or welfare, or a combination thereof."
MINN. Stat. Ann. (West Supp. 1981) 253A.02	"(4) 'Inebriate person' means any person determined as being incapable of managing himself or his affairs by reason of the habitual and excessive use of intoxicating liquors, narcotics, or other drugs." "(20) 'Drug dependent person' means any inebriate person or any person incapable of managing himself or his affairs or unable to function physically or mentally in an effective manner because of the use of psychological or physiological dependency producing drug including alcohol."

TABLE 2.3 STATUTORY DEFINITIONS OF ALCOHOLICS AND DRUG ADDICTS—continued

STATE AND CITATION	STATUTORY PROVISIONS
MISS. Code Ann. (1981) 41-31-1	"(a) An 'alcoholic' shall mean any person who chronically and habitually uses alcoholic beverages to the extent that he has lost the power of self-control with respect to the use of such beverages, or any person who, while chronically under the influence of alcoholic beverages, endangers public morals, health safety or welfare. "(c) 'Alcoholism' shall mean any condition of abnormal behavior resulting directly or indirectly from the chronic and habitual use of alcoholic beverages. "(d) A 'drug addict' shall mean any person who chronically and habitually uses any form of habit-forming drugs, such as opiates and the derivatives thereof, barbiturates, and every tablet, powder, substance, liquid or fluid, patented or not, containing habit-forming drugs if same is capable of being used by human beings and produces drug addiction in any form or degree. "(e) 'Drug addiction' shall mean and include any condition of abnormal behavior or illness resulting directly or indirectly from the chronic and habitual use of habit-forming drugs."
MO. Ann. Stat. (Vernon Supp. 1980) 630.005	"(10) 'Drug abuse,' the use of any drug without compelling medical reason, which use results in a temporary mental, emotional or physical impairment and causes socially dysfunctional behavior, or in psychological or physiological dependency resulting from continued use, which dependency induces a mental, emotional or physical impairment and causes socially dysfunctional behavior. "(1) 'Alcohol abuse,' the use of any alcoholic beverage, which use results in intoxication or in a psychological or physiological dependency from continued use, which dependency induces a mental, emotional or physical impairment and which causes socially dysfunctional behavior."
MONT. Code Ann. (1981) 53-24-103(1)	"'Alcoholic' means a person who has a chronic illness or disorder of behavior characterized by repeated drinking of alcoholic beverages to the extent that it endangers the health, interpersonal relationships, or economic function of the individual or public health, welfare, or safety."
NEB. Rev. Stat. (1976) 83-159	"(1) 'Alcoholic' shall mean any person who habitually uses alcoholic beverages to the extent that he has lost the power of self-control with respect to the use of such beverages, or who is chronically or habitually under the influence of alcoholic beverages and endangers the health, morals, safety, or welfare of himself or any other persons or groups of persons. "(2) 'Alcoholism' shall mean the pathological condition attendant upon the excessive and habitual use of alcoholic beverages."
83-701	"'Drug user' shall mean any person, including a person under eighteen years of age, notwithstanding the provisions of the Juvenile Court Act of the State of Nebraska who uses any habit-forming narcotic drugs so as to endanger the public morals, health, safety, or welfare, or who is so far addicted to the use of such habit-forming narcotic drugs as to have lost the power of self-control with reference to his addiction."
NEV. Rev. Stat. (1981) 458.010	"(2) 'Alcohol and drug abuser' means a person whose consumption of alcohol or other drugs, or any combination thereof, interferes with or adversely affects his ability to function socially or economically. "(3) 'Alcoholic' means any person who habitually uses alcoholic beverages to the extent that he endangers the health, safety or welfare of himself or any other person or group of persons."
458.290	"'[D]rug addict' means any person who habitually takes or otherwise uses any controlled substance as defined in chapter 453 of NRS, other than any maintenance dosage of a narcotic or habit-forming drug administered pursuant to chapter 453 of NRS, to the extent that he endangers the health, safety or welfare of himself or any other person or groups of persons."

TABLE 2.3 STATUTORY DEFINITIONS OF ALCOHOLICS AND DRUG ADDICTS—continued

STATE AND CITATION	STATUTORY PROVISIONS
N.H. Rev. Stat. Ann. (1977) 172:1(XIX)	"'Drug dependent person' means any person who has developed a state of psychic or physical dependence, or both, upon a controlled drug following administration of that drug upon a repeated periodic or continuous basis. No person shall be classified as drug dependent who is dependent: (a) upon a morphine-type drug as an incident to current medical treatment of a demonstrable physical disorder other than drug dependence, or (b) upon amphetamine-type, ataractic, barbiturate-type, hallucinogenic or other stimulant and depressant drugs as an incident to current medical treatment of a demonstrable physical or psychological disorder, or both, other than drug dependence."
172-B:1 (Supp. 1981)	"(I) 'Alcohol abuser' means anyone who drinks to an extent or with a frequency which impairs or endangers his health, or his social and economic functioning, or the health and welfare of others. The class of alcohol abusers includes the smaller class of alcoholics. "(II) 'Alcoholic' means a person suffering from the condition of alcoholism. "(III) 'Alcoholism' means addiction to alcoholic beverages. It is characterized by: (a) Chronic absence of control by the drinker over the frequency or the volume of his alcohol intake; and (b) Inability of the drinker to consistently moderate his drinking practices in spite of the onset of a variety of consequences deleterious to his health or his socio-economic functions."
N.J. Stat. Ann. (West Supp. 1981) 26:2B-8	"'Alcoholic' means any person who chronically, habitually or periodically consumes alcoholic beverages to the extent that: a. such use substantially injuries [sic] his health or substantially interferes with his social or economic functioning in the community on a continuing basis, or b. he has lost the power of self-control with respect to the use of such beverages."
N.M. Stat. Ann. (1979) 43-2-2(A)	"'Alcoholic' means a person who habitually lacks self-control as to the use of alcoholic beverages, or uses alcoholic beverages to the extent that his health is substantially impaired or endangered, or his social or economic function is substantially disrupted."
N.Y. Mental Hyg. Law (McKinney Supp. 1981) 19.03(c)	"1. 'Substance' shall mean: (i) any controlled substance listed in section thirty-three hundred six of the public health law; (ii) any substance listed in section thirty-three hundred eighty of the public health law; (iii) any substance, except alcohol, as listed in the published rules of the division which has been certified to the director by the commissioner of health as having the capability of causing physical and/or psychological dependence. . . . "2. 'Substance abuse' shall mean the repeated use of one or more substances, as defined in this section, except when such substance is used in accordance with a lawful prescription. "3. 'Substance dependence' shall mean the physical or psychological reliance upon a substance as defined in this section, arising from substance abuse or arising from the lawful use of any such substance for the sole purpose of alleviating such a physical or psychological reliance."
(McKinney 1978) 1.03	"(13) 'Alcoholism' means a chronic illness in which the ingestion of alcohol usually results in the further compulsive ingestion of alcohol beyond the control of the sick person to a degree which impairs or destroys his capacity to function normally within his social and economic environment and to meet his civic responsibilities. "(14) 'Alcoholic' means any person who is afflicted with the illness of alcoholism."

TABLE 2.3 STATUTORY DEFINITIONS OF ALCOHOLICS AND DRUG ADDICTS—continued

STATE AND CITATION	STATUTORY PROVISIONS
N.C. Gen. Stat. (1981) 122-36(c)	"The word 'inebriate' shall mean a person habitually so addicted to alcoholic drinks or narcotic drugs or other habit-forming drugs as to have lost the power of self-control and that for his own welfare or the welfare of others is a proper subject for restraint, care, and treatment."
(Supp. 1981) 122-58.22(a)	"A person is an alcoholic if he habitually lacks self control as to the use of alcoholic beverages, or uses alcoholic beverages to the extent that his health is substantially impaired or endangered or his social or economic function is substantially disrupted."
N.D. Cent. Code (1978 & Supp. 1981) 25-03.1-02	"(5) 'Drug addict' means an individual who has a physical or emotional dependence on a drug or drugs which he uses in a manner not prescribed by a physician. "(1) 'Alcoholic individual' means an individual who has lost the power of self-control, exhibits cognitive deficiencies, general confused thinking, or other manifestations of disorientation which show an inability to make judgments about areas of behavior that do not directly relate to his drinking."
OHIO Rev. Code Ann. (Baldwin 1976) 3719.011	"(A) 'Drug of Abuse' means any controlled substance as defined in § 3719.01 of the Revised Code, any harmful intoxicant as defined in § 2925.01 of the Revised Code, and any dangerous drug as defined in § 4729.02 of the Revised Code. "(B) 'Drug dependent person' means any person who, by reason of the use of any drug of abuse, is physically, psychologically, or physically and psychologically dependent upon the use of such drug, to the detriment of his health or welfare. "(C) 'Person in danger of becoming a drug dependent person' means any person who, by reason of his habitual or incontinent use of any drug of abuse, is in imminent danger of becoming a drug dependent person."
3720.01	"(A) 'Alcoholism' means the chronic and habitual use of alcoholic beverages by an individual to the extent that he has lost the power of self-control with respect to the use of such beverages or to the extent that he endangers the health, safety, or welfare of himself or others. "(B) 'Alcoholic' means a person suffering from alcoholism."
OKLA. Stat. Ann. (West Supp. 1981) 63, § 2110.2	"An 'alcohol-dependent person' is one who uses alcoholic beverages to such an extent that it impairs his health, his family life, his occupation and compromises the health and safety of the community."
(West 1979) 43A, § 652.3	"'Drug dependent person' means a person who is using a controlled substance as presently defined in Section 102 of the Federal Controlled Substances Act and who is in a state of psychic or physical dependence, or both, arising from administration of that controlled substance on an intermittent or continuous basis. Drug dependence is characterized by behavioral and other responses which include a strong compulsion to take the substance on a continuous basis in order to experience its psychic effects, or to avoid the discomfort of its absence."

TABLE 2.3 STATUTORY DEFINITIONS OF ALCOHOLICS AND DRUG ADDICTS—continued

STATE AND CITATION	STATUTORY PROVISIONS
OR. Rev. Stat. (1981) 430.405(1)	"'Drug-dependent person' means one who has lost the ability to control the [personal] use of controlled substances or other substances with abuse potential, or who uses such substances or controlled substances to the extent that the health of the person or that of others is substantially impaired or endangered or the social or economic function of the person is substantially disrupted. A drug-dependent person may be physically dependent, a condition in which the body requires a continuing supply of a drug or controlled substance to avoid characteristic withdrawal symptoms, or psychologically dependent, a condition characterized by an overwhelming mental desire for continued use of a drug or controlled substance." (The same definition is found at § 430.306(7) (1981), with the addition of the bracketed word.)
430.306(2)	"'Alcoholic' means any person who has lost the ability to control the use of alcoholic beverages, or who uses alcoholic beverages to the extent that the health of the person or that of others is substantially impaired or endangered or the social or economic function of the person is substantially disrupted. An alcoholic may be physicially dependent, a condition in which the body requires a continuing supply of alcohol to avoid characteristic withdrawal symptoms, or psychologically dependent, a condition characterized by an overwhelming mental desire for continued use of alcoholic beverages."
PA. Stat. Ann. (Purdon Supp. 1980) 71, § 1690.102(b)	"'Drug dependent person' means a person who is using a drug, controlled substance or alcohol, and who is in a state of psychic or physical dependence, or both, arising from administration of that drug, controlled substance or alcohol on a continuing basis. Such dependence is characterized by behavioral and other responses which include a strong compulsion to take the drug, controlled substance or alcohol on a continuous basis in order to experience its psychic effects, or to avoid the discomfort of its absence. This definition shall include those persons commonly known as 'drug addicts.'"
R.I. Gen. Laws (1977) 40.1-4-2(1)	"'Alcoholic' means a person who habitually lacks self-control as to the use of alcoholic beverages, or uses alcoholic beverages to the extent that his health is substantially impaired or endangered or his social or economic function is substantially disrupted."
(Supp. 1981) 21-28.2-1(c)	"'Narcotic addict' means a person who is at the time of examination dependent upon opium, heroin, morphine or any derivative or synthetic drug of that group or any other addictive drug as defined in § 21-28-2, or a depressant or stimulant substance, or who by reason of the repeated use of any such drug is in imminent danger of becoming dependent upon opium, heroin, morphine or any derivative or synthetic drug of that group or any other addictive drug as defined in § 21-28-2, or any person who is or has been so far addicted to the use of such narcotic drugs as to have lost the power of self-control with reference to his addiction, provided, however, that no person shall be deemed a narcotic addict solely by virtue of his taking of any of such drugs pursuant to a lawful prescription issued by a physician in the course of professional treatment for legitimate medical purposes."
S.C. Code Ann. (Law. Co-op. 1976) 44-51-10	"(1) 'Addict' means any person who has the illness known as alcoholism or drug addiction. "(2) 'Alcoholism' means the compulsive use of alcoholic beverages excessively to the extent that he has lost the power of self-control with respect to the use of such beverages. "(3) 'Drug addiction' means the compulsive use of drugs and a dependence on the effects of drugs."
S.D. Codified Laws Ann. (1977 & Supp. 1981) 34-20A-2(1)	"'Alcoholic,' a person who habitually lacks self-control as to the use of alcoholic beverages, or uses alcoholic beverages to the extent that his health is substantially impaired or endangered or his social or economic function is substantially disrupted."

TABLE 2.3 STATUTORY DEFINITIONS OF ALCOHOLICS AND DRUG ADDICTS—continued

STATE AND CITATION	STATUTORY PROVISIONS
TENN. Code Ann. (Supp. 1981) 33-302	"(q) Alcohol abuse—A condition characterized by the continuous or episodic use of alcohol resulting in social impairment, vocational impairment, psychological dependence or pathological patterns of use. "(r) Alcoholism—Alcohol abuse which results in the development of tolerance or manifestations of alcohol abstinence syndrome upon cessation of use. "(s) Drug abuse—A condition characterized by the continuous or episodic use of a drug or drugs resulting in social impairment, vocational impairment, psychological dependence or pathological patterns of use. "(t) Drug dependence—Drug abuse which results in the development of tolerance or manifestations of drug abstinence syndrome upon cessation of use."
TEX. Rev. Civ. Stat. Ann. (Vernon 1958 & Supp. 1981) 5561cc, § 1	"(2) An 'alcoholic' means any person who chronically and habitually uses alcoholic beverages to the extent that he has lost the power of self control with respect to the use of such beverages, or while chronically and habitually under the influence of alcoholic beverages endangers public morals, health, safety or welfare. "(3) 'Alcoholism,' a condition of abnormal behavior or illness leading directly or indirectly to the chronic and habitual use of alcoholic beverages."
UTAH Code Ann. (1978 & Supp. 1981)	
VT. Stat. Ann. (1968 & Supp. 1981) 18, § 8401	"As used in this chapter, 'drug addict' means a person who shows signs of mental illness because of his use of drugs, hallucinogens, stimulants or sedatives or who has an uncontrollable desire for their use or consumption."
18, § 9142	"(1) 'Alcohol abuser' means anyone who drinks to an extent or with a frequency which impairs or endangers his health, or his social and economic functioning, or the health and welfare of others. The class of alcohol abusers includes the smaller class of alcoholics. "(3) 'Alcoholic' means a person suffering from the condition of alcoholism. "(4) 'Alcoholism' means addiction to alcoholic beverages. It is characterized by: (A) chronic absence of control by the drinker over the frequency or the volume of his alcohol intake; and (B) inability of the drinker to consistently moderate his drinking practices in spite of the onset of a variety of consequences deleterious to his health or his socio-economic functioning."
VA. Code (1976 & Supp. 1981) 37.1-203	"As used in this chapter: 1. 'Substance' means both alcoholic beverages and drugs. 2. 'Substance abuse' means the use, without compelling medical reason, of any substance which results in psychological or physiological dependency as a function of continued use in such a manner as to induce mental, emotional or physical impairment and cause socially dysfunctional or socially disordering behavior."
37.1-217A	"'Alcoholic' means a person who: (i) through use of alcohol has become dangerous to the public or himself; or (ii) because of such alcohol use is medically determined to be in need of medical or psychiatric care, treatment, rehabilitation or counseling."
37.1-1(5)	"'Drug addict' means a person who: (i) through use of habit-forming drugs or other drugs enumerated in the Virginia Drug Control Act as controlled drugs, has become dangerous to the public or himself; or (ii) because of such drug use, is medically determined to be in need of medical or psychiatric care, treatment, rehabilitation or counseling."

TABLE 2.3 STATUTORY DEFINITIONS OF ALCOHOLICS AND DRUG ADDICTS—continued

STATE AND CITATION	STATUTORY PROVISIONS
WASH Rev. Code Ann. (1962) 69.32.010	"The term 'narcotic addict' means a person who habitually uses a narcotic drug or drugs."
(1975) 70.96A.020(1)	"'Alcoholic' means a person who habitually lacks self-control as to the use of alcoholic beverages, or uses alcoholic beverages to the extent that his health is substantially impaired or endangered or his social or economic function is substantially disrupted."
W. VA. Code (1980) 27-1A-11	"(c) 'Drug abuser' shall mean a person who is in a state of psychic or physical dependence, or both, arising from the administration of any controlled substance, as that term is defined in chapter sixty-A [§ 60A-1-101 et seq.] of this Code, on a continuous basis. "(a) 'Alcoholic' shall mean any person who chronically and habitually uses alcoholic beverages to the extent that he has lost the power of self-control as to the use of such beverages, or, while chronically and habitually under the influence of alcoholic beverages, endangers public morals, health, safety or welfare."
27-1-4	"An 'inebriate' person is anyone over the age of eighteen years who is incapable or unfit to properly conduct himself or herself, or his or her affairs, or is dangerous to himself or herself or others, by reason of periodical, frequent or constant drunkenness, induced either by the use of alcoholic or other liquors, or of opium, morphine, or other narcotic or intoxicating or stupefying substance."
27-1-11	"'Addiction' means the frequent or constant use of alcohol, narcotic or other intoxicating or stupefying substance which renders the person using such substance incapable of exercising reasonable judgment in the conduct of his affairs or which causes such person to be dangerous to himself or others."
WIS. Stat. Ann. (West 1957 & Supp. 1981) 51.01(1)	"'Alcoholic' means a person who habitually lacks self-control as to the use of alcoholic beverages and uses alcoholic beverages to the extent that his or her health is substantially impaired or by reason of such use is deprived of his or her ability to care for himself or herself, or such person's family. This definition does not apply to § 51.45.
51.45(2)(a)	"'Alcoholic' means a person who habitually lacks self-control as to the use of alcoholic beverages, or uses such beverages to the extent that health is substantially impaired or endangered or social or economic functioning is substantially disrupted.
51.01(8)	"'Drug dependent' means a person who uses one or more drugs to the extent that the person's health is substantially impaired or his or her social or economic functioning is substantially disrupted."
WYO. Stat. (1981)	None.

TABLE 2.4 EMERGENCY DETENTION

STATE	APPLICATION BY: Any Person (1)	APPLICATION BY: Peace Officer (2)	APPLICATION BY: Other Public Official (3)	APPLICATION BY: Mental Health Professional (4)	CERTIFICATION: Medical (5)	CERTIFICATION: Judicial (6)	CERTIFICATION: Other (7)	CONDITION REQUIREMENT: Dangerous to Self or Others (8)	CONDITION REQUIREMENT: Unable to Provide for Basic Physical Needs (9)	DETENTION PLACE: Jail (10)	DETENTION PLACE: Public Mental Health Facility (11)	DETENTION PLACE: Private Mental Health Facility (12)	MAXIMUM PERIOD (13)
ALA. Code (1975 & Supp. 1981)	22-52-1					22-52-7(a)		*fn. 1* 22-52-7(b)		only if no other public facility available to safely detain 22-52-7(b)			probable cause hearing w/in 7 days; hearing w/in 30 days of filing petition 22-52-8(a)
ALAS. Stat. (1979 & Supp. 1981)	any adult 47.30.700	47.30.705			47.30.710			in need of care or treatment 47.30.710(b)	OR AND gravely disabled; in need of care or treatment 47.30.710(b)	correctional facility may be used as emergency evaluation facility if evaluation facility not available 47.30.705	47.30.760	if space available upon acceptance by facility 47.30.760	examination w/in 24 hrs. 47.30.710(a) evaluation for 72 hrs. thereafter 47.30.715
ARIZ. Rev. Stat. Ann. (1974 & Supp. 1981)	person w/knowledge of facts requiring emergency admission 36-524(A)	peace officer 36-525(B)						36-524(C) 36-525(B)			36-524(D) 36-525(B) 36-501(8), (26)	36-524(D) 36-525(B) 36-501(8), (26)	24 hrs. unless petition for ct. ordered evaluation filed 36-527(A) evaluation for less than 72 hrs. 36-530(B)
ARK. Stat. Ann. (1971 & Supp. 1981)	59-1406	any law enforcement officer 59-1406						homicidal or suicidal 59-1406(a)	OR gravely disabled 59-1406(a)		59-1406(a)	*fn. 2* 59-1406(a)	petition filed w/in 72 hrs.; hearing w/in another 72 hrs. 59-1406(a)
CAL. Welf. & Inst. Code (West 1972 & Supp. 1980)		*fn. 3* 5150	other professional person 5150	physician 5150			*fn. 4* 5150	5150	OR 5150 gravely disabled		facility designated by county 5150	facility designated by county 5150	72 hrs. 5150
COLO. Rev. Stat. (1973 & Supp. 1981)	affidavit 27-10-105(b)	27-10-105(1)(a)	professional person 27-10-105(1)(a)			unnecessary if application by peace officer or professional person 27-10-105(b)		27-10-105(1)(a)	OR gravely disabled 27-10-105(1)(a)	if no other suitable place *fn. 5* 27-10-105(1.1)	27-10-105 27-10-102(4.5)	27-10-105 27-10-102(4.5)	72 hrs. 27-10-105(a), (b)
CONN. Gen. Stat. Ann. (West 1975 & Supp. 1981) *fn. 6*	17-183a(b)	17-183a(a)			17-183(a)	probate ct. 17-183a(b) unnecessary if application by police officer		17-183(a) 17-183a	OR gravely disabled 17-183(a) 17-183a		17-183(a) 17-183a	17-183(a) 17-183a	15 days 17-183(a) 72 hrs. unless 15-day emergency certificate issued 17-183a
DEL. Code Ann. (1974 & Supp. 1980)	16, §5122(b)				16, §5122(c)			16, §5122(b)			16, §5122(c)		72 hrs. 16, §5122(d)
D.C. Code Ann. (1981)		21-521	health official 21-521	physician 21-521	psychiatrist on duty at hospital 21-522			21-522			acceptance mandatory 21-522	acceptance discretionary 21-522	48 hrs. unless ct. orders 7-day extension 21-523 21-524
FLA. Stat. Ann. (West 1973 & Supp. 1981)		394.463(1)(b)1, 2	judge 394.463(1)(b)1,2	394.463(1)(b)3	examination by mental health professional 394.463(1)(c), (d)			394.463(1)(a)1	OR in need of care or treatment 394.463(1)(a)2		receiving facility 394.463(1)(b) 394.455(10)	receiving facility 394.463(1)(b) 394.455(10)	48 hrs. 394.463(1)(d)
GA. Code Ann. (1979 & Supp. 1980)	affidavits of at least 2 persons 88-504.2(b)	if person is committing a penal offense 88-504.3		physician certificate 88-504.2(a)		county ct. 88-504.2(b) judicial order required if admission based on affidavits		mentally ill & requiring involuntary treatment 88-504.2 88-504.3 88-501(v)	OR mentally ill & requiring involuntary treatment 88-504.2 88-504.3 88-501(v)		emergency receiving facility 88-504.1	88-504.2 88-504.1	24 hrs. 88-504.4

TABLE 2.4 EMERGENCY DETENTION—*Continued*

STATE	APPLICATION BY				CERTIFICATION			CONDITION REQUIREMENT		DETENTION PLACE			MAXIMUM PERIOD (13)
	Any Person (1)	Peace Officer (2)	Other Public Official (3)	Mental Health Professional (4)	Medical (5)	Judicial (6)	Other (7)	Dangerous to Self or Others (8)	Unable to Provide for Basic Physical Needs (9)	Jail (10)	Public Mental Health Facility (11)	Private Mental Health Facility (12)	
HAWAII Rev. Stat. (1976 & Supp. 1981) *fn. 7*		if person committing an offense; if suicidal 334-59a(1)	attorney, clergyman, state or county employee 334-59a(2)	physician, health or social service professional 334-59a(2), (3)	examination by physician 334-59(b)	334-59a(2)		imminently dangerous to self, others, or property 334-59(d) AND	mentally ill or suffering from substance abuse & in need of care &/or treatment *fn. 8* 334-59(d) 334-1		334-59(a)(1)–(3), (d)	334-59(a)(1)–(3), (d)	48 hrs. 334-59(c)
IDAHO Code (1980 & Supp. 1981)		66-326	if designated examiner finds emergency detention necessary, prosecuting attorney must file petition 66-326(d)		66-326(b), (c)	temporary custody order issued requiring examination by designated examiner w/in 24 hrs. 66-326(b) detention order 66-326(d)		66-326(a) *fn. 9*	gravely disabled *fn. 9* 66-326(d)	*fn. 10* 66-326(b)	*fn. 10* 66-326(b)	*fn. 10* 66-326(b)	*fn. 11*
ILL. Ann. Stat. (Smith-Hurd 1966 & Supp. 1980)	18 yrs. or older 91½, §3-601	91½, §3-606	any ct. 91½, §3-607		qualified examiner 91½, §3-602 §3-603		second certificate after exam by psychiatrist 24 hrs. after admission 91½, §3-610	*fn. 12* 91½, §1-119 §3-602, §3-606 §3-607 OR	91½, §1-119 §3-602, §3-606 §3-607		91½, §3-605	91½, §3-605	*fn. 13* 91½, §3-611
IND. Code Ann. (Burns 1973 & Supp. 1982)	16-14-9.1-7(a)	police officer 16-14-9.1-7(a)	health officer 16-14-9.1-7(a)		16-14-9.1-7(a)(2)	endorsement by judicial officer 16-14-9.1-7		16-14-9.1-7(e) OR	gravely disabled *fn. 14* 16-14-9.1-7(e)		16-14-9.1-7	16-14-9.1-7	72 hrs. 16-14-9.1-7
IOWA Code Ann. (West 1969 & Supp. 1980) *fn. 15*	229.6					229.11		*fn. 16* 229.11 229.22(3) 229.1(2)		only in actual emergency & 24 hrs. max. 229.11(3)	*fn. 17* 229.11(2)	*fn. 17* 229.11(2)	48 hrs. 229.22(4) 5 days (until hearing is held) 229.11
KAN. Stat. Ann. (1976 & Supp. 1980) *fn. 18*	59-2909(c) 59-2912(b)	59-2908 59-2909(b) 59-2912(a)			acceptance at facility after examination by physician 59-2908	59-2912		59-2909(c) 59-2908(a) 59-2912(a)(3), (b)(3)	*fn. 19*	if treatment facility is unwilling or unable to admit 59-2908(b) only if no other facilities available 59-2912(g)	any treatment facility *fn. 20* 59-2908(a) 59-2912(g)	any treatment facility *fn. 20* 59-2908(a) 59-2912(g)	48 hrs. 59-2911 72 hrs. if initiated by peace officer 59-2912(a)(5) until conclusion of hearing if initiated by "any person" 59-2912(b)(3)
KY. Rev. Stat. Ann. (Michie 1977 & Supp. 1980) *fn. 21*	relative, friend, spouse, or guardian 202 A. 050	202 A. 040		202 A. 030 202 A. 050	2 physicians or 1 physician & 1 qualified mental health professional 202 A. 040 202 A. 030	hearing held w/in 48 hrs. 202 A. 050		*fnn. 22, 23* 202 A. 040 202 A. 030 202 A. 050	*fn. 23* 202 A. 040 202 A. 030 202 A. 050 202 A. 010(5)	may be in jail pending hearing 202 A. 040 202 A. 050	202 A. 040 202 A. 030 202 A. 050	202 A. 040 202 A. 030 202 A. 050	7 days 202 A. 040 72 hrs. 202 A. 030 48 hrs. until hearing 202 A. 050
LA. Rev. Stat. Ann. (West 1975 & Supp. 1981)	(detention of minors) 28:57(A)		physician after examination *fn. 24* 28:53(B)			upon petition *fn. 25* 28:53(D)		28:53(B)(2)	28:53(B)(2)			treatment facility 28:53(F)	15 days *fn. 26* 28:53(F)
ME. Rev. Stat. Ann. (1978 & Supp. 1981)	34, §2333	police officer 34, §2333	health officer 34, §2333		physician or clinical psychologist 34, §2333	endorsement 34, §2333		34, §2333 §2251(7) OR	inability to avoid impairment or injury 34, §2333 §2251(7)(c)		34, §2333	34, §2333	*fn. 27* 34, §2333
MD. Ann. Code (1979 & Supp. 1981)	59, §22(b)	59, §22(e)		59, §22(d)		*fn. 28* 59, §22(c)		59, §22(c)			59, §22(a), (f)	59, §22(a), (f)	30 hrs. 59, §22(g)

TABLE 2.4 EMERGENCY DETENTION—*Continued*

STATE	APPLICATION BY				CERTIFICATION			CONDITION REQUIREMENT		DETENTION PLACE			MAXIMUM PERIOD (13)
	Any Person (1)	Peace Officer (2)	Other Public Official (3)	Mental Health Professional (4)	Medical (5)	Judicial (6)	Other (7)	Dangerous to Self or Others (8)	Unable to Provide for Basic Physical Needs (9)	Jail (10)	Public Mental Health Facility (11)	Private Mental Health Facility (12)	
MASS. Ann. Laws (Michie/ Law. Co-op. 1981)	123-12(e)	police officer 123-12(a)		physician 123-12(a)	123-12(a), (e)			*fn. 29* 123-12(a) 123-1	*fn. 29* 123-12(a) 123-1		123-12(a)	123-12(a)	10 days 123-12(a)
MICH. Comp. Laws Ann. (1980 & Supp. 1981)		330.1427(1)						330.1427(1) 330.1401 OR	330.1427(1) 330.1401		330.1429	330.1429	24 hrs. 330.1429
MINN. Stat. Ann. (West 1982)		253A.04(2)	health officer 253A.04(2)	253A.04(1)	if application by health or peace officer 253A.04(2)			253A.04			consent of head of hospital 253A.04	consent of head of hospital 253A.04	72 hrs.; if petition for commitment filed, detention until determination of the matter 253A.04(3)
MISS. Code Ann. (1981)													
MO. Ann. Stat. (Vernon 1979 & Supp. 1980)	632.305(1)	only if likelihood of harm imminent 632.305(3)	mental health coordinator only if likelihood of harm imminent 632.305(3)	632.305(4)		632.05(2)		*fn. 30* 632.305 632.005(9) OR	*fn. 30* 632.305 632.005(9)		mandatory acceptance 632.310	optional acceptance 632.310	96 hrs. 632.305(2), (3)
MONT. Code Ann. (1981)		53-21-129(1)			53-21-129(2)			seriously mentally ill 53-21-129(1) 53-21-102(14)	seriously mentally ill *fn. 31* 53-21-129(1) 53-21-102(14)		53-21-129(3)	53-21-129(3)	until next regular business day 53-21-129(2)
NEB. Rev. Stat. (1976 & Supp. 1981)		83-1020	county attorney 83-1024				peace officer 83-1021 mental health board 83-1028	83-1020	inability to provide for basic human needs 83-1020 83-1009	*fn. 32* 83-1021 83-1028	*fn. 31* 83-1020 83-1028	*fn. 31* 83-1020 83-1028	pending a hearing 83-1026 83-1028
NEV. Rev. Stat. (1981)	to district attorney, who may order detention or apply for emergency hospitalization 433A.160(4)	agent, officer 433A.160(1)		social worker, public health nurse, physician, or psychologist 433A.160(1)	psychiatrist or physician or psychologist 433A.170			433A.170 OR	gravely disabled 433A.170		433A.150(1)	433A.150(1)	2 work days or by ct. order not to exceed 7 days 433A.150(2)
N.H. Rev. Stat. Ann. (1977 & Supp. 1981)	135-B:20(I)				physician 135-B:20(I)	*fn. 33* 135-B:20(II)		135-B:19 OR	lacks capacity to care for own welfare 135-B:19		designated receiving facility 135-B:21 135-B:2(XVI)	135-B:21 135-B:2(XVI)	10 days 135-B:24
N.J. Stat. Ann. (West 1981)				certifying physician 30:4-38			chief executive officer 30:4-38				institution 30:4-38 30:4-23		20 days 30:4-38
N.M. Stat. Ann. (1979 & Supp. 1981)		*fn. 34* 43-1-10A		physician *fn. 35* 43-1-10(B)	admitting physician 43-1-10D			*fn. 36* 43-1-10A 43-1-10B 43-1-3(C)	grave passive neglect *fn. 36* 43-1-10A 43-1-10B 43-1-3(C)	24 hrs. max. *fn. 37* 43-1-10(C)	43-1-10C 43-1-31	43-1-10C 43-1-31	right to hearing w/in 7 days 43-1-10(E)

TABLE 2.4 EMERGENCY DETENTION—*Continued*

STATE	APPLICATION BY: Any Person (1)	APPLICATION BY: Peace Officer (2)	APPLICATION BY: Other Public Official (3)	APPLICATION BY: Mental Health Professional (4)	CERTIFICATION: Medical (5)	CERTIFICATION: Judicial (6)	CERTIFICATION: Other (7)	CONDITION REQUIREMENT: Dangerous to Self or Others (8)	CONDITION REQUIREMENT: Unable to Provide for Basic Physical Needs (9)	DETENTION PLACE: Jail (10)	DETENTION PLACE: Public Mental Health Facility (11)	DETENTION PLACE: Private Mental Health Facility (12)	MAXIMUM PERIOD (13)
N.Y. Mental Hyg. Law (McKinney 1978 & Supp. 1981)	9.39	peace or police officer of state police, authorized police dept., or sheriff's dept. 9.41	any ct. *fn. 38* 9.43		exam by staff physician; independent exam by member of psychiatric staff w/in 48 hrs. of admission 9.39			9.39 9.41			*fn. 39* 9.39 9.41 9.43	*fn. 39* 9.39 9.41 9.43	15 days 9.39
N.C. Gen. Stat. (1981 & Supp. 1981)		law enforcement officer 122-58.18				clerk or magistrate 122-58.18		violent & requires restraint 122-58.18			community or regional mental health facility 122-58.18		pending examination 122-58.18 w/in 24 hrs. *fn. 40* 122-58.6(a)
N.D. Cent. Code (1978 & Supp. 1981)	as part of petition for involuntary treatment 25-03.1-25(2)	25-03.1-25(1)		physician, clinical psychologist, psychiatrist, or mental health professional 25-03.1-25(1)		if by petition for involuntary commitment 25-03.1-25(2)		by petition 25-03.1-25(2) via 25-03.1-25(1), must allege overt act 25-03.1-25(5)		only in actual emergency 24 hrs. max. 25-03.1-25(3)(b)	must accept 25-03.1-25(3)(b) 25-03.1-26(1)	may accept 25-03.1-25(3)(b) 25-03.1-26(1)	by petition: 72 hrs. 25-03.1-25(2) via 25-03.1-25(1): 24 hrs. *fn. 41*
OHIO Rev. Code Ann. (Baldwin 1980 & Supp. 1981)		parole officer, police officer, or sheriff 5122.10		psychiatrist, licensed clinical psychologist, physician, or health officer 5122.10				definition of mentally ill subject to hospitalization 5122.10 5122.01(B)	5122.10 5122.01(B)		5122.10 5122.01(F)	general hospital (24 hrs.) 5122.10	3 days 5122.10
OKLA. Stat. Ann. (West 1979 & Supp. 1981)		43A, §52.1B			physician's endorsement w/in 12 hrs. 43A, §52.1F		written affidavit of person upon whose observations peace officer relied 43A, §52.1C	so mentally ill that emergency action necessary 43A, §52.1A	so mentally ill that emergency action necessary 43A, §52.1A		43A, §51 43A, §52.1D	43A, §51 43A, §52.1D	72 hrs. *fn. 42* 43A, §52.1H
OR. Rev. Stat. (1981)	2 persons *fn. 43* 426.180			physician 426.175(1)	consultation w/another physician 426.175(1) county health officer or 2 physicians 426.180		superintendent of receiving facility 426.190	426.175(1) 426.005(2) emergency 426.180 so mentally ill as to need immediate hospitalization 426.190	426.175(1) 426.005(2) emergency 426.180 so mentally ill as to need immediate hospitalization 426.190		hospital where physician has admitting privileges *fn. 44* 426.175(1) 426.190		5 days 426.175(2) 15 days 426.210
PA. Stat. Ann. (Purdon 1969 & Supp. 1980)		50, §7302(a)		physician 50, §7302(a)	exam by physician w/in 2 hrs. of arrival at facility 50, §7302(b)		optional warrant by county administrator 50, §7302(a)	severely mentally disabled 50, §7302(a) 50, §7301(a), (b)	severely mentally disabled 50, §7302(a) 50, §7301(a), (b)		defined: 50, §7105 50, §7302(a)	defined: 50, §7105 50, §7302(a)	120 hrs. *fn. 45* 50, §7302(d)
R.I. Gen. Laws (1977 & Supp. 1981)	complaint in writing to clerk or justice of district ct. 40.1-5.1-1	police officer *fn. 46* 40.1-5-7		physician, medical director, qualified mental health professional *fn. 45* 40.1-5-7	psychiatrist or physician under his supervision 40.1-5-7	ct. shall issue warrant to appear for examination, designating time & place 40.1-5.1-1		40.1-5-7 40.1-5-2(14) 40.1-5.1-1	restraint necessary for own welfare 40.1-5.1-1		least restraint on liberty 40.1-5-7 40.1-5-2(3) at ct.'s discretion 40.1-5.1-1	least restraint on liberty 40.1-5-7 40.1-5-2(3)	10 days *fn. 47* 40.1-5-7 pending examination (part of regular commitment proceedings) 40.1-5.1-1
S.C. Code Ann. (Law. Co-op. 1976 & Supp. 1981)	44-17-410	*fn. 48*			44-17-410(2)			44-17-410(1)(a)	inability to care for self 44-17-410(2)		4-17-410	4-17-410	*fn. 48* 44-17-410(3)

TABLE 2.4 EMERGENCY DETENTION—*Continued*

	APPLICATION BY				CERTIFICATION			CONDITION REQUIREMENT		DETENTION PLACE			
STATE	Any Person (1)	Peace Officer (2)	Other Public Official (3)	Mental Health Professional (4)	Medical (5)	Judicial (6)	Other (7)	Dangerous to Self or Others (8)	Unable to Provide for Basic Physical Needs (9)	Jail (10)	Public Mental Health Facility (11)	Private Mental Health Facility (12)	MAXIMUM PERIOD (13)
S.D. Codified Laws Ann. (1976 & Supp. 1981)	27A-10-1	27A-10-3			examination w/in 24 hrs. of detention 27A-10-7			27A-10-1		if mental health center not capable of handling person max. of 24 hrs. 27A-10-3	27A-10-3	27A-10-3	5 days *fn. 49* 27A-10-8
TENN. Code Ann. (1977 & Supp. 1981)			any state, county, or municipal officer 33-603(a)	licensed physician or licensed psychologist 33-603(a)	2 required 33-603(a)			33-603(a)			33-603(a)	33-603(a)	5 days 33-603(b)
TEX. Rev. Civ. Stat. Ann. (Vernon 1958 & Supp. 1981)		5547-27(a)	health officer 5547-27(a)	physician 5547-27(b)	5547-28(b)	warrant from magistrate 5547-28(a)		5547-28		*fn. 50* 5547-27(a), (b)	5547-27(a)	5547-27(a)	24 hrs. *fn. 50* 5547-27(a), (b)
UTAH Code Ann. (1978 & Supp. 1981)	a responsible person 64-7-34(1)	64-7-34(2)	mental health officer 64-7-34(2)		by licensed physician or designated examiner must accompany application, unless application by a mental health or peace officer 64-7-34(1)			64-7-34(1), (2)			64-7-34(1)	64-7-34(1)	24 hrs. unless application for involuntary hospitalization has been commenced 64-7-34(3)
VT. Stat. Ann. (1968 & Supp. 1981)	18, §7504(a)	law enforcement officer 18, §7505(a)		18, §7505(a)	18, §7504(a) 18, §7505(e)	18, §7505(a)		*fn. 51* 18, §7504(a) 18, §7505(a) 18, §7508(d) 18, §7101	18, §7504(a) 18, §7505(a) 18, §7101		18, §7504(a) 18, §7508(a)	18, §7504(a) 18, §7508(a)	72 hrs. after emergency exam *fn. 52* 18, §7508(d)
VA. Code (1976 & Supp. 1981)	37.1-67.1					judicial order 37.1-67.1		37.1-67.1 37.1-1(15)	37.1-67.1 37.1-1(15)	only if authorized 37.1-67.1	37.1-67.1	37.1-67.1	72 hrs. 37.1-67.1
WASH. Rev. Code Ann. (1975 & Supp. 1981)	71.05.150(d)(2)	71.05.150(d)(4)			*fn. 53* 71.05.150(d)(2)			71.05.150(d)(2) OR	gravely disabled 71.05.150(a)(2)		71.05.150(d)(2)	71.05.150(d)(2)	72 hrs. *fn. 54* 71.05.150(d)(2)
W. VA. Code (1980 & Supp. 1981)	27-5-2(a)				27-5-3(a) AND	27-5-3(a) 27-5-2(b)(4)	followed by certification of facility w/in 5 days 27-5-3(f)	27-5-2(a)(2) 27-5-3(a)			27-5-3	27-5-3	*fn. 55* 27-5-3
WIS. Stat. Ann. (West 1957 & Supp. 1981)		law enforcement officer 51.15(1)(a)	*fn. 56* 51.15(1)(a)		w/in 24 hrs. only in Milwaukee County 51.15(4)(b)		officer's belief based on overt act or omission 51.15(5)	overt act 51.15 OR	overt act 51.15		51.15(2)(a), (c)	51.15(2)(d)	72 hrs. 51.15(4)(b), (5)
WYO. Stat. (1981 & Supp. 1983)		law enforcement officer 25-3-110(a)		examiner 25-3-110(a) 25-3-101(iv)				recent overt acts, attempts, or threats 25-3-110(a), (b)			hospital or other suitable facility 25-3-220(d)	hospital or other suitable facility 25-3-220(d)	36 hrs. 25-3-110(b)(iii), (c)

FOOTNOTES TABLE 2.4

1. Ala. Code § 22-52-7(b) (Supp. 1981): "No limitations shall be placed upon such person's liberty nor treatment imposed upon such person unless such limitations are necessary to prevent such person from doing substantial and immediate harm to himself or to others or to prevent such person from leaving the jurisdiction of the court."

2. Ark. Stat. Ann. § 59-1406(a) (Supp. 1981): "to a hospital or community mental health center or clinic or state mental health facility."

3. Cal. Welf. & Inst. Code § 5150 (West Supp. 1980). Add: "or member of the attending staff or mobile crisis team."

4. Id.: "Application in writing stating the circumstances under which the person's condition was called to the attention of the officer, member of the attending staff, or professional person, and stating that the officer, member of the attending staff, or professional person has probable cause to believe that the person is, as a result of mental disorder, a danger to others, or to himself or herself, or gravely disabled."

5. Colo. Rev. Stat. § 27-10-105(1.1) (Supp. 1981). Only "if no other suitable place of confinement for treatment and evaluation is available." The person must be transferred to a mental health facility after 24 hours.

6. Conn. Gen. Stat. Ann. §§ 17-183, 17-183a (West Supp. 1981). Connecticut provides for two emergency procedures: 15 days of treatment under a physician's emergency certificate and a 72-hour emergency examination period.

7. Hawaii Rev. Stat. §§ 334-59 to 334-59a (Supp. 1981). Hawaii has three procedures for initiating emergency hospitalization.

8. Id. § 334-1 (1976). Defines "dangerous to self" in terms of attempts to injure oneself or neglect or refusal to take necessary care for one's own physical health and safety.

9. Idaho Code § 66-326 (Supp. 1981):

> (a) . . . a person may be taken into custody by a peace officer if the peace officer has reason to believe that the person's continued liberty poses an imminent danger to that person or others, as evidenced by a threat of substantial physical harm.
>
> . . . .
>
> (d) If the designated examiner finds, in his examination under this section, that the person is mentally ill, and either is likely to injure himself or others or is gravely disabled, the prosecuting attorney shall file, within twenty-four (24) hours of the examination of the person, a petition with the court requesting the patient's detention pending commitment proceedings pursuant to the provisions of section 66-329.

10. Id. § 66-326(b):

> . . . the court shall issue a temporary custody order requring the person to be held in a facility, and requiring an examination of the person by a designated examiner. . . . If necessary to protect against immediate and substantial injury to the proposed patient or others, the court may authorize the proposed patient to be detained in a nonmedical unit used for the detention of individuals charged with or convicted of penal offenses.

Idaho does not provide for the place of custody before the court issues an order for temporary custody.

11. Id. Twenty-four hours before temporary court order; another 24 hours before examination; 24 hours before examiner's report and before prosecuting attorney files a petition; another 5 days detention before hearing.

12. Ill. Ann. Stat. ch. 91½, §§ 1-119, 3-602, 3-606, 3-607 (Smith-Hurd Supp. 1980). "[S]ubject to involuntary admission and requires immediate hospitalization." This means a person who because of his mental illness is likely to physically harm self or others or is unable to provide for basic physical needs.

13. Id. § 3-611. The hospital must file a petition for a court hearing within 24 hours of admission. The court hearing must be held within 5 business days, according to the procedure for a judicial hospitalization order. The patient may be detained pending such proceedings.

14. Ind. Code Ann. § 16-14-9.1-7(e) (Burns Supp. 1982). Mentally ill and either dangerous or gravely disabled and requires continuing care and treatment.

15. Iowa Code Ann. § 229.22 (West Supp. 1980). This section, entitled "emergency procedure," is used only if it appears that a person should be immediately detained due to serious mental impairment but could not be immediately detained by the procedure prescribed in §§ 229.6 and 229.11 because there is no means of immediate access to the district court.

16. Id. §§ 229.11, 229.22, 229.1. Seriously mentally impaired and is likely to physically injure himself or others if not detained. Id. § 229.1(2). "Seriously mentally impaired" means person unable to make responsible decisions regarding treatment who: (a) is likely to physically injure self or others; or (b) is likely to inflict serious emotional injury on members of his or her family or others in close contact with the afflicted person.

17. Id. § 229.11(1): "In the custody of a relative, friend or other suitable person."

18. Kan. Stat. Ann. §§ 59-2909(B), (C), 59-2912 (Supp. 1980). In Kansas persons may be detained at a treatment facility upon an order of protective custody (§ 59-2912), or upon written application of a peace officer (§ 59-2909(B)) or any person (§ 59-2909(C)). However, the latter two avenues must state that an application for an order of protective custody is forthcoming by 5:00 p.m. the next full day the district court is open for business.

19. Id. §§ 59-2902, 59-2908, 59-2909(B)(3), (C)(3). A mentally ill person likely to do physical injury to himself, herself, or others if not immediately detained. According to § 59-2902, dangerous to self may be proved by a person's failure to meet his or her basic physical needs.

20. Id. § 59-2912 (Supp. 1981). Designated treatment facility or any other suitable place, but no person shall be detained in jail unless other facilities are not available. Treatment facility means any mental health clinic, psychiatric unit of a medical

care facility, adult care home, physician or any other institution or individual authorized or licensed by law to give treatment to any patient.

21. Ky. Rev. Stat. Ann. §§ 202A.030, 202A.040, 202A.050 (Michie 1977 & Supp. 1980). Three separate procedures for emergency detention: by medical certificate (§ 202A.030); a peace officer without a warrant, followed by a judicial hearing (§ 202A.040); 48-hour detention by a judge after examining complaint of a friend, relative, spouse, or guardian after 48 hours, a hearing is held (§ 202A.050).

22. Id. § 202A.010(5) (Michie 1977). "Immediate danger" or "immediate threat of danger to self or others" means substantial physical harm or immediate threat of substantial physical harm upon self or others, including actions which deprive self or others of the basic means of survival including provision for reasonable shelter, food, or clothing.

23. Id. §§ 202A.030-050 (Michie 1977 & Supp. 1980). Hospitalization must be the least restrictive alternative.

24. La. Rev. Stat. Ann. § 28:53.2 (West Supp. 1981):

(A) Any parish coroner or judge of a court of competent jurisdiction may order a person to be taken into protective custody and transported to a treatment facility or the office of the coroner for immediate examination when a peace officer or other credible person executes a statement under private signature specifying that, to the best of his knowledge and belief, the person is mentally ill or suffering from substance abuse and is in need of immediate treatment to protect the person or others from physical harm.

25. Id.:

(C) The order for custody shall be effective for twenty-four hours from its issuance and shall be delivered to the director of the treatment facility by the individual who has transported the person. Upon arrival, the person in custody shall determine if the person shall be voluntarily admitted, admitted by emergency certificate, admitted as a non-contested admission, or discharged. The person in custody shall be examined within twelve hours of his arrival at the treatment facility, or be released.

26. Id. § 28:53(A)(2):

A person suffering from substance abuse may be detained at a treatment facility for one additional period, not to exceed fifteen days, provided that a second emergency certificate is executed. A second certificate may be executed only if and when a physician at the treatment facility and any other physician have examined the detained person within seventy-two hours prior to the termination of the initial fifteen day period and certified in writing on the second certificate that the person remains dangerous to himself or others or gravely disabled, and that his condition is likely to improve during the extended period.

27. Me. Rev. Stat. Ann. tit. 34, § 2333 (Supp. 1981). No specified time, but admission must be within 3 days after the date of examination.

28. Judicial review is necessary for any petition not filed by a peace officer, physician, certified psychologist, or local health officer.

29. Mass. Ann. Laws ch. 123, § 1 (Michie/Law. Co-op. 1981):

"Likelihood of serious harm;" (1) a substantial risk of physical harm to the person himself as manifested by evidence of threats of, or attempts at, suicide or serious bodily harm; (2) a substantial risk of physical harm to other persons as manifested by evidence of homicidal or other violent behavior or evidence that others are placed in reasonable fear of violent behavior and serious physical harm to them; or (3) a very substantial risk of physical impairment or injury to the person himself as manifested by evidence that such person's judgement is so affected that he is unable to protect himself in the community and that reasonable provision for his protection is not available in the community.

30. Mo. Ann. Stat. § 632.005(9) (Vernon Supp. 1980):

"Likelihood of serious physical harm" means any one or more of the following:

(a) substantial risk of inflicting serious physical harm on oneself.

(b) substantial risk of harm to self resulting from inability to provide for basic necessities.

(c) substantial risk of inflicting harm on others.

31. Mont. Code Ann. § 53-21-102(14) (1981). "Seriously mentally ill" means suffering from a mental disorder which has resulted in self-inflicted injury or injury to others or the imminent threat thereof or which has deprived the person afflicted of the ability to protect his life or health.

32. Neb. Rev. Stat. § 83-1020 (1976):

When a mental health center or a state hospital, or other government or private hospital, has the capability to detain such an individual in the county in which the individual is found, the individual shall be placed in such facility. When no such facility exists, the individual may be placed in jail.

33. N.H. Rev. Stat. Ann. § 135-B:20(II) (Supp. 1981):

[I]f the person sought to be hospitalized refuses to consent to a mental examination, a petitioner or a law enforcement officer may sign a complaint which shall be sworn before a justice of the peace. . . . if . . . the justice finds that a compulsory mental examination is necessary, the justice may order such an examination.

34. N.M. Stat. Ann. § 43-1-10A (1979):

A peace officer may detain a person for emergency mental health evaluation and care in the absence of a legally valid order from the court only if: (1) the person is otherwise subject to lawful arrest; or (2) the peace officer has reasonable grounds to believe the person has just attempted suicide; or (3) the peace officer, based upon his own observation and investigation, has reasonable grounds to believe that the person, as a result of mental disorder, presents a serious harm to himself or others, and that immediate detention is necessary to prevent such harm.

35. Id. § 43-1-10B:

> An evaluation facility may accept on an emergency basis any person when a licensed physician certifies that such person, as a result of a mental disorder, presents a likelihood of serious harm to himself or others, and that immediate detention is necessary to prevent such harm.

36. Id. § 43-1-3(L):

> "Likelihood of serious harm to oneself" means that it is more likely than not that in the near future the person will attempt to commit suicide or will cause serious bodily harm to himself by violent or other self-destructive means including but not limited to grave passive neglect as evidenced by behavior causing, attempting or threatening the infliction of serious bodily harm to himself.

37. Id. § 43-1-10C:

> Detention facilities shall be used as temporary shelter . . . only in cases of extreme emergency for protective custody, and no person taken into custody under the provisions of the Code shall remain in a detention facility longer than necessary and in no case longer than twenty-four hours. If use of a detention facility is necessary, the proposed client:
>
> (1) shall not be held in a cell with prisoners;
>
> (2) shall not be identified on records used to record custody of prisoners;
>
> (3) shall be provided adequate protection from possible suicide attempts; and
>
> (4) shall be treated with the respect and dignity due every citizen who is neither accused nor convicted of a crime.

38. N.Y. Mental Hyg. Law § 9.43(a) (McKinney 1978):

> Whenever any court of inferior or general jurisdiction is informed . . . that a person is mentally ill and is conducting himself in a manner . . . which is likely to result in serious harm to himself or others as defined in section 9.39, such court shall issue a warrant directing that such person be brought before it. If, when said person is brought before the court, it appears to the court . . . that such person has or may have a mental illness which is likely to result in serious harm to himself or others, the court shall issue a civil order directing his removal to any hospital specified in subdivision (a) of section 9.39 willing to receive such person for a determination by the director of such hospital whether such person should be retained therein pursuant to such section.

39. Id. § 9.41 (McKinney Supp. 1981) (emphasis added):

> Such officer may direct the removal of such person or remove him to any hospital specified in subdivision (a) of Section 9.39 or, pending his examination or admission to any such hospital, temporarily detain any such person in another safe and comfortable place, in which event, such officer shall immediately notify the director of community services or, if there be none, the health officer of the city or county of such action.

40. N.C. Gen. Stat. § 122-58.6(a) (1981): "If the qualified physician finds that the respondent is mentally ill . . . and is dangerous to himself or others . . . he shall hold the respondent at the facility pending the district court hearing."

41. N.D. Cent. Code § 25-03.1-26(1). A person may be detained pending a hearing (set within 72 hours) under § 25-03.1-25(1) if the superintendent or director files a petition with the magistrate within 24 hours of the person's examination.

42. Okla. Stat. Ann. tit. 43A, § 52.1H (West Supp. 1981).

> A person may be detained more than 72 hours only if the facility is presented with a copy of an order of the district court authorizing additional detention. Such order may be entered by the court only after a petition has been filed seeking examination and certification as otherwise provided by law.

43. Or. Rev. Stat. § 426.180 (1981): "If the judge . . . is absent . . . or . . . unable to act and there is no other judge available . . . so that a hearing on an application for commitment cannot be held immediately."

44. Id. § 426.175(3) (1981): "The person shall only be admitted and retained in a hospital or other facility which maintains adequate staff and facilities for care and treatment of the mentally ill and is approved by the division.

45. Pa. Stat. Ann. tit. 50, § 7303(f) (Purdon Supp. 1980): "Upon the filing and service of a certification for extended involuntary emergency treatment, the person may be given treatment in an approved facility for a period not to exceed 20 days.

46. R.I. Gen. Laws § 40.1-5-7 (1977). Any physician who after examining a person has reason to believe that such person is in need of immediate care and treatment, may apply for the emergency certification of such person. The medical director, or any other physician employed by the proposed facility for certification may apply under this subsection if no other physician is available and he or she certifies this fact. In the event that no physician is available, a qualified mental health professional or police officer may make the application for emergency certification to a facility.

47. Id.:

> A person shall be discharged no later than ten (10) days measured from the date of his admission under this section, unless an application for a civil court certification has been filed and set down for hearing under the provisions of §40.1-5-8 of this chapter or the person remains as a voluntary patient pursuant to §40.1-5-6 hereof.

48. S.C. Code Ann. § 44-17-430 (Law. Co-op. 1976 & Supp. 1981). If a person will not willingly submit to examination then a judge may order a peace officer to take that person into custody for twenty-four hours for examination.

> [W]ithin 5 days after the person's admission , . . . the probate court, if it finds the application and certification are valid on their face, may order that the person be detained at the place of his admission, appoint counsel for him if he has not retained counsel and shall fix a date for a full hearing to be held . . . within 20 days from the date of his admission.

Id. § 44-17-410(3) (Law. Co-op. Supp. 1981).

49. S.D. Codified Laws Ann. § 27A-10-8 (Supp. 1981). Within 5 days after the person taken into custody, he or she shall be afforded a hearing to determine whether he or she is mentally ill and in immediate need of treatment.

50. Tex. Rev. Civ. Stat. Ann. art. 5547-27(a), (b) (Vernon Supp. 1981):

> take such person into custody, and immediately transport him to the nearest hospital or other facility deemed suitable by the county health officer, except in no case shall a jail or similar detention facility be deemed suitable unless such jail or detention facility is specifically equipped and staffed to provide psychiatric care and treatment, and make application for his admission, pursuant to the warrant of the magistrate. Such person admitted upon such warrant may be detained in custody for a period not to exceed 24 hours, unless a further written order is obtained from the County Court or Probate Court of such county, ordering further detention.

51. Vt. Stat. Ann. tit. 18, § 7101(17) (Supp. 1981): "In need of treatment" is defined in terms of "dangerous" and "unable to care for self" categories.

52. Id. tit. 18, § 7508(d) (Supp. 1981): "the person's hospitalization may continue for an additional 72 hours, at which time hospitalization shall terminate, unless within that period: . . . (2) an application for involuntary treatment is filed with the appropriate court . . . in which case the patient shall remain hospitalized pending the court's decision on the application."

53. Wash. Rev. Code Ann. § 71.05.150(d)(2) (Supp. 1981). When a mental health professional designated by the county receives information alleging that a person, as a result of a mental disorder, presents a likelihood of serious harm to others or himself, after investigation and evaluation of the specific facts alleged and of the reliability and credibility of the person or persons, if any, providing the information, the mental health professional may take such person, or cause by oral or written order such person to be taken into emergency custody.

54. Id. § 71.05.150(d)(5). If a person is delivered to the evaluation and treatment facility by a peace officer without prior investigation by the mental health professional designated by the county, that person may be held for a maximum of 12 hours. Within 12 hours of his or her arrival, the designated county mental health professional must file a supplemental petition for detention.

55. W. Va. Code § 27-5-3 (1980). Three days if not examined; 5 days if not certified at facility; 10 days before institution of commitment proceedings; 30-day time limitation for conclusion of proceedings.

56. Wis. Stat. Ann. § 51.15(1)(a) (West Supp. 1981): "A law enforcement officer or other person authorized to take a child into custody under ch. 48 may take an individual into custody."

TABLE 2.5 TEMPORARY OR OBSERVATIONAL INSTITUTIONALIZATION

	TEMPORARY OBSERVATIONAL PROCEDURE					PLACE IN REGULAR INSTITUTIONALIZATION PROCEEDINGS			ACTION AFTER OBSERVATION PERIOD				
	Application by			Authorization					By Court			By Institution	
STATE	Health or Welfare Officer (1)	Institution or Physician (2)	Any Person (3)	No. of Medical Certificates (4)	Other Approval (5)	Prior to Final Hearing (6)	After Final Hearing (7)	MAXIMUM PERIOD (8)	Dismissal (9)	Proceed with a Hearing (10)	Commitment Without Further Hearing (11)	Dismissal (12)	Apply for Commitment (13)
ALA. Code (1975 & Supp. 1981)			22-52-1	one 22-52-7	probate judge probable cause hearing 22-52-8	22-52-8				22-52-8(a)			
ALAS. Stat. (1962 & Supp. 1981)			47.30.020	one 47.30.020(2)	head of hospital 47.30.020(2) superior ct. 47.30.030			48 hrs. 47.30.040(b)				47.30.040	47.30.040
ARIZ. Rev. Stat. Ann. (1974 & Supp. 1981)			36-520(A)		screening agency 36-521 superior ct. 36-529	36-533(B)		72 hrs. 36-530(B)				36-531	36-531
ARK. Stat. Ann. (1971 & Supp. 1981)			59-1406			59-1406		hearing must be held w/in 7 days 59-1402 59-1406	59-1406	59-1406			
CAL. Welf. & Inst. Code (West 1972 & Supp. 1981)			5201		prepetition screening agency 5202 judge 5206	5206		72 hrs. 5206	5206	*fn. 1* 5206		5206	*fn. 1* 5206
COLO. Rev. Stat. (1973 & Supp. 1981)			27-10-106(2)		ct. 27-10-106(6)	*fn. 2* 27-10-106(7)		72 hrs. 27-10-106(7)				27-10-106(7)	certify for 3 mos. short-term treatment 27-10-106(7)
FLA. Stat. Ann. (West 1973 & Supp. 1981)			any person, but must have affidavits of 2 others 394.463 (2)(b)(1) OR	certificate of 1 mental health professional 394.463 (2)(b)(2)	judge 394.463(2)	394.467		5 days 394.463(2)(e)				394.463(2)(e)	394.467
GA. Code Ann. (1979 & Supp. 1980)			88-505.2	one 88-505.2(b)	preliminary investigation by county board of health & ct. 88-505.2(a) 88-505.3	88-506.2		5 days 88-505.5(a)				88-505.5(a)(4)	88-505.5(a)(3) 88-506.2
ILL. Ann. Stat. (Smith-Hurd 1966 & Supp. 1980)			18 or over 91½, §3-607 91½, §3-601	one 91½, §3-602		91½, §3-607		24 hrs. 91½, §3-607		91½, §3-607		if no petition for certificate for emergency detention 91½, §3-607	
IND. Code Ann. (Burns 1973 & Supp. 1982)	by order of ct. already having jurisdiction over person 16-14-9.1-8 (b) OR	superintendent of facility 16-14-9.1-8 (a) OR	16-14-9.1-8 (c)	one 16-14-9.1-8 (c)	ct. 16-14-9.1-9 (g)	16-14-9.1-10		90 days *fn. 3* 16-14-9.1-9 (g)				16-14-9.1-9 (h)	apply for additional 90-day temporary commitment *fn. 3* 16-14-9.1-9 (i)

TABLE 2.5 TEMPORARY OR OBSERVATIONAL INSTITUTIONALIZATION—*Continued*

STATE	TEMPORARY OBSERVATIONAL PROCEDURE — *Application by*: Health or Welfare Officer (1)	Institution or Physician (2)	Any Person (3)	*Authorization*: No. of Medical Certificates (4)	Other Approval (5)	PLACE IN REGULAR INSTITUTIONALIZATION PROCEEDINGS: Prior to Final Hearing (6)	After Final Hearing (7)	MAXIMUM PERIOD (8)	ACTION AFTER OBSERVATION PERIOD — *By Court*: Dismissal (9)	Proceed with a Hearing (10)	Commitment Without Further Hearing (11)	*By Institution*: Dismissal (12)	Apply for Commitment (13)
IOWA Code Ann. (1969 & Supp. 1980)					ct. 229.13		229.13	15 days *fn. 4* 229.13	*fn. 4* 229.14(1)		*fn. 4* 229.14		
KAN. Stat. Ann. (1976)					ct. *fn. 5* 59-2918	59-2918		90 days 59-2918	if patient agrees to voluntary treatment 59-2918	otherwise 59-2918		59-2918	
LA. Rev. Stat. Ann. (West 1975 & Supp. 1981)		physician who executes emergency certificate 28:53(B)		one 28:53(B)	independent examination by coroner or deputy w/in 72 hrs. of admission 28:53(G)			15 days 28:53(A)				by coroner 28:53(G)	28:53(H)
MINN. Stat. Ann. (West 1982)					ct. 253A.07(17)		253A.07(17)	60 days 253A.07(17)	*fn. 6* 253A.07(24)	*fn. 6* 253A.07(26)			
MISS. Code Ann. (1981)					ct. 41-21-75		41-21-75	20 days 41-21-81		if patient requests hearing *fn. 7* 41-21-81 41-21-83	if no hearing requested *fn. 7* 41-21-81	any time w/in 20 days 41-21-81	
MO. Ann. Stat. (Vernon 1979 & Supp. 1980)		head of mental health facility 632.330		1; by psychiatrist, physician, or mental health professional 632.330	ct. 632.335			21 days 632.335		to determine whether to grant 90-day extension of detention 632.340			632.340
N.J. Stat. Ann. (West 1981)	police officer 30:4-26.3.			one 30:4-26.3. & certification by admitting physician at hospital 30:4-26.3.	judge 30:4-26.3.			15 days 30:4-26.3.					
N.M. Stat. Ann. (1979)	mental health division 43-1-11(A)	physician or evaluation facility 43-1-11(A)	43-1-11(E)	initial screening report 43-1-11(A) any medical reports then available 43-1-11(E)	district attorney 43-1-11(E)	43-1-12(B)		30 days 43-1-11(C)				43-1-12(G)	43-1-12(A)
PA. Stat. Ann. (Purdon 1969 & Supp. 1980)		treatment facility 50, §7303		examining physician's opinion 50, §7303		50, §7303		20 days 50, §7303				50, §7303	50, §7303
S.D. Codified Laws Ann. (1976)							27A-9-16	14 days; or 30 days in S.D. human services center 27A-9-16					facility administrator advises mental health board & board makes final order 27A-9-16

TABLE 2.5 TEMPORARY OR OBSERVATIONAL INSTITUTIONALIZATION—*Continued*

STATE	TEMPORARY OBSERVATIONAL PROCEDURE					PLACE IN REGULAR INSTITUTIONALIZATION PROCEEDINGS		MAXIMUM PERIOD (8)	ACTION AFTER OBSERVATION PERIOD				
	Application by			*Authorization*					*By Court*			*By Institution*	
	Health or Welfare Officer (1)	Institution or Physician (2)	Any Person (3)	No. of Medical Certificates (4)	Other Approval (5)	Prior to Final Hearing (6)	After Final Hearing (7)		Dismissal (9)	Proceed with a Hearing (10)	Commitment Without Further Hearing (11)	Dismissal (12)	Apply for Commitment (13)
TENN. Code Ann. (1977 & Supp. 1980)	superintendent of treatment center *fn. 8* 33-603(b)			one 33-603(b)	judge makes probable cause finding 33-603(b)			15 days 33-603(c)					33-604(a)
TEX. Rev. Civ. Stat. Ann. (Vernon 1958 & Supp. 1981)			5547-31	two 5547-32	judge 5547-36 5547-38(b)	prerequisite to indefinite commitment procedure 5547-40		90 days 5547-38(b)					
WASH. Rev. Code Ann. (1975 & Supp. 1981)	peace officer may take into custody 71.05.150 (3)	mental health professional 71.05.150 (1)(a)				71.05.150		72 hrs. 71.05.180		71.05.240			71.05.240(4)
W. VA. Code (1980 & Supp. 1981)			27-5-2(a)	one, unless individual has refused 27-5-4(d)	by ct. hearing 27-5-4(k)	27-5-4(k)		6 mos. 27-5-4(k)(1)		may hold hearing 27-5-4(k)(3)			

FOOTNOTES TABLE 2.5

1. A 72-hour evaluation period is a prerequisite to further commitment proceedings. Following evaluation, a person may be certified for a 14-day intensive treatment period (Cal. Welf. & Inst. Code § 5206 (West 1972)), after which application may be made for commitment of 90 days (charted on tables 3.2 and 3.3) Id. §§ 5150, 5250 (Supp. 1982).

2. After a 72-hour court-ordered evaluation, the subject person may be medically certified for a short-term treatment of 3 months. Colo. Rev. Stat. § 27-10-106(7) (1982). Only after such short-term treatment for 5 consecutive months may a petition be filed for the long-term commitment charted on tables 3.2 and 3.3 Id. § 27-10-109(1) (1982).

3. If the person has not already been discharged, 20 days before end of initial or second temporary commitment period, superintendent or physician shall report to the court the mental condition of the patient for purposes of regular commitment proceedings, and the court shall set a hearing date. Ind. Code Ann. § 16-14-9.1-10 (Burns 1983).

4. The chief medical officer of the hospital must report to the court within 15 days of the person's admission, unless an extension of up to 7 days has been granted. Iowa Code Ann. § 229.13 (West Supp. 1983-84). The court acts on the chief medical officer's report. Id. § 229.14 (Supp. 1983-84).

5. If patient requests in writing that hearing be continued for 90 days, the court may make an order of referral for short-term care or treatment.

6. Dismissal after 60 days unless person was committed as mentally ill and dangerous to the public or as a psychopathic personality, in which case a further hearing is held. Minn. Stat. Ann. § 253A.07(24) (Supp. 1982).

7. Within the 20-day period, if the director of the hospital determines the patient needs further hospitalization, he or she shall give written notice to the patient, clerk of the court, and relatives or guardian. Those notified have 30 days to request a hearing. If no request is made, the patient is ordered committed. Miss. Code Ann. § 41-21-81 (1981).

8. Tenn. Code Ann. § 33-603(a) (Supp. 1981):

> Any state, county or municipal officer authorized to make arrests in Tennessee or any licensed physician or licensed psychologist, when all reasonable efforts have been made to contact a licensed physician in the county and no such physician is available to conduct the examination within eight (8) hours of the first effort to contact a licensed physician, who has reason to believe that an individual is mentally ill and, because of this illness, poses a likelihood of serious harm if he is not immediately detained may, without a warrant, take such individual into custody. The phrase "likelihood of serious harm," for this section means (1) a substantial risk of physical harm to the person himself as manifested by evidence of threats of, or attempts at, suicide or serious bodily harm; or (2) a substantial risk of physical harm to other persons as manifested by evidence of homicidal or other violent behavior or evidence that others are placed in reasonable fear of violent behavior and serious physical harm to them.

TABLE 2.6 JUDICIAL INSTITUTIONALIZATION OF MENTALLY ILL PERSONS—PREHEARING PROCEDURES

STATE	APPLICATION BY: Any Person (1)	APPLICATION BY: Limited Group (2)	COURT (3)	CRITERIA FOR INSTITUTIONALIZATION ORDER TO ISSUE — Individual: Dangerous to Self or Others (4)	Individual: Unable to Provide for Basic Needs (5)	Individual: Other (6)	Systemic: No Less Restrictive Alternative (7)	Systemic: Other (8)	SUPPORTING EVIDENCE FOR APPLICATION: No. of Certificates (9)	SUPPORTING EVIDENCE FOR APPLICATION: Other Evidence (10)	PREHEARING MEDICAL EXAMINATION ORDERED BY COURT (11)	DISMISSAL AFTER MEDICAL EXAMINATION (12)	PREHEARING DETENTION (13)	NOTICE OF HEARING: Guardian (14)	NOTICE OF HEARING: Relatives (15)	NOTICE OF HEARING: Attorney (16)	NOTICE OF HEARING: Patient (17)	NOTICE OF HEARING: When (18)
ALA. Code (1975 & Supp. 1981)	22-52-1(a)		probate judge 22-52-1(a)	overt act 22-52-10 AND		mentally ill 22-52-10	22-52-10 (a)(5)	confinement necessary or treatment available 22-52-10			discretionary 22-52-7(c)		upon threat of immediate harm fn. 1 22-52-7(b)				22-52-3	5 days before hearing 22-52-3
ALAS. Stat. (1979 & Supp. 1981)	any adult 47.30.700 (a)		superior 47.30.915 (2)	47.30.735 (c) OR	gravely disabled 47.30.735 (c) AND	mentally ill 47.30.735 (c)	ct. may order less restrictive alternative if program accepts respondent 47.30.735(d)				screening investigation by local mental health professional 47.30.700(a); 72-hr. emergency exam & treatment if ct. finds probable cause 47.30.700(a), 47.30.715			47.30.725(a)	if requested, an adult designated by respondent 47.30.725(a)		47.30.725(a)	when detained for evaluation 47.30.725(a)
ARIZ. Rev. Stat. Ann. (1974 & Supp. 1981)	any responsible person 36-520		superior 36-501(2)	36-540(A), (B) OR	gravely disabled 36-540(C) AND		no other treatment available or appropriate 36-540(A), (B), (C)		affidavits of 2 physicians 36-533(B)		72-hr. max. detention pending exam. 36-521(D)	36-531	36-535				36-536	72 hrs. before hearing 36-536(A)
ARK. Stat. Ann. (1971 & Supp. 1981)	59-1404		probate 59-1402	homicidal or suicidal 59-1409 OR	gravely disabled 59-1409 AND		59-1409 59-1415(A)					59-1406(C)	59-1405				fn. 2 59-1408	w/in 7 days of detention 59-1402(B), (C)
CAL. Welf. & Inst. Code (West 1972)		professional person in charge of facility or designee 5301	superior 5301	to others only 5304 AND				previous 72-hr. evaluation & 14-day certification period 5150, 5213, 5250		affidavits describing behavior in detail 5301	discretionary; psychiatrist or psychologist w/forensic skills 5303.1		continuation of current detention (certification period) 5303			5302	5302	at time petition filed 5302
COLO. Rev. Stat. (1973 & Supp. 1981)		professional in charge of evaluation & treatment 27-10-109 (1)	district (probate in Denver) 27-10-102 (1)	27-10-109 (1)(a) OR	gravely disabled 27-10-109 (1)(a) AND	mentally ill 27-10-109 (1)(a), & refuses voluntary treatment 27-10-109 (1)(b) AND		short-term treatment for 5 consecutive mos. 27-10-109 (1)			discretionary 27-10-111(2)		already detained for short-term treatment 27-10-109 (1)			27-10-109 (2)	27-10-109 (2)	at time petition is filed 27-10-109 (2)
CONN. Gen. Stat. Ann. (West 1975 & Supp. 1981)	17-177(a)		probate 17-177(a)	17-178(c) OR	gravely disabled 17-178(c) AND	mentally ill 17-178(c) AND	17-178(c)				2 physicians, 1 a psychiatrist 17-178(c)		17-183(a)				17-178(a)	reasonable notice 17-178(a)
DEL. Code Ann. (1974 & Supp. 1980)		hospital 16, §5007 (a)	superior or family 16, §5001 (3)	to self, others, or property 16, §5001 OR		unable to make responsible decisions re treatment 16, §5001 AND	16, §5010(2)		psychiatrist's certificate 16, §5007 (a)		discretionary 16, §5008 (4)		16, §5004 §5008 (3)		16, §5008 (2)	16, §5008 (2)	16, §5008 (2)	
D.C. Code Ann. (1981 & Supp. 1982) fn. 3		fn. 4 21-541(a)	superior 21-501	21-545(b) AND		mentally ill 21-545(b)			one 21-541 (a)(1) OR	fn. 5 21-541 (a)(2)	mental health commission 21-542(a)	by commission 21-544	21-528			21-545(a)	21-545(a)	5 days before hearing 21-545(a)
FLA. Stat. Ann. (West 1973 & Supp. 1981)		administrator of treatment facility 394.467(2)	circuit 394.455(19)	394.467 (1)(b) OR	fn. 6 394.467 (1)(b) AND	mentally ill 394.467 (1)(b)			recommendation of 2 health professionals, 1 a physician 394.467(2)	1 of the mental health professionals shall be a witness 394.467(3)	394.463(2)	394.463(2)(d)	394.463(3)	394.467(2)			394.467(2)	

TABLE 2.6 JUDICIAL INSTITUTIONALIZATION OF MENTALLY ILL PERSONS—PREHEARING PROCEDURES—*Continued*

STATE	APPLICATION BY: Any Person (1)	APPLICATION BY: Limited Group (2)	COURT (3)	CRITERIA FOR INSTITUTIONALIZATION ORDER TO ISSUE: Individual: Dangerous to Self or Others (4)	Individual: Unable to Provide for Basic Needs (5)	Individual: Other (6)	Systemic: No Less Restrictive Alternative (7)	Systemic: Other (8)	SUPPORTING EVIDENCE FOR APPLICATION: No. of Certificates (9)	Other Evidence (10)	PREHEARING MEDICAL EXAMINATION ORDERED BY COURT (11)	DISMISSAL AFTER MEDICAL EXAMINATION (12)	PREHEARING DETENTION (13)	NOTICE OF HEARING: Guardian (14)	Relatives (15)	Attorney (16)	Patient (17)	When (18)
GA. Code Ann. (1979 & Supp. 1980)		chief medical officer of evaluating facility 88-506.2	probate 88-501(r)	overt act 88-501(r) OR	so unable to care for own health & safety as to create imminently life-endangering crisis 88-501(r) AND	mentally ill 88-501(r) AND	88-506.2(c)		one fn. 7 88-506.2(a)		patient already in evaluating facility		88-506.2(a)		representatives fn. 8 88-502.18(a)		88-506.2(a)	
HAWAII Rev. Stat. (1976 & Supp. 1981)	334-60(b) (2)(A)		any duly constituted ct. 334-1	to self, others, or property fn. 9 334-60(b)	fn. 9	mentally ill or substance abuse 334-60(b)	in need of treatment & no less restrictive alternative 334-60(b)		one fn. 5 334-60(b) (2)(A)				334-59 (a)(2)	334-60(b) (3)(A)	334-60(b) (3)(A)	334-60(b) (3)(A)	334-60(b) (3)(A)	
IDAHO Code (1980 & Supp. 1981)		fn. 10 66-329(a)	district 66-328	66-329(k)(2) OR	gravely disabled 66-329(k)(2) AND	mentally ill 66-329(k)(1)	66-329(k)		one fn. 5 66-329(c)		1 designated examiner fn. 11 66-329(d)	66-329(d)	66-329(e)	66-329(f)	spouse, next of kin, or friend 66-329(f)		66-329(f)	no min. period between notice & hearing 66-329(f)
ILL. Ann. Stat. (Smith-Hurd 1966 & Supp. 1981)	18 or older 91½, §3-701		county circuit 91½, §3-100	91½, §1-119(1) OR	91½, §1-119(2) AND	mentally ill 91½, §1-119(1), (2)	91½, §3-811		optional fn. 5 fn. 12 91½, §3-702		if no certificate accompanies petition 91½, §3-703			91½, §3-706	91½ §3-706	91½, §3-706	91½, §3-706	
IND. Code Ann. (Burns 1973 & Supp. 1982)		fn. 13 16-14-9.1-10(b)	probate or superior 16-14-9.1-5	16-14-9.1-10(d) OR	gravely disabled 16-14-9.1-10(d) AND	mentally ill, & in need of custody, care, or treatment 16-14-9.1-10(d) AND	16-14-9.1-10(d) 16-14-9.1-1(i)		one 16-14-9.1-8(c)(1) 16-14-9.1-10(b)				inappropriate facility 16-14-9.1-3	to all interested persons 16-14-9.1-10(c)	to all interested persons 16-14-9.1-10(c)	to all interested persons 16-14-9.1-10(c)	16-14-9.1-10(c)	5 days 16-14-9.1-10(c)
IOWA Code Ann. (West 1969 & Supp. 1980)	229.6		district 229.6	229.1(2) AND		seriously mentally impaired 229.13 229.1(2), & lacks capacity to make responsible decisions re treatment 229.1(2)			one fn. 14 229.6(3) OR	1 or more affidavits fn. 14 229.6(3)(b) other corroborative information 229.6(3)(c)	1 or more physicians 229.8(3)(b)	229.10(3)	229.11				229.7	48 hrs. min. 229.7
KAN. Stat. Ann. (1976 & Supp. 1981)	59-2913		district 59-2913	59-2902 OR	59-2902 AND	mentally ill, in need of treatment, & lacks capacity to make responsible decision re treatment 59-2917 59-2902	59-2917		one fn. 5 59-2913		1 physician not mandatory until probable cause hearing unless hearing waived or in custody 59-2914(a)		discretionary 59-2915(a) 59-2912	such persons as the ct. directs 59-2916	such persons as the ct. directs 59-2916	59-2916	59-2916	5 days 59-2916
KY. Rev. Stat. Ann (Michie 1980) fn. 15		friend, relative, spouse, or guardian 202A.060(1)	circuit 202A.060(1)	202A.070 (9)(b) 202A.080 (6)(b) AND		mentally ill 202A.070 (9)(a) 202A.080 (6)(a) AND	202A.070 (9)(c) 202A.080 (6)(c) AND	beneficial treatment available 202A.070 (9)(d) 202A.080 (6)(d)			2 physicians 202A.070(3) 202A.080(2)	202A.070(6) 202A.080(3)	202A.070(5)	202A.070(2)	spouse, parent, or nearest known relative 202A.070(2)		202A.070(2)	
LA. Rev. Stat. Ann. (West 1975 & Supp. 1981)	of legal age 28:54(A)		district 28:54(A)	28:55(E) OR	gravely disabled 28:55(E) AND	substance abuse or mental illness 28:55(E)	28:55(E)	& medically suitable 28:55(E)			discretionary 1 physician 28:54(D)		discretionary 28:54(D)			28:54(C)	28:54(C)	reasonable notice 28:54(C)

TABLE 2.6 JUDICIAL INSTITUTIONALIZATION OF MENTALLY ILL PERSONS—PREHEARING PROCEDURES—*Continued*

STATE	APPLICATION BY: Any Person (1)	APPLICATION BY: Limited Group (2)	COURT (3)	CRITERIA FOR INSTITUTIONALIZATION ORDER TO ISSUE — Individual: Dangerous to Self or Others (4)	Individual: Unable to Provide for Basic Needs (5)	Individual: Other (6)	Systemic: No Less Restrictive Alternative (7)	Systemic: Other (8)	SUPPORTING EVIDENCE FOR APPLICATION: No. of Certificates (9)	Other Evidence (10)	PREHEARING MEDICAL EXAMINATION ORDERED BY COURT (11)	DISMISSAL AFTER MEDICAL EXAMINATION (12)	PREHEARING DETENTION (13)	NOTICE OF HEARING: Guardian (14)	Relatives (15)	Attorney (16)	Patient (17)	When (18)
ME. Rev. Stat. Ann. (Supp. 1981)	34, §2333		district 34, §2334	34, §2334 (5)(A)(1) AND		mentally ill 34, §2334 (5)(A)(1) AND	best available means of treatment 34, §2334 (5)(A)(2) AND	approval of hospital's treatment plan 34, §2334 (5)(A)(3)	1 by physician or psychologist 34, §2333		2 examiners 34, §2334 (3)(A)	34, §2334 (3)(C)	already hospitalized by emergency procedure 34, §2333	34, §2334 (2)(B)	34, §2334 (2)(B)		34, §2334 (2)(A)	72 hrs. 34, §2334 (2)(A)
MD. Ann. Code																		
MASS. Ann. Laws (Michie/Law Co-op. 1981 & Supp. 1982) fn. 16		facility director 123-7(a)	district 123-7(a)	123-8(a)(2) AND		mentally ill 123-8(a)(1)					mandatory 123-12(b)	123-12(b)		123-7(c)	123-7(c)		123-7(c)	14 days of filing of petition 123-7(d)
MICH. Comp. Laws Ann. (1980 & Supp. 1981)	18 yrs. or older 330.1434		probate 330.1400(g)	330.1401(a), (c) OR	330.1401(b) AND	mentally ill 330.1401 OR unable to understand need for treatment 330.1401(c) AND	330.1469 AND	hospital treatment adequate & appropriate 330.1470	1 by physician fn. 17 fn. 5 330.1434(3)		1 or 2 physicians 330.1435(1), (2) fn. 18	330.1435(5)		330.1453(1)	330.1453(1)	330.1453(1)	330.1453(1), (2)	patient: w/in 4 days of petition 330.1453(2) general: earliest practicable 330.1453(1)
MINN. Stat. Ann. (West 1971 & Supp. 1981)	253A.07(1)		probate 253A.07(1)	253A.07 (17)(a) OR	253A.07 (17)(a) AND	mentally ill 253A.07 (17)(a) OR failed to protect self from exploitation 253A.07 (17)(a)	253A.07 (17)(a)		one 253A.07(1)	fn. 5 253A.07(1)	2 examiners, 1 a physician 253A.07(2)		253.07(3)	1 interested person & others as ct. directs 253A.07(9)	1 interested person & others as ct. directs 253A.07(9)	253A.07(9)	253A.07(9)	5 days notice of hearing, 2 days notice of time & date 353A.07(9)
MISS. Code Ann. (1981)	any citizen of state 41-21-65 OR	any relative 41-21-65	chancery 41-21-63(2)	41-21-61(C) OR	41-21-61(C) AND	mentally ill 41-21-61(C)	discretionary 41-21-75				2 physicians or 1 physician & 1 psychologist 41-21-67	41-21-71	41-21-71(2)	41-21-73 OR	2 nearest relatives in county 41-21-73	41-21-73	41-21-73	reasonable time 41-21-73
MO. Ann. Stat. (Vernon 1979 & Supp. 1980)		head of mental health facility 630.330.2	probate 630.335.1	630.335.4	632.335.4 632.005(9) AND	mentally ill 632.335.4	632.335.4	96 hrs. observational detention 632.330.1 632.305	1 by psychiatrist or 1 by physician & 1 by mental health professional 632.330.2(5)				632.335.1			632.335.1	632.335.1	promptly 632.335.1
MONT. Code Ann. (1979)	county attorney upon written request of any person 53-21-121		district 53-21-102(2)	overt act 53-21-102 (5), (14)		seriously mentally ill 53-21-121	53-21-120				1 professional 53-21-123		53-21-124	53-21-121(3)	53-21-121(3)	53-21-121(3)	53-21-121(3)	on or before probable cause hearing 53-21-121(3)
NEB. Rev. Stat.																		
NEV. Rev. Stat. (1981)		fn. 19 433A.200	district 433A.200	433A.310 (1)(b) OR	gravely disabled 433A.310 (1)(b) AND	mentally ill 433A.310 (1)(b)	433A.310(3)		one 433A.200(1)	fn. 5 433A.200(2)	2 physicians or psychologists, at least 1 physician, or a multiple disciplinary team 433A.240		433A.240(2)			433A.220(2)	433A.220(2)	
N.H. Rev. Stat. Ann. (1977 & Supp. 1981)	any responsible person 135-B:27		probate 135-B:3	overt act 135-B:26 135-B:2(XI) AND		mentally ill 135-B:26			one 135-B:28	specific acts of patient, & witnesses thereto 135-B:28	1 psychiatrist 135-B:32		none unless emergency 135-B:31	representative 135-B:7 135-B:30		representative 135-B:7 135-B:30	135-B:7 135-B:30	3 days 135-B:7 w/in 2 days of receipt of petition 135-B:30

TABLE 2.6 JUDICIAL INSTITUTIONALIZATION OF MENTALLY ILL PERSONS—PREHEARING PROCEDURES—*Continued*

STATE	APPLICATION BY		COURT (3)	CRITERIA FOR INSTITUTIONALIZATION ORDER TO ISSUE					SUPPORTING EVIDENCE FOR APPLICATION		PREHEARING MEDICAL EXAMINATION ORDERED BY COURT (11)	DISMISSAL AFTER MEDICAL EXAMINATION (12)	PREHEARING DETENTION (13)	NOTICE OF HEARING				
				Individual			*Systemic*											
	Any Person (1)	*Limited Group* (2)		Dangerous to Self or Others (4)	Unable to Provide for Basic Needs (5)	Other (6)	No Less Restrictive Alternative (7)	Other (8)	*No. of Certificates* (9)	*Other Evidence* (10)				*Guardian* (14)	*Relatives* (15)	*Attorney* (16)	*Patient* (17)	*When* (18)
N.J. Stat. Ann. (West 1981)		interested person *fn. 20* 30:4-27	county or juvenile & domestic relations 30:4-23			mentally ill 30:4-27			two 30:4-29			*fn. 21* 30:4-39	30:4-37, -38		*fn. 21* 30:4-41		*fn. 21* 30:4-41	
N.M. Stat. Ann. (1979)		health dept., physician, or evaluation facility 43-1-11(A) district attorney upon application of any interested person 43-1-11(E)	district 43-1-3(F)	43-1-11 (C)(1) AND		likely to benefit from treatment 43-1-11 (C)(2) AND	least drastic means 43-1-11 (C)(3) AND	prior emergency detention & evaluation 43-1-11(A) district attorney finds reasonable grounds for commitment 43-1-11(E)	initial screening report by evaluating physician 43-1-11(A)	permissible 43-1-11(E)			already detained for evaluation 43-1-11(A)			43-1-11(A)	43-1-11 (A), (E)	5 days 43-1-11(E)
N.Y. Mental Hyg. Law																		
N.C. Gen. Stat. (1981)	122-58.3(a)		district or superior 122-58.3(a)	122-58.7(i) OR	122-58.7(i) 122-58.2 (1)(a)(1) AND	mentally ill 122-58.7(i) AND	122-58.8(b)				1 physician 122-58.3(b)	122-58.4(c)	122-58.4(c) 122-58.6			122-58.5	122-58.5	48 hrs. 122-58.5
N.D. Cent. Code (Supp. 1981)	18 or older 25-03.1-08		county 25-03.1-08	25-03.1-02 (11)(b) OR	25-03.1-02 (11)(b)(3) OR	severely mentally ill 25-03.1-02 (11)(a) AND	25-03.1-21		optional 25-03.1-08(1)	corroborative information & affidavits (optional) 25-03.1-08 (2), (3)	25-03.1-10	25-03.1-11	emergency cases 25-03.1-11	25-03.1-12	spouse or other relatives 25-03.1-12	25-03.1-12	25-03.1-12	earliest possible time 25-03.1-12
OHIO Rev. Code Ann. (Baldwin 1980 & Supp. 1981)	5122.11		probate 5122.01(Q)	5122.01 (B)(1), (2) OR	5122.01 (B)(3) AND	mentally ill 5122.01(B), or in need of & would benefit from treatment & poses grave & immediate risk to substantial rights 5122.01 (B)(4) AND	5122.15(E)		1 psychiatrist or 1 psychologist & 1 physician *fn. 5* 5122.11		1 physician or 1 psychologist & 1 physician 5122.14		5122.11 5122.17	5122.12(B)	spouse, & parents, if a minor 5122.12(B)	5122.12(E)	5122.12(A)	
OKLA. Stat. Ann. (West 1979 & Supp. 1981)		fnn. 22, 23 43A, §54.4(A) §185(A)	district 43A, §54.4(A)	43A, §3(O)(1)	43A, §3 (O)(2) AND	mentally ill 43A, §3(O) AND	43A, §54.9				2 qualified examiners; 1 may be a clinical psychologist 43A, §54.4(F)		probable cause 43A, §54.4(B)	43A, §54.4 (C)(9)	43A, §54.4 (C)(9)	ct. appointed 43A, §54.4(C)	43A, §54.4 (C)(9)	1 day 43A, §54.4(C)
OR. Rev. Stat. (Supp. 1981)	any 2 persons or magistrate or county health officer 426.070		probate *fn. 24* 426.060(1) 426.070(1)	426.005 (2)(a)	426.005 (2)(b) AND	mental disorder 426.005(2)		426.130 (1) & (2)		prehearing investigation by court as to probable cause 426.070(1)	2 physicians or ct.-appointed examiner & 1 physician 426.110		426.070 (3), (5)				citation 426.090	
PA. Stat. Ann. (Purdon 1969 & Supp. 1980)	50, §7304 (c)(1)	facility director where person already subject to involuntary treatment 50, §7304 (b)(1)	common pleas 50, §7304	clear & present danger 50, §7301 (b)(1) overt act or threat 50, §7301 (b)(2)(ii), (iii) OR	50, §7301 (b)(2)(i) AND	mentally ill 50, §7301(a)	50, §7304(f)		physician's name, & substance of opinion, if any 50, §7304 (b)(2), (c)(2)		discretionary 50, §7304 (c)(5)		emergency only 50, §7304 (c)(6)			50, §7304 (c)(4)	50, §7304 (c)(4)	50, §7304 (c)(4) at least 3 days

TABLE 2.6 JUDICIAL INSTITUTIONALIZATION OF MENTALLY ILL PERSONS—PREHEARING PROCEDURES—*Continued*

STATE	APPLICATION BY		COURT	CRITERIA FOR INSTITUTIONALIZATION ORDER TO ISSUE					SUPPORTING EVIDENCE FOR APPLICATION		PREHEARING MEDICAL EXAMINATION ORDERED BY COURT	DISMISSAL AFTER MEDICAL EXAMINATION	PREHEARING DETENTION	NOTICE OF HEARING				
				Individual			Systemic											
	Any Person (1)	*Limited Group* (2)	(3)	Dangerous to Self or Others (4)	Unable to Provide for Basic Needs (5)	Other (6)	No Less Restrictive Alternative (7)	Other (8)	*No. of Certificates* (9)	*Other Evidence* (10)	(11)	(12)	(13)	*Guardian* (14)	*Relatives* (15)	*Attorney* (16)	*Patient* (17)	*When* (18)
R.I. Gen. Laws (1977)		person with whom patient resides, close relative, or public official 40.1-5-8(1)	district 40.1-5-8(1) district 40.1-5.1-1 any justice of supreme ct. 40.1-5.1-9 may appoint 3 commissioners for fact finding 40.1-5.1-9	40.1-5-8(10) so insane as to be dangerous 40.1-5.1-1 welfare of patient or others requires hospitalization or restraint 40.1-5.1-9	restraint & treatment necessary for own welfare 40.1-5.1-1	AND in need of treatment & likely to benefit therefrom 40.1-5-8(10)	40.1-5-8(10)		two 40.1-5-8(3) two, optional 40.1-5.1-2		upon motion or court's discretion 40.1-5-8 (5)(a) optional 40.1-5.1-2	fn. 25 40.1-5-8 (5)(b) 40.1-5.1-12	40.1-5.1-10	40.1-5-8 (4)(b)	40.1-5-8 (4)(b)		40.1-5-8 (4)(b) 40.1-5.1-11	at preliminary hearing 40.1-5-8 (4)(b) due notice 40.1-5.1-11
S.C. Code Ann. (Law. Co-op. 1976 & Supp. 1980)	any interested person or superintendent of institution 44-17-510		probate 44-17-510	44-17-580		mentally ill & needs treatment, or lacks capacity to make responsible decisions re treatment 44-17-580			designated examiner 44-17-510	fn. 5 44-17-510	2 designated examiners, 1 a physician 44-17-530	44-17-540		any interested person 44-17-550	any interested person 44-17-550	44-17-550	44-17-550	5 days 44-17-550
S.D. Codified Laws Ann. (1976 & Supp. 1981)																		
TENN. Code Ann. (1977 & Supp. 1981)		fn. 26 33-604(a)	fn. 27 33-604(a)	likelihood of serious harm 33-604 (d)(2)	AND	mentally ill 33-604 (d)(1)	AND 33-604 (d)(3)		two 33-604(a)	fn. 5 33-604(a)	1 witness must be a physician who examined patient w/in 20 days of hearing 33-604(c)		33-607(b)	parent, guardian, spouse or adult next of kin 33-604(b)	parent guardian, spouse or adult next of kin 33-604(b)		33-604(b)	
TEX. Rev. Civ. Stat. Ann. (Vernon 1958 & Supp. 1981)	5547-41		county 5547-41	5547-52(b)	AND	mentally ill 55-47-52(b)	AND	temporary observation & treatment for 60 days 5547-40	one 5547-42		at least 2 physicians 5547-49(d)		none, unless already a patient or placed in protective custody 5547-47	5547-44	OR 5547-44		5547-44	7 days 5547-44
UTAH Code Ann. (1978 & Supp. 1981)	64-7-36(1)		district 64-7-36(1)	64-7-36 (10)(b)	OR 64-7-36 (10)(b)	AND mentally ill & lacks ability to make rational decisions re treatment 64-7-36 (10)(a), (c)	AND 64-7-36 (10)(d)	AND hospital can provide adequate & appropriate treatment 64-7-36 (10)(e)	one fnn. 5, 28 64-7-36 (1)(a)		2 designated examiners 64-7-36(8)	64-7-36(8)	64-7-36(3)	64-7-36(5)	64-7-36(5)	67-7-36(5)	64-7-36(5)	as soon as practicable 64-7-36(5)
VT. Stat. Ann. (1968 & Supp. 1980)	any interested party 18, §7612(a)		district 18, §7612(b)	18, §7101 (17)	OR 18, §7101 (17)(B)(ii)	AND mentally ill 18, §7101 (17)	AND 18, §7617 (C)	AND treatment must be adequate & appropriate 18, §7617(e)	one 18, §7612 (e)(1)	fn. 5 18, §7612 (e)(2)	1 physician 18, §7614			18, §7613(a)	to any other person ct. believes concerned for patient's welfare 18, §7613	18, §7613(a)	fn. 29 18, §7613 (a), (c)	
VA. Code (1976 & Supp. 1981)	or judge on own motion 37.1-67.1		district 37.1-1(11), 37.1-67.1	37.1-67.3 (a)	OR 37.1-67.3 (b)	AND mentally ill 37.1-67.3	AND 37.1-67.3(C)			sworn petition based on probable cause 37.1-67.1	qualified psychiatrist or physician 37.1-67.3		37.1-67.1				37.1-67.3	

TABLE 2.6 JUDICIAL INSTITUTIONALIZATION OF MENTALLY ILL PERSONS—PREHEARING PROCEDURES—*Continued*

STATE	APPLICATION BY		COURT	CRITERIA FOR INSTITUTIONALIZATION ORDER TO ISSUE					SUPPORTING EVIDENCE FOR APPLICATION		PREHEARING MEDICAL EXAMINATION ORDERED BY COURT	DISMISSAL AFTER MEDICAL EXAMINATION	PREHEARING DETENTION	NOTICE OF HEARING				
				Individual			*Systemic*											
	Any Person (1)	*Limited Group* (2)	(3)	Dangerous to Self or Others (4)	Unable to Provide for Basic Needs (5)	Other (6)	No Less Restrictive Alternative (7)	Other (8)	*No. of Certificates* (9)	*Other Evidence* (10)	(11)	(12)	(13)	*Guardian* (14)	*Relatives* (15)	*Attorney* (16)	*Patient* (17)	*When* (18)
WASH. Rev. Code Ann. (1975 & Supp. 1981)		professional in charge of facility, designee, or designated county mental health professional 71.05.290(1)	superior 71.05.290(1)	71.05.280 (1), (2) OR	gravely disabled 71.05.280(4) AND		71.05.320 AND	72-hr. detention & 14-day intensive treatment 71.05.280	2 physicians or 1 physician & 1 mental health practitioner 71-05.290(2)				71.05.310	71.05.300		71.05.300	71.05.300	
W. VA. Code (1980) *fn. 30*	27-5-2(a)		circuit 27-5-2(b)(2)	27-5-4 (j)(1) AND		mentally ill, retarded, or addicted 27-5-4(j)(1) AND	27-5-4(j)(2)		one 27-5-4(d)(1)	*fn. 5* 27-5-4(d)(2)	27-5-2(b)(4) 27-5-4(f)(1)	27-5-4(f)(3)	until probable cause hearing 27-5-2(b)(4) after 27-5-3	patient's spouse, parents or guardian 27-5-4(e)	patient's spouse, parents or guardian 27-5-4(e)		27-5-4(e)	8 days 27-5-4(e)
WIS. Stat. Ann. (West 1957 & Supp. 1980)	3 adults 51.20(1)(b)		probate 51.20(1)(c)	overt act or threat 51.20(1)(a) OR	51.20 (1)(a) AND	mentally ill, drug dependent, or developmentally disabled 51.20(1)(a) AND	51.20(13)(c)				*fn. 31* 51.20(9)(a), (b)		until probable cause hearing 51.20(2) until full hearing 51.20(8)(b)	51.20(2)	parent 51.20(2)	51.20(2)	51.20(2)	w/in reasonable time 51.20(2)
WYO. Stat. (1981 & Supp. 1982)			district 25-3-101(ii)	by recent overt acts, attempts, or threats 25-3-112(k)	AND	mentally ill 25-3-112(k) AND	25-3-112(k)		one 25-3-112(b)(i)	*fn. 5* 25-3-112 (b)(ii)	1 or more examiners or physicians 25-3-112(f)	25-3-112(g)		25-3-112(e) AND	other persons designated by the court 25-3-112(e)	other persons designated by the court 25-3-112(e)	25-3-112 (e), (g)	as soon as possible 25-3-112(g)

FOOTNOTES TABLE 2.6

1. Ala. Code § 22-52-8(a) (Supp. 1981). If treatment or limitations on liberty are imposed, there must be a probable cause hearing within seven days.

2. Ark. Stat. Ann. § 59-1408 (Supp. 1981). Patient must be served with petition, order for detention or initial evaluation, and statement of rights (including right to be present at hearings). No notice of hearing itself is specifically required. The requirements of due process, however, must be met, which implicitly include notice of the hearing. Von Luce v. Rankin, 588 S.W.2d 445 (Ark. 1979).

3. D.C. Code Ann. § 21-541-21-545 (1981). D.C. has a prehearing examination, then a hearing before a commission, followed by a hearing in court. The latter takes place only if the commission finds the person not sane. Only the court hearing is charted.

4. Id. § 21-541(A): "By his spouse, parent, or legal guardian, by a physician, by a duly accredited officer or agent of the Department of Public Health, or by an officer authorized to make arrests in the District of Columbia."

5. Id. § 21-541(A)(2)(B): "Or a statement by the applicant that the person has refused to submit to an examination." Similar provisions are found in Hawaii Rev. Stat. § 334-60(b)(2)(A) (Supp. 1981); Idaho Code § 66-329(c) (Supp. 1981); Ill. Ann. Stat. ch. 91½, § 3-603 (Smith-Hurd Supp. 1980); Kan. Stat. Ann. § 59-2913 (Supp. 1981); Mich. Comp. Laws Ann. § 330.1434(3) (1980); Minn. Stat. Ann. § 253A.07(1) (West 1982); Nev. Rev. Stat. § 433A.200(2) (1981); Ohio Rev. Code Ann. § 5122.11 (Baldwin Supp. 1981); S.C. Code Ann. § 44-17-510 (Law. Co-op. Supp. 1981); Tenn. Code Ann. § 33-604(a) (Supp. 1981); Utah Code Ann. § 64-8-36.(1)(b) (Supp. 1981); Vt. Stat. Ann. tit. 18, § 7612(e)(2) (Supp. 1981); W. Va. Code § 27-5-4(d)(2) (Supp. 1981); and Wyo. Stat. § 25-3-112(b)(ii) (1981).

6. Fla. Stat. Ann. § 394.467(1)(b)(2) (West Supp. 1981): "In need of care or treatment which, if not provided, may result in neglect or refusal to care for himself, and such neglect or refusal poses a real and present threat of substantial harm to his well-being."

7. Ga. Code Ann. § 88-506.2(a) (Supp. 1980): "Upon recommendation of the Chief Medical Officer of an evaluating facility where the patient has been examined, supported by the opinions of two physicians who have personally examined the patient within the preceeding five days."

8. Id. § 88-502.18(a) (1979). Patient may designate one representative from the following: legal guardian, spouse, an adult child, parent, attorney, adult next of kin, or adult friend. A second representative shall be selected from the same list by the facility.

9. Danger to property, as defined in Hawaii, is an unconstitutional basis for commitment; the Hawaii statute is also unconstitutional in not requiring that danger to self or others be imminent. Suzuki v. Yuen, 617 F.2d 173 (9th Cir. 1980).

10. Idaho Code § 66-329(a) (Supp. 1981). Application may be made by a friend, relative, spouse, guardian, licensed physician, prosecuting attorney, other public official, or director of any facility in which such patient may be.

11. Id. § 66-329(d). Two examiners are required if the individual has refused to submit to an examination prior to the filing of the application.

12. Ill. Ann. Stat. ch. 91½, § 3-604 (Smith-Hurd Supp. 1980). No certificate is required if the petition alleges that it was impossible to have the patient examined, but in such case the patient may not be detained for more than 24 hours unless a certificate is provided to or by the hospital.

13. Ind. Code Ann. § 16-14-9.1-10(b) (Burns Supp. 1982): "By a health or police officer, a friend, relative, spouse, or guardian of the person, the superintendent of an appropriate facility where the person may be found, or a prosecuting attorney."

14. Iowa Code Ann. § 229.6(3) (West Supp. 1980):

a. A written statement of a licensed physician in support of the application; or

b. One or more supporting affidavits otherwise corroborating the application; or

c. Corroborative information obtained and reduced to writing by the clerk of his or her designee, but only when circumstances make it infeasible to comply with, or when the clerk considers it appropriate to supplement the information supplied pursuant to, either paragraph a or b of this subsection.

15. Ky. Rev. Stat. Ann. §§ 202A.070-202A.080 (Michie Supp. 1980). Entries are applicable to both 60-day and 360-day hospitalization procedures.

16. Mass. Ann. Laws ch. 123, § 8A(a) (Michie/Law. Co-op. 1981). Massachusetts provides for commitment of women to an Intensive Care Unit if the court finds that: (1) the woman is mentally ill; (2) the woman has engaged in repeated and recent incidents of serious self-destructive behavior or assaultive behavior as an inpatient at a facility or inmate of a place of detention; (3) the woman cannot be properly treated in any other facility; and (4) there is a substantial likelihood that the woman's condition will continue to cause her to inflict serious harm upon herself or others.

17. Mich. Comp. Laws Ann. § 330.1434(3) (1980): "The petition may also be accompanied by a second certificate. If 2 certificates accompany the petition, at least one of them shall have been executed by a psychiatrist."

18. Id. § 330.1435(1)(2). If petition is accompanied by one certificate, "the court shall order the individual to be examined by a psychiatrist." If petition is not accompanied by a certificate, "by 2 physicians, at least one of whom shall be a psychiatrist."

19. Nev. Rev. Stat. § 433A.200 (1981): "By the spouse, parent, adult children or legal guardian of the person to be treated or by any physician, psychologist, social worker or public health nurse, by a duly accredited agent of the department or by any officer authorized to make arrests in the State of Nevada."

20. N.J. Stat. Ann. § 30:4-27 (West 1981):

A person interested . . . by reason of relationship or marriage, or by the person having the charge or care of such patient, or by the Sheriff, or by the county prosecutor, or by the municipal or county director of welfare or person charged with the care and relief of the poor, or by any chief of police or police captain of any municipality in this State where such patient may be, or by the chief executive officer of any correctional institution, or of any public or private charitable institution or hospital in which the patient may be, or by the Commissioner of Institutions and Agencies.

21. Id. §§ 30:4-39, 30:4-41. The provisions are only in reference to the hospitalization of persons already temporarily confined in institutions.

22. Okla. Stat. Ann. tit. 43A, § 54.4(A) (West Supp. 1981):

Father, mother, husband, wife, brother, sister, guardian or child, over the age of 18 years, of a person alleged to be a person requiring treatment, or the parent, father, mother, guardian or person having custody of a minor child, a physician or person in charge of any facility or correctional institution, or any peace officer within the county in which the person may be found or the district attorney in whose district the person may be found.

23. Id. § 185(A) (West 1979). Oklahoma has separate provisions for commitment to a private facility. Discretion rests primarily with the patient's attending physician, although a court order is necessary to commit the patient.

24. Or. Rev. Stat. §§ 426.060(1), .070(1) (1981): "Any court having probate jurisdiction or, if the circuit court is not the probate court, the circuit court of its jurisdiction has been extended to include commitment of the mentally ill pursuant to ORS 3.275."

25. R.I. Gen. Laws § 40.1-5.1-12 (Supp. 1981). Supreme Court Justice may confirm or disallow commissioners' findings with or without further hearing.

26. Tenn. Code Ann. § 33-604(a) (Supp. 1981): "The parent, guardian, spouse, or a responsible adult relative . . . or by any licensed physician or licensed psychologist, . . . or by any public health or public welfare officer, or by the head of any institution in which the individual may be, or by any officer authorized to make arrests in Tennessee."

27. Id. § 33-604(a):

The courts which have jurisdiction in these proceedings are as follows:

(1) Chancery Court;

(2) Circuit Court;

(3) Juvenile Court in any county having a population of more than [250,000] according to the 1970 federal census of population or any subsequent federal census;

(4) Division II Probate Court in any county having . . . a population of more than [600,000]. . . .

28. Utah Code Ann. § 64-7-36(2) (Supp. 1981): "Prior to issuing a judicial order, the court may require the applicant to consult a mental health facility or may direct a mental health professional from a mental health facility to interview the applicant and the proposed patient to determine the existing facts and report them to the court."

29. Vt. Stat. Ann. tit. 18, § 7613(c) (Supp. 1981). If the court has reason to believe that notice to the proposed patient will be likely to cause injury to the proposed patient or others, it shall direct the proposed patient's counsel to give the proposed patient oral notice prior to written notice under circumstances most likely to reduce likelihood of injury.

30. This procedure is the same as that for administrative hospitalization (cf. Tables 3.4 and 3.5), and either may be used.

31. Wis. Stat. Ann. § 51.20(9) (West Supp. 1981):

(a) 2 licensed physicians specializing in psychiatry, or one licensed physician and one licensed psychologist, or 2 licensed physicians one of whom shall have specialized training in psychiatry, if available, or 2 physicians, to personally examine the subject individual.

(b) If the examiner determines that the subject individual is a proper subject for treatment, the examiner shall make a recommendation concerning the appropriate level of treatment. Such recommendation shall include the level of inpatient facility which provides the least restrictive environment consistent with the needs of the individual, if any, and the name of the facility where the subject individual should be received into the mental health system.

TABLE 2.7 JUDICIAL INSTITUTIONALIZATION OF MENTALLY ILL PERSONS—HEARING AND POSTHEARING PROCEDURES

	HEARING		HEARING HELD BEFORE REFEREE OR FACT-FINDING COMMISSION	CONDUCT OF HEARING		PRESENCE OF PATIENT *fn. 1*			JURY TRIAL		STANDARD OF PROOF *fn. 2*	INSTITUTION'S DISCRETION AS TO ADMISSION		JUDICIAL REVIEW OF HOSPITALIZATION ORDER	PLACE OF TREATMENT		PERIOD OF HOSPITALIZATION	EXTENSION PROVISIONS	
STATE	Mandatory (1)	If Requested by Patient (2)	(3)	Judicial Discretion as to Place (4)	Closed to Public (5)	Mandatory (6)	Unless Harmful (7)	If Requested by Patient (8)	Mandatory if Demanded by Patient (9)	Left to Discretion of Judge (10)	(11)	Suitable Hospital Accommodations Available (12)	Mental Condition (13)	(14)	Public or Private Hospital (15)	Outpatient Treatment *fn. 3* (16)	(17)	Procedure *fn. 4* (18)	Period *fn. 5* (19)
ALA. Code (1975 & Supp. 1981)	22-52-3				open, unless patient requests closed 22-52-9(4)		22-52-9(1)			no jury trial 22-52-9(4)	clear, unequivocal, & convincing 22-52-10(a)			appeal *fn. 6* 22-52-15			not stated		
ALAS. Stat. (1979 & Supp. 1981)	47.30.725 (b)			least likely to harm respondent 47.30.735			47.30.735 (b)(1)			judicial hearing 47.30.715	clear & convincing 47.30.735 (c)					least restrictive alternative 47.30.735 (d)	21 days 47.30.735	jury trial upon request 47.30.745 (c)	90 days 47.30.745 followed by 120 days 47.30.770
ARIZ. Rev. Stat. Ann. (1974 & Supp. 1981)	36-535B			36-539C		36-539B	unless unable for medical reasons 36-539C				clear & convincing *fn. 7* 36-540A, B			36-546	36-540 A to C 36-501.18		varying *fn. 8* 36-540	reapplication 36-542	
ARK. Stat. Ann. (1971 & Supp. 1981)	59-1409		referee 59-1405(c)					right to be present 59-1408(2)			clear & convincing 59-1409			appeal *fn. 9* 59-1402E 59-1423 59-1424	59-1409 59-1401D	59-1415(c) 59-1409	45 days 59-1409	hearing upon petition of 2 psychiatrists 59-1410	120 days 59-1410
CAL. Welf. & Inst. Code (West 1972 & Supp. 1980)	5303					patient kept in custody, but must have counsel 5302, 5303	patient kept in custody, but must have counsel 5302, 5303	patient kept in custody, but must have counsel 5302, 5303	5302						5304		if dangerous to others 90 days 5304	reapplication *fn. 10* 5304	
COLO. Rev. Stat. Ann. (1973 & 1981 Supp.)		in writing 27-107(3)							27-10-109 (3)		clear & convincing 27-10-111 (1)			appeal 27-10-112	27-10-102 (4.5)	written request by patient 27-10-107 (6)	3 mos. 27-10-107	certify to ct.; hearing upon request 27-10-108	3 mos. 27-10-108
CONN. Gen. Stat. Ann. (West 1975 & Supp. 1981)	17-178			*fn. 11* 17-177(a)		17-178(f)					clear & convincing 17-178(c)				17-176		indeterminate w/annual review *fn. 12* 17-178(c), (g)		
DEL. Code Ann. (1974 & Supp. 1980)	16, §5008 (4)				16, §5006 (2)			16, §5006 (2)		no jury 16, §5006 (2)	clear & convincing 16, §5010 (2)		16, §5009	supreme ct. appeal 16, §5013 (a)	least restraint 16, §5010 (2)	least restraint 16, §5010 (2)	6 mos. 16, §5010 (2)	hearing upon notice to ct. 16, §5012	indefinite report to ct. every 6 mos. 16, §5012
D.C. Code Ann. (1981 & Supp. 1982)	21-545(a)		21-542(a)						21-545(a)		*fn. 13*			ct. hearing after commission hearing 21-545 *fn. 14* petition to ct. 21-547	21-545(b) 21-548	*fn. 15* 21-545(b)	indeterminate 21-545(b) patient may file petition 21-546, 21-547 examined every 6 mos. for release 21-548		
FLA. Stat. Ann. (West 1973 & Supp. 1981)	394.467(2)										*fn. 16*	*fn. 17* 394.467 (3)(b)			394.467 (3)(a)	394.463 (2)(e)	max. 6 mos. 394.467 (3)(a)	request ct. order hearing unless waived 394.467(4)	1 yr. 394.467 (4)(f)
GA. Code Ann. (1980 & Supp. 1980)	unless waived 88-506.2(c)											private facility only 88-507.5		appeal to superior ct. 88-506.4 (e)	88-506.2 88-507.5	88-506.2 (c)	max. 6 mos. 88-506.2(d)	medical certification right to hearing 88-506.5(c)	1 yr. max. 88-506.5 (c)(5)

TABLE 2.7 JUDICIAL INSTITUTIONALIZATION OF MENTALLY ILL PERSONS—HEARING AND POSTHEARING PROCEDURES—*Continued*

	HEARING		HEARING HELD BEFORE REFEREE OR FACT-FINDING COMMISSION	CONDUCT OF HEARING		PRESENCE OF PATIENT *fn. 1*			JURY TRIAL		STANDARD OF PROOF *fn. 2*	INSTITUTION'S DISCRETION AS TO ADMISSION		JUDICIAL REVIEW OF HOSPITALIZATION ORDER	PLACE OF TREATMENT		PERIOD OF HOSPITALIZATION	EXTENSION PROVISIONS	
STATE	Mandatory (1)	If Requested by Patient (2)	(3)	Judicial Discretion as to Place (4)	Closed to Public (5)	Mandatory (6)	Unless Harmful (7)	If Requested by Patient (8)	Mandatory if Demanded by Patient (9)	Left to Discretion of Judge (10)	(11)	Suitable Hospital Accommodations Available (12)	Mental Condition (13)	(14)	Public or Private Hospital (15)	Outpatient Treatment *fn. 3* (16)	(17)	Procedure *fn. 4* (18)	Period *fn. 5* (19)
HAWAII Rev. Stat. (1976 & Supp. 1981)	unless waived 334-60 (b)(3)			334-60 (b)(4)(D)			*fn. 18* 334-60 (b)(4)(C)				beyond a reasonable doubt 334-60 (b)(4)(I)	facility must agree 334-60 (b)(4)(I)		appeal & review in family ct. 334-81	334-60 (b)(4)(I)		90 days 334-60 (b)(5)	request ct. order 334-60 (b)(5)	90 days; 180-day extension 334-60 (b)(5)
IDAHO Code (1980 & Supp. 1981)	66-329(f)			66-329(h)			66-329(i)				clear & convincing 66-329(k)			petition for re-examination 66-343	66-329(k)	*fn. 19*	max. 3 yrs. 66-329(k) reviewed in 90 days & then every 120 days 66-331(a)		
ILL. Ann. Stat. (Smith-Hurd 1966 & Supp. 1980)	91½, §3-702			91½, §3-800(a)			91½, §3-806		*fn. 20* 91½, §3-802		clear & convincing 91½, §3-808	private only; if institution agrees w/order 91½, §3-811		right of appeal 91½, §3-816	91½, §3-811	or hospitalization in home of relative or other person 91½, §§3-811, 3-812	max. 60 days 91½, §3-813	petition & 2 certificates; mandatory hearing 91½, §3-813	60 days; 180-day extensions 91½, §3-813
IND. Code Ann. (Burns 1973 & Supp. 1981)	16-14-9.1-10(c)						16-14-9.1-10(c) 16-14-9.1-9(e)	16-14-9.1-10(c) 16-14-9.1-9(e) may be removed if disruptive				16-14-9.1-3		appeal as in other civil cases 16-14-9.1-6	16-14-9.1-10 (d)		indefinite 16-14-9.1-10(d) annual review 16-14-9.1-10(e)		
IOWA Code Ann. (West 1969 & Supp. 1980)	229.8		if referee appointed & no district judge accessible 229.21		*fn. 21* 229.12(2)		*fn. 22* 229.12	right to be present *fn. 22* 229.12			clear & convincing 229.12(3)			appeal to supreme ct. 229.17 if hearing by referee, appeal to trial ct. w/in 7 days 229.21(4)	229.13	ct.-ordered on basis of medical report 229.14(3)	indefinite 229.14(2) report to ct. in 30 days & then every 60 229.15(1)		
KAN. Stat. Ann. (1976 & Supp. 1981)	59-2914(a)			59-2914(a) 59-2917	at ct.'s discretion 59-2917		if patient requests presence, it may not be waived 59-2914(b)	59-2914(b)	59-2917		clear & convincing 59-2917	commitment if institution consents (except state hospital) 59-2917	commitment if institution consents (except state hospital) 59-2917		59-2917	59-2917	indefinite; report to ct. & review every 90 days 59-2917a		
KY. Rev. Stat. Ann. (Michie 1977 & Supp. 1980) *fn. 23*	202A.070 (6) 202A.080 (3)			202A.070 (7) 202A.080 (4)			202A.070 (8) 202A.080 (5)	202A.070 (8) 202A.080 (5)	202A.080 (4)						202A.070 (9) 202A.080 (6)		60 days 202A.070 (9) 360 days 202A.080 (6)	reapplication 202A.070 202A.080 (7)	
LA. Rev. Stat. Ann. (West 1975 & Supp. 1981)	28:54(C)			28:55(A)				28:54(C)			clear & convincing 28:55(E)	28:51		devolutive appeal 28:56(D)	28:55(E)		indeterminate 28:55 review & hearing procedures 28:56		
ME. Rev. Stat. Ann. (1978 & Supp. 1981)	34, §2334 (4)(A)			34, §2334 (4)(B)	closed 34, §2334 (4)(H) ct. may order open upon patient request			34, §2334 (4)(A)			clear & convincing 34, §2334 (5)(A)			appeal only on questions of law 34, §2334 (9)	34, §2334 (6)(A)		4 mos. 34, §2334 (6)(A)	application & hearing 34, §2334 (7)	1 yr. max. 34, §2334 (6)(A)
MD. Ann. Code																			

TABLE 2.7 JUDICIAL INSTITUTIONALIZATION OF MENTALLY ILL PERSONS—HEARING AND POSTHEARING PROCEDURES—*Continued*

STATE	HEARING: Mandatory (1)	HEARING: If Requested by Patient (2)	HEARING HELD BEFORE REFEREE OR FACT-FINDING COMMISSION (3)	CONDUCT OF HEARING: Judicial Discretion as to Place (4)	CONDUCT OF HEARING: Closed to Public (5)	PRESENCE OF PATIENT *fn. 1*: Mandatory (6)	PRESENCE OF PATIENT: Unless Harmful (7)	PRESENCE OF PATIENT: If Requested by Patient (8)	JURY TRIAL: Mandatory if Demanded by Patient (9)	JURY TRIAL: Left to Discretion of Judge (10)	STANDARD OF PROOF *fn. 2* (11)	INSTITUTION'S DISCRETION AS TO ADMISSION: Suitable Hospital Accommodations Available (12)	INSTITUTION'S DISCRETION AS TO ADMISSION: Mental Condition (13)	JUDICIAL REVIEW OF HOSPITALIZATION ORDER (14)	PLACE OF TREATMENT: Public or Private Hospital (15)	PLACE OF TREATMENT: Outpatient Treatment *fn. 3* (16)	PERIOD OF HOSPITALIZATION (17)	EXTENSION PROVISIONS: Procedure *fn. 4* (18)	EXTENSION PROVISIONS: Period *fn. 5* (19)
MASS. Ann. Laws (Michie/Law. Co-op. 1981)	unless waived after consulting counsel 123, §6(b)			123, §5							*fn. 24*			review of questions of law 123, §9(2)	123, §8		6 mos. 123, §8(d)	hearing unless waived 123, §8 mandatory hearing if to Bridgewater 123, §8(d)	1 yr. 123, §8(d) 6 mos. 123, §8(d)
MICH. Comp. Laws Ann. (1980 & Supp. 1981)	right to hearing 330.1453 (2)			in hospital if practicable 330.1456 (1)		unless waived 330.1455			330.1458		clear & convincing 330.1465	330.1468 (2)(b)	330.1468 (2)(b)		330.1468 (2)(a), (b)	330.1468 (2)(c), (d)	60 days 330.1472	petition ct. for order 330.1472 (2)	90 days; next extension may be 90 days or indefinite 330.1472 (2), (3)
MINN. Stat. Ann. (West 1982)	253A.07 (8)			253A.07 (13)	at ct.'s discretion *fn. 25* 253A.07 (12)			right to attend 253A.07 (12)			*fn. 26*	upon consent 253A.07 (17)		review boards 253A.16	253A.07 (17)	ct. shall consider alternative 253A.07 (17)(a)(2)	60 days 253A.07 (17)	ct. order from hospital statement 253A.07 (25) hearing on request if committed as dangerous to public 253A.07 (26)	indefinite 253A.07 (25), (26)
MISS. Code Ann. (1981)	41-21-71 (1)		optional special master in chancery 41-21-75			unless unable 41-21-75					preponderance of evidence 41-21-75			not appealable 41-21-75	41-21-75		20 days observation, diagnosis, & treatment 41-21-81	petition for hearing on need for further treatment 41-21-83	indefinite 41-21-83
MO. Ann. Stat. (Vernon 1979 & Supp. 1980)	632.335.1			632.335.2	patient's choice 632.335.2 (6)		unless disruptive or physically unable 632.335.3		632.335.2 (8)		clear & convincing 632.335.4	facility must agree to accept 632.335.4		appeal 632.430.1 motion for order to stay 632.430.2	632.335.4, 632.005 (11)	632.385	21 days 632.335	hearing 632.340–350 632.355	90 days 632.340 may be followed by 1 yr. 632.355
MONT. Code Ann. (1981)	53-21-122 (3)			53-21-119 (2)(b)			53-21-126 53-21-119 (2)		53-21-125		beyond reasonable doubt re physical facts or evidence; clear & convincing for other matters 53-21-126			appeal to supreme ct. 53-21-131	53-21-102 (6)	53-21-127	3 mos. 53-21-128	petition to ct.; right to hearing 53-21-128	6 mos. 53-21-128
NEB. Rev. Stat. (1976 & Supp. 1981)																			
NEV. Rev. Stat. (Supp. 1981)	433A.220 (1)					433A.290					clear & convincing evidence 433A.310 (1)(b)				433A.330 (1)		6 mos. 433A.310 (2)	reapplication 433A.310	6 mos. 433A.310 (2)
N.H. Rev. Stat. Ann. (1977 & Supp. 1981)	135-B:29				unless patient requests open 135-B:35			right to present evidence 135-B:35			*fn. 27*			petition for release 135-B:40 appeal on record 135-B:35	not stated	135-B:37	2 yrs. 135-B:38	judicial hearing 135-B:38	
N.J. Rev. Stat. (1981)	30:4-42		county adjuster optional 30:4-42				to health of patient or unsafe to produce him *fn. 28* 30:4-41			30:4-42	*fn. 29*			2A:67-13 (e)	30:4-52 to 30:4-59 30:4-27		not stated		

TABLE 2.7 JUDICIAL INSTITUTIONALIZATION OF MENTALLY ILL PERSONS—HEARING AND POSTHEARING PROCEDURES—*Continued*

STATE	HEARING		HEARING HELD BEFORE REFEREE OR FACT-FINDING COMMISSION	CONDUCT OF HEARING		PRESENCE OF PATIENT fn. 1			JURY TRIAL		STANDARD OF PROOF fn. 2	INSTITUTION'S DISCRETION AS TO ADMISSION		JUDICIAL REVIEW OF HOSPITALIZATION ORDER	PLACE OF TREATMENT		PERIOD OF HOSPITALIZATION	EXTENSION PROVISIONS	
	Mandatory (1)	If Requested by Patient (2)	(3)	Judicial Discretion as to Place (4)	Closed to Public (5)	Mandatory (6)	Unless Harmful (7)	If Requested by Patient (8)	Mandatory if Demanded by Patient (9)	Left to Discretion of Judge (10)	(11)	Suitable Hospital Accommodations Available (12)	Mental Condition (13)	(14)	Public or Private Hospital (15)	Outpatient Treatment fn. 3 (16)	(17)	Procedure fn. 4 (18)	Period fn. 5 (19)
N.M. Stat. Ann. (1979)	43-1-11(A)			fn. 30				right to be be present, but may be waived 43-1-11(B)			clear & convincing fn. 31 43-1-11(C)		43-1-12(G)	fn. 32	43-1-11(C)	such non-residential treatment as may be appropriate 43-1-11(D)	30 days 43-1-11(C)	petition for extended commitment 43-1-12	6 mos.; 1 yr. for petition filed after 2 6-mo. periods 43-1-12(C)
N.Y. Mental Hyg. Law (McKinney 1978 & Supp. 1981)																			
N.C. Gen. Stat. (1981)	122-58.7 (a)			122-58.7 (f)	unless patient requests open 122-58.7 (g)	may be waived w/consent of ct. 122-58.7 (d)				fn. 33	clear, cogent, & convincing 122-58.7 (i)	consent if private facility 122-58.8 (c)		right to appeal 122-58.9	122-58.8 (b)	122-58.8 (b)	90 days max. 122-58.8 (b)		
N.D. Cent. Code (1978 & Supp. 1981)	unless waived 25-03.1-19				25-03.1-19			right to attend 25-03.1-09(2)			clear & convincing 25-03.1-19			appeal: review of procedures, findings & conclusions 25-03.1-29	25-03.1-02(16)	25-03.1-21	90 days 25-03.1-22(1) extension 25-03.1-22(2)	petition & certificate; mandatory hearing 25-03.1-22(2)	indefinite 25-03.1-22(2)
OHIO Rev. Code Ann. (Baldwin 1980 & Supp. 1980)	5122.15(A)		referee optional 5122.15(A)		unless counsel & patient request open 5122.15 (A)(5)			5122.15(A) (2)			clear & convincing 5122.15(C)	community facilities 5122.15(D) consent, if not operated by dep't of mental health 5122.15(D)		judicial review of referee's order 5122.15(J) habeas corpus 5122.30	5122.15 (C)(1), (3), (4), (7) 5122.15 (C)(2), (5), (6)	5122.15(C) (6)	90 days 5122.15(C)	application & mandatory hearing: may not be waived 5122.15(H)	hearing every 2 yrs. 5122.15(H)
OKLA. Stat. Ann. (West 1979 & Supp. 1981)	43A, §54.4C						43A, §54.41 fn. 34		43A, §54.4C(4), (9)		clear & convincing 43A, §54.4J				public & private 43A, §54.4, 43A, §3(h) private 43A, §185	43A, §54.9B	indeterminate; annual review 43A, §54.11		
OR. Rev. Stat. (1979 & Supp. 1981)	426.070(3)			426.070(3)		426.070(3)					clear & convincing 426.130			appeal 426.135	fn. 35 426.060(2), (3), (4) fn. 35 426.130(1)	care by relatives fn. 35 426.130(2)	180 days 426.130(3)	medical certification; right to hearing to contest 426.301 426.307	180 days 426.301(3) (c)
PA. Stat. Ann. (Purdon 1969 & Supp. 1980)	50, §7304 (e)		optional mental health review officer 50, §7304 (e)(6)	50, §7304 (e)(6)	if requested by patient or counsel 50, §7304 (e)(4)						clear & convincing 50, §7304(f)				50, §7304 (f) §7103 §7105	50, §7304 (f)	90 days (1 yr. if criminal) charges) 50, §7304 (g)(1)	reapplication fn. 36 50, §7305(a)	180 days (1 yr. if criminal charges) 50, §7305(a)
R.I. Gen. Laws (1977 & Supp. 1980)	40.1-5.1-1 40.1-5.1-11 40.1-5-8		3 commissioners 40.1-5.1-9	fn. 37 40.1-5.1-2 40.1-5-8 (9)(c)		40.1-5.1-1 40.1-5.1-11					beyond reasonable doubt 40.1-5-8 (10)			judicial review of commissioner's report 40.1-5.1-12 right of appeal 40.1-5-8 (11)	40.1-5.1-3 40.1-5.1-12 40.1-5-8	40.1-5-8	6 mos. 40.1-5-8 (10)		
S.C. Code Ann. (Law. Co-op. 1976 & Supp. 1981)	44-17-540			44-17-570	at ct.'s discretion 44-17-570			right to be present may be waived 44-17-570			clear & convincing 44-17-580			on record 44-17-620	44-17-580 44-17-610	44-17-580	not stated re-examination every 6 mos. 44-17-820		

TABLE 2.7 JUDICIAL INSTITUTIONALIZATION OF MENTALLY ILL PERSONS—HEARING AND POSTHEARING PROCEDURES—*Continued*

STATE	HEARING: Mandatory (1)	HEARING: If Requested by Patient (2)	HEARING HELD BEFORE REFEREE OR FACT-FINDING COMMISSION (3)	CONDUCT OF HEARING: Judicial Discretion as to Place (4)	CONDUCT OF HEARING: Closed to Public (5)	PRESENCE OF PATIENT *fn. 1*: Mandatory (6)	PRESENCE OF PATIENT: Unless Harmful (7)	PRESENCE OF PATIENT: If Requested by Patient (8)	JURY TRIAL: Mandatory if Demanded by Patient (9)	JURY TRIAL: Left to Discretion of Judge (10)	STANDARD OF PROOF *fn. 2* (11)	INSTITUTION'S DISCRETION AS TO ADMISSION: Suitable Hospital Accommodations Available (12)	INSTITUTION'S DISCRETION AS TO ADMISSION: Mental Condition (13)	JUDICIAL REVIEW OF HOSPITALIZATION ORDER (14)	PLACE OF TREATMENT: Public or Private Hospital (15)	PLACE OF TREATMENT: Outpatient Treatment *fn. 3* (16)	PERIOD OF HOSPITALIZATION (17)	EXTENSION PROVISIONS: Procedure *fn. 4* (18)	EXTENSION PROVISIONS: Period *fn. 5* (19)
S.D. Codified Laws Ann. (1976 & Supp. 1981)																			
TENN. Code Ann. (1977 & Supp. 1981)	33-604(c)			33-604(c)	at ct.'s discretion 33-604(c)	unless waived by counsel in writing 33-604(c)					clear, unequivocal, & convincing 33-604(d)			regular appeal procedure 33-604(e)	33-604(d)		not stated 90 days after order & every 6 mos. there-after, may request exam 33-609(b) every 6 mos. super-intendent shall order an exam 33-609(d)		
TEX. Rev. Civ. Stat. Ann. (Vernon 1958 & Supp. 1981)	5547-43			5547-49(a)	at ct.'s discretion w/patient's consent 5547-49(c)			right to be present 5547-49(b)	5547-48					appeal to county cts. 5547-54 5547-57	5547-58 5547-59		indefinite if preceded by 60-day observation 5547-52 5547-40		
UTAH Code Ann. (1978 & Supp. 1981)	64-7-36(8)			64-7-36(9)	at ct.'s discretion 4-7-36(9)	waiver for good cause shown (a matter of ct. record) 64-7-36					clear & convincing 64-7-36			rehearing 64-7-36(13)	64-7-36(10) 64-7-28(6)		6 mos. or 64-7-36 (11)(a)	application & hearing 64-7-36(11)	indeter-minate; review every 6 mos. 64-7-36(11)
VT. Stat. Ann. (1968 & Supp. 1981)	18, §7615				at ct.'s discretion 18, §7615(e)			18, §7615(e)			clear & convincing 18, §7616(b)	testimony as to adequate & appropriate treatment 18, §7617(e)	testimony as to adequate & appropriate treatment 18, §7617(e)		18, §7617	18, §7618	90 days 18, §7619	application & hearing 18, §7620, §7621	indeter-minate 18, §7621 (b), (c)
VA. Code (1976 & Supp. 1981)	37.1-67.3			37.1-67.4		37.1-67.3							37.1-70	appeal de novo w/right to a jury 37.1-67.6	37.1-67.3 37.1-1(8)	fn. 38 37.1-67.3 37.1-121	180 days 37.1-67.3	reapplication 37.1-67.3	
WASH. Rev. Code Ann. (1975 & Supp. 1981)	unless waived 71.05.310					71.05.310			71.05.300		clear, cogent, & convincing evidence 71.05.310				71.05.324(1)	71.05.340	90 days max. 71.05.280	petition & hearing 71.05.320(2)	180 days 71.05.320(2)
W. Va. Code (Supp. 1981) *fn. 39*	27-5-4(g) (1)		mental hygiene commissioner (not binding on ct.) 27-5-1(b)	in chambers 27-5-4 (i)(1)		27-5-4(g) (1)					clear, cogent, & convincing 27-5-4(j)(3)			appeal to supreme ct. on verbatim transcript 27-5-5	27-5-4(k) (1)	custody of responsible person 27-5-4(o)	"indeter-minate" expiring in 2 yrs. 27-5-4(k) (1), (4)	exam; hearing if requested 27-5-4(k)(4)	2 yrs. 27-5-4(k)(4)
WIS. Stat. Ann. (West 1957 & Supp. 1981)	51.20(2)		optional commis-sioner 51.21(1)(c)	51.20(5)	right to open; may request closed 51.20(5)				51.20(2)		clear & convincing 51.20(13)(e)			regular appeal to ct. of appeals 51.20(15)	least restrictive facility 51.20(13) (f)	after institutional examination 51.20(13) (dm)	max. 6 mos. 51.20(13) (g)(1) 45 days if unable to provide for needs 51.20(13) (g)(2)	application & hearing 51.20(13) (g)(3) none	not to ex-exceed 1 yr. 51.20(13) (g)(1)
WYO. Stat. (1981)	25-3-112 (g)			25-3-112 (j)	persons not necessary to protect rights of parties excluded 25-3-112 (j)	unless waived 25-3-112 (j)			if requested 25-3-112 (h)	judge may order even if not requested 25-3-112 (h)	clear & convincing 25-3-112 (k)			direct appeal as in civil actions 25-3-124 (c)	25-3-112 (k)		indeter-minate; reexamined every 6 mos. 25-3-120		

FOOTNOTES TABLE 2.7

1. Evans v. Paderick, 443 F. Supp. 583 (E.D. Va. 1977). Constitutional requirement of right to a hearing and right to be present and to participate in due process.

2. Addington v. Texas, 441 U.S. 418 (1979). A clear and convincing standard is required by the Fourteenth Amendment in civil commitment proceedings for an indefinite period.

3. Outpatient treatment at discretion of and ordered by the court unless noted.

4. All extension procedures are initiated by a treating physician or director of the facility as distinguished from the majority of initial commitment proceedings that may be initiated by "any person." Generally the proceedings must be initiated or conducted prior to the expiration of the initial commitment order. In the states that specify a time when the proceedings must be initiated, the provisions range from 10 to 30 days prior to the expiration of the original order.

5. If the extension procedure is a reapplication for an original petition, then the period is the same as the original commitment unless noted.

6. Ala. Code § 22-52-15 (Supp. 1981). De novo in circuit court unless probate judge was learned in the law. In that case appeal is on the record in the court of civil appeals.

7. Ariz. Rev. Stat. Ann. § 36-540A, -540B, -540C (1974 & Supp. 1981). Clear and convincing evidence is required for the commitment of those who are dangerous to self or others but is apparently not required for the commitment of the gravely disabled.

8. Id. § 36-540A, -540B, -540C. Sixty days if danger to self, 180 days if danger to others, one year if gravely disabled.

9. Ark. Stat. Ann. § 59-1402(e) (Supp. 1981): "Appeals from the decision of the referee may be taken as a matter of right to the probate court in the county in which the case was decided." All commitment orders are considered final and appealable. Id. §§ 59-1423, -1424 (Supp. 1981).

10. Cal. Welf. & Inst. Code § 5304 (West Supp. 1980). Grounds for reapplication for treatment if patient has threatened, attempted, or actually inflicted physical harm to another while undergoing treatment.

11. Conn. Gen. Stat. Ann. § 17-177(a) (West Supp. 1981). Hearing is at hospital if the patient is confined there and it would be detrimental to require travel to the court.

12. Id. § 17-188 (West 1975). Court may order for a specified period. See id. § 17-178(g) (West Supp. 1981). At least every two years it shall hold a hearing on need for continued treatment.

13. In re Holmes, 422 A.2d 969 (D.C. 1980). One cannot be civilly committed on a finding supported by less than clear and convincing evidence.

14. In re Walls, 442 F.2d 749 (D.C. Cir. 1971). The court may reject the commission's findings and consider additional evidence.

15. In re Jones, 338 F. Supp. 428 (D.D.C. 1972). Court has the authority to explore alternative courses and facilities both outside and within the hospital for treatment of patient who is involuntarily committed.

16. Reigosa v. State, 362 So.2d 714 (Fla. Dist. Ct. App. 1978). Clear and convincing.

17. Fla. Stat. Ann. § 394.467(3)(b) (West Supp. 1981). The administrator of a treatment facility may refuse admission to any patient who is not accompanied by adequate orders and documentation.

18. Hawaii Rev. Stat. § 334-60(b)(4)(C) (Supp. 1981): "Shall be present unless he waives his right to be present, is unable to attend or creates conditions which make it impossible to conduct the hearing in a reasonable manner."

19. Idaho Code § 66-329(k) (Supp. 1981). The director of the department of health and welfare "shall determine within twenty-four (24) hours the least restrictive available facility consistent with the needs of each patient committed under this section for observation, care, and treatment." Glascoe v. Brassard, 94 Idaho 162, 483 P.2d 924 (1971), interpreted the previous provision, authorizing the director to determine the disposition of each patient at a treatment facility (Idaho Code § 66-329(i) (1980)), to include possible assignment to outpatient treatment centers.

20. Ill. Ann. Stat. ch. 91½, § 3-809 (Smith-Hurd Supp. 1980): "If the court is not satisfied with the verdict of the jury finding the respondent subject to involuntary admission, it may set aside such verdict and order the respondent discharged or it may order another hearing."

21. Iowa Code Ann. § 229.12(2) (West Supp. 1980). Hearing is closed, except that the court may admit persons having a legitimate interest in the hearing.

22. Id. § 229.12:

> The respondent has the right to be present at the hearing. If the respondent exercises that right and has been medicated within twelve hours, or such longer period of time as the court may designate, prior to the beginning of the hearing, . . . the judge shall be informed of that fact and of the probable effects of the medication upon convening of the hearing. . . . Upon motion of the county attorney, the judge may exclude the respondent from the hearing during the testimony of any particular witness if the judge determines that that witness' testimony is likely to cause the respondent severe emotional trauma.

23. Kentucky has two provisions: one for a 60-day commitment and one for a 360-day commitment.

24. Superintendent of Worcester State Hospital v. Hagberg, 372 N.E.2d 242 (1978). Proof beyond a reasonable doubt.

25. Minn. Stat. Ann. § 253A.7(12) (West 1982): "The court may exclude from the hearing any person not necessary for the conduct of the proceedings except those persons to whom notice was given . . . and any other persons requested to be present by the proposed patient."

26. Lausche v. Commission of Public Welfare, 302 Minn. 65, 225 N.W.2d 366, cert. denied, 420 U.S. 993 (1974). Standard of proof beyond reasonable doubt must be employed with regard to initial commitment of allegedly mentally ill person (emphasis added).

27. Proctor v. Butler, 117 N.H. 927, 380 A.2d 673 (1977). Proof beyond a reasonable doubt is required in determinations of mental illness and potential dangerousness under statute establishing likelihood-of-danger criterion for involuntary commitment.

28. Coll v. Hyland, 411 F. Supp. 905 (D.N.J. 1976). New Jersey procedures in civil commitment hearings providing that patient must appear at hearing but may be excused during all or part of testimony for good cause, including testimony by psychiatrist that patient's mental condition would be adversely affected if he or she heard candid and complete testimony, is constitutionally satisfactory; due process is adequately safeguarded by requirement that patient's attorney be present in the few situations where the patient, for his or her own benefit, should be excluded.

29. In re J. W., 44 N.J. Super. 216, 130 A.2d 64 (App. Div.), cert. denied, 132 A.2d 558 (1957). Beyond a reasonable doubt.

30. 1979 Op. Att'y Gen. No. 79-20, cited in N.M. Stat. Ann. § 43-1-13 (Supp. 1981). Absent a showing by the "developmentally disabled" person that his or her substantive rights will be in any way abridged if his or her involuntary commitment hearing is not held at the county seat, the district court is not precluded from adopting the practice of holding such hearings at the commitment facility when, in its discretion, such practice will better serve the public convenience.

31. In re Valdez, 88 N.M. 338, 540 P.2d 818 (1975). Although the highest standard of proof would be desirable, in the civil commitment process proof beyond a reasonable doubt is too stringent. Proof that is clear, cogent, and convincing is the highest standard of proof possible at the current state of the medical arts. On the other hand, preponderance of evidence is "definitely" constitutionally unacceptable.

32. State v. Pernell, 590 P.2d 638 (N.M. Ct. App. 1979). A person involuntarily committed under N.M. Stat. Ann. § 43-1-11 (1979) has a right to appear under N.M. Const. art. VI, § 2, even though no appeal is provided for by statute.

33. Failure to provide a jury trial in involuntary commitment proceedings does not violate the equal protection clause. French v. Blackburn, 428 F. Supp. 1351 (M.D.N.C. 1977), aff'd, 443 U.S. 901 (1979). See also Duncan v. Louisiana, 391 U.S. 145 (1968).

34. Okla. Stat. Ann. tit. 43A, § 54.4I (West Supp. 1981). Patient has right to be present unless harmful or disruptive, but

> The court may not decide in advance of the hearing, solely on the basis of the certificate of the Examining Commission, that the person alleged to be a person requiring treatment should not be allowed nor required to appear. It shall be made to appear to the court based upon clear and convincing evidence that alternatives to exclusion were attempted before the court renders his removal for that purpose or determines that his appearance at such hearing would be improper and unsafe.

35. Or. Rev. Stat. § 426.130 (1981):

> (1) If the mentally ill person is willing and able to participate in treatment on a voluntary basis, and the court finds that he will probably do so, the court shall order the release of the individual and dismiss the case.
>
> (2) If the legal guardian, relative or friend of the mentally ill person requests that he be allowed to care for the mentally ill person . . . in a place satisfactory to the judge, and shows that he is able to care for the mentally ill person, the court may order that the mentally ill person be conditionally released and placed in his care and custody.

36. Pa. Stat. Ann. tit. 50, § 7305(a) (Purdon Supp. 1980). Additional commitment requires a "further finding of a need for continuing involuntary treatment as shown by conduct during the person's most recent period of court-ordered treatment." A person found dangerous to himself or herself is subject to additional commitment only if first released to a less restrictive alternative (not applicable where judge or mental health review officer has determined that such release would not be in the person's best interest).

37. R.I. Gen. Laws § 40.1-5.1-2 (Supp. 1981):

> a certificate signed by 2 practicing physicians . . . which shall declare that said alleged insane person is an invalid or that his condition, mental or physical, is such that he cannot, without serious prejudice to his welfare, be examined in open court, district courts are hereby empowered . . . to hold such examinations at such times and places . . . as shall be most conducive to the health and comfort of the person to be examined.

38. Va. Code § 37.1-121 (Supp. 1981). Director of state hospital may place a committed patient "at board in a suitable family in this state."

39. This procedure is the same as that for administrative hospitalization (table 3.4). It is an alternative to it.

TABLE 2.[illegible] INVOLUNTARY INSTITUTIONALIZATION OF DEVELOPMENTALLY DISABLED PERSONS—PREHEARING PROCEDURES

STATE	TYPE OF DISABILITY (1)	PROCEDURE FOR INVOLUNTARY INSTITUTIONIZATION (2)	APPLICATION BY (3)	COURT (4)	CRITERIA FOR INSTITUTIONALIZATION: Individual: Dangerous to Self or Others (5)	Individual: Unable to Provide for Basic Needs (6)	Individual: Other (7)	Systemic: No Less Restrictive Alternative (8)	Systemic: Other (9)	SUPPORTING EVIDENCE FOR APPLICATION (10)	PREHEARING MEDICAL EXAMINATION ORDERED BY COURT (11)	DISMISSAL AFTER MEDICAL EXAM (12)	PREHEARING DETENTION (13)	NOTICE OF HEARING OR ADMISSION: Guardian (14)	Relative (15)	Attorney (16)	Patient (17)	When (18)
ALA. Code (1975 & Supp. 1981)	mentally retarded 22-52-55(a)	medical certification on judicial order 22-52-55	any responsible person 22-52-55(a)	probate 22-52-55(a)		parents or guardian has failed to provide care 22-52-55(a) AND	in need of treatment 22-52-55 (a), (d) unanimity of physicians' report 22-52-55 (e) AND		available adequate facilities 22-52-54		2 physicians 22-52-55(c)	if physicians don't agree that mentally retarded 22-52-55(d)	22-52-55(b)					
ALAS. Stat. (1979 & Supp. 1981)	developmentally disabled 47.80.900(7)	none																
ARIZ. Rev. Stat. Ann. (1974 & Supp. 1981)	developmentally disabled 8-242 36-560	no judicial admissions except for juvenile offenders 8-242 36-560(F)																
ARK. Stat. Ann. (1977 & Supp. 1981): Adults	developmentally defective 59-1308(C)	judicial commitment for long-term protective custody 59-1308(C)	anyone authorized to take into protective custody 59-1308(C)	probate 59-1308(C)	danger to life or health if remains at residence or in care of parent or guardian 59-1308(C) AND		unable to provide protection from abuse or neglect 59-1308(C) AND	59-1308(C)			59-1308(C)			59-1308(C)	59-1308(C)	59-1308(C)	59-1308(C)	10 days prior to hearing 59-1308(C)
Children	mentally defective 59-1104(a)(7) emotionally disturbed, mentally retarded 59-1132 59-1133	judicial commitment 59-1105	parent or guardian to board; board to ct. 59-1104 59-1105	probate 59-1105(c)		incapable of managing self or affairs 59-1103(2) AND	welfare requires care, training, education of facility 59-1103(2)		adequate facilities 59-1105(a)	board determination of suitability for admission 59-1105(a)	optional 59-1105(c)							
CAL. Welf. & Inst. Code (West 1972 & Supp. 1980)	mentally retarded 6500	judicial commitment 6502	parent, guardian, conservator, probation officer, youth authority, any person designated by ct. 6502	superior 6502	6500 AND			6504.5			ct.-appointed examiner 6504.5		6505, 6506	discretionary 6504	discretionary 6504	conservator discretionary 6504	6504	
COLO. Rev. Stat. (1973 & Supp. 1981)	developmentally disabled 27-10.5-103 27-10.5-104	short-term medical certification 27-10.5-103 long-term medical certification 27-10.5-104	any person (short-term) 27-10.5-103 parent, guardian, or custodian (long-term) 27-10.5-104	district (probate in Denver) 27-10.5-102(3)			suitable for admission; person may benefit from care & treatment 27-10.5-102(13) 27-10.5-103(1) 27-10.5-104(1)			written agreement between facility & applicant 27-10.5-103(3) 27-10.5-104(5)	preadmission evaluation (long-term) 27-10.5-104(4)			notice of admission to ct. 27-10.5-103(4) 27-10.5-104(6)	notice of admission to ct. 27-10.5-103(4) 27-10.5-104(6)			next day 27-10.5-103(4) 27-10.5-104(6)
CONN. Gen. Stat. Ann. (West 1977 & Supp. 1982)	developmentally disabled 19-569d	judicial commitment 19-569d	relative, guardian, commissioner of human resources, selectmen, or welfare dep't head 19-569d(a)	probate 19-569d(a)			mentally retarded, not mentally ill, & has no communicable disease 19-569d				psychologist 19-569d(c)						19-569d(c)	immediately upon filing of application 19-569d(c)

TABLE 2.8 INVOLUNTARY INSTITUTIONALIZATION OF DEVELOPMENTALLY DISABLED PERSONS—PREHEARING PROCEDURES—*Continued*

					CRITERIA FOR INSTITUTIONALIZATION									NOTICE OF HEARING OR ADMISSION				
					Individual			*Systemic*										
STATE	TYPE OF DISABILITY (1)	PROCEDURE FOR INVOLUNTARY INSTITUTIONIZATION (2)	APPLICATION BY (3)	COURT (4)	Dangerous to Self or Others (5)	Unable to Provide for Basic Needs (6)	Other (7)	No Less Restrictive Alternative (8)	Other (9)	SUPPORTING EVIDENCE FOR APPLICATION (10)	PREHEARING MEDICAL EXAMINATION ORDERED BY COURT (11)	DISMISSAL AFTER MEDICAL EXAM (12)	PREHEARING DETENTION (13)	*Guardian* (14)	*Relative* (15)	*Attorney* (16)	*Patient* (17)	*When* (18)
DEL. Code Ann. (1974 & Supp. 1980)	mentally retarded 16, §5522	medical certification 16, §5522	recommendation of mental hygiene clinic or state psychiatrist 16, §5522 (a)(1)	on appeal: chancery 16, §5522(b)	presence in community detrimental to self or community 16, §5522(a)	presence in community detrimental to self or community 16, §5522(a)	presence in community detrimental to self or community 16, §5522(a)			certification by at least 2 physicians 16, §5522(a)								
D.C. Code Ann. (1981)	mentally retarded 6-1924	judicial commitment 6-1924	parent or guardian 6-1924(a)	superior 6-1902(8)			person at least moderately retarded, not competent to refuse commitment if over 14, requires habilitation, & commitment necessary for habilitation 6-1924(b) (1), (2)	6-1924(b)(4)	facility capable of providing habilitation 6-1924(b)(3)	comprehensive evaluation report 6-1943	unless a report included in petition 6-1943					6-1668	6-1668	
FLA. Stat. Ann. (West 1973 & Supp. 1981)	mentally retarded 393.11	judicial commitment 393.11	3-person petition committee (at least 1 physician) 393.11(3)(a)	circuit 393.11(1)	393.11(1) OR	lacks survival & self-care skills 393.11(1) AND	lacks capacity to consent to voluntary 393.11(1) AND	393.11			examining commission of at least 3: physician, psychologist, social worker 393.11(3)(b)							
GA. Code Ann. (1979 & Supp. 1980)	mentally retarded 88-2504	judicial commitment 88-2504	any person 88-2504(a)	probate or juvenile 88-2502 (n)(1), (2)			client requires services & 24-hr. training & parent or guardian has failed or is unable to provide 88-2204	88-2504 (f) AND	bed appropriate to client's needs available 88-2504(f)		comprehensive report of evaluation team 88-2504(b)	88-2504(d)		guardian or representative 88-2504(e)			88-2504(e)	72 hrs. after report filed 88-2504(e)
HAWAII Rev. Stat. (1976 & Supp. 1981)	mentally retarded 333-26	judicial commitment 333-26	adult relative or guardian or authorized government agent 333-26	family 333-26	requires institutional care for own or other's welfare 333-24 AND	incapable of self-support & management 333-24 AND	mentally retarded			1 certificate by physician, psychologist, & social worker 333-26				333-27	parent 333-27		333-27	10 days prior to hearing 333-27
IDAHO Code (1976 & Supp. 1981)	mentally retarded; mentally deficient 56-237(d)	judicial commitment 56-237	friend, relative, spouse, guardian, licensed physician, public officer of a municipality, county, or state, or head of public or private hospital where such person may be 56-237(a)	a ct. of competent jurisdiction 56-237(a)	56-237 (b)(2) AND		mentally retarded or deficient 56-237(h)(1) or is in need of care, custody, or treatment & lacks capacity to make responsible decisions 56-237(h)(3)		56-237(j)	1 certificate from director or written statement from applicant that individual refused to submit to an exam 56-237(a)	if no certificate, at least 2 examiners; if a certificate, at least 1 examiner 56-237(b)	56-237(b)		56-237(d) OR	spouse, parents, other known relative or friend 56-237(d)		unless injurious to patient 56-237(d)	

TABLE 2.8 INVOLUNTARY INSTITUTIONALIZATION OF DEVELOPMENTALLY DISABLED PERSONS—PREHEARING PROCEDURES—*Continued*

STATE	TYPE OF DISABILITY (1)	PROCEDURE FOR INVOLUNTARY INSTITUTION-IZATION (2)	APPLICATION BY (3)	COURT (4)	CRITERIA FOR INSTITUTIONALIZATION: Individual: Dangerous to Self or Others (5)	Individual: Unable to Provide for Basic Needs (6)	Individual: Other (7)	Systemic: No Less Restrictive Alternative (8)	Systemic: Other (9)	SUPPORTING EVIDENCE FOR APPLICATION (10)	PREHEARING MEDICAL EXAMINATION ORDERED BY COURT (11)	DISMISSAL AFTER MEDICAL EXAM (12)	PREHEARING DETENTION (13)	NOTICE OF HEARING OR ADMISSION: *Guardian* (14)	*Relative* (15)	*Attorney* (16)	*Patient* (17)	*When* (18)
ILL. Ann. Stat. (Smith-Hurd 1966 & Supp. 1980)	mentally retarded 91½, §4-500 develop-mentally disabled 91½, §4-300	judicial commitment 91½, §4-500 adminis-trative admission 91½, §4-300	any person 91½, §4-501(a) guardian (or parent if minor) 91½, §4-302	circuit 91½, §4-100 if contested, circuit 91½, §4-307 §4-100	reasonably expected to inflict serious harm on self or others in near future 91½, §4-500		recommen-dation of diagnostic report 91½, §4-304 suitable for admission §4-302	91½, §4-301(a)		optional medical certificate 91½, §4-501(b) diagnostic evaluation of at least 1 physician & 1 psychologist 91½, §34-300	if no certificate filed 91½, §4-502(a)		for exam 91½, §4-504 §4-300(a) §4-306(a)	91½, §4-505 §4-206	91½, §4-505 §4-206	91½, §4-505 91½, §4-307	91½, §4-505 91½, §4-307	
IND. Code Ann. (Burns 1973 & Supp. 1982)	mentally retarded & develop-mentally disabled 16-16-1-1	none																
IOWA Code Ann. (West 1969 & Supp. 1980)	mentally retarded 222.16	judicial commit-222.16	relative, guardian, or reputable citizen of county 222.16	district 222.16	conducive to welfare of person & community 222.17	conducive to welfare of person & community 222.17	conducive to welfare of person & community 222.17				discretionary, 1 physician & 1 psy-chologist 222.28		222.25	222.20 222.19(4)	parents, persons caring for or living w/re-spondent 220.20 220.19(1)		220.20 220.19	
KAN. Stat. Ann. (1976 & Supp. 1981)		none																
KY. Rev. Stat. Ann. (Michie 1978 & Supp. 1980) *fn. 1*	mentally retarded 202B.020	judicial commit-ment same *procedures* as for mentally ill *fn. 1* 202B.020	friend, relative, spouse, or guardian *fn. 1* 202A.060 (1)		immediate AND 202B.070 (9)			202B.070 AND (9)	treatment that can reasonably be expected to benefit available 202B.070 (9)		2 physicians *fn. 1* 202A.070 (3) 202A.080 (2)	*fn. 1* 202A.070 (6) 202A.080 (3)	*fn. 1* 202A.070 (5)	*fn. 1* 202A.070 (2)	*fn. 1* 202A.070 (2)		*fn. 1* 202A.070 (2)	
LA. Rev. Stat. Ann. (West 1975 & Supp. 1981)	mentally retarded 28:398	judicial commit-ment 28:398	relative, spouse, or any person 28:398A	district 28:398A	28:392B AND (4)	28:392(B) (4)		right to least restrictive 28:390(B) (1)		evaluation report, if available & any med-ical records 28:398A	28:398D					28:398C	28:398C	at least 5 days be-fore hearing 28:398C
ME. Rev. Stat. Ann. (1978 & Supp. 1981)	mentally retarded 34, §2651	judicial certification for ad-mission of client not capable of informed consent 34, §2659 -A	dep't of mental health 34, §2659 -A(1)	district 34, §2659 (1)		unable AND to protect self from or avoid physical or psycho-logical impairment 34, §2652 (1)(H)	needs in-stitutional services 34, §2659 -A(4)	34, §2659 AND -A(4)	services available at petitioning facility 34, §2659 -A(4)		34, §2659-A(2)			34, §2659-(A)(2)(B)	34, §2659-A(2)(B)		34, §2659-A(2)(B)	
MD. Ann. Code (1981 & Supp. 1981)	mentally retarded 59A	medical certifica-tion by mental retardation adminis-tration 59A, §10 private facility 59A, §11	guardian or anyone w/legitimate interest in person 59A, §§10, 11	hearing w/in 21 days of admission 59A, §10(f) §11(e)	for protec-tion or adequate care of self or others 59A, §10(b) 59A, §11(b)	for protec-tion or adequate care of self or others 59A, §10(b) 59A, §11(b)		59A, §10(c) 59A, §11(c)			ordered by facility or adminis-tration 59A, §10(b) 59A, §11(b)	59A, §10(c) 59A, §11(c)	59A, §10 59A, §11	notice of hearing to proponent of admission 59A, §10(e) 59A, §11(e)	notice of hearing to proponent of admission 59A, §10(e) 59A, §11(e)		59A, §10(e) 59A, §11(d)	to patient upon admis-sion; to pro-ponent of admission no later than w/in 5 days 59A, §10(e) 59A, §11(d)
MASS. Ann. Laws (Michie/Law. Co-op. 1981 & Supp. 1982)	mentally retarded 123, §1	none																

TABLE 2.8 INVOLUNTARY INSTITUTIONALIZATION OF DEVELOPMENTALLY DISABLED PERSONS—PREHEARING PROCEDURES—*Continued*

STATE	TYPE OF DISABILITY (1)	PROCEDURE FOR INVOLUNTARY INSTITUTION-IZATION (2)	APPLICATION BY (3)	COURT (4)	CRITERIA FOR INSTITUTIONALIZATION — Individual — Dangerous to Self or Others (5)	Unable to Provide for Basic Needs (6)	Other (7)	Systemic — No Less Restrictive Alternative (8)	Other (9)	SUPPORTING EVIDENCE FOR APPLICATION (10)	PREHEARING MEDICAL EXAMINATION ORDERED BY COURT (11)	DISMISSAL AFTER MEDICAL EXAM (12)	PREHEARING DETENTION (13)	NOTICE OF HEARING OR ADMISSION — Guardian (14)	Relative (15)	Attorney (16)	Patient (17)	When (18)
MICH. Comp. Laws Ann. (1980 & Supp. 1981)	mentally retarded *fn. 2* 330.1515 (a)	judicial commitment 330.1515 (a)	any person found suit-able by ct. 330.1516		can be AND reasonably expected to seriously injure self or others in near future 330.1515		overt act 330.1515			names of witnesses 330.1516 (2)	2 examiners 330.1516 (3), (6)	unless both examiners conclude person admittable 330.1516 (7)	330.1516 (5)	330.1517 (2)(c)	330.1517 (2)(c)	330.1517 (2)(c)	330.1517 (2)(c)	as early as practicable & sufficiently in advance 330.1517 (2)(c)
MINN. Stat. Ann. (West 1982)	mentally deficient 253A.07	judicial commit-ment: same *provisions* as for mentally ill 253A.07	any person 253A.07 (1)	probate 253A.07 (1)	attempted OR to harm self or others 253A.07 (17)(b)	253A.07 OR (17)(b)	failed to AND protect self from ex-ploitation 253A.07 (17)(b)	253A.07 (17)(b)		medical certificate or statement that unable to obtain 253A.07(2)	253A.07 (2)		253A.07 (3)	1 interested person 253A.07 (9)	1 interested person 253A.07 (9)	253A.07 (9)	253A.07 (9)	at least 5 days before hearing 253A.07 (9)
MISS. Code Ann. (1981) *fn. 3*	mentally retarded 41-19-11 (b) 41-19-151 (b)	judicial commit-ment: same *procedures* as for mentally ill *fn. 3* 41-19-11 (b) 41-19-151 (b)	any relative or citizen 41-19-11 (b) 41-19-151 (b)	chancery 41-19-11 (b) 41-19-151 (b)	likely to become so OR if left at large 41-19-151 (b) 41-19-11 (b)		needs care, supervision, or control 41-19-151 (b) 41-19-11 (b)				*fn. 3* 41-21-67 (2)	*fn. 3* 41-21-71 (1)	*fn. 3* 41-21-71 (2)	*fn. 3* OR 41-21-73	2 nearest *fn. 3* 41-21-73	*fn. 3* 41-21-73	*fn. 3* 41-21-73	"reasonable" notice *fn. 3* 41-21-73
MO. Ann. Stat. (Vernon 1979 & Supp. 1980)	mentally retarded or develop-mentally disabled 633.120	only emergency detention (procedures as for mentally ill) 633.160			imminent likelihood of serious harm to self or others 633.160													
MONT. Code Ann. (1981)	develop-mentally disabled 53-20-121	judicial commit-ment 53-20-121	any person *fn. 4* 53-20-121	district 53-20-102 (3)			seriously AND develop-mentally disabled 53-20-125 (3)		available community services not adequate 53-20-125 (3)		after finding of probable cause 53-20-122 (3)	53-20-123 (1)	emergency admission 53-20-129	53-20-125	53-20-125		53-20-125	
NEB. Rev. Stat. (1976 & Supp. 1981)	mentally retarded 83-217 83-382	none																
NEV. Rev. Stat. (1981)	mentally retarded 435.123 mentally retarded children 435.030	judicial commit-ment 435.123 adminis-trative 435.030	parent, guardian or other responsible person 435.123 parent, relative, guardian, or nearest friend 435.030(1)	district ct. 435.123	435.128(a) AND	*fn. 5*	mentally AND retarded & in need of institutional training & treatment 435.128	no less AND restrictive alternative consistent w/person's best interests 435.128(c)	appropriate space & programs available at admis-sion site 435.128(b)	1 certificate signed by physician or certified psychologist 435.123	435.125			petitioner 435.128	petitioner 435.128	435.128	435.128	
N.H. Rev. Stat. Ann. (1978 & Supp. 1981)	develop-mentally impaired 171-A	none																
N.J. Stat. Ann. (West 1981)	mentally retarded 30:4-25:1 develop-mentally disabled 30:6D-1	none																
N.M. Stat. Ann. (1979 & Supp. 1981)	develop-mentally disabled 43-1-13	judicial commit-ment 43-1-13	guardian *fn. 6* 43-1-13A	district 43-1-3F	imminent OR likelihood of harm to self or others 43-1-13E	greatly AND disabled & in patient's best interest 43-1-13E		least drastic means 43-1-13E						43-1-13(c)		43-1-13(c)	43-1-13(c)	

TABLE 2.8 INVOLUNTARY INSTITUTIONALIZATION OF DEVELOPMENTALLY DISABLED PERSONS—PREHEARING PROCEDURES—*Continued*

STATE	TYPE OF DISABILITY (1)	PROCEDURE FOR INVOLUNTARY INSTITUTIONIZATION (2)	APPLICATION BY (3)	COURT (4)	CRITERIA FOR INSTITUTIONALIZATION — *Individual* — Dangerous to Self or Others (5)	*Individual* — Unable to Provide for Basic Needs (6)	*Individual* — Other (7)	*Systemic* — No Less Restrictive Alternative (8)	*Systemic* — Other (9)	SUPPORTING EVIDENCE FOR APPLICATION (10)	PREHEARING MEDICAL EXAMINATION ORDERED BY COURT (11)	DISMISSAL AFTER MEDICAL EXAM (12)	PREHEARING DETENTION (13)	NOTICE OF HEARING OR ADMISSION — *Guardian* (14)	*Relative* (15)	*Attorney* (16)	*Patient* (17)	*When* (18)
N.Y. Mental Hyg. Law (McKinney 1978 & Supp. 1981)	mentally retarded 15.27	medical certification 15.27	limited group *fn. 7* 15.27(b)				in need of care & treatment, treatment essential to welfare, & unable to understand need for 15.27 15.01			for admission: 2 physician's certificates or 1 physician & 1 psychologist 15.27(a)					nearest relative 15.29(b)(1)		3 designated by patient 15.29(b(2)	w/in 5 days of admission 15.29(b)
N.C. Gen. Stat. (1981)	mentally retarded 122-58.1	judicial commitment: same provisions as for mentally ill 122-58.1 to 122-58.26	any person 122-58.3(a)	district or superior 122-58.3(a)	122-58.7 (c) OR	122-58.7 (i) 122-58.2 (1)(a)(1)(I) AND	accompanying behavior disorder cause of committable condition 122-58.7(i)	122-58.8(b)			122-58.3(b)	122-58.4(c)	122-58.4(c) 122-58.6			122-58.5	122-58.5	48 hrs. before hearing 122-58.5
N.D. Cent. Code (1978 & Supp. 1981)	mentally deficient 25-04	none																
OHIO Rev. Code Ann. (Baldwin 1980 & Supp. 1981)	mentally retarded 5123.71	judicial commitment 5123.71	not stated 5123.71	probate division of common pleas 5123.71	substantial risk of injury to self 5123.01(L) & at least moderately retarded AND	5123.01(L) OR	at least moderately retarded & needs & susceptible to habilitation 5123.01(L) AND		provision for needs not available in community 5123.01(L)	evaluation report or statement of refusal to submit 5123.71(B)	evaluation report, if not submitted w/application 5123.74		emergency 5123.71(C)	5123.73(A)(2)	5123.73(A)	5123.73(A)(7)	5123.73(A)(1)	after receipt of affidavit 5123.73(A)
OKLA. Stat. Ann. (West 1979 & Supp. 1981)	mentally retarded 43A, §57	none																
OR. Rev. Stat. (1981)	mentally retarded 427.215	judicial commitment 427.235	any 2 persons 427.235(1)	probate, county, or circuit 427.235(1)	427.290 OR	427.290 AND	not receiving care necessary for health, safety, & habilitation 427.290			diagnostic evaluation report of community mental health program for probable cause 427.235(3)	if requested by patient, parent, or guardian 427.270(2)		427.255	if minor or incapacitated 427.245(2)	parent, if minor or incapacitated 427.245(2)		427.245(2)	upon probable cause determination 427.245(2)
PA. Stat. Ann. (Purdon 1969 & Supp. 1980)	mentally retarded *fn. 8* 50, §4406	judicial commit 50, §4406	limited group & any responsible person 50, §4406 (a)(1)	common pleas 50, §4406 (a)			mentally disabled & in need of care & treatment *fn. 8* 50, §4406 (a)			physician certificate or statement of efforts to obtain 50, §4406	after hearing 50, §4406 (a)(4)		50, §4406	notification of parties in interest 50, §4406 (a)(3)	notification of parties in interest 50, §4406 (a)(3)	notification of parties in interest 50, §4406 (a)(3)		
R.I. Gen. Laws (1977 & Supp. 1981)	mentally retarded 40.1-22-9	medical certification 40.1-22-9(1)	director of dep't of mental retardation, relative, guardian 40.1-22-9(1)	if certification objected to: district ct. hearing 40.1-22-9(1)	likelihood of serious harm to self or others (ct.) 40.1-22-10(5)		in need of immediate care & treatment (administrative) 40.1-22-9(1)			physician's certificate 40.1-22-9(1)	if requested by counsel for hearing 40.1-22-10(4)			40.1-22-10(4)	40.1-22-10(4)		40.1-22-10(4)	
S.C. Code Ann. (Law. Co-op. 1976 & Supp. 1981)	mentally retarded 44-21-90	judicial commitment 44-21-90	spouse, relative, guardian, director of facility or dep't of social services 44-21-90	probate or family 44-21-90			mentally retarded & in need of placement in facility 44-21-90				44-21-90			44-21-90	44-21-90		at discretion of ct. 44-21-90	

TABLE 2.8 INVOLUNTARY INSTITUTIONALIZATION OF DEVELOPMENTALLY DISABLED PERSONS—PREHEARING PROCEDURES—*Continued*

STATE	TYPE OF DISABILITY (1)	PROCEDURE FOR INVOLUNTARY INSTITUTION-IZATION (2)	APPLICATION BY (3)	COURT (4)	CRITERIA FOR INSTITUTIONALIZATION: *Individual*: Dangerous to Self or Others (5)	Unable to Provide for Basic Needs (6)	Other (7)	*Systemic*: No Less Restrictive Alternative (8)	Other (9)	SUPPORTING EVIDENCE FOR APPLICATION (10)	PREHEARING MEDICAL EXAMINATION ORDERED BY COURT (11)	DISMISSAL AFTER MEDICAL EXAM (12)	PREHEARING DETENTION (13)	NOTICE OF HEARING OR ADMISSION: *Guardian* (14)	*Relative* (15)	*Attorney* (16)	*Patient* (17)	*When* (18)
S.D. Codified Laws Ann. 1976 & Supp. 1981)	mentally retarded 27B-7-1	adminis-trative commit-ment hearing 27B-7-1	any person 27B-7-2	board of mental retardation 27B-7-1		unable to properly manage or care for self 27B-7-1 AND	care necessary & advisable 27B-7-1				27B-7-3	27B-7-7	if necessary for exam or protection 27B-7-4 27B-7-5			27B-7-8(3)	27B-7-8(3)	upon receipt of petition 27B-7-8(3)
TENN. Code Ann. (1977 & Supp. 1981)	mentally retarded 33-501	none																
TEX. Rev. Civ. Stat. Ann. (Vernon 1958 & Supp. 1981)	mentally retarded 5547-300, §37	judicial commit-ment 5547-300, §37	parent, guardian, or interested person 5547-300, §37(f)	county 5547-300, §37(e)	substantial risk of physical injury to self or others 5547-300, §37(b) OR	5547-300, §37(b) AND		5547-300, §37(b) AND	treatment available at facility 5547-300, §37(b)	diagnosis & evaluation team report, if completed 5547-300, §37(h)	diagnosis & evaluation team report 5547-300, §37(i)		protective custody 5547-300, §37(k)	5547-300, §37(j)	parent of minor 5547-300, §37(j)	5547-300, §37(j)	5547-300, §37(j)	10 days before hearing 5547-300, §37(j)
UTAH Code Ann. (1977 & Supp. 1981)	mentally retarded 64-8-13	judicial commit-ment 64-8-16	any person 64-8-16	district 64-8-16	social menace 64-8-20 OR	unable to properly care for self 64-8-20					64-8-18			subpoena 2 or more persons best acquainted w/patient to testify 64-8-17	subpoena 2 or more persons best acquainted w/patient to testify 64-8-17			
VT. Stat. Ann. (1968 & Supp. 1981)	mentally retarded 18, §8820	judicial commit-ment 18, §8822	interested person *fn. 9* 18, §8822(b)	district 18, §8822 (a)	to self 18, §8828 (c) §8821 AND		in need of treatment 18, §8828 (c) AND	18, §8828 (c) §8821 AND	treatment & habilitation available 18, §8821	medical certificate or statement that patient refused 18, §8822 (c)	18, §8826 (a)	at any stage of proceedings 18, §8823 (c)	emergency 18, §8830	18, §8825 (a)(3)	18, §8825 (a)(3)	18, §8825 (a)(3)	18, §8825 (a)(3)	upon filing of petition 18, §8825 (a)(3)
VA. Code (1976 & Supp. 1981)	mentally retarded 37.1-65.1	judicial certification *fn. 10* 37.1-65.1	parent, guardian, or responsible person 37.1-65.1 (A)	district 37.1-65.1 (c) 37.1-1(11)			incapable of request-ing admis-sion & in need of training & treatment 37.1-65.1 (C3) AND	37.1-65.1 (C3) AND	approval of proposed facility 37.1-65.1 (C3)	prescreening report 37.1-65.1 (B)(i)	37.1-65.1 (C2)		37.1-65.1 (B)	or committee 37.1-65.1 (C)		37.1-65.1 (C)	37.1-65.1 (C)	
WASH. Rev. Code Ann. (1975 & Supp. 1981)	mentally retarded 71.05.040	none																
W. VA. Code (1980) *fn. 11*	mentally retarded 27-5-2(a)(1)	judicial commit-ment: same provisions as for mentally ill 27-5-2	any person 27-5-2(a)	circuit 27-5-2(b)(2)	27-5-4 (j)(1) AND			27-5-4(j)(2)		medical certificate or state-ment of patient's refusal 27-5-4(d)	27-5-2(b)(4) 27-5-4(f)(1)	27-5-4(f)(3)	before prob-able cause 27-5-2(b)(4) after 27-5-3	27-5-4(e)	27-5-4(e)		27-5-4(e)	8 days before hearing 27-5-4(e)
WIS. Stat. Ann. (West 1957 & Supp. 1981)	develop-mentally disabled 51.20	judicial commit-ment: same provisions as for mentally ill 51.20	51.20(1)(b)	probate 51.20(1)(c)	overt act or threat 51.20(1)(b) AND			51.20(13)(c)			51.20(9)(a)		until prob-able cause hearing 51.20(2) until full hearing 51.20(8)(b)	51.20(2)	parent 51.20(2)	51.20(2)	51.20(2)	

TABLE 2.8 INVOLUNTARY INSTITUTIONALIZATION OF DEVELOPMENTALLY DISABLED PERSONS—PREHEARING PROCEDURES—*Continued*

STATE	TYPE OF DISABILITY (1)	PROCEDURE FOR INVOLUNTARY INSTITUTION-IZATION (2)	APPLICATION BY (3)	COURT (4)	CRITERIA FOR INSTITUTIONALIZATION: *Individual* Dangerous to Self or Others (5)	*Individual* Unable to Provide for Basic Needs (6)	*Individual* Other (7)	*Systemic* No Less Restrictive Alternative (8)	*Systemic* Other (9)	SUPPORTING EVIDENCE FOR APPLICATION (10)	PREHEARING MEDICAL EXAMINATION ORDERED BY COURT (11)	DISMISSAL AFTER MEDICAL EXAM (12)	PREHEARING DETENTION (13)	NOTICE OF HEARING OR ADMISSION: *Guardian* (14)	*Relative* (15)	*Attorney* (16)	*Patient* (17)	*When* (18)
WYO. Stat. (1977 & Supp. 1982)	mentally retarded 9-6-642 (a)(viii) 9-6-643	judicial commit-ment 9-6-659	parent, guardian, citizen, superinten-dent, or social service agency 9-6-659(a)	district 9-6-659(a)			facility AND admission would provide most appropriate services for patient 9-6-661(e)		no more appropriate alternatives 9-6-661(e)		preadmission evaluation by training school 9-6-659(c)			all persons given in application & others on ct. order 9-6-660(c), (d)	all persons given in application & others on ct. order 9-6-660(c), (d)		9-6-660(c)(i)	14 days before hearing 9-6-660(c)

FOOTNOTES TABLE 2.8

1. Ky. Rev. Stat. Ann. § 202B.020 (Michie 1980):

Hospitalization for the care and treatment of mentally retarded persons shall be provided by the same procedures as hospitalization of mentally ill persons as provided in KRS chapter 210 and set forth in KRS 202A.020 to 202A.160 and 202A.190, except that:

(1) When the court appoints qualified persons to examine an allegedly mentally retarded respondent such persons shall, where possible, have made a special study of mental retardation;

(2) A qualified mental retardation professional may be substituted for one (1) but not both physicians when certification is required for involuntary hospitalization under this chapter; and

(3) All functions of a hospital as set forth in KRS chapter 202A may be carried out by a mental retardation residential treatment center.

2. Mich. Comp. Laws Ann. § 330.1504 (1980): "An individual with a developmental disability other than mental retardation is eligible for temporary and administrative admission pursuant to sections 508 and 509, but is not eligible for judicial admission."

3. Miss. Code Ann. §§ 41-19-11(B), -15(B) (1981):

[A]ny relative or any citizen of . . . Mississippi may . . . file such affidavit with the Clerk of the Chancery Court. . . . When such affidavit is received by the Chancery Clerk, he shall follow the same procedure for commitment to the North Mississippi Retardation Center as is provided for in the Laws of the State of Mississippi for the commitment of person to the state mental hospitals.

4. Mont. Code Ann. § 53-20-121(1) (1981):

Any person who believes that there is a person who is developmentally disabled and in need of developmental disability services may report the situation to a professional person. If the professional person believes from the facts given to him that the person may be developmentally disabled and in need of developmental disability services, he shall contact the parents or guardian of the person alleged to be developmentally disabled or the person himself. If any of the persons so contacted refuse to cooperate with the professional person and if the professional person believes from all the circumstances of the case that the person may be developmentally disabled and in need of developmental disability services, he shall request the county attorney to file a petition alleging that there is a person in the county who is developmentally disabled and in need of developmental disability services.

5. Nev. Rev. Stat. § 435.030 (1981): "(a) that the child meets the criteria set forth in NRS 435.020; and (b) that the child requires services not otherwise required by law to be provided to him by any other county, political subdivision or agency of this or any other state."

Id. § 435.020:

All mentally retarded children are entitled to benefits under NRS 435.010 to 435.040, inclusive:

1. Who are unable to pay for their support and care;

2. Whose parents, relatives or guardians are unable to pay for their support and care; and

3. If division facilities are to be utilized, whom the division recognizes as proper subjects for services within such division facilities.

6. N.M. Stat. Ann. §§ 43-1-13A, -13B, -13C (1979). A guardian files the initial application with the department or an evaluation facility, which may accept the client for a period of evaluation and treatment not to exceed 14 days. The department or facility may then file a petition with the court for extended residential placement.

7. N.Y. Mental Hyg. Law § 15.27(B) (McKinney 1978). Application by: any person with whom person resides; father, mother, husband, wife, brother, sister, child, or nearest relative; committee or judicially appointed guardian; officer of charitable institution where person resides; director of community services; director of facility where residing; director of division for youth.

8. Pa. Stat. Ann. tit. 50, § 4406 (Purdon Supp. 1980). Tit. 50, § 4406 has been repealed except insofar as it relates to mental retardation or to persons who are mentally retarded.

9. Vt. Stat. Ann. tit. 18, § 8821(3) (Supp. 1981): "'Interested person' means a responsible adult who has a direct interest in a mentally retarded person, and includes but is not limited to a near relative, guardian, public official, social worker, physician, clergyman, or employee of a community mental health agency."

10. Va. Code § 37.1-65.1(D) (Supp. 1981):

Certification of eligibility for admission hereunder shall not be construed as a judicial commitment of such person but shall empower the parent or guardian or other responsible person to admit such person to a facility for the training and treatment of the mentally retarded and shall empower the facility to accept the person as a patient.

11. This procedure is the same as that for administrative hospitalization (cf. tables 3.4 and 3.5), and that procedure may be used alternatively.

TABLE 2.9 INVOLUNTARY INSTITUTIONALIZATION OF DEVELOPMENTALLY DISABLED PERSONS—HEARING AND POSTHEARING PROCEDURES

STATE	HEARING		HEARING HELD BEFORE REFEREE OR FACT-FINDING COMMISSION	CONDUCT OF HEARING		PRESENCE OF PATIENT			JURY TRIAL		STANDARD OF PROOF	INSTITUTION'S DISCRETION AS TO ADMISSION		METHOD OF REVIEW	PLACE OF INSTITUTIONALIZATION			PERIOD OF INSTITUTIONALIZATION	PROVISIONS FOR EXTENSION	
	Judicial Commitment (1)	To Protest Medical Certification or Administrative Commitment (2)	(3)	Judicial Discretion as to Place (4)	Closed to Public (5)	Mandatory (6)	Unless Harmful (7)	If Requested by Patient (8)	Mandatory if Demanded by Patient (9)	Left to Discretion of Judge (10)	(11)	Suitable Hospital Accommodations Available (12)	Mental Condition (13)	(14)	Public (15)	Private (16)	Home of Relatives (17)	(18)	Procedure (19)	Period (20)
ALA. Code (1975 & Supp. 1981)	none: commitment automatic upon unanimous findings by physicians 22-52-55(e)	none: commitment automatic upon unanimous findings by physicians 22-52-55(e)									unanimous conclusion of 2 physicians 22-52-55(e)	22-52-54		exam as often as possible by superintendent of institution; discharge when no longer in need of institutionalization 22-52-57	22-52-50(2)					
ALAS. Stat. (1979 & Supp. 1981)																				
ARIZ. Rev. Stat. Ann. (1974 & Supp. 1980)																				
ARK. Stat. Ann. (1981)	if board determines that child should be admitted by legal commitment only 59-1105(c) 59-1308(c)							presumed able to attend unless guardian certifies otherwise 59-1308(c)			clear & convincing evidence 59-1308(c)	by Colony board (child) 59-1105(a)	by Colony board (child) 59-1105	appeal to a ct. of competent jurisdiction 59-1308(c)	nursing or boarding homes, medical institutions, foster care services, or other appropriate facilities 59-1308(c) Ark. Children's Colony (child) 59-1102	nursing or boarding homes, medical institutions, foster care services, or other appropriate facilities 59-1308(c)	nursing or boarding homes, medical institutions, foster care services or other appropriate facilities 59-1308(c)	status review every 6 mos. 59-1308(c) no discharge until child's condition justifies 59-1109(b)		
CAL. Welf. & Inst. Code (West 1972 & Supp. 1981)	6503			6503	6503										6509	6509				
COLO. Rev. Stat. (1973 & Supp. 1981)		as an objection to long-term admission by medical certification 27-10.5-105						27-10.5-106(4)(b)	27-10.5-106(4)(c)				27-10.5-103 27-10.5-104		27-10.5-102(6)	27-10.5-102(6)		90 days/yr; 30 days consecutive 27-10.5-103(1) indeterminate; first w/in 6 mos. & then annual review 27-10.5-109		
CONN. Gen. Stat. Ann. (West 1977 & Supp. 1981)	19-569d(c)							19-569d (c)(1)			clear & convincing evidence 19-569d(e)				foster or group home, regional center or other least restrictive setting commensurate with need 19-569d(e)	foster or group home, regional center or other least restrictive setting commensurate with need 19-569d(e)	foster or group home, regional center or other least restrictive setting commensurate with need 19-569d(e)	annual review upon request 19-569f(b)		

TABLE 2.9 INVOLUNTARY INSTITUTIONALIZATION OF DEVELOPMENTALLY DISABLED PERSONS—HEARING AND POSTHEARING PROCEDURES—*Continued*

STATE	HEARING		HEARING HELD BEFORE REFEREE OR FACT-FINDING COMMISSION	CONDUCT OF HEARING		PRESENCE OF PATIENT			JURY TRIAL		STANDARD OF PROOF	INSTITUTION'S DISCRETION AS TO ADMISSION		METHOD OF REVIEW	PLACE OF INSTITUTIONALIZATION			PERIOD OF INSTITUTIONALIZATION	PROVISIONS FOR EXTENSION	
	Judicial Commitment (1)	To Protest Medical Certification or Administrative Commitment (2)	(3)	Judicial Discretion as to Place (4)	Closed to Public (5)	Mandatory (6)	Unless Harmful (7)	If Requested by Patient (8)	Mandatory if Demanded by Patient (9)	Left to Discretion of Judge (10)	(11)	Suitable Hospital Accommodations Available (12)	Mental Condition (13)	(14)	Public (15)	Private (16)	Home of Relatives (17)	(18)	Procedure (19)	Period (20)
DEL. Code Ann. (1975 & Supp. 1980)		to appeal commitment 16, §5522 (b)								if requested by patient 16, §5522 (b)	signed certificate 16, §5522 (a)			appeal 16, §5522 (b)	Stockley Center 16, §5522 (a)					
D.C. Code Ann. (1981 & Supp. 1982)	6-1902(4)			conducted as informally as consistent w/orderly procedure 6-1946	unless otherwise requested by patient or counsel 6-1948	right to attend; may be waived by respondent 6-1946					beyond reasonable doubt 6-1924(b) 6-1926(b)	6-1924(c) 6-1926(b)	6-1924(c) 6-1926(b)	appeal 6-1950	facility 6-1902 (13)	facility 6-1902 (13)		fn. 1 ct. hearing every 6 mos. for 2 yrs., then once a yr. 6-1951(a)		
FLA. Stat. Ann. (West 1973 & Supp. 1981)	393.11 (3)(c)					393.11 (3)(c)					clear & convincing evidence 393.11 (3)(c)			appeal 393.11(4) habeas corpus 393.11(5)	residential care 393.11 (3)(e)	residential care 393.11 (3)(e)		indeterminate 393.115		
GA. Code Ann. (1979 & Supp. 1980)	88-2504(e)			88-2502(p)	at client's request 88-2502(p)	may be waived 88-2502(p) 88-2504(f)					clear & convincing evidence 88-2502(p) 88-2504(f)	private facility only 88-2509.5		appeal 88-2503.19	facility 88-2502(f)	facility 88-2502(f)		6 mos. 88-2504(f)	medical certification w/right of review 88-2507(a)	12 mos. 88-2507(b)
HAWAII Rev. Stat. (1976 & Supp. 1981)	333-27					333-27			prohibited 333-26					appeal 333-32 333-27	Waimano Training School 333-26 333-22			60 days, pending certification of a final, indeterminate commitment order 330.30		
IDAHO Code (1976 & Supp. 1981)	56-237(d)			at any suitable place not likely to have harmful effect on individual's health 56-237(e)	ct. authorized to exclude persons not necessary for proceedings 56-237(g)			an opportunity to appear 56-237(g)							to the state dep't of health & welfare which shall determine the disposition of each 56-237 (h)(3)			indeterminate 56-237 (h)(3)		
ILL. Ann. Stat. (Smith-Hurd 1966 & Supp. 1980)	91½, § 4-502(c)	upon petition for review of administrative admission 91½, §4-306 same procedure as judicial admission 91½, §4-307(a)		if possible, at facility where respondent located 91½, §4-600(a)			and waived by counsel 91½, §4-606		commitment verdict may be set aside if ct. dissatisfied 91½, §4-602 91½, §4-609(b)		clear & convincing evidence 91½, §4-608	private facility 91½, §4-609(b)	private facility 91½, §4-609(b)	appeal 91½, §4-613(b) habeas corpus 91½, §4-617	DD facility designated by dep't 91½, §4-609(b)	OR private facility 91½, §4-609(b)	OR nonresidential habilitation 91½, §4-609(b)	180 days 91½, §4-611(a) annual evaluation 91½, §4-310	new petition §4-611 (a), (b)	180 days 91½, §4-611 (a), (b)
IND. Code Ann. (Burns 1973 & Supp. 1982)	16-14-9.1-9			16-14-9.1-9(b)			16-14-9.1-9(e)(3)	ct. can remove if disruptive 16-14-9.1-9(e)(3)				16-14-9.1-1(i)		appeal 16-14-9.1-6	16-14-9.1-1(i)	16-14-9.1-1(i)		90 days 16-14-9.1-9(g)(2)	file a report w/ct. for hearing for additional 90 days 16-14-9.1-9(i) fn. 2	fn. 2
IOWA Code Ann. (West 1969 & Supp. 1981)	222.20 222.21				public, unless otherwise requested, or if judge considers closed hearing in client's best interest 222.27		222.23					222.59(1)	222.59(1)	habeas corpus 222.41	222.31 (2), (3)	222.31(2)		indeterminate petition for discharge may be filed after 6 mos. 222.42		

TABLE 2.9 INVOLUNTARY INSTITUTIONALIZATION OF DEVELOPMENTALLY DISABLED PERSONS—HEARING AND POSTHEARING PROCEDURES—*Continued*

	HEARING		HEARING HELD BEFORE REFEREE OR FACT-FINDING COMMISSION	CONDUCT OF HEARING		PRESENCE OF PATIENT			JURY TRIAL			INSTITUTION'S DISCRETION AS TO ADMISSION			PLACE OF INSTITUTIONALIZATION			PERIOD OF INSTITUTIONALIZATION	PROVISIONS FOR EXTENSION	
STATE	Judicial Commitment (1)	To Protest Medical Certification or Administrative Commitment (2)	(3)	Judicial Discretion as to Place (4)	Closed to Public (5)	Mandatory (6)	Unless Harmful (7)	If Requested by Patient (8)	Mandatory if Demanded by Patient (9)	Left to Discretion of Judge (10)	STANDARD OF PROOF (11)	Suitable Hospital Accommodations Available (12)	Mental Condition (13)	METHOD OF REVIEW (14)	Public (15)	Private (16)	Home of Relatives (17)	(18)	Procedure (19)	Period (20)
KAN. Stat. Ann. (1976 & Supp. 1981)																				
KY. Rev. Stat. Ann. (Michie 1977 & Supp. 1980)	202A.070 (6) 202A.080 (3)			202A.070 (7) 202A.080 (4)			202A.070 (8) 202A.080 (5)	202A.070 (8) 202A.080 (5)	202A.080 (4)			202B.030			mental retardation residential treatment center 202B.030	mental retardation residential treatment center 202B.030				
LA. Rev. Stat. Ann. (West 1975 & Supp. 1981)	28:398(B)							right; may be waived by attorney 28:398(C)							person remanded to dep't of health & human resources for placement 28:398(D)	28:387	substitute family care services 28:419			
ME. Rev. Stat. Ann. (1978 & Supp. 1981)	34, §2659-A (2A)				unless otherwise requested by client 34, §2659-A(3)						clear & convincing 34, §2659-A(4)	certification "empowers" facility to admit 34, §2659-A(5)	certification "empowers" facility to admit 34, §2659-A(5)	appeal to superior ct. on questions of law only 34, §2659-A(8)	facility operated by the dep't of mental health & corrections 34, §2652(E)			certification for max. 2 yrs. 34, §2659-A(6)		
MD. Ann. Code (1979 & Supp. 1981)	w/in 21 days of admission 59A, §10f 59A, §11e							right to call witnesses & present evidence 59A, §10e 59A, §11d						habeus corpus 59A, §13(d) appeal 59A, §14	59A, §10	59A, §11		reevaluation annually 59A, §12(c)		
MASS. Ann. Laws (Michie/Law. Co-op. 1981 & Supp. 1981)																				
MICH. Comp. Laws Ann. (1980 & Supp. 1981)	330.1517			330.1517 (2)(b)				right 330.1517 (3)(a)	330.1517 (3)(b)			public or private facility must agree to accept 330.1518 (2)(b)	public or private facility must agree to accept 330.1518 (2)(b)	habeas corpus 330.1533 review by director of facility every 6 mos. w/ right of hearing 330.1531 annual hearing & petition 330.1532	facility designated by dep't 330.1518 (2)(a), (b)	330.1518 (2)(B)	330.1518 (2)(c) 330.1519	outpatient one yr. 330.1518 (2)(c)		
MINN. Stat. Ann. (West 1982)	253A.07(8)			253A.07(13)	at ct.'s discretion fn. 3 253A.07(12)			right to attend 253A.07(12)			beyond a reasonable doubt fn. 4	upon consent 253A.07(17)		review boards 253A.16	residential training center or hospital 253A.07 (17)(b)	residential training center or hospital 253A.07 (17)(b)	alternative dispositions 253A.07 (17)(b)	60 days unless written statement filed 253A.07 (17)(b), (24) if so, may be indeterminate 253A.07(25)		
MISS. Code Ann. (1972 & Supp. 1980)		41-21-81	optional special master in chancery 41-21-83			unless unable 41-21-83					clear & convincing 41-21-83			appeal as in other civil cases 41-21-83	North & South Miss. Retardation Centers 41-19-11 41-19-15-1			41-21-83		

TABLE 2.9 INVOLUNTARY INSTITUTIONALIZATION OF DEVELOPMENTALLY DISABLED PERSONS—HEARING AND POSTHEARING PROCEDURES—*Continued*

STATE	HEARING: Judicial Commitment (1)	HEARING: To Protest Medical Certification or Administrative Commitment (2)	HEARING HELD BEFORE REFEREE OR FACT-FINDING COMMISSION (3)	CONDUCT OF HEARING: Judicial Discretion as to Place (4)	CONDUCT OF HEARING: Closed to Public (5)	PRESENCE OF PATIENT: Mandatory (6)	PRESENCE OF PATIENT: Unless Harmful (7)	PRESENCE OF PATIENT: If Requested by Patient (8)	JURY TRIAL: Mandatory if Demanded by Patient (9)	JURY TRIAL: Left to Discretion of Judge (10)	STANDARD OF PROOF (11)	INSTITUTION'S DISCRETION AS TO ADMISSION: Suitable Hospital Accommodations Available (12)	INSTITUTION'S DISCRETION AS TO ADMISSION: Mental Condition (13)	METHOD OF REVIEW (14)	PLACE OF INSTITUTIONALIZATION: Public (15)	PLACE OF INSTITUTIONALIZATION: Private (16)	PLACE OF INSTITUTIONALIZATION: Home of Relatives (17)	PERIOD OF INSTITUTIONALIZATION (18)	PROVISIONS FOR EXTENSION: Procedure (19)	PROVISIONS FOR EXTENSION: Period (20)
MO. Ann. Stat. (Vernon 1979 & Supp. 1980)			before a review panel (to review division director's placement) 633.135(3)								preponderance of evidence 633.135(7)	private facility may admit appropriate person 633.120(3)	private facility may admit appropriate person 633.120(3)	subject to administrative procedures 633.135(4)				review of condition every 180 days 633.130(1)		
MONT. Code Ann. (1981)		if requested by patient, parent, guardian, responsible person, or attorney 53-20-123 (2)(b) 53-20-125 (2) ct. initiated 53-20-125 (4)								w/out jury 53-20-123 (2)(b)					residential facility 53-20-125 (3)	residential facility 53-20-125 (3)	community-based course of treatment & habilitation 53-20-125 (3)	ct. order shall specify; max. 1 yr. 53-20-126 (2)	petition for renewal 53-20-128 (1)	
NEB. Rev. Stat. (1976 & Supp. 1981)	83-1127			83-1109							clear & convincing evidence 83-1109			habeas corpus 83-1133(3) appeal 83-1133(4)	Beatrice State Developmental Center or other institution 83-1108	Beatrice State Developmental Center or other institution 83-1108	community-based program 83-1129			
NEV. Rev. Stat. (1981)	435.124					unless unable 435.127(2)									mental retardation center 435.123	mental retardation center 435.123		12 mos. 435.128(2)	administrative officer petitions ct. to renew 435.128(2)	12 mos. 435.128(2)
N.H. Rev. Stat. Ann. (1977)																				
N.J. Rev. Stat. (1981)																				
N.M. Stat. Ann. (1979 & Supp. 1981)	43-1-13C			fn. 5				right 43-1-13D	right 43-1-13D		clear & convincing 43-1-13E		patient if does not require detention, habilitation, or treatment 43-1-13I	right to an expeditious appeal 43-1-13D habeas corpus 43-1-13H	least restrictive placement 43-1-13F	least restrictive placement 43-1-13F	outpatient 43-1-13F	6 mos. 43-1-13E	new commitment hearing unless waived 43-1-13E	6 mos. 43-1-13E
N.Y. Mental Hyg. Law (McKinney 1978)		right to a hearing after involuntary admission on medical certification 15.31										director of a school may receive & retain 15.27(a)	director of a school may receive & retain 15.27(a)	hearing as review of certification commitment 15.31 rehearing if requested (by jury if patient so demands) 15.35	director of a school may receive & retain 15.27(a)	director of a school may receive & retain 15.27(a)	home of relative if able to care 15.31(c)			
N.C. Gen. Stat. (1981)	122-58.7(a)			122-58.7(f)	unless otherwise requested by patient 122-58.7(g)	may be waived with ct. consent 122-58.7(d)				fn. 6	clear, cogent, & convincing 122-58.7(i)	consent if private facility 122-58.8(c)		right to appeal 122-58.9	122-58.8(b)	122-58.8(b) 122-58.19	122-58.8(b) 122-58.19	90 days max. 122-58.8(b)	upon application of chief of medical services, a rehearing 122-58.11(a) after second commitment period, annual review by chief of medical services 122-58.11(e)	180 days 122-58.11(d)
N.D. Cent. Code 1978 & Supp. 1981)																				

TABLE 2.9 INVOLUNTARY INSTITUTIONALIZATION OF DEVELOPMENTALLY DISABLED PERSONS—HEARING AND POSTHEARING PROCEDURES—*Continued*

STATE	HEARING		HEARING HELD BEFORE REFEREE OR FACT-FINDING COMMISSION	CONDUCT OF HEARING		PRESENCE OF PATIENT			JURY TRIAL		STANDARD OF PROOF	INSTITUTION'S DISCRETION AS TO ADMISSION		METHOD OF REVIEW	PLACE OF INSTITUTIONALIZATION			PERIOD OF INSTITUTIONALIZATION	PROVISIONS FOR EXTENSION	
	Judicial Commitment (1)	To Protest Medical Certification or Administrative Commitment (2)	(3)	Judicial Discretion as to Place (4)	Closed to Public (5)	Mandatory (6)	Unless Harmful (7)	If Requested by Patient (8)	Mandatory if Demanded by Patient (9)	Left to Discretion of Judge (10)	(11)	Suitable Hospital Accommodations Available (12)	Mental Condition (13)	(14)	Public (15)	Private (16)	Home of Relatives (17)	(18)	Procedure (19)	Period (20)
OHIO Rev. Code Ann. (Baldwin 1980 & Supp. 1981)	unless waived after probable cause hearing 5123.75(F) probable cause hearing if requested 5123.75		optional referee designated by judge—must be attorney 5123.76(A)		fn. 7 5123.76 (A)(5)			right unless compelling medical necessity renders unable & respondent has not expressed desire to attend 5123.76 (A)(2)			clear & convincing 5123.76(C)	ct. order conditional as to consent of facility, if private 5123.76(D)	ct. order conditional as to consent of facility, if private 5123.76(D)	habeas corpus 5123.88	5123.76 (C)(1)(a)	5123.76 (C)(1)(b) least restrictive 5123.76(E)	other programs 5123.76(C)	90 days 5123.76(C)	application for continued commitment 5123.76(H)	180 days 5123.76 (H)(3)
OKLA. Stat. Ann. (West 1979 & Supp. 1981)																				
OR. Rev. Stat. (1979 & Supp. 1981)	427.245(1)							opportunity to appear 427.245(1)			clear & convincing 427.290			appeal 427.295	commitment to mental health division of dep't of human resources 427.290(3) division assigns best facility 427.300		voluntary treatment if willing & able 427.290(1) care by relative, friend, or guardian 427.290(2)	1 yr. w/ extension provisions 427.290(3)	annual review & certification 427.020	
PA. Stat. Ann. (Purdon 1969 & Supp. 1981)	50, §4406 (a)(3)					50, §4406 (a)(3)(i)								habeas corpus 50, §4425	facility 50, §4102 50, §4406(b)	facility 50, §4102 50, §4406(b)	outpatient 50, §4406			
R.I. Gen. Laws (1977 & Supp. 1981)		if person, parent, guardian, spouse, or next of kin objects to certification 40.1-22-9 (1)			person may request open or closed hearing, ct. has discretion to grant 40.1-22-10 (4)							may admit 40.1-22-9	may admit 40.1-22-9	must be confirmed by team at facility w/in 20 days 40.1-22-9 (1), (2) de novo appeal 40.1-22-10 (6)	40.1-22-3(6)	40.1-22-3(6)		6 mos. 40.1-22-10 (5)	ct. petition 40.1-22-10 (8)	1 yr. 40.1-22-10 (8)
S.C. Code Ann. (Law. Co-op. 1976)	44-21-90			courtroom, person's residence, or other 44-21-90			or person's condition prevents 44-21-90							trial de novo; w/ jury unless waived 44-21-90	S.C. mental retardation dep't informs ct. as to services available 44-21-90			exam of patient after 6 6 mos. & every 6 mos. thereafter 44-17-820		
S.D. Codified Laws Ann. (1976 & Supp. 1981)		may be waived 27B-7-11(6) 27B-7-8(1)		facility or other convenient place 27B-7-8(2)				27B-7-11						habeas corpus 27B-8-4 annual review by facility personnel 27B-8-15 petition for discharge 27B-8-17	facility designated by dep't 27B-7-15 (1)	any private treatment center 27B-7-15 (2)	placement in appropriate programs 27B-7-15 (3) other forms of care & treatment 27B-7-15 (4), 16	until no longer meets the criteria for board-ordered admission 27B-7-22		
TENN. Code Ann. (1977 & Supp. 1981)																				
TEX. Rev. Civ. Stat. Ann. (Vernon 1958 & Supp. 1981)	5547-300, §37(i)				upon showing of good cause by proposed resident or representative 5547-300, §37(m)(1)		5547-300, §37(m)(3)		if demanded by any party 5547-300, §37(m)(2)		beyond reasonable doubt 5547-300, §37(m)(6)			appeal to appropriate ct. of civil appeals 5547-300, §37(p)	community center or residential care facilities 5547-300, §37(o)					

TABLE 2.9 INVOLUNTARY INSTITUTIONALIZATION OF DEVELOPMENTALLY DISABLED PERSONS—HEARING AND POSTHEARING PROCEDURES—*Continued*

	HEARING		HEARING HELD BEFORE REFEREE OR FACT-FINDING COMMISSION	CONDUCT OF HEARING		PRESENCE OF PATIENT			JURY TRIAL			INSTITUTION'S DISCRETION AS TO ADMISSION			PLACE OF INSTITUTIONALIZATION				PROVISIONS FOR EXTENSION	
STATE	Judicial Commitment (1)	To Protest Medical Certification or Administrative Commitment (2)	(3)	Judicial Discretion as to Place (4)	Closed to Public (5)	Mandatory (6)	Unless Harmful (7)	If Requested by Patient (8)	Mandatory if Demanded by Patient (9)	Left to Discretion of Judge (10)	STANDARD OF PROOF (11)	Suitable Hospital Accommodations Available (12)	Mental Condition (13)	METHOD OF REVIEW (14)	Public (15)	Private (16)	Home of Relatives (17)	PERIOD OF INSTITUTIONALIZATION (18)	Procedure (19)	Period (20)
UTAH Code Ann. (1978 & Supp. 81) *fn. 8*	64-8-16					64-8-16					"belief" 64-8-20				Utah State Training School 64-8-20					
VT. Stat. Ann. (1968 & Supp. 1981)	18, §8825 (a)(2)		prehearing determination of less restrictive alternatives 18, §8824(1)		ct. may exclude all people unnecessary to hearing 18, §8827 (b)			"may attend" 18, §8827 (b)			clear & convincing evidence 18, §8823 (b)			application by attorney or person or interested party 18, §8834	Brandon Training School 18, §8828 (c)		18, §8829	indefinite period 18, §8828(c) periodic 2-yr. application for review 18, §8834(b)		
VA. Code (1976 & Supp. 1981)	37.1-65.1(C)			unless objected to by person's attorney 37.1-90		unless waived *fn. 9* 37.1-65.1(c1)	37.1-65.1(c1)								training center for the mentally retarded 37.1-1(23)					
WASH. Rev. Code Ann. (1975 & Supp. 1981)																				
W. VA. Code (1980 & Supp. 1981)	27-5-4 (g)(1)		mental hygiene commissioner (not binding on ct.) 27-5-1 (b)	in chambers 27-5-4 (i)(1)		27-5-4 (g)(1)					clear, cogent & convincing proof 27-5-4 (j)(3)			appeal to supreme ct. on verbatim transcript 27-5-5	27-5-4 (k)(1)	27-5-4 (k)(1)	custody of responsible person 27-5-4(o)	"indeterminate" expiring in 2 yrs. 27-5-4(k) (1), (4)	exam; hearing if requested 27-5-4 (k)(4)	2 yrs. 27-5-4 (k)(4)
WIS. Stat. Ann. (West 1957 & Supp. 1981)	51.20(2)			51.20(5)	right to open; may request closed 51.20(5)				51.20(5)		clear & convincing 51.20 (13)(e)			regular appeal process 51.20(15)	least restrictive facility 51.20 (13)(f)	least restrictive facility 51.20 (13)(f)	outpatient (after institutional examination) 51.20 (13)(dm)	not to exceed 6 mos. 51.20(13) (g)(1) 45 days if unable to provide for needs 51.20 (13)(g)(2)	application & hearing 51.20 (13)(g)(3)	1 yr. 51.20(13) (g)(1)
WYO. Stat. (1977 & Supp. 1982)	9-6-661				all persons not having an interest excluded closed ct. unless jury trial requested 9-6-661(c)		unless independent ct.-appointed physician statement that attendance would injure patient's health & well-being 9-6-661(a)		9-6-661(b)		clear & convincing 9-6-661(e)			appeal to supreme ct. as in civil trial 9-6-662	Wyo. State Training School *fn. 10* 9-6-659 9-6-665	*fn. 10* 9-6-665				

FOOTNOTES TABLE 2.9

1. D.C. Code Ann. § 6-1951 (1981):

> Any decision of the Court ordering commitment of a mentally retarded person to a facility shall be reviewed in a court hearing every six (6) months for two (2) years, and once a year thereafter. The mentally retarded individual shall be discharged unless there is a finding of the following:
>
> (1) The Court determines that the mentally retarded individual has benefitted from the habilitation; and
>
> (2) The facility, its sponsoring agency or the Department of Human Resources demonstrates that continued residential habilitation is necessary for the habilitation program.

2. Ind. Code Ann. § 16-14-9.1-10 (Burns Supp. 1982). Proceedings for regular commitment may be commenced after one or two 90-day commitments. Hearings same as for temporary commitment. Period is indeterminate with an annual review of patient's condition made by the superintendent of the facility filed with the court. Patient may request one hearing per year.

3. Minn. Stat. Ann. § 253A.07(12) (West 1982): "The court may exclude from the hearing any person not necessary for the conduct of the proceeding except those persons to whom notice was given pursuant to subdivision 9 and any other persons requested to be present by the proposed patient.

4. Lausche v. Commissioner of Pub. Welfare, 302 Minn. 65, 225 N.W.2d 366 (1974), cert. denied, 420 U.S. 993 (1975).

5. 1979 Op. Att'y Gen. No. 79-20:

> Absent a showing by the "developmentally disabled" person that his substantive rights have in any way been abridged of his involuntary commitment hearing is not held at the county seat, the district court is not precluded from adopting the practice of holding such hearings at the commitment facility when, it is discretion, such practice would better serve the public convenience.

6. French v. Blackburn, 428 F. Supp. 1351 (M.D.N.C. 1977), aff'd, 443 U.S. 901 (1979). Failure to provide a jury trial in involuntary commitment proceedings does not violate the equal protection clause.

7. Ohio Rev. Code Ann. § 5123.76(A)(5) (Baldwin Supp. 1981): "The hearing may be closed to the public unless counsel for the respondent requests that the hearing be open to the public or, the respondent is a person found not guilty by reason of insanity."

8. Utah has no explicit provisions for a hearing. Rather, the judge conducts a court examination of the proposed patient by a least one physician or psychologist. Utah Code Ann. § 64-8-20 (1978). "The district judge. . . , if he believes the person to be so mentally retarded as to be unable to properly care for himself, or by reason of mental retardation to be a social menace, must make an order that such person be confined in the Utah State Training School."

9. Va. Code § 37.1-65.1(C1) (Supp. 1981):

> He shall be present at any hearing held under this section unless his attorney waives his right to be present and the judge is satisfied by a clear showing and after personal observation that such person's attendance would subject him to substantial risk of physical or emotional injury or would be so disruptive as to prevent the hearing from taking place.

10. Wyo. Stat. § 9-6-665 (Supp. 1982): "If the superintendent determines it is appropriate for the welfare of a resident, the resident may be placed for temporary care and treatment in any public or private hospital, institution or residence in the state which provides services which will benefit the resident."

TABLE 2.10 INVOLUNTARY INSTITUTIONALIZATION OF ALCOHOLICS AND DRUG ADDICTS

	ALCOHOLICS		DRUG ADDICTS	
STATE	In General (1)	Charged with or Convicted of a Crime (2)	In General (3)	Charged with or Convicted of a Crime (4)
ALA. Code (1975 & Supp. 1982)	22-52-1 22-50-1(1)		22-52-1 22-50-1(1)	
ALAS. Stat. (1971 & Supp. 1981)			47.37.190	
ARIZ. Rev. Stat. Ann. (1974 & Supp. 1982)		36-2027		13-3408
ARK. Stat. Ann. (1971 & Supp. 1981)			59-903 to 909	
CAL. Welf. & Inst. Code (West 1972 & Supp. 1982)	14 days 5172	5225	3100-3108	3050 & 3200
COLO. Rev. Stat. (1973 & Supp. 1981)	25-1-311			
CONN. Gen. Stat. Ann. (West 1975 & Supp. 1981)	17-155y		19-495 to 496a	19-498
DEL. Code Ann. (1974 & Supp. 1980)	16 §2213	11 §4210		
D.C. Code Ann. (1973 & Supp. 1981)	24-527		24-603 to 608	
FLA. Stat. Ann. (West 1973 & Supp. 1981)	396.102 396.105	396.131	397.052	
GA. Code Ann. (1979 & Supp. 1981)	88-406.2		88-406.2	
HAWAII Rev. Stat. (1976 & Supp. 1980)	334-60	16-13-6.1-15.1	334-60	16-13-6.1-15.1
IDAHO Code (1980 & Supp. 1983)				
ILL. Ann. Stat. (Smith-Hurd 1966 & Supp. 1980)	91½ §513	1003-3-7		56½ §1410
IND. Code Ann. (Burns 1973 & Supp. 1982) *fn. 1*	16-13-6.1-21		16-13-6.1-21	
IOWA Code Ann. (West 1969 & Supp. 1980)	229.51 to .52		229.51 to .52	204.409
KAN. Stat. Ann. (1976 & Supp. 1982)	65-4032 to 4038			
KY. Rev. Stat. Ann. (1977 & Supp. 1980)			222.430	218A.990 (8(a))
LA. Rev. Stat. Ann. (West 1975 & Supp. 1980)	28:54		28:54	Code of Crim. Pro. Art. 902
ME. Rev. Stat. Ann. (1978 & Supp. 1982)	22, §7120 34, §2334(5) 34, §2551(5)		34, §2334(5) 34, §2334(5) 34, §2551(5)	
MD. Health Gen. Code Ann. (1982 & Supp. 1982)	8-506		9-620	
MASS. Ann. Laws (Michie/Law Co-op 1981 & Supp. 1982)	123 §135			
MICH. Comp. Laws. Ann. (1980 & Supp. 1982)				
MINN. Stat. Ann. (West 1982 & Supp. 1982)	253A.07 253A.02(4)		253A.07 253A.02(4)	
MISS. Code Ann. (1972 & Supp. 1980)	41-31-5		41-31-5	
MO. Ann. Stat. (Vernon 1979 & Supp. 1982)				
MONT. Rev. Code Ann. (1979 & Supp. 1981)	53-24-302			
NEB. Rev. Stat. (1976 & Supp. 1981)			83-702 to 706	
NEV. Rev. Stat. (1981)		458.310		458.310
N.H. Rev. Stat. Ann. (1977 & Supp. 1981)			172:13(III)	172.13
N.J. Stat. Ann. (West 1981) *fn. 1*	30:9-12.21			
N.M. Stat. Ann. (1979)	43-2-9			
N.Y. Mental Hyg. Law (McKinney 1978 & Supp. 1980)				
N.C. Gen. Stat. (1981 & Supp. 1981)	short term 122-58.22 long term 122-58:23 inebriate 122-58.7	14-446	122-58.7	
N.D. Cent. Code (1978 & Supp. 1981)	25-03.1-02 to 30 emergency 25-03.1-25 to 26		25-03.1-02 to 30 emergency 25-03.1-25 to 26	
OHIO Rev. Code Ann. (Baldwin 1980 & Supp. 1980) *fn. 1*				2951.04
OKLA. Stat. Ann. (West 1979 & Supp. 1980)	63, §2128 to 2136		43A, §671 to 675	43A, §682
OR. Rev. Stat. (1981) *fn. 1*				
PA. Stat Ann. (Purdon 1969 & Supp. 1982)				35, §780-118
R.I. Gen. Laws (1977 & Supp. 1982)	40.1-4-12			21-28.2-3 to 8
S.C. Code Ann. (1976 & Supp. 1982)	44-51-30 to 130		44-51-50 to 130	
S.D. Codified Laws Ann. (1976 & Supp. 1980)				
TENN. Code Ann. (1977 & Supp. 1982)	33-806 33-604		33-806 33-604	
TEX. Rev. Civ. Stat. Ann. (Vernon 1958 & Supp. 1980)	5561c-(9)-(12)		5561c-1-(1) to (10)	
UTAH Code Ann. (1978 & Supp. 1981)	78-4-7(j)		78-4-7(j)	
VT. Stat. Ann. (1968 & Supp. 1980)			18 §8402	
VA. Code (1976 & Supp. 1983)	37.1-63 to 67.3		37.1-63 to 67.3	18.2-251 to 252
WASH. Rev. Code Ann. (1975 & Supp. 1982–83)		46.61.515		
W. VA. Code (1980)				
WIS. Stat. Ann. (West 1957 & Supp. 1980)	51.45(13)		51.20	161.47 51.37
WYO. Stat. Ann. (1982 & Supp. 1983)				

FOOTNOTES TABLE 2.10

1. "Voluntary" institutionalization of drug addicts [probation/parole upon agreement of entering for treatment or treatment in lieu of conviction]. See Ind. Code Ann. § 16-13-6.1-22 ((Burns 1973); N.J. Stat. Ann. § 30:6C-6 (West 1981); N.H. Rev. Stat. Ann. § 172:13(IV) (Supp. 1981); Ohio Rev. Code Ann. § 2951.041 (Baldwin 1981); and Or. Rev. Stat. § 426.460 (1983).

TABLE 2.11 INSTITUTIONALIZATION OF MINORS AND OTHER LEGALLY INCOMPETENT PERSONS

STATE	PERSONS SUBJECT TO ADMISSION (1)	APPLICATION BY: Parent or Guardian (2)	APPLICATION BY: Any Adult (3)	PATIENT'S CONSENT REQUIRED (4)	APPROVAL BY: Facility Director (5)	APPROVAL BY: Physician (6)	FORMAL COURT HEARING: Automatic (7)	FORMAL COURT HEARING: Only if Patient Protests (8)	COUNSEL OR GUARDIAN AD LITEM (9)	PERIOD OF INSTITUTIONALIZATION (10)	DISCHARGE: Upon Parent's or Guardian's Request Unless Director Petitions for Involuntary Institutionalization (11)	DISCHARGE: Upon Patient's Request (12)	DISCHARGE: No Longer in Need of Treatment (13)	REVIEW (14)	AGE FOR VOLUNTARY SELF-INITIATED INSTITUTIONALIZATION (15)
ALA. Code (1975 & Supp. 1981)	any mentally retarded resident 22-52-51	or next of kin 22-52-51								as authorized by law 22-52-51	22-52-53		22-52-52		
	mentally ill or retarded minors 12-15-90(a)	12-15-90(a)	12-15-90(a)				juvenile ct. 12-15-30		12-15-90(d) (2)						
ALAS. Stat. (1979 & Supp. 1981)	mentally ill minors 47.30.775		47.30.775 47.30.700			47.30.775 47.30700			esp. in waiver & consent proceedings 47.30.775	21 days 47.30.730 90 days 47.30.740			47.30.780		
	mentally ill minors under 14 47.30.690 (a)	47.30.690 (a)				47.30.690				21 days 47.30.690	47.30.695		47.30.690 (b)		14 or older 47.30.670
ARIZ. Rev. Stat. Ann. (1974 & Supp. 1981)	mentally ill minors 36-518	or next of kin 36-518			36-518								36-519	every 10 days 36-518.01 (A)	14 or older; parent or guardian cosign 36-518(C)
	child w/ mental, emotional, or personality disorder & ward of ct. 8-242.01 (A)	ct. 8-242.01 (A)						14 yrs. or older & danger to self or others or gravely disabled 8-242.01 (C)(2)		specified by ct. 8-242.01 (C)(2) 36-542			8-242.01 (F)	every 30 days 8-242.01 (G)	
ARK. Stat. Ann.															
CAL. Welf. & Inst. Code (West 1972 & Supp. 1981)	mentally disordered minors 6000	or conservator 6000(b)								until majority 6000(b)	or conservator 6000				age of majority 6000
	developmentally disabled 4653 minors 4656	regional center 4653		neither patient nor parent of minor nor conservator of adults objects 4803			objections of minors, parents, or conservators heard by agency procedure 4700	objections of minors, parents, or conservators heard by agency procedure 4700							
COLO. Rev. Stat. (1973 & Supp. 1981)	developmentally disabled minors 27-10.5-103(2)	or custodian 27-10.5-103(2)			facility 27-10.5-103(1), (3)					30 days 27-10.5-103(1)	27-10.5-108(2)(b)		27-10.5-108(1)		18 or older 27-10.5-103(1)
	developmentally disabled minors 27-10.5-104	or custodian 27-10.5-104			facility 27-10.5-104(1), (4)			if patient over 14 or by any interested party 27-10.5-105	27-10.5-106(2)(a) 27-10.5-104(6)(a)	long-term admission 27-10.5-104	27-10.5-108(2)(b)		27-10.5-108(1)	w/in 6 mos. & annually thereafter 27-10.5-109	18 or older 27-10.5-104(1)
CONN. Gen. Stat. Ann. (West 1975 & Supp. 1982)	mentally disordered child 17-205f	17-205f						17-205g	17-205g		17-205f	17-205f		examination annually 17-205g	14 17-205f
	mentally ill child under 16 17-205c		17-205c(a)				17-205c(b)		17-205c(d)	6 mos. 17-205d(e)			17-205d(e)		
DEL. Code Ann. (1974 & Supp. 1980)	mentally retarded minors *fn. 1* 16, §5521 (a)				state mental hygiene clinic 16, §5521 (a)				agency having legal care or custody 16, §5521 (a)						

TABLE 2.11 INSTITUTIONALIZATION OF MINORS AND OTHER LEGALLY INCOMPETENT PERSONS—*Continued*

STATE	PERSONS SUBJECT TO ADMISSION (1)	APPLICATION BY		PATIENT'S CONSENT REQUIRED (4)	APPROVAL BY		FORMAL COURT HEARING		COUNSEL OR GUARDIAN AD LITEM (9)	PERIOD OF INSTITUTION-ALIZATION (10)	DISCHARGE			REVIEW (14)	AGE FOR VOLUNTARY SELF-INITIATED INSTITUTION-ALIZATION (15)
		Parent or Guardian (2)	Any Adult (3)		Facility Director (5)	Physician (6)	Auto-matic (7)	Only if Patient Protests (8)			Upon Parent's or Guardian's Request Unless Director Petitions for Involuntary Institution-alization (11)	Upon Patient's Request (12)	No Longer in Need of Treatment (13)		
D.C. Code Ann. (1981)	mentally ill minors 21-511	or spouse 21-511			21-511	21-511					or spouse 21-512		21-512(b)	periodic 6-1926(a)	18 or older 21-511
	mentally retarded person under 14 6-1926(a)	6-1926(a)					6-1926(a)		6-1926(a) 6-1942		6-1928		6-1930	6-1951	
	mentally retarded incompe-tent per-son 14 or older 6-1924	6-1924(a)					6-1924(a)		6-1924(a) 6-1942		6-1928	if patient has gained competence 6-1928	6-1930	periodic 6-1951	14 or older 6-1922(a)
FLA. Stat. Ann. (West 1973 & Supp. 1982)	mentally ill person 17 or under 394.465 (1)(a)	394.465 (1)(a) 394.467 (1)(a)		394.465	394.465 (1)(a)		informal hearing to determine voluntari-ness of consent 394.465 (1)(b)			394.465 (1)(b) 394.465(5)		394.465 (2)(a)		18 or older 394.465 (1)(a)	
GA. Code Ann. (1980 & Supp. 1981)	mentally ill or retarded child 24A-2601		*fn. 2*		*fn. 3*		*fn. 2*			max. 2 yrs. 24A-2701 (c)					
HAWAII Rev. Stat.															
IDAHO Code (1980 & Supp. 1981)	mentally ill or gravely disabled & under 14 66-318 66-319	66-318 (a)(4), (5)			66-318	designated examiner 66-318 (a)(5)					66-320	w/consent of parent or guard-ian if patient under 16 66-320 (a)(2)	66-319		18 or older *fn. 4* 66-318
	anyone w/o capac-ity to make in-formed de-cisions *re* treatment 66-318 (a)(5)	guardian only 66-318 (a)(5)			66-318(b)	designated examiner 66-318 (a)(5)					66-320	66-320			
ILL. Ann. Stat. (Smith-Hurd 1966 & Supp. 1980)	mentally or emotionally disturbed minor *fn. 5* 91½, §3-503	or person in loco parentis 91½, §3-503			91½, §3-503	91½, §3-503		91½, §§3-505, 3-509	91½, §3-509		91½, §3-508			every 60 days 91½, §3-506	16 or older 91½, §3-502
	develop-mentally disabled & under 18 *fn. 6* 91½, §4-302	or person in loco parentis 91½, §4-302			91½, §4-302			if over 12 91½, §4-503						annual evaluation 91½, §4-310	18 or older 91½, §4-302
IND. Code Ann. (Burns 1973 & Supp. 1982)	mentally ill & under 18 16-14-9.1-2	16-14-9.1-2			16-14-9.1-2(a)						party who filed for admission 16-14-9.1-2(b)		16-14-9.1-2(b)		18 or older 16-14-9.1-2(a) (2)
	develop-mental dis-ability or mental illness *fn. 7* 16-13-20-3 (a)	who has provided residential care for min. of 3 mos. 16-13-20-3 (a)			assist parent or guardian in selecting appropriate facility 16-13-20-3(a), (b)					respite care *fn. 7* 16-13-20-3(a)					
IOWA Code Ann. (West 1969 & Supp. 1981)	mentally ill minor 229.2(1)	or custodian 229.2(1)				chief medi-cal officer 229.2(1)		229.2(1)					229.3		

TABLE 2.11 INSTITUTIONALIZATION OF MINORS AND OTHER LEGALLY INCOMPETENT PERSONS—*Continued*

STATE	PERSONS SUBJECT TO ADMISSION (1)	APPLICATION BY: Parent or Guardian (2)	APPLICATION BY: Any Adult (3)	PATIENT'S CONSENT REQUIRED (4)	APPROVAL BY: Facility Director (5)	APPROVAL BY: Physician (6)	FORMAL COURT HEARING: Auto-matic (7)	FORMAL COURT HEARING: Only if Patient Protests (8)	COUNSEL OR GUARDIAN AD LITEM (9)	PERIOD OF INSTITUTION-ALIZATION (10)	DISCHARGE: Upon Parent's or Guardian's Request Unless Director Petitions for Involuntary Institution-alization (11)	DISCHARGE: Upon Patient's Request (12)	DISCHARGE: No Longer in Need of Treatment (13)	REVIEW (14)	AGE FOR VOLUNTARY SELF-INITIATED INSTITUTION-ALIZATION (15)
KAN. Stat. Ann. (1976 & Supp. 1981)	any person under 18 in need of treatment 59-2905	or person in loco parentis 59-2905			59-2905	director may require 59-2905					59-2907	w/consent of parent, guardian, or person in loco parentis 59-2907	59-2906		over 14 & competent 59-2905
	any inca-pacitated person over 18 *fn. 8* 59-2905 59-3002 59-3006	guardian only 59-2905			59-2905	director may require 59-2905					guardian only 59-2907		59-2906		
KY. Rev. Stat. Ann. (Michie 1977 & Supp. 1980)	unemanci-pated men-tally ill person under 18 202A.020 mentally retarded minor *fn. 9* 202B.020	202A.020 202B.020								until 18 unless patient voluntarily remains or is involun-tarily com-mitted 202A.020(2) 202B.020	*fn. 10* 202A.020(3), (4) 202B.020		202A.020(2) 202B.020		
LA. Rev. Stat. Ann. (West 1975 & Supp. 1982)	mentally ill or substance abusing minor 28:57	or person in loco parentis *fn. 11* 28:57(C)			28:57(C)								28:171(J)	periodic 28:171(Q)	16 or older 28:57(B)
	any mentally retarded person 28:394B	parents only 28:394B			comprehen-sive study made before application 28:394B						28:415	28:415			
ME. Rev. Stat. Ann. (1978 & Supp. 1981–82)															18 or older *fn. 12* 34, §2290
MD. Ann. Code (1979 & Supp. 1981)	mentally disordered person under 18 59, §11	59, §11				59, §11				1 yr. max. 59, §11(g)					16 or older 59, §11
MASS. Ann. Laws (Michie/Law. Co-op. 1981 & Supp. 1982)	mental incompetent or person under 18 in need of care or treatment 123, §10(a)	123, §10(a)			superintendent 123, §10(a)						party who petitioned for admit-tance 123, §11		when in best inter-ests of patient 123, §10(a)		16 or older 123, §10(a)
MICH. Comp. Laws Ann. (1980 & Supp. 1981)	under 18 330.1415	or person in loco parentis 330.1415			330.1415			if over 13 330.1417	hospital assistance in filing objection 330.1417		330.1419(2) 330.1420				18 or older 330.1415(1)
MINN. Stat. Ann.															
MISS. Code Ann. (1981)	mentally ill under 18 41-21-103(1)(c)	parent, guardian, or person in loco parentis 41-21-103(2)(c)		for applica-tions other than by parents or an attorney 41-21-103(2)(b)	41-21-103	2 physicians or 1 physi-cian & 1 psychologist 41-21-103(1)			5 days before peti-tion for discharge may be filed 41-21-103(4)			anyone may file petition for reten-tion—must include 2 medical statements 41-21-103			18 or older 41-21-103(2)(a)
	any incom-petent over 18 41-21-103(2)(d)	guardian only 41-21-103(2)(d)		41-21-103	41-21-103	2 physicians or 1 physi-cian & 1 psychologist 41-21-103(1)			41-21-103(4)			anyone may file petition for reten-tion—must include 2 medical statements 41-21-103			

TABLE 2.11 INSTITUTIONALIZATION OF MINORS AND OTHER LEGALLY INCOMPETENT PERSONS—*Continued*

STATE	PERSONS SUBJECT TO ADMISSION (1)	APPLICATION BY: Parent or Guardian (2)	APPLICATION BY: Any Adult (3)	PATIENT'S CONSENT REQUIRED (4)	APPROVAL BY: Facility Director (5)	APPROVAL BY: Physician (6)	FORMAL COURT HEARING: Automatic (7)	FORMAL COURT HEARING: Only if Patient Protests (8)	COUNSEL OR GUARDIAN AD LITEM (9)	PERIOD OF INSTITUTIONALIZATION (10)	DISCHARGE: Upon Parent's or Guardian's Request Unless Director Petitions for Involuntary Institutionalization (11)	DISCHARGE: Upon Patient's Request (12)	DISCHARGE: No Longer in Need of Treatment (13)	REVIEW (14)	AGE FOR VOLUNTARY SELF-INITIATED INSTITUTIONALIZATION (15)
MO. Ann. Stat. (Vernon 1979 & Supp. 1980)	minor w/ mental disorder other than retardation or developmental disability 632.110(1)	parent or legal custodian 632.110(1)			diagnosis 632.110(1)						632.155(1)	w/consent of person who applied for admission 632.155		every 180 days 632.175	18 or older 632.105
	person declared incompetent by ct. who has mental disorder other than retardation or developmental disability 632.120(1)	guardian only 632.120(1)					after 7 days of institutionalization *fn. 13*			7 days 632.120(2)				every 180 days 632.175	
	mentally retarded minor 633.120(4)	parent or legal custodian 633.120(4)			633.120						person who applied for admission 633.125(1)		633.125(2)		
	mentally retarded adult 633.120(4)	guardian only 633.120(4)			633.120						person who applied for admission 633.125(1)		633.125(2)		
MONT. Code Ann.															
NEB. Rev. Stat.															
NEV. Rev. Stat. (1981) *fn. 14*	minors in need of treatment 433A.140(1)	spouse, parent, or legal guardian 433A.140(1)				admitting personnel 433A.140(2)						433A.140	or no longer danger to others 433A.140		age of majority 433A.140
	mentally retarded children 435.030(1)	parent, relative, guardian, or nearest friend 435.030(1)					county board of commissioners 435.030(1)				435.081(7)				
N.H. Rev. Stat. Ann.															
N.J. Stat. Ann. (West 1981)	mentally ill under 21 30:4-46	or grandparent or adult sibling 30:4-46										*fn. 15*			18 or older 30:4-46
N.M. Stat. Ann. (1978 & Supp. 1982)	mentally disordered minors 43-1-16(A)	43-1-16(C)		signed 43-1-16(C)		review of condition every 60 days 43-1-16(K)			to ascertain & confirm consent initially & every 60 days 43-1-16(F)			43-1-16(J)			12 or older 43-1-16(B)
	mentally disordered or developmentally disabled minors 43-1-16.1(A)		any person 43-1-16.1(B)				43-1-16.1(E)		43-1-16.1(C)	initially up to 60 days then up to 6 mos. 43-1-17				habeas corpus not restricted 43-1-16.1(J)	
N.Y. Mental Hyg. Law (McKinney 1978 & Supp. 1982)	mentally ill & under 16 *fn. 16* 9.13(a)	parent, legal guardian, or next of kin 9.13(a)										or party who applied, person of equal or closer relationship, or mental health information service 9.13(b)			16 or older
	mentally retarded & under 18 15.13(a)	or next of kin 15.13(a)		15.13(a)								or party who applied, person of equal or closer relationship, or mental health information service 15.13(b)		by mental health information service 15.23(a)	

TABLE 2.11 INSTITUTIONALIZATION OF MINORS AND OTHER LEGALLY INCOMPETENT PERSONS—*Continued*

STATE	PERSONS SUBJECT TO ADMISSION (1)	APPLICATION BY: Parent or Guardian (2)	APPLICATION BY: Any Adult (3)	PATIENT'S CONSENT REQUIRED (4)	APPROVAL BY: Facility Director (5)	APPROVAL BY: Physician (6)	FORMAL COURT HEARING: Automatic (7)	FORMAL COURT HEARING: Only if Patient Protests (8)	COUNSEL OR GUARDIAN AD LITEM (9)	PERIOD OF INSTITUTIONALIZATION (10)	DISCHARGE: Upon Parent's or Guardian's Request Unless Director Petitions for Involuntary Institutionalization (11)	DISCHARGE: Upon Patient's Request (12)	DISCHARGE: No Longer in Need of Treatment (13)	REVIEW (14)	AGE FOR VOLUNTARY SELF-INITIATED INSTITUTIONALIZATION (15)
N.C. Gen. Stat. (1981 & Supp. 1981)	minors 122-56.5	or person in loco parentis 122-56.5					w/in 10 days of admission *fn. 17* 122-56.7						*fn. 18*		
	persons adjudicated non compos mentis 122-56.5	guardian or trustee 122-56.5					w/in 10 days of admission 122-56.7								
N.D. Cent. Code (1978 & Supp. 1981)	mentally ill, alcoholic, or drug-addicted minors 25-03.1-04	25-03.1-04				25-03.1-04						25-03.1-06	25-03.1-5		
OHIO Rev. Code Ann. (Baldwin 1980 & Supp. 1981)	mentally ill minor 5122.02(B)	or one having custody 5122.02(B)			may find hospitalization inappropriate 5122.02(B)		on petition of legal rights service, div. of common pleas will determine if hospitalization in person's best interests 5122.02 5123.69(C)				or counsel, spouse, or adult next-of-kin 5122.03	5122.03	or patient refuses treatment 5122.02(C)		18 or older 5122.02(A)
	mentally retarded minor 5123.69(A)	5123.69(A)			w/concurrence of chief program director 5123.69(B)		on petition of legal rights service, div. of common pleas will determine if hospitalization in person's best interests 5122.02 5123.69(C)				or counsel, spouse, or adult next-of-kin 5123.70	5123.70	hospitalization no longer advisable 5123.69(D)	on application or w/consent of party who applied, managing officer may petition ct. to commit 5123.70(A)	18 or older 5123.69
	mentally retarded adult adjudicated incompetent 5123.69(A)	guardian only			w/concurrence of chief program director 5123.69(B)		on petition of legal rights service, div. of common pleas will determine if hospitalization in person's best interests 5122.02 5123.69(C)				or counsel, spouse, or adult next-of-kin 5123.70	5123.70	hospitalization no longer advisable 5123.69(D)	on application or w/consent of party who applied, managing officer may petition ct. to commit 5123.70(A)	18 or older 5123.69
	mentally ill adult adjudicated incompetent 5122.02(B)	guardian or one having custody 5122.02(B)			may find hospitalization inappropriate 5122.02(B)		on petition of legal rights service, div. of common pleas will determine if hospitalization in person's best interests 5122.02 5123.69(C)				or counsel, spouse, or adult next-of-kin 5122.03	5122.03	or patient refuses treatment 5122.02(C)		
OKLA. Stat. Ann. (West 1978 & Supp. 1981)	mentally ill minors 43A, §184	or person having custody 43A, §184										unless attending physician petitions for voluntary hospitalization 43A, §184	attending physician determines 43A, §186		

TABLE 2.11 INSTITUTIONALIZATION OF MINORS AND OTHER LEGALLY INCOMPETENT PERSONS—*Continued*

STATE	PERSONS SUBJECT TO ADMISSION (1)	APPLICATION BY		PATIENT'S CONSENT REQUIRED (4)	APPROVAL BY		FORMAL COURT HEARING		COUNSEL OR GUARDIAN AD LITEM (9)	PERIOD OF INSTITUTION-ALIZATION (10)	DISCHARGE			REVIEW (14)	AGE FOR VOLUNTARY SELF-INITIATED INSTITUTION-ALIZATION (15)
		Parent or Guardian (2)	Any Adult (3)		Facility Director (5)	Physician (6)	Auto-matic (7)	Only if Patient Protests (8)			Upon Parent's or Guardian's Request Unless Director Petitions for Involuntary Institution-alization (11)	Upon Patient's Request (12)	No Longer in Need of Treatment (13)		
OR. Rev. Stat. (1981)	person under 18 who is mentally iill or has nervous disorder 426.220(1)	or adult next of kin 426.220(1)									or adult next of kin 426.220(1)				18 or older 426.220(1)
	mentally retarded minor or mentally retarded in-capacitated adult 427.185	or person entitled to custody 427.185(1)			diagnostic & evaluation service 427.185(3)									annual 427.205	
PA. Stat. Ann. (Purdon 1979 & Supp. 1980)	under 14 & in need of treat-ment 50, §7201	or person in loco parentis 50, §7201		informed, written 50, §7203	or county adminis-trator 50, §7202				if petitioned that hos-pitalization not in minor's best interests 50, §7206(b)		or person in loco parentis may request 50, §7206		50, §7206(c)	any respon-sible party may file for release in minor's best interests 50, §7206(b)	14 or over *fn. 19* 50, §7201
R.I. Gen. Laws (1978 & Supp. 1981)	mentally retarded & under 18 40.1-22-8(1)	director of dep't of mental health in lieu of others 40.1-22-8(1)											when in patient's best interests 40.1-22-8(1)	by family ct. just prior to patient's 18th birthday 40.1-22-8(3)	
S.C. Code Ann. (Law. Co-op. 1976 & Supp. 1981)	mentally ill, under 18, & prop-er subject for treat-ment 44-17-310	44-17-310			44-17-310(2)							14 days notice to parent or guardian if patient under 16 & didn't apply for own ad-mission *fn. 20* 44-17-330(3)	44-17-320		16 or over 44-17-310(1)
S.D. Codified Laws Ann. (1977 & Supp. 1981)	mentally retarded minors 27B-5-1	or person in loco parentis in absence of others 27B-5-4 27B-5-1			if patient suitable 27B-5-4	27B-5-7		hearing if patient over 13 or suitable person protests 27B-5-9	if admission protested 27B-5-11				27B-5-18	annual examination 27B-5-15	
	mentally ill minors 27A-8-2	or person in loco parentis in absence of others 27A-8-2			27A-8-2	27B-5-7		27A-8-5	hospital assistance preparing objection 27A-8-4		27A-8-11 27A-8-13	no longer that which caused	patient's behavior commitment 27A-14-6	27A-8-1	18 or over

TABLE 2.11 INSTITUTIONALIZATION OF MINORS AND OTHER LEGALLY INCOMPETENT PERSONS—*Continued*

STATE	PERSONS SUBJECT TO ADMISSION (1)	APPLICATION BY: Parent or Guardian (2)	APPLICATION BY: Any Adult (3)	PATIENT'S CONSENT REQUIRED (4)	APPROVAL BY: Facility Director (5)	APPROVAL BY: Physician (6)	FORMAL COURT HEARING: Auto-matic (7)	FORMAL COURT HEARING: Only if Patient Protests (8)	COUNSEL OR GUARDIAN AD LITEM (9)	PERIOD OF INSTITUTION-ALIZATION (10)	DISCHARGE: Upon Parent's or Guardian's Request Unless Director Petitions for Involuntary Institution-alization (11)	DISCHARGE: Upon Patient's Request (12)	DISCHARGE: No Longer in Need of Treatment (13)	REVIEW (14)	AGE FOR VOLUNTARY SELF-INITIATED INSTITUTION-ALIZATION (15)
TENN. Code Ann. (1977 & Supp. 1981)	mentally ill & under 16 33-601(a)	or spouse 33-601(a)				33-601(a)				max. 6 mos. per yr. unless approved by admission review committee 33-601(a)	if patient cannot write request 33-601(b)	33-601(b)	33-601(b)		16 or older 33-601(a)
	mentally retarded & under 18 33-501(a)(2)	33-501(a)(2)			33-501(a)								14 days notice to parent or guardian prior to discharge 33-501(b)		18 or over 33-501
	mentally retarded incompetent 33-501(a)(3)	guardian only 33-501(a)(4)			33-501(a)								14 days notice to guardian prior to discharge 33-501(b)		
	mentally retarded person 33-501(a)(4)	spouse, adult relative 33-501(a)(4)			33-501(a)								14 days notice to spouse, adult relative prior to discharge 33-501(b)		
TEX. Rev. Civ. Stat. Ann. (Vernon 1958 & Supp. 1981)	mentally retarded minor or incompetent 5547-300 (29)	parent of minor, guardian of person believed retarded 5547-300 (29)			5547-300 (34)(f)(2)	comprehen-sive diagno-sis & eval-uation 5547-300 (28)	if parent or guardian protests medical evaluation 5547-300 (31)			until age of majority 5547-300 (35)	for safety of public 5547-300 (36)	5547-300 (36)			
	mentally ill person not legally of age 5547-22	or county judge 5547-23		*fn. 21* 5547-23	5547-22					initially at least 10 days 5547-23(c)	5547-24	on patient's behalf or w/patient's consent 5547-24(a)		habeas corpus not restricted 5547-24(b)	person legally of age 5547-23
UTAH Code Ann. (1978 & Supp. 1981)	mentally ill person under 16 64-7-29	64-7-29									64-7-31	may be conditioned on parent or guardian's consent 64-7-31(2)	64-7-30		16 or over 64-7-29
	mentally ill & unable to care for self or social menace 64-8-13	64-8-15			director of family services 64-8-15	affidavit by physician 64-8-15							64-8-8		
VT. Stat. Ann. (1968 & Supp. 1981)	mentally ill person under 14 18, §7503(c)	18, §7503 (b), (c)		written, uncoerced 18, §7503							w/minor's consent 18, §8010(c)	18, §8010(a)	18, §8009 (a), (b)		14 or over 18, §7503(a)
VA. Code															

TABLE 2.11 INSTITUTIONALIZATION OF MINORS AND OTHER LEGALLY INCOMPETENT PERSONS

		APPLICATION BY			APPROVAL BY		FORMAL COURT HEARING				DISCHARGE				
STATE	PERSONS SUBJECT TO ADMISSION (1)	Parent or Guardian (2)	Any Adult (3)	PATIENT'S CONSENT REQUIRED (4)	Facility Director (5)	Physician (6)	Automatic (7)	Only if Patient Protests (8)	COUNSEL OR GUARDIAN AD LITEM (9)	PERIOD OF INSTITUTIONALIZATION (10)	Upon Parent's or Guardian's Request Unless Director Petitions for Involuntary Institutionalization (11)	Upon Patient's Request (12)	No Longer in Need of Treatment (13)	REVIEW (14)	AGE FOR VOLUNTARY SELF-INITIATED INSTITUTIONALIZATION (15)
WASH. Rev. Code Ann. (1982 & Supp. 1982)	mentally ill & under 18 72.23.070 (2)	or other person entitled to custody 72.23.070 (2)		if minor over 13: knowing, voluntary, written consent 72.23.070 (2)	72.23.070 (2)	72.23.070 (2)	if minor over 13 72.23.070		72.23.070	until 18 w/ administrative review every 180 days 72.23.070 (3)(d)	72.23.070 (3)(e)	72.23.070 (3)(e)	72.23.070 (3)(f)		18 or over 72.23.070 (1)
	mentally handicapped minor 72.33.125 (a)	or limited guardian or person or agency entitled to custody 72.33.125 (a)									72.33.140		72.33.170		18 or over 72.33.125 (1)(b)
	mentally handicapped adult 72.33.125 (b)	guardian, limited guardian, or agency entitled to custody 72.33.125 (b)									72.33.140	72.33.140	72.33.170		
W. VA. Code (1980 & Supp. 1981)	person under 18 & mentally ill, retarded, or addicted 27-4-1(a)	27-4-1(b)		if 12 or older 27-4-1(b)	recommendation from facility 27-4-1(c)						27-4-3	if under 12, conditioned on consent of person who applied for admission 27-4-3(b)	27-4-2		over 18 27-4-1(a)
Wis. Stat. Ann. (West 1957 & Supp. 1981)	under 14 & developmentally disabled, drug addicted, alcoholic, or mentally ill 51.13(1)(a)	51.13(1)(a)						51.13(3), (4)	51.13(3)	discharge at 14 unless voluntarily admitted or involuntary commitment proceeding begun 51.13(7)(a)				right to hearing to determine continued appropriateness of admission 51.13(3)(c), (7)(c)	
	minor 14 or over & developmentally disabled, drug addicted, alcoholic, or mentally ill 51.13(1)(b)	& minor *fn. 22* 51.13(1)(b)		must file application w/guardian or parent 51.13(1)(b)	51.13(1)(e)			51.13(3), (4)	51.13(3)			51.13(3) (b), (7)(b)			*fn. 22*
WYO. Stat. (1981 & Supp. 1982)	mentally ill incompetent or minor 25-3-106(b)	25-3-106(b)				application & statement of examiner that person mentally ill 25-3-106(b)					conditioned on patient's consent 25-3-109 (a)(ii)	25-3-109(a)	25-3-108		

FOOTNOTES TABLE 2.11

1. Del. Code Ann. tit. 31, § 5109 (1975). This section provides for the transfer of juveniles already in the custody of the Division of Juvenile Corrections to state institutions for care and treatment when the secretary of the Department of Health and Social Services requests it. Parents or guardians, after notification, may demand a hearing. Del. Code Ann. tit. 16, § 5521(a) (Supp. 1980), entitled "Commitment of arrested person; procedure," deals with these juveniles.

2. Ga. Code Ann. § 24A-1601 (1980). Petitions may be filed alleging deprivation, unruliness, or delinquency; determinations of mental illness may then be made in the course of any hearing.

3. Id. § 24A-2601:

> (a) If, at any time, the evidence indicates that a child may be suffering from mental retardation or mental illness, the court may commit the child to an appropriate institution, agency, or individual for study and report on the child's mental condition.
>
> (b) If it appears from the study and report that the child is committable under the laws of this State as a mentally retarded or mentally ill child, the court shall order the child detained and proceed within 10 days to commit the child to the Georgia Department of Human Resources, Mental Health Division.

4. Idaho Code § 66-318(a)(2) (Supp. 1981):

> Any individual fourteen (14) to eighteen (18) years of age who may apply to be admitted for observation, diagnosis, evaluation, and treatment and the facility director will notify the parent, parents, or guardian of the individual of the admission; a parent or guardian may apply for the individual's release, and the facility director will release the patient within three (3) days . . . of the application for discharge, unless the time period for diagnosis, evaluation, care or treatment is extended.

5. Ill. Ann. Stat. ch. 91½, § 3-504 (Smith-Hurd Supp. 1980). A mentally ill or emotionally disturbed minor may be hospitalized pursuant to emergency procedures upon medical certification as well.

6. Id. ch. 91½, § 4-400(b): "Developmentally disabled persons under 18 years of age and developmentally disabled persons 18 years of age or over who are under guardianship . . . may be admitted for emergency care under § 4-311."

7. Ind. Code Ann. 16-13-20-1 (Burns Supp. 1982). This provision is one of temporary respite care. "Respite care means temporary institutional or noninstitutional care for a developmentally disabled or mentally ill individual who lives at home and is cared for by his family or other caretaker that is provided because the family or caretaker is temporarily unable or unavailable to provide needed care."

8. Kan. Stat. Ann. § 59-3002(1) (1976):

> The term "incapacitated person" shall mean any person who is impaired by reason of mental illness, mental deficiency, physical illness or disability, advanced age, chronic narcotic addiction, chronic intoxication, or other cause to the extent that he or she lacks sufficient understanding or capacity to make or communicate responsible decisions concerning either his or her person or his or her estate.

9. Ky. Rev. Stat. Ann. § 202B.020 (Michie Supp. 1980): "Hospitalization for the care and treatment of mentally retarded persons shall be provided by the same procedures as hospitalization of mentally ill persons as provided in . . . KRS 202A.020 to 202A.160 and 202A.190."

10. Id. §§ 202A.020(3), (4) (Michie 1977). The patient may be detained for up to 72 hours by the certification of two physicians. The patient may be held longer if a petition for involuntary commitment has been filed, but in no case shall the detention period exceed 10 days.

11. La. Rev. Stat. Ann. § 28:57(D) (West Supp. 1981):

> A minor who is eligible for admission . . . and who is in such a condition that immediate hospitalization is necessary, may be admitted upon application of an interested person eighteen years of age or older, when after diligent effort the minor's parent, curator, or person in loco parentis cannot be located. Following the admission of the minor, the director of the treatment facility shall continue efforts to locate the minor's parent, curator, or person in loco parentis. If such person is located and consents in writing to the admission, the minor may be continued to be hospitalized. However, upon notification of the admission, the parent, curator, or person in loco parentis may request the minor's discharge subject to the provisions of Subsection F of this section.

12. Me. Rev. Stat. Ann. tit. 34, § 2290 (1978):

> Any person under the age of 18 years must have the consent of his parent or guardian, and, in the case of an admission to a hospital for the mentally ill other than a private hospital, the consent of the Commissioner of Mental Health & Corrections or his designee. Any such patient shall be free to leave such hospital at any time after adminssion.

13. Mo. Ann. Stat. § 632.120(3) (Vernon Supp. 1980): "If further inpatient services are recommended, the person may remain in the facility only if his guardian is authorized by the court to continue the inpatient hospitalization. The court may authorize the guardian to consent to evaluation, care, treatment, including medication, and rehabilitation on an inpatient basis."

14. Nev. Rev. Stat. § 433A.540 (1981). Treatment for emotionally disturbed children:

> The administrator is authorized to receive any emotionally disturbed child for treatment in a treatment facility or any other division facility . . . if:
>
> (1) The child is committed by court order to the custody of the administrator or to a division facility; or
>
> (2) The child's parent, parents or legal guardian makes application for treatment.

15. A minor who has been admitted to a public or private mental hospital for treatment with his or her parent's signature, pursuant to N.J. Stat. Ann. 30:4-46 (West 1981), has the right to sign himself or herself out on 72 hours notice without parental consent. In re Williams, 140 N.J. Super. 495, 356 A.2d 468 (1976).

16. N.Y. Mental Hyg. Law § 9.13(a) (McKinney Supp. 1981): "If the person is over sixteen and under eighteen years of age, the director may, in his discretion, admit such person either as a voluntary patient on his own application or on the application of the person's parent, legal guardian, next-of-kin."

17. N.C. Gen. Stat. § 122-56.5 Case Notes (1981):

> The admission procedure is permissible. The judicial deference afforded to parental authority along with the parent's interest in being able to seek immediate treatment and the policy encouraging voluntary admissions outweigh any interest the minor may have in pre-admission hearing. However, the continued confinement of a minor based on that procedure requires procedural safeguards consistent with the Due Process Clause. Such procedural due process should be afforded at the earliest possible time.
>
> In re Long, 25 N.C. App. 702, 214 S.E.2d 626, cert. denied, 288 N.C. 241, 217 S.E.2d 665 (1975).
>
> See § 122-56.7.

18. N.C. Gen. Stat. § 122-56.7 Case Notes (Supp. 1981):

> [P]arents who have applied for admission of their minor child to a treatment facility may not later on obtain a discharge of the child prior to judicial determination of the need for further treatment at the treatment facility. Only the court or the treatment facility may release the minor child and only then upon the determination that the child does not need further hospitalization. See opinion of Attorney General to Mary B. Chamblee, Assistant Public Defender, 26th Judicial District, 49 N.C.A.G. 166 (1980).

19. Pa. Stat. Ann. tit. 50, § 7204 (Purdon Supp. 1980):

> Upon the acceptance of an application for examination and treatment by a minor 14 years or over but less than 18 years of age, the director of the facility shall promptly notify the minor's parents, guardian, or person standing in loco parentis, and shall inform them of the right to be heard upon the filing of an objection. Whenever such objection is filed, a hearing shall be held within 72 hours by a judge or mental health review officer, who shall determine whether or not the voluntary treatment is in the best interest of the minor.

20. S.C. Code Ann. § 44-17-330(1) (Law. Co-op. 1976): "Any request for discharge may be denied by the superintendent of a hospital if the request is made sooner than fifteen days after admission."

21. 1980 Tex. Op. Att'y Gen., No. M.W.-180. A minor may be admitted to a mental hospital as a voluntary patient only with the minor's informed consent.

22. Wis. Stat. Ann. § 51.13(1)(c) (West Supp. 1981):

> If a minor 14 years of age or older wishes to be admitted to an . . . inpatient treatment facility but a parent with legal custody or the guardian refuses to execute the application for admission or cannot be found, or if there is no parent with legal custody, the minor or a person acting on the minor's behalf may petition the court assigned to exercise jurisdiction. . . . A copy of the petition and a notice of hearing shall be served upon the parent or guardian at his or her last-known address. If, after the hearing, the court determines that the parent or guardian's consent is unreasonably withheld or that the parent or guardian cannot be found or there is no parent with legal custody, and that the admission is proper under the standards prescribed . . . , it shall approve the minor's admission without the parent or guardian's consent. The court may, at the minor's request, temporarily approve the admission pending hearing on the petition. If a hearing is held under this subsection, no review or hearing under sub. (4) is required.

TABLE 2.12 ADMINISTRATIVE INSTITUTIONALIZATION—PREHEARING PROCEDURES*

STATE	APPLICATION		SUPPLE-MENTARY MEDICAL CERTIFICATION (3)	CRITERIA FOR INSTITUTIONALIZATION ORDER			TYPE OF ADMINISTRATIVE TRIBUNE			QUASI-JUDICIAL POWERS (10)	PREHEARING MEDICAL EXAMINATION (11)	INTERIM DETENTION PENDING HEARING OR REMOVAL TO INSTITUTION (12)	NOTICE OF HEARING				
															Patient		
	By (1)	To (2)		Dangerous or Likely to Cause Injury (4)	In Need of Treatment (5)	Other (6)	Membership (7)	Standing Tribunal (8)	Court Appointment for Each Case (9)				Relatives (13)	Guardian (14)	Mandatory (15)	Attorney (16)	Minimum Notice (17)
NEB. Rev. Stat. (1976 & Supp. 1981)	county attorney 83-1022 83-1024	sheriff, mental health center, or hospital 83-1022 or clerk of district ct. 83-1025		83-1009(1)	unable to care for basic needs 83-1009(2)	no less restrictive alternative 83-1035	lawyer & 2 others; others shall be mental health professionals or lay persons w/interest in mental health issues 83-1018				83-1023 83-1029	pending preliminary hearing 83-1028 pending final hearing 83-1034	parent 83-1027	OR 83-1027	83-1027		
S.D. Codified Laws Ann. (1976 & Supp. 1981)	any person 27A-9-1	state's attorney 27A-9-1	one 27A-9-3	27A-1-1(2)	or lacks capacity to make re-sponsible decisions re ordinary demands of life 27A-1-1(1)	prehearing investigation by state's attorney 27A-9-1	2 & county residents & 1 lawyer or judge 27A-7-1			27A-7-4	27A-9-9				27-A-9-6		5 days prior to hearing 27A-9-6
W. Va. Code (1980 & Supp. 1981) fn. 1	an adult person 27-5-4(b)	mental hygiene commissioner 27-5-4(b)	one 27-5-4(d)(1)	27-5-4(j)(i)		least restrictive alternative 27-5-4(j)(2)	mental hygiene commissioner 27-5-4(i)			27-5-1(b)	27-5-4(f)(1)	27-5-4(f)(2)	27-5-4(e)	27-5-4(e)	27-5-4(e)	7 days notice to counsel 27-5-4(a)	8 days prior to hearing 27-5-4(e)

FOOTNOTES TABLE 2.12

1. This procedure is an alternative to judicial hospitalization (tables 3.2, 3.2A, 3.3 and 3.3A). Those proceedings are the same except that they are held before judges rather than before the mental hygiene commissioner.

TABLE 2.13 ADMINISTRATIVE INSTITUTIONALIZATION—HEARING AND POSTHEARING PROCEDURES

STATE	MANDATORY HEARING (1)	HEARING PLACE		PRESENCE OF PATIENT			RIGHT TO JUDICIAL REVIEW OF INSTITUTIONALIZATION ORDER		ENLARGED STATUTORY PROVISION FOR HABEAS CORPUS (9)	PLACE OF INSTITUTIONALIZATION			PERIOD OF INSTITUTION-ALIZATION (13)	STANDARD OF PROOF (14)
		Courtroom (2)	Discretionary (3)	Mandatory (4)	Mandatory Unless Harmful (5)	If Patient Requests (6)	Hearing Before Judge (7)	Jury on Review (8)		Public (10)	Private (11)	Home of Relative (12)		
NEB. Rev. Stat. (1976 & Supp. 1981)	preliminary hearing if person in custody & final hearing 83-1030		83-1055	83-1056			de novo trial before district ct. 83-1043			83-1038 83-1039			60 days 83-1041	clear & convincing 83-1035
S.D. Codified Laws Ann. (1976 & Supp. 1981)	probable cause finding 27A-9-5 full hearing on the petition 27A-9-5		27A-9-5		reasons shall be noted in the record 27A-9-14				27A-12-4	27-A-9-19	27A-9-19	home of relative or friend when hospital not available 27A-9-20	review after 90 days 27A-10-11	clear & convincing 27A-9-18
W. VA. Code (1980 & Supp. 1981)	27-5-4(e)			27-5-4(g)(1)			ordinary civil appeal 27-5-5			27-5-4(k)	27-5-4(k)		indeterminate; expires after 2 yrs. 27-5-4(k)(4)	clear, cogent, & convincing 27-5-4(j)(3)

TABLE 2.14 INVOLUNTARY INSTITUTIONALIZATION BY MEDICAL CERTIFICATION

		APPLICATION BY					CRITERIA FOR ADMISSION					ADMISSION DISCRETIONARY ON PART OF INSTITUTION AS TO				JUDICIAL REVIEW			RELEASE UPON REQUEST				
							Individual			Systemic													
STATE	LIMIT ON PLACE OF INSTITUTIONALIZATION (1)	Any Person (2)	Health, Welfare, or Peace Officer or Hospital Physician (3)	Attorney, Guardian, Relative, Friend, Spouse, or Person at Whose House Residing (4)	NUMBER OF CERTIFICATES REQUIRED (5)	FURTHER APPROVAL BY (6)	Dangerous to Self or Others (7)	Unable to Provide For Basic Needs (8)	Other (9)	(10)	ADMISSION REPORTED TO (11)	Availability of Suitable Accommodations in Hospital (12)	Mental Condition (13)	Unspecified (14)	PATIENT TOLD OF RIGHT TO OBJECT, RELEASE, OR REVIEW (15)	By Superior Court or Habeas Corpus (16)	Jury on Review (17)	ADMINISTRATIVE RELEASE (18)	Release on Patient's Request (19)	Release on Other's Request (20)	Time After Request (21)	Extension Provision (22)	MAXIMUM PERIOD OF INSTITUTIONALIZATION (23)
ALAS. Stat. (1979)	state-operated or state-designated 47.30. 020		47.30. 020(2)	interested party 47.30. 020(2)	one 47.30. 020(2)		47.30. 020(2) OR		in need of treatment & mentally ill 47.30. 020(2)		legal guardian, parent, spouse, or next of kin, if known report to dep't, superior ct. 47.30. 120			47.30. 020	47.30. 050(b)	superior ct. hearing 47.30. 060 habeas corpus 47.30. 100		47.30. 040(b)	30 days after admission 47.30. 050(a)	30 days after admission 47.30. 050(a)	immediate release unless extension application filed w/in 48 hrs. 47.30. 050(a) (3)	5 or 15 days 47.30. 050(a) (3)	indeterminate 47.30. 040(b)
CAL. Welf. & Inst. Code (West 1972)	county designated 5250(c)		5250(a)		2: agency or facility director & physician 5251	facility providing intensive treatment 5250(c)	5250(a) OR	gravely disabled 5250(a) AND	involuntary AND	previous 72-hr. evaluation period	fn. 1 5253	5250(c)		5250(c)	5252.1 5275 5276	superior ct. review 5276 habeas corpus 5275		5254					14 days 5254
COLO. Rev. Stat. (1973 & Supp. 1981)	designated or approved facility 27-10-107 (1)(c)		detaining facility after emergency or evaluation 27-10-107 (1)		1 physician 27-10-107 (2)		27-10-107(1) OR	gravely disabled 27-10-107 (1) AND	has refused voluntary treatment or reasonable belief patient would not remain if voluntary 27-10-107 (1)	previous 72-hr. ct.-ordered evaluation or emergency detention 27-10-107 (1)	Department of Institutions & 1 person designated by patient 27-10-107 (3) & district ct. 27-10-107 (2)				27-10-107 (3)	district ct. 27-10-107 (6)	27-10-111 (1)						3 mos. 27-10-107 (1) extension for 3 more mos. 27-10-108
D.C. Code Ann. (1973)	public or private 21-513			friend or relative 21-513	one fn. 2 21-513	admitting psychiatrist 21-513			in need of treatment & nonprotesting 21-513				21-513	private only 21-513	21-513				written 21-514		immediate 21-514	if judicial hospitalization proceedings initiated 21-514	
LA. Rev. Stat. Ann. (West 1975 & Supp. 1980)			28:52.3B			director of facility after diagnostic evaluation 28:52.3B			mentally ill or suffering from substance abuse & nonprotesting 28:52.3A					28:52.3A				28:52.3B	written 28:52.3C		72 hrs. 28:52.3C	if judicial or emergency proceedings instituted 28:52.3C	3 mos. 28:52.3D

TABLE 2.14 INVOLUNTARY INSTITUTIONALIZATION BY MEDICAL CERTIFICATION

STATE	LIMIT ON PLACE OF INSTITUTION-ALIZATION (1)	APPLICATION BY			NUMBER OF CERTIFICATES REQUIRED (5)	FURTHER APPROVAL BY (6)	CRITERIA FOR ADMISSION				ADMISSION REPORTED TO (11)	ADMISSION DISCRETIONARY ON PART OF INSTITUTION AS TO			PATIENT TOLD OF RIGHT TO OBJECT, RELEASE, OR REVIEW (15)	JUDICIAL REVIEW		ADMINIS-TRATIVE RELEASE (18)	RELEASE UPON REQUEST				MAXIMUM PERIOD OF INSTITUTION-ALIZATION (23)
							Individual			Systemic													
		Any Person (2)	Health, Welfare, or Peace Officer or Hospital Physician (3)	Attorney, Guardian, Relative, Friend, Spouse, or Person at Whose House Residing (4)			Dangerous to Self or Others (7)	Unable to Provide For Basic Needs (8)	Other (9)	(10)		Availability of Suitable Accommodations in Hospital (12)	Mental Condition (13)	Unspecified (14)		By Superior Court or Habeas Corpus (16)	Jury on Review (17)		Release on Patient's Request (19)	Release on Other's Request (20)	Time After Request (21)	Extension Provision (22)	
MD. Ann. Code (1979 & Supp. 1981) fn. 3	VA hospital or facility licensed by Dep't of Mental Hygiene 59, §12 (a)(1)	59, §12(b)			two 59, §12 (c)(5)	geriatric evaluation unit, if over 65 59, §12 (a)(2)	59, §12 (a)(1) AND		has mental disorder & involuntary 59, §12 (a)(1) AND	least restrictive alternative 59, §12 (a)(1)	Dep't of Mental Hygiene 59, §20			59, §12(b)	told of right to consult attorney 59, §12(c)	ct. review 59, §15 habeas corpus 59, §14	59, §15						indeterminate w/ renewal of certification every yr. 59, §12(e)
MICH. Comp. Laws Ann. (1980 & Supp. 1981)		330.1424 (2)			one 330.1423	hospital psychiatrist 330.1423 330.1430	330.1401 OR	330.1401			ct., relative or guardian, attorney, & 2 designated by patient 330.1431		330.1430		330.1448 (1)	preliminary hearing if requested 330.1450	330.1458	330.1476					
N.Y. Mental Hyg. Law (McKinney 1978)			9.27(b) fn. 4 director of community services or physician designated by him fn. 5 9.37(a)	9.27(b)	two 9.27(a) or certificate of director of hospital 9.37(a)	hospital physician 9.27(e)	9.37(a)		treatment essential to welfare & unable to understand need for treatment 9.01		mental health information service, nearest relative, & 3 others designated by patient 9.29			9.27(a) 9.27(e)		county ct. hearing if requested w/in 60 days of admission 9.31(a)	rehearing with right to jury trial 9.35						60 days; after which ct. order necessary 9.33(a)
R.I. Gen. Laws (1977 & Supp. 1980)				parent, guardian relative, friend 40.1-5.1-8	two 40.1-5.1-8				insane 40.1-5.1-8					40.1-5.1-8									

FOOTNOTES TABLE 2.14

1. Cal. Welf. & Inst. Code § 5253 (West 1972). Hospital admission is reported to the court, the patient's attorney, the district attorney, the public defender, the facility providing intensive treatment, the state department of mental health, and one person designated by the patient.

2. D.C. Code Ann. 21-513 (1973). Referral from a practicing physician is necessary unless the need for immediate admission is apparent to the admitting psychiatrist.

3. Providing for admission by medical certification, was held to violate equal protection in Johnson v. Solomon, 484 F. Supp. 278 (D. Md. 1979).

4. N.Y. Mental Hyg. Law § 9.21(b)(4)-(10) (McKinney 1978). Application may also be executed by the following parties:

(1) an officer of any public or well recognized charitable institution or agency or home in whose institution the person alleged to be mentally ill resides,

(2) the director of community services or social services official, as defined in the social service law, of the city or county in which any such person may be,

(3) the director of the hospital in which the patient is hospitalized,

(4) the director or person in charge of a facility providing care to alcoholics, or substance abusers or substance dependent persons,

(5) the director of the division for youth . . . . ,

(6) . . . a social services official or authorized agency which has . . . care and custody or guardianship and custody of a child over the age of sixteen,

(7) subject to the terms of any court order a person or entity having custody of a child.

5. Id. § 9.37(d) (Supp. 1982):

[I]n counties with a population of less than two hundred thousand, a director of community services who is a licensed psychologist . . . or a certified social worker . . . but who is not a physician may apply for the admission of a patient pursuant to this section without a medical examination by a designated physician if a hospital approved by the commissioner pursuant to section 9.39 of this chapter [for emergency hospitalization] is not located within thirty miles of the patient, and the director of community services has made a reasonable effort to locate a designated examining physician but such a designee is not immediately available and the director of community services after personal observation of the person, reasonably believes that he may have a mental illness which is likely to result in serious harm to himself or others and inpatient care and treatment of such person in a hospital may be appropriate. In the event of an application pursuant to this subdivision, a physician of the receiving hospital shall examine the patient and shall not admit the patient unless he or she determines that the patient has a mental illness for which immediate hospitalization is appropriate and which is likely to result in serious harm to himself or others. If the patient is admitted, the need for hospitalization shall be confirmed by another staff physician within twenty-four hours.

TABLE 2.15 LEGAL COUNSEL IN PROCEEDINGS TO INSTITUTIONALIZE MENTALLY ILL AND DEVELOPMENTALLY DISABLED PERSONS

	MENTALLY ILL				DEVELOPMENTALLY DISABLED			
STATE	Right to Be Represented (1)	Mandatory Court-appointed Counsel if Patient Not Represented (2)	Counsel Publicly Compensated (3)	When (4)	Right to Be Represented (5)	Mandatory Court-appointed Counsel if Patient Not Represented (6)	Counsel Publicly Compensated (7)	When (8)
ALA. Code (1975 & Supp. 1981)	*fn. 1*	if patient lacks funds or mental ability to obtain attorney 22-52-4(a)	state *fn. 2* 22-52-14	upon filing of petition for commitment 22-52-4(a)				
ALAS. Stat. (1979 & Supp. 1981)	47.30.725(d) 47.30.735(b) 47.30.745(a)	47.30.725(d) 47.30.735(b) 47.30.745(d)	if person indigent according to ct. 47.30.905(b)					
ARIZ. Rev. Stat. Ann. (1974 & Supp. 1981)	emergency 36-528D 36-536A	if detained before hearing 36-528D 36-529B 36-536A		3 days before hearing 36-536A "promptly" if taken into custody for evaluation 36-529B				
ARK. Stat. Ann. (1971 & Supp. 1981)	59-1408A1	59-1408B	county pays up to $150, or representation on pro bono basis 59-1408B	immediately upon filing of original petition 59-1408B				
CAL. Welf. & Inst. Code (West 1972 & Supp. 1980)	5206, 5252.1, 5276, 5302	on request 5276 5302	public defender 5276, 5302		6500	6500	person if able 6500	immediately appointed if unrepresented 6500
COLO. Rev. Stat. (1973 & Supp. 1981)	*fn. 3* 27-10-107(5)	27-10-107(5)	judicial department (if eligible) 27-10-127	certification for short-term treatment 27-10-107(5)	if objects to admission or retention 28-10.5-106	if objects to admission or retention 27-10.5-106 (4)(a)	ct. (if indigent) 27-10.5-106 (2)(a)	upon receipt of objection 27-10.5-106 (2)(a)
CONN. Gen. Stat. Ann. (West 1975 & Supp. 1981)	*fn. 4* 17-178(a)	if unable to afford counsel, unless waived w/understanding 17-178(b)	judicial department 17-178(b)		19-569d(c)	19-569d(b)	state, if found mentally retarded; complainant, if not 19-569(e)	immediately upon filing of application 19-569d(b)
DEL. Code Ann. (1974 & Supp. 1980)	*fn. 5* 16, §5006(3)	if patient cannot afford counsel 16, §5006(3)		upon filing of complaint 16, §5008(1)				
D.C. Code Ann. (1981)	21-543	21-543	person's estate or commission on mental health 21-543	counsel granted 5-day recess to prepare case on request 21-543				
FLA. Stat. Ann. (West 1973 & Supp. 1981)	394-467(3)(a)	if patient cannot afford counsel 394-467(3)(a)	county (if indigent) 394.473(1)		393.11(3)(d)	if person cannot afford counsel 393.11(3)(d)	public defender 393.11(3)(d)	20 days before hearing 393.11(3)(d)
GA. Code Ann. (1979 & Supp. 1980)	88.506.2(a)(2)	unless waived in writing 88-506.2(a)(2)	county (if unable to pay) 88-507.2(a)		88-2504(e)(2)	88-2504(e)(2)	county (if unable to pay) 88-2509.2	
HAWAII Rev. Stat. (1976 & Supp. 1981)	334-60(b)(3) (B)(vi)	334-60(b)(3) (B)(vi) 334-60(b)(3) (B)(vii)	public defender 334-60(b)(3) (B)(vi)					
IDAHO Code (1980 & Supp. 1981)	66-329(f), (g)	66-329(g)	county 66-327	upon receipt of application by ct. 66-329(f), (g)				
ILL. Ann. Stat. (Smith-Hurd 1966 & Supp. 1980)	unless makes informed waiver 91½, §3-805	minor: if petition for review 91½, §3-805 91½, §3-509	county (if unable to pay) 91½, §3-805.3	when hearing set 91½, §3-805 minor: upon receipt of petition for review 91½, §3-509	unless makes informed waiver 91½, §4-605	91½, §4-605	county (if unable to pay) 91½, §4-605.3	when hearing set 91½, §4-605
IND. Code Ann. (Burns 1973 & Supp. 1982)	temporary commitment 16-14-9.1-9 (e)(4) 16-14-9.1-10(c)							
IOWA Code Ann. (West 1969 & Supp. 1980)	229.8.1	229.8.1	229.8.1	as soon as practicable after application filed 229.8		222.22	county 222.22	
KAN. Stat. Ann. (1976 & Supp. 1981)	protective custody procedure 59-2912(f) 59-2914(c)	protective custody procedure 59-2912(f) 59-2914(c)	county (applicant if patient not mentally ill) 59-2934	upon filing of application 59-2914				

TABLE 2.15 LEGAL COUNSEL IN PROCEEDINGS TO INSTITUTIONALIZE MENTALLY ILL AND DEVELOPMENTALLY DISABLED PERSONS—*Continued*

	MENTALLY ILL				DEVELOPMENTALLY DISABLED			
STATE	Right to Be Represented (1)	Mandatory Court-appointed Counsel if Patient Not Represented (2)	Counsel Publicly Compensated (3)	When (4)	Right to Be Represented (5)	Mandatory Court-appointed Counsel if Patient Not Represented (6)	Counsel Publicly Compensated (7)	When (8)
KY. Rev. Stat. Ann. (Michie 1977 & Supp. 1980)	60-day 202A.070(7) 360-day 202A.080(4)	60-day 202A.070(7) 360-day 202A.080(4)			same as mentally ill 202B.020	same as mentally ill 202B.020		
LA. Rev. Stat. Ann. (West 1975 & Supp. 1981)	28:54C	28:55B	judiciary funds 28:55C	"as early as possible in every proceeding" 28:55C	28:398B	28:398B		
ME. Rev. Stat. Ann. (1978 & Supp. 1981)	34, §2334.4D	34, §2334.4D			34, §2659-A2D	if indigent 34, §2659-A2D		
MD. Ann. Code (1979 & Supp. 1981)	59, §13(c)			notice of right & availability of legal aid w/in 12 hrs. of involuntary admission 59, §13(c)	59A, §10(e)			
MASS. Ann. Laws (Michie/Law. Co-op. (1981 & Supp. 1981)	123, §5	unless refused 123, §5	state pays all necessary expenses in commitment 123, §33	hearing at least 2 days after counsel appears 123, §5				
MICH. Comp. Laws Ann. (1980 & Supp. 1981)	preliminary probable cause hearing 330.1450(3) 330.1454(1)	may waive after consultation 330.1454(3)	court funds 330.1454(5)	w/in 48 hrs. of petition; w/in 24 hrs. of hospitalization 330.1454(2)	same as mentally ill 330.1517(3)			
MINN. Stat. Ann. (West 1971 & Supp. 1981)	253A.07.15	253A.07.15	county 253A.20.1		253A.07.15	253A.07.15	county 253A.20.1	
MISS. Code Ann. (1981)	41-21-73	may waive 41-21-73	county (if indigent) (if found not in need of treatment, affiant pays) 41-21-79		commitment to S. Miss. Retardation Center same as mental illness procedures 41-19-151(b) 41-21-73	may waive 41-21-73	county (if indigent) (if found not in need of treatment, affiant pays) 41-21-79	
MO. Ann. Stat. (Vernon 1979 & Supp. 1980)	632.335.2(1)	also has right to private counsel of own choosing 632.325(4)	state (if unable to pay) 632.415(2)	w/in 3 hrs. of arrival at facility given notice of identity of appointed attorney 632.320.1(2) if requested, assistance in contacting attorney of own choosing 632.320.1(3)				
MONT. Code Ann. (1981)	may not waive 53-21-119(1) 53-21-115(4)	53-21-116	county 53-21-116	appointed at hearing or trial 53-21-116	same as mentally ill 53-20-112(1), (2)(b) may not waive 53-20-113(1)			
NEB. Rev. Stat. (1976 & Supp. 1981)	83-1049	if indigent 83-1049, 83-1050	public defender 83-1050(2) if none, county 83-1051		83-1109	83-1109	county 83-1132	
NEV. Rev. Stat. (1981)	433A.270	433A.270(1)	county (if indigent) 433A.270(2)	counsel granted 5-day recess to prepare case on request 433A.270(3)				
N.H. Rev. Stat. Ann. (1977 & Supp. 1981)	emergency 135-B:22(I)(a) 135-B:35	right to have counsel appointed if indigent 135-B:22(I)(b)		must be notified of right w/in 12 hrs. 135-B:22(I)	171-A:10(I)	if unable to pay 171-A10(I)	171-A-10(I)	
N.J. Stat. Ann. (West 1981)	opportunity *fn. 6* 30:4-41							
N.M. Stat. Ann. (1979 & Supp. 1981)	minor 43-1-16.1C 43-1-4 43-1-11B	shall be represented 43-1-11B 43-1-4 minor 43-1-16.1C 43-1-4	when indigent 43-1-4(B)		minor 43-1-16.1C 43-1-4 43-1-13D	shall be represented 43-1-13D 43-1-4 minor 43-1-16.1C 43-1-4	when indigent 43-1-4(B)	
N.Y. Mental Hyg. Law (McKinney 1978)	*fn. 7*							
N.C. Gen. Stat. (1981)	122-58.7(c)	if indigent or refuses to retain counsel *fn. 8* 122-58.7(c)			122-58.7(c)	if indigent or refuses to retain counsel 122-58.7(c)		

TABLE 2.15 LEGAL COUNSEL IN PROCEEDINGS TO INSTITUTIONALIZE MENTALLY ILL AND DEVELOPMENTALLY DISABLED PERSONS—*Continued*

	MENTALLY ILL				DEVELOPMENTALLY DISABLED			
STATE	Right to Be Represented (1)	Mandatory Court-appointed Counsel if Patient Not Represented (2)	Counsel Publicly Compensated (3)	When (4)	Right to Be Represented (5)	Mandatory Court-appointed Counsel if Patient Not Represented (6)	Counsel Publicly Compensated (7)	When (8)
N.D. Cent. Code (1978 & Supp. 1979)	25-03.1-13.1	may waive in writing after consultation 25-03.1-13.3	county (if indigent) 25-03.1-13.4	w/in 72 hrs. of service of petition; w/in 24 hrs. of hospitalization 25-03.1-13.2				
OHIO Rev. Code Ann. (Baldwin 1980 & Supp. 1981)	probable cause hearing 5122.141(C) 5122.15(A)(2)	if unable to obtain counsel 5122.15(A)(4) probable cause hearing if unable to obtain counsel 5122.141(C)	5122.43(G)		probable cause hearing 5123.75(B) developmental disabilities or mental retardation 5123.76(A)(2)	if not validly waived 5123.76(A)(3) probable cause hearing if indigent 5123.75(B)	county (reimbursed by state department of mental health & mental retardation) 5123.96(G)	
OKLA. Stat. Ann. (West 1979 & Supp. 1981)	43A, §54.4C	43A, §54.4C	ct. fund (if indigent) 43A, §54.4C7 43A, §54.4E	immediately upon receipt of petition 43A, §54.4C				
OR. Rev. Stat. , (1981)	426.100(1)	unless "expressly, knowingly and intelligently" waived 426.100(2)	county (if indigent) 426.100(3)	when brought before ct. 426.100	427.245	427.265	county (if indigent) 427.265(3)	when brought before ct. 427.265 immediately upon receipt of citation if requested 427.245(2)
PA. Stat. Ann. (Purdon 1969 & Supp. 1980)	fn. 9 50, §7304(e)(1)	extended involuntary emergency treatment 50, §7303(b) 50, §7304(c)(3)	public defender 16, §9960.6(c)	upon determination that petition sets forth reasonable cause 50, §7304(c)(3)	fn. 9 50, §4406			
R.I. Gen. Laws (1977 & Supp. 1981)	40.1-5.1-11	if indigent 40.1-5.1-13	state 40.1-5.1-13		40.1-22-10.4	40.1-22-10.4		
S.C. Code Ann. (Law. Co-op. 1976 & Supp. 1981)	44-17-520	44-17-530		w/in 3 days after petition 44-17-530	44-21-90	44-21-90		
S.D. Codified Laws Ann. (1976 & Supp. 1981)	27A-9-8	upon mandatory petition by patient, representative, or chair of board of mental illness 27A-9-8	county (reimbursed by patient or person legally bound to support, if able) 27A-9-15	at least 72 hrs. before hearing 27A-9-8	27B-7-11		county mental retardation fund 27B-7-12	
TENN. Code Ann. (1977 & Supp. 1981)	33-604(b)	33-604(b)	state (if patient & responsible relatives unable to pay) 33-312	before hearing 10-day extension on request 33-604(b)				
TEX. Rev. Civ. Stat. Ann. (Vernon 1968 & Supp. 1981)	5547-43	5547-43	county (unless committed to private hospital) 5547-14 not less than $25 5547-15		5547-300G, §37(m)(4)	5547-300G, §37(l)	county 5547-300G, §37(l)	10 days before hearing 5547-300G, §37(l)
UTAH Code Ann. (1978 & Supp. 1981)	64-7-36(9)	64-7-36(9)	county 64-7-36(9)	to allow time for consultation before hearing 64-7-36(9)				
VT. Stat. Ann. (1968 & Supp. 1981)	unless emergency proceeding 18, §7111	unless emergency proceeding 18, §7111	state (if patient unable to pay) 18, §7111			18, §8825(a)(1)	department of mental health 18, §8825(b)	upon filing of petition 18, §8825(a)
VA. Code (1976 & Supp. 1981)	37.1-67.3	37.1-67.3	$25 per hearing plus expenses paid by state 37.1-89					
WASH. Rev. Code Ann. (1975 & Supp. 1981)	90 days 71.05.300 upon detention & at 14-day hearing 71.05.200(1)(b)	90 days 71.05.300 14 days 71.05.230(6)	county (if indigent) 71.05.110					
W. VA. Code (1980 & Supp. 1981)	27-5-4(e)	27-5-4(g)(2)	county commission 27-5-4(r)(2)	6 days prior to hearing 27-5-4(g)(2)	27-5-4(e)	27-5-4(g)(2)	county commission 27-5-4(r)(2)	6 days prior to hearing 27-5-4(g)(2)
WIS. Stat. Ann. (West 1957 & Supp. 1980)	51.20(2)	51.20(3)	state public defender 51.20(3) indigency determined by public defender board 977.07(1)	upon filing of petition 51.20(3)	51.20(2)	51.20(3)	state public defender 51.20(3) indigency determined by public defender board 977.07(1)	upon filing of petition 51.20(3)
WYO. Stat. (1977)	25-3-112(g)	25-3-112(g)	county 25-3-116(b)ii if not a state resident, state board of charities 25-3-116(d)					

FOOTNOTES TABLE 2.15

1. Ala. Code § 22-52-4(b) (Supp. 1981): "No statement made or act done in the presence of the probate judge prior to such person obtaining the services of an attorney, by appointment or otherwise, shall be considered by the probate judge in determining whether such person should be committed."

2. Id. § 22-52-14:

> [I]f the petition is denied and the petitioner is not indigent and is not a law enforcement officer or other public official acting within the line and scope of his duties, all costs may be taxed against the petitioner, or if the petition is granted and the person sought to be committed is not indigent, the probate judge may order all costs paid from the estate of the person committed.

3. Colo. Rev. Stat. § 27-10-107(5) (Supp. 1981). Respondent may waive counsel if the waiver is "knowingly and intelligently made in writing and filed with the court by the respondent."

4. Conn. Gen. Stat. Ann. § 17-183(c) (West Supp. 1981). If hearing requested when under emergency hospitalization, right to counsel (provided at state expense if patient unable to pay).

5. Del. Code Ann. tit. 16, § 5011(a) (Supp. 1980). The involuntary patient may knowingly and intelligently waive any right.

6. 100 N.J. Super. 595, 242 A.2d 861 (1968). Counsel should be provided in every judicial commitment proceeding.

7. N.Y. Mental Hyg. Law § 29-09 (McKinney 1978). New York has its Mental Health Information Service (MHIS), with wide-ranging duties to advise the court and the (proposed) patient at various junctures in the commitment process (initially nonjudicial in New York) and once the patient is in the institution. The MHIS, however, is not a patient advocacy agency—it is an arm of the court and its primary responsibility is to the judiciary—nor is it staffed exclusively by lawyers.

8. N.C. Gen. Stat. § 122-58.10 (1981). Counsel assigned to represent indigent defendant continues to be responsible for representation for an appeal and after commitment until released, unless discharged by the court.

9. Commonwealth ex rel. Finken v. Roop, 234 Pa. Super. 155, 339 A.2d 364 (1975), cert. denied, 424 U.S. 960 (1976). By reasonable construction, due process dictates can be incorporated into civil commitment statute so as to require that subject of civil commitment petition be represented by counsel and that the final commitment order follow an evidentiary hearing.

TABLE 2.16 LEGAL COUNSEL IN PROCEEDINGS TO INSTITUTIONALIZE ALCOHOLICS AND DRUG ADDICTS

	ALCOHOLIC					DRUG ADDICT				
		Court-Appointed Counsel if Patient Not Represented					Court-Appointed Counsel if Patient Not Represented			
STATE	*Right to Be Represented* (1)	Mandatory (2)	Mandatory on Patient's Request or if Court Believes Counsel Necessary (3)	*Counsel Publicly Compensated* (4)	*When* (5)	*Right to Be Represented* (6)	Mandatory (7)	Mandatory on Patient's Request (8)	*Counsel Publicly Compensated* (9)	*When* (10)
ALAS. Stat. (1979 & Supp. 1981)	47.37.200(h)		47-37.200(h)							
ARK. Stat. Ann. (1971 & Supp. 1981)						59-906		if unable to pay counsel 59-906		
CAL. Welf. & Inst. Code (West 1972 & Supp. 1982)	judicial review of 14-day certification for intensive treatment 5276	judicial review of 14-day certification: on request 5276		judicial review of 14-day certification: public defender 5276		3104	if unable to pay 3104		public defender or county 3104	
CONN. Gen. Stat. Ann. (West 1975 & Supp. 1981)	17-1552(b)		17-155(b)				if cannot afford counsel 19-495 19-496a(b)			
DEL. Code Ann. (1974 & Supp. 1980)	16, §2213(j)		16, §2213(j)							
D.C. Code Ann. (1981 & Supp. 1983)		24-527(e)				24-604(a)	if unable to obtain counsel 24-604(a)			
FLA. Stat. Ann. (West 1973 & Supp. 1981)	396.102(9)		396.102(9)			397.052(6)		of if ct. believes counsel necessary 397.052(6)		
GA. Code Ann. (1979 & Supp. 1980)	emergency 88-404.6(a) evaluation 88-405.3(a) 88-406.2(a)(2)	*fn. 1*		county (if unable to pay) 88-407.2(a)		emergency 88-404.6(a) evaluation 88-405.3(a) 88-406.2(a)(2)	*fn. 1*		county (if unable to pay) 88-407.2(a)	
HAWAII Rev. Stat. (1976 & Supp. 1981)	suffering from substance abuse 334-60(b)(3)(B)(vi)	suffering from substance abuse 334-60(b)(3)(B)(vi), (vii)		suffering from substance abuse: public defender 334-60(b)(3)(B)(vi)		suffering from substance abuse 334-60(b)(3)(B)(vi)	suffering from substance abuse 334-60(b)(3)(B)(vi), (vii)		suffering from substance abuse: public defender 334-60(b)(3)(B)(vi)	
ILL. Ann. Stat. (Smith-Hurd 1966 & Supp. 1981)	91½, §513(6)									
IND. Code Ann. (Burns 1973 & Supp. 1982) *fn. 2*	16-14-9.1-10(C)					16-14-9.1-10(C)				
IOWA Code Ann. (West & Supp. 1980)		substance abuser: guardian ad litem 229.52					substance abuser: guardian ad litem 229.52			
KAN. Stat. Ann. (1980 & Supp. 1981)	65-4033(C)	65-4036		county 65-4053	upon filing of application 65-4033					
KY. Rev. Stat. Ann. (Michie 1977 & Supp. 1981) *fn. 3*						202A.070(7) 202A.080(4)	202A.070(7) 202A.080(4)			
LA. Rev. Stat. Ann. (West 1975 & Supp. 1981)	suffering from substance abuse 28:54C	suffering from substance abuse 28:55B		suffering from substance abuse: judiciary funds 28:55B	suffering from substance abuse: "as early as possible in every proceeding" 28:55C	suffering from substance abuse 28:54C	suffering from substance abuse 28:55B		suffering from substance abuse: judiciary funds 28:55B	suffering from substance abuse: "as early as possible in every proceeding" 28:55C
ME. Rev. Stat. Ann. (1978 & Supp. 1981)	22, §7120.10 22, §1374.10		22, §7120.10 22, §1374.10							
MD. Health Gen. Ann. Code (1979 & Supp. 1982)						9-605		may be waived 9-605	if individual cannot afford counsel 9-605	at each stage of proceeding 9-605
MINN. Stat. Ann. (West 1971 & Supp. 1981)	(inebriate) 253A.07.15	(inebriate) or county attorney 253A.07.15		(inebriate) county 253A.20.1		(inebriate) 253A.07.15	(inebriate) or county attorney 253.07.15		(inebriate) county 253A.20.1	
MONT. Code Ann. (1981)	53-24-302(3)	if unable to obtain counsel 53-24-302(3)		county 53-24-302(3)						
NEB. Rev. Stat. (1976 & Supp. 1981)						83-702(2)	if unable to pay 83-702(2)			
N.J. Stat. Ann. (West 1981 & Supp. 1983)	30:9-12.21									
N.M. Stat. Ann. (1979 & Supp. 1981)	43-2-9B	if indigent 43-2-9B		43-2-9B 43-1-25	"at all stages of the proceeding" 43-2-9B					
N.C. Gen. Stat. (1981 & Supp. 1981)	122-58.7(c)	if indigent, unless waived 122-58.7(c)				122-58.7(c)	if indigent, unless waived 122-58.7(c)			

TABLE 2.16 LEGAL COUNSEL IN PROCEEDINGS TO INSTITUTIONALIZE ALCOHOLICS AND DRUG ADDICTS—*Continued*

	ALCOHOLIC					DRUG ADDICT				
		Court-Appointed Counsel if Patient Not Represented					*Court-Appointed Counsel if Patient Not Represented*			
STATE	*Right to Be Represented* (1)	Mandatory (2)	Mandatory on Patient's Request or if Court Believes Counsel Necessary (3)	*Counsel Publicly Compensated* (4)	*When* (5)	*Right to Be Represented* (6)	Mandatory (7)	Mandatory on Patient's Request (8)	*Counsel Publicly Compensated* (9)	*When* (10)
N.D. Cent. Code (1978 & Supp. 1981)	25-03.1-13.1	may waive after consultation 25-03.1-13.3 25-03.1-13.2		county (if indigent) 25-03.1-13.4	w/in 72 hrs. of service of petition; w/in 24 hrs. of emergency hospitalization 25-03.1-13.2	25-03.1-13.1	may waive after consultation 25-03.1-13.3 25-03.1-13.2		county (if indigent) 25-03.1-13.4	w/in 72 hrs. of service of petition; w/in 24 hrs. of emergency hospitalization 25-03.1-13.2
OKLA. Stat. Ann. (West 1979 & Supp. 1980)	63, §2130.3	63, §2130.3		ct. (if indigent) 63, §2133C	when judge determines that probable cause exists 63, §2130	43A, §673	if unable to pay counsel 43A, §673			
R.I. Gen. Laws (1977 & Supp. 1981)	40.1-4-12(10)		40.1-4-12(10)			21-28.2-7				
S.C. Code (Law. Co-op. 1976 & Supp. 1981)	44-51-110	discretionary 44-51-110				44-51-110	discretionary 44-51-110			
TENN. Code Ann. (1977 & Supp. 1981) *fn. 4*	33-604(b)	33-604(b)		state (if unable to pay) 33-312	before hearing; 10-day extension on request 33-604(b)	33-604(b)	33-604(b)		state (if unable to pay) 33-312	before hearing; 10-day extension on request 33-604(b)
TEX. Rev. Civ. Stat. Ann. (Vernon 1958 & Supp. 1981)	may be waived 5561c, §9(c)	5561c, §9(c)					5561c-1, §2(c)			
VT. Stat. Ann. (1968 & Supp. 1981) *fn. 5*						18, §7111	18, §7111		state (if unable to pay) 18, §7111	
VA. Code (1976 & Supp. 1981) *fn. 6*	37.1-67.3	37.1-67.3		state 37.1-89		37.1-67.3	37.1-67.3		state 37.1-89	
WASH. Rev. Code Ann. (1975 & Supp. 1981)	70.96A.140(10)		70.96A.140(10)	if unable to pay 70.96A.140(10)						
W. VA. Code (1980 & Supp. 1981)	(addicted) 27-5-4(e)	(addicted) 27-5-4(g)(2)		(addicted) public defender 29-21-15		(addicted) 27-5-4(e)	(addicted) 27-5-4(g)(2)		(addicted) public defender 29-21-15	
WIS. Stat. Ann. (West 1957 & Supp. 1980)	may be waived 51.45(13)(b)2	51.45(13)(d)		state public defender 51.45(13)(b)2 977.07(2)	on receipt of petition 51.45(13)(b)	51.20(2)	51.20(3)		state public defender 51.20(3) 977.07(2)	on filing of petition 51.20(3)
WYO. Stat. Ann. (1977)										

FOOTNOTES TABLE 2.16

1. Ga. Code Ann. § 88-406.2a(2) (Supp. 1980). Mandatory unless waived in writing. Id. § 88-404.6(a) (1979). Emergency—mandatory if can't afford, Id. § 88-405.3(a). Evaluation—mandatory if can't afford, unless waived in writing.

2. Ind. Code Ann. § 16-13-6.1-21 (Burns Supp. 1982): "An individual who is an alcoholic, who is incapacitated by alcohol, or who is a drug abuser may be involuntarily committed to the care of the department by the civil procedure established by IC 16-14-9.1 [16-14-9.1-1 to 16-14-9.1-18—those pertaining to the mentally ill]." See table 3.12.

3. Ky. Rev. Stat. Ann. § 222.430 (Michie Supp. 1980):

(1) Involuntary hospitalization of the drug dependent person, drug addict or person under the influence of drugs . . . shall take place by the same procedures as hospitalization of the mentally ill as provided in KRS Chapters 202A and 210.

(2) All rights guaranteed by KRS Chapters 202A, 202B, and 210 to mentally ill persons shall be guaranteed to the drug dependent person, drug addict and the person under the influence of drugs.

See table 3.12.

4. Tenn. Code Ann. § 33-806 (Supp. 1981). Involuntary hospitalization of drug addicts and alcoholics takes place by the same procedures as hospitalization of the mentally ill; all rights guaranteed to the mentally ill are guaranteed to drug addicts and alcoholics as well. See table 3.12.

5. Vt. Stat. Ann. tit. 18, § 8402 (Supp. 1981): "[A] drug addict may be admitted to a designated hospital and provided with care and treatment in the same manner and under the same conditions as a mentally ill person." See table 3.12.

6. Va. Code § 37.1-1(15) (Supp. 1981): "[P]rovided that, for the purposes of Chapter 2 (§ 37.1-63 et seq.) of this title, the term 'mentally ill' shall be deemed to include any person who is a drug addict or alcoholic." See table 3.12.

7. Wyo. Stat. § 3-1-102 (Supp. 1982). Involuntary hospitalization of alcoholics takes place by the same procedures as hospitalization of the mentally ill, and all rights guaranteed to the mentally ill are guaranteed to alcoholics as well. See table 3.12.

TABLE 2.17 FINANCIAL RESPONSIBILITY FOR MENTALLY ILL PERSONS IN INSTITUTIONS

	PATIENT		FAMILY		COUNTY		STATE	
STATE	Voluntary Admission (1)	Involuntary Admission (2)	Voluntary Admission (3)	Involuntary Admission (4)	Voluntary Admission (5)	Involuntary Admission (6)	Voluntary Admission (7)	Involuntary Admission (8)
ALA. Code (1975 & Supp. 1981)		22-53-20		22-53-1				22-53-3
ALAS. Stat. (1979 & Supp. 1981)	47.30.910(a)	47.30.910(a)	47.30.910(a)	47.30.910(a)			Dep't of Health & Social Services 47.30.910(a)	Dep't of Health & Social Services 47.30.910(a)
ARIZ. Rev. Stat. Ann. (1974 & Supp. 1981)	36-545	36-545.01(B)	private facility only 36-545.03	private facility only 36-545.03 parents, if patient is minor 36-545.01(E)		*fn. 1*	36-545	
ARK. Stat. Ann. (1971 & Supp. 1981)	59-1421	59-1421	person legally liable for patient's support 59-1421	person legally liable for patient's support 59-1421		59-1421	59-1421	
CAL. Welf. & Inst. Code (West 1972 & Supp. 1981)	7275 7279	7275 7279	7275 7279	7275 7279			7275 7279	7275 7279
COLO. Rev. Stat. (1973 & Supp. 1981)	27-12-101	27-12-101	parents, spouse 27-12-101 parents, spouse; parents' liability ends on completing 180-mos. payment or when patient turns 18 27-12-103	parents, spouse 27-12-101 parents, spouse; parents' liability ends on completing 180-mos. payment or when patient turns 18 27-12-103			27-12-101 to 27-12-109	27-12-101 to 27-12-109
CONN. Gen. Stat. Ann. (West 1975 & Supp. 1981)	17-295(c)	*fn. 2* 17-182 17-295(c)	*fn. 3* 17-295(c)	*fn. 2* 17-182 *fn. 3* 17-295(c)			17-295	*fn. 2* 17-182 17-295
DEL. Code Ann. (1974 & Supp. 1980)	16-5127 16-5123	16-5127	*fn. 4* 16-5127(a) 16-5123	*fn. 4* 16-5127(a)				16-5127
D.C. Code Ann. (1981 & Supp. 1982)	21-586(a)	21-586(a)	father, mother, husband, wife, adult children 21-586(a)	father, mother husband, wife, adult children 21-586(a)			district 21-586	district 21-586
FLA. Stat. Ann. (West 1973 & Supp. 1981)	402.33	402.33	spouse, & parents if child is minor 402.33(1)	spouse, & parents if child is minor 402.33(1)			402.33	402.33
GA. Code Ann. §35:(1982) §88:(1979 & Supp. 1980)	35-1105 88-507.7(a)	35-1105 88-507.7(a)	88-507.7(b) spouse, & parents if child is minor 35-1102(d)(2)	88-507.7(b) spouse, & parents if child is minor 35-1102(d)(2)	88-507.7(c)	88-507(c)	Dep't of Human Resources 88-507.7(d)	Dep't of Human Resources 88-507.7(d)
HAWAII Rev. Stat. (1976 & Supp. 1981) *fn. 5*	334-6(b)	334-6(b)	spouse, & parents if child is minor 334-6(b)	spouse, & parents if child is minor 334-6(b)			334-6	334-6
IDAHO Code (1980 & Supp. 1981)	66-354(a)	66-354(a)	*fn. 6* 66-354(a), (b)	*fn. 6* 66-354(a), (b)	66-327(a)	66-327(a)	66-354	66-354 66-327
ILL. Ann. Stat. (Smith-Hurd 1966 & Supp. 1980)	91½, §5-105	91½, §5-105	*fn. 7* 91½, §5-105	*fn. 7* 91½, §5-105	91½, §5-115	91½, §5-115	91½, §5-105 91½, §5-115	91½, §5-105 91½, §5-115
IND. Code Ann. (Burns 1973 & Supp. 1982)	*fn. 8* 16-14-18.1-2(c) 16-14-18.1-3(a)	*fn. 8* 16-14-18.1-2(c) 16-14-18.1-3(a)	*fn. 8* 16-14-18.1-2(c) 16-14-18.1-3(a)	*fn. 8* 16-14-18.1-2(c) 16-14-18.1-3(a)	16-14-18.1-12	16-14-18.1-14	16-14-18.1-5 16-14-18.1-11	16-14-18.1-5 16-14-18.1-11
IOWA Code Ann. (West 1969 & Supp. 1980)	229.41 230.15	*fn. 9* 230.15 229.22	*fn. 9* 230.15	230.15 229.22	230.1 230.20	230.1 230.20	230.1–.30	230.1–.30
KAN. Stat. Ann. (1976 & Supp. 1981)	59-2006	59-2006	spouse, & parents if child is minor 59-2006	spouse, & parents if child is minor 59-2006			59-2006	59-2006

TABLE 2.17 FINANCIAL RESPONSIBILITY FOR MENTALLY ILL PERSONS IN INSTITUTIONS—*Continued*

	PATIENT		FAMILY		COUNTY		STATE	
STATE	Voluntary Admission (1)	Involuntary Admission (2)	Voluntary Admission (3)	Involuntary Admission (4)	Voluntary Admission (5)	Involuntary Admission (6)	Voluntary Admission (7)	Involuntary Admission (8)
KY. Rev. Stat. Ann. (Michie 1977 & Supp. 1980)	210.720(1)	210.720(1)	spouse, & parents if child is minor 210.710(5)	spouse, & parents if child is minor 210.710(5)			210.700–.760	210.700–.760
LA. Rev. Stat. Ann. (West 1975 & Supp. 1981)	28:143 28:22.6	28:143 28:22.6	28:143 28:22.6	28:143 28:22.6			28:143 28:22.6	289:143 28:22.6
ME. Rev. Stat. Ann. (1978 & Supp. 1981)	34, §2512	34, §2512	*fn. 10* 34, §2512	*fn. 10* 34, §2512			34, §2512	34, §2512
MD. Ann. Code art. 59 (1979 & Supp. 1981) art. 43 (1980 & Supp. 1981)	59, §45 43, §601(c)(1)	59, §45 43, §601(c)(1)	spouse; parent, if child is under 18; & child of patient 59, §45 43, §601(c)(1)	spouse; parent, if child is under 18, & child of patient 59, §45 43, §601(c)(1)			59, §45 43, §601	59, §45 43, §601
MASS. Ann. Laws (Michie/Law. Co-op. (1981 & Supp. 1981)	123, §32	123, §32	spouse; parent, if child is minor; or child if over 18 & has sufficient ability 123, §32	spouse; parent, if child is minor; or child if over 18 & has sufficient ability 123, §32			123, §32	123, §32
MICH. Comp. Laws Ann. (1980 & Supp. 1981)	330.1804	330.1804	spouse; parents if child is unmarried minor 330.1804	spouse; parents if child is unmarried minor 330.1804	330.1302 330.1314	330.1302 330.1314	330.1308 330.1309	330.1308 330.1309
MINN. Stat. Ann. (West 1982)	246.51	246.51	spouse; children; parent, if child under 18 246.51	spouse; children; parent, if child under 18 246.51	246.54	246.54	246.51	246.51
MISS. Code Ann. (1981)	41-4-7(e)	41-4-7(e)	41-7-17	41-7-17			41-7-17	41-7-17
MO. Ann. Stat. (Vernon 1979 & Supp. 1980)	630.205	630.205	spouse; parents if child under 18 630.205	spouse; parents if child under 18 630.205			630.205	630.205
MONT. Code Ann. (1979)	53-1-405	53-1-405	spouse; parent, if child under 18 53-1-405	spouse; parent, if child under 18 53-1-405			53-1-405	53-1-405
NEB. Rev. Stat. (1976 & Supp. 1981)	83-352.02	83-352.02	spouse, child, or parent 83-352.02	spouse, child, or parent 83-352.02			*fn. 11* 83-348	*fn. 11* 83-348
NEV. Rev. Stat. (1979)	433A.600 433A.610	433A.600 433A.610	spouse; adult child; parent, if child a minor 433A.600 433A.610	spouse; adult child; parent, if child a minor 433A.600 433A.610			433A.600 433A.610	433A.600 433A.610
N.H. Rev. Stat. Ann. (1977 & Supp. 1981)	126A:51	126A:51	liability of persons other than patient ends after 10 yrs. or when patient reaches majority 126A:51	liability of persons other than patient ends after 10 yrs. or when patient reaches majority 126A:51			*fn. 12* 126A:54	*fn. 12* 126A:54
N.J. Stat. Ann. (West 1981)	30:4-60 30:4-66	30:4-60 30:4-66	spouse; parents, if child under 18 30:4-60 30:4-66	spouse; parents, if child under 18 30:4-60 30:4-66	30:4-60 30:4-68 30:4-73	30:4-60 30:4-68 30:4-73	30:4-60 30:4-69	30:4-60 30:4-69
N.M. Stat. Ann. (1979 & Supp. 1981)	43-1-25	43-1-25					43-1-25	43-1-25
N.Y. Mental Hyg. Law (McKinney 1978 & Supp. 1981)	43.03	43.03	43.03	43.03			43.03	43.03

TABLE 2.17 FINANCIAL RESPONSIBILITY FOR MENTALLY ILL PERSONS IN INSTITUTIONS—*Continued*

STATE	PATIENT Voluntary Admission (1)	PATIENT Involuntary Admission (2)	FAMILY Voluntary Admission (3)	FAMILY Involuntary Admission (4)	COUNTY Voluntary Admission (5)	COUNTY Involuntary Admission (6)	STATE Voluntary Admission (7)	STATE Involuntary Admission (8)
N.C. Gen. Stat. (1981 & Supp. 1981)	*fn. 13* 122-35.47	*fn. 13* 122-35.47			122-35.42	122-35.42	122-35.53	122-35.53
N.D. Cent. Code (1978 & Supp. 1981)	*fn. 14* 25-09-02 25-09-03	*fn. 14* 25-09-02 25-09-03	spouse; parent, if child under 18 *fn. 15* 25-09-04	spouse; parent, if child under 18 *fn. 15* 25-09-04			*fn. 16* 25-09-01	*fn. 16* 25-09-01
OHIO Rev. Code Ann. (Baldwin 1980 & Supp. 1981)	5121.04 5121.06	5121.04 5121.06	spouse; parent, if child under 18 after relative pays charges for 15 yrs., liability ceases 5121.06	spouse; parent, if child under 18 after relative pays charges for 15 yrs., liability ceases 5121.06			5121.01	5121.01
OKLA. Stat. Ann. (West 1979 & Supp. 1981)	43A, §§53, 111	43A, §111	spouse, parents, or child 43A, §§53, 115	spouse, parents, or child 43A, §115			43A, §113	43A, §113
OR. Rev. Stat. (1979 & Supp. 1981)	179.620	426.241(1) 179.620				426.241(1)	179.620	426.241(1) 179.620
PA. Stat. Ann. (Purdon 1969 & Supp. 1980)	50, §4501	50, §4501	parents, if child under 18; spouse for first 120 days of care 50, §4502	parents, if child under 18; spouse for first 120 days of care 50, §4502	50, §4503	50, §4503	50, §4503 50, §4507	50, §4503 50, §4507
R.I. Gen. Laws (1977 & Supp. 1980)	40.1-5-33	40.1-5-33	40.1-5-33	40.1-5-33			40.1-5-33 40.1-5-35	40.1-5-33 40.1-5-35
S.C. Code Ann. (Law. Co-op. 1976 & Supp. 1981)	44-23-1130	44-23-1130	parents or other persons legally re-sponsible 44-23-1130	parents or other persons legally re-sponsible 44-23-1130			44-23-1130	44-23-1130
S.D. Codified Laws Ann. (1976 & Supp. 1981)	27A-13-7	27A-13-7	responsible person or other entity legally liable 27A-13-7	responsible person or other entity legally liable 27A-13-7	27A-13-6	27A-13-6	27A-13-7	27A-13-7
TENN. Code Ann. (1977 & Supp. 1981)	33-402 33-406	33-402 33-406	responsible relatives 33-402 33-406	responsible relatives 33-402 33-406			33-402 33-406	33-402 33-406
TEX. Rev. Civ. Stat. Ann. (Vernon 1958 & Supp. 1981)	5547-14(b)	5547-14(b)	any person or or estate liable for support 5547-14(b)	any person or or estate liable for support 5547-14(b)	5547-14(a)	5547-14(a)	*fn. 17* 5547-14(d)	*fn. 17* 5547-14(d)
UTAH Code Ann. (1978 & Supp. 1981)	64-7-6 64-7-15 64-7-18	64-7-6 64-7-18	spouse, parents, or children 64-7-6 64-7-15	spouse, parents, or children 64-7-6			64-7-6 64-7-15 64-7-20	64-7-6 64-7-20
VT. Stat. Ann. (1968 & Supp. 1981)	18, §§8101, 8108	18, §§8101, 8108	spouse; parents, if child a minor 18, §8101	spouse; parents, if child a minor 18, §8101			18, §8101	18, §8101
VA. Code (1976 & Supp. 1981)	37.1-105	37.1-105	spouse; parents, if child under 18 37.1-105	spouse; parents, if child under 18 *fn. 18* 37.1-105			37.1-105	37.1-105
WASH. Rev. Code Ann. (1975 & Supp. 1981)	71.02.411	71.02.411	71.02.411	71.02.411			71.02.411	71.02.411
W. VA. Code (1980 & Supp. 1981)	27-8-1	27-8-1	spouse; parents, if child uneman-cipated minor 27-8-1	spouse; parents, if child uneman-cipated minor 27-8-1	27-8-2	27-8-2	27-8-1	27-8-1
WIS. Stat. Ann. (West 1980 & Supp. 1981)	46.10(2)	46.10(2)	spouse; parents, if child a minor 46.10(2)	spouse; parents, if child a minor 46.10(2)	46.106	46.106	51.22 46.10(8)(d)	51.22 46.10(8)(d)
WYO. Stat. (1981 & Supp. 1982)	25-3-205	25-3-205	*fn. 19* 25-3-207	*fn. 19* 25-3-207			25-3-209	25-3-209

FOOTNOTES TABLE 2.17

1. Op. Att'y Gen. No. 179-75. Where an individual is undergoing court-ordered psychiatric treatment at a private rather than a county facility and is unable to assume the full cost of care, county is responsible for the portion of the cost that the patient is unable to pay.

2. Conn. Gen. Stat. Ann. § 17-182 (West 1975):

> Any mentally ill person, the expense of whose support is paid by himself or by another person may be committed to any institution for the care of the mentally ill designated by the person paying for such support; and any indigent mentally ill person, not a pauper, . . . shall be committed to any state hospital for mental illness which is equipped to receive him, at the discretion of the court of probate, upon consideration of a request made by the person applying for such commitment.

3. Id. § 17-295(c) (West Supp. 1981):

> Each patient, the husband or wife of such patient and the father and mother of a patient under the age of eighteen years shall be legally liable from the date of admission for support of such patient in such institution in accordance with his ability to pay; except that . . . liability of legally liable relatives as such for a patient in a state humane institution, except a state training school for mentally retarded persons, shall cease when such support has been paid . . . for a period or periods amounting to sixteen years unless earlier terminated as to a patient by attainment by the patient of eighteen.

4. Del. Code Ann. tit. 16, § 5127(a) (1974): "Nothing in this Section shall relieve from liability for support of the patient any person liable under any other law of this State."

5. Hawaii Rev. Stat. § 334-37 (1976): "The administrator of a psychiatric facility operated by the State or a county may accept voluntary contributions for and on behalf of any patient."

6. Idaho Code § 66-354(b) (Supp. 1981): "The following relatives shall be bound by law to provide for the expenses and charges for the commitment, care and treatment of such mentally ill person . . . : husband for the wife, and the wife for the husband; the parent for his or her minor child or minor children, and the children for their parents."

7. Ill. Ann. Stat. ch. 91½, § 5-105 (Smith-Hurd Supp. 1980):

> [T]he liability of each responsible relative for payment of services charges ceases when payments on the basis of financial ability have been made for a total of 12 years for any recipient. . . . No child is liable under this Act for services to a parent. No spouse is liable under this Act for the services to the other spouse who willfully failed to contribute to the spouse's support for a period of 5 years immediately preceeding his admission. No parent is liable under this Act for the services charges incurred by a child after such child reaches the age of majority.

8. Ind. Code Ann. § 16-14-18.1-1 (Burns Supp. 1982): "'Responsible party' means, and includes, the patient, the parents of the patient, the spouse of the patient, and the estates of any and all of them. . . . It does not mean the children of patients or the parents of patients over the age of eighteen (18) years of age."

9. Iowa Code Ann. § 230.15 (West Supp. 1980):

> Mentally ill persons and persons legally liable for their support shall remain liable for the support of such mentally ill. Persons legally liable for the support of a mentally ill person shall include the spouse of the mentally ill person, any person, firm or corporation bound by contract for support of the mentally ill person, and, with respect to mentally ill persons under eighteen years of age only, the father and mother of the mentally ill person. . . . The liability to the county incurred under this section on account of any mentally ill person shall be limited to one hundred percent of the cost of care and treatment of the mentally ill person at a state mental health institute for one hundred twenty days of hospitalization.

10. Me. Rev. Stat. Ann. tit. 34, § 2512 (1978):

> Each patient and the spouse, adult child and parent, jointly and severally, shall be legally liable from the date of admission for the care and treatment of any patient . . . except that a parent shall not be legally liable for care and treatment unless the patient was wholly or partially dependent for support upon such parent at the time of admission. . . . No child of a patient shall be liable for any part of such costs for a parent who willfully failed to support such child prior to the child's 18th birthday . . . The department shall not charge any parent for the care and treatment of a child beyond the child's 18th birthday, or beyond 6 months from the date of admission, whichever occurs later.

11. Neb. Rev. Stat. § 83-348 (1976): State will bear expenses of patients whose legal settlement is outside of the state or unknown.

12. N.H. Rev. Stat. Ann. § 126A54 (Supp. 1981):

> I. Any person transferred to the New Hampshire hospital for observations as to sanity under court order shall be at state expense for the observation period only.
>
> II. Any patient or resident of such institutions defined in RSA 126-A:45 or patient receiving care, treatment or maintenance at the direction of the commissioner of health and welfare who has no means of support and no person chargeable for his support shall be supported by the state.

13. N.C. Gen. Stat. § 122.35.47 (1981): "The area mental health, mental retardation, and substance abuse authority shall make every reasonable effort to collect appropriate reimbursement for its costs in providing mental health services to persons able to pay for service, including insurance or third-party payments. However, no one shall be refused mental health services because of an inability to pay."

14. N.D. Cent. Code. § 25-09-03: Expenses chargeable against estate except for provisions for family hardship.

15. Id. § 25-09-04: "In the event of patient's inability to pay for costs of care and treatment, responsible relative of such patient (spouse, parents or children) . . . shall pay the actual cost incurred by the state . . . or such lesser amount as shall be determined."

16. Id. § 25-09-01: "All of the operational and administrative expense of the state hospital, state school, and San Haven state hospital shall be appropriated from the state treasury."

17. Tex. Rev. Civ. Stat. Ann. art. 5547-14(d) (Vernon 1981): "Neither the county nor the State shall pay any costs for a patient committed to a private hospital."

18. Va. Code § 37.1-105 (1976). "[N]o parent, guardian, spouse or relative shall be liable for any expense which arose from the care, treatment or maintenance furnished to any patient subsequent to institutionalization of such patient in a state hospital for a period of sixty months."

19. Wyo. Stat. § 25-3-207 (1981):

(a) The liability of a spouse for payment of established charges during hospitalization shall terminate at the end of two (2) years of cumulative hospital care. The liability of parents for payment of established charges . . . shall terminate either at the end of two (2) years of cumulative hospital care or when the patient becomes an adult, whichever occurs first.

TABLE 2.18 FINANCIAL RESPONSIBILITY FOR DEVELOPMENTALLY DISABLED PERSONS IN INSTITUTIONS

	RESIDENT		FAMILY		COUNTY		STATE	
STATE	Voluntary Admission (1)	Involuntary Admission (2)	Voluntary Admission (3)	Involuntary Admission (4)	Voluntary Admission (5)	Involuntary Admission (6)	Voluntary Admission (7)	Involuntary Admission (8)
ALA. Code (1975 & Supp. 1981)		22-53-20		22-53-1 22-53-3 22-53-20				22-53-3
ALAS. Stat. (1979 & Supp. 1981)	47.80.150	47.80.150	47.80.150	47.80.150			47.80.150	47.80.150
ARIZ. Rev. Stat. Ann. (1974 & Supp. 1981)	36-562(C)	36-562(C)	parent until child is 18 36-562(B), (C)	parent until child is 18 36-562(B), (C)	36-562(G)	36-562(G)		
ARK. Stat. Ann. (1971 & Supp. 1981)	59-1104(b) 59-1111(a)	59-104(b) 59-1111(a)	59-1104(b) 59-1111(a)	59-1104(b) 59-1111(a)			59-1111(a)	59-1111(a)
CAL. Welf. & Inst. Code (West 1972 & Supp. 1980)	7513.1	7513.1	7513.1	7513.1			7513.1	7513.1
COLO. Rev. Stat. (1973 & Supp. 1981)	27-12-101	27-12-101	parents, spouse; liability of parents ends after payment for 180 mos. or when child turns 18 27-12-101 27-12-103	parents, spouse; liability of parents ends after payment for 180 mos. or when child turns 18 27-12-101 27-12-103			27-12-101 to 109	27-12-101 to 109
CONN. Gen. Stat. Ann. (West 1975 & Supp. 1981)	17-295(c) 17-295a(a)	17-295(c) 17-295a(a)	17-295(c) 17-295a(a)	17-295(c) 17-295a(a)			17-295	17-295
DEL. Code Ann. (1974 & Supp. 1980)	16, §5520(a)	16, §5520(a)	*fn. 1* 16, §5520(a)	*fn. 1* 16, §5520(a)			16, §5520	16, §5520
D.C. Code Ann. (1981 & Supp. 1982)	21-1110	21-1110	21-1111	21-1111			21-1110 21-1111	21-1110 21-1111
FLA. Stat. Ann. (West 1973 & Supp. 1981)	402.33	402.33	402.33	402.33			402.33	402.33
GA. Code Ann. §35: (1982) §88: (1979 & Supp. 1980)	35-1105 88-2509.7	35-1105 88-2509.7	35-1105 88-2509.7	35-1105 88-2509.7	88-2509.7	88-2509.7	35-1105 88-2509.7	35-1105 88-2509.7
HAWAII Rev. Stat. (1976 & Supp. 1981)		333.28	minors only 333.35	parents, until child is 18 333.28				333.28
IDAHO Code (1980 & Supp. 1981)		56-239						56-239
ILL. Ann. Stat. (Smith-Hurd 1966 & Supp. 1980)	91½, §5-105	91½, §5-105	see table 3.13 fn. 7 91½, §5-105	see table 3.13 fn. 7 91½, §5-105	91½, §5-115	91½, §5-115	91½, §5-115	91½, §5-115
IND. Code Ann. (Burns 1973 & Supp. 1982)	16-14-18.1-2(c) 16-14-18.1-3(a)	16-14-18.1-2(c) 16-14-18.1-3(a)	see table 3.13 fn. 8 *fn. 2* 16-14-18.1-2(c) 16-14-18.1-3(a)	see table 3.13 fn. 8 *fn. 2* 16-14-18.1-2(c) 16-14-18.1-3(a)	16-14-18.1-12	16-14-18.1-14	see fn. 2 16-14-18.1-3(a) 16-14-18.1-5 to -11	see fn. 2 16-14-18.1-3(a) 16-14-18.1-5 to -11
IOWA Code Ann. (West 1969 & Supp. 1980)	222.80	222.80	parents if child is under 18 222.78	parents if child is under 18 222.78	222.60	222.60	222.60	222.60
KAN. Stat. Ann. (1976)								
KY. Rev. Stat. Ann. (Michie 1977 & Supp. 1980)	210.720(1)	210.720(1)	spouse; parents, if child is under 18 210.710(5)	spouse; parents, if child is under 18 210.710(5)			210.700–.760	210.700–.760

TABLE 2.18 FINANCIAL RESPONSIBILITY FOR DEVELOPMENTALLY DISABLED PERSONS IN INSTITUTIONS—*Continued*

	RESIDENT		FAMILY		COUNTY		STATE	
STATE	Voluntary Admission (1)	Involuntary Admission (2)	Voluntary Admission (3)	Involuntary Admission (4)	Voluntary Admission (5)	Involuntary Admission (6)	Voluntary Admission (7)	Involuntary Admission (8)
LA. Rev. Stat. Ann. (West 1975 & Supp. 1981)	28:388 28:436	28:388 28:436					28:436	28:436
ME. Rev. Stat. Ann. (1978 & Supp. 1982–83)	34, §2512	34, §2512	see table 3.13 fn. 10 34, §2512	see table 3.13 fn. 10 34, §2512			34, §2516	34, §2516
MD. Ann. Code (1979 & Supp. 1981)	59A, §24	59A, §24	59A, §24	59A, §24			59A, §30	59A, §30
MASS. Ann. Laws (Michie/Law. Co-op. 1981 & Supp. 1982)	123, §32	123, §32					123, §32	123, §32
MICH. Comp. Laws Ann. (1980 & Supp. 1981)	330.1804	330.1804	spouse or parents of unmarried child under 18 330.1804	spouse or parents of unmarried child under 18 330.1804	330.1302 330.1314	330.1302 330.1314	330.1308 330.1309	330.1308 330.1309
MINN. Stat. Ann. (West 1971 & Supp. 1981)	246.51 252.27(2)	246.51 252.27(2)	246.51 252.27(2)	246.51 252.27(2)	246.54 252.27(1)	246.54 252.27(1)	246.51 252.27(1)	246.51 252.27(1)
MISS. Code Ann. (1981)	41-19-13 41-19-153	41-19-13 41-19-153	41-7-71	41-7-71			41-7-71	41-7-71
MO. Ann. Stat. (Vernon 1979 & Supp. 1981)	630.205	630.205	630.205	630.205			630.205	630.205
MONT. Code Ann. (1981)	53-1-405	53-1-405	financially responsible person 53-1-405	financially responsible person 53-1-405			53-1-405	53--1-405
NEB. Rev. Stat. (1976 & Supp. 1981)	83-1132	83-1132	persons legally obligated for support 83-1132	persons legally obligated for support 83-1132	83-1132	83-1132		
NEV. Rev. Stat. (1981) *fn. 3*	435.020(1) 435.360	435.020(1) 435.360	435.020(2) 435.090	435.020(2) 435.090			435.090 435.360	435.090 435.360
N.H. Rev. Stat. Ann. (1977 & Supp. 1981)	*fn. 4* 171-A:16 126-A:51		126-A:51				126-A:54II	
N.J. Stat. Ann. (West 1981)	30:4-165.3	30:4-165.3	30:4-165.3	30:4-165.3	30:4-165.3	30:4-165.3	30:4-165.3	30:4-165.3
N.M. Stat. Ann. (1979 & Supp. 1981)	43-1-25	43-1-25					43-1-25	43-1-25
N.Y Mental Hyg. Law (McKinney 1978 & Supp. 1981)	43.03(a)	43.03(a)	*fn. 5* 43.03(a)	*fn. 5* 43.03(a)			43.03(b)	43.03(b)
N.C. Gen. Stat. (1981 & Supp. 1981)	122-35.47	122-35.47			122-35.42	122-35.42	122-35.47 122-35.53	122-35.47 122-35.53
N.D. Cent. Code (1978 & Supp. 1981)	25-09-02 25-09-03		25-09-04				25-04-05(3) 25-09-01	
OHIO Rev. Code Ann. (Baldwin 1980 & Supp. 1981)	5121.04 5121.06	5121.04 5121.06	spouse; parents, if child under 18 5121.06	spouse; parents, if child under 18 5121.06			5121.01	5121.01
OKLA. Stat. Ann. (West 1979 & Supp. 1981)	43A, §111		parents, spouse, children 43A, §§115, 111				43A, §113	
OR. Rev. Stat. (1981)	179.620 427.195(4) 427.061	179.620 427.061 427.195(4)					179.620 427.195(4) 427.061	179.620 427.061 427.195(4)

TABLE 2.18 FINANCIAL RESPONSIBILITY FOR DEVELOPMENTALLY DISABLED PERSONS IN INSTITUTIONS—*Continued*

	RESIDENT		FAMILY		COUNTY		STATE	
STATE	Voluntary Admission (1)	Involuntary Admission (2)	Voluntary Admission (3)	Involuntary Admission (4)	Voluntary Admission (5)	Involuntary Admission (6)	Voluntary Admission (7)	Involuntary Admission (8)
PA. Stat. Ann. (Purdon 1969 & Supp. 1980)	50, §4501	50, §4501	*fn.* 6 50, §4502	*fn.* 6 50, §4502	50, §§4503, 4505	50, §§4503, 4505	50, §§4507, 4503	50, §§4507, 4503
R.I. Gen. Laws (1977 & Supp. 1981)	40.1-2-4 40.1-3-6 40.1-5-33 40.1-5.2-17	40.1-2-4 40.1-3-6 40.1-5-33 40.1-5.2-17	40.1-2-4 40.1-3-6 40.1-5-33 40.1-5.2-17	40.1-2-4 40.1-3-6 40.1-5-33 40.1-5.2-17	city or town 40.1-3-6	city or town 40.1-3-6	40-5-5 40.1-5.2-11 40.1-5.2-17 40.1-22-21	40-5-5 40.1-5.2-11 40.1-5.2-17 40.1-22-21
S.C. Code (Law. Co-op. 1976 & Supp. 1976)	44-21-260	44-21-260	but no charge for residential services 44-21-260	but no charge for residential services 44-21-260			44-21-260	44-21-260
S.D. Codified Laws Ann. (1976 & Supp. 1981)	27B-9-1	27B-9-1			27B-9-14 27B-9-16	27B-9-14 27B-9-16	27B-9-8 27B-9-20	27B-9-8 27B-9-20
TENN. Code Ann. (1977 & Supp. 1981)	33-402 33-406	33-402 33-406	33-402 33-406	33-402 33-406			33-406	33-406
TEX. Rev. Civ. Stat. Ann. (Vernon 1958 & Supp. 1981)	5547-300, §61(b)	5547-300, §61(b)	5547-300, §61(a)	5547-300, §61(a)			5547-300, §61	5547-300, §61
UTAH Code Ann. (1978 & Supp. 1981)	64-8-8(6)	64-8-8(6)	64-8-8(6) 64-8-9	64-8-8(6) 64-8-9				
VT. Stat. Ann. (1968 & Supp. 1981)								
VA. Code (1976 & Supp. 1981)	37.1-105	37.1-105	37.1-105	37.1-105			37.1-116	37.1-116
WASH. Rev. Code Ann. (1982)	72.33.655	72.33.655					72.33.655	72.33.655
W. VA. Code (1980 & Supp. 1981)	27-8-1	27-8-1	27-8-1	27-8-1	27-8-2	27-8-2	27-8-1	27-8-1
WIS. Stat. Ann. (West 1979 & Supp. 1981)	46.10(2)	46.10(2)	46.10(2)	46.10(2)	46.106	46.106	46.10(8)(d) 51.22(3)	46.10(8)(d) 51.22(3)
WYO. Stat. (1977 & Supp. 1982)	*fn.* 7 9-6-649 9-6-650	*fn.* 7 9-6-649 9-6-650	*fn.* 7 9-6-650	*fn.* 7 9-6-650			9-6-649	9-6-649

FOOTNOTES TABLE 2.18

1. Del. Code Ann. tit. 16, § 5520(a) (Supp. 1980): "Nothing in this section shall relieve from liability for the support of the patient, any person liable under any other law of this State."

2. Ind. Code Ann. § 20-1-6-1(a) (Burns Supp. 1982):

> (a) "Handicapped child" means any child between the ages of three (3) and twenty-one (21) years, inclusive, who because of physical or mental disability, is incapable of being educated properly and efficiently through normal classroom instruction, but who, with the advantage of a special education program, may be expected to benefit from instruction in surroundings designed to further the educational, social or economic status of the child.

Id. § 16-14-18.1-3(a):

> Each patient in a psychiatric hospital and the responsible parties . . . are liable for the payment of the cost of treatment and maintenance of the patient. However, whenever placement of a handicapped child, as defined by IC 20-1-6-1, in a state owned or operated psychiatric hospital is necessary for the provision of a special education for that child, the cost of the child's education program, nonmedical care, and room and board shall be paid by the department of mental health rather than by the child's parents, guardian, or other responsible party.

3. Nev. Rev. Stat. §§ 435.020, .090 (1981), are applicable to financial responsibility for mentally retarded children; id, § 435.360 is applicable to financial responsibility for mentally retarded persons who have attained the age of 18.

4. N.H. Rev. Stat. Ann. § 171A:16 (1977). Clients may be employed "to perform such services as may be determined as not necessarily being beneficial for the care and treatment of any said clients." Client wages "shall be subject to deductions for the costs of care, treatment and maintenance at said school according to RSA 8:39 through 49."

5. N.Y. Mental Hyg. Law § 43.03(a) (McKinney 1978):

> Parents or spouses of parents are not liable for the fees for services rendered to a disabled child under twenty-one years of age, who does not share the common household. . . . [A] child is considered disabled if he/she meets the definition of a . . . disabled child under regulations prescribed by the social security act for medical assistance.

6. Pa. Stat. Ann. tit. 50, § 4502 (Purdon Supp. 1980):

> Upon the mentally disabled person attaining the age of eighteen, . . . the liability under the act of persons owing a legal duty to support him shall cease: Provided, however, that spouses shall remain liable for each other regardless of age except for periods of continuous inpatient care in excess of one hundred and twenty days. Continuous inpatient care . . . shall be any inhospital stay not interrupted by more than one hundred and twenty days.

7. Wyo. Stat. § 9-6-650(c) (Supp. 1982): "Residents who are between the ages of five (5) and twenty-one (21) years of age shall be provided special education and related services at no cost to their parents or estates."

Samuel Jan Brakel

CHAPTER 3

Voluntary Admission

I. INTRODUCTION

The depth of the law's concern with the admission of mentally disabled persons to treatment institutions is illustrated by the fact that even voluntary admission is closely regulated by statute. A typical introductory provision of the state mental health codes is this one found in the Illinois statutes: "A person may be admitted as an inpatient to a mental health facility . . . *only* as provided in this Chapter."[1] The codes then go on to set forth a detailed set of provisions describing the steps and procedures by which a person may on his own initiative seek to enter a mental facility and the rights and restrictions that apply to him once he is in. In this respect, the hospitalization of mentally disabled persons differs markedly from admission to general hospitals for general medical problems, which entails no such statutory practices, procedures, or precautions. The close regulation of mental health admissions may reflect a number of concerns: (1) the fact that mentally disabled persons frequently have only limited capacity to make decisions of this kind, (2) the empirical reality that so-called voluntary admittees are frequently already in custody and are often subjected to subtle pressure, and sometimes overt coercion, in making the decision to admit themselves,[2] and (3) the desire to maximize the chances of treatment success within the facility, manifested by provisions giving the institution power to retain the voluntary patient temporarily, until a considered decision can be made regarding his need for further treatment, to be effected, conceivably, through involuntary commitment.

Admission procedures generally labeled as voluntary come in three types: (1) informal admission procedures, (2) traditional (sometimes called "formal" or "conditional")[3] voluntary admission procedures, and (3) third-party "voluntary" procedures. The informal procedures, in their relative absence of administrative red tape and lack of pre- and postadmission legal constraints to which the person seeking admission is subjected, are the most truly voluntary, but their availability and their use in the various states are limited.[4] The traditional voluntary admission scheme deviates from the pure voluntary model in the retention provisions found in most states as well as in the element of pressure that sometimes accompanies the admission decision. Nonetheless, these procedures are the most heavily used and constitute the classic voluntary admission model. The third-party admission procedures, under which guardians or parents may make the commitment decision and application on behalf of mentally disabled adults and children, are not considered voluntary procedures in this book and are not discussed in this chapter. Whatever the practical merits of these procedures (discussed in chapter 2), they do not meet what we consider to be the primary test of voluntariness—affirmative action and personal application by the person who seeks admission.

Historically, the voluntary admission concept became operational in this country some 100 years ago when (in 1881) the Massachusetts legislature enacted the first provisions of this type.[5] By 1924, 27 additional states had enacted voluntary admission legislation, though diverging widely in substance and scope.[6] Today all states ex-

1. Ill. Ann. Stat. ch. 91½, § 3-200 (Smith-Hurd Supp. 1982) (emphasis added). An exception is made for prisoners who may be transferred to mental health facilities by the Department of Corrections "pursuant to the Unified Code of Corrections." The Illinois law used to be even more emphatic. Prior to the 1979 revisions it said: "No person may be admitted to a hospital as in need of mental treatment or as mentally retarded except as provided in this act." (Ill. Ann. Stat. ch. 91½, § 3-1 (Smith-Hurd Supp. 1970)).

2. See Gilboy & Schmidt, "Voluntary" Hospitalization of the Mentally Ill, 66 Nw. U.L. Rev. 429 (1971); Brakel & South, Diversion from the Criminal Process in the Rural Community: Final Report of the ABF Project on Rural Criminal Justice, 7 Am. Crim. L. Q. 122 (1969), *reprinted as* American Bar Foundation Research Contribution No. 6 (1969).

3. See Gilboy, Informal Admission of Patients to State Psychiatric Institutions, 47 Am. J. Orthopsychiatry 321 (1977).

4. *Id.*

5. A. Deutsch, The Mentally Ill in America: A History of Their Care and Treatment from Colonial Times, (2d ed. 1949).

6. Overholser, The Voluntary Admission Law: Certain Legal and Psychiatric Aspects, 3 Am. J. Psychiatry 475, 476 (1924).

cept Alabama have statutes of this type,[7] and consistent with the increased exchange in information and ideas among the states, there is considerable uniformity. Similar laws exist in numerous foreign countries, particularly the postindustrial societies, and in nations such as Great Britain they have long been the dominant procedure for admission.[8] The basic principles underlying the voluntary admission concept have secured general acceptance, with the questions today reserved for whether the concept is adequately implemented in practice and whether restrictive release procedures may not go too far in undercutting these principles.

Despite conceptual and practical "impurities," the idea of voluntary admission has much to commend itself,[9] and in several states today the *in*voluntary commitment statutes go so far as to require advice on the availability of *voluntary* admission before involuntary procedures may be used.[10] A person who voluntarily seeks admission recognizes his need of mental treatment. He is more prone to cooperate with the treatment staff and to participate conscientiously in the treatment program and therefore more likely to benefit from institutionalization than an unwilling patient. In addition, the availability of voluntary procedures may encourage a person to seek help for his condition early, when the chances of successful treatment are greatest.[11] To delay treatment until the person's condition reaches crisis proportions has several disadvantages in addition to the fact that his prognosis may by then be poor. The response to the crisis is more likely to come in the form of initiation of involuntary commitment procedures, legal steps that leave a public record and generally amount to a more stigmatizing experience than their less formal, voluntary alternatives.[12] Indeed, the involuntary commitment trial, if it comes to that, may be so traumatic as to aggravate the person's mental condition and to increase latent resistance to whatever the hospital staff seeks to do for him. Most of these antitherapeutic consequences are avoided in the voluntary admission process.

The rate of voluntary admissions, which had shown dramatic increases during the decades of the 1950s and 1960s, appears to have stabilized during the 1970s and even shows signs today of a marginal decline. The World Health Organization reported that in 1949 only 13,848 of 138,253—some 10%—of all admissions to state and county mental hospitals in the United States were voluntary.[13] By 1961, the voluntary admission rate had risen to 24%.[14] By 1972, almost half (48.6%) of the admissions in the country were on a voluntary basis.[15] But the most recent (unpublished) statistics (for 1980) show a drop in voluntary admissions to 45.1%.[16] Within these nationwide aggregates, there are major differences on a state-by-state basis. In states such as Illinois and Massachusetts, for example, voluntary admission has been for years and continues today to be the dominant mode of entry into the public mental institutions, with two-thirds and more falling into this category since at least the mid-1970s.[17] By contrast, 1980 statistics for states as disparate as Connecticut and Alaska show a continuing lag in implementation of the voluntary admission concept, with involuntary commitments outnumbering voluntary admissions by 3 to 1.[18] Perhaps the most revealing

7. Arguably, one could include Minnesota along with Alabama as the sole states without voluntary admission statutes. In Minnesota, traditional voluntary admission is limited to drug dependent persons (Minn. Stat. Ann. § 253A.03(2) (West 1982)), while mentally ill and retarded persons who wish to volunteer for admission to the state's mental facilities use the informal admission procedure (§ 253A.03(1)). There have been some slight changes in this scheme since this note was written. See Minn. Stat. Ann. § 253B.04 (West 1982). Maine provides for informal voluntary admission only for the mentally ill (Me. Rev. Stat. Ann. tit. 34, § 2290 (1964)), but formal voluntary procedures obtain for mentally retarded persons (§ 2657).

8. World Health Organization, Hospitalization of Mental Patients: A Survey of Existing Legislation 15 (1955).

9. The voluntary admission approach has been favored by virtually every group concerned with drafting mental health legislation and by both legal and psychiatric patients interests groups. The American Psychiatric Association's "Position Statement on Involuntary Hospitalization of the Mentally Ill" opens up with a plug for voluntary admissions. (See A.D. Brooks, Law, Psychiatry, and the Mental Health System 608-9 (1974).) See also Curran, Hospitalization of the Mentally Ill, 31 N.C.L. Rev. 274 (1952-53), and National Institute of Mental Health, Federal Security Agency, A Draft Act Governing Hospitalization of the Mentally Ill, especially the commentary at 19 (Public Health Service Pub. No. 51, 1952).

10. See, e.g., Colo. Rev. Stat. § 27-10-107(1)(b) (1982), as confirmed in Sisneros v. District Ct., Tenth Judicial Dist., 606 P.2d 55 (Colo. 1980).

11. Early intervention also reduces the financial and human costs associated with mental disability. The longer the disability is allowed to run without an attempt to halt if not reverse the process of deterioration, the greater those costs become.

12. The Ohio law used to provide that if during the course of involuntary proceedings the patient consents to sign in voluntarily, the case will be dismissed and all court records expunged (Ohio Rev. Code Ann. § 5122.31 (Baldwin Cum. Supp. 1978)). This provision has since been replaced by a more general one guarding the confidentiality of all patient's records.

13. World Health Organization, *supra* note 8.

14. American Psychiatric Association and the National Association for Mental Health, Joint Information Service Fact Sheet No. 17, Voluntary and Other Admissions to State Mental Hospitals—1956 and 1961 (Apr. 1962).

15. Division of Biometry and Epidemiology, National Institute of Mental Health, Statistical Note 105, Legal Status of Inpatient Admissions to State and County Mental Hospitals, United States 1972, at 2 (1974).

16. Survey and Reports Branch, Division of Biometry and Epidemiology, National Institute of Mental Health, computer printouts 3 May 1983 (unpublished), at table 1, plane 12, pt. 1-1, State and Country Psychiatric Hospital Inpatient Services.

17. The Illinois data are from the Illinois Dep't of Mental Health and Developmental Disabilities, Mental Health Statistics, Fiscal Year 1976, at 47. The Massachusetts situation is described in Roth, Mental Health Commitment: The State of the Debate, 1980, 31 Hosp. & Community Psychiatry 385, 390, & 395 n.9 (1980), citing Schwitzgebel's Survey of State Civil Commitment Statutes, *in* Civil Commitment and Social Policy (A.L. McGarry ed. 1978).

18. Data sent by the states' mental health and retardation departments in response to author's letter of Nov. 17, 1981. There are indications that jurisdictions lagging in the use of voluntary admission procedures rely heavily on commitment methods occupying the gray area between the voluntary and the involuntary processes. Alaska, e.g., admits a high proportion of its pa-

figures are from California, where there are unmistakable signs of a trend away from voluntary admissions, the number of which has reportedly been cut by 84% while involuntary commitments remain constant.[19] California's commitment scheme is unique, and its movement toward institutionalizing only the most gravely disabled or dangerous—generally poor candidates for voluntary admission—has gone further than in most states. Yet, the latest national statistics together with an analysis of the laws in jurisdictions around the country may portend the development of a similar trend in other states. In contrast to the changing picture for public mental institutions, voluntary admission to psychiatric units of general hospitals has long been the rule, standing at 85.2% of the total admissions there today.[20]

Most states have voluntary admission procedures for developmentally disabled persons and for alcoholics and drug addicts in addition to the statutes' primary target—the mentally ill. The traditional approach was to extend the reach of the statutes covering mentally ill persons to these other groups by defining them as included in the category *mental illness* or by enumerating them as embraced by the statutes. The modern trend, however, has been to enact separate legislation. In a number of states, the "voluntary" admission procedures for developmentally disabled persons are not so much identical as analogous to those for the mentally ill. These procedures are sometimes labeled "administrative," permitting the developmentally disabled person to apply for himself if he is of age and competent but providing for application by the parent or guardian when he is not, in which case the procedure is—by our definition—not voluntary.[21] Voluntary admission provisions for developmentally disabled and retarded persons are charted along with those applying to the mentally ill in table 3.1. Compared with the provisions for the mentally ill, they seem to place somewhat more emphasis on evaluation and diagnosis of the prospective resident and on assuring that appropriate facilities and treatment programs are available, with particular deference to the determination in this regard of the facility's administrator or director. Separate voluntary admission provisions for persons suffering from alcohol or drug addiction are for reasons of space not treated in this book.

II. HOW VOLUNTARY ARE VOLUNTARY ADMISSIONS?

The previous editions of this book referred to voluntary admissions as those that "are initiated by the affirmative action of the patient himself *or of someone empowered by law to act in the patient's behalf*" (emphasis added). The problems with including the italicized alternative under the rubric of "voluntary" procedures were evident even then. Reality had to be ignored in favor of formality: a friend applying for the patient's admission at the latter's request could not be said to effect a voluntary admission because he was not formally empowered to act on the patient's behalf; on the other hand, the parent or legal guardian seeking to commit a child or incompetent adult without the latter's consent, or conceivably against the ward's wishes, was seen to be using the voluntary admission procedure; ironically, if the statute required the third-party application to be supported by evidence of the patient's consent, the procedure was not voluntary but nonprotested involuntary, whereas if consent was ignored and the opportunity to protest not provided for in the statute, the admission did qualify as voluntary. This logic seems too stretched to maintain. In this edition, all third-party-initiated admissions are considered nonvoluntary and are treated in chapter 2. There are enough questions about the voluntariness of patient-initiated admissions.

In a study of voluntary admissions in Illinois, Gilboy and Schmidt[22] found that the majority of persons admitted under the procedure were already in some form of official custody when they "decided" to enter the mental hospital and that many were pressured by the threat of less advantageous alternatives to agree to the suggestion that they sign themselves in. In some 40% of the cases, the admittees were reportedly brought to the hospital by the police, a circumstance that suggests that the alternative to voluntary admission would have been involuntary emergency commitment or placement in jail on a disorderly conduct charge or the like. In slightly more than 10% of the cases, the options were presented to the admittee in the misdemeanor or mental health court: either he could agree to submit to psychiatric observation and care, or alternatively the criminal charge

---

tients on medical certification, many for observation and evaluation. The notion that in states where voluntary admissions are low the majority of disabled persons enter institutions by way of involuntary judicial commitment is demonstrably wrong.

19. Roth, *supra*, note 17, at 390.

20. Survey and Reports Branch, Division of Biometry and Epidemiology, National Institute of Mental Health, computer printouts 6 May 1983 (unpublished), at table 1, plane 12, pt. 1-1, Non-Federal General Hospital Psychiatric Inpatient Services.

21. See, e.g., Ill. Ann. Stat. ch. 91½, § 4-300 (Smith-Hurd Supp. 1982), entitled "Administrative and Temporary Admission of the Developmentally Disabled." Specifically, § 4-302 provides:

> A developmentally disabled person may be administratively admitted to a facility upon application if the facility director of the facility determines that he is suitable for admission. A person 18 years of age or older, if he has the capacity, or his guardian, if he is authorized by the guardianship order of the Circuit Court, may execute an application for administrative admission. Application may be executed for a person under 18 years of age by his parent, guardian, or person in loco parentis.

22. Gilboy & Schmidt, *supra* note 2.

would be pursued, involuntary commitment procedures would be instituted, and/or continued detention in jail would result. If these findings are accurate, a substantial question about the propriety of using voluntary admission procedures arises. Are those voluntary patients who have been "coerced" in effect involuntary patients who are denied the protections to which they are entitled under the involuntary process?

The answer depends on one's perspective. Legal perfectionists will interpret the above findings as clear evidence of abuse of the voluntary process. To those of more practical bent, the conclusion is likely to be less certain. Purity of process, they may recognize, is not attainable in either the medical or the legal world, and least of all where the two intersect. Is there such a thing as an uncoerced decision in any situation? They may further point out that the patients involved do need treatment, that the result is right even if the methods do not conform precisely to the procedural requisites of the law on the books. Or they may discount the legal purists' concern by comparing the hospital admission process favorably with criminal justice decision making and conclude that "coerced" voluntary admission is "probably more voluntary than the 'voluntary' plea of guilty made in the plea-bargaining process of the criminal law."[23] The Illinois legislature, seeking to curb at least the more blatant instances of coercion, has responded by writing an explicit prohibition into the statute against inducing patients to sign voluntary admission papers on the threat of involuntary commitment.[24]

A second challenge to the voluntary admission laws focuses on provisions inhibiting immediate release. A truly voluntary patient should, in this view, be able to walk out of the hospital at will. But instead most of the statutes hedge: typically, the voluntary patient is free to leave only after he gives the hospital staff formal notice of his desire to do so (often required to be in writing) and only several days after the notification, during which interim the hospital may petition for his involuntary commitment and continue to detain him until the case is heard.[25] This may be good policy from the medical point of view and in furtherance of the patient's treatment interests, but it undoubtedly undercuts the meaning of the word *voluntary*.

III. INFORMAL ADMISSION

In response to the criticisms leveled at traditional voluntary admission procedures, a number of states over the years have enacted alternative "informal" admission procedures. Presently, ten states (two more than in 1970) provide for such informal admission.[26] The Illinois statute[27] typifies the modern formulation of this procedure:

> (a) Any person desiring admission to a mental health facility for treatment of a mental illness may be admitted upon his request without making formal application therefor if, after examination, the facility director of the facility considers that person clinically suitable for admission upon an informal basis.
>
> (b) Each patient admitted under this Section shall be informed in writing and orally at the time of admission of his right to be discharged from the facility at any time during the normal daily day-shift hours of operation, which shall include but need not be limited to 9 A.M. to 5 P.M. Such right to be discharged shall commence with the first day-shift hours of operation after his admission.
>
> (c) If the facility director decides to admit a person as a voluntary patient, he shall state in the patient's record the reason why informal admission is not suitable.

The salient features of informal admission are thus (1) entry into the hospital on a simple oral request and (2) release on the same basis. The hospital in turn has the obligation to inform the patient of his right to be discharged on request—a specification contained in most but not all statutes—and it has the power to deny informal admission if the applicant is deemed not suitable. Suitability is ostensibly a clinical criterion and relates specifically to the propriety of admitting the patient on an informal basis, as opposed to by formal voluntary or involuntary process. Realistically, however, the decision is as likely to be made on grounds having to do with the needs of the admitting facility or on the basis of judgments about the patient's decision-making competence, the particular circumstances under which he presents himself (for example, who accompanies him), his general demeanor, his past hospitalization record, and other indicators that are not strictly a part of the clinical diagnosis.[28]

Generally viewed and lauded as the only "truly voluntary" procedure,[29] informal admission nevertheless is only sporadically used in the states where it is available as an alternative to traditional voluntary admission. A study based on 1974-75 data[30] of six of the ten states that have informal provisions showed use of the procedure in two of the three largest states—Illinois and New York—to add up to less than 1% of all admissions. Only

23. R. Slovenko, Psychiatry and Law 204 (1973).
24. Ill. Ann. Stat. ch. 91½, § 3-402 (Smith-Hurd Supp. 1982).
25. See, e.g., Ohio Rev. Code Ann. § 5122.03 (Baldwin 1980).

26. The states are Connecticut, Illinois, Kansas, Louisiana, Maine, Maryland, Michigan, Minnesota, New York, and Washington. See table 3.1, col. 14.
27. Ill. Ann. Stat. ch. 91½, § 3-300 (Smith-Hurd, Supp. 1983).
28. See notes 61 & 62 *infra* and accompanying text.
29. Gilboy, *supra* note 3, at 323.
30. *Id.* at 324 table 1.

in Connecticut, with a 9.3% rate, was there significant use. The rate in Maine was reported at 63.8%, but this is primarily because the traditional voluntary admission alternative is not available for mentally ill persons in that state. It appears that there has been no more than marginal change since this study was done. Illinois statistics for 1981 show informal admissions still at only 2% of the total.[31] By contrast, informal admissions in Great Britain reportedly account for more than 80% of all hospitalizations there.[32]

Several explanations have been offered for the low use of informal admission procedures in this country.[33] The procedures are said in some respects to operate against the hospital staff's interests, sometimes against the patient's interests as well, and in certain cases the public's interests may be disadvantaged. Too facile access to the hospital and release from it, for example, may lead to frivolous use of scarce and expensive medical resources — a consequence detrimental to all concerned. Time, energy, and medications may be expended when they are not really needed or when they can be obtained as easily but more cheaply on an outpatient basis, though the provision for determining the applicant's clinical suitability for informal institutionalization should serve to mitigate this potential. The fact that the patient may walk away at his whim and against medical advice is wasteful when it means that diagnostic and treatment efforts begun cannot be completed successfully. In exercising his freedom to leave, the patient may be harming himself as well. Moreover, the hospital staff's lack of control over the timing of discharge may have additional effects that are less direct but no less serious. Patients sometimes respond only if the staff has some coercive power.[34] Uncontrolled release can be demoralizing for staff working in a setting where ideals of care and service are already difficult enough to live up to. How much effort is a doctor or nurse swamped by the needs of regular patients willing to spend on an informal admittee who walks in one day and may walk out again the next? Moreover, release on demand precludes the opportunity to plan for the patient's aftercare, which is one of the most crucial features in any patient's recovery. Finally, the informal patient, despite his casual legal status, may well be seriously ill, unable to care for himself, and even dangerous to others. The hospital staff's recognition of these conditions creates a duty, and perhaps even a legal obligation,[35] to detain and treat the patient and to protect the public. Such a duty is in obvious conflict with the patient's unfettered right to leave the hospital.[36]

Given the lack of significant experience with and data about informal admissions in this country, it is unclear how large these negatives in fact loom.[37] The experience in Great Britain and in an isolated informal admission state such as Maine suggests that the disadvantages are not that real or at least not serious enough to outweigh some of the obvious therapeutic and administrative benefits of informal admission. But Great Britain is not the United States, and Maine is only one state — a predominantly rural and sparsely populated one — of 50 states. Ultimately, the interpretation of the experience is to a large extent a judgment call, a balancing of variously weighted disadvantages and benefits which submits to no single objective result. The relative dearth of informal admission statutes in this country and the low use of the procedures in the states where they exist indicate that so far the negative side of the scale has been weighted the heavier.

IV. FORMAL PROCEDURES: THE ADMISSION PROCESS

Having touched on the limits of voluntariness in the traditional, formal voluntary admission schemes and some of the pros and cons of the more purely voluntary informal admission alternative, we return to examine the formal procedures in detail.

A. Application

The states' voluntary admission statutes today provide that at a minimum any *adult* person may seek voluntary admission and execute an application to this effect.[38] The trend has been toward lowering the age requirement for a self-initiated application. Most modern statutes pitch it below the age of majority, some specifying 18, 16, or even 14 years as the age at which voluntary

31. Illinois Dep't of Mental Health and Developmental Disabilities, Mental Health Statistics, Fiscal Year 1981, at 66. Since the statistics are not separated according to clinical diagnosis, it is impossible to tell whether developmentally disabled persons are included. The nature of developmental disabilities and the structure of the law (no procedures expressly labeled "informal" for the developmentally disabled) suggest that the informal process is intended primarily for mental illness conditions that may be relieved by brief, episodic institutionalization.

32. Gilboy, *supra* note 3, at 323.

33. *Id.* generally.

34. On the other hand, there is also evidence that coercion reduces the chances of successful psychiatric treatment. Indeed, that theory lies at the heart of the voluntary admission concept. The reconciling argument is that the effects of institutional power exercised over the patient depend on its type and level and the totality of circumstances surrounding the admission decision.

35. See ch. 4, Discharge and Transfer, § VI, Liability for "Wrongful" Discharge, *infra* and cases such as Smith v. United States, 437 F. Supp. 1004 (E.D. Pa. 1977) and Tarasoff v. Regents of Univ. of California, 551 P.2d 334, 131 Cal. Rptr. 14 (1976).

36. Of course the institution can initiate involuntary proceedings against an informal patient who is actively psychotic or judged to be dangerous. But the principles and procedural incentives of informal admission militate against it.

37. Gilboy, *supra* note 3, at 327-28 describes the results of a few studies.

38. See table 3.1, col. 1.

admission on the patient's own petition is possible. The statutes covering voluntary admission of retarded persons—more likely to be separate from mentally ill admissions today than in previous years—tend to set the lowest permissible age. In the District of Columbia, for example, any mentally ill person 18 years or older[39] may apply for admission to the District's mental health facilities, but for the retarded population the relevant age is only 14.[40] Illinois operates with an interesting scheme. Voluntary self-admission is open to any person 16 years or older. The general rule is that to be able to execute an application the applicant must be at least 18,[41] but a specific statutory exception is made for "minors" between the ages of 16 and 18, who by virtue of a separate provision are permitted to execute voluntary admission papers.[42] The law goes on to provide that such minors shall then be treated as adult patients in all relevant respects—that is, subjected to the same restrictions and entitled to the same rights in the institution—except that their parents or guardians must be notified of the admission.[43]

The Illinois scheme exemplifies the new approach to voluntary admissions. The emphasis is on self-initiated and self-executed efforts to gain entry into the hospital. Third-party petitions on behalf of adult patients are not considered voluntary unless requested by the patient.[44] Parents or guardians may still apply for "voluntary" admission of minors,[45] but the law favors the autonomous approach by first stating the minor's right to apply himself and by granting this opportunity at an earlier age than before.[46]

In a growing number of states, the application provisions seek to assure that the admission decision is indeed voluntary by requiring a finding that the applicant understands the nature and implications of his decision.[47] These provisions used to speak in general terms of the patient's mental competency. But today they are more specifically focused. New York's[48] is one of the most elaborate, requiring that the applicant have the ability to understand (1) that the institution to which he is applying for admission is a mental institution, (2) that he is applying for voluntary admission, and (3) what the nature of voluntary status is, including the meaning of provisions governing release and conversion to involuntary status. Maine's statute requires that the conditions for "informed consent" be met, which, as the subsequent definition of the term indicates, means an understanding similar in content and detail to that spelled out in the New York law.[49] Other states are somewhat less specific, requiring simply that the applicant understand the nature of his request (Maryland)[50] or that he have capacity to make a responsible decision (Wyoming).[51] Provisions requiring that the parents or guardians of minors cosign the application (for example, in Delaware)[52] seem more concerned with legal sufficiency than with assuring voluntariness.

A good number of states also require (or encourage by alluding to the option of) medical certification of some sort to support the voluntary application.[53] This is particularly true of the statutes governing the admission of developmentally disabled persons. The rationale is not merely to assure general medical suitability for admission but to promote the best use of resources for applicants who come with a variety of problems and treatment and training needs. The Arizona statute[54] emphasizes this by speaking of the evaluation's aim of finding appropriate placement. In Montana,[55] the certification must include the finding that less restrictive community facilities are not available nearby. And Colorado,[56] recognizing the various needs that patients or any one patient may have, requires certification in the form of a comprehensive mental, physical, social, and educational evaluation.

B. Discretion of Admitting Facility

Mental facilities in most states are granted wide discretion in admitting voluntary patients. The admitting staff's decision may rest on (1) the availability of suitable accommodations and (2) the mental condition of the applicant.[57] A few statutes actually use the term *discretion* in describing the authority of the institution to decide to accept or not accept the voluntary patient.[58] Most state statutes simply say that the institution "*may* admit" or "*may* receive" the applicant[59] (emphasis added). The question of whether suitable accommodations

39. D.C. Code Ann. § 21-511 (1981).
40. *Id.* at § 6-1922.
41. Ill. Ann. Stat. ch. 91½, §§ 3-400, 3-401 (Smith-Hurd Supp. 1983).
42. *Id.* at §§ 3-401, 3-502.
43. *Id.* at § 3-502.
44. *Id.* at § 3-401(2).
45. *Id.* at § 3-503.
46. *Id.* at §§ 3-502, 3-501. By the latter provision, minors as young as 14 may request and obtain *outpatient* services without the need for parental or guardian consent.
47. Table 3.1, col. 1.
48. N.Y. Mental Hyg. Law §§ 9.13(a), 9.17(a), & 15.13(a) (McKinney 1978 & Supp. 1981).
49. Me. Rev. Stat. Ann. tit. 34, §§ 2657-A, 2658-A (Supp. 1983).
50. Md. Ann. Code art. 59A, §§ 10, 11 (1979 & Supp. 1981).
51. Wyo. Stat. Ann. §§ 25-3-106(a) (1981).
52. Del. Code Ann. tit. 16, § 5123(c) (Supp. 1980).
53. Table 3.1, col. 2.
54. Ariz. Rev. Stat. Ann. § 36-560 (Supp. 1981).
55. Mont. Code Ann. § 53-20-120(2) (1981).
56. Colo. Rev. Stat. Ann. § 27-10.5-104(4) (1982).
57. See table 3.1, cols. 6 & 7.
58. E.g., Ind. Code Ann. § 16-14-9.1-2(a) (Burns 1983), Okla. Stat. Ann. 43A, § 53 (1979).
59. See generally table 3.1, cols. 6 & 7.

are available tends to focus, as specified for example in the Iowa statute,[60] simply on whether there is space in the public institutions rather than on the more discrete issue of whether there are treatment or training programs to meet the particular needs of the applicant. The mental condition criterion is spelled out in terms of the applicant's "mental illness," "need of treatment," and the like or in the more impersonal language of "clinical suitability."[61]

A few jurisdictions, such as the District of Columbia,[62] provide that public facilities "*shall* admit" voluntary applicants, if the examination by the admitting physician shows the need for institutionalization, while private institutions "*may* admit" them (emphasis added). The inference that the public facilities are hereby deprived of much discretion is probably false, however. There is plenty of play in the "need for institutionalization" standard. And absent statutory language to the contrary, the discretion to admit based on whether suitable accommodations are available is implicit: no facility is required to admit patients for whom there is no room or no program. The practical meaning of these provisions probably is that public facilities must give formal justification for any refusal to admit while private institutions do not, or when they do, it is a matter of common courtesy rather than legal requirement.

A less defensible exercise of institutional discretion occurs when voluntary applicants are denied admission because staff doctors, for one reason or another, prefer patients to come in on a different legal basis. For example, the institution may favor involuntary commitments because it disapproves of the liberal release rights of the voluntary patient. Or the facility may be concerned about the voluntary patient's right to refuse treatment, or about its ability to collect reimbursement for the cost of care, or about any other management or treatment complications that arise in connection with voluntary status. There is some evidence that the infrequent use of informal admission procedures[63] and of certain emergency admission provisions[64] may be dictated in part by such nonclinical concerns. The overall significant increase in formal voluntary admissions over the past decades argues against the supposition that similar considerations have done much to inhibit use of the formal voluntary procedure.

The notion that applicants for admission to mental facilities have an absolute right to be admitted is extreme. Considerations of physical space, program availability, medical and fiscal priority, residency, and so forth cannot simply be dismissed as irrelevant to the decision whether to admit. At the same time, it is also important to consider the possibility that many applicants for early, voluntary admission will, if turned away, become patients sometime in the future under conditions and circumstances that will make it less likely that they can be helped or that make the provision of help far more costly. Such considerations argue for at least a presumption in favor of admitting the patient when he first seeks treatment on his own initiative.

C. Maintenance of the Voluntary Patient

Access to a public mental facility, whether on a voluntary or involuntary basis, should not be conditioned on the patient's ability to pay. The determination of the patient's ability to finance his institutionalization should be treated as a question separate from that of institutionalization itself. While this is generally accepted policy today, it represents a movement away from the original state of the voluntary admission law: under the earliest statutes, admission of voluntary patients was permitted only if they could pay the costs.[65] The present, more liberal policy is justified not only on humanitarian and medical grounds but on the basis of economics as well. It is less expensive to offer indigent patients voluntary care in the early stages of their illness or when they are still trainable than to risk advancing their disabilities to a point where treatment and training are futile and custodial care, perhaps involuntarily imposed, remains the only alternative.

V. RIGHTS OF THE VOLUNTARY PATIENT IN THE INSTITUTION

An examination of the relevant statutes fails to reveal significant differences between the rights of voluntary patients and those of involuntary patients once they are in the institution. Typically, the statutory provisions that deal with matters such as correspondence, visitation, mechanical restraint, treatment rights, and the exercise of general civil rights refer only to "patients" without differentiating by form of admission. The trend in the laws is toward assuring greater protection in each of these areas and maximizing the opportunity for informed consent for *all* patients.[66] New "rights" such as the right to refuse treatment[67] have generally been as-

60. Iowa Code Ann. § 229.2(z)(a) (West Supp. 1983-84).
61. See table 3.1, col. 7.
62. D.C. Code Ann. § 21-511 (1981).
63. See Gilboy, *supra* note 3.
64. Brakel & South, *supra* note 2.

65. Ross, Hospitalization of the Voluntary Mental Patient, 53 Mich. L. Rev. 353, 368 (1955).
66. See ch. 5, Rights of Institutionalized Persons, *infra* for a detailed discussion of these developments.
67. See Rogers v. Okin, 1478 F. Supp. 1342 (D. Mass. 1979), *modified,* 634 F.2d 650 (1st Cir. 1980); Guardianship of Roe, 421 N.E.2d 40 (Mass. 1981); Mills v. Rogers, 457 U.S. 291 (1982); and Rennie v. Klein, 462 F. Supp. 1131 (D. N.J. 1978), *modified and remanded,* 653 F.2d 836 (3d Cir. 1981).

serted for *in*voluntary patients, mainly because the earlier laws or assumptions were that those patients did not have them. The traditional view was that voluntary patients could refuse treatment and that unwanted treatment could not be imposed, but the patient paid the price for his noncooperation by being immediately discharged from the institution or subjected to incompetency or involuntary commitment proceedings. The modern approach is to be more accommodating to the patient's wishes: today in California, for example, the administrative regulations expressly give to voluntary patients the right to refuse antipsychotic medications.[68]

Whether voluntary and involuntary patients *should* possess similar rights depends in part on whether there is a difference in mental condition between the two classes. If the only difference between these patients is in the willingness to accept treatment coupled with the opportunity to apply for it, then the justification for granting special institutional privileges to one group or withholding them from the other becomes tenuous. There is a superficial logic in (if no hard data for) the supposition that voluntary patients are less disabled than patients who are not aware of their incapacities and who must be forced to undergo treatment, but this logic fails to consider the many diverse social and legal circumstances and personal motivations that bring people to the admission wards of mental facilities. While some involuntary patients, perhaps even the majority of them, may be worse off than most voluntary admittees, there are undoubtedly many cases in which the reverse is true, particularly given differential stages in their treatment or training; to formulate a blanket rule of institutional privileges and entitlements that disadvantages *all* involuntary admittees on the basis of such rough suppositions is difficult to justify. A more tenable argument for granting special rights to voluntary patients is that it might furnish the needed incentive to advance the use of this method of treatment and care. However, such a policy necessarily implies some deprivation to involuntary patients that may not be justifiable on independent grounds.

A 1968 case from New York, *In re Buttonow*,[69] involving a patient converting from involuntary to voluntary status, held that the state's statutory scheme according fewer protections and rights to patients with the latter status was unconstitutional. The specific rights at issue were those of initial and periodic judicial review of the need to be hospitalized, the right to an equal level of assistance from New York's patient counseling system, the Mental Health Information Service, and the requirement of an inquiry into the converting patient's competency to agree to changing his legal status.

A persuasive argument can be made that if rights such as those at stake in *Buttonow* must be equally available for all patients regardless of their legal status, then certainly the same should apply for more obviously status-neutral rights such as the rights to treatment, correspondence, visitation, and so forth. Not everyone may be equally persuaded by the reasoning of the majority in *Buttonow*, however. Judge Breitel, in a partial dissent,[70] pointed out that the differentials in the law affecting voluntary and involuntary patients were quite deliberate and justifiable (why, for example, should a patient who admits himself freely and has a right to release upon request have the same judicial review protections as an involuntary patient?). Some differences in institutional treatment and procedure are justifiable, others are not. The implication of Judge Breitel's dissent is that it depends on the particular rights or protections involved, the purpose for which they exist, and the availability to the population from whom they are withheld of rights and protections that, while perhaps not identical or operative at the same junctures in the process, nonetheless fulfill similar end purposes. Notwithstanding these arguments, the trend in the modern statutes is to expressly provide that voluntary patients shall have the same rights as those who are involuntarily committed.[71]

Some restrictions on a patient's rights are necessary for his medical welfare, whether the patient was voluntarily or involuntarily admitted. Others may exist to serve the institution's general administrative needs, though they may be superfluous for particular patients whose self-management skills are largely intact. Much concern about these restrictions could be eliminated by assuring that hospital authorities exercise their restrictive powers within well-defined limits and that they be subject to the patient's right to be notified of them and, in properly brought instances, to the demand for outside review.[72]

VI. COMPETENCY OF THE VOLUNTARILY INSTITUTIONALIZED PATIENT

The test ordinarily set forth in the statutes to determine an individual's legal capacity to do such things as enter into a contract, execute a conveyance, or exercise the right to vote is whether or not he is "competent," of

68. Cal. Admin. Code tit. 9, § 850.

69. 23 N.Y.2d 385, 244 N.E.2d 677, 297 N.Y.S.2d 97 (1968).

70. 244 N.E.2d 677, 683 (N.Y. 1968).

71. See, e.g., Cal. Welf. & Inst. Code §6006(b) (West 1972). Many states today take the approach of having one "patients' rights" statute that explicitly applies to both voluntary and involuntary patients: e.g., Ark. Stat. Ann. § 59-1416 (Supp. 1983).

72. See ch. 5, Rights of Institutionalized Persons, *infra*.

"sound mind," or "sane."[73] The question that follows is whether or not all patients in mental facilities must be categorized as incompetent or of unsound mind and whether the legal status of being a voluntary or involuntary admittee makes a difference.

A decade or two ago, the presumption and, in many states, the law was that institutionalization was equivalent to a finding of legal incompetency. By 1970, however, this notion of merger of the concepts of institutionalization and incompetency had survived in only a handful of jurisdictions and had been specifically rejected in many others. Today virtually every state has an explicit provision to the effect that institutionalization does not affect competency or even create a presumption of incompetency.[74] The trend has been not only to treat competency as a *separate* issue but as a *separable* issue: mentally disabled persons may be found incompetent to perform certain discrete acts and at the same time retain their legal capacity for all other purposes.[75] To give a telling example: some statutes today require as a predicate for involuntary institutionalization that the disabled person be found incapacitated specifically as to his ability to make a decision on his need of treatment;[76] but even after such a finding is made and the person is institutionalized, substantial support exists for the proposition that he retains competency to refuse any specific treatments the institutional staff wishes to impose.[77]

Among the few concessions to the relationship between competency and institutionalization is the possibility, in some states, of still raising the former issue and having it heard (albeit as a separate issue) during proceedings that decide the latter.[78] This is a concession to logic and economy in situations where the prospective patient shows obvious signs of being incapable of handling certain aspects of life inside or outside the institution. Another is the type of provision, found in the majority of states, which says that without regard to formal competency the patient shall be subject to the general (or "reasonable") rules, regulations, and restrictions of the institution that exist for his "medical welfare."[79] The reasonableness of such provisions depends much on their interpretation and application.

Logically, the entire question of whether institutionalization affects the patient's competency to conduct his personal or business affairs has centered on the involuntary patient. The idea that a patient who was capable of signing himself in would lose or could be presumed to lose his general competency once admitted was always tenuous. A number of states, however, used to have statutes affirming the obvious (perhaps because it was frequently ignored), with New York's being among the most explicit in asserting that "no person admitted to a hospital by voluntary or informal admission shall be deprived of any civil right solely by reason of such admission."[80] Today, the issue is all but moot; such statutes have disappeared to be replaced by provisions, found in one form or another in almost all states, referring to patients in general and disavowing the connection between incompetency and *any* form of institutionalization.[81] There used to be concern when the law and presumptions were less clear that the cloud hanging over the competency of voluntary as well as involuntary patients might discourage persons from seeking voluntary admission. Today, that should be among the least of the voluntary applicant's concerns.

VII. RELEASE

Commonly, a voluntary patient who seeks release must request it in a written application to the institution's authorities. Once this is done, the statutes provide that the release must take place immediately,[82] as soon as practicable,[83] or after a delay of a few days (3 days is typical,[84] but the range goes up to 7 and 15 days).[85] The rationale behind giving the institution a margin of several days is presumably to provide the staff with an opportunity to negotiate for some transitional care or aftercare in the community or, alternatively, to try to

73. See *id.* and ch. 8, Decision-Making Rights over Persons and Property. The trend in the modern law is to differentiate according to the type of activity at issue and the particular capacity required for it, as opposed to making blanket incompetency determinations that affect all civil and business activities.

74. See table 7.2, col. 1.

75. See ch. 8, on Decision-Making Rights over Persons and Property, *infra*.

76. States with statutory provisions to this effect include Alaska, Delaware, Iowa, Kansas, Michigan, South Carolina, Utah, and Wyoming. See ch. 2, Involuntary Institutionalization, *supra* especially table 2.6, and § IIID, text at notes 212-15, and this chapter § VIII, notes 122 & 123.

77. A. E. and R. R. v. Mitchell, No. C-78-466, 5 MDLR 154 (D. Utah June 16, 1980), held to the contrary, but the decision has generated much criticism.

78. See table 8.2, col. 3.

79. Table 8.2, col. 2. The Alaska statute, for example, speaks of restrictions necessary for medical welfare. Alaska Stat. § 47.30.150(a)(3) (1979).

80. N.Y. Mental Hyg. Law § 70-5 (McKinney Supp. 1969).

81. *Id.* at § 33.01 (McKinney 1978).

82. Among the jurisdictions that provide for immediate release are Alaska, California, the District of Columbia (developmentally disabled only; the institution may delay 48 hours for mentally ill patients), Iowa, Maine, Missouri, New Mexico, New York, North Dakota, Ohio, Utah, and West Virginia. See table 3.1, col. 11.

83. States such as Nevada, New Hampshire, and Rhode Island stipulate that the release request must be honored on the day it is made if it is a "normal working" day or "business" day. In Wisconsin, the law provides that the institution may delay discharge only long enough to evaluate the patient's condition. See table 3.1, col. 11.

84. Table 3.1, col. 11.

85. South Dakota permits a 7-day delay for voluntarily admitted developmentally disabled persons (5 days for the mentally ill); Oklahoma allows 15 days. See table 3.1, col. 11.

change the patient's mind, should they feel this is indicated, and to give the patient himself time to reconsider. A margin of 7 days, let alone 15, seems excessive for these purposes.

An all-important qualification to this general release-upon-request scheme is that in the overwhelming majority of states there are specific "extension provisions"[86] or indirect provisos[87] giving the institution authority to detain the patient for an additional period in order to initiate involuntary commitment proceedings in cases where this is deemed necessary and desirable. The Iowa statute[88] is representative in stating that the voluntary patient shall be released "forthwith" upon his request *unless* the chief medical officer of the institution files with the court a certification that the patient is "seriously mentally impaired." The court may then postpone the release for the time necessary to permit commencement of involuntary commitment procedures—a period not to exceed five days unless extended "for good cause shown" by a subsequent court order. Only 15 states[89] do not have extension provisions of this type, and of these, 4[90] nonetheless grant the institution explicit power to initiate involuntary commitment proceedings in the proper cases. This power presumably exists even in the remaining 11 states under the regular involuntary commitment laws, which typically give authority to initiate institutionalization proceedings to public officials and medical professionals when not simply to "any person."[91] The presence of specific extension/detention provisions and the explicit grant of power to initiate commitment in the voluntary admission schemes may serve mainly to give the institution more time and to place it in a legally more defensible position when it seeks to detain the "voluntary" patient who is felt to be not ready for discharge. In giving the institution a continued "hold" over the patient, as it were, these provisions also emphasize that unlike informal admission, formal voluntary admission implies a commitment from the patient to make the most of the treatment program that is offered. In not following through on this commitment, the patient risks his status as a voluntary patient and a considerable measure of his freedom.

The statutes of a few states contain provisions that give the voluntary patient an explicit option to *agree* to commit himself on the institution's treatment terms. In Oregon[92] and Pennsylvania,[93] for example, a patient may contract with the admitting facility to limit his right to release. Normally, voluntary patients in Oregon are entitled to release within 72 hours after they request it, but the institution may condition admission upon agreement with the applicant that he stay in for a definite period and forfeit his right to immediate release upon request. In Pennsylvania, the statute allows the institution and the voluntary applicant to agree that the latter's release may be delayed for up to 72 hours after notice of the desire to be discharged is given, instead of its having to be honored forthwith.[94]

South Carolina[95] and Texas[96] go even farther in this direction with statutory requirements that all voluntary patients shall remain at the institution for treatment for a specified minimum period (15 days and 10 days, respectively). Such requirements may be therapeutically sensible and avoid waste of treatment resources on patients who show insufficient commitment to their rehabilitation, but they also serve to further undermine the "voluntary" admission concept and the goal of encouraging patients to seek treatment with minimal strings attached.

The conservation principle that scarce medical resources not be idly used also extends to concern about their overuse, which in some states has been translated into legislative prescriptions of the maximum time that voluntary patients may remain institutionalized.[97] In Colorado, for example, voluntarily admitted mentally ill patients must have their "status" reviewed at least once every 6 months,[98] while developmentally disabled persons who have been admitted on a voluntary basis are entitled to residential care for no more than 30 consecutive days or a total of 90 days per year.[99] In Illinois, the voluntary patient must reaffirm his desire for treatment 30 days after admission and again every 60 days there-

86. See table 3.1, col. 12.

87. Some states, such as Florida, Kansas, and Montana, do not have specific extension/detention provisions, but they do explicate the power of the institution to initiate involuntary proceedings against the voluntary patient who requests release. Table 3.1, cols. 12 & 15.

88. Iowa Code Ann. § 229.4 (Supp. 1979).

89. California, Colorado, the District of Columbia, Florida, Kansas, Maryland, Montana, Nevada, North Carolina, Oklahoma, Oregon, Pennsylvania, Virginia, Washington, and Wyoming do not have extension provisions. See table 3.1, col. 12.

90. Florida, Kansas, and Montana have provisions giving the institution authority to begin involuntary proceedings despite an absence of specific statutory authority to detain the patient beyond the initial minimum holding period. Wyoming has such a law only for developmentally disabled persons. In Washington a provision of this type exists for a purpose other than to assure continued treatment of a patient who is seen to need this: involuntary commitment proceedings may be initiated when the patient and his relatives cannot pay for the costs of voluntary treatment. Wash. Rev. Code Ann. § 72.23.120 (1982).

91. See ch. 2, Involuntary Institutionalization, *supra*, particularly tables 2.6 & 2.8.

92. Or. Rev. Stat. § 426.220(1) (1981).

93. Pa. Stat. Ann. tit. 50, § 7206(a) (Purdon Supp. 1980).

94. *Id.* The actual language of the statute is that ordinarily a "person in voluntary inpatient treatment may withdraw at any time."

95. S.C. Code Ann. § 44-17-330(1) (1976).

96. Tex. Rev. Civ. Stat. Ann. art. 5547-23(c) (Vernon 1958).

97. See table 3.1, col. 8.

98. Colo. Rev. Stat. Ann. § 27-10-103(5) (1982).

99. *Id.* at § 27-10.5-103(1).

after.[100] An attempt to prevent patients with scant knowledge of their rights and poor communication skills from getting lost on the back wards of the institution may be part of the rationale for such provisions, along with conservation objectives and the goal of assuring that a continuing consensual treatment relationship will be maintained.

Statutory provisions authorizing mental facilities to delay the release of voluntary patients who have requested release have not gone unchallenged. An early case from New Mexico, *Ex parte Romero*,[101] concerned a voluntary patient who sought to secure his immediate release through a writ of habeas corpus in the face of a statute that authorized the detention of voluntary patients for ten days after they notified the hospital, in writing, of their intention and desire to leave. The hospital's position was that by voluntarily seeking admission the patient had in effect contracted to remain in the institution and to receive treatment for ten days after giving notice. The Supreme Court of New Mexico rejected this argument:

> Obviously, it does not require citation of authority that one may not enforce such a contract made with a person he knows to be so disordered in mind as to require treatment in an institution for the treatment of mental diseases.[102]

The rationale for this decision or the decision itself is not likely to find much support today. Current law is to the contrary in several respects. The law on legal incompetency, for one, is more discrete today.[103] The contention that any patient who requests or needs treatment is automatically incompetent to consent to the conditions surrounding his admission and release runs directly counter to the contemporary competency statutes as well as to general legal and medical opinion. More than that, it is directly contrary to the policy underlying the voluntary admission concept, which presumes the applicant's capacity to make decisions of this nature. The aforementioned current provisions in Oregon and Pennsylvania[104] in particular, which permit explicit agreements between the patient and the institution limiting the former's right to release, go directly against the reasoning of the *Romero* case. And admission statutes such as those in South Carolina and Texas,[105] mandating a minimum period of stay for the voluntary patient, are by implication equally out of tune with the *Romero* rationale. Finally, some minimal interlude between the patient's request for release and the facility's response ought to be allowed simply as a matter of public policy. The irony is that the *Romero* court itself, guided by just such practical considerations, made the decree in the case effective two days after it was issued!

Still, underneath the questionable reasoning in *Romero* lie some valid concerns. It has been suggested, for example, that *any* agreement that deprives the individual of his liberty is per se contrary to public policy, unconstitutional, and unenforceable regardless of the individual's competency. This is an extreme position, particularly when applied to invalidate minimal detention periods whose objective is primarily to assure that the next move is a considered one and in accord with the best interests of the patient. But the argument that agreements, express or implied, that limit liberty ought to be subjected to critical scrutiny is sound, and statutes and procedures should be structured in such a way as to assure maximum awareness on the part of the individual of the nature and consequences of the admission decision.

In line with the above objectives, the statutes of an increasing number of states—well over half today[106] as compared with only nine a decade ago—specifically require that a voluntary patient be advised of his right to release and to a clarification or review of his status at admission and periodically thereafter. In addition to the duty to advise, the statutes or administrative regulations in several states impose on the facility authorities a requirement that they assist the patient in the exercise of the right to release. New York's Mental Health Information Service is specifically empowered to render this kind of assistance, and the *Buttonow* case[107] assures that voluntary patients receive a share of it equal to involuntary patients. All this is a long way from where the law stood a number of decades ago, as exemplified in the Connecticut case of *Roberts v. Paine*.[108] In that case the patient alleged conspiracy and false imprisonment, claiming that he was tricked into signing an application for voluntary admission and then detained for a substantial period after he had made an oral request for release. The operative statute at that time required written notice ten days in advance of release. The trial court, in a jury instruction that was upheld on appeal, stated that the law did not impose any obligation on the institution to inform the patient regarding the proper steps for securing release and that even if the institution had *intentionally* concealed this information, no cause of ac-

100. Ill. Stat. Ann. ch. 91½, § 3-404 (Smith-Hurd Supp. 1979).
101. 51 N.M. 201, 181 P.2d 811 (1947).
102. *Id.* at 203, 181 P.2d at 813.
103. See chs. 8 & 9 *infra* on the question of legal competency of mentally disabled persons. Also *In re* Buttonow, 244 N.E.2d 677, 682 (N.Y. 1968), holding that even a person who has been adjudged incompetent retains the capacity to make decisions regarding his institutionalization—in this case, his conversion from involuntary to voluntary patient status.
104. See notes 92 & 93 and accompanying text *supra*.
105. See notes 95 & 96 and accompanying text *supra*.
106. See table 3.1, col. 13.
107. 244 N.E.2d 677 (N.Y. 1968).
108. 124 Conn. 170, 199 A. 112 (1938).

tion would arise. Such an instruction would not be sustained today in any jurisdiction. Notice of, advice on, and assistance in regard to asserting the procedure for release are essential ingredients in giving content to a right that would otherwise be an empty one.

Eleven states by statute,[109] and at least one more by court decision,[110] specify that involuntary commitment proceedings cannot be initiated against a voluntary patient unless or until he requests his release. The intent may be to prevent patients from concerning themselves with the threat of commitment during the course of their treatment. But one wonders whether the provision may not have the effect of making the patients afraid to request release. A more logical justification would be that there is simply no reason to change the legal status of patients so long as they show no intention of leaving. This may not always be true, however. While a change in medical condition need not as a general matter be accompanied by a change in legal status—for example, voluntary patients whose psychiatric condition deteriorates need not necessarily be converted to involuntary patients—it is possible that certain specific concomitants of psychiatric deterioration do make it advisable that the patient's voluntary status be reconsidered. For example, the patient may have become dangerous and be in need of greater institutional restrictions, or uncooperative with the treating staff and responsive only to more coercive treatment methods—situations that might be difficult to reconcile not merely with the voluntary status of the individual patient but with the institution's general treatment of this class of patients. In this light, the provisions prohibiting the initiation of involuntary proceedings prior to a release request by the voluntary patient seem misdirected. Institutional authorities in states without such provisions presumably can initiate commitment proceedings any time they deem proper under the states' regular commitment schemes.

While in the vast majority of states voluntary institutionalization is for an indeterminate period or until such time as the patient is recovered and no longer needs treatment[111] (or decides he no longer wants it and requests release), the statutes of some 14 states specify a definite duration. This latter number is roughly the same as it was a decade ago, but nonetheless there has been a major change in that today all but 2 of these states prescribe *maximum* periods[112] whereas 10 years ago most specified a *minimum* length of stay.[113] The prescribed maximums range from 30 days up to 2 years. The shorter periods typically contemplate a mere review of status or a reaffirmation of the patient's intent to continue treatment as a precondition to further institutionalization, while the statutory vision in prescribing the longer periods is that at or toward their end there must be a full reapplication for admission. The rationales of conserving resources and assuring the maintenance of a consensual treatment relationship which underlie the maximum institutionalization periods have already been noted. An additional point is that the maximums require affirmative action by the patient or the institution to *continue* the former's institutionalization, which may in the long run be in the interest of those patients who are ill equipped to act affirmatively on their *right to release*. Inasmuch as the Constitution does not guarantee an explicit right to treatment[114]—much less treatment beyond a specified time in a particular institution—the provisions limiting treatment to a certain maximum period are on safe legal footing.

Provisions prescribing fixed *minimum* periods of institutionalization for voluntary patients—largely out of vogue today—rest on somewhat less secure legal grounds. Old cases have questioned the competency of the patient to agree to forfeit his liberty for a period of time[115] as well as the authority of the institution to hold anyone against his will absent a court determination[116] or a formal procedure at least ratified by a judicial officer. Today, the challenge would more likely be put in terms of whether the patient was adequately informed of what he was agreeing to, regardless of his competency or the presence of a court order. A substantial effort to apprise the applicant of the conditions of admission should be the standard procedure of any voluntary admission scheme and particularly of those that prescribe minimum periods of institutionalization. Even then, statutory minimums present a conceptual sticking point in the "voluntary" admission idea, and they may be practically counterproductive in that they risk discouraging individuals from seeking treatment on these terms.

109. See table 3.1, col. 15.

110. People v. Hill, 72 Ill. App. 3d 638, 391 N.E.2d 51 (1979); *In re* Meyer, 438 N.E.2d 639 (Ill. App. Ct. 1982).

111. See table 3.1, cols. 8-10.

112. See table 3.1, col. 8.

113. Today only South Carolina and Texas have minimum length of stay provisions. See table 3.1, col. 9.

114. The cases that hint at a constitutionally based right to treatment do so in juxtaposition to the restraint on liberty imposed by involuntary commitment. Donaldson v. O'Connor, 422 U.S. 563 (1975); Addington v. Texas, 441 U.S. 418 (1979); Youngberg v. Romeo, 457 U.S. 307 (1982). Whatever the force of the argument for a right to treatment in that context, it does not extend to persons who seek treatment on their own initiative.

115. *Ex parte* Romero, 51 N.M. 201, 181 P.2d 811 (1947).

116. Barbee v. Kolb, 207 Ark. 227, 179 S.W.2d 701 (1944).

VIII. CONVERSION FROM INVOLUNTARY TO VOLUNTARY STATUS

Whereas much of the discussion surrounding the release of voluntary patients has focused on provisions authorizing the initiation of involuntary procedures against them under given circumstances, a relatively new development in the voluntary admission law is the widespread enactment of provisions authorizing precisely the opposite—conversion from involuntary to voluntary status. Statutes to this effect exist in roughly half the states today.[117] The majority say that the conversion can be accomplished at "any time," though in a few states the opportunity is limited to the emergency detention period[118] or to the time before or pending the involuntary commitment hearing.[119] The statutes that specify when or why it might be proper for an involuntary patient to switch to voluntary status speak generally in terms of the patient's "best interests"[120] or, as in New Hampshire,[121] of his no longer meeting the criteria for involuntary institutionalization. The Florida[122] provision articulates the requirement that the patient undergoing the legal status conversion do so with his "express and informed consent." This protective language raises the question of what is risked, lost, or gained when an involuntary patient becomes a voluntary patient. Obviously, the shift from involuntary to voluntary status does not pose anywhere near as many potential disadvantages for the patient as a change in the other direction, and the legal safeguards surrounding the latter change need not be duplicated for the former. Still, upon attaining voluntary status, the patient may be subjected to a different set of institutional, treatment, review, and release rights, and even his financial obligations to the institution may be altered.[123] The patient should have the capacity to appreciate these changes and, with or without the help of institutional staff or patient advocacy personnel, to assert his new rights and meet his new obligations.

117. See table 3.1, col. 16.
118. Mass. Ann. Laws ch. 123, § 12(c) (Michie/Law. Co-op. 1981).
119. E.g., Mich. Comp. Laws Ann. § 330.1406 (1981).
120. E.g., Fla. Stat. Ann. § 394.465(4) (West Supp. 1981); Ga. Code Ann. § 88-503.5 (1979).
121. N.H. Rev. Stat. Ann. § 135-B:9 (III) (1977 & Supp. 1981).
122. Fla. Stat. Ann. § 394.465(4) (West Supp. 1981).
123. Wash. Rev. Code Ann. § 72.23.120 (1982) states, e.g.:

> Payment of hospitalization charges shall not be a necessary requirement for voluntary admission: *Provided, however*, The department may request payment of hospitalization charges, or any portion thereof, from the patient or relatives of the patient within the following classifications: Spouse, parents, or children. Where the patient or relatives within the above classifications refuse to make the payments requested, the department shall have the right to discharge such patient or initiate proceedings for involuntary hospitalization. The maximum charge shall be the same for voluntary and involuntary hospitalization.

TABLE 3.1 VOLUNTARY ADMISSION OF MENTALLY ILL AND DEVELOPMENTALLY DISABLED PERSONS

STATE	PERSONS WHO MAY APPLY FOR ADMISSION (1)	MEDICAL CERTIFICATION (2)	FURTHER APPROVAL BY (3)	PUBLIC INSTITUTION (4)	PRIVATE INSTITUTION (5)	ADMISSION DISCRETIONARY ON PART OF INSTITUTION AS TO: *Availability of Suitable Hospital Accommodations* (6)	ADMISSION DISCRETIONARY ON PART OF INSTITUTION AS TO: *Mental Condition* (7)	PERIOD: *Definite* Maximum (8)	PERIOD: *Definite* Minimum (9)	PERIOD: *Indefinite* (10)	RELEASE UPON REQUEST (TIME) (11)	EXTENSION PROVISION (12)	TOLD OF RIGHT TO RELEASE OR REVIEW (13)	INFORMAL ADMISSION (14)	PROVISION FOR INVOLUNTARY COMMITMENT OF VOLUNTARY PATIENT (15)	PROVISION FOR CONVERSION FROM INVOLUNTARY TO VOLUNTARY STATUS (16)
ALA. Code																
ALAS. Stat. (1979 & Supp. 1981)	any mentally ill person 14 or older 47.30.670			a treatment facility 47.30.670	a treatment facility 47.30.670					no further need for hospitalization 47.30.680	immediately unless involuntary commitment proceedings begun w/in 48 hrs. 47.30.685				only if patient first requests release 47.30.675(a)(2) 47.30.685	
ARIZ. Rev. Stat. Ann. (1974 & Supp. 1981): Mentally ill	any adult w/a mental or personality disorder or an emotional condition fn. 1 36-518A			evaluation or mental health treatment agency 36-518A state hospital 36-518A	evaluation or mental health treatment agency 36-518A		needs evaluation or will benefit from care & treatment 36-518A			recovered, or no longer benefiting from treatment 36-519A	24 hrs. unless judicial hospitalization proceedings commenced 36-519B	36-519B			36-519B	36-526B 36-531B 36-534 36-542A(1) 36-543A
Developmentally disabled	developmentally disabled adult 36-560(D)	placement evaluation 36-560(G)		facilities operated by licensed, & supervised by, or supported by the dep't 36-559	facilities operated by licensed, & supervised by, or supported by the dep't 36-559	36-560(B)	36-560(H)			36-565(B) 36-566(A)	36-566(A)					
Ark. Stat. Ann. (1971 & Supp. 1981)	any person w/mental illness, disease, or disorder 59-1403 (a)	examination of applicant 59-1403(a)	application signed in presence of 2 witnesses 59-1403(a)				in need of treatment & will be benefited thereby 59-1403(a)			recovery or improvement 59-1403(a)	59-1403B	involuntary commitment proceedings must be commenced; patient must be so advised within 1 hr. of his request 59-1403C			59-1403B	at any time, w/statement signed by staff member & patient's attorney 59-1412
CAL. Welf. & Inst. Code (West 1972 & Supp. 1981) fn. 2	any adult who is suitable for care, treatment or observation 6004			county facility 6004			6004				at any time 6005					
	mentally disordered or developmentally disabled adults 6000(a)			state facility 6000	private facility 6002		6000				at any time 6000					
COLO. Rev. Stat. (1973 & Supp. 1981): Mentally ill	mentally ill person 15 or older 27-10-103 (1), (2), (3)			public agency 27-10-103(1)	private agency 27-10-103(1)			status reviewed at least once every 6 mos. 27-10-103(5)								during 72-hr. involuntary evaluation period 27-10-103(7)
Developmentally disabled	short-term admission of person 18 or older 27-10.5-103(2) long-term admission 27-10.5-104	mental, physical, social, & educational evaluations for long-term admissions 27-10.5-104(4)		facility (for short-term admissions) 27-10.5-103(1) 27-10.5-102(6)	facility (for short-term admissions) 27-10.5-103(1) 27-10.5-102(6)		person may benefit from care & treatment 27-10.5-103(2)(a) 27-10.5-104(2)	max. 30 consecutive days & max. 90 days per yr. (for short-term admissions) 27-10.5-103(1)			w/in 48 hrs. 27-10.5-108(2)(a)		27-10.5-109			

TABLE 3.1 VOLUNTARY ADMISSION OF MENTALLY ILL AND DEVELOPMENTALLY DISABLED PERSONS—*Continued*

STATE	PERSONS WHO MAY APPLY FOR ADMISSION (1)	MEDICAL CERTIFICATION (2)	FURTHER APPROVAL BY (3)	PUBLIC INSTITUTION (4)	PRIVATE INSTITUTION (5)	ADMISSION DISCRETIONARY ON PART OF INSTITUTION AS TO: *Availability of Suitable Hospital Accommodations* (6)	*Mental Condition* (7)	PERIOD: *Definite* Maximum (8)	*Definite* Minimum (9)	*Indefinite* (10)	RELEASE UPON REQUEST (TIME) (11)	EXTENSION PROVISION (12)	TOLD OF RIGHT TO RELEASE OR REVIEW (13)	INFORMAL ADMISSION (14)	PROVISION FOR INVOLUNTARY COMMITMENT OF VOLUNTARY PATIENT (15)	PROVISION FOR CONVERSION FROM INVOLUNTARY TO VOLUNTARY STATUS (16)
CONN. Gen. Stat. Ann. (West 1975 & Supp. 1981):																
Mentally ill	mentally ill person 16 or older 17-176			any hospital for mental illness 17-187(a)	any hospital for mental illness 17-187(a)	may receive 17-187(a)	may receive 17-187(a)				5 days 17-187(a)	15 days where involuntary hospitalization proceedings commenced 17-187(d)	17-187(a)	17-187(b)	after patient requests release 17-187(d)	prior to adjudication of commitment application 17-178(e)
Developmentally disabled	any mentally retarded adult resident of Conn. 19-569l	physician & psychologist 19-569l	commissioner 19-569l	state school, diagnostic center or other facility for mentally retarded persons 19-569l	state school, diagnostic center or other facility for mentally retarded persons 19-569l					until patient will no longer profit from hospitalization 19-569l	7 days 19-569m				19-569 19-569d	
DEL. Code Ann. (1971 & Supp. 1980) *fn. 3*	any mentally ill person; if under 18, legal guardian, spouse, or parents must also sign 16,§5123 (a), (c)	optional: letter from treating physician recommending hospitalization *fn. 4* 16,§5123(b)	subject to payment of charges for care, maintenance, & support 16,§5123(a)	Delaware State Hospital 16,§5123(a)		may admit 16,§5123(a)	may admit 16,§5123(a)			recovered, or hospitalization no longer advisable 16,§5123(d)	5 days 16,§5123(e)	no release where patient otherwise committed or admitted during 5-day period 16,§5123(f)				prior to hearing 16,§5011(b)
D.C. Code Ann. (1981 & Supp. 1982)																
Mentally ill	any mentally ill person 18 or older 21-511	psychiatric examination for public hospital admission 21-511		public hospital 21-511	private hospital 21-511	public hospital shall admit private hospital may admit 21-511	public hospital shall admit private hospital may admit 21-511			recovered, or continued hospitalization no longer beneficial 21-512(b)	48 hrs. 21-512(a)		21-565			
Developmentally disabled	any mentally retarded person 14 or older 6-1922(a)	comprehensive evaluation 6-1922(b)	the ct. 6-1922(c)	facility 6-1922(a)	facility 6-1922(a)	may admit 6-1922(a)	may admit 6-1922(a)			residential care no longer advisable 6-1930	immediate discharge 6-1927					
FLA. Stat. Ann. (West 1973 & Supp. 1981):																
Mentally ill	any mentally ill person 18 or older 394.465(1)(a)			facility 394.465(1)(a) 394.455(8)	facility 394.465(1)(a) 394.455(8)	may be admitted 394.465(1)(a)	evidence of mental illness & suitable for treatment 394.465(1)(a) may be admitted 394.465(1)(a)			sufficiently improved 394.465(2)(a)	3 days or institute release plan approved by patient 394.465(2)(a)		at admission & every 6 mos. 394.465(3)		after patient requests release or revokes consent to treatment 394.465(2)(b), (5)	express & informed consent required; in best interest of patient 394.465(4)
Developmentally disabled	persons eligible for developmentaldisability services 393.065	dep't may screen 393.065(1)	dep't may provide diagnostic evaluation after screening 393.065	facility 393.065 (2)(c)1–7	facility 393.065 (2)(c)1–7		most appropriate, least restrictive & most cost beneficial 393.065(2)(c)			admission no longer appropriate 393.115	hearing upon request for release 393.115	*fn. 5*				
GA. Code Ann. (1979 & Supp. 1980)	any mentally ill person 12 or older; if a minor, parents must consente 88-503.1(a)a)			any facility 88-503.1(a)	any facility 88-503.1(a)	may receive 88-503.1(a)	evidence of mental illness & suitable for treatment 88-503.1(a) may receive 88-503.1(a)			recovered or sufficiently improved 88-503.2	72 hrs. unless involuntary hospitalization proceedings commenced 88-503.3	where involuntary proceedings commenced 88-503.3	88-503.1(b) 88-503.4		88-503.3	chief medical officer thinks in best interest of patient 88-503.5
HAWAII Rev. Stat. (1976 & Supp. 1981)	any mentally ill person 17 or older 334-60(a)			psychiatric facility 334-60(a)(1)	psychiatric facility 334-60(a)(1)	may admit 334.60(a)	may admit 334.60(a)			sufficiently improved 334-60(a)(3)	24 hrs. unless involuntary hospitalization proceedings commenced 334-60(a)(3)	once involuntary proceedings commenced patient may be detained until further ct. order 334-60(a)(3)	at admission & every 6 mos. 334-60(a)(4)		334-60(a)(3)	

TABLE 3.1 VOLUNTARY ADMISSION OF MENTALLY ILL AND DEVELOPMENTALLY DISABLED PERSONS—*Continued*

						ADMISSION DISCRETIONARY ON PART OF INSTITUTION AS TO		PERIOD								
								Definite								
STATE	PERSONS WHO MAY APPLY FOR ADMISSION (1)	MEDICAL CERTIFICATION (2)	FURTHER APPROVAL BY (3)	PUBLIC INSTITUTION (4)	PRIVATE INSTITUTION (5)	*Availability of Suitable Hospital Accommodations* (6)	*Mental Condition* (7)	Maximum (8)	Minimum (9)	*Indefinite* (10)	RELEASE UPON REQUEST (TIME) (11)	EXTENSION PROVISION (12)	TOLD OF RIGHT TO RELEASE OR REVIEW (13)	INFORMAL ADMISSION (14)	PROVISION FOR INVOLUNTARY COMMITMENT OF VOLUNTARY PATIENT (15)	PROVISION FOR CONVERSION FROM INVOLUNTARY TO VOLUNTARY STATUS (16)
IDAHO Code (1980 & Supp. 1981)	any mentally ill emancipated minor or any mentally ill person 18 or older 66-318			any facility 66-318	any facility 66-318	may admit 66-318	may admit 66-318 *fn. 6*			hospitalization no longer appropriate 66-319	66-320(a)	detained up to 3 days for exam & filing of application for continued care 66-320(a)(3)			only after release requested 66-320(b) 66-319	
ILL. Ann. Stat. (Smith-Hurd 1966 & Supp. 1982):																
Mentally ill	any mentally ill person 16 or older 91½,§3-400			mental health facility 91½,§3-400	mental health facility 91½,§3-400	may be admitted *fn. 7* 91½,§3-400	if deemed clinically suitable 91½,§3-400 may be admitted *fn. 7* 91½,§3-400	patient must affirm desire for continued treatment after 30 days & every 60 days thereafter 91½,§3-404		91½,§3-404	5 days unless involuntary hospitalization proceedings commenced 91½,§3-401(b) 91½,§3-403	5 additional days until hearing is held 91½,§3-403	91½,§3-401(b)	91½,§3-300	91½,§3-403	prior to adjudication & w/approval of facility director 91½,§3-801
Developmentally disabled	developmentally disabled person 18 or older 91½,§4-302	91½, §4-300(a) §4-301(b)		mental health facility 91½,§4-300	mental health facility 91½,§4-300	may be admitted 91½,§4-302	may be admitted *fn. 8* 91½,§4-302			*fn. 9* 91½,§4-310	5 days unless involuntary hospitalization proceedings commenced 91½,§4-306	5 additional days until hearing is held 91½,§4-306				
IND. Code Ann. (Burns 1973 & Supp. 1982)	any mentally ill person 18 or older 16-14-9.1-2 (a)(2)			appropriate facility 16-14-9.1-2(a)	appropriate facility 16-14-9.1-2(a)	may, at superintendent's discretion, admit 16-14-9.1-2(a)	mentally ill or has symptoms of mental illness 16-14-9.1-2(a) may, at superintendent's discretion admit 16-14-9.1-2(a)			care not necessary or discharge would contribute to most effective use of facility 16-14-9.1-2(b)	5 days to commence involuntary hospitalization proceedings 16-14-9.1-2(b)	further detention pending hearing 16-14-9.1-2(b)			16-14-9.1-2(b)	
IOWA Code Ann. (West 1969 & Supp. 1979)	any mentally ill adult 229.2(1)			229.2(1)	229.2(1)	availability of space at public hospital 229.2(z)(a) public hospital: shall receive & may admit 229.2(z)(a) private hospital: may receive & may admit 229.2(z)(b)	mentally ill or symptoms of mental illness 229.2(1) public hospital: shall receive & may admit 229.2(z)(a) private hospital: may receive & may admit 229.2(z)(b)			recovered, or hospitalization no longer advisable or discharge would contribute to most effective use of hospital 229.3	forthwith 229.4	5 day postponement of release where involuntary hospitalization proceedings commenced 229.4(3)			after release requested 229.4(3) after departure from hospital without notice 229.5	
KAN. Stat. Ann. (1976 & Supp. 1981)	any mentally ill person 14 or older 59-2905	optional 59-2905		treatment facility 59-2905	treatment facility 59-2905	may be admitted 59-2905	in need of treatment may be admitted 59-2905			treatment no longer advisable 59-2906	3 days 59-2907		59-2905	59-2904	59-2907	prior to hearing 59-2918
KY. Rev. Stat. Ann. (Michie 1977 & Supp. 1980):																
Mentally ill	any mentally ill person 18 or older 202A.020(1)			hospital 202A.020(1)	hospital 202A.020(1)	may admit 202A.020(1)	mentally ill or symptoms of mental illness 202A.020(1) may admit 202A.020(1)			recovered, or hospitalization no longer necessary 202A.020(2)	up to 72 hrs. if involuntary proceedings to be commenced 202A.020(3)	up to 10 days before hearing 202A.020(4)	202A.170(2)		after release requested 202A.020(4)	
Developmentally disabled	any mentally retarded individual *fn. 10* 202B.020			mental retardation residential treatment center 202B.020(3) or hospital 202A.020(1)	mental retardation residential treatment center 202B.020(3) or hospital 202A.020(1)	may admit 202A.010(1)	mentally retarded or symptoms of mental retardation 202A.020(1) may admit 202A.010(1)			recovered, or hospitalization no longer necessary 202A.020(2)	up to 72 hrs. if involuntary proceedings to be commenced 202A.020(3)	up to 10 days before hearing 202A.020	202A.170(2)		after release requested 202A.020(4)	

TABLE 3.1 VOLUNTARY ADMISSION OF MENTALLY ILL AND DEVELOPMENTALLY DISABLED PERSONS—*Continued*

STATE	PERSONS WHO MAY APPLY FOR ADMISSION (1)	MEDICAL CERTIFICATION (2)	FURTHER APPROVAL BY (3)	PUBLIC INSTITUTION (4)	PRIVATE INSTITUTION (5)	ADMISSION DISCRETIONARY ON PART OF INSTITUTION AS TO: *Availability of Suitable Hospital Accommodations* (6)	*Mental Condition* (7)	PERIOD: *Definite* Maximum (8)	Minimum (9)	*Indefinite* (10)	RELEASE UPON REQUEST (TIME) (11)	EXTENSION PROVISION (12)	TOLD OF RIGHT TO RELEASE OR REVIEW (13)	INFORMAL ADMISSION (14)	PROVISION FOR INVOLUNTARY COMMITMENT OF VOLUNTARY PATIENT (15)	PROVISION FOR CONVERSION FROM INVOLUNTARY TO VOLUNTARY STATUS (16)
LA. Rev. Stat. Ann. (West 1975 & Supp. 1981): Mentally ill	any mentally ill person 28:52(A)	admitting physician must deem patient suitable 28:52.2(A)		treatment facility 28:52(A)	treatment facility 28:52(A)	may admit 28:52(A)	mentally ill or substance abuse 28:52(A) may admit 28:52(A)				72 hrs. unless involuntary proceedings commenced 28:52.2(B)	28:52.2(B)	28:52(F)	28:52(A) 28:52.1	after release requested 28:52.2(B)	requires application for writ of habeus corpus 28:52(C) 28:55(J)
Developmentally disabled	any mentally retarded person 28:394	comprehensive diagnosis and evaluation 28:394(B)		residential facility 28:394(B)	residential facility 28:394(B)	28:394(B)	28:394(B)				72 hrs. unless involuntary proceedings commenced 28:415	as long as necessary for commencement of involuntary proceedings 28:415	28:390(B)(9)			
ME. Rev. Stat. Ann. (1978 & Supp. 1981): Mentally ill	*fn. 11*													*fn. 11* 34, §2290		
Developmentally disabled	any mentally retarded person if requirements of informed consent met 34, §2657-A	comprehensive evaluation by inter-disciplinary team 34, §§2654, 2655, 2657-A	director of regional office 34, §2657-A	department-operated facility 34, §2657-A			34, §2655	1 yr.; 30 days prior to termination of 1 yr., new plan may be prepared		when inter-disciplinary team finds client ready for discharge 34, §2661(a)	immediately unless emergency admission pursuant to §2664 instituted 34, §2660	if petition for judicial certification filed, an additional 25 days 34, §2664(a)	34, §2658-A(1)		34, §2664	
MD. Ann. Code (1979 & Supp. 1981): Mentally ill	any mentally disordered person 16 or older 59, §11(a) *fn. 12*		geriatric evaluation unit if person 65 or older 59, §11(b)(2)	any facility 59, §11(a)	any facility 59, §11(a)	may admit 59, §11(a)	mental disorder susceptible of treatment 59, §11(a) may admit 59, §11(a)	one yr.; patient must then execute new application		patient may reapply every yr. 59, §11(f)	3 days 59, §11(d)			59, §11(c)		
Developmentally disabled	any mentally retarded person 18 or older who understands nature of his request 59A, §§10, 11	comprehensive evaluation 59A, §§10(b), 11(b)		appropriate public facility 59A, §10(a)	any private facility 59A, §11(a)	public facility shall approve 59A, §10(c) private facility may admit 59A, §11(c)	public facility shall approve 59A, §10(c) private facility may admit 59A, §11(c)			reevaluation at least once per yr. 59A, §12(c)	3 days 59A, §12(b)		59A, §12			
MASS. Ann. Laws (Michie/Law. Co-op. 1981 & Supp. 1982)	any mentally ill or retarded person 16 or older 123, §10(a)			facility 59, §10(a)	facility 59, §10(a)	may receive & retain 123, §10(a)	in need of care & treatment may receive & retain 123, §10(a)			discharge in patient's best interest 123, §10(a)	within 3 days 123, §11	continued detention if commitment petition filed 123, §11			123, §11	during emergency detention period 123, §12
MICH. Comp. Laws Ann. (1980 & Supp. 1981): Mentally ill	any mentally ill person 18 or older 330.1415(1)			hospital 330.1415	hospital 330.1415		deemed clinically suitable 330.1415			clinically suitable for discharge 330.1476	3 days 330.1419(1)	continued hospitalization if involuntary commitment proceedings commenced 330.1420	330.1416	330.1411 330.1412	330.1420	pending involuntary commitment proceedings 330.1406
Developmentally disabled	any mentally retarded or developmentally disabled person 18 or older 330.1504	330.1510(1)		facility operated or under contract w/a public agency or licensed by state 330.1500(b)	facility operated or under contract w/a public agency or licensed by state 330.1500(b)	may be hospitalized 330.1415	may be hospitalized 330.1415			yrly. reexamination 330.1510(3)	w/in 3 days 330.1512(1)	judicial admission 330.1515	330.1509(3)		judicial commitment 330.1515	

TABLE 3.1 VOLUNTARY ADMISSION OF MENTALLY ILL AND DEVELOPMENTALLY DISABLED PERSONS—*Continued*

STATE	PERSONS WHO MAY APPLY FOR ADMISSION (1)	MEDICAL CERTIFICATION (2)	FURTHER APPROVAL BY (3)	PUBLIC INSTITUTION (4)	PRIVATE INSTITUTION (5)	ADMISSION DISCRETIONARY ON PART OF INSTITUTION AS TO: *Availability of Suitable Hospital Accommodations* (6)	ADMISSION DISCRETIONARY ON PART OF INSTITUTION AS TO: *Mental Condition* (7)	PERIOD: *Definite* Maximum (8)	PERIOD: *Definite* Minimum (9)	PERIOD: *Indefinite* (10)	RELEASE UPON REQUEST (TIME) (11)	EXTENSION PROVISION (12)	TOLD OF RIGHT TO RELEASE OR REVIEW (13)	INFORMAL ADMISSION (14)	PROVISION FOR INVOLUNTARY COMMITMENT OF VOLUNTARY PATIENT (15)	PROVISION FOR CONVERSION FROM INVOLUNTARY TO VOLUNTARY STATUS (16)
MINN. Stat. Ann. (West 1982) *fn. 13*														*fn. 13* 253A.03(1)		
MISS. Code Ann. (1981)	any mentally ill person 18 or older 41-21-103(2)(a)	2 certificates 41-21-103(1)		Miss. State Hosp. or East Miss. State Hosp. 41-21-103(1)		may be admitted 41-21-103(1)	must be deemed suitable for admission 41-21-103(1) may be admitted 41-21-103(1)			condition reviewed every 6 months 41-21-99	5 days 41-21-103(3)	until final ct. order, if involuntary proceedings commenced 41-21-103(3)	41-21-103(4)		41-21-103(3)	
MO. Ann. Stat. (Vernon 1979 & Supp. 1980): Mentally ill	any person 18 or older who has a mental disorder other than mental retardation or developmental disability 632.105			632.105	632.105	public facility shall admit private facility may admit 632.105	public facility shall admit private facility may admit 632.105			in patient care no longer appropriate condition reviewed every 180 days 632.175(1)	immediately 632.150(1)	further detention if involuntary proceedings commenced 632.150(2)			632.150(2)	632.390(3)
Developmentally disabled	any mentally retarded or developmentally disabled adult 633.110(1)	comprehensive evaluation by regional center 633.110(2)		633.115 633.120(3)	633.115 633.120(3)	private facility may admit public facility shall admit 633.120(3)	private facility may admit public facility shall admit 633.120(3)	6 mos. unless otherwise authorized 633.115(4)		evaluation every 180 days 633.130(1)	immediately 633.125(1)	emergency, guardianship or involuntary detention proceedings 633.125(1)				
MONT. Code Ann. (1981): Mentally ill	any mentally ill person 53-21-111	1 certificate 53-21-111(2)		mental health facility 53-21-111(1)	mental health facility 53-21-111(1)			*fn. 14* 53-21-112(3)			5 days 53-21-111(3)		52-21-111(1)		51-21-113(1)	53-21-163
Developmentally disabled	any developmentally disabled person 53-20-120(1)	by professional person that adequate community-based facilities are not available nearby 53-20-120(2)		residential facility 53-20-102(9)	residential facility 53-20-102(9)			30 days (w/out subsequent proceedings before ct.) 53-20-120(2)				ct. proceedings 53-20-120(2) 53-20-121				
NEB. Rev. Stat. (1976 & Supp. 1981)	any mentally ill person 83-1019			83-1019	83-1019						24 hrs. 83-1019	further detention if involuntary proceedings commenced 83-1019				
NEV. Rev. Stat. (1981): Mentally ill	any mentally ill adult 433A.140(1)	if public facility 433A.140(2)		433A.140(1)	433A.140(1)		public facility shall admit if person needs & may benefit from services 433A.140(2)			recovered or improved or services no longer beneficial (if public facility) 433A.140(4)	immediately w/in normal working day (public facility) 433A.140(3)					
Developmentally disabled	any mentally retarded person 18 or older 435.081, 435.007(4)			435.060		435.081	435.081			discharge if in the best interest of person 435.077(2)	435.081(7)				but person must be released upon request pending proceedings 435.081(7)	

TABLE 3.1 VOLUNTARY ADMISSION OF MENTALLY ILL AND DEVELOPMENTALLY DISABLED PERSONS—*Continued*

STATE	PERSONS WHO MAY APPLY FOR ADMISSION (1)	MEDICAL CERTIFICATION (2)	FURTHER APPROVAL BY (3)	PUBLIC INSTITUTION (4)	PRIVATE INSTITUTION (5)	ADMISSION DISCRETIONARY ON PART OF INSTITUTION AS TO: *Availability of Suitable Hospital Accommodations* (6)	ADMISSION DISCRETIONARY ON PART OF INSTITUTION AS TO: *Mental Condition* (7)	PERIOD: *Definite* Maximum (8)	PERIOD: *Definite* Minimum (9)	PERIOD: *Indefinite* (10)	RELEASE UPON REQUEST (TIME) (11)	EXTENSION PROVISION (12)	TOLD OF RIGHT TO RELEASE OR REVIEW (13)	INFORMAL ADMISSION (14)	PROVISION FOR INVOLUNTARY COMMITMENT OF VOLUNTARY PATIENT (15)	PROVISION FOR CONVERSION FROM INVOLUNTARY TO VOLUNTARY STATUS (16)
N.H. Rev. Stat. Ann. (1977 & Supp. 1981): Mentally ill	any mentally ill adult 135-B:9 135-B:11	by admitting physician 135-B:10		facility 135-B:9	facility 135-B:9	*fn. 15* 135-B:9(I)(b), (II)	applicant would benefit from inpatient treatment 135-B:9(I)(a)	2 yrs; must then file new application 135-B:17		no longer benefitting from treatment 135-B:18	same business day 135-B:15	24-hr. restriction may be imposed, w/further detention pursuant to involuntary hospitalization proceedings 135-B:16			135-B:16	if person no longer meets criteria for involuntary hospitalization 135-B:9(III)
Developmentally disabled	any developmentally impaired person 18 or older 171-A:5	comprehensive screening evaluation 171-A:6(II)		state service delivery system *fn. 16* 171-A:4						best interest of client; client can function independently or client has received optimal benefit review after 6 mos. annually thereafter 171-A:8 171-A:11	171-A:7		171-A:15			
N.J. Rev. Stat. (1981): Mentally ill	any mentally ill state resident 18 or older 30:4-46		institution must approve arrangements for payment 30:4-46	30:4-46	30:4-46	shall be admitted 30:4-46	patient requires hospitalization 30:4-46 shall be admitted 30:4-46			recovered, or further treatment undesirable 30:4-48	72 hrs. 30:4-48	further detention if involuntary hospitalization proceedings commenced 30:4-48			30:4-48	
Developmentally disabled	any mentally retarded person over 18 30:4-25.1		commissioner of the dept. 30:4-25.3	functional services 30:4-25.6 30:4-23	functional services 30:4-25.6 30:4-23	wait-listed pending availability if requested 30:4-25.6				earliest appropriate release 30:4-25.7						
N.M. Stat. Ann. (1979)	any mentally disordered or developmentally disabled adult 43-1-14A			residential treatment or habilitation 43-1-14A 43-1-3Q	residential treatment or habilitation 43-1-14A 43-1-3Q						immediately 43-1-14C	up to 5 days additional detention before involuntary hospitalization hearing 43-1-14C			43-1-14C	43-1-12F
N.Y. Mental Hyg. Law (McKinney 1978 & Supp. 1981): Mentally ill	any mentally ill person 18 or older *fn. 17* 9.13(a) 9.17(a)			any hospital 9.13(a)	any hospital 9.13(a)	may receive 9.13(a)	in need of care and treatment; may receive 9.13(a)	written consent to continued stay must be obtained every 120 days 9.19 review by mental health information service every 12 mos. 9.25(a)			immediately (may detain up to 72 hrs. to initiate commitment proceedings) 9.13(b)	detention before hearing for up to 3 days 9.13(b)	9.17(a)(3) 9.19	9.15	9.13 (b)	9.23
Developmentally disabled	any mentally retarded person 18 or older *fn. 18* 15.13(a)	based on examination made w/in 6 mos. of admission 15.05(b)		any school for the mentally retarded 15.13(a) 15.15(a)(1)	any school for the mentally retarded 15.13(a) 15.15(a)(1)	may receive 15.13(a)	may receive 15.13(a)	1 yr. 15.17 15.23		annual written consent for continued stay required 15.17 annual review of status 15.23	promptly (may detain up to 72 hrs. to initiate commitment proceedings) 15.13(b)	detention before hearing for up to 3 days 15.13(b)	15.07 15.17		15.13(b)	

TABLE 3.1 VOLUNTARY ADMISSION OF MENTALLY ILL AND DEVELOPMENTALLY DISABLED PERSONS—*Continued*

						ADMISSION DISCRETIONARY ON PART OF INSTITUTION AS TO		PERIOD								
								Definite								
STATE	PERSONS WHO MAY APPLY FOR ADMISSION (1)	MEDICAL CERTIFICATION (2)	FURTHER APPROVAL BY (3)	PUBLIC INSTITUTION (4)	PRIVATE INSTITUTION (5)	*Availability of Suitable Hospital Accommodations* (6)	*Mental Condition* (7)	Maximum (8)	Minimum (9)	*Indefinite* (10)	RELEASE UPON REQUEST (TIME) (11)	EXTENSION PROVISION (12)	TOLD OF RIGHT TO RELEASE OR REVIEW (13)	INFORMAL ADMISSION (14)	PROVISION FOR INVOLUNTARY COMMITMENT OF VOLUNTARY PATIENT (15)	PROVISION FOR CONVERSION FROM INVOLUNTARY TO VOLUNTARY STATUS (16)
N.C. Gen. Stat. (1981 & Supp. 1981)	any mentally ill person 122-56.3	optional 122-56.3		122-56.3 122-56.4	122-81.1		public facility 122-56.3 private hospital 122-81				72 hrs. 122-56.3		122-56.3			
N.D. Cent. Code (1978 & Supp. 1981): Mentally ill	any mentally ill adult 25-03.1-04			25-03.1-04			mentally ill or symptoms thereof, alcoholic, or drug addict 25-03.1-04			recovered, or treatment no longer advisable 25-03.1-05 clinically suitable for discharge 25-03.1-30(1)	immediately 25-03.1-06	up to 5 days detention for judicial commitment hearing 25-03.1-06	25-03.1-06		25-03.1-06	
Developmentally disabled	any mentally deficient person 25-04-05	comprehensive evaluation w/in 3 mos. of application 25-04-05(1)		state school or other state facility 25-04-05(1)		25-04-05(1)(c)				care, etc., no longer required 25-04-08(1)						
OHIO Rev. Code Ann. (Baldwin 1980 & Supp. 1981): Mentally ill	any mentally ill person 18 or older 5122.02(A)			hospital 5122.02(A)	hospital 5122.02(A)	may be admitted, unless hospitalization is inappropriate 5122.02(B)	may be admitted, unless hospitalization is inappropriate 5122.02(B)			recovered, or hospitalization no longer advisable, or patient refuses to accept treatment 5122.02(C)	forthwith, unless involuntary proceedings commenced w/in 3 days 5122.03(B)	further detention until commitment hearing 5122.03(B)	5122.03(B)		after release requested 5122.03(B)	at any time 5122.15(G)(1)
Developmentally disabled	any mentally retarded person 18 or older 5123.69	comprehensive evaluation 5123.69(B)	managing officer of an institution, w/ concurrence of chief program director 5123.69(B)	any institution 5123.69	any institution 5123.69					institutionalization no longer advisable 5123.69(D)	forthwith, unless involuntary proceedings commence w/in 3 days 5123.70(A)	further detention until commitment hearing 5123.70A			after release requested only 5123.70(B)	
OKLA. Stat. Ann. (West 1979 & Supp. 1981)	any mentally ill person 18 or older 43A, §53 §184			43A, §53	43A, §53 §184	superintendent of any state hospital has discretion to superintendent retain 43A, §53	suitable for care & treatment 43A, §53 receive & of any state hospital has discretion to receive & retain 43A, §53			recovered, or will not benefit from further treatment 43A, §73	15 days 43A, §53					
OR. Rev. Stat. (1981): Mentally ill	any person 18 or older w/mental illness or nervous disorder 426.220(1)			any state hospital 426.220(1)		may admit 426.220(1)	nervous disorder or mental illness; may admit 426.220(1)		fn. 19 426.220(1)		72 hrs. fn. 19 426.220(1)					at any time w/approval of mental health division 426.217
Developmentally disabled	any mentally retarded adult 427.180 427.185	diagnostic evaluation 427.180(1)(b) 427.185(2)	diagnosis & evaluation service 427.190	state training center 427.185(1)		427.180(2)(d)				annual review and certification 427.020(1)						

TABLE 3.1 VOLUNTARY ADMISSION OF MENTALLY ILL AND DEVELOPMENTALLY DISABLED PERSONS—*Continued*

STATE	PERSONS WHO MAY APPLY FOR ADMISSION (1)	MEDICAL CERTIFICATION (2)	FURTHER APPROVAL BY (3)	PUBLIC INSTITUTION (4)	PRIVATE INSTITUTION (5)	ADMISSION DISCRETIONARY ON PART OF INSTITUTION AS TO: *Availability of Suitable Hospital Accommodations* (6)	ADMISSION DISCRETIONARY ON PART OF INSTITUTION AS TO: *Mental Condition* (7)	PERIOD: *Definite* Maximum (8)	PERIOD: *Definite* Minimum (9)	PERIOD: *Indefinite* (10)	RELEASE UPON REQUEST (TIME) (11)	EXTENSION PROVISION (12)	TOLD OF RIGHT TO RELEASE OR REVIEW (13)	INFORMAL ADMISSION (14)	PROVISION FOR INVOLUNTARY COMMITMENT OF VOLUNTARY PATIENT (15)	PROVISION FOR CONVERSION FROM INVOLUNTARY TO VOLUNTARY STATUS (16)
PA. Stat. Ann. (Purdon 1969 & Supp. 1980):																
Mentally ill	any mentally ill person 14 or older *fn. 20* 50, §7201			approved facility 50, §7202	approved facility 50, §7202					treatment is not medically indicated 50, §7206(c)	*fn. 21* 50, §7206(a)		50, §7203			during involuntary detention period 50, §7302(d)(1)
Developmentally disabled	any mentally retarded person over 18 50, §4402 (voluntary admission) §4403 (voluntary commitment)	examination 50, §4402(b) §4403(b)		facility 50, §4402(a) §4102 §4403(a) §4102	facility 50, §4402(a) §4102 §4403(a) §4102	may be admitted 50, §4402(b)	may be admitted 50, §4402(b)	30 days 50, &4403(b)		annual review 50, §4402(d) annual review of successive commitments 50, §4403(d)	at any time upon notice by applicant 50, §4402(c) w/in 10 days notice of patient 50, §4403(c)		every 60 days 50, §4402(d) 50, §4403(d)			
R.I. Gen Laws Ann. (1977 & Supp. 1981) *fn. 22*	any mentally disabled person 18 or older (in presence of 1 witness) 40.1-5-6(1)	examination within 24 hrs. of admission to determine suitability 40.1-5-6(4)		any facility 40.1-5-6(1)	any facility 40.1-5-6(1)		in need of treatment & no suitable alternatives 40.1-5-6(2)	30 days; w/ successive applications for 90-day periods 40.1-5-6(2)		recovered, or discharge will not create likelihood of serious harm 40.1-5-11(1)	1 business day unless commitment proceedings commenced 40.1-5-6(3)	2 additional days pending hearing 40.1-5-6(3)	40.1-5-6(5)		40.1-5-6(3)	
S.C. Code Ann. (Law Co-op. 1976 & Supp. 1981):																
Mentally ill	any mentally ill person 16 or older 44-17-310(1)			hospital 44-17-310	hospital 44-17-310		if person is a proper subject for voluntary admission 44-17-310		15 days 44-17-330(1)	recovered, or detention no longer advisable 44-17-320	forthwith; up to 15 days to file commitment petition 44-17-330(4)	up to 15 additional days prior to hearing 44-17-330(4)	informed at admission, once w/in 6 mos. & annually 44-17-340		44-17-330(4)	
Developmentally disabled	any mentally retarded person 21 or older 44-21-80	examination at at a diagnostic center & certification by dep't. 44-21-40	state commissioner of mental retardation or designee 44-21-60	facilities & services of the dep't 44-21-80 44-21-30(5)		*fn. 23* 44-21-50	*fn. 23* 44-21-50			no longer in need of care, supervision 44-21-100	96 hrs.; up to 15 days to file application for judicial admission 44-21-100	pending a final determination on the application 44-21-100			44-21-100	
S.D. Codified Laws Ann. (1974 & Supp. 1981):																
Mentally ill	any mentally ill person 18 or older 27A-8-1			South Dakota Human Services Center or VA center 27A-8-1		may be hospitalized 27A-8-1	must be deemed clinically suitable 27A-8-1 may be hospitalized 27A-8-1			suitable for discharge 27A-14-1	5 days 27A-8-10	continued detention if involuntary commitment is commenced 27A-8-13	27A-8-14		27A-8-13	
Developmentally disabled	developmentally disabled person 18 or older 27B-5-5, 27B-5-3	preadmission examination 27B-5-7		state facility 27B-1-2(8)						until not in need of care or until adequate alternative available 27B-5-12	7 days 27B-5-16		27B-5-17			
TENN. Code Ann. (1977):																
Mentally ill	any mentally ill person 16 or older 33-601(a)(1)	admitting physician must determine a need for hospitalization 33-601(a)	admissions review committee 33-601(a)	33-601(a)	33-601(a)	33-601(a) public hospital shall admit private hospital may admit 33-601(a)	public hospital shall admit private hospital may admit 33-601(a)			recovered or hospitalization no longer beneficial 33-601(b)	48 hours 33-601(b)	continued detention if involuntary commitment commenced 33-601(b)			33-601(b)	
Developmentally disabled	any mentally retarded person 18 or older 33-501(a)(1)			developmental center 33-501	developmental center 33-501	is authorized to admit 33-501(a) 33-501(a)	is authorized to admit 33-501(a) in need of care & treatment 33-501(a)			in the best interests of the person 33-501(b) 33-502						

TABLE 3.1 VOLUNTARY ADMISSION OF MENTALLY ILL AND DEVELOPMENTALLY DISABLED PERSONS—*Continued*

						ADMISSION DISCRETIONARY ON PART OF INSTITUTION AS TO		PERIOD: Definite								
STATE	PERSONS WHO MAY APPLY FOR ADMISSION (1)	MEDICAL CERTIFICATION (2)	FURTHER APPROVAL BY (3)	PUBLIC INSTITUTION (4)	PRIVATE INSTITUTION (5)	*Availability of Suitable Hospital Accommodations* (6)	*Mental Condition* (7)	Maximum (8)	Minimum (9)	*Indefinite* (10)	RELEASE UPON REQUEST (TIME) (11)	EXTENSION PROVISION (12)	TOLD OF RIGHT TO RELEASE OR REVIEW (13)	INFORMAL ADMISSION (14)	PROVISION FOR INVOLUNTARY COMMITMENT OF VOLUNTARY PATIENT (15)	PROVISION FOR CONVERSION FROM INVOLUNTARY TO VOLUNTARY STATUS (16)
TEX. Rev. Civ. Stat. Ann. (Vernon 1958 & Supp 1981):																
Mentally ill	any mentally ill adult 5547-23(a)			mental hospital 5547-22	mental hospital 5547-22	may admit 5547-22	symptoms of mental illness & will benefit from hospitalization 5547-22 may admit 5547-22		10 days 5547-23(c)	no longer requires hospitalization 5547-80	96 hrs. 5547-25	continued detention if involuntary commitment commenced 5547-25(b)	5547-24(a)		only if release requested 5547-25(b) 5547-26	
Developmentally disabled	any mentally retarded adult 5547-300,§34(c)	comprehensive diagnosis & evaluation 5547-300,§28(a)		residential care facility 5547-300,§34 §3(11)	residential care facility 5547-300,§34 §3(11)	shall be permitted if 5547-300,§34(f)(1)	shall be permitted if 5547,§34(f)(2)				96 hrs. unless application for judicial commitment filed 5547-300,§36	pending a final determination on application 5547-300,§36(c)	5547-300, §§19, 23		5547-300, §36	
UTAH Code Ann. (1978 & Supp. 1981)	any mentally ill person 16 or older 64-7-29			mental health facility 64-7-29	mental health facility 64-7-29	may admit 64-7-29	mentally ill or symptoms thereof; may admit 64-7-29			recovered, or hospitalization no longer advisable 64-7-30	forthwith 64-7-31	release postponed up to 48 hrs. to institute involuntary hospitalization proceedings 64-7-31(3)			only after release requested 64-7-36(4) 64-7-31(3)	
VT. Stat. Ann. (1968 & Supp. 1981)	any mentally ill person 14 or older *fn. 24* 18, §7503(a)			designated hospital 18, §7503	designated hospital 18, §7503	may be admitted 18, §7503	may be admitted 18, §7503			clinically suitable for discharge 18, §8009(a)	*fn. 25* 18, §8010(a)	*fn. 25* 18, §8010(b)	18, §7701		18, §8010(b)	at any time, w/permission of head of hospital 18, §7709
VA. Code (1976 & Supp. 1982)	any mentally ill, mentally retarded, or substance-abusing person 37.1-65	staff physician 37.1-65	community mental health center 37.1-65	state hospital 37.1-65			deemed in need of hospitalization 37.1-65			recovered, not mentally ill, discharge not detrimental to public or patient, or not a proper case for treatment 37.1-98(A)						37.1-67.2
WASH. Rev. Code Ann. (1982 & Supp. 1982):																
Mentally ill	any mentally ill person 18 or older 72.23.070(1)		county mental health professional 72.23.070(2)	72.23.070	72.23.070	72.23.110	suitable for care & treatment 72.23.070	one yr. 72.23.100						72.23.125	where patient fails to pay for voluntary treatment costs 72.23.120	
Developmentally disabled	any handicapped adult 72.33.125(1)(b)	may require affidavit of physician, psychologist, or 1 of each 72.33.125(2)		state programs or services 72.33.125(1)						no longer needs services 72.33.170	48 hrs. 72.33.140	5 days pending hearing for residential custody 72.33.150				
W. VA. Code Ann. (1980 & Supp. 1982)	any mentally ill, mentally retarded, or addicted person over 18 27-4-1(a)		local mental health facility if patient under 18 27-4-1(c)	mental health facility 27-4-1	mental health facility 27-4-1	27-4-1	mentally ill, mentally retarded, or addicted 27-4-1			recovered, or hospitalization no longer advisable 27-4-2	forthwith 27-4-3	20 days detention if involuntary commitment proceedings commenced w/in 96 hrs. 27-4-3(c)			only if release requested 27-4-3(c)	
WIS. Stat. Ann. (West 1957 & Supp. 1981)	mentally ill, developmentally disabled, alcoholic, or drug-dependent adult *fn. 26* 51.10(1) 51.10(2) *fn. 27* 51.10(4m)(a)	*fn. 27* 51.10(4m)(a)(1)	director of treatment facility & community mental health 51.10(1)	inpatient treatment facility 51.10(1)	inpatient treatment facility 51.10(1)	may be admitted 51.10(1)	may be admitted 51.10(1) *fn. 27* 51.10(4)			treatment no longer necessary 51.35(4)(a) discharge in best interest of patient 51.35(4)(c)	only long enough to evaluate individual's condition 51.10(5)(c)	up to 72 hrs. additional detention for probable cause hearing of involuntary commitment 51.10(5)(c)	51.10(5)(a)		51.10(5)(c) 51.15(10)	if facility director approves 51.10(6)

TABLE 3.1 VOLUNTARY ADMISSION OF MENTALLY ILL AND DEVELOPMENTALLY DISABLED PERSONS—*Continued*

STATE	PERSONS WHO MAY APPLY FOR ADMISSION (1)	MEDICAL CERTIFICATION (2)	FURTHER APPROVAL BY (3)	PUBLIC INSTITUTION (4)	PRIVATE INSTITUTION (5)	ADMISSION DISCRETIONARY ON PART OF INSTITUTION AS TO		PERIOD			RELEASE UPON REQUEST (TIME) (11)	EXTENSION PROVISION (12)	TOLD OF RIGHT TO RELEASE OR REVIEW (13)	INFORMAL ADMISSION (14)	PROVISION FOR INVOLUNTARY COMMITMENT OF VOLUNTARY PATIENT (15)	PROVISION FOR CONVERSION FROM INVOLUNTARY TO VOLUNTARY STATUS (16)
						Availability of Suitable Hospital Accommodations (6)	*Mental Condition* (7)	*Definite* Maximum (8)	*Definite* Minimum (9)	*Indefinite* (10)						
WYO. Stat. (1981 & Supp. 1982):																
Mentally ill	any mentally ill adult w/capacity to make responsible application for admission 25-3-106(a)			hospital 25-3-106(a)	hospital 25-3-106(a)	may be admitted 25-3-106(a)	symptoms of mental illness may be admitted 25-3-106(a)			no longer needs hospital treatment 25-3-108	w/in 24 hrs. 25-3-109					
Developmentally disabled	any mentally retarded adult w/sufficient insight or capacity to make responsible application for admission 9-6-657	preadmission evaluation 9-6-655 9-6-657(a)		training school 9-6-657		may be admitted 9-6-657	may be admitted 9-6-657			when appropriately placed in an alternative environment 9-6-664	w/in 20 days unless application for involuntary admission filed 9-6-658	pending ct.'s decision 9-6-658			9-6-658	

FOOTNOTES TABLE 3.1

1. Ariz. Rev. Stat. Ann. § 36-518(c) (Supp. 1981): "A minor fourteen years of age or older may seek voluntary hospitalization. Such application . . . shall be signed by the minor and the parent, guardian or custodian of the minor."

2. California has two voluntary admission procedures, one solely applicable to county mental facilities. The county procedure is set out in §§ 6004, 6005, and the other procedure is set out in § 6000.

3. Del. Code Ann. tit. 16, § 5121 (1974) provides: "the department [of health and social services] may establish, under the direction and supervision of the state hospital, a voluntary admission procedure. . . ." The relationship between this section and the statutorily established procedure in tit. 16, § 5123 is unclear.

4. Id. tit. 16, § 5123(b):

> If the applicant is under the care and treatment of a medical doctor . . . the application shall be accompanied by a letter from the doctor recommending voluntary hospitalization and setting forth a description of the behavior and symptoms of the patient which led him to his decision to recommend voluntary hospitalization. If the applicant is not under the care and treatment of such a medical doctor, he shall not be admitted unless the superintendent (of the Delaware state hospital) first determines that the application has sufficient insight and capacity to make responsible application for voluntary hospitalization.

5. Fla. Stat. Ann. § 393.115(1)(B) (West Supp. 1981): "If the department determines that the resident's continued admission is essential or that the resident is dangerous to himself or others, as documented in the resident's written habilitation plan, he shall remain admitted to residential care provided by the department."

6. Idaho Code § 66-318 (Supp. 1981). Admission may be refused where the facility director finds "that the applicant's welfare and/or the welfare of society are better protected by the admission provisions" of Idaho's commitment procedure.

7. Ill. Ann. Stat. ch. 91½, §§ 3-400, 3-405 (Smith-Hurd Supp. 1980). When admission to a department facility is denied, the person seeking admission shall be given notice of the right to request review of the denial.

8. Id. § 4-312. Developmentally disabled persons have the same right to review denial of admission as mentally ill persons.

9. Id. § 4-310: At least once annually the client shall be evaluated to determine his need for continued residential services. If need for continued residence is indicated, the facility director of the facility shall consult with the person who made application for the admission and shall request authorization for continued residence of the client.

10. Ky. Rev. Stat. Ann. § 202B.020 (Michie Supp. 1980): "Hospitalization for the care and treatment of mentally retarded persons shall be provided by the same procedures as hospitalization of mentally ill persons as provided in KRS Chapter 210 and as set forth in KRS 202A.020 to 202A.160 and 202A.190."

11. Me. Rev. Stat. Ann. tit. 34, § 2290 (1978). Voluntary admissions for the mentally ill is by informal procedure.

12. Md. Ann. Code Art. 59, § 11(B)(1) (1979): "A person may not be admitted under the provisions of this section unless his condition is such that he is able to understand the nature of his request for admission, is able to request his release, and is capable of giving continuous assent to his retention by the facility."

13. Minnesota has only informal voluntary hospitalization for the mentally ill and mentally retarded. The formal voluntary admission is limited to drug-dependent persons. A mentally ill or mentally retarded person informally hospitalized must be released within 12 hours of his or her request.

14. Mont. Code Ann. § 53-21-112(3) (1981): "Unless there has been a periodic review and a voluntary readmission consented to by the minor patient and his counsel, voluntary admission terminates at the expiration of one year."

15. N.H. Rev. Stat. Ann. § 135-B:9(II) (Supp. 1981): "No patient shall be denied admission for inpatient care on a voluntary basis by more than 2 facilities solely on the basis that the facility applied to is not most suited to providing treatment to the applicant, without written approval of the director."

16. Id. § 171-A:4: "comprised of a substantial number of programs and services, including Laconia State School & Training Center, for the care, habilitation, rehabilitation, treatment and training of developmentally impaired persons. Such service delivery system shall be under the supervision of the director."

17. N.Y. Mental Hyg. Law § 9.17(A) (McKinney 1978). Applicant must have ability to understand: "(1) that the hospital to which he is requesting admission is a hospital for the mentally ill; (2) that he is making an application for admission; (3) the nature of the voluntary . . . status . . . and the provisions governing release or conversion to involuntary status."

18. Id. § 15.15(A). Applicant must be notified of and have the ability to understand: "(1) that the school to which he is requesting admission is a school for the mentally retarded; (2) that he is making an application for admission; (3) the nature of the voluntary status and the provisions governing release or conversion to involuntary status."

19. Or. Rev. Stat. § 426.220(1) (1981). A definite period of hospitalization may be imposed as a condition of admission in which case the provision for release within 72 hours of request does not apply.

20. Pa. Stat. Ann. tit. 50, § 7201 (Purdon Supp. 1980): "Any person 14 years of age or over who believes that he is in need of treatment and substantially understands the nature of voluntary treatment."

21. Id. § 7206(A):

> A person in voluntary inpatient treatment may withdraw at any time by giving written notice unless . . . he has agreed in writing at the time of his admission that his release can be delayed following such notice for a period to be specified in the agreement, provided that such period shall not exceed 72 hours.

22. R.I. Gen. Laws § 40.1-5.1-18 (Supp. 1981). Alternate voluntary hospitalization procedure:

> A hospital may receive and retain therein as a boarder and patient any person who is desirous of submitting himself to treatment and who makes a written application therefor, but whose mental condition is not such as to render it legal to grant a certificate of insanity in his case. No such boarder shall be detained for more than 3 days after giving notice in writing to the superintendent of such hospital of his intention or desire to leave such hospital.

23. S.C. Code Ann. § 44-21-50 (Law. Co-op. 1976):

> Mentally retarded individuals admitted to the jurisdiction of the department shall be subject to the following considerations regarding their order of admission:
>
> 1. The relative need of the person for special training, education, supervision, treatment, care or control;
> 2. The impact of the person upon the community and the availability of local resources;
> 3. The ability of the person's family to assimilate him effectively into family life;
> 4. The availability of departmental accommodations and services suitable to the needs of the applicant.

24. Vt. Stat. Ann. tit. 18, § 7503(B) (Supp. 1981). Consent by the applicant "shall include a representation that the person understands that his treatment will involve inpatient status, that he desires to be admitted to the hospital, and that he consents to admission voluntarily, without any coercion or duress."

25. Id § 8010(A): "He shall promptly be released unless he agreed in writing at the time of his admission that his release could be delayed." In that event, the patient may be detained no more than 4 days from receipt of request to leave, during which time, the head of the hospital may apply for involuntary hospitalization. The patient shall then remain hospitalized pending the court's determination of his case. Id. § 8010(B).

26. Wis. Stat. Ann. § 51.10(4) (West Supp. 1981). Criteria for admission: mentally ill or developmentally disabled, or is alcoholic or drug dependent, and has potential to benefit from inpatient care, treatment, or therapy, applicant is not requried to meet standards of dangerousness.

27. Id. § 51.10(4M)(A)(1). A person may also be admitted upon a physician's signed request and held for up to 7 days if he or she fails to indicate a desire to leave the facility, but refuses or is unable to sign an application for admission. Within 7 days there shall be a court hearing to determine whether the patient shall remain in the facility as a voluntary patient, shall be discharged, or shall be the subject of involuntary commitment proceedings.

Samuel Jan Brakel

CHAPTER 4 *Discharge and Transfer*

I. INTRODUCTION

There are three main ways an institutionalized person may be separated from a mental facility: he may be transferred to another institution, he may be released into the community subject to certain conditions such as his continued treatment on an outpatient basis, or he may be granted an unconditional discharge. Death within the institution accounts for a final fraction of separations—some 2% relative to the total "discontinuations" from state and county mental facilities in recent years.[1]

The function of the mental hospital when it was first established as an institution separate and apart from jails was basically custodial. Few patients were discharged as cured or improved; death accounted for most "terminations." This fact, together with the specter of "railroading," stimulated the use of the writ of habeas corpus as a major method of separation from the mental hospital. Since the progress in psychiatric care and habilitation techniques now makes it possible for many patients or residents[2] to improve significantly, perhaps recover completely, or to be trained in basic living skills, discharge procedures have become an increasingly important aspect of the administration of mental institutions while the judicial role has declined.

Up until a decade or two ago, the development of effective discharge procedures was strongly motivated by the overcrowded conditions of mental facilities. Most state institutions consistently operated above their rated bed capacity. Today this population pressure has been significantly reduced and discharge decisions can be more properly focused on what is in the best interests of institutionalized persons.[3]

II. TRANSFERS OF INSTITUTIONALIZED PERSONS

Of the 367,970 "discontinuations"[4] within the state and county mental hospital system in 1981, some 11,500 (roughly 3%) were accounted for by transfers.[5] These were transfers within the state mental health and developmental disabilities systems. Generally, no new admission proceedings need be initiated to validate such transfers. A much smaller, though undetermined, number of transfers entails the movement of patients from state to federal institutions or from a facility in one state to one in another. Transfers within the states or from state to federal institutions are often initiated because the receiving institution has better facilities, programs, or equipment for the patient than the admitting institution. Movements to federal facilities such as

1. Division of Biometry and Epidemiology, National Institute of Mental Health, Statistical Note 156, Michael J. Witkin, Provisional Patient Movement and Selective Administrative Data, State and County Mental Hospitals, by State: United States, 1977, at 26 table 4 (Aug. 1981) [hereinafter cited as Statistical Note 156]. The category of "discontinuations" includes "those persons discharged (excluding death) as well as those placed on long-term leave and transferred to noninpatient components of the same hospital." *Id.* at 20. As of this writing, 1977 is the last year for which relatively complete national statistics are available. Recent estimates for 1981, supplied directly to the American Bar Foundation by the National Institute of Mental Health, show no appreciable change in the percentage of deaths in the institutions since 1977.

2. The term *patients* generally refers to institutionalized mentally ill persons, while *residents* is the preferred designation for developmentally disabled persons in institutions, who are not primarily recipients of medical/psychiatric services. Nonetheless, the term *patients* is used here to cover both groups, since *residents* is too general a word and leads to confusion particularly in the context of "residency provisions" that are part of the laws of admission, discharge, and transfer.

3. This is not to say that ulterior motivations are no longer at play in the discharge policies and practices of the institutions. For one, population pressure continues to be a factor to the extent that applications for admission are far higher today than 15 to 20 years ago. The high turnover of patients made possible by today's improvements in treatment and training methods goes hand in glove with higher admissions and readmissions. Also, tightening state fiscal policies exert pressure on institutions to lower the resident population. But the situation is no longer one of there literally being no space for new admissions.

4. Statistics supplied directly by NIMH.

5. This percentage has decreased somewhat since 1969, the year for which these figures were presented in the previous edition of the book, when it was 5% (24,274 transfers out of 525,584 discontinuations). The 1977 figures were 17,500 transfers out of 415,314 discontinuations—about 4% (see Statistical Note 156, *supra* note 1, at 2).

Veterans Administration Hospitals may be motivated by the desire on the part of the state to shift the cost burden to the federal government. Residential considerations, such as moving the patient closer to home or to his relatives (or occasionally farther from these ties), are sometimes at issue in intrastate transfers. And formal residence requirements, whose underlying considerations may be predominantly economic, are often in the background of *inter*state movements of patients. Many states have detailed statutory schemes covering the admission, treatment, and transfer of nonresident patients.[6] These provisions have undergone considerable change over the years: whereas earlier most of them did no more than bar treatment of nonresidents and call for mandatory transfer, today many of the laws defer to interstate mental health compacts or other reciprocal agreements providing for the retention and treatment of nonresident patients and for their transfer only when it is humane and medically responsible to do so.

There is also a sizable number of transfers back and forth between prisons and mental health facilities, though the majority of these are intraorganizational—i.e., between facilities within the states' departments of corrections rather than from there to and from facilities operated by the departments of mental health—and they are not counted among the "discontinuation" statistics given in the previous paragraph.[7]

The laws of about half the states provide for transfer on the petition of the patient or his representative, which must be approved by the court or by administrative officials,[8] but in the main the transfer decision has been considered a matter of institutional discretion and initiative. Traditionally, institutional transfer, even from one jurisdiction to another, has meant no change in the patient's legal status and has required no new commitment order. Nonetheless, there are limits, and growing limits, on the institution's authority to transfer. The statutes of the majority of states today spell out exclusive conditions or criteria under which transfer may take place, and they provide the patient with an explicit right to object.[9] The criteria most often speak to the medical needs of the patient or his best interests generally, while the patient's right to object finds content in his entitlement to a hearing, administrative or judicial, or some less elaborate form of review.[10] Also, notice of the transfer decision is generally required, with the patient's guardian, his relatives, or the committing court as the most common targets.[11]

The recent case law also emits clear signals that the institution's transfer authority has its limits. The limiting principle that dominates the cases is that when there are significant differences between the sending and receiving facilities, unreviewable administrative transfer is improper and the transferee is entitled to certain basic a priori due process protections—minimally, the right to notice of the authorities' intent to transfer him and the right to an impartial (possibly an adversarial) hearing conducted by an independent decision maker. Because the institutional differences are most obvious when transfers between *systems* are contemplated, the landmark cases have concerned the movement of *prisoners* to mental health facilities. *Baxstrom v. Herold*[12] constitutes the opening salvo, fired as far back as 1966. The Supreme Court of the United States in that instance found a denial of equal protection of the law where an administrative transfer procedure for a mentally ill prisoner *at the expiration of his sentence* failed to provide the same protections afforded to other alleged mentally ill persons under the relevant provisions of the New York code. More recently, in *Vitek v. Jones*[13] in 1980, the Supreme Court held that Nebraska's procedures for transferring prisoners *still under sentence* to mental facilities on the mere recommendation of a physician or psychologist without notice or opportunity to contest the recommendation were wanting on due process grounds.

But transfers *within* the mental health system may require comparable scrutiny today. *Eubanks v. Clarke*,[14] a 1977 case from the Eastern District of Pennsylvania, advanced the proposition that there can be no transfer of an involuntary patient from one mental facility to another that is more restrictive without according the patient a hearing—a requirement that has since found its way into the Pennsylvania statutes[15] as well as those of Ohio[16] and South Carolina.[17] In *Klein v. Califano*,[18] Medicaid patients of a decertified New Jersey nursing home were held to be entitled to similar protections before they could be transferred. Temporary or emergency transfers may still be possible on administrative authority alone.[19] Better considered and more formal

6. See table 4.2
7. See Hartstone, Steadman, & Monahan, *Vitek* and Beyond: The Empirical Context of Prison-to-Hospital Transfers, 45 Law & Contemp. Probs., no. 3, Summer 1982, at 125.
8. See table 4.1 at cols. 2-5.
9. *Id.* at cols. 6-9.
10. *Id.* at cols. 7 & 8.

11. *Id.* at cols. 12 & 13.
12. 383 U.S. 107 (1966).
13. 445 U.S. 480 (1980).
14. 434 F. Supp. 1022 (E.D. Pa., 1977).
15. Pa. Stat. Ann. 50, § 7306(c) (Purdon Supp. 1983).
16. Ohio Rev. Code Ann. § 5122.20 (Baldwin 1982).
17. S.C. Code Ann. § 44-23-210(4) (Law. Co-op.1976).
18. 586 F.2d 250 (3d Cir. 1978).
19. See, e.g., New York *ex rel.* Overton v. Director, Central N.Y. Psychiatric Center, 418 N.Y.S.2d 254 (App. Div. 1979); *In re* Linder, 419 N.Y.S.2d 375 (App. Div. 1979); and Cornell v. Creasy, 491 F. Supp. 124 (N.D. Ohio 1978).

review can then be accorded at the end of the emergency or observational period. Also, expedient transfer procedures should be retained where differences between transferring institutions are minimal and so long as administrative decision makers show evidence that they have considered the patient's social and legal interests as well as his medical interests—for example, his proximity at the receiving facility to family, friends, and (if he has one) his lawyer and the institution's visitation and correspondence provisions regulating access to them. Providing notice of the patient's transfer to these important figures in the patient's life would be among the minimum requirements of an acceptable administrative transfer procedure. Absent built-in assurances and safeguards of this type, the law today is not likely to tolerate the movement of patients on medical or administrative authority alone.

III. DEATH OF INSTITUTIONALIZED PERSONS

The death rate of mentally disabled persons in public (state and county) mental institutions has declined dramatically over the past decade. Whereas death accounted for 7% of the terminations in 1969, it was down to 2% by 1977, where it has remained according to the most recent estimates (1981).[20] By comparison, the death rate within the general population during the year 1977 stood at slightly below 1% (.88).[21]

Mortality rates in public mental facilities were even higher in the decades preceding the 1960s,[22] but the introduction of new therapies[23] and improved general diagnostic and physical maintenance procedures has contributed greatly toward the reduction of the dismal statistics. Another major factor in the decline of the death rate has been the gradual change in the population entering the mental institutions and in the concomitant evolution of new admission and discharge policies. Persons of advanced age who used to constitute a large proportion of the mental hospital population are today increasingly routed or transferred to nursing homes.[24] The dramatic shortening of the average length of stay in state and county mental facilities—only 26 days for 1975 admittees, 23 for 1980[25]—means that the chances of a mentally disabled person's dying while he is institutionalized are significantly reduced. More persons with histories of institutionalization are now dying after discharge from the hospital, in the nursing homes, in community facilities, in the homes of caretakers, family, relatives, in their own living quarters, or on the streets. The deinstitutionalization concept, while in many ways an appropriate response to new medical technologies/procedures and a commendable change in orientation from the days when the mentally disabled were often confined for life, also hides a harsher reality. The death toll has in some measure only been transferred out of the institutions, and today's statistics[26] reveal that in too many cases the mentally disabled person's new freedom to live in the community has in effect meant the freedom to die there.

IV. CONDITIONAL RELEASE

The procedure for conditional release makes it possible for an improved patient to leave the mental facility, although his right to remain "deinstitutionalized" hinges on his compliance with certain conditions. One quite common condition is that he receive outpatient treatment from a local clinic or psychiatrist or perhaps periodically return to the institution for follow-up care. Assuring that the patient continues to take his medication regularly is an important aspect of the aftercare given to many patients today. The patient's failure to adjust to his external circumstances or to comply with any of the general conditions attached to his release may result in his being returned to the institution.

Statutory arrangements providing for conditional release of mentally ill patients exist in some 40 states.[27] A smaller number of states (25) have separate provisions for developmentally disabled and retarded persons.[28] Because of the substantial similarity in structure and underlying principle between the provisions covering mentally ill persons and those addressing conditional

20. Statistical Note 156, *supra* note 1, at 26 table 4. In absolute numbers, the change appears even more dramatic: in 1970, 30,804 patients died in public mental institutions; in 1977, only 9,597. (*Id.* at 11 table C.) NIMH estimates for 1981 were supplied to the American Bar Foundation on request.

21. Bureau of the Census, U.S. Dep't of Commerce, Social Indicators III (Federal Statistical System, Dec. 1980).

22. Malzberg, Rates of Discharge and Rates of Mortality Among First Admissions to the New York Civil State Hospitals, 37 Mental Hygiene 619 (1953), e.g., reports that during the early 1950s in New York 36% of the male first admissions to the state's mental hospitals and 33% of the female first admissions died within three years after admission, with half of these deaths occurring within the first three months.

23. Drug therapies are among the important new treatment methods. The effects on mental functioning and general physical well-being are selective, however. Different drugs are effective for different conditions. Some conditions remain largely unresponsive to any medication or treatment approach.

24. In 1975, only 5% of the admissions to state and county mental hospitals were over 65 years of age, as compared with 28% of the residents. See Office of Program Planning and Coordination, Alcohol, Drug Abuse, and Mental Health Administration, Public Health Service, U.S. Dep't of Health and Human Services, Alcohol, Drug Abuse, and Mental Health National Data Book 54 table 21 (Jan. 1980).

25. *Id.* at 64 table 28. Estimate for 1980 supplied directly by NIMH.

26. Slovenko, The Past and Present of the Right to Treatment: A Slogan Gone Astray, 9 J. Psychiatry & L. 263 (1981), reports that 13% of the patients discharged from New York's state mental hospitals to community facilities were dead within two months!

27. See table 4.3, cols 7-9.

28. See table 4.4.

discharge of developmentally disabled persons, the textual discussion does not go into the details of both. Instead, the discussion concentrates mainly on the provisions for the mentally ill. Readers interested in the differences in detail in the laws covering developmentally disabled persons are advised to compare table 4.3 to 4.4.

The majority of the conditional discharge provisions simply make general reference to the patient's conditional or convalescent status without specifying the conditions[29] (New Jersey's law[30] speaks of "parole," a term more commonly associated with corrections), but a number of state statutes are more explicit. Those of Alaska[31] and Idaho,[32] for example, explicate the patient's obligation to undergo outpatient care. A few states, Missouri[33] is one, speak in terms of conditional release to the "least restrictive environment." The Connecticut statute[34] specifies conditional placement in a boarding home or convalescent hospital. And Colorado's[35] speaks generally of night care, day care, or other outpatient treatment.

The period of conditional release, where specified, is usually one year,[36] at which point there must at the least be a review of the patient's mental state to determine whether discharge is appropriate or whether an extension of conditional status, or even recommitment, is warranted. Michigan,[37] which operates with the common one-year limit, seems to be unique in that it mandates final discharge at that point. In Oregon,[38] Vermont,[39] West Virginia,[40] and Wyoming,[41] the period for which a patient can be kept on conditional status is half a year, and in Ohio[42] it is 90 days with a proviso for possible 90-day extensions up to one year. In Montana,[43] New York,[44] and Washington,[45] the conditional period may not exceed the period for which the patient was initially committed. And in New Mexico[46] there must be at the minimum a reexamination of the conditionally released patient before the original commitment period expires. Provisions specifying the patient's conditional status to be of indefinite duration—formerly on the books in a few states (Alaska and Oregon, for example)—have been repealed. The general consensus is that it is neither necessary nor desirable to keep patients under the threat of reinstitutionalization for indeterminate periods.

Traditionally, the patient's conditional freedom could be revoked upon evidence of generally poor adjustment in the community or upon violation of specific conditions, and he could be reinstitutionalized without the need for new commitment proceedings or formal proceedings of any kind. The theory was that even though the patient might be living with relatives or friends or in a community home, he remained in legal custody of the hospital. Today, the law no longer favors such easy revocation and return. Relying on *Morrissey v. Brewer*,[47] in which the United States Supreme Court held that a basic due process must be applied before a prisoner's parole could be revoked (that is, written notice and at least an informal hearing before a neutral decision maker) several state and federal courts have mandated similar protections for patients conditionally discharged from mental facilities whose return is sought.[48] While not requiring a full duplication of judicial commitment proceedings, the cases make clear that summary revocation without notice or a hearing of any kind will not be condoned. The patient must be provided some forum at which he has a chance to hear and contest the evidence upon which revocation is sought. Only in emergency situations is summary revocation permitted; the patient is then accorded his due process rights after the emergency passes. At least one of the cases[49] suggests that mere extension of the patient's conditional status (as opposed to return to the hospital) requires a hearing. And a case from the criminal area involving an insanity acquittee[50] raises the possibility that the mere violation of a release condition may not suffice as a justification for reinstitutionalization and that a new finding of need of institutionalization or dangerousness is required.

The concept of conditional release is not new. Back in 1920, a commentator described the procedure as

> a means of finishing off the rehabilitative processes

29. See table 4.3, cols. 7–9.
30. N.J. Stat. Ann. § 30:4-107 (West Ann. 1981).
31. Alaska Stat. § 47.30.795 (Supp. 1981).
32. Idaho Code § 66-338 (Supp. 1981).
33. Mo. Ann. Stat. § 632.385 (Vernon Supp. 1980).
34. Conn. Gen. Stat. Ann. § 17-191 (West Supp. 1982).
35. Colo. Rev. Stat. § 27-10-110(1) (1973 & Supp. 1981).
36. See table 4.3, col. 8.
37. Mich. Comp. Laws Ann. § 330.1479 (1980).
38. Or. Rev. Stat. § 426.280 (1981).
39. Vt. Stat. Ann. tit. 18 § 8007 (Supp. 1981).
40. W.Va. Code § 27-7-2 (1980).
41. Wyo. Stat. § 27-10-117 (1977).
42. Ohio Rev. Code Ann. § 5122.22 (Baldwin 1980 & Supp. 1981).
43. Mont. Code Ann. § 53-21-183(1) (1981).
44. N.Y. Mental Hyg. Law § 29.15(b)(1) (McKinney 1978).
45. Wash. Rev. Code § 71.05.340(1) (Supp. 1981).
46. N.M. Stat. Ann. § 43-1-21(A) (1979).
47. 408 U.S. 471 (1972).
48. E.g., Meisel v. Kremens, 405 F. Supp. 1253 (E.D. Pa. 1975); Lewis v. Donahue, 437 F. Supp. 112 (W.D. Okla. 1977); K.B. v. Sprenger, No. 770292 5 MDLR 182 (Minn. Dist. Ct., Hennepin County, Sept. 10, 1980); Flick v. Noot, No. 4-78 Civil 359, 3 MDLR 299 (D. Minn. July 6, 1979); Hamel v. Brooks, No. 78-115, 4 MDLR 97 (D. Or. Dec. 1979); Frederick v. Mulcahy, No. 76-257, 4 MDLR 170 (D. Vt., filed Dec. 16, 1979); and Application of True 645 P.2d 891 (Idaho 1982).
49. Flick v. Noot, No. 4-78 Civil 359, 3 MDLR 299 (D. Minn. July 6, 1979).
50. Cochenour v. Psychiatric Sec. Review Bd., 615 P.2d 1155 (Or. Ct. App. 1980).

> begun under medical supervision in the hospital. From the point of view of . . . reestablishment of the individual in society, it is the only logical means of safely bridging over the gap between hospital care and self-directed life in the community. From the point of view of the hospital management, it does serve to reduce population and thus it diminishes the public expense for the maintenance of the insane. . . .[M]any patients can be discharged under supervision and become self-supporting under these conditions when it would be unsafe to discharge them absolutely from hospital supervision.[51]

In addition to providing a period of transition for the improved patient, the conditional release was also seen to serve as a device for providing noninstitutional care for patients who do not require in-residence treatment. In that vision there is more than a glimmer of the modern-day "least restrictive alternative" concept.[52]

There is no question that the conditional release statutes, and in particular the provisions for outpatient care and timely reexamination that are a part of some of them, constitute enlightened legislation on behalf of mentally disabled persons. But these provisions are of little practical value unless there are adequate outpatient facilities in each jurisdiction that work in close cooperation with the mental institutions. Under ideal circumstances these outpatient facilities would be available in the home community, as returning to the state institution at regular intervals is often difficult for former patients. More than 30 years ago, Albert Deutsch observed:

> Unfortunately, there are some states in which the practice of parole is grossly abused and perverted. In several backward states the parole system is nothing more than a mockery and a sham. Patients are "paroled" without any adequate supervision or follow-up care and protection. Little or no effort is made to follow the progress of the patient after removal from the hospital. Lacking continued psychiatric treatment and advice or the helpful guidance of competent social workers in the critical early period of attempted rehabilitation many a patient who, under proper supervision, might have found adjustment in society, fails to do so and has to be returned to the hospital.[53]

The stituation has improved since that observation was made. There are more and better community facilities today than there were 30 years ago. Staff in the institutions are more aware than ever of the importance of transitional placement and care, and significantly greater resources than before are devoted to planning the patient's posthospitalization route, implementing the plans, and maintaining general liaison with community treatment programs and facilities. But at the same time, much remains to be done. The dumping of mentally disabled patients in blighted areas where flophouses masquerade as community treatment centers is a continuing practice. And well-intentioned policies of deinstitutionalization too often result in leaving expatients to cope with problems in living for which they are wholly unprepared and unequipped.

An increasing number of conditionally released patients today live in foster homes under what are known as family care plans. Under such a plan a socially adjusted patient is maintained by a family at public expense.[54] Although he lives outside the institution, as a conditionally released patient he is considered to be in the constructive custody of the institution. The foster family is expected to provide shelter and apprise the institutional staff of changes in the patient's behavior. This system is more widely practiced than an examination of the statute books would lead one to believe. Between 1965 and 1968, more than $28,000,000 was expended by 22 states for mentally ill or retarded patients boarding with families under such plans.[55] Aggregate figures for recent years are difficult to come by. Also, the available figures do not distinguish between foster care as a transitional arrangement applied after institutionalization or that which is provided in lieu of institutionalization.[56] Unspecified data from select states, however, show continued heavy expenditures for foster care—this despite the fact that foster care is the least expensive type of care compared with other living arrangements. Arizona alone—a state with a small population—spent as much as $1,400,000 for foster care in 1980.[57] The foster care concept appears to be most frequently used for developmentally disabled persons, as distinct from the mentally ill. The costs of foster family care have been estimated to be some 20% less than for

51. Haines, Lessons from the Principles Governing the Parole Procedure in Hospitals for the Insane, 1920 Nat'l Conf. Soc. Work Proc. 159, 160.

52. For some discussion of the concept, see ch. 2, Involuntary Institutionalization, § II A 3(d), Less Restrictive Alternatives and the Deinstitutionalization Movement.

53. A. Deutsch, The Mentally Ill in America: A History of Their Care and Treatment from Colonial Times 438 (2d ed. 1949).

54. The practice is not new. *Id.* at 447-48.

55. Council of State Governments, Action in the States in the Fields of Mental Health, Mental Retardation and Related Areas, at table 10 (1969).

56. See Hitchman & Salomon, Foster Care: An Alternative to Hospitalization (pt. VII) *in* Current Psychiatric Therapies: 1966, at 306 (J. H. Masserman ed. 1966).

57. Information provided to the American Bar Foundation on request. Division of Developmental Disabilities, Annual Report, Arizona Dep't of Economic Security, 1980-81 (1981). Missouri reports that it spends over half-a-million dollars (some $530,000) annually on foster care (Missouri Dep't of Mental Health, Placement Contract Summary, 10-21-81). Florida reports expenditures of $263 per person per month on long-term residential foster care, or some $3,156 per year. But no figures on the number of mentally disabled persons receiving such care were provided.

institutional care, and there is evidence that—whether the result of selection or of the efficacy of the care provided—foster care patients have better physical and mental health than their institutionalized counterparts.[58]

In some states conditional release used to be the only means of justifying continued expenditures for drugs or other necessary therapy once the patient left the institution. Since the patient remained on the books, treatment expenditures were permitted. Separate state and federal funding of community mental health centers and private ways of financing outpatient care should make such intermixing of medical and financial judgments no longer necessary.

V. ABSOLUTE DISCHARGE

The classic discharge procedure consists of a complete termination of the legal relationship between the institution and the patient. Once such a discharge is effected, the former patient may not be returned to the institution without the initiation of a new commitment proceeding.

Even today the belief continues to be widespread that patients in mental facilities are rarely discharged and are left to languish there until death. This perception is based on dated information. While some mentally ill and developmentally disabled persons, particularly the latter, continue to be institutionalized for long periods, even their lifetime, for the vast majority a reverse situation obtains today. For more than a decade discharges from public mental facilities have exceeded admissions,[59] and the large institutions have been emptying, while the average length of stay and the death rate in the institutions are way down from what they were 10 to 20 years ago.[60]

Discharge is considered an administrative function in virtually every state.[61] Normally it is made the responsibility of the superintendents of mental institutions, though a minority of states designate the central state agency as an alternate decision maker.[62] In most states today the administrative decision to release a patient must be reported to the committing court.[63] Twenty-nine states authorize an additional discharge procedure for mentally ill patients by permitting the courts to release a patient upon his application or one made by another interested party.[64] (Separate provisions of this type for the developmentally disabled or retarded exist in 17 jurisdictions).[65] A request for discharge, moreover, may be initiated under a habeas corpus proceeding, but only 11 states explicitly provide for habeas corpus release based on the patient's present mental condition.[66]

A. Administrative Discharge

The institutions' authorities would appear to be best qualified to exercise the major responsibility for discharging involuntary patients. Still appropriate today is the observation made by two legal commentators almost 30 years ago:

> That discharge should be by institutional authorities is entirely logical. It should require no argument to demonstrate that the authorities of the hospital where the patient is under daily supervision and to whom the facts of his previous history and of his mental state are the best known are the persons who should determine his fitness to be returned to the community.[67]

Nonetheless, institutional discharge creates a number of dilemmas. With involuntary institutionalization typically accomplished by judicial process, the resulting division of authority between those responsible for commitment and those responsible for discharge has led to a diversity of policies and sometimes confusion. Not only the formal standards applied by each but the entire outlook on the function and objectives of institutionalization may diverge. It is possible for a person to be

58. Findings of the Medicaid Foster Family Care Pilot Project (1978), *cited in* Stotsky & Stotsky, Nursing Homes: Improving a Flawed Community Facility, 34 Hosp. & Community Psychiatry 238, 241 (1983).

59. The edge in discharges and discontinuations has been maintained up through the recent years, though the differential is diminishing as the residential population seems to be leveling off to some irreducible minimum of around 130,000 to 140,000 patients. In 1976, the number of discontinuations was reported to be 421,461 as against 413,559 additions (Division of Biometry and Epidemiology, National Institute of Mental Health, Statistical Note 153, at 25 table 4 (1976)); in 1977, the respective figures were 415,314 and 414,507 (Statistical Note 156, *supra* note 1, at 26 table 4).

60. See notes 1, 20, 21, & 25 *supra*.

61. Table 4.3 generally. There are isolated exceptions, which may be more an unintended gap in the state's mental disability code than a deliberate and practically acknowledged withholding of authority. For example, the new Arkansas code governing the commitment and discharge of mentally ill persons contains no explicit discharge provisions. Conceivably this is because all commitments under the present Arkansas law are determinate—45 days initially (Ark. Stat. Ann. § 59-1409 (Supp. 1981)) with the possibility of 120-day extensions (§ 59-1410). Whether this means that hospital authorities may not discharge a patient prior to expiration of the commitment term is doubtful, however. The most recently enacted Arkansas provisions for mentally retarded persons do not specify the discharge authority either (Ark. Stat. Ann. §§ 59-1001 to 1019 (1971 & Supp. 1981)), but the old law (§ 59-1109(b) (1971)), presumably still operative, contains a single administrative discharge provision for mentally disabled children committed to the state's "Children's Colony."

62. Table 4.3, cols. 1 & 2. Typically, where the statutes designate the central agency as having discharge authority, it is a power shared with the institution where the patient is receiving treatment. In a few states, however—Idaho, Oregon, and Wisconsin—it is *only* the central agency that has the ultimate discharge power.

63. Table 4.3, cols. 10–12.

64. See table 4.5.

65. Table 4.6.

66. Table 4.5, cols. 15 & 16. This is the count for the statutes governing judicial discharge of the mentally ill. Separate provisions of this type for the retarded exist in four states (table 4.6, cols. 15 & 16.

67. Weihofen & Overholser, Commitment of the Mentally Ill, 24 Tex. L. Rev. 307, 333 (1946).

considered in need of institutionalization by a court and yet at the same time be ready for discharge under the policies and standards guiding the decisions of the institution's authorities. Conversely, a person may be considered ineligible for release by the institution even though the criteria under which he was originally committed no longer apply.

The processing of administrative discharges of involuntary patients is usually the function of the institution. However, eight states give the power to both the institution and the central agency, its board, or its administrator.[68] The institution's authority is dominant nevertheless even in these states, with the central entity serving as a fall-back authority to be used in exceptional events. New York's statutory scheme, for example, posits a lengthy "discharge and conditional release" provision[69] that opens with the statement that "[a] patient may be discharged or conditionally released to the community by the director of a department facility, if, in the opinion of staff familiar with the patient's case history, such patient does not require active in-patient care and treatment."[70] In four full pages the provision then covers various conditional release options, the possibility of court involvement in the decision, the requirement of "written service plans" for all patients no matter what their type of discharge, and so on. Nowhere in this section is there mention of central agency authority; that comes only in a separate section on the "commissioner's power to transfer and discharge patients,"[71] where the last subprovision states that "[t]he commissioner, by order, may discharge any patient in his judgment improperly detained in any facility."

Three states vest the authority to discharge *solely* in the hands of the central agency:[72] in Idaho it is the department director,[73] in Oregon it is the state Division of Mental Health,[74] and in Wisconsin it is the Community Mental Health, Mental Retardation, Alcoholism and Drug Abuse Services Board, organized by the county governments.[75] Locating the power centrally means, of course, that the ultimate decision is made by an agent divorced from the source of the facts. The desirability of this allocation is questionable. It seems unlikely that the opportunity to establish more uniform discharge policies or the attempt to guard against misdirected or prejudicial decisions by local administrators counterbalances the disadvantages of decisions based on insufficient acquaintance with the particular facts or interests at stake. Administrative monitoring by the central agency of the local decision-making process is a better solution.

Since the institution's decision to discharge depends primarily upon the medical status of the involuntary patient, there are no statutory procedures leading to administrative discharge that can be initiated by the patient. In the days when the majority of states provided for indeterminate commitments, the sufficiency of leaving only judicial procedures open to patients who themselves or whose representatives felt they were ready for discharge was sometimes questioned. Today, however, the vast majority of states (39) authorize commitment only for definite durations, and even in those jurisdictions where indefinite commitment continues to be permitted there are explicit provisions for periodic judicial or administrative review[76] so that the patient's mental condition and the need for continued institutionalization are reassessed with sufficient regularity. Whether the practical application of these review procedures is always satisfactory (or necessary, for that matter) is a different question. But it is hard to fault the law as it stands today for failing to provide adequate opportunities to have the question of the patient's discharge considered.

The formal, substantive criteria governing discharge vary from state to state. In some jurisdictions, the standards for administrative release clearly do not match the commitment standards.[77] For example, the state's law may provide that a mentally disabled person can be involuntarily committed only when he is shown to be mentally disabled and dangerous, but the discharge standard in the same state may be simply that the patient no longer needs care and treatment. At least in theory, this could lead to the release of persons who pose a danger to public safety merely because they are not treatable. If this is indeed the practice, there is little justification for it, as one of the two basic purposes of commitment is the protection of society. To deal with this undesired possibility, Minnesota provides that a person found by the committing court to be dangerous or psychopathic shall not be discharged except on order of the commissioner of public welfare (i.e., the central authority) who must be "satisfied that the patient is capable of making an acceptable adjustment in society and . . . [only when he, the commissioner] has received a favorable recommendation to that effect by a majority of [a] special

68. Table 4.3, cols. 1 & 2.

69. N.Y. Mental Hyg. Law § 29.15 (McKinney 1978).

70. *Id.* at § 29.15(a).

71. *Id.* at § 29.11, § 29.11(g).

72. South Carolina used to place this authority centrally but today rests it in the institution (S.C. Code Ann. § 44-17-820 (Law Co-op. Supp. 1981)).

73. Idaho Code § 66-337 (Supp. 1981).

74. Or. Rev. Stat. § 426.300(1) (1981).

75. Wis. Stat. Ann. §§ 51.35(4)(a)(b), 51.42 (West Supp. 1981).

76. See ch. 2, Involuntary Institutionalization, § VC1(f), Period of Institutionalization: Initial Maximums, Review and Extension Procedures.

77. Cf. tables 4.3, cols. 3-6, & 2.6, cols. 4-6.

review board."[78] This fairly stringent safeguard is in effect a liberalization of a more onerous provision that preceded it, under which a dangerous patient could not be released administratively at all but solely on order of a special three-judge court appointed by the state's supreme court.[79]

In contrast to the mismatched criteria, the discharge statutes of 21 states[80] today specify a congruence between the standards for release and those justifying commitment, stating that a patient shall be released when he no longer meets the latter criteria. Such provisions minimize the possibility of conflict between the agents responsible for the mentally disabled person's commitment and those in charge of his rehabilitation and return to the community. They do not obviate it, as basic differences in policy, perspective, and practice may continue to exist in the face of formally matched standards.

Overall, the administrative discharge provisions have undergone major revision over the past decade. At the time the previous edition of this book was being researched (1969), the statutes spoke mostly in terms of the patient's recovery, improvement, or lack of improvement, and the classification scheme used in the book's tables reflected this language. Today, while these old criteria are still found in the statutes of a few states and often can continue to be read into others, the modern criteria tend to be both more specific and more legalistic.[81] The state of no longer meeting the standards that justified commitment—the release standard in 21 jurisdictions—is a legalistic formulation of the patient's condition. So too in some 18 states, to the extent that it mirrors one of the prevailing commitment standards and is concerned with the safety of *others*, is the release criterion of no longer being dangerous or likely to injure oneself or others. The other two main criteria found in the modern discharge provisions—no longer requiring treatment (19 states) and no longer mentally ill (13 states)—are more directly concerned with the patient's medical needs, perhaps as directly as the old recovered/improved/unimproved continuum. The new criteria show considerable overlap and are occasionally difficult to accommodate within the classification scheme we have devised for the tables. In most states, the patient's discharge may be predicated on any one of two or three of the main criteria listed.[82] In states where a single discharge standard is operative, it is usually the most general of the four—no longer requiring or benefiting from treatment—or one that in essence delegates formulation of the standard(s) to a special body, as in New Jersey where discharge shall be "in accordance with the rules and regulations prescribed by the board of managers."[83]

While the principle of administrative decision making suggests that it is a self-contained enterprise not subject to routine review by outside agencies such as the judiciary, the administrative discharge provisions of the vast majority of states do require notice of the release decision to the court.[84] The statutes of some 12 of these states in addition call for notice to relatives, friends, or guardians of the about-to-be-released patient.[85] Eleven states provide that the central mental disability agency also be notified.[86] It has been suggested that such notice provisions, if they are complied with at all, do little more than promote the exercise of futile formality and are of no help in assisting the discharged patient's rehabilitation. The answer to this charge is that the provisions are sound in their objectives, that they would appear to be worth having even if they assisted only a fraction of patients, that an important part of their purpose is the protection of others, and finally that they represent simply good bookkeeping.

Concern about the proper exercise of the discharge function has been a large feature in the literature on mental disability and the law from the early beginnings on. Traditionally, the commentary has come in the form of critiques of institutional reluctance to discharge patients who might by "objective" standards be ready for it. A relatively modern and moderate example comes from a study published in 1968:

> While it cannot be said that the institution acts with improper motives, conditions are often such that patients can, and do, become "lost." For example, in one institution visited a single doctor was responsible for more than 950 patients, and doctor-patient ratios of 1 to 600 were typical in other large institutions.[87]

While less severe today, problems of this type have not been altogether eliminated.[88] The discharge decision is

78. Minn. Stat. Ann. § 253A.15(2)(a) (West 1982).
79. *Id.* at § 253A.15(2) (1971).
80. Table 4.3, cols. 3–6.
81. *Id.* The provisions covering discharge of developmentally disabled persons are similar and can be tabulated within the same categories as those relating to the mentally ill.
82. *Id.*
83. N.J. Stat. Ann. § 30:4-107 (West 1981).
84. Table 4.3, col. 11.
85. Table 4.3, col. 12.
86. Table 4.3, col. 10.
87. R.S. Rock with M.M. Jacobson & R.M. Janopaul, Hospitalization and Discharge of the Mentally Ill 225 (1968).
88. After increasing during the 1960s and early 1970s, the number of psychiatrists in public mental institutions is now declining again. While the number of patients in public institutions has also declined, the number of admissions per year has increased (at least up through the early 1970s; since then there has been a slight decrease). The shortage of psychiatrists thus remains severe. The federal government counts a total of 3,712 psychiatrists in 1978 for 297 reporting institutions, a 14% decline from the number in 1976 and only 1.8% of the total staff in these institutions (Statistical Note 156, *supra* note 1 at 12 table E). A fairly recent statistic on the same point is re-

complicated by the fact that there is often no place for improved patients to go. A study conducted in the 1950s in Texas mental institutions[89] resulted in the estimate that as many as "seventy percent of all the patients don't need to be in a mental hospital." More recently (in 1963), the then superintendent of St. Elizabeths Hospital in Washington, D.C., testified that only "50% of the patients . . . hospitalized required hospitalization in a mental institution."[90] This estimate was updated in 1975 when in the case of *Dixon v. Weinberger*[91] the Court noted that the hospital's own clinical staff conceded that 43% of the inpatients could be treated in "alternative facilities" such as nursing homes, "personal care homes," foster homes, and halfway houses. An action recently brought in a New Jersey appellate court,[92] consolidating nine separate cases, illustrates the same point in the following graphic terms. It involves patients who had been ordered "discharged pending placement" but who have nonetheless remained institutionalized for several years after the order. Some have simply been kept on this interim legal status while others have been recommitted by way of a summary procedure that fails to meet the statutory requirements for commitment. The suit asks the court to clarify the legal meaning of this conditional type of discharge and to provide guidance to the lower courts in the handling of such cases. The case recently made its way to the New Jersey Supreme Court, which ruled that the state "[i]n a proper exercise of its *parens patriae* authority . . . may. . . continue the confinement of such persons on a provisional or conditional basis to protect their essential well-being, pending efforts to foster the placement of these individuals in proper supportive settings outside the institution."[93]

The other side of the coin to unnecessary retention of patients in institutions is discharge *in the absence of* proper placement or aftercare. Among the possible motivations that could lead state systems or institutions into this trap are the desire to create "impressive" release statistics (the supposed signal of impressive care) and the hope of tapping into the federal dollars available for noninstitutional care so as to relieve the pressure on state funds. Statistics and anecdotal information presented earlier[94] show that such discharges do occur on a scale that exceeds the norm of occasional human error to which all decision making is prone. The result is that today there are an increasing number of court cases that challenge not only the administrative decision to retain a patient (calling for the circumscription of that power with judicial safeguards) but also administrative discretion that is exercised summarily in favor of discharge.[95]

B. Judicial Discharge

Going one step beyond providing a judicial check on administrative discharge are statutes locating the actual power to decide in the courts—that is, judicial discharge statutes. Some 27 states today, down from 35 a decade ago, have such provisions as an additional protection of the patient's interests.[96] The judicial proceedings may be initiated on the application of the patient himself, his family, his legal guardian, or any citizen.[97] Eight of the states and the District of Columbia require that the application be accompanied by a medical certificate or at least a mental examination (which may be conducted in the hospital) supporting the contention that the patient is ready for release.[98] In Michigan such supporting evidence is required unless the patient is indigent or the documentation is otherwise unobtainable.[99] Most of the states provide that notice of the application for release be given to the patient's family or guardian and occasionally to his attorney.[100] About half require that the superintendent of the institution be notified specifically.[101] In all but three states, a judicial hearing must be held once the application is properly made.[102] In Arizona,[103] it is within the court's discretion to hold a hearing, as it is in Louisiana,[104] at least when the patient, or someone on his behalf, petitions more than once a year (once in a year the hearing is mandatory). In Iowa,[105] a sworn complaint alleging the improper confinement of a mentally disabled person triggers the appointment of a special commission of inquiry which

ported in Special Article Series: Civil Commitment, 2 MDLR 82, n.68 (1977): that patients in public institutions receive on the average only some three minutes of psychiatric attention per day.

89. Gainfort, How Texas Is Reforming Its Mental Hospitals, 19 The Reporter, Nov. 19, 1956, at 18, 19.

90. Hearings Before the Subcommittee on St. Elizabeths Hospital of the House Comm. on Education and Labor, 88th Cong., 1st Sess., at 23-24 (1963), *cited in* A. Brooks, Law, Psychiatry, and the Mental Health System 725 (1974).

91. 405 F. Supp. 974, 976 (D.D.C. 1975).

92. *In re* S.L., No. A-1734-80T1, 5 MDLR 252 (N.J. Super. Ct. App. Div. appeal docketed Jan. 6, 1981).

93. *In re* Commitment of S.L., 94 N.J. 128, 140, 462 A.2d 1252, 1258 (1983). The decision emphasizes the state's responsibility to expend all reasonable effort in finding proper alternative placement for such patients.

94. See ch. 2, Involuntary Institutionalization, § II A 3(d), Less Restrictive Alternatives and the Deinstitutionalization Movement.

95. E.g., Hildebrand v. Smith, Civil Action No. 77-0399 (E.D. Mich. filed Feb. 18, 1977), in which a class of mentally ill patients and their guardians challenged summary administrative discharge from the hospital to community care homes on the theory that they were thereby deprived of treatment without proper notice or a hearing.

96. See tables 4.5 & 4.6.

97. Table 4.5, cols. 1-3.

98. Table 4.5, col. 6.

99. Mich. Comp. Laws § 330.1485 (1980).

100. Table 4.5, cols. 7 & 8.

101. Table 4.5, col. 8.

102. Table 4.5, col. 9.

103. Ariz. Rev. Stat. Ann. § 36-546(D), (E) (Supp. 1981).

104. La. Rev. Stat. Ann. § 28:56(B) (West Supp. 1981).

105. Iowa Code Ann. § 229.33 (West Supp. 1981).

shall report to the court on the "truth of said allegation." A hearing will ensue if testimony contrary or supplemental to the commission's report is offered.

The criteria for judicial discharge are sufficiently similar to those on which administrative release may be predicated to permit grouping them under the same categories—that the patient is no longer dangerous or likely to cause injury, no longer requires institutional treatment or habilitation, no longer meets the criteria for commitment, or is no longer mentally ill,[106] or not mentally retarded.[107] The legalistic criterion of the patient's no longer meeting the commitment standards figures more prominently in the judicial discharge scheme than in administrative discharge. This is logical enough given that the judicial role is to apply legal criteria, whereas the administrative decision focuses more properly on medical facts. In several states,[108] the statutes contemplate a review of the initial commitment order and instruct the court to release the patient when the confinement is found to have been illegal or irregular. California[109] operates with a set of judicial release criteria which exemplifies the modern trend: the institutional patient shall be discharged if (1) he is no longer dangerous or gravely disabled, or (2) the facility is not equipped to provide treatment for him, or (3) he had not been advised of, or had in fact accepted, voluntary treatment.

Twenty-one states attempt to forestall repetitious and nonmeritorious requests for judicial release by restricting the frequency with which such petitions may be filed.[110] Once a year, once every 6 months, or once in 90 days are the common limitations, the period running either from the initial commitment order or from the last full hearing or review, which in Arizona[111] includes habeas corpus petitions that have been considered. Three states[112] specifically provide for unrestricted applications, stating that the patient may petition "anytime." A small number of states used to require the posting of bond or some other security guaranteeing the patient's future conduct before release could be ordered, but these provisions have been repealed.

All but a couple of states[113] explicitly include within their discharge statutes the right of the patient to seek a writ of habeas corpus as a means of securing his release if he believes he is being improperly detained. Even in the jurisdictions without such provisions the right exists by common law, as this writ has traditionally been available in Anglo-American jurisprudence to any person, including a mentally disabled individual, who asserts that he is being illegally deprived of his liberty.[114] Under the common law the writ is available only to test the legality of the original detention, and most discharge statutes incorporating the right incorporate this limitation.[115] Thus the protection afforded does not extend to a patient who was legally committed at the outset but who later recovered or improved and who may be entitled to release under existing institutional standards.[116] Some courts,[117] however, have broadened the scope of the writ to permit inquiry into the petitioner's current mental condition, and 11 states provide for the same expansion by statute.[118] Under these laws the mental condition of the patient at the time of the habeas corpus proceeding and not the validity of his initial institutionalization serves as the basic criterion for retention or discharge. Finally, in its most recent development, the writ has been used (and sustained) to challenge continued detention of an involuntary patient who is not being provided treatment[119] and to secure the release of a patient from the hospital into the community or his transfer to a community treatment facility under "the least restrictive alternative" doctrine.[120]

How well these two procedures, judicial discharge and habeas corpus, equip the patient to protect himself against the possibility of improper institutionalization is difficult to say. According to the sanguine view, which assumes that the medical staff in the institutions are quite capable of making the discharge decision and have no interest in keeping patients beyond the time during which they stand to profit from treatment, administrative procedures suffice and all other procedures—judicial review, judicial discharge, habeas corpus—are regarded as superfluous.[121] The opposite view is that even the judicial procedures fall short, as patients, typically unrepresented, do not have the wherewithal or initiative to take advantage of them. The

106. Table 4.5, cols. 11–14.

107. Table 4.6, cols. 11–14.

108. Table 4.5, col. 13.

109. Cal. Welf. & Inst. Code § 5276 (West 1972).

110. Table 4.5, col. 5.

111. Ariz. Rev. Stat. Ann. § 36-546(C) (1974 & Supp. 1981).

112. Louisiana, Massachusetts, and Oklahoma. See table 4.5, col. 5, for statutory citations.

113. Table 4.5, cols. 15 & 16.

114. M. Guttmacher & H. Weihofen, Psychiatry and the Law 316 (1952).

115. Table 4.5, cols. 15 & 16.

116. Ross, Commitment of the Mentally Ill: Problems of Law and Policy, 57 Mich. L. Rev. 945, 977 (1959).

117. An early case is Hiatt v. Soucek, 240 Iowa 300, 36 N.W.2d 432 (1949).

118. Table 4.5, col. 16.

119. Rouse v. Cameron, 373 F.2d 451 (D.C. Cir. 1966).

120. Lake v. Cameron, 364 F.2d 657 (D.C. Cir. 1966); Covington v. Harris, 419 F.2d 617 (D.C. Cir. 1969). In *Covington* (at 620–21), the court stated explicitly that habeas corpus was available to challenge the place as well as the period of confinement.

121. Ralph Slovenko appears to be essentially of this view, though he concedes the need for "the ancient writ of habeas corpus" (but no other judicial procedures) to deal with the isolated case of improper commitment or retention. See R. Slovenko, Psychiatry and Law 222 (1973).

occasional patient who does have an attorney may be only slightly better positioned: attorneys are said to be uncomprehending of their role in representing mentally disabled persons and frequently reluctant if not unwilling to press for the patient's discharge in the face of medical opposition.[122] Selective evidence of infrequent use of habeas corpus procedures is cited to demonstrate that patients generally do not avail themselves of judicial discharge procedures and the fraction of patients who do use them, and use them successfully, becomes evidence that there are masses of other patients who should but have not.

Reliable and generalizable data on the use of habeas corpus and other judicial discharge procedures by mental patients do not exist.[123] One is of necessity confined to fragmentary statistics and speculation. That there is wide variation from jurisdiction to jurisdiction appears to be the one certainty. Guttmacher and Weihofen in an old study report that "[i]n some jurisdictions the writ [of habeas corpus] is resorted to almost not at all by mental patients, whereas in others the number of petitions has at times attained such proportions as to call for judicial attention and correction."[124] They go on to cite the District of Columbia experience as an example at one end of the spectrum where one patient had submitted 50 petitions, another 27, and a third 24 in a period of less than five years.[125] The fact that the recent developments in the reach of habeas corpus have come from the District of Columbia's courts[126] suggests that the writ continues to be a potent tool there. Incidental data from a study conducted in California suggest heavy use of the writ, if not overuse, there as well: the study focused on the caseload of a "mental health court in a large metropolitan area [Los Angeles], which hears approximately 1,000 habeas corpus writs per year . . . filed by members of a civilly committed population ten times that size."[127] But between these geographical extremes there are jurisdictions where habeas corpus is for mental patients all but a dead letter.

122. See, e.g., Andalman & Chambers, Effective Counsel for Persons Facing Civil Commitment: A Survey, a Polemic, and a Proposal, 45 Miss. L.J. 43 (1974); Cohen, The Function of the Attorney and the Commitment of the Mentally Ill, 44 Tex. L. Rev. 424 (1966); Klein, My Most Interesting Legal Aid Case: Improper Commitments in Detroit, 15 Briefcase 118-20 (1957). Moore, The Patient and Legal Aid, Search, Oct. 1957, at 6, charging that many lawyers would simply consign all habeas corpus applications from mental hospital patients to the waste basket; Rock, Jacobson, & Janopaul, *supra* note 87, at 234-41.

123. Whatever studies of habeas corpus have been done, quantitative or otherwise, have concentrated almost exclusively on writs filed by prisoners.

124. Guttmacher & Weihofen, *supra* note 114, at 316-17.

125. *Id.* at 317.

126. See notes 119 & 120 *supra.*

127. Warren, Involuntary Commitment for Mental Disorder: The Application of California's Lanterman-Petris-Short Act, 11 Law & Soc'y Rev. 629, 630 (1977).

The level of use of habeas corpus and judicial discharge procedures by mental patients depends on the need that they may have or perceive of such procedures and the help they are able to obtain in pursuing this need. Today these various factors pull in different directions. As the states have moved away from the indeterminate commitment concept toward definite and comparatively short institutionalizations punctuated by mandatory periodic reviews of the patient's condition, the need for a separate set of judicial discharge procedures, including the habeas corpus option, has diminished. On the other hand, there are today more lawyers and more patients' rights advocates willing and able to extend the help most patients require in making release applications to the court. And patients themselves, through formal "rights notification" efforts or simply by general osmosis in an increasingly "belegaled" environment, are today more rights conscious than before. Combine these latter elements with the broadened scope of judicial release procedures—the extension of the habeas corpus inquiry to present mental condition, adequacy of treatment provided, and propriety of the place, time, and restrictiveness of institutionalization—and the potential for greatly increased use of the procedures becomes apparent. Whether this potential is being realized to the point of burdening or overburdening today's courts remains to be determined.

VI. LIABILITY FOR "WRONGFUL" DISCHARGE

While much of the law and the general debate proceeds from the perspective of the need to facilitate the discharge of patients from institutions,[128] there is a growing legal concern with improper institutional decisions to release patients and with the questions of ascribing and assessing liability for such "wrongful" discharge decisions. This concern comes as part of a general increase in legal scrutiny over professional decision making and the growth of professional malpractice (particularly medical malpractice) concepts and the profitability of such claims to plaintiffs and their attorneys. It also stems from developments along the lines of the deinstitutionalization movement and the rise of the least restrictive treatment doctrine, which have put pressure on institutions to release patients at points where in earlier days the decision might have been to retain them and to take greater chances with the patients' ability to survive in the community and adjust to life lived with a sudden exponential increase in freedom. Some of these release decisions have come back to haunt those who

128. This perspective includes concern with unwarranted institutionalization, valid discharge requests resisted by the institution (i.e., improper retention), and the questions of whether there is liability and who is liable for those decisions.

made them: patients, relatives, and bystanders have been hurt, and the damage claims have followed. Discussed more fully in a later chapter,[129] these developments in brief involve some of the following considerations.

A. Sovereign Immunity

From the point of view of a plaintiff trying to succeed against the institution, its staff or against the state in a "wrongful" discharge action, the first hurdle to be vaulted is that of sovereign immunity. To enable it to carry out the functions of regulator, caretaker, service provider—among others—the state may assert (or relinquish for that matter) on behalf of its functionaries the protection of immunity from being sued while they carry out state functions. *Martinez v. California*,[130] in which the United States Supreme Court upheld the immunity of California's prison parole board after a parolee was convicted of murder and the survivors brought an action for damages, supports the rationality of the state's view that concern over legal liability would inhibit state officials in the implementation of the state's programs and concedes the prerogative of the state to create laws that protect its programs from dysfunction and its officials from liability. The case is particularly relevant to the mental disability field because the prisoner was a sex offender who had served part of his time in a state mental hospital. While *Martinez* upheld the absolute immunity of the parole board officials, the state's power to provide for this immunity is not absolute. It is subject to the constraints of the federal constitution,[131] to specific federal statutes granting citizens a right of action against officials who act wrongfully under the color of state law,[132] and to the theory that certain ministerial acts, as opposed to basic policy and planning decisions, may not fall within the grant of immunity covering official action.[133]

B. Negligence and the Duty to Prevent Harm

Assuming the plaintiff clears the immunity hurdle, he must meet a number of other tests before he can succeed against the institutional decision maker. He must establish that the defendant had the duty and the opportunity to prevent the harm that was caused by the release decision.[134] There is no independent constitutional right to be protected by the state from harmful acts committed by fellow citizens.[135] It must be shown that the state assumed a specific obligation that through negligence[136] it failed to carry out. To establish the defendant's negligence the plaintiff has the burden of showing that prevailing standards of care were violated—for example, that the institution failed to conduct a proper medical examination before releasing the patient.[137] And the harm that was caused must have been forseeable in a specific sense[138] and must have been "proximately caused" by the institution's negligence—intervening causal factors, including the lapse of time, may negate the defendant's liability.[139]

C. Conclusion

While the case reports show that suits against public mental facilities for wrongful discharge do succeed on occasion,[140] it is clear that the prevailing law poses heavy burdens on the plaintiff. In an era where much of the legal pressure on institutional decision makers continues to be exerted in the direction of promoting quick discharges and where allegations of malfeasance continue to concentrate on "wrongful" *retentions*, this posture of the law is not necessarily out of line. Doctors and admin-

129. See ch. 10, Provider-Patient Relations: Confidentiality and Liability.

130. 444 U.S. 277 (1980). See also Guess v. State, 157 Cal. Rptr. 618 (Ct. App. 1979), upholding official immunity in a case involving an attempted bank robbery by a community mental health center patient on conditional release from the state hospital.

131. E.g., in *Martinez* the argument was made, though rejected by the Court, that the Fourteenth Amendment's prohibition of the taking of life without due process of law invalidated California's immunity statute.

132. E.g., the federal civil rights act of 1871, 42 U.S.C. § 1983 (1982).

133. A court case sustaining this theory on the particular question of a mental institution's decision to release a patient is Bellavance v. State, 390 So. 2d 422 (Fla. Dist. Ct. App. 1980).

134. Bowers v. DeVito, 686 F.2d 616 (7th Cir. 1982). See also Tarasoff v. Regents of Univ. of California, 551 P.2d 334, 131 Cal. Rptr. 14, (1976).

135. In *Bowers* 686 F.2d 616 (7th Cir. 1982), the federal court dismissed plaintiff's action for precisely this reason: that the individual has no constitutional right to be protected by the state from criminals or madmen. The court suggested, however, that the plaintiff might have an action in the state court under the common law.

136. In Maroon v. State Dep't of Mental Health, 411 N.E.2d 404 (Ind. Ct. App. 1980), however, the court *assumed* negligence on the part of the hospital on the theory of res ipsa loquitur. Liability was found where an escapee from a state institution committed murder and the institution, presumed to have control over the patient, failed to *disprove* negligence.

137. Valenti v. United States, No. 78 C5 198, 6 MDLR 386 (N.D. Ill. July 13, 1982); Ellis v. United States, 484 F. Supp. 4 (D.S.C. 1978).

138. Knight v. Michigan, 297 N.W.2d 889 (Ct. App. 1980); cf. Tarasoff v. Regents of the University of California, 551 P.2d 334, 131 Cal. Rptr. 14, (1976).

139. E.g., Januszko v. State, 391 N.E.2d 297 (N.Y. Ct. App. 1979); Castillo v. United States, 552 F.2d 1385 (10th Cir. 1977). In Doyle v. United States, 530 F. Supp. 1278 (C.D. Cal. 1982), the court ruled that liability was negated by intervening time and distance, where a patient discharged from an Army Hospital in Louisiana went on to commit murder in California one month later. But in Valenti v. United States, No. 78 C5 198, 6 MDLR 386 (N.D. Ill. July 13, 1982), the court found liability even though there was a gap of several months between the patient's release and the offense he committed.

140. See, e.g., the cases reported in issues of the *Mental Disability Law Reporter* over the past few years, including Rum River Lumber Co. v. State, 282 N.W.2d 882 (Minn. 1979); Comiskey v. State, 418 N.Y.S.2d 233 (App. Div. 1979); Smith v. United States, 437 F. Supp. 1004 (E.D. Pa. 1977); Valenti v. United States, No. 78 C5 198, 6 MDLR 386 (N.D. Ill. July 13, 1982); Maroon v. State Dep't of Mental Health, 411 N.E.2d 404 (Ind. Ct. App. 1980); New Hampshire v. Brosseau, No. 82-064, 8 MDLR 128 (N.H. Sup. Ct. Dec. 1, 1983); Durflinger v. Artiles, 673 P.2d 86 (Kan. 1983).

istrators in public mental institutions feel excessively hemmed in by the law as it is. As they see it, in any given case whether they decide to retain or discharge the patient, the potential for legal liability is great enough as it is. Moreover, frequent success in suits for wrongful detention will in the end inhibit the discharge of mentally disabled persons who are ready and entitled to resume life in the community.

TABLE 4.1 TRANSFERS OF MENTALLY DISABLED PERSONS

STATE	TYPE OF DISABILITY (1)	TRANSFER UPON PETITION: Petition by: Patient (2)	Petition by: Other (3)	Approval by (4)	Place of Transfer (5)	TRANSFER AT ADMINISTRATIVE DISCRETION: By Whom (6)	Condition or Criteria (7)	Patient's Right to Object (8)	Place of Transfer (9)	PROVISIONS FOR TRANSFER BETWEEN MENTAL ILLNESS & MENTAL RETARDATION FACILITIES (10)	PROVISIONS FOR TRANSFER TO FEDERAL PROGRAM OR FACILITY (11)	NOTICE OF TRANSFER: Guardian, Spouse, or Relative (12)	Other (13)	PROVISIONS RELATING TO EMERGENCY TRANSFER (14)
ALA. Code (1975 & Supp. 1982)	mentally ill										22-52-13(a)			
	mentally retarded		recommendation of superintendent 22-52-58(b)	board, & ct. having jurisdiction 22-52-58(b)	any state-owned, operated, or supervised psychiatric hospital 22-52-58(b)	board 22-52-58(a)	consistent with training, treatment, hospital, or rehabilitation needs 22-52-58(a)		another institution 22-52-58(a)					
ALAS. Stat. (1979 & Supp. 1981)														
ARIZ. Rev. Stat. Ann. (1974 & Supp. 1981)	mentally ill					director of dep't 36-502(B)	in accordance w/rules made by director, w/ ct. approval 36-502(B)		among mental health evaluation & treatment agencies 36-502(C)		36-548(c)		ct. that ordered commitment 36-548(c)	
	mentally retarded					dep't 36-565(B)	can be better treated in another facility, program, or service 36-565(B)	right to administrative review 36-565(C) 36-563	another mental retardation program or service 36-565(B)			parent & guardian 36-565(c)		
ARK. Stat. Ann. (1971 & Supp. 1981)														
CAL. Welf. & Inst. Code (West 1972 & Supp. 1981)	mentally ill & developmentally disabled		request of relatives or friends 7302 county *fn. 1* 7304	medical directors of both institutions, & of dep't's w/jurisdiction 7302 ct. *fn. 1* 7304	like institution 7302	director of mental health 7300 4122	would be benefitted by transfer 7300 preference to adjoining rather than remote district 7300	right of developmentally disabled to "fair hearing" 4805 "fair hearing" defined 4700 et seq.	another institution in dep't 7300		4123			
COLO. Rev. Stat. Ann. (1973 & Supp. 1981)	mentally ill										27-10-121(1)			
	mentally retarded					dep't of institutions 27-10.5-125(1)	best interests of resident 27-10.5-125(1)	ct. hearing 27-10.5-105, 27-10.5-106 27-10.5-125(2)	any other facility operated by dep't 27-10.5-125(1)			nearest relative or guardian 27-10.5-125(2)	person who applied for patient's admission 27-10.5-125(2)	notice w/in 24 hrs. after transfer 27-10.5-125(3)
CONN. Gen. Stat. Ann. (West 1975 & Supp. 1981)	mentally ill	via petition for release 17-192	representative 17-192	any ct. of probate upon showing of reasonable cause 17-192	any other hospital for mental illness 17-192	agreement of superintendents of the respective institutions 17-193	approval of commissioner 17-193	application for ct. hearing to revoke or modify transfer 17-193	any other hospital for mental illness 17-193				committing ct. 17-193	
(West 1977 & Supp. 1981)	mentally retarded					superintendent of facility 19-569h	person shall remain subject to the control of superintendent of transferring facility 19-569h(a)		training school, regional center, or other facility 19-569h	19-569k(c)			commissioner of mental retardation 19-569h(b)	
						agreement of the superintendents 19-569k(b)			"to any of the other institutions" 19-569k(b)					
DEL. Code Ann. (1974 & Supp. 1980)	mentally ill & mentally retarded 16, §5321					any institution 16, §5324(a)	eligibility 16, §§5324(a), 5321 regulations of the dep't 16, §5324(a)		Governor Bacon Health Center 16, §5324(a)					

TABLE 4.1 TRANSFERS OF MENTALLY DISABLED PERSONS—*Continued*

STATE	TYPE OF DISABILITY (1)	TRANSFER UPON PETITION: Petition by: Patient (2)	Other (3)	Approval by (4)	Place of Transfer (5)	TRANSFER AT ADMINISTRATIVE DISCRETION: By Whom (6)	Condition or Criteria (7)	Patient's Right to Object (8)	Place of Transfer (9)	PROVISIONS FOR TRANSFER BETWEEN MENTAL ILLNESS & MENTAL RETARDATION FACILITIES (10)	PROVISIONS FOR TRANSFER TO FEDERAL PROGRAM OR FACILITY (11)	NOTICE OF TRANSFER: Guardian, Spouse, or Relative (12)	Other (13)	PROVISIONS RELATING TO EMERGENCY TRANSFER (14)
D.C. Code Ann. (1981 & Supp. 1982)	mentally retarded					recommendation by director of facility to ct. 6-1929(a)	beneficial & consistent with habilitation needs; mandatory hearing if to more restrictive environment 6-1929(a) maintenance of family relationships; encouraging visitation 6-1929(a)	request for hearing 6-1929(a)	another facility 6-1929(a)			parent or guardian who petitioned for commitment 6-1929(a)	counsel & mental retardation advocate 6-1929(a)	prompt notice to parent or guardian 6-1929(a) 6-1662(c)
FLA. Stat. Ann. (West 1973 & Supp. 1981)	mentally ill	394.461(3)(a)	guardian 394.461(3)(a)	dep't of health & rehabilitative services, if involuntarily committed 394.461(3)(a)	private facility, if able to pay; or public facility 394.461(3)(a)	dep't 394.461(3)(b)	when medical needs of patient or efficient use of facilities require 394.461(3)(b)	express & informed consent of patient & guardian or representatives required 394.461(3)(b)	another facility of dep't 394.461(3)(b)			guardian or representative 394.461(3)(c)		
GA. Code Ann. (1979 & Supp. 1980)	mentally ill	88-505.7		receiving facility 88-505.7	any other approved evaluating facility 88-505.7							representatives & person who filed original petition 88-505.7	certifying physician & ct. that ordered evaluation 88-505.7	
HAWAII Rev. Stat. (1976 & Supp. 1981)	mentally ill					administrators of sending & receiving facilities 334-71	best interest of patient 334-71	right to hearing after transfer 334-81	another psychiatric facility 334-71		334-72(a)		those specified in current order of commitment 334-71	
IDAHO Code (1980 & Supp. 1981)	mentally ill or mentally retarded					director of dep't or designee 66-334(a)	consistent w/ mental health needs of patient 66-334(a)		another inpatient facility 66-334(a) or other state or private facility 66-334(b)			guardian, parents, spouse, next of kin, or friend 66-334(a), (b)	attorney & committing ct. 66-334(a), (b)	
ILL. Ann. Stat. (Smith-Hurd 1966 & Supp. 1981)	mentally ill	91½, §3-909	attorney, guardian, custodian, or responsible relative 91½, §3-909	ct. 91½, §3-909	different facility or program, or care & custody of different person 91½, §3-909	facility director 91½, §3-908	clinically advisable & consistent with treatment needs 91½, §3-908	righ to hearing 91½, §§3-910 (c), (d)	another dep't facility 91½, §3-908		91½, §3-1003	attorney, guardian, & responsible relative; or parent, guardian, or person who initiated commitment, if a minor 91½, §3-910(a)	committing ct. 91½, §3-1003	91½, §3-910(b)
	developmentally disabled	(nonresidential clients only) 91½, §4-708	attorney, guardian, or nearest adult relative 91½, §4-708 private facility 91½, §4-708 (nonresidential clients only)	ct. 91½, §4-708	a different facility or program of nonresidential services 91½, §4-708	facility director 91½, §4-707	appropriate & consistent w/ habilitation needs 91½, §4-707 close to client's place of residence 91½, §4-707	right fo hearing 91½, §§4-709 (b), (c)	another dep't facility 91½, §4-707			91½, §4-709(a) 91½, §4-206	attorney 91½, §4-709(a)	91½, §4-709(a)
IND. Code Ann. (Burns 1973 & Supp. 1982)	mentally ill, mentally retarded, epilepsy, alcoholism, or addiction 16-14-9.1-1(a)					commissioner 16-14-9.1-17	best interest of patient or other patients; administrative hearing if to more restrictive environment 16-14-9.1-17	petition for administrative hearing 16-14-9.1-17 or petition to set aside transfer 16-14-9.1-17	another hospital or appropriate facility 16-14-9.1-17			guardian, parents, spouse, & attorney 16-14-9.1-17		
IOWA Code Ann. (West 1969 & Supp. 1981)	mentally ill					state director, w/consent of patient or hospitalizing ct. 222.7 chief medical officer 229.15(4)	best interest of patient 229.15(4)	right to hearing 229.15(4)	hospital-school 222.7 different hospital for continued full-time custody 229.15(4)	222.7	229.29		ct. that ordered hospitalization 229.29 229.15(4)	
	mentally retarded					state director 222.7			hospital, school or special unit 222.7	222.7				

TABLE 4.1 TRANSFERS OF MENTALLY DISABLED PERSONS—*Continued*

STATE	TYPE OF DISABILITY (1)	TRANSFER UPON PETITION: Petition by: Patient (2)	TRANSFER UPON PETITION: Petition by: Other (3)	TRANSFER UPON PETITION: *Approval by* (4)	TRANSFER UPON PETITION: *Place of Transfer* (5)	TRANSFER AT ADMINISTRATIVE DISCRETION: *By Whom* (6)	TRANSFER AT ADMINISTRATIVE DISCRETION: *Condition or Criteria* (7)	TRANSFER AT ADMINISTRATIVE DISCRETION: *Patient's Right to Object* (8)	TRANSFER AT ADMINISTRATIVE DISCRETION: *Place of Transfer* (9)	PROVISIONS FOR TRANSFER BETWEEN MENTAL ILLNESS & MENTAL RETARDATION FACILITIES (10)	PROVISIONS FOR TRANSFER TO FEDERAL PROGRAM OR FACILITY (11)	NOTICE OF TRANSFER: *Guardian, Spouse, or Relative* (12)	NOTICE OF TRANSFER: *Other* (13)	PROVISIONS RELATING TO EMERGENCY TRANSFER (14)
KAN. Stat. Ann. (1976 & Supp. 1981)	mentally ill & mentally retarded					director of mental health & retardation services 59-2924	best interest of patient 59-2924		any institution under director's control 59-2924					
KY. Rev. Stat. Ann. (Michie 1977 & Supp. 1981)	mentally ill	secretary shall adopt rules 202A.180	secretary shall adopt rules 202A.180		between hospitals or between hospitals & forensic psychiatric facilities 202A.180(11)						202A.160(1)		hospitalizing ct. 202A.160(1)	
	mentally retarded	secretary shall adopt rules 202B.060	secretary shall adopt rules 202B.060		between hospitals & residential treatment centers, & between residential treatment centers & forensic psychiatric facilities 202B.060(11)									
LA. Rev. Stat. Ann. (West 1975 & Supp. 1981)	mentally ill		joint application of superintendent of private mental institution & guardian 28:94(A)(1)	dep't 28:94(A)	to or from a private mental institution 28:94(A)(1)	dep't 28:94(A)		consent of voluntary patient required 28:94(A)(3)	another mental institution 28:94(A)		28:93			
	mentally retarded	28:411	parent of minor or tutor or curator 28:411 facility to which person has been committed 28:411	client placement division 28:411	from 1 placement to another 28:410	client placement division 28:410		closest relative, tutor, curator, or official advocate may state reasons for opposing transfer 28:410	from 1 placement to another 28:410			parents, tutor, curator, or closest relative 28:410		
ME. Rev. Stat. Ann. (1978 & Supp. 1981)	mentally ill					dep't 34, §2373	consistent with medical needs 34, §2373 maintenance of relationships & encouragement of visits 34, §2373		another hospital in or out of state 34, §2373		34, §2373	guardian, parents, spouse, nearest known relative, or friend 34, §2373	committing ct. 34, §2373	
MD. Ann. Code (1979 & Supp. 1981)	mentally ill					commissioner or authorized representative 59, §17(a)	better care or treatment; safety or welfare of other patients; or likelihood of profiting from care elsewhere 59, §17(a) consent of receiving facility, if private 59, §17(a)		another facility, public or private 59, §17(a)	59, §17A	59, §17(g)	next of kin or guardian 59, §17(c)	committing ct. or proper officer 59, §17(g)	
	mentally retarded					director or designee 59A, §15(a)	better care or treatment; safety or welfare of others; or likelihood of profiting elsewhere 59A, §15(a) consent of receiving facility, if private 59A, §15(a)		another facility, public or private 59A, §15(a)	59A, §15A	59A, §15(d)			

TABLE 4.1 TRANSFERS OF MENTALLY DISABLED PERSONS—*Continued*

STATE	TYPE OF DISABILITY (1)	TRANSFER UPON PETITION: Petition by: Patient (2)	TRANSFER UPON PETITION: Petition by: Other (3)	TRANSFER UPON PETITION: *Approval by* (4)	TRANSFER UPON PETITION: *Place of Transfer* (5)	TRANSFER AT ADMINISTRATIVE DISCRETION: *By Whom* (6)	TRANSFER AT ADMINISTRATIVE DISCRETION: *Condition or Criteria* (7)	TRANSFER AT ADMINISTRATIVE DISCRETION: *Patient's Right to Object* (8)	TRANSFER AT ADMINISTRATIVE DISCRETION: *Place of Transfer* (9)	PROVISIONS FOR TRANSFER BETWEEN MENTAL ILLNESS & MENTAL RETARDATION FACILITIES (10)	PROVISIONS FOR TRANSFER TO FEDERAL PROGRAM OR FACILITY (11)	NOTICE OF TRANSFER: *Guardian, Spouse, or Relative* (12)	NOTICE OF TRANSFER: *Other* (13)	PROVISIONS RELATING TO EMERGENCY TRANSFER (14)
MASS. Ann. Laws (Michie/Law. Co-op. 1981 & Supp. 1982)	mentally ill or mentally retarded					dep't 123, §3	approval of receiving facility's superintendent 123, §3		any other facility dep't finds suitable 123, §3			nearest relative or guardian 123, §3		notice w/in 24 hrs. thereafter 123, §3
MICH. Comp. Laws Ann. (1980 & Supp. 1981)	mentally ill					dep't 330.1407	not detrimental 330.1407	opportunity to appeal 330.1407	any other hospital, or facility of the dep't 330.1407		330.1405	guardian or nearest relative 330.1407	2 persons designated by patient	notice w/in 24 hrs. thereafter 330.1407
	mentally retarded					dep't 330.1536(1)	not detrimental 330.1536(1)	opportunity to appeal 330.1536(2)	any other facility, or hospital operated by dep't 330.1536(1)			nearest relative or guardian 330.1536(2)	2 persons designated by resident 330.1536(2)	notice w/in 24 hrs. thereafter 330.1536 (2), (3)
MINN. Stat. Ann. (West 1971 & Supp. 1981)	mentally ill, mentally deficient, or inebriate					commissioner 253A.14(1)	found dangerous to public or psychopathic personality by committing ct. 253A.14(1)		any other hospital or institution under commissioner's jurisdiction 253A.14(1)	253A.14(1)	253A.08	parent or spouse, or interested person 253A.14(1)	probate ct., if committed, & designated agency 253A.14(1)	
MISS. Code Ann. (1972 & Supp. 1980)	mentally ill										41-21-77			
MO. Ann. Stat. (Vernon 1979 & Supp. 1980)	mentally ill					dept. 632.370(1)	consistent w/ medical needs 632.370(1) maintenance of relationships & encouragement of visits 632.370(1)		another mental health facility 632.370(1)		632.370(2)	upon patient's consent, to parents, spouse, or nearest known relative or friend 632.370	committing ct., last known attorney, & regional mental health coordinator 632.370	
	mentally retarded	630.610(2) 633.145(2)	head of facility 630.610(1) representative, parent of minor, ct., or state or private facility having custody 630.610(2) 633.145(2)	dept 630.610(3) 633.145(2)	to a private mental retardation facility 633.145(2)	division director 633.145(1)	improved habilitation or services, resident's safety & welfare, or closer proximity to family & friends 633.145(1)	consent of resident, guardian, or parent, if a minor, required 633.145(3)	another dep't mental retardation facility 633.145(1)	633.150		guardian or next of kin 633.145(1)		
MONT. Code Ann. (1981)	developmentally disabled	a party who could have requested hearing, if resident admitted w/o hearing 53-20-127(2)	a party who could have requested hearing, if resident admitted w/o hearing 53-20-127(2)	professional person or, if unwilling, by ct. hearing 53-20-127(2)	community-based or residential alternative 53-20-127(1)	professional person in charge of resident 53-20-127(1)	adequate treatment & habilitation, protection or resident & others, or best interests of resident 53-20-127(1)	petition for hearing 53-20-127(1)	community-based alternative or other residential facility 53-20-127(1)			parents or guardian 53-20-127(1), (2)	most recent attorney, responsible person appointed by ct. & ct. that ordered admission 53-20-127(1), (2)	53-20-127(1)
	mentally ill										53-21-133(1)			

TABLE 4.1 TRANSFERS OF MENTALLY DISABLED PERSONS—*Continued*

STATE	TYPE OF DISABILITY (1)	TRANSFER UPON PETITION: Petition by: Patient (2)	TRANSFER UPON PETITION: Petition by: Other (3)	TRANSFER UPON PETITION: Approval by (4)	TRANSFER UPON PETITION: Place of Transfer (5)	TRANSFER AT ADMINISTRATIVE DISCRETION: By Whom (6)	TRANSFER AT ADMINISTRATIVE DISCRETION: Condition or Criteria (7)	TRANSFER AT ADMINISTRATIVE DISCRETION: Patient's Right to Object (8)	TRANSFER AT ADMINISTRATIVE DISCRETION: Place of Transfer (9)	PROVISIONS FOR TRANSFER BETWEEN MENTAL ILLNESS & MENTAL RETARDATION FACILITIES (10)	PROVISIONS FOR TRANSFER TO FEDERAL PROGRAM OR FACILITY (11)	NOTICE OF TRANSFER: Guardian, Spouse, or Relative (12)	NOTICE OF TRANSFER: Other (13)	PROVISIONS RELATING TO EMERGENCY TRANSFER (14)
NEB. Rev. Stat. (1976 & Supp. 1981)	mentally ill					director of public institutions, w/concurrence by receiving facility's superintendent 83-305.03	cannot be properly diagnosed or treated by present facility 83-305.03 temporary transfer only 83-305.03		Nebraska Psychiatric Institute or university hospital 83-305.03					
	mentally retarded					director of public institutions 83-387	when continued residence no longer beneficial 83-387		any other available program or facility 83-387			guardian, parents of minor, or any person authorized to make application for admission 83-387 83-383(1)		
NEV. Rev. Stat. (1979)	mentally ill					administrator 433A.410			another division facility 433A.410		433A.420			
	mentally retarded					administrative officer of division facility 435.085	necessary diagnostic, medical, or surgical services not available w/in division 435.085		a general hospital 435.085					
						administrator 435.077(2)	"administrator shall establish regulations" 435.077(1)		another facility operated by division 435.077(1)					
N.H. Rev. Stat. Ann. (1977 & Supp. 1981)	developmentally disabled	171-A:7	parent or guardian of minor or ward 171-A:7	area agency 171-A:7	"a change in placement" 171-A:7	referral by administrator to area agency 171-A:11(III) 171-A:8(II)		may withdraw or seek change in placement 171-A:7 reviewed by director 171-A:8(IV)	"an appropriate placement" 171-A:8(II)			parent or guardian, if a minor or incompetent 171-A:8(III)		
N.J. Stat. Ann. (West 1981 & Supp. 1982)	mentally ill or mentally retarded		chief executive officer 30:4-83 30:4-84.1	commissioner, in accordance w/rules adopted by state board 30:4-83 30:4-84.1	charitable hospital, or other similar institution 30:4-83 any other mental hospital or functional service 30:4-84.1	commissioner, in accordance w/rules adopted by state board 30:4-83 30:4-84.1	admitted w/o ct. order 30:4-84.1	30:4-84.1	any charitable hospital, or other similar institution 30:4-83 any other mental hospital or functional service 30:4-84.1		30:6B-4	spouse, guardian, parents of minor, or nearest known relative or friend 30:4-83.1		
N.M. Stat. Ann. (1979 & Supp. 1982)														
N.Y. Mental Hyg. Law (McKinney 1978 & Supp. 1981)														
N.C. Gen. Stat. (1981 & Supp. 1981)	mentally disordered		recommendation of director of inpatient services 122-13.1	administrator of appropriate state hospital, on advice of chief of medical services 122-13.1	from Psychiatric Training Research Center at Chapel Hill to a state hospital or institution 122-13.1	dep't of human resources 122-13	such rules & regulations as state commission sees best 122-13		another state hospital or institution under dep't control 122-13		122-14			

TABLE 4.1 TRANSFERS OF MENTALLY DISABLED PERSONS—*Continued*

STATE	TYPE OF DISABILITY (1)	TRANSFER UPON PETITION: Petition by: Patient (2)	TRANSFER UPON PETITION: Petition by: Other (3)	TRANSFER UPON PETITION: *Approval by* (4)	TRANSFER UPON PETITION: *Place of Transfer* (5)	TRANSFER AT ADMINISTRATIVE DISCRETION: *By Whom* (6)	TRANSFER AT ADMINISTRATIVE DISCRETION: *Condition or Criteria* (7)	TRANSFER AT ADMINISTRATIVE DISCRETION: *Patient's Right to Object* (8)	TRANSFER AT ADMINISTRATIVE DISCRETION: *Place of Transfer* (9)	PROVISIONS FOR TRANSFER BETWEEN MENTAL ILLNESS & MENTAL RETARDATION FACILITIES (10)	PROVISIONS FOR TRANSFER TO FEDERAL PROGRAM OR FACILITY (11)	NOTICE OF TRANSFER: *Guardian, Spouse, or Relative* (12)	NOTICE OF TRANSFER: *Other* (13)	PROVISIONS RELATING TO EMERGENCY TRANSFER (14)
N.D. Cent. Code (1978 & Supp. 1981)	mentally ill, alcoholic, or drug addict		parent, brother, sister, child of legal age, or guardian 25-03.1-34(1)	agreement of receiving facility 25-03.1-34(1)	public or private institution 25-03.1-34(1)	superintendent or director of 25-03.1-34(1)	consistent w/ medical needs 25-03.1-34(1) due considera-tion to relation-ship to family, guardian, or friends, & visi-tation 25-03.1-34(1)	right to hearing on the merits 25-03.1-34(3)	another hospi-tal or facility 25-03.1-34(1)		25-03.1-34(2)	guardian, spouse, or next of kin, if known, or chosen friend 25-03.1-34(3)	ct. ordering hospitalization 25-03.1-34(3)	
OHIO Rev. Code Ann. (Baldwin 1980 & Supp. 1981)	mentally ill & developmen-tally disabled					chief of division or designee 5122.20 5123.21	consistent w/ medical needs; consent of pri-vate facility; due considera-tion to wishes of patient; maintenance of relationships & encouragement of visits 5122.20 5123.21	right to hearing if to more restrictive setting, or if patient refuses transfer 5122.20 5123.21	hospital, clinical facility, or other facility offering treatment or services 5122.20 5123.21			guardian, parents, spouse, & counsel, or nearest known relative or friend; custodian of minor fn. 2 5122.20 5123.21		
OKLA. Stat. Ann. (West 1979 & Supp. 1981)	mentally ill & mentally retarded	43A, §188	attending physician, per-son in charge of private facili-ty, relative, or guardian 43A, §188	superintendent of state hospital serving patient's county 43A, §188	from a private institution to a state or federal hospital 43A, §188	director of mental health 43A, §62	agreement be-tween director & board of con-trol of neuro-psychiatric unit 43A, §62		to an institu-tion w/in dep't from neuro-psychiatric unit 43A, §62		43A, §72		committing ct., if transferred to federal facility 43A, §72	
OR. Rev. Stat. (1981)	mentally ill					mental health division 426.060(3) community mental health program director 426.060(4)	for good cause & in best interest of patient 426.060(3) pursuant to rules adopted by division 426.060(4)		another facility 426.060(3) 426.060(4)					
	mentally retarded					the division 427.300(2) community mental health program director 427.300(3)	for good cause & in person's best interest 427.300(2) pursuant to rules adopted by division 427.300(3)	right to appeal before state training center review board 427.300(2)	another facility 427.300(2)			parent, guardian, or person entitled to custody 427.300(2)		
PA. Stat. Ann. (Purdon 1969 & Supp. 1980)	mentally ill					not stated: "may be trans-ferred" 50, §7306(a)	hearing if dis-trict attorney objects 50, §7306(b)	hearing before judge or review officer if transfer consti-tutes greater restraint 50, §7306(c) no transfer of voluntary patient w/o written consent 50, §7207	any approved facility 50, §7306(a)		mental disability 50, §4415		district attorney, committing judge 50, §7306(b)	50, §7306(b)
	mentally retarded, mentally disabled		director of any state-operated facility 50, §4416(a) director of any local facility 50, §4416(a) administrator 50, §4416(b) dep't 50, §4416(c)	dep't 50, §4416(a) administrator 50, §4416(a) dep't 50, §4416(b) administrator 55, §4416(c) committing ct. 50, §4416(d)	any state-oper-ated facility; any local facili-ty; local to state; or state to local 50, §4416(a)–(d)						mental disability 50, §4415	person desig-nated in appli-cation 50, §4416(e)		

TABLE 4.1 TRANSFERS OF MENTALLY DISABLED PERSONS—*Continued*

STATE	TYPE OF DISABILITY (1)	TRANSFER UPON PETITION: Petition by: Patient (2)	Other (3)	Approval by (4)	Place of Transfer (5)	TRANSFER AT ADMINISTRATIVE DISCRETION: By Whom (6)	Condition or Criteria (7)	Patient's Right to Object (8)	Place of Transfer (9)	PROVISIONS FOR TRANSFER BETWEEN MENTAL ILLNESS & MENTAL RETARDATION FACILITIES (10)	PROVISIONS FOR TRANSFER TO FEDERAL PROGRAM OR FACILITY (11)	NOTICE OF TRANSFER: Guardian, Spouse, or Relative (12)	Other (13)	PROVISIONS RELATING TO EMERGENCY TRANSFER (14)
R.I. Gen. Laws (1977 & Supp. 1981)	mental disability					director of transferring facility or designee 40.1-5-32(5)	patient unwilling or unable to pay expenses of facility, in need of immediate care & treatment, & unsupervised presence in community would create imminent likelihood of serious harm 40.1-5-32(5)	consent required unless all criteria met 40.1-5-32(3)	another facility w/in state 40.1-5-32(5)		40.1-5-32(2)			
	insane		trustees of Butler Hospital 40.1-5.1-4	director of mental health, retardation, & hospitals 40.1-5.1-4	from Butler to state hospital for mental diseases 40.1-5.1-4						40.1-5.2-24			
	mentally retarded		person in charge of any state-operated facility fn. 3 40.1-22-18(1), (7) 40.1-22-18(4)	director or designee 40.1-22-18(1), (7) consent of voluntary client 40.1-22-18(3) hearing if no consent 40.1-22-18(6)	any other facility 40.1-22-18(1),						40.1-22-18(2)			
S.C. Code Ann. (Law. Co-op. 1976 & Supp. 1981)	mentally ill & mentally retarded		guardian, parent, spouse, relative, or friend 44-23-210(5)	dep't of mental health fn. 4 44-23-210(5)	another facility 44-23-210(5)	superintendent of facility 44-23-210(4)	consistent w/ medical needs 44-23-210(4)	hearing if to more secure facility 44-23-210(4)	another facility 44-23-210(4)	44-23-210	44-27-30	guardian, attorney, parents or spouse, or nearest known relative, or friend 44-23-210(4) 44-27-30	committing ct. 44-27-30	
S.D. Codified Laws Ann. (1976 & Supp. 1982)	mentally ill					administator of human services center 27A-4-14 board of mental illness of any county 27A-9-24	would benefit from treatment received there 27A-4-14 under board-ordered treatment outside human services center 27A-9-24		veterans' hospital, other private facility, or the mental health center for county where commitment originated 27A-4-14 human services center 27A-9-24					
	mentally retarded					board of charities & corrections 27A-4-13 division of mental health & mental retardation 27B-3-12	not mentally ill but mentally retarded best interest of resident; approval by administrators of sending & receiving facilities 28B-3-10	division directed to consult with immediate family 27B-3-12	from human services center to Redfield State Hospital & School 27A-4-13 any other facility or to state-operated hospital 27B-3-10	27A-4-13		nearest relative or guardian 27A-4-13 27B-3-11	2 persons designated by resident 27A-4-13 27B-3-11	notice w/in 24 hrs. thereafter 27B-3-11 27A-4-13
TENN. Code Ann. (1977 & Supp. 1982)	mentally ill & mentally retarded	"upon proper application" 33-309(d)	"upon proper application" 33-309(d)	sending & receiving facilities 33-309(d)	from (to) a state facility to (from) an accredited private facility 33-309(d)	commissioner 33-309(a) upon superintendent's recommendation 33-309(b)(1)	maintaining relationships; encouraging beneficial visits 33-309(a) better care & treatment elsewhere, in person's best interest, &, if to a more secure facility, substantially likely to injure self or others 33-309(b)	petition for review 33-309(b)(3), (4)	another facility of dep't 33-309(b)	33-309		spouse or parent or adult child & guardian 33-309(b)(2)	committing ct. 33-309(a), (d)	33-309(c)

TABLE 4.1 TRANSFERS OF MENTALLY DISABLED PERSONS—*Continued*

STATE	TYPE OF DISABILITY (1)	TRANSFER UPON PETITION: Petition by: Patient (2)	Other (3)	Approval by (4)	Place of Transfer (5)	TRANSFER AT ADMINISTRATIVE DISCRETION: By Whom (6)	Condition or Criteria (7)	Patient's Right to Object (8)	Place of Transfer (9)	PROVISIONS FOR TRANSFER BETWEEN MENTAL ILLNESS & MENTAL RETARDATION FACILITIES (10)	PROVISIONS FOR TRANSFER TO FEDERAL PROGRAM OR FACILITY (11)	NOTICE OF TRANSFER: Guardian, Spouse, or Relative (12)	Other (13)	PROVISIONS RELATING TO EMERGENCY TRANSFER (14)
TEX. Rev. Civ. Stat. Ann. (Vernon 1958 & Supp. 1981)	mentally ill	5547-74(a)	guardian or friend 5547-74(a)	agreement by head of receiving facility 5547-74(b)	private mental hospital 5547-74	board 5547-73(a) head of private mental hospital 5547-73(b)	whenever deemed advisable 5547-73(a) "for any reason" if patient involuntary 5547-73(b)	consent of voluntary patient required 5547-73(a)	another state mental hospital 5547-73(a) a state mental hospital designated by board 5547-73(b)	5547-75A	5547-75		committing ct. 5547-75 5547-74(c)	
	mentally retarded	5547-300, §40	parent of minor or guardian 5547-300, §40	service provider; administrative hearing if request denied 5547-300, §§40, 41	another facility 5547-300, §40	service provider 5547-300, §39	facility no longer appropriate to needs, or better treatment & habilitation elsewhere 5547-300, §39 prior approval & knowledge of parents or guardian 5547-300, §41(b)	right to administrative hearing 5547-300, §41(a)	another facility 5547-300 §39			parent or guardian 5547-300, §42		5547-300, §38
UTAH Code Ann. (1978 & Supp. 1981)	mentally ill					Utah State Hospital 64-7-3 division of mental health 64-7-41	in need of careful evaluation or treatment at Utah State Hospital, & in interest of person 64-7-3 careful evaluation shows transfer in interest of patient 64-7-41		from any other institution w/in dep't 64-7-3 another mental health facility 64-7-41			guardian, parents, spouse, or nearest known relative or friend 64-7-41		
	mentally retarded					division of family services 64-8-6	when evaluation indicates in person's interest 64-8-6(11), (12)		between Utah State Training School & any other institution of division 64-8-6(11), (12)					
VT. Stat. Ann. (1968 & Supp. 1982)	mentally ill					commissioner 18, §7901	consistent w/ medical needs 18, §7901 maintaining relationships & encouraging beneficial visits; separation of functions & purposes of facilities 18, §7901		between: Vt. state hospital, Brattleboro Retreat, designated hospitals, & training school fn. 5 18, §7901	18, §7901	18, §7903	attorney, guardian, spouse, parents 18, §7901	other interested party 18, §7901	
VA. Code. (1976 & Supp. 1982)	mentally ill & mentally retarded					commissioner 37.1-48 37.1-78.1			any other facility 37.1-48 37.1-78.1	37-1-48	37.1-93			
WASH. Rev. Code Ann. (1982 & Supp. 1982)	mentally ill					dep't 72.23.290	best interests of the patients concerned 72.23.290		among the various state hospitals 72.23.290		72.23.290			
W. VA. Code (1980 & Supp. 1982)	mentally ill, mentally retarded, or alcoholic										27-5-7			
WIS. Stat. Ann. (West 1957 & Supp. 1981)	mentally ill, developmentally disabled, or drug dependent					treatment staff or visiting physician upon periodic reevaluation 51.20(17)	sufficient progress to be entitled to less restrictive facility 51.20(17)		less restrictive facility 51.20(17)				board & committing ct. 51.20(17)	

TABLE 4.1 TRANSFERS OF MENTALLY DISABLED PERSONS—*Continued*

STATE	TYPE OF DISABILITY (1)	TRANSFER UPON PETITION				TRANSFER AT ADMINISTRATIVE DISCRETION				PROVISIONS FOR TRANSFER BETWEEN MENTAL ILLNESS & MENTAL RETARDATION FACILITIES (10)	PROVISIONS FOR TRANSFER TO FEDERAL PROGRAM OR FACILITY (11)	NOTICE OF TRANSFER		PROVISIONS RELATING TO EMERGENCY TRANSFER (14)
		Petition by												
		Patient (2)	Other (3)	Approval by (4)	Place of Transfer (5)	By Whom (6)	Condition or Criteria (7)	Patient's Right to Object (8)	Place of Transfer (9)			Guardian, Spouse, or Relative (12)	Other (13)	
WYO. Stat. (1977 & Supp. 1982)	mentally ill					hospital 25-3-119(a)	best interest of patient 25-3-119(a)	25-3-119 (b)(ii)	another hospital 25-3-119(a)			person responsible for care & custody 25-3-119(b)	ct. 25-3-119(b)	
	mentally retarded					superintendent of training school 9-6-665	appropriate for welfare of resident (temporary care & treatment) 9-6-665	consent of resident & parents or guardian required, or leave of ct. if involuntarily committed 9-6-665	any public or private hospital, institution or residence 9-6-665			parents or guardian 9-6-665	ct., if involuntarily committed 9-6-665	9-6-665

FOOTNOTES: TABLE 4.1

1. Cal. Welf. & Inst. Code § 7304 (West 1972 & Supp. 1981). New adjudication where county seeks to absolve itself of financial liability for patient transferred to state facility in different county.

2. Ohio Rev. Code Ann. § 5122.20 (Baldwin 1980 & Supp. 1981): "Whenever a consenting voluntary patient is transferred, such notification shall be given only at the patient's request." See also id. § 5123.21 ("Resident").

3. R.I. Gen. Laws. § 40.1-22-18(4) (1977 & Supp. 1981): "Transfer from a private facility may only be had with the additional consent or request of the client, guardian, a responsible relative, nearest available friend, or the director."

4. S.C. Code Ann. § 44-23-210(5) (Law. Co-op. 1976 & Supp. 1981): "[U]nless the Department of Mental Health reasonably determines that it would be inconsistent with the medical needs of the person, the transfer shall be made. If the transfer is from a less restricted to a substantially more secure facility, the provisions of paragraph (4) of this section shall govern."

5. Vt. Stat. Ann. tit. 18, § 7901 (1968 & Supp. 1982): "No person may be transferred to a designated hospital unless the head of the hospital or his designee first accepts the patient."

TABLE 4.2 SPECIAL RESIDENCE PROVISIONS APPLICABLE TO INSTITUTIONALIZATION AND DEPORTATION OF MENTALLY DISABLED PERSONS

	ESTABLISHMENT OF RESIDENCE										
STATE	Residence Defined (1)	Time Not Counted (2)	Procedure (3)	Residence Lost by Establishing Residence Elsewhere (4)	ACCEPTANCE OF RESIDENT INSTITUTIONALIZED ELSEWHERE (5)	TREATMENT OF NONRESIDENT (6)	RETURN OF NONRESIDENT TO PLACE OF RESIDENCE (7)	RECIPROCAL INTERSTATE TRANSFER AGREEMENTS AUTHORIZED (8)	UNIFORM ACT FOR EXTRADITION OF PERSONS OF UNSOUND MIND (9)	INTERSTATE COMPACT ON MENTAL HEALTH (10)	SPECIAL PROVISIONS FOR ALIENS (11)
ALA. Code (1977 & Supp. 1982)										22-55-1	
ALAS. Stat. (1979)	person residing state 47.30.340(13)		finding by superior ct. 47.30.070(j)			if hospital head certifies as mentally ill & dangerous or in need of immediate custody & treatment & unable to make responsible decisions re hospitalization 47.30.170(a)		reciprocal treatment agreements also authorized 47.30.170	47.30.410–460	47.30.180	
ARIZ. Rev. Stat. Ann. (1974 & Supp. 1980)											
ARK. Stat. Ann. (1971 & Supp. 1981)					admission to state facility 59-1419					59-801	
CAL. Welf. & Inst. Code (West 1972 & Supp. 1982)	1 yr. continuous residence & adult 4120 minor: 1 yr. continuous residence of parent, guardian, or conservator 4120	time spent in public institution or on leave of absence therefrom; residence not lost by military service 4120		4120	4119		prompt & humane; may defer return for medical reasons 4119	4119			cooperation w/U.S. Bureau of Immigration in arranging deportation of aliens in any state hospitals 4118
COLO. Rev. Stat. (1982)										24-60-1001	
CONN. Gen. Stat. Ann. (West 1975 & Supp. 1980)						30-day admission of indigent 17-293(b) commitment authorized 17-177(a)		transporta- of indigents 17-293(a)		17-258	
DEL. Code Ann. (1974 & Supp. 1982)						if able to pay 16, §5129(a)				16, §6101	
D.C. Code Ann. (1981 & Supp. 1982)	1 yr. immediately prior to filing of commitment petition 21-551(b)						if institution in state of residence willing to accept 21-551(a)			6-1601	
FLA. Stat. Ann. (West 1973 & Supp. 1982)	1 yr. continuously, immediately preceding 394.477				accepted for examination 394.475	pending transfer 394.477 treatment facility shall retain any nonresident who cannot be transferred, w/ approval of dep't of health & rehabilitative services 394.477			941.38–941.42	394.479	
GA. Code Ann. (1978 & Supp. 1982)	legal resident of state 88-501(j)				hospitalized 5 days for examination 88-507.8	as voluntary, paying patient 88-507.3	88-507.3			99-3801 to 3817	
HAWAII Rev. Stat. Ann. (1976 & Supp. 1982)	1 yr. continuous residence or minor child of resident 336-3	time in public institution or on parole therefrom 336-3		336-3	336-2		336-2	return of public charges 336-2	337-337-4	339-1	cooperation w/federal government in arranging for deportation 336-1 may be released to return to native country on condition of remaining away from Hawaii 336-5
IDAHO Code (1980 & Supp. 1981)	"the place where the mentally ill person lives" 66-325	time spent in facility 66-325								66-1201	
ILL. Ann. Stat. (Smith-Hurd 1966 & Supp. 1983)					91½, §5-102	admission subject to laws of Ill. or state w/jurisdiction over patient 91½, §5-102	if arrangements made to receive patient 91½, §5-102	91½, §5-102	91½, §§121–126	91½, §50-1	

TABLE 4.2 SPECIAL RESIDENCE PROVISIONS APPLICABLE TO INSTITUTIONALIZATION AND DEPORTATION OF MENTALLY DISABLED PERSONS—*Continued*

	ESTABLISHMENT OF RESIDENCE										
STATE	Residence Defined (1)	Time Not Counted (2)	Procedure (3)	Residence Lost by Establishing Residence Elsewhere (4)	ACCEPTANCE OF RESIDENT INSTITUTIONALIZED ELSEWHERE (5)	TREATMENT OF NONRESIDENT (6)	RETURN OF NONRESIDENT TO PLACE OF RESIDENCE (7)	RECIPROCAL INTERSTATE TRANSFER AGREEMENTS AUTHORIZED (8)	UNIFORM ACT FOR EXTRADITION OF PERSONS OF UNSOUND MIND (9)	INTERSTATE COMPACT ON MENTAL HEALTH (10)	SPECIAL PROVISIONS FOR ALIENS (11)
IND. Code Ann. (Burns 1973 & Supp. 1982)	1 yr. continuously, immediately prior to application 16-14-10-1		investigation by commissioner if patient believed to be nonresident 16-14-10-3		admission pending commitment 16-14-10-5	if legal settlement cannot be ascertained or because of peculiar circumstances 16-14-10-1	unless impracticable 16-14-10-3	16-14-10-4	other extradition provision 16-14-10-1 16-13-9-1 to -5		
IOWA Code Ann. (West 1969 & Supp. 1983)			determined by ct. when patient found mentally ill 230.2			hospitalized in state hospital 230.5 ct. approval required for involuntary hospitalization 230.7	if condition permits & transfer not inadvisable 230.7			218A.1	
KAN. Stat. Ann. (1981)	1 yr. continuously, prior to application 39-111 minor: same residence as parents 39-111		listed in application for determination of mentally ill person, if known 59-29132			residence requirement for state hospital may be waived if residence unknown or medical emergency requires 39-111	if arrangements made to receive patient 39-110	agreements for arbitration of disuted residence questions 39-110		65-3101	
KY. Rev. Stat. Ann. (Michie 1982)							210.350		other extradition provision 210.340	210.520	
LA. Rev. Stat. Ann. (West 1975 & Supp. 1983)							may return 28:103	28:103	28:501–28:506	28:721	
ME. Rev. Stat. Ann. (1978 & Supp. 1983)										34, §2561	
MD. Ann. Code (1978)									42, §§23–28	41, §§319–334	
MASS. Ann. Laws (Michie/Law. Co-op. 1981 & Supp. 1982)									other extradition provision 123, §20	123, §1	
MICH. Comp. Laws Ann. (1980 & Supp. 1983)										330.1920	
MINN. Stat. Ann. (West 1982 & Supp. 1983)										245.51	
MISS. Code Ann. (1981 & Supp. 1982)							if arrangements made to receive patient 41-21-91				
MO. Ann. Stat. (Vernon 1979 & Supp. 1983)							if arrangements made to receive patient 630.805.1	630.805.2		630.810	
MONT. Code Ann. (1981)						up to 30 days pending return 53-21-134				53-22-101	
NEB. Rev. Stat. (1981 & Supp. 1981)						may be accepted on same terms as private pay patients; must make quarterly payment in advance 83-355				83-801	
NEV. Rev. Stat. (1979)	domicile, place last employed, or place where made home or headquarters 433.434				admission to state facility 433.444(1)			433.444(1)			
N.H. Rev. Stat. Ann. (1978)								indigent insane 135:37		135A:1	

TABLE 4.2 SPECIAL RESIDENCE PROVISIONS APPLICABLE TO INSTITUTIONALIZATION AND DEPORTATION OF MENTALLY DISABLED PERSONS—*Continued*

	ESTABLISHMENT OF RESIDENCE										
STATE	Residence Defined (1)	Time Not Counted (2)	Procedure (3)	Residence Lost by Establishing Residence* Elsewhere (4)	ACCEPTANCE OF RESIDENT INSTITUTIONALIZED ELSEWHERE (5)	TREATMENT OF NONRESIDENT (6)	RETURN OF NONRESIDENT TO PLACE OF RESIDENCE (7)	RECIPROCAL INTERSTATE TRANSFER AGREEMENTS AUTHORIZED (8)	UNIFORM ACT FOR EXTRADITION OF PERSONS OF UNSOUND MIND (9)	INTERSTATE COMPACT ON MENTAL HEALTH (10)	SPECIAL PROVISIONS FOR ALIENS (11)
N.J. Stat. Ann. (West 1981 & Supp. 1983)	continuous residence 1 yr. immediately preceding commitment application 30:4-51 minor: residence that of parents 30:4-49.2, 30:4-49.3 unless employed & independent or married male living away from parents 30:4-49.4 wife: residence that of husband 30:4-49.1	time in institution or residence of family while inmate of institution 30:4-51, 30:4-54 residence not lost by military service if inducted in N.J. 30:4-49.6		continuous absence 1 yr. 30:4-49.6		may be committed in same manner as resident 30:4-31 commitment to state institution pending return 30:4-52	30:4-53			30-7B-1	
N.M. Stat. Ann. (1978 & Supp. 1982)										11-7-1	
N.Y. Mental Hyg. Law (McKinney 1978 & Supp. 1983)	1 yr. continuous residence by patient or, if patient under 16 or mentally retarded, by parent or person having legal custody 67.03(a)	military service not counted toward establishment or loss of residence 67.03(b), (c)		1-yr. absence 67.03(a)			unless agreement provides otherwise or would be undue hardship to patient or family 67.05(b)	agreements for return or treatment of nonresidents 67.05(a)		67.07	reported to federal authorities 67.01
N.C. Gen. Stat. (1981 & Supp. 1981)		residence while mentally ill, inebriate, or under care insufficient to establish residence 122-37	clerk of ct. inquires into residence upon examination proceedings 122-37		admission for 30 days of observation & treatment 122-40	hospitalized in state institution pending return 122-38		122-39		122-99	clerk of ct. promptly notifies governor, who notifies secretary of state w/request to notify representative of patient's country 122-40.1
N.D. Cent. Code (1978 & Supp. 1981)			supervising dep't inquires into residence of one not known to be resident 25-09-10.1			admitted in same manner as resident 25-09-10.1 may be admitted upon payment of full cost of treatment, but not to exclusion of resident 25-02-06	25-09-10.1	25-09.10.1		25-11-01	
OHIO Rev. Code Ann. (Baldwin 1980)										5119.50	
OKLA. Stat. Ann. (West 1979 & Supp. 1983)			director of mental health keeps list of nonresidents 43A, §14.12		admission w/o further proceedings 43A, §59		director of mental health to make "every effort possible" to arrange for transfer 43A, §14.12 43A, §71			43A, §501	
OR. Rev. Stat. (1981)	1 yr. continuous residence 428.210(6)	time spent in hospital or on parole therefrom 428.220(1)(a)		428.210(6)	admission to state hospital 428.230 (2), (3)	physically present in Or. & in need of institutionalization 428.205 may authorize admission of those whose residence cannot be established or of nonresident in sufficient circumstances 428.220(2) (b)	428.230(1)	428.240		428.310	
PA. Stat. Ann. (Purdon 1968 & Supp. 1982)											
R.I. Gen. Laws Ann. (1977 & Supp. 1982)										40.1-9-1	

TABLE 4.2 SPECIAL RESIDENCE PROVISIONS APPLICABLE TO INSTITUTIONALIZATION AND DEPORTATION OF MENTALLY DISABLED PERSONS—*Continued*

STATE	ESTABLISHMENT OF RESIDENCE				ACCEPTANCE OF RESIDENT INSTITUTIONALIZED ELSEWHERE (5)	TREATMENT OF NONRESIDENT (6)	RETURN OF NONRESIDENT TO PLACE OF RESIDENCE (7)	RECIPROCAL INTERSTATE TRANSFER AGREEMENTS AUTHORIZED (8)	UNIFORM ACT FOR EXTRADITION OF PERSONS OF UNSOUND MIND (9)	INTERSTATE COMPACT ON MENTAL HEALTH (10)	SPECIAL PROVISIONS FOR ALIENS (11)
	Residence Defined (1)	Time Not Counted (2)	Procedure (3)	Residence Lost by Establishing Residence Elsewhere (4)							
S.C. Code Ann. (Law. Co-op. 1977 & Supp. 1982)	1 yr. consecutive residence 44-23-10(26)	time in institutions, on parole, or on unauthorized absence therefrom or during military service 44-23-10(26)		44-23-10(26)	admission to state facility 44-13-20	residence requirement may be waived for hardship 44-13-30	unless admitted under interstate compact or supplementary agreement 44-13-30		other extradition provision 44-13-50	44-25-10 44-25-20	federal authorities notified; treatment pending deportation 44-13-40
S.D. Codified Laws Ann. (1976 & Supp. 1982)			attorney general investigates residence upon claim by county that patient improperly charged to it 27A-13-18			charge against state until returned to state of residence 27A-13-19			27A-11-1 to 27A-11-8	27A-6-1	
TENN. Code Ann. (1977 & Supp. 1982)	60 days continuous residence 33-302(h)	time in public institutions or on leave of absence therefrom 33-302(h)		33-302(h)			33-1101		33-1001 to 33-1011	33-1501	
TEX. Rev. Civ. Stat. Ann. (Vernon 1958 & Supp. 1983)	1 yr. continuously 5547-4(n)	time spent in public institution or on furlough therefrom 5547-4(n)		5547-4(n)	5547-16(b)		5547-16	5547-17		5561f	
UTAH Code Ann. (1978 & Supp. 1981)						may be returned to hospital in state or home of relatives or friends; temporary care; admission may be approved by director of division of mental health upon recommendation if in best interest of patient & family 64-7-14					
VT. Stat. Ann. (1968 & Supp. 1982)	1 yr. continuous residence prior to admission or becoming proposed patient 18, §7101 (18)(A) or present intention to make Vt. home for indefinite period 18, §7101 (18)(B)					transfer into Vt. facility to be near relatives or friends—at commissioner's discretion 18, §7902(b)		commissioner may enter into contracts for treatment in other states 18, §7401(6)	18, §§9101–9105	18, §§9001–9014	
VA. Code (1976 & Supp. 1982)	bona fide resident 37.1-1(12)					same proceedings as if resident 37.1-91 may be admitted as paying patient, if no resident excluded thereby 37.1-107	if expedient, as soon as practicable 37.1-91		37.1-172–37.1-178		U.S. immigraation officer notified 37.1-92
WASH. Rev. Code Ann. (1982 & Supp. 1982)	domiciliary residence maintained for 1 yr. preceding commitment w/o receiving assistance from any tax-supported organization 72.25.020	time while inmate of hospital or institution or on parole, escape, or leave of absence therefrom 72.25.020		72.25.020	admission w/o further proceedings; superintendent of institution may discharge or file commitment application w/in 90 days 72.25.020		72.25.020	72.25.020		72.27.010	arrangement w/U.S. Dep't of Interior or Bureau of Immigration for deportation 72.25.010
W. VA. Code Ann. (1980)	residency established for 1 yr. 27-1-8						subject to compact 27-5-4(p)			27-14-1	

TABLE 4.2 SPECIAL RESIDENCE PROVISIONS APPLICABLE TO INSTITUTIONALIZATION AND DEPORTATION OF MENTALLY DISABLED PERSONS—*Continued*

STATE	ESTABLISHMENT OF RESIDENCE: Residence Defined (1)	Time Not Counted (2)	Procedure (3)	Residence Lost by Establishing Residence Elsewhere (4)	ACCEPTANCE OF RESIDENT INSTITUTIONALIZED ELSEWHERE (5)	TREATMENT OF NONRESIDENT (6)	RETURN OF NONRESIDENT TO PLACE OF RESIDENCE (7)	RECIPROCAL INTERSTATE TRANSFER AGREEMENTS AUTHORIZED (8)	UNIFORM ACT FOR EXTRADITION OF PERSONS OF UNSOUND MIND (9)	INTERSTATE COMPACT ON MENTAL HEALTH (10)	SPECIAL PROVISIONS FOR ALIENS (11)
WIS. Stat. Ann. (West 1957 & Supp. 1983)	"the voluntary concurrence of physical presence with intent to remain in a place of fixed habitation. physical presence shall be prima facie evidence of intent to remain" 49.10(12)(c) 51.01(14)					committed to dep't 51.20(13)(a)5			other extradition provision 51.38 51.81–51.85	51.75	
WYO. Stat. Ann. (1982)					25-10-124(a)	board may enter contract for hospitalization of nonresident in Wyo. state hospital when in best interest of state & patient 25-10-124(a)	25-10-124(a)	board may enter contract for hospitalization of resident in another state when in best interest of person & state 25-10-124 (a), (b)		25-10-301	

TABLE 4.3 ADMINISTRATIVE DISCHARGE OF INVOLUNTARILY CONFINED MENTALLY ILL PERSONS

	DISCHARGING AGENCY		ABSOLUTE DISCHARGE—CRITERIA				CONDITIONAL DISCHARGE			NOTICE OF DISCHARGE TO		
STATE	Institution (1)	Central Agency (2)	No Longer Dangerous to or Likely to Injure Self or Others (3)	No Longer Requires Treatment (4)	No Longer Meets Criteria (5)	No Longer Mentally Ill (6)	Provision for Conditional Discharge (7)	Period of Conditional Discharge (8)	Adminis-trative Return (9)	Central Agency (10)	Court (11)	Relative, Friend, or Guardian (12)
ALA. Code (1975 & Supp. 1981)												
ALAS. Stat. (1979 & Supp. 1981)	47.30.780		47.30.780				conditional on receipt of outpatient care 47.30.795		47.30.795(c)		47.30.780	
ARIZ. Rev. Stat. Ann. (1974 & Supp. 1981)	36-543A		or no longer gravely disabled 36-543A *fn. 1*								36-543B	
ARK. Stat. Ann. (1971 & Supp. 1981)												
CAL. Welf. & Inst. Code (West 1972 & Supp. 1982)	5254, 5305, 7105		5305	7105		improved sufficiently to leave 5254	5258				5305	conservator 5359
COLO. Rev. Stat. (1973 & Supp. 1981)	professional in charge of treatment 27-10-110(1)			has received sufficient benefit from treatment to leave 27-10-110(1)			night care, day care, or other prior to termination 27-10-110(1)				27-10-110(1)	
CONN. Gen. Stat. Ann. (West 1977 & Supp. 1982)	17-191						placement in boarding home or convalescent hospital 17-191		17-191			
DEL. Code Ann. (1974 & Supp. 1980)	*fn. 2* 16-5009 16, §5131					*fn. 2* 16, §§5009, 5131	convalescent status *fn. 2* 16, §5131(c)	annual review *fn. 2* 16, §5131(d)	*fn. 2* 16, §5132		16, §5009	
D.C. Code Ann. (1981 & Supp. 1982)	*fn. 3* 21-546 21-548		if reexami-nation requested 21-546		21-548							
FLA. Stat. (West 1973 & Supp. 1982)	394.469				*fn. 1* 394.469		convalescent status 394.469(3)	one yr. 394.469(3)	394.469(3)		394.469(2), (3)	394.469(2), (3)
GA. Code Ann. (1979 & Supp. 1980)	88-506.6(b)			88-506.6(b)	defined 88-501(v) *fn. 1* 88-506.6(b)						88-506.6(b)	representa-tives 88-506.6(b)
HAWAII Rev. Stat. (1976 & Supp. 1981)	or physician responsible for patient 334-76				334-76					those specified in commitment order 334-76	those specified in commitment order 334-76	those specified in commitment order 334-76
IDAHO Code (1980 & Supp. 1981)		66-337	66-337(b)		66-337	66-337(b)	receipt of outpatient care or other 66-338	reexamine after 1 yr. 66-338(a)	*fn. 4* 66-339		66-337(a)	66.337(a)
ILL. Ann. Stat. (Smith-Hurd 1966 & Supp. 1980)	91½, §3-902				no longer subject to to involuntary admission *fn. 1* 91½, §3-902(b)		temporary release 91½, §3-902(e)				and state's attorney, if patient regarded as continuing threat to community 91½, §3-902(d)	91½, §3-903(a)
IND. Code Ann. (Burns 1973 & Supp. 1981)	superin-tendent 16-14-16-2			whenever mental & physical con-dition of patient justifies discharge 16-14-16-2			convalescent leave 16-14-16-2				16-14-9.1-18 16-14-15-3 16-14-16-3	
IOWA Code Ann. (West 1969 & Supp. 1981)	chief medical officer 229.16	state director 226.18	state director: can be cared for w/o dan-ger to others & benefit to patient 226.18	facility OR 229.16		state director 226.18	convalescent leave 229.15(4) 226.23	state director: one yr. 226.23			229.15(4) 229.16	
KAN. Stat. Ann. (1976 & Supp. 1981)	59-2924 head of facility			59-2924			convalescent status 59-2924	treatment reexamined annually 59-2924	59-2924		59-2925	patient & attorney 59-2925
KY. Rev. Stat. Ann. (Michie 1977 & Supp. 1980)	authorized staff physician 202A.171				202A.171		convalescent status 202A.181		202A.181		notice of convalescent status 202A.181	

TABLE 4.3 ADMINISTRATIVE DISCHARGE OF INVOLUNTARILY CONFINED MENTALLY ILL PERSONS—*Continued*

	DISCHARGING AGENCY		ABSOLUTE DISCHARGE—CRITERIA				CONDITIONAL DISCHARGE			NOTICE OF DISCHARGE TO		
STATE	Institution (1)	Central Agency (2)	No Longer Dangerous to or Likely to Injure Self or Others (3)	No Longer Requires Treatment (4)	No Longer Meets Criteria (5)	No Longer Mentally Ill (6)	Provision for Conditional Discharge (7)	Period of Conditional Discharge (8)	Adminis-trative Return (9)	Central Agency (10)	Court (11)	Relative, Friend, or Guardian (12)
LA. Rev. Stat. Ann. (West 1975 & Supp. 1981)	public 28:96 private 28:96.1	28:97	sufficiently recovered & no harm will result 28:96A 28:96.1A	should no longer be detained 28:97			conditional discharge 28:56(G) convalescent status 28:100.1	one yr. con-ditional discharge 28:56(G) annual review of con-valescent status 28:100.1	28:56(G) 28:100.1		28:56(G)	28:96(F) 28:96.1(D) 28:97
ME. Rev. Stat. Ann. (1978 & Supp. 1981)	34, §2374				34, §2374		convalescent status 34, §2375		34, §2375	34, §2374		34, §§2374, 2375
MD. Ann. Code (1979 & Supp. 1981)	59, §18	59, §18	& patient or others able to provide care 59, §18 OR		for com-mitment	not mentally disordered 51, §18	conditional release 59, §18(b)	annual ex-amination 59, §§18(b), 12(e)		59, §20		
MASS. Ann. Laws (Michie/ Law. Co-op. 1981 & Supp. 1981)	public 123, §4			123, §4			interim community leave 123, §4					
MICH. Comp. Laws Ann. (1980 & Supp. 1981)	director of facility 330.1476			clinically suitable for discharge 330.1476(1) OR	330.1476(2)		leave or absence 330.1479	discharge after 1 yr. 330.1479	330.1408		330.1476(3) 330.1479	
MINN. Stat. Ann. (West 1971 & Supp. 1981)	hospital head 253A.15(1)	commissioner of public welfare, if committed as dangerous to public 253A.15(2)	can make acceptable adjustment to society, if committed as dangerous to public 253A.15(2)	253A.15(1)			provisional discharge 253A.15(1) 253A.15(2)	1 yr., unless extended 253A.15(4)	253A.15(7)	253A.15(11)	253A.15(9)	253A.15(11)
MISS. Code Ann. (1981)	director of state hospital 41-21-87		& can no longer benefit from treat-ment 41-21-87(b) OR	41-21-87(a)			convalescent status 41-21-87(c)	discretionary discharge after 1 yr. 41-21-87(c)			41-21-87	
MO. Ann. Stat. (Vernon 1979 & Supp. 1980)	632.385(1) 632.390(1)		632.390(1) OR			632.390(1)	conditional release to least restric-tive environ-ment 632.385		hearing, upon request 632.385(5)	mental health coordinator 632.390(2)	632.390(2) 632.385(3)	
MONT. Code Ann. (1981)	53-21-163 53-21-181				53-21-163		receipt of outpatient care 53-21-183	may not exceed period of commitment 53-21-183(1)	53-21-183(3)		53-21-181 53-21-183(5)	
NEB. Rev. Stat. (1976 & Supp. 1981)	state hospital 83-340	mental health board 83-1046	may be safely & properly dis-charged 83-340.01		83-1046	cured 83-340	convalescent leave 83.340.01 change to less restric-tive alterna-tive 83-1046			county board of mental health 83-340.01		
NEV. Rev. Stat. (1981)	evaluation team of 2 mental health professionals 433A.390(2)		& no longer gravely dis-abled 433A.390(2)(a) OR			433A.390(2)(a)	convalescent leave 433A.380				433A.390(2)(b)	
N.H. Rev. Stat. Ann. (1977 & Supp. 1981)	135-B:39(I)			135-B:39(I)							135-B:39	
N.J. Stat. Ann. (West 1981)	30:4-107		discharge in accordance with rules of board of managers or freeholders 30:4-107	discharge in accordance with rules of board of managers or freeholders 30:4-107	discharge in accordance with rules of board of managers or freeholders 30:4-107	discharge in accordance with rules of board of managers or freeholders 30:4-107	parole & parole in family care 30:4-107		30:4-107			
N.M. Stat. Ann. (1979 & Supp. 1982)	43-1-21						convalescent status 43-1-21	reexamine prior to end of com-mitment period 43-1-21	43-1-21			
N.Y. Mental Hyg. Law (McKinney 1978 & Supp. 1981)	29.15	29.11(g)	improperly detained in facility 29.11(g)	improperly detained in facility 29.11(g) 29.15	improperly detained in facility 29.11(g)	improperly detained in facility 29.11(g)	conditional release 29.15	remainder of authorized detention period 29.15(b)(1)	29.15(e)	*fn. 5* 29.15(n)		

TABLE 4.3 ADMINISTRATIVE DISCHARGE OF INVOLUNTARILY CONFINED MENTALLY ILL PERSONS—*Continued*

	DISCHARGING AGENCY		ABSOLUTE DISCHARGE—CRITERIA				CONDITIONAL DISCHARGE			NOTICE OF DISCHARGE TO		
STATE	Institution (1)	Central Agency (2)	No Longer Dangerous to or Likely to Injure Self or Others (3)	No Longer Requires Treatment (4)	No Longer Meets Criteria (5)	No Longer Mentally Ill (6)	Provision for Conditional Discharge (7)	Period of Conditional Discharge (8)	Administrative Return (9)	Central Agency (10)	Court (11)	Relative, Friend, or Guardian (12)
N.C. Gen. Stat. (1981 & Supp. 1981)	122-58.13(A)			no longer in need of hospitalization 122-58.13(A)			conditional release 122-58.13(A)	30 days 122-58.13(A)	122-58.13(A)		122-58.13(A)	
N.D. Cent. Code (1978 & Supp. 1981)	25-03.1-30	25-03.1-30			25-03.1-30(2)		less restrictive form of treatment, upon ct. order 25-03.1-30(6)				25-03.1-30(3)	
OHIO Rev. Code Ann. (Baldwin 1980 & Supp. 1981)	5122.21				5122.21(A)		trial visit 5122.22	90 days w/ 90-day extensions 5122.22	5122.22	public hospital notifies 5122.23	5122.21(B)	
OKLA. Stat. Ann. (West 1979 & Supp. 1981)	attending physician: private institution 43A, §186 43A, §73(G) 43A, §73		discharge OR not detrimental to public or injurious to patient 43A, §73 (A)(2), (G)	will not OR benefit from further treatment, if private institution 43A, §186(2)		recovered 43A, §§73 (A)(1), 186(1)	convalescent leave status 43A, §§73B, 186 transfer to outpatient status 43A, §73C	private & public: 12 mos. 43A, §73 (A)3, (G) private: 6 mos. 43A, §186			43A, §§73E, 186	
OR. Rev. Stat. Stat. (1981)		426.300(1)				*fn.* 6 426.300(1)	trial visit 426.280	up to 180 days 426.280	426.290		426.300(1)	
PA. Stat. Ann. (Purdon 1969 & Supp. 1980)	50, §7304(g)(3)			not severely mentally disabled & in need of treatment 50, §7304(g)(3)	defined: 50, §7304 (g)(3), (a)							
R.I. Gen. Laws (1977 & Supp. 1981)	40.1-5-11		40.1-5-11(1)(c) OR			40.1-5-11(1)(b)						
S.C. Code Ann. (Law. Co-op. 1976 & Supp. 1981)	44-17-820				44-17-820		conditional discharge upon approval & conditions of dep't of mental health 44-17-830			44-17-820	44-17-820 44-17-830	anyone who has requested notification 44-17-820
S.D. Codified Laws Ann. (1976 & Supp. 1981)	27A-14-2 27A-14-6				behavior no longer that that caused admission 27A-14-2 27A-14-6		provisional discharge 27A-14-2	not beyond original commitment period 27A-14-4		27A-14-3 27A-14-4	27A-14-6	
TENN. Code Ann. (1977 & Supp. 1981)	33-609(b) 33-609(d)				*fn.* 7 33-609(b) 33-609(d)						33-609(b) 33-609(d)	admission applicant 33-609(d)
TEX. Rev. Civ. Stat. Ann. (Vernon 1958 & Supp. 1981)	5547-80(a)			no longer requires hospitalization 5547-80(a)			furlough 5547-79	18 mos. 5547-80(b)	5547-79		5547-80(e)	
UTAH Code Ann. (1978 Supp. 1981)	64-7-42				64-7-42		conditional release of improved patient 64-7-43	exam after 1 yr. 64-7-43	64-7-43(2)	64-7-42	64-7-42	
VT. Stat. Ann. (1968 & Supp. 1981)	18, §§7802, 8009	board of mental health 18, §7802		not in need of further treatment 18, §§7802, 8009(b)			conditional discharge 18, §8007	*fn.* 8 6 mos.; may be extended 18, §8007	18, §8008		18, §8009(b)	*fn.* 9 18, §8009(b)
VA. Code (1976 & Supp. 1982)	37.1-98 37.1-99		discharge OR not detrimental to public or injurious to patient 37.1-98(A)(3) 37.1-99		not a proper OR case for treatment 37.1-98(A)(4) 37.1-99	or recovered 37.1-98(A)(1), (2) 37.1-99	convalescent status public: 37.1-98(B) private: 37.1-99					
WASH. Rev. Code Ann. (1962, 1975 & Supp. 1981)	71.05.330		71.05.330				conditional release w/out patient care 71.05.340	not to exceed period of commitment 71.05.340(1)	for 5 days before hearing for 71.05.340(3)		71.05.330 71.05.340(4) 72.23.180	state hospital 72.23.180
W. VA. Code (1980 & Supp. 1982)	27-7-1			can no OR longer benefit from treatment 27-7-1	27-7-1		convalescent status 27-7-2 *fn.* 10 release as unimproved 27-7-3	6 mos. 27-7-2	27-7-4		27-7-1 27-7-2 27-7-3	
WIS. Stat. Ann. (West 1957 & Supp. 1981)		51.35(4)(a), (b)			51.35(4)(a), (b)						51.35(4)(f)	

TABLE 4.3 ADMINISTRATIVE DISCHARGE OF INVOLUNTARILY CONFINED MENTALLY ILL PERSONS—*Continued*

STATE	DISCHARGING AGENCY		ABSOLUTE DISCHARGE—CRITERIA				CONDITIONAL DISCHARGE			NOTICE OF DISCHARGE TO		
	Institution (1)	Central Agency (2)	No Longer Dangerous to or Likely to Injure Self or Others (3)	No Longer Requires Treatment (4)	No Longer Meets Criteria (5)	No Longer Mentally Ill (6)	Provision for Conditional Discharge (7)	Period of Conditional Discharge (8)	Adminis-trative Return (9)	Central Agency (10)	Court (11)	Relative, Friend, or Guardian (12)
WYO. Stat. (1977 & Supp. 1981)	25-3-120				25-3-120		convalescent status 25-3-121	6 mos. 25-3-121(c)	25-3-121(b)	25-3-120(b)	25-3-120(b) 25-3-121(a)	25-3-120(b)

FOOTNOTES: TABLE 4.3

1. Ariz. Rev. Stat. Ann. § 36-543(A) (Supp. 1981). Discharge or transfer to voluntary status if requested. Also, Fla. Stat. Ann. § 394.469 (West Supp. 1981); Ga. Code Ann. § 88-506.6(b)(2) (1979); and Ill. Ann. Stat. ch. 91½, § 3-902(b) (Smith-Hurd Supp. 1980).

2. Del. Code Ann. tit. 16, §§ 5131-5132 (1974). Discharge provisions apply to persons admitted under 16-5125, which has been repealed. However, 16-5131 and 16-5132 have not been repealed.

3. D.C. Code Ann. § 21-546 (1981). Upon request of patient, attorney, legal guardian, spouse, parent, or other nearest adult relative for examination of mental condition.

4. Idaho Code §§ 66-339, -340 (Supp. 1981). Rehospitalization of patient conditionally released upon request of any two designated examiners, the prosecuting attorney, or a judge of court. Patient may appeal to court within 30 days.

5. N.Y. Mental Hyg. Law § 29.15(n) (McKinney Supp. 1981). The administrator of the facility shall notify when appropriate the local social services commissioner and the appropriate state and local mental health representatives of discharge or conditional release.

6. Or. Rev. Stat. § 426.300(1) (1981). Division may discharge a patient when no longer mentally ill or the transfer to voluntary status is in the best interest of treatment of the patient.

7. Tenn Code Ann. § 33-609 (Supp. 1981).

8. Vt. Stat. Ann. tit. 18, § 8007(b) (Supp. 1981). A conditional discharge may extend for 6 months but shall not exceed 60 days unless a longer period will materially improve the availability of a program of treatment which is an alternative to hospitalization.

9. Id. § 8009(b). Notice of discharge to certifying physician and anyone who was notified at the time the patient was hospitalized.

10. W. Va. Code § 27-7-3 (1980). Release as unimproved to responsible person. No discharge given until patient has returned to facility for examination and determination that patient is no longer in need of hospitalization.

TABLE 4.4 ADMINISTRATIVE DISCHARGE OF INVOLUNTARILY CONFINED DEVELOPMENTALLY DISABLED PERSONS

STATE	DISCHARGING AGENCY		ABSOLUTE DISCHARGE CRITERIA				CONDITIONAL DISCHARGE			NOTICE OF DISCHARGE TO			RIGHT TO OBJECT TO DISCHARGE (13)
	Institution (1)	Central Agency (2)	No Longer Dangerous to Self or Others (3)	No Longer Needs Residential Treatment or Care (4)	No Longer Meets Criteria for Commitment (5)	Not Mentally Retarded (6)	Provision for (7)	Period of Conditional Discharge (8)	Adminis-trative Return (9)	Central Agency (10)	Court (11)	Relative, Friend, or Guardian (12)	
ALA. Code (1975 & Supp. 1981)	*fn. 1* 22-52-57			22-52-57			placement on leave 22-52-57	such time as superintendent may prescribe 22-52-57	conditions of leave set by superintendent 22-52-57				
ALAS. Stat.													
ARIZ. Rev. Stat. Ann. (1974 & Supp. 1981)		36-565 36-566		program no longer appropriate to needs 36-565(B) client has necessary independent living skills 36-566(A)								client, parent, guardian 30 days notice 36-565(C)	client, parent, guardian right to administrative review 36-565(C)
ARK. Stat. Ann. (1971 & Supp. 1981)	discharge from Ark. Children's Colony: Superintendent 59-1109(b) AND	board 59-1109(b)			condition justifies discharge 59-1109(b)		permit to visit 59-1108	specified by permit 59-1108	59-1108		59-1109(b)		
CAL. Welf. & Inst. Code (West Supp. 1981)	7352.5, 7357, 7359, 7362 OR	7362	*fn. 2* 7359 7362(b) OR	*fn 2* 7362(a)	recovered 7357		leave of absence 7352.5			7357, 7359			
COLO. Rev. Stat. (1973 & Supp. 1981)	27-10.5-108			can no longer benefit from care & treatment 27-10.5-108						dep't of social services 27-10.5-108		person who made application for admission 27-10.5-108	
CONN. Gen. Stat. Ann. (1977)		commissioner of mental retardation 19-569l		patient will not profit from a further stay 19-569l									
DEL. Code Ann.													
D.C. Code Ann. (1981 & Supp. 1982)	director 6-1930			residential care no longer advisable 6-1930									*fn. 3*
FLA. Stat. Ann. (West 1973 & Supp. 1981)		Dep't of Health & Rehabilitative Services—hearing upon application of resident, parent, guardian, or dep't 393.115	*fn. 4* 393.115(b) OR	continued admission not essential *fn. 4* 393.115(b)									
GA. Code Ann. (1979 & Supp. 1980)	88-2508(b)			88-2508(b)							88-2508(b)	client & client's representatives 14 days prior to discharge 88-2508(b)	
HAWAII Rev. Stat. Ann. (1976 & Supp. 1981)		director of health (conditional release only) 333-31					& temporary leave 333-31	annual review temporary leave 120 days 333-31	333-31				
IDAHO Code													

TABLE 4.4 ADMINISTRATIVE DISCHARGE OF INVOLUNTARILY CONFINED DEVELOPMENTALLY DISABLED PERSONS—*Continued*

	DISCHARGING AGENCY		ABSOLUTE DISCHARGE CRITERIA				CONDITIONAL DISCHARGE			NOTICE OF DISCHARGE TO			
STATE	Institution (1)	Central Agency (2)	No Longer Dangerous to Self or Others (3)	No Longer Needs Residential Treatment or Care (4)	No Longer Meets Criteria for Commitment (5)	Not Mentally Retarded (6)	Provision for (7)	Period of Conditional Discharge (8)	Adminis-trative Return (9)	Central Agency (10)	Court (11)	Relative, Friend, or Guardian (12)	RIGHT TO OBJECT TO DISCHARGE (13)
ILL. Ann. Stat. (Smith-Hurd 1966 & Supp. 1980)	facility director 91½, §4-701(b)				91½, §4-701(b)		temporary release 4-701(d) 4-702	1 yr. unless extended for 1 more yr. 4-702(b)	w/consent of ct., if judicially admitted; or person who executed appli-cation, if administrative admission 4-702(c)		state's attorney of county in which client resided prior to admission 4-701(c)	client, if over 12, attorney, guardian, & applicant for initial admission 4-704(a)	client, attorney, guardian, & applicant for initial admis-sion hearing at facility upon objection 4-704
IND. Code Ann.													
IOWA Code Ann.													
KAN. Stat. Ann.													
KY. Rev. Stat. Ann. (Michie 1977 & Supp. 1980)	authorized staff physician 202B.020 202A.120		202A.120 202B.020 OR	can no longer benefit from treatment 202B.020 202A.120	OR	202B.020 202A.130	convalescent status 202B.020 202A.130		202B.020 202A.130		notice of convalescent status 202B.020 202A.130		
LA. Rev. Stat. Ann. (West 1975 & Supp. 1981)	superintendent (leaves of absence) 28:417	client place-ment division (only for dis-charge after 1 yr. leave) 28:414		discharge after 1 yr. leave w/o treatment 28:414			leave of absence 28:417	set by superintendent 28:417	28:417				closest relative, tutor, or offi-cial advocate 28:412
ME. Rev. Stat. Ann. (1964 & Supp. 1981)	interdisci-plinary team 34, §2660(2) AND	regional office 34, §2660(2)			prepared for discharge fn. 5 34, §2660(2), 2661		34, §2661(2)						
MD. Ann. Code (1979 & Supp. 1981)		public facility 59A, §16	59A, §16(a)			59A, §16(a)	59A, §16(b)	any basis of duration 59A, §16(b)					
MASS. Ann. Laws (Michie/Law. Co-op. 1981 & Supp. 1981)	superintendent 123, §4			123, §4									
MICH. Comp. Laws Ann. (1980 & Supp. 1981)	director of facility 330.1525(1)			suitable for discharge 330.1525(1)	330.1525(2)		procedures for for leaves or absences to be established by facility or dep't 330.1528	after 1 yr. of authorized leave of ab-sence, resi-dent shall be discharged 330.1528	fn. 6 330.1537(1)(b)		330.1525(3) 330.1528		
MINN. Stat. Ann. (West 1971 & Supp. 1981)	253A.15(1) OR	if committed as dangerous to public 253A.15(2)	capable of making an acceptable adjustment to society, if found dan-gerous by committing ct. 253A.15(2) OR	253A.15(1)			provision discharge 253A.15(1), (2)	1 yr. unless extended 253A.15(4)	253A.15(7)	253A.15(11)	253A.15(9)	253A.15(11)	
MISS. Code Ann. (1981)	fn. 7 no procedures for discharge												

TABLE 4.4 ADMINISTRATIVE DISCHARGE OF INVOLUNTARILY CONFINED DEVELOPMENTALLY DISABLED PERSONS—*Continued*

	DISCHARGING AGENCY		ABSOLUTE DISCHARGE CRITERIA				CONDITIONAL DISCHARGE			NOTICE OF DISCHARGE TO			
STATE	Institution (1)	Central Agency (2)	No Longer Dangerous to Self or Others (3)	No Longer Needs Residential Treatment or Care (4)	No Longer Meets Criteria for Commitment (5)	Not Mentally Retarded (6)	Provision for (7)	Period of Conditional Discharge (8)	Adminis-trative Return (9)	Central Agency (10)	Court (11)	Relative, Friend, or Guardian (12)	RIGHT TO OBJECT TO DISCHARGE (13)
MO. Ann. Stat. (Vernon 1979 & Supp. 1980)	*fn. 8* 633.125 633.130		633.125(3) AND	facility does not offer program for resident's needs or does not provide least restrictive environment 633.125(3) OR		*fn. 9* 633.125(2)					copy of evaluation 633.130(3)		resident, parent, or guardian 633.125
MONT. Code Ann. (1981)	53-20-127(1)		53-20-127 AND	*fn. 10* 53-20-127							15 days before release 53-20-127(1)	& attorney & resident 15 days before release 53-20-127(1)	any of parties notified may petition court for hearing 53-20-127(1)
NEB. Rev. Stat. (1976 & Supp. 1981)	83-1131			discharge desirable for needs of the client 83-1131								to the client & client's representative 83-1131	any party notified, may request administrative hearing 83-1131
NEV. Rev. Stat. (1981)		associate administrator for mental retardation 435.077(2)		best interest of person 435.077(2)			convalescent leave 435.077(2)				10 days notice before discharge 435.077(3)		
N.H. Rev. Stat. Ann.													
N.J. Stat. Ann.													
N.M. Stat. Ann. (1979 & Supp. 1981)	*fn. 11* 43-1-13(I)			*fn. 11* 43-1-13(I)			convalescent status 43-1-21		43-1-21(B)				
N.Y. Mental Hyg. Law													
N.C. Gen. Stat. (1981 & Supp. 1981)	122-58.13(A)			122-58.13			122-58.13(A)	30 days 122-58.13(A)	122-58.13(A)		122-58.13(A)		
N.D. Cent. Code (1978 & Supp. 1981)	25-04-08(1)			25-04-08(1)						director of county social service board & director of state social service board 25-04-08.1 AND	25.04-08.1 OR	25-04-08.1	
OHIO Rev. Code Ann. (Baldwin 1980)	5123.79				institutionalization no longer appropriate 5123.79(A)		trial visit 5123.80	automatic discharge after 1 yr. continuous trial visit 5123.80(E)	5123.80(C), (D)		5123.79(A)		
OKLA. Stat. Ann. (West 1954)	43A, §73		43A, §73(A)(2) AND	who will not benefit by further treatment 43A, §73(B)			convalescent leave 43A, §73(B)	automatic discharge after 12 mos. convalescent leave 43A, §73(A)(3)	43A, §73(F)(2)		w/in 48 hrs. prior to discharge 43A, §73(E)		

TABLE 4.4 ADMINISTRATIVE DISCHARGE OF INVOLUNTARILY CONFINED DEVELOPMENTALLY DISABLED PERSONS—*Continued*

STATE	DISCHARGING AGENCY		ABSOLUTE DISCHARGE CRITERIA				CONDITIONAL DISCHARGE			NOTICE OF DISCHARGE TO			RIGHT TO OBJECT TO DISCHARGE (13)
	Institution (1)	Central Agency (2)	No Longer Dangerous to Self or Others (3)	No Longer Needs Residential Treatment or Care (4)	No Longer Meets Criteria for Commitment (5)	Not Mentally Retarded (6)	Provision for (7)	Period of Conditional Discharge (8)	Adminis-trative Return (9)	Central Agency (10)	Court (11)	Relative, Friend, or Guardian (12)	
OR. Rev. Stat. (1979)		427.300(2)		427.300(2)								& resident 15 days before dis-charge 427.300(2)	resident, parent, guardian, or person entitled to custody may appeal discharge 427.300(2)
PA. Stat. Ann. (Purdon 1969)		50, §4420		50, §4420			leave of absence 50, §4419	1 yr. unless extended; after 3 yrs. becomes dis-charge 50, §4419	50, §4419(b)				
R.I. Gen. Laws Ann. (1977 & Supp. 1981)	40.1-22-11 40.1-22-16		40.1-22-16	40.1-22-11 OR	substantially improved 40.1-22-16(1)(a)	40.1-22-16(1)(b)	interim com-munity leave 40.1-22-11		40.1-22-11				
S.C. Code Ann. (Law. Co-op 1976)		44-21-100		44-21-100 OR		44-21-100	conditional release to spouse, parent, guardian, rela-tive, or suit-able person 44-21-100	periods & conditions set by commissioner 44-21-100					
S.D. Codified Laws Ann. (1976)	27B-7-22 OR	discharge on hearing of mental health board at peti-tion of resi-dent 27B-8-17			27B-7-22 27B-8-17		leave of absence 27B-8-24	after 1 yr. of continuous leave of absence, client shall be discharged 27B-8-24	27B-8-25	county board of retardation & county auditor 27B-7-22 27B-8-24			
TENN. Code Ann. (1977 & Supp. 1981)	33-504 33-501(b)			in the patient's best interest 33-501(b) or if resident will be cared for properly by person or family able to do so 33-504			33-504	when superin-tendent deter-mines resident may safely be released, he may grant absolute dis-charge 33-504	33-504			14 days notice to parent, guard-ian, spouse, or relative who applied for patient's admission 33-501(b)	
TEX. Rev. Civ. Stat. Ann. (Vernon 1958 & Supp. 1981)	5547-300, §§38–40 5547-300, §45			placement no longer appropriate to patient's needs or bet-ter treatment elsewhere 5547-300, §39 OR		discharge w/no further hearings 3547-300, §38	leave of absence or furlough 5547-300, §45				5547-300, §47	client & or guardian 30 days notice 5547-300, §42	client, parent, guardian: administrative hearing *fn. 12* 5547-300, §42
UTAH Code Ann.													
VT. Stat. Ann. (1968 & Supp. 1981)		commissioner of mental health 18, §8833 18, §8834					conditional discharge 18, §8833 visit permit, max. 6 mos. 18, §8832		18, §8833				
VA. Code (1976 & Supp. 1982)	37.1-98 37.1-99		37.1-98(A) 37.1-99 OR	37.1-98(A) 37.1-99 OR		37.1-98(A) 37.1-99	convalescent status 37.1-98B 37.1-99						

TABLE 4.4 ADMINISTRATIVE DISCHARGE OF INVOLUNTARILY CONFINED DEVELOPMENTALLY DISABLED PERSONS—*Continued*

	DISCHARGING AGENCY		ABSOLUTE DISCHARGE CRITERIA				CONDITIONAL DISCHARGE			NOTICE OF DISCHARGE TO			
STATE	Institution (1)	Central Agency (2)	No Longer Dangerous to Self or Others (3)	No Longer Needs Residential Treatment or Care (4)	No Longer Meets Criteria for Commitment (5)	Not Mentally Retarded (6)	Provision for (7)	Period of Conditional Discharge (8)	Adminis-trative Return (9)	Central Agency (10)	Court (11)	Relative, Friend, or Guardian (12)	RIGHT TO OBJECT TO DISCHARGE (13)
	WASH. Rev. Code Ann.												
W. VA. Code (1980 & Supp. 1981)	27-7-1			can no longer benefit from hospitali-zation 27-7-1 OR	27-7-1		convalescent status 27-7-2 release as unimproved *fn. 13* 27-7-3	absolute discharge after 6 mos. con-valescent status 27-7-2	27-7-4	county mental hygiene commissioner 27-7-2	27-7-1 27-7-2 27-7-3		
WIS. Stat. Ann. (West 1957 & Supp. 1981)		51.35(4)(a), (b)			51.35(4)(a), (b)		home visit, leave for education or employment 51.35(8)(a)	15 days 51.35(8)(a)	51.35(8)(b)		51.35(4)(f)		
WYO. Stat.													

FOOTNOTES: TABLE 4.4

1. Ala. Code § 22-52-57 (1975). Superintendent shall discharge pursuant to the rules and regulations of the board of mental health.

2. Cal. Welf. & Inst. Code § 7362 (West Supp. 1981):

The medical superintendent of a state hospital . . . may on his own motion, and shall on the order of the State Department of Mental Health, discharge any patient who comes within any of the following descriptions:

(a) Who is not a proper case for treatment therein.

(b) Who is developmentally disabled or is affected with a chronic harmless mental disorder.

3. D.C. Code Ann. § 6-1930 (1981): "If the resident, the resident's parent or guardian, the resident's counsel, or the mental retardation advocate objects to the discharge, he or she may file a petition with the Court requesting a hearing in accordance with the procedures set forth. . . . The resident shall not be discharged prior to the hearing."

4. Fla. Stat. Ann. § 393.115(b) (West Supp. 1981): "If the department determines that the resident's continued admission is essential or that the resident is dangerous to himself or others, . . . he shall remain admitted to residential care provided by the department."

5. Me. Rev. Stat. Ann. tit. 34, § 2661(2) (Supp. 1981). Whenever an interdisciplinary team finds that the client may be ready for discharge, the team may recommend placement in the community and shall develop a prescriptive program plan to insure that the client's needs are met.

6. Mich. Comp. Laws Ann. § 330.1537 (1980):

(1) An individual is subject to being returned to a facility if:

. . . .

(b) He has left the facility without authorization, or has refused a lawful request to return to the facility while on authorized leave or other authorized absence from the facility.

. . . .

(3) An opportunity for appeal shall be provided to any individual returned over his objection from any authorized leave in excess of 10 days, and the individual shall be notified of his right to appeal.

7. Miss. Code Ann. §§ 41-19-11(b), 41-19-151(b) (1981). The commitment provisions for mentally retarded persons found in these sections refer to the procedures for commitment of the mentally ill for use in committing the mentally retarded. Although no discharge provisions are provided in the mental retardation code, the discharge procedures for the mentally ill may be applicable (see table 4.1).

8. Mo. Ann. Stat. § 633.135(5) (Vernon Supp. 1980): "Any resident of a mental retardation facility who is age eighteen or older and who does not have a legal guardian shall not be discharged unless probate court approval is obtained to confirm that the resident is not in need of the care, treatment or programs now being received in the mental retardation facility."

9. Id. § 633.125(2), (3). Consent of resident, parent, if patient is a minor, or guardian is required for discharge. If consent is not offered, must have court determination.

10. Mont. Code Ann. § 53-20-127 (1981): "If . . . there exist sufficient community-based alternatives to provide adequate treatment and habilitation for the resident and adequate protection of the life and physical safety of the resident and others . . . then he may release the resident to such community-based alternative."

11. N.M. Stat. Ann. § 43-1-13(I) (1979): "No developmental disabilities treatment or habilitation facility is required to detain, treat or provide services to a client when the client does not appear to require such detention, treatment or habilitation."

12. Tex. Rev. Civ. Stat. Ann. art. 5547-300, § 42 (Vernon Supp. 1981): "The client and parent or guardian shall be given 30 days notice of the proposed transfer or discharge under this subchapter. The client and parent or guardian shall also be informed of the right to an administrative hearing for the purpose of contesting the proposed transfer or discharge." The provision for a hearing and an appeal from the hearing to county court is in id. § 43. The client, parent, or guardian may also request a discharge and initiate the hearing procedure. Id. § 40.

13. W. Va. Code § 27-7-3(1980). Release as unimproved to responsible person. No discharge given until patient has returned to facility for examination and determination that patient is no longer in need of hospitalization.

TABLE 4.5 JUDICIAL DISCHARGE OF INVOLUNTARILY CONFINED MENTALLY ILL PERSONS

STATE	APPLICATION BY			COURT WITH JURISDICTION	RESTRICTION ON PETITION FREQUENCY	MEDICAL CERTIFICATION IN SUPPORT OF PETITION	NOTICE OF HEARING TO		HEARING	NO. OF COURT-APPOINTED MEDICAL EXAMINERS	CRITERIA FOR DISCHARGE				HABEAS CORPUS	
	Patient (1)	Family or Guardian (2)	Anyone (3)	(4)	(5)	(6)	Family or Guardian (7)	Superintendent of Institution (8)	(9)	(10)	No Longer Dangerous or Likely to Cause Injury (11)	No Longer Requires Treatment (12)	No Longer Meets Criteria for Commitment (13)	No Longer Mentally Ill (14)	Provision for (15)	Determination of Mental Condition at Time of Writ (16)
ALA. Code (1978 & Supp. 1981)															15-21-3	
ALAS. Stat. (1979 & Supp. 1981)																
ARIZ. Rev. Stat. Ann. (1974 & Supp. 1981)	36-546(A)		anyone acting on patient's behalf 36-546(A)	superior 36-546(D)	60 days after treatment order or hearing on writ of habeas corpus 36-546(C)				judicial discretion 36-546(D), (E)						36-546(A)	
ARK. Stat. Ann. (1971 & Supp. 1981)															59-1424	
CAL. Welf. & Inst. Code (West 1972 & Supp. 1981)	fn. 1 5275		any person acting on patient's behalf 5275	superior ct. 5276					mandatory 5276		& no longer gravely disabled 5276 OR	facility not equipped to provide treatment 5276 OR	had not been advised of, or had accepted voluntary treatment 5276		5275	5276
COLO. Rev. Stat. (1973 & Supp. 1981)															27-10-113	
CONN. Gen. Stat. Ann. (West 1975 & Supp. 1981)	17-178(g) 17-192	representative 17-192	judge appoints commission on information of wrongful confinement 17-200	probate 17-178 17-192 superior 17-200	1 yr. 17-178(g) not stated 17-192 6 mos. 17-200		17-192	17-192	mandatory 17-178(g) 17-192 commission appointed by judge 17-200			confinement no longer beneficial or advisable 17-200 OR	not legally detained 17-200 17-178(g) 17-192 OR	17-200	17-201	
DEL. Code Ann. (1974 & Supp. 1981)															16, §5013 (b)	16, §5013 (b)(2)
D.C. Code Ann. (1981 & Supp. 1982)	21-546	attorney, guardian, spouse, parent, nearest relative 21-546		U.S. District Ct. (D.C.) 21-546	6 mos., or 90 days after commitment 21-546	examination in hospital 21-546					21-546				21-549	
FLA. Stat. Ann. (West 1973 & Supp. 1981)															394.459(10)	
GA. Code Ann. (1979 & Supp. 1980)															88-502.14(a)	
HAWAII Rev. Stat. (1976 & Supp. 1981)	334-81	or friend 334-81	responsible person 334-81	family ct. 334-81	6 mos. 334-85				mandatory 334-83			334-84	OR admission is not regular 334-84			
IDAHO Code (1980 & Supp. 1981)	66-343	friend, attorney, family 66-343		district 66-343	1 yr., or 4 mos. after commitment 66-343		66-329(f) 66-343		mandatory 66-329 66-343	two 66-329(d) 66-343			66-343		66-347	

TABLE 4.5 JUDICIAL DISCHARGE OF INVOLUNTARILY CONFINED MENTALLY ILL PERSONS—*Continued*

STATE	APPLICATION BY						NOTICE OF HEARING TO				CRITERIA FOR DISCHARGE				HABEAS CORPUS	
	Patient (1)	Family or Guardian (2)	Anyone (3)	COURT WITH JURISDICTION (4)	RESTRICTION ON PETITION FREQUENCY (5)	MEDICAL CERTIFICATION IN SUPPORT OF PETITION (6)	Family or Guardian (7)	Superintendent of Institution (8)	HEARING (9)	NO. OF COURT-APPOINTED MEDICAL EXAMINERS (10)	No Longer Dangerous or Likely to Cause Injury (11)	No Longer Requires Treatment (12)	No Longer Meets Criteria for Commitment (13)	No Longer Mentally Ill (14)	Provision for (15)	Determination of Mental Condition at Time of Writ (16)
ILL. Ann. Stat. (Smith-Hurd 1966 & Supp. 1980)	91½, §3-900(a)		on patient's behalf 91½, §3-900(a)	county ct. where patient resides or is found 91½, §3-900(a)	after first petition, only w/ leave of ct. 91½, §3-901(c)		attorney, & at least 2 of any other persons designated by patient 91½, §3-901(a)	or person having custody 91½, §3-901(a)	mandatory 91½, §3-901				not subject to involuntary admission 91½, §3-901(b)		91½, §3-905	
IND. Code Ann. (Burns 1973 & Supp. 1982)	16-14-9.1-10(g)	representative 16-14-9.1-10(g)			once a yr., unless ct. finds good cause 16-14-9.1-10(g)		counsel & other interested parties 16-14-9.1-10(g)		mandatory 16-14-9.1 10(g)				review of commitment 16-14-9.1-10(g)		16-14-9.1-14	
IOWA Code Ann. (West 1969 & Supp. 1981)			229.31	district ct. in county of settlement or hospital 229.31	6 mos. 229.36				if testimony is offered 229.33					not seriously mentally impaired 229.33	229.37	229.37
KAN. Stat. Ann. (1976 & Supp. 1981)	59-2923		59-2923	district 59-2923	6 mos. after initial order & once every 6 mos. thereafter 59-2923		attorney & other persons as ct. directs 59-2916	59-2923	mandatory 59-2923 59-2917					reasonable doubt of mental illness 59-2923	59-2938	
KY. Rev. Stat. Ann. (Michie 1977)															202A.070 (10) 202A.080 (7)	
LA. Rev. Stat. Ann. (West 1975 & Supp. 1981)				ct. issuing commitment order 28:56(A)	any time 28:56(B)				ct. discretion; mandatory, once a yr. 28:56(B)				involuntary status should not be continued 28:56(B)		28:56(F)	
ME. Rev. Stat. Ann. (1978 & Supp. 1981)															34, §2255	
MD. Ann. Code (1979 & Supp. 1981)	59, §15(a)		any person w/legitimate interest in patient's welfare 59, §15(a)	equity ct. 59, §15(a)	once a yr., unless accompanied by affidavit showing improvement subsequent to last trial 59, §15(g)	if filed w/in 1 yr. of last petition 59, §15(g)			trial by jury upon request 59, §15(c)		inpatient care unnecessary for protection of self or others 59, §15(d) OR			no mental disorder 59, §15(d)	59, §14	
MASS. Ann. Laws (Michie/Law. Co-op. 1981 & Supp. 1981)			123, §9(b)	justice of superior ct. 123, §9(b)	none 123, §9(b)		such other persons as judge considers proper 123, §9(b)	123, §9(b)	mandatory 123, §9(b)		no likelihood of serious harm if released 123, §9(b) OR			123, §9(d)		
MICH. Comp. Laws Ann. (1980 & Supp. 1981)	330.1985			probate ct. 330.1400(g)	once a yr. 330.1485	physician's report unless indigent or unobtainable 330.1485			right to hearing 330.1485	1 physician, if no report w/application 330.1485		330.1485 (a)(1)			330.1486	

TABLE 4.5 JUDICIAL DISCHARGE OF INVOLUNTARILY CONFINED MENTALLY ILL PERSONS—*Continued*

	APPLICATION BY						NOTICE OF HEARING TO				CRITERIA FOR DISCHARGE				HABEAS CORPUS	
STATE	Patient (1)	Family or Guardian (2)	Anyone (3)	COURT WITH JURISDICTION (4)	RESTRICTION ON PETITION FREQUENCY (5)	MEDICAL CERTIFICATION IN SUPPORT OF PETITION (6)	Family or Guardian (7)	Superintendent of Institution (8)	HEARING (9)	NO. OF COURT-APPOINTED MEDICAL EXAMINERS (10)	No Longer Dangerous or Likely to Cause Injury (11)	No Longer Requires Treatment (12)	No Longer Meets Criteria for Commitment (13)	No Longer Mentally Ill (14)	Provision for (15)	Determination of Mental Condition at Time of Writ (16)
MINN. Stat. Ann. (West 1971 & Supp. 1981)			253A.19(1)	committing ct. 253A.19(1)			counsel & such others as ct. directs 253A.19(2)	253A.19(2)	mandatory 253A.19(2)	two 253A.19(3)		253A.19 (1), (5) OR		253A.19(1), (5)	253A.21(3)	
MISS. Code Ann. (1981)															41-21-89	
MO. Ann. Stat. (Vernon 1979 & Supp. 1980)	632.400	guardian, parent, spouse, relative, or attorney 632.400		"the court which has jurisdiction" 632.005(3)	fn. 2 632.400			632.400 632.340(2)	mandatory 632.400 632.340(2)				632.400 632.340		632.435	
MONT. Code Ann. (1981)																
NEB. Rev. Stat. (1976 & Supp. 1981)																
NEV. Rev. Stat. (1981)															433.464	
N.H. Rev. Stat. Ann. (1977 & Supp. 1981)	135-B:40			probate of county where admitted, or residence 135-B:40		135-B:40	patient & representative 135-B:40 135-B:30		mandatory 135-B:40	one 135-B:40 135-B:32			no longer in need of involuntary admission 135-B:40		135-B:41	
N.J. Stat. Ann. (West 1981 & Supp. 1981) fn. 3															30:4-24.2 (h)	
N.M. Stat. Ann. (1979 & Supp. 1982)	43-1-12(D)	or friend 43-1-12(D)		district 43-1-12(D)	60 days 43-1-12(D)		patient & attorney 43-1-12(D) 43-1-12(A)		mandatory, jury trial if requested 43-1-12(D) 43-1-12(B)				reexamination of commitment order 43-1-12(D)		43-1-12(E)	
N.Y. Mental Hyg. Law (McKinney 1978 & Supp. 1981)	9.31(a)	or friend 9.31(a)	mental health information service 9.31(a)	supreme ct. or county ct. 9.31(b)	w/in 60 days of admission on medical certification 9.31(a)	9.31(a)	& patient, applicant, & mental health service 9.31(c)	9.31(c)	mandatory 9.31(a)				not in need of retention 9.31(c) OR	9.31(c)	33.15	33.15(b)
N.C. Gen. Stat. (1981 & Supp. 1981)																
N.D. Cent. Code (1978 & Supp. 1981)	25-03.1-31			county 25-03.1-02 (2)	w/in 7 days of receipt of periodic review report 25-03.1-31	25-03.1-31			right to 25-03.1-31	one, if patient indigent, or unable to obtain 25-03.1-31		25-03.1-31	defined: 25-03.1-02 (11)		25-03.1-40 (11)	
OHIO Rev. Code Ann. (Baldwin 1980 & Supp. 1981)	5122.15(H)		patient's counsel 5122.15(H)	probate ct. 5122.15(H)	180 days after last full hearing fn. 4 5122.15(H)				mandatory 5122.15(H)				5122.15(H)		5122.30	fn. 5 5122.30

TABLE 4.5 JUDICIAL DISCHARGE OF INVOLUNTARILY CONFINED MENTALLY ILL PERSONS—*Continued*

	APPLICATION BY						NOTICE OF HEARING TO				CRITERIA FOR DISCHARGE				HABEAS CORPUS	
STATE	Patient (1)	Family or Guardian (2)	Anyone (3)	COURT WITH JURISDICTION (4)	RESTRICTION ON PETITION FREQUENCY (5)	MEDICAL CERTIFICATION IN SUPPORT OF PETITION (6)	Family or Guardian (7)	Superintendent of Institution (8)	HEARING (9)	NO. OF COURT-APPOINTED MEDICAL EXAMINERS (10)	No Longer Dangerous or Likely to Cause Injury (11)	No Longer Requires Treatment (12)	No Longer Meets Criteria for Commitment (13)	No Longer Mentally Ill (14)	Provision for (15)	Determination of Mental Condition at Time of Writ (16)
OKLA. Stat. Ann. (West 1979 & Supp. 1981)	43A, §54.11(B)		patient's counsel 43A, §54.11(B)	ct. in county where patient is located or committing ct. 43A, §54.11(B)	any time 43A, §54.11(B)		patient's attorney 43A, §54.11(B)	43A, §54.11(B)							43A, §99	43A, §99
OR. Rev. Stat. (1981) *fn. 6*															426.380	
PA. Stat. Ann. (Purdon 1969 & Supp. 1980) *fn. 7*															50, §7113	
R.I. Gen. Laws (1977 & Supp. 1981) *fn. 8*	40.1-5.2-5		40.1-5.2-5	supreme ct. justice, who shall appoint a commission 40.1-5.2-5			patient 40.1-5.2-6		exam. by commissioners *fn. 9* 40.1-5.2-6, 7					*fn. 10* 40.1-5.2-5	40.1-5-12 40.1-5.2-10	40.1-5.2-10
S.C. Code Ann. (Law Co-op. 1976 & Supp. 1981)	44-17-630		44-17-630	probate ct. 44-17-630	once each 6 mos. 44-17-630	44-17-630 44-17-510	& any other interested person 44-17-630 44-17-520		mandatory 44-17-630 44-17-540				reexamination of commitment order 44-17-630		44-23-230	
S.D. Codified Laws Ann. (1976 & Supp. 1981)															27A-12-4	27A-12-4
TENN. Code Ann. (1977 & Supp. 1981)	33-609				90 days after initial order, & once every 6 mos. after 33-609(b)	physician's report 33-609(b)			testimony of physicians 33-609(c)				33-609(b)		33-316 33-303	33-316
TEX. Rev. Civ. Stat. Ann. (Vernon 1958 & Supp. 1981)	5547-82(a)		next friend, w/patient's consent 5547-82(a)	ct. of hospital county 5547-82(a)	1 yr. after initial commitment, 2 yrs. thereafter 5547-82(g)	hospital certificate 5547-82(c)		5547-82(b)	mandatory 5547-82			no longer requires hospitalization as mentally ill 5547-82(f)			5547-85	
UTAH Code Ann. (1978 & Supp. 1981)	64-7-45	64-7-45		ct. of hospital or residence 64-7-45	6 mos. 64-7-45		64-7-45		mandatory 64-7-36 64-7-45	two 64-7-36 64-7-45			reexamination of hospitalization order 64-7-45		64-7-49	
VT. Stat. Ann. (1968 & Supp. 1981)	18, §7801 (a)			district ct. of hospital 18, §7801 (a)			attorney, guardian 18, §7613 18, §7801 (b)		mandatory 18, §7613 18, §7801 (b)	one 18, §7612 18, §7801 (b)		18, §7801 (c)			18, §8005	
VA. Code (1976 & Supp. 1982)															37.1-103	37.1-103
WASH. Rev. Code (Ann. 1975 & Supp. 1981)															71.05.480	
W. VA. Code																
WIS. Stat. Ann. (West 1957 & Supp. 1981)	51.11(1)	or friend 51.11(1)		ct. of hospital county or county from which committed 51.11(1)	1 yr. 51.11(8)		51.11(4)	51.11(4)	mandatory 51.11(4) jury trial on request 51.11(5)	two 51.11		51.11(5)			782.01(2)	782.01(2)
WYO. Stat. (1977 & Supp. 1982)															25-3-124(c)	

FOOTNOTES: TABLE 4.5

1. Cal. Welf. & Inst. Code § 5275 (West 1972). Procedure initiated by habeas corpus.

2. Mo. Ann. Stat. § 632.400 (Vernon Supp. 1980). "Any respondent ordered detained for ninety-day or one-year periods of involuntary treatment under this chapter shall be entitled to a reexamination of the order for his detention."

3. N.J. Stat. Ann. § 30:4-107.4(3) (West 1981). Provides that discharges may be effected by court order but does not provide any procedures or criteria.

4. Ohio Rev. Code Ann. § 5122.15(H) (Baldwin Supp. 1981). The court may grant a full hearing within 180 days of the patient's last full hearing, if the application is "supported by an affidavit of a psychiatrist or licensed clinical psychologist."

5. Id. § 5122.30: "No person may bring a petition for a writ of habeas corpus that alleges that a person involuntarily detained pursuant to this chapter is no longer mentally ill subject to hospitalization by court order unless the person shows that the release procedures of division (H) of §5122.15 of the Revised Code are inadequate or unavailable."

6. Or. Rev. Stat. § 426.301 (1981). Oregon does not have a provision for application to the court for discharge. However, if the institution certifies the patient for further commitment after the initial period, the patient has a right to protest and have a hearing.

7. Pa. Stat. Ann. tit. 50, § 7113 (Purdon Supp. 1980): "Actions requesting damages, declaratory judgment, injunction, mandamus, writs of prohibition, habeas corpus, including challenges to legality of detention or degree of restraint, and any other remedies or relief granted by law may be maintained in order to protect and effectuate the rights granted under this act."

8. R.I. Gen. Laws § 40.1-5.2-5 (Supp. 1981). The procedure charted (other than habeas corpus) applies only to the persons committed under the provisions of chapter 5.1.

9. Id. § 40.1-5.2-6-7. The commissioners appointed by the Supreme Court justice must personally examine the patient outside of the presence of anyone connected with the institution (40.1-5.2-7). The patient has the right to "confer with counsel, to produce evidence, and to be present at the inquisiton." Id. § 40.1-5.2-6.

10. Id. § 40.1-5.2-4. A person committed by a supreme court justice may be discharged by a supreme court justice, although such person is not restored to sanity, upon the written recommendation of the trustees and superintendent.

TABLE 4.6 JUDICIAL DISCHARGE OF INVOLUNTARILY CONFINED DEVELOPMENTALLY DISABLED PERSONS

	APPLICATION BY						NOTICE OF HEARING TO				CRITERIA FOR DISCHARGE				HABEAS CORPUS	
STATE	Patient (1)	Family or Guardian (2)	Other (3)	COURT WITH JURISDICTION (4)	RESTRICTION ON PETITION FREQUENCY (5)	MEDICAL CERTIFICATION IN SUPPORT OF PETITION (6)	Family or Guardian (7)	Superintendent of Institution (8)	HEARING (9)	NO. OF COURT-APPOINTED MEDICAL EXAMINERS (10)	No Longer Dangerous to Self or Others (11)	No Longer Needs Residential Care or Treatment (12)	No Longer Meets Criteria for Commitment (13)	Not Mentally Retarded (14)	Provision for (15)	Determination of Mental Condition at Time of Writ (16)
CONN. Gen. Stat. Ann. (West 1977 & Supp. 1980)	19-569f(b)			probate ct. 19-569f(b)	1 yr. after original order & once a yr. thereafter 19-569f(b)			& commissioner of mental retardation 19-569f(b)	w/in 10 days of filing of request 19-569f(b)				review of original order of placement 19-569f(b)			
DEL. Code Ann. (1974)	16, §5522(b)	family 16, §5522(b)		chancery 16, §5522(b)	right to appeal commitment at any time 16, §5522(b)				may have jury trial on whether patient is mentally retarded 16, §5522(b)					16, §5522(b)		
D.C. Code Ann. (1981 & Supp. 1983)	6-1928	parent or guardian 6-1928		superior ct. 6-1928 6-1902(8)	mandatory ct. review of commitment every 6 mos. for 2 yrs. & once a yr. thereafter 6-1951				hearing to determine competence, if patient petitions fn. 1 6-1928 mandatory ct. hearing to review commitment 6-1951			patient not benefited from habilitation or continued habilitation not necessary 6-1951	patient has competence to make decision to leave fn. 1 6-1928		6-1974(b)	
FLA. Stat. Ann. (West 1973 & Supp. 1980)	no judicial														393.115(c)	
HAWAII Rev. Stat. (1976)		parent, for removal of director as guardian 333-46.5	interested person 333-46.5	family ct. 333-46.5	mandatory review by committee at least annually 333-44.5											
ILL. Ann. Stat. (Smith-Hurd 1966 & Supp. 1980)	91½, §4-705(a)		any person 91½, §4-705(a)	circuit ct. 91½, §4-100	every 60 days unless leave of ct. 91½, §4-706(b)	clinical psychologist or physician 91½, §4-705(b)	& client 91½, §§4-706 (a), 4-206	91½, §4-706(a)	w/in 7 days of receipt of petition 91½, §4-706(a)	1, if no certificate in support of petition 91½, §4-705(c)			91½, §4-706(b)		91½, §4-617	
IOWA Code Ann. (West Supp. 1980)	222.42		any person 222.42	committing ct. if in private facility; ct. of county of facility if public 222.42	6 mos. after commitment 222.42		interested parties 222.44	222.44	222.45		relative or friends willing to care for patient & no harmful consequences likely to result 222.43(3) OR	client able to care for self 222.43(2) OR		222.43(1)	222.41	
KY. Rev. Stat. Ann. (Michie 1977 & Supp. 1980)															202B.020 202A.070(10) 202A.080(7)	
LA. Rev. Stat. Ann. (West 1975 & Supp. 1980)	28:411	parent of minor or tutor or curator 28:411	facility 28:411	committing ct. 28:413(B)									fn. 2			
MD. Ann. Code (1979)	59A, §14(a)		anyone w/ legitimate interest in patient's welfare 59A, §14(a)	equity ct. of county of residence or county where confined 59A, §14(a)	yrly unless accompanied by affidavit & accepted by ct. 59A, §14(g)				hearing & right to jury trial 59A, §14		59A, §14(d) OR (2)			59A, §14(d)(1)	59A, §13	
MICH. Comp. Laws Ann. (1980)	330.1531 330.1532		someone on resident's behalf 330.1531	probate ct. of residence of patient 330.1500(f)	may challenge 6-mo. review reports 330.1531 may also petition ct. annually 330.1532	330.1532	& attorney 330.1531 330.1532 330.1517(1)(c)		mandatory 330.1531 unless physician report concludes resident still meets criteria 330.1532	1, if no report w/petition 330.1532			330.1531 330.1532		330.1533	
MINN. Stat. Ann. (West 1971)			any interested person 253A.19(1)	committing ct. 253A.19(1)			counsel & others as directed by ct. 253A.19(2)	& commissioner 253A.19(2)	mandatory 253A.19(2)	1 physician & 1 person skilled in ascertainment of mental deficiency 253A.19(3)		253A.19(1), (5)	OR	253A.19(1), (5)	253A.21(3)	

TABLE 4.6 JUDICIAL DISCHARGE OF INVOLUNTARILY CONFINED DEVELOPMENTALLY DISABLED PERSONS—*Continued*

	APPLICATION BY						NOTICE OF HEARING TO				CRITERIA FOR DISCHARGE				HABEAS CORPUS	
STATE	Patient (1)	Family or Guardian (2)	Other (3)	COURT WITH JURISDICTION (4)	RESTRICTION ON PETITION FREQUENCY (5)	MEDICAL CERTIFICATION IN SUPPORT OF PETITION (6)	Family or Guardian (7)	Superintendent of Institution (8)	HEARING (9)	NO. OF COURT-APPOINTED MEDICAL EXAMINERS (10)	No Longer Dangerous to Self or Others (11)	No Longer Needs Residential Care or Treatment (12)	No Longer Meets Criteria for Commitment (13)	Not Mentally Retarded (14)	Provision for (15)	Determination of Mental Condition at Time of Writ (16)
MISS. Code Ann. (1972 & Supp. 1980)															41-21-151(b) 41-21-89	
MO. Ann. Stat. (Vernon 1979 & Supp. 1980)			fn. 3 633.135(5)	probate 633.135(5)					probate ct. "approval" of discharge 633.135(5)			resident w/o legal guardian 633.135(5)				
MONT. Code Ann. (1981)			person who could have requested hearing at admission 53-20-127(2)				53-20-127(2) 53-20-125		if person in charge of resident refuses to authorize release 53-20-127(2)							
NEB. Rev. Stat. (1976 & Supp. 1981)	habeas corpus 83-1133(3)		habeas corpus: any person 83-1133(3)	habeas corpus: any ct. of competent jurisdiction 83-1133(3)											83-1133(3)	
NEV. Rev. Stat. (1979)															433.464	
N.M. Stat. Ann. (1979 & Supp. 1982)	43-1-13(G)	guardian, parent, spouse, relative, or friend 43-1-13(G)		district ct. or commissioner appointed by ct. 43-1-13(G) 43-1-13(F)	60 days after admission & once every 60 days thereafter 43-1-13(G)		43-1-13(C), (G)						reexamination of involuntary referral 43-1-13(G)		43-1-13(H)	
N.Y. Mental Hyg. Law (McKinney 1978)	15.35	father, husband, mother, wife, or child 15.35		supreme ct. justice, other than justice presiding over original order 15.35	w/in 30 days after any order denying release or authorizing retention 15.35				jury trial unless waived 15.35			15.35	OR	15.35		
OHIO Rev. Code Ann. (Baldwin 1980)			director of private institution or facility or probate ct. 5123.79(B)	probate ct. of residence or institution 5123.79(B)					5123.79(B)				rehearing to determine advisability of continued institutionalization 5123.79(B)		5123.88	
OKLA. Stat. Ann. (West 1979)	no commitment														43A, §99	43A, §99
OR. Rev. Stat. (1979)															427.031(2)(h)	
PA. Stat. Ann. (purdon 1969)	habeas corpus 50, §4426(a)		habeas corpus: anyone 50, §4426(a)												50, §4426	50, §4426(b)(2)
R.I. Gen. Laws (1977 & Supp. 1981)	40.1-22-17(2)			district ct.; or family ct. if under 18 40.1-22-17(2)					if provisions for review of detention are not available 40.1-22-17(2)			40.1-22-17(2)				
S.D. Codified Laws Ann. (1976)															27B-8-4	27B-8-4
TENN. Code Ann. (1977 & Supp. 1981)	no commitment														33-316	33-316
TEX. Rev. Civ. Stat. Ann. (Vernon 1958 & Supp. 1980)	no judicial discharge														5547-300(48) (48)	
VT. Stat. Ann. (1968 & Supp. 1981)	18, §8834		commissioner of mental health, attorney, or interested party fn. 4 18, §8834(b)	district ct. 18, §8834(a)	6 mos. after commitment; annually thereafter fn. 4 18, §8834(b)		& attorney 18, §8834(c)		w/in 10–30 days after receipt of application or medical report 18, §8834(c)	1 or more; discretionary 18, §8834(c)			18, §8834(e), (f)			
WIS. Stat. Ann. (West 1957 & Supp. 1982)	51.11(1)	or friend 51.11(1)		ct. of hospital county or county where committed 51.11(1)	once per yr. 51.11(8)		51.11(4)	51.11(4)	mandatory 51.11(4) jury trial on request 51.11(5)	two 51.11		51.11(5)				

TABLE 4.6 JUDICIAL DISCHARGE OF INVOLUNTARILY CONFINED DEVELOPMENTALLY DISABLED PERSONS—*Continued*

STATE	APPLICATION BY			COURT WITH JURISDICTION (4)	RESTRICTION ON PETITION FREQUENCY (5)	MEDICAL CERTIFICATION IN SUPPORT OF PETITION (6)	NOTICE OF HEARING TO		HEARING (9)	NO. OF COURT-APPOINTED MEDICAL EXAMINERS (10)	CRITERIA FOR DISCHARGE				HABEAS CORPUS	
	Patient (1)	Family or Guardian (2)	Other (3)				Family or Guardian (7)	Superintendent of Institution (8)			No Longer Dangerous to Self or Others (11)	No Longer Needs Residential Care or Treatment (12)	No Longer Meets Criteria for Commitment (13)	Not Mentally Retarded (14)	Provision for (15)	Determination of Mental Condition at Time of Writ (16)
WYO. Stat. (1977 & Supp. 1981)	9-6-661(f)	9-6-661(f)	superintendent 9-6-664(a) 9-6-661	district ct. 9-6-659(a)					discretionary, but no discharge w/o 9-6-661(f)			placement in a less restrictive environment available & appropriate 9-6-661(f) 9-6-664(a)				

FOOTNOTES: TABLE 4.6

1. D.C. Code Ann § 6-1928 (1981). If the parent or guardian who petitioned for the initial commitment requests the resident's discharge, the court shall discharge the resident if based on consultation with the resident, and his or her counsel, the court determines that the resident consents to the release.

2. La. Rev. Stat. Ann. § 28:413B (West Supp. 1980) (effective until Aug. 1, 1983). See id. §§ 28:407-:410 (West Supp. 1982) for provisions after Aug. 1, 1983: "A mentally retarded person committed in accordance with this Chapter shall be discharged only upon order of the committing court."

3. Mo. Ann. Stat. § 633.135(5) (Vernon Supp. 1980): "Any resident of a mental retardation facility who is age eighteen or older and who does not have a legal guardian shall not be discharged unless probate court approval is obtained to confirm that the resident is not in need of the care, treatment or programs now being received in the mental retardation facility."

4. Vt. Stat. Ann. tit. 18, § 8834(h) (Supp. 1981): "Application for judicial review shall be made to the commissioner of the department of mental health if no application has been made pursuant to this section, within the preceding two years."

Barbara A. Weiner

CHAPTER 5 *Rights of Institutionalized Persons*

I. INTRODUCTION

Until the 1970s it was taken for granted that entrance into a mental health facility meant leaving one's rights at the door and submitting oneself to total control by the facility staff. Typically the disabled were housed in large state institutions, in dormitory-like settings, lacking privacy and any means of mitigating the effects of institutionalization.[1] All aspects of the disabled's daily life were strictly regulated from what he wore to how or with whom he was permitted to communicate.[2] The notions that the disabled should have some control over his life while institutionalized and that he had a right to participate in treatment decisions were only rarely, if ever, put into practice.

The decade of the 1970s brought about major changes in the rights of mentally disabled persons. The past two editions of this book were in part devoted to setting out the legal changes needed to properly protect the disabled while institutionalized.[3] This edition documents how most of those recommendations offered in the last edition have become reality, at least in the law if not in practice. These changes resulted from a recognition of the detrimental effects of institutionalization[4] and an understanding that the constitutional protections so often taken for granted by most citizens should also apply to the mentally disabled.[5]

These changes spanned all aspects of the care and treatment of the mentally disabled—from guaranteeing due process protections before civil commitment[6] to providing for a recognition of the rights of the disabled while in the community.[7] Similar to the civil rights movement, which made great strides during the 1960s, the movement to guarantee the rights of mental patients was greatly advanced during the 70s. The legal changes were accomplished through class action lawsuits,[8] and partly as a result of these lawsuits, numerous state mental health codes were modified to provide recognition of the rights of the disabled.[9]

Today, entering into a mental health facility no longer means leaving one's rights at the door. Now, in theory at least, the disabled in institutions have largely the same civil rights and legal protections afforded to the rest of society.[10]

The revolution in recognizing the rights of institutionalized mentally disabled persons began with *Wyatt v. Stickney*,[11] a case filed in October 1970 as a class action on behalf of persons involuntarily confined for

1. See, e.g., E. Cumming & J. Cumming, Closed Ranks: An Experiment in Mental Health Education (1957); A. Deutsch, The Shame of the States (1948), one of the earliest classic works documenting problems with state mental hospitals; E. Goffman, Asylums: Essays on the Social Situation of Mental Patients and Other Inmates (1961), the classic study of the life in a state mental hospital; Joint Commission on Mental Illness and Health, Action for Mental Health: Report of the Joint Commission on Mental Illness and Health (1961), documenting the problems with state mental hospitals.

2. See L. Sturm, The Mental Hospital Nightmare (1973), documenting experiences of an employee at a Montana state mental hospital.

3. S.J. Brakel & R.S. Rock, The Mentally Disabled and the Law (rev. ed. 1971); F.T. Lindman & D.M. McIntyre, The Mentally Disabled and the Law (1961).

4. See references cited in note 1 *supra*. See also L. Bachrach, Deinstitutionalization: An Analytical Review and Sociological Perspective (1977); L. R. Jones & R. Parlour, *Wyatt v. Stickney*: Retrospect and Prospect (1981).

5. See, e.g., Dowben, Legal Rights of the Mentally Impaired, 16 Houston L. Rev. 833 (1979); B.J. Ennis & R.D. Emery, The Rights of Mental Patients (rev. ed. 1978); P.R. Friedman, Legal Rights of Mentally Disabled Persons (1979); Fry, The Mentally Retarded Citizen's Civil Rights, 47 UMKC L. Rev. 185 (1978); Schoenfeld, A Survey of Constitutional Rights of the Mentally Retarded, 32 Sw. L.J. 605 (1978).

6. See ch. 2, Involuntary Institutionalization, *supra*.

7. See ch. 11, Rights and Entitlements in the Community, *infra*.

8. Pennhurst State School & Hosp. v. Halderman, 451 U.S. 1 (1981); Welsch v. Likins, 550 F.2d 1122 (8th Cir. 1977); Dixon v. Weinberger, 405 F. Supp. 974 (D.D.C. 1975); Lessard v. Schmidt, 349 F. Supp. 1078 (E.D. Wis. 1972), *vacated and remanded on other grounds*, 414 U.S. 473 (1974), *on remand*, 379 F. Supp. 1376 (E.D. Wis. 1974), *vacated*, 421 U.S. 957 (1975); Wyatt v. Stickney, 344 F. Supp. 373 (M.D. Ala. 1972).

9. See the tables at the end of this chapter and compare them with the tables for the same chapter in the last edition. Many more states now have delineated in greater detail the rights of the disabled.

10. Weiner, Decade of Litigation Has Led to Redefinition of Patients' Rights, Hospitals, May 1, 1981, at 67.

11. 344 F. Supp. 373 (M.D. Ala. 1972).

mental treatment at Bryce Hospital in Alabama and expanded in August 1971 to include residents of Partlow State School and Hospital, a facility for the mentally retarded, and of Spearcy, the one other Alabama facility for the mentally ill. With testimony taken from this country's leading experts on mental health and retardation to establish minimum medical and constitutional requirements for public institutions, amici included the American Orthopsychiatric Association, the American Psychological Association, the American Civil Liberties Union, the American Association on Mental Deficiency, and the United States government. As a result of the extensive hearings and the amici briefs, the court entered two orders, one relating to the treatment of the mentally ill and the other to the treatment and habilitation of the mentally retarded.[12] An appendix to each of these orders set out the minimum standards the court considered constitutionally necessary to treat the mentally ill or provide adequate habilitation to the mentally retarded.[13] These standards governed all aspects of institutional life from the actual physical conditions to the rights of the patient. Many of those concepts became the foundation for challenges to institutional conditions in other states,[14] and the rights guaranteed to the patient in *Wyatt* have now been adopted by many states as part of their mental health codes,[15] often in the same language Judge Johnson used in *Wyatt*. Appendix A at the end of this chapter contains those key standards formulated in the *Wyatt* appendixes.

In the succeeding sections considerable attention is devoted to case law grounded on the federal Constitution. The due process and equal protection clauses of the Fourteenth Amendment are primary guarantors of individual rights and liberties against infringements by state and local governmental entities. They are paralleled by the due process clause of the Fifth Amendment, which has been interpreted as embodying an equal protection guarantee[16] and is applicable to actions of the federal government. The due process clauses essentially require that government act fairly, which entails both substantive and procedural limitations. The equal protection clause guarantees that similarly situated people are to be treated similarly.

It is important to understand that these constitutional provisions do not apply to the actions of private entities. Thus, abuses in private mental institutions usually cannot be attacked as violations of the Constitution. Even the receipt of governmental monies, whether in contracts or grants, will by itself not sufficiently intertwine the private institution with the governmental provider of funds to engage constitutional provisions.[17] However, it must be remembered that federal and state statutory laws may, and often do, impose requirements on institutions both private and public. The private nature of an institution in a given situation will not free it from the demands and limitations of these laws.

This chapter documents the development and present state of the rights of the institutionalized mentally disabled person in 15 areas. Additionally, issues relating to confidentiality between the patient and his doctor are discussed in chapter 10, "Provider-Patient Relations: Confidentiality and Liability," and rights relating to treatment are discussed in chapter 6, "Treatment Rights." Traditional issues covered in the previous editions, such as communication, property, and financial rights, remain important. Concepts only beginning to be discussed at the time of the last edition, such as provision of humane care and treatment in the least restrictive setting, are now well accepted principles. Over the decade as a whole, substantial advances were made in the rights of the institutionalized mentally disabled.

II. COMMUNICATION

Limitations commonly have been placed on communications between institutionalized mentally disabled individuals and persons outside the institution. When such restrictions are imposed by governmental facilities, constitutional considerations come into play, and federal and state statutes may regulate the extent to which private as well as public facilities may isolate patients from the outside world and, correlatively, the extent to which they may bar access by outsiders to the patients.[18]

Communication by patients may occur in a variety of forms and contexts: letters mailed to family, friends, attorneys, public officials, and others; personal contact

12. *Id.* and 344 F. Supp. 387 (M.D. Ala. 1972).

13. See *id.* at 378–82 & 395–407 for appendixes on, respectively, the mentally ill and the mentally retarded, *reprinted in part* in appendix A at the end of this chapter.

14. See, e.g., O'Connor v. Donaldson, 422 U.S. 563 (1975); Halderman v. Pennhurst State School & Hosp., 612 F.2d 84 (3d Cir. 1979), *rev'd in part and remanded*, 451 U.S. 1 (1981); Eckerhart v. Hensley, 475 F. Supp. 908 (W.D. Mo. 1979); Davis v. Balson, 461 F. Supp. 842 (N.D. Ohio 1978); New York State Ass'n for Retarded Children, Inc. v. Carey, 393 F. Supp. 715 (E.D.N.Y. 1975); Welsch v. Likins, 373 F. Supp. 487 (D. Minn. 1974), 550 F.2d 1122 (8th Cir. 1977).

15. As this chapter shows, *Wyatt* set the initial standards in many areas. Because the appendixes to *Wyatt* were so comprehensive and were based on extensive hearings, numerous cases and states adopted the *Wyatt* language. Compare the tables in this chapter with the *Wyatt* appendix.

16. See, e.g., Bolling v. Sharpe, 347 U.S. 497 (1954).

17. See, e.g., Greenya v. George Washington Univ., 512 F.2d 556 (D.C. Cir.), *cert. denied*, 423 U.S. 995 (1975); Junior Chamber of Commerce of Kansas City, Mo. v. Missouri State Junior Chamber of Commerce, 508 F.2d 1031 (8th Cir. 1975); Junior Chamber of Commerce of Rochester, Inc. v. United States Jaycees, 495 F.2d 883 (10th Cir.), *cert. denied*, 419 U.S. 1026 (1974).

18. Jackson v. Metropolitan Edison Co., 419 U.S. 345 (1974). See also Note, State Action: Theories for Applying Constitutional Restrictions to Private Activity, 74 Colum. L. Rev. 656 (1974).

with visitors; and telephone conversations. Both the means of communication and the receiver of the message are considered in assessing the legitimacy of institutional constraints on the disabled. Likewise, the roles and the means of communication are legally relevant factors in considering restrictions on outsiders' access to the institutionalized mentally disabled.

A. Statutory Protections and Limitations

Communication rights of the disabled are governed by state laws in many ways.[19] The previous edition of this book noted that all but 10 states had enacted statutory provisions concerning patient correspondence and more than half the states had adopted provisions relating to visitation.[20] Since 1971, 5 additional states have enacted laws to guarantee the institutionalized disabled's ability to communicate with those outside the institution,[21] and 38 states have enacted laws specifically providing access to telephones.[22]

With 3 exceptions,[23] the states have adopted statutes guaranteeing the disabled person's general right to communicate by mail.[24] Almost all the states, however, permit some restrictions to be imposed, most commonly specifying as adequate justification "good cause"[25] or the medical welfare of the patient[26] — terms potentially subject to expansive interpretation by institutional personnel. Some states permit bans on mail communication when the correspondence is likely to be harassing or harmful to someone[27] — again, considerably malleable standards. In contrast to these broad qualifications on the rights of the disabled, 2 states require a court order before placing restrictions on communication by mail,[28] and approximately half the states require documentation on the patient's chart.[29] While this latter reporting requirement may not seem to substantively affect the freedom of administrators to control the communications of institutionalized persons, it may in itself avert abuses that might otherwise occur.

Obviously, a statutorily created right to communicate by mail would be hollow without the availability of paper, writing implements, and/or stamps. Accordingly, approximately half the states have a statutory provision for reasonable access to writing materials and to postage.[30] However, what is "reasonable" is usually not defined, leaving room for both magnanimity and chariness on the part of staff. In the rest of the states lacking such provisions, the right to communicate may indeed be a hollow one.

Visitation by noninstitutionalized persons, another very important mechanism for communication by the institutionalized, is generally guaranteed in all but 5 states.[31] Again, however, a number of these laws contain restrictions, often imposed for "good cause"[32] or for protection of the patient's health.[33] Abuse of these restrictions is checked in approximately half the states by requirements for reporting any restrictions on the person's chart.[34] In addition, 21 states permit attorneys to visit without any restrictions,[35] and 15 states authorize unrestricted visitation by clergy.[36]

At least 3 states have addressed the question of conjugal visits.[37] The statute enacted in Ohio is typical. It guarantees "[t]he right to social interaction with members of either sex, subject to adequate supervision, unless such social interaction is specifically withheld under a patient's written treatment plan."[38] New Jersey provides for "suitable opportunities for interaction with members of the opposite sex, with adequate supervision."[39] Whether any of these statutes make it possible for the patient to "interact" freely in conjugal visits cannot be known without observation. One way to provide the disabled with privacy is to permit them off-grounds passes or weekend furloughs.

Access to the telephone, another means for communication outside the institution, is particularly important for the institutionalized who cannot write and for those whose family and friends find visitation difficult because of the location of the facility or its rules and regulations. The telephone thus may be important

19. See table 5.1.
20. Brakel & Rock, *supra* note 3, at 155.
21. See table 5.1, cols. 1-9.
22. See table 5.1, cols. 17 & 18.
23. Alabama, Mississippi, and West Virginia.
24. See table 5.1, col. 1.
25. See table 5.1, col. 2, e.g., California, Colorado, Indiana, Kansas, Louisiana, Nebraska, New Jersey, and New Mexico.
26. See table 5.1, col. 2,, e.g., Maryland, Massachusetts, Minnesota, Missouri, North Dakota, Ohio, Oklahoma, South Carolina, Texas, Utah, Vermont, and Wyoming.
27. See *id.*, e.g., Delaware, Florida, Illinois, Iowa, Michigan, Nevada, New Hampshire, New York, and Washington.
28. Georgia and Nebraska.
29. See table 5.1, col. 3.
30. See table 5.1, col. 5.
31. See table 5.1, col. 10; exceptions are Alabama, Mississippi, Pennsylvania, Virginia, and West Virginia.
32. See table 5.1, col. 11,, e.g., California, Colorado, District of Columbia, Indiana, Kansas, Louisiana, Massachusetts, New Jersey, New Mexico, and Wisconsin.
33. See *id.*, e.g., Connecticut, Maine, Minnesota, Missouri, North Dakota, Oklahoma, South Carolina, and Texas.
34. See table 5.1, col. 12.
35. See *id.*, e.g., Colorado, Connecticut, District of Columbia, Idaho, Indiana, Kansas, Maine, Maryland, Massachusetts, Michigan, Minnesota, Missouri, Montana, New Jersey, New Mexico, North Carolina, Ohio, Pennsylvania, Rhode Island, Utah, and Vermont.
36. See table 5.1, col. 15, e.g., Arkansas, Colorado, Connecticut, District of Columbia, Louisiana, Maine, Maryland, Massachusetts, Minnesota, Missouri, Montana, New Mexico, Pennsylvania, Utah, and Vermont.
37. Kan. Stat. Ann. § 59-2929(a)(3) (1976 & Supp. 1982); N.J. Stat. Ann. § 30:4-24.2(e)(10) (West 1981); Ohio Rev. Code Ann. § 5122.29(1) (Baldwin 1980 & Supp. 1981).
38. Ohio Rev. Code Ann. § 5122.29(I) (Baldwin 1980 & Supp. 1981).
39. N.J. Stat. Ann. § 30:4-24.2(f)(10) (West 1981).

for maintaining contact with family and friends and reinforcing their support.

Thirty-eight states and the District of Columbia guarantee by statute the disabled's right of access to the telephone[40] but again, as in the statutes concerning mail and visitors, with restrictions and generally for the same types of reasons[41] Limitations on telephone communication make the most sense when aimed at preventing the patient from harassing someone who has complained about previous harassment. Unlike the mail situation in which an unwilling recipient can request the post office not to deliver a letter from a particular sender, he has no way of preventing an unwanted telephone call. Setting aside this rational restriction on the use of the telephone, the right to communicate is meaningless if the patient has no access to a telephone or if there is only a pay phone and he has no funds, but few statutes take up the question of use of a free phone or funds to make calls.[42]

B. Constitutional Parameters

Insofar as a statute provides an institutionalized mentally disabled individual with an unrestricted ability to communicate, the occasion for considering constitutional claims regarding communication is unlikely to occur. Barring unreasonable interpretation of the statute by an administrator, the disabled will have nothing to complain about. Should an administrator too narrowly construe such a statute, however, or should there be no statutorily created right, or should the statute be deemed to be insufficiently protective, constitutionally based claims may well arise.

Such claims may evoke one or more of several constitutional considerations. The first is grounded in the First Amendment guarantee of freedom of speech and press. While this amendment literally protects only against abridgements of those freedoms by the federal government, the Fourteenth Amendment's due process clause has been read as incorporating the First Amendment's guarantees, thereby making them applicable to the states and to subordinate governmental entities, that is, counties, school boards, departments of mental health, and so on.[43]

It was not until the twentieth century that the Supreme Court began to systematically construe the First Amendment. The dominant trend is that while the right to speak freely is not absolute, restrictions on this right will be viewed with searching scrutiny by the courts, with a very strong predisposition for striking down limitations on speech. Embodied in this principle is the perception that it is better to incur the risks that may accompany certain types of speech than squelch speech before it is uttered; if indeed that speech turns out to be undeserving of constitutional protection as in the cases of libel, obscenity, or fighting words, the speaker can be punished after the fact. Thus, prior restraints will almost never be allowed by the courts.[44]

A second constitutional consideration is the claim of the press to have access to institutionalized persons and for the patients to be able to communicate with the press. It has been contended that because of their unique role in preserving free communication in our society generally, the news media have a right to command access to facilities from which the rest of the public may be barred. Justice Stewart was the primary Supreme Court proponent of this view,[45] and while it has not captured a majority there, it remains an argument that must be considered in many specific instances involving access to, or by, the news media.

A third constitutional concern is couched in the language of privacy. In recent years the Supreme Court has recognized an ill-defined constitutional right of privacy that includes freedom from government intrusion into, or restrictions on, the intimacies of the sexual life of adult heterosexuals, particularly insofar as married couples are concerned in the prevention of conception,[46] the decision to bear children or terminate pregnancy;[47] the decision to marry;[48] and the structuring of the nuclear family and families made up of closely related individuals.[49] The right of privacy comes into play particularly in institutional visitation.

Finally, constitutional rights may be abrogated in instances where an institution restricts communication between an institutionalized individual and his attorney.[50]

1. First Amendment Rights

The primary case law affecting the right of institutionalized individuals to use the mails has been developed in the context of persons confined in prisons.[51] Yet its relevance to mentally disabled persons and facilities housing them is clear. The leading case is *Procunier v. Martinez* (1974),[52] in which the United States Supreme

40. See table 5.1, col. 17.

41. See table 5.1, col. 18.

42. *Id.*

43. See, e.g., Malloy v. Hogan, 378 U.S. 1 (1964) (self-incrimination in a state criminal proceeding).

44. See, e.g., New York Times Co. v. United States, 403 U.S. 713 (1971) (Pentagon Papers); Near v. Minnesota, 283 U.S. 697 (1931).

45. Stewart, "Or of the Press," 26 Hastings L.J. 631 (1975), which recorded some of the remarks Justice Stewart made in the November 1974 Yale Law School Speech.

46. Griswold v. Connecticut, 381 U.S. 479 (1965).

47. Roe v. Wade, 410 U.S. 113 (1973).

48. Zablocki v. Redhail, 434 U.S. 374 (1978).

49. Moore v. East Cleveland, 431 U.S. 494 (1977).

50. See this chapter § XIV, Access to Counsel, *infra.*

51. See Procunier v. Martinez, 416 U.S. 396 (1974); Pell v. Procunier, 417 U.S. 817 (1974).

Court articulated standards to be applied relating to the regulation of prison inmate correspondence, as follows:

> First, the regulation or practice in question must further an important or substantial government interest unrelated to the suppression of expression. Prison officials may not censor inmate correspondence simply to eliminate unflattering or unwelcome opinions or factually inaccurate statements. Rather they must show that a regulation authorizing mail censorship furthers one or more of the substantial governmental interests of security, order and habilitation. Second, the limitation on First Amendment freedoms must be no greater than is necessary or essential to the protection of the particular governmental interest involved. Thus, a restriction on inmate correspondence that furthers an important or substantial interest in penal administration will nevertheless be invalid if its sweep is unnecessarily broad.[53]

If persons convicted of crimes serious enough to warrant their incarceration in penal institutions do not fully lose the protection of the First Amendment, it necessarily follows that institutionalized mentally disabled persons likewise may invoke a constitutionally guaranteed right to freedom of speech, as all the courts that have addressed the issue have uniformly recognized. In *Wyatt v. Stickney*[54] a federal district court affirmed "an unrestricted right to send sealed mail,"[55] eliminating any restriction on the grounds that the recipient does not wish to receive the communication. In *Davis v. Balson*[56] a federal district court accordingly held that letters addressed to "strange people," such as the Pope and the Queen of England, could not be barred, reasoning that no legitimate governmental interest was furthered by the restriction.[57]

Given this case law, and particularly the *Procunier* holding that institutional officials may not censor correspondence simply to eliminate unwelcome opinions or inaccurate statements,[58] there is reason to question the constitutionality of those statutes, noted earlier, that authorize restrictions on mail deemed to be harassing in nature.

Different considerations arise in the context of restrictions on incoming mail. Sometimes, it is contended that the medical needs of the patient militate against unfettered receipt of mail. In *Wyatt* the court expressed approval of a restriction imposed for such purposes, stating:

> Patients shall have a right to receive sealed mail from others, except to the extent that the Qualified Mental Health Professional responsible for formulation of a particular patient's treatment plan writes an order imposing special restrictions on receipt of sealed mail.[59]

At the same time, the *Wyatt* court sought to limit the scope of allowable limitations on mail by requiring that the restriction could continue only if it were "renewed after each periodic review of the treatment plan." In addition, the court banned any restrictions on mail sent by the patient's attorney, private physician, the courts, government officials, and mental health professionals.[60]

Administrators of mental health facilities, like prison officials, have sought to justify opening incoming mail as necessary to prevent the introduction of contraband into the institution. Two federal courts have addressed this question and have partially upheld the institutions' position, looking to their interests in maintaining security.[61] However, both courts sought to provide protection for the patients' rights by requiring that they be present when the mail was opened in order to assure that it was not read.[62] Thus, in *Davis v. Balson* the court stated:

> The presence of the patient when his mail is opened is the only effective means known to this Court to insure that such mail is not read, which defendants concede would be constitutionally impermissible. In the Court's view, the opening of mail in the patient's presence poses only an administrative problem for the institution, and not a true security problem.[63]

Given both *Procunier* and those two lower court decisions, there is reason to question the validity of those state statutes that authorize restrictions on incoming mail on such vague grounds as "good cause" and that make no provision for the person's presence when mail is opened.

Apart from personal correspondence, censorship issues may also arise with regard to bans on magazines, books, and other publications. A number of courts have addressed such bans in the context of claims made by prisoners.[64] They consistently affirm that prisoners have First Amendment rights that cannot idly be taken away, and they often have ruled for the prisoner plaintiffs.[65] In

52. 416 U.S. 396 (1974).
53. *Id.* at 413.
54. 344 F. Supp. 373 (M.D. Ala. 1972).
55. *Id.* at 379.
56. 461 F. Supp. 842 (N.D. Ohio 1978).
57. *Id.* at 862-63.
58. Procunier v. Martinez, 416 U.S. at 413.
59. 344 F. Supp. 373, 379-80 (M.D. Ala. 1972).
60. *Id.* at 379. See in this chapter appendix A *infra* for the detailed *Wyatt* provisions on mail.
61. Davis v. Balson, 461 F. Supp. 842 (N.D. Ohio 1979); Eckerhart v. Hensley, 475 F. Supp. 908 (W.D. Mo. 1979).
62. 461 F. Supp. at 864; 475 F. Supp. at 925.
63. 461 F. Supp. at 865.
64. See, e.g., Frazier v. Donelon, 381 F. Supp. 911 (E.D. La. 1974); Theriault v. Blackwell, 437 F.2d 76 (5th Cir. 1971), *cert. denied*, 402 U.S. 953 (1971).

a case that addressed this issue for mental patients, a federal district court gave limited administrative discretion to instances where "the qualified mental health professional responsible for formulation of a particular patient's treatment plan writes an order imposing special restrictions on the use of reading matter."[66]

The problem, of course, in any regulatory scheme short of absolute freedom of the disabled to send and receive communications is the potential for abuse. This is so whether the restriction is categorical (e.g., no mail may be received from the person's wife) or involves an item-by-item review. Nonetheless, it is not likely that the courts would be prepared to hold that institutionalized mentally disabled persons have an absolute right of communication, free from any supervision by institutional personnel. The particular needs and weaknesses of the disabled and the particular needs of the institution must be taken into account. The task, then, for institutional staff, lawyers, legislators, and judges is to accommodate these varying needs with the undeniable thrust of the First Amendment, which embodies the proposition that freedom of speech must be accorded extraordinary protection.

Vague restrictions, defined in terms of "good cause," "medical need," "institutional security," and the like, are of particularly dubious constitutional validity. That statutes embodying such terms have not yet been struck down is no assurance that, when ultimately challenged, they will survive. Indeed, given the Supreme Court's often expressed special distaste for vesting in government employees standardless discretion to censor and to restrict First Amendment rights,[67] the likelihood is that they will not. Restrictions that constrain scrutiny should at most be allowable only where there is reasonable cause to believe that receipt of a given item or correspondence to or from a given individual will pose a clear and present danger to the institutionalized individual or the institution. The burden must be on the administration to justify the imposition of the restriction by specifically detailing the nature of that danger. This standard, derived from First Amendment case law enunciated in other contexts,[68] rests on protection of speech.

The concept of freedom of the press is also embodied within the First Amendment. Traditionally, journalists have played an important role in alerting society to conditions in both state mental health facilities and the prisons. It can be argued that this "watchdog" role entitles the press to special access to institutions. However, such claims raised in the context of prisons, addressed by the Supreme Court on at least two occasions, have been denied.[69] Any similar challenges to the policies of mental institutions may bring similar results.

2. The Right of Privacy

Although not specifically provided for in the Constitution or Bill of Rights, the Supreme Court's vaguely defined notion of the right of privacy protecting people in their family and intimate heterosexual relationships[70] may apply in the mental health setting. A measure of privacy is vital for a disabled person's efforts to communicate with his family, by visitation or telephone.

In the constitutional challenges to restrictive visitation and telephone policies, the courts have recognized the significance of the disabled being able to maintain contact with those outside the institution while often not identifying any specific constitutional source for this right. For example, in *Davis v. Watkins*[71] a federal district court ruled—without specifying the constitutional basis for its holding—that "[p]atients' telephone calls shall not be monitored" and that "[p]atients in the hospital shall have unrestricted right to visitation, at all reasonable times, including the right to visit with their own children."[72] At the same time, however, the court qualified this broad ruling by sanctioning restrictions if they were imposed by the qualified mental health professional responsible for the patient, in a written order stating the reasons for the restrictions.[73]

However, it can be assumed that the right of privacy has provided some of the impetus for the recognition of these rights, especially in any rules or regulations interfering with family relationships.[74]

3. Other Constitutional Issues

While 21 states provide that the institutionalized person is entitled to unrestricted access to his attorney,[75] the

65. See, e.g., Finney v. Arkansas Board of Correction, 505 F.2d 194 (8th Cir. 1974); LeVier v. Woodson, 443 F.2d 360 (10th Cir. 1971); Goldsby v. Carnes, 365 F. Supp. 395 (N.D. Mo. 1973); Jones v. Wittenberg, 323 F. Supp. 93 (N.D. Ohio 1971), *aff'd*, 456 F.2d 854 (6th Cir. 1972); Landman v. Royster, 333 F. Supp. 621 (E.D. Va. 1971); Palmigiano v. Travisono, 317 F. Supp. 776 (D.R.I. 1970).

66. Davis v. Watkins, 384 F. Supp. 1196, 1208 (N.D. Ohio 1974).

67. See, e.g., Smith v. Goguen, 415 U.S. 566 (1974); Kunz v. New York, 340 U.S. 290 (1951); Saia v. New York, 334 U.S. 558 (1948).

68. See, e.g., Pell v. Procunier, 417 U.S. 817 (1974).

69. See, e.g., Houchins v. KQED, Inc., 438 U.S. 1 (1978); Pell v. Procunier, 417 U.S. 817 (1974).

70. See, e.g., Roe v. Wade, 410 U.S. 113 (1973); Eisenstadt v. Baird, 405 U.S. 438 (1972); Griswold v. Connecticut, 381 U.S. 479 (1965).

71. 384 F. Supp. 1196 (N.D. Ohio 1976).

72. *Id.* at 1208.

73. *Id.*

74. Significantly, the Supreme Court has recognized the importance of maintaining family ties in Moore v. East Cleveland, 431 U.S. 494, 503 (1977), which challenged an ordinance that defined "family" very narrowly for zoning purposes. The Court noted that the decisions of the Supreme Court established that the Constitution protects the sanctity of the family.

75. See table 5.1, col. 14.

rest have no statutes relating to attorney access. Yet even where the mentally disabled person's right of access to counsel has not been expressly recognized, an institution would be hard pressed to deny an attorney access to his institutionalized client, for the right to access to one's attorney has been well established within the prison setting.[76] One court that has addressed the issue has held that the institution should make it possible for a patient to make as many telephone calls as necessary to obtain an attorney.[77]

Other courts have considered access to the telephone and visitation rights on other grounds. In *Eckerhart v. Hensley*,[78] which involved a challenge to conditions at a Missouri state hospital, the court found that the severe restrictions on visitors and the effective prohibition on the use of the telephone were "so restrictive as to constitute punishment and [were] therefore violative of patients' rights under the due process clause of the fourteenth amendment."[79] In reaching its conclusion the court asserted that

> [t]hese severe restrictions isolate patients from the outside world and constitute an excessive and arbitrary response to a legitimate interest in institutional security. . . . Visitation and telephone contacts are important to maintain ties in the community outside the mental hospital. To impose so complete a limitation on outside contact deprives patients of needed support from family, friends and other resources in the community.[80]

In a Wisconsin case[81] involving a challenge to the constitutionality of a state hospital's visitation policies, a federal district court ruled that a policy limiting the amount of time each visitor could spend with the patient was unreasonable.[82] This conclusion was based on the fact that the state could provide no justification for limiting allocation of available visiting hours to certain people.

III. RELIGIOUS FREEDOM

The freedom to practice one's religion or to refrain from religious practice is embodied in the First Amendment. Nonetheless, some states have felt the need to specifically protect this right by statutes addressing the institutionalized mentally disabled.[83] Such statutes are particularly important insofar as persons who are hospitalized in private mental health facilities are concerned, inasmuch as the First Amendment's strictures apply only to governmental entities.

Approximately half the states have enacted religious freedom clauses or clauses protecting the right to treatment through spiritual means[84] as part of their mental health codes in sections that address the rights of the disabled generally. The provisions vary from Rhode Island's brief guarantee of the right to "religious freedom"[85] and North Dakota's right "to participate in religious worship of choice"[86] to more extensive language recognizing both the right to practice one's religion and to abstain from religious practice, such as New Jersey's statute providing the patient with the right "to practice the religion of his choice or abstain from religious practices" with the further stipulation that "[p]rovisions for such worship shall be made available to each person on a nondiscriminatory basis."[87] New Mexico has perhaps the most detailed statute:

> Each resident client shall have the right to follow or abstain from the practice of religion. The supervised residential facility shall provide appropriate assistance in this connection including reasonable accommodations for religious worship and transportation to nearby religious services. Clients who do not wish to participate in religious practice shall be free from pressure to do so or to accept religious beliefs.[88]

Ohio has even recognized the right "to services and sacred texts that are within the reasonable capacity of the institution to supply."[89] In addition to these specific statutes, 15 states have guaranteed the institutionalized disabled the right to unrestricted visitation from the clergy.[90]

There are no reported cases addressing infringements of the religious freedom of the mentally disabled. In the analogous institutional setting of prisons, however, a number of cases have been litigated regarding inmates' religious practices.[91] The courts, including the Supreme Court, have been careful to affirm the rights of prisoners to practice their religion, so long as a heavy burden is not placed on the correctional facility,[92] with some cases

76. See this chapter § XIV, Access to Counsel, *infra*.
77. Davis v. Watkins, 384 F. Supp. 1196, 1207 (N.D. Ohio 1976).
78. 475 F. Supp. 908 (W.D. Mo. 1979).
79. *Id.* at 925.
80. *Id.*
81. Schmidt v. Schubert, 422 F. Supp. 57 (E.D. Wis. 1976).
82. *Id.* at 58.
83. See table 5.2, col. 9.

84. *Id.*
85. R.I. Gen. Laws § 40.1-5-5(d) (Supp. 1980).
86. N.D. Cent. Code § 25-03.1-40(9) (Supp. 1981); see also N.C. Gen. Stat. § 122-55.2(b)(7) (1981).
87. N.J. Stat. Ann. § 30:4-24.2(e)(11) (West 1981); see also Mo. Ann. Stat. § 630:115.1(5) (Vernon 1979).
88. N.M. Stat. Ann. § 43-1-6(C) (1979).
89. Ohio Rev. Code Ann. § 5122.29(H) (Baldwin 1980).
90. See table 5.1, col. 15.
91. Cruz v. Beto, 405 U.S. 319 (1972); Hoggro v. Pontesso, 456 F.2d 917 (10th Cir. 1972); Banks v. Havener, 234 F. Supp. 27 (E.D. Va. 1964); Brown v. Peyton, 437 F.2d 1228 (4th Cir. 1971); Williford v. California, 217 F. Supp. 245 (N.D. Cal. 1963).
92. See, e.g., Cruz v. Beto, 405 U.S. 319 (1972); Brown v. Peyton, 437 F.2d 1228 (4th Cir. 1971). See also Barnett v. Rodgers, 410 F.2d 995 (D.C. Cir. 1969); Cooper v. Pate, 378 U.S. 546 (1964); Jackson v. Godwin, 400 F.2d 529 (5th Cir. 1968).

considering specifics of practice such as appearance[93] and diet.[94]

Certainly, if they were to address the issue of religious freedom, the courts should be no less vigilant in protecting the rights of the mentally disabled than they have been in the case of incarcerated criminal offenders.

IV. THE RIGHT TO BE PRESUMED COMPETENT

A declaration of incompetency carries with it very serious legal consequences in addition to the stigmatization that so often attaches.[95] The incompetent individual is divested of a number of significant civil rights, including the right to vote, marry, enter into contracts, hold a driver's license, and be eligible for civil service employment and professional licensure. His freedom to make important personal decisions, such as choice of residence and refusal or acceptance of medical treatment, is often denied, and he is deprived of the ability to manage his financial assets and to determine their disposition, whether by will or otherwise.

The withdrawal of these civil rights is grounded on the notion that the incompetent is unable to adequately make the decisions involved in each of those areas of activity. Hardly a new idea, the notion of declaring the "insane" individual incompetent to protect his estate so that it would not be dissipated has a long history, predating the perceptions that hospitalization and treatment are possible and proper for the mentally ill and the retarded.[96] What is relatively new is a changed perception, reflected in statutes and judicial decisions, as to the wisdom of imposing such deprivations. No longer is involuntary hospitalization tantamount to an automatic declaration of incompetency.[97]

The previous edition of this book dealt with the common merging of incompetency with hospitalization. At the time of its publication, several states had statutes equating involuntary hospitalization with a finding of incompetency, and others, such as Wisconsin, provided that hospitalization, both voluntary or as a consequence of commitment, raised a rebuttable presumption of incompetency for the duration of the hospitalization.[98] While a number of states provided that at the time of the civil commitment hearing there could be a separate finding of incompetency, in some of them, at least, such a finding was a foregone conclusion.

Today, involuntary hospitalization rarely results in an automatic declaration of incompetency either formally or effectively. This is the result of statutory changes beginning in the 1960s and accelerated by decisions in patients' rights cases litigated during the 1970s. In the landmark decision of *Wyatt v. Stickney*,[99] for example, the court order provided:

> No person shall be deemed incompetent to manage his affairs, to contract, to hold professional or occupational or vehicle operator's licenses, to marry and obtain a divorce, to register and vote, or to make a will *solely* by reason of his admission or commitment to the hospital.[100]

This language finds analogues in a number of state statues such as Hawaii's, which provides:

> No presumption of insanity or legal incompetency shall exst with respect to any patient by reason of his admission to a psychiatric facility . . . . The fact of the admission shall not in itself modify or vary any civil right of any such person, including but not limited to civil service status or rights relating to the granting, forfeiture, or denial of a license, permit, privilege, or benefit pursuant to any law, or the right to dispose of property, execute instruments, make purchases, enter into contractual relationships and to vote.[101]

The states that previously had made a finding of involuntary hospitalization synonomous with a finding of incompetence have changed their laws so that the latter finding does not automatically follow the former.[102] Most state statutes now specifically provide that there is no presumption of incompetency attaching to involuntary hospitalization[103] and that incompetency must be determined in a separate hearing.[104]

Notwithstanding this liberalization, in some states various restrictions continue to attach to the involuntarily hospitalized patient who for certain purposes, at

93. A number of courts have upheld prisoners' rights to grow hair or wear beards for religious reasons. See, e.g., Shabazz v. Barnauskas, 598 F.2d 345 (5th Cir. 1979); Burgin v. Henderson, 536 F.2d 501 (2d Cir. 1976).

94. On the other hand, the courts have been less receptive to the claim that the failure to provide pork-free diets for Muslim prisoners is an unconstitutional infringement of freedom of religion. Their answer to his claim has been that the institutions need not provide special foods; rather, the offended inmates simply can refrain from eating the food—an option obviously already available, in any event, and one that certainly does not leave the hungry prisoner with any useful alternative. See, e.g., Elam v. Henderson, 472 F.22 582 (5th Cir. 1973), *cert. denied*, 414 U.S. 868 (1973); Anderson v. Wolff, 468 F.2d 252 (8th Cir. 1972); Childs v. Pegelow, 321 F.2d 487, 490 (4th Cir. 1963), *cert. denied*, 376 U.S. 932 (1964); X. (Bryant) v. Carlson, 363 F. Supp. 928 (E.D. Ill. 1973).

95. See ch. 7, Incompetency, Guardianship, and Restoration.

96. 2 L. Shelford, A Practical Treatise on the Law Concerning Lunatics, Idiots and Persons of Unsound Mind 7 (1833). See also 2 J. Reeves, History of English Law, 307–8 (1814).

97. See 29 Am. Jur. Insane and Other Incompetent Persons § 32 (1960).

98. See Brakel & Rock, *supra* note 3, at 253, 254, 273 table 8.2, 278.

99. 344 F. Supp. 373 (M.D. Ala. 1972).

100. *Id.* at 379 (emphasis in original).

101. Hawaii Rev. Stat. § 334-61 (Supp. 1981).

102. See Colo. Rev. Stat. § 27-10-104 (1973 & Supp. 1982); Ohio Rev. Code Ann. § 5122.301 (Baldwin Supp. 1981); W. Va. Code § 27-5-9(a) (1980).

103. See table 7.2, col. 1, e.g., California, Colorado, Georgia, Hawaii, New Jersey, New York, Oklahoma, Rhode Island, South Carolina, Vermont, Virginia, Washington, and Wyoming.

104. See table 7.2, col. 3, e.g., Connecticut, Illinois, Louisiana, and Ohio.

least, is deemed incompetent to make decisions. Usually these are restrictions on the patient's freedom to refuse treatment and to manage his funds while hospitalized.

Thus, a few state laws specifically provide that although the person is not considered legally incompetent, he may nevertheless be found incompetent in treatment matters,[105] so that, for example, he does not have the right to "refuse treatment during such commitment or detention."[106] In a few states, the facility superintendent is authorized to consent to emergency medical care for the disabled;[107] in others, the hospital can place limitations on the person's rights if these would serve his medical welfare.[108] Such constraints on the disabled are understandable, and perhaps likely to increase, given the difficulties attendant upon having to obtain a specific declaration of incompetency each time an institutionalized mentally disabled person refuses to consent to a particular feature of the medical regimen. On the other hand, given the growing debate concerning the right of the mentally disabled to refuse treatment, particularly medication,[109] these constraints may be viewed to constitute an unwarranted erosion of this right.

Three states have adopted provisions permitting hospital personnel to manage the disabled's funds in limited circumstances and for limited amounts.[110] This reflects the belief that although the person may not have been declared incompetent, during the institutionalization he is deemed incapable of handling his funds.

One may be tempted to dismiss concerns over the rights of the involuntarily hospitalized as irrelevant or at least overblown. To speak of preserving the freedom to enter into contracts, or to vote, or to hold a driver's license for the severely retarded and for the seriously psychotic, for instance, risks emphasizing form over substance, for in reality these individuals may not be interested in exercising such freedoms, at least while institutionalized, or they may indeed be incapable of pursuing them. That argument, however, entails the very dangers that the recent statutes and decisions such as *Wyatt v. Stickney* were designed to avert. For the truly mentally deficient or deranged individual, a declaration of incompetency may be secured. It is by insisting on a formal declaration of incompetency, with the procedural safeguards that accompany such a declaration, that we can assure that persons who are institutionalized but who can make, at least in certain areas, adequately informed choices will be allowed to do so.

V. VOTING RIGHTS

Although most citizens take for granted the opportunity to vote in local and national elections, this is a right often denied to the institutionalized mentally disabled. The right to vote is important to the mentally disabled in keeping him in touch with what is going on outside the institution and enhancing "normalization."[111] While disenfranchisement of the mentally disabled was common in the past,[112] today statutes in a number of states secure the vote to such individuals.[113] Even absent the existence of such a statute, the United States Constitution limits the ability of a governmental body to preclude persons such as the mentally disabled from participating in the electoral process.

The constitutional dimensions of voting are different for state and federal elections. There is no constitutional right *per se* to vote in the states, and conceivably a state could establish a system of selection of public officials by a means other than popular election. In fact, of course, every state has established a system of choosing certain officers by vote of the populace. What the Supreme Court has established is that when a state or a subordinate governmental entity does establish an electoral system, there arises a right, based on the Fourteenth Amendment's equal protection clause, to be treated equally in terms of access to the franchise.[114]

This does not bar the states from imposing qualifications for eligibility to vote, and indeed such regulations of the franchise involving duration of residency, literacy, competency, and age are still common. Today, the Twenty-Sixth Amendment bars setting age restrictions higher than 18 years. As to voting restrictions based on other grounds, the Supreme Court has generally looked with disfavor on state restrictions that tend to disenfranchise those who are assumed to have an insufficient interest in an issue of concern in the election or its outcome, while it has been more sympathetic to barriers imposed in the name of assuring that those who vote are competent to do so.[115] Accordingly, a ban on persons

105. See Vt. Stat. Ann. tit. 18, § 7706 (1968 & Supp. 1982).

106. See Wis. Stat. Ann. § 51.59 (West 1957 & Supp. 1982).

107. See, e.g., Ariz. Rev. Stat. Ann. § 36-512 (1974). See also Minn. Stat. Ann. § 253A.17(8) (West 1982).

108. See Utah Code Ann. § 64-7-48(1)(c) (1978 & Supp. 1981).

109. See ch. 6, Treatment Rights, *infra* for a full discussion of treatment issues. See also Rogers v. Okin, 634 F.2d 650 (1st Cir. 1980); Rennie v. Klein, 462 F. Supp. 1131 (D.N.J. 1978), *modified and remanded*, 653 F.2d 836 (3d Cir. 1981).

110. N.Y. Mental Hyg. Law 29.28 (McKinney 1978); N.D. Cent. Code §§ 25-01.1-19 to -20 (1978); Va. Code § 37.1-28 (1976 & Supp. 1980). See table 7.2, col. 2. See also table 5.2, col. 5.

111. Klein & Grossman, Voting Pattern of Mental Patients in a Community State Hospital, 3 Community Mental Health J. 149 (1967).

112. See Lindman & McIntyre, *supra* note 3, at 291-96.

113. Usually in a general statement providing that a patient's rights will not be restricted merely because of admission to a mental health facility. See table 5.5.

114. Harper v. Virginia Bd. of Elections, 383 U.S. 663 (1966).

115. Compare Kramer v. Union Free School Dist., 395 U.S. 621 (1969) with the dicta in Gray v. Sanders, 372 U.S. 368, 380-81 (1963).

not possessing property, and therefore allegedly not bearing a sufficient economic investment in the community to have an interest in the question of property taxes, was struck down as violative of equal protection,[116] while literacy tests have been upheld as constitutional, at least as long as they are not used in a discriminatory manner so as to favor one group over another.[117]

Typically, the courts will apply very strict scrutiny to restrictions on the right to vote, placing upon the governmental body imposing the restriction the burden of proving that it has a compelling interest for so doing and that the means used to achieve that interest are the narrowest possible.[118] However, the law in this area is not uniform, as some other cases apply a much weaker test for measuring the constitutionality of voting restrictions, only asking whether such bars are rational.[119]

In the past the mentally disabled were usually regarded as unqualified to vote, simply by virtue of their being institutionalized.[120] Such a simplistic view no longer holds. Civil commitment, which in the past typically carried with it automatic loss of the right to vote, today no longer suffices to disqualify the disabled from voting, unless he is specifically declared incompetent.[121] Many states have enacted statutes expressly providing that an order for involuntary hospitalization does not mean that the person is legally incompetent and that the patient retains all his rights, including the right to vote.[122] In *Manhattan State Citizens' Group, Inc. v. Bass*[123] a federal district court held that a statute prohibiting those who had been involuntarily committed to mental institutions from voting was unconstitutional insofar as it was applied to persons who were involuntarily committed to hospitals by court order but who had not been adjudged incompetent. The court pointed out that "[c]ommitment proceedings should not be confused with competency proceedings" and further stated:

> When one is declared incompetent, the court has found that person unable to conduct any of his personal or business affairs. Presumably, this includes the ability to cast a rational vote. One who has merely been committed, however, is in quite a different position. The principal issue in a commitment proceeding is a medical one: does the person to be committed have a mental illness for which hospitalization is essential and is the person's judgment so impaired that he does not understand his need for hospitalization. A finding that a person lacks understanding about his mental illness and need for hospitalization is not determinative of his ability to vote intelligently.[124]

In this case New York did not meet the burden of proving that the restriction was narrowly tailored to meet a compelling state interest: instead the statute disenfranchised persons who might well be capable of making intelligent voting choices.[125]

A finding of mental illness and subsequent commitment to a mental hospital may not even raise a presumption of incompetency anymore. According to the Massachusetts court that decided *Boyd v. Board of Registrars of Voters in Belchertown* in 1975,[126] residents of a state facility for mentally retarded persons who had not been adjudicated incompetent or placed under guardianship could not be precluded from registering to vote merely because of the fact that they resided in the facility.[127] The court perceived a legally relevant distinction between placing an incompetent person unable to manage his affairs under guardianship and placing him in, or allowing him to admit himself to, a mental health facility.

There remains the problem that access to the ballot box will be impossible unless a voting booth is set up within the confines of the institution or absentee ballots are made available. As of 1976 every state except Louisiana permitted absentee voting by disabled persons.[128] Case law suggests that even in the absence of such statutes, the refusal to provide absentee ballots would be found unconstitutional if challenged—at least it has been in instances involving other persons not physically present to vote, albeit not institutionalized.[129] More directly, a federal district court held in *McGill v. Alton*[130] that officials responsible for conducting elections may not refuse to allow institutionalized mentally disabled persons to vote by absentee ballot.

One question in voting law that may affect the institutionalized individual is determining his place of residence. Often, communities that have large institutions populated by persons coming from other geographical areas (such as universities) have looked askance at the prospect of deeming these individuals residents lest they vote as a bloc and in effect take over the local community. Efforts by local communities to fence out college students who in fact satisfy statutorily set local residency requirements for eligibility to vote

116. Kramer v. Union Free School Dist., 395 U.S. 621 (1969).
117. Lassiter v. Northampton Election Bd., 360 U.S. 45 (1959).
118. Dunn v. Blumstein, 405 U.S. 330 (1972).
119. Salyer Land Co. v. Tulare Lake Basin Water Storage Dist., 410 U.S. 719 (1973).
120. See 29 Am. Jur. Insane and Other Incompetent Persons § 32 (1960); see also this chapter § IV, The Right to Be Presumed Competent, *supra*.
121. See references cited in note 120 *supra*.
122. *Id.* See also Wyatt v. Stickney, 344 F. Supp. 373 (M.D. Ala. 1972).
123. 524 F. Supp. 1270 (S.D.N.Y. 1981).
124. *Id.* at 1273, 1274–75.
125. *Id.* at 1271.
126. 334 N.E.2d 629 (Mass. 1975).
127. *Id.* at 632.
128. Exercising a Right, 1 MDLR 237 (1976).
129. O'Brien v. Skinner, 414 U.S. 524 (1974).
130. No. 74-1164, 1 MDLR 19 (W.D. Pa. Jan. 26, 1976).

have been successfully challenged under the equal protection clause,[131] and presumably the same result would obtain if a community sought to exclude institutionalized mentally disabled persons who otherwise met the residency requirements for voting. In any event, even in a small community in which the institutionalized persons constitute a significant percentage of the hypothetical voting age population, it is doubtful that fears of bloc voting would be justified. A 1967 study of the voting patterns of acute and chronically mentally ill hospitalized patients and their potential effect on a community if they actually voted found their voting patterns similar to those of "normal" voters in the district and thus having no significant effect on the election results in the event that all psychiatric patients in a community hospital were indeed allowed to vote.[132]

VI. HUMANE CARE

The idea that a mentally disabled person is entitled to humane care and treatment while institutionalized seems so obvious as not to be worthy of comment. In fact, however, the history of treatment of mentally disabled persons in this country shows that numerous institutions have failed to meet even minimally acceptable standards of decency. Descriptions of the depersonalization of institutional life and gross deficiencies in the physical environment have generated an awareness of the possibility of harmful psychological effects from long-term placement in state facilities.[133] In response, a number of state legislatures, as well as courts, have affirmatively mandated, by statute or decree, minimal standards of care. As in other patients' rights areas, the court in *Wyatt v. Stickney*[134] was in the vanguard in addressing the issues; it provided that:

> A patient has a right to a humane psychological and physical environment within the hospital facilities. These facilities shall be designed to afford patients with comfort and safety, promote dignity, and ensure privacy. The facilities shall be designed to make a positive contribution to the efficient attainment of the treatment goals of the hospital.[135]

This right encompasses the total institutional situation, from the quality of the physical plant to the hands-on care given to the disabled person.

Other courts have followed *Wyatt*, holding that the disabled person has a constitutional right to minimally adequate treatment, which includes a humane physical and psychological treatment environment[136] as well as protection from harm. One court ruled that the state "shall take every precaution to prevent the physical or psychological abuse, neglect or mistreatment of state residential facility residents and shall promptly investigate, document and take corrective action with respect to each and every alleged incident of abuse."[137] A Mississippi federal district court recognized a constitutional right to protection from harm that guaranteed minimum standards of custodial care.[138] Another court that examined conditions at a state hospital found that confining committed patients in locked cells without toilets or sinks for long periods violated the Eighth Amendment's cruel and unusual punishment clause.[139]

Most state legislatures likewise have recognized a need for the disabled to be treated in a humane environment. Approximately 35 states have enacted provisions for affording care in a safe, secure, and humane environment.[140] Some states, such as Wisconsin,[141] have adopted in their statutes the language used by the *Wyatt* court. Other states have enacted simple statements, such as "[a] resident is entitled to mental health services suited to his condition and to a safe, sanitary, and humane living environment."[142] One of the more explicit statutes is Florida's:

> Each patient in a facility shall receive treatment suited to his needs, which shall be administered skillfully, safely, and humanely with full respect for his dignity and personal integrity. Each patient shall receive such medical, vocational, social, educational, and rehabilitation services as his condition requires to bring about an early return to his community.[143]

The Maine legislature, perhaps more candid about the likelihood of compliance with hortatory statutory statements, provided: "Every patient shall be entitled to

131. See, e.g., Note, Student Voting and Apportionment: The "Rotten Boroughs" of Academia, 81 Yale L.J. 35 (1971); see also Applying Equal Protection to Bona Fide Residence Requirements, 59 Iowa L. Rev. 671 (1974).

132. Klein & Grossman, *supra* note 111, at 150–52.

133. See Goffman, *supra* note 1, and books and articles cited in notes 1–4 *supra*.

134. 344 F. Supp. 373 (M.D. Ala. 1972).

135. *Id.* at 381.

136. Eckerhart v. Hensley, 475 F. Supp. at 908 (W.D. Mo. 1979); Davis v. Watkins, 384 F. Supp. 1196 (N.D. Ohio, 1974); Welsch v. Likins, 373 F. Supp. 487, 497 (D. Minn. 1974).

137. Medley v. Ginsberg, No. 78-2099 CH, 5 MDLR 393 (S.D.W Va. Oct. 8, 1981).

138. Vanderzeil v. Hudspeth, Civ. Act. No. J76-262(R), 1 MDLR 450 (S.D. Miss. Feb. 11, 1977).

139. Flakes v. Percy, 511 F. Supp. 1325 (W.D. Wis. 1981). This is, however, a minority view. Most courts base a constitutional violation on the Fourteenth Amendment. The Eighth Amendment is generally believed to apply only to penal situations.

140. See National Association of State Mental Health Program Directors, Status Paper on Current Mental Health Legislation (1979); table 6.1, cols. 1–3; see also Lyon, Levine & Zusman, Patients' Bills of Rights: A Survey of State Statutes, 6 MDLR 178, 185 (1982) [hereinafter cited as Patients' Bills of Rights].

141. Wis. Stat. Ann. § 51.61(1)(m) (West 1957 & Supp. 1982).

142. Mich. Comp. Laws Ann. § 330.1708 (1980). For similar law, see Kan. Stat. Ann. § 59-2927 (1976 & Supp. 1982).

143. Fla. Stat. Ann. § 394.459(3)(a) (West 1973 & Supp. 1982).

humane care and treatment and, to the extent that facilities, equipment and personnel are available, to medical care and treatment in accordance with the highest standards accepted in medical practice."[144]

Whether statutory guarantees of humane care and treatment and emphasis on respect for the patient's privacy and dignity have, without more, any impact on the reality of institutional life is debatable. On balance, such statements at the least serve as expressions of society's concern. Perhaps they are also bench marks for institutional staff in their day-to-day work and for judges in cases challenging substandard institutional conditions.

VII. LEAST RESTRICTIVE ALTERNATIVE

Obviously institutionalization of any kind involves some curtailment of individual freedom, for the institution will have needs that conflict with the notion that each person within that institution is to be free to do what he wishes, when he wishes, in the manner he wishes. Not surprisingly, the claimed needs of the institution, articulated by its administrators and staff, are likely to be put forth aggressively in the face of claims by the institutionalized to individual rights and privileges. It is in the nature of institutions to impose rules in the first instance and to then exalt conformity to them as a good transcending the claimed needs and wishes of the group served by the institution.

The legal counterpoint to this institutional urge for conformity and control is the concept of the least restrictive alternative, which holds that restrictions on liberty should be confined to the minimum necessary to establish the espoused governmental or administrative objective sought to be accomplished by the fact of institutionalization. This concept has many applications in the area of mental health law and today is widely accepted by both the courts[145] and the state legislatures.[146] Initially inseparably linked to the right to treatment or habilitation[147] and used to challenge the fact of institutionalization itself,[148] the least restrictive alternative concept has been expanded to form the basis for challenges to the type of institution in which treatment is provided[149] and to the limits placed on the liberties of the institutionalized.[150] It has also been relied on as legal justification for the asserted right to refuse certain treatments[151] and has further served as the basis for demanding that alternative placements in the community be developed for the developmentally disabled and the mentally ill.[152]

This section will explore the development of the least restrictive alternative concept and its application as it affects the rights of the mentally disabled in institutions. The concept as it is applied to civil commitment is discussed in more detail in chapter 2, "Involuntary Institutionalization," and as applied to the right to treatment and the refusal of treatment, in chapter 6, "Treatment Rights," and as the basis for deinstitutionalization in chapter 11, "Rights and Entitlements in the Community."

A. Development Through Case Law

The concept of least restrictive alternative had its basis in *Shelton v. Tucker,*[153] a United States Supreme Court decision in 1960 addressing a challenge to a state statute that required school teachers to reveal all their organizational associations for the past five years. The Court said:

> [E]ven though the government purpose be legitimate and substantial, that purpose cannot be pursued by means that broadly stifle fundamental personal liberties when the end can be more narrowly achieved. The breadth of legislative abridgement must be viewed in the light of less drastic means of achieving the same basic purpose.[154]

The first case in the mental health area to recognize the concept was *Lake v. Cameron* in 1966.[155] Mrs. Lake, who was 60 years old, suffered from a chronic brain syndrome associated with aging, was somewhat senile, demonstrated poor memory, and was considered a danger to herself in that she had a tendency to wander about the streets and was not competent to care for herself. Chief Judge Bazelon, speaking for a plurality of the federal District of Columbia Circuit Court of Appeals, held that before Mrs. Lake could be committed to an institution the lower court must make judicial "inquiry into 'other alternative courses of treatment.' "[156]

144. Me. Rev. Stat. Ann. tit. 34, § 2252 (1978).

145. See cases cited in notes 147–52 *infra*.

146. See table 6.1, col. 3.

147. See Halderman v. Pennhurst State School & Hosp., 612 F.2d 84 (3d Cir. 1979); Lake v. Cameron, 364 F.2d 657 (D.C. Cir. 1966), Dixon v. Weinberger, 405 F. Supp. 974 (D.D.C. 1975), Wyatt v. Stickney, 344 F. Supp. 373 (M.D. Ala. 1972).

148. Lake v. Cameron, 364 F.2d 657 (D.C. Cir. 1966); Dixon v. Weinberger, 405 F. Supp. 974 (D.C. Cir. 1975).

149. See, e.g., Covington v. Harris, 419 F.2d 617 (D.C. Cir. 1969); Eubanks v. Clarke, 434 F. Supp. 1022 (E.D. Pa. 1977).

150. See Eubanks v. Clarke, 434 F. Supp. 1022. See also Davis v. Watkins, 384 F. Supp. 1196 (N.D. Ohio 1974); Wyatt v. Stickney, 344 F. Supp. 373 (M.D. Ala. 1972).

151. See Rennie v. Klein, 653 F.2d 836 (3d Cir. 1981); Rogers v. Okin, 634 F.2d 650 (1st Cir. 1980).

152. See, e.g., Welsch v. Likins, 373 F. Supp. 487 (D. Minn. 1974); Dixon v. Weinberger, 405 F. Supp. 974 (D.D.C. 1975); Halderman v. Pennhurst State School & Hosp., 612 F.2d 84 (3d Cir. 1979), *rev'd in part and remanded*, 451 U.S. 1 (1981).

153. 364 U.S. 479 (1960).

154. *Id.* at 488.

155. 364 F.2d 657 (D.C. Cir. 1966).

156. *Id.* at 661.

The court said: "The alternative course of treatment or care should be fashioned as the interests of the person and of the public require in a particular case. Deprivations of liberty solely because of dangers to the ill persons themselves should not go beyond what is necessary for their protection."[157] The court then placed the obligation on the state to bear the burden of exploring all possible alternatives. In a concurring opinion Judge Skelly Wright took the position that although some provision for Mrs. Lake's safety was required under the statute, full-time involuntary confinement was not a permissible alternative. He said:

> The record shows only that Mrs. Lake is somewhat senile; that she has a poor memory, has wandered on a few occasions, and is unable to care for herself at all times. This evidence makes out a need for custodial care of some sort, but I cannot accept the proposition that this showing automatically entitles the Government to compel Mrs. Lake to accept its help at the price of her freedom.[158]

In his dissent Warren Burger, then a judge on the D.C. Court of Appeals, argued that the court was improperly ordering the district court "to perform functions normally reserved to social agencies" and that the petitioner should have the burden of presenting alternatives to the court.[159] (Ironically, at the rehearing by the district court no suitable alternatives could be found.)[160]

The 1966 *Lake* decision came early in the movement for deinstitutionalization,[161] when the concept of deinstitutionalization was recognized as a goal by the mental health community[162] but had not yet been translated into the reality of alternative placements that truly provided community mental health care.

In 1969 the same Court of Appeals for the District of Columbia Circuit expanded the least restrictive alternative doctrine in *Covington v. Harris*[163] to apply to placement within the hospital. The decision, again written by Judge Bazelon, recognized a constitutional basis for the concept of least restrictive alternative[164] as well as a statutory basis in the District's mental health statutes. The case arose out of a habeas corpus petition by James Covington seeking transfer from the maximum security pavilion of St. Elizabeths hospital to a less restrictive ward. Convicted in 1942 of second degree murder and released after serving 14 years in prison, Covington had shortly thereafter been charged with another murder, at which time he was found incompetent to stand trial because of an IQ of 38 and accordingly was confined at St. Elizabeths. Eventually, the criminal charges were dismissed and he was civilly committed. After ten years of confinement in the maximum security unit, where he came to be considered a model patient, his doctor requested that he be placed in a less restrictive unit. Subsequently, an incident arose that resulted in questions about whether he was taking his medication and was fully following the rules of the unit. After this incident it was determined that his transfer to another unit should not be considered for at least a year, and Covington then filed his habeas action. The court said:

> The principle of the least restrictive alternative is equally applicable to alternate dispositions *within* a mental hospital. It makes little sense to guard zealously against the possibility of unwarranted deprivations prior to hospitalization, only to abandon the watch once the patient disappears behind hospital doors. The range of possible dispositions of a mentally ill person within a hospital, from maximum security to outpatient status, is almost as wide as that of dispositions without.[165]

Concerned about the reasons for Covington's being denied transfer to a less restrictive unit, the court pointed out that "[i]n these circumstances it is fair to ask the hospital how appellant can ever demonstrate his readiness for a less pervasive confinement: What evidence of improvement are they looking for?" The court wanted to be sure that the appellant did not become a "non-person, deprived of any rights to minimally rational treatment within the hospital because he murdered once and may have murdered again."[166]

Emphasizing the importance of looking at the therapeutic objective of hospitalization, the court reasoned that since "treatment is an essential justifying purpose of any civil commitment, a 'permissible . . . decision' to confine a patient under maximal restrictions cannot be made without consideration of its therapeutic consequences," and it then went on to require that on remand to the lower court the hospital "explain either why maximum security confinement does not impair appellant's prospects for the promptest rehabilitation, or that he is so dangerous as to require such impairment."[167] Given its reasoning, *Covington* provided the foundation not only for challenging what type of unit one was placed on in the hospital—from a very secure one to one with an open-door policy—but also for questioning the privi-

157. *Id.* at 660 (notes omitted).
158. *Id.* at 662-63.
159. *Id.* at 663-64.
160. Lake v. Cameron, 267 F. Supp. 155 (D.D.C. 1967).
161. The movement for deinstitutionalization began in the 1960s but was at a highpoint of activity by the early 1970s. Deinstitutionalization continues to be the goal today. See generally ch. 11, Rights and Entitlements in the Community.
162. See Joint Commission on Mental Illness & Health, *supra* note 1.
163. 419 F.2d 617 (D.C. Cir. 1969).
164. *Id.* at 623.
165. *Id.* at 623-24 (emphasis in original).
166. *Id.* at 628.
167. *Id.* at 625-26.

leges one had while hospitalized, including grounds passes, home visits, and so on.

In *Wyatt v. Stickney*[168] the federal district court addressed the concept of least restrictive alternative as it applied to both the mentally ill and the mentally retarded. In the appendix to the portion dealing with the mentally ill, the court held that "[p]atients have a right to the least restrictive conditions necessary to achieve the purposes of commitment."[169] The findings relating to the retarded were more extensive: the appendix required that "[n]o person shall be admitted to the institution unless a prior determination shall have been made that residence in the institution is the least restrictive habilitation setting feasible for that person."[170] This case was the first to recognize that civil commitment of the retarded required habilitation to occur as a matter of constitutional right.[171] To implement the requirement that habilitation occur, the court ordered:

> Residents shall have a right to the least restrictive conditions necessary to achieve the purposes of habilitation. To this end, the institution shall make every attempt to move residents from (1) more to less structured living; (2) larger to smaller facilities; (3) larger to smaller living units; (4) group to individual residence; (5) segregated from the community to integrated into the community living; (6) dependent to independent living.[172]

The concepts embodied in this paragraph became the goals of the major cases seeking deinstitutionalization of the retarded.[173]

Expanding on the arguments raised in *Wyatt*, advocates for the mentally retarded have sought to use the right to treatment or habilitation in the least restrictive setting as the vehicle for forcing states to develop community-based treatment programs. In *Welsch v. Likins*[174] a class action suit in 1974 challenged the lack of treatment and the conditions at six state facilities for the retarded and requested the court to order the state of Minnesota to develop treatment/habilitation alternatives to placement in these institutions. The court held that due process required that civilly committed retarded persons be provided minimally adequate treatment designed to afford the residents a "realistic opportunity to be cured or to improve . . . [their] mental condition."[175] The court further asserted that "[t]he due process clause does no more than require that State officials charged with obligations for the care and custody of civilly committed persons make good faith attempts to place such persons in settings that will be suitable and appropriate to their mental and physical conditions while least restrictive of their liberties."[176] In broad terms, the court indicated that it was unconstitutional to institutionalize the borderline or mildly retarded, since presumably they should be able to function in community settings.

In 1975 in another class action, *Dixon v. Weinberger*,[177] patients at St. Elizabeths Hospital argued that under the mental health code of the District of Columbia they had a right to placement in alternative facilities in the community. The hospital staff admitted that approximately 43% of the patients could be cared for and treated in alternative facilities, defined to include, but not limited to, nursing homes, personal care homes, foster homes, and halfway houses. The court held that the statute at issue required that the patients at St. Elizabeths receive "suitable care and treatment under the least restrictive conditions as such conditions are required in an individual case consistent with the purposes of the Act," which would include placement in alternative facilities."[178] The court then found that both the District of Columbia and the federal government (because of its role in governing the District) had responsibility for providing such care and treatment. The decision did not address whether there was a constitutional basis for its funding; instead it relied on the 1964 Hospitalization of the Mentally Ill Act, a local law aimed at returning the mentally ill to the community through care and treatment.

In *Eubanks v. Clarke* (1977),[179] a Pennsylvania federal district court addressed the issue of whether a civilly committed mental patient's constitutional rights were violated when he was transferred from a minimum security hospital, Philadelphia State Hospital, to Farview, the state's maximum security facility, without notice or a hearing. The plaintiff, Aaron Eubanks, had been sent to Farview without a hearing or an opportunity to tell his side of the story, after an altercation with another patient, and he remained there for 20 months before being returned to Philadelphia State Hospital. The testimony revealed that Farview was a maximum security hospital in which little treatment occurred. The court declared that "[t]he purpose of civil commitment in Pennsylvania

168. 344 F. Supp. 373, 387 (M.D. Ala. 1972).
169. *Id.* at 379.
170. *Id.* at 387, 396.
171. *Id.* at 390.
172. *Id.* at 396. See in this chapter appendix A *infra* containing the *Wyatt* court's provisions on habilitation.
173. See Welsch v. Likins, 373 F. Supp. 487 (D. Minn. 1974); Halderman v. Pennhurst State School & Hosp., 446 F. Supp. 1295 (E.D. Pa. 1977), *aff'd in part and remanded in part,* 612 F.2d 84 (3d Cir. 1979); see also ch. 11, Rights and Entitlements in the Community, *infra.*
174. 373 F. Supp. 487 (D. Minn. 1974).
175. *Id.* at 499, quoting Wyatt v. Stickney, 325 F. Supp. 781, 784 (M.D. Ala. 1971).
176. 373 F. Supp. at 502.
177. 405 F. Supp. 974 (D.D.C. 1975).
178. *Id.* at 979.
179. 434 F. Supp. 1022 (E.D. Pa. 1977).

is care and treatment." It went on to say: "While such commitment involves a tremendous loss of fundamental freedoms, the state may not infringe those freedoms more than is necessary to achieve its compelling interests." The court said:

> [W]here a state has varying available facilities for the mentally ill which differ significantly in the amount of restrictions on the rights and liberties of the patients, due process requires that the state place individuals in the least restrictive setting consistent with legitimate safety, care and treatment objectives.[180]

Finding "that constitutional liberty interests are implicated in transfers from minimum to maximum security state mental hospitals," the court required that a hearing be held, with the burden placed on the state to show by a preponderance of evidence that placement at Farview was necessary and that there was no "less restrictive facility to which the patient could be committed."[181]

Without the means to implement the concept, judicial enunciations of the least restrictive alternative are of little value. In two 1978 cases aimed at assuring placement of the mentally disabled in the community, elaborate consent decrees were entered into specifically defining how their objectives were to be accomplished.[182] In *Wuori v. Zitnay* the decree established standards for community care and treatment for the mentally retarded residents of Maine's Pineland Center and set forth precisely how needed community facilities for the retarded were to be developed.

In *Brewster v. Dukakis*[183] the decree provided:

> A comprehensive mental health and retardation system consists of three distinct components: (1) residential environments which are the least restrictive and more normal settings appropriate for each resident or client; (2) nonresidential treatment, training, and support programs which are geographically separate from community residences and which provide the major daily activity for those clients whose residential environment does not provide the total treatment program, as well as for other members of the plaintiff class who live independently in the community; and (3) management services to adequately develop, coordinate, administer, monitor, and evaluate this network of environments and programs.[184]

The decree specified the numbers of patients to be placed in the community from various facilities and the way the community placement system would operate, providing that "[r]esidents and clients are entitled to live in the least restrictive, most normal residential alternative and to receive appropriate treatment, training, and support suited to their individual needs."[185]

In a 1974 case analyzing the rights of delinquent and anti-social juveniles to treatment, the Texas federal district court in *Morales v. Turman*[186] stated that an inquiry into the least restrictive alternative is hollow if there are in fact no alternatives to institutionalization. The court held:

> The state may not circumvent the Constitution by simply refusing to create any alternatives to incarceration; it must act affirmatively to foster such alternatives as now exist only in rudimentary form (foster homes, supervised probation and parole), and to build new programs suited to the needs of the hundreds of its children that do not need institutional care. . . .[187]

Even decrees such as those in *Wuori* and *Brewster* may not assure more than paper success for prevailing plaintiffs. Critical problems of implementation remain. The first has been that of finding the funds to develop alternative placements. Although community care is generally less expensive than hospitalization, there remains a need to maintain some institutional beds, with the costs of these increasing yearly. A second problem follows from the sometime resistance of public employee unions, whose members view the development of less restrictive settings and the correlative closure or contraction of institutional facilities as job-threatening events. Accordingly, political pressures are exerted to maintain the institutions. Such pressures are also engendered by the local communities in which the institutions are located for whom such facilities may be a dominant economic resource. Conversely, a third problem is that of finding communities willing to accept nursing homes and group homes within their boundaries. Community resistance has proved to be a major obstacle, with many communities adopting exclusionary zoning laws to keep out nonfamily living arrangements.[188] As a result, much of the placement of the deinstitutionalized has been in decaying urban neighborhoods that have come to be characterized as "psychiatric ghettos."[189] Finally, there is the continuing danger that so-called alternative placements will turn out to be as restrictive as any major state institution—notwithstanding their denominations

180. *Id.* at 1028.

181. *Id.* at 1028–29.

182. Wuori v. Zitnay, No. 75-80-SD, 2 MDLR 693, 729 (D. Me. July 14, 1978); see also Brewster v. Dukakis, C.A. No. 76-4423-F, 3 MDLR 44 (E.D. Mass. Dec. 6, 1978). See ch. 11, Rights and Entitlements in the Community, *infra* for a more extended discussion of these cases.

183. C.A. No. 76-4423-F, 3 MDLR 44 (E.D.Mass. 1978).

184. *Id.* at 46.

185. *Id.*

186. 383 F. Supp. 53 (E.D. Tex. 1974), *vacated,* 535 F.2d 864 (5th Cir. 1976), *reinstated,* 430 U.S. 322 (1977).

187. 383 F. Supp. at 125.

188. See ch. 11, Rights and Entitlements in the Community, esp. § VI A, Exclusionary Zoning and Restrictive Covenants.

189. See Talbott, Deinstitutionalization: Avoiding the Disasters of the Past, 30 Hosp. & Community Psychiatry 621, 622 (1979).

as community centers, nursing homes, halfway houses, and the like.

B. Statutory Requirements

With the revision of many state mental health codes in the 1970s the concept of least restrictive alternative has come to be embodied in statutory prescriptions of most states.[190] The *Wyatt* concepts of humane care and treatment pursuant to an individualized treatment plan in the least restrictive setting served as the foundation for those statutory changes.[191] Today 36 states require that involuntary commitment be the least restrictive available alternative for an institutionalization order to issue, and 26 states require that patients receive, while institutionalized, the least restrictive form of treatment.[192] A typical statute, that of Illinois, provides that "[a] recipient of services shall be provided with adequate and humane care and services in the least restrictive environment, pursuant to an individual service plan."[193]

The federal Mental Health Systems Act of 1980 included a patients' bill of rights section,[194] encouraging a right to appropriate treatment and related services in that setting most supportive and least restrictive of the individual's liberty. While most of the act has been repealed,[195] this section remains. However, it is only a recommendation to the states and there is no enforcement component. A recent analysis of the state laws found that 19 states had a provision quite like the one in the act and that an additional 28 states were in partial conformity with this section.[196] Only Alabama, Mississippi, and Oregon had no provision addressing the issue of treatment in the least restrictive environment.

In most statutes, the concept envisions an inquiry into whether there are alternatives to hospitalization, rather than into what levels of restrictiveness are available within the institution. However, the concept's reach can be extended to the latter issue. In addition, the least restrictive idea can be applied to treatment modalities, given that some therapies are more restrictive and entail a greater deprivation of freedom than others.

Precise wording aside, the statutes make it clear that most states at least recognize the importance of the least restrictive alternative. Whether this translates into alternative placement and types of treatments remains to be seen. There is not yet the claim that the concept has resulted in a meaningful consideration of other alternatives, since in most communities too few good alternatives exist.

C. The Mental Health Professional's Perspective

Concepts such as "deinstitutionalization" and "normalization" were developed during the high point of the community mental health movement in the 1960s.[197] This movement focused attention on the need and desirability of providing mental health services in the community rather than in large state institutions, which typically were located in remote areas and often did little more than warehouse the disabled.[198] Deinstitutionalization was based on the notion that the disturbed or retarded person is "normalized" in treatment integrated with community-based mental health services, thus reducing the need to be placed in a large state institution. The legal underpinning for the concepts of normalization and deinstitutionalization is the constitutional requirement that treatment be provided in the least restrictive setting necessary to accomplish treatment objectives.

Many within the mental health profession question whether deinstitutionalization, however laudable as a goal, has worked as promised.[199] There is legitimate grounds for asking whether the least restrictive alternative concept needs some better definition so that the restrictiveness of a given setting can be more accurately measured.[200] As one commentator has noted, the "policies of deinstitutionalization and the right to the least restrictive treatment alternative are relatively straightforward in principle. However, their implementation is both complex and controversial."[201]

190. See tables 2.6, col. 7, & 6.1, col. 3.

191. See tables 2.6, col. 7, & 6.1, cols. 2 & 3.

192. See tables 2.6, col. 7, & 2.8, col. 8. See also cases cited in note 152 *supra*.

193. Ill. Ann. Stat. ch. 91½, § 2-102(a) (Smith-Hurd 1966 & Supp. 1981).

194. Pub. L. No. 96-398, § 501, 94 Stat. 1564, 1598 (1980) (codified at 42 U.S.C. § 9501 (1982)).

195. Omnibus Budget Reconciliation Act of 1981, Pub. L. No. 97-35, 95 Stat. 357 (1981).

196. Patients' Bills of Rights, *supra* note 140, at 181-84.

197. See Joint Commission on Mental Illness and Health, *supra* note 1, which described conditions at state hospitals and emphasized why treatment in the community was important. See also W. Wolfensberger, B. Nirge, S. Olshansky, R. Penske, & P. Roos, The Principle of Normalization in Human Services (1972).

198. For a good review of the rights of the retarded, see the fourth issue of 31 Stan. L. Rev. 541-829 (1979), esp. Herr, The New Clients: Legal Services for the Mentally Retarded, at 553; Ewing, Health Planning and Deinstitutionalization: Advocacy Within the Administrative Process, at 679; and Ferleger & Boyd, Anti-Institutionalization: The Promise of the *Pennhurst* Case, at 71.

199. See Alternatives to Mental Hospital Treatment (L.I. Stein & M.A. Test eds. 1978); see also State Mental Hospitals: What Happens When They Close (P.I. Ahmed & S.C. Plog eds. 1976); Lamb & Goertzel, The Long-Term Patient in the Era of Community Treatment, 34 Archives Gen. Psychiatry 679 (1977).

200. Bachrach, Is the Least Restrictive Environment Always the Best? Sociological and Semantic Implications, 31 Hosp. & Community Psychiatry 97 (1980); Killebrew, Harris, & Kruckeberg, A Conceptual Model for Determining the Least Restrictive Treatment-Training Modality, 33 Hosp. & Community Psychiatry 367 (1982); Ransohoff, Zachary, Gaynor, & Hargreaves, Measuring Restrictiveness of Psychiatric Care, 33 Hosp. & Community Psychiatry 361 (1982).

201. See Ransohoff, Zachary, Gaynor, & Hargreaves, *supra* note 200, at 362.

Part of the controversy concerns who should be held responsible for ensuring that an individual receives minimally restrictive placement or treatment. Who should have the duty to try to locate other alternatives—the treatment staff, the courts, or the mental health advocates or attorneys? This question was in part raised by *Lake v. Cameron*[202] as discussed earlier. If no placement alternatives exist, is it the duty of the state mental health agency to redirect its limited funds to create alternatives, or is it the duty of the legislatures to provide more funds so that the full range of alternatives from outpatient care to inpatient treatment can exist? These are some of the practical issues that compound the problems created by the concept.

Some mental health professionals believe that a "linear" concept of restrictiveness does not apply in mental health treatment and that "[t]he law must come to acknowledge that more treatment does not always mean a greater degree of limitation of individual freedoms," as one commentator put it.[203] They believe that the judiciary, in embracing the least restrictive alternative concept, has unduly focused on the physical facade of treatment settings and has failed to consider important differences in modes of treatment as well as differences in the individual needs of each patient. Concerns have been raised about the validity of the assumption that being outside the institution is automatically a less restrictive form of treatment.[204] Which is more restrictive: being hospitalized in a minimum security unit of a state hospital with grounds privileges and weekend passes, or being confined in a nursing home with no grounds and no opportunity to leave?

In an official statement on the adequacy of treatment, the American Psychiatric Association has stated: "The definition of treatment and the appraisal of its adequacy are matters for medical determination. Final authority with respect to interpreting the law on the subject rests with the courts."[205] This statement reflects the belief on the part of many mental health professionals that when the courts rule that certain settings are too restrictive, they go beyond their proper role by presuming to adjudge the quality and legitimacy of certain treatments, determinations that should instead be left to the mental health professionals working in this area.[206]

The tension generated by the concept of the least restrictive alternative likely will continue, and grow, as litigation proliferates and as state mental health departments seek to juggle shrinking budgets, political pressures, court decrees, and statutory prescriptions for expansion of alternative placements. Although the concept of the least restrictive setting is now well accepted by both the courts and the states,[207] what is less restrictive still is not always self-evident[208] and deinstitutionalization has not clearly resulted in more freedom or a better quality of life for the disabled.[209]

Acceptance of the least restrictive alternative concept should provide the impetus for states to explore developing real alternatives, which provide quality care in settings that maximize the disabled's opportunity for liberty. This process has begun, but not enough has yet been done to provide a full range of meaningful treatment alternatives. It is to be hoped that the recognition of a constitutional basis for this right will force the development of truly impressive alternative sites for treatment, or of more liberty within those existing facilities that presently deliver services to the disabled.

VIII. PERIODIC REVIEW

Although an individual's initial confinement in a mental health facility may be justified, the changes in circumstance during the course of hospitalization may render further confinement invalid or even unconstitutional.[210] Periodic review of the patient's mental condition serves to determine if the basis for hospitalization continues to exist, thereby ensuring that the patient's deprivation of freedom lasts only so long as is necessary to serve the state's interest in safety, care, and treatment.[211]

Not only does review help determine whether the pa-

202. 364 F.2d 657 (D.C. Cir. 1966). See text at notes 157–60.

203. Appelbaum, Least Restrictive Environment: Some Comments, Amplification, 31 Hosp. & Community Psychiatry 420 (1980).

204. Bachrach, *supra* note 200; see also Chambers, Community-Based Treatment and the Constitution: The Principle of the Least Restrictive Alternative, *in* Alternatives to Mental Hospital Treatment, *supra* note 199, at 23.

205. Council of the American Psychiatric Association, Official Action: Position Statment on the Question of Adequacy of Treatment, 123 Am. J. Psychiatry 1458 (1967).

206. Ransohoff, Zachary, Gaynor, & Hargreaves, *supra* note 200, at 362; see also Glazer, Towards an Imperical Judiciary? 41 Pub. Interest 104 (1975).

207. See in this chapter § VII A, Development Through Case Law, *supra* and table 2.6.

208. Even within the mental health community there is disagreement on this matter. E.g., some would argue that chemical restraints are less restrictive than physical restraints, while others take the opposition position.

209. See Wolfensberger, Nirge, Olshansky, Penske, & Roos, *supra* note 197. See also Bassuk & Gerson, Deinstitutionalization and Mental Health Services, Sci. Am., Feb. 1978, at 46; Borus, Deinstitutionalization of the Chronically Mentally Ill, 305 New Eng. J. Med. 339 (1981); Etzioni, No Place to Go, Washington Monthly, Dec. 1978, at 46–48; Lamb, What Did We Really Expect from Deinstitutionalization? 32 Hosp. & Community Psychiatry 105 (1981); Lehman, Ward, & Linn, Chronic Mental Patients: The Quality of Life Issue, 139 Am. J. Psychiatry 1271 (1982); Scull, Deinstitutionalization and the Rights of the Deviant, 37 J. Soc. Issues, No. 3, 1981, at 6; Talbott, *supra* note 189.

210. See, e.g., O'Connor v. Donaldson, 422 U.S. 563 (1975).

211. See, e.g., Ennis & Emery, *supra* note 5, at 127. See also Eubanks v. Clarke, 434 F. Supp. 1022, 1027 (E.D. Pa. 1977).

tient continues to meet the standards for involuntary hospitalization,[212] but it also serves to determine whether the disabled person should be placed in a less restrictive setting,[213] and it may alert the staff to the need for a change in the treatment plan or for transfer to a different type of facility that can better meet the treatment or habilitation needs of the patient.[214] Requiring the staff to examine why the person was institutionalized, whether he continues to need institutionalization, and what is being done for him protects the disabled person from getting "lost" in the institution or being subjected to inadequate or inappropriate treatment.[215]

Thirty-one states and the District of Columbia have statutes pertaining to periodic examination of patients,[216] of which 25 specify the frequency of examinations, ranging from once every 30 days to once a year.[217] Some states have established separate review timetables for the mentally ill and for the developmentally disabled.[218] which often results in the developmentally disabled being reviewed less frequently than the mentally ill.[219] Although most statutes do not distinguish between children and adults for review purposes, some mental health professionals believe that children should be reviewed more frequently to assure that they are institutionalized for the shortest period necessary to accomplish their treatment goals[220] since the impact of institutionalization is likely to be more profound for children.[221]

Twelve jurisdictions permit review upon the petition of the disabled or someone acting in his behalf.[222] Review also might be permitted as required by "good medical practice."[223] In addition to the statutes setting forth the physical review of the person, 35 states require periodic review of the patients' records by the facility staff.[224] It is unclear what a review of the record will accomplish without an accompanying review of the disabled.

The failure of some states to provide for regular or any monitoring of the disabled's condition is inconsistent with the principle of assuring that the mentally disabled individual be treated in the least restrictive setting or manner necessary to accomplish the treatment or habilitation goals established for him. If the disabled person receives only an annual personal examination or record check, he could remain for many months in a setting or regimen that is not justified by his clinical condition. This is particularly likely to occur now that modern drug therapies can achieve rapid improvements for the mentally ill.[225]

Although periodic review remains important, it is less important than in the past since most states today permit only commitment orders of limited duration.[226] Thus extended commitment can be achieved only by periodic recommitment, which is in effect a guarantee of "periodic review." Some states even require that the "voluntariness" of the patients who have been voluntarily admitted must be reconfirmed after a period of time.[227]

IX. PATIENT TRANSFERS

It is not uncommon that during the course of institu-

212. See ch. 2, Involuntary Institutionalization, for a discussion of the criteria for civil commitment.

213. See discussion of the least restrictive alternative in § VII of this chapter *supra*, ; see also Strauss, Due Process in Civil Commitment and Elsewhere, *in* The Mentally Retarded Citizen and the Law 456 (M. Kindred ed. 1976).

214. For example, some facilities may have specialized programs for the deaf, the blind, or those with a diagnosis of both mental illness and mental retardation; thus a transfer would be beneficial. A review also permits checking on medication and determining if the proper dosage has been prescribed.

215. Many states require an individual treatment plan. See table 5.2. See also Evans v. Washington, 459 F. Supp. 483, 485 (D.D.C. 1978); to ensure habilitative care in the alternative least restrictive of individual liberty, the court enjoined the institution to develop an individualized habilitation program in accordance with treatment and to provide an annual periodic review of the plan and program with the opportunity for the patient and parent/guardian to participate in such review.

216. See table 6.1, cols. 4-6, e.g., Alabama, Arizona, Arkansas, California, Colorado, Delaware, District of Columbia, Hawaii, Idaho, Illinois, Indiana, Louisiana, Maine, Maryland, Massachusetts, Michigan, Minnesota, Mississippi, Missouri, Montana, New Mexico, New York, Ohio, Pennsylvania, South Carolina, South Dakota, Tennessee, Texas, Utah, West Virginia, Wisconsin, and Wyoming.

217. See table 6.1, col. 5, e.g., Arkansas, Delaware, District of Columbia, Idaho, Illinois, Indiana, Louisiana, Maine, Maryland, Massachusetts, Michigan, Minnesota, Mississippi, Missouri, Montana, New Mexico, New York, South Carolina, South Dakota, Tennessee, Texas, West Virginia, Wisconsin, and Wyoming.

218. See table 6.1, cols. 4-6.

219. See, e.g., Montana, which provides that the mentally ill must be examined every 90 days (Mont. Code Ann. § 53-21-162(5) (1981)), and that the developmentally disabled be examined six months after admission and at least annually thereafter (Mont. Code Ann. § 53-20-148(7) (1981)). Ill. Ann. Stat. ch. 91½, § 3-404 (Smith-Hurd Supp. 1981), provides for review after the first 30 days and then after 60 days for the mentally ill, while only providing for an annual review for the developmentally disabled in § 4-310.

220. M.L. Hutt & R.G. Gibby, The Mentally Retarded Child: Development, Education, and Treatment 337 (3d ed. 1976); Menolascino, Primitive, Atypical and Abnormal Behaviors, *in* Mental Health Services for the Mentally Retarded, 96 (E. Katz ed. 1972).

221. Mercer, Patterns of Family Crisis Related to Reacceptance of the Retardate, 71 Am. J. Mental Deficiency 19 (1966); H.B. Robinson & N.M. Robinson, The Mentally Retarded Child: A Psychological Approach 531 (1965).

222. See table 6.1, col. 6, e.g., Alabama, Arkansas, California, Colorado, District of Columbia, Hawaii, Ohio, Pennsylvania, Tennessee, Texas, Utah, and Wisconsin.

223. See table 6.1, col. 6, e.g., Alaska.

224. See, table 6.1, cols. 8 & 9, e.g., Alabama, Colorado, Delaware, Florida, Georgia, Hawaii, Illinois, Indiana, Iowa, Kansas, Louisiana, Maryland, Massachusetts, Michigan, Minnesota, Mississippi, Missouri, Montana, Nebraska, Nevada, New Mexico, New York, North Carolina, North Dakota, Ohio, Oklahoma, Oregon, Pennsylvania, Rhode Island, South Dakota, Texas, Vermont, Virginia, West Virginia, and Wyoming.

225. See ch. 6, Treatment Rights, § II A, Psychotropic Medication.

226. See table 2.7.

227. See table 2.6. See, e.g., Ill. Ann. Stat. ch. 91½, § 3-304 (Smith-Hurd Supp. 1981), which provides for reaffirmation of voluntary status every 30 days.

tionalization, transfer of the disabled from one facility to another will be considered. There can be a number of reasons for transfer, including: changed treatment needs of the person; improved financial circumstances of the disabled, enabling him to move to a private facility; deteriorated financial circumstances, necessitating movement to a state facility; determination that the disabled was wrongly placed initially; better matching of treatment needs with institutional capabilities, such as in the case of transfer of a deaf person to a facility equipped to deal with hearing impaired individuals; placement nearer to the person's family; and removal of the disabled to his state of residence.

Sometimes, a transfer will be welcomed by the disabled person and/or his family, but this will not always be the case. Consequently, the question of statutory and judicial constraints upon the freedom of institutions to transfer unwilling people to other institutions is a part of the matrix to be addressed in considering the rights of the mentally disabled.

A. Statutory Provisions

Almost all states have some statutory provisions regulating transfers, varying in both scope and the procedures mandated before someone can be transferred.[228] All but seven states[229] have statutes making a person's transfer a matter of administrative discretion.[230] The criteria most frequently used to justify transfer include "best interests" of the patient,[231] "clinically or medically advisable,"[232] "consistent with mental health needs,"[233] or "not detrimental" or "for any reason."[234] These criteria are sufficiently vague to allow institutional administrators broad discretion. Most of the states require that notice of the transfer be given to a relative, guardian, or committing court.[235] Fourteen states provide that formal approval must be obtained before the transfer can occur.[236]

Transfers typically occur as a result of administrative decision rather than decisions by the disabled or their families. When a person wishes to be transferred from the state system to a private facility and the private facility is willing to take him, the transfer will occur easily. The problems arise when the person is in a state facility and the state proposes to transfer him to another state facility to which he does not want to go. Since the prior edition of this book was published in 1971, more states have enacted statutes recognizing that an institutionalized mentally disabled person has some procedural rights before a transfer can occur.[237] Thirty-two states now provide a method for the patient to object to being transferred, usually accomplished through an administrative hearing or in rare instances a judicial hearing. Three states[238] provide for a judicial hearing when the transfer is to a more restrictive setting.

In addition to state laws covering intrastate transfers, 44 states and the District of Columbia have enacted the Interstate Compact on Mental Health, which governs the interstate transfer of the mentally disabled.[239] This compact was developed as a result of a meeting called by the Council of State Governments in 1955, where it was noted that the number of persons repatriated to other states equalled the number received from other states within a given period. The Compact provides a legally based administrative mechanism for the transfer of the mentally disabled to their home states. The Compact emphasizes the importance of the patient's welfare in that it, rather than his place of residence per se controls the placement decision.[240] A specific provision protecting the rights of the patient when a transfer is requested provides:

> Whenever the compact administrator receives a request for the transfer of a patient from an institution in this State to an institution in another party state, and he determines that the transfer is in the best interest of the patient, he shall give notice of the proposed transfer to the patient, the spouse of the patient, the parents of the patient and the adult children of the patient. This notice shall also notify such people of the right, if requested, to a court hearing on the proposed transfer and shall contain a request for a written consent from such people for the transfer. The notice shall be in writing, and the respondents shall be given 14 days from the date of mailing of the notice to consent or object to the transfer, or to request a court hearing. No transfer shall be made if there is any such written objection or request made to the compact administrator except upon order of the court after hearing. However, no transfer shall be made if the compact administrator receives such writ-

228. See table 4.1.

229. See Arkansas, Georgia, Kentucky, Mississippi, New Mexico, New York, and West Virginia.

230. See table 4.1, cols. 6-9.

231. See table 4.1, col. 7, e.g., Colorado, Hawaii, Indiana, Iowa Kansas, Oregon, South Dakota, Utah, Washington, and Wisconsin.

232. See table 4.1, col. 7, e.g., Alabama, Louisiana, Maine, Maryland, North Dakota, Ohio, South Carolina, and Vermont.

233. *Id.*, e.g., Alaska, District of Columbia, Indiana, and Illinois.

234. *Id.*, e.g., California, Michigan, and Texas.

235. See table 4.1, cols. 12 & 13.

236. See table 4.1, col. 4, e.g., Florida, Georgia, Louisiana, Maine, Montana, New Hampshire, New Jersey, North Carolina, North Dakota, Ohio, Rhode Island, South Carolina, Tennessee, and Texas.

237. See table 4.1, col. 8.

238. Ohio Rev. Code Ann. §§ 5122.20, 5123.21 (Baldwin 1980 & Supp. 1981); Pa. Stat. Ann. tit. 50, § 7306(c) (Purdon Supp. 1983); S.C. Code Ann. § 44-23-210(4) (Law. Co-op. 1976 & Supp. 1981).

239. The nonmembers are Arizona, California, Mississippi, Nevada, Utah, and Virginia.

240. For an example of the full compact, see, e.g., Ky. Rev. Stat. §§ 210.520 to 210.550 (Michie 1977 & Supp. 1982) or N.J. Stat. Ann. §§ 30:7B-1 to-18 (West 1981).

> ten objections from all such people. No transfer shall be made of a patient order hospitalized by any court unless written notice of the proposed transfer has been given to that court.[241]

Pursuant to the compact in Illinois, for example, approximately 40 people per year are transferred to other states, and 30 are transferred into the state.[242] That is, there does not tend to be a large disbalance between numbers entering and leaving states. However, it may be that as more and more states encounter budgetary difficulties, some will try to find a way to close the doors to the mentally disabled from other jurisdictions.

There is also an Interstate Compact on the Mentally Disordered Offender,[243] but it has not been widely adopted and is rarely used. The transfer rights of the mentally disordered offender are discussed in chapter 12, "Mental Disability and the Criminal Law." Issues in transferring the mentally disabled person from a mental health facility to a community facility are discussed under the rubric of discharge in chapter 4, "Discharge and Transfer."

B. Case Law

Many of the statutes governing patient transfers may need to be revised in light of recent cases setting out the due process rights of patients before transfer to a maximum security facility[244] or from a prison to a mental hospital.[245] In *Vitek v. Jones* in 1980,[246] the United States Supreme Court held that the due process clause of the Fourteenth Amendment applied in transfers from prisons to mental hospitals. The Court recognized that although the prisoner was confined under a prison sentence, this "did not authorize the State to classify him as mentally ill and subject him to involuntary psychiatric treatment without affording him additional due process protections."[247] Reasoning that the stigmatizing consequences of a confinement in a mental hospital constituted an additional deprivation of liberty sufficient to entitle the prisoner to procedural protections, the Court went on to endorse most of the protections the district court had held to be applicable. These included (1) notice of the proposed transfer, (2) a hearing, with the prisoner present, to present and consider evidence, including witnesses, (3) an independent decision maker, and (4) a written statement by the fact-finder of the evidence relied on and the reasons for transfer.[248] The Court did not require the automatic appointment of an attorney.

The matter of a hearing had come up in a federal district court in 1977 in *Eubanks v. Clarke*,[249] which involved a schizophrenic patient who was transferred from a minimum security facility to a maximum security facility after an altercation with another patient. The transferee was not notified of the reason for the transfer and was given no opportunity to confront the authorities. In ruling on the patient's challenge to his transfer, the court held that a constitutionally protected liberty interest was implicated in transfers from minimum to maximum security hospitals, stating: "The Due Process Clause of the fourteenth amendment entitles an involuntarily committed mental patient to a hearing when transferred to a hospital where conditions are substantially more restrictive."[250]

A hearing is usually not necessary when the transfer is to a less secure facility or involves a move from one minimum security facility to another, according to the state court in *In re Guzan* (1979).[251] The *Guzan* court interpreted a Pennsylvania statute regarding court approval of transfers to require that while in all transfer cases the committing court's approval for transfer was necessary, a real hearing was required only when the transfer was to a setting where the conditions were substantially more restrictive.[252]

With the mentally ill patient's average length of stay less than a month in public facilities today,[253] transfers are as a practical matter less likely to occur now than in the past. However, for many of the longer term patients, that is, chronically ill individuals, the retarded residents, and the mentally disordered offenders, the potential for transfer remains. Often, the issue will arise as a result of the closing of a facility where many of the residents have lived for years. Large-scale transfers today also occur as part of the continuing thrust to return the mentally disabled to the community, which may involve little more than substituting one type of institutional environment—for example, nursing homes or so-called halfway houses—for mental health facilities. The disabled who do not want such transfers or seem reluctant to accept them will need an opportunity to voice their objections in an impartial hearing.

241. Ill. Ann. Stat. ch. 91½, § 50-5 (Smith-Hurd 1966 & Supp. 1981).

242. This is according to Muriel Reitz, director of Interstate Compact Services for Illinois, who has held that position for more than a decade.

243. See e.g., Ill Ann. Stat. ch. 91½, § 50-21 (Smith-Hurd 1966 & Supp. 1981).

244. Eubanks v. Clarke, 434 F. Supp. 1022 (E.D. Pa. 1977).

245. Vitek v. Jones, 445 U.S. 480 (1980).

246. *Id.*

247. *Id.* at 494.

248. *Id.* at 494–95.

249. 434 F. Supp. 1022 (E.D. Pa. 1977).

250. *Id.* at 1029. For analogous types of cases see discussion in this chapter § VII, Least Restrictive Alternative, *supra*.

251. 405 A.2d 1036 (Pa. Commw. Ct. 1979).

252. *Id.* at 1038.

253. Office of Program Planning and Coordination, Alcohol, Drug Abuse, and Mental Health Administration, Public Health Service, U.S. Dep't of Health and Human Services, The Alcohol, Drug Abuse, and Mental Health National Data Book 64 table 28 (Jan. 1980) [hereinafter cited as National Data Book].

X. RESTRAINTS AND SECLUSION

The use of physical restraints and seclusion are two commonly accepted practices in many institutions for the mentally ill and the retarded. Clearly controversial—in the mental health community as well as in legal circles—these practices have been justified as necessary in certain circumstances. However, significant restrictions on their use have been imposed by both courts and state legislatures in response to real and potential abuses. Those who view these practices as useful regard these restrictions, which typically take the form of procedural requirements, as troublesome interferences with the need for treatment flexibility. On the other hand, those who view restraints and seclusion as punitive and inappropriate will deem anything short of total prohibition inadequate. Neither of these polar positions, total staff freedom or total prohibition, is acceptable. What is needed, rather, is compromise and accommodation of some of the concerns of both sides, with the interests of the patient the critical determinant.

A. Restraints

Physical restraints, sometimes called *mechanical restraints*, physically incapacitate the person by means such as tying him to his bed or a chair with straps, "poseys," sheets, or otherwise. Other means of restriction include cuffs or mitts on the hands and, formerly, straitjackets, which are seldom used today.

To the lay person, such restraints often appear cruel and punitive, and even those trained in mental health disagree over the wisdom of using them. Condemnation of their use by mental health professionals is not new.[254] Nonetheless, most mental facilities continue to resort to restraints on at least some occasions, and there is respectable professional opinion supporting such occasional discrete use. Rosen and DiGiacomo have set forth guidelines on the appropriate use of restraints, and while they were addressing the psychiatric patient, their list is generally applicable to institutionalized mentally retarded individuals as well:

> The primary indication for the use of restraints is the control of violent behavior occurring during the course of a psychotic illness which cannot be adequately controlled with psychosocial techniques and/or medications. When violence takes the form of self-destructive behavior as in a severe mood disorder, restraints must be used to protect the patient from his impulses until definitive treatment of his illness takes effect.
>
> . . .
>
> [Restraints should be used when there is] marked agitation, thought disorder, or severe confusion in a patient whose physical condition prevents or seriously limits the use of antipsychotic medication.
>
> . . .
>
> [Restraints may be appropriate in] the presence of hyperactivity, insomnia, decreased food and fluid intake, and grossly impaired judgment particularly when these symptoms are accompanied by regressed, socially unacceptable behavior.
>
> . . .
>
> [The use of restraints might be indicated as] a joint effort by both the patient and therapist to reduce the disruptive effects of excessive external stimuli.
>
> . . .
>
> The final indication [for the use of restraints is when the patient requests them].[255]

Rosen and DiGiacomo further assert that a patient should be removed from restraints when there has been a decrease in restlessness and anxiety, stabilization of mood, increased attention span and orientation, and improvement in reality testing and judgment with a decrease in hallucinations, delusions, and violent impulses. Patients' rights advocates may question the broadness of these criteria and whether they truly represent the least restrictive way of meeting the needs of the disabled.

Actual practice, of course, does not necessarily accord with this scheme. A major Canadian study of the use of restraints in facilities for both the mentally ill and the developmentally disabled reported that they were primarily employed as a means to control violent behavior but also found that they were used in facilities for the retarded to prevent self-abuse and self-mutilation and for behavior modification purposes.[256] One study indicated that physical restraints were used when there were violations of the rules on a psychiatric unit of a general hospital.[257]

254. J. Connolly's Treatment of the Insane Without Mechanical Restraints (1865) was the first book to reject the use of mechanical restraints and advocated the use of kindness and patience and the end of the prison-like aspects of the institutions. These views were regarded more as pious opinion than as useful guidelines and were met with vigorous opposition in America. (F.G. Alexander & S.T. Selesnick, The History of Psychiatry: An Evaluation of Psychiatric Thought and Practice from Prehistoric Times to the Present (1966); R. Hunter & I. Macalpine, Three Hundred Years of Psychiatry 1535-1860: A History Presented in Selected English Texts (corrected reprint ed. 1982 of 1963 ed.).) The first superintendent of Columbus Hospital in Columbus, Ohio, in 1838 wrote that restraint was seldom required if the patient was treated with "kindness and forbearance." See Martin, Inside the Asylum, Sat. Evening Post, Nov. 10, 1965, at 130.

255. Rosen & DiGiacomo, The Role of Physical Restraint in the Treatment of Psychiatric Illness, 39 J. Clinical Psychiatry 228 (1978) (notes omitted).

256. Guirguis & Durost, The Role of Mechanical Restraints in the Management of Disturbed Behaviour, 23 Canadian Psychiatric Ass'n J. 212 (1970).

257. Soloff, Physical Restraint and the Nonpsychotic Patient: Clinical and Legal Perspectives, 40 J. Clinical Psychiatry 302 (1979).

The general consensus today is that restraints are a measure of last resort, reserved for the disruptive patient who is unresponsive to verbal or chemical intervention.[258] Abuses do occur however. Restraints have served as a means of punishing the institutionalized and as a means for staff to vent frustration or avoid contact with the disabled. These abuses have prompted several judicial decisions and statutes to govern the use of restraints.

B. Seclusion

Seclusion involves placing a person in isolated confinement. Most institutions have set aside a specific room for this purpose, generally securely built, small and often unfurnished, or furnished in a way designed to assure that the person does not injure himself. The typical seclusion room has a locked door with an observation window, and in some institutions it is a padded cell.

Seclusion has been justified as serving three acceptable goals for the psychiatric patient: containment, isolation, and a decrease in sensory input. Gutheil elaborates on these goals, as follows:

> *Containment*
>
> The core of this principle is the restriction of a patient's movement to a place that is safe in two senses of the word: the patient is safe from both self-injury and the possibly damaging consequences of injury to others, . . . and the ward is safe from the patient's out-of-control actions and impulses. This two-fold element of safety plays the largest role in the feeling of reassurance that the patient in seclusion experiences. . . .
>
> *Isolation*
>
> This second principle addresses the particular vulnerability of the seriously ill to a variety of forms of pathological intensity in relationships. . . . [T]he isolation from relationships provided by seclusion may serve as an oasis—perhaps the only oasis—of relief from this interpersonal torment.
>
> *Decrease in Sensory Input*
>
> This [third] principle represents the "quiet" in "quiet room" . . . .The uniformity and consistency of the sensory input in seclusion produce a relative monotony that provides welcome relief from the sensory overload supplied by even a quiet ward to patients in those clinical states for which seclusion is most useful.[259]

Seclusion, or "time out," rooms may also be used for retarded individuals, but sometimes for the mentally ill as well, as part of a behavior modification regimen.[260] "Inappropriate" behavior by the disabled leads to placement in the seclusion room to provide an avoidance incentive for appropriate behavior. While behavior modification programs have generated considerable controversy, they do appear to be successful with some retarded and autistic children.[261]

While the use of such rooms is generally accepted,[262] some mental health professionals regard the practice negatively.[263] The intense impact of the seclusion experience has been documented;[264] it is definitely not an innocuous aspect of life in a mental institution. Like the use of restraints, isolation of the person in a seclusion room is generally regarded as an intervention of last resort, to be used only when all less restrictive alternatives have failed or are known to be of no avail in the circumstances.[265]

While most facilities for the mentally disabled, including psychiatric units of general hospitals, have isolation or seclusion rooms,[266] there have been few studies analyzing how seclusion is actually used. A recent study of a psychiatric unit of a general hospital[267] found that seclusion was most often used during the night and morning shift changes, which was attributed to patient and staff anxiety accompanying the staff departures and arrivals. The study also noted that there was an increased use of seclusion when there were more patients on the unit, which it suggested could be attributed to increased stimulation or lack of staff to provide more appropriate, personalized attention for particularly needful patients.[268] Another study found that "behavior disruptive to the therapeutic environment" was the most frequent reason given for placing patients in the seclu-

258. *Id.* See also Rosen & DiGiacomo, *supra* note 255, at 231.

259. Gutheil, Observations on the Theoretical Bases for Seclusion of the Psychiatric Inpatient, 135 Am. J. Psychiatry 325, 326 (1978).

260. For a more detailed description of behavior modification see ch. 6, Treatment Rights, *infra*. Ayllon & Azrin, The Measurement and Reinforcement of Behavior of Psychotics, 8 J. Experimental Analysis Behav. 357 (1965); Lovaas, Koegel, Simmons, & Long, Some Generalization and Follow-up Measures on Autistic Children in Behavior Therapy, 6 J. Applied Behav. Analysis 131 (1973); J. Wolpe & A.A. Lazarus, Behavior Therapy Techniques (1966).

261. See also Baer & Guess, Receptive Training of Adjectival Inflections in Mental Retardates,4 J. Applied Behav. Analysis 129 (1979); B.S. Brown, L.A. Wienckowski, & S.B. Stolz, Behavior Modification: Perspective on a Current Issue (DHEW Pub. No. (ADM) 75-202, 1975).

262. See M. Day & E. Semrad, Schizophrenic Reactions (ch. 11), *in* A. Nicholi, The Harvard Guide to Modern Psychiatry 236–37 (1978); Gutheil, *supra* note 259; The Psychiatric Uses of Seclusion and Restraint (K. Tardiff ed. 1984).

263. See Greenblatt, Seclusion as a Means of Restraint, Psychiatric Opinion, Feb. 1980, at 13, for a documentation of some of the problems with use of selection; Mattson & Sacks, Seclusion: Uses and Complications, 135 Am. J. Psychiatry 1210 (1978); Van Putten, Milieu Therapy: Contraindications? 29 Archives Gen. Psychiatry 640 (1973).

264. Fitzgerald & Long, Seclusion in the Treatment and Management of Severely Disturbed Manic and Depressed Patients, 11 Perspectives Psychiatric Care 59 (1973).

265. Wadeson & Carpenter, Impact of the Seclusion Room Experience, 163 J. Nervous & Mental Disease 318 (1976).

266. See Gutheil, *supra* note 259, at 327.

267. Schwab & Lahmeyer, The Uses of Seclusion on a General Hospital Psychiatric Unit, 40 J. Clinical Psychiatry 228 (1979).

268. *Id.* at 231.

sion room.[269] While how frequently seclusion rooms are used in state mental health facilities is unknown, it can be assumed that it varies from facility to facility depending on the institution's "philosophy," its staffing, and the applicable state laws and regulations.

C. Case Law

The use of restraints or seclusion within facilities for the mentally disabled has prompted several legal challenges in facilities both for the mentally ill[270] and for the mentally retarded.[271] Often they have been made within the context of lawsuits attacking a wide range of alleged abuses within the hospital and attempting to establish a whole panoply of rights for the disabled.[272] Most cases have cited specific examples of abusive use of restraints or seclusion.[273] In general the cases hold, or through consent decrees provide, that restraints or seclusion can be used only when the disabled person could harm himself or others and there is no less restrictive alternative available to control this danger.[274] Other common elements in the decisions are that (1) restraints and seclusion may be imposed only pursuant to written order, (2) such orders must be confined to limited time periods, (3) the patient's condition must be charted at regular time intervals, and (4) if orders are extended beyond the initial period, the extension must be authorized by a doctor, often with review by the medical director or superintendent required. Many of these requirements are now also found in state statutes.[275]

Again, *Wyatt v. Stickney*[276] first set forth limitations, on which other courts have often based their rulings. In *Wyatt*, which dealt with the rights of the mentally ill, the federal district court held that patients had a right to be free from physical restraint and isolation and that except for emergency situations patients might be physically restrained or placed in isolation only on a written order explaining the rationale for such action. The court went on to elaborate conditions and requirements for the use of such orders and for administering the restraint or isolation.[277]

Some courts have been even more restrictive than *Wyatt* as to who can order the restraints or seclusion and as to the length of time for which a patient can be restrained or secluded. In *Davis v. Balson*[278] the federal district court recognized that the patient had a protected liberty interest in not being restrained and that before restraint or isolation could occur, certain procedural safeguards had to be followed. The court held that the patient was entitled to: (1) written notice of the charges 24 hours prior to a hearing, (2) a hearing to call witnesses on his behalf, (3) a written statement of the findings of fact and the evidence relied upon, (4) assistance from another resident or a member of the staff if the patient was illiterate or the issues complex, and (5) an impartial decision maker.[279] The court did not address the question of compliance with, or waiving of, these requirements in an emergency necessitating the immediate use of restraints or seclusion. This seems somewhat absurd given that restraints are generally employed in an emergency when the person is agitated. Since their use is temporary, it is unlikely that 24 hours later the circumstances will be the same, thus requiring restraints.

In *Eckerhart v. Hensley*[280] the federal district court did address the emergency situation. In an overall less stringent view than the *Davis* court holding it concluded that notice and hearing requirements were inappropriate not only in emergency situations but generally. While acknowledging that "a *medical* decision to physically restrain or isolate a mental patient involves no less an extraordinary deprivation of liberty than does the use of punitive isolation in a prison,"[281] the *Eckerhart* court reasoned:

> A requirement of advance notice and hearing is not at all appropriate to the medical decision to use seclusion or restraints. Such a decision often is made under conditions of emergency, in which an agitated patient presents an immediate danger to himself or others. However, this Court concludes that minimal due process requires at least that the *medical* decision to utilize physical restraints or seclusion be made in a context designed to protect the patient from an arbitrary deprivation of personal liberty.[282]

The court concluded that the policy of the defendant hospital gave due consideration to the important liberty

269. Mattson & Sacks, Seclusion: Use and Complications, 135 Am. J. Psychiatry 1210 (1978).

270. See Rogers v. Okin, 478 F. Supp. 1342 (D. Mass. 1979); Eckerhart v. Hensley, 475 F. Supp. 908 (W.D. Mo. 1979); Davis v. Balson, 461 F. Supp. 842 (N.D. Ohio 1978); Davis v. Watkins, 384 F. Supp. 1196 (N.D. Ohio 1974); Wyatt v. Stickney, 344 F. Supp. 373 (M.D. Ala. 1973); Negron v. Ward, 74 Civ. 1480, 1 MDLR 191 (S.D.N.Y. July 13, 1976).

271. Youngberg v. Romeo, 457 U.S. 307 (1982); New York State Ass'n for Retarded Children, Inc. v. Carey, 393 F. Supp. 715 (E.D.N.Y. 1975); Welsch v. Likins, 373 F. Supp. 487 (D. Minn. 1974); Wyatt v. Stickney, 344 F. Supp. 387 (M.D. Ala. 1972).

272. See cases cited in notes 270 & 271 *supra*.

273. See Davis v. Balson, 461 F. Supp. 842 (N.D. Ohio 1978); Eckerhart v. Hensley, 475 F. Supp. 908 (W.D. Mo. 1979); Rogers v. Okin, 478 F. Supp. 1342 (D. Mass. 1979); and New York State Ass'n for Retarded Children, Inc. v. Carey, 393 F. Supp. 715 (E.D.N.Y. 1975).

274. See cases cited in notes 270 & 271 *supra*.

275. See table 6.2, cols. 9-11.

276. 344 F. Supp. 373 (M.D. Ala. 1972).

277. *Id.* at 380. See in this chapter appendix A *infra*, reprinting details of the *Wyatt* court's stipulations on restraint and isolation.

278. 461 F. Supp. 842, 876 (N.D. Ohio 1978).

279. *Id.* at 878.

280. 475 F. Supp. 908 (W.D. Mo. 1979).

281. *Id.* at 926 (emphasis in original).

282. *Id.* (emphasis in original).

interest at stake and that it provided adequate means of assuring against the arbitrary deprivation of liberty. The hospital's policy included the following: (1) a requirement that restraint and/or seclusion not be imposed without an order signed by a doctor, (2) the limiting of such restraints and seclusion to 20 minutes in emergency situations when no doctor's order could be immediately obtained, (3) a requirement that the patient be observed every 15 minutes, (4) a general 24-hour limit on the use of restraints, and (5) a mechanism for reviewing the initial decision by the hospital superintendent. On the facts before it, the *Eckerhart* court concluded that these safeguards were not observed.[283] It also found that although hospital policy prohibited the use of restraints or seclusion for disciplinary purposes, they were in fact being so used. If restraint and seclusion were to be used for disciplinary purposes, the Court went on, the hospital had to comply with the due process requirements set forth in *Wolff v. McDonnell,*[284] a prisoners' rights decision by the United States Supreme Court in 1974. *Wolff* required that the following procedures be observed: (1) written notice of the violation in advance of the hearing, (2) a written statement by the fact-finder of the evidence relied upon and of the reasons for the disciplinary action, and (3) an opportunity for the prisoner to call witnesses and present other evidence in his defense, when this would not be unduly hazardous to institutional security.[285]

Allegations of abusive use of restraints and seclusion have also been a major element in suits challenging institutional practices.[286] Like concern has generated statutory limitations to the effect that restraints and seclusion are not to be used as punishment.[287] Even with such laws on the books, abuses occur. In *New York State Association for Retarded Children, Inc. v. Carey* (1975)[288] the consent decree included a provision with language typically found in both the statutes and other consent decrees in this area. The decree provided:

> Physical restraints shall be employed only when absolutely necessary to prevent a resident from seriously injuring himself or others. Restraints shall never be employed as punishment, for the convenience of staff, or as a substitute for programs. In any event, restraints may only be applied if alternative techniques have failed (such failure to be documented in the resident's records) and only if such restraints impose the least possible restriction consistent with their purposes.[289]

Such a provision of course does not guarantee that abuses do not occur but rather establishes that any abuses constitute a violation of the law and, consequently, potential liability. By initiating various procedural and charting requirements, the courts hope to have the staff seriously think about and fully justify their use of restraints or seclusion.

Negron v. Ward[290] in 1976 produced one of the most extensive and restrictive consent decrees on this subject. It required the physician to write the order and mandated review by the director of the facility or the senior administrative physician if the disabled was to be restrained or secluded for more than four hours. Patients in restraints or seclusion were to be released every two hours. If the patient made no overt gestures threatening serious injury to himself or to others, restraints or seclusion could not be reimposed unless a doctor certified in writing that such release would be harmful. Probably the most unique requirement of the decree was that if the inmate was restrained for more than 48 hours, a qualified psychiatrist who was not employed by the hospital had to examine the inmate and make a written report indicating whether continued restraint or seclusion was justified.[291]

Some of the cases challenging restraint and seclusion practices in mental retardation facilities have made a distinction between the use of these procedures for control of threatened or actual violent behavior and their use for behavior modification purposes. For example, in the *Wyatt* case, which looked at conditions at Partlow State School and Hospital, the court held:

> Seclusion, defined as the placement of a resident alone in a locked room, shall not be employed. Legitimate "time out" procedures may be utilized under close and direct professional supervision as a technique in behavior-shaping programs.[292]

The acceptability of using restraints or seclusion for the purposes of training was also recognized by the United States Supreme Court in 1982 in *Youngberg v. Romeo,*[293] which involved a challenge to the practices at Pennhurst State School and Hospital in Pennsylvania. The Court held that residents could not be restrained except to assure their safety or in certain undefined cir-

283. *Id.* at 927.

284. 418 U.S. 539 (1974).

285. Eckerhart v. Hensley, 475 F. Supp. 908, 928 (W.D. Mo. 1979).

286. Rogers v. Okin, 634 F.2d 650 (1st Cir. 1980), *vacated and remanded,* Mills v. Rogers, 457 U.S. 291 (1982); Rogers v. Commissioner, 458 N.E.2d 308 (1983); Negron v. Ward, 74 Civ. 1480, 1 MDLR 191 (S.D.N.Y. July 13, 1976); Pennhurst State School & Hosp. v. Halderman, 451 U.S. 1 (1981), *on remand,* 673 F.2d 647 (3d Cir. 1982), *rev'd,* 104 S. Ct. 900 (1984); Youngberg v.Romeo, 457 U.S. 307 (1982).

287. See table 6.2, cols. 9–11.

288. 393 F. Supp. 715 (E.D.N.Y. 1975).

289. See Texts, 1 MDLR 65 (1976), for a reprint of the full consent decree, which was approved by the court at 393 F.Supp. 715 (E.D.N.Y. 1975).

290. 74 Civ. 1480, 1 MDLR 191 (S.D.N.Y. July 13, 1976).

291. *Id.* at 191.

292. Wyatt v. Stickney, 344 F. Supp. 387, 400 (M.D. Ala. 1972).

293. 457 U.S. 307 (1982).

cumstances "to provide needed training."[294] As has been noted, these types of practices have proven quite effective for the severely retarded when used as part of a consistent behavior modification program.[295] *Youngberg v. Romeo*[296] involved a 33-year-old profoundly retarded plaintiff, Nicholas Romeo, who had the mental capacity of an 18-month-old child. He had been admitted to Pennhurst State School and Hospital on the petition of his mother when she felt she could no longer care for him or control his violence. While at Pennhurst, Romeo suffered injuries on at least 63 occasions, some of which were self-inflicted. Romeo's lawyers claimed that the due process clause of the Fourteenth Amendment entitled their client to safe conditions of confinement, freedom from bodily restraints, and affirmative efforts at training or habilitation. The Supreme Court, in analyzing these claims, recognized that Romeo had a liberty interest in safety and freedom from bodily restraint but indicated that these interests were not absolute and to some extent were even in conflict. The Court explained:

> In operating an institution such as Pennhurst, there are occasions in which it is necessary for the State to restrain the movement of residents—for example, to protect them as well as others from violence. Similar restraints may also be appropriate in a training program. And an institution cannot protect its residents from all danger of violence if it is to permit them to have any freedom of movement.[297]

The Court then asserted:

> The State also has the unquestioned duty to provide reasonable safety for all residents and personnel within the institution. And it may not restrain residents except when and to the extent professional judgment deems this necessary to assure such safety or to provide needed training. In this case, therefore, the State is under a duty to provide respondent with such training as an appropriate professional would consider reasonable to ensure his safety and to facilitate his ability to function free from bodily restraints.[298]

The Court also held that decisions made by the appropriate professionals as to when to restrain would be presumptively considered correct.[299] This case is a landmark decision for the retarded because for the first time the Supreme Court recognized a limited right to treatment and habilitation, with the goal of trying to teach the resident to be able to control his behavior so that he would not have to be restrained. While viewed as a first step in the right direction by advocates for the developmentally disabled, the *Youngberg* decision is also one to be appreciated by mental health professionals to the extent that the Court recognized that the professionals, rather than the courts, are best able to determine the needs of the residents, including when restraint is proper.

D. Statutory Requirements

Most states have enacted statutes regulating the use of restraints at least to some extent,[300] generally specifying the circumstances under which restraints can be used, most often those in which the disabled person presents a risk of harm to himself or others.[301] Some states also permit the use of restraints for therapeutic or treatment purposes.[302] A few states as well as the District of Columbia require that the restraints be prescribed by a doctor.[303] Four states ban "unnecessary" restraint or seclusion,[304] 5 states preclude the use of restraints for punishment or staff convenience,[305] and 11 states permit use only upon a determination by the head of the treatment facility or his designee that the patient's medical needs require it.[306] Those states that do not have statutes concerning the use of restraints usually have administrative regulations on the matter. Administrative regulations are likely to further elaborate on the procedures to be followed when restraints are employed even in those states that have statutory law on the subject.

Statutory regulation of the use of seclusion is far less common. Only about half the states have laws relating to seclusion.[307] Nine states recognize that it may be used for treatment or some therapeutic purpose;[308] 18 specify that seclusion can be employed to prevent the person from harming himself or others.[309] Colorado prohibits the use of seclusion, but permits a "time out" proce-

294. *Id.* at 324.
295. See Brown, *supra* note 261, and accompanying text.
296. 457 U.S. 307 (1982).
297. *Id.* at 320
298. *Id.* at 324.
299. *Id.* at 323.

300. See table 6.2, col. 9.
301. *Id.*, e.g., Alaska, Arizona, Arkansas, Colorado, Connecticut, District of Columbia, Florida, Georgia, Hawaii, Idaho, Illinois, Indiana, Kansas, Louisiana, Massachusetts, Michigan, Minnesota, Missouri, Montana, New Jersey, New York, North Carolina, Oregon, Pennsylvania, South Dakota, and Wyoming.
302. *Id.*, e.g., Arizona, District of Columbia, Georgia, Hawaii, Indiana, Louisiana, North Carolina, and Wisconsin.
303. See *id.*, e.g., Connecticut,Nevada, and New York.
304. *Id.*, e.g., Arkansas, California,North Dakota, and Virginia. See also Cal. Welf. & Inst. Code 5325.1(c) (West 1972 & Supp. 1981); N.D. Cent. Code § 24-03.1-4 (1978 & Supp. 1981).
305. See Illinois, Louisiana, Montana, New York, and South Dakota.
306. See table 6.2, cols. 8-10, and laws of Alaska, Arizona, Colorado, Connecticut, District of Columbia, Idaho, Minnesota, Ohio, Oregon, South Carolina, and Vermont.
307. See table 6.2, col. 10.
308. See *id.*, e.g., Arizona, Hawaii, Indiana, Louisiana, Maine, Michigan, Missouri, North Carolina, Ohio, and Tennessee.
309. See *id.*

dure.[310] The District of Columbia and Montana have similar provisions on behalf of the developmentally disabled.[311] Idaho prohibits seclusion of developmentally disabled persons entirely.[312]

The majority of the states with laws regulating seclusion and/or restraint require some type of documentation of their usage.[313]

XI. FINANCIAL FREEDOM AND RESPONSIBILITY

Many of the institutionalized disabled have some financial assets from past wages or salaries, investments, governmental or private benefits, aid from family or friends, and so forth. Legal questions arise concerning the disabled's access to and use of these funds, the limits that may be put on his control of funds, the role of a representative payee or guardian, and the responsibility of the institutionalized person or his representative payee, family, or guardian to pay for the services rendered to the patient.

A. Patient's Control of Funds

Almost half the states[314] have enacted statutes concerning the institutionalized mentally disabled person's control of his funds. These laws mainly fall into two categories: (1) statutes recognizing the right to enter into contractual relationships and thus spend money freely, and (2) statutes governing the use of funds within institutions. Those statutes that recognize that a person who has not been declared incompetent has the right to enter into contractual relationships and to spend his money as he wishes usually express the freedom from institutional control in a general statement, often at the beginning of statutory sections addressing a whole range of rights of the institutionalized person.[315]

Modern case law and statutes make it clear that these provisions are for persons who have not been declared incompetent.[316] The provision in Louisiana's statute is typical:

> No patient in a treatment facility . . . shall be deprived of any rights, benefits, or privileges guaranteed by law, the Constitution of the state of Louisiana, or the Constitution of the United States solely because of his status as a patient in a treatment facility. These rights, benefits, and privileges include, but are not limited to . . . the right to enter contractual relationships and to manage property.[317]

Such affirmative statutory statements have been prompted by the former assumption that admission to a mental health facility was equivalent to legal incompetency.[318]

The second group of statutes addressing the disabled's control of funds relates to the use of those funds within the institution. Only 32 states have statutes dealing with the disabled person's control of funds within the institution.[319] Typically, these statutes provide that the individual may spend "reasonable amounts" or may have "small sums" for use in buying food, toiletry goods, and other items sold at the institution's canteen. Arizona's statute, for example, provides that the patient be permitted to keep and "be allowed to spend a reasonable sum of his or her own money for his own needs and comforts."[320] California's provision is that the patient "be allowed to spend a reasonable sum of his or her own money for canteen expenses and small purchases."[321] Connecticut's statute is somewhat more restrictive, vesting control in the institution's administration so that the patient has the right "in such manner *as determined by the facility* to spend a reasonable sum of his or her own money for canteen expenses and small purchases."[322]

Of course, these two groups of statutes are not mutually exclusive. Some states have both types, recognizing a general right of the disabled to control his funds but limiting the amount of funds that may be spent within the institution itself[323] and setting out the circumstances under which the institution may exercise control over the funds.[324] Typically such provisions are phrased in terms of preventing medical harm to the patient.[325]

By regulation or statute most states now have a formal means of accounting for funds, whereby the disabled can deposit his funds in a personal account and receive periodic reports, thus both providing access to the funds by the disabled person and preventing loss and theft.

B. Funds Managed by a Representative Payee or Guardian

Most patients who are mentally ill will not have been adjudicated incompetent and indeed are capable, at least to some extent, of managing their assets. But on relatively infrequent occasions a mentally ill person is declared incompetent. This may occur when the person is in a manic state of manic-depressive illness or is

310. Colo. Rev. Stat. § 27-10.5-115(5) (1973 & Supp. 1982).
311. D.C. Code Ann. § 6-1970(d) (1981); Mont. Code Ann. § 53-20-146(3) (1981).
312. Idaho Code § 66-412(2) (1980 & Supp. 1983).
313. See table 6.2, col. 11.
314. See table 5.2, col. 3.
315. See, e.g., District of Columbia, Kentucky, Louisiana, and Mississippi.
316. See ch. 7, Incompetency, Guardianship, and Restoration.
317. La. Rev. Stat. Ann. tit. 28, § 171 (West 1975 & Supp. 1982).
318. For further discussion of incompetency see ch. 7, Incompetency, Guardianship, and Restoration.
319. See table 5.2, col. 3.
320. Ariz. Rev. Stat. Ann. § 36-507(5) (Supp. 1982).
321. Cal. Welf. & Inst. Code 5325(a) (West 1972 & Supp. 1981).
322. Conn. Gen. Stat. Ann. § 117-206i(a) (West 1975 & Supp. 1981) (emphasis added).
323. See Louisiana.
324. See table 5.2, col.5.
325. Connecticut, Pennsylvania, and Washington.

chronically ill and there is little hope of his responding to treatment sufficiently to make him capable of managing his funds.

For many such patients, the family will manage whatever funds are available until the person is discharged from the hospital. In cases of persons who are chronically mentally ill or who are rehospitalized frequently, and who receive benefits such as Social Security disability, Social Security income, or veterans' benefits, a *representative payee* may be appointed to manage the funds.[326]

A representative payee is a person appointed by the benefit provider to accept the beneficiary's checks and to spend the funds on his behalf when it has been determined that the beneficiary is incapable of handling his own funds. Thus, the representative payee is a type of guardian, but only for the limited purpose of handling the funds from the particular agency. Family members, friends, or employees of the institutional provider may be the representative payee.

Compared with mentally ill persons, mentally retarded institutionalized individuals are more likely to be intellectually unable to make financial decisions. If these persons are profoundly or severely retarded, there can be little question that any assets they have will need management. In instances where the resident is entitled to benefits, the guardian is often the representative payee. In any case, the representative payee has the responsibility of acting in the resident's best interest in managing and utilizing the funds to the disabled person's benefit.[327]

It is in the context of the representative payee that the major problems in access to funds have arisen. Litigation occurs most frequently in the situation in which an employee of the institution serves in this capacity but is merely a conduit to transfer funds from the disabled person to the state treasury. When a family member serves as the payee, friction may arise from the disabled's feeling—perhaps correctly—that the family is interested only in his benefits and not in his welfare.

Today, every state has some statutory provision establishing a payment system for the cost of care rendered by mental institutions.[328] A traditional scheme has the hospital superintendent serve as the representative payee to receive, in the name of the disabled, benefits he is entitled to from a federal or state agency, most frequently the Social Security Administration or the Veterans Administration. Upon receipt of the payment, the representative payee will credit the amount received against the amount the person owes for his care in the institution. The funds thus go directly back to the state, with the disabled having no opportunity to decide on a different allocation of his money. This practice has resulted in litigation over what rights the person retains when a representative payee is appointed and over what limits there are on state employees who act as representative payees.

A typical fact pattern was presented in *McAuliffe v. Carlson*,[329] in which Connecticut's Commissioner of Finance and Control was made the representative payee for persons confined in state mental facilities and used the funds to reimburse the state for expenses thus incurred. In a challenge to this practice the court found that the Commissioner's automatic appointment as a conservator for the disabled violated due process and that by diverting patients' funds for liabilities that were not constitutionally required, the Commissioner violated his fiduciary duties.[330]

The federal courts have diverged on just what procedural rights a person has when a representative payee is to be appointed. The Court of Appeals for the Tenth Circuit, in *McGrath v. Weinberger*,[331] addressed the issue of whether the Social Security Administration's procedures for appointment of a representative payee violated the due process clause in the failure to give prior notice to the recipient, in that he was not given an opportunity to contest the determination. In this case family members acted as the representative payees. The court held that notice and a hearing before a representative payee was appointed was not required, basing its decision on the United States Supreme Court's decision in *Mathews v. Eldridge*,[332] which held that due process was not violated by terminating benefits without an evidentiary hearing. The *McGrath* court said: "It would be an unwarranted departure on our part to hold that due process requires prior notice and an opportunity for a hearing where there has been no termination of benefits." The court went on to state:

> We believe that the risk of an erroneous deprivation of the beneficiary's interest in the free use of his benefits appears to be relatively slight. The determination of incompetency to manage benefits is based primarily on evaluations by psychologists and staff members who have observed the beneficiary. It would be unwarranted conjecture on our part to speculate that such evaluations reflect anything other than a sincere determina-

326. Both the Social Security Administration and the Veterans Administration have developed simple procedures for the appointment of a representative payee.

327. The issue of guardianship is discussed at length in ch. 7, Incompetency, Guardianship, and Restoration.

328. See Kapp, Residents of State Mental Institutions and Their Money (or the State Giveth and the State Taketh Away), 6 J. Psychiatry & L. 287, 305 (1978). Also see Doe v. Vermont, No. S-14-80W, 7 MDLR 320 (Washington County Super. Ct., Vt. May 23, 1983).

329. 386 F.Supp. 1245 (D. Conn. 1975).

330. *Id.* at 1245, 1249.

331. 541 F.2d 249 (10th Cir. 1975).

332. 424 U.S. 319 (1975).

tion that the best interests of the beneficiary would be served by appointing a representative payee to manage the financial affairs of the beneficiary.[333]

In *Tidwell v. Weinberger*[334] a three-judge federal panel was presented with the same issue, that is, whether an evidentiary hearing is required before a representative payee is appointed, but unlike *McGrath*, in which family members served as the representative payee, in this case the superintendent of the state mental health facility filled that role. The court refused to declare, as requested by the plaintiffs, that the superintendent could *never* properly be named as representative payee. It also refused to find that the disabled were constitutionally entitled to an evidentiary hearing regarding the appointment. However, the court did recognize certain lesser rights, including (1) notice to the patient that a determination to appoint a representative payee was to be made, (2) access by the patient to all materials used in making the determination, (3) an opportunity for the patient to submit materials in his own behalf, and (4) where a representative payee was actually appointed, notice of such action and of the beneficiary's right to challenge the decision.[335]

In *Vecchione v. Wohlgemuth*,[336] the Court of Appeals for the Third Circuit struck down a Pennsylvania statute that permitted appropriating Social Security checks without a hearing. In January 1973, Elvira Vecchione had filed a class action complaint on behalf of mental patients who had not been adjudicated incompetent, challenging a Pennsylvania law that permitted the state to take their property in satisfaction of the costs of their care without a prior or subsequent hearing on the correctness of the state's assessment. A three-judge federal district court held that the Pennsylvania statute was unconstitutional on its face and enjoined its application, and the state was ordered to return to Vecchione all her assets.[337] Seven months later, a class member moved to hold the defendants in contempt for violating the original decree by continuing to appropriate his Social Security checks without a hearing, which was resolved with the defendants entering into a consent decree in which they agreed to restore to the patients all funds that had been withheld pursuant to the invalid statutory procedure. However, the defendants then stalled and claimed that the attorneys who negotiated the consent decree were not authorized to enter into such a decree, and they moved for the court to vacate or modify it. The district court denied the defendant's motion and refused to stay its order pending appeal.

On appeal the Court of Appeals for the Third Circuit rejected the defendants' arguments as to the consent decree's alleged invalidity.[338] The court concluded that neither "the unwillingness of the Commonwealth to return the 9.1 million dollars . . . [nor] the unwillingness of the Pennsylvania courts to entertain proceedings which would meet due process standards" would justify vacating the district court's order.[339] Following this decision the district court entered an order implementing its original decree. The order set forth procedures for assuring that patients receive their funds back, including accrued interest from the date of the original order. The thrust of the order was to make sure that when the bills for care were presented, there would be no duress, harassment, or unfair collection methods used to secure payment for the costs of hospital care. For example, no correspondence could be initiated regarding the bills until at least ten days after the moneys were refunded.

Although one might have assumed that after all this litigation activity in *Vecchione* the problems would have been eliminated, a subsequent Pennsylvania state court case showed that state officials were still being appointed as representative payees and that this was considered legally satisfactory under Pennsylvania law. In *Tartaglia v. Pennsylvania*[340] the trial court upheld the decision of a hearing officer not to modify or abate a bill accumulated by a mentally retarded former resident of a state institution. The court distinguished this situation from *Vecchione* by finding that the representative payee, who was the state's bookkeeper, had not violated the fiduciary duty delineated in *Vecchione* since he did not actually collect the bill for the state and the plaintiff had not demonstrated that her representative payee had neglected her needs by not expending more money for her care in the institution.

Although state statutes usually do not address the representative payee issue, the trend in practice seems to be to at least provide the disabled person with some due process protections when a representative payee is appointed, along the lines set forth in the *Tidwell* case. Tension likely will continue between the rights of the disabled to receive his benefits and decide how they are

333. 541 F.2d at 253.

334. Tidwell v. Weinberger, Nos. 73-C-3104 & 74-C-183, 1 MDLR 192 (N.D. Ill., June 28, 1976).

335. See also Federal Courts Refuse to Require Prior Hearing in Designating "Representative Payees" for Disability Benefits, 1 MDLR 192 (1976). After the initiation of the case the Social Security Administration developed regulations for handling the appointment of the representative payee, which gave the patient greater rights.

336. 558 F.2d 150 (3d Cir. 1977), where the three-judge district court held the statutes unconstitutional, and 426 F. Supp. 1297 which denied motion to vacate consent decree.

337. 377 F. Supp. 1361 (E.D. Pa. 1974).

338. Vecchione v. Wohlgemuth, 558 F.2d 150 (3d Cir. 1977).

339. *Id.* at 159.

340. Tartaglia v. Commwealth Dep't of Pub. Welfare, 416 A.2d 608 (Pa. Commw. Ct. 1980).

spent and the institution's need to find a way to collect compensation for services provided.

C. The Patient's Responsibility to Pay for His Care

Statutes asserting the right of access to funds are meaningless if all the disabled person's funds are used to offset the costs of his care. Today, every state has some statutory scheme for delineating the extent of private responsibility for the costs of care in state mental institutions.[341] These provisions and the resulting litigation are discussed more extensively in chapter 2, "Involuntary Institutionalization," in its concluding section on liability for costs. This chapter will provide a brief overview of the claims a state may have on the funds of an institutionalized mentally disabled person.

All states by statute provide that the disabled is responsible for the costs of his care. These provisions make no distinction between "voluntary" and committed persons.[342] Costs may be determined by a variety of methods, and each state has a procedure for assessing liability based on the costs he incurred and the disabled's ability to pay. In many states liability can extend to the person's family.[343] The statutes usually specify the family members who may be liable and the extent of their liability. Some states make only the spouse liable for adult recipients of care; other states may include parents and even children. In a few states liability is limited to the disabled person or his estate.[344]

In most cases there is little prospect of recovering the full cost of the care from the disabled or his family. Most enforcement of repayment consists of seeking assignment of benefits the person receives from third-party payers or direct reimbursements from the disabled's estate. Several states require residents, as a condition for remaining in the institution, to assign in writing to the state the right to any benefits—up to the cost of maintenance or treatment—which they are entitled to receive from third-party payers, such as private or public insurers.[345] When authorized by statute, the institution can attempt to collect directly from the family members who are designated as responsible for care.[346]

The laws often set a maximum that a person can be charged[347] or for which relatives will be responsible,[348] and in some states they limit the duration of financial liability.[349] Chiefly, there are two ways the state may try to collect. The representative payee option, favored when the mentally ill were institutionalized for extended periods, is now used mainly for the chronically ill and the mentally retarded. The other method is to file a civil suit to enforce payment of the debt,[350] a cumbersome process that may result in only a small return.

Few will dispute the need of the states to find some means, other than complete dependence on taxpayer appropriations, to pay for the care they render, but debate continues over how much the disabled person should pay, which family members should be responsible for the bill, and what methods the state will use to collect this money, and whether collection efforts are worth their return.

XII. PERSONAL POSSESSIONS

In the past persons institutionalized in state facilities were usually denied the right to retain personal possessions, including sometimes their own clothing. More recently, the general trend toward making institutions more humane and "normal" has resulted in greater control by the disabled over personal items. As many mental health codes have been revised in recent years, they have included explicit sections on patient's rights, including typically a provision that guarantees the disabled the right to his personal possessions.[351] Roughly half the states have enacted such provisions. Usually these provisions specifically address the right of the disabled to wear his own clothes. Some also provide for the right to keep some possessions, including toilet articles. A growing number of states provide that the disabled shall be given individual storage space for their private use.[352]

The statutes vary from the simple to the detailed. For example, North Carolina's statute provides only that the patient shall retain the right to "[k]eep and use his own clothing and personal possessions."[353] Ohio recognizes that if the person does not have his own clothes he should be "provided an adequate allowance for or allotment of neat, clean, and seasonable clothing."[354] The same provision adds that the patient has a right to "maintain his personal appearance according to his own personal

341. Kapp, *supra* note 328, at 305, for an article explaining patient payment laws; see also tables 2.17 & 2.18.

342. Kapp, *supra* note 328, at 306. See also Chill v. Mississippi Hosp. Comm., 429 So. 2d 574 (Miss. 1983); and Virginia Dep't of Mental Health & Mental Retardation v. Jenkins, 297 S.E.2d 692 (Va.1982), which upheld payment by involuntarily committed patients or their families.

343. See table 2.17: all states but New Mexico, North Carolina, and Oregon hold the family partly responsible.

344. New Mexico, North Carolina, and Oregon.

345. See Kapp, *supra* note 328, at 306, e.g., Florida, Indiana, and Maryland.

346. See table 2.17.

347. See ch. 2, Involuntary Institutionalization, § VI, Liability for the Costs of Institutionalization.

348. E.g., Delaware, Florida, Indiana, Maryland, Massachusetts, Nevada, New Jersey, New York, and Pennsylvania.

349. See ch. 2, Involuntary Institutionalization, § VI, Liability for the Costs of Institutionalization, and table 2.17.

350. See Kapp, *supra* note 328, at 309. Sections 417 and 517 of the MDLR document cases relating to payment issues.

351. See table 5.2, col. 2.

352. See, e.g., Ariz. Rev. Stat. Ann. § 36-508 (1974 & Supp. 1981).

353. N.C. Gen. Stat. § 122-55.2(b)(5) (1981).

354. Ohio Rev. Stat. § 5122.29(F)(1) & (2) (Baldwin 1980 & Supp. 1981).

taste, including head and body hair."[355] These provisions are typically counterbalanced by others that authorize the treatment staff to limit possession of certain items. Two rationales are offered. First, certain types of property, such as razors, scissors, knives, and other sharp instruments, which may pose a danger to the disabled or to others may not be routinely banned but rather restricted under specific circumstances or on certain units because of the nature of the person's illness. Second, property such as television sets, expensive clothing, or other costly items may be excluded from the institution because of concern about theft.

Typical of statutes aimed at these problems is Montana's, which provides:

> Patients have a right to wear their own clothes and to keep and use their own personal possessions, including toilet articles, except insofar as such clothes or personal possessions may be determined by a professional person in charge of the patient's treatment plan to be dangerous or otherwise inappropriate to the treatment regimen. The facility has an obligation to supply an adequate allowance of clothing to any patients who do not have suitable clothing of their own. Patients shall have the opportunity to select from various types of neat, clean, and seasonable clothing. Such clothing shall be considered the patient's throughout his stay at the facility. The facility shall make provision for the laundering of patient clothing.[356]

The concept of guaranteeing the patient the general right to use his clothes and personal items, with limitations set by the staff, first received judicial endorsement in *Wyatt v. Stickney*,[357] which provided:

> Patients have a right to wear their own clothes and to keep and use their own personal possessions except insofar as such clothes or personal possessions may be determined by a Qualified Mental Health Professional to be dangerous or otherwise inappropriate to the treatment regimen.[358]

In *Davis v. Watkins*,[359] which addressed the rights of institutionalized mentally retarded residents, the court enunciated elaborate provisions relating to clothing, including a requirement of clothing that would make it possible for the patients to "go out-of-doors in inclement weather, to go for trips or visits appropriately dressed, and to make normal appearances in the community." The order further provided for the daily dressing of nonambulatory residents and the use of suitable clothing for incontinent residents that would "foster comfortable sitting, crawling, and/or walking, and toilet training."[360]

It is now well recognized that it is important for the disabled to have possession of, and control over, his belongings while institutionalized and for him to feel he has some choice over what occurs in his life, even if it involves only what he wears each day.

XIII. PATIENT WORKERS

A. Past Practices

Use of patient workers within facilities for the mentally ill and mentally retarded was an accepted practice until the mid-1970s. For example, a study, conducted in 1972, of 154 institutions, which included 76% of the then existing public facilities for the retarded, found that 32,180 of 150,000 residents were participating in a work program.[361] Thirty percent of these workers received no pay at all, and an additional 50% received less than $10.00 a week. An earlier 1969 study in Pennsylvania indicated that two-thirds of the working residents in that state were performing tasks deemed essential to the maintenance of the institution, resulting in savings to the state of over $10 million a year.[362]

The institutionalized mentally disabled in large state mental institutions commonly provided a variety of services, including such activities as housekeeping in the wards, grounds maintenance, laundry duty, cooking, and farming. Typically, these resident-workers were engaged in work of little therapeutic value.[363] They received little or no financial compensation, with this being justified on the theory that work was part of the treatment program and thus did not constitute employment deserving of compensation.

Not only was much of the work nontherapeutic, but access to grounds privileges or release from the institution might be denied if the disabled refused to cooperate by not doing his scheduled tasks. There was also the risk that institutions would be reluctant to release people who had become so proficient in their tasks that they seemed too "valuable" to lose.[364] These patterns were detailed in *Downs v. Department of Public Welfare*,[365] a federal district court ruling:

> Almost invariably, the labor is non-therapeutic. Some of the forced labor includes repairing outdoor benches,

355. *Id.* at subsec. (3).
356. Mont. Code Ann. § 53-21-142(6) (1981).
357. 344 F. Supp. 373 (M.D. Ala. 1972).
358. *Id.* at 380 (M.D. Ala. 1972). See in this chapter appendix A *infra*, containing additional *Wyatt* provisions on clothing.
359. Davis v. Watkins, 384 F. Supp. 1196, 1209 (N.D. Ohio 1974).
360. *Id.* at 1209.
361. Friedman, The Mentally Handicapped Citizen and Institutional Labor, 87 Harv. L. Rev. 567, 568 (1974).
362. Pennsylvania Dep't of Public Welfare, Calculation of Implied Savings for Nine State Schools and Hospitals as a Consequence of Utilization of Unpaid Patient Labor (June 17, 1969).
363. See, e.g., Sloan & Levitt, Patient Workers, 13 Mental Retardation 22 (1975); See also Dale v. State, 355 N.Y. S. 484. (1974).
364. See Friedman, *supra* note 361.
365. 368 F. Supp. 454 (E.D. Pa. 1973).

sewing rag rugs, repair work in an electrical shop, furniture repair and refinishing, delivering messages, selling food in the snack bar, dishwashing, janitorial work, grounds maintenance, and car washing. The source of coercion is said to be the boredom of institutional life and the belief of patients that it will be advantageous to them to appear to cooperate with the institution.

> . . . Coercion results from deprivation of the right to leave the ward on "grounds" privileges or being otherwise restricted.[366]

Nonethless, there were justifications—over and above the monetary savings to the institution—to be offered for the use of resident labor. The practice of using resident workers for understaffed state hospitals has been defended as a fair and equitable pact mutually beneficial to both parties and as an opportunity for secure work with limited demands not readily found in the society at large.[367]

Other justifications[368] for resident labor include the habilitative effect in developing new skills to help economic self-sufficiency, development of a sense of routine, a means for the resident to contribute to the costs of his care,[369] and relief from the boredom of doing nothing. However, these arguments have not been accepted in the courts, which have recognized that "institutional peonage," as compulsory uncompensated work programs have been called, today is permissible only in strictly limited circumstances.

B. Challenges To Resident Labor

Legal attacks on "institutional peonage" have been based on (1) the Thirteenth Amendment, (2) the minimum wage provisions of the Fair Labor Standards Act (FLSA), and (3) the patient's right to treatment.

1. The Thirteenth Amendment

The Thirteenth Amendment to the United States Constitution prohibits involuntary servitude. Institutional peonage, it has been argued, is tantamount to involuntary servitude because it involves the use of laborers who receive neither compensation nor therapeutic benefit. Although the courts have generally acknowledged that the Thirteenth Amendment is relevant to the issue, they have failed to adequately delineate what would suffice to establish a violation of the Amendment's prohibition, and they have refused to hold that all uses of unpaid resident labor are prohibited.[370] The cases indicate that at the least, the patient must show that the work was done involuntarily and he must be able to refute state arguments that it serves a compelling governmental interest.[371] Whether the laborer is compensated is not by itself dispositive of the voluntariness issue, but adequate compensation will create a strong presumption of voluntary consent to the labor performed.[372] The decisions generally acknowledge that the state can require certain types of unpaid labor, such as personal housekeeping functions,[373] as well as work that is genuinely therapeutic.[374] An illustrative case is *Jobson v. Henne* (1966),[375] in which the Court of Appeals for the Second Circuit stated:

> We assume that even though the purpose of the Thirteenth Amendment was to proscribe conditions of 'enforced compulsory service of one to another,' . . . the states are not thereby foreclosed from requiring that a lawfully committed inmate perform without compensation certain chores designed to reduce the financial burden placed on a state by its program of treatment for the mentally retarded, if the chores are reasonably related to a therapeutic program, or if not directly so related, chores of a normal house keeping type and kind.[376]

2. The Fair Labor Standards Act

The Fair Labor Standards Act (FLSA) was passed by the Congress in 1938[377] to improve the economic position of workers by establishing minimum wages and setting maximum hours of work, which if exceeded required overtime pay. In 1966 the act was amended to extend coverage to include nonfederal hospitals and institutions for the mentally disabled.[378] These amendments made no distinction between the patient and nonpatient but simply provided that covered work included "activities performed . . . by any person or persons" in the operation of an institution for the mentally ill or retarded.[379] Provision was made, however, for payment of less than the minimum wage to workers who because of a mental or physical handicap were unable to work at a full productive level.

366. *Id.* at 458-59.

367. A. Ludwig, Treating the Treatment Failures: The Challenge of Chronic Schizophrenia 52 (1971).

368. See, e.g., Schoenfeld, *supra* note 5, at 627.

369. Kapp, *supra* note 328, at 303.

370. See Jobson v. Henne, 355 F.2d 129 (2d Cir. 1966); Downs v. Department of Pub. Welfare, 368 F. Supp. 454 (E.D. Pa. 1973); Wyatt v. Stickney, 344 F. Supp. 373 (M.D. Ala. 1972); Johnston v. Ciccone, 260 F. Supp. 553 (W.D. Mo. 1966); Tyler v. Harris, 226 F. Supp. 852 (W.D. Mo. 1964).

371. See Friedman, *supra* note 361, at 579-84, for a discussion of the Thirteenth Amendment issues. See also Ferleger, Loosing the Chains: In-Hospital Civil Liberties of Mental Patients, 13 Santa Clara Law. 447, 447-83 (1973).

372. See Heflin v. Sanford, 142 F.2d 798, 799 (5th Cir. 1944), which said "[i]t is not uncompensated service, but involuntary servitude which is prohibited by the Thirteenth Amendment."

373. See Jobson v. Henne, 355 F.2d 129, 132 (2d Cir. 1966).

374. *Id.* See also Wyatt v. Stickney, 344 F. Supp. 373 (M.D. Ala. 1972).

375. 355 F.2d 129 (2d Cir. 1966).

376. *Id.* at 132.

377. Ch. 676, 52 Stat. 1060 (1938) (codified as amended at 29 U.S.C. §§ 201-219 (1982)).

378. 29 U.S.C. 203(d), (r), & (s) (1982).

379. *Id.*

In 1973, in *Souder v. Brennan*,[380] a federal district court ruled that the FLSA minimum wage and overtime provisions applied to resident workers at nonfederal hospitals, homes, and institutions for the mentally ill and retarded.[381] The court reasoned:

> Economic reality is the test of employment and the reality is that many patient-workers perform work for which they are in no way handicapped and from which the institution derives full economic benefit. So long as the institution derives any consequential economic benefit the economic reality test would indicate an employment relationship rather than mere therapeutic exercise. To hold otherwise would make therapy the sole justification for thousands of positions as dishwashers, kitchen helpers, messengers and the like.[382]

Accordingly, the court ordered the secretary of labor to implement reasonable enforcement efforts to apply the statutory provisions to the applicable institutionalized workers.[383]

The *Souder* decision spurred further suits by disabled workers seeking back wages, overtime compensation, and sometimes damages.[384] Many of these suits never reached the merits but were dismissed on other grounds, including failure to satisfy the statute of limitations, lack of court jurisdiction, and sovereign immunity. In addition, the Supreme Court's ruling in *Employees of the Department of Public Health and Welfare v. Department of Public Health and Welfare of Missouri*[385] that the Eleventh Amendment to the Constitution barred a federal court from granting relief under the FLSA against a nonconsenting state presented a major problem for enforcement of the FLSA 1966 amendments.

Some regarded *Souder* and the resultant federal regulations[386] issued by the Department of Labor pursuant to the court's order as a great victory for the mentally disabled.[387] Clearly, change was effected. Many states chose to discontinue the use of disabled workers, rather than pay for the labor,[388] and other states provided the required pay for their workers.[389] Some decried the decision because it resulted in eliminating work as therapy.[390]

Today, *Souder* and the regulations issued pursuant to the court's order are no longer viable, for in 1976 the Supreme Court in *National League of Cities v. Usery*[391] overruled its earlier decision in *Maryland v. Wirtz*,[392] which had upheld the 1966 FLSA amendments making the minimum wage applicable to state institutions. The Court in *Usery* held that the statutory amendments exceeded congressional power under the Constitution's commerce clause[393] and that they violated the Tenth Amendment to the Constitution by virtue of their displacing the states' freedom to structure internal operations in areas of governmental functioning traditionally reserved to the states.[394]

Although *Usery* did not specifically involve state mental institutions, since the decision the secretary of labor has not sought to enforce the regulations promulgated pursuant to *Souder*,[395] apparently reasoning that *Usery* had effectively rendered them unconstitutional. However, although there is support for this reading, there is also some room for disagreement on several grounds. First, there was no majority opinion in *Usery*: Justice Blackmun simply concurred to provide the fifth vote necessary to form a majority and espoused a balancing test whereby a sufficiently strong federal interest could override the states' freedom from regulation. Conceivably, if Congress were to now adopt a specific amendment to the FLSA directed toward institutional peonage, with adequate supporting data establishing the detriments of the practice and the need of patients for federal protections, that amendment would survive attack. Second, *Usery* immunizes the states only from commerce clause–based laws that impair integral or essential governmental functions, and arguably the state has no particular need or integral function at stake that would be imperiled by a requirement that patient workers be paid for their labor. Third, subsequent rulings have narrowed the *Usery* decision, signaling a possible retreat by the Supreme Court from the range of areas in which it is willing to embrace states' rights under the Tenth Amendment.[396]

380. 367 F. Supp. 808 (D.D.C. 1973).
381. *Id.* at 812.
382. *Id.* at 813.
383. *Id.* at 815.
384. Kapp, *supra* note 328, at 295.
385. 411 U.S. 279 (1973).
386. Regulations at 29 C.F.R. 524 (1982).
387. See, e.g., Sloan & Levitt, *supra* note 363.
388. See Perlin, The Right to Voluntary, Compensated, Therapeutic Work as Part of the Right to Treatment: A New Theory in the Aftermath of *Souder*, 7 Seton Hall L. Rev. 298, 300 (1976). States that eliminated patient workers included California, Illinois, Indiana, Kentucky, Michigan, New Jersey, North Dakota, Vermont, and Virginia; see also From Peonage to Pay (pts. 2 & 4), 5 Behav. Today 331 (1974), 6 Behav. Today 351 (1975).
389. See Perlin, *supra* note 388. See also Alabama, Connecticut, Idaho, Kansas, Massachusetts, North Carolia, Rhode Island, and South Dakota.
390. See Lebar, Worker-Patients: Receiving Therapy or Suffering Peonage? 62 A.B.A.J. 219 (1976); Safier, Patient Work Under Fair Labor Standards: The Issues in Perspective, 27 Hosp. & Community Psychiatry 89 (1976); Schwartz, Expanding a Sheltered Workshop to Replace Nonpaying Patient Jobs, 27 Hosp. & Community Psychiatry 98 (1976).
391. 426 U.S. 833 (1976).
392. Maryland v. Wirtz, 392 U.S. 183 (1968).
393. U.S. Constitution, art. I, § 8.
394. National League of Cities v. Usery, 426 U.S. 833 (1976).
395. See Kapp, *supra* note 328, at 299.
396. See, e.g., Federal Energy Regulatory Comm'n v. Mississippi, 456 U.S. 742 (1982); United Transp. Union v. Long Island R.R. Co., 455 U.S. 678 (1982); Hodel v. Virginia Surface Mining & Reclamation Ass'n, 452 U.S. 264 (1981).

Since no state or lower federal court has yet directly addressed the relevance of *Usery* to patient labor, the ultimate significance of decision in this context remains an open question.

3. The Right to Treatment

In the late 1960s the concept that an institutionalized mentally disabled person had a constitutionally based right to receive treatment was first enunciated[397] and soon received endorsement in numerous courts.[398] An argument can be made that institutional labor that displaces beneficial activity and provides no therapeutic advantage violates the patient's right to treatment. The corollary of this, i.e., that the disabled are entitled to meaningful work which is therapeutic and compensated, has also been articulated.[399]

The first case to adopt the theory that disabled persons could not be forced to work unless their labor served therapeutic ends was *Wyatt v. Stickney*.[400] The federal district court in *Wyatt* held that the right to treatment generally proscribed institutions from requiring patients to perform labor involving the operation and maintenance of the institution, presumably because "nontherapeutic . . . work assignments . . . constituted dehumanizing factors contributing to the degeneration of the patients' self-esteem."[401] The court held:

> Privileges or release from the hospital shall not be conditioned upon the performance of labor covered by this provision. Patients may voluntarily engage in such labor if the labor is compensated in accordance with the minimum wage laws of the Fair Labor Standards Act.[402]

In *Davis v. Balson*[403] a federal district court in Ohio also held that "forced participation in work programs or work assignments which are considered by professionals in the field to be countertherapeutic is violative of the patient's constitutional right to treatment."[404] Thus, both in *Davis* and *Wyatt* the courts set restrictions on what a resident could do. Both courts, however, did permit requiring the resident to perform the tasks of personal housekeeping.[405]

Today, the occasions for challenging institutional peonage have been greatly reduced by the fact that few institutions still engage in this type of activity. The more likely challenge comes from the opposite direction, that is, that a person while institutionalized has a right to engage in work that is therapeutic and sufficiently meaningful and productive to merit compensation.[406] Such a claim in fact was litigated in a case resulting from New Jersey's decision to terminate the use of patient workers. In the consent decree of *Schindenwolf v. Klein*,[407] New Jersey committed itself to employ or involve in vocational rehabilitation programs 25% of the patients in five state facilities.

The *Schindenwolf* consent decree recognized that "[i]nstitutional work assignments must not impede the residents' movement towards discharge and shall be monitored in such a way as to prevent inappropriate institutionalization . . . [and that] [i]nstitutional assignments should neither be created nor maintained for the sole purpose of providing residents with activity."[408] Under this decree patients could still be required to perform personal housekeeping functions without compensation. New Jersey is one of the few states that has officially recognized the importance of patient work programs. It is unlikely, given shrinking state budgets and powerful employee labor unions resistant to competition, whether an experiment such as *Schindenwolf* will be repeated soon in other jurisdictions.

C. The Current Situation

Today approximately half the states have laws guaranteeing the institutionalized mentally disabled compensation for work.[409] Ironically, however, success in combatting the use of residents for uncompensated nontherapeutic work has led to a total termination or rejection of work activities in many states. *Souder v. Brennan*,[410] which was a major victory for those advocating an end to institutional peonage, was in another sense a defeat. State budgetary constraints and public employee demands to end the use of competitive mentally disabled workers have created a situation where the states are inhibited from establishing meaningful work programs for their residents. While the regulations

397. Birnbaum, The Right to Treatment, 46 A.B.A. J. 499 (1966).

398. Rouse v. Cameron, 373 F.2d 451 (D.C. Cir. 1966); Wyatt v. Stickney, 344 F. Supp. 373 (M.D. Ala. 1972); O'Connor v. Donaldson, 422 U.S. 573 (1975); Halderman v. Pennhurst State School & Hosp., 446 F. Supp. 1295 (1975), *aff'd in part, rev'd and remanded in part,* 612 F.2d 84 (3d Cir. 1979), *rev'd in part and remanded,* 451 U.S. 1 (1981); Youngberg v. Romeo, 457 U.S. 307 (1982).

399. See Perlin, *supra* note 388, setting forth the arguments for patients' constitutional right to compensated work. These arguments were the basis of a successful consent decree in Schindenwolf v. Klein, No. L41293-75 P.W., 5 MDLR 60 (N.J. Super. Ct., Mercer County Dec. 22, 1980), in which the defendants agreed to provide work for 25% of patients at five state facilities. The plaintiffs were represented by Perlin in this action.

400. 344 F. Supp. 373 (M.D. Ala. 1972).

401. *Id.* at 375.

402. *Id.* at 381. See in this chapter appendix A *infra* for other *Wyatt* provisions governing labor.

403. 461 F. Supp. 842 (N.D. Ohio 1978).

404. *Id.* at 852.

405. Wyatt v. Stickney, 344 F. Supp. 373, 381 (M.D. Ala. 1972); Davis v. Balson, 461 F. Supp. 842, 852, 857 (N.D. Ohio 1978).

406. See Perlin, *supra* note 388.

407. No. L 41293-75 P.W., 5 MDLR 60 (N.J. Super. Ct., Mercer County Dec. 22, 1980).

408. *Id.* at 63.

409. See Patients' Bills of Rights, *supra* note 140, at 200.

410. 367 F. Supp. 808 (D.D.C. 1973).

promulgated in response to *Souder* left room for programs in which the disabled could be compensated at less than the minimum wage, based on their productivity,[411] few state institutions have developed such programs.[412] Even after the decision in *National League of Cities v. Usery*,[413] which apparently freed the states from FLSA constraints, few if any states have reverted to utilizing resident workers.

Experienced mental health clinicians agree that therapeutic work "enhances the patient's self-esteem as a member of a work-oriented society," since the person "knows that what he is doing has value."[414] It has been noted that offering appropriate and purposeful work is an effective way to mitigate the dangerous effects of institutionalization. "In the case of a newly admitted acutely ill patient, it modifies the tendency for a 'person' to erode into a 'patient,'" observes one mental health professional, while for "chronically ill residents, it can serve as a pivotal force in rehabilitation."[415] Additionally, training provided in the hospital can help lead to outpatient training programs or jobs.

The public policy problem is to find a way to offer meaningful compensated programs to patients, while not displacing other employees and not reverting to past abuses. One attorney has suggested developing programs to compensate the disabled with some part of that compensation used to offset the expenses of his care.[416] To protect against abuses he suggests setting a limit on what percentage of wages could go toward setting off institutional charges. He pointed out that payment of wages, even if immediately recouped by the state, would let the resident know that he was earning his room and board and was not a mere ward of the state, thus providing "a sense of accomplishment, self-respect, and dignity of considerable therapeutic worth."[417] Wages could also provide the disabled worker with such tangible benefits as eligibility for Social Security, worker's compensation, and retirement benefits.[418]

Whether more states will find an incentive to develop meaningful work programs for the institutionalized disabled person remains to be seen. The need for programs to provide the disabled with a sense of worth and the ability to learn skills that can be utilized for self support upon release from the institution is clear.

411. Special Minimum Wages for Handicapped Workers in Competitive Employment, 29 C.F.R. § 524 (1982).
412. See Perlin, *supra* note 388, at 300.
413. 426 U.S. 833 (1976).
414. D. H. Clark, Social Therapy in Psychiatry 80-81 (1974).
415. Schwartz, *supra* note 390, at 99-100 (1976).
416. Kapp, *supra* note 328, at 304.
417. *Id.*
418. *Id.* at 305, and Schoenfeld, *supra* note 5, at 62.

XIV. ACCESS TO COUNSEL

That the state mental health facility of the 1980s is much different from that of 1970 is in large part due to the recognition and vindication of individual rights that previously were unrecognized or, even if given lip service, were left unprotected and therefore infringed. The expansion of patients' rights and the correlative changes in institutions are in no small measure due to the efforts of attorney advocates for the mentally disabled. These advocates fought for a recognition of the rights of the disabled in the courts, state legislatures, Congress, and even the news media. To sustain the achievements of the 1970s and keep the rights of the institutionalized secure, the mentally disabled must have access to legal services.

In addition to the legal problems specifically related to institutionalization, the mentally disabled have many of the same types of problems noninstitutionalized people experience, such as marital problems, financial problems, family difficulties, and so on. When they are institutionalized, however, they are less likely to have access to counsel to help them solve these problems. This section will explore why institutionalized persons may need counsel, the present availability of counsel, proposals for the delivery of legal services to institutionalized persons, the concerns of mental health professionals with legal services provided to patients, and the conflicts presented for the providers of those services.

A. Representation by an Attorney

The courts have recognized that due process requires legal counsel in any civil commitment proceeding in which the liberty of the individual is at stake and the likelihood of institutionalization exists.[419] Although most courts and state legislatures[420] have recognized a right to counsel for adults to civil commitment proceedings, the Supreme Court did not extend this right to minors when their parents seek to involuntarily commit them.[421] An individual subject to detention on grounds of mental illness not only has a right to legal counsel in the abstract but is entitled in many jurisdictions to appointed counsel if he indicates he is unable to afford an attorney.[422] Further, the individual has the right to effective assistance of counsel at all significant stages of the commitment process.[423]

419. *In re* Barnard, 455 F.2d 1370 (D.C. Cir. 1971); Heryford v. Parker, 396 F.2d 393, 396 (10th Cir. 1968); Lessard v. Schmidt, 349 F. Supp. 1078 (E.D. Wis. 1972); Dixon v. Attorney Gen., 325 F. Supp. 966, 974 (M.D. Pa. 1971).
420. See table 2.15.
421. Parham v. J.R., 442 U.S. 584 (1979); Secretary of Pub. Welfare v. Institutionalized Individuals, 442 U.S. 640 (1979).
422. Lessard v. Schmidt, 349 F. Supp. 1078, 1099 (E.D. Wis. 1972). See also table 2.15.
423. Lynch v. Baxley, 386 F. Supp. 378, 389 (M.D. Ala. 1974); see also Meachum v. Fano, 427 U.S. 215, 222 (1976).

In the past a guardian ad litem was sometimes appointed to represent a mentally disabled person in legal proceedings. According to some decisions, such an appointee does not satisfy the requirement of representation by counsel. A guardian ad litem does not generally perceive his role as an advocate for the client, his function being more in the nature of an evaluator of what would be in the best interest of his client.[424] However, at least one federal court has held that the appointment of a guardian ad litem will satisfy the right to counsel if the guardian is a licensed attorney and occupies a true adversary position.[425]

Although juveniles are entitled to be represented by counsel at delinquency hearings,[426] they have not been given this right when mental health treatment is sought.[427] In 1979 in *Parham v. J.R.*[428] the United States Supreme Court was presented with the issue of determining what due process rights minors were entitled to when their parents sought to "voluntarily" commit them to state mental hospitals. The Court rejected the notion that representation by an attorney as well as other aspects of a full-blown adversarial proceeding were necessary. Instead, the Court held:

> In general, we are satisfied that an independent medical decisionmaking process . . . will protect children who should not be admitted; we do not believe the risks of error in that process would be significantly reduced by a more formal, judicial-type hearing.[429]

Once a person is institutionalized, his claim to a right to counsel greatly diminishes, as does the likelihood of his having access to an attorney. However, the need for legal services does not necessarily stop once the commitment proceeding is concluded. The disabled may encounter problems while they are in the institution—some having legal dimensions—and, as mentioned, they are not immune from the civil legal problems common to the noninstitutionalized.

The extent to which the mentally disabled are entitled to counsel remains unclear. In 1980 in *Vitek v. Jones*[430] the United States Supreme Court held that prisoners who were being transferred to a state mental hospital *were not automatically* entitled to the appointment of counsel. Even so, a plurality of the Court noted that:

> A prisoner thought to be suffering from a mental disease or defect requiring involuntary treatment probably has an even greater need for legal assistance, for such a prisoner is more likely to be unable to understand or exercise his rights. In these circumstances it is appropriate that counsel be provided to indigent prisoners whom the State seeks to treat as mentally ill.[431]

B. Availability of Counsel

The right to counsel is hollow if no attorneys are available to provide the services. Every state acknowledges a right to representation by counsel for allegedly mentally ill individuals in civil commitment proceedings.[432] Most statutes provide for the mandatory appointment of counsel for indigents who want representation. Separate statutes guaranteeing these rights to mentally retarded persons exist in slightly more than half the states.[433]

Much of the legal advocacy for the mentally disabled has been undertaken by legal services attorneys funded under the Legal Services Corporation Act of 1974, which provides that priority should be given to handicapped individuals or others experiencing particular difficulty in obtaining legal representation.[434] These attorneys have won some significant victories, often in class action lawsuits challenging the procedures for commitment and the rights of the disabled once hospitalized. However, there always has been a persistent lack of adequate resources, and drastic cutbacks in the Legal Services Corporation's budget make it even less likely that adequate resources will be available in the future for legal services for the mentally disabled.

The Congress in the past recognized the special needs of the developmentally disabled for advocacy, in 1975 passing the Developmentally Disabled Assistance and Bill of Rights Act,[435] which provided for the creation of protection and advocacy services for the developmentally disabled.[436] These systems, which were established in every state with federal funds, have provided substantial assistance to their constitutents.[437] As with the Legal Services Corporation, the cutback in funds in legal advocacy for the developmentally disabled is likely to drastically reduce the ability to deliver even the inadequate level of services that had been provided in the past. Other federal legislation providing for the recovery

424. Lessard v. Schmidt, 349 F. Supp. 1078, 1099 (E.D. Wis. 1972).
425. Lynch v. Baxley, 386 F. Supp. 378, 389 (M.D. Ala. 1974).
426. *In re* Gault, 387 U.S. 1 (1967).
427. Parham v. J.R., 442 U.S. 584 (1979).
428. *Id.*
429. *Id.* at 613.
430. Vitek v. Jones, 445 U.S. 480 (1980).
431. *Id.* at 497.
432. See table 2.15.
433. See tables 2.15 & 2.16; see also Herr, *supra* note 198; Mickenberg, The Silent Clients: Legal and Ethical Considerations in Representing Severely and Profoundly Retarded Individuals, 31 Stan. L. Rev. 625 (1979).
434. Pub. L. No. 93-355, 88 Stat. 378 (1974) (codified as amended at 42 U.S.C. § 2996f(a)(2)(C) (1982)).
435. Pub. L. No. 94-103, 89 Stat. 486 (1975) (codified as amended in scattered sections primarily of 42 U.S.C. (1982)).
436. *Id.* at § 203, 89 Stat. 504 (codified as amended at 42 U.S.C. § 6012).
437. U.S. General Accounting Office, How Federal Developmental Disabilities Programs Are Working: Report to the Subcommittee on the Handicapped, Senate Committee on Labor and Human Resources by the Comptroller of the United States, GAO Report HRD-80-43 (Feb. 20, 1980).

of attorneys' fees in certain cases has also encouraged some attorneys to fight for the mentally disabled.[438]

Only a few states have systematically addressed the advocacy needs of the mentally disabled. New York has the most noteworthy program with its provision of legal and social services through its Mental Health Information Service, which initially served only the mentally ill but recently extended its services to the developmentally disabled.[439] New Jersey, also has a strong program. In most jurisdictions, however, there are only scattered programs, leaving the mentally disabled in the main underrepresented.[440]

Several cases have challenged restrictions on attorneys' access to patients and have been settled through consent decrees, with access generally allowed but subject to specific restrictions as to when and under what circumstances an attorney may meet with a patient.[441] Approximately 20 states have provisions that appear to give the institutionalized an unrestricted right to be visited by their attorneys.[442] However, there are often limitations. In Arizona, for example, persons confined in mental health facilities may have their statutory right to counsel denied for "good cause" by the individual in charge of the agency.[443] The Arizona statute does not define "good cause."

Wyatt v. Stickney[444] also recognized the importance of access to legal services. The consent decree in that federal district court case provided that "[p]atients shall have an unrestricted right to visitation with attorneys."[445] For the more severely retarded person, access to counsel is greatly limited by the patient's reduced level of functioning, which may make it impossible for him to know what his rights are, if they are being violated, and how to contact an attorney. It is equally difficult for the attorney to identify the needs of such a client.[446] An additional problem may arise from the fact that an incompetent person has no capacity to contract with an attorney. If he has no guardian and if there is not a specific advocacy group providing services, it may be impossible for such a person to hire a lawyer. In the case where a guardian has been appointed, the guardian may have no interest in upsetting the status quo and arranging for legal representation.

As has been touched on in the discussion of communication, many states have statutes governing access to mail.[447] Some of these laws provide that mail to or from an attorney cannot be opened or censored.[448] A typical statute of this nature reads:

> [a]ll letters addressed by a recipient to . . . licensed attorneys at law must be forwarded at once to the persons to whom they are addressed without examination by the facility authorities. Letters in reply . . . [also] must be delivered to the recipient without examination by the facility authorities.[449]

There is little case law concerning the hospitalized patients' communications with attorneys by mail. But some prison cases are relevant. In *Guajardo v. Estelle*[450] the court held that outgoing mail to attorneys was to be sent uninspected but that incoming mail was subject to inspection for contraband in the presence of the inmate.[451] This reasoning has been applied to patients at Ohio's maximum security mental health facility.[452]

The interception of a mental patient's telephone call with her attorney was held to be a violation of the right to privacy in *Gerrard v. Blackman*.[453] The court in this case held that conversations between a client and lawyer not only were private but might be privileged.[454] The right to communicate in relatively unrestricted fashion with counsel is well established. The problems of the institutionalized mentally disabled, however, concern their awareness of this right and the accessibility of attorneys.

C. Proposals for the Delivery of Legal Services

Guaranteeing the mentally disabled access to attorneys poses a problem not only of finding an attorney who will represent the disabled but also of finding funds to pay for that representation. With the passage of the Developmentally Disabled Assistance and Bill of Rights Act of 1975,[455] protection and advocacy systems were re-

438. Civil Rights Attorney's Fees Awards Act of 1976, Pub. L. No. 94-559, 90 Stat. 2641 (1976) (codified at 42 U.S.C. §§ 1981, 1988 (1982)); Equal Access to Justice Act, Pub. L. No. 96-481, 94 Stat. 2325 (1980) (codified as amended at 5 U.S.C. § 504 (1982)); § 504 of the Rehabilitation Act of 1973, 87 Stat. 394 (codified as amended at 29 U.S.C. § 794 (1982)). For a more thoughtful discussion of how these acts have affected legal services for the mentally disabled see ch. 11, Rights and Entitlements in the Community.

439. Gupta, New York's Mental Health Information Service: An Experiment in Due Process, 25 Rutgers L. Rev. 405 (1971).

440. American Bar Association Commission on the Mentally Disabled, Report to the Board of Governors of the ABA (June 1982).

441. Becker v. Hobby Horse Ranch School, No. 79-303, 4 MDLR 112 (D. Ariz. 1979); Cypen v. Burton, No. 80-6183-Civ. ALH, 4 MDLR 417 (S.D. Fla. July 25, 1980); and DeVito v. Murphy, No. 79 Ch 2369, 3 MDLR 247 (Ill. Cook County Cir. Ct. May 1, 1979).

442. See table 5.1, col. 14.

443. Ariz. Rev. Stat. Ann. § 36-514(1) (1974 & Supp. 1982).

444. 344 F. Supp. 373 (M.D. Ala. 1972).

445. *Id.* at 379. See in this chapter appendix A *infra* for other *Wyatt* provisions on communication with attorneys.

446. Mickenberg, *supra* note 433.

447. See table 5.1, col. 1.

448. See table 5.1, col. 8.

449. Ill. Ann. Stat. ch. 91½, § 2-103(c) (Smith-Hurd 1966 & Supp. 1979).

450. 580 F.2d 748 (5th Cir. 1978).

451. *Id.* at 758.

452. Davis v. Balson, 461 F. Supp. 842, 865 (N.D. Ohio 1978).

453. 401 F. Supp. 1189 (N.D. Ill. 1975).

454. *Id.* at 1193.

455. Pub. L. No. 94-103, 89 Stat. 486 (1975).

quired of all states receiving funds under the act.[456] These programs, which were designed to protect and advocate the rights of persons with developmental disabilities, were set up in every state to meet the legal needs of the developmentally disabled. As in the case of other legal aid programs, funding for the protection and advocacy systems is being drastically reduced, thus returning the developmentally disabled to a situation of greatly limited access to advocates.

Brakel has suggested placing "ombudsman-like" lawyers full time on the premises of mental institutions "to help assess the priorities and allocate services in the light of concrete circumstances and in line with available professional and also nonprofessional resources."[457] As a result of studies he has conducted for the American Bar Foundation of the delivery of legal services to the mentally disabled, he has concluded that those legal aid programs that are willing to negotiate with the hospital, rather than sue, are the most effective in meeting the needs of their clients. This has led Brakel to endorse a generally nonadversarial posture for hospital-based attorneys.[458] In response to Brakel, one commentator has suggested that the decision to function as a traditional adversary or in the best interests of the client cannot be made in a vacuum but should depend on the specific complaint that is being addressed, the condition of the client, and the nature of the institution.[459] Although some attorneys, particularly in Legal Services programs, have criticized Brakel's approach,[460] other commentators, including mental health professionals, support it.[461]

New York's Mental Health Information Service, an in-hospital agency that acts as a vehicle for communication between hospital personnel and patients, and between the patients and the court,[462] has achieved recognition for providing effective legal and social services for the mentally disabled.[463] Not having to always act on an adversarial basis may enhance the value of such a service,[464] with more open communication with hospital staff being less threatening to the staff and therefore likely to achieve resolutions of problems without resort to litigation. In addition to suggestions for ombudsman services[465] and for the development of in-house legal services,[466] it has been proposed that the lawyer become part of the hospital team and act in a number of roles, which would include serving as an interdisciplinary mediator to facilitate the efforts of other professionals and acting as an adjunct therapist, using legal counseling skills to complement the therapeutic strategies.[467]

D. The Adversary Versus the Best Interest of the Client Conflict

Just as criminal defendants are entitled to have attorneys articulate their desire for freedom, the mentally ill are also entitled to advocates to prevent their loss of freedom.[468] A conflict that often confronts the attorney participating in civil commitment proceedings is the role he is required to assume in representing his client. A lawyer representing the mentally ill is faced with the choice between acting as a defense attorney for a person who is confronted with the possible loss of his freedom or acting as a benevolent figure who seeks to achieve a ruling that would be in the best interests of the client, whatever the client's own expressed desires.[469] A graphic statement of the dilemma faced was presented by one public defender, who explained:

> When a public defender finds himself in this situation he is put in the position of playing "God." The humane thing for him to do is to yield in cases in which he feels the patient is actually ill. While I feel my role as an advocate, I also feel a moral responsibility for the welfare of the patient. I do not feel that I am really qualified to judge whether a person is mentally ill and then, on the basis of this personal analysis, to defend him either strenuously or half-heartedly. Yet I am constantly called upon to make just this determination and do in fact make it. My personal judgments do affect my defense of a patient. I do not like being put in this position. It is just too much responsibility on the public defender's shoulders.[470]

456. *Id.* at § 203, Protection and Advocacy of Individual Rights, 89 Stat. 504 (codified as amended at 42 U.S.C. § 6012 (1982)).

457. Brakel, The Role of the Lawyer in the Mental Health Field, 1977 A.B.F. Res. J. 467, 474.

458. Brakel, Legal Aid in Mental Hospitals, 1981 A.B.F. Res. J. 21.

459. Woody, Comment, The Lawyer in the Mental Health Field: Beyond Brakel, 1979 A.B.F. Res. J. 211, 213.

460. Brakel, Schwartz, & Fleischner, Legal Advocacy for Persons Confined in Mental Hospitals, 5 MDLR 274 (1981).

461. Appelbaum, Paternalism and the Role of the Mental Health Lawyer, 34 Hosp. & Community Psychiatry 211 (1983).

462. Epstein & Lowinger, Do Mental Patients Want Legal Counsel? 45 Am. J. Orthopsychiatry 88 (1975).

463. See Gupta, *supra* note 439, for a nice review of this system.

464. Verkuil, The Ombudsman and the Limits of the Adversary System, 75 Colum. L. Rev. 845, 850 (1975).

465. See Brakel, *supra* note 457; Verkuil, *supra* note 464; also Broderick, A One-Legged Ombudsman in a Mental Hospital: An Over-the-Shoulder Glance at an Experimental Project, 22 Cath. U.L. Rev. 517 (1973).

466. White, Protection Following Commitment: Enforcing the Rights of Persons Confined in Arizona Mental Health Facilities, 17 Ariz. L. Rev. 1090 (1975).

467. Woody, *supra* note 459, at 212. This interesting idea has not received much discussion.

468. Andalman & Chambers, Effective Counsel for Persons Facing Civil Commitment: A Survey, a Polemic, and a Proposal, 45 Miss. L.J. 43 (1974).

469. Note, The Role of Counsel in the Civil Commitment Process: A Theoretical Framework, 84 Yale L.J. 1540 (1975). This article describes cases involving claims of ineffective assistance of counsel to demonstrate that confusion exists over the role of the attorney in the civil commitment process. See also Miller, Role of the Attorney in the Mental Health Process, *in* The Mental Health Process 462 (F.W. Miller, R.O. Dawson, G.E. Dix, & R.I. Parnas eds. 1976), for a good discussion of the issues in this area.

Cohen spells out extensively what the attorney is required to do in representing the mentally disabled, which includes a thorough study of all the records, meetings with the proposed patient, his family, and friends, exploration of available community resources, and attempting to explain to his client the legal consequences of a commitment; he suggests that the lawyer must become a mediator between the sociomedical model and the legal model in order to reach a satisfying resolution of a case.[471]

Many in the mental health community who do not agree with the goals of advocacy for the mentally disabled believe that advocacy that tries to avoid civil commitment, or results in the disabled's ability to refuse treatment, is against the best interests of the patient. This viewpoint was typically expressed in 1978 by a physician:

> Championing issues such as individual liberties, "least restrictive" treatment environments, more narrowly defined criteria for involuntary admission to psychiatric hospitals, these advocates have transplanted theories and practices from our system of criminal justice to the in-patient psychiatric treatment facilities and programs for the mentally ill. They are frequently unaware of psychiatric and medical realities. They have inadvertently increased, rather than diminished, pain and anguish to the mentally ill and their families and forced the psychiatrist into a therapeutically nihilistic procrustean bed, which severely restricts his treatment options.[472]

One of the best known critics of the efforts of attorneys and their effects on the patient and the psychiatric profession is Alan Stone, who has served as president of the American Psychiatric Association. It is his view that lawyers and the courts have taken on the role of telling psychiatrists how to practice their profession.[473] He reflects the views of many mental health professionals in his exposition of "the myth of advocacy":

> Where we want the best treatment setting for our patients, they want the least restrictive alternative. Where we want careful treatment planning and continuity of care, they want immediate deinstitutionalization and maximum liberty. Where we are concerned about access to treatment, they are concerned about stigma and the right to refuse treatment. Where we are trying to salvage what is salvageable in the state hospital system, they are trying to close down the state hospital system. Where we want to advocate the medical model, they want to advocate the legal model.[474]

Many of those who have advocated for the rights of the mentally disabled have done so because they have been shocked by the conditions they found, or heard about, in state mental hospitals. They have also felt that psychiatrists too often dictate to the patient the care they believe he needs. Whether the level of advocacy has always been appropriate, or whether it may at times have been counterproductive, is open to debate. The fact, however, is that today the mentally disabled have specific legal rights that in a lawful society cannot be ignored, but must be protected. Legal advocates for the mentally disabled have brought many positive changes to the mental health system.

XV. THE MENTALLY DISABLED AS RESEARCH SUBJECTS

Few would question the value of human research to our society. Clearly, the only way to find cures for the ills of mankind is to experiment to find the reasons for the illness and test the potential cures. The issue is under what circumstances the mentally disabled should serve as research subjects in the search for answers.

Until the early 1970s it was accepted practice to use the institutionalized — the mentally disabled, prisoners, and nursing home patients — as research subjects. These groups presented unique research opportunities because of the researcher's ability to carefully control and monitor the subject and his environment and to find subjects who willingly or unwillingly could participate in studies. The research projects, which ranged from the nonintrusive to the very intrusive, included a wide variety of studies aimed at obtaining information on medical and psychological problems. Few bothered to question the propriety of using the mentally disabled for these purposes.

By the early 1970s the public's attention was focused on certain research projects that were difficult to categorize as anything but abusive. For example, it was disclosed that some retarded residents at Willowbrook State Hospital in New York had been deliberately infected with viral hepatitis and that many of the residents then contracted this illness.[475] It was also revealed that 22 geriatric patients at the Jewish Chronic Disease Hospital were injected with foreign cancer cells without

470. See Miller, *supra* note 469, at 467 n.3, quoting R.S. Rock, with M.A. Jacobson & R.M. Janopaul, Hospitalization and Discharge of the Mentally Ill 157-60 (1968).

471. Cohen, The Function of the Attorney and the Commitment of the Mentally Ill, 44 Tex. L. Rev. 424, 451-53, 456 (1966).

472. Shwed, Protecting the Rights of the Mentally Ill, 64 A.B.A. J. 565 (April 1978).

473. Stone, The Myth of Advocacy, 30 Hosp. & Community Psychiatry 819, 822 (1979).

474. *Id.* at 819.

475. The Willowbrook research is described in The Case of Willowbrook State Hospital, Research Symposium on Ethical Issues in Human Experimentation Proc. (Urban Health Affairs Program, N.Y.U. Medical Center, 1972).

their knowledge or consent.[476] These and other revelations generated concern about the use of unconsenting mentally disabled persons for *any* research purposes. In 1974 the Congress created the National Commission for the Protection of Human Subjects of Biomedical and Behavioral Research to address the issues raised by research on the institutionalized.[477] The establishment of this commission and other indications of heightened concern have resulted in a body of restrictions on when the mentally disabled can be the subjects of a research protocol as well as a series of measures to protect the disabled when they do participate in research.

A. Types of Research on the Mentally Disabled

The National Commission for the Protection of Human Subjects of Biomedical and Behavioral Research conducted a survey in 1974 to determine the type of research being done on the mentally disabled and who was doing it. Reporting that the research might be biomedical, behavioral, or biobehavioral, it found that the trend was to focus on the interaction of the physiological and behavioral processes. It observed that studies of the institutionalized mentally infirm "may involve interventions that benefit the subjects directly, may be designed to contribute knowledge about the class of subjects, or may be unrelated to the conditions of the mental infirmity."[478]

The largest sponsor of research on the mentally disabled is the National Institute of Mental Health (NIMH). Over 60% of NIMH's research is aimed at the causes and prevention of mental illness, with another 20% aimed at amelioration.[479] The Veterans Administration is the second largest sponsor of research relating to the mentally disabled. Most of the federally sponsored research relating to mental retardation is conducted under the auspices of the National Institute of Child Health and Human Development.[480] Other federal agencies as well as state agencies also support research into varying aspects of mental illness or retardation. Additionally, research in these areas receives private support, often from drug companies testing new medications or from private foundations more generally concerned about the causes or treatment of mental retardation and mental illness.

B. Benefits of Research to the Mentally Disabled

The Commission found that research that might benefit the disabled included studies to improve existing methods of biomedical or behavioral therapy and to develop new educational and training methods. A sizeable portion of the research was designed to produce knowledge about various disabilities, the factors underlying or precipitating them, and the accompanying biobehavioral changes. Other research involved looking at placement alternatives for the disabled, including evaluations of halfway houses, community living arrangements, and the general success of "deinstitutionalization."

Research on the mentally ill has made it possible to develop drugs to relieve many of the symptoms of their illness. Indeed, development of chemical therapies to alleviate the symptoms of the major mental illnesses has created a revolution in the mental health field, making possible the deinstitutionalization of many mental patients and greatly reducing average length of stay for those who are still hospitalized.[481] Similarly, although not as dramatic, research in the area of mental retardation has led to new training and "habilitation" methods that enable many retarded persons to live in noninstitutional environments. Research has also led to a greater understanding of the causes of retardation.[482]

C. Ethical Issues in Using the Mentally Disabled for Research

In human research, it is the subject alone who is at risk, while the benefits may accrue to others.[483] When is it appropriate to use the mentally disabled as research subjects? Clearly, if the research poses a low risk to the

476. Hyman v. Jewish Chronic Disease Hosp., 15 N.Y.2d 317, 206 N.E.2d 338 (1965).

477. National Research Service Award Act of 1974, Pub. L. No. 93-348, §§ 201 to 205, 88 Stat. 342, 348 (1974). See 42 U.S.C. § 289*l*-1 note (1982) for history of this commission and limitations on research.

478. U.S. Dep't of Health, Education, & Welfare, Protection of Human Subjects: Research Involving Those Institutionalized as Mentally Infirm; Report and Recommendations for Public Comment, 43 Fed. Reg. 11,328, 11,336 (Mar. 17, 1978) [hereinafter cited as Protection of Human Subjects, Report and Recommendations].

479. Based on data obtained from the Program Analysis Branch of NIMH.

480. Protection of Human Subjects, Report and Recommendations, *supra* note 478, at 43 Fed. Reg. 11,337.

481. See ch. 6, Treatment Rights, *infra* for a general discussion of the benefits of medication. In 1975 average length of stay had been reduced to 26 days. (National Data Book, *supra* note 253, at 64 table 28.)

Although no "cure" has been found, with the help of a variety of drugs the schizophrenic can now often live in the community, and the most debilitating effects of the manic-depressive's illness can be controlled with the use of lithium carbonate. Goldberg, Schooler, Hogarty, & Roper, Prediction of Relapse in Schizophrenic Outpatients Treated by Drug and Sociotherapy, 34 Archives Gen. Psychiatry 171 (1977); Goldstein, Rodnick, Evans, May, & Steinberg, Drug and Family Therapy in the Aftercare of Acute Schizophrenics, 35 Archives Gen. Psychiatry 1169 (1978); Kane, Quitkin, Rifkin, Ramos-Lorenzi, Nayak, & Howard, Lithium Carbonate and Imipramine in the Prophylaxis of Unipolar and Bipolar II Illness, 39 Archives Gen. Psychiatry 1065 (1982); Peselow, Dunner, Fieve, & Lautin, Lithium Prophylaxis of Depressions in Unipolar, Bipolar II, and Cyclothymic Patients, 139 Am. J. Psychiatry 747 (1982).

482. See, e.g., A. Milunsky, The Prevention of Genetic Disease and Mental Retardation (1975); B. Schlanger, Mental Retardations (1973); M. McCormack, Prevention of Mental Retardation and Other Developmental Disabilities (1980).

483. Ritts, A Physician's View of Informed Consent in Human Experimentation, 36 Fordham L. Rev. 631, 634 (1968).

disabled person, with a high likelihood of direct benefit to him, then the research can be justified, assuming a valid consent can be obtained. The controversies arise regarding the use of the disabled for research when there is no prospect of direct benefit to them. The belief that each of us owes society a duty to bear minor risks for the benefit of the general welfare has been the justification for using the institutionalized mentally disabled for research that does not directly benefit them or does not seek a cure for their illness.[484] An easier case can be made for research on the causes and treatment of mental disturbance, as such work can be done only on those in fact suffering from such disturbance.

A narrower position has been taken by the American Bar Association Commission on the Mentally Disabled. The Commission recommended:

> The proposed research should relate directly to the "etiology, pathogenesis, prevention, diagnosis, or treatment" of mental disability, and should seek only such information as cannot be obtained from other types of subjects.
>
> The information sought in research on institutionalized mentally disabled individuals must be of high potential significance for the advancement of acknowledged goals in the diagnosis, prevention, or treatment of mental . . . disability. The value of such information must, at a minimum, clearly outweigh the risks to which the subjects are exposed.[485]

Others suggest that research should never involve incompetent persons if it does not hold out the prospect of direct benefit to the individuals on whom the research is conducted.[486]

A major ethical concern is the subject's ability to give a truly informed consent — a special problem in the case of the mentally disabled. Assignment of a value to the exposure to possible stress or harm as a result of the research is another issue that must be considered in deciding whether to permit research on human subjects. Finally, in many experimental research programs the ethical dilemma arises of having to withhold potentially beneficial experiences from members of the control group.

484. H.T. Engelhardt, Jr., Basic Ethical Principles in the Conduct of Biomedical and Behavioral Research Involving Human Subjects, submitted to the National Commission for the Protection of Human Subjects of Biomedical and Behavioral Research (Dec. 1975); McCormick, Commentary, Experimental Subjects: Who Should They Be? 235 J. A.M.A. 2197 (1976); R. Veatch, Three Theories of Informed Consent: Philosophical Foundations and Policy Implications, Submitted to the National Commission for the Protection of Human Subjects of Biomedical and Behavior Research (Feb. 2, 1976).

485. The Statement of the American Bar Association Commission on the Mentally Disabled Before the National Human Experimentation Group is *reprinted in* 1 MDLR 156-57 (1976) (note omitted).

486. P. Ramsey, The Patient as Person: Explorations in Medical Ethics 14 (1970).

The ethical controversy over experimentation with human subjects has been sparked in part by the fact that the psychological and medical professions and the legal community have viewed the issues in different ways.[487] The doctor may uphold experimentation to find a cure for the affliction, while the lawyer seeks to protect his particular client-patient from potential mental or bodily harm. The National Commission for the Protection of Human Subjects of Biomedical and Behavioral Research identified three principles that the Commission members felt should underlie the conduct of research involving human subjects: respect for persons, beneficence, and justice.[488] The principle of "respect for persons," that is that people should be allowed to make and pursue their own decisions so long as basic conditions of information, communication, and voluntariness can be met, embodies the concept of informed consent. "Beneficence," which means that subjects must be protected from harm and that there must be positive benefits from the research, involves a risk-benefit analysis to determine whether the possible good justifies the risk of harm.[489] "Justice," which means social justice as well as individual justice, considers the selection of classes of subjects, specifically whether those institutionalized as mentally infirm should be research subjects and, if so, under what conditions, and it demands proper selection and information procedures for the individual.[490]

Based on these concepts the Commission proposed regulations to protect the mentally disabled who would be the subject of research.[491] These guidelines clarify some of the problems inherent in research involving the mentally disabled and seek to ensure the integrity of the disabled person.

D. The Problems of Consent

Assuming that it has been determined appropriate to conduct a particular research study on the mentally disabled, the question still remains whether the individual research subject has the capacity to consent to participate in that project. It is well accepted today that individuals selected as research subjects must be aware that they are subjects and must give knowing consent to their participation in the research program, which applies to nonintrusive as well as intrusive research. Generally the criteria for true consent are (1) sufficient information to enable the subject to make an "informed deci-

487. Schultz, The Boston State Hospital Case: A Conflict of Civil Liberties and True Liberalism, 139 Am. J. Psychiatry 183 (1982).

488. Protection of Human Subjects, Report and Recommendations, *supra* note 478, at 43 Fed. Reg. 11,343-44.

489. *Id.* at 11,343-44.

490. *Id.* at 11,344.

491. *Id.* at 11,329-44.

sion," (2) absence of coercion to ensure the "voluntariness" of the decision, and (3) the subject's competency to make the decision.[492]

1. Competency to Consent

There are two types of competency: (1) legal competency and (2) clinical competency.

Legal competency is at issue when a person has been declared judicially incompetent or is a minor. Every state has a procedure for declaring a person legally incompetent,[493] which is based on a finding that the individual is incapable of managing his assets and is unable to make personal decisions regarding his care and welfare. Underlying reasons for incompetency include mental illness, retardation, senility, and a comatose condition. Most mentally ill persons have not been declared incompetent, and properly so since most mentally ill persons are capable, when their illness is under control, of making decisions relating to their welfare. The institutionalized mentally retarded, however, are more likely to have been declared legally incompetent. Some would argue that the severity of their retardation renders them unable to make competent decisions about their daily needs, although others would debate the limits of their decision-making ability.

Clinical competency means that the person understands what he is being asked to consent to. Frequently, even though a mentally ill person has not been declared legally incompetent, he may be clinically incompetent. This situation is most likely to exist at the time of admission, when the person may be in a psychotic state and has not yet begun to respond to treatment. Many institutionalized mentally retarded persons are considered to be clinically incompetent.

In order to be able to give valid consent to participate in a research program, a person should be both legally and clinically competent. A signed consent form from someone who is severely retarded or is actively psychotic is as valueless as no consent. Without legal and clinical competence the only way to obtain a valid consent is through substituted consent given by a guardian or in a court order.[494] If a person is clinically incompetent and his consent is needed, he has to be declared legally incompetent and a guardian should be appointed to make decisions for him. If the person has already been declared legally incompetent, there should be a guardian who is to act in his best interest. In the case of a child, a guardian should provide the consent. However, special protections are to be taken before a child can be a research subject.[495]

2. Informed Consent

The concept of informed consent was first developed for use in the medical/surgical setting. It was based on the view that the patient has the right to self-determination as to what is to be done with his body. First espoused judicially in 1914,[496] the concept did not gain wide attention and acceptance until the disposition of two medical cases in 1972.[497] In the research setting, the doctrine of informed consent requires that the research subject understand what he is being asked to consent to, what his participation will involve, and the potential risks and benefits to him. Obtaining an "informed consent" has become routine procedure both in medical practice and in research. The procedure serves to protect not only the patient from unwanted treatment but also the clinician or the investigator from legal liability.[498]

Studies have indicated that patients do not always comprehend the information contained in consent forms, as it is often phrased in medical and legal terms that a lay person does not understand.[499] Additionally, the information given to the research subject is often not complete[500] and his assent to the experimental procedure is thus based on an incomplete understanding of the nature and potential consequences of the experiment. A valid consent requires full opportunity and knowledge to evaluate the options available and the possible risks associated with each option.[501]

Even when it appears that a legally satisfactory "informed consent" has been obtained, one must question whether the person really understood what he consented to. A study conducted in a Massachusetts mental hospital found that only 8.4% of the patients surveyed could correctly indicate the name of at least one medication they were taking, its dosage schedule, and its in-

492. Appelbaum, Mirkin, & Bateman, Empirical Assessment of Competency to Consent to Psychiatric Hospitalization, 138 Am. J. Psychiatry 1170 (1981); also in Kaimowitz v. Department of Mental Health, No. 73-19434-AW, 1 MDLR 147 (Cir. Ct. of Wayne County, Mich. July 10, 1973) the court considered the three basic elements of informed consent to be competency, knowledge, and voluntariness.

493. See ch. 7, Incompetency, Guardianship, and Restoration, *infra*.

494. *Id.*

495. See, e.g., Human Subjects Research (R. Greenwal, M. Ryan, & J. Mulvihill eds. 1982), esp. ch. 11 by O'Sullivan, Studies Involving Children; Lewis, Comments on Some Ethical, Legal, and Clinical Issues Affecting Consent in Treatment, Organ Transplants, and Research in Children, 20 J. Am. Acad. Chld Psychiatry 581 (1981).

496. Schloendorff v. Society of N.Y. Hosp., 211 N.Y. 125, 105 N.E. 92, 93 (1914).

497. Canterbury v. Spence, 464 F.2d 772 (D.C. Cir. 1972); Cobbs v. Grant, 502 P.2d 1 (Cal. 1972).

498. Cassileth, Zupkis, Sutton-Smith, & March, Informed Consent—Why Are Its Goals Imperfectly Realized? 302 New Eng. J. Med. 896, 899 (1980). Eight percent of the patients in the reported study viewed consent forms as a protection for the physician.

499. See, e.g., Ingelfinger, Editorial, Informed (But Uneducated) Consent, 287 New Eng. J. Med. 465–66 (1972); Grundner, On the Readability of Surgical Consent Forms, 302 New Eng. J. Med. 900 (1980).

500. Ingelfinger, *supra* note 499.

501. Canterbury v. Spence, 464 F.2d 772, 780 (D.C. Cir. 1972).

tended effect.[502] In this patient population, 54.7% showed no understanding at all of the drugs they were taking. When the mentally retarded residents were excluded from the analysis, 47% of the remaining patients had no understanding of their medication.[503] Another study focused on the competency of patients voluntarily admitted at the Massachusetts Mental Health Center.[504] Half the newly admitted patients did not think they required hospitalization, and only 46% acknowledged the existence of psychiatric problems.[505] These results raise questions about the ability of the mentally disabled to give informed consent which are not easily answered.

3. Voluntariness

In addition to the requirements that the patient have the capacity to consent and that he give an informed consent, the individual must give his consent voluntarily. Only when all three of these elements are present is the consent valid. It is often assumed that the subject's signature on an "informed consent form" to participate in an experimental procedure establishes that the person made a voluntary choice, free of coercion. Though the institutionalized mentally disabled person may not necessarily have a voluntary relationship with his doctor, it is taken for granted that the paper opportunity to give or withhold consent establishes the free choice of the patient. In fact, however, experimental practices often arise in inherently coercive settings.[506]

Confinement is one of the variables that can affect the voluntariness of a person's acts.[507] The confined person may be motivated to act in a certain way because of a desire to secure freedom, to please the persons in charge, or to gain acceptance in his group.[508] In one of the leading cases on whether involuntarily committed patients can give informed consent, a Michigan state court in *Kaimowitz v. Department of Mental Health*[509] held in 1973 that an involuntarily detained mental patient could not be given an informed consent for experimental psychosurgery.[510] In this case, "John Doe," who had been convicted as a sexual psychopath in 1955 for the murder and rape of a student nurse who was working in the state hospital where he was confined, was asked to participate in an experiment to determine if surgery on the amygdaloid portion of the limbic system of his brain would help control his aggression in the institution. Doe gave his "informed consent." His parents also consented. The decision was reviewed by two separate internal review committees, one a scientific review committee and the other the human rights review committee. All agreed that the surgery could take place.

The plans for this surgery became known to Kaimowitz, a legal aid attorney, who filed suit on behalf of Doe, challenging both his confinement and the planned experiment. The court ruled that Doe should be released but felt nonetheless that they should address the issue of whether an involuntarily detained patient could give an informed consent for experimental psychosurgery:

> Although an involuntarily detained mental patient may have a sufficient I.Q. to intellectually comprehend his circumstances . . . the very nature of his incarceration diminishes the capacity to consent to psychosurgery. He is particularly vulnerable as a result of his mental condition, the deprivation stemming from involuntary confinement, and the effects of the phenomenon of "institutionalization."[511]

Doe had testified in court about how extraordinary it was for him to be approached by one of the doctors and how unusual it was to be consulted about his preference. The court found:

> [t]he involuntarily detained mental patient is in an inherently coercive atmosphere even though no direct pressures may be placed upon him. He finds himself stripped of customary amenities and defenses. Free movement is restricted. He becomes part of communal living subject to the control of the institutional authorities. . . .
>
> The inherently coercive atmosphere to which the involuntarily detained mental patient is subjected has bearing upon the voluntariness of his consent.[512]

The court concluded that an involuntarily detained mental patient can never give informed and adequate consent to experimental psychosurgery.[513]

Although it deals with consent to experimental psychosurgery, *Kaimowitz* raises the question of whether

502. Geller, State Hospital Patients and Their Medication—Do They Know What They Take? 139 Am. J. Psychiatry 611, 614 (1982) (251 patients at Northampton hospital were surveyed).

503. *Id.* at 614.

504. Appelbaum, Mirkin, & Bateman, *supra* note 492.

505. *Id.* at 1174.

506. Goldstein, For Harold Lasswell: Some Reflections on Human Dignity, Entrapment, Informed Consent, and the Plea Bargain, 84 Yale L.J. 683, 696 (1975).

507. Friedman, Legal Regulation of Applied Behavior Analysis in Mental Institutions and Prisons, 17 Ariz. L. Rev. 39, 82 (1975).

508. Martin, Arnold, Zimmerman, & Richart, Human Subjects in Clinical Research—A Report of Three Studies, 279 New Eng. J. Med. 1426, 1427 (1968).

509. No. 73-19434-AW, 1 MDLR 147 (Cir. Ct. of Wayne County, Mich. July 10, 1973). Although not reported in official legal reporters, the *Kaimowitz* case is widely known in both the mental health and the prison rights area. It is *reported in part in* The Mental Health Process, *supra* note 469, at 567, and *in* State Court Bars Experimental Brain Surgery, 2 Prison L. Rep. 433 (1973), and *reprinted in* A.D. Brooks, Law, Psychiatry, and the Mental Health System 902 (1974).

510. Kaimowitz, *in* The Mental Health Process, *supra* note 469, at 573.

511. *Id.* at 574.

512. *Id.* at 575.

513. *Id.* at 576.

institutionalized persons can give voluntary consent to *any* proposition. Confinement of an indefinite duration clearly has some effect on how free an individual feels to reject the suggestions of the staff of the hospital. This is particularly true when he thinks that consent to what is suggested will speed the day when he will be released from confinement. At the very least, consent from the institutionalized mentally disabled must be very carefully scrutinized.[514]

Some of the same pressures that influence the mentally disabled to consent to experimental research may also be exerted on family members or guardians who are asked to provide a consent. For example, the desire for the disabled's release may cause the consentor to agree to try any procedure in the hope that the patient will be cured. Other personal reasons may motivate the acts of the guardians, including wanting to appear cooperative with the staff in hopes of assuring good treatment for the disabled. Thus, one must question when it is appropriate to permit a third party to consent on behalf of the disabled. In *Kaimowitz* the court did not permit a guardian to consent, stating that "[t]he guardian or parent cannot do that which the patient, absent a guardian, would be legally unable to do."[515]

Generally, the consensus is that the courts should recognize the right of the competent disabled person to consent or refuse to consent to be a research subject and that guardians should be able to give substituted approval for the incompetent person. However, in the circumstances where there is a high risk, with little potential benefit, the question of the validity of the consent must be closely examined. It has been suggested that any third-party consent should be permitted only when there is a potential benefit to the patient from the experimental procedure.[516]

514. Thorough analysis of a disabled person's ability to consent calls for assessment of the effect his mental disability has on his decision-making ability. Geller has shown that significant differences in understanding of treatment procedures may be, alternatively, functions of diagnosis, age, and length of stay in the hospital. Geller, *supra* note 502, at 614 (1982). Model tests for competency to consent to treatment tend to focus on objectively ascertainable behavior rather than on inferred mental status. See Roth, Meisel, & Lidz, Tests of Competency to Consent to Treatment, 134 Am. J. Psychiatry 279, 280 (1977). These findings suggest that evaluations of a mentally disabled person's condition must be made at routine intervals as well as prior to experimental procedures.

Appelbaum and Roth have recommended that when an assessment of competency is conducted in a nonemergency setting, more than one evaluation should be made, and they have proffered elaborate standards for assessing clinical competency which include considering the following: (1) the psychodynamic elements of the patient's personality, (2) the accuracy of the historical information conveyed by the patient, (3) the accuracy and completeness of the information disclosed to the patient, (4) the stability of the patient's mental status over time, and (5) the effect of the setting in which consent is obtained. Appelbaum & Roth, Clinical Issues in the Assessment of Competency, 138 Am. J. Psychiatry 1462, 1466 (1981).

515. The Mental Health Process, *supra* note 469, at 575.

516. Protection of Human Subjects, Report and Recommendations, *supra* note 478, at 43 Fed. Reg. 11,329, 11,347.

E. Case and Statutory Law

Concern on the part of courts and legislatures about the use of the mentally disabled as human research subjects has resulted in numerous decisions and statutes aimed at protecting the disabled, grounded on the First and Eighth Amendments to the Constitution and the right of privacy.

Research on the disabled should not infringe on the patient's First Amendment right to be free from interference with his mental processes.[517] As the *Kaimowitz* court found, "[i]f the First Amendment protects the freedom to express ideas, it necessarily follows that it must protect the freedom to generate ideas. Without the latter, the former is meaningless."[518] The potential for violation of this principle arises in any experiment that might interfere with the thought processes of the individual, including chemical or surgical alteration of his brain.

The cruel and unusual punishment clause of the Eighth Amendment is engaged when proposed research is likely to be harmful or makes use of aversive conditioning techniques that operate on the behavioral principle of negative reinforcement, which induces discomfort in the subject in order to change or modify behavior. In a number of cases courts have held that a specific technique used in certain circumstances violated the Eighth Amendment.[519] Among the more notable are cases in which the aversive conditioning technique involved inducing vomiting to curtail future minor rules infractions.[520]

The constitutionally derived right of privacy forms another basis for challenge to some research programs. The *Kaimowitz* court said:

> Intrusion into one's intellect, when one is involuntarily detained and subject to control of institutional authorities, is an intrusion into one's constitutionally protected right of privacy. If one is not protected in his thoughts, behavior, personality and identity, then the right to privacy becomes meaningless.[521]

It is possible for a person to waive his constitutional rights as a research subject. A valid waiver can exist, however, only when it is entered *competently, knowingly*, and *voluntarily*.[522]

517. Mackey v. Procunier, 477 F.2d 877, 878 (9th Cir. 1973); Kaimowitz v. Department of Mental Health, No. 73-19434-AW, 1 MDLR 147 (Cir. Ct. of Wayne County,Mich. July 10, 1973).

518. Kaimowitz, 1 MDLR at 147.

519. Mackey v. Procunier, 477 F.2d 877, 878 (9th Cir. 1972); Wyatt v. Hardin, No. 3195-N, 1 MDLR 55 (M.D. Ala. Feb. 28, 1975, *modified* July 1, 1975); Knecht v. Gillman, 488 F.2d 1136 (8th Cir. 1973).

520. See Knecht v. Gillman, 488 F.2d 1136 (8th Cir. 1973).

521. See Kaimowitz *in* The Mental Health Process, *supra* note 469, at 577. See also Schloendorff v. Society of N.Y. Hosp., 211 N.Y. 125, 105 N.E. 92 (1914).

The landmark case of *Wyatt v. Stickney*[523] in 1972 elaborated standards for assessing research on the disabled, including the right not to be subjected to experimental research without express, informed consent, review and approval of the research by the institution's Human Rights Committee before such consent could be sought, and determination of compliance "with the principles of the Statement on the Use of Human Subjects for Research of the American Association on Mental Deficiency and with the principles for research involving human subjects required by the United States Department of Health, Education and Welfare for projects supported by the agency."[524]

The decree agreed to by the parties in the 1975 case of *New York State Association for Retarded Children, Inc. v. Carey*,[525] involving conditions at Willowbrook State School, produced one of the broadest judicial prohibitions on research which the court linked to the context of a particular institution:

> Because of the necessity to concentrate on the basic programmatic needs of Willowbrook residents and the history of experimentation at Willowbrook, no physically intrusive, chemical, or bio-medical research or experimentation shall be performed at Willowbrook or upon members of the plaintiff class. This standard, however, recognizes the possibility that such research or experimentation, under proper safeguards, may be appropriate for persons who are not members of the [plaintiff] class, in other facilities or programs.[526]

Currently 20 states have statutes pertaining to experimental research and treatment.[527] Though some of these statutes specifically state that the patient has a right to refuse to participate in experimentation,[528] others only vaguely deal with the issue, some simply referring to federal regulations as the guidelines to be used when assessing the validity of research procedures.[529]

The regulations proposed by the National Commission for the Protection of Human Subjects of Biomedical and Behavioral Research have never been codified.[530] However, there are other regulations requiring that recipients of federal funds have the research approved by a human investigation committee or an institutional review board,[531] with the result that such committees (also referred to in *Wyatt*) now exist at virtually all academic institutions and medical centers in the United States conducting research on human subjects. These multidisciplinary committees, which according to the federal regulations must have at least one lay representative, do a risk-benefit analysis of all proposed research within the institution before deciding which projects should be undertaken.[532]

F. Conclusion

The task of the law is to attempt to resolve the conflict between preserving the rights of the mentally disabled and the desire to increase knowledge and improve treatment.[533] The key is to find a balance so that important research can occur which holds out the best hope for understanding the causes of mental disability and finding treatments while protecting the rights of the disabled to participate or refuse to participate in the proposed research. At a minimum, the mentally disabled should no longer be asked to participate in intrusive research aimed at learning about problems that do not directly relate to their disability.

XVI. THE RIGHT TO AN EDUCATION

Education is considered basic to our democratic system in that it instills values and teaches skills in writing and reading which are integral to the functioning of a political system grounded on the exercise of choice by its citizenry. Until recently there was little recognition of the need to provide an education to the institutionalized mentally ill or mentally retarded child (let alone to the adult).[534] It was assumed that a child who required hospitalization for a mental illness was too disturbed to learn, and one who was institutionalized as a result of retardation was so limited in his abilities that any attempt at education would be futile.[535]

522. Statement of the American Bar Association Commission on the Mentally Disabled Before the National Human Experimentation Group, 1 MDLR 155-56 (1976) (emphasis added). For a more extensive discussion of the right to consent or refuse consent see ch. 6, Treatment Rights, *infra*.

523. 344 F. Supp. 387 (M.D. Ala. 1972).

524. *Id.* at 401-2. See in this chapter appendix A *infra* for further *Wyatt* stipulations on research and experimentation.

525. 393 F. Supp. 715 (E.D.N.Y. 1975).

526. See texts, 1 MDLR 65 (1976), for the full consent decree, including this provision.

527. Patients' Bills of Rights, *supra* note 140, at 188. See also table 6.2, col. 3.

528. Ark. Stat. Ann. § 59-1416(15) (1971 & Supp. 1982): Patient's rights should specifically include but are not limited to the following: to refuse to participate in human experimentation research projects.

529. See, e.g., Cal. Welf. & Inst. Code § 5325.1(i) (West 1972 & Supp. 1981): A right to be free from hazardous procedures, also Colo. Rev. Stat. § 27-10-116(2)(d) (1973 & Supp. 1981): the department shall adopt regulations to assure that each agency or facility providing evaluation, care, or treatment shall require the following: conduct according to the guidelines contained in the regulations of the federal government and the department with regard to clinical investigations, research experimentation, and testing of any kind.

530. Protection of Human Subjects, Report and Recommendations, *supra* note 478, at 43 Fed. Reg. 11,328.

531. Protection of Human Subjects, 45 C.F.R. § 1, 46.103 § 46.101 (1984).

532. *Id.* at § 46 generally and esp. §§ 46.107 to 46.111.

533. Nelson & Grunebaum, Ethical Issues in Psychiatric Follow-Up Studies, 128 Am. J. Psychiatry 1358 (1972).

534. The congressional hearings conducted as part of the Education for All Handicapped Children Act of 1975 estimated that one million handicapped children were entirely excluded from public education. See H.R. Rep. No. 94-332, 94th Cong., 1st Sess. (1975).

535. Begab, The Major Dilemma of Mental Retardation: Shall We Prevent It? (Some Social Implications of Research in Mental Retardation), 78 Am. J. Mental Deficiency 519 (1974); Hungerford, DeProspo, & Rosen-

The Constitution makes no explicit mention of education, and the Supreme Court, even though it has recognized the virtues of schooling,[536] has refused to find implicit in the Constitution any entitlement to an education.[537] Nonetheless, most courts ruling on the issue have inferred such an entitlement, including the handicapped, from the fact that all state laws make school attendance mandatory for children and that parents may be held legally responsible for failure to see that their children comply with these laws.[538]

Congress first addressed the problem of educating the handicapped in 1966 when it amended the Elementary and Secondary Education Act of 1965 to establish a grant program "for the purpose of assisting the States in the initiation, expansion, and improvement of programs and projects . . . for the education of handicapped children."[539] Yet, when the previous edition of this book was published in 1971 some states still denied the severely disabled child access to any educational services,[540] while many others showed no concern whether educational services reached the mentally disabled child.[541]

Two landmark federal district court decisions in 1972 recognized that handicapped children should be given access to public education. In *Mills v. Board of Education*[542] and *Pennsylvania Association for Retarded Children v. Commonwealth of Pennsylvania* (*PARC*),[543] the courts held that handicapped children were denied due process by not having the opportunity for a public education that was statutorily guaranteed to all children in a specified age group. Recognition of the critical role that education might play in helping a disabled child to achieve some self-sufficiency as an adult has led parents and other advocacy groups to fight for educational programs for the mentally disabled.

A. The Education for All Handicapped Children Act

Such group pressure together with the litigation precedents of *Mills* and *PARC* provided the impetus for Congress to pass the Education for All Handicapped Children Act in 1975.[544] This act provides local school districts with federal funds to assure free programs for handicapped children and requires that an individualized educational program be developed for all handicapped children between the ages of 3 and 21. But Congress prescribed no guidelines for school officials and did not specify the meaning of "individualized" programs and took the general view that education is a local concern and that local educators should have flexibility in developing their programs.[545]

One of the most frequent areas of litigation engendered by the act is what constitutes "appropriate" education: in the absence of guidelines the courts have attempted to make this determination. In a broad range of judicial definitions of the services necessary for local school districts to provide for handicapped children,[546] one consistent theme has been that "appropriate" education must be determined on an individual case-by-case basis.[547] In *Springdale School District No. 50 v. Grace*[548] the federal Court of Appeals for the Eighth Circuit held that the state had no duty to provide the best education, only an appropriate education.[549] The Court of Appeals for the Third Circuit has required that the education program be tailored to the special needs of each child rather than fitting the child into an inflexible education program.[550]

In 1982 the United States Supreme Court held in *Board of Education v. Rowley*[551] that "[a]ccording to the definitions contained in the Act, a 'free appropriate public education' consists of educational instruction specially designed to meet the unique needs of the handicapped child, supported by such services as are necessary to permit the child 'to benefit' from the instruction."[552] The Court made clear that "the intent of the

zweig, Education of the Mentally Handicapped in Childhood and Adolescence, 57 Am. J. Mental Deficiency 214 (1952).

536. See, e.g., Brown v. Board of Educ., 347 U.S. 483 (1954).

537. See, e.g., San Antonio Independent School Dist. v. Rodriguez, 411 U.S. 1 (1973); McInnis v. Shapiro, 293 F. Supp. 327 (N.D. Ill. 1968), *aff'd sub nom.* McInnis v. Ogilivie, 394 U.S. 322 (1969); Plyler v. Doe, 102 S. Ct. 383 (1982).

538. See, e.g., Mills v. Board of Educ., 348 F. Supp. 866 (D.D.C. 1972); Pennsylvania Ass'n for Retarded Children v. Commonwealth, 334 F. Supp. 1257 (E.D. Pa. 1971), *modified*, 343 F. Supp. 279 (E.D. Pa. 1972).

539. Pub. L. No. 89-750, § 161, 80 Stat. 1191, 1204 (1966).

540. See Brakel & Rock, *supra* note 3.

541. See, e.g., D.C. Code Ann. § 31-203 (1970), which allowed exclusion of child who "is found mentally and physically unable to profit from . . . school." See Basic Rights of the Mentally Handicapped, Mental Health Law Project (1973).

542. 348 F. Supp. 866 (D.D.C. 1972).

543. 343 F. Supp. 279 (E.D. Pa. 1972).

544 Pub. L. No. 94-142, 89 Stat. 773 (1975) (codified at 20 U.S.C. §§ 1232, 1401, 1405, 1406, 1411-20, & 1453 (1982)). A more detailed discussion of this act and a consideration of the impact of other legislation and cases on the rights of the mentally disabled child to an education are in ch. 11, Rights and Entitlements in the Community, *infra*.

545. See H.R. Rep. No. 94-332, *supra* note 534.

546. Armstrong v. Kline, 476 F. Supp. 583 (E.D. Pa. 1979), held sufficient to make handicapped person independent and self-sufficient; Rowley v. Board of Educ., 632 F.2d 945, 948 (2d Cir. 1980), held full potential commensurate with opportunity provided to nonhandicapped children; Kruelle v. New Castle County School Dist., 642 F.2d 687 (3d Cir. 1981), held maximization of learning potential.

547. Battle v. Pennsylvania, 629 F.2d 269, 280 (3d Cir. 1980); Anderson v. Thompson, 495 F. Supp. 1256, 1266 (E.D. Wis. 1980). In *Armstrong* and *Battle*, the board of education had applied the 180-day rule to handicapped children. This was an administrative policy that set a limit of 180 days of instruction per year for handicapped and nonhandicapped children. In ruling against the applicability of the rule, the courts held that equality of education was not the goal of the act and was incompatible with the act's emphasis on the individual needs of the handicapped child.

548. 656 F.2d 300 (8th Cir. 1981).

549. *Id.* at 304.

550. Battle v. Pennsylvania, 629 F.2d 269, 280 (3d Cir. 1980).

551. 458 U.S. 176 (1982).

552. *Id.* at 188-89.

Act was more to open the door of public education to handicapped children on appropriate terms than to guarantee any particular level of education once inside."[553] The decision was a blow to those who had hoped to use the act to establish that handicapped children were entitled to an education that maximized each child's potential, commensurate with the opportunities provided other children, a view the Court rejected explicitly.[554]

B. The Act Applied to the Residential Setting

The act defines special education as "specially designed instruction, at no cost to parents or guardians, to meet the unique needs of a handicapped child, including classroom instruction, instruction in physical education, home instruction, and instruction in hospitals and institutions."[555] Since the intent of the act was to make education available to all handicapped children, it is meant to apply to those who are institutionalized. The lack of adequate educational services for children in institutions has traditionally meant that mentally disabled children have had to sacrifice their educational opportunities in order to meet their treatment needs.[556]

In the residential setting one major issue is separating treatment from education to determine who is responsible for which costs. In 1981 in *Kruelle v. New Castle County School District*[557] the Court of Appeals for the Third Circuit began by holding that what constitutes appropriate education for the nonhandicapped could not be presumed to satisfy the unique needs of handicapped children; thus equality of services was not the test for determining whether an appropriate education was being provided by the state. The *Kruelle* court then addressed whether the state's educational obligations included provisions for treatment and whether the treatment could be segregated from the educational process, questions also dealt with earlier by a federal district court in *North v. District of Columbia Board of Education*.[558] Both courts found that the emotional and physical needs of the children were closely interwoven with their educational needs and that the difficulty in segregating these needs was the basis for holding the boards of education responsible for the services even though they were provided in the institution.

The overall impact of the cases interpreting the act has been to improve the availability of education services to the mentally disabled child. Because in the institutional setting the definition of education has been broadened to include aspects of treatment, the act has indirectly also expanded the treatment rights of children living in residential facilities, affording them year-round habilitation services provided by the state.[559]

Without a survey of the programs of individual states, it is difficult to know what type of education the disabled child who is institutionalized is receiving. The need for educational programs in institutions is today well recognized. What form that educational program will take, who will provide it, and how well it will be financed, however, are determinations that will vary from state to state. The importance of the passage of the Education for All Handicapped Children Act was the recognition that *all* handicapped children are entitled to some form of education. However, generally the states have a long way to go before it can be said that the institutionalized disabled child is receiving an education that is aimed at maximizing his potential.

XVII. CONCLUSION

Since the filing of *Wyatt v. Stickney*[560] in 1970 a revolution has occurred in affirming the rights of the mentally disabled, carried out through numerous court cases as well as major legislative change. There have also been drastic changes in the patterns of institutionalization. The patient population since 1970 has been cut in half,[561] with the average length of stay for the mentally ill reduced from 44 days to less than 25 days.[562] Although 26 state facilities were closed, 45 new facilities were built during the 1970s.[563] The total spent for state mental hospital treatment programs doubled from $2 billion to $4 billion, with corresponding increases being spent for treatment in the private psychiatric hospital setting.[564] While admissions have risen, the overall effect remains that substantially more money is being spent per patient than before. Additionally, the emphasis on deinstitutionalization and the least restrictive alternative has resulted in shifting mental health care into the community with greatly increased spending for community services.[565]

553. *Id.* at 192.
554. *Id.* at 198.
555. 20 U.S.C. § 1401(16) (1982).
556. J.P. Wilson, The Rights of Adolescents in the Mental Health System, 155, 158 (1978).
557. 642 F.2d 687, 693 (3d Cir. 1981).
558. 471 F. Supp. 136 (D.D.C. 1979).
559. See Case Law Developments, 1 MDLR 125 (1976).
560. 325 F. Supp. 781 (M.D. Ala. 1971).
561. Division of Biometry and Epidemiology, National Institute of Mental Health, Statistical Note 139, C.A. Taube & R.W. Redick, Provisional Data on Patient Care Episodes in Mental Health Facilities 1975 (Aug. 1977).
562. Division of Biometry and Epidemiology, National Institute of Mental Health, Statistical Note 144, M. Wittin, State and Regional Distribution of Psychiatric Beds in 1976 (Feb. 1978).
563. Schnibbe, Changes in State Mental Health Service System Since *Wyatt*, *in* Jones & Parlour, *supra* note 4, at 176.
564. National Association of State Mental Health Program Directors (NASMHPD), State Report: State Government Management of Programs for the Mentally Disabled (Jan. 1974).
565. See Schnibbe, *supra* note 563.

This revolution has resulted in a set of well-defined rights for mentally disabled persons who are institutionalized. The vast majority of states today have specific, often elaborate, patients' rights provisions in their state statutes.[566] Some require posting a copy of those rights in the institution.[567] Thirty-five states have established explicit standards for a safe, secure, and humane environment.[568] Forty-two provide for care in the least restrictive setting.[569] At least 30 states require comprehensive individualized treatment plans,[570] and the vast majority of states have statutory limitations on the use of restraints and seclusion.[571] These developments represent major advances in the rights of the mentally disabled.

In addition to all the activity at the state legislative level and in the courts, the United States Congress in 1980 passed the Mental Health Systems Act, which included a patients' bill of rights section.[572] Although the bill of rights provision was merely a recommendation to the states, it chronicled the rights recognized in *Wyatt* and many other courts and state legislatures during the 1970s.[573] Most of the act was repealed by the Omnibus Budget Reconciliation Act of 1981,[574] but the patients' rights section was left intact. In addition the Civil Rights of Institutionalized Persons Act was passed in 1980,[575] which permits the United States Justice Department to initiate legal actions against state mental health facilities in which "egregious or flagrant conditions [exist] which deprive such persons of any rights, privileges, or immunities secured or protected by the Constitution or laws of the United States causing such persons to suffer grievous harm."[576] These two acts are further proof of the nationwide concern that has arisen during the past decade for the rights of the mentally disabled.

At the end of this chapter in the previous edition in 1971, a series of recommendations were posited to establish and protect certain basic rights for the hospitalized mentally disabled. These recommendations and more have today become the law. The challenge for the 1980s is to assure that the legal victories documented in this chapter are not merely paper victories but are the actual practice in the facilities for the mentally disabled.

566. See survey of these provisions, Patients' Bills of Rights, *supra* note 140, at 178-201.

567. *Id.* See also in this chapter table 5.2, col. 12.

568. Patients' Bills of Rights, *supra* note 140, at 185-87, table 2A, Treatment Rights.

569. *Id.* See also in this book ch. 6, Treatment Rights, table 6.1, col. 3, *infra*.

570. Patients' Bills of Rights, *supra* note 140, at 185-87, table 2A, Treatment Rights. See also in this book ch. 6, Treatment Rights, table 6.1, col. 3, *infra*.

571. Patients' Bills of Rights, *supra* note 140, at 197-99 and in this book ch. 6, Treatment Rights, table 6.2, cols. 9-11, *infra*.

572. See Pub. L. No. 96-398, § 501, 94 Stat. 1564, 1598 (1980) (codified at 42 U.S.C. § 9501 (1982)).

573. See this chapter for documentation of both cases and statutes with recognized rights of the disabled. Note tables at the end of this chapter.

574. Pub. L. No. 97-35, 95 Stat. 357 (1981).

575. Pub. L. No. 96-247, 94 Stat. 349 (1980) (codified at 42 U.S.C. § 1997 (1982)).

576. *Id.* at § 3, 94 Stat. 350 (codified at 42 U.S.C. § 1997a).

APPENDIX A

Wyatt v. Stickney[1]

MINIMUM CONSTITUTIONAL STANDARDS FOR ADEQUATE TREATMENT OF THE MENTALLY ILL

. . . .

II. *Humane Psychological and Physical Environment*

1. Patients have a right to privacy and dignity.

2. Patients have a right to the least restrictive conditions necessary to achieve the purposes of commitment.

3. No person shall be deemed incompetent to manage his affairs, to contract, to hold professional or occupational or vehicle operator's licenses, to marry and obtain a divorce, to register and vote, or to make a will *solely* by reason of his admission or commitment to the hospital.

4. Patients shall have the same rights to visitation and telephone communications as patients at other public hospitals, except to the extent that the Qualified Mental Health Professional responsible for formulation of a particular patient's treatment plan writes an order imposing special restrictions. The written order must be renewed after each periodic review of the treatment plan if any restrictions are to be continued. Patients shall have an unrestricted right to visitation with attorneys and with private physicians and other health professionals.

5. Patients shall have an unrestricted right to send sealed mail. Patients shall have an unrestricted right to receive sealed mail from their attorneys, private physicians, and other mental health professionals, from courts, and government officials. Patients shall have a right to receive sealed mail from others, except to the extent that the Qualified Mental Health Professional responsible for formulation of a particular patient's treatment plan writes an order imposing special restrictions on receipt of sealed mail. The written order must be renewed after each periodic review of the treatment plan if any restrictions are to be continued.

6. Patients have a right to be free from unnecessary or excessive medication. No medication shall be administered unless at the written order of a physician. The superintendent of the hospital and the attending physician shall be responsible for all medication given or administered to a patient. The use of medication shall not exceed standards of use that are advocated by the United States Food and Drug Administration. Notation of each individual's medication shall be kept in his medical records. At least weekly the attending physician shall review the drug regimen of each patient under his care. All prescriptions shall be written with a termination date, which shall not exceed 30 days. Medication shall not be used as punishment, for the convenience of staff, as a substitute for program, or in quantities that interfere with the patient's treatment program.

7. Patients have a right to be free from physical restraint and isolation. Except for emergency situations, in which it is likely that patients could harm themselves or others and in which less restrictive means of restraint are not feasible, patients may be physically restrained or placed in isolation only on a Qualified Mental Health Professional's written order which explains the rationale for such action. The written order may be entered only after the Qualified Mental Health Professional has personally seen the patient concerned and evaluated whatever episode or situation is said to call for restraint or isolation. Emergency use of restraints or isolation shall be for no more than one hour, by which time a Qualified Mental Health Professional shall have been consulted and shall have entered an appropriate order in writing. Such written order shall be effective for no more than 24 hours and must be renewed if restraint and isolation are to be continued. While in restraint or isolation the patient must be seen by qualified ward personnel who will chart the patient's physical condition (if it is compromised) and psychiatric condition every hour. The patient must have bathroom privileges every hour and must be bathed every 12 hours.

8. Patients shall have a right not to be subjected to experimental research without the express and informed consent of the patient, if the patient is able to give such consent, and of his guardian or next of kin, after opportunities for consultation with independent specialists and with legal counsel. Such proposed research shall first have been reviewed and approved by the institution's Human Rights Committee before such consent shall be sought. Prior to such approval the Committee shall determine that such research complies with the principles of the Statement on the Use of Human Subjects for Research of the American Association on Mental Deficiency and with the principles for research involving human subjects required by the United States Department of Health, Education and Welfare for projects supported by that agency.

9. Patients have a right not to be subjected to treatment procedures such as lobotomy, electro-convulsive treatment, adversive reinforcement conditioning or other unusual or hazardous treatment procedures without their express and informed consent after consultation with counsel or interested party of the patient's choice.

10. Patients have a right to receive prompt and adequate medical treatment for any physical ailments.

11. Patients have a right to wear their own clothes and keep and use their own personal possessions except insofar as such clothes or personal possessions may be determined by a Qualified Mental Health Professional to be dangerous or otherwise inappropriate to the treatment regimen.

12. The hospital has an obligation to supply an adequate allowance of clothing to any patients who do not have suitable clothing of their own. Patients shall have the opportunity to select from various types of neat, clean, and seasonable clothing. Such clothing shall be considered the patient's throughout his stay in the hospital.

13. The hospital shall make provisions for the laundering of patient clothing.

14. Patients have a right to regular physical exercise several times a week. Moreover, it shall be the duty of the hospital to provide facilities and equipment for such exercise.

15. Patients have a right to be outdoors at regular and frequent intervals, in the absence of medical considerations.

16. The right to religious worship shall be accorded to each patient who desires such opportunities. Provisions for such worship shall be made available to all patients on a nondiscriminatory basis. No individual shall be coerced into engaging in any religious activities.

17. The institution shall provide, with adequate supervision, suitable opportunities for the patient's interaction with members of the opposite sex.

18. The following rules shall govern patient labor:

A. *Hospital Maintenance* No patient shall be required to perform labor which involves the operation and maintenance of the hospital or for which the hospital is under contract with an outside organization. Privileges or release from the hospital shall not be conditioned upon the performance of labor covered by this provision.

1. Excerpts reprinted from Wyatt v. Stickney, 344 F. Supp. 373, 379–86 appendix A (1972), and 344 F. Supp. 387, 395–407 appendix A (1972). These provisions have served as models for subsequent cases and regulations.

Patients may voluntarily engage in such labor if the labor is compensated in accordance with the minimum wage laws of the Fair Labor Standards Act, 29 U.S.C. § 206 as amended, 1966.

B. *Therapeutic Tasks and Therapeutic Labor*

(1) Patients may be required to perform therapeutic tasks which do not involve the operation and maintenance of the hospital, provided the specific task or any change in assignment is:

a. An integrated part of the patient's treatment plan and approved as a therapeutic activity by a Qualified Mental Health Professional responsible for supervising the patient's treatment; and
b. Supervised by a staff member to oversee the therapeutic aspects of the activity.

(2) Patients may voluntarily engage in therapeutic labor for which the hospital would otherwise have to pay an employee, provided the specific labor or any change in labor assignment is:

a. An integrated part of the patient's treatment plan and approved as a therapeutic activity by a Qualified Mental Health Professional responsible for supervising the patient's treatment; and
b. Supervised by a staff member to oversee the therapeutic aspects of the activity; and
c. Compensated in accordance with the minimum wage laws of the Fair Labor Standards Act, 29 U. S.C. § 206 as amended, 1966.

C. *Personal Housekeeping* Patients may be required to perform tasks of a personal housekeeping nature such as the making of one's own bed.

D. Payment to patients pursuant to these paragraphs shall not be applied to the costs of hospitalization.

. . . .

IV. *Individualized Treatment Plans*

25. Each patient shall have a comprehensive physical and mental examination and review of behavior status within 48 hours after admission to the hospital.

26. Each patient shall have an individualized treatment plan. This plan shall be developed by appropriate Qualified Mental Health Professionals, including a psychiatrist, and implemented as soon as possible—in any event no later than five days after the patient's admission. Each individualized treatment plan shall contain:

a. a statement of the nature of the specific problems and specific needs of the patient;
b. a statement of the least restrictive treatment conditions necessary to achieve the purposes of commitment;
c. a description of intermediate and long-range treatment goals, with a projected timetable for their attainment.
d. a statement and rationale for the plan of treatment for achieving these intermediate and long-range goals;
e. a specification of staff responsibility and a description of proposed staff involvement with the patient in order to attain these treatment goals;
f. criteria for release to less restrictive treatment conditions, and criteria for discharge;
g. a notation of any therapeutic tasks and labor to be perfomred by the patient in accordance with Standard 18.

27. As part of his treatment plan, each patient shall have an individualized post-hospitalization plan. This plan shall be developed by a Qualified Mental Health Professional as soon as practicable after the patient's admission to the hospital.

28. In the interests of continuity of care, whenever possible, one Qualified Mental Health Professional (who need not have been involved with the development of the treatment plan) shall be responsible for supervising the implementation of the treatment plan, integrating the various aspects of the treatment program and recording the patient's progress. This Qualified Mental Health Professional shall also be responsible for ensuring that the patient is released, where appropriate, into a less restrictive form of treatment.

29. The treatment plan shall be continuously reviewed by the Qualified Mental Health Professional responsible for supervising the implementation of the plan and shall be modified if necessary. Moreover, at least every 90 days, each patient shall receive a mental examination from, and his treatment plan shall be reviewed by, a Qualified Mental Health Professional other than the professional responsible for supervising the implementation of the plan.

30. In addition to treatment for mental disorders, patients confined at mental health institutions also are entitled to and shall receive appropriate treatment for physical illnesses such as tuberculosis. In providing medical care, the State Board of Mental Health shall take advantage of whatever community-based facilities are appropriate and available and shall coordinate the patient's treatment for mental illness with his medical treatment.

. . . .

V. *Miscellaneous*

35. Each patient and his family guardian, or next friend shall promptly upon the patient's admission receive written notice, in language he understands, of all the above standards for adequate treatment. In addition a copy of all the above standards shall be posted in each ward.

MINIMUM CONSTITUTIONAL STANDARDS FOR ADEQUATE HABILITATION OF THE MENTALLY RETARDED

. . . .

II. *Adequate Habilitation of Residents*

1. Residents shall have a right to habilitation, including medical treatment, education and care, suited to their needs, regardless of age, degree of retardation or handicapping condition.

2. Each resident has a right to a habilitation program which will maximize his human abilities and enhance his ability to cope with his environment. The institution shall recognize that each resident, regardless of ability or status, is entitled to develop and realize his fullest potential. The institution shall implement the principle of normalization so that each resident may live as normally as possible.

3a. No person shall be admitted to the institution unless a prior determination shall have been made that residence in the institution is the least restrictive habilitation setting feasible for that person.
b. No mentally retarded person shall be admitted to the institution if services and programs in the communtiy can afford adequate habilitation to such person.
c. Residents shall have a right to the least restrictive conditions necessary to achieve the purposes of habilitation. To this end, the institution shall make every attempt to move residents from (1) more to less structured living; (2) larger to smaller facilities; (3) larger to smaller living units; (4) group to individual residence; (5) segregated from the community to integrated into the community living; (6) dependent to independent living.

4. No borderline or mildly mentally retarded person shall be a resident of the institution. For purposes of this standard, a borderline retarded person is defined as an individual who is functioning between one and two standard deviations below the mean on a stan-

dardized intelligence test such as the Stanford Binet Scale and on measures of adaptive behavior such as the American Association on Mental Deficiency Adaptive Behavior Scale. A mildly retarded person is defined as an individual who is functioning between two and three standard deviations below the mean on a standardized intelligence test such as the Stanford Binet Scale and on a measure of adaptive heavior such as the American Association on Mental Deficiency Adaptive Behavior Scale.

5. Residents shall have a right to receive suitable educational services regardless of chronological age, degree of retardation or accompanying disabilities or handicaps.

a. The institution shall formulate a written statement of educational objectives that is consistent with the institution's mission as set forth in Standard 2, *supra*, and the other standards proposed herein.

b. School-age residents shall be provided a full and suitable educational program. Such educational program shall meet the following minimum standards:

	Mild	Moderate	Severe/ Profound
(1) Class Size	12	9	6
(2) Length of school year (in months)	9-10	9-10	11-12
(3) Minimum length of school day (in hours)	6	6	6

6. Residents shall have a right to receive prompt and adequate medical treatment for any physical ailments and for the prevention of any illness or disability. Such medical treatment shall meet standards of medical practice in the community.

III. *Individualized Habilitation Plans*

7. Prior to his admission to the institution, each resident shall have a comprehensive social, psychological, educational, and medical diagnosis and evaluation by appropriate specialists to determine if admission is appropriate.

a. Unless such preadmission evaluation has been conducted within three months prior to the admission, each resident shall have a new evaluation at the institution to determine if admission is appropriate.

b. When undertaken at the institution, preadmission diagnosis and evaluation shall be completed within five days.

8. Within 14 days of his admission to the institution, each resident shall have an evaluation by appropriate specialists for programming purposes.

9. Each resident shall have an individualized habilitation plan formulated by the institution. This plan shall be developed by appropriate Qualified Mental Retardation Professionals and implemented as soon as possible but no later than 14 days after the resident's admission to the institution. An interim program of habilitation, based on the preadmission evaluation conducted pursuant to Standard 7, *supra*, shall commence promptly upon the resident's admission. Each individualized habilitation plan shall contain:

a. a statement of the nature of the specific limitations and specific needs of the resident;

b. a description of intermediate and long-range habilitation goals with a projected timetable for their attainment;

c. a statement of, and an explanation for, the plan of habilitation for achieving these intermediate and long-range goals;

d. a statement of the least restrictive setting for habilitation necessary to achieve the habilitation goals of the resident.

e. a specification of the professionals and other staff members who are responsible for the particular resident's attaining these habilitation goals;

f. criteria for release to less restrictive settings for habilitation, including criteria for discharge and a projected date for discharge.

. . . .

IV. *Humane Physical and Psychological Environment*

15. Residents shall have a right to dignity, privacy and humane care.

16. Residents shall lose none of the rights enjoyed by citizens of Alabama and of the United States solely by reason of their admission or commitment to the institution, except as expressly determined by an appropriate court.

17. No person shall be presumed mentally incompetent solely by reason of his admission or commitment to the institution.

18. The opportunity for religious worship shall be accorded to each resident who desires such worship. Provisions for religious worship shall be made available to all residents on a nondiscriminatory basis. No individual shall be coerced into engaging in any religious activities.

19. Residents shall have the same rights to telephone communication as patients at Alabama public hospitals, except to the extent that a Qualified Mental Retardation Professional responsible for formulation of a particular resident's habilitation plan (see Standard 9, *supra*) writes an order imposing special restrictions and explains the reasons for any such restrictions. The written order must be renewed semiannually if any restrictions are to be continued. Residents shall have an unrestricted right to visitation, except to the extent that a Qualified Mental Retardation Professional responsible for formulation of a particular resident's habilitation plan (see Standard 9, *supra*) writes an order imposing special restrictions and explains the reasons for any such restrictions. The written order must be renewed semiannually if any restrictions are to be continued.

20. Residents shall be entitled to send and receive sealed mail. Moreoever, it shall be the duty of the institution to facilitate the exercise of this right by furnishing the necessary materials and assistance.

21. The institution shall provide, under appropriate supervision, suitable opportunities for the resident's interaction with members of the opposite sex, except where a Qualified Mental Retardation Professional responsible for the formulation of a particular resident's habilitation plan writes an order to the contrary and explains the reasons therefor.

22. *Medication:*

a. No medication shall be administered unless at the written order of a physician.

b. Notation of each individual's medication shall be kept in his medical records (Standard 14(i) *supra*). At least weekly the attending physician shall review the drug regimen of each resident under his care. All prescriptions shall be written with a termination date, which shall not exceed 30 days.

c. Residents shall have a right to be free from unnecessary or excessive medication. The resident's records shall state the effects of psychoactive medication on the resident. When dosages of such are changed or other psychoactive medications are prescribed, a notation shall be made in the resident's record concerning the effect of new medication or new dosages and the behavior changes, if any, which occur.

d. Medication shall not be used as punishment, for the convenience of staff, as a substitute for a habilitation program, or in quantities that interfere with the resident's habilitation program.

. . . .

23. Seclusion, defined as the placement of a resident alone in a locked room, shall not be employed. Legitimate "time out" procedures may be utilized under close and direct professional supervision as a technique in behavior-shaping programs.

24. Behavior modification programs involving the use of noxious or aversive stimuli shall be reviewed and approved by the institution's Human Rights Committee and shall be conducted only with the express and informed consent of the affected resident, if the resident is able to give such consent, and of his guardian or next of kin, after opportunities for consultation with independent specialists and with legal counsel. Such behavior modification programs shall be conducted only under the supervision of and in the presence of a Qualified Mental Retardation Professional who has had proper training in such techniques.

25. Electric shock devices shall be considered a research technique for the purpose of these standards. Such devices shall only be used in extraordinary circumstances to prevent self-mutilation leading to repeated and possibly permanent physical damage to the resident and only after alternative techniques have failed. The use of such devices shall be subject to the conditions prescribed in Standard 24, *supra*, and Standard 29, *infra,* and shall be used only under the direct and specific order of the superintendent.

26. Physical restraint shall be employed only when absolutely necessary to protect the resident from injury to himself or to prevent injury to others. Restraint shall not be employed as punishment, for the convenience of staff, or as a substitute for a habilitation program. Restraint shall be applied only if alternative techniques have failed and only if such restraint imposes the least possible restriction consistent with its purpose.

a. Only Qualified Mental Retardation Professionals may authorize the use of restraints.
   (1) Orders for restraints by the Qualified Mental Retardation Professionals shall be in writing and shall not be in force for longer than 12 hours.
   (2) A resident placed in restraints shall be checked at least every 30 minutes by staff trained in the use of restraints, and a record of such checks shall be kept.
   (3) Mechanical restraints shall be designed and used so as not to cause physical injury to the resident and so as to cause the least possible discomfort.
   (4) Opportunity for motion and exercise shall be provided for a period of not less than ten minutes during each two hours in which restraint is employed.
   (5) Daily reports shall be made to the superintendent by those Qualified Mental Retardation Professionals ordering the use of restraints, summarizing all such uses of restraint, the types used, the duration, and the reasons therefor.

b. The institution shall cause a written statement of this policy to be posted in each living unit and circulated to all staff members.

. . . .

28. The institution shall prohibit mistreatment, neglect or abuse in any form of any resident.

a. Alleged violations shall be reported immediately to the superintendent and there shall be a written record that:
   (1) Each alleged violation has been thoroughly investigated and findings stated;
   (2) The results of such investigaiton are reported to the superintendent and to the commissioner within 24 hours of the report of the incident. Such reports shall also be made to the institution's Human Rights Committee monthly and to the Alabama Board of Mental Health at its next scheduled public meeting.

b. The institution shall cause a written statement of this policy to be posted in each cottage and building and circulated to all staff members.

29. Residents shall have a right not to be subjected to experimental research without the express and informed consent of the resident, if the resident is able to give such consent, and of his guardian or next of kin, after opportunities for consultation with independent specialists and with legal counsel. Such proposed research shall first have been reviewed and approved by the institution's Human Rights Committee before such consent shall be sought. Prior to such approval the institution's Human Rights Committee shall determine that such research complies with the principles of the Statement on the Use of Human Subjects for Research of the American Association on Mental Deficiency and with the principles for research involving human subjects required by the United States Department of Health, Education and Welfare for projects supported by that agency.

30. Residents shall have a right not to be subjected to any unusual or hazardous treatment procedures without the express and informed consent of the resident, if the resident is able to give such consent, and of his guardian or next of kin, after opportunities for consultation with independent specialists and legal counsel. Such proposed procedures shall first have been reviewed and approved by the institution's Human Rights Committee before such consent shall be sought.

31. Residents shall have a right to regular physical exercise several times a week. It shall be the duty of the institution to provide both indoor and outdoor facilities and equipment for such exercise.

32. Residents shall have a right to be outdoors daily in the absence of contrary medical considerations.

TABLE 5.1 COMMUNICATION

STATE	CORRESPONDENCE: General Freedom of Corre-spondence (1)	Restrictions (2)	Restrictions Recorded (3)	Censorship (4)	Writing Material & Postage Furnished (5)	Unrestricted as to: Central Agency (6)	Public Official (7)	Counsel (8)	Other (9)	VISITATION: General Freedom of Visitation (10)	Restrictions (11)	Restrictions Recorded (12)	Unrestricted as to: Family & Friends (13)	Counsel (14)	Clergy (15)	Physician (16)	TELEPHONE: General Freedom to Use Telephone (17)	Restrictions (18)
ALA. Code (1975 & Supp. 1982)																		
ALAS. Stat. (1979 & Supp. 1981)	47.30.840 (6)									at reasonable times 47.30.840 (5)							reasonable access 47.30.840 (7)	
ARIZ. Rev. Stat. Ann. (1974 & Supp. 1981)	right to communi-cation of develop-mentally disabled 36-551.01(q) 36-514(3)				36-514(3)					develop-mentally disabled 36-551.01(q) 36-514.1	reasonable limitations by head of agency 36-514(1)						reasonable access between 9:00 a.m. & 9:00 p.m. 36-514(2)	on request of person being called 36-514(2)
ARK. Stat. Ann. (1971 & Supp. 1981)	59-1416(6)				59-1416(6)					59-1416(4)			during established visiting hours 59-1416(20)		in private 59-1416(20)	59-1416(17)	reasonable access 59-1416(5)	
CAL. Welf. & Inst. Code (West 1972 & Supp. 1981)	5325(e)	for good cause 5326	5326		5325(e)					each day 5325(c)	for good cause 5326	5326					reasonable access 5325(d)	for good cause 5326
COLO. Rev. Stat. Ann. (1973 & Supp. 1981)	develop-mentally disabled: 27-10.5-117(2), (3) 27-10-117 (1)(a)	for good cause 27-10-117(2) 27-10.5-111(3)	27-10-117(2) 27-10.5-111(3)		staff assistance in writing & mailing 27-10-117 (1)(b) develop-mentally disabled 27-10.5-117(7)					develop-mentally disabled: right to communi-cate freely & privately 27-10.5-117(1) 27-10.5-117(5) 27-10-117 (1)(d)	for good cause 27-10-117(2) develop-mentally disabled 27-10.5-111(3)	27-10-117(2) 27-10.5-111(3)		at any time 27-10-117 (1)(d)	at any time 27-10-117 (1)(d)	at any time 27-10-117 (1)(d)	ready access 27-10-117 (1)(c) develop-mentally disabled reasonable access 27-10.5-117(5)	for good cause 27-10-117(2) 27-10.5-111(3)
CONN. Gen. Stat. Ann. (West 1975 & Supp. 1981)	17-206g(a)	*fn. 1* 17-206h(f)	17-206g(c)	incoming mail returned to sender w/ explanation if medically harmful 17-206g(c)	17-206g(b)					regular visiting hours *fn. 2* 17-206h(a)	if medically harmful *fn. 1* 17-206h(d)	17-206h(d)		at any rea-sonable time 17-206h(c)	at any rea-sonable time 17-206h(c)	at any rea-sonable time 17-206h(c)	17-206g(d)	if makes obscene or threatening calls *fn. 1* 17-206g(e) or if medi-cally harmful (written ex-planation to family & per-sons regularly called) *fn. 1* 17-206g(f)
DEL. Code Ann. (1974 & Supp. 1980)	general freedom of communi-cation *fn. 3* 16, §5161(3) procedures established providing full opportunity for corres-pondence 16, §5161(3)	to protect safety & welfare of other patients & avoid serious harassment to others 16, §5161(3)								general free-dom of com-munication 16, §5161(3) frequent & convenient opportunities for visitation 16, §5161(3)	to protect safety & welfare of other patients & avoid serious harassment to others 16, §5161(3)						general free-dom of com-munication 16, §5161(3) reasonable access to telephone 16, §5161(3)	to protect safety & welfare of other patients & avoid serious harassment to others 16, 5161(3)

TABLE 5.1 COMMUNICATION—*Continued*

	CORRESPONDENCE									VISITATION							TELEPHONE	
							Unrestricted as to						*Unrestricted as to*					
STATE	*General Freedom of Corre-spondence* (1)	*Restrictions* (2)	*Restrictions Recorded* (3)	*Censorship* (4)	*Writing Material & Postage Furnished* (5)	Central Agency (6)	Public Official (7)	Counsel (8)	Other (9)	*General Freedom of Visitation* (10)	*Restrictions* (11)	*Restrictions Recorded* (12)	Family & Friends (13)	Counsel (14)	Clergy (15)	Physician (16)	*General Freedom to Use Telephone* (17)	*Restrictions* (18)
D.C. Code Ann. (1981 & Supp. 1982)	communication by sealed mail or otherwise 21-561(a)(1) mentally retarded 6-1965(b)			incoming 21-561(b)	mentally retarded: plus reasonable assistance 6-1965(b)			21-561(a)(2)	personal physician 21-561(a)(2)	mentally retarded 6-1965(a)	mentally ill reasonable rules 21-561(c) mentally retarded: by physician for good cause 6-1965(a)		mentally retarded: parents or guardian, at any reasonable time 6-1965(a)	mentally retarded: at any reasonable time 6-1965(a)	mentally retarded: at any reasonable time 6-1965(a)	mentally retarded: at any reasonable time 6-1965(a)	mentally retarded: reasonable access 6-1965(b)	reasonable rules regarding use of telephone & telegraph 21-561(c)
FLA. Stat. Ann. (West 1973 & Supp. 1981)	general freedom of communication 394.459(5)(a) freedom of correspondence 394.459(5)(b) mentally retarded 393.13(3)(c)(1)	if likely to be harmful to patient or others 394.459(5)(a) mentally retarded 393.13(3)(c)(1)	394.459(5)(c)	if reason to believe contents may be harmful 394.459(5)(b) mentally retarded 393.13(3)(c)(1)						general freedom of communication 394.459(5)(a) mentally retarded 393.13(3)(c)(3)	if likely to be harmful to patient or others 394.459(5)(a) least restrictive possible, reasonable rules 394.459(5)(d)	394.459(5)(c)					general freedom of communication 394.459(5)(a) mentally retarded 393.13(3)(c)(2)	if likely to be harmful to patient or others 394.459(5)(a) least restrictive possible, reasonable rules 394.459(5)(d)
GA. Code Ann. (1979 & Supp. 1982)	general freedom of correspondence 88-502.7(a) 88-502.7(b)	outgoing mail may be temporarily restricted by ct. order 88-502.7(d)-(f)	notice of order; right to hearing whenever restricted 88-502.7(f) 88-502.7(g)	incoming, if reason to believe contents may be dangerous 88-502.7(c)			88-502.7(f)	88-502.7(f)		88-502.7(a)	reasonable regulations 88-502.7(h)						general freedom of communication 88-502.7(a)	reasonable regulations 88-502.7(h)
HAWAII Rev. Stat. (1976 & Supp. 1981)	uncensored communication 334E-2(6)									uncensored communication 334E-2(6)							uncensored communication 334E-2(6)	
IDAHO Code (1980 & Supp. 1981)	communication by sealed mail or otherwise 66-346(a)(1)	by director of facility 66-346(c)	66-346(c)		66-346(a)(1)		committing ct. 66-346(b)			at all reasonable times 66-346(a)(2)	by director of facility 66-346(c)	66-346(c)		at any time 66-346(a)(5) 66-346(c)				
ILL. Ann. Stat. (Smith-Hurd 1966 & Supp. 1981)	convenience ensured 91½, §2-103 (a) 91½, §2-103	to protect against harm, harassment, or intimidation 91½, §2-103 (c)			91½, §2-103 (a)	91½, §2-103 (c)	governor, state legislator, attorney general, judge, state's attorney 91½, §2-103 (c)	91½, §2-103 (c)		reasonable times & places 91½, §2-103 91½, §2-103 (b)	to protect against harm, harassment, or intimidation 91½, §2-103 (c)						reasonable times & places 91½, §2-103 91½, §2-103 (b)	to protect against harm, harassment, or intimidation 91½, §2-103 (c)
IND. Code Ann. (Burns 1973 & Supp. 1982)		by regula-tions, because of inconsistency w/approved program design, or for good cause 16-14-1.6-3(b)	notice to patient & guardian or advocate 16-14-1.6-3(c)		16-14-1.6-3(a)(2)			"contact" 16-14-1.6-2(a)(4)	"contact" w/private practitioner 16-14-1.6-2(a)(4)		by regula-tions, because of inconsistency w/approved program design, or for good cause 16-14-1.6-3(b)	notice to patient & guardian or advocate 16-14-1.6-3(c)		16-14-1.6-2(a)(4)		16-14-1.6-2(a)(4)		by regula-tions, because of inconsistency w/approved program design, or for good cause 16-14-1.6-3(b)
IOWA Code Ann. (West 1969 & Supp. 1981)	mentally ill fn. 4 mentally retarded 222.8	offensive character 222.8				222.8	state or local 222.8			all reasonable opportunity & facility for communication w/friends 222.8							all reasonable opportunity & facility for communication w/friends 222.8	
KAN. Stat. Ann. (1976 & Supp. 1981) fn. 5	59-2929(a)(2)	for good cause 59-2929(b) right to mail any correspon-dence not violating postal regulations not to be restricted	59-2929(b)	opened & examined in patient's presence 59-2929(a)(2)			secretary of social & rehabilitation services, head of treatment facility, any ct. 59-2929(a)(8)	59-2929(a)(8)	physician 59-2929(a)(8)	each day 59-2929(a)(4)	for good cause 59-2929(b)	59-2929(b)	conjugal visits if facilities available 59-2929(a)(3) may be restricted	at all times 59-2929(a)(9)		at all times 59-2929(a)(9)	59-2929(a)(2)	for good cause 59-2929(b)

TABLE 5.1 COMMUNICATION—*Continued*

	CORRESPONDENCE									VISITATION							TELEPHONE	
						Unrestricted as to							*Unrestricted as to*					
STATE	*General Freedom of Correspondence* (1)	*Restrictions* (2)	*Restrictions Recorded* (3)	*Censorship* (4)	*Writing Material & Postage Furnished* (5)	Central Agency (6)	Public Official (7)	Counsel (8)	Other (9)	*General Freedom of Visitation* (10)	*Restrictions* (11)	*Restrictions Recorded* (12)	Family & Friends (13)	Counsel (14)	Clergy (15)	Physician (16)	*General Freedom to Use Telephone* (17)	*Restrictions* (18)
KY. Rev. Stat. Ann. (Michie 1982)							mentally ill & mentally retarded secretary for human resources 210.220	mentally ill & mentally retarded 210.220		mentally ill & mentally retarded 202A.191(e) 202B.050			mentally retarded 202B.060(5)					
LA. Rev. Stat. Ann. (West 1975 & Supp. 1981)	28:171(c)	sufficient cause 28:171(c)	written notice to counsel & next of kin or responsible party 28:171(c)		28:171(c)			28:171(c)		reasonable times & places may be established 28:171(c)	sufficient cause 28:171(c)	written notice to next of kin or responsible party 28:171(c)			in private at all times 28:171(c)	28:171(n)	reasonable times & places may be established 28:171(c)	sufficient cause 28:171(c)
ME. Rev. Stat. Ann. (1978 & Supp. 1982)		hospital regulations 34, §2254(1)				34, §2254(1)	ct. ordering hospitalization 34, §2254(1)	34, §2254(1)	clergy 34, §2254(1)		if definitely contraindicated by patient's medical condition 34, §2254(2)			at any reasonable time 34, §2254(2)	at any reasonable time 34, §2254(2)			
MD. Health-Gen. Code Ann. (1982 & Supp. 1982)	mentally ill 10-701(a)	any reasonable limitation on access to writing materials 10-701(a)(1)	either to access, or if physician believes another individual should be present when writing 10-701(c)	under direction of addressee 10-701(a)(2)	10-701(a)(1)					10-702(a)(3)		as well as refusals to see visitors 10-702(b),(c)		reasonable hrs. 10-702(a)(1) 10-702(c)(2)	reasonable hrs. 10-702(a)(2) 10-702(c)(2)		at all reasonable hrs. 10-701(b)	upon written notice of unwillingness to receive calls 10-701(b)
MASS. Ann. Laws (Michie/Law. Co-op. 1981 & Supp. 1981)		when in person's best interest 123, §23		superintendent may open 123, §23	123, §23		123, §23 governor, commissioner, any public elected official	123, §23	123, §23 personal physician, clergyman, immediate family	reasonable times 123, §23	when not in best interest 123, §23	123, §23		123, §23	123, §23	123, §23	reasonable access 123, §23	
MICH. Comp. Laws Ann. (1980 & Supp. 1981)	mentally ill 330.1726(1)	if essential to prevent patient from violating law or being substantially & seriously harmed 330.1726(4)	330.1726(8)		330.1726(2)		ct. 330.1726(7)	330.1726(7)	when involves matters which are or may be the subject of legal inquiry 330.1726(7)	reasonable times & places 330.1726(1) 330.1726(3)	to prevent substantial & serious harm to patient 330.1726(6)	330.1726(8)		others when involves matters which are or may be the subject of legal inquiry 330.1726(7)			reasonable times & places fn. 6 330.1726(3) 330.1726(1)	if essential to prevent patient from violating law or being substantially & seriously harmed 330.1726(4) on complaint of person called 330.1726(5)
MINN. Stat. Ann. (West 1982)		if required by patient's medical welfare 253A.17(5) subject to review by commissioner of public welfare	253A.17(5)		253A.17(4)	any official agency 253A.17(2)	governor, commissioner of public welfare, ct. 253A.17(2)	communication by sealed mail or any other means 253A.17(2)	communication w/physician by sealed mail or any other means 253A.17(2) single selected correspondent 253.17(3)	253A.17(6)	if necessary for patient's medical welfare; by general rules of hospital 253A.17(6)			at all reasonable times 253A.17(6)	at all reasonable times 253A.17(6)	at all reasonable times 253A.17(6)		
MISS. Code Ann. (1981 & Supp. 1982)																		
MO. Ann. Stat. (Vernon 1979 & Supp. 1982)	630.110.1(3)	if inconsistent w/treatment 630.110.1	630.110.2			630.110.4	ct. w/jurisdiction 630.110.4	630.110.4		at reasonable times 630.110.1(4)	if inconsistent w/treatment 630.110.1	630.110.2		in private, at reasonable times 630.110.3	in private, at reasonable times 630.110.3	in private, at reasonable times 630.110.3	reasonable access 630.110.1(5)	if inconsistent w/treatment 630.110.1

TABLE 5.1 COMMUNICATION—*Continued*

STATE	CORRESPONDENCE									VISITATION							TELEPHONE	
	General Freedom of Correspondence (1)	Restrictions (2)	Restrictions Recorded (3)	Censorship (4)	Writing Material & Postage Furnished (5)	Unrestricted as to: Central Agency (6)	Public Official (7)	Counsel (8)	Other (9)	General Freedom of Visitation (10)	Restrictions (11)	Restrictions Recorded (12)	Unrestricted as to: Family & Friends (13)	Counsel (14)	Clergy (15)	Physician (16)	General Freedom to Use Telephone (17)	Restrictions (18)
MONT. Code Ann. (1981)	developmentally disabled 53-20-142 53-21-142(4)	incoming 53-21-142(4) on order of person responsible for formulating patient's treatment plan			staff assistance in writing & mailing 53-21-142(5)	53-21-142(4)	cts. & government officials 53-21-142(4)	53-21-142(4)	physician, professional person 53-21-142(4)	same rights as patients at public hospitals 53-21-142(3)	on order of person responsible for formulating 53-21-142(3) patient's treatment plan			53-21-142(3)	53-21-142(3)	& other professional persons 53-21-142(3)	same rights to reasonable access as patients at public hospitals 53-21-142(3)	on order of person responsible for formulating patient's treatment plan 53-21-142(3)
NEB. Rev. Stat. (1981)	83-1066(4)	on ct. order for good cause, unless patient consents 83-1067								83-1066(4)	on ct. order for good cause, unless patient consents 83-1067						83-1066(4)	on ct. order for good cause, unless patient consents 83-1067
NEV. Rev. Stat. (1981)	packages not considered correspondence 433.482(5)	to protect health & safety of patient or others 433.534(1)	433.534(1)		433.482(5)					each day 433.482(3)	to protect health & safety of patient or others 433.534(1)	433.534(1)					reasonable access 433.482(4)	
N.H. Rev. Stat. Ann. (1977 & Supp. 1981)	general freedom of communication 135-B:45 developmentally disabled 171-A:14(II)	if substantial reason to believe contents may be harmful; lapse after 7 days unless renewed 135-B:45	135-B:45		developmentally disabled 171-A:14(II)					general freedom of communication 135-B:45 developmentally disabled 171-A:14 (III)	if harmful or by reasonable regulations; lapse after 7 days unless renewed 135-B:45 developmentally disabled 171-A:14(III)	developmentally disabled: & subject to review of human rights committee 171-A:14(III)					developmentally disabled: reasonable access 171-A:14(IV) general freedom of communication 135-B:45	if harmful or by reasonable regulations; lapse after 7 days unless renewed 135-B:45 developmentally disabled 171-A:14(IV)
N.J. Stat. Ann. (West 1981 & Supp. 1982)	30:4-24.2e(7)	for good cause, if program director feels it is imperative 30:4-24.2g(1)	30:4-24.2g(1) written notice to patient, attorney, guardian, & dep't 30:4-24.2g(3)		30:4-24.2e(7)		right to communicate w/cts. not restricted 30:4-24.2g(1)	right to communicate not restricted 30:4-24.2g(1)	right to communicate w/physician not restricted 30:4-24.2g(1)	each day 30:4-24.2e(5)	for good cause, if program director feels it is imperative 30:4-24.2g(1)	written notice to patient, attorney, guardian, & dep't 30:4-24.2g(1) 30:4-24.2g(3)		right to communicate not restricted 30:4-24.2g(1)		right to communicate not restricted 30:4-24.2g(1)	reasonable access 30:4-24.2e(6)	for good cause, if program director feels it is imperative 30:4-24.2g(1)
N.M. Stat. Ann. (1979 & Supp. 1982)	43-1-6(B)	by physician for good cause 43-1-6(B)			assistance in writing & mailing on request, w/o charge if indigent 43-1-6(B)		ct. 43-1-6(B)	43-1-6(B)		daily, hrs. limited only in interest of effective treatment & reasonable efficiency 43-1-6(A)	by physician for good cause 43-1-6(A)			at any reasonable time, w/reasonable cause 43-1-6(A)	at any reasonable time, w/reasonable cause 43-1-6(A)	or psychologist or social worker 43-1-6(A) at any reasonable time w/reasonable cause	reasonable access 43-1-6(B)	by physician for good cause 43-1-6(B)
N.Y. Mental Hyg. Law (McKinney 1978 & Supp. 1982)	general freedom of communication 33.05(b) 33.05(a)	to assure safety & welfare of patients & avoid serious harassment to others 33.05(a)				33.05(a)	33.05(a)	33.05(a)	clergy 33.05(a)	frequent & convenient opportunities 33.05(b) general freedom of communication 33.05(a)	to assure safety & welfare of patients & avoid serious harassment to others 33.05(a)						reasonable access 33.05(b) general freedom of communication 33.05(a)	to assure safety & welfare of patients & avoid serious harassment to others 33.05(a)
N.C. Gen Stat. (1981 & Supp. 1981)	122-55.2(a)(1)				staff assistance 122-55.2(a)(1)			unrestricted contact 122-55.2(a)(2)	unrestricted contact w/physician 122-55.2(a)(2)	at least 6 hrs. daily between 8:00 a.m. & 9:00 p.m., at least 2 of which after 6:00 p.m. 122-55.2(b)(2)	by professional responsible for patient's treatment plan 122-55.2(d)	written notice to patient's next of kin or guardian 122-55.2(d)		122-55.2(a)(2), (d)		122-55.2(a)(2	122-55.2(b)(1)	by professional responsible for patient's treatment plan 122-55.2(d)

TABLE 5.1 COMMUNICATION—*Continued*

	CORRESPONDENCE									VISITATION							TELEPHONE	
						Unrestricted as to							*Unrestricted as to*					
STATE	*General Freedom of Corre-spondence* (1)	*Restrictions* (2)	*Restrictions Recorded* (3)	*Censorship* (4)	*Writing Material & Postage Furnished* (5)	Central Agency (6)	Public Official (7)	Counsel (8)	Other (9)	*General Freedom of Visitation* (10)	*Restrictions* (11)	*Restrictions Recorded* (12)	Family & Friends (13)	Counsel (14)	Clergy (15)	Physician (16)	*General Freedom to Use Telephone* (17)	*Restrictions* (18)
N.D. Cent. Code (1978 & Supp. 1981)	25-03.1-40(6)	by treating physician, psychiatrist, or clinical psychologist if in patient's best interest 25-03.1-41	25-03.1-41							25-03.1-40(5)	by treating physician, psychiatrist, or clinical psychologist if in patient's best interest 25-03.1-41	25-03.1-41 (Supp. 1979)					25-03.1-40(5)	by treating physician, psychiatrist, or clinical psychologist if in patient's best interest 25-03.1-41
OHIO Rev. Code Ann. (Baldwin 1980 & Supp. 1982)	general freedom of communication 5122.29(D),(E) mentally retarded & developmentally disabled 5123.84	specifically restricted in patient's treatment plan for clear treatment reasons 5122.29(D)	in treatment plan 5122.29(D)		assistance in writing on request 5122.29(E) mentally retarded & developmentally disabled 5123.84(D)			general freedom of communication w/counsel or legal rights service personnel 5122.29(C)	general freedom of communication w/physician or psychologist unless prior ct. restriction 5122.29(C)	at reasonable times general freedom of communication 5122.29(D) mentally retarded & developmentally disabled 5123.84(B)	specifically restricted in patient's treatment plan for clear treatment reasons 5122.29(D)	in treatment plan 5122.29(D)		or personnel of legal rights service at reasonable times 5122.29(C) mentally retarded & developmentally disabled 5123.84(B)		or psychologist unless prior ct. restriction; at reasonable times 5122.29(C) mentally retarded & developmentally disabled 5123.84(B)	reasonable access 5122.29(D)(2) general freedom of communication 5122.29(D) mentally retarded & developmentally disabled 5123.84(C)	specifically restricted in patient's treatment plan for clear treatment reasons 5122.29(D)
OKLA. Stat. Ann. (West 1979 & Supp. 1982)	43A, §93	for patient's welfare; may appeal to ct. 43A, §93	43A, §93			43A, §93	director of mental health, committing ct., & other cts. 43A, §93	43A, §93	physician 43A, §93	43A, §93	for patient's welfare; may appeal to ct. 43A, §93	43A, §93					43A, §93	for patient's welfare; may appeal to ct. 43A, §93
OR. Rev. Stat. (1981)	mentally retarded 427.031(2)(a) 426.385(1)(a)				mentally retarded 427.031(2)(f) 426.385(1)(f)					freedom of communication in person 426.385(1)(a) mentally retarded 427.031(2)(a)							reasonable access 426.385(1)(a) mentally retarded 427.031(2)(a)	
PA. Stat. Ann. (Purdon 1969 & Supp. 1982)	reasonable opportunities 50, §4423(5)	director's discretion 50, §4423(5)			50, §4423(5)	50, §4423(1)	director of facility, committing ct., governor 50, §4423(1)	50, §4423(1)	family 50 §4423(1)					50, §4423(1)	50, §4423(2)	representative of dep't of public welfare 50, §4423(1)		
R.I. Gen. Laws (1977 & Supp. 1982) *fn. 7*	mentally retarded 40.1-22-12						*fn. 7*			mentally retarded, except during illness or incapacity 40.1-22-13				*fn. 7*				
S.C. Code Ann. (Law. Co-op. 1976 & Supp. 1982)	44-23-1030(1)	if medically necessary 44-23-1030	44-23-1030			44-23-1030	committing ct. 44-23-1030	44-23-1030	legal guardian, physician, clergy 44-23-1030	44-23-1030(2)	if medically necessary 44-23-1030	44-23-1030					44-23-1030(1)	if medically necessary 44-23-1030
S.D. Codified Laws Ann. (1976 & Supp. 1982)	27A-12-2(4) 27B-8-2(4)				27A-12-2(4) 27B-8-2(4)					regular visiting hrs. 27A-12-2(4) 27B-8-2(4)							access between 9:00 a.m. & 8:00 p.m. 27A-12-2(4) 27B-8-2(4)	
TENN. Code Ann. (1977 & Supp. 1982)				incoming if necessary for patient's medical welfare 33-306(a)			communication by sealed mail or otherwise w/cts. (subject to censorship) 33-306(a)(2)	communication by sealed mail or otherwise 33-306(a)	communication by sealed mail or otherwise w/physician 33-306(a) & w/minister, family (subject to censorship) 33-306(a)(2)	regular visiting hrs. 33-306(a)(1)	reasonable rules 33-306(a)							reasonable rules for use of telephone & telegraph 33-306(a)

TABLE 5.1 COMMUNICATION—*Continued*

STATE	CORRESPONDENCE									VISITATION							TELEPHONE	
						Unrestricted as to							Unrestricted as to					
	General Freedom of Corre-spondence (1)	Restrictions (2)	Restrictions Recorded (3)	Censorship (4)	Writing Material & Postage Furnished (5)	Central Agency (6)	Public Official (7)	Counsel (8)	Other (9)	General Freedom of Visitation (10)	Restrictions (11)	Restrictions Recorded (12)	Family & Friends (13)	Counsel (14)	Clergy (15)	Physician (16)	General Freedom to Use Telephone (17)	Restrictions (18)
TEX. Rev. Civ. Stat. Ann. (Vernon 1958 & Supp. 1982)	general freedom of communication 5547-86(a)(3) mentally retarded 5547-300(25)	general rules & regulations of hospital; restrictions necessary for patient's welfare 5547-86(a)	5547-86(b)			5547-86(a)(4)	cts. & attorney general 5547-86(a)(4)	5547-86(a)(4)		mentally retarded 5547-300(25) 5547-86(a)(1)	general rules & regulations of hospital; restrictions necessary for patient's welfare 5547-86(a)						general freedom of communication 5547-86(a)(3) mentally retarded 5547-300(25)	general rules & regulations of hospital; restrictions necessary for patient's welfare 5547-86(a)
UTAH Code Ann. (1978 & Supp. 1981)	communication by sealed mail or otherwise 64-7-48(1)(a)	general rules & regulations of facility; restrictions necessary for patient's welfare 64-7-48(1)	64-7-48(2)			64-7-48(3)	committing ct. 64-7-48(3)	64-7-48(3)		64-7-48(1)(b)	general rules & regulations of facility; restrictions necessary for patient's welfare 64-7-48(1)	64-7-48(2)		64-7-48(3)	64-7-48(3)			
VT. Stat. Ann. (1968 & Supp. 1982)	communication by sealed mail or otherwise 18, §7705(a) (1)	general rules & regulations of hospital; restrictions necessary for medical welfare 18, §7705(a)				18, §7705(b)	commissioner, committing judge 18, §7705(b)	18, §7705(b)	clergy 18, §7705(b)	18, §7705(a) (2)	general rules & regulations of hospital; restrictions necessary for medical welfare 18, §7705(a)			at all reasonable times 18, §7710	at all reasonable times 18, §7710		18, §7705(a) (2)	general rules & regulations of hospital; restrictions necessary for medical welfare 18, §7705(a)
VA. Code (1976 & Supp. 1983)	37.1-84.1(7)	may be limited by adjudicated legal incompetence 37.1-84.1																board shall issue rules & regulations 37.1-84.1
WASH. Rev. Code Ann. (1975 & Supp. 1982)	71.05.370(6)	if danger to patient or others 71.05.370			71.05.370(6)					at reason-able times 71.05.370(4)	if danger to patient or others 71.05.370						reasonable access 71.05.370(5)	if danger to patient or others 71.05.370
W. VA. Code Ann. (1980 & Supp. 1983																		
WIS. Stat. Ann. (West 1957 & Supp. 1982)	51.61(1)(c)		51.61(1)(c)	if reason to believe contains contraband or dangerous objects 51.61(1)(c)	51.61(1)(c)		cts. & government official 51.61(1)(c)	51.61(1)(c)	physicians & psychologists 51.61(1)(c)	each day 51.61(1)(f)	for cause or when medically or therapeutically contraindicated 51.61(2)	notice to patient & opportunity for review 51.61(2)					w/in reason-able limit 51.61(1)(p)	for cause or when medically or therapeutically contraindicated 51.61(2)
WYO. Stat. Ann. (1982 & Supp. 1983)	communication by sealed mail or otherwise 25-10-120 (a)(i) mentally retarded 25-5-132 (c)(i)	general rules & regulations of hospital 25-10-120(b) as part of individual program plan 25-5-132	25-10-120(b) 25-5-132				governor 25-5-132 (d)(v)	25-10-120(b)	parent, guardian, or guardian ad litem 25-5-132 (d)(v)	25-10-120 (a)(ii) mentally retarded 25-5-132 (c)(viii)	general rules & regulations of hospital 25-10-120(b) as part of individual program plan 25-5-132(c)	25-10-120(b) 25-5-132(c)					mentally retarded 25-5-132 (c)(vii)	as part of individual program plan 25-5-132(c)

FOOTNOTES: TABLE 5.1

1. Conn. Gen. Stat. Ann. § 17-206h(f) (West Supp. 1981): "No restriction of any patient's rights to send and receive mail, make and receive telephone calls, or receive visitors shall be made in any manner, or for any reasons, other than prescribed in sections 17-206g and this section."

2. Id. § 17-206h(b) (West 1975). If the patient's family cannot visit during regular visiting hours, a mutually convenient weekly two hour period is scheduled.

3. Del. Code Ann. tit. 16, § 5161(3) (Supp. 1980): "Correspondence initiated to others by the patient shall be sent along promptly without being opened."

4. Every patient has the right to:

> [i]n addition to protection of his constitutional rights enjoyment of other legal, medical, religious, social, personal and working rights and privileges which he would enjoy if he were not so hospitalized or detained, so far as is possible consistent with effective treatment of that person and of the other patients of the hospital. If the patient's rights are restricted, the physician's direction to that effect shall be noted on the patient's record. The department of social services shall . . . establish rules setting forth the specific rights and privileges to which persons so hospitalized or detained are entitled.

Iowa Code Ann. § 229.23(3) (West Supp. 1981).

5. Kan. Stat. Ann. § 59-2910(a) (1976):

> During a 72-hour emergency observation or protective custody period, the patient shall be allowed to communicate by reasonable means with a reasonable number of persons and to consult privately with an attorney, personal physician, and at least one member of his or her family. The patient must be immediately informed of his or her right to contact legal counsel and next of kin.

6. Mich. Comp. Laws Ann. § 330.1447 (1980). Patients hospitalized pending medical certification or examination are allowed to make a reasonable number of telephone calls (at least two). If the patient has insufficient funds, at least two calls must be allowed at the expense of the hospital.

7. Rhode Island grants the mental health advocate the right to privately communicate, by mail or orally, with a patient. R.I. Gen Laws § 40.1-5-24(1) (Supp. 1982). The patient's freedom to communicate with the directors of health and of mental health, retardation, and hospitals may not be restricted unless the directors consent, and the patient must be afforded "every facility for making such communications." Id. The patient has the right to confer with counsel if a petition for release from commitment under chapter 5.1 is submitted. Id. § 40.1-5.2-6.

TABLE 5.2 PROPERTY AND PERSONAL RIGHTS OF INSTITUTIONALIZED PERSONS

STATE	TYPES OF PATIENTS COVERED (1)	CONTROL OF PATIENTS' PROPERTY — Patients' Property Rights: Personal Possessions (2)	Spending Money (3)	Disposition of Property (4)	ADDITIONAL RIGHTS OF INSTITUTIONALIZED PATIENTS: Institutional Control (5)	Diet (6)	Employment (7)	Exercise (8)	Religion (9)	Privacy for Personal Needs (10)	EXPLANATION OF RIGHTS UPON ADMISSION (11)	NOTICE OF RIGHTS POSTED (12)
ALA. Code (1975 & Supp. 1982)	all forms of mental or emotional illness *fn. 1* 22-50-1											
ALAS. Stat. (1979 & Supp. 1981)	mentally ill 47.30.825 developmentally disabled 47.80.900 (6), (7)	47.30.840(4)	47.30.840(4)	47.30.835(a)	reasonable protections to safeguard possessions & provide storage 47.30.840 (2), (3)				47.30.835(a)		if patient does not understand English 47.30.855	47.30.855
ARIZ. Rev. Stat. Ann. (1974 & Supp. 1981)	mentally ill (mentally disordered) 36-501(17) developmentally disabled 36-551(10)	& individual storage space 36-507(4), (5) 36-551.01(Q)	36-507(5)	36-506(A)	if necessary to protect safety of patient or others 36-507(5) if involuntarily committed & w/o guardian 36-508		compensation if not therapeutic 36-510 fair compensation 36-551.01(I)		36-514(4)		36-551.01(P)	in English & Spanish 36-504(A)
ARK. Stat. Ann. (1971 & Supp. 1981)	mentally ill 59-1403 59-1404	& individual storage space 59-1416(3) 59-1416(1)	59-1416(2)		unless dangerous to patient, because acutely suicidal or agitated 59-1416(1)			59-1416(26)	59-1416(25)	right to refuse being photographed for medical purposes 59-1416(16)		59-1416(28)
CAL. Welf. & Inst. Code (West 1972 & Supp. 1981)	mentally ill & mentally retarded 5325	private storage space 5325(a), (b)	reasonable sum 5325(a)		reasonable precautions to safeguard possessions 5156, 7278			5325.1(h)	5325.1(e)	5325.1(b)	in language or modality accessible to patient 5325(i)	in the predominant language of the community 5325
COLO. Rev. Stat. (1973 & Supp. 1981)	mentally ill 27-10-101 developmentally disabled 27-10.5-101	27-10-117(1)(e) 27-10.5-121(1)	27-10-117(1)(e) reasonable amounts 27-10.5-121(3)		denial of rights for good cause by professional providing treatment 27-10-117(2) denial of rights for proper purposes of treatment by professional or ct. 27-10.5-111(3) custody when essential for medical & safety reasons 27-10.5-121(1)		compensation in accordance w/ min. wage laws; no involuntary labor other than personal housekeeping 27-10.5-118	recreation 27-10.5-112(1)	27-10.5-116		right to explanation 27-10.5-123	27-10-117(5)
CONN. Gen. Stat. Ann. (West 1975 & Supp. 1981)	mentally disordered 17-206a	& individual storage space 17-206i(a)	reasonable sum 17-206i(a)	17-206b	rights denied if superintendent finds medically harmful 17-206i(a)					17-206c		17-206i(c)
DEL. Code Ann. (1974 & Supp. 1980)	mentally ill 16, §5125 mentally retarded 16, §§5522(a), 5161(a)	16, §5161(a)(4)			temporarily for patient's protection 16, §5161(a)(4)		entitled to therapeutic work programs; not covered by workmen's compensation or unemployment insurance 16, §5161(a)(5)		treatment by spiritual means through prayer 16, §5161(a)(8)			in English & Spanish 16, §5161(a)

TABLE 5.2 PROPERTY AND PERSONAL RIGHTS OF INSTITUTIONALIZED PERSONS—*Continued*

STATE	TYPES OF PATIENTS COVERED (1)	CONTROL OF PATIENTS' PROPERTY — *Patients' Property Rights*				ADDITIONAL RIGHTS OF INSTITUTIONALIZED PATIENTS					EXPLANATION OF RIGHTS UPON ADMISSION (11)	NOTICE OF RIGHTS POSTED (12)
		Personal Possessions (2)	Spending Money (3)	Disposition of Property (4)	*Institutional Control* (5)	*Diet* (6)	*Employment* (7)	*Exercise* (8)	*Religion* (9)	*Privacy for Personal Needs* (10)		
D.C. Code Ann. (1981 & Supp. 1982)	mentally ill 21-501 et seq.			21-564							written statement to patient, & spouse, parents, or nearest adult relative 21-565	
	mentally retarded 6-1961 et seq.	reasonable, including locked storage space 6-1965(d)			record kept of all possessions 6-1965(d)	nourishing, well-balanced, varied, & appetizing; special diet on doctor's order 6-1965(f)	may be required to do habilitative & housekeeping tasks not involving operation or maintenance of facility 6-1971	reasonable daily opportunities 6-1965(e)	right to follow or abstain 6-1965(c)	reasonable privacy in sleeping & hygiene practices 9-1965(d)		
FLA. Stat. Ann. (West 1973 & Supp. 1981)	mentally ill 394.459	clothing & personal effects 394.459(6)			temporary custody when required for medical & safety reasons 394.459(6)							
	mentally retarded 393.13(1)	clothing & personal effects 393.13(3)(d)	held by dep't in compliance w/ 402.17(2), (7) 393.13(3)(d)(1)		temporary custody for medical & safety reasons 393.13(3)(d)		compliance w/ federal wage & hr. laws 393.13(3)(k)	as prescribed by habilitation plan 393.13(3)(h)	religious freedom & practice 393.13(3)(b)	dignity, privacy, & humane care 393.13(3)(a)	393.13(5)	393.13(3)(l)(4)
GA. Code Ann. (1979 & Supp. 1982)	mentally ill 88-501 et seq.	right to personal effects shall be respected 88-502.8		reasonable efforts to assure safety 88-502.8	temporary custody when for medical reasons 88-502.8		shall be assisted in finding suitable employment outside facility if such will aid treatment 88-502.10					
	mentally retarded 88-2501 et seq.	right to personal effects shall be respected 88-2503.8		reasonable efforts to assure safety 88-2503.8	temporary custody for medical reasons 88-2503.8							
HAWAII Rev. Stat. (1976 & Supp. 1981)	mentally ill, drug abuse, & alcoholism 334-61			334-61	if administrator applies for show cause order against patient's right 334-61 administrator may deposit in financial institution small amounts of cash that come into his hands & apply all or part to benefit (but not to maintenance in facility) of patient 334-23	adequate diet 334E-2(14)	work & fair compensation 334E-2(16)	physical exercise & recreation 334E-2(13)		privacy, respect, & personal dignity 334E-2(3)	right to knowledge of rights withheld by ct. or law 334E-2(12), (a)(20)	right of access to written rules & regulations 334E-2(1)
IDAHO Code (1980 & Supp. 1982)	mentally ill 66-300 et seq.	including toilet articles & clothes 66-346(a)(3)	reasonable sum for canteen expenses & small purchases 66-346(a)(3)	66-346(a)(6)	patient's trust fund 66-501, 502 director may restrict patient's right to spending money & personal possessions 66-346(c)						66-346(d)	prominently in all facilities 66-346(d)
	developmentally disabled 66-412	66-412(3)(e)	66-412(3)(e)	66-312(3)					66-412(3)(g)		66-412(5)	66-412(5)

TABLE 5.2 PROPERTY AND PERSONAL RIGHTS OF INSTITUTIONALIZED PERSONS—*Continued*

STATE	TYPES OF PATIENTS COVERED (1)	CONTROL OF PATIENTS' PROPERTY — *Patients' Property Rights*: Personal Possessions (2)	Spending Money (3)	Disposition of Property (4)	*Institutional Control* (5)	ADDITIONAL RIGHTS OF INSTITUTIONALIZED PATIENTS: *Diet* (6)	*Employment* (7)	*Exercise* (8)	*Religion* (9)	*Privacy for Personal Needs* (10)	EXPLANATION OF RIGHTS UPON ADMISSION (11)	NOTICE OF RIGHTS POSTED (12)
ILL. Ann. Stat. (Smith-Hurd 1966 & Supp. 1981)	mentally ill & developmentally disabled 91½, §1-101 et seq.	91½, §2-104	91½, §2-105		to protect patient or others from harm 91½, §2-104		if consistent w/services plan; wages if of any economic benefit 91½, §2-106		services by spiritual means through prayer 91½, §2-102(b)		orally & in writing 91½, §2-200(a)	conspicuously in public areas 91½, §2-200(a)
IND. Code Ann. (Burns 1973 & Supp. 1982)	mentally ill & developmentally disabled 16-14-1.6-1	& clothes 16-14-1.6-3 (a)(1)	reasonable amount 16-14-1.6-3 (a)(1)		rights conditioned on consistency w/treatment program; dep't regulations; may be denied for good cause 16-14-1.6-3(b) if rights waived 16-14-1.6-5				16-14-1.6-2(3)			duty of administrator to ensure access 16-14-1.6-11
IOWA Code Ann. (West 1969 & Supp. 1981)	mentally ill *fn. 6* mentally retarded 222.84		to purchase personal incidentals, desires, & comforts 222.85		personal deposit fund 222.84, 85						229.23(3)	
KAN. Stat. Ann. (1976 & Supp. 1981)	mentally ill 59-2901	including clothes & toilet articles 59-2929(a)(1)	59-2929(a)(1)	property rights 59-2930	for good cause 59-2929(b) reasonable rules & regulations 59-2930		right to refuse involuntary labor & to be paid for work other than personal housekeeping 59-2929(a)(5)		rights as a citizen 59-2930		orally & in writing 59-2929(a)(10)	
KY. Rev. Stat. Ann. (Michie 1982)	mentally ill & mentally retarded 202A.006 et seq. 202B.050	right to maintain, keep, & use 202A.191(d) 202B.060(4)	right to maintain, keep, & use 202A.191(d) 202B.060(4)				right to payment for work performed for hospital 202A.191(f) or residential treatment center 202B.060(6)		religious instruction & ministration 210.130			
LA. Rev. Stat. Ann. (West 1975 & Supp. 1981)	mentally ill or substance abuse 28:2(17)	including clothes & toilet articles, unless medically inappropriate 28:171(G)	reasonable sum for canteen expenses & small purchases 28:171(G)	right to enter contractual relationships & manage property 28:171(A)	deposit of patients' funds 28:172, 173		at useful occupation, depending on patient's condition & facilities 28:171(H) right to sell products of personal labor at director's discretion 28:171(I)	interest earned on funds deposited for patients shall be expended by institution for recreational purposes 28:173		28:171(A)		
	mentally retarded 28:380	28:392(B)(3)						28:392(B)(7)	28:392(B)(6)			
ME. Rev. Stat. Ann. (1978 & Supp. 1982)	mentally ill 34, §2254(3) mentally retarded 34, §2603			*fn. 7* 34, §2254(3)			all civil rights *fn. 7* 34, §2254(3)	all civil rights *fn. 7* 34, §2254(3)	all civil rights *fn. 7* 34, §2254(3) treatment by spiritual means alone 34, §2603	all civil rights *fn. 7* 34, §2254(3)		

TABLE 5.2 PROPERTY AND PERSONAL RIGHTS OF INSTITUTIONALIZED PERSONS—*Continued*

STATE	TYPES OF PATIENTS COVERED (1)	CONTROL OF PATIENTS' PROPERTY — *Patients' Property Rights*			ADDITIONAL RIGHTS OF INSTITUTIONALIZED PATIENTS						EXPLANATION OF RIGHTS UPON ADMISSION (11)	NOTICE OF RIGHTS POSTED (12)
		Personal Possessions (2)	Spending Money (3)	Disposition of Property (4)	*Institutional Control* (5)	*Diet* (6)	*Employment* (7)	*Exercise* (8)	*Religion* (9)	*Privacy for Personal Needs* (10)		
MD. Health-Gen. Code Ann. (1982 & Supp. 1982)	mentally retarded 7-601 et seq. mentally ill 10-101(f)			right to receive, hold, & dispose of property may not be deprived solely because of commitment 7-603 right to receive, hold, & dispose of property 10-703						right to receive respect & privacy in an individually developed program 7-601(a)(5)	copy of policy given to individual & guardian, next of kin, or sponsoring agency 7-601(b)(2)	conspicuously in a public place 7-601(b)(1)
MASS. Ann. Laws (Michie/Law. Co-op. 1981 & Supp. 1981)	mentally ill & mentally retarded 123, §23	including toilet articles & clothes 123, §23	reasonable sum for canteen expenses & small purchases 123, §23	123, §27	superintendent may deposit patient funds in bank							
MICH. Comp. Laws Ann. (1980 & Supp. 1981)	mentally ill & developmentally disabled 330.1401 330.1501	all personal property 330.1728(1)	entitled to easy access, except where unreasonably dissipated 330.1730	entitled to receive, possess, & use all personal property 330.1728(1)	to prevent theft, loss, or destruction; physicial harm; for compelling treatment reasons or effective functioning of facility 330.1728(4) dep't may safekeep or deposit patient money 330.1730, 1732				right to treatment by spiritual means 330.1704(2)			
MINN. Stat. Ann. (West 1982)	mentally ill, mentally retarded, & chemically dependent 246.01 253B.02				care & custody of all moneys of inmates 246.151(1)		compensation not less than 25% min. wage 246.151(1)		253B.03(4)			
MISS. Code Ann. (1981 & Supp. 1982)	mentally ill 41-21-61(c) mentally retarded 41-19-1			41-21-101								
MO. Code Ann. (1979 & Supp. 1982)	all mental disabilities 630.005 et seq.	& clothes 630.110(1)(1)	reasonable sum for canteen & small purchases 630.110(1)(2)		if inconsistent w/care & treatment 630.110(1)	nourishing, well-balanced, & varied 630.115(1)(13)	right to not participate in nontherapeutic labor 630.116(1)(4)	physical exercise & outdoor recreation 630.110(1)(7)	right to attend or not attend services 630.115(1)(5)		630.125	in residential & activity areas 630.125(3)
MONT. Code Ann. (1981)	developmentally disabled 53-20-101 mentally ill 53-21-101	& clothes 53-20-142(7) & clothes 53-21-142(6)	reasonable sum 53-21-142(7)		if dangerous to self or others 53-20-142(7) if dangerous to self or others 53-21-142(6)	nourishing, well-balanced diet 53-20-142(12) right to min. recommended daily allowance 53-21-142(12)	compensation 53-20-164 53-21-167	several times a week 53-20-142(13) several times a week 53-21-142(9)	53-20-142(11) 53-21-142(8)	dignity, privacy, & humane care 53-20-142(1) privacy & dignity 53-21-142(1), (13)	in language patient understands 53-21-168	in each ward 53-21-168

TABLE 5.2 PROPERTY AND PERSONAL RIGHTS OF INSTITUTIONALIZED PERSONS—*Continued*

STATE	TYPES OF PATIENTS COVERED (1)	CONTROL OF PATIENTS' PROPERTY — *Patients' Property Rights*: Personal Possessions (2)	*Patients' Property Rights*: Spending Money (3)	*Patients' Property Rights*: Disposition of Property (4)	CONTROL OF PATIENTS' PROPERTY: *Institutional Control* (5)	ADDITIONAL RIGHTS OF INSTITUTIONALIZED PATIENTS: *Diet* (6)	*Employment* (7)	*Exercise* (8)	*Religion* (9)	*Privacy for Personal Needs* (10)	EXPLANATION OF RIGHTS UPON ADMISSION (11)	NOTICE OF RIGHTS POSTED (12)
NEB. Rev. Stat. (1981)	mentally ill dangerous persons 83-1001	private storage space for personal possessions 83-1066(5)			by ct. order, for good cause, or by waiver 83-1067		compensation in accordance w/ Fair Labor Standards Act 83-1066(7)		to engage or refuse to engage in worship & political activity 83-1066(6)	reasonably private living conditions 83-1066(5)		
NEV. Rev. Stat. (1981)	mentally ill & mentally retarded 433.003(1)	including clothes & toilet articles, unless used to endanger self or others 433.482(1)			correspondence identified as containing check payable to client for safekeeping 433.482(5)(b) personal deposit fund 433.539		compensation 433.524				by means administrator may dsignate by regulation 433.482 mentally ill: written statement in simple language 433A.350	in all facilities providing service 433.482
N.H. Rev. Stat. Ann. (1977 & Supp. 1981)	mentally ill 135-B:1 developmentally impaired 171-A:14	all legal rights, unless adjudicated incompetent 135-B:42 including clothes & toilet articles 171-A:14(IV)	all legal rights, unless adjudicated incompetent 135-B:42 for canteen & other purchases 171-A:14(IV)	all legal rights, unless adjudicated incompetent 135-B:42 contract or manage affairs 171-A:14(I)	all legal rights, unless adjudicated incompetent 135-B:42 denial for good cause; subject to review by human rights committee 171-A:14(IV)		wages subject to deductions for cost of care; such services as not necessarily therapeutic if mandated by Fair Labor Standards Act 171-A:16			individual dignity 135-B:42 individual dignity 171-A:14(I)		in every treatment facility 135-B:46 in every program w/in delivery system 171-A:15
N.J. Stat. Ann. (West 1981 & 1982)	mentally ill, mentally retarded, or tuberculosis 30:4-33	including clothes, toilet articles, & storage space 30:4-24.2(e)(3)	reasonable sum for canteen expenses & small purchases 30:4-24.2(e)(3)		for good cause for 30 days, subject to renewal 30:4-24.2(g)(2)			several times a week 30:4-24.2(e)(8)	to practice or abstain 30:4-24.2(e)(11)	privacy & dignity 30:4-24.2(e)(1)	written notice w/in 5 days of admission 30:4-24.2(b)	in all facilities providing services 30:4-24.2(d)
N.M. Stat. Ann. (1979 & Supp. 1982)	mentally ill & developmentally disabled 43-1-1 et seq.	reasonable storage space 43-1-6(D)				nourishing, well-balanced, varied, & appetizing 43-1-6(F)		reasonable daily opportunities 43-1-6(E)	follow or abstain, including reasonable accommodations & transportation 43-1-6(C)	reasonable privacy in sleeping & hygiene practices 43-1-6(D)		
N.Y. Mental Hyg. Law (McKinney 1978 & Supp. 1982)	mentally ill & mentally retarded 9.07 15.07 33.01 et seq.	right to retain 33.07(a)			temporary custody 33.07(a) interest received to accrue to patient 33.07(c), (d)		dep't shall encourage employment as part of care or release & promote training for gainful employment 33.09(a) compensation 33.09(b), (c)				9.07(a) 15.07(a)	at places throughout the hospital 9.07(b) 15.07(b)
N.C. Gen. Stat. (1981 & Supp. 1981)	mentally ill, mentally retarded, or substance abuse 122-1 et seq.	& clothing 122-55.2(b)(5)	reasonable sum 122-55.2(b)(8)	unless adjudicated incompetent 122-55.2(c)	on written restriction in treatment plan up to 60 days; subject to renewal 122-55.2(d)			several times a week 122-55.2(b)(4)	122-55.2(b)(7)	dignity, privacy, & humane care 122-55.1		

TABLE 5.2 PROPERTY AND PERSONAL RIGHTS OF INSTITUTIONALIZED PERSONS—*Continued*

STATE	TYPES OF PATIENTS COVERED (1)	CONTROL OF PATIENTS' PROPERTY: Patients' Property Rights: Personal Possessions (2)	Spending Money (3)	Disposition of Property (4)	ADDITIONAL RIGHTS OF INSTITUTIONALIZED PATIENTS: *Institutional Control* (5)	*Diet* (6)	*Employment* (7)	*Exercise* (8)	*Religion* (9)	*Privacy for Personal Needs* (10)	EXPLANATION OF RIGHTS UPON ADMISSION (11)	NOTICE OF RIGHTS POSTED (12)
N.D. Cent. Code (1978 & Supp. 1981)	mentally ill, alcoholic, or drug addict 25-03.1-02(11)	& clothing 25-03.1-40(7)		all civil rights 25-03.1-40(11)	if treating physician issues written restriction in best interests of patient; review & renewal procedure in 14 days 25-03.1-41 bond for funds in trust 25-01.1-19, 20			regular outdoor opportunities 25-03.1-40(8)	25.03.1-41(9)	dignity & respect 25-03.1-40(3)		
OHIO Rev. Code Ann. (Baldwin 1980 & Supp. 1982)	mentally ill 5122.01 et seq.	clothes & personal effects; personal possessions, including toilet articles; storage space 5122.29(F)(1), (4), (5)	reasonable sum for expenses & small purchases 5122.29(F)(6)				no compulsory labor involving operation, support, or maintenance of hospital, or for which there is outside contract; prevailing wage rate for voluntary labor 5122.28		including right to services & sacred texts 5122.29(H)	privacy & dignity 5122.29(B) reasonable privacy, including both periods & places 5122.29(G)	w/in 24 hrs. of admission, according to rules established by legal rights service 5122.27(G) written list 5122.29(A)	
	mentally retarded & developmentally disabled 5123.02 et seq.	retains all rights not specifically denied by statute 5123.81	retains all rights not specifically denied by statute 5123.81	retains all rights not specifically denied by statute 5123.81	retains all rights not specifically denied by statute 5123.81		no compulsory labor involving operation or maintenance of institution, or under outside contract 5123.81 5123.87					
OKLA. Stat. Ann. (West 1979 & Supp. 1982)	mentally ill or mentally retarded 43A, §2					sufficient & wholesome 43A, §91	43A, §191.1					
OR. Rev. Stat. (1981)	mentally ill 426.005 et seq.	including clothing, toilet articles, private storage 426.385(1)(b), (c), (e)	make purchases 426.385(1)(m)	426.385(1)(m)	if adjudicated incompetent 426.385(1)(m)		no compulsory routine labor tasks except as essential for treatment 426.385(1)(j) reasonable compensation except for housekeeping 426.385(1)(k)		426.385(1)(d)		simple & clear statement 426.395	in each room frequented by patients 426.395
	mentally retarded 427.005 et seq.	including clothing, toilet articles, private storage 427.031(2)	make purchases 427.031(1)	427.031(1)	if adjudicated incompetent 427.031(1)		no compulsory routine labor tasks except those essential for treatment; reasonable compensation except for housekeeping 427.031(2) (i), (j)		427.031(2)(d)		encouraged & assisted to understand & exercise their rights 427.031(2)	in all facilities housing residents 427.031(2)

TABLE 5.2 PROPERTY AND PERSONAL RIGHTS OF INSTITUTIONALIZED PERSONS—*Continued*

STATE	TYPES OF PATIENTS COVERED (1)	CONTROL OF PATIENTS' PROPERTY — *Patients' Property Rights* — Personal Possessions (2)	Spending Money (3)	Disposition of Property (4)	ADDITIONAL RIGHTS OF INSTITUTIONALIZED PATIENTS — *Institutional Control* (5)	*Diet* (6)	*Employment* (7)	*Exercise* (8)	*Religion* (9)	*Privacy for Personal Needs* (10)	EXPLANATION OF RIGHTS UPON ADMISSION (11)	NOTICE OF RIGHTS POSTED (12)
PA. Stat. Ann. (Purdon 1969 & Supp. 1982)	mentally retarded 50, §4401(a) mentally ill 50, §7102		right to expend or send home proceeds of labor 50, §4423(4)				insofar as patient may benefit & facility can furnish 50, §4423(3)		unless particular minister or ministration interferes w/administration or security or care & welfare of patient 50, §4423(2)			
R.I. Gen. Laws (1977 & Supp. 1982)	insane 40.1-5.1-1 mentally disabled 40.1-5-3(1)	including clothes & toilet articles 40.1-5-5(g)					gainful occupation insofar as condition permits 40.1-5-5(i)		40.1-5-5(6)(d)	privacy & dignity 40.1-5-5(6)(a)		conspicuously in all wards & public rooms 40.1-5.2-22
S.C. Code (Law. Co-op. 1976 & Supp. 1982)	mentally ill or mentally retarded 44-23-10 et seq.	including clothes, individual storage space 44-23-1030(3), (4)	reasonable sum 44-23-1030(3)	unless adjudicated incompetent 44-23-1040(1)	as required by patient's medical needs 44-23-1030 inventory of stored possessions 44-23-1050		right to refuse nontherapeutic employment 44-23-1060					
S.D. Codified Laws Ann. (1976 & Supp. 1982)	mentally ill 27A-1-1 et seq. mentally retarded 27B-1-1 et seq.	such as variety store items, clothes, & toilet articles 27A-12-2(3), (5) 27B-8-2(3), (6)	unless conservator appointed 27A-12-2(3) 27A-8-2(3)		if essential to prevent violation of law or substantial & serious physical or mental harm 27A-12-2 27B-8-2		operation & maintenance only if voluntary, in accordance w/labor laws, & integral part of treatment plan 27A-12-23 27A-12-24	at least 2 hrs. per day 27A-12-2(3) 27B-8-2(3)	right to treatment through spiritual means 27A-12-22 27B-8-22 27A-12-9 27B-8-8	individual privacy & dignity 27A-12-1 27B-8-1	written copy 27A-12-3 27B-8-3	in every ward 27A-12-3 27B-8-3
TENN. Code Ann. (1977 & Supp. 1982)	mentally ill, mentally retarded 33-306			unless adjudicated incompetent 33-306(e)							written statement 33-306(h)	
TEX. Rev. Civ. Stat. Ann. (Vernon 1958 & Supp. 1982)	mentally ill 5547-4(g) mentally retarded 5547-300(5)	personal property 5547-300(25)					fair compensation 5547-300(13)		5547-86(a)(2)		orally informed, plus written statement 5547-300(23)	
UTAH Code Ann. (1978 & Supp. 1981)	mentally ill 64-7-7			unless adjudicated incompetent 64-7-48(1)(c)	as necessary for welfare of patient 64-7-48(1)				right to visit w/clergy of patient's choice 64-7-48(3)			64-7-48(5)
VT. Stat. Ann. (1968 & Supp. 1982)	mentally ill, mentally retarded 18, §7101 et seq.			unless adjudicated incompetent 18, §7705(a)(3)	as necessary for medical welfare or needs of patient 18, §7705(a)				patient's clergyman admitted at all reasonable times 18, §7710			excerpts from relevant statutes 18, §7701
VA. Code (1976 & Supp. 1983)	all mental disabilities 37.1-1 et seq.	board shall promulgate rules 37.1-84.1	board shall promulgate rules 37.1-84.1		commissioner authorized to receive & expend social security, etc., payments 37.1-28	board shall promulgate rules 37.1-84.1	board shall promulgate rules 37.1-84.1		board shall promulgate rules 37.1-84.1			

TABLE 5.2 PROPERTY AND PERSONAL RIGHTS OF INSTITUTIONALIZED PERSONS—*Continued*

STATE	TYPES OF PATIENTS COVERED (1)	CONTROL OF PATIENTS' PROPERTY — *Patients' Property Rights* — Personal Possessions (2)	Spending Money (3)	Disposition of Property (4)	ADDITIONAL RIGHTS OF INSTITUTIONALIZED PATIENTS — *Institutional Control* (5)	*Diet* (6)	*Employment* (7)	*Exercise* (8)	*Religion* (9)	*Privacy for Personal Needs* (10)	EXPLANATION OF RIGHTS UPON ADMISSION (11)	NOTICE OF RIGHTS POSTED (12)
WASH. Rev. Code Ann. (1975 & Supp. 1982)	mentally disordered 71.05.020(2)	including clothes & storage space, except when deprivation essential to protect resident or others 71.05.370 (1, 3)	reasonable sum for canteen expenses & small purchases 71.05.370(2)	unless adjudicated incompetent 71.05.370(8)	superintendent acts as custodian 72.23.230							in all facilities, institutions, & hospitals providing services 71.05.370
W. VA. Code (1980 & Supp. 1983)	mentally ill, mentally retarded & addicts 27-5-9(a)			unless adjudged incompetent 27-5-9(a)							27-5-9(f)	
WIS. Stat. Ann. (West 1957 & Supp. 1982)	mentally ill, developmentally disabled, alcoholism, or drug dependency 51.61(1)	clothing, storage space 51.61(1)(q), (r)			for cause after review by director, if medically or therapeutically contraindicated 51.61(2)		right to refuse labor of financial benefit to facility; may voluntarily perform such labor if therapeutic & compensated 51.61(1)(b)		to worship w/in facility if clergyman of patient's denomination available; freedom from coerced engagement in religious activities 51.61(1)(l)	facilities designed to promote dignity & ensure privacy 51.61(1)(m) reasonable privacy in such matters as toileting & bathing 51.61(1)(s)	orally & in writing 51.61(1)(a)	in each patient area 51.61(1)(a)
WYO. Stat. (1982 & Supp. 1983)	mentally ill 25-10-101 et seq.								right to treatment, in good faith, by spiritual means alone, unless incompetent or clear & convincing evidence of mental illness from recent overt acts 25-10-120(d)			
	mentally retarded 25-5-103	including toilet articles & clothes 25-5-132(c)(ii), (iii)	25-5-132(c)(iv)		as part of individual program plan 25-5-132(c)				to participate or refuse to participate 25-5-132(d)(iv)	in matters such as toileting & bathing 25-5-132(c)(vi)	orally & in writing 25-5-132(b)	

FOOTNOTES: TABLE 5.2

1. The provisions charted in this column grant patients within institutions the right to be treated in the least restrictive manner consistent with their treatment needs. These provisions are distinct from the ones charted in table 3.2. Those direct courts to order commitment only when the treatment proposed is the least restrictive means of treating the condition by virtue of which the proposed patient meets the commitment criteria.

2. Ala. Code § 22-50-1(1) (1975): "including, but not limited to, alcoholism, drug addiction, epilepsy or mental retardation."

3. Del. Code Ann. tit. 16, § 5161(a)(1) (Supp. 1982)): "Each patient shall receive care and treatment suited to his needs and skillfully, safely and humanely administered with full respect for his dignity and personal integrity."

4. Del. Code Ann. tit. 16 § 5502 (Supp. 1982):

> Mentally retarded persons have the right to proper medical care and physical restoration and to such education, training, and habilitation and guidance as will enable them to develop their abilities and potentials to the fullest possible extent no matter how severe their disability may be.

5. Fla. Stat. Ann. § 394.459(4) (Supp. 1983):

> Each patient in a facility shall receive treatment suited to his needs which shall be administered skillfully, safely, and humanely with full respect for his dignity and personal integrity. Each patient shall receive such medical, vocational, social, educational, and rehabilitative services as his condition requires to bring about an early return to his community.

6. Iowa Code Ann. § 229.23(3) (West Supp. 1981):

> In addition to protection of his constitutional rights, enjoyment of other legal, medical, religious, social, political, personal and working rights and privileges which he would enjoy if he were not so hospitalized or detained, so far as is possible consistent [sic] with effective treatment of that person and of the other patients of the hospital.

7. Me. Rev. Stat. Ann. tit. 34, § 2254(3) (Supp. 1982):

> Except to the extent that the head of the hospital or residential care facility determines that it is necessary for the medical welfare of the patient to impose restrictions, and unless a patient has been adjudicated incompetent and has not been restored to legal capacity and except where specifically restricted by other statute or regulation, but not solely because of the fact of admission to a mental hospital or residential care facility for the mentally ill, to exercise all civil rights, including but not limited to, civil service status, the right to vote, rights relating to the granting, renewal, forfeiture or denial of a license, permit, privilege or benefit pursuant to any law, and the right to enter contractual relationships and to manage his property. . . . Any limitations . . . and the reasons for such limitations shall be made a part of the clinical record of the patient.

8. N.H. Rev. Stat. Ann. § 135-B:43 (1977):

> Every mentally ill person has a right to adequate and humane treatment including such psychological, medical, vocational, social, educational or rehabilitative services as his condition requires to bring about an improvement in condition within the limits of modern knowledge.

9. N.H. Stat. Ann. § 171A:13 (Supp. 1981):

> Every developmentally impaired client has a right to adequate and humane habilitation and treatment including such psychological, medical, vocational, social, educational or rehabilitative services as his condition reqires to bring about an improvement in condition within the limits of modern knowledge.

TABLE 5.3 PENALTIES FOR UNWARRANTED INSTITUTIONALIZATION AND DENIAL OF RIGHTS

						LIABILITY		GOOD-FAITH IMMUNITY	
STATE	TYPE OF DISABILITY (1)	UNWARRANTED INSTITUTION-ALIZATION (2)	DENIAL OF PATIENT'S RIGHTS (3)	MALTREATMENT OR ABUSE (4)	OTHER (5)	Criminal (6)	Civil (7)	Any Person (8)	Limited Group (9)
ALA. Code (1975 & Supp. 1982)	all forms of mental or emotional illness *fn. 1* 22-50-1(1)				violation of mental health code 22-50-23	$50 per day for each day of violation 22-50-23			
ALAS. Stat. (1979 & Supp. 1981)	mentally ill 47.30.655	47.30.815(c)				felony 47.30.815(c)		47.30.815(a)	
					denial of a civil right 47.30.835(a)	crime of interference w/constitutional rights (class A misdemeanor) 47.30.835(a) 11.76.110(c)			
ARIZ. Rev. Stat. Ann. (1974 & Supp. 1981)	mentally ill (disorder) 36-501(17)	36-515(B)				class 1 misdemeanor 36-515(B)		36-515(A)	
			36-516				$1,000 or, if greater, 3x actual damages 36-516	"knowing violation" 36-516	
				harsh or cruel treatment or neglect of duty 36-517		class 2 misdemeanor 36-517			
	develop-mentally disabled 36-569		36-551.01(R)	improper, abusive treatment or neglect 36-569		class 2 misdemeanor 36-569(B)	petition for redress 36-551.01(R)		
ARK. Stat. Ann. (1971 & Supp. 1981)	mentally incompetent 59-601 mentally ill 59-1403 59-1404		right to legal counsel & lawyer referral services to enforce rights 59-1416(27)	striking, beating, abusing, intimidating, assaulting, or physically chastising 59-601(a)		report submitted to prosecuting attorney if board feels criminal laws violated 59-601(b)	dismissal from employment 59-601(b)	59-1414(b)	
	mentally deficient or mentally retarded 59-602			abuse or ridcule 59-602(a)		misdemeanor—$100 or 6 mos. or both 59-602(a)		crime requires willfulness 59-602(a)	
CAL. Welf. & Inst. Code (West 1972 & Supp. 1981)	mentally ill (disorder) 5150 et seq.		by physician 5326.9(c)				$5,000 per *intentional* violation, &/or revocation of license 5326.9(b), (c) $1,000 per *knowing* violation 5326.9(d) other civil remedies 5326.9(e)	fines require intent or knowledge 5326.9	
COLO. Rev. Stat. (1973 & Supp. 1982)	develop-mentally disabled 27-10.5-101				violation of code 27-10.5-134		civil cause of action 27-10.5-134		
CONN. Gen. Stat. Ann. (West 1975 & Supp. 1981)	mentally ill 17-184	17-184				$1,000 or 5 yrs. or both 17-184		crime requires willfulness or malice 17-184	
	mentally disordered, unless incom-petent 17-206b		any personal property, or civil rights 17-206b				injunctive relief or civil action for damages 17-206k		

TABLE 5.3 PENALTIES FOR UNWARRANTED INSTITUTIONALIZATION AND DENIAL OF RIGHTS—*Continued*

STATE	TYPE OF DISABILITY (1)	UNWARRANTED INSTITUTION-ALIZATION (2)	DENIAL OF PATIENT'S RIGHTS (3)	MALTREATMENT OR ABUSE (4)	OTHER (5)	LIABILITY Criminal (6)	 Civil (7)	GOOD-FAITH IMMUNITY Any Person (8)	 Limited Group (9)
DEL. Code Ann. (1974 & Supp. 1980)	mentally ill 16, §5161		patients' bill of rights 16, §§5161, 5162			enforceable by the attorney general or by any interested citizen 16, §5162	enforceable by the attorney general or by any interested citizen 16, §5162		
		16, §5133(a)	16, §5133(a)			$500 or 1 yr. or both 16, §5133(a)		crime requires willfulness 16, §5133(a)	
D.C. Code Ann. (1981 & Supp. 1982)	mentally ill 21-591	21-591	21-591			$5,000 &/or 3 yrs. 21-591			
	mentally retarded 6-1973		6-1973	6-1970			action to compel rights; $25 per day in violation 6-1973(a), (b)	6-1973(d)	
FLA. Stat. Ann. (West 1975 & Supp. 1980)	mentally retarded 393.13(1)		393.13(4)				liable for damages 393.13(4)	if w/o negligence 393.13(4)	
	mentally ill 394.459		394.459(13)				liable for damages 394.459(13)	if w/o negligence 394.459(13)	
GA. Code Ann. (1979 & Supp. 1980)	all those covered by public health code 88-301				violation of provisions of public health title 88-301	misdemeanor 88-301	injunctive relief 88-302		re admission & discharge of the mentally ill *fn. 2* 88-502.23
HAWAII Rev. Stat. (1976 & Supp. 1981)	mentally ill, drug addiction, or alcoholism 334-1	or discharge 334-24							
IDAHO Code (1980 & Supp. 1981)	mentally ill 66-300 et seq.		civil rights, right to be visited by attorney, & right to refuse specific modes of treatment 66-346(c)	denial of humane care & treatment 66-344	other code violations 66-349	$500 & 1 yr. 66-349		if w/o gross negligence 66-341	director may abridge right to refuse treatment in emergency or if patient incompetent 66-346(c)
ILL. Ann. Stat. (Smith-Hurd 1966 & Supp. 1981)	mentally ill or develop-mentally disabled 91½, §6-102	91½, §6-102		maltreatment 91½, §6-102	other code violations 91½, §6-102	class A misdemeanor 91½, §6-102		if w/o negligence 91½, §6-102	
IND. Code Ann. (Burns 1973 & Supp. 1980)	mentally ill 16-14-9.1-12	16-14-9.1-12 (a)	16-14-9.1-12 (b)	physical abuse 16-14-9.12(b)				w/o malice or negligence *fn. 3* 16-14-9.1-12	
				abuse, mal-treatment, or neglect 16-14-1-2(a)		class B misdemeanor 16-14-1-2(a)			
					failure to report vio-lations 16-14-1-2(b)	class C infraction 16-14-1-2(b)			
IOWA Code Ann. (West 1969 & Supp. 1981)	mentally retarded 222.47	222.47				guilty of a fraudulent practice 222.47		crime requires malice 222.47	
	mentally ill 229.38			unnecessary cruelty or official misconduct 229.38		"a serious misdemeanor" 229.38			

TABLE 5.3 PENALTIES FOR UNWARRANTED INSTITUTIONALIZATION AND DENIAL OF RIGHTS—*Continued*

STATE	TYPE OF DISABILITY (1)	UNWARRANTED INSTITUTION-ALIZATION (2)	DENIAL OF PATIENT'S RIGHTS (3)	MALTREATMENT OR ABUSE (4)	OTHER (5)	LIABILITY Criminal (6)	LIABILITY Civil (7)	GOOD-FAITH IMMUNITY Any Person (8)	GOOD-FAITH IMMUNITY Limited Group (9)
KAN. Stat. Ann. (1976 & Supp. 1981)	mentally ill 59-2901	for a corrupt consideration or advantage, or through malice 59-2932				class A misdemeanor 59-2932		if w/o negligence 59-2932	
					violation of confidentiality of records 59-2931(b)	class C misdemeanor 59-2931(b)		willfulness required 59-2931(b)	
KY. Rev. Stat. Ann. (Michie 1977 & Supp. 1980)	mentally retarded 210.005 202B.990	210.991(1) 202B.990(1)	any right accorded under this chapter 210.991(2) 202B.990(2) 202B.050			$5,000 or 5 yrs. or both 210.991(2)		202B.990 willfulness required 210.991	
			correspondence or religious instruction 210.990(2)				$25 to $100 210.990(2)		
					violation of confidentiality of records 202B.990(3)	class A misdemeanor 202B.990(3)			
	mentally ill 202A.990	202A.990(1) (a)	any right under chapter 202A.990(1) (b)			$5,000 or 5 yrs. or both 202A.990(1)			those w/in scope of official duties 202A.200
					violation of confidentiality of records 202A.990(2)	class A misdemeanor 202A.990(2)			
LA. Rev. Stat. Ann. (West 1975 & Supp. 1981)	mentally ill or mentally retarded 28, §181 28, §448	28, §181 28, §448				$1,000 or 1 yr. or both 28, §181 28, §448		"unlawfully, willfully, maliciously, & w/o reasonable cause" 28, §181 28, §448	
				maltreatment 28, §182 28, §449		$500 &/or 6 mos. 28, §182 28, §449			
ME. Rev. Stat. Ann. (1978 & Supp. 1981)	mentally ill 34, §2250 et seq.	34, §2259	rights under chapter 34, §2259			$100–$1,000 &/or 1–5 yrs. 34, §2259		offense requires willfulness 34, §2259	
MD. Ann. Code (1979 & Supp. 1981)	mentally ill 59, §1A	59, §21(a), (b)	"interference" w/rights 59, §52		violation of provisions re patients' records 59, §21(b)	misdemeanor; $5,000 &/or 2 yrs. 59, §21(a), (b) 59, §52	for damages, if violations were willful 59, §21(c)	"knowing false application" 59, §21(a) "knowingly interferes" w/rights 59, §52	informers (except abusers) immune from civil liability 59, §52A(d)
	mentally ill or mentally retarded 59, §36 59A, §23	by a private facility 59, §36(a) 59A, §23(a)				license suspended or revoked & $5,000 &/or 1 yr. for participants; $10,000 fine against facility if unlicensed 59, §36 59A, §23	59, §36(c) 59A, §23(c)	"knowing participation" 59, §36 59A, §36	
MASS. Ann. Laws (Michie/Law Co-op 1981 & Supp. 1981)	mentally ill or mentally retarded 123, §1 et seq.	123, §22							civil immunity for physicians, qualified psychologists, & police officers 123, §22
MICH. Comp. Laws Ann. (1980 & Supp. 1981)	mentailly ill, mentally retarded, alcoholism, or substance abuse 330.1116(a)			physicially, sexually, or otherwise abused 330.1722(1)		facility shall cooperate in prosecuting 330.1722(3)	injunctive & other civil relief 330.1722(4)		peace officer, if w/o gross negligence or willful misconduct 330.1427b

TABLE 5.3 PENALTIES FOR UNWARRANTED INSTITUTIONALIZATION AND DENIAL OF RIGHTS—*Continued*

STATE	TYPE OF DISABILITY (1)	UNWARRANTED INSTITUTION-ALIZATION (2)	DENIAL OF PATIENT'S RIGHTS (3)	MALTREATMENT OR ABUSE (4)	OTHER (5)	LIABILITY: Criminal (6)	LIABILITY: Civil (7)	GOOD-FAITH IMMUNITY: Any Person (8)	GOOD-FAITH IMMUNITY: Limited Group (9)
MINN. Stat. Ann. (West 1971 & Supp. 1981)		253A.21(1)				gross misdemeanor; $500 or 1 yr. 253A.21(1)		253A.21(2)	
MISS. Code Ann. (1972 & Supp. 1980)	mentally ill 41-21-61(c)	41-21-107		41-21-107	any other violation of code 41-21-107	misdemeanor; $500–$1,000 &/or 1 yr. 41-21-107		41-21-105(1)	civil immunity for board members, directors, or those acting w/in scope of employment, unless willful or malicious 41-21-105(2)
	mentally retarded 41-19-155	41-19-155(1)				$200 &/or 1 yr. 41-19-155		"knowingly" 41-19-155(1)	
MO. Ann. Stat. (West 1972 & Supp. 1980)	mental disorders other than mentally retarded or developmentally disabled 632.005(1)	632.440 632.445						petitioners for commitment 632.445	public officials, if w/o gross negligence 632.440
	all mental disabilities 630.005 et seq.			630.155		class A misdemeanor 630.155(2)	disqualification from employment by dep't of mental health 630.170		
MONT. Code Ann. (1981)	developmentally disabled 53-20-101			53-20-163			duty upon facility to investigate all alleged violations 53-20-163		
NEB. Rev. Stat. (1981)	mentally ill 83-356 83, 1001			wanton severity, harshness, or cruelty 83-356		class V misdemeanor 83-356	damages 83-356		
		83-1069(1)	83-1069(2)		breach of confidentiality of records 83-1069(3)	class II misdemeanor 83-1069	83-1069	"willfully" 83-1069(1)	83-312
NEV. Rev. Stat. (1979)	mentally ill 433A.750	433A.750 (1)(a), (2)	433A.750 (1)(b)			1–6 yrs. &/or $5,000 433A.750			public officer or employee, unless negligence resulted in bodily harm 433A.740
	mentally ill or mentally retarded 433.003(1)			433.554(1)(a)		misdemeanor 433.554(1)	5 yrs. disqualification from state employment 433.554(2)	"willfully abuses" 433.554(1)(a)	
			433.534(1)(a)			board may investigate 433.534(3)(a)	board may seek remedies on behalf of client 433.534(3)(c) failure to report abuse is ground for dismissal 433.534(1)		
N.H. Rev. Stat. Ann. (1977 & Supp. 1981)									

TABLE 5.3 PENALTIES FOR UNWARRANTED INSTITUTIONALIZATION AND DENIAL OF RIGHTS—*Continued*

STATE	TYPE OF DISABILITY (1)	UNWARRANTED INSTITUTION-ALIZATION (2)	DENIAL OF PATIENT'S RIGHTS (3)	MALTREATMENT OR ABUSE (4)	OTHER (5)	LIABILITY Criminal (6)	LIABILITY Civil (7)	GOOD-FAITH IMMUNITY Any Person (8)	GOOD-FAITH IMMUNITY Limited Group (9)
N.J. Stat. Ann. (West 1981 & Supp. 1982)	mentally ill, mentally retarded, or tuberculosis 30:4-33	30:4-33				misdemeanor 30:4-33			chief executive officer, in granting consent to treatment 30:4-7.5
N.M. Stat. Ann. (1979 & Supp. 1982)	mentally ill & developmentally disabled 43-1-1 et. seq.	43-1-23					right to petition for redress 43-1-23		
N.Y. Mental Hgy. Law (McKinney 1978 & Supp. 1981)									
N.C. Gen. Stat. (1981 & Supp. 1981)	mentally ill, mentally retarded, substance abuse 122-35.40B				negligence or tort 122-35.40B(a)		area authority may waive governmental immunity for negligence or tort of agent by securing liability insurance 122-35.40B(a)		area authority may budget funds for paying civil judgments against agents, if agents acted w/o fraud, corruption, or actual malice 122-35.40C(b)
	mentally ill or mentally retarded 122-51	by husband, wife, guardian, or physician 122-51					122-51		
N.D. Cent. Code (1978 & Supp. 1981)	mentally ill, alcoholism, or drug abuse 25-03.1-42	25-03.1-42(3)			fulfilling an obligation or discretionary responsibility under this chapter 25-03.1-42(2)	class A misdemeanor 25-03.1-42(3)		25-03.1-42(1)	physician, psychiatrist, clinical psychologist, mental health professional, employee, or peace officer, if w/o negligence 25-03.1-42(2)
OHIO Rev. Code Ann. (Baldwin 1980 & Supp. 1981)	mentally ill 5122 et seq.	5122.34						criminal & civil immunity 5122.34	
	mentally retarded 5123.91 et seq.							if not subject to any criminal provisions, & if acted reasonably 5123.91	

TABLE 5.3 PENALTIES FOR UNWARRANTED INSTITUTIONALIZATION AND DENIAL OF RIGHTS—*Continued*

STATE	TYPE OF DISABILITY (1)	UNWARRANTED INSTITUTION-ALIZATION (2)	DENIAL OF PATIENT'S RIGHTS (3)	MALTREATMENT OR ABUSE (4)	OTHER (5)	LIABILITY Criminal (6)	LIABILITY Civil (7)	GOOD-FAITH IMMUNITY Any Person (8)	GOOD-FAITH IMMUNITY Limited Group (9)
OKLA. Stat. Ann. (West 1979 & Supp. 1981)	mentally ill or mentally retarded 43A, §2	43A, §131				misdemeanor; $1,000 &/or 1 yr. 43A, §131		requires malice 43A, §131	
				assault, beat, batter, abuse, or use mechanical restraints w/o authority 43A, §134		felony; $500 &/or 5 yrs. 43A, §134			crime requires malice, & applies only to officers or employees of hospitals 43A, §134
					superintendent's failure to report maltreatment 43A, §135	misdemeanor 43A, §135			
		false certificate by physician 43A, §139				misdemeanor; $500 &/or 1 yr. 43A, §139			
OR. Rev. Stat. (1981)	mentally ill 426.070	notification & investigation 426.070(1), (2)							program director, petitioners, health officer, physician, magistrate, & peace or probation officer, if on probable cause & w/o malice 426.070(1), (2)
		emergency hospitalization 426.175(4)							physician, hospital, or judge, if on probable cause & w/o malice 426.175(4)
					disclosure of records 179.507		actual damages or $500; punitive damages if intentional 179.507		
PA. Stat. Ann. (Purdon 1969 & Supp. 1980)	all mental disabilities 50, §4605	false statement by physician 50, §4605(4) 50, §4605(6)	50, §4605(4)		disclosure of records 50, §4605(5)	misdemeanor; $1,000 &/or 1 yr. 50, §4605		requires willfulness; 4605(4) requires knowledge 4605(6)	
	mentally ill 50, §7103		50, §7113				damages & all legal remedies 50, §7113		administrator, director of facility, physician, peace officer, or other authorized person, if w/o willful misconduct or gross negligence 50, §7114(a) complete immunity for judge or mental health review officer 50, §7114(b)
R.I. Gen. Laws (1977 & Supp. 1981)	mentally retarded 40.1-22-1	40.1-22-25				$5,000 or 5 yrs. 40.1-22-25		crime requires willfulness 40.1-22-25 40.1-22-26 40.1-5.1-19	
			40.1-22-26			$2,000 or 2 yrs. 40.1-22-26			
	insane 40.1-5.1-1	by physician 40.1-5.1-19				$5,000 or 5 yrs. 40.1-5.1-19			
					violation of code provisions 40.1-5.1-23		$20 40.1-5.1-23		
	all mental disabilities 40.1-5-3(1)	40.1-5-38				$5,000 or 5 yrs. 40.1-5-38		crime requires willfulness 40.1-5-38 40.1-5-39	
			40.1-5-39			$2,000 or 2 yrs. 40.1-5-39			

TABLE 5.3 PENALTIES FOR UNWARRANTED INSTITUTIONALIZATION AND DENIAL OF RIGHTS—*Continued*

STATE	TYPE OF DISABILITY (1)	UNWARRANTED INSTITUTION-ALIZATION (2)	DENIAL OF PATIENT'S RIGHTS (3)	MALTREATMENT OR ABUSE (4)	OTHER (5)	LIABILITY Criminal (6)	LIABILITY Civil (7)	GOOD-FAITH IMMUNITY Any Person (8)	GOOD-FAITH IMMUNITY Limited Group (9)
S.C. Code Ann. (Law. Co-op. 1976 & Supp. 1981)	mentally retarded 44-21-20				fn. 4 44-21-560		suspension, denial, or revocation of license 44-21-560		
	mentally ill or mentally retarded 44-23-10 et seq.	44-23-240	44-23-1070			$1,000 &/or 1 yr. 44-23-240		offense requires willfulness 44-23-240 44-23-1070	
S.D. Codified Laws Ann. (1976 & Supp. 1982)	mentally ill 27A-1-1 et seq.; & mentally retarded 27B-1-1 et seq.	unlawful confinement 27A-1-4 27B-1-7 hospitalized by unauthorized means 27A-1-5				class 1 misdemeanor 27A-1-4 27B-1-7 class 6 felony 27A-1-5		"intentionally & wrongfully" 27A-1-5	
					neglect of duty under code 27A-1-6 27B-1-8	class 1 misdemeanor 27A-1-6 27B-1-8	damages 27A-1-6 27B-1-8	offense requires intentional neglect 27A-1-6 27B-1-8	
TENN. Code Ann. (1977 & Supp. 1982)	mentally retarded or mentally ill 33-303 et seq.	33-304(a)(1), (b)	33-304(a)(2)			$5,000 &/or 5 yrs. 33-304(a)		if reasonable & w/o negligence 33-304(c)	
		supplying false information 33-305				misdemeanor 33-305			
TEX. Rev. Civ. Stat. Ann. (Vernon 1958 & Supp. 1981)	mentally ill 5547-2	5547-19				misdemeanor; $5,000 &/or 2 yrs. 5547-19		if reasonable & w/o negligence 5547-18	
					knowing violation of code 5547-20	misdemeanor $5,000 &/or 1 yr. 5547-20			
	mentally ill or mentally retarded 5561h				breach of confidentiality of records 5561h(5)		damages & injunctive relief 5561h(5)		
	mentally retarded 5547-300	w/intent to do harm 5547-300(63)				class B misdemeanor 5547-300(63)		offense requires intent of knowledge 5547-300(63)	
			5547-300(64)			$100–$5,000 if willful; $100–$1,000 if reckless 5547-300(64)			
					release of confidential information 5547-300(64)		$1,000 or treble damages 5547-300(64)		
UTAH Code Ann. (1978 & Supp. 1981)	mentally ill 64-7-7	64-7-21		undue restraint, wanton severity or cruelty, or abuse 64-7-22		class B misdemeanor 64-7-21 64-7-22	damages 64-7-21 64-7-22		
					willful violation of other provisions of mental health code 64-7-26	class C misdemeanor 64-7-26			
VT. Stat. Ann. (1968 & Supp. 1982)	mentally ill or mentally retarded 18, §7101 et seq.	18, §7104 (1), (3)	18, §7104(2)		disclosure of confidential information 18, §7103(c)	$500 &/or 1 yr. 18, §7104 18, §7103(c)		offense requires willfulness 18, §7104	
VA. Code (1976 & Supp. 1982)	all mental disabilities 37.1-1 et seq.	knowingly & maliciously 37.1-154		maltreat or misuse 37.1-150		class 1 misdemeanor 37.1-155			
WASH. Rev. Code Ann. (1975 & Supp. 1981)	mentally disordered 71.05.020(2)	71.05.500 detention for more than the allowable number of days 71.05.510					damages 71.05.510	71.05.500	fn. 5 71.05.120

TABLE 5.3 PENALTIES FOR UNWARRANTED INSTITUTIONALIZATION AND DENIAL OF RIGHTS—*Continued*

STATE	TYPE OF DISABILITY (1)	UNWARRANTED INSTITUTION-ALIZATION (2)	DENIAL OF PATIENT'S RIGHTS (3)	MALTREATMENT OR ABUSE (4)	OTHER (5)	LIABILITY Criminal (6)	LIABILITY Civil (7)	GOOD-FAITH IMMUNITY Any Person (8)	GOOD-FAITH IMMUNITY Limited Group (9)
W. VA. Code (1980 & Supp. 1982)	mentally ill, mentally retarded, or alcoholism 27-12-1	27-12-1		tease, pester, annoy, or molest 27-12-3		misdemeanor; $500 &/or 1 yr. 27-12-1 $10–$100 or 6 mos. 27-12-3		offense requires malice 27-12-1	
WIS. Stat. Ann. (West 1957 & Supp. 1981)	all mental disorders & developmental disabilities 51.001(1)		51.61(7)				$100 per violation; $500–$1,000 if willful, &/or injunction; action against state 51.61(7)		
WYO. Stat. (1982 & Supp. 1983)	mentally ill 25-10-101 et seq. mentally retarded 25-5-103	25-10-126(a)	25-10-126(b)		release of confidential records from training school 25-5-131(c)	felony $5,000 &/or 5 yrs. 27-10-126(a) misdemeanor; $750 &/or 6 mos. 25-10-126(b) misdemeanor; $500 &/or 6 mos. 25-5-131(c)		crime requires willfulness 25-10-126(a) 25-10-126(b) 25-5-131(c)	

FOOTNOTES: TABLE 5.3

1. Ala. Code § 22-50-1(1) (1975): "including, but not limited to, alcoholism, drug addition, epilepsy or mental retardation."

2. Ga. Code Ann. § 88-502.23 (1979): "Any physician, peace officer, attorney, health official, or hospital official, agent, or employee."

3. Ind. Code Ann. § 16-14-9.1-12(b) (Burns 1983): "This immunity does not permit any person to physically abuse a patient nor deprive a patient of any personal or civil rights except according to the provisions of this chapter."

4. S.C. Code Ann. § 44-21-560 (Law. Co-op. 1976):

   (1) Failure to establish or maintain proper standards of care and service as prescribed by the Department.

   (2) Conduct or practices detrimental to the health or safety of residents, students, or employees of any such facilities or programs.

   (3) Violations of any provisions under this article or the rules and regulations promulgated hereunder.

5. Wash. Rev. Code Ann. § 71.05.120 (1975):

   No officer of a public or private agency, nor the superintendent, professional person in charge, his professional designee, or attending staff of any such agency, nor any public official performing functions necessary to the administration of this chapter, nor peace officer responsible for detaining a person pursuant to this chapter, nor any county designated mental health professional shall be civilly or criminally liable for performing his duties pursuant to this chapter with regard to the decision of whether to admit, release, or detain a person for evaluation and treatment: Provided, that such duties were performed in good faith and without gross negligence.

Barbara A. Weiner

CHAPTER 6 Treatment Rights

I. INTRODUCTION

The establishment of a right to treatment or habilitation in the case law and statutes of the various states was one of the main developments in mental disability law during the 1970s. The cases often came in the form of class action suits challenging the conditions of institutionalization and urging the creation of an environment in which treatment or habilitation could occur. While the United States Supreme Court has so far refrained from explicitly endorsing a general right to treatment for institutionalized persons, numerous lower courts and the majority of state legislatures have formalized this basic guarantee.

In the late 1970s patient advocates also began a push for a right to refuse treatment, in particular a right to refuse medication. Although at first blush the right to refuse seems contrary to a right to treatment, it need not be. The power to involuntarily commit a person for treatment presupposes the obligation to create an environment in which such treatment is forthcoming. But the right of an institutionalized person to an environment enhancing his treatment does not in itself abrogate his right to bodily autonomy. A person who retains legal competency should retain at least a limited option to participate in treatment decisions and to refuse particularly those treatment modes that carry a risk of harmful side effects.

This chapter describes the various treatment techniques and their potential side effects, sketches the development of the legal right to treatment and habilitation, reviews the concept of informed consent, and examines the newly emerging right to refuse treatment.

II. TYPES OF TREATMENT

Beginning in the late nineteenth century Dorothea Dix crusaded to create hospital-like institutions that would provide the "insane" with humane treatment.[1] It was felt that such hospitals would provide "an ideal testing ground" for new theories of treatment, including "moral treatment"[2] and "milieu therapy."[3] Typically, these institutions were far removed from urban areas with the stresses of everyday life. Long hospitalizations of years or even decades became common. But with the introduction of psychotropic drugs in the 1950s, a revolution in the treatment of the mentally ill has taken place, greatly altering the pattern of institutionalization.

The institutionalization of the mentally retarded followed a similar path. In the first part of the twentieth century families with no hope that their retarded children would ever be able to lead useful lives came to abandon them to state institutions.[4] Many mentally retarded persons spent almost their entire lives in institutions, often considered their final home. In the past two decades, however, there has been a dramatic change in attitude toward the retarded and, accordingly, in their treatment. Today, the emphasis is on teaching such individuals the skills that will help them live in the community.

A. Psychotropic Medication

In 1952 Delay, Deniker, and Harl ushered in a new era in the treatment of psychiatric disorders when they discovered the effectiveness of chlorpromazines in controlling acute psychotic episodes.[5] Discovery of other psychotropic drugs followed. Today, these drugs are

1. See, e.g., Mora, Historical and Theoretical Trends in Psychiatry, *in* 1 Comprehensive Textbook of Psychiatry 4, 72 (H.I. Kaplan, A.M. Freedman, & B. J. Sadock 3d ed. 1980) [hereinafter cited as Comprehensive Textbook].

2. *Id.* at 48.

3. Abroms, Defining Milieu Therapy, 21 Archives Gen. Psychiatry 553 (1969).

4. See, e.g., W. Wolfensberger, The Origin and Nature of Our Institutional Models, *in* Changing Patterns in Residential Services for the Mentally Retarded 59, 120-36 (President's Committee on Mental Retardation, 1969) [hereinafter cited as Changing Patterns].

5. Davis, Antipsychotic Drugs, *in* 3 Comprehensive Textbook, *supra* note 1, at 2257.

the most frequently prescribed class of medications worldwide[6] and account for 25% of all prescription drugs used in the United States.[7] Psychotropic drugs may be classified into four categories, based on the conditions they are intended to treat: (1) antipsychotic drugs (major tranquilizers), for schizophrenia and related psychoses, (2) antidepressant drugs for biochemical depression, (3) lithium for the treatment of manic-depressive illness, and (4) antianxiety drugs for situational and neurotic anxiety.[8]

1. Antipsychotic Drugs

The introduction of antipsychotic drugs in the 1950s had a profound effect on the treatment of schizophrenia. Today, many schizophrenic patients can be treated with antipsychotic medications without needing to be hospitalized, and for those who are hospitalized, the length of stay is usually brief, often less than 20 days. These drugs are now considered the treatment of choice for schizophrenics, and in combination with other therapies they permit many of them to remain in or return to the community.[9] Antipsychotic drugs do not cure schizophrenia; they only control its symptoms. The drugs have a normalizing effect, lessening typical symptoms such as hallucinations and delusions, decreasing agitation and hyperactivity, and ameliorating disordered thought and perception, emotional and social withdrawal, paranoid ideation, and personal neglect.[10] There are numerous types of antipsychotic medications, each with different properties and different advantages and disadvantages.[11] Some of the more common trade names are Haldol, Mellaril, Navane, Prolixin, and Thorazine.

Although these drugs provide many benefits in the treatment of mental illness, they may also produce adverse side effects, most commonly blurred vision, dryness of the throat and mouth, constipation, urinary retention, heart palpitations, dizziness, and fainting.[12] Additionally, there may be negative effects on the reproductive system, including for women amenorrhea (the absence of menstruation), false positive pregnancy tests, increased libido, and breast engorgement. For men there may be decreased libido, excessive development of the male mammary glands, inhibition of ejaculation, and sexual impotence.[13]

Probably the most common as well as most detrimental side effects produced by antipsychotic drugs are the neurological syndromes manifested by what is known in medical parlance as *extrapyramidal* effects (having to do with the brain structure affecting bodily movements). These fall into three categories: the parkinsonian syndrome, dyskinesias, and akathesia. The parkinsonian syndrome consists of a mask-like face, tremor at rest, rigidity, shuffling gait, and general motor retardation. The dyskinesias may consist of a broad range of bizarre movements of the tongue, face, and neck. Akathesia is a motor restlessness making it difficult to sit still in one place. Parkinsonian syndrome and akathesia may be alleviated by lowering the dosage of the antipsychotic drugs or taking the person off the drugs completely. Additionally, antiparkinsonian drugs may alleviate the problem.[14]

However, the person who shows signs of dyskinesia may be suffering from tardive dyskinesia, a syndrome for which there is no known effective treatment.[15] There is no direct correlation between the amount of medication taken, the duration of treatment, and the development of tardive dyskinesia. Although reduction or total withdrawal of the medication may reduce the involuntary movements, this will not always be the case. For the mentally ill person who benefits from control of his symptoms through antipsychotic medication, the threat of tardive dyskinesia creates an agonizing dilemma. The very medication that enables him to live a relatively normal life carries with it the potential for causing irreversible extrapyramidal symptoms that will at the very least cause embarassment. Yet the discontinuation of the medication may result in a relapse into active psychosis and the need for institutionalization.[16]

2. Antidepressant Drugs

In the late 1950s two classes of drugs were discovered which proved effective in the treatment of biochemically caused depression—the tricyclic antidepressants and the MAO inhibitors. These drugs do not generally have a

6. Symonds, Mental Patients' Right to Refuse Drugs: Involuntary Medication as Cruel and Unusual Punishment, 7 Hastings. Const. L.Q. 701, 704 (1980).

7. Winick, Psychotropic Medication and Competence to Stand Trial, 1977 A.B.F. Res. J. 769, 778-79.

8. For a good description of the use of psychotropic drugs see Comprehensive Textbook, *supra* note 1; see also G. Usdin & J. Lewis, Psychiatry in General Medical Practice (1979); Symonds, *supra* note 6, at 704-11, which contains a very good description of the uses and effects of psychotropic drugs in terms a nonmedical person can easily understand.

9. Davis, Organic Therapies, *in* 3 Comprehensive Textbook, *supra* note 1, at 2257.

10. American Medical Association, Dep't of Drugs, AMA Drug Evaluations 420 (3d ed. 1977) [hereinafter cited as AMA Drug Evaluations].

11. See Davis, *supra* note 9, at 2261-63 for a comprehensive discussion of the various types of antipsychotic medications.

12. R. Sample, G. DiGregoria, & R. Wicks, Psychopharmacologic Drugs: A Pocket Reference 16-17 (1978); see also Davis, *supra* note 9, at 2273-86.

13. *Id.* See also Hollister, Human Pharmacology of Antipsychotic and Antidepressant Drugs *in* 8 Annual Rev. of Pharmacology 491, 500 (H.W. Elliott, W.C. Cutting, & R.H. Dreisbach eds. 1968).

14. Davis, *supra* note 9, at 2280-81.

15. Wettstein, Tardive Dyskinesia and Malpractice, 1 Behav. Sci. & L. 85, 86 (1983).

16. With the recognition of tardive dyskinesia as a potential side effect of antipsychotic medications, the drug manufacturers are placing great emphasis on developing a safer drug without such potential side effects.

euphoric or stimulant effect on the normal person or the person whose depression is not biochemical in origin.[17] Treatment of the psychotically depressed person with antidepressants will result in a marked lessening of the depression within three to ten days,[18] a change that often enables the person to resume normal activities.

Unfortunately both types of depressants can have adverse side effects. The MAO inhibitors, which seem to produce the more serious negative consequences, have been documented as causing damage to the liver, brain, and cardiovascular system, and they may also result in very high blood pressure, acute cardiac failure, and intracranial bleeding. Less severe symptoms include dry mouth, constipation, impotence, tremors, insomnia, and skin rashes.[19] The user may also experience emotional confusion, mild mania, and, occasionally, hallucinations.[20] Given the range and potential seriousness of their side effects, the MAO inhibitors are being used less and less frequently.

The tricyclic antidepressants, considered much safer as well as more effective than the MAO inhibitors, are today the most widely used for biochemically caused depression.[21] But even these drugs, which include Tofranil, Elavil, and Norpramin, may produce some of the same side effects as the antipsychotic medications and some others, including dry mouth, rapid heart beat, fainting, vomiting, constipation, blurred vision, an aggravation of certain types of glaucoma, undue sweating, weakness, fatigue, headache, and a rapid tremor of the tongue.[22]

3. Lithium

Although the benefits of lithium in the treatment of manic patients was discovered in 1949, it was not until 1970 that the Food and Drug Administration approved the drug's use in the United States. Generally exhibiting an elated mood, excess energy, grandiosity, and hyperactivity in a manic state, manics typically exhibit very bad judgment as a result of their greatly exaggerated ideas of their abilities. Treatment with lithium makes it possible to combat current episodes of manic illness and to prevent future manic and depressive relapses.[23] The benefits of the drug seem unrelated to age, sex, or the duration of the disorder.

Lithium usage must be monitored carefully, however, a task that can be accomplished through blood tests. Generally, persons with cardiovascular, renal, and central nervous system pathology are poor candidates for the drug. For the rest of those who may benefit from its use, the most common side effects include muscle weakness, hand tremors, abdominal cramps, nausea, diarrhea, fatigue, sleeplessness, and weight gain.[24]

4. Antianxiety Drugs

For more than 20 years physicians have used drugs to treat anxiety in their patients.[25] Some of these drugs, such as Valium and Librium, have become widely used, and questions have been raised about the frequency with which they are prescribed.[26] These drugs are used not only for persons who have been labeled "mentally ill" but also for patients who are having difficulty in coping with personal and/or professional pressures and as a result are experiencing such symptoms as insomnia, fatigue, short temper, and inability to concentrate, as well as physical discomforts.[27] The drugs often have a sedative or hypnotic primary effect, and major side effects include a slowed reaction time with its potential for serious consequences if the drugs are combined with alcohol.[28] Overuse can lead to chronic confusion and to addiction. For these reasons it is recommended that antianxiety drugs be prescribed only for short periods and that the underlying causes of the stress or anxiety be explored, with efforts concentrating on changing those environmental factors producing the anxiety.[29]

5. Conclusion

The introduction of psychotropic medications has revolutionized the treatment of the mentally ill, vastly diminishing the number of persons needing institutionalization and significantly relaxing the terms of confinement for those who are institutionalized. These drugs have become the first treatment choice for the major mental illnesses; unfortunately, in some instances, they are the only type of treatment offered. Instances of overuse and abuse of psychotropic medications in psychiatric facilities—particularly state institutions—are now well documented.[30] The abuse of these

17. Davis, *supra* note 9, at 2290.
18. AMA Drug Evaluations, *supra* note 10, at 360.
19. L.S. Goodman & A. Gilman, The Pharmacological Basis of Therapeutics 182 (5th ed. 1975).
20. Davis, *supra* note 9, at 2302.
21. Sample, DiGregoria, & Wicks, *supra* note 12, at 30.
22. Davis, *supra* note 9, at 2298.
23. Fieve, Lithium Therapy, *in* 3 Comprehensive Textbook, *supra* note 1, at 2348.
24. Davis, *supra* note 9, at 2351, 2291-92.
25. *Id.* at 2349.
26. Davis, Minor Tranquilizers, Sedatives, and Hypnotics, *in* 3 Comprehensive Textbook, *supra* note 1, at 2316.
27. M. Lipton & K. Jobson, Psychopharmacology, *in* Usdin & Lewis, *supra* note 8, at 592.
28. Davis, *supra* note 9, at 2317.
29. Lipton & Jobson, *supra* note 27, at 593.
30. See Rennie v. Klein, 462 F. Supp. 1131 (D.N.J. 1978); see also Davis v. Hubbard, 506 F. Supp. 915, 926-29 (N.D. Ohio 1980); see also Brooks, The Constitutional Right to Refuse Antipsychotic Medications, 8 A.A.P.L. Bull.

medications and their potential for serious adverse side effects have caused patient advocates to challenge the medication practices in some facilities. Perhaps the most controversial area of litigation in mental health today concerns the institutionalized person's right to refuse medication.[31] Some courts[32] and some legislatures[33] have already recognized this right. The controversy is likely to continue at least until treatments having no side effects can be developed for the mentally ill.

B. Psychotherapy

Psychotherapy, sometimes referred to as "talk therapy," is defined in a standard textbook as:

> [a] form of treatment for mental illness and behavioral disturbances in which a trained person establishes a professional contract with the patient and through definite therapeutic communication, both verbal and nonverbal, attempts to alleviate the emotional disturbance, reverse or change maladaptive patterns of behavior, and encourage personality growth and development.[34]

It has been charged that because of understaffing, state hospitals provide little psychotherapy and rely heavily on psychotropic drugs.[35] This is probably true, but defenders of the state institutions argue that persons who are so disturbed as to require institutionalization generally do not respond to psychotherapy until the immediate symptoms of their illness are alleviated. Indeed, today, psychiatric hospitalization is largely limited to the most disturbed individuals, and in the institutional setting medication is the first course of treatment, with psychotherapy sometimes added in conjunction with the medication treatment. As a result, most psychotherapy occurs in the outpatient setting, where an individual seeks help from a private therapist or a mental health clinic.

Unlike medication, which can be prescribed only by physicians, psychotherapy can be conducted by a wide range of mental health professionals, including psychiatrists, psychologists, and social workers. Psychotherapy may take different forms and be brief—10 to 15 sessions—or long term.[36] It may be individualized or conducted in groups or in the form of family therapy.

C. Electroconvulsive Therapy

Discovered in 1938, electroconvulsive therapy (ECT) has been employed to alleviate the symptoms of mental illness. Initially used primarily for the treatment of schizophrenia, ECT was after a few years found to be very successful in treating depression,[37] and until the introduction of psychotropic medications, it was widely used in treating the institutionalized mentally ill. However, almost from the beginning, questions have been raised about the appropriateness of its use—whether it actually served as a mechanism for treatment or, as some cases suggest, for punishment as well.[38] Today, drug therapy is usually tried first, ECT being reserved only for the refractory cases. In some instances, however, such as a severe life-threatening depression, ECT will be the procedure of first choice.[39] It is considered to be appropriate for some types of depression, for catatonia,[40] and for certain cases of schizophrenia.[41]

ECT is administered in a hospital to a sedated patient who has received muscle relaxants to prevent contractions during the convulsions, which if uncontrolled could result in bone fractures. An anesthesiologist controls the breathing of the patient with a respirator. Electrodes are attached to the person's temple and an electrical current of between 70 and 150 volts is administered for between .1 and 1.0 seconds. The resulting seizure—which is considered the therapeutic agent—lasts from 30 to 40 seconds. The patient returns to consciousness within about five minutes after the convulsion. The standard course of ECT treatment for depression is six to nine sessions, administered three times per week.[42] "The effect of ECT in endogenous depressions," reports one textbook, "is one of the most spectacular therapeutic responses in medicine."[43] Usually, the relief comes after as few as four treatments.

Except for bone fractures, which can result if ECT is administered without muscle relaxants, the only other

179, 188 (1980); Rhoden, The Right to Refuse Psychotropic Drugs, 15 Harv. C.R.-C.L.L. Rev. 363, 367 (1980).

31. See discussion in this chapter § VI A, The Right to Refuse Medication, *infra*.

32. See *id.* for the cases that have now recognized a right to refuse medication.

33. See table 6.2, cols. 12–15.

34. See 3 Comprehensive Textbook, *supra* note 1, at 3352.

35. See Symonds, *supra* note 6, at 702.

36. See 3 Comprehensive Textbook, *supra* note 1, at 3314, 3350. Brief therapy is more likely to be aimed at alleviating a specific problem. Long-term psychotherapy or psychoanalysis will have the broader goals of bringing about a better understanding of the self and changes in personality to achieve more personal satisfaction.

37. Kalinowsky, Convulsive Therapy, *in* 3 Comprehensive Textbook, *supra* note 1, at 2339.

38. See discussion in this chapter in § VI B, The Right to Refuse ECT, *infra*. Also see Plotkin, Limiting the Therapeutic Orgy: Mental Patients' Right to Refuse Treatment, 72 Nw. U.L. Rev. 461, 471–74 (1978).

39. Kalinowsky, *supra* note 37, at 2339.

40. American Psychiatric Association Task Force on Electroconvulsive Therapy, Electroconvulsive Therapy: Report of the Task Force on Electroconvulsive Therapy 161 (1978) [hereinafter cited as A.P.A. Task Force on Electroconvulsive Therapy].

41. P.R.A. May, Treatment of Schizophrenia: A Comparative Study of Five Treatment Methods 267 (1968); see also M. Fink, Convulsive Therapy: Theory and Practice 32 (1979).

42. See Tenenbaum, ECT Regulation Reconsidered, 7 MDLR 149 (1983), for a good description of how ECT is administered and its benefits.

43. Kalinowski, *supra* note 37, at 2339.

complication appears to be some memory loss in some cases.[44] Unlike psychotropic medications, ECT comes with few contraindications for its use: it is thus especially promising for people who are unable to take drugs because of cardiac, kidney, or other medical problems.[45]

Notwithstanding its effectiveness and its relative medical safety, ECT remains a controversial treatment outside the psychiatric community.[46] In part, this can be attributed to its past history of abuse within psychiatric facilities. When introduced it was used randomly for all types of patients and without muscle relaxants, which resulted in serious bone fractures. Although it now is used with muscle relaxants and only for specific types of mental illnesses, ECT still retains its negative image for the general public, which may lack understanding of its benefits as well as be concerned about the uncertainty over why it has a therapeutic effect.

D. Psychosurgery

Psychosurgery is defined in a standard textbook as

> surgical intervention to sever fiber connecting one part of the brain with another or to remove, destroy, or stimulate brain tissue with the intent of modifying or altering disturbances of behavior, thought content, or mood for which no organic pathological cause can be demonstrated by established tests and techniques.[47]

Psychosurgery began in the United States with the first prefrontal lobotomy in 1937. This procedure eliminated aggressive and assaultive behavior in previously intractable patients, and within a short period of time the procedure was widely adopted. Initial enthusiasm waned, however, as some of the detrimental effects became apparent. Aside from a troubling mortality rate of up to 5%, many of the patients, while no longer manifesting aggression, exhibited other unacceptable behaviors. These included signs of irreversible brain damage, loss of initiative, profound apathy, varying degrees of intellectual deterioration, and the loss of previously acquired mechanical and intellectual skills. Some people were left in vegetative states so severe that they needed constant, total care. As a result, by the mid-1950s prefrontal lobotomization was abandoned as a treatment procedure for mentally disabled persons.[48]

The use of other psychosurgical procedures continues to be the subject of study and debate,[49] though they are rarely performed.[50] Surgical techniques of great precision have been developed, but their use is limited to experimental situations. Psychosurgery today is clearly a treatment of last resort, and whatever promise it has seems to be confined to depressed patients who have not responded to medication or ECT.[51] The procedure is apparently of little or no value for schizophrenics and may even hasten their deterioration.

The future of psychosurgery as a viable treatment procedure is uncertain. To the extent that discrete parts of the brain can be identified as causing particular aberrant types of behavior, use of the more refined surgical techniques that have been developed by neurosurgeons may be appropriate. However, given past abuse and the potentially radical and irreversible consequences of psychosurgery, it is likely that even today's refined procedures will be considered acceptable only in rare and specific circumstances and that they will be performed only on a strictly controlled basis.

E. Habilitation and Normalization

Over the past two centuries society's view of mentally retarded persons and their learning potential has oscillated. The beginning of the nineteenth century saw the publication of the work of Itard, who wrote of his five-year effort to educate Victor, the "Wild Boy of Aveyron."[52] Illustrating that a highly structured, creative, and individualized approach could achieve remarkable results, Itard's work formed the underpinnings for the creation of state-supported schools in the United States to train mentally retarded persons.[53] These schools emphasized training the person to develop skills to live a more independent life. However, by the end of the nineteenth century retardation had come to be identified with defects in the brain,[54] a position associated with waning hopes for educating the retarded.

In the first three decades of the twentieth century three events severely set back the case for educating the

44. Fink, *supra* note 41, at 49.

45. Kalinowsky, *supra* note 37, at 2338.

46. This is reflected not only in the law review articles that oppose the use of ECT but also in the statutes that regulate its use. See discussion in this chapter § V B, The Right to Refuse ECT, *infra*.

47. Donnelly, Psychosurgery, *in* 3 Comprehensive Textbook, *supra* note 1, at 2342.

48. *Id.* at 2343.

49. L.B. Kalinowsky & H. Hippius, Pharmacological, Convulsive and Other Somatic Treatments in Psychiatry 336 (1969). Also see E. Valenstein, The Psychosurgery Debate (1980), for probably the most comprehensive book on this subject.

50. Donnelly, The Incidence of Psychosurgery in the United States 1971–73, 135 Am. J. Psychiatry 1476 (1978), in which he estimated that far fewer than 200 operations have occurred since 1973. Because of legislative protections in many states this number is likely to be much larger than would be expected in 1983.

51. Donnelly, *supra* note 47, 2345.

52. See generally H. Lane, The Wild Boy of Aveyron (1976). Itard took Victor, who was considered severely retarded and had been abandoned by his family in the forest, and trained him through sensory input and habit training. He was very successful in changing the child, who had previously behaved like an animal, into a more normal child.

53. Wolfensberger, *supra* note 4, at 63.

54. L. Kanner, A History of the Care and Study of the Mentally Retarded (1964).

retarded. The first was the introduction in the first decade of the Binet intelligence test, which purported to provide a rapid assessment of intelligence and made the case study methodology of the psychiatrist expendable in cases where retardation was an issue.[55] Secondly, in 1912 Goddard published a monograph that attributed mental retardation to a fixed genetic disorder not amenable to treatment.[56] Finally, the concept of psychoanalysis was introduced into the United States in 1912; psychiatrists generally found its practice more professionally interesting than addressing the problems presented by the mentally retarded and consequently largely abandoned any efforts to work with the retarded, even though institutions for the retarded were, and continued to be, based primarily on a medical model.[57] The result of these developments, as a group of commentators observed, was that the "focus of sheltering the retarded from society was drastically altered to one of protecting society from the retarded."[58] This shift was reflected in the passage of restrictive legislation, such as bans on marriage and mandatory sterilization statutes.

It was not until the early 1960s that society's response to mentally retarded persons came out of this dark age, with emphasis shifting from institutionalization back to the concepts of normalization and habilitation. Today, the word *treatment* is not used in the context of the mentally retarded, because they are not ill but rather developmentally delayed. Emphasis has shifted away from the medical model to a developmental model that recognizes that each retarded person is in a state of change that can be positively influenced by environmental factors.[59]

Habilitation aims to remedy the delayed learning processes so as to develop the maximum growth potential of the individual by the acquisition of self-help, language, personal, social, educational, vocational, and recreational skills.[60] It encompasses (1) a detailed developmental assessment of the retarded individual's ability to cope with personal social expectations at the differing developmental stages of his life, (2) a survey of the physical, motor, language, social, and intellectual components of his functioning, and (3) the provision of the specific services needed to effectively alter the deficits identified by the developmental assessment.[61] To be most effective, habilitation must begin early in the person's life,[62] making early identification of mental retardation of paramount importance.

The concept of "normalization" for mentally retarded persons was first expressed in North America by Wolfensberger, and he and Nirje have been its most active and articulate spokesmen.[63] Based on the view that the mentally retarded person, when placed in a normal environment, will attempt to live up to normal expectations, the normalization approach emphasizes a positive view of what can be accomplished to help him reach his maximum developmental potential. Proponents of normalization take the view that the retarded person should be furnished with patterns of life that correlate as closely as possible to what is accepted for the rest of society. Thus, the large state institution is an inappropriate environment; if some type of institutionalization is necessary, it should occur in a more family-like setting.[64] Support services are geared toward maximizing the possibility that the retarded individual will stay with his family and be "mainstreamed" with the rest of society.[65]

The concepts of normalization and habilitation have revolutionized the treatment of the mentally retarded. The future outlook for someone diagnosed as "mentally retarded" is much brighter today than it was ten years ago. The trend now is to abolish large state institutions and provide support services within the family setting or in small-group living homes.[66] Legislation has been passed recognizing the value of educating the retarded within the public school system whenever possible.[67] The question remains, however, whether sufficient resources will be provided to accomplish these goals.

55. See Mason, Menolascino, & Galvin, Mental Health: The Right to Treatment for Mentally Retarded Citizens: An Evolving Legal and Scientific Interface, 10 Creighton L. Rev. 124, 130-32 (1976), which gives a good description of the history of the treatment of the retarded and the impact of the Binet test.

56. H. Goddard, The Kallikak Family (1912), *discussed in* Mason, Menolascino, & Galvin, *supra* note 55, at 131.

57. See, e.g., Mason, Menolascino, & Galvin, *supra* note 55, at 121-32.

58. *Id.* at 130.

59. *Id.* at 138-141.

60. G.S. Baroff, Mental Retardation: Nature, Cause and Management (1974).

61. See Mason, Menolascino, & Galvin, *supra* note 55, at 139.

62. W. Wolfensberger, B. Nirje, S. Olshansky, B. Perske, & P. Roos, The Principle of Normalization in Human Services 130 (1972).

63. *Id.* See also Wolfensberger, The Principle of Normalization and Its Implications to Psychiatric Services, 127 Am. J. Psychiatry 291 (1970); B. Nirje, The Normalization Principle and Its Human Management Implications *in* Changing Patterns, *supra* note 4.

64. See Wolfensberger, Nirje, Olshansky, Perske, & Roos, *supra* note 62.

65. F.J. Menolascino, Challenges in Mental Retardation: Progressive Ideology and Services 263-93 (1977); P.C. Chinn, C.J. Drew, & D.R. Logan, Mental Retardation: A Life Cycle Approach 224-28 (1975); D. Sabatino, Resource Rooms: The Renaissance in Special Education, *in* Mental Retardation: Social and Educational Perspectives 156-66 (C. Drew, M. Hardman, & H. Bluhm eds. 1977).

66. Tuoni, Deinstitutionalization and Community Resistance by Zoning Restrictions, Mass. L. Rev. 125-26 (1981); see also Mason, Menolascino, & Galvin, *supra* note 55, at 143.

67. See Education for All Handicapped Children Act of 1975, Pub. L. No. 94-142, 89 Stat. 773 (1975) (codified as amended at 20 U.S.C. §§ 1232, 1401, 1405, 1406, 1411-1420, & 1453 (1982)); Rehabilitation Act of 1973, Pub. L. No. 93-112, 87 Stat. 355 (1973) (codified as amended at 29 U.S.C. §§ 701-792 (1982)).

F. Behavior Modification

Behavior modification has long been recognized as a treatment option for both the mentally ill and the mentally retarded.[68] It is felt that many of the most promising techniques for training retarded persons in particular involve some combination of various behavior modification techniques.[69] Roos has found that these techniques can "free individuals from crippling behavior, enabling them to interact more meaningfully with their environment and thereby enhancing their opportunities to develop their human qualities."[70]

Behavior modification or behavior therapy has been defined as a "treatment modality that focuses on overt and objectively observable behavior and uses various conditioning techniques derived from learning theory to modify the patient's behavior directly. Behavior therapy aims exclusively at symptomatic improvement, without addressing psychodynamic causation."[71] Based on the principle that people are influenced by the consequences of their behavior, behavior modification techniques are intended to improve self-control by strengthening individual skills, abilities, and independence.[72] The procedures require identifying both the problem behavior and the desirable response. Such an approach is useful only for solving specific problems as opposed to bringing about general adjustment to life. Unlike other types of therapy, behavior modification has results that are relatively changeable.[73]

Not one technique but a family of techniques, behavior modification includes positive reinforcement, aversive control, overcorrection, and systematic desensitization.[74]

Positive reinforcement involves the giving of a reward, such as money, food, praise, and attention, to develop and maintain new behavior. Positive reinforcers are withheld to decrease the frequency of undesired behavior.

Aversive control techniques subjecting the individual to sensory or emotional experiments are justified as mechanisms to help reduce the person's desire to engage in inappropriate behavior.[75] This type of technique seems to work well with addictions, certain sexual behaviors, and life-threatening behaviors, such as self-mutilation.[76] Administering low-level electrical shocks is one of the most commonly used aversive control techniques. Another approach is the removal of positive reinforcers, such as a loss of privileges. Sometimes a "time-out" procedure is used, in which an already institutionalized person is placed in isolation following inappropriate action. Aversive control techniques have been severely criticized, especially when used on the mentally disabled. While aversive control will continue to be part of behavior modification programs, some of the more offensive techniques, such as the use of nausea-inducing drugs, have resulted in lawsuits[77] and are likely to fade from practice.

Overcorrection is a technique that seems to be particularly effective in eliminating aggressive and disruptive behavior among institutionalized persons.[78] Combining both positive reinforcement and aversive control to discourage the inappropriate behavior, this technique teaches the person not only to remedy the situation but to "overcorrect" it. For example, if a person turns over his bed, then he will have to straighten up not only his bed but also all other beds on the unit.

Systematic desensitization involves the gradual, progressive exposure of the individual to feared situations, thereby enabling him to learn to relax and conquer his fears through familiarization with the feared object or experience.

Facilities for the mentally disabled will continue to employ a variety of behavior modification techniques because they have been shown to be effective and do not produce the same side effects accompanying other treatment methods that are intrusive of the patient's body. For retarded persons these techniques are likely to continue to be the major methods used to help develop his social skills.

G. Restraints and Seclusion

The use of physical restraints and/or seclusion is widely accepted in facilities for both the mentally ill and the mentally retarded. Yet their value as a treatment method has been questioned by both mental health professionals and patient advocates. Abuse of these techniques has led to litigation and legislation strictly governing the circumstances under which they may be utilized.[79]

68. B.S. Brown, L.A. Wienckowski, & S.B. Stolz, Behavior Modification: Perspective on a Current Issue, (DHEW Pub. No. (ADM) #75-202, 1975).

69. Roos, Reconciling Behavior Modification Procedures with the Normalization Principle, *in* Wolfensberger, Nirje, Olskansky, Perske, & Roos, *supra* note 62, at 137-48.

70 *Id.* at 146.

71. See 3 Comprehensive Textbook, *supra* note 1, at 3313.

72. See Brown, Wienckowski, & Stolz, *supra* note 68, at 1.

73. *Id.* at 2.

74. *Id.* at 4-9 for a good description of how these techniques work.

75. See, e.g., S. Rachman & J. Teasdale, Aversion Therapy and Behavior Disorders (1969).

76. *Id.* See also Bucher, Some Ethical Issues in the Therapeutic Use of Punishment in Advances in Behavior Therapy (R. Rubin & C. Franks eds. 1969).

77. See Knecht v. Gillman, 488 F.2d 1136 (8th Cir. 1973).

78. Foxx & Azrin, Restitution: A Method of Eliminating Aggressive-Disruptive Behavior of Retarded and Brain Damaged Patients, 10 Behav. Research & Therapy, 15 (1972); see also Webster & Azrin, Required Relaxation: A Method of Inhibiting Agitative-Disruptive Behavior of Retardates, 11 Behav. Research & Therapy 76 (1973).

79. See ch. 5, Rights of Institutionalized Persons, § X, Restraints and Seclusion, *supra*.

Physical restraints may involve the total physical incapacitation of the person or the incapacitation of parts of the person's body, such as his arms or legs. Methods include tying the person to his bed or to a chair with straps or restraining his hands with mitts. Restraints may be used for the purposes of behavior modification, that is, treatment or habilitation, or to prevent the person from harming himself or others.[80] At times restraints have been inappropriately used to punish an institutionalized person for his behavior.

Seclusion that involves placing the individual in isolated confinement may also be used as part of a behavior modification program or to prevent injury to self or others. The theory is that isolation has a calming effect, enabling the person thereafter to better deal with his surroundings.[81] The typical facility has a specially designed "seclusion" or "time out" room, small in size and either unfurnished or furnished in a way to assure that the disabled person does not injure himself. There is usually a small window in the door to permit observation.

There are very specific clinical indications for the use of either seclusion or restraints. When a person is being restrained or secluded he needs to be carefully monitored to make sure no harm comes to him.

III. THE RIGHT TO TREATMENT

In 1960 Birnbaum first proposed that the courts recognize a constitutionally protected right to treatment for institutionalized mentally ill persons based on notions of substantive due process.[82] Viewing institutionalization without treatment in mental health facilities as tantamount to criminal incarceration, he reasoned:

> [I]f repeated court decisions constantly remind the public that medical care in public mental institutions is inadequate, not only will the mentally ill be released from their mental prisons, but, it is believed that public opinion will react to force the legislatures to increase appropriations sufficiently to make it possible to provide adequate care and treatment so that the mentally ill will be treated in mental hospitals.[83]

Birnbaum's thesis provided the foundation for later judicial developments making this right to treatment a reality.

A. The Case Law

Rouse v. Cameron was the first decision in which a court gave substance to a constitutionally based right to treatment, stating that "[t]he purpose of involuntary hospitalization is treatment, not punishment."[84] Authored by Judge Bazelon, this ruling addressed the issue of whether a person acquitted by reason of insanity and then automatically committed to a mental institution had a right to treatment. Although a District of Columbia statute provided the actual basis for the court's holding that there was such a right, Judge Bazelon implied that even in the absence of specific statutory authority the absence of treatment might raise constitutional concerns. The court in dicta expressed three bases of possible constitutional infirmity. The first concerned the lack of procedural safeguards provided when a criminal defendant was automatically committed upon a finding of not guilty by reason of insanity. Second, the court questioned the propriety of the fact that the acquittee could be institutionalized in a mental facility longer than he could be imprisoned if sentenced. Rouse at most could have been sentenced to a year in prison, whereas under the mandatory commitment statute he was subject to indefinite institutionalization and had in fact been confined for four years at the time of the litigation. While the difference in the duration of confinement was justified by the need for treatment, the court suggested that the state's failure to provide treatment undercut this justification and raised due process and equal protection problems. Finally, the court suggested that "[i]ndefinite confinement without treatment of one who has been found not criminally responsible may be so inhumane as to be 'cruel and unusual punishment.'"[85]

The *Rouse* court then addressed what would be required of the hospital, concluding that "[t]he hospital need not show that the treatment will cure or improve him, but only that there is a bona fide effort to do so."[86] Despite its grounding on a statute whose effect applied only within the jurisdiction in which the case was decided—the District of Columbia—the *Rouse* decision became the analytical starting point for all subsequent right to treatment cases.[87]

A federal district court in 1972, in *Wyatt v. Stickney*,[88] gave the first decision squarely holding that

80. See Rosen & DiGiacomo, The Role of Physical Restraint in the Treatment of Psychiatric Illness, 39 J. Clinical Psychiatry 228 (1978).

81. See Gutheil, Observations on the Theoretical Bases for Seclusion of the Psychiatric Inpatient, 135 Am. J. Psychiatry, 325, 326 (1978).

82. Birnbaum, The Right to Treatment, 46 A.B.A. J. 499, 503 (1960). This is considered the seminal work on the right of the mentally ill to treatment.

83. *Id.* at 503.

84. 373 F.2d 451, 452 (D.C. Cir. 1966).

85. *Id.* at 453. This was based on the United States Supreme Court's decision in Robinson v. California, 370 U.S. 660 (1962).

86. 373 F.2d at 456.

87. Wyatt v. Stickney, 325 F. Supp. 781 (M.D. Ala. 1971), which was the first case to cite *Rouse* in recognizing a right to treatment. See also Donaldson v. O'Connor, 493 F.2d 507 (5th Cir.1974), which also relied in part on *Rouse*.

88. 344 F. Supp. 373 (M.D. Ala. 1972).

there was a constitutionally based right to treatment for involuntarily civilly committed patients. The ruling resulted from a class action suit challenging the conditions within Alabama's mental institutions. Most of the patients in the class had been committed through noncriminal proceedings "without the constitutional protections afforded defendants in criminal proceedings." Holding that when patients were committed for treatment purposes they unquestionably had a "constitutional right to receive such individual treatment as will give each of them a realistic opportunity to be cured or to improve his or her mental condition," the court noted that the purpose of involuntary hospitalization for treatment purposes was treatment and not mere custodial care or punishment, and that treatment was the only justification, from a constitutional standpoint, that allowed civil commitment to mental institutions.[89] In a subsequent ruling on the same case the court, after hearing weeks of expert testimony, defined the minimum standards for constitutionally adequate treatment: (1) a humane psychological and physical environment, (2) qualified staff in numbers sufficient to administer adequate treatment, and (3) individualized treatment plans.[90] Although *Wyatt* announced a constitutional right to treatment, the court did not articulate a clear theory on which this right was based.

It was not until the Court of Appeals for the Fifth Circuit decided *Donaldson v. O'Connor*[91] in 1974 that such a constitutional basis was specifically set forth. The case of Kenneth Donaldson presented a fact pattern typical of the situation attacked in a number of class action lawsuits seeking to secure reform of state mental institutions.[92] In 1957, at the age of 50, Donaldson was committed as a "paranoid schizophrenic" to the Florida State Hospital. Fourteen and one-half years later—still institutionalized—Donaldson initiated the suit that was eventually to be heard by the United States Supreme Court.[93] Donaldson was a Christian Scientist and because of his religious beliefs refused medication and ECT. However he was denied other forms of therapy, including grounds privileges and occupational therapy.[94] Testimony revealed that there was only one psychiatrist for nine hundred patients and that Donaldson never even spoke to him.[95] During most of his institutionalization Donaldson was kept in a locked room with other patients, most of whom were mentally ill criminals. At no point did a review of his records suggest that he posed a danger either to himself or to others.

From the beginning Donaldson felt he was institutionalized unjustifiably. He wrote to state officials, filed numerous writs of habeas corpus in the Florida courts, and tried desperately to get someone to address his plight.[96] A group that worked with former mental patients from Minnesota inquired about the possibility of Donaldson's being released to their care. This proposal was rejected. A college friend of Donaldson's made continual attempts to have Donaldson released to his care. Each time, the hospital imposed conditions for release that, once met, only resulted in the imposition of new conditions. Finally, the friend gave up, since it was clear the hospital would not release Donaldson.[97]

Ultimately, Donaldson filed suit in federal court against the director of the Florida State Hospital and others who were responsible for his care. A jury found that Donaldson's rights had been violated and awarded damages, both compensatory and punitive, against two of the defendants who had been primarily responsible for his care. On appeal the Court of Appeals held "that the Fourteenth Amendment guarantees involuntarily civilly committed mental patients a right to treatment, and that the evidence (in the trial court) was sufficient to support the verdict" finding defendants guilty of violating Donaldson's rights.[98] In reaching this conclusion the court articulated the constitutional analysis that justified the recognition of a constitutionally based right to treatment.

Beginning by noting that civil commitment involved the kind of massive curtailment of liberty with which the due process clause is concerned, the court then set forth a two-part theory for recognizing a constitutionally-based right to treatment, relying on developments in other areas of the law and on court decisions from all levels of courts including the United States Supreme Court.[99] The first part, often referred to as the "rational relationship" test, distinguishes between persons who have been civilly committed based on the state's police

89. 325 F. Supp. 781, 784 (M.D. Ala. 1971).

90. 344 F. Supp. 373 (M.D. Ala. 1972). The components of each of these elements were detailed; they are *reprinted in part in* ch. 5, Rights of Institutionalized Persons, appendix A.

91. 493 F.2d 507 (5th Cir. 1974), *vacated and remanded,* 422 U.S. 563 (1975).

92. The ease with which Donaldson was admitted to the hospital and the fact that there was no periodic review were typical of conditions existing in the 1950s and 1960s. In this book chapter 2, Involuntary Institutionalization, sets forth the legal developments in this area, and chapter 5, Rights of Institutionalized Persons, traces the development of the other rights now guaranteed to the institutionalized mentally disabled.

93. O'Connor v. Donaldson, 422 U.S. 563 (1975).

94. Donaldson v. O'Connor, 493 F.2d 507, 513-14 (5th Cir. 1974).

95. *Id.* at 515. Over a ten-year period Donaldson testified that he spent no more than three hours in total speaking to a psychiatrist.

96. See Baldwin, O'Connor v. Donaldson: Involuntary Civil Commitment and the Right to Treatment, 7 Colum. Hum. Rts. L. Rev. 573, 576 (1975), for a review of the facts and implications of this case.

97. 493 F.2d at 516, 517.

98. *Id.* at 510.

99. The court reviewed cases from four major areas: habeas corpus petitions, nonpenal sex offender and defective delinquent laws, treatment issues cases such as Rouse v. Cameron, and cases challenging institutional conditions. (*Id.* at 520-25.)

power as dangerous to others and those, like Donaldson, who had been committed based on a *parens patriae* rationale of being in need of treatment and unable to care for themselves. The court found that if "the rationale for confinement is the 'parens patriae' rationale that the patient is in need of treatment, the due process clause requires that minimally adequate treatment be in fact provided. This in turn requires that, at least for the nondangerous patient, constitutionally minimum standards of treatment be established and enforced."[100] It follows that if the purpose of commitment is treatment yet in fact no treatment is occurring, the nature of the commitment bears no reasonable relationship to its purpose and the due process clause is violated.

The second part, deemed the "quid pro quo" theory, does not distinguish between those who are committed under the police power and those committed under the parens patriae rationale. The theory is that due process requires the state to extend treatment as the quid pro quo for its right to deprive individuals of their liberty in noncriminal proceedings. This theory requires that treatment be provided even to dangerous mentally ill individuals, whose basis for commitment is to prevent dangerous acts. In the event such individuals are untreatable, the theory as specified by the court still requires "minimally adequate habilitation and care, beyond the subsistence level of custodial care that would be provided in a penitentiary."[101]

In 1975 the United States Supreme Court heard the *Donaldson* case and backed away from the Court of Appeals for the Fifth Circuit's holding. While in *O'Connor v. Donaldson* the Court unanimously agreed that Donaldson should have been released,[102] it refrained from ruling that an involuntarily confined mentally ill person has a right to treatment.[103] The Court held that "a State cannot constitutionally confine without more a nondangerous individual who is capable of surviving safely in freedom by himself or with the help of willing and responsible family members or friends" and that a "finding of 'mental illness' alone cannot justify a State's locking a person up against his will and keeping him indefinitely in simple custodial confinement."[104] In a footnote, however, the Court noted that this case did not concern the right or adequacy of treatment but rather the propriety of confinement.[105] To emphasize this point, the Court instructed the appeals court on remand to consider only the issue of monetary liability, adding: "Of necessity our decision vacating the judgment of the Court of Appeals deprives that court's opinion of precedential effect, leaving this Court's opinion and judgment as the sole law of the case."[106]

Buttressing the narrowing effect of the Supreme Court ruling, Chief Justice Burger's concurring opinion devoted 10 pages of his 12-page concurrence to the proposition that the Fifth Circuit's analysis regarding a right to treatment had "no basis in the decision of this Court."[107] Thus, in his view, *O'Connor v. Donaldson* "only describes a combination of factors which compels release. It articulates no detailed constitutional criteria for either initial commitment or continued confinement."[108] Consequently, the right to treatment articulated by the Court of Appeals seemingly suffered an early death. Despite this, the ruling has provided other courts with a reasoned analysis to affirm such a right.[109]

Commentary following the Supreme Court's decision explored the limits of *Donaldson* and its meaning for the delivery of mental health services.[110] The decision was a disappointment to those who had hoped to see the highest Court recognize a constitutional right to treatment. Nonetheless, the Court's majority opinion did not reject such a right, leaving the door open for lower courts to affirm it on a jurisdiction-by-jurisdiction basis. Since *Donaldson*, the Supreme Court has not reconsidered the question of whether the institutionalized mentally ill have a right to treatment, but it has recognized a very limited right to treatment and habilitation for the mentally retarded, based on a constitutionally protected liberty interest in safety and freedom.[111]

B. Eighth Amendment Basis for a Right to Treatment

While the initial case law on the right to treatment has by and large emphasized that the right is founded in

100. *Id.* at 521.
101. *Id.* at 522.
102. 422 U.S. 563, 576, (1975).
103. *Id.* at 573. The court in reversing the Fifth Circuit opinion found the lower court's decision needlessly broad and remanded for a finding of the defendant's liability in light of its decision in Wood v. Strickland, 420 U.S. 308 (1975), which dealt with the scope of qualified immunity of state officials under § 1983.
104. 422 U.S. 575-76.

105. *Id.* at 574 n.10.
106. *Id.* at 577-78 n.12.
107. O'Connor v. Donaldson, 422 U.S. 563, 580 (1975); see at 578-98 for the concurrence.
108. Baldwin, *supra* note 96, at 589.
109. See, e.g., Santana v. Collazo, 533 F. Supp. 966 (D.P.R. 1982); Garrity v. Gallen, 522 F. Supp. 171 (D.N.H. 1981).
110. *Id.* See also Kopolow, A Review of Major Implications of the *O'Connor v. Donaldson* Decision, 133 Am. J. Psychiatry 379 (1976); Lipscomb, "Without More": A Constitutional Right to Treatment? 22 Loyola L. Rev. 373 (1975-76); Lottman, Whatever Happened to Kenneth Donaldson? 1 MDLR 288 (1977); Mancilla, The Right to Treatment Case—That Wasn't, 30 U. Miami L. Rev. 486 (1976); Spece, Preserving the Right to Treatment: A Critical Assessment and Constructive Development of Constitutional Right to Treatment Theories, 20 Ariz. L. Rev. 1 (1978).
111. Romeo v. Youngberg, 457 U.S. 307 (1982), which is discussed in this chapter in § IV, The Right to Habilitation, *infra*.

the due process clause of the Fourteenth Amendment, even the very first case, *Rouse v. Cameron*,[112] suggested that there may be a violation of the Eighth Amendment's cruel and unusual punishment clause when treatment is not provided.[113] In support of this view, Judge Bazelon, the author of the *Rouse* opinion, cited the Supreme Court's decision in *Robinson v. California*,[114] holding that the Eighth Amendment forbids a state from criminally punishing someone for a condition or status—in that case, the status of being a narcotics addict. Confining a mentally ill person without providing treatment, according to this argument, comes close to punishing him for the status of being mentally ill.

The question whether the Eighth Amendment applies outside the criminal justice context has been addressed in other cases. In *Ingraham v. Wright*,[115] which involved the paddling of school children for disciplinary purposes, the Court suggested that although the Eighth Amendment did not apply in that situation it "may have force in other settings."[116] The Court elaborated by adding that for the amendment to be applicable there must, first of all, be "punishment," and second it must be "sufficiently analogous" to criminal punishment in terms of the way and setting in which it is administered.[117] The analogy for involuntary institutionalization in a mental facility is that there is a massive loss of liberty, almost complete control of the daily life of the person, and dependence on the institution for the provision of all of one's basic needs. In addition, the mentally ill, like prisoners, are stigmatized by their status as deviants and by the very fact of having been institutionalized. Still, these realities do not in themselves render confinement in a mental institution equivalent to criminal punishment, and the courts have generally held the Eighth Amendment's proscriptions to be inapplicable to the mental health setting.[118] The amendment can be invoked in right to treatment cases only by prisoners seeking treatment within correctional institutions.

C. Present Status

Today, the right to treatment is statutorily recognized by the majority of states.[119] Furthermore, the right appears to be widely accepted by state officials and mental health treatment providers. There remains a significant problem, however, of translating the legal right to treatment into the reality of meaningful medical care. Budgetary constraints still limit the programs available to the mentally disabled. While most mental institutions today are providing far better care and treatment than they did a decade or two ago, the base line from which progress is measured is very low.

IV. THE RIGHT TO HABILITATION

Whereas the law speaks of the right to treatment for the mentally ill, for the retarded the common phrase is the right to habilitation. Though the terms *habilitation* and *treatment* are sometimes used interchangeably, as discussed earlier, habilitation is distinguished by its association with the developmental model, whose aim is the remediation of the delayed learning processes of the mentally retarded individual. To habilitate a person means to develop his maximum growth potential in terms of self-help, language, personal, social, educational, vocational, and recreational skills.[120] Treatment for mental illness, based on the medical model, is by contrast aimed at a defined malcondition. Although the distinction may seem one largely of language, its importance lies in its accentuation of the fact that the mentally ill and the mentally retarded are different in terms of etiology, symptomatology, and needs. For the mentally retarded, skills training is the key to making life in the community possible.

Suits seeking to establish a right to habilitation initially invoked "right to treatment" rhetoric.[121] Indeed the legal theories are the same, but what is required to implement habilitation of the retarded is usually very different from the treatment requirements of the mentally ill, as has been suggested earlier in the distinction between treatment and habilitation. Although both populations require properly maintained environments and adequate staff, staff functions and programs goals differ. A major thrust of today's right to habilitation litigation is to require programs in a community setting rather than in a large, isolated state institution, where habilitation, to the extent that it is equated with preparation for community living, is unlikely to occur.[122]

Initially, institutionalization of the mentally retarded was based on the parens patriae concept of caring for those who could not care for themselves.[123] The mental-

112. 373 F.2d 451 (D.C. Cir. 1966).
113. *Id.* at 453.
114. 370 U.S. 660 (1962).
115. 430 U.S. 651 (1977).
116. *Id.* at 669.
117. *Id.* at 671 n.37.
118. See generally Comment, Right to Treatment for the Civilly Committed: A New Eighth Amendment Basis, 45 U. Chi. L. Rev. 731 (1978); also Bell v. Wolfish, 441 U.S. 520 (1979).
119. See table 6.1, col. 1.

120. Mason, Menolascino, & Galvin, *supra* note 55, at 139-40. See notes 77-80 *supra* and accompanying text.
121. See, e.g., Wyatt v. Stickney, 344 F. Supp. 387 (M.D. Ala. 1972), and Welsch v. Likins, 373 F. Supp. 487 (D. Minn. 1974).
122. See Wolfensberger, Nirje, Olshansky, Persky, & Roos, *supra* note 62. See also text accompanying notes 78-83 *supra*.
123. See Mason, Menolascino, & Galvin, *supra* note 55 at 128-30.

ly retarded were committed to large state institutions, thereby relieving their families of the responsibility of caring for them. Typically, these facilities were overcrowded and understaffed, and they offered no more than a place to eat and sleep.[124] The conditions described in *Halderman v. Pennhurst State School and Hospital*[125] are a graphic example of life in a state facility for the mentally retarded in the 1970s. Pennhurst had 1,230 residents, whose average length of stay at the institution was 21 years. Forty-three percent had had no family contact in the 3 years preceding the initiation of the lawsuit. The average resident received one psychological evaluation each year and one vocational adjustment services report every ten years. Residents enjoyed no privacy, sleeping in large dormitories, spending their waking hours in a large day room and eating in a group setting. The average resident received only 1½ hours of programming per day and none on the weekends. It took years to move to the top of waiting lists for participation in the limited educational and vocational programs. As a result, the abilities of many of the residents admitted to Pennhurst actually declined during their institutionalization. Pennhurst was not the worst of the facilities for the mentally retarded: at the time the suit was begun, it had undergone a major upgrading and it was in fact providing more services for its residents than many other state facilities.[126] Yet Pennhurst reflected much of what was wrong in the traditional state institution, and the facts developed in the litigation strengthened the case of those who believed that habilitation/normalization could not occur in such a setting.[127]

A. The Case Law

Wyatt v. Stickney[128] provided the seminal formulation of a constitutional right to habilitation for the mentally retarded person involuntarily confined in a state facility. The court defined "habilitation" as "the process by which the staff of the institution assists the resident to acquire and maintain those life skills which enable him to cope more effectively with the demands of his own person and to his environment and to raise the level of his physical, mental, and social efficiency."[129] With this standard in mind, the court asserted that as "the only constitutional justification for civilly committing a mental retardate . . . is habilitation, it follows ineluctably that once committed such a person is possessed of an inviolable constitutional right to habilitation."[130] The court then set forth the minimum conditions necessary to create an environment where habilitation can occur. These included 49 detailed provisions falling into three broad categories or requirements: (1) a humane psychological and physical environment, (2) qualified staff in numbers sufficient to administer adequate treatment, and (3) individualized treatment plans.[131]

While the court did not delineate the basis for a constitutional right to habilitation, the Fifth Circuit did so in *Donaldson v. O'Connor*[132] and *Wyatt v. Aderholt,*[133] enunciating a right to treatment and habilitation based on the due process clause of the Fourteenth Amendment—a constitutional grounding reiterated in subsequent cases.[134] In *Welsch v. Likins*, for example, the court held "that due process requires that civil commitment for reasons of mental retardation be accompanied by minimally adequate treatment designed to give each committed person 'a reasonable opportunity to be cured or to improve his or her mental condition.'"[135] In addition to stating the constitutional basis, the court held that the statutory law of Minnesota also mandated treatment to be provided in a setting least restrictive of the person's liberties.[136]

The right to treatment cases do not impose upon the state an affirmative obligation to provide services to the mentally disabled. Once the state undertakes to intervene in the lives of mentally disabled persons, however, it can only do so in a constitutionally permissible manner.[137] Cases such as *Wyatt v. Stickney* prescribe detailed standards for institutions in order to give content to the patients' right to treatment and

124. *Id.* See also B. D. Sales, D. M. Powell, R. Van Duizend, & Associates, Disabled Persons and the Law (1982).

125. 446 F. Supp. 1295, 1302-11 (E.D. Pa. 1977).

126. Pennhurst had reduced its population from 4,000 in the 1960s to 1,230 residents at the time of the suit. All acknowledged that major improvements had occurred, yet it was agreed that the facility did not meet minimum standards for the habilitation of its residents.

127. See, Wolfensberger, Nirje, Olshansky, Persky, & Roos, *supra* note 62, at 28. See generally ch. 5, Rights of Institutionalized Persons, *supra* for a discussion of the specific rights that were addressed as part of class action lawsuits challenging the conditions within the state institutions.

128. 344 F. Supp. 387 (M.D. Ala. 1972).

129. *Id.* at 395.

130. *Id.* at 390.

131. *Id.* at 395-407, which is appendix A, Minimum Constitutional Standards for Adequate Habilitation of the Mentally Retarded. These standards are *reprinted in part in* this book in ch. 5, Rights of Institutionalized Persons, app. A, Minimum Constitutional Standards Set Out in *Wyatt* Appendixes, *supra*.

132. 493 F.2d 507 (5th Cir. 1974); see discussion in previous section on the right to treatment.

133. 503 F.2d 1305 (5th Cir. 1974); in Wyatt the court reaffirmed its quid pro quo theory that habilitation had to be provided as the jurisdiction for depriving someone of liberty. See p. 1314.

134. See, e.g., Welsch v. Likins, 373 F. Supp. 487 (D. Minn. 1974); Davis v. Watkins, 384 F. Supp. 487 (D. Minn. 1974); Gary W. v. State of Louisiana, 437 F. Supp. 1209 (E.D. La. 1976); Halderman v. Pennhurst State School & Hosp., 446 F. Supp. 1295 (E.D. Pa. 1977).

135. 373 F. Supp. 487, 499 (D. Minn. 1974), quoting Wyatt v. Stickney, 325 F. Supp. at 784.

136. 373 F. Supp. at 500, 502.

137. See *id.* at 498-99 (D. Minn. 1974).

habilitation.[138] In *Halderman v. Pennhurst State School and Hospital*, however, the court ruled that "minimally adequate habilitation *cannot* be provided in [an institutional setting].[139]

The *Halderman* court heard extensive testimony on the conditions at Pennhurst State School and on the improvements that could be made if the principles of normalization and habilitation were conscientiously applied. On the basis of this evidence the court found:

> [W]henever a state accepts retarded individuals into its facilities, it cannot create or maintain those facilities in a manner which deprives those individuals of the basic necessities of life. . . .
>
> Once admitted to a state facility, the residents have a constitutional right to be provided with minimally adequate habilitation under the least restrictive conditions consistent with the purpose of the commitment.[140]

Finding that the right could not be implemented in the Pennhurst institution, the court ordered that the institution be closed and appropriate community facilities be developed for its residents. The court thus accepted the argument that segregating the retarded from the community and sheltering them in a total control environment was antithetical to "normalization" and inimical to the opportunity to realize full developmental potential.[141]

The landmark district court ruling in *Halderman* did not stand long. The court had identified three bases for the right to habilitation: the Fourteenth Amendment of the federal constitution, Pennsylvania statutory law, and § 504 of the Rehabilitation Act of 1973. On review the Court of Appeals for the Third Circuit affirmed the district court's statutory analysis, but it took pains to avoid the constitutional issue. It reversed the part of the lower court's decision that banned all future admissions to Pennhurst and that required the eventual closing of the facility.[142] In sustaining the right to habilitation, the appellate court found alternate grounds in the Developmentally Disabled Assistance and Bill of Rights Act,[143] § 6010 of which provides:

> Congress makes the following findings respecting the rights of the person with developmental disabilities:
>
> 1) Persons with developmental disabilities have a right to appropriate treatment, services, and habilitation for such disabilities;
>
> 2) The treatment, services, and habilitation for a person with developmental disabilities should be designed to maximize the developmental potential of the person and should be provided in the setting that is least restrictive of the person's liberty;
>
> 3) The Federal Government and the States both have an obligation to assure that public funds are not provided to any institution . . . that
>
> A. does not provide treatment, services, and habilitation which are not appropriate to the needs of such persons . . . .[144]

Review of *Halderman* by the United States Supreme Court resulted in a further trimming of the initial holding, and it dealt a major setback for those who hoped for an unequivocal recognition of a constitutional right to habilitation. In the same way that the Supreme Court made it clear in *O'Connor v. Donaldson*[145] that it was not recognizing a constitutionally based right to treatment, the Court in *Pennhurst State School and Hospital v. Halderman*[146] refused to announce a constitutional right to habilitation. It did not support the statutory analysis of the circuit court.[147] Justice Rehnquist, in writing the majority opinion, held that § 6010 of the Developmentally Disabled Assistance and Bill of Rights Act did not confer upon the institutionalized mentally retarded a right to appropriate treatment, whether in the least restrictive environment or elsewhere.[148] The Court reviewed the legislative history of the act and interpreted § 6010 as merely expressing a preference for certain kinds of treatment. The dissent on the other hand, written by Justice White and joined by Justices Brennan and Marshall, read the legislative history as confirming that the right of the developmentally disabled to habilitation in the least restrictive environment indeed was statutorily demanded. The majority's decision means, however, that today there is no federally enforceable statute that guarantees the mentally retarded a right to habilitation.[149]

In 1982 the United States Supreme Court in *Youngberg v. Romeo*[150] addressed the substantive rights of in-

138. 344 F. Supp. 387 (M.D. Ala. 1972); see also Davis v. Watkins, 384 F. Supp. 1196 (N.D. Ohio 1974).

139. 446 F. Supp. 1295, 1318 (E.D. Pa. 1977) (emphasis added). This ruling was limited by subsequent rulings: *aff'd in part, rev'd and remanded in part,* 612 F.2d 84 (3d Cir.1979), *rev'd in part and remanded,* 451 U.S.1 (1981).

140. 446 F. Supp. at 1319.

141. *Id.* at 1318; see also Mason, Menolascino, & Galvin, *supra* note 55, at 156–57.

142. 612 F.2d 84 (3d Cir. 1979).

143. 42 U.S.C. § 6010 (1976).

144. *Id.*

145. 422 U.S. 563 (1975).

146. 451 U.S. 1 (1981).

147. *Id.* at 11.

148. *Id.* at 20–27.

149. On remand the Third Circuit affirmed the original relief based on state law grounds (673 F.2d 647 (3d Cir.1982)). The Supreme Court reversed, holding that the Eleventh Amendment's sovereign immunity principle prohibits a federal district court from ordering Pennsylvania officials to conform their conduct to state law. (104 S. Ct. 900 (1984)). The case has again been remanded to the Third Circuit. See also 8 MPDLR 7 (1984) for a further discussion of this case.

150. 457 U.S. 307. See extended discussion of this case in ch. 5, Rights of Institutionalized Persons, § X, Restraints and Seclusion.

voluntarily committed mentally retarded persons. Nicholas Romeo was a profoundly retarded 33-year-old man who had the mental capacity of an 18-month-old child. Following his father's death, Romeo was admitted upon his mother's petition to Pennhurst State School, based on her inability to control her son's violence. Between the time he was admitted and the date of suit, Romeo was injured on at least 63 occasions. In his class action lawsuit, his attorneys argued that he had a constitutionally protected liberty interest in safety, freedom of movement, and training within the institution and that his rights were violated when the defendants failed to provide constitutionally required adequate conditions of confinement.

The Supreme Court held that the due process clause of the Fourteenth Amendment provided Romeo with a liberty interest that required "the State to provide minimally adequate or reasonable training to ensure safety and freedom from undue restraint."[151] It reasoned that "[i]f it is cruel and unusual punishment to hold convicted criminals in unsafe conditions, it must be unconstitutional to confine the involuntarily committed—who may not be punished at all—in unsafe conditions."[152] The Court went on to recognize "that there is a constitutionally protected liberty interest in safety and freedom from restraint, training may be necessary to avoid unconstitutional infringement of those rights."[153] It then defined, in exceedingly vague terms, the minimally adequate training required by the Constitution as "such training as may be reasonable in light of respondent's liberty interests in safety and freedom from unreasonable restraints."[154] The Court further held that "[i]n determining what is 'reasonable'—in this and in any case presenting a claim for training by a State—we emphasize that courts must show deference to the judgment exercised by a qualified professional. . . . the decision, if made by a professional, is presumptively valid . . . ."[155]

The unanimous *Romeo* decision gives only scant support for the right to habilitation. The ruling falls far short of the sweeping district court decision in *Halderman*. While the Court did hold that training is required in some circumstances, it mandated only that minimum amount that would enable the individual to avoid danger and unnecessary restraint. Even this limited guarantee is undercut by the Court's strong deference to the professional caretaker's judgment. Whether *Romeo* will be viewed by lower courts as setting constitutional maxima beyond which they will not venture or only as articulating minima which will form the foundation for a more expansive view of habilitation rights remains to be seen.

B. The Present Status

The notion that the institutionalized mentally retarded are entitled to habilitation and normalization has become well accepted. Twenty-five states mandate this by statute.[156] The trend in most states is to develop small group living arrangements for the mentally retarded, closer to the "normal" environment.[157] However, both the economic and the political costs of changing to community-based care are high, and the new facilities come with their own defects and inadequacies.[158]

V. INFORMED CONSENT

The informed consent doctrine gained judicial recognition as far back as 1914,[159] but significant refinement of the doctrine did not come until 1972 in two cases involving surgery.[160] It has long been accepted that a competent medical patient has a right to refuse treatment based on his own views or judgments. The doctrine of informed consent merely shifts the burden of obtaining information toward the treatment provider, holding that prior to treatment the patient must be apprised of the diagnosis, the nature of the contemplated treatment, the risks inherent in such treatment, his prognosis with and without the treatment, and any possible alternative approaches to alleviate the problem. The provision of this information will not by itself render an ensuing consent to treatment valid, for in addition to being informed, a patient must be both legally and clinically competent and must give his consent voluntarily and knowingly.[161] The informed consent doctrine furthers the well-accepted proposition that each individual has a right to decide what will be done with his body, at least insofar as the exercise of this right does not infringe upon the rights of others.

151. *Id.* at 319.
152. *Id.* at 315-16.
153. *Id.* at 318 (note omitted).
154. *Id.* at 322.
155. *Id.* at 322-23 (notes omitted).

156. See table 6.1, col. 1.
157. L. Lippman & S. Meyers, Community Organization of Mental Health Services for the Mentally Retarded *in* Mental Health Services for the Mentally Retarded 235 (E. Katz ed. 1972).
158. See ch. 11, Rights and Entitlements in the Community.
159. See opinion of Justice Cardozo in Schloendorff v. Society of N.Y. Hosp., 211 N.Y. 125, 105 N.E. 92, 93 (1914). "Every human being of adult years and sound mind has a right to determine what shall be done with his own body; and a surgeon who performs an operation without his patient's consent commits an assault, for which he is liable in damages."
160. Canterbury v. Spence, 464 F.2d 772 (D.C. Cir. 1972), and Cobbs v. Grant, 502 P.3d 1 (Cal. 1972).
161. See ch. 5, Rights of Institutionalized Persons, § X V D 2, Informed Consent, for an extensive discussion of the elements necessary for an informed consent. See also ch. 8, Decision-making Rights over Persons and Property, for additional discussion on informed consent.

It is only since the late 1970s that the argument has been made that the mentally disabled should have a similar right to make an informed decision, which could result in their rejecting treatment and/or habilitation.[162] Proponents of this position acknowledge that the exercise of this right may result in an individual's refusing treatment that would be beneficial to him, but they find this risk outweighed by the value of giving mentally disabled persons free choice.[163] They point out that the mentally disabled cannot automatically be presumed to be incompetent[164] and that some treatment or habilitation methods are harmful, exposing the clients to lasting adverse consequences.[165]

VI. THE RIGHT TO REFUSE TREATMENT

The recently evolving notion that an institutionalized mentally disabled person has a right to refuse treatment is perhaps the most divisive issue confronting the mental health field in the 1980s. It pits the medical and legal professions against each other in a way that accentuates their differing orientations while it fails to address the larger problems of the quality of care provided in the institutions. For the health care provider the medical best interests standard guides his decisions, with the goal being to maximize life and promote health.[166] The attorney, on the other hand, is responsible for advocating what his competent client desires, even if what he desires may not appear to be in his "best medical interests." If the client is incompetent, the attorney must try to ascertain what his client would have desired had he been competent, and he then must advocate that position. This obligation is complicated by the fact that in some cases the line between competency and incompetency is an unclear one with the client appearing competent to decide some issues but not others.

Assertion of a right of the mentally ill or mentally retarded to refuse treatment is complicated by the fact of their mental disability. In contrast to the assumption of competency governing the medical patient's participation in treatment decisions, an assumption of incompetency in part has dictated the treatment received by the institutionalized mentally disabled, who have been thought to have no right to engage in decisions relating to their care once they were institutionalized. Until recently it was not even questioned that the institution should decide care without consulting either the disabled or his family. Even the passage in the 1970s of the laws stating that the mentally disabled were to be considered competent unless declared otherwise in a separate proceeding[167] did not change institutional practices, since the disabled were considered clinically—albeit not legally—incompetent and accordingly could have no say in their treatment. The cases challenging a patient's right to refuse medication best illustrate the arguments set forth to establish a right to refuse treatment generally.

A. The Right to Refuse Medication

Since the introduction of psychotropic drugs in the 1950s, the treatment of institutionalized mentally ill persons has been revolutionized: today these medications constitute the primary treatment in facilities for the mentally ill.[168] Moreover, the tranquilizing effects of these medications have led to their extensive use in facilities for the mentally retarded,[169] as well as in juvenile detention facilities.[170]

Abuses of these medications in the institutional setting are well documented.[171] In a case in 1980, *Davis v. Hubbard*, the use of psychotropic drugs was described as follows:

> Psychotropic drugs are not only overprescribed; they are also freely prescribed. They are prescribed by both licensed and unlicensed physicians. Both licensed and unlicensed physicians regularly prescribe drugs for any patient in the institution without regard to whether he is personally assigned to the patient or whether he has even seen the patient. It is not unusual for attendants to recommend a certain dosage or increased dosage. Such recommendations are often accepted by the physician without having examined the patient. Further, when dealing with an especially disturbed patient, attendants can obtain additional medication by submitting appropriate forms to the pharmacy when there is no physician available. . . . Nonetheless, patients are generally not given the opportunity to refuse psychotropic drugs, although roughly 85% of the patients are capable of rationally deciding whether to consent to their use.[172]

162. See, e.g., Plotkin, *supra* note 38; Rhoden, *supra* note 30, Psychotropic Drugs, 15 Harv. C.R.-C.L.L. Rev. 363 (1980).

163. Brooks, *supra* note 30, at 192.

164. See ch. 5, Rights of Institutionalized Persons, § IV, The Right to Be Presumed Competent, and ch. 8, Decision-making Rights over Persons and Property, for an extensive discussion of the informed consent doctrine and its application to the mentally disabled.

165. See this chapter § II, Types of Treatment, for a description of side effects.

166. See Summary and Analysis, 6 MDLR 63 (1982).

167. See ch. 5, Rights of Institutionalized Persons, § IV, The Right to Be Presumed Competent, which discusses the change in laws on incompetency during the past decade. In almost every state the mentally disabled person is considered competent unless there is a separate hearing declaring him incompetent.

168. See this chapter § II, Types of Treatment, which discusses the uses of these medications.

169. Comment, The Forcible Medication of Involuntarily Committed Mental Patients with Antipsychotic Drugs—Rogers v. Okin, 15 Ga. L. Rev. 739 (1981) [hereinafter cited as Comment, The Forcible Medication].

170. See e.g., Morales v. Turman, 535 F.2d 864 (5th Cir. 1976), and Gary W. v. State of Louisiana, 437 F. Supp. 1209 (E.D. La. 1976).

171. See Rhoden, *supra* note 30.

172. 506 F. Supp. 915, 926-27 (N.D. Ohio (1980).

The institution portrayed above unfortunately merely exemplified the situation existing in many mental institutions during the 1970s. Questions have justifiably been raised as to whether these drugs were being used for control or punishment rather than treatment. Frequently, abuses of psychotropic medications have seemed to be the way the facility coped with inadequate staffing. Concern about the common inappropriate use of psychotropic medications and the fact that these medications can produce serious side effects has led attorneys for the mentally disabled to seek judicial recognition of a right by the institutionalized disabled to refuse medication. This issue, more than any other in the mental health field, has brought mental health professionals and advocates for the mentally disabled into sharp conflict.

Proponents of this right have primarily relied on constitutional law claiming that an individual's bodily integrity and personal autonomy is invaded by the forced use of medication. They further emphasize that civilly committed persons are legally competent, unless specifically found not to be, and thus have the legal right to determine what medical and psychiatric treatments they will receive. Finally, they point to the potentially irreversible side effects that may come from psychotropic medications.

The arguments presented by mental health professionals against a right to refuse medication have been summarized by Brooks: (1) the cost of procedural implementation will be inappropriately high, (2) valuable personnel and resources will be diverted away from treatment toward due process procedures, and (3) the care and treatment of the mentally ill will be adversely affected.[173] Brooks points out that we do not have sufficient data to support these arguments.

The claims of proponents have relied primarily on the Fourteenth Amendment and on both state statutes and state common law. Because the right to refuse medication goes to the very core of institutional functions, some mental health professionals have objected vociferously.[174] Some have come forward with proposals that embody recognition of a limited right to refuse medication while at the same time providing for a corresponding ability of the institution to medicate the person over his objections in certain instances.[175]

173. Brooks, *supra* note 30, at 201-13.

174. See, e.g., Feldman, Why Can't We Decide What's Best for Our Mentally Ill Patient? 7 Legal Aspects of Medical Practice 28 (1979); Gutheil, Editorial, In Search of True Freedom: Drug Refusal, Involuntary Medication and "Rotting with Your Rights On," 137 Am. J. Psychiatry 327 (1980); Perr, Effect of the *Rennie* Decision on Private Hospitalization in New Jersey: Two Case Reports, 138 Am. J. Psychiatry 774 (1981).

175. See, e.g., Mills, The Rights of Involuntary Patients to Refuse Pharmacotherapy: What is Reasonable? 8 A.A.P.L. Bull. 313 (1980); Roth, A Commitment Law for Patients, Doctors and Lawyers, 136 Am. J. Psychiatry 1121 (1979).

1. Constitutional Basis

(a) Freedom of religion

The courts have recognized that practicing the tenets of one's religion can dictate a "best interest" antithetical to getting well, and they have generally honored such decisions.[176] Thus, when a person rejects medication in a nonemergency situation based on his religious principles, the courts will honor that rejection so long as the person is competent and the religion is a recognized one and not simply part of his delusional system.

The First Amendment's guarantee of freedom of religion served as the basis for the first suit regarding an institutionalized mentally ill person's right to refuse medication. In *Winters v. Miller*[177] the court was presented with the claim of a 59-year-old practicing Christian Scientist who upon admission to Bellevue Hospital refused to have her blood pressure taken because of her religious beliefs and objected to being given medication for the same reason. Her objections were ignored, and the medication was administered both orally and intramuscularly. In concluding that Winters had a cause of action the court emphasized that since she had not been declared incompetent her religious views had to be recognized.[178]

A more unique fact pattern was presented in *In re Boyd*,[179] in which the issue was whether the court could authorize a hospital to administer psychotropic drugs to a person who had been adjudicated *incompetent* but who had previously rejected any use of medication on religious grounds. The appellate court remanded the case to the trial court for a determination of what position the petitioner would have taken if she had been competent to give her views as a Christian Scientist. The court acknowledged the traditional rule against forcing a competent person to submit to treatment in the absence of a compelling state interest, and it noted the "traditional deference given the First Amendment right to the free exercise of religion."[180] The appellate court instructed that (1) when the individual's life was not at stake, as here, (2) when prior to incompetence the person objected absolutely to medical care on religious grounds, and (3) when the evidence demonstrated strong adherence to the tenets of that faith and there was no evidence of vacillation, the trial court should conclude that the individual would reject treatment.[181]

176. The courts will generally not force Jehovah's Witnesses to have blood transfusions even though not having them will result in their dying. See, e.g., *In re* Osborne, 294 A.2d 372 (D.C. 1972); *In re* Brooks' Estate, 32 Ill. 2d 361, 205 N.E.2d 435 (1965).

177. 446 F.2d 65 (2d Cir. 1971), *cert. denied*, 404 U.S. 985 (1971).

178. *Id.* at 68, 71.

179. 403 A.2d 744 (D.C. 1979).

180. *Id.* at 750.

181. *Id.* at 751.

This type of analysis was also used by another court to prevent the guardian of an incompetent mentally ill outpatient from forcing his ward to take medication over the ward's religious objection.[182]

(b) A liberty interest

The primary constitutional basis for recognizing the right of the mentally disabled to refuse medication is the individual's interest in liberty, as protected by the due process clause of the Fourtheenth Amendment. While the Supreme Court has recognized a number of liberty interests, the one of particular relevance here is the right to privacy, taking the form of freedom from bodily intrusion. The two leading cases in this area are *Rennie v. Klein*[183] and *Rogers v. Okin*.[184]

(1) Rennie v. Klein □□ In December 1977, John Rennie, an involuntarily committed mental patient at Ancora Psychiatric Hospital in New Jersey, filed suit in federal district court against the hospital and the state Department of Human Services, alleging that the hospital's practice of forcibly medicating him with psychotropic drugs was unconstitutional.[185] At one time a flight instructor and a pilot, he began to experience mental problems in 1971, which became serious when his twin brother died in a plane crash in 1973. From 1973 until the time the case was heard, Rennie was frequently hospitalized, having been diagnosed as a schizophrenic and also as a manic-depressive. While hospitalized he was given numerous psychotropic medications, which had noticeable adverse side effects.

In concluding that Rennie had a right to refuse unwanted medications, the trial court invoked "the emerging right of privacy" "broad enough to include the right to protect one's mental processes from governmental interference" and "to establish an individual's autonomy over his own body"; holding "that the right to refuse treatment extends to patients in non-emergent circumstances," the court stated that [o]nly where the government shows some strong countervailing interest can the right to refuse be qualified."[186] Three factors were to be considered in determining whether it was proper to override the patient's refusal: the state's police power, the state's parens patriae power, and the state's efforts at selecting the least restrictive alternative. The court noted that "[t]he fact that the patient is dangerous in free society may give the state power to confine, but standing alone it does not give the power to treat involuntarily."[187] The significance of the liberty interest at stake required at least a hearing before medication could be administered over the patient's objection in nonemergency situations.

The Court of Appeals for the Third Circuit, sitting en banc, heard the appeal in the *Rennie* case.[188] The court agreed with the lower court that giving medication over the patient's objection infringed the patient's liberty interest, but it rejected the district court's requirements relating to a hearing, the use of patient's advocates, and an independent psychiatrist to review the decision.[189] It held that the procedure New Jersey had established, requiring a series of informed consultations and reviews to determine from a medical standpoint whether administration of the drug is necessary as well as the least intrusive means of treating the individual, was sufficient to meet due process protections.[190]

Subsequently, the United States Supreme Court heard arguments in the case[191] but did not render an opinion, remanding the case for further consideration in light of its intervening decision in *Romeo v. Youngberg*.[192] The Third Circuit held that dangerous mentally ill patients who have been involuntarily committed may be administered antipsychotic drugs "whenever, in the exercise of professional judgment such an action is deemed necessary to prevent the patient from endangering himself or others."[193] The court then upheld New Jersey's regulatory scheme for reviewing a patient's refusal of medication.[194]

(2) Rogers v. Okin □□ *Rogers v. Okin* followed a pattern similar to that in *Rennie*: a broad recognition of the right to refuse treatment by the district court,[195] a narrowing of the decision by the Court of Appeals,[196] and a remand by the United States Supreme Court.[197] *Rogers* began in 1975 as a class action suit on behalf of

182. Guardianship of Roe, 421 N.E.2d 40 (Mass. 1981).

183. 462 F. Supp. 1131 (D.N.J. 1978), *remanded,* and 476 F.Supp. 1294 (D.N.J. 1979), *vacated and remanded,* 653 F.2d 836 (3d Cir. 1981), *vacated and remanded,* 458 U.S. 1119 (1982), 720 F.2d 266 (3d Cir. 1983). The 1983 Third Circuit decision is the final holding in this case and it recognizes the right of a patient to refuse medication and accepts New Jersey's procedures for overriding the patient's refusal.

184. 478 F. Supp. 1342 (D. Mass.1979), *aff'd in part, rev'd in part,* Rogers v. Okin, 634 F.2d 650 (1st Cir. 1980), *vacated and remanded sub nom.* Mills v. Rogers, 457 U.S. 291 (1982), Rogers v. Commissioner of Dep't of Mental Health, 458 N.E.2d 308 (Mass. 1983) (on remand) (the court upheld the right of a patient to refuse medication; this was the final decision in this case).

185. See 462 F.Supp. at 1135-36 for Rennie's history and at 1138-41 for his diagnosis, his treatment, and the side effects of the medication incuding dry mouth, blurred vision, and uncontrollable tremors.

186. *Id.* at 1144.

187. *Id.* at 1145.

188. 653 F.2d 836 (3d Cir. 1981).

189. *Id.* at 844, 849, 850.

190. *Id.* at 851.

191. 458 U.S. 1119 (1982).

192. 457 U.S. 307 (1982) (*Romeo* is discussed in this ch. in § IV, The Right to Habilitation, *supra*).

193. Rennie v. Klein, 720 F.2d 266, 269 (3d Cir. 1983).

194. *Id.* at 270. The full meaning of this opinion is difficult to assess, as there were three separate concurring opinions and one dissent. All the justices appeared, however, to accept that the judgment of the treating professional is presumed valid unless the evidence demonstrated a substantial departure from accepted practice.

195. 478 F. Supp. 1342 (D. Mass. 1979).

196. Rogers v. Okin, 634 F.2d 650 (1st Cir. 1980).

197. Mills v. Rogers, 457 U.S. 291 (1982).

patients at Boston State Hospital who claimed that their constitutional rights were being violated by their being given medication over their objections and by the use of seclusion in nonemergency situations. The district court held that competent patients had a constitutionally protected right to decide for themselves whether to submit to such treatments.[198] The court reasoned that involuntarily committed mental patients were considered competent under state law unless declared otherwise and that this, combined with their right of privacy, gave them the right to make decisions regarding their treatment. The court further held that when a patient was declared incompetent, his guardian would have the authority to make treatment decisions.[199] Refusal of treatment could be overridden by the state only in an emergency, which was narrowly defined as a "situation in which a failure to do so would result in a substantial likelihood of physical harm to that patient, other patients, or to staff members of the institution."[200]

On appeal, the Court of Appeals for the First Circuit recognized "an intuitively obvious proposition: a person has a constitutionally protected interest in being left free by the state to decide for himself whether to submit to the serious and potentially harmful medical treatment that is represented by the administration of antipsychotic drugs."[201] This proposition was said to flow from the due process clause of the Fourteenth Amendment, "as part of the penumbral right to privacy, bodily integrity, or personal security."[202] The essential question presented was whether, upon commitment to a state mental institution, this interest was overridden by legitimate state interests under its parens patriae and police powers. In analyzing the police power interest the court held:

> The state's purpose in administering drugs forcibly must be to further its police power interests, i.e., the decision must be the result of a determination that the need to prevent violence in a particular situation outweighs the possibility of harm to the medicated individual. Thus, medication cannot be forcibly administered solely for treatment purposes absent a finding of incompetency. . . . Additionally, reasonable alternatives to the administration of antipsychotics must be ruled out. . . . Finally, given the interests involved, the Fourteenth Amendment requires the imposition of procedures whereby the necessary determinations can be made with due process.[203]

In *Rogers, as in all other cases* in which the plaintiffs have attempted to establish a right to refuse medication, both sides agreed that the state could override the patient's objection to medication in an emergency. A major issue was how to define "emergency." The Court of Appeals regarded the district court's "likelihood of serious harm" standard as impractical.[204] It held that the varying interests of particular patients in refusing antipsychotic medication had to be balanced against the equally varying interests of patients—and the state—in preventing violence, with an ad hoc decision, to be made by the state physicians, following from this balancing. By its deference to state physicians to determine when the appropriate circumstances existed to override the patient's refusal, this ruling clearly broadened the definition of "emergency."

As regards the state's parens patriae power, the appellate court held that absent an emergency, a judicial determination of incompetency to make treatment decisions must be made before the state may rely on its parens patriae powers to forcibly medicate a patient. However, once this is accomplished, the state is not required to seek the guardian's approval for each decision to administer antipsychotic drugs. Instead, a general medication program must be worked out, based on what the individual himself would have been likely to consent to if he were competent.[205]

Subsequently, this case was argued before the United States Supreme Court. The Court, however, did not address the merits. It vacated the Court of Appeals decision[206] and remanded it for reconsideration in light of the Massachusetts Supreme Court's decision *Guardianship of Roe*,[207] in which the state court had recognized that an incompetent mentally ill patient may have a right to refuse medication based on a constitutional right to privacy and on the common law.[208] The Massachusetts Supreme Judicial Court held that in the absence of an emergency, any person who has not been adjudicated incompetent has a right to refuse antipsychotic medication. Incompetent persons have a similar right that has to be exercised through a substantial judgment treatment plan that is reviewed and approved by the court.[209]

(3) Significance of Rennie *and* Rogers □□ Until the Supreme Court addresses directly whether an involuntarily hospitalized mental patient has a right to

198. 478 F.Supp. at 1367.
199. *Id.* at 1354.
200. *Id.* at 1365.
201. Rogers v.Okin, 634 F.2d 650, 653 (1st Cir. 1980).
202. *Id.* at 653.
203. *Id.* at 656.
204. *Id.* at 658.
205. *Id.* at 659-61.
206. Mills v. Rogers, 457 U.S. 291 (1982).
207. 421 N.E.2d 40 (Mass. 1981).
208. *Id.* at 42.
209. Rogers v. Commissioner of Dep't of Mental Health, 458 N.E. 2d 308, 314-15 (Mass. 1983). The reasoning follows the logic of the *Guardianship of Roe* case.

refuse medication and the contours of such a right, the decisions reached by the lower courts on remand in *Rennie* and *Rogers* suggest how other courts may define such a right. While both cases recognized the right of a patient to refuse medication absent an emergency, each took a different approach to defining the extent of that right and determining who had the final decision-making authority when the right to refuse medication was to be exercised.

In *Rennie*, the Third Circuit very closely followed the Supreme Court's decision in *Youngberg v. Romeo*,[210] holding that whether a dangerously mentally ill person had a right to refuse medication "must be the product of the medical authorities' professional judgment, such judgment and the resulting decision to administer medication will be presumed valid unless it is a substantial departure from accepted professional judgment, practice or standards."[211] The opinion seemed to reject the "least intrusive means test" that the court had articulated earlier[212] and upheld the New Jersey three-step procedure for administering medications over a patient's refusal.[213] This decision sustained the requirement of mental health professionals that only they can and should determine when an emergency exists and when and whether it required forced intervention.

In contrast, the Massachusetts Supreme Judicial Court in *Rogers* gave the courts, rather than physicians, the ultimate authority to override a refusal of medication.[214] Unlike *Rennie*, which was based on constitutional principles, *Rogers* was based on the interpretation of the laws of Massachusetts.[215] It is also exceptional in its requirement that a guardian for an incompetent person seek court approval before overriding the ward's decision to refuse medication. Although *Rogers* makes the courts the ultimate decision makers, it defines "emergency" broadly,[216] thereby giving the physicians considerable leeway in giving medication in "emergency" situations.

It will take years before the impact of these decisions will be fully known. For patients' rights advocates satisfaction can be derived from the almost universal recognition of the right of the patient to refuse medication absent an emergency. They may even argue that since the Supreme Court in *Romeo* did recognize a limited constitutionally based right to treatment, there is now support for the position that involuntary institutionalization cannot lead to a patient losing his right to refuse treatment. Indeed, it could further be argued that the remanding of *Rogers* in light of *Guardianship of Roe*, which was a strong patients' rights decision, and the remanding of *Rennie* in light of *Romeo*, in which for the first time the Supreme Court recognized a limited right to treatment, lead to the conclusion that the Court believes the mentally disabled do have a liberty of interest in refusing medication and are entitled to some protection of that interest.

(4) Other decisions □□ In addition to *Rennie* and *Rogers*, a number of other decisions have addressed the right to refuse medication. For example, in *In re K.K.B.*[217] the Supreme Court of Oklahoma held that legally competent adults involuntarily committed to state mental hospitals had a right to refuse medication[218] based on a constitutional right of privacy. In *Davis v. Hubbard*[219] an Ohio court was presented with arguments similar to those in *Rennie* and *Rogers*, with the state relying on its police and parens patriae power to justify overriding the rights of the disabled to refuse medication. The court rejected the notion that these powers automatically permitted the state to medicate institutionalized mentally ill persons against their will.[220] It held that there cannot be "forced drugging of a patient for the purpose of 'doing good' *absent* a determination that the person is not capable of rationally deciding what is good for himself."[221] Based on a liberty interest analysis, the court said that the state's interest "must be sufficiently grave and imminent" to justify the "significant invasion of fundamental interests that the

210. 457 U.S. 307 (1982).

211. Rennie v. Klein, 720 F.2d 266, 269 (3d Cir. 1983), quoting Youngberg v. Romeo, 457 U.S. at 323.

212. The "least intrusive means" test had been expressed in Rennie v. Klein, 653 F.2d 836 (3d Cir. 1981). Since this decision was made up of four separate concurring opinions it is difficult to know the full status of the "least intrusive means" test. Of the nine members of the panel, four clearly accepted it, four clearly rejected it, and one judge was equivocal.

213. This provides for (1) the physician's informing the patient of his condition and discussing and exploring the risks and benefits of the treatment and alternative treatments; (2) review by the treatment team, with the patient present, if his condition permits, and (3) if he continues in his refusal, a review and decision by the medical director of the hospital. "Similarly the Second Circuit Court of Appeals has upheld a nonjudicial review process for persons in New York refusing antipsychotic medication before they are committed. The court accepted a procedure which required review by three levels of medical personnel other than the treating physician." 8 MPDLR 86-87 (1984), reporting Project Release v. Prevost, 722 F.2d 960 (2d Cir. 1983).

214. 458 N.E.2d 308 (Mass. 1983).

215. *Id.* at 312-15.

216. *Id.* at 321, applying the same definition of emergency as that for administering medication over the person's objection. "Emergency" exists when "there is the occurrence or serious threat of extreme violence, personal injury, or attempted suicide."

217. 609 P.2d 747 (Okla. 1980).

218. *Id.* at 751.

219. 506 F. Supp. 915 (N.D. Ohio 1980).

220. *Id.* at 935. See also Jamison v. Farabee, No. C 780445WHO, 7 MDLR 436 (N.D. Cal. Apr. 26, 1983), in which a consent decree was entered guaranteeing patients at Napa State Hospital in California substantial rights to refuse medication. Their refusal could be overridden by the staff only in an emergency or in the event that the patient was substantially deteriorating. An elaborate procedure was adopted to assure protection of the rights of the patient.

221. 506 F. Supp. at 936 (emphasis in original).

forced use of psychotropic drugs represents."[222] The court then gave a very narrow standard for when the state could override a patient's refusal:

> As a constitutional minimum, . . . the state must have at least probable cause to believe that the patient is *presently* violent or self-destructive, and in such condition presents a present danger to himself, other patients or the institution's staff before it may disregard the patient's interests in refusing treatment.[223]

The most recent case to recognize the right of involuntary patients to refuse medication came as a result of a consent decree in *Jamison v. Farabee*[224] after five years of litigation. In *Jamison* the state of California agreed to recognize that involuntary committed patients at Napa State Hospital had a substantial right to refuse medication but held that this right was qualified and could be overridden in an emergency or when the patient was "substantially deteriorating." The decree established precise procedures to be followed in overriding the patient's refusal of medication. In addition a protocol was developed for selecting independent reviewers[225] as well as incorporating into the consent decree the general prescribing policies of the medical staff.[226] This type of approach is likely to serve as a model for other states attempting to define the limits of the mentally disabled person's right to refuse medication.

There is only one recent case in which a court rejected the argument that the plaintiffs had a right to refuse medication. In *A.E. and R.R. v. Mitchell*,[227] the court held that involuntarily committed patients could not make this decision, since by virtue of the Utah commitment statute they were considered incompetent to make any treatment decisions. The case is exceptional in part because of the commitment statute used in Utah, which requires a finding that the person lacks the ability to engage in rational decision making regarding the acceptance of mental treatment, is replicated in only a small minority of states. The view in most states is that a finding of mental illness or involuntary hospitalization does not mean that the person is incompetent to make decisions, including decisions relating to treatment of his mental illness.

(c) Freedom of thought

The argument that forced medication of the mentally disabled over their objection violates a First Amendment right to freedom of thought has been made in a number of cases.[228] The district court in *Rogers v. Okin*[229] accepted this contention, stating:

> Whatever powers the Constitution has granted our government, involuntary mind control is not one of them, absent extraordinary circumstances. The fact that mind control takes place in a mental institution in the form of medically sound treatment of mental disease is not, itself, an extraordinary circumstance warranting an unsanctioned intrusion on the integrity of a human being.[230]

The *Rogers* court stands alone, thus far, in protecting freedom of the patient's thinking processes based on a First Amendment right. Other courts have recognized the importance of being able to think as one desires, even if the individual's thoughts are disordered, but have founded this on a liberty interest protected by the Fourteenth Amendment.[231] For example, in *Davis v. Hubbard*[232] the court said:

> [W]e need not rest the protection of a person's interest in being free to use his mind as he so desires on the First Amendment. It is enough to observe that "the power to control men's minds" is wholly inconsistent not only with "the philosophy of the first amendment but with virtually any concept of liberty."[233]

The pure mental autonomy argument is that disabled persons should be permitted to think psychotic thoughts. As one commentator has described the argument, it "asserts that any intent forcibly to change a patient's ideas on the grounds that they are 'disordered' or his perceptions on the grounds that they are 'deluded' violates his first amendment right to generate disordered and deluded thoughts."[234] The broader argument would be that the imprecise nature of psychiatry should not be permitted to override an individual's constitutional interests. The courts have been reluctant to recognize such a First Amendment right because this would trigger a strict scrutiny test of the actions of the state, forcing it to show a compelling need to justify any intervention made in the lives of mentally

222. *Id.*

223. *Id.* at 935 (emphasis in original).

224. No. C789445WHO, 7 MDLR 436 (N.D. Cal. Apr. 26, 1983).

225. Exhibit B Protocol for Selection of Independent Reviewers is part of the consent decree and can be obtained from the Legal Resource Center of the *Mental and Physical Disability Law Reporter*.

226. Exhibit C is part of the consent decree and can be obtained from the Legal Resource Center, *supra* note 225.

227. No. C78-466, 5 MDLR 154 (D. Utah June 16, 1980).

228. See, e.g., Rogers v. Okin, 478 F. Supp. 1342 (D. Mass. 1979); Rennie v. Klein, 462 F. Supp. 1131 (D.N.J. 1978); Davis v. Hubbard, 506 F. Supp. 915 (N.D. Ohio 1980).

229. 478 F. Supp. 1342 (D. Mass. 1979).

230. *Id.* at 1367.

231. See, e.g., Rennie v. Klein, 462 F. Supp. 1131, 1143-44 (D.N.J. 1978); Davis v. Hubbard, 506 F. Supp. 915, 933 (N.D. Ohio 1980); also Rogers v. Okin, in which the Third Circuit declined to address the First Amendment argument, 634 F.2d at 654 n.2.

232. 506 F. Supp. 915 (N.D. Ohio 1980).

233. *Id.* at 933, quoting in part from the United States Supreme Court's decision in Stanley v. Georgia, 394 U.S. 557, 565-66 (1964).

234. Comment, Madness and Medicine: The Forcible Administration of Psychotropic Drugs, 1980 Wis. L. Rev. 497, 513-14 (1980).

disabled persons.[235] "[If] recognized, the first amendment claim should stand as the most significant barrier protecting involuntary mental patients against state imposition of mind-altering drugs."[236]

(d) The Eighth Amendment

Involuntary institutionalization in a mental hospital has been compared to imprisonment: in both settings the person loses his liberty, is separated from family and friends, is stigmatized by the fact of institutionalization, and must rely on the state for satisfaction of all his basic needs.[237] Some legal commentators have suggested that the forced administration of medication over the patient's objection violates the cruel and unusual punishment clause of the Eighth Amendment.[238] In order for the courts to recognize an Eighth Amendment violation in the context of a mental institution, it would have to be shown that the medication was being used not for treatment but for punishment.[239] Thus far, this argument has not succeeded in right to refuse medication cases, although it has been in a case challenging behavior modification principles.[240]

2. *Statutory Basis*

Increased sensitivity to the rights of the mentally disabled, and specific concerns about the use of medication, have led 20 states to enact provisions relating to the administration of medication in facilities for the mentally disabled.[241] A small number of states specifically recognize the right of voluntary patients to refuse medication.[242] A number of states provide generally that there shall be no excessive or unnecessary use of medication,[243] or that it shall not be used for punishment purposes. Even in some of the states that specifically grant the patient the right to refuse medication, the refusal can be overridden if necessary to prevent injury.[244]

There are only a few cases in which courts have addressed refusals to accept medication under these statutes. One Colorado court based the patient's right to refuse medication, absent a finding of incompetency or an emergency, on general protections accorded in the state's law that protected the rights of the mentally disabled rather than on a specific statute granting a right to refuse medication.[245] The few other decisions have been concerned with procedural issues rather than the substance of the state statutes.[246]

3. *The Common Law*

In light of the Supreme Court's dispositions in *Romeo v. Youngberg*,[247] *Mills v. Rogers*,[248] and *Rennie v. Klein*,[249] the constitutional status of a right of the mentally disabled to refuse medication is unclear. Combined with the relative lack of statutory law on this issue, this makes the common law arguments supporting this right very significant. The common law tort of battery and one of its remote descendants—the doctrine of informed consent—have provided the nonmentally ill with a right to bodily autonomy which prohibits unwanted medical or surgical procedures except under very limited circumstances.[250] These common law concepts are now being recognized as affording the mentally disabled the same protection as is enjoyed by those whose competency is not in doubt.

Were mentally disabled individuals unable to engage in rational decision making, these common law precedents would be be much less amenable to application to the mental health setting. While in the past the mentally disabled were presumed to be incompetent, the modern law is more refined with the majority of states specifically providing by statute that a finding of need for involuntary hospitalization does not constitute a finding of incompetency.[251] The law in this respect is supported

235. See, e.g., West Virginia State Bd. of Educ. v. Barnette, 319 U.S. 624, 639 (1943); see also discussion in Comment, The Forcible Medication, *supra* note 169, Rhoden, *supra* note 30, at 388-96, for a discussion of the right to privacy.

236. See Comment, The Forcible Medication, *supra* note 169, at 760.

237. Symonds, *supra* note 9, at 723, which provides an excellent discussion of the Eighth Amendment issues. This article also concisely presents the types of medications used for mental patients and their side effects.

238. See, e.g., *id.*; Plotkin, *supra* note 38, at 494.

239. See Ingraham v. Wright, 430 U.S. 651, 664 (1977). in which the Supreme Court held that the Eighth Amendment was "designed to protect those convicted of crimes." However, in a footnote the court implied that it was reserving judgment on whether the amendment applied to mental institutions (at 666 n.37).

240. Knecht v. Gillman, 488 F.2d 1136 (8th Cir. 1973).

241. See table 6.2, cols. 12-15.

242. See table 6.2, col. 13, e.g., Arizona, Connecticut, Indiana, New Hampshire, New Jersey, and West Virginia. See also Callahan & Longmire, Psychiatric Patients' Right to Refuse Psychotropic Medication: A National Survey, 7 MDLR 494 (1983), for a very thorough review of the patient's rights in this area. The study found that in all the states and the District of Columbia, there was no right to refuse medication in 6 jurisdictions and that 45 recognized a qualified right for all patients.

243. See table 6.2, col. 14, e.g., Arkansas, California, Colorado, Montana, New Jersey, New Mexico, North Carolina, North Dakota, Ohio, and Wisconsin.

244. See table 6.2, col. 14, e.g., Illinois, Michigan, and Nebraska.

245. Goedecke v. State Dep't of Institutions, 603 P.2d 123 (Colo. 1979).

246. People v. Freeman, 636 P.2d 1334 (Colo. 1981), which modified an order relating to the type of medication used; and Wolfe v. Maricopa County Gen. Hosp., 619 P.3d 1041 (Ariz. 1980), which held that if a person had been committed for 25 days for treatment he could not be held longer than 25 days even though he had refused medication, without another petition for hospitalization.

247. 457 U.S. 307 (1982).

248. 457 U.S. 291 (1982).

249. 458 U.S. 1119 (1982).

250. See in this chapter § V, Informed Consent, *supra*. See also A Common Law Remedy for Forcible Medication of the Institutionalized Mentally Ill, 82 Colum. L. Rev. 1720 (1982), for a very good discussion of this area [hereinafter cited as A Common Law Remedy].

251. See ch. 5, Rights of Institutionalized Persons, § IV, The Right to Be Presumed Competent.

by the psychiatric literature pointing out that there is no necessary relationship between hospitalization and the ability to make rational decisions.[252] The sticking point is that in practice most staff in mental institutions continue to view the mentally disabled as clinically, even if not legally, incompetent. As one article has pointed out, "[i]n psychiatry the entire edifice of involuntary treatment is erected on the supposed incompetency of some people to voluntarily seek and consent to needed treatment."[253] Given such a perspective, institutional staff will remain likely to administer medication notwithstanding their charges' rejection of it.

Proponents of using common law doctrine as a basis for recognizing, and vindicating, the right of the mentally disabled to refuse medication argue that the disabled, if they are competent, should have the same protections as do other persons seeking medical care.[254] Just as courts rendering common law decisions reject compelling competent adults to involuntarily undergo medical or surgical procedures—at least if their refusal does not imminently threaten the health of others who are themselves helpless[255] so too, it is contended, the mentally disabled should be free from forced treatment. Even the fact that an individual's refusal of treatment may seem unwise and counter to his own interests should not justify overriding his decision.[256] This is so, it is argued, even for mentally disabled individuals who are the only ones who can balance whether the benefits of medication in alleviating the symptoms of their illness outweigh the adverse effects and permanent damage that may result.

Other counter arguments rely on the state's parens patriae and police powers. The latter speaks especially to emergency situations where an individual poses a danger to himself or others. Whatever the reach of this power, there is no reason why in emergencies every attempt should not be made to treat the person in the least restrictive manner. In some cases this may mean physically, rather than chemically, restraining him; in others, perhaps, just the opposite.

When the state undertakes to use its parens patriae powers, it is acting to protect the person and the interests of the person who cannot care for himself. If the person is mentally disabled and has been declared legally incompetent, it is presumably the guardian who may then consent to treatment. In the case of *Guardianship of Roe*,[257] however, the Massachusetts Supreme Court held that even a declaration of incompetency and a decision by the guardian to consent to medication were not sufficient to justify administering medication over the ward's refusal. The trial court was instructed to consider the incompetent's refusal and order it overridden only on the finding that if the ward had been competent, he would have agreed to the treatment.[258] The *Roe* court further concluded that absent an emergency it would not force medication on an incompetent outpatient who before having been declared incompetent had refused medication and who, subsequent to the declaration of incompetency, continued in that refusal. The court, quoting a law review analysis, said:

> "While psychotropic drugs may play a significant role in the treatment of psychiatric disorders, there is no wisdom in permitting their continued indiscriminate use upon unconsenting persons or upon persons who are uninformed as to their potential consequences."[259]

As for the outpatient who refuses medication and poses a danger to others, he faces the choice—the *Roe* court opined—between being civilly committed or taking medication that will alleviate the symptoms of his illness.[260]

Roe is thus far the only decision recognizing that an incompetent mentally ill person may have a right to refuse medication without having a religious basis for that refusal. *Roe* is unique in the review process it establishes because it requires the court, rather than the guardian, to make the substituted decision about refusal of medication. Other decisions have honored a person's medication refusal based on the common law but have suggested that this refusal could be overridden if the person were declared incompetent.[261]

Much will be gained if the right to refuse treatment is seen in its proper context. It was noted in *Rogers v. Okin* that during the course of the litigation only 12 patients out of 1,000 actually refused medication.[262] Moreover, Appelbaum and Gutheil, perhaps the strongest critics of

252. L.R. Tancredi & A.E. Slaby, Ethical Policy in Mental Health Care: The Goals of Psychiatric Intervention 104 (1977).

253. Roth, Meisel, & Lidz, Tests of Competency to Consent to Treatment, 134 Am. J. Psychiatry 279 (1977).

254. See A Common Law Remedy, *supra* note 250, at 1746; see also Plotkin, *supra* note 38, at 485-90.

255. The courts have required persons to undergo medical treatment even when against their religious beliefs if they would die with minor children, see Raleigh Fitkin-Paul Morgan Memorial Hosp. v. Anderson, 201 A.2d 537 (N.J. 1964), *cert. denied,* 377 U.S. 985 (1964); *In re* President & Directors of Georgetown College, Inc., 331 F.2d 1000 (D.C. Cir.), *cert. denied,* 377 U.S. 978 (1964).

256. See, e.g., Lane v. Candura, 376 N.E.2d 1232 (Mass. 1978).

257. 421 N.E.2d 40 (Mass. 1981).

258. *Id.* at 56-59.

259. *Id.* at 53, quoting Plotkin, *supra* note 38, at 478-79.

260. *Id.* at 61.

261. See, e.g., Goedecke v. State Dep't of Institutions, 603 P.2d 123 (Colo. 1979); see also *In re* K.K.B., 609 P.2d 747 (Okla. 1980); see also Parry, Summary and Analysis of Right to Refuse Psychotropic Medication, 8 MPDLR 82-85 (1984), for most recent update on refusal of medication cases.

262. Rogers v. Okin, 478 F. Supp. 1342, 1369 (D. Mass. 1979).

the right to refuse, have found that virtually all refusers subsequently accept medication without having been harmed by their previous refusal.[263] Perhaps the issue has generated more heat than is deserved. As Mark Mills, former Commissioner of Mental Health in Massachusetts, has stated:

> It is important to remind oneself that much of what is wrong with mental health care has little to do with the right to refuse treatment. Inequities in funding, inadequacies in training, misallocation of resources, and deficiencies in knowledge (about mental illness) all make present treatment less than ideal.[264]

B. Right to Refuse ECT

Treatment in the form of electroconvulsive therapy (ECT) evokes for the general public an image of a person with electrodes attached to his head, who is shocked into a zombie-like state. This image comes in part from Ken Kesey's book, *One Flew over the Cuckoo's Nest*, later made into a movie, in which the hero was placed in a mental hospital for criminal behavior and then given ECT when he refused to conform to the hospital regimen.[265] It is also the result of nonfictional exposes in the 1950s and early 1960s of the occasional use of ECT in state mental hospitals under inappropriate circumstances or for inappropriate purposes. In fact, ECT today is recognized in the psychiatric community as a valid treatment that is quite appropriate for certain conditions, most notably depression.[266] Improved techniques for administering ECT mean that it is no longer accompanied by unpleasant side effects, and some would argue that it is less intrusive and less likely to cause harm than psychotropic medications.[267]

Because memories of its earlier procedures and abuses linger on, it is not uncommon to find state regulation of ECT.[268] Most such statutes provide that ECT can be administered if an informed consent is obtained from the patient.[269] Many provisions specifically give the patient a right to refuse its use.[270]

Most of the past furor over ECT has subsided. Since the treatment is used infrequently, as compared with psychotropic medication, it is unlikely that there will be much further case law development in this area. The same constitutional and common law arguments set forth to establish the right of the mentally disabled to refuse medication can also be used to justify a recognition of the right of the disabled to refuse ECT. As of now there are only a few cases addressing the regulation of ECT, *Wyatt v. Stickney* being one of the first decisions to require an informed consent for the procedure.[271] Pursuant to the original *Wyatt* order, more stringent requirements were established for ECT, including prior approval by a committee composed of mental health professionals and lay people.[272] In a different case in which ECT was administered to a minor without parental consent, the court rejected the parents' claim that this constituted cruel and unusual punishment, since ECT had been given specifically for treatment purposes after other treatments tried had failed.[273] The court did declare, however, that thereafter ECT could not be administered without the consent of the parents unless a court ordered it.[274] Another case that addressed the issue of involuntary administration of ECT held that it could not be given without the patient's consent, absent an emergency or a declaration of incompetency.[275] Finally, in a challenge to a California law regulating the use of ECT from the other side, where the claim was that the regulations were too restrictive, the court upheld most of the regulations, reasoning that the state had a legitimate interest in seeing that these procedures "are performed under circumstances insuring maximum safety for the patient."[276]

C. Right to Refuse Psychosurgery

Psychosurgery remains an experimental and hazardous procedure presenting many risks and only unclear benefits.[277] Lobotomy, the most common type of psychosurgery associated with state mental institutions, has not been used since the 1950s. Past abuses and in particular an experiment proposed in the early 1970s in Michigan, the *Kaimowitz* case, to use psychosurgery on certain institutionalized disabled persons resulted in many states passing laws protecting the mentally dis-

263. Appelbaum & Gutheil, Drug Refusal: A Study of Psychiatric Inpatients, 137 Am. J. Psychiatry 340 (1980).

264. Mills, *supra* note 175, at 315.

265. K. Kesey, One Flew over the Cuckoo's Nest: A Novel (1962).

266. A.P.A. Task Force on Electroconvulsive Therapy, *supra* note 40.

267. See, e.g., Tenenbaum, *supra* note 42, at 153–54 (1983).

268. See table 6.2, esp. col.3.

269. See table 6.2, cols. 3 & 5. See also Tenenbaum, *supra* note 42, at 151. Note the laws of California, Connecticut, Delaware, Illinois, Louisiana, Mississippi, North Carolina, North Dakota, New Jersey, New York, Oregon, South Dakota, and Wisconsin.

270. See table 6.2, cols. 5 & 3. See also Tenenbaum, *supra* note 42, at 151. Note the laws of Alaska, Arkansas, Iowa, Kentucky, Massachusetts, and South Carolina. In November 1982, Berkeley, California, approved a referendum making the use of ECT a misdemeanor, thus effectively making it unlikely that ECT would be used since it carried criminal sanction and would be considered negligence per se if a civil suit were brought. See Summary & Analysis, 6 MDLR 366 (1982).

271. 344 F. Supp. 373, 380 (M.D. Ala. 1972).

272. Wyatt v. Hardin, No. 3195-N, 1 MDLR 55 (M.D. Ala. Feb. 28, 1975, *modified* July 1, 1975).

273. Price v. Sheppard, 239 N.W.2d 905 (Minn. 1976).

274. *Id.* at 913.

275. Gundy v. Pauley, No. 80-CA-1737-MR, 5 MDLR 321 (Ky. Ct. App. Aug. 21, 1981).

276. Aden v. Younger, 57 Cal. 3d 662, 678 (1976).

277. See in this chapter § II D, Psychosurgery, *supra*.

abled from such procedures.[278] There is today a great deal more commentary than actual cases of psychosurgery.[279]

Although most of the states have enacted laws restricting the use of psychosurgery,[280] these restrictions may be phrased in terms of "brain surgery," "lobotomy," or other "experimental" and "hazardous" procedures. Most of the laws provide that psychosurgery may not be performed without the patient's informed consent, thereby foreclosing at least in this context the debate on whether the mentally disabled individual can refuse treatment. Other states require that if the person is incompetent, psychosurgery may be performed only upon a court order.[281] A few provide for a detailed internal review procedure. Oregon probably has the most protective scheme, requiring approval by a review board before psychosurgery can be performed.[282]

The most important decision on the subject is *Kaimowitz v. Department of Mental Health*,[283] which involved proposed experimental surgery on the amygadloid portion of the limbic system of the brain for the purpose of determining if a diminution of aggression could be achieved thereby. The procedure was approved by two review committees, but only one patient, "John Doe," was found to meet the criteria for the research program. Doe had been committed 17 years earlier as a result of murdering a student nurse at a state mental institution while he was a patient there. The Court stated: "Psychosurgery should never be undertaken upon involuntarily committed populations, when there is a high-risk low-benefits ratio as demonstrated in this case. This is because of the impossibility of obtaining fully informed consent from such populations."[284] The court went on to explain that involuntarily detained mental patients could not give a voluntary informed consent for experimental psychosurgery in part because institutionalization militated against it, inasmuch as release or other benefits might be contingent on their cooperation. The court also held that neither a guardian nor a parent could give the requisite substitute consent.[285]

Only a few other courts have addressed questions regarding psychosurgery. In *Wyatt v. Stickney* the original court order required an informed consent as a precondition to psychosurgery.[286] Subsequent modification of that order totally prohibited psychosurgery, lobotomy, or other unusual, hazardous or intrusive surgical procedures thereby paralleling the result in *Kaimowitz*.[287] In *Aden v. Younger*,[288] a California court upheld the stringent review procedures on psychosurgery adopted by the California legislature. The rare use of psychosurgery makes it unlikely that there will be further case law developments.

D. Right Not to Participate in Behavior Modification Programs

As mentioned earlier, behavior modification consists of a series of techniques employed to alter specific behavior, and the techniques take various forms[289] and may be used in a variety of settings, including mental institutions, prisons, and classrooms. Some of them, such as aversive conditioning, raise serious questions of appropriateness and effectiveness.[290]

Several lawsuits have challenged the use of behavior

278. See table 6.2, esp. col. 3. In addition, the case of Kaimowitz v. Department of Mental Health, No. 73-19434-AW, 1 MDLR 147 (Cir. Ct. Wayne County, Mich. July 10, 1973), sets out the facts that caused concern about the use of psychosurgery. This case is discussed in more detail in notes 283-85 and accompanying text *infra*.

279. See, e.g., Comment, Psychosurgery and the Involuntarily Confined, 24 Vill. L. Rev. 949 (1979); Medical Experimentation: A Symposium on Behavior Control, 13 Duq. L. Rev. 673 (1973); Plamondon, Psychosurgery: The Rights of Patients, 23 Loy. L. Rev. 1007 (1977); Zakowski, Psychosurgery, J. Legal Med., Apr. 1976, at 26.

280. See table 6.2, esp. col. 3.

281. See table 6.2, cols. 3 & 7, e.g., California, Connecticut, Delaware, Missouri, Montana, North Carolina, Ohio, South Dakota, Vermont, and Wisconsin.

282. Or. Rev. Stat. § 426.385(2) (1983).

283. No. 73-19434-AW, 1 MDLR 147 (Cir. Ct. Wayne County, Mich. July 10, 1973. Although not published in official legal reporters, the *Kaimowitz* case is widely known in both the mental health and the prison rights areas. It is *reported in part in* The Mental Health Process 567 (F.W. Miller, R.O. Dawson, B.E.Dix, & R.I. Parnas eds. 1976) and *in* State Court Bars Experimental Brain Surgery, 2 Prison L. Rep. 433 (1973), and *reprinted in* A.D. Brooks, Law, Psychiatry, and the Mental Health System 902 (1974).

284. See The Mental Health Process, *supra* note 283, at 571. The discussion generated by the *Kaimowitz* case helped spur the creation of the National Commission for the Protection of Human Subjects of Biomedical and Behavioral Research, which recommended a ban on psychosurgery on prisoners, children, and certain mental patients. The Commission also set forth stringent guidelines for the use of psychosurgery. These were to a large extent adopted as regulations by the U.S. Department of Health, Education, and Welfare. U.S. Dep't of Health, Education, & Welfare, Protection of Human Subjects: Use of Psychosurgery in Practice and Research: Report and Recommendations for Public Comment, 42 Fed. Reg. 26,318 (May 23, 1977).

285. *Id.* at 573-75.

286. 344 F. Supp. 373, 380 (M.D. Ala. 1972).

287. Wyatt v. Hardin, No. 3195-N, 1 MDLR 55 (M.D. Ala. Feb. 28, 1975 *modified* July 1, 1975).

288. 57 Cal. 3d 662 (1976).

289. See in this chapter § II F, Behavior Modification, *supra* for a more extensive discussion.

290. Restraints and seclusion, for example, sometimes are used for behavior modification purposes. Since these measures are discussed extensively in chapter 5, Rights of Institutionalized Persons, this discussion will not include the regulation of restraints and seclusion. See, e.g., Burns, Behavior Modification as a Punishment, 22 Am. J. Juris. 19 (1977); Friedman, Legal Regulation of Applied Behavior Anaysis in Mental Institutions and Prisons, 17 Ariz. L. Rev. 39 (1975); Selva, Treatment as Punishment, 6 New Eng. J. Prison L. 265 (1980); Shapiro, Legislating the Control of Behavior Control: Autonomy and the Coercive Use of Organic Therapies, 47 S. Cal. L. Rev. 237 (1974); Viewpoints on Behavioral Issues in Closed Institutions, 17 Ariz. L. Rev. (1975).

modification techniques within prisons and mental institutions,[291] most commonly the aversive conditioning variety, in which an unpleasant experience or sensation is imposed each time the individual exhibits inappropriate behavior. Particular targets of the litigation have been the administration of electrical shocks and drugs that cause nausea and vomiting. One of the issues has been whether the objective is indeed behavior modification or rather punishment that is disproportionate to the violation of the rules. *Knecht v. Gillman*[292] provides a graphic example:

> The drug [apomorphine] was administered by intramuscular injection by a nurse after an inmate had violated the behavior protocol established for him by the staff. Dr. Loeffelholz testified that the drug could be injected for such pieces of behavior as not getting up, for giving cigarette against orders, for talking, for swearing, or for lying. Other inmates or members of the staff would report on these violations of the protocol and the injection would be given by the nurse without the nurse or any doctor having personally observed the violation and without specific authorization of the doctor. . . . The inmate was taken to a room near the nurse's station which contained only a water closet and there given the injection. He was then exercised and within about fifteen minutes he began vomiting. The vomiting lasted from fifteen minutes to an hour.[293]

The Court of Appeals for the Eighth Circuit held that this constituted cruel and unusual punishment in violation of the Eighth Amendment, and it prohibited the use of apomorphine for treatment except under very specific circumstances, which included allowing the inmate to withdraw consent to its use at any time.[294]

Since most behavior modification techniques do not seem offensive or abusive, there is relatively little regulation of their use. A few states regulate aversive techniques,[295] while more numerous states have laws regulating restraint and seclusion.[296] With the exception of a few challenges to the use of token economies,[297] there has been almost no litigation in this area over the last few years.

VII. CONCLUSION

The rights to treatment and habilitation are now generally recognized, although there remain sharp disagreements over their precise content. Translating these legal rights into meaningful programs for the mentally disabled is a task for the coming decade. Institutionalization of the disabled without corresponding programs that seek to alleviate their disability should no longer be tolerated. The clinical knowledge to provide meaningful treatment and habilitation is much more extensive today than in decades past, but what remains lacking is a full commitment of resources to accomplish these tasks. Additionally, there needs to be a frank acknowledgement that these tasks cannot always, or even generally, be accomplished in the large state institutions that have traditionally housed the mentally disabled. For many mentally disabled persons noninstitutional care and treatment is more appropriate and beneficial.

It is likely that during the coming decade there will be a growing recognition of at least a limited right to refuse treatment, based on the rights guaranteed to all citizens by the Constitution, the common law, and state statutes. An extension of the right to refuse treatment, specifically medication, will necessitate some hard choices, however. The assumption of full personal autonomy for persons whose decision-making competence is questionable may conflict with their right to treatment, particularly their right to be treated in the least restrictive setting. There will need to be a careful balancing between the right of the individual to choose and the right of the state to care and protect. The individual's right to choose may even conflict with his own best interest. A fair balance, however, should at least grant the individual the right to refuse treatment in those circumstances where his decision is knowing and rational.

291. See, e.g., Clonce v. Richardson, 379 F. Supp. 338 (W.D. Mo. 1974); Mackey v. Procunier, 477 F.2d 877 (9th Cir. 1973). Knecht v. Gillman, 488 F.2d 1135 (8th Cir. 1973).

292. 488 F.2d 1136 (8th Cir. 1973).

293. *Id.* at 1137.

294. *Id.* at 1140. See also Comment, Recent Developments in Behavior Modification, 60 Neb. L. Rev. 363 (1981); Plotkin, *supra* note 38; The Right Against Treatment: Behavior Modification and the Involuntarily Committed, 23 Cath. U.L. Rev. 774 (1974), for a discussion of the possibility of Eighth Amendment violations.

295. See, e.g., Kan. Stat. Ann. 59-2929 (6) (1976) and Ohio Rev. Code Ann. 5122.27 (Baldwin 1980).

296. See table 6.2, cols. 9-11.

297. See, e.g., Goodwin v. Shapiro, 545 F. Supp. 826 (D.N.J. 1982).

TABLE 6.1 TREATMENT RIGHTS AND REVIEW OF TREATMENT NEEDS

	TREATMENT RIGHTS			EXAMINATION OF PATIENT			REVIEW OF PATIENT RECORDS			
					Periodic					
STATE	*To Treatment in General* (1)	*Individualized Treatment Plan* (2)	*Least Restrictive Alternative fn. 1* (3)	*Upon Admission* (4)	Specified Frequency (5)	As Practicable (6)	*Frequency* (7)	*Treatment Plan Review* (8)	*Administrative Review for Discharge* (9)	*Report to Court* (10)
ALA. Code (1977 & Supp. 1982)							as often as ordered by judge, but at least every 90 days 22-52-12(b)			22-52-12(b)
ALAS. Stat. (1980 & Supp. 1982)		mentally ill 47.30.825(1) developmentally disabled habilitation plan 47.80.120				as often as consistent w/ good medical practice 47.30.220				
ARIZ. Rev. Stat. Ann. (1974 & Supp. 1982–83)	mentally ill (mentally disordered): physical & psychiatric care 36-511	mentally ill (mentally disordered): written treatment program plan based on individual needs 36-511(B)(1) developmentally disabled: written program plan 36-551.01(J) periodic review thereof 36-551.01(K)	developmentally disabled 36-551.07		each 90 days; full physical annually 36-511					
ARK. Stat. Ann. (1971 & Supp. 1981)	prompt medical care & treatment (mentally ill & mentally retarded) 59-1416(24)		offer of another modality of care (mentally ill & mentally retarded) 59-1416(22)	w/o undue delay 59-1407 59-1416(12)		at intervals thereafter 59-1416(12)				
CAL. Welf. & Inst. Code (West 1972 & Supp. 1983)	treatment services that promote potential independence 5325.1		5325.1	w/in 3 days 7251		from time to time 7251				
COLO. Rev. Stat. (1982)	medical treatment, recreation, training, & psychological & social services suited to needs (developmentally disabled) 27-10.5-111(2)	suited to individual needs (mentally ill) 27-10-116(1)(a) developmentally disabled 27-10.5-113(2)	mentally ill 27-10-116(1)(a)	w/in 6 mos. of admission (developmentally disabled only) 27-10.5-109		at least annually thereafter (developmentally disabled only) 27-10.5-109	w/in 6 mos. of admission & at least annually thereafter (developmentally disabled only) 27-10.5-109	developmentally disabled only 27-10.5-109		
CONN. Gen. Stat. Ann. (West 1975 & Supp. 1983–84)	humane & dignified treatment 17-206(c)	specialized treatment plan suited to disorder 17-206(c)						each facility develops own written policy 17-215(c)		monthly list of all involuntary patients, w/date & type of last review 17-178(g)
DEL. Code Ann. (1974 & Supp. 1982)	suited to patient's needs (mentally ill) *fn. 3* 16, §5161(a)(1) mentally retarded *fn. 4* 16, §5502	mentally ill 16, §5161(a)(2)(e)			at least every 6 mos. 16, §5131 physical examination annually 16, §5161(a)(2)		6 mos. after admission & every 6 mos. thereafter 16, §5012(b)			16, §5012(b)
D.C. Code Ann. (1981 & Supp. 1983)	medical & psychiatric care & treatment (mentally ill) 21-562 6-1961(a) habilitation program (mentally retarded) 6-1961(b)	individual habilitation plan (mentally retarded) 6-1964(a)	mentally retarded 6-1963		at least every 6 mos. 21-548	at written request of patient, attorney, guardian, or relative 21-546(a)		annually 6-1964		
FLA. Stat. Ann. (West 1973 & Supp. 1983)	medical, vocational, social, educational, & rehabilitative (mentally ill) *fn. 5* 394.459(4) treatment for mental & physical ailments & prevention of them (mentally retarded) 393.13(3)(f)	mentally ill 394.459(2)(e) individual habilitative program (mentally retarded) 393.13(3)(e)	mentally retarded 394.459(2)(b)	physical exam w/in 24 hrs. (mentally ill) 394.459 (2)(c)			review at least semiannually; revision annually (developmentally disabled) 393.065	habilitation plan for developmentally disabled 393.065		
GA. Code Ann. (1979 & Supp. 1982)	mentally ill: care & treatment suited to needs 88-502.4(a) mentally retarded: habilitation services not denied 88-2503.3 suited to needs 88-2503.4(a)	mentally ill: individualized service plan 88-501(w) mentally retarded: individualized program plan 88-2502(i)	mentally ill 88-502.4(a) mentally retarded 88-2503.4(a)	as soon as possible 88-502.4(e)			at regular intervals 88-506.6(a)	individual service plan reviewed & modified 88-506.6(a)		
HAWAII Rev. Stat. (1976 & Supp. 1982)		written 334E-2(7)		exam w/in 60 days of admission (mentally retarded) 333-30		periodic (mentally ill) 334-35(2)	periodic (mentally ill) 334-35(2)	mentally ill 334-35(2)		results of exam (mentally retarded) 333-30

TABLE 6.1 TREATMENT RIGHTS AND REVIEW OF TREATMENT NEEDS—*Continued*

	TREATMENT RIGHTS			EXAMINATION OF PATIENT			REVIEW OF PATIENT RECORDS			
					Periodic					
STATE	*To Treatment in General* (1)	*Individualized Treatment Plan* (2)	*Least Restrictive Alternative fn. 1* (3)	*Upon Admission* (4)	Specified Frequency (5)	As Practicable (6)	*Frequency* (7)	*Treatment Plan Review* (8)	*Administrative Review for Discharge* (9)	*Report to Court* (10)
IDAHO Code (1980 & Supp. 1983)		developmentally disabled 66-413	developmentally disabled 66-412(3)(b)	as soon as practicable 66-333	at end of first 90 days; every 120 days thereafter 66-337					exam results 66-337
ILL. Ann. Stat. (Smith-Hurd 1966 & Supp. 1983–84)	humane treatment 91½, §2-102	individual service plan 91½, §2-102(a)	91½, §2-102		developmentally disabled evaluated at least annually 91½, §4-310		not less than every 30 days 91½, §3-209 60-day intervals for voluntary patients 91½, §3-404 every 30 days (developmentally disabled) 91½, §4-309(c)	mentally ill 91½, §3-209, §3-404 habilitation plan (developmentally disabled) 91½, §4-309		treatment plan filed w/in 30 days of admission (mentally ill) 91½, §3-814 habilitation plan filed w/in 60 days (developmentally disabled) 91½, §4-612
IND. Code Ann. (Burns 1983)	humane care & protection 16-14-1.6-2(2)				review care & treatment at least annually 16-14-9.1-10(e)		review care & treatment at least annually 16-14-9.1-10(e)			review filed 16-14-9.1-10(e)
IOWA Code Ann. (West 1969 & Supp. 1983)	as indicated by sound medical practice 229.23			w/in 15 days 229.13			w/in 30 days of hospitalization & at 60-day intervals thereafter 229.15			229.15
KAN. Stat. Ann. (1976 & Supp. 1981)	humane treatment consistent w/accepted ethics & practice 59-2927						at end of each 90-day treatment period 59-2917a			summary of medical records 59-2917a
KY. Rev. Stat. Ann. (Michie 1982)		mentally ill 202A.196 mentally retarded 202B.050	202B.060(12)	review committee 202A.196(1)						
LA. Rev. Stat. Ann. (West 1975 & Supp. 1983)	treatment & habilitative services (mentally retarded) 28:391(A)	mentally ill 28:171(Q) mentally retarded 28:390(B)(5)	mentally retarded 28:390(B)(1) 28:390(B)(4)		at least every 6 mos. 28:96(B)		at least after 30, 90, 180 days; & every 180 days thereafter 28:171(Q)	28:171(Q)		
ME. Rev. Stat. Ann. (1978 & Supp. 1982–83)		ct. must be satisfied w/plan before commitment (mentally ill) 34, §2334(5)(A)(3)		w/in 24 hrs. 34, §2372	at least annually 34, §2374					
MD. Health-Gen. Code Ann. (1982 & Supp. 1982)	treatment & services (mentally retarded) 7-601(2)	mentally ill: written plan 10-705 mentally retarded: written treatment plan 7-605(a) individualized habilitation plan 7-504(c)(2)	mentally retarded 7-601(2)				reevaluated at least annually (mentally retarded) 7-606 at least annually & when patient's status changes (mentally ill) 10-707	periodically reevaluate (mentally retarded) 7-605 periodically update (mentally ill) 10-705		
MASS. Ann. Laws (Michie/Law. Co-op. 1981 & Supp. 1983)				123, §4	once during first 3 mos.; once during second 3 mos.; annually thereafter 123, §4		upon admission; once during first 3 mos.; once during second 3 mos.; annually thereafter 123, §4	123, §4	123, §4	
MICH. Comp. Laws Ann. (1980 & Supp. 1983–84)		written plan 330.1712	freedom of movement not restricted more than necessary 330.1744		at least annually (mentally retarded) 330.1510(3)		every 6 mos. (mentally ill) 330.1482 every 6 mos. (mentally retarded) 330.1531	kept current & modified when indicated 330.1712	mentally ill 330.1482 mentally retarded 330.1531	w/in 5 days of review (mentally ill) 330.1483 w/in 5 days of review (mentally retarded) 330.1531
MINN. Stat. Ann. (West 1982 & Supp. 1983)		written plan 253B.03(7)		as soon as practicable 253A.07(23)	appearance before review board on request; board visit at least every 6 mos. 253A.16 physical exam at least annually 253A.17(7)		at least quarterly 253A.17(9)	253A.17(9)		
MISS. Code Ann. (1972 & Supp. 1980)				during first mo. (mentally retarded) 41-19-107	at least every 6 mos. (mentally ill) 41-21-99 during first 2 yrs.; during first 5 yrs. (mentally retarded) 41-19-107		at least every 6 mos. (mentally ill) 41-21-99 during first 2 yrs.; during first 5 yrs. (mentally retarded) 41-19-107	mentally retarded 41-19-107	mentally ill 41-21-99	

TABLE 6.1 TREATMENT RIGHTS AND REVIEW OF TREATMENT NEEDS—*Continued*

	TREATMENT RIGHTS			EXAMINATION OF PATIENT			REVIEW OF PATIENT RECORDS			
					Periodic					
STATE	*To Treatment in General* (1)	*Individualized Treatment Plan* (2)	*Least Restrictive Alternative fn. 1* (3)	*Upon Admission* (4)	Specified Frequency (5)	As Practicable (6)	*Frequency* (7)	*Treatment Plan Review* (8)	*Administrative Review for Discharge* (9)	*Report to Court* (10)
MO. Ann. Stat. (Vernon 1979 & Supp. 1983)	humane care & treatment 630.115(1)	individualized habilitation plan (mentally retarded) 630.005(1)(15) individualized rehabilitation plan (alcohol or drug abuse) 630.005(1)(16) mentally disordered or mentally ill 630.005(1)(17)	630.115(10)		at least once every 180 days (mentally ill) 632.375		at least once every 180 days 632.175 633.130		condition of each patient to be reviewed (mentally ill) 632.175 mentally retarded 633.130	exam results (mentally ill) 632.375
MONT. Code. Ann. (1981)	for physical ailments (mentally ill) 53-21-142(1)	individualized habilitation plan (developmentally disabled) 53-20-148(4) mentally ill 53-21-162(2)	mentally ill 53-21-142(2)	w/in 48 hrs. (mentally ill) & again w/in 30 days of admission 53-21-162(1) 53-21-163	6 mos. after admission & at least annually thereafter (developmentally disabled) 53-20-148(7) mental exam at least every 90 days (mentally ill) 53-21-162(5)		monthly (developmentally disabled) 53-20-148(7) continuous review, revision every 90 days (mentally ill) 53-21-162(5)	habilitation plan (developmentally disabled) 53-20-148(7) mentally ill 53-21-162(5) 30 days after admission 53-21-163		
NEB. Rev. Stat. (1981 & Supp. 1983)	83-1066(2)	individualized program plan (mentally retarded) 83-1111					at least every 90 days for 1 yr.; every 6 mos. thereafter 83-1045			progress reports to mental health board 83-1045
NEV. Rev. Stat. (1981)	medical, psychological & rehabilitative care 433.484	individualized written plan of treatment & training services 433.494(1)					review at least once every 3 mos.; modification when indicated 433.494(2)	433.494(2)		
N.H. Rev. Stat. Ann. (1977 & Supp. 1981)	medical, psychological, vocational, social, & rehabilitative services (mentally ill) *fn. 8* 135B:43 medical, psychological, vocational, educational, social, or rehabilitative services (developmentally impaired) *fn. 9* 171-A:13	mentally ill 135B:44 individualized service plan (developmentally impaired) 171-A:12		w/in 14 days 171-A:6(II)				continually 171-A:12		
N.J. Stat. Ann. (West 1981 & Supp. 1983–84)	medical care & other professional services in accord w/professional standards 30:4-24.1		to achieve purposes of treatment 30:4-24.2(e)(2)							
N.M. Stat. Ann. (1978 & Supp. 1982)	mentally ill 43-1-7 habilitation plan (developmentally disabled) 43-1-8 education (minors) 43-1-18	developmentally disabled & mentally ill 43-1-7 individualized habilitation plan (developmentally disabled) 43-1-8	least drastic means (mentally ill) 43-1-7 mentally retarded 43-1-8	43-1-6(G)	at least once every 6 mos. thereafter 41-1-6(G)		as circumstances require 43-1-9(D)	revision of individualized treatment plan 43-1-9(D)		
N.Y. Mental Hyg. (McKinney 1978 & Supp. 1982–83)	education (children) 33.11 33.03(a)	included in patient's clinical records 33.03(5)	respect for dignity & personal integrity 33.03(a)		at least annually 33.03(b)(1)		29.13	29.13		
N.C. Gen. Stat. (1981 & Supp. 1981)	treatment & prevention of mental & physical ailments 122-55.6	treatment or habilitation plan 122-55.6					annually 122-58.11(e)		15 days before end of first & second treatment periods 12-58.11(a), (e)	122-58.11(e)
N.D. Cent. Code (1978 & Supp. 1981)	treatment & prevention of mental & physical ailments 25-03.1-40(1)		25-03.1-40(2)				6 mos. after admission & annually thereafter 25-03.1-31		25-03.1-31	w/in 5 days of review 25-03.1-31
OHIO Rev. Code Ann. (Baldwin 1982 & Supp. 1982)	mentally ill: for physical disease or injury 5122.27(E), (F) programs designed to facilitate return to community 5122.27(F)(5)	written treatment plan consistent w/evaluation, diagnosis, prognosis, & goals (mentally ill) 5122.27(B) written habilitation plan consistent w/comprehensive evaluation, diagnosis, prognosis, & goals (mentally retarded & developmentally disabled) 5123.85(B)	consistent w/treatment plan (mentally ill) 5122.27(F)(2)	w/in 24 hrs. of admission 5122.19		during 90-day treatment period 5122.15(F) as frequently as practicable 5122.21(A)	at least every 90 days 5122.27(D)	5122.27(D)		

TABLE 6.1 TREATMENT RIGHTS AND REVIEW OF TREATMENT NEEDS—*Continued*

	TREATMENT RIGHTS			EXAMINATION OF PATIENT			REVIEW OF PATIENT RECORDS			
					Periodic					
STATE	*To Treatment in General* (1)	*Individualized Treatment Plan* (2)	*Least Restrictive Alternative fn. 1* (3)	*Upon Admission* (4)	Specified Frequency (5)	As Practicable (6)	*Frequency* (7)	*Treatment Plan Review* (8)	*Administrative Review for Discharge* (9)	*Report to Court* (10)
OKLA. Stat. Ann. (West 1979 & Supp. 1982–83)		43A, §3(S)					at least annually 43A, §54.11(A)		43A, §54.11(A)	
OR. Rev. Stat. (1981)		written, kept current (mentally ill) 426.385(g) annual plan of care (mentally retarded) 427.020					annually (mentally retarded) 427.020	"plan of care" (mentally retarded) 427.020 written treatment plan kept current w/ patient's progress (mentally ill) 426.385		report to state training center review board (mentally retarded) 427.020
PA. Stat. Ann. (Purdon 1969 & Supp. 1983–84)		mentally ill 50, §7107		mentally ill 50, §7205	at least every 30 days (mentally ill) 50, §7108(a)	upon request (mentally retarded) 50, §4423	at least annually (mentally retarded) 50, §4403 50, §4404 at least every 30 days (mentally ill) 50, §7108(a)	mentally ill 50, §7108(a)	mentally retarded 50, §4403 50, §4404	
R.I. Gen. Laws (1977 & Supp. 1981)	necessary for & appropriate to condition for which admitted 40.1-5-9	mentally disabled 40.1-5-9	statement of least restrictive alternative included in treatment plan 40.1-5-9(b)				at least monthly 40.1-5-5(7) committee review at least every 90 days 40.1-5-10(2)	40.1-5-5(7)	40.1-5-10(2)	
S.C. Code Ann. (Law. Co-op. 1976 & Supp. 1982)				w/in 15 days 44-17-650	at least once every 6 mos. 44-17-820					
S.D. Codified Laws (1976 & Supp. 1982)	for physical illness 27A-12-18	individualized program for education & training 27B-12-11 27A-12-11	27B-8-14	w/in 48 hrs. (mentally ill) 27A-12-10 w/in 48 hrs. (mentally retarded) 27B-8-9	w/in 15 days of admission (mentally ill) 27A-12-15 at least once annually (mentally retarded) 27B-5-15		periodically (mentally ill) 27A-12-13 discharge review after 90 days 27A-12-16 annually (mentally retarded) 27B-8-15	mentally ill 27A-12-13	mentally ill 27A-12-16 mentally retarded 27B-8-15	review results filed w/admitting board w/in 5 days 27B-8-15
TENN. Code Ann. (1977 & Supp. 1982)	medical care & other professional services to extent available 33-306(b) education & training 33-306(c)			as soon as practicable 33-609(a)	at least every 6 mos. 33-609(d)	upon written request after 90 days of hospitalization but not more than every 6 mos. 33-609(b)				
TEX. Rev. Civ. Stat. Ann. (Vernon 1958 & Supp. 1982–83)	educational services including those provided by Tex. Education Code (mentally retarded) 5547-300(8)	individualized habilitation plan 5547-300(16)	including group homes, family living, & living alone (mentally retarded) 5547-300 (7), (15)		at least every 6 mos. 5547.77 prior to release (mentally ill) 5547-78	after petition by patient or next friend (mentally ill) 5547-82	at least annually (mentally retarded) 5547-300 (D)(17)	individualized habilitation plan (mentally retarded) 5547-300 (D)(17)		release examiner reports to ct. 5547-78
UTAH Code Ann. (1978 & Supp. 1981)	medical care in accordance w/accepted standards 64-7-46					as frequently as practicable 64-7-42				
VT. Stat. Ann. (1968 & Supp. 1983)							at least every 6 mos. 18, §7802		18, §7802	
VA. Code (1976 & Supp. 1983)	treatment or training 37.1-84.1(2)		37.1-84.1	w/in 24 hrs. 37.1-70			30, 60, 90 days; every 6 mos. thereafter 37.1-84.2		review of progress toward discharge 37.1-84.2	
WASH. Rev. Code Ann. (1975 & Supp. 1983–84)	adequate care 71.05.360(2)	individual treatment 71.05.360(2)								petition must be filed to hold for more than 90 days 91.05.320(2)
W. VA. Code (1980 & Supp. 1983)	27-5-9(b)	27-5-9(e)			psychiatric exam every 3 mos.; physical exam every 6 mos. *fn. 1* 27-5-9(c)		periodically consistent w/patient exams *fn. 1* 27-5-9(d)	*fn. 1* 27-5-9(d)		
WIS. Stat. Ann. (West 1957 & Supp. 1982–83)	treatment, rehabilitation, & educational services 51.61(3)(f)		51.61(3)(e)	w/in 30 days 51.20(17)	3 mos. later & at least once each 6 mos. thereafter 51.20(17)	upon petition of patient, guardian, relative, friend, or any person providing treatment 51.20(16)(a)				
WYO. Stat. (1983 & Supp. 1983)		mentally retarded 25-5-116			at least every 6 mos. 25-10-116					if patient no longer requires hospitalization 25-10-116

FOOTNOTE: Table 6.1

1. W. Va. Code § 27-5-9(d) (1980): "Failure to accord the patient the requisite periodic examinations or treatment plan and reevaluations shall entitle the patient to release."

TABLE 6.2 RESTRICTIONS ON TREATMENT OF INSTITUTIONALIZED PERSONS

STATE	TYPES OF PATIENTS COVERED (1)	LIMITATIONS ON PERIOD COVERED BY RESTRICTIONS (2)	MAJOR MEDICAL TREATMENT: Type of Treatment Restricted (3)	MAJOR MEDICAL TREATMENT: Medical Condition (4)	MAJOR MEDICAL TREATMENT: Consent or Approval by: Patient (5)	Consent or Approval by: Parent, Guardian, or Next of Kin of Minor or Incompetent (6)	Consent or Approval by: Court (7)	Consent or Approval by: Other (8)	MECHANICAL RESTRAINTS AND SECLUSION: Conditions for Use: Restraint (9)	Conditions for Use: Seclusion (10)	Reasons For Use Part of Record (11)	MEDICATION: Same Conditions as Restraint or Seclusion (12)	MEDICATION: Right to Refuse (13)	MEDICATION: No Excessive or Unnecessary Use (14)	MEDICATION: Other (15)	RESTRICTION AS TO AVERSIVE THERAPY (16)
ALA. Code (1975 & Supp. 1982)	all forms of mental or emotional illness, including mental retardation 22-50-1															
ALAS. Stat. (1979 & Supp. 1982)	mentally ill 47.30.825 47.30.660		electroconvulsive therapy 47.30.825(5) psychosurgery 47.30.825(6) surgery 47.30.825(7)	true medical emergency fn. 1 47.30.825(7)	may knowingly withhold consent on religious grounds 47.30.825 (5)–(7)	legal guardian 47.30.825(6)	if patient lacks substantial capacity 47.30.825(5) after hearing w/full due process 47.30.825(6)	professional person or designee, if time will not permit consent or ct. order 47.30.825(7)	likely to harm self or others unless restrained 47.30.825(C)	likely to harm self or others unless restrained 47.30.825(C)				47.30.825(4)	in patient's best interest or to prevent serious harm to others 47.30.825(4)	absolute right to accept or refuse 47.30.825(5)
ARIZ. Rev. Stat. Ann. (1974 & Supp. 1982)	mentally disordered 36-501(17)		any & all medical treatment 36-512 brain surgery 36-540(H) no psychosurgery, insulin shock, or electroshock 36-561(A)	true medical emergency 36-512 OR	36-512 36-540(H)	legal guardian 36-540(H) AND	36-540(H)	medical director, if time will not permit appropriate judicial authority 36-512	emergency for safety of person or others or as part of written plan 36-513	emergency for safety of person or others or as part of written plan 36-513	36-513	36-513 OR	consent 36-513			
	developmentally disabled 36-551(10)													36-551.01(O)	no experimental drugs 36-561(A)	in accordance w/rules & regulations of dep't & individual program plan 36-561(B)
ARK. Stat. Ann. (1971 & Supp. 1981)	mentally ill 59-1403, 59-1404	initial 72-hour commitment 59-1415(b)(2) 45- or 180-day commitment 59-1415(b) (3 & 4)	no electroconvulsive therapy or psychosurgery 59-1415(b)(2) psychosurgery 59-1415(b)(3) electroconvulsive therapy 59-1415(b)(3)	clear & convincing proof that treatment is necessary 59-1415(b)(3) OR	right to refuse 59-1416(8) 59-1416(7)		probate 59-1415(b)(3)		except as reasonably necessary to protect person or others 59-1415(a) no excessive or unnecessary use 59-1416(23)	no excessive or unnecessary use 59-1416(23)		59-1416(23)		59-1416(23)	only if effects do not exceed 72 hrs. 56-1415(b)(2) short- & long-acting medication may be used 59-1415(b)(4) fn. 2 59-1416(23)	
CAL. Welf. & Inst. Code Code (West 1972 & Supp. 1981)	mentally ill & mentally retarded 5325		psychosurgery 5326.6 convulsive (involuntary patients) 5326.7 convulsive (voluntary patients) 5326.75- convulsive (minors) 5326.8	all other treatment modalities exhausted, & this mode least drastic 5326.6(c) all reasonable treatment modalities considered, & this mode least drastic 5326.7(a) all reasonable treatment modalities considered, & this mode least drastic 5326.7(a) deemed life-saving treatment in emergency & patient over 12 but under 16 5326.8	right to refuse 5326.6(a) 5325(g) right to refuse 5325(d), (f) 5326.85 right to refuse 5325(d), (f) 5326.85 5326.8 5326.7(d) AND	of patient's choosing & consent, if person can be reached 5326.6(b) notice, unless party unavailable or patient does not so desire 5326.7(c) notice, unless party unavailable or patient does not so desire 5326.7(c) notice 5326.7(c)		fn. 3 5326.6(c), (d) patient's attorney or public defender agrees w/capacity to consent 5326.7(e) fn. 4, 5 5326.7(a), (b), (f) psychiatrist or neurologist verifies capacity to consent 5326.75(b) not permitted if under 12 5326.8	no unnecessary or excessive use 5325.1(c)	no unnecessary or excessive use 5325.1(c)		5325.1(c)		5325.1(c)	fn. 2 5325.1(c)	

TABLE 6.2 RESTRICTIONS ON TREATMENT OF INSTITUTIONALIZED PERSONS—*Continued*

			MAJOR MEDICAL TREATMENT						MECHANICAL RESTRAINTS AND SECLUSION			MEDICATION				
					Consent or Approval by				Conditions for Use							
STATE	TYPES OF PATIENTS COVERED (1)	LIMITATIONS ON PERIOD COVERED BY RESTRICTIONS (2)	*Type of Treatment Restricted* (3)	*Medical Condition* (4)	Patient (5)	Parent, Guardian, or Next of Kin of Minor or Incompetent (6)	Court (7)	Other (8)	Restraint (9)	Seclusion (10)	*Reasons For Use Part of Record* (11)	*Same Conditions as Restraint or Seclusion* (12)	*Right to Refuse* (13)	*No Excessive or Unnecessary Use* (14)	*Other* (15)	RESTRICTION AS TO AVERSIVE THERAPY (16)
COLO. Rev. Stat. (1982)	mentally ill 27-10-101		surgery 27-10-116(2)(a)	nature of consent, by whom given, & under what conditions determined by dep't regulations 27-10-116(2)(a)	nature of consent, by whom given, & under what conditions determined by dep't regulations 27-10-116(2)(a)	nature of consent, by whom given, & under what conditions determined by dep't regulations 27-10-116(2)(a)	nature of consent, by whom given, & under what conditions determined by dep't regulations 27-10-116(2)(a)	physician's order 27-10-116(2)(b)								
	developmentally disabled 27-10.5-101		organs removed for transplantation 27-10.5-114(8)	physician rendering emergency care or treatment to any resident 27-10.5-114(10) OR	27-10.5-114(8)	resident may implicitly or explicitly object 27-10.5-114(8)			absolutely necessary to prevent injury to self or others 27-10.5-115(7)	prohibited; "time out" procedures only 27-10.5-115(5)	restraint 27-10.5-115(8)		experimental research or hazardous treatment procedures 27-10.5-114(7) unless physician rendering emergency care or treatment to	fn. 2 27-10.5-114 (4), (5)	written order of physician 27-10.5-114(2)	consent of resident or legal guardian, after consultation w/disinterested expert & approval by review board 27-10.5-115(6) any resident 27-10.5-114(10)
CONN. Gen. Stat. Ann. (West 1975 & Supp. 1982)	mentally disordered 17-206a		medical or surgical procedures; psychosurgery; shock therapy 17-206d(b), (d)	extremely critical, & delay harmful 17-206d(b), (c) OR	17-206d(b), (d) fn. 6	17-206d(b) OR	after hearing, if no reasonable alternative 17-206d(d)	physician appointed by committing ct. 17-206d(b) opinion of head of hospital & 2 physicians that consent impossible 17-206d(d)	imminent physical danger to patient or others, & ordered by physician 17-206e(a)	imminent physical danger to patient or others, & ordered by physician 17-206e(a)	17-206e(a)		if voluntary patient & condition not extremely critical 17-206d(a), (c)		not to be used as substitute for habilitation program 17-206e(b)	
DEL. Code Ann. (1974 & Supp. 1982)	mentally ill & mentally retarded 16, §5161(a) 16, §5125 16, §5522(a)		surgery, electric shock, or experimental drugs & treatment 16, §5161 (a)(2)(d)		16, §5161 (a)(2)(d)	guardian 16, §5161 (a)(2)(d)		order of staff member, based on appropriate examination 16, §5161 (a)(2)(c)								
D.C. Code Ann. (1981 & Supp. 1983)	mentally ill 21-501 *et seq.* mentally retarded 6-1901 *et seq.*		no psychosurgery, convulsive therapy, or experimental treatment 6-1966	emergency surgery, if delay in obtaining consent would create grave danger 6-1967 AND		6-1967 OR		chief medical officer, if others cannot reasonably be contacted 6-1967	prescribed by physician 21-563 absolutely necessary to prevent seriously injuring self or others, & alternatives have failed 6-1970(a)	"time out" only 6-1970(d)	21-563 6-1970(b)		experimental research 6-1969	6-1965(h)	physician's order *fn. 2* 6-1965(h)	no behavior modification using aversive stimuli or deprivation of rights 6-1966
FLA. Stat. Ann. (West 1973 & Supp. 1982)	mentally ill 394.459		any 394.459(3)(a) surgery requiring general anesthetic or electro-convulsive treatment 394.459(3)(b)	emergency & least restrictive 394.459(3)(a) OR emergency, life-saving surgery, & permission cannot be obtained *fn. 1* 394.459(3)(b)	or written 394.459(3)(a), (b) OR	written 394.459(3)(b)	after hearing to determine competency to consent 394.459(3)(a) hearing, if appropriateness contested by physician 394.459(3)(c)									
	mentally retarded 393.13(1)		experimental medical treatment or necessary surgery 393.13(3)(f)(6)	emergency care, if delay would endanger health 393.13(3)(f)(8)	393.13(3)(f)(6)	393.13(3)(f)(6)	hearing, if appropriateness contested by physician 393.13(3)(f)(7)		emergency, to prevent imminent injury to self or others, least restrictive alternative 393.13(3)(l)	barred enclosures considered restraints 393.13(3)(l)(2)	daily reports to chief administrator 393.13(3)(l)			393.13(3)(f)(1)	physician's order *fn. 2* 393.13(3)(f)(1)	use of noxious or painful stimuli prohibited 393.13(3)(j)(1)

TABLE 6.2 RESTRICTIONS ON TREATMENT OF INSTITUTIONALIZED PERSONS—*Continued*

			MAJOR MEDICAL TREATMENT						MECHANICAL RESTRAINTS AND SECLUSION			MEDICATION				
					Consent or Approval by				Conditions for Use							
STATE	TYPES OF PATIENTS COVERED (1)	LIMITATIONS ON PERIOD COVERED BY RESTRICTIONS (2)	*Type of Treatment Restricted* (3)	*Medical Condition* (4)	Patient (5)	Parent, Guardian, or Next of Kin of Minor or Incompetent (6)	Court (7)	Other (8)	Restraint (9)	Seclusion (10)	*Reasons For Use Part of Record* (11)	*Same Conditions as Restraint or Seclusion* (12)	*Right to Refuse* (13)	*No Excessive or Unnecessary Use* (14)	*Other* (15)	RESTRICTION AS TO AVERSIVE THERAPY (16)
GA. Code Ann. (1979 & Supp. 1983)	mentally ill 88-2903 88-501 et seq.		any surgical medical treatment or procedures 88-2904	emergency, person authorized to consent not readily available, & delay could jeopardize life or health 88-2905 88-502.6(e)	OR right to refuse 88-2904 88-2907	or spouse 88-2904			solely for providing effective treatment & protecting safety of patient & others 88-502.5(a) absolutely necessary to prevent serious injury 88-502.5(b)	solely for providing effective treatment & protecting safety of patient & others 88-502.5(a)	88-502.5(b)	88-502.5(a)	except where physician determines refusal would be unsafe to patient or others 88-502.6(b)		no quantities that interfere w/treatment program 88-502.5(a)	
HAWAII Rev. Stat. (1976 & Supp. 1982)	mentally ill 334E-1		any nonemergency treatment 334E-1	emergency situations 334E-2(a)(9)	OR 334E-1	334E-1	OR ct. order 334E-2(a)(9)		necessary to prevent injury to self or others, part of treatment plan, or necessary to preserve rights of patients or staff 334E-2(a)(24)	necessary to prevent injury to self or others, part of treatment plan, or necessary to preserve rights of patients or staff 334E-2(a)(24)			experimentation 334E-2(a)(10)			
IDAHO Code (1980 & Supp. 1983)	mentally ill 66-300 et. seq.		specific modes of treatment 66-346(a)(4)	emergency, at determination of director 66-346(c)	OR right to refuse 66-346(a)(4)			director, in emergency or if ct. has determined patient lacks capacity to consent 66-346(c)	necessary to safety of patient or others *fn. 1* 66-345	necessary to safety of patient or others *fn. 1* 66-345	66-345					
	developmentally disabled 66-412		specific modes of treatment or habilitation 66-412(4)	emergency, at determination of director 66-412(4)	OR right to refuse 66-412(4)	right to refuse 66-412(4)		director, in emergency or if ct. finds consent impossible 66-412(4)	necessary for safety of patient or others 66-412(2)	prohibited 66-412(2)	66-412(2)					
ILL. Ann. Stat. (Smith-Hurd 1966 & Supp. 1982)	mentally ill & developmentally disabled 91½, §1-101 et seq.		electroconvulsive or unusual, hazardous, or experimental services or psychosurgery 91½, §2-110	emergency when delay involved w/obtaining consent would endanger life or health 91½, §2-111	OR 91½, §2-110	91½, §2-110		physician may determine in emergency whether recipient capable of informed consent 91½, §2-111	therapeutic measure to prevent harm to self or others; not for punishment or discipline, nor for convenience of staff *fn. 1* 91½, §2-108 91½, §2-109	therapeutic measure to prevent harm to self or others; not for punishment or discipline, nor for convenience of staff *fn. 1* 91½, §2-108 91½, §2-109	91½, §2-201(c)		except where necessary to prevent serious harm to self or others 91½, §2-107			
IND. Code Ann. (Burns 1983)	mentally ill & developmentally disabled 16-14-1.6-1		any 16-14-1.6-7		right to refuse, if voluntary 16-14-1.6-7		may petition for consideration of program, if involuntary 16-14-1.6-7		necessary to prevent danger of abuse or injury to self or others, or as a measure of therapeutic treatment 16-14-1.6-6	necessary to prevent danger of abuse or injury to self or others, or as a measure of therapeutic treatment 16-14-1.6-6	16-14-1.6-6		if voluntary, or to petition committing ct. for consideration if involuntary 16-14-1.6-7			
IOWA Code Ann. (West 1969 & Supp. 1982)	mentally ill 229.23 mentally retarded 222.1 et seq.		shock treatment 229.23(2)		right to refuse 229.23(2)	next of kin or guardian may override patient's refusal 229.23(2)							chemotherapy, unless necessary to preserve patient's life or physical injury to self or others 229.23(2)			

TABLE 6.2 RESTRICTIONS ON TREATMENT OF INSTITUTIONALIZED PERSONS—*Continued*

			MAJOR MEDICAL TREATMENT						MECHANICAL RESTRAINTS AND SECLUSION			MEDICATION				
					Consent or Approval by				Conditions for Use							
STATE	TYPES OF PATIENTS COVERED (1)	LIMITATIONS ON PERIOD COVERED BY RESTRICTIONS (2)	*Type of Treatment Restricted* (3)	*Medical Condition* (4)	Patient (5)	Parent, Guardian, or Next of Kin of Minor or Incompetent (6)	Court (7)	Other (8)	Restraint (9)	Seclusion (10)	*Reasons For Use Part of Record* (11)	*Same Conditions as Restraint or Seclusion* (12)	*Right to Refuse* (13)	*No Excessive or Unnecessary Use* (14)	*Other* (15)	RESTRICTION AS TO AVERSIVE THERAPY (16)
KAN. Stat. Ann. (1976 & Supp. 1981)	mentally ill 59-2901	48 hrs. prior to each 90-day review of commitment order 59-2916a all other periods of commitment 59-2928	no therapy which may adversely affect preparation for or outcome of hearing 59-2916a psychosurgery, electroshock, or hazardous treatment procedures 59-2929(a)(6)	unless necessary to sustain life or protect patient or others 59-2916a	59-2929(a)(6)	59-2929(a)(6)			to prevent bodily injury to patient or others *fn. 1* 59-2928	to prevent bodily injury to patient or others *fn. 1* 59-2928	59-2928		experimental 59-2929(a)(6)		none, unless necessary to sustain life or protect self or others or not adversely influential at hearing 59-2916a	none w/o consent 59-2929(a)(6)
KY. Rev. Stat. Ann. (Michie 1982)	mentally ill 202A.006 et seq. mentally retarded 202B.050		any 202A.191(c) 202B.060(3) intrusive 202A.191(g) 202B.060(7)		202A.191(c) 202A.191(g) OR		after de novo determination of appropriateness 202A.196(3) AND	recommendation of review committee 202A.196(2)	no unreasonable use 202A.191(h) secretary shall adopt rules & regulations 202B.060(10)	no unreasonable use 202A.191(h) secretary shall adopt rules & regulations 202B.060(10)						
LA. Rev. Stat. Ann. (West 1975 & Supp. 1982)	mentally ill or substance abuse 28:2(17) mentally retarded 28:380		major surgical procedures or electroshock 28:171(F) no prefrontal lobotomies solely for mental or emotional illness 28:171(O)	life threatening emergency, determined by director in consultation w/2 physicians 28:171(F) OR			after hearing 28:171(F)		as therapy or to prevent harm to self or others; not for punishment, discipline, or staff convenience 28:171(D), (E)	as therapy or to prevent harm to self or others; not for punishment, discipline, or staff convenience 28:171(D), (E)					physician responsible for all ordered prescriptions, no nonmedical reasons for use 28:171(P)	
ME. Rev. Stat. Ann. (1978 & Supp. 1982)	mentally ill 34, §2251 et seq. mentally retarded 34, §2601 et seq.								*fn. 1* 34, §2253	*fn. 1* 34, §2253						
MD. Health-Gen. Code Ann. (1982 & Supp. 1982)	mentally ill 10-101(f) mentally retarded 7-601 et seq.		any 7-602(d)(1)(ii)		right to refuse, unless medically inadvisable 7-602(d)(1)(ii)				minimal, & authorized by physician in record as for clearly medical need 7-601(a)(4)			chemical restraints 7-601(a)(4)	unless medically inadvisable 7-602(d)(1)(ii)			
MASS. Ann. Laws (Michie/Law. Co-op. 1981 & Supp. 1982)	mentally ill & mentally retarded 123, §23		lobotomy & shock 123, §23 no psychosurgery or electroshock if patient in Intensive Care Unit for Women 123, §23		right to refuse; may be denied for good cause 123, §23	required, even if patient competent 123, §23			occurrence or serious threat of extreme violence, personal injury, or attempted suicide *fn. 1* 123, §21 nonchemical restraints permissible for 8 hrs. if physician unavailable 123, §21		123, §21	chemical restraints 123, §21				

TABLE 6.2 RESTRICTIONS ON TREATMENT OF INSTITUTIONALIZED PERSONS—*Continued*

STATE	TYPES OF PATIENTS COVERED (1)	LIMITATIONS ON PERIOD COVERED BY RESTRICTIONS (2)	MAJOR MEDICAL TREATMENT						MECHANICAL RESTRAINTS AND SECLUSION			MEDICATION				RESTRICTION AS TO AVERSIVE THERAPY (16)
					Consent or Approval by				Conditions for Use							
			Type of Treatment Restricted (3)	*Medical Condition* (4)	Patient (5)	Parent, Guardian, or Next of Kin of Minor or Incompetent (6)	Court (7)	Other (8)	Restraint (9)	Seclusion (10)	*Reasons For Use Part of Record* (11)	*Same Conditions as Restraint or Seclusion* (12)	*Right to Refuse* (13)	*No Excessive or Unnecessary Use* (14)	*Other* (15)	
MICH. Comp. Laws Ann. (1980 & Supp. 1982)	mentally ill & developmentally disabled 330.1401 330.1501	no chemotherapy on day before or day of full ct. hearing unless patient consents or necessary to prevent physical injury to self or others 330.1718(2)	surgery, convulsive, or coma producing 330.1716(1)	life threatened, & no time to obtain consent 330.1716(2) OR	330.1716(1)(a)	330.1716(1) (b, c) OR	after hearing 330.1716(3)		to prevent physical harm to self, others, or substantial property damage, upon physician's order, unless emergency 330.1740 330.1742	to prevent physical harm to self, others, or substantial property damage, upon physician's order, unless emergency 330.1740 330.1742 clinical or therapeutic benefit 330.1742(2)	330.1740(9) 330.1742(9)		unless necessary to prevent physical injury to self or others 330.1718(1)		ct. order, after hearing 330.1718(1)	
MINN. Stat. Ann. (West 1982 & Supp. 1982)	chemically dependent, mentally ill, or mentally retarded 253B.02		any medical or surgical treatment, other than for mental illness, mental retardation, or chemical dependence 253B.03(6)	to preserve life or health of patient 253B.03(6)	253B.03(6)(1)	even if not adjudicated but head of facility deems patient incompetent 253B.03(6)(2), (3)	after hearing to establish incompetency 253B.03(6)(3)	head of facility in emergency, if can't locate person to give consent 253B.03(6)(5)	necessary for safety of patient or others *fn. 1* 253B.03(1)		253B.03(1)					
MISS. Code Ann. (1981 & Supp. 1982)	mentally ill 41-21-61(c) mentally retarded 41-19-1															
MO. Stat. Ann. (Vernon 1979 & Supp. 1982)	all mental disabilities 630.005 et. seq.		hazardous or surgical 630.115(11), (12) no experimental research on involuntary patients 630.115(1)(8) electroconvulsive 630.130(1) no electroconvulsive therapy ever for persons solely mentally retarded 630.130(5) psychosurgery 630.133	clear & convincing evidence that therapy will improve or cure disorder for substantial time period w/o serious functional harm, & no less drastic alternative 630.130(3) OR	right to refuse 630.115(11) 630.130(1), (2) 630.133(1)	required to obtain ct. order after full hearing 630.115(11) 630.130(4) same procedures as for electroconvulsive 630.133(1)	patient may request impartial review if surgery irreversible or treatment hazardous, except in life-preserving emergency 630.115(11), (12) after full evidentiary hearing 630.130(3)		necessary to protect self or others *fn. 1* 630.175(1)	necessary to protect self or others *fn. 1* 630.175(1)	630.175(2)	chemical restraints 630.175(1)				
MONT. Code Ann. (1981)	mentally ill 53-21-101 developmentally disabled 53-20-101		experimental research 53-21-147 53-20-147 shock devices considered experimental for developmentally disabled 53-20-146(6) lobotomy, aversive reinforcement, or other unusual or hazardous treatment procedures 53-21-148 53-20-146(1)	to prevent self-mutilation 53-20-146(6)	after opportunity to consult w/independent specialists & counsel 53-21-147(1) 53-20-147(1) after consultation w/counsel, ct.-appointed guardian, friend, & interested party of patient's choice 53-21-148 53-20-146(1)	after opportunity to consult w/independent specialists & counsel 53-21-147(1) 53-20-147(1) AND		mental disabilities board of visitors 53-21-147(2) 53-20-147(2) one of those consulted must also consent, along with patient's counsel 53-21-148	professional person's written order, unless emergency situation where patient likely to harm self or others, & no less restrictive means 53-21-146 upon professional person's order; necessary to prevent injury to developmentally disabled resident or others; not as punishment or for convenience; least restrictive alternative 53-20-146(2)	professional person's written order, unless emergency situation where patient likely to harm self or others, & no less restrictive means 53-21-146 "time out" only for developmentally disabled 53-20-146(3)				53-21-145 53-20-145	written order of physician *fn. 2* 53-21-145 53-20-145	aversive reinforcement conditioning only after informed consent following consultation w/counsel, guardian, friend appointed by ct., & interested party of patient's choice 53-21-148 53-20-146(4) not permissible solely for institutional convenience for developmentally disabled 53-20-146(5)

TABLE 6.2 RESTRICTIONS ON TREATMENT OF INSTITUTIONALIZED PERSONS—*Continued*

STATE	TYPES OF PATIENTS COVERED (1)	LIMITATIONS ON PERIOD COVERED BY RESTRICTIONS (2)	MAJOR MEDICAL TREATMENT: Type of Treatment Restricted (3)	MAJOR MEDICAL TREATMENT: Medical Condition (4)	MAJOR MEDICAL TREATMENT: Consent or Approval by: Patient (5)	MAJOR MEDICAL TREATMENT: Consent or Approval by: Parent, Guardian, or Next of Kin of Minor or Incompetent (6)	MAJOR MEDICAL TREATMENT: Consent or Approval by: Court (7)	MAJOR MEDICAL TREATMENT: Consent or Approval by: Other (8)	MECHANICAL RESTRAINTS AND SECLUSION: Conditions for Use: Restraint (9)	MECHANICAL RESTRAINTS AND SECLUSION: Conditions for Use: Seclusion (10)	MECHANICAL RESTRAINTS AND SECLUSION: Reasons For Use Part of Record (11)	MEDICATION: Same Conditions as Restraint or Seclusion (12)	MEDICATION: Right to Refuse (13)	MEDICATION: No Excessive or Unnecessary Use (14)	MEDICATION: Other (15)	RESTRICTION AS TO AVERSIVE THERAPY (16)
NEB. Rev. Stat. (1981)	mentally ill dangerous 83-1001 mentally retarded 83-1101		any 83-1066(3)	to prevent injury to self or others or to substantially improve mental illness 83-1066(3) OR	right to refuse 83-1066(3)											
NEV. Rev. Stat. (1981)	mentally ill & mentally retarded 433.003(1)		any 433.484(1)(a)	accident or acute illness or condition & delay would endanger health 433.484(1)(d) OR	433.484 (1)(a)(1)	433.484 (1)(a)(2), (3)		consultation w/other physicians if proposed emergency care unusual, experimental, or infrequently used in routine practice 433.484(1)(e)	prescribed by physician 433.484(2)		433.484(2)					
N.H. Rev. Stat. Ann. (1977 & Supp. 1981)	mentally ill 135-B:1 developmentally impaired 171-A:1												voluntary patient may withdraw from any specific form of treatment 135-B:15			
N.J. Stat. Ann. (West 1981 & Supp. 1983)	mentally ill, mentally retarded, or TB 30:4-23		experimental research, shock treatment, psychosurgery, or sterlization 30:4-24.2(d)(2)		after consultation w/counsel or interested party of patient's choice 30:4-24.2(d)(2)		hearing to determine necessity if patient adjudicated incompetent 30:4-24.2(d)(2)		emergency involving substantial property damage or attempt to harm self or others, & no less restrictive alternative fn. 1 30:4-24.2(d)(3)	emergency involving substantial property damage or attempt to harm self or others, & no less restrictive alternative fn. 1 30:4-24.2(d)(3)	30:4-24.2(d)(3)		voluntary patients 30:4-24.2(d)(1)	30:4-24.2(d)(1)	written order of physician fn. 2 30:4-24.2(d)(1)	
N.M. Stat. Ann. (1979)	mentally ill & developmentally disabled 43-1-1 et seq.		psychosurgery, convulsive, experimental, or behavior modification 43-1-15(A)		43-1-15(A)		hearing following petition to allow substitute consent by treatment guardian 43-1-15(B)	consultation w/physician, attorney, & interested friends or relatives 43-1-15(B)					emergency administration of psychotropic medication w/o consent if necessary to protect client from serious harm & no less drastic means 43-1-15(F)	43-1-6(I)	written order of physician fn. 2 43-1-6(I)	no behavior modification w/o proper consent 43-1-15(A)
N.Y. Mental Hyg. Law (McKinney 1978 & Supp. 1982)	mentally ill & mentally retarded 33.01 et seq.		surgery, shock, major medical in in the nature of surgery, or experimental drugs or procedures 33.03(b)(4)		subject to regulations of commissioner 33.03(b)(4)				to prevent serious injury to self or others; less restrictive techniques inappropriate or insufficient; & not for punishment or staff convenience 33.04(b) camisole or restraining sheet only 33.04(c)		33.04(d), (g)					
N.C. Gen. Stat. (1981 & Supp. 1981)	mentally ill, mentally retarded, or substance abuse 122-1 et seq.		electroshock, experimental drugs or procedures, or nonemergency surgery 122-55.6		122-55.6	122-55.6			to prevent abuse or injury to self or others or as measure of therapeutic treatment 122-55.3	to prevent abuse or injury to self or others or as measure of therapeutic treatment 122-55.3	122-55.3			122-55.6	written order of physician fn. 2 122-55.6	

TABLE 6.2 RESTRICTIONS ON TREATMENT OF INSTITUTIONALIZED PERSONS—*Continued*

STATE	TYPES OF PATIENTS COVERED (1)	LIMITATIONS ON PERIOD COVERED BY RESTRICTIONS (2)	MAJOR MEDICAL TREATMENT						MECHANICAL RESTRAINTS AND SECLUSION			MEDICATION				RESTRICTION AS TO AVERSIVE THERAPY (16)
					Consent or Approval by				Conditions for Use							
			Type of Treatment Restricted (3)	*Medical Condition* (4)	Patient (5)	Parent, Guardian, or Next of Kin of Minor or Incompetent (6)	Court (7)	Other (8)	Restraint (9)	Seclusion (10)	*Reasons For Use Part of Record* (11)	*Same Conditions as Restraint or Seclusion* (12)	*Right to Refuse* (13)	*No Excessive or Unnecessary Use* (14)	*Other* (15)	
N.D. Cent. Code (1978 & Supp. 1981)	mentally ill, alcoholic, or drug addict 25-03.1-02 (11)	24 hrs. before a discharge or commitment hearing 25-03.1-16 pending a discharge of commitment hearing in general 25-03.1-16 all other times 25-03.1-40	medication any form of treatment 25-03.1-16 experimental research, psychosurgery, electroconvulsive, or aversive reinforcement conditioning 25-03.1-40 (12), (13)		right to refuse unless necessary to prevent bodily harm to self or others or imminent deterioration of condition 25-03.1-16 25-03.1-40 (12), (13)	25-03.1-40 (12), (13)		treating physician's judgment that treatment in patient's best interest, & compatible w/dep't regulations 25-03.1-41	right to be free from unnecessary restraint & isolation 25-03.1-40(4)	right to be free from unnecessary restraint & isolation 25-03.1-40(4)	25-03.1-41		right to be free from effects, unless discontinuance would hamper preparation of & participation in proceedings 25-03.1-16	25-03.1-40(10)		no aversive reinforcement conditioning w/o consent of patient or guardian 25-03.1-40(13)
OHIO Rev. Code Ann. (Baldwin 1980 & Supp. 1982)	mentally ill 5122.01 et seq. mentally retarded & developmentally disabled 5123.02 et seq.		sterilizations, unusually hazardous procedures, psychosurgery 5122.271(B) 5123.86(B) surgery 5122.271(C) 5123.86(C) convulsive therapy 5122.271(E) does not include defibrillation 5122.271(G)(2) 5123.86(G)(2)	emergency, & delay would endanger health or life 5122.271(D), (E)(1) 5123.86(E)(1)	OR right to refuse AND 5122.271 (A)(1), (2), (4)–(6), (B) 5123.86(A)(1), (2), (4)–(6)	or if patient physically or mentally unable to receive information required for consent 5122.271 (C), (E)(2) 5123.86 (C), (E)(2)	unless voluntary & competent in nonpublic hospital 5122.271(B) if incompetent & no legal guardian, following recommendation of chief medical officer & physician 5123.86(C) 5122.271(C) if emergency 5122.271(E)(1) 5123.86(E)(1)	chief medical officer or attending physician in emergency 5123.271(D) 5123.86(C) chief medical officer & 2 licensed physicians 5122.271(E)(1) 5123.86(E)(1)	or by patient's individual physician in nonstate hospital *fn. 1* 5122.27(F)(7)	or by patient's individual physician in nonstate hospital *fn. 1* 5122.27(F)(7)				5122.27(F)(6)		*fn. 7* 5122.271(F) 5123.86(F)
OKLA. Stat. Ann. (West 1979 & Supp. 1982)	mentally ill or mentally retarded 43A, §2		any major operation advisable or necessary 43A, §96	grave emergency, to prevent serious consequences or death 43A, §96	OR	by notification, whether or not patient competent 43A, §96			*fn. 1* 43A, §92		43A, §92					
OR. Rev. Stat. (1981)	mentally ill 426.005 et seq. mentally retarded 427.005 et seq.		potentially unusual or hazardous treatment procedures, including electroshock 426.385(2)		426.385(2) OR			for good cause by director after consultation w/independent physician 426.385(2)	*fn. 1* 426.385(3) determined by chief medical officer or designee as required for safety & welfare of self or others 427.031(4)		426.385(3) 427.031(4)					
PA. Stat. Ann. (Purdon 1969 & Supp. 1982)	mentally retarded 50, §4401(a) mentally ill 50, §7102								or necessary to prevent harm to self or others *fn. 1* 50, §4422							
R.I. Gen. Laws (1977 & Supp. 1982)	mentally disabled 40.1-5-3(1)								*fn. 8* 40.1-5-5(6)(l)							
S.C. Code (1976 & Supp. 1982)	mentally ill or mentally retarded 44-23-10 et seq.		any treatment not recognized as standard psychiatric treatment; lobotomy 44-23-1010 shock treatment 44-23-1010		right to refuse AND 44-23-1010	whether incompetent or not 44-23-1010		statement by superintendent or designated physician that treatment necessary if patient incompetent 44-23-1010	authorized as necessary by physician, or emergency, e.g., threat of extreme violence, personal injury, or attempted suicide 44-23-1020	authorized as necessary by physician, or emergency, e.g., threat of extreme violence, personal injury, or attempted suicide 44-23-1020	44-23-1020					corporal punishment or any form of physical coercion; same criteria as restraints & seclusion 44-23-1020

TABLE 6.2 RESTRICTIONS ON TREATMENT OF INSTITUTIONALIZED PERSONS—*Continued*

STATE	TYPES OF PATIENTS COVERED (1)	LIMITATIONS ON PERIOD COVERED BY RESTRICTIONS (2)	MAJOR MEDICAL TREATMENT: *Type of Treatment Restricted* (3)	MAJOR MEDICAL TREATMENT: *Medical Condition* (4)	MAJOR MEDICAL TREATMENT: *Consent or Approval by*: Patient (5)	MAJOR MEDICAL TREATMENT: *Consent or Approval by*: Parent, Guardian, or Next of Kin of Minor or Incompetent (6)	MAJOR MEDICAL TREATMENT: *Consent or Approval by*: Court (7)	MAJOR MEDICAL TREATMENT: *Consent or Approval by*: Other (8)	MECHANICAL RESTRAINTS AND SECLUSION: *Conditions for Use*: Restraint (9)	MECHANICAL RESTRAINTS AND SECLUSION: *Conditions for Use*: Seclusion (10)	MECHANICAL RESTRAINTS AND SECLUSION: *Reasons For Use Part of Record* (11)	MEDICATION: *Same Conditions as Restraint or Seclusion* (12)	MEDICATION: *Right to Refuse* (13)	MEDICATION: *No Excessive or Unnecessary Use* (14)	MEDICATION: *Other* (15)	RESTRICTION AS TO AVERSIVE THERAPY (16)
S.D. Codified Laws Ann. (1976 & Supp. 1982)	mentally ill 27A-1-1 et seq.		surgery & other medical procedures 27A-12-19 experimental research, hazardous procedure, surgery or electro-convulsive 27A-12-20	life threatened & no time to obtain consent or ct. order 27A-12-19 OR	27A-12-20(1)	27A-12-20 (2, 3)	psychosurgery or convulsive; after hearing if no one eligible to consent can be found 27A-12-20	experimental research or hazardous procedures conducted in manner prescribed by board of charities & corrections 27A-12-21 *fn. 9* 27B-8-2	written order of mental health professional, or emergency when harm to self or others likely & no less restrictive means 27A-12-6	written order of mental health professional, or emergency when harm to self or others likely & no less restrictive means 27A-12-6		chemical restraints 27A-12-6			treatment shall not consist solely of drug therapy unless supported by sufficient medical opinion 27A-12-11	
	mentally retarded 27B-1-1 et seq.		drugs, electric shock, insulin shock, psychosurgery, research 27B-8-2(1) surgery & other medical procedures 27B-8-19	life threatened & no time to obtain consent or ct. order 27B-8-19 OR	right to refuse 27B-8-2(1) 27B-8-20(1)	27B-8-20 (2, 3)	psychosurgery or convulsive; after hearing if no one eligible to consent can be found 27B-8-20	no experimental or hazardous procedure unless conducted in manner prescribed by board of charities & corrections 27B-8-21	absolutely necessary to protect resident from injuring self or others, or as part of an approved behavioral program; not as punishment, for convenience, or as substitute for treatment 27B-8-5.1				27B-8-2(1)	facility may not use chemical restraint excessively, as punishment, for staff convenience, or as substitute for activities or treatment 27B-8-5.3	facility may not use chemical restraint excessively, as punishment, for staff convenience, or as substitute for activities or treatment 27B-8-5.3	behavior modification *fn. 10* 27B-8-5.4 to 27B-8-5.7
TENN. Code Ann. (1972 & Supp. 1982)	mentally ill & mentally retarded 33-302		standard treatment, including surgery 33-307(a) convulsive for minors 33-320(a) no lobotomies or surgery for intervention or alteration of mental, emotional, or behavioral disorders of minors 33-320(f)	necessary for welfare of patient 33-307(a) life-saving emergency *fn. 11* 33-320(h) AND OR	surgery 33-307(a)	surgery 33-307(a)	after hearing showing necessary for minor's health & safety 33-320(a)	corroborative testimony of independent psychiatrist 33-320(d)	required by patient's medical or treatment needs 33-306(d)	required by patient's medical or treatment needs 33-306(d)	33-306(d)					
TEX. Rev. Civ. Stat. Ann. (Vernon 1958 & Supp. 1982)	mentally ill 5547-4(g)								prescribed by physician 5547-71		5547-71					
	mentally retarded 5547-300(5)		no unusual or hazardous procedures, experimental research, organ transplantation, or non-therapeutic surgery 5547-300(24) (c)											5547-300(21)	physician's prescription *fn. 2* 5547-300(21)	
UTAH Code Ann. (1978 & Supp. 1981)	64-7-7								*fn. 1* 64-7-47		64-7-47				determined by physician as required by patient's needs 64-7-47	
VT. Stat. Ann. (1968 & Supp. 1983)	mentally ill & mentally retarded 18, §7101 et seq.		surgical operation 18, §7708	requires operation or would promote possibility of discharge 18, §7708	18, §7708 AND	or attorney 18, §7708 AND		superintendent 18, §7708	*fn. 1* 18, §7704		18, §7704					

TABLE 6.2 RESTRICTIONS ON TREATMENT OF INSTITUTIONALIZED PERSONS—*Continued*

			MAJOR MEDICAL TREATMENT						MECHANICAL RESTRAINTS AND SECLUSION			MEDICATION				
					Consent or Approval by				*Conditions for Use*							
STATE	TYPES OF PATIENTS COVERED (1)	LIMITATIONS ON PERIOD COVERED BY RESTRICTIONS (2)	*Type of Treatment Restricted* (3)	*Medical Condition* (4)	Patient (5)	Parent, Guardian, or Next of Kin of Minor or Incompetent (6)	Court (7)	Other (8)	Restraint (9)	Seclusion (10)	*Reasons For Use Part of Record* (11)	*Same Conditions as Restraint or Seclusion* (12)	*Right to Refuse* (13)	*No Excessive or Unnecessary Use* (14)	*Other* (15)	RESTRICTION AS TO AVERSIVE THERAPY (16)
VA. Code (1976 & Supp. 1983)	all mental disabilities 37.1-1 et seq.	while appeal pending 37.1-85	experimental or investigational research 37.1-84.1(4) hazardous treatment or irreversible surgery 37.1-84.1(5) any treatment 37.1-85	emergency; procedures required for preservation of health 37.1-84.1(5) to protect patient's life, health, or safety 37.1-85	37.1-84.1(4)	guardian or committee 37.1-84.1(4)	may prohibit treatment 37.1-85	right to impartial review before implementation 37.1-84.1(5) doctor of any hospital 37.1-85	no unnecessary physical restraints & isolation 37.1-84.1(6)	no unnecessary physical restraints & isolation 37.1-84.1(6)						
WASH. Rev. Code Ann. (1975 & Supp. 1982)	mentally disordered 71.05.020(2)		no psychosurgery under any circumstances 71.05.370(9) shock treatment or surgery 71.05.370(7)	emergency life-saving surgery 71.05.370(7) OR	71.05.370(7) OR		after full hearing 71.05.370(7)									
W. VA. Code (1980 & Supp. 1983)	mentally ill, mentally retarded, or addiction 27-5-9(a) 27-4-1(a)		any course of treatment 27-4-4(b)		voluntary patients 27-4-4(b)						mechanical restraints; involuntary patients 27-5-9(e)					
WIS. Stat. Ann. (West 1957 & Supp. 1982)	mentally ill, developmentally disabled, alcoholism, or drug dependency 51.61(1)	prior to final commitment order 51.61(1)(g) at any time 51.61(1)(h)	all medication & treatment 51.61(1)(g) experimental research 51.61(1)(j) psychosurgery or other drastic treatments, including electroconvulsive 51.61(1)(k)		right to refuse 51.6(1)(g) after consultation w/independent specialists & counsel 51.61(1)(j) after consultation w/counsel & guardian 51.61(1)(k)			review by institution's research & human rights committee & by dep't 51.61(1)(j)	emergency situations or part of treatment program; less restrictive measures ineffective or feasible *fn. 1* 51.61(1)(i)	emergency situations or part of treatment program; less restrictive measures ineffective or feasible *fn. 1* 51.61(1)(i)			except as ordered by ct. or necessary to prevent serious physical harm to self or others 51.61(g) if member of recognized religion whose tenets prohibit such unless ordered by ct. or to prevent serious physical harm as evidenced by recent overt act 51.61(1)(h)	51.61(1)(h)	ct. order finding medication therapeutic, won't interfere w/proceedings, & probable cause to believe patient not competent to refuse 51.61(1)(g) physician's order *fn. 2* 51.61(1)(h)	
WYO. Stat. (1982 & Supp. 1983)	mentally ill 25-10-101 et seq. mentally retarded 25-5-103		major surgery 25-5-130(a) psychosurgery or other drastic procedures 25-5-132 (d)(iii) experimental research 25-5-132 (d)(ii)	emergency or parent or guardian cannot be located 25-5-130(b) OR	25-5-130 (a)(i) 25-5-132 (d)(iii) may consult w/counsel & medical specialists 25-5-132 (d)(ii)	25-5-130 (a)(i) 25-5-132 (d)(iii) 25-5-132 (d)(ii)	25-5-132(d) 25-4-132(d)		*fn. 1* 25-10-119 emergency situations as necessary to protect self or others 25-5-132 (c)(v) less restrictive measures ineffective 25-5-133(a)	emergency situations as necessary to protect self or others 25-5-132 (c)(v) less restrictive measures ineffective 25-5-133(a)	25-10-119 25-5-133(a)			unless authorized by ct., guardian, or parent 25-5-132(d)	physician's order *fn. 2* 25-5-133(b)	

FOOTNOTES TO TABLE 6.2

1. Use must be approved by head of hospital or designee, based on determination that patient's medical needs require it:

Alas. Stat. § 47.30.14 (1979)
Fla. Stat. Ann. § 394.459(3)(b) (West Supp. 1980)
Idaho Code Ann. § 66-345 (1980)
Ill. Ann. Stat. ch. 91½, §§ 2-108(d), -109(c) (Smith-Hurd Supp. 1979)
Kan. Stat. Ann. § 59-2928 (1976)
Me. Rev. Stat. Ann. tit. 34, § 2253 (1978)
Mass. Ann. Laws ch. 123, § 21 (Michie/Law. Co-op. 1981)
Minn. Stat. Ann. § 253B.03(1) (West 1971)
Mo. Ann. Stat. § 630.175(1) (Vernon Supp. 1980)
N.J. Stat. Ann. § 30:4-24.2(d)(3) (West 1981)
Ohio Rev. Code Ann. § 5122.27(F)(7) (Baldwin 1980)
Okla. Stat. Ann. tit. 43A, § 92 (West 1979)
Or. Rev. Stat. § 426.385(3) (1979)
Pa. Stat. Ann. tit. 50, § 4422(2) (Purdon 1969)
Utah Code Ann. § 64-7-47 (Supp. 1979)
Vt. Stat. Ann. tit. 18, § 7704 (1968)
Wis. Stat. Ann. § 51.61(1)(i) (West Supp. 1980)
Wyo. Stat. § 25-10-119 (1977).

2. Medication shall not be used as punishment for patients, for convenience of staff, or in quantities that interfere with the treatment program:

Ark. Stat. Ann.. § 59-1416(23) (Supp.1983)
Cal. Welf. & Inst. Code § 5325.1(c) (West Supp. 1980)
Colo. Rev. Stat. § 27-10.5-114(5) (Supp. 1980)
D.C. Code Ann. § 6-1965(h) (1973)
Fla. Stat. Ann. § 393.13(f)(1) (West Supp. 1980)
Mont. Code Ann. §§ 53-20-145, 53-21-145 (1979)
N.C. Gen. Stat. § 122-55.6 (1981)
N.J. Stat. Ann. § 30:4-24.2(d)(1) (West 1981)
N.M. Stat. Ann. § 43-1-6(I) (1979)
Tex. Civ. Stat. Ann. § 5547-300(21) (Vernon 1958)
Wis. Stat. Ann. § 51.61(1)(h) (West Supp. 1980)
Wyo. Stat. § 25-5-133(b) (1977)

3. Cal. Welf. & Inst. Code § 5326.6 (West Supp. 1980):

(c) The attending physician gives adequate documentation entered in the patient's treatment record of the reasons for the procedure, that all other appropriate treatment modalities have been exhausted and that this mode of treatment is definitely indicated and is the least drastic alternative available for the treatment of the patient at the time. Such statement in the treatment record shall be signed by the attending and treatment physician or physicians.

(d) Three physicians, one appointed by the facility and two appointed by the local mental health director, two of whom shall be either board certified or eligible psychiatrists or board certified or eligible neurosurgeons, have personally examined the patient and unanimously agree with the attending physician's determinations pursuant to subdivision (c) and agree that the patient has the capacity to give informed consent. Such agreement shall be documented in the patient's treatment record and signed by each such physician.

Psychosurgery shall in no case be performed for at least 72 hours following the patient's written consent. Under no circumstances shall psychosurgery be performed on a minor.

4. Id. § 2326.7(a):

(a) The attending or treatment physician enters adequate documentation in the patient's treatment record of the reasons for the procedure that all reasonable treatment modalities have been carefully considered, and that the treatment is definitely indicated and is the least drastic alternative available for this patient at this time. Such statement in the treatment record shall be signed by the attending and treatment physician or physicians.

5. Id. § 2326.7:

(b) A review of the patient's treatment record is conducted by a committee of two physicians, at least one of whom shall have personally examined the patient. One physician shall be appointed by the facility and one shall be appointed by the local mental health director. Both shall be either board-certified or board-eligible neurologists. This review committee must unanimously agree with the treatment physician's determinations pursuant to subdivision (a). Such agreement shall be documented in the patient's treatment record and signed by both physicians. . . .

> (f) If either the attending physician or the attorney believes that the patient does not have the capacity to give a written informed consent, then a petition shall be filed in superior court to determine the patient's capacity to give written informed consent. The court shall hold an evidentiary hearing after giving appropriate notice to the patient, and within three judicial days after the petition is filed. At such hearing the patient shall be present and represented by legal counsel. If the court deems the above-mentioned attorney to have a conflict of interest, such attorney shall not represent the patient in this proceeding.

6. Conn. Gen. Stat. Ann. § 17-206d(e) (Supp. 1983-84). "No public or private facility shall request or require blanket consent to all procedures as a condition of admission or treatment."

7. Ohio Rev. Code Ann. § 5122.271(F), § 5123.86(F) (Baldwin 1980). Major aversive behavior modification not to be used unless patient continues behavior destructive to self or others after other forms of therapy have been attempted. Such therapy must be approved by behavior modification committee and may not be applied to a voluntary patient without consent.

8. R.I. Gen. Laws § 40.1-5-5(6)(l) (1977). Right to have the least possible restraint imposed consistent with affording patient the care and treatment necessary and appropriate to patient's condition.

9. S.D. Codified Laws Ann. § 27B-8-2 (1976). "Reasonable limitations may be placed on these rights if each limitation is essential in order to prevent the resident from violating a law or to prevent substantial and serious physical or mental harm to the resident or other residents, and if each limitation is documented in the patient's record and approved by the administrator or his designee."

10. Id. § 27B-8-5.5 (Supp. 1982)

> Behavior modification programs involving the use of aversive stimuli or time out devices shall be:
>
> 1. Reviewed and approved by the human rights committee;
>
> 2. Conducted only with the consent of the affected resident's parents or legal guardian; and
>
> 3. Described in written plans that are kept on file. [§ 27B-8-5.5]
>
> For time out purposes, time out devices and aversive stimuli may not be used for longer than one hour, and then only during the behavior modification program and only under the supervision of the programmer.

Id. § 27B-8-5.7.

11. Tenn. Code Ann. § 33-320(h) (1977 & Supp. 1982):

> Affidavit from a child psychiatrist . . . stating that (1) the minor is fourteen years of age or older; (2) his life is in imminent peril; (3) all other accepted methods of treatment have been exhausted; (4) the minor is suffering from a psychosis or mania which has resulted in acute physical exhaustion or starvation bordering on serious collapse; (5) electroconvulsive or convulsive therapy is necessary to save the minor's life due to potential suicide, or to prevent irreparable injury resulting from conditions such as starvation, dehydration, or physical exhaustion bordering on serious collapse to the extent such conditions are life threatening; and (6) there is insufficient time to complete the procedure provided by subsections (b), (c) and (d) of this section, and therefore treatment prior to a court hearing is necessary.

John Parry

CHAPTER 7 *Incompetency, Guardianship, and Restoration*

I. INTRODUCTION

The three most significant legal mechanisms affecting the personal and property decision-making rights of mentally disabled persons are involuntary commitment, incompetency, and guardianship. In this chapter, two of these legal constructs—incompetency and guardianship[1]—are discussed fully, along with the process of restoring citizenship rights to individuals once they are no longer incompetent or in need of a guardian. In addition, the interrelationship between involuntary commitment and incompetency, and general limitations on the ward's decision-making rights once incompetency is established, will be reviewed. The primary focus of each discussion will be the history, theory, and mechanisms of the law. The next chapter, "Decision-making Rights over Persons and Property," will review specific personal and property rights retained or withdrawn from incompetent individuals and individuals with less than full mental capacities.

II. HISTORICAL BACKGROUND AND DEFINITIONS

Incompetency proceedings are of a much earlier origin than hospitalization proceedings. For example, in Rome in the first century B.C., elaborate provisions were made for the protection of the property of the mentally disabled, while none at all existed for their person. This pattern was followed in England and also in colonial America, where several of the colonies passed legislation designed to protect the estates of "insane persons" long before the colonial governments became concerned with the personal welfare of the mentally disabled.[2]

No institution for the care of the mentally disabled existed in England until long after the Norman Conquest. Guardianship of the mentally disabled in medieval England was the function of the lord of the manor, who was charged with protecting their proprietary and personal interests. This guardianship actually applied to both the person and the property of the insane, but the chief reason for its existence was apparently proprietary, stemming from the desire to prevent the mentally disabled from becoming a public burden or dissipating their assets to the detriment of their heirs.

It would seem that originally this guardianship, or *tutorship* as it was called, was applicable only to mentally deficient persons.[3] By the beginning of the fourteenth century, however, guardianship was expanded to include mentally ill persons and was formally recognized as a duty of the Crown.[4]

The king's guardianship was exercised through the Lord Chancellor, by virtue of a special commission issued to him by the Crown rather than by the general authority of the chancery court. In exercising the power, the Chancellor held an inquisition to determine the condition of the mentally disabled person and to appoint a committee for his person and property if he was adjudged an "idiot" or a "lunatic." It was the further duty of the chancery court to supervise and control the conduct of such a committee.

In the United States responsibility for incompetents was deemed to be vested in the people. Either by inheritance from the common law or by expressed constitutional and statutory provisions, jurisdiction over the person and property of incompetents was assumed by the courts of equity.[5]

1. For additional discussion of the concept and function of guardians see in this chapter § VIII, Incompetency and Guardianship, and § IX, Special Guardianship or Related Situations, *infra*.
2. A. Deutsch, The Mentally Ill in America: A History of Their Case and Treatment from Colonial Times 40 (2d ed. 1949).
3. 2 L. Shelford, A Practical Treatise on the Law Concerning Lunatics, Idiots and Persons of Unsound Mind 7 (1833); 2 J. Reeves, History of English Law 307-8 (1814). In this context, "mentally deficient" is equivalent to "mentally retarded."
4. De Praerogativa Regis, 17 Edw. 2, cs. 9, 10 (1324).
5. For a general history see 29 Am. Jur. Insane and Other Incompetent Persons § 32 (1960).

The doctrine of *parens patriae*, which obligates the state to care for the vulnerable and the less fortunate, provides both the primary philosophical justification and the legal basis for our guardianship laws.[6] More recently, the principle that the state should exercise its power against the individual only so far as is absolutely necessary[7] has made the individual circumstances of the ward an important basis for state action.[8] Thus, incompetency and guardianship are often viewed in gradations that attempt to approximate the range of capacities enjoyed by mentally disabled persons.

From a legal standpoint *incompetency* is a term that largely defines when the state may take actions that limit an individual's right to make decisions about his person or property based on his mental disability. The limitations may be so broad as to deprive the individual of the right to make any binding legal decisions, or the limitations may be applied more narrowly to one group of decisions, such as financial matters, or to one specific decision, such as driving a car. To a large extent, jurisdictions define the term differently to fit their own views about the capacities or incapacities of mentally disabled persons and others who may be included among those individuals who need this type of protection or assistance from the state.

Guardianship is a related concept that often defines how the incompetency determination is to be implemented. Guardianship is the most inclusive method of substituted decision making for individuals for whom it has been judicially determined that they cannot act for themselves. Depending upon the jurisdiction and the circumstances, the substitution may be complete, covering all legal decisions, or it may be limited to one or more aspects of a person's life. In addition, there are other mechanisms available for assigning limited substituted decision-making powers, such as the *representative payee*, who is the recipient and caretaker for certain specified financial transactions, or the *guardian ad litem*, who represents the individual's interest in one judicial action.

Key distinctions are made in the law among types of guardianship dispositions. Traditionally, guardianships were divided into actions that affected property interests, known as *guardianships of the estate*, and actions that affected personal interests, known as *guardianships of the person*. A plenary guardian controlled both types of interests. Such distinctions represented early legislative recognition that incompetency in one area of decision making did not necessarily mean the person was incompetent in other areas. These basic types of guardianship are still reflected in the law today, but at the same time legislatures and courts have recognized that other distinctions must be made to better differentiate individual capacities. Plenary guardianship is often viewed as a disposition of last resort. What constitutes a limited guardianship, however, is still evolving. Many jurisdictions make categorical limitations similar to, although more sophisticated than, the estate versus personal interests of old. Other jurisdictions have moved toward individualized guardianship dispositions reflecting the particular needs of the incapacitated person and the circumstances of the situation, thus relieving the person of a specified decision-making responsibility only if it is absolutely necessary.

Restoration is the judicial process for returning some, or often all, decision-making rights to the individual by changing the individual's legal status from incompetent to competent.

Legal competency, whatever its definition may be in a particular jurisdiction, is usually quite different from *clinical competency*,[9] which according to one description addresses "cognitive functioning or, more precisely, the extent to which cognitive functioning is 'minimally adequate' in the areas of word knowledge, recent and remote memory, perceptual accuracy or reality testing, abstraction, and judgment as it is applied to both the personal and social spheres."[10] Competency criteria from this psychological point of view "imply some specific basis from which the contents of a stimulus field are received and processed fairly accurately; and that processing is, in turn, translated in such a way as to make decision actions commensurate with the purpose and nature of the legal procedure."[11]

Clinical competency, by its definition, also suggests a distinction between the criteria that should be applied in evaluating persons who are mentally ill and persons who are mentally retarded, brain damaged, or otherwise permanently mentally incapacitated. Mentally ill

6. Regan, Protective Services for the Elderly: Commitment, Guardianship, and Alternatives, 13 Wm. & Mary L. Rev. 569 (1972); Rothman, The State as Parent: Social Policy in the Progressive Era, *in* Doing Good: The Limits of Benevolence 67-70 (W. Gaylin, I. Glasser, S. Marcus, & D.J. Rothman eds. 1978); B.D. Sales, D.M. Powell, R. Van Duizend, & Associates, Disabled Persons and the Law 459 (1982).

7. Shelton v. Tucker, 364 U.S. 479 (1960); Keiter, A Preliminary Review of Wyoming's Revised Civil Commitment Procedures, 17 Land & Water L. Rev. 531, 535 (1982).

8. Comment, The Eighth Amendment Right to Treatment for Involuntarily Committed Mental Patients, 61 Iowa L. Rev. 1057, 1069-70 (1976) [hereinafter cited as Comment, The Eighth Amendment]; Keiter, *supra* note 7, at 538, 540-47; White, Protection Following Commitment: Enforcing the Rights of Persons Confined in Arizona Mental Health Facilities, 17 Ariz. L. Rev. 1090 (1976).

9. For a more detailed examination of clinical competency, see ch. 5, Rights of Institutionalized Persons, § XV D, The Problems of Consent.

10. Exner, Diagnosis Versus Description in Competency Issues, 347 Annals N.Y. Acad. Sci. 20 (1980).

11. *Id.* at 20.

persons may be clinically incompetent, but because of the "temporary" nature of their disability they may improve to the point that they can make rational decisions. Persons who are clinically incompetent because of a permanent mental incapacity such as profound mental retardation or irreversible coma never become clinically competent unless, of course, the diagnostic procedures were inadequate or applied incorrectly.

III. INCOMPETENCY AND INVOLUNTARY COMMITMENT COMPARED

The laws governing incompetency and restoration often do not recognize or incorporate the aforementioned clinical concepts or do so incompletely, which may create a number of serious theoretical and practical problems. Nowhere are such difficulties more obvious than in the jurisdictions that fail to clearly distinguish incompetency from involuntary commitment criteria. In 1971 when the previous edition of this book was published, and even more so in the years before that, the two concepts of incompetency and commitment were commonly merged and confused.[12] What would happen in most instances is that following institutionalization no guardians would be appointed, so the residents would be unable, both practically and legally, to exercise rights of citizenship. Figure 1 shows how the two concepts were viewed then and how they are viewed today. While in many states significant distinctions have been made between the legal mechanisms used to determine incompetency and to order involuntary commitment, the separation is far from complete. At their present stages of legal evolution, the two legal terms, depending on the jurisdiction, are defined differently, moving from the traditional lack of separation toward a complete separation more consistent with clinical competency. The chart also reflects a realignment of individual and state interests with the strong emergence of such concepts as the least restrictive alternative state action and substituted decision making, which give greater consideration to the views and values of the incompetent person.

A. Tests Applied

In the 1971 edition, incompetency tests generally linked the inability to care for one's property or personal affairs to a specified disability that did not necessarily have to encompass a cognitive incapacity. Commitment was statutorily predicated on the existence of most of the same disabling conditions but was linked in different jurisdictions to separate social concerns: either dangerousness to self or others or the need for treatment.

A major practical problem developed because it was both clinically and judicially unclear who should be categorized as incompetent persons unable to care for themselves or as committable persons in need of treatment. Where no meaningful distinction could be made, the difference between incompetency and involuntary commitment became arbitrary, and the same disabled person could be placed under guardianship, involuntarily committed, or both given a guardian and committed. This determination was based not on an individual's clinical conditions but on the type of proceeding or proceedings that were instituted against him. While the concept of dangerousness was substantially differentiated from the need for treatment or the ability to care for oneself or one's property, there were still problems in determining when dangerousness existed and in distinguishing dangerousness to self from an inability to properly care for oneself.

Today, some states retain the inability to care for one's property or person as a criterion for finding incompetency.[13] What has happened in a number of other jurisdictions, however, is the emergence of criteria that reorient the judicial process of making incompetency determinations more toward clinical notions of competency. A number of jurisdictions now employ criteria that minimize the importance of the results of an individual's decision and instead examine the ability of the individual to go through the cognitive process of making rational decisions. At least 16 states have adopted the Uniform Probate Code, or a close variant thereof, which defines an incapacitated person as an individual so impaired that he "lacks sufficient understanding or capacity to make or communicate responsible decisions concerning his person."[14] The benefit of such a system is that in theory it accounts for eccentricities and variations in individual choice and tries to avoid viewing decision making from the perspective of the substituted decision maker alone. In addition, as we shall see, the Uniform Probate Code standard and its progeny are more clearly distinguishable from civil commitment criteria both in language and in purpose. The difficulty is establishing functional judicial criteria that can be used to accurately measure cognitive functioning.

Current involuntary commitment standards place a far greater priority on proof of dangerousness as the pri-

12. S.J. Brakel & R.S. Rock, The Mentally Disabled and the Law 251 (rev. ed. 1971).

13. See table 7.3, col. 7.

14. See National Conference of Commissioners on Uniform State Law, Uniform Probate Code § 5 at 203 (4th ed. 1975) [hereinafter cited as Uniform Probate Code].

Eleven states have adopted the Uniform Probate Code Statute: Alaska, Arizona, Colorado, Hawaii, Idaho, Montana, Nebraska, New Mexico, North Dakota, Oregon, and Utah. In addition, a number of the states including Kansas, Maine, Maryland, Pennsylvania, and West Virginia use similar language in their formulations. See Sales, Powell, Van Duizend, & Associates, *supra* note 6, at 469-75.

Fig. 1. Incompetency and involuntary commitment compared in 1971 and 1983

	1971 Edition		*1983*	
	Incompetency	Hospitalization	Incompetency	Involuntary Commitment
Test	unable to care properly for one's property or person because of one of the following conditions:	dangerous to self or others, or in need of treatment, because of one of the following conditions:	a. unable to properly care for one's property or person or b. unable to make rational decisions concerning his person:	dangerous to self or others or Gravely disabled/unable to provide for basic needs
Applicable to cases of	mental illness mental deficiency drug addiction alcoholism senility physical disability spendthrifts	mental illness mental deficiency drug addiction alcoholism epilepsy	a. mental illness mental retardation/developmental disability physical disability advancing age alcoholism drug addiction or b. any infirmity	mental illness mental retardation/developmental disability alcoholism drug addiction
Purposes	protect estate from dissipation and provide protection for persons unable to care for themselves	removal from society for protection of the individual or of society and/or for treatment of the illness	a. to protect the best interests of the individual or b. make the decision the individual would have made if rational	removal from society for protection of the individual or of society or care of severely disabled
Limitations			least restrictive alternative	no custodial confinement
Primary rights affected	civil rights	freedom to be at large	decision-making rights/civil rights	liberty
Comparable to	legal status of a minor	person removed from society for a contagious disease	a. legal status of minor or b. legal status of a released offender	person removed from society for a contagious disease

mary determinant of the need for civil confinement.[15] A secondary trend reveals that the need for treatment standard for commitment is being replaced by a standard that requires either the presence of a grave disability or an inability to provide for one's basic needs.[16]

The new statutory alignments of incompetency and commitment criteria have produced three distinguishable systems for controlling the actions and movements of mentally disabled persons. First, nearly half the jurisdictions limit involuntary commitment to dangerous individuals and apply incompetency proceedings only as a method of protecting individuals who suffer impaired judgment or are unable to properly care for themselves.[17] In these jurisdictions, the overlap between the two different methods of judicial control is narrowed because the purposes are largely distinct, although in one respect the confusion remains. Mentally disabled persons may be both legally dangerous to themselves and incompetent in jurisdictions that use a competency standard that includes the ability to care for oneself. Again, which type of proceeding will be applied may depend more on the person who initiates the judicial action than on the appropriateness of the disposition.[18] Where competency criteria only measure the ability to make a decision, the statutory purpose is sufficiently distinct from commitment to theoretically justify two entirely separate judicial proceedings with different dispositions.

A second group of states has commitment statutes that apply both to gravely disabled citizens or persons unable to provide for their basic needs and incompetency provisions that cover individuals who are unable to

15. See ch. 2, Involuntary Institutionalization, esp. table 2.6, col. 4.

16. See ch. 2, Involuntary Institutionalization, esp. table 2.6, col. 5.

17. In this group we are focusing on jurisdictions that have restricted involuntary commitment to dangerous individuals.See table 2.6, col. 4, & table 7.3, cols. 5-7.

18. If an individual in fact meets both criteria, then what normally happens is that the initial proceedings will determine the type of disposition since in most jurisdictions commitment and competency proceedings are separate.

care for their property or person.[19] This type of system provides for a great deal of discretion on the part of the person initiating the proceedings because of the wide overlap among the various classes of disabilities covered by the two methods of judicial control. As a result, it is quite possible for the most appropriate disposition to be precluded on the questionable theory that institutionalization proceedings generally are a better protective alternative for severely incapacitated persons than guardianship proceedings.

A third type of statutory arrangement is found in jurisdictions that simply reject the protective services rationale for competency criteria and use as a threshold requirement the ability to make a rational decision.[20] In those states, there is no overlap in purpose or coverage with any of the applicable commitment standards, whether the commitment standards deal with dangerousness, need for care, or grave disability. Instead, there may be a protection gap in which the state is precluded from attending to nondangerous individuals who are not irrational legally but who, according to medical criteria, need involuntary care or treatment. From one point of view, the gap may be evidence of a noncaring or medically ignorant society, while from another perspective such noninvolvement may be applauded for allowing individuals the freedom to make their own decisions.

B. Persons Covered by the Applicable Tests

As the applicable tests for incompetency and commitment evolved, the types of incapacities that were linked to those tests have changed but not significantly. At the time of the last edition of this book, the major categories of persons covered by incompetency statutes included those who were mentally ill, mentally deficient, drug addicted, or alcoholic. Involuntary commitment was applicable to the same groups, except that persons with epilepsy were also included. In addition, a number of states covered persons in their incompetency provisions who were described as senile, physically disabled, or spendthrifts.

During the past decade, the incompetency categories have been broadened somewhat and the terminology changed to accommodate what are perceived to be more appropriate labels. *Mental illness, physical disability, alcoholism,* and *drug addiction* are commonly used terms, while the designation of *spendthrift* is rarely employed.[21] What has also happened, however, is the rapid expansion of the notion that protective services such as guardianship should be applied to "any impairment" as long as the person is in need of assistance.[22] In other words, the individual's functioning level should be determinative regardless of the impairment category the person falls into. This minimizes the potential danger of service neglect found in other states that use standards that link applicable tests to specified conditions or incapacities. The major problem with this functional approach is that it is possible to be overly paternalistic. State-sanctioned "protection" may do more harm than good, particularly where these laws are applied to people who are eccentric, unpopular, or wealthy by petitioners who are self-interested or prejudiced. Linking specific categorizations to the test at least ensures that there is a medically recognizable incapacity present. Some states have done better than others in fine tuning their legislation so that both gaps in coverage and unnecessary intrusions are minimized.

One popular approach is for states to adopt the Uniform Probate Code,[23] which defines an "incapacitated person" as "any person who is impaired by reason of mental illness, mental deficiency, physical illness or disability, advanced age . . . or other cause (except minority) to the extent that he lacks sufficient understanding or capacity to make or communicate responsible decisions concerning his person."[24] These statutes go on to define personal and property guardianships but, except for in Idaho, do not have a mechanism for limited guardianships.[25]

Connecticut includes a person who is either incapable of managing his own affairs or "incapable of caring for one's self." In both instances such a person must have "a mental, emotional or physical condition resulting from mental illness, mental deficiency, physical illness or disability, advanced age, chronic use of drugs or alcohol or confinement."[26]

The American Bar Association's Commission on the Mentally Disabled in its own model statute prepared in 1979 uses an entirely functional approach that distinguishes between "partially disabled" and "disabled persons" and limits the applicable definitions to adults, providing separate definitions for children:

> (1) "Partially Disabled persons" means adults whose ability to receive and evaluate information effectively and/or communicate decisions is impaired to the extent that they lack the capacity to manage at least some of

19. Examples of states that do this are: Arkansas, Connecticut, Florida, Illinois, Indiana, Mississippi, Missouri, Nevada, Ohio, Oklahoma, Pennsylvania, Vermont, Virginia, Washington, Wisconsin, and Wyoming. See tables 7.1 & 2.6.

20. See Uniform Probate Code, *supra* note 14.

21. See table 7.3, cols. 8-14. The spendthrift concept is used only in Massachusetts and Wisconsin.

22. *Id.* Twenty-five states apply this type of provision.

23. See states listed *supra* in note 14. Sales, Powell, Van Duizend, & Associates, *supra* note 6, at 469-75 examine the adoption of the Uniform Probate Code (*supra* note 14) in the states.

24. Uniform Probate Code, *supra* note 14, at § 5-103(7).

25. Idaho Code 56-239 (Supp. 1984).

26. Conn. Gen. Stat. Ann. § 45-70a(c)-(d) (Supp. 1980).

their financial resources and/or meet at least some of the essential requirements for their physical health or safety without court-ordered assistance or appointment of a limited personal guardian or limited conservator.

(2) "Disabled persons" means adults whose ability to receive and evaluate information effectively and/or to communicate decisions is impaired to such an extent that they lack the capacity to manage their financial resources and/or to meet essential requirements for their physical health or safety even with court-ordered assistance or the appointment of a limited personal guardian or limited conservator.[27]

West Virginia is the only state that uses a functional definition and allows for limited guardianship as well. Its legislation includes any "person unable to care for his physical well-being." Such an inability is shown by: substantial risk of physical harm to self as evidenced by conduct demonstrating that he is dangerous to himself, notwithstanding poor judgment; inability to manage business affairs; and inability to know and appreciate the nature and effect of business transactions, notwithstanding poor judgment.[28]

Other changes have been primarily symbolic. For example, the terms *mental retardation* or *developmental disability* have generally replaced the more derogatory term *mental deficiency,* and *advancing age* is used instead of *senility.* Terms like "idiot," "imbecile," and "depraved" have largely disappeared.

Similarly the conditions or incapacities leading to institutionalization have changed little in substance, but changes in terminology mirror the trend of using more appropriate labels.

C. Underlying Purposes

In the past, guardianship was intended first and foremost to be a means of preventing mentally disabled individuals from dissipating their estates and, secondarily, to protect persons who were unable to care for themselves. Institutionalization was viewed as a medical action and referred to as "hospitalization." The need for treatment was one justification for confinement. The other was the protection of society or the individual from harm.[29]

Today, preventing the dissipation of a person's estate is not as important a factor in determining the need for a guardian as it once was. In fact, all factors that measure the effects of a person's decisions on others have been reduced in their importance. What is gaining prominence instead are factors that measure a person's cognitive ability to make a lawful decision, regardless of the economic effect it may have on others. Concurrently, incompetency dispositions have been influenced by the emergence of the doctrine of the least restrictive alternative, which limits state action on behalf of individuals to those actions that meet state interests as unobtrusively as possible.[30]

The major justification for involuntary commitment remains the protection of society or the incapacited individual. Need for treatment by itself generally is not sufficient to uphold incarceration. Even in those states that do not limit their criteria to dangerousness, there must be clear and convincing evidence of a severe disabling mental condition.[31] More importantly, the United States Supreme Court, while not going so far as demanding the wholesale application of the least restrictive alternative disposition, ruled that custodial confinement was inappropriate for individuals capable of surviving safely in freedom by themselves or with the help of willing and responsible family members or friends.[32]

D. Primary Rights Affected

In the years preceding the 1971 edition of this book, the primary rights affected by incompetency determinations included the broad spectrum of rights identified with citizenship such as voting, marriage, driving, or civil service employment.[33] At one time, an incompetent person would lose all or many rights automatically. In the past 20 years, the trend in the law has moved toward requiring courts to examine rights separately to determine whether or not a person has lost the capacity to exercise each particular right.[34]

While civil commitment has always affected liberty interests, there is strong support for making liberty the exclusive issue to be resolved at commitment proceedings and for reserving judgment on other rights until a formal incompetency proceeding has been held.[35]

E. Legal Status

Incompetency status in many jurisdictions still resem-

27. *Published in* Sales, Powell, Van Duizend, & Associates, *supra* note 6, at 535-36.

28. W. Va. Code § 27-11-1 (d)(1)-(2) (1980 & Supp. 1984).

29. Brakel & Rock, *supra* note 12, at 251.

30. See table 7.3, col. 1. Colorado, Minnesota, and New Hampshire specifically require that the appointment of a guardian be the least restrictive alternative. There are also legal decisions and judicial theories that strongly support the principle. See Comment, The Eighth Amendment, *supra* note 8; Frolik, Plenary Guardianship: An Analysis, a Critique and a Proposal for Reform, 23 Ariz. L. Rev. 599, 660 (1981); Peters, Teply, Wunsch, & Zimmerman, Administrative Civil Commitment: The Nebraska Experience and Legislative Reform Under the Nebraska Mental Health Commitment Act of 1976, 10 Creighton L. Rev. 243 (1976); Preface in Sales, Powell, Van Duizend, & Associates, *supra* note 6, at xv; Tieger & Kresser, Civil Commitment in California: A Defense Perspective on the Operation of the Lanterman-Petris-Short Act, 28 Hastings L.J. 1407 (1977).

31. See tables 2.6 & 2.8.

32. O'Connor v. Donaldson, 422 U.S. 563 (1975).

33. Brakel & Rock, *supra* note 12, at 250-65.

34. See references in note 30 *supra*.

35. See table 7.2. Only eight states allow the two proceedings to be held together.

bles the status of a minor. Yet minors have won a number of important procedural and substantive rights in the past 20 years that elevate their positions with respect to their parents, guardians, and the state. Many mentally disabled persons who have been found incompetent similarly find themselves with more discrete limitations on their right to make various decisions. In some jurisdictions incompetent persons have more rights than children do. Although the analogy is not perfect, incompetents in those states more closely resemble released criminal offenders who may be denied specified rights or privileges but generally may exercise most rights and privileges of citizenship.

IV. DISTINCT LEGAL CONCEPTS

The authors of this book's second edition observed in 1971 that most statutes failed to make proper distinctions between incompetency and involuntary commitment. Many provisions employed terms such as "insane," "lunatic," "idiocy," and the like to describe either or both incompetency and the need for commitment.[36]

Remnants of the old law still are found in a few statutes that fail to adequately distinguish between incompetency and commitment proceedings[37] and in a greater number of provisions that make the distinction but nonetheless permit institution administrators to deny rights that were never withheld by a court.[38]

A primary justification for giving such unbridled power to the states and their agents has been to protect the incapacitated individual. Also, the delegation of this power and discretion is seen as a means for promoting other important societal interests, such as the financial solvency of merchants and other individuals who make legal transactions, the convenience of family members, and the protection of the members of the community from physical harm.

In the past decade, there has been a noticeable shift toward the individualization of legal remedies to address various degrees of diminished capacity. The most significant change has been the relationship between involuntary commitment and personal rights of citizenship. Previously, as reflected in the second edition of this book, only a small handful of jurisdictions specifically stated that competency was not affected by involuntary hospitalization. Numerous states made competency determinations an essential part of the commitment process allowing state institutions to severely limit the rights of residents to control their property or conducting pro forma guardianship proceedings to achieve similar ends. All too often, people who were institutionalized were effectively deprived of many, if not all, of their rights of citizenship.

What the law has been moving closer to is judicial and legislative recognition that while incompetency and involuntary commitment determinations are both methods of social control, they are most useful where they are "distinct legal concepts determining separate issues and leading to different results."[39] Involuntary commitment largely has become a measure of last resort applicable to situations that present a serious and often an immediate danger to the mentally disabled person or the community.[40] Commitment still may be used to compel care or treatment for nondangerous severely mentally disabled individuals, but these applications have been curtailed or eliminated in recent years causing frustration for many mental disability professionals.[41]

Presently, 42 jurisdictions specify that an individual's competency is not affected by institutionalization,[42] and even the 9 states that lack such a provision do not require competency to be resolved at a commitment proceeding. Eighteen jurisdictions, however, still employ statutes that give institution officials broad authority to interfere with individual rights in order to facilitate normal institutional operations.

Incompetency and guardianship hearings still may focus on almost any considerations relevant to a person's decision-making capabilities,[43] including in certain instances the need for institutionalization.[44] In the past the law usually allowed all or nothing determinations to be made so that if a specified threshold were reached, a significant group of or even all decision-making rights were withheld. Now the tendency is to tailor guardianship dispositions to the individual needs of the proposed ward. No more liberty is withheld or decision-making rights curtailed than is necessary to resolve the particular problem or problems under consideration.[45] This may mean doing as little as appointing a representative payee to cash a ward's social security check or as much as appointing a guardian to authorize institutionalization and major psychiatric treatment.

36. Brakel & Rock, *supra* note 12, at 251. The legal concepts and problems raised by blurring them remain much the same as reported in the previous edition of this book at 250–55, on which this section relies heavily.

37. See table 7.2. Alabama, Delaware, Florida, Kentucky, Maryland, Nebraska, Nevada, and Pennsylvania have no such provision that formally separates the proceedings.

38. Table 7.2, col. 2. Seventeen states have such statutes.

39. Brakel & Rock, *supra* note 12, at 250.

40. See discussion in ch. 2, Involuntary Institutionalization, *supra*.

41. See ch. 5, Rights of Institutionalized Persons, § XIV D The Adversary Versus the Best Interest of the Client Conflict.

42. Table 7.2, col. 1.

43. Table 7.1.

44. *Id.* California in particular has a determination that allows guardians to institutionalize their wards.

45. See references in note 30 *supra*; see also *In re* Boyer, 636 P.2d 1085 (Utah 1981); Guardianship of Roe, 421 N.E.2d 40 (Mass. 1981).

V. MAKING INCOMPETENCE A PREREQUISITE FOR INVOLUNTARY COMMITMENT

Although a vast majority of jurisdictions recognize the distinct purposes served by incompetency and involuntary commitment and separate the two proceedings, two states have enacted hybrid legislation attempting in different ways to promote the availability of treatment or habilitation by making a finding of incompetency a prerequisite for involuntary commitment.

California's Lanterman-Petris-Short Act of 1969 allows a guardian to commit a ward without further due process deliberations, if a special type of incompetency hearing has been held that in theory is supposed to "end the inappropriate, indefinite and involuntary commitment" of mentally disordered and chronically alcoholism-impaired persons.[46] The substantive standard limits such a drastic action to persons who are gravely disabled as a result of a mental disorder.[47] According to the California courts, this does not include an individual who is "capable of surviving safely in freedom by himself or with the help of willing and responsible family members or friends or third parties"[48] as set out in *O'Connor v. Donaldson*.[49] In addition, all determinations under the statute must be individualized so they are "necessary in light of all the relevant facts,"[50] and they must follow rigorous hearing procedures.[51]

The major conceptual problem with the California approach, which in other ways is praiseworthy, is that the justifications for commitment diminish as time passes by before the conservator admits the ward into a facility. What is most relevant at the time of admission is the ward's present mental status and ability to care for himself, which may have changed if there was a significant delay between the incompetency proceedings and the commitment. This deficiency is not necessarily cured by a periodic commitment review, or habeas corpus relief, although any additional harm can be corrected in the future when a review is conducted. In addition, once conservators are appointed under this provision, they wield considerable power in all aspects of the ward's life. It is unlikely, unless someone cares enough to petition the court, that the relationship between conservator and ward will be modified, even if circumstances change.

Utah statutorily incorporates an incompetency determination into its involuntary commitment standard in order to facilitate treatment decisions within state institutions. Under this formulation a person may be institutionalized and relieved of the right to make personal medical decisions if all the following criteria are met:[52] the patient is mentally ill and dangerous, which includes an inability to provide the basic necessities of life; the patient is unable to make rational decisions regarding treatment; there is no less restrictive alternative placement; and the facility can provide adequate and appropriate individualized treatment. A federal court, after reviewing the statute, concluded that state institutional staff could forcibly administer psychotropic medications to unwilling inmates since the issue of the resident's abilities to consent to treatment had been resolved at the commitment hearings.[53]

Conceptually, this approach suffers from the same type of timeliness problem as the California statute. The relevant inquiry concerning a patient's decision-making ability should be made at the time the treatment is offered, not at some prior hearing. Also, the presumption remains that commitment is needed when the patient's status is next reviewed, and overcoming this presumption is the only way to successfully challenge forcible treatment. Moreover, although no court has decided the matter, the formulation appears to require the questionable result that patients who can demonstrate they have regained their capacities to make rational decisions must be released from civil commitment even if they are mentally ill and dangerous.

VI. VOLUNTARY THIRD-PARTY COMMITMENT[54]

Significant disputes arise when guardians assert that the scope of their powers includes the right to "voluntarily" commit their wards. One aspect of this assertion of power, dealing with minors, has been resolved by the United States Supreme Court.[55] The justices held that parents or legal guardians could voluntarily admit their charges into an institution but only if the state afforded the children minimal due process protections. While these safeguards fall well short of a full judicial hearing, they do require that the final decision be made by a neutral medical fact-finder who may be the admitting physician. How this decision affects minors without guardians is not entirely clear. On the one hand, the Court emphasized the fact that at periodic medical reviews mandated by the applicable state statutes, the childrens' rights were protected adequately and there was no need for an adversary hearing. On the other

46. Cal. Welf. & Inst. Code § 5001(a) (West 1979).

47. Estate of Roulet, 590 P.2d 1, 152 Cal. Rptr. 425 (1979).

48. Estate of Davis v. Treharne, 124 Cal. App. 3d 313, 177 Cal. Rptr. 369, 370 (1981).

49. 422 U.S. 563 (1975).

50. Estate of Davis v. Treharne, 124 Cal. App. 3d 313, 177 Cal. Rptr. 369, 370 (1981).

51. Estate of Roulet, 590 P.2d 1, 152 Cal. Rptr. 425 (1979).

52. Colyar v. Third Judicial Dist. Ct., 469 F. Supp. 424 (D. Utah 1979).

53. A.E. & R.R. v. Mitchell, No. C-78-466, 5 MDLR 154 (D. Utah June 16, 1980).

54. For a full discussion of this topic see ch. 2, Involuntary Institutionalization.

55. Parham v. J.R. 442 U.S. 584 (1979); and Secretary of Pub. Welfare v. Institutionalized Juveniles, 442 U.S. 640 (1979).

hand, the Court placed a great deal of weight on the traditional authority of parents and legal guardians as decision makers for their children. Moreover, with respect to children who were wards of the state, the justices suggested that greater procedural protections might be necessary at the initial commitments.

Due process requirements for adults facing voluntary commitments by their guardians seem to be set somewhere between the limited safeguards enjoyed by minors and the full panoply of protections that attach to involuntary admissions. One view is that adults who have guardians are in an analogous position to minors and should receive no further due process than a review by a neutral fact-finder.[56] However, this view may be challenged because the analogy breaks down, in at least two respects: the traditional abhorrence courts have for interfering with parental authority is not a factor in adult-guardian relationships, and as a practical matter, guardians—particularly those for adults—may have a far more distant relationship with their wards than parents have with their children.

Recent decisions indicate that the courts are moving closer to a consensus that would strictly limit, if not eliminate, the authority of guardians to admit their adult wards into institutions. Guardians in Illinois and Washington may never voluntarily commit a nonconsenting ward.[57] The only legal procedure available is to file a petition for involuntary civil commitment. Similarly, the Arkansas Supreme Court ruled that while it was proper for a temporary guardian to commit her nonprotesting mother into a hospital for treatment, once the ward requested to leave the hospital the state had to either release her or provide her with a full due process hearing.[58] In Massachusetts, the Supreme Judicial Court concluded that even though appointment of a guardian is based on a determination that the ward is mentally ill and unable to care for himself, commitment will not go forward unless there is also a finding that there is a likelihood of serious harm to the proposed ward or others and this is proved beyond a reasonable doubt.[59] As was discussed earlier, in California before a conservator can be appointed with the power to commit, there has to be proof beyond a reasonable doubt that the proposed ward is gravely disabled, and even after such a hearing, in theory the original court has continuing oversight jurisdiction to make sure the least restrictive environment is maintained.[60] Finally, an appeals court in the District of Columbia found that a mentally retarded resident in a community program who was under the care of the city's department of human services was improperly transferred to an institution. Prior notice to the individual and court approval was necessary, even though the resident was reportedly hallucinating and in need of more restrictive care.[61]

VII. ADMINISTRATIVE REGULATIONS IN THE INSTITUTION

In order for an institution to function, certain rules and regulations need to be established. Many are needed to protect the residents; others are essential or convenient for administrative purposes. As a practical matter, every institution does impose limitations that go beyond the fact of confinement itself. Seventeen states have statutes that specify what restrictions may be employed.[62] It may be a requirement that residents follow institution rules, permission to take action in emergencies, or authority to control the residents' property. Thirty-four states have no provision, thus leaving the matter to the institutions themselves or the courts.

It is convenient to divide administrative regulations into three categories for the purpose of analysis: (1) regulations governing personal or property rights of residents which have nothing or little to do with the internal operations of an institution, such as prohibitions against driving a car once the person is released, making a contract, or voting, for example; (2) regulations clearly affecting the institution's competent administration, such as regulations designed to prevent violence among the residents, minimize opportunities for suicide, protect staff from assaults, maintain the physical health of the other residents, or otherwise control emergency situations;[63] and (3) regulations addressing administrative concerns that may or may not be deemed to be necessary to the smooth functioning of an institution, such as limiting associations with people outside the institution, requiring residents to do certain chores, restricting opportunities for voting, and compelling psychiatric treatment.

Generally speaking, category 1 regulations that may already be illegal should be eliminated, regulations in category 2 should be and are allowed if they are carried out in the least intrusive manner possible consistent with dealing with such emergencies, and those in category 3 should be closely examined by legislatures in the context

56. See discussion in ch. 4, Discharge and Transfer.

57. *In re* Gardner, 121 Ill. App. 3d 7, 459 N.E. 2d 17 (1984); *In re* Limited Guardianship of Anderson, 564 P.2d 1190 (Wash. Ct. App. 1977).

58. Von Luce v. Rankin, 588 S.W.2d 445 (Ark. 1979).

59. Doe v. Doe, 385 N.E.2d 995 (Mass. 1979).

60. Estate of Roulet, 590 P.2d 1, 152 Cal. Rptr. 425 (1979); *In re* Gandolfo, 185 Cal. Rptr. 911 (Ct. App. 1982).

61. *In re* Williams, No. 83-135, 8 MPDLR 90 (D.C. Ct. App. Jan. 9, 1984).

62. Table 7.2, col. 2.

63. Rennie v. Klein, 653 F.2d 836 (3d Cir. 1981); Rogers v. Okin, 634 F.2d 650 (1st Cir. 1980); Banos v. Crosland, No. 80-2677, 5 MDLR 35 (D.D.C. Dec. 11, 1980); *In re* KKB, 609 P.2d 747 (Okla. 1980); Davis v. Hubbard, No. C-73-205, 4 MDLR 396 (N.D. Ohio Sept.6, 1980).

of real life situations to determine each regulation's legality and desirability.

The right to refuse treatment is the 1980s administrative issue that is creating the most litigation and concern.[64] In a nonemergency, the courts generally require that certain due process protections be afforded before medical decision-making rights are withheld.[65] Usually the purpose of the proceedings is to determine whether the residents are able to make these decisions for themselves and if not, how these decisions will be made. Where residents are able to make their own decisions the question is whether the interests of the institution outweigh the individual interests involved. If the residents are incompetent, their so-called best interests become primary, although it is still debated from whose point of view the best interests are to be evaluated—the resident's or society's. Recent Supreme Court cases lend support for the view that, whatever the standard, the staff are in a better position than the courts to decide what should be done to carry out the law appropriately within an institution.[66] The exceptions would seem to be where noninstitutional concerns are regulated or where fundamental interests of the individuals such as the right to control one's body or enjoy certain areas of privacy are unnecessarily restricted.[67]

VIII. INCOMPETENCY AND GUARDIANSHIP

Twenty years ago one of the major inadequacies in the commitment laws was the merger of incompetency with institutionalization.[68] Since then, there has been a steady movement to completely separate the two questions.[69] Today incompetency and guardianship have been merged together much the way incompetency and institutionalization used to be. Incompetency is a judicial status, while guardianship is the primary disposition that arises from that status. The new alignment or merger of the two concepts promotes the best interests of the individual by allowing sufficient flexibility for courts to adequately address individual circumstances. Unfortunately, institutions are filled with individuals who are legally incompetent or have diminished capabilities and have no legal guardians.[70] Some, perhaps most, were institutionalized when incompetency was a by-product of commitment and no guardian was appointed.[71] A number are presumed competent by the law and are either incompetent in fact[72] or have been deprived of their rights as if they were incompetent.[73] Others are "voluntary" residents who always were or are now incompetent.

The solution to many of these competency problems of institution residents is to provide separate guardianship proceedings for every involuntarily committed individual whether they have been institutionalized for many years or are facing confinement for the first time. In addition, "voluntarily" admitted residents should be given hearings when their competency to provide proper consent is seriously questioned. Yet such solutions are not without their own problems. Arguments against this type of an approach are based on several very different practical concerns. There is no denying that there would be a substantial cost associated with the providing of hearings for so many people, even if some hearings were combined with commitment proceedings as is now possible in only 8 states.[74] From a different vantage point, civil libertarians and others argue that automatic proceedings of this nature may do more harm than good. They explain that there would be an irresistible bureaucratic tendency to provide pro forma hearings, as is commonly the practice already with commitment hearings, and there would not be enough guardians available to handle the present need, much less a substantially increased volume of cases.[75]

As persuasive as these considerations may be, they do not undercut the fundamental need that remains unfulfilled for decision-making assistance to persons confined in institutions. While in confinement, the resident is at

64. In addition to the cases cited *supra* in note 63, see Clites v. State, 322 N.W.2d 917 (Iowa Ct. App. 1982); Ford v. Second Judicial Dist. Ct.; 635 P.2d 578 (Nev. 1981); *In re* Freeman, 636 P.2d 1334 (Colo. Ct. App. 1981); Gundy v. Pauley, No. 80-CA-1737-MR, 5 MDLR 321 (Ky. Ct. App. Aug. 21, 1981); Hanes v. Ambrose, 437 N.Y.S.2d 784 (App. Div. 1981); G.A. v. Public Health Trust of Dade County, No. 80-2924, 5 MDLR 179 (S.D. Fla. filed Oct. 28, 1980); A.E. & R.R. v. Mitchell, No. C-78-466, 5 MDLR 154 (D. Utah June 16, 1980); *In re* FHD, 80-042, No. HDY 2400-80, 5 MDLR 41, (N.J. Dep't of Human Servs. Oct. 10, 1980); Wolfe v. Maricopa County Gen. Hosp., 619 P.2d 1041 (Ariz. 1980).

65. Rennie v. Klein, 653 F.2d 836 (3d Cir. 1981); Rogers v. Okin, 634 F.2d 650 (1st Cir. 1980).

66. Youngberg v. Romeo, 457 U.S. 307 (1982); Parham v. J.R., 442 U.S. 584 (1979); Bell v. Wolfish, 441 U.S. 520 (1979).

67. Rennie v. Klein, 653 F.2d 836 (3d Cir. 1981) (right to refuse medication); Rogers v. Okin, 634 F.2d 650 (1st Cir. 1980) (right to refuse treatment); Manhattan State Citizens Group, Inc. v. Bass, 524 F. Supp. 1270 (S.D.N.Y. 1981).

68. R.C. Allen, E.Z. Ferster, & H. Weihofen, Mental Impairment and Legal Incompetency 37 (1968).

69. Table 7.2.

70. Sherman, Guardianship: Time for a Reassessment, 49 Fordham L. Rev. 350, 367 n.112 (1980).

71. Power, Cigarettes, Cokes and Candy: Must Mental Patients Beg? 2 District Law 25, 35, 38 (1978); Zenoff, Civil Incompetency in the District of Columbia, 32 Geo. Wash. L. Rev. 243, 257 (1963).

72. Power, *supra* note 71, at 35.

73. R. Burgdorf, The Legal Rights of Handicapped Persons, 523-26 (1980); Comment, Guardianship of Adults with Mental Retardation: Towards a Presumption of Competence, 14 Akron L. Rev. 321, 331 (1980) [hereinafter cited as Comment, Guardianship of Adults]; Ferleger, Loosing the Chains: In-Hospital Civil Liberties of Mental Patients, 13 Santa Clara Law. 447 (1973); Horstmann, Protective Services for the Elderly: The Limits of Parens Patriae, 40 Mo. L. Rev. 225, 231-35 (1975).

74. Table 7.2, col. 3. Moreover, even fewer states determine all aspects of guardianship in all situations. Georgia, Iowa, and Michigan are examples of states that do.

75. Comment, Guardianship of Adults, *supra* note 73, at 327; cf. Sherman, *supra* note 70, at 353-54, 359 n.60.

the mercy of the institutional environment in which neglect and abuse may be frequent occurrences.[76] There also have been numerous instances in which residents' funds have been mismanaged or spent without proper authority.[77]

Guardianship proceedings, whether they are to serve the interests of a person inside or outside an institution, should address the specific needs of the individual so that the deprivation of decision-making authority inherent in the appointment of a guardian is strictly limited to those needs. This in fact represents the trend in several jurisdictions and is recommended in much of the recent literature. As a result, the conceptualization of incompetency as a threshold determination that affects all decision making is being revised to encompass only limited areas of decision making or conduct where that is more appropriate. Is the person able to vote? Can the senior citizen handle major financial transactions? Is the mentally ill mother's disability temporary? A serious problem remains, however, because while the laws have changed, in many instances the judicial practice of ordering full incompetency has not.

Full guardianship is generally needed only where there has been profound and irreversible mental or cognitive incapacity and it is likely a number of decisions will have to be made for the individual. Such a situation is likely to occur if the person is severely brain damaged, comatose, profoundly mentally retarded, or occasionally if the person is chronically mentally ill. Otherwise, some less drastic alternative is probably needed to address either the temporary or the limited nature of the problem.

The traditional view of incompetency is heavily influenced by the medical and the protective service models of care.[78] Under both these systems the individual is seen as a person who needs assistance; professional staff are best able to determine what assistance is necessary and how it should be delivered. Once the gross determination of need is established, the consumer of the service (the mentally disabled person) loses control of the situation. When the social service or medical system responds to this need it is assumed that the intentions are benevolent *and* that the results are beneficial, which frequently is the case.

A critical weakness in both models is that too often neither accounts for the individualized needs of the person in the initial decision-making process. Moreover, in too many instances more harm is done than good or less good is done than is desirable. On the other hand, one should be reluctant to conclude that there should be no intervention, although this is the conclusion of a few.[79] The total absence of involuntary assistance may be an even more gross distortion of the needs of the individual. For example, there is an overriding need to provide discrete, substitute consent mechanisms that can address the situation where medical treatment is indicated but the patient's ability to consent is questionable or where he is clearly incompetent. Answers must be more precise in order to keep pace with technical or theoretical advancements. This is true whether advancements are in science or the delivery of social services. Just as in many instances modern brain surgeons have discarded the scalpel in favor of the laser beam, courts and legislators need to replace outmoded legal concepts that were once useful for making determinations about mentally disabled people with new concepts that are designed to examine individual needs and individual rights. In the area of incompetency and guardianship this means employing concepts of limited, partial, or temporary guardianship when, and if, intervention is called for following an incompetency determination. It also means providing supportive services that will allow individuals to provide for themselves without the necessity of legal intervention. Generally, when services are provided competently and in good faith, voluntary social programs work far more efficiently than litigation.[80]

A. Initiation of Guardianship Proceedings

Guardianship proceedings, with some exceptions, may be initiated by "any interested person."[81] Forty-five states use this or similar language, although Florida requires three "citizens" to make the application, and South Carolina specifies that the parents of mentally retarded individuals must give their consent. Two of the 5 remaining states, New Jersey and West Virginia, have no provision, Alabama provides that a friend or relative may make the application, and Massachusetts and

76. Dewey, Imprisonment of the Mentally Ill: An Inquiry into the Deprivation of Civil Liberties Under Ohio Laws and Procedures, 1 Cap. U.L. Rev. 1 (1972); Ferleger, *supra* note 73; Shaffer, Introduction to Symposium: Mental Illness, the Law and Civil Liberties, 13 Santa Clara Law. 369, 370 n.2, 371 (1973).

77. Ferleger, *supra* note 73, at 456.

78. For a review and critique of these care models, see Special Article Series: Guardianship, 2 MDLR 443 (1978); Sales, Powell, Van Duizend, & Associates, *supra* note 6, at 461-66, Frolik, *supra* note 30.

79. George J. Alexander, however, goes almost that far. He has written that "every human being of adult years, *regardless* of his state of mind, has a right to determine what shall be done with his own body" if he "is able to communicate his preferences no matter how 'unnatural' or unpopular they may be" (from Alexander's foreword to A Future Without Guardianships, an unpublished paper prepared by G.H. Ishi & C.F. Beraldo for the American Bar Association Commission on the Legal Problems of the Elderly, 1982). See also Alexander, On Being Imposed upon by Artful or Designing Persons—The California Experience with Involuntary Placement of the Aged, 14 San Diego L. Rev. 1083 (1977).

80. See discussion in ch. 11, Rights and Entitlements in the Community. See also A Future Without Guardianships, *supra* note 79.

81. Table 7.3, col. 2.

Rhode Island allow a state or local official and a friend or relative to apply. In 29 states alleged incompetent persons may initiate proceedings for themselves. Only 12 jurisdictions specify that a state or local official may file an application, and Ohio is alone in stating that a court may begin a proceeding on its own motion.

An incidental means by which a guardianship proceeding can be initiated is at a commitment hearing.[82] This is possible in only 8 states, and 2 of those states have significant restrictions. Three statutes address only property concerns during the period of commitment. Twelve states provide for the appointment of temporary guardians in emergency situations.

These methods of initiating guardianship proceedings generally produce litigation in only two situations: over requirements for standing where there is no statutory provision and where there are mass appointments of guardians for residents of state institutions. The limited amount of litigation over such procedures probably is less a reflection of satisfaction with the status quo than the realization that in comparison with other aspects of guardianship initiation is relatively unimportant in most circumstances.

In New Jersey, which has no statute, standing is limited by common law rule to "a relative or a person with a legal or equitable interest in the subject of the action."[83] Thus, one court held that a mere friend could not bring the matter to the court's attention.[84] A year later, however, another New Jersey court determined that the state office on aging could petition the court to appoint a guardian for an 82-year-old woman who was found wandering in the streets.[85] The reasoning was that anyone could bring such an action since the courts must always protect the rights of the incompetent person. The only discernible difference between the two rulings was the respective court's judgment concerning the proposed ward's best interests, which leaves future petitioners in that state without much guidance, other than if a person appears to need assistance the courts may decide to hear a petition of a friend or concerned party. The New Jersey cases illustrate the dilemma facing courts and legislatures in other jurisdictions—how to protect the person in need without unnecessarily stigmatizing or inconveniencing the person who is not in need by bringing him into court against his wishes.

A well-publicized case in New York involving an infant born with spina bifida who was denied corrective surgery demonstrates the limits on third parties initiating guardianship proceedings and the potential danger to the initiator. The state's highest court ruled that a private individual without direct interest or knowledge of alleged child neglect could not bring an action on behalf of the child.[86] Moreover, in trying to have himself appointed as guardian ad litem in federal court, the petitioner was fined for harassing the parents who were the natural guardians.[87]

For different reasons, litigation has also occurred when guardianship proceedings have been initiated en masse in institutions. The Florida health department filed applications for two thousand mentally retarded adults who were unable to consent to residential care to prevent them from being released from a state institution.[88] The New Hampshire Supreme Court decided that the state was responsible for obtaining guardians for all incompetent, indigent residents of state institutions whenever an incompetency determination was made.[89] In Michigan, a mass guardianship hearing for more than one hundred institutionalized mentally retarded persons was overturned because the 75-minute hearing did not conform with minimal due process.[90] The appeals court ordered the petitions to be reheard so that the state facility could still serve those who could not consent to services. These outcomes suggest that there is a need to insure that consent will be given by a duly appointed individual, but a shortage of resources makes it difficult to do so properly.

In addition to initiating the proceeding, the petitioner also must file in the correct court, although not all jurisdictions make a specific designation legislatively. In 17 states the statutes designate a probate court, in 9 a district court, in 8 a circuit court, and in 8 others a county court.[91]

B. Notice of Proceedings and Presence in Court

After the proceedings have been initiated, notice must be given to the proposed ward concerning the action that is about to be taken. All but three states—Alabama, Louisiana, and Mississippi—have some statutory requirements concerning notification,[92] and constitutional due process considerations make it more than likely that notice is mandatory in some form in those

82. Table 7.2, col. 3, & table 7.3.

83. *In re* Tierney, 421 A.2d 610, 611 (N.J. 1980), *In re* Oswald, 28 A.2d 299 (N.J. Ch. 1942).

84. *In re* Tierney, 421 A.2d 610 (N.J. 1980).

85. *In re* Bennett, 434 A.2d 1155 (N.J. 1981).

86. Weber v. Stony Brook Hosp., 52 U.S.L.W. 2267 (N.Y. Ct. App. Oct. 28, 1983).

87. Washburn *ex rel.* Baby Jane Doe v. Abrams, No. 83-CV1711, 8 MPDLR 112 (N.D.N.Y. Jan. 20, 1984).

88. Davis v. Page, No. 77-2731, 2 MDLR 386 (Fla. Cir. Ct. Leon County Jan. 4, 1978).

89. *In re* Gamble & Cummings, 394 A.2d 308 (N.H. 1978).

90. Michigan Ass'n for Retarded Citizens v. Wayne County Probate Judge, No. 77-535, 2 MDLR 364 (Mich. Ct. App. Nov. 9, 1977).

91. Table 7.3, col. 1.

92. *Id.*

three states as well.[93] Furthermore, it seems only fair that our legal system provide the proposed ward with meaningful notice and a duly appointed or recognized representative.[94]

What constitutes proper notice changes with the situation and the particular jurisdiction.[95] Forty-eight states mandate that the respondent be contacted directly regardless of the person's mental condition. Thirty-nine jurisdictions specify that the nearest relative must be informed. Nineteen designate the person with care and custody of the individual as the recipient of notice. Atypically, North Carolina specifically singles out the guardian ad litem as the person appointed to act on behalf of the alleged incompetent person throughout the legal proceedings. In most jurisdictions but certainly not all, someone close to the proposed ward must be notified; this requirement is based on the reasonable assumption that the respondent may have limited capacity to understand the meaning of the legal document that sets out the place, time, and kind of proceeding that has been scheduled. Normally where the individual or a representative cannot understand the document and does not attend the hearing, notice is defective, and the entire proceedings may be void or voidable.[96]

The issue of proper notice may be confused in jurisdictions that provide for a waiver of the respondent's right to be present at the hearing.[97] There may be only a subtle difference between faulty notice and constructive waiver of the right to attend, especially where the person who initiates the proceedings is the person caring for the respondent.[98] Where waivers are allowed, the court should confront the proposed incompetent person directly to make sure the waiver is knowingly and intelligently made. If a court appearance would seriously disturb the person, then an interview could be arranged in the judge's chambers or some less threatening environment. For all intents and purposes, a waiver in this situation is equivalent to an admission of incompetency. For this reason, Texas does not permit recognition of a waiver of service of process in proceedings to declare a person of unsound mind. Actual service must be completed before the courts may maintain proper jurisdiction over the proposed ward.[99] A similar requirement has been made by an appeals court in Ohio.[100]

The proposed ward's presence in court is mandatory in 15 states, subject either to the court's general discretion or to a review of the patient's condition.[101] There also is a general right to attend competency hearings in 24 states and a right to a closed hearing in 23 states. Similar to what one finds in civil commitment hearings,[102] a practical tension exists between the right to be directly confronted when the legal system is contemplating a fundamental deprivation of rights and the desire not to worsen the person's mental condition in the process. Unfortunately, in some jurisdictions excusing the respondent's attendance has become a routine practice leading to serious abuses of judicial authority, most notably the conduct of proceedings that lack any substance.[103]

Although notice must be written and "should give intelligent information of the nature of the proceeding,"[104] this does not mean that the proposed incompetent persons have been fairly apprised of the actions that have been initiated on their behalf. Notification is often highly technical and not very informative when reviewed by the educated layperson. Moreover, even if the respondents understand the legal documents, there still may not be enough time to contact an attorney and properly prepare for the hearing. Of the 24 states that bother to specify the amount of time that is minimally necessary, 16 provide for prior notice ranging between three and ten days.[105] Where there is no specific provision, most courts require reasonable notice, but reasonableness allows for considerable interpretation.[106] In Pennsylvania some kind of notice is always required, but who is to receive notice is left up to the trial judge's discretion.[107]

C. Other Due Process Considerations

There is no significant dispute over the right to a hear-

93. *In re* Hruska's Guardianship, 298 N.W. 664 (Iowa 1941); Trapnell v. Smith, 205 S.E.2d 875 (Ga. Ct. App. 1974); Shanklin v. Boyce, 204 S.W. 187 (Mo. 1918). See also Frolik, *supra* note 30, at 637: "A fundamental respect for procedural values requires that adequate notice of the guardianship hearing be given to the alleged incompetent."

But see Walker v. Graves, 125 S.W.2d 154 (Tenn. 1939), which said that guardianship is intended to preserve property for the ward and thus notice is not constitutionally required.

94. See ch. 2, Involuntary Institutionalization, § V CII(c), Notice of Proceedings and Opportunity to Be Heard.

95. Table 7.3, cols. 17-21.

96. 39 Am. Jur. 2d Guardian and Ward § 41 (Law Coop. 1968 & Supp. 1982).

97. See table 7.3 col. 21; 39 Am. Jur. 2d Guardian and Ward § 44 (Law Coop. 1968 & Supp. 1982). Waiver may be by statute, by case law in which consent to the appointment of a guardian constitutes a waiver, and by attendance at the hearing.

98. A number of courts have held that the incompetent person is incapable of warning notice in guardianship proceedings. Guardianship of Walters, 231 P.2d 473 (Cal. 1951); Inhabitants of Winslow v. Inhabitants of Troy, 53 A. 1008 (Me. 1902); Glenn v. Rich. 147 P.2d 849 (Utah 1944).

99. Dyers v. Walls, 645 S.W.2d 317 (Tex. Ct. App. 1982).

100. *In re* Guardianship of Corless, 440 N.E.2d 1203 (Ohio Ct. App. 1982). See also Nigg v. Smith, 415 So. 2d 108 (Ala. 1982).

101. Table 7.4, cols. 5-7.

102. See ch. 4, Discharge and Transfer, *supra*..

103. Mitchell, Involuntary Guardianship for Incompetents: A Strategy for Legal Services Advocates, 12 Clearinghouse Rev. 451, 454 (1978).

104. 44 C.J.S. Insane Persons § 40 (1945 & Supp. 1982).

105. Table 7.3, col. 20.

106. See 44 C.J.S. Insane Persons § 40(f)(0) (1945 & Supp. 1982); Muller v. De Vries, 188 N.W. 885 (Iowa 1922).

107. *In re* Kafic, 439 A.2d 1235 (Pa. Super. Ct. 1982).

ing as part of the guardianship proceedings.[108] Forty-eight states and the District of Columbia provide for it statutorily, and in Louisiana and Rhode Island, which have no provision, the same result applies by basic constitutional considerations.[109]

The right to legal representation at the hearing is a firmly established although not a universal principle.[110] Thirty-four states provide for legal counsel, 36 make a guardian ad litem available either in every situation or where one is necessary, and 26 require or give the court discretion to appoint counsel where the person is unrepresented. As was discussed earlier, constitutional concerns may make the availability of counsel to indigent persons mandatory.[111]

Jury trials are not mandatory, except in 5 states, but juries must be provided if requested in 23 jurisdictions, or as in Wyoming, when it is in the best interests of the alleged incompetent person.[112] Texas clearly states that there is no right to a jury trial, while 26 other jurisdictions have no applicable provision.[113]

Relatively few states dictate the standard of proof that must be used in competency proceedings.[114] Of the 13 that do, 9 require clear and convincing evidence, although Vermont uses a lesser standard in certain situations. New Hampshire demands proof beyond a reasonable doubt. Only Louisiana, which requires proof that satisfies the judge, and North Carolina, which uses the greater weight of the evidence, have lesser standards. Whether constitutional mandates provide for clear and convincing evidence largely depends on one's reading of *Addington v. Texas*,[115] a United States Supreme Court decision that applied that standard to civil commitment hearings. The Court's emphasis on the deprivation of liberty involved in institutionalization may distinguish commitment from incompetency proceedings, except where the guardian has the power to voluntarily commit the ward without a separate hearing. On the other hand, the stigma and fundamental interests involved in guardianship may well provide an independent basis for the higher standard of proof. Many courts and scholars have supported this analysis;[116] a few have not.[117]

The recent trend is to require a higher standard of proof. The Alaska Supreme Court, for example, remanded a case because the lower court failed to indicate that it had applied the clear and convincing evidence standard when appointing a guardian.[118] Similarly, Missouri courts require this intermediate standard.[119] Moreover, in California where guardians may commit their wards to institutions, the standard is proof beyond a reasonable doubt in recognition of the threat "to a person's liberty and dignity on a massive scale."[120]

D. Supporting Medical Evidence

In many states the statutes provide for certification or examination as a condition precedent to an incompetency determination. Generally, either the certification process or examination must be carried out by a physician.[121] The wisdom of this approach is highly questionable given the fact that diagnosis and evaluation of mental disorders has undergone dramatic changes over the years. It used to be generally true that doctors cared for every physical or mental disorder.[122] More recently, doctors' roles have been changing and at least two treatment models are competing with the medical model for prominence. A therapeutic model is used by many psychologists, clinical social workers, and psychiatrists to treat mentally ill patients,[123] and a developmental model is used by a number of professionals, in addition to the three groups just listed, to manage and care for mentally retarded and other developmentally disabled persons.[124] At the same time, most general physicians have little training or experience handling psychiatric or developmental disorders.[125]

An approach superior to accepting submissions of expert evidence only from physicians would be to qualify professionals based on their actual training and experi-

108. Table 7.4, col. 1.

109. Corr v. Mattheis, 407 F. Supp. 847 (D.R.I. 1976); Haughton Elevator Div. v. State, 367 So. 2d 1161 (La. 1979).

110. Table 7.4, cols. 2-4.

111. Sherman, *supra* note 70, at 361; Burgdorf, *supra* note 73, at 591 (1980); Mitchell, *supra* note 103; at 457.

112. Table 7.4, col. 10.

113. *Id.* A number of cases have held there is no constitutional right to a jury trial in these proceedings. Ward v. Booth, 197 F.2d 963 (9th Cir. 1952). Scherz v. Peoples National Bank, 218 S.W.2d 86 (Ark. 1949); *In re* Bundy, 186 P. 811 (Cal. Dist. Ct. App. 1919).

114. Table 7.4, col. 11.

115. 441 U.S. 418 (1979).

116. *In re* Mills, 250 Wis. 401, 27 N.W.2d 375, (1947); *In re* Guardianship of Frank, 137 N.W.2d 218 (N.D. 1965); Regan, *supra* note 6, at 588; Sherman, *supra* note 70, at 357(1980).

117. Cal. Prob. Code § 1751 (West 1972); Horstman, *supra* note 73, at 254-55 (1976).

118. *In re* O.S.D., 672 P.2d 1304 (Alaska 1983).

119. *In re* Richard, 655 S.W.2d (Mo. Ct. App. 1983).

120. Estate of Roulet, 590 P.2d 1, 152 Cal. Rptr. 425 (1979).

121. Table 7.3, cols. 15 & 16.

122. Deutsch, *supra* note 2, at 15, 21-22, 65; Comment, Appointment of Guardians for the Mentally Incompetent, 1964 Duke L. Rev. 341, 346; cf. *In re* Guardianship of Tyrrell, 92 Ohio L. Abs. 253 (P. Ct.), *aff'd* (Ohio App. 1962), *app. dismissed* for lack of debatable constitutional question, 174 Ohio St. 552, 190 N.E.2d 687 (1963); DeCain, Commitment Procedures and the Non-Mentally Ill, 33 N.Y. St. B.J. 151, 152 (1961).

123. L.U. Brammer, Therapeutic Psychology: Fundamentals of Counseling and Psychotherapy (2d ed. 1968).

124. Comment, Guardianship of Adults, *supra* note 73, at 322 n.10; Comment, The Constitutional Right to Treatment Services for the Noncommitted Mentally Disabled, 14 U.S.F.L. Rev. 675, 677 (1980).

125. J.M. May, A Physician Looks at Psychiatry, 133 (1958).

ence rather than their degree. This is done in several states already.[126]

The difference between certification and examination in practical terms is the thoroughness of the evaluation and the opportunity for cross-examination. Certification merely requires an out-of-court conclusion as to whether the alleged incompetent person meets the legal criteria established in a given jurisdiction.[127] The supporting documentation may be minimal. A court-ordered examination usually includes substantial documentation, is delivered in the form of a report, and is subject to cross-examination. A New York court held that an incompetency determination leading to guardianship could not be based on a physician's affidavit even though all parties concurred. The issue of competency had to be presented to the court as a triable issue of fact based on medical evidence.[128] Twelve jurisdictions use certification, while 34 states now require a court-ordered exam.

E. Criteria for Appointing a Guardian

The authority to find a person incompetent and to appoint a guardian is based on a number of legal criteria that differ from state to state. The most prominent difference exists between jurisdictions that focus on general mental status and those that specifically measure the ability to function in society.[129] Twenty-seven statutes include a requirement that there be some kind of mental condition present. Twenty-one jurisdictions use "incompetency" as a criterion for the appointment of a guardian, and 21 predicate it on "incapacity." In addition, 41 statutes require that the incompetency or incapacity stem from a mental illness or deficiency.

Under either a status or a functional test of incompetency it is likely the Oklahoma Supreme Court would have still ruled that the parents of an 18-year-old congenitally deaf woman could not use the state's guardianship statute to force their daughter to leave the Kingdom Come Ministry, a Christian religious group. Despite a lower court ruling that found her "judgmentally immature" and as a result incompetent, the higher court pointed to the court record, which showed she was of above average intelligence, held part-time jobs, and was a registered voter and licensed driver. The court also observed that the daughter's deafness may have created special needs but that she was trained to cope with her communication difficulties, which made her "'capable of understanding and acting with discretion in the ordinary affairs of life.'"[130]

Seventeen jurisdictions add a "best interests" requirement of some type. In the statutes' words, the appointment must be "necessary and desirable," the person must be "in need of supervision," or the appointment must be in the individual's "best interest." Two states—Minnesota and New Hampshire—also require that there be no less restrictive alternative dispositions available, a criterion that is recognized as a constitutional requirement by certain courts and scholars[131] and as a desirable provision by many others[132] where important individual interests are at stake.

Courts will refuse to approve the appointment of a guardian for a mentally disordered person if a guardian is unnecessary. For example, an Illinois appeals courts upheld a trial court's decision to deny a guardianship petition for a proposed ward who suffered from physical disability and "mental peculiarities" when the evidence showed that the individual involved was able to manage his person and estate.[133] A daughter who had been appointed her father's conservator in Illinois was allowed to serve as her father's California representative payee in applying for his social service benefits,[134] while in another California case a guardianship was set aside because the lower court never determined whether with family members of friends a proposed ward could meet his own needs.[135]

Another factor differentiating appointment criteria is the listing of impairments that are included in the applicable definitions of incompetency.[136] The conditions most often specified are in order of frequency: mental retardation or developmental disability (44 states), mental illness (41), advancing age (35), alcoholism (34), drug addiction (30), and physical disability (29).

In addition, there are several less important but nevertheless noteworthy quirks in the way states define

126. Table 7.3, cols. 15 & 16. Connecticut, Georgia, Hawaii, Kentucky, and Vermont.

127. *Id.*

128. *In re* Von Bulow, 22 Misc. 2d 129, 470 N.Y.S.2d 72 (Sup. Ct. 1983).

129. Table 7.3, cols. 15 & 16.

130. *In re* Guardianship of Pollin, 675 P.2d 1013 (Okla. 1984).

131. Covington v. Harris, 419 F.2d 657 (D.C. Cir. 1969); Lake v. Cameron, 364 F.2d 657 (D.C. Cir. 1966); Wyatt v. Stickney, 344 F. Supp. 387 (M.D. Ala. 1972), *aff'd in part, remanded in part sub nom.* Wyatt v. Aderholt, 503 F.2d 1305 (5th Cir. 1974); Davis v. Watkins, 384 F. Supp. 1196 (N.D. Ohio 1974); Comment, Guardianship of Adults, *supra* note 73, at 329.

132. Sales, Powell, Van Duizend, & Associates, *supra* note 6, at xv; Frolik, *supra* note 30, at 653; Special Article Series: Summary of Substantive Issues, 2 MDLR 68-69 (1977); Developmentally Disabled Assistance and Bill of Rights Act of 1975, Pub. L. No. 94-103, § 201 (codified at 42 U.S.C. § 6010 (1982)); Education for All Handicapped Children Act of 1975, Pub. L. No. 94-142 (codified as amended at 20 U.S.C. §§ 1232, 1401, 1405, 1406, 1411-20, & 1453 (1982)); Comment, Involuntary Civil Commitment: The Inadequacy of Existing Procedural and Substantive Protections, 28 U.C.L.A. L. Rev. 906, 910 (1981); Colley, The Education for All Handicapped Children Act (EHA): A Statutory and Legal Analysis, 10 J.L. & Educ. 137, 148 (1981).

133. Estate of Galvin v. Galvin, 112 Ill. App. 3d 677, 445 N.E.2d 1223 (1983).

134. Holiway by Karriem v. Woods, 192 Cal. Rptr. 445 (Ct. App. 1983).

135. Plumer v. Early, 190 Cal. Rptr. 578 (Ct. App. 1983).

136. Table 7.1.

impairments or the impaired:[137] Connecticut, Georgia, and Maryland statutes still state that institutionalized persons are included by virtue of their confinement; despite the fact that the term *developmentally disabled* is widely accepted, only 5 jurisdictions use the term in their guardianship statutes; Mississippi and North Carolina are the only states to specify that advancing age is not an included impairment;[138] and 9 states exclude all minors from coverage.[139]

F. Nature of Guardianship and Powers of Guardians

Although almost every state establishes a general threshold beyond which incompetency is proven and before which it is not, the nature of guardianship is often separated into property and personal interests. In most states it is also limited by the circumstances of the individual and tempered by the opportunity of choosing a temporary or emergency proceeding as an alternative to a permanent guardianship proceeding. The confluence of these trends indicates a movement of the law toward individualized determinations with significantly more flexibility in the possible results. On the other hand, there are still considerable problems to overcome before such individualization is universally incorporated into the law of guardianship and then implemented.

As will be discussed in more detail in the next chapter, the guardian, once appointed, may have substantial, sometimes almost exclusive, authority over the ward, depending on the nature of the substitute consent relationship that is established.[140] In a guardianship of the person a guardian's duties may cover almost any aspect of the ward's day-to-day decision making that does not directly involve financial decisions, including fundamental concerns such as institutionalization, medical treatment, and housing. A conservatorship or guardianship of the property operates similarly but is exclusively concerned with decisions about the ward's property and income such as initiating and cancelling contracts or other financial transactions, managing bank accounts, trusts or real property interests, paying debts, guarding against fraud or mistake, and, if necessary, initiating litigation. Plenary guardianship encompasses decisions over both the person and the person's estate.

The personal guardian, because of the considerable degree of intimacy associated with many of the life decisions of the ward, is more apt to be a relative or a friend. More recently a state agency or representation of such an agency may be involved in the absence of a suitable acquaintance. Often the conservator of an estate is a banker, some other professional financial manager, an attorney, or an institution empowered to protect both the individual interest of the ward and the broader financial interests of the state and local community.

Whether the guardian is of the person or of the estate, the guardianship relationship may be specificially limited by statute to those aspects of the ward's life which clearly need attention. A limited guardianship has been defined as a relationship where the guardian is "assigned only those duties and powers which the individual is incapable of exercising."[141] Such a provision has been endorsed by the American Bar Association and enacted in at least 20 states.[142] Most states have provisions that specify the scope and procedures that limit a guardianship so that no more decision-making power is assumed than is justified by the actual mental, physical, or adaptive limitations of the individual.[143] States set out assigned duties and powers of a guardian and indicate that the court may decide not to include all the duties and power that are listed.[144] A few states require consideration of the less restrictive alternatives.[145]

Only in a few states do guardians have what is essentially unrestricted authority, because more often than not, potentially serious intrusions into the rights of the ward such as institutionalization, sterilization, abortion, electroconvulsive shock therapy, and the administration of psychotropic drugs in nonemergency situations require court approval.[146] Twenty-five states, however, do statutorily provide for proceedings that determine all personal and property rights at the same time.[147] In fact, in 14 states the guardian has the same powers, rights, and duties as the parent of an unemancipated minor. Twenty jurisdictions make competency determinations about property matters in separate proceedings. In fact, there are far more statutes that allow guardians to man-

137. *Id.*

138. *Id.* See also Morgan v. Potter, No. 25657, 3 MDLR 109 (Ct. of Common Pleas, Ohio May 11, 1978).

139. Table 7.1.

140. Frolik, *supra* note 30, at 602-3; Mitchell, *supra* note 103 at 460-61.

141. Sales, Powell, Van Duizend, & Associates, *supra* note 6, at 462.

142. *Id.* According to the authors' compilation in 1978, Connecticut, Florida, Idaho, Illinois, Kentucky, Maine, Maryland, Michigan, New York, North Carolina, South Carolina, South Dakota, Texas, Virginia, Washington, West Virginia, and Wisconsin had this type of provision.

Since then the *Mental Disability Law Reporter* has reported that at least three other states—Alabama, Arkansas, and Nebraska—have enacted such legislation into law. 7 MDLR 134, 278 (1983).

143. Sales, Powell, Van Duizend, & Associates, *supra* note 6, at 462. They indicate that 11 states fall into this category. They are: Connecticut, Florida, Idaho, Illinois, Kentucky, New York, South Carolina, Texas, Washington, West Virginia, and Wisconsin. In addition, 3 states—Alabama, Arkansas, and Nebraska—have more recently enacted legislation that falls into this category. 7 MDLR 134, 278 (1983)

144. Sales, Powell, Van Duizend, & Associates, *supra* note 6, at 462, list Maine, Michigan, North Carolina, South Dakota, and Virginia.

145. *Id.*; only Maryland is listed. In addition, table 7.4, col. 19, notes Colorado requires the least restrictive alternative.

146. See discussion in ch. 8, Decision-making Rights over Persons and Property, *infra*.

147. Table 7.4, cols. 16-19.

age property concerns exclusively than statutes that allow guardians to manage only personal matters.

Whether the guardianship is of the person, the estate or both, the guardian's powers may be substantially curtailed by judicial review[148] or, in a few states, by statute. For example, Colorado, Minnesota, and New Hampshire statutorily limit the choices of a guardian by requiring adherence to the principle of the least restrictive alternative in deciding the type of guardianship that will be established, while Michigan and Tennessee legislatures allow courts to create limited or partial guardianships tailored to the needs of the individual.

In addition, there may be limitations on the scope of the guardianship in specific provisions circumscribing the authority of guardians or in provisions that give discretion to judges.[149] It should be pointed out, however, that a study conducted in 1978 by the American Bar Association found that in six states that have such provisions the limited approach was rarely used.[150] Whether this has changed in past years has not been a subject of further study, although there are indications in the cases that courts are more willing to apply certain kinds of equitable limits regardless of the applicable statutory requirements.[151]

Finally, as will be discussed in more detail in a later section, 33 jurisdictions provide for temporary or emergency guardianships that cover periods of time that range between 30 days and 6 months.[152] This gives authorities the flexibility to deal with an emergent or limited problem in strictly measured time frameworks while providing the proposed ward with some due process—substantially less than the requirements in a regular guardianship hearing. The danger is that curtailed due process allows certain types of abuses to occur more easily, such as the use of pro forma proceedings, representation by unprepared attorneys, or undue influence from the community.

G. Appointment of a Guardian

Once the need for a guardian has been established and the guardian's role defined, the appointment process is carried out by the court. Generally, three types of criteria are applied: eligibility standards, disqualifying factors, and priority setting. Yet even when these criteria are measured, they are not necessarily determinative because there are few statutory guidelines to be followed and considerable judicial discretion in appointing an appropriate guardian.

Most of the states provide broad eligiblility standards that allow "competent," "suitable," "qualified," or "any" adults to serve as guardians.[153] A significant number of states have no provision, and a small handful use special structures such as a committee or commission. Eighteen jurisdictions restrict appointments by disqualifying various categories of individuals, particularly service providers, convicted felons, judges, suspended or disbarred lawyers, spouses, and guardians ad litem. While disqualifying statutes are rare, those establishing preferences are not. About half the states favor the nearest relative, 17 consider the ward's stated preference, and a few look at what is termed the ward's best interest.

Much of the substantive input depends on the discretionary review of probate judges. Normally, courts of appeal will challenge that discretion only in instances of clear abuse.[154] An important factor in virtually every case, regardless of the statutory provisions, "is [the] best interest and well-being of the incompetent."[155] In fact, it is the paramount concern in many decisions,[156] although the determination is often subjective and differs among jurisdictions.

One factor that indicates the ward's best interests may be in jeopardy is the presence of a conflict of interest between the ward and the proposed guardian.[157] The conflict need not be illegal in order for the court to disqualify the proposed guardian. Simple indebtedness to the incompetent person may be enough to remove a person from consideration as an appropriate guardian.[158] Disqualification, however, can mean that a complete stranger will be appointed over a spouse or close relative.[159]

A demonstrable intimacy between the ward and the proposed guardian is an important positive factor in appointments, especially if there is more than one quali-

148. American Bar Association Section of Real Property, Probate and Trust Law, Limited Guardianship: Survey of Implementation Considerations, 15 Real Prop., Prob. & Tr. J. 544, 545 n.6 (1980) [hereinafter cited as Limited Guardianship: Survey]; Comment, Limited Guardianship for the Mentally Retarded, 8 N.M.L. Rev. 31, 239 (1978).

149. Table 7.4.

150. M.T. Axilbund, Substituted Judgment for the Disabled: Report of an Inquiry into Limited Guardianship, Public Guardianship and Adult Protective Services in Six States (A.B.A. Comm'n on the Mentally Disabled, July 1979).

151. Courts have been influenced by equitable principles such as the least restrictive alternative and best interests of the ward. See discussion.

152. Table 7.5, col. 10.

153. Table 7.4, cols. 12 & 13.

154. 39 Am. Jur. 2d Guardian and Ward § 27 (Law. Coop. 1968 & Supp. 1982).

155. *In re* Estate of Vicic, 79 Ill. App. 3d 383, 398 N.E.2d 420, 420 (1979). See also 39 Am. Jur. 2d Guardians and Ward § 31 (Law. Coop. 1968 & Supp. 1982).

156. 39 Am. Jur. 2d Guardians and Ward § 31 (Law. Coop. 1968 & Supp. 1982). *In re* Walsh's Estate, 223 P.2d 322 (Cal. Dist. Ct. App. 1950); Kelsey v. Green, 37 A. 679 (Conn. 1897); *In re* Guardianship of Howard, 349 P.2d 547 (N.M. 1960); Application of Cicero, 421 N.Y.S.2d 965 (1979).

157. 44 C.J.S. Insane Persons § 42; *In re* Voshake's Guardianship, 189 A.753 (Pa. Super. Ct. 1937).

158. *In re* Lyon's Guardianship, 299 N.W. 322 (Neb. 1941).

159. *In re* Tepen, 599 S.W.2d 533 (Mo. Ct. App. 1980).

fied guardian available.[160] Close relatives are ordinarily thought to be "most solicitous of the incompetent's welfare," but in the absence of a statute the final decision remains within the sound discretion of the court,[161] even if there is no evidence that an available family member is unqualified.[162] In Montana one sister was chosen as guardian over another sister because the evidence showed that the eventual guardian had visited her incapacitated sister often and was supported in her application by two other siblings. The other sister who was already the representative payee had shown little personal concern for her sick sister.[163] In New York even though family members may be interested in serving, it is within a court's discretion to choose a nonfamily member.[164]

Another major factor in determining the ward's best interests is the "fitness" of the proposed guardian.[165] In many instances, these factors are very subjective in nature, again requiring probate judges to exercise much discretion. Fitness has been measured in terms of moral character,[166] in-state residence,[167] age or physical condition,[168] proposed plans for the ward's welfare,[169] professional qualifications,[170] experience in managing finances equivalent to the ward's estate,[171] and religious beliefs where the ward is a minor.[172]

In North Carolina, the appointment of a guardian of the estate is so routine that it is handled by the court clerk following an incompetency hearing.[173] The standard for judicial review is similar to appellate review in other states—whether the appointment is "manifestly unsupported by reason."[174]

H. Limitations on the Powers of the Guardian

Besides using the discretion inherent in guardianship,[175] courts have a number of means at their disposal to restrict the powers of the guardian. Some of these devices are outlined specifically in the statutes; others are possible through broad equitable considerations. In addition, through petitions for removal of the guardian or restoration of competency or accounting for assets, there are ways in which the ward and interested third parties can ask the courts to change the status quo and correct inequities caused by the guardian.

Two common statutory provisions that have been enacted to protect the ward's interests are continued court supervision following appointment of a guardian and the posting of bond to insure there will be funds on hand if the guardian errs. Periodic judicial review is required in some form by 30 states[176] and discretionary review as the interests of justice dictate is also common.[177] In 43 jurisdictions the judge has the discretion to make the guardian post bond where money interests are at stake, such as in New York where a court made a conservator post $3 million, a figure corresponding to that value of the portion of the estate the conservator would not inherit.[178]

Courts will also limit the scope of the guardian's powers where abuses to the ward are possible. The same New York court that required the large bond also gave detailed instructions to the spouse who was serving as the conservator because the court had qualms about her appointment.[179] It specified that the husband's sons would be paid $6,000 a year support and that the wife could not make art purchases because she was inexperienced in that field. To a lesser extent, courts will take into consideration the rights of third parties interested in the guardianship arrangements,[180] for example, the sons in the New York case.

In all types of guardianship proceedings, the overriding concern should be the ward's best interests. In structuring the fiduciary relationship a number of courts tailor the duties of a guardian to the actual needs of the ward.[181] To do otherwise would be constitutionally suspect and inconsistent with the least restrictive alternative.[182]

After the relationship has been legally formed, the courts may retain jurisdiction and take steps, short of restoring the ward's capacity or removing the guardian, to modify or negate the guardian's decisions. In their role as parens patriae courts may intercede whenever the welfare of the ward is threatened by the guardian's ac-

160. Ferry v. Powers, 433 N.E.2d 1250 (Mass. App. Ct. 1982).
161. 39 Am. Jur. 2d Guardian and Ward § 29 (Law. Coop. 1968 & Supp. 1982).
162. *In re* Scurlock, 455 N.Y.S.2d 131 (App. Div. 1982).
163. *In re* Guardianship of Nelson, 663 P.2d 316 (Mont. 1983).
164. *In re* Scurlock, 455 N.Y.S.2d 131 (App. Div. 1982).
165. 39 Am. Jur. 2d Guardian and Ward § 32 (Law. Coop. 1968 & Supp. 1982).
166. Guardianship of Pankey, 38 Cal. App. 3d 919 (Dist. Ct. App. 1974); *In re* Fujimoto, 226 P. 505 (Wash. 1924).
167. Speight v. Knight, 11 Alan 461 (1847).
168. *In re* Estate of Vicic, 79 Ill. App. 3d 383, 398 N.E.2d 420 (1979). Also 39 Am. Jur. 2d Guardian and Ward § 32 (Law. Coop. 1968 & Supp. 1982).
169. *In re* Estate of Vicic, 79 Ill. App. 3d 383, 398 N.E.2d 420 (1979).
170. *Id.*
171. *In re* Ramos, 445 N.Y.S.2d 891 (Sup. Ct. Bronx County 1981).
172. 39 Am. Jur. 2d Guardian and Ward § 34 (Law. Coop. 1968 & Supp. 1982); *In re* Waite, 180 N.W. 159 (Iowa 1920).
173. *In re* Bidstrup, 285 S.E.2d 304 (N.C. Ct. App. 1982).
174. *Id.* at 304.
175. Tables 7.3, 7.4, & 7.5.
176. Table 7.4, col. 20.
177. *Id.*
178. *In re* Salz, 436 N.Y.S.2d 713 (App. Div. 1981).
179. *Id.*
180. 44 C.J.S. Insane Persons § 42 (1945 & Supp. 1982). *In re* Cooper, 94 N.Y.S. 270 (App. Div. 1905).
181. Guardianship of Bassett, 385 N.E.2d 1024 (Mass. App. Ct. 1975); *In re* Boyer 636 P.2d 1085 (Utah 1981); Limited Guardianship: Survey, *supra* note 148, at 556 n.124 (1980).
182. In addition to references cited in note 181 *supra*, see Fazio v. Fazio, 378 N.E.2d 951 (Mass. 1978).

tions or neglect. Moreover, as an officer of the court the guardian is always subject to judicial supervision.[183] Court intervention is most common where financial transactions are made on the ward's behalf, although it may occur in personal matters as well. The applicable definition of the ward's best interests depends upon the circumstances and the jurisdiction. Two major themes run through the case law: the more traditional assessment of what would most benefit the ward from the standpoint of the decision maker[184] and the more recently developed notion of attempting to ascertain what the ward would decide if competent to do so.[185]

The second type of standard appeals to one's sense of justice if free choice is the primary value. Yet, determining what someone else would have wanted is not necessarily easier and at times can be more difficult than deciding what is best in a particular situation. In addition, viewed from either a theoretical or a practical basis, what the ward might prefer may not be in the ward's interest. For example, suppose the ward would favor an outcome that benefits a close relative at his own expense. Sometimes the results appear to be benign; other times they raise questions. One of the most common examples in which courts do not intercede is a gift.[186] A much more troublesome application of the standard based on what the ward would want done is the donation of a ward's kidney to an ailing family member.[187] However, anytime a guardian will receive a monetary or psychic benefit from the decision, the potential for overreaching is present, whether the situation involves a gift of money or life, institutionalization, or sterilization. (A more complete discussion of the legal nature of these problems is found in the next chapter.)

Where the courts do establish that a decision goes against the best interest of the ward or that some other impropriety exists, broad equitable powers can be applied to make adjustments and to prevent further indiscretions or mistakes. One option is to request an accounting of the financial transactions that have been made and charge the guardian for all unjustified losses of the ward's income.[188] These assessments may be done on a regular basis. Another option is to simply cancel the transaction and bring the parties back to their relative financial status when the improper transaction was made.[189]

One of the most powerful tools at a court's disposal is the option, in appropriate circumstances, of removing the guardian and replacing him with someone who is more suitable, adhering to the same standards that were used to appoint the original guardian.[190] A threshold requirement, however, is that the first guardian must have been legally unqualified to continue, even in the face of persuasive evidence that another person would be better.[191] Frequently, in removal proceedings financial misdealings are the major issue. For example, a North Carolina appeals court removed a guardian who violated his fiduciary duty by renting land from his incompetent mother and paying her significantly less than fair market value.[192] In a more difficult factual situation a divided Louisiana appeals court was confronted with a curator who spent $80,000 of the ward's $158,000 estate for a 24-hour guard service. The bank was removed because to the majority the bank's actions had been financially "imprudent."[193]

Guardians also directly or indirectly may be penalized for their actions. A conservator in Indiana forfeited compensation for his services after a court found that as the ward's attorney he convinced his charge to sign a contract for legal services and a will, both of which benefited the conservator's law firm.[194] Similarly, a New York conservator had to give up the possibility of inheriting from her ward's estate when it was discovered she advised her ward to renounce her will.[195] But in some jurisdictions conflict of interest or mismanagement by itself may be insufficient reason to penalize the guardian. An appeals court in Wisconsin would not assess costs against a guardian without evidence of fraud, bad faith, or deliberate dishonesty.[196]

Closely related to the idea of a court's taking actions against a guardian for misbehavior is permitting a court to decide how to compensate guardians for various types of services rendered. Sometimes the difference between the two types of decisions is subtle, such as where the

183. 44 C.J.S. Insane Persons § 49 (1945 & Supp. 1982).

184. Estate of Hymes, 424 N.Y.S.2d 608 (N.Y. County Sur. Ct. 1979); Conservatorship of Bradlee, 415 A.2d 1144 (N.H. 1980).

185. *In re* Jones, 401 N.E.2d 351 (Mass. 1980). See also, for a case review, Rohan, Caring for Persons Under a Disability: A Critique of the Role of the Conservator and the "Substitution of Judgment Doctrine," 52 St. John's L. Rev. 1 (1977).

186. Rohan, *supra* note 185; *In re* Estate of Fairbairn, 392 N.Y.S.2d 152 (App. Div. 1977); *In re* Trott, 288 A.2d 303 (N.J. Super. Ct. Ch. Div. 1972).

187. Little v. Little, 576 S.W.2d 493 (Tex. Civ. App. 1979); Strunk v. Strunk, 445 S.W.2d 145 (Ky. Ct. App. 1969).

188. *In re* Estate of Bradshaw, 606 P.2d 578 (Okla. 1980); Estate of Weber v. Hampshire, 81 Ill. App. 3d 257, 401 N.E.2d 245 (1980); Harbaugh v. Myron Harbaugh Motor, Inc., 597 P.2d 18 (Idaho 1979).

189. Marshall v. Kleinman, 438 A.2d 1199 (Conn. 1982); Strain v. Rossman, 614 P.2d 102 (Or. Ct. App. 1980); Bolik v. Cole, 271 S.E.2d 540 (N.C. Ct. App. 1980); Conservatorship of Bradlee, 415 A.2d 1144 (N.H. 1980).

190. Estate of Rumoro v. Leoni, 90 Ill. App. 3d 383, 413 N.E.2d 70 (1980); *In re* Guardianship of Lake, 644 P.2d 1368 (Kan. Ct. App. 1982); Ahlman v. Wolf, 413 So. 2d 787 (Fla. Dist. Ct. App. 1982).

191. Freeman v. Chaplic, 446 N.E.2d 1369 (Mass. 1983).

192. Parker v. Barefoot, 300 S.E. 2d 571 (N.C. Ct. App. 1983).

193. *In re* Ronstrom, 436 So. 2d 588 (La. Ct. App. 1983).

194. Briggs v. Clinton County Bank & Trust Co., 452 N.E.2d 989 (Ind. Ct. App. 1983).

195. *In re* Rossi, 455 N.Y.S. 2d 505 (Sup. Ct. Spec. Terms 1982).

196. *In re* Guardianship and Estate of P.A.H., 340 N.W.2d 577 (Wis. Ct. App. 1983).

guardian's actions are questionable ethically. Other times, a dispute is so squarely centered on the nature of the services, that the decision has to be made on the basis of whether services actually benefited the ward. The Illinois Supreme Court affirmed compensation for guardians who provided the ward with emotional support and nothing else.[197] A dissent at the intermediate appellate level noted that such a broad compensation theory was a radical departure from the past precedents.[198] On the other hand, another Illinois court refused to repay a conservator for repairs he ordered for his ward's property. Because the expense was large and no prior authorization had been obtained from the court, the guardian's good faith defense was not persuasive, given the harm to the ward's estate.[199]

IX. SPECIAL GUARDIANSHIP OR RELATED SITUATIONS

Special guardianship-like relationships are available to meet special circumstances. Nine of the most important will be discussed below: (1) the successor to a natural guardian by testamentary appointment, (2) temporary or emergency appointment, (3) guardians ad litem, (4) guardians for minors, (5) public guardians, (6) guardians for physically disabled persons, (7) representative payees, (8) living wills, and (9) adult protective services. In each instance, the general rules of guardianship are modified in order to address a particular societal concern.

A. Testamentary Guardian

In almost every jurisdiction a form of testamentary guardianship is recognized in which parents or spouses acting as natural guardians may determine their successors by deed or will.[200] This is primarily a mechanism to allow parents to care for their minor children should the parents die. It also has specific relevance to the law of the mentally disabled in the following circumstances: where a minor child is disabled, where an adult child is disabled, where a spouse is the guardian of an incapacitated person, or where a guardian becomes incapacitated.

Generally, the common law does not provide for the appointment of a testamentary guardian.[201] There must be a statute from which the testator's authority derives. If the statute is generally worded, the power of appointment is exclusively with the father[202] and no one has the power to appoint a successor for an adult child, even if the child is disabled.[203] In many jurisdictions, however, the rights of the mother have been recognized in subsequent legislation.[204]

The appointment of a guardian by will is given effect by the judicial system in three basic ways. Most frequently the will is analogous to a statutory appointment preference and is considered as a request or nomination. Generally, the probate court may overrule the testator if to do so would improve the welfare of the ward,[205] but in a few states the nomination is binding on the courts.[206] In order to change the guardian there must be a removal proceeding after the appointment is recognized. Many states combine the two methods by allowing the testator to appoint a guardian by will but establishing a court confirmation process.

Where the statutes specify a preference, spouses are most often mentioned as the successors to the original guardian.[207] Normally, no preference is specified, which means that in the absence of a will or a deed indicating an individual as the successor, guardianship will be determined at an open hearing. Of the 12 states that establish a priority among the testators, 11 give first preference to the spouse. North Carolina provides that the will with the latest date will be given priority. In 10 jurisdictions testamentary guardianship can be terminated upon the written objection of the ward or in Michigan and North Carolina upon judicially following a guardian's dismisssal or a ward's restoration.

Testamentary guardianship allows parents in the event of their death or disability to provide for their disabled children, whether the children are minors or adults. The same relationship is applied to spouses who are guardians for their disabled husbands or wives. Like a living will, the testamentary guardianship preserves the parents' or spouse's decision about their loved ones. However, to avoid abuses or mistakes courts at least should review each appointment to determine whether the ward's interests are being well-served. This type of review is already statutorily required in many states.[208]

B. Temporary or Emergency Guardians

Thirty-four states provide a mechanism for tempo-

197. *In re* Estate of Donnelly, 98 Ill. 2d 24, 455 N.E.2d 88 (1983).

198. *In re* Estate of Donnelly, 111 Ill. App. 3d 1035, 445 N.E.2d 49 (1983).

199. Parsons v. Estate of Wambaugh, 110 Ill. App. 3d 374, 442 N.E.2d 571 (1982).

200. 39 Am. Jur. 2d Guardian and Ward § 11 (Law. Coop. 1968 & Supp. 1982); 39 C.J.S., Guardian and Ward § 15 (1976 & Supp. 1982).

201. *Id.*

202. 39 Am. Jur. 2d Guardian and Ward § 12 (Law. Coop. 1968 & Supp. 1982).

203. *Id.* See Hemphill v. Smith, 91 So. 337 (Miss. 1922).

204. 39 Am. Jur. 2d Guardian and Ward § 11 (Law. Coop. 1968 & Supp. 1982).

205. *Id.* at § 15; Note, The Appointment of Guardians by Will: A Comparison of Vermont's Statutory Provisions with the Provisions of the Uniform Probate Code, 4 Vt. L. Rev. 275, 276, 277 (1979).

206. See references cited in note 205 *supra*.

207. Table 7.5, col. 14.

208. *Id.*

rary or emergency guardianship[209] which is normally used when a guardian dies suddenly or is incapacitated while the process of appointing a permanent guardian is under way or when a non-life-threatening emergency arises, such as the need for treatment that requires prompt action. Due to the limited nature of the relationship and the need for quick action, procedural requirements are lessened, and considerable discretion both in the appointment of an interim guardian and in the continuing review of the ward's situation is left to the courts.[210]

Two sets of criteria normally are used for the appointment of a guardian in these circumstances.[211] One statutory mechanism operates where there is no guardian and an incompetent or incapacitated person is facing an emergency situation. The other type of appointment process is initiated where the present guardian is inadequate and the immediate welfare of the ward is threatened.

Fifteen jurisdictions state that notice to the individual or his representative is not required.[212] Five states leave notice to the court's discretion, and Pennsylvania requires notice when it is feasible. Only 6 states make notice mandatory, and 20 jurisdictions have no applicable statutes.

The maximum duration of an emergency or temporary guardianship varies considerably with the jurisdictions.[213] Twelve states limit appointment to the time the guardianship hearing is held or a permanent guardian is appointed, 8 set durational limits between 30 and 90 days depending on the jurisdiction, 8 others provide for a maximum of 6 months, and 2 leave it up to the court's discretion.

Only 12 states provide a forum in which to raise objections to the temporary appointment process.[214] In general, hearings take place if there is an objection by an interested party.

While most of the legal controversies surrounding emergency or temporary guardianships involve the need for substituted consent to provide medical or psychiatric treatment to incompetent or unwilling patents (an issue thoroughly addressed in other chapters),[215] an emerging problem is the authority of courts to permit parents or relatives to be temporary guardians so they may remove their emancipated or adult children from groups that are considered to be religious or political cults. In such a situation the allegation is not that the children are mentally incompetent in a traditional sense but that they are acting incompetently due to the influence of others. A federal court in Oklahoma, for example, granted a petition to a father who wished to be appointed temporary guardian in order to forcibly deprogram his son, even though there was no judicial finding that the son was mentally ill. The Tenth Circuit recognized the potential for abuse in such a situation and reversed: "The [lower court] judge considered the guardianship order to be for the purpose of determining whether the son had been brainwashed in the monastery . . . an objective which, of course, is not provided for in any Oklahoma statute."[216] This case underscores the need for careful judicial review in temporary or emergency guardianship proceedings, with strict adherence to existing statutory standards. In addition, those states that have no temporary mechanism should make it clear what role, if any, the judiciary is to play where indefinite guardianship is inappropriate.

C. Guardians Ad Litem

Thirty-six states provide a guardian ad litem automatically or as it is necessary[217] to ensure that the proposed incompetent person is protected during the course of litigation. The scope of the guardian's responsibilities is limited to making all decisions regarding legal proceedings on behalf of the ward. The issue may be appointment of a guardian, or it may concern other important interests such as involuntary commitment, right to life, sterilization, or termination of parental rights.[218] More often than not, guardians ad litem are attorneys who are representing the ward in court and assume the added responsibilities until the proceedings conclude.

Recent cases suggest that the authority of the guardian ad litem will be strictly circumscribed by statutory authority and the needs of the litigation. The appointment of a guardian ad litem against the wishes of the proposed ward was held to be reversible error by one court,[219] while a second court found that notification to such a guardian did not constitute notice to the ward where there was no statute that permitted this type of substituted service.[220] In Nebraska a guardian ad litem was unable to waive his client's rights in a parental termination hearing without first proving to the court that waiver was appropriate,[221] while in New Jersey there was

209. *Id.*
210. 44 C.J.S. Insane Persons § 38 (1945 & Supp. 1982).
211. Table 7.5.
212. *Id.*
213. *Id.*
214. *Id.*
215. See ch. 8, Decision-making Rights over Persons and Property, *infra*.
216. Taylor v. Gilmartin, 686 F.2d 1346, 1352 (10th Cir. 1982).
217. Table 7.4, col. 4.
218. Nebraska v. Rima, 310 N.W.2d 138 (Neb. 1981); Wilmington Medical Center, Inc. v. Severns, 433 A.2d 1047 (Del. 1981); *In re* A.W., 637 P.2d 366 (Colo. 1981); State v. Ladd, 433 A.2d 294 (Vt. 1981).
219. State v. Ladd, 433 A.2d 294 (Vt. 1981).
220. Kadota v. Hosogai, 608 P.2d 68 (Ariz. Ct. App. 1980).
221. Nebraska v. Rima, 310 N.W.2d 138 (Neb. 1981).

no authority under any circumstance for a guardian ad litem to file for divorce on behalf of a ward since divorce was too personal a decision for someone else to initiate.[222] Finally, a Florida court decided that a guardian ad litem had to limit her investigations to the case she was appointed to handle for the ward[223] since all of the ward's other concerns were beyond her authority.

D. Guardians for Minors

Since a child's age and the absence of a guardian are usually the only criteria needed to justify the appointment of a guardian for a minor,[224] the existence of a mental disability is normally unnecessary in the appointment process. A child is presumed to be incompetent unless the presumption is overcome by proof of marriage, adulthood, or legal emancipation. In contrast adults are presumed to be competent until they are adjudicated incompetent. Also, the scope of the guardian's authority is often broader where the ward is a child because of the deference traditionally accorded to the parent-child relationship.[225] Although parents may commit their children to institutions without a prior due process hearing, it is disputed whether a hearing can be dispensed with if the ward is an adult.[226] Moreover, while the courts may attach many limits to a guardianship if the ward is an adult, this is done less frequently if the ward is a child.

E. Public Guardians

A survey conducted in 1978 indicated that 12 states had empowered public guardians to provide guardianship services when no suitable private individuals were available.[227] Typically, public guardians are bound by the same laws as other guardians.[228] In six of the states the powers are plenary, and in six they are limited.[229] All but two jurisdictions place both personal and estate interests under the public guardian's control.[230] Five jurisdictions cover minors as well as adults.

In many states the public guardian is a full-time state or county official.[231] In some places the guardians are appointed on a case-by-case basis through a local or state office and paid a reasonable rate for their services.[232] This latter method shifts the monitoring responsibility for guardianships from the courts to a public agency that may be involved in providing other services to the ward, creating a potential conflict of interest.

A primary function of many public guardians is to act as a case manager coordinating services needed by the ward. In four jurisdictions there is legislation mandating that the guardian insure that the ward receives necessary habilitative or treatment services.[233] These dual responsibilities in which the guardian is both a case manager coordinating services and the person who monitors the delivery of services to the ward create another potential conflict of interest.[234]

Other problems with public guardianship also have been identified in the literature, including underutilization,[235] the opposite problem of creating clients to justify the office's existence,[236] and the difficulty of distinguishing the role of the public guardian from general protective services.[237] With respect to this last problem, a California appeals court had to instruct the public guardian that less restrictive facilities were more consistent with both the stated and the actual interests of a gravely disabled, mentally retarded ward.[238]

One way to address many of the stated objections about public guardianship is to make the guardian an independent, nonprofit, nongovernmental agency that does not provide other services. The guardian would serve as a protector of the client without being unduly influenced by other state interests, such as protection of society, reducing expenditures, or serving as a case manager. Such an agency could provide guardianship services itself sells or train and monitor relatives, friends, or members of the community to perform those duties.

F. Guardians for Physically Disabled Persons

In a few jurisdictions guardians may be appointed for persons found to be physically incompetent.[239] Two recent cases illustrate two approaches that may be used to protect the interests of physically disabled persons who have serious functional limitations. A Florida appeals court reversed a lower court that failed to appoint a guardian for an 87-year old man who was found to be physically incapacitated because the lower court believed it had no discretion in the matter.[240] The higher court disagreed, finding that the statutory language required that a personal guardian be appointed for a

222. *In re* Jennings, 453 A.2d 572 (N.J. Super. Ct. Ch. Div.1981).
223. *In re* Jensen, 405 So. 2d 1074 (Fla. Ct. App. 1981).
224. Sales, Powell, Van Duizend, & Associates, *supra* note 6, at 464.
225. Parham v. J.R., 442 U.S. 584 (1979).
226. *Id.*
227. Sales, Powell, Van Duizend, & Associates, *supra* note 6, at 474, 475.
228. *Id.* at 474, 475, 480, 494, 495, 499, 501.
229. *Id.* at 480. Plenary—Arizona, California, Georgia, Ohio, Oregon, and Tennessee; Limited—Colorado, Delaware, Illinois, Maine, Minnesota, and North Carolina.
230. *Id.* at 500.
231. *Id.*
232. *Id.* at 494-95.
233. *Id.*
234. Frolik, *supra* note 30, at 645-46.
235. Axilbund, *supra* note 150, at iii.
236. Frolik, *supra* note 30, at 646.
237. Axilbund, *supra* note 150.
238. *In re* Gandolfo, 185 Cal. Rptr. 911 (Ct. App. 1982).
239. E.g., Florida, Fla. Stat. Ann. § 744.331(9) (West Supp. 1984), and Ohio, Ohio Rev. Code Ann. § 2111.02 (Baldwin 1976 & Supp. 1984).
240. *In re* Sepe, 421 So. 2d 27 (Fla. Dist. Ct. App. 1982).

"physically incompetent" person regardless of the man's mental capacity or his stated preferences. In an Ohio case, however, mental status was relevant. A guardian was found to be inappropriate for a physically incompetent person who had not given his consent.[241] Furthermore, according to the same statute, physically disabled persons were permitted to select their own guardians.

A third approach, which is by far the most common, is to provide guardians only for mentally incompetent persons. While this may be preferable to compulsory guardianship for certain categories of physically incompetent persons, it falls short in comparison with the alternative of allowing mentally competent disabled persons to determine for themselves what is in their best interests.

G. Representative Payees

Many institutionalized persons and certain disabled individuals in the community are unable because of their isolation or their physical and mental limitations to properly handle third-party benefits used for their care, such as social security, veterans benefits, and pensions. Since these benefits are their only substantial assets or income, and a formal incompetency determination would be unnecessary or lead to an overly intrusive resolution of the problem, a system has been established to appoint a representative payee to make payments on behalf of the incapacitated person. Often the person is the individual who operates the institution, nursing home, or board and care home that houses the disabled individual. While this may be very convenient for all parties concerned, it also raises concerns about misuse of funds and overpayments to the facility. In the institutional context, particularly, there have been documented instances where funds were spent inappropriately.[242]

H. Living Wills

A living will allows competent persons to specify before they become incompetent what medical treatment they wish to receive or to refuse if they are seriously ill. This is especially important with regard to the use of extraordinary life-sustaining measures and equipment for dying or comatose individuals. According to a recent review of legislation, 13 states and the District of Columbia have enacted "right to die" statutes since 1976, and 22 other jurisdictions are considering such legislation.[243] Although jurisdictions have established very different procedures for invoking and revoking a living will, they all provide a means by which a person may direct what will happen to him if a catastrophic illness occurs. "Whether or not a living will must be followed by medical personnel in a state without a right-to-die law is uncertain," reports this study.[244] (This problem is discussed in the next chapter.) However, in general, even in states without a statute, a specific declaration by the individual will positively influence most courts, particularly those courts that view substituted consent as an effort to most closely approximate the wishes of the patient.[245] In theory, of course, there is no reason why the scope of living wills should be confined to serious medical illness, although to date, other areas of concern to incompetent persons, such as housing or financial management, have not been addressed in living will legislation.

I. Adult Protective Services

One alternative to traditional guardianship is protective services ostensibly provided to incapacitated persons so that they may live safely and humanely in the community without more restrictive legal intervention. The clients who benefit from such services include elderly, mentally ill, and developmentally disabled persons. Adult protective services is a legislative mechanism that allows the state through its caseworkers to provide "a coordinated system of social and health services"[246] without appointing a guardian or relying on civil commitment. In some instances the threat of guardianship or commitment is used as a means to compel the acceptance of those services that the providers determine are needed. The legislation is a hybrid that responds to a variety of social concerns by allowing a range of actions from limited judicious intervention to de facto guardianship, depending on the jurisdiction and the individual circumstances. However, as one study notes, "adult protective services, as an integrated and inter-professional concept, is sufficiently new so that legal concepts and bounds are only beginning to develop."[247]

It should be pointed out that certain commentators and legislators view almost all the mechanisms described in this section along with regular guardianship services and certain voluntary private mechanisms such as estate planning as part of the protective services scheme.[248] This broad definition, while functionally useful in other contexts, fails to sufficiently highlight the distinguishing thrust of the basic adult protective services approach, which is it seems to provide alternatives to guardianship

241. *In re* Guardianship of Gallagher, 441 N.E.2d 593 (Ohio Ct. App. 1981).

242. See ch. 5, Rights of Institutionalized Persons, *supra*.

243. Cohn, The Living Will from the Nurse's Perspective, 11 Law, Medicine and Health Care 121-24 (1983).

244. *Id.* at 122.

245. See ch. 8, Decision-making Rights over Persons and Property, *infra*.

246. J.J. Regan, Protecting the Elderly: The New Paternalism, 32 Hastings L.J. 1111, 1112 (1982).

247. Center for Research and Advanced Study, University of Southern Maine, Improving Protective Services for Older Americans 5 (1982) [hereinafter cited as Improving Protective Services].

248. *Id.* at 1-7.

and commitment while allowing for "involuntary" intervention. The concept should be broad enough to encompass specific community services that are available and necessary as alternatives to plenary guardianship and commitment, while recognizing that various other services should be independent of the protective services scheme to the extent that they can be provided voluntarily outside the protective services model.

The protective services model gives the social service workers the authority to provide a range of community services and where necessary, to do so without the informed consent of the client. A recent Colorado enactment[249] of a protective services bill underscores the way such legislation can be used as a threat. The bill declares that any disabled adult who is subjected to abuse, exploitation, or neglect is entitled to a range of community services. If the adult refuses to comply and accept the identified services, then the county social services director may petition the courts to order the services provided or initiate guardianship proceedings.[250] In addition, there is always the possibility that overzealous caseworkers will use nonlegal means or the threat of court action to encourage or even compel the client to submit to the state's protection.

Problems identified with this kind of legislation, while many,[251] are particularly significant in three areas. First, the language used to define the individuals to be protected may be under- or overinclusive.[252] A judgment about whether this is in fact the case depends on the services that are to be provided and the due process safeguards that are followed. Second, in some legislation there are almost no limits on the permissible range of services that may be included—"casework, medical care, legal services, fiscal management and 'guardianship services and placement services'"[253] are all identified in Ohio's legislation, for example. This means that while services can be tailored to fit individual needs, they can also be compelled en masse at the discretion of the state agencies. Third, in many instances due process protections are insufficient either because they do not exist statutorily or because they are not obeyed to the letter of the law.[254] In essence, the legal problems are very similar to those discussed in reference to guardianship and commitment. The difference is that the concept of adult protective services is far less susceptible to precise definition, often including or excluding people and services depending on legislative preference. Each protective services system must be evaluated on its own terms at least until there is agreement as to what the concept should mean and how it is differentiated from guardianship and commitment. In the meantime, as one leading commentator points out, a moratorium should be placed on involuntary interventions and resources rechanneled into voluntary assistance programs. "If the agency comes to realize that involuntary intervention is no longer possible, the incidence of uncooperative clients may tend to decrease and the need for involuntary intervention may drop dramatically." [255] In addition, states should review their current legislation "to eliminate substantive and procedural defects . . . [and] focus their efforts on creating legal mechanisms whereby the citizen can make binding arrangements for control of his or her person and property in advance of the onset of any mental incapacity."[256]

X. RESTORATION TO COMPETENCY

Restoration is a legal determination that individuals who have been adjudged incompetent are now able to manage their business and personal affairs adequately. The law presumes that persons who are adjudicated incompetent remain so. In order for wards to regain their competent status they normally must vindicate themselves in a separate judicial proceeding or, in a few states, be discharged from a mental institution.[257] This second method is a holdover from the time when it was common to merge commitment and competency hearings. It avoids the need to prevail in a hearing that may be even more difficult than challenging an assertion of incompetency in the first instance. However, in many instances the facts are clear-cut and the restoration decision is made without controversy. A Louisiana petitioner was found incapable of caring for either his person or his property where the evidence revealed that the ward still suffered from a manic-depressive disorder, organic brain syndrome, diabetes, obesity, and hypertension.[258] On the other hand, an Arkansas appeals court found the evidence insufficient to continue a guardianship in the face of testimony the ward had cared for herself for more than 12 years and had shown that she understood how to manage her property.[259]

A. Initiation of Restoration Proceedings

In the situation most common today where restoration is not automatic upon discharge from an institu-

249. Colorado Senate Bill 59, 8 MPDLR 145 (1984).

250. *Id.*

251. See Regan, *supra* note 246. Regan discusses many potential benefits and problems of this type of legislative scheme in the specific context of the elderly in what is, to date, the most comprehensive legal treatment of the subject.

252. *Id.* at 1122-26.

253. Improving Protective Services, *supra* note 247, at 6-7, describing Ohio statutes § 5101.60(N).

254. Regan, *supra* note 246, at 1117-22.

255. *Id.* at 1131.

256. *Id.*

257. Table 7.6, cols. 1, 19, & 20.

258. *In re* Aaron, 434 So. 2d 624 (La. Ct. App. 1983).

259. *In re* Estate of Lemley, 653 S.W.2d 141 (Ark. Ct. App. 1983).

tion, there must be a formal initiation process carried out by the ward, a relative, or an interested party.[260] Thirty-nine jurisdictions permit wards to apply for restoration themselves. Forty jurisdictions state essentially that anyone with an interest in the matter may initiate proceedings on behalf of the ward. California is unique because the legislature enacted a statute that provides for automatic restoration unless the conservator applies for reappointment. A number of other states require periodic review of guardianships,[261] while Illinois and Virginia specify that the court of proper jurisdiction may initiate the proceedings on its own.[262] There is also substantial legal authority for the view that courts that decide that a person is incompetent automatically retain jurisdiction until restoration.[263] In New York a friend of the conservatee had no standing to seek any changes in conservatorship because the only legitimate remedy was to seek the conservator's removal.[264]

No matter who begins the restoration process, active support by the guardian appears to be a critical element in persuading the fact-finder. In most instances, the court begins with the perception that the ward is still incompetent.[265]

The place restoration applications are to be filed differs depending on the state. Especially if the original incompetency court retains jurisdiction, the proper forum is usually the same court that would handle an incompetency proceeding.[266] Most jurisdictions in fact follow this approach. A few states include courts of general jurisdiction or equity as well.

B. Due Process Considerations

The statutes of most states require that one or more persons closely involved in the restoration be notified of the time, place, and nature of the proceedings.[267] The designated individuals most frequently are the guardians, close relatives, and the wards themselves. Several jurisdictions leave the matter to the court's discretion, while 13 states have no applicable statutory provisions. More so even than with the original incompetency determination, there is a lingering perception that restoration is not an adversary proceeding but a medical judgment. As a result, notice to the wards or their closest relatives has been held not to be constitutionally required, and its absence has not constituted a jurisdictional defect.[268]

Only 25 of the states have a provision governing the ward's presence in court.[269] Twenty-one states indicate that the ward either may be present or should be present, while 3 other jurisdictions specify that attendance should be waived if it would not be safe for the ward. Mississippi mandates that all interested parties be present in court. In all but 6 states there are statutes that require a formal restoration hearing, although in Alabama the requirement obtains only if the proceedings must be contested and in Texas it obtains only if the facts are doubtful. Rhode Island retains the medical emphasis and appoints a commission to examine the ward in the "hospital." Only 14 jurisdictions provide the incompetent person with a jury trial by right, 2 make a jury trial mandatory, and 3 make it optional with the court. Thirty-one states have no special provision concerning jury requirements. Nearly half the jurisdictions have statutes that require supporting evidence to accompany a restoration petition. Eight use a verified petition, 6 indicate that some kind of medical certificate is necessary, and a number of jurisdictions use some variation of a petition or certificate.

It is not altogether clear when a restoration petition may be filed for the first time and how frequently it may be filed thereafter. Only a few states have a provision that addresses either one of these issues.[270] Those provisions that exist vary greatly, indicating that depending on the jurisdiction the first petition may be filed after six months, after a year, or anytime. Thereafter, the waiting period is usually six months, although Georgia specifies two years.

Finally, although only 12 states have a specific appeals mechanism that covers restoration hearings, there is strong case law support for the proposition that general appeals statutes allow for restoration proceedings.[271]

C. Effect of Restoration

Complete restoration of incompetent persons is provided for by statute in 46 jurisdictions;[272] many of those provisions allow for partial restoration as well,[273] meaning that certain limits may be placed on the ward's activities. Typically, however, the ward is returned to full citizenship, the guardian is discharged, and the court's jurisdiction is extinguished.[274] It should be noted that

260. Table 7.6, cols. 1, 19, & 20.
261. Table 7.4, col. 20, & table 7.6.
262. Table 7.6.
263. State *ex rel.* Martin v. Superior Ct. of King County, 172 P. 257 (Wash. 1918); 41 Am. Jur. 2d Incompetent Persons § 26 (Law. Coop. 1968).
264. *In re* Wais, 464 N.Y.S.2d 634 (Sup. Ct., Albany County 1983).
265. Mitchell, *supra* note 103, at 456.
266. Table 7.6, cols. 5 & 6.
267. *Id.*
268. 41 Am. Jur. 2d Incompetent Persons § 26 (Law. Coop. 1968).
269. Table 7.6, col. 14.
270. *Id.*
271. 41 Am. Jur.2d Incompetent Persons § 30 (Law. Coop. 1968).
272. *Id.*
273. Table 7.6, col. 20.
274. *Id.*

most courts have held that restoration in one state is merely grounds for restoration in another state and not res judicata in any jurisdiction on the issue of competency with respect to other business affairs or parties that were not part of the original proceedings.[275] This leaves the individual and the financial community uncertain of the effects of restoration. Moreover, an individual who has been restored is generally not entitled to have the original judgment of incompetency expunged unless there was a mistake in the original proceedings.

Whether every incompetent person may apply for restoration is unclear. Only 18 jurisdictions use restoration proceedings that specify all incompetent persons.[276] Texas limits its provisions to persons of unsound mind and drunkards, while a substantial majority of states have no provision. In any event, certain categories of incompetent persons probably will never be restored since their conditions make it unlikely that significant improvements will occur as measured by the incompetency criteria. Many, if not most, developmentally disabled individuals fall in this group. It may be, however, that some of those people were mistakenly categorized to begin with and never should have been found incompetent. For them, restoration is at least theoretically possible on the grounds that they never were incompetent. As a practical matter, reversing the original judgment is usually harder than restoring a person to competency, given the strong presumption that the legal proceedings were correct. Thus, it makes sense for restoration to be available universally.

D. Restoration Merged with Discharge

In the past, when institutionalization and competency proceedings were merged together, so were restoration and discharge from the institution.[277] Today, restoration based upon discharge is available in only eight states.[278] Merger of the two concepts is confusing, especially where discharge is conditional or is required for some reason other than that the person has regained his mental competency. In the vast majority of states where incompetency and involuntary commitment are viewed separately, restoration is also separate from discharge, as it should be if conceptual consistency is to be maintained. Discharge from the institution is only one factor in proving restoration, and institutionalization is only one factor denying restoration. If significant doubts arise concerning the ward's legal competency, the ward should be given an automatic restoration hearing to avoid subsequent legal uncertainties.

275. 41 Am. Jur. 2d Incompetent Persons § 28 (Law. Coop. 1968).
276. *Id.*
277. Brakel & Rock, *supra* note 12, at 262–63.
278. Table 7.6, col. 1.

TABLE 7.1 STATUTORY DEFINITIONS OF INCOMPETENTS AND OTHER PERSONS SUBJECT TO GUARDIANSHIP

STATE AND CITATION	STATUTORY PROVISIONS
ALA. Code (1977) 26-2-40	"The court of probate shall have the authority and the duty to appoint guardians for persons of unsound mind residing in the county having an estate, real or personal, and of persons of unsound mind residing without the state, having within the county property requiring the care of a guardian."
(Supp. 1980) 26-2-1	"The term 'person of unsound mind' . . . includes idiots, lunatics or the insane."
26-7A-1	"Any probate court . . . may appoint a curator to take charge of, manage and conserve the property of any person . . . who shall become physically incapacitated, or feebleminded or epileptic or so mentally or physically defective by reason of age, sickness, use of drugs . . . that he or she is unable to take care of his or her property, and in consequence thereof, is liable to dissipate or lose the same, or to become the victim of designing persons."
ALAS. Stat. (1972) 13.26.005(1)	"'incapacitated person' means any person who is impaired by reason of mental illness, mental deficiency, physical illness or disability, advanced age, chronic use of drugs, chronic intoxication or other cause . . . to the extent that he lacks sufficient understanding or capacity to make or communicate responsible decisions concerning his person."
13.26.110	"The court may appoint a guardian . . . if it is satisfied that the person for whom a guardian is sought is incapacitated."
ARIZ. Rev. Stat. Ann. (1975) 14-5101	"'Incapacitated person' means any person who is impaired by reason of mental illness, mental deficiency, mental disorder, physical illness or disability, advanced age, . . . or other cause, except minority, to the extent that he lacks sufficient understanding or capacity to make or communicate responsible decisions concerning his person."
ARK. Stat. Ann. (Supp. 1981) 57-601(c)(2)	"'An incompetent' is any person who is . . . incapable by reason of insanity, mental illness, inbecility, idiocy, senility, habitual drunkenness, excessive use of drugs, or other mental incapacity, either of managing his property or caring for himself."
CAL. Welf. & Inst. Code (West 1956 & Supp. 1980) 1801	"(a) A conservator of the person, may be appointed for a person who is unable properly to provide for his or her personal needs for physical health, food, clothing, or shelter, except as provided for such person as described in subdivision (d) [limited conservators for developmentally disabled adults]. "(b) A conservator of the estate may be appointed for a person who is substantially unable to manage his or her own financial resources or resist fraud or undue influence, except as provided for such person as described in subdivision (d). Substantial inability may not be proved solely by isolated incidents of negligence or improvidence. "(c) A conservator of the person and estate may be appointed for a person described in subdivisions (a) and (b)."
3603	"When reference is made . . . to 'incompetent person,' the reference shall be deemed to include 'a person for whom a conservator may be appointed.'"

TABLE 7.1 STATUTORY DEFINITIONS OF INCOMPETENTS & OTHERS SUBJECT TO GUARDIANSHIP—continued

STATE AND CITATION	STATUTORY PROVISIONS
COLO. Rev. Stat. (1973 & Supp. 1980) 15-14-101(1)	"'Incapacitated person' means any person who is impaired by reason of mental illness, mental deficiency, physical illness, or disability, advanced age, chronic use of drugs, chronic intoxification, or other cause (except minority) to the extent that he lacks sufficient understanding or capacity to make or communicate responsible decisions concerning his person."
15-14-204(2)	"The court may appoint a guardian . . . if it is satisfied that the person for whom care is sought is incapacitated and that the appointment is necessary or desirable as a means of providing continuing care and supervision of the incapacitated person."
CONN. Gen. Stat. Ann. (West Supp. 1980) 45-70a	"(a) 'Conservator of the estate' means a person; legally authorized state official, or private . . . corporation . . . appointed by the court of probate . . . to supervise the financial affairs of a person found incapable of managing his or her own affairs or of a person who voluntarily asks for a conservator of the estate. "(b) 'Conservator of the person' means a person . . . appointed by the probate court . . . to supervise the personal affairs of a person found incapable of caring for himself or herself or of a person who voluntarily asks for the appointment of a conservator of the person. "(c) 'Incapable of caring for one's self' means a mental, emotional or physical condition resulting from mental illness, mental deficiency . . . which results in the person's inability to provide medical care for physical and mental health needs, nutritious meals, clothing, safe and adequately heated and ventilated shelter, personal hygiene and protection from physical abuse or harm and which results in endangerment to such person's health. "(d) 'Incapable of managing his or her affairs' . . . prevents that person from performing the functions inherent in managing his or her affairs, and the person has property which will be wasted or dissipated unless proper management is provided, or that funds are needed for the support, care or welfare of the person or those entitled to be supported by such person."
DEL. Code Ann. (1979) 3701	"The Court . . . shall have the care of mentally ill persons . . . so . . . as to appoint trustees for such persons to take charge of them and manage their estates."
3914	"Guardian may be appointed for person, not mentally ill, who by reason of advanced age or mental infirmity or physical incapacity is unable properly to manage and care for his person or property and as a consequence is in danger of dissipating or losing such property or of becoming the victim of designing persons."
D.C. Code Ann. (1973) 21, §501	"'Mental illness' means a psychosis or other disease which substantially impairs the mental health of a person."
21, §1501	"When an adult . . . is unable, by reason of advanced age, mental weakness not amounting to unsoundness of mind, mental illness . . . or physical incapacity, to properly care for his property the [court] . . . may . . . appoint a fit person to be conservator of his property."
FLA. Stat. Ann. (West Supp. 1980) 744.102	"An incompetent is a person who, because of minority, mental illness, mental retardation, senility, excessive use of drugs or alcohol, or other physical or mental incapacity, is incapable of either managing his property or caring for himself, or both."

TABLE 7.1 STATUTORY DEFINITIONS OF INCOMPETENTS & OTHERS SUBJECT TO GUARDIANSHIP—continued

STATE AND CITATION	STATUTORY PROVISIONS
GA. Code Ann. (Supp. 1981) 49-601	"(a) A probate judge may appoint guardians over the person of adults who are incapacitated by reason of mental illness, mental retardation, mental disability . . . or other cause to the extent that such adults lack sufficient understanding or capacity to make significant responsible decisions concerning their persons or to the extent that they are incapable of communicating them. "(b) A probate judge may appoint guardians over the property of adults who are incapacitated by reason of mental illness, mental retardation, mental disability, advanced age, physical illness or disability, chronic use of drugs or alcohol, detention by a foreign power, disappearance, or other cause to the extent that such adults are incapable of managing their estates and that such appointment is necessary because such property will be either wasted or dissipated unless proper management is provided, or such property is needed for the support, care, or well-being of such adults or those entitled to be supported by such adults."
HAWAII Rev. Stat. (1976) 560:5	"(1) 'Guardianship proceeding' is a proceeding to appoint a guardian of the person for an incapacitated person or a minor. "(2) 'Incapacitated person' means any person who is impaired by reason of mental illness, mental deficiency, physical illness or disability, advanced age, chronic use of drugs, chronic intoxication, or other cause (except minority) to the extent that he lacks sufficient understanding or capacity to make or communicate responsible decisions concerning his person."
IDAHO Code (1979) 15-5-101(a)	"'Incapacitated person' means any person who is impaired by reason of mental illness, mental deficiency, physical illness or disability, advanced age, chronic use of drugs, chronic intoxication, or other cause (except minority) to the extent that he lacks sufficient understanding or capacity to make or communicate responsible decisions concerning his person."
15-5-304	"The court may appoint a guardian as requested if it is satisfied that the person for whom a guardian is sought is incapacitated and that the appointment is necessary or desirable as a means of providing continuing care and supervision of the person of the incapacitated person."
ILL. Ann. Stat. (Smith-Hurd 1978 & Supp. 1980) 110½, §11a-2	"'Disabled person' means a person 18 years or older who (a) because of mental deterioration or physical incapacity is not fully able to manage his person or estate, or (b) is mentally ill or developmentally disabled and who because of his mental illness or developmental disability is not fully able to manage his person or estate, or (c) because of gambling, idleness, debauchery or excessive use of intoxicants or drugs, so spends or wastes his estate as to expose himself or his family to want or suffering."
110½, §11a-3(a)	"Upon the filing of a petition . . . the court may adjudge a person to be a disabled person and may appoint (1) a guardian of his person, if because of his disability he lacks sufficient understanding or capacity to make or communicate responsible decisions concerning the care of his person, or (2) a guardian of his estate, if because of his disability he is unable to manage his estate or financial affairs, or (3) a guardian of his person and of estate."
IND. Code Ann. (Burns Supp. 1980) 29-1-18-1	"(a) A 'guardian' or 'conservator' is one appointed by a court to have the care and custody of the person or of the estate, or of both, if an incompetent." "(c) An 'incompetent' or 'disabled person' is a person who is: (1) under 18; or (2) incapable by reason of insanity, mental illness, mental retardation, senility, habitual drunkenness, excessive use of drugs, old age, infirmity, disappearance, or other incapacity, of either managing his property or caring for himself or both."

TABLE 7.1 STATUTORY DEFINITIONS OF INCOMPETENTS & OTHERS SUBJECT TO GUARDIANSHIP—continued

STATE AND CITATION	STATUTORY PROVISIONS
IOWA Code Ann. (West Supp. 1980) 633.3(22)	"Incompetent includes any person who has been adjudicated by a court to be incapable of managing his property, or caring for his own person, or both."
633.552	"The petition for appointment of a guardian shall state the following information . . . (2) That the proposed ward is . . . incapable of caring for his own person."
633.566	"The petition for the appointment of a conservator shall state the following information . . . (2) That the proposed ward . . . is incapable of managing his property."
KAN. Stat. Ann. (1976) 59-3002	"(1) The term 'incapacitated person' shall mean any person who is impaired by reason of mental illness, mental deficiency, physical illness or disability, advanced age . . . or other cause to the extent that he or she lacks sufficient understanding or capacity to make or communicate responsible decisions concerning either his person or his estate. "(2) The term 'guardian' shall mean any person who has been appointed by a court of competent jurisdiction to exercise control over the person of an incapacitated person or of a minor."
KY. Rev. Stat. (Michie Supp. 1980) 203.010(2)	"'Incompetency' or 'incompetent person' shall apply to a person of unsound mind who from confirmed bodily infirmity is unable to make known to others by speech, sign or otherwise his thoughts or desires and by reason thereof is unable to manage his estate, or one whose mind because of mental illness or infirmity or old age has become so disabled as to render him unable to manage his estate."
LA. Rev. Stat. Ann. (West 1952) 389	"No person . . . who is subject to an habitual state of imbecility, insanity or madness, shall be allowed to take care of his own person and administer his estate, although such person shall, at all times, appear to have the possession of his reason."
ME. Rev. Stat. Ann. (1981) 18-A, §5-101	"'Incapacited person' means any person who is impaired by reason of mental illness, mental deficiency, physical illness or disability, chronic use of drugs, chronic intoxication, or other cause . . . to the extent that he lacks sufficient understanding or capacity to make or communicate responsible decisions concerning his person."
18-A, §5-304	"The court may appoint a guardian as requested if it is satisfied that the person for whom a guardian is sought is incapacitated and that the appointment is necessary or desirable as a means of providing continuing care and supervision of the person of the incapacitated person."
MD. Ann. Code (1974) 13-201(c)	"A guardian shall be appointed if the court determines that (1) The person is unable to manage his property and affairs effectively because of physical or mental disability, senility, or other mental weakness, disease, habitual drunkenness, addiction to drugs, imprisonment, compulsory hospitalization, confinement, detention by a foreign power, or disappearance."
MASS. Ann. Laws (Michie/Law. Co-op. 1981) 16, 16B	"A conservator may be appointed for a mentally retarded person or person who by reason of advanced age, mental weakness or physical incapacity is unable to properly care for his property."
201, §6	"A guardian may be appointed for a mentally ill person incapable of taking care of himself by reason of mental illness . . . .
201, §6A	"A guardian may be appointed for a person mentally retarded to the degree that he is incapable of making informed decisions with respect to the conduct of his personal and financial affairs."
201, §8	"A guardian may be appointed for a person who, by excessive drinking, gaming, idleness, or debauchery of any kind, so spends, wastes or lessens his estate as to expose him and his family to want or suffering. Such person may be adjudged a spendthrift.

TABLE 7.1 STATUTORY DEFINITIONS OF INCOMPETENTS & OTHERS SUBJECT TO GUARDIANSHIP—continued

STATE AND CITATION	STATUTORY PROVISIONS
MICH. Comp. Laws Ann. (1980) 700.8	"'Legally incapacitated person' means a person, other than a minor, who is impaired by reason of mental illness, mental deficiency, physical illness or disability, chronic use of drugs, chronic intoxication, or other cause . . . to the extent that the person lacks sufficient understanding or capacity to make or communicate responsible decisions concerning his or her person."
700.44	"The court may appoint a guardian . . . if it is satisfied by clear and convincing evidence that the person for whom a guardian is sought is a legally incapacitated person."
MINN. Stat. Ann. (West Supp. 1981) 525.54	"(2) For purpose of guardianship or conservatorship of the person 'incapacitated person' means any adult person who is impaired by reason of mental condition to the extent that he lacks sufficient understanding or capacity to make or communicate responsible decisions concerning his person, and who has demonstrated deficits in behavior which evidences his inability to meet essential requirements for his health or safety. "(3) For purpose of guardianship or conservatorship of the estate of an adult, 'incapacitated person' means any adult person who is impaired by reason of mental condition to the extent that he lacks sufficient understanding or capacity to make or communicate responsible decisions concerning his estate or financial affairs, and who has demonstrated deficits in behavior which evidences his inability to manage his estate."
MISS. Code Ann. (1973) 93-13-131	"Guardian may be appointed for habitual drunkard, habitual user of cocaine, opium or morphine."
(Supp. 1980) 93-13-111	"Guardian may be appointed for a person in need of mental treatment and incapable of taking care of his person and property."
93-13-121	"Guardian shall be appointed for a person incompetent to manage his or her estate."
MO. Ann. Stat. (Vernon Supp. 1980) 475.010	"(1) A 'guardian' is one appointed by the court to have the care and custody of the person or of the estate, or of both, of a minor or of an incompetent." "(3) An 'incompetent' is any person who is incapable by reason of insanity, mental illness, imbecility, idiocy, senility, habitual drunkenness, excessive use of drugs, or other incapacity, of either managing his property or caring for himself or both."
MONT. Code Ann. (1981) 72-5-101	"'Incapacitated person' means any persons who is impaired by reason of mental illness, mental deficiency, physical illness or disability, advanced age, chronic use of drugs, chronic intoxication, or other cause to the extent that he lacks sufficient understanding or capacity to make or communicate responsible decisions concerning his person or which cause has so impaired the person's judgment that he is incapable of realizing and making a rational decision with respect to his need for treatment."
72-5-316	"The court may appoint a guardian . . . if it is satisfied that the person for whom a guardian is sought is incapacitated."
NEB. Rev. Stat. (1979) 30-2601	"'Incapacitated person' mans any person who is impaired by reason of mental illness, mental deficiency, physical illness or disability, advanced age, chronic use of drugs, chronic intoxication, or other cause . . . to the extent that he lacks sufficient understanding or capacity to make or communicate responsible decisions concerning his person."
NEV. Rev. Stat. (1979) 159.019	"'Incompetent' includes any person who, by reason of mental illness, mental deficiency, advanced age, disease, weakness of mind or any other cause, is unable, without assistance, properly to manage and take care of himself or his property."

TABLE 7.1 STATUTORY DEFINITIONS OF INCOMPETENTS & OTHERS SUBJECT TO GUARDIANSHIP—continued

STATE AND CITATION	STATUTORY PROVISIONS
N.H. Rev. Stat. Ann. (Supp. 1979) 464-A:2(VIII) & (IX)	"A guardian may be appointed for the person and estate of an incapacitated person."
464-A:2(XI)	"'Incapacity' shall mean any person who has suffered, is suffering or is likely to suffer substantial harm due to an inability to provide for his personal needs for food, clothing, shelter, health care or safety or an inability to manage his or her property or financial affairs."
N.J. Stat. Ann. (West Supp. 1981) 3A:6-16.10(c)	"'Mental incompetent' means a person who is impaired by reason of mental illness or mental deficiency to the extent that he lacks sufficient capacity to govern himself and manage his affairs. The term 'mental incompetent' is also used to designate a person who is impaired by reason of physical illness or disability, chronic use of drugs, chronic alcoholism or other cause to the extent that he lacks sufficient capacity to govern himself and manage his affairs."
N.M. Stat. Ann. (1978) 45-5-101(F)	"'[I]ncapacitated person' means any person who is impaired by reason of mental illness, mental deficiency, physical illness or disability, advanced age, chronic use of drugs, chronic intoxification or other cause, except minority, to the extent that he lacks sufficient understanding or capacity to make or communicate responsible decisions concerning his person or management of his affairs."
45-5-304	"The court may appoint a guardian . . . if it finds that the person for whom a guardian is sought is incapacitated and that the appointment is necessary or desirable as a means of providing continuing care and supervision of the person of the incapacitated person."
N.Y. Mental Hyg. Law (McKinney 1978 & Supp. 1980) 78.01	"The Supreme Court, and the county courts outside the City of New York, have jurisdiction over the custody of a person and his property if he is incompetent to manage himself or his affairs by reason of age, alcohol abuse, mental illness, or other cause, or is a patient . . . who is unable adequately to conduct his personal or business affairs. As used in this article, the term 'patient' shall mean a person who has been lawfully committed or admitted to any facility for the mentally ill or mentally retarded. . . . In exercising such custody, the court may appoint a committee of the person or a committee of the property, who may be the same or different individuals."
N.C. Gen. Stat. (1976 & Supp. 1979) 35-1.7(11)	"The term 'incompetent adult' means an adult who lacks sufficient capacity to make or communicate important decisions concerning his person, family, or property because of mental illness, mental retardation, epilepsy, cerebral palsy, or autism. "The term 'incompetent child' means a minor who, other than by reason of his minority, is impaired to the extent that he lacks sufficient capacity to make or communicate important decisions concerning his person, family, or property because of mental illness, mental retardation, epilepsy, cerebral palsy, or autism."
35-2	"[The clerk] shall . . . appoint a guardian of any person . . . found to be inebriate or incompetent by inquisition of a jury . . ., provided, where the person is found to be incompetent from want of understanding to manage his affairs, by reason of physical and mental weakness on account of old age and/or disease and/or other like infirmities, the clerk may appoint a trustee instead of guardian."

TABLE 7.1 STATUTORY DEFINITIONS OF INCOMPETENTS & OTHERS SUBJECT TO GUARDIANSHIP—continued

STATE AND CITATION	STATUTORY PROVISIONS
N.D. Cent. Code (1976) 30.1-26-01(1)	"'Incapacitated person' means any person who is impaired by reason of mental illness, mental deficiency, physical illness or disability, advanced age, chronic use of drugs, chronic intoxification, or other cause (except minority) to the extent that he lacks sufficient understanding or capacity to make or communicate responsible decisions concerning his person."
30.1-28-04	"The court may appoint a guardian as requested if it is satisfied that the person for whom a guardian is sought is incapacitated and that the appointment is necessary or desirable as a means of providing continuing care and supervision of the incapacitated person."
OHIO Rev. Code Ann. (Baldwin 1978 & Supp. 1980) 2111.01(D)	"'Incompetent' means any person who by reason of advanced age, improvidence, or mental or physical disability or infirmity, chronic alcoholism, mental retardation, or mental illness, is incapable of taking proper care of himself or his property or fails to provide for his family or other persons for whom he is charged by law to provide, or any person confined to a penal institution within this state."
2111.02	"When found necessary, the probate court . . . shall appoint a guardian of the person, the estate, or both, of a minor, or incompetent."
OKLA. Stat. Ann. (West 1965 & Supp. 1980) 58, §851	"When it is represented to the court upon verified petition . . . that any person is insane, or from any cause mentally incompetent to manage his property, the court shall cause notice . . . of th time and place of hearing the case."
58,§852	"If after a full hearing and examination . . . it appears to the judge of the county court that the person in question is incapable of taking care of himself and managing his property, he may appoint a guardian of his person and estate."
58, §852	"Words 'mentally incompetent,' 'incompetent' and 'incapable,' in this section and §851 . . . mean person who, though not insane is, by reason of old age, disease, weakness of mind, or from other cause, unable or incapable, unassisted, of properly taking care of himself or managing his property, and who by reason thereof would be likely to be deceived or imposed upon by artful or designing persons. In re Guardianship of Bogan, Okl., 441 P.2d 972 (1968)."
OR. Rev. Stat. (1979) 126.003(4)	"'Incapacitated person' means a person who is unable, without assistance, to properly manage or take care of himself or his personal affairs."
126.107	"The court may appoint a guardian as requested if the court is satisfied that: (1) the person for whom a guardian is sought is incapacitated; and (2) the appointment is necessary or desirable as a means of providing continuing care and supervision of the person of the incapacitated person."
PA. Stat. Ann. (Purdon 1975 & Supp. 1980) 20, §5501	"'Incompetent' means a person who, because of infirmities of old age, mental illness, mental deficiency or retardation, drug addiction or inebriety: (1) is unable to manage his property, or is liable to dissipate it or become the victim of designing persons; or (2) lacks sufficient capacity to make or communicate responsible decisions concerning his person."
20, §5511	"(a) The court, upon petition and a hearing at which good cause is shown, may find a person domiciled in the Commonwealth to be incompetent and appoint a guardian or guardians of his person or estate. "(b) The court may find a person not domiciled in the Commonwealth, having property in the Commonwealth, to be incompetent and may appoint a guardian of his estate."

TABLE 7.1 STATUTORY DEFINITIONS OF INCOMPETENTS & OTHERS SUBJECT TO GUARDIANSHIP—continued

STATE AND CITATION	STATUTORY PROVISIONS
R.I. Gen. Laws (1969) 33-15-8	"A probate court may appoint a guardian of the person and estate, or of the person or estate, of any idiot, lunatic, or person of unsound mind, of any habitual drunkard, or of any person who from excessive drinking, gaming, idleness or debauchery of any kind, or from want of discretion in managing his estate, so spends, wastes, or lessens his estate or is likely so to do, that he may bring himself or his family to want or suffering, or may render himself or family chargeable upon the town for support."
S.C. Code Ann. (Law. Co-op. 1976) 21-19-10	"The judge of probate shall have jurisdiction in relation to the appointment and removal of guardians of the person of minors and persons who are mentally incompetent."
21-19-200	"When it shall appear to the satisfaction of the probate court of the county in which any person resides that such person is a mentally retarded person, defined . . . as any person, other than a mentally ill person primarily in need of mental health services, whose intellectual deficit and adaptive level of behavior require for his benefit, or that of the public, special training, education, supervision, treatment, care or control in his home or community, or in a service facility or program under the control and managemnt of the Department of Mental Retardation, who requires in his best interests the appointment of a guardian of the person or of the property or both, the court is authorized . . . to appoint such guardian."
44-23-10(19)	"'Guardian' or 'legal guardian' means a person who legally has the care and management of the person of one who is not sui juris."
S.D. Codified Laws Ann. (1976) 27B-6-1	"If the courty board determines that a person is mentally retarded, not receiving proper care and education, and there is no responsible relative to take custody of the person on petition for guardianship, the board shall notify the board of social services who may petition for letters of guardianship."
30-27-6	"The circuit court, when it appears necessary or convenient, may appoint a guardian of the person and estate, or either, of a minor or of a person who is mentally ill or for any cause mentally or physically incompetent to manage his own property, such person being hereafter . . . referred to as an incompetent."
TENN. CODE Ann. (1977 & Supp. 1980) 34-502	"An 'incompetent' . . . shall be construed to be any person who has been, or shall be, by a proper judgment or decree of a court of this state, having jurisdiction, in a proceeding brought for that purpose, declared to be of unsound mind, and for whom a legal guardian has been appointed."
34-12-203	"If a person by reason of advanced age or physical incapacity or mental weakness is incapable of managing his own estate, the county court, or the probate court in counties having such a court, of the county wherein such person resides may, upon the petition of such person or of one or more of his friends or relatives, appoint a conservator to have charge and management of the property of such person, and if the court deems it advisable, also to have charge and custody of the person subject to the direction of the appointing court."
TEX. Rev. Civ. Stat. Ann. (Vernon 1958 & Supp. 1980) 5547-4(l)	"'Mentally incompetent person' means a mentally ill person whose mental illness renders him incapable of caring for himself and managing his property and financial affairs."

TABLE 7.1 STATUTORY DEFINITIONS OF INCOMPETENTS & OTHERS SUBJECT TO GUARDIANSHIP—continued

STATE AND CITATION	STATUTORY PROVISIONS
UTAH Code Ann. (1978 & Supp. 1979) 75-1-201	"(16) 'Guardian' means a person who has qualified as a guardian of a minor or incapacitated person pursuant to testamentary or court appointment but excludes one who is merely a guardian ad litem. "(18) 'Incapacitated person' means any person who is impaired by reason of mental illness, mental deficiency, physical illness or disability, advanced age, chronic use of drugs, chronic intoxification, or other cause (except minority) to the extent that he lacks sufficient understanding or capacity to make or communicate responsible decisions concerning his person." "(24) 'Minor' means a person who is under 18 years of age."
VT. Stat. Ann. (1974 & Supp. 1980) 14, §3061(1)	"'Mentally disabled person' means a person who has been found to be: (a) at least eighteen years of age; and (b) mentally ill or mentally retarded; and (c) unable to manage, without the supervision of a guardian, some or all aspects of his personal care or financial affairs."
14, §3068(f)	"If upon completion of the hearing and consideration of the record the court finds that the petitioner has proved by clear and convincing evidence that the respondent is mentally disabled, it shall enter judgment specifying the powers . . . and the duties of the guardian."
33, §3604	"Protective supervision or guardianship of the person may be provided to any mentally retarded person who: (1) is at least 18 years of age, (2) is in need of supervision and protection for his own welfare or the public welfare, and (3) is not a resident of a state school or hospital or is to be discharged from a state school or hospital at such time as guardianship or protective supervision is ordered."
VA. Code (1976 & Supp. 1981) 37.1-128.01	"'Legally incompetent' means a person who has been adjudicated incompetent by a circuit court because of a mental condition which renders him incapable of taking care of his person or handling and managing his estate."
37.1-128.02(A)	"On petition of any person to the circuit court of a county or city in which resides or is located any person who because of mental illness or mental retardation is incapable of taking care of his person or handling and managing his estate, the court, after reasonable notice . . . shall hold a hearing to determine if a committee should be appointed."
37.1-128.04	"'Legally incapacitated' when used in reference to a person means that the person has been adjudicated incapacitated by a circuit court because of a mental or physical condition which renders him, either wholly or partially, incapable of taking care of himself or his estate."
37.1-128.1(A)	"On petition of any person to the circuit court of a county or city, in which resides or is located any person who by reason of mental illness or mental retardation has become incapable, either wholly or partially, of taking care of himself or his estate, the court, after reasonable notice to such . . . person of the hearing and his right to be present, shall hold a hearing to determine whether a guardian should be appointed."
WASH. Rev. Code Ann. (1967 & Supp. 1980) 11.88.010(1)	"The superior court of each county shall have power to appoint guardians for the persons and estates, or either thereof, of incompetent persons, and guardians for the estates of all such persons who are nonresidents of the state but who have property in such county needing care and attention. "An 'incompetent' is any person who is either: (a) under the age of majority . . . or (b) incompetent by reason of mental illness, developmental disability, senility, habitual drunkenness, excessive use of drugs, or other mental incapacity, of either managing his property or caring for himself or both."

TABLE 7.1 STATUTORY DEFINITIONS OF INCOMPETENTS & OTHERS SUBJECT TO GUARDIANSHIP—continued

STATE AND CITATION	STATUTORY PROVISIONS
WIS. Stat. Ann. (West 1980) 880.01	"(3) 'Guardian' means one appointed by a court to have care, custody and control of the person of a minor or an incompetent or the management of the estate of a minor, an incompetent or a spendthrift. "(4) 'Incompetent' means a person adjudged by a court of record to be substantially incapable of managing his property or caring for himself by reason of infirmities of aging, developmental disabilities, or other like incapacities. "(7) 'Minor' means a person who has not attained the age of 18 years. "(9) 'Spendthrift' means a person who because of the use of intoxicants or drugs or of gambling, idleness or debauchery or other wasteful course of conduct is unable to attend to business or thereby is likely to affect the health, life or property of himself or others so as to endanger the support of himself and his dependents or expose the public to such support."
W. VA. Code (1980 & Supp. 1981) 27-11-1	"(a) The county commission of a person's residence may appoint a committee for a person found to be incompetent. Any finding of incompetency . . . shall be made separately and at a different proceeding from any finding of mental retardation or addiction."
27-11-1	"(d) Upon completion of the hearing . . . the county commission may find that (i) the individual is unable to manage his business affairs, or (ii) the individual is unable to care for his physical well-being, or (iii) both, and is therefore incompetent, or (iv) that the person is competent. Evidence of mere poor judgment or of different life style shall not be competent evidence upon which to base a finding of incompetency."
WYO. Stat. (1977) 3-2-301	"The district court of each county, or the judge thereof, may appoint a guardian for the person and estate, or either of them, of mentally incompetent or incompetent persons who reside or have estates within the county, and who have no legally appointed guardian in this state. As used in this Act . . . 'mentally incompetent person' shall mean an individual who is unable, unassisted, to properly manage and take care of himself or his property or both as a result of mental illness, mental deficiency or mental retardation; and 'incompetent person' shall mean an individual who is unable, unassisted, to properly manage and take care of himself or his property as the result of the infirmities of advanced age, physical disability, disease, alcoholism, or addiction to drugs."

TABLE 7.2 RELATIONSHIP BETWEEN INVOLUNTARY INSTITUTIONALIZATION AND LEGAL COMPETENCY

STATE	COMPETENCY NOT AFFECTED BY INVOLUNTARY INSTITUTIONALIZATION (1)	LIMITATIONS ON COMPETENCY DURING INVOLUNTARY INSTITUTIONALIZATION (2)	INCOMPETENCY MAY BE DETERMINED AT INSTITUTIONALIZATION HEARING (3)	APPOINTMENT OF GUARDIAN		
				Conditional (4)	Of Property (5)	Of Person (6)
ALA. Code (1975 & Supp. 1980)						
ALAS. Stat. (1979 & Supp. 1982)	not a judicial determination of incompetency 47.30.070	subject to general rules of hospital restrictions necessary for medical welfare 47.30.150(a)(3) not competent to consent to treatment unless head of hospital so determines 47.30.070(e), 47.30.130(b)				
ARIZ. Rev. Stat. Ann. (1974 & Supp. 1982)	not a determination of legal incompetency 36-506A	consent not necessary to emergency medical care 36-506A, 36-512	evidence & tentative finding (sufficient to authorize investigation) on need for guardianship of gravely disabled 36-539B, 36-540D	if ct. finds at hospitalization hearing that patient gravely disabled & in need of immediate guardianship, temporary guardian may be appointed 36-540E		
ARK. Stat. Ann. (1971 & Supp. 1981)	not incompetent per se 59-1422					
CAL. Welf. & Inst. Code (West 1972 & Supp. 1983)	no presumption of incompetence 5331					
COLO. Rev. Stat. (1973 & Supp. 1982)	competency retained unless specifically stated otherwise in order by ct. 27-10-104					
CONN. Gen. Stat. Ann. (West 1975 & Supp. 1982)	competence retained unless found incompetent in separate proceeding; finding of incompetency specifically states which rights incompetent to exercise 17-206b					
DEL. Code Ann. (1974 & Supp. 1980)						
D.C. Code Ann. (1981 & Supp. 1982)	21-564					
FLA. Stat. Ann. (West 1973 & Supp. 1980)		if adjudicated incompetent 394.459(1)	394.467(3)(a)	guardian advocate appointed if person incompetent to consent to treatment 394.467(3)(a)		394.467(3)(a)
GA. Code Ann. (1979 & Supp. 1980)	not considered incompetent 88-502.1			2 representatives or guardian ad litem designated upon admission 88-502.18 or before hearing on ct.-ordered evaluation 88-505.3(a)		
HAWAII Rev. Stat. Ann. (1976 & Supp. 1980)	no presumption of insanity or legal incompetency 334-61	administrator of facility applies to ct. for show cause order if wishes to restrict patient's exercise of any civil right 334-61	334-60(b)(4)(J)			
IDAHO Code (1980 & Supp. 1981)	unless limited by prior ct. order 66-346(a)(6), (c)			if patient has property that cannot be cared for while patient hospitalized, guardian ad litem appointed pending further guardianship or conservatorship proceedings 66-329(n)	66-329(n)	
ILL. Ann. Stat. (Smith-Hurd 1966 & Supp. 1983)	no presumption of incompetency unless so determined in separate proceeding 91½, §2-101					
IND. Code Ann. (Burns 1973 & Supp. 1980)	section shall not be construed as validating otherwise voidable act of person incompetent at time of act but not so judicially declared 16-14-1.6-4(a), (b)			ct.'s discretion 16-14-9.1-10(f)		
IOWA Code Ann. (West 1969 & Supp. 1983)	neither equivalent to nor raises presumption of incompetency 229.27(1)			advocate appointed upon counsel's withdrawal or at end of hospitalization hearing 229.19(2)		
KAN. Stat. Ann. (1976 & Supp. 1981)	59-2930	head of facility may make reasonable rules 59-2930				

TABLE 7.2 RELATIONSHIP BETWEEN INVOLUNTARY INSTITUTIONALIZATION AND LEGAL COMPETENCY—*Continued*

STATE	COMPETENCY NOT AFFECTED BY INVOLUNTARY INSTITUTIONALIZATION (1)	LIMITATIONS ON COMPETENCY DURING INVOLUNTARY INSTITUTIONALIZATION (2)	INCOMPETENCY MAY BE DETERMINED AT INSTITUTIONALIZATION HEARING (3)	APPOINTMENT OF GUARDIAN		
				Conditional (4)	Of Property (5)	Of Person (6)
KY. Rev. Stat. Ann. (Michie 1982)				in all cases 210.405(2)		
LA. Rev. Stat. Ann. (West 1975 & Supp. 1983)	no presumption of incompetency unless determined in separate proceeding from judicial determination of involuntary commitment 28:171B					
ME. Rev. Stat. Ann. (1978 & Supp. 1983)	34, §2254(3)	restrictions necessary for patient's medical welfare 34, §2254(3)				
MD. Ann. Code (1979 & Supp. 1982)						
MASS. Ann. Laws (Michie/Law. Co-op. 1981 & Supp. 1983)	not deemed incompetent 123, §25					
MICH. Comp. Laws Ann. (1980 & Supp. 1983)	neither finding nor presumption of legal incompetence 330.1489 copies of this provision given to patients 330.1490		if petition filed for declaration of legal incompetence & appointment of guardian 330.1491	if question raised at hearing & appointment appropriate 330.1492	330.1492	330.1492
MINN. Stat. Ann. (West 1982 & Supp. 1983)	253A.18(1)		may be joint incompetency & hospitalization proceedings 253A.18(2)	if person to be committed appears incompetent & is minor or owns property 253A.18		
MISS. Code Ann. (1972 & Supp. 1980)	neither presumption nor adjudication of incompetency 41-21-101					
MO. Ann. Stat. (Vernon 1979 & Supp. 1983)	not deemed incompetent 630.120					
MONT. Code Ann. (1981)	no legal disability unless specifically stated in ct. order 53-21-141(1)	insofar as necessary to detain patient 53-21-141(1)	ct. may make order imposing specific disabilities on patient committed for 3 mos. or more 53-21-141(2)	may appoint conservator for period of involuntary commitment 53-21-141	53-21-141(2)	
NEB. Rev. Stat. (1976)						
NEV. Rev. Stat. (1981)	433A.460(1)					
N.H. Rev. Stat. Ann. (1978)	135-B:42	if adjudicated incompetent 135-B:42		in all cases 135-B:42		
N.J. Stat. Ann. (West 1981 & Supp. 1983)	no presumption of incompetence 30:4-24.2c patient given statement of this provision upon departure 30:4-24.2c			action for appointment of guardian if appears on final hearing that patient has property, no arrangements made for payment, & no action brought to appoint guardian 30:4-65	30:4-65	
N.M. Stat. Ann. (1979 & Supp. 1982)	not basis for finding of incompetence 43-1-5					
N.Y. Mental Hyg. Law (McKinney 1978 & Supp. 1983)	not finding of incompetency 29.03 cannot be deprived of any civil rights 33.01	commissioner of mental health may authorize director of facility to obtain up to $5,000 of patient's property if patient has no committee (or, on discharge if has committee) & to disburse this money toward patient's expenses 29.23				
N.C. Gen. Stat. (1981 & Supp. 1981)	but act of patient in fact incompetent not validated 122-55.2(c)					
N.D. Cent. Code (1970 & Supp. 1981)						
OHIO Rev. Code Ann. (Baldwin 1980)	unless adjudicated incompetent in judicial proceeding other than hospitalization proceeding 5122.301			judge may appoint special guardian of patient's estate, unless guardian of patient's estate already appointed 5122.41	5122.41	

TABLE 7.2 RELATIONSHIP BETWEEN INVOLUNTARY INSTITUTIONALIZATION AND LEGAL COMPETENCY—*Continued*

STATE	COMPETENCY NOT AFFECTED BY INVOLUNTARY INSTITUTIONALIZATION (1)	LIMITATIONS ON COMPETENCY DURING INVOLUNTARY INSTITUTIONALIZATION (2)	INCOMPETENCY MAY BE DETERMINED AT INSTITUTIONALIZATION HEARING (3)	APPOINTMENT OF GUARDIAN Conditional (4)	Of Property (5)	Of Person (6)
OKLA. Stat. Ann. (West 1979 & Supp. 1983)	no presumption of incompetency 43A, §64	superintendent of institution w/in dep't guardian of patients committed there for purpose of retaining them 43A, §95	43A, §65	if person found mentally incompetent but not in need of hospitalization, judge of county ct. must issue order adjudging person mentally incompetent & must appoint guardian of person & estate 43A, §65	43A, §65	43A, §65
OR. Rev. Stat. (1981)	not considered incompetent by virtue of admission 426-295(1)					
PA. Stat. Ann. (Purdon 1969 & Supp. 1982)		unless guardian appointed or helpful to patient to manage own property, revenue agent takes custody of patient's property 50, §4424				
R.I. Gen. Laws (1977 & Supp. 1979)	person admitted under ch. 5 of tit. 40.1 not thereby deemed incompetent 40.1-5-5(8)					
S.C. Code Ann. (Law Co-op. 1977 & Supp. 1982)	no presumption of incompetency; no rights denied w/o specific ct. order 44-17-580					
S.D. Codified Laws Ann. (1976 & Supp. 1981)						
Tenn. Code Ann. (1977 & Supp. 1981)						
TEX. Rev. Civ. Stat. Ann. (Vernon 1958 & Supp. 1983)	judicial determination that person mentally ill or admission or commitment not adjudication of mental competency 5547-83(b)		ct. or jury shall determine whether person mentally incompetent 5547-51(a)(3)			
UTAH Code Ann. (1978 & Supp. 1981)	64-7-48(1)(c)	subject to general rules of facility & restrictions necessary for patient's medical welfare 64-7-48(1)				
VT. Stat. Ann. (1968 & Supp. 1982)	no presumption of legal incompetence 18, §7706	subject to general rules of facility & restrictions necessary for welfare of patient or hospital 16, §7705(a)(3) lack of presumption of legal incompetence does not apply to treatment matters 18, §7706				
VA. Code (1976 & Supp. 1982)	no presumption of incompetency, legal incapacity 37.1-87	commissioner authorized to receive & expend social security & retirement benefits on behalf of patients 37.1-28				
WASH. Rev. Code Ann. (1975 & Supp. 1984)	no presumption of incompetency 71.05.450	if danger created 71.05.370(8)				
W. Va. Code Ann. (1980 & Supp. 1982)	does not of itself relieve patient of legal capacity 27-5-9(a)	if adjudicated incompetent 27-5-9(a)				
WIS. Stat. Ann. (West 1957 & Supp. 1983)	51.59	not authorized to refuse treatment 51.59				
WYO. Stat. (1982 & Supp. 1982)	no presumption as to competency nor cause for guardianship 25-10-121					

TABLE 7.3 INITIATION OF GUARDIANSHIP PROCEEDINGS

	APPLICATION BY				CRITERIA FOR COURT-ORDERED APPOINTMENT OF GUARDIAN										SUPPORTING EVIDENCE		NOTICE OF PROCEEDING				PROVISIONS FOR WAIVER OF NOTICE TO RESPONDENT OR SUBSTITUTE SERVICE
					Legal Status			Included Impairments													
STATE	Court (1)	Any Person (2)	Alleged Incompetent (3)	Other (4)	Incompetent (5)	Incapacitated (6)	Other (7)	Mental Illness (8)	Mental Deficiency (9)	Physical Disability (10)	Advancing Age (11)	Alcoholism (12)	Drug Addiction (13)	Other (14)	Medical Certification (15)	Court-Ordered Examination (16)	Respondent (17)	Relatives (18)	Other (19)	When (20)	(21)
ALA. Code (1975 & Supp. 1982)	probate 26-2-40			relatives or friends 26-2-42(a)			unsound mind 26-2-45 26-2-1	lunacy or insanity 26-2-1	idiocy 26-2-1												
ALAS. Stat. (1972 & Supp. 1981)	superior 13.06.050(5)	interested person 13.26.105(a)	13.26.105(a)			13.26. 113(c) AND	alternatives to full guardianship unfeasible 13.26.113(f)							any except minority 13.26.005(1)		expert & visitor 13.26.106(c)	13.26.135 (a)(1)	spouse, parents, & adult children 13.26.135 (a)(1) closest adult relative 13.26.135 (a)(3)	person having care & custody 13.26.135 (a)(2)	upon appointment of visitor 13.26.107 (a)(2)	
ARIZ. Rev. Stat. Ann. (1975 & Supp. 1981)	superior 14-1201(7)	interested person 14-5303(A)	14-5303(A)			14-5304 AND	necessary & desirable for continuing care & supervision 14-5304	or disorder 14-5101(1)	14-5101(1)	or illness 14-5101(1)	14-510(1)	14-5101(1)	14-5101(1)	any except minority 14-5101(1)		physician & visitor 14-5303(B)	14-5309 (A)(1)	spouse, parents, & adult children 14-5309 (A)(1) closest adult relative 14-5309 (A)(3)	person having care & custody 14-5309 (A)(2)		waiver ineffective unless present at hearing or confirmed by visitor 14-5309(B)
ARK. Stat. Ann. (1979 & Supp. 1981)	probate 57-604(a)	57-609			57-614(a) AND		desirable to protect interests of incompetent 57-614(b)	or insanity 57-601(c)(2)	imbecility or idiocy 57-601(c)(2)		senility 57-601(c)(2)	57-601 (c)(2)	57-601 (c)(2)	under majority 57-601(c)(1) detained by foreign power or disappeared 57-601(c)(3)	sworn testimony or evidence of 1 or more qualified medical witness 57-615(b)	57-615(b)	if over 14 57-611(b)(1)	parents of minor, spouse, or or nearest competent relative 57-611(b)	57-611(b)	3 days before hearing 57-611(c)	•57-611(a)(2)
CAL. Prob. Code (West 1981 & Supp. 1981)		interested person or friend 1820(a)(5)	1820(a)(1)	spouse, relative, or interested public entity or officer 1820(a)(2)–(4)	see table 7.1 3603 1801										of inability to attend hearing 1825(b)	if unwilling or unable to attend hearing 1826	citation 1823(a)	spouse & relatives 1822(b)(1), (2)	1822(c)–(f)	15 days before hearing 1822(a) citation w/in 30 days 1824	
COLO. Rev. Stat. (1973 & Supp. 1981)	district; probate in Denver 15-10-201(8)	interested person 15-14-303(1)	15-14-303(1)			15-14-302(2) AND	necessary & desirable for continuing care & supervision 15-14-304(2)	15-14-101(1)	15-14-101(1)	or illness 15-14-101(1)	15-14-101(1)	15-14-101(1)	15-14-101(1)	any except minority 15-14-101(1)		physician 15-14-303(3) visitor 15-14-303(2)	15-14-309 (1)(a)	spouse, parents, & adult children 15-14-309 (1)(a) closest adult relative 15-14-309 (1)(c)	person having care & custody 15-14-309 (1)(b)		waiver ineffective unless present at hearing or confirmed by visitor 15-14-309(2)
CONN. Gen. Stat. Ann. (West 1981)	probate 45-70b(a) 45-78b	45-70b(a)		parents, or interested person w/consent of parents 45-78b		incapable of managing affairs or of caring for self 45-70d(c)	incapable of managing affairs or of caring for self 45-70d(c) mentally retarded 45-78b 45-78a	45-70a(c), (d)	45-70a(c), (d)	or illness 45-70a(c), (d)	45-70a(c),(d)	45-70a(c), (d)	45-70a(c), (d)	confinement 45-70a(c), (d)	2 physicians or 1 physician & 1 psychologist 45-78a	45-70d(a)	45-70c(a) (1)(A)	spouse 45-70c(a) (1)(B) children, parents, or brothers & sisters 45-70c(a) (2)(F)	person in charge of hospital, nursing home, or institution 45-70c(a) (1)(A), (2), (3)	7 days before hearing & w/in 30 days of application 45-70c(a)	
DEL. Code Ann. (1979 & Supp. 1980)	chancery 12, §3914(a)	fn. 1 12, §3914(a)	12, §3914(a)	fn. 1 12, §3914(a)			unable to manage & care for person & property 12, §3914(a)	specifically excluded 12, §3914(a)		12, §3914(a)	12, §3914(a)			mental infirmity 12, §3914(a)			12, §3914(b)		such others as ct. may deem desirable 12, §3914(b)		notice waived if petitioner also respondent 12, §3914(b)

TABLE 7.3 INITIATION OF GUARDIANSHIP PROCEEDINGS—*Continued*

STATE	APPLICATION BY: Court (1)	APPLICATION BY: Any Person (2)	APPLICATION BY: Alleged Incompetent (3)	APPLICATION BY: Other (4)	CRITERIA FOR COURT-ORDERED APPOINTMENT OF GUARDIAN — Legal Status: Incompetent (5)	Legal Status: Incapacitated (6)	Legal Status: Other (7)	Included Impairments: Mental Illness (8)	Included Impairments: Mental Deficiency (9)	Included Impairments: Physical Disability (10)	Included Impairments: Advancing Age (11)	Included Impairments: Alcoholism (12)	Included Impairments: Drug Addiction (13)	Included Impairments: Other (14)	SUPPORTING EVIDENCE: Medical Certification (15)	SUPPORTING EVIDENCE: Court-Ordered Examination (16)	NOTICE OF PROCEEDING: Respondent (17)	NOTICE OF PROCEEDING: Relatives (18)	NOTICE OF PROCEEDING: Other (19)	NOTICE OF PROCEEDING: When (20)	PROVISIONS FOR WAIVER OF NOTICE TO RESPONDENT OR SUBSTITUTE SERVICE (21)
D.C. Code Ann. (1981 & Supp. 1982)	superior 21-1501 21-1301	21-1501		relatives 21-1501			unable to properly care for property 21-1501	21-1501		21-1501	21-1501	21-1301	21-1301	mental weakness not amounting to unsoundness 21-1501			21-1502(a)		such others as ct. directs 21-1502(a)	14 days before hearing 21-1502(a)	
FLA. Stat. Ann. (West 1964 & Supp. 1981)	circuit 744.102(15)	any 3 citizens 744.331(2)(b)	744.331(2)(c)	medical director of institution 744.331(2)(d) relatives fn. 2 744.331(2)(a)	744.331(9)			744.102(5)	mentally retarded 744.102(5)	744.102(5)	senility 744.102(5)	744.102(5)	744.102(5)	minority 744.102(5)	if applicant is alleged incompetent 744.331(2)(c)	examining committee 744.331(5)(a)	744.331(4)	1 or more members of family 744.331(4)	such persons as ct. may direct 744.331(4)		
GA. Code Ann. (1979 & Supp. 1982)	probate 49-606(a)(1)	interested person 49-606(a)(1)	49-606(a)(1)	dep't of human resources 49-606(a)(1)		49-601(a), (b)		or disability 49-601	mentally retarded 49-601	or illness 49-601	49-601	49-601	49-601	detention by foreign power 49-601(b) 49-601	physician or applied psychologist 49-606(a)(3)	physician or applied psychologist 49-606(c)	49-606(d)(1)		attorney 49-606(d)(1)	10 days before hearing 49-606(d)(1)	
HAWAII Rev. Stat. (1976 & Supp. 1981)	family 560:5-102	interested person 560:5-303(a)	560:5-303(a)			560:5-304		560:5-101(2)	560:5-101(2)	or illness 560:5-101(2)	560:5-101(2)	560:5-101(2)	560:5-101(2)	except minority 560:5-101(2)		physician & family ct. officer 560:5-303(b)	560:5-309 (a)(1)	spouse, parents, & adult children 560:5-309 (a)(1) closest adult relative 560:5-309 (a)(3)	person w/care & custody 560:5-309 (a)(2)		waiver ineffective unless present at hearing or confirmed by visitor 560:5-309(b)
IDAHO Code (1979 & Supp. 1981)	district 15-1-201(6)	interested person 15-5-303(a)	15-5-303(a)			15-5-304 AND	necessary & desirable for continuing care & supervision 15-5-304	15-5-101(a)	15-5-101(a)	or illness 15-5-101(a)	15-5-101(a)	15-5-101(a)	15-5-101(a)	except minority 15-5-101(a)		physician & visitor 15-5-303(b)	15-5-309 (a)(1)	spouse, parents, & adult children 15-5-309(a)(1) closest adult relative 15-5-309(a)(3)	person w/care & custody 15-5-309(a)(2)		waiver ineffective unless present at hearing or confirmed by visitor 15-5-309(b)
ILL. Ann. Stat. (Smith-Hurd 1978 & Supp. 1981)		reputable person 110½, §11a-3(a)	110½, §11a-3(a)				disabled 110½, §§11a-3(a), 12(b)	110½, §11a-2(b)	developmentally disabled 110½, §11a-2(b)	incapacity 110½, §11a-2(a)	mental deterioration 110½, §11a-2(a)	110½, §11a-2(c)	110½, §11a-2(c)	gambling, idleness, or debauchery 110½, §11a-2(c)	report 110½, §11a-9(a)	110½, §§11a-9(b), 11(c)	110½, §11a-10(e)		those whose names appear in petition 110½, §11a-10(f)	14 days before hearing 110½, §11a-10(e), (f)	
IND. Code Ann. (Burns 1972 & Supp. 1982)	probate, & mental health division of municipal ct. 29-1-18-4	29-1-18-11	29-1-18-11					or insanity 29-1-18-1 (c)(2)	mentally retarded 29-1-18-1(c)(2)		senility or old age 29-1-18-1(c)(2)	29-1-18-1 (c)(2)	29-1-18-1 (c)(2)	other incapacity 29-1-18-1(c)(2)			if over 14 29-1-18-14 (c)(1)		person having care & custody 29-1-18-14 (c)(2) any other person directed by ct. 29-1-18-14 (c)(3)	3 days before hearing 29-1-18-14(c)	29-1-18-14(c)
IOWA Code Ann. (West 1964 & Supp. 1981)	district 633.3(9) 633.10(3)	633.552 633.566	633.557 633.572		633.3(22)	incapable of caring for self or managing property 633.552(2) 633.566(2)	incapable of caring for self or managing property 633.552(2) 633.566(2)										633.554 633.568				
KAN. Stat. Ann. (1976 & Supp. 1981)	district 59-3005	59-3009				59-3013		59-3002(1)	59-3002(1)	or illness 59-3002(1)	59-3002(1)	59-3002(1)	59-3002(1)	other cause 59-3002(1)		investigation 59-3011(A)(1), & psychological testing 59-3011(B)(5) 59-3010(A)(6)	59-3012	spouse or natural guardian 59-3012	attorney & such others as ct. directs 59-3012	5 days before hearing 59-3012	to head of psychiatric hospital if hospitalized 59-3012
KY. Rev. Stat. Ann. (Michie 1977 & Supp. 1980)	circuit 203.012(1)	reputable resident of county 203.012(1)			203.012(1)			or infirmity 203.010(2)		confirmed bodily infirmity 203.010(2)	203.010(2)					2 physicians or 1 physician & 1 psychologist 203.015(1)	203.016		all others named in petition 203.016		

TABLE 7.3 INITIATION OF GUARDIANSHIP PROCEEDINGS—*Continued*

	APPLICATION BY				CRITERIA FOR COURT-ORDERED APPOINTMENT OF GUARDIAN										SUPPORTING EVIDENCE		NOTICE OF PROCEEDING				PROVISIONS FOR WAIVER OF NOTICE TO RESPONDENT OR SUBSTITUTE SERVICE
					Legal Status			Included Impairments													
STATE	Court (1)	Any Person (2)	Alleged Incompetent (3)	Other (4)	Incompetent (5)	Incapacitated (6)	Other (7)	Mental Illness (8)	Mental Deficiency (9)	Physical Disability (10)	Advancing Age (11)	Alcoholism (12)	Drug Addiction (13)	Other (14)	Medical Certification (15)	Court-Ordered Examination (16)	Respondent (17)	Relatives (18)	Other (19)	When (20)	(21)
LA. Civ. Code Ann. (West 1952 & Supp. 1981)	judge of domicile or residence 392	any stranger 391		every relation, husband or wife 390		mental incapacity 389 393	physical infirmity 422	insanity or madness 389	imbecility 389	422				any infirmity 422		393					
ME. Rev. Stat. Ann. (1981 & Supp. 1981)	probate 18-A, §1-201(5)	18-A, §5-303(a)	18-A, §5-303(a)			18-A, AND §5-304	necessary & desirable for continuing care & supervision 18-A, §5-304	18-A, §5-101(1)	18-A, §5-101(1)	or illness 18-A, §5-101(1)		18-A, §5-101(1)	18-A, §5-101(1)	except minority 18-A, §5-101(1)		physician & visitor 18-A, §5-303(b)	18-A, §5-309(a)(1)	spouse, parents, & adult children 18-A, §5-309(a)(1) closest adult relative 18-A, §5-309(a)(3)	person w/care & custody 18-A, §5-309(a)(2)		waiver ineffective unless present at hearing or confirmed by visitor 18-A, §5-309(b)
MD. Ann. Code (1977 & Supp. 1981) MD. Est. & Trusts Code Ann. §13-101 et seq. (1979 & Supp. 1981)	circuit 13-105(b) 13-101(b)	interested person rule R71(a)	rule R77(a)(2)					disability or other weakness 13-201 (c)(1) rule R73(b)(1)	disability or other weakness 13-201 (c)(1) rule R73(b)(1)	disease 13-201 (c)(1) rule R73(b)(1) disability rule R73(b)(1)	senility 13-201 (c)(1) rule R73(b)(1)	13-201 (c)(1) rule R73(b)(1)	13-201 (c)(1) rule R73(b)(1)	compulsory hospitalization, confinement, detention by foreign power, disappearance 13-201 (c)(1)	2 physicians rule R73(b)(1)		interested persons designated by ct. rule R74(b)	interested persons designated by ct. rule R74(b)	interested persons designated by ct. rule R74(b)		
MASS. Ann. (Michie/Law. Co-op. 1981 & Supp. 1981)	probate 201, §1		for a conservator 201, §16	parent, 2 relatives or friends, mayor, corporation, or dep't of mental health 201, §6 agency of human services office 201, §§6A, 16B relative or dep't of public welfare 201, §8			mentally ill, mentally retarded, or spendthrift 201, §1	201, §1	mentally retarded 201, §1	for conservatorship 201, §1	for conservatorship 201, §1			spendthrift 201, §1	201, §6A	201, §§6, 6A	201, §§7, 9, 17	husband of spendthrift 201, §9	dep't of mental health 201, §7	7 days before hearing 201, §§7, 9, 17	
MICH. Comp. Laws Ann. (1980 & Supp. 1981)	probate 330.1600 (d)	interested person 330.1609 (1)	330.1609 (1)				developmentally disabled & totally w/o capacity to care for self or estate 330.1618 (5)		mentally retarded 330.1600 (e)(iii)(A)					cerebral palsy, autism, epilepsy 330.1600 (e)(iii)(A) dyslexia 330.1600 (e)(iii)(c)	330.1612 (1)	if report does not accompany petition 330.1612 (3)	330.1614 (3)	presumptive heirs 330.1614 (3)	preparer of report, director of facility where residing, guardian ad litem, & counsel 330.1614 (3)		
MINN. Stat. Ann. (West 1975 & Supp. 1981)	probate 525.011	525.541	525.541			525.551 (5)(b)(1)	in need of supervision & protection & no less restrictive alternatives 525.551 (5)(b)(2), (3)										525.55(1)	spouse, parents, adult children, siblings, next of kin 525.55(1)	administrative head of hospital or institution; such others as ct. directs 525.55(1)	14 days before hearing 525.55(1)	

TABLE 7.3 INITIATION OF GUARDIANSHIP PROCEEDINGS—*Continued*

	APPLICATION BY				CRITERIA FOR COURT-ORDERED APPOINTMENT OF GUARDIAN										SUPPORTING EVIDENCE		NOTICE OF PROCEEDING				PROVISIONS FOR WAIVER OF NOTICE TO RESPONDENT OR SUBSTITUTE SERVICE
					Legal Status			Included Impairments													
STATE	*Court* (1)	*Any Person* (2)	*Alleged Incompetent* (3)	*Other* (4)	Incompetent (5)	Incapacitated (6)	Other (7)	Mental Illness (8)	Mental Deficiency (9)	Physical Disability (10)	Advancing Age (11)	Alcoholism (12)	Drug Addiction (13)	Other (14)	*Medical Certification* (15)	*Court-Ordered Examination* (16)	*Respondent* (17)	*Relatives* (18)	*Other* (19)	*When* (20)	(21)
MISS. Code Ann. (1972 & Supp. 1981)	chancery 93-13-121 93-13-123 93-13-125 93-13-131	interested party (unsound mind) 93-13-125	incompetent 93-13-121	guardian of incompetent 93-13-121 relative or friend of unsound person, drunkard, or drug addict 93-13-123, 125,131	93-13-121 OR		unsound mind 93-13-123, 125, or drunkard or drug addict 93-13-131				excluded 93-13-121	93-13-131	93-13-131		director of hospital where confined 93-13-125	fn. 3 93-13-121					
MO. Ann. Stat. (Vernon 1956 & Supp. 1981)	probate Const. 1945, art. 5, §16	475.060			475.090			or insanity 475.010 (3)	imbecility or idiocy 475.010 (3)		senility 475.010 (3)	475.010 (3)	475.010 (3)				475.075 (2)	spouse 475.075 (2)		reasonable time before hearing 475.075 (2)	
MONT. Code Ann. (1981)	district 72-1-103 (7)	interested person 72-5-315 (1)	72-5-315 (1)			72-5-316(1) AND	necessary to meet essential requirements for physical health or safety 72-5-316 (1)	72-5-101 (1)	72-5-101 (1)	or illness 72-5-101 (1)	72-5-101 (1)	72-5-101 (1)	72-5-101	except minority 72-5-101		physician & visitor 72-5-315 (3)	72-5-314 (1)(a)	spouse, parents, & adult children 72-5-314 (1)(a) closest adult relative 72-5-314 (1)(c)	person w/care custody 72-5-314 (1)(b)		waiver ineffective unless present at hearing or confirmed by visitor 72-5-314 (2)
NEB. Rev. Stat. (1979 & Supp. 1981)	county 30-2209 (5)	interested person 30-2619 (a)	30-2619(a)			30-2620 AND	necessary or desirable for continuing care & supervision 30-2620	30-2601 (1)	30-2601 (1)	or illness 30-2601 (1)	30-2601 (1)	30-2601 (1)	30-2601 (1)	except minority 30-2601 (1)		physician & visitor 30-2601 (1)	30-2625 (a)(1)	spouse, parents, & adult children 30-2625 (a)(1) closest adult relative 30-2625 (a)(3)	person w/care & custody 30-2625 (a)(2)		waiver ineffective unless present at hearing or confirmed by visitor 30-2625(b)
NEV. Rev. Stat. (1981)	159.015	159.044	159.044(1)	governmental agency or nonprofit organization 159.044 (1)	159.054			159.019	or weakness of mind 159.019	disease 159.019	159.019			any other cause 159.019			159.047	spouse & adult children, or parent, brother, or sister 159.047 (2)(a)(1)	person w/care, custody, or control 159.047 (2)(a)(2)	20 days before hearing 159.0475 (1)	
N.H. Rev. Stat. Ann. (1968 & Supp. 1981)	probate 464-A:2 (IV)	interested person 464-A:4 (I)	464-A:4(I)	relative of public official 464-A:4 (I)		464-A:9 (III)(a) AND	necessary to continuing care & supervision, no available alternatives, least restrictive form of intervention 464-A:9 (III)(b)–(d)										464-A:5(I)	464-A:5 (IV)(a)	proposed guardian; medical director where patient in institution 464-A:5 (IV)	14 days before hearing 464-A:5 (I), (IV)	
N.J. Stat. Ann. (West 1953 & Supp. 1982); N.J. Rules (1982)	superior 3B:12-25 county or superior R.4:83-1				3B:12-25 R.4:83-1			insanity, lunacy, or unsound mind R.4:83-1 3B:1-2	idiocy R.4:83-1 3B:1-2	or illness 3B:1-2		3B:1-2 R.4:83-1	3B:1-2		2 reputable physicians R.4:83-2 (b), (c)	R.4:83-4(b)	R.4:83-4(a)	spouse, adult children, & parents R.4:83-4(a)	person w/care or custody, & such others as ct. directs R.4:83-4(a)	20 days before hearing R.4:83-4(a)	ct. may, for good cause, shorten or dispense w/notice R.4:83-4(a)

TABLE 7.3 INITIATION OF GUARDIANSHIP PROCEEDINGS—*Continued*

	APPLICATION BY				CRITERIA FOR COURT-ORDERED APPOINTMENT OF GUARDIAN										SUPPORTING EVIDENCE		NOTICE OF PROCEEDING				PROVISIONS FOR WAIVER OF NOTICE TO RESPONDENT OR SUBSTITUTE SERVICE
					Legal Status			*Included Impairments*													
STATE	*Court* (1)	*Any Person* (2)	*Alleged Incompetent* (3)	*Other* (4)	Incompetent (5)	Incapacitated (6)	Other (7)	Mental Illness (8)	Mental Deficiency (9)	Physical Disability (10)	Advancing Age (11)	Alcoholism (12)	Drug Addiction (13)	Other (14)	*Medical Certification* (15)	*Court-Ordered Examination* (16)	*Respondent* (17)	*Relatives* (18)	*Other* (19)	*When* (20)	(21)
N.M. Stat. Ann. (1978 & Supp. 1982)	district 45-5-302	interested person 45-5-303(A)	45-5-303 (A)			45-5-101(F) AND	necessary or desirable for continuing care & supervision 45-5-101 (F)	45-5-101(F)	45-5-101(F)	or illness 45-5-101 (F)	45-5-101(F)	45-5-101(F)	45-5-101(F)			physician & visitor 45-5-303 (B)	45-5-309 (A)(1)	45-5-309 (A)(2)	person w/care & custody 45-5-309 (A)(3)		waiver ineffective unless present at hearing or confirmed by visitor 45-5-309 (B)
N.Y. Mental Hyg. Law (McKinney 1978 & Supp. 1981)	supreme ct., & county cts. outside NYC 78.01 78.03(b)	78.03(a)		social services official 78.03(a)	78.01 AND		would not be in person's best interest to appoint conservator 78.02	78.01			78.01	78.01		patient at facility for mentally ill or mentally retarded 78.01			unless ct. orders otherwise 78.03(d)	spouse 78.03(d)	distributees & person w/whom respondent resides 78.03(d)		
N.C. Gen. Stat. (1976 & Supp. 1981)	clerk of superior ct. 35-1.8(a) 35-2	35-1.10 35-2			from want of understanding to manage own affairs 35-2 35-1.16(f) OR		inebriate 35-2	35-1.7(11)	mentally retarded 35-1.7(1)		excluded 35-1.8(b)			cerebral palsy, autism, epilepsy 35-1.7(1)			35-1.13	spouse, adult children, or next of kin, or persons acting in loco parentis 35-1.13	guardian ad litem or counsel appointed by clerk 35-1.13		
N.D. Cent. Code (1976 & Supp. 1981)	county 30.1-01-06(6)	interested person 30.1-28-03(1)	30.1-28-03(1)			30.1-28-04 AND	necessary or desirable for continuing care & supervision 30.1-28-04	30.1-26-01(1)	30.1-26-01(1)	or illness 30.1-26-01(1)	30.1-26-01(1)	30.1-26-01(1)	30.1-26-01(1)	except minority 30.1-26-01(1)		physician & visitor 30.1-28-03(2)	30.1-28-09(1)(a)	spouse, parents, & adult children 30.1-28-09(1)(a) closest adult relative 30.1-28 09(1)(c)	person w/care & custody 30.1-28-09(1)(b)		waiver ineffective unless present at hearing or confirmed by visitor 30.1-28-09(2)
OHIO Rev. Code Ann. (Baldwin 1978 & Supp. 1981)	probate 2111.02	interested party 2111.02		ct.'s own motion 2111.02	2111.02			mental disability or infirmity, mentally retarded, or mentally ill 2111.01(D)	mental disability or infirmity, mentally retarded, or mentally ill 2111.01(D)	or infirmity 2111.01(D)	2111.01(D)	2111.01(D)		improvidence 2111.01(D)			2111.04 (B)(1)	next of kin 2111.04 (B)(2)		3 days before appointment 2111.04	waiver prohibited 2111.04 (B)(2)
OKLA. Stat. Ann. (West 1965 & Supp. 1981)	county 58, §1			relative or friend 58, §851	58, §851 OR	incapable of taking care of self & managing property 58, §852 OR	insane 58, §851	weakness of mind see table 8.1		disease see table 8.1	old age see table 8.1			see table 8.1			58, §851	known near relative, not the petitioner 58, §851		5 days before hearing 58, §851	
OR. Rev. Stat. (1981)	probate 126.003 (2)	interested person 126.103 (1)	126.103 (1)			126.107 (1)	necessary or desirable for continuing care & supervision 126.107 (2)									physician & visitor 126.103 (3), (4)	126.127 (1)	spouse, parents, & adult children 126.127 (1) closest adult relative 126.127 (3)	person w/care & custody 126.127 (2)	10 days before hearing 126.103 (2) 126.007 (1)	waiver 126.013
PA. Cons. Stat. Ann. (Purdon 1975 & Supp. 1980)		interested person 20, §5511 (a)						20, §5501	or mentally retarded 20, §5501		20, §5501	inebriety 20, §5501	20, §5501			physician 20, §5511 (c)	20, §5511 (a)	all who are sui juris 20, §5511 (a)	such others as ct. may direct 20, §5511 (a)		

TABLE 7.3 INITIATION OF GUARDIANSHIP PROCEEDINGS—*Continued*

STATE	APPLICATION BY: Court (1)	APPLICATION BY: Any Person (2)	APPLICATION BY: Alleged Incompetent (3)	APPLICATION BY: Other (4)	CRITERIA FOR COURT-ORDERED APPOINTMENT OF GUARDIAN: Legal Status: Incompetent (5)	Legal Status: Incapacitated (6)	Legal Status: Other (7)	Included Impairments: Mental Illness (8)	Included Impairments: Mental Deficiency (9)	Included Impairments: Physical Disability (10)	Included Impairments: Advancing Age (11)	Included Impairments: Alcoholism (12)	Included Impairments: Drug Addiction (13)	Included Impairments: Other (14)	SUPPORTING EVIDENCE: Medical Certification (15)	SUPPORTING EVIDENCE: Court-Ordered Examination (16)	NOTICE OF PROCEEDING: Respondent (17)	NOTICE OF PROCEEDING: Relatives (18)	NOTICE OF PROCEEDING: Other (19)	NOTICE OF PROCEEDING: When (20)	PROVISIONS FOR WAIVER OF NOTICE TO RESPONDENT OR SUBSTITUTE SERVICE (21)
R.I. Gen. Laws (1969 & Supp. 1981	probate 33-15-8			relative, friend, or director of public welfare 33-15-8			see table 8.1	lunatic or person of unsound mind 33-15-8	idiot 33-15-8			33-15-8		gaming, idleness, or debauchery 33-15-8			if in asylum 33-15-9 33-15-17	by publication; next of kin of minor 33-15-17	33-15-8	upon filing petition 33-15-8 14 days before any action 33-15-17	33-15-9
S.C. Code Ann. (Law. Co-op. 1976 & Supp. 1981)	probate 21-19-10	w/consent of parents (mentally retarded) 21-19-200 interested person (incompetent) 21-23-20		parents of mentally retarded fn. 4 21-19-200 21-23-20	21-19-10	OR	mentally retarded 21-19-200										by publication 21-23-10	by publication 21-23-10	by publication 21-23-10	once a week for 2 weeks 21-23-10	
S.D. Codified Laws Ann. (1976 & Supp. 1982)	circuit 30-27-5 county board of mental retardation 27B-6-1	other person fn. 5 30-27-11 responsible individual 27B-6-1	minor over 14 30-27-11	relative 30-27-11 secretary of social services 30-27-11	30-27-6		mentally retarded & not receiving proper care or education 27B-6-1	30-27-6						for any cause mentally or physically incompetent 30-27-6				such relatives as ct. directs 30-27-15	person w/care & custody & such others as ct. directs fn. 5 30-27-15	manner & method to be determined by ct. 30-27-15	may be dispensed with for good cause 30-27-15
TENN. Code Ann. (1977 & Supp. 1982)	chancery, circuit, law & equity, or probate 34-12-102 (3) county, probate or chancery 34-12-203	interested person 34-12-104 (a)	34-12-104 (a) 34-12-203	friend or relative 34-12-203			disabled 34-12-110 (a) incapable of managing estate 34-12-203	34-12-102 (1) mental weakness 34-12-203	developmentally disabled 34-12-102 (1) mental weakness 34-12-203	illness or injury 34-12-102 (1) incapacity 34-12-203	34-12-102 (1) 34-12-203			other incapacity 34-12-102 (1)		physician selected from list of 3 submitted by adversary counsel 34-12-108 (a) 2 reputable physicians 34-12-205	34-12-105 (a) 34-12-204	parent or guardian, if a minor; person most closely related 34-12-105 (a), (b) husband, wife, descendants, ascendants, & next of kin 34-12-204	person, institution or agency w/care & custody 34-12-105 (b)	7 days before appointment 34-12-204	to guardian ad litem if personal service would be a futile act 34-12-105 (a)
TEX. Prob. Code Ann. (Vernon 1980 & Supp. 1981)	county judge 415 county ct. 111	415 111		county officer 415	109(c)		unsound mind or habitual drunkard 418	unsound mind 114(a) 418				habitual drunkard 114(a) 418					notice by posting 418, 420, 130 by citation 130(c)	notice by posting 418, 420 130	notice by posting 418, 420 130		citation not required if judged unsound or drunkard w/in prior 6 mos. 130(d)
UTAH Code Ann. (1978 & Supp. 1981)	district 75-1-201 (5)	interested person 75-5-303 (1)	75-5-303 (1)			75-5-304	necessary or desirable for continuing care & supervision 75-5-304	75-1-201 (18)	75-1-201 (18)	or illness 75-1-201 (18)	75-1-201 (18)	75-1-201 (18)	75-1-201 (18)	except minority 75-1-201 (18)		physician & visitor 75-5-303 (2)	75-5-309 (1)(a)	spouse, parents, & adult children 75-5-309 (1)(a) closest adult relative 75-5-309 (1)(c)	person w/care & custody 75-5-309 (1)(b) testamentary guardian 75-5-309 (1)(d)		waiver ineffective unless present at hearing or confirmed by visitor 75-5-309 (2)
VT. Stat. Ann. tit. 14: (1974 & Supp. 1982) tit. 33: (1980 & Supp. 1982)	probate 14, §3062 district 33, §3603	interested person 14, §3063 fn. 6 33, §3605		state's attorney fn. 6 33, §3605			mentally retarded & in need of supervision & protection 33, §3604	14, §3061 (1)(B)	mentally retarded 14, §3061 (1)(B) mentally disabled 14, §3068 (f)							mental health professional 14, §3067 comprehensive evaluation 33, §3606	14, §3064 (a) 33, §3607	spouse or nearest relative 14, §3064 (a) spouse or nearest relative 33, §3607	counsel & such others as ct. directs 14, §3064 (a) counsel, state's attorney, & such others as ct. directs 33, §3607	10 days before hearing 14, §3064 (a) 10 days before hearing 33, §3607	

TABLE 7.3 INITIATION OF GUARDIANSHIP PROCEEDINGS—*Continued*

	APPLICATION BY				CRITERIA FOR COURT-ORDERED APPOINTMENT OF GUARDIAN										SUPPORTING EVIDENCE		NOTICE OF PROCEEDING				PROVISIONS FOR WAIVER OF NOTICE TO RESPONDENT OR SUBSTITUTE SERVICE
					Legal Status			Included Impairments													
STATE	Court (1)	Any Person (2)	Alleged Incompetent (3)	Other (4)	Incompetent (5)	Incapacitated (6)	Other (7)	Mental Illness (8)	Mental Deficiency (9)	Physical Disability (10)	Advancing Age (11)	Alcoholism (12)	Drug Addiction (13)	Other (14)	Medical Certification (15)	Court-Ordered Examination (16)	Respondent (17)	Relatives (18)	Other (19)	When (20)	(21)
VA. Code (1976 & Supp. 1982)	circuit 37.1-128. 02(A) 37.1-128. 1(A)	37.1-128. 02(A) 37.1-128. 1(A)			37.1-128. 02(A)	37.1-128. 1(A)	incapable of taking care of self or handling & managing estate 37.1-128. 02(A)	37.1-128. 02(A) 37.1-128. 1(A)	mentally retarded 37.1-128. 02(A) 37.1-128. 1(A)							comprehensive evaluation 37.1-128. 02(A) 37.1-128. 1(A)	37.1-128. 02(A) 37.1-128. 1(A)			reasonable notice 37.1-128. 02(A) 37.1-128. 1(A)	
WASH. Rev. Code Ann. (1967 & Supp. 1981)	superior 11.88.010 (1)	interested person or entity 11.88.030 (1)			11.88.010 (1)			11.88.010 (1)	develop-mentally disabled 11.88.010 (1)		senility 11.88.010 (1)	11.88.010 (1)	11.88.010 (1)	other mental incapacity 11.88.010 (1)		physician's report 11.88.045 (3)	if over 14 11.88.040 (1)	parent of minor, & spouse 11.88.040 (2)	person w/whom respondent resides 11.88.040 (3)	10 days before hearing fn. 7 11.88.040	may be waived by all parties but respondent 11.88.040
W. VA. Code (1980 & Supp. 1982)	county commission 27-11-1(a)				27-11-1(d)											27-11-1(d)	27-11-1(b)	spouse or adult next of kin 27-11-1(b)		10 days before hearing 27-11-1(b)	
WIS. Stat. Ann. (West 1981)	circuit 880.02	880.07(1)		relative or or public official 880.07(1)	880.03 OR		spendthrift 880.03		develop-mentally disabled 880.01(4)		880.01(4)			other like incapacities fn. 8 880.01 (4), (8)			880.08 (1), (2)	presumptive adult heirs 880.08(1)	existing guardian; counsel; person w/custody 880.08(1)	10 days before hearing 880.08 (1), (2)	
WYO. Stat. (1977 & Supp. 1982)	district 3-2-101	interested party 3-2-302(a)		relative or friend 3-2-302(a)	or mentally incompetent 3-2-301			3-2-301	or retardation 3-2-301	or disease 3-2-301	3-2-301	3-2-301	3-2-301		if presence at hearing injurious or impossible 3-2-303(a)		3-2-305(a) 3-2-302(a)	spouse & children, or parents, brothers & sisters, or nearest known relatives 3-2-305(a) 3-2-302 (a)(i)(A)	person w/care or institution w/custody 3-2-305(a) 3-2-302 (a)(i)(B)	10 days before hearing 3-2-305(a)	

FOOTNOTES: Table 7.3

1. Del. Code Ann. tit. 12, § 3914(a) (1981): "mother, father, brother, sister, husband, wife, child, next of kin, creditor, debtor, any public agency or, in the absence of such person or persons or public agency or the refusal or inability to act, any other person."

2. Fla. Stat. Ann. § 744.331(2)(a) (West Supp. 1980): "The mother, father, brother, sister, husband, wife, adult child, or next of kin of the alleged incompetent."

3. Miss. Code Ann. § 93-13-121 (Supp. 1980):

> Upon the return day of the process, the Chancellor, . . . or the court . . . shall cause the applicant to appear in person and then and there examine such applicant and all interested parties, and if after such examination the Chancellor . . . or the court . . . be of the opinion that the applicant is incompetent to manage his or her estate, then it shall be the duty of the court to appoint a guardian of the estate.

4. S.C. Code Ann. § 21-23-20 (Law. Co-op. 1976): "The application for the appointment of the judge of probate as . . . Guardian . . . shall be made by the father, mother, husband, brother, executor, administrator or other person interested in the minor or mentally incompetent person."

5. S.D. Codified Laws Ann. § 27B-6-7 (1976): "If the county board determines that a person is mentally retarded, not receiving proper care and education, and there is no responsible relative to take custody of the person or petition for guardianship, the board shall notify the board of social services who may petition for letters of guardianship."

6. Vt. Stat. Ann. tit. 33, § 3605 (1980): "Any interested person with knowledge of the facts alleged may request the state's attorney having jurisdiction to file a petition with the district court alleging that person is mentally retarded and in need of protective supervision or guardianship of the person. The state's attorney shall file the petition unless it clearly appears that the petition will be insufficient to support an action under this chapter."

7. Wash. Rev. Code Ann. § 11.88.040(3) (Supp. 1980): "The court for good cause may reduce the number of days of notice, but in every case, at least three days notice shall be given."

8. Wis. Stat. Ann. § 880.01(8) (West 1980): "'Other like incapacities' means those conditions incurred at any age which are the result of accident, organic brain damage, mental or physical disability, continued consumption or absorption of substances, producing a condition which substantially impairs an individual from providing for his own care or custody."

TABLE 7.4 CONDUCT AND RESULTS OF GUARDIANSHIP PROCEEDINGS

		LEGAL REPRESENTATION			PRESENCE IN COURT			HEARING CLOSED TO PUBLIC	JURY TRIAL		STANDARD OF PROOF	PROVISIONS FOR PRIORITY AND PREFERENCE IN APPOINTMENT				NATURE OF GUARDIANSHIP				CON-TINUED COURT SUPER-VISION	GUARDIAN TO POST BOND	
STATE	HEARING (1)	Right to Counsel (2)	Appoint-ment Unrep-sented (3)	Guardian Ad Litem (4)	Mandatory Attendance (5)	Except When Harmful (6)	Right to Attend (7)	(8)	Mandatory (9)	Upon Request (10)	(11)	Eligibility (12)	Disquali-fied Parties (13)	Priority Among Eligible Parties (14)	Attention to Re-spondent's Preference (15)	Of Person or Proper-ty or Both (16)	Same Powers, Rights & Duties as Parent of Unemanci-pated Child (17)	Separate Proceeding For Protec-tion of Property (18)	Other (19)	(20)	Amount Set at Judge's Discretion (21)	Statutory Guideline (22)
ALA. Code (1975 & Supp. 1982)	26-2-42(a)		guardian ad litem 26-2-42(b) 26-2-46	appointed when unrep-resented 26-2-42(b) 26-2-46	if consistent w/health or safety 26-2-43				26-2-43				judge 26-7-1	nearest re-lationship, & person who will best man-age estate 26-2-49					sheriff, if no other suitable person applies & qualifies 26-2-50	annual settlement of estate 26-4-9	not less than 2 times value of estate 26-3-1	not less than 2 times value of estate 26-3-1
ALAS. Stat. (1972 & Supp. 1981)	13.26.106(a)	13.26.106(b)	13.26.106(b)	13.26.112			unless so disruptive that pro-ceedings cannot rea-sonably continue 13.26.113(5)	if requested 13.26.113(4)		entitled to 13.26.113(6)	clear & convincing evidence 13.26.113(b)	any compe-tent person or suitable insitution 13.26.145		patient's nominee, spouse, adult child, parent, relative, private or-ganization, public guardian 13.26.145(d)	13.26.113(g)		13.26.150	13.26.165			conserva-tors only fn. 1 13.26.215	conserva-tors only fn. 1 13.26.215
ARIZ. Rev. Stat. Ann. (1975 & Supp. 1981)	14-5303(B)		guardian ad litem 14-5303(B)	appointed when unrep-resented 14-5303(B)			14-5303(B)	if requested 14-5303(B)		entitled to 14-5303(B)		any compe-tent person 14-5311(A)		spouse, adult child, parent, relative, nominee 14-5311(B)			14-5312	14-5401			conservators only fn. 1 14-5411(A)	conservators only fn. 1 14-5411(A)
ARK. Stat. Ann. (1971 & Supp. 1981)	57-615			not neces-sary to proceeding 57-611(c)	at ct.'s discretion 57-615(b)							corporation 57-607(d) adult resident of sound mind 57-607(a)	convicted, unpardoned felon 57-607(a) sheriff, clerk, judge, or deputy 57-607(g)	due regard to requests of parents, spouse, & to blood or marriage 57-608 (a), (c), (d)	if a minor 14 or older 57-608(b)	57-616				periodic reports at ct.'s direction 57-624(a)	57-617	$1,000 for guardian of person 57-617
CAL. Prob. Code (West 1981 & Supp. 1981)	1822(a)	1823(b)(6)	1823(b)(6)		unless out of state, medically unable, or not contesting 1825(a)	serious & immediate physiologi-cal damage 1825(c)				1823(b)(7) 1827			spouse, if action brought for separation, divorce, etc. 1813	spouse, adult child, parent, brother or sister, other eligible person or entity 1812(b)	unless respondent's nominee is not in best interests 1810	conservator 1801 (a)–(c)				biennial ct. review 1850(a)	2320(a)(1)	
COLO. Rev. Stat. (1973 & Supp. 1981)	15-14-303 (2)	15-14-303 (5)(a)	15-10-403 (5)(a), (b) 15-14-303 (5)(c)	15-10-403 (5)(c)			15-14-303 (4)	if requested 15-14-303 (4)		15-14-303 (4)		any competent person 21 or older or suitable institution 15-14-311 (1)		spouse, anticipatory nominee, adult child, parent, relative, caretaker's nominee 15-14-311 (2)	anticipatory nominee 15-14-311 (2)(b)		15-14-312 (1)	15-14-401	no less restrictive alternative means 15-14-304 (1)		conserva-tors only fn. 1 15-14-411	conserva-tors only fn. 1 15-14-411
CONN. Gen. Stat. Ann. (West 1981)	45-70c(a) if over 18 45-78d(b)	45-70c(b)(2)	45-70c(b)(2)				45-70c(b)(2)				clear & convincing evidence 45-70d(c)	any qualified person, authorized public official, or corporation 45-70d(d)			unless not in person's best interests 45-70d(d)	conservator of estate or person 45-70d(c) 45-78b				annual accounting before ct., if requested 45-75(c)	45-70d(f)	
DEL. Code Ann. (1979 & Supp. 1980)	12, §3914(b)	entitled to represen-tation 12, §3914(b)														12, §3914(c)				biennial accounting 12, §3943	ct. may order waiver 12, §3914(h)	

TABLE 7.4 CONDUCT AND RESULTS OF GUARDIANSHIP PROCEEDINGS—*Continued*

		LEGAL REPRESENTATION			PRESENCE IN COURT				JURY TRIAL			PROVISIONS FOR PRIORITY AND PREFERENCE IN APPOINTMENT				NATURE OF GUARDIANSHIP					GUARDIAN TO POST BOND	
STATE	HEARING (1)	Right to Counsel (2)	Appointment Unrepsented (3)	Guardian Ad Litem (4)	Mandatory Attendance (5)	Except When Harmful (6)	Right to Attend (7)	HEARING CLOSED TO PUBLIC (8)	Mandatory (9)	Upon Request (10)	STANDARD OF PROOF (11)	Eligibility (12)	Disqualified Parties (13)	Priority Among Eligible Parties (14)	Attention to Respondent's Preference (15)	Of Person or Property or Both (16)	Same Powers, Rights & Duties as Parent of Unemancipated Child (17)	Separate Proceeding For Protection of Property (18)	Other (19)	CONTINUED COURT SUPERVISION (20)	Amount Set at Judge's Discretion (21)	Statutory Guideline (22)
D.C. Code Ann. (1981 & Supp. 1982)	21-1502(a)	*fn. 2* annot. to 21-1502		"may appoint" 21-1502(b)	for alcoholics or drug addicts 21-1301											conservator of estate 21-1503 or person 21-1506			committee for alcoholics or drug addicts 12-1301		12-1503	personal property & yearly rental value of estate (alcoholics & drug addicts) 12-1302
FLA. Stat. Ann. (West 1964 & Supp. 1981)	744.331(4)	744.331(4)	744.331(4)									any resident who is sui juris 744.309 (1)(a) related nonresident 744.309 (2) trust company, bank, or corporation 744.309 (5), (6)	any judge, unless related by blood, marriage, or adoption 744.309 (1)(b) ex-felons or incapable persons *fn. 3* 744.309 (4)	next of kin, testamentary designee 744.312 (2) may be contested 744.344	744.312 (3)(a)	744.344				annual examination by physician 744.364 (1)	744.351 (3), (4)	*fn. 4* 744.351 (3), (5)
GA. Code Ann. (1979 Supp. 1982)	49-606(d) (1)	49-606(b) (2)(B)	49-606(b) (2)(B)	at judge's discretion 49-606(b) (2)(D)	appearance may be waived upon good cause 49-606(e) (1)			upon request & for good cause 49-606(e) (1)			clear & convincing evidence 49-606(e) (4)	any person 49-602(a) corporation 49-602(b)		anticipatory nominee, spouse, adult child, parent, guardian while a minor, relative, director of family services, county *fn. 5* 49-602	anticipatory nominee 49-602(c) (1) 49-606(e) (5)	49-603 49-604 49-606(f) (1)				annual report to ct. 49-603(b) (10) such other provisions as ct. deems proper 49-606(f) (1)(H)–(J)		a like bond as required for guardians of property of minors (guardian of property only) 49-604(1)
HAWAII Rev. Stat. (1976 & Supp. 1981)	560:5-303 (b)			if interests inadequately represented 560:5-303 (b)			560:5-303 (b)	discretionary 560:5-303 (b)				any competent person or nonprofit agency or corporation 560:5-311 (a)		spouse, adult child, parent, relative, nominee *fn. 6* 560:5-311 (b)			560:5-312	560:5-401		annual reports to ct. 560:5-308A	conservators 560:5-411	
IDAHO Code (1979 & Supp. 1981)	15-5-303 (b)	15-5-303 (b)	guardian ad litem 15-5-303 (b)	appointment when unrepresented 15-5-303 (b)			15-5-303 (b)	if requested 15-5-303 (b)				any competent person or suitable institution 15-5-311 (a)		spouse, adult child, parent, relative, nominee 15-5-311 (b)			15-5-312	15-5-401			conservators only *fn. 1* 15-5-411	conservators only *fn. 1* 15-5-411
ILL. Ann. Stat. (Smith-Hurd 1978 & Supp. 1981)	110½, §11a-10(a)	110½, §11a-11(a)	if interests best served 110½, §11a-10(b)	if necessary for protection, or reasonably informed decision on petition 110½, §11a-10(a)	unless excused upon good cause 110½, §11a-11(a)			upon request 110½, §11a-11(a)		110½, §11a-11(a)		any adult of sound mind, public agency, not-for-profit or trust corporation 110½, §11a-5	ex-convicts, or agency providing residential services to ward 110½, §11a-5	at discretion of ct. 110½, §11a-12(d)	anticipatory designee 110½, §11a-6 due consideration 110½, §11a-12(d)	110½, §11a-8				annual report to ct. 110½, §11a-17(b)	110½, §12-2	

TABLE 7.4 CONDUCT AND RESULTS OF GUARDIANSHIP PROCEEDINGS—*Continued*

STATE	HEARING (1)	LEGAL REPRESENTATION			PRESENCE IN COURT			HEARING CLOSED TO PUBLIC (8)	JURY TRIAL		STANDARD OF PROOF (11)	PROVISIONS FOR PRIORITY AND PREFERENCE IN APPOINTMENT				NATURE OF GUARDIANSHIP				CON-TINUED COURT SUPER-VISION (20)	GUARDIAN TO POST BOND	
		Right to Counsel (2)	Appointment Unrepresented (3)	Guardian Ad Litem (4)	Mandatory Attendance (5)	Except When Harmful (6)	Right to Attend (7)		Mandatory (9)	Upon Request (10)		Eligibility (12)	Disqualified Parties (13)	Priority Among Eligible Parties (14)	Attention to Respondent's Preference (15)	Of Person or Property or Both (16)	Same Powers, Rights & Duties as Parent of Unemancipated Child (17)	Separate Proceeding For Protection of Property (18)	Other (19)		Amount Set at Judge's Discretion (21)	Statutory Guideline (22)
IND. Code Ann. (Burns 1972 & Supp. 1982)	29-1-18-19		"may appoint" 29-1-18-19	not necessary 29-1-18-14 (c)		29-1-18-19				29-1-18-19		any public agency or charitable organization; persons or corporate fiduciary most suitable & willing to serve 29-1-18-9 29-1-18-10		due regard to will, request by spouse, relationship, & assets 29-1-18-10	due regard *fn. 7* 29-1-18-10	29-1-21(a)			1 or 2 guardians 29-1-21(a)		may reduce amount 29-1-18-22 (b)	value of estate & income from estate 29-1-18-22 (a)
IOWA Code Ann. (West 1964 & Supp. 1981)	633.555 633.569			if physician certifies as mentally incompetent to conduct defense R. Civ. P. 13, 14						633.555 633.569		qualified or suitable person 633.559 633.571				guardian of person 633.556		conservator 633.570			*fn. 8* 633.633	
KAN. Stat. Ann. (1976 & Supp. 1981)	59-3010 (A)(1)	59-3010 (A)(3)	preference to attorney who has represented respondent before 59-3010 (A)(3)		at ct.'s discretion 59-3011 (B)(2)	59-3010 (A)(2)		all unnecessary persons 59-3013		or commission 59-3012 (1)(D) 59-3013		1 or more suitable persons 59-3013		nominee of natural guardian 59-3014(2)		guardian or conservator or both 59-3013				annual account by conservator 59-3029	may be waived if no property 59-3014(2)	
KY. Rev. Stat. Ann. (Michie 1977 & Supp. 1980)	203.022(1)	203.014	203.014			203.018			203.022(2)							committee 203.032			dep't. for human resources 210.290(1)		not required from dep't. of human resources 210.290(1)	not required from dep't. of human resources 210.290(1)
LA. Civ. Code Ann. (West 1952 & Supp. 1981)			if confined (discretionary) 391	provisional administrator if proper for preservation & administration of estate 394							to the satisfaction of judge 393					curator of person & property 404				ct.-appointed superintendent 424 visits by judge 425		
ME. Rev. Stat. Ann. (1981 & Supp. 1981)	18-A, §5-303(b)	18-A, §5-303(b)	guardian ad litem 18-A, §5-303(b)	appointment when unrepresented 18-A, §5-303(b)			18-A, §5-303(b)	upon request 18-A, §5-303(b)				any competent person or suitable institution 18-A, §5-311(a)	facility licensed under 22, §§1817, 7801 18-A, §5-311(c)	respondent's nominee, spouse, adult child, parent, relative, caretaker's nominee 18-A, §5-311(b)			18-A, §5-312	18-A, §5-401			conservators only *fn. 1* 18-A, §5-411	conservators only *fn. 1* 18-A, §5-411
MD. Ann. Code of 1957 (1977 & Supp. 1981) MD. Est. & Trusts Code Ann. §13-101 *et seq.* (1974 & Supp. 1981)	rule R77(b)		discretionary rule R76 see also rule 205(e)(2)						unless waived rule R77(b)							rule 278(a)		13-201(a)		annual accounting rule V74 13-209		13-208 rule V73
MASS. Ann. Laws (Michie/ Law. Co-op. 1981 & Supp. 1981)	201, §§6, 6A, 8, 16B			discretionary *fn. 9* annot. to 201, §6A									*fn. 10* 201, §6A			person & property 201, §§6, 6A, 8		201, §16B				201, §§12, 19 205, §1

TABLE 7.4 CONDUCT AND RESULTS OF GUARDIANSHIP PROCEEDINGS—*Continued*

STATE	HEARING (1)	LEGAL REPRESENTATION			PRESENCE IN COURT			HEARING CLOSED TO PUBLIC (8)	JURY TRIAL		STANDARD OF PROOF (11)	PROVISIONS FOR PRIORITY AND PREFERENCE IN APPOINTMENT				NATURE OF GUARDIANSHIP				CON-TINUED COURT SUPER-VISION (20)	GUARDIAN TO POST BOND	
		Right to Counsel (2)	Appoint-ment Unrep-sented (3)	Guardian Ad Litem (4)	Mandatory Attendance (5)	Except When Harmful (6)	Right to Attend (7)		Mandatory (9)	Upon Request (10)		Eligibility (12)	Disquali-fied Parties (13)	Priority Among Eligible Parties (14)	Attention to Re-spondent's Preference (15)	Of Person or Proper-ty or Both (16)	Same Powers, Rights & Duties as Parent of Unemanci-pated Child (17)	Separate Proceeding For Protec-tion of Property (18)	Other (19)		Amount Set at Judge's Discretion (21)	Statutory Guideline (22)
MICH. Comp. Laws Ann. (1980 & Supp. 1981)	330.1614(1)	330.1615(1)	330.1615(2)	if necessary to represent best interests & assist counsel 330.1616		330.1617(4)		upon request 330.1617(3)		330.1617(1)	clear & convincing evidence 330.1618(5)	any suitable person or agency, including a private association 330.1628(1)	dep't. of mental health or any other agency directly providing services 330.1628(1)		due consideration 330.1628(2)	330.1618(5)			partial guardianship preferred 330.1602(2)	annual report to ct. 330.1631(2)	330.1632 704.3	
MINN. Stat. Ann. (West 1975 & Supp. 1981)	525.55(1)	525.55(2)	if requested 525.55(2)		525.551(1)		525.55(2)				clear & convincing evidence 525.54(1)	1 or 2 suitable & competent persons 525.54(1)		most suitable & best qualified person 525.551(5)	525.544	1 or 2 persons as general guardians or conservators 525.551(5)				annual accounting 525.58(1)	525.551(6)	
MISS. Code Ann. (1972 & Supp. 1981)	93-13-121 93-13-131				93-13-121 93-13-131											for drunkards & drug addicts 93-13-131		93-13-121 93-13-123, 125		annual account filed w/ct. 93-13-121		
MO. Ann. Stat. (Vernon 1956 & Supp. 1981)	475.075(1)	475.075(3)	475.075(3)				475.075(2)			of either party 475.075(1)		any adult, charitable organization, or corporation 475.055(1)	judge, sheriff, deputy, clerk, minor, person of unsound mind, drunkard, or addict 475.055(2)	spouse 475.050		person & property 475.090					475.100(1)	at least 2 times value of estate & yearly income from estate 475.100(1)
MONT. Code Ann. (1981)	72-5-315(2)	72-5-315(2)	guardian ad litem 72-5-315(2)	appointment when unrepresented 72-5-315(2)			72-5-315(4)	w/o jury upon request 72-5-315(4)		72-5-315(4)		any competent person or suitable institution 72-5-312(1)		nominee, spouse, adult child, parent, relative, friend, private corporation 72-5-312(2)			72-5-321(2)	72-5-401			conservators only fn. 1 72-5-411	conservators only fn. 1 72-5-411
NEB. Rev. Stat. (1979 & Supp. 1981)	30-2619(b)	30-2619(b)	guardian ad litem 30-2619(b)	appointment when unrepresented 30-2619(b)			30-2619(b)	upon request 30-2619(b)				any competent person or suitable institution 30-2627(a)	owner or employee of institution for mentally or physically handicapped 30-2627(a)	spouse, adult child, parent, relative, nominee 30-2627(b)			30-2628(a)	30-2630			conservators only fn. 1 30-2640	conservators only fn. 1 30-2640
NEV. Rev. Stat. (1981)	159.047(1)	159.048(4)	159.048(4)		except for good cause, if in state 159.0535(1)		159.048(3)					any qualified person or entity 159.059	incompetent, minor, ex-felon, suspended or disbarred lawyer, nonresident 159.059	parents 159.061	anticipatory request 159.061(1)	159.055(2)(a)				annual report to ct. 159.081(1)	159.065(1)	
N.H. Rev. Stat. Ann. (1968 & Supp. 1981)	464-A:5(I)	464-A:6(I)	464-A:6(I)			464-A:8(I), (II)		unless otherwise requested 464-A:8(VII)			beyond reasonable doubt 464-A:8(IV)	any competent person; bank or trust company 464-A:10	institution or agency providing care & custody 464-A:10			464-A:9(III)		464-A:13		annual account 464-A:26(V), 36 biennial report 464-A:35	464-A:21	
N.J. Stat. Ann. (West 1953 & Supp. 1982) N.J. Rules (1982)	R.4:83-4(a)	R.4:83-4(a)	R.4:83-4(a)		at ct. or plaintiff's discretion R.4:83-5	R.4:83-5	R.4:83-4(a)			3B:12-24 R.4:83-4(a)				spouse, next of kin, other proper person R.4:83-6(c) spouse, heirs 3B:12-25		3B:12-25	3B:12-56				R.4:83-6(c)	

TABLE 7.4 CONDUCT AND RESULTS OF GUARDIANSHIP PROCEEDINGS—*Continued*

STATE	HEARING	LEGAL REPRESENTATION			PRESENCE IN COURT			HEARING CLOSED TO PUBLIC	JURY TRIAL		STANDARD OF PROOF	PROVISIONS FOR PRIORITY AND PREFERENCE IN APPOINTMENT				NATURE OF GUARDIANSHIP				CONTINUED COURT SUPERVISION	GUARDIAN TO POST BOND	
	(1)	Right to Counsel (2)	Appointment Unrepresented (3)	Guardian Ad Litem (4)	Mandatory Attendance (5)	Except When Harmful (6)	Right to Attend (7)	(8)	Mandatory (9)	Upon Request (10)	(11)	Eligibility (12)	Disqualified Parties (13)	Priority Among Eligible Parties (14)	Attention to Respondent's Preference (15)	Of Person or Property or Both (16)	Same Powers, Rights & Duties as Parent of Unemancipated Child (17)	Separate Proceeding For Protection of Property (18)	Other (19)	(20)	Amount Set at Judge's Discretion (21)	Statutory Guideline (22)
N.M. Stat. Ann. (1978 & Supp. 1982)	45-5-303(B)	45-5-303(B)	guardian ad litem 45-5-303(B)	appointment when unrepresented 45-5-303(B)			45-5-303(B)	upon request 45-5-303(B)		entitled to 45-5-303(B)		any competent person or suitable institution 45-5-311(A)		spouse, adult child, parent, relative, nominee 45-5-311(B)			45-5-312	45-5-401			conservators only *fn. 1* 45-5-411(A)	conservators only *fn. 1* 45-5-411(A)
N.Y. Mental Hyg. Law (McKinney 1978 & Supp. 1981)	or trial 78.03(e)	78.03(e)		if not represented by counsel 78.03(e)						by any party 78,03(e)		committee 78.01				committee 78.01				no power to act except on ct. authorization (property only) 78.15(a)	78.09(a)	not less than value & 2 yrs. expected income of estate 78.09(a)
N.C. Gen. Stat. (1976 & Supp 1981)	35-1.16(b) 35-2	35-1.16(a)	*fn. 11* OR 35-1.16(a)	*fn. 11* 35-1.16(a) 35-2				open, unless otherwise requested 35-1.16(d)	35-2	or on clerk's own motion 35-1.16(c)	greater weight of evidence 35-1.16(f)	individual, domestic corporation, or disinterested public agent 35-1.28(a)		individual, domestic corporation, or disinterested public agent 35-1.29		person & property, unless clerk orders otherwise 35-1.16(g)(2) 35-1.7(7)		trustee 35-2		status reports 35-1.31	35-1.19	no bond required from guardian of person 35-1.19
N.D. Cent. Code (1976 & Supp. 1981)	30.1-28-03(2)	30.1-28-03(2)	guardian ad litem 30.1-28-03(2)	appointment when unrepresented 30.1-28-03(2)			30.1-28-03(2)	upon request 30.1-28-03(2)				any competent person or suitable institution 30.1-28-11(1)		spouse, adult child, parent, relative, nominee 30.1-28-11(2)			30.1-28-12(1)	30.1-29-01			conservators only *fn. 1* 30.1-29-11	conservators only *fn. 1* 30.1-29-11
OHIO Rev. Code Ann. (Baldwin 1978 & Supp. 1981)	2111.04	2111.02		if under legal disability 2111.23								any person, association or corporation 2111.01(A)	administrator or executor of will, where ward has interest 2111.09			unless a corporation *fn. 12* 2111.02 2111.06, 2111.10						
OKLA. Stat. Ann. (West 1965 & Supp. 1981)	58, §851				58, §851											person & property 58, §852		conservatorship 58, §890.1		annual inventory of estate 58, §871	58, §§853, 776	same as for guardian of minor 58, §853
OR. Rev. Stat. (1981)	126.103(2)	126.103(2)	ct. "may" appoint 126.103(2)				126.103(5)	upon request 126.103(5)					incompetent, minor, suspended or disbarred lawyer, judge, ex-felon *fn. 13* 126.045, 126.050	due regard to anticipatory nominee, blood, or marriage 126.035	anticipatory nominee 126.035(1)		126.137(1)	126.157			conservators only *fn. 13* 126.237(1)	conservators only *fn. 13* 126.237(1)
PA. Cons. Stat. Ann. (Purdon 1975 & Supp. 1980)	20, §5511 (a)	if in state mental hospital or center for mentally retarded *fn. 14* annot. to 20, §5511	if in state mental hospital or center for mentally retarded *fn. 14* annot. to 20, §5511	not necessary to proceeding 20, §5511 (a)		or outside of state 20, §5511 (a)(i),(ii)		upon request 20, §5511 (a)		20, §5511 (a)						person or estate 20, §5511 (a)				accounting whenever ct. directs 20, §5531	having regard to value of personal estate 20, §5515 (3)	
R.I. Gen. Laws (1969 & Supp. 1981)				if in asylum for insane 33-15-9												33-15-8				annual account 33-15-26	33-17-1	
S.C. Code Ann. (Law. Co-op. 1976 & Supp. 1981)	for appointment of judge as guardian 21-23-30												corporations, unless nonprofit & empowered by state 21-19-240	judge, only if no willing, fit, competent, & responsible person found 21-23-10		mentally retarded 21-19-200			judge to act as guardian of estate of incompetent 21-23-10	annual account of estate 21-19-140 annual report 21-23-80		2 times value of estate; 1½ times for corporate guardians 21-19-40

TABLE 7.4 CONDUCT AND RESULTS OF GUARDIANSHIP PROCEEDINGS—*Continued*

STATE	HEARING (1)	LEGAL REPRESENTATION: Right to Counsel (2)	LEGAL REPRESENTATION: Appointment Unrepresented (3)	LEGAL REPRESENTATION: Guardian Ad Litem (4)	PRESENCE IN COURT: Mandatory Attendance (5)	PRESENCE IN COURT: Except When Harmful (6)	PRESENCE IN COURT: Right to Attend (7)	HEARING CLOSED TO PUBLIC (8)	JURY TRIAL: Mandatory (9)	JURY TRIAL: Upon Request (10)	STANDARD OF PROOF (11)	PROVISIONS FOR PRIORITY AND PREFERENCE IN APPOINTMENT: Eligibility (12)	PROVISIONS FOR PRIORITY AND PREFERENCE IN APPOINTMENT: Disqualified Parties (13)	PROVISIONS FOR PRIORITY AND PREFERENCE IN APPOINTMENT: Priority Among Eligible Parties (14)	PROVISIONS FOR PRIORITY AND PREFERENCE IN APPOINTMENT: Attention to Respondent's Preference (15)	NATURE OF GUARDIANSHIP: Of Person or Property or Both (16)	NATURE OF GUARDIANSHIP: Same Powers, Rights & Duties as Parent of Unemancipated Child (17)	NATURE OF GUARDIANSHIP: Separate Proceeding For Protection of Property (18)	NATURE OF GUARDIANSHIP: Other (19)	CONTINUED COURT SUPERVISION (20)	GUARDIAN TO POST BOND: Amount Set at Judge's Discretion (21)	GUARDIAN TO POST BOND: Statutory Guideline (22)
S.D. Codified Laws Ann. (1976 & Supp. 1982)	30-27-14			at ct.'s discretion 30-26-2	at ct.'s discretion 30-27-17											30-27-11				accounting whenever ct. directs 30-27-30(3)	30-27-30	
TENN. Code Ann. (1977 & Supp. 1982)	34-12-104 (c) 34-12-205	34-12-106 (a)	34-12-106 (a)	if ct. determines advisable 34-12-106 (a) to present respondent's interests at hearing 34-12-205			except when harmful 34-12-107 (4)			34-12-107 (1)		any suitable person or any parent 34-12-109 (a)	dep'ts of mental health & mental retardation 34-12-109 (b)			conservator 34-12-207	34-12-207		limited & limited standby guardian 34-12-110	annual report to ct. 34-12-114 (b)	34-12-116 34-12-208	no bond if no control over property 34-12-116 like that of guardians of minor 34-12-208
TEX. Prob. Code Ann. (Vernon 1980 & Supp. 1981)	417	ct. "may" appoint attorney ad litem 113A		417	416		right to appear & contest 113, 115		417	no right to jury 115			minors, persons of notorious conduct, incompetent parties, debtors of estate 110	spouse, next of kin, other qualified person 109(c)		418 116					420 193	
UTAH Code Ann. (1978 & Supp. 1981)	75-5-303(2)	75-5-303(2)	ct. "may" appoint 75-5-303(2)	ct. "may" appoint 75-5-303(2)			75-5-303(2)	closed w/o jury upon request 75-5-303(2)		75-5-303(2)		any competent person or suitable institution 75-5-311(1)		spouse, adult child, parent, relative, nominee 75-5-311(2)			75-5-312	75-5-401			conservators only fn. 1 75-5-411	conservators only fn. 1 75-5-411
VT. Stat. Ann. tit. 14: (1974 & Supp. 1982) tit. 33: (1980 & Supp. 1982)	14, §3064(a) 33, §3607	14, §3065 33, §3608	14, §3065 33, §3608	if unable to communicate w/counsel 14, §3066			14, §3068(a) 33, §3609(a)	ct. may exclude any unnecessary person 14, §3068(b) 33, §3609(a)			clear & convincing evidence 14, §3068(f) a fair preponderance of evidence 33, §3609(e)	competent adults 14, §3072(a) commissioner 33, §3610	guardian ad litem; employee or operator of facility where residing 14, §3072(a)	consideration to location, relationship, ability, & conflicts of interest 14, §3072(b)	14, §3072(b) (1)	total or limited guardian 14, §§3069, 3070 appointment of commissioner as guardian 33, §3610				annual report to ct. 14, §3076 annual review 33, §3614	14, §2751	
VA. Code (1976 & Supp. 1982)	37.1-128.02 (A) 37.1-128.1 (A)			37.1-128.02 (B) 37.1-128.1 (B)			37.1-128.02 (A), (B) 37.1-128.1 (A), (B)			37.1-128.02 (A) 37.1-128.1 (A)	clear & convincing evidence 37.1-128.02 (A) clear & convincing evidence 37.1-128.1 (A)	committee 37.1-128.02 (A) suitable person 37.1-128.1 (A)			due regard 37.1-128.1 (A)	committee 37.1-128.02 (A) 37.1-128.1 (A)			sheriff, if no guardian appointed w/in 7 days of hearing 37.1-128.1 (B)		37.1-128.02 (B) 37.1-135 37.1-128.1 (B) 37.1-135	
WASH. Rev. Code Ann. (1967 & Supp. 1981)	11.88.040	11.88.045 (1)	11.88.045 (1)	11.88.090 (2)	may be waived by ct. for good cause 11.88.040			11.88.040		11.88.045 (2)	clear, cogent & convincing evidence 11.88.045 (2)				11.88.090 (3)(b)(iv)	person, trust company, national bank, or nonprofit corporation 11.88.030 (1)				annual account 11.92.040 (2) intermediate accounts 11.92.050	11.88.100	
W. VA. Code (1980 & Supp. 1982)	27-11-1(b)		guardian ad litem 27-11-1(b)	appointment when unrepresented 27-11-1(b)		27-11-1(b)						committee 27-11-1(d)				committee 27-11-1(e)					27-11-2	
WIS. Stat. Ann. (West 1981)	880.08	880.33 (2)(a)(1)	if requested or if justice so requires 880.33 (2)(a)(1)	880.33 (2)(a)(1)	if able 880.08(1)					880.33 (2)(a)(1)	clear & convincing evidence 880.33(4)			parents, other suitable individual, corporation 880.09(2)	anticipatory nominee 880.09(7)	880.02, 03, 12				inventory & account 880.191	guardian of estate only 880.13	

TABLE 7.4 CONDUCT AND RESULTS OF GUARDIANSHIP PROCEEDINGS—*Continued*

		LEGAL REPRESENTATION			PRESENCE IN COURT				JURY TRIAL			PROVISIONS FOR PRIORITY AND PREFERENCE IN APPOINTMENT				NATURE OF GUARDIANSHIP					GUARDIAN TO POST BOND	
STATE	HEARING (1)	Right to Counsel (2)	Appointment Unrepsented (3)	Guardian Ad Litem (4)	Mandatory Attendance (5)	Except When Harmful (6)	Right to Attend (7)	HEARING CLOSED TO PUBLIC (8)	Mandatory (9)	Upon Request (10)	STANDARD OF PROOF (11)	Eligibility (12)	Disqualified Parties (13)	Priority Among Eligible Parties (14)	Attention to Respondent's Preference (15)	Of Person or Property or Both (16)	Same Powers, Rights & Duties as Parent of Unemancipated Child (17)	Separate Proceeding For Protection of Property (18)	Other (19)	CONTINUED COURT SUPERVISION (20)	Amount Set at Judge's Discretion (21)	Statutory Guideline (22)
WYO. Stat. (1977 & Supp. 1982)	3-2-304(a)	3-2-305(b)	ct. may, in the exercise of sound discretion, appoint legal counsel 3-2-305(b)	if person has relatives (minors) whose interests are inadequately protected or represented 3-2-305(d)		3-2-304(a)	3-2-306		w/o jury unless ct. deems in best interests of alleged incompetent 3-2-306	w/o jury unless ct. deems in best interests of alleged incompetent 3-2-306						3-2-306		conservator, if instutionalized 3-2-309		annual account 3-2-206	3-2-108(a)	

FOOTNOTES: TABLE 7.4

1. Alas. Stat. § 13.26.215 (1980):

> Unless otherwise directed, the bond shall be in the amount of the aggregate capital value of the property of the estate in his control plus one year's estimated income minus the value of securities [and cash] deposited under arrangements requiring an order of [by] the court for their removal and the value of any land which the fiduciary, by express limitation of power, lacks power to sell or convey without court authorization.

See Ariz. Rev. Stat. Ann. § 14-5411(A) (Supp. 1981); Colo. Rev. Stat. § 15-14-411 (Supp. 1980); Idaho Code § 15-5-411 (Supp. 1980); Me. Rev. Stat. Ann. tit. 18-A, § 5-411; Mont. Code Ann. § 72-5-411(2) (1981); Neb. Rev. Stat. § 30-2640 (1981) (similar language); N.M. Stat. Ann. § 45-5-411(A) (1980) (similar language); N.D. Cent. Code § 30.1-29-11 (Supp. 1981) (similar language); Or. Rev. Stat. § 126.237(1) (1980); and Utah Code Ann. § 75-5-411 (Supp. 1981).

2. Annot. to D.C. Code Ann. § 21-1502 (Supp. 1981): "Person for whose estate appointment of a conservator is sought may select private counsel of his own choice to advocate his position in opposition to appointment of a conservator. Mazza v. Pechacek (1956, 233 F.2d 666, 98 U.S. App. D.C. 175)."

3. Fla. Stat. Ann. § 744.309(4) (West Supp. 1980): "No person who has been convicted of a felony or who, from sickness, intemperance, or want of understanding, is incapable of discharging the duties of a guardian shall be appointed to act as guardian."

4. Id. § 744.351:

> (3) The penal sum of a guardian's bond shall be fixed by the court, and it must be in an amount not less than the full amount of the cash on hand and on deposit belonging to the ward, plus the value of the notes and bonds owned by the ward that are payable to bearer. . . .
>
> . . . .
>
> (5) Banks and trust companies authorized by law to be guardians shall not be required to file bonds.

5. Ga. Code Ann. § 49-602(b) (Supp. 1981):

> [F]or good cause shown, in writing, the court may pass over a person having a preference and appoint a person having a lower preference or no preference or, in appointing a proper guardian, may appoint a corporation having general trust powers of the court finds such person or corporate fiduciary to be substantially more qualified and such appointment to be clearly in the best interests of the ward.

6. Hawaii Rev. Stat. § 560:5-311(b): "The family court, for good cause, may pass over a person having priority and appoint a person having less or no priority."

7. Ind. Code Ann. § 29-1-18-10 (Burns Supp. 1980): "Due regard to: (1) any request made by one for whom a guardian is being appointed by reason of old age, infirmity, or other incapacity, other than insanity, mental illness, mental retardation, senility, habitual drunkenness, or excessive use of drugs; (2) any request for the appointment contained in a will or other written instrument."

8. Iowa Code Ann. § 633.633 (West Supp. 1980): "[A] guardian shall not be required to give bond unless the court, for good cause, finds that the best interests of the ward require a bond."

9. Annot. to Mass. Ann. Laws ch. 201, § 6A (Michie/Law. Co-op. 1981):

> Probate Court is a court of superior and general jurisdiction, has equity jurisdiction, and can act in all matters relating to guardianship, including the power to appoint . . . a guardian ad litem in order to protect the interests of a person in a proceeding before it. Superintendent of Belchertown State School v. Salkewicz (1977) 373 Mass. 728, 370 N.E.2d 417.

10. Id.: "The court shall not . . . appoint as guardian [of a mentally retarded person] any person or organization which, in its opinion, has an interest, responsibilities or powers which would render such person or organization unable to perform the duties of guardian in the best interest of the mentally retarded person."

11. N.C. Gen. Stat. § 35-1.16(a) (Supp. 1979):

> The respondent is entitled to be represented by counsel of his own choice or by court-appointed counsel or guardian ad litem . . . . If the respondent for whom counsel has been appointed seeks to waive the right to counsel and if the clerk determines at the hearing on the petition that he lacks capacity to waive the right . . . but does not want counsel, the clerk shall appoint a guardian ad litem.

12. Ohio Rev. Code Ann. § 2111.10 (Baldwin Supp. 1980): "Any appointment of a corporation as guardian shall apply to the estate only and not to the person, except that a nonprofit corporation . . . that has a contract with the Department of Mental Retardation and Developmental Disabilities to provide protective services may be appointed as a guardian of the person of a mentally retarded or other developmentally disabled person."

13. Or. Rev. Stat. § 126.050(1) (1980):

> A person nominated as guardian or conservator who has been convicted of a felony shall inform the court of the conviction. The conviction shall not disqualify the nominee . . . unless the court finds that the facts underlying the conviction are such as to give rise to a reasonable belief that such person will be unfaithful to or neglectful of his trust or that the appointment will not be in the best interests of the . . . protected person.

14. Annot. to Pa. Stat. Ann. tit. 20, § 5511 (Purdon Supp. 1980): "(3) The alleged incompetent and his guardian shall be represented by counsel, and unless private estate counsel exists or is appointed by the Court of Common Pleas, the court administrator shall take necessary steps to insure that such counsel is provided." (Applies only to patients of state mental hospital or state center for the mentally retarded.)

TABLE 7.5 TEMPORARY, EMERGENCY, AND TESTAMENTARY APPOINTMENT OF GUARDIANS

	SUCCESSOR TO NATURAL GUARDIAN BY TESTAMENTARY APPOINTMENT			TEMPORARY OR EMERGENCY GUARDIANSHIP							
				Criteria For Appointment							
STATE	*Appointment by Whom* (1)	*Priority Among Testators* (2)	*Termination Upon* (3)	Incompetent or Incapacitated (4)	No Guardian and Emergency Exists (5)	Present Guardian Inadequate (6)	Immediate Welfare Needs of Person (7)	Other (8)	*Notice* (9)	*Maximum Duration* (10)	*Right to Object* (11)
ALA. Code (1975 & Supp. 1982)											
ALAS. Stat. (1972 & Supp. 1981)	parent or spouse 13.26.095 (a), (b)	spouse 13.26.095(b)	written objection by ward 13.26.095(d)				in need of immediate services & not capable of procuring them 13.26.140(a)		immediately upon filing petition 13.26.140(a)	until end of guardianship proceeding 13.26.140(e)	
ARIZ. Rev. Stat. Ann. (1975 & Supp. 1981)	parent or spouse 14-5301 (A), (B)	spouse 14-5301(B)	written objection by ward 14-5301(D)	14-5310	AND 14-5310	OR 14-5310	AND 14-5310		not required 14-5310	6 mos. 14-5310	
ARK. Stat. Ann. (1971 & Supp. 1981)				57-620	AND		57-620		not required 57-620	90 days 57-620	
CAL. Prob. Code (1981 & Supp. 1981)						if powers suspended 2250(e)		good cause 2250(b)	5 days before appointment 2250(c)	pending hearing on conservatorship 2250(c)	
COLO. Rev. Stat. (1973 & Supp. 1981)	parent or spouse 15-14-301 (1), (2)	spouse 15-14-301	written objection by ward 15-14-301(4)	15-14-310	AND 15-14-310	OR 15-14-310	AND 15-14-310		not required 15-14-310	6 mos. 15-14-310	
CONN. Gen. Stat. Ann. (West 1981)				45-72(a), (b)			45-72(b)	certificate of 2 physicians 45-72(b)	waived 45-72(c)	30 days 45-72(a)	hearing, if in respondent's best interests 45-72(c)
DEL. Code Ann. (1979 & Supp. 1980)											
D.C. Code Ann. (1981 & Supp. 1982)								necessary for protection of estate 21-1505	not required 21-1505	until permanent conservator appointed or until sooner discharged 21-1505	
FLA. Stat. Ann. (West 1964 & Supp. 1981)											
GA. Code Ann. (1979 & Supp. 1982)				gravely incapacitated 49-608			or estate 49-608(a)	affidavits of 2 physicians 49-608(b)	immediate 49-608(c)(6)	45 days 49-608(e)	emergency hearing before ct. 49-608(c)(2)
HAWAII Rev. Stat. (1976 & Supp. 1981)	parent or spouse 560:5-301	spouse 560:5-301		560:5-310	AND 560:5-310		560:5-310			90 days 560:5-310	
IDAHO Code (1979 & Supp. 1981)	parent or spouse 15-5-301 (a), (b)	spouse 15-5-301(b)	written objection by ward 15-5-301(d)	15-5-310	AND 15-5-310	OR 15-5-310	AND 15-5-310		not required 15-5-310	6 mos. 15-5-310	
ILL. Ann. Stat. (Smith-Hurd 1978 & Supp. 1981)	by parent at ct.'s discretion 110½, §11a-16			disabled 110½, §11a-4			or estate 110½, §11a-4		such as ct. may prescribe 110½, §11a-4	60 days or until regular appointment 110½, §11a-4	right to revoke appointment 110½, §11a-4
IND. Code Ann. (Burns 1972 & Supp. 1982)	not stated *fn. 1* 29-1-18-10(2)			29-1-18-24			29-1-18-24		none, unless ordered by ct. 29-1-18-14(a)	60 days 29-1-18-24	
IOWA Code Ann. (West 1964 & Supp. 1981)									such as ct. shall prescribe 633.558 633.573	such as ct. shall prescribe 633.558 633.573	appointment follows a hearing 633.558 633.573
KAN. Stat. Ann. (1976 & Supp. 1981)											
KY. Rev. Stat. Ann. (Michie 1977 & Supp. 1980)											
LA. Civ. Code Ann. (West 1952 & Supp. 1981)								preservation of movables & administration of estate (administrator *pro tempore*) 394		pending interdiction 394	
ME. Rev. Stat. Ann. (1981 & Supp. 1981)	parent or spouse 18-A, §5-301 (a), (b)	spouse 18-A, §5-301(b)	written objection by ward 18-A, §5-301(d)	18-A, §5-310	AND 18-A, §5-310	OR 18-A, §5-310	AND 18-A, §5-310		not required 18-A, §5-310	6 mos. 18-A, §5-310	
MD. Est. & Trusts Code Ann. (1974 & Supp. 1981)				disabled 13-203(a)			immediate, substantial, & irreparable injury to applicant or respondent 13-203(b)	preservation & application of property (by ct.) 13-203(a)	immediate 13-203(b)	pending appointment proceeding 13-203(a)	by guardian or interested person 13-203(d)
MASS. Ann. Laws (Michie/Law. Co-op. 1981 & Supp. 1981)				mentally ill, mentally retarded, or spendthrift 201, §14			201, §14		discretionary 201, §14	until otherwise ordered by supreme ct., or until appointment of permanent guardian 201, §14	

TABLE 7.5 TEMPORARY, EMERGENCY, AND TESTAMENTARY APPOINTMENT OF GUARDIANS—*Continued*

	SUCCESSOR TO NATURAL GUARDIAN BY TESTAMENTARY APPOINTMENT			TEMPORARY OR EMERGENCY GUARDIANSHIP							
				Criteria For Appointment							
STATE	*Appointment by Whom* (1)	*Priority Among Testators* (2)	*Termination Upon* (3)	Incompetent or Incapacitated (4)	No Guardian and Emergency Exists (5)	Present Guardian Inadequate (6)	Immediate Welfare Needs of Person (7)	Other (8)	*Notice* (9)	*Maximum Duration* (10)	*Right to Object* (11)
MICH. Comp. Laws Ann. (1980 & Supp. 1981)	parent who has been appointed as guardian 330.1642(2)		ct. dismissal 330.1642(2)	develop-mentally disabled 330.1607(1)	emergency circumstances 330.1607(1)		330.1607(1)			pending appeal or action for appointment 330.1607(1)	hearing w/in 14 days 330.1607 (2)–(4)
MINN. Stat. Ann. (West 1975 & Supp. 1981)											
MISS. Code Ann. (1972 & Supp. 1981)											
MO. Ann. Stat. (Vernon 1956 & Supp. 1981)											
MONT. Code Ann. (1981)	parent or spouse 72-5-302 (1), (2)	spouse 72-5-302(2)	written objection by ward 72-5-304	72-5-317(1)	AND 72-5-317(1)	OR 72-5-317(2)	AND 72-5-317(2)		not required 72-5-317(2)	6 mos. 72-5-317(2)	
NEB. Rev. Stat. (1979 & Supp. 1981)	parent or spouse 30-2617 (a), (b)	spouse 30-2617(b)	written objection by ward 30-2617(d)	30-2626	AND 30-2626	OR 30-2626	AND 30-2626		not required 30-2626	6 mos. 30-2626	
NEV. Rev. Stat. (1981)				159.052(1)	AND		159.052(1)	AND petitioner made good faith effort to give notice 159.052(1)		10 days; may be extended to 30 days upon hearing 159.052	
N.H. Rev. Stat. Ann. (1968 & Supp. 1981)				464-A:12(I)(a)	AND			in need of temporary guardianship & regular proceedings inappropriate 464-A:12(II) (a), (c)	464-A:12(II)	60 days 464-A:12(II)	hearing: same protections as for appointment of permanent guardian 464-A:12(IV)
N.J. Stat. Ann. (West 1953 & Supp. 1982)	parent of unmarried incompetent, or spouse 3B:12-30							testamentary guardian appointed, but ward not yet adjudicated incompetent 3B:12-32	3B:12-30	until determination of issue of mental incompetency 3B:12-32	
N.M. Stat. Ann. (1978 & Supp. 1982)	parent or spouse 45-5-301 (A), (B)	spouse 45-5-301(B)	written objection by ward 45-5-301(D)	45-5-310(A)	AND no guardian 45-5-310(A)	OR 45-5-310(A)	AND 45-5-310(A)		not required 45-5-310(A)	6 mos. 45-5-310(A)	
N.Y. Mental Hyg. Law (McKinney 1978 & Supp. 1981)				incompetency proceeding pending 78.03(f)	AND			temporary receiver needed to preserve estate 78.03(f)		pending adjudication of incompetency 78:03(f)	
N.C. Gen. Stat. (1976 & Supp. 1981)	any person authorized to appoint testamentary guardian for minor may direct such person to petition for continuation before ward reaches majority 35-1.41	will w/latest date 33-2	restoration 35-1.39	incompetency proceeding pending 35-1.15(a), (e)			imminent or foreseeable danger to physical well-being 35-1.15(b)		prompt service 35-1.15(c)	45 days; 45-day extension upon good cause 35-.1-15(d)	hearing w/in 15 days of service 35-1.15(c)
N.D. Cent. Code (1976 & Supp. 1981)	parent or spouse 30.1-28-01 (1), (2)	spouse 30.1-28-01(2)	written objection by ward 30.1-28-01(4)	30.1-28-10	AND 30.1-28-10	OR 30.1-28-10	AND 30.1-28-10		not required 30.1-28-10	6 mos. 30.1-28-10	
OHIO Rev. Code Ann. (Baldwin 1978 & Supp. 1981)											
OKLA. Stat. Ann. (West 1965 & Supp. 1981)											
OR. Rev. Stat. (1981)				126.133	AND 126.133	OR 126.133	AND 126.133		not required 126.133	"a specified period" 126.133	
PA. Stat. Ann. (Purdon 1975 & Supp. 1980)	*fn.* 2 20, §5515(2)			20, §5513	AND			nonappointment will result in irreparable harm to person or estate 20, §5513	only such notice as appears to be feasible 20, §5513	such time as ct. shall direct 20, §5513	same type of hearing as for permanent guardianship 20, §5513
R.I. Gen. Laws (1969 & Supp. 1981)				guardianship application pending or on appeal 33-15-10	AND			if ct. deems proper 33-15-10	such notice as ct. directs 33-15-10	until guardianship application adjudicated or until discharged by ct. 33-15-11	appeal from appointment prohibited 33-15-11
S.C. Code Ann. (Law. Co-op. 1976 & Supp. 1981)				pending guardianship 21-19-50	AND			upon ex parte petition 21-19-50	not required 21-19-50	pending legal citation 21-19-50	
S.D. Codified Laws Ann. (1976 & Supp. 1982)											
TENN. Code Ann. (1977 & Supp. 1982)											

TABLE 7.5 TEMPORARY, EMERGENCY, AND TESTAMENTARY APPOINTMENT OF GUARDIANS—*Continued*

STATE	SUCCESSOR TO NATURAL GUARDIAN BY TESTAMENTARY APPOINTMENT			TEMPORARY OR EMERGENCY GUARDIANSHIP — *Criteria For Appointment*							
	Appointment by Whom (1)	*Priority Among Testators* (2)	*Termination Upon* (3)	Incompetent or Incapacitated (4)	No Guardian and Emergency Exists (5)	Present Guardian Inadequate (6)	Immediate Welfare Needs of Person (7)	Other (8)	*Notice* (9)	*Maximum Duration* (10)	*Right to Object* (11)
TEX. Prob. Code Ann. (Vernon 1980 & Supp. 1981)				person of unsound mind, or common or habitual drunkard 131(a)	AND			interest of person or estate requires immediate appointment 131(a)	appointment made w/o notice or citation 131(b)	if contested, pendency of contest 131(e); otherwise, such time as appears in interest of estate or person 131(c), (d)	same provisions as for permanent guardianship *fn. 3* 113 133(b)
UTAH Code Ann. (1978 & Supp. 1981)	parent or spouse 75-5-301 (1), (2)	spouse 75-5-301(2)	written objection by ward 75-5-301(4)	75-5-310(1)	AND 75-5-310(1)	OR 75-5-310(1)	AND 75-5-310(1)		not required 75-5-310(1)	30 days 75-5-310(1)	hearing w/in 5 days 75-5-310(2)
VT. Stat. Ann. (1974 & Supp. 1982)				petition for guardianship filed 14, §3081(a)	BUT		adherence to procedure would cause serious & irreparable harm to physical health or financial interests 14, §3081(a)	adherence to procedure would cause serious & irreparable harm to physical health or financial interests 14, §3081(a)	unless clearly appears from facts or testimony that immediate harm will result 14, §3081(c)	pendency of petition 14, §3081(b)	hearing at earliest possible date 14, §3081 (b), (c)
VA. Code (1976 & Supp. 1982)											
WASH. Rev. Code Ann. (1967 & Supp. 1981)											
W. VA. Code (1980 & Supp. 1982) *fn. 4*											
WIS. Stat. Ann. (West 1981)				spendthrift or incompetent 880.15(1)	AND		880.15(1)		not required 880.15(1)	60 days, unless further extended by ct. order 880.15(1)	no appeal from order permitted 880.15(1)
WYO. Stat. (1977 & Supp. 1982) *fn. 5*											

FOOTNOTES: TABLE 7.5

1. Ind. Code Ann. § 29-1-18-10(a) (Burns Supp. 1981): "The court shall appoint as guardian or coguardian of an incompetent the person, persons or corporate fiduciary or any combination thereof most suitable and willing to serve, having due regard to: . . . (2) any request for the appointment contained in a will or other written instrument."

2. It is unclear whether Pennsylvania law permits appointment of guardians for incompetents by will. Pa. Stat. Ann. tit. 20, § 5515(2) (Purdon Supp. 1980) declares that state provisions for appointment "by conveyance" of guardians of minors (*id.*, § 5115) shall apply to incompetents as well, but § 5115 speaks only of conveyances by deed, gift inter vivos, and insurance. Yet *id.* § 5122(a), also applicable to incompetents, (see *id.* § 5515(4)), includes among "guardian[s] named in conveyance" a guardian "appointed by or in accordance with the terms of a will."

3. Tex. Prob. Code Ann. § 113 (Vernon 1980): "Any person has the right to appear and contest the appointment of a particular person as guardian, or to contest any proceeding which he deems injurious to the ward . . . ." But, "A jury trial verdict, and judgement . . . shall not be prerequisite to . . . appointment . . . ; nor shall it be necessary that such person be present at the trial." *Id.* at § 115.

4. W. Va. Code § 27-11-1(b) (Supp. 1981):

Notwithstanding any requirement hereof to the contrary such hearing may proceed without the presence of the individual alleged to be incompetent if

(1) proper notice has been served upon the party alleged to be incompetent . . . , and

(2) a duly licensed physician shall have certified in writing and upon affidavit that he or she has examined such individual and that such individual is physically unable to appear at such hearing or that such an appearance would likely impair or endanger the health of such individual, or

(3) such individual refuses to appear, and

(4) upon the specific written findings by such commission of facts as will justify a hearing without the presence of such individual as provided in this subsection.

5. Wyo. Stat. § 3-2-309 (1977):

If it shall appear that the estate of the ward requires no management by a guardian but consists primarily of income essential to the said person's subsistence and that the said person is admitted to a public or private institution, the court may, in lieu of appointing a guardian, designate the superintendent or director of such institution to serve as conservator of such funds.

TABLE 7.6 INDEPENDENT RESTORATION PROCEEDINGS

STATE	RESTORATION MERGED WITH DISCHARGE (1)	APPLICATION BY			COURT		SUPPORTING EVIDENCE			NOTICE TO			HEARINGS (13)	PRESENCE IN COURT (14)	JURY TRIAL				RESTORATION		FREQUENCY OF RESTORATION APPLICATIONS (21)	APPEALS (22)	APPLICABLE TO ALL INCOMPETENTS (23)
		Ward (2)	Relative (3)	Anyone (4)	Incompetency Court (5)	Other (6)	Medical Certificate (7)	Verified Petition (8)	Other (9)	Guardian (10)	Relatives (11)	Others (12)			Mandatory (15)	Optional (16)	Right of Incompetent (17)	Right of Others (18)	Full (19)	Partial (20)			
ALA. Code (1977 & Supp. 1982) fn. 1		26-2-5		by next friend 26-2-51	probate 26-2-51		2 physicians or 2 competent persons 26-2-51			26-2-52		the person at whose instance original inquisition made 26-2-52	if contested by guardian or other person 26-2-53	if consistent w/ ward's health or safety 26-2-53 26-2-43	fn. 2 26-2-53				26-2-54				
ALAS. Stat. (1972 & Supp. 1982)		13.26. 125(b)		any person interested in welfare or guardian 13.26. 125(b)						13.26. 135	spouse, parents, & adult children 13.26. 135	person alleged to be incapacitated 13.26. 135	13.26. 125(a)	right to be present, remain silent 13.26. 113(a)			13.26. 113(a)(6)						
ARIZ. Rev. Stat. Ann. (1975 & Supp. 1983)		14-5307 (B)		any person interested in ward's welfare 14-5307	14-5313	ct. where ward resides 14-5313				14-5309	spouse, parents, & adult children 14-5309	person alleged to be incapacitated 14-5309	14-5307 (C) 14-5303 (B)	14-5303 (B)			14-5303				no petition in first yr. 14-5307 (B)		
ARK. Stat. Ann. (1971 & Supp. 1981)				57-643.1	57-643 57-643.1			57-643.1				such notice as ct. may require 57-643.(b)	ct. shall cause facts to be inquired into fn. 3 57-643.1						57-643 57-643.2				
CAL. Prob. Code §§1822, 1862 et seq.: (1981 & Supp. 1983) CAL. Welf. & Inst. Code §535 et seq.: (1972 & Supp. 1983)		conservator or conservatee 1861 application for reappointment only by existing temporary conservator; unless made, conservatorship terminates after 1 yr., & ct. will so decree 5361	spouse or any relative 1861 application for reappointment only by existing temporary conservator; unless made, conservatorship terminates after 1 yr., & ct. will so decree 5361	any interested person or friend 1861 application for reappointment only by existing temporary conservator; unless made, conservatorship terminates after 1 yr., & ct. will so decree 5361	superior 5361 fn. 4		2 physicians or licensed psychologists 5361			conservator if not the petitioner 1862 conservator 5362	spouse & other relatives 1822	conservatee if not the petitioner 1862 1822(c), (f) conservatee & his attorney, & the person in charge of the facility in which he resides fn. 5 5362	1863 5350, 5362	may appear 1863			right to request; judge may or may not reject petition 5362		1863(b) 5362		one per 6 mos. 5364		
COLO. Rev. Stat. (1974 & Supp. 1982)		15-14-307		any interested person 15-14-307	15-14-313	ct. where ward resides 15-14-313	fn. 6 15-14-307 (4)			& ward 15-14-309	spouse & parents 15-14-309		15-14-307 15-14-303	entitled to be present 15-14-303			entitled to trial by jury 15-14-303		15-14-307				
CONN. Gen. Stat. Ann. (West 1981 & Supp. 1982)					probate 45-77					ct. prescribes 45-77	ct. prescribes 45-77	ct. prescribes 45-77	45-77						45-77			fn. 7 45-288	45-77
DEL. Code Ann. (1979 & Supp. 1982)		12, §3914 (e)		having sufficient interest 12, §3914 (e)	chancery 12, §3914 (e)								if guardianship appears to the ct. to be no longer necessary 12, §3914						12, §3914 (e)				12, §3914 (e)
D.C. Code Ann. (1981 & Supp. 1982)		21-1504			district 21-1504														21-1504				21-1504
FLA. Stat. (West 1964 & Supp. 1983)			relative, spouse, or friend 744.464 (4)		744.464 (2)	ct. of county where person lives 744.464 (4)	744.464 (1)(a)			744.464 (4)(b)		744.464 (4)(b)	744.464 (4)(b)						744.464 (4)(c)(2)				

TABLE 7.6 INDEPENDENT RESTORATION PROCEEDINGS—*Continued*

	RESTORATION MERGED WITH DISCHARGE	APPLICATION BY			COURT		SUPPORTING EVIDENCE			NOTICE TO				PRESENCE IN COURT	JURY TRIAL				RESTORATION		FREQUENCY OF RESTORATION APPLICATIONS		APPLICABLE TO ALL INCOMPETENTS
STATE	(1)	Ward (2)	Relative (3)	Anyone (4)	Incompetency Court (5)	Other (6)	Medical Certificate (7)	Verified Petition (8)	Other (9)	Guardian (10)	Relatives (11)	Others (12)	HEARINGS (13)	(14)	Mandatory (15)	Optional (16)	Right of Incompetent (17)	Right of Others (18)	Full (19)	Partial (20)	(21)	APPEALS (22)	(23)
GA. Code Ann. (1976 & Supp. 1982)	if guardian appointed 49-605(a)	49-609(a)		any interested person 49-609(a) fn. 8	probate 49-609(a)		fn. 9 49-609(b)			49-609(d)		ward 49-609(d)	fn. 9 49-609(b)	49-606(e)					49-609(a)(5)	49-609(a)(4)	none w/in 2 yrs. after application dismissed 49-610	49-611	
HAWAII Rev. Stat. (1976 & Supp. 1982)		560:5-307(b)		any person interested in ward's welfare 560:5-307	family ct. 560:5-313	family ct. where ward resides 560:5-313				ward 560:5-309	spouse, parents, grandparents, & adult children 560:5-309		560:5-307(c) 560:5-303	560:5-303					560:5-307				
IDAHO Code (1979 & Supp. 1981)	15-1818	15-5-307		any person interested in ward's welfare 15-5-307	15-5-313	ct. where ward resides 15-5-313				& ward 15-5-309	spouse, parents, & adult children; if no other, closest adult relative 15-5-309		15-5-307(e) 15-5-303	entitled to be present 15-5-303			upon request 15-5-307(d)	upon request 15-5-307(d)	15-5-307				
ILL. Ann. Stat. (Smith-Hurd 1978 & Supp. 1983)	fn. 10	110½, §11a-20		on behalf of disabled person; ct. may make its own motion 110½, §11a-20						or ward unless also the petitioner 110½, §11a-20		notice given to ward unless also the petitioner 110½, §11a-20	110½, §11a-21	110½, §11a-21			110½, §11a-21		110½, §11a-21	110½, §11a-21			
IND. Code Ann. (1972 & Supp. 1982)		29-1-18-48		29-1-18-48	probate 29-1-18-47								29-1-18-48								no new petition w/in 6 mos. 29-1-18-48		
IOWA Code Ann. (West 1964 & Supp. 1983)		633.679			probate 633.10														633.679		every 6 mos. 633.680		633.679
KAN. Stat. Ann. (1976 & Supp. 1981)		59-3027		59-3027	district 59-3027	or to which venue transferred 59-3027				59-3012	natural guardian(s), spouse 59-3012	attorney, custodian; conservator, others as directed by ct. 59-3012	59-3013				59-3013		59-3027		not until 6 mos. after hearings 59-3027	59-2401 (19)	59-3033
KY. Rev. Stat. Ann. (Michie 1977 & Supp. 1980)		or guardian 203.024(1)	spouse 203.024(1)	next friend 203.024(1)	circuit 203.024(1)			affidavit 203.024(1)		if not petitioner 203.024(1)	if not petitioner 203.024(1)	county attorney & committee, if any 203.024(1) spouse	203.024(2)			203.024(2)		ct. 203.024(2)	203.024(3)				203.024(1)
LA. Code Civ. Proc. Ann. (West 1961 & Supp. 1983) fn. 25													summary trial 4546	4547								4548	
ME. Rev. Stat. Ann. (1981 & Supp. 1983)		18A, §5-307(b)		any person interested in ward's welfare 18A, §5-307(b)	18A, §5-313	18A, §5-313				18A, §5-309	spouse, parents, & adult children, or closest adult relative 18A, §5-309	ward 18A, §5-309	18A, §5-307 18A, §5-303	right to be present 18A, §5-303									
MD. Ann. Code. (1974)		13-221	the guardian 13-221	any interested person 13-221																			

TABLE 7.6 INDEPENDENT RESTORATION PROCEEDINGS—*Continued*

STATE	RESTORATION MERGED WITH DISCHARGE (1)	APPLICATION BY			COURT		SUPPORTING EVIDENCE			NOTICE TO			HEARINGS (13)	PRESENCE IN COURT (14)	JURY TRIAL				RESTORATION		FREQUENCY OF RESTORATION APPLICATIONS (21)	APPEALS (22)	APPLICABLE TO ALL INCOMPETENTS (23)
		Ward (2)	Relative (3)	Anyone (4)	Incompetency Court (5)	Other (6)	Medical Certificate (7)	Verified Petition (8)	Other (9)	Guardian (10)	Relatives (11)	Others (12)			Mandatory (15)	Optional (16)	Right of Incompetent (17)	Right of Others (18)	Full (19)	Partial (20)			
MASS. Ann. Laws (Michie/ Law. Co-op. 1981 & Supp. 1983)		201, §13			probate 201, §13						heirs apparent or pre-sumptive, including spouse, if any 201, §13	7 days notice to dep't of mental health 201, §13							201, §13				201, §13
MICH. Comp. Laws Ann. (1980 & Supp. 1983)		700.447(2)		a person interested in ward's welfare 700.447(2)	700.457	ct. in county where ward resides 700.457				& ward 700.451 (a), (b)	spouse, parents, & adult children 700.451(a)		700.447(3) 700.443(2)	entitled to be present 700.443(2)			700.443(2)		700.447(3)				
MINN. Stat. Ann. (West 1975 & Supp. 1983)	253A.19	or guar-dian or conservator 525.61		525.61	525.61					525.61	spouse, parents, adult children, siblings, next of kin 525.55	ward 525.61	525.61						525.61	525.61		525.71(14)	525.61
MISS. Code Ann. (1973 & Supp. 1982)				93-13-151	chancery 93-13-151				fn. 11 93-13-151				93-13-151	"all interested parties" 93-13-151					93-13-151				93-13-151
MO. Ann. Stat. (1956 & Supp. 1983)		475.360	475.360	475.360	probate 475.360			475.360					475.360						475.365(1)			475.365(3)	475.360
MONT. Code Ann. (1981)		72-5-325		72-5-325	72-5-323	ct. where ward resides 72-5-323							72-5-325 72-5-315	entitled to be present 72-5-315			72-5-315		72-5-325				
NEB. Rev. Stat. (1981)		30-2623(b)		any person interested in ward's welfare 30-2623(b)	30-2629	ct. where ward resides 30-2629				& ward 30-2625	spouse, parents, & adult children 30-2625		30-2623(c) 30-2619(b)	entitled to be present 30-2619(b)					30-2623(c)				
NEV. Rev. Stat. (1979)	certificate of dis-charge signed by state hos-pital chief establishes presumption of legal capacity 41.300			41.320		district 41.310		"petition" 41.320				as ct. may order 41.320	41.310						fn. 12 41.300 41.310				41.300 41.310 41.320
N.H. Rev. Stat. Ann. (1968 & Supp. 1981)		464A:39		454A:39	probate 464A:2IV	probate ct. where ward resides 464A:2IV							464A:39 464A:8	464A:8	464A:8				464A:39				464A:39
N.J. Stat. Ann. (West 1981) & Rules Governing the Courts of the State of New Jersey (1981)		rule 4:83-7		some interested person rule 4:83-7	superior 3A:6-43			complaint verified by affidavit rule 4:83-7	facts evi-dencing return to competency rule 4:83-7				rule 4:83-7			rule 4:83-7			rule 4:83-7 3A:6-43				rule 4:83-7 3A:6-43
N.M. Stat. Ann. (1978 & Supp. 1982)		45-5-307		45-5-307	district 45-5-307 45-5-101(B)					45-5-309	spouse, parents, & adult children, or at least 1 of closest adult relatives 45-5-309	ward 45-5-309	45-5-307 45-5-303	entitled to be present 45-5-303			45-5-303		45-5-307				45-5-307

TABLE 7.6 INDEPENDENT RESTORATION PROCEEDINGS—*Continued*

	RESTORATION MERGED WITH DISCHARGE	APPLICATION BY			COURT		SUPPORTING EVIDENCE			NOTICE TO			HEARINGS	PRESENCE IN COURT	JURY TRIAL				RESTORATION		FREQUENCY OF RESTORATION APPLICATIONS	APPEALS	APPLICABLE TO ALL INCOMPETENTS
STATE	(1)	Ward (2)	Relative (3)	Anyone (4)	Incompetency Court (5)	Other (6)	Medical Certificate (7)	Verified Petition (8)	Other (9)	Guardian (10)	Relatives (11)	Others (12)	(13)	(14)	Mandatory (15)	Optional (16)	Right of Incompetent (17)	Right of Others (18)	Full (19)	Partial (20)	(21)	(22)	(23)
N.Y. Mental Hyg. Law (McKinney 1978 & Supp. 1983)	78.27(b)				78.27														78.27				78.27
N.C. Gen. Stat. (1976 & Supp. 1981)		or guardian 35-1.39		any interested person 35-1.39	clerks of superior ct. 35-1.8					guardian & ward unless one is petitioner 35-1.39		any other parties to proceedings 35-1.39	35-1.39				35-1.39		35-1.39			right of appeal 35-1.39	35-1.39
N.D. Cent. Code (1976 & Supp. 1981)		30.1-28-07		30.1-28-07	30.1-28-05					or ward 30.1-28-09	spouse, parents, & adult children 30.1-28-09		30.1-28-07 30.1-28-03	entitled to be present 30.1-28-03					30.1-28-07				30.1-28-07
OHIO Rev. Code Ann. (Baldwin 1978 & Supp. 1982)		5122.38		5122.38	probate 2111.47 5122.38			5122.38		& ward 2111.47 5122.38	spouse 5122.38	person who applied for appointment 2111.47 5122.38	5122.38						2111.47 5122.38				
OKLA. Stat. Ann. (West 1965 & Supp. 1983)		or guardian 58, §854	58, §854	friend 58, §854	county 58, §854			58, §854		58, §854	spouse; father or mother 58, §854		58, §854						*fn. 13* 58, §854 58, §855				58, §854
OR. Rev. Stat. (1981)	*fn. 14* 426.295(3)	*fn. 13* 126.123 426.295(3)	426.295(3)	126.123 426.295(3)	126.143 426.295(3)	ct. in state where ward resides 126.143				& ward 126.127	spouse, parents, & adult children 126.127		126.123 126.103	may be present 126.103					126.123 426.295(3)				126.123
PA. Stat. Ann. (Purdon 1975 & Supp. 1982)		not stated	not stated	20, §5517	ct. of common pleas, orphans' ct. division 20, §712(2) county ct. 20, §5512				"good cause" 20, §5513			such notice as ct. shall direct 20, §5517	20, §5517						20, §5517				20, §5517
R.I. Gen. Laws (1977 & Supp. 1982)		40.1-5.2-5		anyone in ward's behalf 40.1-5.2-5		justice of supreme ct. 40.1-5.2-5						person confined as insane 40.1-5.2-5	commission shall examine patient in hospital 40.1-5.2-7	right to be present at the inquisition 40.1-5.2-6					40.1-5.2-8				
S.C. Code Ann. (Law. Co-op. 1977)		or guardian 44-23-800		ward's committee if any 44-23-800		probate ct. of county where ward resides 44-23-800	report of 2 designated examiners, 1 a licensed physician 44-23-800			& ward 44-23-800	or friend 44-23-800	counsel 44-23-800	44-23-800	right to appear 44-23-800					44-23-810			44-23-820	
S.D. Codified Laws Ann. (1976 & Supp. 1982)		or guardian 30-31-3	w/in 3d degree 30-31-3	friends 30-31-3	county 30-31-3					30-31-4	next of kin 30-31-4	next of kin 30-31-4	30-31-5						30-31-6	30-31-7			30-31-3
TENN. Code Ann. (1977 & Supp. 1982)		or conservator 34-12-212 the disabled person 34-12-112		an interested 3d party; any interested person 34-12-112	county, probate, or chancery ct. 34-12-212					conservator; person for whom conservator appointed 34-12-212	spouse, descendants, ascendants, & next of kin, except where ward is himself the petitioner 34-12-212		34-12-212 34-12-112	right to attend, unless good cause shown 34-12-107			34-12-112 34-12-107		34-12-212 34-12-112	34-12-212 34-12-112		34-12-107	

TABLE 7.6 INDEPENDENT RESTORATION PROCEEDINGS—*Continued*

STATE	RESTORATION MERGED WITH DISCHARGE (1)	APPLICATION BY Ward (2)	APPLICATION BY Relative (3)	APPLICATION BY Anyone (4)	COURT Incompetency Court (5)	COURT Other (6)	SUPPORTING EVIDENCE Medical Certificate (7)	SUPPORTING EVIDENCE Verified Petition (8)	SUPPORTING EVIDENCE Other (9)	NOTICE TO Guardian (10)	NOTICE TO Relatives (11)	NOTICE TO Others (12)	HEARINGS (13)	PRESENCE IN COURT (14)	JURY TRIAL Mandatory (15)	JURY TRIAL Optional (16)	JURY TRIAL Right of Incompetent (17)	JURY TRIAL Right of Others (18)	RESTORATION Full (19)	RESTORATION Partial (20)	FREQUENCY OF RESTORATION APPLICATIONS (21)	APPEALS (22)	APPLICABLE TO ALL INCOMPETENTS (23)
TEX. Prob. Code (Vernon 1980): §§3, 426 TEX. Rev. Civ. Stat. Ann. (Vernon 1958 & Supp. 1983): §§5547—83	"presumption until discharged" 5547-83(a)			426(a)	"court" includes both county ct. exercising probate jurisdiction & ct. especially created; district ct. 3(g)				guardian to appear 426(a)	426(a)			if facts doubtful 426(b)			if facts doubtful 426(b)			426(b)				only to persons adjudged of unsound mind or habitual drunkards 426(b)
UTAH Code Ann. (1978 & Supp. 1981)		75-5-307		any person interested in ward's welfare 75-5-307	75-5-313	ct. where ward resides 75-5-313				& ward 75-5-309	spouse, parents, & adult children 75-5-309		75-5-307 75-5-303	entitled to be present at hearing 75-5-303			entitled to trial by jury 75-5-303		75-5-307				
VT. Stat. Ann. (1974 & Supp. 1982)				any interested person 14, §3077	14, §3077	ct. where venue lies 14, §3077					spouse or nearest relative 14, §3064	counsel of ward 14, §3064 such other persons as ct. directs 14, §3064 petitioner 14, §3064	14, §3077 14, §3068	may attend 14, §3068					14, §3077	14, §3077		14, §3080	
VA. Code (1976 & Supp. 1982)		37.1-134.1			circuit ct. 37.1-134.1					37.1-134.1	committee 37.1-134.1		37.1-134.1						37.1-134.1				
WASH. Rev. Code Ann. (1967 & Supp. 1984)					11.88.140							such notice as ct. requires 11.88.140							11.88.140			11.96.010	
W. VA. Code (1980 & Supp. 1982)		27-11-1(g)		27-11-1(g)	county commission 27-11-1(g)			27-11-1(b)			spouse or adult next of kin, if not petitioner 27-11-1(b)	ward, if not petitioner 27-11-1(b)	27-11-1(b)	attendance mandatory unless affidavit or finding of facts shows presence is unnecessary or health endangering 27-11-1(b)					27-11-1(g)			27-11-1(g)	
WIS. Stat. Ann. (1958 & 1980 Special Pamph.) *fn. 15*		or guardian 880.34(4)		880.34(4)	880.34(4)								880.34(4)	880.34(4)			880.34(4)		880.34(4)	880.34(4)			
WYO. Stat. Ann. (1977 & Supp. 1982)		or guardian 3-2-310(a)	or friend 3-2-310(a)		3-2-310(a)		affidavit prima facie evidence of mental competency of such person 3-2-311 3-2-310(b)			3-2-311	spouse & children, if any, & if more, to parents & siblings 3-2-311		3-2-311						3-2-311				

FOOTNOTES: TABLE 7.6

1. Ala. Code § 26-2-55 (1977). There is another brief procedure which is not on the chart. If the guardian becomes satisfied that his ward has been restored to sanity and is capable of managing his estate, and the probate judge views, from the proof and facts stated, such representation as correct, the judge must make an order discharging the guardian and restoring the estate to the ward.

2. Id. § 26-2-53 (1977). Not necessary if neither guardian nor person instituting incompetency proceedings contests the application.

3. Ark. Stat. Ann. § 57-643 (Supp. 1981). Deals with the adjudication of the ward's competency. Secs. 57-643.1 and 57-643.2 deal with the restoration to sanity of a person of unsound mind or habitual drunkenness. These provisions are not part of the probate code.

4. Cal. Welf. & Inst. Code § 5352.6 (West Supp. 1983) The court may terminate conservatorship if the individualized treatment plan goals have been met and the person is no longer gravely disabled according to the progress review mental health director and the county officer providing conservatorship investigation.

5. Id. § 5362(a): "If the conservator is a private party, the clerk of the superior court shall also notify the mental health director and the county officer providing conservatorship investigation."

6. Colo. Rev. Stat. § 15-14-307(4) (1974). Where appointment of guardian was based on the incapacitated person being adjudicated mentally ill, mentally deficient, etc., the court may terminate the appointment upon the filing of a petition supported by a certified copy of an order of competency.

7. Conn. Gen. Stat. Ann. § 45-288 (Supp. 1982). Appeal may be taken from any order, denial, or decree of the probate court by any "aggrieved" party.

8. Ga. Code Ann. § 49-609(b) (Supp. 1981). Hearing procedures are the same as those for the adjudication of incompetency, except the court may dismiss the petition prior to hearing if after reviewing the evaluation report the court finds there is not probable cause to believe that there are grounds for modification or termination of the guardianship. Petition must be accompanied by affidavit of two persons who have knowledge of the ward or of a licensed physician or of a licensed applied psychologist.

9. Id. § 49-609(a). Upon the probate court's own motion after review of the guardianship reports.

10. Ill. Ann. Stat. Ch. 3, § 906 (Smith-Hurd 1966 & Supp. 1980). Outlines a procedure for restoration to legal competence which includes a notice of discharge as supporting evidence for the petition.

11. Miss. Code Ann. § 690-9-14 (1973 & Supp. 1982). The statute does not say who may file the application, only that "upon the filing of a proper petition therefor supported by such proof as the chancellor may deem sufficient" the proper chancery court may adjudicate.

12. Nev. Rev. Stat. § 159.191(3) (1979). A guardianship is terminated on orders of the court if the court determines that the guardianship is no longer necessary. If the guardianship is of the person and estate, the court may order the guardianship terminated as to the person, the estate, or the person and estate.

13. Okla. Stat. Ann. tit. 58, § 855 (West 1965 & Supp. 1983). Whenever a guardian for an incompetent is discharged by the proper court by final order thereof, and no other guardian has been appointed for such person, such person shall be presumed to be fully restored and shall be presumed to be fully capable and competent to make contracts and transact any and all business as though said person had never been declared to be incompetent.

14. Or. Rev. Stat. § 426.295 (1981). When a person committed to a state hospital has been declared incompetent and is discharged from the hospital, the superintendent of the hospital shall advise the court which entered the order of incompetency whether or not on the basis of medical evidence the person is competent. If the superintendent advises that the person is not competent, upon petition of the person, his guardian, relative, creditor, or other interested person, the court shall hold a hearing to determine whether or not the discharged person is competent.

15. Wis. Stat. Ann. § 880.34(1) (West Supp. 1980). Wisconsin also has a provision for review of the competency of an incompetent upon reaching the age of majority.

John Parry

CHAPTER 8 *Decision-making Rights Over Persons and Property*

I. INTRODUCTION

Mentally disabled persons often do not enjoy the same personal and property rights as other citizens. In theory, as the previous edition of this book reported, our laws treat mentally disabled people differently in order to provide adequate protection to the person, his family, and those with whom he or his guardian must necessarily deal.[1] In practice, many of our legal strictures go well beyond what is necessary to protect the interests of the individual, the state, or other concerned parties.

Mentally disabled persons may be deprived of their rights of citizenship because they are labeled and categorized by terms that generally connote mental incapacity but which fail to reveal an individual's abilities—"incompetent," "idiot," "insane," "in need of guardianship," "institutional resident" or "mentally retarded." Once the label is attached by the courts or the community, rights may be withheld en masse or simply presumed inapplicable. In this process, the logical step of matching the specific abilities of the individual with the functional capabilities society has determined as being necessary to exercise a particular right or privilege is eliminated or applied ignorantly, usually to the disadvantage of the mentally disabled person.

On occasion, other societal interests may be compromised unnecessarily. As a result of misunderstanding and discrimination, mentally disabled persons sometimes become the beneficiaries of rights, privileges, entitlements, and services they do not need, deserve, or want. There is a financial cost to communities that underestimate the abilities of disabled persons and, in so doing, provide questionable programs and services. In addition, certain citizens discover after they allegedly have been civilly harmed by a mentally disabled person that otherwise available opportunities to redress their grievances are severely limited or that a good faith financial transaction with a mentally disabled person is void or voidable because of the existence of special legal considerations that go too far to protect mentally disabled persons.

The old legal order provided that persons who were found incompetent or were institutionalized, placed under guardianship, or simply known to be mentally deficient were thereby deprived of almost all their rights and accorded no more decision-making authority than an unemancipated child and less autonomy than a prisoner. Once identified as mentally disabled, these individuals were not permitted to execute legal documents, such as contracts or wills, engage in business or professional activities, drive a car, vote, hold public office, serve on juries, marry, be parents to their children, own a gun, make medical decisions, or in many instances travel outside of an institution. If they were aliens, they could not immigrate legally or obtain citizenship.

The old legal order also mandated that the state as *parens patriae* provide special and often essential benefits to mentally disabled persons, but all too frequently the necessary mechanisms were missing to guarantee the proper implementation of the laws. The proposed benefits included protection from abuse, exploitation, or negligence; provision of minimal essential services such as shelter, food, and medical care; provision of entitlements such as veterans' benefits, pensions, workers' compensation, and tax deductions; avoidance of certain obligations such as military service; and the ability to overturn certain legal transactions or avoid legal liability.

This special legislation for mentally disabled citizens—whatever benefits it might bestow—suffered, and often continues to suffer, from more than one of the deficiencies listed below:

1. It compromises the fundamental notion that all citizens are equal before the law by creating a legal ap-

1. S.J. Brakel & R.S. Rock, The Mentally Disabled and the Law 303 (rev. ed. 1971).

paratus that has one set of standards for "normals" and another set of standards for mentally disabled persons.

2. It perpetuates the perception that incompetency is by itself a sufficiently compelling state concern to justify the deprivation of fundamental rights without further due process.
3. It incorporates an all or nothing view of rights protection that ignores the common sense view that suggests rights require different skill levels to be exercised competently.
4. It fails to specify whether formal legal adjudication is required before rights can be restricted.
5. It fails to specify how rights are to be exercised if a person is adjudicated incompetent and no guardian is appointed.
6. It fails to indicate whether persons who are in fact incompetent but have not been adjudicated incompetent may exercise their rights.
7. It fails to set out what due process protections are to be provided before specific rights are suspended.
8. It has no specified process for restoring rights if there has been no adjudication of incompetency.
9. It either does not specify or curtails en masse the rights of civilly committed individuals.

While all these statutory deficiencies persist—more so in some jurisdictions than in others—the modern law is improving as it moves toward new ideals grounded in contemporary views about how best to measure and restrict human behavior.

One of the guiding principles is a version of the social contract which suggests that with respect to personal and property rights of mentally disabled persons there should be no special restrictions or benefits unless a particular need is established precisely and the need is addressed in ways that are consistent with the interests of the individual and the health, safety, and welfare of the community. To accomplish this, the law should make finer discriminations between the needs of the individual and the needs of society. The presumption should be that mentally disabled persons are able to function normally unless there are demonstrable circumstances that dictate otherwise. Each right or privilege that is curtailed and each benefit bestowed should be evaluated in light of the individual's situation, not as part of a collection of rights that are withheld from or of benefits granted to a group of people who share certain characteristics. As one author who is now a federal appellate judge explained, "[t]he law presently has no scientific or other basis on which to presume that any mentally retarded individual cannot do any or all things well. Only an individual's capacity to do specific things can be judged." Broadly worded laws thus are suspect, this commentator asserts, "when they place categorical disqualifications and restrictions on persons. . . . Each person's capacities must be judged individually before he can be denied rights of citizenship or humanity."[2] Legal standards should be applied to all persons, not just to those who are defined as mentally disabled. For example, such standards are seen today in a number of jurisdictions that restrict voting, driving, or jury service only if it is proved that a specified level of understanding or physical skill necessary to exercise a particular right or privilege is absent.[3] These competency standards are applied to all persons regardless of mental disability, thus making incapacity labels largely irrelevant legally.

Some of the most serious ethical and legal problems are associated with obtaining informed consent from mentally disabled persons for various types of medical, psychiatric, and habilitative services as well as research. The medical and social service models often do not coexist well with the principle of self-determination. Even if the law could adequately identify who is not competent to make medical decisions, the problem remains who shall decide what services the incompetent person should receive and according to what standards. Much of the law in this area is an uncertain mix of paternalistic judgments by others of what is in the best interests of the patient and of adversarial judgments based on perceptions of what the patient appears to want. Establishing a consensus is often difficult because the philosophical principles underlying the two methods of decision making are diametrically opposed and the competing interests of several professions, particularly of doctors and lawyers, are frequently at stake.

In 1971 the authors of this book determined that the loss of the total bundle of personal and property rights was unnecessary and undesirable for the great majority of the mentally ill. That principle that is no less valid today now also applies to developmentally disabled persons. Intervention by the state which unduly restricts or eliminates the exercise of any right or privilege of citizenship is a form of discrimination. Justification for this type of discrimination should be specific to the particular individual and to the particular right at issue, and it should be substantial.

II. PARTICIPATION IN THE LEGAL SYSTEM

More so perhaps than in any other country, participation in the legal system plays a major role in the personal and property rights of American citizens. Access to the courts is an overriding concern for mentally disabled persons who wish to redress civil grievances and citizens

2. Wald, Basic Personal and Civil Rights, *in* The Mentally Retarded Citizen and the Law 5 (M. Kindred, J. Cohen, D. Penrod, & T. Schaeffer eds. 1976).

3. See table 8.1.

who may have claims against a mentally disabled person. The courts can operate as both a shield and a sword depending on whether the mentally disabled person is the plaintiff or the defendant. The judiciary may serve as the approval mechanism for certain financial transactions, and other transactions may be invalidated, if one of the parties is mentally disabled.

A. Access to the Courts

A majority of states have legislation governing the capacity of mentally disabled persons to gain access to or be brought into court. The applicable statutes determine who can sue or be sued, whether a guardian ad litem must be appointed, what methods of serving process are available, whether time limits on suits will be extended, and whether default judgments are prohibited.

Early common law prohibited "idiots" and "lunatics" from instituting suits in their own behalf since they lacked the requisite reason and understanding. However, by the time of Lord Coke, the common law rule had been changed to allow lunatics to maintain suits. In most jurisdictions today, a person who is legally incompetent may sue or be sued through his guardian or some other legal representative,[4] even though the same person might not be tried in a criminal proceeding.[5] Only eight states have no provision allowing such suits.[6] If there has never been an incompetency adjudication, the general rule is that the person is competent to sue or be sued. Thirty-nine jurisdictions make the appointment of a guardian ad litem mandatory where a person is actually incompetent and sometimes where his or her competency is merely questionable. Maryland provides for discretionary appointment through the court.[7]

Modern authorities generally regard the requirement that a guardian sue or be sued for the incompetent person as a protection of the interests of the incompetent person rather than as a limitation on his or her capacity to institute suit.[8] Major problems may arise where there has been an incompetency adjudication and no guardian has been appointed or where the person is not incompetent but has been civilly committed. In all but ten states there is legislation that permits the appointment of a guardian ad litem for an incompetent person.[9] However, for individuals who are civilly committed, access to the courts may be restricted by institutional rules and regulations and by the residents' lack of awareness that they have a cause of action or defense to an action against them. Of course, confinement merely accentuates a more universal problem. Without proper guidance, mentally disabled persons who are living in the community may also fail to choose the most appropriate legal response, even when they are legally competent.

An essential step in such legal proceedings is the service of process notifying the defendant that he or she is being sued. Without proper service a court has no jurisdiction. Where the person to be served is incompetent all but ten states have special provisions to cover that situation. Thirty-six jurisdictions specify that a guardian or, if there is no guardian, the person who has custody or with whom the incompetent person resides must be served.[10] Two other states designate a representative who may be the guardian. Twenty-three jurisdictions require that incompetent persons themselves be served. Even in the states without a statute, some kind of substituted service is generally provided for.

Persons who are institutionalized may receive service through their guardian or, more commonly, through the superintendent of the institution.[11] Only nine states mandate service directly upon the institutionalized person. Thirty-six states have no such applicable legislation, meaning that in many instances service of mentally disabled institutionalized individuals will be governed by legislation that applies to everyone.

Incompetent persons are often exempted from the application of two elements of legal process — the statute of limitations and default judgments.

Recognizing the fact that incompetent persons probably will be unaware of their legal rights or obligations, many jurisdictions have enacted statutes that will extend the life of a civil suit, within reason, until after the person's disability ends. Some extend the time limits beyond the point at which the incompetent person's sanity is restored, typically by one to five years or at least during the period of incompetency.[12] Others extend the filing time to some arbitary period of time after which incompetent persons forfeit their right to bring suit. Pennsylvania is the only state that specifies the statute of limitations will not be extended. It should be noted, however, that the chief justice of the Nebraska Supreme Court has pointed out that "any effort by the legislature to bar a cause of action before it has been discovered, or in the exercise of reasonable diligence could be discovered, would be to deny a class of persons both equal protection of the law and due process in violation of both their state and federal constitutional rights."[13] Nebraska has an absolute exception to the statute of limitations for those who are

4. *Id.*
5. Commissioner of Social Servs. v. Patricia A., 432 N.Y.S.2d 137 (N.Y. County Fam. Ct. 1980).
6. See table 8.1.
7. Md. Est. & Trusts Code Ann. § 13-704 (Cum. Supp. 1984).
8. 29 Am. Jur. Insane and Other Incompetent Persons § 117 (1960).
9. *Id.*
10. See table 8.1.
11. *Id.*
12. *Id.*
13. Sacchi v. Blodig, 341 N.W. 2d 326 (Neb. 1983) (concurring opinion by Chief Justice Krivosha).

"insane," a term that means "'a condition of mental derangement as actually to bar the sufferer from comprehending rights which he is otherwise bound to know.'" Thus, a contrary state provision allowing lawsuits for only ten years after the disputed event occurred was found to be "neither absolute nor unconditional" as applied to a mental patient.[14]

By and large, state statutes separate causes of action, and accordingly the time limits applied to these actions, into three categories: personal matters, real property claims, and other types of suits. With each category the time limits are different.[15]

Mentally disabled defendants also are protected from summary actions taken against them in ex parte proceedings. Twenty-nine states prohibit courts from granting default judgments against incompetent persons who are unrepresented by either an attorney or a guardian.[16]

B. Financial Transactions

1. Contracts and Conveyances

"Perhaps no branch of jurisprudence is more tenuous or spectral than that dealing with one's mental capacity to contract," observed the Arkansas Supreme Court in 1942.[17] Little has happened since then to invalidate that court's assessment.

Under the early common law it was permissible to claim mental disability in order to avoid any contractual obligations that occurred during the period the disability existed. Subsequently the view developed that no one, mentally disabled or recovered, could assert his inability to avoid an act while mentally disabled.[18] The strength of either of these absolute approaches was their predictability. However, the search for fairness gave birth to the modern view that adopts no absolute positions with respect to the right to negate obligations incurred by a mentally disabled person. The determination to void a contractual obligation is dependent on a number of factors calculated to acknowledge the interests of both parties to a transaction. While this approach holds the promise of promoting equity in individual cases, it also creates difficulties in judicial interpretaion and general consistency.

Most jurisdictions apply different standards depending on whether the contract[19] or conveyance is executed before or after a court adjudication of incompetency.[20] Prior to such an adjudication a substantial majority hold that there is a continuing presumption that every person is able to contract or make a conveyance. The person seeking to set aside a transaction because of mental disability has the burden of proof.[21] If it is met, both contracts[22] and conveyances[23] are voidable at the option of the mentally disabled person. A minority of states, based on the earliest common law, still hold that contracts of incompetent persons, whether the individuals have been formally adjudicated incompetent or not, are absolutely void.[24] As the United States Supreme Court reasoned more than one hundred years ago in *Dexter v. Hall*,[25] there cannot be a contract where there is no meeting of the minds.

Twelve jurisdictions provide that where there has been an adjudication of incompetency or a guardian has been appointed, the incompetent person or the ward has no power to contract.[26] Most make the contracts void; a few make them voidable at the option of the incompetent person. The primary justification for the majority view is that it would be extremely inconvenient and often unfair to make the guardian go to court each time a transaction was made by the ward.[27] If there is no guardian, the contract may also be void[28] or more frequently voidable on the basis of the common law.[29] The latter result stems from the belief that if individuals are incompetent and have no one to act on their own behalf they should be able to make transactions for their own benefit.

Regardless of whether the incompetent person has a guardian or has been adjudicated incompetent, there is substantial authority that there must be something more than proof of incapacity in order to cancel a transaction. The burden is on incapacitated persons to establish that the other party knew of the incompetency[30] or knew of the incompetency and acted in bad faith.[31] Other authority, however, places the burden on the

14. *Id.*
15. See table 8.1.
16. *Id.*
17. Waggoner v. Atkins, 162 S.W.2d 55 (Ark. 1942).
18. 2 W. Blackstone, Commentaries 291 (1983).
19. Negotiable instruments are treated as ordinary contracts in this section.
20. See table 8.1.
21. Cohen v. Crumpacker, 586 S.W.2d 370 (Mo. Ct. App. 1979), Owen v. Owen, 376 So. 2d 26 (Fla. Dist. Ct. App. 1979); *In re* Estate of DeKoekkoek, 76 Ill. App. 3d 795, 395 N.E.2d 113 (1979); *In re* Estate of Head, 615 P.2d 271 (N.M. Ct. App. 1980); Taylor v. Avi, 415 A.2d 894 (Pa. Super. Ct. 1979). See also 41 Am. Jur. 2d Incompetent Persons § 131 (1968).
22. See references cited in note 21 *supra*. See also table 8.1
23. Note, Real Property—Validity of Conveyances by Mental incompetents (*Brown v. Khoury*, Mich., 1956), 3 Wayne L. Rev. 73, 74 (1956).
24. Comment, The Mentally Ill and the Law of Contracts, 29 Temp. L.Q. 380, 383 (1956) [hereinafter cited as Comment, The Mentally Ill].
25. 82 U.S. (15 Wall.) 9 (1872).
26. See table 8.1.
27. Annot., 7 A.L.R. 568, 594 (1920).
28. 2 S. Williston, A Treatise on the Law of Contracts § 251 (3d ed. 1959).
29. Rubenstein v. Dr. Pepper Co., 228 F.2d 528 (8th Cir. 1955); 2 Williston, *supra* note 28, § 251.
30. Schaps v. Lehner, 55 N.W. 911 (Minn. 1893); Fidelity Financial Services, Inc. v. McCoy, 392 So.2d 118 (La. Ct. App. 1980); 41 Am. Jur. 2d Incompetent Persons § 131 (1968).
31. Schaps v. Lehner, 55 N.W. 911 (Minn. 1893); 41 Am. Jur. 2d Incompetent Persons § 131 (1968).

nondisabled parties to show that their actions were taken in good faith and they did not know of the incompetency.[32] A North Carolina case demonstrates that the burden on the complaining party may be substantial even where the other party is under guardianship. A state appellate court dismissed an annulment action filed by a bank, which was managing a ward's estate, because there was insufficient evidence showing that at the time of the marriage the ward did not understand the special nature of the marriage contract.[33]

Where there has been a formal adjudication of incompetency[34] or a showing of continuous or chronic insanity,[35] there is a general presumption that incompetency exists until the person is judicially restored. This is usually considered to be a rebuttable presumption that can be overcome by the party asserting the validity of the transaction by showing the existence of a lucid interval or restoration in fact.[36] However, in the North Carolina case discussed above, the court declared that incompetency does not make a marriage contract void and the burden is on the person challenging the validity of the contract.[37]

In the not so distant past, institutionalized patients or residents were frequently deprived of their right to contract because their confinement constituted an automatic adjudication of incompetency. Today this is rare,[38] though some states still provide for automatic independent incompetency hearings for institutionalized persons. Moreover, the administrative regulations or unofficial operating procedures within an institution may place significant restrictions on residents' contractual abilities. As a practical matter, many parties will be reluctant to contract with a person inside an institution because of the higher potential for serious legal complications. Yet, in the majority of states that have statutes that provide that any person is presumed to be competent absent a formal adjudication to the contrary there is a corollary presumption that the person can make a contract.

Although only 12 jurisdictions have statutes that make mentally disabled persons liable for goods and services that are necessary to maintain their basic health safety and welfare (known as *necessaries*),[39] Williston concludes that all jurisdictions make everyone liable for the actual value, as opposed to the agreed price, of necessaries.[40] Most controversies arise over the definition of what constitutes a necessary. This principle of law is frequently extended to make mentally disabled persons responsible for necessaries purchased by or on behalf of their spouses or families who are in need and entitled to support.[41]

In sum, the ability to contract is distinguishable from the question of whether a person is incompetent generally. No matter who has the burden of proof, the tests for measuring the propriety of a contract are more specific. They include the following: the ability to understand the nature and consequences of the transaction,[42] the ability to act in a reasonable manner in relation to the transaction,[43] ability to understand the character of the transaction,[44] and the ability to understand or agree to the contract.[45] Even if the person is incompetent a contract may be valid. As one older case points out, insanity does not make one incompetent to contract unless "the subject-matter of a contract . . . is so connected" with an insane delusion "as to render the affected party incapable of understanding."[46]

2. Wills

All but three states have legislation governing mental capacity to make a will.[47] Forty-six jurisdictions require that a person be of "sound mind," "sound mind and memory" or "sane mind." Georgia disqualifies those who "want [meaning lack] capacity," and Maryland mandates that a person be legally competent. Testamentary capacity is the ability to make a will and provides a means by which property may be passed from the owner at death to specified beneficiaries or heirs in accordance with the person's stated desires and preferences.

In the sixteenth century the Wills Act granted testamentary capacity to everyone regardless of mental status or condition.[48] Soon the act was amended so that it excluded "idiots" or persons with "insane memory."[49] This established the foundation for the modern statutes that

32. 41 Am. Jur. 2d Incompetent Persons § 131 (1968); Hull v. Louth, 10 N.E. 270 (Ind. 1887); Riggs v. American Tract Soc'y, 84 N.Y. 330 (1881); Ipock v. Atlantic & N.C.R. Co., 74 S.E. 352 (N.C. 1912).

33. Geitner v. Townsend, 312 S.E.2d 236 (N.C. Ct. App. 1984).

34. Comment, The Mentally Ill, *supra* note 24, at 384.

35. 41 Am. Jur. 2d Incompetent Persons § 131 (1968); Zeigler v. Coffin, 123 So. 22 (Ala. 1929); Trish v. Newell, 62 Ill. 196 (1871); Corbit v. Smith, 7 Iowa 60 (1858); Lambert v. Powell, 24 So. 2d 773 (Miss. 1946).

36. See references cited in note 35 *supra*. See also Comment, The Mentally Ill, *supra* note 24, at 384.

37. Geitner v. Townsend, 312 S.E.2d 236 (N.C. App. Ct. 1984).

38. See ch. 7, Incompetency, Guardianship, and Restoration, *supra* for further discussion of incompetency and guardianship regulations affecting the right to contract.

39. See table 8.1.

40. 2 Williston, *supra* note 28.

41. *Id.*

42. Restatement (Second) of Contracts § 15 (1964); 41 Am. Jur. 2d Incompetent Persons § 71.

43. Restatement (Second) of Contracts § 15 (1964).

44. 41 Am. Jur. 2d Incompetent Persons § 71 (1968).

45. *Id.*

46. Weller v. Copeland, 120 N.E. 578 (Ill. 1918).

47. See table 8.1.

48. 32 Hen. 8, c.1 (1540).

49. Green, Public Policies Underlying the Law of Mental Incompetency, 38 Mich. L. Rev. 1189, 1203-4 (1940).

require "sound mind and memory" to make a will. The operative language in the statutes on wills is often similar to the terminology used in civil commitment or incompetency legislation, but testamentary capacity is further defined in the case law by the following elements:

1. Testators must have a general, although not necessarily a comprehensive, understanding of the nature and extent of the property they wish to bequeath.[50]
2. Testators must know the nature of the act they wish to perform to the extent that they understand the instrument they are executing is a legally operative will.[51]
3. Testators must recognize the names and identity of their beneficiaries, including familial relationships or the other reasons why these individuals should be included in the will.[52]
4. Testators must have sufficient mind and memory to indicate that they intended to distribute their estate in the way they specified.[53]
5. Testators must be able to integrate all the requisite elements so that they may appreciate the relationship of these elements to each other.[54]

Another factor that is mentioned frequently is the ability to recollect the decision that has been made.[55] However, there is authority that imperfect memory by itself will not establish testamentary incompetency.[56]

There are two basic kinds of public policy considerations supporting the need to prove testamentary capacity exists in order for a will to be valid. First, under the *parens patriae* power the state has an interest in protecting mentally disabled persons "from testamentary acts which would not be undertaken had the person a full understanding of those acts and their consequences."[57] Second, society has an interest in the rights of family members and other individuals who may have a moral or legal claim on the testator to ensure they are not excluded unfairly as beneficiaries.[58]

Because testamentary capacity is supported by particular policy considerations and fulfills specialized purposes in the law, it is readily distinguishable from incompetency or the capacity to make a contract. Thus, persons under guardianship or in institutions may retain their testamentary capacity despite prior legal adjudications governing other aspects of their decision-making rights, including adjudications of incompetency.[59]

Clearly not every instance of mental unsoundness will interfere with the ability to make a will. In fact, mental illness or mental retardation by themselves are legally insufficient to meet the general test of testamentary incapacity. The comprehension level required to exercise the basic right to make a will is low.[60] Thus, while one Pennsylvania court concluded that a testator with the intellectual functioning of a five-year-old child could not devise his estate,[61] most courts examine the person's capabilities in relation to the substantive criteria described earlier rather than the nature of the mental disability itself.[62] Under the more popular approach a will made by a person with an insane delusion may be valid.[63]

Generally, the existence of another type of incapacity or even an adjudication of incompetency is an inconclusive indication of testamentary incapacity and will be treated as a rebuttable presumption of incapacity.[64] The same is true for prior guardianship determinations.[65] However, in the words of a New Mexico court, in those instances where there has been a formal adjudication before the will is made "the burden of proof is upon the proponent of the will to rebut the presumption or inference of incapacity, from such record; and it is said that very clear evidence is required to rebut such presumption."[66]

Institutionalization has less or the same probative value regarding the issue of testamentary capacity as an adjudication of incompetency.[67] It may not raise any kind of presumption or may be used merely as probative evidence. Very occasionally institutionalization constitutes a prima facie case of testamentary incapacity. Nevertheless, the administrative regulations or informal policies within an institution may prevent or discourage residents from making valid wills. Even though the one known case to review the validity of such a will con-

50. B.D. Sales, D.M. Powell, R. Van Duizend & Associates, Disabled Persons and the Law ch. 1.3, Testamentary Capacity 55, (1982); Weihofen, Mental Incompetency to Make a Will, 7 Nat. Resources J. 89, 89–94 (1967).

51. See references cited in note 50 *supra*.

52. *Id.*

53. *Id.*

54. Sales, Powell, Van Duizend, & Associates, *supra* note 50, at 55; Note, Psychiatric Assistance in the Determination of Testamentary Capacity, 66 Harv. L. Rev. 1116, 1116–17 (1953).

55. 1 W. Page, Treatise on the Law of Wills § 132 (1941).

56. Sehr v. Lindemann, 54 S.W. 537 (Mo. 1899).

57. Sales, Powell, Van Duizend, & Associates, *supra* note 50, at 54.

58. *Id.*

59. *In re* Will of Maynard, 307 S.E.2d 416 (N.C. Ct. App. 1983).

60. Sales, Powell, Van Duizen, & Associates, *supra* note 50, citing Weihofen (and cases cited therein), *supra* note 50, at 89–94.

61. *In re* Estate of Glesenkamp, 107 A.2d 731 (Pa. 1954).

62. Sales, Powell, Van Duizend, & Associates, *supra* note 50, at 55.

63. Roller v. Kurtz, 6 Ill.2d 618, 129 N.E.2d 693 (1955).

64. *In re* Armijo's Will, 261 P.2d 833, (N.M. 1953) (citing 2 Page, Wills, *supra* note 55, at § 807).

65. Sales, Powell, Van Duizend, & Associates, *supra* note 50, at 55 (citing Weihofen, *supra* note 50, at 93).

66. *In re* Armijo's Will, 261 P.2d 833, 837 (N.M. 1953) (citing 2 Page, Wills, *supra* note 55, at § 807); see also Dean v. Jordan, 79 P.2d 331 (Wash. 1938); *In re* Hall's Estate, 195 P.2d 612 (Kan. 1948).

67. Sales, Powell, Van Duizend, & Associates, *supra* note 50, at 55 (citing Weihofen, *supra* note 50, at 94).

cluded that the will was valid,[68] the chilling effect of the institutional environment seems obvious given the need for a competent witness and legal assistance to complete a will.

The predominant view is that contractual and testamentary capacities are different, although a few courts have treated them as the same[69] or have held that a contract requires less capacity than a will.[70] Maryland and the District of Columbia are the only jurisdictions that require that a testator have contractual capacity in order to make a valid will.[71]

In many ways testamentary competency may be the easiest type of capacity to establish.[72] Among other reasons for this is that the person's status or condition is rarely determinative, the same criterion applies to everyone regardless of mental disability, and the process is flexible enough to account for individual differences. Nevertheless, critics point out the difficulty in making a judicial decision concerning the intent or capacity of a testator who at the time the will is reviewed has, of course, passed away: "Because capacity cases are often decided on little more than conjecture, a growing tendency has developed for dissatisfied relatives to contest testamentary capacity on a 'what-do-we-have-to-lose' basis, oftentimes without any real basis in fact."[73] With "the usual lack of reliable information on which the court can base an opinion as to capacity," they observe,[74] hearings can easily degenerate into a battle of psychiatric experts who must answer hypothetical questions concerning the capacity of someone most of them have never examined. Even in the rare instance that a prior examination takes place, the examination is probably conducted by a general practitioner and is not in close time proximity to the will's execution. Faced with unreliable information, the court may simply decide the matter based on its own view of the reasonableness of the testamentary disposition, ignoring the disputable evidence of the testator's intent. This, it is argued, is "completely at odds with the long-recognized doctrine that a will may be 'as eccentric, as injudicious or as unjust as caprice, frivolilty or revenge can dictate.'"[75] Yet, where the testator's intent is unknown, it may well be preferable to use an objective albeit arbitrary standard than to guess at intent.

A frequently mentioned solution is for a lawyer to arrange for a professional evaluation of a testator's mental capacity at the time the will is executed if a question is likely to be raised.[76] The objective of the evaluation would be to obtain information admissible in court to explain the testator's condition in relation to the legal standards applicable in the governing jurisdiction. Since most states admit diagnoses and evaluations of patients as exceptions to the hearsay rule,[77] the person who conducted the exam would not even have to be present in court. Where undue influence by the beneficiary is an issue, courts could use the evaluation to measure the testator's intent and, in many instances, the reasons the testator made the decision.[78] Not infrequently the mere fact that expert testimony will be forthcoming would deter frivolous or dubious claims.

Arguments against such examinations are the cost to the testator and the concern that the examiners and not the courts would become the real final arbiters of testamentary claims. There is also the possibility that these examinations might raise questions about the testator's capacity that otherwise would have never been raised.[79] Of course, raising such questions might well lead to a fairer and more realistic determination.

III. BUSINESS AND PROFESSIONAL ACTIVITIES

To be successful in many business or professional activities or even to be hired and retained in certain jobs, people must be licensed professionally, licensed to drive, or able to establish an agency relationship with a client. For the mentally disabled person, obtaining or retaining permission from the proper authorities to legally undertake or continue these business-related activities may pose major difficulties.

A. Professional Licensing

Every jurisdiction in the United States has legislation in place that limits occupational licensing for mentally disabled persons.[80] All but two states deny licenses to specified professional types who are mentally incapacitated, and many have provisions to suspend or revoke

68. *In re* Alexieff's Will, 94 N.Y.S.2d 32 (Sur. Ct. 1949), *aff'd*, 277 A.D. 790, 97 N.Y.S.2d 532 (1950) *motion for leave to appeal denied*, 277 A.D. 901, 98 N.Y.S.2d 582 (1950).

69. Hanks v. McNeal Coal Corp., 168 P.2d 256, 260 (Colo. 1946).

70. *In re* Good's Estate, 274 S.W.2d 900, 902 (Tex. Civ. App. 1955).

71. Md. Ann. Code, art. 93, § 349 (1964); D.C. Code Ann. § 18-102 (1967).

72. Sales, Powell, Van Duizend, & Associates, *supra* note 50, at 56 (citing *In re* Safer's Will, 242 N.Y.S.2d 445 (1963)).

73. *Id.* (citing Epstein, Testamentary Capacity, Reasonableness and Family Maintenance: A Proposal for Meaningful Reform, 35 Temp. L.Q. 231, 232 (1962)).

74. Sales, Powell, Van Duizend, & Associates, *supra* note 50.

75. *Id.* at 57 (quoting from Schneider v. Vosburgh, 106 N.W. 1129 (Mich. 1906)).

76. Hulbert, Probate Psychiatry—A Neuro-Psychiatric Examination of Testator from the Psychiatric Viewpoint, 25 Ill. L. Rev. 288 (1930); Sales, Power, Van Duizend, & Associates, *supra* note 50, at 56; Stephens, Probate Psychiatry—Examination of Testamentary Capacity by a Psychiatrist as a Subscribing Witness, 25 Ill. L. Rev. 276, 277-78 (1930).

77. Sales, Powell, Van Duizend, & Associates, *supra* note 50, at 56.

78. Stephens, *supra* note 76.

79. Sales, Powell, Van Duizend, & Associates, *supra* note 50, at 57 (citing Singer & Krohn, Insanity and Law 343 (1924)).

80. See table 8.2.

the licenses of certain professionals who become disabled. Thirty-one states place members of specified professions on probation if they are having mental problems.

The stated purposes of most of these statutes is to protect the public from unprofessional conduct or, less frequently, to restore the stricken individual to mental health. More often than not the legislation specifies that particular professions will police themselves. The experience of lawyers and doctors raises questions about the wisdom of this latter approach, although there is some evidence that no better system is available.[81] In any approach the task is to identify persons who can no longer function adequately in their professional roles before harm comes to their clients or patients without unfairly penalyzing those professionals. Normally, no action is taken until a disability is revealed in the application process or a dissatisfied client files a formal complaint.[82] Experience shows that both doctors and lawyers are extremely reluctant to identify colleagues who are mentally disabled. It is only recently that these two professions established uniform standards to guide their members when confronted with disabled colleagues. Even today, the legal profession's Model Code of Professional Responsibility makes only general reference to the problem,[83] and the medical profession often employs strictly voluntary programs for dealing with impaired physicians.[84] States in regulating all professions use different criteria and operate their oversight functions through boards with disciplining capacities that vary with the jurisdiction and the professional group that is involved. Professionals who are institutionalized, of course, normally would have little practical opportunity to conduct their business.

In addition to sometimes failing to protect the public, the legislative schemes used to license mentally disabled persons may be unfair to the job applicant or the employee or of questionable relevancy. For example, a divided Florida Supreme Court agreed that the state's bar examiners could refuse to process a bar admission application until the applicant disclosed his entire history of psychological and medical treatment, which included releasing all his confidential records. The state had a compelling interest in ensuring that practicing lawyers were fit, and that interest outweighed the individual's privacy. A dissenting judge found the inquiry for information too broad; he would have limited the inquiry to what was relevant to the applicant's present health.[85] It is common for the statutes to apply terms such as "insane," "unsound mind," "incompetence," "mentally ill," "not mentally capable," and "mental condition renders practice unsafe" without specifically defining the terms.[86] Only rarely do jurisdictions even require a prior adjudication of incompetency or mental illness. Nor does there seem to be any rhyme or reason beyond politics to the selection of professions that are covered in the licensing statutes. Alabama, for example, regulates nurses, pharmacists, doctors, physical therapists, chiropractors, and pilots but has no statutory provisions governing lawyers, chauffeurs, dentists, or nursing home operators. Massachusetts, on the other hand, regulates physical therapists, physicians, tax collectors, and any registered profession. Moreover, states commonly apply different concepts of mental disability to different professions within the same state. Thus, a doctor might have to be "insane," a lawyer "of unsound mind," and an architect "not mentally capable." Often those disparities are due to the fact that each of the professions has a substantial but clearly different input into the legislative process which ultimately determines coverage.

A comparison of the two most-written-about professions—law and medicine—is instructive. Lawyers in 48 jurisdictions must adhere to the Model Code of Professional Responsibility, which offers little guidance to the public, the disciplinary board, or to the lawyer. In essence, lawyers must either withdraw from a case if they are too disabled to continue or face disbarment or some lesser penalty. Not only is this unfair if the person is not responsible for the actions and is penalized, but it also may be fruitless since there is only an ethical consideration with no penalty to motivate other members of the bar to identify unqualified lawyers. In at least 32 states the Code is supplemented by disciplinary rules[87] that are generally independent of the state statutes regulating other professions.[88] Only a small fraction of states will even allow the existence of a mental disability to be used as a defense for professional misconduct by a lawyer, wary of the possibility that the defense would be misused in ways that would create problems similar to the insanity defense.[89] A few states consider mental disability to be

81. McDonald, In Search of New Remedies: Mentally Disabled Doctors and the Practice of Medicine, 3 MDLR 428 (1979); Skoler & Klein, Mentally Troubled Lawyers: Client Protection and Bar Discipline, 3 MDLR 131 (1979).

82. See references cited *supra* in note 81

83. American Bar Association Model Code of Professional Responsiblity DR2-110 1979.

84. McDonald, *supra* note 81, at 428.

85. Florida Bd. of Bar Examiners Re: Applicant, 443 So. 2d 71 (1983).

86. See table 8.2.

87. Skoler & Klein, *supra* note 81, at 134.

88. See table 8.2.

89. Skoler & Klein, *supra* note 81, at 143. See also ch. 12, Mental Disability and the Criminal Law, esp. § III C, The American Standards: Their Development and Rationale, *infra* for a discussion of the continuing debate over the insanity defense.

a mitigating circumstance but will not excuse the misconduct.[90]

According to a review of legislation made in 1979,[91] doctors are regulated in almost every state and in 34 states are regulated by state medical associations. Where the physician's "reasonable skill and safety" are called into question the governing board is usually allowed to act. First, a medical examination is ordered to assess fitness. The emphasis is not on punishment but on rehabilitation and protection of the public. Frequently, physicians are given the option of voluntarily undergoing treatment before formal charges are brought against them. In most instances, every effort is made to maintain "as much of the doctor's professional activities as his impairment will allow." Nevertheless, according to this report, severe difficulties remain: "Not only is it still difficult to identify physicians who have mental problems, but there is no accurate method of judging success since statistics are generally unavailable with regard to the number of doctors . . . who are rehabilitated by the new mechanisms and the number of patients who are actually harmed before or during the rehabilitative process."[92] Not always are the procedures voluntary. In Florida, an appeals court, unpersuaded by a physician's Fifth Amendment privilege against self-incrimination, upheld a regulating body's direction that the doctor submit to a psychiatric examination. Despite the possibility of license revocation, the proceedings are not considered to be penal in nature; thus the Fifth Amendment privilege did not apply.[93]

The overall picture of professional licensing of mentally disabled persons is curious because there really are few consistent patterns. While more than 20 professions are included in the statutes collectively, only 10 receive frequent mention: in addition to attorneys and doctors, statutes often include pharmacists, nurses, physical therapists, psychologists, chiropractors, dentists, nursing home operators, and chauffeurs.[94] Professions or businesses such as social workers, school bus drivers, teachers, real estate brokers, cosmetologists, and private detectives receive occasional mention.

The mental conditions or statuses that trigger the use of the licensing sanctions are divided into four general categories: "mentally ill," "not mentally capable," "mental condition renders practice unsafe," and "adjudicated incompetent or mentally ill."[95] None or as many as all four categories may be applicable to a given profession. Different categories are applicable to different professions within the same state. However, across the states there is some consistency in the application of categories to various professions. For example, most often the standard for nursing home administrators is whether they are "mentally ill," for nurses it is whether they are mentally incapable, for physicians whether their mental condition renders it safe to practice, and for physical therapists whether there has been a formal adjudication of mental illness or incompetency.

Similar structures are used whether the applicable sanction is denial of license, suspension or revocation of license, or probation.[96] Which sanction will be applied depends on the state and the profession involved. In many jurisdictions license denial, suspension, and revocation are all used to regulate a given profession. Probation and other options are found less frequently.[97]

To a significant extent, this piecemeal approach to professional licensing reflects the influence and inclinations of various professions in different states and a willingness to allow professions to police themselves. A problem is that in the process clients or patients may be harmed needlessly, they may have no effective mechanism for redressing their grievances, and the mentally disabled professional may be unfairly deprived of a means to earn a livelihood.

B. Driver's Licenses

For many individuals, driving is a personal privilege granted by the state which holds high importance in their daily lives.[98] On the other hand, the fact that fifty thousand people are killed in traffic accidents each year[99] and many more are injured attests to the need to better regulate licensing to prevent drivers from harming others and themselves. As a result, there are statutes in every state that directly or indirectly restrict the operation of a motor vehicle, and all of them cover mentally disabled persons. Forty-six states and the District of Columbia have legislation that disqualifies such persons.[100] Five jurisdictions have legislation that gives general authority to restrict the licenses of anyone for good cause.[101]

The theoretical boundaries governing enactment of licensing statutes for mentally disabled drivers are established by the predominant view that there should be ab-

90. Skoler & Klein, *supra* note 81, at 141.

91. McDonald, *supra* note 81, at 429, 435.

92. *Id.* at 435.

93. Boedy v. Department of Professional Regulation, Bd. of Medical Examiners, 444 So. 2d 503 (Fla. Dist. Ct. App. 1984).

94. See table 8.2.

95. See *id.*, cols. 1-4.

96. Table 8.2, cols.1-4, 5-8, & 9-12.

97. Twenty states have no such statute.

98. R.C. Allen, E.Z. Ferster, & H. Weihofen, Mental Impairment and Legal Incompetency 345 (1968); Sales, Powell, Van Duizen, & Associates, *supra* note 50, at ch. 1.8, Driver Licensing, 113.

99. Allen, Ferster, & Weihofen, *supra* note 98 (citing U.S. Dep't of Transportation, 1977 Highway Safety Act Report).

100. See table 8.3.

101. Sales, Powell, Van Duizend, & Associates, *supra* note 50.

solute disqualifications for certain categories of individuals—mentally ill, institutionalized, insane, incompetent, or feebleminded[102]—and the contrary belief that "[a]nyone who can pass a driving test ought to receive his license; anyone who cannot should not."[103] In between these extremes there are many different approaches to the problem which do not deny driving privileges based on a condition or status, unless it can be shown that a person's ability to drive is affected, nor do they ignore the fact that a licensed driver may be very dangerous if he or she is an alcoholic, uses drugs, or suffers from hallucinations or delusions. One exemplary model statute recognizes that certain regulation is necessary but advises that "in order to deprive an individual of the driving privilege, it is incumbent on the state to illustrate a real, not conjectural, link between the individual's particular disability and an impaired ability to safely operate a vehicle."[104]

Existing laws, however, disqualify various categories of mentally disabled persons from driving, as well as persons suffering from disabilities such as epilepsy, alcoholism, or drug addiction. The most frequently enacted statutes cover individuals who are mentally disabled and unable to drive or adjudicated disabled and not restored.[105] Other provisions disqualify people who are mentally disabled,[106] institutionalized,[107] certified unable to drive by an institution superintendent[108] or for good cause.[109] In addition, almost every state has legislation that allows the department of motor vehicles to restrict driving privileges of anyone who is an unsafe driver, is unable to understand highway and traffic signs, and cannot exercise reasonable control over a vehicle.[110]

In addition to refusing to license certain types of individuals, states have legislation that subjects licensed drivers to revocation, suspension, or restriction of their driving privilege.[111] The categories of mentally disabled persons who are included are similar and sometimes identical to those who are subject to license denial in the first instance.

Although no one has a constitutional right to a driver's license, the Supreme Court has ruled that a state cannot suspend a license of a driver for being in an accident without first making a determination of who is at fault.[112] Several state statutes and a few courts require a due process hearing before a license can be denied, suspended, or revoked.[113] Most states, however, have no special review procedure, much less an automatic hearing. What process is due has not been thoroughly tested constitutionally.

How capricious certain state systems can be is illustrated by such anomalies as allowing individuals who have repeatedly had accidents while under the influence of alcohol to drive but denying the privilege to persons with controlled epilepsy who have nearly perfect driving records.[114] This occurs even though there are no reliable data linking any known disease or condition, except alcoholism, to increased accidents.[115]

Certain reforms of the existing law seem justified. A study by the American Bar Association's Commission on the Mentally Disabled has identified three elements that should be included in a good piece of legislation: licensing should be based on functional ability to drive and not a determination of whether a person belongs to a particular category of people, determinations should be made individually according to established procedures, and each person should have a meaningful opportunity to challenge adverse determinations in administrative hearings.[116] These are reasonable recommendations that should be incorporated into state statutes.

C. Agency, Representative, and Fiduciary Matters

While incompetent individuals usually may not appoint agents to act on their behalf, incompetent agents in some circumstances may represent a client. This seeming paradox is explained by the nature of the agency relationship.

The principal for whom the agent acts must have the necessary capacity to contract with the agent.[117] Moreover, for the action of the agent to be valid the principal must understand what it is that is being done.[118] If a principal cannot act for himself an agent cannot do so unless that agent is appointed by the courts.[119] The same is true if the principal becomes incompetent after the agency relationship is established.[120] In either situation,

102. See table 8.3.
103. Wald, *supra* note 2, at 23.
104. Sales, Powell, Van Duizend, & Associates, *supra* note 50, at 114.
105. See table 8.3.
106. E.g., Delaware, District of Columbia, Pennsylvania, and Vermont.
107. E.g., Nebraska, New York, and Oregon.
108. Wisconsin.
109. Sales, Powell, Van Duizend, & Associates, *supra* note 50, at 114.
110. *Id.* at 114.
111. See table 8.3.
112. Bell v. Burson, 402 U.S. 535 (1971).
113. See table 8.3; Tolbert v. McGriff, 434 F. Supp. 682 (M.D. Ala. 1976); Rodriguez v. Miera, No. 78-194P, 2 MDLR 565 (D.N.M. Apr. 11, 1978) (consent judgment).
114. Ormond v. Garrett, 175 S.E.2d 371 (N.C. Ct. App. 1970); Geen v. Foschio, No. Civ. 82-83B (C), 6 MDLR 253 (W.D.N.Y. May 4, 1982); Rodriguez v. Miera, No. 78-194P, 2 MDLR 565 (D.N.M. Apr. 11, 1978) (consent judgment).
115. Allen, Ferster, & Weihofen, *supra* note 98, at 345 n.10.
116. Sales, Powell, Van Duizend, & Associates, *supra* note 50.
117. 2A C.J.S. Agency § 28 (1972 & Supp. 1982).
118. *Id.*
119. 3 Am. Jur. 2d Agency § 12 (1962 & Supp. 1982); Mitchell v. State, 176 So. 743 (Miss. 1937).
120. Restatement of Agency §§ 122, 133 (1958).

however, there are recognized exceptions. There is authority for the position that an agent's actions may be voidable by the principal but not necessarily void since the agent does not always lose the authority to act for the principal.[121] Courts also have held that a contract entered into by an agent can be ratified or disaffirmed by the incompetent person after competency is restored or by the incompetent person's estate at his or her death.[122]

Nearly 30 years ago, the suggestion was made that people should be allowed to appoint agents temporarily or permanently to act on their behalf in the event the principal became incompetent.[123] Like a living will, the designation would allow the incompetent principal's intentions to be carried out.

On the other hand, provided persons are not clearly mentally ill, they may function as agents.[124] If the principal realizes the agent is incompetent and nevertheless permits the agent to act on his or her behalf there is authority for the position that the capacity of the agent will be conclusively presumed.[125] There is even authority for the view that the principal is responsible regardless since he guarantees the capacity of an agent by approving the appointment.[126]

In addition to placing limitations on agency relationships, state statutes prohibit certain mentally disabled persons from becoming or acting as representatives or fiduciaries.[127] All but 9 states have legislation that disqualifies individuals from functioning as personal representatives of an estate if they are variously stated "imbeciles," "of unsound mind," "incompetent," "insane," "mentally ill," "adjudicated incompetent," or "unable to discharge their duties" or for other reasons. Similar legislation governs guardians and conservators in 41 states and fiduciaries or trustees in 23 others.

IV. PRIVILEGES AND DUTIES OF CITIZENSHIP

Every person has the privilege and the duty to participate in certain activities normally associated with citizenship—voting, holding political office, jury duty, and testifying in court. To the extent that one may become stigmatized or alienated from society, one who is denied the opportunity to participate in these essential activities loses more than the opportunity to exercise these privileges.

A. Right to Vote

Although voting may be the most basic privilege and duty in a democratic society, all but ten states prohibit certain classes of mentally disabled persons from exercising their franchise.[128] Twenty-four jurisdictions deny the franchise to "idiots," "insane persons," "mentally incompetent persons," or "those of unsound mind." Fifteen states and the District of Columbia disqualify only individuals who are formally adjudicated incompetent or who are placed under guardianship. Oklahoma denies the vote only to mentally retarded persons who have been adjudicated incompetent. Maryland and Missouri do not allow institutionalized persons to vote.[129]

With the exception of persons in institutions, there are substantial problems enforcing any of these provisions. Fourteen jurisdictions have no formal enforcement mechanism at all.[130] Most either allow the ballot to be challenged by an interested citizen or provide for cancellation of the person's registration. A few require the person's name to be removed from the voter roles. Since in most cases someone must identify the mentally disabled persons and make the situation known to the proper officials, the number of sanctions meted out is minimal.

When viewed as a body of law, state restrictions of the voting rights of mentally ill and mentally retarded individuals suffer not only because they may not be good social policy but because they pose significant constitutional problems.[131] Numerous complaints about the constitutionality of these franchise restrictions have been lodged: the most persuasive are that they interfere with the exercise of a fundamental right without enforcing a compelling state interest,[132] they suffer from both over- and underinclusivity,[133] and they often use unacceptably vague standards.[134]

Voting repeatedly has been held to be a fundamental right.[135] In order for states to properly exercise their power to establish voter qualifications in state and feder-

121. 2A C.J.S. Agency § 28 (1972 & Supp. 1982); Parton v. Robinson, 574 S.W.2d 679 (Ky. Ct. App. 1978).

122. Silver v. United States, 498 F. Supp. 610 (N.D. Ill. 1980).

123. Wynn, Management of Infants' and Incompetents' Property, 1 A.B.A. Sec. Real Prop., Prob. & Tr. Proc. 96 (pt. I, 1956).

124. 2A C.J.S. Agency § 29 (1972 & Supp. 1982); Sims v. Slovin, 207 A.2d 597 (Del. Ch. Ct. 1965), *aff'd*, 213 A.2d 903 (Del. 1965).

125. 3 Am. Jur. 2d Agency §§ 13, 16 (1962 & Supp. 1982).

126. *Id.*

127. See table 8.3.

128. See *id.*: Colorado, Illinois, Indiana, Kansas, Michigan, New Hampshire, North Carolina, Pennsylvania, Tennessee, and Vermont.

129. New York's law was struck down as unconstitutional because there was no determination of incompetency: Manhattan State Citizens' Group, Inc. v. Bass, 524 F. Supp. 1270 (S.D.N.Y. 1981).

130. See table 8.3.

131. Note, Mental Disability and the Right to Vote, 88 Yale L.J. 1644 (1979) [hereinafter cited as Note, Mental Disability]; Sales, Powell, Van Duizend, & Associates, *supra* note 50, ch. 1.7, Voting Rights 105; Allen, Ferster, & Weihofen, *supra* note 98, at 364-67.

132. Note, Mental Disability, *supra* note 131, at 1647-56; Sales, Powell, Van Duizend, & Associates, *supra* note 50, ch. 1.7, at 105-6.

133. See references cited in note 132 *supra*.

134. Sales, Powell, Van Duizend, & Associates, *supra* note 50, at 107.

135. See, e.g., Bullock v. Carter, 405 U.S. 134 (1972); Reynolds v. Sims, 377 U.S. 533, 561-62 (1964).

al elections,[136] they must be able to satisfy a two-pronged classification test.

The first prong examines the stated or implicit purpose(s) of their restrictions. The most supportable reason is the desire "to exclude from electoral participation persons incapable of making rational voting decisions." The question is whether this is compelling when measured against the individual interests of mentally disabled persons to vote. Although the Supreme Court has never answered this question definitively, commentators seem to agree that while in practice the restrictions are badly flawed, the concept of restricting the vote based on some kind of competency test is constitutionally sound.[137]

This does not mean, however, that these statutes are necessarily constitutional. The second prong, which asks whether the legislative enactment is "narrowly drawn to express only the legitimate interest at stake,"[138] is frequently in doubt. Statutes can be overinclusive or underinclusive depending on the circumstances. Assuming for the moment there is no vagueness problem, statutes that take away the franchise because of a condition or status that describes some form of mental impairment or institutional confinement are too broad since many, or at least some, of the individuals included by the label are fully capable of voting.[139] Similarly, legislation that restricts the franchise only for persons adjudicated incompetent or placed under guardianship may also be overinclusive, since the incapacity at issue in those adjudications may have little to do with the capacity to vote.[140] In fact, at least ten states do not recognize a necessary relationship between mental disability and voting.[141]

At the same time, it has been noted, some "disfranchisement mechanisms are underinclusive because they do not focus on the critical factor: capacity for rationality. . . . Some persons incapable of voting rationally will not fit into any of the statutory categories."[142]

Another major deficiency with such legislation is vagueness. The statutes do not reveal a sound basis for determining who is or is not prohibited from casting a ballot. Terms such as "idiot," "insane," "unsound mind," and "imbecile" have little meaning even in common usage. "Mental illness" or "mental retardation" are only better terms if they are defined according to acceptable medical practice and are translatable into understandable legal standards. Even "adjudicated incompetent" or "placed under guardianship" may be confusing where the terms are equated with commitment.[143]

If competency requirements are to be used, the standards should not be based on any definition of mental disability. The practical difficulties in establishing a constitutionally permissible structure and basic fairness dictate using an approach that focuses on the characteristics of voting. The disqualification requirements, whatever they are, should apply to all voters or to no voters.[144] In addition, persons in institutions who are qualified to vote should be given assistance in registering and casting their ballots. However, such assistance should be nonpartisan and monitored for possible partisan indiscretions where assistance is given to large numbers of people such as those in an institution. In a 1984 case reviewed by the Fourth Circuit, authorities became alarmed when all the absentee ballots from the residents of a nursing home registered votes for a straight Democratic ticket.[145]

B. Holding Political Office

Although many of the same problems associated with voting reappear with respect to holding public office, depending upon the jurisdiction legislation governing this latter right may be substantially different. While only 4 states have no applicable statute,[146] many of the existing statutes only apply restrictions to selected offices. The provisions that do disqualify office seekers do so in two ways. They may require a person to be a qualified voter or deny eligibility to those who have been adjudicated incompetent, or who are "insane," "idiots," "incompetents," "of unsound mind" or "medically unfit." Some jurisdictions use both types of disqualification in combination.

Thirty-one jurisdictions mandate that an officeholder be qualified to vote.[147] Seventeen apply the requirement to any state officeholder, and 24 specify particular offices. In all, 28 states have no mechanism for disqualifying mentally disabled persons from every state office. Instead the coverage is selective, affecting such positions as judgeships or important executive offices. The 23 statutes that apply restrictions to all those seeking or

136. U.S. Const. art. I, § 2 cl. 1.

137. Note, Mental Disability, *supra* note 131, at 1651.

138. Sales, Powell, Van Duizend, & Associates, *supra* note 50, at 105; see, e.g., Roe v. Wade, 410 U.S. 113 (1973).

139. See Note, Mental Disability, *supra* note 131.

140. *Id.*

141. See table 8.3; see also Klein & Grossman, Voting Competence and Mental Illness, *in* American Psychological Association, 76th Annual Convention Proc. 701, 702 (pt. 3, 1968).

142. Note, Mental Disability, *supra* note 131, at 1659.

143. Sales, Powell, Vạn Duizend, & Associates, *supra* note 50, at ch. 1.7.

144. A project of the American Bar Association Commission on the Mentally Disabled suggests the following language for those states that want to use a competency test: "Any person who is able to provide the information, whether orally, in writing, through an interpreter or interpretive device or otherwise, which is reasonably required of all persons seeking to register to vote, shall be considered a qualified voter of this state." Sales, Powell, Van Duizend, & Associates, *supra* note 50, at 111.

145. United States v. Odom, 736 F.2d 104 (4th Cir.1984).

146. See table 8.3.

147. *Id.*

holding public office usually cover only individuals who have been adjudicated incompetent.

There are good reasons for applying restrictions on holding or seeking public office to everyone or no one at all. At the very least, all qualified voters should be allowed to hold office. Moreover, it is not merely facetious to suggest, as some have done, that there should be no automatic disqualifications, since "anyone who can survive a political campaign certainly ought to be able to hold office."[148] The voters should be allowed to choose for themselves who is competent to serve them.

C. Jury Duty

The restrictions applied to jury duty are frequently very different from but may be the same as those used for voting and holding public office. Eleven jurisdictions disqualify nonvoters,[149] 22 use the standard "incapable of rendering satisfactory service due to mental disability" or a closely similar formulation, and many more disqualify individuals who are of "unsound mind," have been adjudicated incompetent, or are under guardianship.

Although arguably none of the statutes uses language that is ideally suited for the task of restricting jury duty, the 22 states that focus on a person's ability to render satisfactory service are preferable conceptually because they link mental disability with a specific capacity. Other provisions focus exclusively on the existence of a particular status or condition.

D. Testifying in Court

The capacity of someone to testify in court is not regulated by statute. In general, testimony will be permitted because there is a strong presumption in common law that any person has the ability to testify.[150] Very young children may give testimony if the judge believes the testimony will be truthful. Mentally disabled persons may testify on a similar basis. For example, a mentally retarded man was able to testify against the person who had robbed him because the trial court was satisfied that the witness had enough intelligence to understand the oath and to provide a reasonably accurate account of what happened.[151] Similarly, a mentally retarded rape victim with a mental age of six or seven was allowed to testify against her attacker because she knew the difference between the truth and a lie, even though she was not always responsive to the questions that were directed to her on the witness stand.[152] On appeal, a trial court's decision about a witness's competency to testify will be disturbed only if there is a clear abuse of discretion.[153]

Not infrequently, the uncertain capacity of certain mentally disabled persons to testify has a chilling effect on the legal system. There are probably many instances where the prosecution will not go ahead with a case if a lay witness is mentally disabled and lacks credibility on the stand. In addition, mentally disabled persons may not be able to persuade a lawyer to file suit on their behalf where the plaintiff's credibility on the stand will be an important factor in the case.

V. INFORMED CONSENT AND MEDICAL CARE

In recent years there has been substantial conflict between certain patients and their advocates who want to refuse medical care and physicians who believe they have a professional duty to protect patients from harming themselves, sometimes irrespective of the individual's personal wishes. A reasonable resolution of this intense dispute often depends more on views about individual choice and the obligations of society than on empirical data, which are scarce. No matter how the available information is analyzed and how one goes about measuring the differences among competing values, a resolution frequently demands that a choice be made between the value of individual decision making on the one hand and the best interests of the patient as reflected in the physician's Hippocratic Oath on the other hand. This need to make an ultimate choice often brings lawyers and doctors into conflict.[154] Each profession predisposes its members toward certain values that promote specific aspects of their professional roles. In one instance, it is advocacy of the client's point of view, and in the other, it is protection of the patient's mind and body.

Although psychiatrists are by no means in agreement about how the issue of the right to refuse mental health treatment should be resolved, in most instances their proposed solutions emphasize the need to make sure patients receive the care and treatment that will make them well. The leading medical view, endorsed by the American Psychiatric Association, in certain respects mirrors the Utah civil commitment statute discussed in the preceding chapter.[155] The association's model law requires the court to find that the involuntary patient not only is severely mentally ill and treatable but also "lacks the capacity to make an informed decision con-

148. See Wald, *supra* note 2, at 25.
149. See table 8.3.
150. New York v. Rensing, 199 N.E.2d 489 (N.Y. 1964). People v. Spencer, 119 Ill. App. 3d 971, 457 N.E.2d 473 (1983); Stafford v. State, 455 N.E.2d 402 (Ind. Ct. App. 1983).
151. People v. Freshley, 451 N.Y.S.2d 73 (App. Div. 1982).
152. Louisiana v. Peters, 441 So. 2d 403 (La. Ct. App. 1983).
153. People v. Freshley, 451 N.Y.S.2d 73 (App. Div. 1982); Jones v. Alabama, 439 So. 2d 1338 (Ala. Crim. App. 1983).
154. Summary and Analysis, 6 MDLR 62-66 (1982).
155. See ch. 7, Incompetency, Guardianship, and Restoration, § V, Making Incompetence a Prerequisite for Involuntary Commitment, *supra*.

cerning treatment." Voluntary patients, for whom there has been no adjudication of incompetency, retain the "right to refuse treatment," but they may be discharged if they do so.[156]

Earlier criticisms that were made about the Utah statute also apply to the model statute proposed by the American Psychiatric Association. Briefly, the validity of a past determination concerning present capacity to make medical decisions diminishes over time, and potentially dangerous patients may be able to win their release from civil commitment if they can show they have regained their capacity to make their own decisions. In addition, a fellow psychiatrist warns that clinicians should be most reluctant to resort to legal means to override patients' wishes. In the context of refusing antipsychotic medication, he views the problem as one to be worked out between the patient and the doctor in the therapeutic relationship. He argues that patients' refusals are often related to legitimate concerns that need to be explored by both parties without an adversarial struggle.[157]

The doctrine of informed consent—which in theory strives for voluntary, knowing, and competent decision making—provides the conceptual boundaries within which the right to refuse treatment issues are waged. One major problem with evaluating informed consent is that only a relatively few studies have determined what information is used or required in patient decision making, and many of those have serious limitations.[158] The most comprehensive and acclaimed study to date suggests that for a variety of structural reasons informed decision making rarely takes place as it was intended to function:

> It is not unduly harsh to conclude that current informed consent policy has been a dismal failure in the settings we studied, at least when measured against the loftier goals of the doctrine. We simply did not witness a consistent pattern of behavior by staff members that was directed toward providing patients with adequate information on the basis of which they might make intelligent decisions; nor did we witness much enthusiasm by patients for making decisions when they were given the opportunity to do so.[159]

It should be noted, however, that even this study was small in scope, focusing on just three units—an evaluation center, a research ward, and an outpatient clinic—associated with the same university hospital. More reliable empirical data are necessary before it would be prudent to recommend fundamental changes in the nature of informed consent as it is presently constituted.

To a significant extent, the law has chosen to make the individual's point of view the primary consideration, despite loud protests from the medical profession. Whether this is due in part to the fact that lawyers have a significant impact on the development of the law may be debated. Nevertheless, a hallmark of American democracy is the right of individuals to determine for themselves what is or is not in their best interests. Stated in another way, idiosyncratic individuals are generally allowed to follow the counsel of their own minds, even if their decisions are viewed by the majority as being unreasonable. Exceptions exist where human life and, to a lesser extent, significant property interests are endangered. In addition, a therapeutic privilege may allow mental disability professionals to withhold certain information if it would be demonstrably harmful to the patient.[160]

A. Voluntary, Knowing, and Competent Consent

United States law requires consent to be voluntary, knowing, and competent.[161] Since voluntariness encompasses the element of free choice, consent is not present where there has been an influence on the decision maker that makes the freedom meaningless, such as threat of force, coercion, fraud, duress, deceit, or some other type of over-reaching.[162]

The second requirement that consent be knowing focuses on the amount and the quality of information that is necessary to make an informed decision. In the context of treatment the concept of informed consent is less than 30 years old.[163] Legally, informed consent replaced the notion that doctors could obtain valid consent by providing nothing more than their opinion that medical procedures should be carried out. Today, most jurisdictions demand substantial disclosure or something akin

156. Stromberg Stone, A Model State Law on Civil Commitment of the Mentally Ill, 20 Harv. J. on Legis. 275, 282 (1983).

157. Appelbaum, Can Mental Patients Say No to Drugs? New York Times Magazine, Mar. 21, 1982, at 46.

158. The deficiencies in the existing empirical data are reviewed in a recent study. See C.W. Lidz, A. Meisel, E. Zerubavel, M. Carter, R.M. Sestak, & L.H. Roth, Informed Consent: A Study of Decisionmaking in Psychiatry 24-32 (1984).

159. *Id.* at 326.

160. *Id.* at 18-19. The strength of such a defense is somewhat uncertain because of the paucity of case law on the subject.

161. R. Burgdorf, The Legal Rights of Handicapped Persons 525-27 (1980); Kaimowitz v. Dep't of Mental Health, No. 73-19434-AW, 1 MDLR 147 (Cir. Ct. of Wayne County, Mich. July 10, 1973), *reprinted in* A.D. Brooks, Law, Psychiatry, and the Mental Health System 902 (1974); Katz, Disclosure and Consent in Psychiatric Practice: Mission Impossible? *in* Law and Ethics in the Practices of Psychiatry 91-118 (C.K. Hofling ed. 1981); A.J. Rosoff, Informed Consent: A Guide for Health Care Providers (1981).

162. Burgdorf, *supra* note 161, at 526; see also Kaimowitz v. Dep't of Mental Health, No. 73-19434-AW, 1 MDLR 147 (Cir. Ct. of Wayne County, Mich. July 10, 1973).

163. According to several authors, the notion of informed consent was first recognized in a 1957 judicial decision by the California Court of Appeals in Salgo v. Stanford Univ. Bd. of Trustees, 317 P.2d 170 (1957). See Katz, *supra* note 161, at 93; Rosoff, *supra* note 161, at 33.

to it. "Why it took such a long time to appreciate that there was something wrong with leaving patients so completely in the dark about diagnostic procedures and therapeutic interventions is an intriguing question," observes one commentator—"and so is the question as to why two judges suddenly challenged such omissions in the late 1950's."[164]

The nature of the disclosure that is necessary was defined in the landmark decision *Natanson v. Kline*,[165] which applied what has become known as the professional community standard or the "old rule."[166] Realizing that there had to be certain limitations on the volume of information a doctor was obligated to communicate to the patient, the *Natanson* court linked the physician's obligation to what it described as normal standards of medical practice. In order to recover for negligent nondisclosure, the plaintiff must prove that the accepted professional standard was not met. Most frequently, the standard is measured by the level of medical practice in a particular specialty area.[167] In a few jurisdictions the even more difficult evidentiary requirement that measures the standard of practice in a geographical area is used.[168]

Although most statutes have no legislation governing informed consent standards, of those that do, 11 retain some form of the old rule.[169] One major practical problem is proving that the standard was violated, since the burden of proof is normally on the patient and physicians are reluctant to testify against their colleagues. Even in the few states that do require the physician to provide expert testimony, once a prima facie case is made, the patient must still rebut the expert's testimony.

Largely because patients do have much difficulty in finding experts who are willing to testify, other approaches have been developed and followed. What has been accepted as an alternative in several state statutes and many court decisions is the "reasonable patient" standard.[170] This so-called modern rule "focuses on the informational needs of an average, reasonable patient rather than on professionally established standards of disclosure."[171] The seminal case in this area, *Canterbury v. Spence*,[172] emphasized the right of patients to make their own determinations about medical treatment.[173] In order to carry out the right of self-determination, patients must be given sufficient information to understand the risks and evaluate the available options open to them.

A number of jurisdictions either mix their approaches or fail to resolve conflicts between the old and the new rules.[174] Eleven states, including at least three jurisdictions that have accepted the professional community standards approach,[175] include provisions requiring substantial information to be conveyed to the patient about any medical procedure. Three states specify that a patient has a right to refuse treatment.[176]

A number of medical organizations have supported statutes that counteract the need for disclosure, limit liability, or place the final decision making about negligence in the hands of physicians. Twenty-one states presently have such legislation.[177]

According to ten state statutes and the case law in this area, physicians will not be liable for nondisclosure in emergency situations.[178] In fact, informed consent is normally waived altogether if obtaining the consent would place the patient at risk of serious physical or mental injury.[179] Some courts merely require that treatment be needed to "alleviate great pain and suffering, even though the threat of irreversible harm is not present."[180]

A variety of defenses also exist. None are found in great numbers in the statutes, but they are more commonly found in the case law.[181] In certain jurisdictions liability variously will be denied if (1) the undisclosed information is common knowledge,[182] (2) there has been a waiver by the patient,[183] (3) information is withheld to prevent psychological harm to the patient,[184] (4) there is a written and signed consent form,[185] (5) a reasonable, prudent person would have undergone the procedure anyway,[186] (6) there was no expert medical testimony,[187] or (7) the risk to the patient was insubstantial.[188] In addition, seven states create a rebuttable presumption that

164. Katz, *supra* note 161, at 93.
165. 350 P.2d 1093 (Kan. 1960).
166. Rosoff, *supra* note 161, at 34-38.
167. *Id.*; Ficklin v. MacFarlane, 550 P.2d 1295 (Utah 1976); Bly v. Rhoads, 222 S.E.2d 783 (Va. 1976).
168. Rosoff, *supra* note 161, at 36. Arizona, Idaho, Michigan, and Mississippi are cited as examples of states that use the more restrictive standard.
169. *Id.*
170. *Id.* at 38-41.
171. *Id.* at 38.
172. 464 F.2d 772 (D.C. Cir. 1972).
173. *Id.* at 780.
174. Rosoff, *supra* note 161, at 38-41.
175. Florida, Kentucky, and North Carolina.
176. Georgia, Minnesota, and Utah.
177. Rosoff, *supra* note 161, at 38-41.
178. *Id.*
179. *Id.* at 14-19.
180. *Id.* at 16.
181. *Id.*
182. Delaware, New York, and Vermont.
183. Delaware, New York, Utah, and Vermont.
184. Delaware, Minnesoa, New York, Oregon, Utah, and Vermont.
185. Florida and Georgia.
186. Delaware, Nebraska, New York, North Carolina, North Dakota, Utah, and Vermont.
187. New Hampshire and Vermont.
188. Vermont.

disclosure is proper where a written consent form has been signed,[189] and Arizona precludes claims of common law assault and battery in medical malpractice litigation.

Two states, Hawaii and Texas, have delegated authority to medical boards allowing them to determine what constitutes acceptable disclosure practices for each type of procedure. The strength of this approach is that it establishes a definable standard for the doctor to obey and provides the patient with a suitable means of redressing alleged instances of malpractice. The danger is that the medical boards may be overly protective of their colleagues.

The third requirement that there be a competent decision addresses the level of cognitive functioning necessary to give a valid consent. The concept has been discussed in detail in the previous chapter, and that discussion will not be repeated here.[190] It should be recalled, however, that competency may have a different meaning from one jurisdiction to the next.

The competency requirement, whatever it may be, applies to the informed consent of mentally disabled persons to any social service they may need, including psychiatric or habilitative care. Generally, there are three possible alternative dispositions for incompetent persons who are unable to provide informed consent: (1) take no action until the incompetent person is able to give consent, (2) allow the service provider to make the decision, or (3) appoint a substitute consent giver. Implicit in these options is the fact that informed consent has been accepted as a desirable requirement. There is a fourth option that is similar to allowing the service provider to provide consent. This is to reject the concept of informed consent and to allow the physician to make the decision in all situations. The common law of battery, which precludes unauthorized touching, and of assault, which precludes even a threatening approach,[191] make the fourth alternative largely impractical without legislative intervention. In addition, legislative solutions may be limited by the constitution. The United States Supreme Court, for example, has recognized that the "personal right to privacy . . . is broad enough to encompass a woman's decision whether or not to terminate her pregnancy."[192]

The extreme alternatives of taking no action or transferring all decision-making power to the attending physician are straightforward albeit inelegant and arbitrary concepts. Substituted decision making, on the other hand, is fraught with ambiguity despite the fact that it has been accepted in 13 states and much of the case law.[193] To begin with, once a decision has been made whether the substitute consent giver is to be the permanent guardian or a person appointed to make one treatment decision, the legal authority diverges as to what constitutes a proper decision. Two legal positions are put forward most prominently. Should a decision reflect what most people would decide in the same situation? Or should it reflect the best possible approximation of what a particular individual would decide if he or she were able to do so? While the law has been consistent in favoring freedom of choice for competent citizens,[194] many courts have backed away from this principle if the person for whom the decision is to be made is incompetent. Instead they often favor the best interest standard. Without resolving the more fundamental issue of whether the best interest standard should be applied to everyone regardless of mental abilities, it is troubling to see similar applications of the law create two standards, one for "normals" and one for persons who are mentally disabled. What makes matters worse is that the existing law of informed consent, as applied to mentally disabled individuals, is riddled with inconsistencies. Often the degree of control or regulation bears little relationship to the actual intrusiveness or seriousness of the procedure. For example, the law generally establishes more or equally rigorous consent requirements for both sterilization and electroconvulsive shock therapy treatments than for the withholding of life support systems for profoundly disabled or terminally ill patients. Similarly, competent mentally disabled persons living with their parents or residing in institutions may have no more decision-making rights on any of these questions than an adjudicated incompetent person.

While it may not be desirable to rank different types of treatment according to intrusiveness or some other measure since each case has its own particular circumstances to consider, the lack of consistency is evident in recent decisions. The law governing informed consent as applied to mentally disabled persons is disparate, determined more by the development of legal attitudes with respect to each particular type of procedure than by a coherent view of decision-making processes.

B. Life-threatening Decisions: Adults and Children

The most drastic intervention is the decision to terminate life. The moral responsibility for such a decision, if

189. Idaho, Iowa, Louisiana, North Carolina, Ohio, Texas, and Washington,

190. See ch. 7, Incompetency, Guardianship, and Restoration, § II, Historical Background and Definitions.

191. Rosoff, *supra* note 161, at 3.

192. Roe v. Wade, 410 U.S. 113, 152 (1973).

193. Rosoff, *supra* note 161, at 75–185.

194. See Kaimowitz v. Dep't of Mental Health, No. 73-1943-AW, 1 MDLR 147 (Cir. Ct. of Wayne County Mich. July 10, 1973); Katz, *supra* note 161; Rosoff, *supra* note 161.

it is to be made at all, is great, and the outcome should be founded on well-articulated principles that support the interests of the mentally disabled individual and reflect a strong social consensus as well. Because of the moral complexity of those decisions and the competing values involved, it is hardly surprising that the laws governing euthanasia and the right to die are inexact and inconsistent.

The modern law on this issue may be traced to 1975. In that year Karen Ann Quinlan came to the attention of the courts when she became comatose permanently after ingesting drugs. Her father sought court sanction to remove her from a mechanical respirator, but initially failed when the lower court refused to designate him as her guardian.[195] Following a special appeal, the Supreme Court of New Jersey ruled unanimously that the father should be authorized to give substituted consent for his daughter in order to withdraw extraordinary life-sustaining treatment.[196] The court's reasoning began with the proposition that if competent the patient would have had a constitutional right under notions of privacy[197] to decline medical treatment, even if death would result.[198] Since she was unable to make that decision for herself, her guardian could substitute his decision for hers by consulting with responsible physicians and then attempting to divine his daughter's preference. But the standard was somewhat elusive. The court seemed to be less concerned with what the daughter would have done than reflecting a consensus of responsible physicians that there was no "reasonable possibility" that she would become conscious again and of the recommendation by both the treating physicians and the guardian to discontinue the life-supporting apparatus. Significantly, the physicians who made up the ethics committee disagreed with the treating physicians about the ultimate decision. In part, the outcome was a battle of experts, and a decision was not made on the basis of clear facts. Even after the issue was legally resolved, Karen Ann Quinlan, although comatose, survived for eight years without mechanical assistance.

At the very least, the *Quinlan* case indicated that courts would be willing, in certain circumstances, to approve the termination of life-support systems of a brain-damaged person. Based considerably on the New Jersey Supreme Court's reasoning, a substantial if not wholly satisfactory area of law has developed. It is a mistake, however, to assume that all of the subsequent cases involved the balancing of the same basic principles. There are substantial differences depending on circumstances such as a variety of possible legal analyses and whether the patient is comatose as in the *Quinlan* case, mentally ill, mentally retarded, or a minor with a mental impairment.

1. Comatose Adults

Even with respect to individuals who are considered comatose the law is neither certain nor uniform. A Tennessee court, for example, diverged from the *Quinlan* rationale by ruling that further treatment for an unconscious woman in a vegetative state would not be authorized without the consent of her family.[199] The decision, similar to the *Quinlan* case, recognized that at a certain point the patient's right of bodily privacy would overcome the state's interest in preserving her life artificially. However, the court rejected any attempts to divine the patient's preference in this situation and instead based its ruling not to authorize an unnatural invasion of her body on an evaluation of her best interests. In the same opinion, the court made a helpful distinction between the criminal act of euthanasia, or mercy killing, which involves a positive action that leads to a patient's death, and the withdrawal of extraordinary life-support systems that do not benefit the patient, which involves a negative act with no criminal or civil liability implications.

While the Tennessee chancery court focused on the differences between an action and an omission, most other courts that have reviewed the matter have been able to distinguish withdrawal of life support from mercy killing by focusing on the existence or absence of court approval. Normally, prosecutors and courts are reluctant to find criminal liability for what is viewed as a moral dilemma. Two California physicians were not guilty of conspiracy to commit murder because the judge found that their decision to turn off life-support equipment "was not an unlawful failure to perform a duty."[200] Moreover, the California legislature had failed to give proper evidence on such matters.[201]

In Delaware,[202] the supreme court determined that even without specific legislative direction a chancery court applying the principles of equity could appoint a guardian for a comatose patient who would then be allowed to recommend termination of life-sustaining medical equipment. However, the court would make the final decision after reviewing the evidence in a full

195. *In re* Quinlan, 137 N.J. Super. 227 (1975).

196. *In re* Quinlan, 70 N.J. 10, 355 A.2d 647, *cert. denied sub nom.* Garger v. N.J., 429 U.S. 922 (1976).

197. See Roe v. Wade, 410 U.S. 113 (1973); Griswold v. Connecticut, 381 U.S. 479 (1965).

198. *In re* Quinlan, 355 A.2d 647 (N.J. 1976).

199. Dockery v. Dockery, No. 51439, 1 MDLR 453 (3d Ch. Div., Pt. 2, Hamilton County, Tenn. Feb. 11, 1977).

200. Barber v. Superior Ct. of California, Los Angeles County, 195 Cal. Rptr. 484 (Cal. Ct. App. 1983).

201. *Id.*

202. Severns v. Wilmington Medical Center, Inc., 421 A.2d 1334 (Del. 1980).

hearing. On remand from the high court, the Delaware chancery court relied on statements made by the patient before her car accident which indicated that she wished to die with dignity if she were ever unable to care for herself. Based on these prior expressions, the petition to cease extraordinary care was granted.

Prior expressions, as related in testimony by friends and relatives, that a comatose patient had often stated that she did not want to be placed on a life-support system convinced an Ohio court to allow the woman's husband to carry out her wishes.[203] Since medical science had created a new state of human existence "minimal human life sustained by man-made life supports . . . [society] . . . must now devise and fashion rules and parameters for that existence."[204]

The Florida Supreme Court recently went a significant step further by holding that individuals who are properly involved in the execution of a living will[205] on behalf of a comatose patient—guardians, consenting family members, physicians, and hospital personnel—should be absolved from all civil and criminal liability if they in good faith terminate extraordinary life-support systems for the patient, even without obtaining prior court approval. Good faith is shown if three physicians certify that the patient is in a permanent vegetative state, there is no reasonable prospect that the patient will regain cognitive brain function, and he is being sustained only through extraordinary life-sustaining measures. The court disagreed with the *Quinlan* case, dismissing the necessity of even a hospital ethics committee review of such a decision. Only where there is disagreement among the primary parties or evidence of wrongdoing or malpractice is judicial intervention warranted following the initiation of a proper petition.[206]

A federal court in California determined that a terminally ill war veteran who had lapsed into a coma retained his right to die where he had recently requested, while he was still competent to do so, that his artificial respirator be detached from his body.[207] The fact that his wife and child opposed disconnecting the respirator did not outweigh the clear, previous expression of the patient's right to privacy.

Unfortunately, the evidence of the patient's prior intentions is not always so clear. In New York a previous expression supported in court by clear and convincing proof led to the cessation of life-sustaining measures for a comatose patient.[208] However, absent such clarity New York's case law is somewhat muddled. In the same decision, involving a different plaintiff, the court ruled that a mother's wishes for her son, combined with the son's fatal condition and his significant fear, were insufficient justifications to halt his blood transfusions. It should be noted that the doctrine of substituted consent was not rejected, merely refashioned to fit the situation where the patient had never considered the right to die before becoming incompetent.

In an earlier New York decision, an appeals court had allowed a friend to decide that a patient should die, based on the friend's hearsay testimony concerning the patient's previous expressions which was admitted in the furtherance of justice.[209] The state's highest court affirmed, and declined to review the issue of substituted consent, noting that the patient previously had made the decision for himself.[210] In Connecticut a court determined that even though a semicomatose multiple sclerosis patient had never in her life expressed an opinion about "the use of extraordinary life support systems on patients with no reasonable hope of recovery," her family could act as her substitute decision maker and discontinue her treatment where the attending physician and two other doctors unanimously concurred about the patient's condition and the family acted in good faith as evidenced by the absense of contrary interests.[211] This substitute decision, ruled the court, most closely matched what the patient would have wanted done if she had been able to make the decision herself.

2. Mentally Disabled Adults

Where the patient is mentally disabled but not comatose the right to die takes on added complications, although of course there are obvious similarities and opportunities to apply common principles. Three differences stand out. Courts must first determine whether the patient is in fact incompetent and, if so, whether the patient has provided or can provide any indications about his or her feelings about that termination issue. Because the person is not comatose, of course, the argument that the patient is legally dead will have no applicability. In this type of situation where the quality of life rather than its existence is at issue, the judiciary should proceed very cautiously. Yet, based on a comparison of existing cases, which admittedly are relatively few in number, the courts seem to have been more willing to

203. Leach v. Akron Gen. Medical Center, 426 N.E.2d 809 (Ohio Ct. Com. Pl. 1980).

204. *Id.*

205. See ch. 7, Incompetency, Guardianship, and Restoration, § IX H, Living Wills, *supra* for a definition and description of a living will.

206. John F. Kennedy Memorial Hosp. v. Bludworth, 452 So. 2d 921 (Fla. 1984).

207. Foster v. Tourtellotte, No. Civ. 81-5046-RMT(AAX), 6 MDLR 15 (C.D. Cal. Nov. 16, 1981.

208. *In re* Storar, 420 N.E.2d 64 (N.Y. 1981).

209. Eichner v. Dillon, 426 N.Y.S.2d 517 (App. Div. 1980).

210. *In re* Storar, 420 N.E.2d 64 (N.Y. 1981).

211. Foody v. Manchester Memorial Hosp., 40 Conn. Supp. 127 (Super. Ct. 1984).

terminate extraordinary care for patients who are mentally disabled than for comatose patients. It is unlikely that this is due to deliberate discrimination, although insensitivity by those underestimating the potential for abuse may play a role to the extent that broad principles are laid down without proper consideration of how they might be applied by some other court in different situations.

The Supreme Judicial Court of Massachusetts in the seminal case of *Superintendent of Belchertown v. Saikewicz*[212] ordered chemotherapy withheld from a 67-year-old profoundly mentally retarded resident of a state institution who was suffering from leukemia. The right to privacy outweighed the need for medical treatment. Specifically, the limited extension of life possible if chemotherapy were used was less persuasive than the fact that the patient had an incurable illness, would suffer substantial side effects and discomfort, and might experience considerable fear because of his lack of understanding about what was happening. Conceptually, the court established the rationale that in order to decline the treatment, there had to be substituted consent based not on the patient's best interests but on his actual interests and preferences. Substituted judgment as it is known should be made by the judiciary and not by an ethics committee or some "other group purporting to represent the 'morality and conscience of our society.'"[213]

Three years later, the same court attempted to clarify somewhat the perception that there was an absolute requirement that courts review such matters.[214] While in general it is undesirable to shift the ultimate responsibility from the judiciary, noted the court, doctors could end life-prolonging care on their own initiative but would be subject to liability if they were wrong. According to the facts of that case, the wife and son of a mentally ill man who were acting as his guardians had the authority to withhold hemodialysis used to treat the man's kidney failure. The critical factor in approving substituted judgment was a finding that the ward if competent would not have elected to undergo any more treatment. An expression of intent by the ward was not essential in arriving at this conclusion. In addition, several other factors were cited by the court as important: corroboration by his wife of 55 years, support by a closely knit family, medical testimony that the prognosis was hopeless and hemodialysis constituted a significant bodily intrusion, and the absence of countervailing state interest. Tragically, the proceedings took over a year to conclude, by which time the patient had already died.

As was described previously, a New York court in assessing the need for blood transfusions to sustain the life of a terminally ill profoundly retarded adult refused to permit a court-ordered termination of the treatments, denying a request of the patient's mother.[215] The mother's belief that the transfusions would be painful and traumatic and the fact the son had contracted terminal cancer were insufficient reason not to extend his life. The issue of substituted consent was left in limbo.

The substituted judgment doctrine as applied to mentally disabled or comatose adults has substantial support. In addition to these court decisions, a March 1983 report by a presidential commission, *Deciding to Forgo Life-sustaining Treatment*,[216] endorsed the concept wholeheartedly. Where it differed with the holdings of many courts was in its support of the view that the ultimate decisions should be made by the guardians and the treating physicians with a review by an intrahospital ethics committee. The report assumed that medical institutions, not courts, are best able to make these decisions, particularly in terms of understanding medical issues and in making immediate decisions.

While there is little doubt that courts have been slow to respond in certain situations, there are mechanisms available to speed up the legal process such as those used in death row cases in the criminal area. Moreover, courts can allow hospital authorities to proceed on their own where there is a legitimate emergency. This is commonly done in other medical decision-making areas already. Before a shift is made away from court review, several considerations should be addressed carefully: courts are structured and judges trained to gather and assess technical information; constitutional issues that are inherently involved in substituted judgment are particularly well-suited for judicial resolution; the family and patient's viewpoint may be submerged under the weight of medical decision making; and the public may have less input into the moral and ethical decisions about how life is to be valued and who should receive increasingly overutilized extraordinary care resources when hospitals establish the criteria and with the family's or the guardian's input make the final decision.

A closely related issue is the person who is clearly competent legally but who may decide during a period of great despair brought on by catastrophic illness or disability that life is no longer worthwhile. What is the judi-

212. Superintendent of Belchertown State School v. Saikewicz, 370 N.E.2d 417 (Mass. 1977).

213. *Id.* at 435.

214. *In re* Spring, 405 N.E.2d 115 (Mass. 1980).

215. *In re* Storar, 420 N.E.2d 64 (N.Y. 1981).

216. President's Commission for the Study of Ethical Problems in Medicine and Biomedical and Behavioral Research, Deciding to Forego Life-sustaining Treatment (March 1983), *reported in* Summary and Analysis, 7 MDLR 213 (1983).

ciary's role in allowing the patient to demand that a physician or hospital carry out the person's wishes? Two recent cases suggest that courts may be more reluctant to affirm such choice where the person is still competent than if he is incompetent to decide and legal standards provide little direction in such situations. A California court ruled that while being treated in a hospital a completely quadriplegic patient had no right to demand cessation of forced feeding where to do so would have a devastating effect on hospital morale; once she was discharged, however, that was a different matter.[217] In New York a lower court would not allow a competent, quadriplegic patient to petition the court in advance of her hospitalization to direct the medical staff to allow her to refuse treatment and food at her discretion.[218] The action was premature. The idea of a competent person taking her life may be psychologically more troubling to sitting judges than an incompetent person being allowed to die with the help of family and friends.

3. Children and Infants

Decisions regarding life and death are often made more difficult when disabled infants and children are the patients because (1) the interests of the parents or guardians may conflict with the child's interests, (2) the child's potential for physical and social development may be uncertain, and (3) the issues are often obscured by broader right-to-life arguments. As a result, even where the overriding circumstances and philosophical considerations are the same for adults and minors, the outcomes may be different.

Perhaps, no case better illustrates the potential danger in assuming that parents and children necessarily share identical interests than the multiyear litigation surrounding Phillip Becker in California.[219] There a Down's Syndrome child required surgery in order to repair a congenital heart defect. The evidence indicated that without an operation Phillip's life would be shortened considerably. His parents, who had placed him into an institution six days after he was born and visited him rarely, ignored the best medical opinions and decided to withhold permission for the operation. To many, including the two foster parents who had befriended Phillip, the natural parents' decision was unconscionable. Phillip was denied the opportunity to live to his fullest potential because he was a mentally retarded child.

In 1979, a juvenile court, applying traditional notions of parent-child relationships, rejected efforts to make Phillip a ward of the court so that permission could be given for the surgery. Despite this setback the foster parents initiated proceedings to obtain limited guardianship over Phillip without totally severing his ties to his real parents. Without resolving the issue of surgery, a superior court granted the petition and awarded custody to the psychological parents over the objections of the biological parents. The court placed the best interests of the child over the rights of the biological parents where the evidence demonstrated that the parenting had been detrimental in the past. Without that finding of detriment, the court would have found for the natural parents regardless of the child's other interests. Once the detriment was established, however, the court willingly substituted the judgment of what Phillip would want based on his demonstrated affection for his foster parents.

On appeal the decision was upheld,[220] but the appeals court observed that the long delay in resolving this matter, in part because of the need to overcome the strong deference to parental control, may have made the original concern for life-prolonging surgery moot by increasing the risk of surgery to an arguably unacceptable level. Fortunately, the surgery was performed successfully.

Where no parents or family are involved the courts may apply the doctrine of substituted judgment differently. The highest court in Massachusetts, for example, affirmed an order by a juvenile court not to use extraordinary efforts to extend the life of an infant with a fatal heart disease.[221] Because the child was incompetent due to age and had no responsible guardian, the lower court correctly attempted "to act on the same motives and considerations as would have moved the child."[222] The court did not have to "reach a level of moral certainty"; clear and convincing evidence was judged to be sufficient.

Nevertheless the court's analysis was clouded by two factors. First, there was the implication in the opinion that a different assessment would have been made if the parents had been available and they had challenged the medical judgments. The decision might be left to them and to the physicians, even though the same court in another opinion involving an incompetent adult noted it would be extremely reluctant to shift responsibility away from the judiciary.[223] Second, all the original parties to the suit, including the attending physicians, concluded

217. Bouvia v. County of Riverside, No. 159780, 8 MPDLR 377 (Cal. App. Dep't Super. Ct. Dec. 16, 1983).

218. A.B.V.C., 477 N.Y.S. 2d 281 (App. Div. 1984).

219. *In re* Phillip B., 156 Cal. Rptr. 48 (Ct. App. 1979), Guardianship of Becker, No. 101981, 5 MDLR 326 (Cal. App. Dep't Super. Ct., Santa Clara County Aug. 7, 1981) (discussed in Summary and Analysis, 5 MDLR 315-16), Guardianship of Phillip B., 188 Cal. Rptr. 781 (Ct. App. 1983).

220. Guardianship of Phillip B., 188 Cal. Rptr. 781 (Ct. App. 1983).

221. Custody of a Minor, 434 N.E.2d 601 (Mass. 1982).

222. 434 N.E.2d at 609.

223. *In re* Spring, 405 N.E.2d 115 (Mass. 1980).

later that heroic measures should be employed.[224] The medical experts not involved in the baby's care felt otherwise.

Another set of legal responses was generated by the death by starvation of an Indiana infant known as "Baby Doe."[225] According to newspaper reports, the parents of a Down's Syndrome infant decided to withhold consent for an operation to correct a stomach blockage that prevented the baby from digesting food property. Although the extent of the infant's retardation could not be predicted at that early an age, the likelihood of a successful operation was very high. "The Indiana judiciary from the trial court to the state supreme court, agreed that surgery would not be ordered by them over the express, contrary wishes of the parents. . . . Due to the nonintervention, Baby Doe died of starvation."[226]

In response to the state judiciary's deference to the wishes of the parents, a coalition of groups advocating for handicapped children and the right to life for newborns convinced the federal government to promulgate rules under § 504 of the Rehabilitation Act of 1973[227] that would address the problem with what was viewed by many medical authorities as draconian measures that intruded upon the smooth operation of hospitals. A federal court agreed and overturned the regulations citing administrative due process violations such as the failure to demonstrate the need for a full-scaled investigation and inspection of medical records each time a tip was received anonymously. Nevertheless, given the broad swathe of the federal handicapped discrimination statute, it is likely that some kind of regulations were contemplated by the statute's language, although such a conclusion has been questioned legally.[228] Assuming the regulations cover handicapped infants, their effects are limited by court decisions that prohibit overburdensome accommodations to the needs of the handicapped.[229] Based on other reported decisions, there is reason to proceed with extreme caution in sanctioning the withholding of life-sustaining care to disabled infants or children for any reason unless one obtains prior court approval. On the other hand, court approval may not be that difficult to obtain if the infant or child is seriously ill and the courts address only the procedural aspects and not the merits of such cases.

In a second case, "Baby Jane Doe," New York's highest court refused to grant a petition to an interested citizen who sought to compel proper care and treatment for a severely disabled infant born with spina bifida, microcaphaly, and hydrocephalus where the parents were against further medical intervention.[230] The justices found that the petitioner had no personal knowledge about the infant's situation and that the parents had a constitutionally protected interest in making the treatment decision in consultation with their physicians. In a related decision in the same case, a federal court similarly refused to allow the United States Justice Department to review the infant's medical records in order to determine whether there had been a violation of § 504 of the Rehabilitation Act which prohibits discrimination against handicapped persons.[231] The court held that the New York courts had properly settled the matter, and it would not allow the federal government to second-guess the state courts. In dicta, the court asserted that the provisions under § 504 did not apply to this type of situation because there was no discrimination but merely a defensible medical choice, even though without the benefit of medical documentation it was difficult if not impossible for the court to legally assess the propriety of the parents' choice.

The United States Court of Appeals for the Second Circuit subsequently affirmed the decision, but on broader grounds. It expanded the holding with the determination that § 504 does not "apply to treatment decisions involving defective newborn infants." The appeals court viewed as an essential condition of § 504 that the plaintiff be "otherwise qualified" for services and found that such a condition was inapplicable to medical decisions to initiate corrective surgery or administrative actions to initiate litigation by the hospital on the plaintiff's behalf. It stressed the difficulty in differentiating between a decision based on "bona fide medical judgment" and an act of discrimination. Moreover, the majority noted that nothing in the legislative history of the act indicated that the Congress specifically intended § 504 to apply to treatment decisions involving handicapped babies. A dissenting opinion, however, concluded that the majority had completely misunderstood § 504. The dissent seems to hold the better position. While it is true that Congress never specifically considered applying § 504 to handicapped infants, it is also true, and more relevant, that in enacting such a broad statute neither house discussed the necessity of excluding infants from its coverage.[232]

224. Custody of a Minor, 434 N.E.2d 601 (Mass. 1982).

225. Summary and Analysis, 6 MDLR 135-37 (1982). The reports came from newspaper accounts because the court sealed the records.

226. 6 MDLR at 135.

227. American Academy of Pediatrics v. Heckler, 561 F. Supp. 395 (D.D.C. 1983).

228. See discussion *infra* at notes 230-32 and surrounding text, which suggests handicapped infants may not be covered.

229. See Southeastern Community College v. Davis, 442 U.S. 397 (1979).

230. Weber v. Stony Brook Hosp., 52 U.S.L.W. 2267 (N.Y. Ct. App. Oct. 28, 1983).

231. United States v. University Hosp., 575 F. Supp. 607 (E.D.N.Y. 1983).

232. United States v. University Hosp. 729 F.2d 144, 154-56, 161-63 (2d Cir. 1984) (J. Winter dissenting).

In any case, regardless of the applicability of § 504, Congress in the Child Abuse Amendments of 1984 specifically addressed the obligations of physicians and the states in preventing the withholding of treatment from infants born with mental or physical impairments. Two major initiatives were detailed in the legislation. First, only in three exceptional circumstances may a treating physician withhold "medically-indicated treatment":

> "(3) the term 'withholding of medically indicated treatment' means the failure to respond to the infant's life-threatening conditions by providing treatment (including appropriate nutrition, hydration, and medication) which, in the treating physician's or physicians' reasonable medical judgment, will be most likely to be effective in ameliorating or correcting all such conditions, except that the term does not include the failure to provide treatment (other than appropriate nutrition, hydration, or medication) to an infant when, in the treating physician's or physicians' reasonable medical judgment, (A) the infant is chronically and irreversibly comatose; (B) the provision of such treatment would (i) merely prolong dying, (ii) not be effective in ameliorating or correcting all of the infant's life-threatening conditions, or (iii) otherwise be futile in terms of the survival of the infant; or (C) the provision of such treatment would be virtually futile in terms of the survival of the infant and the treatment itself under such circumstances would be inhumane."

Second, each state's child protection services agency must develop a system to handle reports of medical neglect of these infants including legal remedies where the law is violated.[233]

C. Organ Donation

Given the speed with which medical advances are made today, the ethical considerations relating to organ donation take on far greater significance than in the past. When the donor is mentally disabled the potential for abuse of the individual's rights is ever present. To date, the legal system has been faced with this problem only rarely. In two reported decisions, state courts in both Texas and Kentucky authorized the parents of incompetent children to consent to surgery that removed one of the child's kidneys so that it could be implanted into the body of a brother or sister.[234] In each case, the courts discussed the doctrine of substituted judgment in relation to what the incompetent person would have done if he or she had not been disabled. At the same time, they also assessed the broader interests involved in the transfer. The critical factor turned out to be the psychological benefits the child would receive by helping a loved one. The Texas court also listed a number of other factors that were persuasive such as the consent of the parents, no evidence of undue pressure from family members, the brother's need for the kidney, the minimal danger to the ward, and the due process protections of a hearing and the appointment of an attorney.

Despite the careful judicial analysis, it would appear likely that the donation was approved based on a consensus that the sibling without a kidney needed the kidney more than the mentally disabled child. Strictly from the viewpoint of the donor's health, the child's best interest would be served better by retaining the kidney. While the decision may seem reasonable given all the circumstances, the application of the substituted judgment doctrine in other more ambiguous situations may lead to abuses where the mentally disabled child is caught between conflicting loyalties to family members and society. Moreover, as medical technology moves forward both the types and numbers of organ donation disputes will inevitably increase. Thus, it is important for legislatures and in their absence courts to establish guidelines that can be applied to a variety of transplant situations.

D. Psychosurgery

In the previous edition of this book the recommendation was made that before psychosurgery be permitted there be minimal protections of notice, consent, and documentation of the need for surgery; at that time, this edition observed that there was little or no legislative attention to how far mental hospitals might go in administering treatments involving danger to the patient. Since then there has been a strong movement to abolish psychosurgery entirely.[235] Few practitioners today believe that it is medically justified, given the risks and the limited benefits. the National Commission for the Protection of Human Subjects of Biomedical and Behavioral Research recommended that psychosurgery be banned on prisoners, children, and mental patients who are involuntarily institutionalized or adjudicated incompetent.[236]

Case law and state legislation have also placed significant restrictions on the use of psychosurgery. At the fed-

233. Pub. L. No. 98-457, §§ 121, 122, 1984 U.S. Code Cong. & Ad. News (98 Stat.) 1749, 1752-53 (to be codified at 42 U.S.C. § 5101). See also Joint Explanatory Statement of the Committee of Conference, H. Conference Rep. No. 1038, 98th Cong., 2d Sess., *reprinted in* 1984 U.S. Code Cong. & Ad. News 2947, 2948-49, 2969-71 (see 130 Cong. Rec. S9317-29 (daily ed. July 26, 1984) for introduction and discussion of amendments).

234. Little v. Little, 576 S.W.2d 493 (Tex. Civ. App. 1979); Strunk v. Strunk, 445 S.W.2d 145 (Ky. Ct. App. 1969).

235. See ch. 6, Treatment Rights, § VI C, The Right to Refuse Psychosurgery, and ch. 5, Rights of Institutionalized Persons, § XV, The Mentally Disabled as Research Subjects, *supra*.

236. U.S. Dep't of Health, Education, & Welfare, Protection of Human Subjects: Use of Psychosurgery in Practice and Research: Report and Recommendations for Public Comment, 42 Fed. Reg. 26,318, 26,330 (May 23, 1977).

eral level, recipients of federal funding are not absolutely precluded from using this medical procedure because the rules were promulgated but never codified. However, various states have enacted limiting legislation banning the use of psychosurgery on persons under 18,[237] requiring informed consent[238] and requiring that its use be "definitely indicated."[239]

Two legal decisions establish absolute judicial limitations on institutionalized patients. In 1973 a Michigan court concluded that there was no possibility that a confined inmate could make an informed choice about psychosurgery.[240] Three years later an Alabama federal court banned lobotomies, psychosurgery, and any other unusual, hazardous, or intrusive surgical procedures designed to alter or affect a patient's mental condition.[241] Within an institution voluntariness is necessarily compromised and good information may be scarce.

On the other hand, a California court ruled that states had a right to regulate such procedures as long as it was done clearly and the opportunity for psychosurgery was not precluded altogether.[242]

E. Sterilization

Although sterilization is covered in considerable detail in chapter 9, "Family Laws," it is important in this chapter on decision making to note that mainly because of large-scale abusive sterilization programs of the mentally retarded and other institutionalized persons in the past, the procedure is heavily regulated today. In fact, in many jurisdictions it is considerably more difficult in terms of the present legal procedures and standards to arrange for the sterilization of a mentally disabled person than to terminate the life of the same person by discontinuing extraordinary care.[243]

A number of states that have no statutes governing sterilization absolutely preclude the procedure absent the existence of informed consent. Courts in these jurisdictions have ruled that there is no equitable authority to authorize such a drastic intervention without express approval of the legislature.[244] No such legislatively derived authority has been required in denying permission to withhold life-sustaining treatment.

Many jurisdictions that rule there is this type of inherent equitable judicial discretion require the courts to follow rigid and detailed procedural and substantive safeguards, particularly a prior finding of medical necessity.[245] Typically, the petitions are granted only in "the rare and unusual case that sterilization is in the best interests of the retarded person."[246] Some critics maintain that these requirements make approval almost impossible.[247]

In the past, there was legislation that required that certain mentally disabled or institutionalized persons be sterilized. Today's legislation, where it exists, protects mentally disabled persons by requiring procedures to ensure voluntariness or substituted consent mechanisms such as guardianship.

F. Elective Surgery

The need to obtain informed consent for surgery may increase if there is no immediate threat to an individual's health and welfare. Yet, since the medical consequences of elective surgery are by definition not as serious, the procedural restrictions and applicable legislation are less common.

In nonemergency situations the courts are split over the type of substituted consent requirements that should obtain and when they should be applied. Generally, although not always, the courts are hesitant to order elective surgery unless the person is incompetent and the surgery is consistent with what the person would want if competent to decide.

A New Jersey court appointed a special guardian to approve the amputation of an incompetent man's foot, because even though the man's surgery was considered elective his life would soon be in danger if the surgery was not performed.[248] By contrast, a third New York court refused to appoint a guardian to approve amputation where there was a genuine dispute about the operation's medical necessity and the man expressed an unwillingness to go ahead with the surgery.[249] Another New York court approved cosmetic surgery for a mentally retarded adult in order to enhance his opportunity for human development.[250] In the absence of parents to provide consent, the court "must decide what its ward

237. Legislative and Regulatory Developments, 1 MDLR 135, 138 (1976).

238. *Id.* at 275.

239. *Id.*

240. Kaimowitz v. Dep't of Mental Health, No. 73-19434-AW (Cir. Ct. of Wayne County, Mich. July 10, 1973).

241. Wyatt v. Hardin, No. 3195-N, 1 MDLR 55, 56 (MD. Ala. Feb., 1975, *modified* July 1, 1975).

242. Doe v. Younger, No. 4 Civ. 14407, 1 MDLR 119 (Cal. Ct. App., 4th Dist. Apr. 23, 1976).

243. See discussion in this chapter in § V B, Life-threatening Decisions: Adults and Children, *supra*.

244. Hudson v. Hudson, 373 So. 2d 310 (Ala. 1979), Guardianship of Tulley, 146 Cal. Rptr. 266 (1978); *In re* S.C.E., 378 A.2d 144 (Del. Ch. 1977); A.L. v. G.R.H., 325 N.E.2d 501 (Ind. Ct. App. 1975); Holmes v. Powers, 439 S.W.2d 579 (Ky. 1968); *In re* M.K.R., 515 S.W.2d 467 (Mo. 1974) (en banc); Frazier v. Levi, 440 S.W.2d 393 (Tex. Civ. App. 1969).

245. Wentzel v. Montgomery Gen. Hosp., 293 Md. 685 (1982); *In re* C.D.M., 627 P.2d 607 (Alaska 1981), *In re* Hayes, 608 P.2d 635 (Wash. 1980), *In re* Grady, 426 A.2d 467 (N.J. 1981), *In re* Guardianship of Eberhardy, 307 N.W.2d 881 (Wis. 1981).

246. *In re* Hayes, 608 P.2d 635, 640 (Wash. 1980).

247. *Id.* (for concurring opinion, see 4 MDLR 154 (1979)).

248. *In re* Schiller, 372 A.2d 360 (N.J. Super. Ct. Ch. Div. 1977).

249. *In re* Nemser, 273 N.Y.S.2d 624 (1966).

250. *In re* Weberlist, 360 N.Y.S.2d 783 (Sup. Ct., N.Y. County 1974).

would choose, if he were in a position to make a sound judgment."[251] The procedure was approved because the ward's appearance kept him from fulfilling his social and educational potential. He was hydrocephalic and had a cleft palate and webbed fingers. Where a patient's preference against elective hip surgery had been previously stated, a New York court refused to approve a psychiatric hospital's petition to order surgery without proof of the woman's present incompetence to decide for herself.[252]

G. Electroconvulsive Shock Therapy

One of the more perplexing decision making issues is the use of electroconvulsive shock therapy (ECT), which is discussed in detail in chapter 6, "Treatment Rights." Like sterilization, ECT is more tightly regulated than the right to a natural death because ECT has a reputation for frequent abuse. Unlike sterilization, however, ECT can be a life-saving intervention, and its outright denial is potentially more harmful than its use. To deprive mentally disabled persons of the right either to accept what competent professional opinion believes to be the best available alternative treatment in certain specific situations or to refuse what a significant minority believe is nothing more than psychiatric abuse undermines respect for individual decision making. As with the issue of treatment with psychotropic drugs, which is discussed later, the right to accept or refuse treatment inevitably clashes unless the law clearly defines the proper limits of each.

With respect to ECT assiduous attempts have been made to resolve these differences, and despite the rhetoric there is more consensus than there is disagreement. Yet those who hold more extreme views on either side are strident and uncompromising. Juxtaposed are those who insist ECT should be outlawed in all its forms and all its uses[253] and those who view treatment decisions, including ECT, as strictly medical.[254]

Two developments have negated many of the abuses of the past. First, ECT is recommended by doctors only when a limited number of psychiatric conditions are present,[255] and new protocols governing the administration of ECT have substantially eliminated many of the undesirable side effects and the chances of serious injury.[256] As a result, stricter standards for legal liability have been established that reflect improved medical knowledge. Second, all but 13 states and the District of Columbia have legislation that regulates either ECT or some other more generalized psychiatric procedures.[257] Typically the legislation fits into one of two general categories: some kind of right to refuse treatment or a requirement that there be informed consent. Either type of statute may refer to ECT specifically or to treatment generally.

Legislation that abolishes or effectively eliminates all opportunities to use ECT is subject to legal challenge. Recently, a city ban on the procedure in Berkeley was overturned as unconstitutional.[258] A few years ago, a restrictive California statute that both provided a right to refuse ECT and required informed consent was struck down for invasion of privacy, vagueness, and due process deficiencies.[259] Currently, only Colorado and Ohio still have statutes that include both types of provisions, but each statute has broad exceptions,[260] such as situations in which if the patient's life is endangered.[261]

Generally, persons who are not adjudicated incompetent have a right to refuse ECT either by statute or case law. Legal disputes tend to focus on the definition of competency because legal competency is often different from what is viewed as clinically desirable by medical practitioners.

Although a few respected authorities decry any notion of informed consent as an invalid legal concept,[262] most psychiatrists would prefer to see informed consent and the regulation of ECT handled as an internal professional problem without interference from the legislatures or the courts.[263] Yet while the medical profession is protected from many forms of liability, final control remains with legislatures and the judiciary. The perception that ECT is overregulated is supported by comparisons with more serious types of intervention such as termination of life, organ transplants, and life-threatening surgery. The perception that regulation is still necessary is supported by a history of ECT abuses generally and abuses to mentally disabled persons specifically.

251. 360 N.Y.S.2d at 787.

252. Hanes v. Ambrose, 437 N.Y.S.2d 784 (App. Div. 1981).

253. L. Frank, History of Shock Treatment (self-published ed. 1978); J. Friedberg, Shock Treatment Is Not Good for Your Brain (1976). Also in Berkeley, California, voters passed a referendum banning the use of ECT within the city limits for any purpose (Summary and Analysis, 6 MDLR 363, 366 (1981)).

254. See, e.g., Stone, Recent Mental Health Litigation: A Critical Perspective, 134 Am. J. Psychiatry 273 (1977); Tenenbaum, ECT Regulation Reconsidered, 7 MDLR 148-49 (1982).

255. Tenenbaum, *supra* note 254, at 149; Scovern & Kilmann, Status of Electroconvulsive Therapy: Review of the Outcome Literature, 87 Psychological Bull. 260 (1980).

256. 1968 American Psychiatric Association Task Force on Electroconvulsive Therapy 164 [hereinafter cited as A.P.A. Task Force]; Tenenbaum, *supra* note 254, at 148-49; S. Halleck, Law in the Practice of Psychiatry: A Handbook for Clinicans 97 (1980).

257. Tenenbaum, *supra* note 254, at 149-51.

258. Northern California Psychiatric Soc'y v. City of Berkeley, No. 566778-3 (Cal. Super. Ct. Sept. 14, 1983).

259. Aden v. Younger, 57 Cal. App. 3d 662 (1976).

260. Tenenbaum, *supra* note 254, at 149-51.

261. *In re* William M., 3 MDLR 184 (Ohio, Franklin County Ct. of C.P. Probate Div. Mar. 15, 1979).

262. See, e.g., Stone, *supra* note 254; Tenenbaum, *supra* note 254.

263. See A.P.A. Task Force, *supra* note 256.

H. Psychotropic Medication

The forced administration of psychotropic medication to any one inidividual may or may not be as serious an intrusion as ECT (it would depend on the circumstances), but its routine application to mentally and developmentally disabled individuals in institutions throughout the United States has made its use even more controversial.

The clinical revolution in psychiatry is due more than anything else to the development of drugs that can maintain patients in the community and replace other forms of institutional care and treatment. Unfortunately, in too many instances, widespread use has made institutions depend on drugs to keep their programs functioning smoothly, costs down, and patients in control. In addition, there has been the emergence in the medical literature of serious, unexpected side effects—one in particular that has caused substantial permanent damage for a few long-term users is known as tardive dyskenesia.[264]

The legal system has responded to the difficult task of balancing individual, social and professional interests by creating a system of laws that are often most notable for their controversy, ambiguity, and inconsistency. The United States Supreme Court so far has been unwilling to enter the fray, preferring instead to leave responsibility to the lower courts.[265] However, despite the many differences among courts reviewing the right to refuse medication issue, certain legal principles are achieving consensus support. There now exists a qualified constitutional right to refuse psychotropic or antipsychotic medication, except in a legitimate emergency where staff may compel medication. In nonemergencies, nondangerous competent individuals, even involuntary psychiatric hospital patients, usually have an absolute right to refuse treatment. In those instances where a patient's right to refuse can be overridden, significant due process safeguards must be present. At a minimum these protections should include an independent medical review to ensure that professional judgment is being exercised properly and that the patient's point of view is being recognized in the decision-making process. Certain states such as Massachusetts go much further and require a full judicial hearing.

When a patient's competency is questionable, or incompetency in fact has been determined judicially, the element of substituted consent is introduced. The case law suggests that a guardian, hospital staff, or the judiciary may become the final decision maker depending on the jurisdiction. The standards to be used by the decision maker fall into two familiar categories: the best interests of the patient from the perspective of an informed decision maker and what the patient himself would want if he were competent to make the choice. (For another review of the law see chapter 6, "Treatment Rights.")

Generally, if compulsory medication is part of an institution's program of treatment, certain state statutes[266] and court decisions[267] indicate that there are institutional interests that outweigh individual concerns of involuntarily committed residents. Voluntarily admitted persons usually have an absolute right to refuse treatment,[268] but the courts also hold that those who refuse may be asked to leave the institution.[269]

Although a number of courts have established an absolute right of competent patients to refuse psychotropic drugs in nonemergency situations,[270] a majority of the decisions either reject this approach entirely or place limitations on the patient's ability to exercise the right. Certain courts have held that treatment is for the hospital to determine.[271] Others require that an independent determination be made that medical treatment is necessary[272] or that the person's health is deteriorating.[273] A few courts have restricted the application of the right to more powerful drugs,[274] or linked it specifically to the free exercise of religion.[275] One court has allowed the institution staff to determine competency, thus bypassing a formal adjudication entirely.[276]

Two recent decisions involving patients who are legally competent represent the leading substantive standards. In *Rennie v. Klein*,[277] the Third Circuit found that dangerous mentally ill patients who have been involuntarily committed may be given antipsychotic drugs

264. Rosoff, *supra* note 161, at 239-40.

265. Mills v. Rogers, 457 U.S. 291 (1982).

266. See, e.g., Conn. Gen. Stat. Ann. § 17-206d (West 1975 & Supp. 1982) (consent is not required); La. Rev. Stat. Ann. § 28:5211 (West 1975 & Supp. 1983) (consent is not required); and Or. Rev. Stat. (1981) (medication sole responsibility of physician).

267. See, e.g., A.E. & R.R. v. Mitchell, No. C-78-466, 5 MDLR 154 (D. Utah June 16, 1980); Rennie v. Klein, 653 F.2d 836 (3d Cir. 1981); Rogers v. Okin, 634 F.2d 650 (1st Cir. 1980).

268. However, according to a 1977 review of state statutes, only New Jersey provides for a statutory right to refuse treatment for voluntary patients. Practice Manual: Right to Refuse Treatment Under State Statutes, 2 MDLR 240, 241 (1977). See also Stone, The Right of the Psychiatric Patient to Refuse Treatment, 4 J. Psychiatry & L. 515 (1976).

269. See, e.g., Rogers v. Okin, 634 F.2d 650 (1st Cir. 1980).

270. Davis v. Hubbard, 506 F. Supp. 915 (N.D. Ohio 1980); *In re* K.K.B., 609 P.2d 747 (Okla. 1980); Rogers v. Okin, 478 F. Supp. 1342 (D. Mass. 1979), *modified,* 634 F.2d 650 (1st Cir. 1980) (the First Circuit diluted the right substantially).

271. *In re* A.E. & R.R. v. Mitchell, No. C-78-466, 5 MDLR 154 (D. Utah June 16, 1980).

272. Rennie v. Klein, 653 F.2d 836 (3d Cir. 1981).

273. Rogers v. Okin, 634 F.2d 650 (1st Cir. 1980).

274. 634 F.2d 650 (psychotropic medication only).

275. Dyer v. Brooks, No. 93758, 1 MDLR 122 (Or. Cir. Ct., Marion County June 10, 1976).

276. Rennie v. Klein, 653 F.2d 836 (3d Cir. 1981).

277. Rennie v. Klein, 720 F.2d 266 (3d Cir.1983).

whenever professionals conclude it is necessary to prevent the patient from endangering himself or others.

Based on state law, the Massachusetts Supreme Judicial Court held that in the absence of an emergency any person who has not been adjudicated incompetent has a right to refuse antipsychotic medication.[278] The Massachusetts court, however, viewed emergency more broadly than many other jurisdictions. In addition to the traditional definition under the police power which encompasses actions where a patient poses an imminent threat of harm to himself or others, the court recognized that under the state's parens patriae power patients could be forcibly treated "to prevent the 'immediate, substantial, and irreversible deterioration of a serious mental illness'"[279] where even the smallest delay would be intolerable. But, in order to continue treating such an individual the medical staff would be obliged to seek judicial approval.

Regardless of what a state may use as its substantive standard, there is widespread adherence to certain minimal due process safeguards in implementing those standards, ranging from provision of an independent decision maker to a full judicial hearing.[280]

In any due process review it is difficult to accurately evaluate stated institutional concerns such as maintaining order, patient welfare, and financial constraints. There is often a thin line between what is being done for staff convenience and what is actually necessary for the smooth operation of the institution. Barring an absolutist approach to the determination of a substantive standard, these types of factual determinations are crucial. According to a recent Supreme Court decision, the law requires a fact-finder to accept professional judgments as correct unless the challenging party shows that those judgments diverge substantially from accepted standards of practice.[281] It has been argued that the Court was referring to a narrow range of institutional decisions, but the language of the opinion and subsequent lower court interpretations refute this position. For example, the Court of Appeals for the Third Circuit accepted the position that in an institution or hospital setting the judgment of the treating professionals should be presumed valid, but the nine justices disagreed about which factors must be considered, including whether professionals must choose treatment alternatives that satisfy the state's interests in the least intrusive manner possible. Four panel members clearly endorsed the least restrictive means test, four clearly rejected the test, and one judge did not state his position.[282]

Although medication abuses occur in almost every institutional setting, it is important to distinguish residents who are mentally ill from residents who are mentally retarded or otherwise developmentally disabled. Whereas the use of drugs is accepted in psychiatric hospitals as treatment in most instances, their use on developmentally disabled persons usually is not for treatment purposes. Rather, medication is often administered in order to control and sedate mentally retarded residents.[283] The law is now only beginning to recognize liability for professional malpractice in the administration of drugs within an institution. A recent case resulted in a $760,000 award to a mentally retarded resident of an Iowa institution where the unmonitored application of certain drugs led to personal injuries including long-term overmedication.[284]

For mentally disabled individuals in the community the issues surrounding forcible treatment are somewhat different. While persons have an absolute right to refuse medication as long as they are competent and there is no emergency,[285] the state may either institutionalize such persons if their conditions deteriorate or threaten to do so in order to encourage them to accept treatment. In addition, a few courts release individuals from commitment conditionally and retain the right to recommit the resident if they discontinue their medication. At least one state supreme court, however, has refused to allow compulsory outpatient treatment unless the patient meets existing standards for involuntary commitment.[286]

If the mentally disabled person is incompetent, there is no emergency, and informed consent cannot be given directly, a substitute decision maker may consent to the administration of medication. Who is to accept the role as the substitute and what standards are to be used to make the decision about drug treatment still trouble the courts. Sometimes only a duly appointed guardian may provide the necessary consent.[287] In other jurisdictions institution staff may make the decision by themselves[288] or following an informal hearing,[289] the authority may be

278. Rogers v. Commissioner of Dep't of Mental Health, 390 Mass. 489, 458 N.E.2d 308 (1983).

279. 458 N.E.2d at 311.

280. Rennie v. Klein, 720 F.2d 266 (3d Cir. 1983). See also Johnson v. Solomon, 484 F. Supp. 278 (D. Md. 1979); Davis v. Hubbard, 506 F. Supp. 915 (N.D. Ohio 1980); A.E. & R.R. v. Mitchell, No. C-78-466, 5 MDLR 154 (D. Utah June 16, 1980).

281. Youngberg v. Romeo, 457 U.S. 307 (1982).

282. Rennie v. Klein, 720 F.2d 266 (3d Cir. 1983). See also Association for Retarded Citizens of North Dakota v. Olson, 561 F. Supp. 495 (D.N.D. Aug. 31, 1982).

283. Clites v. State, 322 N.W.2d 917 (Iowa Ct. App. 1982).

284. *Id.*

285. Guardianship of Roe, 421 N.E.2d 40 (Mass. 1981).

286. *In re* Cross, 662 P.2d 828 (Wash. 1983).

287. *In re* K.K.B., 609 P.2d 747 (Okla. 1980).

288. *In re* Fussa, No. 66110, 1 MDLR 332 (P. Ct., Hennepin County, Minn. June 4, 1976).

289. Rennie v. Klein, 653 F.2d 836 (3d Cir. 1981); Davis v. Hubbard, 506 F. Supp. 915 (N.D. Ohio 1980).

shared with a treating physician,[290] or the courts may be required to make the final decision.[291] Yet, it should be noted that wherever the legal decision-making authority resides, a facility normally develops its own informal procedures to "encourage" those who "need" medication to take that medication. Community outpatient programs with less control over their clients attempt to establish certain incentives and reminders that will avoid the necessity of rehospitalizing a client.

Obtaining substituted consent for an institutionalized person is essentially the same process as for anyone else. The main difference is that the administrative assessment mechanism is not always used when it should be. Again, the legal standards emphasize either the best interests of the person or the closest approximation of what the person would want if he or she were competent to decide. As has been discussed previously, with certain notable exceptions,[292] most recent decisions concerning substitute consent have adopted some kind of procedure that attempts to view the medical decision from the viewpoint of the patients or residents.[293] The District of Columbia Court of Appeals applied the concept of substituted judgment to a severely mentally ill woman who because of her religious beliefs as a Christian Scientist refused to take medication. Her religious convictions outweighed expert opinion about her medical best interests. Two other United States appeals courts have made similar rulings. The United States Court of Appeals for the First Circuit required "treatment decisions as the individual himself would were he competent to do so" in lieu of consent from the individual or his guardian.[294] The Third Circuit mandated an individualized medical determination and a careful review of the patient's perspective along with the needs of the state.[295]

For mentally disabled persons living in the community the substitute decision maker is normally the guardian. One notable exception, however, is Massachusetts, where the state's highest tribunal ruled that the administration of antipsychotic drugs in a nonemergency situation is not a matter to be decided by a legal guardian. Courts must decide, based on what patients would choose for themselves if they were faced with a choice between compulsory medication or possible subsequent involuntary commitment.[296]

290. Rogers v. Okin, 634 F.2d 650 (1st Cir. 1980).

291. *In re* Boyd, 403 A.2d 744 (D.C. 1979).

292. See *In re* K.K.B., 609 P.2d 747 (Okla. 1980) (informed decision by guardian); Johnson v. Solomon, 484 F. Supp. 278 (D. Md. 1979) (therapeutically required for minors).

293. *In re* Boyd, 403 A.2d 744 (D.C. 1979).

294. Rogers v. Okin, 634 F.2d 650 (1st Cir. 1980).

295. Rennie v. Klein, 653 F.2d 836 (3d Cir. 1981).

296. Guardianship of Roe, 421 N.E.2d 40 (Mass. 1981).

I. Conclusion

The doctrines of informed consent and substituted decision making are neither convenient nor conceptually appealing for many providers of services whose first obligation is to ensure that the patient or client is cared for in the best possible circumstances as perceived by the provider. The creation of judicial standards to make decisions that traditionally have been made by doctors and other professionals is often viewed as an unnecessary intrusion. Inconsistent legal applications of inconsistent legal standards increase this resistance.

In spite of these legitimate concerns, informed consent and substituted decision making are essential to individual autonomy, one of our society's most cherished values. In the context of medical decision making, as in other endeavors, the law is defined in ways that favor the free exercise of idiosyncratic behavior over paternal involvement. As perplexing as the issue of informed consent can be when it involves people whose capacity to comprehend is often limited or fluctuating, much of the rancor about its implementation can be minimized. Doctors and other service professionals need to be as willing to accept individualism from their patients as they do for their own professional interests. Perhaps more importantly, lawyers and judges must provide a legal matrix for rationally evaluating a whole host of treatment decisions that require a delicate balancing of medical need with sometimes competing interests of the patient, the family, and the state—all in the context of different levels of patient competency. Currently, the law for each type of treatment procedure emphasizes disparate judicial and institutional decision making based on the almost independent evolution of legal values and social considerations.

VI. RECORDS AND PERSONAL INFORMATION

As applied, the law governing confidentiality of medical records and information makes mentally disabled persons both the beneficiaries and the victims of their unique status. In order to ensure that mentally disabled persons obtain the care and treatment they need, certain information between patient and therapist is protected as confidential or privileged, even where its dissemination could serve legitimate and benefical purposes. At the same time, patients or recipients of services that are provided outside the therapeutic relationship may be subject to invasions of their privacy by any one of a number of third parties who are able to establish a legal right to the information or simply are able to secure information because there are no practical means available to ensure that confidentiality is maintained. Moreover, somewhat ironically, in legal or administrative proceedings that recipients initiate against various service providers, recipients may be denied access to their own personal files as a result of laws, regulations, or practices ostensibly designed to protect them from harm.

Today, as technology foments rapid changes in the uses of information, the law is unable to keep pace. The problem is magnified with respect to confidentiality and information access for mentally disabled persons since the governing principles of law are still variable and, as a whole, confusing.

The law approaches confidentiality from two vantage points: as a privilege that protects the disclosure of certain types of information[297] and as a right that protects against certain invasions of individual privacy.[298] Neither approach as applied to the private communications between patients and their therapists is found in the common law.[299] In addition, the statutory law on the subject is often construed narrowly to promote free access to relevant information, especially in the courtroom, and certain constitutional principles governing privacy interests are limited by overriding state concerns.

A. Therapist-Patient Privilege

The first legislative effort to protect therapist-patient communications has been traced back to an 1828 New York statute that covered private communications between doctors and their patients.[300] The purpose was to encourage persons in need of medical assistance to seek professional help. Today, at least 49 states have enacted some type of privilege that limits the disclosure of the private communications between therapists and patients.[301] An overwhelming majority of the statutes cover all types of medical practitioners, not just therapists. For this reason, only a handful of states have been persuaded that a specific statute for psychiatrist-patient communications is necessary, while more than 20 states have enacted legislation protecting communications between nonphysician psychologists and their patients. A number of states have covered other types of therapists as well, such as licensed social workers. In addition, therapist-patient communications may be protected by the attorney-client privilege in certain circumstances where the therapist is working with the attorney in a case.[302] (For a review of the therapist-patient privilege from the therapist's point of view, see chapter 10.)

In each of these situations, the privilege is confined to information divulged within an established professional therapy relationship. These privileges have been divided into four broad categories, based on the way the actual scope of the therapeutic relationship is determined.[303] First, there are statutes that define their scope by the kind of conduct engaged in by the therapist. It is the specific activity that is protected—diagnosis, prescription, treatment, or the like—not the professional who carries out the therapy. Second, there are statutes that consider the degree of confidentiality that is involved. These statutes normally include all communications that arise naturally out of a therapeutic relationship and make all such communications confidential. Third, there is legislation that examines the nature of the information sought from the therapist to determine whether the information is uniquely a work product of the therapist. If, for example, the information could have been obtained by a lay person as easily as the professional involved, the material would not be protected. Fourth, there are statutes that cover only those communications that are made to one or more designated types of professionals. The same communications made to other professionals might be excluded by definition. More often than not, however, the statutory bases for the privilege are mixed so that, for example, the type of professional and the kind of information are both specified.

All privileges in a general sense balance the right of individuals to have private communications in relationships that serve a larger public interest against the legitimate needs of society to have access to that information in a court of law. Outside of the courtroom none of the cited privileges apply. Dean Wigmore established four minimal criteria that must be present to justify limiting a court's access to relevant information,[304] all of which apply to the therapeutic relationship: (1) the communications are made in a situation in which both parties have an expectation of confidentiality, (2) confidentiality is essential if the relationship between therapist and patient is to be complete and satisfactory, (3) the therapeutic relationship is one that should be fostered by society, and (4) in many instances, the injury caused by disclosure of therapeutic information would outweigh the benefit gained by improving the judicial result.

297. Saltzburg, Privileges and Professionals: Lawyers and Psychiatrists, 66 Va. L. Rev. 597 (1980).

298. Note, Privacy in Personal Medical Information: A Diagnosis, 33 U. Fla. L. Rev. 394 (1981) [hereinafter cited as Note, Privacy].

299. Saltzberg, *supra* note 297, at 616.

300. *Id.*

301. See ch. 10, Provider-Patient Relations: Confidentiality and Liability, *infra* for specific numbers and citations. Also see Ferster, Statutory Summary of Physician-Patient Privileged Communications Laws, *in* Readings in Law and Psychiatry 239–49 (R.C. Allen, E.Z. Ferster, & J.B. Rubin eds. 1975).

302. Annot., 44 A.L.R.3d 24, 45 (1972).

303. *Id.* at 34–39 § 2(a).

304. 8 J. Wigmore, Evidence § 2380a (J.T. McNaughton rev. ed. 1961).

The fact that the therapist-patient privilege seems to meet Wigmore's criteria has provided no guarantee that it would be applied uniformly. Courts as a rule do not like to grant such privileges and interpret those statutes that do very narrowly. The law is clear that in order to be considered protected there must be specific legislative intent to make such communications confidential.[305] Thus, information that appears by statute or by circumstance to be more public than part of a protected professional relationship will usually be disclosable. For example, the Oregon Supreme Court, narrowly construing a confidentiality statute, allowed a treating physician to testify about his patient's ability to prepare for and function in a trial.[306] Similarly, the Washington Supreme Court permitted a psychiatrist to testify at a commitment hearing where his patient was not told that the communications with the psychiatrist were solely for treatment purposes and that there was a constructive waiver of the privilege in order to protect the patient.[307] However, the Minnesota Supreme Court used common sense to determine that group therapy is not a public event.[308] Even though third parties were involved, all the participants were part of the therapeutic process.

Generally, the privilege is intended for the benefit of the patients or clients since they would be the individuals harmed by the disclosures. Therefore, they should be able to determine whether to assert or waive the privilege. Not suprisingly, because of a number of factors this process is not always as easy as it sounds. To begin with, patients may not want to waive confidentiality with respect to specific portions of the communications between themselves and their therapists. Either all of the information is confidential or none of it is. In Maryland, an appeals court refused to allow a patient to assert the privilege in one lawsuit after he had waived the privilege in a virtually identical lawsuit filed in another state.[309] Another problem occurs where the therapist attempts to assert the privilege on the patient's behalf.[310] Often, where this is allowed, a question arises as to whether the real interests are those of the patient or those of the therapist. Such a conflict is raised when a therapist or a facility is being investigated for fraud or some other crime or regulatory violation. The patient's confidentiality may be at stake, but so is the therapist's career or livelihood.[311]

Where the privilege is present, there are a number of circumstances, beyond the limits of the privilege itself, that create substantial legal exceptions. Arguably some of these exceptions turn the protection of confidentiality into an ever-growing liability by permitting medical information to be used against the mentally disabled person's interests.

The best-known exception is applied by statute or case law whenever patients are involved in litigation and introduce their mental condition as an issue in a case. The "patient-litigant" exception, as it is called, is premised on the view that no one should be allowed to make a claim or assert a defense based on their mental condition and then hide behind the disability in order to deny the other party and the court access to evidence that would refute that claim or defense.[312] This ruling is found frequently in criminal cases where the insanity defense or defense of diminished capacity is raised. The main problem with the exception is the lack of fairness with which it is applied by courts who are predisposed against allowing the privilege in the first place.[313] Sometimes, the circumstances are ambiguous enough that it is uncertain whether the patient's mental condition is an issue. For example, an appeals court in Illinois determined that the patient-litigant exception was present where the patient testified against a defendant in an administrative employment discharge proceeding and the patient was the victim.[314] Other times, the circumstances do not clearly indicate when in the proceedings the patient's mental condition becomes an issue.[315] In terms of litigation strategy, determinations about timing can be important.

A related but broader exception is limited only to criminal proceedings. Certain statutes "make a blanket exception for all criminal proceedings" or whenever an exception would support the interests of justice.[316] However, at least one court has ruled that waiver of the right that is compelled in a criminal trial does not constitute a waiver in a subsequent civil suit concerning the same patient in a related matter.[317] Others allow disclosures of communications by court-appointed psychiatrists since the results are intended for use in the courtroom and are not intended to promote treatment per se.[318] California

305. Shah, Privileged Communications, Confidentiality and Privacy, *in* Readings in Law and Psychiatry, *supra* note 301, at 236.

306. State v. O'Neill, 545 P.2d 97 (Or. 1976.)

307. State Dep't of Social & Health Servs. v. Latta, 601 P.2d 520 (Wash. 1979).

308. Minnesota v. Andring, 342 N.W.2d 128 (Minn. 1983).

309. Hamilton v. Verdow, 414 A.2d 914 (Md. 1980).

310. Smith v. Superior Ct., 118 Cal. App. 3d 136, 173 Cal. Rptr. 145 (1981); State Dep't of Social & Health Servs. v. Latta, 601 P.2d 520 (Wash. 1979).

311. The interests of mental disability professionals in matters of confidentiality are discussed in detail in ch. 10, Provider-Patient Relations: Confidentiality and Liability, *infra*.

312. Annot., 44 A.L.R.3d 24 (1972).

313. Paul, Confidentiality and Patient's Records: Balancing the Interests of Society and the Individual, 7 J. Psychiatry & L. 49 (1979).

314. Laurent v. Brelji, 74 Ill. App. 3d 214, 392 N.E.2d 929 (1979).

315. Annot., 44 A.L.R.3d 24, 50 (1972).

316. *Id.* at 51.

317. Novak v. Rathnam, 119 Ill. App. 3d 847, 457 N.E.2d 158 (1983).

318. 44 A.L.R.3d; see also State v. Taylor, 283 S.E.2d 761 (N.C. 1981).

limits the use of the privilege in criminal cases to psychiatrists and licensed psychologists, excluding other professionals even if they work in the same office as a privileged professional.[319]

Beyond the criminal sphere, disclosure may be compelled where the information is needed to satisfy what is loosely termed the interests of justice. Often this occurs where the competing interest involves the welfare of a child, such as child custody, abuse, or neglect proceedings.[320] Even if disclosure is privileged courts have ordered parents to submit to mental examinations in order to get to the "truth."[321] Other courts have suspended the privilege in civil commitment proceedings[322] where disclosures have been made to a court-appointed psychiatrist in probate proceedings[323] or in situations where the patient is testifying as an adverse witness.[324]

Privileges also may be waived by the patients either expressly or by implication or by their guardians or representatives if they are incompetent. An express waiver by competent persons may be necessary in order to gain access to records or information for themselves or others. Implicit waivers are often found to exist where patients have introduced their mental condition into litigation.[325] The most difficult situation may occur when a third party attempts to assert the privilege on behalf of an incompetent patient. Assuming that the individual wishing to assert the privilege has been legally recognized as the proper party to do so, the primary concern is the possible existence of a conflict of interest.[326] For example, if a guardian decides to involuntarily commit an incompetent ward, the different interests may be difficult to sort out. To a significant extent, the rights of the patient would change depending on the court measured the patient's interests from the patient's point of view or from the viewpoint of a reasonable person. The same kind of conflict in viewpoints could also arise at proceedings to appoint a guardian or to decide whether a person is incompetent. Generally, however, a person may not provide substituted consent where he has interests adverse to those of the patient.

B. Right to Privacy

Early common law did not recognize invasion of privacy as a tort.[327] The theory was developed in a much-discussed law review article by Samuel Warren and Louis Brandeis at the turn of the century.[328] At first the concept was limited to physical intrusions upon persons or property and later was extended to include "reputation, intangible property, and emotional tranquillity."[329] Today, the common or statutory law of almost every state allows a person to bring suit where his confidences are broken by invasions of privacy, but there are always distinct limits. Normally, such a tort requires a "'public disclosure of private facts.'"[330] If the person is not readily identifiable or the disclosure is not made to the general public, there may be no tortious invasion. Recently, at least one state has rejected such a limited approach and has applied the concept to any unwarranted invasion of privacy.[331] A number of jurisdictions narrow the scope of such a tort to the appropriation of a person's name or likeness for commercial purposes without prior consent.[332] Even where such appropriations are proved, the case may fail because the interest is viewed as insignificant or the court believed consent was implied.[333]

Some statutes recognize an action against a therapist or other professional who discloses confidences in violation of "statutorily established standard of conduct."[334] This may be a testimonial privilege that limits disclosure to specific stituations or a statute on professional licensing. In certain situations patients may sue a therapist for breach of a fiduciary relationship or contract. At the same time, a number of jurisdictions through their case law and statutes require therapists to disclose information to an intended victim or the authorities when a patient reveals he or she is going to commit a violent crime. The problems experienced by therapists who are liable for both disclosing and failing to disclose information is discussed in detail in chapter 10, "Provider-Patient Relations: Confidentiality and Liability."

A federal constitutional privacy right is potentially the broadest yet the most unsettled legal theory supporting confidentiality of communications. The typical dispute occurs when the mentally disabled person wishes to keep information secret and the state maintains it has a legitimate reason for using the information. Assuming a privacy interest exists, the court must determine the importance of the individual interest as compared with the

319. People v. Gomez, 185 Cal. Rptr. 155 (Ct. App. 1982).

320. *In re* Parental Rights of PP 648 P.2d 512 (Wyo. 1982); *In re* Doe, 649 P.2d 510 (N.M. Ct. App. 1982); Moosa v. Abdalla, 178 So. 2d, 273 (La. 1965).

321. Barker v. Barker, 440 P.2d 137 (Idaho 1968).

322. *In re* R., 641 P.2d 704 (Wash. 1982).

323. James v. Brown, 629 S.W.2d 781 (Tex. Ct. App. 1981).

324. State v. Civil Servs. Employees Ass'n, Inc., 430 N.Y.S.2d 510 (Erie County Sup. Ct. 1980); Civil Ser. Employees Ass'n v. Director, Manhattan Psychiatric Center, 420 N.Y.S.2d 909 (App. Div. 1979).

325. See H. Weihofen, Mental Disorder as a Criminal Defense 300 (1954).

326. Annot., 44 A.L.R.3d 24 (1972).

327. Note, Privacy, *supra* note 298, at 402.

328. Warren & Brandeis, The Right to Privacy, 4 Harv. L. Rev. 193 (1890).

329. Note, Privacy, *supra* note 298, at 403.

330. *Id.* at 404.

331. Horne v. Patton, 287 So. 2d 824 (Ala. 1973).

332. Note, Privacy, *supra* note 298, at 404; see also Barber v. Time, Inc., 159 S.W.2d 291 (Mo. 1942); Fla. Stat. § 540.08(1) (1979).

333. Delan v. Delan, 458 N.Y.S.2d 608 (App. Div. 1983).

334. Note, Privacy, *supra* note 298, at 406.

asserted state interest. A right to privacy of medical and social service data and documents is most frequently found under the Fourth Amendment's expectation of privacy. Arguably there are also protected interests under the due process clause of the Fifth and Fourteenth Amendments' protections of life, liberty, and property as well as under what has become known as the penumbral guarantees of privacy of the First, Third, Fourth, Fifth, and Ninth Amendments articulated in *Griswold v. Connecticut*.[335] A few courts have found fundamental privacy rights at issue when mental health records are revealed.[336] In order to justify their disclosure the state must demonstrate a compelling interest and use the least intrusive method available to review the records.[337]

Similar privacy concerns are protected in several state constitutions. Florida, California, and Alaska are among those that offer such protections.[338]

C. Access to Records or Information by Third Parties

Despite the existence of a variety of privacy and confidentiality protections and provisions, it still is possible for third parties to gain access to information about a person's mental condition. As has been discussed, courts and parties to litigation are able to puncture the privileges in a variety of ways. The effect is minimized somewhat because most courts are careful to restrict the use of such information so that it will be admissible only when it is relevant and necessary[339] and will be shown only to those who really need to see it. In addition, a number of jurisdictions provide for inspection only by court order,[340] and many of those states require the inspection to be made in the judge's chambers.[341]

Outside the courtroom, mentally disabled persons should be concerned about disclosures. Unauthorized disclosures to third parties occur because it is unlikely that patients or clients will ever discover the breaches. Also, as the need for records becomes more widespread, as technologies keep changing, and as the need for personal information becomes more valuable, abuses are harder to control.[342] Moreover, most disclosures are not even illegal, because the law covers only certain situations. Particularly widespread are uses of information by insurance firms and government agencies that provide health benefits or by agencies that seek to regulate dangerous behavior by controlling driving, gun ownership, drug abuse, child abuse, and violent crime.

Both private insurers, such as Blue Cross–Blue Shield or health maintenance organizations, and governmental insurance programs, such as Medicare, Medicaid, or CHAMPUS, have valid reasons for wanting to have access to mental health records. The purpose may be to conduct an audit, program evaluation, or a fiscal review or to prevent fraud.[343] The countervailing concerns are how to control that access so that only the information necessary to achieve the stated purpose is used, only a limited number of people view the information, and the patient or client has an opportunity to challenge the disclosure of information and correct misinformation. In the past few years, there have been legal and legislative efforts to remedy these problems,[344] although the primary concern has been with the inviolability of the "traditional" therapist-patient relationship rather than with the actual condifentiality interests of the patients or clients per se.

Some argue psychiatric information should not be used to facilitate social control. While there are legitimate reasons for governmental agencies to want to identify incompetent drivers, irresponsible gun owners, drug and child abusers, and violent criminals, there are other significant interests at stake: the privacy of the individual, the social good of encouraging mentally disabled persons to seek out the treatment they need, and the conceivable threat to society if governmental institutions were to use psychiatry to create a police state.

D. Access by the Patient/Client

Until recently, mentally disabled patients or clients frequently were left unprotected from invasions of their privacy and breaches of their confidences. Ironically the same individuals were unable to obtain their records for their own use. Many therapists and other managers of confidential information traditionally have been unwilling to provide patients with access in order to protect the patients or third parties who provided the information from harm or liability.[345] The best interests of the pa-

335. 381 U.S. 479 (1965).

336. Hawaii Psychiatric Soc'y v. Ariyoshi, No. CV79-0113, 7 MDLR 229 (D. Hawaii Dec. 27, 1982); Whalen v. Roe, 429 U.S. 589 (1977); Merriken v. Cressman, 364 F. Supp. 913 (E.D. Pa. 1973); *In re* B., 394 A.2d 419 (Pa. 1978) (only two justices supported this particular theory).

337. Hawaii Psychiatric Soc'y v. Ariyoshi, No. CV79-0113, 7 MDLR 229 (D. Hawaii Dec. 27, 1982).

338. Note, Privacy, *supra* note 298, at 421.

339. Bell v. State, 385 So. 2d 78 (Ala. Crim. App. 1980); People v. Phipps, 79 Ill. App. 3d 532, 398 N.E.2d 650 (1979); State v. Tsavaris, 382 So. 2d 56 (Fla. Dist. Ct. App. 1980).

340. Doe v. Beal, No. 76-1396, 2 MDLR 387 (E.D. Pa. Dec. 6, 1977); Hess v. Hess, No. 73-7139, 2 MDLR 26 (Cir. Ct., Winnebago County, Ill. Feb. 4, 1977).

341. Civil Serv. Employees Ass'n, Inc. v. Soper, 431 N.Y.S.2d 909 (Sup. Ct. 1980); Laurent v. Brelji, 74 Ill. App. 3d 214, 392 N.E.2d 929 (1979).

342. See Beigler, Privacy and Confidentiality, *in* Law and Ethics in the Practice of Psychiatry (C.K. Hofling ed. 1981).

343. Paul, *supra* note 313, at 50.

344. See Beigler, *supra* note 342; Paul, *supra* note 313; American Psychiatric Association, Official Action: Model Law on Confidentiality of Health and Social Service Records, 136 Am. J. Psychiatry 137 (1979) [hereinafter cited as A.P.A. Model Law on Confidentiality]; District of Columbia Mental Health Information Act of 1978, 25 D.C. Reg. 5055 (1978).

345. See Beigler, *supra* note 342.

tient, as viewed by the patient, may come in conflict with the view of the patient's best interests held by the therapist, who would be influenced by concerns about malpractice implications of access, control of patients, and increased competition for the patient's dollar.

Patients, in addition, are increasingly concerned about personal interests that may be compromised by faulty records and records containing information that may stigmatize or subject them to discrimination. In response to these concerns the law has changed and continues to change.

On the federal level, the Buckley Amendment permits students and their parents or guardians to view student records.[346] If the record contains potentially harmful medical information, a professional of the student's choice reviews and interprets the information for the student. A similar approach is set out by the American Psychiatric Association, which recommends that potentially harmful information be submitted to a "clinical mediator" who will decide what should be done with the information.[347] If the patient is dissatisfied with the decision, he may ask a court to review the material in chambers. Legislation in a number of states provides patients with access by allowing them to waive confidentiality entirely or by providing a system for them or a representative to review the records.[348]

The results of litigation have been somewhat mixed. The federal courts, for example, have denied access to a former patient who wanted to use her records in order to document her experiences in a book[349] because that purpose was considered illegitimate. Similarly, a court in North Carolina ruled that prison inmates had no common law right to inspect their own medical records.[350]

However, purposes justifying access have been recognized as appropriate by the courts. The United States Court of Appeals for the Fifth Circuit decided that the Social Security Administration erred by refusing to send a claimant her medical and psychological records so that she could use them to prove she was eligible for benefits.[351] A federal court granted a prisoner access to conflicting psychiatric reports concerning his competency to stand trial.[352] In Florida, a patient was permitted access to medical information where the hospital failed to show that a disclosure would harm the patient.[353] A New York court decided that a patient's psychiatric records had to be revealed to a third party where the patient gave his permission and the records were relevant to pending litigation.[354] Several courts have ruled that patient records must be opened to lawyers or advocacy agencies representing the general interests of mentally disabled persons in a particular facility.[355]

Closely related to the issue of access is expungement of records by former patients where they have been institutionalized improperly or have been discharged as recovered. Normally, if this is done it is done by statutory interpretation. In Pennsylvania, a patient's prior commitment to a mental hospital was declared unconstitutional, but he was unable to expunge the records because the court concluded that there was a legitimate state purpose in retaining the records for possible future treatment.[356] A New York court refused to expunge records in similar circumstances where the legislature provided instead for their sealment.[357] Subsequent Pennsylvania cases have held that an illegal commitment does provide the necessary grounds for expungement in order to protect the patient's reputation.[358] Similarly, two New Jersey decisions found that a statute that provides for expungement of records of recovered institutional patients applied to persons discharged as improved[359] and to discharged persons who still were liable to the state for the cost of their care.[360]

VII. IMMIGRATION TO THE UNITED STATES

Perhaps no area of American law discriminates against a subgroup of mentally disabled persons more than the alien and immigration statute set out in the McCarran-Walter Act of 1952.[361] As amended, this legislation governs admission into and deportation from the United States. According to its mandates, virtually every mentally ill or developmentally disabled alien is affected.

Specifically, the act makes the following classes of aliens ineligible to receive visas and subjects for subsequent deportation if admitted mistakenly: aliens who are mentally retarded, insane, or afflicted with a psychopathic personality, a sexual deviation, or a mental

346. Family Educational Rights and Privacy Act of 1974, Pub. L. No. 93-380, § 513(a), 88 Stat. 571 (1974) (codified as amended at 20 U.S.C. § 1232g (1982)).

347. A.P.A. Model Law on Confidentiality, *supra* note 344.

348. Paul, *supra* note 313.

349. Gotkin v. Miller, 379 F. Supp. 859 (E.D.N.Y. 1974), *aff'd*, 514 F.2d 125 (2d Cir. 1975).

350. Baugh v. Woodard, 287 S.E.2d 412 (N.C. Ct. App. 1982).

351. Thorton v. Schweiker, 663 F.2d 1312 (5th Cir. 1981).

352. United States v. Dannon, 481 F. Supp. 152 (W.D. Okla. 1979).

353. Sullivan v. Florida, 352 So. 2d 1212 (Fla. Dist. Ct. App. 1977).

354. Cynthia B. v. New Rochelle Hosp. Medical Center, 50 U.S.L.W. 2683 (N.Y. App. Div. May 3, 1982).

355. E.g., *In re* Residents of Los Lunas Hosp. & Training School, No. 111-Misc., 2 MDLR 710 (N.M. Dist. Ct., Valencia County Feb. 13, 1978).

356. Souder v. Watson, Civ. Act. No. 74-279, 2 MDLR 388 (M.D. Pa. Dec. 20, 1977).

357. Wade v. Department of Mental Hygiene, 418 N.Y.S.2d 154 (App. Div. 1979).

358. Wolfe v. Beal, 384 A.2d 1187 (Pa. 1978).

359. *In re* Expungement of Commitment Records of D.G., No. 2X-77, 3 MDLR 18 (Essex County Juv. & Dom. Rel. Ct. Aug. 1, 1977).

360. *In re* Expungement of Commitment Records of H., No. 1X-77, 2 MDLR 28 (Juv. & Dom. Rel. Ct., Essex County, N.J. Mar. 8, 1977).

361. Immigration and Nationality Act & Pub. L. No. 414, ch. 477, § 241, 66 Stat. 163, 251 (1952).

defect; narcotic drug addicts or chronic alcoholics; and aliens who have had one or more attacks of insanity or have a physical defect, disease, or disability that may affect the ability of the person to earn a living.[362] In addition, immigrants may be deported if they were excludable at the time they entered the country[363] or if within five years of their entry they either become public charges or are institutionalized and cannot show that their mental or physical disabilities did not predate their entry.

The initial decision to deny a mentally disabled alien a visa is based solely on the certification of a medical officer, which may be appealed to a special board of medical officers.[364] At the board certification proceeding, the alien may call at least one expert medical witness, but the burden of proof is on the alien to show that he or she is eligible for a visa.[365] Appeal from the board's decision is available only for those certified as physically ineligible.[366] Mentally ineligible individuals have no further recourse.

Before a visiting alien may be deported there must be a hearing, and while the defendant may obtain an attorney there is no requirement that one be provided.[367]

Although there have been few decisions interpreting the immigration and deportation laws as they are applied to mentally disabled persons, it is clear that courts do not side with commentators who believe significant aspects of the procedures are unconstitutional.[368] The statute and the case law suggest that there are few effective judicial deterrents to arbitrary or discriminatory actions against handicapped aliens.

The United States Supreme Court recognized that Congress can exclude all classes of undesirables from this country[369] and can make rules that deny admission to individuals who possess characteristics deemed by the legislators to be undesirable.[370] This was reinforced by the United States Court of Appeals for the Second Circuit, which concluded that Congress has broad discretion to establish administrative procedures for determining entry and deportation.[371]

The seminal Supreme Court case in this area held that as long as the immigration regulations focused on the characteristics of aliens at the time they were about to enter the United States and not subsequent conduct, the void for vagueness doctrine was inapplicable to such regulations.[372] Thus, a homosexual who had been living in this country could be deported because of his prior homosexual behavior. In addition, the Court determined that in establishing the category of persons with psychopathic personality Congress was not using a clinically accurate term and specifically intended to include homosexuals and sexual deviates.

In recent years, the immigration laws have gained notoriety in the way they have been applied to homosexuals[373] and to Cuban refugees who unexpectedly fled en masse to southern Florida.[374] In both instances, the provisions regarding mentally disabled persons were used to exclude or to attempt to exclude them. In the case of the Cubans, many of the refugees were interned for indefinite periods of time as they waited for deportation hearings or were caught between being deported and having no homeland to which they could return.[375] Even after five years many remain interned.

Two federal circuit courts of appeal have reaffirmed that mentally disabled aliens are subject to the exclusionary provisions of the immigration and naturalization laws if the aliens are medically certified as unfit due to psychopathic personality or sexual deviation.[376] However, the appellate courts disagreed that whether homosexual aliens could be similarly excluded without medical certificates.[377] Since 1979 the surgeon general has removed homosexuality from the list of certifiable medical conditions; thus, if a medical certificate is required there would be no means of applying the immigration or deportation laws consistent with due process.

The threat of deportation, however, is still placed on every alien who comes into the United States and subsequently requires institutionalization or community-

362. *Id.* (current version codified at 8 U.S.C. § 1182(a) (1982)).

363. *Id.* at 8 U.S.C. § 1251(a)(1); E. Lowenstein, The Alien and the Immigration Law: A Study of 1,446 Cases Arising Under the Immigration and Nationalization Laws of the United States (1972).

364. F.L. Auerbach, Immigration Laws of the United States 202–3 (1955).

365. *Id.* at 83.

366. *Id.* at 202–3.

367. Mentally Disabled Cuban Refugees: The U.S. Moves for Deportation, 4 MDLR 273 (1980) [hereinafter cited as Mentally Disabled Cuban Refugees].

368. Notes and Comments, Limitations on Congressional Power to Deport Resident Aliens Excludable as Psychopaths at Time of Entry (*United States ex rel. Leon v. Murff,* 2d Cir., 1957), 68 Yale L.J. 931 (1959); The Immigration and Nationality Act and the Exclusion of Homosexuals: *Boutilier v. INS* Revisited, 2 Cardozo L. Rev. 359 (1981) [hereinafter cited as The Immigration and Nationality Act and the Exclusion of Homosexuals].

369. Rosenberg v. Fleuti, 374 U.S. 449 (1963).

370. Boutilier v. Immigration & Naturalization Serv., 387 U.S. 118 (1967).

371. United States *ex rel.* Wulf v. Esperdy, 277 F.2d 537 (2d Cir. 1960).

372. Boutilier v. Immigration & Naturalization Serv., 387 U.S. 118 (1967).

373. The Immigration and Nationality Act and the Exclusion of Homosexuals, *supra* note 368.

374. Mentally Disabled Cuban Refugees, *supra* note 367.

375. Art Harris, Wash. Post, Aug. 17, 1981, at A 1 b; Peter McGrath, Newsweek, Feb. 1, 1982, at 28.

376. Hill v. Immigration & Naturalization Serv., 52 U.S.L.W. 2165 (9th Cir. Sept. 7, 1983); *In re* Petition of Longstaff, No. 82-1218, 7 MDLR 458 (5th Cir. Sept. 28, 1983).

377. Hill v. Immigration and Naturalization Serv., 52 U.S.L.W. 2165 (9th Cir. Sept. 7, 1983) (medical certificate was necessary); *In re* Petition of Longstaff, No. 82-1218, 7 MDLR 458, (5th Cir. Sept. 28, 1983) (medical certificate was unnecessary).

based services to treat a mental disability.[378] As a result, aliens with mental illness or a developmental disability may be reluctant to seek out treatment when it is needed, and if they do request services they may face community opposition that could eventually lead to retaliatory deportation. In Pennsylvania, one county attempted unsuccessfully to deny outpatient habilitative services to a mentally retarded adult "solely due to her status as an alien."[379] Although a federal court decided that such a denial was a violation of the equal protection laws, there would be little to stop the plaintiff from being deported since her mental retardation by definition preceded her immigration.

VIII. SPECIAL BENEFITS

While it has been shown that there are numerous ways in which mentally disabled persons may be subjected to harmful discrimination in the exercise of their personal and property rights, there are also a number of special benefits that society bestows on mentally disabled persons as a result of their condition. Together, the liabilities and the benefits make up a sociolegal structure in which this group of American residents must function on a day-to-day basis. The effects of this structure may be measured on two levels: how the special benefits and the harmful discriminatory treatment affects mentally disabled persons and how the results of those actions affect society as a whole. In this section the focus is an overview of the legal and legislative developments that provide assistance to mentally disabled persons and, it is hoped, help to maximize their potential for normal, independent living.

Many of the federal and state programs for mentally disabled persons are discussed in chapter 11, "Rights and Entitlements in the Community." They include programs for income assistance, disability payments, social security retirement, education, medical care, workers' compensation, housing, and employment. For the most part, these are not comprehensive programs in the sense that everybody in need is served and everyone served is left without major needs. Instead, the programs tend to provide mere subsistence for many, more than subsistence for some, and far less than subsistence for others. Oftentimes, political choices that favor certain subgroups over others as well as the inherent difficulty in distributing any resource fairly account for these differentials in coverage. Without those resources, however, many mentally disabled persons would not live even at a bare subsistence level. Such is the problem that threatens numerous mentally disabled who recently were cut off from or unable to qualify for social security benefits because of shifting eligibility standards.[380]

Private insurance is also discussed in the chapter on community entitlements. While mental disabilities are not given the same social priority as many physical ills, there are numerous ways of obtaining insurance that will pay for some if not all the costs of care and treatment for mental disabilities. Moreover, there are a number of mechanisms that parents, relatives, and the mentally disabled persons themselves may implement that can support the needs of mentally disabled persons. Estate planning, tax shelters, and insurance mechanisms can all be used to obtain desired results immediately or sometime in the future.

Several benefits, however, will not be covered in other chapters: veterans' benefits, tax incentives, and avoidance of legal obligations and liability. In each instance, the legislative or legal preference identifies mentally disabled persons as the recipients of some advantage or opportunity that the rest of society does not normally receive.

A. Veterans' Benefits

Ever since post-traumatic stress disorder (PTSD) has been recognized as a mental illness and, in some instances, even a valid defense in criminal actions,[381] particularly for veterans of the Vietnam War, the support for mental disability benefits for veterans has increased in strength. The Reagan administration pushed hard for additional benefits including higher disability payments and reimbursement for drugs and medicines.[382]

Mental disorders have long been accepted, going back to both world wars and the Korean War, as justifiable reasons for awarding veterans' disability payments.[383] In each war that the United States has fought in this century, special programs were established to ameliorate psychiatric conditions that resulted from combat. Ironically, none has been more successful than the program established during the Vietnam War, which relied on "a limited tour of duty, frequent 'rest and relaxation,' and . . . modern military psychiatry."[384] Unfortunately, because of stigma and widespread disenchantment associated with the war, many veterans returned to

378. Deportation is legal if the government can establish that the mental condition preceded the person's entry into this country.

379. Wong v. Bucks County, Pennsylvania, No. 81-1331, 6 MDLR 89 (E.D. Pa. Feb. 8, 1982).

380. See ch. 9, Family Laws, *infra*.

381. Note, Post-Traumatic Stress Disorder—Opening Pandora's Box? 17 New Eng. L. Rev. 91, 91 (1981) [hereinafter cited as Note, Post-Traumatic Stress Disorder]; see American Psychiatric Association, Diagnostic and Statistical Manual of Mental Disorders (DSM III,) 236 (3d ed. 1980) See also discussion in ch. 12, Mental Disability and the Criminal Law, § III C 7, New Concepts to Excuse from Criminal Responsibility, *infra*.

382. No End of Plans to Boost Veterans' Benefits, U.S. News & World Rep., Mar. 1, 1982, at 39.

383. Note, Post-Traumatic Stress Disorder, *supra* note 381, at 94–97.

384. *Id.* at 99–100.

face unusually harsh social and personal pressures that helped to trigger mental disorders years later.

These new developments complicate an already difficult disability claims system under the Veterans Administration. In the previous editions of this book, it was noted that disbursement of funds was often linked through state statutes to a showing that the potential recipient was incompetent. This meant that veterans were automatically deprived of many rights if they wanted to receive benefits, including the appointment of guardians to handle their estates. Today, most laws define eligibility in terms of the existence of a mental disorder, but with the recognition of delayed reactions to wartime they stress that the timing of the onset of the disability is crucial to the awarding of benefits. Was the disorder brought on by the war or by other intervening factors? Acceptance of post-traumatic stress disorder or post-Vietnam syndrome has ameliorated the problem to a certain extent, but disagreements continue to occur over eligibility. Not infrequently, veterans in need have not received proper assistance. The Veterans' Health Care Amendments of 1979 partially addressed this need by entitling all Vietnam-era veterans to a general mental and psychological assessment to determine if they required counseling in order to readjust to civilian life.[385] Those that did, qualified for outpatient services at Veterans Administration facilities. A year later, Congress increased the availability of rehabilitation services to veterans who suffered service-connected disability that was incurred or aggravated after September 16, 1940.[386] The emphasis in this legislation is living independently in the community. In addition, a majority of states have tax exemptions for mentally disabled veterans on various items of property, most significantly their homes.[387] A total exemption or exemptions of $2,000, $5,000, or $10,000 are not uncommon.

In measurable ways mentally disabled veterans are receiving benefits that they would not receive if they were not mentally disabled, but usually at the cost of having been psychologically scarred by the experience of serving in the armed forces. Thus, veterans' "benefits" of this kind are more properly viewed as just compensation for injuries sustained in military service for one's country.

B. Payment of Taxes

Veterans are not the only mentally disabled individuals who receive tax breaks or incentives. Similar tax programs are commonly available through state and federal government. Whereas veterans receive generous preferences with respect to property taxes, all mentally disabled persons may receive a variable assortment of other deductions. Fewer than half the states even offer nonveterans' property tax deductions, and many of those that do offer less beneficial arrangements.[388] A small number of statutes are strictly applied to the physically disabled.

With respect to income tax payments, however, about half of the states provide preferences for mentally disabled persons and normally such preferences are available to all according to the severity of their disability.[389] Some of the incentives do not go to the disabled person directly but are provided to the people who care for that person. A substantial number of the statutes are aimed at promoting either housing or care for the disabled person in the home. In addition, there are state tax statutes that give percentage reductions on federal assistance payments. Recently, a number of pieces of legislation have been filed in state legislatures that are intended to promote independent living.[390] Whether these good intentions will be realized or not is uncertain.

The most important tax advantages are contained in the federal Internal Revenue Service regulations. since federal tax savings are substantially more than state taxes in most instances. A number of the deductions or credits are ones offered to everyone but affect mentally disabled persons or their custodians to a greater extent because their expenses are higher. The $1,800 maximum tax credit available to parents for child and dependent care while they are working, medical expense deductions for a dependent living at home, or dependent exemptions for students living in school or in an institution are examples of such tax advantages. Other tax preferences are aimed directly at the mentally disabled person or the custodian and are not offered to the nondisabled public. These include: deductions for expenses of a person living in a group home or other community setting, costs for individualized training and transportation related to that training, $1,500 for adopting a special needs child, medical expenses for attending a sheltered workshop, institution, or special program, transportation for visiting one's child in a residential program, and income from supplemental security income. In addition, all taxpayers may take a deduction for charitable contributions they make to mentally disabled persons or the programs serving disabled per-

385. Pub. L. No. 96-22, 93 Stat. 47 (1979). (codified as amended at 38 U.S.C. § 1501 (1982)).

386. Veterans' Rehabilitation and Education Amendments of 1980, Pub. L. No. 96-466, 94 Stat. 2171, 2173 (1980) (codified as amended at 38 U.S.C. § 150 (1982)).

387. Commerce Clearing House, State Tax Guide (1979).

388. *Id.*

389. *Id.*

390. See Legislative Filings in Brief in all issues of MDLR from 1970 on.

sons and for the value of services contributed to charitable organizations on a volunteer basis.[391]

A number of states exempt mentally disabled and/or incompetent persons from paying poll taxes, but this is more of a stigma than a privilege since the amount is relatively insignificant and the exemption is based on the premise that these individuals should not have to pay if they are to be denied their franchise.

As was noted in the previous edition, certain jurisdictions extend the period for redeeming property that will be sold for unpaid taxes if the person is suffering from a mental disability at the time of the sale. This is done to protect incompetent persons who have no guardian but do have assets to pay their taxes and fail to make payments because they lack the necessary understanding of what is happening to them. It also protects mentally disabled persons with an illness that prevents them from earning the income necessary to pay their taxes. In fact, redemption proceedings may be tolled without a statute because of a 1956 Supreme Court decision, *Covey v. Town of Somers*,[392] which on constitutional due process grounds invalidated a redemption sale where the owner "was wholly unable to understand the nature of the proceedings against her property . . . and . . . the town authorities knew her to be an unprotected incompetent."[393] Moreover, a 1966 West Virginia statute goes one step further by tolling the redemption for one year automatically after the removal of the disability but in no event for longer than twenty years.[394] This is based on the rationale for invalidating lawsuits against mentally disabled persons discussed below.

C. Legal Actions

As discussed previously, the mentally disabled person's involvement in the court system may produce instances of harmful discrimination or benign protection.[395] In those situations in which the incapacity can be used as a sword or shield for the mentally disabled person who is participating in the judicial system, it can be said that the person is receiving a special benefit or consideration that others do not receive. This may occur where someone attempts to sue a mentally disabled person or where mentally disabled persons attempt to negate an unfavorable financial transaction or contract by tolling the statute of limitations and asserting their incapacity as an affirmative claim.

In eight jurisdictions there is no provision that allows a legally incompetent person to be sued.[396] Where it is allowed, suit must be filed against the guardian or representative.[397] Persons who are incompetent but who have never been adjudicated incompetent or whose competency is questionable must have a guardian ad litem in most jurisdictions.[398] Another major obstacle to a suit against a mentally disabled person is service-of-process requirements without which the court has no jurisdiction.[399] Most states make some special arrangements that require service upon the guardian or a person close to the incompetent person. No state denies the opportunity for proper service entirely.

Normally, states have provisions that toll the governing statute of limitations,[400] but the lengths of time are different depending on the type of suit that is contemplated. More than one-half the states will not allow a court to grant a default judgment against an unrepresented incompetent person.

The justifications for each of these statutes is the unfairness of taking legal action against a person who is unable to comprehend what is going on and is not represented by someone who does. This of course makes sense, but only if such provisions are not abused. A skillful attorney can use these provisions on behalf of a mentally disabled client to get something more than a reasonable delay such as a complete dismissal of a judgment. Moreover, a plaintiff may have a legitimate grievance that cannot be carried through because of the legal complications involved in initiating a suit against a mentally disabled person.

A mental disability can also be used as a sword for the incapacitated person to invalidate any number of otherwise legal transactions or as a defense in certain lawsuits. Usually, such an action is taken in order to prevent a miscarriage of justice against a person who was incapacitated. Sometimes, the law becomes an avenue to assert one's interests over the interests of another who is not mentally disabled. Whether it is a contract, conveyance, or will that is involved, the law is complicated enough that the outcome may often depend more on the comparative knowledge of the attorneys than on the rightfulness of the claim. The intricacies of the law with respect to these financial transactions are covered at the beginning of this chapter.

391. 1983 Income Tax Guide, Focus, Jan. 1983, at 5-8.
392. 351 U.S. 141 (1956).
393. *Id.* at 147.
394. W. Va. Code Annot. § 11A-4-34 (1966).
395. See in this chapter § II, Participation in the Legal System, *supra.*
396. See table 8.1.
397. 29 Am. Jur. Insane and Other Incompetent Persons § 117 (1960).
398. See ch. 7, Incompetency, Guardianship, and Restoration, § IX, Special Guardianship or Related Situations, *supra.*
399. See table 8.1.
400. *Id.*

TABLE 8.1 PERSONAL AND PROPERTY RIGHTS OF MENTALLY DISABLED PERSONS

	CONTRACTS			CAPACITY TO MAKE A WILL (Must Be of "Sound Mind")	CIVIL SUITS		EFFECT OF MENTAL DISABILITY ON PROCEDURAL RIGHTS					
							Service of Process		No Default Against Unrepresented Incompetent	Extension of Time Limitation on Actions		
STATE	Persons with No Power to Contract (1)	Validity of Contracts (2)	Liability for Necessaries (3)	(4)	Capacity to Sue and Be Sued (5)	Appointment of Guardian Ad Litem (6)	Incompetents (7)	Institutionalized Patients (8)	(9)	Personal Actions (10)	Real Property Actions (11)	Other (12)
ALA. Code (1975 & Supp. 1982) R. Civ. P.		contracts of insane void 8-1-170 exception for real property actions 8-1-171-72	guardian 8-1-170 6-7-102		representative may sue or defend for incompetent, or may sue by next friend rule 17(c) mother or wife of person confined in mental institution may sue or defend in his name 6-7-1	mandatory; incompetents rule 17(c),(d)	service on incompetent & guardian; if no guardian then on person w/whom incompetent lives rule 4(c)	service on superintendent if no guardian rule 4(c)	rule 55(b)(2)	insane persons: 3 yrs. after termination of disability but limitation may not exceed 20 yrs. 6-2-8	insane persons: 3 yrs. after termination of disability but limitation may not exceed 20 yrs. 6-2-8	insane persons: 3 yrs. after termination of disability but limitation may not exceed 20 yrs. 6-2-8
ALAS. Stat. (1972 & Supp. 1982)				13.11.150						incompetent by reason of mental illness: time of disability is not part of time limitation, however limitation shall not be extended more than 2 yrs. 09.10.140	incompetent by reason of mental illness: time of disability is not part of time limitation, however limitation shall not be extended more than 2 yrs. 09.10.140	incompetent by reason of mental illness: time of disability is not part of time limitation, however limitation shall not be extended more than 2 yrs. 09.10.140
ARIZ. Rev. Stat. Ann. (1975 & Supp. 1983) R. Civ. P.				14-2501	representative of incompetent may sue or defend on incompetent's behalf rule 17(g)	mandatory for incompetent not represented in action rule 17(g)	& persons adjudicated insane—on person & guardian; if no guardian, then on person & other person ct. designates rule 4(d)(4)		rule 55(b)		unsound mind: time of limitation after removal of disability 12-528	other actions: time of limitation after removal of disability 12-502 action against state: insane or incompetent, 2 yrs. after disability ceases 12-822
ARK. Stat. Ann. (1971 & Supp. 1982) R. Civ. P.		contracts entered into prior to incompetency are enforcible 57-628		60-401	guardian must sue or defend on behalf of incompetent; if no guardian, incompetent may sue by next friend or guardian ad litem rule 17(b) guardian of estate must sue or defend all actions to charge or benefit estate 57-627	rule 17(b)	persons adjudged to be of unsound mind—service on guardian; if no guardian, service on spouse or person caring for or living w/incompetent rule 4(d)(3)	service on guardian & superintendent rule 4(d)(3)	no judgment against rule 17(b)		non compos mentis: 3 yrs. after coming of sound mind 37-101	insane: 3 yrs. after removal of disability 37-226
CAL. Civ. Code 38–40 Civ. Proc. Code 328, 352, 272, 416.70 Prob. Code 20 (West)	persons of unsound mind after adjudication of incapacity 40 persons entirely w/o understanding 38	contract subject to recession if 1 party of unsound mind, but not entirely w/o understanding 39	38	20	an incompetent shall appear by a guardian or guardian ad litem who shall have the power to compromise, agree to order, satisfy judgment, or discharge claim against the incompetent fn. 1 372	372	service of process on person under guardianship or conservatorship is by service on guardian or conservator 416.70				insane: limitation runs from removal of disability but shall not exceed 20 yrs. 328	insane: limitation runs from removal of disability 352
COLO. Rev. Stat. (1973 & Supp. 1982) R. Civ. P.	if deprived of right by ct. finding 27-10-125			15-11-501	representative may sue or defend on incompetent's behalf rule 17(c)	rule 17(c)	serve conservator of person under conservatorship rule 4(e)(3)		rule 55(b)(2)	insane persons: limitation runs from removal of disability 13-80-114	insane persons: limitation runs from removal of disability 13-80-114	insane persons: limitation runs from removal of disability 13-80-114
CONN. Gen. Stat. Ann. (West 1977 & Supp. 1982)		pending application for appointment of conservator, not valid w/o ct. approval 45-73(a)		45-160				serve superintendent & commissioner fn. 2 4-68(f)			non compos mentis entry upon land: 5 yrs. 52-575	simple contracts: 3 yrs. 52-576
DEL. Code Ann. (1974 & Supp. 1982) Super. Ct. Civ. P.	persons under guardianship of property w/regard to such property 12, §3914(f)				representative may sue or defend on behalf of incompetent rule 17(c)	rule 17(c)	serve trustee or guardian if w/in state or adult person w/whom incompetent lives fn. 3 rule 4(f)		rule 55(b)(1), (2)	3 yrs. after removal of disability 10, §8116	10 yrs. after removal of disability 10, §7903	

TABLE 8.1 PERSONAL AND PROPERTY RIGHTS OF MENTALLY DISABLED PERSONS—*Continued*

STATE	CONTRACTS			CAPACITY TO MAKE A WILL	CIVIL SUITS		EFFECT OF MENTAL DISABILITY ON PROCEDURAL RIGHTS					
							Service of Process		No Default Against Unrepresented Incompetent	Extension of Time Limitation on Actions		
	Persons with No Power to Contract (1)	Validity of Contracts (2)	Liability for Necessaries (3)	(Must Be of "Sound Mind") (4)	Capacity to Sue and Be Sued (5)	Appointment of Guardian Ad Litem (6)	Incompetents (7)	Institutionalized Patients (8)	(9)	Personal Actions (10)	Real Property Actions (11)	Other (12)
D.C.Code Ann. (1981) Fed. R.C.P.		void if made after filing for conservatorship 21-1507	contracts for necessaries made after filing for conservatorship not void 21-1507		rule 17	rule 17	personal service on incompetent & on committee 13-333		rule 55		non compos mentis: 5 yrs. after removal of disability 12-302(b)	all other actions w/in time limitation after removal of disability 12-301(a)
FLA. Stat. Ann. (West 1970 & Supp. 1982) R. Civ. P.				732.501	incompetent may sue or defend by guardian or, if none, by next friend or guardian ad litem rule 1.210(b)	rule 1.210(b)	read process to incompetent & person caring for him; also serve guardian ad litem & legal guardian, if any 48.041		unless previous ct. order that no representative necessary rule 1.500(e)	statute of limitations is tolled by adjudicated incompetency before cause of action accrued 95.051(d)	statute of limitations is tolled by adjudicated incompetency before cause of action accrued 95.051(d)	statute of limitations is tolled by adjudicated incompetency before cause of action accrued 95.051(d)
GA. Code Ann. (1977 & Supp. 1982)	adjudged insane, lunatic, or non compos mentis 20-206	void if adjudicated insane or incompetent; voidable if not so adjudicated 20-206	20-206	capable unless under some legal disability arising from want of capacity fn. 4 113-201	incompetent may sue or defend by guardian or, if none, by next friend or guardian ad litem 81A-117(c)	81A-117(c)	serve insane person & guardian or trustee 81-212			limitation runs from removal of disability fn. 5 3-801	limitation runs from removal of disability fn. 5 3-801	limitation runs from removal of disability fn. 5 3-801
HAWAII Rev. Stat. (1970 & Supp. 1982)				560:2-501				serve patient, guardian, & administrator of facility; administrator may not accept for patient 334-62		insane: limitation runs from removal of disability 657-13	insane: 5 yrs. after disability removed 657-34	
IDAHO Code (1963 & Supp. 1982) R. Civ. P.	insane person after adjudication of incapacity 32-108 no capacity if entirely w/o understanding 32-106	subject to rescission if made before adjudication of incapacity 32-107	idiots 32-106	15-2-501	incompetent may sue or defend by guardian or, if none, by next friend or guardian ad litem rule 17(c) insane or incompetent party must appear by guardian 5-306	rule 17(c)	adjudicated incompetent: serve guardian or, if none, competent adult family member; serve incompetent unless ct. orders otherwise rule 4(d)(3)	serve superintendent if no guardian & serve person unless ct. orders otherwise rule 4(d)(3)	rule 55(b)(2)		insane: limitation runs from removal of disability but action shall be instituted w/in 5 yrs. after disability ceases 5-213	insane: disability tolls statute but not for more than 6 yrs. 5-230
ILL. Stat. Ann. (Smith-Hurd 1966 & Supp. 1982)		contract w/person under plenary guardianship or adjudged unable to contract is void against that person or estate 110½, §11a-22		sound mind & memory 110½, §4-1						incompetent: 2 yrs. after removal of disability 83, §22	insane or mentally ill: 2 yrs. after removal of disability 83, §9	products liability & medical malpractice: limitation runs from removal of disability 83, §22.1 83, §22.2
IND. Code Ann. (Burns 1972 & Supp. 1982) R. Trial P. 4.2., 17 R. Civ. P. 55(B)		contract for a sale or conveyance executed by previously adjudged incompetent void 29-1-18-41 enforcible if entered into prior to incompetency 29-1-18-42		29-1-5-1	incompetent may sue or defend in own name, or in own name by guardian ad litem or next friend, or by ct.-appointed representative rule 17(c) guardian of estate prosecutes all actions for ward 29-1-18-37	mandatory if not represented rule 17(c)	serve next friend or guardian ad litem; if none, ct.-appointed representative; if none, serve incompetent & custodian rule 4.2(B)		rule 55(B)	2 yrs. after removal of disability 34-1-2-5	2 yrs. after removal of disability 34-1-2-5	2 yrs. after removal of disability 34-1-2-5
IOWA Code Ann. (West 1969 & Supp. 1982) R. Civ. P.		presumption of fraud in all contracts made after filing of petition for conservatorship 633.638		633.264	judicially adjudged incompetent may sue by guardian, or ct.-appointed guardian, shall defend by guardian ad litem rule 12, 13	rule 13, 14	adjudged incompetent: serve guardian rule 56.1(c)	rule 56.1(d)(e)	no judgment against unrepresented adjudged incompetent or person confined in mental institution rule 13	mentally ill: 1 yr. after termination of disability 614.8	mentally ill: 1 yr. after termination of disability 614.8	mentally ill: 1 yr. after termination of disability 614.8
KAN. Stat. Ann. (1976 & Supp. 1982)				59-601	representative of incapacitated person may sue or defend or, if none, may sue by next friend or guardian 60-217(c)	60-217(c)	serve guardian, conservator, or competent family member w/whom incompetent lives & person unless ct. orders otherwise 60-304(c)	serve guardian, conservator, or superintendent & person unless ct. orders otherwise 60-304(c)	60-255		incapacitated person: 2 yrs. after removal of disability, but no action more than 23 yrs. after cause accrues fn. 6 60-508(a)	incapacitated person: 1 yr. after removal of disability, but no action more than 8 yrs. after cause accrues 60-515(a)

TABLE 8.1 PERSONAL AND PROPERTY RIGHTS OF MENTALLY DISABLED PERSONS—*Continued*

	CONTRACTS			CAPACITY TO MAKE A WILL	CIVIL SUITS		EFFECT OF MENTAL DISABILITY ON PROCEDURAL RIGHTS					
							Service of Process		No Default	Extension of Time Limitation on Actions		
STATE	*Persons with No Power to Contract* (1)	*Validity of Contracts* (2)	*Liability for Necessaries* (3)	(Must Be of "Sound Mind") (4)	*Capacity to Sue and Be Sued* (5)	*Appointment of Guardian Ad Litem* (6)	Incompetents (7)	Institutionalized Patients (8)	*Against Unrepresented Incompetent* (9)	Personal Actions (10)	Real Property Actions (11)	Other (12)
KY. Rev. Stat. Ann. (Michie 1970 & Supp. 1982) R. Civ. P.				394.020	action for person of unsound mind shall be brought by guardian or committee rule 17.03(2)	if person defendant & has no guardian rule 17.03(2) rule 4.04(3)	serve in order of preference: 1. guardian 2. father or mother 3. person having custody of individual 4. appointed guardian ad litem rule 4.04(3)				3 yrs. after removal of disability 413.020	w/in time limited after removal of disability 413.170
LA. Civ. Code Ann. (West 1952 & Supp. 1982) Code Civ. P.	insane 31	contracts of insane persons void 1788 contract enforceable if suit brought by person on his representative when disability shall cease 1791		1475	mental incompetent has no capacity to sue or be sued; curator enforces rights & is proper defendant fn. 7 Code Civ. P. 684, 733		serve representative Code Civ. P. 1235			no prescriptions against persons under interdiction 3522	no prescriptions against persons under interdiction 3522	no prescriptions against persons under interdiction 3522
ME. Rev. Stat. Ann. (1981) R. Civ. P.				18-A, §2-501	incompetent may sue or defend by guardian or, if none, by next friend or guardian ad litem rule 17(b)	rule 17(b)	serve guardian or competent adult family member w/whom incompetent lives & incompetent unless ct. orders otherwise rule 4(d)(3)	serve director & incompetent unless ct. orders otherwise rule 4(d)(3)	rule 55(b)(2)		mentally ill: 10 yrs. after removal of disability 14, §807	mentally ill: civil actions, actions against sheriff, contract actions for balance due; w/in time limitations after removal of disability 14, §853
MD. Ann. Code (1974 & Supp. 1982)				legally competent to make a will Est. & Trusts 4-101	guardian shall appear, answer, & defend for a party under a disability 203(b), 205d, 205e	ct. may appoint attorney for a defendant under a disability if there is no guardian rules 205d, 205e	serve disabled person on the parent or guardian, or other person rule 119			mental incompetents: lesser of 3 yrs. or time of limitation after removal of disability, unless statute has more than 3 yrs. to run Cts. & Jud. Proc. 5-201	mental incompetents lesser of 3 yrs. or time of limitation after removal of disability, unless statute has more than 3 yrs. to run Cts. & Jud. Proc. 5-201	mental incompetents lesser of 3 yrs. or time of limitation after removal of disability, unless statute has more than 3 yrs. to run Cts. & Jud. Proc. 5-201
MASS. Ann. Laws (Michie/ Law. Co-op. 1981) R. Civ. P.				191, §1	guardian shall represent ward in all suits unless a guardian ad litem appointed 201, §37 rule 17(b)	rule 17(b)			rule 55(b)	w/in time of limitation after removal of disability 260, §7		
MICH Comp. Laws Ann. (1980 & Supp. 1982) *fn. 8*				700.121			service on judicially declared incompetent by serving guardian 600.1913(1)(c)			insane: 1 yr. after removal of disability if person entitled to make an entry or bring an action under 18 600.5851	insane: 1 yr. after removal of disability if person entitled to make an entry or bring an action under 18 600.5851	insane: 1 yr. after removal of disability if person entitled to make an entry or bring an action under 18 600.5851
MINN. Stat. Ann. (West 1975 & Supp. 1982) R. Civ. P.		contracts made by ward after filing of petition *lis pendens* & appointment of guardian are void 525.543	525.543	524.2-501	incompetent may sue or defend by representative rule 17.02	mandatory if no representative rule 17.02		serve patient & chief executive officer of institution rule 4.03(a)		insane: suspension of statute until removal of disability; extension not to exceed 1 yr. after removal fn. 6 541.15	insane: suspension of statute until removal of disability; extension not to exceed 1 yr. after removal fn. 6 541.15	foreclosure sale: insane: 5 yrs. after removal of disability 580.20
MISS. Code Ann. (1972 & Supp. 1982)				sound & disposing mind 91-5-1	guardian may sue for debts of ward 93-13-38 nonresident guardian may sue for ward's property 93-13-183		person judicially declared of unsound mind: serve person & guardian 13-3-45	13-3-45 fn. 9		unsound mind: w/in times limited after removal of disability (not to extend more than 21 yrs.) 15-1-59	unsound mind: 10 yrs. after removal of disability 15-1-7 adverse possession not to be extended more than 31 yrs. 15-1-13	medical malpractice: 2 yrs. after removal of disability 15-1-36

TABLE 8.1 PERSONAL AND PROPERTY RIGHTS OF MENTALLY DISABLED PERSONS—*Continued*

	CONTRACTS			CAPACITY TO MAKE A WILL	CIVIL SUITS		EFFECT OF MENTAL DISABILITY ON PROCEDURAL RIGHTS					
							Service of Process			*Extension of Time Limitation on Actions*		
STATE	*Persons with No Power to Contract* (1)	*Validity of Contracts* (2)	*Liability for Necessaries* (3)	(Must Be of "Sound Mind") (4)	*Capacity to Sue and Be Sued* (5)	*Appointment of Guardian Ad Litem* (6)	Incompetents (7)	Institutionalized Patients (8)	*No Default Against Unrepresented Incompetent* (9)	Personal Actions (10)	Real Property Actions (11)	Other (12)
MO. Ann. Stat. (Vernon 1956 & Supp. 1982) R. Civ. P.		contract of person found to be incom- -etent or of unsound mind invalid w/o consent of guardian & ct. 475.345		474.310	guardian of estate shall prosecute & defend w/actions in behalf of or against ward 473.130(3)	for mentally infirm failure to do so does not invalidate proceeding rule 52.02(k), (m)	guardian & incompetent 506.150			w/in time limitations after removal of disability 516.170 inapplicable to medical malpractice 516.170 516.105 *fn. 10*	insane: 3 yrs. after removal of disability 516.030 *fn. 10*	
MONT. Ann. Code (1981) R. Civ. P.	person entirely w/o understanding 28-2-202	contract of person of unsound mind but not entirely w/o understanding is subject to recission 28-2-203	28-2-202 28-2-204	72-2-301	representative may sue or defend for incompetent or, if none, then next friend or guardian ad litem rule 17(c) *fn. 1*	rules 4(D)(2)(d), 17(c)	persons adjudged of unsound mind: serve guardian or appointed guardian ad litem; serve person as directed by ct. rule 4(D)(2)(d)		rule 55(b)(2)	seriously mentally ill: time of disability not part of time limited, however limitation shall not be extended more than 5 yrs. or more than 1 yr. after disability ceases 27-2-401 *fn. 11*	seriously mentally ill: time of disability not part of time limited, however limitation shall not be extended more than 5 yrs. or more than 1 yr. after disability ceases 27-2-401 *fn. 11*	seriously mentally ill: time of disability not part of time limited, however limitation shall not be extended more than 5 yrs. or more than 1 yr. after disability ceases 27-2-401 *fn. 11*
NEB. Rev. Stat. (1979 & Supp. 1982)				30-2326							insane: 20 yrs. after accrual of action, but no longer than 10 yrs. after removal of disability 25-213	w/in time limitations after removal of insanity 25-213
NEV. Rev. Stat. (1974 & Supp. 1982) R. Civ. P.	persons judicially determined insane 43.300			133.02	representative may sue or defend for for incompetent; if none, incompetent may sue by guardian ad litem rule 17(c)	rule 17(c)	serve guardian & person judicially declared of un- sound mind rule 4(d)(4)		rule 55		insane: time of disability not part of time limited, but no action shall ex- tend more than 2 yrs. after disability ceases 11.180.2	insane—all other claims: time of dis- ability not part of time limitation 11.250.2 *fn. 12*
N.H. Rev. Stat. Ann. (1974 & Supp. 1982)				of sane mind 551:1						mentally incompetent persons: 2 yrs. after removal of disability 508:8	5 yrs. after removal of disability 508:3	
N.J. Rev. Stat. (1981) Civ. Practice R.				3A:2A-3	represented by guardian or appointed guardian ad litem rule 4:26-2(a)	rule 4:26-2(b)	on guardian or adult member of household & incompetent unless ct. orders otherwise rule 4:4-4(b)	on director of institution & incom- petent unless ct. orders otherwise rule 4:4-4(b)	rule 6:6-3		adverse possession— person of unsound mind: 5 yrs. after removal of disability 2A:14-32	insane—all other actions: w/in time limits after removal of disability 2A:14-21
N.M. Stat. Ann. (1978 & Supp. 1982) R. Civ. P.				45-2-501	representative may sue or defend on behalf of incompetent & if none by next friend or guardian ad litem rule 11(c)	power of guardian ad litem to compromise & agree to judgment rule 11(c) 38-4-15	insane or incompetent: service on guardian of estate or guardian of person, if appointed; if none, on person 38-1-12 rule 4(e)(8)		rule 55(b)		unsound mind: 1 yr. after removal of disability 37-1-21 37-1-28	all other actions: 1 yr. after termina- tion of disability 37-1-10
N.Y. (McKinney 1978 & Supp. 1982)	Civ. Proc. Law §§309, 1201–1203 Est. Powers & Trusts §3-1.1 Mental Hyg. Law 72.25(c)	to extent permitted by ct. contracts of conservator are voidable by conservator 72.25(c)		sound mind & memory 3-1.1	person judicially declared incompetent shall appear by committee or by guardian ad litem 1201	1202	judicially declared incompetent: serve committee & incompetent, unless ct. orders otherwise 309(b)		or unless 20 days days have expired since appointment of guardian ad litem 1203	insane: *if time limita- tion more than 3 yrs. then shall extend for 3 yrs. after dis- ability ceases *if less than 3 yrs., shall extend for period of limitation after disability, ceases *not to extend more than 10 yrs. after accrual of action	insane: *if time limita- tion more than 3 yrs. then shall extend for 3 yrs. after dis- ability ceases *if less than 3 yrs., shall extend for period of limitation after disability, ceases *not to extend more than 10 yrs. after accrual of action	insane: *if time limita- tion more than 3 yrs. then shall extend for 3 yrs. after dis- ability ceases *if less than 3 yrs., shall extend for period of limitation after disability, ceases *not to extend more than 10 yrs. after accrual of action

TABLE 8.1 PERSONAL AND PROPERTY RIGHTS OF MENTALLY DISABLED PERSONS—*Continued*

	CONTRACTS			CAPACITY TO MAKE A WILL (Must Be of "Sound Mind")	CIVIL SUITS		EFFECT OF MENTAL DISABILITY ON PROCEDURAL RIGHTS					
							Service of Process		No Default Against Unrepresented Incompetent	Extension of Time Limitation on Actions		
STATE	Persons with No Power to Contract (1)	Validity of Contracts (2)	Liability for Necessaries (3)	(4)	Capacity to Sue and Be Sued (5)	Appointment of Guardian Ad Litem (6)	Incompetents (7)	Institutionalized Patients (8)	(9)	Personal Actions (10)	Real Property Actions (11)	Other (12)
N.C. Gen. Stat. (1976 & Supp. 1982)				31-1	incompetent must appear & defend by guardian or guardian ad litem §1A-1, rule 17(b)	1A-1, rule 17(c)	serve guardian if known 1A-1, rule 4(j)(1) serve appointed guardian ad litem if *known* incompetent w/no guardian 1A-1, rule 4(j)(2)		1A-1, rule 55(b)		insane: 3 yrs. after removal of disability 1-17	insane: w/in time limitations after removal of disability 1-17
N.D. Cent. Code (1976 & Supp. 1982) R. Civ. P.	person entirely w/o understanding 14-01-01 person of unsound mind after incapacity has been judicially determined 14-01-03	contract of person of unsound mind not entirely w/o understanding before judicial determination of incapacity is subject to recission 14-01-02	14-01-01	30.1-08-01	representative may sue or defend for incompetent; if none, by next friend or guardian ad litem rule 17(b)	rule 17(b)	serve guardian ad litem, guardian, or both rule 4(d)(2)(C)		rule 55(a)(3)	insane: disability not part of time limited 28-01-25 28-01-30 28-01-31	insane: time of limitation after removal of 28-01-14	mentally ill-tax redemption: 2 yrs. 57-26-04
OHIO Rev. Code Ann. (Baldwin 1978 & Supp. 1982) R. Civ. P.				sound mind & memory 2107.02	guardian may sue or defend on behalf of incompetent; otherwise incompetent may sue by next friend or defend by guardian ad litem rule 17(B)		guardian or incompetent if no guardian rule 4.2(3)	superintendent rule 4.2(5)	rule 55(A)		unsound mind: 10 yrs. after removal of disability 2305.04	unsound mind: time of limitation after removal of disability 2305.16 *fn. 6*
OKLA. Stat. Ann. (West 1970 & Supp. 1982) Ct. R. & P.	persons of unsound mind 15, §11; 15, §24; 15, §16 person entirely w/o understanding 15, §22	rescission of contracts made by persons of unsound mind 15, §23	15, §22	84, §41 *fn. 13*	guardian must appear & represent ward in all suits *fn. 1* 58, §§803–804		guardian of insane or incompetent person (probate procedure) 58, §810				2 yrs. after disability is removed rule 12, §94	other actions 1 yr. after removal of disability rule 12, §96
OR. Rev. Stat. (1979 & Supp. 1982) R. Civ. P.	ct. may enter into contracts for incapacitated persons 126.217 similar power may be conferred on conservator 126.343			112.225	if incapacitated, appears by guardian or conservator; if none, by ct.-appointed guardian ad litem rule 27(B)	rule 27(B)	serve person & conservator or guardian or, if none, guardian ad litem rule 7(D)(3)(a)					12.160(2) 12.170 12.180
PA. Stat. Ann. (Purdon 1981) R. Civ. P.	adjudged incompetents 20, §5524			20, §2501	incompetent shall be represented by a guardian or guardian ad litem rule 2053 see generally rules 2051–2075	rules 2056, 2059, 2060	serve guardian or incompetent rule 2055		rule 2057	insanity does not extend the time limited for commencement of actions 42, §5533	insanity does not extend the time limited for commencement of actions 42, §5533	insanity does not extend the time limited for commencement of actions 42, §5533
R.I. Gen. Laws (1969 & Supp. 1982) R. Civ. P.		void after appointment of guardian & recording 33-15-13	33-15-13	sane mind 33-5-2	by representative or, if none, by next friend or guardian ad litem rule 17(c)	R. Civ. P. 17(c)	serve incompetent & guardian or conservator rule 4(d)(2)		rule 55(b)	unsound mind: time of limitation after removal of disability 9-1-19	unsound mind: time of limitation after removal of disability 9-1-19	medical malpractice: 1 yr. after removal of mental incompetency 9-1-14.1(a)
S.C. Code Ann. (Law Co-op. 1974 & Supp. 1982)				21-7-10	person shall appear by guardian ad litem in action by or against 15-5-310	15-5-360	on committee or guardian & dependent personally 15-9-490	superintendent shall file copy in permanent record of patient 15-9-510		insane: disability not part of time limited, but period cannot be extended more than 5 yrs. or more than 1 yr. after disability ceases 15-3-40	insane: disability not part of time limited, but period cannot be extended more than 5 yrs. or more than 1 yr. after disability ceases 15-3-40	insane: disability not part of time limited, but period cannot be extended more than 5 yrs. or more than 1 yr. after disability ceases 15-3-40
S.D. Codified Laws Ann. (1976 & Supp. 1982)	persons entirely w/o understanding 27A-2-1(1976) person of unsound mind whose incapacity judicially determined 27A-2-3	a contract of person of unsound mind, but not entirely w/o understanding made before incapacity judicially determined is subject to recission 27A-2-2	person entirely w/o understanding 27A-2-1	29-2-3	representation by guardian, if none, by guardian ad litem 15-6-17(c) *fn. 1*	15-6-17(c)	serve guardian or person having custody & incompetent person 15-6-4(d)(6)	serve guardian or superintendent & incompetent person 15-6-4(d)(6)	15-6-55(b)		mentally ill: 10 yrs. after disability ceases 15-3-14	mentally ill—actions generally: time of disability not part of time limited, but no extension of more than 5 yrs. or 1 yr. after disability ceases 15-2-22

TABLE 8.1 PERSONAL AND PROPERTY RIGHTS OF MENTALLY DISABLED PERSONS—*Continued*

	CONTRACTS			CAPACITY TO MAKE A WILL	CIVIL SUITS		EFFECT OF MENTAL DISABILITY ON PROCEDURAL RIGHTS					
							Service of Process			Extension of Time Limitation on Actions		
STATE	Persons with No Power to Contract (1)	Validity of Contracts (2)	Liability for Necessaries (3)	(Must Be of "Sound Mind") (4)	Capacity to Sue and Be Sued (5)	Appointment of Guardian Ad Litem (6)	Incompetents (7)	Institutionalized Patients (8)	No Default Against Unrepresented Incompetent (9)	Personal Actions (10)	Real Property Actions (11)	Other (12)
TENN. Code Ann. (1977 & Supp. 1982) R. Civ. P.	if conservator for person incapable of managing estate, not person's contractual powers obligations same as minor's 34-12-20	if conservator for person incapable of managing estate, not person's contractual powers obligations same as minor's 34-12-20		32-102	representative may sue or defend on behalf of incompetent, if none, incompetent & may sue by next friend rule 17.03	service rule 4.04(2) mandatory, if defending party rule 17.03	resident guardian or conservator of incompetent; if not known, serve parent w/custody or person having control; if none, serve guardian ad litem rule 4.04(2)		rule 55	unsound mind: 3 yrs. or time of limitation after removal of disability, whichever is less 28-1-106	unsound mind: 3 yrs. or time of limitation after removal of disability, whichever is less 28-1-106	unsound mind: 3 yrs. or time of limitation after removal of disability, whichever is less 28-1-106
TEX. Prob. Code Ann. art. 57 Rev. Civ. State Ann. arts. 1984 5518.3, 5535 (Vernon 1980 & Supp. 1981) R. Civ. P.				57	lunatics, idiots, non compos mentis who have no guardian may sue by next friend rule 44	mandatory if lunatic, idiot, or non compos mentis is defendant w/o guardian or represented by someone who appears to have adverse interests rule 173				person of unsound mind: time of disability not part of time limited 5518.3, 5535	person of unsound mind: time of disability not part of time limited 5518.3, 5535	person of unsound mind: time of disability not part of time limited 5518.3, 5535
UTAH Code Ann. (1975 & Supp. 1982) R. Civ. P.				75-2-501	insane or incompetent person must appear by general guardian or guardian ad litem rule 17(b)	rule 17(b)	serve guardian of person of unsound mind rule 4(e)(3)		only judgments entered by clerk rule 55(b)	*fn. 14*	insane: time of limitation after removal of disability 78-12-21 *fn. 14*	products liability: disability does not toll statute 78-15-3
VT. Stat. Ann. (1974 & Supp. 1981) R. Civ. P.		void after filing an application w/probate ct. & appointment of guardian 14, §2689	14, §2689	14, §1	representative may sue or defend on behalf of incompetent; if none, incompetent may sue by next friend or guardian ad litem rule 17(b)	rule 17(b)	serve guardian or competent adult family member w/whom incompetent resides serve incompetent unless ct. orders otherwise rule 4(d)(1)(ii)	serve director or chief executive officer serve incompetent unless ct. orders otherwise rule 4(d)(1)(ii)	rule 55(b)	insane: time of limitation after removal of disability 12, §551(a)	insane: time of limitation after removal of disability 12, §551(a)	insane: time of limitation after removal of disability 12, §551(a)
VA. Code (1980 & Supp. 1981)				64.1-47		persons under disability: mandatory unless already represented by attorney; if interests of justice require, appointment even if person has an attorney 8.01-9				unsound mind: time of limitation after removal of disability *fn. 15* 8.01-229(1)	unsound mind: time of limitation after removal of disability *fn. 15* 8.01-229(1)	unsound mind: time of limitation after removal of disability *fn. 15* 8.01-229(1)
WASH. Rev. Code Ann. (1962 & Supp. 1980)				11.12.010	insane party to an action shall appear by guardian; if none, or guardian is improper person, by guardian ad litem 4.08.060	insane: if plaintiff, on application of relative or friend; if defendant, on relative or friend, or, if none, on application of any party to action 4.08.060	on guardian 4.28.080(12)				recovery of real estate: 3 yrs. after removal of disability 4.16.070	4.16.190
W. VA. Code (1966 & Supp. 1981) R. Civ. P.	an adjudged incompetent may be deprived of right to contract 27-11-1			41-1-1 41-1-2	representative may sue or defend on behalf of incompetent; if none, incompetent may sue by next friend	rule 17(c)	on incompetent if over 14, & guardian or committee; if none, then father, mother, or guardian ad litem rule 4(d)(2), (3)		rule 55(2)	insane: time of limitation after becoming sane, total time not to exceed 20 yrs. 55-2-15	5 yrs. after insanity ceases; total time not to exceed 20 yrs. 55-2-3 55-2-4	ejectment actions: 3 yrs. after removal of disability 55-4-27
WIS. Stat. Ann. (West 1971 & Supp. 1981)		if guardian appointed, contracts of insane, or incompetent persons shall be void 880.215	880.215	853.01	mental incompetent may be represented by an attorney, general guardian, or guardian ad litem 803.01(3)	if has guardian, none appointed unless general guardian has interests adverse to incompetent 803.01(3)	on person under disability & guardian or guardian ad litem; if person of under 14, serve parent or guardian or person having care or control; otherwise serve guardian ad litem 801.11(2)			insane: 2 yrs. after removal of disability, however period of limitation may not be extended more than 5 yrs. 893.16	insane: 2 yrs. after removal of disability, however period of limitation may not be extended more than 5 yrs. 893.16	insane: 2 yrs. after removal of disability, however period of limitation may not be extended more than 5 yrs. 893.16

TABLE 8.1 PERSONAL AND PROPERTY RIGHTS OF MENTALLY DISABLED PERSONS—*Continued*

	CONTRACTS			CAPACITY TO MAKE A WILL	CIVIL SUITS		EFFECT OF MENTAL DISABILITY ON PROCEDURAL RIGHTS					
							Service of Process		No Default	Extension of Time Limitation on Actions		
STATE	Persons with No Power to Contract (1)	Validity of Contracts (2)	Liability for Necessaries (3)	(Must Be of "Sound Mind") (4)	Capacity to Sue and Be Sued (5)	Appointment of Guardian Ad Litem (6)	Incompetents (7)	Institutionalized Patients (8)	Against Unrepresented Incompetent (9)	Personal Actions (10)	Real Property Actions (11)	Other (12)
WYO. Stat. (1981) R. Civ. P.				2-6-101	representative may sue or defend on behalf of incompetent; if none, may sue by next friend or guardian ad litem rule 17(c)	rule 17(c)	serve guardian, or if none, serve person having legal control or guardian ad litem rule 4(d)(2)		rule 55	other than real actions 3 yrs. after removal of disability 1-3-114	10 yrs. after removal of disability 1-3-104	workman's compensation: statute tolled as long as mental incompetent has no guardian 27-12-505

FOOTNOTES: TABLE 8.1

1. A person of unsound mind, of whatever degree, is civilly liable for a wrong done by him or her, but is not liable in exemplary damages unless at the time of the act he/she was capable of knowing that it was wrongful. Cal. Civ. Code § 41 (West 1954); Mont. Code Ann. § 21-7-711 (1981); Okla. Stat. Ann. tit. 15, §§ 25-26 (West 1972), and S.D. Codified Laws Ann. 27A-2-4 (1976).

2. Conn. Gen. Stat. Ann. § 4-68(f) (West 1969). Superintendent shall deliver a copy to the confined person.

3. Del. Super. Ct. Civ. P. 4(f) (1974). Service on incompetent nonresident is in the same manner as on a competent nonresident.

4. Ga. Code Ann. § 3-802 (1975). If disability occurs after accrual of right, limitation shall cease to operate during its continuance.

5. Id. §§113-201 to 113-205 (1975).

> Every person may make a will, unless laboring under some legal disability arising either from a want of capacity or a want of perfect liberty of action.
>
> An incapacity to contract may coexist with a capacity to make a will. The amount of intellect necessary to constitute testamentary capacity is that which is necessary to enable the party to have a decided and rational desire as to the disposition of his property. His desire must be decided, or distinguished from the wavering, vacillating fancies of a distempered intellect. It must be rational, as distinguished from the ravings of a madman, the silly pratings of an idiot, the childish whims of imbecility, or the excited vagaries of a drunkard.
>
> An insane person generally may not make a will. A lunatic may during a lucid interval. A monomaniac may make a will, if the will is in no way the result of or connected with his monomania. In all such cases it must appear that the will speaks the wishes of the testator, unbiased by the mental disease with which he is affected.
>
> Eccentricity of habit or thought does not deprive a person of the power of making a will; old age and weakness of intellect resulting therefrom does not, of itself, constitute incapacity. If that weakness amounts to imbecility, the testamentary capacity is gone. In cases of doubt as to the extent of this weakness, the reasonable or unreasonable disposition of his estate should have much weight in the decision of the question.

6. Disability not only when action accrues but arising during running of limitation will give rise to an extension. Kan. 60-508(a) (1976) (real property); Minn. 541.15 (Supp. 1980) and Ohio 2305.16 (1980).

7. La. Code Civ. Proc. Ann. art. 733 (1960): "If an incompetent has no curator, but is interdicted, or committed to or confined in a mental institution, the action shall be brought against him, but the court shall appoint an attorney at law to represent him."

8. Mich. Comp. Laws Ann. § 600.5851(2) (1968 & Supp. 1981): "The term insane as employed in this chapter means a condition of mental derangement such as to prevent the sufferer from comprehending rights he is otherwise bound to know and is not dependent on whether or not the person has been judicially declared to be insane."

9. Miss. Code Ann. § 13-3-45 (1972). If the superintendent certifies that the person is mentally incapable of responding to process, service is not required. Such certification endorsed on the process shall serve in lieu of service.

10. Mo. Ann. Stat. § 516.180 (Vernon 1949 & Supp. 1980). At the death of a person under disability the cause of action survives for one year.

11. Mont. Code Ann. §§ 27-2-401, 27-2-211(3) (1981). The extension of time for persons under disability does not apply to actions for forfeiture or penalty against shareholders or directors of corporations.

12. Nev. Rev. Stat. § 11.280 (1979). On an action to recover an estate the time limitation extends one year after removal of any disability to sue.

13. Okla. Stat. Ann. tit. 15, § 24 (West 1970 & Supp. 1982): "After his incapacity has been judicially determined, a person of unsound mind can make no conveyance or other contract, nor designate any power, nor waive any right, until his restoration to capacity is judicially determined. But if actually restored to capacity, he may make a will, though his restoration is not thus determined."

14. Utah Code Ann. § 78-12-36 (1977). If mentally incompetent and without legal guardian, the time of disability is not part of time limited for commencement of action.

15. Va. Code § 8.01-237 (1977 & Supp. 1981). Disabilities shall not extend right to make entry on or bring action to recover land for more than 25 years after such right first accrued.

Id. § 8.01-229(2)(b) (1977). If person becomes of unsound mind after cause of action accrues, that period of disability is not computed as part of the limitation period unless a guardian or committee is appointed.

TABLE 8.2 ENGAGEMENT IN OCCUPATIONS

STATE	DENIAL OF LICENSE fn. 1				SUSPENSION OR REVOCATION OF LICENSE fn. 1				PROBATION				RESTRICTIONS OR LIMITATIONS ON LICENSE (13)	OTHER ACTIONS fn. 2 (14)
	Mentally Ill (1)	Not Mentally Capable (2)	Mental Condition Renders Practice Unsafe (3)	Adjudicated Incompetent or Mentally Ill (4)	Mentally Ill (5)	Not Mentally Capable (6)	Mental Condition Renders Practice Unsafe (7)	Adjudicated Mentally Ill or Incompetent (8)	Mentally Ill (9)	Not Mentally Capable (10)	Mental Condition Renders Practice Unsafe (11)	Adjudicated Mentally Ill or Incompetent (12)		
ALA. Code (1977 & Supp. 1982)		nurse (mentally incompetent) 34-21-25		counselor 34-8A-16(b) physical therapist 34-24-217(6)	pilot (mental derangement) 33-4-46	nurse 34-21-25 pharmacist 34-23-33(7)	chiropractor 34-24-166(23)	counselor 34-8A-16 optometrist 34-22-23(6) physical therapist 34-24-217(6)		pharmacist 34-23-33(7)				
ALAS. Stat. (1982 & Supp. 1982)	nurse 08.68.270(7)	nurse 08.68.270(7)		physical therapist 08.84.120(7)	nurse 08.68.270(7)	dental hygienist 08.32.160(6) dentist 08.36.315(7)(D) nurse 08.68.270(7) optician 08.71.170(6)(C) chiropractor 08.20.170(a)(7)(C) nursing home administrator 08.70.155(6)(C) optometrist 08.72.240(7)(D) pharmacist 08.80.261(7)(D) psychologist 08.86.204(7)(D) veterinarian 08.98.235(7)(C)		of if voluntarily committed: medical doctor or osteopath 08.64.332		chiropractor 08.20.170(a)(7)(C) physical therapist 08.84.120(7) nursing home administrator 08.70.155(6)(C) optometrist 08.72.240(7)(D) pharmacist 08.80.261(7)(D) psychologist 08.86.204(7)(D) veterinarian 08.98.235(7)(C)				mentally ill bank corporator removed from office 06.15.050
ARIZ. Rev. Stat. Ann. (1976 & Supp. 1982)	nurse 32-1632(2) 32-1637(2)	chiropractor 32-921A4	medical doctor 32-1423(5)	chauffeur 28-413A5		dentist or dental hygienist 32-1263(3) denturist 32-1297.07A3 medical doctor 32-1451A pharmacist 32-1927A5	homeopathic physician 32-2934A	physical therapist or physical therapist assistant 32-2042C 32-2001A8(d) 32-2001A3 psychologist 32-2081(4)		dentist or dental hygienist 32-1263(3) denturist 32-1297.07A3 medical doctor 32-1451H pharmacist 32-1927(5)	homeopathic physician 32-2935B1	physical therapist or physical therapist assistant 32-2042 32-2001A8(d) 32-1001A3 psychologist 32-2081(4)		

TABLE 8.2 ENGAGEMENT IN OCCUPATIONS—*Continued*

	DENIAL OF LICENSE *fn. 1*				SUSPENSION OR REVOCATION OF LICENSE *fn. 1*				PROBATION					
STATE	Mentally Ill (1)	Not Mentally Capable (2)	Mental Condition Renders Practice Unsafe (3)	Adjudicated Incompetent or Mentally Ill (4)	Mentally Ill (5)	Not Mentally Capable (6)	Mental Condition Renders Practice Unsafe (7)	Adjudicated Mentally Ill or Incompetent (8)	Mentally Ill (9)	Not Mentally Capable (10)	Mental Condition Renders Practice Unsafe (11)	Adjudicated Mentally Ill or Incompetent (12)	RESTRICTIONS OR LIMITATIONS ON LICENSE (13)	OTHER ACTIONS *fn. 2* (14)
ARK. Stat. Ann. (1979 & Supp. 1981)	pharmacist or druggist 72-1040(4)	nurse 72-760(5)		private investigator or security services contractor 71-2135(5) polygraph examiner 71-2217(10) chiropractor 72-441(5) pharmacist or druggist 72-1040(4) veterinarian 72-1144(2) physical therapist or physical therapist assistant 72-1328(g) inhalation therapist 72-1613(g) medical doctor (also if voluntarily admitted or found mentally ill by 3 psychiatrists) 72-613(k) chauffeur 75-309(5)	pharmacist or druggist 72-1040(4) dentist or dental hygienist 72-560(3)	nurse 72-760(5)		architect 71-310(1)(j) polygraph examiner 71-2217(10) landscape architect 71-2905(h) chiropractor 72-441(5) pharmacist or druggist 72-1040(4) veterinarian 72-1144(2) physical therapist or physical therapist assistant 72-1328(g) inhalation therapist 72-1613(g) dentist or dental hygienist (if deemed detrimental to patients) 72-560(3) also if voluntarily admitted or found mentally ill by 3 psychiatrists: medical doctor 72-613(k) and physician's trained assistant 72-2015 mandatory suspension: cosmetologist, electrologist, or manicurist 71-874						

TABLE 8.2 ENGAGEMENT IN OCCUPATIONS—*Continued*

STATE	DENIAL OF LICENSE fn. 1				SUSPENSION OR REVOCATION OF LICENSE fn. 1				PROBATION				RESTRICTIONS OR LIMITATIONS ON LICENSE (13)	OTHER ACTIONS fn. 2 (14)
	Mentally Ill (1)	Not Mentally Capable (2)	Mental Condition Renders Practice Unsafe (3)	Adjudicated Incompetent or Mentally Ill (4)	Mentally Ill (5)	Not Mentally Capable (6)	Mental Condition Renders Practice Unsafe (7)	Adjudicated Mentally Ill or Incompetent (8)	Mentally Ill (9)	Not Mentally Capable (10)	Mental Condition Renders Practice Unsafe (11)	Adjudicated Mentally Ill or Incompetent (12)		
CAL. Bus. & Prof. Code (West 1974 & Supp. 1983)							psychologist or psychological assistant 2967 podiatrist 2497	social worker 9023 clinical social worker 9051			podiatrist 2497		may not use alcoholic beverage license if incompetent 23102	
COLO. Rev. Stat. (1978 & Supp. 1982)	pharmacist, assistant pharmacist 12-22-125(2)(a)(I)	architect 12-4-115(1)(c) psychiatric technician 12-42-113(1)(c)	medical doctor 12-36-116, 12-36-117(1)(o) nurse 12-38-117(1)(j)	child health associate, psychologist, physical therapist (if ct. order specifically finds incapacity to practice) 12-31-110(1)(f) 12-43-111(1)(g) 12-41-118(1)(g) social worker 12-63.5-114(1)(d)	pharmacist, assistant pharmacist 12-22-125(2)(a)(I)	architect 12-4-115(1)(c) psychiatric technician 12-42-113(1)(c)	physician or podiatrist 12-36-118, 12-36-117(1)(o) nurse 12-38-117(1)(j)	teacher (ct. order must specifically find incapacity to teach) 22-60-110(2)(a) social worker 12-63.5-114(1)(d) chiropractor, medical doctor, podiatrist (ct. order must specifically find incapacity to practice) 12-33-117(5) 12-36-118(8) nurse (automatic suspension) 12-38-119(1) child health associate, physical therapist, veterinarian, psychologist (if ct. order specifically finds incapacity to practice) 12-31-110(1)(f) 12-41-118(1)(g) 12-64-111(1)(w) 12-43-111(1)(e)			physician or podiatrist 12-36-118, 12-36-117(1)(o) nurse 12-38-117(1)(j)	child health associate, physical therapist (if ct. order specifically finds incapacity to practice) 12-31-110(1)(f) 12-41-110(1)(g)		

TABLE 8.2 ENGAGEMENT IN OCCUPATIONS—*Continued*

	DENIAL OF LICENSE *fn. 1*				SUSPENSION OR REVOCATION OF LICENSE *fn. 1*				PROBATION					
STATE	Mentally Ill (1)	Not Mentally Capable (2)	Mental Condition Renders Practice Unsafe (3)	Adjudicated Incompetent or Mentally Ill (4)	Mentally Ill (5)	Not Mentally Capable (6)	Mental Condition Renders Practice Unsafe (7)	Adjudicated Mentally Ill or Incompetent (8)	Mentally Ill (9)	Not Mentally Capable (10)	Mental Condition Renders Practice Unsafe (11)	Adjudicated Mentally Ill or Incompetent (12)	RESTRICTIONS OR LIMITATIONS ON LICENSE (13)	OTHER ACTIONS *fn. 2* (14)
CONN. Gen. Stat. Ann (West 1969 & Supp. 1982)	natureopath 20-40 sanitarian 20-361(a)				physician 20-13(c)(2) nurse 20-99(b)(4) osteopath 20-20(2) dentist 20-114(9) chiropractor 20-29 natureopath 20-40 practitioner of healing arts 20-45 podiatrist 20-59(7) optometrist 20-133(7) optician 20-154 psychologist 20-192 veterinarian 20-202(10) embalmer or funeral director 20-227(8) barber 20-238 hairdresser or cosmetician 20-263 hypertrichologist 20-271 hearing aid dealer 20-404(a)(13) speech pathologist or audiologist 20-414(a)(4)	physical therapist 20-73(a)			osteopath 20-20(2) chiropractor 20-29 natureopath 20-40 podiatrist 20-59(7) nurse 20-99(b)(3) dentist 20-114(9) optometrist 20-133(7) optician 20-154 psychologist 20-192 veterinarian 20-202(10) embalmer or funeral director 20-227(8) barber 20-238 hairdresser or cosmetician 20-263 hypertrichologist 20-271 hearing aid dealer 20-404(a)(13) speech pathologist or audiologist 20-414(a)(4)				physician 20-13(c)(2)	
DEL. Code Ann. (1981 & Supp. 1982)	cab driver 21, §2763	nurse 24, §1921(a)(5) pharmacist 24, §2526(a)(2)	podiatrist 24, §510(a)(7) medical doctor or osteopath 24, §1731(a)(1)	podiatrist 24, §510(a)(8) medical doctor or osteopath 24, §1741(a)(8) cab driver 21, §§2763, 2707(a)(4) chauffeur 21, §2707(a)(4)		nurse 24, §1921(a)(5) pharmacist 24, §2526(a)(2)	podiatrist 24, §510(a)(7) medical doctor or osteopath 24, §1741(a)(7)	podiatrist 24, §510(a)(8) medical doctor or osteopath: automatic suspension 24, §1741(a)(8) veterinarian 24, §3313(b)(2)(3)			medical doctor or osteopath 24, §1741(a)(7)		pharmacist 24, §1921(a)(5)	
D.C. Code Ann. (1981)	physical therapist 2-1703.11(6)	nurse 2-1702.12(6)		psychologist 2-1704.11(4) 2-3308.6		nurse 2-1702.12 physical therapist 2-1703.11		psychologist 2-491(D) engineer 2-2308(p)(6)						

TABLE 8.2 ENGAGEMENT IN OCCUPATIONS—*Continued*

	DENIAL OF LICENSE *fn. 1*				SUSPENSION OR REVOCATION OF LICENSE *fn. 1*				PROBATION					
STATE	Mentally Ill (1)	Not Mentally Capable (2)	Mental Condition Renders Practice Unsafe (3)	Adjudicated Incompetent or Mentally Ill (4)	Mentally Ill (5)	Not Mentally Capable (6)	Mental Condition Renders Practice Unsafe (7)	Adjudicated Mentally Ill or Incompetent (8)	Mentally Ill (9)	Not Mentally Capable (10)	Mental Condition Renders Practice Unsafe (11)	Adjudicated Mentally Ill or Incompetent (12)	RESTRICTIONS OR LIMITATIONS ON LICENSE (13)	OTHER ACTIONS *fn. 2* (14)
FLA. Stat. Ann. (West 1981 & Supp. 1982) *fn. 3*	acupuncturist 468.325(2)(b) 468.325(1)(a) real estate broker or salesperson 475.25(1)(l) nurse 464.008(1)(b)		physician 458.331(1)(s) 458.331(2) osteopath 459.015(1)(5) 459.015(2) chiropractor 460.413(1)(r) 460.413(2)(a) podiatrist 461.013(1)(s) 461.013(2)(a) optometrist 463.016(1)(p) 463.016(2)(a) nurse 464.018(1)(h) 464.018(2)(a) pharmacist 465.016(1)(d)3 465.016(1)(m) 465.016(2)(a) dentist 466.028(1)(t) 466.028(2)(a) nursing home administrator 468.1755(1)(l) 468.1755(2)(a) veterinarian 474.214(1)(i) 474.214(2)(a) real estate broker or salesperson 475.25(1)(m) optician 484.014(1)(t) 484.014(2)(a)	dentist 466.028(1)(dd) 466.028(2)(a) engineer 471.033(1)(a) 471.033(3)(a) land surveyor 472.033(1)(a) 472.033(3)(a) accountant 473.323(1)(a) 473.323(3)(a) veterinarian 474.214(1)(a) 474.214(2)(a) real estate broker or salesperson 475.25(1)(a) 475.25(1)(m) architect 481.225(1)(a) 481.225(3)(a) landscape architect 481.325(1)(a) 481.325(3)(a) clinical laboratory personnel 483.21(6) physical therapist 486.091(6) chauffeur 322.05(5)(1975)	acupuncturist 468.325(2)(h) 468.325(1)(a)2,3 real estate broker (suspension during temporary derangement) or salesperson 475.25(1)(i)		physician 458.331(1)(s) 458.331(2)(b) osteopath 459.015(1)(s) 459.015(2)(b) chiropractor 460.413(1)(r) 460.413(2)(b) podiatrist 461.013(1)(s) 461.013(2)(b) optometrist 463.016(1)(p) 463.016(2)(b) nurse 464.018(1)(h) 464.018(2)(b) pharmacist 465.016(1)(d)3 465.016(1)(m) 465.016(2)(b) dentist 466.028(1)(t) 466.028(2)(b) nursing home administrator 468.1755(1)(l) 468.1755(2)(b) veterinarian 474.214(1)(i) 474.214(2)(b) real estate broker or salesperson 475.25(1)(m) optician 484.014(1)(t) 484.014(2)(b)	any licensed profession 455.227(1)(d) dentist 466.028(1)(dd) 466.028(2)(b) engineer 471.033(1)(a) 471.033(3)(b) land surveyor 472.033(1)(a) 472.033(3)(b) accountant 473.323(1)(a) 473.323(3)(b) veterinarian 474.214(1)(a) 474.214(2)(b) real estate broker or salesperson 475.25(1)(a) 475.25(1)(m) architect 481.225(1)(a) 481.225(8)(b) landscape architect 481.325(1)(a) 481.325(3)(b) clinical laboratory personnel 483.21(6) physical therapist 486.091(6)	acupuncturist 468.325(2)(h) 468.325(1)(b)		physician 458.331(1)(s) 458.331(2)(f) osteopath 459.015(1)(s) 459.015(2)(f) chiropractor 460.413(1)(r) 460.413(2)(f) podiatrist 461.013(1)(s) 461.013(2)(f) optometrist 463.016(1)(p) 463.016(2)(e) nurse 464.018(1)(h) 464.018(2)(e) pharmacist 465.016(1)(d)3 465.016(1)(m) 465.016(2)(e) dentist 466.028(1)(t) 466.028(2)(e) nursing home administrator 468.1755(1)(l) 468.1755(2)(e) veterinarian 474.214(1)(i) 474.214(2)(e) optician 484.014(1)(t) 484.014(2)(e)	dentist 466.028(1)(dd) 406.028(2)(e) engineer 471.033(1)(a) 471.033(3)(c) land surveyor 472.033(1)(a) 472.033(3)(e) accountant 472.323(1)(a) 472.323(3)(e) veterinarian 474.214(1)(a) 474.214(2)(e) architect 481.225(1)(a) 481.225(3)(e) landscape architect 481.325(1)(a) 481.325(3)(e)	mentally ill acupuncturist 468.325(1)(a)2, (2)(h) clinical laboratory personnel adjudicated incompetent 483.21(6) if practice unsafe because of mental illness: physician 458.331(1)(s),(2)(c) osteopath 459.015(1)(s),(2)(c) podiatrist 461.013(1)(s),(2)(c) chiropractor 460.413(1)(r),(2)(c) dentist 466.028(1)(t),(2)(f) nursing home administrator 468.1755(1)(l),(2)(f)	
GA. Code Ann. (1979 & Supp. 1982)	nursing home administrator 84-4903(a)(3)	barber 84-428(a)(5) recreation administrator, supervisor, or leader 84-5915(a)	dentist 84-724(a)(10),(11) physician 84-916(a)(13) private detective or private security 84-6510(a)(3) licensed practical nurse 84-6808(a)(10)	physician 84-916(a)(12) physical therapist 84-3020(a)(2) orthotist 84-7214(g) licensed practical nurse 84-6808(a)(9)		barber 84-428(a)(5) recreation administrator supervisor, or leader 84-5915(a)	dentist 84-724(a)(10),(11) 84-724(b)(3),(5) physician 84-916(a)(13) 84-916(b)(1)(iii),(v) registered nurse 84-1004(vii),(viii) private detective or private security 84-6510(a)(5), (b)(3),(5) licensed practical nurse 84-6808(a)(10), (b)(3),(5) pharmacist 79A-408(A)(1)(b)	physician 84-916(a)(12) registered nurse 84-1004(b)(vii) veterinarian 84-1509(2) physical therapist 84-3020(a)(2) licensed practical nurse 84-6808(a)(10) orthotist 84-7219(g) pharmacist 79A-408(4)			dentist 84-724(a)(10),(11) 84-724(b)(6) physician 84-916(a)(13) 84-916(b)(2) registered nurse 84-1004(vi) private detective or private security 84-6510(a)(5), (b)(6) licensed practical nurse 84-6808(a)(10), (b)(7)		if practice unsafe because of mental condition: dentist 84-724(a)(10),(11) 84-724(b)(4) physician 84-916(a)(13), (b)(1)(iv) registered nurse 84-1004(vii) private detective or private security 84-6510(a)(5), (b)(4) licensed practical nurse 84-6808(a)(10), (b)(4)	
HAWAII Rev. Stat. (1976 & Supp. 1982)		nurse 457-12(a)(5) pilot 462A-8(4) radiologic technologist 466J-8(2) veterinarian 471-10(a),(b)(5) boxer, etc. 440-12			physician 453-8(8)(5) naturopath 455-6(2)(H)	nurse 457-12(a)(5) pilot 462A-8(4) radiologic technologist 466J-8(2) veterinarian 471-10(b)(5)		funeral authority 441-23(5) real estate broker or salesperson 467-14(15)	physician 453-8.2(1)				physician practicing while mentally unstable 453-8(8)	

TABLE 8.2 ENGAGEMENT IN OCCUPATIONS—*Continued*

STATE	DENIAL OF LICENSE fn. 1				SUSPENSION OR REVOCATION OF LICENSE fn. 1				PROBATION				RESTRICTIONS OR LIMITATIONS ON LICENSE (13)	OTHER ACTIONS fn. 2 (14)
	Mentally Ill (1)	Not Mentally Capable (2)	Mental Condition Renders Practice Unsafe (3)	Adjudicated Incompetent or Mentally Ill (4)	Mentally Ill (5)	Not Mentally Capable (6)	Mental Condition Renders Practice Unsafe (7)	Adjudicated Mentally Ill or Incompetent (8)	Mentally Ill (9)	Not Mentally Capable (10)	Mental Condition Renders Practice Unsafe (11)	Adjudicated Mentally Ill or Incompetent (12)		
IDAHO Code (1979 & Supp. 1981)		nurse 54-1412(a)(6) 54-1407(a)(3) 54-1408(a)(3)		accountant 54-217(12) architect 54-305(1)d chauffeur 49-309(5) (1980)	engineer or surveyor 54-1220(b)	nurse 54-1412(a)(6)	physician 54-1832(a)	chauffeur 49-309(5) (1980) accountant 54-217(12) architect 54-305(1)d real estate broker or salesperson 54-20408(b) veterinarian 54-2112(2)					mentally unfit nurse 54-1412(a)(6) physician so mentally ill that unable to practice w/reasonable skill & safety 54-1832(a)	
ILL. Ann. Stat. (Smith-Hurd 1978 & Supp. 1983)	nursing home administrator 111, §§3604, 3606(c)			physician, midwife, or person licensed to treat human ailments 111, §4433(24) engineer 111, §5124(4) real estate broker or salesperson 111, §5732(c) school bus driver 95½, §6-106.1 (a)(14)		barber 111, §1653(g)	barber 111, §1653(g)	barber 111, §1653 dentist or dental hygienist 111, §2222-3(c) funeral director or embalmer 111, §2830 nursing home administrator 111, §3620 pharmacist 111, §4041 physical therapist 111, §4216 physician, midwife, or person licensed to treat human ailments 111, §1433 podiatrist 111, §4922 engineer 111, §5124(4) psychologist 111, §5316 real estate broker or salesperson 111, §5732(c) shorthand reporter 111, §6120 social worker 111, §6315				physician, midwife, or person licensed to treat human ailments 111, §4433(24)		
IND. Code Ann. (Burns 1982 & Supp. 1982)	health facility administrator 25-19-1-3(a)(1)				attorney rules, Admission & Discipline 23, §3(b)			dentist 25-14-19(2) psychologist 25-33-1-13(a)(3)						
IOWA Code Ann. (West 1972 & Supp. 1983)	nursing home administrator 135E.3(1)		chauffeur 321.177(7)	chauffeur 321.177(5)			physician, surgeon, or osteopath 148.6(1)(h) nurse 152.10(1)(h)	physician, surgeon, or osteopath 148.6(1)(f) nurse 152.10(1)(f)						
KAN. Stat. Ann. (1981)		nurse 65-1120(5) mental health technician 65-4209(c)	podiatrist 65-2006(a)(13)	physical therapist 65-2912(h)		nurse 65-1120(5) pharmacist 65-1627(a)(7) mental health technician 65-4209(c)	podiatrist 65-2006(a)(13) practitioner of healing arts 65-2836(m)	physical therapist 65-2912(h)		pharmacist 65-1627(a)(7)			mentally incompetent nurse 65-1120(5) if unable to practice w/reasonable skill & safety because of mental condition: podiatrist 65-2006(a)(13) practioner of healing arts 65-2836(m)	attorney transferred to disability inactive statous if adjudicated incompetent or committed 7-124b, R.220(a)

TABLE 8.2 ENGAGEMENT IN OCCUPATIONS—*Continued*

	DENIAL OF LICENSE fn. 1				SUSPENSION OR REVOCATION OF LICENSE fn. 1				PROBATION					
STATE	Mentally Ill (1)	Not Mentally Capable (2)	Mental Condition Renders Practice Unsafe (3)	Adjudicated Incompetent or Mentally Ill (4)	Mentally Ill (5)	Not Mentally Capable (6)	Mental Condition Renders Practice Unsafe (7)	Adjudicated Mentally Ill or Incompetent (8)	Mentally Ill (9)	Not Mentally Capable (10)	Mental Condition Renders Practice Unsafe (11)	Adjudicated Mentally Ill or Incompetent (12)	RESTRICTIONS OR LIMITATIONS ON LICENSE (13)	OTHER ACTIONS fn. 2 (14)
KY. Rev. Stat. Ann. (Michie 1983)	physician or osteopath ("emotionally unstable") 311.570(2)(d) registered nurse 314.041(1) practical nurse 314.051(1)	physical therapist 327.070(11)	podiatrist 311.480(9) physician or osteopath 311.595(7) cosmetologist 317A.140(1)(c) barber 317.590(1)(b)	physician or osteopath 311.570(2)(e) physical therapist 327.070(8) deception examiner 329.070(8) engineer or land surveyor 322.050		physical 327.070(11)	podiatrist 311.480(9) physician or osteopath 311.595(7) dentist 313.130(7) dental specialist 313.460 barber 317.590(1)(b) cosmetologist 317A.140(1)(c)	physical therapist therapist 327.070(8) deception examiner 329.070(8)		physical therapist 327.070(11)	physician or osteopath 311.595(7) pharmacist 315.127(5)	physical therapist 327.070(8)	physician or osteopath if continued practice dangerous because of mental condition 311.595(7)	teacher's contract terminated for mental disability 161.790(1)(b)
LA. Rev. Stat. Ann. (West 1974 & Supp. 1983)	continued practice by mentally ill cosmetologist 37:513(4)	registered nurse 37:921F practical nurse 37:969A(4)(e)	medical doctor or midwife 37:1285(25)	medical doctor or midwife 37:1285(21) physical therapist 37:2413(3) social worker 37:2713A(5)	continued practice by mentally ill cosmetologist 37:513(4)	registered nurse 37:921F practical nurse 37:969A(4)(e)	medical doctor or midwife 37:1285(25)	medical doctor or midwife 37:1285(21) veterinarian 37:1526(2) physical therapist 37:2413(5) social worker 37:2713A(5)			medical doctor or midwife 37:1285(25)	medical doctor or midwife 37:1285(21) physical therapist 37:2413(5)	medical doctor or midwife if committed, interdicted, or unable to practice w/reasonable skill & safety because of mental illness or deficiency 37.1285(21),(25)	attorney suspended if interdicted, committed, or mentally incapacitated 37: ch. 4 app. 15, §9
ME. Rev. Stat. Ann. (1978 & Supp. 1983)	chiropractor 32, §503(3)E psychologist 32, §3837	nurse 32, §2105(1)E polygraph examiner 32, §716(1)O		contract security company 32, §9411(3)	chiropractor 32, §503(3)E denturist 32, §1100-E(5)F physician's assistant 32, §3270-C(1)F physician 32, §3286 psychologist 32, §3837	nurse 32, §2105(1)E osteopath 32, §2591(1)J physical therapist 32, §3117(2)C veterinarian 32, §4864(5-A) animal technician 32, §4865-A(5) substance abuse counselor 32, §6217-A(3) social worker 32, §7059(2)C polygraph examiner 32, §7161(1)O	dentist 32, §1091(1)G physician's assistant 32, §3270-C(2)	osteopath 32, §2591(1)I		osteopath 32, §2591(1)J veterinarian 32, §4864(5-A) animal technician 32, §4865-A(5)		osteopath 32, §2591(1)I		
MD. Ann. Code (1980)		pharmacist 43, §266A(c)(1)(xvi)		electrologist 43, §555B-23(a)(3)		physician 43, §130(h)(18) pharmacist 43, §266A(c)(1)(xvi) optometrist 43, §378(a)(15) podiatrist 43, §490(b)(11),(e) dentist 32, §11(a),(e) dental hygienist 32, §32(e)		electrologist 43, §555B-23(a)(3) social worker 43, §869(a)(4)		physician 43, §130(h)(18) optometrist 43, §378(a)(15) podiatrist 43, §490(b)(11),(e)				
MASS. Ann. Laws (Michie/Law. Co-op. 1975 & Supp. 1983)				physical therapist 112, §23k(d)	physician (if practices while mentally unstable) 112, §5(d) any registered profession 112, §61			physical therapist 112, §23k(d)						insane tax collector may be removed 60, §96

TABLE 8.2 ENGAGEMENT IN OCCUPATIONS—*Continued*

STATE	DENIAL OF LICENSE fn. 1				SUSPENSION OR REVOCATION OF LICENSE fn. 1				PROBATION				RESTRICTIONS OR LIMITATIONS ON LICENSE (13)	OTHER ACTIONS fn. 2 (14)
	Mentally Ill (1)	Not Mentally Capable (2)	Mental Condition Renders Practice Unsafe (3)	Adjudicated Incompetent or Mentally Ill (4)	Mentally Ill (5)	Not Mentally Capable (6)	Mental Condition Renders Practice Unsafe (7)	Adjudicated Mentally Ill or Incompetent (8)	Mentally Ill (9)	Not Mentally Capable (10)	Mental Condition Renders Practice Unsafe (11)	Adjudicated Mentally Ill or Incompetent (12)		
MICH. Comp. Laws Ann. (1980 & Supp. 1983)	school bus driver 257.316a	chauffeur 257.303(1)(f)	health professional 331.16221(b)(iii) 331.16226 physician's assistant 333.17086(1)	health professional 331.16221(b)(iv) 331.16226 physician's assistant 333.17086(1) chauffeur 257.303(1)(e)			health professional 331.16221(b)(iii) 331.16226 physician's assistant 333.17086(1) chauffeur 257.303a(1) 257.320	health professional 331.16221(b)(iv) 331.16226 physician's assistant 333.17086(1)				health professional 331.16221(b)(iv) 331.16226 physician's assistant 333.17086(1)	health professional if mentally unable to practice safely & competently, or if adjudicated incompetent 331.16221(b)(iii),(iv) 331.16226 physician's assistant 333.17086(1) chauffeur if has mental infirmity or disability rendering driving unsafe 257.320	
MINN. Stat. Ann. (West 1970 & Supp. 1983)	registered nurse 148.211(1)(b) practical nurse 148.291(1)(b)	chiropractor 148.10(1)(7) dentist, dental hygienist, or dental assistant 150A.08(1)(7) pharmacist 151.06(1)(6)(k)	physician 147.021(1)(l)	physician 147.021(1)(j)		chiropractor 148.10(1)(7) dentist, dental hygienist, or dental assistant 150A.08(1)(7) pharmacist 151.06(1)(6)(k)	physician 147.021(1)(j)	physician 147.021(1) veterinarian 156.081 subd. 3					physician unable to practice w/reasonable skill & safety because of mental condition 147.021(1)(j) chiropractor subject to advanced mental disability 148.10(1)(7) dentist, dental hygienist, or dental assistant subject to advanced mental disability 150.A.08(1)(7)	mentally ill teacher suspended & may be discharged 125.12(7), (8)
MISS. Code Ann. (1973 & Supp. 1982)	nursing home administrator 73-17-11(a)(3)	nurse 73-15-29(i)		physical therapist 73-23-59(d) polygraph examiner 73-29-31(10) psychologist 73-31-21(a)(8)	veterinarian 73-39-19(a)	nurse 73-15-29(e) physician 73-25-53(a) veterinarian 73-39-19(a)	physician 73-25-53(a)	physical therapist 73-23-59(d) polograph examiner 73-29-31(10) psychologist 73-31-21(a)(8) veterinarian 73-39-19(a)	veterinarian: "prohibition" 73-39-19(a)	veterinarian: "prohibition" 73-39-19(a)		veterinarian: "prohibition" 73-39-19(a)	physician unable to practice w/reasonable skill or safety because of mental illness 73-25-53(a)	attorney so mentally ill that unable to practice competently suspended until reinstated by ct. order 73-3-347 73-3-349
MO. Ann. Stat. (Vernon 1966 & Supp. 1983)		nurse 335.066(2)(9)	medical doctor 334.100(1)(15) pharmacist 338.055(2)(9)	architect, engineer, or land surveyor 327.441(2)(9) dentist 332.321(1)(2)(9) chauffeur 302.060(5) nurse 335.066(2)(9)		nurse 335.060(9)	medical doctor 334.100(1)(2)(9) pharmacist 338.055(2), (3)	architect, engineer, or land surveyor 327.441(2)(9)(3) dentist 332.321(1)(2)(9)(3)				pharmacist 338.055(2)(3)(9) medical doctor 334.100(2)(12)(9)		teacher removed if mental condition incapacitates to instruct or associate w/children 168.114(1)(1) 168.221(3) school employee removed if mental condition incapacitates from properly performing duties or associating w/children 168.281(2)(1)
MONT. Code Ann. (1981)	nursing home administrator 37-9-301(1)(a)	nurse 37-8-441(4)	acupuncturist 37-13-311(3)	chauffeur 61-5-105(5) physical therapist 37-11-321(7) acupuncturist 37-13-311(2)		dentist or dental hygienist 37-4-321(1) nurse 37-8-441(4) radiologic technologist 37-14-321(3)	physician 37-3-323(1)(a), (4)(a), (b) chiropractor 37-12-322(1)(a), (4)(a), (b) acupuncturist 37-13-311(3)	physician 37-3-323(1)(a), (4)(a), (b), (7) physical therapist 37-11-321(7) chiropractor 37-12-322(1)(b), (4)(a), (b) acupuncturist 37-13-311(2)		dentist or dental hygienist 37-4-321	physician 37-3-323(1)(a) (4)(d) chiropractor 37-12-322(1)(a), (4)(d) acupuncturist 37-13-311(3) 37-13-312(2)(d)	physician 37-3-323(1)(a), (4)(d) chiropractor 37-12-322(1)(b), (4)(d) acupuncturist 37-13-311(2) 37-13-312(2)(d)		

TABLE 8.2 ENGAGEMENT IN OCCUPATIONS—*Continued*

STATE	DENIAL OF LICENSE *fn. 1*				SUSPENSION OR REVOCATION OF LICENSE *fn. 1*				PROBATION				RESTRICTIONS OR LIMITATIONS ON LICENSE (13)	OTHER ACTIONS *fn. 2* (14)
	Mentally Ill (1)	Not Mentally Capable (2)	Mental Condition Renders Practice Unsafe (3)	Adjudicated Incompetent or Mentally Ill (4)	Mentally Ill (5)	Not Mentally Capable (6)	Mental Condition Renders Practice Unsafe (7)	Adjudicated Mentally Ill or Incompetent (8)	Mentally Ill (9)	Not Mentally Capable (10)	Mental Condition Renders Practice Unsafe (11)	Adjudicated Mentally Ill or Incompetent (12)		
NEB. Rev. Stat. (1981 & Supp. 1982)	emergency medical technician or paramedic 71-5522(5)	nurse if attempts to practice when performance interfered w/by mental illness, deterioration, or disability 71-1132.29(4) nursing home administrator 71-2045.02(b)		health professional 71-147(7) health profession 71-1163(2)	71-1162.5(c)	teacher or school administrator 79-1234(9) health professional 71-147(7) 71-161.12 health professional if practices while ability impaired by mental disability 71-147(6) medical doctor 71-11625(c) nursing home administrator 71-2045.02(6)		health professional 71-147(7) 71-161.17(2) veterinarian 71-1,163(2)		health professional 71-147(7) 71-155(3) if practices while ability impaired by mental disabilty 71-147(6) 71-155(3)			health professional: if practices while ability impaired by mental disability 71-147(6) or if mental incapacity determined by lawful means 71-147(7) or if not qualified because of mental illness, deterioration, or disability 71-161.12 medical doctor if not qualified because of mental illness, deterioration, or disability 71-1,104.02	
NEV. Rev. Stat. (1981)		professional nurse 632.220(5) practical nurse 632.320(5) nursing facility administrator (not "emotionally capable") 654.150(1) attorney Sup. Ct. R. 51(6)	practitioner of traditional oriental medicine 634A.170(8)	optician 637.150(1) physical therapist 640.160(7)		professional nurse 632.220(5) practical nurse 632.320(5) osteopath or osteopathic physician's assistant 633.111(2) 633.511(5) 633.651(2)(d), (e) optometrist 636.295(b) teacher or school administrator 391.330(3)	physician or physician's assistant 630.022(2) 630.301(5) 630.352(2)(d), (e) practitioner of traditional oriental medicine 634A.170(8)	optician 637.150(1) pharmacist (or if voluntarily admitted) 639.211 physical therapist 640.160(7) psychologist (or if voluntarily admitted) 641.330 shorthand reporter 656.270			physician or physician's assistant 630.022(21) 630.301(5) 630.352(2)(a) osteopath or osteopathic physician's assistant 633.111(2) 633.511(5) 633.651(2)(a)		physician or physician's assistant if unable to practice safely & skillfully because of impaired mental capability 630.022(2) 630.301(5) 630.352(2)(c) osteopath or osteopathic physician's assistant if unable to practice safely & skillfully because of impaired mental capability 633.111(2) 633.511(5) 633.651(2)(c)	attorney transferred to disability inactive status if adjudicated incompetent or committed Sup. Ct. R. 117 (1) or if incapable because of mental infirmity or illness Sup. Ct. R. 117(2) teacher may be suspended, dismissed, or not reemployed & school administrator may be demoted, suspended, dismissed, or not reemployed because of mental incapacity 391.312(1)(f)
N.H. Rev. Stat. Ann. (1966 & Supp. 1981)	dentist or dental hygienist 317-A:171	nurse 326-B:12I(f)			dentist or dental hygienist 317-A:171 hawker or peddler 320:14(4) medical doctor 329:17VI, 329:17VII(b), (c) rehabilitation counselor 332-F:9II(a)	chauffeur 262:40 nurse 326-B:121(f) physical therapist or physical therapist's assistant 328-A:91		medical doctor 329:17-a psychologist 330-A:14(d) veterinarian 332-B:14II(f)		nurse 326-B:12I(f)			insane or psychiatrically disordered medical doctor 329:17VI, VII(b)	insane dentist or dental hygienist may be required to submit to treatment or to practice under direction 317-A:17II(e), (g) insane or psychiatrically disordered medical doctor may be required to submit to treatment or to practice under direction 329:17VI, VII(d), (f)
N.J. Stat. Ann. (West 1978 & Supp. 1983)		medical practitioner 45:9-16(d)	pharmacist or assistant pharmacist 45:14-12	medical practitioner 45:9-16(a) pharmacist or assistant pharmacist 45:14-12	pilot or deputy pilot 12:8-19c	medical practitioner 45:9-16(d)	pharmacist or assistant pharmacist 45:14-12	medical practitioner 45:9-16(a) pharmacist or assistant pharmacist 45:14-12						

TABLE 8.2 ENGAGEMENT IN OCCUPATIONS—*Continued*

STATE	DENIAL OF LICENSE fn. 1				SUSPENSION OR REVOCATION OF LICENSE fn. 1				PROBATION				RESTRICTIONS OR LIMITATIONS ON LICENSE (13)	OTHER ACTIONS fn. 2 (14)
	Mentally Ill (1)	Not Mentally Capable (2)	Mental Condition Renders Practice Unsafe (3)	Adjudicated Incompetent or Mentally Ill (4)	Mentally Ill (5)	Not Mentally Capable (6)	Mental Condition Renders Practice Unsafe (7)	Adjudicated Mentally Ill or Incompetent (8)	Mentally Ill (9)	Not Mentally Capable (10)	Mental Condition Renders Practice Unsafe (11)	Adjudicated Mentally Ill or Incompetent (12)		
N.M. Stat. Ann. (1978 & Supp. 1981)		nurse 61-3-28A(5) pharmacist 61-11-20A(8)		chiropractor 61-4-101 dentist or dental hygienist 61-5-14A(2) psychologist 61-9-13A(7) physical therapist 61-12-12B nursing home administrator 61-13-13F polygrapher 61-26-9D	physician 61-7-3A	nurse 61-3-28A(5) pharmacist 61-11-20A(8)		chiropractor 61-4-101 dentist or dental hygienist 61-5-14(2) physician 61-6-29A psychologist 61-9-13A(7) physical therapist 61-12-12B nursing home administrator 61-13-13F veterinarian or person holding artificial insemination or pregnancy diagnosis permit 61-14-13A(2) polographer 61-26-9D	physician 61-7-3A, 61-7-8c(1)				physician 61-7-3A	
N.Y. Educ. Law (McKinney 1972 & Supp. 1983)					physician's assistant or specialist's assistant 6544(1)(c)	any licensed profession, if practice while ability impaired by mental disability 6509(3), 6511(2), (3)								removal of teacher for mental disability 3012(2)(b), 3014(2)(b)
N.C. Gen. Stat. (1981 & Supp. 1981)	nursing home administrator 90-278(1)a	dentist 90-41(a)(7) optometrist 90-121.2(a)(7) podiatrist 90-202.8(a)(7) dental hygienist 90-229(a)(13)	architect 83A-15(2)b medical doctor 90-14(5) dentist 90-41(a(7)) pharmacist or assistant pharmacist 90-65(a)(6) optometrist 90-121.2(a)(7) podiatrist 90-202.8(a)(7) dental hygienist 90-229(a)(13)	medical doctor 90-14(10) dentist 90-41(a)(7) optometrist 90-121.2(a)(7) podiatrist 90-202.8(a)(7) dental hygienist 90-229(a)(13) physical therapist 90-270.36(5) 90.270.26(2)		dentist 90-41(a)(7) optometrist 90-121.2(a)(7) nurse 90-171.5(7) podiatrist 90-202.8(a)(7) dental hygienist 90-229(a)(13)	architect 83A-15(2)b medical doctor 90-14(5) dentist 90-41(a)(7) pharmacist or assistant pharmacist 90-65(a)(6) optometrist 90-121.2(a)(7) podiatrist 90-202.8(a)(7) dental hygienist 90-229(a)(13)	engineer or land surveyor 89C-21(a)(5) medical doctor 90-14(10) dentist 90-41(a)(7) optometrist 90-121.2(a)(7) veterinarian 90-187.8(2) podiatrist 90-202.8(a)(7) dental hygienist 90-229(a)(13) physical therapist 90-270.36(5) 90-270.26(2)		dentist 90-41(a)(7) optometrist 90-121.2(a)(7) podiatrist 90-202.8(a)(7) dental hygienist 90-229(a)(13)	dentist 90-41(a)(7) optometrist 90-121.2(a)(7) podiatrist 90-202.8(a)(7) dental hygienist 90-229(a)(13)	dentist 90-41(a)(7) optometrist 90-121.2(a)(7) podiatrist 90-202.8(a)(7) dental hygienist 90-229(a)(13)		attorney transferred to inactive status if mental incompetence interferes w/practice 84-28(e) career teacher may be dismissed, demoted, or employed on part-time basis because of mental incapacity 115-142(e)(1)e public school employees must certify freedom from mental disease impairing ability to perform duties beginning employment 115-143 mentally unfit pilot retired from active service 76-12, 76-68
N.D. Cent. Code (1978 & Supp. 1981)	chiropractor 43-06-15(3) nursing home administrator 43-34-03(1)		physician 43-17-31(5) nurse 43-12.1-14(6)	psychologist 43-32-27(6) physical therapist 43-26-11(5)	chiropractor 43-06-15(3)	physician 43-17.1-07(5) pharmacist 43-15-10(1)(f)	physician 43-17-31(5) nurse 43-12.1-14(6)	psychologist 43-32-27(6) dentist 43-28-18(3)			nurse 43-12.1-14(6)		physician 43-17.1-07(5)	

TABLE 8.2 ENGAGEMENT IN OCCUPATIONS—*Continued*

	DENIAL OF LICENSE fn. 1				SUSPENSION OR REVOCATION OF LICENSE fn. 1				PROBATION					
STATE	Mentally Ill (1)	Not Mentally Capable (2)	Mental Condition Renders Practice Unsafe (3)	Adjudicated Incompetent or Mentally Ill (4)	Mentally Ill (5)	Not Mentally Capable (6)	Mental Condition Renders Practice Unsafe (7)	Adjudicated Mentally Ill or Incompetent (8)	Mentally Ill (9)	Not Mentally Capable (10)	Mental Condition Renders Practice Unsafe (11)	Adjudicated Mentally Ill or Incompetent (12)	RESTRICTIONS OR LIMITATIONS ON LICENSE (13)	OTHER ACTIONS fn. 2 (14)
OHIO Rev. Code Ann. (Baldwin 1979 & Supp. 1983)	(insane) chauffeur's license 4507.08(B)		physician 4731.22(B)(16)	veterinarian 4741.22(P) psychologist 4732.17(I) physical therapist 4755.47(D) emergency medical technican 4731.85(D) physician 4731.22(B)(16) nurse 4723.28			physician 4731.22(16)	emergency medical technician 4731.85(D) psychologist 4732.17(I) chiropractor 4734.11 physician 4731.22(B)(16) 4731.221 veterinarian 4741.22(P) chauffeur's license 4507.161 dispensing optician 4725.53(E) physical therapist 4755.47(D) nurse 4723.28						
OKLA. Stat. Ann. (West 1971 & Supp. 1983)	chauffeur's license 47, §6-207			chauffeur's license 47, §6-103(5) polygraph examiner 59, §1468(10) physical therapist 59, §887.13 osteopath 59, §637(h) nurse 59, §567.8	chauffeur's license 47, §6-207 physician 59, §516 chiropractor 59, §167	attorney 5, ch. 1, App. 1, Art. II, §§1, 2	physician 59, §503 59, §509(16) podiatrist 59, §148	polygraph examiner 59, §1468(10) physical therapist 59, §887.13 veterinarian 59, §698.14(5) osteopath 59, §637(h) nurse 59, §567.8 pharmacist 59, §353.26(f) dental hygienist 59, §328.33(g) dentist 59, §328.32(l)				pharmacist 59, §353.26(f)		
OR. Rev. Stat. (1981)		chauffeur's license 482.130(1)(b) emergency medical technician 677.680(10) clinical social worker 675.540(4) psychologist 675.070(1)(f)		physical therapist 688.140(7) chiropractor 684.100(1)(e) nursing home administrator 678.780(1)(c)	physician 677.190(14), (21)	emergency medical technician 677.680(10) clinical social worker 675.540(4) psychologist 675.070(1)(f)	chauffeur's license 482.450(1)(c) nurse 678.111(1)(f)	chiropractor 684.100(1)(e) dentist 679.165 physical therapist 688.140(7) nursing home administrator 678.780(1)(c) radiologic technologist 688.525(6) physician 677.190(14), (21) 677.225(1)(a) occupational therapist 675.300(2)			nurse 678.111(1)(i)			dismissal of teacher for mental incapacity 342.865
PA. Stat. Ann. (Purdon 1968 & Supp. 1982)		pharmacist 63, §390-3(2) podiatrist 63, §42.16(6)	physician 63, 421.15(5) osteopath 63, §271.15(5) optometry 63, §244.7(7)	physical therapist 53, §1311(A)(7)		practical nurse 63, §666 pharmacist 63, §390-5 podiatrist 63, §42.16(6)	physician 63, 421.15 osteopath 63, §271.15(5) optometrist 63, §244.7(7) nurse 63, §224(2)	physical therapist 63, §1311(A)(7) psychologist 63, §1209 physician 63, 421.14						

TABLE 8.2 ENGAGEMENT IN OCCUPATIONS—*Continued*

STATE	DENIAL OF LICENSE fn. 1 Mentally Ill (1)	Not Mentally Capable (2)	Mental Condition Renders Practice Unsafe (3)	Adjudicated Incompetent or Mentally Ill (4)	SUSPENSION OR REVOCATION OF LICENSE fn. 1 Mentally Ill (5)	Not Mentally Capable (6)	Mental Condition Renders Practice Unsafe (7)	Adjudicated Mentally Ill or Incompetent (8)	PROBATION Mentally Ill (9)	Not Mentally Capable (10)	Mental Condition Renders Practice Unsafe (11)	Adjudicated Mentally Ill or Incompetent (12)	RESTRICTIONS OR LIMITATIONS ON LICENSE (13)	OTHER ACTIONS fn. 2 (14)
R.I. Gen. Laws (1976 & Supp. 1982)	chauffeur 31-10-3(5)	psychologist 5-44-18(4) physical therapist 5-40-13(3) social worker 5-39-16(4) nurse 5-34-28(5)	acupuncturist 5-37.2-15(8)			physician 5-37.1-5(20) 5-37.1-13 psychologist 5-44-18(4) physical therapist 5-40-13(3) social worker 5-39-16(4) nurse 5-34-24(e) barber 5-27-28(j)	chauffeur 31-11-7(5) acupuncturist 5.37.2-15(8) barber 5-27-28(j)						physician 5-37.1-5 5-37.1-13	
S.C. Code Ann. (Law. Co-op. 1977 & Supp. 1982)	nursing home administrator 40-35-30(3) private detective 40-17-80			veterinarian 40-69-140 polygraph examiner 40-53-180 physical therapist 40-45-200(7) engineer, land surveyor 40-21-340(6)			dentist or dental hygienist 40-15-190(1) chiropractor 40-9-90(5)	veterinarian 40-69-140 polygraph examiner 40-53-180 physician 40-47-200 physical therapist 40-45-200(7) engineer, land surveyor 40-21-340(6)					physician 40-47-200(6) chiropractor 40-9-90(5)	
S.D. Codified Laws Ann. (1977 & Supp. 1982)			nurse 36-9-49 36-9-49.1 physical therapist 36-10-38 36-10-40 physician 36-4-28				social worker 36-26-32(5) physical therapist 36-10-38 36-10-40 nurse practitioner or midwife 36-9A-32 nurse 36-9-49.1 physician 36-4-29 36-4-30(12)	life support personnel 36-4B-33 physician 36-4-32 physician's assistants 36-4A-40						
TENN. Code Ann. (1982 & Supp. 1982)		nurse 63-752(a)(5)	physician 63-618(a)(18) dentist, dental hygienist, registered dental assistant 63-554(a)(9)	veterinarian 63-1224(24) osteopath 63-912(a)(18)		pharmacist 63-1020(e) mandatory: nurse 63-752(a)(5)	mandatory: physician 63-618(a)(18) mandatory: dentist, dental hygienist, registered dental assistant 63-554(a)(9)	veterinarian 63-1224(24) mandatory: osteopath 63-912(a)(18)					physician limit or restrict 63-618(a)(18)	
TEX. Rev. Civ. Stat. Ann. (Vernon 1976 & Supp. 1983)			podiatrist 4570(d)(15) physician 4495(16)	hearing aid dispenser 4566-1.10 optometrist 4552-4.04 pharmacist 4542a(12e) nurse 4525(10) physical therapist 4512e(7) chiropractor 4512b(14a) commerical operator or chauffeur 6687b(4)	licensed vocational nurse 4528c(10)		podiatrist 4573(a) psychologist 4512c(23f) physician 4495(16)	hearing aid dispenser 4566-1.10 commercial operator or chauffeur 6687b(30) optometrist 4552-4.04(4) dentist 4549(a) pharmacist 4542a(12e) nurse 4525(10) physical therapist 4512e(19a) chiropractor 4512b(13)						

TABLE 8.2 ENGAGEMENT IN OCCUPATIONS—*Continued*

	DENIAL OF LICENSE fn. 1				SUSPENSION OR REVOCATION OF LICENSE fn. 1				PROBATION					
STATE	Mentally Ill (1)	Not Mentally Capable (2)	Mental Condition Renders Practice Unsafe (3)	Adjudicated Incompetent or Mentally Ill (4)	Mentally Ill (5)	Not Mentally Capable (6)	Mental Condition Renders Practice Unsafe (7)	Adjudicated Mentally Ill or Incompetent (8)	Mentally Ill (9)	Not Mentally Capable (10)	Mental Condition Renders Practice Unsafe (11)	Adjudicated Mentally Ill or Incompetent (12)	RESTRICTIONS OR LIMITATIONS ON LICENSE (13)	OTHER ACTIONS fn. 2 (14)
UTAH Code Ann. (1973 & Supp. 1981)		nurse-midwife mentally incom-petent 58-44-8(e)		chauffeur's license 41-2-5(4) nurse 58-31-14(e)		nurse-midwife mentally incom-petent 58-44-8(e) dental hygienist 58-7-2 58-7-16	chauffeur's license 41-2-19(3) chiropractor 58-12-52(3)(a) physician 58-12-35(3)	nurse 58-31-14(e) chiropractor (license auto-matically suspended upon adjudication) 58-12-52(2) physician (license auto-matically suspended upon adjudication) 58-12-35(2)						
VT. Stat. Ann. (1975 & Supp. 1983)		nurse 26, §1582(6) dentist or hygienist 26, §809(19) school bus driver 23, §1282	chiropractor 26, §505	polygraph examiner 26, §2908(10)		school bus driver 23, §1282 nurse 26, §1582(6) physician 26, §1354(20)	dentist or hygienist 26, §809(19) chiropractor 26, §505(5)	polygraph examiner 26, §2908(10)					physician conditions & limitations on license 26, §1354, 26, §1361	
VA. Code (1982)		pharmacist 54-524.22:1(d) chauffeur's license 46.1-361	physician 54-316 nurse 54-367.32	veterinarian 54-786.4		pharmacist 54-524.22:1	optometrist 54-388 54-367.32 physician 54-316(5) dental hygienist 54-200.18 dentist 54-187	veterinarian 54-786.4(1)			nurse 54-367.32(j) physician 54-316(5)			
WASH. Rev. Code Ann. (1978 & Supp. 1984)			registered nurse 18.88.230(5)	physical therapist 18.74.080(5) osteopath 18.57.170 18.57.180 nursing home administrator 18.52.120(5)			registered nurse 18.88.230(5)	chiropractor 18.26.030 18.26.210(15) physical therapist 18.74.080(5) physician 18.72.275(2) osteopath 18.57.185 nursing home administrator 18.52.120(5) dentist 18.32.550 pharmacist 18.64.160(5)						
W. VA. Code (1980 & Supp. 1982)	pharmacist 30-5-7	practical nurse 30-7A-10 professional nurse 30-7-11 teacher 18A-3-1 accountant 30-9-9(F)		physician 30-3-14(21)	pharmacist 30-5-7 teachers (mental defect) 18A-3-6	accountant 30-9-9(f) practical nurse 30-7A-10 professional nurse 30-7-11(e)		physical therapist 30-20-10(s) veterinarian 30-10-12						
WIS. Stat. Ann. (West 1974 & Supp. 1983)		nurse 441.07(c) electrologist 458.08			dentist or dental hygienist 447.07(7) patient in mental hospital	nurse 441.07(c)		designer of engineering systems 443.13					designer of engineering systems 443.13	
WYO. Stat. (1977 & Supp. 1982)		nurse 33-21-115	physician 33-26-129(b)(ii) optometrist 33-10-110(a)(v)(b)	veterinarian 33-30-212(a)(ii) physical therapist 33-25-111(vi)		nurse 33-21-115(a)(iv)	physician 33-26-129(b)(ii) optometrist 33-10-110(a)(v)(b)	veterinarian 33-30-212(a)(ii) physical therapist *shall* be suspended 33-25-111(vi)						

FOOTNOTES: TABLE 8.2

1. Denial, suspension, or revocation of a license on grounds of mental impairment is usually at the discretion of a professional board; typical language is "[t]he board may refuse to issue or renew a license or may suspend or revoke the license of any licensee if." Mont. Code Ann. § 37-15-321(1) (1981). But in some occupations or certain circumstances a license must be denied to a mentally disabled person or if granted must be revoked or suspended. Examples of mandatory denial provisions are in the health care professions and in professions that involve driving, e.g., Va. Code § 54-367.32 (Supp. 1981) (nurse); Ill. Ann. Stat. ch. 95½, § 6-106.1(a)(14) (Smith-Hurd Supp. 1980) (school bus driver). Provisions for the mandatory suspension of the licenses of health care professionals during their period of mental incapacity are also common, e.g., Ga. Code § 84-916(a)(12) (Supp. 1981) (physician); Colo. Rev. Stat. § 12-38-119(1) (Supp. 1980) (nurse).

2. Ethical Consideration 1-6 of the ABA Code of Professional Responsibility provides that lawyers should be diligent in taking steps to see that persons disqualified by mental or emotional instability are not licensed as lawyers or, if licensed, are not permitted to practice. Lawyers should assist such persons in being licensed or restored to practice after their disqualification has ended.

3. But see the Florida "Regulatory Sunset Act," Fla. Stat. Ann. § 11.61 (West 1961 & Supp. 1982). The Sunset Act provides, in part: "That no profession, occupation, business, industry or other endeavor be subject to regulation by the state unless such regulation is necessary to protect public health, safety, or welfare from significant and discernable harm or damage and that the police power of the state be exercised only to the extent necessary for that purpose."

4. All of the following provisions have been repealed, effective July of 1986.

TABLE 8.3 OTHER RIGHTS AFFECTED BY MENTAL DISABILITY

	VOTING		DRIVING			HOLDING PUBLIC OFFICE			DISQUALIFICATION FROM REPRESENTATIVE AND FIDUCIARY FUNCTIONS		
							Other Disqualifications				
STATE	*Persons Disqualified* (1)	*Enforcement* (2)	*Persons Disqualified* (3)	*Enforcement* (4)	JURY DISQUALIFICATIONS (5)	*Must Be Qualified Voter* (6)	From All Offices (7)	From Specified Offices (8)	*Personal Representative of Estate* (9)	*Guardian or Conservator* (10)	*Fiduciary or Trustee* (11)
ALA. Code (1975 & Supp. 1982)	all idiots or insane persons const. art. VIII, §182	challenge by any person 17-12-1	adjudged insane, idiot, imbecile, or feeble-minded & not restored or certified by hospital on release 32-6-7(5) mental disability will prevent exercising reasonable & ordinary control over vehicle 32-6-7(6)		challenge for cause if of unsound mind 12-6-150(9)	any state office 36-2-1(a)(1)	idiots or insane 36-2-1(a)(3) adjudication of insanity vacates office 36-9-3	governor's duties performed by officer next in succession if governor decreed of unsound mind const. art. V, §128 vacancy in office of attorney general, state auditor, secretary of state, treasurer, superintendent of education, or commissioner of agriculture & industries if ascertained by Supreme Ct. to be of unsound mind const. art. V, §136	may be removed for imbecility 43-2-290(1)	guardian may be removed for imbecility 26-6-2(a)(4)	*fn. 1* 35-5-8
ALAS. Stat. (1962 & Supp. 1982)	judicially determined to be of unsound mind const. art. V, §2 15.05.040		dep't has determined from medical evidence that person cannot drive safely because of mental disability *fn. 2* 28.15.031(4), (5)		not of sound mind 09.20.010(4)	legislator const. art. II, §2 governor const. art. III, §2 lieutenant governor const. art. III, §7 member of state board or commission 39.05.100			removed when becomes incapable of discharging duties *fn. 3* 13.16.295(b) 13.16.285	*fn. 4* 13.26.145(a) *fn. 5* 13.26.120	*fn. 1* 45.60.0611
ARIZ. Rev. Stat. Ann. (1975 & Supp. 1982)	under guardianship, non compos mentis or insane const. art. VII, §2	registration canceled when insanity legally established 16-165(A)(3) may not register 16-101(4)	*fn. 2* 28-413(5)		not qualified for voter registration 21-201	any office const. art. VII, §15	office deemed vacant if holder adjudicated insane 38-291(2)		*fn. 3* 14-3609	*fn. 4* 14-5311A *fn. 5* 14-5306	*fn. 1* 44-2077(D)
ARK. Stat. Ann. (1976 & Supp. 1981)	idiot or insane person const. art. III, §5	challenge 3-714	*fn. 2* 75-309(5)		idiot or insane 39-102(b)	any office const. art. XIX, §3 justice of the peace const. art. VII, §41			unsound mind 62-2201(b)(2) incompetency terminates appointment 62-2203.1 62-2203	guardian of incompetent must be of sound mind 57-607(a) may be removed if mentally incompetent 57-621, 62-2203 conservator 57-704	*fn. 1* 50-907

TABLE 8.3 OTHER RIGHTS AFFECTED BY MENTAL DISABILITY—*Continued*

STATE	VOTING: *Persons Disqualified* (1)	VOTING: *Enforcement* (2)	DRIVING: *Persons Disqualified* (3)	DRIVING: *Enforcement* (4)	JURY DISQUALIFICATIONS (5)	HOLDING PUBLIC OFFICE: *Must Be Qualified Voter* (6)	HOLDING PUBLIC OFFICE: *Other Disqualifications* From All Offices (7)	HOLDING PUBLIC OFFICE: *Other Disqualifications* From Specified Offices (8)	DISQUALIFICATION FROM REPRESENTATIVE AND FIDUCIARY FUNCTIONS: *Personal Representative of Estate* (9)	DISQUALIFICATION FROM REPRESENTATIVE AND FIDUCIARY FUNCTIONS: *Guardian or Conservator* (10)	DISQUALIFICATION FROM REPRESENTATIVE AND FIDUCIARY FUNCTIONS: *Fiduciary or Trustee* (11)
CAL. Codes (West 1977 & Supp. 1981)	mentally incompetent const. art II, §4	registration canceled when insanity legally established Elec. 701(b)	unable to drive safely because of disability, disease, or disorder Veh. 12805(e)(2) license issued if mental defect does not affect ability to exercise reasonable & ordinary control in driving Veh. 12806(a)	suspension or revocation Veh. 13359	not in possession of natural faculties or not of ordinary intelligence Civ. Proc. 198(2) grand juror: not in possession of natural faculties, not of ordinary intgelligence, or not of sound judgment Penal 893(a)(2)		office becomes vacant if adjudicated mentally incapacitated Gov't 1770(b)	public officer or employee having powers of peace officer if mental or emotional condition might adversely affect exercise of powers Gov't 1031(f) judge may be retired for disability which seriously interferes w/performance of duties & is or is likely to become permanent const. art. VI, §18(c)(1)	adjudication of incompetence disqualifies Prob. 401, 420	removal for incapacity to suitably perform duties Prob. 2650(c)	trustee's office vacated when conservator or guardian appointed for own estate or person *fn. 1* Civ. 2281(1)(c) Civ. 1161(a)
COLO. Rev. Stat. Ann. (1973 & Supp. 1982)	*fn. 6*		inability to operate motor vehicle because of mental incompetence *fn. 2* 42-2-119(1)(b) 42-2-103(2)(d)	cancellation 42-2-119(1)(b) mandatory revocation if ct. determines person mentally incompetent & enters order specifically finding person incapable of safely operating motor vehicle 42-2-122(1)(h)	incapable of rendering satisfactory jury service because of mental disability 13-71-109(c)				*fn. 3* 15-12-609	*fn. 5* 15-14-306	*fn. 1* 11-50-108
CONN. Gen. Stat. Ann. (West 1970 & Supp. 1981)	mentally incompetent 9-12(a)		if suffers from any disease that might affect operation of motor vehicle, may be required to demonstrate capability or to provide medical certificate; license refused to person incapable of driving safely 14-36(b)	license refused or limited 14-36(b)	permanent disability impairing capacity to serve 51-217 not an elector 51-217	any office const. art. VI, §10 governor const. art. IV, §5 lieutenant governor const. art. IV, §6	commissioner of administrative services may reject any application for job as state employee, if applicant medically unfit to perform duties effectively 5-221(a)		executor incapable of accepting such trust 45-168(a)	testamentary trustee or guardian may be removed by ct. if becomes incapable, unless will provides otherwise 45-263(c)	vacancy when trustee becomes incapable *fn. 1* 45-84 fiduciary may be removed by ct. if becomes incapable 45-263(a) 45-107(b) testamentary trustee or guardian may be removed by ct. if becomes incapable, unless will provides otherwise 45-263(c)

TABLE 8.3 OTHER RIGHTS AFFECTED BY MENTAL DISABILITY—*Continued*

	VOTING		DRIVING			HOLDING PUBLIC OFFICE			DISQUALIFICATION FROM REPRESENTATIVE AND FIDUCIARY FUNCTIONS		
							Other Disqualifications				
STATE	*Persons Disqualified* (1)	*Enforcement* (2)	*Persons Disqualified* (3)	*Enforcement* (4)	JURY DISQUALIFICATIONS (5)	*Must Be Qualified Voter* (6)	From All Offices (7)	From Specified Offices (8)	*Personal Representative of Estate* (9)	*Guardian or Conservator* (10)	*Fiduciary or Trustee* (11)
DEL. Code Ann. (1974 & Supp. 1980)	idiot or insane person const. art. V, §2 15, §1701	refuse registration const. art. V, §4 names of persons disqualified from voting removed by board of elections 15, §1702 any person may move before judge to remove name of disqualified voter 15, §1706	adjudged mentally ill, idiot, imbecile, or feeble-minded, unless restored to competency by judicial decree or hospital superintendent's certificate, or unless dep't satisfied that competent to drive safely fn. 7 21, §2707(b)(4), (5)	may be immediately suspended if mental infirmities or disabilities render driving unsafe 21, §2733(a)(3) revocation upon hearing 21, §2733(b) if may not be mentally qualified, evaluation & report by medical advisory board, followed by suspension or restriction of license or further exam. 21, §2724	incapable, by reason of mental infirmity, to render satisfactory jury service 10, §4506(b)(4)			lieutenant governor acts as governor if governor incapable because of mental disability const. art. III, §20	mentally incapacitated person 12, §1508		fn. 1 12, §4507
D.C. Code Ann. (1973 & Supp. 1978)	adjudged mentally incompetent 1-1102(c)	denial of registration 1-1107(b)(1)	not mentally qualified 40-301(a)(1)	suspension or revocation for mental incapacity 40-302(a)	same as federal jurors 11-1901 incapable of rendering satisfactory jury service because of mental infirmity 28 U.S.C. §1865(b)(4)		developmentally disabled may be examined to assure that meet min. qualifications 1-337.2		mentally ill or under conservatorship 20-351(a)(2), (3) executor must be legally competent 20-301(a)(1)		
FLA. Stat. Ann. (West 1976 & Supp. 1980)	adjudicated mentally incompetent const. art. VI, §4 adjudicated mentally incompetent & competency not legally restored 97.041(3)(a)	proof of qualifications may be required upon registration 97.041(2) challenge by any elector or watcher 101.111	fn. 2 322.05(5)	ct. shall require surrender of all licenses when adjudicated mentally incompetent 322.2505	not registered elector 40.01	legislator const. art. III, §15(c) lieutenant governor, cabinet minister const. art. IV, §5(b) justice or judge const. art. V, §8	final adjudication that mentally incompetent creates vacancy in office 114.01(1)(k)	lieutenant governor acts as governor during governor's mental incapacity const. art. IV, §3(b) justice or judge may be retired for permanent disability that seriously interferes w/performance of duties const. art. V, §12(f) upon recommendation of 2/3 of judicial qualifications commission const. art. V, §12(f)	mentally unable to perform duties 733.303(1)(b) removed for adjudication of incompetency or mental incapacity 733.504(1), (2)	guardian of incompetent must be sui juris 744.309(1)(a) disqualified if incapable from sickness or want of understanding 744.309(4) guardian may be removed for insanity or other incompetency 744.474(4)	fn. 1 710.08

TABLE 8.3 OTHER RIGHTS AFFECTED BY MENTAL DISABILITY—*Continued*

STATE	VOTING: *Persons Disqualified* (1)	VOTING: *Enforcement* (2)	DRIVING: *Persons Disqualified* (3)	DRIVING: *Enforcement* (4)	JURY DISQUALIFICATIONS (5)	HOLDING PUBLIC OFFICE: *Must Be Qualified Voter* (6)	HOLDING PUBLIC OFFICE: *Other Disqualifications* From All Offices (7)	HOLDING PUBLIC OFFICE: *Other Disqualifications* From Specified Offices (8)	DISQUALIFICATION FROM REPRESENTATIVE AND FIDUCIARY FUNCTIONS: *Personal Representative of Estate* (9)	DISQUALIFICATION FROM REPRESENTATIVE AND FIDUCIARY FUNCTIONS: *Guardian or Conservator* (10)	DISQUALIFICATION FROM REPRESENTATIVE AND FIDUCIARY FUNCTIONS: *Fiduciary or Trustee* (11)
GA. Code Ann. (1980 & Supp. 1981)	idiots & insane persons const. 2-501	denial of registration const. 2-501 probate judge files list w/registrars of those who appear to be disqualified by adjudication of idiocy or insanity 34-621 challenge by any elector 34-628	cannot drive safely because of mental disability *fn. 2* 68B-203(6)4, 6	revocation w/o hearing if so incapacitated by disease or mental disability that incompetent to drive 68B-307(a)2	not "intelligent" 59-106 challenge for cause in felony case: idiot or lunatic 59-804.3 grand juror: idiot, lunatic, or insane 59-201		unsound mind 89-101(5) office vacated 89-501(4)	office of elected executive officer declared vacant if unable to perform duties because of permanent mental disability const. 2-2901a justice or judge may be retired for disability seriously interfering w/performance of duties, which is, or is likely to become permanent const. 2-1203(b)	administrator must be of sound mind & laboring under no disability 113-1202	may not be appointed guardian of incapacitated adult if adjudged incapacitated 49-602(e)	*fn. 1* 48-307
HAWAII Rev. Stat. Ann. (1976 & Supp. 1980)	non compos mentis const. art. II, §2	name removed by clerk 11-23 challenge by voter 11-25	unable to drive safely because of mental disability 286-104(4) ordered hospitalized or committed, unless certified mentally competent by director of health 286-104(6)	suspension w/o hearing if mental infirmities make driving unsafe; revocation or further suspension after hearing 286-119	incapable of rendering satisfactory jury service because of mental disability 612-4(3)	legislator const. art. III, §6 governor const. art. V, §1 lieutenant governor const. art. V, §2	may not be discriminated against because of mental handicap if can perform efficiently & not hazardously 78-2		*fn. 3* 560:3-609	*fn. 4* 560:5-311(a) *fn. 5* 560:5-306	*fn. 1* 553-7
IDAHO Code Ann. (1980 & Supp. 1981)	under guardianship, idiotic, or insane const. art. VI, §3 34-403	not registered 34-412 challenge 34-1111	*fn. 2* 49-309(5)	suspension w/o hearing if mental disability prevents exercise of reasonable & ordinary control over motor vehicle 49-330(a)3(1) revocation or further suspension after hearing 49-330(d)	under guardianship, idiotic, or insane const. art. VI, §3 incapable of rendering satisfactory jury service because of mental disability 2-209(2)(c)	legislator const. art. III, §6 prosecuting attorney const. art. V, §18 district judge const. art. V, §23	under guardianship, idiotic, or insane const. art. VI, §3		*fn. 3* 15-3-609	*fn. 4* 15-5-311(a) *fn. 5* 15-5-306	*fn. 1* 68-807
ILL. Ann. Stat. (Smith-Hurd 1971 & Supp. 1980)	*fn. 8*	challenge by legal voter 46, §§17-10, 18-5	*fn. 2* 95½, §6-103(5) unable to drive safely because of mental disability 95½, §6-103(8)	suspension or revocation 95½, §6-206(a)18	infirm or not in possession of natural faculties 78, §2 grand juror: same 78, §9			judge may be suspended or retired if mentally unable to perform duties const. art. VI, §15(e)(2)	of unsound mind or adjudged disabled person 110½, §§6-13(a), 9-1 removed if adjudged subject to involuntary admission or disabled person 110½, §63-2(a)(2)	of unsound mind or adjudged disabled person: guardian of minor 110½, §11-3(a) guardian of disabled adult 110½, §11a-5(a)	*fn. 1* 110½, §207
IND. Code Ann. (Burns 1972 & Supp. 1981)			*fn. 2* *fn. 7* 9-1-4-30(d), (e)		incompetence cause for challenge of juror in criminal case 35-37-1-5(a)(8) incompetent grand juror discharged 35-34-2-3(c)(7)			justice or judge may be removed for disability seriously interfering w/performance of duties and/or likely to become permanent const. art. VII, §11	unsound mind 29-1-10-1(b)(2) may be removed if becomes mentally incompetent 29-1-10-6	guardian must be qualified to serve as personal representative 29-1-18-9	trustee must be of sound mind & have legal capacity 30-4-2-11(a)

TABLE 8.3 OTHER RIGHTS AFFECTED BY MENTAL DISABILITY—*Continued*

STATE	VOTING		DRIVING		JURY DISQUALIFICATIONS	HOLDING PUBLIC OFFICE			DISQUALIFICATION FROM REPRESENTATIVE AND FIDUCIARY FUNCTIONS		
							Other Disqualifications				
	Persons Disqualified (1)	*Enforcement* (2)	*Persons Disqualified* (3)	*Enforcement* (4)	(5)	*Must Be Qualified Voter* (6)	From All Offices (7)	From Specified Offices (8)	*Personal Representative of Estate* (9)	*Guardian or Conservator* (10)	*Fiduciary or Trustee* (11)
IOWA Code Ann. (West 1966 & Supp. 1980)	idiot or insane person const. art. II, §5	registration canceled on notice by district ct. clerk that person legally determined incompetent or severely retarded 48.31 challenge by any person 48.15	adjudged incompetent because of mental illness & not restored 321.177(5) unable to drive safely because of mental disability 321.177(7)	examined if dep't believes mentally incompetent 321.186 suspension 321.210(4) revocation 321.211	not of sound judgment 607.1					must qualify as fiduciary 633.633	disqualified as fiduciary if mentally ill or retardate 633.63
KAN. Stat. Ann. (1976 & Supp. 1980)			*fn. 2* 8-237(e)		under adjudication of incompetency 43-158 may be excused if so mentally infirm that unequal to ordinary jury duty 43-159(a)			justice or judge may be retired for incapacity const. art. III, §15	executor must be legally competent 59-701 administrator must be competent 59-705	conservator removed for incapacity 59-3029	fiduciary may be removed if becomes incapacitated *fn. 1* 59-1711 38-907
KY. Rev. Stat. Ann. (Michie 1980 & Supp. 1983)	idiots & insane persons const. §145.1 116.025	purged 116.115, 116.125, 116.127 not registered 116.045(1)	adjudged insane or mentally retarded & not restored by judicial decree or hospital superintendent's certificate *fn. 7* 186.440(5), (6)	suspension if mental infirmities render unsafe to drive 186.570(1)(c)	incapable of rendering effective jury service because of mental disability 29A.080(2)(d)			judge or justice may be retired for disability const. §121 may not be special local peace officer if adjudged mentally disabled 61.360(1)(c) may not be special law enforcement officer if adjudicated mentally disabled & not restored 61.906(1)(d)	removed if insane 395.160(1)	insane guardian removed 387.090(1)	incompetent fiduciary removed *fn. 1* 395.325(2) mentally disabled fiduciary removed 395.325(2) 385.071
LA. Rev. Stat. Ann. (West 1979 & Supp. 1980)	interdicted after being judicially declared mentally incompetent 18:102(1)	not registered 18:102(1) clerk of ct. transmits copy of judgment of interdiction for mental incompetence to registrar 18:172 challenge on affidavit of 2 voters 18:196 challenge by commissioner, watcher, or voter 18:565A		suspension, cancellation, or revocation if afflicted w/such mental infirmities or disabilities as would constitute grounds for refusal of license 32:414D(8), E	under interdiction or incapable because of mental infirmity La. Code Crim. Proc. Ann. art. 401 13:3041	legislator const. art. III, §4(A) executive officer: governor, lieutenant governor, secretary of state, attorney general, treasurer, commissioner of agriculture, commissioner of insurance, superintendent of education, commissioner of elections const. art. IV, §2 justice of the peace 13:2581.1 constable 13.2581.2B 33:1731 legislative auditor 24:511A			interdicted or mentally incompetent La. Code Civ. Pro. Ann. art. 3097(2)	may not be appointed tutor if interdicted or mentally incompetent La. Code Civ. Pro. Ann. art. 4231(2)	

TABLE 8.3 OTHER RIGHTS AFFECTED BY MENTAL DISABILITY—*Continued*

STATE	VOTING		DRIVING		JURY DISQUALIFICATIONS (5)	HOLDING PUBLIC OFFICE			DISQUALIFICATION FROM REPRESENTATIVE AND FIDUCIARY FUNCTIONS		
	Persons Disqualified (1)	*Enforcement* (2)	*Persons Disqualified* (3)	*Enforcement* (4)		*Must Be Qualified Voter* (6)	*Other Disqualifications* From All Offices (7)	*Other Disqualifications* From Specified Offices (8)	*Personal Representative of Estate* (9)	*Guardian or Conservator* (10)	*Fiduciary or Trustee* (11)
ME. Rev. Stat. Ann. (1981)	under guardianship for reasons of mental illness const. art. II, §1 21, §245(1)	removed from voting list 21, §102-A(3)			incapable of rendering satisfactory jury service because of mental disability 14, §1211			president of senate or speaker of house exercises powers & duties of governor when governor unable from mental disability const. art. V, §15	*fn. 3* 18-A, §3-609	*fn. 4* 18-A, §5-311(a) *fn. 5* 18-A, §5-306	*fn. 1* 33, §1007
MD. Ann. Code (1980)	under care or guardianship for mental disability const. art. I, §4	not registered 33, §3-4(d) challenge by any voter 33, §3-16	*fn. 2* Transp. §16-103.1		not qualified to vote or incapable of rendering satisfactory jury service because of mental infirmity Cts. & Jud. Proc. §8-207	governor const. art. II, §5 lieutenant governor 41, §15D(b) judge const. art. IV, §2 attorney general const. art. V, §4		office of governor or lieutenant governor becomes vacant if 3/5 of general assembly & ct. of appeals determine unable to perform duties because of mental disability const. art. II, §6(b)	appointment terminated by judicial determination of disability Est. & Trusts §6-304	appointment of guardian terminated by judicial decree of legal disability Est. & Trusts §13-220(c)	*fn. 1* Est. & Trusts §13-307
MASS. Ann. Laws (Michie/Law. Co-op. (1980 & Supp. 1981)	under guardianship const. articles of amendment art. III, §105 51, §1	must state not under guardianship in affidavit 51, §36 examined & stricken from register if not qualified 51, §§47B, 49			not qualified to vote 234, §1 234A, §11(1) in Middlesex county: incapable of rendering satisfactory jury service because of mental disability 234A, §11(5)		*fn. 9*	judicial officers may be retired because of mental disability const. pt. 2, ch. 3, art. I, §82 amended by Articles of Amendment art. LVIII, §188 art. XCVIII, §244 assistant clerk may be removed if incapacitated by mental disability 211A, §6 treasurer's duties performed by first deputy treasurer when treasurer incapacitated by mental illness 10, §4	must be competent 192, §4 193, §1 may be removed if insane 195, §11	may be removed if mentally ill 201, §33	insane trustee may be removed 203, §12
MICH. Comp. Laws Ann. (1980 & Supp. 1980)			mental disability prevents exercise of reasonable & ordinary control over vehicle 257.303(f) adjudged mentally incompetent & not judicially declared competent 257.303(e)	investigation, examination, and suspension, revocation or restriction if mental infirmity or disability renders driving unsafe 257.320 superintendent of hospital notifies dep't that person under care for mental illness; license suspended until notifies dep't condition no longer exists 257.303a	not mentally able to carry out functions of juror 600.1307a(1)(c)					*fn. 4* *fn. 5* 700.454(1) 700.446	*fn. 1* 554.457

TABLE 8.3 OTHER RIGHTS AFFECTED BY MENTAL DISABILITY—*Continued*

STATE	VOTING: Persons Disqualified (1)	VOTING: Enforcement (2)	DRIVING: Persons Disqualified (3)	DRIVING: Enforcement (4)	JURY DISQUALIFICATIONS (5)	HOLDING PUBLIC OFFICE: Must Be Qualified Voter (6)	HOLDING PUBLIC OFFICE: Other Disqualifications: From All Offices (7)	HOLDING PUBLIC OFFICE: Other Disqualifications: From Specified Offices (8)	DISQUALIFICATION FROM REPRESENTATIVE AND FIDUCIARY FUNCTIONS: Personal Representative of Estate (9)	Guardian or Conservator (10)	Fiduciary or Trustee (11)
MINN. Stat. Ann. (West (1975 & Supp. 1980)	under guardianship, insane, or not mentally competent const. art. VII, §1	report by probate judge 201.15 not registered 201.061 challenge by any registered voter 201.231	adjudged legally incompetent because of mental illness or deficiency and not restored to capacity *fn. 7* 171.04(5), (9)	suspension w/o hearing if adjudged incompetent to drive; revocation or extended suspension upon hearing 171.18(5)	incapable of rendering satisfactory jury service because of mental disability 593.41(2)(5) cause for objection to grand juror that insane 625.54(4)	any elective office const. art. VII, §6 legislator const. art. IV, §6		judge may be retired for disability that seriously interferes w/performance of duties or is likely to become permanent 490.16(3) office of probate judge declared vacant if insane or incapacitated by mental disability 525.072 incapacitated supreme ct. justice retired 490.025(1) mentally incapacitated district judge retired 490.101(2)	*fn. 3* 524.3-609		*fn. 1* 527.07
MISS. Code Ann. (1972 & Supp. 1981)	idiots & insane persons const. art. XII, §241 23-5-85		adjudged mental disability & not restored to mental competency 63-1-9(f) unable to operate vehicle safely because of mental disability 63-1-9(d)		not qualified elector 13-5-1	any office const. art. XII, §250 sheriff 19-25-3 legislator const. art. IV, §§41, 42 county judge 9-9-5	office vacated if found of unsound mind by inquest 25-5-1	justice or judge may be removed for mental disability seriously interfering with performance of duties which is or is likely to become permanent const. art. VI, §177A	unsound mind 91-7-65 91-7-35		*fn. 1* 91-19-17
MO. Rev. Stat. (1980)	person who has guardian because of mental incapacity or who is involuntarily confined in a mental institution by adjudication const. art. VIII, §2 adjudged incompetent 115.133(2)	report by probate clerk of those adjudicated incompetent & not restored 115.195(3) not registered 115.135 name stricken 115.193	adjudged of unsound mind & not restored to competency 302.060(5)		incapable of performing duties of juror because of mental illness or infirmity 494.020(6) not "sober and intelligent" 494.010	legislator const. art. III, §§4, 6 judge const. art. V, §21 sheriff 57.010	office deemed vacant if adjudicated incompetent 475.350	commissioner of supreme ct. or ct. of appeals retired for permanent mental infirmity 476.445	unsound mind 473.117(1)(2) letters revoked if becomes of unsound mind 473.140	may not be guardian if of unsound mind 475.055(2) guardian removed if becomes of unsound mind 475.110 473.140	*fn. 1* 404.070
MONT. Code Ann. (1979)	unsound mind as determined by ct. const. art. IV, §2	registration canceled 13-2-402(3) challenge by elector 13-2-404	*fn. 2* 61-5-105(5)		not registered elector on most recent list 3-15-301	any public office const. art. IV, §3	office becomes vacant upon determination that incumbent mentally ill 2-16-501(2)		*fn. 3* 72-3-522	*fn. 4* 72-5-312(1) *fn. 5* 72-5-324	trustee discharged by judgment that of unsound mind *fn. 1* 72-23-504(5) 72-26-402
NEB. Rev. Stat. (1979 & Supp. 1981)	non compos mentis const. art. VI, §2 32-1048	challenge 32-217	committed to state institution *fn. 10* 60-419	*fn. 10* 60-419	incapable of rendering satisfactory jury service because of mental disability 25-1601(1)	legislator const. art. III, §8 chief justice or judge of supreme ct. const. art. V, §7 24-202(d)		judge may be retired for mental disability which seriously interferes with performance of duties and which is or is reasonably likely to become permanent 24-709	*fn. 3* 30-2452	*fn. 4* 30-2627(a) *fn. 5* 30-2622	*fn. 1* 38-1007

TABLE 8.3 OTHER RIGHTS AFFECTED BY MENTAL DISABILITY—*Continued*

	VOTING		DRIVING			HOLDING PUBLIC OFFICE			DISQUALIFICATION FROM REPRESENTATIVE AND FIDUCIARY FUNCTIONS		
							Other Disqualifications				
STATE	*Persons Disqualified* (1)	*Enforcement* (2)	*Persons Disqualified* (3)	*Enforcement* (4)	JURY DISQUALIFICATIONS (5)	*Must Be Qualified Voter* (6)	From All Offices (7)	From Specified Offices (8)	*Personal Representative of Estate* (9)	*Guardian or Conservator* (10)	*Fiduciary or Trustee* (11)
NEV. Rev. Stat. (1981)	idiot or insane person const. art. II, §1	registration canceled if insanity legally established 293.540(2) challenge by registered voter 293.303	not able to drive safely because of mental disability *fn. 2* 483.250(4), (6)	if mentally incompetent to drive, suspension w/o hearing 483.470(1)(e)	rendered incapable by mental infirmity 6.010 not qualified elector const. art. IV, §27	any office const. art. XV, §3 281.040 governor const. art. V, §3 223.010(2) lieutenant governor const. art. V, §17 224.010(2) secretary of state const. art. V, §19 225.010(2) treasurer const. art. V, §19 226.010(2) controller const. art. V, §19 227.010(2) attorney general const. art. V, §19 228.010(2) supreme ct. justice 12.020(3) clerk of supreme ct. 2.210(2) legislator 218.010(1) district judge 3.060(3) justice of the peace 4.010	vacancy on ct. finding of confirmed insanity of incumbent 283.040(1)(c)	justice or judge may be retired for mental disability which prevents proper performance of duties and is likely to be permanent const. art. VI, §21(6)(b)	adjudged incompetent to execute duties because of want of understanding 138.020(1)(c) 139.010(3)	incompetent may not be guardian 159.059(1) ct. may remove guardian who has become mentally incompetent 159.185(1)(a)	*fn. 1* 167.080
N.H. Rev. Stat. Ann. (1979)			mentally improper or incompetent to drive 262:40	suspension 262:40	deemed mentally unfit by ct. 500-A:20			insane state treasurer removed 6:19 supreme ct. justice retired for permanent disability 490:2(I) superior ct. justice retired for permanent disability 491:2	removed if unfit or unsafe because of infirmity of mind 553:10	guardian of incapacitated person must be competent 469-A:10	insane trustee of estate may be removed 564:9 *fn. 1* 463-A:7
N.J. Rev. Stat. Ann. (West 1970 & Supp. 1981)	idiot or insane person const. art. II, §6 19:4-1(1)	name stricken by ct. 19:33-1 peremptory order by superintendent of elections refusing permission to vote 19:32-15			mental disability prevents from properly serving as juror 2A:69-1		vacancy in office when appears insane & committed 52:14-13	supreme ct. justice or superior ct. judge may be removed if so incapacitated as to prevent performing duties const. art. VI, §6 ¶5 tax ct. judge may be retired 2A:3A-17			fiduciary may be removed if of unsound mind or mentally incapacitated for transaction of business 3A:11-4e
N.M. Stat. Ann. (1978 & Supp. 1981)	idiots & insane persons const. art. VII, §1	ct. files certificate w/county clerk upon determining insanity 1-4-26 county clerk cancels registration 1-4-24	mental disability or disease renders unable to drive safely & not restored to health 66-5-5E		incapable because of mental illness or infirmity 38-5-1 38-5-11B(1)	elective office const. art. VII, §2A			*fn. 3* 45-3-609	*fn. 4* 45-5-311A *fn. 5* 45-5-306	*fn. 1* 46-7-7

TABLE 8.3 OTHER RIGHTS AFFECTED BY MENTAL DISABILITY—*Continued*

STATE	VOTING: *Persons Disqualified* (1)	VOTING: *Enforcement* (2)	DRIVING: *Persons Disqualified* (3)	DRIVING: *Enforcement* (4)	JURY DISQUALIFICATIONS (5)	HOLDING PUBLIC OFFICE: *Must Be Qualified Voter* (6)	HOLDING PUBLIC OFFICE: *Other Disqualifications* From All Offices (7)	HOLDING PUBLIC OFFICE: *Other Disqualifications* From Specified Offices (8)	DISQUALIFICATION FROM REPRESENTATIVE AND FIDUCIARY FUNCTIONS: *Personal Representative of Estate* (9)	DISQUALIFICATION FROM REPRESENTATIVE AND FIDUCIARY FUNCTIONS: *Guardian or Conservator* (10)	DISQUALIFICATION FROM REPRESENTATIVE AND FIDUCIARY FUNCTIONS: *Fiduciary or Trustee* (11)
N.Y. Laws (McKinney 1978 & Supp. 1980)	adjudged incompetent or committed & not thereafter adjudged competent or released Elec. 5-106(6)	registration canceled Elec. 5-400(4) challenge Elec. 5-218 8-502		permissive suspension or revocation if mentally disabled or committed to dep't of mental hygiene Veh. & Traf. 510.3(b)	not in possession of natural faculties or incapable of rendering satisfactory jury service because of mental infirmity Jud. 510(3) not intelligent Jud. 510(5)		office becomes vacant on ct. order or judgment declaring incumbent incompetent Pub. Off. 30(1)(f)	judge may be retired for mental disability const. art. VI, §22			disqualified as fiduciary if incompetent or incapable because of want of understanding *fn. 1* Sur. Ct. Proc. Act 707(1)(b),(e) 711(2) Est. Powers & Trusts 7-4.6
N.C. Gen. Stat. (1978 & Supp. 1981)			*fn. 7* 20-9(e) adjudged insane, idiot, imbecile, or feebleminded & not restored 20-9(d)	on notice by clerk of ct. that person adjudicated incompetent, commissioner of motor vehicles revokes license unless satisfied person competent to operate vehicle safely 20-17.1	not mentally competent, adjudged non compos mentis 9-3			lieutenant governor serves as acting governor during mental incapacity of governor const. art. III, §3(2), (4) see also 147-11.1 justice, judge, magistrate, or clerk may be removed for mental incapacity const. art. IV, §17	adjudged incompetent and remains under disability 28A-4-2	guardian removed where would be legally disqualified as administrator 33-9(4)	successor trustee may be appointed upon incapacity of trustee 36A-33
N.D. Cent. Code (1980 & Supp. 1981)	declared mentally incompetent & order not rescinded const. art. II, §2 under guardianship; non compos mentis or insane; to be denied right to vote must have guardian appointed by ct. upon finding of incompetence or incapacitation due to mental illness or defect 16.1-01-04(5)		not able to drive safely because of mental disability *fn. 2* 39-06-03(4), (7)		incapable of rendering satisfactory jury service because of mental disability 27-09.1-08(2)d	any office 44-01-01 governor, lieutenant governor const. art. V, §3 legislator const. art. IV, §§4, 10	office becomes vacant if incumbent adjudged mentally ill 44-02-01(2)	judge may be retired for disability seriously interfering with performance of duties which is or is likely to become permanent 27-23-03(3) supreme ct. or district judge retired for mental disability 27-05-03.1 another assigned to hear cause when justice or judge mentally incapacitated const. art. VI, §11	*fn. 3* 30.1-17-09	*fn. 4* 30.1-28-11(1) *fn. 5* 30.1-28-06	trustee discharged by judgment that of unsound mind *fn. 1* 59-02-20-1960 47-24-07
OHIO Rev. Code Ann. (Baldwin 1975 & Supp. 1980)	idiot or insane person const. art. V, §6	probate judge notifies board of elections of those adjudicated incompetent to vote 3503.18 not registered 3503.7 registration canceled 3503.18	*fn. 7* 4507.08(B)	suspension if adjudged mentally incompetent to hold license 4507.161	not elector 2313.06	any office const. art. XV, §4 county judge 1907.051		judge may be retired for permanent mental disability preventing proper discharge of duties 2701.12(B) judge may be suspended w/o pay when mental disability will prevent proper discharge of duties indefinitely 2701.12(c)			final account if sole fiduciary becomes incapacitated 2109.26

TABLE 8.3 OTHER RIGHTS AFFECTED BY MENTAL DISABILITY—*Continued*

	VOTING		DRIVING			HOLDING PUBLIC OFFICE			DISQUALIFICATION FROM REPRESENTATIVE AND FIDUCIARY FUNCTIONS		
							Other Disqualifications				
STATE	*Persons Disqualified* (1)	*Enforcement* (2)	*Persons Disqualified* (3)	*Enforcement* (4)	JURY DISQUALIFICATIONS (5)	*Must Be Qualified Voter* (6)	From All Offices (7)	From Specified Offices (8)	*Personal Representative of Estate* (9)	*Guardian or Conservator* (10)	*Fiduciary or Trustee* (11)
OKLA. Stat. (West 1976 & Supp. 1980)	adjudged mentally incompetent, until judicially declared competent 26, §4-101(2) mentally retarded 26, §4-101(3)	registration canceled; county clerk prepares monthly list of persons adjudged mentally incompetent 26, §4-120(5) not registered 26, §4-101(2), (3)	afflicted with mental disease that would impair driving ability *fn. 2* 47, §6-103(5), (8)	cancellation, at discretion of commissioner, if person may temporarily lose control of vehicle because of mental disease 47, §6-207	not qualified elector, of sound mind & discretion 38, §28	legislator const. art. V, §17 governor, lieutenant governor, secretary of state, state auditor & inspector, attorney general, treasurer, superintendent of public instruction const. art. VI, §3 supreme ct. justice const. art. VII, §2 ct. of criminal appeals judge 20, §31 district judge const. art. VII, §8(g) ct. of appeals judge 20, §30.9			adjudged incompetent for want of understanding 58, §102(3) 58, §126(3) removed if incompetent to act 58, §§234, 235	guardian may be removed if becomes insane or otherwise incapable 58, §875	*fn. 1* 60, §407
OR. Rev. Stat. (1979)	idiot or mentally diseased const. art. II, §3	challenge 247.550, 247.560, 254.415	admitted to state institution & found mentally ill or mentally retarded, unless restored *fn. 7* 482.120(2) 482.130(1)(b)	suspension w/o hearing if mental infirmities or disabilities render driving unsafe 482.450(1)(c) revocation or extension of suspension upon hearing 482.450(2) if history of mental disability or disease, may be required to demonstrate that qualified to safely operate motor vehicle 482.240	not of sound mind 10.030(1)(d)	ct. of appeals judge 2.540(2) justice of the peace 51.240 constable 51.450	office becomes vacant if adjudged mentally diseased 236.010(f)	judge may be retired if becomes so mentally incapacitated that unable to discharge duties 1.310	incompetent 113.095(1) removed 113.195(1)	incompetent 126.045(1)	*fn. 1* 126.856 126.860
PA. Stat. Ann. (Purdon 1977 & Supp. 1980)			reported mental disability or disorder *fn. 2* 75, §1503(4), (5)	those authorized to treat required to report mental disabilities or disorders affecting ability to drive safely 75, §1518 examined & license recalled if not mentally qualified 75, §1519	incapable of efficient jury service because of mental infirmity 42, §4502(2)			judge may be retired for disability seriously interfering w/performance of duties 42, §3331	adjudged lunatic 20, §3182(2) incompetent because of mental incapacity & incompetency likely to continue 20, §3182(3)	guardian of minor removed on same grounds as personal representative 20, §5131(1) guardian of incompetent removed on same grounds as personal representative 20, §5515(6)	trustee removed on same grounds as personal representative *fn. 1* 20, §7121(1) incompetent fiduciary 20, §3324 20, §5308

TABLE 8.3 OTHER RIGHTS AFFECTED BY MENTAL DISABILITY—*Continued*

STATE	VOTING		DRIVING		JURY DISQUALIFICATIONS (5)	HOLDING PUBLIC OFFICE			DISQUALIFICATION FROM REPRESENTATIVE AND FIDUCIARY FUNCTIONS		
	Persons Disqualified (1)	*Enforcement* (2)	*Persons Disqualified* (3)	*Enforcement* (4)		*Must Be Qualified Voter* (6)	*Other Disqualifications* From All Offices (7)	*Other Disqualifications* From Specified Offices (8)	*Personal Representative of Estate* (9)	*Guardian or Conservator* (10)	*Fiduciary or Trustee* (11)
R.I. Gen. Laws (1969 & Supp. 1981)	adjudicated non compos mentis const. articles of amendment art. XXXVIII, §1	challenge 17-1-3.1 name stricken 17-10-7	unable to operate vehicle safely because of mental disability *fn. 2* 31-10-3(5), (8)	suspension w/o hearing if incompetent to drive safely because of mental disability; revocation, extension, or modification of suspension upon hearing 31-11-7(a), (b)	not qualified elector 9-9-1	any civil office const. articles of amendment art. XXXIX, §1		governor, lieutenant governor, secretary of state, attorney general, treasurer replaced if insane or otherwise incapacitated const. articles of amendment art. XI, §3 election to replace legislator if insane or otherwise incapacitated const. articles of amendment art. XI, §6 judge retired for mental disability interfering w/performance of duties 8-16-9 law enforcement officer must pass psychological examination 42-28.3-1	incompetent 33-8-4	guardian removed if incapable because of insanity 33-15-18	
S.C. Code Ann. (Law. Co-op. 1976 & Supp. 1980)	mentally incompetent 7-5-120(5)(a)	not registered 7-5-120(5)(a)	*fn. 2* 56-1-40(4)	examination if dep't has good cause to believe incompetent or otherwise not qualified because of mental disability; suspension, revocation, or restriction 56-1-270	not qualified elector const. art. V, §18 mental infirmities prevent efficient jury service 14-7-820	legislator const. art. III, §7 any office const. art. XVII, §1		judge may be removed for disability seriously interfering w/performance of duties which is or is likely to become permanent const. art. V, §13		guardian of mentally retarded person or minor replaced if becomes incapacitated 21-19-230, 21-19-250	*fn. 1* 35-3-80
S.D. Codified Laws Ann. (1980 & Supp. 1981)	mental incompetence const. art. VII, §2	not registered 12-4-1 clerk of ct. reports names of persons declared mentally incompetent 12-4-18 challenge 12-4-23	*fn. 2* 32-12-32	suspension after opportunity for hearing if mentally incompetent to drive 32-12-49(3)	not of sound mind 16-13-10	legislator const. art. III, §3 justice, judge, person presiding over ct. of limited jurisdiction const. art. V, §6 magistrate or clerk acting as magistrate 16-12A-5			suspension & removal if incompetent to act 30-14-4 30-14-5	guardian removed if becomes mentally ill or otherwise incapable 30-27-42	*fn. 1* 55-10-29, 55-10-31, 55-10-34
TENN. Code Ann. (1980)			unable to operate vehicle with safety because of mental disabilities *fn. 2* 55-7-105(a)(5), (7)		unsound mind 22-1-102		office vacated by adjudication of insanity of incumbent 8-48-101(7)	additional treasurer serves when treasurer incapacitated 8-5-202			trustee removed if lunatic or non compos mentis *fn. 1* 35-117 35-808

TABLE 8.3 OTHER RIGHTS AFFECTED BY MENTAL DISABILITY—*Continued*

STATE	VOTING		DRIVING		JURY DISQUALIFICATIONS	HOLDING PUBLIC OFFICE			DISQUALIFICATION FROM REPRESENTATIVE AND FIDUCIARY FUNCTIONS		
							Other Disqualifications				
	Persons Disqualified (1)	*Enforcement* (2)	*Persons Disqualified* (3)	*Enforcement* (4)	(5)	*Must Be Qualified Voter* (6)	From All Offices (7)	From Specified Offices (8)	*Personal Representative of Estate* (9)	*Guardian or Conservator* (10)	*Fiduciary or Trustee* (11)
TEX. Rev. Civ. Stat. Ann. (Vernon 1967 & Supp. 1980)	idiots & lunatics const. art. VI, §1 Elec. 5.01	not registered Elec. 5.10a challenge Elec. 5.17a, 8.09	adjudged insane, idiot, imbecile, or feeble-minded & not restored *fn. 7* 6687b(4), (6), (8)	revocation by finding of ct. that mentally incompetent 6687b(30)	not of sound mind 2133(2) insanity cause for challenge Crim. Proc. 35.16(a)4	legislator const. art. III, §§6, 7		judge or justice may be retired or removed for disability seriously interfering w/performance of duties which is or is likely to become permanent const. art. V, §1-a special commissioner appointed to assist civil appeals judge totally disabled by mental illness 1813(b) district or county officer removed by district ct. if has become unfit because of serious mental defect 5970, 5972(a)	incompetent Prob. 78(b)	incompetent not appointed as guardian Prob. 110(c) removed Prob. 222(b)(5)	incompetent trustee removed *fn. 1* 7425b-42 5923-101(7)
UTAH Code Ann. (1978 & Supp. 1981)	mentally incompetent const. art. IV, §6		adjudged mentally incompetent & not restored *fn. 7* 41-2-5(4), (5)	suspension w/o hearing if mental infirmities or disabilities render unsafe to drive 41-2-19(a)(3) revocation or extension of suspension upon hearing; suspension becomes revocation after 1 yr. 41-2-19(b)	not capable of rendering satisfactory jury service 78-46-8(2)(c)	legislator const. art. VI, §5 governor, lieutenant governor, auditor, treasurer, attorney general const. art. VII, §§1, 3		justice, judge or justice of peace may be retired for disability seriously interfering w/performance of duties which is or is likely to become permanent 78-7-29	*fn. 3* 75-3-609	*fn. 4* 75-5-311(1) *fn. 5* 75-5-306	
VT. Stat. Ann. (1978 & Supp. 1980)	not "of a quiet and peaceable behavior" const. ch. II, §42		mentally unfit 23, §603		grand juror: not "judicious" R. Crim. P. 6(a)				removed if becomes insane or otherwise incapable 14, §917	mentally disabled guardian of minor removed 14, §3001 guardian of mentally disabled person must be competent 14, §3072(a)	insane or otherwise incapable trustee removed 14, §2314
VA. Code Ann. (1980 & Supp. 1981)	adjudicated mentally incompetent & not restored const. art. II, §1 24.1-42	not registered 24.1-47 petition to ct. by 3 qualified voters 24.1-63 challenge 24.1-133	adjudged legally incompetent or mentally ill & not restored *fn. 7* 46.1-360 46.1-361(a)		adjudicated mentally incompetent 8.01-338(1) mentally retarded or mentally ill 8.01-338(3) 8.01-2(6)	any elective office const. art. II, §5 24.1-167 legislator const. art. IV, §4 governor const. art. V, §3 lieutenant governor const. art. V, §13		judge retired for disability seriously interfering w/performance of duties which is or is likely to be permanent const. art. VI, §10			trustee replaced if becomes incapable because of mental disability 26-48(2)

TABLE 8.3 OTHER RIGHTS AFFECTED BY MENTAL DISABILITY—*Continued*

STATE	VOTING		DRIVING		JURY DISQUALIFICATIONS (5)	HOLDING PUBLIC OFFICE			DISQUALIFICATION FROM REPRESENTATIVE AND FIDUCIARY FUNCTIONS		
							Other Disqualifications				
	Persons Disqualified (1)	*Enforcement* (2)	*Persons Disqualified* (3)	*Enforcement* (4)		*Must Be Qualified Voter* (6)	From All Offices (7)	From Specified Offices (8)	*Personal Representative of Estate* (9)	*Guardian or Conservator* (10)	*Fiduciary or Trustee* (11)
WASH. Rev. Code Ann. (1976 & Supp. 1980)	idiots & insane persons const. art. VI, §3	challenge 29.59.010	adjudged mentally ill, insane, or incompetent & not restored unless ct. finds can operate vehicle safely 46.20.031(5) unable to operate vehicle safely because of mental disability 46.20.031(8)	suspension 46.20.291(1)(d) restricted license if demonstrate that proper person to operate vehicle 46.20.041	not in full possession of faculties & of sound mind 2.36.070(3) mental defect 2.36.110	any office const. amendment 31; 42.04.020 legislator const. art. II, §7 justice of the peace 3.04.040 3.34.060(1)		judge may be retired for disability seriously interfering w/performance of duties which is or is likely to become permanent const. amendment 71	unsound mind 11.36.010 removed if incompetent to act 11.28.250	unsound mind disqualifies domiciliary guardian 11.88.020(2)	*fn. 1* 21.24.070
W. VA. Code (1981)	unsound mind const. art. IV, §1	not registered 3-2-2 challenge 3-2-29	*fn. 2* 17B-2-3(5)		idiots & lunatics 52-1-2	any office const. art. IV, §4					*fn. 1* 36-7-7
WIS. Stat. Ann. (West 1981)	under guardianship, non compos mentis, or insane const. art. III, §2 under guardianship or adjudicated incapable of understanding objective of elective process 6.03(3)	challenge 6.48, 6.92, 6.925, 6.935, 6.93	adjudged mentally ill or mentally deficient & not restored by ct., certificate of superintendent of institution, or examination *fn. 7* 343.06(5), (7)		infirm or not possessed of natural faculties 756.01(1)	legislator const. art. IV, §6 governor or lieutenant governor const. art. V, §2 judge const. art. VII, §10(1)	office deemed vacant if incumbent adjudged insane 17.03(6)	lieutenant governor serves as acting governor while governor incapable from mental disease const. art. V, §7	removed if becomes incompetent 857.15		*fn. 1* 880.67
WYO. Stat. (1980 & Supp. 1981)	idiots & insane persons const. art. VI, §6	county clerk investigates qualifications upon registration 22-3-105 registration canceled 22-3-115(a)(iv) challenge 22-15-104(a)(i)	adjudged mentally incompetent & not restored 31-7-108(b)(iii) unable to operate vehicle safely because of mental disability 31-7-108(b)(v)	cancelation upon report of medical advisory board that mentally incompetent to drive 31-7-121(d)	not in possession of natural faculties & of ordinary intelligence 1-11-101(a)(ii)	any civil or military office const. art. VI, §15 governor const. art. VI, §2 secretary of state, auditor, treasurer, superintendent of public instruction const. art. IV, §11 justice of the peace 5-4-201(b) county ct. judge 5-5-112(a)(i) commissioner or adjunct commissioner of county ct. 5-5-164 municipal judge 5-6-103 examiner 9-2-403 attorney general 9-2-502 state planning coordinator 9-2-701		secretary of state acts as governor if governor becomes incapable because of mental disease const. art. IV, §6	removed if becomes incompetent 2-3-123	guardian removed if becomes insane or otherwise incapable 3-2-113	*fn. 1* 34-13-107

FOOTNOTES: TABLE 8.3

1. Custodian of minor's property removed when he or she becomes legally incapacitated. Ala. Code § 35-5-8 (1975 & Supp. 1980); Alas. Stat. § 45.60.061 (1980); Ariz. Rev. Stat. Ann. § 44-2077 (1967 & Supp. 1980); Ark. Stat. Ann. § 50-907 (1971); Cal. Civ. Code § 1161 (West 1954 & Supp. 1980); Colo. Rev. Stat. Ann. § 11-50-108 (1973 & Supp. 1981); Conn. Gen. Stat. Ann. § 45-107 (West 1960 & Supp. 1980); Del. Code Ann. tit. 12 §4507 (1979); Fla. Stat. Ann. § 710.08 (West 1969 & Supp. 1980); Ga. Code Ann. § 48-307 (1979); Hawaii Rev. Stat. Ann. § 553-7 (1976 & Supp. 1980); Idaho Code Ann. § 68-807 (1980); Ill. Ann. Stat. ch. 110½, § 207 (Smith-Hurd 1978); Kan. Stat. Ann. § 38-907 (1973); Ky. Rev. Stat. Ann. § 385 (Michie 1972 & Supp. 1980); Me. Rev. Stat. Ann. tit. 33, § 1007 (1978); Md. Est. & Trusts Code Ann. § 13-307 (1974 & Supp. 1981); Mich. Comp. Laws Ann. § 554.457 (1967 & Supp. 1980); Minn. Stat. Ann. § 527.07 (1975); Miss. Code Ann. § 91-19-17 (1972 & Supp. 1982); Mo. Ann. Stat. § 404.070 (Vernon 1979); Mont. Code Ann. § 72-26-402 (1979); Neb. Rev. Stat. § 38-1007 (1978 & Supp. 1981); Nev. Rev. Stat. § 167.080 (1981); N.H. Rev. Stat. Ann. § 463-A:7 (1968); N.M. Stat. Ann. § 46-7-7 (1978); N.Y. Est. Powers & Trusts Law § 7-4.6 (McKinney 1967 & Supp. 1980); N.D. Cent. Code § 47-24-07 (1978); Okla. Stat. tit. 60, § 407 (West 1971); Or. Rev. Stat. §§ 126.856, -860 (1979); Pa. Stat. Ann. tit. 20, § 5308 (Purdon 1975); S.C. Code Ann. § 35-3-80 (Law. Co-op. 1976 & Supp. 1980); S.D. Codified Laws Ann. §§ 55-10-29, -31, -34 (1980); Tenn. Code Ann. § 35-808 (1977); Tex. Rev. Civ. Stat. Ann. Art. 5923-101(7) (Vernon 1962 & Supp. 1980); Wash. Rev. Code Ann. § 21.24.070 (1978); W.Va. Code § 36-7-7 (1966 & Supp. 1981); Wis. Stat. Ann. § 880.67 (West 1981); and Wyo. Stat. § 34-13-107 (1980 & Supp. 1981).

2. License not to be issued to a person ajudged to be afflicted with or suffering from a mental disability or disease and not restored to competency. Alas. Stat. § 28.15.031(4) (1978); Ariz. Rev. Stat. Ann. § 28-413(5) (1976); Ark. Stat. Ann. § 75-309(5) (1979); Colo. Rev. Stat. § 42-2-103(2)(d) (1973); Fla. Stat. Ann. § 322.05(5) (1975); Ga. Code Ann. § 68B-203(b)(4) (1980); Idaho Code § 49-309(5) (1980); Ill. Ann. Stat. ch. 95½, § 6-103(5) (Smith-Hurd 1971 & Supp. 1980); Ind. Code Ann. § 9-1-4-30(d) (Burns 1980); Kan. Stat. Ann. § 8-237(e) (1975 & Supp. 1980); Md. Transp. Code Ann. § 16-103.1 (1977); Mont. Code Ann. § 61-5-105(5) (1979); Nev. Rev. Stat. § 483.250(4) (1981); N.D. Cent. Code § 39-06-03(4) (1980); Okla. Stat. Ann. tit. 75, § 1503(4) (West 1977); Pa. Stat. Ann. tit. 75 §1503(4)(5) (Purdon 1977); R.I. Gen. Laws § 31-10-3(5) (1968); S.C. Code Ann. § 56-1-40(4) (Law. Co-op. 1976); S.D. Codified Laws Ann. § 32-12-32 (1976); Tenn. Code Ann. § 55-7-105(a)(5) (1980); and W.Va. Code Ann. § 17B-2-3(5) (1974).

3. Appointment of a conservator for the estate of personal representative terminates his appointment as personal representative. Alas. Stat. § 13.16.285 (1972); Ariz. Rev. Stat. Ann. § 14-3609 (1975); Colo. Rev. Stat. § 15-12-609 (1979); Hawaii Rev. Stat. § 560:3-609 (1976 § Supp. 1980); Idaho Code § 15-3-609 (1979); Me. Rev. Stat. Ann. tit. 18-A, § 3-609 (1981); Minn. Stat. Ann. §524.3-609 (West 1975); Mont. Code Ann. § 72-3-522 (1979); Neb. Rev. Stat. § 30-2452 (1979); N.M. Stat. Ann. § 45-3-609 (1978); N.D. Cent. Code § 30.1-17-09 (1976); and Utah Code Ann. § 75-3-609 (1978).

4. Guardian of incapacitated person must be competent. Alas. Stat. § 13.26.145(a) (1972); Ariz. Rev. Stat. Ann. § 14-5311A (1975); Colo. Rev. Stat. § 15-14-311(1) (Supp. 1980); Hawaii Rev. Stat. § 560:5-311(a) (1976); Idaho Code § 15-5-311(a) (1979); Me. Rev. Stat. Ann. tit. 18-A, § 5-311(a) (1981); Mich. Comp. Laws Ann. § 700.454(1) (1980 & Supp. 1980); Mont. Code Ann. § 72-5-312(1) (1979); Neb. Rev. Stat. § 30-2627(a) (1979); N.M. Stat. Ann. § 45-5-311A (1979); N.D. Cent. Code § 30.1-28-11(1) (1976); and Utah Code Ann. § 75-5-311(1) (1978).

5. The authority and responsibility of a guardian terminates upon a determination of his or her incapacity. Alas. Stat. § 13.26.120 (1972 & Supp. 1980); Ariz. Rev. Stat. Ann. § 14-5306 (1975); Colo. Rev. Stat. § 15-5-306 (1979); Hawaii Rev. Stat. Ann. § 560:5-306 (1979); Idaho Code § 15-5-306 (1980); Me. Rev. Stat. Ann. tit. 18-A, § 5-306 (1981); Mich. Comp. Laws Ann. § 700.446 (1980); Mont. Code Ann. § 72-5-324 (1983); Neb. Rev. Stat. § 30-2622 (1979); N.M. Stat. Ann. § 45-5-306 (1979); N.D. Cent. Code § 30.1-20-06 (1976); and Utah Code Ann. § 75-5-306 (1978).

6. Colo. Rev. Stat. 1-2-103(5) (1980): "No person confined in a state institution for the mentally ill shall lose his right to vote because of such confinement."

7. A license shall not be issued to a person whose mental disability or disease prevents the exercise of reasonable and ordinary control over a motor vehicle. Del. Code Ann. tit. 21, § 2707(b)(5) (1979); Ind. Code Ann. § 9-1-4-30(e) (Burns 1980); Ky. Rev. Stat. Ann. § 186.440(6) (Michie 1980); Minn. Stat. Ann. § 171.04(9) (West 1960 & Supp. 1980); N.C. Gen. Stat. § 20-9(e) (1978 & Supp. 1980); Ohio Rev. Code Ann. § 4507.08(B) (Baldwin 1975 & Supp. 1980); Or. Rev. Stat. § 482.130(1)(b) (1979); Tex. Rev. Civ. Stat. Ann. Art. 6687b (4)(8) (Vernon 1977); Utah Code Ann. § 41-2-5(5) (1970 & Supp. 1981), Va. Code § 46.1-361(a) (1980); and Wis. Stat. Ann. § 343.06(7) (West 1971).

8. Illinois has no statutory or constitutional disqualification for mental incapacity. The Illinois Supreme Court has held that the vote of a person non compos mentis should not be received, but that it is sufficient if the voter knows what he or she is doing. Welsh v. Shumway, 232 Ill. 54, 75-76, 83 N.E. 549, 558 (1907).

9. Mass. Ann. Laws ch. 31, §47 (Michie/Law. Co-op. 1973 & Supp. 1981). Massachusetts provides for the temporary appointment of mentally retarded persons to civil service positions, with the approval of the Massachusetts rehabilitation commission. Such appointments become permanent and tenured after three years.

10. License of person committed to state institution revoked; license of person voluntarily admitted to state institution not revoked unless superintendent certifies that person not competent to drive. Neb. Rev. Stat. § 60-419(1) (1978). To be relicensed, such person must pass an examination and furnish "a certificate of competence to operate a motor vehicle" from the superintendent of the institution. Id. § 60-419(4).

Samuel Jan Brakel

CHAPTER 9 *Family Laws*

I. INTRODUCTION

Mental disability may prevent or hinder the afflicted person from functioning in normal domestic relationships. Laws have been passed to prevent or lessen domestic disruption by forbidding mentally disabled persons to marry, providing for divorce or annulment on grounds of mental disability latently manifest, limiting or terminating the right of mentally disabled parents to care for their children, and—in the extreme—abrogating their right to have children.

II. MARRIAGE OF MENTALLY DISABLED PERSONS

A. Development of the Law

Prohibitions against the marriage of mentally disabled persons appear in the common law.[1] The law's concern with this topic may be attributed to two separate policies: (1) preventing the creation of a marital contract where one of the partners is incapable of understanding the nature of the relationship and (2) preventing reproduction by persons whose issue may become a public charge. The first of these policies is the older and has played a more prominent part in the legislation. The latter concern over propagation of the mentally disabled—which has also led to laws authorizing their sterilization—stems from the more recent eugenics movement of the 1920s and 1930s. It is reflected today in the statutes of only a few states, as the movement itself has been largely discredited.[2]

Sufficient mental capacity to consent is a prerequisite for a valid marriage by statute and at common law.[3] Although no general test of capacity is universally recognized, the usual test is the person's ability to understand the nature of the marriage relation and the duties and obligations involved. The law in most jurisdictions makes a distinction between this capacity and the person's competence to contract generally.[4]

States opposing the marriage of mentally disabled persons for eugenic reasons adhere to the theory that mental illness and deficiency are hereditary and that it is the state's duty to prevent their perpetuation. The rationale is apparent in provisions that make an exception to the general prohibition to marry in cases where the mentally disabled person has been sterilized or when the person, if a woman, is over 45 years of age (past childbearing age) or, if a man, is marrying a woman over 45. In 1970, provisions of this kind were on the books in eight states. Only three retain them today.[5] Michigan has a unique statute that allows a mentally disabled person to marry if he can show by means of a two-physician medical certification that he is cured and that there is no probability that he will transmit the earlier defects.[6] A number of other states today provide for exceptions to the marital prohibition on vaguer grounds, such as if a judge decides it is in the best interests of the applicant and the public,[7] or if the commissioner of public welfare,[8] the superintendent of the mental facility (in case

1. See Annot., 28 A.L.R. 631 (1924); Annot., 82 A.L.R.2d 1040 (1962) and Later Case Service (1979 & Supp. 1982).

2. See generally tables 9.1 & 9.5. Discussion of the statutory details ahead—particularly the repeal of eugenics-based provisions in several states—indicates the demise of eugenics theories as an important influence on legislation.

3. See references cited in note 1 *supra*.

4. Roether v. Roether, 180 Wis. 24, 191 N.W. 576 (1923). But see Knight v. Radomski, 414 A.2d 1211 (Me. 1980), which comes close to making an equation between general contractual capacity and capacity to marry. The real issue addressed in the case was, however, the reach of a guardianship, the guardian being the one to seek annulment of a marriage entered into by his ward without his consent.

5. North Carolina continues to exempt from the marital prohibition mentally disabled persons who have been sterilized (N.C. Gen. Stat. § 51-12 (1976)). North Dakota and Virginia use the age criterion. (N.D. Cent. Code § 14-03-07 (Supp. 1981), applying to persons "institutionalized as severely retarded"; Va. Code § 20-46(2) (1983), applying to "legally incompetent" persons, a switch from the former "insane" persons). See generally table 9.1, col. 2.

6. Mich. Comp. Laws Ann. § 551.6 (1967).

7. Pa. Stat. Ann. ch. 48, § 1-5(d) (Purdon Supp. 1980).

8. Minn. Stat. Ann. § 517.03 (West Supp. 1981).

the person is institutionalized),[9] or the guardian[10] gives written consent.

While ostensibly scientific, eugenic theories can in fact draw only scant support from available medical evidence. The role of heredity in many types of mental illness and deficiency remains unclear. Environmental and organic causes often interact in the development of mental disability in a particular person. Whether a person succumbs to a genetic susceptibility may depend on the interaction of a variety of outside circumstances. Organic disabilities are differentially disabling in different persons, and intensive training can often greatly ameliorate the disabled person's life. Medication—an organic treatment approach—has shown remarkable successes when administered to persons whose disabilities are triggered by, if not predominantly rooted in, environmental factors. More specifically, there are many "healthy" carriers of mental disability, while disabled parents may produce children who are perfectly well. Indeed, it has been estimated that some 90% of inheritable mental disability is passed on by persons who are not themselves disabled.[11]

Humane social theory, perhaps more than scientific argument, also figures in the decline of the eugenics movement. As a society, we are no longer so quick to discount the capabilities and needs of the mentally disabled. Whether they are adult and our concern is with their capacity as parents, or whether they are newborn and we envision the quality of life ahead of them, the guiding premise for dealing with the problems they may have or face is the intrinsic worth of each disabled individual. Harsh Darwinian theories, commanding only scant scientific support, are a poor basis for denying mentally disabled persons fundamental rights such as the right to marry and have children.

In recent years the argument against marriages of mentally disabled persons has shifted from heredity to environment. Evidence has been adduced to show that such persons, whether their condition is inherited/inheritable or not, are unfit parents and should not be permitted to bear or rear children. Given these new grounds, the laws limiting the domestic relations rights of the mentally disabled continue to find broad support in the legislatures and among the public.

B. Persons Prohibited from Marrying

The states have been slow to modernize statutes prohibiting marriage of the mentally disabled. In describing the persons affected by these laws, many states retain archaic and offensive designations on the order of "idiots," "lunatics," "imbeciles," the "insane," the "weak-minded," and so forth.[12] These provisions would be improved—as has been acomplished in states such as Iowa[13] and Maine[14]—by a switch to more acceptable language such as "mentally ill" or "mentally retarded" persons.

Modernizing the language does not remedy a more basic defect—the unscientific character and the overbreadth of the statutes.[15] Mental illness and deficiency come in many forms and afflict persons with widely varying degrees of severity. Both the scientific and the legal bases for denying the right to marry and attendant rights to the broad groups presently described in the statutes are lacking. The provisions ought to be more specifically focused on the capacity to enter into the marriage relationship. A number of states have taken this step by identifying "persons adjudged incompetent"[16] or "persons under guardianship," either solely or in addition to the broader designations, as subject to the marital prohibition. It could be argued that even the incompetency designation is too broad in that the competence to marry is different from the capacity to make other decisions and to embark on other ventures in life. At least one state—Nebraska[17]—avoids this criticism by specifying incompetence to enter into the marriage contract. The problem with that language may be that it is tautological and, if unaccompanied by references to the underlying mental disability, unhelpful to the decision maker.

A few states refer to patients or institutionalized persons as (among) those who are prohibited from marrying.[18] The rationale for such provisions may have as much to do with the practical problems of institutional management which could result from marriages of or

9. Del. Code Ann. tit. 13, § 101(b)(2) (1981).

10. Conn. Gen. Stat. Ann. § 46b-29 (West Supp. 1981).

11. A. Deutsch, The Mentally Ill in America: A History of Their Care and Treatment from Colonial Times 373-74 (2d ed. 1949). On the more general proposition that only a very small portion of mental retardation is attributable to hereditary factors, see Mental Retardation: An Annual Review (H.I. Kaplan, A.M. Freedman, & B.J. Sadock 3d ed. 1980), esp. Cytryn & Lourie, ch. 36, Mental Retardation 2484-2537.

12. See table 9.1, col. 1.

13. Iowa Code Ann. § 595.3(5) (West 1981).

14. Me. Rev. Stat. Ann. tit. 19, § 32 (Supp. 1981).

15. A commentator writing in the 1930s launched an attack on these statutes which still has considerable validity:

> The totally unscientific character of the statutes dealing with a scientific subject in this modern age of scientific enlightenment is revealed in connection with the inconsistent . . . statements defining the classes of incompetents. . . . There are all degrees of mental incapacity; and many varieties of insanity, some curable, some incurable; some acquired and some hereditary. Perhaps these defy legal description or definition, but it is certain that their different degrees and characteristics have hardly been recognized at all by the legislation of the Nation in dealing with the marriage problem.

C.G. Vernier, 1 American Family Laws: A Comparative Study of the Family Law of the Forty-Eight States, Alaska, the District of Columbia, and Hawaii (to Jan. 1, 1931) 190 (1931).

16. E.g., Connecticut, Iowa, New Jersey, and South Carolina. See table 9.1, col. 1, for statutory citations.

17. Neb. Rev. Stat. § 42-107 (1978).

18. E.g., Delaware: Del. Code Ann. tit. 13, § 101(b)(2) (1981).

among patients as with any judgments about the general desirability of allowing mentally incapacitated persons to marry and have children.

C. Methods of Enforcement

The effectiveness of the various statutes prohibiting marriage of persons with mental infirmities is highly questionable. Only 10 states—down from 20 a decade ago—currently have any enforcement machinery.[19] Typically, the statutes provide for criminal punishment, mostly minor fines or short jail sentences.[20] Michigan, however, exacts a fine of up to $1,000 or a state prison term of one to five years. This heavy punishment applies to "any person of sound mind who shall intermarry with such insane person or idiot . . . or who shall advise, aid, abet, cause, procure or assist in procuring any such marriage."[21] The punitive measures usually also apply to the incompetent person himself and often to the clerk or whichever official is in charge of the licensing process or the solemnizing of marriage contracts.[22] In Kentucky, the clerk who knowingly issues a license to persons barred by the statute from marrying shall be removed from office.[23] Some states require that a medical certificate avowing the absence of the prohibited condition be produced before any marriage license can be issued,[24] while in others persons who were once institutionalized or adjudged insane by a court may marry only upon production of a medical certificate that they are cured.[25] The antiquity, not to mention the offensiveness, of some of these laws is pointedly illustrated in Michigan's case, where the relevant statute includes a provision for the "validation of White-African marriages."[26]

It has been concluded that statutes designed to prevent marriages of persons with mental disabilities have in fact prevented very few such marriages[27] and that they have "proved worthless, chiefly because of the lack of adequate provision for the identification or diagnosis of the mental status of applicants for marriage licenses."[28] There is a real difficulty: in the absence of an affirmative requirement for marriage applicants to produce evidence of mental competence, how is the state to find out that the requisite capacity is lacking? Kansas used to have a provision explicitly requiring the county clerk to ask the applicants if they had ever been adjudicated "an incapacitated person," and if so, whether they had been restored.[29] But absent such a statutory instruction, officials can hardly be expected to raise the issue. One Texas clerk, queried on the point during a study, is reported to have replied: "Are you serious? How can I ask a person if he's crazy?"[30]

Many states do not specifically prohibit marriage of the mentally disabled but instead provide for annulment or divorce on grounds of mental disability.[31] Of course, the threat of a severed marriage is not an effective deterrent to one who is incapable of understanding the marriage relationship, nor is dissolution an effective enforcement measure when it is dependent upon the voluntary initiative of one of the parties to the disapproved relationship. The objective of the divorce and annulment provisions is to provide relief from an intolerable relationship; it is neither their design nor their intent to function in a deterrent or prohibiting capacity.

The dearth of effective enforcement provisions may suggest that the states are not serious about prohibiting and perhaps not convinced of the need for or desirability of preventing the marriage of mentally disabled persons. If the states truly wanted to control marriages considered inadvisable, they could take more decisive action. One of the more effective, if perhaps Orwellian, methods would be to check all applications for marriage licenses against a central record file for all incompetent and institutionalized persons. In New Hampshire, such procedures were in effect prior to 1961. All public and private schools were required to report annually the names of all epileptic, imbecile, feeble-minded, idiotic, or insane pupils who had left school or had become 14 years of age during the preceding year. Also, the state hospitals and the state school for the retarded were required to file the names of all patients discharged or paroled.[32] These requirements were repealed, however, in 1961. Rightly, it would seem, the costs in terms of the intrusion on personal privacy, in the possible undermining of the doctor-patient relationship, in the potential for discouraging persons from seeking voluntary treatment, and the possibility of outright abuse of the information were seen to outweigh the marginal benefits of a guaranteed detection/prohibition system.

D. Institutionalized Persons

While persons outside institutions have been shown to be rarely affected by the laws regulating or prohibiting marriage of the mentally disabled, the situation appears to be quite different for patients in mental facilities. As mentioned, the statutes of several states specifically in-

19. See table 9.1, col. 3.
20. *Id.*
21. Mich. Comp. Laws Ann. § 551.6 (1967).
22. Table 9.1, col. 3.
23. Ky. Rev. Stat. Ann. § 402.990 (Michie 1982).
24. E.g., N.C. Gen. Stat. § 51-9 (Supp. 1981).
25. E.g., Mich. Comp. Laws Ann. § 551.6 (1967 & Supp. 1984).
26. *Id.*
27. R.C. Allen, E.Z. Ferster, & H. Weihofen, Mental Impairment and Legal Incompetency 299 (1968).
28. Deutsch, *supra* note 11, at 377.
29. Kan. Stat. Ann. §§ 23-121 & 22-123 (1964 & Supp. 1968).
30. Allen, Ferster, & Weihofen, *supra* note 27, at 303.
31. Table 9.1, cols. 4 & 5.
32. See Allen, Ferster, & Weihofen, *supra* note 27, at 304.

clude institutionalized persons in their description of persons prohibited from marrying.[33] Combined with lack of interest on the part of patients and institutional policies against the marriage of patients, these prohibitions appear to be quite effective, if not absolute. A 1968 study updated in 1975 summarized the marital prospects of institutionalized persons this way:

> Patients in mental hospitals seem to have little interest in getting married while they are at the hospital. Most of the hospitals report that patients do not ask for permission to marry, and they knew of no instances in which a patient had married during a visit at home. Only two of the hospitals would permit a patient to marry. One, a private hospital, said that it exercises no control to prevent the marriage of a patient "on privileges." The other, a state hospital, reported that some of its patients do marry while they are living at the hospital. A doctor may counsel a patient against marrying for therapeutic reasons, but there is no articulated policy at the hospital forbidding marriage. In fact, a doctor may advise a patient to marry even though legally incompetent, in the case of a woman who is pregnant and wants to legitimatize her child.
>
> None of the hospitals interfere with the marriages of patients who are on conditional release. If the hospital is seeing the person on an outpatient basis, it may recommend that the marriage be postponed for therapeutic reasons, but it will not prohibit the marriage or take steps to prevent or annul it.
>
> Patients in institutions for the mentally retarded show a much greater interest in getting married. Some institutions reported that patients have run away to get married and several reported that patients marry while on home leave. One institution will discharge the patient if he marries unless an annulment is initiated by the family or guardian, but the others will allow the patient to remain in the institution and will not attempt to annul the marriage. A few of the institutions reported that they sometimes grant permission for patients to marry. The decision is based on whether the hospital thinks the person is competent to marry, not on his legal status.[34]

III. DIVORCE AND ANNULMENT

If a marriage is contracted in spite of the mental disability of one of the partners, or such disability develops or is discovered only after the marriage has been entered into, the law provides various procedures for dissolving the relationship. On the other hand, the presence of a mental disability may also protect the afflicted person in a divorce action brought against him, or he himself may be barred from suing for a dissolution.

A. Legal Effect of Prohibited Marriages

The legal effect of prohibited marriages varies from state to state. In most states, such a marriage is "voidable," meaning that one or both of the partners, a guardian, or some other authorized representative may bring a court action to have the marriage annulled by reason of the preexisting mental incapacity.[35] In a minority of jurisdictions, the marriage is statutorily declared "void" or even "absolutely void." Nonetheless, a number of these states provide for annulment procedures,[36] somewhat of a conceptual anomaly since the presence of such procedures implies that the relationship is in fact "voidable." Absent such procedures—Michigan, for one, has none—the word *void* apparently means what it says, though it would seem that legal certainty on this score is achieved only in the states of Maine[37] and Wyoming,[38] where provisions exist explicitly stating that no court decree is necessary to confirm the null status of such a marriage.

Theoretically, a void marriage ought to raise serious questions about the spouses' rights to property and the legitimacy of children of the marriage, but in fact the strict logical conclusions are often avoided. About half the states today have provisions asserting the legitimacy of children of such marriages.[39] Wyoming provides that legitimacy shall be presumed.[40] California explicates that it is the existence of the parent-child relationship that controls the issue of legitimacy, regardless of the legal status of the marriage.[41] And the Georgia statute goes so far as to prohibit annulment of the marriage if there are children.[42] Only Rhode Island goes against the grain, specifying that the children of marriages of "idiots and lunatics" (deemed "absolutely void") are *il*legitimate.[43] Other logical consequences of prohibited marriages are often avoided as well. A study published in the late 1960s summed up the situation as follows:

> It is not at all certain . . . that even in those states [which use the language of voidness] the courts would inexorably apply all the orthodox consequences of voidness. The statutes themselves frequently make an exception by declaring that children of such void marriages shall nevertheless be legitimate. Others specifically forbid attack on the marriage after the death of the parties. Although, logically, a void marriage cannot be ratified, only one court seems to have denied the right to ratify, and that court later reversed itself.[44]

33. Table 9.1, col. 1.
34. Readings in Law and Psychiatry 436 (R.C. Allen, E.Z. Ferster, & J.G. Rubin eds. 1975).

35. See table 9.1, cols. 4 & 5.
36. See table 9.1, cols. 6–8.
37. Me. Rev. Stat. Ann. tit. 19, §§ 32 & 631 (1981).
38. Wyo. Stat. § 20-2-101(a) (1977).
39. Table 9.1, col. 12.
40. Wyo. Stat. § 20-2-117 (1977).
41. Cal. Civ. Code § 7002 (West 1983).
42. Ga. Code Ann. § 53-601 (1982).
43. R.I. Gen. Laws § 15-1-5 (1981).

Considerable variation exists with regard to who may institute annulment proceedings. Most states today provide that "either party" may bring the action[45]—a decade ago only a minority of states did so. In some jurisdictions, only the "injured" or "aggrieved" partner has the right to sue for annulment. On the face of it, it is not clear whether this is the disabled or the nondisabled spouse. A few states clearly extend the right only to the incapacitated party, in a couple of cases only after he is restored. No state today gives the right only and unequivocally to the partner who is well. In a good number of states, relatives, friends, guardians, other legally authorized representatives, or legal counsel may also petition for annulment. Again, theoretically, if a marriage is "void" under the statute, either partner as well as interested third parties should be able to assert the defect. But generally the logic has not been so extended. Designation of who may sue for dissolution bears little relationship to whether the statutes deem such marriages void or voidable. Also, with isolated exceptions,[46] the courts have refused to allow voidness to deprive spouses of such marriages of the dissolution and survivorship rights accorded to persons who contracted legal marriages.[47]

There are some limitations in the statutes on the right to sue for annulment. Some 16 states[48] bar the action if the parties cohabited after restoration of the disabled partner or, as in Virginia,[49] after the nondisabled party gained knowledge of the spouse's disability. In addition, in some 3 states[50] the right to an annulment is forfeited if the spouse had knowledge of the partner's mental incapacity or, as in Texas,[51] if he or she should have known. Many states also set time limits on when the action for annulment may be brought: so many days (90 is typical) after the petitioner obtains knowledge of the disability, a year (typically) or two after the marriage was entered into, or any time before the death of the disabled partner.[52] The burden of proving incapacity is on the party seeking the annulment, the general presumption being that both parties were capable.[53] The determining fact is the mental condition at the time of the marriage ceremony rather than the condition prior to, or subsequent to, the marriage, even though the interval may be very short.[54]

44. Allen, Ferster, & Weihofen, *supra* note 27, at 307 (notes omitted).
45. See table 9.1, cols. 6-8, for this assertion and those immediately following in the same paragraph.
46. See Allen, Ferster, & Weihofen, *supra* note 27, at 307-8.
47. *Id.*
48. See table 9.1, cols. 9-11.
49. Va. Code § 20-89.1(c) (1983).
50. Table 9.1, cols. 9-11.
51. Tex. Fam. Code § 2.45(b)(2) (Vernon 1975).
52. Table 9.1, col. 11.
53. 35 Am. Jur. Marriage § 113 (1941).

B. Postnuptial Mental Disability

Divorce is designed to dissolve marriages for postnuptial causes, annulment for causes existing at the time of the marriage.[55] Postnuptial *mental illness* is usually the only type of mental disability for which a divorce may be granted, as other types of mental disability such as mental retardation tend to be present from the time of birth or early childhood.[56]

Postnuptial mental illness as a ground for divorce in this country has had a slow growth. It is a matter of academic dispute whether Arkansas, in a statute of 1843, or Washington, in 1886, was the first state to permit divorce for postnuptial mental illness.[57] In 1931 only 13 states were reported to have statutory provisions allowing divorce for postnuptial mental illness.[58] Fifteen years later 26 states had such statutes.[59] At the present time the number is up to 30—a total that has not changed over the past decade and a half, however.[60]

Mental disability as a ground for divorce has always been the subject of much controversy. It has been objected to not only by those who are generally opposed to divorce but also by those who recognize the need for

54. In Littreal v. Littreal, 253 S.W.2d 247 (Ky. 1952), where a wife brought a separate maintenance action and the husband's representatives sought an annulment on the ground that the husband had been adjudicated incompetent prior to the marriage, the court denied the annulment on the ground that the prior adjudication merely raised a presumption that the incapacity continued thereafter. It was the court's view that the presumption as to the validity of the marriage is so strong that a presumption of incompetency would not overcome it unless the marriage ceremony and the incompetency decree were reasonably simultaneous. Similarly in Forbis v. Forbis, 274 S.W.2d 800 (Mo. Ct. App. 1955), it was the opinion of the court that a person's being of unsound mind 11 months after a marriage did not necessarily mean that the condition had existed at the time of the marriage.
55. McCurdy, Insanity as a Ground for Annulment or Divorce in English and American Law, 29 Va. L. Rev. 771, 774 (1943).
56. In the annulment case of Knight v. Radomski, 414 A.2d 1211 (Me. 1980), discussed in note 4 *supra*, the ward's disability (severe brain damage with paralysis and change of personality) was, however, incurred later in life, resulting from his being struck by an automobile while jogging. The marriage—with his treating psychologist—was contracted after the accident, indeed after his being declared mentally incompetent, the latter fact constituting the basis for the conservator's (his father) action to have the marriage annulled.
57. Gordon, Insanity and Divorce, 5 J. Crim. L. & Crim. 544-48 (1914-15); F.J. Stimson, American Statute Law § 6201 (1886); 2 Vernier, *supra* note 15, at § 72 (1932); Comment, Divorce: Statutory Abolition of Marital Fault, 35 Cal. L. Rev. 99, 105 (1947) [hereinafter cited as Comment, Divorce].
58. 2 Vernier, *supra* note 15, at § 72 (1932).
59. F.H. Keezer, On the Law of Marriage and Divorce, § 451 (J. Morland 3d ed. 1946).
60. See table 9.2, col. 1. Two qualifications are in order regarding this total. (1) The constancy of the count of states having such laws is somewhat misleading, as it is a function of the fact that over the recent years a number of states have added such laws while a corresponding number of other states have dropped them. (2) In a few cases it is difficult to say whether a state does or does not have such a law; for example, the New Hampshire law merely states that "the insanity of the libelee may be considered by the court in determining whether a divorce should be granted, [but that] such insanity shall not constitute a defense to a libel for divorce." N.H. Rev. Stat. Ann. § 458:12 (1969 & Supp. 1979).

divorce in some cases but believe it should be restricted to situations in which there is "fault" on the part of one spouse. One of the general arguments is as follows:

> A concealed hereditary taint, which breaks out after marriage, is sometimes made cause of divorce by our legislatures. . . . and yet devoted kindness and forbearance not only afford the surest hope of restoring the sufferer, diseased in mind or body, to health once more, but may bring the highest blessings to the patient spouse. The constancy of husband and wife to one another in sickness or health, in accordance with the marriage vow, is the crown of matrimony.[61]

A more direct attack is delivered by another writer:

> One objection to making insanity a ground for divorce is that not only is there absence of fault but renunciation of duty for mere misfortune. . . . Another objection is that if insanity is made a ground for divorce why should not any other disease if it results similarly in irreparable disruption of the cohabitational aspects of the marriage. A distinction may perhaps be found in the fact that insanity unlike other diseases results in substantial change in personality.[62]

The growth of the concept of divorce without "fault" seems to be in part responsible for the increase in the number of states permitting divorce on account of mental disability. The movement to substitute the "forward-looking" consideration of "cooperation" for the outdated principle of "guilt" has gained strength in many countries. "Nowhere," say its proponents, "is the justification for such a change of attitude more obvious than in the law of divorce. . . . Countries which refuse to impose a business partnership on an unwilling party do not hesitate to impose on unwilling spouses this most intimate of human relations."[63]

Divorce on the ground of mental illness can, of course, be characterized as divorce without "fault."[64] Other reasons for the acceptance of the mental illness ground have been put forth as follows: "[t]he possibility of defective offspring, the apparent unfairness of considering a person legally married whose spouse is incurably insane, and the effect upon other persons not responsible for the unfortunate situation have been factors in bringing about this attitude."[65]

None of these arguments is new. Many were propounded 50 or 60 years ago. Given the stagnation over the past 15 years in the number of states allowing divorce on the ground of mental disability, it appears that their power to convert has diminished.

There is substantial similarity among the statutes of the 30-odd states today that allow postnuptial mental disability as a ground for divorce. All but a few states[66] require the condition to have persisted for a specified period—three years is the most common, with Maine's[67] seven years the longest—which in most jurisdictions refers to time spent in a mental institution. In some states, such as Kansas[68] and Utah,[69] the time is calculated from the formal adjudication of mental illness or mental incapacity. A trend toward reducing the length of time during which the illness/confinement must have persisted is discernible: since 1970, several states have eliminated the reference to time altogether, and in a number of other states the requirement has been reduced from five to three or two years.

Fewer statutes than a decade or two ago require the condition to be incurable, though this prognosis may still be implied in the references to "insanity" and the rather lengthy confinement requirements.[70] Kansas[71] and Oklahoma[72] stipulate the more moderate criterion of "poor prognosis for recovery." The language in Pennsylvania is "no reasonable prospect" of discharge.[73] And the Texas statute[74] speaks in terms of a disabled spouse who is not likely to adjust and who will probably suffer a relapse. Delaware's statute[75] is an example of the modern outlook: it speaks of the marriage as being irretrievably broken, characterized by separation of the partners as a result of the mental illness. A large majority of states require that the allegation of the disability be supported by medical evidence.[76]

There are some problems with the criteria set by the statutes under which mental disability may serve as a ground for divorce. Length of institutionalization or incurability as indicated by length of confinement is an imperfect standard. Given the inadequacy of treatment programs in many public institutions, the length of time a person spends in such an institution is from a purist's view not a good measure either of his curability or of his

61. 2 J. Schouler, A Treatise on the Law of Marriage, Divorce, Separation and Domestic Relations 1787 (1921).

62. McCurdy, *supra* note 55, at 804-5.

63. Silving, Divorce Without Fault, 29 Iowa L. Rev. 527, 557 (1944), *cited in* Keezer, *supra* note 59, at § 451 n.10.

64. Comment, Divorce, *supra* note 57, at 105-6.

65. Keezer, *supra* note 59, at § 450 (note omitted). Since divorce is technically appropriate only in cases of postnuptial disability—i.e., forms of mental disturbance the person was not obviously born with—the eugenic argument may be least persuasive in this context. On the other hand, divorce may be appropriate on the theory that the home environment with a mentally ill parent is damaging to a child's development. See Anthony, A Clinical Evaluation of Children with Psychotic Parents, 126 Am. J. Psychiatry 177 (1969).

66. The exceptions are California, Delaware, the District of Columbia, and Utah. See table 9.2, cols. 3 & 4.

67. Me. Rev. Stat. Ann. tit. 19, § 691(1)(I) (1964).

68. Kan. Stat. Ann. § 60-1601(7) (1976).

69. Utah Code Ann. § 30-3-1(9)(a) (1976).

70. See table 9.2, col. 2.

71. Kan. Stat. Ann. § 60-1601(7) (1976 & Supp. 1981).

72. Okla. Stat. Ann. ch. 12, § 1271(12) (West 1961).

73. Pa. Stat. Ann. tit. 23, § 201(b) (Purdon Supp. 1980).

74. Tex. Fam. Code § 3.07 (Vernon 1975).

75. Del. Code Ann. ch. 13, § 1505(b)(3) (1975).

76. Table 9.2, cols. 5 & 6.

ability to function in a marital situation. On the other hand, some practical realities, not necessarily contemplated by the writers of the statutes, provide support for the criteria: (1) lengthy institutionalization today (in an era of generally very brief confinements) is a more valid indicator of serious disability than it might have been in earlier times; (2) the connection between length of confinement and capacity to continue the marriage relationship is valid in the unfortunate sense that extended institutionalization often results in the loss of social functioning skills and in the sense that it indicates the reality of an extended separation between the partners, which no doubt is relevant to the survival of the marriage relationship. Perhaps questions from the opposite end are today more telling: with the drastically reduced stays of patients, brought about by virtue of new social and financial policy as much as by medical advancements, it appears at least equally tenuous to equate a patient's discharge with curability or recovery, and it is even more doubtful whether the discharge criterion has any bearing on whether the marriage relationship should be forced to continue in opposition to the desire of the plaintiff spouse.

Only a few cases touch on these problems.[77] A California case[78] denied divorce to the plaintiff husband where the wife had entered the hospital as a voluntary patient rather than being confined under order of court. It is difficult to see why the legal status of the afflicted spouse should be determinative of whether divorce is or is not appropriate. Decisions in Kansas[79] and North Carolina[80] come closer to dealing with the relevant problems, indicating that curability is the primary issue while length of institutionalization—either as an independent criterion or as evidence of incurability—is of lesser import. These cases held that the statutory requisite regarding length of confinement did not necessarily mean a continuous period of confinement: intervening periods of outpatient treatment or parole (especially when such intervals are *not* spent with the "sane" spouse) do not operate to preclude the granting of divorce.

California used to have a provision—since repealed—requiring that for purposes of the divorce statute the mentally ill spouse be confined within the state.[81] In *Dribin v. Superior Court*,[82] the plaintiff, in a divorce suit seeking a California decree, offered in evidence a deposition from the Minnesota State Hospital stating that the "defendant was incurably insane."[83] The plaintiff urged that the California requirement of confinement within the state was unconstitutional because there would seem to be no logical reason for such discrimination and the restriction amounted to discrimination on the basis of state citizenship. The Supreme Court of California decided that this was not an arbitrary requirement:

> The legal concept of "insanity" may well vary considerably in the different jurisdictions and in different applications of the term . . . (. . . "'insanity' is a broad, comprehensive, and generic term, of ambiguous import, for all unsound and deranged conditions of the mind"). In this state a definition of such concept in respect to civil proceedings has been expressly set forth . . . and in addition . . . [the] code . . . throws about an alleged insane or incompetent person various safeguards by way of notice, service of process, hearing, evidence, jury trial, etc., before an adjudication of insanity and commitment therefor may be made. . . . The Legislature in requiring proof of confinement in California may have had in mind that the same safeguards might not be afforded before adjudication and confinement in other jurisdictions.[84]

Following the *Dribin* holding, there was concern that similar problems would arise with frequency throughout the country. This prospect has not materialized, however.[85] Perhaps—despite our population's increasing mobility—the *Dribin* type of factual situation remains a rare occurrence. The decision is not likely to be followed today in any event. The law of divorce, with its increasing emphasis on evidence of irretrievable breakdown of the marriage relationship, will cause the courts to look more toward the *effects* of institutionalization and separation upon the marriage, regardless of the procedural diversities among jurisdictions or institutions that may stand in the background. And the laws of residence, increasingly giving way to the principle of equal rights and entitlements for *all* citizens,[86] are no longer so likely to be interpreted to thwart parties from achieving a divorce when there is unrefuted evidence of

77. See Annot., 15 A.L.R.2d 1135-37 (1951) and Later Case Service (1973).

78. Riggins v. Riggins, 139 Cal. App. 2d 712, 294 P.2d 751 (1956).

79. Katz v. Katz, 191 Kan. 500, 382 P.2d 331 (1963).

80. Mabry v. Mabry, 243 N.C. 126, 90 S.E.2d 221 (1955).

81. Cal. Civ. Code § 108 (West 1954 & Supp. 1967).

82. 37 Cal. 2d 345, 231 P.2d 809 (1951).

83. The statute under consideration required that the incurably insane spouse be confined in a California institution for a period of at least three consecutive years before divorce was to be allowed. The couple in that case had married in the state of Illinois and had separated two and one-half years later. Subsequently, the defendant was adjudged "insane" in Minnesota on the application of her mother. At the time of the divorce suit, she had been a patient in the Minnesota State Hospital for more than five years.

84. 37 Cal. 2d at 349, 231 P.2d at 813-14.

85. Shelton v. Shelton, 209 Ga. 454, 74 S.E.2d 5 (1953), is one of the few cases seconding the *Dribin* view.

86. In the mental disability field in particular, the Interstate Compact on Mental Health and similar reciprocal statutes regarding the transfer of patients among the states explicitly place the patient's therapeutic interests over traditionally dominant state administrative and economic interests. See Council of State Governments, The Interstate Compact on Mental Health: What It Is and Does (rev. ed. Dec. 1968); also see in this book ch. 4, Discharge and Transfer, esp. table 4.2, and ch. 5, Rights of Institutionalized Persons, *supra*. See in the welfare rights area Shapiro v. Thompson, 394 U.S. 618 (1969).

irreparable disruption of the communal aspects of the marriage.

Most of the states permitting divorce on the ground of mental disability make provision for the future support of the disabled person.[87] These provisions fall into two categories — one under which the statutes unequivocally state that the divorce shall not relieve the petitioning party from support obligations, the other comprising provisions that allow the court discretion to award support and maintenance payments to the defendant spouse. The discretionary statutes are slightly more common than the mandatory ones.[88] They are not mutually exclusive: California[89] has a statute that requires continued support and then gives the court discretion to order it and to determine the proper amount. Arkansas has a provision that requires the court to order the plaintiff to provide for the disabled spouse's care and maintenance for as long as he or she may live.[90] A similar provision in California, which in addition required the plaintiff to prove ownership sufficient to meet this requirement before the divorce could be granted, was declared unconstitutional years ago in the same *Dribin* case discussed above. The court held that the statute created an unreasonable class discrimination between persons of different financial resources.[91]

A good majority of states today require the appointment of a *guardian ad litem* to represent the disabled spouse in the divorce proceedings, and a few even provide for legal counsel, particularly where the defendant is indigent and has no other representation.[92] Many states do not require personal service of process on the mentally disabled person, providing instead for substitute service on the guardian or the proper hospital authority,[93] who may in a few states decide, in the best interest of the patient, that he not be personally notified. Thus the defendant may be totally ignorant of the divorce proceeding. Whether this is ever desirable has been a point of debate and even some litigation. It may be argued that some patients are in no position to appreciate the proceedings, that little is gained by the vigorous contest to preserve a marriage unwanted by at least one of the parties, and that the guardianship provisions are adequate to protect the financial and property rights of the disabled partner. The argument on the other side — which seems to have found favor in the courts[94] — is that the marriage relationship is quintessentially personal and that notice of proceedings to dissolve it, let alone the decision to contest its dissolution, cannot be delegated.

87. Table 9.2, cols. 7 & 8.

88. *Id.*

89. Cal. Civ. Code § 4510(b) (West 1983).

90. Ark. Stat. Ann. § 34-1202(8) (Supp. 1981).

91. Dribin v. Superior Ct., 37 Cal. 2d 345, 348, 231 P.2d 809, 812 (1951):

> No compelling necessity has been found by the Legislature or suggested to us for generally denying divorce to the poor and making it available to the wealthy. Here the state has guarded against financial dependency of the insane spouse by providing that the divorce of an insane spouse does not relieve the other spouse of "any obligation imposed by law as a result of the marriage for the support" of the insane spouse . . . [I]n view of such provision, the additional requirement of proof of possession of financial ability appears arbitrary. . . . Since full liability for support perdures, after divorce as during marriage, and since the court can exact security as in any case according to the means of the spouse securing the decree, the only basis left for the classification is wealth as against poverty. In this application it is not a valid classification.

92. Table 9.2, cols. 9 & 10.

93. See table 8.1, cols. 7 & 8.

C. Mental Disability as a Defense in Divorce Actions

The question of mental disability as a defense to divorce arises most commonly in jurisdictions that do not recognize postnuptial mental disability as a ground for divorce. In those states, the disability may work in the opposite direction: it may be asserted as a fact that will bar a divorce based on misconduct that occurred during the incapacitation. The defense is introduced primarily in cases where divorce is sought on the grounds of cruelty, desertion, separation, or adultery. In those jurisdictions where postnuptial mental disability is a valid ground, the defense, if recognized at all, will generally have only a temporary effect since a divorce may subsequently be granted, after a statutory waiting period.[95]

Many courts have taken the view that if the nature of the mental disability is such that it deprives the defendant of the ability to differentiate right from wrong or to understand the nature and consequences of his acts, he may not be held legally accountable for behavior that would otherwise be grounds for divorce, any more than he could be held accountable for it in a criminal action.[96] It appears that a rule akin to the *M'Naghten* test for criminal responsibility is applied, for if the defendant knows the difference between right and wrong, mental disability is no defense to the divorce action even though the defendant acted under compulsion from a diseased mind.[97]

94. See, e.g., Munden v. Munden, No. 1-279 A56 (Ind. Ct. App. Dec. 26, 1979) (divorce by default ruled invalid where papers were served on hospital personnel (the statistician) and patient may never have received personal notice); *In re* Jennings, 453 A.2d 572 (N.J. Super. Ct. Ch. Div. 1981) (court refuses to appoint mother of comatose, incompetent adult as guardian so she could bring divorce action on son's behalf against wife for alleged adultery; divorce held to personal remedy, not susceptible of being delegated to guardian under any circumstances (background in instant case included $600,000 malpractice award to son rendered incompetent as a result of complications during routine surgery and mother's intervention and allegations against wife coming after the accident and award)); Clark v. Clark, 372 So. 2d 814 (La. Ct. App. 1979) (default separation judgment set aside, even though personal service on hospital patient, but failure to appoint attorney in face of indications of patient's incompetence).

95. See generally Annot., 19 A.L.R.2d 144 (1951), and Later Case Service (1982). A couple of recent cases are Gipson v. Gipson, 379 So. 2d 1171 (La. Ct. App. 1980), and Hoehn v. Hoehn, 418 N.E.2d 648 (Mass. App. Ct. 1981). In *Hoehn*, the defense, asserted in a divorce action on grounds of cruel and unusual treatment, was rejected by the court because the spouse, though acting bizarre, also had periods of obvious lucidity.

96. E.g., Cosgrove v. Cosgrove, 217 N.E.2d 754 (Mass. 1966); Fansler v. Fansler, 344 Mich. 569, 75 N.W.2d 1 (1956).

It has been argued that since divorce is a civil action, it is curious to insist upon the right-and-wrong standard of criminal responsibility and that the standards of civil hospitalization would be more appropriate.[98] This line of reasoning is not entirely convincing: if "fault" is indeed the basis for divorce, then absence of fault, as a defense, could well be appropriately predicated on a formula involving knowledge of right and wrong. The better point may be that "fault" is a dubious standard in divorce actions, whether disproved by criminal or by civil criteria. According to this view, the focus should be on the degree or type of mental disability and its effects on the marriage (including the children) in determining whether dissolution or continuation of the relationship would be in the best interest of the parties to it (and of the state, which sees its function as preserving the institution of marriage generally).

D. The Right of a Mentally Disabled Spouse to Sue for Divorce

Whereas in the case of prenuptial mental disability most states allow the disabled party to seek annulment,[99] in cases where the disability developed subsequent to the marriage only one jurisdiction—Alabama—grants the mentally disabled spouse (as well as the "sane" party) the right to seek divorce.[100] This right exists in Alabama by judicial interpretation[101] of a statute that contains only a general provision such as is found in all states allowing a guardian of an incompetent person to sue or be sued for his charge. Massachusetts used to have an express statutory provision[102] giving the guardian or next friend, appointed by the court for that purpose, the power to file an action for divorce on behalf of a mentally disabled person, but this statute was repealed in 1975.

The vast majority of the courts that have been confronted with the question of the right of a mentally ill person to sue for divorce have held that a guardian or next friend may *not* maintain the action.[103] It has been held that general statutes giving the guardian, committee, or next friend the power to sue do not apply to divorce actions, on the theory that a divorce is so personal that it cannot be maintained by a person who is not a party to the marriage. Another line of reasoning is that a petition in a divorce proceeding must be personally verified and mentally ill persons are incapable of doing this.[104]

The courts in a few states have carved out special exceptions to this general rule. A California decision[105] permitted an action for divorce where the spouse, although under a conservatorship, did retain an ability to exercise judgment and expressed a clear desire for dissolution of the marriage. And a Washington case[106] held that the guardian of an incompetent person could sue for divorce where the grounds for it would originally have justified annulment (lack of capacity, force, or fraud) but where divorce had since been ruled to be the exclusive remedy.

Since mentally ill persons often see things in an entirely different light when they recover or regain their balance, the proposal to permit them to sue for divorce must be considered with caution. On the other hand, denial of the right to sue for divorce may result in considerable hardship to the disabled spouse, as, for example, in situations where the "sane" partner is left in physical control of property owned by the disabled spouse and uses it to the latter's detriment.

IV. CHILD CUSTODY, SUPPORT, ADOPTION, AND TERMINATION OF PARENTAL RIGHTS

A major concern inherent in the law's regulation of marriages involving mentally disabled persons centers on the capacity of such persons to provide support and care for the children that may result. This section treats the issues of child custody/support and adoption/termination, with a heavy emphasis on the latter issue, which in the past decade has drawn fast-increasing judicial and legislative attention.

97. See cases cited *supra* in note 96. See also F.V. Harper, Problems of the Family 706-8 (rev. ed. 1962).

98. Another view on the subject is found in the position of some English judges that the purpose of divorce is not to punish the defendant for offenses but to protect the offended spouse against violation of his marital rights. It is immaterial to the offended party that his marital partner was mentally incapable of understanding the legal consequences of the acts being cited as grounds for divorce. According to this view, mental illness is never a defense to an action for divorce. This view has not been favored by American courts. Annot., 19 A.L.R.2d 144, 148 (1951).

99. See table 9.1, col. 6. In some states, a divorce action can be based on such prenuptial mental disability. See table 9.1, cols. 4 & 5. See also Jones v. Minc, 77 Wash. 2d 381, 462 P.2d 927 (1969), discussed *infra* in text surrounding note 106.

100. There are in addition a couple of cases (one quite dated) from New York and California (the latter interpreting preterritorial Hawaiian law)—which may be aberrational in these jurisdictions—seemingly supportive of the Alabama position. See McRae v. McRae, 43 Misc. 2d 252, 250 N.Y.S.2d 778 (1964), and McGrew v. Mutual Life Ins. Co., 132 Cal. 85, 64 P. 103 (1901).

101. Campbell v. Campbell, 242 Ala. 141, 5 So. 2d 401 (1941).

102. Mass. Ann. Laws ch. 208, § 7 (Law. Co-op 1955, 1981).

103. Annot., 19 A.L.R.2d 144, 182-83 (1951); Annot., 6 A.L.R.3d 681 (1966 & Supp. 1982). Two recent cases affirming the traditional doctrine that the incompetent spouse cannot sue for himself are G.A.S. v. S.I.S., 407 A.2d 253 (Del. Fam. Ct. 1978) and Brice-Nash v. Brice-Nash, 615 P.2d 836 (Kan. Ct. App. 1980). See also cases cited in note 94 *supra*.

104. Annot., 149 A.L.R. 1284, 1285-86 (1944).

105. *In re* Marriage of Higgason, 10 Cal. 3d 476, 516 P.2d 289 (1973).

106. Jones v. Minc, 77 Wash. 2d 381, 462 P.2d 927 (1969). See also Quada v. Quada, 396 S.W.2d 232 (Tex. Civ. App. 1965), a case in which the incapacitated husband was allowed to bring an action for divorce by next friend where the wife was the legal guardian.

A. Child Custody and Support

Evidence of a disabled parent's inability to care for a child may lead to a transfer of custody to the nondisabled spouse, where the couple is separated, or to an agency of the state or to individuals who are not the child's natural parents, where both natural parents are disabled or where the option of giving custody to the other natural parent is unavailable for other reasons. The state statutory law of custody today uniformly defers to the best interest of the child, and where it is modeled after the Uniform Marriage and Divorce Act—as it is in many states—the law provides that a determination of this interest shall include consideration of "the mental and physical health of all individuals involved."[107] The transfer of custody is conceptually a less final decision than transfer by adoption —sometimes it is explicitly a temporary measure—with the result that the legal standards and safeguards applicable to the custody decision tend to be less rigorous than those surrounding the adoption/termination process.

Two recent cases coming to opposite conclusions on whether custody should be transferred provide a good measure of the content of the standards. In *Price v. Price*,[108] where the husband, separating from his disabled spouse, claimed custody over the children, the court held that the wife's mental illness and formal legal incompetency for general purposes did not suffice as a matter of law to deprive her of the right to custody of the children. Incompetence to rear children is a specific issue that must be specifically alleged and proved in a custody case. It cannot be inferred from the fact of general mental or even legal incapacity. The case of *In re C.L.M.*,[109] on the other hand, involving the transfer of custody from the natural mother to the state, emphasizes the reversibility of custody decisions (as distinguished from adoptions) and the consequent propriety of making the former decisions on softer standards. Thus the court approved giving custody to the state on the mere basis of evidence of the mother's incapacity to provide necessary and proper care. The court stated that the custody change could properly be construed as a preventative measure: actual harm to the child or actual neglect need not be shown, as this adverse *potential* was implicit in the mother's general incapacity.[110]

Child custody and support questions can also arise in connection with the *child's* mental disability. One issue that has come to the fore in recent litigation is the validity of statutes requiring parents to give up custody of their disabled children to the state in order for the latter to receive residential care provided by the state. Two New York cases decided in 1982[111] have struck down that state's version of such laws. Another important related question has to do with the responsibility of the parent(s) to provide for financial support of a disabled child once that child reaches majority. Two recent cases on that point[112] indicate the current judicial view that the responsibility is a continuing one at least when the disabled person continues to reside at home. Financial liability for an *institutionalized* person appears to be a different matter, as the recent legal trend there is in the direction of extinguishing parental responsibility when the child reaches majority.[113]

B. Adoption and Termination of Parental Rights

1. Historical Background

Adoption dates back to biblical times.[114] In both England and the United States, however, adoption is not part of the common law but is based entirely upon statutes. Massachusetts enacted the first adoption statute in the United States in 1851; England did not have a provision on the subject until 1926.[115]

The power of the state legislature to provide for adoption is universally recognized, and the welfare of the child is considered the primary objective. Consent of the natural parents or surviving parent to an adoption proceeding is quite uniformly required in the statutes of the various states and lies at their very foundation.[116]

Parental consent is not required, however, in cases where the conduct of the parents has been deleterious to the welfare of the child.[117] Early statutes dispensed with

107. See, e.g., Ill. Ann. Stat. ch. 40, § 602 (Smith-Hurd 1980). The commentary to this statute cites § 402 of the Uniform Marriage and Divorce Act (9A U.L.A.) as the source from which this language derives.

108. 255 S.E.2d 652 (N.C. Ct. App. 1979).

109. 625 S.W.2d 613 (Mo. 1981).

110. Whether these two cases are reconcilable is difficult to say. They are certainly very different in tone, thereby providing a nice illustration of the outer limits of the law on custody. The cases on the substantive standards for custody change also raise the question of procedural standards, in particular the standard of proof that must be met before an allegation can be accepted by the courts as fact and as the basis for awarding custody to one party or the other. The recent case of *In re* Calkins, 96 Ill. App. 3d 74, 420 N.E.2d 861 (1981), held that parental unfitness to retain custody must be proved by *clear and convincing* evidence. See further discussion of this issue in § IV B, Adoption and Termination of Parental Rights, *infra*.

111. Joyner v. Dumpson, 533 F. Supp. 233 (S.D.N.Y. 1982), and *In re* Davis, 452 N.Y.S.2d 1007 (Fam. Ct. 1982). These decisions were recently reversed, however, in Lowry *ex rel.* Joyner v. Dumpson, 712 F.2d 770 (2d Cir. 1983), the court holding that since the New York statute required the temporary transfer of custody for *all* children in the program, the statute did not discriminate against handicapped children.

112. Wilkinson v. Wilkinson, 585 P.2d 599 (Colo. Ct. App. 1978); Kamp v. Kamp, No. 5514, 6 MDLR 171 (Wyo. Sup. Ct. Jan. 28, 1982).

113. See ch. 2, Involuntary Institutionalization, § VI, Liability for the Costs of Institutionalization.

114. The adoption of Moses by Pharoah's daughter is described in Exodus 2:10.

115. Note, Due Process Rights of Mentally Ill Parents in Nonconsensual Adoptions, 30 Ind. L.J. 431, 433 n.9 (1954-55).

116. 1 Am. Jur. Adoption of Children §§ 4, 36 (1936).

117. In such cases the issue is, more precisely speaking, not one of obtain-

consent only when there was parental misconduct such as abandonment, neglect, or cruelty.[118] In more recent times, nonconsensual adoptions have been extended to include cases where the parents of the children to be adopted are mentally disabled. This extension has probably resulted from the view that mentally disabled persons are incapable of consenting to adoption of their children.[119] Presently, there are 28 states with statutes that specifically include mental disability as a ground for dispensing with the need for parental consent to adoption.[120] In the remaining jurisdictions, the mental disability of the parent may be an element that proves the broader criterion of "parental incapacity" or the parent's inability to function in "the best interest of the child."

Adoption of children of mentally disabled parents involves two separate issues or sets of circumstances. One situation concerns parents who may be willing to have their children adopted but who because of mental disability are incapable of giving valid legal consent. Statutory authorization for consent by a friend or relative in such instances is aimed at securing the legality of transfer of parental rights and serves mainly to protect the rights of the adopting parents. In the other situation, involving parents who may *not* want to have their parental rights abrogated or whose consent is not considered, the parent's mental disability is cause for a petitioner (the state, a welfare agency, the "sane" parent, etc.) to seek a transfer of parental custody. The question is thus one of unfitness for parenthood, analogous to parental delinquency, and what is sought is legal justification for *termination* of the rights of the natural parents. The distinction is often obscured in the literature on the subject, as it is in the statutory provisions.[121]

Authorizing adoption without the consent of the mentally disabled parent, and even more so termination against parental wishes, is a very difficult decision to make, involving a delicate problem of balancing interests as between parent and child. The requisite scientific knowledge about mental disability—its nature, duration, curability—as well as the sociological knowledge about what ultimately is best for parents or children which would give decision makers confidence in the substantive correctness of their decisions is wanting. As a result, perhaps, there has been a heavy emphasis on decision-making *procedure*—not merely to minimize the chance of error but to legitimize, as it were, decisions that are based on inadequate knowledge of what is really right or best.

2. Present State of the Law: Statutes and Cases

The laws permitting the adoption of children of the mentally disabled without the parents' consent have undergone significant change during the past decade. Some six states that did not have provisions at all in 1970 have now enacted them. In addition, many of the statutes today seek to make the distinction between nonconsensual adoption and termination of parental rights, where few did so before. About half the states have distinct provisions to address the two issues, sometimes in widely separated sections of the statute books.[122] The remaining states, however, operate with only one provision whose objective is unclear and whose suitability for addressing either one or both situations is often ambiguous.

In theory, keeping the two issues separate should not be too difficult. To authorize an adoption where parents may well want to give consent but are mentally incapable of doing so, the decision maker would require proof of that fact only—the incapacity—by way of a formal adjudication of incompetence generally or, preferably, a finding of incompetence more specifically related to the question of giving up the children. In termination proceedings, on the other hand, a different set of facts would have to be established (and a finding of decisional incompetence, though it might in many cases be justified, would not be required): at minimum, parental unfitness (the inability to care for the children), harm to the children (or at least the potential for it) if they remain with the parent(s), and the probability that the unfitness to provide care and support will persist for the foreseeable future. The statutory schemes of only some of the states conform to this theoretical model.[123] Many deviate substantially.

In the statutes of some seven states,[124] a legal termina-

---

ing consent to *adoption* but one of forced *termination* of the parent-child relationship. The distinction is important, and legal standards and procedures, which often do not reflect the distinction, should do so.

118. See Keal v. Rhydderck, 317 Ill. 231, 148 N.E. 53 (1925).

119. 1 Am. Jur. Adoption of Children § 36 (1936); 45 A.L.R.2d 1379 (1956).

120. See table 9.3.

121. The literature in general is not extensive in this area. Recent pertinent articles include: Galliher, Jr., Termination of the Parent-Child Relationship: Should Parental I.Q. Be an Important Factor? 1973 Law & Soc. Order 855, and Note, The Law and The Problem Parent: Custody and Parental Rights of Homosexual, Mentally Retarded, Mentally Ill and Incarcerated Parents, 16 J. Fam. L. 797 (1977-78); Symposium: The Impact of Psychological Parenting on Child Welfare Decision-making, 12 N.Y.U. Rev. L. & Soc. Change No. 3 (1983-84). One of the most useful contributions is Goldstein, Freud, & Solnit's revision and further development of their earlier work (Beyond the Best Interests of the Child (1973)) in Before the Best Interests of the Child (1979).

122. See table 9.3.

123. E.g., Arizona, Arkansas, Nebraska, North Carolina, and North Dakota have statutes that conform substantially to this model. See table 9.3 for citations and abbreviated paraphrasings of the language contained in the provisions.

124. Connecticut, Delaware, Idaho, Montana, New Hampshire, New Jersey, and South Carolina. See table 9.3 for citations.

tion of parental rights must precede the filing of an adoption petition. The propriety of nonconsensual adoption is thus predicated on a finding of unfitness to fulfill parental responsibilities. In a number of other states, the adoption statutes speak of the parents' unfitness to rear children[125] or of dispensing with parental consent when this is in the *child's* best interest.[126] Both types of statutes are potentially confusing: for nonconsensual adoption to be authorized it need only be shown that the parent was incapable of consenting, his or her fitness as a parent and the child's interest being relevant only to the distinct question of whether the state should actively intervene and terminate the parental rights.

The adoption/termination statutes also address the nature of the parent's disability, its duration or the prognosis for recovery, and its impact on the parent's capacity to provide care for the child or children. There are a number of common phrasings that appear in the statutes of several states. The language of the North Dakota statute is typical in several respects. Termination in that state is warranted where

> by reason of physical or mental incapacity the parent is unable to provide necessary parental care for the minor, and the court finds that the conditions and causes of the behavior, neglect, or incapacity are irremediable or will not be remedied by the parent, and that by reason thereof the minor is suffering or probably will suffer serious physical, mental, moral, or emotional harm. . . .[127]

Some statutes are more explicit in describing the mental incapacity. Arizona's,[128] for example, alludes to mental illness, mental deficiency, or a history of chronic abuse of dangerous drugs, controlled substances, or alcohol. Other variations concern the medical prognosis, with several statutes speaking in terms of persistence of the disability for the "foreseeable future"[129] and others making reference to the incapacity lasting for a "prolonged [or] indeterminate period."[130] A couple of states—Delaware[131] and Kentucky[132]—specifically require that the finding of incapacity be supported by medical evidence or certification, but any of the other statutes—particularly those that predicate adoption/termination on a judicial finding of parental incompetency—may well require the same in practice. In Wisconsin the disabled parent must be presently, and for a cumulative period of at least two years within the past five, institutionalized in a mental facility.[133]

Previous editions of this book commented on the dearth of litigation, particularly appellate litigation, in the area of adoptions/terminations involving mentally disabled parents. This situation has changed dramatically. Case law reviews, aggregating mental disability litigation over the past year or so, report dozens of adoption/termination cases, many of them appealed to the highest state courts, on procedural issues, substantive criteria, or close factual situations.[134] Today the statutory law comes supplemented by a substantial body of case law, interpreting its reach and requirements and assessing its constitutional validity.

One of the rare, early cases—but still an important one—was the 1954 *Nabstedt* case[135] from Illinois addressing the constitutionality of that state's adoption statute. The statute provided that the parent must have been mentally ill for a period of three years and required that two qualified physicians selected by the court testify that the parent was not expected to recover in the foreseeable future. The law also authorized the court appointment of a guardian ad litem to represent the parent and to consent to adoption. The principal attack on the statute was based on the argument that it violated the substantive due process requirement of the Fourteenth Amendment because of the possibility that the parent might be restored to reason but could not regain the custody and companionship of the child. The court conceded the possibility but considered it too remote to invalidate the law and concluded:

> The concern of the legislature for the interest of the parent shows in its requirement that the mental illness must have continued for a period of three years and must, in the opinion of two qualified physicians, be such that there will not be recovery in the foreseeable future. . . . [W]e note that a majority of the statutes of other States do not contain a requirement that insanity must have existed for a prescribed period of time before the entry of an adoption decree. Nor are they so strict in their requirements concerning medical evidence as to the permanent character of the mental illness.[136]

Illinois has since dispensed with this three-year requirement.[137] Most other states have followed suit in eliminating provisions that are geared to a definite time. They survive only in Wisconsin, where the requirement relates to time spent in an institution.[138] The modern stat-

125. E.g., Miss. Code Ann. § 93-17-7 (Supp. 1981).
126. E.g., Iowa Code Ann. § 600.7(4) (West 1981).
127. N.D. Cent. Code § 14-15-19(3) (1981).
128. Ariz. Rev. Stat. Ann. § 8-533(B)(3) (Supp. 1981).
129. E.g., Del. Code Ann. tit. 13, § 1103(4) (1981).
130. Neb. Rev. Stat. § 43-209(5) (1978).
131. Del. Code Ann. 13, § 1103(4) (1981).
132. Ky. Rev. Stat. Am. § 208C.090(2)(a) (Michie 1982).
133. Wis. Stat. Ann. § 48.415(3) (West Supp. 1981).

134. The six issues of the 1982 volume of the *Mental Disability Law Reporter* (6 MDLR 1982) report no fewer than 45 adoption/termination cases involving mentally disabled parents.
135. People *ex rel.* Nabstedt v. Barger, 3 Ill.2d 511, 121 N.E.2d 781 (1954).
136. *Id.* at 514, 121 N.E.2d at 784.
137. The modern provisions are premised on the prognosis of no recovery "in the foreseeable future." Ill. Ann. Stat. ch. 4, § 9.1-8(e) (Smith-Hurd 1975), and ch. 40, § 1510(e) (Smith-Hurd 1980 & Supp. 1984).
138. Wis. Stat. Ann. § 48.415(3) (West Supp. 1981).

utes focus more on prognosis than on the history of the parent's disability.

The *Nabstedt* case also dealt with the question of adequate notice. Though the "insane" parent in *Nabstedt* had been personally served, counsel argued that the statute was void for failing to *require* such notice. The court responded that notice was indeed constitutionally required in petitions of the first instance but that it was *not* required in "supplemental petitions," where the court had continuing jurisdiction over the case on the basis of a prior decree involving guardianship. The soundness of this dictum may be questioned in view of the fact that many years may elapse (four years in the *Nabstedt* case) between the appointment of a guardian and the petition for adoption: the natural parent should be entitled to dispute the presumption of continued unfitness.[139] The statutes of most states fail to provide explicitly for the kinds of procedural protections that constitute or are argued to be basic "due process" in other decisional contexts—notice, the right to a hearing, the right to counsel or other representation, the right to confrontation, and other evidentiary rules. The case law, however, goes a good way toward filling this gap.

Litigation concerning the substantive standard that must be met before parental rights may be terminated has firmly established that a mere finding of mental disorder is not enough. There must be a specific showing that the disorder renders the parent unfit to rear children, and statutes failing to require this have been struck down,[140] while trial court decisions that have not fully followed the mandate of statutes that do contain the requirement have been reversed.[141] Even confinement in a mental institution has in at least one jurisdiction been held to be an insufficient ground in and of itself to support termination, the court reasoning that the attendant separation between parent and child would support a transfer of custody but not a final severing of the parent-child relationship.[142] The courts and many statutes also require an express consideration of the child's interests to supplement the parental unfitness criterion, but the cases have stopped short of requiring a finding of actual abuse of the child before a termination order can be issued.[143] That the untenable parent-child relationship must persist for the foreseeable future is one other dominant theme in the termination cases.[144]

The rigor with which these various substantive prerequisites must be proved is one of the main procedural questions that have recently occupied the courts in adoption/termination cases. An emerging consensus that the standard of proof should be at least one of "clear and convincing evidence"—the same as the civil commitment proceedings[145]—was just in 1982 given the imprimatur of the United States Supreme Court in the case of *Santosky v. Kramer.*[146] The Court held that New York's Family Court Act's provision for parental termination was unconstitutional for merely requiring proof by a "preponderance of the evidence" that the child is "permanently neglected."

Another major issue concerns the appointment of guardians ad litem or legal counsel for parents faced with the possibility of having their childrearing rights judicially terminated. The United States Supreme Court has issued a recent opinion that, while not directly concerned with mentally disabled parents, is nonetheless closely relevant. *Lassiter v. Department of Social Services of Durham County*[147] involved an indigent mother imprisoned for second-degree murder whose parental rights the county agency sought to terminate. While the evidence of parental neglect and unfitness in this case was clear, there was no question of mental disorder. The state court found for the agency, and the mother appealed on the ground that the state, despite her indigence, had not provided counsel for her. The United States Supreme Court, using the interest-balancing formula of *Mathews v. Eldridge*,[148] held in favor of the state. The Court reasoned that while the parental interest in retaining the right to rear their children was very strong and could in some cases override the state's interest in conserving its legal services resources, the circumstances of the case were not such as to dictate the conclusion that due process had been violated because of the state's failure to furnish counsel. It would seem that the mental disability of the parent would further weight the scales in favor of a requirement to provide for at least some kind of assistance—a guardian ad litem or some other competent representative, if not licensed legal counsel.

139. See Child Saving Inst. v. Knobel, 372 Mo. 609, 37 S.W.2d 920 (1931). See also Annot, 76 A.L.R. 1077, 1079 (1932).

140. See Helvey v. Rednour, 86 Ill. App. 3d 154, 408 N.E.2d 17 (1980).

141. E.g., State *ex rel.* E. & B. v. J.T., 578 P.2d 831 (Utah 1978). Though the facts supported a finding of parental unfitness, the court reversed the trial judge's decision because it was based only on a showing of mental disability and failed to include an explicit showing of parental unfitness as required by Utah Code Ann. § 78-3a-48 (1977 & Supp. 1981).

142. Williams v. Mashburn, 602 P.2d 1036 (Okla. 1979).

143. *In re* David B., 5 Fam. L. Rep. (BNA) 2531 (Cal. 5th Dist. Ct. App. Mar. 28, 1979).

144. See, e.g., *In re* Young, 600 P.2d 1312 (Wash. Ct. App. 1979); *In re* Brendendick, 74 Ill. App. 3d 946, 393 N.E.2d 675 (1979); New Mexico Health & Social Servs. Dep't v. Smith, 600 P.2d 294 (Ct. App. 1979); *In re* Sylvia M. & Alicia M., 443 N.Y.S.2d 214 (App. Div. 1981); *In re* Holley, 308 N.W.2d 341 (Neb. 1981); *In re* Castillo, 632 P.2d 855 (Utah 1981); *In re* D.L.R., 432 A.2d 196 (Pa. 1981).

145. Addington v. Texas, 441 U.S. 418 (1979).

146. 455 U.S. 745 (1982). The clear and convincing standard is a minimum standard and does not affect the validity of state laws requiring a higher burden. E.g., New Hampshire v. Robert H., No. 78-090 (Merrimack County Prob. Ct. Oct. 30, 1978): petition for termination of parental rights must be proved "beyond a reasonable doubt."

147. 452 U.S. 18 (1981).

148. 424 U.S. 319 (1975). See also ch. 2, Involuntary Institutionalization, particularly note 39, for some elaboration of the *Mathews* case.

That the state may at present not be required to appoint legal counsel in these cases does not mean it is not desirable. Where legal services for mentally disabled persons are available, placing a high priority on providing aid in termination cases is certainly not out of order. In making the priority assessment, consideration should be given to the availability and role of guardians, particularly guardians ad litem appointed for the very purpose of looking after the disabled parent's interests in litigation. There are a number of cases on the powers of the guardian ad litem in termination cases. One, from South Carolina,[149] underscores the special trust relationship of such a guardian to the disabled parent, a relationship that is different from the one between legal counsel and client. The case held that the state cannot terminate the parental rights of alleged incompetent parents without appointing a guardian ad litem; this, despite the fact that the parents did have appointed legal counsel. While avowedly different from the attorney role, the precise powers and role of the guardian ad litem are not always clear, however. A Tennessee case[150] holds that the guardian ad litem can give substitute consent for an adoption, but a Nebraska case[151] suggests the opposite, holding that the guardian ad litem may not waive the substantive rights of the parents.

The Nebraska decision also makes a procedural point in favor of full hearings in termination cases. A recent New York case[152] mandates the presence of the parent where no showing of the need to exclude him or her is made. It also supports the allegedly disabled parent's entitlement to a recent psychiatric examination. In sum, while there may be uncertainty about the thrust of all this litigation or disagreement with the results in individual cases, it would be difficult to contend today that the procedural and substantive rights of mentally disabled parents in adoption/termination cases have gone unattended by the courts. The subject richly merits such critical attention. Mental problems figure in a significant percentage of the adoption/termination cases where direct consent cannot be obtained.[153] The right to parenthood is fundamental. Mentally disabled parents whom the law singles out as potentially incapable of fulfilling parental responsibilities are at the same time entitled to every protection the law affords before the threat implied in this identification is carried out.

C. Adoption and the Disabled Child

While the focus of much of the law and discussion of adoption has been on the consequences of parental disability, there are also legal effects when the *child* is mentally disabled. Two contrasting concepts are operative today. (1) The older, negative tradition permits the legal annulment of adoptions when the child, subsequent to the adoption, is recognized as suffering from a preexisting mental disability. (2) The newer, more positive laws come from an opposite perspective. Their intent is to foster the adoption of mentally disabled children by providing financial subsidies to the adopting parents. A few states, paradoxically, have both types of laws on the books.[154]

1. Annulment of Adoptions

At the writing of the previous edition of this book in 1970, there were seven states with statutory provisions allowing the annulment of an adoption if the child developed a mental disability—or as the terms went, feeble-mindedness, insanity, or epilepsy—as a result of a condition existing prior to the adoption and of which the adopting parents had no notice. Today, only three states—California, Maine, and Missouri—retain laws of this type. Missouri's statute[155] represents the old formulation and still speaks in terms of feeble-mindedness and epilepsy. California's[156] is a modernized version in that it refers to *evidence* of the child's *developmental disability* or *mental illness*. Not only is this the modern lexicon of disabilities, but the reference to *evidence* of disability acknowledges that the statute's concern is with the *symptoms* of a mental defect that predated the adoption but that were recognized only subsequent to it. Maine's statute[157] simply permits annulment for "good cause." In each state, the legislature's decision to retain these annulment laws has not kept it from enacting subsidization provisions whose objective is to promote adoption of mentally disabled children.[158]

The California and Missouri statutes specify that the annulment action be brought within five years of the

149. South Carolina Dep't of Social Servs. v. McDow, 280 S.E.2d 208 (1981).

150. Tennessee Dep't of Human Servs. v. Ogle, 617 S.W.2d 652 (Ct. App. 1981).

151. *In re* Interest of Burbanks, 310 N.W.2d 138 (Neb. 1981).

152. *In re* Guardianship of Daniel Aaron D., 403 N.E.2d 451 (N.Y. 1980).

153. Relative to grounds such as abandonment, mental disability as a ground for terminating parental rights without consent may seem to be an infrequent occurrence. Still, a New York survey done in the 1960s reported that mental illness precluded obtaining parental consent in 12% of the cases (Allen, Ferster, & Weihofen, *supra* note 27, at 321).

154. E.g., California and Maine. See notes 156 & 157 *infra* and table 9.4 for statutory citations.

155. Mo. Rev. Stat. § 453.130 (1977). The extent to which the Missouri law is dated is revealed, among other things, by its provision that one other ground for annulment of the adoption is when the child is found to be "a member of a race, the members of which are prohibited by the laws of this state from marriage with members of the race to which the parents by adoption belong." The Missouri legislature repealed this law in 1982 (shortly after the initial draft of this chapter was completed).

156. Cal. Civ. Code § 227b (West 1982).

157. Me. Rev. Stat. Ann. ch. 19, § 538 (1981).

158. See table 9.4.

adoption decree—a proviso that was typical when these laws were more prevalent. The time limit evidences the intent of the statutes to reach only inherited conditions. It may be asked on the one hand whether five years is not excessively long in this regard. On the other hand, the entire effort to make a distinction between inheritable mental disabilities and noninheritable ones is probably futile, while making the child's status and future depend on such a distinction appears even less defensible.

The disregard in the statutes for the rights of the child is a general problem. The old laws, like Missouri's,[159] made no provision as to the nature of the proof required, failed to provide for a guardian ad litem for the child, and neglected to provide for the disposition of the child whose adoption was annulled. California's statute is an improvement at least in the latter two respects. It provides that when the mental disability is such "that the child cannot be relinquished to an adoption agency on the grounds that the child is considered unadoptable" "it shall be the duty of the clerk of the superior court of the county wherein the [annulment] action is brought to immediately notify the State Department of Social Services," which "shall file a full report with the court and shall appear before the court for the purpose of representing the adopted child."[160]

2. *Subsidizing Adoptions*

Thirty-nine jurisdictions today have statutes providing for financial subsidies to parents who adopt children with mental disabilities.[161] These laws have several objectives: (1) they serve as a general incentive for the adoption of hard-to-place children, (2) they help defray the costs of special care that such children may need, including medical costs,[162] and (3) they make it possible to avoid institutionalizing such children. Data on how well these objectives are being met are hard to come by, but just having these laws on the books, particularly as compared with the annulment provisions, comes as a breath of fresh air.

V. THE RIGHT TO BEAR (OR NOT TO BEAR) CHILDREN

The earlier editions of this book contained a separate chapter on eugenic sterilization of the mentally disabled in which the emphasis was on laws permitting the performance of this procedure without the consent of the disabled individual and possibly against his will. This is an outdated focus. "Involuntary sterilizations"—in the strict sense of these words—are today rarely performed. The eugenic rationale is no longer generally accepted or deemed acceptable. And many states have drastically altered, if not repealed, laws that did allow sterilization on this basis.

Nonetheless, the sterilization issue remains an important and controversial one, deserving of significant coverage in a book such as this. Whatever the present practices, the effects of past practices are still with us. Furthermore, some 14 states today retain laws that permit nonconsensual sterilizations. In other states, the requisite consent may be acquired from persons other than the individual who is to be sterilized, raising at least a potential question about the "voluntariness" of the procedure when used under these circumstances. The eugenic rationale has been supplanted by "environmental" and financial justifications—that the mentally disabled are unfit parents and that we ought to prevent them from adding to the welfare rolls—which command considerable, if not always overt, support. And, most significantly, the opposite side of the issue has begun to receive attention: how can disabled and incompetent persons who *want* to be sterilized (or in whose best interest it is in the judgment of their representatives) obtain sterilization in an era of gun-shy medical and judicial officials loath to assume authority in a field abandoned (as it is in a number of jurisdictions) by the lawmakers? Issues of personal "hygiene" and the right to be sexually active without the consequences of pregnancy are at the core of this new focus. Recognizing this other side—as the title of this section does—suggests that the sterilization issue is really the broader one of "procreative choice." It also suggests new complexity and controversy: there is an unavoidable tension between the objective of protecting the incompetent from unwanted or unnecessary sterilization and that of giving them the option to choose the procedure as the means for preventing conception.

A. Sterilization as a Medical Procedure

Sterilization is the surgical means by which either males or females are rendered incapable of reproduction. The operation is much more serious in women than in men. In females the surgeon must do an abdominal operation, removing segments of the fallopian tubes (salpingectomy) and tying the cut ends. In men the operation is relatively simple. Small scrotal skin incisions are made, segments of the vas deferens are removed (vasectomy), and the proximal ends of the vas are tied. Neither operation interferes with the desire for sexual intercourse or with its gratification.[163] Sterilization op-

159. Repealed in 1982.

160. Cal. Civ. Code § 227b (West 1982).

161. See table 9.4, where these statutes are set out.

162. See, e.g., N.Y. Soc. Serv. Law §§ 450 to 458 (McKinney 1983); *In re* Adoption of Crane, 417 N.Y.S.2d 629 (Putnam County Fam. Ct. 1979).

163. Deutsch, *supra* note 11, at 371.

erations are effective in nearly 100% of the cases: failure actually to sterilize occurs in 1-2% of operations performed on both males and females. Salpingectomy is at present irreversible, although research to effect reversibility is continuing. Vasectomy is reversible on occasion.[164]

Sterilization may be performed for a variety of purposes: (1) therapeutic reasons, such as the cure or treatment of certain diseases or malfunctions, or the preservation of the health of a woman when it can be reasonably calculated by competent medical authority that pregnancy or childbirth would be fatal or seriously damaging to the woman's physical (or—a more recent inclusion—psychological) well-being; (2) socioeconomic reasons, prompting increasing numbers of persons today to undergo the operation as the most effective and convenient method of limiting the family or avoiding the family situation altogether (i.e., "birth control," in the popular meaning of that term); (3) eugenic reasons, applying to mentally disabled persons in particular as a method for preventing the birth of defective children and to deflect the threat to the "welfare of the race" that is seen to accompany uncontrolled propagation;[165] and (4) "management" reasons, centering on reducing the burdens and level of care for mentally disabled persons, who—without the potential complications of pregnancy—are able to live lives with a greater measure of social freedom and personal responsibility, permitting in an increasing number of instances their maintenance in the free community, in community-based facilities, or in other settings least restrictive of their liberty. As mentioned, the original eugenic rationale is largely discredited today and is being replaced by the management rationale or by less benign arguments that the mentally disabled are unfit parents and that this parental unfitness would result in children who, even when not defective themselves, will become a public burden. A final rationale for sterilization, no longer condoned today, is the punitive one: a number of states used to authorize the involuntary sterilization of persons identified as hereditary criminals and sex offenders.[166]

164. Comment, Sterilization: A Continuing Controversy, 1 U.S.F.L. Rev. 159 (1966) [hereinafter cited as Comment, Sterilization]; J.H. Landman, Human Sterilization: The History of the Sexual Sterilization Movement (1932); M. Woodside, Sterilization in North Carolina: A Sociological and Psychological Study (1950).

165. American Neurological Association, Committee for the Investigation of Eugenical Sterilization, Eugenical Sterilization: A Reorientation of the Problem (1936) [hereinafter cited as Am. Neur. Ass'n Committee, Eugenical Sterilization]; Cook, Eugenics or Euthenics, 37 Ill. L. Rev. 287 (1943).

166. See O'Hara & Sanks, Eugenic Sterilization, 45 Geo. L.J. 20 (1956). California, Delaware, Georgia, Idaho, Iowa, Oklahoma, Oregon, Utah, and Wisconsin used to provide for compulsory sterilization of "hereditary criminals"; California, Georgia, Idaho, Iowa, Michigan, and Oregon included in their statutes such groups as sex offenders and syphilitics.

B. The History of Sterilization

Until the end of the nineteenth century sterilization was impractical because castration, the only method known at the time, caused undesirable changes in secondary sex characteristics and was considered too radical an operation to use for eugenic reasons. In the last decade of the century, however, Dr. Harry C. Sharpe of the Indiana State Reformatory—the prison location is indicative—developed a method of sterilizing males (vasectomy), and at about the same time the now-standard method of sterilizing females (salpingectomy) was developed in France.[167]

The United States was the pioneer in the field of sterilization legislation, but this lead came only after much legislative and judicial opposition.[168] Although the first bill on the subject was introduced in a state legislature almost immediately after the perfection of the new surgical techniques, it was 30 years before the constitutionality of compulsory sterilization of the mentally disabled was sustained by the United States Supreme Court in 1927.[169]

The first sterilization bill was introduced in 1897 in the state of Michigan, but it was defeated.[170] In 1905, the Pennsylvania legislature passed a bill "for the prevention of idiocy," which has been summarized as follows:

> It provided that upon enactment, "it shall be compulsory for each and every institution in the State, entrusted. . . . with the care of idiots. . . . to appoint" a neurologist and a surgeon "to examine the mental and physical condition of the inmates." If this examination showed that there was "no probability of improvement of the mental condition of the inmate" and "procreation is inadvisable," the surgeon was authorized "to perform such operation for the prevention of procreation as shall be decided safest and most effective."[171]

The bill was vetoed by the governor, who returned it with this message:

> "This Bill has, what may be called with propriety, an attractive title. If idiocy could be prevented by an Act of Assembly, we may be quite sure that such an act would have long been passed and approved in this State, and . . . in all civilized countries. . . . The nature of the operation is not described, but it is such an operation as they shall decide to be safest and most effective. It is plain that the safest and most effective methods of pre-

167. *Id.*

168. Landman, The History of Human Sterilization in the United States—Theory, Statute, Adjudication, 23 Ill. L. Rev. 463 (1929).

169. Buck v. Bell, 274 U.S. 200 (1927).

170. O'Hara & Sanks, *supra* note 166, at 22.

171. Challener, The Law of Sexual Sterilization in Pennsylvania, 57 Dick. L. Rev. 298 (1952).

venting procreation would be to cut the heads off the inmates, and such authority is given by the Bill to this staff of scientific experts."[172]

Indiana finally enacted the first compulsory sterilization law in 1907.[173] Even before 1907, superintendents of mental hospitals in several states were secretly having mentally deficient persons sterilized. In fact, it is asserted that Dr. Sharpe, who perfected the vasectomy operation, secretly and illegally sterilized several hundred males at the Indiana State Reformatory before the passage of the Indiana law.[174] The Indiana statute was later declared unconstitutional,[175] as were other similar statutes that came before the courts prior to 1925.[176]

In 1925 the highest courts of Michigan[177] and Virginia[178] held that the sterilization statutes of their respective states were constitutional. Two years later the constitutionality of the Virginia statute was upheld by the United States Supreme Court in *Buck v. Bell.*[179]

In the ten years following this Supreme Court decision, 20 states passed sterilization laws, many of these resembling the Virginia statute.[180] In all, 32 states at one point had sterilization statutes. This number has today been reduced to 19[181] as a result of court rulings that the statutes were unconstitutional or of direct legislative repeal. Of these remaining 19, most have undergone substantial revision in their scope and procedures since they were first enacted.

Opposition to the sterilization laws has come in the form of both medical and legal criticism. In 1965 the Board of Directors of the Association for Voluntary Sterilization, formerly known as the Human Betterment Association, "unanimously voted that this Association is opposed to compulsion of any kind [in regard to sterilization], either directly or implicit."[182] In April 1969, the American Civil Liberties Union Board of Directors adopted a similar policy statement.[183] More significantly perhaps, opposition is shown in the decline in actual application of the sterilization laws. The number of sterilizations has decreased steadily during the past 50 years. Reaching a peak during the 1920s and 1930s, sterilizations performed pursuant to the statutes dropped to a low of 467 in 1963.[184] A mail survey conducted in late 1981 suggests that involuntary sterilizations performed under the applicable legislation and on the authority of the state departments of mental health and retardation have today dwindled to a negligible number.[185] Many states reported they had ceased to collect information on this matter, some simply saw no need to respond, and all of those that did answer indicated that there had been no such sterilizations in the past "several" years, the most recent reported instance being in 1972.[186] Nonetheless, the legislation remains on the books in many states, the legal fallout from earlier sterilization programs is only now beginning to appear, and serious questions have been raised about "consensual" sterilization.

C. Sterilization Today

Scientific findings throwing doubt on the validity of eugenic reasons for targeting the mentally disabled for sterilization, the development of contraceptive alternatives, and an increased awareness of the rights of mentally disabled persons generally combined with a number of well-publicized scandals have resulted in major changes in the statutes authorizing sterilization, in the type and frequency of litigation brought to contest or assert sterilization authority, and in sterilization practices.

1. The Statutes

At the publication in 1971 of the last edition of this book, 26 states retained laws authorizing sterilization of mentally disabled persons, all but 5 allowing the procedure to be performed on nonconsenting subjects. Today, the total number is down to 19 states, of which 14 still permit sterilization without the subject's consent.[187]

172. Pennsylvania, Vetoes by the Governor of Bills Passed by the Legislature, Session of 1905, at 26, *cited in* Challener, *supra* note 171, at 299 n.1.

173. 1907 Ind. Acts ch. 215, *cited in* O'Hara & Sanks, *supra* note 166, at 22 n.17.

174. Deutsch, *supra* note 11, at 370.

175. Williams v. Smith, 190 Ind. 526, 131 N.E. 2 (1921).

176. Smith v. Board of Examiners of Feeble-Minded, 85 N.J.L. 46, 88 A. 963 (1913); Haynes v. Lapeer Circuit Judge, 201 Mich. 138, 166 N.W. 938 (1918); *In re* Thomson, 103 Misc. 23, 169 N.Y.S. 638 (Sup. Ct. 1918), *aff'd mem. sub nom.* Osborn v. Thomson, 185 App. Div. 902, 171 N.Y.S. 1094 (3d Dep't 1918).

177. Smith v. Command, 231 Mich. 409, 204 N.W. 140 (1925). This decision upheld 1923 Mich. Pub. Acts No. 285, which authorized the sterilization of mentally deficient persons but did not include mentally ill persons.

178. Buck v. Bell, 143 Va. 310, 130 S.E. 516 (1925), *aff'd,* 274 U.S. 200 (1927). This decision upheld 1924 Va. Pub. Acts ch. 394, which, like the Michigan statute, authorized the sterilization of mentally deficient persons and did not include mentally ill persons.

179. 274 U.S. 200 (1927).

180. Notes and Legislation, Human Sterilization, 35 Iowa L. Rev. 251, 253 n.12 (1950).

181. See table 9.5.

182. Letter to the American Bar Foundation from the Association for Voluntary Sterilization, Inc. (John R. Rague, Executive Director, July 7, 1969).

183. *Id.*.

184. *Id.*

185. The survey was conducted by the American Bar Foundation as part of a larger inquiry into the state of mental disability law and practices in the various states. Letters were sent to the departments of mental health and developmental disability in each state. Though the overall response rate, and particularly response to the sterilization question, was less than complete, the results are at the least suggestive of the national patterns and trends.

186. South Carolina was the only jurisdiction responding with specific numbers, reporting that there had been no sterilizations since 1972, when five were performed. Most of the other states responding generalized that there had been no sterilizations in "recent years" or in the "recent past."

187. See table 9.5, col. 13.

At least 2 of the states requiring consent[188] permit the procedure to be performed on the substituted consent of a relative or guardian when the subject is not competent to give it himself. Apart from the numbers of states involved, there have been major changes in the coverage of the laws and in the rigor of the procedures that must be observed before the statutory authority can take effect.

The majority of the sterilization statutes include in their scope the mentally ill and the developmentally disabled (or retarded).[189] A recent development, which applies in some 8 states,[190] has been to restrict this coverage to mentally disabled persons who are formally incompetent or under guardianship. In about an equal number but different set of states,[191] the statutes apply only to mentally disabled persons in institutions—an older qualification. Many of the old sterilization statutes included epileptics among the persons targeted for the procedure, but today only 3 states still extend their coverage to this group.[192] A number of states today specify that minors are not subject to sterilization under the statute or, alternatively, only if consent for the procedure is obtained from the parents or guardian.[193] The Oklahoma statute[194] has a limit at the other end of the age spectrum: only males under 65 and females under 47 come within its authority.

Most of the statutes today make explicit the rationale(s) upon which sterilization may be authorized.[195] The majority of these premise it (typically in combination with one or two other bases) on the subject's "best interests"[196]—a modern feature. A common formulation speaks of the "welfare of [both] the patient and society."[197] The statutes of 9 states still adhere to the eugenic rationale, providing that one of the reasons for a sterilization order may be to prevent mentally disabled offspring.[198] Six are (also) concerned with the ability of mentally disabled persons to function as parents.[199] And in 3 states,[200] the authority to order sterilization may be predicated on the prospect that the subject would require public aid if she were to bear a child or further children. Finally, about half the statutes contain references to the subject's medical welfare.[201] These are diverse in content, ranging from privisos about the incurability of the subject's mental disability[202] to the specific concern that the sterilization procedure not be detrimental to the subject's health.[203] Connecticut's statute[204] represents the modern prototype. Essentially an elaboration of the "best interest" rationale, it requires a finding that (a) less drastic alternative contraceptive methods are unworkable or inapplicable, (b) the patient is capable of reproduction, (c) the patient has the capability and opportunity for sexual activity, and (d) procreation would endanger the life or severely impair the health of the patient.

Persons who may apply for a sterilization order typically include the superintendent of the institution (in case the subject is institutionalized) and the parents or guardian.[205] Others include the subject himself or herself,[206] a concession to the fact that the procedure may be desired by the person who will undergo it, and/or persons such as the county welfare director,[207] the prosecuting attorney,[208] a physician,[209] or any interested party.[210]

The most significant new feature of the statutes is the lengthy array of procedural protections that have been written into them. The majority of statutes today explicitly require that notice of the application for a sterilization order be given to various concerned parties, including typically the subject himself or herself, parents or guardians if the subject is a minor or incompetent, and to the spouse (if the patient is married) or his nearest relatives.[211] Oregon requires that the public defender be notified.[212] Time requirements are universal, with the length ranging from 7 to 30 days between the notification and the hearing on the application.[213] In 12 states, a valid application for sterilization must be accompanied

188. Me. Rev. Stat. Ann. tit. 34, § 2461 (1978); N.J. Stat. Ann. § 30:6D-5(a)(4) (West 1981).

189. See table 9.5, cols. 1 & 2. Because heredity figures more dominantly in developmental disabilities than in mental illness, both the early practices and the more recent legal controversies have involved primarily persons with one of the former types of disability.

190. Table 9.5, col. 4.

191. Table 9.5, col. 5.

192. Delaware, Mississippi, and South Carolina. See table 9.5, col. 3, for the statutory citations.

193. Table 9.5, cols. 6, 11, & 12.

194. Okla. Stat. Ann. tit. 43A, § 341 (West 1979).

195. Table 9.6, cols. 5-9.

196. Table 9.6, col. 8.

197. *Id.*

198. Table 9.6, col. 5.

199. Table 9.6, col. 6.

200. Georgia, Idaho, and Oklahoma. See table 9.6, col. 7, for statutory citations.

201. Table 9.6, col. 8.

202. E.g., Ga. Code Ann. § 84-933(b)(1)(1979); Idaho Code § 39-3901(a) (1977).

203. E.g., Miss. Code Ann. § 41-45-9 (Supp. 1982). The statutes of Oklahoma and South Carolina contain similar language. See table 9.6, cols. 8 & 9, for specific citations.

204. Conn. Gen. Stat. Ann. § 45-78w and p(d) (West 1981).

205. Table 9.5, cols. 7-9.

206. Table 9.5, col. 9.

207. Minn. Stat. Ann. § 256.08 (West 1971 & Supp. 1981); N.C. Gen. Stat. § 35-37 (1976 & Supp. 1981).

208. Idaho Code § 39-3903 (a) (1977 & Supp. 1981).

209. Me. Rev. Stat. Ann. tit. 34 § 2461 (1978); Or. Rev. Stat. § 436.025 (1981).

210. Conn. Gen. Stat. § 45-78 (1981); Or. Rev. Stat. § 436.025 (1981).

211. Table 9.5, cols. 14-16.

212. Or. Rev. Stat. § 436.041 (2) (1981).

213. Table 9.5, col. 17.

by medical certification.[214] In several states, as many as three professionals—some combination of physicians, psychologists, hospital superintendents, or social workers—must attest to the medical propriety of the procedure applied for.[215] In Kentucky,[216] the medical involvement is not only for the purpose of examination but to provide counseling to the subject who is to undergo the sterilization. Even at that, some states require further approval/review by hospital or social services personnel or a special committee composed of such staff.[217]

Eleven states require a court hearing before sterilization may be performed;[218] 4 provide for an administrative board to decide whether the procedure is to be authorized or not.[219] Six states do not specifically provide for a hearing.[220] Three of these have notice provisions—requiring notification to the parties concerned 20 or 30 days before the sterilization is to be performed.[221] Absent a clear right to a hearing, it is difficult to see what the purpose of the notice requirement is. In 10 states, the patient has a right to be present at the hearing by statute;[222] in 2 of these the patient's presence is mandatory *per se*, in the others only if he requests it. Sixteen states provide for a right to counsel, some requiring the appointment of an attorney if the subject is indigent.[223] Eight mandate the appointment of a guardian ad litem.[224]

A number of states have enacted additional protections in the form of waiting periods subsequent to the sterilization order,[225] stays pending appeal,[226] and general provisions for judicial review.[227] Assuming all these statutory requirements are indeed observed, it can be concluded that sterilization of mentally disabled persons today ensues only after a most deliberate decision-making process in which the subjects' procreative rights are thoroughly safeguarded. The rights of others participating in the process also receive protection. Most statutes today contain provisions holding medical personnel and other persons "legally participating" immune from liability.[228]

214. Table 9.5, col. 18.
215. *Id.*
216. Ky. Rev. Stat. Ann. § 212.343 (Michie 1977 & Supp. 1980).
217. Table 9.5, col. 19.
218. Table 9.6, col. 1.
219. Table 9.6, col. 2.
220. Table 9.6, cols. 1 & 2.
221. Del. Code Ann. tit. 16, § 5701(c) (1973); Me. Rev. Stat. Ann. tit. 34, § 2464 (1978); Ark Stat. Ann. § 59-501(E)(b) (1971). In Delaware, the notice goes only to the husband or wife, parent or guardian, or the person with whom the patient last resided—not specifically to the patient himself.
222. Table 9.6, col. 3.
223. Table 9.6, col. 4.
224. Table 9.6, col. 15.
225. Table 9.6, col. 10.
226. Table 9.6, col. 12.
227. Table 9.6, col. 11.
228. Table 9.6, cols. 13 & 14. Several states stipulate that such immunity obtains only in the absence of negligence. The well-known United States Supreme Court case of Stump v. Sparkman, 435 U.S. 349 (1978), affirms the principle of judicial immunity in the sterilization context.

2. The Case Law

(a) Substantive due process □□ In the leading sterilization case, *Buck v. Bell*,[229] the United States Supreme Court held that sterilization of a mentally deficient woman who had a mentally deficient mother as well as a mentally deficient daughter did not violate substantive due process.

Proceeding on the assumption—a plausible one on the facts of the particular case—that the defects were hereditary, Justice Holmes, speaking for the Court, said that the statute was a valid exercise of the state's police power and compared it with statutes requiring compulsory vaccination. With regard to this comparison, it is interesting to note that when the constitutionality of the vaccination statute was upheld in Massachusetts in 1903—later affirmed by the United States Supreme Court—the Massachusetts Supreme Judicial Court said:

> If a person should deem it important that vaccination should not be performed in his case, and the authorities should think otherwise, it is not in their power to vaccinate him by force, and the worst that could happen to him under the statute would be the payment of the penalty of $5.[230]

One obvious argument is that the Massachusetts vaccination statute and the Virginia sterilization statute are not analogous because "[s]o far as concerns liberty there would appear to be a real difference between assessing a fine and compelling submission."[231] A further objection to the analogy is that the scientific findings relating the prevention of smallpox with vaccination are far more conclusive than the highly controverted claim that mental disorders are largely hereditary. Finally, there is no comparison in terms of bodily intrusion between scratching the skin and what, particularly for women, is an intricate surgical procedure.

Justice Holmes also made another analogy in *Buck v. Bell*, to the effect that if the nation can call upon its best citizens to sacrifice their lives in time of war, it should be able to ask a lesser sacrifice of those who are a burden to it. This analogy has been criticized on the ground that there is "a necessity and an urgency that causes us to sacrifice men in self-defense which is wholly lacking in the case of eugenic sterilization."[232] Also the idea of forced military service in itself is not beyond controversy in a civilized society.

229. 143 Va. 310, 130 S.E. 516 (1925), *aff'd*, 274 U.S. 200 (1927).
230. Commonwealth v. Pear, 183 Mass. 242, 66 N.E. 719, 722 (1903), *aff'd sub nom.* Jacobson v. Massachusetts, 197 U.S. 11 (1905).
231. Gest, Eugenic Sterilization: Justice Holmes vs. Natural Law, 23 Temp. L.Q. 306, 308 n.3 (1950).
232. O'Hara & Sanks, *supra* note 166, at 29-30.

Even before *Buck v. Bell,* the dangers inherent in the logic of compulsory sterilization were discerned by the Supreme Court of New Jersey:

> There are other things besides physical or mental diseases that may render persons undesirable citizens, or might do so in the opinion of a majority of a prevailing Legislature. Racial differences, for instance, might afford a basis for such an opinion in communities where that question is unfortunately a permanent and paramount issue.[233]

The issue of whether the eugenic theories that underlay the old sterilization statutes are upheld by scientific evidence was not raised in *Buck v. Bell.* Justice Holmes's assertion that "three generations of imbeciles are enough"[234] left little doubt about the Court's assumptions, however. Subsequent sterilization cases were decided on similar assumptions.[235] Along with *Buck v. Bell* these decisions show the danger of generalizing from what might appear as overwhelming evidence in the particular case.

Recent critics of *Buck v. Bell* have argued that compulsory sterilization violates substantive due process regardless of the validity of eugenic theories or the effectiveness of such practices. Their position is that the right to parenthood or the right of procreation generally is a fundamental liberty that can be restricted only on the basis of a compelling state or public interest, hardly satisfied by the marginal contribution to the public welfare that might result from compulsory sterilization.[236] A line of United States Supreme Court cases going back to the mid-1960s can be read to provide support for this position. In *Griswold v. Connecticut* (1965),[237] the Court, invoking a constitutionally protected right to privacy,[238] upheld the right of competent married adults to choose to use contraceptives in the face of a Connecticut statute that made it a crime for any person to use any drug or device to prevent conception. Subsequent decisions extended this right to unmarried persons[239] and to minors.[240] *Roe v. Wade*[241] established the right of an adult individual to choose to have an abortion, a holding that was broadened in *Planned Parenthood of Missouri v. Danforth,*[242] where the Court sustained the right to choose the *method* of abortion and struck down Missouri's blanket requirement that all minors obtain parental consent before being permitted to have a pregnancy terminated. *Ruby v. Massey,*[243] a federal district court decision involving parents who sought to have the sterilization procedure performed on their severely mentally retarded children, brings the argument quite close to the issue at hand. The court ruled that the option to choose contraceptive *sterilization* is constitutionally protected the same as the right to select any other fertility or birth control device or procedure, including abortion. While *Massey* and the foregoing cases affirm the individual's procreative right in a negative sense, sustaining the use of various measures to prevent conception and birth in various circumstances, there is potential support in them for a positive assertion of the procreative right and for the position that substantive due process prohibits state infringement of this right without the subject's knowing, voluntary consent.

(b) Equal protection □□ In 1918 two sterilization statutes were successfully attacked on the grounds that they applied only to inmates of public institutions and therefore violated the Fourteenth Amendment's guarantee of equal protection of the laws.[244] However, in 1925 in *Buck v. Bell* the Virginia Supreme Court of Appeals, holding to the contrary that a law applying solely to inmates in state institutions did not violate this clause, said that "there can be no discrimination . . . since the woman on the outside, if in fact feeble-minded, can, by the process of commitment, and afterwards a sterilization hearing, be sterilized under the act."[245] When the United States Supreme Court considered the case,[246] it also decided that there was no denial of equal protection. In ruling on this question, the Court stated:

> [T]he law does all that is needed when it does all that it can, indicates a policy, applies it to all within the lines,

233. Smith v. Board of Examiners of Feeble-Minded, 85 N.J.L. 46, 88 A. 963, 966 (1913).

234. 274 U.S. 200, 207 (1927).

235. E.g., State v. Troutman, 50 Idaho 673, 299 P. 668 (1931), in which the Idaho Supreme Court said that there was "no doubt in our minds that heredity plays a controlling part in the blight of feeble-mindedness" (670). The defendant in this case was himself a "congenital defective"; his mother, father, five brothers, and six sisters were also feeble-minded; his mother's sister had seven children, three of whom were feeble-minded; and one of these had ten children, all ten of whom were similarly disabled.

236. E.g., Gest, *supra* note 231; Burgdorf & Burgdorf, The Wicked Witch Is Almost Dead: *Buck v. Bell* and the Sterilization of Handicapped Persons, 50 Temp. L.Q. 995 (1977); Ross, Sterilization of the Developmentally Disabled: Shedding Some Myth-Conceptions, 9 Fla. St. U.L. Rev. 599 (1981).

237. 381 U.S. 479 (1965).

238. Individual privacy as a constitutional right was first suggested in a dissent by Justice Brandeis in Olmstead v. United States, 277 U.S. 438 (1928), a wire-tapping case. There is of course no specific mention of a right to privacy in the federal Constitution, but it has been said to materialize from the "shadows" of the various Constitutional amendments (Whalen v. Roe, 429 U.S. 589 (1977)) or to be part of the "penumbra" of specific guarantees of the Bill of Rights (Griswold v. Connecticut, 381 U.S. 479 (1965)).

239. Eisenstadt v. Baird, 405 U.S. 438 (1972).

240. Carey v. Population Servs. Int'l, 431 U.S. 678 (1977).

241. 410 U.S. 113 (1973).

242. 428 U.S. 52 (1976).

243. 452 F. Supp. 361 (D. Conn. 1978).

244. Haynes v. Lapeer Circuit Judge, 201 Mich. 138, 166 N.W. 938 (1918); *In re* Thomson, 103 Misc. 23, 169 N.Y.S. 638 (Sup. Ct. 1918), *aff'd mem. sub nom.* Osborn v. Thomson, 185 A.D. 902, 171 N.Y.S. 1094 (3d Dep't 1918).

245. 143 Va. 310, 130 S.E. 516, 520 (1925), *aff'd,* 274 U.S. 200 (1927).

246. 274 U.S. 200 (1927).

and seeks to bring within the lines all similarly situated so far and so fast as its means allow. Of course so far as the operations enable those who otherwise must be kept confined to be returned to the world, and thus open the asylum to others, the equality aimed at will be more nearly reached.[247]

The majority of the sterilization statutes today are broader in their application, including mentally disabled persons who may be legally incompetent but "at large."[248] Of the present 19 statutes, only 7 are aimed solely at institutionalized persons.[249]

In 1942 the United States Supreme Court struck down an Oklahoma sterilization statute on grounds that it violated the equal protection clause.[250] This statute applied to habitual criminals, and its constitutional flaw was that it excepted embezzlers. Today, such a statute would fall on substantive due process and cruel and unusual punishment grounds as well.

(c) Cruel and unusual punishment □□ The ostensible justification for laws authorizing compulsory sterilization is that they exist for the protection of society or even to protect the persons who are the target of these laws from themselves. Where they were aimed at the criminal population or elements of this population, the underlying punitive intent of the laws has been more readily perceived. On this basis, the laws are vulnerable to attack for violating the Eighth Amendment's prohibition against cruel and unusual punishment. One of the earliest state court cases on the issue[251] rejected this challenge, holding that a compulsory vasectomy was not cruel in a case where the defendant was adjudged guilty of the statutory rape of a girl under the age of ten years. Two federal court cases,[252] coming only a few years after the state decision, did accept the Eighth Amendment argument. While conceding that the sterilization procedure may not be cruel in the physical sense, the courts in these cases characterized the operation as degrading, humiliating, and productive of mental suffering and therefore *legally* cruel.

Sterilization statutes aimed at mentally disabled persons are not intended to inflict punishment.[253] Whether or not one is willing to accept this absence of punitive intent at face-value, the fact remains that the effects of degradation, humiliation, and mental anguish are as apt to result when the subject of compulsory sterilization is a mentally disabled person as when the subject is one convicted of a crime.

(d) Procedural due process □□ Justice Holmes, prior to stating in *Buck v. Bell* that the "attack is not upon the procedure but upon the substantive law," delivered himself of the dictum that under the Virginia law involved "[t]here can be no doubt that so far as procedure is concerned the rights of the patient are most carefully considered."[254] He then gave the following detailed description of the procedure set out in the statute:

> The superintendent first presents a petition to the special board of directors of his hospital or colony, stating the facts and the grounds for his opinion, verified by affidavit. Notice of the petition and of the time and place of the hearing in the institution is to be served upon the inmate, and also upon his guardian, and if there is no guardian the superintendent is to apply to the Circuit Court of the County to appoint one. If the inmate is a minor notice also is to be given to his parents if any with a copy of the petition. The board is to see to it that the inmate may attend the hearings if desired by him or his guardian. The evidence is all to be reduced to writing, and after the board has made its order for or against the operation, the superintendent, or the inmate, or his guardian, may appeal to the Circuit Court of the County. The Circuit Court may consider the record of the board and the evidence before it and such other admissible evidence as may be offered, and may affirm, revise, or reverse the order of the board and enter such order as it deems just. Finally any party may apply to the Supreme Court of Appeals, which, if it grants the appeal, is to hear the case upon the record of the trial in the Circuit Court and may enter such order as it thinks the Circuit Court should have entered.[255]

Up until recently, most sterilization statutes offered substantially less protection of the patient's rights than the Virginia statute. But legal challenges were few and far between, and those that were brought achieved mixed success.[256] The past decade, however, has produced a major upgrading in the procedural rigor of the laws, both on legislative initiative[257] and through the courts in jurisdictions where the legislature lagged or, by

247. *Id.* at 208.

248. Table 9.5, cols. 1-6. E.g., Del. Code Ann. 16, § 5701 (1973 & Supp. 1980).

249. *Id.*

250. Skinner v. Oklahoma *ex rel.* Williamson, 316 U.S. 535 (1942).

251. State v. Feilen, 70 Wash. 65, 126 P. 75 (1912).

252. Davis v. Berry, 216 F. 413 (S.D. Iowa 1914), *rev'd for mootness,* 242 U.S. 468 (1916); Mickle v. Henrichs, 262 F. 687 (D. Nev. 1918).

253. E.g., *In re* Cavitt, 182 Neb. 712, 157 N.W. 2d 171 (1968); Smith v. Command, 231 Mich. 409, 204 N.W. 140 (1925) (specifically disavowing punishment as an end).

254. 274 U.S. 200, 207 (1927).

255. *Id.* at 206-7.

256. Some of the old cases are: Brewer v. Valk, 204 N.C. 186, 167 S.E. 638 (1933); Williams v. Smith, 190 Ind. 526, 131 N.E. 2 (1921) (statutes struck down for failure to provide for notice and a full hearing); Garcia v. State Dep't of Institutions, 36 Cal. App. 2d 152, 97 P.2d 264 (1939) (statute upheld even though no notice and hearing requirements); State *ex rel.* Smith v. Schaffer, 126 Kan. 607, 270 P. 604 (1928) (no right to appeal from sterilization order issued by administrative board).

257. See generally table 9.5.

repealing the existing statutory provisions without replacing them, abandoned the field altogether.[258]

In *Wyatt v. Aderholt* (1974),[259] Judge Johnson of the United States District Court for the Middle District of Alabama, noting that sterilizations continued to be performed by the state's health authorities despite the fact that Alabama's sterilization statute had been judicially declared unconstitutional, in effect rewrote the statute, ordering that henceforth the procedure could be performed "only where the full panoply of constitutional protections has been accorded to the individuals involved."[260] The court spelled out the following procedural requirements to be part of this "panoply." (1) The director of the institution, in recommending the procedure for the patient, would have to do so in a written report evaluating the patient, giving the reasons for the proposed sterilization and detailing the steps taken to inform the patient of the proposed operation. (2) A special review committee would make a written, documented review of the director's recommendation based on: (a) consideration of appropriate medical, social, and psychological information on the patient, (b) a personal interview with the patient, (c) interviews with other concerned individuals such as relatives of the patient, and (d) a finding by the committee that the sterilization is appropriate and necessary beyond "any doubt." (3) The review committee's decision would be given to patient's counsel and be open to review by the institution's human rights committee and the court. (4) The patient must be represented throughout the proceedings by legal counsel.

Subsequent court decisions have elaborated on and refined the scheme of procedural protections that apply in sterilization proceedings. As procedure shades into substantive standards—*what* must be alleged, shown, reviewed as opposed to how or who must do it—the courts in some states have fully assumed the legislative function. The case of *In re Guardianship of Hayes*,[261] filling the statutory void that existed in the state of Washington, is a good example. The court prescribed the following "sterilization guidelines":

> The decision can only be made in a superior court proceeding in which (1) the incompetent individual is represented by a disinterested guardian ad litem, (2) the court has received independent advice based upon a comprehensive medical, psychological, and social evaluation of the individual, and (3) to the greatest extent possible, the court has elicited and taken into account the view of the incompetent individual.
>
> Within this framework, the judge must first find by clear, cogent and convincing evidence that the individual is (1) incapable of making his or her own decision about sterilization, and (2) unlikely to develop sufficiently to make an informed judgment about sterilization in the foreseeable future.
>
> Next, it must be proved by clear, cogent and convincing evidence that there is a need for contraception. The judge must find that the individual is (1) physically capable of procreation, and (2) likely to engage in sexual activity at the present or in the near future under circumstances likely to result in pregnancy, and must find in addition that (3) the nature and extent of the individual's disability, as determined by empirical evidence and not solely on the basis of standardized tests, renders him or her permanently incapable of caring for a child, even with reasonable assistance.
>
> Finally, there must be no alternatives to sterilization. The judge must find that by clear, cogent and convincing evidence (1) all less drastic contraceptive methods, including supervision, education and training, have been proved unworkable or inapplicable, and (2) the proposed method of sterilization entails the least invasion of the body of the individual. In addition, it must be shown by clear, cogent and convincing evidence that (3) the current state of scientific and medical knowledge does not suggest either (a) that a reversible sterilization procedure or other less drastic contraceptive method will shortly be available, or (b) that science is on the threshold of an advance in the treatment of the individual's disability.[262]

These "guidelines" are as detailed as any of the statutory prescriptions existing in other jurisdictions, and they represent the very latest in procedural "progressivism."[263]

258. See *In re* Marcia R., No. C267-75 Rc, 4 MDLR 258 (Vt. Super. Ct., Rutland County June 11, 1980) for one of the most recent cases in which a state sterilization statute was invalidated for providing inadequate procedural protections. Where there is no statute, much of the controversy in the litigation centers on whether courts have inherent power to authorize sterilizations or whether the authority derives only from a specific legislative grant of such power. The cases go both ways, with decisions such as Guardianship of Tulley, 83 Cal. App. 3d 698, 146 Cal. Rptr. 226 (1978), *cert. denied,* 440 U.S. 967 (1979), holding that courts have no subject matter jurisdiction over the issue in the absence of express legislative authorization, and cases such as *In re* Guardianship of Hayes, 608 P.2d 635 (Wash. 1980), and *In re* Grady, 426 A.2d 467 (N.J. Sup. Ct. 1981), coming to the opposite conclusion based on the general powers granted to courts under the state constitution or on their inherent parens patriae powers.

259. 368 F. Supp. 1383 (M.D. Ala. 1974).

260. *Id.* at 1384.

261. 608 P.2d 635 (Wash. 1980). The court in developing its sterilization guidelines noted the assistance of the amicus brief filed by the Mental Health Law Project as well as the directives provided by cases such as Wyatt v. Aderholt, 368 F. Supp. 1383 (M.D. Ala. 1974), and North Carolina Ass'n for Retarded Children v. North Carolina, 420 F. Supp. 451 (M.D.N.C. 1976).

262. 608 P.2d at 641 (subsection numbers omitted). Cf. *In re* A.W., 637 P.2d 366 (Colo. 1981); *In re* C.D.M., 627 P.2d 607 (Alaska 1981); *In re* Penny N., 414 A.2d 541 (N.H. 1980); *In re* Moe, 385 Mass. 555, 432 N.E.2d 712 (1982); Wentzel v. Montgomery Gen. Hosp., 293 Md. 685 (1982); *In re* Grady, 426 A. 2d 467 (N.J. 1981); *In re* Marcia R., No. C267-75 Rc, 4 MDLR 258 (Vt. Super. Ct., Rutland County June 11, 1980).

263. See note 261 *supra* and table 9.5.

3. New Theories and Trends

In terms of performance of the procedure on unwilling persons confined in institutions, sterilization today is no longer a "problem." Scientific,[264] moral,[265] religious,[266] and legal[267] challenges—some launched more than half a century ago—to the theories particularly the eugenic theories, that were once thought to justify compulsory sterilization of the mentally disabled, have in the past two decades made their effects felt both on the statutory provisions authorizing such practices and on the practices themselves. A considerable part of the controversy today has been reduced to addressing past wrongs for which the remedy is sought only now that the collective social consience and the legal resources have been brought around to focus on these wrongs. For example, suit was filed in 1980 in a federal district court in Virginia to seek redress for the surviving members of the class of 7,500 patients who were sterilized in that state between the year 1924 and 1972 under involuntary or nonconsensual circumstances.[268]

Today, sterilizations are performed overwhelmingly, if not exclusively, with the consent of the subject. This does not mean all problems associated with the procedure have disappeared; but the concerns are different. A main concern is whether procedures that are labeled voluntary are in fact so. In the classic situation where the person who is to undergo the operation is mentally incapable of giving valid informed consent, the objective of the law is to elicit valid substituted consent and to erect the necessary standards and protections to ensure that the ultimate decision is medically justified and in other respects in the subject's best interest. Presumably, a decision made in accordance with these requirements would square with the patient's own decision if he were competent to make it. It goes without saying that both the laws and the practices occasionally fall short of this ideal.[269]

Certain special situations raise the problem of assuring true voluntariness more starkly than others. The "voluntary" sterilization of young children under statutes that specify no minimum age[270] and its performance on institutionalized persons who give consent as a condition of discharge[271] have long drawn the attention of critics. The situations and cases that have come under scrutiny date from the 1960s, and it may be that the "problem"—in terms of quantitative significance—has abated today. Nonetheless, the potential for such abuse of the concept of voluntariness remains, particularly as the rationales for the procedure shift from eugenics to parenthood and public welfare considerations. The fact that some of the cases involved persons of normal mental competence[272] and that some of the statutes aimed at the mentally *in*competent—an infinitely more vulnerable group—endorse these new rationales[273] shows that there is no reason to be complacent.

Recently, the Health Research Group—a public interest organization formed by Ralph Nader—sought to focus public attention on what it perceived as abuses in Medicaid-funded sterilizations and hysterectomies.[274]

264. E.g., Myerson, Certain Medical and Legal Phases of Eugenic Sterilization, 52 Yale L.J. 618 (1943); Am. Neur. Ass'n, Committee, Eugenical Sterilization, *supra* note 165; Deutsch, *supra* note 11, at 373-74. These works show that questions have long been raised regarding the role of heredity in perpetuating mental disabilities, including mental deficiency or retardation. While acknowledging evidence that mentally deficient persons are more likely to produce subnormal children than persons of normal intelligence, the reports stress that there are many other causes for mental deficiency and that even the most drastic programs for inhibiting propagation among the mentally deficient would have only very limited effect on the overall "problem." Other long-standing contentions are that:

> (1) There is nothing to indicate that mental disease and mental defect are increasing, and from this standpoint there is no evidence of a biological deterioration of the race.
> (2) The reputedly high fecundity of the mentally defective groups . . . is a myth based on the assumption that those who are low in the cultural scale are also . . . biologically defective.
> . . . .
> (4) Nothing in the acceptance of heredity as a factor in the genesis of any condition considered by this report excludes the environmental agencies of life as equally potent, and in many instances as even more effective.

Findings of the American Neurological Association Committee *as reported in* Ferster, Eliminating the Unfit—Is Sterilization the Answer? 27 Ohio St. L.J. 591, at 602-3 (1966).

265. See, e.g., Deutsch, *supra* note 11, at 373.

266. Pope Pius XI, Casti Connubii: Encyclical Letter on Christian Marriage (1930), *in* The Papal Encyclicals in Their Historical Context 235, 236 (1956). The Roman Catholic Church's official position against sterilization, and particularly against involuntary sterilization, remains as firm today.

267. See case citations in notes 256, 258, & 262 *supra*.

268. Poe v. Lynchburg Training School & Hosp., No. 80-0172 (L) (W.D. Va. filed Dec. 29, 1980). The named plaintiff in this case is a man sterilized in 1952 while on furlough from the institution. Allegedly, his consent to the procedure was obtained by the authorities' telling him he would be circumcised.

269. See tables 9.5 & 9.6 for a summary of the statutes and their shortcomings and the cases in note 262, *supra*, for evidence of practices that depart from the ideal. By the scheme used in this book for classifying voluntary commitments—i.e., only those that are initiated by and consented to by the prospective patient himself—sterilization performed on someone else's initiative and substituted consent is not voluntary sterilization.

270. See Ferster, *supra* note 264, reporting that 30% of North Carolina's sterilizations from 1962 through 1964 were performed on children between the ages of 10 and 19.

271. See *In re* Cavitt, 182 Neb. 712, 157 N.W. 2d 171 (1968), upholding the constitutionality of a Nebraska statute providing for the sterilization of mentally defective persons as a prerequisite for parole or release from a state institution. See also Am. Neur. Ass'n, Committee, Eugenical Sterilization, *supra* note 165, at 7:

> [T]he word *voluntary* is frequently a mere subterfuge, in that it is often a condition of discharge from the institution that the patient be sterilized, and consequently the individual involved is in the position of being confined or confinable until he gives his consent for sterilization, which hardly makes the bargain free and equal and nullifies the real meaning of the word voluntary.

272. See discussion of the cases of *In re* Andrade and *In re* Hernandez in Comment, Sterilization, *supra* note 164.

273. See table 9.6, cols. 5-9.

274. See Medicaid Sterilization Rules Violated: Group, 67 A.B.A.J. 1249 (1981).

Citing figures showing that no less than 110,619 such procedures were performed in 1980 at government expense, the group charged that the federal regulations enacted to assure the making of voluntary and considered decisions to submit to the operations were routinely violated at the state level. The violations included noncompliance with the 30-day "cooling off" period, with the requirement that the subject be at least 21 years of age, and with the necessity of obtaining valid, signed consent. The government's response to the charges was that the matter was largely not of substance but of incomplete compliance with the *reporting* requirements.

The concern over voluntariness can be overdone, however, to a point where the true problem becomes one of the inability on the part of legal representatives to consent to, for courts or administrative boards to authorize, for medical professionals to dare to perform, and thus for individuals to obtain sterilizations that are clearly desired by them or their guardians, medically indicated, and generally in the individuals' best interest. Some recent cases illustrate that this state of affairs has been attained in some jurisdictions and show what the judicial response to it has been. In the New Jersey case of *In re Grady*,[275] the state supreme court considered the situation where the parents of a mentally disabled young woman sought, with the advice of their doctor, to have sterilization performed on their daughter so as to enable her to live life with some measure of independence and free of the risk of conception and the complications of birth and childrearing which she would be unable to handle. Because of her disability, the daughter was unable to give personal consent. The hospital refused to perform the operation on the parents' substituted consent.

The *Grady* court noted that the case presented neither a question of voluntary sterilization nor one of compulsory sterilization, but an in-between situation where personal consent was unobtainable and third-party consent the only alternative. The court recognized that there was a right to be sterilized[276] as well as a right to procreate[277] and the inevitable tension that existed between the two. Holding that courts had inherent power to authorize sterilization even in the absence of specific statutory provisions on the subject,[278] the *Grady* decision went one step further and found that the operation in cases such as the one before it could be performed *only* on judicial authority, not merely on medical recommendation and individual, substituted consent.[279] The court therefore remanded the case for reconsideration by the court below on the question of whether the operation would indeed be in the young woman's best interest. In deciding, the lower court was directed to observe a series of standards and procedures not unlike those announced in the Washington case of *In re Guardianship of Hayes*.[280]

Courts in other states have faced similar situations. One of the more notable instances was in Wisconsin, where in the case of *In re Guardianship of Eberhardy*[281] the state supreme court held that even though the judiciary had plenary constitutional power to authorize sterilizations, the complexity of the public policy considerations required that the legislature be given an opportunity to conduct hearings first and to formulate legislation in the area and that the courts refrain from entertaining petitions of this nature until the legislature had had its say. The Wisconsin legislature had only recently repealed the existing compulsory sterilization statute and had chosen not to replace it with new sterilization legislation. The *Eberhardy* decision was the subject of a strongly critical comment in the 1982 *Wisconsin Law Review* to the effect that the court's unwarranted deference to legislative initiative had robbed mentally disabled individuals of their "fundamental constitutional right to choose sterilization."[282] Such commentary is a long way from writings focusing on the evils of sterilization that have been the standard fare of law journals for years.

D. "Wrongful Life" and "Wrongful Birth" Actions

The birth of a disabled child is the kind of personal misfortune that often leads parents toward an effort to fix the "blame" outside the environment within their own immediate control and sometimes to seek legal re-

275. 426 A.2d 467 (N.J. 1981).

276. The court cited Hathaway v. Worcester City Hosp., 475 F. 2d 701 (1st Cir. 1973); Ruby v. Massey, 452 F. Supp. 361 (D. Conn. 1978); Peck v. Califano, 454 F. Supp. 484 (D. Utah 1977); and Ponter v. Ponter, 135 N.J. Super. 50, 342 A.2d 574 (Ch. Div. 1975).

277. See discussion accompanying notes 237–43 *supra*.

278. The courts have divided on the existence of this inherent authority. Some of the cases in accord with *In re* Grady include: *In re* C.D.M., 627 P.2d 607 (Alaska 1981); *In re* Guardianship of Hayes, 608 P.2d 635 (Wash. 1980); *In re* Penny N., 414 A.2d 541 (N.H. 1980); *In re* Guardianship of Eberhardy, 102 Wis. 2d 539, 307 N.W.2d 881 (1981); *In re* Moe, 385 Mass. 555, 432 N.E. 2d 712 (1982).

Some cases holding the contrary are: Hudson v. Hudson, 373 So. 2d 310 (Ala. 1979); Guardianship of Tulley, 83 Cal. App. 3d 698, 146 Cal. Rptr. 226 (1978), *cert. denied*, 440 U.S. 967 (1979); *In re* S.C.E., 378 A.2d 144 (Del. Ch. 1977); A.L. v. G.R.H., 163 Ind. App. 636, 325 N.E.2d 501 (1975); Holmes v. Powers, 439 S.W.2d 579 (Ky. 1968); *In re* Interest of M.K.R., 515 S.W.2d 467 (Mo. 1974) (en banc); Frazier v. Levi, 440 S.W.2d 393 (Tex. Civ. App. 1969).

279. In this respect, the decision goes against the holding of the well-known case of *In re* Quinlan, 70 N.J. 10, 355 A.2d 647, *cert. denied sub nom.* Garger v. N.J., 429 U.S. 922 (1976), where the court held that the life-support decision was best made by allowing the family and guardian to render their best judgment without judicial interference.

280. 608 P.2d 635 (Wash. 1980).

281. 102 Wis. 2d 539, 307 N.W.2d 881 (1981).

282. Comment, *In re Guardianship of Eberhardy:* The Sterilization of the Mentally Retarded, 1982 Wis. L. Rev. 1199, 1201.

dress (damages) to alleviate their hurt, expiate the sense of responsibility or even guilt that such a misfortune may (subconsciously) produce, and cover the very real and extraordinary expenses that raising a disabled child may bring. The legal profession has not been unreceptive to this urge, and thus there has come in recent years a surge of litigation against medical practitioners for failing to identify the potential for, or failing to give proper counsel or take the requisite operational steps to prevent, the birth of disabled children.[283] These legal actions have become known as "wrongful birth" or "wrongful life"[284] actions. Occasionally, there have even been actions for "wrongful conception,"[285] where parents out of prior experience or from family history have realized the special risk they would incur in producing (further) offspring and have submitted to sterilization procedures to avoid this risk. Where the procedures have been unsuccessful and conception (and birth) have occurred nonetheless, suit has been brought based on the alleged negligent performance of the procedure by the practitioners involved.

Actions for wrongful birth have generally been sustained, given the right facts.[286] Those for wrongful life generally have not.[287] The issue of how to measure damages is a major aspect of the cases, sometimes a controlling one to the extent that some courts have thrown out wrongful life actions on grounds that assessing the negative value of the life of a disabled child is an impossible task.[288] More commonly, the wrongful life action has been rejected simply as being against public policy.[289] Any life is assumed to be better than no life.

The cases involve children with physical as well as mental disabilities at birth, and not infrequently both. An action for wrongful conception ("failed sterilization") would theoretically apply even if the child was born healthy (and presumably even if the pregnancy was terminated prior to birth—for the costs incurred until termination or in inducing termination), but the motivation to bring suit is stronger if the unwanted child is disabled.[290]

The tragedy of lives lived under the burden of mental disability cannot be undone by money, though the law often seems to assume it can be. The legal assessment of blame is not a cure, though that too is often forgotten. There may be specific expenses to be borne and paid for with the help of resources beyond those possessed by the afflicted family. Whether the determination of who is responsible for this financial help is best made by way of an assessment of who is legally "at fault" is an old question that remains open to debate in many contexts.

283. E.g., Robak v. United States, 658 F.2d 471 (7th Cir. 1981).

284. Curlender v. Bio-Science Laboratories, 106 Cal. App. 3d 811, 165 Cal. Rptr. 477 (1980).

285. E.g., Ochs v. Borrelli, 445 A.2d 883, 884 (Conn. 1982).

286. E.g., Robak v. United States, 658 F.2d 471 (7th Cir. 1981); Becker v. Schwartz, 46 N.Y.2d 401, 386 N.E.2d 807 (1978); Speck v. Finegold, 268 Pa. Super. 342 (1979); Berman v. Allan, 404 A.2d 8 (N.J. Super. Ct. 1979); Schroeder v. Perkel, 432 A.2d 834 (1981); Turpin v. Sortini, 174 Cal. Rptr. 128 (Ct. App. 1981); Phillips v. United States, 508 F. Supp. 537 (D.S.C. 1980).

287. See cases cited *supra* in note 286. Typically, both the wrongful birth and the wrongful life claims are made in the same case. Among the few decisions to sustain the latter are Curlender v. Bio-Science Laboratories, 106 Cal. App. 3d 811, 165 Cal. Rptr. 477 (1980); Harbeson v. Parke-Davis, Inc., 656 P.2d 483 (Wash. 1983); and Procanik v. Cillo, 478 A.2d 755 (N.J. 1984). Despite the judicial disinclination to recognize wrongful life actions, the parameters of liability are expanding in other ways—new grounds for liability are pressed (breach of implied contract, negligence, including failure to provide genetic counseling, failure to inform the parents of procedures for detecting abnormality, failure to properly perform the detection tests, etc.) along with more liberal theories for recognizing and assessing damages (parental pain and suffering, medical care costs for the projected life span of the disabled child)—so that ultimately it may make little difference whether the rubric of wrongful life or birth is used. The distinction may be so much legal semantic play to begin with. For further reading on the topic, see Bernstein, Damage Awards for Wrongful Birth and Wrongful Life, Hospitals, Mar. 1, 1982, at 65: Warren, The Law of Human Reproduction: An Overview, 3 J. Legal Med. 1 (1982); Zaslow, Wrongful Conception, Wrongful Birth, and Wrongful Life—The Parameters of Liability, Legal Aspects Med. Prac., May 1982, at 6-7.

288. See generally Phillips v. United States, 508 F. Supp. 537 (D.S.C. 1980). The case contains a good summary of the arguments and decisions against the wrongful life claim.

289. *Id.*

290. In Ochs v. Borrelli, 445 A.2d 883 (Conn. 1982), the child conceived and born after the unsuccessful sterilization suffered from an orthopedic disability, as did her two older siblings.

TABLE 9.1 MARRIAGE AND MENTAL DISABILITY

STATE	DESCRIPTION OF PERSONS PROHIBITED FROM MARRYING (1)	EXCEPTION TO PROHIBITION (2)	ENFORCEMENT OF PROHIBITION (3)	STATUS OF MARRIAGE OF MENTALLY DISABLED PERSONS: Void (4)	STATUS OF MARRIAGE OF MENTALLY DISABLED PERSONS: Voidable/Annulment Provisions (5)	PERSONS AUTHORIZED TO PETITION FOR JUDICIAL ANNULMENT: Spouse (6)	PERSONS AUTHORIZED TO PETITION FOR JUDICIAL ANNULMENT: Guardian or Next Friend of Mentally Disabled Party (7)	PERSONS AUTHORIZED TO PETITION FOR JUDICIAL ANNULMENT: Other Persons (8)	LIMITATIONS ON ABILITY TO OBTAIN ANNULMENT: Barred if Parties Freely Cohabited After Restoration of Mental Capacity (9)	LIMITATIONS ON ABILITY TO OBTAIN ANNULMENT: Barred if Petitioning Party Had Knowledge of Disability at Time of Marriage (10)	LIMITATIONS ON ABILITY TO OBTAIN ANNULMENT: Time Limits (11)	LEGITIMACY OF CHILDREN OF VOID OR VOIDABLE MARRIAGES (12)
ALA. Code (1975 & Supp. 1981)												
ALAS. Stat. (1977 & Supp. 1981) *fn. 1*					if either party incapable of consenting for want of sufficient understanding 25.05.031 if either party of unsound mind 09.55.090(2)	party under disability 25.05.031 not stated 09.55.090(2)			09.55.090(2)			
ARIZ. Rev. Stat. Ann. (1976 & Supp. 1981)												
ARK. Stat. Ann. (1971 & Supp. 1981)					void from time declared by ct. if either party incapable of consenting for want of understanding 55-106							
CAL. Civ. Code (West 1970 & Supp. 1981)	imbecile or insane 4201				annulment if 1 party of unsound mind at time of marriage 4425(c)	injured party 4426(c)		relative or conservator of party of unsound mind 4426(c)	4425(c)		before death of either party 4426(c)	parent-child relationship regardless of marital status 7002
COLO. Rev. Stat. (1973 & Supp. 1981)					ct. decree of invalidity if either party lacked the capacity to consent 14-10-111(1)(a)	either aggrieved party 14-10-111(2)(a)	legal representative of party lacking ability to consent 14-10-111(2)(a)				w/in 6 mos. of obtaining knowledge of condition 14-10-111(2)(a)	legitimate 14-10-111(4)
CONN. Gen. Stat. Ann. (West 1978 & Supp. 1981)	persons under conservatorship or guardianship 46b-29	written consent of conservator or guardian 46b-29			annulment if void or voidable under laws of Conn. or state where marriage performed 46b-40(b)							
DEL. Code Ann. (1981)	persons of unsound mind 13, §101(b)(1) patient in mental hospital 13, §101(b)(2)	patient in mental hospital, if patient files certificate stating fitness to marry, signed by superintendent of institution 13, §101(b)(2)	guilty party or parties: $100 fine or 30 days upon default 13, §102		annulment if marriage was prohibited & void as person of unsound mind or patient in mental hospital 13, §1506(a)(7) 13, §101	either party 13, §1506(b)(4)		appropriate state official or child of either party 13, §1506(b)(4)			before death of either party or prior to final settlement of estate 13, §1506(b)(4)	legitimate 13, §1506(c)
D.C. Code Ann. (1981 & Supp. 1982)	idiot or person adjudged to be lunatic 30-103				marriage of idiot or person adjudged to be lunatic void from decree 30-103 annulment if marriage contracted during insanity of either party 16-904(d)(2)	party capable of contracting may not petition 30-104	30-104		16-904(d)(2)			legitimate 16-908

TABLE 9.1 MARRIAGE AND MENTAL DISABILITY—*Continued*

STATE	DESCRIPTION OF PERSONS PROHIBITED FROM MARRYING (1)	EXCEPTION TO PROHIBITION (2)	ENFORCEMENT OF PROHIBITION (3)	STATUS OF MARRIAGE OF MENTALLY DISABLED PERSONS: Void (4)	STATUS OF MARRIAGE OF MENTALLY DISABLED PERSONS: Voidable/ Annulment Provisions (5)	PERSONS AUTHORIZED TO PETITION FOR JUDICIAL ANNULMENT: Spouse (6)	PERSONS AUTHORIZED TO PETITION FOR JUDICIAL ANNULMENT: Guardian or Next Friend of Mentally Disabled Party (7)	PERSONS AUTHORIZED TO PETITION FOR JUDICIAL ANNULMENT: Other Persons (8)	LIMITATIONS ON ABILITY TO OBTAIN ANNULMENT: Barred if Parties Freely Cohabited After Restoration of Mental Capacity (9)	LIMITATIONS ON ABILITY TO OBTAIN ANNULMENT: Barred if Petitioning Party Had Knowledge of Disability at Time of Marriage (10)	LIMITATIONS ON ABILITY TO OBTAIN ANNULMENT: Time Limits (11)	LEGITIMACY OF CHILDREN OF VOID OR VOIDABLE MARRIAGES (12)
FLA. Stat. Ann. (West 1973 & Supp. 1981) *fn. 1*												
GA. Code Ann. (1982)	persons not of sound mind 53-102			marriages of persons unable to contract (of unsound mind) are void 53-104	annulment of marriage of persons unable to contract if no children 53-601	either party 53-602	53-603					no annulment if children 53-601
HAWAII Rev. Stat. (1976 & Supp. 1981)					annulment if 1 party lacked mental capacity to consent 580-21(4) 580-26	either party 580-26	580-26		580-26			legitimate 580-27
IDAHO Code (1963 & Supp. 1981)					annulment if 1 party of unsound mind at time of marriage 32-501(3)	injured party 32-502(3)	32-502(3)	relative 32-502(3)	32-501(3)		any time before death of either party 32-502(3)	legitimate 32-503
ILL. Ann. Stat. (Smith-Hurd 1980) *fn. 1*					ct. order of invalidity if either party lacked capactity to consent 40, §301(1)	either party 40, §302(a)(1)	legal representative 40, §302(a)(1)				no later than 90 days after petitioner obtained knowledge of condition & before death of parties 40, §302(a)(1), (b)	legitimate 40, §303
IND. Code Ann. (Burns 1980 & Supp. 1982)	persons adjudged of unsound mind 31-1-3-3		solemnization in violation of code is class C infraction 31-1-1-6	void if either party insane or idiotic at time of marriage 31-1-1-2	voidable if either party incapable of contracting from want of understanding 31-1-7-6	party incapable of contracting 31-1-7-6						legitimate 31-1-7-6
IOWA Code Ann. (West 1981 & Supp. 1981)	mentally ill or retarded, mental retardate or under guardianship as incompetent 595.3(5)				annulment where either party mentally ill or retarded at time of marriage 598.29(4)	either party 598.30						legitimate 598.31
KAN. Stat. Ann. (1981 & Supp. 1981)												
KY. Rev. Stat. Ann. (Michie 1972 & Supp. 1980)	person adjudged mentally disabled 402.020(1)		fines for aiding, abetting, solemnizing, or issuing license for prohibited marriage, clerk knowingly issuing license removed from office 402.990	void if a party adjudged mentally disabled 402.020(1)								
LA. Rev. Stat. Ann. (West 1975 & Supp. 1981)												

TABLE 9.1 MARRIAGE AND MENTAL DISABILITY—*Continued*

STATE	DESCRIPTION OF PERSONS PROHIBITED FROM MARRYING (1)	EXCEPTION TO PROHIBITION (2)	ENFORCEMENT OF PROHIBITION (3)	STATUS OF MARRIAGE OF MENTALLY DISABLED PERSONS: Void (4)	STATUS OF MARRIAGE OF MENTALLY DISABLED PERSONS: Voidable/Annulment Provisions (5)	PERSONS AUTHORIZED TO PETITION FOR JUDICIAL ANNULMENT: Spouse (6)	PERSONS AUTHORIZED TO PETITION FOR JUDICIAL ANNULMENT: Guardian or Next Friend of Mentally Disabled Party (7)	PERSONS AUTHORIZED TO PETITION FOR JUDICIAL ANNULMENT: Other Persons (8)	LIMITATIONS ON ABILITY TO OBTAIN ANNULMENT: Barred if Parties Freely Cohabited After Restoration of Mental Capacity (9)	LIMITATIONS ON ABILITY TO OBTAIN ANNULMENT: Barred if Petitioning Party Had Knowledge of Disability at Time of Marriage (10)	LIMITATIONS ON ABILITY TO OBTAIN ANNULMENT: Time Limits (11)	LEGITIMACY OF CHILDREN OF VOID OR VOIDABLE MARRIAGES (12)
ME. Rev. Stat. Ann. (1981 & Supp. 1981)	mentally ill or mentally retarded person 19, §32			marriage of mentally ill or mentally retarded person void w/o legal process 19, §§631, 632								legitimate children of parent capable of contracting marriage 19, §633
MD. Ann. Code (1957 & Supp. 1981)												
MASS. Ann. Laws (Michie/Law. Co-op. 1981 & Supp. 1981)	insane person, idiot, feeble-minded person committed to institution 207, §5				annulment if marriage invalid for incapacity to contract marriage 207, §14 207, §5	either party 207, §14						legitimate children of parent capable of contracting marriage 207, §16
MICH. Comp. Laws Ann. (1967 & Supp. 1981)	insane or idiotic; persons confined as or adjudged feeble-minded, imbecilic, or insane 551.6	if expatient files certificates of 2 physicians stating person cured & no probability of transmitting to offspring 551.6	max. $1,000 or 1–5 yrs. in state prison to any person of sound mind who marries prohibited person or abets any such marriage 551.6	marriage solemnized when either party insane or idiot absolutely void 552.1								legitimate 552.1
MINN. Stat. Ann. (West 1969 & Supp. 1981)	mentally deficient persons committed to the guardianship or conservatorship of the commissioner of public welfare 517.03	marriage on written consent of commissioner of public welfare 517.03		marriages of mentally deficient persons under guardianship or conservatorship w/o written consent of commissioner 518.01	voidable if 1 party lacked capacity to consent 518.02(a)	either party 518.05(a)	legal representative 518.05(a)			518.02(a)	no later than 90 days after petitioner obtained knowledge of condition & before death of either party 518.05(a)	
MISS. Code Ann. (1972 & Supp. 1981)	insane or imbecile 93-1-5(f)				annulment for idiocy or insanity of either or both parties 93-7-3(b)	either party 93-7-3(b)	of insane person 93-7-3(b)				if guardian or next friend; w/in 6 mos. after marriage 93-7-3(b)	legitimate 93-7-5
MO. Ann. Stat. (Vernon 1977 & Supp. 1981)	insane, feeble-minded, or mentally imbecile 451.020		misdemeanor for state official issuing license 451.020	marriages of insane, feeble-minded, or mentally imbecile are absolutely void 451.020								
MONT. Code Ann. (1979) *fn. 1*					ct. decree of invalidity if a party lacked the capacity to consent 40-1-402(1)(a)			any petitioner 40-1-402(2)(a)			w/in 1 yr. of obtaining knowledge of mental incapacity or infirmity 40-1-402(2)(a) before death of either party 40-1-402(2)	legitimate 40-1-402(4)

TABLE 9.1 MARRIAGE AND MENTAL DISABILITY—*Continued*

STATE	DESCRIPTION OF PERSONS PROHIBITED FROM MARRYING (1)	EXCEPTION TO PROHIBITION (2)	ENFORCEMENT OF PROHIBITION (3)	STATUS OF MARRIAGE OF MENTALLY DISABLED PERSONS: Void (4)	STATUS OF MARRIAGE OF MENTALLY DISABLED PERSONS: Voidable/ Annulment Provisions (5)	PERSONS AUTHORIZED TO PETITION FOR JUDICIAL ANNULMENT: Spouse (6)	PERSONS AUTHORIZED TO PETITION FOR JUDICIAL ANNULMENT: Guardian or Next Friend of Mentally Disabled Party (7)	PERSONS AUTHORIZED TO PETITION FOR JUDICIAL ANNULMENT: Other Persons (8)	LIMITATIONS ON ABILITY TO OBTAIN ANNULMENT: Barred if Parties Freely Cohabited After Restoration of Mental Capacity (9)	LIMITATIONS ON ABILITY TO OBTAIN ANNULMENT: Barred if Petitioning Party Had Knowledge of Disability at Time of Marriage (10)	LIMITATIONS ON ABILITY TO OBTAIN ANNULMENT: Time Limits (11)	LEGITIMACY OF CHILDREN OF VOID OR VOIDABLE MARRIAGES (12)
NEB. Rev. Stat. (1978 & Supp. 1981)	parties legally incompetent to enter marriage contract 42-107			void when either party is insane or mentally incompetent to enter marriage relation 42-103	annulment of void marriage 42-119 annulment when either party mentally ill or mentally retarded at time of marriage 42-374(4)	either party 42-119	42-375	parent 42-375	42-375			legitimate 42-377
NEV. Rev. Stat. (1979)					annulment if 1 party incapable of assenting for want of understanding 125.330(1)				125.330(2)			legitimate 125.410(2)
N.H. Rev. Stat. Ann. (1977 & Supp. 1981)												
N.J. Stat. Ann. (1968 & Supp. 1982)	persons currently adjudicated mentally incompetent 37:1-9		illegal issuance of marriage license misdemeanor 37:1-11		voidable if 1 party lacked capacity to marry for want of understanding 2A:34-1(d)							
N.M. Stat. Ann. (1978 & Supp. 1982)												
N.Y. Dom. Rel. Law. (McKinney 1977 & Supp. 1981)					voidable if 1 party incapable of consenting for want of understanding 7(2) voidable & annulment if a party incurably mentally ill for 5 yrs. or more 7(5), 140(f) annulment if either party mentally retarded or mentally ill 140(c)	either party 140(f) mentally ill party after restored to reason or other party 140(c)	next friend at ct.'s discretion 140(c)	someone on behalf of party 140(f) relative who has interest to avoid marriage 140(c)		140(c)		legitimate 24(1)
N.C. Gen. Stat. (1976 & Supp. 1981)	persons adjudged idiot, imbecile, mental defective, or of unsound mind on recommendation of 1 or more practicing psychiatrists 51-12	sterilized persons 51-12	requirement of health certificate stating that applicant mentally competent for license 51-9 violation of prohibition by person charged w/enforcement is misdemeanor 51-13	void if 1 party AND incapable of contracting for want of understanding 50-4 51-3	prohibited marriages declared void on suit 50-4 voidable if 1 party incapable of contracting for want of understanding 50-4 51-3	either party 50-4			no marriage followed by cohabitation & issue shall be declared void after death of either party 51-3	no marriage followed by cohabitation & issue shall be declared void after death of either party 51-3	no marriage followed by cohabitation & issue shall be declared void after death of either party 51-3	

TABLE 9.1 MARRIAGE AND MENTAL DISABILITY—*Continued*

				STATUS OF MARRIAGE OF MENTALLY DISABLED PERSONS		PERSONS AUTHORIZED TO PETITION FOR JUDICIAL ANNULMENT			LIMITATIONS ON ABILITY TO OBTAIN ANNULMENT			
STATE	DESCRIPTION OF PERSONS PROHIBITED FROM MARRYING (1)	EXCEPTION TO PROHIBITION (2)	ENFORCEMENT OF PROHIBITION (3)	Void (4)	Voidable/ Annulment Provisions (5)	Spouse (6)	Guardian or Next Friend of Mentally Disabled Party (7)	Other Persons (8)	Barred if Parties Freely Cohabited After Restoration of Mental Capacity (9)	Barred if Petitioning Party Had Knowledge of Disability at Time of Marriage (10)	Time Limits (11)	LEGITIMACY OF CHILDREN OF VOID OR VOIDABLE MARRIAGES (12)
N.D. Cent. Code (1971 & Supp. 1981)	institutionalized as severely retarded 14-03-07	woman over 45; man marrying woman over 45 14-03-07	violation of provisions of chapter is class A misdemeanor 14-03-28		annulment when either party was of unsound mind 14-04-01(3)	injured party 14-04-02(3)	14-04-02(3)	relative of party of unsound mind 14-04-02(3)	14-04-01(3)		before death of either party 14-04-02(3)	legitimate 14-04-03
OHIO Rev. Code Ann. (Baldwin 1976 & Supp. 1981)					annulment if either party has been adjudicated mentally incompetent 3105.31(c)	aggrieved party 3105.32(c)	3105.32(c)	relative of party adjudicated incompetent 3105.32(c)	after being restored to competency 3105.31(c)		before death of either party 3105.32(c)	legitimate 3105.33
OKLA. Stat. Ann. (West 1961 & Supp. 1981)					voidable if either party incapable of contracting for lack of understanding 12, §1283	incapable party 12, §1283	12, §1283	parent of incapable party 12, §1283	cohabitation after incompetency ceases(?) is defense 12, §1283			legitimate 12, §1283
OR. Rev. Stat. (1981)					voidable & grounds for annulment if either party incapable of consenting for want of understanding 106.030, 107.015				annulment barred if contract later ratified 107.015			
PA. Stat. Ann. (Purdon 1965 & Supp. 1980)	insane, weak-minded, of unsound mind, or under guardianship as of unsound mind 48, §1-5(d)	if judge of orphan's ct. decides in best interest of applicant & public to issue license 48, §1-5(d)		void if either party incapable of consenting by reason of insanity or serious mental disorder 23, §204(a)(3)	annulment of marriage void because either party incapable of consenting by reason of insanity or serious mental disorder 23, §§203, 204(b)	either party 23, §203			not void 23, §204(a)			
R.I. Gen. Laws (1969 & Supp. 1981)	idiots & lunatics 15-1-5			marriages of idiots & lunatics absolutely void 15-1-5	relief by divorce action for void marriages 15-5-1							illegitimate 15-1-5
S.C. Code Ann. (Law. Co-op. 1976 & Supp. 1981)	mentally incompetent persons 20-1-10				ct. of common pleas has authority to determine issues affecting the validity of marriage 20-1-510							
S.D. Codified Laws Ann. (1976 & Supp. 1981)					annulment if either party of unsound mind at time of marriage 25-3-2	injured party 25-3-2	25-3-2	relative of party of unsound mind 25-3-2	25-3-2		before death of either party 25-3-2	legitimate 25-3-3
TENN. Code Ann. (1977 & Supp. 1981)	insane or imbecile 36-411											

TABLE 9.1 MARRIAGE AND MENTAL DISABILITY—*Continued*

STATE	DESCRIPTION OF PERSONS PROHIBITED FROM MARRYING (1)	EXCEPTION TO PROHIBITION (2)	ENFORCEMENT OF PROHIBITION (3)	STATUS OF MARRIAGE OF MENTALLY DISABLED PERSONS: Void (4)	STATUS OF MARRIAGE OF MENTALLY DISABLED PERSONS: Voidable/ Annulment Provisions (5)	PERSONS AUTHORIZED TO PETITION FOR JUDICIAL ANNULMENT: Spouse (6)	PERSONS AUTHORIZED TO PETITION FOR JUDICIAL ANNULMENT: Guardian or Next Friend of Mentally Disabled Party (7)	PERSONS AUTHORIZED TO PETITION FOR JUDICIAL ANNULMENT: Other Persons (8)	LIMITATIONS ON ABILITY TO OBTAIN ANNULMENT: Barred if Parties Freely Cohabited After Restoration of Mental Capacity (9)	LIMITATIONS ON ABILITY TO OBTAIN ANNULMENT: Barred if Petitioning Party Had Knowledge of Disability at Time of Marriage (10)	LIMITATIONS ON ABILITY TO OBTAIN ANNULMENT: Time Limits (11)	LEGITIMACY OF CHILDREN OF VOID OR VOIDABLE MARRIAGES (12)
TEX. Fam. Code (Vernon 1975 & Supp. 1981)					voidable & subject to annulment if either party at time of marriage lacked mental capacity to consent §2.45(a), (b)	either party §2.45(a), (b)	in ct.'s discretion §2.45(a)		§2.45(a), (b)	or should have known §2.45(b)(2)	before death of parties §2.47	
UTAH Code Ann. (1976 & Supp. 1981)					annulment on grounds existing at common law fn. 1 30-1-17.1(2)							legitimate 30-1-17.2
VT. Stat. Ann. (1968 & Supp. 1981)	persons non compos mentis 18, §5142(3)		max. fine $20 for clerk knowingly violating provision 18, §5143		voidable & may be annulled if either party idiot or lunatic at time of marriage 15, §512	lunatic, after restored to reason 15, §514(c)	next friend at ct.'s discretion 15, §514(d)	relative of idiot or lunatic 15, §514(a), (b)	lunatic, after restored to reason 15, §514(c)		relative of idiot or lunatic, during life of either party 15, §514(a), (b) next friend, during life of both parties 15, §514(d)	legitimate 15, §520
VA. Code (1975 & Supp. 1982)	insane persons 20-46(2) persons adjudged insane or feeble-minded & admitted as patients to institutions 20-47	woman over 45; man if marrying woman over 45 20-46(2)	$100 maximum &/or 90 days 20-46(7) person who marries admitted insane or feeble-minded patient $500 &/or 6 mos. 20-47		void from time so declared by ct. when either party lacked capacity to consent because of mental incapacity or infirmity 20-45.1(b) annulment of above 20-89.1(a)	either party 20-89.1(a)			after knowledge of mental condition 20-89.1(c)		w/in 2 yrs. of marriage 20-89.1(c)	
WASH. Rev. Code Ann. (1961 & Supp. 1981)					voidable if either party incapable of consenting for want of understanding 26.04.130 ct. decree of invalidity of marriage if a party lacked mental capacity to consent 26.09.040 (4)(b)(i)	either party 26.09.040(1)(a)	guardian 26.09.040(1)(a)				both parties must be living 26.09.040(1)	legitimate 26.09.040(5)
W. VA. Code (1980 & Supp. 1982)					voidable if marriage solemnized when either party insane, feeble-minded, idiot, or imbecile 48-2-1 annulment of above 48-2-2	either party 48-2-2	committee 48-2-11					

TABLE 9.1 MARRIAGE AND MENTAL DISABILITY—*Continued*

STATE	DESCRIPTION OF PERSONS PROHIBITED FROM MARRYING (1)	EXCEPTION TO PROHIBITION (2)	ENFORCEMENT OF PROHIBITION (3)	STATUS OF MARRIAGE OF MENTALLY DISABLED PERSONS: Void (4)	STATUS OF MARRIAGE OF MENTALLY DISABLED PERSONS: Voidable/ Annulment Provisions (5)	PERSONS AUTHORIZED TO PETITION FOR JUDICIAL ANNULMENT: Spouse (6)	PERSONS AUTHORIZED TO PETITION FOR JUDICIAL ANNULMENT: Guardian or Next Friend of Mentally Disabled Party (7)	PERSONS AUTHORIZED TO PETITION FOR JUDICIAL ANNULMENT: Other Persons (8)	LIMITATIONS ON ABILITY TO OBTAIN ANNULMENT: Barred if Parties Freely Cohabited After Restoration of Mental Capacity (9)	LIMITATIONS ON ABILITY TO OBTAIN ANNULMENT: Barred if Petitioning Party Had Knowledge of Disability at Time of Marriage (10)	LIMITATIONS ON ABILITY TO OBTAIN ANNULMENT: Time Limits (11)	LEGITIMACY OF CHILDREN OF VOID OR VOIDABLE MARRIAGES (12)
WIS. Stat. Ann. (West 1980)					annulment if a party lacked capacity to consent because of mental incapacity or infirmity 767.03(1)	either party 767.03(1)	legal representative 767.03(1)				w/in 1 yr. of obtaining knowledge of condition 767.03(1) & before death of either party	
WYO. Stat. (1977)				void when either party mentally incompetent at time of marriage; no ct. decree necessary 20-2-101(a)	annulment on grounds of mental incompetency 20-2-101(e)	mentally incompetent person, if restored to reason 20-2-101(e)	20-2-101(e)		20-2-101(e)			legitimacy presumed following dissolution 20-2-117

FOOTNOTE: TABLE 9.1

1. See 51 A.L.R. 852 (1927).

TABLE 9.2 DIVORCE AND MENTAL DISABILITY

STATE	MENTAL DISABILITY AS GROUNDS FOR DIVORCE fn. 1 (1)	CRITERIA FOR DISABILITY TO FUNCTION AS GROUNDS FOR DIVORCE: Incurable Condition (2)	CRITERIA: Duration of Condition (3)	CRITERIA: Period of Confinement in Institution (4)	REQUIRED MEDICAL EVIDENCE: Testimony (5)	REQUIRED MEDICAL EVIDENCE: Examination (6)	CONTINUING FINANCIAL LIABILITY OF PETITIONING SPOUSE: Divorce shall not Relieve Petitioning Party from Support Obligations (7)	CONTINUING FINANCIAL LIABILITY OF PETITIONING SPOUSE: Court Discretion to Award Support and Maintenance to Defendant (8)	GUARDIAN AD LITEM APPOINTED BY COURT (9)	COURT-APPOINTED COUNSEL (10)
ALA. Code (1975 & Supp. 1982)	30-2-1(8)	hopelessly & incurably insane 30-2-1(8) AND		5 successive yrs. 30-2-1(8)	certified statement under oath of superintendent of institution or assistant 30-2-1(8)					
ALAS. Stat. (1980 & Supp. 1981)	09.55.110(8)	mental illness 09.55.110(8) AND		at least 18 mos. 09.55.110(8)			09.55.110(8)			
ARK. Stat. Ann. (1962 & Supp. 1981)	34-1202(8)	husband & wife have lived apart for 3 yrs. by reason of incurable insanity of 1 34-1202(8) AND	has been adjudged insane 34-1202(8) AND	commitment for 3 yrs. 34-1202(8)	proof of incurable insanity shall be supported by evidence of 2 physicians: physician of community and/ or superintendent 34-1202(8)		ct. shall require plaintiff to provide for care & maintenance of insane defendant as long as he/she may live 34-1202(8)		service upon appointed guardian ad litem if no acting guardian 34-1202	
CAL. Civ. Code (West 1970 & Supp. 1981)	4506(2)	insanity 4506(2)			competent medical or psychiatric testimony 4510(a)		4510(b) AND	4510(b)	mandatory appointment if insane spouse has no guardian or if spouse bringing action is guardian 4510(c)	guardian ad litem may be district attorney or county counsel 4510(c)
CONN. Gen. Stat. Ann. (1978 & Supp. 1981)	46b-40(c)(10)			legal confinement for mental illness at least 5 of 6 yrs. preceding complaint 46b-40(c)(10)	testimony of ct.-appointed examiners fn. 2 46b-47(c)	on motion of either party, ct. shall appoint 2 or more psychiatrists (not on staff of state hospital) to examine & report to ct. 46b-47(c)		46b-85	mandatory if adverse party has no conservator or conservator does not appear in ct. 46b-47(b)	
DEL. Code Ann. (1975 & Supp. 1980)	13, §1505(b)(3)		marriage is irretrievably broken; characterized by separation caused by mental illness 13, §1505(b)(3)					13, §1512(a)(2)		
D.C. Code Ann. (1981 & Supp. 1982)	at time of marriage w/o knowledge of partner 16-904(2)									
FLA. Stat. Ann. (West 1969 & Supp. 1981)	61.052(1)(b)		3 yrs. adjudged mental incompetent 61.052(1)(b)					61.052(1)(b)	mandatory if incompetent has no general guardian 61.052(1)(b)	
GA. Code Ann. (1980 & Supp. 1981)	30-102(2) 30-102(11)	mental illness 30-102(11) & confinement 30-102(11) OR	mental incapacity at time of marriage 30-102(2)	2 yrs. immediately preceding action & adjudged or certified mentally ill 30-102(11)	certified statement under oath of superindent physican appointed by ct. 30-102(11)		30-102(11)		if no guardian ad litem shall be appointed & served 30-102(11)	

TABLE 9.2 DIVORCE AND MENTAL DISABILITY—*Continued*

STATE	MENTAL DISABILITY AS GROUNDS FOR DIVORCE fn. 1 (1)	CRITERIA FOR DISABILITY TO FUNCTION AS GROUNDS FOR DIVORCE			REQUIRED MEDICAL EVIDENCE		CONTINUING FINANCIAL LIABILITY OF PETITIONING SPOUSE		GUARDIAN AD LITEM APPOINTED BY COURT (9)	COURT-APPOINTED COUNSEL (10)
		Incurable Condition (2)	Duration of Condition (3)	Period of Confinement in Institution (4)	Testimony (5)	Examination (6)	Divorce shall not Relieve Petitioning Party from Support Obligations (7)	Court Discretion to Award Support and Maintenance to Defendant (8)		
HAWAII Rev. Stat. (1976 & Supp. 1981)								580-49		
IDAHO Code (1963 & Supp. 1981)	32-603(7) 32-801	permanent & incurable insanity 32-801 AND		3 yrs. 32-801				as in other divorce cases 32-801	mandatory 32-802	county attorney shall appear & defend 32-803
IND. Code Ann. (Burns 1980 & Supp. 1982)	31-1-11.5-3(a)(4)	insanity 31-1-11.5-3(a)(4) AND	2 yrs. 31-1-11.5-3(a)(4)							
IOWA Code Ann. (West 1950 & Supp. 1981)							598.17			
KAN. Stat. Ann. (1976 & Supp. 1981)	60-1601(7)	poor prognosis for recovery 60-1601(7) AND	adjudication of mental illness or incapacity w/o restoration for more than 3 yrs. 60-1601(7) OR	3 yrs. 60-1601(7)	finding by 2 of 3 ct.-appointed physicians of poor prognosis for recovery 60-1601		60-1601(7)			
ME. Rev. Stat. Ann. (1964 & Supp. 1981)	19, §691(I)			mental illness requiring confinement for 7 yrs. 19, §691(I)					mandatory 19, §691	
MD. Ann. Code (1981 & Supp. 1981)	16, §26	permanent & incurable insanity 16, §26		3 yrs. 16, §26	testimony of 2 or more physicians competent in psychiatry 16, §26			if plaintiff is husband 16, §26		mandatory if defendant has no guardian; discretionary if defendant has guardian Md. R. P., R.572 §b
MASS. Ann. Laws (Michie/Law. Co-op. 1981 & Supp. 1982)									mandatory for insane defendant 208, §15	
MISS. Code Ann. (1972 & Supp. 1981)	93-5-1(8), (12)	insanity 93-5-1(12) AND	insanity or idiocy at the time of marriage, if petitioning party did not know of infirmity 93-5-1(8)	3 yrs. 93-5-1(12)		examination & affidavits of finding by hospital superintendent & 1 other physician, both recognized authorities on mental disease 93-5-1(12)	(12) AND	93-5-1(12)	if no legal guardian 93-5-1(12)	
NEB. Rev. Stat. (1978)								42-362	mandatory for either party if mentally ill 42-362	
NEV. Rev. Stat. (1981)	125.010(1)		insanity for 2 yrs. 125.010(1)		ct. shall require corroborative evidence 125.010(1)		125.010(1)			
N.H. Rev. Stat. Ann. (1968 & Supp. 1981)	fn. 3						458:12		ct. may appoint for mentally ill libelee 458.12	

TABLE 9.2 DIVORCE AND MENTAL DISABILITY—*Continued*

STATE	MENTAL DISABILITY AS GROUNDS FOR DIVORCE *fn. 1* (1)	CRITERIA FOR DISABILITY TO FUNCTION AS GROUNDS FOR DIVORCE: Incurable Condition (2)	Duration of Condition (3)	Period of Confinement in Institution (4)	REQUIRED MEDICAL EVIDENCE: Testimony (5)	Examination (6)	CONTINUING FINANCIAL LIABILITY OF PETITIONING SPOUSE: Divorce shall not Relieve Petitioning Party from Support Obligations (7)	Court Discretion to Award Support and Maintenance to Defendant (8)	GUARDIAN AD LITEM APPOINTED BY COURT (9)	COURT-APPOINTED COUNSEL (10)
N.J. Stat. Ann. (West 1952 & Supp. 1981)	2A:34-2(f)			institutionalization for mental illness for 24 mos. 2A:34-2(f)						
N.M. Stat. Ann. (1978)									mandatory appointment of attorney as guardian ad litem for insane spouse 40-4-10	
N.C. Gen. Stat. (1976 & Supp. 1981)	*fn. 4* 50-5(6)	insanity 50-5(6) AND	3 yrs. living apart because of insanity of 1 spouse 50-5(6) AND	3 yrs. or proof of insanity for 3 yrs. 50-5(6)	testimony of 2 physicians, 1 being staff member of institution or psychiatrist 50-5(6)			if insane defendant has insufficient income to provide for self, ct. shall require plaintiff to do so for defendant's lifetime 50-5(6)	mandatory if defendant has no general guardian 50-5(6)	
N.D. Cent. Code (1981)	14-05-03(7)	14-05-03(7) AND	insanity for 5 yrs. & affected w/any psychosis 14-05-03(7) AND	5 yrs. 14-05-03(7)		examination by 3 physicians who are authorities on mental disease; superintendent & 2 ct.-appointed must agree that person is incurable 14-05-03(7)				
OHIO Rev. Code Ann. (Baldwin 1976)	3105.01(K)			4 yrs. 3105.01(K)						
OKLA. Stat. Ann. (West 1961 & Supp. 1981)	12, §1271(12)	insanity w/ poor prognosis for recovery 12, §1271(12) AND		5 yrs. 12, §1271(12)		examination by 3 physicians, superintendent & 2 ct.-appointed; 2 of 3 must agree on poor prognosis for recovery 12, §1271(12)	successful party shall not be relieved of contributing to support of defendant 12, §1271(12)		mandatory 12, §1271(12)	
PA. Stat. Ann. (Purdon 1955 & Supp. 1980)	23, §201(b)	no reasonable prospect of discharge during next 3 yrs. 23, §201(b) AND		insanity or serious mental disorder that resulted in confinement for 3 yrs. 23, §201(b)	certificate of superintendent & statement of treating physician 23, §201(b)					
R.I. Gen. Laws (1969 & Supp. 1981)	*fn. 5* 15-5-1 15-1-5		idiocy or lunacy at time of mariage 15-5-1 15-1-5							
S.C. Code Ann. (Law. Co-op. 1976 & Supp. 1981)				*fn. 6*						

TABLE 9.2 DIVORCE AND MENTAL DISABILITY—*Continued*

STATE	MENTAL DISABILITY AS GROUNDS FOR DIVORCE *fn. 1* (1)	CRITERIA FOR DISABILITY TO FUNCTION AS GROUNDS FOR DIVORCE			REQUIRED MEDICAL EVIDENCE		CONTINUING FINANCIAL LIABILITY OF PETITIONING SPOUSE		GUARDIAN AD LITEM APPOINTED BY COURT (9)	COURT-APPOINTED COUNSEL (10)
		Incurable Condition (2)	Duration of Condition (3)	Period of Confinement in Institution (4)	Testimony (5)	Examination (6)	Divorce shall not Relieve Petitioning Party from Support Obligations (7)	Court Discretion to Award Support and Maintenance to Defendant (8)		
S.D. Codified Laws Ann. (1976)	at ct.'s discretion 25-4-18	incurable, chronic mania or or dementia 25-4-18 AND	5 yrs. 25-4-18 AND	5 yrs. under ct. or board order 25-4-18						
TEX. Fam. Code (Vernon 1975 & Supp. 1981)	3.07	not likely to adjust or will probably suffer a relapse 3.07 AND		at least 3 yrs. 3.07(1)						
UTAH Code Ann. (1976 & Supp. 1981)	30-3-1(9)	permanent & incurable insanity 30-3-1(9) AND	duly adjudged insane prior to action 30-3-1(9)(a)		testimony of competent witness 30-3-1(9)(b)	either party may request that defendant be examined by 2 or more physicians 30-3-1(9)		as in other divorce actions 30-3-1(9)	mandatory 30-3-1(9)	county attorney to defend insane party
VT. Stat. Ann. (1972 & Supp. 1982)	15, §551(6), 631	insanity 15, §631 AND		5 yrs. 15, §631				15, §635	mandatory 15, §632	state's attorney shall defend 15, §633
VA. Code (1975 & Supp. 1982)	*fn. 7*								if insane defendant has no committee 20-91(9)(a)	
WASH. Rev. Code Ann. (1961 & Supp. 1981)	when either party shall be incapable of consenting to marriage because of insufficient understanding 26.08.020(1)									
W. VA. Code (1980 & Supp. 1982)	48-2-4(8)	permanent & incurable insanity 48-2-4(8) AND		3 yrs. 48-2-4(8)	competent medical testimony 48-2-4(8)			48-2-4(8)		
WYO. Stat. (1977 & Supp. 1981)	20-2-105	insanity 20-2-105(a) AND		2 yrs. 20-2-105(a)				as in other divorce actions 20-2-105(d)	mandatory 20-2-105(b)	county attorney shall appear & defend 20-2-105(c)

FOOTNOTES: TABLE 9.2

1. Almost all states now have "no fault" divorce provisions. Of all the states that do not have some provision for mental illness as a grounds for divorce, only New York and Illinois do not have "no-fault divorce." See Ill. Ann. Stat. 40, § 401 (Smith-Hurd 1981) and N.Y. Dom. Rel. § 170 (McKinney 1977).

2. Conn. Gen. Stat. Ann. § 46-40 (West 1978). Testimony of no physicians other than court-appointed examiners shall be received at trial.

3. N.H. Rev. Stat. Ann. § 458:12 (1969): "Although the insanity of the libelee may be considered by the court in determining whether a divorce should be granted, such insanity shall not constitute a defense to a libel for divorce."

4. N.C. Gen. Stat. § 50-5(6) (1976): "In all actions brought under this subdivision, if the jury finds as a fact that the plaintiff has been guilty of such conduct as has conduced to the unsoundness of mind of the insane defendant, the relief prayed for shall be denied."

5. Divorce for any marriage that is void or voidable (R.I. Gen. Laws § 15-5-1 (1977)). Marriage where either party is an idiot or lunatic at time of marriage is void (id. § 15-1-5).

6. S.C. Code Ann. § 20-3-10 (Law. Co-op. 1976). In general a separation of over one year entails a right to divorce. Confinement in a mental institution might cause such a separation.

7. Va. Code § 20-91(9)(a) (1975). In a divorce on grounds that the parties have lived separate and apart for one year, the action is not barred if either party has been adjudged insane before or after such separation.

TABLE 9.3 EFFECT OF PARENT'S MENTAL DISABILITY ON PARENT-CHILD RELATIONSHIP *fn. 1*

STATE	ADOPTION: CONSENT OF PARENT NOT NECESSARY IF (1)	TERMINATION OF PARENT-CHILD RELATIONSHIP IF (2)
ALA. Code (1975 & Supp. 1982)	parent insane or otherwise incapacitated from giving consent 26-10-3	
ALAS. Stat. (1975 & Supp. 1981)	parent judicially declared incompetent or mentally defective & ct. dispenses w/parent's consent 20.15.050(a)(6)	
ARIZ. Rev. Stat. Ann. (1974 & Supp. 1981)	parent declared incompetent 8-106(A)(1)(a)	parent unable to discharge parental responsibilities because of mental illness, mental deficiency, or history of chronic abuse of alcohol or dangerous drugs & reasonable grounds to believe condition will be prolonged 8-533(B)(3)
ARK. Stat. Ann. (1971 & Supp. 1981)	parent judicially declared incompetent or mentally defective & ct. dispenses w/parent's consent 56-207(a)(6)	mental incapacity makes parent unable to provide necessary care for minor, & ct. finds incapacity irremediable, & thus minor will probably suffer serious harm 56-220-(c)(2)
CAL. Civ. Code (West 1954 & Supp. 1981)		
COLO. Rev. Stat. (1973 & Supp. 1981)		
CONN. Gen. Stat. Ann. (West 1975 & Supp. 1981)	consent of natural parent not necessary if rights as statutory parent have been terminated 45-61(i)	parents, from mental deficiency, were & will be unable to provide child w/care necessary to well-being 17-43(a)
DEL. Code Ann. (1981)	if parent legally incompetent by virtue of insanity or feeble-mindedness, legal termination of parental rights must precede filing petition for adoption 13, §908(1)(b)	ct. finds parent mentally incompetent &, from evidence of 2 qualified ct.-appointed psychiatrists, unable to discharge parental responsibilities in foreseeable future *fn. 2* 13, §1103(4)
D.C. Code Ann. (1981)	ct. finds after hearing that consents are withheld contrary to child's best interests 16-304(e)	
FLA. Stat. Ann. (West 1969 & Supp. 1981)	parent judicially declared incompetent for whom restoration of competency medically improbable 63-072(3)	
GA. Code Ann. (1981 & Supp. 1981)	where parent insane or otherwise incapacitated from surrendering such rights & ct. thinks adoption in child's best interest 74-405(a)	
HAWAII Rev. Stat. (1976 & Supp. 1981)	parent judicially declared mentally ill or mentally retarded & found by ct. incapable of giving consent to adoption of child 578-2(c)(1)(G)	any parent found by ct. to be mentally ill or mentally retarded & incapable of giving consent to adoption of child or of providing now & in foreseeable future care necessary child's well-being 571.61(b)(1)(F)
IDAHO Code (1979 & Supp. 1980)	parental rights have been judicially terminated 16-1504	parent unable to discharge parental responsibilities because of mental illness or mental deficiency & reasonable grounds to believe the condition will be prolonged & be injurious to child's well-being 16-2005(d)
ILL. Ann. Stat. (Smith-Hurd 1980)	parent adjudicated incompetent from mental impairment, subject to involuntary admission, or mentally retarded; ct. finds that parent will not recover in foreseeable future, ct. may appoint state's attorney guardian ad litem to represent parent, & state's attorney shall have authority to consent to adoption 40, §1510	
IND. Code Ann. (Burns 1980 & Supp. 1982)	parent judicially declared incompetent or mentally defective & ct. dispenses w/parent's consent 31-3-1-6(9)(5)	
IOWA Code Ann. (West 1950 & Supp. 1981)	ct. determines in best interests of child & adoptive parent(s) that any particular consent unnecessary to granting adoption petition 600.7(4)	
KAN. Stat. Ann. (1976 & Supp. 1981)	consent by 1 parent if other is incapable of giving consent 59-2102(3) rights of parents have been legally terminated 59-2102(5)	child deprived, i.e., lacks care necessary for other than financial reasons 38-824, 38-802
KY. Rev. Stat. Ann. (Michie 1977 & Supp. 1980)	parent adjudged mentally disabled not less than 1 yr. prior to filing adoption petition 199.500(1)(a)	professionally certified emotional or mental illness or mental deficiency of parent rendering parent consistently unable to care for child for extended periods 208C.090(2)(a)
LA. Rev. Stat. Ann. (1965 & Supp. 1981)		
ME. Rev. Stat. Ann. (1964 & Supp. 1981)	parent judged unwilling or unable to undertake such responsibility 19, §532	
MD. Ann. Code (1957 & Supp. 1981)	ct. finds consents are withheld contrary to the child's best interest 16, §74	
MASS. Ann. Laws (Michie/Law. Co-op. 1981 & Supp. 1982)	ct. finds adoption in child's best interests 210, §3(a)(ii)	
MICH. Comp. Laws Ann. (1968 & Supp. 1981)	ct.-appointed guardian of mentally incompetent parent given authority by ct. to consent in parent's stead 710.28(1), 710.43(1)	
MINN. Stat. Ann. (West 1971 & Supp. 1981)		
MISS. Code Ann. (1972 & Supp. 1981)	ct. concludes from evidence that parent mentally unfit to rear child 93-17-7	parent's condition makes parent unable to provide minimally acceptable care of child & unlikely to change w/in reasonable time 93-15-103(3)(d)(i)

TABLE 9.3 EFFECT OF PARENT'S MENTAL DISABILITY ON PARENT-CHILD RELATIONSHIP *fn. 1—Continued*

STATE	ADOPTION: CONSENT OF PARENT NOT NECESSARY IF (1)	TERMINATION OF PARENT-CHILD RELATIONSHIP IF (2)
MO. Ann. Stat. (Vernon 1977 & Supp. 1981)	parent adjudged incompetent 453.040(1)	
MONT. Code Ann. (1981)	parental rights have been judicially terminated 40-8-111(1)(a)(vi)	parent so emotionally or mentally ill, or mentally deficient that unlikely to care for needs of child 41-3-609(2)(a)
NEB. Rev. Stat. (1943 & Supp. 1978)	parent incapable of consenting 43-104(3)(d)	parents unable to discharge parental responsibilities because of mental illness or deficiency & reasonable grounds to believe condition will be prolonged 43-209(5)
NEV. Rev. Stat. (1979 & Supp. 1981)	parent adjudged insane for 2 yrs. & ct. satisfied by proof that such insanity incurable 127.040(2)	
N.H. Rev. Stat. Ann. (1977 & Supp. 1981)	parental rights have been judicially terminated 170-B:6II	mental deficiency or mental illness makes parent incapable of giving child proper care for period of time detrimental to child 170-C:5IV
N.J. Stat. Ann. (West 1976 & Supp. 1982)	parental rights have been judicially terminated 9:3-46(a)	ct. finds parent mentally incompetent 9:2-19
N.M. Stat. Ann. (1978)	parent has been judicially declared incompetent or mentally defective & if ct. dispenses w/parent's consent 40-7-7(E)	parent neglects or abuses child 40-7-4
N.Y. Dom. Rel. Law (McKinney 1977 & Supp. 1981)	parent by reason of mental illness or mental retardation, presently & for foreseeable future unable to provide proper care for child 111(2)(c)	
N.C. Gen. Stat. (1981 & Supp. 1981)	ct. finds parent unable to give valid consent because adjudged mentally incompetent 48-9(d)	parent incapable, from mental retardation or illness, organic brain syndrome, or any degenerative mental condition, of providing proper care for child throughout its minority *fn. 3* 7A-289.32(7)
N.D. Cent. Code (1981)	parent adjudged incompetent or mentally defective if ct. dispenses w/parent's consent 14-15-06(1)(f)	physical or mental incapacity make parent unable to provide necessary care for minor & ct. finds conditions irremediable & thus likely to seriously harm minor 14-15-19(3)(b)
OHIO Rev. Code Ann. (Baldwin 1981 & Supp. 1981)	parent judicially declared incompetent & guardian of parent found by ct. to be withholding consent unreasonably 3107.07(E)	
OKLA. Stat. Ann. (West 1966 & Supp. 1980)	parent has been judicially deprived of custody 10, §60.6(2)	child deprived from acts or omissions resulting from parent's continuing condition, & termination in child's best interests *fn. 4* 10, §1130(3)
OR. Rev. Stat. (1979 & Supp. 1981)	parent adjudged mentally ill or mentally deficient & remains so at time of adoptive proceedings, & ct. finds child's welfare will be promoted by adoption 109.322	parent unfit by reason of conduct or condition seriously detrimental to child; such conduct or condition includes emotional or mental illness, or mental deficiency that makes parent unable to care for the child for extended periods 419.523(2)
PA. Stat. Ann. (Purdon 1955 & Supp. 1981)		repeated & continued incapacity of parent has deprived child of care necessary to well-being 23, §2511(a)(2)
R.I. Gen. Laws (1977 & Supp. 1980)		prolonged emotional or mental illness, mental deficiency, or institutionalization make it improbable parent can care for child for extended period 15-7-7(b)(1)
S.C. Code Ann. (Law Co-op. 1976 & Supp. 1980)	parental rights have been judicially terminated 20-7-1710	child abandoned, i.e., parent has been judicially determined to be so mentally ill or retarded that can never function as parent 20-7-1570(2)(b)
S.D. Codified Laws Ann. (1976 & Supp. 1980)	parent adjudged an habitual drunkard or mentally incompetent 25-6-4(3)	
TENN. Code Ann. (1977 & Supp. 1981)	parent incompetent to give consent; guardian ad litem shall be appointed for incompetent parent to give or withhold consent 36-108	
TEX. Rev. Civ. Stat. Ann. (Vernon 1975 & Supp. 1981)	affidavit of relinquishment appointing Tex. Dep't Human Resources or authorized agency managing conservator of child 16.03(d)	adoption by others 16.03(d) parent petition & child's best interest 15.01 child's best interest 15.02(2)
UTAH Code Ann. (1977 & Supp. 1981)	parent judicially deprived of custody on account of cruelty, neglect, or desertion or has released control to an agency 78-30-4(1)	best interest of child; emotional or mental illness or mental deficiency render parent incapable of caring for child 78-3a-48(a)(ii)
VT. Stat. Ann. (1974 & Supp. 1981)	parent incompetent to have care & custody of minor 15, §435(5)	
VA. Code (1982)	ct. finds consents unobtainable or withheld contrary to child's best interests 63.1-225(C)	child neglected or abused 16.1-279
WASH. Rev. Code Ann. (1961 & Supp. 1981)		petition of parent being deprived 26.32.032
W. VA. Code (1980 & Supp. 1982)	if 1 parent insane, only the consent of other parent required; if both parents insane, consent of legal guardian, or person having legal custody, or suitable person appointed by ct. as child's next friend 48-4-1(b)(1)	

TABLE 9.3 EFFECT OF PARENT'S MENTAL DISABILITY ON PARENT-CHILD RELATIONSHIP *fn. 1—Continued*

STATE	ADOPTION: CONSENT OF PARENT NOT NECESSARY IF (1)	TERMINATION OF PARENT-CHILD RELATIONSHIP IF (2)
WIS. Stat. Ann. (West 1979 & Supp. 1981)		parent presently, & for at least 2 of last 5 yrs., an inpatient because of mental illness or developmental disability; & condition likely to continue indefinitely; & child not being provided w/adequate care by relative or guardian 48.415(3)
WYO. Stat. (1977 & Supp. 1982)	parent adjudged incompetent or insane; consent of parent's guardian to adoption sufficient 1-22-109(a)(viii)	child has been abused & neglected, family has refused rehabilitative treatment, & child's heath & safety endangered 14-2-309(a)(iii)

FOOTNOTES: TABLE 9.3

1. While on the one hand encouraging adoptions of mentally disabled children by providing subsidies to adopting parents (table 7.4), California and Missouri also allow the adoption of a child to be annulled if, within five years of the adoption the child develops a mental disability. Cal. Civ. § 2270 (Supp. 1980); Mo. Ann. Stat. § 453.130 (Vernon 1977). Maine allows an adoption annulled if "good cause" is shown. Me. Rev. Stat. Ann. 19, § 538 (1981).

2. Del. Code Ann. tit. 13, § 1101(4) (1981). Mentally incompetent shall be interpreted as referring to a parent who is unable to understand and discharge the natural and regular obligations of care and support of a child by reason of mental illness, psychopathology, mental retardation, or mental deficiency.

3. N.C. Gen. Stat. § 7A-289.33 (1981). Child's right to inheritance is not terminated by severance.

4. Okla. Stat. Ann. art. 10, § 1101(d) (West 1973). The term "deprived child" means a child who does not have the proper parental care or guardianship.

TABLE 9.4 SUBSIDIES FOR ADOPTION OF MENTALLY DISABLED CHILDREN

STATE AND CITATION	STATUTORY PROVISIONS
ALA. Code (1975 & Supp. 1981) 26-10-22	The state department of pensions and securities shall administer a program of subsidized adoptions for children certified as eligible. "'[C]hild' means a child or a minor as defined by Alabama statute, who is (a) in the permanent custody of a public or voluntary licensed child-placing agency, (b) legally free for adoption and (c) in special circumstances because he is not likely to be adopted by reason of one or more conditions, such as: (1) Physical or mental disability, (2) Emotional disturbance, (3) Recognized high risk of physical or mental disease."
ALAS. Stat. (1975) 20-15.190	"A handicapped minor in the permanent custody of the department in a foster home for not less than one year may not be denied the opportunity for a permanent home if the achievement of this depends on continued subsidy by the state."
ARIZ. Rev. Stat. Ann. (1974 & Supp. 1980) 8-141	The Department of Economic Security shall establish a program to subsidize the adoption of eligible children. "'[C]hild' means any person under the age of eighteen years who is legally free for adoption . . . who otherwise may not be adopted because of any of the following special circumstances: (1) Physical or mental disability, (2) Emotional disturbance, (3) High risk of physical or mental disease."
ARK. Stat. Ann. (1971 & Supp. 1981) 56-131	Public financial subsidies are provided for adoption of children certified as eligible by the Division of Social Services. "[C]hild means a minor as defined by Arkansas Statute, who is: (a) a dependent of a public child-placing agency; and (b) legally free for adoption; and (c) in special circumstances. . . . (2) a child who is not likely to be adopted by reason of one [1] or more conditions, such as: A. physical or mental disability; B. emotional disturbance; C. recognized high risk of physical or mental disease."
CAL. Welf & Inst. Code (West 1980)[1] 16116	The county responsible for providing foster care for a child shall provide financial aid to the adoptive family of a hard-to-place child. "[A] 'hard-to-place' child is a child who is disadvantaged because of adverse parental background, or a handicapped child. . . . "It is the purpose of this chapter to encourage and promote the placement in adoptive homes of children who because of their . . . mental, or emotional or medical handicaps . . . have become difficult to place in adoptive homes."
COLO. Rev. Stat. (1973) 26-7-101(2)	The department of social services may make payments for adoption of a child with special needs. "'Child with special needs' means a child with a special, unusual, or significant physical or mental handicap, or emotional disturbance, or such other condition which acts as a serious barrier to his adoption."
CONN. Gen. Stat. Ann. (West 1975 & Supp. 1980) 17-44a	Special need and periodic subsidies are provided to the adopting parents of hard-to-place children. "[A] 'hard-to-place' child is a child who is a ward of the commissioner of children and youth services or is to be placed by a licensed child-placing agency and is difficult to place in adoption because of . . . a physical or mental handicap."

TABLE 9.4 SUBSIDIES FOR ADOPTION OF MENTALLY DISABLED CHILDREN—continued

STATE AND CITATION	STATUTORY PROVISIONS
D.C. Code Ann. (1973) 3-115(2)(A)	"The term 'child with special needs' includes any child who is difficult to place in adoption because of . . . physical or mental condition. . . . A child for whom an adoptive placement has not been made within six months after he is legally available for adoptive placement shall be considered a child with special needs within the meaning of this section."
IDAHO Code (1976) 56-802(1)	Financial aid provided to families adopting a "Hard to place child," that is, a child who is difficult to place for adoption because of "mental, emotional or medical handicap."
IND. Code Ann. (Burns 1980) 31-3-3-1(b)	The department of public welfare may be ordered to pay aid for adoption of a hard-to-place child. "[A] 'hard to place' child is a child who is disadvantaged because of . . . physical, mental, or medical handicaps."
IOWA Code Ann. (West 1981) 600.17	"The department of social services shall . . . provide financial assistance to any person who adopts a physically or mentally handicapped, older, or otherwise hard-to-place child."
KAN. Stat. Ann. (1973 & Supp. 1980) 38-322	"Before a child may become eligible for adoption support under this act, it shall be necessary that: (a) The child shall be or have been a child hard to place in adoption due to attitudes of society toward his: . . . mental, emotional or physical handicap."
KY. Rev. Stat. Ann. (Michie 1977) 199.555(1)	Payment of subsidy to adoptive parents of hard-to-place children. "'[H]ard to place children' means those children for whom adoptive homes are difficult to find because of a physical handicap, a mental condition, or the age of the child."
LA. Rev. Stat. Ann. (West 1950 & Supp. 1980) 46:1790(B)	"The department may make payments to the adoptive parents on behalf of a child placed for adoption . . . whenever: (1) The child, because of physical or mental condition, . . . or other serious impediments or special needs, is considered a child that is difficult to place for adoption."
ME. Rev. Stat. Ann.[2] (1981) 19, §541	"The Department of Human Services is authorized to subsidize the adoption of children in its care or custody who are legally eligible for adoption and who are physically or mentally handicapped, emotionally disturbed."
MD. Ann. Code (1981) 16, §88A	The local department of social services shall establish a program of subsidization for the adoption of hard-to-place children. "'[C]hild' means a minor as defined by State law, who is legally free for adoption and for whom a determination has been made by the local department of social services, that a cash subsidy, medical assistance or medical care is necessary to assure his adoption because of special circumstances such as: (1) Physical or mental disability; (2) Emotional disturbance; (3) Recognized high risk of physical or mental disease."
MICH. Comp. Laws Ann. (1976 & Supp. 1980) 400.115f(2)	"(a) The minimum requirements for certification for a support subsidy are: (i) the adoptee was in foster care for not less than 4 months before certification. (ii) A reasonable effort has failed to identify a person qualified and willing to adopt without subsidy . . . (iii) Certification for a support subsidy has been made by the office before the petition for adoption. "(b) The minimum requirements for certification for a medical subsidy are that the expenses to be covered by the medical subsidy are necessitated by a physical, mental, or emotional condition of the adoptee which existed or the cause of which existed before the adoption petition was filed or certification was established, which ever occurred first."

TABLE 9.4 SUBSIDIES FOR ADOPTION OF MENTALLY DISABLED CHILDREN—continued

STATE AND CITATION	STATUTORY PROVISIONS
MINN. Stat. Ann. (West 1971 & Supp. 1980) 259.40(4)	Subsidy payments to families of children certified as eligible. "Eligibility conditions . . . (a) A placement agency has made reasonable efforts to place the child for adoption without subsidy, but has been unsuccessful; or (b) The child's licensed foster parents desire to adopt the child and it is determined by the placing agency that: . . . (2) Due to the child's characteristics or circumstances it would be difficult to provide the child an adoptive home without subsidy."
MISS. Code Ann. (1972 & Supp. 1980) 93-17-55	Supplemental benefits are provided to assure adoption of eligible children. "'[C]hild' shall mean a minor as defined by Mississippi law who is: (a) a dependent of a public or voluntary licensed child-placing agency; (b) legally free for adoption; and (c) in special circumstances whether [sic]: . . . (ii) because he is not likely to be adopted because of one (1) or more of the following handicaps: (A) severe physical or mental disability, (B) severe emotional disturbance, (C) recognized high risk of physical or mental disease, or (D) any combination of these handicaps."
MO. Ann. Stat.[3] (Vernon 1977 & Supp. 1980) 453.073(1)	"This authorization [for subsidy payments] shall pertain to those children previously considered unadoptable, those suffering from physical handicaps or mental retardation."
MONT. Code Ann. (1979) 53-4-303	Subsidies are provided for adoption of children who are certified as hard to place. "'Hard-to-place child' means a minor, as defined by 41-1-101, who is a dependent of a public or voluntary licensed child-placing agency, legally free for adoption, and if not likely to be adopted because of: (a) physical or mental disease or disability; (b) recognized high risk of physical or mental disease or disability."
NEB. Rev. Stat. (1978) 43-117	"The Department of Public Welfare may make payments as needed in behalf of a ward of the department with special needs after the legal completion of his adoption."
NEV. Rev. Stat. (1981) 127.186	"(1) The welfare division of the department of human resources, or a child-placing agency licensed by the welfare division . . . may consent to the adoption of a child under 18 years of age with special needs as to . . . physical or mental problems. "(2) The welfare division may grant financial assistance . . . for maintenance and for preexisting physical and/or mental conditions to the adoptive parents."
N.H. Rev. Stat. Ann. (1977 & Supp. 1979) 170-F:2(I)	Subsidy payments are to be made by the Director of the Division of Welfare to adoptive parents on behalf of hard-to-place children. "'Hard-to-place child' means a child in or likely to be placed in a foster home who is found by the director to be legally free for, but difficult to place in, adoption because of physical or other reasons, including, but not limited to, physical or mental handicap, emotional distress."
N.J. Stat. Ann. (West 1981) 30:4C-46	"The Bureau of Children's Services or its successor, the Division of Youth and Family Services may make payments to adoptive parents on behalf of a child placed for adoption by the bureau whenever: a. the child because of physical or mental condition . . . falls into the category of a child hard to place for adoption."

TABLE 9.4 SUBSIDIES FOR ADOPTION OF MENTALLY DISABLED CHILDREN—continued

STATE AND CITATION	STATUTORY PROVISIONS
N.M. Stat. Ann. (1978) 40-7-27B	The health and social services department may make payment to adoptive parents on behalf of a difficult-to-place child. "[A] 'difficult to place child' means a child who is physically or mentally handicapped, emotionally disturbed."
N.Y. Soc. Serv. Law (McKinney 1976 & Supp. 1980) 451	Maintenance and medical subsidies are provided for the adoption of handicapped and hard-to-place children. "(2) 'Handicapped child' shall mean a child who possesses a specific physical, mental or emotional condition or disability of such severity or kind which, in accordance with regulations of the department, would constitute a significant obstacle to the child's adoption. "(3) 'Hard to place child' shall mean a child, other than a handicapper [sic] child, . . . (c) who possesses or presents any personal or familial attribute, condition, problem or characteristic which, in accordance with regulations of the department, would be an obstacle to the child's adoption."
N.C. Gen. Stat. (1976) 48-39.1	"A fund, to be known as the 'State Fund for Adoptive Children with Special Needs,' shall be created from appropriations made by the General Assembly and from grants of the federal government when made available to the State. This fund shall be used exclusively for the purpose of meeting the needs of adoptive children who are physically or mentally handicapped, older, or otherwise hard to place for adoption."
OHIO Rev. Code Ann. (Baldwin 1980) 5153.16(N)(3)	The county children's services board shall enter into agreements before adoption to make payments as needed in behalf of children with special needs. "'[C]hild with special needs' means a child or sibling group that is difficult to place because of . . . mental or emotional conditions . . . and is or in all probability would become dependent upon the resources of the State, county, or sources other than adoptive parents."
OR. Rev. Stat. (1979) 418.330(1)(a)	Payments to adoptive parents when the division determines: "The child has special needs because of a handicap to adoptive placement by reason of his physical or mental condition."
PA. Stat. Ann. (Purdon 1968 & Supp. 1980) 62, §772	Subsidies are provided for the adoption of children certified as eligible. "'Eligible child' means a child in the legal custody of local authorities where parental rights have been terminated . . . and such child has been in foster placement for a period of not less than six months and where the child has been shown to be a difficult adoption placement because of a physical and/or mental handicap, emotional disturbance."
R.I. Gen. Laws (1970 & Supp. 1980) 15-7-25	"The state shall make funds available through the department of social and rehabilitative services for special reimbursement to adoptive parents in matters of placement of handicapped or hard to place children."
S.C. Code Ann. (Law Co-op. 1976 & Supp. 1980) 15-45-320	Supplemental benefits are provided for the adoption of children certified by the Department of Social Services as eligible. "'[C]hild' means a minor as defined by South Carolina law who is: (A) a dependent of a public or voluntary licensed child-placing agency, (B) legally free for adoption, and (C) in special circumstances . . . (2) because he is not likely to be adopted because of one or more of the following handicaps: (a) Physical or mental disability. (b) Emotional disturbance. (c) Recognized high risk of physical or mental disease."

TABLE 9.4 SUBSIDIES FOR ADOPTION OF MENTALLY DISABLED CHILDREN—continued

STATE AND CITATION	STATUTORY PROVISIONS
TEX. Hum. Res. Code Ann. (Vernon 1980) 47.001	The Department of Human Resources shall provide financial assistance for adoption of hard-to-place children. "'[H]ard-to-place child' means a child who is three years of age or older and who is difficult to place in an adoptive home because of . . . physical, mental, or emotional handicap."
VA. Code (1980 & Supp. 1981) 63.1-238.1(b)	Maintenance and special need subsidy payments are provided to adoptive parents of children with special needs. "'Child with special needs' shall mean any child in the custody of a local board of public welfare or social services which has the authority to place the child for adoption . . . for whom it has been determined that it is unlikely that the child will be adopted within a reasonable period of time due to one or more factors including, but not limited to: 1. Physical, mental or emotional condition existing prior to adoption; 2. Hereditary tendency, congenital problem or birth injury leading to substantial risk of future disability."
WASH. Rev. Code Ann. (1962 & Supp. 1980) 74.13.109	"Disbursements . . . shall be made . . . for the purpose of supporting the adoption of children in, or likely to be placed in, foster homes or child caring institutions who are found by the secretary to be difficult to place in adoption because of physical or other reasons; including, but not limited to, physical or mental handicap, emotional disturbance."
W. VA. Code (1980) 49-2-17	"From funds appropriated to the department of welfare, the commissioner shall establish a system of assistance for facilitating the adoption of children who are dependents of the department or a child welfare agency licensed to place children for adoption, legally free for adoption and in special circumstances either because they: . . . (b) Are not likely to be adopted by reason of one or more of the following conditions: (1) They have a physical or mental disability; or (2) They are emotionally disturbed."
WIS. Stat. Ann. (West 1979) 48.975	"(2) The department may subsidize an adoption only when it has determined that such assistance is necessary to assure the child's adoption. "(3) (b) A medical assistance subsidy shall be sufficient to pay expenses due to a physical, mental or emotional condition of the child which is not covered by a health insurance policy insuring the child or the parent."
WYO. Stat. (1977 & Supp. 1981) 1-22-115(a)	"The division of public assistance and social services may grant subsidy payments to the adoptive parent of a child . . . if, at the time the child is placed for adoption: . . . (iv) The child has special needs as determined by the division."

FOOTNOTES: TABLE 9.4

1. Cal. Civ. Code 227b (West 1954 & Supp. 1980). Annulment of adoption if within 5 years of decree, child shows evidence of a developmental disability or mental illness as a result of conditions prior to adoption to such an extent that the child cannot be relinquished to an adoption agency on the grounds that the child is considered unadoptable, and of which conditions the adopting parent(s) had no knowledge or notice prior to the decree.

2. Me. Rev. Stat. Ann. 19, §538 (1981). Annulment of adoption allowed if "good cause" is shown.

3. Mo. Rev. Stat. 453.130 (1977). Annulment of adoption allowed if within 5 years after adoption the child develops feeblemindness or epilepsy (repealed in 1982).

TABLE 9.5 STERILIZATION—PREHEARING PROCEDURES

	PERSON COVERED BY STERILIZATION STATUTE						APPLICATION BY			CONSENT REQUIRED				NOTICE					
STATE	Mentally Retarded (1)	Mentally Ill (2)	Epileptic (3)	Incompetent (4)	Person in State Institution (5)	Age Requirements (6)	Institution Superintendent (7)	Parent or Guardian (8)	Other (9)	Person Subject to Sterilization (10)	Parent or Guardian (11)	Other (12)	STERILIZATION WITHOUT CONSENT (13)	Patient (14)	Parent or Guardian (15)	Other (16)	When (17)	MEDICAL CERTIFICATES (18)	FURTHER APPROVAL BY (19)
ARK. Stat. Ann. (1971 & Supp. 1981): Judicial procedure	59-501 (A)(3) OR	59-501 (A)(3) AND		59-501 (A)(3)		over 14; notice to parents of minors 59-501 (E)		59-501 (D)					59-501	if over 14 59-501 (E)(b)(1)	parent of minor; guardian if any 59-501 (E)(b)	spouse or nearest relative 59-501 (E)(b)	20 days before hearing 59-501 (E)(b)	two 59-501 (G)(1)	
Medical certification	59-502 (B) OR	59-502 (B) AND		59-502 (B)		parent may seek sterilization of minor 59-502 (B)		59-502 (B)					59-502					three 59-502 (D)	hospital review committee 59-502 (E)
COLO. Rev. Stat. (1973 & Supp. 1981)	voluntary 27-10.5-128 involuntary 27-10.5-129 AND					over 18 27-10.5-128		27-10.5-129(1)	person 27-10.5-130 person 27-10.5-129(1)	fn. 1 27-10.5-128(1) AND	27-10.5-128(1) AND	27-10.5-128(1) psychiatrist or psychologist and a mental retardation worker	27-10.5-129	27-10.5-129(2)	27-10.5-129(2)		not less than 10 days before hearing 27-10.5-129(2)	two 27-10.5-130(1)	
CONN. Gen. Stat. (West 1981 & Supp. 1981)				persons under guardianship or conservatorship 45-78q OR	sterilization only w/informed consent 45-78q	18 & over 45-78q	director of institution or attending physician fn. 2 45-78r	45-78x	patient or interested party fn. 2 45-78r	informed consent fn. 3 45-78q OR			persons under guardianship or conservatorship 45-78q 45-78x 45-78y	45-78s	45-78s		at least 7 days prior to hearing 45-78s	three 45-78u	
DEL. Code Ann. (1973 & Supp. 1980)	16, §5701 (a) OR	16, §5701 (a) OR	16, §5701 (a) AND		or "at large" 16, §5701	none stated							16, §5701		16, §5701 (c)	husband or wife 16, §5701 (c)	30 days before sterilization performed 16, §5701 (c)	examination by physician, alienist, & institution superintendent fn. 4 16, §5701 (a)	Dep't of Health & Social Services 16, §5701 (b)
GA. Code Ann. (1979 & Supp. 1980)	or brain damaged 84-933 (b)(i) AND			84-933 (b)(i)		adult or minor 84-933 (b)(i)	board of health 84-933 (c)(i)	84-933 (c)(i)			patient or guardian ad litem 84-933 (c)(i)							two 84-933 (c)(ii)	medical staff of hospital 84-933 (c)(iii)
IDAHO Code (1977 & Supp. 1981)	39-3901 (a) AND			39-3901 (a)		past age of puberty 39-3901 (a)	health & welfare director 39-3903 (a)	39-3903 (a)	prosecuting attorney 39-3903 (a)		39-3903 (a) OR	health & welfare director 39-3903 (a)						two 39-3903 (d)	
KY. Rev. Stat. Ann. (Michie 1977 & Supp. 1980)	mentally disabled 212.345	mentally disabled 212.345				consent of parent or guardian if minor 212.345	no application fn. 5	no application fn. 5	no application fn. 5	212.345 OR	guardian if adult; parent or guardian if minor & unmarried 212.345							physician required to provide counseling to person 212.343	
ME. Rev. Stat. Ann. (1978 & Supp. 1981)	feeble-minded 34, §2461 feeble-minded 34, §2462 OR	34, §2462 AND			34, §2462		medical staff of institution fn. 6 34, §2462		physician suggests advisability of to patient 34, §2461	if capable of consenting 34, §2461 OR	nearest relative or guardian if incapable of consenting 34, §2461		34, §2462	34, §2464	34, §2464	husband or wife 34, §2464	30 days before sterilization 34, §2464	two fn. 7 34, §2461	

TABLE 9.5 STERILIZATION—PREHEARING PROCEDURES—*Continued*

	PERSON COVERED BY STERILIZATION STATUTE						APPLICATION BY			CONSENT REQUIRED				NOTICE					
STATE	Mentally Retarded (1)	Mentally Ill (2)	Epileptic (3)	Incompetent (4)	Person in State Institution (5)	Age Requirements (6)	Institution Superintendent (7)	Parent or Guardian (8)	Other (9)	Person Subject to Sterilization (10)	Parent or Guardian (11)	Other (12)	STERILIZATION WITHOUT CONSENT (13)	Patient (14)	Parent or Guardian (15)	Other (16)	When (17)	MEDICAL CERTIFICATES (18)	FURTHER APPROVAL BY (19)
MINN. Stat. Ann.: Institutionalized mentally ill (West 1971)		involuntarily hospitalized patients only 256.08 AND			hospitalized for at least 6 mos. 256.08				commissioner of public welfare 256.08	256.08									hospital superintendent, physician, & psychologist 256.08
Mentally retarded (1971 & Supp. 1980)	252A.13					parental consent if minor 252A.13 (3), (4)				unless right to consent restricted 252A.13 AND	parental consent if minor 252A.13 (3) OR							physician, psychologist & social worker 252A.13 (4)	
Persons under guardianship (1975 & Supp. 1981)	525.56 (3), (4)(c) AND OR			525.56(3)		minors under guardianship: same procedure 525.619 (c)		guardian 525.56 (3), (4)(b)				consent of commissioner of public welfare (& parent, if minor) 252A.13 (4)	525.56 (3), (4)(b)		525.56 (3), (4)(b)	525.56 (3), (4)(b) 525.55	spouse, adult children, siblings, next of kin 525.56 (3), (4)(b) 525.55	one 525.56 (3), (4)(b) physician, psychologist, & social worker if minor 525.56 (3), (4)(c)	
MISS. Code Ann. (1972)	41-45-1 OR	41-45-1 OR	41-45-1 AND		41-45-1	notice to parents if minor 41-45-5	41-45-1						41-45-1	41-45-5	guardian 41-45-5 parent if minor 41-45-5 OR	next of kin 41-45-5	30 days before petition for sterilization filed w/board of trustees 41-45-5		
N.J. Stat. Ann. (West 1981 & Supp. 1982)	developmentally disabled 30:6D-5(a)(4) AND				any institution 30:6D-5(a)	consent of guardian ad litem if minor 30:6D-5(a)(4)		30:6D-5(a)(4)	30:6D-5(a)(4) patient	if competent adult 30:6D-5(a)(4) OR	guardian ad litem if minor, incompetent, or mentally deficient 30:6D-5(a)(4)								
N.C. Gen. Stat. (1976 & Supp. 1981)	35-36 35-37 OR	35-36 35-37			not in state institution 35-37 35-36		35-36		county director of social services 35-37				35-43	35-41	guardian or guardian ad litem 35-41 OR	next of kin 35-41	at least 20 days before hearing 35-41		
OKLA. Stat. Ann. (West 1979 & Supp. 1981)	43A, §341 OR	43A, §341 AND			43A, §341 AND	males under 65 & females under 47 43A, §341	43A, §342						43A, §342	43A, §342	guardian or guardian ad litem; parent of infant 43A, §342		not less than 10 days before application filed 43A, §342		
OR. Rev. Stat. (1981)	436.070 OR	436.070							any 2 persons or any doctor 436.025	436.700 AND	guardian, spouse, next known kin, or friend in that order 436.100 OR		*fn. 8* 436.100 436.125	436.041 (1)	guardian, spouse, next known kin, or friend 436.041 436.090	public defender 436.041 (2)	at least 20 days prior to hearing 436.041 (1)		
S.C. Code (Law Co-op. 1976 & Supp. 1981)	44-47-10 OR	hereditary form of insanity 44-47-10 OR	44-47-10 AND		44-47-10		44-47-10						44-47-50	44-47-20	44-47-20	child, brother, or sister 44-47-20	not less than 30 days before application made 44-47-20		
UTAH Code Ann. (1978 & Supp. 1981) *fn. 9*	64-10-1 AND			adjudicated mental incompetent 64-10-1 AND	64-10-1	notice to parents of minor 64-10-3	64-10-1						64-10-4	64-10-3			30 days before hearing 64-10-3		
VA. Code (1978 & Supp. 1981)	mentally disabled 54-325.10	mentally disabled 54-325.10 AND		adjudicated incompetent or incapable of consent, if 18 or over 54-325.11 (4)		14–18 54-325.10 18 & over 54-325.9 54-325.11				if capable of informed consent 54-325.9 OR			if incapable of consent or 14–18 yrs. old 54-325.10 54-325.11	54-325.10 (2) 54-325.11 (2)	both if age 14–15 54-325.10 (2) guardian; parent if no spouse 54-325.11 (2)	spouse 54-325.10 (2) 54-325.11 (2)			

TABLE 9.5 STERILIZATION—PREHEARING PROCEDURES—*Continued*

STATE	PERSON COVERED BY STERILIZATION STATUTE						APPLICATION BY			CONSENT REQUIRED			STERILI-ZATION WITHOUT CONSENT (13)	NOTICE				MEDICAL CERTIFI-CATES (18)	FURTHER APPROVAL BY (19)
	Mentally Retarded (1)	Mentally Ill (2)	Epileptic (3)	Incom-petent (4)	Person in State In-stitution (5)	Age Re-quirements (6)	Institu-tion Superin-tendent (7)	Parent or Guardian (8)	Other (9)	Person Subject to Sterili-zation (10)	Parent or Guardian (11)	Other (12)		Patient (14)	Parent or Guardian (15)	Other (16)	When (17)		
W. VA. Code (1980 & Supp. 1982)				person declared mentally incompetent 27-16-1			27-16-1	27-16-1					27-16-1	27-16-1			at least 15 days prior to hearing 27-16-1	examination by physi-cian & psy-chologist 27-16-1	

FOOTNOTES: TABLE 9.5

1. Colo. Rev. Stat. § 27-10.5-132 (Supp. 1981): "Consent to sterilization shall be made neither a condition for release from any institution nor a condition for the exercise of any right, privilege or freedom."

2. Conn. Gen. Stat. Ann. § 45-78r (West 1981). An application for a determination of a person's ability to give informed consent to a sterilization procedure may be filed by the person seeking sterilization, by the director of the institution, or by an interested party and shall state the reason for seeking such determination.

3. Id. § 45-78w. The court determines issues of informed consent. If the court finds a patient incompetent to consent it may only order sterilization if it is in the "best interests" of the patient.

4. Del. Code Ann. tit. 16, § 5702(b). If the mental defective is at large, the examining commission should be 2 physicians and one alienist.

5. Ky. Rev. Stat. § 212.345 (Michie Supp. 1980). The Kentucky statute requires written informed consent for nontherapeutic sterilizations in all cases. This does not entail any application to, or determination by, a court or administrative body.

6. Me. Rev. Stat. Ann. tit. 34, § 2462 (Supp. 1981). The medical staff of the institution recommend the sterilization of a patient to the department of mental health and corrections.

7. Id. tit. 34, § 2463. The department sends a written order to proceed with sterilization to the superintendent, if it approves of the recommendation.

8. Or. Rev. Stat. § 436.110 (1981). If there is no consent, the patient may request a board rehearing within 30 days. Failure to request rehearing shall be conclusively deemed the equivalent of consent, as though expressly given.

9. Utah Code Ann. § 64-10-1 (1978). The procedure charted is for sterilization or asexualization.

TABLE 9.6 STERILIZATION—HEARING AND POSTHEARING PROCEDURES

STATE	HEARING AGENCY Court (1)	HEARING AGENCY Adminis-trative (2)	PRESENCE OF PATIENT (3)	RIGHT TO COUNSEL (4)	REASON FOR STERILIZATION Prevent Mentally Disabled Offspring (5)	REASON FOR STERILIZATION Patient Unable to Care for Children (6)	REASON FOR STERILIZATION Patient Would Require Public Aid (7)	REASON FOR STERILIZATION Best Interests of Patient (8)	REASON FOR STERILIZATION Other (9)	WAITING PERIOD AFTER STERILI-ZATION ORDER (10)	JUDICIAL REVIEW (11)	APPEAL STAYS STERILI-ZATION ORDER (12)	MEDICAL PERSONNEL IMMUNE FROM LIABILITY (13)	OTHERS IMMUNE FROM LIABILITY (14)	GUARDIAN AD LITEM APPOINTED (15)
Ark. State Ann. (1971 & Supp. 1981): Judicial procedure Medical certification	59-501(b) no hearing	 no hearing	fn. 1 59-501(G)(2)	59-501(G)(2)					fn. 2 59-501(A)(3) 59-502(D)		59-501(K)	59-501(K)	59-501(L) 59-502(G)		mandatory 59-501(F)
COLO. Rev. Stat. (1973 & Supp. 1981)	27-10.5-129(1)		mandatory 27-10.5-129(3)	counsel appointed if indigent 27-10.5-129(4)					fn. 3 27-10.5-130(1)				voluntary sterilization 27-10.5-128(1)(a)		
CONN. Gen. Stat. (1973 & Supp. 1981)	45-78q		mandatory 45-78v	counsel appointed 45-78t				fn. 4 45-78w 45-78p(d)							
DEL. Code Ann. (1973 & Supp. 1980)	no hearing	no hearing							fn. 5 16, §5701(b)						
GA. Code Ann. (1979 & Supp. 1980)	84-933(c)(i)			right to counsel 84-933(c)(vi)	84-933(b)(i)	84-933(b)(i)	84-933(b)(i)		irreversibly & incurably mentally incompetent 84-933(b)(i)		de novo trial w/right to jury 84-933(c)(v)	84-933(c)(v)	84-935.1	other persons legally participating 84-935.1	consent by parent or guardian ad litem 84-933(c)(i)
IDAHO Code (1977 & Supp. 1981)	39-3903		right to be present 39-3903(e)	represented by counsel at all stages 39-3903(b)		39-3901(a)	39-3901(a)	if childless could live outside institution 39-3901(a)	irreversibly & incurably retarded 39-3901(a)	until time for appeal expires 39-3904	39-3904	39-3904	w/o negligence 39-3908	other persons legally partici-pating w/o negligence 39-3908	
KY Rev. Stat. Ann. (Michie 1977 & Supp. 1980)	no hearing	no hearing								24-hr. waiting period after informed consent 212.347					
ME. Rev. Stat. Ann. (1978 & Supp. 1981)	no hearing	no hearing			34, §2461 34, §2463			therapeutic treatment 34, §2461		30 days to appeal to superior ct. 34, §2465	34, §2465	34, §2466	w/o negligence 34, §2468	superintendent or other persons legally partici pating w/o negligence 34, §2468	
MINN. Stat. Ann.: Institutionalized mentally ill (West 1971) Mentally retarded (1971 & Supp. 1981) Persons under guardianship (1975 & Supp. 1981)	no hearing if consent is by commissioner 252A.13(4) 525.56(3), (4)(b)	no hearing		counsel appointed unless provided by others 252A.13(4) counsel appointed 525.56(3), (4)(b)				252A.13(4) 525.56(3), (4)(b)	consideration of medical risks & alternative methods 252A.13(4) consideration of medical risks & alternative methods 525.56(3), (4)				256.09		
MISS. Code Ann. (1981)		board of trustees 41-45-3	if desired or requested 41-45-7	right to be represented by counsel 41-45-7	41-45-9			promotes welfare of inmate & society 41-45-9	sterilization not detrimental to health 41-45-9	30 days 41-45-9	41-45-11	41-45-13	41-45-17	institution director or other persons legally partici-pating 41-45-17	if no guardian or next of kin 41-45-5
N.J. Stat. Ann. (West 1981 & Supp. 1982)	30:6D-5(a)(4)		on petition of party alleging necessity of or guardian ad litem 30:60-5(a)(4)	counsel appointed 30:60-5(a)(4)											consent of appointed guardian ad litem necessary 30:60-5(a)(4)
N.C. Gen. Stat. (1976 & Supp. 1981)	no hearing unless requested 35-43		right to be present 35-43	counsel at all stages of proceeding 35-45	35-39(3)	35-39(3)		35-39(1)	for public good 35-39(2)		right to jury at de novo trial 35-44	35-44	35-48	other persons legally participating 35-48	notice to guard-ian or guardian ad litem 35-41

TABLE 9.6 STERILIZATION—HEARING AND POSTHEARING PROCEDURES—*Continued*

STATE	HEARING AGENCY		PRESENCE OF PATIENT (3)	RIGHT TO COUNSEL (4)	REASON FOR STERILIZATION					WAITING PERIOD AFTER STERILIZATION ORDER (10)	JUDICIAL REVIEW (11)	APPEAL STAYS STERILIZATION ORDER (12)	MEDICAL PERSONNEL IMMUNE FROM LIABILITY (13)	OTHERS IMMUNE FROM LIABILITY (14)	GUARDIAN AD LITEM APPOINTED (15)
	Court (1)	Administrative (2)			Prevent Mentally Disabled Offspring (5)	Patient Unable to Care for Children (6)	Patient Would Require Public Aid (7)	Best Interests of Patient (8)	Other (9)						
OKLA. Stat. Ann. (West 1979 & Supp. 1981)		board of affairs 43A, §342	if desired or requested 43A, §342	43A, §342	43A, §341		43A, §341	promotes welfare of patient & society 43A, §342	may be sterilized w/o detriment to health 43A, §342	30 days 43A, §342	43A, §343	43A, §343	43A, §345	superintendent or other persons legally participating 43A, §345	if no guardian 43A, §342
OR. Rev. Stat. (1981)		state board of social protection 436.010		public defender 436.056	436.070(1)	436.070(1)			*fn.* 6 436.050	30 days to request rehearing 436.115	rehearing by board; after rehearing patient may seek judicial review *fn.* 7 436.125	436.115	436.035	applicant, board members, or other persons legally participating 436.035	
S.C. Code (Law. Co-op. 1976 & Supp. 1981)		department of health & environmental control 44-47-30	right to attend if desired 44-47-30	right to be represented by counsel 44-47-30	44-47-50(a)			promotes welfare of inmate & society 44-47-50(c)	may be sterilized w/o detriment to health 44-47-50(b)	30 days 44-47-50	44-47-60	44-47-60	44-47-100	superintendent or other persons legally participating 44-47-100	mandatory 44-47-30
UTAH Code Ann. (1978 & Supp. 1981) *fn.* 8	64-10-1			counsel appointed upon filing of petition of impecuniosity 64-10-3					a compelling state interest requires sterilization or asexualization 64-10-4		64-10-10	64-10-10	*fn.* 9	*fn.* 9	if no guardian 64-10-3
VA. Code (1978 & Supp. 1981)	54-325.11(1) 54-325.10			counsel appointed 54-325.10(2) 54-325.11(2)		54-325.12(A)(4)			*fn.* 10 54-325.12(A)	30 days 54-325.10(7) 54-325.11(7)			w/o negligence 54-325.14		
W. VA. Code (1980 & Supp. 1982)	27-16-1		right to be present 27-16-1	counsel appointed 26-16-1	27-16-1(2)	27-16-1(3)			no alternative contraceptive method feasible 27-16-1	60 days 27-16-1	27-16-2	27-16-2	except for negligence 27-16-3		

FOOTNOTES: TABLE 9.6

1. Ark. Stat. Ann. § 59-501(G)(2) (1971). Incompetent entitled to appear at hearing, unless two medical witnesses certify to the court that appearance would result in extreme danger to himself or others.

2. Id. § 59-501(A)(3) (Supp. 1981). It must be proved:

(i) he is incapable of caring for himself by reason of mental retardation, mental illness, imbecility, idiocy, or other mental incapacity; and

(ii) manifests sexual inclinations which make it probable that he will procreate children unless he be rendered incapable of procreation; and

(iii) there is no probability that his condition will improve so that he will become capable of caring for himself.

3. Colo. Rev. Stat. § 27-10.5-130(1) (Supp. 1981). If a mentally retarded person's competency to give consent to sterilization is denied by the doctor from whom he seeks sterilization, he may petition the court for sterilization. The only issue for the court's determination is the competency to give consent. If the court determines that the person is incompetent to give consent, the court shall order that no sterilization be performed.

4. Conn. Gen. Stat. Ann. § 45-78p(d) (West 1981). "Best interest":

(1) less drastic alternative contraceptive methods unworkable or inapplicable

(2) patient is capable of reproduction

(3) patient has capability and opportunity for sexual activity

(4) procreation would endanger the life or severely impair the health of the patient.

Even if the court finds sterilization to be in the patient's "best interests," he or she can still refuse sterilization if capable of understanding the nature of the refusal.

5. Del. Code Ann. tit. 16, § 5701(b). If the examination commission unanimously finds "procreation inadvisable," then with the consent of the department of health and social services, sterilization may be performed.

6. Or. Rev. Stat. § 436.050 (1981). The board must also find no probability that the condition of the patient will improve to such an extent as to eliminate the need for sterilization.

7. Id. § 436.125. If there is no consent after rehearing, the patient may seek judicial review. Failure to seek judicial review shall be conclusively deemed the equivalent of consent, as though expressly given.

8. Utah Code Ann. § 64-10-1 (1978). The procedure charted is for sterilization or asexualization.

9. Id. § 64-10-12. Performing, encouraging, or assisting in operation to destroy the power to procreate contrary to this chapter is a felony.

10. Va. Code § 54-325.12(A) (1978). It must be proven that:

(1) there is a current need for contraception and pregnancy would not usually be intended by such person if such person were competent and engaging in sexual activity under similar circumstances

(2) no reasonable alternative method of contraception exists

(3) the proposed method of sterilization conforms to standard medical practice and can be carried out without unreasonable risk to life and health of the patient.

11. W. Va. Code § 27-16-1 (1980). An initial hearing is held to determine whether circumstances warrant a continuation of incompetent status. If so, a hearing for sterilization is held.

Barbara A. Weiner

CHAPTER 10 Provider-Patient Relations: Confidentiality and Liability

Unlike the other chapters of this book, which address the rights of the mentally disabled within institutions or in the community, this chapter focuses on interests of both the patient and the therapist which arise out of the therapeutic relationship: confidentiality and the liability of mental health professionals. Each area has become more complicated during the past decade, and each is of vital concern to both the provider and the patient.

Our society has increasingly come to recognize the importance of privacy and confidentiality generally. Concern about who has access to treatment and habilitation records, particularly those of the mentally disabled, has heightened awareness of the importance of confidentiality. The stigma that still attaches to those who are labeled "mentally ill" or "mentally retarded" has required more vigilance on the part of mental health professionals to be accurate in what is recorded and to be careful about to whom and under what circumstances information is released. The section on confidentiality highlights the state of the law and current issues, with particular attention to the laws of privilege.

The liability of the mental health professional as a result of his interactions with the disabled is an issue of great concern to therapists. Fears of being sued as a result of services they have provided burden many mental health professionals and also other health care providers. New areas of liability, such as those resulting from the duty to warn, have increased mental health professionals' nervousness about their work. This section of the chapter highlights the areas of potential liability.

I. CONFIDENTIALITY

A. The Importance of Confidentiality

"As asepsis is to surgery, so is confidentiality to psychiatry," testified one mental health professional before the United States Congress.[1] Considered the *sine qua non* for successful psychiatric treatment, confidentiality is essential to the therapeutic relationship.[2] More than two decades ago Goldstein and Katz described the problems that would be created by a lack of confidentiality:

> Even under optimum conditions of confidentiality, it is difficult for the patient to confide his thoughts and feelings to another person. If to that difficulty is added the possibility of disclosure at some future date, it can be expected that he will not speak freely and that his concern about the other implications of treatment will be reinforced.[3]

It is even clearer that once in treatment, all patients would be affected by the absence of confidentiality. Every person, however well motivated, has to overcome resistances to therapeutic exploration. These resistances seek support from every possible source, to which could be added the possibility of unwanted disclosure. At best, the possibility of disclosure will prolong treatment; at worst, it will make thorough exploration of emotional conflicts impossible.[4] The patient's statements may reveal to his therapist much more than he intends or realizes. As Guttmacher and Weihofen have observed: "The psychiatric patient confides more utterly than anyone else in the world. He exposes to his therapist not only what his words directly express; he lays bare his en-

1. Citizens Privacy Protection Act: Hearings Before the Subcommittee on the Constitution of the [Senate] Committee on the Judiciary [on S. 3162 and S. 3164], 95th Cong., 2d Sess. 223, 255 (1978) (Testimony of Jerome S. Beigler, M.D., Chairman of the American Psychiatric Association, Committee on Confidentiality, Aug. 22, 1978). Beigler explained:

> Just as a surgeon cannot operate unless he has optimum aseptic conditions without a potential for infection, similarly, a psychiatrist cannot work unless he has the absolute confidentiality of the patient, because some of the things that a patient says are very personal and could not be disclosed unless he were assured of the confidentiality.

Id. at 226.

2. Group for the Advancement of Psychiatry, Confidentiality and Privileged Communication in the Practice of Psychiatry 85 (formulated by the Committee on Psychiatry and the Law) Rep. No. 45, 1960 [hereinafter cited as GAP Report].

3. Goldstein & Katz, Psychiatrist-Patient Privilege: The GAP Proposal and the Connecticut Statute, 118 Am. J. Psychiatry 733, 734 (1962).

4. *Id.* at 734-35.

tire self, his dreams, his fantasies, his sins, and his shame."[5]

Often those who need mental health services are particularly reluctant to seek professional help. In part, this stems from the stigma attached to being labeled "mentally ill" or "emotionally disturbed." Many of those who recognize their need for mental health services also recognize the possible negative career, social, and economic consequences of seeking that assistance if it became generally known. These consequences can include inability to obtain a job or a promotion, inability to obtain life insurance, and social ostracism. Additionally, a history of having been treated for mental illness can have adverse consequences in litigation in which the person is a plaintiff, a defendant, or a witness.[6] As Jerome Beigler, one of the nation's leading advocates of confidentiality for the mentally disabled, has stated:

> Because the material disclosed to a psychiatrist includes information relevant to a patient's relationships to the whole outside world, the psychiatrist becomes the repository of information valuable to many third parties, such as insurance carriers, legal adversaries, law-enforcement agencies, and employers. To the extent that such information is disclosed without the patient's consent, the reliability of the physician-patient relationship is eroded, and the ability of a physician to help his or her patient is impaired.[7]

Understandably, the person entering into a therapeutic relationship expects that what he reveals to the therapist will be kept secret. Notwithstanding its being critically important, confidentiality in the mental health setting is never absolute. Under certain circumstances, the law demands that the therapist subordinate the confidentiality entrusted to him.[8] In other instances, the professional ethics of the therapist himself may require him to reveal information.[9]

B. Privileged Communications

"Privilege statutes" are the most common manifestations of the states' concern with protecting information revealed by the patient to the therapist. To encourage full disclosure to a therapist, these statutes provide that what has been disclosed in the therapeutic setting cannot be revealed without the patient's consent. However, "privileged communication" refers only to information that is at issue in litigation.[10] The matter of privilege arises only when the bearer of the privileged communication is asked a question that would cause him to divulge that information. These statutes do not govern access by third parties in the nonlitigation setting, nor are they absolute in the litigation contest; each statute provides exceptions as to when information revealed during the therapeutic relationship may be revealed in the courtroom.

1. Development of Privilege Laws

The earliest and most widely accepted privilege rests in the attorney-client relationship and dates back to the 1500s. Initially, the justification for the confidentiality of this relationship was that the honor and oath of the barrister or solicitor forbade disclosure of the client's secrets.[11] While this justification—which is really only an assertion—was rejected in the 1700s on the premise that the truth-seeking nature of judicial proceedings could not tolerate the withholding of information, a new theory evolved to support the need for privilege. This was that lawyers cannot effectively represent their clients unless fully advised of all facts and that without a privilege available to foreclose public disclosure the client would not be willing to divulge to his attorney all relevant information.[12] The attorney-client privilege, which is the only privilege recognized by the common law,[13] today is statutorily protected in every state.

In addition to the attorney-client privilege, all states have recognized the priest-penitent privilege, which is rooted in the need for secrecy in religious confessions.[14] This privilege has been made applicable to all clergy and is based on the First Amendment right to the free exercise of religion.[15] Furthermore, all states also recognize a marital privilege, which prohibits one spouse from testifying against the other except when one is suing or has committed a criminal act against the other. This privilege is based on the concept that open communication is essential for promoting marital harmony.[16]

2. The Physician-Patient Privilege

Initially, the Hippocratic Oath prohibited physicians only from voluntarily revealing the secrets of their patients. Were a physician to be called to testify in a court

5. M.S. Guttmacher & H. Weihofen, Psychiatry and the Law 272 (1952).

6. Special Article Series: Therapeutic Confidentiality, 2 MDLR 337, 338 (1977); J. Robitscher, The Powers of Psychiatry (1980).

7. J.S. Beigler, Statement of the American Psychiatric Association, Before the U.S. House of Representatives, Committee on Government Operations, Subcommittee on Government Information and Individual Rights (Apr. 9, 1979), *reprinted in* 79 N.Y. State J. Med. 2088 (Dec. 1979).

8. See in this chapter § II B, The Duty to Warn, *infra*.

9. *Id.*

10. McCormick's Handbook of the Law of Evidence, § 72 (E.W. Cleary 2d ed. 1975) [hereinafter cited as McCormick's Handbook].

11. M. Radin, The Privilege of Confidential Communication Between Lawyer and Client, 16 Calif. L. Rev. 487 (1927).

12. 8 J. Wigmore, Evidence in Trials at Common Law, § 229 (J.T. McNaughton rev. ed. 1961).

13. *Id.*

14. *Id.* § 2394 & 2395r.

15. *Id.* See also § 2395 (Supp. 1981).

16. McCormick's Handbook, *supra* note 10, at 161–62.

proceeding, he would in that setting be required to reveal the confidences entrusted to him, the Oath notwithstanding. Thus, in the first known English case involving the testimony of a physician who raised the issue of whether he was required to disclose his professional confidences, it was stated:

> If a surgeon was voluntarily to reveal these secrets, to be sure, he would be guilty of a breach of honor and of great indiscretion; but to give that information in a court of justice which by the law of the land he is bound to do, will never be imputed to him as any indiscretion whatsoever.[17]

Today, this common law view has largely been consigned to history, inasmuch as 34 states and the District of Columbia have adopted statutes that guarantee invocation of the physician-patient privilege in judicial settings.[18] Additionally, with the exceptions of Rhode Island and South Carolina, the remaining states at least make provision for a narrower psychiatrist-patient privilege or a psychotherapist-patient privilege.[19] Both the general physician-patient statutes and the narrower laws typically reject an absolutist position; they usually contain specific exceptions abrogating the availability of the privilege in specified circumstances.[20]

3. Privilege Laws: Criteria and Justification

At the heart of the American legal system is the concept that through the adversarial process, ultimately culminating in a trial, the full truth will emerge and justice will prevail. Privilege laws, by insulating some information from disclosure no matter how relevant or even critical it may be in a given litigation setting, obviously conflict with this quest for truth. These laws, then, are the result of a balancing process, the legislatures having determined that the protection of certain relationships is more important than an unbridled quest for the accurate outcome in judicial proceedings. Not surprisingly, the merits of privilege laws, the appropriate criteria to be utilized in their drafting, and their proper limits all have occasioned much debate.[21] Thus, for example, a recent major preoccupation of several professional groups including nonpsychiatric mental health professionals,[22] newsmen,[23] and accountants[24] has been to have privilege laws expanded to include them.

The criteria often cited as determining when a privilege is justified were enunciated in the early 1940s by Dean John Wigmore:

> (1) The communications must originate in a *confidence* that they will not be disclosed.
> (2) This element of *confidentiality must be essential* to the full and satisfactory maintenance of the relation between the parties.
> (3) The *relation* must be one which in the opinion of the community ought to be sedulously *fostered*.
> (4) The *injury* that would inure to the relation by the disclosure of the communications must be *greater than the benefit* thereby gained for the correct disposal of the litigation.[25]

There is a general consensus that the attorney-client and priest-penitent relationships satisfy these criteria. There is some dispute, however, as to whether the criteria are met in the context of the physician-patient relationship.

The justification for the privilege is the special need for privacy inherent in the physician-patient setting. This position has been stated as follows:

> Patients depend on doctors for special counseling and personal attention, and they need a zone of privacy to seek this help. Because medicine involves intimate facts about one's body, health, and mind, the privacy of this treatment and counseling should be protected. The unhappy prospect of disease, sickness, and injury should not be aggravated by a rule that freely allows public disclosure in court papers and open trials of medical procedures and the facts surrounding medical treatment.[26]

Wigmore, the preeminent expert in evidence law, took a negative position, as have others.[27] Wigmore maintained that illnesses were generally publicly known and disclosable without shame (except in the case of

17. The Duchess of Kingston Trial, 20 How. St. Trials 355 (1776), which was a bigamy case.

18. See table 10.1; see also Shuman & Weiner, The Privilege Study: An Empirical Examination of the Psychotherapist-Patient Privilege, 60 N.C.L. Rev. 893, 926 (1982).

19. See table 10.1.

20. See in this chapter § 1 C, Exceptions to the Psychotherapist-Patient Privilege, *infra*. In contrast, the attorney-client and priest-penitent privileges, which exist in every state, do not contain exceptions.

21. See, e.g., Fisher, The Psychotherapeutic Professions and the Law of Privileged Communications, 10 Wayne L. Rev. 609 (1964); Paul, Confidentiality and Patients' Records: Balancing the Interests of Society and the Individual, 7 J. Psychiatry & L. 49 (1979); Slovenko, Psychiatry and a Second Look at the Medical Privilege, 6 Wayne L. Rev. 175 (1960); GAP Report, *supra* note 2.

22. Delgado, Underprivileged Communications: Extension of the Psychotherapist-Patient Privilege to Patients of Psychiatric Social Workers, 61 Calif. L. Rev. 1050 (1973); Geiser & Rheingold, Psychology and the Legal Process: Testimonial Privileged Communications, 19 Am. Psychologist 831 (1967).

23. Branzburg v. Hayes, 408 U.S. 665 (1972); Marburger, More Protection for the Press: The Third Circuit Expands the Fair Report Privilege, 43 U. Pitt. L. Rev. 1143 (1982).

24. D.Y. Causey, Duties and Liabilities of the CPA 150 (rev. ed. 1976); Note, Protecting the Auditor's Work Product from the IRS, 1982 Duke L.J. 604; Robinson & Stoltenberg, Privilege and Accountants' Workpapers, 68 A.B.A. J. 1248 (1982).

25. 8 Wigmore, *supra* note 12, § 2285 at 527 (Supp. 1981) (emphasis in original).

26. Saltzburg, Privileges and Professionals: Lawyers and Psychiatrists, 66 Va. L. Rev. 597, 618-19 (1980).

27. Wigmore, *supra* note 12, § 2285 at 527 (Supp. 1981).

"loathsome disease") and that the doctor-patient relationship thus did not give rise to a nondisclosure privilege. Moreover, he argued that confidentiality was not essential to the relationship: as a practical matter patients rarely refrained from disclosing information because of fear of revelation by the doctor in a courtroom.[28] By contrast, the attorney-client relationship often arose for the very reason that a client wanted to avert, was involved in, or anticipated litigation. Finally, Wigmore contended that the injury to the physician-patient relationship deriving from disclosure did not outweigh the social benefit to be gained by having full access to all evidence in the litigation setting.

There are other considerations besides Wigmore's criteria. It has been pointed out that few patients are even aware of a confidentiality interest when they visit their doctors, and even if they were, few would lie to their doctors out of fear that the information given would be used as evidence in court.[29] As early as 1906 legal commentators questioned whether the privilege was essential for encouraging medical treatment.[30] Others have simply contended that the privilege interferes with the proper conduct of litigation by obstructing the quest for truth[31] — a position that, of course, would wipe out all provider-client privileges. Revealingly, the Advisory Committee on the Federal Rules of Evidence has refused to adopt a general doctor-patient privilege as a rule of evidence for the federal courts.[32]

While the wisdom of general physician-patient privilege laws is thus subject to open dispute, there is greater agreement that a privilege for communications between the patient and his therapist does meet the Wigmore criteria and is necessary for encouraging persons to enter into and remain in psychotherapy.

4. The Psychotherapist-Patient Privilege

(a) The need for a special privilege

People today commonly seek the assistance of the mental health professional both for transitory situational problems such as marital difficulties and depression arising from the death of a close friend or relative, the end of a significant relationship, or loss of a job and for treatment of major mental illnesses such as schizophrenia. Yet, though it is much more socially acceptable than it was in the past to seek mental health services, for many people there still is a stigma attached to needing this type of help, even for less serious situational problems. When full-scale psychiatric or institutional treatment is sought, the stakes are even higher, since the adverse consequences of disclosure of serious mental illness can be particularly severe. Confidentiality, then, is in most instances a necessary corollary to therapy. Moreover, from the therapist's perspective, confidence in the possibility of helping patients, and hence the efficacy of the therapy, is totally dependent on being able to assure patients that what they reveal will be kept confidential.[33]

As a result of the increased demand for remedial services for various mental or emotional problems, there has been a considerable expansion in the types of professionals who provide them. Initially, such services could be obtained only from psychiatrists and clinical psychologists. Today, social workers, psychiatric nurses, clergymen, and school guidance counselors may deal with psychological problems as a formal part of their role. Insofar as they do so, a strong argument can be made that at least for confidentiality purposes they should be considered mental health professionals along with psychiatrists and psychologists. As other professionals have assumed counseling and therapeutic roles, there has been a move to pass privilege statutes, which were originally designed just for the psychiatrist-patient relationship, extending coverage to a much broader group of providers.

In a detailed analysis of whether the psychotherapist privilege meets the Wigmore criteria,[34] Slovenko has argued:

> (1) First of all, communications to a psychiatrist during the course of treatment are of a confidential and secret nature. The very essence of psychotherapy is confidential personal revelations about matters which the patient is and should be normally reluctant to discuss. . . .
>
> The patient's communications to the psychiatrist always originate in a confidence that they will not be divulged. . . .
>
> (2) The inviolability of that confidence is essential to the achievement of the purpose of the relationship. . . .
>
> (3) The psychiatrist-patient relationship is one that should be fostered. . . .
>
> (4) The information if revealed would produce far few-

28. *Id.*
29. Saltzburg, *supra* note 26, at 617.
30. Purrington, An Abused Privilege, 6 Colum. L. Rev. 388, 396 (1906).
31. Chafee, Privileged Communications: Is Justice Served or Obstructed by Closing the Doctor's Mouth on the Witness Stand? 52 Yale L.J. 607, 616 (1943).
32. Proposed Fed. R. Evid. 504 advisory committee note, 56 F.R.D. 183, 240, 242 (1972).
33. See, e.g., Beigler, Psychiatric Confidentiality and the American Legal System: An Ethical Conflict, *in* Psychiatric Ethics 224 (S. Bloch & P. Chodoff eds. 1981); GAP Report, *supra* note 2, at 92; Goldstein & Katz, *supra* note 3, at 734.
34. Although Wigmore himself had only caustic criticism for the medical privilege, he never addressed the issue of psychotherapist privilege. See also Foster, An Overview of Confidentiality and Privilege, 4 J. Psychiatry & L. 393, 397 (1976).

er benefits to justice than the consequent injury to the entire field of psychiatry.[35]

These arguments are difficult to refute. Today, only Wigmore's fourth criterion, that is, consideration of whether the injury from disclosure will be greater than the benefit gained for the litigation process, generates much discussion. While it has been argued that "[t]reatment of the mentally ill is too important, and the assurance of confidentiality too central to it, to risk jeopardizing the whole because of the relevance of some patients' statements to some legal proceedings,"[36] the countervailing viewpoint, that is, that psychiatric information is particularly important in some legal proceedings, is also persuasive. These competing considerations have resulted in exceptions being grafted onto the privilege laws.

(b) Various forms of privilege statutes

Privilege statutes relevant to our discussion take one of four forms: (1) general physician-patient privilege, (2) psychiatrist-patient privilege, (3) psychologist-patient privilege, and (4) psychotherapist-patient privilege.

(1) General physician-patient privilege□□The physician-patient privilege is the most common source of protection against disclosure of psychotherapeutic communications in the absence of specific privilege statutes for psychiatrists or psychotherapists. It applies, however, only to communications made to physicians and not to other types of mental health professionals. Since psychiatrists are physicians, this privilege does cover them and their patients. The statutes, operative in 34 states and the District of Columbia,[37] generally provide that a physician shall not disclose any of his patient's communications that were necessary to enable the physician to treat the patient. Some more broadly protect any communications made in the course of treatment.[38] Although courts generally do not make distinctions based on whether the privilege is invoked by a general physician or by a psychiatrist, a few cases have extended the reach of the statutes to communication between any *psychotherapist* and his patient.[39]

(2) Psychiatrist-patient privilege□□The psychiatrist-patient privilege is specifically recognized in the statutes of at least 7 states.[40] In most of the remaining jurisdictions the protection in such communication is subsumed under the rubric of the general physician-patient privilege.[41] Typically, the specific states protect communications between the patient and his psychiatrist from disclosure without the patient's permission, except in certain circumstances. A good example of the general coverage and the exceptions is the Kentucky statute:

> (2) Except as hereinafter provided, in civil and criminal cases, in proceedings preliminary thereto, and in legislative and administrative proceedings, a patient, or his authorized representative, has a privilege to refuse to disclose, and to prevent a witness from disclosing, communications relating to diagnosis or treatment of the patient's mental condition between patient and psychiatrist, or between members of the patient's family and the psychiatrist, or between any of the foregoing and such persons who participate, under the supervision of the psychiatrist, in the accomplishment of the objectives of diagnosis or treatment.
>
> (3) There shall be no privilege for any relevant communications under this section:
>
> (a) When a psychiatrist, in the course of diagnosis or treatment of the patient, determines that the patient is in need of admission to or commitment to a hospital for care of the patient's mental illness;
>
> (b) If a judge finds that the patient, after having been informed that the communications would not be privileged, has made communications to a psychiatrist in the course of a psychiatric examination ordered by the court provided that such communications shall be admissible only on issues involving the patient's mental condition;
>
> (c) In a civil proceeding in which the patient introduces his mental condition as an element of his claim or defense, or, after the patient's death, when said condition is introduced by any party claiming or defending through or as a beneficiary of the patient, and the judge finds that it is more important to the interests of justice that the communication be disclosed than that the relationship between the patient and psychiatrist be protected.[42]

(3) Psychologist-patient privilege□□A specific psychologist-patient privilege has been adopted in 26 states and the District of Columbia.[43] In 9 other states, the psychologist is covered under a psychotherapist privilege statute.[44] South Carolina is the only state having no confidentiality provision at all for either medical or mental health communications. In some states the psychologist privilege appears to be as broad as the attorney privilege. For example, Georgia provides:

35. Slovenko, *supra* note 21, at 184–92.
36. Goldstein & Katz, *supra* note 3, at 735.
37. See table 10.1 and Shuman & Weiner, *supra* note 18.
38. See, e.g., Ark. Stat. Ann. § 28-1001, Unif. R. Evid. 503 (1979); Colo. Rev. Stat. § 13-90-107(d) (1973); Idaho Code § 9-203(4) (Supp. 1981); Wash. Rev. Code Ann. § 5.60.060(4) (Supp. 1981).
39. See Horan & Guerrini, Developing Legal Trends in Psychiatric Malpractice, 9 J. Psychiatry & L. (1981); also Annot., 44 A.L.R.3d 24–162 (1972), for a very thorough discussion of privilege as it relates to psychotherapy.
40. Alabama, Connecticut, Georgia, Kentucky, Maryland, Michigan, and Tennessee.
41. See table 10.1, cols. 1 & 2.
42. Ky. Rev. Stat. Ann. § 421.215(2) & (3) (Michie 1972).
43. See table 10.1, col. 1.
44. *Id.*

> The confidential relations and communications between a licensed applied psychologist and client are placed on the same basis as those provided by law between attorney and client; and nothing in this chapter shall be construed to require any such privileged communication to be disclosed.[45]

Psychologist privilege provisions are usually located in psychologist licensing provisions. They are typically qualified, often in different parts of the state's law such as the evidence rules, by three common exceptions to the privilege: for civil commitment, court-ordered examinations, and the patient-litigant.[46]

(4) Psychotherapist-patient privilege□□Thirteen states have privilege provisions specifically applicable to the psychotherapist-patient relationship.[47] In most of these states the psychotherapist is defined to include psychiatrists and licensed psychologists.[48] As with other privilege statutes, the three common exceptions apply.[49]

In addition to these formally designated "psychotherapist privilege" statutes, some states also have privilege laws specifically identifying other providers of mental health services. At least 8 states now recognize a privilege for social workers.[50] Some states specifically include nurses,[51] while others recognize marriage and family counselors[52] and school counselors.[53] Probably the broadest definition of a therapist is contained in the Illinois statute:

> a psychiatrist, physician, psychologist, social worker, or nurse providing mental health or developmental disabilities services or any other person not prohibited by law from providing such services or from holding himself out as a therapist if the recipient reasonably believes that such person is permitted to do so.[54]

This definition could encompass pastoral counselors, school counselors, and all those who have been trained to provide mental health services. The extension of the privilege to these nontraditional mental health professionals is premised on the perception that they are all performing a therapeutic function and that the privilege is designed to protect therapeutic relationships, distinctions based on status notwithstanding.

There may be some danger of abuse of the privilege by those who cloak themselves in the legal garb of therapeutic relationships. There is some risk in expanding the privilege so far as to unduly undermine the truth-seeking function of the judicial process. Irrespective of the titles or credentials of service providers, there is a need to determine whether an individual claiming the privilege is indeed performing a true therapeutic role. The objective of the law should be to define the privilege as precisely as possible in terms of the function performed and the services rendered,[55] with a concurrent concern for the patient's expectation of confidentiality.

5. *Who Holds the Privilege*

The right of privilege protects the interest of the patient and is designed to promote the seeking of mental health services rather than the quest for truth in the litigation process. Its goal is to encourage open disclosure in treatment while preventing unwanted disclosure in the courtroom. The privilege generally belongs only to the patient, who is the one to decide whether it will be exercised or waived:

> [T]he patient's secret and potentially self-damaging communications are regarded as if they were his possession, like material things that can be owned (for example, money). Thus, his "property-right" is protected by tradition and law. By the same token, since the "secrets" are the patient's, he may give them away, should he wish to.[56]

While in theory patient's control seems appropriate, in fact the merits and drawbacks of such control are complicated and debatable. It may be psychologically detrimental, for example, for a patient to learn of the contents of his therapist's report. Yet, unless he is apprised of the information, he will not be able to make an informed decision to assert or to waive the privilege. Whether detrimental to him or not, it remains the case that in most instances it is the patient who is the one who can assert or waive the privilege.

Most states specifically define who has the right to assert the privilege, often including a provision for the transfer of the privilege to a guardian executor when the privilege holder has been declared incompetent or has died.[57] While the potentially harmful effect of a waiver

45. Ga. Code Ann. § 84-3118 (1981).
46. See table 10.1.
47. See *id.*, col. 1, e.g., Arkansas, California, Delaware, Florida, Illinois, Maine, Massachusetts, New Mexico, North Dakota, Oklahoma, Oregon, South Dakota, and Texas.
48. The majority of these states have adopted proposed Rule 504 of the Federal Rules of Evidence. Rule 504 was never enacted by Congress, the consensus of the legislators being that state law should govern on these issues.
49. See, e.g., Del. Unif. R. of Evid. 503.
50. See Delgado, *supra* note 22, which argues why privilege should be extended to social workers. See table 10.1.
51. See table 10.1.
52. See, e.g., Cal. Evid. Code § 1010(e) (West Supp. 1985).
53. See, e.g., Ark. Stat. Ann. § 71-5214 (1979 & Supp. 1981); Ky. Rev. Stat. Ann. § 421.216 (Michie Supp. 1984); S.D. Codified Laws Ann. § 19-13-21.1 & -21.2 (1979).
54. Ill. Ann. Stat. ch. 91½, § 802(9) (Smith-Hurd Supp. 1984).
55. Louisell, The Psychologist in Today's Legal World: Part II, 41 Minn. L. Rev. 731 (1957).
56. Szasz, The Problem of Privacy in Training Analysis, 25 Psychiatry 195, 196 (1962).
57. Many privilege statutes will permit the guardian or legal representative to exert the privilege.

argues for deeming a waiver effective only when the patient voluntarily and affirmatively gives up his privilege, in *City of San Francisco v. Superior Court of San Francisco*[58] the court held that the statutory physician-patient privilege was waived if the patient did not claim it.[59] According to this decision, a waiver may occur by virtue of inaction on the patient's part. By contrast, in situations where the patient was not a party to the immediate action or was not present to assert the privilege, some courts have asserted the privilege sua sponte on behalf of the patient.[60]

It has been urged that the psychotherapist-patient privilege should belong to the therapist as well as the patient to assure that the patient's best interests are fully protected.[61] This position received much attention as a result of two California cases in which psychiatrists refused to reveal information concerning former patients who were involved in litigation.[62] In *In re Lifschutz*[63] the psychiatrist refused to release any records or answer any questions about a patient he had seen in therapy ten years earlier. During the course of the litigation, a personal injury case, the patient had revealed that he had been treated by Lifschutz, but he neither expressly asserted nor waived the confidentiality privilege. Lifschutz, who was held in contempt for refusing to obey a court order to disclose requested information, made three arguments in his appeal. He contended that the order infringed on his own constitutional right of privacy. Additionally, he argued that requiring a psychotherapist to reveal confidences would unconstitutionally impair the practice of his profession. This claim was based on two concepts: (1) the impairment was so severe as to constitute an unconstitutional "taking" of a valuable property right, that is, the doctor's right to practice psychotherapy, and (2) compelled disclosure of any psychotherapeutic communication would render his continued practice of psychotherapy impossible and thus would restrict the realm of available treatment. Finally, Lifschutz maintained that he was denied equal protection of the laws because the California clergyman-penitent privilege, unlike the psychotherapist-patient privilege, was absolute.

The California Supreme Court rejected all of Lifschutz's arguments, arguing that "[t]he psychotherapist . . . cannot assert his patient's privilege if that privilege has been waived or if the communication in question falls within the statutory exceptions to the privilege."[64] Here, by his having raised the issue of pain and suffering in a personal injury case—an issue involving his mental state—the former patient fell within the patient-litigant exception.[65]

Thus far, arguments for extending the psychotherapist privilege to the therapist have met with favorable response only in Illinois, where a confidentiality provision has been enacted providing that "a recipient, and a therapist on behalf and in the interest of a recipient, has the privilege to refuse to the disclose and to prevent the disclosure of the recipient's records or communications."[66] One benefit of the right of the therapist to assert the privilege is that the therapist can protect the patient who inadvertently waives the privilege.[67] However, the Illinois statute does not give the therapist an absolute privilege: after an in-camera inspection the court may force disclosure when the patient has raised the issue of his mental health in civil litigation.[68] Thus, with the narrow exception of Illinois, the law recognizes the privilege as only belonging to the patient.

C. Exceptions to the Therapist-Patient Privilege

As indicated, each state that grants a privilege also specifies exceptions to the privilege. Most commonly these exceptions arise in the context of suspected child abuse cases, when civil commitment is sought and when the patient raises his mental condition as a claim or defense in a civil or criminal proceeding. Additionally, there is no privilege when a court-ordered examination occurs and when the courts are called upon to determine the validity of wills. Arguably, these exceptions can go so far as to practically swallow up the privilege. Slovenko maintains that "[i]n every jurisdiction, the exceptions and implied waivers are so many and so broad that it is difficult to imagine a case in which the privilege applies."[69] This section will set forth the most common exceptions to the privilege laws, except for those arising in criminal cases, which are discussed in chapter 12.

1. Child Abuse

Most states by statute require that professionals who deal with children report any cases of suspected child

58. 231 P.2d 26 (Cal. 1951).
59. *Id.* at 29.
60. Annot., 44 A.L.R.3d 24, 57 (1972).
61. Note, The Psychiatrist-Patient Privilege in Illinois, 10 Loy. U. Chi. L.J. 55 (1979) [hereinafter cited as Note, Psychiatrist-Patient Privilege]; R. Slovenko & G.L. Usdin, Psychotherapy, Confidentiality and Privileged Communication (1966).
62. *In re* Lifschutz, 467 P.2d 557, 85 Cal. Rptr. 829 (1970), and Caesar v. Mountanos, 542 F.2d 1064 (9th Cir. 1976), *cert. denied*, 430 U.S. 954 (1976).
63. 467 P.2d 557, 85 Cal. Rptr. 829 (1970).
64. *Id.* at 566.
65. *Id.* at 567. See also Caesar v. Mountanos, 542 F.2d 1064 (9th Cir. 1976).
66. Ill. Ann. Stat. ch. 91½, § 810(a) (Smith-Hurd Supp. 1984).
67. Note, Psychiatrist-Patient Privilege, *supra* note 61, at 537.
68. Ill. Ann. Stat. ch. 91½, § 810(b) (Smith-Hurd Supp. 1984).
69. Slovenko, Psychotherapist-Patient Testimonial Privilege: A Picture of Misguided Hope, 23 Cath. U.L. Rev. 649, 652 (1974).

abuse and/or neglect.[70] The duty to report suspected child abuse is imposed on the psychotherapist in 42 states and the District of Columbia.[71] In most of these jurisdictions immunity from suit for "good faith" reporting accompanies these reporting requirements.[72]

For the therapist who is treating an abusive or neglectful parent, whose problems may have led him to seek therapy, this reporting requirement may seem countertherapeutic. Moreover, particular difficulties may arise when the therapist believes that intervention by the state probably will not lead to a better situation for the child, given that such intervention is often at best a mixed blessing.[73] The therapist may be of the view that the best hope for the child is to provide help for the parent and that such help can be given only if the parent is free to share with his therapist his thoughts, fears, and actions. Moreover, the therapist might argue that others will be in a position to report the abuse—that is, family members, neighbors, the pediatrician, or the school—while he is the only one in a position to help the parent overcome his or her problems and thereby bring an end to the abusive behavior itself. Obviously, these difficulties admit of no clear resolution. There is no reported case in which a court has been called upon to essay the task of resolving the conflicting interests at stake.

2. Civil Commitment

Most hospitalizations for mental illness, if one includes those to private facilities, are voluntary. However, in a minority of instances an individual will either not recognize or not admit the seriousness of his illness and will resist hospitalization. In such situations civil commitment proceedings may be instituted.[74] Often, the person most knowledgeable about the patient's illness and his need for hospitalization will be his therapist. For this reason, in approximately half the states and the District of Columbia the general privilege may be overridden in cases where civil commitment is sought.[75] Delaware's law is typical: "There is no privilege under this rule for communications relevant to an issue in proceedings to hospitalize the patient for mental illness, if the physician or psychotherapist in the course of diagnosis or treatment has determined that the patient is in need of hospitalization."[76]

From the therapist's professional perspective this exception to the patient-therapist privilege should be easy to accept. His breach of the confidential relationship is undertaken to serve, rather than undermine, the patient's best interests. Additionally, it is likely that the therapist will not have to reveal many, if any, confidences at the civil commitment hearing. Instead, he will be able to rely on his general observations and examination of the patient. In this way the therapist can try to obtain for the patient the level of services he needs while still maintaining the therapeutic relationship. Of course, the patient may not always appreciate the therapist's claimed concern for his best interests. Nonetheless, the civil commitment exception is, at bottom, justifiable in terms of society's needs, the patient's interests, and the therapist's professional ethics.

3. Court-ordered Examinations

There are many times when courts, in both civil or criminal matters, seek the expert advice of a mental health professional—usually a psychiatrist or psychologist—as to an issue raised at trial. Such instances can involve evaluations of the litigants as well as of witnesses. For example, a court may be interested in assuring that a witness is emotionally stable before deciding whether to permit his testimony. Likewise, a court may need to determine the extent of emotional damage in a personal injury claim, or the best placement for a child who is the subject of a custody dispute, or the competency of a defendant to stand trial in a criminal proceeding.

Approximately half the states set forth an exception to the psychotherapist-patient privilege for court-ordered examinations.[77] Typical of this exception is the one enacted in New Mexico:

> If the judge orders an examination of the mental or emotional condition of the patient, communications made in the course thereof are not privileged under this rule with respect to the particular purpose for which the examination is ordered unless the judge orders otherwise.[78]

70. Besharov, The Legal Aspects of Reporting Known and Suspected Child Abuse and Neglect, 23 Vill. L. Rev. 458 (1977–78); Butz, Lawyering for the Abused Child: "You Can't Go Home Again," 29 U.C.L.A. L. Rev. 1216 (1982); Fraser, A Glance at the Past, a Gaze at the Present, a Glimpse at the Future: A Critical Analysis of the Development of Child Abuse Reporting Statutes, 54 Chi.-Kent L. Rev. 641 (1977–78); Note, The Child's Right to "Life, Liberty, and the Pursuit of Happiness": Suits by Children Against Parents for Abuse, Neglect, and Abandonment, 34 Rutgers L. Rev. 154 (1981); Note, Unequal and Inadequate Protection Under the Law: State Child Abuse Statutes, 50 Geo. Wash. L. Rev. 243 (1982).

71. See table 10.1, col. 3. Exceptions are Alaska, Arizona, Florida, Rhode Island, Texas, and Vermont.

72. See table 10.1, col. 5. J. Monahan, Predicting Violent Behavior: An Assessment of Clinical Techniques (1981).

73. J. Goldstein, A. Freud, & A.J. Solnit, Before the Best Interests of the Child 25 (1979).

74. See in this book ch. 2, Involuntary Institutionalization, for a full discussion of the standards for civil commitment and the right of the person when commitment is sought.

75. See table 10.1, col. 9.

76. Del. Code Ann. tit. 16, Unif. R. Evid. 503(d)(1) (1981).

77. See table 10.1, col. 8.

78. N.M. Stat. Ann. R. Evid. 504(d)(2) (1983), which was modeled on the proposed federal rules and adopted by numerous states.

With or without the exemption, the danger of disclosure of confidential information is limited, since court-ordered examinations typically will not be conducted by the individual's treating therapist. Additionally, good practice requires the examiner to notify the person that the evaluation is being conducted pursuant to a court order and that statements made during the examination may be contained in the report to the court or revealed during testimony.[79] Thus, a court-ordered examination will not usually present a true violation of the therapeutic relationship, since it is unlikely that any relationship would have formed.

4. Patient-Litigant Exception

Introduction into litigation of a claim or defense of mental or emotional illness may subject to disclosure any previous treatment undergone by the claimant or defendant. This would be the patient-litigant exception to the therapist-patient privilege of confidentiality. Twenty-two states and the District of Columbia specifically provide for this exception.[80] Typical is Delaware's statute:

> There is no privilege under this rule as to a communication relevant to an issue of the physical, mental or emotional condition of the patient in any proceeding in which he relies upon the condition as an element of his claim or defense or, after the patient's death, in any proceeding in which any party relies upon the condition as an element of his claim or defense.[81]

Even in those states that have not enacted a specific patient-litigant statutory exception, the courts will usually find that an exception to confidentiality exists, reasoning that by raising the issue of mental or emotional condition the claimant has brought into question his mental health and that justice requires making all relevant facts known.

The patient-litigant exception raises real problems. "When a person becomes a psychiatric patient, he potentially impairs his prior legal rights," observes Beigler.[82] Fear of disclosure may cause potential litigants to avoid seeking legal redress, even when they have justifiable claims, or to acquiesce to otherwise unwarranted settlements out of fear of public disclosure of the past treatment.

When the patient-litigant exception is raised, it does not automatically follow that all previous records will be admitted into the proceeding. The court will admit as evidence only what is relevant or material to the case. Disclosure is required only as to the mental condition put into issue; no other aspects of the patient-litigant's personality will have to be revealed. However, the burden rests on the patient to show that a given communication is not directly related to the issue he has tendered to the court. He will have to reveal to the court to some extent the nature of the psychotherapeutic communications if he is to convince the court that they are not at issue in the matter before it.

The five most common occasions in which the patient-litigant exception comes into play are: (1) child custody disputes, (2) malpractice actions against the therapist, (3) personal injury actions, (4) workers' compensation claims, and (5) will contests.

(a) Child custody disputes □□ The guiding legal principle in child custody disputes is that it is the court's duty to protect the "best interests of the child."[83] To make this determination, courts are permitted to consider the physical and emotional health of both the children and the parents. Many state statutes provide that the parent's present mental illness or a history of it is relevant to the custody decision, and court cases reflect this assertion. Frequently, one spouse will attempt to introduce evidence of the other's past psychiatric hospitalization and/or treatment. In general, the courts will be more interested in learning of the opposing parent's present adjustment. If one parent is in treatment, the court may compel disclosure of the nature and extent of that treatment.[84]

Even when neither parent raises the issue of the other's mental health, the court can do so on its own motion. Occasionally, the court will order an evaluation of the entire family by a therapist or a social service agency to determine how the child's best interests can best be served. This evaluation may reveal previous emotional problems, leading the court to seek disclosure of the earlier records. Generally, however, the courts are sensitive to the risk of discouraging people from seeking therapy, and they recognize that many people seek counseling immediately before or at the time of the breakup of their marriage.

(b) Malpractice cases □□ When an individual sues his therapist for malpractice he automatically opens up the issue of his treatment. The question before the court then is whether the appropriate standard of care was provided. Without detailed revelations of what occurred during treatment there is no way to evaluate

79. Rappeport, Differences Between Forensic and General Psychiatry, 139 Am. J. Psychiatry 331 (1982); R. Sadoff, Forensic Psychiatry: A Practical Guide for Lawyers and Psychiatrists 25 (1975).

80. See table 10.1.

81. Del. Code Ann. tit. 16, Unif. R. Evid. 503(d)(3) (1981).

82. Beigler, *supra* note 33, at 224.

83. Every state now uses the standard of "best interest of the child" when determining custody matters. See Freed & Foster, Family Law in the Fifty States: An Overview, 17 Fam. L.Q. 365, 415 (1984); Unif. Marriage & Divorce Act § 402, 9a U.L.A. 197–98 (1979) (setting out the "best interest of the child" standard).

84. See Annot., 44 A.L.R.3d 24, 64–69, for cases where this was an issue.

whether the therapist has been negligent. A few states specifically provide for an exception to the privilege in a malpractice action,[85] but in most states this is covered under the general patient-litigant exception.[86]

(c) Personal injury suits □□ The most frequent occasion for application of the patient-litigant exception is in personal injury suits in which a litigant raises a claim or defense of mental or emotional injury. One of the first questions that will be asked by the opposing party's attorney during discovery is whether the litigant is receiving, or has received, treatment for a mental or emotional illness or any type of counseling. If the answer is affirmative, the attorney will try to discover the extent of that treatment by subpoenaing the records and by taking the deposition of the treating therapist. The burden will be upon the litigant to show that his past history is not relevant and is thus beyond the proper scope of discovery.

The patient-litigant exception attempts to balance an individual's need for privacy when seeking mental health services against the need for the court to know all the facts relevant to its decision. Knowledge of a person's history of treatment for mental or emotional problems can greatly affect the assessment of the extent of the injury the plaintiff may have incurred. It may be, for example, that contrary to the plaintiff's claim that his emotional problems were caused by the defendant's negligence, in reality his emotional imbalance preceded the allegedly negligent or wrongful act. In justifying the patient-litigant exception one court explained that it:

> strikes a proper balance between the conditional right of privacy encompassing the psychotherapist-patient relationship and the state's compelling need to insure the ascertainment of the truth in court proceedings. The plaintiff has placed her mental and emotional condition in issue. By raising this issue she herself has breached the confidential relationship and made her emotional problems known to the public. Having so acted, the patient and her psychiatrist should not now be permitted to rely upon an absolute privilege which would preclude a proper determination of the truth of the plaintiff-patient's allegations.[87]

The argument *against* breaching the confidentiality of the therapeutic relationship is based on the belief that a personal injury claimant is in fact unlikely to feign illness for the purpose of increasing his damages award. To routinely force a therapist to disclose confidential information would sacrifice confidentiality for many blameless people in the name of averting the false claims of a few. On balance it may be better to try to preserve the therapeutic relationship and not impose a double penalty upon a person who has been injured, that is, disclosure of his therapeutic confidences on top of the injury itself. This can be accomplished, as it often is, by appointing a nontreating expert to examine the claimant to determine the validity of his claim—this procedure is feasible, for while confidentiality is essential to successful treatment,[88] it is less essential for purposes of making a ready diagnosis that relates to present condition and not the desire to change behavior. While the testimony of the treating therapist is sometimes valuable—particularly in so far as the therapist can provide a perspective on the individual before the injury occurred and on any changes resulting from the injury—the testimony of the appointed expert will usually be adequate for the purposes of the litigation.[89]

To minimize the breach of confidentiality and to assure that only relevant and material matters are opened up to scrutiny, the court can also at the outset limit the scope of discovery. In Illinois, which has adopted a model confidentiality act, prior to disclosure there must be an in-camera inspection, and the court must determine that the evidence is relevant, probative, not unduly prejudicial, and otherwise clearly admissible.[90] The court must further determine that other evidence would be demonstrably unsatisfactory and that disclosure is more important to the interests of substantial justice than is protection from injury to the therapist-recipient relationship. This statutorily mandated balancing best protects the interests of all the parties in the litigation; it is matched by a trend in court decisions rejecting complete disclosure in favor of similarly limited disclosure.[91]

Another issue is whether a claim of "pain and suffering" is sufficient to invoke the patient-litigant exception. Such claims are often made in personal injury suits. Typically, the plaintiff has not experienced any emotional injury beyond that caused by the trauma of the event. In a few jurisdictions it is now specified that a claim based on "pain and suffering" in and of itself does not bring into play the patient-litigant exception, unless the litigant raises the issue of his mental condition in some other specific fashion.[92]

85. See table 10.1, col. 14; see also Ill. Ann. Stat. ch. 91½, § 810(a)(3) (Smith-Hurd Supp. 1984).

86. The number of suits brought against mental health professionals is small compared with suits brought against physicians generally. Malpractice is discussed at length in this chapter at § II A, Malpractice by Mental Health Professionals, *infra*.

87. Caesar v. Mountanos, 542 F.2d 1064, 1070 (9th Cir. 1976) (note omitted), referring to § 1016 of the California Evidence Code as interpreted in *In re* Lifschutz, 467 P.2d 557, 85 Cal. Rptr. 829 (1970).

88. See GAP Report, *supra* note 2, at 93.

89. This in fact was suggested by Judge Hufstedler in her dissent in Caesar v. Mountanos, 542 F.2d at 1070, 1074–75.

90. Ill. Ann. Stat. ch. 91½, § 810(b) (Smith-Hurd Supp. 1984).

91. See Annot., 44 A.L.R.3d 24, 97–107, for cases in this area.

92. See Ill. Ann. Stat. ch. 91½, § 810(a)(1) (Smith-Hurd Supp. 1984); District of Columbia Mental Health Information Act of 1978, tit. V, D.C. Code Ann. § 6-2041 (1981).

(d) Workers' compensation cases □□ Workers' compensation laws, providing a type of insurance for the employee who is injured on the job, have been enacted in every state.[93] The goal of these statutes is to compensate employees for work-related injuries without forcing resort to the courts for a determination of negligence and of the amount of recompense.[94] The acts are administered by workers' compensation boards that rule on the extent of the injury or disability. The amounts recoverable are set by a predetermined schedule.[95]

By applying for workers' compensation the employee gives up his right to file a civil action against the employer.[96] To succeed in a workers' compensation claim the employee must prove that the injury was job related and that his damages were directly related to the injury. Initially, employees could recover for emotional illness only if they had also been physically injured.[97] Today, however, a risk of danger without any actual physical harm having been experienced may be sufficient to support a finding that a job-related psychological injury was suffered by the employee.[98] In a case that dates from 1941, an employee was permitted to recover for the emotional trauma she suffered from having seen a fellow worker electrocuted, which rendered her unable to work.[99]

When an employee claims mental or emotional illness, he places his mental condition in issue, and the patient-litigant exception will usually permit discovery of his previous treatment. The workers' compensation boards take the same view as the courts in personal injury actions, that is, that the information, when relevant, will be discoverable and admissible.

(e) Will contests □□ In some instances, the concept of confidentiality may die with the patient, as in a will contest where efforts are made to set aside a contract entered into by a decedent. The writer of a will must be able to understand the nature and extent of his property and the natural objects of his bounty.[100] Since a will speaks only at death, it is not until that time that the question of the testator's competence can be raised. The issue is whether at the time of writing the will (rather than at the time of death) the testator was mentally competent. There is a legal presumption that unless the testator had been declared legally incompetent, he will be presumed to have been competent.[101] Overcoming this presumption is a heavy burden for the challenger to the will. To meet this burden, the challenger may try to introduce either the testimony or records of the therapist who treated the testator.

Nine states have enacted specific exceptions to the confidentiality privilege whereby a waiver of the privilege is permitted in a dispute over a will or other property document.[102] As in other types of litigation, matters that the courts determine to be irrelevant or immaterial will still be inadmissable. Most courts are hesitant to set aside wills, and unless a bequest seems plainly irrational they are unlikely to admit the therapist's testimony. This reluctance is buttressed by the fact that challengers can accomplish their goals without having to impinge on psychotherapist-patient confidentiality by calling as witnesses other individuals who knew the testator and his mental state at the time of writing the will. A testator can himself help forestall breaches of confidentiality following his death by videotaping his act of affirming and then signing the will and by securing affidavits from reliable individuals as to his understanding of his actions at that time. Such corroborative evidence of mental stability will provide justification for the court's refusal to breach the privilege.

D. Criticisms of Privilege Laws

Although it has been forcefully argued that privilege laws are crucial for encouraging individuals to seek mental treatment,[103] there is reason to question whether these laws really have an effect on the number of persons seeking treatment and on what is revealed during therapy. A few studies have analyzed the practical effects of psychotherapist-patient privilege laws.[104] The most recent analysis, by Shuman and Weiner, has examined the impact of the enactment in Texas of a psychotherapist-patient privilege statute.[105] The authors sent questionnaires to therapists, persons in treatment, law persons, and judges to determine the effect of the law. In addition, they analyzed Blue Cross–Blue Shield records to see if the number of claims for psychiatric treatment

93. E. Blair, Reference Guide to Workmen's Compensation Law (1968).

94. S. Horowitz, Injury and Death Under Workmen's Compensation Laws 72 (1944).

95. *Id.* at 382.

96. *Id.* at 316.

97. Joseph, Causation in Workers' Compensation Mental Disability Cases: The Michigan Experience, 27 Wayne L. Rev. 1079 (1981); Mussoff, Determining the Compensability of Mental Disabilities Under Workers' Compensation, 55 S. Cal. L. Rev. 193 (1981-82).

98. Horowitz, *supra* note 94, at 95.

99. Burlington Mills Corp. v. Hagood, 177 Va. 204, 13 S.E.2d 291 (1941).

100. W.D. Rollison, The Law of Wills 101 (1939).

101. *Id.* at 102.

102. See table 10.1, col. 11.

103. Foster, Illinois: A Pioneer in the Law of Mental Health Privileged Communications, 62 Ill. B.J. 668 (1974); GAP Report, *supra* note 2; Slovenko, *supra* note 21.

104. See, e.g., Note, Where the Public Peril Begins: A Survey of Psychotherapists to Determine the Effect of *Tarasoff*, 31 Stan. L. Rev. 165 (1978) [hereinafter cited as Survey of Psychotherapists]; Notes and Comments, Functional Overlap Between the Lawyer and Other Professionals: Its Implications for the Privileged Communications Doctrine, 71 Yale L.J. 1226 (1962); Shuman & Weiner, *supra* note 18, at 898; Suarez & Balcanoff, Massachusetts Psychiatry and Privileged Communication, 15 Archives Gen. Psychiatry 619 (1966).

105. See Shuman & Weiner, *supra* note 18.

increased, a consequence they theorized would ensue if privilege laws in fact encouraged people to seek therapy. The authors concluded that the "existence of the privilege is consequential in the inception and conduct of a therapeutic relationship for only a small percentage of individuals who might consider psychotherapy for the treatment of an emotional problem."[106] They found that since most people were unaware of the privilege statute, it could not affect their seeking therapy. The analysis of the Blue Cross–Blue Shield data did not reveal an increased incidence of psychiatrist's services sought after the privilege law was passed. On the other hand, the researchers found evidence that the knowledge that the therapist would keep information confidential was felt by the patients to be very important.[107]

Critics of privilege laws have pointed out that neither Canada[108] nor Great Britain[109] has such laws. Slovenko has argued that "the statutory privilege as a guideline is much sound and fury signifying nothing."[110] He contends:

> The privilege is a venture that gains nothing. The practice in states where there is no physician-patient privilege or psychotherapist-patient privilege is the same as in states where there is a privilege. . . . The harm done, though, by privilege laws is that the privilege gives an undue sense of importance to communications in psychotherapy.[111]

Slovenko concludes that the concept of privilege should be abandoned as a means of determining whether communications made during psychotherapy should be disclosed. He believes that the standard guidelines in evidentiary matters of materiality and relevancy protect against intervention in the therapeutic relationship, at least to the extent that it "would unfairly be a source of regret for patient."[112]

E. Licensure Requirements

In addition to specific therapist-patient privilege statutes, there are confidentiality provisions in numerous states' statutes setting forth requirements for professional licensure. Most commonly, these laws concern psychologists and social workers. These licensing laws usually contain the same exceptions for breaching confidentiality as do the privilege statutes. In some states, however, the licensure law provides coverage that is not provided by the privilege statute.

F. Nonstatutory Protections of Confidentiality

In addition to privilege and licensure statutes guaranteeing confidentiality, there are three other potential sources for protecting patient-therapist communications. These are (1) the ethics of the mental health professional, (2) the common law, and (3) the constitutional right of privacy.

1. The Ethics of the Mental Health Professional

The notion that a physician has an ethical obligation to keep the patient's communications confidential has been codified since the fourth century B.C. in that part of the Hippocratic Oath that states: "All that may come to my knowledge in the exercise of my profession . . . or in daily commerce with men, which ought not to be spread abroad, I will keep secret and will never reveal."[113]

The primary providers of mental health care—psychiatrists, psychologists, social workers, and psychiatric nurses—are all governed by professional codes of ethics, each of which contains a provision emphasizing the importance of confidentiality.[114] Although not carrying the weight of law, these codes establish standards of conduct that members of those professions are expected to uphold.

In elaborating on the principles of ethics adopted by the American Medical Association, the American Psychiatric Association (APA) states:

> Psychiatric records, including even the identification of a person as a patient, must be protected with extreme care. . . . Because of the sensitive and private nature of the information with which the psychiatrist deals, he must be circumspect in the information that he chooses to disclose to others about a patient. The welfare of the patient must be a continuing consideration.[115]

The APA commentary concludes:

> When the psychiatrist is ordered by the court to reveal the confidences entrusted to him by patients he may comply or he may ethically hold the right to dissent within the framework of the law. When the psychiatrist is in doubt, the right of the patient to confidentiality and, by extension, to unimpaired treatment, should be given priority. The psychiatrist should reserve the right to raise the question of adequate need for disclosure. In the event that the necessity for legal disclosure is demon-

106. *Id.* at 927.
107. *Id.* at 918–26.
108. Dickens, Legal Protection of Psychiatric Confidentiality, 1 Int'l J. L. & Psychiatry 255, 260 (1978).
109. 30 Halsbury & Laws of England, Medicine, Pharmacy, Drugs and Medical Procedures § 19 (4th ed. 1980).
110. Slovenko, *supra* note 69, at 658.
111. *Id.* at 658–59.
112. *Id.* at 673.
113. Steadman's Medical Dictionary (23d ed. 1976).
114. American Psychological Association, Ethical Standards of Psychologists 53 (1953); National Association of Social Workers, Profession of Social Work: Code of Ethics (adopted Oct. 13, 1960, and amended Apr. 11, 1967), *in* 2 Encyclopedia of Social Work 958–59 (6th ed. 1971).
115. American Psychiatric Association, Official Actions: The Principles of Medical Ethics with Annotations Especially Applicable to Psychiatry, 130 Am. J. Psychiatry 1057, 1063 (1973) [hereinafter cited as A.P.A. Annotations].

strated by the court, the psychiatrist may request the right to disclosure of only that information that is relevant to the legal question at hand.[116]

2. The Common Law

Traditionally, the only privilege existing under the common law was the attorney-client privilege. However, at least two states have recognized a common law privilege for therapist-patient communications.[117] In a 1952 case seeking damages for alienation of affection, an Illinois court refused to order the claimant's wife's psychiatrist to testify or to release the hospital records relating to her treatment.[118] In Alaska, also, a common law privilege has been created in the state supreme court decision in *Allred v. State*.[119] The *Allred* trial court had admitted into evidence statements made by the defendant to his drug abuse counselor, who had visited him in jail shortly after his arrest. The Alaska Supreme Court analyzed the Wigmore criteria for determining when a privilege should be attached and reasoned that the psychotherapeutic relationship satisfied each of these criteria. It concluded by recognizing a general common law privilege, belonging to the patient, which protects communications made to psychotherapists during the course of treatment. The court then articulated a test to determine when this privilege should apply: (1) when the communication was made to a psychiatrist or a licensed psychologist and (2) when the communication was made in the course of psychotherapeutic treatment or during examinations or diagnostic interviews that might reasonably lead to psychotherapeutic treatment.[120] In applying the test to the facts before it, the *Allred* court concluded that the privilege should not apply because the statements had not been made to a psychiatrist or psychologist and because they had not been made in the course of psychotherapeutic treatment.[121] With many states having enacted privilege statutes it is unlikely that other courts will follow the Alaska example and enunciate a common law privilege for therapeutic relationships.

3. The Constitutional Right of Privacy

In *Griswold v. Connecticut*[122] the United States Supreme Court enunciated an ill-defined, yet potentially expansive, constitutional right of privacy. Looking to the implications emanating from the First, Third, Fourth, Fifth, Ninth, and Fourteenth Amendments to the Constitution, Justice Douglas, who authored the *Griswold* majority opinion, held that there was a right of married couples to be free from the strictures of a state law banning the sale and use of contraceptives.[123] Because there were several concurring opinions in which justices who ostensibly agreed with Justice Douglas set forth analyses and rationales departing from the majority opinion in which they joined, it is difficult to delineate the exact scope of the *Griswold* decision. It is safe to say, however, that the ruling clearly sets forth the basis for establishing a constitutionally protected right of privacy extending far beyond the marital relationship and the use of contraceptives in that relationship. Indeed, later decisions building on *Griswold* confirm this perception; cases such as *Eisenstadt v. Baird*,[124] involving the use of contraceptives by unmarried people, *Roe v. Wade*,[125] regarding the woman's right to seek an abortion, and *H.L. v. Matheson*,[126] on parental notification requirements for minors seeking abortions, go well beyond the *Griswold* situation.

In *Griswold*, Justice Douglas deplored the intrusiveness necessarily involved in enforcing the Connecticut contraceptive ban, whereby police would be searching marital bedrooms for evidence of use of the banned items. This concern laid the basis for later courts to extract from *Griswold* wider privacy rights such as a freedom from governmental acquisition of intimate information about individuals and a freedom from government disclosure of personal information. In *Whalen v. Roe*, for example, Justice Stevens, writing for the Court 12 years after the Connecticut case, summarized the import of *Griswold* and succeeding rulings by observing that these cases had "in fact involved at least two different kinds of interests. One is the individual interest in avoiding disclosure of personal matters, and another is the individual interest in independence in making certain kinds of important decisions."[127]

The logical connection of these holdings to claims of confidentiality in the mental health setting is easy to discern. Here, too, there is intimate information at issue, and here, too, the individual's concern is to insulate the information from governmental acquisition and dissemination. The Supreme Court has not yet addressed privacy claims in this context. The closest it has come is in *Whalen v. Roe*, which involved a challenge to a state law requiring doctors to report all prescriptions written

116. *Id.*
117. Alaska and Illinois.
118. Binder v. Russell, Civil Docket No. 52 C 2535 (Cir. Ct. of Cook County (1953), *discussed in* Foster, *supra* note 103, at 668.
119. 554 P.2d 411 (Alaska 1976).
120. *Id.* at 421.
121. *Id.* at 418–19. The court distinguished between counseling and psychotherapy, defining psychotherapy as the "use of psychological means to modify mental and emotional disorders of a serious, disabling nature" and counseling as assisting the client in making "more effective use of his present resources."
122. 381 U.S. 479 (1965).
123. *Id.* at 484.
124. 405 U.S. 438 (1972).
125. 410 U.S. 113 (1973).
126. 450 U.S. 398 (1981).
127. 429 U.S. 589, 599–600 (1977).

for dangerous drugs. The Court upheld the statute but only because of the protections contained in the particular law before it. Justice Stevens emphasized that the law at issue barred the disclosure of the identity of the patients, and he left open the question of the legitimacy of disclosure systems involving less stringent security measures:

> We are not unaware of the threat to privacy implicit in the accumulation of vast amounts of personal information in computerized data banks or other massive government files. . . . Recognizing that in some circumstances . . . [the] duty [to avoid unwarranted disclosures] arguably has its roots in the Constitution, nevertheless, New York's [procedures] . . . evidence a proper concern with, and protection of, the individual's interest in privacy. We therefore need not, and do not, decide any question which might be presented by the unwarranted disclosure of accumulated private data—whether intentional or unintentional—or by a system that did not contain comparable security provisions.[128]

At least one legal commentator has argued that a constitutional right of privacy should extend to mental health records,[129] and a number of courts have agreed.[130] In *In re "B,"* the Supreme Court of Pennsylvania reversed the contempt citation of a psychiatrist who refused to release the treatment records of a woman whose son was involved in the dispositional phase of a delinquency proceeding.[131] As part of the juvenile court's efforts to determine the placement of B, the mother was interviewed, and it was learned that she had had several psychiatric hospitalizations. The juvenile court ordered production of the records. The refusal and subsequent contempt citation led to the higher court's holding that the mother had a constitutionally based right to prevent disclosure of her records. The court recognized that although this might make it more difficult for courts to obtain information they might desire, "[t]he individual's right of privacy . . . must prevail."[132]

In *Hawaii Psychiatric Society v. Ariyoshi*[133] a federal district court struck down a Hawaiian Medicaid statute that permitted the seizure and examination of the clinical notes of psychotherapists. Grounding its decision on a constitutionally protected right of privacy, the court concluded that although the Medicaid fraud investigator had a compelling state interest in ensuring compliance with the state Medicaid law, this interest was inadequate to override the intrusion into an individual's reasonable expectation of privacy.[134] This court later stated:

> The disclosure of a patient's innermost thoughts, feelings, conduct, and beliefs is, quite simply, not justified by the State's interest in verifying the necessity or performance of psychotherapeutic treatments, in preventing fraud, or in catching those who commit fraud. In short, the court concludes, the State could implement a statutory scheme that would strike a more appropriate balance between preserving the integrity of the Medicaid program and minimizing any intrusion on an individual's right to confidentiality.[135]

G. Breaches of Confidentiality

1. *Affirmative Duty by the Therapist*

In some situations a therapist is required by law or by the ethics of his profession to disregard confidentiality expectations. These are (1) when the therapist acts pursuant to the mandate of child abuse reporting statutes,[136] (2) when the therapist deems it necessary to seek the civil commitment of the patient,[137] and (3) when there is a duty to warn others of potential danger from the patient.[138] Each of these situations is discussed in more detail in other parts of this chapter.

2. *Waivers of Confidentiality by the Patient*

Not infrequently an individual will waive the confidentiality of his records, as, for example, when he is seeking to obtain health insurance benefits or in an employment situation. Before the therapist releases the information, however, he should inform the patient of its substance and scope, thereby enabling the patient to make an informed decision whether to authorize disclosure. The therapist should also apprise the patient of the extent to which disclosure might be detrimental to him, if adverse consequences indeed are a possibility. Regardless of any limits imposed by the patient, the therapist is under an ethical duty to only disclose that information that is relevant, and nothing more.[139]

(a) Release in the employment situation Typically, the fact of past or ongoing treatment for mental

128. *Id.* at 605-6.

129. Smith, Constitutional Privacy in Psychotherapy, 49 Geo. Wash. L. Rev. 1 (1980).

130. Roe v. Ingraham, 403 F. Supp. 931 (S.D.N.Y. 1975); *In re* B, 394 A.2d 419 (Pa. 1978); Hawaii Psychiatric Soc'y v. Ariyoshi, 481 F. Supp. 1028 (D. Hawaii 1979).

131. 394 A.2d 419, 426 (Pa. 1978).

132. *Id.* at 426.

133. 481 F. Supp. 1028 (D. Hawaii 1979).

134. 481 F. Supp. at 1038.

135. Hawaii Psychiatric Soc'y v. Ariyoshi, No. CV79-0113, 7 MDLR 229 (D. Hawaii Dec. 27, 1982).

136. See extensive discussion in this chapter § I C 1, Child Abuse, *supra*.

137. See § I C 2, Civil Commitment, *supra*; see also ch. 2, Involuntary Institutionalization, which sets forth the civil commitment standards.

138. See extensive discussion in this chapter § II B, The Duty to Warn, *infra*.

139. See A.P.A. Annotations, *supra* note 115, which provide that "[t]he continuing duty of the psychiatrist to protect the patient includes fully apprising him of the connotations of waiving the privilege of privacy."

problems will put a job applicant at a disadvantage compared with competitors for the job who do not have a history of seeking such treatment. Yet it is common for job application forms, particularly for jobs that require security clearances, to inquire whether the applicant has been treated for a mental illness. Even if an affirmative answer does not immediately disqualify the applicant, it often leads the employer to dig deeper into the applicant's history. He may seek release of the applicant's treatment record or a report from the treating therapist. It could lead to psychological testing of the applicant as a predicate to his being hired and perhaps to other intrusive inquiries.

It may also happen that an employee, long after being hired, voluntarily requests a leave of absence to receive treatment, or that the employer takes the initiative of encouraging the employee to seek such treatment for emotional problems. In order to return to work, the individual will then often have to reveal his records or have a report submitted by his treating therapist. In addition, the employer may require the company's doctor or psychologist to determine if the employee is emotionally able to return to his former position. In either event, the fact of treatment will be known to the employer and may affect future job assignments or promotions.[140]

It is a rare situation where the fact of an employee's past treatment for a mental illness will not affect, at least subtly if not overtly, the employer-employee relationship. Consequently, some employees may forgo making health insurance claims under a company plan for fear that their claims for reimbursement will become known to their employer.[141]

(b) Release to insurance companies □ □ The most common release of information about mental health treatment is that made to insurance companies by therapists based on the patient's voluntary consent given in the course of his efforts to qualify for reimbursement of the costs of treatment.[142] The health insurer, of course, needs proof that the claim is a valid one, and the standard insurance reimbursement form requires the patient to authorize the provider of services, that is, the therapist, to release all records and other information relating to the patient's treatment. This may create a conflict for the therapist, however, who will feel the need to keep records that are sufficiently detailed to document the treatment needs but that may also contain the kind of personal information whose release to outsiders would be detrimental to the patient. The patient's interests may be particularly jeopardized if the information disclosed to the insurance company is fed into the Medical Data Bank, to which all insurance companies have access.[143] Instances of misuse of such information are well documented:[144] knowledge of psychiatric treatment, for example, has been put to questionable use in assessing eligibility for automobile insurance and life insurance. Indeed, it has been noted that some civil service employees, military personnel, corporate executives, and politicians avoid using their insurance coverage to pay for mental health services because of the risk of damage to their careers by disclosure of treatment.[145]

A number of innovative programs have set limits on the amount of information the insurer receives.[146] Yet the misuse of information released to insurance companies remains one of the more serious threats to the confidentiality of the patient-therapist relationship.

3. Group Therapy

Group therapy is used in a wide variety of settings, ranging from inpatient psychiatric settings, to outpatient programs that provide help for special problems such as alcoholism and drug addiction, to adult and child guidance clinics. When a person agrees to participate in group therapy, he waives confidentiality at least insofar as revealing information to other members of the group is concerned. However, participants in group therapy expect that each member of the group can rely on all the other members to keep what is revealed strictly confidential.[147] Even so, from a strict legal perspective, there remains a substantial question whether members of a group can be forced to testify in court or otherwise reveal information disclosed by fellow members during the group sessions. A few commentators have suggested that there is a need for a formal confidentiality privilege in the group therapy situation,[148] but it has been recognized in only a few jurisdictions.[149] Thus far, there are

140. Beigler, Privacy and Confidentiality *in* Law and Ethics in the Practice of Psychiatry 70 (C.K. Hofling ed. 1980) [hereinafter cited as Law and Ethics].

141. *Id.*

142. Grossman, Insurance Reports as a Threat to Confidentiality, 128 Am. J. Psychiatry 64 (1971).

143. Westin, Brief Effort at Clarifying the Policy Analysis of "Confidentiality" Issues in Health Care (paper presented at the Conference on Confidentiality of Health Records, Key Biscayne, Fla., Nov. 6-9, 1974), *reprinted in* Confidentiality: Report of the Conference on Confidentiality of Health Records (N. Davis Spingarn ed. 1975) [hereinafter cited as Conference on Confidentiality of Health Records].

144. Britton, Rights to Privacy in Medical Records, 3 J. Legal Med., July/Aug. 1975, at 30, 31.

145. See Beigler, supra note 140.

146. See *id.* at 73-77, which describes these programs.

147. J. Moreno, Code of Ethics for Group Psychotherapy and Psychodrama (Psychodrama and Group Psychotheraphy Monograph No. 31, 1962).

148. See, e.g., Notes, Group Therapy and Privileged Communication, 43 Ind. L. J. (1967); Cross, Privileged Communications Between Participants in Group Psychotherapy, 1970 Law & Social Order 191. D.C. Code Ann. § 6-2002(b) (1981) and Ill. Rev. Stat. ch. 91½, § 810(a)(1) (1981) are probably the only statutes that impose a duty on all the participants of group therapy and impose a penalty for revealing confidential information.

149. Minnesota v. Andring, 342 N.W.2d 128 (Minn. 1983).

no reported instances of group members being compelled to testify about confidences revealed in therapy.

H. Disclosure of Records

Today, third-party payments and computerization by insurance carriers, health providers, and governmental agencies have made the handling of personal medical information a complex matter. There are least four risks[150] associated with the collection of health records:[151] (1) the centralization of information from widely divergent sources creates serious problems of information accuracy, (2) civil liberties are threatened by potential unregulated information surveillance by government agencies, (3) governmental and private informa tion-gathering agencies may go beyond the current levels of inquiry and begin to demand even more sensitive information, and (4) there is increasing use of recorded information and third-party evaluations of past performance as the bases for making important decisions about people instead of personal, individualized assessment of present capacities. These dangers are exacerbated by problems with the accuracy of the records. The possibilities of professional and clerical errors, of substantive mistakes in information obtained from the patient, and of misfiling and illegibility compound the potential damage that may be caused by use of medical records for purposes other than treatment.[152]

Since the problems associated with information are not only ongoing but likely to increase, the task at hand is to work out a means of balancing the individual's control over disclosure of personal information and the needs of society for the data on which to base decisions about individual situations and to formulate public policies.[153] All jurisdictions except Minnesota and New Mexico have enacted statutes to protect the confidentiality of patient records.[154] Most of these statutes are specifically concerned with records relating to the identification, commitment, and treatment of patients in state mental hospitals.[155] This section will emphasize some of the issues relating to treatment records.

1. Patient's Access to Records

Thirty-one states and the District of Columbia[156] have enacted statutes covering the patient's access to records. Typically, these laws do not give open-ended access. Most make access conditional on the patient's mental health status: the patient's right to see his records is foreclosed if the information would be detrimental to his mental health or its disclosure to him would not be in his best interests.[157] Furthermore, some statutes provide that the patient must show "good cause" in order to see his records;[158] others provide that the patient may have "reasonable" access.[159] In almost half the states the patient does not have a specific right to see his records, even though other persons or agencies do have such access, that is, his representative,[160] insurance companies,[161] and various other persons and entities in a variety of circumstances.[162]

Several arguments support patient access to records. By being able to review his records, the patient has the opportunity to verify their accuracy.[163] Patient access also can enhance continuity of care when the patient moves and seeks out a new treatment provider. Finally, patient access serves to facilitate protection of his privacy interests by enabling him to make an adequately informed decision before he permits disclosure of his records.[164]

The primary argument against access is couched in terms of solicitude for the patient who, it is contended, should be shielded from information in his record that may be disturbing to him. Assessment of the validity of this concern is difficult. The literature reports no instances of harm in states where patients have been afforded access to their records. To the contrary, a measure of openness may provide a means for the patient and therapist to further discuss the therapist's impressions and views.[165]

A few courts have addressed the issue of patient access to records. The leading case is *Gotkin v. Miller*,[166] in which the Court of Appeals for the Second Circuit flatly denied a former mental patient access to her records. The court rejected arguments that the denial of the records constituted a deprivation of liberty under the Four-

150. The Conference on Confidentiality of Health Records, *supra* note 143, brought together mental health providers, data specialists, medical record administrators and lawyers to discuss the issue and develop guidelines.

151. See Miller, The Assault on Privacy, *reprinted as* part of Conference on Confidentiality of Health Records, *supra* note 143.

152. Britton, *supra* note 144.

153. Westin, *supra* note 143.

154. See table 10.2

155. *Id.*, col. 2.

156. See table 10.2.

157. See *id.*

158. See, e.g., Tenn. Code Ann. § 68-11-304 (1983).

159. See, e.g., Idaho Code § 66-346(a)(7) (Supp. 1983) and Miss. Code Ann. § 41-9-65 (1981).

160. See table 10.2.

161. Usually to obtain insurance coverage, the person must sign a waiver, which will give the insurance company access to the entire record.

162. See table 10.2 for other circumstances in which the record will be released.

163. Kaiser, Patient's Rights of Access to Their Own Medical Records: The Need for New Law, 24 Buffalo L. Rev. 317 (1975).

164. *Id.* at 327.

165. When the author was an attorney for the Illinois Department of Mental Health and Developmental Disabilities, the facilities were hesitant about permitting patients to see their records. However, when the law was observed and a therapist sat with the patient and explained what was in the record, the results never seemed to be negative and were often positive, sometimes dispelling the patient's concerns about what was being said about him.

166. 514 F.2d 125 (2d Cir. 1975).

teenth Amendment[167] and that she was deprived of her property without due process of law.[168]

2. *Statutory Access by Others*

The statutes designed to assure the confidentiality of mental health records usually provide for certain exceptions.[169] In most states these statutes apply only to public facilities, agencies, or practitioners.[170] In the private setting, the release of records is usually governed by statutes relating to medical records in general or by other broader confidentiality provisions, including the privilege statutes discussed in detail earlier.[171]

Table 10.2 sets forth the various exceptions contained in the mental health record confidentiality statutes. Twenty-eight states and the District of Columbia allow a patient's attorney access to the patient's mental health records.[172] Two of them give the attorney unrestrained access, not requiring the patient's permission.[173] The most common confidentiality exception permits release of information concerning treatment from one treatment provider to another.[174] About one quarter of the states have provisions for record disclosure when a question regarding a patient's mental condition arises after his death.[175] Additionally, 30 states allow limited disclosure for research purposes, usually requiring that the patient's anonymity be protected.[176]

3. *The Records of Minors*

The issue of the confidentiality of minors' records is especially complicated. In order to develop the therapeutic relationship, the therapist needs to obtain the confidence of the child, and this may be possible only if he promises not to disclose information to parents. But the parents usually will want to know how the child is doing and what they can do to help. Since the child is their responsibility, they may feel they have a right to know what is occurring in therapy. More than that, it is often desirable to involve the parents in the treatment process so that therapeutic gains with the child will not be compromised by the parents' own problems or by the continuation of their earlier negative parental practices and attitudes.

It is possible for the therapist to reach a compromise without breaching expectations of confidentiality. The therapist can make clear to both the child and the parents the types of communication he will have with each,[177] thereby enabling all concerned to know what to expect and what the limitations are.

There is also the question of who has the right to consent to release of a child's records. Illinois, which has a broad confidentiality law, provides that for children 12 years of age or older both the youngster and the parents must consent. If the child refuses, then the therapist may not make a disclosure unless he makes a separate determination that it would be in the child's best interests.[178] This law has much to commend it, although some advocates of children's rights have argued that too much discretion is reposed in the therapist.

Another question is when parents are entitled to access to the child's treatment records. There are situations when it may be detrimental to the child for the parents to see the records, for example, in instances where the child has made negative comments about a parent or has revealed behavior of which parents are unaware. In one of the few instances in which the question has been litigated, the trial court refused a parent access to her daughter's records, in part because the guardian ad litem testified that disclosure would be against the child's best interests.[179]

4. *Disclosure in Publications*

The statutes and ethical considerations that prohibit disclosure of records also prohibit the therapist from disclosing communications made by the patient in scientific writings and teaching situations without the patient's consent. Indeed, the Group for the Advancement of Psychiatry has taken the official position that the psychiatrist's ethical duty to the patient has priority over scientific objectives. If clinical material cannot be sufficiently disguised to protect the patient's identity, it should not be published or presented to students in teaching situations.[180] Whatever the official ethical pronouncements about the conditions of securing consent, there remains a question about whether a therapist can in reality obtain a truly voluntary consent to disclosure for publication from a patient who is still in treatment and in a relationship of dependence on the therapist. At the very least, the therapist should wait for completion of the therapy and then request permission to publish, with

167. *Id.* at 129.
168. *Id.* at 128.
169. See table 10.2, cols. 9-11.
170. See table 10.2; see also Ill. Ann. Stat. ch. 91½, § 802(6) (Smith-Hurd Supp. 1984) and R.I. Gen. Laws § 40.1-5-26 (1977) for statutes not limited to state mental health facilities.
171. See in this chapter § I B 4(b), Various Forms of Privilege Statutes, *supra*.
172. See table 10.2, col. 14.
173. See, e.g., Vt. Stat. Ann. tit. 18, § 7103(b) (1968); Va. Code § 8.01-413 (Supp. 1983).
174. See table 10.1, col. 7.
175. See table 10.1, e.g., California, Connecticut, Illinois, Indiana, Kansas, Louisiana, New Jersey, New York, Ohio, and Vermont.
176. See table 10.2, col. 9.
177. Slovenko & Usdin, *supra* note 61, at 72.
178. Ill. Ann. Stat. ch. 91½, § 805(a) (Smith-Hurd Supp. 1984).
179. *In re* J.C.G., HDCC-8-76, 1 MDLR 264 (Super. Ct. Hudson County, N.J. Nov. 16, 1976).
180. GAP Report, *supra* note 2, at 110.

the former patient having had an opportunity to read the proposed publication before giving consent. Even with permission, the therapist still has the duty not to disclose anything that might reveal the patient's identity.

Case law is sparse in this area. One notable decision is *Doe v. Roe*,[181] which involved a book published by a psychiatrist in which he reported verbatim the thoughts, feelings, and fantasies communicated by a patient during therapy, which had terminated eight years before. The patient sued, seeking an injunction and damages, basing his claim on a state statute barring physicians from disclosing patients' confidences and on the implied promise of confidentiality that every physician makes to his patients. The psychiatrist contended that the public's interest in the scientific value of the publication outweighed the patient's privacy interest. The court held that though the guarantee of confidentiality was not absolute and might be subordinated to other compelling interests, in this case the educational needs of the medical profession did not override the duty of confidentiality.[182] The court enjoined any distribution of the book, including its dissemination to the scientific community.[183]

I. Protecting Confidentiality: New Models

We have seen several respects in which the present laws relating to the confidentiality of mental health treatment are unsatisfactory, if not flawed. The major problems reside primarily in four areas: (1) the excessive qualifications of the privilege statutes that often seem to strip them of any value, (2) the broadness of what can presently be discovered or will be released once consent is given, (3) the inability of patients in many states to gain access to their own records, and (4) the general difficulty of protecting confidentiality interests without penalties for those who violate confidentiality. A number of model laws have been either enacted or suggested to cure these deficiencies.[184] The two most comprehensive are the Illinois Mental Health and Developmental Disabilities Confidentiality Act[185] and the American Psychiatric Association's Model Law on Confidentiality of Health and Social Service Records.[186] The Illinois law was enacted after years of work by the Governor's Commission for Revision of the Mental Health Code, a blue-ribbon panel composed of mental health professionals, lawyers, judges, and laypersons. At the same time that Illinois was working on this reform, the APA's Task Force on Confidentiality of Children's and Adolescents' Clinical Records and its Committee on Confidentiality were developing a model statute. Some of the same people were involved in drafting both the Illinois law and the APA model, and consequently many of the provisions are similar in intent, if not in exact wording. The District of Columbia is thus far the only jurisdiction to adopt this model law.

1. Limitations of the Privilege Statutes

The privilege statutes are limited in protecting confidentiality because of the narrowness of their application. Typically, they come into play only in the litigation setting. Often, they are applicable only to psychiatrists and psychologists and so afford no protection for confidentiality in the work of other mental health professionals. Both the APA and the Illinois models embody comprehensive protections for confidentiality rather than simply a list of privileges. Both models use a very broad definition of "therapist."[187]

The extensive exceptions to the privilege statutes and particular concern about the impact of the patient-litigant exception led Illinois to further attempt to balance the interests of justice against the right of the individual to confidentiality as follows:

> Records and communications may be disclosed in a civil, criminal or administrative proceeding in which the recipient introduces his mental condition or any aspect of his services received for such condition as an element of his claim or defense, if and only to the extent the court in which the proceedings have been brought, or, in the case of an administrative proceeding, the court to which an appeal or other action for review of an administrative determination may be taken, finds, after in camera examination of testimony or other evidence, that it is relevant, probative, not unduly prejudicial or inflammatory, and otherwise clearly admissable; that other satisfactory evidence is demonstrably unsatisfactory as evidence of the facts sought to be established by such evidence; and that disclosure is more important to the interests of substantial justice than protection from injury to the therapist/recipient relationship or to the recipient or other whom disclosure is likely to harm. Except in a criminal proceeding in which the recipient, who is accused in that proceeding, raises the defense of insanity, no record or communication between a therapist and a recipient shall be deemed relevant for purposes of this subsection, except the fact of treatment, the cost of services and the ultimate diagnosis unless the

181. 400 N.Y.S.2d 668 (App. Div. 1977).

182. *Id.* at 677.

183. *Id.* at 679.

184. See American Psychiatric Association, Official Action: Model Law on Confidentiality of Health and Social Service Records, 136 Am. J. Psychiatry 137 (1979) [hereinafter cited as A.P.A. Model Law on Confidentiality]; Report: Governor's Commission for Revision of the Mental Health Code of Illinois (1976).

185. Ill. Ann. Stat. ch. 91½, § 801 (Smith-Hurd Supp. 1984).

186. A.P.A. Model Law on Confidentiality, *supra* note 184, at 138–44.

187. See, e.g., Illinois statute's definition set out in text at note 54 *supra*.

party seeking disclosure of the communication clearly establishes in the trial court a compelling need for its production.[188]

Not only does this provision carefully circumscribe what may be disclosed, but it also places the burden on the party seeking disclosure to prove why more than the fact of treatment, the diagnosis, and the cost of treatment should be disclosed.

Another criticism of the privilege statutes is that they give the privilege only to the patient; the therapist has no right to exert it. The cases of *In re Lifschutz*[189] and *Caesar v. Mountanos*,[190] mentioned earlier, heightened concern within the psychiatric community over the therapist's ability to protect the patient.[191] The Illinois statute responds to this concern by giving the therapist the privilege to refuse to disclose and prevent the disclosure of the patient's records or communications,[192] a privilege that can be overridden only by the court.

2. Limiting What Is Disclosed

The most novel approach to preventing harmful disclosure is the concept of "personal notes." These are defined in the Illinois statute as:

> (1) information disclosed to the therapist in confidence by other persons on condition that such information would never be disclosed to the recipient or other persons;
> (2) information disclosed to the therapist by the recipient which would be injurious to the recipient's relationships to other persons, and
> (3) the therapist's speculations, impressions, hunches, and reminders.[193]

The act then provides that:

> A therapist is not required to but may, to the extent he determines it necessary and appropriate, keep personal notes regarding a recipient. Such personal notes are the work product and personal property of the therapist and shall not be subject to discovery in any judicial, administrative or legislative proceeding or any proceeding preliminary thereto.[194]

Thus, the therapist can maintain two sets of records: one containing the diagnosis and any specific treatment, test results, correspondence, and billing information, and another, which may be more extensive, consisting of personal notes. The former may be subject to discovery, but the latter never will be. This scheme is in part modeled on the attorney work product rule, which prohibits discovery of attorney's notes. More than any other concept in the model acts, the concept of personal notes assures protection for the patient since it enables the therapist to insulate from disclosure much of the day-to-day, personal information transmitted to him by the patient.

While the personal notes concept became part of the Illinois law in 1979, it is still not widely known or used, particularly in the nonprivate treatment setting.[195] Even so, the statute has been successfully used on at least two occasions to prevent the discovery of therapists' notes, once in a criminal case and once in a malpractice case.[196]

The Illinois and APA models further bar the use of blanket consent forms[197] and, in addition, limit disclosure to what is relevant to the purposes *as determined by the therapist*.[198] Thus, if information is to be provided for treatment purposes, the therapist will disclose only that information he believes essential to another treatment provider. The APA model alone also limits what may be disclosed by the therapist to insurance companies, and it prohibits subsequent disclosure by insurance companies to others, including other insurance carriers.[199] If it is true—as alleged—that insurance carriers are among the major violators of patients' confidentiality, the enactment of these provisions should considerably advance patients' privacy interests.

3. Patient's Access to Records

As discussed earlier, almost half the states do not permit the patient to have access to his record. The Illinois and the APA models take the opposite position, though with some provisos as to when full access ought not to be granted.[200] The law also gives the patient an opportunity to raise questions about the accuracy of the information in the record.[201] Finally, it gives children 12

188. Ill. Ann. Stat. § 810(a)(1) (Smith-Hurd Supp. 1984); see also A.P.A. Model Law on Confidentiality, *supra* note 184, § 4(2), at 136.

189. 467 P.2d 557, 85 Cal. Rptr. 829 (1970).

190. 542 F.2d 1064 (9th Cir. 1976).

191. For more extensive discussion see in this chapter § I B 3, Privilege Laws: Criteria and Justification, *supra*.

192. See discussion of precise formulation of Ill. Ann. Stat. ch. 91½, § 810(a) (Smith-Hurd Supp. 1984), in this chapter at note 66 and surrounding text *supra*.

193. *Id.* at § 802(4); the A.P.A. model is very similar.

194. *Id.* at § 803(b); the A.P.A. model is very similar.

195. The author conducted an informal survey of therapists—psychiatrists, psychologists, and social workers—and found that most were not familiar with the concept. Those who were familiar with it used the personal notes only in their private practices and not within the inpatient hospital setting or the outpatient clinic, although these notes can be maintained in both settings.

196. These were trial court decisions in Cook County, which were not appealed.

197. See Ill. Ann. Stat. ch. 91½, § 805(c); see A.P.A. Model Law on Confidentiality, *supra* note 184, § 3(a), at 139.

198. See § 805(c) of the Illinois statute.

199. See §§ 15 & 16, at 143, of the APA model.

200. See § 12(a) of the APA model; see also §§ 804(a)(1) & (2) of the Illinois statute.

201. See § 12(c) of the APA model; see also § 804(c) of the Illinois statute.

years of age and older the right to see their records and to consent or to withhold consent to their release.[202]

4. Penalties for Improper Disclosure

Both the Illinois law and the APA model statute provide that a knowing and willful violation of its provisions constitutes a misdemeanor.[203] Both acts also provide for civil remedies. Under the Illinois statute "[a]ny person aggrieved by a violation of this Act may sue for damages, an injunction, or other appropriate relief."[204] The statute further authorizes the award of reasonable attorney's fees and costs.[205]

J. Conclusion

To the individual seeking help for a mental disability, the importance of confidentiality cannot be underestimated. But with the increased computerization of all types of data, including mental health records, and the expansion of third-party payment schemes, the likelihood is greatly increased that knowledge of the treatment will become known to those outside the therapeutic relationship, including employers and insurance carriers. The sensitive nature of mental health records makes it imperative that they be accurate and limited to what is essential for treatment purposes.

Given the stigma associated with mental disability, it is essential that people be free to seek mental health services without fear that their having sought this kind of help will come back to haunt them in another setting. More states need to enact broader provisions that protect the confidentiality of mental health records and that give the disabled person himself access to these records. The patient should also have a right to question the contents of his record, and his questions or disagreements should be noted and become part of the record. Blanket information release forms should be prohibited, and the recipient of the mental health services should be told under what circumstances and for what purposes certain information may be released. He should have the right to withdraw any previously given consent. Finally, any release of information should be limited strictly to what is necessary for the purposes of the disclosure.

II. LIABILITY OF MENTAL HEALTH PROFESSIONALS

Although litigation against the mental health professional is still rare, lawsuits seeking to establish the civil liability of mental health professionals are increasing.[206] Not only are the numbers of suits growing but so are the theories whereby aggrieved individuals can seek to hold the therapist liable. New liability concepts include the therapist's duty to warn a potential victim of harm from a patient, provider liability for negligently discharging from the hospital someone who then commits a violent act, and treatment staff liability for infringements of the patient's civil rights in the treatment setting. Simultaneously with the expansion of liability in these areas, in other areas the law has provided the mental health professional with more protection: most notable are statutes permitting good faith breaches of confidentiality.[207]

Most litigation is brought against psychiatrists. Psychologists, who are rarely sued, face the greatest risk of liability when doing evaluations that may be used in the litigation setting.[208] There are not yet any reported cases involving social workers,[209] but they also face potential liability for misdiagnosis, breach of confidentiality, and improper evaluations.[210] Despite the relatively small number of suits so far, concern about legal liability "has affected, both positively and negatively, the treatment offered and the conditions under which it is offered," according to two mental health professionals, who suggest that the possibility of malpractice action has had an impact on the "psychological security" of mental health professionals.[211]

A. Malpractice by Mental Health Professionals

1. Overview

Malpractice suits are based on the premise that the defendant professional was negligent in performing his duty. Three elements must be proven to establish negligence: (1) a duty, (2) breach of that duty, and (3) injury resulting from that breach. To establish that a duty existed, the plaintiff must show that there existed a professional relationship between him and the professional. This is most frequently a contractual relationship in

202. See § 804(a)(2) of the Illinois statute and § 3 of the APA model.
203. See § 816 of the Illinois statute and § 10(b) of the APA model.
204. See § 815 of the Illinois statute and see also § 10(a) of the APA model.
205. Ill. Ann. Stat. Ch. 91½, § 815 (1979).

206. See, e.g., Twardy, The Issue of Malpractice in Psychiatry, 25 Med. Trial Technique Q. 161 (1978), which discusses a study by the American Medical Association in which only 48 of 1,566 malpractice cases involved psychiatric malpractice; Slawson, Psychiatric Malpractice: The California Experience, 136 Am. J. Psychiatry 650 (1979).

207. See, e.g., Cal. Evid. Code § 1024 (West 1966 & Supp. 1982); Mass. Ann. Laws ch. 233, § 20B(a) (Michie/Co-op 1974).

208. See, e.g., Wright, Psychologists and Professional Liability (Malpractice) Insurance: A Retrospective Review, 36 Am. Psychologist 1485, 1487 (1981).

209. Watkins & Watkins, Malpractice in Clinical Social Work: A Perspective on Civil Liability in the 1980's, 1 Behav. Sci. & L. 55 (1983).

210. *Id.* at 60, which also lists other potential areas of social worker liability including (1) failure to warn of a client's dangerousness, (2) assault and battery on the client as a result of therapeutic encounters, (3) abandonment and termination of treatment, and (4) poor or incomplete record keeping resulting in the "loss" of children in the foster care bureaucracy.

211. Cavanaugh & Rogers, Malpractice, 1 Behav. Sci. & L. 7 (1983).

which services are provided in exchange for fees. However, a duty may exist even in the absence of a traditional contractual relationship, such as when an individual is receiving treatment in a public mental health facility and the state pays for the care.[212]

To establish a breach of duty, the plaintiff must show that the prevailing standards of care within the defendant's particular profession were not met. Thus, the plaintiff, if suing a psychologist, must show a breach of the standards applicable in the psychological field rather than those applicable to, say, psychiatrists or social workers. In order to prevail, the plaintiff must establish that his claimed injury is the direct result of a breach of those standards.

Usually, expert testimony will be needed to establish the standards of the profession and to show that the mental health professional deviated from those standards. One who holds himself out as a specialist will be held to a higher standard of care than the nonspecialist. Thus, a psychiatrist is held to a higher standard insofar as the treatment of mental illness is concerned than a general physician, and a child psychiatrist will be held to a higher standard than a general psychiatrist in a case involving the evaluation or treatment of a child. This nexus between specialization and standard of care can generate complications, as there are more than 200 schools of psychiatric therapy. For example, the question may be whether a psychiatrist who is not psychoanalytically trained should be expected to meet the same standards as one who is. Furthermore, specialists in one type of treatment or therapy should arguably not be able to serve as expert witnesses in cases involving a different mode of therapy.[213]

There are cases in which no expert testimony is needed to establish deviation from the standards or negligence. These cases are based on the doctrine of *res ipsa loquitur*, which literally means "the thing speaks for itself." This doctrine requires that four elements be present: (1) a harm that rarely occurs in the absence of negligence, (2) the defendant's exclusive control of the instrumentality that caused the injury, (3) no contribution by the plaintiff to the bad result, and (4) the defendant's sole possession of the information regarding what actually occurred. Typical cases in the medical area involve such occurrences as surgical instruments left inside a patient or removal of the wrong limb. In the psychiatric area, the courts have not required expert witnesses when the plaintiff alleges having had sexual relations during therapy,[214] having been beaten by the therapist,[215] or, in the case of a person on suicide precautions, having been permitted near an open window out of which he jumped.[216]

If liability is established, the plaintiff, in order to recover monetary compensation, must still prove damages. In cases involving mental health treatment this will often be hard to do since it is difficult to place a determinable dollar value on psychological injury unaccompanied by physical injury.[217] It has been suggested that the difficulty in proving damages helps explain the comparatively few suits against mental health professionals.[218]

2. Common Sources of Malpractice Suits

(a) Suicide Suicide is a major cause of death in the United States.[219] It is also the leading cause of suits against psychiatrists and psychiatric facilities.[220] In these cases the establishment of the defendant's negligence typically turns on the foreseeability of the suicide and on the precautions taken (or not taken) to prevent that suicide. Therapists have been held liable for failure to diagnose suicidal risks and for failure to take steps to prevent harm once the risk is known.[221] The plaintiff must establish that the therapist or hospital's actions or inaction were the proximate cause of death; mere errors in judgment are not sufficient to create liability. Thus, for liability to be established it must be shown that the defendant, as a reasonable professional, should have been aware of the suicide risk posed by the deceased and that he failed to take proper precautions to protect the

212. McCoid, The Care Required of Medical Practitioners, 12 Vand. L. Rev. 549, 555 (1959).

213. Comment, The Psychologist as Expert Witness: Science in the Courtroom? 38 Md. L. Rev. 539 (1979).

214. See, e.g., Cooper v. Board of Medical Examiners, 49 Cal. App.3d 931, 123 Cal. Rptr. 563 (1975).

215. See, e.g., Hammer v. Rosen, 165 N.E.2d 756 (N.Y. 1960).

216. See, e.g., Meier v. Ross General Hosp., 445 P.2d 519, 71 Cal. Rptr. 903.

217. Rothblatt & Leroy, Avoiding Psychiatric Malpractice, 9 Cal. W.L. Rev. 260, 264 (1973).

218. *Id.* at 260; Tarshis, Liability for Psychotherapy, 30 Faculty L. Rev. 75 (1972).

219. Holinger, Self-Destructiveness Among the Young: An Epidemiological Study of Violent Deaths, 27 Int'l J. of Social Psychiatry 277 (1981).

220. As one group of commentators has said:

> In contrast to the almost passive acceptance of a potential for fatal outcome in physical disease, the mentally ill patient is not expected to die. This position may be held by the family and friends in the face of repeated self-inflicted assaults on life, the gravity of which may far exceed those complications which would normally prepare a family for the possibility of death.

Slawson, Flinn, & Schwartz, Legal Responsibility for Suicide, 48 Psychiatric Q. 50, 51 (1974).

The tentative results of a five-year study (1974–78) by the American Psychiatric Association of contacts between the psychiatrist and his insurance company reveal that "suicide appears to be the single factor most frequently associated with psychiatric malpractice claims." Slawson & Guggenheim, Psychiatric Malpractice: A Review of the National Loss Experience, 141 Am. J. Psychiatry 979, 980 (1984). Most of the suits are against the hospital, although the negligence of the mental health professional will be asserted as part of the suit. See also Beresford, Professional Liability of Psychiatrists, 21 Def. L.J. 123, 157 (1972).

221. See, e.g., Annot., 17 A.L.R. 4th 1128 (1982), for a good survey of the cases in this area.

deceased from harming himself. Because of the great difficulty in predicting suicide, liability will be found only in those rare situations where indications of risk were overwhelming.[222]

An example of a "judgment error" is described in *Katz v. State*.[223] The defendant institution's staff had determined that the patient did not seem suicidal, even though they had been informed of previous suicide attempts. The patient, after being placed on a unit with minimal restrictions, escaped and then committed suicide. The court held that mere error in medical judgment regarding the patient's suicide risk was not sufficient to hold the facility liable. By contrast, where the staff itself recognizes that a patient is suicidal and specifies that he should be kept on "suicide precautions" or "always attended," liability will result if he is then permitted access to a means of escape or to dangerous devices such as knives or razors.[224]

The problem presented to the treatment staff is how to protect the patient while at the same time not wholly restraining his liberty. It is generally recognized that it is psychologically beneficial to subject a patient to as few restraints as possible;[225] this is legally mandated as well, according to the concept of least restrictive alternative.[226] Moreover, some persons will succeed in committing suicide, no matter how stringent the precautions.[227] Liability, then, typically will be imposed only in the most egregious cases.

(b) Negligent administration of somatic therapy □□ The second most frequent basis for liability is the negligent administration of somatic (nonverbal) therapies. The early suits in the 1950s raised the issue of liability as a result of physical injuries suffered from the improper administration of insulin shock therapy and electroconvulsive therapy (ECT) and the use of wet-pack treatments.[228] Today, suits more often result from the improper prescribing or monitoring of medication. Suits arising out of the alleged negligent administering of somatic therapy may involve claims (1) that the psychiatrist failed to warn the patient of the risks inherent in the treatment, (2) that he failed to respond to the patient's complaints during or after the therapy, (3) that he was negligent in the administration of the therapy, or (4) that he committed some act outside the scope of treatment.[229] Since somatic therapies can result in physical injuries, they pose probably the greatest risk of liability and damage awards.

Until recent decades, the administration of electroconvulsive therapy (ECT) created the highest risk of liability for the therapist. Indeed, a 1954 law review article noted that malpractice carriers were reluctant to insure physicians and hospitals administering ECT.[230] Claims resulting from the administration of ECT today are rare,[231] however. This is in part because of the use of muscle relaxants that greatly reduce the likelihood of physical injury during ECT treatments. Another factor is that ECT is now administered infrequently, the procedure having been replaced in many instances by medication therapy.[232] Other earlier therapies that generated suits, such as insulin shock and wet packs, are no longer used.

Liability for the negligent administration of medication may be based on several theories, including: (1) prescription of a contraindicated medication, (2) prescription of the wrong dosage, or lack of careful monitoring of the patient's reaction to the medication, (3) failure to do a physical examination and/or to ascertain the patient's medical history and his potential for allergic reactions, and (4) failure to give warning regarding possible side effects of the medication.

It is now known that the use of neuroleptic medications can cause a clinical syndrome known as tardive dyskinesia, which is characterized by involuntary movements.[233] There is no known correlation, however, between the amount of medication taken, the duration of treatment, and the development of the syndrome. Nor is there any known cure, although reduction or elimination of the medication sometimes reduces the involuntary movements. While few suits have been brought, and fewer have succeeded, tardive dyskinesia is likely to be the basis for an increasing amount of litigation in the

222. See, e.g., Beresford, *supra* note 220; Dawidoff, The Malpractice of Psychiatrists: Malpractice in Psychoanalysis, Psychotherapy and Psychiatry 131 (1973).

223. 46 Misc. 2d 61, 258 N.Y.S.2d 912 (Ct. Cl. 1965).

224. See, e.g., Meier v. Ross General Hosp., 445 P.2d 519, 71 Cal. Rptr. 903 (1968), which involved the patient's being placed in a second-floor unit with an open window; see also the cases cited in Annot., 11 A.L.R. 4th 1128 (1982).

225. Wedge, Changing Perceptions of Mental Health, 48 Mental Hygiene 22 (1964).

226. See ch. 5, Rights Of Institutionalized Persons, § VII, Least Restrictive Alternative, *supra*.

227. Fishalow, The Tort Liability of the Psychiatrist, 3 A.A.P.L. Bull. 191, 204 (1975).

228. Morse, The Tort Liability of the Psychiatrist, 19 Baylor L. Rev. 208 (1967).

229. Horan & Milligan, Recent Developments in Psychiatric Malpractice, 1 Behav. Sci. & L. 23, 28 (1983).

230. Rebein, Liability for Injury Caused by "Shock" Treatment, 2 Kan. L. Rev. 393 (1954).

231. The initial results of the American Psychiatric Association's five-year study show liability claims as a result of ECT is very rare. Slawson & Guggenheim, *supra* note 220.

232. Scovern & Kilmann, Status of Electroconvulsive Therapy: Review of the Outcome Literature, 87 Psychological Bull. 260 (1980).

233. See Wettstein, Tardive Dyskinesia and Malpractice, 1 Behav. Sci. & L. 85, 86 (1983) for the most thorough article relating to tardive dyskinesia and its potential for malpractice liability for therapists. See in this book ch. 6, Treatment Rights, for a discussion of medications and their side effects.

future.[234] So long as the therapist forewarns the patient of the risk and obtains an informed consent regarding the prescription of neuroleptic medication, he will minimize the chances of being found liable.

(c) Negligent diagnosis Another potential source of liability for mental health professionals is negligent diagnosis. For the psychiatrist these cases most frequently involve failure to recognize that a patient is likely to commit suicide or erroneous diagnoses of the illness.[235] Psychologists may also face liability for misinterpreting the results of psychological tests, which may have serious consequences in the employment setting, child custody disputes, and the disposition of criminal offenders.[236] Although liability for negligent diagnosis has thus far been only rarely established, there is increasing discussion of liability for failures of this type, in particular the failure to predict the dangerousness of a patient.[237]

(d) Sexual activity with a patient Although therapist-patient sexual liaisons have generated considerable publicity, the number of suits in which it has been alleged that the therapist engaged in sexual relations with the patient actually is small, albeit increasing.[238] Perhaps the most discussed case is *Zipkin v. Freeman*.[239] The plaintiff initially sought treatment for headaches that were thought to be psychosomatic. Although the headaches disappeared after two months, the doctor convinced the patient to remain in treatment. They became lovers, and the plaintiff left her family and moved into an apartment near the doctor's office. She invested in the doctor's business ventures and at his suggestion filed suit against family members.[240] When she threatened to leave him, he threatened to have her committed. Ultimately, the by-then disaffected patient sued her therapist. While holding the defendant liable for damages, the court also found that the transference was a part of psychotherapy and that the misuse of it was deemed an abuse of "professional services," which would be covered by the terms of the defendant's malpractice policy.[241]

The case of *Hartogs v. Employers Mutual Liability Insurance Co. of Wisconsin*[242] reached an opposite result, the court holding that the insurance company *did not* have to cover a psychiatrist who had been held liable in a suit brought by a patient as a result of his having had sexual intercourse with her. The court said that the therapist knew that his "fornication therapy" was undertaken for his own personal satisfaction and was not part of any legitimate treatment program. As such, he could not invoke the protection of his medical malpractice insurance policy.[243]

In addition to facing personal monetary liability, the therapist in these cases also risks the criminal charge of rape[244] and loss of his professional license.[245] It is likely that future courts will find sexual relations with a patient as actionable per se.[246] Courts will stress the fiduciary relationship that exists between the therapist and the patient and characterize the sexual activity as a betrayal of the patient's trust and an "unfair capitalization on the patient's transference feelings."[247]

(e) Improper psychotherapy To date, there are no reported cases involving malpractice by mental health professionals in which purely verbal therapy is the stated cause of harm. This is in part because of the difficulty of associating verbal therapy with demonstrable injury. It also may be the result of the therapist's ability to help the patient deal with negative feelings, including those toward the therapist. In either event, unless the therapy involved some unique approach not considered acceptable by professional standards, it would be difficult to prove that the therapist was at fault in his treatment of the patient. An unsatisfactory result is in itself not sufficient for a finding of malpractice.

(f) Informed consent Malpractice suits can be brought against mental health professionals for failure to obtain the patient's informed consent to the treatment, although to date these suits have been very rare.[248] Informed consent presupposes a competent patient who knowingly and voluntarily approves his treatment.[249] In order to establish malpractice, the plaintiff would have to show that a proper consent was not ob-

234. Wettstein, *supra* note 233, at 90, 91, in which he reports knowledge of four cases.

235. Fishalow, *supra* note 227, at 194.

236. Cohen, The Professional Liability of Behavioral Scientists: An Overview, 1 Behav. Sci. & L. 9, 18 (1983); Kahn & Taft, The Application of the Standard of Care Doctrine to Psychological Testing, 1 Behav. Sci. & L. 71 (1983).

237. See in this chapter § II B, the Duty to Warn, and § II C, Negligent Discharge, *infra*.

238. Trent & Muhl, Professional Liability Insurance and the American Psychiatrist, 132 Am. J. Psychiatry 1312 (1975). Both the American Psychiatric Association and the American Psychological Association take the view that having sexual relations with a patient is improper under any circumstances.

239. 436 S.W.2d 753 (Mo. 1969).

240. *Id.* The reported case does not indicate why she filed suit against her family members.

241. *Id.* at 764.

242. 391 N.Y.S.2d 962 (Sup. Ct. Spec. Term 1977).

243. *Id.* at 964. Now many insurance policies specify that they do not cover unethical behavior.

244. Horan & Guerrini, *supra* note 39, at 75.

245. See, e.g., Solloway v. Department of Professional Regulation, 421 So. 2d 573 (Fla. Dist. Ct. App. 1982); Cooper v. Board of Medical Examiners, 49 Cal. App. 3d 931, 123 Cal. Rptr. 563 (1975).

246. See Horan & Milligan, *supra* note 229, at 30.

247. T.G. Gutheil & P.S. Applebaum, Clinical Handbook of Psychiatry and the Law 153 (1982).

248. The American Psychiatric Association's study (Slawson & Guggenheim, *supra* note 220) found that claims based on lack of informed consent were the least frequent claims to malpractice insurance carriers.

249. The doctrine of informed consent is discussed in greater detail in ch. 7, Incompetency, Guardianship, and Restoration, *supra*.

tained prior to the treatment procedure, that some harm resulted, and that if he had been fully informed he would have chosen not to proceed. The dispute in consent cases generally focuses on assessing what constitutes "informed" consent. How much detail of possible risk the therapist should have provided must generally be established by expert testimony. The relative dearth of cases on the issue may be attributable to the fact that the majority of mental health treatments are not inherently risky.

3. Why Malpractice Suits Are Uncommon

Probably one of the primary reasons for the relatively small amount of malpractice litigation against mental health professionals[250] is the imprecision of diagnosis and treatment of mental and emotional disorders, making it exceedingly difficult to establish a standard of proper care against which to measure unsuccessful treatments. Inasmuch as there are more than 200 types of therapy,[251] establishing that one approach was the one and only correct way to proceed is very problematic. When this is combined with the absence of physical injury, the problem of proving that the treatment or lack thereof proximately caused the harm and the difficult task of measuring damages make a rather forbidding legal scenario for the potential plaintiff.

Already mentioned has been the transference phenomenon,[252] which may lead a patient to view his therapist as a friend and make him reluctant to find fault with the treatment, much less to initiate legal proceedings. In addition, because of possible negative reactions by employers, friends, and family, few people are willing to open up to public view their emotional problems and the fact that they sought mental treatment. Thus, even in blatant cases of malpractice, such as the therapist's having sexual relations with the patient, the latter may be reluctant to institute legal action. Finally, the aggrieved patient may realize, or be so counseled by his attorney, that success in the legal action will ultimately boil down to the patient's word against the therapist's, with the former's most likely to be considered the less credible.

B. The Duty to Warn

It is a well-recognized legal principle that in the absence of a specific statutory provision to the contrary, there generally is no affirmative duty and thus no liability for failure to control the behavior of another or to warn a third person of another's threat.[253] There are two exceptions to this rule: where there is a special duty—usually a custodial relationship—between the party considered responsible and the one considered dangerous, and where the party considered responsible expressly undertakes to warn the endangered third party but fails to do so adequately.[254] In *Tarasoff v. Regents of the University of California* the California Supreme Court in two decisions—*Tarasoff I*[255] and *Tarasoff II*[256]—enunciated a new common law duty to warn, applicable to mental health professionals whose patients constitute a threat to third parties, even when the patient is being seen on an outpatient basis and there is no true custodial relationship.

While *Tarasoff* has generated an outpouring of commentary by attorneys and mental health professionals alike, the ruling in fact reflected what probably already existed as an ethical obligation. Even before the decisions, the Principles of Ethics of the American Medical Association stated:

> A physician may not reveal the confidences entrusted to him in the course of medical attendance, or the deficiencies he may observe in the character of patients, unless he is required to do so by law or unless it becomes necessary in order to protect the welfare of the individual or of the community.[257]

In its annotation accompanying these Principles the American Psychiatric Association took the position that "[p]sychiatrists at times may find it necessary, in order to protect the patient or the community from imminent danger, to reveal confidential information disclosed by the patient."[258] Moreover, a number of states have encouraged, although they have not required, therapists to abide by this ethical obligation by enacting exceptions to their therapist-patient confidentiality statutes, immunizing the therapist from liability that might otherwise exist under these laws if he in good faith believes, and so reports, that his patient or others are in danger.[259]

Tarasoff commands particular attention because it

250. Rothblatt & Leroy, *supra* note 217, at 265; Slawson & Guggenheim, *supra* note 220. See, e.g., Comment, The Liability of Psychiatrists for Malpractice, 36 U. Pitt. L. Rev. 108 (1974); Fink, Medical Malpractice: The Liability of Psychiatrists, 48 Notre Dame Law. 693 (1973); Fishalow, *supra* note 227.

251. R. Herink, The Psychotherapy Handbook (1980).

252. Fishalow, *supra* note 227, at 192.

253. See Restatement (Second) of Torts § 315 (1965); W.L. Prosser, Handbook of the Law of Torts § 356 (4th Ed. 1971).

254. See Restatement (Second) of Torts §§ 315-20 (1965). Typically mental institutions and prisons are considered responsible for keeping dangerous people locked away so they will not harm society. See in this chapter § II C, Negligent Discharge, *infra*.

255. 529 P.2d 553, 118 Cal. Rptr. 129 (1974) [hereinafter cited as Tarasoff I].

256.51 P.2d 334, 131 Cal. Rptr. 14 (1976) [hereinafter cited as Tarasoff II].

257. A.P.A. Annotations, *supra* note 115, at 1059.

258. *Id.* at 1063 (annotation to § 9 of the AMA Principles of Medical Ethics).

259. See, e.g., Note, Medical Malpractice—Psychotherapist's Liability to Third Persons for Violent Acts of Patient, 55 N.D.L. Rev. 253 (1979).

creates a *legally* enforceable duty to warn, the breach of which may expose the therapist to civil liability for damages.

1. The Tarasoff Decisions

In October 1969, Prosenjit Poddar, a graduate student at the University of California, fatally shot and stabbed Tatiana Tarasoff, a fellow student who earlier had spurned his romantic overtures. Following her rejection of him, Tarasoff had left the country. During her absence, Poddar on nine occasions saw two therapists, a psychiatrist and a psychologist, at the University of California's Student Health Service in Berkeley. Both therapists diagnosed Poddar as an acute paranoid schizophrenic. During his last therapy session Poddar alluded to his intention to kill Tarasoff. His therapist requested Poddar's assurance that he would not take any such action; he further implied that he would take steps to prevent Poddar from doing any harm to the woman.[260] Poddar then angrily left the session and did not return subsequently for treatment. The therapist notified the campus police for the purpose of initiating involuntary commitment proceedings.[261] However, the police, after investigating the matter and receiving Poddar's promise that he would stay away from Tarasoff, concluded that civil commitment proceedings were not justified.[262] A few weeks later, the woman returned from abroad. Poddar attempted to contact her daily; she refused to see him; ultimately, Poddar did continue to see her and killed her.

At his trial the jury concluded that Poddar had been sane at the time of the killing and that he had not been suffering from diminished capacity.[263] His murder conviction later was reversed, however, on technical grounds relating to the instructions given to the jury by the trial court judge.[264] As a result of information revealed during the course of the trial, Tarasoff's family filed suit against the University of California, the two therapists, and the campus police, seeking damages based on the theory that Tarasoff had been due a warning as to Poddar's danger to her and that the failure to so warn her constituted actionable negligence.

Both the trial court and the intermediate appellate court in the civil case ruled that the Tarasoff family had failed to state an actionable cause of action. However, the California Supreme Court reversed, holding that a cause of action could be maintained against the therapist and the police for failing to warn the victim.[265] Subsequently, the case was reargued before the court. In the second *Tarasoff* ruling the court excluded the police from liability.[266] But it reaffirmed its reasoning that there exists a special relationship between a psychotherapist and his patient which engenders affirmative duties to third persons who are endangered by the patient and that the failure to take action may expose the therapist to liability. The court held:

> When a therapist determines, or pursuant to the standards of his profession should determine, that his patient presents a serious danger of violence to another, he incurs an obligation to use reasonable care to protect the intended victim against such danger. The discharge of this duty may require the therapist to take one or more of various steps, depending upon the nature of the case. Thus, it may call for him to warn the intended victim or others likely to apprise the victim of the danger, to notify the police, or to take whatever other steps are reasonably necessary under the circumstances.[267]

The court went on to make clear that the standard of care typically applied in malpractice suits would apply here as well:

> Obviously we do not require that the therapist, in making that determination, render a perfect performance; the therapist need only exercise "that reasonable degree of skill, knowledge, and care ordinarily possessed and exercised by members of [that professional specialty] under similar circumstances." Within the broad range of reasonable practice and treatment in which professional opinion and judgment may differ, the therapist is free to exercise his or her own best judgment without liability; proof, aided by hindsight, that he or she judged wrongly is insufficient to establish negligence.[268]

The court summarized its holding by stating that "the therapist owes a legal duty not only to his patient, but also to his patient's would-be victim and is subject in both respects to scrutiny by judge and jury."[269]

Subsequently, the University of California reached a settlement with the Tarasoffs for an undisclosed amount, making unnecessary a final determination whether the therapist had in fact failed to meet the standard of care set forth by the California Supreme Court.[270]

260. For a good description of the facts in both the civil and the criminal cases, see Winslade, Psychotherapeutic Discretion and Judicial Decision: A Case of Enigmatic Justice *in* The Law-Medicine Relation: A Philosophical Exploration 139-57 (J.M. Healey & H.T. Tristram eds. 1981).

261. People v. Prosenjit Poddar, 518 P.2d 342, 111 Cal. Rptr. 910 (1974).

262. Tarasoff's brother Alex was Poddar's roommate. Ironically, he was aware of the threats but did not take them seriously.

263. People v. Prosenjit Poddar, 518 P.2d at 344, 111 Cal. Rptr. at 912.

264. *Id.* at 350, 111 Cal. Rptr. at 918.

265. Tarasoff I, 529 P.2d 553, 118 Cal. Rptr. 129 (1974).

266. Tarasoff II, 551 P.2d 334, 352-53, 131 Cal. Rptr. 14, 32-33 (1976).

267. *Id.* at 340, 131 Cal. Rptr. at 32.

268. *Id.*

269. *Id.* at 345-46.

270. See Merton, Confidentiality and the "Dangerous" Patient: Implications of *Tarasoff* for Psychiatrists and Lawyers, 31 Emory L.J. 263, 295 (1982).

2. *Contours of the Duty to Warn*

The *Tarasoff II* court relied upon an article by Fleming and Maximov,[271] which began by describing the facts surrounding the Tarasoff killing and concluded that a legal duty to warn pertained to the psychotherapist. In reaching that conclusion, they asserted that "by entering into a doctor-patient relationship the therapist becomes sufficiently involved to assume some responsibility for the safety, not only of the patient himself, but also of any third person whom the doctor knows to be threatened by the patient."[272] Obviously, this duty to warn creates conflict for the therapist, who is engaged in a confidential relationship with his patient. The two authors, writing before the *Tarasoff II* decision, had suggested four guidelines designed to avert too-easy breach of confidentiality:

- the therapist should secure a second professional opinion as to the potential dangerousness of the patient;
- the therapist should not take any action until the danger is imminent;
- when the danger is imminent the therapist should select the form of intervention which is least harmful to the patient's interests;
- the therapist at the outset of treatment should warn the patient of the circumstances in which he would feel compelled to breach confidentiality.[273]

The *Tarasoff II* court subsequently put the matter this way:

> Weighing the uncertain and conjectural character of the alleged damage done the patient by such a warning against the peril to the victim's life, we conclude that professional inaccuracy in predicting violence cannot negate the therapist's duty to protect the threatened victim.
>
> The risk that unnecessary warnings may be given is a reasonable price to pay for the lives of possible victims that may be saved.[274]

In justifying its refusal to honor a therapist-patient privilege, the court stated that "[t]he protective privilege ends where the public peril begins."[275]

3. *Arguments Against a Duty to Warn*

Neither Fleming and Maximov's guidelines nor the less carefully constructed *Tarasoff II* opinion resolves basic issues involved in placing a legal duty on the therapist to warn third parties of dangers posed by patients. In addition to the criticism that the Fleming and Maximov reasoning reflects an undue optimism regarding the therapist's ability to control his patient in the outpatient setting,[276] two other arguments have been put forth that point to the unworkability of imposing a duty to warn. These are: first, that therapists are unable to predict dangerousness, and second, that the breach of confidentiality required by a warning is destructive to the therapeutic relationship.

(a) Inability to predict dangerousness□□The belief that a therapist can predict dangerousness has been widely accepted by legislatures and is the foundation for many civil commitment statutes[277] as well as for release provisions of criminal commitment laws.[278] Yet there is strong evidence to indicate that mental health professionals are unable to predict dangerousness[279] and that their success rate may be no better than that arrived at by tossing a coin.[280] Indeed, just a few months before the first *Tarasoff* decision a task force of the American Psychiatric Association (APA) concluded that "neither psychiatrists nor anyone else have reliably demonstrated an ability to predict future violence or 'dangerousness.' Neither has any special psychiatric expertise in this area been established."[281]

Studies reveal that there are many "false positives" when therapists attempt to predict dangerousness, meaning many more people are predicted to be violent in the future than actually will be.[282] Dangerousness "is a way of describing the probable outcome of interaction between a person and the environment or social situation in which that person functions. To predict violent behavior is to speculate about someone's future response

271. Fleming & Maximov, The Patient or His Victim: The Therapist's Dilemma, 62 Calif. L. Rev. 1025 (1974).

272. *Id.* at 1030-31.

273. *Id.* at 1065-66.

274. 551 P.2d at 346, 131 Cal. Rptr. at 26.

275. *Id.* at 347.

276. See, e.g., Dix, *Tarasoff* and the Duty to Warn Potential Victims, *in* Law and Ethics, *supra* note 140; Sloan & Klein, Psychotherapeutic Disclosures: A Conflict Between Right and Duty, 9 Toledo L. Rev. 57 (1977); Stone, The *Tarasoff* Decisions: Suing Psychotherapists to Safeguard Society, 90 Harv. L. Rev. 358 (1976).

277. The notion that a person is "dangerous to self or others" is contained in most civil commitment laws. See in this book ch. 2, Involuntary Institutionalization; *supra*; see also Weissbourd, Involuntary Commitment: The Move Toward Dangerousness, 15 J. Mar. L. Rev. 83 (1982).

278. Once someone is considered "no longer dangerous" he will be eligible for release. See in this book ch. 12, Mental Disability and the Criminal Law, for a discussion of release provisions for persons found not guilty by reason of insanity.

279. Diamond, The Psychiatric Prediction of Dangerousness, 123 U. Pa. L. Rev. 439 (1974); Monahan, *supra* note 72; Rubin, Prediction of Dangerousness in Mentally Ill Criminals, 27 Archives Gen. Psychiatry 397 (1972); Steadman & Keveles, The Community Adjustment and Criminal Activity of the Baxstrom Patients: 1966-70, 129 Am. J. Psychiatry 304 (1972).

280. Ennis & Litwack, Psychiatry and the Presumption of Expertise: Flipping Coins in the Courtroom, 62 Calif. L. Rev. 639 (1974).

281. American Psychiatric Association Task Force on Clinical Aspects of the Violent Individual, Rep. No. 8, Clinical Aspects of the Violent Individual 28 (1974).

282. See Monahan, *supra* note 72; also Steadman & Keveles, *supra* note 279.

to a complex of variables, any one of which may or may not occur."[283] Psychiatrists argue that "dangerousness" is a legal construct, not a medical one, and a poorly defined construct at that.[284] Thus, if therapists must satisfy a duty to warn, they will be warning many more people than the number who actually face danger. The social cost implications of this—fostering a climate of fear and distrust—may be significant. So long as our understanding of violent behavior is crude and there is no reliable method of predicting future violence, liability based on a failure to warn a potential victim is both impractical and unjust.

(b) Confidentiality and the therapeutic relationship☐ This chapter began with an extensive discussion of the importance of confidentiality to the therapeutic relationship.[285] Confidentiality is particularly important to the patient with thoughts of violence.

As one group of experts has pointed out:

> [A]s a class, patients willing to express to psychiatrists their intention to commit crime are not ordinarily likely to carry out that intention. Instead, they are making a plea for help. The very making of such pleas affords the psychiatrist his unique opportunity to work with patients in an attempt to resolve their problems. Such resolutions would be impeded if patients were unable to speak freely for fear of possible disclosure at a later date in a legal proceeding.[286]

It has been suggested that at the outset of therapy the therapist explain the confidential nature of the relationship and the circumstances under which he may have to breach confidences revealed in therapy,[287] which puts the patient on notice and permits the therapist to feel free to breach confidentiality when the situation fits the circumstances outlined. The counter argument to such a priori admonitions is that they may discourage those most in need of help from seeking it and will inhibit full revelation of feelings and thoughts, which is crucial for successful psychotherapy.[288]

Furthermore, a warning actually delivered by the therapist to a third party can itself generate negative results. It may in fact trigger the feared violent action from the patient, who, when he learns of the warning, takes action to "live up to" the therapist's expectations.[289] Or the intended victim, in response to the warning, may take preemptive action against the patient, thus precipitating needless tragedy since the patient may not have actually carried out the threat.[290] For these reasons, many in the therapeutic community oppose the duty to warn.[291]

4. Post-Tarasoff Cases

Since the *Tarasoff* decision a number of suits have been brought attempting to impose liability on therapists who, it is argued, should have known that an individual posed a danger to others. The plaintiffs in some of these suits have attempted to extend the duty to warn to a wide variety of nontherapeutic agents, including attorneys,[292] probation and parole officers,[293] and even the owner of a massage parlor.[294] The cases that have followed the *Tarasoff* logic have generally held that the duty is owed only when there is an identifiable victim.[295]

A case with a fact pattern almost identical to *Tarasoff* is *McIntosh v. Milano*,[296] in which the parents of a girl killed by a person in outpatient therapy brought suit against the therapist, a Dr. Milano, claiming he owed a duty to warn of the danger his patient posed to their daughter. Lee Morganstein, the patient, had been under treatment with Milano for more than two years before the murder. During the treatment he revealed that he carried a knife to frighten people or scare them away. He also discussed his feelings for Peggy McIntosh, the victim, and told the therapist how he had once shot a BB gun at a car that he believed belonged to McIntosh's boyfriend, since he was upset that she was going on a date. As a result of the information revealed during the criminal trial, the plaintiffs felt Milano was negligent in his duty to their daughter.

283. See Merton, *supra* note 270, at 299.
284. *Id.*
285. See in this chapter § I A, The Importance of Confidentiality, *supra*.
286. Goldstein & Katz, *supra* note 3, at 739.
287. Roth & Meisel, Dangerousness, Confidentiality, and the Duty to Warn, 134 Am. J. Psychiatry 508, 510 (1979); see also Fleming & Maximov, *supra* note 271, at 1057.
288. Stone, *supra* note 276, at 369.
289. See brief of amicus curiae at Schneider v. Vine St. Clinic, 77 Ill. App. 3d 946, 397 N.E.2d 194 (1979).
290. Griffith & Griffith, Duty to Third Parties, Dangerousness, and the Right to Refuse Treatment: Problematic Concepts for Psychiatrist and Lawyer, 14 Cal. W.L. Rev. 241, 254 (1978).
291. See Sloan & Klein, *supra* note 276, at 72; also Merton, *supra* at 270; Roth & Meisel, *supra* note 287, at 510.
292. See Hawkins v. King County Dep't of Rehabilitative Servs., 24 Wash. App. 338, 602 P.2d 361 (1979). At the bail hearing the attorney who was warned by a psychiatrist that his client was mentally ill and dangerous did not advise the court of these facts. The court held that the duty of counsel to be loyal to his client overrode the disclosure of information that would be detrimental to the client's interest.
293. See, e.g., Thompson v. County of Alameda, 614 P.2d 728, 167 Cal. Rptr. 70 (1980), which involved the release into the community of a dangerous juvenile. The court held that there is no duty to warn the community of the release of a dangerous individual. See also Semler v. Psychiatric Inst. of Washington, D.C., 538 F.2d 121 (4th Cir. 1976), in which a probation officer was held liable for not following a court order relating to release. This case would be more appropriately discussed as a negligent release case.
294. See Mangeris v. Gordon, 580 P.2d 481 (Nev. 1978), which rejected the notion that the manager of a massage parlor owed a duty to warn of harm, particularly when there was no foreseeable victim.
295. See, e.g., Brady v. Hopper, 570 F. Supp. 1333 (D. Col. 1983); Leedy v. Hartnett, 510 F. Supp. 1125 (M.D. Pa. 1981); Cole v. Taylor, 301 N.W.2d 766 (Iowa 1981); Cairl v. State, 323 N.W.2d 20 (Minn. 1982); McIntosh v. Milano, 403 A.2d 500 (N.J. 1979).
296. 403 A.2d 500 (N.J. 1979).

As in the *Tarasoff* case, the initial suit was dismissed on the belief that there was no valid claim stated against the defendant. However, the New Jersey Supreme Court reinstated the case, following the reasoning of *Tarasoff*. The Court said:

> [A] psychiatrist or therapist may have a duty to take whatever steps are reasonably necessary to protect an intended or potential victim of his patient when he determines, or should determine, in appropriate factual setting and in accordance with the standards of his profession established at trial, that the patient is or may present a probability of danger to that person, . . .[297]

The case was sent back to the lower court for trial, the state supreme court observing that there remained "a factual question which should be presented to a jury as to whether, based on expert testimony, defendant breached the appropriate duty in this case."[298] At the trial Dr. Milano was exonerated from liability.[299]

In *Leedy v. Hartnett*,[300] the defendant, Hartnett, had discharged himself from a Veterans Administration hospital and notified the hospital that he was staying with the Leedys. He had a prior history of numerous hospitalizations and of many violent outbursts during these hospitalizations. On the night of the harm to the plaintiffs all the parties went out to celebrate Hartnett's birthday. He drank more than 24 bottles of beer and also took 400 milligrams of Thorazine, an antipsychotic drug. Sometime after the Leedys went to sleep, they were beaten. Although they did not see their attacker, the police found no signs of forced entry, and it was assumed that Hartnett was the aggressor. The Leedys sued the Veterans Administration, but the court ruled for the defendant, reasoning:

> In order for the rule of liability announced in *Tarasoff* to be kept within workable limits, those charged with the care of potentially dangerous people must be able to know to whom to give warnings. When, as in *Tarasoff* and *McIntosh*, a particular victim can be identified, there is good reason to impose upon psychiatrists or custodians a duty to warn the intended victim of the danger posed by the person under their care. On the facts of this case, however, Hartnett did not pose any danger to the Leedys different from the danger he posed to anyone with whom he might be in contact when he became violent.[301]

Following similar logic, the Minnesota Supreme Court in *Cairl v. State of Minnesota* held "that if a duty to warn exists, it does so only when specific threats are made against specific victims."[302] The case involved an institutionalized retarded child who had a long history of setting fires. Released to his mother for Christmas vacation, he set a fire in which one of his sisters was killed and another was seriously injured. The plaintiffs sought to hold the boy's institutional custodian liable. In rejecting liability based on the failure-to-warn theory, the court opined that the mother was well aware of her son's history and that the staff had no duty to issue any warnings.[303]

Three cases have expanded on the identifiable victim theory by holding that a duty may also exist when there is an identifiable *class* of victims.[304] In *Lipari v. Sears Roebuck*,[305] a federal diversity action was brought against Sears for selling a gun to a mentally ill person who subsequently used it to shoot into a crowded barroom, killing one person and injuring another. Sears joined the Veterans Administration in the action, based on the patient's having been treated and released from the V.A. The court concluded that under Nebraska precedents "the therapist/patient relationship gives rise to an affirmative duty for the benefit of third persons," asserting that "[t]his duty arises only when, in accordance with the standards of his profession, the therapist knows or should know that his patient's dangerous propensities present an unreasonable risk of harm to others."[306] It reasoned:

> [T]he risk created by the V.A.'s negligence was such that, under the circumstances, the V.A.'s employees could have reasonably foreseen an unreasonable risk of harm to the Liparis or a class of persons of which the Liparis were members. . . . To satisfy this standard, the plaintiff need not prove that the V.A.'s employees knew the identity of the plaintiff or her decedent.[307]

The case was eventually settled out of court with a substantial award paid to the plaintiffs by both Sears and the Veterans Administration.[308]

Similarly, the California Supreme Court in *Thompson v. County of Alameda* asserted that "[i]n those instances in which the released offender poses a predicta-

297. *Id.* at 511–12.
298. *Id.* at 515.
299. Conversation with defense attorney after the trial, which confirmed that Milano was found by a jury not to have violated any duties owed to third parties.
300. 510 F. Supp. 1125 (M.D. Pa. 1981).
301. *Id.* at 1130.

302. 323 N.W.2d 20, 26 (Minn. 1982). See also Furr v. Spring Grove State Hosp., 454 A.2d 414 (Md. 1983), in which the court dismissed a suit where the parents of a murdered child claimed the hospital was liable for the release of the murderer and not warning of the danger posed by the patient. The court found there had to be a "readily identifiable" victim for liability to be imposed.
303. See Cairl v. State, 323 N.W.2d 20, 26 (Minn. 1982).
304. Lipari v. Sears Roebuck, 497 F. Supp. 185 (D. Neb. 1980); Thompson v. County of Alameda, 167 Cal. Rptr. 70, 614 P.2d 728 (1980); Petersen v. State, 671 P.2d 230 (Wash. 1983).
305. 497 F. Supp. 185 (D. Neb. 1980).
306. *Id.* at 191, 193.
307. *Id.* at 194–95.
308. Conversation with the attorney for the plaintiff.

ble threat of harm to a named or readily identifiable victim or group of victims who can be effectively warned of the danger, a releasing agent may well be liable for failure to warn such persons."[309] *Thompson* involved the release of a juvenile offender who was considered to have "extremely dangerous and violent propensities regarding young children."[310] Within 24 hours of being released the juvenile killed a child in the neighborhood. The court, however, found no liability in this particular case, concluding "that public entities and employees have no affirmative duty to warn of the release of an inmate with a violent history who has made *nonspecific threats of harm directed at nonspecific victims*."[311]

The most expansive Court interpretation of the therapist's duty to warn or to take some action to protect unidentifiable victims came in 1983 in *Petersen v. State*,[312] in which the Washington Supreme Court following *Lipari* held that a physician at a state hospital had a duty to protect anyone who might foreseeably be endangered by the former patient's drug-related behavior.[313] Five days after his discharge from a state hospital to which he had been committed, the former patient, Larry Knox, caused an automobile accident, injuring the plaintiff and damaging her automobile. Known to have a history of drug abuse, particularly of angel dust, and on probation for a second burglary conviction consequent to which he had been required to receive counselling, Knox had continued to exhibit bizarre behavior while under treatment, including self-mutilation and, just the day before expiration of his commitment, driving his car erratically on the hospital grounds while out on a pass. Each time the doctor concluded that his behavior was due to a schizophrenic-like reaction to drugs.

The plaintiff brought suit against the state, arguing that the hospital's failure to extend the commitment was the proximate cause of her injuries and that it had negligently treated the patient by failing to protect her from his dangerous tendencies. The Washington Supreme Court concluded that the psychiatrist incurred a duty to take reasonable precautions to protect anyone who might foreseeably be endangered by the patient's drug-related mental problems. In essence the court held the psychiatrist liable for failure to seek further civil commitment.[314]

Petersen not only expands the liability of mental health professionals to anyone who might foreseeably be injured by a mental patient but also raises the issue of at what point therapists are obligated to try to prevent drug-induced behavior. Obviously, the intake of drugs in the hospital setting can be controlled, or at least the resultant behavior monitored, but once someone with a long drug history is discharged, there is nothing the therapist can do to prevent further ingestion of the drugs, short of being with the person 24 hours a day. Whether other courts will follow the reasoning of the Washington Supreme Court remains to be seen. It is too early to tell the full implications of this decision.

The question of whether the therapist has a duty to warn family members that a patient is likely to harm himself or commit suicide has also been litigated. In *Bellah v. Greenson*, the court declined to extend *Tarasoff* "where the risk of harm is self-inflicted harm or mere property damage."[315] The court felt that notifying the parents of their adult daughter's mental state would have been an inappropriate violation of confidentiality. While this limitation on *Tarasoff* should provide some comfort to therapists, the families in these cases are not precluded from bringing a malpractice action based on negligent treatment.

A novel fact situation was presented in *Cole v. Taylor*,[316] in which the plaintiff claimed her therapist had a duty to warn her former husband of the danger she posed to him. The plaintiff murdered her former husband and was convicted. The Supreme Court of Iowa rejected this patently outrageous claim, stating that it had not adopted the *Tarasoff* rationale, and that if it were to do so, it would not apply in this case since the duty to warn runs to the victim, not the patient.[317]

While it is safe to say that *Tarasoff* and subsequent cases will provide the basis for further suits against therapists for failure to warn identifiable potential victims, thus far that duty has not been extended to cases where the patient poses a potential danger to the general public. As was pointed out in *Thompson v. County of Alameda*:

> We are skeptical of any net benefit which might flow from a duty to issue a generalized warning of the probationary release of offenders. In our view, the generalized warnings sought to be required here would do little to increase the precautions of any particular members of the public who already may have become conditioned to locking their doors, avoiding dark and deserted streets, instructing their children to beware of strangers and taking other precautions.[318]

Even if the defendant's duty to warn is established, the plaintiff still has the difficult task of proving at trial that the therapist violated the standards of his profession.

309. 614 P.2d 728, 738, 167 Cal. Rptr. 70, 80 (1980).
310. *Id.* at 730, 167 Cal. Rptr. at 72.
311. *Id.* at 735, 167 Cal. Rptr. at 80 (emphasis in original).
312. 671 P.2d 230 (Wash. 1983).
313. *Id.* at 237.
314. *Id.* at 241–43.
315. 81 Cal. App. 3d 614, 622, 146 Cal. Rptr. 535, 540 (1978).
316. 301 N.W.2d 766 (Iowa 1981).
317. *Id.* at 768.
318. 614 P.2d 728, 736, 167 Cal. Rptr. 70, 78 (1980).

The plaintiff must establish shortcomings in the course of therapy between the therapist and the aggressor,[319] which without access to the treatment records will be difficult to do. The alternative of proving general negligence, as in a malpractice action, will be no easier. Thus, the burdens on the plaintiff are substantial and success is likely in only the most blatant cases.

5. Impact on Mental Health Professionals

The initial response to the *Tarasoff* decision by mental health professionals was one of great concern. Some therapists protested that they were being asked to become "gatekeepers of the criminal justice system" and wondered "When does the healer become the informer?"[320] Others felt that they were damned if they warned and damned if they did not, since liability could occur both for a breach of confidentiality and for a failure to warn.[321] Clearly, the *Tarasoff* decision has generated anxiety and confusion among many mental health professionals.[322] In a survey of California psychiatrists and psychologists conducted four years after *Tarasoff*, it was found that "[o]ver half the therapists reported an increased fear of being sued for failure to exercise their *Tarasoff* duty to warn properly, and a similar number reported feeling greater anxiety in dealing with patients because of *Tarasoff*."[323] The surveyors further reported:

> Most of the therapists surveyed thought that patients will withhold information important to treatment if they believe the therapist may breach confidentiality. One-fourth of the respondent therapists reported actually observing their patients' reluctance to discuss their violent tendencies when informed of the possibility of an exception to absolute confidentiality. The survey also revealed, however, that almost 70% of the therapists believed confidentiality could justifiably be breached in some circumstances. The survey uncovered evidence that therapists have traditionally acted on this belief: A substantial percentage of the respondents report having breached confidentiality by giving warnings about a potentially dangerous patient even before the *Tarasoff* decision.[324]

The surveyors further found that after *Tarasoff* many therapists changed the way they kept their records, with the goal of avoiding legal liability. The study concluded:

> [I]mposing on therapists a *legal* duty to warn, as opposed to the traditionally discretionary professional duty, has had potentially detrimental effects on psychotherapy. Therapists report feeling serious anxiety because of their uncertainty about the scope of their new duty to warn. More specifically, many therapists report altering the character of their dialogue with their patients by focusing their own clinical attention as well as their patients' attention on the patients' capacity for violent behavior and the possibility of breaches in confidentiality to respond to the risk of such behavior.[325]

Numerous articles have been written to advise therapists of what actions they should take when faced with a patient they believe poses a danger.[326] These range from the initiation of civil commitment proceedings[327] to involving the potential victim in the treatment.[328] Roth and Meisel make a number of suggestions, including:

> 1. Since actual violence is relatively rare among psychiatric patients, especially those with no history of previous violence, it is prudent to rely on the odds and not warn. . . .
>
> 2. Before entering into a treatment contract the therapist should inform the patient of the confidential nature of the relationship and the various circumstances under which confidentiality might have to be breached. . . .
>
> 3. Even when danger seems imminent there are a number of social or environmental manipulations which may be agreed upon by the doctor and patient that reduce the patient's dangerousness without compromising confidentiality. For example, other persons may be brought into the therapy or it may be insisted that the patient rid himself of lethal weapons.
>
> 4. . . . When disclosing information about the patient to others, the physician must attempt to obtain the patient's permission to do so and should reveal the disturbing information about the patient in his presence.
>
> 5. The psychiatrist's need to act should always be assessed in light of the impact of the proposed intervention

319. The therapist has no right or duty to release his treatment records to a third party. Without access to the records it will be difficult for the plaintiffs to prove their case. In *McIntosh* and *Tarasoff* detailed information came out at the criminal trial which provided the basis for the civil suits. See, e.g., Comment, Discovery of Psychotherapist-Patient Communications After *Tarasoff*, 15 San Diego L. Rev. 265 (1978), for a good discussion of this issue; see also Mavroudis v. Superior Ct. of San Mateo County, 102 Cal. App. 3d 594, 162 Cal. Rptr. 724 (1980), which permitted an in-camera review of therapists' records to determine if a duty to warn parents arose out of therapists' relationship with their son.

320. Everstine, Everstine, Heymann, True, Frey, Johnson, & Seiden (members of the Committee on Privacy and Confidentiality of the California State Psychological Association), Privacy and Confidentiality in Psychotherapy, 35 Am. Psychologist 828, 839 (1980).

321. Brooks, Mental Health Law: The Right to Refuse Treatment, 4 Administration in Mental Health 94, 96 (1977); see also Roth & Meisel, *supra* note 287, and Stone, *supra* note 276.

322. Appelbaum, *Tarasoff*: An Update on the Duty to Warn, 32 Hosp. & Community Psychiatry (1981); Survey of Psychotherapists, *supra* note 104.

323. Survey of Psychotherapists, *supra* note 104, at 187.

324. *Id.* at 183.

325. *Id.* at 190.

326. For general article on concerns of mental health professionals and a review of the cases see Bursten, Dimensions of Third Party Protection, 6 A.A.P.L. Bull. 405 (1978); Knapp & Vandecreek, *Tarasoff*: Five Years Later, 13 Professional Psychology 511 (1982).

327. See Stone, *supra* note 276.

328. Wexler, Patients, Therapists and Third Parties: The Victimological Virtues of *Tarasoff*, 2 Int'l J.L. & Psychiatry 1 (1979).

> on future therapy with the patient and in light of the likelihood of success in preventing violence. If the probability of compromising future therapy is great and/or if the likelihood of the success of the intervention is slight, the psychiatrist may prefer to rely on the odds and to hope for the best, rather than warning a potential victim or attempting to hospitalize the patient involuntarily.[329]

When a therapist is in doubt about whether his patient poses a danger, he would be well advised to seek another opinion. This not only may help the therapist clarify the issue and confirm his impressions, but also will provide documentation, should he be sued for either his actions or his inactions. It must also be kept in mind that *Tarasoff* and subsequent decisions did not confine the options available to the therapist to that of warning the potential victim. The court held that to discharge the duty the therapist may "take one or more of various steps, depending upon the nature of the case. Thus it may call for him to warn the intended victim or others likely to apprise the victim of the danger, to notify the police, or to take whatever steps are reasonably necessary under the circumstances."[330] In this way the therapist may find a way to protect the victim while at the same time maintaining some prospect of keeping intact the therapeutic relationship.

In the decade since the *Tarasoff I* decision, the question of its practical significance is still open. There is no documentation that as a result of the case therapists have issued warnings, with lives consequently being saved. Nor is there hard evidence to support the belief that imposition of a legal duty to warn has in fact eroded therapeutic relationships and discouraged people in need of treatment from seeking therapy. Clearly, however, the duty to warn cases have heightened the concerns of mental health professionals and perhaps made them more cautious in treating people who they believe are dangerous.

C. Negligent Discharge

The so-called negligent discharge of a patient is today also an actionable wrong. Cases involving this claim typically arise when the discharged mental patient kills or injures someone shortly after release from the hospital. It is claimed in the ensuing lawsuit that the facility was aware of the danger the patient posed to the victim and that the patient's discharge was the proximate cause of the harm to the victim. These cases can be distinguished from the "duty to warn" cases just discussed in two ways. For one, duty-to-warn cases have involved people in outpatient treatment, where the therapist has relatively little control over the individual. Negligent discharge cases involve persons who were institutionalized and whose release from the institution was completely under the control of the hospital staff. Secondly, negligent discharge cases are predicated on the claim that through the facility's affirmative act of releasing the patient the injury to the third party occurred. By contrast, in duty-to-warn cases liability is based on the inaction of the therapist, who failed to take affirmative steps to warn of a danger.

While most negligent discharge cases have been brought against public institutions, private psychiatric facilities also have been held liable.[331] Most often the victim is a family member—frequently a spouse or former spouse.[332] Courts had recognized the concept of negligent discharge long before the duty-to-warn concept was adopted in *Tarasoff*.[333] The typical fact pattern is illustrated by *Merchants National Bank and Trust Co. of Fargo v. United States*,[334] which involved a Mr. Newgard, who was treated at a Veterans Administration hospital after having been civilly committed. The hospital was aware of his wife's fear of him and also aware of the strong negative feelings he had toward her. The hospital gave Newgard a temporary leave to live and work on a ranch, but the owners of the ranch were given no information or instructions regarding him. One weekend he left the ranch and killed his wife. The court concluded that the Veterans Administration had been negligent in releasing the patient and that the release was the cause of Mrs. Newgard's death.[335] In a similar case the United States was held liable for negligently discharging from a military hospital an airman who was permitted to go back on duty without any restrictions, putting him in a position to obtain a pistol that he used to kill his former wife.[336] As in the Newgard case, the hospital was aware of the airman's anger toward his former wife and of her fears of him. The court found that the negligent discharge and the negligence of the United States Air Force in permitting the man to obtain a gun were the proximate causes of the victim's death.[337]

There are also cases in which mental health facilities have been held liable for not fully informing courts of

329. See Roth & Meisel, *supra* note 287, at 509–10 (notes omitted).
330. Tarasoff II, 551 P.2d 334, 340, 131 Cal. Rptr. 14, 20 (1976).

331. See, e.g., Bradley Center Inc. v. Wessner, 250 Ga. 199, 296 S.E.2d 693 (1982).
332. See, e.g., Merchants Nat'l Bank & Trust Co. v. United States, 272 F. Supp. 409 (D.N.D. 1967) (killed wife); Underwood v. United States, 356 F.2d 92 (5th Cir. 1966) (killed former wife); Hicks v. United States, 511 F.2d 407 (D.C. Cir. 1975) (killed wife). Bradley Center, Inc. v. Wessner, 250 Ga. 199, 296 S.E.2d 693 (1982) (killed wife and her lover).
333. See, e.g., Underwood v. United States, 356 F.2d 92 (5th Cir. 1966), which was decided 10 years before the *Tarasoff II* decision.
334. 272 F. Supp. 409 (D.N.D. 1967).
335. *Id.* at 418.
336. Underwood v. United States, 356 F.2d 92 (5th Cir. 1966).
337. *Id.* at 99.

the decision to release a patient. In *Semler v. Psychiatric Institute of Washington, D.C.*,[338] the defendants were treating John Steven Gilreath under a court order that required judicial approval for release from confinement. The court had approved weekend passes but was never asked to approve the man's discharge. One month after his release Gilreath killed a young woman, in circumstances similar to the earlier charge of abducting a woman which had led to his commitment. The court found that "the breach of the court order was the proximate cause of the plaintiff's loss."[339]

Hicks v. United States[340] is a similar case, except that the release was court approved. The finding of negligence was based on the hospital's failure to adequately inform the court of the patient's mental condition and history at the time the discharge was recommended. The patient, a Mr. Morgan, had been committed as a result of criminal charges pressed by his wife after Morgan had beaten her and threatened to kill her. These threats and beatings had occurred on numerous previous occasions. Morgan was released from the hospital and within five weeks he killed his wife. On appeal, the appellate court agreed with the lower court's finding that the negligence of the hospital in not fully informing the court of Morgan's condition was a substantial factor contributing to the release and the subsequent events which proximately caused Mrs. Morgan's death.[341]

In other cases, plaintiffs have been unsuccessful because they were unable to prove that the injury was proximately caused by the negligence of the hospital. In some of these cases there was a long lapse in time between the discharge and the injury.[342] In others, the courts have found that the actions of the facility in discharging the person were appropriate.[343] Obviously, a facility cannot guarantee that every person who is released will not do harm to himself or others.

D. Other Grounds for Liability

There are at least three other bases on which to predicate the mental health professional's liability. These are: (1) breach of confidentiality, (2) false imprisonment, and (3) deprivation of civil rights.

1. Breach of Confidentiality

When a therapist breaches his patient's expectations of confidentiality, real harm may be done to the patient. Although actual financial loss may not be suffered, the emotional damage may be quite severe. There are four theories under which recovery from a therapist for breach of confidentiality may be pursued:[344] (1) breach of contract, (2) invasion of privacy, (3) malpractice, and (4) breach of a statutory duty. Perhaps because of the difficulty of proving damages, few suits have been brought.

2. False Imprisonment

False imprisonment is an intentional tort founded on the claim that the therapist deprived his patient of freedom in an unjustified manner. A few decades ago actions against therapists for false imprisonment were relatively common and served as a means to secure the freedom of the patient.[345] These actions are now rare, in part because most of today's statutes grant the therapist immunity when he moves for civil commitment, at least so long as he acts in good faith.

3. Civil Rights Actions

Since the late 1960s, a growing number of class action lawsuits have been brought challenging the practices and procedures in state mental health facilities. These suits, alleging deprivations of rights guaranteed by the United States Constitution, often seek systemic changes in the institutions and sometimes in the state mental health systems as a whole.[346] They are typically brought under § 1983 of title 42 of the United States Code, which authorizes causes of action for deprivation under color of law "of any rights, privileges, or immunities secured by the Constitution and laws."[347] In many of these suits state employee defendants are sued in both their official and individual capacities and damages are sought. For

338. 538 F.2d 120 (4th Cir. 1976), *cert. denied*, 429 U.S. 827 (1976).

339. *Id.* at 126. It has been argued that in *Semler* strict liability was imposed for failure to follow the court order rather than for any negligence on the part of the hospital staff. See Comment, Psychotherapists' Liability for the Release of Mentally Ill Offenders: A Proposed Expansion of the Theory of Strict Liability, 126 U. Pa. L. Rev. 204 (1977).

340. 511 F.2d 407 (D.C. Cir. 1975).

341. *Id.* at 421.

342. See, e.g., Januszko v. State, 47 N.Y.2d 744, 391 N.E.2d 297 (1979), which held the state was not liable for the death of a daughter who had been released from a state hospital five months earlier; Bowers v. DeVito, 686 F.2d 616 (7th Cir. 1982), which denied recovery for a murder by a former mental patient (plaintiffs claimed a violation of civil rights of the deceased, which was rejected by the court); Doyle v. United States, 530 F. Supp. 1278 (C.D. Cal. 1982), which held that the U.S. Army was not liable in discharging a serviceman who, more than a month after seeing an Army psychiatrist and two days and 1,000 miles after his release from the Army, killed a college security guard.

343. See Knight v. State, 99 Mich. App. 226, 297 N.W.2d 889 (1980), in which a mentally retarded man was placed on work-convalescent status and worked on a farm. He allegedly burned the barn, and the farm owners sued the state for negligent release and misrepresentation based on the fact that he may have set a fire ten years earlier, as a child. The court concluded that the act was unforeseeable and the placement decision was consistent with good psychological practice.

344. See, e.g., Eger, Psychotherapists' Liability for Extrajudicial Breaches of Confidentiality, 18 Ariz. L. Rev. 1061 (1976), for a thorough article discussing the various theories under which damages can be received for breaching confidentiality.

345. Morse, *supra* note 228.

346. See ch. 5, Rights of Institutionalized Persons, for a documentation of these suits and their success.

347. 42 U.S.C. § 1983 (1981).

the mental health professional, especially members of the line staff as opposed to those in the administrative hierarchy, such suits create considerable anxiety, as well as resentment. Indeed, § 1983 actions have been described as "one of the most powerful stimuli to the pervasive sense of paranoia about the legal profession that exists in psychiatry today."[348]

Many mental health professionals consider such suits as personal affronts, while most mental health attorneys view them as merely another tool for bringing about needed and proper changes in deficient and unconstitutionally conducted state mental health facilities. Whatever the relative perceptions, the fact is that these suits have been very successful in establishing the rights of the mentally disabled[349] and that the mental health practitioner who acted in good faith has remained immune from liability. As the United States Supreme Court stated in *Youngberg v. Romeo*:[350]

> [L]iability may be imposed only when the decision by the professional is such a substantial departure from accepted professional judgment, practice, or standards as to demonstrate that the person responsible actually did not base the decision on such a judgment. In an action for damages against a professional in his individual capacity, however, the professional will not be liable if he was unable to satisfy his normal professional standards because of budgetary constraints; in such a situation, good-faith immunity would bar liability.[351]

This case should now make it possible for responsible mental health professionals who work in state facilities to feel that they can do the best they can for the residents of the facility without fear of being held individually liable for shortcomings that may occur because of budgetary or other systemic constraints.

E. Conclusion

The mental health professional's concern about liability for his actions or inactions is no doubt well based. The multiplicity of statutory and constitutional grounds available to plaintiffs who claim harm creates a particular sense of unease for those who work in the public institutional setting. Expanding theories of liability and the publicity associated with resultant litigation have no doubt changed the way some mental health professionals conduct their practices, that is, some are more cautious today in accepting patients with a history of violence, others more conservative in discharging from the institution someone who may have been dangerous upon admission. Whether these changes have been beneficial for mentally disabled persons or for society as a whole is difficult to determine. The positive note for the mental health professional is that when suits have been brought, the courts have generally been sensitive to the difficulties inherent in the delivery of mental health services. They have been deferential to clinical judgment exercised in accordance with professional norms, and as for practitioners in the public sector in particular, they have been sensitive to the systemic and financial constraints under which the work must be performed. As a result, actual findings of liability have been minimized.

348. Gutheil & Appelbaum, *supra* note 247, at 173, 174.
349. See ch. 5, Rights of Institutionalized Persons.
350. 457 U.S. 307 (1982).
351. *Id.* at 323 (note omitted).

TABLE 10.1 CONFIDENTIALITY OF COMMUNICATIONS BETWEEN PATIENT AND THERAPIST

	CONFIDENTIALITY BETWEEN PATIENT AND		EXCEPTIONS													
			Child Abuse													
STATE	Psychologist (1)	Physician (2)	Duty to Report (3)	Exclusion of Privilege (4)	Good Faith Immunity (5)	With Consent of Patient (6)	Communications w/other Treatment Providers (7)	Court-Ordered Examination of Patient (8)	Commitment Proceedings (9)	Mental Condition as a Claim or Defense by Patient (10)	Pertains to Validity of a Property Document (11)	Competency Proceedings (12)	If Patient Dangerous to Self or Others (13)	Malpractice Suits (14)	Reveals Intent to Commit a Crime or Harmful Act (15)	Other (16)
ALA. Code (1975 & Supp. 1982)	34-26-2	psychiatrist 34-26-2	26-14-3	26-14-10	person removing child, making report, or participating in judicial proceedings 26-14-9											
ALAS. Stat. (1962 & Supp. 1982)	08.86.200					written 08.86.200	08.86.200									
ARIZ. Rev. Stat. Ann. (1978 & Supp. 1982)		criminal proceedings 13-4062(4) civil proceedings 12-2235				13-4062(4) waived if patient testifies concerning them 12-2236		pending insanity plea 13-3993								
ARK. Stat. Ann. (1979 & Supp. 1981) Uniform Rules of Evidence	psychotherapist 28-1001 social worker 71-28-22 counselor 71-5214 psychologist 72-1516	28-1001 R.503	42-808	42-815	persons making report, photographing or removing child in good faith 42-814			28-1001 R.503(d)(2)	28-1001 R.503(d)(1)	28-1001 R.503(d)(3)						knife or gunshot wounds 42-501 disabled adult abuse duty to report 59-1305 disabled adult abuse 59-1305
CAL. Evid. Code (West 1972 & Supp. 1981)	psychotherapist 1014									1016 1023	1021 1022	1025	1024	breach of duty arising from psychotherapist relationship 1020		therapy sought as aid in crime or tort 1027 in a child's best interests 1027
COLO. Rev. Stat. (1973 & Supp. 1981)	13-90-107(g) 12-43-120 social worker 12-63.5-115(1)	13-90-107	19-10-104	19-10-112 12-63.5-115 (2)(c)	19-10-110	13-90-107 may offer as a witness 13-90-108 12-63.5-115(2) 12-63.5-115 (2)(a)	13-90-107(d) (IV)							13-90-107(d) (I) 12-63.5-115 (2)(a)	12-62.5-115 (2)(b)	
CONN. Gen. Stat. Ann. (West 1975 & Supp. 1981)	52-146(c)	psychiatrist 52-146d	17-38a		17-38h	52-146c 52-146d 52-146e(b)	52-146f(a)	52-146c(a) 52-146f(d)	52-146f(b)	52-146c(b) 52-146f(e)		52-146f(d)	52-146f(b)			after death, if more important than confidentiality 52-146c(b) name, address, & fee—for collection 52-146f(c)
DEL. Code Ann. (1974 & Supp. 1980) Rules of Evidence	psychotherapist R.503	R.503	16-903	16-908 R.503(4)	16-906			R.503(d)(2)	R.503d(1)	R.503(d)(3)						when mental incompetent needs a guardian R.503(4)
D.C. Code Ann. (1981 & Supp. 1982)		14-307(a)	2-1352	2-1355	2-1354	14-307			21-583 21-503	14-307(b)(2)		juvenile delinquent 14-307(b)(2)		14-307(b)(1)		
FLA. Stat. Ann. (West 1979 & Supp. 1981)	or psychotherapist 90.503					90.503(2)		90.503(4)(b)	90.503(4)(a)	90.503(4)(c)		90.503(4)(a)				
GA. Code Ann. (1982 & Supp. 1982)	84-3118	psychiatrist 38-418 (5785)	74-111		74-111											
HAWAII Rev. Stat. (1968 & Supp. 1981)																
IDAHO Code (1977 & Supp. 1981)	social worker 54-3213 54-2314	9-203(4)		9-203(4)(A)		9-203(4)					9-203(4)(B)			9-203(4)(C)		

TABLE 10.1 CONFIDENTIALITY OF COMMUNICATIONS BETWEEN PATIENT AND THERAPIST—*Continued*

STATE	CONFIDENTIALITY BETWEEN PATIENT AND		EXCEPTIONS													
			Child Abuse													
	Psychologist (1)	*Physician* (2)	Duty to Report (3)	Exclusion of Privilege (4)	Good Faith Immunity (5)	*With Consent of Patient* (6)	*Communications w/other Treatment Providers* (7)	*Court-Ordered Examination of Patient* (8)	*Commitment Proceedings* (9)	*Mental Condition as a Claim or Defense by Patient* (10)	*Pertains to Validity of a Property Document* (11)	*Competency Proceedings* (12)	*If Patient Dangerous to Self or Others* (13)	*Malpractice Suits* (14)	*Reveals Intent to Commit a Crime or Harmful Act* (15)	*Other* (16)
ILL. Ann. Stat. (Smith-Hurd 1966 & Supp. 1981) *fn. 1*		51, §5.1		51, §5.1(7) 23, §2054		51, §5.1(3) 23, §2059				physical or mental condition an issue 51, §5.1(4)	51, §5.1(5)	51, §5.1(2)			when directly relevant to a homicide trial 51, §5.1(1) in criminal abortion trial 51, §5.1(6)	
IND. Code Ann. (Burns 1980 & Supp. 1982)	25-33-17	34-1-14-5	31-6-11-3	31-6-11-8	31-6-11-7						will 25-33-1-17(4)	25-33-1-17(2)		against psychologist 25-33-1-17(3)	homocide trials 25-33.1-17(1)	
IOWA Code Ann. (West 1950 & Supp. 1981)		622.10	232.70	232.74	232.73	622.10								622.10		
KAN. Stat. Ann. (1980)	74-532		38-717	38-719	38-718				60-427(c)(1)	60-427(d)	60-427(c)(2, 3)	60-427(c)(1)				services sought for illegal aid 60-427(f) waived by contract or previous disclosure 60-437
KY. Rev. Stat. Ann. (Michie 1972 & Supp. 1982)	social worker 335.170	psychiatrist 421.215(2) 213.200	*fn. 2* 199.335 335.170(7)	*fn. 2* 199.335(7)	*fn. 2* 199.335(6)	335.170(1)		421.215(3)(b) 335.170(4)	421.215(3)(b)	421.215(3)(c)			contemplation of crime or harmful act 335.170(2)	licensee is defendant 335.170(5)		if communication indicates patient victim of crime 335.170(3) state employees 335.170(6)
LA. Rev. Stat. Ann. (West 1977 & Supp. 1981)	health care provider 13:3734 social worker 37.23	health care provider 13:3734	14:403	14:403(F)	14:403(E)			15:476			13:3734			13:3734(c)(2) 13:3734(c)(4) good faith immunity 13:3734(c)(5)		workmen's compensation action 13:3734(c)(3) good faith immunity 13:3734(c)(5)
ME. Rev. Stat. Ann. (1964 & Supp. 1982)		social worker 32, §7005 school counselor 20, §806 health maintenance organization 24A, §4224	32, §4011	22, §4015	22, §4014											
MD. Cts. & Jud. Proc. Code Ann.; MD. Evid. Code Ann. (1980 & Supp. 1982)	CJP 9, §109	psychiatrist 9, §109	Evid. 27, §35A	Evid. 27, §35A	Evid. 27, §35A(j)	right to refuse CJP 9-109(b)		CJP 9-109(d)(2)		CJP 9-109(d)(3)(i)		CJP 9-109(d)(1)		CJP 9-109(4)		after death beneficiary may waive CJP 9-109(d)(3)(ii)
MASS. Ann. Laws (Michie/Co-op 1974 & Supp. 1982)	psychotherapist 233, §20B social worker 112, §135		19, §51A	119, §51A information pertaining to child custody cases 112, §135(d),(e)	119, §51A	233, §20B 112, §135(a)		233, §20B(b)	233, §20B(a)	233, §20B(d)			233, §20B(a)	233, §20B(f) 112, §135(a)	112, §135(a)	child custody 233, §20B(e) insurance beneficiary may waive 112, §135(a)
MICH. Comp. Laws Ann. (1980 & Supp. 1981)	psychologist 330.1750	600.2157 psychiatrist 330.1750	722.623		722.625	330.1750(2)		330.1750(3)(e)		330.1750(3)(a)		330.1750(3)(c)		600.2157		heirs may waive 600.2157
MINN. Stat. Ann. (West 1975 & Supp. 1981)	595.02(7)	nurse 595.02(7) 595.02(4)	626.556	626.556(8)	666.556(4)											beneficiary may waive to obtain insurance 595.02(5)
MISS. Code Ann. (1972 & Supp. 1982)	73-31-29	13-1-21	43-21-353	97-5-39(6)	43-21-355									13-1-21		cancer 13-1-21
MO. Ann. Stat. (Vernon 1966 & Supp. 1981)	337.055	491.060(5)	210.115	210.140	210.135											

TABLE 10.1 CONFIDENTIALITY OF COMMUNICATIONS BETWEEN PATIENT AND THERAPIST—*Continued*

	CONFIDENTIALITY BETWEEN PATIENT AND		EXCEPTIONS													
			Child Abuse													
STATE	*Psychologist* (1)	*Physician* (2)	Duty to Report (3)	Exclusion of Privilege (4)	Good Faith Immunity (5)	*With Consent of Patient* (6)	*Communications w/other Treatment Providers* (7)	*Court-Ordered Examination of Patient* (8)	*Commitment Proceedings* (9)	*Mental Condition as a Claim or Defense by Patient* (10)	*Pertains to Validity of a Property Document* (11)	*Competency Proceedings* (12)	*If Patient Dangerous to Self or Others* (13)	*Malpractice Suits* (14)	*Reveals Intent to Commit a Crime or Harmful Act* (15)	*Other* (16)
MONT. Code Ann. (1981)	26-1-807	26-1-805	41-3-201	41-3-201(4)	41-3-203	26-1-805										
NEB. Rev. Stat. (1979)	physician (including psychologists) 27-504	27-504	28-711	28-714	28-716	privilege to refuse 27-504(2)		27-504(4)(a)	27-504(4)(a)	27-504(4)(c)						
NEV. Rev. Stat. (1981)	doctor (including psychologists) 49.215	doctor (including social workers) 49.215	200.502	200.506	200.505			49.245(2)	49.245(1)	49.245(3)						attempts to procure illegal drugs 49.245(5)
N.H. Rev. Stat. Ann. (1978 & Supp. 1981)	330-A:19	329:26	169:40	169:43	169:42											
N.J. Stat. Ann. (West 1972 & Supp. 1982)	45:14B-28	2A:84A-22.2	9:6-8.10	2A:84A-22.5	9:6-8.13				2A:84A-22.2	2A:84A-22.4	2A:84A-22.3(b)					physicians aid sought to aid in crime/tort 2A:84A-22.6
N.M. Stat. Ann. (1978 & Supp. 1981) Rules of Evidence	psychotherapist *fn. 3* 61-9-18 R.504					right to refuse R.504		R.504(d)(2)	R.504(d)(1)	R.504(d)(3)						voluntary disclosure waives privilege R.511
N.Y. Soc. Serv. Law; N.Y. Civ. Proc. Law (1964 & Supp. 1981)	C.P. 4507 social worker C.P. 4508	physician, nurse C.P. 4504	S.S. 413 C.P. 4508(3)		S.S. 413, 419	C.P. 4508(1)								C.P. 4508(4)	C.P. 4508(2)	post mortem C.P. 4504(b)
N.C. Gen. Stat. (1981 & Supp. 1981)	8-53.3	8-53	7A-543	7A-551	7A-550											
N.D. Cent. Code (1981) Evidence Rules		R.501 & 503	50-25.1-03	50-25.1-10	50-25.1-09											
OHIO Rev. Code Ann. (Baldwin 1981)	4732.19	2317.02B	2151.421		2151.421	2317.02B				2317.02B	2317.02B					
OKLA Stat. Ann. (West 1980 & Supp. 1981)	psychotherapist 12, §2503	12, §2503	21, §846	21, §848	21, §847	privilege to refuse to disclose 12, §2503		12, §2503(D)(2)	12, §2503(D)(1)	12, §2503(D)(3)						
OR. Rev. Stat. (1981)	psychotherapist 40.230R. 504 clinical social worker 40.240R. 504-4	nurse 40.240R. 504-2 40.235R. 504-1	40.240R. 504-4	child abuse ct. proceedings 418.775		privilege to refuse to disclose 40.230R. 504(2) right to claim privilege 40.235R. 504-1 40.240R. 504-2 40.240R. 504-4(1)		40.230R. 504(4)(a) 40.235R. 504-1 40.250R. 504-4(5)		40.230R. 504(4)(b)				40.240R. 504-4(2)	40.250R. 504-4	
PA. Stat. Ann. (Purdon 1982)	school psychologist 42, §5945	42, §5929	11, §2204	11, §2222	11, §2211											applies only to civil matters 42, §5929
R.I. Gen. Laws (1977 & Supp. 1983)	health care information 5-37.3-4	health care information 5-37.3-4				5-37.3-4	5-37.3-4			5-37.3-4				5-37.3-4(8)	5-37.3-4(4)	
S.C. Code Ann. (Law. Co-op. 1976 & Supp. 1981)																

TABLE 10.1 CONFIDENTIALITY OF COMMUNICATIONS BETWEEN PATIENT AND THERAPIST—*Continued*

STATE	CONFIDENTIALITY BETWEEN PATIENT AND		EXCEPTIONS													
			Child Abuse													
	Psychologist (1)	*Physician* (2)	Duty to Report (3)	Exclusion of Privilege (4)	Good Faith Immunity (5)	*With Consent of Patient* (6)	*Communications w/other Treatment Providers* (7)	*Court-Ordered Examination of Patient* (8)	*Commitment Proceedings* (9)	*Mental Condition as a Claim or Defense by Patient* (10)	*Pertains to Validity of a Property Document* (11)	*Competency Proceedings* (12)	*If Patient Dangerous to Self or Others* (13)	*Malpractice Suits* (14)	*Reveals Intent to Commit a Crime or Harmful Act* (15)	*Other* (16)
S.D. Codified Laws Ann. (1977 & Supp. 1982)	psycho-therapist 19-13-7R. 503(b)	19-13-7R. 503(b)	26-10-10 26-10-11	26-10-14	26-10-15			19-13-10R. 503(d)(2)	19-13-9R. 503(d)(1)	19-13-11R. 503(d)(1)						
TENN. Code Ann. (1980 & Supp. 1982)		psychiatrist 24-1-207							24-1-207(3)	24-1-207(1)						in interests of justice 24-1-207(2)
TEX. Rev. Civil Stat. Ann. (Vernon 1958 & Supp. 1982)	mental health professional 5561h(2)(a)	medical or mental health professional 5561h(2)(a)				5561h(4)(a)(2), (b)(4)	5561h(4)(b)(6)	5561h(4)(a)(4)						5561h(4)(a)(1)	imminent danger 5561h(4)(b)(1)	for fee collection 5561(4)(a)(3), (b)(5)
UTAH Laws (1978 & Supp. 1981)	social worker 58-25-8 58-35-10	58-24-8(4)		58-35-10(3)		58-35-10(1)								58-35-10(4)	crime only 58-35-10(2)	
VT. Stat. Ann. (1973 & Supp. 1982)	mental health professional 12, §1612	physician, registered professional, registered nurse 12, §1612									12, §1612(c)(3)					
VA. Code (1980 & Supp. 1982)	psychologist, counselor, social worker 8.01-400.2	8.01-399	63.1-248.3	63.1-248.11 8.01-400.2 63.1-248.5	63.1-248.5	practitioner of the healing arts, including psychologists 8.01-399 8.01-400.2				8.01-400.2 8.01-399						necessary to administer justice 8.01-400.2 effort to procure illegal drugs 8.01-394
WASH. Rev. Code Ann. (1962 & Supp. 1981)	18.83.110	5.60.060(4)	26.44.030	26.44.060(3)	26.44.060(1)											
W.VA. Code (1980 & Supp. 1982)	treatment providers 27-3-1(a)	treatment providers 27-3-1(a)	49-6A-2	49-6A-7	49-6A-6	written 27-3-2	27-3-1(b)(5)	27-3-1(b)(2) & 27-6A-1	27-3-1(b)(1) & 27-5-2 27-5-3 27-5-4				27-3-1(b)(4)			by ct. order 27-3-1(b)(3)
WIS. Stat. Ann. (West 1975 & Supp. 1982)	905.04(2)	905.04(2)	48.981	905.04(e)	48.981(4)	right to refuse 905.04(2)		905.04(4)(b)	905.04(4)(a)	905.04(4)(c)						paternity cases 905.04(4)(g) homocide cases 905.04(4)(g)
WYO. Stat. (1977 & Supp. 1982)		1-12-101(a)(i)	14-3-205	14-3-210	14-3-209	1-12-101(a)(i)										to counteract patient's voluntary testimony 1-12-101(a)(i)

FOOTNOTES: TABLE 10.1

1. Ill. Ann. Stat. ch. 51, § 5.1 (Smith-Hurd 1966 & Supp. 1981): "In the event of a conflict between the application of this section and the Mental Health and Developmental Disabilities Confidentiality Act (Chapter 91½, § 801 et seq.), enacted by the 80th General Assembly, to a specific situation, the provisions of the Mental Health and Developmental Disabilities Confidentiality Act shall control."

2. Ky. Rev. Stat. Ann. (Michie 1972 & Supp. 1982). Repealed effective July 15, 1984.

3. N.M. Stat. Ann. § 61-9-18 (1978 & Supp. 1981). Effective until July 1, 1986.

TABLE 10.2 CONFIDENTIALITY OF PATIENT RECORDS

					EXCEPTIONS TO CONFIDENTIALITY OF RECORDS													
STATE	TYPES OF PATIENTS COVERED (1)	SCOPE OF COVERAGE (2)	PATIENT'S RIGHT TO SEE RECORDS (3)	CONFIDENTIALITY & PATIENT ACCESS AFTER DISCHARGE (4)	Upon Court Order (5)	With Consent of Patient or Guardian (6)	During Court-ordered Examination of Patient (7)	Communication with Other Patient Providers (8)	Research Uses (9)	To Claim Benefits (10)	To Protect Patient Against Risk of Injury (11)	Competency Proceedings (12)	Law Enforcement Agencies (13)	Patient's Counsel (14)	Patient's Family (15)	Crimes By/Against Patient (16)	Institutionalization Proceedings (17)	Other (18)
ALA. Code (1975 & Supp. 1982)	all forms of mental or emotional illness *fn. 1* 22-50-1	all information compiled in attending or treating any patient 22-50-62			for the promotion of justice 22-50-62		22-50-62		if anonymity protected 22-50-61					in criminal case if examination ordered 22-50-62				
ALAS. Stat. (1979 & Supp. 1981)	recipients of community mental health services 47.30.590	dep't shall adopt regulations to safeguard records & information about recipients 47.30.590						if in patient's best interest 47.30.590										
	institutionalized mentally ill 47.30.825	photos 47.30.840(1) information & records obtained in course of evaluation or treatment 47.30.845	"may be copied & disclosed" 47.30.845(2)	patient may move to have records expunged 47.30.850	47.30.840(1) 47.30.845(3)	47.30.845(2)		47.30.845(1)	if anonymity assured 47.30.845(4)				to secure return of patient if on unauthorized absence 47.30.845(6)				if necessary 47.30.845	division of corrections 47.30.845(5)
ARIZ. Rev. Stat. Ann. (1974 & Supp. 1981)	mentally ill (mentally disordered) 36-501(17)	photos 36-507(2) all information & records 36-509	unless contraindicated by physician 36-507(3)		36-507(2) 36-509(4)	36-509(2)		36-509(1)	if anonymity ensured 36-509(5)				to secure return of patient on unauthorized absence 36-509(7)	36-509(3)				dep't of corrections 36-509(6)
	developmentally disabled 36-551(10)	all information & records 36-568.01(A)			36-568.01 (A)(3)	36-568.01 (A)(1)		36-568.01 (A)(4)		36-568.01 (A)(2)	36-568.01 (A)(5)	36-568.01 (A)(6)						other state agencies or bodies for official purposes 36-568.01 (A)(7)
ARK. Stat. Ann. (1971 & Supp. 1981)	mentally ill 59-1403, 59-1404	all communications & records 59-1416(14)	right to obtain complete information re diagnosis & treatment 59-1416(13)															"proper authorization" 59-1416(14)
CAL. Welf. & Inst. Code (1972 & Supp. 1981)	persons involuntarily hospitalized 5355	all records & information 5328			as necessary to the administration of justice 5328(f)	5328(a), (b), (d) to employers 5328.9	following conviction of crime 5328(k)	5328(a)	upon signing an oath of confidentiality 5328(e) 5329	5328(c), (i)		5328(a)	for protection of elective officers & their families 5328(g); sex offenders 5328.01 5328.2	5328(j)	if authorized by patient 5328.1			to coroner 5328.8
COLO. Rev. Stat. (1973 & Supp. 1981)	mentally ill 27-10-101	photos 27-10-117(4) all information & records 27-10-120(1)			27-10-117(4) 27-10-120 (1)(f)	27-10-120 (1)(b)		27-10-120 (1)(a)	upon oath of confidentiality 27-10-120 (1)(d)	27-10-120 (1)(c)						upon premises of any facility 27-10-120(2)		
	developmentally disabled 27-10.5-101	information re admission, care & treatment 27-10.5-120	27-10.5-120			27-10.5-120 (2)			if anonymity protected 27-10.5-120 (3)					27-10.5-120 (2)	parents 27-10.5-120 (2)			
CONN. Gen. Stat. Ann. (West 1975 & Supp. 1981)	mentally disordered 17-206a		4-104 17-206i(d)	access in connection w/litigation related to hospitalization 17-206i(b)														
	patients of psychiatrists 52-146(d)	all records & information re diagnosis & treatment 52-146(d)				52-146(d)	52-146f(d)	52-146f(a)			52-146f(b)	52-146f(d)				52-146f(e)		

TABLE 10.2 CONFIDENTIALITY OF PATIENT RECORDS—*Continued*

STATE	TYPES OF PATIENTS COVERED (1)	SCOPE OF COVERAGE (2)	PATIENT'S RIGHT TO SEE RECORDS (3)	CONFIDENTIALITY & PATIENT ACCESS AFTER DISCHARGE (4)	EXCEPTIONS TO CONFIDENTIALITY OF RECORDS													
					Upon Court Order (5)	With Consent of Patient or Guardian (6)	During Court-ordered Examination of Patient (7)	Communication with Other Patient Providers (8)	Research Uses (9)	To Claim Benefits (10)	To Protect Patient Against Risk of Injury (11)	Competency Proceedings (12)	Law Enforcement Agencies (13)	Patient's Counsel (14)	Patient's Family (15)	Crimes By/Against Patient (16)	Institutionalization Proceedings (17)	Other (18)
DEL. Code Ann. (1974 & Supp. 1980)	mentally ill 16, §5125 mentally retarded 16, §5522(a) 16, §5161(a)	all records & information re admission, legal status, care, & treatment 16, §5161 (a)(7)			16, §5161 (a)(7)(a)	16, §5161 (a)(7)(c)		if transferred to institution outside dep't of mental health 16, §5161 (a)(7)(d)						16, §5161 (a)(7)(b)				
D.C. Code Ann. (1981 & Supp. 1982)	mentally ill 21-562	all records re care & treatment 21-562	available to attorney or personal physician, upon patient's written authorization	records preserved until discharge 21-562				personal physician 21-562						upon patient's authorization 21-562				
	mentally retarded 6-1961 et seq.	all records 6-1972	6-1972			6-1972								6-1972	parent 6-1972			
FLA. Stat. Ann. (West 1973 & Supp. 1981)	mentally ill 394.459	data pertaining to admission & such other information that may be required by dep't 394.459(9)	exception for psychiatric hospital records 458.16		394.459 (9)(b)	394.459(9)		394.459 (9)(c)						394.459 (9)(a)				
	mentally retarded 393.13(1)	data pertaining to admission & such other information that may be required by dep't 393.13(3) (m)(1)	393.13(3) (m)(4)		excluding matters privileged by other provisions of law 393.13(3) (m)(2)(b)	393.13(3) (m)(2)(a)		393.13(3) (m)(2)(c)	if anonymity protected 393.13(3) (m)(2)(d)					if designated by patient 393.13(3) (m)(2)(a)				
GA. Code Ann. (1979 & Supp. 1982)	mentally ill 88-501 et seq.	data pertaining to admission & such other information that may be required by dep't 88-502.12(a)	88-502.12 (a)(7)		88-502.12 (a)(8)	88-502.12 (a)(2)		when necessary for treatment 88-502.12 (a)(1), (4) bona fide emergency 88-502.12 (a)(6)					in course of criminal investigation (identity & address) 88-502.12 (a)(9)	if patient consents 88-502.12 (a)(5)	parent, if appropriate 88-502.12 (a)(2)		88-502.12 (b)	
HAWAII Rev. Stat. (1976 & Supp. 1981)	mental illness, drug abuse, & alcoholism 334-1 et seq.	all certificates, applications, records, & reports 334-5	if not clearly adverse to patient's interests 334-5		if necessary to conduct of proceedings & in public interest 334-5(3)	334-5(1)	if necessary to conduct of proceedings 334-5(3)					if necessary to conduct of proceedings 334-5(3)			if not clearly adverse to patient's interests 334-5		if necessary to conduct of proceedings & in public interest 334-5(3)	by hospital administrator if necessary to carry out chapter 334-5(2)
IDAHO Code (1980 & Supp. 1981)	mentally ill 66-300 et seq.	all certificates, applications, records & reports identifying patient 66-348(a)	reasonable access 66-346(a)(7)		66-348(a)(3)	66-348(a)(1)												necessary to carry out provisions of act 66-348(a)(2)
Ill. Ann. Stat. (Smith-Hurd 1966 & Supp. 1981)	mentally ill & developmentally disabled 91½, §1-101 et seq.	all records, except personal undisclosed notes by therapist 91½, §§803, 802(7)	including right to an interpretation & to dispute contents 91½, §804,	confidential after death until representative & therapist consent to disclosure 91½, §805(e)	after death 91½, §805(e)	91½, §§804, 805		91½, §809	if anonymity preserved 91½, §807	91½, §806			if recipient in custody 91½, §809(4) secret service or dep't of law enforcement 91½, §812	91½, §809(3)	unless patient or therapist objects 91½, §804 (a)(4)	as a claim or defense 91½, §810(1) 91½, §812.1		if therapist or agency audited, etc., so long as personally identifiable data removed 91½, §807
IND. Code Ann. (Burns 1973 & Supp. 1982)	mentally ill & developmentally disabled 16-14-1.6-1	all information obtained & maintained in course of providing services 16-14-1.6-8(b)	unless denied or limited by service provider for good cause 16-14-1.6-8(c)	no limitation or denial of access permitted 16-14-1.6-8(c)		16-14-1.6-8 (b), (d), (g)	16-14-1.6-8 (e)(5)	16-14-1.6-8 (e)(1)	in accordance w/regulations of dep't 16-14-1.6-8 (e)(4)	16-14-1.6-8 (e)(2)		16-14-1.6-8 (e)(5)	reporting of abuse 16-14-1.6-8 (e)(5) inadmissible in any legal proceeding w/o consent 16-14-1.6-8(f)	16-14-1.6-8 (e)(3)		16-14-1.6-8 (e)(5)	16-14-1.6-8 (e)(5)	protection & advocacy service commission 16-14-1.6-8 (e)(3)

TABLE 10.2 CONFIDENTIALITY OF PATIENT RECORDS—*Continued*

					EXCEPTIONS TO CONFIDENTIALITY OF RECORDS													
STATE	TYPES OF PATIENTS COVERED (1)	SCOPE OF COVERAGE (2)	PATIENT'S RIGHT TO SEE RECORDS (3)	CONFIDENTIALITY & PATIENT ACCESS AFTER DISCHARGE (4)	Upon Court Order (5)	With Consent of Patient or Guardian (6)	During Court-ordered Examination of Patient (7)	Communication with Other Patient Providers (8)	Research Uses (9)	To Claim Benefits (10)	To Protect Patient Against Risk of Injury (11)	Competency Proceedings (12)	Law Enforcement Agencies (13)	Patient's Counsel (14)	Patient's Family (15)	Crimes By/Against Patient (16)	Institutionalization Proceedings (17)	Other (18)
IOWA Code Ann. (West 1969 & Supp. 1981)	mentally ill 229.24	records relating to examination, custody, care, & treatment 229.25			for good cause 229.24(1) 229.25(2)	to any designated person 229.24(2) w/waiver 229.25(1)		w/client waiver 229.25(1)	if anonymity preserved 229.25(3)					w/client waiver 229.25(1)				
KAN. Stat. Ann. (1976 & Supp. 1981)	mentally ill 59-2901	ct., treatment, & medical records 59-2931(a)	59-2931 (a)(2)(B)	same rules for patients & former patients 59-2931	59-2931 (a)(2)(C)	unless deemed injurious to welfare by head of facility 59-2931 (a)(2)(A)	59-2931 (a)(2)(D)	head of facility may release information if necessary to treatment 59-2931 (a)(2)(B)	upon pledge of confidentiality 59-2931 (a)(2)(B)					in any proceedings under act 59-2931 (a)(2)(D)	next of kin 59-2931 (a)(2)(B)		upon ct. order if otherwise admissible, or by request of counsel 59-2931 (a)(2)(C), (D)	accreditation agency pledging confidentiality 59-2931 (a)(2)(B)
KY. Rev. Stat. Ann. (Michie 1982)	mentally ill & mentally retarded 202A.006 et seq. 202B.050	ct. records in commitment proceedings 202A.091(1)	upon ct. order, or pursuant to 202A.016 *fn. 2* 202A.091(1)	motion to expunge 202A.091(2)	following motion by any person 202A.091(3)		*fn. 2* 202A.091(1)							*fn. 2* 202A.091(1)			*fn. 2* 202A.091	
		all applications, certifications, records & reports directly or indirectly identifying patient 210.235			210.235(4)	210.235(1)									or friends, of information as to patient's medical condition 210.235(4)			to carry out provisions of KRS & rules & regulations of dep'ts & agencies of state or U.S. 210.235 (2), (3)
LA. Rev. Stat. Ann. (West 1982)	mentally ill 40:2013.3			post-mortem 40:2013.3 40:2014.1										after discharge 40:2013.3 40:2014.1	heirs or near relative 40:2013.3, 40:2014.1			
	all patients in public hospitals or institutions 44:7(A)	charts, records, reports, documents, & other memoranda 44:7(A)			if relevant to any judicial proceeding 44:7(C)			governing authority of hospital may make rules 44:7(B)	governing authority of hospital may make rules 44:7(B) anonymously encoded abstract furnished to cancer registry 44:7(E)			if relevant 44:7(C)				if relevant 44:7(C)	44:7(C)	
ME. Rev. Stat. Ann. (1978 & Supp. 1982)	mentally ill 34, §1-B	orders of commitment, medical & administrative records, applications, & reports 34, §1-B	34, §1-B(3)		subject to Me. Rules of Evidence, Rule 503 34, §1-B(3)	34, §1-B(1)		training programs 34, §1-B(3)	34, §1-C(1)	34, §1-B(3)			to carry out investigatory function of the protection & advocacy agency for the developmentally disabled 34, §1-B(2)		spouse or next of kin 34, §1-B(3)		34, §1-B(2)	to carry out statutory functions of dep't 34, §1-B(2)
MD. Health-Gen. Code Ann. (1982 & Supp. 1982)	mentally retarded 7-601 et seq.	all information required by code or administration 7-610(a)(2)	w/in 14 days of request *fn. 3* 7-611 7-612(b)(2)–(4)		7-612 (c)(4)(iv)	7-612(a)		7-612(c)(2)	*fn. 4* 7-612(c)	*fn. 4* 7-612(c)			state-designated protection & advocacy agency 7-612 (b)(1)(iii)	7-612 (b)(1)(ii)	parent or guardian, unless patient requests otherwise 7-612 (b)(1)(i)			*fn. 4* 7-612(c)
	mentally ill 10-101(f)	all information required by title or administration 10-709(a)(2)																director, or designee 10-709(c)
MASS. Ann. Laws (Michie/Law. Co-op. 1981 & Supp. 1981)	mentally ill or mentally retarded 123, §1 et seq.	records of admission, treatment, & periodic review 123, §36	when in best interests of patient 123, §36(3)		123, §36(1)	to attorney 123, §36(2)								123, §36(2)				

TABLE 10.2 CONFIDENTIALITY OF PATIENT RECORDS—*Continued*

STATE	TYPES OF PATIENTS COVERED (1)	SCOPE OF COVERAGE (2)	PATIENT'S RIGHT TO SEE RECORDS (3)	CONFIDENTIALITY & PATIENT ACCESS AFTER DISCHARGE (4)	EXCEPTIONS TO CONFIDENTIALITY OF RECORDS													
					Upon Court Order (5)	With Consent of Patient or Guardian (6)	During Court-ordered Examination of Patient (7)	Communication with Other Patient Providers (8)	Research Uses (9)	To Claim Benefits (10)	To Protect Patient Against Risk of Injury (11)	Competency Proceedings (12)	Law Enforcement Agencies (13)	Patient's Counsel (14)	Patient's Family (15)	Crimes By/Against Patient (16)	Institutionalization Proceedings (17)	Other (18)
MICH. Comp. Laws Ann. (1980 & Supp. 1981)	mentally ill 330.1401	information pertinent to services & legal status, & that acquired in course of providing services 330.1748(1)	if not detrimental 330.1748 (5)(b)		330.1748 (4)(a)	if not detrimental to patient or others 330.1748 (5)(b)		w/consent of patient or guardian 330.1748 (5)(a)	provided subject is not likely to be harmed 330.1748 (6)(b)	330.1748 (6)(a)	330.1748 (6)(c)			w/patient's consent 330.1748 (4)(c)			to prosecuting attorney 330.1748 (4)(b)	legislative subpoena 330.1748 (4)(a)
MINN. Stat. Ann. (West 1982)																		
MISS. Code Ann. (1981 & Supp. 1982)	patients at any hospital 41-9-61(c)	all hospital records except ordinary business & accreditation records 41-9-61(b) 41-9-67	reasonable access upon good cause 41-9-65					attending medical personnel, upon good cause 41-9-65						personal representative or heirs, upon good cause shown 41-9-65	personal representative or heirs, upon good cause shown 41-9-65			
	mentally ill 41-21-97	hospital records at state institutions 41-21-97			if mental condition is a matter of inquiry 41-21-97		fn. 5 41-21-97			41-21-97		fn. 5 41-21-97	county or district attorney, or attorney general in official capacity 41-21-97	41-21-97			fn. 5 41-21-97	
MO. Ann. Stat. (Vernon 1979 & Supp. 1982)	all mental disabilities 630.005 et seq.	all information & records compiled by facility 630.140(1)	630.110(1)(6)		630.140(3)(7)	630.140 (2), (3)	fn. 6 630.140 (3)(5)	630.140 (3)(2)	if anonymity preserved 630.140 (3)(4)	630.140 (3)(3)		fn. 6 630.140 (3)(5)		630.140(2)	notified of hospital & cost 630.145	child abuse or neglect 630.140 (3)(9)	fn. 6 630.140 (3)(5)	
MONT. Code Ann. (1981)	developmentally disabled 53-20-101	all information in resident's records 53-20-161(1)	53-20-161(1)		53-20-161 (1)(a)	53-20-161(1)									53-20-161(1)			federal or state law, or dep't of social & rehabilitation services rules 53-20-161 (1)(h)
	mentally ill 53-21-101	all information & records obtained in course of providing any service 53-21-166			as necessary to the administration of justice 53-21-166 (5), (6)	fn. 7 53-21-166(2)		between qualified professionals in provision of services or referral 53-21-166(1)	oath of confidentiality 53-21-166(4)	53-21-166(3)								mental disabilities board of visitors 53-21-166(7)
NEB. Rev. Stat. (1981)	mentally ill dangerous persons 83-1001	all records 83-1068	may be denied by ct. order if adverse to mental state 83-1068		83-1068(5)	83-1068(6)								83-1068(2)				mental health board 83-1068(4)
NEV. Rev. Stat.	mentally ill & mentally retarded 433.003(1)		& to be informed at regular intervals of status & progress 433.504															
	mentally ill 433A.010 et seq.	information pertaining to admission, legal status, treatment, & habilitation plan 433A.360			433A.360(2)	or parent, to physicians, attorneys, & social workers 433A.360(1)		when administrator deems necessary for proper care 433A.360(3)	if abstracted to protect identity 433A.360(4)	433A.360(5)				w/written consent of patient, guardian, or parents 433A.360(1)				prosecution of mandamus proceeding 49.245(4)
N.H. Rev. Stat. Ann. (1977 & Supp. 1981)	mentally ill 135-B:1 developmentally disabled 171-A:1																	

TABLE 10.2 CONFIDENTIALITY OF PATIENT RECORDS—*Continued*

					EXCEPTIONS TO CONFIDENTIALITY OF RECORDS													
STATE	TYPES OF PATIENTS COVERED (1)	SCOPE OF COVERAGE (2)	PATIENT'S RIGHT TO SEE RECORDS (3)	CONFIDENTIALITY & PATIENT ACCESS AFTER DISCHARGE (4)	Upon Court Order (5)	With Consent of Patient or Guardian (6)	During Court-ordered Examination of Patient (7)	Communication with Other Patient Providers (8)	Research Uses (9)	To Claim Benefits (10)	To Protect Patient Against Risk of Injury (11)	Competency Proceedings (12)	Law Enforcement Agencies (13)	Patient's Counsel (14)	Patient's Family (15)	Crimes By/Against Patient (16)	Institutionalization Proceedings (17)	Other (18)
N.J. Stat. Ann. (West 1981 & Supp. 1982)	mentally ill, mentally retarded, or tuberculosis 30:4-33	all certificates, applications, records, & reports 30:4-24.3			necessary for conduct of proceeding & nondisclosure contrary to public interest 30:4-24.3(3)	30:4-24.3(1)		personal physician 30:4-24.3				to carry out provisions of 2A:82-41 et seq. 30:4-24.3(2)		30:4-24.3	relative or friend 30:4-24.3			to carry out provisions of act 30:4-24.3(2)
N.M. Stat. Ann. (1979 & Supp. 1982)	mentally ill & developmentally disabled 43-1-1 et seq.		43-1-19(D)			43-1-19(A)		to extent practice, employment, or training requires 43-1-19 (B)(1)	title searchers, upon authorization of clerk of district ct. 43-1-19(H)	43-1-19 (B)(4)	clear & substantial risk of imminent serious physical injury or death 43-1-19 (B)(2)							federal statute or regulation 43-1-19(G)
N.Y. Mental Hyg. Law (McKinney 1978 & Supp. 1982)	all patients (mentally ill & mentally retarded) 33.01 et seq.	all matters relating to admission, legal status, care, & treatment 33.13(a)		petition to seal records 33.14 (a)(1)(b)	33.13(c)(1)	& commissioner 33.13 (c)(4)(ii)		w/consent of patient & commissioner 33.13 (c)(4)(i) mental health information service 33.13(c)(2)	statistical information for dep't (identification not required) 33.13(b)	w/consent of commissioner 33.13(c)(5)			to locate missing persons in criminal matter, w/consent of commissioner 33.13(c)(5)				attorney representing patient 33.13(c)(3)	firearms control board 33.13(c)(5)
N.C. Gen. Stat. (1981 & Supp. 1981)	mentally ill, mentally retarded, or substance abuse 122-1 et seq.	any information, record, report, case history, or memo 122-8.1(a)			122-8.1(a)		criminal cases 122-8.1(a)	122-8.1(c)	if anonymity preserved 122-8.2							report of mental examination of defendant 122-8.1(a)	122-8.1(b)	
N.D. Cent. Code (1978 & Supp. 1981)	mentally ill, alcoholic, or drug addict 25-03.1-02 (11)	all information & records 25-03.1-43		may petition for expungement 25-03.1-45	25-03.1-43(4)	25-03.1-43(2)		upon written consent 25-03.1-43(1)	if anonymity assured & consent given 25-03.1-43(5)				when necessary to return A.W.O.L. patients 25-03.1-43(7)	unless patient specifically withholds consent 25-03.1-43(3)			25-03.1-43	director of state hospital if patient is prison transfer 25-03.1-43(6)
	mentally retarded 25-16-07	records of a treatment or care center 25-16-17			25-16-07(1)								25-16-07(2)		or legal guardian 25-16-07(3)			any other legally constituted boards or agencies serving interests of residents 25-16-07(2)
OHIO Rev. Code Ann. (Baldwin 1980 & Supp. 1982)	mentally ill 5122.01 et seq.	all certificates, applications, records, & reports, other than ct. journal or docket entries 5122.31	unless specifically restricted in treatment plan for clear treatment reasons 5122.31(E)		5122.31(D)	if in best interests of patient 5122.31(A)		5122.31(F)		insurers 5122.31(C)								legal rights service 5122.31(B) 5123.60
	mentally retarded & developmentally disabled 5123.02 et seq.	all certificates, applications, records, & reports other than ct. journal or docket entries 5123.89(A)				if in best interests of patient 5123.89 (A)(1)		to mental health facility, if managing officer for institution records in best interest 5123.89 (A)(3)										
OKLA. Stat. Ann. (West 1979 & Supp. 1982)	mentally ill or mentally retarded 43A, §2	all records 43A, §18(10)	access in malpractice suit 76, §19		43A, §18(10)			of institution, that superintendent shall designate 43A, §18(10)										consent of director 43A, §18(10)

TABLE 10.2 CONFIDENTIALITY OF PATIENT RECORDS—*Continued*

					EXCEPTIONS TO CONFIDENTIALITY OF RECORDS													
STATE	TYPES OF PATIENTS COVERED (1)	SCOPE OF COVERAGE (2)	PATIENT'S RIGHT TO SEE RECORDS (3)	CONFIDENTIALITY & PATIENT ACCESS AFTER DISCHARGE (4)	Upon Court Order (5)	With Consent of Patient or Guardian (6)	During Court-ordered Examination of Patient (7)	Communication with Other Patient Providers (8)	Research Uses (9)	To Claim Benefits (10)	To Protect Patient Against Risk of Injury (11)	Competency Proceedings (12)	Law Enforcement Agencies (13)	Patient's Counsel (14)	Patient's Family (15)	Crimes By/Against Patient (16)	Institutionalization Proceedings (17)	Other (18)
OR. Rev. Stat. (1981)	all patients receiving health care services 192.525 179.505(1)	medical history 192.525 histories, records, x-rays, reports, charts, & other accounts 179.505(2)	192.525 unless an immediate & grave detriment to treatment 179.505 (7)(a)			179.505(3)		179.505(6)	including program evaluation, peer review, & financial audits, if identity not disclosed 179.505 (4)(b)	insurer 192.525 179.505(4) (b & c)			clear & immediate danger to others or to society 179.505(10)			inadmissible unless patient voluntarily produces evidence making records relevant 179.505(9)		rights may be limited only to benefit patient 192.525
PA. Stat. Ann. (Purdon 1969 & Supp. 1982)	mentally ill 50, §7103	all documents concerning person in treatment 50, §7111			in course of proceedings authorized by act 50, §7111(3)			50, §7111(1)	if identity undisclosed 50, §7111	county administrator 50, §7111(2)			Pa. Drug & Alcohol Abuse Control Act 50, §7111				50, §7111(3)	federal rules, statutes, & regulations, where treatment undertaken in federal agency 50, §7111(4)
R.I. Gen. Laws (1977 & Supp. 1982)	mentally disabled 40.1-5-3(1)	all information & records 40.1-5-26			40.1-5-26(7)	40.1-5-26(1)	40.1-5-26(2)	40.1-5-26(2)	& program evaluation; oath of confidentiality 40.1-5-26(6) anonymous statistical data 40.1-5-30	40.1-5-26(4)	where life or health in immediate jeopardy 40.1-5-26(5)	in communications between qualified medical or mental health professionals in course of ct. proceedings 40.1-5-26(2)	unauthorized disappearances 40.1-5-28	40.1-5-27	40.1-5-27	in communications between qualified medical or mental health professionals in course of ct. proceedings 40.1-5-26(2)	in communications between qualified medical or mental health professionals in course of ct. proceedings 40.1-5-26(2)	
S.C. Code Ann. (Law. Co-op. 1976 & Supp. 1982)	mentally ill & mentally retarded 44-23-10 et seq.	all certificates, applications, records, & reports 44-23-1090			necessary for conduct of proceeding & nondisclosure contrary to public interest 44-23-1090 (3)	44-23-1090 (1)					if public safety is involved 44-23-1090 (6)		44-23-1090 (5)	44-23-1090	relatives 44-23-1090			state or federal agencies in furthering welfare of patient or family 44-23-1090 (4) to carry out provisions of code 44-23-1090 (2)
S.D. Codified Laws Ann. (1976 & Supp. 1982)	mentally ill 27A-1-1 et seq. mentally retarded 27B-1-1 et seq.	complete statistical & medical record, & other information acquired in providing services 27A-12-25 27A-12-26 27B-8-27 27B-8-28	if not detrimental to recipient or others 27A-12-28(2) 27B-8-30		or subpoenas of legislature 27A-12-27(1) 27B-8-29(1)	if not detrimental to recipient or others 27A-12-28(2) 27B-8-30		w/consent 27A-12-28(1)	evaluation, training, or accreditation 27A-12-29 (2, 3) 27B-8-31	at discretion of holder 27A-12-29(1) 27B-8-31		prosecuting attorney 27A-12-27(2) 27B-8-29(2)		w/patient's consent 27A-12-27(3) 27B-8-29(3)			prosecuting attorney 27A-12-27(2) 27B-8-29(2)	when necessary to comply with law or discharge responsibility 27A-12-27 (4), (5) 27B-8-29 (4), (5)
TENN. Code Ann. (1977 & Supp. 1982)	mentally retarded or mentally ill 33-306	all petitions, applications, certificates, records, & reports 33-306(j)			necessary for conduct of proceeding & nondisclosure contrary to public interest 33-306(j)(3)	33-306 (j)(1)						necessary to carry out provisions of chs. 3–8 of title 33-306(j)(2)	child abuse reporting & investigation 33-306(j) 37-1203 37-1206		or relatives or friends 33-306(j)		necessary to carry out provisions of chs. 3–8 of title 33-306(j)(2)	necessary to carry out provisions of chs. 3–8 of title 33-306(j)(2)

TABLE 10.2 CONFIDENTIALITY OF PATIENT RECORDS—*Continued*

STATE	TYPES OF PATIENTS COVERED (1)	SCOPE OF COVERAGE (2)	PATIENT'S RIGHT TO SEE RECORDS (3)	CONFIDENTIALITY & PATIENT ACCESS AFTER DISCHARGE (4)	EXCEPTIONS TO CONFIDENTIALITY OF RECORDS													
					Upon Court Order (5)	With Consent of Patient or Guardian (6)	During Court-ordered Examination of Patient (7)	Communication with Other Patient Providers (8)	Research Uses (9)	To Claim Benefits (10)	To Protect Patient Against Risk of Injury (11)	Competency Proceedings (12)	Law Enforcement Agencies (13)	Patient's Counsel (14)	Patient's Family (15)	Crimes By/Against Patient (16)	Institutionalization Proceedings (17)	Other (18)
TEX. Rev. Civ. Stat. Ann. (Vernon 1958 & Supp. 1982)	mentally ill 5547-4(g)	hospital records which directly or indirectly identify a former, present, or proposed patient 5547-87(a)		if deceased, consent by executor or next of kin 5547-87 (a)(1)	necessary for conduct of proceeding & nondisclosure contrary to public interest 5547-87 (a)(3)	5547-87(a)(1)									or relatives or friends 5547-87(b)			necessary to carry out provisions of code 5547-87 (a)(2) board or head of hospital determines
	any mental disorder 5561h (1)(b)	professional records 5561h (2)(b)			5561h(4)	written waiver 5561h(4)		5561h(4)	if identity undisclosed 5561h(4)	5561h(4)	imminent injury 5561h(4)		imminent injury 5561h(4)			malpractice & other suits against MD 5561h(4)		disclosure in patient's best interest 5547-87 (a)(4)
	mentally retarded 5547-300(5)	records of identity, diagnosis, evaluation, or treatment 5547-300(57)	unless qualified professional signs statement that disclosure not in best interest of patient 5547-300 (57)(b)	if deceased, consent by executor, spouse, or next of kin 5547-300 (57)(b)	for good cause 5547-300 (57)(c)(3)	5547-300 (57)(b)		emergencies, or other governmental treatment agencies 5547-300 (57)(c, f)	& audits, if identity concealed 5547-300 (57)(c)(2)		bona fide medical emergency 5547-300 (57)(c)(1)		no record may be used to initiate, substantiate, or help investigate criminal charge against patient 5547-300		parent, guardian, relative, or friends 5547-300 (57)(i)	to investigate claims of abuse or denial of rights 5547-300 (57)(c)(4)		
UTAH Code Ann. (1978 & Supp. 1981)	mentally ill 64-7-7	all certificates, applications, records, & reports 64-7-50(1)			necessary for conduct of proceedings & nondisclosure contrary to public interest 64-7-50 (1)(c)	64-7-50(1)(a)								unlimited access, w/ patient consent 78-25-25	or relatives or friends 64-7-50(2)		necessary to carry out provisions of act 64-7-50 (1)(b)	necessary to carry out provisions of act 64-7-50 (1)(b)
VT. Stat. Ann. (1968 & Supp. 1982)	mentally ill or mentally retarded 18, §7101 et seq.	all certificates, applications, records, & reports 18, §7103(a)			necessary for conduct of proceeding & nondisclosure contrary to public interest 18, §7103 (a)(3) 18, §7103(a)	18, §7103 (a)(1)		physician 18, §7103(b)						18, §7103(b)	18, §7103(b)		necessary to carry out provisions of this part 18, §7103 (a)(2)	necessary to carry out provisions of this part 18, §7103 (a)(2) interested party or clergyman 18, §7103(b)
VA. Code (1976 & Supp. 1983)	all mental disabilities 37.1-1 et seq.	medical & mental records 37.1-84.1(8)	consistent w/ condition & sound therapeutic treatment 37.1-84.1(8) unless injurious to patient's health 8.01-413											unlimited access 8.01-413				
WASH. Rev. Code Ann. (1975 & Supp. 1982)	mentally disordered 71.05.020(2)	all information records 71.05.390			as necessary to administration of chapter 71.05.390(6)	to a professional person, not employed by facility or responsible for patient 71.05.390(1) 71.05.390(3)		operator of outpatient facility 71.05.390 (1), (2)	&/or program evaluation, upon oath of confidentiality 71.05.390(5)	71.05.390(4)		71.05.390(1)	or public health officers to regain custody 71.05.390 (7)(c)	71.05.390(8)		not admissible in any legal proceeding outside chapter w/o consent 71.05.390		
W. VA. Code (1980 & Supp. 1983)	mentally ill, mentally retarded, or addiction 27-5-9(a)	clinical record at mental health facility 27-5-9(e)			27-5-9 (e)(1)	& of director 27-5-9 (e)(3)(iii)		w/consent of patient & director 27-5-9 (e)(3)(ii)		w/consent of of patient & director 27-5-9 (e)(3)(i)				27-5-9 (e)(2)				

TABLE 10.2 CONFIDENTIALITY OF PATIENT RECORDS—*Continued*

					EXCEPTIONS TO CONFIDENTIALITY OF RECORDS													
STATE	TYPES OF PATIENTS COVERED (1)	SCOPE OF COVERAGE (2)	PATIENT'S RIGHT TO SEE RECORDS (3)	CONFIDENTIALITY & PATIENT ACCESS AFTER DISCHARGE (4)	Upon Court Order (5)	With Consent of Patient or Guardian (6)	During Court-ordered Examination of Patient (7)	Communication with Other Patient Providers (8)	Research Uses (9)	To Claim Benefits (10)	To Protect Patient Against Risk of Injury (11)	Competency Proceedings (12)	Law Enforcement Agencies (13)	Patient's Counsel (14)	Patient's Family (15)	Crimes By/Against Patient (16)	Institutionalization Proceedings (17)	Other (18)
WIS. Stat. Ann. (West 1957 & Supp. 1982)	mentally ill, developmentally disabled, alcoholism, or drug dependency 51.61(1) 51.30(1)(b)	all treatment records 51.61(1)(n) 51.30(1)(b)	access to nonmedication records may be restricted by director 51.30 (4)(d)(1) right to challenge accuracy 51.30(4)(f) 51.61(1)(n)	access 51.30 (4)(d) (2, 3)	51.30 (4)(b)(4)	51.30(4)(a)		51.30(4)(b) (5, 6, 7, 9)	if identity remains confidential 51.30 (4)(b)(3) audits 51.30 (4)(b)(1)	billing & collection purposes 51.30 (4)(b)(2) to coordinate services 51.30 (4)(b)(15)	part of records necessary to meet medical emergency 51.30 (4)(b)(8)		unauthorized absence 51.30 (4)(b)(13) correctional institution, probation or parole officer 51.30 (4)(b) (10, 12)	or guardian ad litem 51.30 (4)(b)(11)	parents, children, or spouse 51.30 (4)(b)(13)		51.30(4)(b) (11, 14)	
WYO. Stat. (1982 & Supp. 1983)	mentally ill 25-10-101 et seq.	records & reports 25-10-122(a)			necessary for conduct of proceedings & nondisclosure contrary to public interest 25-10-122 (a)(iii)	25-10-122 (a)(i)		25-10-122 (a)(iv)									necessary to carry out act 25-10-122 (a)(ii)	necessary to carry out act 25-10-122 (a)(ii)
	mentally retarded 25-5-103	all records 25-5-131(a)	superintendent may provide access 25-5-131 (b)(i)	same provisions apply to former resident 25-5-131(b)	in camera inspection, unless public disclosure necessary; superintendent may provide access 25-5-131 (b)(iv)	superintendent may provide access 25-5-131 (b)(iii)		superintendent may provide access to subject's physician or surgeon 25-5-131 (b)(ii) employees of training school 25-5-131 (b)(v)						superintendent may provide access to guardian, guardian ad litem, or attorney 25-5-131 (b)(i)				

FOOTNOTES: TABLE 10.2

1. Ala. Code § 22-50-1(1) (1975): "including, but not limited to, alcoholism, drug addiction, epilepsy or mental retardation."

2. Ky. Rev. Stat. Ann. § 202A.016 (Michie 1982): "In all proceedings under this chapter, it shall be the duty of the county attorney to assist the petitioner and represent the interest to the Commonwealth and to assist the court in its inquiry by the presentation of evidence."

3. Md. Health-Gen. Code Ann. § 7-611 (1982): "Within 14 days after a mentally retarded individual asks a facility for information about its records on that individual, the facility shall advise the individual, in writing, about the records and the procedures for their disclosure." "If the facility refuses to disclose a record . . . the administrative head of that facility shall apply, within 10 working days after the refusal, to the circuit court for the county where the facility is located for an order to permit the administrative head to continue to refuse disclosure to the mentally retarded individual." Id. § 7-612(b)(4).

4. Id. § 7-612(c):

Additional disclosure. A facility shall disclose a record that is sought:

(1) By the staff of the facility to carry out a purpose for which the record is kept;

. . . .

(3) By the Director or a representative of the Director; and

(4) By a person to further the purposes of:

(i) a medical review committee;
(ii) an accreditation board or commission;
(iii) a licensing agency that is authorized by statute to review records;
(iv) a court order;
(v) a representative of the Division of Reimbursement of the Department;
(vi) an auditor of the Department; or
(vii) an auditor of the Division of Audits of the Department of Fiscal Services.

5. Miss. Code Ann. § 41-21-97 (1981): "by any court in which the mental condition of the patient is or has been a matter of inquiry or question."

6. Mo. Ann. Stat. § 630.140.3 (Vernon Supp. 1982): "(5) To the courts as necessary for the administration of chapter 211, 475, 552 or 632, RSMo; . . . . (8) To the attorney representing petitioners and to mental health coordinators, but only to the extent necessary to carry out their duties under chapter 632, RSMo."

7. Mont. Code Ann. § 53-21-166(2) (1981): "except that nothing in this section shall be construed to compel a physician, psychologist, social worker, nurse, attorney, or other professional person to reveal information which has been given to him in confidence by members of a patient's family."

John Parry

CHAPTER 11 *Rights and Entitlements in the Community*

I. FEDERAL MENTAL DISABILITY LEGISLATION

The 1970s marked a substantial movement forward in federal efforts to provide care, treatment, rehabilitation, and community services to mentally and developmentally disabled persons. While in practice the shift from institutional care to semiindependent living in the community has fallen well short of the projections by advocates of this movement, the impetus of the law in many respects is now behind deinstitutionalization and community-based services, leaving behind the pre-1970s system in which mentally disabled persons could look forward to little more than humane custodial care if they were fortunate and inexcusable abuses if they were not. Admittedly the law, by nature conservative, moves slowly, yet once the direction is set on a new course, it can provide a steady and powerful pressure for reform. Such a reformation has happened in the past 15 years as many of the traditional and outmoded legal principles that governed the rights and privileges of mentally disabled persons have been discarded or recast to fit a different theoretical perspective that shapes the obligations of society to this often isolated, neglected, and vulnerable population. Thus even though powerful social and economic forces still resist the positive direction set by the courts and many legislatures and serious problems in implementing new theory have been documented in the social science literature, the system that once was is no longer in place, significant improvements can be identified, and new and enduring problems are receiving more attention now than they could have 20 years ago. Whether this progress is continued, slowed, halted, or redefined—and any of these choices is a possibility in the mid-1980s—the legal developments of the recent past probably have precluded a return to the old ways of ignoring the rights and abilities of mentally disabled persons.

For this legal reform to take hold in the mental disability area, significant federal involvement was a necessary ingredient. Six major federal statutes and their key provisions provided a foundation for the federal government's community-oriented initiatives, so this is where the chapter begins. A certain amount of repetition will be necessary later to give readers a sense of both the complete picture and the important technical details affecting particular rights and entitlements. Much like the tables in other chapters, this brief legislative review can serve as a reference section, but it is also an introduction to the community movement that has changed the ways in which our society attempts to fill the needs and guarantee the rights of mentally disabled persons.

A. Mental Retardation Facilities and Community Mental Health Centers Construction Act of 1963

With enactment in 1963 of the Mental Retardation Facilities and Community Mental Health Centers Construction Act,[1] Congress set into motion a movement to secure community-based care and treatment of mentally disabled persons. In providing the federal seed money, Congress concluded that large state and county institutions that isolated mentally ill persons should be supplanted by a system of community-oriented treatment programs.[2] Based on a mathematical formula that took into account population and need, money was allocated to every state that developed a comprehensive mental health plan indicating state priorities for services in each "catchment" area to be served by the community mental health centers. Each center had to provide care and treatment, including free or low-cost services to indigent persons, to anyone who lived within designated geographic boundaries. At a bare minimum, a qualify-

1. Pub. L. No. 88-164, 77 Stat. 282 (codified as amended in scattered sections of 42 U.S.C., with notes on history at §§ 2681 to 2696 (1982)).

2. House Comm. on Interstate and Foreign Commerce, Mental Retardation Facilities and Community Mental Health Centers Construction Act of 1963, H. Rep. No. 694, 88th Cong., 1st Sess., *reprinted in* 1963 U.S. Code Cong. & Ad. News 1054, 1065.

ing center had to be equipped to handle inpatient, outpatient, partial hospitalization, emergency care, and consultant and education services for between 75,000 and 200,000 persons.[3]

Subsequently, amendments passed in 1965 added funds for initial staffing by professional and technical personnel in both existing and soon-to-be-constructed centers.[4] The 1968 amendments authorized the construction of specialized facilities to treat alcohol and narcotic addiction and provided up to 2% of any center's funding for program administration.[5]

The 1970 amendments diverged from the original focus on start-up costs: finding that state and local contributions were inadequate to maintain operations, Congress increased funding and made long-term federal commitments.[6] The old programs were maintained, one new program serving children was added,[7] and the federal share of construction projects in traditionally underserved urban and rural areas was increased to a maximum of 90%.[8]

Funds to underserved areas continued to be expanded with the enactment of a series of health law amendments in 1975.[9] The Special Health Revenue Sharing Act of 1975[10] specified a number of new funding requirements for community mental health centers concerning organization, operations, provision of services, coordination with other programs, integration of services, community and citizen involvement, quality assurance, and governing bodies. The Community Mental Health Centers Amendments of 1975[11] funded a new national center to conduct research into the medical, social, and legal aspects of rape and rape prevention[12] and increased from 5 to 12 the requisite services each center must provide. The new services included programs for children, the aged, and alcohol and drug abusers, and screening, follow-up care, and transitional community-based services.

Since 1975 the Community Mental Health Centers program has been extended twice with only slight modifications, requiring a few additional services such as halfway houses and new transitional services.[13] A more ambitious funding package known as the Mental Health Systems Act[14] was prepared by the Carter administration, largely as a result of the recommendations of the President's Commission on Mental Health. It stressed the effective use of available resources, development of community-based services for the most underserved and needy, including the chronically mentally ill, minimal use of institutions, care in the least restrictive settings, and preventive mental health. Moreover, the act established a bill of rights, similar to the one that had already been passed on behalf of developmentally disabled persons, and a limited advocacy system.[15]

Soon after the Mental Health Systems Act became law, and before it could be fully implemented, the Reagan administration passed the Omnibus Budget Reconciliation Act of 1981, which in reorganizing a number of social programs did away with most of the Carter legislation and replaced it with a simple extension of the Community Mental Health Centers Act but kept an advisory bill of rights to guide the states.[16] Recently, the Senate Labor Committee's Subcommittee on the Handicapped reported a bill concerning the funding of an advocacy system for mentally ill persons.[17]

B. Rehabilitation Act of 1973

The federal government's commitment to community programming was broadened to include additional disability groups through the Rehabilitation Act of 1973 as amended by the Rehabilitation, Comprehensive Services, and Developmental Disabilities Amendments of 1978.[18] The amended act includes seven parts designed to develop and implement "comprehensive and coordinated programs of vocational rehabilitation and independent living."[19] The intended beneficiaries are handicapped individuals who are defined in two different ways depending on the provisions applicable to them. First, in the titles having to do with funding vocational rehabilitation services, "handicapped" includes any person who by reason of physical or mental disability is substantially handicapped with respect to employment and who can reasonably be expected to benefit from the services that

3. National Institute of Mental Health Report, History of Community Mental Health Centers Program (April 1980) [hereinafter cited as NIMH Rep. (1980)].

4. Mental Retardation Facilities and Community Mental Health Centers Construction Act Amendments of 1965, Pub. L. No. 89-105, 79 Stat. 427.

5. Pub. L. No. 90-574, 82 Stat. 1005, 1006-12 (1968).

6. Community Mental Health Centers Amendments of 1970, Pub. L. No. 91-211, 84 Stat. 54; Developmental Disabilities Services and Facilities Construction Amendments of 1970, Pub. L. No. 91-517, 84 Stat. 1316.

7. Pub. L. No. 91-211, § 401, 84 Stat. 60 (1970).

8. *Id.* § 104, 84 Stat. at 55.

9. Pub. L. No. 94-63, 89 Stat. 304 (1975) (amending the Public Health Service Act and related health laws).

10. Pub. L. No. 94-63, §§ 101 & 102, 89 Stat. 304 (1975).

11. *Id.*, §§ 301-303, 89 Stat. at 308 (1975).

12. National Center for the Prevention and Control of Rape, Pub. L. No. 94-63, § 303 pt. D, 89 Stat. 328 (1975) (current version codified at 42 U.S.C. § 9511 (1982)).

13. Community Mental Health Centers Extension Act of 1978, Pub. L. No. 95-622, Title I, 92 Stat. 3412 (1978); Joint Resolution (to amend the Public Health Service Act and related health laws), Pub. L. No. 96-32, § 8(a)(1) & (2), 93 Stat. 82, 85 (1979).

14. Pub. L. No. 96-398, 94 Stat. 1564 (1980).

15. *Id.* § 501, 94 Stat. at 1598 (codified at 42 U.S.C. 9501 (1982)).

16. Pub. L. No. 97-35, 95 Stat. 357, 560 (1981).

17. S. 974. Reported to Subcommittee on the Handicapped June 6, 1985.

18. Rehabilitation Act of 1973, Pub. L. No. 93-112, 87 Stat. 355 (codified in scattered sections of 29 U.S.C. §§ 701 to 794). The 1978 Amendments are described in this chapter in § I D, Developmental Disabilities Act Amendments of 1978, *infra*.

19. 29 U.S.C.A. § 701 (Supp. 1985).

are provided.[20] Second, under the titles bestowing legal rights, "handicapped" refers to any person who has, is regarded as having, or has a record of having a physical or mental impairment that substantially limits one or more of his major life activities.[21] The second definition specifically excludes alcoholics and drug abusers from coverage under the employment discrimination provisions of Title V.

1. Vocational Rehabilitation Services

Title I aims to engage handicapped individuals in gainful employment by authorizing funding for basic vocational rehabilitation services.[22] To qualify, a state must submit a plan detailing how it plans to use existing rehabilitative services, comply with the Architectural and Transportation Barriers Act of 1968 to make public buildings and programs accessible to handicapped persons, and coordinate activities with the services provided under the Education for All Handicapped Children Act.[23]

Similar to other legislation with a community focus, the title establishes a means for assessing the needs and implementing the services for recipients. The administering agency is responsible for preparing an individualized written rehabilitation program for each eligible client, which includes long-range rehabilitation goals, intermediate objectives, specific services that need to be provided, and criteria to measure and evaluate progress.[24] A variety of individualized services may be included as long as they are intended to help mentally or physically disabled persons become employable.[25]

The Rehabilitation Amendments of 1984[26] continue the program at least through 1987 and add one important new feature—an advocacy system for vocational rehabilitation clients. Beginning October 1, 1984, each participating state must create a client assistance program to help clients obtain the benefits available to them under the act. Each program must have the authority to pursue legal, administrative, and other remedies.[27]

Under Title II, funds are authorized for research and training that facilitate independent living.[28]

2. Employment and Other Forms of Discrimination

The Rehabilitation Act's most important rights provisions are contained in Title V, which prohibits employment and nonemployment discrimination against handicapped persons. These provisions, especially after the passage of the 1978 amendments, are analogous to the discrimination prohibitions found in the 1964 Civil Rights Act and amendments which protect other minority groups.

Section 501 mandates each federal agency to establish and implement an affirmative action program plan to provide for "adequate hiring, placement, and advancement opportunities for handicapped individuals."[29] Section 502 establishes the Architectural and Transportation Barriers Compliance Board, which is empowered to investigate and oversee efforts to make public buildings and transportation accessible to all handicapped persons.[30]

Section 503, one of the two most used provisions in this title, governs all employment under federal contracts; it states that in any contract with the federal government which exceeds $2,500, the contracting party "shall take affirmative action to employ and advance in employment qualified handicapped individuals."[31] Any handicapped individual who "believes" a contractor has failed to comply with the provision may file a complaint with the U.S. Department of Labor, which will investigate and take appropriate action.[32] As will be elaborated later, the meaning of § 503 is subject to judicial interpretation in a number of areas including the right of private parties to file suit, definition of qualified handicapped employees, and exhaustion of administrative remedies.

The most relied on provision in Title V is § 504, which demands nondiscrimination in federal grants and programs and governs employment and nonemployment claims. It states:

> No otherwise qualified handicapped individual in the United States . . . shall, solely by reason of his handicap, be excluded from the participation in, be denied the benefits of, or be subjected to discrimination under any program or activity receiving Federal financial assistance or under any program or activity conducted by any Executive agency or by the United States Postal Service.[33]

In order to implement this deceptively simple provision, each federal department was instructed to promulgate separate regulations governing its area of authority. The most relied upon regulations have come from the U.S. Department of Health and Human Services (formerly

20. 29 U.S.C. § 706(7)(A)(1982).
21. 29 U.S.C. § 706(7)(B).
22. 29 U.S.C. § 720(a).
23. 29 U.S.C. § 721.
24. 29 U.S.C. § 722.
25. 29 U.S.C. § 723.
26. Pub. L. No. 98-221, 98 Stat. 17 (1984) (codified at 29 U.S.C. § 701 and scattered sections thereafter).
27. 29 U.S.C.A. § 732 (Supp. 1985).
28. 29 U.S.C. § 760 (1982).
29. 29 U.S.C. § 791(b).
30. 29 U.S.C. § 792.
31. 29 U.S.C. § 793(a).
32. 29 U.S.C. § 793(b).
33. 29 U.S.C. § 794.

the Department of Health, Education, and Welfare) regulating employment, program accessibility, education, postsecondary education, and social services. As with § 503, subsequent judicial interpretations have expanded the meaning of § 504 and its regulations. Some of the most notable disputes are waged over the existence of a private right of action, particularly in employment cases, the difference between discrimination and affirmative action, and definition of recipients under the act.

Section 505 was created by the 1978 amendments in order to better define the available remedies in Title V and to provide for attorneys' fees.[34] As a result of these changes, employees or applicants for employment can make private legal complaints under §§ 501 and 504 and rely on procedures contained in Title VI of the 1964 Civil Rights Act. This so-called improvement turned out to be a mixed blessing, as the more precise definition complicated standing in § 504 employment cases. In addition, the section provides that "[i]n fashioning an equitable or affirmative action remedy . . . a court may take into account the reasonableness of the cost of any necessary work place accommodation, and the availability of alternatives . . . in order to achieve an equitable and appropriate remedy." Also "the court, in its discretion, may allow the prevailing party, other than the United States, a reasonable attorney's fee as part of the costs."[35]

3. *Independent Living for Unemployable Handicapped Persons*

Title VII establishes a program designed to provide comprehensive services to severely handicapped persons who do not have employment potential in order to help place them into independent living situations in the community.[36] One notable aspect of the program is the funding of centers for independent living which bring together a continuum of services in one location, including counseling, advocacy, and many other social services.[37]

C. Education for All Handicapped Children Act of 1975

The first federal legislation to implement the goal of full educational opportunities for handicapped children, the Education of the Handicapped Amendments of 1974,[38] was superseded by the Education for All Handicapped Children Act of 1975 (EAHCA)[39] and except for some minor amendments has not been changed since then, although it was interpreted by final regulations published in 1977.[40]

According to the act's "statement of findings and purpose" there were more than eight million handicapped children in the United States in 1975, more than half of whom did "not receive appropriate educational services which would enable them to have full equality of opportunity" and of whom one million handicapped children were excluded entirely. It was Congress's stated intention

> to assure that all handicapped children have available to them . . . a free appropriate public education which emphasizes special education and related services designed to meet their unique needs, to assure that the rights of handicapped children and their parents or guardians are protected, to assist States and localities to provide for the education of all handicapped children, and to assess and assure the effectiveness of efforts to educate handicapped children.[41]

"Handicapped children" means "mentally retarded, hard of hearing, deaf, speech impaired, visually handicapped, seriously emotionally disturbed, orthopedically impaired, or other health impaired children, or children with specific learning disabilities, who by reason thereof require special education and related services." Other important terms, discussed in subsequent sections and defined generally in the act, are "special education," "related services," "free appropriate public education," and "individualized education program."[42]

In addition to providing relatively modest sums of money to the states electing to participate in the program, the act establishes stringent eligibility requirements.[43] In order to qualify for funding, each state must take responsibility for guaranteeing that the state and the local school districts comply with specific standards. These include six basic areas of concern.

First, the act established that all handicapped children ages 3 through 21 had to have access to free appropriate public education by September 1, 1980, unless the state had an incompatible law, in which case the provision of services for children ages 3 through 5 and 18 through 21 would be governed by preexisting state law.[44]

Second, by October 1, 1977, the states had to establish policies and procedures that govern the identification, evaluation, or placement of each handicapped child and minimally include the following: (1) prior

34. 29 U.S.C. § 794a.
35. 29 U.S.C. § 794a.
36. 29 U.S.C. § 796.
37. 29 U.S.C. § 796e.
38. Pub. L. No. 93-380, §§ 611, 614(a), 88 Stat. 576, 580 (1974).
39. Pub. L. No. 94-142, 89 Stat. 773 (codified as amended at 20 U.S.C. §§ 1232, 1401, 1405-6, 1411-20, 1453 (1982) [hereinafter cited as EAHCA].
40. 34 C.F.R. § 300 (1984) (originally 42 Fed. Reg. 42,476 (Aug. 23, 1977), redesignated at 45 Fed. Reg. 77,368 (Nov. 21, 1980)).
41. 20 U.S.C. § 1400(b) & (c) (1982).
42. 20 U.S.C. § 1401(1). See in this chapter § IV, Education of Mentally Disabled Children, *infra* for the courts' interpretations of these terms.
43. 20. U.S.C. § 1412.
44. 20 U.S.C. § 1412(2)(B).

notice of any change in placement, (2) an opportunity for the parents or guardian to examine all relevant records and to obtain an independent educational evaluation of the child, (3) the right to an impartial due process hearing conducted by the state, the intermediate, or the local education agency in front of a hearing officer who is not employed by the agency or unit involved in the education or care of the child, (4) if an intermediate or local education agency conducts the hearing, the right of any aggrieved party to appeal to a state agency that will conduct an impartial review of the first hearing, (5) the right, at the original administrative hearing, of parents to have legal counsel and use experts, to present evidence, subpoena, confront, and cross-examine witnesses, to have a record of the proceedings, and to have written findings of fact supporting the decision, (6) the right of any aggrieved party to file a civil suit in federal or state court, and (7) the right of either party to insist that the handicapped child remain in the then current educational placement until all the proceedings are completed.[45]

Third, to the greatest extent possible, handicapped children should be educated with children who are not handicapped, whether or not they are in public or private institutions or other care facilities.[46]

Fourth, the tests and procedures used to evaluate a handicapped child should not be racially or culturally discriminatory, should be administered in the child's native language, where possible, and should not be based on any single criterion.[47]

Fifth, each child must have a written individualized education program (IEP) that is reviewed annually by the parents, teachers, and a school district designee and encompasses a child's performance level, short- and long-term goals, specific services that are to be provided, and specific criteria for measuring progress.[48]

Sixth, handicapped children who are referred to or are placed in private schools should be guaranteed the same rights to a free appropriate special education and related services as public school children.[49]

The act also mandates participating states to make comprehensive plans to develop and train the necessary instructional support personnel.[50]

It should be noted that much of the meaning of the act has come from the implementing regulations and from the administrative and judicial interpretations following its enactment. Moreover, most courts read the provisions in conjunction with the regulations implemented under § 504 of the Rehabilitation Act.

45. 20 U.S.C. § 1415(b), (c), & (d).
46. 20 U.S.C. § 1412(5)(B).
47. 20 U.S.C. § 1412(5)(C).
48. 20 U.S.C. §§ 1412(4), 1413(a), 1414(a)(5).
49. 20 U.S.C. §§ 1413(a)(4), 1414(a) & (b).
50. 20 U.S.C. §§ 1413(a)(3), 1414(a)(1)(C)(i).

D. Developmental Disabilities Act Amendments of 1978

As amended in 1978, the Developmentally Disabled Assistance and Bill of Rights Act (Developmental Disabilities Act)[51] serves severely disabled persons whose needs cannot be met by the Education for All Handicapped Children Act, the Rehabilitation Act, and other programs. In addition to providing services, the act attempts to reduce or eliminate the need for institutional care and to protect the legal and human rights of eligible persons.[52]

One major change from the 1970 and 1975 developmental disabilities acts is in the definition of "developmentally disabled." The previous legislation used a categorical approach that covered persons with mental retardation, epilepsy, and cerebral palsy[53] and later, autism.[54] In the 1978 amendments the term "developmentally disabled" was redefined on a strictly functional basis to include any disorder that is a "severe, chronic disability," demonstrated by limitations in performing accepted social roles and tasks, "attributable to a mental or physical impairment . . . manifested before the person attains age twenty-two" and "likely to continue indefinitely." In order to be included, a person must have "substantial functional limitations in three or more . . . areas of major life activity . . . [which reflect] the person's need for . . . lifelong . . . individually planned and coordinated" services.[55]

Under the amended act each client who is served must have written an individualized habilitation plan that states long-term habilitation goals and intermediate objectives with "measurable indices of progress" and that provides for a program coordinator who will implement that plan.[56] Included also is a statement of rights that sets out guidelines for states to follow in providing care and habilitation, including a controversial right to "appropriate treatment, services, and habilitation" in "the

51. Rehabilitation, Comprehensive Services, and Developmental Disabilities Amendments of 1978, Pub. L. No. 95-602, 92 Stat. 2955 (1978) [hereinafter cited as Developmental Disabilities Act Amendments of 1978], amending the Developmental Disabilities Services and Facilities Construction Amendments of 1970 and the Developmentally Disabled Assistance and Bill of Rights Act of 1975 (codified as amended in scattered sections of 29 and 42 U.S.C. (1982)). Title V of the Pub. L. No. 95-602, 92 Stat. 3003 (1978), is also called the Developmentally Disabled Assistance and Bill of Rights Act.
52. 42 U.S.C. § 6000 (1982).
53. Developmental Disabilities Services and Facilities Construction Amendments of 1970, Pub. L. No. 91-517, 84 Stat. 1316. The term also included neurological conditions clearly related to mental retardation.
54. Developmentally Disabled Assistance and Bill of Rights Act of 1975, Pub. L. No. 94-103, 89 Stat. 497. The term also included a disabling condition closely related to mental retardation and mentioned dyslexia in particular.
55. The new definitions of the 1978 Developmental Disabilities Act Amendments are reported in 3 MDLR 121 (1979) (current version at 42 U.S.C. § 6001(7) (1982)).
56. 42. U.S.C. § 6011(b) (1982).

setting that is least restrictive of the person's personal liberty."[57]

One of the novel aspects of this legislation was the establishment in 1978 of a mandatory protection and advocacy system in each participating state. According to the amended law, the systems may be different but they all must be independent of direct service providers, contain provisions for securing legal representation for those clients needing such help, and otherwise advocate for the rights of developmentally disabled persons in their state.[58] This advocacy provision provided the prototype for other client protection provisions in federal handicap legislation.

E. Civil Rights of Institutionalized Persons Act of 1980

In the Civil Rights of Institutionalized Persons Act[59] in 1980, Congress, moved by widespread support from a number of interested groups, gave the U.S. Department of Justice formal authority to initiate and intervene in litigation intended to secure the constitutional and federal rights of institutionalized persons, including mentally disabled institution residents. Although the Justice Department had participated in such litigation for a number of years, the need for the act was demonstrated after two federal appellate decisions created significant doubt whether litigation by the DOJ was appropriate without Congress's express approval.[60] However, advocates for a states' rights position convinced Congress the legislature should move cautiously, if at all, with the result that a number of restrictive conditions were placed on the attorney general and the Justice Department in order to ensure that meaningful efforts would be made to resolve all disputes without going to court. The legislative history of the act notes the importance of federal involvement:

> One measure of a nation's civilization is the quality of treatment it provides persons entrusted to its care. The past decade has borne testimony to the growing civilization of this country through its commitment to the adequate care of its institutionalized citizens. Nowhere is that commitment more evident than in the actions of the United States Justice Department.[61]

Nevertheless, some advocates are questioning the federal government's resolve in light of the relatively few actions brought so far and the Justice Department's emphasis on bringing about institutional change through negotiation, trade-offs, and compromise without litigation.

In the act, "institutionalized persons" are defined as those persons who live in facilities or institutions "owned, operated, or managed by" or providing services on behalf of a state or political subdivision of a state.[62] In addition to people in jails and prisons, this includes residents "who are mentally ill, disabled, or retarded, or chronically ill or handicapped" or who live in facilities" providing skilled nursing, intermediate or long-term care, or custodial or residential care."[63] Specifically excluded are private facilities whose only nexus with the state is through licensing procedures or receipt of certain federal funds such as under Title XIX of the Social Security Act.[64]

In order to assert discretionary authority to initiate civil actions, the attorney general must, by a certification process, satisfy several requirements: (1) he must have reasonable cause to believe the state "is subjecting persons residing in or confined to an institution . . . to egregious or flagrant conditions . . . causing such persons to suffer grievous harm," (2) the deprivation must be "pursuant to a pattern or practice of resistance to the full enjoyment of . . . rights, privileges, or immunities" secured by the Constitution or the laws of the United States, and (3) the civil action may be instituted only to obtain such equitable relief "as may be appropriate to insure the minimum corrective measures necessary to insure the full enjoyment of such rights, privileges, or immunities."[65] Attorneys' fees and costs may be awarded by the court.[66]

The restrictions on federal action include: (1) a certification system requiring the attorney general to personally verify that the governor of the state has been given 49 calendar days of prior written notification of the alleged conditions, supporting facts giving rise to the conditions, and the minimum measures that would remedy the situation, (2) advance notice by at least seven days before an action is commenced in which the attorney general must verify he has notified the appropriate state authorities, "made a reasonable good faith effort to consult with the Governor" and the attorney general of the state about how to correct those conditions, and attempted to resolve the matter first by negotiation, persuasion, and conciliation.[67]

Similar stipulations govern the attorney general's intervention in an action initiated by others. The differences are that the attorney general must have "reason-

57. 42 U.S.C. § 6012.

58. Pub. L. No. 95-602, Title V, § 508, 92 Stat. 3003, 3007–8 (1978) (codified as amended at 42 U.S.C. § 6012).

59. Pub. L. No. 96-247, 94 Stat. 349 (1980) (codified at 42 U.S.C. §§ 1997 to 1997j).

60. S. Rep. No. 416, 96th Cong., 2d Sess. 1, *reprinted in* 1980 U.S. Code Cong. & Ad. News 787.

61. *Id.* (note omitted).

62. 42 U.S.C. § 1997(1)(A) (1982).

63. 42. U.S.C. § 1997(1)(B)(i).

64. 42 U.S.C. § 1997(2).

65. 42 U.S.C. § 1997a(a).

66. 42 U.S.C. § 1997a(b).

67. 42 U.S.C. § 1997b(a).

able cause to believe" that there is a violation of the type defined in the initiation section above and that 90 days have passed since the action was filed, unless the court shortens that period "in the interests of justice." The certification process is largely the same, although the time limit for giving notice to the state is only 15 days and notification need be made only once. The prevailing party, other than the United States, may recover attorneys' fees and costs.[68]

As a general matter, the legislation indicates that the provisions of the act do not expand or restrict the authority of the parties to enforce their legal rights independent of this legislation.[69]

F. Social Security Benefits

A broad array of entitlements is provided under the Social Security Act, of which the programs providing the greatest financial support to mentally disabled persons are the income assistance programs for aged, blind, and disabled persons, the children's program, and the Medicare and Medicaid programs for needy individuals.

1. Income Assistance for the Needy Disabled

In 1972 Congress enacted amendments to the Social Security Act, which among other things authorized benefits for permanently and totally disabled persons.[70] Unlike previously funded programs, this program placed the disabled into one assistance category with blind and aged persons.[71] The legislation also authorized states to establish a Supplemental Security Income (SSI) program if they wished to provide additional assistance to eligible individuals.[72] The regular assistance program is entirely federally funded, whereas SSI is funded by the states except for administrative costs, which the federal government assumes.[73]

Mentally disabled individuals are eligible to receive benefits under both assistance schemes if the resident state chooses to participate in the SSI portion and if the applicants meet two criteria. The first criterion is financial need, which changes almost every year (under the basic program only the most needy qualify for benefits). The second criterion is meeting the definition of "disabled," which is an inability "to engage in any substantial gainful activity by reason of a medically determinable physical or mental impairment which is expected to last, or has lasted, for 12 months or can be expected to end in death."[74] As will be discussed in more detail later, significant controversy in recent years has surrounded the federal government's regulations to implement the criteria to apply for and continue benefits. Theoretically, mentally impaired persons can be gainfully employed but eligible under another category if they are blind, over 65, under 21, or married to an eligible person.

The benefits under the basic program are gauged to place the eligible person just over the poverty line. The supplemental income, the guidelines for which are established by each state that chooses to participate, provides benefits that go beyond bare subsistence.

Disabled individuals are normally referred to the state's agency that administers vocational rehabilitation services. Social Security Disability applicants are obligated to accept any services offered, unless there is good cause to refuse; otherwise, they may lose their eligibility for benefits.[75]

Another amendment in 1976, popularly called the Keys Amendment, put into effect a system for the federal government to regulate the living standards in institutions, foster homes, or group living arrangements that provide services to a significant number of SSI recipients.[76] The areas of regulation are admission policies, safety, sanitation, and protection of civil rights, and the facilities covered are those that provide both room and board and continuous protective oversight including medical treatment. Specifically excluded are Medicaid- or Medicare-certified facilities.[77] Enforcement is provided by the state agency designated for that purpose, which is also responsible for establishing standards to be used in that state.[78] Necessary procedures include inspections, provision of technical assistance, a warning system that allows deficient facilities to comply, and notification to residents whose facility has been cited out of compliance.

2. Maternal and Child Health Services

The Social Security Act with its amendments also establishes a special program for maternal and child health services "to reduce infant mortality and the incidence of preventable diseases and handicapping conditions among children."[79] Within this program there is funding for research into genetic diseases including certain types of mental retardation and rehabilitation assistance for persons under 16. In order to participate,

68. 42 U.S.C. § 1997c.
69. 42 U.S.C. § 1997j.
70. Pub. L. No. 92-603 (current version codified at 42 U.S.C. § 1351 (1982)).
71. H. Rep. No. 231, 92d Cong., 2d Sess., *reprinted in* 1972 U.S. Code Cong. & Ad. News 4989, 4992.
72. 42 U.S.C. § 1381.
73. H. Rep. No. 231, *supra* note 71, 1972 U.S. Cong. & Ad. News at 4989, 4992.
74. *Id.* at 5013.
75. *Id.* at 5014.
76. Pub. L. No. 94-566, § 505(d), 90 Stat. 2687 (1976). Regulations at 45 C.F.R. § 1397.1 (1984).
77. 45 C.F.R. §§ 1397.20, 1397.5.
78. 45 C.F.R. 1397.10.
79. 42 U.S.C. § 701(A)(2) (1982).

each state must prepare a state plan that specifies coordination efforts with other state and local programs and how it intends to make expenditures.[80]

3. Medical Assistance for the Needy Disabled

Health Insurance for Aged and Disabled under the Social Security Act is commonly referred to as Medicare.[81] It "provides basic protection against the costs of hospital, related post-hospital, home health services, and hospice care" to individuals who are 65 or older or who are disabled for not less than 24 months as defined in the statute.[82] Severe limitations are placed on inpatient psychiatric services, which among other things are restricted to a total of 190 days during a lifetime.[83] Certain specified home health services, including intermittent skilled nursing care and therapies of different kinds,[84] are reimbursable under Medicare, but the criteria for eligibility are stringent. In 1985 the Health Care Financing Administration issued a final rule that may help to encourage states to participate in the option of providing home and community-based services to specified population groups.[85] A separate part of the program is a voluntary supplementary assistance plan with specified deductibles and coinsurance premiums, intended to allow disabled persons to pay monthly premiums in order to obtain additional coverage that goes beyond meeting extraordinary health expenses.[86]

Medicaid provides services to dependent children and aged, blind, and disabled individuals "whose income and resources are insufficient to meet the costs of necessary medical services." Assistance is also provided in the form of "rehabilitation and other services to help such . . . individuals attain or retain capability for independence or self-care.[87] In general, those eligible are the categorically needy who receive benefits under the Social Security Income Assistance programs;[88] however, states do have the option to include other needy individuals such as patients in hospitals who have been excluded from the income assistance program, as long as they are not under 65 or over 21 and are not living in mental institutions. States may also include aged, blind, or disabled persons or children who have enough income to cover daily expenses but do not have enough to pay for medical care. Many jurisdictions cover both the categorically and the medically needy.[89]

In addition to a wide range of inpatient hospital services, diagnosis, screening, and home health services that are mandatory, states may choose to provide any number of other services, such as inpatient psychiatric care for children and the aged and services in intermediate care facilities.[90]

Under existing law, Medicaid recipients have what is known as the "freedom of choice," which means that any institution, agency, organization, or person holding itself out as qualified to perform a service must provide medical assistance to Medicaid recipients.

II. MENTALLY ILL AND DEVELOPMENTALLY DISABLED PERSONS: TWO DISTINCT POPULATIONS

As a result of a series of changes in the identification, care, treatment, and habilitation of mentally disabled residents of institutions that began in the 1950s, two distinct, albeit interrelated, service delivery systems have evolved: one for mentally ill persons and the other for mentally retarded and other developmentally disabled persons. Although it would be incorrect to state that similarities between mentally ill and developmentally disabled persons no longer exist in the rights and services they receive, distinctions are even more important in explaining how these rights and entitlements have been refocused to serve community-oriented objectives such as limiting institutionalization, fostering deinstitutionalization, and providing a whole range of supportive services to each of these populations.

A. Profiles of the Two Populations

1. Mentally Ill Persons

According to general estimates by the President's Commission on Mental Health published in 1978, 15% of the population of the United States, or approximately 34 million people, were in need of mental health care services.[91] Of those, only a relatively small number received inpatient or outpatient services in any given year. The National Institute of Mental Health reported that in 1977 there were 6,392,979 patient-care episodes, which included patients who experienced more than one episode.[92] The vast majority of the mentally ill appeared to receive either limited care from general prac-

80. 42 U.S.C. § 705.

81. Health Insurance for the Aged Act, Pub. L. No. 89-97, 79 Stat. 290 (1965).

82. 42. U.S.C. § 1395c (1982).

83. 42 U.S.C. § 1395d(b)(3).

84. 42 U.S.C. § 1395f(a)(2)(D).

85. Medicaid Program; Home and Community-Based Services, 50 Fed. Reg. 10,013 (Mar. 13, 1985).

86. 42 U.S.C. § 1395j.

87. 42 U.S.C. § 1396.

88. Senate Comm. on Finance, Social Security Amendments of 1965, S. Rep. No. 404, 89th Cong., 1st Sess., *reprinted in* 1965 U.S. Code Cong. & Ad. News 1943.

89. 42 U.S.C.A. 1396a(a)(10)(A) (Supp. 1985).

90. *Id.*

91. 2 Task Panel Reports Submitted to The President's Commission on Mental Health 4 (1978) [hereinafter cited as President's Commission].

92. Goldman, Adams, & Taube, Deinstitutionalization: The Data Demythologized, 34 Hosp. & Community Psychiatry 129, 131 table 1 (1983).

titioners who were not adequately trained in the mental health field[93] or no care at all. More startling, perhaps, only 1,816,613 of the patient-care episodes occurred in inpatient facilities.[94] While the total number of episodes has increased significantly since 1955, the actual number of residents in public hospitals during the period from 1955 to 1980, representing most institutionalized mental patients, dropped from 558,922 to 137,810.[95] This apparent inconsistency can be explained by several developments: individuals who would never have received care previously were obtaining services in the community from outpatient providers, fewer patients were receiving long-term custodial care in state and county hospitals, and the number of short-term inpatient care episodes had increased,[96] particularly as reflected in the rate of readmissions of former patients.[97]

While many noninstitutional services such as housing, legal aid, and income maintenance are being used by mentally ill persons who no longer receive inpatient medical care,[98] many of those most in need of psychiatric care have been either "transinstitutionalized"[99] into nursing homes and board-and-care facilities or "dumped" into the community. What we have instead of successful deinstitutionalization with well-funded community programs are many seriously flawed institutional and community programs competing for dwindling resources, with the demand for those resources steadily increasing as more people seek care.[100]

2. *Developmentally Disabled Persons*

The first definition of developmental disability included only four conditions—mental retardation, epilepsy, cerebral palsy, and autism. A revision of the definition in 1978 dissolved the four specified categories and identified a single group based on functional level: "severely and permanently disabled."[101] This change reduced the population that was eligible for federal support. Depending on how the definition is interpreted and what method is used to make the estimates, there are between 2 and 3 million developmentally disabled persons, of which the largest single subpopulation (between 35% and 50%) is the mentally retarded.[102] In addition, there are approximately 5.9 million mentally disabled persons with a diagnosis of mildly retarded, who are not included in the newer federal developmentally disabled category.

Only a small proportion of developmentally disabled persons live in public residential institutions, and most of those individuals are found in facilities for the mentally retarded. These facilities have shown a steady decline in total population since 1967, when there were 195,000 residents, up to 1978, when the number decreased to 139,432.[103] According to the National Association for Retarded Citizens, most mentally retarded persons live at home. In addition, 80,000 mentally retarded persons have been identified as living in nursing homes and intermediate care facilities and 55,000 in small community residences with 20 or fewer persons.[104]

B. Nature of the Services Received: Treatment versus Habilitation

Competing philosophies underlying care and treatment constitute a critical difference between the two populations. In the not so distant past, the entire system of care for mentally disabled persons was one dimensional. Whether persons were mentally ill, mentally retarded, or severely physically disabled, they were generally regarded as patients, and if care or treatment was provided at all, it was for the most part involuntary care provided by physicians in state hospitals. The terminology used in the previous editions of this book reflected the medical model.

Today, however, both the system of care and the terminology have changed: social service, developmental, self-help, and medical models are all present. The individuals who need mental disability services are variously referred to as "patients," "inmates," "residents," "recipients," or "clients." The professionals who provide the services may be physicians, psychiatrists, administrators, psychologists, social workers, or habilitation and rehabilitation specialists or there may be no professionals at all, only concerned people trying to help each other. The location for services may be hospitals, institutions, facilities, community programs, or family homes. Most services today are supposed to be provided on a voluntary basis, except in institutions where invol-

93. President's Commission, *supra* note 91, at 427.

94. Goldman, Adams, & Taube, *supra* note 92, at 131.

95. *Id.* at 132 table 2.

96. *Id.* at 131 table 1.

97. Stromberg & Stone, A Model State Law on Civil Commitment of the Mentally Ill, 20 Harv. J. on Legis. 275, 278 (1983).

98. Chambers, Alternatives to Civil Commitment of the Mentally Ill: Practical Guides and Constitutional Imperatives, 70 Mich. L. Rev. 1107, 1117 (1972).

99. U.S. General Accounting Office, Returning the Mentally Disabled to the Community: Government Needs to Do More (1977) [hereinafter cited as G.A.O. Rep.].

100. Bachrach, Commentary, 34 Hosp. & Community Psychiatry 105 (1983).

101. E. Golloy, Summary Report on the Implications of Modifying the Definition of a Developmental Disability (report submitted to Office of Developmental Disabilities, U.S. Dep't of Health & Human Services, June 1981). See in this chapter § I D, Developmental Disabilities Act Amendments of 1978, *supra* for a review of the evolution of the definition in legislation.

102. Golloy, *supra* note 101, at 15 (estimated total of 2,812,000 in 1976–77); statistics provided in telephone interview with National Association for Retarded Citizens (1983) (2 million).

103. Braddock, Deinstitutionalization of the Retarded: Trends in Public Policy, 32 Hosp. & Community Psychiatry 607 (1981).

104. K. Lakin, R.E. Bruininks, D. Doth, B. Hill, & F. Hauber, Sourcebook on Long-Term Developmentally Disabled People 1 (Sept. 1982).

untary care is the general rule. From these divergent theories of care have emerged two related but distinguishable systems: one for the mentally ill, who are usually treated within a system with a distinctly medical orientation, and the other for the developmentally disabled, who are more often than not habilitated within a system that has adopted a developmental model stressing the learning of life skills. Both systems, however, depend on work carried out by a wide assortment of social service personnel and are influenced by the desire of some patients and clients not to be cared for at all by either system.

1. Mentally Ill Persons

Since World War I, the delivery of mental health services has evolved from a system based on large, public institutions as the chief provider of psychiatric services.[105] Historically these state hospitals were overcrowded, understaffed, and poorly financed.[106] Somatic therapies, individual and group psychotherapy, psychosurgery, and some attention to individualized treatment plans were introduced in the 1940s, but even this selective use of more intensive personal care was largely replaced in the mid-1950s by the widespread use of tranquilizing and antipsychotic drugs. This later development marked the beginning of a decrease in the number of persons hospitalized in state mental institutions over the next 25 years.

In 1963, noting the nation's long-term neglect of mentally ill (and mentally retarded) persons, Congress enacted legislation "to provide for early diagnosis, and continuous and comprehensive care, in the community, of those suffering from these disorders."[107] This legislation launched the construction of community mental health centers by the federal government in conjunction with the states. As the underlying philosophy has changed from an institutional to a community focus,[108] the medical model has become less dominant. Although providing treatment is still the primary justification for funding mental health services, there has arisen a more pluralistic system of public and private, inpatient and outpatient, and institutional and community-based care[109] delivered by a more diverse group of professional staff.[110] According to one leading epidemiologist, these developments threaten to cause the disintegration of publicly supported psychiatric services.[111]

In reaction to this phenomenon, certain medical experts are calling for the psychiatric profession to take a more central role in the care and treatment of the mentally ill,[112] for example, by improving clinical treatment or by acting "as the coordinators of patient care,"[113] since psychiatry, they point out, is the only discipline that provides training in the biological, psychological, and social aspects of human behavior.[114] These beneficent justifications for the control of treatment services are mixed with practical considerations of viability and economic growth of the profession. Through the leadership of Alan Stone, a past president of the American Psychiatric Association and a Harvard Law School professor, psychiatrists have asserted themselves politically with well-financed efforts at lobbying, influencing the media, and litigation to overcome perceived attacks by lawyers, nonmedical mental health professionals, former patients, and the public. While it is too early to assess the outcomes of these outreach efforts, one trend is firmly established. The people and groups representing the mentally ill have become fragmented in part because certain mental health professionals view compulsory treatment as the greatest unmet need, and many former patients and advocates want no treatment to be provided at all or else provided only on a voluntary basis.

2. Developmentally Disabled Persons

At the beginning of the 1960s the plight of severely mentally retarded and severely disabled persons was probably even more disturbing than the situation in which the severely mentally ill found themselves. Individuals who have come to be known as the developmentally disabled were warehoused in large public institutions without treatment and subjected to a battery of abuses.[115] The psychiatric advances in the 1940s and 1950s largely passed them by, and when tranquilizing drugs came into use they were administered to them routinely and, in many instances, inappropriately.

The community-oriented awakening for mentally retarded persons as for mentally ill persons began with the passage of the Mental Retardation Facilities and Community Mental Health Centers Construction Act of 1963.[116] However, the major thrust for the mental retar-

105. Goldman, Adams, & Taube, *supra* note 92, at 130.

106. NIMH Rep. (1980), *supra* note 3 at 3, 4.

107. Preface to *id.* at iii; see in this chapter § I A, Mental Retardation Facilities and Community Mental Health Centers Construction Act of 1963, *supra*.

108. L. Bachrach, Deinstitutionalization: An Analytical Review and Sociological Perspective (1977).

109. Goldman, Adams, & Taube, *supra* note 92, at 130.

110. Winslow, Changing Trends in CMHCs: Keys to Survival in the Eighties, 33 Hosp. & Community Psychiatry 273 (1982).

111. Mollica, From Asylum to Community: The Threatened Disintegration of Public Psychiatry, 308 New England J. Med. 367 (1983).

112. *Id.*; Winslow, *supra* note 110.

113. Winslow, *supra* note 110, at 276.

114. *Id.*; Mollica, *supra* note 111. See also Beigel, Sharfstein, & Wolfe, Toward Increased Psychiatric Presence in Community Mental Health Centers, 30 Hosp. & Community Psychiatry 763 (1979).

115. For one of the best observations of such abuses, see S.S. Herr, Rights and Advocacy for Retarded People 9-28 (1983).

116. See in this chapter § I A *supra* for a description of this act.

dation portion of the act came, not from the treating professionals, but from parents and the National Association for Retarded Children with its local affiliates.[117] Their common objective was to depopulate large institutions but to do so by providing living situations in less restrictive surroundings. This they did by creating a movement, incorporating in part both the civil rights and Ralph Nader's consumerism movements, bringing together parents, relatives, and service providers to stop abuse and neglect, first at the state and local levels and then nationally.

The theoretical underpinning for such a widespread challenge of the existing system was imported from Sweden and called the "normalization principle" by its American adapter, Wolf Wolfensberger.[118] In the place of a medical model of care, he advocated the socialization of disabled individuals according to the developmental model—"the utilization of means which are as culturally normative as possible, in order to establish and/or maintain personal behaviors and characteristics which are as culturally normative as possible."[119] To accomplish this, he urged parents, relatives, friends, and care providers to work together in advocacy on behalf of mentally retarded persons to secure political and legislative changes and, where necessary, to engage in litigation.

Spurred on by the adoption of the United Nations Declaration on the Rights of the Mentally Retarded in 1971, the coalition of advocates supporting mentally retarded individuals grew rapidly as interest groups representing other severely disabled persons joined forces and adopted the normalization principle. Congress took notice of this political power base and enacted legislation providing services and rights protection for those who were termed *developmentally disabled* persons.[120] At this juncture their interests became severable from the interests of the mentally ill, who received services from other federal funding sources, principally the National Institute of Mental Health. Further differences in philosophy and political strategies along with funding decisions led to differences in services that arguably have favored the developmentally disabled.[121]

C. Avoiding Institutionalization

Separable from the deinstitutionalization movement per se are developments that have made it possible for many mentally disabled persons to avoid institutionalization altogether. Paradoxically, avoiding institutionalization can provide the greatest opportunity for disabled persons to be integrated into society, but it can also create the greatest threat of their being lost or mistreated in the process.

The most obvious legal constraints on institutionalization are the changes in civil commitment which have made involuntary confinement far more difficult to accomplish than before. (These laws are examined in chapters 2 and 3 and focus most on the mentally ill.) In addition several other important sociolegal factors have influenced the number and types of persons who are institutionalized, factors that are somewhat different for mentally ill and for developmentally disabled persons.

Most prominent are the combined efforts to promote programs of prevention and early intervention into the conditions that cause mental illness or developmental disabilities, especially legislative and philanthropic efforts that provide funding for research. Because of the distinctive nature of mental illnesses that are often curable and of developmental disabilities that are almost always permanent cognitive and physical conditions, legislative interventions have been founded on different premises. Nevertheless, out of political shortsightedness most public health concepts of prevention and early intervention for either group have often failed to capture the attention of legislatures, which respond more readily to crises than to long-term social problems. Those born with or afflicted with any mental disorder are a weak constituency for asserting rights and obtaining services for themselves and future generations of mentally disabled persons.[122]

The legislation doing the most to reduce the need for institutionalization, particularly for developmentally disabled children, has been the Education for All Hand-

117. The Myths of Deinstitutionalization: Policies for the Mentally Disabled 98-103 (Westview Special Studies in Health Care and Medical Science, Halpern, Sockett, Binner, & Mohr eds. 1980 [hereinafter cited as Myths of Deinstitutionalization]. In 1980 the National Association for Retarded Children changed its name to National Association for Retarded Citizens.

118. W. Wolfensberger, B. Nirje, S. Olshansky, R. Perske, & P. Roos, The Principle of Normalization in Human Services (1972).

119. *Id.* at 28.

120. See current codification of the definition at 42 U.S.C. § 6001(7) (1982). For the evolving definition through legislation in the 1970s see in this chapter § I D, Developmental Disabilities Act Amendments of 1978, esp. notes 51-55 and surrounding text, *supra*.

121. Wolfensberger attributes the disparities between the services and rights received by the two groups—the mentally ill and the developmentally disabled—to dynamic and innovative changes in the management of and attitudes toward mental retardation. While the habilitation of mentally retarded individuals generally involves attainable, realistic goals, the treatment of mentally ill people is wedded unnecessarily to an often dysfunctional medical model bounded by its traditional approach. In addition, he concludes that vigorous citizen advocacy supporting mentally retarded consumers and apathy among those who represented the mentally ill contributed to differential results. Wolfensberger, *supra* note 118, ch. 8.

Other commentators have cited the superior legal, political, and financial position of advocacy groups supporting the developmentally disabled, more positive community attitudes toward the developmentally disabled, and the advantages of using intelligence scores to diagnose mentally retarded individuals instead of the inconclusive diagnostic labels used to classify mentally ill persons. Myths of Deinstitutionalization, *supra* note 117; Biklen, The Case for Deinstitutionalization, 10 Soc. Pol'y, May/June 1979, at 48, 49.

122. Herbert, The Politics of Prevention, 10 Am. Psychological Monitor, May 1979, at 7.

icapped Children Act of 1975 (EAHCA), which covers handicapped children between the ages of 3 and 21.[123] The act expresses a strong and deliberate preference for mainstreaming and normalization over institutionalization, and both parents and children are provided with due process procedures for individually obtaining the broad array of entitlements Congress intended.

Another factor contributing to lower institutionalization rates is the availability, albeit limited, of financing and social services, such as estate planning, income maintenance, education, employment, housing, and medical care, to properly support some disabled individuals in the community. Again the movement to provide such services has been led by groups supporting developmentally disabled persons.

D. Deinstitutionalization

Deinstitutionalization is an ideology supporting community-based noninstitutional care and a realignment of the service delivery system to provide a continuum of care from the home to the institution as well as to depopulate institutions.[124] The implementation of this ideology has led to the movement of many mentally ill and developmentally disabled persons from large institutional settings to smaller community-based facilities, transitional living situations, group homes, and sometimes the streets and flophouses of large urban areas. The origins of this movement can be traced to the 1950s and the practical impetus provided by the treatment revolution in the mental health field. Major breakthroughs in psychopharmacology, the popularization of treatment in the community, and a nascent awareness of the deprivation of the rights of mentally disabled persons in large institutions helped make deinstitutionalization a legitimate goal.[125]

1. Mentally Ill Persons

With the reform of the 1950s coming primarily from professional intervention and legislative change on behalf of the mentally ill, it was not surprising that the mentally ill, rather than the developmentally disabled, were the first to move out of the public institutions in large numbers. Litigation initiated in the late 1960s to promote the right to treatment, without which it was argued there was no justification for confinement,[126] soon gave rise to friction between the mental health providers who supported the right to treatment and institutional reform and former mental patients who became convinced that all psychiatric treatment was an extension of institutional abuses.[127] For more radical patients, complete deinstitutionalization and the right to refuse all treatments have become major objectives, leading toward the goal of nonintervention by the state, except for the provision of basic social services and income maintenance received by all people in need.

The benefits of deinstitutionalization have been bittersweet for mentally ill persons as a group. While there has been a precipitous decline in the number of residents of large public institutions, much of the outflow has led to reinstitutionalization into nursing homes, large board and care facilities, prisons, and jails.[128] Reinstitutionalization, however, has also meant less restrictive and better surroundings for many mentally ill people as nursing homes and board and care facilities have been improved through active federal and state involvement.[129] For the mentally ill patients who have been released directly into the community, freedom has not necessarily led to an improved quality of life. A large number of these people, particularly the chronically mentally ill, are reported to have been dumped into the streets, cheap hotels, or boarding homes in very poor neighborhoods and without proper follow-up care and support services.[130]

At the same time, the vigorous emphasis on community programming has brought care, treatment, and services to an expanding segment of noninstitutionalized mentally ill individuals who might otherwise have been bypassed by the mental health system.[131] Moreover, some reformers argue that mentally ill individuals who are ignored by the state are better off than they would be attended to by overworked staff in large institutions.[132] Practically, however, nonintervention is hardly a satisfactory option for an increasing number of chronically mentally ill patients. Recent reviews in the literature tentatively support the contention of advocates that with adequately funded and designed programs, it is possible to maintain even severely ill patients in the community.[133] Further support for this position comes from the ex-

123. See in this chapter § I C *supra* for a description of the EAHCA.

124. Bachrach, *supra* note 100; see also Bachrach, A Conceptional Approach to Deinstitutionalization, 29 Hosp. & Community Psychiatry 573 (1978).

125. Bachrach, *supra* note 108; S.P. Segal & U. Aviram, The Mentally Ill in Community-Based Sheltered Care: A Study of Community Care and Social Integration (1978).

126. See in this chapter § III, Deinstitutionalization and Community Placements, *infra*.

127. Miller, History of the Psychiatric Inmates' Liberation Movement, Madness Network News, Summer 1983, No. 2, at 14.

128. Goldman, Adams, & Taube, *supra* note 92, at 131 table 1; Felton & Shinn, Ideology and Practice of Deinstitutionalization, 37 J. Soc. Issues, No. 3, 1981, at 158, 161.

129. G.A.O. Rep., *supra* note 99.

130. Bassuk & Gerson, Deinstitutionalization and Mental Health Services, 238 Sci. Amer., Feb. 1978, at 46.

131. Goldman, Adams, & Taube, *supra* note 92, at 131 table 1.

132. Szasz, Voluntary Medical Hospitalization: An Unacknowledged Practice of Medical Fraud, *in* Medicine, Law, and Public Policy 403 (N.N. Kittrie, H.L. Hirsch, & G. Wegner eds. 1975).

133. H. Lamb, Deinstitutionalization and the Homeless Mentally Ill, 35 Hosp. & Community Psychiatry 899, 906 (1984).

perience of the other population, developmentally disabled persons.

2. Developmentally Disabled Persons

In addition to benefiting from those federal policies that have favored deinstitutionalization, developmentally disabled persons have been affected more positively than negatively by litigation on behalf of the mentally ill. Major class actions, some stretching over many years, stimulated changes in state policies, helping to establish community-centered service delivery systems.[134] In the most notable case involving a single plaintiff, the Supreme Court not only concluded that the Constitution prohibited the warehousing of mentally disabled citizens but diluted the immunity against personal liability that protected doctors, administrators, and other institutional staff.[135] Yet for all the successes, plaintiffs' lawyers have failed more often than not with the fundamental argument that holds that without proper treatment or habilitation the state loses its justification for involuntarily confining mentally disabled persons. Either the argument has been rejected[136] or, more frequently, the courts' solutions have denied a wholesale release policy in favor of specific institutional changes.[137]

For developmentally disabled persons, the deinstitutionalization movement has progressed toward its goal of institutional depopulation at a slower rate than for mental patients but with superior planning and organization, which have led to community transitions with fewer problems and placements with better supportive services.

E. Maintenance and Support in the Community

It was the politically powerful coalition of groups for the developmentally disabled which emerged in the mid-1970s that was largely responsible for the passage of two of the decade's most significant pieces of mental disability legislation: the Education for All Handicapped Children Act of 1975 and the Developmentally Disabled Assistance and Bill of Rights Act in 1975.[138] Modeled after the consent decrees in litigation initiated on behalf of mentally retarded children who had been denied equal educational opportunities,[139] the EAHCA provided a whole range of services, gave parents numerous due process protections, and created a powerful impetus for integrating disabled children into the public school systems. The Developmentally Disabled Assistance and Bill of Rights Act provided essential services, including an advocacy system, in each of the 50 states and the District of Columbia.

Toward the end of the decade, representatives of developmentally disabled persons initiated lawsuits to establish community-based facilities and homes as alternatives to institutionalization,[140] and they were among the first to challenge restrictive zoning ordinances and private covenants that blocked the establishment of group homes. Advocates of the disabled were also successful in convincing states and municipalities to enact ordinances eliminating discrimination in housing, employment, and public accommodations. Only occasionally did such legislation include protections for mentally ill persons.

In addition, from only a few isolated legal aid programs at the beginning of the 1970s,[141] several different publicly funded systems of legal representation for the mentally disabled have developed, including the Legal Services and public defender networks and a small number of private public interest attorneys practicing in discrete areas of disability law. Moreover, there is a federally funded protection and advocacy system in every state, although in most instances the clientele is limited to developmentally disabled persons. However, collectively even these legal advocacy services for mentally disabled persons have experienced some decline in the 1980s without ever coming close to achieving adequate representation for either group.

III. DEINSTITUTIONALIZATION AND COMMUNITY PLACEMENTS

While employment, education, housing, and income maintenance help sustain the mentally disabled person in the community, deinstitutionalization is the legal process that permits and encourages many disabled individuals to be in the community in the first place. The process involves a movement from the institution into a community setting or transitional stops in between, following a series of legal judgments on matters such as an individual's mental and physical status, his ability to

134. Brewster v. Dukakis, No. 76-4423-F (E.D. Mass. filed Dec. 15, 1976). A final consent was signed two years later: No. 76-4423-F, 3 MDLR 44 (E.D. Mass. Dec. 6, 1978). On the basis of a state plan entitled "Community-Based Residential Services for Mental Health Clients," Massachusetts has shifted from an institution-based delivery system to one oriented toward community services. Practice Manual: Community-Based Residential Services for Mental Health Clients, 3 MDLR 150 (1979).

135. O'Connor v. Donaldson, 422 U.S. 563 (1975).

136. New York State Ass'n for Retarded Children, Inc. v. Carey, 393 F. Supp. 715 (E.D.N.Y. 1975). Chief Justice Burger has been a leading critic of the "quid pro quo" theory of justifying the right to treatment. See his concurring opinions in both O'Connor v. Donaldson, 422 U.S. 563 (1975), and Youngberg v. Romeo, 457 U.S. 307 (1982).

137. Youngberg v. Romeo, 457 U.S. 307 (1982); Welsch v. Likins, 373 F. Supp. 487 (E.D. Minn. 1974), *aff'd*, 550 F.2d 1122 (8th Cir. 1977); Wyatt v. Aderholt, 503 F.2d 1305 (5th Cir. 1974).

138. See in this chapter §§ I C and I D for description of this legislation.

139. Pennsylvania Ass'n for Retarded Children v. Commonwealth, 343 F. Supp. 279 (E.D. Pa. 1972); Mills v. Board of Educ., 348 F. Supp. 866 (D.D.C. 1972).

140. Halderman v. Pennhurst State School & Hosp., 446 F. Supp. 1295 (E.D. Pa. 1977).

141. S. S. Herr, The New Clients: Legal Services for Mentally Retarded Persons, 31 Stan. L. Rev. 553 (1979).

care for himself, his perceived dangerousness to society, and the availability and adequacy of resources in the community.

The right to treatment or habilitation in the least restrictive setting, a concept that fosters deinstitutionalization, presumes a continuing responsibility of the state to provide basic care and shelter and other necessary services while retaining the minimum amount of control over the individual necessary for the welfare of the individual and of the state. When, as is inevitable, these interests conflict, the legal system must determine how, by whom, and according to which standards and procedures the interests of the individual and of the state should be balanced.

Although similar legal standards apply to both mentally ill and developmentally disabled persons in the deinstitutionalization process, there are significant differences in the legal results based on each group's special needs, the circumstances in which they find themselves, and public perceptions about the nature of their disabilities. As has been noted already, developmentally disabled persons, in part because of superior organizing and planning, have had less difficulty in making the transition from the institution into the community.

A. United States Constitution

Many jurisdictions have moved from the view in the 1950s that the state could best decide what to do with a person who was mentally disabled as long as those actions did not produce some gross infringement of rights, to the view that mentally disabled individuals are entitled to a range of services provided to them in the least restrictive manner possible.[142] Yet substantial doubts remain because the Supreme Court has been equivocal in its response to these issues, particularly the right to be treated or else released.[143]

What the Supreme Court decided, in the 1975 landmark case of *O'Connor v. Donaldson*,[144] was the right of a nondangerous individual not to be warehoused: "A State cannot constitutionally confine without more a nondangerous individual who is capable of surviving safely in freedom by himself with the help of willing and responsible family members or friends."[145] Seven years later in *Youngberg v. Romeo*,[146] the Justices added that although the adequacy of professional care in an institution should be presumed, in order to exercise reasonable professional judgment the state had the responsibility of providing "minimally adequate training" within an institution "as may be reasonable in light of . . . liberty interests in safety and freedom from unreasonable restraints."[147] Given these two constitutional principles, there is a logically compelling argument that minimally adequate treatment or habilitation is constitutionally mandated in order to allow those confined individuals who are or will be able to leave to do so safely. Yet as will be seen, so far the logic has not been persuasive to many courts.

The parameters for courts' recent deinstitutionalization concerns were set out clearly in Justice Stewart's majority opinion in *O'Connor v. Donaldson*:

> Specifically, there is no reason now to decide whether mentally ill persons dangerous to themselves or to others have a right to treatment upon compulsory confinement by the State, or whether the State may compulsorily confine a nondangerous, mentally ill individual for the purpose of treatment.[148]

Despite the Court's silence in *Donaldson*, other courts have rendered enlightening although conflicting decisions further defining these two principles, and the Supreme Court has indirectly touched on them in other cases. In *Jackson v. Indiana*[149] the Supreme Court concluded that a pretrial detainee who had been adjudicated incompetent to stand trial could not be incarcerated indefinitely without meeting the procedural requirements of criminal conviction or civil commitment. Due process demands no less than a rational relationship between the nature and the duration of involuntary confinement.[150] A 1983 decision, *Jones v. United States*,[151] changed the Court's emphasis significantly: dangerous behavior may be indicated by small crimes against property as well as by violence, and the presumption of continuing dangerousness, at least for an insanity acquittee, may continue for a year or more.[152]

A number of courts have concluded that civilly confining without treatment a mentally disabled person who is dangerous would in many situations be tantamount to indefinite or even permanent incarceration.[153]

142. Halderman v. Pennhurst State School & Hosp., 446 F. Supp. 1295 (E.D. Pa. 1977); B.D. Sales, D.M. Powell, R. Van Duizend, & Associates, Disabled Persons and the Law xv (1982).

143. In 1960 Morton Birnbaum first articulated the right to be treated or be released. See Editorial, A New Right, 46 A.B.A. J. 516 (1960). Since then a number of courts have adopted the principle, but the United States Supreme Court has not decided one way or the other. However, Chief Justice Burger in a concurring opinion in O'Connor v. Donaldson, 422 U.S. 563 (1975), observed "there is no historical basis for imposing such a limitation on state power." *Id.* at 582.

144. 422 U.S. 563 (1975).

145. *Id.* at 576.

146. 457 U.S. 307 (1982).

147. *Id.* at 322.

148. 422 U.S. 563, 573 (1975).

149. 406 U.S. 715 (1972).

150. *Id.* at 738.

151. 103 S. Ct. 3043 (1983).

152. *Id.* at 3049-53.

153. Jackson v. Indiana, 406 U.S. 715 (1972); Ohlinger v. Watson, 652 F.2d 775 (9th Cir. 1980); Brown v. Warden, Great Meadow Correctional Facility, 682 F.2d 348 (2d Cir. 1982); People v. Nunn, 108 Ill. App. 3d 169, 438 N.E.2d 1342, 1345 (1982).

Thus, either confinement must be limited to the sentence a person would have received if he had been subject to criminal prosecution, or the inmate is entitled to sufficient treatment to provide a reasonable opportunity of being released into the community. Even in *Jones* the Supreme Court pointed out that "the purpose of commitment following an insanity acquittal, like that of civil commitment, is to treat the individual's mental illness *and* protect him and society from his potential dangerousness."[154]

The Supreme Court's statement in *Jones* also seems to suggest that without dangerousness there can be no forced confinement since both the availability of treatment and the protection of society constitute necessary justifications for commitment. Although the Court's view of dangerousness seems to be very broad, encompassing most if not all antisocial acts toward others[155] and, as has been mentioned, dangerousness to oneself, the Court has previously ruled that nondangerous mentally ill persons cannot be warehoused if they are able to live by themselves or with assistance in the community.[156] At the same time, mentally retarded individuals, no matter how dismal their prospects for development, are at least entitled to minimally adequate training to reduce restraints on their freedom.[157] Together these cases suggest that nondangerous, mentally disabled persons must be released into the community if they are presently able to exist on their own with whatever services are available; if they are presently unable to survive in the community, they must be given a minimally adequate opportunity to be habilitated or rehabilitated so that they may be released. Who is or is not dangerous is a matter still disputed.

Also unclear is whether, as is asserted by some, the states are constitutionally obligated to provide supportive services in the community to allow disabled individuals to be transferred out of institutions. In the seminal case, *Halderman v. Pennhurst State School and Hospital* (1977),[158] a federal district court found a constitutional right to minimal habilitation or treatment in the least restrictive environment for mentally retarded residents of a large institution. Constitutional deficiencies as well as violations of federal and state law formed the basis for directing the commonwealth of Pennsylvania to provide community living arrangements for most of the residents of Pennhurst.

Despite the fact that the case was reversed on other grounds,[159] the opinion has been cited favorably by a number of courts[160] and has led to a recent consent decree over *Pennhurst* calling for the closing of the institution and the placement of all its residents into community facilities or settings.[161] In a 1984 decision the United States Court of Appeals for the Second Circuit ruled that New York had to provide each mental patient with the opportunity to improve his health and regain his liberty. Moreover, while professional care may be presumed to be adequate if an institution has been accredited, this status does not settle the issue if contrary evidence is presented.[162]

Other courts, however, have found no constitutional basis for a right to habilitation in the least restrictive setting, much less an obligation to actually provide specific community services.[163] One California appeals court has gone so far as to state that an assumption by officials that community care is preferable to institutional living may violate the right of competent individuals to decide for themselves what level of care is most appropriate.[164] Similarly, a lawsuit in Ohio has been filed on behalf of former residents of a mental retardation facility who allegedly want to be reinstitutionalized rather than remain in the community without the proper services.[165] In addition, a 1983 New Jersey decision ruled that residents who are no longer dangerous and are able to live in the community may be kept in an institution temporarily if there are no adequate community placements available and the state makes good faith efforts to find or create such placements.[166]

The United States, through the Department of Justice, has filed a brief in the Third Circuit arguing that both constitutionally and under federal law, mentally retarded—and it would be reasonable to assume by analogy mentally ill—citizens have no right to be placed in the community based on the least restrictive alternative principle or any other rationale.[167] In determining whether the minimal constitutional standards of *Youngberg v. Romeo* have been met, advised DOJ, courts should consider only whether reasonable professional judgment was

154. 103 S. Ct. at 3051 (emphasis added).

155. *Id.* In a concurring opinion in O'Connor v. Donaldson, 422 U.S. 563 (1975), Chief Justice Burger used the term "significant antisocial acts" to describe the level of dangerousness necessary for confinement, at 582–83.

156. O'Connor v. Donaldson, 422 U.S. 563. (1975).

157. Youngberg v. Romeo, 457 U.S. 307 (1982).

158. 446 F. Supp. 1295 (E.D. Pa. 1977).

159. Pennhurst State School & Hosp. v. Halderman, 451 U.S. 1 (1981).

160. E.g., Philipp v. Carey, 517 F. Supp. 513, 518 (N.D.N.Y. 1981); Medley v. Ginsberg, 492 F. Supp. 1294, 1301 (S.D.W. Va. 1980).

161. Halderman v. Pennhurst State School & Hosp., No. 74-1345 (E.D. Pa. filed July 23, 1984).

162. Woe v. Cuomo, 729 F.2d 96 (2d Cir. 1984).

163. Garrity v. Gallen, 522 F. Supp. 171 (D.N.H. 1981).

164. *In re* Borgogna, 121 Cal. App. 3d 937, 175 Cal. Rptr. 588 (1981).

165. Balanced Mental Health Laws, Inc. v. Ohio Dep't of Mental Retardation & Development Disabilities, No. 83 CV-04-233, 7 MDLR 241 (Ohio C.P. Franklin County filed Apr. 19, 1983).

166. *In re* Commitment of S.L., No. A-47, 7 MDLR 378 (N.J. Sup. Ct. July 20, 1983).

167. Halderman v. Pennhurst State School & Hosp., No. 78-1490, 8 MPDLR 296 (3d Cir. filed Apr. 24, 1984).

exercised in making the placement for or providing services to disabled clients. This approach has been used by the United States Court of Appeals for the Second Circuit in *Society for Good Will to Retarded Children, Inc. v. Cuomo*,[168] overruling a federal court that had issued a comprehensive deinstitutionalization order. It found no constitutional right to be placed in the community or any other less restrictive setting unless a failure to do so would constitute a substantial departure from accepted professional judgment.

Matters become even more complicated when the parents oppose deinstitutionalization and there is no direct evidence that the children are actually being abused or neglected in their residential setting. The Third Circuit underscored the judiciary's ambivalence by acknowledging that parents do not have an absolute constitutional right to bring up their children but do have a substantial interest that must be considered by any court that is making a disposition about placements.[169] Absent a showing of abuse or neglect, the parents' interests may be subject to governmental interference only if a significant contrary state interest is identified. This viewpoint is not conclusive, however, particularly since only one of the three justices hearing the case endorsed that part of the opinion and since other courts have disputed this type of reasoning because it does not sufficiently acknowledge the independent interests of the child. The Fifth Circuit in *Wyatt v. Aderholt* determined that it would be immoral for the state or the judiciary to assume that the parents are the true clients of the institutions.[170] Such a view was also supported recently by a federal district court in Texas, which refused to give parents a veto power to prevent their children from being removed from a state institution as a part of a class action settlement.[171] Moreover, the Supreme Court recognized limited rights of children to object to institutionalization when it determined that at the very least there must be an independent decision-making process whenever admissions and continued commitment of children are at issue.[172]

While substantive due process arguments have led to inconsistent outcomes, it was hoped that equal protection theories supporting community-based placements and services would be substantially strengthened by two recent (but short-lived) federal court of appeals decisions involving zoning restrictions.[173] Both circuits held that mentally disabled persons in pursuit of important community services, such as housing, were to be viewed as a quasi-suspect class and that denial of their claimed entitlements had to be reviewed using heightened judicial scrutiny.

Under a heightened scrutiny rationale it could have been persuasively argued that states had to demonstrate substantial reasons before they could deny training and other services to mentally disabled clients either inside institutions or in community programs, if the same services were available to similarly situated groups of individuals. As a result of a controversial 6-to-3 decision by the United States Supreme Court in July 1985 any such argument is going to be far more difficult to make successfully. In *City of Cleburne v. Cleburne Living Center, Inc.*,[174] a fragile majority held that mentally retarded persons were not a quasi-suspect class and thus not constitutionally deserving of heightened scrutiny. However, as pointed out by four dissenters and implicitly demonstrated in a different way by two justices who wrote a special concurring opinion, the traditional rational relationship test was given a new vitality in the thorough way in which the majority opinion applied the test to the given circumstances.[175]

B. Federal Law

Four federal statutes in varying proportions have provided the avenues for most of the deinstitutionalization litigation initiated on behalf of mentally disabled children and adults: the Education for All Handicapped Children Act (EAHCA), § 504 of the Rehabilitation Act, the Developmental Disabilities Act, and the Civil Rights of Institutionalized Persons Act. These statutes are complemented by § 1983 of the Civil Rights Act, providing individual relief, and by the Community Mental Health Centers Construction Act, which has influenced the national deinstitutionalization movement without providing much opportunity for direct judicial intervention.[176]

1. Education for All Handicapped Children Act (EAHCA)

Although limited to handicapped children and adolescents, EAHCA[177] influences the deinstitutionalization process in two ways. First, it mandates that handicapped students be mainstreamed into the least restrictive educational setting whenever possible.[178] This legal pre-

168. 737 F.2d 1239 (2d Cir. 1984).
169. Halderman v. Pennhurst State School & Hosp., 707 F.2d 702 (3d Cir. 1983).
170. 503 F.2d 1305 (5th Cir. 1974).
171. Lelsz v. Kavanagh, No. S-74-95-CA, 7 MDLR 379 (E.D. Tex. July 21, 1983), *appeal dismissed*, 710 F.2d 1040 (5th Cir. 1983).
172. Parham v. J.R., 442 U.S. 584 (1979).
173. J.W. v. City of Tacoma, 720 F.2d 1126 (9th Cir. 1983); Cleburne Living Center, Inc. v. City of Cleburne, 726 F.2d 191 (5th Cir. 1984).
174. No. 84-468 (U.S. Sup. Ct. July 1, 1985).
175. *Id.* This decision and two federal appeals court decisions preceding it are discussed in this chapter in an examination of zoning issues in § VI A 1, Constitutional Requirements, *infra*.
176. In Medley v. Ginsberg, 492 F. Supp. 1294 (S.D.W. Va. 1980), the court upheld a private right of action to pursue violations of the Community Mental Health Centers Construction Act under § 1983 of the Civil Rights Act.
177. See in this chapter § I C *supra* for a description of this legislation.
178. 20 U.S.C. § 1412(5)(B) (1982).

sumption, when applied in the context of high cost of institutional care, encourages the use of regular, public school education over residential placements or private schools for the handicapped.[179] Second, the EAHCA can provide for education and life skills training for children remaining inside institutions[180] to enable some of them to break out of the institutional cycle and live relatively successfully in the community.

Since most of the cases defining either educational obligation have been decided after 1980, use of EAHCA can be expected to be heavier in the future, especially now that other promising legal avenues have been effectively limited or even foreclosed.[181] To date, EAHCA has been used to compel deinstitutionalization in a number of ways: as leverage to achieve a negotiated settlement allowing a mentally retarded child to enter a school program with nonhandicapped children,[182] as an avenue for parents to have their handicapped child placed in an appropriate public school program even though the court concluded that the public placement was not necessarily the best placement,[183] as a means of transferring a mentally retarded adolescent from a developmental center to a school that would provide "contact with nonhandicapped students to the maximum extent consistent with an appropriate education,"[184] and, most commonly, as an argument by local and state officials that children should be placed in public schools, not private institutions.[185] In addition, decisions based on entitlements to services under the EAHCA have provided some children in institutions with much of the programming they need to be deinstitutionalized appropriately,[186] such as basic skills training or other services closely related to education. Nevertheless, despite the federal law's certain preference for obtaining the least restrictive outcome possible, EAHCA does support residential placements in some circumstances, when there is no other appropriate setting. Generally, courts are most likely to make such a ruling if the parents or guardians favor the more restrictive situation.[187]

2. Section 504 of the Rehabilitation Act

Section 504's[188] initial promise for providing the most potent legal theory to promote deinstitutionalization has been reduced significantly, although a few judicial interpretations are still pending, and newer legal theories supporting community services have been litigated successfully using § 504. The initial promise of this provision for plaintiffs was found in its broad scope of coverage (including all handicapped individuals), the existence of a private right of action, and the heavy financial involvement of the federal government in the care of mentally disabled persons, making many programs subject to the mandates of the law.

The first decision to interpret § 504 in the context of deinstitutionalization was the 1977 case *Halderman v. Pennhurst State School and Hospital.*[189] A federal district court judge not only ruled that the federal handicapped discrimination statute was intended to provide all mentally retarded residents of institutions with minimally adequate habilitation in the least restrictive environment[190] but stunned institutional staffs by concluding that a large institution like Pennhurst with its numerous deficiencies could not possibly provide the necessary level of services. The court ordered Pennhurst to close and the state to provide suitable community living arrangements for each resident based on individualized habilitation plans. It appointed a special master to supervise the day-to-day implementation of the court's order. Eventually the Supreme Court reversed and remanded the case twice, but on other grounds.[191]

After the initial *Pennhurst* opinion came a number of class action deinstitutionalization suits using § 504 as at least one of the major legal theories.[192] Before these cases

179. In the following recent cases, parents' efforts to place their children in private residential facilities were denied in favor of public school placements: Hessler v. Maryland Bd. of Educ., 700 F.2d 134 (4th Cir. 1983); Flavin v. Connecticut Bd. of Educ., 553 F. Supp. 827 (D. Conn. 1982); Lang v. Braintree School Comm., 545 F. Supp. 1221 (D. Mass. 1982); Harrell v. Wilson County Schools, 293 S.E.2d 687 (N.C. Ct. App. 1982).

180. Thornock v. Evans, No. 78704, 7 MDLR 234 (Idaho Dist. Ct. Apr. 4, 1983); Christopher T. v. San Francisco Unified School Dist., 553 F. Supp. 1107 (N.D. Cal. 1982); Stacey G. v. Pasadena Indep. School Dist., 547 F. Supp. 61 (S.D. Tex. 1982).

181. See in this chapter § III B 2, Section 504 of the Rehabilitation Act, and § III B 3, Developmental Disabilities Act Amendments of 1978, *infra*.

182. Selelyo v. Drury, No. C-3-78-369, 5 MDLR 241 (S.D. Ohio Apr. 30, 1981).

183. Springdale School Dist. # 50 v. Grace, 693 F.2d 41 (8th Cir. 1982).

184. Campbell v. Talladega County Bd. of Educ., 518 F. Supp. 47 (N.D. Ala. 1981).

185. See discussion in this chapter § IV H 3, The Least Restrictive Education Alternative, *infra*.

186. Three recent cases are typical. The state of West Virginia extinguished a lawsuit by agreeing to provide hospitalized children who were mentally ill with at least as many hours of education each day as nonhandicapped students. Medley v. Ginsberg, 492 F. Supp. 1294 (S.D.W. Va. 1982). A federal court in Colorado ruled that the state had to provide children in state institutions with an appropriate education. Association for Retarded Citizens in Colorado v. Frazier, 517 F. Supp. 105 (D. Colo. 1981). A federal court in New Hampshire concluded that institutionalized children had to be given the same educational opportunities as handicapped students in public schools. Garrity v. Gallen, 522 F. Supp. 171 (D.N.H. 1981).

187. Gladys J. & Laura J. v. Pearland Indep. School Dist., 520 F. Supp. 869 (S.D. Tex. 1981); Christopher T. v. San Francisco Unified School Dist., 553 F. Supp. 1107 (N.D. Cal. 1982).

Note that in Board of Educ. v. Rowley, 458 U.S. 176 (1982), the presumption is in favor of the local school officials' decisions.

188. See in this chapter § I B 2, Employment and Other Forms of Discrimination, *supra*, for a description of Title V of the Rehabilitation Act.

189. 446 F. Supp. 1295 (E.D. Pa. 1977).

190. *Id.* at 1319–20.

191. Pennhurst State School & Hosp. v. Halderman, 451 U.S. 1 (1981).

192. Area V Developmental Disabilities Bd. v. Brown, No. 543060-2, 5 MDLR 180 (Cal. Super. Ct. Alameda County filed Feb. 27, 1981); Spangler v. Throne, B-80-238, 5 MDLR 107 (D. Conn. Dec. 30, 1980); Kentucky Ass'n for Retarded Citizens v. Conn, No. C-770048, 1 MDLR 456 (W.D. Ky. filed

were decided, however, the United States Supreme Court in 1979 issued *Southeastern Community College v. Davis*,[193] which restricted the substantive scope of § 504. The Court foreclosed mandatory affirmative action but warned federal financial recipients that they could not practice de facto discrimination by applying very rigid determinations to their services and programming. Some program adjustments are necessary to accommodate handicapped individuals as long as the modifications are not overly burdensome to the administration of the program or activity.

Exactly how *Davis* is to be applied to *Pennhurst* and its progeny is not entirely clear. The United States Court of Appeals for the Sixth Circuit found no legislative mandate for state deinstitutionalization under § 504, agreeing with the lower court that such a substantial change in programming would constitute affirmative action.[194] Similarly, the Eighth Circuit found that handicapped residents of residential facilities could be legally excluded from adult day programs in Iowa funded in part by the federal government.[195] The suspension of state regulations that allocate services between residential and nonresidential clients would be too much of a burden under § 504. Other federal courts have looked at the statute somewhat differently. One court distinguished reasonable accommodation from affirmative action: § 504 mandated neither deinstitutionalization of a training school nor the provision of services in the least restrictive manner available[196] but required individualized treatment plans to maximize the potential of each resident. Taking a comparatively extreme view of the requirements after *Davis*, another federal court found that a quadriplegic adult was entitled to home health care services rather than services in a nursing home[197] and asserted that unnecessary institutionalization constituted illegal discrimination. *Davis* was distinguished on the ground that the client could actually benefit from the home services without undue financial or administrative burdens to the state.

What the post-*Davis* cases suggest is that certain beneficial services may be required under the federal discrimination statute where their implementation will create only minor burdens on the system. Most reasonable programming that will help residents leave the institution would fall within that definition. Services in the community, however, are not absolutely required even if they are provided to other groups. They would seem to be necessary only if the available evidence showed that the individual client would benefit and the added burden on the state was modest. Of course, where actual discrimination is proven, § 504 would be applicable in any case. The difficulty is that discrimination has been hard to prove, especially where courts mistakenly have insisted that discrimination must be intentional. Since the United States Supreme Court has ruled that such a requirement is not part of the act, at least not in all circumstances,[198] a new wave of litigation will have to define exactly what proof is required in different situations.

Nevertheless, a June 1985 Supreme Court decision has added a new and significant limitation to all § 504 litigation. As will be discussed later in the employment section of this chapter, a narrow 5-to-4 majority concluded that receipt of funding under the Rehabilitation Act was insufficient by itself to create a waiver of a state's Eleventh Amendment immunity.[199] A state's waiver of immunity which would allow it to be sued for illegal discrimination under § 504 must be manifested unambiguously.

3. Developmental Disabilities Act Amendments of 1978

The Developmental Disabilities Act Amendments of 1978 is another piece of federal legislation that created high expectations for advocates and great concern for institution administrators and state officials.

The first major decision utilizing this act was the United States Court of Appeals for the Third Circuit's review of the *Pennhurst* case.[200] Avoiding the constitutional questions, the Third Circuit relied exclusively on the Developmental Disabilities Act and state law to find an individual right to habilitation in the least restrictive alternative setting. Focusing on § 6010 of the act, known as "the bill of rights," the majority opinion retreated from the view that a large institution is unconstitutional on its face, finding instead a presumption favoring deinstitutionalization but reasoning that individual situations had to be reviewed independently to make sure that each person's particular needs were identified and met.

Most of the other courts called upon to interpret the Developmental Disabilities Act agreed with the basic thrust of the opinion set forth by the Third Circuit.[201]

June 2, 1977); Knott v. Hughes, No. Y-80-2832, 4 MDLR 412 (D. Md. filed Oct. 27, 1980); Zerega v. Okin, 79-1895-Z, 3 MDLR 408 (D. Mass. filed Sept. 17, 1979).

193. 442 U.S. 397 (1979).

194. Kentucky Ass'n for Retarded Citizens v. Conn, 674 F.2d 582 (6th Cir. 1982).

195. Plummer v. Branstad, 731 F.2d 574 (8th Cir. 1984).

196. Garrity v. Gallen, 522 F. Supp. 171 (D.N.H. 1981).

197. Lynch v. Maher, 507 F. Supp. 1268 (D. Conn. 1981).

198. Alexander v. Choate, 105 S. Ct. 712 (1985). The Supreme Court discussed the issue of intentional discrimination in the context of a Medicaid case. The Court's unanimous opinion favorably cited legislative history that Congress intended to rectify past harms resulting from the effects of discrimination as well as by design. *Id.* at 718–20.

199. Atascadero State Hosp. v. Scanlon, No. 84-351 (U.S. Sup. Ct. June 28, 1985).

200. Halderman v. Pennhurst State School & Hosp., 612 F.2d 84 (3d Cir. 1979) (en banc).

201. A state appellate court in Indiana held that good faith efforts to utilize available resources were insufficient where the level of treatment fell below what was necessary to provide a mentally retarded, emotionally disturbed

The primary case opposing the Third Circuit's reasoning in *Pennhurst* was *Kentucky Association for Retarded Citizens v. Conn*[202] in 1980. Whatever may have been intended under the federal law, ruled the federal district court, it never included mandatory deinstitutionalization of a medium-sized facility that complied with appropriate licensing standards and did nothing more egregious than isolate residents from the mainstream of society in a facility with institutional characteristics. The court believed that Congress wanted the states to determine funding patterns for community programs and that the act's emphasis, therefore, was on appropriate care, not necessarily services outside the institution.

A majority of the Supreme Court justices reviewing *Pennhurst* endorsed the reasoning of the Kentucky case, not only rejecting the Third Circuit's interpretation but issuing the most restrictive view of the act to date.[203] The majority reasoned that because Congress exercised its authority under the spending powers of article I, section 8, of the Constitution rather than section 5 of the Fourteenth Amendment, the plaintiffs representing the residents had to show that Congress had made an explicit statement or had unambiguously intended to obligate the states to provide appropriate habilitation in the least restrictive setting. In reviewing the act, the Court found no express language or deliberate intention to create such an obligation in § 6010, which simply recommended policy objectives regarding residents' rights in what was termed "precatory language."[204] In addition, the Supreme Court could find no other provision in the act that created a right to appropriate treatment or habilitation in the least restrictive setting for mentally retarded persons. In a subsequent opinion, a federal court characterized the bill of rights section as one that "creates no rights whatsoever."[205]

What is left, according to four justices, were the limited protections contained in other sections of the act.[206] In one of the very few interpretations coming after the Supreme Court's historic opinion, a federal court found a privately enforceable right to action in other provisions of the act, yet limited enforcement to compelling the secretary of the U.S. Department of Health and Human Services to perform her statutory duty of withholding funds but specifically disallowing private injunctive relief for damages.[207]

4. Civil Rights of Institutionalized Persons Act

The fourth statute, the Civil Rights of Institutionalized Persons Act,[208] allows the Justice Department, subject to certain restrictions, to intervene or initiate actions on behalf of residents where there has been an administrative finding that an institution has engaged in a pattern of abuse. While the act has the potential to provide both mentally ill and developmentally disabled residents of facilities and hospitals with an indirect federal remedy, so far the Justice Department has filed only a few pleadings in intervention, the Attorney General believing that where possible it is preferable to leave these matters to the states.[209] In one of the few actions that has reached settlement the state of Indiana agreed to improve conditions at two mental hospitals, but the agreement was premised on a narrow reading of the constitutional arguments.[210]

5. Section 1983 of the Civil Rights Act

Complementing the four previously discussed federal statutes is § 1983 of the Civil Rights Act,[211] which provides the potential for limited, indirect relief. In *Maine v. Thiboutot*[212] in 1980 the Supreme Court determined that in general § 1983 entitled individuals to bring lawsuits whenever their "rights, privileges, or immunities" are violated under the Constitution or any federal statute. Furthermore, the prevailing party may recover attorney's fees and costs at the court's discretion.

This general rule, however, has two limitations, upheld by the Supreme Court in *Pennhurst State School and Hospital v. Halderman*, which severely restrict the application of § 1983 to deinstitutionalization issues: there must be an enforceable right (in this context the Developmental Disabilities Act merely provides assurances), and no § 1983 relief will be available where the

resident with a reasonable opportunity to change the behavior that required institutionalization in the first place. In essence there had to be a specific plan in place designed to allow him to be moved into the community. *In re* Ackerman, 409 N.E.2d 1211 (Ind. Ct. App. 1980).

Similarly, a federal court in South Dakota ruled that the requirement that individualized treatment be provided under the act obligated the state to pay for a private, out-of-state residential placement for a 24-year-old mentally retarded woman. Henkin v. South Dakota Dep't of Social Servs., 498 F. Supp. 659 (D.S.D. 1980).

202. 510 F. Supp. 1233 (W.D. Ky. 1980).

203. Pennhurst State School & Hosp. v. Halderman, 451 U.S. 1 (1981).

204. *Id.* at 18.

205. Wong v. Bucks County, No. 81-1331, 6 MDLR 89 (E.D. Pa. Feb. 8, 1982).

206. Pennhurst State School & Hosp. v. Halderman, 451 U.S. at 22 (concurring and three dissenting opinions).

207. Garrity v. Gallen, 522 F. Supp. 171 (D.N.H. 1981).

208. See in this chapter § I E *supra* for a description of this legislation.

209. Summary and Analysis, 7 MDLR 3, 5–8 (1983); Staff Report on the Institutionalized Mentally Disabled and a Response of the Justice Department, 9 MPDLR 154–57 (1985). An example of such a pleading is in Davis v. Henderson, 535 F. Supp. 407 (E.D. Pa. 1982), in which the department filed on behalf of inmates at an institution for the criminally insane in Louisiana.

210. United States v. Indiana, No. IP 84-411 C, 8 MPDLR 320 (S.D. Ind. Apr. 6, 1984).

211. The Civil Rights Act of 1871, 42 U.S.C. § 1983.

212. 448 U.S. 1 (1980).

213. Pennhurst State School & Hosp. v. Halderman, 451 U.S. 1 (1981); Middlesex County Sewerage Auth. v. National Sea Clammers Ass'n, 453 U.S. 1 (1981).

statute itself mandates an exclusive remedy.[213] One federal court reached the conclusion that under the Developmental Disabilities Act there could be no § 1983 civil rights action because the existence of limited administrative relief constituted an exclusive remedy.[214] Similarly, courts have found that the EAHCA has an exclusive remedy with respect to § 1983 through its elaborate series of due process protections.[215] While no decisions have been reached under the Civil Rights of the Institutionalized Act, there would appear to be an exclusive remedy as well in the form of federal legal intervention. Under § 504 the problem is the same since there already is a private remedy that is as broad as § 1983 with regard to nonemployment claims.[216]

Section 1983 can also be used if legitimate constitutional claims are raised. Two obstacles to such claims are the need to prove state action exists and then to identify constitutionally mandated deinstitutionalization or community services that have been withheld.

6. Community Mental Health Centers Construction Act

Since the first federal legislative expression of a preference for community-based care and treatment, the Community Mental Health Centers Construction Act of 1963,[217] the government has spent millions of dollars to construct over 760 community centers around the country,[218] serving nearly 30% of all outpatient and almost 5% of all inpatient episodes reported each year.[219] But recent review of the program suggests that the act has not really led to widespread deinstitutionalization of mentally ill persons into community-based programs. Chronically mentally ill persons spend less time in institutional settings, but short-term patient episodes are increasing and many chronic patients are placed into nursing homes, boarding homes, and hotels, or more disturbingly, are left to walk the streets.

Almost no litigation has been filed under this act since neither the original legislation nor its numerous amendments included any kind of private right of action.

C. State Law

The deinstitutionalization of developmentally disabled or mentally ill individuals is mandated or substantially encouraged at the state level by statutes, legal decisions interpreting those statutes, and consent decrees.

1. State Statutes

In many states an inequity in the statutory protections for mentally ill persons and developmentally disabled persons can be attributed in part to the perception that mentally ill individuals are more likely to engage in violent or unpredictable behavior as well as to superior organizing for legislative change by advocates and friends of developmentally disabled persons.[220]

Nearly half the states have statutes that require habilitation, normalization, or the provision of services in the least restrictive setting for developmentally disabled or mentally retarded individuals.[221] The statutes differ a great deal as to their coverage and their specific requirements. Most of the existing statutes have mandatory provisions; a few simply state general public policy.[222] Four states have provisions that constitute expressions of public policy without directly mandating the least restrictive services. For example, South Carolina, which is representative of the four states, mandates resources to allow mentally retarded individuals to live in the com-

214. Garrity v. Gallen, 522 F. Supp. 171 (D.N.H. 1981).

215. Anderson v. Thompson, 658 F.2d 1205 (7th Cir. 1981); Davis v. District of Columbia Bd. of Educ., 530 F. Supp. 1215 (D.D.C. 1982).

216. Miener v. Missouri, 673 F.2d 969 (8th Cir. 1982); Meyerson v. Arizona, 526 F. Supp. 129 (D. Ariz. 1981).

217. See in this chapter § I A, Mental Retardation Facilities and Community Mental Health Centers Construction Act of 1963, *supra*.

218. W. Winslow, *supra* note 127, at 273.

219. Goldman, Adams, & Taube, *supra* note 92, at 131. (In 1977, the 2 million episodes accounted for 27.2 percent of the outpatient and 4.2 percent of the inpatient episodes. By 1980 the centers handled 25 million episodes.)

220. See in this chapter § II, Mentally Ill and Developmentally Disabled Persons: Two Distinct Populations, *supra*.

221. Alaska Stat. § 47.80.110 (1984); Cal. Welf. & Inst. Code § 4502(a) (West 1984). Colo. Rev. Stat. § 27-10.5-101(a) & (b) (1982); Del. Code Ann. tit. 16, §§ 5501, 5504 (1983); D.C. Code Ann. §§ 6-1961(b), 6-1962, 6-1963 (1981); Fla. Stat. Ann. § 393.13(2)(d)(7) (West 1985); Ga. Code Ann. § 31-8-101, 31-8-108 (1982); Hawaii Rev. Stat. § 333E-1 (1976); Idaho Code § 39-4605 (Supp. 1984); Ill. Ann. Stat. ch. 91½ § 2-102(a) (Smith-Hurd Supp. 1984); La. Rev. Stat. Ann. § 28.390(B)(1), (2), & (3) (West Supp. 1985); Md. Health-Gen. Code Ann. § 7-601(a)(2) (Supp. 1981); Minn. Stat. Ann. § 253B (West Supp. 1982); Mo. Ann. Stat. § 630.115(1) (Vernon Supp. 1982); N.H. Rev. Stat. Ann. § 171-A:12 II(e) (1978); N.D. Cent. Code § 25-01.2-02 (Supp. 1983); Pa. Stat. Ann. tit. 50, §§ 4201(1)(4), 4301(e)(3) (Purdon 1969); S.C. Code Ann. § 44-21-20 (Law. Co-op. 1985); Tex. Rev. Civ. Stat. Ann. art. 5547-300(7)(11)(15) (Vernon Supp. 1981); Vt. Stat. Ann. tit. 18, § 8824 (Supp. 1984); Wis. Stat. Ann. § 51.61(1)(e) (West Supp. 1984); Wyo. Stat. § 35-1-625(a)(1) (Supp. 1984).

222. Delaware includes only mentally retarded individuals who are entitled to live with families or foster parents and to participate in community activities, unless it can be shown that institutional care is necessary, in which case the living situation must be made as normal as possible. Idaho states that developmentally handicapped persons are to receive treatment in a manner that is not more restrictive than is necessary for their own protection or the protection of society. Maryland provides that mentally retarded persons who are receiving services from the state must receive those services in the least restrictive available environment. Two states require administrative determinations before placements may be made. In Massachusetts there must be periodic reviews of mentally retarded individuals living in institutions to consider all possible alternatives to residential care. Vermont directs the commissioner of mental health to make sure that there are no less restrictive alternatives available for any placement of a mentally retarded person. Minnesota and Nebraska both require the courts to make sure that there are no alternatives to judicial commitment that are less restrictive when ordering placements for mentally retarded individuals. Similar requirements have been found in Pennsylvania's law. Wyoming is unique in the sense that its statute only applies to program providers under contract to the state. These contract recipients must individualize services so that each person served will receive the least restrictive treatment consistent with his needs. See statutes listed *supra* in note 221.

munity where it is feasible for them to do so.[223] Of the remaining 28 states, 10 limit the principle of providing the least restrictive services to residents of institutions[224] or developmentally disabled persons receiving services in a facility.[225] One state limits its least restrictive requirements to treatment procedures.[226] Nine other states specifically provide for care, treatment, or habilitation but with no requirement that it be in the least restrictive setting.[227] Two states support but do not mandate community placement.[228] Finally, 6 states place no statutory conditions on care and treatment,[229] although of course minimal constitutional standards apply.

For the mentally ill, by comparison, only 14 states have statutes that require or encourage services in the least restrictive environment.[230] Of those, only 3 create a certain entitlement to community services or deinstitutionalization.[231] One state makes it state policy to secure the least restrictive alternative placement.[232] Of the remaining 10 states, 6 provide an indeterminate right to treatment in the least restrictive setting,[233] 2 have a policy that supports deinstitutionalization or community services indirectly,[234] and 2 have a procedure for reviewing alternatives to hospitalization.[235]

Thirty-six states lack any kind of right to mental health treatment in the least restrictive available setting. Of these, 13 states provide for treatment in the hospital or institutional setting,[236] 13 require treatment and nothing more,[237] and 10 have no applicable statute.[238]

Thirteen of the 14 states with statutes that actively encourage deinstitutionalization for the mentally ill also have similar coverage for developmentally disabled persons.[239] Only 1 state[240] extends such coverage to the mentally ill alone, while 10 states extend such coverage only to the developmentally disabled.[241] In 27 states there is no explicit mandate to provide or encourage deinstitutionalization for either the mentally ill or the developmentally disabled, although in most of those states there are statutes that might indirectly support the goal of providing comprehensive community services. Seventeen states, for example, require facilities serving either the mentally ill or the developmentally disabled to furnish care and treatment in the least restrictive setting possible.[242] Five of those states have statutes covering both the mentally ill and the developmentally disabled populations.[243]

Also, according to a survey conducted in an American Bar Association project, more than 115 programs

223. In the District of Columbia, the applicable statute announces an intent to secure habilitation in the least restrictive setting for each mentally retarded individual. A similar provision in Florida states the legislature's intent to be guided by principles of normalization, to establish community services, and to provide institutional care in the least restrictive setting. Hawaii's statute pronounces deinstitutionalization of the developmentally disabled as a major goal of the state. See statutes listed *supra* in note 221.

224. Ariz. Rev. Stat. Ann. § 36-551.01(C) (Supp. 1984); Ky. Rev. Stat. Ann. §§ 202B.040, 202B.060 (Michie 1982); Me. Rev. Stat. Ann. tit. 34, § 2147(2)(D) (1978); Mont. Code Ann. 53-20-148(1) & (2) (1983); N.M. Stat. Ann. § 43-1-7 (1979); Okla. Stat. Ann. tit. 43A, § 622(5) (West Supp. 1984); Or. Rev. Stat. § 427.031(3) (Supp. 1983); S.D. Codified Laws § 27B-8-11, 14 (1984); Va. Code § 37.1-84.1(6) (1984).

225. N.J. Stat. Ann. § 30:6D-9 (West 1981).

226. Nev. Rev. Stat. § 433.494(1) (1983).

227. Conn. Gen. Stat. Ann. § 19a-469(b) (West Supp. 1985); Ind. Code Ann. § 16-14-1.6-2 (Burns 1983); Mich. Stat. Ann. § 14.800(704)(1) (Callaghan 1980); Mich. Comp. Laws Ann. § 330.1708 (1980); Neb. Rev. Stat. § 83-1,141 (Supp. 1981); N.Y. Ment. Hyg. Law § 33.03 (McKinney 1978); Ohio Rev. Code Ann. § 5123.01 (Page 1981 & Supp. 1984); Tenn. Code Ann. § 33-5-201 (1984); Utah Code Ann. § 64-7-46 (1978 & Supp. 1983); W. Va. Code § 27-5-9 (1980).

228. R.I. Gen. Laws § 40.1-21-1 (1984); Wash. Rev. Code Ann. ch. 71.20.010 (1975).

229. Alabama, Arkansas, Iowa, Kansas, Mississippi, and North Carolina.

230. Alaska Stat. § 47.30.655(2) (1982); Cal. Welf. & Inst. Code § 5325.1(a) (West 1984); Colo. Rev. Stat. § 27-10-101(a) & (b) (1982); Ga. Code Ann. § 37-3-162(a) (1982); Hawaii Rev. Stat. § 334-35(1) (1976); Ill. Ann. Stat. ch. 91½, § 2-102(a) (Smith-Hurd Supp. 1984); Ky. Rev. Stat. Ann. 202A.196 (Michie 1982); Me. Rev. Stat. Ann. tit. 34, § 3003(2)(A) (Supp. 1984); Mass. Gen. Laws Ann. ch. 123, § 4(3) (West Supp. 1985); Minn. Stat. Ann. § 253B.09(1) (West 1982); Mo. Ann. Stat. § 630.115(1) (Vernon 1979 & Supp. 1983); Pa. Stat. Ann. tit. 50, § 7102 (Purdon Supp. 1985); Vt. Stat. Ann. tit. 18, § 7703 (Supp. 1984); Wis. Stat. Ann. § 51.61(3)(e) (West Supp. 1984).

231. Colo. Rev. Stat. § 27-10-101(a) & (b) (1982); District of Columbia by judicial interpretation in Dixon v. Weinberger, 405 F. Supp. 974 (D.D.C. 1975); Wis. Stat. Ann. § 51.61(3)(e) (West Supp. 1984).

232. Ga. Code Ann. § 37-3-162(a) (1982).

233. Alaska Stat. § 47.30.655(2) (1982); Cal. Welf. & Inst. Code § 5325.1(a) (West 1984); Ill. Ann. Stat. ch. 91½, § 2-102(a) (Smith-Hurd Supp. 1984); Me. Rev. Stat. Ann. tit. 34, § 3003(2)(A) (Supp. 1984); Mo. Ann. Stat. § 630.115(10) (Vernon 1979 & Supp. 1983); Pa. Stat. Ann. tit. 50, § 7102 (Purdon Supp. 1985).

234. Hawaii Rev. Stat. § 334-35(1) (1976); Vt. Stat. Ann. tit. 18, § 7703 (Supp. 1984).

235. Mass. Gen. Laws Ann. ch. 123(3) (West Supp. 1985); Minn. Stat. Ann. § 253B.09(1) (West Supp. 1985).

236. Fla. Stat. Ann. § 394.459(2)(b) (West Supp. 1985); Mont. Code Ann. 53-21-142(2) (1983); Neb. Rev. Stat. 83-1044 (1981); Nev. Rev. Stat. § 433.494(1) (1983); N.J. Stat. Ann. § 30:4-24.2(e)(2) (West 1981); N.M. Stat. Ann. § 43-1-7 (1978 & Supp. 1982); N.C. Gen. Stat. § 122-55.1 (1981); N.D. Cent. Code Ann. § 25-03.1-40(1)-(3) (1978); Ohio Rev. Code Ann. § 5122.27(F) (Baldwin 1982 & Supp. 1982); Okla. Stat. Ann. tit. 43A, § 622(5) (West Supp. 1981); R.I. Gen. Laws § 40.1-5-9 (1984); S.D. Codified Laws § 27A-12-11 (1976 & Supp. 1982); Va. Code § 37.1-84.1(6) (1984).

237. Ariz. Rev. Stat. Ann. § 36-511(A) (Supp. 1984); Conn. Gen. Stat. Ann. § 17-206(c) (West 1975 & Supp. 1983–84); Del. Code Ann. tit. 16, § 5161(a)(i) (1974 & Supp. 1982); Ind. Code Ann. § 16-14-1.6-2 (Burns 1983); Iowa Code Ann. § 229.23 (West Supp. 1983); Kan. Stat. Ann. § 59-2927 (1976 & Supp. 1981); La. Rev. Stat. Ann. § 28-171(Q) (West 1983); Mich. Comp. Laws Ann. § 330.1708 (1980); N.H. Rev. Stat. Ann. § 135B.43 (1977 & Supp. 1981); N.Y. Mental Hyg. Law § 33.03 (McKinney 1978 & Supp. 1982–83); Tenn. Code Ann. § 33-306(b) (1977 & Supp. 1982); Utah Code Ann. § 64-7-46 (Supp. 1981); W. Va. Code § 27-5-9 (1980 & Supp. 1983).

238. Alabama, Arkansas, Idaho, Maryland, Mississippi, Oregon, South Carolina, Texas, Washington, and Wyoming.

239. Alaska, California, Colorado, Georgia, Hawaii, Illinois, Kentucky, Massachusetts, Minnesota, Missouri, Pennsylvania, Wisconsin, and Vermont.

240. Maine.

241. Delaware, Florida, Idaho, Louisiana, Maryland, Nebraska, North Dakota, South Carolina, Texas, and Wyoming.

242. Arizona, Florida, Kentucky, Maine, Montana, Nebraska, Nevada, New Jersey, New Mexico, North Carolina, North Dakota, Ohio, Oklahoma, Oregon, Rhode Island, South Dakota, and Virginia.

243. Montana, New Mexico, Oklahoma, South Dakota, and Virginia.

throughout all the states serve some portion of the noninstitutional housing needs of mentally disabled adults.[244] Many additional programs undoubtedly exist for children.

2. Legal Decisions Interpreting State Law

Although there has been relatively little litigation involving state deinstitutionalization or community services statutes, actions based on state law are becoming more prevalent with the limitations on legal redress based on constitutional law or federal statutes, but a 1982 United States Supreme Court decision may dramatically alter that trend.

Once again the *Pennhurst* case is involved.[245] The Third Circuit, after being reversed by the Supreme Court on the issue of the applicability of the Developmental Disabilities Act to deinstitutionalization,[246] reinstated its original order based on state law.[247] State and county officials were told to provide habilitation for mentally retarded citizens in the least restrictive setting including substantial services in the community. In an earlier decision, *In re Schmidt*, the Pennsylvania Supreme Court had determined that state law required that services be provided if they would eliminate the need for institutionalization, even if the services would have to be provided for a long period of time. In subsequent decisions the *Pennhurst* lower court ordered proper funding of community services to habilitate mentally retarded children and an advocacy program for children without parents to speak on their behalf.[248]

Nevertheless, the Supreme Court reversed and remanded the entire case to be reheard on constitutional and federal statutory grounds, finding a violation of the principle of sovereign immunity. In a 5-4 decision, the majority ruled that a federal court could not use state law against state officials to compel them to provide suitable community living arrangements for the residents and former residents of Pennhurst. Public policy considerations having to do with the administration of the federal court system "cannot override the constitutional limitation on the authority of the federal judiciary to adjudicate suits against a State." The four justices who joined the dissent were severely critical of what they termed a "remarkable result" based on "an equally remarkable misapplication of the ancient doctrine of sovereign immunity." In a completely unprecedented holding, noted the dissent, "the Court concludes that Pennsylvania's sovereign immunity prevents a federal court from enjoining the conduct that Pennsylvania itself has prohibited."[249]

Before the second *Pennhurst* case, the deinstitutionalization of mentally ill patients also had been judically mandated based on state law. In *Dixon v. Weinberger*,[250] a federal court concluded that a District of Columbia mental health statute created a right to be placed in the least restrictive appropriate facility or living situation and an obligation on the part of the local government to provide such placements even where they did not currently exist.

New York State's highest court concluded that despite notions of sovereign immunity articulated by the United States Supreme Court, deinstitutionalized mentally ill persons and those persons awaiting release into suitable community programs might proceed against the state by seeking declaratory relief in a mandamus action.[251] It found a justifiable distinction between "a court's imposition of its own policy determination upon its governmental partners and its mere declaration and enforcement of the individual's rights that have already been conferred by the other branches of government."[252] Moreover, the fact that the state might have to expend money to provide required services was not a proper defense to a legal action such as this. However, the court emphasized that how New York decided to meet its obligations was not a subject for courts to determine in a mandamus action.

Two 1985 decisions from California set out broad parameters for that state's provision of community services. In one case, a lower court, in rejecting the novel theory that professional standards of acceptable practices constitutionally require treatment in the least restrictive setting for chronically mentally ill persons, indicated that plaintiffs might have done better under California law.[253] More importantly, the state's supreme court determined that a state statute entitled developmentally disabled persons to supportive services needed to carry out their individual program plan as long as appropriations existed to pay for those services.[254]

In addition, several other cases dealt with states' obli-

244. State Laws and Programs Serving Elderly Persons and Disabled Adults (excerpted from: Board and Care Report: An Analysis of State Laws and Programs Serving Elderly Persons and Disabled Adults by ABA Commission on the Mentally Disabled and ABA Commission on the Elderly), 7 MDLR 158, 161-72 (1983).

245. Halderman v. Pennhurst State School & Hosp., 673 F.2d 647 (3d Cir. 1982).

246. Pennhurst State School & Hosp. v. Halderman, 451 U.S. 1 (1981).

247. *In re* Schmidt, 429 A.2d 631 (Pa. 1981).

248. Halderman v. Pennhurst State School & Hosp., 555 F. Supp. 1142 (E.D. Pa. 1982).

249. Pennhurst State School & Hosp. v. Halderman, 104 S. Ct. 900, 922 (1984) (Stevens, J., dissenting, joined by Brennan, Marshall, & Blackmun, J.J.).

250. 405 F. Supp. 974 (D.D.C. 1975).

251. Klostermann v. Cuomo, 463 N.E.2d 588 (N.Y. 1984).

252. *Id.* at 593.

253. Mental Health Ass'n v. Deukmejian, No. CA 000 540, 9 MPDLR 199 (Cal. Super. Ct. L.A. County Apr. 12, 1985).

254. Association for Retarded Citizens v. Department of Developmental Servs., No. S.F. 24761, 9 MPDLR 199 (Cal. Sup. Ct. Mar. 21, 1985).

gations,[255] but their effect is tempered not only by sovereign immunity but by other decisions suggesting that the individual's choice may supersede state policy on deinstitutionalization. It has already been held that a competent resident may choose to remain in an institution[256] and that the interests of incompetent persons in living within an institution or the community must be evaluated on an individual basis.[257]

3. Consent Decrees

A number of states under the threat of extended litigation have entered into consent decrees that serve much the same function as state policy on deinstitutionalization and community programming.[258] In many instances, however, there have been enforcement problems and subsequent disagreements between the parties.[259] In the 1970s many courts tried to force the states to make good faith efforts at compliance[260] including the appropriation of necessary funds.[261] In the 1980s circumstances are changing, and the courts are more reluctant to be initiators of action. To begin with, the United States Supreme Court has indicated that professional judgments should be presumed to be valid, absent strong evidence to the contrary.[262] Other courts are consistently deferring to professional expertise.[263] Second, courts are recognizing limits to deinstitutionalization which had gone unnoticed or had been thought unimportant before. For example, in the long-running Willowbrook consent decree, the Court of Appeals for the Second Circuit ruled the decree had to be modified to account for the fact that only large community residences had space available for deinstitutionalized residents.[264] Third, states are becoming more aware of the need to ensure that proper transitional services and community support programs are in place before deinstitutionalization begins. Two recent decrees provide considerable detail about precisely how the process will be carried out,[265] including in one of those decrees a plan for the establishment of case managers both in the institution and the community, clinical reviews for each patient, and the provision of a full continuum of residential and support services.[266] This decree is summarized in the *Mental and Physical Disability Law Reporter.* (See appendix A.)

Finally, two recent consent decrees, although acknowledging the fact that not all residents are ready to be deinstitutionalized and that some may never be, have attempted to improve institutional conditions for those who remain and encourage community placements for clients who are ready to leave. While one decree strives to promote the normalization principle by replicating the living situations of ordinary people in the community and making numerous institutional improvements for those who remain,[267] the other decree explicitly recognizes that significant obstacles remain in the way of community living including zoning restriction, community resistance, and financing on the state and federal levels which preclude or discourage proper funding.[268] These obstacles were persuasive despite overwhelming testimony that "the overall cost of care for a client living in the community was never more than, and is generally significantly less than, that in an institution such as the Center."[269]

255. While ruling on the due process rights of a mentally ill patient who was being transferred to a substantially more restrictive hospital setting, a federal district court in 1977 pieced together several sections of the Pennsylvania mental health act and found a right to adequate treatment in the least restrictive facility. Eubanks v. Clarke, 434 F. Supp. 1022 (E.D. Pa. 1977). In Kentucky, a federal court ruled that voluntary residents of a mental retardation facility were entitled to be released on request, while involuntary residents were entitled to the "least restrictive alternative mode of treatment" that was available. Kentucky Ass'n for Retarded Citizens v. Conn, 510 F. Supp. 1233, 1233 (1980). A New Hampshire federal court concluded that mentally retarded training school residents did not have a right to be deinstitutionalized but that state law obligated the state to provide a comprehensive array of community residences and programs. Garrity v. Gallen, 522 F. Supp. 171 (D.N.H. 1981). In Idaho, a state court decided that the state not only had to provide community placements and supportive services if they were needed but also had to pay for them where no federal funds were available. Woods v. Idaho Dep't of Health & Welfare, No. 74139, 6 MDLR 46 (Idaho Dist. Ct. Ada County Oct. 27, 1981).

256. *In re* Borgogna, 121 Cal. App. 3d 937, 175 Cal. Rptr. 588 (1981).

257. Halderman v. Pennhurst State School & Hosp., 612 F.2d 131 (3d Cir. 1979).

258. E.g., Brewster v. Dukakis, No. 76-4423-F, 3 MDLR 44 (E.D. Mass. Dec. 6, 1978); Spangler v. Thorne, B-80-238, 5 MDLR 107 (D. Conn. Dec. 30, 1980); Welsch v. Noot, No. 4-72 Cir. 451, 5 MDLR 155 (D. Minn. Sept. 15, 1980); Sidles v. Delaney, No. C75-300A, 1 MDLR 19 (N.D. Ohio Apr. 26, 1976); *In re* Shepard, 4 MDLR 29 (Vt. Washington County Dist. Ct. Aug. 31, 1979); New York State Ass'n for Retarded Children, Inc. v. Carey, 393 F. Supp. 715 (E.D.N.Y. 1975).

259. For example, there has been frequent litigation in Brewster v. Dukakis, 520 F. Supp. 882 (D. Mass. 1981), *modified*, 675 F.2d 1 (1st Cir. 1982), *original order vacated and remanded*, 687 F.2d 495 (1st Cir. 1982), *on remand*, 544 F. Supp. 1069 (D. Mass. 1982); and New York State Ass'n for Retarded Children, Inc. v. Carey, 706 F.2d 965 (2d Cir. 1983), *partly aff'g and partly rev'g* 551 F. Supp. 1165, 631 F.2d 162 (2d Cir. 1980), *rev'g* 492 F. Supp. 1110, 612 F.2d 644 (2d Cir. 1979), *aff'g* 466 F. Supp. 479, 596 F.2d 27 (2d Cir. 1979), *aff'g* unspecified Dist. Ct. Order, 492 F. Supp. 1099 (E.D.N.Y. 1980), 466 F. Supp. 487 (E.D.N.Y. 1979), 456 F. Supp. 85 (E.D.N.Y. 1978).

260. See all the cases listed in note 259 *supra*.

261. New York State Ass'n for Retarded Children, Inc. v. Carey, 456 F. Supp. 85 (E.D.N.Y. 1978).

262. Youngberg v. Romeo, 457 U.S. 307 (1982).

263. New York State Ass'n for Retarded Children, Inc. v. Carey, (2d Cir. 1983); Association for Retarded Citizens of North Dakota v. Olson, 516 F. Supp. 495 (D.N.D. 1982); Scott v. Plante, 691 F.2d 634 (3d Cir. 1982).

264. New York State Ass'n for Retarded Children, Inc. v. Carey, 706 F.2d 956 (2d Cir. 1983).

265. Deckard v. Cerro Gordo County, No. 1C81-3014, 6 MDLR 374 (N.D. Iowa Sept. 8, 1982); Caswell v. Secretary of Health & Human Servs., No. 77-0488-C-V-W-8, 7 MDLR 221 (W.D. Mo. Feb. 8, 1983).

266. Caswell v. Secretary of Health & Human Servs., No. 77-0488-C-V-W-8, 7 MDLR 221 (W.D. Mo. Feb. 8, 1983).

267. Lelsz v. Kavanaugh, No. 5-74-95-CA, 7 MDLR 379 (E.D. Tex. July 21, 1983), *appeal dismissed*, 710 F.2d 1040 (5th Cir. 1983).

268. Society for Good Will to Retarded Children, Inc. v. Cuomo, 572 F. Supp. 1300 (E.D.N.Y. 1983).

269. *Id.* at 1339.

IV. EDUCATION OF MENTALLY DISABLED CHILDREN

A. Introduction

In the development of community-based rights and entitlements for mentally disabled persons during the 1970s, unprecedented attention was devoted to the educational needs of all handicapped children.[270] When the previous edition of this book was published in 1971, several states still explicitly denied educational services to severely disabled children[271] if a determination was made by school officials that in their judgment a handicapped child, particularly one who was mentally retarded, could not profit from an education.[272] Many other states did so de facto by ignoring the inadequate education received by the vast majority of severely handicapped children.[273] As a whole, educational systems throughout the United States neglected handicapped students in shameful ways,[274] comparable to the warehousing of the disabled in institutions.

During the past 10 years, significant steps have been taken by states and the federal government to eliminate many of the worst problems and generally improve other less serious deficiencies, but a substantial number of handicapped children are still not receiving an appropriate education,[275] and the momentum for improving special education services may be waning.[276]

B. Constitutional Bases for the Right to Education

Several major legal decisions have identified constitutional bases for the right to a free appropriate education[277] which arguably establish an independent basis for educational services, should federal and state legislative enactments be repealed or substantially modified.

The United States Constitution does not require that the states educate their citizens,[278] but once a state creates an entitlement to public education the constitutional requirements of equal protection and due process influence how the services are to be administered.[279]

Since state-funded education is a statutory or constitutional entitlement in each of the 50 states,[280] an education may not be denied to any class of children, including the mentally disabled, without substantial justification and a due process procedure that insures that each child is actually a legitimate member of the class that is legally denied services.[281] The standards have been elaborated in several cases.

In 1973 in *San Antonio Independent School District v. Rodriguez*,[282] the Supreme Court declared that a general right to education was not fundamental. While the case involved nonhandicapped children, the implications for handicapped children were clear. States need only provide a minimal justification for excluding children from public schools instead of the higher justification required when fundamental interests are involved.[283] The other justification for applying the strictest scrutiny, the existence of a suspect class of individuals, has rarely been applied to mentally disabled persons,[284] although certain legal commentators concluded that mentally disabled individuals obviously met the criteria by being both an isolated and a discriminated-against minority.[285]

Between the minimum justification requirement and strict scrutiny, however, lies a third, intermediate standard. Used in cases addressing important but not fundamental rights, this standard requires a state to demonstrate that its legislative scheme is substantially related to achieving an important governmental objective. In 1982, in *Plyler v. Doe*[286] the Supreme Court applied this standard to the education of children whose parents were illegal aliens, determining that while education was not

270. In large measure this was due to the passage of the Education for All Handicapped Children Act; see in this chapter § III B 1.

271. Legal Rights of the Mentally Handicapped (B.J. Ennis, P.R. Friedman, & B. Gitlin eds., 1973).

272. E.g., D.C. Code Ann. § 31-203 allows exclusion of a child who "is found mentally or physically unable to profit from . . . school."

273. Weintraub & Abeson, Appropriate Education for All Handicapped Children: A Growing Issue, 23 Syracuse L. Rev. 1037 (1972).

274. *Id.* They reported that in 1972 one million handicapped children were totally excluded from educational services.

275. A report authored by representatives from 13 advocacy groups, the Education Advocates Coalition, concluded that hundreds of thousands of handicapped children were being denied the "appropriate" education guaranteed under federal law. The report was based on a six-month investigation of the educational services provided in ten states and the District of Columbia. Items of Interest: Advocacy Coalition Says Educational Services for Disabled Not Being Enforced, 4 MDLR 203 (1980).

276. *Id.* See also Summary and Analysis, 6 MDLR 137 (1982) concerning the Reagan administration's proposed changes in the federal law designed to reduce the impact on the states and localities. S. Vitto & R. Soskin, Mental Retardation: Its Social and Legal Context 62-69 (1985).

277. Pennsylvania Ass'n for Retarded Children v. Commonwealth, 343 F. Supp. 279 (E.D. Pa. 1972); Mills v. Board of Educ., 348 F. Supp. 866 (D.D.C. 1972); Panitch v. Wisconsin, 371 F. Supp. 955 (E.D. Wis. 1977); Kruse v. Campbell, 431 F. Supp. 180 (E.D. Va. 1977); Frederick L. v. Thomas, 419 F. Supp. 960 (E.D. Pa. 1976).

278. San Antonio Indep. School Dist. v. Rodriguez, 411 U.S. 1 (1973); Plyler v. Doe, 457 U.S. 202 (1982).

279. Plyler v. Doe, 457 U.S. 202 (1982).

280. Note, The Right to Education: A Constitutional Analysis, 44 U. Cin. L. Rev. 796, 804 (1975).

281. Plyler v. Doe, 457 U.S. 202 (1982).

282. 411 U.S. 1 (1973).

283. *Id.* But see Plyler v. Doe, 457 U.S. at 202, which concluded that an intermediate standard showing a substantial relationship must be used.

284. Benham v. Edwards, 678 F.2d 511, 515-16 (5th Cir. 1982). Note, Mental Illness: A Suspect Classification? 83 Yale L.J. 1237, 1268 (1974); see Burgdorf & Burgdorf, A History of Unequal Treatment: The Qualifications of Handicapped Persons as a "Suspect Class" Under the Equal Protection Clause, 15 Santa Clara Law. 855, 910 (1974); but see Kruse v. Campbell, 431 F. Supp. 180 (E.D. Va. 1977) (indigent handicapped children suspect class); Fialkowski v. Shapp, 405 F. Supp. 946 (E.D. Pa. 1975) (mentally retarded children may constitute suspect class).

285. See Burgdorf & Burgdorf, *supra* note 284.

286. 457 U.S. 202 (1982).

fundamental, it did have special importance. Moreover, to determine what was a substantial government interest, it instructed courts to look past the limited boundaries of the school district or the state and measure the impact nationwide.[287] In that context, the majority concluded that the cost of educating these particular children was not a sufficient reason to deny them an educational opportunity.[288] Applying those standards to children whose parents are not in this country illegally, it seems clear that mentally handicapped children are entitled to no less from the Constitution, although the balancing process would differ in accounting for their special circumstances.

State legislation that limits special educational services for handicapped children would likely meet a substantial relationship test if the limitations were in response to excessive costs per student or administrative difficulties threatening the overall education program,[289] but at the same time unless a state could show that a child was uneducable[290] there would be little or no justification for spending less on a handicapped student than on a nonhandicapped student.[291] The problem for profoundly mentally retarded children is the possibility that states could successfully exclude them by demonstrating that any educational effort would be futile. Such precedents have already been upheld in New Jersey[292] and Ohio,[293] and Chief Justice Burger maintains that a profoundly mentally retarded resident may be denied habilitative services where expert administrators have determined that such services would be wasteful.[294]

Two ground-breaking cases established an independent right to education for handicapped children and also provided a detailed blueprint of procedural protections for subsequent federal legislation—*Pennsylvania Association for Retarded Children v. Commonwealth*[295] and *Mills v. Board of Education*.[296] In both decisions, the federal courts derived a right to education for handicapped children from the statutory obligation to provide an education to all state residents within a specified age group.[297] By denying handicapped children an equal opportunity to share in this entitlement without providing them with a hearing and other procedures, the states were denying these students due process.[298] The courts ordered detailed due process protections that were later adopted to a significant extent in the EAHCA and § 504 regulations.[299]

Subsequent decisions also found an equal education was mandatory absent rational explanations for not providing minimal services to particular classes of handicapped children.[300] Some courts, however, have held that the Constitution provides a right to a minimally adequate education as opposed to a particular grade level[301] or what is termed an appropriate education.[302]

What an "equal" education is remains somewhat ambiguous, although the Supreme Court has settled the question of what balancing test should be applied in making a determination. All the constitutionally based opinions have held that nothing more than an equal education is necessary. Moreover, equality was frequently viewed in strictly mathematical terms measuring dollars spent per child without taking into consideration the individual needs of each child. Two state statutes still exclude uneducable mentally disabled children from public education entirely,[303] although a determination of who is not educable may well differ from one expert to another.

C. Federal Statutes

The major impetus for states to address the needs of handicapped children was the passage of two federal statutes, the Education for All Handicapped Children Act in 1975 and the Rehabilitation Act of 1973, particularly its § 504. In all but one state[304] it was not long before statutes were enacted or modified to bring those jurisdictions into compliance with federal requirements.

287. *Id.* at 210-15.

288. *Id.* at 227-30.

289. San Antonio Indep. School Dist. v. Rodriguez, 411 U.S. 1 (1973); Fialkowski v. Shapp, 405 F. Supp. 946 (E.D. Pa. 1975); Levine v. New Jersey Dep't of Institutions & Agencies, 418 A.2d 229 (N.J. 1980).

290. See Levine v. New Jersey Dep't of Institutions & Agencies, 418 A.2d 229 (N.J. 1980); Cuyahoga County Ass'n for Retarded Children & Adults v. Essex, 411 F. Supp. 46 (N.D. Ohio 1976). (In both cases the funding difference was justified.)

291. Pennsylvania Ass'n for Retarded Children v. Commonwealth, 343 F. Supp. 279 (E.D. Pa. 1972); Mills v. Board of Educ., 348 F. Supp. 866 (D.D.C. 1972); Frederick L. v. Thomas, 419 F. Supp. 960 (E.D. Pa. 1976); Panitch v. Wisconsin, 444 F. Supp. 320 (E.D. Wis. 1977).

292. Levine v. New Jersey Dep't of Institutions & Agencies, 418 A.2d 229 (N.J. 1980).

293. Cuyahoga County Ass'n for Retarded Children & Adults v. Essex, 411 F. Supp. 46 (N.D. Ohio 1976).

294. Youngberg v. Romeo, 457 U.S. 307, 329-31 (1982) (concurring opinion).

295. 343 F. Supp. 279 (E.D. Pa. 1972).

296. 348 F. Supp. 866 (D.D.C. 1972).

297. Pennsylvania Ass'n for Retarded Children v. Commonwealth, 343 F. Supp. 279 (E.D. Pa. 1972); Mills v. Board of Educ., 348 F. Supp. 866 (D.D.C. 1972).

298. Pennsylvania Ass'n for Retarded Children v. Commonwealth, 343 F. Supp. 279, 273 (E.D. Pa. 1972); Mills v. Board of Educ., 348 F. Supp. 866 (D.D.C. 1972).

299. 45 C.F.R. §§ 84.31 to 84.38 (1984).

300. Kruse v. Campbell, 431 F. Supp. 180 (E.D. Va. 1977); Panitch v. Wisconsin, 444 F. Supp. 320 (E.D. Wis. 1977).

301. Fialkowski v. Shapp, 405 F. Supp. 946 (E.D. Pa. 1975).

302. Frederick L. v. Thomas, 419 F. Supp. 960 (E.D. Pa. 1976).

303. Levine v. New Jersey Dep't of Institutions & Agencies, 418 A.2d 229 (N.J. Sup. Ct. 1980); Cuyahoga County Ass'n for Retarded Children & Adults v. Essex, 411 F. Supp. 46 (N.D. Ohio 1976).

304. New Mexico is the only state that is not eligible to participate in this federal program. See New Mexico Ass'n for Retarded Citizens v. New Mexico, 678 F.2d 847 (10th Cir. 1982).

1. Education for All Handicapped Children Act (EAHCA)

The central requirement of EAHCA is a "free appropriate public education" for "all handicapped children."[305] The most vexing problem has been this requirement's lack of specificity: initial case decisions that attempted to interpret the phrase established wide parameters for legal maneuverings. At one extreme were interpretations demanding the maximization of each child's learning potential[306] or the most appropriate education possible.[307] At the other extreme, courts settled for anything that would provide the child with "a reasonable chance" to acquire skills needed to function in society through educational strategies that have proven successful in the past.[308] The most cited definition was set out by a federal district court in 1980 in *Rowley v. Board of Education*: the "opportunity to achieve . . . [one's] full potential commensurate with the opportunity provided to other children."[309]

But in 1982 in *Board of Education v. Rowley*, a divided Supreme Court disagreed with this definition, finding that Amy Rowley was not entitled to a sign language interpreter to help her maximize her educational potential.[310] The Court held instead that states must provide sufficient personalized instruction and supportive services to insure that each child actually benefits from the individualized education program (IEP) prepared for that child. Moreover, in order to insure that the child will be able "to benefit" from the instruction, an education must meet existing state standards and approximate the grade levels used in regular public schools. The IEP must enable a child placed in a regular public school classroom to achieve passing marks and advance from grade to grade. Even though a dissenting opinion suggests that the Court majority's opinion will do little to improve educational standards,[311] such an interpretation is unduly pessimistic from the point of view of the handicapped child, for the majority's language implies a considerable state obligation to individualize educational planning and to make sure that each child keeps pace with his classmates. Outside the regular public classroom the state's obligations are less settled. As the Court noted, "[i]t is clear that the benefits obtainable by children at one end of the spectrum will differ dramatically from those obtainable by children at the other end, with infinite variations in between."[312] There is no one test that can be applied to all children covered by the act. In a footnote the Court indicated that the "basic floor" for any child could be no less than the opportunity "to achieve a reasonable degree of self-sufficiency."[313]

After *Rowley*, an "appropriate education for handicapped students" is something less than the best education available and even less still than the opportunity to achieve one's full potential to the same degree as other children. Before that decision, courts were often swayed by the parents' conception of an appropriate education. The United States Court of Appeals for the Eighth Circuit, for example, in *Springdale School District #50 v. Grace*[314] upheld what it acknowledged was less appropriate than another available placement because the less appropriate placement was consistent with the parents' wishes and the mainstreaming requirement. In the same year, a federal district court in the Eighth Circuit accepted a more restrictive residential setting because it met the unique needs of the child and was consistent with the parents' wishes.[315] As a result of the Supreme Court's opinion, however, courts will have to acknowledge the expertise of the local school authorities.[316] In fact, the Eighth Circuit in rehearing the *Springdale School District* case affirmed the original decision but did so by citing the superior judgment of the state administrators.[317]

Certainly meeting a child's individual needs will be a crucial consideration in subsequent decisions. A previous interpretation by the Third Circuit seems to capture the spirit of the Supreme Court opinion by affirming the idea of an education sufficient to make a child independent and self-sufficient but insisting that state authorities, in the first instance, have enough flexibility to individualize program plans in a reasonable manner.[318]

2. Section 504 of the Rehabilitation Act

Section 504 of the Rehabilitation Act of 1973 prohibits discrimination based on mental or physical handicaps in federally assisted programs[319] and allows any person identified as handicapped to bring a private action.[320]

305. 20 U.S.C. § 1412(1) & (2) (1982). See in this chapter § I C *supra* for a description of the EAHCA.

306. Kruelle v. Biggs, 489 F. Supp. 169 (D. Del. 1980), *aff'd*, Kruelle v. New Castle County School Dist., 642 F.2d 687 (3d Cir. 1981).

307. Dewalt v. Burkholder, No. 80-0014-A, 3 Education for the Handicapped L. Rep. 551:550 (E.D. Va. Mar. 13, 1980).

308. Rettig v. Kent City School Dist., 539 F. Supp. 768, 769 (N.D. Ohio 1981).

309. 483 F. Supp. 528, 534 (S.D.N.Y. 1980).

310. 458 U.S. 176, 203-4.

311. *Id.* at 212-18 (White, J., dissenting, joined by Brennan & Marshall, J.J.).

312. *Id.* at 202.

313. *Id.* at 201 n.23.

314. 494 F. Supp. 266 (W.D. Ark. 1980), *aff'd*, 656 F.2d 300 (8th Cir. 1981).

315. Gladys J. & Laura J. v. Pearland Indep. School Dist., 520 F. Supp. 869 (S.D. Tex. 1981).

316. Board of Educ. v. Rowley, 458 U.S. 176, 207-8 (1982). See also Hines v. Pitt County Bd. of Educ., 497 F.Supp. 403 (E.D.N.C. 1980); Battle v. Pennsylvania, 629 F.2d 269 (3d Cir. 1980).

317. Springdale School Dist. # 50 v. Grace, 693 F.2d 41 (8th Cir. 1982).

318. Battle v. Pennsylvania, 629 F.2d 269 (3d Cir. 1980).

319. See in this chapter § I B *supra* for a description of this act.

320. Akers v. Bolton, 531 F. Supp. 3300 (D. Kan. 1981).

In *Hairston v. Drosick* (1976)[321] a federal district court held that the deliberate exclusion of a physically disabled child from a normal classroom environment "without a bona fide educational reason" violated the act, since a denial must be justified by "compelling" educational needs. "School officials must make every effort to include such children within the regular public classroom situation, even at great expense to the school system."[322] A year later, another federal district court rejected the argument that § 504 applied only to employment and vocational training programs and found that educational opportunities were specifically recognized by Congress when it enacted the statute.[323]

In 1979, however, came a major change in direction after the Supreme Court issued a narrow interpretation of § 504 in *Southeastern Community College v. Davis.*[324] A unanimous Court determined that federal recipients could impose reasonable physical qualifications on handicapped individuals. Individuals with handicaps that precluded them from meeting legitimate program or activity requirements might be denied access or admittance unless reasonable modifications could be made to accommodate their shortcomings. "Reasonable" meant without imposing "undue financial and administrative burdens" upon the recipients of federal funds.[325]

No decision since *Davis* has denied that § 504 requires an appropriate education for handicapped children where such an education is offered to nonhandicapped children. What is ambiguous is the extent to which schools must make program modifications to serve the special needs of special children. Perhaps the most important case in this regard was litigated in New Mexico, the only state that until recently elected not to receive funding under the EAHCA.[326] A federal court ruled that the state had violated § 504 when it created a funding option for local school districts which permitted special education funds to be used for nonrelated programs. The state's failure to adequately finance programs and hire qualified personnel for handicapped children was tantamount to a direct violation whether or not the discriminatory effect was intended. The court noted that *Davis* could be distinguished in this situation because it dealt with postsecondary education. The United States Court of Appeals for the Tenth Circuit reversed the matter for further consideration of the difference between illegal discrimination and affirmative action.[327] The appeals court observed that an outright refusal to modify a program might constitute illegal discrimination if the handicapped plaintiffs were prevented from realizing the same benefits that would normally accrue to nonhandicapped children. The more children that were denied services the more likely it was that a § 504 violation had occurred.

A number of courts and administrative bodies have used § 504 as a justification for requiring education services.[328] A federal district court in Colorado ruled that the § 504 restriction in *Davis* was inapplicable where a handicapped child could realize the same benefits as a nonhandicapped child merely by attending an appropriate education program.[329] Using the same rationale, the Court of Appeals for the Eleventh Circuit ruled that Georgia could not limit all educational programs to 180 days if the handicapped student actually needed education year round.[330] Under § 504 certain services must be provided to serve the special needs of handicapped children.[331] Reasonable modifications upheld by the courts include sustaining the level of education necessary to guarantee that a child will receive a diploma of some kind[332] or providing a self-contained classroom in a centralized location in the county for learning disabled children,[333] but not providing residential care at a private facility.[334]

In 1984, however, the United States Supreme Court set out a new restriction by ruling that where § 504 and the EAHCA are coextensive in terms of their coverage, the remedies found under § 504 may not be applied to enlarge the EAHCA remedies.[335] The court left open the question of what remedies would be available if it were found that only § 504 applied to a particular situation. Thus, both the scope of § 504's coverage and its available remedies are less than certain when used to further the educational opportunities of handicapped children. Moreover, as was discussed earlier in the chapter, states retain their immunity to suit under § 504 unless they

321. 423 F. Supp. 180 (S.D. W. Va. 1976).

322. *Id.* at 184.

323. Kruse v. Campbell, 431 F. Supp. 180 (E.D. Va. 1977); § 111(a) of the Rehabilitation Act Amendments of 1974, Pub. L. No. 93-516, 88 Stat. 1617, 1619 (defining handicapped individual for purposes of Titles IV & V).

324. 442 U.S. 387 (1979).

325. *Id.* at 412.

326. New Mexico Ass'n for Retarded Citizens v. New Mexico, 495 F. Supp. 391 (D.N.M. 1980).

327. New Mexico Ass'n for Retarded Citizens v. New Mexico, 678 F.2d 847 (10th Cir. 1982).

328. Mauk v. Idaho Dep't of Educ., No. 10801042, 5 MDLR 171 (OCR Region 10 Dec. 31, 1980); Ladson v. Board of Educ., 615 F.2d 1369 (D.C. Cir. 1980); North v. District of Columbia Bd. of Educ., 471 F. Supp. 136 (D.C. 1979).

329. Association for Retarded Citizens in Colorado v. Frazier, 517 F. Supp. 105 (D. Colo. 1981).

330. Georgia Ass'n of Retarded Citizens v. McDaniel, 716 F.2d 1565 (11th Cir. 1983).

331. Association for Retarded Citizens in Colorado v. Frazier, 517 F. Supp. 105 (D. Colo. 1981); Georgia Ass'n of Retarded Citizens v. McDaniel, 511 F. Supp. 1263 (N.D. Ga. 1981).

332. Board of Educ. v. Ambach, 436 N.Y.S.2d 564 (Sup. Ct. 1981).

333. Pinkerton v. Moye, 509 F. Supp. 107 (W.D.W. Va. 1981).

334. Colin K. v. Schmidt, 536 F. Supp. 1375 (D.R.I. 1982).

335. Smith v.Robinson, 104 S. Ct. 3457 (1984).

have demonstrated a clear intention to waive their immunity.

D. State Law

Many jurisdictions enacted special education statutes before the federal legislation came into existence, and afterward every state except New Mexico revised its statutes to make them consistent with EAHCA.[336]

One of the first cases to recognize statutory educational rights of handicapped children, *Mills v. Board of Education* in 1972, stated that children who were "unable mentally or physically to profit from attendance at school" were entitled by law to "specialized instruction adapted to [their] needs."[337] The jurisdiction's interest in conserving limited financial resources was tempered by the requirement that funds be spent equitably so that educational "inadequacies" did not "bear more heavily on the 'exceptional' or handicapped child than the normal child."[338] The state of Maryland required comprehensive special educational services several years before the federal legislation went into effect.[339] Local school boards were obliged to "make some other appropriate provision" for mentally retarded children who were too disabled to be instructed in regular public schools, and all handicapped children had to receive services that would help them "achieve their full potential."[340] Connecticut provided a free, appropriate public education for all mentally retarded children, regardless of the severity of their condition.[341]

Legal disputes about the educability of mentally handicapped children have focused almost entirely on severely mentally retarded children; those with mental illness or less severe retardation have rarely been the subjects of blanket exclusions by the states. The New Jersey Supreme Court, for example, concluded in 1980 that universal public education mandated in the state constitution did not cover mentally retarded children who were "subtrainable" since their needs could be satisfied by minimal custodial care.[342] Yet two years later the same court ruled that institutionalized children had, under New Jersey statutes, a right to individualized education and habilitation in the least restrictive setting.[343]

Two important 1984 decisions extended special educational opportunities by relying on state law. The United States Court of Appeals for the First Circuit held that "states are free to elaborate procedural and substantive protections for the disabled child that are more stringent than those contained in the [federal] Act."[344] Thus, the Massachusetts Supreme Judicial Court found that a 21-year-old brain-damaged student was entitled by state law to a public education that provided him with the "maximum possible development,"[345] a standard that exceeded the United States Supreme Court's interpretation of a free appropriate education in *Rowley*. Similarly, a learning disabled child was denied due process when federal hearing procedures were used in a situation where Massachusetts's regulations provided significantly more protections for the child.[346]

E. Malpractice Theory

A final legal basis used to argue in favor of the provision of appropriate educational services is malpractice founded on traditional tort theory. Its essence is the recovery of monetary damages after an appropriate education has been denied because of negligence by the school authorities.[347] One reported decision awarded damages under this theory,[348] but it was reversed on appeal.[349] The Montana Supreme Court apparently authorized a lower court to award damages for educational malpractice involving the misplacement of a child into a class for mentally retarded children.[350] Although three dissenting justices decried the decision because it endorsed educational malpractice, a concurring justice stated that the case did not concern negligence but rather the violation of mandatory statutes and procedural due process.

A far greater number of decisions, however, have summarily rejected the malpractice theory as either against public policy or extremely difficult to ascertain fairly, or both.[351] Appellate courts in New York[352] and

336. New Mexico Ass'n for Retarded Citizens v. New Mexico, 495 F. Supp. 391 (D.N.M. 1980).

337. Mills v. Board of Educ., 348 F. Supp. 866 (D.D.C. 1972).

338. *Id.* at 876.

339. Moore & Bulman, Recent Changes in the Law Affecting Educational Hearing Procedures for Handicapped Children, 7 U. Balt. L. Rev. 41 (1977).

340. Maryland Ass'n for Retarded Citizens v. Maryland, No. 77676 (Baltimore County Cir. Ct. May 3, 1974).

341. Connecticut Ass'n for Retarded Citizens v. State Bd. of Educ., No. H-77-122, 3 MDLR 109 (D. Conn. 1978).

342. Levine v. New Jersey Dep't of Institutions & Agencies, 418 A.2d 229 (N.J. 1980).

343. New Jersey Ass'n for Retarded Citizens, Inc. v. New Jersey Dep't of Human Servs., 445 A.2d 704 (N.J. 1982).

344. Town of Burlington v. Department of Educ., 736 F.2d 773, 784-85 (1st Cir. 1984). See also Eberle v. Board of Pub. Educ., 444 F. Supp. 41 (W.D. Pa. 1977).

345. Stock v. Massachusetts Hosp. School, 467 N.E.2d 448, 453 (Mass. 1984).

346. Town of Burlington v. Department of Educ., 736 F.2d 773 (1st Cir. 1984).

347. Hoffman v. Board of Educ., 410 N.Y.S.2d 99 (App. Div. 1978); D.S.W. v. Fairbanks North Star Borough School Dist., 628 P.2d 554 (Alaska 1981).

348. Hoffman v. Board of Educ., 410 N.Y.S.2d 99 (App. Div. 1978).

349. Hoffman v. Board of Educ., 400 N.E.2d 317 (N.Y. 1979).

350. B.M. v. State, 649 P.2d 425 (Mont. 1982).

351. Peter W. v. San Francisco Unified School Dist., 60 Cal. App. 3d 814, 131 Cal. Rptr. 854 (1976); Donohue v. Copiague Union Free School Dist., 391 N.E.2d 1352 (N.Y. 1979); Smith v. Alameda County Social Servs. Agency, 90 Cal. App. 3d 929, 153 Cal. Rptr. 712 (1979); D.S.W. v. Fairbanks North Star Borough School Dist., 628 P.2d 554 (Alaska 1981); Tubell v. Dade County Pub. Schools, 419 So. 2d 388 (Fla. Dist. Ct. App. 1982); Doe v. Board of Educ., No. 125, 7 MDLR 83 (Md. Ct. App. Dec. 22, 1982).

California[353] did not wish to interfere with the professional judgment of school officials in educational matters, while the Alaska Supreme Court did not want to award monetary relief where declaratory relief that would correct the lack of proper educational services would be more effective.[354]

F. Requirements for Related Services

A variety of services necessary for a handicapped child to benefit from a special education have been required under EAHCA and to a lesser extent § 504[355] and state law.[356] These "related services,[357] as they are called, include many essential components of an individualized education program: transportation to and from schools,[358] transportation necessary to carry out another related service or extracurricular activity,[359] a self-contained classroom,[360] surrogate parents,[361] and foster placement.[362] A number of "related services" that courts have ordered are especially important for children with mental handicaps: therapy, counseling and other psychological services, residential placements,[363] specially adapted classrooms for children with brain injuries,[364] and training and counseling for the parents of a disabled child.[365]

What constitutes a related service under the EAHCA and § 504 has been addressed by the United States Court of Appeals for the Fifth Circuit in *Tatro v. Texas* (1980)[366] and by the Supreme Court in *Board of Education v. Rowley* (1982).[367] Under the EAHCA states must provide those supportive services that will help handicapped children take advantage of their special individualized education, but related services are not required when a child does not need a special education, the related service is not closely associated with the education program, or the service is one that can be provided only by a physician. Under § 504, related services are required where children would otherwise be unable to "realize the principal benefits" of their educational programs.[368]

Under the EAHCA regulations, a state agency must pay for legitimate related services even in situations where the agency does not have to pay for the education.[369] Thus, an Idaho court ruled that the state had to provide an aide for a handicapped child who was being educated in a private school at the insistence of his parents.[370] Because the interpretation is so broad, the educational related services requirement also enables children to obtain a variety of psychological services at state expense. There is substantial legal support for the proposition that therapy and counseling must be provided to emotionally disturbed youngsters, even if the state statute specifically rejects the provision of such services.[371] However, because the regulations also specify that services rendered by a physician are excludable,[372] cases have held that psychiatric services are not "related services" if they are provided as treatment and not for diagnosis or evaluation.[373] Other cases have upheld counseling in an out-of-state residential facility,[374] therapy that was part of the child's individual education plan,[375] and a residential placement for two emotionally disturbed children.[376] Moreover, even the distinction between treatment and nontreatment is somewhat tenuous, as indicated by a 1983 case that held psychotherapy in a hospital setting for an emotionally disturbed child was fundable under the EAHCA.[377]

352. Hoffman v. Board of Educ., 400 N.E.2d 317 (N.Y. 1979).

353. Smith v. Alameda County Social Servs. Agency, 90 Cal. App. 3d 929, 153 Cal. Rptr. 712 (1979).

354. D.S.W. v. Fairbanks North Star Borough School Dist., 628 P.2d 554 (Alaska 1981).

355. Mitchell v. Board of Educ., 414 N.Y.S.2d 923 (App. Div. 1979); *In re* M.W., No. S1979-1, 3 MDLR 251 (Ga. Floyd County Bd. of Educ. Mar. 6, 1979).

356. Casement v. Douglas County School Dist., No. 4935, 4 MDLR 38 (Colo. Dist. Ct. Douglas County Oct. 25, 1979); Anderson v. Thompson, 495 F. Supp. 1256 (E.D. Wis. 1980).

357. 20 U.S.C. § 1401(7).

358. Mitchell C. v. Board of Educ., 414 N.Y.S.2d 923 (App. Div. 1979).

359. Policy Memorandum of July 30, 1978, HEW Office for Civil Rights § 504 Digest of Significant Case-related Policy Clarification Memoranda, 4 MDLR 89 (1980) [hereinafter cited as Civil Rights Policy Clarification Memoranda].

360. Pinkerton v. Moye, 509 F. Supp. 107 (W.D.W. Va. 1981).

361. Although no case has specifically found an entitlement to have surrogate parents provided, Connecticut agreed as a result of a class action to provide such services. Tina A. v. Shedd, No. H 80-462, 4 MDLR 403 (D. Conn. 1980).

362. Department of Social Servs. v. Ryder, 425 N.Y.S.2d 944 (Rockland County Fam. Ct. 1980).

363. Kruelle v. New Castle County School Dist., 642 F.2d 687 (3d Cir. 1981).

364. Espino v. Besteiro, 520 F. Supp. 905 (S.D. Tex. 1981).

365. Stacey G. v. Pasadena Indep. School Dist., 547 F. Supp. 61 (S.D. Tex. 1982).

366. 625 F.2d 557 (5th Cir. 1980).

367. 458 U.S. 176 (1982).

368. Tatro v. Texas, 625 F.2d at 564.

369. 20 U.S.C. § 1401(17) (1982).

370. Thornock v. Evans, No. 78704, 7 MDLR 234 (Idaho Dist. Ct. Apr. 4, 1983).

371. 20 U.S.C. § 1401(17). "Psychological services" are specifically identified as "related services" in the act. Montana's highest court ordered the state to pay for counseling provided in an out-of-state residential facility. *In re* "A" Family, 602 P.2d 157 (Mont. 1979). In Illinois a federal district court ruled that therapy was not excludable as a medical treatment as long as it was part of the child's educational plan. Gary B. v. Cronin, No. 79C5383, 4 MDLR 26 (N.D. Ill. June 10, 1980). Also Daniels v. Kendrick, No. 16, 165-79-5, 3 MDLR 423 (Tex. Dist. Ct. Nacogdoches County May 24, 1979). And two emotionally disturbed children compelled the city of San Francisco to provide the children with a free residential placement despite the contention that they had noneducational problems. Christopher T. v. San Francisco Unified School Dist., 553 F. Supp. 1107 (N.D. Cal. 1982).

372. 20 U.S.C. § 1401(17) (1982).

373. Darlene L. v. Illinois State Bd. of Educ., 568 F. Supp. 1340 (N.D. Ill. 1983); McKenzie v. Jefferson, 566 F. Supp. 404 (D.D.C. 1983).

374. *In re* "A" Family, 602 P.2d 157 (Mont. 1979).

375. Gary B. v. Cronin, No. 79C5383, 4 MDLR 26 (N.D. Ill. June 10, 1980).

376. Christopher T. v. San Francisco Unified School Dist., 553 F. Supp. 1107 (N.D. Cal. 1982).

377. T.G. v. Board of Educ., 576 F. Supp. 420 (D.N.J. 1983).

In addition, services are not related unless they are educational in a general sense,[378] although as can be understood from the cases discussed above, the lines of demarcation are confusing when treatment is concerned. Also, in certain circumstances services may be modified to save money,[379] as, for example, where transportation must always be provided but the child is required to travel a long distance if such travel is not harmful.[380]

What will be mandated as a required, related service is determined to a large extent by the actions of the local authorities who prepare the individualized educational program (IEP). If the service is not included in the IEP, the parent must show that the service is needed to enable the child to benefit from his education. Under this standard, many of the services that courts have ordered in the past would be required today, although some, such as interpreter services for the deaf, would be questionable and in-service training for the parents might well be precluded.[381] However, in many instances the local experts may support the need for a particular service and include it in the IEP. If this occurs, the child and the parents may be in a stronger position than they were before *Rowley* was decided. In order to challenge the local decision, the state must oppose the education plan agreed upon by a consensus of the individuals who know the child best. The act's presumption in favor of the IEP would work for the benefit of the parents.

The Fifth Circuit affirmed an order to provide catheterization services so that a seven-year-old child could attend an early childhood development class rather than receive home services or be placed in a residential institution.[382] Even though the related service was not specifically identified in the IEP, the fact that the local authorities identified the special class as necessary was enough to make the catheterization necessary as well. The United States Supreme Court in a 1984 decision agreed, reaffirming much of what was implied in previous cases with respect to "related services." A unanimous Court indicated that the key factors were whether the child would be able to benefit from her free appropriate education without the special service and whether the service could be provided without the intervention of a physician.[383] It also pointed to other factors in the federal act that ensured school systems would not be overly burdened by providing "related services," including the limitation of eligibility to children who met the definition of handicapped and the fact that expensive equipment was not required.

G. Requirements for Intensive Programming

Another source of controversy in defining an appropriate education is the amount of education that should be provided for each child. How many hours of instruction each day? How many days of instruction each year? Up to what age? In general, the amount of instruction required is related to the individual needs of the child. Such intensive programming often is referred to as "compensatory education," a term that insofar as it suggests that a past deprivation is being corrected is misleading since the case law usually mandates extra instruction whenever it is needed.

The primary justification for awarding compensatory education was established in 1979 in the landmark case *Armstrong v. Kline*,[384] in which the United States Court of Appeals for the Third Circuit upheld a lower court decision that eviscerated Pennsylvania's 180-day limitation on educational programming for handicapped children and emphasized the overriding need to tailor each education program to the child's needs. Such an inflexible policy that gave every child the same amount of services was found to be incompatible with the federal education law (EAHCA). Other federal appellate courts have made the same ruling,[385] and none has disagreed with the decision.

Using largely the same reasoning as *Armstrong*, a federal district court concluded that an unwritten policy that denied mentally handicapped children educational services beyond the normal school year also was impermissible.[386] As was the case in the lower court opinion in *Kline*, the major consideration was whether the child's skills would regress during the summer months.[387] Several federal courts using the same rationale have ruled that summer school is required under § 504.[388]

Although most of the reported decisions on this subject deal with summer schooling, it seems clear from previous court decisions and administrative rulings that

378. Board of Educ. v. Rowley, 458 U.S. 176 (1982).

379. Mitchell C. v. Board of Educ., 414 N.Y.S.2d 923 (App. Div. 1979).

380. Pinkerton v. Moye, 509 F. Supp. 107 (W.D.W. Va. 1981).

381. Rettig v. Kent City School Dist., 720 F.2d 463 (6th Cir. 1983).

382. Tatro v. Texas, 703 F.2d 823 (5th Cir. 1983).

383. Irving Indep. School Dist. v. Tatro, 104 S. Ct. 3371 (1984), *aff'g* Tatro v. Texas, 625 F.2d 557 (5th Cir. 1980).

384. 476 F. Supp. 583 (E.D. Pa. 1979), *remanded sub nom.* Battle v. Pennsylvania, 629 F.2d 269 (3d Cir. 1980).

385. Georgia Ass'n of Retarded Citizens v. McDaniel, 716 F.2d 1565 (11th Cir. 1983); Crawford v. Pittman, 708 F.2d 1028 (5th Cir. 1983).

386. Georgia Ass'n of Retarded Citizens v. McDaniel, 511 F. Supp. 1263 (N.D. Ga. 1981), *aff'd*, 716 F.2d 1565 (11th Cir. 1983).

387. A federal district court in Wisconsin accepted the *Kline* approach to a large extent but added that compensatory education would not be appropriate unless it was necessary to prevent irreparable harm. Anderson v. Thompson, 495 F. Supp. 1256 (E.D. Wis. 1980), *aff'd on other grounds*, 658 F.2d 1205 (7th Cir. 1981).

388. Such services are basic to the concept of nondiscrimination and not to be viewed as "extensive modifications" inconsistent with Davis (Phipps v. New Hanover County Bd. of Educ., 551 F. Supp. 732, 734 (E.D.N.C. 1982), since children in these cases can benefit from the extra programming and the time extension does not change the size of the services that are provided. Georgia Ass'n of Retarded Citizens v. McDaniel, 716 F.2d 1565 (11th Cir. 1983).

handicapped children cannot be given less than a full day of instruction and that they are entitled to related services that extend their instruction beyond the normal school day if necessary.[389]

An obvious justification for awarding compensatory education under EAHCA is to make up for a previous mistake by the state or localities, such as delays,[390] inappropriate education,[391] or discrimination.[392] According to the United States Court of Appeals for the Tenth Circuit, a mentally retarded student in Oklahoma was able to receive schooling until he was 21 despite a state regulation limiting education to 12 years.[393] In Nebraska only children age 3 to 21 are affected by EAHCA according to the interpretation of the state's supreme court, which then made the questionable ruling that a mentally handicapped child who required additional programming beyond his twenty-first birthday to compensate for the school district's past mistakes was not entitled to such services.[394]

Recent appellate decisions suggest states may have to provide extra programming to handicapped students who have not been given proper notice and opportunity to pass competency exams for graduation.[395] While such exams are probably legal, one court held that 18 months was not sufficient time to prepare,[396] while the other court held that 3 years was more than adequate.[397] According to the United States Court of Appeals for the Seventh Circuit, deficient procedures could be remedied by giving the handicapped students additional schooling or allowing them to graduate.[398]

Conversely, Massachusetts's highest court ruled that school officials could not hasten the process of providing necessary educational services to a brain-damaged student by giving him a diploma that he had not earned.[399] By acting improperly the school district had to provide the student with compensatory education beyond the age of 22 if such services would be appropriate.

Since all cases now must be read within the limits established by the Supreme Court in *Rowley*, it is likely that additional education to prevent regression or irreparable harm or to remedy previous harm is required as long as it is contained in the IEP.[400] The case for services beyond what is called for in the IEP is more difficult to make without proof of discrepancies in the IEP formulation.

H. Plaintiff's Due Process Protections

Procedural due process is the legal mechanism through which substantive entitlements become actual benefits. With respect to educational services for handicapped children, this may mean more or less is delivered than what appeared to be promised in the federal and state statutes. The rules of the game are often more significant than the substance of the entitlements.

Under the complex federal statutes and state laws now governing the education of all handicapped children, the plaintiff's due process protections are extensive. Of particular importance are those covering: (1) the proper classification of children as handicapped, (2) the development of an individualized education program for each child, (3) the obligation, where possible, to mainstream children into the least restrictive appropriate public school setting, (4) the right to an administrative hearing, (5) the procedures to be used at that hearing, (6) the right to appeal an adverse decision, and (7) the standard of review for the courts.

There are, in addition, two types of due process questions that occur so frequently they deserve separate mention: (8) disciplinary actions, particularly suspension and expulsion, against children whose handicapping conditions include behavioral disturbance, and (9) financial disputes between parents and school officials or between school officials in more than one political jurisdiction.

1. Classification as Handicapped

The conduct of evaluations for the placement of handicapped children often raises two kinds of issues: the validity of classification procedures generally applied to all children and the legitimacy of applying cer-

389. Board of Educ. v. Rowley, 458 U.S. 176 (1982); policy memorandum of Apr. 23, 1979, Civil Rights Policy Clarification Memoranda, *supra* note 359 (transportation for extracurricular activities must be provided).

390. The city of Boston was ordered to give extended special education services to every child who experienced unnecessarily long delays in the implementation of their programs. Allen v. McDonough, No. 14948, 4 MDLR 402 (Mass. Sup. Ct. Suffolk County Aug. 19, 1980).

391. A mentally retarded adolescent in Alabama was entitled to education that extended two years past his twenty-first birthday to compensate for the inappropriate education he had received previously. Campbell v. Talledega County Bd. of Educ., 518 F. Supp. 47 (N.D. Ala. 1981).

392. The U.S. Department of Education's Office of Civil Rights ruled that a 22-year-old man was entitled to remedial educational services under § 504 in order to overcome the effects of past discrimination. *In re* Richard F., No. 01-80-1047, 4 MDLR 337 (E.D.O.C.R. June 16, 1980).

393. Helms v. Independent School Dist. No. 3, No. 82-C-752-C, 7 MDLR 397 (N.D. Okla. Aug. 29, 1983), *aff'd*, 750 F.2d 820 (10th Cir. 1984).

394. Adams Central School Dist. v. Deist, 334 N.W.2d 775 (Neb. 1983). Similarly, an Oregon appeals court found that a speech- and language-impaired child 4½ years old was too young under that state's age formulation to receive special education. Stewart *ex rel.* Stewart v. Salem School Dist. 243, 670 P.2d 1048 (Or. Ct. App. 1983). Oregon's age limit of 6 to 21 was grandfathered in by the regulations implementing the act. 34 C.F.R. § 300.300(b)(3) (1984) states a school district does not have to provide a service until a child is 6 unless it already serves 50% or more of the children in the child's age group with the same disability.

395. Brookhart v. Illinois State Bd. of Educ., 697 F.2d 179 (7th Cir. 1983); Board of Educ. v. Ambach, 458 N.Y.S.2d 680 (App. Div. 1982).

396. Brookhart v. Illinois State Bd. of Educ., 697 F.2d 179 (7th Cir. 1983).

397. Board of Educ. v. Ambach, 458 N.Y.S.2d 680 (App. Div. 1982).

398. Brookhart v. Illinois State Bd. of Educ. 697 F.2d 179 (7th Cir. 1983).

399. Stock v. Massachusetts Hosp. School, 467 N.E.2d 448 (Mass. 1984).

400. 458 U.S. 176 (1982).

tain procedures to minority children, particularly children who are black or Hispanic and subject to racial and cultural bias.

Demonstrating that a child is actually handicapped in order to determine who is entitled to special services is normally a problem of underinclusion, a failure to identify the handicap or the child with the handicap.[401] Under federal law, an emotional disturbance constitutes a mental handicap where it is both serious and due to mental illness.[402] However, social maladjustment by itself is not a handicapping condition. Thus, a child who is unable to cope with the crime, violence, drugs, and sexual permissiveness in his high school environment because of a childhood trauma is not entitled to a special education.[403]

No child, no matter what behavior is being manifested, will be considered mentally handicapped until after school officials have completed their evaluation. As a result, there is no entitlement to services before the evaluation is done.[404] Moreover, as held by the United States Court of Appeals for the Eleventh Circuit in 1983, once a child has been placed into a regular classroom with the parents' permission, the issue of whether the child is handicapped becomes moot and no relief may be sought.[405]

The automatic segregation of severely mentally retarded children into a program without an evaluation has been determined to be a violation of both EAHCA and § 504.[406] Even a more flexible formula, allowing learning disabled children to receive services if their expected achievement exceeded by 50% their actual achievement, was initially struck down.[407]

Sometimes classification procedures produce mistakes or ambiguous results that are reflected in subsequent legal proceedings. A Pennsylvania girl, for example, was alternately identified as mentally retarded and brain damaged. The significance of the label was that as a brain-damaged child she would be entitled to placement in a private residential facility while as a mentally retarded child she would remain in special public school programs. The court overruled the state, agreeing with the parents that the child was brain injured.[408] In another case, the United States Court of Appeals for the Fifth Circuit found that a father of six children, all of whom allegedly had been misplaced in classes for mentally retarded students, stated a cause of action under § 504 but that he could not collect damages unless he proved the discrimination that led to the misclassification was intentional.[409] Misclassification can also lead to lawsuits for monetary damages based on tort theory, but as was discussed earlier, most courts have automatically rejected educational malpractice as being against public policy.

Misclassification involving alleged racial discrimination has prompted considerable litigation. In such cases, normally, the problem is overinclusion of children with minority backgrounds into various classes for mentally handicapped students. In one of the earliest decisions, a federal district court in Mississippi ruled in 1977 that black children had been placed in special education classes pursuant to racially and culturally discriminatory testing procedures in violation of EAHCA.[410] The state was required to revamp its tests to insure that black children were not overrepresented in these classes.[411]

Another testing controversy for minority children is the use of intelligence quotient (IQ) tests. In a decision of first impression in 1979, *Larry P. v. Riles*, a federal district court in California concluded that the standardized tests employed by the city of San Francisco unlawfully discriminated against black children who, based on their low scores, had been segregated into special classes for mentally retarded students.[412] The resulting overrepresentation of black children in these special classes violated two legal principles. First, the IQ tests were racially and culturally biased, had never been validated, and had a "discriminatory impact" on black children by stigmatizing them and leading to their placement into inferior classes. Thus, federal statutes—EAHCA, § 504, and Title VI of the 1964 Civil Rights Act—were violated. Second, the testing procedures the school system used perpetuated discrimination and demonstrated the system's intent to segregate by the way it selected and used the tests that violated constitutional equal protection standards.[413] Recently the United States Court of Appeals for the Ninth Circuit upheld the result and reasoning of the lower court.[414]

401. U.S. Bureau of Education for the Handicapped, Progress Toward a Free Appropriate Education (Jan. 1979).

402. 20 U.S.C. § 1401(1) (1982), 34 C.F.R. § 300.5(a) (1984); Johnpoll v. Elias, 513 F. Supp. 430 (E.D.N.Y. 1980).

403. Johnpoll v. Elias, 513 F. Supp. 430 (E.D.N.Y. 1980).

404. Mrs. A.J. v. Special School Dist. No. 1, 478 F. Supp. 418 (D. Minn. 1979).

405. Powell v. Defore, 699 F.2d 1078 (11th Cir. 1983).

406. Pehowski v. Blatnik, No. 78-0030-W(H), 4 MDLR 174 (N.D.W. Va. Apr. 14, 1980).

407. Riley v. Ambach, 508 F. Supp. 1222 (E.D.N.Y. 1980). However, on appeal the decision was reversed for failure to properly exhaust administrative remedies. Riley v. Ambach, 668 F.2d 635 (2d Cir. 1981).

408. Levy v. Commonwealth, Dep't of Educ., 399 A.2d 159 (Pa. Commw. Ct. 1979).

409. Carter v. Orleans Parish Pub. Schools, 725 F.2d 261 (5th Cir. 1984).

410. Mattie T. v. Halloday, No. DC 75-31-s, 2 MDLR 177 (N.D. Miss. July 28, 1977).

411. Mattie T. v. Halloday, No. DC 75-31-s, 3 MDLR 98 (N.D. Miss. Jan. 26, 1979).

412. Larry P. v. Riles, 495 F. Supp. 926 (N.D. Cal. 1979).

413. *Id.* at 988.

414. Larry P. v. Riles, No. 80-4027, 8 MPDLR 302 (9th Cir. Jan. 23, 1984).

A very different conclusion was reached by a federal district court that reviewed the use of IQ tests in the Chicago school system. None of the statutory or constitutional provisions cited in *Riles* were found to be violated as long as the tests were used with other substantive criteria.[415] Because the plaintiffs were unable to show that the testing procedures were culturally unfair, legally no test bias existed. The court left open the possibility the result could be reconciled with *Riles* based on the factual differences in the two cases.

The United States Court of Appeals for the Second Circuit may have undercut the usefulness of Title VI for plaintiffs in these discrimination cases by overruling a lower court that had found statutory violations in New York City's method for placing black and Hispanic students in classes for the emotionally disturbed.[416] For discrimination to constitute a violation, stated the appeals court, it must be purposeful, which is rarely proven in court. However, this view was challenged by the Ninth Circuit in the *Riles* case, which required only a finding of discriminatory effect.[417]

2. Individualized Educational Program (IEP)

The EAHCA requires that every child have a written individualized education program that is reviewed annually. The child, the parents, school staff, and another individual designated by the school system must participate in the development of a program that includes evaluations of the child's performance level, a statement of immediate and long-term goals, indication of specific services that will be provided, and criteria that measure progress.[418]

The implementation of an IEP raises many questions for parents and school systems alike. The U.S. Department of Education issued a paper addressing 60 questions that have been asked concerning the IEP,[419] and there have also been numerous court interpretations.

The individual education needs of the student must be the primary implementation consideration.[420] According to the United States Court of Appeals for the Third Circuit, "school officials and parents [are] relatively unconstrained in creating individualized education programs (IEPs) for handicapped children."[421] Many of the requirements for services are initiated by the evaluation. If they are not contained in the plan, changes may be necessary. In Alabama, a federal court ruled that an IEP had to be written to provide age-appropriate training in living and vocational skills, recreation and social adjustment, significantly more contact with nonhandicapped students, summer instruction, and services past the plaintiff's twenty-first birthday.[422]

The Supreme Court has indicated that preparation of the IEP is the most critical part of the process for determining an appropriate education. Adequate compliance with procedures prescribed for developing an IEP "would in most cases assure much if not all of what Congress wished in the way of substantive content in an IEP"[423] and therefore satisfy the requirements for an appropriate education. In the words of the Fifth Circuit, the Supreme Court recognized that

> [t]he IEP is the educational blueprint that specifies how the child is to be taught, sets goals and determines how progress is to be measured. . . . [and] [a]s such . . . is the primary vehicle for implementing the requirements of the EAHCA, which has placed primary responsibility for formulating handicapped children's education in the hands of state and local school agencies in cooperation with each child's parents.[424]

This emphasis not only reduces the involvement of the courts but may well encourage greater cooperation between the parties at the planning stage.

In an important 1985 decision, Justice Rehnquist, writing for a unanimous Supreme Court, reemphasized the need for cooperative planning by defining the IEP as

> a comprehensive statement of the educational needs of a handicapped child and the specially designed instruction and related services to be employed to meet those needs § 1401(19). The IEP is to be developed jointly by a school official qualified in special education, the child's teacher, the parents or guardian, and, where appropriate, the child.[425]

3. The Least Restrictive Education Alternative

The earliest right-to-education cases endorsed the principle of providing services that constituted the least restrictive appropriate educational alternatives.[426] This concept, incorporated under EAHCA, was interpreted to mean that handicapped children have the right to be

415. Parents in Action on Special Educ. (PASE) v. Harmon, 506 F. Supp. 831 (N.D. Ill. 1980).

416. Lora v. Board of Educ., 623 F.2d 248 (2d Cir. 1980).

417. Larry P. v. Riles, No. 80-4027, 8 MPDLR 302 (9th Cir. Jan. 23, 1984).

418. 20 U.S.C. §§ 1412(4), 1413(a)(11), 1414(a)(5) (1982).

419. Education Department Issues IEP Interpretation, 5 MDLR 196 (1981).

420. *Id.* See also Battle v. Pennsylvania, 629 F.2d 269 (3d Cir. 1980); Howard S. v. Friendswood Indep. School Dist., 454 F. Supp. 634 (S.D. Tex. 1978).

421. Kruelle v. New Castle County School Dist., 642 F.2d 687, 691 (3d Cir. 1981).

422. Campbell v. Grisett, No. 79-M-277, 5 MDLR 168 (N.D. Ala. Mar. 31, 1981).

423. Board of Educ. v. Rowley, 458 U.S. 176, 206 (1982).

424. Tatro v. Texas, 703 F.2d 823, 830 (5th Cir. 1983).

425. School Committee of the Town of Burlington v. Department of Educ., No. 84-433, 9 MPDLR 203, 204 (U.S. Sup. Ct. Apr. 29, 1985).

426. Pennsylvania Ass'n for Retarded Children v. Commonwealth, 343 F. Supp. 279 (E.D. Pa. 1979); Mills v. Board of Educ., 348 F. Supp. 866 (D.D.C. 1972).

educated, to the maximum extent appropriate, with children who are not handicapped.[427] Whenever it is possible to provide the child with an appropriate education in a normalized environment, the state must do so, even where such a placement conflicts with the parents' stated wishes.[428]

The most common litigation in the early years, however, was brought by parents or guardians challenging their child's placement after the state had refused to mainstream the child in the public school. The least restrictive alternative and the requirement of an individualized education precluded using inflexible rules to categorize or place groups of handicapped student.[429]

Nevertheless, there are limits to a normalized education. An inappropriate placement is improper no matter how few restrictions it might impose on the student,[430] and an appropriate placement need not be the best possible education. Thus, a federal court in Missouri upheld that state's system of placing all severely handicapped children in separate schools as long as the school districts' interdisciplinary teams determine that such a placement is appropriate for the individual student.[431] Once what is minimally appropriate is determined, however, the least restrictive principle is the dominant factor,[432] even if the parents strongly favor a more segregated or isolated education program for their child.[433] Frequently, school systems view the requirement for the most normal setting possible as a means to avoid funding expensive private school or residential placements. At the same time, some parents view institutionalization as a better alternative for their own interests. In the past three years there has been considerable litigation in which parents have sought to place their children into private residential facilities against the recommendations of the local school authorities,[434] but parents have lost more than their share of these decisions both on the merits and because of procedural considerations having to do with maintaining the status quo during the pendency of legal proceedings.

4. Administrative and Judicial Hearing Procedures

EAHCA requires that every participating state agree to establish procedures and guidelines that enable parents or guardians to challenge the identification, evaluation, institutionalization, or program placement of their handicapped child. Among other things, these requirements include prior notice if there is to be a change in the child's program, parental access to relevant school records, an administrative hearing to air complaints, appeal to a higher state authority and to the federal or state courts, and the right of the child and the school district to maintain the existing placement while all the procedures are being exhausted.[435]

The major difficulty in providing adequate notice is determining when a change in program has occurred. At times it is not self-evident. Certainly if a child is excluded from the classroom entirely[436] or his educational program is discontinued[437] the parents are entitled to notice and procedural protections. However, modifications that do not necessarily affect the nature of the program are viewed differently. A change in physical location alone is not enough to trigger the procedural safeguards unless the move is from one school district to another.[438] The United States Court of Appeals for the Second Circuit concluded that there had been no change in placement in the transfer of handicapped children from an experimental program to a regular program in the same district even though the new placement did not duplicate the innovative curriculum at the old school and the transfer itself had been poorly planned. In the words of the court, "strong policy considerations support a restrictive interpretation."[439]

427. 20 U.S.C. § 1412(5)(B) (1982).

428. Shanberg v. Commonwealth, Secretary of Educ., 426 A.2d 232 (Pa. Commw. Ct. 1981); Fitz v. Intermediate Unit § 29, 403 A.2d 138 (Pa. Commw. Ct. 1979); Savka v. Commonwealth, Dep't of Education, 403 A.2d 142 (Pa. Commw. Ct. 1979).

429. E.g., in one case a school district's placement of all severely mentally retarded students into segregated schools was found to violate federal law. Pehowski v. Blatnik, No. 78-0030-W(H), 4 MDLR 174 (N.D.W. Va. Apr. 14, 1980). Similarly, a school district could not use administrative difficulties as a justification for not providing the most normalized appropriate education. *In re* Paul P., No. 114, 3 MDLR 187 (Pa. Secretary of Educ. Spec. Educ. App. Sept. 26, 1978). According to an agreement reached by the city of Roanoke with the U.S. Office of Civil Rights for the Department of Education, the least restrictive education for mentally retarded children should include classrooms in regular public schools, integrated transportation services, and shared use of the playground facilities. *In re* Roanoke City Pub. Schools, No. 03801083, 5 MDLR 241 (E.D.O.C.R. Dep't of Educ. Aug. 17, 1980).

430. Dewalt v. Burkholder, No. 80-0014-A, 3 Education for the Handicapped L. Rep. 551:550 (E.D. Va. Mar. 13, 1980).

431. St. Louis Developmental Disabilities Treatment Center Parents Ass'n v. Mallory, 591 F. Supp. 1416 (W.D. Mo. 1984).

432. Springdale School Dist. § 50 v. Grace, 656 F.2d 300 (8th Cir. 1981).

433. Shanberg v. Commonwealth, Secretary of Educ., 426 A.2d 232 (Pa. Commw. Ct. 1981); Fitz v. Intermediate Unit § 29, 403 A.2d 138 (Pa. Commw. Ct. 1981); Savka v. Commonwealth, Dep't of Educ., 403 A.2d 142 (Pa. Commw. Ct. 1979).

434. Smrcka v. Ambach, 555 F. Supp. 1227 (E.D.N.Y. 1983); Cain v. Yukon Pub. Schools, Dist. 1-27, 556 F. Supp. 605 (W.D. Okla. 1983); Hessler v. State Bd. of Educ., 700 F.2d 134 (4th Cir. 1983); Flavin v. Connecticut Bd. of Educ., 553 F. Supp. 827 (D. Conn. 1982); Manecke v. School Bd., 553 F. Supp. 787 (M.D. Fla. 1982).

435. 20 U.S.C. § 1415 (1982).

436. Hairston v. Drosick, 423 F. Supp. 180 (S.D.W. Va. 1976).

437. Leon R. v. Bulliard, Civ. No. H-76-327, 3 MDLR 27 (D. Conn. Sept. 20, 1978).

438. Policy memorandum of Apr. 20, 1979, Civil Rights Policy Clarification Memoranda, *supra* note 359, at 90; Brown v. District of Columbia Bd. of Educ., No. 78-1646, 3 Education for the Handicapped L. Rep. 551:101 (D.D.C. Sept. 13, 1978).

439. Concerned Parents and Citizens for the Continuing Education at Malcolm X (PS 79) v. New York City Bd. of Educ., 629 F.2d 751, 755 (2d Cir. 1980).

The initial administrative hearing must be conducted by a hearing officer who is not an employee of an agency that is involved with the child's education.[440] This rule has excluded, for example, members of the school board,[441] the director of the department of education,[442] and employees of the department of education.[443] The subsequent administrative review by the state of the local decision must also meet a test of impartiality.[444] Courts have differed on whether employees of the state education department may conduct these reviews, depending on the court's view of the employee's involvement in the special education process.[445] Only aggrieved parties may appeal administrative decisions to the courts.[446] Thus, where a school district received a favorable ruling it could not make an appeal concerning the definition of an appropriate placement.[447]

Both state and federal courts have jurisdiction over civil actions brought under EAHCA without regard to the amount in controversy. The federal statute directs the court to receive the records from the administrative proceedings, hear additional evidence at the request of either party, and adopt the preponderance of the evidence standard in reaching a decision.[448] At least one lower court has held that while there should be a thorough judicial review, special deference should be accorded to the findings of the administrative agencies.[449] The Supreme Court put forward a very similar position recently when it determined that de novo judicial review under the EAHCA is intended to guarantee that the procedures set out in the act have been followed correctly, leaving the actual educational methodology to the local and state agencies.[450] Typical is a decision in which the United States Court of Appeals for the Sixth Circuit remanded for reconsideration a lower court decision not to mainstream a severely mentally retarded child when both the administrative hearing officer and the Ohio school board had determined that the child needed some interaction with nonhandicapped children.[451] The federal district courts must give due weight to the state proceedings. Courts may countermand the states in only two situations: when the statutory procedures have not been complied with and when the IEP is not reasonably calculated to provide the child with educational benefits.[452]

As stated in the act, "[d]uring the pendency of any proceedings conducted pursuant to this section, unless the State or local educational agency and the parents or guardian otherwise agree, the child shall remain in the then current educational placement."[453] This applies whether the appeal occurs at the administrative level or in the courts. Usually, this requirement has been advantageous for the handicapped child and the parents. Occasionally, it has favored the education authorities, particularly where parents attempt to unilaterally place their children in residential facilities and recover reimbursement.[454] In Delaware, parents recovered tuition to pay for the continued education of a child with multiple handicaps at a private facility while the appeals process was being completed.[455] The same result was achieved in Massachusetts, even though the program had changed its name and was under new management.[456] Similarly, a California court ordered the state to maintain a child in a special academy, after he was supposed to have graduated, because the appeal was in progress.[457] In each of these cases the courts ordered the state to maintain the current educational placement even when there were changed circumstances. Conversely the Fourth Circuit ruled that parents could not recover tuition where they had unilaterally removed their child from the current placement, even if later it turned out that the private placement the parents selected was the appropriate one.[458]

Other circuits agreed with this basic rule but tempered it somewhat by noting that a unilateral placement before the completion of administrative proceedings would be appropriate in exceptional circumstances such as when the child's health is in danger or the school district has acted in bad faith.[459] In addition, one court ruled that where the placement was made and not objected to by the school district for two years, the placement was to be considered the current one even if it originally was made improperly by the parents.[460]

440. 20 U.S.C. § 1415(b)(1)(B) (1982).

441. Campochiaro v. Califano, No. H-78-64, 2 MDLR 558 (D. Conn. May 18, 1978).

442. Robert M. v. Benton, 622 F.2d 370 (8th Cir. 1980).

443. Smith v. Cumberland School Comm., No. 76-510, 3 MDLR 329 (D.R.I. May 29, 1979).

444. 20 U.S.C. § 1415(c).

445. Smith v. Cumberland School Comm., No. 76-510, 3 MDLR 329 (D.R.I. May 29, 1979).

446. 20 U.S.C. § 1415 (e)(2).

447. Baker v. Butler Pub. School Dist., No. 79-629-W, 4 MDLR 265 (W.D. Okla. May 22, 1980).

448. 20 U.S.C. § 1415(e)(2).

449. Laura M. v. Special School Dist. No. 1, 79 Civ. 123, 3 Education for the Handicapped L. Rep. 552:152 (D. Minn. Jan. 21, 1980).

450. Board of Educ. v. Rowley, 458 U.S. 176 (1982).

451. Roncker v. Walter, 700 F.2d 1058 (6th Cir. 1983).

452. Board of Educ. v. Rowley, 458 U.S. 176 (1982).

453. 20 U.S.C. § 1415(e)(3) (1982).

454. See cases cited in note 434 *supra*.

455. Grymes v. Delaware Bd. of Educ., No. 79-55, 5 MDLR 95 (D. Del. Jan. 7, 1981).

456. Abrahamson v. Hershman, No. 80-2513-K, 5 MDLR 93 (D. Mass. Jan. 30, 1981).

457. Cox v. Fouts, No. N13288, 4 MDLR 175 (Cal. Sup. Ct. San Diego County Jan. 8, 1980).

458. Stemple v. Board of Educ., 623 F.2d 893 (4th Cir. 1980). See also Marvin H. v. Austin Indep. School Dist., 714 F.2d 1348 (5th Cir. 1983).

459. Anderson v. Thompson, 658 F.2d 1205 (7th Cir. 1981); Adams Central School Dist. v. Deist, 334 N.W.2d 775 (Neb. 1983); Mountain View-Los Altos Union High School Dist. v. Sharron B.H., 709 F.2d 28 (9th Cir. 1983).

460. Christopher N. v. McDaniel, 569 F. Supp. 291 (N.D. Ga. 1983).

However, *Doe v. Brookline School Committee*,[461] decided by the United States Court of Appeals for the First Circuit, added a major twist to the direction of litigation when there is a dispute about changes in the current educational placement. That court determined that while a case is on appeal either party may seek to modify an existing educational program by filing a motion for a preliminary injunction and that if the requirements for a preliminary injunction are met, the status quo will be changed.

The trend noted in *Doe* of looking at the equities of the situation, as opposed to focusing solely on procedures, provided the basis for a 1985 Supreme Court decision. In *School Committee of Town of Burlington v. Department of Education*,[462] the Court set to rest many of the past controversies in this area by ruling that as long as parents ultimately prevail, they will be entitled to reimbursement, even in those instances in which they changed the child's placement on their own initiative; should they fail in court, however, then not only will parents not be able to obtain reimbursement, but the state or school district may seek reimbursement from the parents for any funds it mistakenly expended on the child's tuition while the matter was being resolved. Although such a state of equilibrium should breed caution on both sides, it is the parents, particularly parents with limited financial resources, who stand to be inhibited most by this judicial outcome.

5. Disciplinary Actions: Suspension and Expulsion

Intense controversy often results when school officials attempt to suspend or expel handicapped students who create disciplinary problems. Most courts have ruled that if the behavior is related to the handicapping condition, normally an emotional problem, EAHCA requires that full due process be afforded before the penalty of suspension or expulsion can be meted out other than as a temporary measure. Under no circumstances may students be entirely deprived of an educational program if their behavior was due to their handicap, although if students are dangerous they can be removed from the public school setting for as long as necessary.

Both nonhandicapped and handicapped students are entitled to certain due process protections before they may be disciplined, but once the process has been concluded whatever disciplinary action that is appropriate is permitted.[463] Courts have held that under both EAHCA and § 504 and their implementing regulations handicapped children deserve special consideration if their handicap is the cause of their behavioral problem. Even before the federal legislation, one federal court specifically precluded the use of expulsion or long-term suspension for any handicapped child.[464]

Stuart v. Nappi[465] in 1978 was the first major decision based on the federal legislation. In response to a motion for a preliminary injunction filed by a learning disabled high school student with limited intelligence and with emotional difficulties, a federal district court established four requirements under the EAHCA which as applied prohibited the girl's summary expulsion from school. (1) Students are entitled to an appropriate education, which she probably had not received. If there was a "causal relationship between plaintiff's academic program and her anti-social behavior," then disciplinary measures would not be justified. (2) Students are entitled to remain in their present placement until after the appeals process is exhausted, unless the student or some other students are being endangered, in which case there would be a temporary suspension during the appeals process. (3) Students have the right to be educated in the least restrictive environment whenever possible, which might be "circumvented if schools are permitted to expel handicapped children. An expulsion has the effect not only of changing a student's placement, but also of restricting the availability of alternative placements." (4) Expulsion "is inconsistent with the procedures established by the Handicapped Act for changing the placement of disruptive children. The Handicapped Act prescribes a procedure whereby disruptive children are transferred to more restrictive placements when their behavior significantly impairs the education of other children."[466]

Subsequent decisions have adopted the *Stuart v. Nappi* approach, and two courts have specifically concluded that § 504 by itself prohibits expulsion whenever the disruptive behavior is triggered by a handicap[467] or by the school's lack of resources to deal with the handicap.[468]

In a second major decision, *S-I v. Turlington*, the Court of Appeals for the Fifth Circuit defined due process entitlements under both EAHCA and § 504.[469] By way of affirming a preliminary injunction ordered by the lower court, the federal court of appeals ruled that school officials may not presume that the student's misconduct and his handicap are unrelated simply because the student understands the difference between right and wrong and does not suffer from a serious emotional

461. 722 F.2d 910 (1st Cir. 1983).
462. No. 84-433, 9 MPDLR 203 (U.S. Sup. Ct. Apr. 29, 1985).
463. Goss v. Lopez, 419 U.S. 565 (1975).
464. Mills v. Board of Educ., 348 F. Supp. 866 (D.D.C. 1972).
465. 443 F. Supp. 1235 (D. Conn. 1978).
466. *Id.* at 1241-43.
467. Sherry v. New York State Educ. Dep't, 479 F. Supp. 1328 (D.N.Y. 1979).
468. Doe v. Koger, 480 F. Supp. 225 (N.D. Ind. 1979).
469. 635 F.2d 342 (5th Cir. 1981).

disturbance. Given the remedial nature of the two federal provisions involved, state and local officials have the burden of going forward with the evidence that a student's misconduct is an outgrowth of a handicapping condition. If they do not, they must assume the conduct and the handicap are related and provide the student with an appropriate alternative placement in the least restrictive setting possible.[470]

Both the Fifth Circuit decision and a later Sixth Circuit decision agree that handicapped children can be expelled as long as there is not a "complete cessation of educational services during an expulsion period"[471] and the proper procedures are followed in changing the placement.[472] Temporary suspensions require less stringent protections—notice, an explanation of the evidence against the handicapped child, and an opportunity to refute that evidence.

6. Tuition Reimbursement and Financial Disputes

Procedural disputes over tuition reimbursement and financial obligations generate considerable litigation in the education law area whether the parties are the parents and the school authorities or squabbling jurisdictions within the same state or different states. What many people would label as procedural technicalities, as opposed to questions of merit, often have significant impact on the legal results in these disputes.

Even before the Education for All Handicapped Children Act became effective, several states passed laws that enabled handicapped children to obtain tuition reimbursement.[473] In 1980, the Connecticut Supreme Court, relying on a state statute that apportioned educational costs between the state and the local school district, ordered parents who had unilaterally placed their son into a private school to be reimbursed because the state subsequently ratified the appropriateness of the placement and the locality admitted that the public school system could not meet the child's needs.[474] Under the EAHCA, tuition reimbursement is required for all authorized placements and certain placements that are not authorized.[475]

In other situations, however, procedural requirements may result in the parents losing their petitions for reimbursement. A most noteworthy case, ***Stemple v. Board of Education,***[476] decided by the United States Court of Appeals for the Fourth Circuit before the Supreme Court's contrary ruling in the *Burlington* case discussed earlier, denied financial support to parents who had unilaterally placed their multiply handicapped child in a private school while the administrative appeals process was under way. Most United States circuit courts of appeals that interpreted this provision concluded that no reimbursement was possible if the status quo was disrupted by the parents before final deliberations were completed.[477] Parents also lost reimbursement claims when they unilaterally placed their child in an out-of-state school[478] or an in-state private school[479] instead of the designated public school placement, when they waited too long to make the necessary request for funding,[480] when they refused to allow their child to be evaluated for placement,[481] or when they failed to establish the

470. *Id.*; *In re* Austin Indep. School Dist., No. 06791572, 4 MDLR 403 (OCR HEW Aug. 1980).

471. S-1 v. Turlington, 635 F.2d at 348; Kaelin v. Grubbs, 682 F.2d 595, 600 (6th Cir. 1982).

472. Although some courts have diverged from the *Nappi* reasoning, those decisions preceded the two federal appeals court decisions above. The Iowa Supreme Court found no conflict between the school districts' expulsion powers and their duty to provide education to all handicapped children, although it ruled that before expulsion could be used there had to be a showing that no reasonable alternative placement was available. Southeast Warren Community School Dist. v. Department of Pub. Instruction, 285 N.W.2d 173 (Iowa 1979). In Minnesota, a federal court concluded since there were limited federal protections for nonhandicapped students, students could be expelled until they had been formally identified as handicapped. Mr. A.J. v. Special School Dist. No. 1, 478 F. Supp. 418 (D. Minn. 1979). Officials in South Carolina attempted to bypass the education law by bringing students into juvenile court on delinquency petitions. The strategy was successful in a case where the parents' suit under EAHCA was dismissed for failing to exhaust administrative remedies. Charles J. v. Johnson, No. 79-236 (D.S.C. 1979). It was unsuccessful where a judge dismissed the delinquency petition and reprimanded the school officials for bringing a handicapped child before the court. Garrett v. McAnville, CA No. 79-1470 (D.S.C. 1979).

473. In Rhode Island, which obligated its mental health department to pay for the care and treatment of emotionally disturbed children (R.I. Gen. Laws § 40.1-7-4(1) & (5)), an autistic child obtained educational services at a private day care center based on expert testimony that the child should be categorized as emotionally disturbed rather than mentally retarded. Naughton v. Goodman, 363 A.2d 1345 (R.I. 1976). A similar statute intended for deaf and blind children in New York was upheld over a challenge by a mentally handicapped child since it was rational for the legislature to conclude that one group was more educable than the other. Levy v. City of New York, 382 N.Y.S.2d 13, 345 N.E.2d 556 (1976). In Illinois, however, a statute that limited reimbursement for public education of mentally retarded children to $2,500 violated the state constitution, which provided for universal free education. Elliot v. Board of Educ., 64 Ill. App. 3d 229, 380 N.E.2d 1137 (1978).

474. Manchester Bd. of Educ. v. Connecticut Bd. of Educ., 41 Conn. L.J. 35, 35 (Conn. 1980).

475. A federal district court in Delaware stated that a school district had to show that it presently had the ability to meet a handicapped child's needs in a public program before it could properly deny full reimbursement to parents who placed their child in a private school. Grymes v. Madden, 672 F.2d 321 (3d Cir. 1982). Evidence that the district would develop a suitable plan later was not persuasive. In New York a reimbursement petition was not deemed to be premature even though it was filed before the school year began; the right to a free public education was considered more important than adhering to the procedural limitation. *In re* Laura A., 419 N.Y.S.2d 40 (Fam. Ct. 1979).

476. Stemple v. Board of Educ., 623 F.2d 893 (4th Cir. 1980).

477. *Id.*; Stacey G. v. Pasadena Indep. School Dist., 695 F.2d 949 (5th Cir. 1983); Anderson v. Thompson, 658 F.2d 1205 (7th Cir. 1981); Meiner v. Missouri, 673 F.2d 969 (8th Cir. 1982); Powell v. Defore, 699 P.2d 1078 (11th Cir. 1983).

478. Dubner v. Ambach, 426 N.Y.S.2d 164 (App. Div. 1980).

479. Plitt v. Madden, 413 A.2d 867 (Del. 1980).

480. *In re* Sharon R., No. H-1205, 4 MDLR 329 (N.Y. Queens County Fam. Ct. July 14, 1980); *In re* Lape, 437 N.Y.S.2d 509 (Fam. Ct. 1981).

481. Welsch v. Commonwealth, Dep't of Educ., 400 A.2d 234 (Pa. Commw. Ct. 1979).

placement was the current state-designated placement.[482]

There was, however, an exception to the general rule that parents cannot recover damages if the status quo was changed by either party. This occurred when there was a risk to the health of the child or school officials acted in bad faith.[483] Similarly, the United States Court of Appeals for the First Circuit held that in certain circumstances when it turned out that school officials were correct about a child's placement, the state or locality could seek reimbursement from the parents.[484] This, of course, put the parents in a difficult position because of the possibility of later losing on appeal and finding themselves responsible for the tuition costs. The First Circuit, unlike other courts of appeal that addressed this problem, took the view that whoever ultimately was at fault, whether it was the school district or the parents, should bear the financial burden. Thus, it disagreed with the Fourth Circuit's reasoning in *Stemple* that parents may never unilaterally remove a child from a placement and recover tuition. The preferable rule as articulated by the First Circuit in *Town of Burlington v. Department of Education*[485] is to award parents reimbursement unless the school system has the capacity to implement an appropriate IEP and in fact proposes to do so.

In 1985, the First Circuit's position was upheld by the United States Supreme Court, which, among other findings, made two points very clearly:[486] (1) reimbursement is distinctly different from awarding prospective damages under the EAHCA and thus permissible in certain situations, and (2) the party that ultimately prevails on the merits of such a dispute, regardless of any unilateral actions taken by either party, is entitled to reimbursement for funds wrongfully expended. It is the equity of the entire circumstances and not the adherence to procedures which determines entitlements to reimbursements.

Disagreements between states over payment also is of concern to the jurisdictions and the parents who must await reimbursement. In many instances, arbitrary rules are applied simply to avoid disputes, such as in North Dakota and New Hampshire, where the state supreme courts in almost identical circumstances arrived at opposite conclusions about who was responsible for educating children who moved from one district to another.[487]

The United States Supreme Court may have placed a serious limitation on the actions of some parents or guardians by allowing states to establish residency requirements that preclude education benefits for children who move into a local district for the sole purpose of attending school.[488] Such a rationale had been used previously to sustain a state lower court decision denying free tuition to a handicapped child who failed to meet the school district's residency requirements.[489]

Sometimes disputes arise between the states and the local school districts which result in unnecessary delays in the provision of appropriate educational services or the recovery of legitimate payments for services rendered.[490] In either situation it is the parents and the child who are most harmed by the disputes.

I. Procedural Limitations for Plaintiffs Under the EAHCA and § 504

As much as the EAHCA and § 504 can be seen as effective mechanisms for promoting the rights of handicapped children and their parents and guardians, there are legal protections for defendants in both pieces of legislation, which sometimes present what seem to be unreasonable limitations, complications, or potential pitfalls for plaintiffs who seek judicial relief. Three such

482. Zvi D. v. Ambach, 694 F.2d 904 (2d Cir. 1982).

483. Anderson v. Thompson, 658 F.2d 1205 (7th Cir. 1981); Adams Central School Dist. v. Deist, 334 N.W.2d 775 (Neb. 1983).

484. Doe v. Brookline School Comm., 722 F.2d 910 (1st Cir. 1983).

485. 736 F.2d 773 (1st Cir. 1984).

486. School Comm. of the Town of Burlington v. Department of Educ., No. 84-433, 9 MPDLR 203 (U.S. Sup. Ct. Apr. 29, 1985).

487. The North Dakota Supreme Court determined that a handicapped child who became a ward of the state was a resident of the district in which the wardship was begun. *In re* G.H., 218 N.W.2d 441 (N.D. 1974). Thus the original district was responsible for educating the child even though the child was attending a private school in another district. The opposite conclusion was reached by the New Hampshire Supreme Court, which determined that the district in which a child was presently residing, regardless of the reason why, was responsible for educating the child. *In re* Juvenile Case 1089, 398 A.2d 65 (N.H. 1979). A New York appeals court ruled that any county that initially provided reimbursement prior to January 1, 1974, was obligated to continue to assume that responsibility. Quogue Union Free School Dist. v. County of Suffolk, 424 N.Y.S.2d 261 (App. Div. 1980). In Illinois an appellate court ruled that financing was the responsibility of the school district where the children's parents resided, even where the children who were mentally retarded lived in a residential facility in another district. William C. v. Board of Educ., 71 Ill. App. 3d 783, 390 N.E.2d 479 (1979).

488. Martinez v. Bynum, 461 U.S. 321 (1983).

489. Connelly v. Gibbs, 112 Ill. App. 3d 257, 445 N.E.2d 477 (1983).

490. The Rhode Island Supreme Court determined that while the local educational agencies were responsible for educational expenses of emotionally disturbed children, the state mental health department was responsible for those services that "complement rather than supplement" treatment. Smith v. Cumberland School Comm., 415 A.2d 168 (R.I. 1980). An Illinois federal district court castigated the local and state agencies for their squabblings over financial responsibility which led to the "disgraceful" result of depriving a handicapped child of a free appropriate education for many months. Parks v. Pavkovic, 557 F. Supp. 1280 (N.D. Ill. 1983). In North Carolina an appeals court stated that the parents had no standing to sue for reimbursement since the county and state departments of human resources were the actual parties in conflict, although the state was still ultimately responsible for providing the child with an appropriate public education. Linder v. Wake County Bd. of Educ., 273 S.E.2d 735 (N.C. Ct. App. 1981). Finally, a Pennsylvania court ruled that a local school district could recover tuition from a private residential facility for education services the district provided to a handicapped child whose parents resided in New Jersey; education was part of the services the parents were paying the private facility to provide to the child. Nelson v. Tuscarora Intermediate Unit No. 11, 426 A.2d 1234 (Pa. Commw. Ct. 1981).

limitations are in the areas of private right of action, the Eleventh Amendment, and exhaustion of administrative remedies.

1. Private Right of Action

There is no disagreement that EAHCA provides a private right of action for injunctive or declaratory relief.[491] Similarly, all of the courts that have examined the question of injunctive or declaratory relief under § 504 have found a private right of action for handicapped children.[492] One court found that Congress did not intend to provide direct enforcement by individuals, but that finding was in a situation where the plaintiffs had failed to properly exhaust their administrative remedies.[493] With respect to § 504, the Supreme Court by refusing to address the issue of a private right of action in the 1979 case of *Southeastern Community College v. Davis*[494] left some room for doubt, despite almost unanimous judicial opinions favoring the existence of individual relief. Any further doubts should be removed now that the Supreme Court has found a private right to action for damages under § 504 for intentional employment discrimination.[495] It may be assumed that if there is any kind of private right for damages there must be a corresponding right for injunctive or declaratory relief, for damage actions are less favored in the law.

Substantial doubt remains, however, over collecting monetary damages. Under EAHCA federal appellate court decisions have ruled that either the statute affords no monetary relief[496] or it does so only in "exceptional circumstances" such as where the health of the child was jeopardized or school officials acted in bad faith.[497] At the federal district court level, there are at least two cases holding that monetary damages may be awarded under the EAHCA[498] and one federal appeals court decision allowing damages in the form of reimbursement for tuition.[499]

Until recently there had been considerable support for awarding monetary damages under § 504 generally, including a Supreme Court opinion dealing with intentional employment discrimination.[500] However, in a 1984 decision, *Smith v. Robinson*, the Supreme Court concluded that no remedies were available under § 504 for claims made coextensively with the EAHCA and that the question of remedies where the EAHCA was not applicable would have to be decided in a subsequent case.[501]

2. Eleventh Amendment

Even if monetary damages are permissible under the EAHCA or § 504, recovery may be precluded by the Eleventh Amendment: "The judicial power of the United States shall not be construed to extend to any suit in law or equity, commenced or prosecuted against one of the United States by citizens of another State, or by citizens or subjects of any foreign State." The Court of Appeals for the Eighth Circuit has so held for claims asserted against the state, its agencies and departments, and those state employees working in their official capacities.[502] Other courts generally agree, although there are exceptions and areas of disagreement in some jurisdictions.[503]

A state may waive its immunity if it does so persuasively[504] either through a statutory enactment[505] or by a

491. Board of Educ. v. Rowley, 458 U.S. 176 (1982).

492. Miener v. Missouri, 673 F.2d 969 (8th Cir. 1982); Boxall v. Sequoia Union High School Dist., 464 F. Supp. 1104 (N.D. Cal. 1979); Patton v. Dumpson, 498 F. Supp. 933 (S.D.N.Y. 1980); Rowley v. Board of Educ., 632 F.2d 945 (2d Cir. 1980), *rev'd on other grounds*, 458 U.S. 76 (1982).

493. Sherer v. Waier, 457 F. Supp. 1039 (W.D. Mo. 1977).

494. 442 U.S. 397 (1979).

495. Consolidated Rail Corp. v. Darrone, 104 S. Ct. 1248 (1984).

496. Miener v. Missouri, 673 F.2d 969 (8th Cir. 1982). See also Hines v. Pitt County Bd. of Educ., 497 F. Supp. 403 (E.D.N.C. 1980); Loughran v. Flanders, 470 F. Supp. 110 (D. Conn. 1979).

497. Anderson v. Thompson, 658 F.2d 1205, 1206 (7th Cir. 1981).

498. Boxall v. Sequoia Union High School Dist., 464 F. Supp. 1104 (N.D. Cal. 1979); Carter v. Indep. School Dist. No. 6, 550 F. Supp. 172 (W.D. Okla. 1981). Note that certain courts will award tuition reimbursement differentiating this type of payment from compensatory or punitive damages. See this chapter § IV H 6, Tuition Reimbursement and Financial Disputes, *supra*.

499. Doe v. Brookline School Comm., 722 F.2d 910 (1st Cir. 1984).

500. Consolidated Rail Corp. v. Darrone, 104 S. Ct. 1248 (1984).

501. 104 S. Ct. 3457 (1984). The Court of Appeals for the Eighth Circuit has held that monetary damages are available "as a necessary remedy for discrimination" because the existing administrative remedies are of little value to the individual; it asserted that "the right to seek money damages for civil rights violations is an accepted feature of the American judicial system." Miener v. Missouri, 673 F.2d 969 (8th Cir. 1982). Although one federal district court has endorsed this approach (Patton v. Dumpson, 498 F. Supp. 933 (S.D.N.Y. 1980)), other courts have reached a variety of different conclusions. Boxall v. Sequoia Union High School Dist., 464 F. Supp. 1104 (N.D. Cal. 1979); Sherer v. Waier, 457 F. Supp. 1039 (W.D. Mo. 1977). The Eighth Circuit subsequently limited its holding so that individuals bringing actions under both EAHCA and § 504 could seek monetary relief only where there were exceptional circumstances. Monahan v. Nebraska, 687 F.2d 1164 (8th Cir. 1982). The Fifth Circuit decided that no damages were available unless intentional discrimination could be demonstrated. Marvin H. v. Austin Indep. School Dist., 714 F.2d 1348 (5th Cir. 1983). The Seventh Circuit took the extreme view that no damages were ever recoverable because the EAHCA affords plaintiffs with an exclusive remedy that should not be altered when a § 504 claim is added. Timms v. Metropolitan School Dist., 718 F.2d 212, *amended*, 722 F.2d 1310 (7th Cir. 1983) (reaching same result on partially different grounds). And a federal court in Illinois took a more moderate approach, concluding that damages would be recoverable if the plaintiffs could show that the alleged discrimination involved a service that was not available to nonhandicapped children. William S. v. Gill, 572 F. Supp. 509 (N.D. Ill. 1983).

502. Miener v. Missouri, 673 F.2d 969 (8th Cir. 1982).

503. Stemple v. Board of Educ., 464 F. Supp. 258 (D. Md. 1979). Stubbs v. Kline, 463 F. Supp. 110 (W.D. Pa. 1978); M.R. v. Milwaukee Pub. Schools, 495 F. Supp. 864 (E.D. Wis. 1980). See also Edelman v. Jordan, 415 U.S. 651 (1974), the leading case dealing with sovereign community.

504. Miener v. Missouri, 673 F.2d 969 (8th Cir. 1982); Hark v. School Dist., 505 F. Supp. 727 (E.D. Pa. 1980).

505. Rainey v. Tennessee Dep't of Educ., No. A-3100, 1 MDLR 336 (Chancery Ct. Davidson County Jan. 28, 1977).

clear indication from Congress evidenced by an express provision, a formal intention to have the states abrogate, or substantial legislative history.[506] States' mere agreement to participate in a federal program will not be considered an abrogation without something more specific in the legislation.[507] Such specificity has been held to be missing in the EAHCA[508] and § 504.[509]

Courts have taken the position, however, that the immunity of state officials for constitutional violations is not absolute but is qualified for officials who knew or should have known of the violation.[510] In addition, state officials who are acting in their individual capacities outside the scope of their official duties are not protected by the Eleventh Amendment.[511] Moreover, a number of courts have issued injunctions that would impose indirect financial obligations upon the state by forcing it to correct a violation,[512] which is *prospective* as opposed to *retrospective* relief. Finally, if the state deliberately disobeys an injunction, the courts may issue a contempt citation and possibly an accompanying fine since the federal judiciary is preeminent over the state in these matters.[513]

3. Exhaustion of Administrative Remedies

Generally, plaintiffs must exhaust administrative remedies before they may file suit in federal court, although no exhaustion is necessary if it would be futile. Although the general rule is clear, its application to EAHCA and § 504 is not, especially where a suit is brought under both statutes at once.

A number of special education lawsuits have been dismissed because plaintiffs failed to properly exhaust administrative remedies.[514] At the same time, more than a few plaintiffs have avoided dismissal by showing that exhaustion was futile in their particular situation,[515] the available remedies would be inadequate,[516] the state's procedures fail to conform to state law,[517] or the action is part of a § 1983 Civil Rights claim.[518] One plaintiff avoided dismissal because he had already exhausted administrative remedies once and the court concluded that it was unnecessary to repeat the process each year to challenge the new individualized educational program.[519]

While most courts have concluded that exhaustion is required under the EAHCA unless some special circumstance makes the requirement unreasonable, a number of courts in reviewing § 504 have held that exhaustion is not required because meaningful administrative remedies do not exist at the federal level to vindicate personal rights.[520] This view was supported by the U.S. Department of Labor, the administering agency, which stated that a private right of action would help them to implement the law effectively,[521] and it is also supported by the existence of two analogous enforcement schemes under Title IX of the Social Security Act and under Title VI of the Civil Rights Act, which do not require exhaustion.[522]

A few court cases have required exhaustion under § 504,[523] although only one of these cases dealt with handicapped children.[524] In those jurisdictions that require exhaustion, it is still possible to bypass the requirement by also filing under § 1983 of the Civil Rights Act, which requires no exhaustion,[525] but relief may be used only to redress certain types of violations that are not covered by the EAHCA § 504.[526]

Another possibility would be to file under both EAHCA and § 504. Courts have split on the question of exhaustion where a complaint is based on both federal acts,[527]

506. Miener v. Missouri, 673 F.2d 969 (8th Cir. 1982); Hark v. School Dist., 505 F. Supp. 727 (E.D. Pa. 1980).

507. Miener v. Missouri, 673 F.2d 969 (8th Cir. 1982).

508. *Id.;* Hark v. School Dist., 505 F. Supp. 727 (E.D. Pa. 1980); Stubbs v. Kline, 463 F. Supp. 110 (W.D. Pa. 1978); Stemple v. Board of Educ., 464 F. Supp. 258 (D. Md. 1979).

509. Miener v. Missouri, 673 F.2d 969 (8th Cir. 1982). But see contra Akers v. Bolton, 531 F. Supp. 300 (D. Kan. 1981).

510. Fialkowski v. Shapp, 405 F. Supp. 946 (E.D. Pa. 1975); O'Connor v. Donaldson, 422 U.S. 563 (1975); Wood v. Strickland, 420 U.S. 308 (1975).

511. Stubbs v. Kline, 463 F. Supp. 110 (W.D. Pa. 1978); M.R. v. Milwaukee Pub. Schools, 495 F. Supp. 864 (E.D. Wis. 1980); Scheuer v. Rhodes, 416 U.S. 232 (1974).

512. M.R. v. Milwaukee Pub. Schools, 495 F. Supp. 864 (E.D. Wis. 1980).

513. Rainey v. Tennessee Dep't of Educ., No. A-3100, 1 MDLR 336 (Chancery Ct. Davidson County Jan. 28, 1977).

514. Harris v. Campbell, 472 F. Supp. 51 (E.D. Va. 1979); Sessions v. Livingston Parish School Bd., 501 F. Supp. 251 (M.D. La. 1980); Riley v. Ambach, 668 F.2d 635 (2d Cir. 1981); Timms v. Metropolitan School Dist., 722 F.2d 1310 (7th Cir. 1983).

515. Association for Retarded Citizens in Colorado v. Frazier, 517 F. Supp. 105 (D. Colo. 1981); Monahan v. Nebraska, 645 F.2d 592 (8th Cir. 1981); Medley v. Ginsberg, 492 F. Supp. 1294 (S.D.W. Va. 1980).

516. Monahan v. Nebraska, 645 F.2d 592 (8th Cir. 1981); Loughran v. Flanders, 470 F. Supp. 110 (D. Conn. 1979).

517. Association for Retarded Citizens in Colorado v. Frazier, 517 F. Supp. 105 (D. Colo. 1981); Campochiaro v. Califano, No. H-78-64, 2 MDLR 558 (D. Conn. May 18, 1978).

518. Medley v. Ginsberg, 492 F. Supp. 1294 (S.D.W. Va. 1980).

519. Selelyo v. Drury, 508 F. Supp. 122 (S.D. Ohio 1980).

520. Adashunas v. Negley, 626 F.2d 600 (7th Cir. 1980); Patton v. Dumpson, 498 F. Supp. 933 (S.D.N.Y. 1980); Association for Retarded Citizens in Colorado v. Frazier, 517 F. Supp. 105 (D. Colo. 1981).

521. Amicus curiae brief in Whitaker v. Board of Higher Educ., 461 F. Supp. 99 (E.D.N.Y. 1978); Patton v. Dumpson, 498 F. Supp. 933 (S.D.N.Y. 1980).

522. Medley v. Ginsberg, 492 F. Supp. 1294 (S.D.W. Va. 1980); Cannon v. University of Chicago, 441 U.S. 677 (1979).

523. Harris v. Campbell, 472 F. Supp. 51 (E.D. Va. 1979); Lloyd V. Regional Transp. Auth., 548 F.2d 1277 (7th Cir. 1977); Doe v. New York Univ., 442 F. Supp. 522 (S.D.N.Y. 1978).

524. Phipps v. New Hanover County Bd. of Educ., 551 F. Supp. 732 (E.D. N.C. 1982).

525. Pushkin v. Regents of the Univ. of Colorado, 658 F.2d 1372 (10th Cir. 1981).

526. Smith v. Robinson, 104 S. Ct. 3457 (1984). See also Calhoun v. Illinois State Bd. of Educ., 550 F. Supp. 796 (N.D. Ill. 1982).

527. One court has ruled that a person does not have to exhaust both administrative remedies where exhaustion requirements have been fulfilled un-

but as has been mentioned, remedies will be limited to those available under the EAHCA.

J. Attorneys' Fees

An important consideration in the provision of competent legal representation to handicapped children and their parents, especially for those plaintiffs who lack the financial resources to pay for an attorney, is the availability of attorneys' fees for the prevailing party in an education lawsuit. In the past it was possible to recover a fee award in a number of jurisdictions under a variety of federal statutes. The 1984 decision by the United States Supreme Court in *Smith v. Robinson* greatly limits such recoveries, largely resolving the questions that had arisen over attorneys' fees.[528] This decision reaffirmed that the EAHCA does not provide for attorneys' fees and determined that in a suit filed under the EAHCA there can be no recovery of such fees under either the Civil Rights Act or the Rehabilitation Act.

The majority opinion precluded attorneys' fees under § 1988 of the Civil Rights Act for two reasons. First, the due process claim upon which the § 1983 civil rights claim was based could not have been maintained independently of the EAHCA. Second, even if it were independent the plaintiffs would not have been entitled to an award because their claim had no bearing on the substantive claim on which the plaintiffs had prevailed. In essence, when different claims are presented based on different facts and legal theories, and the plaintiffs prevail only on a claim that provides for no attorneys' fees, fees will not be awarded on a separate constitutional claim brought under § 1983, except to the extent plaintiffs actually prevail under the § 1983 theory.[529]

The Court also found that in a case such as this "where . . . whatever remedy might be provided under § 504 is provided with more clarity and precision under the EHA [EAHCA], a plaintiff may not circumvent or enlarge on the remedies available under the EHA by resort to § 504." The opinion specifically stated that it did "not address a situation where the EHA is not available or where § 504 guarantees substantive rights greater than those available under the EHA.[530] Here it was determined that the § 504 claim added nothing to the petitioners' substantive right to a free appropriate public education.

Where attorneys' fees under the Rehabilitation Act are appropriate they may be awarded even if the case is settled or a consent decree is entered. The test according to one court is whether or not a party has vindicated his or her rights, which may be nothing more than obtaining an additional hour of summer school instruction for a child.[531] Fees may also be awarded for prevailing in administrative proceedings, or they may be made a part of the settlement or consent decree,[532] in which case no statutory support is required.

Three justices dissented from the Supreme Court's opinion in *Smith v. Robinson*, citing the majority's faulty analysis that created the ironic circumstance that will force handicapped children to pay the costs of having the courts interpret "a statute wholly intended to promote the educational rights of those children."[533] In particular the dissenters were dismayed by the majority's violation of the principle of statutory construction that states "conflicting statutes should be interpreted so as to give effect to each but to allow a later-enacted, more specific statute to amend an earlier, more general statute only to the extent of the repugnancy between the two statutes."[534] Thus, while it was clear that Congress intended that claimants under the EAHCA exhaust administrative remedies under that act before seeking redress in court, this did not mean they intended to preclude persons from using § 504 or § 1983 in all education-related matters involving handicapped children. Section 505 of the Rehabilitation Act and § 1988 of the Civil Rights Act were passed to provide attorneys' fees in all cases involving the deprivation of rights under each of the applicable acts. The majority's decision, argued the dissent, implies that Congress created an exception under § 505 and § 1988 only for handicapped children.

Nevertheless, one important exception already has been noted in two U.S. Court of Appeals decisions

---

der the education law. Boxall v. Sequoia Union High School Dist., 464 F. Supp. 1104 (N.D. Cal. 1979). Several courts have indicated, however, that while both administrative remedies need not be exhausted, there must be exhaustion of administrative remedies under the EAHCA, for otherwise the education procedures would be meaningless. Phipps v. New Hanover County Bd. of Educ., 551 F. Supp. 732 (E.D. N.C. 1982); Riley v. Ambach, 668 F.2d 635 (2d Cir. 1981); Calhoun v. Illinois State Bd. of Educ., 550 F. Supp. 796 (N.D. Ill. 1982). A third court found that under no circumstances will exhaustion of § 504 satisfy the requirements of the EAHCA. Akers v. Bolton, 531 F. Supp. 300 (D. Kan. 1981).

528. 104 S. Ct. 3457 (1984).

Before 1984, there was a distinct split whether decisions that were wholly or in part based on the EAHCA allowed for the recoupments of fees. According to a number of decisions the EAHCA did not provide for such awards. Tatro v. Texas, 516 F. Supp. 968 (N.D. Tex. 1981); Anderson v. Thompson, 495 F. Supp. 1256 (E.D. Wis. 1980); Hines v. Pitt County Bd. of Educ., 497 F. Supp. 403 (E.D. N.C. 1980). Other decisions suggested that where the defendants acted in bad faith, fee awards might be appropriate. Benner v. Negley, 725 F.2d 446 (7th Cir. 1984); Timms v. Metropolitan School Dist., 718 F.2d 212, *amended*, 722 F.2d 1310 (7th Cir. 1983) (reaching same result on partially different grounds).

In addition, some courts awarded attorneys' fees under other, related federal statutes.

529. Smith v. Robinson, 104 S. Ct. at 3467-70.

530. *Id.* at 3474.

531. Hilden v. Evans, No. 80-511-RE, 5 MDLR 27 (D. Or. Nov. 5, 1980).

532. Allen v. McDonough, No. 14948, 4 MDLR 404 (Mass. Sup. Ct. Suffolk County May 25, 1979); Alley v. Anne Arundel County Bd. of Educ., No. K-79-2211, 4 MDLR 179 (D. Md. Apr. 29, 1980).

533. 104 S. Ct. at 3474, 3479 (1984) (Brennan, J., dissenting, joined by Marshall & Stevens, J.J.).

534. *Id.* at 3476.

because of the high court's language suggesting that an independent due process claim may lead to an award of attorney's fees if it is brought independently of the EAHCA claim.[535]

K. Implementation of a Court Order or Consent Decree

If the plaintiffs are successful, strategies for implementing the decision or decree become of primary concern. As in other areas of civil rights, moving state bureaucracies can be difficult, particularly where implementation involves a large class of individuals. The three most frequently used implementation tools in recent times have been consent decrees, special masters, and contempt of court citations.

Consent decrees between the parties and approved by the courts, used by themselves or in combination with other methods to encourage obedience, have the advantage of representing an understanding rather than being a direct order. Two of the first major education cases were settled through the use of consent decrees, one before an order was issued[536] and one afterwards.[537] The difference is that in the former situation the defendants admitted no liability and reached a negotiated settlement[538] whereas in the latter situation there was a judicial finding of wrongdoing.[539]

Special masters may be appointed to monitor the implementation process for the court and to hold hearings to attempt to settle disputes as they arise.[540] Often courts will allow the state an opportunity to implement the decree through the state's own administrative resources before stepping in with a master,[541] and sometimes the master will be appointed at the beginning of the implementation process.[542]

Contempt of court citations against the state or state officials are normally employed only when the state is extremely resistant.[543] Issuing a contempt citation usually indicates a long and slow implementation process. In the District of Columbia, for example, the court has now spent more than ten years trying to enforce the requirements it originally set down in *Mills v. Board of Education* in 1972.[544]

V. LEGALLY ENFORCEABLE EMPLOYMENT OPPORTUNITIES

While employment cannot be the answer for the financial needs of all mentally disabled persons, the social investment necessary to make them employable is worthwhile even if the training process requires the teaching of new skills. Unfortunately, in addition to overcoming the effects of their disabilities, mentally impaired persons have to overcome the high unemployment rate and the stigma of their handicaps in order to earn a legitimate employment opportunity. Although some people are successful, overall the results are not encouraging. Mentally disabled applicants or employees have been found to face "outright refusal by employers to hire them; self-doubts created by prejudice; and rigid physical [or mental] examinations, the validity of which is accepted by employers without question."[545] This type of discrimination has been fought with limited success through litigation, legislation, and affirmative action proposals.

A. Constitutional Requirements

The United States Constitution provides only limited protection against employment discrimination. Normally, private employers are effectively outside the scope of constitutional requirements, except in the rare instances where their business is so entangled with the government that their actions are considered to be the actions of the state.[546] However, in those relatively few instances where "state action" is involved, particularly with governmental or public employers, discrimination on the basis of mental handicaps is subject to the prohibitions imposed by due process, equal protection, and the right to privacy.[547]

Due process arguments under the Fifth and Fourteenth Amendments have been successful where there is an entitlement to or even an expectation of employment.[548] If a property interest can be established, then

535. Teresa Diana P. v. Alief Indep. School Dist., 744 F.2d 484 (5th Cir. 1984); Rose v. Nebraska, No. 83-2678, 9 MPDLR 138 (8th Cir. Nov. 26, 1984).

536. Pennsylvania Ass'n for Retarded Children v. Commonwealth, 343 F. Supp. 279 (E.D. Pa. 1972).

537. Mills v. Board of Educ., 348 F. Supp. 866 (D.D.C. 1982).

538. Pennsylvania Ass'n for Retarded Children v. Commonwealth, 343 F. Supp. 279 (E.D. Pa. 1972); see also P-1 v. Shedd, No. 78-58, 3 MDLR 167 (D. Conn. Mar. 23, 1979).

539. Mills v. Board of Educ., 348 F. Supp. 866 (D.D.C. 1972); Mattie T. v. Halloday, No. DC 75-31-S (N.D. Miss. Jan. 26, 1979).

540. Gary W. v. Louisiana, 601 F.2d 240 (5th Cir. 1979); P-1 v. Shedd, No. 78-58, 3 MDLR 167 (D. Conn. Mar. 23, 1979).

541. Gary W. v. Louisiana, 601 F.2d 240 (5th Cir. 1979); P-1 v. Shedd, No. 78-58, 3 MDLR 167 (D. Conn. Mar. 23, 1979).

542. P-1 v. Shedd, No. 78-58, 3 MDLR 167 (D. Conn. Mar. 23, 1979).

543. Mills v. Board of Educ., 348 F. Supp. 866 (D.D.C. 1972); Rainey v. Tennesee Dep't of Educ., No. A-3100, 1 MDLR 336 (Tenn. Ch. Ct. Davidson County Jan. 28, 1977).

544. Mills v. Board of Educ., No. 1939-71, 4 MDLR 267 (D.D.C. June 18, 1980).

545. Weiss, Equal Employment and the Disabled: A Proposal, 10 Colum. J.L. & Social Probs. 457, 458 (1974).

546. Comment, The Equal Protection and Due Process Clauses: Two Means of Implementing "Integrationism" for Handicapped Applicants for Public Employment, 27 DePaul L. Rev. 1169, 1173–74 (1978) [hereinafter cited as Comment, The Equal Protection and Due Process Clauses].

547. Legal Issues in State Mental Health Care: Proposals for Change: Discrimination, 2 MDLR 510, 510–11 (1978) [hereinafter cited as Legal Issues: Discrimination].

548. Comment, The Equal Protection and Due Process Clauses, *supra* note 546, at 1189–90.

the mentally disabled individual may rightfully challenge any denial of employment, limitation of benefits, or dismissal that fails to comply with minimal due process.[549] Due process prohibits the use of irrebuttable presumptions of mental unfitness[550] and inflexible policies that deny employment to or adversely affect the employability of a person based on the existence of a mental impairment without providing the individual with the opportunity to demonstrate an ability to do the job competently.[551]

Equal protection standards, of which there have been basically three, have not substantially affected employment discrimination based on mental handicap. The strictest standard, which requires the state to demonstrate a compelling interest before it may properly use special criteria for employing or dismissing mentally disabled persons, is not generally applicable to employees.[552] Very few courts have found that the mentally disabled are members of a requisite vulnerable and insular minority entitled to special protection under the Constitution, nor have they found that employment is a fundamental concern.[553] As a general rule, courts have been far more likely to apply less strict standards where employment issues are at stake.[554]

Both the intermediate and the rational relationship tests have been interpreted in ways that give the "state" the benefit of the doubt as to the legitimacy of the identified governmental objective[555] if minimal due process is followed. Moreover, a very recent United States Supreme Court decision makes it clear that strict and heightened scrutiny will no longer be applicable to mentally disabled persons.[556]

The same kinds of limitations are found under a right to privacy action where a job applicant complains that an employer asked about his mental health history.[557] The legal propriety of such an inquiry is determined by a standard that measures the importance of the liberty interest against the governmental objective involved.[558] Rarely have courts found that mentally disabled plaintiffs possess fundamentally important privacy interests that need special protection from governmental incursions.[559]

B. Federal Statutes

One major factor accounting for the relative success or failure of various legal steps taken against employment discrimination has to do with the status of the employer. Public employers, particularly those in government, have become more responsive to the employment needs of handicapped workers than most private employers. Arguably this is so not only because of the less competitive setting provided by public employers, but also because of the additional obligations created by federal and state legislation.

The full force of the Rehabilitation Act of 1973 is focused on employment through Title V, especially §§ 504, 503 and 501.[560] A "handicapped" person, in the current codification, is defined as one "who (i) has a physical or mental impairment which substantially limits one or more of such person's major life activities, (ii) has a record of such an impairment, or (iii) is regarded as having such an impairment."[561]

Each of the sections under Title V differs in terms of the requirements it imposes on employers who are financially connected with the federal government: § 504 prohibits discrimination in programs or activites that are recipients of federal assistance;[562] § 503 requires federal contractors to take affirmative steps to hire the handicapped;[563] and § 501 is an affirmative action program for handicapped applicants to federal jobs or employees working for the federal government.[564]

This crucial federal legislation has been legitimately described as "the greatest step taken by the federal government to guarantee equal employment to the dis-

549. Davis v. Bucher, 451 F. Supp. 791 (E.D. Pa. 1978). See also Gurmankin v. Costanzo, 556 F.2d 184 (3d Cir. 1977) [blind teacher]; American Bar Association Commission on the Mentally Disabled, Prohibiting Discrimination Against Developmentally Disabled Persons 23 (1978) [hereinafter cited as A.B.A. Comm'n, Prohibiting Discrimination].

550. Irrebuttable presumption of physical incompetence of pregnant teachers found to violate due process by United States Supreme Court in Cleveland Bd. of Educ. v. La Fleur, 414 U.S. 632 (1974); A.B.A. Comm'n, Prohibiting Discrimination, *supra* note 549.

551. Davis v. Bucher, 451 F. Supp. 791 (E.D. Pa. 1978); A.B.A. Comm'n, Prohibiting Discrimination, *supra* note 549; Lang, Employment Rights of the Handicapped, 11 Clearinghouse Rev. 703 (1977). See also Gurmankin v. Costanzo, 556 F.2d 184 (3d Cir. 1977).

552. See Comment, The Equal Protection and Due Process clauses, *supra* note 546, at 1174–76.

553. *Id.*

554. Legal Issues: Discrimination, *supra* note 547, at 511. See, e.g., Arnett v. Kennedy, 416 U.S. 134 (1974); Cafeteria Workers v. McElroy, 368 U.S. 886 (1961); Wieman v. Updegroff, 344 U.S. 183 (1952).

555. See Weiss, *supra* note 545, at 468–70.

556. City of Cleburne v. Cleburne Living Center, Inc., No. 84-468 (U.S. Sup. Ct. July 1, 1985).

557. Legal Issues: Discrimination, *supra* note 547, at 511; Doe v. Syracuse School Dist., 508 F. Supp. 333 (N.D.N.Y. 1981); 45 C.F.R. § 84.14 (1984).

558. Duffy, Privacy vs. Disclosure: Balancing Employee and Employer Rights, 7 Employee Rel. L.J. 594 (1982).

559. *Id.*

560. Rehabilitation Act of 1973. Pub. L. No. 93-112, 87 Stat. 355, 390, 393–94 (1973) (§§ 504, 503, & 501 codified as amended at 29 U.S.C. §§ 794, 793, 791 (1982) respectively).

561. Codified at 29 U.S.C. § 706(7)(B) (1982). To the original definition of a handicapped individual was added a limiting second sentence: "For purposes of sections 793 and 794 of this title as such sections relate to employment, such term does not include any individual who is an alcoholic or drug abuser whose current use of alcohol or drugs prevents such individual from performing the duties of the job in question or whose employment, by reason of such current alcohol or drug abuse, would constitute a direct threat to property or the safety of others."

562. 29 U.S.C. § 794.

563. 29 U.S.C. § 793.

564. 29 U.S.C. § 791.

abled,"[565] but at the same time the provisions may be criticized for their loopholes, exceptions, and enforcement difficulties.

Unlike Title VII of the Civil Rights Act, which does not apply to the handicapped, the Rehabilitation Act regulates only private employers who are recipients of federal funds or contracts, although disability groups have unsuccessfully attempted to expand Title VII to include handicapped individuals.[566] In addition to this common fundamental characteristic, each of the three provisions has its own peculiar limitations as well.

1. Section 504

A general private right of action under § 504 is virtually a certainty.[567] In 1984, the United States Supreme Court in *Consolidated Rail Corporation v. Darrone*[568] ruled that there is a private right specifically to recover back pay for intentional employment discrimination.[569] Logic would dictate that this at least means handicapped individuals may also bring lawsuits for injunctive and declaratory relief for employment discrimination since damage actions are the least favored in the law.[570] What constitutes the present status with respect to nonintentional employment discrimination claims for damages is still uncertain. The lower courts have been split over the issue of damages in § 504 cases generally, but more recently the trend, especially as reflected in education cases, has been to allow such suits.[571] The Court of Appeals for the Ninth Circuit ruled that an administrative law judge had erred in not awarding back pay to an employee who had proved he had been the victim of unintentional handicap discrimination. The court noted that if the employer wished to use employment criteria to exclude a handicapped person, the criteria had to be directly connected with and substantially promote business and safe performance. Otherwise, the necessary discrimination was shown and damages for back pay could be awarded.[572]

The Supreme Court's decision in the *Darrone* case also settled one of the most vexing procedural problems facing litigants in employment discrimination cases under § 504 by finding that handicapped job applicants or employees who wish to file suits do not have to demonstrate that a primary objective of the federal funds received by their employers is to provide employment.[573] It is enough that the employers receive federal funds. Prior to this decision, many lower courts, including a substantial majority of the United States circuit courts of appeals that had reviewed the question, were convinced that a contrary ruling was correct.[574] In *Trageser v. Libbie Rehabilitation Center, Inc.* (the leading case until *Darrone*), decided just after the 1978 amendments to the act became effective, the United States Court of Appeals for the Fourth Circuit had concluded that those amendments wholly incorporated the remedies, procedures, and rights of Title VI of the Civil Rights Act, including the provision in § 604 that prohibits legal actions "except where a primary objective of the Federal financial assistance is to provide employment."[575] Courts of Appeal in the Second, Fifth, Seventh, Eighth, and Ninth Circuits adopted the reasoning of *Trageser*.[576] The Third and Eleventh Circuits, most commentators,[577] and a unanimous Supreme Court were persuaded that Congress had no intention of reducing preexisting rights by including Title VI protections because the express purpose of the amendment was to "*expand* the remedies available under the Act," not to reduce existing rights in a "deft, unheralded maneuver."[578] The language, legislative history, and executive agency interpretation of the amendment supported their position.[579]

The elimination of the primary objective requirement for individual lawsuits also eliminates similar con-

565. A.B.A. Comm'n, Prohibiting Discrimination *supra* note 549, at 3, citing Weiss, *supra* note 545, at 466.

566. A law review article in 1974 recommended that Title VII be expanded to insure equal employment for the handicapped. Weiss, *supra* note 545.

567. A vast majority of courts that have addressed the question recognize a private remedy. See, e.g., Prewitt v. United States Postal Serv., 662 F.2d 292 (5th Cir. 1981); Coleman v. Darden, 595 F.2d 533 (10th Cir. 1979); Rogers v. Frito Lay, Inc., 611 F.2d 1074 (5th Cir. 1980); Doe v. Syracuse School Dist., 508 F. Supp. 333 (N.D.N.Y. 1981); Camenisch v. University of Texas, 616 F.2d 127 (5th Cir. 1980); Coleman v. Casey County Bd. of Educ., 510 F. Supp. 301 (W.D. Ky. 1980); Reynolds v. Ross, 25 Fair Empl. Prac. Cas. (BNA) 462 (N.D.N.Y. 1981).

568. 104 S. Ct. 1248 (1984).

569. Although the Supreme Court initially declined to uphold a private right of action in Southeastern Community College v. Davis, 442 U.S. 397 (1979), it recently found a private right for monetary damages where intentional employment discrimination was alleged. Consolidated Rail Corp. v. Darrone, 104 S. Ct. 1248 (1984).

570. J. Parry, Summary, Analysis and Commentary, 8 MPDLR 262 (1984).

571. *Id.* Miener v. Missouri, 673 F.2d 969 (8th Cir. 1982); Manecke v. School Bd., 553 F. Supp. 78 (M.D. Fla. 1982). See contra Timms v. Metropolitan School Dist., 718 F.2d 212, *amended*, 722 F.2d 1310 (7th Cir. 1983) (reaching same result on partially different grounds).

572. Bentivegna v. United States Dep't of Labor, 694 F.2d 619 (9th Cir. 1982).

573. Consolidated Rail Corp. v. Darrone, 104 S. Ct. 1248 (1984).

574. Trageser v. Libbie Rehabilitation Center, 590 F.2d 87 (4th Cir. 1978), *cert. denied*, 47 U.S.L.W. 3811. Carmi v. Metropolitan St. Louis Sewer Dist., 620 F.2d 672 (8th Cir. 1980); Simpson v. Reynolds Metals Co., 629 F.2d 1226 (7th Cir. 1980); Brown v. Sibley, 650 F.2d 760 (5th Cir. 1981); United States v. Cabrini Medical Center, 639 F.2d 908 (2d Cir. 1981); Scanlon v. Atascadero State Hosp., 677 F.2d 1271 (9th Cir. 1982).

575. 590 F.2d 87 (4th Cir. 1978).

576. See cases listed in note 574 *supra*.

577. Jones v. Metropolitan Atlanta Rapid Transit Auth., No. 81-7746, 6 MDLR 314 (11th Cir. Aug. 6, 1982); Le Strange v. Consolidated Rail Corp., 687 F.2d 767 (3d Cir. 1982).

578. Hart v. County of Alameda, 485 F. Supp. 66, 72 (N.D. Cal. 1979) (emphasis in original).

579. Consolidated Rail Corp. v. Darrone, 79 L.Ed. 2d 568, 104 S. Ct. 1248 (1984).

cerns about which level of funding (the state, the institutions, or the individual program) is primary for the purpose of ascertaining who is a recipient of federal employment monies.[580] However, the more general problem of determining what is a program or activity receiving federal financial assistance is not yet resolved. At the end of the *Darrone* opinion there was a brief discussion of that issue. Citing *Grove City College v. Bell*,[581] another Supreme Court decision issued on the same day, the Court stated that it was obvious to them that the program or activity "language limits the ban on discrimination to the specific program that receives federal funds" as opposed to being applicable to an entire institution, office, or corporation if one of its program or activities is funded.[582] What remained unclear to the justices was the precise distinction between the broader and more narrow entities, which in most instances would be determined on a case by case basis. In *Grove City* the federal financial aid office was the recipient and not the entire college because the mere fact that the federal assistance augmented the college's general operating budget was not determinative. There had to be something greater than a ripple effect alone which would allow for a more exact measurement of the federal funds' influence on the larger entities' economic situation and its actual relationship to the federal government. Justices Brennan and Marshall dissented[583] in *Grove City* because they were convinced that the applicable federal regulations made no distinction between an institution and its programs or activities as long as the institution benefited from the monies. Justice Stevens concurred in order to point out that the majority's discussion of the program or activity requirement was unnecessary to the decision and ill advised based as it was on inadequate evidence at trial.[584] In reaction to the decision, unsuccessful legislation was filed in both houses of Congress in 1984 to make it clear that in all three pieces of civil rights legislation including § 504 the receipt of federal aid means both direct and indirect assistance.[585] The bills had substantial congressional support but reportedly were opposed by the Department of Justice on behalf of the United States government. In 1985 new legislation was submitted, one version similar to the 1984 legislation and the other version more agreeable to the Justice Department, which would limit the legislation's applicability to educational institutions.[586]

In addition to the questions about receipt of federal assistance, employment discrimination suits are subject to all the other § 504 limitations previously discussed in the education section: the disputed need to exhaust administrative remedies, narrow definitions of otherwise qualified handicapped persons, and the potential nonavailability of monetary damages.

What all the uncertainties add up to is that despite the significant litigation in this area, only a few decisions have upheld employment discrimination complaints filed by mentally or developmentally disabled persons.

Three § 504 cases are different because they were decided before the 1978 amendments became effective and, as a result, indicate the potential scope of the legislation now that *Trageser* has been overruled. In those decisions former drug users overturned a policy of the City of Philadelphia which denied them employment solely on the basis of their past drug abuse,[587] a professor in an alcohol rehabilitation program was able to maintain a discrimination action relating to his university tenure,[588] and a man with a history of epilepsy obtained a restraining order so that he would not be denied the opportunity to take an entrance exam for admission to the Michigan police academy.[589]

Two nonemployment discrimination cases are important because the principles are directly applicable to the employment situation. In one, a woman seeking readmission to medical school after having taken a leave of absence to deal with a serious psychiatric problem was able to sue the university.[590] However, other limitations attendant to § 504 prevented her from obtaining a preliminary injunction so that she could be readmitted during the pendency of the legal proceedings.[591] The Court of Appeals for the Second Circuit concluded that she was not "an otherwise qualified handicapped person."[592] Even though the trial court held that more likely than not she would be a successful student, the appeals court ruled that the university did not have to accept the substantial risk that she might still fail to meet the requisite stan-

580. Sabol v. Board of Educ., 510 F. Supp. 892 (D.N.J. 1981); Brown v. Sibley, 650 F.2d 760 (5th Cir. 1981); Miller v. Abilene Christian Univ., 517 F. Supp. 437 (N.D. Tex. 1981); Simon v. St. Louis County, 497 F. Supp. 141 (E.D. Mo. 1980); Guertin v. Hackerman, 496 F. Supp. 593 (S.D. Tex. 1980).

581. 104 S. Ct. 1211 (1984). The case dealt with sex discrimination under Title IX, which has a provision that is similar in language to § 504.

582. 104 S. Ct. at 1248, 1255 (1984).

583. 104 S. Ct. at 1211, 1226-37.

584. *Id.* at 1225.

585. S. 2568 and H.R. 5490, *described in* 8 MPDLR 416 (1984).

586. S. 431 — the Civil Rights Restoration Act of 1985 — and its companion bill H.R. 700 would define program or activity to mean all operations of an entity receiving federal assistance, while S. 272 and its companion bill H.R. 2061 would limit its scope to educational institutions receiving federal funding. 9 MPDLR 143, 223-24 (1985).

587. Davis v. Bucher, 451 F. Supp. 791 (E.D. Pa. 1978).

588. Whitaker v. Board of Higher Educ., 461 F. Supp. 99 (E.D.N.Y. 1978).

589. Fast v. Ross, Civ. No. G-78-775, 3 MDLR 34 (W.D. Mich. Dec. 11, 1978).

590. Doe v. New York Univ., 666 F.2d 761 (2d Cir. 1981). Since the case did not involve employment directly, the limitations in Trageser v. Libbie Rehabilitation Center, 590 F.2d 87 (4th Cir. 1978), did not apply.

591. Doe v. New York Univ., 666 F.2d at 761, 779.

592. *Id.* at 762.

dards. Normally, the burden is upon the applicant to show that she is either qualified despite her handicap or as well qualified as applicants who were admitted into the program. The exception is where the defendants fail to even rebut the original inference of discrimination, in which case a plaintiff would automatically prevail.

In the other case,[593] a doctor was denied admittance into a psychiatric residency program because he had multiple sclerosis. Here discrimination was found by the lower court and affirmed by the United States Court of Appeals for the Tenth Circuit because the doctor established a prima facie case that he was qualified for the residency program apart from his handicap and was rejected under circumstances that indicated the judgment was made on the basis of his handicap. He met the requisite academic standards by having earned an M.D. degree and obtaining a letter from the dean of the medical school he attended indicating satisfactory performance. The defendants in turn did not meet their burden of showing that he was rejected for reasons other than his handicap. Both the Second and the Tenth Circuits agreed that intentional discrimination did not have to be demonstrated and used similar standards to determine whether the plaintiffs were otherwise qualified handicapped persons. However, the two courts differed on the emphasis to be placed on being minimally qualified. The Second Circuit focused on the differences of the plaintiff that created a risk, and the Tenth Circuit was persuaded by the doctor's satisfactory record.

A 1985 United States Supreme Court decision provides strong support for the view that in order to prove handicap discrimination under § 504, a plaintiff need not necessarily show that the defendant acted purposefully. In the context of a Medicaid dispute, a unanimous Court found the effects of benign neglect to be covered along with those of invidious discrimination. "While we reject the boundless notion that all disparate-impact showings constitute prima facie cases under § 504, we assume without deciding that § 504 reaches at least some conduct that has an unjustifiable impact upon the handicapped." In reviewing the application of this provision to future disputes, the justices reemphasized the value of the notion of reasonable accommodation.[594]

Another even more recent Supreme Court decision, however, *Atascadero State Hospital v. Scanlon*,[595] added a new and potentially substantial limitation to all § 504 litigation. A 5-to-4 majority opinion written by Justice Powell found that the state of California had not waived, nor had Congress waived, California's Eleventh Amendment immunity. In order for any state to complete such a waiver there must be a clear manifestation of intent to do so since as a constitutional matter such an abrogation of state power by the federal judiciary cannot be viewed lightly. Thus, an applicant for employment at a California state mental hospital who was physically handicapped could not bring suit against the state or its officials under § 504. Justice Brennan, writing for the four dissenters, presented a lengthy and detailed analysis supporting their belief that "the Court's Eleventh Amendment doctrine diverges from text and history virtually without regard to underlying purposes or genuinely fundamental interests."[596]

Only a few cases have been decided, since the 1978 amendments became effective, in which mentally or developmentally disabled plaintiffs have avoided a summary dismissal by demonstrating they had stated a proper cause of action under § 504. In one case, a man who had suffered a nervous breakdown in the air force and then applied for a teaching position was entitled to summary relief because the job application included a question about whether he had ever had a nervous breakdown or had been a recipient of psychiatric treatment.[597] Federal regulations expressly prohibit the use of preemployment application inquiries concerning the existence, nature, or severity of a handicap.[598]

In a second case, a nursing assistant with epilepsy was able to win back his job after being medically disqualified from his position with the Veterans Administration. The court found that he was otherwise qualified because his condition did not interfere with his duties or prevent him from fully performing his job. Thus, he was entitled to a reasonable accommodation that would not be overly burdensome to the hospital such as supervising his medication levels while he worked or giving him a clerical position. He received $15,000 in back pay as well as his old job.[599]

The United States Court of Appeals for the Fifth Circuit affirmed a lower court that had overturned a jury verdict in favor of a psychiatric worker suffering from severe emotional problems.[600] The jury had awarded her $25,000 in damages after she had been terminated from her position, but the trial court ruled that the evidence failed to support a violation under § 504. There was a reasonable basis for finding the nurse was not otherwise qualified based on her suicidal tendencies over a long

593. Pushkin v. Regents of Univ. of Colorado, 658 F.2d 1372 (10th Cir. 1981).

594. Alexander v. Choate, 105 S. Ct. 712, 720 (1985).

595. 53 U.S.L.W. 4985 (U.S. Sup. Ct. June 28, 1985).

596. *Id.* (dissenting opinion) at 4989.

597. Doe v. Syracuse School Dist., 508 F. Supp. 333 (N.D.N.Y. 1981).

598. *Id.*; 45 C.F.R. § 84.14 (1984).

599. Smith v. Administrator of Veterans Affairs, 32 Fair Empl. Prac. Cas. (BNA) 986 (C.D. Cal. 1983).

600. Doe v. Region 13 Mental Health-Mental Retardation Comm'n, 704 F.2d 1402 (5th Cir. 1983).

period of time, her past hospitalization for her problems, and evidence that her condition was deteriorating.

2. Section 503

A number of courts have found a private right of action under § 503.[601] Among the arguments persuading them are the following: § 503 should be interpreted the same as other antidiscrimination statutes that provide private remedies,[602] after § 503 was passed a number of people in Congress stated that it had intended to create a private right of action,[603] the 1978 amendments assumed the existence of private litigation in passing an attorneys' fees amendment,[604] and the federal administrative agency in charge of enforcing § 503 stated that the existence of a private remedy reinforced the administrative scheme.[605]

Nevertheless, most courts, including all the federal circuit courts that have ruled on the question, disagree that a private remedy is available.[606] They counter with the following arguments: § 503 is an affirmative action covenant intended to promote general public interests over the interests of the members of a specific group,[607] congressional expressions subsequent to § 503's passage were not persuasive regarding what was meant at the time of its enactment, only minimal weight should be given to the fact that the 1978 amendments provided for attorneys' fees since they can be awarded for administrative work, and the existence of an express administrative remedy, coupled with the absence of language about a private remedy, suggested that a private remedy was inconsistent with the administrative enforcement scheme.

Even in those jurisdictions that recognize individual relief under § 503, there are other requirements that must be met before a plaintiff can proceed to the merits of a complaint.

One limitation, the exhaustion of administrative remedies, has not proved to be an unmovable obstacle in practice. Those jurisdictions that accept the notion of a private § 503 remedy have been receptive to arguments that exhaustion is futile or unnecessary.[608] Often the issue is never raised.[609] Two different New York plaintiffs, both with epilepsy, made successful challenges to hiring and employment practices of federal contractors and were not required to pursue administrative relief first. One federal district court explained that because the U.S. Department of Labor had such a backlog of cases there was no assurance that any complaint would be decided within a reasonable amount of time and that in any case there were no provisions for individual relief.[610] The other federal district court noted that "neither the participation of the aggrieved individual nor individual relief is provided by the administrative remedies."[611]

Another potential limitation is the intended scope of the provision, since the Department of Labor has ruled that § 503 applies to federal contractors only when they are working on contracts or projects that are directly funded with federal money.[612] Apparently, the contractor can legally discriminate or fail to incorporate affirmative action guidelines in those projects that are not receiving federal money.

In addition, not even all handicapped plaintiffs are covered. Only those individuals who have a "substantial handicap to employment" fall within the statute.[613] Especially with mental impairments, the substantial requirement could prove to be troublesome since the concept of a substantial mental impairment is difficult to evaluate using traditional psychiatric diagnosis.[614]

If a private right of action is foreclosed under § 503, the individual complainant does have the option of requesting the U.S. Department of Labor to conduct an investigation.[615] Where a violation is proved, among the

601. E.g., California Paralyzed Veterans Ass'n v. F.C.C., 496 F. Supp. 125 (C.D. Cal. 1980); Clarke v. FELEC Servs., Inc., 489 F. Supp. 165 (D. Alaska 1980).

602. Analysis that follows is taken from Summary and Analysis, 4 MDLR 71-72 (1980), which compares Rogers v. Frito Lay, Inc., 611 F.2d 1074 (5th Cir. 1980); Chaplin v. Consolidated Edison Co. of N.Y., 482 F. Supp. 1165 (S.D.N.Y. 1980), and the dissent in *Rogers*.

603. Summary and Analysis, *supra* note 602, at 71-72.

604. *Id.*; see also House Comm. on Educ. & Labor, H. Rep. No. 1149, Rehabilitation, Comprehensive Services, and Development Disabilities Amendments of 1978, 95th Cong., 2d Sess., 2, 21, *reprinted in* 1978 U.S. Code Cong. & Ad. News 7312, 7313, 7332.

605. Summary and Analysis, *supra* note 602.

606. Painter v. Horne Bros., 710 F.2d 143 (4th Cir. 1983); Hoopes v. Equifax, Inc., 611 F.2d 134 (6th Cir. 1979); Rogers v. Frito Lay, Inc., 611 F.2d 1074 (5th Cir. 1980), *cert. denied*, 449 U.S. 889 (1980); Simpson v. Reynolds Metals Co., 629 F.2d 1226 (7th Cir. 1980); Brown v. Sibley, 650 F.2d 760 (5th Cir. 1981); Davis v. United Air Lines, 662 F.2d 120 (2d Cir. 1981); Coleman v. Noland Co., 21 Fair Empl. Prac. Cas. (BNA) 1248 (W.D. Va. 1980); EE Black Ltd. v. Marshall, 23 Fair Empl. Prac. Cas. (BNA) 1253 (D. Hawaii 1980); Reynolds v. Ross, 25 Fair Empl. Prac. Cas. (BNA) 462 (N.D.N.Y. 1981).

607. Summary and Analysis, *supra* note 602.

608. Chaplin v. Consolidated Edison Co. of N.Y., 482 F. Supp. 1165 (S.D.N.Y. 1980); Davis v. United Air Lines, 25 Fair Empl. Prac. Cas. (BNA) 565 (E.D.N.Y. 1980), *rev'd*, 662 F.2d 120 (2d Cir. 1981).

609. Clarke v. FELEC Servs., Inc., 489 F. Supp. 165 (D. Alaska 1980); California Paralyzed Veterans Ass'n v. F.C.C., 496 F. Supp. 125 (C.D. Cal. 1980).

610. Chaplin v. Consolidated Edison Co. of N.Y., 482 F. Supp. 1165 (S.D.N.Y. 1980).

611. Davis v. United Air Lines, 25 Fair Empl. Prac. Cas. (BNA) 565, 567 (E.D.N.Y. 1980), *rev'd*, 662 F.2d 120 (1981) [no private right of action under § 503].

612. Office of Federal Contract Compliance Program. Western Elec. Co., No. 80-OFCCP-29, 5 MDLR 171 (U.S. Dep't of Labor Mar. 4, 1981).

613. 29 U.S.C. § 706(6)(A) (1982); EE Black Ltd. v. Marshall, 23 Fair Empl. Prac. Cas. (BNA) 1253 (D. Hawaii 1980).

614. Diagnostic terms are categorized into "mental disorders" and other conditions that are not mental disorders. The severity of the disorder does not determine whether or not it is included. The nature of the condition does. See Spitzer, Williams, & Skodal, DSM-111: The Major Achievements and an Overview, 137 Am. J. Psychiatry 151 (1980).

615. 29 U.S.C. § 793(b) (1982). (The regulation containing the complaint procedures are at 41 C.F.R. § 60-741.26 (1984).

remedies open to the government is the cancellation of the existing contract or withholding of future contracts.[616] However, the individual complainant could not be compensated unless the employer did so as part of a settlement agreement.[617] In the unusual event that the individual is illegally prevented from filing an administrative action, the Court of Appeals for the Fifth Circuit has ruled that under the provisions of *Maine v. Thiboutot*[618] a person may file a § 1983 civil rights action.[619] Yet no court has found that an administrative backlog constitutes such an illegal deprivation. In those jurisdictions where a § 503 private action is permitted, a companion § 1983 action would be more practical since the requisite interference with a federal right is circumscribed more broadly, encompassing both judicial and administrative relief.[620]

Finally, the United States Court of Appeals for the Eleventh Circuit cited § 503 as the obstacle to a handicapped individual's recovering against an employer for not living up to its contractual affirmative action obligations. The doctrine of federal preemption precluded state relief under Alabama's third-party beneficiary contract law that normally allows a third party to sue if he is bound by the failure of some of the contracting parties to live up to the agreement. The contract between the employer and the federal government was governed exclusively by the § 503 regulations.[621]

3. Section 501

Section 501, a provision of Title V which has been the subject of minimal litigation, requires federal agencies to promote affirmative action.[622] One example of such a program is the "excepted" service appointment process that allows mentally disabled and other handicapped applicants to bypass the normal competitive selection procedures under the Civil Service laws. The major source of contention under this program has been the absence of job tenure protection for individuals doing work that is similar to the work of individuals hired competitively. Two federal courts of appeals have ruled that the government must provide a rational explanation for denying employment benefits to a disabled person hired through excepted service. The Court of Appeals for the District of Columbia Circuit decided that § 501 at the very least provided handicapped employees with the right to "evenhanded treatment" and perhaps something more.[623] A ruling that mentally impaired employees could not obtain equal job status after a substantial period of time would pose a greater threat than granting a limited privilege under the merit system. Similarly, the Eighth Circuit found a constitutional equal protection violation where a mentally retarded employee was summarily fired from an excepted service position that would have provided job tenure if it had been held by a nonretarded competitively hired employee.[624] Recently a federal court in the District of Columbia concluded that the excepted service program as applied to former mental patients who were hired as housekeepers at St. Elizabeths Hospital violated § 501. The class of employees was doing exactly the same work as other housekeepers in the competitive service but did not receive the same benefits, nor did they have any means of converting to competitive status without starting over again as new employees.[625]

Section 501 also affords protections for handicapped employees who require special accommodations to do their jobs competently. A mentally retarded janitor at the United States Air Force Academy was ordered reinstated with back pay after he was unfairly fired for not remembering his duties.[626] A reasonable accommodation was to provide him with a written list of tasks he could carry with him. However, if an employee or job applicant is not qualified, no duty to accommodate exists.[627] Thus, a postal worker who suffered from post-traumatic stress disorder could not win reinstatement to his position where he had accumulated a poor work and attendance record. The federal court also noted that the United States Postal Service's policy of allowing a past poor record to be overcome by most recent employment was a reasonable accommodation.[628]

4. Other Federal Actions

Individual federal agencies may have regulations in place which govern specific aspects of employment which appear to differ from the thrust of Title V of the Rehabilitation Act.[629] For example, in a 1978 decision that was later vacated and remanded a federal judge upheld the validity of United States Postal Service regulations that automatically disqualified individuals with epilepsy and other convulsive disorders from employ-

616. 41 C.F.R. § 60-741.28(d) & (e) (1984).
617. Wolff, Protecting the Disabled Minority: Rights and Remedies Under Sections 503 and 504 of the Rehabilitation Act of 1973, 22 St. Louis U.L.J. 25, 50-51 (1978).
618. 448 U.S. 1 (1980).
619. Brown v. Sibley, 650 F.2d 760 (5th Cir. 1981).
620. *Id.* According to the Fifth Circuit the right to redress under § 1983 is defined by the scope of the right secured by the federal statute.
621. Howard v. Uniroyal, Inc., 719 F.2d 1552 (11th Cir. 1983).
622. 29 U.S.C. § 791(b) (1982).
623. Shirey v. Devine, 670 F.2d 1188, 1201 (D.C. Cir. 1982).
624. Fowler v. United States, 633 F.2d 1258 (8th Cir. 1980).
625. Allen v. Heckler, 35 Fair Empl. Prac. Cas. (BNA) 281 (D.D.C. 1984).
626. *In re* Roberts, 4 MDLR 427 (E.E.O.C. Sept. 1980).
627. 29 C.F.R. § 1613.704 (1984).
628. Boyd v. U.S. Postal Serv., 32 Fair Empl. Prac. Cas. (BNA) 1217 (W.D. Wash. 1983).
629. Sections 503 and 504 do not apply to federal agencies.

ment as postal clerks and letter carriers.[630] In a more recent case, Federal Aviation Administration regulations were interpreted so that a history of epilepsy or certain severe mental illness constituted an absolute disqualification for the position of airline pilot except in extenuating circumstances such as recovery from alcoholic addiction where the FAA has allowed exemptions that are consistent with the "public interest."[631]

Also, federal statutes can be useful in securing vocational rehabilitation services that may lead eventually to employment. Both § 504 and Title I of the Rehabilitation Act have been used in this regard.[632] However, the cases have mostly concerned physically as opposed to mentally disabled persons. Under § 504 all handicapped individuals are entitled to equal vocational rehabilitation opportunities because the vocational programs are federally funded.[633] In addition, Title I either by itself or through § 1983 litigation has been found to create certain entitlements.[634] A state that accepts a client for vocational rehabilitation is obligated to provide the services set out in the person's rehabilitation plan.[635] Thus a client whose paranoid schizophrenia was in remission was able to bring suit to obtain financial aid for law school tuition but lost because he failed to show that his disability was a "substantial handicap" to employment and that he was severely handicapped.[636]

Finally, while many commentators have pointed out that the Civil Rights Act should apply to handicapped individuals, there is little basis in the law itself to support the contention that the act as presently considered was meant to include the handicapped. The United States Court of Appeals for the Tenth Circuit held that an employee who claimed that he was demoted and then discharged from his position in a real estate insurance firm because he disclosed he had multiple schlerosis had no private cause of action under § 1985(3) of the Civil Rights Act. There was nothing in the legislation "to give any encouragement whatever to extend § 1985 to classes other than those involved in the strife in the South in 1871."[637] Any change to include mentally or physically disabled persons in the act's coverage would require congressional action, and, in fact, for several years now disability groups have been lobbying Congress to effectuate such a result.

C. State Law

Two broad categories of statutes largely define the state-protected employment rights of mentally disabled individuals: (1) general prohibitions against specified kinds of discrimination and (2) eligibility criteria for workers' compensation, which will be discussed later.

As table A shows, although some 46 states and the District of Columbia do have statutes prohibiting discrimination against job applicants and employees on the basis of handicap or disability,[638] only 32 states have statutes that apply specifically to mental disabilities. The other 14 states and the District of Columbia limit their coverage to the physically disabled.

TABLE A
Number of State Statutes Prohibiting Discrimination in Employment, Housing, and Public Accommodations*

Statutory Coverage by Area

Class	Employment	Housing	Public Accommodations
Physically disabled	14	19	30
Mentally disabled	1	1	0
Both physically and mentally disabled	31	13	7
Total no. of states	46	33	37

Administrative Procedure by Area

Administrative Procedure	Employment	Housing	Public Accommodations
Investigation	34	23	21
Administrative hearing	33	22	21
Ordering compliance	33	21	21
Total no. of states	40	31	31

*See table 11.1 for details on statutes and their codification.

While federal handicap discrimination legislation is normally tied to the receipt of federal funds, most state statutes encompass private as well as state-funded employment.[639] Beyond this tendency, however, there is lit-

630. Counts v. U.S. Postal Serv., 17 Fair Empl. Prac. Cas. (BNA) 1161 (N.D. Fla. 1978).

631. 14 C.F.R. §§ 67.13 to 67.17 (1985); 14 C.F.R. § 11.27(e) (1985); Delta Airlines v. United States, 490 F. Supp. 907 (N.D. Ga. 1980).

632. Jones v. Illinois Dep't of Rehabilitation Servs., No. 81-1267, 6 MDLR 389 (7th Cir. Sept. 27, 1982); Schornstein v. New Jersey Div. of Vocational Rehabilitation Servs., 688 F.2d 824 (3d Cir. 1982) (decision without published opinion, *aff'g*, 519 F. Supp. 773 (D.N.J. 1981)); Ryans v. New Jersey Comm'n for the Blind & Visually Impaired, 542 F. Supp. 841 (D.N.J. 1982).

633. Jones v. Illinois Dep't of Rehabilitation Servs., No. 81-1267, 6 MDLR 389 (7th Cir. Sept. 27, 1982); Schornstein v. New Jersey Div. of Vocational Rehabilitation Servs., 688 F.2d 824 (3d Cir. 1982).

634. Schornstein v. New Jersey Div. of Vocational Rehabilitation Servs., 688 F.2d at 824; Ryans v. New Jersey Comm'n for the Blind & Visually Impaired, 542 F. Supp. 841 (D.N.J. 1982).

635. Schornstein v. New Jersey Div. of Vocational Rehabilitation Servs., 688 F.2d at 824.

636. Martin v. Commonwealth, Dep't of Labor & Industry, 461 A.2d 1351 (Pa. Commw. Ct. 1983).

637. Wilhelm v. Continental Title Co., 720 F.2d 1173, 1176 (10th Cir. 1983).

638. See table 11.1, col. 1.

639. See table 11.1, cols. 2 & 3. However, Mississippi prohibits employment discrimination against the physically handicapped in state governmental or state-funded employment and South Dakota limits its coverage to public employment.

tle uniformity in the scope of these state statutes. Arizona, for example, prohibits discrimination against any individual who is undergoing mental health treatment. Thirty-one states generally prohibit employment discrimination against persons with mental or physical disabilities.[640] Two states, Pennsylvania and Wisconsin, prohibit discrimination based on any handicap,[641] while Texas limits its protective coverage to the physically handicapped and the mentally retarded.[642]

Some statutes offer little or no guidance in defining "mental disability," while others are more specific but not necessarily more clear, covering either general categories such as "mental handicap" or "impairment"[643] or levels of functioning such as "substantial handicap."[644] Ohio, has the most detailed definition, which emphasizes both duration and functional abilities: "a medically diagnosable, abnormal condition which is expected to continue for a considerable length of time, whether correctable or uncorrectable by good medical practice, which can reasonably be expected to limit the person's functional ability."[645]

The reluctance of some legislatures to treat the handicapped as they do other groups covered by discrimination statutes has led to the adoption of special qualifications that may negatively affect the employability of mentally disabled persons who are included as a subclass of the handicapped.[646] The most popular is the "bona fide occupational qualification," which limits coverage to those handicaps that are "unrelated to a person's ability to perform the duties of a particular job."[647] Another qualification technique, which is used in Indiana, requires that the person be certified as handicapped before the terms of the statute can even be applied.[648] An uncertified individual, no matter how severely mentally disabled, would not be covered.

640. See table 11.1, col. 1.

641. See table 11.1, cols. 2 & 3; Pa. Stat. Ann. tit. 43, § 955 (Purdon Supp. 1985); Wis. Stat. Ann. §§ 101.22, 111.32 (West 1974 & Supp. 1984).

642. Tex. Rev. Civ. Stat. Ann. art. 5221K(5) (Vernon 1985).

643. Connecticut makes it unlawful to discriminate on the basis of an individual's present or past history of mental disorder, mental retardation, or physical disability, the covered conditions including any "impairment . . . from bodily injury, organic processes or changes or from illness." Conn. Gen. Stat. Ann. § 46a.60 & § 1-1f (West Supp. 1985). Maine defines mental or physical handicap as "disability [or] infirmity . . . as determined by a physician, or, in the case of mental handicap, by a psychiatrist or psychologist, as well as any other health or sensory impairment which requires special education, vocation rehabilitation or related services." Me. Rev. Stat. Ann., tit. 5, § 4553 (7-A) (West 1979).

644. Iowa and Indiana focus on the extent of the disability or handicap, requiring an impairment to be substantial. Iowa Code Ann. § 601A.2(11) (West 1975) ("substantial handicap"), Ind. Code Ann. § 22-9-1-3(q) (Burns 1983) ("substantial disability").

645. Ohio Rev. Code Ann. §§ 4112-01(A)(13) (Page 1980).

646. A.B.A. Comm'n, *supra* note 549, at 9.

647. *Id.*

648. Ind. Code Ann. § 22-9-1-13(e) (Burns Supp. 1977).

The kinds of employment practices prohibited because of discrimination against mentally disabled persons vary according to the jurisdiction. Certain state statutes have general prohibitions that leave considerable discretion in the hands of the administering agencies or, on occasion, the courts. More recent legislation will usually explain with some specificity the kinds of practices that are unlawful.[649] A number of states make it illegal for an employer to use preemployment inquiries that require individuals to reveal the existence or nature of their disabilities in the initial application process.[650] More often, statutes set out broad prohibitions against discrimination such as "in the hire, apprenticeship, tenure, conditions or privileges of employment."[651] A few states will not allow notices of employment that attempt to preclude or include certain handicapped individuals.[652]

As with most other discrimination provisions at the state or local levels, the major problem involves enforcement of the noble words of prohibition. While most states do have some kind of administrative compliance procedure,[653] a number withhold the authority to investigate complaints, conduct formal hearings, or issue orders of compliance.[654] In many states the allocated resources are too meager to allow complaints to be handled effectively or, for that matter, to provide sufficient outreach to encourage the victims of discrimination to file their complaints.[655] A private right of action for judicial enforcement usually is not an available option and where it is, the need to exhaust administrative remedies coupled with frequently heavy backlogs of cases make such private suits impractical. Nevertheless, a few cases among thousands of complaints do receive federal review, with varying results.[656]

649. See table 11.1, cols. 2 & 3.

650. *Id.*, e.g., Minnesota and Pennsylvania.

651. *Id.*, e.g., Ohio and Pennsylvania.

652. *Id.*, e.g., New Hampshire and Ohio.

653. See table 11.1.

654. *Id.*, e.g., Florida, Hawaii, and Illinois.

655. A.B.A. Comm'n, Prohibiting Discrimination, *supra* note 549, at 9-10.

656. A woman with epilepsy used the Colorado statute to successfully challenge a hospital's policy of automatically excluding job applicants with particular disabilities. Silverstein v. Sisters of Charity of Leavenworth Health Servs. Corp., 614 P.2d 891 (Colo. Ct. App. 1979). In West Virginia, the state's highest tribunal found that a coal miner's civil rights had been violated when he was denied employment solely because he had taken medication to treat his depression. Hurley v. Allied Chem. Corp., 262 S.E.2d 757 (W.Va. 1980). Perhaps the most intriguing court interpretation of a state statute governing hiring practices was made by an appeals court in Florida, which upheld a ruling that a blind man was entitled to employment as an elementary school physical education teacher on a trial basis to determine whether his handicap would prevent satisfactory job performance. Zorick v. Tynes, 372 So. 2d 133 (Fla. Dist. Ct. App. 1979). Presumably, the limited benefit of the doubt that was extended to the blind man in this case would also be extended to other disabled persons covered under the statute.

Disputes over the interpretation of state statutes have produced few court decisions focusing on the dismissal of mentally disabled employees. In the two

D. Workers' and Unemployment Compensation

Workers' compensation statutes are "laws providing for compensation for loss resulting from the injury, disablement, or death of workmen through industrial accident, casualty or disease . . . ."[657] Although the laws differ among jurisdictions, they share two basic features. Each statute provides no-fault compensation regardless of tort liability, and each statute sets out a definite schedule of payments based on the loss of earning power. Moreover, in most jurisdictions there is a presumption that doubts concerning the scope and application of these compensation statutes should be resolved in favor of those who claim to be beneficiaries.

One of the most controversial areas of compensation — payments for mental or nervous disorders — has inherent difficulties for those trying to substantiate or refute such claims with acceptable medical evidence and also provokes a lingering prejudice toward those who would file claims invoking the stigma of mental illness. As a general rule, benefits may be awarded where a mental disorder results from a physical injury on the job such as a severe neurotic-depressive reaction to a back injury or a hysterical neurosis attributable to a physical injury that caused a disabling psychosomatic condition.[658] Disagreements arise far more frequently when the mental or nervous disorder finds its origin in a work-related emotional stimulus.[659] Several viewpoints are expressed in the caselaw interpreting different state statutes.

The more traditional legislation states that there must be a physical basis for the condition or there can be no compensation, since by definition there has to be a physical injury or physical trauma.[660] To provide compensation would encourage employers not to hire "persons of delicate psychic constitution" for fear of having to pay out disability benefits.[661] Under this theory, numerous claims have been denied in circumstances that might have led to compensation in other jurisdictions. Such denials have included: a teacher who suffered a nervous breakdown attributable to harassment by her students,[662] a sales clerk who had a heart attack brought on by emotional stress,[663] a woman who suffered a disabling psychological injury as a result of an emotional trauma arising from an argument with her superiors,[664] and an employee who attributed her nervous breakdown to employment stress.[665] The Kansas Supreme Court's interpretation of legislation that limited recovery to a "change in physical structure of the body" obviously excluded mental injuries but also was accompanied with further restrictions on mental conditions arising from physical trauma. The court held that a plant worker who was permanently mentally disabled after coming to the scene where his coworker and friend's head had been crushed in a die press could not recover any compensation. Moreover, in discussing the state law the justices observed that there was no entitlement unless the mental condition was directly traceable to the physical injury, it resulted from the nature and requirements of the employment, and no uncontrollable external forces were the intervening cause of the mental harm.[666]

A second view, adhered to in many of the more recent cases, allows compensation, although with limitations, if the stimulus is emotional. The prevailing rationale is that the availability of compensation should not be related exclusively to the nature of the cause but should also reflect the nature of the disability.[667] Courts are divided, however, whether the stimulus must be a sudden, unexpected occurrence or simply unexpected.[668] There is a consensus in these cases that normal, everyday stress, even if it becomes disabling, either should never be compensated or should be compensated only if causation can be proved convincingly.[669] The Oregon Supreme Court found that a sheriff's deputy could be compensated for anxiety and depressive neurosis where job stress was shown to be the major contributing cause of his condition and the causation was demonstrated by objective

cited examples, both plaintiffs had epilepsy, which like mental illness is a condition that can remain hidden for a long time and can be controlled. A Wisconsin man was improperly fired as a welder because the employer could not meet the burden of showing that the employee was not able to do his job satisfactorily. Chicago & North Western R.R. v. Labor & Indus. Review Comm'n, 283 N.W. 2d 603 (Wis. Ct. App. 1979). A different legal approach was applied by the Iowa Civil Rights Commission, which stressed reasonable accommodation. The Commission reinstated with back pay a cafeteria worker who had been fired after she experienced a grand mal seizure on the job; the employer erred by not attempting to find a position with less dangerous duties for her to perform. Harkin v. Foods, Inc., No. Cp 03-77-4339, 4 MDLR 260 (Iowa Civil Rights Comm'n May 15, 1980).

657. 81 Am. Jur. 2d Workmen's Compensation § 1 (1976).

658. Fayne v. Fieldcrest Mills, Inc., 282 S.E.2d 539 (N.C. Ct. App. 1981); Paulson v. Idaho Forest Indus., Inc., 591 P.2d 143 (Idaho 1979).

659. 81 Am. Jur. 2d Workmen's Compensation §§ 225-27 (1976); 97 A.L.R.3d 161-200 (1980).

660. See references in note 659 *supra*.

661. Hanson Buick, Inc. v. Chatham, 292 S.E.2d 428, 430 (Ga. Ct. App. 1982).

662. Williams v. Hillsborough County School Bd., 389 So. 2d 1218 (Fla. Dist. Ct. App. 1980).

663. Szymanski v. Halle's Dep't Store, 407 N.E.2d 502 (Ohio 1980).

664. Brady v. Royal Mfg. Co., 160 S.E.2d 424 (Ga. Ct. App. 1968).

665. Samson v. Southern Bell Tel. & Tel. Co., 205 So. 2d 496 (La. Ct. App. 1967).

666. Followill v. Emerson Elec. Co., 674 P.2d 1050 (Kan. 1984).

667. Ditler v. Workers' Compensation Appeals Bd., 13 Cal. App. 3d 803, 182 Cal. Rptr. 839 (1982) (psychiatric injury due to job transfer); Royal State Nat'l Ins. Co. v. Labor & Indus. Relations Appeal Bd., 487 P.2d 278 (Hawaii 1971).

668. 81 Am. Jur. 2d Workmen's Compensation §§ 225-27.

669. Loh Lin v. Burroughs Corp., 427 N.Y.S.2d 78 (App. Div. 1980); School Dist. #1 v. Department of Indus., Labor, & Human Relations, 215 N.W.2d 373 (Wis. 1974).

criteria that measured actual as opposed to imagined problems on the job.[670]

The most inclusive statutes compensate employees for all accidents or diseases that result from: "the nature of the employment." These states treat work-related mental stress or injury identically to work-related physical injury. Hawaii's highest court applied the test of whether the injury reasonably appeared to have flowed from the conditions of employment and ruled in favor of a man who received a psychogenic injury in the workplace.[671] At least four other state appeals courts have held that a mental illness is a compensable occupational disease where a preexisting mental health problem was aggravated by job stress.[672] In two of those decisions, the courts were willing to compensate widows whose husband had committed suicide as long as the widows could establish a direct relationship between the workplace environment and their husband's death.[673] A few cases have ruled that workers' compensation may be paid for a mental disability caused by an emotional stimulus that was not sudden.[674] Certain courts award compensation only if the mental injury is susceptible to some sort of "scientific" measurement.[675] Finally, a few courts have allowed compensation for mental disorders as occupational diseases where it can be shown either that the disorder was a disease[676] or that a disease contributed to the deterioration of a separate mental condition.[677]

In addition to compensation for injuries on the job, every state also has temporary compensation for persons who are unemployed involuntarily, without good reason. The issue of voluntariness inevitably involves cases of mentally disabled persons who left work but did not do so voluntarily because they were unable to understand the consequences of their actions. For example, an Iowa court of appeals found that a sales clerk who suffered a nervous breakdown did not leave voluntarily when she was hospitalized and unaware of the reason for her unexcused absence until several months had passed.[678] A Pennsylvania court affirmed an award to a claimant who due to job stress had a compelling medical reason for voluntarily terminating her employment.[679] However, the United States Court of Appeals for the District of Columbia ruled that a woman was not eligible for compensation because she voluntarily resigned from her position after her employer initiated involuntary psychiatric retirement proceedings. Her resignation was seen as a desire to avoid airing her problems in public, and her disability was found to be unrelated to her work.[680]

E. Collective Bargaining Agreements

An individual who is hired for union employment is protected against certain kinds of on-the-job discrimination by the collective bargaining agreement between the employer and the employees. Arbitrators are called upon to decide whether the provisions of the agreement are being applied correctly, apart from any consideration of whether the employer may also be violating a law.[681] The agreement will cover discipline, suspension, firing or layoff, demotion or denial of promotion, and transfer.[682] What it will not specify in most instances is how to address the special problems posed by mental disabilities, especially mental illness:[683] "in spite of the seemingly increased acceptance of rehabilitation by the

670. McGarrah v. State Accident Ins. Fund Corp., 675 P.2d 159 (Or. 1983).

671. Royal State Nat'l Ins. Co. v. Labor & Indus. Relations Appeal Bd., 487 P.2d 278 (Hawaii 1971).

672. *In re* Compensation of Gygi, 639 P.2d 655 (Or. Ct. App. 1982); Lopucki v. Ford Motor Co., 311 N.W.2d 338 (Mich. Ct. App. 1981); Thompson v. Lenoir Transfer Co., 268 S.E.2d 534 (N.C. Ct. App. 1980); Hughes v. Webster Parish Pub. Jury, 414 So. 2d 1353 (La. Ct. App. 1982).

673. Lopucki v. Ford Motor Co., 311 N.W.2d 338 (Mich. Ct. App. 1981); Thompson v. Lenoir Transfer Co., 268 S.E.2d 534 (N.C. Ct. App. 1980).

674. Maine's highest court, relying on a Wisconsin decision (School District # 1 v. Department of Indus., Labor, & Human Relations, 215 N.W.2d 373 (Wis. 1974)), made gradual mental injury compensable where claimants were subjected to unusual stress or there was clear and convincing evidence that ordinary stress produced the injury. Townsend v. Maine Bureau of Pub. Safety, 404 A.2d 1014 (Me. 1979). An Arizona court refused to distinguish the event that caused the injury from the disabling condition. Fireman's Fund Ins. Co. v. Industrial Comm'n, 579 P.2d 555 (Ariz. 1978). If the condition is unexpected then the injury is an accident and can be compensated, even if the stimulus is not sudden. In Michigan, the state supreme court sustained an award for cumulative emotional harm despite evidence that the claimant had psychiatric problems that predated and were unrelated to his job and that there were no unusual aspects to his position. Carter v. General Motors Corp., 106 N.W.2d 105 (Mich. 1960).

675. In Georgia, the court would not award payment for a gradual mental injury, but it would compensate employees for occupational diseases caused by employment-related hazards. As a result, benefits could be extended to a claimant with paranoid schizophrenia if he could demonstrate that the condition was a disease. Sawyer v. Pacific Indem. Co., 233 S.E.2d 227 (Ga. Ct. App. 1977). Similarly, a psychological disability that was produced by a sudden and severe emotional shock, but with no accompanying physical injury, was compensable in Illinois, if the event could be traced to a definite time and place. Pathfinder Co. v. Industrial Comm'n, 62 Ill. 2d 556, 343 N.E.2d 913 (1976). In another state, compensation was denied because there was no "distinct psychiatric injury." Thomas v. Commonwealth, Workmen's Compensation Appeal Bd., 423 A.2d 784 (Pa. Commw. Ct. 1980).

676. Sawyer v. Pacific Indem. Co., 233 S.E.2d 227 (Ga. Ct. App. 1977).

677. McMahon v. Anaconda Co., 678 P.2d 661 (Mont. 1984). The worker developed psychological problems over his work environment after being exposed to certain pollutants.

678. Quenot v. Iowa Dep't of Job Serv., 339 N.W.2d 624 (Iowa Ct. App. 1983).

679. Central Data Center v. Commonwealth Unemployment Compensation Bd. of Review, 458 A.2d 335 (Pa. Commw. Ct. 1983).

680. Hill v. District of Columbia Dep't of Employment Servs., 467 A.2d 134 (D.C. 1983).

681. Spencer, The Developing Notion of Employer Responsibility for the Alcoholic, Drug-Addicted or Mentally Ill Employee: An Examination Under Federal and State Employment Statutes and Arbitration Decisions, 53 St. John's L. Rev., 659, 685 (1979).

682. *Id.* at 645 n.90.

683. Marmo, Alcoholism, Drug Addiction, and Mental Illness: The Use of Rehabilitative Remedies in Arbitration, 32 Labor L.J. 491-97 (1981).

broader society in recent years," observes one commentator, "contracts negotiated in recent years are no more likely to contain provisions dealing with rehabilitation than were agreements negotiated 20 years ago."[684] Nevertheless, many arbitrators have introduced the notion of rehabilitation into the collective bargaining process.

Arbitration decisions indicate that a mental disability, whether it be mental illness, drug addiction, or alcoholism, may be viewed as an acceptable excuse for otherwise punishable behavior, a mitigating factor, or of no consequence whatsoever. Recently, it has often come to depend on a balancing of interests presented by the disabled employee, the employer, other employees, and the public. Such a balancing of interests is more common in cases of mental illness and alcoholism than for drug addiction, which is treated more harshly.[685]

In a few cases mental disability has been cited as an acceptable excuse for behavior if the employees seek professional help for their problems. For example, arbitrators have concluded that it "would be a cruel and undeserved penalty" to discharge an employee who was chronically absent because of mental problems,[686] or to deny sick pay to a teacher who failed to report to work because of stress and anxiety associated with the Three Mile Island nuclear accident.[687] In other decisions, arbitrators have ordered employers to reinstate a police officer who had a severe psychiatric condition that was being controlled by medication[688] and a steelworker who successfully completed an alcohol rehabilitation program.[689]

Not infrequently, a mental disability will be considered a mitigating factor in assessing unacceptable job behavior. Thus an employee who was discharged for excessive absenteeism and tardiness was reinstated because he voluntarily enrolled in an alcohol rehabilitation program, for which he was given an unpaid leave of absence.[690] Similarly, a woman who left work against the orders of her supervisor succeeded in reducing her termination to a suspension on the ground that she suffered a bout with depression.[691] In two other decisions, arbitrators refused to fire employees who failed to take job fitness tests but recommended less severe disciplinary measures if the employees subsequently agreed to take the examinations.[692]

In a large number of cases, the existence of a mental disability does not mitigate the outcome of the disciplinary proceedings, such as those in which it is found that there is no evidence of actual discrimination[693] or deliberate falsification of job application by withholding information about psychiatric care,[694] or that there is evidence of willful and purposeful destruction of company property,[695] failure to seek professional help after receiving a leave of absence,[696] failure to be rehabilitated after a reasonable period of time,[697] violent outbursts that frightened coworkers,[698] extremely hazardous work conditions,[699] or failure to ascertain side effects of taking medication.[700]

F. Sheltered Workshops

A number of mentally disabled individuals, particularly those who are developmentally disabled, participate in employment programs known as "sheltered workshops" as well as in other community employment situations that are partially or largely therapeutic in nature. The major source of legal contention in these employment situations is determining the proportions of the work that are compensable employment and noncompensable therapy. In addition, the rate of compensation is often subject to legal challenge.

Section 14 of the 1966 Amendments to the Fair Labor Standards Act of 1938[701] provides for the issuance of special wage certificates to mentally and physically handicapped workers who cannot produce as much as regular workers. After certification they can be paid a proportion of the minimum wage based on their individual productivity levels. The certified proportion may not be less than half the normal minimum wage and must be commensurate with wages paid to nonhandicapped workers in the immediate vicinity for the same type,

684. *Id.* at 492.
685. Spencer, *supra* note 681, at 710, 711.
686. *In re* Babcock & Wilcox Co. v. United Steelworkers Local 4396, 72 Lab. Arb. (BNA) 1073 (1979) (Mullin, Arb.).
687. Penn Manor School Dist. 73 v. Penn Manor Educ. Ass'n, Lab. Arb. (BNA) 1227 (1979) (Crawford, Arb.).
688. City of Fenten v. International Bhd. of Teamsters Local 129, 76 Lab. Arb. (BNA) 355 (1981) (Roumell, Arb.).
689. Bethlehem Steel Corp. v. United Steelworkers Local 2610, 74 Lab. Arb. 322 (1979) (Strongin, Arb.).
690. St. Joe Minerals Corp. v. United Steelworkers Local 8183, 73 Lab. Arb. (BNA) 1193 (1979) (McDermott, Arb.).
691. Clevepak Corp. v. United Paperworkers Int'l Union Local 1106, 73 Lab. Arb. (BNA) 641 (1979) (Archer, Arb.).
692. City of Charlevoix v. Michigan Law Enforcement Union, Teamsters Local 129, 76 Lab. Arb. (BNA) 753 (1981) (Daniel, Arb.); Southern California Rapid Transit Dist. v. Amalgamated Transit Union Div. 1277, 76 Lab. Arb. (BNA) 144 (1980) (Sabo, Arb.).
693. Porcelain Metals Corp. v. International Bhd. of Teamsters Local 89, 73 Lab. Arb. (BNA) 1133 (1979) (Roberts, Arb.).
694. United States Steel Corp. v. United Steelworkers Local 5030, 74 Lab. Arb. (BNA) 354 (1980) (Dybeck, Arb.).
695. Allis-Chalmers Corp. v. United Steelworkers Local 1958, 73 Lab. Arb. (BNA) 1230 (1979) (Goetz, Arb.).
696. Johns-Manville Prods. Corp., v. International Union UAW & Local 1073, 76 Lab. Arb. (BNA) 845 (1981) (Kates, Arb.).
697. Monsanto Co. v. United Steelworkers Local 12610, 76 Lab. Arb. (BNA) 509 (1981) (Thomson, Arb.).
698. Appleton Elec. Co. v. International Bhd. of Elec. Workers Local 031, 76 Lab. Arb. 167 (1981) (Roomkin, Arb.).
699. ASARCO, Inc. v. International Chem. Workers Union Local 700, 76 Lab. Arb. (BNA) 163 (1981) (Grooms, Arb.).
700. New York Wire Mills Corp. v. United Steelworkers Local 7560, 76 Lab. Arb. (BNA) 232 (1981) (Le Winter, Arb.).
701. Pub. L. No. 89-601, 29 U.S.C. § 214(c)(1) (1982).

quality, and quantity of work. The rationale behind this provision is to make handicapped workers competitive with nonhandicapped workers in the employment market place.

Another provision found in the 1966 amendments establishes a certification procedure for severely handicapped individuals in "work activities centers" (sheltered workshops) that allows payment of wages below 50% of the minimum wage if the compensation is an equitable representation of the individual's productivity.[702] The assumption underlying the creation of the centers was that the work product was inconsequential when compared with the therapeutic benefits provided to severely impaired clients.

A 1976 decision by the United States Supreme Court, *National League of Cities v. Usery*,[703] cast doubt about the applicability of these amendments to state and local governments by ruling that the Tenth Amendment prohibited regulation of traditional governmental functions of the states. While most commentators and the federal government concluded that the decision encompassed the governmental function of state institutions,[704] it was equally clear to them that the decision did not affect privately run workshops such as Goodwill, which are beyond the reach of government. The United States Court of Appeals for the Sixth Circuit ruled that a private corporation in a contractual relationship with the state of Tennessee to provide services to mentally retarded persons was subject to the Fair Labor Standards Act's minimum wage and overtime provisions because the necessary state indicators were not present. Contractors are clearly differentiable from the state itself where there is no joint responsibility for employment decisions.[705]

In addition, whether sheltered workshops might be covered by collective bargaining agreements depended on the nature of the employment situation. Once again, the work-therapy dichotomy appeared to be crucial. A Goodwill enterprise was not eligible where its prime purpose was to provide rehabilitation for persons unable to compete in private industry.[706] On the other hand, the Court of Appeals for the Sixth Circuit approved a National Labor Relations Board decision to assert its jurisdiction over a workshop for visually impaired persons where the workshop displayed significant economic purpose and more closely resembled a traditional for-profit business enterprise than a rehabilitative therapeutic workshop.[707]

Nevertheless, despite the strong academic and scholarly support for the outcome in *National League of Cities*, it was overruled in 1985 by a sharply divided United States Supreme Court. To the surprise of many Court watchers, a 5-to-4 majority ruled that the Fair Labor Standards Act applied to all public or private employers involved in interstate transactions including those employers engaged in such traditional state functions as hospitals, schools, and mass transit. The four dissenters promised to reverse the outcome as soon as possible.[708]

VI. LEGALLY MANDATED HOUSING OPPORTUNITIES FOR FOR THE MENTALLY DISABLED

Over the past ten years, substantive legal developments have improved housing opportunities for mentally disabled persons, although not without leaving major problems still to be solved. Although loopholes remain in the patchwork of legal restrictions and entitlements, the new system serves the needs of mentally disabled clients better than the much looser structure it replaced, which relied almost entirely on overburdened families and inadequate institutional care.

Recently, significant strides have been taken in overcoming exclusionary zoning and restrictive covenants (in the past an impenetrable barrier to placing disabled persons in residential neighborhoods) and also in promoting construction or creation of new housing through legislation and litigation. Although less than half of the jurisdictions protect the mentally disabled against discrimination in housing and what legislation does exist is often difficult to enforce properly, more such laws are in place today than ever before.

Most of the recent activities in housing for the disabled have been at the local level. At the federal level, the broad prohibitions in § 504 of the Rehabilitation Act covering discriminatiuon against the handicapped in federally assisted programs have, according to available evidence, had only a slight effect on housing. Other federal programs have created housing units for mentally disabled persons, but they were never intended to meet the total need.

A. Exclusionary Zoning and Restrictive Covenants

1. Constitutional Requirements

702. 29 U.S.C. § 214(c)(3)(A) & (B) (1982).

703. 426 U.S. 833 (1976).

704. Institutionalized Patient Workers and Their Right to Compensation in the Aftermath of *National League of Cities v. Usery*, 22 B.C.L. Rev. 511 (1981) [hereinafter cited as Institutionalized Patient Workers]; Townsend v. Clover Bottom Hosp. & School, 560 S.W.2d 623 (Tenn. 1978).

705. Skills Dev. Servs., Inc. v. Donovan, 728 F.2d 294 (6th Cir. 1984).

706. Goodwill Indus. of Southern California v. Local Freight Drivers, 231 N.L.R.B. 49 (1977).

707. Cincinnati Ass'n for the Blind v. NLRB, 672 F.2d 567 (6th Cir. 1982).

708. Garcia v. San Antonio Metropolitan Transit Auth., 105 S. Ct. 1005, 1021, 1038 (1985) (Powell, J., dissenting, joined by Burger, O'Connor, & Rehnquist, J.J.), *rev'g and remanding* National League of Cities v. Usery, 426 U.S. 833 (1976).

A well-established tradition in Anglo-American law favors the unencumbered use of land. Before this century the only restriction on land use came through the common law of nuisance, which prohibited unreasonable practices that diminished the value of neighboring lands. But with industrial growth and urbanization in the late nineteenth century, the common law of nuisance proved to be inadequate to cope with the competing public welfare needs of the community and the economic needs of business and industry, and local governments proposed zoning ordinances that governed specified uses of land in designated areas.[709]

The conflict between those who favored the unencumbered use of land and those who wanted restrictions that would promote specific community values reached the United States Supreme Court in the 1926 landmark case, *Village of Euclid v. Ambler Realty Company.*[710] In *Euclid* a property owner objected to a local zoning ordinance that limited his realty to residential uses, claiming that the municipality's restriction amounted to a taking of his property without due process of law. The Supreme Court, however, disagreed, holding that zoning restrictions were permissible forms of governmental regulation unless they were "clearly arbitrary and unreasonable, having no substantial relation to the public health, safety, morals, or general welfare."[711]

The Court defined the boundaries of *Euclid* two years later in two cases. In *Nectow v. Cambridge,*[712] it struck down a clearly arbitrary ordinance that bore no relationship to the common good, finding that the prohibition against business uses left the owner with no practical use of his land since all the adjacent property was zoned for industrial purposes. *Washington ex rel. Seattle Title Trust Co. v. Roberge,*[713] presented a zoning dispute similar to a group home dispute: the city ordinance would permit only homes of charity for children and old people in a specified district, if two-thirds of the property owners within 400 feet of the proposed home gave their written consent. The Court concluded that the restriction was unconstitutional since the owners could withhold their consent for any reason and there was no evidence that the home would have a negative impact on the community.

Nearly 50 years later, a different type of exclusionary device, ostensibly to protect the traditional family structure, was upheld in *Village of Belle Terre v. Boraas.*[714] Six college students who were sharing a house unsuccessfully challenged an ordinance that allowed only families to live in the neighborhood. The students could not meet the definition of family—"[o]ne or more persons related by blood, adoption, or marriage, living and cooking together as a single housekeeping unit."[715] The constitutionality of the restriction was upheld because it did not infringe upon a fundamental protection—the right to travel, due process, association, privacy, or equal protection. The police power, explained the Supreme Court, is certainly broad enough to enable municipalities to create "zones where family values, youth values, and the blessings of quiet seclusion and clean air make the area a sanctuary for people."[716]

The police power, of course, is not unlimited. In *Moore v. City of East Cleveland*[717] the Court rejected a narrowly defined notion of family and ruled that there must be something more than a tenuous relationship to the common good to justify a zoning restriction. Mrs. Moore, her son, and two grandsons had been prohibited from living together because the grandsons were cousins and not brothers. Only the son's son, not the cousin, was part of the family. It was improper, wrote the Court, to force people "to live in certain narrowly defined family patterns."[718] Furthermore, observed Justice Stevens in a concurring opinion, *Belle Terre* was not determinative since it was "primarily concerned with the prevention of transiency in a small, quiet suburban community."[719] Stevens was quoting from *City of White Plains v. Ferraioli,*[720] a case in which a New York appeals court concluded that a group home with a married couple, two natural children, and ten foster children constituted a single family unit.

Within the legal boundaries established by *Belle Terre* and *Moore*, existing laws and policies governing zoning have gone in different directions, although the trend has been toward expanding opportunities for housing.[721] It should be noted that separate legal arguments arise when the property restriction is a covenant that is part of the deed.[722] These restrictive covenants, as they are called, are private agreements that specify or prohibit certain land uses.[723]

Recently, for a period of less that two years, it ap-

709. R.M. Anderson, American Law of Zoning 6 (2d ed. 1978 & Supp. 1982); P.J. Rohan, Zoning and Land Use Controls ch. 1 at 3 (1978 & Supp. 1979).
710. 272 U.S. 365 (1926).
711. *Id.* at 395.
712. 277 U.S. 183 (1928).
713. 278 U.S. 116 (1928).
714. 416 U.S. 1 (1974).
715. *Id.* at 2.
716. *Id.* at 9.
717. 431 U.S. 494 (1977).
718. *Id.* at 506.
719. *Id.* at 519 n.15.
720. 34 N.Y.2d 300, 313 N.E.3d 756 (1974).
721. See discussion in this chapter § VI A, of cases throughout, Exclusionary Zoning and Restrictive Covenants. Also A.A. Rathkopf & D.A. Rathkopf, The Law of Zoning and Planning § 17A.05, Operation of Group Homes in Single Family Districts (1977 & Supp. 1982).
722. See discussion in this chapter § VI A 6, Restrictive Covenants, *infra*.
723. C.M. Haar & L. Liebman, Property and Law 824 (1977).

peared that equal protection standards governing zoning regulations for mentally disabled persons were changing significantly. Citing the United States Supreme Court in the 1982 case *Plyler v. Doe*[724]—a decision that applied heightened judicial scrutiny to the education of children with parents who were illegal aliens—the Ninth and Fifth Circuits concluded that the same intermediate equal protection review had to be applied to zoning regulations that limit housing for mentally disabled persons.[725] This standard required more than the traditional rational relationship test applied in the past to local housing statutes, although not the strictest scrutiny reserved for racial minorities. As stated by the Ninth Circuit, "a court must look more carefully to determine whether the decision to deny a permit is related to the *substantial* state interest that justifies the discriminatory classification. Unless it specifically serves such an interest, the permit denial is arbitrary and violates due process."[726] In the Ninth Circuit case, zoning criteria were overturned because they were applied to deny a permit based only on community opposition without specific evidence of potential harm to the neighborhood. Similarly, the Fifth Circuit struck down a requirement that all "hospitals for the insane or feebleminded, or alcoholic or drug addicts" obtain a special permit as applied to a group home for mentally retarded persons. The court asserted: "giving the city council complete discretion to bar all group homes is too dangerous" because there "is too great a potential for blanket discrimination."[727]

But despite the appealing nature of the arguments in favor of an intermediate standard for mentally disabled persons because of their long history of isolation, abuse, and deprivations, a 6-3 majority of the United States Supreme Court in *City of Cleburne v. Cleburne Living Center, Inc.*[728] dismissed the Fifth Circuit's equal protection analyses. Justice White's opinion for the Court concluded that mentally retarded persons, similar to persons who are mentally ill, elderly, physically disabled, or infirm, did not have the group characteristics associated with those classes of people for whom strict or heightened scrutiny had been extended previously. While it is undeniable that mentally retarded persons have a tragic history, two other factors are even more significant in terms of an equal protection analysis, according to this decision: (1) the class of mentally retarded persons is composed of individuals with very different needs, and (2) the fact that federal and state legislation has been enacted on their behalf indicates clearly that mentally retarded persons are not a politically helpless minority. Nevertheless, in applying the rational relationship test to the Cleburne City zoning ordinance, the Court went further than it had in examining situations involving social and economic legislation and determined that the ordinance as applied in these circumstances was constitutionally deficient.

A vitriolic dissent by Justice Marshall, who was joined by two other justices, found the majority's analysis to be deficient in two major ways: (1) mentally retarded persons are indistinguishable from historically disadvantaged groups such as blacks and women who also are made up of very different types of people and have been the beneficiaries of legislative efforts on their behalf and (2) the Court may have stated that heightened scrutiny was inapplicable to the Cleburne zoning case, but in fact a higher order of scrutiny was applied than had been used in previous Court examinations of social and economic legislation.[729] The significance of this possible higher rational relationship analysis was enhanced in a concurring opinion by Justice Stevens joined by Chief Justice Burger, which suggested that there are no separate, distinguishable equal protection standards, only a continuum of different analyses applied to the specific circumstances of the group involved.[730]

Even if one counts only the five Justices who either dissented or concurred with a separate opinion, a majority of the Court seems to favor an equal protection analysis that would distinguish mentally disabled persons based on their unique circumstances. Moreover, the entire Court appears to acknowledge that in presuming that the legislatures have acted constitutionally, the courts must at least review the rationale behind a policy to make sure that it is legitimate and if so, that it is legitimate as applied to the group in question.

2. State Statutes Governing Group Homes

The best way to avoid litigation is for the state legislatures to expressly determine what group home policy the localities must follow. As shown in table 11.2, to date, 21 states have enacted such legislation.[731] In an overwhelming number of court decisions, where the state statute and the local ordinance conflict the state statute

724. 487 U.S. 202 (1982).

725. J.W. v. City of Tacoma, 720 F.2d 1126 (9th Cir. 1983); Cleburne Living Center, Inc. v. City of Cleburne, 726 F.2d 191 (5th Cir. 1984).

726. J.W. v. City of Tacoma, 720 F.2d 1126, 1131 (9th Cir. 1983) (emphasis added) (note omitted).

727. Cleburne Living Center, Inc. v. City of Cleburne, 726 F.2d 191, 194, 201 (5th Cir. 1984).

728. No. 84-468 (U.S. Sup. Ct. July 1, 1985).

729. *Id.* (dissenting and concurring opinion of Justice Marshall).

730. *Id.* (concurring opinion of Justice Stevens).

731. Rathkopf & Rathkopf, *supra* note 721, § 17A.05 at n.45 lists Arizona, California, Colorado, Connecticut, Idaho, Maryland, Michigan, Minnesota, Montana, Nevada, New Jersey, New Mexico, New York, Ohio, Rhode Island, South Carolina, Tennessee, Vermont, Virginia, and Wisconsin. Also 30 Me. Stat. Ann. § 4962-A (West 1984).

In addition, North Carolina, Nevada, and Utah (everywhere except exclusively single-family districts). See table 11.2.

has been preeminent.[732] In the absence of home rule provisions that insulate local governments, the courts have uniformly held that legislatures may establish statewide zoning policies as long as the policies are substantially related to one or more legitimate governmental objectives.[733] Over the past ten years, the legislative thrust has been to expand opportunities for community living for disabled persons,[734] in large measure to overcome in many areas what was a total exclusion of group homes. But there remains the danger of a backlash reaction to restrict community living opportunities, for absent state provisions to the contrary, there are only broad constitutional and common law limitations on the types of local zoning legislation that can be enacted.

Existing legislative enactments to create group homes can be broadly grouped into three categories, although state statutes may fall into more than one category. First, there is the most basic statute that without any other conditions directs localities to accept specifically described group homes in residential areas by defining them as family-living situations. The legal disputes such statutes engender do not center on the definition of "family" but rather on whether the local statute is in conflict with the state statute and if not, whether the home meets the established characteristics of an exempted group home,[735] such as the number of residents allowed. Only two states have this type of statute.

A second type of statute also prescribes that localities accept certain types of group homes but adds conditions for the builder to meet. In addition to complying with the general descriptive characteristics of an exempted home, the residence must be licensed by the state[736] and/or meet specified dispersal requirements that are intended to eliminate the "ghetto" effect of overconcentration of group homes in any one area.[737] Fifteen jurisdictions have this kind of statute.[738]

A third category of legislation delegates authority to localities so they may require special use permits on certain types of homes. Builders must meet a series of conditions precedent to the issuance of any permit,[739] such as specific health, safety, or compatibility-of-use requirements,[740] or in the case of Idaho, dispersal requirements.[741] While local governments need not create variances from general zoning statutes by allowing special use permits, once they do these mechanisms must follow specified criteria and be applied in the same way to all applicants. Thus in Omaha, Nebraska, a requirement that all facilities providing therapy and counseling must obtain a special exception could not be reasonably applied to group homes whose residents received outpatient care at two local hospitals.[742] Nor could the city of Des Moines, Iowa, withhold a special use permit for the construction of an apartment building for elderly and handicapped persons by refusing to grant an unrelated parking variance.[743] Moreover, if a stated criterion is very general for a special use permit, courts have placed the burden of proving the inappropriateness of a proposed use on the zoning authorities once the other more specific criteria have been met. In Florida, for example, the zoning board failed to show that the public interest was not being served by allowing foster parents to bring a fourth developmentally disabled child into their home.[744]

732. Costley v. Caromin House, Inc., 313 N.W.2d 21 (Minn. 1981); Region 10 Client Management, Inc. v. Town of Hampstead, 424 A.2d 207 (N.H. 1980); Mental Health Ass'n of Union County v. City of Elizabeth, 434 A.2d 688 (N.J. Super. Ct. 1981); Mongony v. Bevilacqua, 432 A.2d 661 (R.I. 1981); City of Los Angeles v. California Dep't of Health, 63 Cal. App. 3d 473, 133 Cal. Rptr. 771 (1976).

In California, the state supreme court concluded that the state constitution's right to privacy precluded any statute that interfered with the right of a group of individuals to live together. City of Santa Barbara v. Adamson, 610 P.2d 436, 164 Cal. Rptr. 539 (1980). An exception is Ohio, where the state supreme court found that the statute violated the state constitution's delegation of powers to the municipalities. Garcia v. Siffrin Residential Ass'n, 407 N.E.2d 1369 (Ohio 1980); Brownfield v. State, 407 N.E.2d 1365 (Ohio 1980).

733. E.C. Yokley, The Law of Subdivisions 11 (1963). Moreover, in 1983 a Michigan appeals court determined that despite home rule, the state's Adult Foster Care Facility Licensing Act, which exempts foster care facilities for six or fewer persons from the requirements of local zoning ordinances, was constitutional. City of Livonia v. Department of Social Servs., 333 N.W.2d 151 (Mich. Ct. App. 1983).

734. Rohan, *supra* note 709, at 3-12 and 3-122.

735. For example, the Rhode Island Supreme Court ruled that the state law defining six or fewer mentally retarded persons living in a community residence as a "family" superseded any inconsistent local regulations. Mongony v. Bevilacqua, 432 A.2d 661 (R.I. 1980). See R.I. Gen. Laws § 45-24-22 (1980). Tennessee, the only other state that has enacted such a statute, defines up to eight mentally or physically disabled persons as a single family. Tenn. Code Ann. § 13-24-102 (Michie 1980).

736. Arizona, California, Colorado, Connecticut, Maryland, Michigan, Minnesota, Montana, New Mexico, New York, Ohio, South Carolina, and Wisconsin; Rathkopf & Rathkopf, *supra* note 721, § 17A-38 at n.51.

737. Arizona, Colorado, Michigan, Minnesota, North Carolina, Ohio, South Carolina, Vermont, and Wisconsin; Rathkopf & Rathkopf, *supra* note 721, § 17A-38 at n.53.

738. Arizona, California, Colorado, Connecticut, Maryland, Michigan, Minnesota, Montana, North Carolina, New Mexico, New York, Ohio, South Carolina, Vermont, and Wisconsin; Rathkopf & Rathkopf, *supra* note 721, § 17A-38 at nn.51, 53.

739. California, Colorado, Idaho, Maine, Michigan, Montana, New Mexico, New York, and South Carolina; Rathkopf & Rathkopf, *supra* note 721, § 17A.05[2][c] at n.48.

740. Rathkopf & Rathkopf, *supra* note 721, § 17A.05[2][c] at n.48.

741. *Id.* at n.51. In Maine, for example, localities are given the option of making a state-approved group home "for 8 or fewer mentally handicapped or developmentally disabled persons" either a permitted single-family residential use or a conditional use. 30 Me. Stat. Ann. § 4962-A (West 1984). If the locality selects the option of making it a conditional use, the local zoning board must establish a hearing process. At that hearing, the board is limited to five reasons for denying an application of a qualifying group home: traffic safety, "pedestrian circulation," access to community services, and conformance to housing codes and to density requirements.

742. Nebraska Methodist Hosp. v. City of Omaha, No. 83-0-534, 8 MPDLR 35 (D. Neb. Oct. 7, 1983).

743. Jorgensen v. Board of Adjustment, 336 N.W.2d 423 (Iowa 1983).

744. Forsyth v. Board of Comm'rs, No. 83-4986, 6 MDLR 409 (Fla. Cir. Ct. Oct. 22, 1982). Similarly, a New York appeals court placed the burden on the objecting town to present specific and convincing evidence that a small

Even when no special use permit has been granted, group homes and other community living situations may become legitimate over time if no one objects soon enough. Continuing, nonconforming, preexisting uses have been legitimized as part of the tradition of favoring the free use of property. Moreover, they have been approved where the use has been changed insubstantially.[745]

If builders of group homes and other housing for mentally disabled clients do not have to obtain special permits, they may still have to overcome limitations found in the exemptions, which allow different types of community living arrangements to operate in residential areas. First, each statute normally specifies the type of resident for which the statute is intended.[746] Sometimes it will include certain disabled populations and exclude others. Every existing group home statute includes mentally retarded individuals, and most also include other developmentally disabled individuals.[747] However, most of them do not specifically include mentally ill persons or those with alcohol or drug-related problems.[748] Second, each statute specifies the maximum number of residents for a family or residential use.[749] A common limit is 6 or 8 individuals, not including houseparents, for a single-family district,[750] but as many as 14 disabled individuals are permitted in some states.[751] As a general rule, more residents are allowed in multiple-family districts, where the range extends as high as 16 persons.[752] Third, the statutes indicate what type of community residence is acceptable.[753] In addition to the familiar designation of "group homes," states use terms such as "residential facility," "family care home," "foster home," "community resident facility," and "any type of residence."

3. State Policy

Even where there is no explicit statute or regulation governing community residences, a state may have related statutes or general policies favoring or encouraging their establishment or take the public position that federal regulation requires the state to implement such policies.[754] Unlike the explicit statutes above, state policies do not necessarily preempt reasonable local regulations,[755] although in most instances courts have gone out of their way to rule favorably in support of the need for more community housing opportunities. In a few states, courts have taken a policy expression that only indirectly affects group homes, such as the creation of educational opportunities or community housing alternatives, and have found the necessary intent to overrule local restrictions.[756] Without the existence of an express state policy, certain courts have favored local authorities, even as against the preferences of state governments.[757]

---

residential program could substantially change the nature and character of the community. Town of Hempstead v. Commissioner, N.Y. Office of Mental Retardation & Developmental Disabilities, 453 N.Y.S.2d 32 (App. Div. 1982).

745. A Pennsylvania court decided that a hospital that had been a nonconforming use could now be void as a psychiatric facility because both were treating illnesses. Collins v. Zoning Hearing Bd. of Wilkes-Barre, 465 A.2d 53 (Pa. Commw. Ct. 1983). And in New York, an appeals court ruled that property that previously had been a nonconforming use—a school for 50 children—could then be turned into a 12-bed mental health facility. Village of Westbury v. Prevost, 467 N.Y.S.2d 70 (App. Div. 1983).

746. American Bar Association Commission on the Mentally Disabled, Zoning for Community Residences (1978) [hereinafter cited as A.B.A. Comm'n, Zoning]; 2 Rathkopf & Rathkopf, *supra* note 721; § 17A.05[2][c] at 17A-37.

747. A.B.A. Comm'n, Zoning, *supra* note 746, at 6-8.

748. In addition to the previously discussed social factors accounting for their relatively more successful advocacy, representatives of developmentally disabled persons have been more active in the communities and have been more successful in preventing neighborhood disturbances than have advocates for mentally ill persons.

749. A.B.A. Comm'n, Zoning, *supra* note 746, at 6.

750. *Id.* See, e.g., Arizona, California, Colorado, Maryland, and Minnesota.

751. *Id.* See, e.g., New Jersey, New Mexico, South Carolina, and New York.

752. *Id.* See, e.g., Arizona, Minnesota, Ohio, and Wisconsin.

753. *Id.*

754. 2 Rathkopf & Rathkopf, *supra* note 721, § 17A.05[2][b][u].

755. The New Hampshire Supreme Court found that the state's deinstitutionalization statute created a state policy in favor of placing developmentally disabled individuals into small community-based homes and that this policy preempted local zoning ordinances because the intent to do so was clear. Region 10 Client Management, Inc. v. Town of Hampstead, 424 A.2d 207 (N.H. 1980). Similarly, agreements by New York state and county governments to encourage the establishment of halfway houses for recovering alcoholics outweighed any community opposition absent health, safety, or welfare considerations to the contrary. Alcoholism Servs. of Erie County, Inc. v. Common Council, 453 N.Y.S.2d 390 (App. Div. 1982) (mem.). A methadone clinic in Illinois could operate where the evidence established a clinic was consistent with public policy and the use was not dissimilar to offices for doctors and dentists already in the neighborhood. Village of Maywood v. Health, Inc., 104 Ill. App. 3d 948, 433 N.E.2d 1951 (1982).

756. Massachusetts's policy of banning local ordinances that place restrictions on land that is to be used for educational purposes has been interpreted as protecting the establishment of group homes for emotionally disturbed adolescents (Schonnings v. People's Church Home, Inc., No. 7188, 2 MDLR 17 (Sup. Ct. Worcester, Mass. Jan. 28, 1977) and former mental patients (Zorek v. Attleboro Area Human Servs., Inc., No. 2450 (Mass. Sup. Ct. Nov. 1975)). In *New York v. 11 Cornwell Company* a federal judge concluded in part that the state had a constitutional obligation to provide community alternatives to institutionalization based on the United States Supreme Court's decision in *O'Connor v. Donaldson* prohibiting the warehousing of mental patients. Thus neighbors who conspired to deny housing to mentally disabled residents were in violation of the Civil Rights Act. New York v. 11 Cornwell Co., 508 F. Supp. 273 (E.D.N.Y. 1981), *aff'd*, 695 F.2d 34 (2d Cir. 1982); O'Connor v. Donaldson, 422 U.S. 563 (1975).

757. An Alabama court ruled that even if there had been a state policy promoting deinstitutionalization, a point it did not decide, reasonable zoning restrictions governing the establishment of a small group home would be permissible. Civitans Care, Inc. v. Board of Adjustment, 437 So. 2d 540 (Ala. Civ. App. 1983). Similarly, a New Jersey statute that merely encouraged the development of outpatient mental health services was insufficient reason to overrule local regulation. Township of Washington v. Central Bergen Community Mental Health Center, Inc., 383 A.2d 1194 (N.J. Super. Ct. 1978). In New York the construction of two drug rehabilitation centers was halted: one subject to reasonable local criteria (Ibero-American Action League, Inc. v. Palma, 47 A.D.2d 998, 366 N.Y.S.2d 747 (1975)) and the other to an ordinance that did not unduly interfere with the state's objectives (People v. Renaissance Project, Inc., 36 N.Y.2d 65, 324 N.E.2d 355 (1975)).

4. Governmental Immunity

As sovereign powers, states are immune from local zoning regulations unless the immunity is waived.[758] The issue becomes more complicated, however, in the usual situation where the group home is one, two, or more administrative steps removed from the state.[759] Two situations are most common in reported litigation: the community residence is operated by a state agency or a state agency contracts with another party who is reimbursed for providing the service. The legal test is whether the state legislature intended to give agencies immunity and if so, whether in the contract situation the immunity extends to the contracting party.

In the case law, courts have adopted two approaches in applying the test. The first approach examines the specific intent and the general relationship between the state and the community home. The New Jersey Supreme Court in *Berger v. State*[760] had no difficulty concluding that the necessary relationship was established, where the state department of institutions had been statutorily assigned the responsibility of caring for children who could not be properly cared for in their own homes. Other cases have also established intent by demonstrating the existence of a governmental as opposed to a proprietary purpose in running a group residence.[761] However, intent is not enough if the necessary relationship with the state does not exist. In a contractual arrangement this may present a difficult interpretive problem. For example, the Maine Supreme Court rejected immunity claims where no special state involvement was present in the contract,[762] and in New Jersey a court held that there could never be immunity unless a state agency was directly involved.[763]

The second approach courts use attempts to balance the public and local interests.[764] Yet the Florida Supreme Court noted that it would use the balancing approach only if there was no clear indication of legislative intent.[765] Where the second approach has been used, the results have been mixed. A New York case allowed governmental interest to prevail as long as the implementation process diminished local interests as little as necessary,[766] while Ohio's highest court struck down the state's zoning statute in favor of local interests.[767]

5. Fitting Within the Definition of "Family"

The most frequently litigated zoning issue is a given community living arrangement's conformance with a municipality's definition of a single-family or residential use. The criteria for making such a judgment vary from jurisdiction to jurisdiction, but certain indices are cited more frequently than others.[768] Without question small group homes with stable living situations are most favored.[769]

The typical ordinance that defines "family" unambiguously restricts the members to persons related by blood, marriage, or adoption[770] or to a specified number of unrelated individuals.[771] Despite *Belle Terre's* approval of such ordinances,[772] many courts have looked past the literal definition and instead found that the disputed nonfamily living arrangement was encompassed by the actual purpose of the statute.[773]

Of course, where ambiguity does exist, the courts generally rule that the property owners should be able to use their land for community homes. The prevailing view is that the scope of a family should not be limited to the traditional structure unless the statute does so explicitly.[774] Often the most important factor is the existence of a single housekeeping unit as opposed to a number of unrelated boarders.[775] A single unit has been found to exist where the group home has shared household activities,[776] live-in houseparents who head the household,[777] residents who share common interests,[778] closely supervised residents,[779] residents who plan to stay permanently,[780] and residents whose numbers are closely restricted.[781]

758. Rathkopf & Rathkopf, *supra* note 721, § 17A.05[2][b][u].

759. Lippincott, "A Sanctuary for People": Strategies for Overcoming Zoning Restrictions on Community Homes for Retarded Persons, 31 Stan. L. Rev. 767, 776 (1979).

760. 364 A.2d 993 (N.J. 1976).

761. Conners v. New York State Ass'n of Retarded Children, Inc., 370 N.Y.S.2d 474 (Sup. Ct. Spec. Term 1975); Rathkopf & Rathkopf, *supra* note 721, § 17A.05[2][b][u].

762. Penobscot Area Housing Dev. Corp. v. City of Brewer, 434 A.2d 14 (Me. 1981).

763. Township of Washington v. Central Bergen Community Mental Health Center, Inc., 383 A.2d 1194 (N.J. Super. Ct. Law Div. 1978).

764. Lippincott, *supra* note 758, at 777; Rathkopf & Rathkopf, *supra* note 721, § 17A.05[2][b[u].

765. Hillsborough Ass'n for Retarded Citizens, Inc. v. City of Temple Terrace, 332 So. 2d 610 (Fla. 1976).

766. Conners v. New York State Ass'n of Retarded Children, Inc., 370 N.Y.S.2d 474 (Sup. Ct. Spec. Term 1975).

767. Garcia v. Siffrin Residential Ass'n, 407 N.E.2d 1369 (Ohio 1980).

768. Summary and Analysis, 6 MDLR 3-7 (1982).

769. Rathkopf & Rathkopf, *supra* note 721, § 17A.05[2][b][i].

770. Region 10 Unit Management, Inc. v. Town of Hampstead, 424 A.2d 207 (N.H. 1980).

771. Hopkins v. Zoning Hearing Bd., 423 A.2d 1082 (Pa. Commw. Ct. 1980).

772. Village of Belle Terre v. Boraas, 416 U.S. 1 (1974).

773. Hopkins Zoning Hearing Bd., 423 A.2d 1082 (Pa. Commw. Ct. 1980); Hessling v. City of Broomfield, 563 P.2d 12 (Colo. 1977); City of White Plains v. Ferraioli, 34 N.Y.2d 300, 313 N.E.2d 756 (1974).

774. P. Rohan, *supra* note 709, ch. 3 at 98-100.

775. *Id.* ch. 3 at 102-7.

776. Costley v. Caromin House, Inc., 313 N.W.2d 21 (Minn. 1981); City of West Monroe v. Ouachita Ass'n for Retarded Children, Inc., 402 So. 2d 259 (La. Ct. App. 1981).

777. Costley v. Caromin House, Inc., 313 N.W.2d 21 (Minn. 1981).

778. City of West Monroe v. Ouachita Ass'n for Retarded Children, Inc., 402 So. 2d 259 (La. Ct. App. 1981).

779. Mongony v. Bevilacqua, 432 A.2d 661 (R.I. 1981).

780. Costley v. Caromin House, Inc., 313 N.W.2d 21 (Minn. 1981).

781. In each of the cases mentioned in notes 776-77 *supra* which had a single housekeeping unit, the number of residents was limited to six individuals.

The few courts that have concluded a small group home does not constitute a single housekeeping unit have cited the absence of live-in parents,[782] the lack of permanency in the living situation,[783] involvement of professional staff in the household activities,[784] medical care given in the home[785] and other institutional characteristics.[786] One recent case in Alabama found that a group home with six developmentally disabled adults and two resident managers was in conflict with a local zoning ordinance that limited housing to family-only occupancy. Since there was no preempting state legislation, the court concluded the stated criterion was applied properly because the managers were paid on salary and the residents received meals as in a rooming house.[787]

6. Restrictive Covenants

Restrictive covenants raise many of the same kinds of legal questions restrictive zoning ordinances do, with the major difference being that a covenant is in the nature of a private contract and as a rule does not carry the imprimatur of the state. In California, where group homes are encouraged by statute, courts are unwilling to overrule restrictive covenants, even though the same courts will preempt local zoning ordinances.[788] However, California seems to be an aberration. Most courts will be persuaded by strong expressions of contrary public policy because restrictive covenants are disfavored as encumbrances on the free use of land.[789] Even where there is no directly contrary state policy that preempts restrictive covenants, many courts will demand that the purpose of the covenant be unambiguous. A Delaware court determined that a private restriction on the deed referred to the structure of the building and not the proposed usage.[790] Thus, homes with eight developmentally disabled persons and houseparents may have been used differently from single family dwellings, but because the physical structures were the same the house was consistent with the covenant. The court warned that a less ambiguous covenant would have prevailed. Nevertheless, using liberal interpretations to find that small group homes for mentally disabled adults were included within the covenants' definition of family, the supreme courts of North Carolina[791] and Minnesota[792] were persuaded by such indications as live-in houseparents, shared household duties, the absence of institutional qualities, and the permanent nature of the living situations.

7. Factors in Addition to Zoning Restrictions

A 1983 survey by the General Accounting Office[793] suggested that while combating legal impediments to zoning was important, the major remaining obstacles to community housing for mentally disabled clients were formidable. In order of importance the obstacles included: (1) insufficient funding to pay for the start-up costs and continued operations of viable community alternatives, (2) an insufficient number of suitable housing units situated near community services and transportation networks, (3) community resistance, especially if no meaningful efforts had been made to educate people in the neighborhood of the purpose of group homes, (4) burdensome administrative requirements of basic federal entitlement programs such as Medicaid and SSI that support the residents, and (5) heightened prejudice toward mentally disabled persons, in particular those who were mentally ill as opposed to residents who were developmentally disabled.

B. State Housing Discrimination Statutes

Currently, most states have statutes that prohibit housing discrimination against the handicapped.[794] As shown in table 11.1, they vary greatly in the scope of their coverage, particularly as they affect mentally disabled persons. To begin with, protecting the handicapped against housing discrimination has received relatively less legislative attention than discrimination in employment and public accommodations.[795] Those

782. Penobscot Area Housing Dev. Corp. v. City of Brewer, 434 A.2d 14 (Me. 1981).

783. *Id.*

784. Garcia v. Siffrin Residential Ass'n, 407 N.E.2d 1369 (Ohio 1980).

785. Brownsdale Int'l Ltd. v. Board of Adjustments, 208 N.W.2d 121 (Wis. 1973).

786. *Id.*

787. Civitans Care, Inc. v. Board of Adjustment, 437 So. 2d 540 (Ala. Civ. App. 1983).

788. Seaton v. Clifford, 24 Cal. App. 3d 46, 100 Cal. Rptr. 779 (1972).

789. The Michigan Supreme Court and a lower court in Minnesota both found that state policies favoring the construction of group homes should not be deterred by restrictive covenants with contrary aims. Bellarmine Hills Ass'n v. Residential Systems Co., No. CR24-78, 3 MDLR 187 (Mich. Sup. Ct. Feb. 7, 1979); Alexander v. Minnesota Jewish Group Homes, Inc., No. 746834, 3 MDLR 36 (Minn. 4th Jud. Dist. Ct. July 26, 1978). Similarly, a New York policy of encouraging community residences for mentally disabled persons preempted a restrictive covenant (Crane Neck Ass'n, Inc. v. New York City of Long Island County Servs. Group, 460 N.Y.S.2d 69 (App. Div. 1983), *aff'd*, 460 N.E.2d 1336 (1984)), even though a court in the same judicial department had four years earlier upheld the same kind of covenant (Tytell v. Kaen, N.Y.L.J., June 11, 1979, at 12 col. 3, 3 MDLR 249 (Bronx County Sup. Ct. June 11, 1979)).

790. Cain v. Delaware Sec. Invs., No. 7236, 7 MDLR 384 (Del. Ch. Ct. Aug. 11, 1983).

791. J.T. Hobby & Son, Inc. v. Family Homes of Wake County, Inc., 274 S.E.2d 174 (N.C. 1981).

792. Costley v. Caromin House, Inc., 313 N.W.2d 21 (Minn. 1981).

793. An Analysis of Zoning and Other Problems Affecting the Establishment of Group Homes for the Mentally Disabled (GAO/HRD-83-14), 7 MDLR 376 (1983).

794. Table 11.1, A.B.A. Comm'n, Prohibiting Discrimination, *supra* note 549. These materials in the state survey were updated in 1983 for this book, but the format was developed by the Commission on the Mentally Disabled.

795. See table 11.1, col. 1. Thirty-three states have some kind of housing discrimination statute for the disabled as compared with 46 states that have employment provisions and 37 that have public accommodation provisions.

states that have legislation prohibiting discriminatory practices in housing tend to do so as part of a comprehensive statute that also prohibits discrimination in employment and public accommodations. More importantly, more than half the housing discrimination statutes cover the physically disabled but not those with mental disabilities.[796] Only 14 states even have statutory protections against housing discrimination on the basis of mental disability. Those 14 statutes also tend to limit their coverage to specific housing problems: refusing to transact real property including rentals, sales and leasing, placing unfair conditions or privileges on housing transactions, publishing notices that discourage certain groups of individuals from applying, and withholding financial assistance when it is to be used to buy, construct, or rehabilitate real property for mentally disabled persons.

As with many other discrimination statutes, those protecting the mentally handicapped against housing discrimination are difficult to enforce. Although most do have some kind of administrative enforcement procedure, they vary in their levels of effectiveness. Twenty-nine states do not have investigation capabilities or hearing procedures, have inadequate resources to handle complaints effectively, or have inadequate mechanisms to get victims of discrimination to file complaints. Some states invoke misdemeanor criminal penalties that have proven to be ineffective. Very few states allow private lawsuits for injunctive or monetary relief, and those that do so usually require that administrative remedies be exhausted first. Since most administrative procedures are backlogged, suits are discouraged, with the result that there has been almost no litigation by mentally disabled persons involving housing discrimination.[797]

At the very least, what is needed is inclusion of mentally and physically disabled persons in the proposed Fair Housing Act Amendments of 1983,[798] which would be the most direct and effective way of addressing inconsistent state coverage and enforcement. In addition, new approaches should be tried in order to supplement discrimination statutes. In New Jersey, for example, the state enacted a Senior Citizens and Disabled Protected Tenancy Act,[799] which protects disabled persons and others against evictions when condominium conversions are contemplated. As protected tenants they cannot be evicted for a specified period of time, and rent increases are also regulated. The United States Court of Appeals for the Third Circuit upheld the statute even where it was applied retroactively. Finding that there were no constitutional violations since any impairment on the right to contract was insubstantial, the state had a legitimate interest in protecting the welfare of its citizens, and the owners received compensation in the form of rent.[800] The power of the state to use land and property for public purposes recently was given a broad interpretation by the United States Supreme Court[801] suggesting strongly that many innovative solutions to inadequate housing are constitutionally permissible.

C. Section 504

Within its broad scope, § 504 of the Rehabilitation Act includes protection of mentally handicapped individuals from discrimination in housing projects that receive federal financial assistance.[802] To date, the U.S. Department of Housing and Urban Development (HUD) has not issued the regulations required to fully implement the statute.[803] So far the very few housing opinions decided by courts under § 504 involve admittance into public housing projects. Handicapped individuals may be eligible under a housing program specifically for the handicapped or under a program that includes the handicapped as one of the eligible groups.[804]

A 1984 New Jersey case holds that mentally ill persons seeking restitution for alleged discrimination in section 202 housing have a cognizable claim under § 504.[805] However, the federal court that decided the case noted the secretary of the federal department in charge of the program must be given broad discretion to distribute

796. *Id.* Nineteen of the 33 statutes cover only physical disabilities.

797. Review of the *Mental and Physical Disability Law Reporter* and federal and state reporting services found almost no cases.

798. U.S. Attorney General William French Smith recommended such an expansion in a speech before the American Bar Association's House of Delegates in 1983 (Annual Meeting of the American Bar Association, Atlanta, Ga., Aug. 1983).

799. N.J. Stat. Ann. § 2A:18-61.22 (West Supp. 1984). "Disabled tenant" is defined in § 2A:18-61.24(b).

800. Troy Ltd. v. Renna, 727 F.2d 287 (3d Cir. 1984).

801. Hawaii Housing Auth. v. Midkiff, 104 S. Ct. 2321 (1984).

802. Majors v. Housing Auth., 652 F.2d 454 (5th Cir. 1981); Morphis v. Dallas Housing Auth., No. CA3-80-0830-G, 4 MDLR 330 (N.D. Tex. July 2, 1980).

803. On June 15, 1983, HUD published a notice of proposed rulemaking for the implementation of § 504. 48 Fed. Reg. 27,529 (1983) (to be codified at 24 C.F.R. pt. 8).

804. According to two cases, § 504 does limit exclusions on the basis of mental impairments.

In one court opinion, a Dallas man with cerebral palsy obtained a preliminary injunction against a public housing project, ordering the defendants to reserve an apartment for him while they prepared and submitted specific tenant selection criteria for determining whether handicapped individuals were capable of independent living. The direct implication of the order was that the plaintiffs would ultimately suceed on the merits if reasonable criteria were applied. Morphis v. Dallas Housing Auth., No. CA3-80-0830-G, 4 MDLR 330 (N.D. Tex. July 2, 1980).

Another opinion involved a lawsuit by a woman who had formed an emotional dependence on her dog. She filed suit against a public housing project that would not allow anyone to have pets. The action was successful, not because the project was guilty of discrimination by enforcing the rule but because § 504 required this type of minimal concession to accommodate her special needs. Majors v. Housing Auth., 652 F.2d 454 (5th Cir. 1981).

805. Edge v. Pierce, Jr., No. 82-51, 8 MPDLR 387 (D.N.J. May 22, 1984).

housing and support services consistent with the purpose of the program, which is to create independent living situations. More dependent persons might be properly excluded, and the opportunities for the mentally ill might be justifiably different from those opportunities provided for elderly and physically handicapped persons.

At the very least, however, there must be bona fide reasons for excluding mentally disabled individuals from public housing and other federally funded housing projects. Moreover, while affirmative action is not required, certain modifications must be made to accommodate mentally disabled persons in those housing programs. Nevertheless, it should be emphasized that because most housing is privately financed, § 504 is of limited value in this area of mental disability law.

D. Federal Housing Programs for the Disabled

Federal housing assistance programs for the handicapped specifically include those who are mentally impaired.[806] In 1979, however, it was reported that there was "surprisingly little federally funded housing" for this category of people.[807] Since then HUD's Office of Independent Living, supported by the requirements of § 504, has increased somewhat the number of housing opportunities through the implementation of three different programs.

The assisted-housing program (§ 8) under the United States Housing Act of 1937 provides rent subsidies for a wide variety of existing housing options,[808] including small group homes and other independent, semi-independent, or supervised living situations for handicapped individuals. To qualify, the person must be poor and handicapped, which is defined as having an impairment that is of indefinite duration, substantially interferes with independent living, and would be improved by more suitable housing.[809] An attendant or nurse may live in only if it is essential to the care and well-being of the handicapped individual.

The elderly and handicapped housing loan program under § 202 of the Housing Act of 1959 provides direct loan assistance to nonprofit organizations that construct or substantially rehabilitate rental housing for the handicapped.[810] New construction is approved only if HUD determines there is a shortage of suitable housing in that area. HUD has used this program to encourage the establishment of more group homes and small apartment complexes.[811]

Finally, HUD has used the general public housing program,[812] in combination with the requirements of § 504, to increase the opportunities for mentally disabled persons in low-income public housing. The eligibility criteria parallel the requirements in § 8 housing.[813]

VII. FINANCING COMMUNITY LIVING

For those mentally disabled persons who are not employed and want to live outside of an institution, financial assistance becomes an overwhelming concern.[814] Whether unemployment is a temporary or a long-term problem, the individual must be financed by alternative means, such as through family, friends, preexisting savings, insurance, or public assistance. Without adequate financial support suitable community living becomes difficult or impossible. Moreover, the level of support that is available largely defines the lifestyle that is possible for that individual.

The problem of financing needed services is particularly severe for disabled adults for two important reasons. Major programs such as the Education for All Handicapped Children Act are intended only for children, and adults are far less likely, due both to the law and demography, to have relatives who are responsible for their care. The system's bias is toward protecting children while permitting dependent adults to fend for themselves.

A. Private Financing

The most desirable financing for both the individual mentally disabled person and society is private contributions from family and friends or from foundations, which minimize both stigma for the individual and the public debt. Two methods for making the most of available private funds are estate planning and the use of various insurance plans. However, even with recent advances in these two types of funding mechanisms substantial gaps in coverage remain.

1. Estate Planning

Basically, estate planning is a comprehensive planning process for anticipating immediate or future financial needs. The key to success is examining the total set of circumstances that will apply or might apply to an individual's situation during his lifetime. Until very recently, however, estate plans for parents of mentally disabled children or the mentally disabled children

806. 42 U.S.C. § 1437a(b)(3) (1982).

807. Practicing Law Institute, Legal Rights of Mentally Disabled Persons: Federal Housing Programs for the Mentally Disabled 1743 (1979) [hereinafter cited as P.L.I., Legal Rights].

808. 42 U.S.C.A. § 1437f (section 8 lower-income housing assistance); § 1437f(p) (shared housing for elderly and handicapped) (Supp. 1985).

809. 42 U.S.C. § 1437(b)(3) (1982).

810. 12 U.S.C. § 1701q (1982).

811. P.L.I., Legal Rights, *supra* note 807, at 1748.

812. 42 U.S.C. § 1437a(b)(3) (1982).

813. P.L.I., Legal Rights, *supra* note 807, at 1749.

814. See this chapter § V, Legally Enforceable Employment Opportunities, *supra*.

themselves were ignored by the legal profession and advocacy groups.[815] Now the importance of planning is being recognized,[816] and efforts are being made to insure the financial stability of many more mentally disabled individuals.

A fundamental objective of estate planning for mentally disabled beneficiaries is obtaining a result that integrates the private resources of the individual with governmental benefits.[817] A nettlesome problem is anticipating the amount of governmental benefits and how those benefits will be affected by different estate planning arrangements. Three main categories of governmental assistance need to be considered: (1) benefits provided to designated individuals without regard to other available income or assets, such as social security retirement benefits, Medicare for the aged, and educational services for handicapped children; (2) benefits available only to individuals who meet specified financial eligibility requirements such as SSI, Medicaid, and Legal Services, and (3) benefits available without regard to income or assets but reimbursable to the entity that provided the funds or services at a rate proportional to the individual's assets and income, such as care at a residential facility. The last two categories make planning difficult since available income in either category reduces or eliminates potential benefits and increases the individual's financial obligations. Although hiding available resources is not illegal and according to the leading law review article on the subject should not be viewed as "morally reprehensible,"[818] the fact remains that such a maneuver could be a financial drain on society, may negatively affect other disabled individuals who depend on the same limited benefits, and comes in conflict with the normalization principle to the extent that society generally devalues recipients of governmental services.

The desirability of seeking a guardianship arrangement for incompetent mentally disabled individuals should be considered carefully by attorneys at the beginning of the planning process as this can affect both the practical and the legal aspects of the final financial arrangements. Not surprisingly there is considerable disagreement about how attorneys should go about resolving the guardianship question, especially determining whether clients will actually be better off with a judicial resolution of the problem.

There are several financial arrangements to choose from. For the disabled person who does not have sufficient assets to make an estate plan worthwhile, the most financially rewarding plan may be to dissipate resources through disinheritance and other legal means so that there will be no available resources to eliminate or reduce governmental support. Second, for the moderately disabled person with good employment potential, a gift might be the desirable option, although the requisite circumstances that make this option worthwhile would occur only rarely. Third, a bequest could be made to a relative or custodian conditioned with instructions to take care of the disabled person—a high-risk option in that it creates a moral obligation that may not be legally enforceable.

The preferable alternative in many circumstances is the creation of a trust, particularly where larger estates are involved. Although trusts may be structured in many different ways, there are essentially two kinds. A mandatory trust establishes a precise method of distributing income which cannot be changed by the trustee. The potential weakness of this approach is that new circumstances can reduce the benefits of the trust arrangement to the disabled individual. A discretionary trust, often the more sensible approach, can be created with strong precatory language that gives a clear explanation of the purpose of the trust so that courts can interpret the terms as they were intended to function. This permits a trustee to react to unforeseen events and protect the beneficiary's interests, for example, by avoiding situations where available income will make the beneficiary ineligible for needed federal or state assistance. In the words of one commentator, "[g]ifts to a disabled child which reduce the child's state or federal aid are not gifts to the child: they are gifts to the state or federal government."[819] The architect of a trust may also wish to include a standard that requires the trustee to make a distribution when specified situations arise or for specific purposes: "in case of emergency," "in an extraordinary event," "for support," "for care and maintenance," or for "educational needs." Whether the trust is mandatory or discretionary, it may be structured so that the benefits run to the individual at the benefactor's death or during the lifetime of the benefactor.[820] A living trust is amendable by the benefactor until he or she dies and provides funds for the care of disabled person immediately.[821]

815. Effland, Trusts and Estate Planning, *in* Mentally Retarded Citizens and the Law 116 (M. Kindred, J. Cohen, D. Penrod, & T. Schaeffer eds. 1976).

816. Frolik, Estate Planning for Parents of Mentally Disabled Children, 40 U. Pitt. L. Rev. 305 (1979); Center for Law and Health Sciences, Estate Planning for Parents of Persons with Developmental Disabilities (May 1982).

817. Frolik, *supra* note 816, at 305. The suggestions in the rest of this section on estate planning are for the most part developed in detail in Frolik's article, esp. at 312-30.

818. *Id.* at 322.

819. *Id.* at 315.

820. Effland, *supra* note 815.

821. Baker & Karol, Employee Insurance Benefit Plans and Discrimination on the Basis of Handicap, 27 DePaul L. Rev. 1013 (1978).

A 1984 issue of the National Association of State Mental Retardation Program Directors' newsletter lists ten different programs around the country that help disabled individuals and their families with future financial planning including one that has life insurance to use for children once their parents die.[822]

2. Insurance

An important means of providing private financing for mentally disabled persons is through careful use and drafting of insurance policies. The purpose may be to protect the disabled person directly against health risks or loss of income or to enable parents or friends to provide income to the disabled person after their death through the use of life insurance. However, with regard specifically to third-party payments for care and treatment, a book written under the auspices of the American Psychiatric Association concludes

> treatments for mental disorders are not reimbursed by third-party payers in the same degree or manner as general medical disorders. Although the coverage of psychiatric care has improved during the 50-year history of health insurance in the United States, private insurance to cover the cost of psychiatric care is only about half as available to cover general medical costs.[823]

Although there are no precise statistics on the subject, insurance companies routinely treat mentally disabled individuals differently from other applicants, sometimes because of actuarial tables that show that the individual is a higher risk, other times because of misperceptions or invidious discrimination. "Little or no regard has been given to the correlation of their disabilities with the increase risk they are perceived to represent," observes one commentator.[824] The result is that mentally disabled individuals frequently pay higher premiums, are ineligible for coverage, or are excluded from recovering benefits when they do file a claim.[825] Moreover, some employers are reluctant to hire disabled persons "because of the increased insurance costs" to their businesses if the health plans are company supported.[826]

Federal, state, or local statutes, some enforceable in court, make certain types of public discrimination illegal.[827] However, since currently employers are the source of most private insurance,[828] special legislation may be necessary in addition to discrimination statutes in order to encourage companies to spread the insurance risk to a larger segment of the population that includes persons with various mental disabilities.

Among the considerations in providing insurance coverage is competence to make a contract.[829] The ability of incompetent individuals to make an insurance contract is not settled in the law,[830] although there is no such problem with group insurance since the contract is between the employer and the insurer. A second concern is whether the disabled individual may give a valid release in order to accept payment in satisfaction of a claim. Again the law provides no uniform answer to whether a person needs to be competent to collect. Certain jurisdictions make the insurance contract voidable by the incompetent person, but it would not be automatically void. The presence of temporary or limited legal guardians would resolve either one of these contractual difficulties, but as is detailed in a previous chapter, the availability of guardians for this purpose at best is uncertain.[831]

Some of the most vigorously contested underwriting concerns are associated with health and long-term disability insurance policies in which one claim can cost the insurance company thousands or perhaps several millions of dollars.[832]

Numerous companies provide private health insurance. From the perspective of mentally disabled persons, questions about the scope of coverage are crucial. Who is eligible? Will services that are needed to treat an ongoing or newly discovered disability be valid under the policy?

Statistics describing the actual numbers and categories of mentally disabled individuals with insurance policies are incomplete, whether the person is mentally ill or mentally retarded. Among the reasons is an understandable hestitancy on the part of many individuals to divulge this information and the availability of group insurance plans that do not require disclosure. It is generally accepted, however, that many mentally disabled persons go without health and disability coverage.[833]

A study conducted in 1979 supports the observation made earlier that private health insurance coverage for mental illness is widespread, although not necessarily comprehensive as measured against other medical serv-

822. New Directions, No. 5, May 1984.

823. S. Sharfstein, S. Muszynski, & E. Myers, Health Insurance and Psychiatric Care: Update and Appraisal 1 (1984).

824. *Id.* at 1013, 1014.

825. *Id.*; Senn v. Old Am. Ins. Corp., 120 F. Supp. 422 (E.D.S.C. 1954).

826. Baker & Karol, *supra* note 821, at 1014.

827. For example, in Chrysler Outboard Corp. v. Wisconsin Dep't of Indus., Labor & Human Relations, 14 Fair Empl. Prac. Cas. (BNA) 344 (Wis. Cir. Ct. 1976), an employer was prohibited from denying employment to an applicant with leukemia where the employer explained his decision in terms of the applicant's higher risk of absenteeism and the employer's higher costs in insuring him. See also, discussion *supra* on employment discrimination.

828. Sharfstein, Muszynski, & Myers, *supra* note 823, at 8-9.

829. The issue of competence generally is covered in ch. 7, Incompetency, Guardianship, and Restoration.

830. Effland, *supra* note 815, at 147.

831. See in this book ch. 7, Incompetency, Guardianship, and Restoration, *supra*.

832. Baker & Karol, *supra* note 821, at 1019.

833. *Id.*; Mentally Retarded Citizens and the Law, *supra* note 815.

ices provided to individual patients.[834] In 1969 the Social Security Administration estimated that 63 percent of the population had some inpatient mental health coverage and 37 percent had some outpatient services covered under private insurance plans.[835] Today, at least 11 state legislatures have enacted statutes mandating some type of coverage for mental disorders. Fourteen additional states provide for optional coverage.

Despite certain inroads, substantial gaps in services remain. A study released in 1983 reported that 25 states and the District of Columbia did not provide for any kind of coverage.[836] In addition, one of the major sticking points in the promotion of legislation for national health insurance has been the proposed inclusion of psychiatric services. Even where limited services are available in private policies, legal disputes arise over the length of time a person may be hospitalized and still be protected,[837] whether there can be reimbursement for inpatient care at a public psychiatric hospital,[838] and what type of professional is qualified to deliver reimbursable services.[839] Moreover, insurers and employers continue to be concerned about the absence of precise information on key points about mental illness and treatment, such as the nature and causes of mental illness, forms of treatment that should be used, and the incidence and duration of services that are utilized in treatment.[840] Without answers to these and other questions insurers may be reluctant to broaden coverage because the assignment of risk has no proper foundation. Thus, two major insurance companies challenged Massachusetts's mandatory mental health insurance law, arguing that it came in conflict with the federal requirements under the Employee Retirement Income Security Act (ERISA), which covers all but a few specifically mentioned employee benefit plans. Massachusetts's highest court determined that an exception under the federal act for state regulation of insurance made the mandatory state statute valid,[841] but strong language in a 1983 United States Supreme Court case, *Shaw v. Delta Air Lines, Inc.*,[842] seemed to suggest that Massachusetts had made too broad an interpretation of the exception. In the New York case, a state law that required employers to provide the same benefits for pregnancy as for other nonoccupational disabilities was struck down.

Somewhat surprisingly, a unanimous United States Supreme Court affirmed the Massachusetts Supreme Judicial Court in 1985,[843] upholding the state law that required insurance companies to provide minimum mental health benefits in employee health care plans that cover hospital and surgical expenses. Neither the federal Employee Retirement Income Security Act of 1974 nor the National Labor Relations Act preempted state regulation in this area. As a result, more states will be encouraged to broaden rather than narrow their involvement in the regulation of insured mental disability care. Nevertheless, other obstacles remain in the way of more universal insurance availability.

A conflict between the psychiatric and the psychological professions over qualifications has already worked its way through the Supreme Court. A 5-4 majority held that a group health plan subscriber who was denied reimbursement for the costs of her treatment with a clinical psychologist had standing to sue under the Clayton Antitrust Act.[844] The patient alleged that the insurer had conspired with the psychiatric profession to limit reimbursement to treatment that was supervised by and billed through a physician. Such allegations, if proved, constitute an antitrust violation. Similar conflicts have also arisen between various public or private insurers and clients of other nonmedical professionals.[845]

The availability of insurance coverage for developmentally disabled persons is a separate problem. According to a 1976 review of state statutes, 33 jurisdictions had some kind of legislation pertaining to health insurance for mentally retarded individuals.[846] Many of these laws, noted the author, were based on model legislation prepared jointly by the National Association for Retarded Children and the Health Insurance Association of America. The basic thrust of the draft bill was to prevent insurers from dropping developmentally disabled children from the family or group policy when the children reached the age of majority. This coverage would protect adult children who were unable to sustain themselves through employment and were thus dependent on others for support and maintenance. In order to protect the insurance companies, the disabled person or their family would have the burden of establishing both the necessary degree of incapacity and dependence.

There remain several major obstacles to establishing a comprehensive system of private health insurance for developmentally disabled persons. First, 18 states do not have any substantive insurance legislation protecting this group of individuals. Second, treatment and habili-

834. Practice Manual: Private Health Insurance Benefits: Alcoholism, Drug Abuse and Mental Illness, 4 MDLR 52 (1980).

835. Sharfstein, Muszynski, & Myers, *supra* note 823, at 91 table 23.

836. *Id.*

837. Coliseum House Hosp. v. Bonis, 396 So. 2d 495 (La. Ct. App. 1981).

838. Bernard B. v. Blue Cross & Blue Shield of Greater N.Y., 528 F. Supp. 125 (S.D.N.Y. 1980).

839. Blue Shield of Va. v. McCready, 457 U.S. 465 (1982).

840. Sharfstein, Muszynski, & Myers, *supra* note 823, at 13.

841. Attorney Gen. v. Travelers Ins. Co. 463 N.E.2d 548 (Mass. 1984).

842. 103 S. Ct. 2890 (1983).

843. Metropolitan Life Ins. Co. v. Massachusetts, 105 S. Ct. 2380 (1985), *aff'g* Att'y Gen. v. Travelers Ins. Co., 463 N.E.2d 548 (Mass. 1984).

844. Blue Shield of Va. v. McCready, 457 U.S. 465 (1982).

845. See, e.g., reimbursement under federal Medicaid program discussed in this chapter § VII B, Public Financial Support, *infra*.

846. Fallman, Insurance, *in* Mentally Retarded Citizens and the Law, *supra* note 815, at 150.

tation are not always fully reimbursable. For example, the costs normally associated with educating, training, or taking care of disabled individuals are not included unless these costs are part of the active treatment, and direct medical care is often excluded if it is provided inside an institution which is not a regularly licensed hospital. Third, eligibility for individual health insurance will often depend on the perceived severity of the disability. Severely or profoundly mentally retarded persons, as a general rule, are totally excluded as are individuals who are inside institutions, incompetent, or not self-supporting. Less disabled individuals may be eligible for coverage, but they may have fewer benefits. Fourth, while the precise availability of group health insurance is a subject of dispute among the experts, there is a consensus that individuals who are in the lower socioeconomic levels of society are underserved.[847]

In order to supplement workers' compensation, many insurance companies offer protection against loss of income through both group and individual plans. However, since most coverage is group oriented, many mentally disabled individuals who are not full-time employees are excluded. A few individuals might otherwise qualify for individual insurance coverage, but if they are disabled to begin with, many companies will not allow them to purchase policies or will raise their premiums. Usually, mildly mentally retarded individuals may obtain this kind of insurance under standard premiums. As the degree of retardation or mental illness becomes more severe, the selection criteria typically will become increasingly more difficult for the applicant.[848]

Finally, life insurance can produce income for mentally disabled individuals who are named as beneficiaries by their parents, relatives, or friends. The main legal issue is the beneficiary's competence to give a valid release for the payment of benefits. Where there is a legitimate concern about the person's capacity, a guardian or conservator may have to be appointed.[849] In this situation, a temporary or limited guardian is all that is necessary.

B. Public Financial Support

Several federally funded public insurance income maintenance programs can be used by mentally disabled individuals in the community. No one program covers every need. For many mentally disabled persons the federal programs could make community living a feasible arrangement, but for others at high risk the community alternative may turn out to be undesirable even with federal contributions.

Programs providing income maintenance and basic services fall into two categories: those that identify mentally disabled individuals as intended recipients and those that provide support to mentally disabled individuals along with nondisabled individuals if they meet financial eligibility criteria.

1. Social Security

Since 1974 the most important assistance program for mentally disabled citizens has been Supplemental Security Income for the Aged, Blind, and Disabled (SSI)[850] and its implementing regulations.[851] Before SSI was enacted there were separate programs for each named group of individuals which were administered according to state standards. Supplemental Security Income consolidated these assistance programs, placed the administrative responsibilities in the hands of the federal government, and established uniform eligibility criteria applicable for every state in the Union.[852]

A major requirement for applicants is demonstrating financial need and taking all appropriate steps to apply for and obtain any other benefits to which they are entitled.[853] Generally inmates or residents of public institutions are excluded from receiving benefits,[854] unless the facility is a community residence that serves no more than 16 clients.[855] Because of such financial exclusions the program provides assistance mostly to those individuals who have few other sources of income or accumulated assets. For many mentally disabled persons, the program can mean the difference between institutionalization and living in the community at varying levels of comfort and satisfaction.

A complementary Social Security program furnishes disability insurance benefits to mentally disabled individuals who become impaired while they are employed or who simply reach retirement age.[856] This legislation is intended to protect workers and their dependents from the risk of loss of income due to the insured's old age, death, or disability.[857]

Mentally disabled persons qualify for Social Security if their impairments are so severe that they are unable to do the work that they were engaged in previously, they are unable to undertake other substantial gainful activities, or their identified impairments have lasted or are

847. *Id.* at 145-51.
848. *Id.* at 157.
849. *Id.* at 161.

850. 42 U.S.C. §§ 1381 to 1383c (1982). See in this chapter § I F 1, Income Assistance for the Needy Disabled, *supra* for a description of the program.
851. 20 C.F.R. § 416 (1984).
852. Berliner, Supplemental Security Income: A Practical Overview, 13 Clearinghouse Rev. 934 (1980).
853. 42 U.S.C. §§ 1382(a) & (e)(2), 1382a(a)(2)(B).
854. 42 U.S.C. § 1382(e)(1)(A).
855. 42 U.S.C. § 1382(e)(1)(C).
856. 42 U.S.C. §§ 301 to 433; 70 Am. Jur. 2d § 1.
857. 42 U.S.C. §§ 301 to 433 (1976 & Supp. IV 1980); 70 Am. Jur. 2d § 4.

expected to last more than 12 months or are fatal.[858] Children who are under 18 qualify for SSI if they have a comparably severe mental disability. Their mental disabilities must also preclude undertaking "any substantial gainful activity" and must have endured 12 months. Under this standard persons must not only be unable to do their previous work assignments but also lack the ability to do other work anywhere in the United States, once age, education, and work experience are taken into consideration.[859] For eligible individuals, the amount of the allowance is determined by assuming that the person has attained the statutory retirement age.[860]

In deciding if a person is disabled under the Social Security Act, whether it is under the disability insurance program or SSI, courts have proceeded under certain basic interpretive principles. First, the act is viewed as a remedial statute that must be construed broadly and applied liberally in favor of the claimants.[861] Thus courts have ruled in favor of claimants who submitted evidence of subjective symptoms of mental illness[862] or evidence that they were unable to control their temper.[863]

Second, despite these liberal court constructions, applicants must still meet the burden of proving their claims.[864] This cannot be done by showing the mere existence of a psychological disorder because the condition must be severe enough to substantially interfere with employment.[865] The actual standard, which varies according to the cases, may require something less than a preponderance of the evidence[866] or require something that approximates proof beyond a reasonable doubt.[867]

Third, if the claimants do come forward with substantial evidence showing they are unable to return to work and the evidence is not refuted, then the burden shifts, and the government, if it wants to deny the benefit, must show that other jobs are available for that particular individual.[868] To do this, it must prove the claimant retains a residual functional capacity to perform work,[869] but it does not have to show that the individual could actually be hired.[870]

Fourth, the use of expert medical testimony will often be determinative in the courtroom. While it is clear that the claimants are not required to present medical evidence if they can show that subjective symptoms exist,[871] they are in a much stronger position if they do. If the claimant goes forward with substantial testimony from a physician, the government can only refute that evidence with another medical opinion.[872] If claimants do not present medical testimony, the claimants must relate their subjective symptoms to a "medically determinable impairment."[873]

Fifth, on appeal the standard of review is whether the administrative law judge's decision was reasonable.[874] Even if the courts would have weighed the evidence differently, this by itself is not enough to change the result.

Finally, the law states that once the claimant has become a recipient, the government, if it determines to cut off the benefits, has the burden of showing that the individual is no longer disabled.[875]

Since 1980, when new administrative policies were implemented, there has been a concerted effort by the executive branch to institute a fundamental change in the eligibility criteria for mentally disabled persons under the Social Security program. In order to be considered disabled, an applicant had to be medically impaired to such an extent that he was completely unable to work.[876] This new evaluation process established a five-step series of requirements for eligibility[877] which was especially difficult for mentally impaired claimants. Claimants under 50 years of age who did not have one of the listed severe disorders or did not meet one of the other criteria were presumed to have sufficient residual work capacity to undertake some kind of substantial gainful employment and thus were ineligible for benefits. Chronically mentally ill patients in particular maintained that the process as applied to them was illegal and shortsighted because while they were unable to hold down jobs for the most part, they were also precluded from receiving Social Security. As a result, a number of patients who needed SSI to prevent reinstitutionalization were cut off the eligibility roles even though they managed to exist in the community only by taking psychotropic medications and relying on various support networks.

Several lawsuits were filed challenging the new system; two led to court decisions that preceded congres-

858. 42 U.S.C. § 1382c(a)(3)(A) & (B).
859. 42 U.S.C. § 423(d)(2)(A).
860. 42 U.S.C. § 423(a)(2).
861. Berliner, *supra* note 852.
862. Stanley v. Schweiker, 529 F. Supp. 236 (E.D.N.Y. 1981).
863. Schmidt v. Harris, 498 F. Supp. 1181 (W.D. Mo. 1980).
864. Scharlow v. Schweiker, 655 F.2d 645 (5th Cir. 1981); Blalock v. Richardson, 483 F.2d 773 (4th Cir. 1972).
865. Sitar v. Schweiker, 671 F.2d 19 (1st Cir. 1982).
866. Jeralds v. Richardson, 445 F.2d 36 (7th Cir. 1971).
867. Blalock v. Richardson, 483 F.2d 773 (4th Cir. 1972).
868. Brenem v. Harris, 621 F.2d 688 (5th Cir. 1980); Meneses v. Secretary of Health, Educ. & Welfare, 442 F.2d 803 (D.C. Cir. 1971).
869. Berry v. Schweiker, 675 F.2d 464 (2d Cir. 1982); Brenem v. Harris, 621 F.2d 688 (5th Cir. 1980).
870. Herridge v. Richardson, 464 F.2d 198 (5th Cir. 1972).
871. Woodard v. Schweiker, 668 F.2d 370 (8th Cir. 1981); Stanley v. Schweiker, 529 F. Supp. 236 (E.D.N.Y. 1981).
872. Aquino v. Harris, 516 F. Supp. 265 (E.D. Pa. 1981).
873. Ware v. Schweiker, 651 F.2d 408 (5th Cir. 1981).
874. Lizotte v. Secretary of Health & Human Servs., 654 F.2d 127 (1st Cir. 1981).
875. McCoy v. Secretary of Health & Human Servs., 532 F. Supp. 359 (S.D. Ohio 1981).
876. 42 U.S.C. § 423(d)(2)(A) (1982).
877. 20 C.F.R. §§ 404.1545(c) & 416.945(c) (1984).

sional reform. A federal court in Minnesota issued a preliminary injunction temporarily halting the administration's evaluation process as it was being applied to mentally ill persons.[878] In the court's view there was a substantial probability that the existing policies would be ruled improper because they precluded an individual assessment of a person's mental condition as it related to the person's ability to engage in substantial gainful activity. The new procedures when judged against the act, implementing regulations, and case law were found to be "arbitrary, capricious, irrational, and an abuse of discretion."[879] On appeal the United States Court of Appeals for the Eighth Circuit substantially affirmed the lower court, differing only with the scope of relief granted to the plaintiffs. Those who were denied benefits as a result of the incorrect procedures had to be reinstated until new procedures were implemented.[880] Similarly, a federal court in New York, later upheld by the United States Court of Appeals for the Second Circuit, concluded the same procedures for determining eligibility for Social Security were improper, reinstated claimants' benefits until proper standards were developed, and indicated that those who were denied benefits unfairly would be entitled to retroactive reimbursement.[881]

Before other cases could work their way through the judicial system, Congress enacted the Social Security Disability Benefits Reform Act of 1984,[882] which reemphasized due process rights thought to exist before the Reagan administration began reinterpreting the regulations. Most importantly for mentally ill persons, the act prohibited the termination of benefits for existing recipients unless there is substantial evidence of medical improvement in either a claimant's impairment or combination of impairments and that claimant now is able to engage in substantial gainful activity.[883] This revised scheme places the burden of proving ineligibility on the government, although to what extent depends on the adoption of final regulations and subsequent court interpretation.

Recently, the United States Supreme Court reiterated the principle that even though courts may declare governmental actions illegal, they must proceed carefully in fashioning relief that may interfere with professional judgments. Thus, even though one class of Social Security disability claimants were able to show that there had been long delays in providing hearings, a federal district court in Vermont, affirmed by a federal circuit court of appeals, was reversed and criticized when it established specific deadlines for the department to follow in the future.[884]

As with many legal problems in the mental disability area, the Social Security laws' applications seem to be less restrictive for mentally retarded or developmentally disabled persons than for mentally ill persons. "The irremediable, life-long nature of retardation generally leads to a swifter, favorable disposition of disability claims, in contrast to claims based on mental illness," explains one commentator, but pointing out that "adjudication of these claims can pose the same vocational issues as any other disability case, due to the varying degrees of retardation and the impact of early intervention on the acquisition of academic, social, and vocational skills."[885]

In addition, mentally retarded persons may share common administrative obstacles with other mentally disabled persons. For example, in a federal case from New York, involving all mentally impaired recipients of Social Security benefits who were being automatically reviewed to determine continued eligibility, the court preliminarily enjoined the government from terminating benefits unless it first contacted the recipients in person to make sure they understood what they needed to do to respond to the review. Before the injunction was ordered many different types of mentally disabled persons had been losing their payments because they were unable to properly respond to the administrative investigation.[886]

2. Income Maintenance

General income maintenance programs for indigent persons include Aid to Families with Dependent Children (AFDC) and food stamps. The AFDC program authorizes federal payments of funds to states that have approved plans for providing aid and services to needy families and children.[887] The protected class under the statute is the dependent child, who is defined as a child deprived of parental support or care by reason of death, continued absence, or physical or mental incapacity of a parent. In order to be eligible there also must be a showing of financial need. The Food Stamp Act gives financially eligible households an opportunity to buy stamps that have greater food purchasing value than their purchase price in order to promote a nutritionally adequate diet for those in need.[888]

878. Mental Health Ass'n of Minn. v. Schweiker, No. 4-82-Civ.-83, 7 MDLR 18 (D. Minn. Dec. 22, 1982).

879. *Id.*

880. Mental Health Ass'n of Minn. v. Heckler, No. 83-1263, 7 MDLR 455 (8th Cir. Nov. 4, 1983).

881. City of New York v. Heckler, 578 F.Supp. 1109 (E.D.N.Y. 1984), *aff'd*, 742 F.2d 729 (2d Cir. 1984).

882. Pub. L. No. 98-460, 98 Stat. 1794 (1984).

883. Polaski v. Heckler, 751 F.2d 943 (8th Cir. 1984).

884. Day v. Schweiker 685 F.2d 19 (1982), *vacated and remanded sub nom.* Heckler v. Day, 104 S. Ct. 2249 (1984).

885. Practice Manual: Social Security Disability Benefits: Legal Issues for Mentally Disabled Claimants, 4 MDLR 438, 441 (1980).

886. Schisler v. Heckler, 574 F. Supp. 1538 (W.D.N.Y. 1983).

887. 42 U.S.C. §§ 601 to 610 (1982).

888. 7 U.S.C. §§ 2011 to 2025.

Two other federally assisted programs encourage states to provide adequate supplies of food to young children: the National School Lunch Program[889] and the Child Nutrition Act.[890]

3. Medical Assistance and Nutrition

A broad range of medical assistance is provided to mentally disabled citizens through Medicaid, Medicare, and maternal and child health care. Medicaid enables states to furnish medical assistance to families with dependent children and to aged, blind, or disabled individuals.[891] It is an open-ended program that reimburses the states based on a percentage of expenditures they incur pursuant to their state plans. One stated purpose of the legislation is to furnish rehabilitation and other services to help families and individuals attain or retain the capacity for independence and self-care in the community.

While Medicaid does provide a source of funds for some mentally disabled persons living in the community, it is also true that Medicaid through its program for intermediate care facilities (ICF)[892] has stood as a strong disincentive to deinstitutionalization. According to the Center for Human Policy in Syracuse, pouring billions of dollars into what has been described as inadequate and segregated care left little money targeted by the states for noninstitutional community-based services for mentally retarded persons.[893] Similar complaints can be made on behalf of groups representing chronically mentally ill persons. Part of the problem may have been rectified by an amendment that provides a mechanism for states to request that Medicaid funding be diverted for such services as respite care, homemakers, case management, habilitation, and personal care—all of which can be provided in the home or in semiindependent living situations.[894] Thus, the state of Idaho has enacted a program of reimbursement for personal care services for Medicaid recipients in their homes as alternatives to nursing home and ICF placements.[895] However, there are serious drawbacks, in addition to the fact that there is no guarantee that states will in fact request such monies. First, states may exclude those individuals for whom there is an expectation that home and community-based services would be more expensive than the Medicaid services the individual would otherwise receive. Second, the state may elect to provide these services to a limited group of eligible individuals rather than all eligible individuals. Third, no payments may be used for room and board.[896]

At the same time, Congress has explicitly declined to permit the use of any Medicaid funds for custodial care and treatment of mentally disabled persons if they are between the ages of 21 and 65, regardless of the type of facility that may be offering the services. The United States Court of Appeals for the Second Circuit upheld the disallowance of funds against the state of Connecticut, which had used Medicaid payments to provide custodial support to patients in a rest home that had been properly certified as an ICF.[897] The Court of Appeals for the Eighth Circuit disagreed, determining that the federal government could not disallow Medicaid payments to three community residential facilities without making sure the required services were in fact custodial.[898] The overall character of a facility was not the proper basis for denying funds for particular services.

A unanimous United States Supreme Court recently affirmed the Second Circuit's interpretation that based on the overall character of a facility, an intermediate care facility may be viewed as an institution for mental disease and thus be ineligible for Medicaid reimbursement.[899]

In addition, the justices were unanimous in another opinion that the state of Tennessee did not violate § 504 of the Rehabilitation Act by reducing the number of inpatient hospital days per year for all its Medicaid recipients.[900]

Also, it should be noted that under Medicaid alcohol and drug dependencies are not reimbursable mental disorders.[901] Moreover, even clients with eligible disorders may be denied reimbursement if the services they receive are not provided by a physician. Several decisions from New York, for example, have resulted in reimbursement denials for services performed by nonphysicians, such as ancillary psychiatric personnel working

889. 42 U.S.C. §§ 1752 to 1766.

890. 42 U.S.C. §§ 1771 to 1785.

891. 42 U.S.C. §§ 1396 to 1396p. It is also known as Title XIX of the Social Security Act.

892. § 1396d(c) & (d).

893. Center for Human Policy, Title XIX and Deinstitutionalization: The Issue for the 80s (1981). Also Herr, *supra* note 115, at 95.

894. Pub. L. No. 97-35, § 2176, 95 Stat. 809, 812 (1981) (codified as amended at 42 U.S.C. § 1396n (c)(4)(B) (1982)).

895. Peret v. Purse, No. 79505, 7 MDLR 269 (Idaho Dist. Ct. 1982).

896. 42 U.S.C. § 1396n (c); Health Care Financing Administration Final Rule, Medicaid Program; Home and Community-Based Services, 50 Fed. Reg. 10,013 (Mar. 13, 1985).

897. Connecticut v. Heckler, No. 245, (2d Cir. Mar. 10, 1983). Also Granville House, Inc. v. Department of Health & Human Servs., 550 F. Supp. 628 (D. Minn. 1982).

898. Noot *ex rel.* Minnesota v. Heckler, 718 F.2d 852 (8th Cir. 1983).

899. Connecticut Dep't of Income Maintenance v. Heckler, 105 S. Ct. 2210 (1985), *aff'g* 731 F.2d 1052 (1984).

900. Alexander v. Choate, 105 S. Ct. 712 (1985).

901. Granville House, Inc. v. Department of Health & Human Servs., 550 F. Supp. 628 (D. Minn. 1982).

under the direction of a medical doctor[902] or a psychologist.[903]

Medicare is both a general program of medical insurance for the aged, blind, and disabled designed to provide protection against extraordinary health expenses[904] and insurance that provides for the cost of medical services not covered by the first part.[905] The second program is a voluntary supplemental system in which participants pay monthly premiums and are subject to certain deductibles and exclusions. Recently, for example, the regulations were changed so that the need for occupational therapy would no longer create an entitlement to home health services.[906]

Maternal and child health care is provided by the Special Supplemental Food Program for Women, Infants, and Children (WIC) and grants for Maternal and Child Health Services. WIC was created in 1978 to help pregnant, postpartum-syndrome-affected, or breast-feeding women, infants, and young children from families with inadequate incomes who were at special risk with respect to physical and mental impairments arising out of inadequate nutrition or health care.[907] The program provides food supplements and nutrition education to eligible persons. State plans for serving maternal and child health needs are federally funded if they include programs aimed at reducing (1) the incidence of mental retardation and other handicapping conditions associated with childbearing and (2) infant and maternal morbidity and mortality.[908]

4. Title XX

Title XX of the Social Security Act[909] reimburses states for achieving a number of goals, several of which directly promote community living for mentally disabled persons: (1) preventing or reducing inappropriate institutional care by providing for community-based care, home-based care, or other forms of less intensive care, (2) achieving or maintaining economic self-support, and (3) achieving or maintaining self-sufficiency. In addition, it seeks to prevent or remedy neglect, abuse, or exploitation of children and adults unable to protect their own interests and to preserve and reunite families.

5. Section 504

Because so much of the funding of community living programs for mentally ill, mentally retarded, and other developmentally disabled persons originates in federal programs that may or may not be supplemented by state treasuries, § 504 is beginning to play an important role in determining an equitable distribution of these services. The general principle is quite simple—individuals may not be denied access to federally funded programs and activities on the basis of their handicaps. As in other service areas, implementation of the principle is not without its difficulties.

While there seems to be overwhelming legal support for a general private right of action for handicapped individuals under § 504, one federal court, even after the Supreme Court's decision in *Conrail v. Darrone*, has indicated its indecision about applying this provision to social welfare assistance programs such as Aid to Families of Dependent Children. The court incorrectly asserted that "in each of the reported decisions wherein a party has invoked the protection of section 794 [§ 504], the alleged discrimination against a handicapped individual occurred in the workplace."[910] As a result, the parties were asked to brief the issue of a private right of action. Given the fact that numerous courts have found a private right outside the context of employment, such as under Title XX funding for adult care services, Medicare and Medicaid, veterans' benefits, and vocational rehabilitation services, a ruling on the merits was unnecessarily delayed. Other remedies have been initiated by federal agency investigations.

Even more recently, the Supreme Court unanimously decided *Alexander v. Choate*,[911] which provided expansive language describing the opportunities for plaintiffs to prove the existence of handicap discrimination. In the context of upholding a Tennessee plan to reduce Medicaid coverage, the Court found that purposeful discrimination is not an absolute requirement for a claim to be justiciable and embraced reasonable accommodation as a workable judicial concept that requires something more than no program or activity modifications and something less than affirmative action.

In light of *Choate* and *Darrone* and several lower federal court decisions[912] there is every reason to believe

902. Yapalater v. Bates, 494 F. Supp. 1349 (S.D.N.Y. 1980), *aff'd*, 644 F.2d 131 (2d Cir. 1981).

903. Kai v. Blum, 440 N.Y.S.2d 91 (App. Div. 1981).

904. 42 U.S.C. § 1395c (1982).

905. 42 U.S.C. § 1395i(2).

906. Omnibus Budget Reconciliation Act of 1981, Pub. L. No. 97-35, § 2176 (adding waiver provision for Home and Community-Based Services for Certain Individuals) (codified at 42 U.S.C. § 1915(c) (1982)), *reported in* Summary and Analysis, 5 MDLR 299, 304 (1981).

907. Child Nutrition Amendments of 1978, Pub. L. No. 95-627, 92 Stat. 3603 (codified as amended at 42 U.S.C. §§ 1771, 1786).

908. 42 U.S.C.A. §§ 701 to 709 (Supp. 1985); 42 C.F.R. § 51a (1981) (incorporated by reference in ch. 1.420 of Dep't of Health & Human Services Grants Administration Manual, notice in 46 Fed. Reg. 47,938, 47,941 (Sept. 30, 1981).

909. 42 U.S.C. §§ 1397 to 1397f.

910. Ayres v. Dempsey, No. 81-72047, 8 MPDLR 413 (E.D. Mich. Mar. 27, 1984).

911. 105 S. Ct. 712 (1985).

912. The United States Court of Appeals for the Eighth Circuit allowed residents of an ICF to bring suit about Title XX funding for adult care services under § 504 but found no violation since Iowa's state government was providing similar services in the ICF and reserving adult care for people who were

that § 504 will continue to be used by mentally handicapped persons to obtain needed community services despite the difficulties in overcoming procedural obstacles inherent in the legislation. Still, as has been noted, those states that have not explicitly waived their immunity to suit and those states' officials are beyond the reach of § 504.

VIII. LEGAL REPRESENTATION AND ADVOCACY SERVICES

Legal representation and advocacy are community services that often determine whether other services and rights and entitlements are provided. For individuals who are mentally disabled, the availability of or entitlement to effective advocates is especially important, given clients' vulnerability and potential communication problems. Except where fundamental liberty interests are involved, however, courts have not found a general right to counsel or legal representation. The limited services that do exist for mentally disabled persons tend to be the result of legislation or equal protection litigation. To a lesser extent representation is encouraged by the legal profession's stated responsibility to serve the legal needs of all individuals, including people who cannot pay for legal services.

In addition to legal advocacy carried out by lawyers, there are many other components of the "advocacy spectrum"[913] that supplement and complement the work of lawyers but generally are not addressed in litigation that seeks to expand access to advocacy services in the community. Stanley Herr, who has studied advocacy for mentally retarded persons over a period of several years, describes self-advocacy, human rights advocacy committees, and internal advocacy—each with different characteristics and purposes. Noting that there are many service professionals who mistakenly consider themselves to be advocates because they help mentally disabled people obtain services or because they perform case management functions, Herr distinguishes between advocacy and satisfying service needs.[914] The reason for making such a distinction becomes obvious when an organization that is supposed to provide an entitlement also is responsible for advocating for a client who is trying to obtain the services the organization is supposed to be providing. Similarly when a state agency is performing the dual roles of advocacy and service delivery, conflicting loyalties may be inevitable.

A. Constitutional Mandates

The right to counsel has been established in criminal proceedings. Generally, courts also recognize a right to counsel in civil commitment hearings[915] and guardianship proceedings,[916] the rationale being that even though no criminal matter is at stake, a compelling circumstance involving the liberty or decision-making interests of the individual is at issue. Yet beyond those situations there is no certain constitutional right to representation for mentally disabled persons. With respect to the institutional setting, the Supreme Court has ruled that a prisoner who is being transferred to a mental hospital need not be represented by an attorney as long as the prisoner has a qualified, independent advocate, who may be a psychiatrist or other mental health professional.[917] Similarly, a child who is admitted "voluntarily" by a parent, guardian, or the state is entitled to no more than an independent administrative review of the admission papers.[918]

When such constitutional principles are applied in the community context there are very few situations in which the mentally disabled person has a right to an attorney. One likely exception is mentally disabled parents who face termination of their parental rights. The Supreme Court has held that there is no automatic right to counsel for indigent parents in parental termination

---

not already receiving services. Plummer v. Branstsad, 731 F.2d 574 (8th Cir. 1984). A lower federal court in Texas determined that Medicare and Medicaid payments constituted federal financial assistance under § 504, thus giving the federal government the go-ahead to investigate whether hearing impaired persons were receiving proper inpatient and emergency treatment. United States v. Baylor Univ. Medical Center, 564 F. Supp. 1495 (N.D. Tex. 1983). A private right of action under § 504 for Medicaid assistance was acknowledged by a federal court in New Hampshire, but the case was dismissed. The asserted remedy would necessarily invoke affirmative action for a Down's Syndrome child trying to obtain services under a program intended for those children who were black or without parental support. Duquette v. Dupuis, 582 F. Supp. 1365 (D.N.H. 1984). In Tennessee an army veteran was able to bring a private § 504 action against the Veterans Administration for denying him and other veterans extensions to complete their education where they were physically or mentally unable to continue. Tinch v. Waters, 573 F. Supp. 346 (E.D. Tenn. 1983). A California appeals court overturned a state regulation that prohibited payments for protective supervision services provided to totally disabled persons by the clients' housemates as a violation of § 504 and the state's program to help disabled individuals avoid institutionalization. Miller v. Woods, 148 Cal. App. 3d 862, 196 Cal. Rptr. 69 (1983). Finally, the United States Court of Appeals for the First Circuit dismissed a § 504 claim filed by a client who was dissatisfied with the rehabilitation services he was receiving, citing Eleventh Amendment immunity and the lack of a due process violation, but the opinion did not deny that the plaintiff had a right to file his private action. Ciampa v. Massachusetts Rehabilitation Comm'n, 718 F.2d 1 (1st Cir. 1983).

913. Herr, *supra* note 115, at 213.

914. *Id.* at 213–19.

915. Lessard v. Schmidt, 349 F. Supp. 1078 (E.D. Wis. 1972); Heryford v. Parker, 396 F.2d 393 (10th Cir. 1968); *In re* Barnard, 455 F.2d 1370 (D.C. Cir. 1971); *In re* Moyer, 263 So. 2d 286 (Fla. Ct. App. 1972); State *ex rel.* Memmel v. Mundy, 249 N.W.2d 573 (Wis. 1977).

916. In every jurisdiction an individual for whom guardianship is sought has a right to retain counsel. Because of the traditional notion that guardianship is not an adversarial process, however, few states have guaranteed this right by providing court-appointed counsel. See R. Burgdorf, The Legal Rights of Handicapped Persons 591–92 (1980), for list of state statutes and further discussion.

917. Vitek v. Jones, 445 U.S. 480 (1980).

918. Parham v. J.R., 442 U.S. 584 (1979).

hearings,[919] because in the absence of a "potential deprivation of physical liberty" there is a presumption that appointed counsel is unnecessary.[920] Nevertheless, the majority indicated that this presumption would be overcome where there was a substantial risk of an erroneous decision because of parents' inability to represent themselves and a compelling countervailing individual interest. For the typical mentally disabled parent the problems inherent in self-representation are obvious. In addition, the Supreme Court has frequently documented the importance of parental rights.

A related constitutional argument that has been used successfully to promote access to legal services is identified with the First Amendment. Without acknowledging a right to representation, the First Circuit ruled that an advocacy organization has standing to sue to communicate with mentally retarded residents of a state training school without restrictions. The court observed, "it is now clear that such advocacy organizations have first amendment rights which, in appropriate circumstances, may permit them to seek out clients and initiate litigation."[921] Moreover, the court asserted, "subject only to reasonable time, place and manner restrictions the . . . attorneys should have unlimited access."[922]

B. Federal Statutes

The major impetus for the provision of counsel or legal advocacy services to mentally disabled clients in the community can be traced to relatively recent federal initiatives. To begin with, there are three separate pieces of federal legislation that provide for either discretionary or mandatory fee awards to the prevailing parties in suits likely to involve disabled clients— the Civil Rights Attorneys' Fees Awards Act, § 505 of the Rehabilitation Act, and the Equal Access to Justice Act. In addition, through the Legal Services Corporation and the Developmental Disabilities Act Amendments of 1978, handicapped clients have three significant programs that address different legal needs.

1. Civil Rights Attorneys' Fees Awards Act of 1976

Although under the American Rule attorneys' fees are not generally recoverable,[923] the Civil Rights Act as amended in the Civil Rights Attorney's Fees Awards Act of 1976 provides for discretionary fee awards to prevailing parties in litigation involving vindication of civil rights or § 1988 of the Civil Rights code.[924] With a few notable exceptions,[925] § 1983 of the code pertains to violations of any rights secured by the Constitution and federal statutes.[926] The act's legislative history shows strong support for attorneys' fees to be provided to public interest attorneys and organizations,[927] and even though courts do have discretion, they may withhold fees only in special circumstances. Operating as a public interest law firm is not the kind of circumstance that necessitates the elimination or reduction of fee awards.[928] At the same time, prevailing defendants may recover only where the plaintiffs instituted a suit frivolously or in bad faith.[929] In this judicial climate, lawyers representing mentally disabled clients have prospered. Most successful attorney fee claims under § 1988 for mentally disabled clients have involved civil commitment[930] and other institutional representation such as the right to treatment,[931] humane care,[932] and freedom to manage and control one's own property.[933] In addition, there have been awards associated with community-based litigation. In the *Pennhurst* case, plaintiffs received $64,000 after successfully instituting a contempt of court proceeding against Pennsylvania for refusing to pay a special master to oversee the implementation of community living arrangements.[934] In Massachusetts plaintiffs were awarded $385,000 in fees for their contributions in obtaining and carrying out a consent decree defining the provision of community mental health services.[935]

Despite these plaintiff victories, the award of attorneys' fees is anything but routine. The most contested issue is the determination of who has prevailed in a lawsuit. A federal court in North Dakota awarded $500,000 to attorneys who played a "provocative role" in a lawsuit against a state institution for mentally retarded persons by negotiating a favorable settlement for their clients.[936] The defendants' arguments that there had been no court ruling and they had acted in good faith in achiev-

919. Lassiter v. Dep't of Social Servs., 452 U.S. 18 (1981).

920. *Id.* at 31.

921. Developmental Disabilities Advocacy Center, Inc. v. Melton, 689 F.2d 281 (1st Cir. 1982).

922. *Id.* at 284.

923. Alyeska Pipeline Serv. Co. v. Wilderness Soc'y, 421 U.S. 240 (1975).

924. Pub. L. No. 94-559, § 2, 90 Stat. 2641 (codified as amended at 42 U.S.C. §§ 1981, 1988 (1982)).

925. In Pennhurst State School & Hosp. v. Halderman, 451 U.S. 1 (1981), the Supreme Court held that the application of § 1983 to statutory violations depends on (1) whether private enforcement of the statute was foreclosed by Congress and (2) whether the statute at issue created enforceable rights under § 1983.

926. Maine v. Thiboutot, 448 U.S. 1 (1980).

927. Larson, Attorney's Fees Under the Civil rights Attorney's Fees Awards Act of 1976, 15 Clearinghouse Rev. 309, 314 (1981).

928. *Id.* at 314; New York Gaslight Club, Inc. v. Carey, 447 U.S. 54, 70 n.9 (1980).

929. Larson, *supra* note 927, at 311.

930. Suzuki v. Yuen, 507 F. Supp. 819 (D. Hawaii 1981).

931. Gary W. v. Louisiana, 622 F.2d 804 (5th Cir. 1980).

932. New York State Ass'n for Retarded Children, Inc. v. Carey, 456 F. Supp. 85 (E.D.N.Y. 1978).

933. Vecchione v. Wohlgemuth, 481 F. Supp. 776 (E.D. Pa. 1979).

934. Halderman v. Pennhurst State School & Hosp., 533 F. Supp. 649 (E.D. Pa. 1982).

935. Brewster v. Dukakis, 544 F. Supp. 1069 (D. Mass. 1982).

936. Association for Retarded Citizens of N. D. v. Olson, 561 F. Supp. 495 (D.N.D. 1982).

ing the final result were irrelevant. All but $50,000 of the award was affirmed by the United States Court of Appeals for the Eighth Circuit. The reduction was based on the conclusion that the trial phase of the case could have been presented in less time.[937]

A 1983 Supreme Court decision, *Hensley v. Eckerhart,*[938] established certain parameters on court interpretations of prevailing parties. A 5-4 majority concluded that as a general rule, attorneys' fees under § 1988 should be reduced in situations where the plaintiffs are only partially successful. Considerable discretion is given to the lower courts to fashion equitable awards as long as plaintiffs meet the threshold requirement of being successful on any significant issue which is "degree of success obtained,"[939] not a rigid mathematical formula. The Supreme Court suggested two kinds of tests: if the claims are based on divergent facts and legal theories, only time spent on the successful claims may generate an award; if the successful and unsuccessful claims are intertwined, a full recovery does not depend on the lawyers prevailing on every issue but is precluded where the success is clearly limited, even if the claims are interrelated, relevant, and raised in good faith. Four dissenting justices found the Court's opinion to be inconsistent with the broader purposes of § 1988, which they noted was intended to encourage attorneys to file civil rights actions in behalf of clients whose rights have been violated, and they argued that attorneys should be awarded full compensation based on the actual market value of their services so that other lawyers would be motivated to handle similar cases.[940]

Two subsequent federal cases have in one instance expanded and in another instance narrowed the scope of *Hensley v. Eckerhart.* A district court in North Carolina allowed the plaintiffs to recover full attorneys' fees of $88,000 for time expended litigating integrally related right-to-treatment claims, not all of which were successful.[941] What persuaded the court that the Supreme Court's standard had been met were evidence of substantial relief obtained in a matter of considerable importance and the lawyer's ethical duty to litigate all reasonable claims. Yet in Nebraska a federal court determined that no fees could be awarded for prevailing in an administrative action implementing a deinstitutionalization consent decree.[942] The distinction was that § 1988 applies only to judicial actions. This decision is consistent with an earlier federal district court case in Minnesota that also rejected fees for administrative relief but suggested fees would have been forthcoming if the original action had been filed in federal court.[943]

Beyond determining who has prevailed in a lawsuit, courts also need to determine whether to adhere to the prevailing market rates in awarding fees or to make a special adjustment. For a long time there was uncertainty as to the proper method for ascertaining special circumstances that would call for a reduction or addition to the basic award. Much of that uncertainty has been resolved by a 1984 Supreme Court decision in *Blum v. Stenson*[944] which held that such adjustments could be made in certain exceptional circumstances, although lingering uncertainty over standards of proof necessary to justify bonuses and the risk incurred in contingent-fee cases suggest that other cases will come before the courts, probably sooner rather than later.[945]

A number of plaintiffs have attempted to mix § 1983 claims with claims under the Education for All Handicapped Children Act (EAHCA) in order to recover attorneys' fees in education suits. As was discussed earlier in the section on education, this legal maneuver has been largely unsuccessful. By and large, courts have followed the United States Court of Appeals for the Seventh Circuit and determined that no fees may be awarded because the EAHCA provides for an exclusive enforcement system of its own that would be undercut by additional avenues of relief.[946] To permit attorneys' fees in this situation where the EAHCA provides all conceivable dam-

937. Association for Retarded Citizens of North Dakota v. Olson, 713 F.2d 1384 (8th Cir. 1983).

938. 461 U.S. 424 (1983).

939. *Id.* at 436.

940. *Id.* at 441, 442, 447 (Brennan, J., concurring in part and dissenting in part, joined by Marshall, Blackmun, & Stevens).

941. Willie M. v. Hunt, No. C-C-79-294-M (W.D.N.C. June 2, 1983).

942. Horacek v. Thone, 710 F.2d 496 (8th Cir. 1983).

943. Derheim v. Hennepin County Bureau of Social Servs., 524 F. Supp. 1321 (D. Minn. 1981).

944. 104 S. Ct. 1541 (1984).

945. *Id.* Attorneys for the New York Legal Aid Society sought attorneys' fees under the Civil Rights Attorney's Fees Awards Act of 1976 after successfully litigating a civil rights action on behalf of Medicaid recipients who had had their benefits terminated improperly. A lower court awarded the attorneys the prevailing market rate and added a bonus of 50% for the complexity of the case, the quality of the representation, the great benefit achieved, and the riskiness of success. A court of appeals affirmed, and the defendants applied for and were granted certiorari by the Supreme Court on the question of whether the prevailing market rate much less a bonus should be used to calculate the award for a publicly funded litigation unit. A majority of the Court found that Congress intended for the prevailing market rate to be applied to public interest and private attorneys alike in order to attract competent counsel without producing unwarranted windfalls to attorneys in these cases. However, the exceptional circumstances necessary to justify a bonus were inadequately supported by the evidence. The burden was on the plaintiffs to show that "the quality of service rendered was superior to that one reasonably should expect in light of the hourly rates charged and that the success was 'exceptional.'" Normally, the novelty and complexity of a case and the quality of representation will be reflected in the number of billable hours and the hourly rate so that no upward adjustment will be necessary. The same is true for the benefits achieved. With respect to the riskiness of litigation there was no independent evidence that the risk was not ordinary even though it was a contingent-fee case. A concurring opinion disagreed with this one point, observing that the risk of not receiving a fee should always be a proper basis for an upward fee adjustment.

946. Anderson v. Thompson, 658 F.2d 1205 (7th Cir. 1981). See also Tatro v. Texas, 516 F. Supp. 968 (N.D. Tex. 1981); Smith v. Cumberland School Comm., 703 F.2d 4 (1st Cir. 1983); Hurry v. Jones, 560 F. Supp. 500 (D.R.I. 1983).

ages would make § 1983 nothing more than a conduit for recovering attorneys' fees with no substantive impact on the litigation.[947] This view has been affirmed by the United States Supreme Court in a 1984 decision.[948] On the other hand, a Rhode Island federal court, without challenging this rationale directly, awarded attorneys' fees for work in the course of preparing for a state education administrative hearing because exhaustion of administrative remedies was an essential precondition to filing for judicial relief.[949]

2. Section 505 of the Rehabilitation Act

Plaintiffs have had a much easier time recovering attorneys' fees under §§ 501, 503, and 504 of the Rehabilitation Act, even where the claims are mixed with other legal theories including the EAHCA. Section 505 specifically provides for the recovery of fees for prevailing parties under Title V of the Rehabilitation Act of 1973.[950] However, in the education context, the EAHCA may provide an exclusive remedy in relation to § 504 so recovery may be precluded.[951]

3. Equal Access to Justice Act

Another means of obtaining attorneys' fees is to be involved in a lawsuit in which the opposing party is the United States. Prevailing private parties are entitled to attorneys' fees under the Equal Access to Justice Act[952] whenever the federal litigants cannot prove that their legal position was substantially justified.[953]

Two federal cases involving Social Security Disability claimants are illustrative. The United States Court of Appeals for the Eighth Circuit awarded attorneys' fees where the government had denied benefits despite uncontradicted subjective and medical evidence of pain and severe back problems and no evidence that the claimant was fit to work. Attorneys' fees were awarded to the claimant's pro bono counsel in order to provide "a strong incentive" for public interest representation of indigent clients.[954] In the second decision, a federal court in Georgia ruled that the Equal Access to Justice Act was applicable to Social Security cases since fees against the government were not authorized elsewhere but that in the circumstances of this case no fee was warranted. Instead, the lawyer had to recover his fee from the past-due benefits.[955]

4. Legal Services Corporation

As much as the federal attorneys' fees statutes may promote the provision of legal counsel in specific situations, there are many types of legal problems of mentally disabled clients that extend beyond the reach of these statutes. This is why federal programs that provide general legal assistance to this population are still very much needed.

The most comprehensive system of legal representation was established by the Legal Services Corporation Act of 1974.[956] The Corporation is a private, nonmembership, nonprofit organization designed to provide financial support for legal assistance in noncriminal proceedings involving persons otherwise unable to afford representation.

Full access to legal services by poor, mentally disabled persons has never become a reality, even though the act provided that priority service was to be given to individuals such as the handicapped who experience special problems or particular difficulties obtaining legal representation[957] and even though § 504 and its regulations clearly state that federal programs must be "readily accessible to and usable by handicapped persons."[958] As a result of two administrative complaints filed against the Legal Services Corporation[959] and the outcry by advocates nationwide,[960] a concerted effort was made to be more open to handicapped clients. However, this change in attitude did not occur until 1981, and by then the Legal Services Corporation itself was under siege and facing dramatic cutbacks in funding.[961] In the future, it appears that the opportunities for mentally disabled clients under the Legal Services Corporation Act will depend on the level of funding from federal and state sources and on administrative decisions on how to distribute these limited funds.

5. Developmental Disability Protection and Advocacy System

Similarly, representation and advocacy services pro-

947. Anderson v. Thompson, 658 F.2d 1205 (7th Cir. 1981); Smith v. Cumberland School Comm., 703 F.2d 4 (1st Cir. 1983).

948. Smith v. Robinson, 104 S. Ct. 3457 (1984).

949. Turillo v. Tyson, 535 F. Supp. 577 (D.R.I. 1982). See also Monahan v. Nebraska, 687 F.2d 1164 (8th Cir. 1982) (awarded attorneys' fees where plaintiff was successful under EAHCA but not successful under § 1983).

950. 29 U.S.C. § 794a (1982).

951. Patsel v. District of Columbia Bd. of Educ., 530 F. Supp. 660 (D.D.C. 1982); Davis v. District of Columbia Bd. of Educ., 530 F. 1215 (D.D.C. 1982).

952. Pub. L. No. 96-481, 94 Stat. 2325 (1980) (codified as amended at 28 U.S.C. § 2412 (1982)).

953. National Legal Aid and Defender Association, Commentary: The Equal Access to Justice Act, 15 Clearinghouse Rev. 1021 (1982).

954. Cornella v. Schweiker, 728 F.2d 978, 986 (8th Cir. 1984).

955. Tant v. Heckler, 577 F. Supp. 448 (N.D. Ga. 1983).

956. Pub. L. No. 93-355, 88 Stat. 378 (1974) (codified as amended at 42 U.S.C. §§ 2996 to 2996(l) (1982)).

957. 42 U.S.C. § 2996f(a)(2)(C).

958. 45 C.F.R. § 1624.5(b) (1984).

959. *In re* Clifford (Legal Servs. Corp. Region 2 filed Jan. 3, 1980); Colorado Developmental Disabilities Council v. Colorado Rural Legal Servs., 5 MDLR 34 (Legal Services Corp. Region VIII filed Sept. 8, 1980).

960. Mental Health Law Project, Federal Regulations Open Legal Doors to Handicapped Clients, 14 Clearinghouse Rev. 1157 (1981).

961. Summary and Analysis, 5 MDLR 75, 77 (1981).

vided by the 50 statewide protection and advocacy systems created under the Developmental Disabilities Act Amendments of 1978[962] will depend heavily on funding decisions. Since 1978, these advocacy systems have provided substantial assistance to their constituents.[963] Efforts to create a parallel system for mentally ill clients have been largely unsuccessful, producing only limited federal funding for the establishment of model programs.[964] However, the Protection and Advocacy for Mentally Ill Persons Act of 1985 has been submitted for consideration in the Senate and seems to have substantial support.[965]

6. *Client Assistance Under the Rehabilitation Amendments of 1984*

In February 1984, amendments to the Rehabilitation Act authorized client assistance programs in each of the 50 states to advise and aid clients in obtaining vocational rehabilitation services. Modeled on the successful developmental disability protection and advocacy system, these new programs must also have the authority to pursue legal, administrative, and other remedies to protect the rights of handicapped clients.[966]

C. State Efforts

1. *Criminal Representation*

Criminal representation for mentally disabled persons is handled by public defender and assigned counsel systems that serve all indigent criminal defendants. In the public defender system a group of lawyers provide legal representation as public employees through a contractual agreement. In the assigned counsel system, local attorneys in private practice are appointed by the court to provide service on a case by case basis.[967] While public defenders may provide some civil representation in commitment matters, generally they do not provide it for other civil issues.[968]

2. *Civil Representation*

Civil representation at the state level is a somewhat haphazard affair depending on the inclinations of the various state legislatures and follow-up implementation. Most states provide counsel in cases involving civil commitment, competency, and guardianship because there is or appears to be a constitutional obligation to do so. Numerous states contribute money in order to supplement federal programs such as the Legal Services Corporation and the developmental disability protection and advocacy systems. These programs represent clients in a wide range of civil legal matters. Nevertheless, as the American Bar Association's Commission on the Mentally Disabled has noted, this scattered coverage still leaves many mentally disabled individuals wanting for representation.[969] Moreover, the prognosis for improved coverage, or even sustaining the status quo, is poor, given the recent contraction of Legal Services programs.[970]

D. Private Bar Initiatives

Under Canon 2 of the old American Bar Association Model Code of Professional Responsibility and in the recently adopted Model Rules of Professional Conduct, individual lawyers have an obligation to assist the legal profession in making counsel available.[971] In the past, with regard to mentally disabled persons and other clients who were comparably disadvantaged, the basic responsibility for providing legal representation to those who were unable to pay ultimately rested on the individual attorney. As long as the practitioner was able to provide the client with competent representation, he was obligated not to let the inability to pay or the unattractiveness of the assignment deter him from tendering employment.[972] Under the new Model Rules of Professional Conduct lawyers are encouraged to provide pro bono services, although they cannot be disciplined for failing to do so.[973]

By and large, private bar initiatives on behalf of the mentally disabled have not been comprehensive, even though past efforts have led to the establishment of local and state bar committees or projects in more than half the states.[974] Two recurring problems have been noted. First, the subject matter is difficult and the financial rewards are perceived to be even more limited than they really are.[975] Second, the attorney-client relationship is

962. 42 U.S.C. § 6012 (1982).

963. Items of Interest (report of U.S. General Accounting Office, How Federal Developmental Disabilities Programs Are Working), 4 MDLR 202 (1980).

964. Summary and Analysis: The Federal Budget and Its Effect on Programs for Disabled Persons, 5 MDLR 299 (1981).

965. S. 974, 9 MPDLR 224 (1985).

966. Pub. L. No. 98-221, 98 Stat. 20 (codified at 29 U.S.C. 732 (1982)).

967. National Legal Aid and Defender Association, The Other Side of Justice: A Report of the National Defender Survey 1971 (1973).

968. Standards for Defender Services, NLADA Briefcase, Apr.-May 1977, at 83-86.

969. American Bar Association Commission on the Mentally Disabled, Report to the Board of Governors of the American Bar Association (June 1982) [hereinafter cited as A.B.A. Comm'n Report to the Board].

970. *Id.*

971. Model Code of Professional Responsibility Canon 2 at 5 (as amended Aug. 1980); Model Rules of Professional Conduct (1983).

972. Model Code of Professional Responsibility EC 2-25, EC 2-26, & EC 2-27 at 8-9.

973. Model Rules of Professional Conduct Rule 6.1 (1983).

974. Mental and Developmental Disabilities Directory of Legal Advocates 14-16 (1982).

975. The federal statutes for attorneys' fees cover numerous cases. In addition, many parents and clients have resources to pay a fee even if a contingent fee arrangement is not possible in a given situation. As a result, a number of lawyers are making representation under the EAHCA a significant part of their practice.

hard to establish where clients have problems communicating because of their disability or their medication and attorneys are apprehensive about the unpredictability of their clients.[976]

Existing models for delivering private bar assistance to underserved clients take three forms: the judicare model with a staff component, the contract arrangement with private law firms, and the organized pro bono model. The first model uses private attorneys who are willing to take reduced fees to provide services on a fee-for-service basis. Small administrative staffs check client eligibility, make referrals to the attorneys on the panels, review and pay attorney bills, provide emergency backup services, and represent clients on major impact litigation.[977] In the contract law firm model, an existing staff attorney program is supplemented with attorneys selected from private practice to provide specialized services, either in a subject area that requires special expertise or in a geographic area that is underserved. The contract attorneys usually accept clients on a reduced fee-for-service basis.[978]

The organized pro bono model, which typically operates as a supplement to existing staff programs, depends on attorneys who represent clients for no compensation other than incidental costs incurred while providing services. These attorneys are supported by staff attorneys and paralegals who perform intake and referral services, who sometimes provide training and technical assistance to the pro bono attorneys, and who maintain quality control and handle case followup.[979]

E. Competent Representation

Just as important as the methods for delivering legal services to the mentally disabled in the community is the level of competency with which they are delivered. Much of the literature on this subject focuses on civil commitment and institutional representation.[980] Little has been written about the noninstitutional settings in which a significant amount of litigation occurs.

There are two fundamental concerns for the attorney and the client. First, how does the attorney best understand what it is the mentally disabled client wants done in a particular situation? Second, if the client is partially or wholly incapacitated, whose definition of interest should prevail—the actual or substituted expression of interests by or for the client or the best interests of the client as perceived by the attorney?

The beginning of the process is to try to ascertain what it is that the client really wants, for no matter how the client's interests are defined, that information is crucial to any kind of competent representation. There are few formal guidelines for attorneys in matters as subjective as these. The overriding professional obligation as stated by the ABA Model Rules of Professional Conduct is "the lawyer shall as far as reasonably possible, maintain a normal client-lawyer relationship with the client."[981] This is based on the assumption that most clients, including many who are mentally disabled, are capable of making decisions on important matters when they are "properly advised and assisted." Even a legally incompetent client "often has the ability to understand, deliberate upon, and reach conclusions about matters affecting the client's own well-being."

Whenever an attorney represents a disabled person with impaired judgment, he takes on "additional duties," but according to the Model Rules of Professional Conduct he must act with restraint: "A lawyer may seek the appointment of a guardian or take other protective action with respect to a client, only when the lawyer reasonably believes that the client cannot adequately act in the client's own interest." In the commentary, the Model Rules indicate that where the client suffers a disability and "has no guardian or legal representative, the lawyer often must act as de facto guardian. Even if the person does have a legal representative, the lawyer should as far as possible accord the represented person the status of client, particularly in maintaining communication." To a large extent, the new Model Rules suggest that the legal profession has resolved the question of which interests should be represented by requiring lawyers to listen to clients and by giving clients the benefit of the doubt when judging whether they understand what their best interests might be.

Once attorneys have taken appropriate steps, either through their own resources or the resources of others, to understand what it is the mentally disabled client wants, or to understand as much as the client's condition permits, attorneys must decide how to represent those interests. If what the client desires is clear and reasonable, the decision is obvious—do what the client wants "within the bounds of the law."[982] Only if it is clearly irrational

976. Luckasson & Ellis, Representing Institutionalized Mentally Retarded Persons, 7 MDLR 49-54 (1983); Costello, Representing the Medicated Client, 7 MDLR 55-56, 62 (1983).

977. Swanson, Judicare: An LSC Regional Director Takes a Look, 37 NLADA Briefcase, Nov. 1980, at 97-101; Vogt, The Legal Services Corporation Delivery Systems Study and the Role of the Private Bar, 37 NLADA Briefcase, Nov. 1980, at 88-89.

978. See references cited in note 977 *supra*.

979. *Id.*

980. Brakel, Legal Aid in Mental Hospitals, 1981 A.B.F. Res. J. 21 (1981); Brakel, Fleischner, & Schwartz, Legal Advocacy for Persons Confined in Mental Hospitals, 5 MDLR 274 (1981); Practice Manual: The Attorney's Role at the Commitment Hearing: Guidelines and Practical Considerations, 2 MDLR 427 (1978) [hereinafter cited as Practice Manual, Attorney's Role].

981. Model Rules of Professional Conduct Rule 1.14, Client Under a Disability, comment at 52 (1983).

982. Model Code of Professional Reponsibility Canon 7, A Lawyer Should Represent a Client Zealously Within the Bounds of the Law (as amended Aug. 1980); Lessard v. Schmidt, 349 F. Supp. 1078 (E.D. Wis. 1972).

do the new rules of conduct leave the matter to professional judgment. In the past, commentators generally supported one of two alternative approaches. Either lawyers should follow their own preferences in determining what the client's best interests are or they should, as closely as possible, do what the client would want done if he or she were competent to decide.[983] In making the latter judgment the opinions of the client and his relatives, friends, or acquaintances will carry considerable weight, in that order of preference. With the new Model Rules, a lawyer's judgment in such circumstances is even more narrowly circumscribed. Moreover, where the client's interests are fundamental or extremely important, as with civil commitment or competency determinations, the state legislatures or the courts may step in and further define lawyers' obligations to their clients.

F. Conclusion and Overview

While there are numerous potential avenues for generating legal representation for mentally disabled persons, together they are fundamentally inadequate in several important aspects. A recent study of Florida's system of delivering legal assistance to mentally and developmentally disabled persons noted five problems shared by systems nationwide.[984] Each of these general deficiencies has been cited and discussed by other commentators, whose findings are consistent with those that follow.

First, the quantity of available resources remains limited, and recent federal and state cutbacks in funding threaten to dilute that limited capacity even further. The most widespread institutional mechanism for providing legal services to the poor, the Legal Services Corporation, does "not specifically serve persons with mental disabilities" despite a clear federal mandate to do so, report specialists in the field, and as its funds are slashed and its continued existence threatened, prospects for representation of mentally disabled persons "can only diminish."[985] On the positive side, legal assistance for the developmentally disabled is still in place, and disabled children with unfulfilled educational needs have often found advocates.

Second, those within institutions who as a group are cited as having the most serious legal needs are also the most isolated from existing advocacy programs. In a few notable instances, public institutions have on-site advocacy programs, but a significant majority do not, and many of the institutions today are privately run facilities. Furthermore, existing programs are unable to identify the actual legal needs of their potential clients, lack the resources to do anything more than selective advocacy, and are often attacked from both sides of the political spectrum as not properly representing the interests of the clients.[986] At the same time, because there have been no comprehensive studies of the actual availability of community legal services for the mentally disabled, it is difficult to determine whether in fact the situation has improved. Also, it is unlikely, except in isolated cases, that the "street people" who are receiving almost no other social services are being legally represented.

Third, pro bono activity by individual lawyers likewise appears to be extremely limited, with prospects for improvement uncertain.[987] The Model Rules of Professional Conduct that was approved in 1983 rejected mandatory pro bono obligations for attorneys.[988] Instead, the Rules indicated that such activity was "expected" to be carried out as a part of an attorney's practice. Since mentally disabled clients are often perceived as being among the most troublesome and difficult of clients, there is every reason to be concerned that they will receive less pro bono attention than other poor individuals.

Fourth, the private bar beyond its pro bono efforts has been unable to generate enough legal activity in this area to make a sustained and substantial difference, despite some notable contributions by the American Bar Association and a number of local and state bar associations. The problems seem even more intractable when compared with other areas of legal representation because of such factors as the lack of experience within the legal profession in dealing with the special communication and legal problems of these clients, the perception that most litigation in this area will not sustain a general practice, and the absence of available expert technical support by other professions.[989]

Finally, there are a number of reasons to question the general competency of the legal representation that is provided, particularly legal services within an institution or at civil commitment and guardianship proceedings, which have been the subject of much criticism.[990] The most serious problems are inadequate preparation,[991] a tendency to overlook individual representation

983. Brakel, *supra* note 980; Developments in the Law: Civil Commitment of the Mentally Ill, 87 Harv. L. Rev. 1190 (1974); Practice Manual: Preparation and Trial of a Civil Commitment Case, 5 MDLR 201, 203-5 (1981); Practice Manual: Attorney's Role, *supra* note 980, Practice Manual: Handling the Civil Commitment Case, 2 MDLR 430 (1978).

984. Nelson, Schmidt, & Miller, The Legal Needs of the Mentally and Developmentally Disabled—A Florida Study, 6 MDLR 418-24 (1982).

985. *Id.* at 422.

986. See references listed in note 983 *supra*.

987. Nelson, Schmidt, & Miller, *supra* note 984, at 423.

988. Model Rules of Professional Conduct Rule 6.1, Pro Bono Publico Service.

989. A.B.A. Comm'n Report to the Board, *supra* note 969.

990. See references listed in note 983 *supra*; Nelson, Schmidt, & Miller, *supra* note 984, at 423.

991. Nelson, Schmidt, & Miller, *supra* note 984, at 424.

in favor of class advocacy, and conflicting values between a disabled client's stated or assumed position and the attorney's perception of what is actually in the client's best interest.[992] At the same time, since there are few reports about the level of representation in the community, there is no reason to assume the situation is generally better with respect to community-based representation. This is especially true with respect to those mentally ill individuals who have reportedly been "dumped" into the community and ignored.

992. See references listed in note 980 *supra*.

APPENDIX A

COMPREHENSIVE CONSENT DECREE ON PLACEMENT IN LESS RESTRICTIVE COMMUNITY SETTING[1]

In a federal district court in Missouri, a comprehensive consent decree settled a class action suit filed to obtain care and treatment in the least restrictive environment for residents of a large, state mental institution. The agreed-upon plan for gradual deinstitutionalization included a uniform system for clinically reviewing inpatients, providing individualized treatment plans, and referring patients to the department of mental health's community placement branch. Clinicians are designated as case managers and advocates for each patient within the hospital, and other staff perform similar functions for individuals when they are placed in the community. The provision of a continuum of residential and support services is the responsibility of the department of mental health and the hospital.

The 75-page consent decree, which contains a number of significant provisions, is highlighted in this appendix.

Overview: Introduction, Goals, and Objectives

While the state defendants did not admit any wrong-doings or violations of the law, they agreed "with the concept that mental patients should be treated and cared for in the least restrictive facilities and settings appropriate to the individual needs of each patient, within the parameters of financial resources and responsible fiscal management and subject to the availability of non-institutional community settings appropriate to the patients concerned." They also agreed to pay $17,500 in attorneys' fees to Legal Aid of Western Missouri, which represented the plaintiffs.

The parties agreed that "a successful community placement program consists of at least six components":

> 1. An assessment methodology relying primarily on clinical judgment, but augmented by a reliable and valid objective instrument to determine the ongoing needs and number of Hospital residents who are in need of placement in community facilities and programs;
> 2. An effective system to coordinate the hospital treatment teams, the Office of Community Placement staff, the Community Support field staff, and private service providers . . . ;
> 3. Appropriate preplacement and transitional living programs and services for patients to develop or redevelop those skills necessary for community living;
> 4. An adequate number of appropriate community placements;
> 5. An adequate number of trained staff to provide necessary services for Hospital and community placement programs;
> 6. The provision of services . . . and the monitoring of these services to upgrade and maintain the quality of the programs and services and to prevent unnecessary or inappropriate rehospitalization of persons residing in community facilities or receiving community-based services.

In order to improve available mental health services, the parties agreed to follow certain principles: (1) services should be individualized and based on a person's "level of psychosocial functioning"; (2) they "should be provided in the least restrictive environment appropriate to the provision of necessary care and treatment"; and (3) they should follow the principles of normalization so that former inpatients can "live as normally as possible in the community," supported by "appropriate treatment, habilitative, rehabilitative, social, recreational and occupational services . . . ." Patients should be placed "in the most home-like facility possible."

The defendants have a number of specific responsibilities, which include the following:

1. Assess each patient's need for community-based residential services using clinical judgment "augmented by a valid and reliable instrument";
2. Determine each patient's eligibility for public benefits;
3. Provide each patient with a written individualized treatment plan (ITP);
4. Allow each patient to participate in the development of the plan;
5. Assign both hospital and community patients a case manager;
6. Provide each patient with notice and an opportunity to object or agree to a proposed community placement;
7. Limit nursing home placements to situations that meet specified criteria;
8. Place patients only into licensed or certified programs and facilities;

1. Excerpts and summaries from Caswell v. Secretary of U.S. Dep't of Health & Human Servs., No. 77-0488-C-V-W-8, 7 MDLR 221 (W.D. Mo. Feb. 8, 1983).

9. Develop and maintain sufficient residential facilities and support services to meet patients' needs for independent living, semi-independent living, and supervised living in community residential facilities;

10. Develop and implement a program and process providing for quarterly review of the needs and progress of each patient who is placed in the community ("Said review shall address the appropriateness of the patient's current placement and services, the patient's potential for placement in a less restrictive setting, and appropriateness for referral to other support services");

11. Seek necessary appropriations "in good faith and with utmost speed" if additional funding is needed.

Patient Evaluation and Needs Assessment

In order to promote the ultimate goal of discharge of the patient and successful integration or reintegration into the community, the defendants shall clinically evaluate each patient "on an ongoing basis to determine which services should be provided to assist the individual to achieve and maintain appropriate community living skills, consonant with the wishes of that individual."

Within 72 hours of admission, each hospital patient shall have "an initial treatment plan prepared by an interdisciplinary professional team," which shall assess "psychiatric, social, and medical needs." If the person remains in the hospital for more than 10 days, a master ITP must be prepared and reviewed regularly, in no event less frequently than every 3 months. This plan shall include "an assessment of psychiatric, psychological, social, cultural, educational, vocational, and medical needs" as well as a discharge plan. The chief of staff shall conduct a concurrent review "to aid in the prevention of unnecessary hospitalization by identifying patients who do not meet clinically acceptable criteria for inpatient care."

For persons who remain more than 60 days, the hospital shall use a survey instrument to identify those patients so their need for continued hospitalization may be reviewed to "provide an overall picture of the composite needs of the Hospital population" and to "provide the basis for assessing current program capabilities and for planning for the provision of services."

Philosophy of Care-giving Process

The philosophy of the hospital's care-giving process "is that every patient shall be given the opportunity to achieve maximum improvement in his or her condition in the least restrictive environment possible. In all cases, return to community living is the goal of hospital treatment." Moreover, it is the policy and practice of the department and hospital "that each patient shall be allowed the opportunity to participate directly in the development and implementation of his individualized treatment plan (ITP)."

Hospital Case Management

"Throughout the course of inpatient hospitalization, a responsible clinician . . . shall be designated to assure that each component of the individualized treatment plan is carried out." This person "shall assume an administrative role in initiating, coordinating and integrating treatment planning for the patient, and in assuring that the patient's medical chart contains qualitatively and quantitatively appropriate documentation relating to the patient's condition and treatment." In addition, the case manager shall maintain regular scheduled contact with the patient in order to explain treatment planning and implementation, provide support and advocacy services, answer the client's questions, and assess the client's satisfaction. "The functions performed by the Casemanager shall not detract from, compromise, nor replace the ethical and legal responsibilities assumed by professional staff involved in the treatment of the patient."

Preplacement Coordinator

Services for patients who have been returned to the hospital from the community, and who have been hospitalized for 90 or more days, shall be coordinated by a preplacement coordinator. This individual shall be a credentialed mental health proessional and

> shall participate with the inpatient treatment team in reviewing the patient's treatment and programs. The overlap between the functions of the Hospital Casemanager and those of the Pre-placement Coordinator is designed to assure continuity of care, prevent slippage of the patient's skills, and accomplish adequate staff monitoring during the patient's transition from inpatient to outpatient status.

The primary task of the preplacement coordinator is "to assure that each patient is being provided those care, treatment and habilitation services necessary to minimize the patient's inhospitalization and to maximize the potential for successful outplacement."

Community Placement Case Management

The community placement case manager who may also be the preplacement coordinator shall by him or herself, or with the cooperation of the preplacement coordinator: (1) "set a date for placement" of each patient, (2) "insure that the patient and proposed providers have access to all the data on which the placement recommendation is based," (3) "obtain agreement or disapproval with the proposed placement from the patient," and (4) help the patient visit the proposed facility and program whenever it is practical to do so. In addition, this person shall be primarily responsible for developing and implementing the community ITP and monitoring the patient's progress on a quarterly basis.

Hospital Referral and Outplacement Systems

Following a hospital referral, a patient is eligible for placement into the community by the community placement office. After the initial placement the case manager for community placement shall monitor the progress of the patient monthly for four months. Thereafter, there must be a quarterly review. Any change in mental or physical condition, incident or accident must be documented.

The department "shall establish an impartial review procedure . . . to enable clients to voice their objections, if any, to proposed transfers from a less restrictive community placement or service provider to another which is more restrictive." At this review, the patient may withhold consent to a proposed transfer, unless the delay would threaten his or her physical or mental health.

Hospital Support Programs and Transitional and Support Programs in the Community

Hospital support programs are divided into day care programs "for persons who are living at home or in the community but are still in need of rehabilitation," and outplacement follow-up "to provide patients with continuing training and reinforcement to help them further develop skills which are specific for their individual living situation and surrounding community," and transitional living programs "designed to improve the patient's transition to the community and to minimize the potential for rehospitalization."

The transitional living program shall teach each patient the following skills needed for living in the community: self-care such as personal hygiene, food preparation, and nutrition; coping skills, such as maintenance of a healthy and safe living environment; money management and use of community resources; and communication skills, such as use of the telephone, decision-making, and problem solving.

General Placement Criteria

Before nursing care will be used, a patient must have a physician's certification of need for skilled or intermediate nursing care, and there must be demonstrable evidence that the patient needs nursing care and that those needs cannot be met in a less restrictive environment.

Financial Assistance Eligibility Determination

Within 30 days of admission, each patient shall be subjected to a financial needs assessment, including the patient's eligibility for government benefits. This assessment will be repeated before the patient is placed in the community.

Provision of Community-based Facilities and Services

In order to achieve placements that are in the least restrictive setting and "most conducive to achieving the quality of life patients deserve," the defendants are committed to "provide an appropriate level of supervision and good quality care; . . . residential placements shall be in small, homelike, normal environments"; support services necessary to sustain community living shall be made available; and "a variety of residential and programmatic opportunities sufficient to permit matching of individual patients with the most appropriate residential and service setting possible" shall be offered. In addition, the defendants are to discourage "over-concentration of community residences for mentally disabled persons in particular geographical areas of the State."

Types of Community-based Residential Facilities

"Independent living is a residential setting appropriate for persons who either by themselves or with family help are capable of performing activities of daily living . . . , managing household affairs . . . , functioning in the community . . . , and supporting themselves through public benefits, employment or other private means."

"Semi-independent living means living alone, with friends or with a group of compatible persons in an apartment house, with assistance and training in daily living activities, home management and community skills provided . . . by persons who do not live in the residence."

"Supervision in a family-sized setting means residential care in an apartment, house, or DMH licensed group home including one adult living in the home who is responsible for providing assistance with the tasks of daily living, supervision, meals, lodging and rehabilitative care to the residents."

"Supervision in a large setting means meals, lodging, personal supervision and assistance in the tasks of daily living provided in a DMH licensed boarding home with more than three residents."

"Supervision and rehabilitative care in a large setting means meals, lodging, personal supervision and rehabilitative care . . . provided in a licensed DMH boarding home with more than three residents."

"Nursing care means residential care and the services of professionally trained nurses and other professional personnel, under the direction of a licensed physician provided in Medicare/Medicaid certified, DMH licensed, or DMH certified nursing homes, to persons with somatic ailments or disabilities which cannot be adequately cared for on other than an inpatient basis."

"Nursing and rehabilitative care means residential nursing and psychiatric rehabilitative care provided in licensed nursing homes."

Community Mental Health Services

Community mental health services shall include the following:

1. Quarterly patient evaluations and assessments;
2. Twenty-four-hour-telephone counseling service;
3. Day treatment program including a range of therapeutic interventions;
4. Day activity program including a range of rehabilitative and training activities;
5. Drug therapy providing prescribed medication and monitoring services;
6. Community education and consultation to community groups about deinstitutionalization and available services; and
7. Medical care services.

Community Placement Office

Before every placement is finalized, the patient must be notified and have an opportunity to object. Incompetent patients and minors must agree through their legal guardians with the placement. The patient or representative may appeal administratively if they disagree.

If the condition of a facility or program constitutes a potential health or safety hazard, the staff of the community placement office shall notify the operator and give him or her 10 days to correct the problem. If this is not done, the office shall begin to remove patients as soon as possible.

Intervention by Case Managers to Protect Patients' Rights

Patients may need the help of departmental personnel to intercede on their behalf to assure equity and the protection of their rights. Such interventions could occur in the form of *case-specific intervention,* in which the case manager influences the human services system in order to respond to patients' needs, and/or *class-specific intervention,* in which the case manager influences human services systems "to change in response to documented deficiencies in their capacity to serve and nurture."

TABLE 11.1 PROHIBITIONS AGAINST DISCRIMINATION IN EMPLOYMENT, HOUSING, AND PUBLIC ACCOMMODATIONS

STATE	TYPE OF DISCRIMINATION (1)	PERSONS COVERED Handicapped Generally (2)	Mentally Handicapped (3)	INVESTIGATION (4)	ADMINISTRATIVE HEARING (5)	AUTHORITY TO ORDER COMPLIANCE (6)	APPEAL (7)	PENALTY (8)
ARIZ. Rev. Stat. Ann. (1974 & Supp. 1982)	employment; housing 36-506(B)(1), (3)		36-506(B)(1), (3)					36-516(B) *fn. 1*
CONN. Gen. Stat. Ann. (West Supp. 1982)	employment 46a-60	physically handicapped or retarded 46a-60 46a-61		46a-83	46a-84	46a-86	46a-95(i)	46a-95(d)
D.C. Code Ann. (1981)	employment 1-607.2	physically or developmentally disabled 1-607.2						$300 fine &/or 90 days 6-1506
FLA. Stat. Ann. (West 1973 & Supp. 1983)	employment 23.167	23.167		23.167(11)(a)	23.167(13)			2d degree misdemeanor 413.08(5)
GA. Code Ann. (1982)	employment 66-504	66-502-3		54-122(3)	54-122(5)	54-122(1)		misdemeanor 54-9910
HAWAII Rev. Stat. (1976 & Supp. 1980)	public employment 78-2	78-2						
IDAHO Code (1976 & Supp. 1982)	public employment 56-707	56-707						
ILL. Ann. Stat. (Smith-Hurd 1979 & Supp. 1983–84)	employment 68, §2-102 housing 68, §3-102	68, §1-103(I), (Q)						
IND. Code Ann. (Burns 1981 & Supp. 1982–83)	employment, housing, public accommodations 22-9-1-2 16-7-5.5-2	22-9-1-2 22-9-1-3(G), (L)		22-9-1-11	29-9-1-6(J)(1)	22-9-16(K)(1)	22-9-16(K)(2)	
IOWA Code Ann. (West 1975 & Supp. 1983–84)	employment 601A.6 housing 601A.8 public accommodations 601A.7	601A.6 601A.7 601A.8		601A.5	601A.5	601A.15(2)	601A.15(1)	601A.7
LA. Rev. Stat. Ann. (West 1982)	employment 46:2253 46:2254	retardation or physiological disorder 46:2253 46:2254						
ME. Rev. Stat. Ann. (1979 & Supp. 1982–83)	employment 5, §4572, housing 5, §4582 public accommodations 5, §4592	5, §4572, 5, §4582 5, §4592		5, §4612(1)	5, §4612(3), (4) *fn. 2*	5, §4613(2)		$100 in 1st case; $250 on 2d order; $1,000 on 3d & subsequent orders
MD. Ann. Code (1972 & Supp. 1982)	employment 49B, §14 housing 49B, §20 public accommodations 49B, §5			49B, §10	49B, §11	may file suit in equity ct. 49B, §12		determined by equity ct. 49B, §26
MASS. Gen. Laws Ann. (West Supp. 1982)	employment 149, §24K public accommodations 272, §98	149, §24K 272, §98						$25–200 fine 149, §24K up to $300 or 1 yr.
MICH. Comp. Laws Ann. (1982 & Supp. 1982–83)	employment 37.1202, 37.1206 housing 37.1052 public accommodations 37.1302	37.1103(a)		37.2602	37.2602	37.2605	37.2606	
MINN. Stat. Ann. (West 1959 & Supp. 1983)	employment, housing, public accommodations 363.03 (subds. 1, 2, 3) *fn. 3*			363.06 (subd. 4)(1) 363.05 (subd. 1)(9)	363.05 (subd. 1)(18)	363.091 363.06 (subd. 4)(3)	363.072 363.06 (subd. 4)(1)	misdemeanor 363.101

TABLE 11.1 PROHIBITIONS AGAINST DISCRIMINATION IN EMPLOYMENT, HOUSING, AND PUBLIC ACCOMMODATIONS—*Continued*

STATE	TYPE OF DISCRIMINATION (1)	PERSONS COVERED: Handicapped Generally (2)	PERSONS COVERED: Mentally Handicapped (3)	INVESTIGATION (4)	ADMINISTRATIVE HEARING (5)	AUTHORITY TO ORDER COMPLIANCE (6)	APPEAL (7)	PENALTY (8)
MO. Ann. Stat. (Vernon 1962 & Supp. 1983)	employment 296.020 housing 213.105 public accommodations 314.010(1)	296.010 213.100(5) 314.010(2)		296.040 213.120(2) 314.060(2)	296.040(2) 213.120(4) 314.060(4)	296.040(7) 213.120(7) 314.060(9)	296.040(11) 213.120(9) 213.127 314.060(11)	
MONT. Code Ann. (1981)	employment 49-2-303 housing 49-2-305 public accommodations 49-2-304			49-2-504	49-2-505	49-2-506		misdemeanor: max. fine $500, 6 mos., or both 49-2-601
NEB. Rev. Stat. (1977 & Supp. 1981)	employment 48-1104 to 48-1107	48-1104 to 48-1107		48-1117(1) 48-1118	48-1117(2) 48-1119	48-1119(3)	48-1120	
N.J. Stat. Ann. (West 1976 & Supp. 1982)	employment, housing, public accommodations 10:5-4.1 10:5-12	10:5-14	10:5-15 10:5-16			10:5-14.1 10:5-17 10:5-19	10:5-21	*fn. 4*
N.M. Stat. Ann. (1978 & Supp. 1981)	employment, housing, public accommodations 28-1-7(A)-(G)	28-1-2(K)	28-1-10(B)		28-1-10(A), (B) 28-1-11	28-1-12	28-1-13	
N.Y. Exec. Law (McKinney 1982 & Supp. 1982-83)	employment, housing, public accommodations 296(1), (1a), (2), (2a), (5)	292(21)		297(2)	297(4)	297(4c), (6)	297-a 298	*fn. 5*
N.C. Gen. Stat. (1978 & Supp. 1979)	employment 143-422.2 168-6 housing 168-9 public accommodations 168-2 168-3	168-1		143-422.3	143-422.3	143-422.3		
OHIO Rev. Code Ann. (Baldwin 1970 & Supp. 1977)	employment, housing, public accommodations 4112.02(A)-(G)	4112.02		4112.05(B)	4112.05(B)	4112.05(G)	4112.06(A)	misdemeanor 4112.99
OKLA. Stat. Ann. (West 1966 & Supp. 1982-83)	employment 25, §1302 public accommodations 25, §1401	25, §1301		25, §1503	25, §1503	25, §1505	25, §1506	
OR. Rev. Stat. (1973 & Supp. 1981)	employment, housing, public accommodations 659.425(1), (2) 659.430	659.425		659.050	659.060	659.060(3) 659.070		*fn. 6*
R.I. Gen. Laws (1978 & Supp. 1982)	employment 28-5-7	28-5-7		28-5-13	28-5-18	28-5-24	28-5-28	
TENN. Code Ann. (1973 & Supp. 1977)	employment 8-50-103	8-50-103						misdemeanor 8-50-103
TEX. Hum. Res. Code Ann. (Vernon 1976 & Supp. 1981)	employment 121.003(f)	121.003(f)						misdemeanor $100-300 fine 4419e(6) *fn. 7*
UTAH Code Ann. (1966 & Supp. 1981)	employment 34-35-6	34-35-6		34-35-7(3)	34-35-7(6)	34-35-7(12)	34-35-8	
VT. Stat. Ann. (1968 & Supp. 1981)	employment 21, §495	21, §495(d)						
WASH. Rev. Code Ann. (1962 & Supp. 1983-84)	employment 49.60.180-200 *fn. 8*	49.60.180		49.60.120 49.60.240	49.60.240	49.60.250 49.60.260	49.60.270	*fn. 9*
W. VA. Code (1980 & Supp. 1982)	employment, housing, public accommodations 5-11-9(a)-(g)	5-11-3(f)		5-11-10	5-11-10	5-11-10 5-11-11	29A-5-4	
WIS. Stat. Ann. (West 1974 & Supp. 1982-83)	employment 111.321 housing 101.22	111.32 101.22		111.36(1) 101.22(4)(a)	111.36(3) 101.22(4)(b), (c)	111.36(3)(b) 101.22(4)(c)	111.37 101.22(5)	

FOOTNOTES: TABLE 11.1

1. Ariz. Rev. Stat. Ann. § 36-516(b) (1974). Violation of a person's right not to be discriminated against in employment and housing gives that person a cause of action for "greater of either $1,000 or 3 times the amount of actual damages."

2. Me. Rev. Stat. Ann. tit. 5, § 4612(3), (4) (1979 & Supp. 1982-83). There is no provision for a formal hearing; informal resolution is sought through conference, conciliation, and persuasion. If conciliation efforts fail, the Human Rights Commission shall file a civil action seeking appropriate relief.

3. Minn. Stat. Ann. § 363.03 (subds. 4, 5) (West Supp. 1983). Discrimination in providing public service or education is also prohibited.

4. N.J. Stat. Ann. § 10:5-38 (West 1983-84). Any individual who has been discriminated against and any organization that represents the interests of individuals who have been discriminated against shall have standing in courts of law to institute actions to enforce the law against discrimination.

5. N.Y. Exec. Law § 297(9) (McKinney Supp. 1982-83). Any person claiming to be aggrieved by an unlawful discriminatory practice shall have a cause of damages and other appropriate remedies.

6. Ore. Rev. Stat. §§ 659.435, 659.105 (1981). As made applicable to violations of the civil rights of the physically and mentally handicapped by the above statutes, gives an aggrieved person a cause of action against the violator for damages sustained and for exemplary damages as may be reasonable.

7. Tex. Hum. Res. Code § 121.004(b) (Vernon Supp. 1982-83). "Handicapped Person" who has also been deprived of his civil liberties by a person, firm or other organization may maintain a civil cause with a conclusive presumption of at least $100 of damages to the handicapped person.

8. Wash. Rev. Stat. Ann. § 50.12.210 (Supp. 1983-84).

> It is the policy of the state of Washington that persons with physical handicaps shall be given equal opportunities in employment. The legislature recognizes that handicapped persons have faced unfair discrimination in employment. For these reasons the state employment service division of the employment security department shall give particular and special attention to those persons with physical, mental, or sensory handicaps which substantially limit one or more of their major life functions . . . . Particular and special attention service shall include but not be limited to particular and special attention in counseling, referral, notification of job listings in advance of other persons, and other services of the employment service division.

9. Id., § 49.60.030(2). Any aggrieved person shall have a civil action in a court to enjoin further violations, to recover actual damages, or both together with cost of suit and any other remedy authorized by the United States Civil Rights Act of 1964.

TABLE 11.2 ZONING OF COMMUNITY FACILITIES FOR DEVELOPMENTALLY DISABLED PERSONS

STATE	TYPE OF COMMUNITY FACILITY (1)	RESIDENTS Number (2)	RESIDENTS Type (3)	ZONE IN WHICH PERMITTED (4)
ARIZ. Rev. Stat. Ann. (1974 & Supp. 1982–83)	residential facility 36-582	6 plus staff (max. 8 total) 36-582 7 or more 36-582	developmentally disabled 36-582 developmentally disabled 36-582	single-family residential 36-582 any zone where residential buildings of similar size permitted 36-582
CAL. Welf. & Inst. Code (West 1972 & Supp. 1983)	family care, foster or group home 5115, 5116	6 or less 5115, 5116	mentally disordered or otherwise handicapped persons or dependent & neglected children 5115, 5116	all residential zones, including for single-family dwellings 5115, 5116
COLO. Rev. Stat. (1982)	group home 30-28-115	8 30-28-115	developmentally disabled 30-28-115	all forms of residential zoning, including single-family residential 30-28-115
CONN. Gen. Stat. (West 1977 & Supp. 1983–84)	community residence 8-3e	6 or less 8-3e	mentally retarded 8-3e	single-family residential 8-3e
IDAHO (1980 & Supp. 1983)	home 67-6531	8 or less 67-6531	mentally &/or physically disabled handicapped 67-6531	single-family dwelling 67-6531
ME. Rev. Stat. Ann. (1980 & Supp. 1982–83)	community living use 30, §4692-A(2)	8 or less 30, §4692-A(2)	developmentally disabled 30, §4692-A(2)	single-family residential areas 30, §4692-A(1)
MD. Health Gen. Code Ann. (1982)	public group home 7-318 private group home 7-416	4 to 8 7-318 7-416	mentally retarded 7-318 developmentally disabled 7-416	*fn. 1* all residential zones (private group home) 7-416
MICH. Comp. Laws Ann. (1980 & Supp. 1983–84)	residential facility 125.286a(2)	6 or less 125.286a(2)	in need of supervision or care 125.286a(2)	single-family 125.286a(2)
MINN. Stat. Ann. (West Supp. 1983)	residential facility 462.357(7), (8) 245.812	6 or less; 10, if day care only 462.357(7) 245.812 7 to 16 462.357(8)	mentally retarded, physicially handicapped 462.357	single-family residential 462.357(7) 245.812 multifamily residential 462.357(8)
MONT. Code Ann. (1981)	community residential 76-2-314	8 or less 76-2-314	developmentally disabled or handicapped 76-2-313	all residential zones including single-family 76-2-314
N.J. Stat. Ann. (West 1981 & Supp. 1983–84)	group home 30:4C-2(m)	12 or less 30:4C-2(m)	children 30:4C-2(m)	*fn. 2*
N.M. Stat. Ann. (1978 & Supp. 1981)	community residences 3-21-1(c)	10 or less 3-21-1(c)	mentally ill or developmentally disabled 3-21-1(c)	single-family & all other residential uses 3-21-1(c)
N.Y. Mental Hyg. Law (McKinney 1978 & Supp. 1982–83)	community residential facility for disabled 41.34(f)	4 to 14 41.34(f)	mentally disabled 41.34(a)(1)	a family unit for purposes of local laws & ordinances 41.34(f)
OHIO Rev. Code Ann. (Baldwin 1982)	group home 5123.19 family home 5123.19	9 to 16 5123.19 1 to 8 5123.19	developmentally disabled 5123.19 developmentally disabled 5123.19	multifamily residential zone 5123.19 any residential zone, including single-family 5123.19
R.I. Gen. Laws (1977 & Supp. 1982)	community residences 45-24-22 group homes 45-24-22	6 or less 45-24-22 8 or less 45-24-22	retarded children or adults 45-24-22 mentally disabled 45-24-22	all local zoning requirements waived 45-24-22
S.C. Code Ann. & Regulations (Law. Co-op. 1976 & Supp. 1982)	boarding home serving developmentally disabled 88-110	based on accomodations 44-21-525	developmentally disabled 88-110	single-family 44-21-525
TENN. Code Ann. (Vernon 1980 & Supp. 1982)	residence of retarded or handicapped 13-24-102	8 or less 13-24-102	mentally or physically handicapped 13-24-101	single-family 13-24-102
VT. Stat. Ann. (1968 & Supp. 1982)	community care or group home 24, §4409(d)	6 or less 24, §4409(d)	developmentally disabled or physicially handicapped 24, §4409(d)	single-family 24, §4409(d)

TABLE 11.2 ZONING OF COMMUNITY FACILITIES FOR DEVELOPMENTALLY DISABLED PERSONS —*Continued*

STATE	TYPE OF COMMUNITY FACILITY (1)	RESIDENTS Number (2)	RESIDENTS Type (3)	ZONE IN WHICH PERMITTED (4)
VA. Code (1976 & Supp. 1983)	family care, foster, or group home 15.1-486.2	not specified 15.1-486.2	mentally retarded & other developmentally disabled 15.1-486.2	appropriate private residential districts 15.1-486.2
WIS. Stat. Ann. (West 1979 & Supp. 1982–83)	community-based residential facility 46.03(22)	8 or less; 15 or less 50.01	not specified 50.01	any deed covenant limiting use to single- or 2-family residences 50.01

FOOTNOTES: TABLE 11.2

1. Md. Health Gen. Code § 7-318 (1982). The statute is somewhat unclear with regard to public group homes. Although the public group home is exempt from any local zoning rule or regulation, public group homes may not be located in any area prohibited by the local zoning law. However, for the purposes of the mental retardation law and zoning, the public group home "conclusively shall be deemed a single family residential use, permitted in all residential zones."

2. N.J. Stat. Ann. § 40:55D-66.1 (West Supp. 1983-84): "Community residences for the developmentally disabled . . . shall be permitted use in all residences of a municipality, and the requirements therefore shall be the same as for single family dwelling units." (Provided however, that residences housing large numbers of developmentally disabled persons may be required to obtain conditional use permits.)

Barbara A. Weiner

CHAPTER 12 *Mental Disability and the Criminal Law*

I. INTRODUCTION

Deeply engrained in the American legal tradition of criminal justice is the proposition that a person who has committed a crime while suffering from a mental disorder or defect should be relieved of criminal liability. The question of the defendant's mental disability, or "insanity," may be raised at any point during the criminal trial. It can even affect the pretrial decision to prosecute and the tactical decisions of both the prosecution and the defense. It can also influence posttrial decisions, including the choice of whether the offender is sentenced to a correctional facility or placed for treatment in a mental institution. While the complexities inherent in the practical application of this tradition cannot be avoided by semantic sleight of hand, it is nonetheless helpful to recognize that the term *insanity* as used in the statutes and cases is a legal construct with no medical counterpart: it narrowly treats only the question whether the accused possessed the requisite mental state for criminal responsibility for his actions.[1] Even at that, considerable controversy remains about the precise formulation of the legal tests of responsibility, which have continued to evolve and which remain entangled in conflicting philosophies, assumptions, medical opinion, and changing sociopolitical conditions and perspectives.

Distinct from the matter of criminal responsibility is the question of *competency* to participate in the legal process. Rooted in the common law and incorporated in the constitutional protection of due process is the proposition that an accused may not be tried or sentenced while "incompetent." While the insanity defense has received more attention from the media and has inflamed public debate, the issue of competency, or what has sometimes been called "present insanity," affects far greater numbers of mentally disabled defendants,[2] and some consider this issue the most significant mental health inquiry pursued in the criminal justice process.[3] Since the previous edition of this book there has been increased recognition of the detrimental consequences of a finding of incompetency for the defendant, which has resulted in an increasing number of challenges to the state procedures for hospitalizing incompetent defendants and to provisions permitting indeterminate hospitalization without resolution of the criminal charges. As with the concept of criminal responsibility, the question of present competency engages conflicting philosophies and varying standards for application to individual cases, and it raises both substantive and procedural questions at each stage of the criminal process.

Even for the defendant who is determined competent to stand trial and found guilty, the issue of mental disability may arise at sentencing. Particularly controversial at this stage are questions concerning the role of the mental health professional and uses of information revealed during the psychiatric evaluation. The convicted person's mental disability may affect the conditions of his incarceration/institutionalization as well as his rights

1. "[T]he divergence between law and psychiatry is caused in part by the legal fiction represented by the words 'insanity' or 'insane,' which are a kind of lawyer's catchall and have no clinical meaning." J. Biggs, The Guilty Mind: Psychiatry and the Law of Homicide 117 (1955). See also A.S. Goldstein, The Insanity Defense 9 (1967).

2. For example, a 1979 study estimated that out of more than two million felony and misdemeanor cases disposed of in the state and federal courts 6,420 were institutionalized because they were incompetent to stand trial, as compared with 1,625 who were there as a result of being found not guilty by reason of insanity. Steadman, Monahan, Hartstone, Davis, & Robbins, Mentally Disordered Offenders: A National Survey of Patients and Facilities, 6 Law & Hum. Behav. 31, 33 (1982).

It has been estimated that as many as 9,000 persons a year are found incompetent, a figure that reflects that not all of them are institutionalized or that a percentage of those who are institutionalized are discharged after relatively brief periods. H.J. Steadman, Beating A Rap? Defendants Found Incompetent to Stand Trial 4 (1979). In Illinois, for example, approximately 300 people a year are found incompetent, while only about 40 are found not guilty by reason of insanity (statistics kept by the Illinois Dep't of Mental Health & Developmental Disabilities, Statistical Branch, Springfield, Illinois).

3. See, e.g., A.A. Stone, Mental Health and Law: A System in Transition 201 (Crime & Delinquency Series, DHEW No. ADM 76-176, 1976).

within the correctional or mental health system or those attendant upon his transfer from one system to the other.

An area that has diminished in importance is the set of special laws for the detection and treatment of mentally disordered sex offenders or sexual psychopaths. Because of growing doubt about the existence in reality of such a distinct homogeneous category of disability, over the past decade many of these laws have been repealed or have ceased to be used.

This chapter reviews the origins, historical development, and current status of the criminal law as it relates to the mentally disabled, and it assesses the sentencing and treatment consequences for the mentally disabled defendant who is found to be "incompetent," "insane," or sexually psychopathic.

II. COMPETENCY TO PARTICIPATE IN THE CRIMINAL JUSTICE PROCESS

A. Introduction: The Rationale

Four principles have been advanced to explain the need to suspend criminal proceedings against an accused who is found to lack or is suspected of lacking the mental capacity to understand the nature of the proceedings against him.[4] First, safeguarding the accuracy of the proceedings requires full cooperation with the accused in getting all the facts relevant to a case, particularly when he is the only party aside from the complainant who has knowledge of the facts. Second, ensuring procedural fairness depends on an accused's having the basic capacity to exercise the rights accorded to him in the process by society, which include the rights to choose and assist counsel, to act as a witness in one's own behalf, and to confront opposing witnesses. This means that an accused must not only be aware of the facts and capable of communicating them but also be able to help counsel in the presentation of a defense, understand his role in the proceedings, and have some grasp of the substantive and tactical options open to him or his attorney. Third, the integrity and dignity of the legal process and general respect for our judicial and law enforcement systems would be undermined by the spectacle of trying an incapacitated defendant. Fourth, achieving the objectives of punishment or sentencing, whether they be retribution, rehabilitation, or deterrence, depends on the defendant's comprehending the punishment and the reasons for its imposition. In sum, the trial, adjudication, sentence, or execution of a person charged with a criminal offense, while insane, is a violation of due process of law.[5]

Because it is often missed by practitioners in both the legal and the psychiatric professions, it is important to keep in mind the conceptual distinction between competency to participate in the criminal justice process and criminal responsibility. Competency concerns only the defendant's present ability to assist in his defense and understand the process he is involved in or the punishment he receives, whereas criminal responsibility concerns only the mental state of the defendant at the time of the commission of the crime, which may have been months or years before the trial. Thus, a defendant may be competent to stand trial but be found not criminally responsible for his acts. Conversely, he could be adjudged incompetent but once restored to competency be held responsible for his criminal actions. Finally, he could be declared incompetent and once restored to competency be found not criminally responsible.

Although questions of competency may arise at any stage of the criminal justice process, in practice competency is most critical and most frequently raised at the trial stage.

B. Competency to Stand Trial

1. Introduction

The issue of competency to stand trial dominates criminal cases involving mentally disabled defendants because of the ease with which it is raised by the defense, by the prosecution, and by the court and because of the consequences it may have for the defendant and the proceedings in general. Unless the competency question is raised frivolously, the trial is suspended and a mental evaluation is ordered. A finding of incompetency poses several possible negative consequences for the defendant: (1) having bail revoked or denied, (2) being hospitalized, in some cases for a longer period than if he had been convicted of the charge, and (3) being stigmatized with the label of "mentally ill" or "mentally defective."

2. Development of the Standard

Present formulations of the concept of competency to stand trial derive from the basic, if imprecise, common law doctrine that an accused may not be tried while "insane."[6] United States Supreme Court decisions have indicated that an accused is constitutionally entitled to a

4. Note, Incompetency to Stand Trial, 81 Harv. L. Rev. 454, 456 (1967); also Smith, Competency: Symposium on Forensic Psychiatry, 6 Psychiatric Clinics of North America 635 (1983), for historical development of competency rules.

5. Pizzi, Competency to Stand Trial in Federal Courts: Conceptual and Constitutional Problems, 45 U. Chi. L. Rev. 21 (1977); also Porter v. Estelle, 709 F. 2d 944, 949 (5th Cir. 1983); United States v. Voice, 627 F. 2d 138, 140 (8th Cir. 1980); Youtsey v. United States, 97 F. 937, 942 (6th Cir. 1899), which is one of the earliest cases discussing the due process implications of the competency issue.

6. W. Blackstone, Commentaries 24, 395 (9th ed. 1783); Annot., 3 A.L.R. 94 (1919).

determination of competency to stand trial. That is, if because of mental disability a defendant cannot recall events, produce evidence, or comport himself within the limits of proper courtroom demeanor, he is in effect denied the constitutionally guaranteed rights accorded to all defendants in criminal trials—assisting counsel, testifying in his own behalf, and confronting adverse witnesses.[7]

In *Dusky v. United States*[8] in 1960 the United States Supreme Court articulated the test for determining the defendant's competency to stand trial: "whether he [the defendant] has sufficient present ability to consult his lawyer with a reasonable degree of rational understanding and whether he has a rational as well as factual understanding of the proceedings against him."[9] This standard, which reflects common law notions of competency, has today been codified in the vast majority of states.[10] While the *Dusky* case did not hold that lack of competency must be due to a mental illness or defect, 37 states specifically require a finding of mental disease or defect as a prerequisite for establishing incompetency.[11] Illinois and Hawaii provide that an accused can be found incompetent as a result of either a mental *or* a physical disability. Fourteen states follow *Dusky's* unspecified standard.[12]

Dusky has been criticized for the lack of precision in its language,[13] which leaves considerable room for disagreement in its application to a given set of facts. A number of courts since *Dusky* have been faced with the problem of articulating what the standard means functionally.[14] One of the more detailed definitions, provided by a federal district court in 1961 in *Wieter v. Settle*,[15] sets out the following characteristics of a competent defendant:

> (1)that he has mental capacity to appreciate his presence in relation to time, place and things; (2) that his elementary mental processes be such that he apprehends (i.e. seizes and grasps with what mind he has) that he is in a Court of Justice, charged with a criminal offense; (3)that there is a Judge on the Bench; (4) a Prosecutor present who will try to convict him of a criminal charge; (5) that he has a lawyer (self-employed or Court-appointed) who will undertake to defend him against that charge; (6) that he will be expected to tell his lawyer the circumstances, to the best of his mental ability, (whether colored or not by mental aberration) the facts surrounding him at the time and place where the law violation is alleged to have been committed; (7) that there is, or will be, a jury present to pass upon evidence adduced as to his guilt or innocence of such charge; and (8) he has memory sufficient to relate those things in his own personal manner:—such a person from consideration of legal standards, should be considered mentally competent to stand trial under criminal procedure, lawfully enacted.[16]

3. Reasons for Raising the Issue of Competency

(a) Due process □□ Because proceeding against an accused person while he is incompetent violates due process, the defense, the prosecution, and the court all have an obligation to assure that the issue is explored at whatever point in the proceedings the defendant shows evidence of mental imbalance. The defense attorney's most obvious interest is to assure that his client can understand the nature of the proceedings and assist in the defense. The prosecutor clearly has a duty to see to it that the trial proceeds properly as well as an interest in not being reversed on appeal for having ignored telling evidence of the defendant's lack of competency.

The judge's responsibility was affirmed by the United States Supreme Court as far back as 1966 in *Pate v. Robinson*, holding that the trial judge had to explore the issue sua sponte when the evidence before him raised "a '*bona fide doubt*' as to a defendant's competence to stand trial."[17] In *Robinson* the trial court was presented with a defendant who had killed his common law wife and infant son and whose history included frequent bizarre and violent behavior as well as attempted suicide. The Illinois Supreme Court upheld the trial court's decision not to address the issue of competency, noting the defendant's mental alertness and apparently adequate level of understanding at trial. However, the Supreme Court reversed, stating that "this reasoning offers no justification for ignoring the uncontradicted testimony of Robinson's history of pronounced irrational behavior."[18]

7. Pate v. Robinson, 383 U.S 375 (1966); Bishop v. United States, 350 U.S. 961 (1956).
8. 362 U.S. 402 (1960).
9. *Id.* at 402.
10. See table 12.1, cols. 6-9. As early as 1899 in Youtsey v. United States, 97 F. 937 (6th Cir. 1899), the court adopted medical testimony in competency proceedings and began to examine the specific skills that constitute competency. A few years later in United States v. Chisolm, 149 F. 284, 289, 290 (S.D. Ala. 1906) the court held that the questions to be answered in a competency inquiry are: "Does the mental impairment of the prisoner's mind . . . disable him . . . from fairly presenting his defense . . . ?" and further "Is the mind of the defendant at the bar . . . so far from normal and so impaired by disease as to make it improper and unjust to keep him on trial . . . ?"
11. See table 12.1, cols. 6-9.
12. District of Columbia, Florida, Georgia, Indiana, Maine, Maryland, Nebraska, Nevada, New Hampshire, New Jersey, New Mexico, Oklahoma, Tennessee, and Vermont. See table 12.1.
13. Group for the Advancement of Psychiatry, 2 Misuse of Psychiatry in the Criminal Courts: Competency to Stand Trial 881 (Rep. No. 89, 1974) [hereinafter cited as GAP Competency Report].
14. See, e.g., Morrow v. State, 443 A.3d 108 (Md. 1982); State v. Austad, 641 P.2d 1373 (Mont. 1982); State v. Heger, 326 N.W.2d 855 (N.D. 1982).
15. 193 F. Supp. 318 (W.D. Mo. 1961).
16. *Id.* at 321, 322.
17. 383 U.S. 375, 385 (1966) (emphasis in orginial).
18. *Id.* at 385-86.

What degree of doubt must exist about the defendant's competency before an examination and hearing are required? While *Pate v. Robinson* spoke of "bona fide doubt" and "uncontradicted testimony," the modern rule in the federal courts is that a proper motion for a competency evaluation cannot be denied if there is "reasonable cause" to believe that the accused is incompetent.[19] Presumably, the same standard applies to the judge's obligation to raise the issue on his own. The practice in most courts is to grant an examination and to hold a hearing whenever there is some evidence to indicate the possibility of incompetency. In noting when a competency evaluation should be ordered, Judge Bazelon of the United States Court of Appeals for the District of Columbia Circuit stated in *Mitchell v. United States*[20] in 1963:

> It cannot reasonably be supposed that Congress intended to require the accused to produce, in order to get a mental examination, enough evidence to prove that he is incompetent or irresponsible. That is what the examination itself may, or may not, produce. If the accused already had such evidence there would be little need for the examination.[21]

Thus, if the information about competency raises a reasonable doubt as to the defendant's competency, the denial of an examination and hearing would be a denial of due process.[22]

(b) Strategic uses of competency issue □□ In some cases both the defense and the prosecution may desire an examination for reasons that have little to do with the defendant's ability to participate in the trial process. Requesting a competency evaluation may hold strategic advantages for the defense, who may use it as a foundation for a defense of mitigating circumstances or to avoid the risk and rigors of an insanity plea.[23] There has been considerable controversy over the appropriateness of the prosecutor's raising the issue, centering, among other things, on the fact that doing so usually prevents pretrial release of the accused.[24] Whatever the motives of either the defense or the prosecution for raising the incompetency plea, it almost always has the effect of delaying or interrupting the trial process. In addition, the issue is sometimes used as a device to get a psychiatric examination for consideration in plea bargaining or sentencing.[25]

Because the defendant continues to be detained while the criminal proceedings are suspended, some view the examination as a kind of "preventive detention,"[26] that is, confinement without any finding of guilt or need of treatment or consent to it. From the opposite perspective comes the charge that the defendant is being given "psychiatric immunity."[27] Both perspectives hint at some of the constitutional issues implicated.

A recent study of statutes and cases relating to competency to stand trial suggested that the motion for a competency evaluation should detail the behaviors that the defendant is alleged to have exhibited and how these might relate to his ability to understand the charges or assist his counsel.[28] Doing so would clarify the basis for raising the issue of competency for the trial court and would also create an unambiguous record for the reviewing court on appeal.

4. Competency to Plead Guilty

It has traditionally been presumed that competency to stand trial means competency to participate in all phases of the trial process, including such pretrial activities as deciding how to plead, participating in plea bargaining, and deciding whether to assert or waive the right to counsel. In 1973 the United States Court of Appeals for the Ninth Circuit ruled in *Sieling v. Eyman* that a hearing must be held to determine the defendant's ability to plead guilty "[w]here the question of a defendant's lack of mental capacity lurks in the background."[29] Here the court's standard differed from the one set forth in *Dusky*, which concerned competency to stand trial. *Sieling* adopted the dissent of Judge Hufstedler in an earlier Ninth Circuit case, *Schoeller v. Dunbar*,[30] in which she wrote:

> A defendant is not competent to plead guilty if mental illness has substantially impaired his ability to make a reasoned choice among the alternatives presented to him and to understand the nature of the consequences of his plea.[31]

Other courts have rejected the notion of having a specific competency standard for pleading guilty, different from the standard for standing trial.[32] In *Allard*

19. United States v. Bodey, 547 F. 2d 1383 (9th Cir. 1977); United States v. Nichelson, 550 F. 2d 502 (8th Cir. 1977); Rose v. United States, 513 F. 2d 1251 (8th Cir. 1975).
20. 316 F. 2d 354 (D.C. Cir. 1963).
21. *Id.* at 360.
22. People v. Hays, 54 Cal. App. 3d 755, 126 Cal. Rptr. 770 (1976).
23. Slovenko, The Developing Law on Competency to Stand Trial, 5 J. Psychiatry & L. 165, 196 (1977).
24. Eisenstadt, Mental Competency to Stand Trial, 4 Harv. C.R.-C.L. L. Rev. 379, 384, 410 (1968), which discusses why a prosecutor might want a person to be found incompetent (as a means of institutionalizing him for a lengthy period).
25. Slovenko, *supra* note 23, at 196.
26. *Id.* at 167.
27. *Id.*
28. Roesch & Golding, Competency to Stand Trial ch. 7 (1980).
29. 478 F.2d 211, 214 (9th Cir. 1973).
30. 423 F.2d 1183 (9th Cir. 1970).
31. *Id.* at 1194.
32. Allard v. Helgemoe, 572 F.2d 1 (1st Cir. 1978); People v. Heral, 62 Ill. 2d 329, 342 N.E.2d 34 (1976); Commonwealth v. Leate, 327 N.E.2d 866 (Mass. 1966).

v. Helgemoe in 1978,[33] the United States Court of Appeals for the First Circuit concluded that while the waiver of rights involved in entering a guilty plea needed to be closely examined, the *Dusky* standard was a functional one that would cover the considerations involved in pleading guilty.[34]

5. Competency to Waive Counsel

The possibility that a person who is competent to stand trial may at the same time be incompetent to make the decision to waive his right to counsel was raised by the United States Supreme Court's brief per curiam decision in 1966 in *Westbrook v. Arizona*.[35] The defendant, convicted of murder and given the death penalty, had waived his right to counsel after being found competent to stand trial, but on appeal he argued that he was incompetent to represent himself. Observing that no hearing or inquiry had been held on his competence to waive his constitutional right to the assistance of counsel, the Supreme Court asserted:

> "The constitutional right of an accused to be represented by counsel invoked, of itself, the protection of a trial court, in which the accused—whose life or liberty is at stake—is without counsel. This protecting duty imposes the serious and weighty responsibility upon the trial judge of determining whether there is an intelligent and competent waiver by the accused."[36]

The language suggests that if the defendant wishes to proceed pro se, the trial court must first determine whether the defendant is competent to stand trial and then, separately, whether he is competent to waive his right to counsel. *Westbrook* is an affirmation of the observation made earlier by the Supreme Court in *Massey v. Moore*[37] that a defendant "might not be insane in the sense of being incapable of standing trial and yet lack the capacity to stand trial without benefit of counsel."[38] The justification for this distinction flows from the difference between capability of cooperating with one's attorney and the greater complexities involved in making for oneself the decisions the attorney would otherwise make.[39]

It is unclear whether a defendant has a *right* to represent himself if the court determines he is incompetent to do so. Presumably he does not, since by definition his incompetency deprives him of the capacity to represent himself or to decide that he can. The *Westbrook* ruling would indicate that the trial court should carefully scrutinize a request for pro se representation by a defendant; if the court concludes the defendant is mentally incompetent, the request should be denied and an attorney should be appointed to represent him.

6. The Competency Examination

(a) Conduct of the evaluation

Once the question of competency has been raised and found valid, the court orders an examination. The site of the evaluation, the choice of examiner, and the examination itself may raise constitutional questions.

(1) Site of the evaluation □□ Typically a competency evaluation is performed in a maximum security hospital to which the defendant has been committed by the court for observation for a period typically ranging from 30 to 90 days.[40] The statutes of 18 states *require* these evaluations to be done on an inpatient basis.[41] The duration and setting of the confinement make it easy to understand why those concerned with the needs and rights of defendants see it as a type of preventive detention.

There is a growing trend, however, to perform competency evaluations on an outpatient basis. Approximately 17 states provide for this possibility by law.[42] In large urban areas, these evaluations may be performed by court clinics, often located in the criminal court buildings or nearby. While the defendant is thus not hospitalized, he usually remains incarcerated in a correctional facility because of inability to make bail. Use of outpatient competency evaluations is supported by research data indicating that the narrow issues of the defendant's capacity to understand the charges and to assist his counsel can usually be determined in a brief examination.[43] Considerations of cost efficiency and of due process provide added support for outpatient eval-

33. 572 F.2d 1 (1st Cir. 1978).

34. In another case on the issue, the Illinois Supreme Court held that "a finding of competency to stand trial necessarily involves a finding that, with the advice and assistance of counsel, defendant is capable of waiving some or all of his constitutional rights, whether by a plea of guilty or during the course of his trial." People v. Heral, 62 Ill. 2d 329, 342 N.E.2d 34, 37 (1976).

35. 384 U.S. 150 (1966).

36. *Id.* at 150, quoting Johnson v. Zerbst, 304 U.S. 458, 465 (1938), Carnley v. Cochran, 369 U.S. 506 (1962).

37. 348 U.S. 105 (1954).

38. *Id.* at 108.

39. Silten and Tullis have depicted the greater competence required of a defendant without counsel:

> The defendant who waives counsel will be alone when it becomes necessary to decide whether to testify or to decide matters involving trial procedures and strategy. He must therefore be able to determine the alternatives available to him during the proceeding, to evaluate these choices, and to decide for himself what action to take. He will not have guidance from an attorney and cannot depend upon the court to provide the assistance he would receive if he had counsel. In this situation, it is clear that the defendant must have greater powers of comprehension, judgment, and reason than would be necessary to stand trial with the aid of an attorney.

Silten & Tullis, Mental Competency in Criminal Proceedings, 28 Hastings L.J. 1053, 1068 (1977).

40. See table 12.1, cols. 13 & 14.

41. See table 12.1, col. 13.

42. *Id.*

43. Roesch & Golding, *supra* note 28, at 204.

uations as opposed to institutionalization in hospitals for the criminally insane.

(2) The evaluator □□ Almost every state statute specifies who the evaluator must be and how many evaluations must be performed.[44] Twenty states require that the evaluation be done only by a psychiatrist. Some require a general physician and/or a psychiatrist, and some have recognized the qualifications of other mental health professionals, particularly Ph.D. clinical psychologists, to conduct the competency evaluations. It has also recently been suggested that the decision be made by a competency screening panel, which would include in addition to mental health professionals, an attorney who would be in the best position to determine the defendant's understanding of the legal process and his ability to cooperate with counsel.[45] Some statutes provide for general referral of the defendant to the state mental health agency for an evaluation.[46] Where statutes are not specific about what type of mental health professional should perform the evaluation, the usual practice is to select a psychiatrist.[47]

Ten states require that more than one evaluation be done.[48] Even in the absence of such a statutory requirement, the defense or the prosecution, when not satisfied with one evaluation, may request another by an outside expert in contemplation of a contested competency hearing.

(3) The evaluation□□ Although the evaluation is ostensibly restricted to determining the defendant's present understanding of the trial process and his ability to assist his attorney, studies have found that psychiatrists often misunderstand the test of incompetency, confusing it with the test for criminal responsibility,[49] or that they deliberately resist such artificially compartmentalized mental inquiries.[50]

At present no standard evaluation format is in widespread use, in part because no state requires that the evaluator be specific in reporting his findings or the methodology used in reaching his conclusions. Attempts have been made to develop structured screening devices. The most notable is the work of A. Louis McGarry, M.D., who has developed a competency screening test to assess all possible legal grounds for a finding of competency.[51] McGarry explains that the instrument "is expressed as a series of thirteen ego functions related to what is required of a defendant in criminal proceedings in order that he may adequately cope with and protect himself in such proceedings."[52]

McGarry's test has been criticized by both attorneys and mental health professionals. Brakel has argued that it measures not so much competency to stand trial as an acceptance of prevailing ideologies (as opposed to practices) of the criminal justice system.[53] A survey has found that the McGarry instrument is often used "as a structuring device rather than a definitive determiner of competency: the instruments are frequently not scored but are used rather to articulate the standards for competency."[54] However, even where the McGarry test is not used, there are indications that experienced forensic examiners develop questioning formats that resemble it because of their general familiarity with McGarry's work and other relevant legal literature.[55]

(b) Some special mental functioning problems

Certain disabilities may be found or claimed that may dramatically affect the decision of the evaluator. These include mental retardation, amnesia, and dependence on medication to function competently.

(1) Mental retardation □□ Although debate continues over the social bias inherent in measuring intelligence and in assigning the label "mentally retarded," the disability of mental retardation remains a fact.[56] It has been defined as a condition characterized as "significantly subaverage intellectual functioning existing concurrently with deficits in adaptive behavior, and manifested during the developmental period."[57]

44. See table 12.1, col. 11.

45. Roesch & Golding, Treatment and Disposition of Defendants Found Incompetent to Stand Trial: A Review and a Proposal, 2 Int'l J. L. & Psychiatry 366 (1969).

46. See table 12.1, col. 11.

47. This is in part because psychiatrists have traditionally been the ones to become involved in these issues; only in recent years have legislatures included nonmedical people such as clinical psychologists to perform the competency evaluation.

48. See table 12.1, col. 11.

49. See Note, Incompetency to Stand Trial, *supra* note 4, at 470; also Poythress & Stock, Competency to Stand Trial: A Historical Review and Some New Data, 8 J. Psychiatry & L. 131 (1980); Comment, An End to Incompetency to Stand Trial, 13 Santa Clara Law. 560, 563 (1973).

50. The Group for the Advancement of Psychiatry has framed the problem of the competency evaluation for psychiatrists:

> It may be helpful for the psychiatrist to set the problems of competency before himself in this way: After a careful psychiatric examination, he might ask himself, has mental illness or disease affected the patient's mental status such that it would in some general way interfere with his understanding of the legal issues? His capacity to recall and disclose significant information? His ability to consult and communicate with his lawyer?

See GAP Competency Report, *supra* note 13, at 897.

51. A.L. McGarry (Harvard University Laboratory of Community Psychiatry), Competency to Stand Trial and Mental Illness (Crime and Delinquency Issues Series, DHEW Pub. No. HSM73-9105, 1973).

52. *Id.* at 5.

53. Brakel, Presumption, Bias, and Incompetency in the Criminal Process, 1974 Wis. L. Rev. 1105 (1974).

54. Schreiber, Assessing Competency to Stand Trial: A Case Study of Technology Diffusion in Four States, 6 A.A.P.L. Bull. 439, 452 (1978).

55. *Id.*

56. J.S. Coleman with E.Q. Campbell, C.J. Hobson, J. McPartland, A.M. Mood, F.D. Weinfeld, & R.L. York, Equality of Educational Opportunity (1966); Loretan, The Decline and Fall of Group Intelligence Testing, Teachers College Rec. 10 (1967).

57. Manual on Terminology and Classification in Mental Retardation 148 (American Association on Mental Deficiency, Special Pub. No. 2) (H.J. Grossman ed. 1977).

The disproportionate number of mentally retarded persons in the penal system, with estimates ranging from 10 to 25% of all prisoners being retarded,[58] leads to the question why there are not more pretrial challenges to competency. One reason may be that often attorneys do not recognize that their client is retarded.[59] If the issue is raised, the report by the mental health professional is likely to include an IQ score, which may measure the person's mental aptitude but will afford little insight into his ability to communicate and his functional skills. Not infrequently, courts have simply observed that the defendant's IQ is below normal and then stated that this does not mean he is incompetent.[60] In the case of the mildly retarded defendant, the line between competency and incompetency is indeed likely to be elusive.[61] One commentator has suggested that not until detailed guidelines of the mental and physical skills necessary for a finding of incompetency are formulated will it be possible for judges to relate the effects of mental defect to the issue of competency.[62] Clearly an evaluation that speaks only in general terms of mental illness or mental retardation is not sufficient to establish that a person is incompetent. The evaluator must go on to apply this finding to the defendant's ability to meet the legal standard for competency to stand trial.

Special problems are presented when the mentally retarded person wants to enter a guilty plea.[63] In 1976 in *United States v. Masthers*[64] Judge Bazelon, writing for the United States Court of Appeals for the District of Columbia Circuit, observed that [t]he impropriety of reliance on personal observation is highlighted in the case of a retarded defendant."[65] Specialists have pointed out that retardation is not always readily recognized by the untrained observer or official:[66] retarded persons may appear a "little slow" or be "very agreeable" to suggestions, often possessing a compliant nature that makes them eager to please in a difficult situation,[67] and they sometimes adapt to the stigma of their disability by wearing a "cloak of competence" to hide their handicap from the world.[68]

The average defense attorney has no particular understanding of mental retardation or training in identifying its symptoms.[69] His inexpertise may be compounded by insufficient expertise on the part of the evaluator. In most instances, evaluations are performed by psychiatrists rather than clinical psychologists, who as a rule are better trained in differentiating retardation from normal functioning.[70] Inadequate identification may in turn be compounded by inadequate response in known cases. As two commentators have pointed out: "The ability of the retarded citizen accused of a crime to aid in his own defense may be as much a function of the attorney's familiarity with and ability to relate to retarded persons as of the person's own tested competence."[71]

(2) Amnesia □□ Loss of memory about a particular event or period of time, due to either physical or psychic trauma,[72] may affect the defendant's ability to participate in the trial process. One is considered to be suffering from amnesia when there is general memory loss, more than forgetfulness as to a few of the details.[73] When a defendant claims amnesia, a court must make three determinations: whether the defendant has the condition, the extent of the condition, and its effect on the defendant's ability to assist his attorney. Although the testimony of medical experts is crucial to verify the presence of amnesia, there is no objective test to measure the memory of another person.[74] Moreover, amnesia is easily feigned.[75]

The courts that have addressed claims of amnesia have asserted that the fact that a defendant is an amne-

58. Brown & Courtless, The Mentally Retarded in Penal and Correctional Institutions, 124 Am. J. Psychiatry 1164 (1968). See also Haggerty, Kane, & Udall, An Essay on the Legal Rights of the Mentally Retarded, 6 Fam. L.Q. 59 (1972); Brelje, An Overview of Incarceration, *in* Rehabilitation and the Retarded Offender (P.L. Browning ed. 1976).

59. See Alperin, Jones, Moschella, & Teahan, Representation of a Mentally Retarded Criminal Defendant, 64 Mass. L. Rev. 106 (1979); also Mickenberg, Competency to Stand Trial and the Mentally Retarded Defendant: The Need for a Multi-Disciplinary Solution to a Multi-Disciplinary Problem, 17 Cal. W.L. Rev. 367 (1981).

60. The Accused Retardate, 4 Colum. Hum. Rts. L. Rev. 245, 246 (1972).

61. See Mickenberg, *supra* note 59, at 382.

62. *Id.* at 407.

63. See Note, Competence to Plead and the Retarded Defendant: *United States v. Masthers*, 539 F.2d 721 (D.C. Cir. 1976), 9 Conn. L. Rev. 176 (1976); Hays & Ehrlich, Ability of the Mentally Retarded to Plead Guilty, 1975 Ariz. St. L.J. 66 (1975).

64. 539 F.2d 721 (D.C. Cir. 1976).

65. *Id.* at 728.

66. See Alperin, Jones, Moschella, & Teahan, *supra* note 59; also The Accused Retardate, *supra* note 60.

67. R.B. Edgerton, The Cloak of Competency: Stigma in the Lives of the Mentally Retarded (1967).

68. *Id.*

69. Indeed in *Masthers* the defense counsel, in raising the issue of competency after sentencing, argued:

> [H]e was misled by defendant's attitude and manner into believing that defendant understood the proceedings and the consequences of his plea of guilty. Defendant appeared to be agreeable to all suggestions, *nodding* to counsel as though he understood counsel's explanation.

539 F.2d 721, 727 (D.C. Cir. 1976) (emphasis in original; note omitted).

70. Because psychologists, unlike psychiatrists, have been trained in measuring intellectual assessment, they are better able to assess the cognitive abilities required in determining competency to stand trial for retarded defendants.

71. Ravenel & Bush, A Legal Framework: An Outsider's Perspective, *in* Rehabilitation and the Retarded Offender, *supra* note 58.

72. Note, Amnesia: The Forgotten Justification for Finding an Accused Incompetent to Stand Trial, 20 Washburn L.J. 289, 301 (1981) [hereinafter cited as Note, Amnesia].

73. Purver, Annotation, Amnesia as Affecting Capacity to Commit a Crime or Stand Trial, 46 A.L.R. 3d 544 (1972).

74. See Note, Amnesia, *supra* note 72, at 301.

75. See Purver, *supra* note 73, at 548; Lennox, Amnesia, Real and Feigned, 10 U. Chi. L. Rev. 298 (1943).

siac does not necessarily preclude a fair trial and that the affliction by itself does not render someone incompetent.[76] This is not to say that amnesia is legally irrelevant; instead, the problem for the courts has been to try to define *when* amnesia should render someone incompetent.

In a leading case in this area in 1968, *Wilson v. United States*,[77] the United States Court of Appeals for the District of Columbia Circuit was faced with a defendant who suffered amnesia as a result of brain injuries from an automobile accident that occurred in a high-speed auto chase as he fled the scene of the crime. The court set out six factors to be considered by the trial court in deciding whether the amnesia affected the defendant's competency.

> (1) The extent to which the amnesia affected the defendant's ability to consult with and assist his lawyer.
> (2) The extent to which the amnesia affected the defendant's ability to testify in his own behalf.
> (3) The extent to which the evidence in suit could be extrinsically reconstructed in view of the defendant's amnesia. Such evidence would include evidence relating to the crime itself as well as any reasonably possible alibi.
> (4) The extent to which the Government assisted the defendant and his counsel in that reconstruction.
> (5) The strength of the prosecution's case. Most important here will be whether the Government's case is such as to negate all reasonable hypotheses of innocence. If there is any substantial possibility that the accused could, but for his amnesia, establish an alibi or other defense, it should be presumed that he would have been able to do so.
> (6) Any other facts and circumstances which would indicate whether or not the defendant had a fair trial.[78]

The *Wilson* court also held that the trial court should make written findings setting out the bases for a conclusion that the defendant's amnesia did not prevent him from receiving a fair trial.[79]

The thinking of the courts in amnesia cases seems to be that although a defendant is entitled to a fair trial, he is not necessarily entitled to a "perfect trial."[80] Numerous cases have found the defendant to be competent although he suffered brain damage as a result of an accident.[81] Some courts have felt that the defendant with amnesia is no more handicapped than the defendant who claims he was insane at the time of the crime, or very intoxicated, or completely drugged.[82] Yet in those instances those conditions might be a defense to the crime, since they affected the defendant's ability to form intent. No courts recognize amnesia as the basis for a defense to a crime,[83] because the amnesia that occurs after a crime can have no effect on a defendant's motives or behavior at the time he committed the criminal act. Most courts appear to take the functional approach of the *Wilson* case to determine whether the defendant's amnesia interferes with his present ability to consult with his lawyer with a reasonable degree of understanding and whether he has a rational as well as a factual comprehension of the proceedings.[84]

(3) Medication□□ The psychotropic medications developed in the 1950s to relieve or at least control the symptoms of many mental illnesses[85] are today often given to defendants hospitalized because of incompetence to stand trial, but with considerable confusion about the legal, if not the medical, effects of the drugs. Some courts have held that these medications create a "chemical sanity" unacceptable for participation at trial.[86]

76. See, e.g., Notes and Comments, Amnesia: A Case Study in the Limits of Particular Justice, 71 Yale L.J. 109 (1961); also State v. McClendon, 437 P.2d 421 (Ariz. 1968); State v. Pugh, 283 A.2d 537 (N.J. Super. Ct. App. Div. 1971); Commonwealth *ex rel.* Cummins v. Price, 218 A.2d 758 (Pa. 1966); United States v. Sermon, 228 F. Supp. 972 (W.D. Mo. 1964).

77. 391 F.2d 460 (D.C. Cir. 1968).

78. *Id.* at 463-64 (note omitted).

79. *Id.*

80. State v. McClendon, 437 P.2d 421 (Ariz. 1968).

81. See, e.g., State v. Austad, 641 P.2d 1373 (Mont. 1982); Reagon v. State, 251 N.E.2d 829 (Ind. 1969), *cert. denied*, 397 U.S. 1042 (1970); Wilson v. United States, 391 F.2d 460 (D.C. Cir. 1968). In one case the court reasoned:

> Many times in a trial of a criminal case evidence is lost, a material witness dies, or, as in this case, the defendant has amnesia as to certain events or a time. Still such handicaps from a defendant's point of view cannot prevent a trial from taking place eventually.

Reagon v. State, 251 N.E.2d at 831. Yet one must question how much assistance an amnesiac defendant can give his attorney and whether a fair trial can occur.

82. See, e.g., Commonwealth *ex rel.* Cummins v. Price, 218 A.2d 758, 763 (Pa. 1966).

83. See, e.g., Purver, *supra* note 73; also State v. Bridges, 468 P.2d 604 (Ariz. Ct. App. 1970); United States v. Sullivan, 406 F.2d 180 (2d Cir. 1969); Taylor v. State, 199 So. 2d 694 (Ala. Ct. App. 1967).

84. See Purver, *supra* note 73, at 544. Some commentators have suggested distinguishing between permanent and temporary amnesia. A defendant with temporary amnesia might be found incompetent because of the prospect that his memory, and thus competency, will quickly be restored, whereas for a defendant whose amnesia is considered permanent, the trial should proceed since postponing it would diminish the recall of other witnesses and thus reduce the chances that the defendant would get a fair trial. Koson & Robey, Amnesia and Competency to Stand Trial, 130 Am. J. Psychiatry 588 (1973); see Note, Amnesia, *supra* note 72. Unfortunately, there seems to be no medical way to determine when amnesia is temporary or permanent.

One law review note has suggested that the issue is not whether the defendant is competent to stand trial, which often requires a finding of mental disease or defect, but whether he will be able to obtain a fair trial. Note, Amnesia, *supra* note 72, at 304. Since assurance of fairness is a basic reason for limiting prosecutions only to competent defendants, it does not really matter how the issue is characterized.

85. D.W. Goodwin & S.B. Guze, Psychiatric Diagnosis (3d ed. 1984); Anderson & Kuehnle, Strategies for the Treatment of Acute Psychosis, 229 J. A.M.A. 1884 (1974). See in this book ch. 6, Treatment Rights, § II A, Psychotropic Medication.

86. Bushman & Reed, Tranquilizers and Competency to Stand Trial, 54 A.B.A. J. 284-87 (1968).

A survey conducted in 1976 showed that 13 states had a policy forbidding a defendant to proceed to trial if his "competency" was achieved through medication.[87] Today all of these states have changed their policies to acknowledge that competency as a result of medication is legally appropriate.[88] There have also been a number of court decisions that have recognized that legal competency can be attained by the use of medication.[89] Resolving the question of whether the court is seeing the "true person" is futile from a practical perspective. Today, the argument that there should be no trial while the defendant is on medication rarely succeeds.[90]

According to the Group for the Advancement of Psychiatry (GAP), the vast majority of persons found incompetent to stand trial could be restored to competency and so maintained as long as they remain on psychoactive drugs.[91] GAP has suggested that the judge and attorneys be told "(1) that the defendant is appearing under the influence of drugs, and (2) the type of drug administered to the defendant, the dosage, and the effect the drug has on the defendant's demeanor."[92] This information is likely to be useful for the conduct of the trial as well as for disposition.

One of the problems faced by the courts is that defendants who are competent while in the hospital on a regimen of medication and other treatments often "decompensate" when they are returned to the jail in preparation for trial: the medications are discontinued and the symptoms of the mental illness return. By the time the defendant appears in court he is once again incapable of participating in the trial and must be sent back to the hospital for reevaluation and treatment. This situation, sometimes repeated several times for a particular defendant, causes delays in trials in many states.

In 1971 in *State v. Maryott*,[93] a court addressed the situation of a defendant's refusing to take medication that would render him competent. The court held that the forced administration of medication was a violation of due process. However, at least one commentator has made a strong argument for the proposition that forced administration of medication in this circumstance is appropriate and that the state has a right to assert its interest in assuring the "accuracy, dignity, and apparent fairness of the criminal process."[94] Whether the recent recognition of the right of civilly committed mental patients to refuse medication[95] will be extended to incompetent defendants is unclear.

(c) Constitutional issues

The competency inquiry raises the constitutional issues of right to bail and the privilege against self-incrimination.

(1) Bail □□Although the Constitution does not guarantee release on bail in all cases, there is a federal statutory right to bail in noncapital cases,[96] and most states have enacted similar provisions. The purpose of setting bail is to increase the likelihood, if not to assure, that the defendant will appear for trial. If the defendant is certain to appear, then theoretically no bail need be imposed. This theory is glaringly violated in cases where the issue of competency is raised. Although only one state by statute[97] specifically provides for denial or revocation of bail during the competency evaluation, such denial or revocation is common practice in many states. Where the evaluations must be performed on an inpatient basis, there is not much choice,[98] but where they can be conducted on an outpatient basis, there should be no automatic denial of bail.[99] The ideal approach would be simply to consider the defendant's mental difficulties as one of the factors in the decision to grant bail.[100]

In most cases the defense attorney will want to urge that the competency evaluation be conducted on an outpatient basis,[101] which will enable the accused who can make bail to remain in the community. There are times, however, when the defense attorney may not want an outpatient evaluation: for example, if his client needs treatment immediately and it can be provided while he is being evaluated in the hospital, or when the client cannot make bail and where in the attorney's judgment the general conditions at the mental hospital are better than the jail, which is often the case.[102]

(2) Self-incrimination □□The Fifth Amendment commands that "no person . . . shall be compelled in any criminal case to be a witness against himself." Yet because an adequate competency evaluation will generally involve discussion of the pending charges, a defendant is quite likely to make statements that can be used against

87. Winick, Psychotropic Medication and Competence to Stand Trial, 1977 A.B.F. Res. J. 769, 775. This article provides a comprehensive discussion of the issues raised relating to use of medication to achieve competency.
88. See table 12.1, col. 10.
89. People v. Dalfonso, 24 Ill. App. 3d 748, 321 N.E.2d 379 (1974); State v. Hampton, 218 So. 2d 311 (La. 1969).
90. See Slovenko, *supra* note 23, at 177.
91. See GAP Competency Report, *supra* note 13, at 901.
92. *Id.* at 904.
93. 492 P.2d 239 (Wash. Ct. App. 1971).
94. See Winick, *supra* note 87, at 814.
95. See ch. 6, Treatment Rights, § VI A, The Right to Refuse Medication.
96. The Bail Reform Act of 1966, Pub. L. No. 89-465 (codified as amended in scattered sections of 18 U.S.C. §§ 3141 to 3152 (1982 & Supp. 1984). Section 3146 provides for release in noncapital cases unless release will not assure the defendand's appearance at trial.
97. South Dakota.
98. See table 12.1, col. 13.
99. Kaufman, Evaluating Competency: Are Constitutional Deprivations Necessary? 10 Am. Crim. L. Rev. 465, 473 (1972).
100. See Stone, *supra* note 3, at 209.
101. Golten, Role of Defense Counsel in the Criminal Commitment Process, 10 Am. Crim. L. Rev. 385, 390 (1972).
102. *Id.*

him. Such statements could be used against the defendant in at least three ways: (1) when the evaluator testifies at trial and repeats confessions or admissions of fact implicating the defendant in the crime with which he is charged, (2) when the prosecutor uses the statements to impeach the defendant's credibility in case he testifies at trial, and (3) when the prosecution, prior to trial, uses the information (available through discovery) to add to his knowledge of the defendant.[103]

The potential of disclosures can handicap preparation and presentation of an adequate defense. While the defendant's attorney may recognize that he needs a psychiatric evaluation of his client, he must also take into account the possibility that admissions the client makes during the evaluation may ultimately be made known to the court or the jury, with adverse consequences for the defense.[104] This same problem can arise, of course, when the defendant is examined pursuant to court order by an independent expert or by a psychiatrist for the prosecution.

Confronted with the claim that disclosure of information revealed in the context of a psychiatric examination violates the self-incrimination guarantee, courts have used a number of rationales to justify compelled examinations and introduction of the information revealed during the examination at trial. Primarily, they have relied on specific statutory authorizations, enacted in some states, which provide for a waiver of the privilege against self-incrimination when incompetency to stand trial or the insanity defense is raised.[105]

Numerous states by statute and several by court decision provide that the statements made during the competency evaluation cannot be used to prove the defendant's guilt.[106] The theory is that the defendant's compulsory submission to a psychiatric evaluation does not jeopardize his right against self-incrimination so long as use of the results of the evaluation is limited to the issue of his competency to stand trial.[107] Furthermore, the results of the competency evaluation may not be used to determine either criminal responsibility or the sentence, since the evaluation is designed only for the determination of competency.[108]

In 1981 in *Estelle v. Smith*,[109] the United States Supreme Court endorsed an argument made in 1972[110] when it held that the defendant's right to counsel had been violated because his attorney had not been given notice that the competency evaluation would be used as part of the sentencing process. The Court said: "Respondent was denied the assistance of his attorneys in making the significant decision of whether to submit to the examination and to what end the psychiatrist's findings could be employed."[111]

Recently, additional calls have been made for strict limitations on the use of psychiatric evaluations.[112] The American Bar Association Standing Committee on Association Standards for Criminal Justice has urged that the results of a defense-initiated examination not be discoverable unless it is introduced by the defense at trial and that the defense attorney and the evaluator be obliged to explain to the defendant the nature and purpose of the evaluation and the potential consequences of participating or refusing to participate in the exam.[113] While the adoption of this position would enable the defendant to protect himself by limiting what he reveals, it might at the same time defeat the defense counsel's goal of exploring all available defenses by operating as a kind of self-censorship.

It is accepted practice by forensic evaluators for the defendant to be advised of the purpose of the competency evaluation and of how his statements will be used.[114] A related issue that remains to be resolved through litigation or legislation is whether the defense attorney or the "defense psychiatrist" has a right to be present at the "impartial" examination.

7. The Competency Hearing: Burden and Standard of Proof

Once the examination has been completed and the report(s) filed, the court must decide whether the de-

103. Berry, Self-Incrimination and the Compulsory Mental Examination: A Proposal, 15 Ariz. L. Rev. 919, 929 (1973).

104. The issues raised by this potential violation of the privilege against self-incrimination by disclosure in a compulsory psychiatric examination are similar in the case of the insanity defense. For additional issues, see discussions *infra* in subsection on procedural issues in raising the insanity defense and in the section on sentencing the mentally disabled convicted offender. See also Griffith & Griffith, The Patient's Right to Protection Against Self-Incrimination During the Psychiatric Examination, 13 Toledo L. Rev. 269, 272 (1982).

105. The Fifth Amendment and Compelled Psychiatric Examinations: Implications of *Estelle v. Smith*, 50 Geo. Wash. L. Rev. 275, 288 (1982) [hereinafter cited as The Fifth Amendment and Compelled Psychiatric Examinations]; Note, Protecting the Confidentiality of Pretrial Psychiatric Disclosures: A Survey of Standards, 51 N.Y.U. L. Rev. 409, 421 (1976). See also table 12.6, col. 8, since most states that protect someone being evaluated who raises an insanity defense also protect statements made during a competency evaluation.

While it may seem fair and justifiable to allow for a compelled examination when a defendant raises a mental competency issue, the disclosure of the information gained by the psychiatrist is understandably troubling in light of the existence of the privilege against self-incrimination.

106. Texas, Tex. Crim. Proc. Code Ann. § 46:02(3)(g) (Vernon 1979); Ill. Ann. Stat. ch. 38, § 104-14 (Smith-Hurd 1980); United States v. Alvarez, 519 F.2d 1036 (3d Cir. 1975).

107. Pizzi, *supra* note 5, at 43–47 (1977).

108. United States v. Driscoll, 399 F.2d 135 (2d Cir. 1968); United States v. Alvarez, 519 F.2d 1036 (3d Cir. 1975); Estelle v. Smith, 451 U.S. 454 (1981).

109. 451 U.S. 454 (1981).

110. See Golten, *supra* note 101, at 397.

111. 451 U.S. at 471.

112. Criminal Justice Mental Health Standards (1st Tent. Draft 1983).

113. *Id.* § 7-3.3 at 74–75 and § 7-3.6 at 89-90.

114. R. Sadoff, Forensic Psychiatry: A Practical Guide for Lawyers and Psychiatrists 25 (1974).

fendant is competent to continue with the trial process. It has been estimated that some 25% of the defendants who raise the issue of competency to stand trial are declared incompetent.[115] In 24 states the decision may be reached just on the basis of the expert's report.[116] If either of the parties or the court itself has a disagreement with the report, a hearing will be held.[117] Studies have shown that the court follows the expert's recommendation in over 90% of the cases.[118] Even the contested hearings are usually brief, typically less than 20 minutes.[119] Three states require a jury to decide the competency question, and eight others make it optional.[120]

The questions of who has the burden of proof or what the standard of proof is in determining competency are specifically addressed in only a few of the state statutes. Some statutes specify that the state has the burden of proving the defendant's competency once the issue has been raised,[121] while others place the burden on the defendant.[122] The compromise position recommended by the American Bar Association is that the party raising the issue should have the burden of going forward with the proof.[123] Nine state statutes specify a "preponderance of evidence" standard,[124] and case law seems to confirm this as the proper standard for the competency inquiry.[125] However, in light of the Supreme Court's decision in 1979 in *Addington v. Texas*,[126] holding that at least a clear and convincing evidence standard should be used for civil commitment proceedings, it might be argued that this more rigorous standard should apply to a competency determination as well, since a finding of incompetency often results in hospitalization. Thus far, however, there have been no court decisions to this effect, and only one statute[127] requires use of the clear and convincing evidence standard.

115. See Steadman, *supra* note 2, at 38. This has also been supported by an informal poll I conducted of court clinics in Cleveland, Baltimore, and Chicago. See note 2 *supra* in this chapter for an indication of total numbers involved.

116. See table 12.3, col. 8.

117. See table 12.2, col. 4.

118. See Steadman, *supra* note 2, at 54.

119. *Id.* at 47.

120. See table 12.1, col. 17. This is required by Alabama, Florida, and South Dakota. California, Illinois, Kansas, New Mexico, Oklahoma, Tennessee, Texas, and Washington make it optional.

121. See table 12.1, col. 18, and also Ill. Ann. Stat. ch. 38, § 104-11 (Smith-Hurd 1982).

122. See table 12.1 and also, e.g., State v. Aumann, 265 N.W.2d 316, 320 (Iowa 1978).

123. Criminal Justice Mental Health Standards, *supra* note 112, § 7-4.8. See also Col. Rev. Stat. § 16-8-111(2) (1975 & Supp. 1982).

124. See table 12.1, col. 17.

125. State v. Aumann, 265 N.W.2d 316 (Iowa 1978); United States v. DiGilio, 538 F.2d 972, 988 (3d Cir. 1978), and accompanying case citations.

126. 441 U.S. 418 (1979).

127. Okla. Stat. Ann. tit. 22, § 1175.4(B) (West Supp. 1984).

C. Disposition of the Incompetent Defendant

1. Basis for and Duration of Hospitalization

During the past decade the question of what happens to the defendant *after* he is declared incompetent has been reexamined, spurred by cases publicizing the plight of defendants who had been held in state hospitals for lengthy periods, sometimes longer than if they had been tried, convicted, and sentenced.[128] Commentators deplored this situation as a violation of the accused's constitutional rights.[129] The 1972 decision by the United States Supreme Court in *Jackson v. Indiana*, holding that an incompetent defendant could be confined no longer than reasonably necessary to determine whether he would attain competency within the foreseeable future,[130] provided the impetus for many states to rewrite their statutes to include similar limits on the length of time that defendants could be kept confined while incompetent. In addition, 20 states have enacted statutory provisions allowing for the resolution of certain procedural issues relevant to the trial notwithstanding the defendant's incompetency.[131]

Prior to *Jackson v. Indiana* a declaration of incompetency was often the functional equivalent of commitment to a state mental hospital, but without the standards that limit civil commitment having been met.[132] Where the accused was retarded or had organic brain syndrome, both of which are incurable disabilities, such commitments were tantamount to life sentences since the person was committed until he "recovered his sanity" or "was restored to competency."[133] Not infrequently mentally ill defendants languished for life in state mental institutions where treatment, much less successful treatment, was rarely provided. To the extent that the accused was separated from society and kept in a maximum security environment, such results may have been satisfactory to the prosecution. If the criminal case against the defendant was solid, even the defense might be satisfied, as the conditions of confinement and the treatments provided—however inadequate—might

128. Foote, A Comment on Pre-trial Commitment of Criminal Defendants, 108 U. Pa. L. Rev. 832 (1960), discusses Clarence Coons, who was charged with murder. His codefendant was set free, while he spent 10 years institutionalized as incompetent; United States *ex rel.* Wolfersdorf v. Johnston, 317 F. Supp. 66 (S.D.N.Y. 1970), which involved an 86-year-old man who was charged with murder and considered incompetent to stand trial for 20 years.

129. See Burt & Morris, A Proposal for the Abolition of the Incompetency Plea, 40 U. Chi. L. Rev. 66 (1972); also Golten, *supra* note 101, at 401; Kaufman, *supra* note 99, at 467; Gobert, Competency to Stand Trial: A Pre- and Post-*Jackson* Analysis, 40 Tenn. L. Rev. 659 (1973).

130. 406 U.S. 715, 716 (1972).

131. See table 12.1, col. 20.

132. See ch. 2, Involuntary Institutionalization, § V C, Extended Commitment Procedures, for discussion of the civil commitment standards.

133. A.R. Matthews, Mental Disability and the Criminal Law: A Field Study 89 (1970).

nonetheless be better than those afforded in the state prison. Technically, the problem with using an incompetency finding as a sentencing alternative, of course, was that the defendant had never been found guilty.

In *Jackson* the Supreme Court was confronted with the case of a mentally retarded deaf mute who was charged with two purse snatchings, found incompetent, and committed under Indiana law until he "regained his sanity." The Court held:

> [A] person charged by a State with a criminal offense who is committed solely on account of his incapacity to proceed to trial cannot be held more than the reasonable period of time necessary to determine whether there is a substantial probability that he will attain that capacity in the foreseeable future. If it is determined that this is not the case, then the State must either institute the customary civil commitment proceeding that would be required to commit indefinitely any other citizen, or release the defendant. Furthermore, even if it is determined that the defendant probably soon will be able to stand trial, his continued commitment must be justified by progress toward that goal.[134]

The Court did not specify what a "reasonable period" was. Although a fair reading would suggest that a finding of incompetency without more could not be sufficient ground for commitment beyond a brief observational period, almost half the states and the District of Columbia still permit indefinite hospitalization based solely on a finding of incompetency.[135] The remaining states permit hospitalization of incompetent defendants only for specified periods, ranging from six months to five years, or for a period limited to determining the likelihood of recovery of competency. In a number of jurisdictions the commitment period is limited to the maximum period the defendant could have served if he had been sentenced. Both the longer specified periods and those based on the sentence equivalent are difficult to square with the *Jackson* rationale.

2. Place of Treatment

Traditionally, once a person was found incompetent he was sent to a maximum security hospital even though neither the charges against him nor his past behavior necessarily warranted this type of security. Some cases and statutes now require that an individual determination be made regarding the most appropriate place for the incompetent defendant to be institutionalized.[136] Commentaries on proposals for reform and the rights of the incompetent suggest that in a significant number of instances outpatient treatment is safe and appropriate.[137]

Wexler has pointed out that given the right to bail and the concept of least restrictive institutionalization and considering that an adjudication of incompetency does not ordinarily involve a showing of dangerousness, the mandatory secure confinement of all defendants who are found incompetent "is bad policy, bad psychology, and perhaps bad law."[138] The statutory trend is in accord with this observation, as a growing number of states provide for the institutionalization of incompetent defendants in civil hospitals,[139] while at least three provide for outpatient evaluation and treatment.[140] Four states permit the conditional release of the incompetent defendant.[141]

3. Right to a Speedy Trial and Proposals for Change

Traditionally, a declaration of incompetency meant total suspension of the criminal proceedings. In effect, one commentator has observed, this constitutes a "tradeoff between the sixth amendment right to a prompt disposition of the charges; and the (sixth amendment) right to be able to confront one's accusers and assist in one's own defense."[142] The Sixth Amendment guarantee to a speedy trial is based on three premises: (1) a defendant is deemed innocent and thus should not be incarcerated until proven guilty, (2) the trial should be held when the evidence is fresh and most illuminating, and (3) the defendant's anxiety caused by a pending criminal charge ought to be minimized.[143]

As early as 1960 Foote proposed a provisional trial in which the incompetent defendant would be given the opportunity to test the merits of the case against him.[144] In 1972 in *Jackson v. Indiana* the Supreme Court noted the desirability of permitting some of the proceedings to go forward, including consideration of certain preliminary defenses and pretrial motions, despite the defendant's incompetency.[145] Among the most discussed proposals is one by Burt and Morris suggesting that "no trial may be delayed longer than six months solely because of a defendant's incompetency" and that even during the defendant's incompetency the trial should proceed with

134. 406 U.S. at 738.
135. See table 12.1, col. 22; Roesch & Golding, *supra* note 28, at 121-26.
136. See, e.g., Johnson v. Brelje, 525 F. Supp. 183 (N.D. Ill. 1981).

137. See Roesch & Golding, *supra* note 28.
138. D. Wexler, Criminal Commitments and Dangerous Mental Patients: Legal Issues of Confinement, Treatment, and Release 40 (NIMH Crime and Delinquency Issues: A Monograph Series, No. ADM 76-331, 1976).
139. See table 12.1, col. 23.
140. See, e.g., Cal. Penal Code § 1370(a)(2) (West 1982); Ill. Ann. Stat. ch. 38, § 104-17(b) (Smith-Hurd 1981); and Tex. Crim. Proc. Code Ann. 46.02(5)(d) (Vernon 1979).
141. See e.g., Arkansas, Florida, Hawaii, and Oregon.
142. See Golten, *supra* note 101, at 404.
143. *Id.* at 404; Burt & Morris, *supra* note 129, at 104; Kaufman, *supra* note 99. Also see references cited in notes 128 & 129 *supra*.
144. See Foote, *supra* note 128, at 841.
145. 406 U.S. at 740-41 (1972).

special provisions and motions that could lead to an eventual dismissal of the charges.[146] Furthermore, to guard the rights of the defendants, the prosecution should be required to provide complete pretrial discovery and meet a particularly heavy burden of proof, while the jury should be given special instructions.[147] Since Burt and Morris's proposal in 1972, numerous additional suggestions have been made,[148] all embodying two basic concepts: (1) there must be a limit on the amount of time a person can be confined while incompetent to stand trial, and (2) the trial should go forward provisionally despite the defendant's incompetency.

The result of these proposals would be to drastically reduce the adverse consequences of being found incompetent. They would: (1) eliminate indefinite commitment, (2) provide the opportunity to raise selected procedural issues, possibly leading to dismissal of the charges, (3) give the incompetent defendant the opportunity to raise the more obvious substantive defenses, possibly resulting in acquittal, (4) help assure that the trial was held while witnesses were available and their memories still accurate, and (5) set a limit on the amount of time the defendant would be in the legal limbo of being an accused without a decision on the charges.

While no state has adopted these proposals in full, several states have gone part way. The most widely adopted reform permits evidence to be presented and objections to be made on matters for which the incompetent defendant's presence is not crucial.[149] Another, enacted in several states, permits a trial in which only a not-guilty finding is recognized.[150] As regards the disposition, at least five states now require a probable cause hearing before the defendant can be hospitalized as incompetent.[151] The trend toward statutory change in these directions is likely to continue.

4. Restoration

Most incompetent defendants today are restored to competency in a relatively short period of time,[152] usually with the help of medication. For the defendant whose incompetence is due to retardation or chronic brain syndrome, however, there continues to be little likelihood of recovery. Almost every state by statute provides a mechanism for informing the criminal court of the mental status of the defendant.[153] In most states it is the responsibility of the superintendent of the confining hospital or the director of the state mental health agency to notify the court of the defendant's progress toward competency. In 17 states the defendant is given the explicit right to petition for a rehearing on his competency. In 23 states the prosecution may request a rehearing and/or the court may order one.[154]

The prevailing practice in most states is for the attorneys on both sides to stipulate upon appropriate evidence that the defendant is restored to competency, with a hearing held only if one of the parties so requests.[155] The criteria for restoration are the same as those that determine the initial competency decision, that is, whether the individual is fit to proceed to trial.

5. Disposition After Restoration

Once the defendant is restored to competency the criminal proceedings resume. When the defendant has been institutionalized for a long period of time, the common practice, if he is convicted or pleads guilty, is to sentence him to an equivalent period and then to "credit" the time during which he was hospitalized. This may be part of a plea bargain in which the prosecution's motive in assenting to the disposition is the difficulty of obtaining a conviction in open court because the witnesses are no longer available and in which the defense attorney's motive is the fact that his client will not have to spend any more time institutionalized. Another frequent outcome in cases of lengthy hospitalization is an outright dismissal of the charges.[156] This may be followed by a civil commitment proceeding, depending on the nature of the crime, the publicity surrounding it, and whether the defendant appears to meet the civil commitment criteria.

D. Competency to Be Sentenced

During the period between the guilty verdict and sentencing, the competent defendant may decompensate mentally and become incompetent. It has been suggested that sentencing one who does not comprehend the meaning of the sentence would serve no retributive effect and would be futile.[157] Although slippage back into incompetency at this point is a rare occurrence, it has been statutorily addressed by many states.[158] The test for com-

146. Burt & Morris, *supra* note 129, at 86, 93–95.

147. *Id.* at 76.

148. See Roesch & Golding, *supra* note 28, at 117 for a summary of the major proposals.

149. E.g., Hawaii, Illinois, Massachusetts, Michigan, West Virginia, and Wisconsin.

150. See, e.g., Illinois and Texas.

151. Delaware, Hawaii, Idaho, Minnesota, and Ohio.

152. In many states a person is often restored to competency within three months as a result of psychotropic medication. An Illinois study found that there was a positive correlation between the length of hospitalization and the seriousness of the crime. The more serious the crime, the longer the hospitalization. See Cuneo, Brelje, Randolph, & Taliana, Seriousness of Charge and Length of Hospitalization for the Unfit Defendant, 10 J. Psychiatry & L. 163 (1982).

153. See table 12.2, cols. 1–3.

154. See table 12.2 col. 3.

155. See table 12.2, col. 4.

156. See table 12.2, col. 7.

157. See Note, Incompetency to Stand Trial, *supra* note 4, at 456.

158. See table 12.3.

petency to be sentenced is similar to that for competency to stand trial.[159] The emphasis is on the defendant's capacity to tell his attorney about factors that would mitigate his sentence or would refute aggravating circumstances brought up by the prosecution, as well as on his understanding of the punishment.

As at earlier stages in the trial process, questions of competency to be sentenced can be raised by the defense, the prosecution, and the court. The proceedings for determining restoration to competency are essentially the same as for competency to stand trial.

E. Incompetency and the Death Penalty

In 1976 the United States Supreme Court, in five separate plurality opinions, rejected the contention that the death penalty in and of itself constituted cruel and unusual punishment.[160] This cleared the way for states to design laws meeting the standards established by the Court for the constitutional application of the penalty.[161] In the following seven years more than 1,250 persons were sentenced to death,[162] although a de facto moratorium on executions persisted and has only recently been broken.[163] Of the 39 states that authorize the use of the death penalty,[164] all adopt the common law prohibition against execution of the insane.[165]

1. The Standard and Its Rationale

Rationales for prohibiting executions of the insane include the following: (1) the insane person could not assist in explicating reasons for a stay of execution,[166] (2) executing an insane person would not serve the goals of either general deterrence or retribution,[167] and (3) the execution of a prisoner unable to reflect on his situation would deprive him of the opportunity to make peace with his God.[168]

Most states do not specify a standard for determining the capital prisoner's incompetency.[169] The common law test was whether the condemned was aware of his conviction and his impending fate.[170] It has been suggested that the Eighth and Fourteenth Amendments require a standard of insanity tailored to the specific rationale of the execution and the needs of the prisoner.[171] Such a test would require in the prisoner an understanding of the nature, the purpose, and the extent of his punishment, an awareness of any facts making his punishment unjust, and the ability to convey such information to his attorney.[172]

The Supreme Court has not addressed what the standard for staying an execution should be in the case of an offender of questionable competency. However, in *Rees v. Peyton, Penitentiary Superintendent*[173] in 1966, the Court refused to allow a condemned prisoner of questionable competency to abandon legal efforts to save his life until there had been an adequately informed judicial determination that he was competent to do so.[174] The standard the *Rees* Court used before accepting a withdrawal of an appeal of the death sentence was the existence of a mental disease or defect that substantially affected his capacity either to appreciate his present position or to make a rational choice whether to continue or abandon further litigation.[175] By analogy, this case suggests that a like standard would apply to stays of execution.

2. Procedures

Although the states do not specify a substantive standard for determining when an execution should be stayed due to incompetency, almost half the states have statutes specifying the procedures to be used when the condemned prisoner is thought to be insane.[176] In these states, the prison warden generally makes the initial evaluation of the credibility of the prisoner's insanity claim[177] and then notifies either a state court judge or a state executive officer,[178] who initiates a proceeding to evaluate the prisoner's claim more formally. Whether the prison warden has discretion in forwarding such a claim or whether he must always respond when the prisoner or his counsel raises a claim is unclear. If the pris-

159. See table 12.3, col. 4; also e.g., Commonwealth v. Edward, 450 A.2d 15 (1982); and Weissman, Determinate Sentencing and Psychiatric Evidence: A Due Process Examination, 27 St. Louis U.L.J. 347 (1983).

160. Roberts v. Louisiana, 428 U.S. 325 (1976); Woodson v. North Carolina, 428 U.S. 280 (1976); Jurek v. Texas, 428 U.S. 262 (1976); Proffitt v. Florida, 428 U.S. 242 (1976); Gregg v. Georgia, 428 U.S. 153 (1976).

161. See table 12.4.

162. U.S. Dep't of Justice, Bureau of Justice Statistics, (July 1983).

163. As of May 1985 there had been only 30 executions since the Supreme Court's decisions in 1976.

164. See table 12.4.

165. See *id.* col. 3; also Blackstone, *supra* note 6, at 395–96; E. Coke, Third Institute 4 (London 1809) (1st ed. London, 1644); 1 W. Hawkins, 1 A Treatise of the Pleas of the Crown bk. 1, ch. 1, § 3 at 2 (6th ed. London 1788) (1st ed. London, 1716).

166. Blackstone, *supra* note 6.

167. Coke, *supra* note 165; Hazard & Louisell, Death, the State, and the Insane: Staying of Execution, 9 U.C.L.A. L. Rev. 381 (1962), which provides a thorough analysis of the common law reasoning.

168. Hazard & Louisell, *supra* note 167.

169. See table 12.4, col. 3.

170. See Hazard & Louisell, *supra* note 167, at 394 n.44.

171. Note, Insanity of the Condemned, 88 Yale L.J. 533, 561 (1979), which reviews the procedures used to consider due process issues raised by executing the incompetent.

172. *Id.* at 562.

173. 384 U.S. 312 (1966).

174. See also Gilmore v. Utah, 429 U.S. 1012 (1976); also see Note, The Eighth Amendment and the Execution of the Presently Incompetent, 32 Stan. L. Rev. 765 (1980) [hereinafter cited as Note, The Eighth Amendment].

175. 384 U.S. at 313–14.

176. See table 12.4; also Note, Insanity of the Condemned, *supra* note 171.

177. See table 12.4, col. 1.

178. See table 12.4, col. 2.

oner is found to be insane in the formal proceedings, the execution is stayed until he regains sanity.[179]

With more offenders being sentenced to death, there will likely be more challenges based on the prisoner's alleged insanity, invoking the cruel and unusual punishment clause of the Eighth Amendment and the due process clause of the Fourteenth Amendment, which have traditionally been relied on in death penalty cases.[180] On each of the three occasions that it has reviewed constitutional attacks on state procedures deferring execution of insane prisoners, the Supreme Court has upheld the constitutionality of those procedures that vested in a state administrative official the determination of whether the person was insane.[181] The Court rejected the notion that the defendant was entitled to a special judicial hearing on the issue. However, these three cases rely heavily on the common law, with the last two decisions explicitly deferring to the Court's 1897 opinion in the first case, *Nobles v. Georgia*.[182] In light of more recent Supreme Court decisions articulating the standards and procedures due process requires before the state can deprive a person of liberty,[183] these older precedents no longer seem altogether compelling. As a note in a 1979 law review suggested, "[a]t the very least, the due process clause requires that a condemned prisoner be provided notice of when and how his insanity claim will be reviewed and a hearing in order to review that claim prior to execution."[184]

III. THE INSANITY DEFENSE

A. Introduction

The insanity defense, the legal construct that relieves an accused of criminal responsibility for his conduct, is interwoven with ancient and enduring principles of morality and justice and with varying intuitive and philosophical notions of human nature. The Anglo-American legal tradition is grounded on the premise that persons are normally capable of free and rational choice between alternative acts and that one who chooses to harm another is thus morally accountable and liable to punishment. If, however, a person for any reason lacks the capacity to make rational choices or to conform his behavior to the moral and legal demands of society, traditionally he has been relieved of criminal responsibility and liability for his actions. Thus, as one commentator has expressed it, the "insanity defense marks the transition from the adequate man the law demands to the inadequate man he may be."[185]

Other, more specific rationales for the insanity defense flow from theories of retribution, deterrence, and rehabilitation which are at the heart of the Anglo-American system of criminal justice. Under the retributive theory, in which the criminal owes the community a measure of suffering comparable to that which he has knowingly and wilfully inflicted, the accused's insanity precludes the formation of such criminal intent and the consequent determination that he is blameworthy and deserving of punishment. The deterrent theory, which holds that the function of the criminal law is to force people to conform to social norms through establishment of a criminal code describing the prohibited conduct and sanctions imposed for engaging in such conduct, works only when men can understand the code and its potential sanctions. A person lacking the required intelligence, reasoning ability, and foresight capacity to understand the code or its sanctions will not be deterred by them, and neither the prospect nor the infliction of punishment serves a purpose. Likewise, there is no prospect of achieving rehabilitation through punishment of a person who was unable to appreciate the nature of his actions or their wrongfulness.

A precise and widely accepted definition of legal insanity, however, continues to elude the legal system after more than a century of controversy, modification, and refinement of successive tests of criminal responsibility. Predictably, the controversy over the insanity defense intensifies each time it is successfully used in a highly publicized case, and it is usually followed by a spate of legislative proposals for statutory change.[186] The current debate over the insanity defense embraces calls for abolishing the defense, creating a compromise guilty-

179. See table 12.4, col. 4.

180. See Note, The Eighth Amendment, *supra* note 174.

181. Nobles v. Georgia, 168 U.S. 398 (1897); Solesbee v. Balkcom, 339 U.S. 9 (1950); Caritativo v. California, 357 U.S. 549 (1958) *per curiam*. In *Nobles v. Georgia* and *Solesbee v. Balkcom,* the official was the governor of Georgia; in *Caritativo v. California,* it was the prison warden. In *Solesbee v. Belkcom* the Court said: "to require judicial review every time a convicted defendant suggested insanity would make the possibility of carrying out a sentence depend upon the 'fecundity in making suggestion after suggestion of insanity.'" 339 U.S. at 12.

182. 168 U.S. 398 (1897).

183. See, e.g., Jackson v. Indiana, 406 U.S. 715 (1972); *In re* Winship, 397 U.S. 358 (1970); Baxstrom v. Herold, 383 U.S. 107 (1966).

184. See Note, Insanity of the Condemned, *supra* note 171, at 553.

185. Goldstein, *supra* note 1, at 18. For other historical surveys of the insanity defense, see A.D. Brooks, Law, Psychiatry and the Mental Health System 111 (1974); H. Fingarette, The Meaning of Criminal Insanity 7 (1972).

186. Most recently, sharp public debate has been provoked by the jury verdict finding John Hinckley not guilty by reason of insanity of attempted assassination by shooting of President Ronald Reagan in 1981 (United States v. Hinckley, 525 F. Supp. 1342 (D.D.C. 1981)). Following the *Hinckley* decision, 27 bills were introduced in the United States Congress to abolish the insanity defense or to change it, and numerous state legislatures changed or considered changing their laws. The Subcommittee on Criminal Law of the Senate Judiciary Committee held hearings two days after the verdict. Limiting the Insanity Defense: Hearings on S. 818, S. 1106, S. 1558, S. 1995, S. 2572, S. 2658, & S. 2669 Before the Subcomm. on Criminal Law of the Senate Comm. on the Judiciary, 97th Cong., 2d Sess. (1982) [hereinafter cited as Senate Subcomm. Hearings on Limiting the Insanity Defense]. Legislatures in Alabama, Alaska, Delaware, Georgia, and Pennsylvania among others introduced bills to change the insanity defense or to adopt a guilty but mentally ill verdict.

but-mentally-ill verdict, narrowing the standard for a successful assertion of the defense, shifting the burden of proof to the defendant, instituting procedural changes to make the determination of the defense more "fair," limiting the role of expert witnesses, and creating new, more secure, or otherwise reformed treatment programs for insanity acquittees.

Heavy media coverage of sensational cases in which the insanity defense is raised creates the impression that the defense is a common feature in criminal cases. Although insanity can be asserted as an affirmative defense to a crime in all but three states in the United States,[187] it is in fact rarely used and even more rarely successful.[188] As indicated earlier, the number of cases in which the insanity defense is invoked, let alone those in which it succeeds, is dwarfed by the vast number of cases resulting in a finding of present incompetency.[189]

Traditionally, the defense was raised almost exclusively in murder cases to avoid capital punishment. Today, while the defense is still most likely to be raised and to be successful in murder and attempted murder cases,[190] its application has been extended to a much wider variety of criminal cases including misdemeanors. Partly as a result, the dispositional consequences for a person who succeeds with the defense have changed drastically.[191] Whereas traditionally the insanity acquittee was likely to spend the remainder of his life in a mental hospital, today a significant portion of insanity acquittees are hospitalized only a short time. The early calls for abolition of the insanity defense stemmed from the feeling that long-term confinement in hospitals for the criminally insane was even worse than lengthy imprisonment. Today, calls for changes in the insanity defense, or its abolition, are often based on the perception that too many undeserving defendants are succeeding with the defense and getting off too lightly, leaving society inadequately protected.[192]

An understanding of the current status or recent modification of the insanity defense must rest on an appreciation of its history.

B. Origins of the Insanity Defense

The doctrine of *mens rea*, or "the guilty mind," holding that criminal intent must accompany a physical act for it to constitute punishable wrongdoing,[193] has ancient origins.[194] The biblical Hebrews made a distinction between intentional and unintentional crimes: neither children nor insane persons were held criminally responsible for their acts, nor did they have to compensate their victims.[195] Greek philosophers beginning with Plato came to believe that free will made it possible for an in-

187. Idaho, Montana, and Utah; see Idaho Code 18-107 (1982); Mont. Code Ann. § 713 (1979); Utah Code Ann. 76-2-305 (1983). See table 12.5, col. 1.

188. Less than 1% of all felony prosecutions result in an acquittal by reason of insanity. See, e.g., Criss & Racine, Impact of Change in Legal Standard for Those Adjudicated Not Guilty by Reason of Insanity, 1975-1979, 8 A.A.P.L. Bull. 261, 264 (1980), which found the insanity defense was raised in .11% of cases where the person was arrested for an index offense; Petrilia, The Insanity Defense and Other Mental Health Dispositions in Missouri, 5 Int'l J. L. & Psychiatry 81 (1982); Phillips & Pasewark, Insanity Plea in Connecticut, 8 A.A.P.L. Bull. 335 (1980).

189. See note 2 *supra* for the comparative statistics on incompetency pleas and the insanity defense. See in this chapter § III D 2, At Trial, *infra* for detailed statistics on use of the insanity defense.

190. The more frequent invocation of the insanity defense in these settings may be due to the hope of avoiding severe, possibly capital, punishment, and its relative success may be attributable to the fact that criminal acts of this severity are more often committed in a state of mental derangement or at least without planning or deliberation than are lesser crimes. See, e.g., Steadman, Keitner, Braff, & Arvanites, Factors Associated with a Successful Insanity Plea, 140 Am. J. Psychiatry 401 (1983), which indicates that of those found NGRI in their New York study, 27% were charged with murder; Testimony of Stuart B. Silver, M.D., *in* Senate Subcomm. Hearings on Limiting the Insanity Defense, *supra* note 186, at 374, which showed in Maryland 25% for murder and 25% for attempted murder. Statistics kept by the Illinois Department of Mental Health reveal that 38% of the NGRIs were charged with murder and 20% with attempted murder in 1981-82, according to Daniel Cuneo, Director of Research, Chester Mental Health Center, Chester, Ill. See Phillips & Pasewark, *supra* note 188, at 237-38, which reveals that 28% were charged with murder and 36% with assault; also Criss & Racine, *supra* note 188, at 265, which revealed 29.6% charged with murder, 17.9% charged with attempted murder, and 13.4% were charged with serious assaults.

Successful insanity defense pleas occur frequently in cases involving the killing of family members. Women who kill their children are disproportionately represented, probably because there is medical support for the view that such women, in cases where the crime is committed shortly after childbirth, suffer from postpartum psychosis. See, e.g., W. Carnahan, The Insanity Defense in New York 54-55 (produced for the N.Y. Dep't of Mental Hygiene, 1978); Criss & Racine, *supra* note 188, at 263; Petrilia, *supra* note 188, at 95-96; Fourth Annual Report of the Isaac Ray Center (Rush-Presbyterian-St. Luke's Medical Center, Chicago, Illinois) (1983).

Comparing the population of insanity acquittees in hospitals throughout the United States with the general prison population, it is evident that the former group has a significantly greater percentage of women and whites and that it is older. See articles cited *supra* in this note; Criss & Racine, *supra* note 188, at 263; and Isaac Ray Center Annual Report, *supra*, at 8. Many of the acquittees, moreover, have had no prior serious involvement with the law, though they may have had a number of previous psychiatric hospitalizations. See Pasewark, Insanity Plea: A Review of the Research Literature, J. Psychiatry & L. 357, 370 (1981); Petrilia, *supra* note 188, at 84.

These statistics suggest that the use and the success of the insanity defense have a more rational basis than some alarmists would have us believe.

191. See information and references in note 190 *supra*; Rogers & Bloom, Characteristics of Persons Committed to Oregon's Psychiatric Review Board, 10 A.A.P.L. Bull. 155, 158 (1982), which shows 25% of the cases of nonresponsibility in Oregon are for misdemeanor offenses.

192. See Morris, Psychiatry and the Dangerous Criminal, 41 So. Cal. L. Rev. 514 (1968), and 127 Cong. Rec. E.5365 (daily ed. Nov. 17, 1981) (statement of Sen. Ashbrook) for profiles of debate over the insanity defense in different periods.

193. Most felonies have an intent element, and many such as murder require specific intent before one can be convicted of a crime. For example, murder is defined in Illinois as follows: "A person who kills an individual without lawful justification commits murder if, in performing the acts which cause the death: (1) He either *intends* to kill or do great bodily harm. . . ." Ill. Ann. Stat. ch. 38, § 9-1(a) (Smith-Hurd Supp. 1984) (emphasis added).

194. Gerber, Is the Insanity Test Insane? 20 Am. J. Jur. 3 (1975). This article provides a good review of the insanity defense.

195. The Talmud provides: "It is an ill thing to knock against a deaf mute, an imbecile, or a minor. He that wounds them is culpable, but if they wound others they are not culpable. For with them only the act is of consequence while the intention is of no consequence." Quen, Anglo-American Criminal Insanity—An Historical Perspective, 10 J. Hist. Behav. Sci. 313 (1974).

dividual to be responsible for the good and evil in his life.[196] Aristotle believed that an individual was morally responsible if with knowledge of the circumstances and freedom from external compulsion he deliberately chose to commit a specific act.[197] In the sixth century, the Code of Justinian recognized the principle that children and insane persons could not be held responsible for their acts and also formulated the beginnings of a "heat of passion" test in which punishment was mitigated for one who committed homicide in a brawl.[198]

In England, by the time of Elizabeth I, these legal concepts had developed into the doctrine that insane persons and children were exempted from punishment for their acts because they could not comprehend the morality of what they had done.[199] However, although an individual exempt from moral responsibility was not punished in the traditional way of, say, losing an arm for stealing or his life for killing, he was not set free. He would be restrained in some manner—he would be sent to a mental institution for the "criminally insane," usually to spend the rest of his life.

From this English doctrine an Anglo-American legal tradition of criminal irresponsibility continued to evolve.

C. The American Standards: The Development and Rationale

1. Introduction

The insanity defense standard as it has developed over the course of American history has had as a constant four basic elements: (1) presence of mental disease, (2) presence of defect of reason, (3) lack of knowledge of nature or wrongfulness of the act, and (4) incapacity to refrain from the act.[200] While the relative emphasis placed on the latter three elements has varied, the consistent core of the insanity defense has been the existence of a mental disease. The defendant who raises the insanity defense, in any form, explains one commentator, "tries to shift the responsibility from himself to something called 'mental disease,' which kept him from being what he appeared to be, a man committing a crime with a full measure of culpability."[201]

2. M'Naghten Rule

Until the 1960s the standard used in the vast majority of the states was the M'Naghten test, a formulation that grew out of the first English case in which the developing medical science of psychiatry played a role. In this celebrated 1843 trial for the murder of an aide to the prime minister, Daniel M'Naghten was found totally insane. The verdict resulted in a parliamentary inquiry and a judicial response thereto, which became the official M'Naghten rules.[202] The lord chief justice pronounced the test:

> [T]he jurors ought to be told in all cases that every man is to be presumed to be sane, and to possess a sufficient degree of reason to be responsible for his crimes, until the contrary be proved to their satisfaction; and that to establish a defence on the ground of insanity, it must be clearly proved that, at the time of the committing of the act, the party accused was labouring under such a defect of reason, from disease of the mind, as not to know the nature and quality of the act he was doing; or, if he did know it, that he did not know he was doing what was wrong.[203]

For more than one hundred years this standard, also known as the "right or wrong" test, has been used throughout the United States. Today, it remains the law in about one-third of the states in its original form, while in several other states it has been modified, either by statute or by case law, with the addition of an "irresistible impulse" test.[204] The five elements of the rule—defect of reason, disease of the mind, knowing, nature and quality of the act, and wrong—have not been adequately or consistently defined in either the statutes or the cases. But the consensus of legal scholars is that they mean something on the order of the following: "defect of reason" is a substantial defect in capacity for rational conduct and a pathological condition of the mind; "disease of the mind" means psychosis; "to know" means recognizing that what one was doing was wrong or understanding the nature and quality of one's act; "wrong" means that the act was illegal or contrary to the law or that it was in contravention to the actor's private morality.[205] "Nature and quality of the act" has not been

196. Plato, The Republic 350 (Conford trans. 1945).
197. Aristotle, The Nicomachean Ethics 48 (Book III) (Ross trans. 1980).
198. Dig. Just. 4.8.8.2.
199. See Gerber, *supra* note 194, at 114.
200. See Fingarette, *supra* note 185, at 19.
201. Goldstein, *supra* note 1, at 18–19.

202. M'Naghten's Case, 10 Clark & Fin. 200, 8 Eng. Rep. 718, 720–24 (1843). Daniel M'Naghten, a Glasgow woodturner, in 1843 shot and killed Edward Drummond, the secretary to the British prime minister, Robert Peel, while suffering from the delusion that Peel and the pope were conspiring against him. To protect himself, M'Naghten had decided to kill Peel but instead shot Drummond, whom he mistook for Peel. Nine medical witnesses, relying heavily on Dr. Isaac Ray's contemporary text on forensic psychiatry (A Treatise on the Medical Jurisprudence of Insanity (1983 repr. of 1838 ed.)), testified to the court that M'Naghten was totally insane. The jury accepted their judgment, and M'Naghten spent the remainder of his life at Broadmoor, a mental institution. Following a great public outcry over the possible consequences of the precedent set by M'Naghten's acquittal, the House of Lords put to the common law judges five hypothetical questions about trying persons who committed crimes while afflicted with an insane delusion. The judges' answers to these questions resulted in the adoption of the M'Naghten standard in Great Britain.
203. M'Naghten's case, 8 Eng. Rep. at 722.
204. See table 12.5, col. 5.
205. See Brooks, *supra* note 185, at 142–45.

subjected to sufficient analysis to produce a commonly shared interpretation.

In its emphasis on the defendant's lack of cognitive ability, the M'Naghten standard has been criticized for being too narrow and for excusing too few people, and it has been argued that in its grounding on outdated theories of human behavior it denies the courts the available insights of modern psychology.[206]

3. The Irresistible Impulse Test

Never used as the sole standard and lacking a uniform definition, the irresistible impulse test has evolved to broaden the scope of the M'Naghten test. In essence, the concept recognizes that an individual may know the nature and quality of his act and may be aware that it is wrong but may nonetheless be driven to commit the act out of an overpowering compulsion that has roots in a mental disability.[207] The concept rests on four assumptions: (1) that certain mental diseases may impair volition or self-control while leaving cognition relatively unimpaired, (2) that use of the M'Naghten test alone would not find persons suffering from such diseases insane, (3) that the law should make the insanity defense available to such persons, and (4) that no matter how broadly it is construed the M'Naghten test will not reach certain areas of serious mental disability.[208]

The irresistible impulse modification of the M'Naghten test is statutory in four states,[209] but in most states it has been defined by the case law.[210]

4. Durham Rule

In 1954 in *Durham v. United States*,[211] the United States Court of Appeals for the District of Columbia Circuit espoused a new conception of criminal responsibility, holding simply that "an accused is not criminally responsible if his unlawful act was the product of mental disease or mental defect."[212] With this test, known as "the Durham rule," "the New Hampshire rule,"[213] and sometimes "the product rule," the court explicitly rejected both the right-wrong test of the M'Naghten rule and its modification by the irresistible impulse test,[214] and in their place offered a flexible definition of mental disease or defect to permit psychiatric testimony unbound by narrow or psychologically inapposite legal questions.

Despite, or perhaps as a result of, a number of well-known inquiries into its impact,[215] the test never gained acceptance in the legal community: it was adopted only in the District of Columbia, Maine, and New Hampshire.[216] In 1972 in *United States v. Brawner*, the Court of Appeals for the District of Columbia Circuit itself rejected *Durham* in a decision that adopted the American Law Institute's formulation of the standard of criminal responsibility.[217] Despite its failure to command significant formal support, *Durham* did much to spur discus-

206. See Goldstein, *supra* note 1, at 47.

207. In 1929 in *Smith v. United States*, the United States Court of Appeals for the District of Columbia outlined a more modern, medically based test to remedy the shortcomings of the older test of insanity:

> The modern doctrine is that the degree of insanity which will relieve the accused of the consequences of a criminal act must be such as to create in his mind an uncontrollable impulse to commit the offense charged. This impulse must be such as to override the reason and judgment and obliterate the sense of right and wrong to the extent that the accused is deprived of the power to choose right from wrong. The mere ability to distinguish between right and wrong is no longer the correct test either in civil or criminal cases, where the defense of insanity is interposed. The accepted rule in this day and age, with the great advancement in medical science as an enlightening influence on this subject, is that the accused must be capable, not only of distinguishing between right and wrong, but that he was not impelled to do the act by an irresistible impulse, which means before it will justify a verdict of acquittal that his reasoning powers were so far dethroned by his diseased mental condition as to deprive him of the will power to resist the insane impulse to perpetrate the deed, though knowing it to be wrong.

36 F.2d 548, 549 (D.C. Cir. 1929).

208. See Goldstein, *supra* note 1, at 67.

209. See table 12.5, col 6.

210. As indicated in the previous edition of this book in 1971, the irresistible impulse test probably had its genesis in 1834 in Ohio in State v. Thompson, Wright's Ohio Rep. 617 (1834) (see Clark v. State, 12 Ohio Rep. 483 (1843); Blackburn v. State, 23 Ohio 146 (1872)), and progressively evolved into the modern form in subsequent decisions in other states: Commonwealth v. Rogers, 48 Mass. 500 (1844); Commonwealth v. Mosler, 4 Pa. 264 (1846); State v. Felter, 25 Iowa 67 (1868). For debate over the origins of the test in these cases, see R.M. Perkins, Criminal Law, 759-60 (1948); H. Weihofen, Mental Disorder as a Criminal Defense 85-89 (1954); Annot., 70 A.L.R. 659 (1931); and Annot., 173 A.L.R. 391 (1948).

For development of the test in case law since the 1971 edition of this book, see, e.g., Clark v. State, 266 S.E.2d 466 (Ga. 1980); State v. Hamann, 285 N.W. 2d 180 (Iowa 1979); Herron v. State, 287 So. 2d 759 (Miss. 1974), *cert. denied*, 417 U.S. 972 (1974).

211. 214 F.2d 862 (D.C. Cir. 1954).

212. *Id.* at 874-75.

213. The test was known as "the New Hampshire rule" because of its adoption in New Hampshire in 1869. State v. Pike, 49 N.H. 399 (1869).

214. In reversing the conviction of Monte Durham for housebreaking and petit larceny, the court said:

> We find that as an exclusive criterion the right-wrong test is inadequate in that (a) it does not take sufficient account of psychic realities and scientific knowledge, and (b) it is based upon one symptom and so cannot validly be applied in all circumstances. We find that the "irresistible impulse" test is also inadequate in that it gives no recognition to mental illness characterized by brooding and reflection and so relegates acts caused by such illness to the application of the inadequate right-wrong test. We conclude that a broader test should be adopted.

214 F.2d at 874.

215. In the four years before *Durham* was implemented there were 34 people acquitted for reason of insanity; in the four years after the rule there were 150. President's Commission on Crime in the District of Columbia, Report 534 (1966). For initial commentary on the *Durham* criteria, see Comments on Recent Cases: Criminal Law—Insanity Defense—The Durham Rule, 40 Iowa L. Rev. 652 (1955); Goldstein, *supra* note 1; Krash, The Durham Rule and Judicial Administration of the Insanity Defense in the District of Columbia, 70 Yale L.J. 905 (1960-61); Note, Criminal Law: A Significant Development in the Law Relating to Insanity as a Defense to Crime, 1955 Wis. L. Rev. 506 (1955); Tuchler, Century of Progress: The Durham Case, Int'l J. Forensic Sci. 41 (1956); Wechsler, The Criteria of Criminal Responsibility, 22 U. Chi. L. Rev. 367 (1955).

216. Durham v. United States, 214 F.2d 862 (D.C. Cir. 1954); Me. Rev. Stat. Ann. tit. 15, § 102 (repealed 1975); State v. Pike, 49 N.H. 399 (1869) (the law was not codified but adopted 85 years before *Durham* by this case).

217. 471 F.2d 969 (D.C. Cir. 1972). For an extensive discussion of this case, see Symposium: *United States v. Brawner*,, 173 Wash. U.L.Q. 17 (1973). See this chapter § III C 6, The American Law Institute (ALI) Test *infra*.

sion of what type of test could be devised for determining criminal responsibility which would avoid both the narrowness of the M'Naghten rule and the overbreadth of alternative formulations seeking to cure this defect.[218]

5. Diminished Responsibility or Capacity

In 1949 in *People v. Wells*[219] the California Supreme Court introduced into American jurisprudence the concept of diminished responsibility or diminished capacity, another approach to broaden the scope of the M'Naghten rule then in use in California.[220] This concept did not completely excuse someone from criminal responsibility but recognized mental illness as a mitigating factor in certain instances. The court broke new ground by holding that evidence of reduced mental capacity tending to show absence of any mental state essential to the alleged crime should be accepted by the trial court in determining guilt, whether or not an insanity plea was entered.

The diminished capacity or responsibility concept has been used primarily when the defendant is charged with first-degree murder: it is seen as a way to mitigate the harsh penalty by permitting psychiatric testimony concerning the defendant's mental condition at the time of the act and his capacity for deliberation and premeditation in forming the requisite intent to commit the crime.[221] Thus, in a first-degree murder case the defense attorney may introduce psychiatric testimony showing that his client could not appreciate the nature of his act, which could lead to a reduction of the grade of the crime to second-degree murder or manslaughter—offenses that carry a lesser sentence.

The diminished responsibility concept has developed along two theoretical lines.[222] The first focuses on the specific states of mind essential to the various grades of murder: though not amounting to legal insanity, the evidence of mental abnormality may indicate the absence of a specific mental element of a crime, despite the presence of general criminal intent. This approach thus retains the specific intent doctrine but expands the scope of evidence permitted to establish lack of the requisite mental state. The second approach, introduced in 1964 in *People v. Wolff*,[223] also calls for an inquiry into the defendant's mental state but focuses on his ability to understand the moral and social values underlying the laws and attempts to determine the defendant's ability to "maturely and appreciatively reflect" on his acts.[224]

The diminished responsibility or capacity concept has been criticized for being too difficult to apply, leading to uneven and inequitable outcomes.[225] Legal commentators have pointed out that given a similar set of facts, courts respond in widely different ways to consideration of diminished capacity.[226] Although some form of the concept has been used over time by 15 states, it has failed to capture major support and has even lost the support it previously enjoyed.[227] Criticism from the legal community and growing use of the American Law Institute test in jurisdictions that had previously embraced the diminished capacity concept have resulted in calls for its abandonment.[228]

6. The American Law Institute (ALI) Test

In the 1950s the American Law Institute (ALI) drafted a provision in its Model Penal Code to respond to criticisms of both the M'Naghten and the Durham rules.[229] The two-part test devised by the ALI provides:

> A person is not responsible for criminal conduct if at the time of such conduct as a result of mental disease or defect he lacks substantial capacity either to appreciate the criminality [wrongfulness] of his conduct or to conform his conduct to the requirements of law.
>
> As used in this Article, the terms "mental disease or defect" do not include an abnormality manifested only by repeated criminal or otherwise anti-social conduct.[230]

The ALI approach differs from the M'Naghten rule in three respects. First, the ALI test substitutes the concept

218. Acheson, *McDonald v. United States:*: The Durham Rule Redefined, 51 Geo. L.J. 580 (1963); Halleck, The Insanity Defense in the District of Columbia—a Legal Lorelei, 49 Geo. L.J. 294 (1960); Watson, Durham Plus Five Years: Development of the Law of Criminal Responsibility in the District of Columbia, 116 Am. J. Psychiatry 289 (1959).

219. 33 Cal. 2d 330, 202 P.2d 53 (Cal. 1949).

220. See Brooks, *supra* note 185, at 200-201. See generally at 200-209 for application, interpretation, and evaluation of the concept.

221. *Id.*

222. H. Fingarette & A.F. Hasse, Mental Disabilities and Criminal Responsibility 119-20 (1979).

223. 394 P.2d 959, 40 Cal. Rptr. 271 (1964).

224. Fingarette & Hasse, *supra* note 222, at 120. Also People v. Goedecke, 423 P.2d 777, 781 (Cal. 1967).

225. See Comment, A Punishment Rationale for Diminished Capacity, 18 U.C.L.A. L.Rev. 561 (1971) [hereinafter cited as Comment, A Punishment Rationale]; also Fingarette & Hasse, *supra* note 222, at 131.

226. See Comment, A Punishment Rationale, *supra* note 225, at 567-72, which contrasts cases in which each defendant exhibited the same mental incapacity at the time of the crime but in which each court responded differently to whether it would consider diminished capacity.

227. See Fingarette & Hasse, *supra* note 222, at 117 n.1. Indeed, in the state of its origin, California, the use of diminished capacity has been abolished by state statute, largely in response to a notorious decision in which the defendant, charged with killing the mayor of San Francisco and a county supervisor, was found guilty by a jury of voluntary manslaughter rather than first-degree murder, after testimony that he had been experiencing mental stress aggravated by chemical imbalances resulting from his sporadic large intakes of "junk food" (the "Twinkie defense"). Cal. Penal Code § 28(b) (West 1981).

228. See Fingarette & Hasse, *supra* note 222, at 131.

229. Hall, Mental Disease and Criminal Responsibility—M'Naghten Versus Durham and the American Law Institute's Tentative Draft, 33 Ind. L.J. 212 (1958). In United States v. Brawner, 471 F.2d 969 (D.C. Cir. 1972), the court explicitly replaced the Durham rule with the ALI test. See note 217 and surrounding text *supra*.

230. Model Penal Code § 4.01 (1962), 10 U.L.A. 490-91 (1974).

of "appreciation" for cognitive understanding in the definition of insanity, thus introducing an effective and more personalized approach for evaluating the nature of a defendant's knowledge or understanding. Second, the ALI definition does not insist that the defendant totally lack appreciation of the nature of his conduct but asks instead that he lack "substantial capacity for such appreciation." Finally, it incorporates a volitional approach to insanity, thus adding an independent criterion for insanity— the defendant's inability to control his actions.

The ALI test is perceived to have numerous advantages over either M'Naghten or Durham.[231] Most notably, it encourages adjudication based on reality and the practical experience of psychiatrists by recognizing that both the volitional and the cognitive processes of an individual may be impaired. It also moves from the absolute requirement of total incapacity, required by M'Naghten, toward a more realistic substantial incapacity standard. Finally, it encourages maximum input from the expert witnesses while leaving the ultimate decision making to the jury.[232]

In making it clear that "mental disease or defect" does not include behavior manifested by repeated antisocial activity, the second part of the ALI test alleviates the problem with the Durham rule observed in the District of Columbia, where courts in some cases accepted a diagnosis of "sociopath" as sufficient to excuse a defendant from criminal responsibility, since at that time the psychiatric manual in use listed "sociopathic personality disturbance" as an illness. Since then the term *sociopath* has lost all official standing, and the nomenclature for repeated or chronic antisocial behavior has changed.[233]

Except for the explicit exclusion of sociopathy, the ALI test does not define the "mental disease or defect" that it says must be a cause of the incapacity, but the phrase has been defined by the case law. Many courts have relied on the definition articulated in 1962 in *McDonald v. United States*,[234] even though that decision was written with the Durham rule in view. The *McDonald* court defined mental disease or defect as "any abnormal condition of the mind which substantially affects mental or emotional processes and substantially impairs behavior controls."[235] Thus, to succeed with an insanity defense the defendant must prove that he was suffering from some type of mental disease or defect, generally one accepted and recognized as such by the psychiatric profession.[236] Having proved the existence of a mental disease or defect, the defendant must further prove that it impaired his judgment so that he could not conform his conduct to the requirements of the law.

The ALI test has met with favorable response and has been adopted in about half the states.[237] Of these states a majority have adopted the test verbatim. Some others have made slight modifications, such as removing the word "substantial"[238] and substituting other phrases such as "is unable" or "lacks capacity,"[239] and other states have modified the test by using a term other than "appreciate."[240] Some states have tried to provide better understanding of "mental disease or defect" by elaborating on its meaning.[241] Hawaii has expanded the concept by adding that the lack of criminal responsibility may be due to a physical as well as a mental disease.[242]

Although widely accepted, the ALI test is not without its critics, who feel that it excuses too many people from responsibility.[243] Such criticism has resulted in renewed calls for abolition of the insanity defense, a return to a narrower standard such as M'Naghten, and other modifications.[244]

7. New Concepts to Excuse from Criminal Responsibility

Even under the broader ALI test, most medical evaluators believe that a defendant's illness must be of considerable magnitude to excuse him from criminal responsibility. Usually, this has meant that there must be a finding of psychosis. In the past few years, however, a number of new "disorders" or "syndromes" have been

231. See opinion of J. Kaufman in United States v. Freeman, 357 F.2d 606, 622-25 (2d Cir. 1966); also United States v. Brawner, 471 F.2d 969 (D.C. Cir. 1972).

232. United States. v. Brawner, 471 F.2d at 1002; United States v. Freeman, 357 F.2d at 622.

233. Sociopathy, defined in the first edition of the psychiatrists' diagnostic manual at the time of the Durham rule, is now referred to as an "Antisocial Personality Disorder" (301.70), which is characterized by a history, beginning before the age of 15, "of continuous and chronic antisocial behavior in which the rights of others are violated." "Adult Antisocial Behavior," which embraces many of the same symptoms but cannot be shown to have a childhood onset, is classified in the category "Conditions Not Attributable to a Mental Disorder." American Psychiatric Association, Diagnostic and Statistical Manual of Mental Disorders 6, 317-19, 331-32 (3d ed. 1980) [hereinafter cited as DSM—III]; for a discussion of the debate surrounding this diagnostic category, see J. Robitscher, The Powers of Psychiatry 169-70 (1980).

234. 312 F.2d 847 (D.C. Cir. 1962).

235. *Id.* at 851.

236. DSM—III, *supra* note 233, catalogs the mental disorders and their characteristics.

237. See table 12.5, col. 7.

238. *Id.*, specifically Arkansas, Missouri, and Washington.

239. See, e.g., State *ex rel.* Krutzfeldt v. District Ct. of 13th Jud. Dist., 515 P.2d 1312, 1316 (Mont. 1973).

240. Pegues v. United States, 415 A.2d 1374 (D.C. App. 1980) used term *recognize*; State v. Staten, 247 N.E.2d 293 (Ohio 1969) used term *knew*, as did Graham v. State, 566 S.W.2d 941 (Tex. Crim. App. 1978).

241. See table 12.5, col. 7, specifically Maryland and Michigan.

242. Hawaii Rev. Stat. 704-400 (1976 & Supp. 1982).

243. See Halpern, The Insanity Defense: A Judicial Anachronism, 7 Psychiatric Annals 41 (1977); K. Menninger, The Crime of Punishment (1968); T.S. Szasz, Law, Liberty, and Psychiatry: An Inquiry into the Social Uses of Mental Health Practices (1963).

244. See Bonnie, Morality, Equality, and Expertise: Renegotiating the Relationship Between Psychiatry and the Criminal Law, 12 A.A.P.L. Bull. 5 (1984). See also references cited in notes 192 and 243 *supra*.

brought forward as warranting excuse from responsibility under the insanity defense. These include post-traumatic stress disorder, pathological gambling, and premenstrual syndrome.

(a) Post-traumatic stress disorder □□ Post-traumatic stress disorder (PTSD), since officially recognized as a mental illness by the psychiatric profession, strikes survivors of traumatic events, such as natural disasters, plane crashes, and wartime combat, who may reexperience elements of the trauma in dreams, uncontrollable and emotionally intrusive images, dissociative states of consciousness, and unconscious behavioral reenactments of the traumatic situation.[245] PTSD has received the most attention in cases involving Vietnam veterans who raise the condition as the basis for an insanity defense,[246] in which it is argued that the defendant engaged in criminal behavior as a result of a stressful event that caused him to revert to the behavior he exhibited under conditions of war in Vietnam.[247]

An insanity defense based on PTSD is most plausible and is most likely to be successful in cases in which the defendant exhibited behavior during the crime indicating that he was reliving his war experience.[248] In cases where the defense is less plausible, it will still provide the attorney with an opportunity to present a wide range of evidence contrasting the defendant's behavior before and after the war, in the hopes of getting a conviction for a lesser offense or a lighter sentence.[249] Because of its relatively recent recognition as an "illness," there are as yet few reported cases involving PTSD as a defense.[250] This situation may change, particularly given the concept's potential for extension to other kinds of cases, such as those involving women who have committed criminal acts after being raped.[251]

(b) Pathological gambling □□ Pathological gambling, an impulse disorder classified as a mental illness by the psychiatric profession in 1980, is characterized by an inability to control gambling which results in disruption of the gambler's daily life.[252] The disorder has served as the basis for raising an insanity defense in a few federal and state trials in which the defendant was charged with forgery or embezzlement.[253] Although it is clear that the defendant can distinguish right from wrong, it is argued that the illness makes it impossible for him to conform his conduct to the requirements of the law.

Initially some courts accepted the pathological gambling theory as a basis for an insanity defense. The following factors appear to have been influential: (1) the cases involved a very persuasive psychiatric expert,[254] and (2) the accused were "white-collar" defendants with no previous criminal history, leaving mental aberration as the only plausible explanation for their behavior.[255] More recently, it appears that the tide has turned, with a number of federal district courts specifically excluding pathological gambling as a basis for an insanity defense.[256]

245. DSM—III, *supra* note 233, at 236–38.

246. This has been the subject of numerous media accounts. See Erlinder, Post-Traumatic Stress Disorder, Vietnam Veterans and the Law: A Challenge to Effective Representation, 1 Behav. Sci. & Law 32 (1983), for a list of several of the cases raising this defense.

247. For a description of the various symptoms of dissociative states of consciousness and behavioral reenactments of the combat trauma and the process through which they might lead to criminal behavior (such as shooting a police officer or taking hostages), see Wilson & Zigelbaum, The Vietnam Veteran on Trial: The Relation of Post-Traumatic Stress Disorder to Criminal Behavior, 1 Behav. Sci. & L. 70, 73–75 (1983). This article describes how the veteran may enter into a "survivor mode of functioning" that results in an altered state of consciousness and the use of survival skills learned in the Vietnam War.

248. See Erlinder, *supra* note 246, for a description of some of the cases. See, e.g., State v. Heads, No. 106 (1st Jud. Dist. Ct. Caddo Parish, La. Oct. 1981), in which the defendant murdered his sister-in-law's husband for no logical reason in a way that appeared as though he were reenacting a war experience. He had recently learned that his wife planned to leave him.

249. It has been estimated that 25% to 35% of those Vietnam veterans who saw heavy combat have been arrested for criminal charges. House Comm. on Veterans' Affairs, 96th Cong., 1st Sess., Presidential Review Memorandum on Vietnam Era Veterans, Oct. 10, 1978 (Comm. Print 38 (1979)). Thus if this defense should be used frequently for combat veterans it could open a wide range of testimony. See also Erlinder, *supra* note 246.

For a discussion of the problems presented for the psychiatrist involved in evaluating a defendant who raises PTSD as a defense, see Lipkin, Scurfield, & Blank, Post-Traumatic Stress Disorder in Vietnam Veterans: Assessment in a Forensic Setting, 1 Behav. Sci. & L. 63 (1983); also Apostle, The Unconsciousness Defense as Applied to Post Traumatic Stress Disorder in a Vietnam Veteran, 8 A.A.P.L. Bull. 426 (1980); Walker, Viet-Nam Combat Veterans with Legal Difficulties: A Psychiatric Problem? 138 Am. J. Psychiatry 1384 (1981).

250. There are not, at the date of this writing, any appellate cases in this area. For a list of the major cases see Erlinder, *supra* note 246, at 33.

251. Burgess, Rape Trauma Syndrome, 1 Behav. Sci. & L. 97 (1983).

252. See DSM—III, *supra* note 233, at 291–92. The gambling must compromise, disrupt, or damage family, personal, and vocational pursuits. There are specific ways the illness is manifested and excludes people who gamble because of antisocial personality disorder.

253. These cases, not officially reported, include the following trials in which pathological gambling as the basis for the insanity defense was raised: People v. Dube, No. 5260-80 (N.Y. County); State v. Campanaro, (Sup. Ct. of N.J.); No. 632-79 (Crim. Div., Union County, Ind.); United States v. Bertolone, No. Cr. 80-67 (U.S. Dist. Ct. Buffalo, N.Y.); United States v. McGee, No. Cr. 78-80 (U.S. Dist. Ct. Las Vegas, Nev.); State v. Lafferty, No. 44359 (Conn. Super. Ct. June 5, 1981). *Reported in* McGarry, Pathological Gambling: A New Insanity Defense, 11 A.A.P.L. Bull. 301, 305 (1983).

254. In three successful cases the expert witness was Robert Custer, M.D., a pioneer in the development of this diagnosis and its treatment within the Veterans Administration.

255. See McGarry, *supra* note 253, at 305..

256. See, e.g., United States v. Torniero, 570 F. Supp. 721 (D. Conn. 1983); United States v. Lewellyn, 723 F.2d. 615 (8th Cir. 1983). Acceptance of pathological gambling as a basis for the insanity defense would have disturbing and widespread implications. If it is recognized that the pathological gambler knew right from wrong but could not conform his conduct to the requirements of law and therefore should be exculpated, then the same type of argument could be used to excuse other types of criminal behavior that the defendant demonstrates was perpetrated to satisfy the demands of his illness. For example, it could easily be imagined that a drug addict engaged in crime to support his drug habit would be likely to make the same arguments. Another troubling feature of pathological gambling is the probability that the defendant would not be committable to a mental hospital. For a commentary

(c) Premenstrual syndrome □□ Unlike PTSD and pathological gambling, what has been called "premenstrual syndrome" imbalances, thought by some to cause sudden mood shifts resulting in violent behavior,[257] has not been defined as a mental illness by the American psychiatric community.[258] However, in a handful of criminal cases in Europe it has served as the basis for excusing women from criminal responsibility,[259] which has led to speculation that under certain circumstances it could form the basis for a successful insanity defense in the United States, although there are as yet no reported cases in which such an attempt has been made.[260] But the prospects for success are dubious, given the vagueness of the condition and its symptoms. First, there is still considerable dispute as to whether a condition definable as a premenstrual syndrome even exists, let alone whether it should be acknowledged for purposes of determining criminal responsibility. The existing studies have succeeded in ascribing criminal behavior to the menstrual cycle only after the fact. It has also been pointed out that many of the symptoms characterizing the syndrome are not uniquely associated with women but rather are often experienced by both men and women while under stress.[261] Second, public policy implications in giving legal recognition to the syndrome are troubling, given that this would conflict with, among other things, political efforts—championed particularly by women's groups—to refute arguments that women behave unpredictablv because of their menstrual cycle.

8. Guilty but Mentally Ill (GBMI)

Dissatisfaction with the insanity defense combined with the belief that it cannot constitutionally be abolished has led numerous states to seek a compromise verdict called "guilty but mentally ill" (GBMI).[262] The underlying reason for creating the GBMI verdict is to decrease the number of people found not guilty by reason of insanity. Michigan, the first state to adopt this verdict, did so in 1975.[263] Since then, approximately 20% of the states have followed suit, most of those in direct response to the Hinckley verdict of 1981.[264]

The GBMI verdict takes two forms. One type is the Michigan law, the model for most of the other states adopting the verdict. Following the presentation of the insanity defense, there are four possible verdicts: (1) not guilty, (2) guilty, (3) not guilty by reason of insanity (NGRI), or (4) guilty but mentally ill. For a verdict of guilty but mentally ill it must be proven that the defendant (1) is guilty of the offense charged, (2) was mentally ill when he committed the offense, but (3) was not legally insane at the time he committed the offense.[265] While most states require proof of each of these elements beyond a reasonable doubt, Alaska and Kentucky provide that guilt must be proven beyond a reasonable doubt but that only a preponderence of evidence is needed to establish mental illness at the time the crime was committed.[266]

The other version of the GBMI verdict excludes the insanity defense and thus leaves only three possible verdicts: (1) not guilty, (2) guilty, or (3) guilty and suffering from a mental disease or defect. As of May 1985, Montana was the only state to have adopted this form of the GBMI verdict.[267] Under the Montana statute, if the mental state element of a crime is not proven, an evaluation may be ordered to determine if the defendant is "not guilty by reason of lack of mental state."[268] Apparently, this version of the law also permits an initial finding of guilty with a finding at the sentencing stage that the defendant needs mental treatment.

At the time of the adoption of the GBMI law in Michi-

---

on this issue see Comment, Beating the Odds: Compulsive Gambling as an Insanity Defense—*State v. Lafferty,* 14 Conn. L. Rev. 341, 365 (1982).

257. D'Orban & Dalton, Violent Crime and the Menstrual Cycle, 10 Psychological Med. 353 (1980).

258. Premenstrual Syndrome is not recognized in DSM—III, *supra* note 233.

259. In at least four criminal cases in England and one in France, premenstrual syndrome constituted the basis for excusing a woman for criminal responsibility. Dalton, Cyclical Criminal Acts in Premenstrual Syndrome, The Lancet, Nov. 15, 1980, at 1070-71.

260. Women on Trial: New Defense, Nat'l L. J., Feb. 15, 1982, at 1; PMS Case Ends with Guilty Plea, Nat'l. L.J. Nov. 15, 1982, at 36.

261. See Horney, Menstrual Cycles and Criminal Responsibility, 2 Law & Hum. Behav. 25-26 (1978), for a good discussion of whether the symptoms really form a unique syndrome and the flaws in the existing studies that have identified premenstrual syndrome. It has been pointed out that some of the symptoms include feeling "bloated," constipation, diarrhea, insomnia, or sleeping all day.

262. See table 12.5, col. 8, e.g., Alaska, Delaware, Georgia, Illinois, Indiana, Kentucky, Michigan, Montana, New Mexico, Pennsylvania, South Dakota, Utah, and Vermont.

263. Mich. Comp. Laws Ann. § 768.36(3) (1968 & Supp. 1982), Mich. Stat. Ann. § 28.1059 (Supp. 1983-84). In part the Michigan law was adopted because of a state court decision in People v. McQuillan, 221 N.W.2d 569 (Mich. 1974), which held that insanity acquittees had to be treated the same as other persons where civil commitment was sought. This decision resulted in the release of 79% of the confined insanity acquittees, two of whom committed an additional violent act, one a murder and the other a brutal rape. Project: Evaluating Michigan's Guilty But Mentally Ill Verdict: An Empirical Study, 16 J. L. Reform, 77-79 (1982) [hereinafter cited as Project].

264. Before the Hinckley verdict, Georgia, Illinois, Indiana, and Michigan had enacted GBMI, in part in response to defendants raising the insanity defense in crimes that outraged the public. The remaining states adopted the verdict after the jury verdict finding Hinckley not guilty by reason of insanity. Although it appears that by fall 1983 the move to adopt GBMI verdicts had slowed down, it is likely to be revived in those states where a crime occurs which enrages the public when the defendant raises and/or succeeds with the insanity defense.

265. See, e.g., Mich. Stat. Ann. § 28.1059 (Supp. 1983-84); N.M. Stat. Ann. § 31-9-3 (Supp. 1983). The wording is usually identical in each of the state GBMI laws.

266. Alaska Stat. § 12.47.040(b) (1980 & Supp. 1982); Ky. Rev. Stat. Ann. § 504.130 (Baldwin 1975 & Supp. 1982).

267. Mont. Code Ann. §§ 46-14-201, 46-14-210 (1981).

268. Mont. Code Ann. § 46-14-301 (1981).

gan, it was argued that the verdict would decrease the number of persons acquitted by reason of insanity while at the same time assuring treatment of the "guilty" mentally ill within the correctional setting.[269] Each defendant found guilty but mentally ill would be evaluated upon entry into the correctional system and be provided the mental health services indicated by the evaluation.[270] In addition, the law made it possible to mandate outpatient treatment for the convicted person as part of a sentence of probation or upon release on parole.

The GBMI has been criticized on a number of accounts: the overlapping definitions[271] raise questions about whether a jury or an expert witness can understand clearly the distinction between being guilty but mentally ill and not guilty by reason of insanity;[272] juries will misuse the verdict as a compromise device, finding someone guilty but mentally ill when a finding of not guilty by reason of insanity might have been more appropriate;[273] the verdict is a legal hoax or fraud,[274] a political response to public outrage about a particular case, and it gives the illusion that something positive has been done when in reality there has been little if any change in what happens to criminal defendants pleading mental incapacity;[275] the verdict is potentially harmful to the defendant who raises the insanity defense and then is found GBMI.[276]

While successful legal challenges have not yet been mounted against the GBMI verdict, the concept is susceptible to attack in three areas: the possibility that the defendant's constitutional rights are violated by his being denied the ability to invoke the insanity defense; the possibility that jury instructions cannot be framed to meaningfully and coherently distinguish between the insanity defense standard and the guilty but mentally ill standard; and the lack of treatment programs available within the correctional facility to which the person found GBMI is sentenced.

Because Michigan has had a GBMI verdict for the longest period of time, and all forensic evaluations are done at the Center for Forensic Psychiatry in Ann Arbor, the Michigan experience affords the best setting for evaluating the GBMI verdict. The two primary goals of the GBMI law in Michigan—to decrease the number of persons acquitted by reason of insanity and to simplify jury instructions—have not been achieved. Since 1976 the number of persons found NGRI has remained essentially constant,[277] suggesting that defendants who would formerly have received an acquittal by reason of insanity are still likely to do so. As for those receiving the GBMI verdict, 60% have done so through the plea bargaining process. An additional 20% have been found GBMI in bench trials.[278] Only a very small percentage of defend-

269. See, e.g., Robey, Guilty But Mentally Ill, 6 A.A.P.L. Bull. 374, 379-80 (1978).

270. Under the Michigan model, once a person has been found guilty but mentally ill the court may impose any sentence that the defendant could have received by virtue of being found guilty. Only Delaware and Kentucky require that persons found GBMI be given treatment that can be provided either within the correctional system or by transfer to the state mental health system. Del. Code Ann. tit. 11, § 408(b) (Supp. 1984); Ky. Rev. Stat. Ann. § 504.250 (Baldwin 1975 & Supp. 1982).

If, under the Montana law, the defendant is found not guilty by reason of lack of mental state, the defendant can be committed to the state mental hospital. The defendant may also introduce his mental condition at sentencing, and he can be given any sentence the judge believes is appropriate, including sentencing to the state mental hospital for a period not to exceed the maximum sentence the defendant could have received had he been convicted of the crime.

271. E.g., in Illinois "insanity" is defined as follows: "A person is not criminally responsible for conduct if at the time of such conduct, as a result of mental disease or defect, he lacks substantial capacity either to appreciate the criminality of his conduct or to conform his conduct to the requirements of law." Ill. Ann. Stat. ch. 38, § 6-2(a) (Smith-Hurd 1977 & Supp. 1983-84). "Guilty but mentally ill" means a person who, at the time of the commission of a criminal offense, was not insane but was suffering from a mental illness, and who is not relieved of criminal responsibility for his conduct and may be found guilty but mentally ill. For the purposes of this section "mental illness" or "mentally ill" means a substantial disorder of thought, mood, or behavior that afflicted a person at the time of the commission of the offense and impaired that person's judgment, but not to the extent that he was unable to appreciate the wrongfulness of his behavior or was unable to conform his conduct to the requirements of law." *Id.* at § 6-2(c) & (d).

272. The Constitutionality of Michigan's Guilty But Mentally Ill Verdict, 12 U. Mich. J.L. Ref. 188 (1978), in which the author points out:

> To be found GBMI, a defendant must have been mentally ill, but not legally insane, when he committed the offense. Yet it is hard to imagine "a substantial disorder of thought or mood which significantly impairs judgment, behavior, capacity to recognize reality, or ability to cope with the ordinary demands of life" that may not also be a substantial incapacity "either to appreciate the wrongfulness of . . . conduct or to conform . . . conduct to requirements of law."

Id. at 196 (notes omitted; ellipses in original). This description incorporates both the insanity and guilty but mentally ill standards.

273. Comment, Guilty But Mentally Ill: An Historical and Constitutional Analysis, 53 J. Urb. L. 474, 492 (1976).

274. This view has been taken by both legal scholars and practicing criminal attorneys in news media accounts. See, e.g., B.A. Weiner, Guilty But Mentally Ill: New Plea in Criminal Cases Fools Public, Chicago Sun-Times, Aug. 5, 1981, at 52 col. 1; Interview with Barbara Weiner, AMA News, Aug. 6, 1982, at 3.

275. The GBMI verdict does not guarantee treatment for the defendant while incarcerated. Although incarcerated persons are entitled to some level of medical and psychiatric treatment, it could be provided by existing laws. In People v. McLeod, 258 N.W.2d 214 (Mich. Ct. App. 1979), the trial court recognized a right to receive treatment, which the court held could not occur in the prison system. But many states have provisions for transfer from the correctional system to the mental health system for mentally ill inmates. See also Criminal Justice Mental Health Standards, *supra* note 112, 7-10.3 Commentary, and in this chapter § V D, Treatment, *infra*.

276. A label of GBMI may preclude the prisoner's placement in more open prison programs such as prison camps and also may negatively influence a parole board's decision on parole. Blunt & Stock, Guilty But Mentally Ill: The Michigan Experience 11 (paper presented at the Annual Meeting of the American Academy of Psychiatry and Law, Portland, Or., Oct. 1983). (This unpublished paper can be obtained by writing to the authors at the Center for Forensic Psychiatry, P.O. Box 2040, Ann Arbor, Mich. 48106.)

For the prisoner who is inappropriately labeled "mentally ill," adjustment in prison may be more difficult because he will be stigmatized by this designation.

277. Blunt & Stock, *supra* note 276, at 8. Michigan finds an average of 54 people NGRI a year, or 7% of those who raise the defense.

278. Smith & Hall, Evaluating Michigan's Guilty But Mentally Ill Verdict: An Empirical Study, 16 U. Mich. J.L. Ref. 77, 94 (1982).

ants receive this verdict through jury trials. Apparently, the most important determinant of whether someone will be acquitted by reason of insanity or found GBMI is the recommendation of the Center for Forensic Psychiatry.[279] A study done by the staff of the center concluded with the following assessment:

> It seems that the GBMI verdict is a superfluous one as it pertains to mental health treatment. It has had virtually no impact on the number of NGRI adjudications or the handling of persons after the NGRI verdict. It does have potential for positive use in the mandatory mental health treatment of those placed on probation, and does give the trier of fact an alternative verdict. The verdict appears to be an attempt to recognize diminished capacity or responsibility without any diminished sentence or significant rights to treatment beyond those granted to all prisoners in the State of Michigan.[280]

Whether this assessment will be true for the other states that have adopted this verdict will become known only in time. At this point, the Michigan experience appears to support claims by critics that the GBMI verdict is not needed,[281] that it accomplishes little,[282] and that despite widespread touting of GBMI as an answer to controversial insanity verdicts, it in fact avoids few or none of the perceived problems of the traditional defense. The one apparent advantage in the GBMI approach—the possibility for mandating outpatient treatment upon return to the community—is offset by the fact that many of those found GBMI have no mental illness that is amenable to treatment.[283]

9. Abolition

Proposals for modifications of the insanity test have been accompanied periodically by calls for outright abolition of the defense.[284] Historically, the constitutionality of eliminating the defense has always been dubious.[285] Before 1930, three states had tried to abolish the defense; their laws were struck down on grounds of violation of the right to a jury trial and/or of due process.[286] The reasons or theories offered for abolition of the insanity defense have varied according to different theories of criminal justice.[287]

The early proposals, growing out of the belief that long-term confinement in hospitals for the criminally insane was inhumane, tended to regard inquiry into the offender's state of mind as futile and advocated focusing instead on how to rehabilitate and treat the offender.[288] Other proposals, in recognition of the significant changes in use of the defense and disposition of the insanity acquittee, tend to emphasize deterrence and protection of society. Thus, Norval Morris has suggested that the best use of psychiatric resources would be in the prevention and treatment of crime rather than in determinations of legal culpability.[289] He elaborates that "[t]he accused's mental condition should be relevant [only] to the question of whether he did or did not, at the

279. *Id.* at 97. In 96% of the cases in which the defendant was later found guilty or GBMI, the Forensic Center had previously determined that he did not meet the requirements for an insanity defense.

280. Blunt & Stock, *supra* note 276, at 11.

281. Judges and juries are continuing to find defendants NGRI at least as often as they did before the GBMI alternative, and the evidence suggests that they are rarely entering the verdict when they would previously have found the person NGRI. Unpublished statistics for Illinois reveal a 15% increase in the number of NGRIs since 1981, when the GBMI law became effective. In that two-year period approximately 100 people were found GBMI, according to Daniel Cuneo, Director of Research, Chester Mental Health Center, Chester, Ill.

282. Preliminary indications from Illinois reveal that the GBMI verdict is most frequently stipulated to, often as part of a plea bargain, where the defendant may have faced the death penalty. (Information secured by telephone survey of prosecutors from the largest Illinois counties.) Except in death penalty cases there is no logical reason for a defense attorney to stipulate to a GBMI finding, since care for mentally ill prisoners in Illinois is given within the Department of Corrections, as appears to be the case in most states that have enacted a GBMI statute.

283. An analysis by the Center for Forensic Psychiatry in Michigan determined that almost all the people found GBMI were sociopaths and thus not suffering from an illness amenable to treatment. Blunt & Stock, *supra* note 276.

284. In 1911 Dr. William White proposed abandonment when he recommended that the jury be confined to determining if the accused were the true transgressor. M.S. Guttmacher, The Role of Psychiatry in Law 93 (1968).

285. See Weihofen, *supra* note 210, at 477-80 for a discussion of the constitutional aspect.

286. In 1909 the state of Washington adopted a statute that provided that insanity at the time of the crime would no longer be a defense that could be raised by the defendant, but the statute left it within the power of the trial court, sitting without a jury, to find the accused insane at the time of commission of the offense and order him to a mental institution. Rem. & Bal. Code § 2259 (1909 Wash. Laws ch. 249, § 7). This law was struck down as a violation of the defendant's right to a jury trial. State v. Strasburg, 60 Wash. 106, 110 P. 1020 (1910).

In 1928 Mississippi enacted a provision to the effect that insanity was not a defense to murder; on conviction the defendant would be imprisoned for life, except that the governor could transfer him to a hospital for the insane if his condition warranted it. Miss. Code 1930 ch. 75, §§ 1327 & 1328 (1928 Miss. Laws). The Mississippi Supreme Court held that the statute violated due process. Sinclair v. State, 132 So. 581 (Miss. 1931).

Also in 1928 Louisiana enacted a law providing that in the case of a plea of insanity, the defendant was to be tried before a "lunacy commission," which could commit him if he were found insane. If he was found sane, a trial would be ordered and the defendant would be precluded from reraising the insanity defense. Act No. 17 Ex. Sess. 1928, amending Code of Crim. Proc. art. 268. The Louisiana Supreme Court struck down the statute as violating due process and the right to a jury trial. State v. Lange, 123 So. 639 (La. 1929).

287. See in this chapter § III A, Introduction, *supra*.

288. Wootton advocated that the mens rea (guilty mind) concept be discarded and that the individual's mental state be considered only at the posttrial disposition, with the choices ranging from immediate release to various types of hospitalization. B. Wootton, Crime and the Criminal Law chs. 2 & 3 (1963). Hart, on the other hand, argued that the mens rea concept should be retained but that a mental abnormality did not by itself negate it. Medical testimony would be permitted only at the posttrial disposition. H.L.A. Hart, The Concept of Law (1961).

289. Morris, Psychiatry and the Dangerous Criminal, 41 S. Cal. L. Rev. 514, 515 (1968). See app. at 544 for a summary of several of the arguments advanced for abolishing the defense of insanity. For another proposal see Shwedel & Roether, The Disposition Hearing: An Alternative to the Insanity Defense, 49 J. Urb. L. 711 (1972).

time of the act, have the prohibited *mens rea* of the crime of which he is charged."[290] Justice Weintraub of the New Jersey Supreme Court had similarly written that psychiatric testimony should be limited to the issue of mens rea.[291]

The most recent legislative efforts to abolish the insanity defense followed public outcry over the verdict in the *Hinckley* case in 1981.[292] In April 1982, Idaho became the first state in recent times to abolish the insanity defense. Its new law provides that "[m]ental condition shall not be a defense to any charge of criminal conduct" and states that "nothing herein is intended to prevent the admission of expert evidence on the issues of mens rea or any state of mind which is an element of the offense, subject to the rules of evidence."[293] The states of Montana and Utah have since followed suit.[294]

Proponents of the position set forth in the Idaho statute point out that there is no constitutional requirement that an affirmative defense of mental disability shall exist. But while modern abolitionists propound eliminating the insanity defense in the traditional sense, they accept retaining the concept of mens rea,[295] which is thought to make the new scheme both workable and impervious to constitutional attack. They also keep intact the concept of free will. Thus the person who "truly" did not know what he was doing, that is, one who could not form the requisite criminal intent, would still be excused from criminal responsibility while the tradition of absolving from blame and punishment only those who are "truly" not blameworthy would be preserved. Psychiatric testimony would be permitted to determine the defendant's ability to form the required mental state of criminal intent. There would be only two available verdicts, guilty and not guilty. The person found not guilty because he lacked the requisite mental state would not automatically be subjected to posttrial commitment proceedings. If psychiatric treatment was seen to be necessary or desirable, separate civil commitment proceedings would have to be initiated.

This newest abolitionist position, like earlier abolition efforts, has been criticized as an extreme and unwarranted reversal of hundreds of years of moral and legal history, a constitutionally dubious overreaction to one contemporary controversial verdict.[296] Some critics have pointed out that unless the courts broadly interpret "knowledge or intent," under the Idaho model a defendant operating under severe psychotic delusions and only minimally aware of his actions may nonetheless be found guilty. Thus, if a mother killed her child under the delusion that God had asked her to make this sacrifice, she would appear to be guilty under the abolitionist position because she had the intent to kill her child. Yet, by hypothesis, this would be the act of an insane woman whose psychotic state rendered her unable to understand the criminality of her act. The abolitionist approach thus threatens to foreclose, in cases whose facts argue compellingly to the contrary, the exercise of humane moral judgment that has distinguished our criminal law heritage.

10. Narrowing of the Standard

With the passage of the Comprehensive Crime Control Act in October 1984,[297] the federal government followed a trend set by legislative and professional organizations rejecting the ALI standard in favor of a narrower approach that excluded the volitional element in consideration of the insanity defense. The new federal law defines insanity to mean "[t]hat, at the time of the commission of the acts constituting the offense, the defendant, as a result of a severe mental disease or defect, was unable to appreciate the nature and quality of the wrongfulness of his acts."[298] A direct result of the Hinckley verdict, this change followed the adoption of a narrower standard by both the American Bar Association and the National Conference of Commissioners on Uniform State law.

The resolution approved by the House of Delegates of the American Bar Association (ABA) in February 1983 was a rejection of the ALI test that it had accepted in principle since 1975. This resolution stated:

> The ABA approves, in principle, a defense of nonresponsibility for crime which focuses solely on whether the defendant as a result of mental disease or defect was unable to appreciate the wrongfulness of his or her conduct at the time of the offense charged.[299]

290. Morris, *supra* note 289, at 518.

291. See concurring opinion in State v. Lucas, 152 A.2d 50 (N.J. 1959).

292. See note 186 *supra* for a summary of efforts following the *Hinckley* decision.

293. Idaho Code § 18-207 (1974 & Supp. 1984).

294. See Mont. Code Ann. 46-14-201 (1981); Utah Code Ann. 76-2-305 (1978 & Supp. 1983). The Montana Supreme Court has upheld the statute that abolished the insanity defense by concluding that it did not violate the Eighth Amendment proscription against cruel and unusual punishment or the due process clause. State v. Korell, 620 P.2d 992 (Mont. 1984).

295. See Testimony of Idaho Attorney General David H. Leroy, *in* Senate Subcomm. Hearings on Limiting the Insanity Defense, *supra* note 186, at 308-11, in which he describes how the law works and why it can withstand constitutional attack. On December 6, 1983, the American Medical Association House of Delegates adopted the position that the special defense of insanity should be abolished. See Report of Board of Trustees, 251 J.A.M.A. 2967 (1984).

296. See Criminal Justice Mental Health Standards, *supra* note 112, § 7-6.1 commentary at 262; American Psychiatric Association Statement on the Insanity Defense, 140 Am. J. Psychiatry 681, 683-84 (1983) [hereinafter cited as A.P.A. Statement]; Bonnie, The Moral Basis of the Insanity Defense, 69 A.B.A. J. 194-95 (1983).

297. Pub. L. No. 98-473, 98 Stat. 1837 (1984).

298. *Id.* § 402, 98 Stat. at 2057, which amends 18 U.S.C. to add § 20 Insanity Defense.

As justification for considering only the cognitive element and eliminating the volitional, the ABA committee asserted that (1) "the 'appreciation of wrongfulness' formula is sufficiently broad to take into account the morally significant effects of severe mental disorder," and (2) "any independent volitional inquiry involves a significant risk of 'moral mistakes' in the adjudication of criminal responsibility."[300] Although the ABA concedes that the current insanity defense was not being abused, it proposed this new test to avoid the mistakes that could sometimes arise out of consideration of the volitional element. The standard does away with the irresistible impulse approach and other volitional or "control" aspects of expert testimony. The commentary to the standard argues that this approach is in line with current clinical expertise and avoids the problem of "vague or broad interpretations of the term 'mental disease.'"[301]

Although the ABA proposal has been viewed by some to be a return to the M'Naghten test, it is likely to prove broader in application since use of the word *appreciate* still leaves room for psychiatric expertise on the defendant's mental or emotional condition. This nuance has been pointed out by Richard Bonnie, who suggested the narrower insanity defense standard that the ABA endorsed;[302] he has written that under this proposal the defendant's ability to "appreciate the wrongfulness of his conduct" will be broad enough to encompass all cases of severe psychotic deterioration.[303] The American Psychiatric Association has not taken a definitive position on what form the insanity defense standard should take. The APA agrees with Bonnie, however, that the ABA standard will continue to permit relevant psychiatric testimony in the "great majority of cases where criminal responsibility is at issue."[304]

Perhaps the proposal most likely to have the broadest impact is the Model Insanity Defense and Post-Trial Disposition Act,[305] adopted by the National Conference of Commissioners on Uniform State Laws in 1984. This act provides that "[a]n individual is not criminally responsible if at the time of the alleged offense, as a result of mental illness or defect, the individual was substantially unable to appreciate the wrongfulness of the alleged conduct."[306] Although not a return to the M'Naghten standard, it clearly narrows the ALI standard initially adopted by the Commissioners.[307] This act, which will serve as a model for those states considering changes in their insanity defense laws, is particularly important because it addresses not only the standard but also a wide range of procedural issues in a comprehensive approach to the commitment and discharge of insanity acquittees.

There has not been enough time to subject these proposals for a narrower standard to the kind of critical scrutiny that earlier modifications, such as the abolitionist position or guilty-but-mentally ill proposals, have received. Yet one can anticipate questions about whether changing the words will really eliminate the volitional aspect from consideration by evaluators or whether that is even desirable. If it is granted that the insanity defense is not being abused and is raised successfully in only a very small percentage of cases, then one must question the practical significance in addition to the theoretical merit of changing the defense.

11. Current Status: In Defense of the Insanity Defense

Recent proposals to change or abolish the insanity defense may be criticized for ignoring the history of the defense and its purposes within the Anglo-American criminal justice system. Three decades ago the English Royal Commission on Capital Punishment said:

> We make one fundamental assumption, which we should hardly have thought it necessary to state explicitly. . . . It has for centuries been recognized that, if a person was, at the time of his unlawful act, mentally so disordered that it would be unreasonable to impute guilt to him, he ought not to be held liable to conviction and punishment under the criminal law. Views have changed and opinions have differed, as they differ now, about the standards to be applied in deciding whether an individual should be exempted from criminal responsibility for this reason, but the principle has been accepted without question.[308]

This statement still carries considerable weight today. It is unlikely that the United States Supreme Court will permit the insanity defense to be abolished or allow the

299. Criminal Justice Mental Health Standards, *supra* note 112, § 7-6.1 at 261. See in this chapter § III C 6, The American Law Institute (ALI) Test, *supra* to compare the texts of the two standards. The action by the House of Delegates was contrary to the position of the ABA committee, which had been established specifically to develop criminal justice mental health standards. The 1983 resolution was passed in response to pressure from legislation introduced in the Congress and state legislatures in response to the Hinckley verdict.

300. Criminal Justice Mental Health Standards, *supra* note 112, at 264.

301. *Id.* at 265.

302. Testimony of Richard Bonnie, *in* The Insanity Defense: Hearings on S. 818, S. 1106, S. 1558, S. 2669, S. 2672, S. 2678, S. 2745, & S. 2780 Before the Senate Comm. on the Judiciary, 97th Cong., 2d Sess. 258 (1982) [hereinafter cited as Senate Judiciary Comm. Hearings on the Insanity Defense].

303. Bonnie, *supra* note 296, at 197.

304. A.P.A. Statement, *supra* note 296, at 681, 685.

305. This act was the result of three years of work by the Commissioners, begun before the Hinckley verdict was rendered. 11 U.L.A. 144 (Supp. 1985).

306. *Id.* § 201 Standard for Absence of Criminal Responsibility, 11 U.L.A. at 147.

307. Section 4.02 of the Model Penal Code was the work of the Uniform Law Commissioners, 10 U.L.A. 491 (1974).

308. Royal Commission on Capital Punishment, 1949-53, Report, Cmd. No. 8932, at 98 (1953).

concept to be so narrowed that the defendant's rational knowledge and understanding of the prohibited act are not considered essential to establishing the mens rea.[309] State courts, in examining the constitutionality of bifurcated trials in which the state of mind or insanity issue is heard separately, have held it to be a fundamental principle of criminal law that the intent or knowledge forming the mental element of the offense must be "sane" intent and "sane" knowledge.[310] Without a showing of sanity as to these elements the prosecution can only establish that prohibited acts have occurred, and not that a crime has been committed.

As one leading psychiatrist has pointed out in defending the insanity defense:

> The contradiction between this experience of being without choice and the moral intuition of free will is one of the inescapable contradictions of human existence. That contradiction is expressed and denied by the insanity defense. The insanity defense is the exception that "proves" the rule of law. . . . the insanity defense does more than test the law; it *demonstrates* that all other criminals had free will—the ability to choose between good and evil—but that they choose evil and therefore deserve to be punished.[311]

A just society must have the ability to express compassion and exercise moral judgment so as to excuse those rare individuals who could not comprehend the wrongfulness of their actions. This vision of law has led civilized societies for centuries and will likely continue to sustain resistance to demands to abolish the insanity defense in the future.

D. Procedural Issues

In all but two states[312] the defendant who raises an insanity defense thereby admits that he committed the physical act of the crime with which he is charged. His argument is that he did not possess the intent required to make that act punishable as a crime. In most states the insanity defense is an affirmative defense or special plea,[313] which must be raised before the trial begins. Often state laws will spell out that the prosecution must be given written notice that the defense will be raised; some statutes also set forth the time limits within which notice must be given. Once the defense is raised, the defendant must submit to a mental evaluation.

1. The Evaluation

(a) Conduct of the evaluation □□ As in the case of competency evaluations, the statutes covering evaluations related to the insanity defense usually prescribe who is to do the examinations. Typically, they designate a physician and/or psychiatrist, but in some states they may also allow a psychologist.[314] A number of statutes require that pending the examination the defendant be hospitalized,[315] frequently in the same facility where persons alleged or found incompetent to stand trial are being evaluated and/or treated. Some statutes limit the length of hospitalization.[316] In some states the defendant is examined on an outpatient basis and is brought to the examiner from the jail or seen while free on bond. Since the insanity defense does not raise the issue of present mental status but only the defendant's mental state at the time of the crime, invocation of the defense does not in and of itself justify forced hospitalization to do the evaluation.

In many states the court appoints impartial experts to conduct the evaluation. If the defendant is dissatisfied with the evaluators selected or with the results of the evaluation, he has the right in most states to seek his own independent examination,[317] and in some jurisdictions the prosecution has the same option. In practice, most evaluations produce no conflict in expert opinion, or the defendant accepts the conclusion of the court-appointed psychiatrist.[318]

(b) Self-incrimination □□ The psychiatric examination that is triggered by invocation of the insanity defense poses the same risk of violating the Fifth Amendment privilege against self-incrimination as the examination for incompetency, and the rationales for running this risk as well as the remedies to protect the defendant's privilege are generally the same.[319] Statutes in a number of states provide for a waiver when either the insanity de-

309. Robitscher & Haynes, In Defense of the Insanity Defense, 31 Emory L.J. 9 (1982); also see discussion in this chapter in § III D 2.a., Burden and Standard of Proof, *infra*.

310. See, e.g., State *ex rel.* Boyd v. Green, 355 So. 2d 789, 793 (Fla. 1978); Sanchez v. State, 567 P.2d 270 (Wyo. 1977); State v. Shaw, 471 P.2d 715 (Ariz. 1970).

311. Stone, The Insanity Defense on Trial, 33 Hosp. & Community Psychiatry 636, 640 (1982).

312. Louisiana and Maine. See La. Code Crim. Proc. Ann. art. 650 (West 1981); Me. Rev. Stat. Ann. tit. 17-A, § 40(1) (1981).

313. See table 12.5, col. 1.

314. For description of conduct of the evaluation for competency, see this chapter II B(6), The Competency Evaluation, and accompanying notes *supra*. See table 12.6, col. 1. Over the past decade several states have added psychologists as acceptable examiners. See, e.g., Alabama, California, Illinois, Minnesota, and Oregon.

315. See table 12.6, col. 3.

316. See table 12.6, col. 4.

317. See table 12.6, col. 7.

318. Studies have shown that when the court appoints the expert, the court agrees with the expert in 93% of the cases. Steadman, Keitner, Braff, & Arvanites, *supra* note 190.

319. See in this chapter notes 103-14 and accompanying text on self-incrimination *supra* and § IV, Sentencing the Mentally Disabled Convicted Offender, *infra* for detailed consideration of how disclosures by the defendant in court-ordered examinations can be used against him by the court or the jury.

fense or the incompetency to stand trial issue is raised.[320] Many statutes provide that statements made by the defendant during the evaluation are admissible only on the issue of his mental state and not on the matter of his guilt or innocence.[321] Even in states without such laws, most forensic examiners feel compelled to warn defendants of the purposes of the evaluation and of how their statements may be used by the court.[322] The defendant's privilege against self-incrimination is thus protected either by a statute limiting the use of the examination or by the practice of examiners' warnings.

2. At Trial

In 49 jurisdictions the only issue at trial, once the insanity defense is raised, is proving or disproving the defendant's criminal responsibility. In the 2 states that permit a combined plea of not guilty and insanity, the act must first be proven before the sanity issue is considered.[323] As has been pointed out, the insanity defense is rarely raised and even more rarely successful.[324] A study conducted in 1978 estimated that out of more than two million felony and misdemeanor cases disposed of in the state and federal courts that year, only 1,600 defendants were institutionalized as a result of successful insanity pleas.[325] Studies indicate that between 10% and 25% of defendants who raise the defense are successful,[326] with the primary predictor of success being the pretrial evaluator's assessment that the person was psychotic at the time of the crime.[327]

(a) Burden and standard of proof □ □ The uniform rule in all jurisdictions is that a defendant is presumed sane until he places his sanity in issue. At that point the defendant assumes the burden of showing a reasonable basis for raising the insanity defense. Once that burden is met, there is a split in the jurisdictions as to who bears the burden of proof and what standard is to be used.[328] In approximately half the states, the prosecution has the burden of proving beyond a reasonable doubt that the defendant was sane. The remainder of the jurisdictions and all federal courts place on the defendant the burden of proving by a preponderance of the evidence that he was insane.[329]

Proposals have been made to shift the burden to the defendant in those instances where insanity and mens rea can be separately identified, with the defendant bearing the burden as to the first issue and the prosecution continuing to have the burden of proving all elements of the crime, including the defendant's criminal intent.[330] The shifting of the burden of proof for insanity has generated controversy, and the constitutionality of doing so is unclear, given the seemingly contradictory decisions of the United States Supreme Court.[331]

Some commentators[332] have suggested that the ruling case is the 1975 decision, *Mullaney v. Wilbur*,[333] which addressed a Maine statute that placed on the defendant the burden of proving by a preponderance of evidence that he was guilty of manslaughter, rather than murder, because he committed the act "in the heat of passion on

320. See table 12.6, col. 8.

321. *Id.*

322. See Sadoff, *supra* note 114, at 25; Rappeport, Differences Between Forensic and General Psychiatry, 139 Am. J. Psychiatry 331 (1982).

323. Louisiana and Maine.

324. See note 188 and accompanying text *supra* in this chapter.

325. Steadman, Monahan, Hartstone, Davis, & Robbins, *supra* note 2, at 33. While not every defendant acquitted by reason of insanity is hospitalized, the vast majority are, and so these figures are at least roughly indicative of the total number of pleas that succeed. This same study found that there were 3,140 people institutionalized as a result of being found NGRI: this reflects the total institutionalized NGRI population, while the 1,600 figure represents those acquitted in a given year.

326. Steadman, Keitner, Braff, & Arvanites, *supra* note 190, at 403, which estimates that 25% of those who raise the insanity defense are successful. Criss & Racine, *supra* note 188, finds that 10% of those who raise the issue in Michigan are successful. Only a small number of states keep statistics on the issue, and comparable statistics are rarer. An informal poll conducted by the author in court clinics in Baltimore, Chicago, Cleveland, Michigan, and Oregon indicates that the clinics recommend the person is not criminally responsible in 10% to 25% of the cases they evaluate for this purpose.

327. See, e.g., Steadman, Keitner, Braff, & Arvanites, *supra* note 190, at 402; Petrilia, *supra* note 188, at 93.

328. See table 12.6, cols. 9-13.

329. The burden was on the prosecution in all federal courts until the law was changed in November 1984.

330. See Criminal Justice Mental Health Standards, *supra* note 112, § 7-6.9.

331. See Davis v. United States, 160 U.S. 469 (1895); Leland v. Oregon, 343 U.S. 790 (1952); and Mullaney v. Wilbur, 421 U.S. 684 (1975).

In *Davis* the Court held that "the burden of proof . . . is never upon the accused to establish his innocence or to disprove the facts necessary to establish the crime for which he is indicted"; rather, "[i]t is on the prosecution from the beginning to the end of the trial and applies to every element necessary to constitute the crime." The Court explained that "his guilt cannot be said to have been proved beyond a reasonable doubt—his will and his acts . . . charged—if the jury, upon all the evidence, have a reasonable doubt whether he was legally capable of committing a crime, or (which is the same thing) whether he willfully, deliberately, unlawfully, and of malice aforethought took the life of the deceased." 160 U.S. at 487, 488. Yet in *Leland* the Court upheld an Oregon statute requiring the prosecution to prove every element of the crime beyond a reasonable doubt while at the same time placing on the defendant the burden of establishing his insanity beyond a reasonable doubt. 343 U.S. at 799. The apparent conflict between the two decisions is reconcilable since the Oregon law clearly delineated between the elements of the crime and the issue of insanity. Varga, Due Process and the Insanity Defense: Examining Shifts in the Burden of Persuasion, 53 Notre Dame Law. 123, 128 (1977). In *Leland* the jury was given clear instructions that the prosecution had to prove both the physical act and the required mental state, and then once that was proven the defendant was required to prove his insanity. In *Leland* the insanity defense was viewed as having no significant relationship to the elements of the crime, while in *Davis* the insanity defense went directly to the issue of whether the defendant could form the required mental state.

Leland appears to be aberrational, since in other cases, in addition to *Davis*, the Court has required proof beyond a reasonable doubt.

332. See Eule, The Presumption of Sanity: Bursting the Bubble, 25 U.C.L.A. L. Rev. 637, 677 (1978), which provides a comprehensive examination of the burden of proof in insanity defense cases and a good historical overview of the development of the burden of pursuasion; Note Constitutional Limitations on Allocating the Burden of Proof of Insanity to the Defendant in Murder Cases, 56 Boston U.L. Rev. 499, 500 (1976).

333. 421 U.S. 684 (1975).

sudden provocation." The Court held that "the Due Process Clause requires the prosecution to prove beyond a reasonable doubt the absence of the heat of passion on sudden provocation when the issue is properly presented in a homicide case."[334]

Commentators who believe the insanity defense is constitutionally mandated but who share dissatisfaction with its present form have suggested that shifting the burden of proof to the defendant to prove—typically by a preponderance of the evidence—that he was insane would resolve many of the complaints against the defense. They have argued that for the prosecution to have to prove beyond a reasonable doubt that the defendant was sane is too difficult a burden, especially when there is a conflict in psychiatric testimony and the judge or jury thus almost inevitably will have more than minor doubts about the defendant's mental state.[335] Recent proposals in jurisdictions following the ALI standard for insanity have been accompanied by the argument that switching the burden to the defendant in ALI jurisdictions can be justified as the "*quid pro quo* for the greater latitude implicit" when the volitional element is included as part of the insanity defense.[336] Correlatively, this shift of the burden would not apply in those jurisdictions using a narrower insanity defense standard.

Accordingly, the American Bar Association's Criminal Justice Mental Health Standards committee has recommended a burden-shifting procedure in the following situations:

> (b) Once evidence of insanity has been introduced at trial, the burden of persuasion should be allocated as follows:
>
> (i) in jurisdictions utilizing any test for insanity which focuses solely on whether the defendant, as a result of mental disease or was unable to know, understand or appreciate the wrongfulness of his or her conduct at the time of the offense charged, the prosecution should have the burden of disproving the defendant's claim of insanity beyond a reasonable doubt;
>
> (ii) in jurisdictions utilizing the ALI-Model Penal Code test for insanity, the defendant should have the burden of proving the claim of insanity by a preponderance of the evidence.
>
> (c) Nothing contained in paragraph (b) above relieves the prosecution of its burden of proving beyond a reasonable doubt all elements of the offense charged including the mental state required for the offense charged.[337]

Two justifications exist for shifting the burden in ALI jurisdictions in particular: (1) mistakes are more likely to be made in the administration of the insanity defense in jurisdictions using the volitional element of the ALI test, and (2) since this risk of mistake is greatly reduced when only a cognitive test is employed, the risk of error should be upon the prosecution.[338]

The ABA proposal has been adopted by a few states,[339] and others may follow. However, because it is apparently only in the exceptional case that the burden of proof is a critical factor,[340] a shift in the burden will probably not reduce substantially the number of successful insanity pleas.

(b) The role of the expert witness □□ Some of the debate over the insanity defense has centered on the role of the expert witness. One issue is whether the defendant is entitled to a psychiatric evaluation when the insanity defense is raised. Questions have been raised about the ability of anyone, no matter how well trained or experienced professionally, to know what the state of mind of the defendant was at the time of the crime. This has led to calls for limiting the testimony and general contribution of the psychiatric expert to the dispositional phase of the hearing.[341]

334. *Id.* at 704 (1975). The argument that *Mullaney* overturned *Leland* is buttressed by the Court's decision in *In re Winship*, relating to juvenile proceedings, where the Court said:

> Lest there remain any doubt about the constitutional stature of the reasonable-doubt standard, we explicitly hold that the Due Process Clause protects the accused against conviction except upon proof beyond a reasonable doubt of every fact necessary to constitute the crime with which he is charged.

397 U.S. 358, 364 (1970).

335. See, e.g., Bonnie, *supra* note 296, at 196; also Criminal Justice Mental Health Standards, *supra* note 112, § 7-6.9 & commentary. Support for such a change was fueled by jurors in the Hinckley case, who, following their rendering of a NGRI verdict as to the attempted assassination of President Reagan, testified before the United States Senate Judiciary Committee. They reported that they had been left confused by the conflicting expert testimony in the case as well as by the jury instructions and that because of the reasonable doubt standard they felt they had no alternative but to acquit the defendant. See Senate Subcomm. Hearings on Limiting the Insanity Defense, *supra* note 186, at 60–155, which includes the comments of jurors.

336. Criminal JusticeMental Health Standards, *supra* note 112, § 7-6.9 commentary at 293.

337. *Id.* The commentary accompanying this proposal suggested that the Supreme Court's decision in Davis v. United States, 160 U.S. 469 (1895), was only supervisory and thus does prohibit a shift in the burden of persuasion. Additionally, it was their view that the Court's decision in Leland v. Oregon, 343 U.S. 790 (1952), which upheld the defendant's carrying the burden of persuasion in an insanity defense case, was a sufficient basis for believing this was a constitutionally permissible approach.

338. Criminal Justice Mental Health Standards, *supra* note 112, at 293.

339. E.g., Ill. Ann. Stat. ch. 38, § 3-2 (Smith-Hurd Supp. 1983–84), which went into effect Jan. 1, 1984; Vt. Stat. Ann. tit. 13, § 4801(b) (Supp. 1983); Wyo. Stat. 7-11-305(b) (1977 & Supp. 1984).

340. There are no empirical studies or data showing that a person is more or less likely to be acquitted by reasons of insanity in those states where he bears the burden as compared with states where the burden is on the prosecution.

341. See, e.g., Bartholomew & Milte, The Reliability and Validity of Psychiatric Diagnoses in Courts of Law, 50 Australia L.J. 450 (1976); Diamond, Criminal Responsibility of the Mentally Ill, 14 Stan. L. Rev. 59 (1967); *id.*, The Psychiatrist as Advocate, 1 J. Psychiatry & L. 18 (1973); Ennis & Litwack, Psychiatry and the Presumption of Expertise: Flipping Coins in the Courtroom, 62 Calif. L. Rev. 693 (1974); Halpern, The Fiction of Legal Insanity and the Misuse of Psychiatry, 2 J. Legal Medicine 19 (1980); Menninger, *supra* note 243; Morse, Crazy Behavior, Morals, and Science: An Analysis of

In 1985, the United States Supreme Court in *Ake v. Oklahoma*[342] decisively recognized that under certain circumstances a defendant has an absolute right to a psychiatric evaluation when the insanity defense *is* being raised. The Court held that

> when a defendant has made a preliminary showing that his sanity at the time of the offense is likely to be a significant factor at trial, the Constitution requires that a State provide access to a psychiatrist's assistance on this issue, if the defendant cannot otherwise afford one.[343]

The Court was presented with the case of George Ake who was charged with first degree murder and shooting with intent to kill. At his arraignment, the trial court found his behavior so bizarre that a psychiatric evaluation was ordered to determine his competency to stand trial. He was found to be incompetent and committed to a state hospital. Six weeks later he was found by a state psychiatrist to be competent as long as he remained on his medication.[344] At the pretrial conference Ake's attorney indicated that the insanity defense would be raised, and he requested a psychiatric evaluation at the state's expense because Ake was indigent. The trial court denied his motion, and its decision was affirmed by the Oklahoma Court of Criminal Appeals.[345] At the trial on the issue of guilt, Ake's only defense was insanity. There were no expert witnesses on either side to testify as to Ake's behavior at the time of the killings. He was found guilty by the jury. At the sentencing proceeding the state asked for the death penalty. The prosecution established future dangerousness by relying on the testimony of the state psychiatrist who during the guilt determination phase of the trial had testified that Ake was a danger to society.[346] Ake had no expert witnesses to rebut this testimony or to introduce mitigating evidence. The jury sentenced Ake to death.

Writing for the majority, Justice Marshall concluded that "the governmental interest in denying Ake the assistance of a psychiatrist is not substantial, in light of the compelling interest of both the State and the individual in accurate dispositions." The Court pointed out that in circumstances where the defendant's mental condition is critical to the issue of criminal culpability "the assistance of a psychiatrist may well be crucial to the defendant's ability to marshal his defense. It rejected the state's assertion that it would be extraordinarily burdened if it had to provide Ake and all other defendants in his situation with psychiatric assistance, pointing out that at least 40 states as well as the federal government had already recognized the right of a defendant to a competent psychiatric evaluation.[347]

The Court found that the foregoing led inexorably to the following conclusion:

> [W]ithout the assistance of a psychiatrist to conduct a professional examination on issues relevant to the defense, to help determine whether the insanity defense is viable, to present testimony, and to assist in preparing the cross-examination of a State's psychiatric witnesses, the risk of an inaccurate resolution of sanity issues is extremely high. With such assistance, the defendant is

Mental Health Law, 51 S. Cal. L. Rev. 527 (1978); J. Ziskin, Coping with Psychiatric and Psychological Testimony (3d ed. 1981).

Dr. Bernard Diamond has been one of the leading critics of the role of the psychiatrist in the courtroom. Other psychiatrists too have criticized their role in the courtroom: they have cited the harm done to their profession by its involvement in highly publicized cases, particularly when psychiatric opinion is divided, suggesting that psychiatry is an unrefined, even primitive, discipline without scientific or intellectual rigor, and some have argued that courtroom appearances degrade the profession and that testimony in insanity defense cases constitutes an improper use of psychiatric knowledge. In addition to Diamond's articles cited *supra*, see Szasz, *supra* note 243; Watson, On the Preparation and Use of Psychiatric Expert Testimony: Some Suggestions in an Ongoing Controversy, 6 A.A.P.L. Bull. 226 (1978); Wettstein, In Search of a Verdict, Illinois Psychiatric Examiner 2 (1982).

342. 105 S. Ct. 1087 (1985). In an 8-to-1 opinion the Court reversed the Oklahoma Court of Criminal Appeals for not granting the defendant access to a psychiatric evaluation.

343. *Id.* at 1092.

344. *Id.* at 1091. The psychiatrist stated that Ake would need to continue receiving 200 milligrams of Thorazine, an antipsychotic medication, three times a day if he were to remain competent for trial.

345. *Id.* The motion was denied, based on United States *ex rel.* Smith v. Baldi, 344 U.S.. 561 (1953). The Supreme Court rejected *Smith* as a basis for not providing a psychiatric examination, emphasizing that since its 1953 decision there had been an "increased commitment to assuring meaningful access to the judicial process." 105 S. Ct. at 1098.

346. 105 S. Ct. at 1092.

347. *Id.* at 1095. The Court pointed out that in 18 U.S.C. § 3006A, the Criminal Justice Act, the federal government provides that individual defendants shall receive the assistance of all experts necessary for an adequate defense. In a note the Court set forth those states that also provided for access to a psychiatric expert:

> See Ala. Code § 15-12-21 (Supp. 1984); Alaska Stat. Ann. § 18.85.100 (1981); Ariz. Rev. Stat. Ann. § 13-4013 (1978) (capital cases; extended to noncapital cases in *State v. Peeler,* 126 Ariz. 254, 614 P.2d 335 (App. 1980)); Ark. Stat. Ann. § 17-456 (Supp. 1983); Cal. Penal Code Ann. § 987.9 (West Supp. 1984) (capital cases, right recognized in all cases in *People v. Worthy,* 109 Cal. App. 3d 514, 167 Cal. Rptr. 402 (1980)); Colo. Rev. Stat. § 18-1-403 (Supp. 1984); *State v. Clemons,* 168 Conn. 395, 363 A.2d 33 (1975); Del. Code Ann. Tit. 29 § 4603 (1983); Fla. Rule Crim. Proc. 3.216; Haw. Rev. Stat. §802-7 (Supp. 1983); *State v. Olin,* 103 Idaho 391, 648 P.2d 203 (1982); *People v. Watson,* 36 Ill. 2d 228, 221 N.E. 2d 645 (1966); *Owen v. State,* 272 Ind. 122, 396 N.E.2d 376 (1979) (trial judge may authorize or appoint experts where necessary); Iowa Rule Crim. Proc. 19; Kan. Stat. Ann.§ 22-4508 (Supp. 1983); Ky. Rev. Stat. §§ 31.070, 31.110, 31.185 (1980); *State v. Madison,* 345 So.2d 485 (La. 1977); *State v. Anaya,* 456 A.2d 1255 (Me. 1983); Mass. Gen. Laws Ann., ch. 621, § 27C(4) (West Supp. 1984–1985); Mich. Comp. Laws Ann. § 768.20a(3) (Supp. 1983); Minn. Stat. § 611.21 (1982); Miss. Code Ann. § 99-15-17 (Supp. 1983); Mont.Code Ann. § 46-8-201 (1983); *State v. Suggett,* 200 Neb. 693, 264 N.W.2d 876 (1978) (discretion to appoint psychiatrist rests with trial court); Nev. Rev. Stat. § 7.135 (1983); N.H. Rev. Stat. Ann. § 604-A:6 (Supp. 1983); N.M. Stat. Ann. §§ 31-16-2, 31-16-8 (1984); N.Y.County Law § 772-c (McKinney Supp. 1984-1985); N.C. Gen. Stat. § 7A-454 (1981); Ohio Rev. Code Ann. § 2941.51 (Supp. 1983); Ore. Rev. Stat. § 135.055(4) (1983); *Commonwealth v. Gelormo,* — — — Pa. Super. — — —, — — —, and n.5, 475 A.2d 765, 769, and n.5 (1984); R.I. Gen. Laws § 9-17-19 (Supp. 184); S.C. Code §17-3-80 (Supp. 1983); S.D. Codified Laws § 23A-40-8 (Supp. 1984); Tenn. Code Ann. § 40-14-207 (Supp. 1984); Tex. Code Crim. Proc. Ann., Art. § 26.05 (Vernon Supp. 1984); Utah Code Ann. § 77-32-1 (1982); Wash. Rev. Code §§ 10.77.020, 10.77.060 (1983) (*see also State v. Cuningham,* 18 Wash. App. 517, 569 P.2d 1211 (1977); W. Va. Code § 29-21-14(e)(3) (Supp. 1984); Wyo. Stat. §§ 7-1-108; 7-1-110; 7-1-116 (1977).

Id. at 1094–95.

> fairly able to present at least enough information to the jury, in a meaningful manner, as to permit it to make a sensible determination.[348]

The Court observed that since the defendant's mental condition would not be an issue in every criminal proceeding, psychiatric assistance would be limited to those cases "[w]hen the defendant is able to make an ex parte threshold showing to the trial court that his sanity is likely to be a significant factor in his defense." Although the Court recognized that the psychiatrist must be competent to "assist in evaluation, preparation, and presentation of the defense," there is nothing in the opinion which suggests that there is a "constitutional right to choose a psychicatrist"[349] or that the defendant is entitled to more than one evaluation, until he finds a psychiatrist who will render an opinion favorable to him. The Court clearly limits the defendant to one competent psychiatrist.

The Court then addressed Ake's right to a psychiatrist for the sentencing phase of the hearing, when future dangerousness was at issue. It concluded that for this purpose as well Ake would be entitled to a psychiatric evaluation.

Although not specifically decided, the notion that the right to a psychiatric evaluation arises in all criminal cases in which the mental state of the defendant is a significant element is indirectly supported by the *Ake* case. It can be inferred not only from the broad wording of the majority opinion but also from the fact that Chief Justice Burger in his concurrence and Justice Rehnquist in his dissent discussed limiting this right to capital cases.[350] For all intents and purposes then, the *Ake* decision ends the debate about whether mental health professionals have a role in insanity defense hearings.

The debate, however, may shift to subsidiary questions. Some commentators have suggested that if psychiatrists and psychologists are to continue to participate in criminal trials,[351] they should be permitted only to testify about behavior they observe rather than venture suppositions about the past or the future.[352] The ABA, in its Criminal Justice Mental Health Standards, has suggested that the mental health expert be prohibited from offering opinions on the ultimate legal issue in the case.[353] This position was adopted by the Congress in amending Federal Rules of Evidence to prohibit the expert witness from testifying his opinion on "whether the defendant did or did not have the mental state or condition constituting an element of the crime charged or of a defense thereto."[354] The rationale behind this restriction is that whatever test of insanity is used, the basic inquiry is not a scientific or clinical assessment but rather a moral and social judgment about the defendant's actions, measured by the community's sense of justice and ethics and balanced by the need to exert social control.[355]

A number of forensic psychiatrists have discussed steps to improve the quality of their evaluations and to bring the maximum amount of relevant data to bear on the legal questions at issue.[356] Others have emphasized such simple and straightforward changes as better courtroom preparation and more candor about the limitations of their expertise.[357]

(c) Raising the insanity defense over the defendant's objection □□ There will be times when an insanity defense will appear indicated or advantageous to everyone involved but the defendant. Reasons the defendant may not want to raise the defense include: (1) fear that an insanity acquittal will result in commitment to a mental hospital for a longer period than if he were imprisoned, (2) objection to the quality of treatment and type of confinement he may be subject to in a mental institution, (3) the desire to avoid the stigma of being labeled "insane," (4) the desire to avoid the collateral consequences of being found insane, which may result in loss of the right to obtain a driver's license and may affect other legal rights, and (5) denigration of what the defendant views as a political or religious act.[358]

A number of courts have been forced to address the question of whether a defendant with indications of mental difficulties may forego the defense, typically in cases where the issue of competency to stand trial has been raised and resolved in favor of competency or

348. 105 S. Ct. at 1096.

349. *Id.* at 1097. The Court limits its holding to a competent psychiatrist and does not provide for a psychiatrist of the defendant's choice.

350. *Id.* at 1099.

351. See Ennis & Litwack, *supra* note 341; Ziskin, *supra* note 341.

352. See Morse, *supra* note 341.

353. See Criminal Justice Mental Health Standards, *supra* note 112, § 7-6.6, which provides:

> Expert opinion testimony as to how the development, adaptation and functioning of the defendant's mental processes may have influenced his conduct at the time of the offense charged should be admissible. Opinion testimony, whether expert or lay, as to whether or not the defendant was criminally responsible at the time of the offense charged should not be admissible.

354. Fed. R. Evid. 704(b), which was amended as part of the Comprehensive Crime Control Act of 1984, Pub. L. No. 98-473, § 406, 98 Stat. 1837, 2068.

355. Holloway v. United States, 148 F.2d 665, 666 (D.C. Cir. 1945). This limitation is not opposed by the American Psychiatric Association; see A.P.A. Statement, *supra* note 296, at 686.

356. Rogers, Wasyliw, & Cavanaugh, Evaluating Insanity: A Study of Construct Validity, 8 Law & Hum. Behav. 293 (1984); Rogers, Dolmetsch, & Cavanaugh, An Empirical Approach to Insanity Evaluations, 37 J. Clinical Psychology 683 (1981).

357. Bonnie & Slobogin, The Role of Mental Health Professionals in the Criminal Process: The Case for Informed Speculation, 66 Va. L. Rev. 427 (1980).

358. See Frendak v. United States, 408 A.2d 364, 376-77 (D.C. 1979).

where the defendant has been restored to competency.[359] In 1965 in *Whalem v. United States*, the leading case, the United States Court of Appeals for the District of Columbia held that a defendant "may, if he wishes, refuse to raise the issue of insanity, but he may not, in a proper case, prevent the court from injecting it."[360] The court reasoned that the trial judge must refuse "to allow the conviction of an obviously mentally irresponsible defendant, and when there is sufficient question as to a defendant's mental responsibility at the time of the crime, that issue must become part of the case."[361]

The problem under *Whalem* is determining when the trial judge should sua sponte raise the insanity defense. In 1977 in *United States v. Robertson*[362] the federal district court set out a number of factors to consider:

> the quality of the evidence supporting the insanity defense; the defendant's wish in the matter; the quality of defendant's decision not to raise the defense; the reasonableness of defendant's motives in opposing presentation of the defense; and the Court's personal observations of the defendant throughout the course of the proceedings against him.[363]

Some have argued that a determination of competency to stand trial is sufficient to require the court to honor the defendant's desire not to raise the insanity defense.[364] In rejecting this argument, and at the same time modifying *Whalem*, in 1979 the District of Columbia Court of Appeals said in *Frendak v. United States*:[365]

> We hold that the trial judge may not force an insanity defense on a defendant found competent to stand trial *if* the individual intelligently and voluntarily decides to forego that defense. In reaching this result, however, we further hold that the court's finding of competency to stand trial is not, in itself, sufficient to show that the defendant is capable of rejecting an insanity defense; the trial judge must make further inquiry into whether the defendant made an intelligent and voluntary decision.[366]

(d) The insanity defense in juvenile proceedings ☐ ☐
The Supreme Court has not yet decided whether the insanity defense can be asserted in juvenile proceedings, but a series of rulings it has delivered assuring juveniles most of the same rights adults have in criminal trials[367] suggest that possibility.

In the first state case addressing the issue, the Supreme Court of Wisconsin concluded that the concept of criminal responsibility was relevant to juvenile proceedings,[368] and a number of other state courts have ruled similarly since.[369] In contrast, the District of Columbia Court of Appeals has rejected the right to interpose the insanity defense in juvenile delinquency proceedings, holding that due process and equal protection are not violated because juvenile proceedings are essentially fact-finding proceedings and do not determine criminal responsibility.[370] The purpose of a juvenile hearing, the court said, is "to determine the treatment required to rehabilitate" the youngster, as to which the inquiry mandated by the insanity defense would be superfluous. The court did assert, however, that it is "an indispensable element of fundamental fairness that a mentally ill child offender be accorded the same opportunity for psychiatric treatment and ultimate release as a similarly situated adult."[371]

Questions about the use of the insanity defense in juvenile proceedings require an inquiry into the broader purposes of juvenile justice. Mounting evidence that the system is failing to meet its primary goal of rehabilitation[372] and realization that a finding of "delinquency"

359. See, e.g., Bruning, The Right of the Defendant to Refuse an Insanity Plea, A.A.P.L. Bull. 238 (1975); Whalem v. United States 346 F.2d 812 (D.C. Cir. 1965); United States v. Ashe, 427 F.2d 626 (D.C. Cir. 1970); United States v. David, 511 F.2d 355 (D.C. Cir. 1975); United States v. Robertson, 430 F. Supp. 444 (D.D.C. 1977); Frendak v. United States, 408 A.2d 364 (D.C. 1979); State v. Khan, 417 A.3d 585 (N.J. Super. Ct. App.Div. 1980).

360. 346 F.2d 812, 818 (D.C. Cir. 1965).

361. *Id.*

362. 430 F. Supp. 444 (D.D.C. 1977).

363. *Id.* at 446.

364. See cases cited in note 359 *supra.*

365. 408 A.2d 364 (D.C. 1979).

366. *Id.* at 367 (emphasis in original).

In a 1980 New Jersey case, a defendant charged with a homicide wanted to invoke a claim of self-defense as the motive for his killing another man, while the psychiatrists believed that the crime resulted from a paranoid delusional system. The court suggested that a bifurcated trial be held, with the issue of sanity tried first. If the defendant was found insane, that verdict would end the case. If he was not, the jury would then address his self-defense argument. State v. Khan, 417 A.2d 585, 592 (N.J. Super. Ct. App. Div. 1980).

367. This line of rulings began with a holding that a child had a right to an attorney when a decision was being made as to whether he would be tried as a juvenile or an adult. Kent v. United States, 383 U.S. 541 (1966). In *In re Gault*, 387 U.S. 1 (1967), the Court extended to juvenile proceedings the minimal due process rights afforded to adults, including the right to notice of the charges, right to counsel, right to confront and cross-examine witnesses, and the privilege against self-incrimination. The landmark *Gault* decision also paved the way for the decision that the beyond a reasonable doubt standard applies in juvenile proceedings (*In re* Winship, 397 U.S. 358 (1970)) and for the decision that the double jeopardy clause of the Constitution likewise applies (Breed v. Jones, 421 U.S. 519 (1975), which reaffirmed *Gault* in recognizing that juvenile proceedings were considered criminal in nature since they could result in deprivation of liberty).

368. *In re* Winburn, 145 N.W.2d 178, 184 (Wis. 1966).

369. See, e.g., State *in re* R.G.W., 342 A.2d 869 (N.J. Super Ct. App. Div. 1975), *aff'd*, 358 A.2d 473 (N.J. 1976); State *ex rel.* Causey, 363 So. 2d 472 (La. 1978); People v. Superior Ct., Humboldt County, 95 Cal. App. 3d 380, 157 Cal. Rptr. 157 (1979); *In re* Two Minor Children, 592 P.2d 166 (Nev. 1979).

370. *In re* C.W.M., 407 A.2d 617, 622 (D.C. 1979).

371. *Id.* at 622–23.

372. See, Guggenheim, Abolishing the Juvenile Justice System, 15 Trial 22 (1977); Paulsen, The Problems of Juvenile Courts and the Rights of Children (1975); Shepherd, Challenging the Rehabilitative Justification for Indeterminate Sentencing in the Juvenile Justice System: The Right to Punishment, 21 St. Louis U.L.J. 12 (1977).

seriously stigmatizes the juvenile and often results in a loss of liberty[373] create a strong argument for allowing the insanity defense into juvenile delinquency proceedings.[374]

E. Disposition of the Persons Found Not Guilty by Reason of Insanity (NGRI)

1. Introduction

In the past, the finding of not guilty by reason of insanity (NGRI) usually resulted in long-term, if not permanent, confinement of the defendant in an isolated state hospital for the criminally insane, where the general conditions might well be as bad as those in prison and with treatment no more forthcoming.[375] Such a disposition would satisfy the more immediate public interests, as represented by the prosecution.

The advent of psychotropic medication radically changed methods for treatment for the mentally ill[376] and made it possible to return many of the institutionalized mentally ill to the community.[377] The least restrictive alternative doctrine[378] and other reforms of the mental health movement, embraced by both courts and legislatures with respect to civil commitment, have been argued to be equally relevant to mentally ill offenders, including those found incompetent to stand trial,[379] those committed or transferred after prison terms,[380] and those found not guilty by reason of insanity.[381] Some commentators have concluded that the United States Supreme Court decision in *Jackson v. Indiana* (1972),[382] which held impermissible the differential treatment in the commitment of those incompetent to stand trial as compared with those committed under a civil standard, should be extended to those found not guilty by reason of insanity.[383] The successful assertion of this theory in a couple of court cases resulted in the release of insanity acquittees to the community at the discretion of a hospital administrator.[384] However, a 1983 decision by the United States Supreme Court in *Jones v. United States*[385] struck down this line of reasoning by permitting insanity acquittees to be treated differently from all other persons with respect to civil commitment, although not without dissent. Debate on this issue continues.

Today, the laws relating to the disposition of the insanity acquittee are in a state of flux. In a few states, there are no special provisions for the disposition of the insanity acquitee;[386] in others, the law governs all dispositional alternatives.[387] At the completion of the previous edition of this book, when insanity acquittees still tended to be hospitalized for long periods, there was little public concern with their release. Today, however, with earlier releases and reports in the media of a number of sensational instances of ill-advised release, the public demands assurance that the insanity acquittee who is discharged will at least receive continued treatment and supervision under court order. In the legal community, also, there appears to be a growing consensus that stricter standards are necessary for the disposition of the insanity acquittee. A number of states and the United States Congress are now considering new procedures[388] in three areas: the commitment criteria, the discharge process, and mandatory outpatient treatment. Some working model programs instituting these changes will provide a base for assessment and further development.

2. The Commitment Standard

State statutes dealing with the disposition of persons acquitted by reason of insanity are of four basic types.

373. See *In re* Gault, 387 U.S. 1 (1967); also *In re* Winship, 397 U.S. 358 (1970).

374. Harrington & Keary, The Insanity Defense in Juvenile Delinquency Proceedings, 8 A.A.P.L. Bull. 272 (1980).

375. See E. Goffman, Asylums: Essays on the Social Situation of Mental Patients and Other Inmates (1961), a classic account of the plight of the mental patient in a large state institution.

376. Goodwin & Guze, *supra* note 85. Anderson & Kuehnle, Strategies for the Treatment of Acute Psychosis, 229 J. A.M.A. 1884 (1975); L. Grinspoon, J. Ewalt, & R.R. Shader, Schizophrenia—Pharmacotherapy and Psychotherapy (1972).

377. Bassuk & Gerson, Deinstitutionalization and Mental Health Services, 238 Sci. Am., Feb. 1978, at 46-53; Etzioni, No Place to Go, Washington Monthly, Dec. 1976, at 42.

378. See, e.g., Lake v. Cameron, 364 F.2d 657 (D.C. Cir. 1966)., *cert. denied*, 382 U.S. 863 (1965); Welsch v. Likins, 373 F. Supp. 487 (D. Minn. 1974); Lessard v. Schmidt, 349 F. Supp. 1078 (E.D. Wis. 1972), *vacated and remanded on other grounds*, 414 U.S. 473 (1974); Dixon v. Attorney Gen., 325 F. Supp. 966 (M.D. Pa. 1971). Also see in this book ch. 5, Rights of Institutionalized Persons, § VII, Least Restrictive Alternative.

379. Jackson v. Indiana, 406 U.S. 715 (1972).

380. Baxstrom v. Herold, 383 U.S. 107 (1966).

381. United States v. Ecker, 543 F.2d 178 (D.C. Cir. 1976); Bolton v. Harris, 395 F.2d 642 (D.C. Cir. 1968).

382. 406 U.S. 715 (1972).

383. See German & Singer, Punishing the Not Guilty: Hospitalization of Persons Acquitted by Reason of Insanity, 29 Rutgers L. Rev. 1011 (1976); Powell v. Florida, 579 F.2d 324 (5th Cir. 1978); Benham v. Edwards, 678 F.2d 511 (5th Cir. 1982).

384. At that time many states provided that upon civil commitment the insanity acquittee should be treated the same as other mental patients. See, e.g., Ill. Ann. Stat. ch. 38, § 1005-2-4 (Smith-Hurd 1977 & Supp. 1983-84); also table 12.7, col. 9.

385. 103 S. Ct. 3043 (1983).

386. See, e.g., Idaho; also those states that move for regular civil commitment in table 12.7, cols. 1 & 2, and ch. 2, Involuntary Institutionalization, *supra*.

387. See table 12.7 and the laws of Illinois, Maryland, and Oregon.

388. See Senate Subcomm. Hearings on Limiting the Insanity Defense, *supra* note 186, and Senate Judiciary Comm. Hearings on the Insanity Defense, *supra* note 302. These hearings resulted in changes in the insanity defense in federal cases codified in the Comprehensive Crime Control Act of 1984, Pub. L. No. 98-473, 98 Stat. 1837. In addition, 12 states adopted guilty-but-mentally-ill laws as of December 1984 or made other modifications. As of June 1984 the reverberations of the *Hinckley* case were still being felt with various legislatures still considering changes in the insanity defense.

The first approach, formerly followed by the federal courts, has no special provisions: the insanity acquittee is treated like any other defendant found not guilty, and the court has no hold on him.[389] The second type provides for automatic commitment of the acquittee for a period of evaluation to determine if he is a candidate for civil commitment, followed by a hearing to determine need for continued hospitalization.[390] The third provides for automatic commitment, with no set procedure or date for determining the need for continued hospitalization.[391] The fourth type provides for a hearing immediately after the verdict in which commitment must be predicated on an affirmative finding that the acquittee is mentally ill and/or dangerous.[392]

The statutes vary in their approach to the duration of commitment. In most states, to be discharged the acquittee must be found by hospital doctors or by the court to be no longer in need of mental treatment or no longer dangerous.[393] In some states the acquittee is to be released when he no longer meets the civil commitment criteria.[394] A number of states specify that the person cannot be held longer than the period for which he could be imprisoned had he been convicted and received the maximum sentence for the crime of which he was accused.[395] If he is to be retained after that, it must be through regular civil commitment. Some states set limits on the amount of time the acquittee can be subject to court-supervised outpatient care.[396]

In a few states where commitment of a person acquitted by reason of insanity is mandatory, the commitment is indeterminate and is based on information gathered at the criminal trial, with no separate evidence or further hearing required. In other states, the automatic commitment is only for an evaluation period, usually lasting from 30 to 90 days, to be followed by a full commitment hearing.[397]

Usually the rules governing life within the mental hospital are set by the state mental health agency,[398] but states with separate criminal commitment procedures often have statutory provisions that place special restrictions on the insanity acquittee and on the hospital's power to grant him certain measures of freedom. In some states, prior court approval is required for conditional departures from the hospital, such as off-grounds passes or home visits.[399] The acquittee may be required to be hospitalized in a specific institution, typically the mental health agency's maximum security facility.[400]

State and federal courts have diverged in their holdings regarding the constitutional propriety of these dispositional procedures, particularly on the matter of indefinite confinement of the insanity acquittee without the due process protections afforded to civil committees.[401]

Jones v. United States[402] presented to the Supreme Court for the first time the issue of what procedural and substantive rights an insanity acquittee is entitled to before being committed to a mental institution. In *Jones* the defendant pleaded not guilty by reason of insanity to stealing a jacket from a department store, a misdemeanor under the laws of the District of Columbia for which

389. Senate Subcomm. Hearings on the Insanity Defense, *supra* note 186. Effective October 1984, elaborate provisions were adopted by the Congress for insanity acquittees. See Comprehensive Crime Control Act of 1984, Pub. L. No. 98-473, 98 Stat. 1837. Also see Nevada, Pennsylvania, and South Carolina.

390. See table 12.7, cols. 1 & 2, e.g., Arizona, Connecticut, Georgia, Maryland, Massachusetts, Michigan, Nebraska, New York, Rhode Island, Tennessee, and West Virginia.

391. See table 12.7, col. 2, e.g., Colorado, District of Columbia, Kansas, Louisiana, Maine, and Missouri.

392. See *id.*, e.g., Iowa, Louisiana, South Dakota, Virginia, Washington, and Wyoming.

393. See table 12.7, col. 7; e.g., Alabama, Arizona, Colorado, Connecticut, Delaware, Iowa, Kansas, Louisiana, Maine, Minnesota, Montana, Nebraska, New York, and Oregon.

394. *Id.*, e.g., District of Columbia and Georgia.

395. See table 12.7, col. 16, e.g., Alaska, Connecticut, Illinois, Michigan, Oregon, Washington, and Wisconsin.

A few studies have looked at the length of hospitalization of insanity acquittees and have found that they are hospitalized much longer than persons who are civilly committed. But civil commitments today are very brief, averaging three to four weeks. Braff, Arvanites, & Steadman, in Detention Patterns of Successful and Unsuccessful Insanity Defendants, 21 Criminology 439 (1983), studied insanity acquittals in the Buffalo, N.Y., area between 1970 and 1980. The study showed that the average length of hospital stay for the insanity acquittee was 1,031 days, which contrasted with the average 1,253 days of imprisonment for the defendant who was unsuccessful in his insanity defense plea. In Illinois the average length of stay for a civilly committed mental patient was 20 days, while for a NGRI acquittee after being acquitted the average length of stay was 25.3 months in 1982, according to Daniel Cuneo, Director of Research, Chester Mental Health Center, Chester, Ill. See also Criss & Racine, *supra* note 188, at 262, which found 55.6% of the insanity acquittees were discharged after their 60-day diagnostic evaluation, while the remainder stayed for varying periods.

Studies have also found that the more serious the crime charged the longer the acquittee's hospitalization. See, e.g., Pasewark, *supra* note 190, at 378; Braff, Arvanites, & Steadman, *supra* at 445. A Maryland study looked at the length of hospitalization for insanity acquittees in several consecutive years and found it to vary from a low of 749 days in 1981 to a high of 961 days in 1982. See Testimony of Silver, *supra* note 190. In 1979 the average length of stay was 880 days, and in 1980 it was 912 days.

In Illinois in 1982 insanity acquittees were hospitalized for an average of 25.3 months until discharge. If the time spent hospitalized as a result of incompetency to stand trial were to be added to these totals, the average time spent hospitalized was 54.2 months. These Illinois statistics, which have not yet been published, were provided by Daniel Cuneo, of the Chester Mental Health Center, *supra*.

396. See table 12.7, col. 16, e.g., Arkansas, Hawaii, Illinois, Maryland, Michigan, and Wisconsin.

397. See table 12.7, col. 2.

398. See table 5.2 in ch. 5, Rights of Institutionalized Persons.

399. See, e.g., Conn. Gen. Stat. Ann. § 53a-47 (West 1972 & Supp. 1982); also Ill. Ann. Stat. ch. 38, § 1005-2-4(a) (Smith-Hurd 1977 & Supp. 1983-84).

400. See, e.g., Conn. Gen. Stat. Ann. § 53a-47 (West 1972 & Supp. 1982).

401. It has long been recognized that in the context of civil commitment the due process clause guarantees a right to notice of the proceedings, the right to cross-examination, a trial by jury, and periodic review. See ch. 2, Involuntary Institutionalization.

402. 103 S. Ct. 3043 (1983).

the maximum prison term was one year. He was acquitted by reason of insanity and automatically committed to St. Elizabeths hospital. At the required hearing held 50 days after his commitment, it was determined that Jones was still mentally ill. Another hearing on his need for continued hospitalization was held one year after the initial commitment. Because he had been institutionalized for a longer period than he could have been imprisoned, upon conviction, Jones demanded that he either be released or be recommitted pursuant to civil commitment procedures, which afford a jury trial and require proof by clear and convincing evidence of mental illness and dangerousness. He argued that at a minimum he could only be civilly committed pursuant to the clear and convincing evidence standard that is applicable in civil commitment proceedings in the District of Columbia and that had been accepted by the Supreme Court in *Addington v. Texas*[403] as the minimum evidentiary standard in civil commitment hearings. The Court, in a 5-to-4 decision, rejected Jones's arguments and held that "[t]he preponderance of the evidence standard comports with due process for commitment of insanity acquittees."[404]

The Court thus struck down one line of reasoning in two earlier Supreme Court decisions, *Baxstrom v. Herold*[405] and *Jackson v. Indiana*,[406] which taken together seemed to establish the proposition that all mentally ill offenders for whom civil commitment is sought must be treated alike.[407] The rationale underlying those cases and similar lower court holdings was that a person who has committed past criminal acts is not necessarily presently dangerous and that there is no justifiable basis for statutory schemes that treat as a special class persons who have been involved with the criminal justice system.[408]

In *Jones*, the Supreme Court rejected that reasoning:

> [There are] important differences between the class of potential civil-commitment candidates and the class of insanity acquittees that justify differing standards of proof. The *Addington* Court expressed particular concern that members of the public could be confined on the basis of "some abnormal behavior which might be perceived by some as symptomatic of a mental or emotional disorder, but which is in fact within a range of conduct that is generally acceptable." . . . But since automatic commitment under [D.C. law] follows only if the *acquittee himself* advances insanity as a defense and proves that his criminal act was a product of his mental illness, there is good reason for diminished concern as to the risk of error. More important, the proof that he committed a criminal act as a result of mental illness eliminates the risk that he is being committed for mere "idiosyncratic behavior."[409]

The Court concluded that concerns critical to their earlier decision in *Addington* were diminished or absent in the case of insanity acquittees and that therefore there was no reason for adopting the same standard of proof in both cases.

In his dissent, Justice Brennan disagreed with this distinct treatment of insanity acquittees, arguing that a finding of not guilty by reason of insanity is "backward-looking, focusing on one moment in the past, while commitment requires a judgment as to the present and future."[410] He would have permitted some differentiation between insanity acquittees and civil committees at the time of initial hospitalization but felt that at some point the distinction must end, specifically at the end of the period that would have been the maximum sentence the petitioner could have received, after which the government would have to carry the burden of proof for authorizing continued retention by clear and convincing evidence.

The *Jones* decision goes further than any prior lower court decision in limiting the rights and due process pro-

403. 441 U.S. 418 (1979).

404. 103 S. Ct. at 3051.

405. 383 U.S. 107 (1966).

406. 406 U.S. 715 (1972). In *Baxstrom v. Herold* the Court struck down a New York statutory scheme that permitted convicted persons to be civilly committed at the end of their prison term without being granted the same due process protections as other civil committees (383 U.S. at 107). In *Jackson v. Indiana* the Court held unconstitutional an Indiana law that provided for the automatic and indefinite commitment of incompetent defendants until they regained sanity. The Court held that this violated the equal protection clause because the incompetent defendant was condemned "to permanent institutionalization without the showing required for commitment or the opportunity for release" (406 U.S. at 730).

407. This argument was found persuasive by the New Jersey Supreme Court in State v. Krol, 344 A.2d 289 (N.J. 1975), which struck down that state's automatic commitment provisions for insanity acquittees. In reviewing both the *Baxstrom* and *Jackson* decisions, the court said:

> While neither of these cases deal specifically with the problems of involuntary commitment of persons acquitted by reason of insanity, the Supreme Court in these opinions has plainly attempted to enunicate a broad principle—that the fact that the person to be committed has previously engaged in criminal acts is not a constitutionally acceptable basis for imposing upon him a substantially different standard or procedure for involuntary commitment. The labels "criminal commitment" and "civil commitment" are of no constitutional significance.

344 A.2d at 297. A few other courts have required the same type of commitment proceedings for insanity acquittees as other civil committees. See, e.g., Benham v. Edwards, 678 F.2d 511 (5th Cir. 1982); Jackson v. Foti, 670 F.2d 516 (5th Cir. 1982); Powell v. Florida, 579 F.2d 324 (5th Cir. 1978); People v. McQuillan, 221 N.W.2d 569 (Mich. 1974). The rationale for this is a recognition that the acquittal by reason of insanity relates back to the defendant's mental illness at the time of the crime, while the civil commitment hearing relates to a person's present mental illness and dangerousness. "Simply stated, the criminal trial looks toward the past, the civil commitment hearing and criteria look toward the future," it was asserted in Benham v. Edwards, 678 F.2d at 518.

408. See Note, Commitment Following an Insanity Acquittal, 94 Harv. L. Rev. 605, 610 (1981) [hereinafter cited as Note, Commmitment]; German & Singer, *supra* note 383. See, e.g., Harris v. Ballone, 681 F.2d 225 (4th Cir. 1982); Warren v. Harvey, 632 F.2d 925 (2d Cir. 1980); United States v. Ecker, 543 F.2d 178 (D.C. Cir. 1976); *In re* Jones, 612 P.2d 1211 (Kan. 1980); *In re* Lewis, 403 A.2d 1115 (Del. 1979); State v. Kee, 510 S.W.2d 477 (Mo. 1974).

409. 103 S. Ct. at 3051 (emphasis in original; notes and citations omitted).

410. *Id.* at 3056.

tections afforded to insanity acquittees. In some of the earlier cases the automatic commitment of insanity acquittees had been upheld for the limited purpose of an evaluation.[411] In others, courts had sustained a looser standard for commitment.[412] Yet no court prior to *Jones* had permitted an indefinite confinement without the procedural protections and substantive standards applied to civil committees. Moreover, the *Jones* decision involved an insanity acquittee charged with a nonviolent act, thus negating the underlying logic in earlier lower court decisions which premised this differential treatment of insanity acquittees on the individual's demonstrated violent history.[413] (Not surprisingly, there have been numerous suggestions that special commitment proceedings for insanity acquittees apply only to those who are charged with violent acts.)[414]

No litigation has as yet been reported on the validity of special in-hospital restrictions posed by some state statutes on insanity acquittees. It is likely, however, that these restrictions will in the near future be challenged on equal protection and due process grounds, just as the distinct commitment and discharge procedures for insanity acquittees have been.[415] Whether the logic of *Jones* will be applied to in-hospital restrictions remains to be seen.

The reasoning in *Jones* has been subjected to strong criticism. Although the Court specifically recognized that the petitioner could not be punished because he had not been convicted, it nonetheless sanctioned his prolonged hospitalization, potentially longer than if he had entered the mental health system via either civil commitment or transfer from a correctional facility.[416] One commentator has referred to decisions of this kind as reflecting the "cleanup doctrine," whereby mistakes made in the criminal justice process are rectified in subsequent commitment proceedings.[417] Acceptance of a lower standard of proof for insanity acquittees, he argues, "is at odds with the premises of the insanity defense" and conceals "the deeply felt but seldom acknowledged belief that insanity acquittees deserve something approaching punishment for their actions."[418] If no distinction is made between insanity acquittees committing violent acts and those committing nonviolent acts, the rights that were assured in *O'Connor v. Donaldson*[419] to nondangerous individuals are categorically denied to nondangerous insanity acquitees. By not establishing a reasonable time within which the insanity acquittee must be accorded the same rights accorded to persons who are civilly committed, the *Jones* decision seems to approve the "punishment" of persons who succeed with the insanity defense.

Recommendations that special commitment statutes be enacted for violent insanity acquittees[420] are based on the presumption that a person who has committed a violent act poses an evident risk to society. Such statutes

411. *In re* Jones, 612 P.2d 1211 (Kan. 1980); People v. De Anda, 114 Cal. App. 3d 480, 170 Cal. Rptr. 830 (1980); People v. Froom, 108 Cal. App. 3d 820, 166 Cal. Rptr. 786 (1980); People v. Salas, 165 Cal. Rptr. 82 (1980); *In re* Torsney, 394 N.E.2d 262 (N.Y. 1979).

412. See, e.g., Harris v. Ballone, 681 F.2d 225 (4th Cir. 1982); Warren v. Harvey, 632 F. 2d 925 (2d Cir. 1980); Williams v. Superintendent, Clifton T. Perkins Hosp. Center, 406 A.2d 1302 (Md. 1979).

413. Most notable is Warren v. Harvey, 632 F.2d 925 (2d Cir. 1980), which permitted commitment of an insanity acquittee under a preponderance of evidence standard:

> The obvious difference between insanity acquittees and other persons facing commitment is the fact that the former have been found, beyond a reasonable doubt, to have committed a criminal act. Insanity acquittees thus have "proved" themselves a danger to society at one time. Nonacquittees, in contrast, have not been found by any factfinder to have harmed society as a result of their mental illness. This difference, we believe, gives rise to considerations which justify a lesser standard of proof to commit insanity acquittees than to commit other persons.

632 F.2d at 931. In further expressing the rationale for its decision, the *Warren* court set forth reasoning that has been used by other courts, as well, to justify different commitment procedures:

> Appellant in the instant case was tried and found by a jury to have killed another human being. He escaped punishment solely because he successfully pled that he was insane. He cannot fairly be said to occupy the same position as, for example, a man who has never harmed anyone in his life but who faces civil commitment because he may have dangerous propensities due to a mental disease. We do not believe the Constitution compels the state to shoulder the same burden of proof in order to commit persons in such situations.

632 F.2d at 932. For cases from which *Warren* elaborated its rationale, see cases cited in notes 411 & 412 *supra*. The reasoning of these cases has been criticized for ignoring the fact that numerous individuals who enter the mental health system have a history of past criminal violence and may be entering the system as a condition of bail, at the end of their prison term, or as an alternative to having criminal charges placed against them.

Several who have proposed changes in the disposition process have suggested that there is valid justification for differentiating insanity acquittees who were charged with violent crimes from all other persons who may need involuntary treatment in a mental institution. See, e.g., Criminal Justice Mental Health Standards, *supra* note 112, § 7-7.3; Weiner, Not Guilty by Reason of Insanity: A Sane Approach, 56 Chi.-Kent L. Rev. 1057 (1980), containing Model Legislation for Proceedings After Being Found Not Guilty by Reason of Insanity (at 1072–75).

414. See German & Singer, *supra* note 383; Note, Rules for An Exceptional Class: The Commitment and Release of Persons Acquitted of Violent Offenses by Reason of Insanity, 57 N.Y.U. L. Rev. 281 (1982) [hereinafter cited as Note, Rules].

415. In instances where the defendant was acquitted by reason of insanity for a nonviolent offense or a misdemeanor, the rationale for distinguishing them from other civilly committed persons does not hold up. See reasoning in *Warren v. Harvey* described in note 413 *supra*; also see German & Singer, *supra* note 383.

416. 103 S. Ct. at 3043. In *Vitek v. Jones*, 445 U.S. 480 (1980), the Supreme Court established elaborate procedures to be followed before transfer from a prison to a mental hospital. And in an affirmation of Baxstrom v. Herold, 383 U.S. 107 (1966), it held that someone to be held beyond his prison sentence would have to be subjected to the normal civil commitment procedures. For those who are civilly committed in most states there is a maximum length of time before that commitment must be periodically reviewed. If the committee does not continue to meet the involuntary hospitalization standard with the same standard and burden of proof then he must be discharged. See ch. 2, Involuntary Institutionalization, for further discussion.

417. See Note, Commitment Following an Insanity Acquittal, 94 Harv. L. Rev. 605, 618 (1981).

418. *Id.* at 620.

419. 422 U.S. 563 (1975).

420. See Criminal Justice Mental Health Standards, *supra* note 112, §§ 7-7.1 to 7-7.3; also Weiner, *supra* note 413.

separating violent from nonviolent mentally ill persons in both placement and treatment would have the advantage both of breaking down the popular association of all mentally persons with violent acts and of assuring the public that appropriately careful treatment and discharge procedures were being followed in cases involving acquittees who might be dangerous.

The proposed legislation would include the following two basic elements: (1) automatic commitment for an evaluation period and (2) a broader standard for commitment. The mandatory evaluation period, typically 30 days in duration, would be to determine present mental status and treatment needs.[421] Although this may be substantially longer than the period required for prospective civil committees, it can be justified on grounds that the acquittee's past violent behavior requires a more comprehensive evaluation.[422] Additionally, in contrast to the ordinary civil committee, whose overt signs of mental illness have brought him to the attention of the mental health system, the insanity acquittee may have his illness sufficiently under control to be found competent to stand trial, thus making more thorough evaluation necessary to determine not only his present mental status but also what his future treatment needs might be. This approach has been adopted legislatively by some ten states[423] and upheld by the courts.[424] The broader commitment standard would focus to a greater extent on *future* dangerousness;[425] a finding that an acquittee was not *presently* dangerous or in need of hospitalization—the typical civil commitment standard—would not necessarily bar his commitment.

The American Bar Association's Criminal Justice Mental Health Standards propose such an approach, which it outlines as follows:

> [T]he court may order the acquittee to be committed if it finds by clear and convincing evidence that the acquittee:
>
> (i) is currently mentally ill or mentally retarded; and, as a result,
> (ii) poses a substantial threat of serious bodily harm to others.
>
> (c) The court may not commit the acquittee unless it finds, beyond a reasonable doubt, that the acquittee committed the criminal act for which he or she was acquitted by reason of insanity, or unless the trier of fact made such a finding at the acquittee's criminal trial. The commitment court shall evaluate the relevance of the criminal act to the proposed commitment in light of the amount of time which has passed since its occurrence, and the possibility that the acquittee's confinement may have prevented the commission of other overt acts posing a serious threat of bodily harm to others.
>
> (d) If the court concludes that the only reason the acquittee does not meet the standard for commitment. . . is the effect of treatment or habilitation currently being received, the acquittee may be committed unless the court is persuaded by a preponderance of the evidence that the acquittee will continue to receive such treatment or habilitation following release for as long as the treatment or habilitation is required.[426]

Although the ABA proposal prescribes stricter commitment standards than do most other similar proposals, it is based on the same recognition that the psychotic symptoms of many insanity acquittees may be in remission at the end of the trial as a result of pretrial treatment with medication. An evaluation immediately after the trial risks failing to ascertain the true extent of the acquittee's illness, which could result in a premature release decision.[427] Upon return to the community, the acquittee, following a pattern common in mental illness cases, may stop taking his prescribed medication and deteriorate. In the case of insanity acquittees in particular, the fear is that with deterioration will come a repetition of violent behavior.

3. The Discharge Process

The discharge decision is made in one of three ways:[428] (1) on an application to the court for the acquittee's release by the superintendent of the state hospital or the director of the state mental health agency, (2) on the acquittee's own application or by someone petitioning the court on his behalf, or (3) by the direct decision of the appropriate hospital authorities or the state men-

421. Criminal Justice Mental Health Standards, *supra* note 112, § 8-7.2; Weiner, *supra* note 413, at 1072.

422. Criminal Justice Mental Health Standards, *supra* note 112, § 7-7.2 commentary.

423. Arizona, Connecticut, Georgia, Illinois, Maryland, Michigan, Nebraska, Rhode Island, Virginia, and West Virginia. See table 12.7, cols. 1 & 2.

424. See, e.g., Jones v. United States, 103 S. Ct. 3043 (1983); Warren v. Harvey, 632 F.2d 925 (2d Cir. 1980); Locklear v. Hultine, 528 F. Supp. 982 (D. Kan. 1981); Benham v. Edwards, 678 F.2d 511 (5th Cir. 1982).

425. E.g., the Model Insanity Defense and Post-Trial Disposition Act provides: "If the court finds that the individual is mentally ill or defective and that there is a substantial risk, as a result of mental illness or defect, that the individual will commit a criminal act of violence threatening another person with bodily injury or property damage and that the individual is not a proper subject for conditional release, it shall order the individual committed to [a mental hospital or other suitable facility designated by the commissioner of mental health] for custody and treatment." § 903(d)(2), 11 U.L.A. 162 (Supp. 1985). This eliminates the civil commitment standard of the need for present likelihood of dangerousness or serious bodily harm, thus providing a much broader commitment standard.

426. See Criminal Justice Mental Health Standards, *supra* note 112, § 7-7.4.

427. See Weiner, *supra* note 413, at 1072–73, which suggests that if the person does not meet the civil commitment criteria, at least he be found to be in need of "involuntary hospitalization" if the person is reasonably expected to pose a danger to himself or others because of a mental illness.

428. See table 12.7, cols. 6–10.

tal health agency.[429] Regardless of who initiates or makes the discharge decision, the release criteria in the vast majority of states are that the patient no longer need hospitalization[430] and no longer pose a danger to others. Most states require special court approval before discharge of the insanity acquittee.[431] In some states a discharge hearing is held only when either the court or the prosecution disagrees with the hospital's discharge recommendation. In other states the court hearing is automatic[432] upon a petition for discharge, with the states varying as to whether the hearing is before the court that heard the criminal case[433] or the court that normally has jurisdiction over civil commitment matters.[434]

In some of the states that require court approval for the discharge decision, the statutes provide that one or more qualified medical examiners must examine the acquittee and report to the court whether he is ready for discharge. Once the issue is before the court, the states divide over who has the burden of proving whether the acquittee is an appropriate candidate for release. In some states the acquittee has the burden.[435] In other states, the burden is on whoever petitioned for discharge, which could be the acquittee, his representative, or the mental health or hospital official.[436] Finally, some states put the burden on those disagreeing with the petition for discharge to prove that the acquittee should *not* be released. If the discharge petition is denied, most states provide that there cannot be another hearing for a certain period of time, ranging from six months to a year.

The requirement of court approval for discharge contrasts with the treatment of the civilly committed patient, who can be discharged at the discretion of a hospital administrator when it is determined that the patient no longer needs hospitalization. In addition to approving the discharge decision, the courts in several states have the authority to condition the release on the acquittee's participation in an outpatient program or some similar requirement.[437]

Suits have been brought challenging on equal protection grounds the courts' authority to become involved in the discharge process, but the courts have universally rejected this argument by noting the fact that the insanity acquittee committed a violent act.[438] In *United States v. Ecker* in 1976, for example, the court said:

> "Equal protection does not require that all persons be dealt with identically, but it does require that a distinction made have some relevance to the purpose for which the classification is made," i.e., "a reasonable justification." [Insanity acquittees] . . . are treated differently from civil commitees because they are an "exceptional class of people" who have "already unhappily manifested the reality of anti-social conduct."[439]

Even courts requiring the civil standard for commitment have approved different procedures for discharge of the insanity acquittee who has committed a violent act.[440] The rationales for these decisions include the acquittee's dangerousness as demonstrated by the past violent act, the fact that he has been confined in a "secure" environment since his apprehension, and the staff's consequent inability to predict how he will react to the stresses of returning to the community or whether he will continue to take his medication.[441]

The provisions in some states today, stipulating that the insanity acquittee cannot be hospitalized under the criminal commitment statute for a period longer than the maximum sentence for the crime with which he was charged, are not constitutionally required, as *Jones v. United States* makes clear:

> There simply is no necessary correlation between severity of the offense and length of time necessary for recovery. The length of the acquittee's hypothetical criminal

429. See ch. 2, Involuntary Institutionalization. This occurs in those states where the insanity acquittee is treated the same as other civil committees.

430. See table 12.7, col. 7, and states where the person is treated the same as other civil committees.

431. See table 12.7, col. 9; also *In re* Harris, 617 P.2d 739 (Wash. 1980), which reaffirmed the rational basis for handling civil and criminal committees differently, even for property crimes.

432. See table 12.7, col. 9.

433. E.g., Illinois, Minnesota, Missouri, Nebraska, Ohio, and Rhode Island.

434. E.g., California, Colorado, Florida, Louisiana, Montana, New Jersey, Virginia, Washington, West Virginia, and Wyoming.

435. See table 12.7, col. 11, e.g., Alaska, District of Columbia, Connecticut, Kansas, Louisiana, Montana, and Virginia.

436. E.g., California, Georgia, Hawaii, Oregon, and Utah.

437. See table 12.7, cols. 13–15.

438. See, e.g., United States v. Ecker, 543 F.2d 178 (D.C. Cir. 1976), *cert. denied*, 429 U.S. 1063 (1977); Alter v. Morris, 536 P.2d 630 (Wash. 1975); State v. Alto, 589 P.2d 402 (Alaska 1979); *In re* Harris, 617 P.2d 739 (Wash. 1980).

439. 543 F.2d 178, 196 (D.C. Cir. 1976); see also other cases listed in note 438 *supra*.

440. See Powell v. Florida, 579 F.2d 324 (5th Cir. 1978); Benham v. Edwards, 678 F.2d 511 (5th Cir. 1982); State v. Krol, 344 A.2d 289 (N.J. 1975).

441. In upholding the commitment and release provisions of the Connecticut law relating to insanity acquittees, the United States Court of Appeals for the Second Circuit noted in *Warren v. Harvey*:

> His acquittal on grounds of insanity constituted proof beyond a reasonable doubt that he once had been a danger to society. While the insanity acquittal did not constitute dispositive proof of present dangerousness, it was substantial evidence that appellant remained a danger to society. . . .One means of demonstrating that an individual poses a "danger to himself or others" is to show that he has "a propensity to commit criminal acts." . . . Certainly past commission of a criminal act must be accorded considerable weight in determining the existence of a "propensity to commit criminal acts."

632 F.2d 925, 934 (2d Cir. 1980). The court went on to state:

> Furthermore, the lack of evidence that appellant has engaged in more recent violent acts or threats must be viewed in light of the fact that he has been in custody ever since he killed his neighbor. It obviously is more difficult for a man who is in jail or confined to a mental hospital to translate his violent propensities into actual conduct than it is for a man who is free to act as he pleases.

Id.

sentence therefore is irrelevant to the purposes of his commitment.

We hold that when a criminal defendant establishes by a preponderance of the evidence that he is not guilty of a crime by reason of insanity, the Constitution permits the Government, on the basis of the insanity judgment, to confine him to a mental institution until such time as he has regained his sanity or is no longer a danger to himself or society.[442]

Other differences in the discharge provisions for insanity acquittees could take the form of restrictions on the hospital's discretion to release the patient. The discharge decision would be made by a court under some proposals[443] or by a board similar to a parole board under others.[444] Under either model, once the hospital staff believes the individual no longer needs hospitalization, the hospital administrator would be required to petition the discharging authority for discharge of the acquittee. In addition, the acquittee himself could also petition for discharge. The goals of this type of discharge process are (1) to take the pressure off the mental health professionals and (2) to provide a broader scope of review that considers both the treatment needs of the acquittee and the potential impact of his release on the public.

Although today more than half the states require court approval of the discharge decision,[445] the approving court is not necessarily the one that originally heard the case. In model legislation elaborated for dealing with the insanity acquittee, I have suggested that the approval come from the criminal court that heard the case, because that court would be most familiar with the acquittee's history and prior violent behavior and thus in the best position to fully comprehend the consequences of a discharge.[446] If the court is not confident that discharge is appropriate at a particular time, it can order intermediate measures, such as off-grounds passes and weekend passes, to test the acquittee's ability to handle graduated degrees of freedom. For these provisions to be effective, the court must in addition have the authority to order follow-up care after discharge from the mental institution.

Where the authority to discharge resides in an entity similar to a parole board, this agency would consist of a multidisciplinary group of individuals who are not employees of the state mental health agency. This is the approach taken in Oregon,[447] and it has been endorsed by the American Psychiatric Association.[448] The board retains continuing jurisdiction over the acquittee for a specific period while he is in the community and has the authority to order rehospitalization.

Whichever approach is taken, it is likely that more states will remove from the mental health agency the discharge decision because of fear that the changes in laws and treatment methods that have greatly reduced the length of institutionalization for civil committees will result in the premature return of the insanity acquittee to the community.

4. Discharge Conditions: Mandatory Outpatient Treatment

In most of the states in which the insanity acquittee is released from the hospital at the hospital's discretion, there are no further requirements imposed upon him. In states where court approval must be obtained for the discharge decision, the statutes divide as to the nature of the release, the majority providing for both conditional and unconditional discharge and a few permitting only unconditioned release.[449] Where an option exists, unconditional discharge is ordered only when it is determined that the acquittee no longer poses a danger and is no longer in need of treatment. In cases of conditional discharge, the court continues to have some hold over the individual in order to monitor his behavior or to assure continued treatment. The conditions that can be imposed include mandatory outpatient care by mental health professionals, requirements to participate in drug or alcohol rehabilitation programs, or restrictions similar to probation or parole orders, such as prohibitions on drinking, taking drugs, or possessing a gun. In Louisiana and New Hampshire the acquittee is actually under the jurisdiction of a parole officer. A few statutes specify that the release conditions apply for a certain number of years, five being typical,[450] though they usually also permit the acquittee to petition for earlier termination of these conditions.

Another way to try to assure that the insanity acquittee's mental illness is kept under control and thus to protect the public is to require that the acquittee participate in outpatient care under the discharging authority, be it a court or a board.[451] Several courts have suggested

442. 103 S. Ct. 3043, 3052 (1983) (note and sec. number omitted).

443. See Criminal Justice Mental Health Standards, *supra* note 112, § 7-7; also Weiner, *supra* note 413, at 1071-73.

444. See A.P.A. Statement, *supra* note 296.

445. See table 12.7, col. 9.

446. See Weiner, *supra* note 413, at 1071.

447. See Or. Rev. Stat. §§ 161.319 to .351 & §§ 161.385 to .395 (1981). For a good description of how the board works see Bloom & Bloom, Disposition of Insanity Defense Cases in Oregon, 9 A.A.P.L. Bull. 93 (1981).

448. See A.P.A. Statement, *supra* note 296, at 687.

449. See table 12.7.

450. E.g., Arkansas, Hawaii, Illinois, Maryland, Michigan, Oregon, and Wisconsin.

451. See Model Insanity Defense and Post-Trial Disposition Act § 903(d)(2), which provides: "If the court finds that the risk that the individual will commit an act of violence threatening another person with bodily injury or property damage will be controlled adequately with supervision and treatment if the individual is conditionally released and that necessary supervision

the need for such a system.[452] The care provided could include the whole spectrum of treatments, including individual psychiatric therapy, drug and alcohol rehabilitation programs, and chemotherapy. Critical to the success of such programs is management by qualified mental health professionals who can both monitor progress and assure compliance with treatment recommendations.[453]

The discharging authority should have the power to order the acquittee into a specific program and to require staff to report on his progress. It is often helpful if the patient knows that the discharging authority can and will impose sanctions if he does not keep his appointments or fails to follow the rules and regulations of the treatment program.[454] A number of states give general authority of this kind to a court or parole type of board. Three states—Maryland, Illinois, and Oregon—have programs specifically designed for treatment of the insanity acquittee. While not conclusive, the experience of these programs suggests that with treatment and careful monitoring, the insanity acquittee is indeed less likely to become involved in new violent behavior than general statistics would predict.[455] What preliminary evidence on these programs also shows, however, is that even with good outpatient care, a proportion of the acquittees will deteriorate to a point of needing rehospitalization, even if only for a temporary period.[456]

This type of mandatory outpatient care system requires a group of mental health professionals who are familiar with the criminal justice system, who can deal comfortably with patients who have a history of violent behavior, who can maintain general contact with the discharging authority, and who can count on support from the discharging authority in imposing sanctions. Such a program can achieve a proper balance between the rights of the acquittees to be treated in the least restrictive environment and the rights of the community to be protected from those with a known potential for causing serious harm.

5. Working Models of Programs for Insanity Acquittees

Although the laws of many states permit special treatment of insanity acquittees, only a few states have developed special treatment programs.[457] The oldest and most comprehensive such program is Maryland's, established in 1967. A substantially similar program was adopted in Illinois in 1978. A new model was developed in 1978 in Oregon. These programs embody many of the proposed reforms in the laws governing the disposition of insanity acquittees.

(a) The Maryland model □□ Since 1967 Maryland has had special statutes relating to insanity acquittees.[458] Upon a finding of not guilty by reason of insanity, the acquittee is automatically committed for a brief period of evaluation to determine if he meets a civil commitment standard. If he does, he is committed to Perkins State Hospital, which will begin a program

---

and treatment are available, it shall order the individual released subject to conditions the court considers appropriate for the protection of society." 11 U.L.A. 162 (Supp. 1985). The new federal law also permits the conditional release of insanity acquittees under a court order. See Comprehensive Crime Control Act of 1984, Pub. L. No. 98-473, § 403, 98 Stat. 1837, 2057 (to be codified at 18 U.S.C. § 4243(f)(2)(A) (1984)). See also Weiner, *supra* note 413, at 1071; A.P.A. Statement, *supra* note 296, at 687; Criminal Justice Mental Health Standards, *supra* note 112, § 7-7.4(d), which does not require mandatory outpatient care but does permit it.

452. The courts have also expressed concern about the discharged individual's receiving appropriate aftercare:

> The disposition must be individualized with the focus on the offender, not the offense he committed, although such offense can serve as an indication of the harm the patient is capable of inflicting. Perhaps most important is the establishment of psychiatric outpatient care. . . .
>
> The success of conditional release depends, to a large extent, upon the adequacy of the supervisory controls imposed by the courts to insure the public safety. The most obvious condition for safeguarding the community against a repetition of criminal behavior is a careful follow-up and required attendance for psychiatric treatment over a long period of time.

State v. Krol, 344 A. 2d 289, 303 (N.J. 1975).

453. Careful management by mental health professionals is particularly important when the treatment includes medication, since careful monitoring is essential to ensure that the right dosages are being given and that the medication is being taken. Cavanaugh, Wasyliw, & Rogers, Treatment of Mentally Disordered Offenders, *in* Psychiatry (J. Cavenar ed. 1985).

454. The acquittee could be held in contempt by a court for violating its initial order, and the court or parole board may move for rehospitalization of the acquittee if his clinical condition warrants it. The choice between treatment as an outpatient or as an inpatient will encourage the acquittee to follow the rules and treatment recommendations so that he can remain an outpatient.

455. See discussion of these programs in this chapter in § III E 5, Working Models of Programs for Insanity Acquitees, *infra*. The Isaac Ray Center, which is the Illinois outpatient program for insanity acquittees, reports that their patients have not been involved in repeated violent behavior. Cavanaugh & Wasyliw, Adjustment of the Not Guilty by Reason of Insanity (NGRI) Outpatient: An Intitial Report, 30 J. Forensic Sci. 24 (1985). The Maryland program also reports very little repeated violent activity among its outpatients. Spodak, Silver, & Wright, Criminality of Discharged Insanity Acquittees: Fifteen Year Experience in Maryland Reviewed, 12 A.A.P.L. Bull. 373, 376 (1984).

The experience of the Oregon program, operated under the Psychiatric Security Review Board, is reported in a number of articles, including: Bloom & Bloom, *supra* note 445; Rogers & Bloom, *supra* note 191. Rogers and Bloom reported in 1983 that 13% (39 persons of 295) who were on conditional release under the PSRB were charged with new crimes, of which only 5% were felonies, the rest being misdemeanors. Rogers, Bloom, & Mason, Oregon's New Insanity Defense System: A Review of the First Five Years—1978–1982 (paper presented at the Annual Meeting of the American Academy of Psychiatry and Law, Portland, Or., Oct. 1983). See also Bloom, Rogers, & Mason, After Oregon's Insanity Defense: A Comparison of Conditional Release and Hospitalization, 5 Int'l J.L. & Psychiatry 391 (1982).

It should be borne in mind that violence is what is called a low-base-rate behavior—that is, it occurs infrequently and cannot be predicted well. This, as well as continued treatment, primarily with medication, may explain why there are so few violent incidents among these treated insanity acquittees.

456. The Illinois experience indicates that about 20% of the patients need rehospitalization each year. Sixth Annual Report, Issac Ray Center, Chicago, Ill. Maryland shows a slightly lower rehospitalization rate (Testimony of Silver, *supra* note 190). The figures have not yet been compiled for Oregon.

457. See table 12.7, cols. 9, 10, & 13.

458. Md. Ann. Code art. 59, §§ 27 & 28 (1979 & Supp. 1982).

designed to assess his treatment needs and to gradually introduce him to increased amounts of freedom to determine his ability to handle this responsibility.[459] The program at Perkins permits the acquittee to have day passes and allows for employment either on the grounds of the hospital or in a nearby community. When the acquittee has demonstrated his ability to handle a significant measure of freedom and responsibility, the hospital staff will petition the court for his conditional release. Upon release the acquittee participates in mandatory outpatient programs under the supervision of the staff at Perkins. In some cases the acquittee will live in a halfway house run by the Perkins staff in the city of Baltimore.[460] This mandatory outpatient care is designed to last for five years, with staff able to petition for an additional five-year period.[461] At any point after the first three months of commitment, however, the acquittee is entitled to petition the court for release from the program.

The Maryland program embodies several suggested reforms: (1) there is an automatic commitment for a period of evaluation, (2) the acquittee cannot be discharged from the hospital without court approval, and (3) the court can order outpatient care. Moreover, the outpatient care is provided by an experienced staff familiar with treating violent offenders, and the halfway house — open to some of the acquittees — facilitates careful monitoring of the patient in the community.

Because of the quality of care and the careful monitoring guaranteed by the Maryland program, criminal recidivism and repeated violent activity are minimized.[462] After seven years of operation of a similar model in Illinois, there had been no insanity acquittee in the outpatient program who became involved in repeated violent activity.[463] To guard against undue optimism, however, it should be noted that the Illinois program accepts only carefully selected acquittees whose violent behavior was clearly a manifestation of their illness.

(b) The Oregon model □□ In January 1978, Oregon began a unique experiment providing for a Psychiatric Security Review Board (PSRB) to assume responsibility for making decisions on the disposition of insanity acquittees.[464] This five-person board, consisting of a psychiatrist, a psychologist, a lawyer, a person familiar with parole and probation, and a lay citizen, has authority over all insanity acquittees who are determined by the court to have a mental disease or defect and to present a substantial danger to others.[465] The board supervises the acquittee for a period equal to the maximum sentence he could have received had he been convicted, and it determines whether the person is institutionalized, placed in the community with conditions, or discharged from its jurisdiction.[466] The board is responsibile for ensuring that those persons released to the community are adequately supervised and treated and that they are rehospitalized if they deteriorate.

The main reform features of the Oregon model are: (1) a broader standard than that for civil commitment applies for deciding whether the acquittee comes under the board's jurisdiction, (2) release cannot occur without board approval, and (3) mandatory treatment can be ordered as a condition of release. This model differs from Maryland's in that the deciding authority rests with five people rather than with one judge and that the treatment options are provided in different settings rather than by one program. The PSRB can arrange for treatment in any number of programs, a feature needed because of Oregon's geographical size and, unlike in Maryland, the extension of its jurisdiction to misdemeanants who are acquitted by reason of insanity.[467]

Initially designed as a four-year experiment, the Psychiatric Security Review Board was considered successful enough to become permanent in 1981.[468] During a five-year period, of 295 people conditionally released under the PSRB's authority only 6% were involved in new felony charges.[469] This type of success, along with the board's ability to generate important data on insanity acquittees, has led some influential groups to endorse this model.[470]

Proponents of moving to a board system, as distinct from leaving the responsibility with the judiciary, have argued that the "trial courts' retention of jurisdiction over n.g.i. [NGRI] cases was inadequate." Because courts do not have the staff to deal with or to arrange for supervi-

459. For a description of the Maryland program, see Weiner, *supra* note 413, at 1076-78, and Spodak, Silver, & Wright, *supra* note 453, also.

460. Goldmeier, Sauer, & White, A Halfway House for Mentally Ill Offenders, 134 Am. J. Psychiatry 45 (1977).

461. Md. Ann. Code §§ 12-115 & 12-121 1984).

462. See Testimony of Silver, *supra* note 190, at 383, which showed that in a survey of 72 patients for five years 76% of the patients were not rearrested, and 97.5% of the patients had no serious complications. Those who were rearrested were often arrested for misdemeanors such as traffic violations rather than for violent crimes. Also see Spodak, Silver, & Wright, *supra* note 455.

463. See Cavanaugh & Wasyliw, which describes an outpatient program for insanity acquittees and a two year study of their patients. Of 44 insanity acquittees in treatment, 67% had been charged with murder or attempted murder, and none had engaged in repeated violent criminal activity.

464. Or. Rev. Stat. §§ 161.319 to .351 & §§ 161.385 to .395 (1981).

465. Or. Rev. Stat. § 161.327(2)(a) (1981).

466. Rogers & Boom, *supra* note 191.

467. In Oregon, for example, 24% of the people under the PSRB's control were acquitted of misdemeanors. See Bloom, Rogers, & Mason, *supra* note 455, at 398. In both Maryland and Illinois it is very rare that an insanity defense would be raised for a misdemeanor charge.

468. See Or. Rev. Stat. § 161.327 (1981).

469. Rogers, Bloom, & Mason, *supra* note 455.

470. See A.P.A. Statement, *supra* note 296, at 687.

sion and treatment, such a system poses an undue risk to the community.[471]

Whether a state adopts a model similar to Maryland's, as did Illinois, or whether it uses the Oregon model, it is clear that there are advantages to developing a systematic approach for addressing the problems raised by persons acquitted by reason of insanity. It is likely that during the coming decade major changes will occur in both state laws and state treatment programs.

IV. SENTENCING THE MENTALLY DISABLED OFFENDER

A. Introduction

The issue of the defendant's mental disability, usually associated with competency to stand trial or invocation of the insanity defense, may also arise at the time of sentencing. As discussed earlier, mental disability can be found to make a defendant incompetent to serve a sentence and thus cause its imposition to be postponed. Mental disability may also be considered in determining the sentence for a defendant who is well enough to stand trial and be convicted. In this context, the same questions arise about self-incrimination in the psychiatric evaluation and the role of the psychiatric expert,[472] but with the additional complications inherent in the attempt to predict future danagerousness.

B. Self-Incrimination

Disclosure of information during a psychiatric evaluation conducted at any stage of the process can be detrimental to the defendant at sentencing. For example, if the psychiatric report reveals that the defendant feels no regret for the crime, the judge may feel obliged to impose the harshest punishment available.[473] The propriety of this was addressed by the Supreme Court in 1981 in *Estelle v. Smith*,[474] the most notable case to explore both the Fifth Amendment privilege against self-incrimination and the Sixth Amendment right to counsel in the context of a mental evaluation. Information and impressions gained during a competency evaluation served as the basis for the psychiatrist's concluding that the defendant had no remorse or sorrow for his acts and was likely to commit other similar crimes. The psychiatrist's testimony introduced during the sentencing phase of the trial to determine whether the defendant should be given the death penalty resulted in the imposition of that penalty. At no time had the defendant or his attorney been warned that the statements made during the competency evaluation might be used for sentencing purposes.

Reasoning that the Fifth Amendment privilege applies to the sentencing phase of trial as well as the guilt-determination phase, the Court held that "[a] criminal defendant, who neither initiates a psychiatric evaluation nor attempts to introduce any psychiatric evidence, may not be compelled to respond to a psychiatrist if his statements can be used against him at a capital sentencing proceeding."[475] This holding specifically did not address what limitations, if any, there might be on the introduction of the defendant's statements in a noncapital case.

In addressing the Sixth Amendment right to counsel in the context of a psychiatric evaluation, the Court observed that "because [a] layman may not be aware of the precise scope, the nuances, and the boundaries of his Fifth Amendment privilege, the assertion of that right 'often depends upon legal advice from someone who is trained and skilled in the subject matter.'"[476] Since the situation in *Smith* was literally a matter of life and death, the Court concluded that "a defendant should not be forced to resolve such an important issue without 'the guiding hand of counsel.'"[477] Commentators have gone further, suggesting that defense counsel be present during any psychiatric evaluation in order to assure the protection of the client's rights.[478]

C. Fitting the Sentence to the Criminal

"The history of criminal sentencing laws reflects a shifting focus between letting the punishment fit the crime and letting the punishment fit the criminal," observes one commentator.[479] In those instances in which the judge has discretion as to the sentence imposed, heavy emphasis often will be placed on the presentence report as a device for aiding an informed exercise of that discretion. The report may include an evaluation by a mental health professional, who will have attempted to determine the defendant's present mental status and his future dangerousness. The evaluator may in addition have recommended alternatives to incarceration, such as diversion into a drug or alcohol rehabilitation program, a sex offender program, or treatment on either an inpatient or an outpatient basis for mental illness.

Recently, a committee of the American Bar Association recommended that evidence of mental illness or mental retardation be a mitigating factor in sentencing

471. Bloom & Bloom, *supra* note 447, at 95.

472. See in this chapter notes 103–14 with accompanying text and notes 319–22 with accompanying text *supra*.

473. The Fifth Amendment and Compelled Psychiatric Examinations, *supra* note 105, at 294.

474. 451 U.S. 454 (1981).

475. *Id.* at 468.

476. *Id.* at 471, quoting Maness v. Meyers, 419 U.S. 449, 466 (1975).

477. 451 U.S. at 471, quoting Powell v. Alabama, 287 U.S. 45, 69 (1932).

478. Golten, *supra* note 101, at 297 (1972).

479. Dershowitz, The Role of Psychiatry in the Sentencing Process, 1 Int'l J.L. & Psychiatry 63, 76 (1978).

any convicted offender.[480] Further, the committee suggested that mental disability should "not be used as an excuse for imprisonment where probation would otherwise be appropriate and reasonable."[481] The availability of effective treatment programs gives the court the latitude to divert from incarceration those defendants who can be helped and whose crime and past behavior do not merit imprisonment.

Although there are questions about the mental health professional's role in the sentencing process in any case,[482] the controversy is heightened in death penalty cases.[483] In a series of cases decided in 1976, the United States Supreme Court rejected the notion that the death penalty per se constituted cruel and unusual punishment.[484] This left the way open for the states to reenact capital sentencing provisions, as long as they conformed to the standards set forth by the Court. Some statutes[485] as well as the American Law Institute's Model Penal Code specifically provide that evidence of a mental disability should be a mitigating factor in weighing imposition of the death penalty.[486] Other states do not specifically refer to mental disability as a mitigating factor but do provide for consideration of mitigating factors in general.[487] In *Lockett v. Ohio,*[488] a 1978 decision, the Supreme Court held that the sentencer should "not be precluded from considering, *as a mitigating factor,* any aspect of a defendant's character or record and any of the circumstances of the offense that the defendant proffers as a basis for a sentence less than death."[489] Since a mental disability may interfere with an individual's ability to think rationally, it would seem appropriate that evidence of a mental disability be considered when the death penalty is at issue.[490]

D. Predicting Future Dangerousness

A more controversial question concerns the admission of testimony by mental health professionals on the future dangerousness of the defendant being sentenced. This issue has been framed most sharply in the context of sentencing decisions made by the state court in Texas, which has a statute, approved by the Supreme Court,[491] providing that one of the issues to be resolved by the jury in a death penalty case is "whether there is a probability that the defendant would commit criminal acts of violence that would constitute a continuing threat to society."[492] Texas prosecutors frequently have called upon psychiatrists to testify on defendants' future dangerousness.[493] In some instances such testimony has been based on a psychiatric evaluation of the defendant, but in other cases the testimony has been based on hypothetical questions, uninformed by a direct evaluation of the defendant.

In 1983 in *Barefoot v. Estelle,*[494] the Supreme Court for the first time addressed squarely whether psychiatric testimony could be admitted during the sentencing phase of the hearing on the issue of the defendant's future dangerousness. In *Estelle v. Smith,*[495] the Court had held that without a warning of the possible uses of the evaluation to the defendant, the psychiatrist could not testify as to future dangerousness at the death penalty hearing when he had only examined the defendant for competency to stand trial. Invoking the Eighth and Fourteenth Amendments, Barefoot argued that admission of psychiatric predictions of dangerousness of a person's future conduct was unconstitutional because of the unreliability of such predictions. The Court was also asked to bar hypothetical questions directed to a psychiatrist who had not examined the defendant. The Court rejected both points, despite the support they received from the American Psychiatric Association in an amicus brief. The Court stated that it was "not persuaded that such testimony is almost entirely unreliable and that the factfinder and the adversary system will not be competent to uncover, recognize, and take due account of its shortcomings."[496] The Court added:

> Psychiatric testimony predicting dangerousness may be countered not only as erroneous in a particular case but as generally so unreliable that it should be ignored. If

480. Criminal Justice Mental Health Standards, *supra* note 112, § 7-9.4.

481. *Id.* § 7-9.5 commentary at 358.

482. American Psychiatric Association, Report of the Task Force on the Role of Psychiatry in the Sentencing Process (1984); Menninger, *supra* note 243, at 139.

483. See, e.g., Dix, The Death Penalty,"Dangerousness," Psychiatric Testimony, and Professional Ethics, 4 Am. J. Crim. L. 151 (1977); *id.*, Participation by Mental Health Professionals in Capital Murder Sentencing, 1 Int'l J.L. & Psychiatry 283 (1978) and *id.,* Psychiatric Testimony in Death Penalty Litigation, 5 A.A.P.L. Bull. 287 (1978).

484. Gregg v. Georgia, 428 U.S. 153 (1976); Proffitt v. Florida, 428 U.S. 242 (1976); Jurek v. Texas, 428 U.S. 262 (1976); Woodson v. North Carolina, 428 U.S. 280 (1976); and Roberts v. Louisiana, 428 U.S. 325 (1976).

485. See, e.g., Fla. Stat. Ann. § 921.141(6)(b) & (c) (West Supp. 1982) and Ohio Rev. Code Ann. § 2929.04(B)(3) & (7) (Page 1982).

486. Model Penal Code § 210.6(4)(g), 410 U.L.A. 537 (1974).

487. See, e.g., Ga. Code Ann. § 17-10-30(b) (1982) and Okla. Stat. Ann. tit. 21, § 701.10 (West 1983).

488. 438 U.S. 586 (1978).

489. *Id.* at 587 (emphasis in original).

490. See in this chapter § II E, Incompetency and the Death Penalty, *supra* for a discussion of the rationale behind the death penalty.

491. Jurek v. Texas, 428 U.S. 262 (1976).

492. Tex. Crim. Proc. Code Ann. § 37.071(b)(2) (Vernon 1981).

493. James Grigson, who was involved in both the *Smith* and the *Barefoot* cases, has often been used by the prosecution to predict future dangerousness. He has been nicknamed "Dr. Death." For reference to his role in these cases see Dix, The Death Penalty, *supra* note 483; W.J. Winslade & J.W. Ross, The Insanity Plea 159 (1983) (containing chapter entitled "James Grigson: 'The Hanging Psychiatrist'").

494. 103 S. Ct. 3383 (1983).

495. 451 U.S. 454 (1981). See discussion of Court's holding on use of information disclosed in evaluation with respect to competency in § II B 6(c)(2), Self-Incrimination, *supra.*

496. 103 S. Ct. at 3377.

the jury may make up its mind about future dangerousness unaided by psychiatric testimony, jurors should not be barred from hearing the views of the State's psychiatrists along with opposing views of the defendant's doctors.[497]

As for hypothetical questions posed to nonexamining psychiatrists, the Court asserted that there was "no constitutional barrier to applying the ordinary rules of evidence governing the use of expert testimony."[498]

Justices Blackmun, Brennan, and Marshall dissented, emphasizing that psychiatrists accurately predict dangerousness in only one in three cases at best. The dissenters reasoned that while "[o]ne may accept this in a routine lawsuit for money damages, ... when a person's life is at stake— no matter how heinous his offense— a requirement of greater reliability should prevail."[499] The dissent reiterated the concerns of the psychiatrists' amicus brief and of other commentators about the misuse of this testimony:

> It is impossible to square admission of this purportedly scientific but actually baseless testimony with the Constitution's paramount concern for reliability in capital sentencing. Death is a permissible punishment in Texas only if the jury finds beyond a reasonable doubt that there is a probability the defendant will commit future acts of criminal violence. The admission of unreliable psychiatric predictions of future violence offered with unabashed claims of "reasonable medical certainty" or "absolute" professional reliability, creates an intolerable danger that death sentences will be imposed erroneously.[500]

Dix has suggested guidelines for mental health professionals who continue to testify in capital cases.[501] He believes that following these guidelines, which provide for revealing the extent of the evalutor's knowledge about the defendant and the law and the empirical basis for his predictions, would make the judge or jury sufficiently aware of the likelihood of inaccuracy in predictions of future dangerousness. He may be overly sanguine, however: predictions of dangerousness made by doctors carrying professional titles and the other trappings of expertise still may continue to have an impact on the jury out of proportion to their reliability.

V. MENTALLY DISABLED PRISONERS

A. Introduction

Mentally disabled persons are disproportionately represented in the correctional system. Of the some 6.2 million people who pass through this country's jails each year, it is estimated that 600,000 of them are seriously mentally ill.[502] Other studies have concluded that anywhere from 9% to 23% of those confined in jails awaiting trial are psychotic or suffering from schizophrenia.[503] If drug- and alcohol-dependent persons and those diagnosed with character disorders were included in these estimates, the percentage of persons who suffer from some type of "mental" disability would range from 40% to 90% of the total jail population.[504] Estimates of the number of convicted felons[505] who are mentally ill range from 14% considered psychotic to as high as 50% when behavior disorders are included.[506] Thus, while the drastic ranges in the estimates reveal considerable diagnostic uncertainties, even the lower figures confirm that mentally disabled persons form a substantial portion of the population of this nation's detention and correction facilities.

B. Criminalization of the Mentally Ill

With the advent of more stringent standards for involuntary civil commitment,[507] it has been contended that more and more mentally ill persons are ending up in jails and prisons[508] or on the "forensic" wards of hospitals as incompetent to stand trial, including increasing numbers of defendants with only misdemeanor charges.[509] While the behavior of many of these defendants may be inappropriate, disturbing enough to warrant arrest on disorderly conduct charges[510] and at least suggestive of an underlying mental problem, it is not classically psychotic or sufficiently dangerous to warrant hospitalization by today's civil commitment standards.

497. *Id.* (note omitted).
498. *Id.* at 3400.
499. *Id.* at 3406.
500. *Id.* at 3410-2 (note omitted).
501. Dix, The Death Penalty, *supra* note 483.

502. National Coalition for Jail Reform, Washington, D.C. Jails are for persons who are awaiting trial or have been sentenced to less than a year of imprisonment.
503. R. Goldfarb, Jails: The Ultimate Ghetto (1975); Mental Health Services for Adults on Probation/Parole and in Jails: Addendum to 1980 Milwaukee County, Wis. 51.411.437 Plan, July 1979, at 5-6.
504. D. Wood, The Mentally Retarded and Mentally Ill in Our Nation's Jails (prepared for the National Coalition for Jail Reform, Washington, D.C., Oct. 1979); W.C. Eckerman, A Nationwide Survey of Mental Health and Correctional Institutions for Adult Mentally Disordered Offenders, for the National Institute of Mental Health (DHEW Pub. No. (HSM) 73-9018, 1972).
505. Persons found guilty of a felony and sentenced to more than one year of imprisonment are incarcerated in the nation's prisons.
506. Prison Mental Health Care Can Be Improved by Better Management and More Effective Federal Aid: Report to Congress by the Comptroller General of the United States 2 (GAO Report GGD-80-11, Nov. 1979).
507. See ch. 2, Involuntary Institutionalization, *supra*.
508. Lamb & Grant, The Mentally Ill in an Urban County Jail, 39 Archives Gen. Psychiatry 17 (1982); Whitmer, From Hospitals to Jails: The Fate of California's Deinstitutionalized Mentally Ill, 50 Am. J. Orthopsychiatry 65 (1980); Zitrin, Hardestry, Burdock, & Drossman, Crime and Violence Among Mental Patients, 133 Am. J. Psychiatry 142 (1976).
509. Dickey, Incompetency and the Nondangerous Mentally Ill Client, 16 Crim. L. Bull. 22 (1980).
510. Adler, From Hospital to Jail: New Challenges to the Law-Enforcement Process, 17 Crim. L. Bull. 319 (1981).

Studies of the so-called criminalization of mentally ill behavior have found that this phenomenon closely follows changes in civil commitment laws.[511] They suggest that tightening up the civil commitment statutes will not necessarily result in a lower rate of institutionalization of mentally disabled persons but will merely change the place of institutionalization.[512] Moreover, misdemeanants who are hospitalized frequently spend more time institutionalized than if convicted.[513]

C. Mentally Retarded Prisoners

Mentally retarded offenders (those with IQs of 70 or less) represent approximately 9.5% of the prison population according to national estimates,[514] with some states' statistics classifying up to 29% of the prison population as retarded.[515] The majority of such prisoners in the corrections system are only mildly retarded (IQ between 55 and 70). Few studies have systematically analyzed the retarded offender. One Missouri study found retarded offenders to be generally older than other prisoners and less educated, with an average of two to three fewer years of formal education.[516] Another national study, done in 1970, found that retarded offenders were accused of crimes against persons in 57% of criminal cases, as compared with a national average of 27% for all other offenders. Mentally retarded persons were also found to be disproportionately represented in homicide cases, being charged three times more frequently with a homicide than nonretarded persons.[517] The meaning of such statistics is unclear: they may indicate only that retarded persons are more likely to be caught and convicted of violent crimes rather than that they are more prone to violence.

It has also been noted that mentally retarded offenders confess more easily and plead guilty more often[518] than do the nonretarded offenders. They may also be easier to convict because at trial their mental condition may hamper their ability to remember details, locate witnesses, and testify credibly. When convicted, adult retarded offenders tend to be incarcerated longer, spending an average of 6.9 years in prison compared with 3.9 years for the nonretarded.[519] This may be the result of their being convicted of more violent crimes combined with the fact that they lack job skills and thus will be less able to formulate reasonable parole plans. Retarded offenders also have a higher recividism rate: 30%, as compared with an estimated average for nonretarded offenders of 20%.[520]

Within the prison, the retarded offenders often present unique problems. Many have passive-dependent personalities that make them prone to be victimized, abused, and coerced to a greater extent than other inmates.[521] They also have more adaptive problems, have difficulty in understanding prison rules and regulations, and may act out in frustration. Even so, many retarded prisoners are apparently not recognized as such by correctional officials.[522]

D. Treatment

In 1976 in *Estelle v. Gamble*[523] the United States Supreme Court ruled that the constitutional prohibition against cruel and unusual punishment obligates the government to provide medical care for those it incarcerates.[524] Lower courts have expanded upon the *Estelle* ruling to include mental health care. In *Bowring v. Godwin*[525] the Court of Appeals for the Fourth Circuit recognized the right of a prison inmate to psychiatric and psychological treatment. The court held:

> [A prisoner] is entitled to psychological or psychiatric treatment if a physician or other health care provider, exercising ordinary skill and care at the time of observation, concludes with reasonable medical certainty (1) that the prisoner's symptoms evidence a serious disease or injury; (2) that such disease or injury is curable or may be substantially alleviated; and (3) that the potential for harm to the prisoner by reason of delay or the denial of

511. One study that looked at the so-called criminalization of mentally ill behavior found that after California tightened its civil commitment standards, the mentally ill patients discharged from Napa State Hospital were five times more likely to be arrested than before. Sosowsky, Crime and Violence Among Mental Patients Reconsidered in View of the New Legal Relationship Between the State and the Mentally Ill, 135 Am. J. Psychiatry 33 (1978). Along similar lines, a Wisconsin study found that after a change in the state civil commitment law, the rate of commitment of persons found incompetent to stand trial on misdemeanor charges rose from 28% to 42% of the state hospital population. Dickey, *supra* note 509, at 31.

512. Dickey, *supra* note 509, at 40.

513. An Illinois study, e.g., found that misdemeanants were hospitalized as incompetent to stand trial for an average of 10.5 months—considerably longer than the average sentence for a disorderly conduct charge. In the course of such comparisons, however, it should not be forgotten that these misdemeanants may have had real treatment needs and thus may have profited from their hospitalization. Cuneo, Brelje, Randolph, & Taliana, *supra* note 152.

514. M. Santamour & B. West, The Mentally Retarded Offender and Corrections 16 (Study for National Institute of Law Enforcement, Law Enforcement Assistance Administration, U.S. Dep't of Justice, Aug. 1977).

515. *Id.* at 17: Georgia 27%; South Carolina 29%. Also see M. Kindred, J. Cohen, D. Penrod, & T. Schaeffer, Corrections ch. 21, The Mentally Retarded Citizen and the Law (1976).

516. Missouri Association for Retarded Citizens, Mentally Retarded Offenders with Recommendations for a State-Wide System of Services (study for Missouri Dep't of Public Health, 1976).

517. Brown & Courtless, The Mentally Retarded Offender, *in* Readings in Law & Psychiatry 586 (R. Allen, E. Ferster, & J. Rubin, eds. 1975).

518. Santamour & West, *supra* note 514, at 5.

519. Wood, *supra* note 504, at 3.

520. *Id.*

521. R. Urbank, Project Grant: Deinstitutionalization Services for Mentally Retarded Youthful Offenders (N. C. Dep't of Corrections, Apr. 1979).

522. See Santamour & West, *supra* note 514, at 22, 25.

523. 429 U.S. 97 (1976).

524. *Id.* at 104.

525. 551 F.2d 44 (4th Cir. 1977).

care would be substantial. The right to treatment is, of course, limited to that which may be provided upon a reasonable cost and time basis and *the essential test is one of medical necessity and not simply that which may be considered merely desirable.*[526]

Other courts have gone further. In a case challenging conditions in Alabama's prisons the court ordered that mental health professionals be hired to provide at least minimum standards of mental health care within the correctional system.[527] Additionally, the court required that inmates who needed care in facilities for the mentally ill or retarded be transferred to those facilities.[528] A 1982 federal district court decision required that a separate facility be constructed to treat the most severely mentally disturbed inmates in the Arkansas correctional system. The court reasoned that "persons who are severely sick simply cannot be held in custody unless they are provided with necessary medical services. Mental health treatment is clearly a necessary medical service in certain cases."[529]

It appears that adequate provision of medical services to prisoners often comes only as a result of a class action suit, media coverage of an inmate suicide, an exposé of inhumane conditions, or some such dramatic event. Absent such external pressures, adequate mental care is not likely to be provided for. Studies of staff/inmate ratios for state prisons have revealed ratios as low as 1:521 for psychologists and 1:676 for psychiatrists.[530] The mental health professional is often viewed with ambivalence by correctional staff and inmates alike; among the reasons is that such professionals are in the conflicted position of serving the prisoner and the state at the same time.

Arguably, the best solution is to entirely remove prisoners with mental problems from the prison setting. The National Coalition for Jail Reform and other groups have articulated some of the obvious reasons why the mentally disabled do not belong behind bars: prisons are not equipped and prison staffs are not trained to recognize, handle, or treat these individuals, who are often disciplined for behavior resulting from their mental disability.[531]

Short of wholesale removal of mentally disabled persons from our jails and prisons, certain intermediate steps are worth considering. Suggestions include the establishment of screening systems and of at least minimal treatment facilities within the correctional system.[532] Another possibility is vesting the state mental health agency with the responsibility and authority for providing services to the prisoners, either in the prison itself or, more ideally, in a separate facility.[533]

E. Transfer Rights

Until the United States Supreme Court's decision in *Vitek v. Jones*[534] in 1980, many states permitted the transfer of inmates from correctional systems to mental health systems simply on the basis of a finding by a physician or a psychologist that the individual needed treatment that could not be provided within the prison setting.[535] The decision to transfer was viewed as an administrative prerogative of the correctional agency, with the inmate seldom having a choice in the matter. Although the provision of needed health services would appear to be an obvious benefit to the individual, in fact, there are also disadvantages to being transferred to a state mental institution. Among the more notable disadvantages may be the ineligibility for "good time" credits that reduce a prisoner's length of incarceration, and the delay or denial of parole based on the belief that if the individual cannot function in prison he is unlikely to be able to cope in society.[536] Additionally, some stigma may attach to the inmate who spends time on a mental health ward: he is considered not only bad but mad. He also may be subjected to treatment against his wishes as well as more restrictions than he faced in the prison.

The Supreme Court's decision in 1966 in *Baxstrom v. Herold*,[537] which required that prisoners subject to civil commitment at the end of their prison terms had to be

526. *Id.* at 47-48 (emphasis added).

527. Pugh v. Locke, 406 F. Supp. 318, 333 (M.D. Ala. 1976).

528. *Id.*

529. Finney v. Mabry, 534 F. Supp. 1026, 1037 (E.D. Ark. 1982).

530. National Institute of Law Enforcement and Criminal Justice, Law Enforcement Assistance Administration, U.S. Dep't of Justice, National Manpower Survey of Criminal Justice System 66 (vol. 6, Criminal Justice Manpower Planning, 1977).

The recruitment and retention of psychiatric staff in prisons is made difficult by such factors as low prestige and low salary in the positions, distance from urban areas, and frustration from having the people they try to help stay in prison. Speiglman, Prison Psychiatrists and Drugs: A Case Study, 7 Crime & Social Justice 25 (1977).

531. M. Churgin, Mental Health Services and the Inmates: Problems and Considerations, *in* 2 Prisoners' Rights Sourcebook 295 (I. Robbins ed. 1980), for a good review of the issues in this area. Also see materials of National Coalition of Jail Reform, Washington, D.C.

532. National Advisory Commission on Criminal Justice Standards and Goals, Corrections 374 (1973), *cited in* Special Article Series: Mental Health Services for Prisoners, 2 MDLR 666, 667 (1978).

533. Criminal Justice Mental Health Standards, *supra* note 112, §§ 7.9 & 7.10, which provide a mechanism for treatment by the state mental health agency, and the commentary notes on the advantages of this process.

Control by the mental health agency could have the effect of improving the competence and morale of mental health professionals, who would feel professionally more comfortable within a mental health agency career track. This also has the benefit that the mental health professional would not be situated in a conflicted position with responsibilities both to his patient and to his patient's keepers. It also makes it more likely that a higher quality of treatment will be provided and a broader range of treatment options available.

534. 445 U.S. 480 (1980).

535. Churgin, The Transfer of Inmates to Mental Health Facilities, *in* Mentally Disordered Offenders: Perspectives from Law and Social Science 215 (J. Monahan & H. Steadman eds. 1983) [hereinafter cited as Mentally Disordered Offenders].

536. *Id.* at 208.

537. 383 U.S. 107 (1966).

provided the same procedures as other civil committees, paved the way for the assertion that transfer of inmates from prisons to mental institutions raised constitutionally protected liberty interests. Based on *Baxstrom*, two federal circuit courts subsequently found that due process required that prisoners who were to be transferred to mental health facilities had to be accorded certain procedural protections substantially the same as those applied in civil commitment cases.[538] Both cases granted prisoners substantially the same procedures granted to nonprisoners when civil commitment was sought. In *United States ex rel. Schuster v. Herold*,[539] for example, decided in 1969, the United States Court of Appeals for the Second Circuit was faced with an individual who in 1941 had expressed the view that prison officials were corrupt and subsequently had been transferred to Dannemora State Hospital for the Criminally Insane when a physician certified that he was "paranoid." Schuster remained at Dannemora for more than 20 years, at which point he would have been eligible for parole had he not been transferred.[540] The court held that prisoners "must be afforded substantially the same procedural safeguards as are provided in civil commitment proceedings, including proper examination, a hearing upon notice, periodic review of the need for commitment, and trial by jury."[541]

Schuster served as the foundation for other decisions in which prisoners successfully challenged transfers to mental institutions.[542] Ultimately, the Supreme Court in 1980 in *Vitek v. Jones*[543] sustained the reasoning of these cases. The Court stated:

> A criminal conviction and sentence of imprisonment extinguish an individual's right to freedom from confinement for the term of his sentence, but do not authorize the State to classify him as mentally ill and to subject him to involuntary psychiatric treatment without affording him additional due process protections.[544]

Recognizing the prisoner's right to notice and to an adversary hearing conducted by an independent decision maker, the 5 to 4 majority further held that the prisoner had to be allowed to examine and cross-examine witnesses and that he was entitled to a written statement by the fact-finder of the evidence relied upon and the reasons for the transfer.[545] Although the court did not mandate an attorney for transfer hearings, it did recognize the desirability of having one:

> A prisoner thought to be suffering from a mental disease or defect requiring involuntary treatment probably has an even greater need for legal assistance, for such a prisoner is more likely to be unable to understand or exercise his rights. In these circumstances, it is appropriate that counsel be provided to indigent prisoners whom the State seeks to treat as mentally ill.[546]

Recently, the American Bar Association recommended that in addition to guaranteeing the rights established in *Vitek*, states adopt procedures permitting voluntary transfers for those inmates not contesting the move and entitling transferred inmates to continue to earn good time credits and be eligible for parole on the same basis they would enjoy in prison.[547]

An issue that has rarely been addressed by the courts or by legislation is the rights of a person who refuses transfer back to the prison from the mental institution. There are reasons both for and against checks on administrative discretion in these decisions: in being transferred back to prison the inmate may or may not shed the label and stigma of being mentally disabled, he may or may not be cured and be able to survive in the prison, and he may or may not prefer the hospital environment.[548] Two courts that have addressed the issue have reached opposite results on the applicability of the due process clause in those retransfer situations.[549]

VI. SEXUAL PSYCHOPATH LAWS

A. Introduction

In 1937 Michigan adopted the first so-called sexual psychopath law.[550] This marked the beginning of a trend that peaked in the mid-1960s, by which time more than half the states had adopted laws providing special legal and medical treatment, including in some instances special facilities for persons with abnormal sexual propensities manifested through criminal behav-

538. United States *ex rel.* Schuster v. Herold, 410 F.2d 1071 (2d Cir. 1969), *cert. denied*, 396 U.S. 847 (1969); and Matthews v. Hardy, 420 F.2d 607 (D.C. Cir. 1969), *cert. denied*, 397 U.S. 1010 (1970).

539. 410 F.2d at 1071.

540. *Id.* at 1073.

541. *Id.* at 1073.

542. See, e.g., United States *ex rel.* Souder v. Watson, 413 F. Supp. 711 (M.D. Pa. 1976); Sites v. McKenzie, 423 F. Supp. 1190 (N.D.W. Va. 1976); Evans v. Paderick, 443 F. Supp. 583 (E.D. Va. 1977); Harmon v. McNutt, 587 P.2d 537 (Wash. 1978).

543. 445 U.S. 480 (1980).

544. *Id.* at 493-94.

545. *Id.* at 495-96.

546. *Id.* at 496-97.

547. Criminal Justice Mental Health Standards, *supra* note 112, §§ 7-10.3 & 7-10 generally for transfer rights; § 7-10.10.

548. M. Churgin, *supra* note 531, at 309.

549. Cruz v. Ward, 558 F.2d 658 (2d Cir. 1977), which held the transfer was within the discretion of the correctional and mental health authorities; Burchett v. Bower, 355 F. Supp. 1278 (D. Ariz. 1973), which found a judicial hearing necessary if the person was transferred over his objections.

550. Pub. Act No. 196, 1937 Mich. Pub. and Local Acts at 305; Criminal Sexual Psychopathic Persons Act of 1939, No. 165, Mich. Comp. Laws §§ 480.501 to 480.509 (1948) (repealed in 1966 by Pub. Act No. 267, effective Mar. 10, 1967). Michigan's sexual psychopath statute was repealed in its entirety and the legal category of criminal sexual psychopath abolished by Public Act 143, effective Aug. 1, 1968.

ior.[551] These laws were viewed as alternatives to criminal processing and imprisonment for this group of offenders. Referred to by various names, including "sexual psychopath laws," "sexually dangerous persons acts," and "mentally disordered sex offenders acts," these laws had the dual goals of removing the sex offender from the community and treating him.[552]

More recently, a contrary trend has taken hold: since 1976, 13 states have repealed their laws,[553] and another 12 have greatly modified them,[554] the primary modification being to make treatment voluntary to the prisoner.[555] In all, as of 1984, sexual psychopath laws exist in only 16 states and the District of Columbia.[556] Of these jurisdictions, only 6 actually enforce the laws in more than isolated cases.[557]

In this section the phrase *sexual psychopath laws* refers to all laws that treat sex offenders or sexually dangerous persons as a separate category subject to procedures different from those followed in either the criminal justice or the civil commitment process.

B. Profile of the Person Committed Under Sexual Psychopath Laws

A number of studies have examined the effects of sexual psychopath laws, and four studies have analyzed aspects of the California program (the nation's largest), providing a rough profile of the typical committee.[558] One found that the majority of subjects were sentenced following a plea bargain.[559] The other studies showed that the determination and treatment of a defendant as a "mentally disordered sex offender" was based primarily on his social history related in the presentence probation report rather than on clinical observation.[560] Involvement in sexual activity with a child or a previous history of being charged with sex offenses proved to be the key factors correlating with a defendant's being determined to be a mentally disordered sex offender.[561]

Two other studies have compared persons committed under sexual psychopath laws with those sent to prison after being convicted of sex offenses.[562] Analyzing data from California and Wisconsin, these studies found that persons committed under the sexual psychopath laws were usually older and more likely to be white than other offenders and had been involved in sexual offenses against children.[563] Yet other research has shown that (in 1978) 6% of all mentally ill offenders admitted to state mental health facilities were there because of sexual psychopath laws.[564]

It is not clear whether the information gained from the California experience can be generalized to other states that have programs for sexual psychopaths. But, with the widespread repeal or modification of these laws, there will be a dramatic decline in the number of persons committed as sexual psychopaths.

C. Procedures

Each statute defines the sexual psychopath somewhat differently.[565] The common features are that he has been convicted of, or has pleaded guilty to, a sex crime and in addition has a history of sexual-acting-out behavior, usually of a threatening or violent nature. Most of the statutes are aimed at persons who engage in sexual activity with children. Most specify a standard to the effect that the person be mentally ill and/or dangerous. Generally, the statutes come into play only at the time of sentencing, when a finding of sexual psychopathy and resultant need of treatment may be an alternative to standard prison sentencing.

551. Group for the Advancement of Psychiatry, Psychiatry and Sex Psychopath Legislation: The 30s to the 80s at 861 (formulated by the Committee on Psychiatry and Law, Rep. No. 98, 1977) [hereinafter cited as GAP Sex Psychopath Report]. See also S.J. Brakel & R.S. Rock, The Mentally Disabled and the Law 341 n.1 (rev. ed. 1971), reporting that 28 states had sexual psychopath laws.

552. *Id.* at 854.

553. Alabama, Florida, Indiana, Iowa, Minnesota, Mississippi, Missouri, Oklahoma, Pennsylvania, Rhode Island, Vermont, Virginia, and Wisconsin.

554. California, Connecticut, Kansas, Maryland, Nebraska, New Hampshire, New Jersey, Oregon, Tennessee, Utah, Washington, and Wyoming.

555. See, e.g., Md. Ann. Code art. 31B, §§ 8 to 13 (Supp. 1980), which provides that the offender must volunteer or consent to treatment to remain in the program. See also Çal. Welf. & Inst. Code §§ 6300 to 6330 (West 1979 & Supp. 1981), which provides that if an offender convicted of a sex offense receives a prison sentence of three years or more, at the beginning of the third year prior to release the offender can be evaluated for treatment, and if he is found to need it and consents to treatment then he will be transferred to a state hospital for treatment.

556. See table 12.8.

557. The author conducted an informal survey of the states with sexual psychopath laws and found that they were being used on a regular basis only in Massachusetts, Nebraska, New Jersey, Oregon, and Washington. Florida has a large treatment program, but it is a voluntary one. The other states that have such laws rarely, if ever, invoke them.

558. See, e.g., Dix, Differential Processing of Abnormal Sex Offenders: Utilization of California's Mentally Disordered Sex Offender Program, 67 J. Crim. L. & Criminology 233 (1976); M.L. Forst, Civil Commitment and Social Control (1978); Konecni, Mulcahy, & Ebbesen, Prison or Mental Hospital: Factors Affecting the Processing of Persons Suspected of Being "Mentally Disordered Sex Offenders," *in* New Directions in Psycholegal Research (P.D. Lipsitt & B.D. Sales eds. 1980); Sturgeon & Taylor, Report of a Five-Year Follow-Up Study of Mentally Disordered Sex Offenders Released from Atascadero State Hospital in 1973, 4 Crim. Just. J. (Western State Univ.) 31 (1980).

559. See Forst, *supra* note 558, at 121.

560. See Dix, *supra* note 558, at 236.

561. See Monahan & Davis, Mentally Disordered Sex Offenders, *in* Mentally Disordered Offenders, *supra* note 535, at ch. 6, which provides a brief review of each of the studies discussed in this section. Also see studies by Dix, *supra* note 558, and Konecni, Mulcahy, & Ebbesen, *supra* note 558.

562. See Sturgeon & Taylor, *supra* note 558, which compared 260 mentally disordered sex offenders in California with a group of 122 persons convicted of sexual crimes. See also Pacht & Cowden, An Exploratory Study of Five Hundred Sex Offenders, 1 Crim. Just. & Behav. 13 (1974), which compared 380 persons committed under the Wisconsin sexual psychopath law with 121 persons given prison sentences who had been evaluated under that law.

563. Also see Monahan & Davis, *supra* note 561, at 195.

564. Steadman, Monahan, Hartstone, Davis, & Robbins, *supra* note 2, at 34 (1982).

565. See table 12.8.

In some states a person may be committed under a sexual psychopath law without having been convicted of a crime.[566] Nonetheless, there is usually a criminal charge in the background, or at least an arrest, and it is the prosecution who must initiate the sexual psychopath proceedings. In the past, commitment under both these "preconviction" statutes and the "postconviction" schemes was typically for an indeterminate period. However, today only five jurisdications still permit indefinite confinement, and of these only one uses its law with any frequency.[567] Commitment absent a criminal conviction can only be to a mental institution. But imprisonment—limited to the statutory maximum for the crime or for an indeterminate period—continues to be an option under some of the postconviction sexual psychopath statutes. The standard for release is a medical finding that the person is "fully recovered" or improved sufficiently so that he "no longer presents a danger to others."

D. Procedural Challenges

When first enacted, sexual psychopath laws were generally viewed as civil in nature. This meant that statutory definitions of the applicable offenses or offenders and procedural rights were not as rigorous as those required in criminal proceedings. Early challengers to the laws alleged that they were unconstitutionally vague and that the difference in treatment of sexual psychopaths and of other offenders violated equal protection. These contentions were brushed aside by the United States Supreme Court in the 1940 case of *Minnesota ex rel. Pearson v. Probate Court*.[568] Twenty-seven years later, however, the Court in *Specht v. Patterson*,[569] took a far more critical line: while sexual psychopath proceedings may be ostensibly civil in nature, the reality that they could lead to indeterminate institutionalization entitles a person subject to these proceedings to certain fundamental protections, including the right to "be present with counsel, have an opportunity to be heard, be confronted with witnesses against him, have the right to cross-examine and to offer evidence of his own." Furthermore, "there must be findings adequate to make meaningful any appeal that is allowed."[570]

Specht did not go so far as to specify the standard of proof applicable in sexual psychopath proceedings. The United States Court of Appeals for the Seventh Circuit, however, following the Supreme Court's reasoning in *In re Winship*,[571] which applied the beyond a reasonable doubt standard of proof to juvenile proceedings, has held that standard applicable to the Illinois Sexually Dangerous Persons Act.[572] Other courts have followed with identical holdings.[573] In addition to the equal protection and due process reasoning used in *Specht* and other cases to upgrade the procedural safeguards for alleged sexual psychopaths, one court has accepted the contention that the laws, at least as administered in Oregon, violated the cruel and unusual punishment clause of the Eighth Amendment.[574] The declining use of the sexual psychopath laws may in part reflect the view that the programs are too vulnerable to legal attack or at least that they are not worth the continual litigation that they stimulate.

E. Treatment

One of the original goals of the sexual psychopath laws was to provide treatment. At the time of their enactment it was believed that mental health professionals could identify a specific mental disability called sexual psychopathy that made persons suffering from this disability more likely to commit dangerous sex offenses and that treatment made improvement and cure possible.[575]

The literature of the past decade has pointed out, however, that these laws were enacted with few or no data to support the premise of existence of a broad category of people known as "sexual psychopaths" who can be treated successfully.[576] The Group for the Advancement of Psychiatry (GAP) has stated that the category lacks clinical validity and that sexual psychopathy is not a psychiatric diagnosis.[577] Its report points out that individuals may engage in sexually inappropriate behavior for a number of reasons, some relating to illness and others not, and concludes that using sexual psychopathy as a common denominator to prescribe treatment is fatally flawed.[578]

Today, it is generally recognized that sex offenders do not constitute a homogeneous group of people. Their personalities are as diverse as those of the general population, and they vary in their dangerousness, the frequency with which they commit illegal sexual acts, and the types of victims they select.[579] There is no treatment

566. See also the laws of District of Columbia, Illinois, and Minnesota.

567. See, e.g., Colorado, District of Columbia, Illinois, Massachusetts, and Minnesota. Massachusetts is the only state that uses the law for more than very isolated cases.

568. 309 U.S. 270 (1940).

569. 386 U.S. 605 (1967).

570. *Id.* at 610.

571. 397 U.S. 358, 364 (1970).

572. United States *ex rel.* Stachulak v. Coughlin, 520 F.2d 931 (7th Cir. 1975).

573. People v. Burnick, 535 P.2d 352, 121 Cal. Rptr. 488 (1975); People v. Pembrock, 62 Ill. 2d 317, 342 N.E.2d 28 (1976). For commentary on these cases see Comment, Due Process Requires Proof Beyond Reasonable Doubt for Commitment of Sex Offenders, 1975 Wash. U.L.Q. 1092 (1975); Comment, Dangerousness, Reasonable Doubt and Preconviction Psychopath Legislation, 1 S. Ill. U.L.J. 218 (1970).

574. Ohlinger v. Watson, 652 F.2d 775, 777 (9th Cir. 1980).

575. See GAP Sex Psychopath Report, *supra* note 551, at 840.

576. See Monahan & Davis, *supra* note 561, at 326.

577. See GAP Sex Psychopath Report, *supra* note 551, at 840, 935.

578. *Id.* at 858-60.

579. Quinsey, Prediction of Recidivism and the Evaluation of Treatment Programs for Sex Offenders, *in* Sexual Aggression and the Law 29 (S. Simon-Jones ed. 1983).

that would apply to all persons designated as "sexual psychopaths."

Prisons that have special programs for sex offenders usually employ behavioral techniques to try to change the offender's behavior so that upon release he will channel his sexual drive toward a mutually consenting heterosexual relationship.[580] There are, however, almost no postrelease programs to reinforce the techniques employed in the institution, and there have been no follow-up studies to determine if these treatment programs have any lasting effect once the person is returned to the community.

During the past decade research has been conducted in a handful of states to determine if there is an objective way to measure what type of stimulus causes a person to become aroused and whether there are workable methods that can change sexual arousal patterns so that they will occur only in "appropriate" circumstances.[581] These programs may employ behavior modification techniques, psychotherapy, and/or drug treatments.[582] The results of this new research are only beginning to be reported; no long-term follow-up studies have as yet been done.[583]

There are a few treatment programs that use antiandrogen drugs to treat certain male sex offenders as well as individuals who, while not having been charged with any legal offense, exhibit inappropriate sexual activity.[584] These drugs, which suppress the serum testerone level and thus have the effect of decreasing sexual fantasy and desire, are apparently more effective in eliminating sexually dangerous behavior than other types of therapy.[585]

As yet, there has been so little work done with these drugs in the United States that few clinicians are aware of them. Their use for the purpose of rehabilitating offenders has not been approved by the U.S. Food and Drug Administration, thus severely limiting the settings in which research, experimentation, and treatment can be attempted.[586] Wider experience with the drug in Europe, supported by a few case studies conducted in the United States and Canada, seems to suggest that this treatment may be quite successful for at least certain types of sex offenders.[587]

F. Constitutional Problems Presented by Lack of Treatment

Sexual psychopath laws were premised on the existence of a group of individuals whose behavior justified their isolation and treatment as mentally disordered persons, or "sexual psychopaths." The persistence of significant uncertainty about the capacity to identify such persons or to provide successful medical treatment for them has eroded the justification for their separate legal treatment. As early as 1966 in *Millard v. Cameron*[588] the United States Court of Appeals for the District of Columbia Circuit held that indefinite confinement under a sexual psychopath law was justified only upon a theory of therapeutic treatment[589] and that the reality of "'[l]ack of treatment destroys any otherwise valid reason

580. The behavioral approaches include a variety of techniques. they will first identify the specifics of the problem, considering the targets and circumstances of inappropriate sexual activity, and then formulate an individual treatment program. Usually, there will be training in developing heterosocial skills and sex education, and there may also be self-assertiveness training to overcome a poor self-image. Finally, there may be techniques specifically aimed at changing the inappropriate sexual arousal patterns, which may include the use of slides and video or audio tapes and possibly the administration of mild electrical shocks to reinforce the proper response. Finally, some programs may try to help the offender develop alternative ways of handling his sexual drive so that he does not engage in illegal sexual activity.

For discussion of behavior treatment programs for sex offenders, see, e.g., Abel, Becker, & Skinner, Aggressive Behavior and Sex, 3 Sexuality 133 (1980); Abel, Blanchard, & Becker, An Integrated Treatment Program for Rapists, *in* Clinical Aspects of the Rapist (R.T. Rada ed. 1978); Bradford, The Hormonal Treatment of Sexual Offenders, 11 A.A.P.L. Bull. 159 (1983); Marshall, Abel, & Quinsey, The Assessment and Treatment of Sexual Offenders, *in* Sexual Aggression and the Law, *supra* note 579; Money & Bennett, Postadolescent Paraphilic Sex Offenders: Antiandrogenic and Counseling Therapy, 10 Int'l J. Mental Health 122 (1981); Quinsey, *supra* note 579; Whitman & Quinsey, Heterosocial Skill Training for Institutionalized Rapists and Child Molesters, 13 Canadian J. Behav. Sci. 105 (1981).

581. See, e.g., Abel, Barlow, Blanchard, & Guild, The Components of Rapists' Sexual Arousal, 34 Archives Gen. Psychiatry 895 (1977), which describes the use of penile measures to determine erection responses of rapists to various stimuli. These types of measures are being used for other groups of sex offenders to determine what they respond to and if they have responded to treatment by having erections only under sexually appropriate circumstances. See also Quinsey & Chaplin, Penile Responses to Nonsexual Violence Among Rapists, 9 Crim. Just. & Behav. 372 (1982).

582. See Marshall, Abel, & Quinsey, *supra* note 580; Bradford, *supra* note 580; Money & Bennett, *supra* note 580.

583. The primary work in this area is being done at Johns Hopkins University in Baltimore under the direction of John Money, Ph.D., and Leonard Berlin, M.D., and at the Sexual Behavior Clinic of the New York Psychiatric Institute under the direction of Gene Abel, M.D. In Canada most of the research is being done by Penetanguishene Mental Health Center in Ontario under the direction of Vernon Quinsey, Ph.D., who is using behavioral techniques, and at the Royal Ottawa Hospital under the direction of John Bradford, M.D., who is also using antiandrogen treatments.

584. The few programs in the United States offering treatment with antiandrogens include the Johns Hopkins University School of Medicine in Baltimore, the Issac Ray Center of Rush-Presbyterian-St. Luke's Medical Center in Chicago, and a few individual practitioners around the country. There is also a program at the Royal Ottawa Hospital in Ottawa, Canada.

585. See Bradford, *supra* note 580; Money, Paraphilia and Abuse-Martyrdom: Exhibitionism as a Paradigm for Reciprocal Couple Counseling Combined With Antiandrogen, 7 J. Sex & Marital Therapy 115 (1981); Cooper, A Placebo-Controlled Trial of the Antiandrogen Cyproterone Acetate in Deviant Hypersexuality, 22 Comprehensive Psychiatry 458 (1981). Kelly & Cavanaugh, Treatment of the Sexually Dangerous Patient, *in* 21 Current Psychiatric Therapies 101 (J.H. Masserman ed. 1982).

586. Upjohn Laboratories, which produces Depo-Provera, the antiandrogen currently used for treating sex offenders in the United States, has not sought FDA approval for this purpose, in part because of the costs involved in obtaining approval for what is perceived to be a limited market. Lack of FDA approval makes clinicians hesitant to use the drug for fear of liability.

587. See Kelly & Cavanaugh, *supra* note 585, at 102; Bradford, *supra* note 580, at 165.

588. 373 F.2d 468 (D.C. Cir. 1966).

589. *Id.* at 473.

for differential consideration of the sexual psychopath.'"[590]

The question of differential consideration arises in cases in which the individual is committed for an indefinite period as a sexual psychopath whereas he would probably have spent less time incarcerated if committed under the criminal laws.

The United States Court of Appeals for the Ninth Circuit, reviewing a challenge to the Oregon sex offenders statute, recently asserted:

> Adequate and effective treatment is constitutionally required because, absent treatment, appellants could be held indefinitely as a result of their mental illness, while those convicted and sentenced under statutes governing the State sodomy offense need only serve the fifteen-year maximum term.[591]

The court went on to hold that "[t]he rehabilitative rationale is not only desirable, but it is constitutionally required,"[592] and ordered the petitioners transferred to a facility where they could receive treatment. The court said:

> Constitutionally adequate treatment is not that which must be provided to the general prison population, but that which must be provided to those committed for mental incapacity. "At the least, due process requires that the nature and duration of the commitment bear some reasonable relation to the purpose for which the individual is committed."[593]

Thus, the practice of incarcerating a sex offender for a period longer than if he had been sentenced, with no meaningful treatment provided, probably cannot withstand constitutional attack.[594] The lack of successful treatment methods or programs constitutes a basic condemnation of the sexual psychopath laws, since the very justification for such legislation was that sex offenders should be treated rather than punished. Practically speaking, the lack of treatment, or the availability of only unproven experimental treatment, has led many prosecutors to conclude that it is preferable to seek conviction and sentence of sex offenders under the criminal law than to resort to the constitutionally suspect sexual psychopath laws.

G. Move for Repeal

Growing awareness that there is no specific group of individuals who can be labeled sexual psychopaths by acceptable medical standards and that there are no proven treatments for such offenders has led such professional groups as the Group for the Advancement of Phychiatry,[595] the President's Commission on Mental Health,[596] and, most recently, the American Bar Association Committee on Criminal Justice Mental Health Standards[597] to urge that these laws be repealed.

590. *Id.*, quoting F.T. Lindman & D.M. McIntrye, The Mentally Disabled and the Law 308 (1961).

591. Ohlinger v. Watson, 652 F.2d 775, 778 (9th Cir. 1980).

592. *Id.* at 777.

593. *Id.* at 778, also citing Jackson v. Indiana, 406 U.S. 715, 738 (1972).

594. The Supreme Court's decision in Jones v. United States, 103 S. Ct. 3043 (1983), raises questions of whether the Court would strike down as unconstitutional sexual psychopath laws that permit indeterminate sentences or sentences that are longer than the prison term for the given offense of which the person could have been convicted, even if it were shown that no adequate treatment was being provided. In *Jones* the court upheld institutionalizing insanity acquittees for as long as they needed treatment without requiring that at some point, such as when their criminal sentence would have expired, they be held pursuant to the civil commitment procedures and standards. The Court said: "There simply is no necessary correlation between severity of the offense and length of time necessary for recovery. The length of the acquittee's hypothetical criminal sentence therefore is irrelevant to the purposes of his commitment" (*Id.* at 3052). This decision seems to fly in the face of the Court's earlier decisions in Baxstrom v. Herold, 383 U.S. 107 (1966), and Humphrey v. Cady, 405 U.S. 504 (1972), and leaves unclear whether the rational behind *Jones* would apply only to insanity acquittees or might be extended to others who might be "mentally ill" and be incarcerated under special statutes because of their criminal behavior.

595. GAP Sex Psychopath Report, *supra* note 551, at 843.

596. 4 Task Panel Reports, Submitted to the a President's Commission on Mental Health 1978 at 1461 (1978).

597. Criminal Justice Mental Health Standards, *supra* note 112, § 7.8-1.

TABLE 12.1 INCOMPETENCY TO STAND TRIAL

STATE	ISSUE RAISED BY				REQUIRED CONDITION	CRITERIA FOR CONDITION (*fn. 1*)				COMPETENT IF FIT BECAUSE OF OR IN SPITE OF MEDICATION
						Lacks Capacity to		*Because of Mental Disease or Defect*		
	Judge upon (1)	*Prosecutor* (2)	*Defendant* (3)	*When* (4)	(5)	Understand Proceedings (6)	Assist in Defense (7)	(8)	*Other* (9)	(10)
ALA. Code (1982)	reasonabledoubt as to sanity 15-16-21 or written report of 3 specialists or superintendent of state hospital in capital cases 15-16-22(a)			any time after indictment in capital cases 15-16-22(a) while confined & under indictment in felony cases 15-16-21	insane 15-16-21	*fn. 2* annot. to 15-16-21	OR *fn. 2* annot. to 15-16-21			
ALAS. Stat. (1968 & Supp. 1982)		attorney general 12.47.100(b)	12.47.100(b)	after arrest & before imposition of the sentence or before expiration of probation 12.47.100(b)	incompetent to proceed 12.47.100	12.47.100(b)	OR 12.47.100(b)	12.47.100(b)		12.47.110(d)
ARIZ. R. Crim. P.		any party rule 11.2	any party rule 11.2	any time after information filed or indictment returned rule 11.2	incompetent rule 11.1	rule 11.1	OR rule 11.1	mental illness or defect rule 11.1		
ARK. Stat. Ann. (1976 & Supp. 1983)			41-604(1)	earliest practicable time *fn. 3* 41-604(1)	lacks fitness to proceed 41-603	41-603	OR 41-603	41-603		
CAL. Penal Code (West 1970 & Supp. 1983)	doubt as to mental competence, & conference w/defense counsel 1368(a)		1368(a), (b)	during pendency of action & prior to judgment 1368(a)	mentally incompetent 1367	1367	OR in a rational manner 1367	mental disorder or developmental disability 1367		
COLO. Rev. Stat. (1978 & Supp. 1982)	reason to believe incompetent 16-8-110(2)(a)	16-8-110(2)(b)	16-8-110(2)(b)	on or before commencement of proceeding 16-8-110(2)(b)	incompetent to proceed 16-8-110(1)	16-8-102(3)	OR 16-8-102(3)	16-8-102(3)		
CONN. Gen. Stat. Ann. (West 1960 & Supp. 1983–84)	54-56d(c)	54-56d(c)	54-56d(c)	any time during proceeding 54-56d(c)	not competent 54-56d(c)	54-56d(a)	OR 54-56d(a)			
DEL. Code Ann. (1979 & Supp. 1982)				whenever ct. satisfied 11, §404(a)	too mentally ill to stand trial 11, §404	11, §404(a)	OR give evidence or instruct counsel on own behalf 11, §404(a)	11, §404(a)		
D.C. Code Ann. (1973)	own observations or prima facie evidence submitted 24-301(a)			prior to imposition of sentence 24-301(a)	unsound mind or mentally incompetent 24-301(a)	24-301(a)	OR 24-301(a)			
FLA. Stat. Ann. (West 1973 & Supp. 1983)					incompetent to stand trial 916.12(1)	*fn. 5* 916.12(1)	OR *fn. 5* 916.12(1)			psychotropic medication 916.12(2)

COURT-ORDERED EXAMINATION				DISPOSITION ON BASIS OF EXAMINER'S REPORT	JUDICIAL HEARINGS	JURY TRIAL	STANDARD OF PROOF	DISPOSITION IF UNFIT TO PROCEED				
By Whom (11)	*Defendant's Physician Permitted to Attend* (12)	*Hospitalization Pending Examination* (13)	*Maximum Duration* (14)	(15)	(16)	(17)	(18)	*Suspension of Proceedings* (19)	*Continuation Where Personal Participation Unnecessary* (20)	*Commitment* (21)	*Duration of Commitment* (22)	*Other* (23)
physician, if confined 15-16-20 commission on lunacy, if charged w/capital offense 15-16-22(a)		15-16-22(b)	as long as necessary for examination 15-16-22(b)	in capital cases 15-16-22(d)		15-16-21		15-16-21		15-16-21	until restored to right mind 15-16-21	
psychiatrist 12.47.100(b)		or other suitable facility 12.47.100(b)	a reasonable time 12.47.100(b)	12.47.100(b)	12.47.100(b)		preponderance of evidence 12.47.110(a)	12.47.110(a)		12.47.110(a)	90 days 12.47.110(a)	
if reasonable grounds exist, by 2 mental health experts rule 11.3(a), (b)	rule 11.3(c)	not unless necessary rule 11.3(d)	30 days rule 11.3(d)		rule 11.5(a)			rule 11.5(a)		if restoration probable w/in reasonable time rule 11.5(b) (3)	6 mos. rule 11.5(b) (3)	civil commitment or release if restoration improbable rule 11.5(b) (2)
psychiatrist or director of state hospital 41-605(2)		discretionary 41-605(2), (3)	30 days; longer if necessary 41-605(2)(d)	41-606	if report contested 41-606			41-607(1)	41-608	41-607(1)	until restoration of fitness to proceed 41-607(1)	conditional release if not dangerous 41-607(1)
psychiatrist or psychologist & any other expert *fn. 4* 1369(a)	*fn. 4* 1369(a)	discretionary 1369(a)			1368(b) OR	1369(e)	preponderance of evidence & unanimous jury 1369(f)	1370(a)(1) 1370.1(a)(1)		1370(a)(1)(i) 1370.1(a) (1)(A)	3 yrs. 1370(c)(1) 1370.1(c)(1)	outpatient status 1370(a)(1)(i) 1370.1(a) (1)(A) reexamination 1370(a)(2) 1370.1(a)(2)
if available information inadequate 16-8-111 (1), (2)		discretionary 16-8-111(2)		preliminary finding on available evidence 16-8-111(1)	at either party's request 16-8-111(2)		preponderance of evidence 16-8-111(2)	mistrial 16-8-111(3)		16-8-112(2)	until competent to proceed 16-8-112(2) not in excess of max. sentence for offense charged 16-8-114(5)	
psychiatrist(s) or commissioner of mental health either by a clinical team of psychiatrist & clinical psychologist & psychiatric social worker or by 1 or more psychiatrists 54-56d(d)	counsel may observe exam & ct. may authorize psychiatrist, clinical psychologist, or psychiatric social worker selected by defendant to be present at exam 54-56d(d)			54-56d(g)	54-56d(g)			54-56d(g) OR		54-56d(g)	placement for rendering competent may not exceed max. sentence 54-56d(i)	
					11, §404(a)			if hearing indicates state does not have a prima facie case 11, §404(a)	entitled to hearing on whether case prima facie 11, §404(a)	11, §404(a)	until capable of standing trial 11, §404(a)	
superintendent of mental hospital or chief psychiatrist of general hospital 24-301(a)		24-301(a)	reasonable period designated by ct. 24-301(a)	24-301(a)	if accused or government objects 24-301(a)			24-301(a)		24-301(a)		
2 or 3 experts, 1 appointed by state 916.11(1), (2)		in appropriate local facility 916.11(1)						916.13(1)		916.13(1)	until competent or no longer meets criteria for commitment 916.13(1)	conditional release 916.17(1)

TABLE 12.1 INCOMPETENCY TO STAND TRIAL*—*Continued*

STATE	ISSUE RAISED BY				REQUIRED CONDITION (5)	CRITERIA FOR CONDITION (fn. 1)				COMPETENT IF FIT BECAUSE OF OR IN SPITE OF MEDICATION (10)
						Lacks Capacity to		Because of Mental Disease or Defect (8)	Other (9)	
	Judge upon (1)	*Prosecutor* (2)	*Defendant* (3)	*When* (4)		Understand Proceedings (6)	Assist in Defense (7)			
GA. Code Ann. (1983 & Supp. 1983)			27-1502(a)	upon arraignment 27-1501	mentally incompetent 27-1502(a)					
HAWAII Rev. Stat. (1968 & Supp. 1982)	reason to doubt fitness to proceed 704-404(1)					704-403	OR 704-403	physical or mental disease, disorder or defect 704-403		
IDAHO Code (1979 & Supp. 1983)	reason to doubt fitness to proceed 18-211(1)					18-210	OR 18-210	18-210		
ILL. Ann. Stat. (Smith-Hurd 1980 & Supp. 1983–84)	bonafide doubt 38, §104-11(a)	38, §104-11(a)	38, §104-11(a)	any appropriate time before plea entered or before, during, or after trial 38, §104-11(a)	unfit 38, §104-10	38, §104-10	OR 38, §104-10	mental or physical condition 38, §104-10		38, §104-21(a) special provisions or assistance 38, §104-22(a)
IND. Stat. Ann. (Burns 1979 & Supp. 1983)	reasonable grounds 35-36-3-1(a)			any time before final submission to ct. or jury 35-36-3-1(a)		35-36-3-1(a)	AND 35-36-3-1(a)			
IOWA Code Ann. (West 1979 & Supp. 1983–84)				any stage of proceeding 812.3	incapacitated 812.4	812.3	OR 812.3	mental disorder 812.3	appreciating the charge 812.3	
KAN. Stat. Ann. (1980 & Supp. 1982)	reason to believe incompetent 22-3302(1)	22-3302(1)	22-3302(1)	after arraignment & before sentencing 22-3302(1)	incompetent to stand trial 22-3301(1)	22-3301(1)(a)	OR 22-3301(1)(b)	22-3301(1)		
KY. Rev. Stat. Ann. (Michie 1975 & Supp. 1982)	reasonable grounds to believe incompetent 504.100(1)			on arraignment, or during any stage of proceedings 504.100(1)	incompetent 504.090	504.060(3)	OR 504.060(3)	as result of mental condition 504.060(3)		
LA. Code Crim. Proc. (West 1981 & Supp. 1983); LA. Rev. Stat. Ann. §28:59 (West 1975 & Supp. 1983)	own motion 642(a)	642(a)	642(a)	at any time 642	mental incapacity to proceed 641	641	OR 641	641		fn. 6 649.1
ME. Rev. Stat. Ann. (1980 & Supp. 1982–83)	ct. may order 15, §101				incompetent to stand trial 15, §101					
MD. Ann. Code (1979 & Supp. 1982)			59, §23	prior to or during trial 59, §23	incompetent to stand trial 59, §23	59, §23	OR 59, §23			

COURT-ORDERED EXAMINATION				DISPOSITION ON BASIS OF EXAMINER'S REPORT (15)	JUDICIAL HEARINGS (16)	JURY TRIAL (17)	STANDARD OF PROOF (18)	DISPOSITION IF UNFIT TO PROCEED				
By Whom (11)	*Defendant's Physician Permitted to Attend* (12)	*Hospitalization Pending Examination* (13)	*Maximum Duration* (14)					*Suspension of Proceedings* (19)	*Continuation Where Personal Participation Unnecessary* (20)	*Commitment* (21)	*Duration of Commitment* (22)	*Other* (23)
						trial by special jury 27-1502(a)		27-1502		transfer to dep't of human resources 27-1502(a)	90 days; 9 more mos. if recovery probable in near future 27-1502(b), (d)	civil commitment if recovery improbable in near future 27-1502(c)
3 examiners, at least 1 psychologist & 1 psychiatrist 704-404(2)	704-404(2)	704-404(2)	30 days; longer if ct. deems necessary 704-404(2)	704-405	if contested 704-405			74-406(1)	special post-commitment hearing 74-407	74-406(1)	so long as unfitness shall endure 74-406(1)	conditional release 74-406(1)
psychiatrist or psychologist 18-211(1)	18-211(1)	18-211(1)	60 days; longer if ct. deems necessary 18-211(1)	18-212(1)	if report contested 18-212(1)			18-212(2)	special post-commitment hearing 18-212(3)	18-212(2)	so long as unfitness shall endure 18-212(2)	
38, §104-13 (a), (b)	38, §104-13 (e)	38, §104-13 (c)	7 days; 7 more on good cause 38, §104-13 (c)		38, §104-16 (a)	on motion of ct. or either party, except when raised after trial has begun 38, §104-12	preponderance of evidence (on state) 38, §104-11 (c)	38, §104-23	pretrial motions 38, §104-11 (d) discharge hearing 38, §104-25	38, §104-17 (b), (c)	90 day hearings 38, §104-20 (a) subject to max. sentence for offense 38, §104-25 (f)(5)	outpatient treatment 38, §104-17 (b), (c)
2 psychiatrists 35-36-3-1(a)					35-36-3-1(a)			ct. shall delay or continue the trial 35-36-3-1(b)	ct. shall delay or continue the trial 35-36-3-1(b)	35-36-3-1(b)	6 mos. 35-36-3-3	civil commitment 35-36-3-3 35-36-3-4
					812.3			812.4		if release will endanger public peace or safety 812.4	6 mos. 812.5	civil commitment proceedings 812.5
2 physicians 22-3302(3)		22-3302(3)	60 days; 60 more for good cause 22-3302(3)		22-3302(1), (2)	discretionary 22-3302(3)		22-3302(1)		22-3303(1)	90 days; 6 mos. if recovery substantially probable 22-3303(1)	civil commitment if recovery improbable 22-3303(1)
psychiatrist or psychologist 504.100(1)				504.100(3)	504.100(3)			504.040(1)		504.110	60 days or until competent 504.110	if not substantial probability of recovery of competency ct. shall conduct civil commitment proceeding 504.110(2)
not stated; mental exam ordered on reasonable doubt as to capacity 643		ct. may order appearance at exam 644(C)		report examined by a sanity commission of 2 or 3 physicians 644(A)	647			648(A)		648(A)	as long as lack of capacity continues, up to max. sentence for offense 648(A), (B)	release or civil commitment if won't be competent in foreseeable future 648(B) 28:59(B)
at least 1 psychiatrist or psychologist & further exam if indicated by commissioner of mental health 15, §101		15, §101	60 days 15, §101	15, §101	on motion of defendant or ct. 15, §101			"the court . . . shall continue the case until . . . defendant is deemed competent to stand trial" 15, §101	"the court . . . shall continue the case until . . . defendant is deemed competent to stand trial" 15, §101	15, §101(1)	1 yr. 15, §101(1) hearing after 30 days to determine whether competent or recovery probable 15, §101(1)	charges dismissed & release or civil commitment if recovery improbable in foreseeable future 15, §101(1)
Dep't of Mental Hygiene, on good cause 59, §23		discretionary; may be conducted on outpatient basis except in capital cases 59, §23		59, §23	59, §23			59, §23	upon defense counsel's election 59, §24(a)	or bail or ROR 59, §24(a)		

TABLE 12.1 INCOMPETENCY TO STAND TRIAL—*Continued*

STATE	ISSUE RAISED BY: *Judge upon* (1)	*Prosecutor* (2)	*Defendant* (3)	*When* (4)	REQUIRED CONDITION (5)	CRITERIA FOR CONDITION (*fn. 1*): *Lacks Capacity to* Understand Proceedings (6)	Assist in Defense (7)	*Because of Mental Disease or Defect* (8)	*Other* (9)	COMPETENT IF FIT BECAUSE OF OR IN SPITE OF MEDICATION (10)
MASS. Ann. Laws (Michie/ Law. Co-op. 1981 & Supp. 1983)	doubt whether competent 123, §15(a)	123, §15(d)	123, §15(d)	any time after indictment or issuance of complaint 123, §15(a)	not competent to stand trial 123, §15(b)			mental illness or defect 123, §15(b)		
MICH. Comp. Laws Ann. (1980 & Supp. 1983–84)	own motion 330.2024	330.2024	330.2024	by ct. rule 330.2024	incompetent to stand trial 330.2020(1)	330.2020(1) OR	330.2020(1)	mental condition 330.2020(1)		psychotropic drugs or other medication 330.2020(2) 330.2030(4)
MINN. R. Crim. P. (West 1979 & Supp. 1982)	own motion 20.01, subd. 2	20.01, subd. 2	20.01, subd. 2	during the pending proceedings 20.01, subd. 2	incompetent to proceed 20.01, subd. 1	20.01, subd. 1 OR	20.01, subd. 1	while mentally ill or deficient 20.01, subd. 1		
MISS. Code Ann. (1972 & Supp. 1982)	own motion 99-13-11	99-13-11	99-13-11				99-13-11	mental condition in question 99-13-11		
MO. Ann. Stat. (Vernon 1953 & Supp. 1983)	reasonable cause 552.020(2)	552.020(2)	552.020(2)		lacks mental fitness to proceed 552.020(8)	552.020(1) OR	552.020(1)	552.020(1)		
MONT. Code Ann. (1983)			46-14-221(1)		lacks fitness to proceed 46-14-221(2)	46-14-103 OR	46-14-103	46-14-103		
NEB. Rev. Stat. (1979)		29-1823	29-1823	any time prior to trial 29-1823	mentally incompetent to stand trial 29-1823					
NEV. Rev. Stat. (1981)	doubt as to sanity of defendant 178.405			between indictment & judgment 178.405	insane 178.400					
N.H. Rev. Stat. Ann. (1977 & Supp. 1981)	notification by either party 135:17	135:17	135:17	after indictment or awaiting action of grand jury 135:17						
N.J. Stat. Ann. (West 1981 & Supp. 1983–84)	reason to doubt fitness 2C:4-5(a)	2C:4-5(a)	2C:4-5(a)		lacks fitness to proceed 2C:4-6(b)	2C:4-4(a) OR	2C:4-4(a)			
N.M. Stat. Ann. (1978); N.M. R. Crim. P. (1980 & Supp. 1983)	own motion 31-9-1 rule 35(b)(1)	motion 31-9-1 rule 35(b)(1)	motion 31-9-1 rule 35(b)(1)	any stage of proceedings rule 35(b)(1)	mental incompetency 31-9-1				incompetent to stand trial 31-9-1 rule 35(b)(2)	

COURT-ORDERED EXAMINATION				DISPOSITION ON BASIS OF EXAMINER'S REPORT	JUDICIAL HEARINGS	JURY TRIAL	STANDARD OF PROOF	DISPOSITION IF UNFIT TO PROCEED				
By Whom (11)	*Defendant's Physician Permitted to Attend* (12)	*Hospitalization Pending Examination* (13)	*Maximum Duration* (14)	(15)	(16)	(17)	(18)	*Suspension of Proceedings* (19)	*Continuation Where Personal Participation Unnecessary* (20)	*Commitment* (21)	*Duration of Commitment* (22)	*Other* (23)
1 or more physicians 123, §15(a)		whenever practicable, at courthouse or place of detention 123, §15(a)		further observation at state hospital for 20 days 123, §15(b)	if ct. not satisfied by examiner's reports as to competence, or at either party's request 123, §15(d)		preponderance of evidence 123, §15(d)	unless case dismissed 123, §15(d)		release w/or w/o bail 123, §16(a) 123, §17(c)	40–50 days 123, §16(a)	civil commitment 123, §16 (b), (c)
personnel of facility certified by dep't of mental health 330.2026(1)		if defendant fails to make self available or if necessary to exam 330.2026 (1), (3)	release upon completion of exam 330.2026(4)		330.2030(1)			330.2022(1)	pretrial motions, by either party 330.2022(2) taking & preserving of evidence 330.2022(3)	if recovery w/in 15 mos. or 1/3 max. sentence substantially probable 330.2032(1) bail or ROR 330.2036	15 mos. or 1/3 max. sentence 330.2034(1)	civil commitment if recovery improbable 330.2031 330.2034(3)
psychiatrist or psychologist or physician experienced in field 20.01, subd. 2 (3)	20.01, subd. 2 (3)	20.01, subd. 2 (3)	60 days 20.01, subd. 2 (3)	20.01, subd. 3	if either party objects to report 20.01, subd. 3			20.01, subd. 4 (2)	by defense counsel 20.01, subd. 7 probable cause hearing 20.01, subd. 2 (2)	civil commitment proceedings 20.01, subd. 4 (2)		dismissal of misdemeanor charges 20.01, subd. 4 (2)
psychiatrist 99-13-11												
1 or more private psychiatrists, or designees of dep't of mental health 552.020(2)			w/in 60 days except on good cause 552.020(2)	552.020(7)	if either party contests opinion based on report 552.020(7)			552.020(8)		552.020(8)	for so long as unfitness endures 552.020(8)	
psychiatrist 46-14-202 (1)	46-14-202 (2)	46-14-202 (2)	60 days; longer if ct. deems necessary 46-14-202 (2)	46-14-221 (1)	if either party contests report 46-14-221 (1)			46-14-221 (2), (3)	by defense counsel 46-14-221(4)	46-14-221 (2)	so long as unfitness endures 46-14-221 (2)	
such medical, psychiatric, or psychological exam as judge deems warranted 29-1823					if judge deems necessary 29-1823			29-1823		29-1823	until disability removed 29-1823	
2 physicians, 1 a psychiatrist 178.415(1)					178.415(2)			178.425(3)		178.425(1)	until returned OR for trial or judgment 178.425(2)	until a ct. orders release 178.425(2)
psychiatrist 135:17		outpatient basis only 135:17	30 days 135:17		135-30-a							
psychiatrist agreed to by ct., prosecutor, & defendant 2C:4-5(a)	2C:4-5(a)(2)	2C:4-5(a)(2)	30 days; 15 more on showing of particular need 2C:4-5(a)(2)	2C:4-6(a)	if report contested or if no report 2C:4-6(a)			2C:4-6(b)	by defense counsel 2C:4-6(f)	2C:4-6(b)	such period during which recovery substantially probable in foreseeable future 2C:4-6(b) dismissal of charges thereafter 2C:4-6(c)	outpatient placement or release 2C:4-6(b)
on motion of defendant 31-9-1 rule 35(c)					if reasonable doubt as to competency rule 35(b)(2)	if raised during trial; submission to separate jury if raised prior to trial discretionary rule 35(b)(2)		mistrial rule 35(b) (3), (4)		where appropriate rule 35(b)(3)		

TABLE 12.1 INCOMPETENCY TO STAND TRIAL—*Continued*

STATE	ISSUE RAISED BY				REQUIRED CONDITION (5)	CRITERIA FOR CONDITION (*fn. 1*)				COMPETENT IF FIT BECAUSE OF OR IN SPITE OF MEDICATION (10)
						Lacks Capacity to		*Because of Mental Disease or Defect* (8)	*Other* (9)	
	Judge upon (1)	*Prosecutor* (2)	*Defendant* (3)	*When* (4)		Understand Proceedings (6)	Assist in Defense (7)			
N.Y. Crim. Proc. Law (McKinney 1971 & Supp. 1982–83)	opinion that defendant may be incapacitated 730.30(1)			any time after arraignment & before imposition of sentence 730.30(1)	incapacitated person 730.10(1)	730.10(1)	OR 730.10(1)	730.10(1)		
N.C. Gen. Stat. (1978 & Supp. 1981)	own motion 15A-1002(a)	15A-1002(a)	15A-1002(a)	at any time 15A-1002(a)	incapacity to proceed 15A-1001(a)	15A-1001(a)	OR 15A-1001(a)	mental illness or defect 15A-1001(a)	comprehend own situation in reference to proceeding 15A-1001(a)	
N.D. Cent. Code (1976 & Supp. 1981)	reason to doubt fitness to proceed 12.1-04-06				lacks fitness to proceed 12.1-04-08	12.1-04-04	OR 12.1-04-04	12.1-04-04		
OHIO Rev. Code Ann. (Baldwin 1979 & Supp. 1983)	own motion 2945.37(A)	2945.37(A)	2945.37(A)	before or after trial begun 2945.37(A)	incompetent to stand trial 2945.37(A)	2945.37(A)	OR 2945.37(A)	mental condition 2945.37(A)		2945.37(A) 2945.38(A)
OKLA. Stat. Ann. (West 1958 & Supp. 1982–83)	own motion 22, §1175.2(A)	22, §1175.2(A)	22, §1175.2(A)	at any time 22, §1175.2(A)	incompetent 22, §1175.1 (1), (2)	22, §1175.1(1)	OR 22, §1175.1(1)		includes incompetence due to physical disability 22, §1175.1(1)	
OR. Rev. Stat. (1981)	reason to doubt fitness 161.360(1)			before or during trial 161.360(1)	incompetent 161.360(2)	161.360(2)(a)	OR 161.360(2) (b), (c)	161.360(2)		
PA. Stat. Ann. (Purdon 1969 & Supp. 1983–84)		attorney for commonwealth & warden or other official w/custody 50, §7402(c)	50, §7402(c)		incompetent 50, §7402(a)	substantially unable to 50, §7402(a)	OR substantially unable to 50, §7402(a)			
R.I. Gen. Laws (1977 & Supp. 1982)	reason to suspect incompetent 40.1-5.3-3(b)			any time before imposition of sentence 40.1-5.3-3(b)	mentally incompetent to stand trial 40.1-5.3-3 (a)(3)	40.1-5.3-3 (a)(3)	OR 40.1-5.3-3 (a)(3)			
S.C. Code (Law. Co-op. 1976 & Supp. 1980)	reason to believe not fit 44-23-410			at any time 44-23-410	not fit to stand trial 44-23-410	44-23-410	OR 44-23-410	lack of mental capacity 44-23-410		
S.D. Codified Laws Ann. (1979 & Supp. 1982)	may impanel jury if it appears defendant incompetent 23A-10A-4	23A-10A-3		upon indictment, trial, or sentencing 23A-10A-4	mentally incompetent to proceed 23A-10A-8	23A-10A-1	OR 23A-10A-1			

COURT-ORDERED EXAMINATION				DISPOSITION ON BASIS OF EXAMINER'S REPORT	JUDICIAL HEARINGS	JURY TRIAL	STANDARD OF PROOF	DISPOSITION IF UNFIT TO PROCEED				
By Whom (11)	*Defendant's Physician Permitted to Attend* (12)	*Hospitalization Pending Examination* (13)	*Maximum Duration* (14)	(15)	(16)	(17)	(18)	*Suspension of Proceedings* (19)	*Continuation Where Personal Participation Unnecessary* (20)	*Commitment* (21)	*Duration of Commitment* (22)	*Other* (23)
2 psychiatrists 730.20(1)	730.20(1)	if necessary 730.20 (2), (3)	30 days; 30 more if satisfied as to necessity 730.20(4)	730.30 (2), (3), (4)	upon own motion or motion of either party or if examiners not unanimous 730.30 (2), (3), (4)			misdemeanor indictments dismissed 730.50(1)	by defense 730.60(4)	final order of observation or commitment 730.50(1)	90 days if charged with misdemeanor; 1 yr. for felonies 730.50(1)	order of retention prior to expiration of term of commitment 730.50(2) may not serve more than ⅔ max. sentence 730.50(5)
discretionary; 1 or more experts 15A-1002 (b)(1)		discretionary 15A-1002 (b)(2)	60 days 15A-1002 (b)(2)	civil commitment proceedings may be instituted 15A-1002 (b)(2)(a)	15A-1002 (b)(3)			15A-1001(a)	15A-1001(b)	civil commitment proceedings 15A-1003(a)		
psychiatrist 12.1-04-06		12.1-04-06	30 days; 30 more on ct. order 12.1-04-06	12.1-04-07	if report contested 12.1-04-07			12.1-04-08	by defense 12.1-04-09	12.1-04-08	reasonable time necessary to determine whether recovery in foreseeable future substantially probable, not to exceed 3 yrs. or max. sentence 12.1-04-08	
1–3 evaluations at forensic or other center 2945.371(A) psychiatrist or psychologist 2945.371(F)		discretionary 2945.371 (B), (C)	20 days 2945.371 (B), (C)		if raised before trial; for good cause if after trial begun 2945.37(A)		preponderance of evidence 2945.37(A)		probable cause hearing 2945.38(C)	if substantial probability of competency w/in 1 yr. 2945.38(D)	15 mos. or 1/3 (max). sentence 2945.38(D)	civil commitment 2945.37 (C)
doctors or appropriate technicians 22, §1175.3 (D)		discretionary 22, §1175.3 (D)	ct. shall impose reasonable time limitation 22, §1175.3 (D)		pre-examination hearing (probable cause as to incompetency) 22, §1175.3 (A) 22, §1175.4 (A)	on request 22, §1175.2 (B)(2) if necessary or on request 22, §1175.4 (B)	doubt as to competency 22, §1175.3 (D) clear & convincing evidence 22, §1175.4 (B)	22, §1175.2(A)		if capable of achieving competency in reasonable period 22, §1175.6 (2) 22, §1175.7 (1)		civil commitment 22, §1175.6(3) involuntary commitment proceedings 22, §1175.6 (3), or outpatient assistance 22, §1175.6 (4)
psychiatrist 161.365(1)		161.365(2)	30 days 161.365(2)	161.370(1)	if finding contested 161.370(1)			161.370(2)	by defense 161.370(5)	161.370(2)	so long as such unfitness shall endure 161.370(2), subject to max. sentence or 5 yrs. 161.370(3)	conditional release 161.370 (2)
at least 1 psychiatrist *fn.* 7 50, §7402 (e)(2) 50, §7402(d)	50, §7402(f)	outpatient basis, unless otherwise authorized in act 50, §7402 (e)(1)		w/in 20 days 50, §7402(g)	*fn.* 7 50, §7402(d) 50, §7403		on moving party by clear & convincing evidence 50, §7403(a)	50, §7403(b)	50, §7403(b)	60 days involuntary treatment if not severely mentally disabled 50, §7402(b) if recovery probable 50, §7403(d)	for so long as such incapacity persists 50, §7403(b) max. sentence or 10 yrs., whichever less 50, §7403(f)	discharge 50, §7403(g)
1 or more physicians 40.1-5.3-3 (b)				if report finds competent 40.1-5.3-3 (d)	unless both parties assent in writing to finding of competency 40.1-5.3-3 (d)			40.1-5.3-3	40.1-5.3-3 (k)	or custody of guardian 40.1-5.3-3 (e)	2/3 of most serious sentence 40.1-5.3-3 (f)	civil commitment 40.1-5.3-3 (e)(4)
2 examiners designated by dep't of mental health or retardation 44-23-410 (1)		44-23-410 (2)	15 days; 15 more if necessary 44-23-410 (2)		44-23-430				by defense 44-23-440	if likely to become fit in foreseeable future 44-23-430 (3)	60 days; civil commitment thereafter 44-23-430 (3)	civil commitment or release 44-23-430 (2), (3)
appropriate state facility 23A-10A-3						23A-10A-4		23A-10A-8		23A-10A-8	until mentally competent to proceed 23A-10A-8	

TABLE 12.1 INCOMPETENCY TO STAND TRIAL—*Continued*

STATE	ISSUE RAISED BY				REQUIRED CONDITION (5)	CRITERIA FOR CONDITION (*fn. 1*)				COMPETENT IF FIT BECAUSE OF OR IN SPITE OF MEDICATION (10)
	Judge upon (1)	*Prosecutor* (2)	*Defendant* (3)	*When* (4)		*Lacks Capacity to* Understand Proceedings (6)	Assist in Defense (7)	*Because of Mental Disease or Defect* (8)	*Other* (9)	
TENN. Code Ann. (1977)	own motion 33-708(a)	33-708(a)	33-708(a)		incompetent to stand trial 33-708(b)			mental illness 33-708(b)		
TEX. Code Crim. Proc. Ann. (Vernon 1979 & Supp. 1982–83)	own motion before trial 46.02(2)(a) evidence from any source during trial 46.02(2)(b)		before trial 46.02(2)(a)	before or during trial 46.02(2)	incompetent to stand trial 46.02(1)(a)	46.02(1)(a)(2)	OR 46.02(1)(a)(1)			
UTAH Code Ann. (1978 & Supp. 1982)	directing prosecutor to file petition 77-15-4	77-15-3(2)	or person having custody 77-15-3(2)		incompetent to proceed 77-15-1	77-15-2(1)	OR 77-15-2(2)	77-15-2		
VT. Stat. Ann. (1974 & Supp. 1983)	reason to believe not competent 13, §4817(b) 13, §4814	13, §4817(b) 13, §4814	13, §4817(b) 13, §4814	any time before, during, or after trial 13, §4814(a)	incompetent to stand trial 13, §4817(a)					
VA. Code (1983)		exam on request of commonwealth 19.2-168.1	19.2-168	any time after retention of counsel & before end of trial 19.2-169.1	insane or feebleminded 19.2-167	included in psychiatrist report 19.2-169.1(D)	AND included in psychiatrist report 19.2-169.1(D)			19.2-169.1(E)
WASH. Rev. Code Ann. (1980 & Supp. 1983–84)	reason to doubt competency 10.77.060(1)	10.77.060(1)	10.77.060(1)	any time prior to judgment 10.77.090(1)	incompetency 10.77.010(6) 10.77.050	10.77.010(6)	OR 10.77.010(6)	10.77.010(6)		10.77.090(5)
W. Va. Code (1980 & Supp. 1983)	belief that defendant may be incompetent 27-6A-1(a)			any stage of proceedings after indictment or issuance of warrant 27-6A-1(a)	incompetent to stand trial 27-6A-1(a)	27-6A-2(b)	OR 27-6A-2(b)	mental illness, mental retardation, or addiction 27-6A-1(a)		
WIS. Stat. Ann. (West 1971 & Supp. 1983–84)	reason to doubt defendant's competency 971.14(1)			only if probable that defendant committed offense, or after a preliminary examination or guilty verdict 971.14(1)	lacks competency to proceed 971.14(5)	971.13	OR 971.13	971.13		971.14(5)(d)
WYO. Stat. (1977 & Supp. 1983)	reasonable cause 7-11-303(a)	7-11-303(a)	7-11-303(a)	any stage of proceeding 7-11-303(a)	unfit to proceed 7-11-303(a)	*fn. 8* 7-11-302(a)	AND *fn. 8* 7-11-302(a)	mental illness or deficiency 7-11-302(a)	*fn. 8* 7-11-302(a)	

COURT-ORDERED EXAMINATION				DISPOSITION ON BASIS OF EXAMINER'S REPORT (15)	JUDICIAL HEARINGS (16)	JURY TRIAL (17)	STANDARD OF PROOF (18)	DISPOSITION IF UNFIT TO PROCEED				
By Whom (11)	*Defendant's Physician Permitted to Attend* (12)	*Hospitalization Pending Examination* (13)	*Maximum Duration* (14)					*Suspension of Proceedings* (19)	*Continuation Where Personal Participation Unnecessary* (20)	*Commitment* (21)	*Duration of Commitment* (22)	*Other* (23)
after hearing, by community health center or private practitioner 33-708(a)		if outpatient evaluation impossible 33-708(a)	30 days 33-708(a)		33-700(b)	upon demand by either party 33-708(b)				judicial hospitalization proceedings 33-708(b) 33-604	indeterminate 33-708(c)	
disinterested experts 46.02(3)(a)		if defendant fails to submit 46.02(3)(b)	21 days 46.02(3)(b)			if ct. finds evidence to support finding 46.02(4)(a)	prepon derance of evidence 46.02(1)(b)	46.02		upon hearing as to necessity 46.02(4)(a) if competency probable in foreseeable future 46.02(5)(a)	60 days to 18 mos. 46.02(5)(a)	bail or outpatient treatment 46.02 (5)(d)
2 or more alienists 77-15-5(2) (b)		77-15-5(2) (a)	30 days 77-15-5(2) (a)		77-15-5(1)			77-15-5(6)		77-15-6	until competent to proceed 77-15-6	
psychiatrist 13, §4814(a)		13, §4815(a)	60 days 13, §4815(b) 15 day extensions 13, §4815(c)		13, §4817(b)			13, §4817(a)				
at least 1 psychiatrist, or qualified psychologist 19.2-169.1 (A)				treatment ordered by ct. 19.2-169.2			preponderance of evidence 19.2-169.1			treatment ordered by ct. 19.2-169.2	6-mo. periods 19.2-169.3 (B) up to max. sentence for offense charged or 5 yrs. 19.2-169.3(C)	
2 experts 10.77.060 (1)	10.77.060 (2)	10.77.060 (1)	15 days 10.77.060 (1)	10.77.090 (1)	following 90-day period 10.77.090 (2)	if demanded by judge or either party 10.77.090 (2)	preponderance of evidence 10.77.090 (2)	if dangerous & recovery probable w/in reasonable period 10.77.090 (1), (3)	10.77.090 (4)	10.77.090 (1)	90 days 10.77.090 (1)	dismissal of charges, & release or civil commitment 10.77.090 (3)
1 or more psychiatrists, or psychiatrist & psychologist 27-6A-1(a)		after exam for further observation 27-6A-1(b)	20 days; 20 more on physician's request & ct. order 27-6A-1(b)	27-6A-1(d)	if requested by counsel or ordered by ct. 27-6A-1(d)		preponderance of evidence 27-6A-1(d) 27-6A-2(b)			if recovery w/in 6 mos. substantially likely 27-6A-2(b)	6 mos.; 3 mos. more on request of chief medical officer 27-6A-2(b)	dismissal of charges & civil commitment proceedings if recovery w/in 6 mos. unlikely 27-6A-2(c), (d) release w/or w/o bail 27-6A-7
physician 971.14(2)		971.14(2)	30 days 971.14(2)	971.14(4)	if neither party contests finding 971.14(4)			971.14(5)	by defense 971.14(6)	971.14(5)	24 mos., so long as making progress toward competency 971.14(5)	civil commitment 971.14(5)
designated examiner 7-11-303(b)		or outpatient basis 7-11-303(b)	30 days 7-11-303(b)	7-11-303(f)	if neither party contests finding 7-11-303(f)			7-11-303(g)	by defense 7-11-303(j)	7-11-303(g)	time reasonably necessary to determine whether recovery substantially probable 7-11-303(g)	civil commitment 7-11-303 (g)

FOOTNOTES: TABLE 12.1

1. In federal cases, the Supreme Court has long approved a test of incompetence that inquires into whether a criminal defendant "has sufficient present ability to consult with his lawyer with a reasonable degree of rational understanding—and whether he has a rational as well as factual understanding of the proceedings against him." See, e.g., Dusky v. United States, 362 U.S. 402, 402 (1960). In Pate v. Robinson, 383 U.S. 375 (1966), the Court held that a state court's failure to invoke statutory procedures adequate to protect a defendant's right not to be tried or convicted while incompetent to stand trial deprived him of his due process right to a fair trial. Although Pate did not address the central issue of whether the procedure prescribed by Ill. Rev. Stat., ch. 38, § 104-2 (Smith-Hurd 1963) was constitutionally mandated, subsequent dictum in Drope v. Missouri, 420 U.S. 162 (1975), suggests that the criteria enumerated in Dusky may be "fundamental to an adversary system of justice." Id. at 171-72 (following statement that "[i]t has long been accepted that a person whose mental condition is such that he lacks capacity to understand the nature and object of the proceedings against him, to consult with counsel, and to assist in preparing his defense may not be subjected to trial"). Because Missouri's statutes, as was true of Illinois's in Pate, "jealously guard" a defendant's right to a fair trial, Mo. Ann. Stat. §552.020(1) (Vernon 1969) (adopting language similar to the federal test), the Supreme Court avoided the issue. 420 U.S. at 173. See also Davis v. Alabama, 545 F.2d 460 (5th Cir.), cert. denied, 431 U.S. 957 (1977), and Franklin v. United States, 589 F.2d 192 (5th Cir. 1979).

2. Alabama courts have adopted the majority view that a criminal defendant must have an understanding of the proceedings against him and an ability to communicate with his attorney in preparing his defense before he may be proceeded against criminally. See, e.g., Edgerson v. State, 53 Ala. App. 581, 302 So. 2d 556 (1974), cited with approval in Holland v. State, 376 So. 2d 796, 801 (Ala. Crim. App.), cert. denied, 376 So. 2d 802 (Ala. 1979). See also Annot. to Ala. Code §15-16-21 (1975 & Supp. 1981). Unlike the Model Penal Code formulation, Alabama's court-created standard does not seem to rely upon a prerequisite finding of mental disease or defect.

3. Ark. Stat. Ann. § 41-604(2) (1977): "Failure to notify the prosecutor within a reasonable time before the trial date shall entitle the prosecutor to a continuance."

4. Cal. Penal Code § 1369 (West 1970 & Supp. 1980):

> In any case where the defendant or the defendant's counsel informs the court that the defendant is not seeking a finding of mental incompetence, the court shall appoint two psychiatrists, licensed psychologists, or a combination thereof. One of the psychiatrists or licensed psychologists may be named by the defense and one may be named by the prosecution.

5. Fla. Stat. Ann. § 916.12 (Supp. 1980): "does not have sufficient present ability to consult with his lawyer with a reasonable degree of rational understanding or if he has no rational, as well as factual, understanding of the procedings against him."

6. La. Code Crim. Proc. Ann. art. 649.1 (West 1981):

> When a person is returned to the committing court from an institution pursuant to Article 649 [see table 12.2] pending a sanity hearing, and the superintendent of the committing institution deems it necessary that the patient receive prescribed medication, it shall be the duty of the chief administrative officer of the parish jail to make such medication available . . . until such time as the coroner or another physician finds that the medication or . . . dosage is no longer necessary.

7. Pa. Stat. Ann. tit. 50, § 7402(d) (Purdon 1969 & Supp. 1980):

> The court, either on application or on its own motion, may order an incompetency examination at any stage in the proceedings and may do so without a hearing unless the examination is objected to by the person charged with a crime or by his counsel. In such event, an examination shall be ordered only after determination upon a hearing that there is prima facie question of incompetency.

8. Wyo. Stat. § 7-11-302(a) (1977) (emphasis added):

> [L]acks the capacity to:
>
> (i) comprehend his position;
>
> (ii) understand the nature and object of the proceedings against him;
>
> (iii) conduct his defense in a rational manner; AND
>
> (iv) cooperate with his counsel to the end that any available defense may be interposed.

TABLE 12.2 RECOVERY OF COMPETENCY TO PROCEED WITH TRIAL

	APPLICATION BY					DISPOSITION			
STATE	Mental Health Official (1)	Defendant (2)	Other (3)	JUDICIAL HEARING (4)	CRITERIA (5)	Criminal Proceedings Resumed (6)	Dismissal of Charges (7)	Other (8)	CRITERIA FOR NOT RESUMING PROCEEDINGS (9)
ALA. Code (1982)	hospital superintendent 15-16-21				restored to right mind 15-16-21	15-16-21			
ALAS. Stat. (1968 & Supp. 1982)	custodian 12.47.120(a)			12.47.120(a)	mentally competent to understand nature of proceedings & assist in defense 12.47.120(b)	12.47.120			
ARIZ. R. Crim. P.	11.6(a)	11.6(a)	automatically on expiration of term of commitment 11.6(a)	11.6(a)	competent 11.6(c)	11.6(c)	OR 11.6(e)		discretion of ct. 11.6(e)
ARK. Stat. Ann. (1976 & Supp. 1983)	report on defendant's fitness due w/in 1 yr. 41-607(2)(a) director of state hospital 41-607(3)	41-607(3)	ct. or prosecuting attorney 41-607(3)	discretionary 41-607(2)(b) if requested 41-607(3)	fit to proceed 41-607(2)(b), (3)	41-607(2)(b), (3)	OR 41-607(3)	conditional release or involuntary hospitalization 41-607(3)	unjust because so much time elapsed since commitment 41-607(3)
CAL. Penal Code (West 1970 & Supp. 1983)	county or regional mental health director or director of facility 1372(a)(1) outpatient treatment staff 1374			1372(c)	mentally competent 1372(a)(1) 1374	1374 1372	OR1385	credit on sentence for time spent in facility 1375.5	in furtherance of justice 1385
COLO. Rev. Stat. (1975 & Supp. 1982)	head of institution or treating physician 16-8-113(1)	16-8-117	ct. or prosecuting attorney 16-8-113(1) review hearing every 6 mos. 16-8-114.5(2)	16-8-113(1)	restored to competency (preponderance of evidence) 16-8-113(2), (5)	16-8-114(1)		credit on sentence for time confined 16-8-114(1) release or civil commitment proceedings 16-8-114.5(2)	substantial probability of not being restored to competency in forseeable future 16-8-114.5(2)
CONN. Gen. Stat. Ann. (West 1960 & Supp. 1983–84)	7 days prior to hearing, when defendant is competent; when defendant will probably not regain competency during placement 54-56d(j)		review w/in 90 days 54-56d(k)	54-56d(k)	competent 54-56d(k)	54-56d(k)	54-56d(l)	civil commitment 54-56d(l)	
DEL. Code Ann. (1979 & Supp. 1982)					capable of standing trial 11, §404(b)	11, §404(b)		remission against sentence of all or part of time committed 11, §404(b)	
D.C. Code Ann. (1973)	superintendent 24-301(b) 24-303			if accused or government objects 24-301(b)	restored to mental competency 24-301(b)	24-301(b)			
FLA. Stat. Ann. (West 1973 & Supp. 1983)									
GA. Code Ann. (1983 & Supp. 1983)	dep't of human resources 27-1502(e)			if contested by accused 27-1502(f)	mentally competent 27-1502(e)	27-1502(e)	OR 27-1502(e)		
HAWAII Rev. Stat. (1968 & Supp. 1982)	director of health 704-406(2)	704-406(2)	prosecutor, or ct. on own motion 704-406(2)	if requested 704-406(2)	fit to proceed 704-406(2)	704-406(2)	OR 704-406(2)		unjust because so much time elapsed since commitment or conditional release 704-406(2)
IDAHO Code (1979 & Supp. 1983)	director of dep't 18-212(2)		ct. on own motion or prosecutor 18-212(2)	if requested 18-212(2)	fit to proceed 18-212(2)	18-212(2)	OR 18-212(2)		unjust because so much time elapsed since commitment 18-212(2)
ILL. Ann. Stat. (Smith-Hurd 1980 & Supp. 1983–84)	supervisor of treatment 38, §104-20(a)		90-day hearings 38, §104-20(a)	w/o jury 38, §104-20(a)	fit to stand trial or plead 38, §104-20-(a)			matter set for trial 38, §104-20(b) time spent in custody credited against sentence 38, §104-24	

TABLE 12.2 RECOVERY OF COMPETENCY TO PROCEED WITH TRIAL—*Continued*

STATE	APPLICATION BY: Mental Health Official (1)	APPLICATION BY: Defendant (2)	APPLICATION BY: Other (3)	JUDICIAL HEARING (4)	CRITERIA (5)	DISPOSITION: Criminal Proceedings Resumed (6)	DISPOSITION: Dismissal of Charges (7)	DISPOSITION: Other (8)	CRITERIA FOR NOT RESUMING PROCEEDINGS (9)
IND. Code Ann. (Burns 1979 & Supp. 1983)	superintendent of institution 35-36-3-2				ability to understand proceedings & assist in defense 35-36-3-2	35-36-3-2			
IOWA Code Ann. (West 1979 & Supp. 1983–84)	812.5				can effectively assist in defense 812.5	812.5	OR 812.5		
KAN. Stat. Ann. (1980 & Supp. 1982)			ct. on reasonable grounds 22-3303(3)	22-3303(3)	competent 22-3303(3)	22-3303(3)		time spent in public institution may be credited against sentence 22-3303(4)	
KY. Rev. Stat. Ann. (Michie 1975 & Supp. 1982)	psychologist or psychiatrist treating defendant 504.110(1)			504.110(a)	competent to stand trial 504.110(a)	504.110(3)			
LA. Rev. Stat. Ann. §15:211 (West 1981 & Supp. 1983) LA. Code Crim. Proc. arts. 641 et seq. (West 1981 & Supp. 1983)	staff shall review defendant's records at least yrly. 15:211 report of superintendent 649(A)	649(C)	district attorney 649(C)	w/in 30 days given prima facie showing of present capacity 649(A), (C)	mental capacity to proceed 649(E)	649(E)			
ME. Rev. Stat. Ann. (1980 & Supp. 1982–83)	institutional report at end of 30 days, 60 days, & 1 yr. 15, §101(1)			15, §101(1)	competent to stand trial 15, §101	15, §101	if incompetent but recovery improbable in foreseeable future 15, §101(1)	civil commitment 15, §101(1)	
MD. Ann. Code (1979 & Supp. 1982)	yrly. recommendation by dep't 59, §24(b)	59, §24(a)	ct. on own motion 59, §24(a)	may reconsider question 59, §24(a)	competent to stand trial 59, §24(a)	59, §23	59, §24(b)	conditional release 59, §28	so much time elapsed since finding of incompetency as to render it unjust *fn. 1* 59, §24(b)
MASS. Ann. Laws (Michie/Law. Co-op. 1981 & Supp. 1983)	periodic review by superintendent or medical director 123, §17(a)	123, §17(a)		123, §17(a)	competent to stand trial 123, §17(a)	123, §17(a)			at any appropriate time, ct. may release defendant w/or w/o bail 123, §17(c)
MICH. Comp. Laws Ann. (1980 & Supp. 1983–84)	90-day treatment reports by medical supervisor 330.2038(1)			330.2040(1)	competent to stand trial 330.2040(3)	330.2040(3)	OR 330.2044(1)	credit for time spent in custody 330.2042	charges dismissed after 15 mos. or on prosecutor's decision not to prosecute 330.2044(1)
MINN. R. Crim. P. (West 1979 & Supp. 1982)	periodic reports by person charged w/ supervision 20.01[5]	20.01[5]	prosecutor, or ct. on own motion 20.01[5]	20.01[5]	competent to proceed 20.01[5]	20.01[5]	OR except when charged with murder 20.01[6]	credit for time spent in confinement 20.01[9]	charges dismissed after 3 yrs. unless prosecutor files notice of intention to prosecute 20.01[6]
MISS. Code Ann. (1972 & Supp. 1982)									
MO. Ann. Stat. (Vernon 1953 & Supp. 1983)	director of dep't 552.020(9)	writ of habeas corpus 552.020(9)	state 552.020(9)	552.020(9)	mentally fit to proceed 552.020(9)	552.020(9)	OR 552.020(9)		so much time elapsed since commitment that resumption unjust 552.020(9)
MONT. Code Ann. (1983)	director of dep't of institutions 46-14-222	46-14-222	county attorney, or ct. on own motion 46-14-222	if requested 46-14-222	fit to proceed 46-14-222	46-14-222	OR 46-14-222	civil commitment 46-14-222	so much time elapsed since commitment that resumption unjust 46-14-222
NEB. Rev. Stat. (1979)									
NEV. Rev. Stat. (1981)	administrator of division 178.450(1)			sanity commission of 3 physicians 178.455	*fn. 2* 178.460(1)	178.460(1)			

TABLE 12.2 RECOVERY OF COMPETENCY TO PROCEED WITH TRIAL—*Continued*

STATE	APPLICATION BY Mental Health Official (1)	Defendant (2)	Other (3)	JUDICIAL HEARING (4)	CRITERIA (5)	DISPOSITION Criminal Proceedings Resumed (6)	Dismissal of Charges (7)	Other (8)	CRITERIA FOR NOT RESUMING PROCEEDINGS (9)
N.H. Rev. Stat. Ann. (1977)									
N.J. Stat. Ann. (West 1981 & Supp. 1983–84)	commissioner 2C:4-6(d)	2C:4-6(d)	prosecutor, or ct. on own motion 2C:4-6(d)	if requested 2C:4-6(d)	fit to proceed 2C:4-6(d)	2C:4-6(d)	if time elapsed adequate 2C:4-6(c)	civil commitment 2C:4-6(c)	
N.M. Stat. Ann. (1978)	31-9-1			issue of competency redetermined 31-9-1	see table 11.2(a)				
N.Y. Crim. Proc. Law (McKinney 1971 & Supp. 1982–83)	superintendent of institution 730.60(2)			on motion of either party or ct. 730.60(2) 730.30(2)	no longer incapacitated 730.60(2)		730.60(5)		continuously confined for 2 yrs., consistent w/ends of justice, & not necessary to protection of public or treatment of defendant 730.60(5)
N.C. Gen. Stat. (1978 & Supp. 1981)	custodian institution or individual 15A-1006		ct. on own motion 15A-1007(b)	15A-1007	capacity to proceed 15A-1006	15A-1004(e) UNLESS	15A-1004(e)		recovery unlikely, confined for max. period of sentence, or 10 yrs. elapsed since determination of incapacity (5 yrs. for misdemeanors) 15A-1008
N.D. Cent. Code (1976 & Supp. 1981)				if requested 12.1-04-08	fit to proceed 12.1-04-08	12.1-04-08	12.1-04-08	civil commitment 12.1-04-08	max. term of sentence elapsed or obvious that defendant won't regain fitness 12.1-04-08
OHIO Rev. Code Ann. (Baldwin 1979 & Supp. 1983)	reports every 90 days, when defendant regains competence or it becomes clear he will not 2945.38(E)			2945.38(F)	competent to stand trial 2945.38(F)	2945.38(F)	2945.38(G)	sentence credited by time spent on issue 2945.38(I)	prosecutor files notice of intention not to prosecute, or found finally incompetent 2945.38(G)
OKLA. Stat. Ann. (West 1958 & Supp. 1982–83)	medical supervisor 22, §1175.8			22, §1175.8	competent 22, §1175.8	22, §1175.8			
OR. Rev. Stat. (1981)	superintendent of hospital 161.370(2)	161.370(2)	ct. on own motion, or prosecutor 161.370(2)	if requested 161.370(2)	fit to proceed 161.370(2)	161.370(2)	OR 161.370(2)	civil commitment 161.370(2) remission of sentence by time committed 161.370(4)	so much time elapsed that resumption unjust 161.370(2)
PA. Stat. Ann. (Purdon 1969 & Supp. 1983–84)		50, §7403(e)	attorney for commonwealth, or ct. on own motion 50, §7403(e)		competent to proceed 50, §7403(e)	50, §7403(e)	OR 50, §7403(e)		unjust by reason of passage of time 50, §7403(e)
R.I. Gen. Laws (1977 & Supp. 1982)	director, every 6 mos. 40.1-5.3-3(g)	40.1-5.3-3(h)		40.1-5.3-3(i)	competent 40.1-5.3-3(i)	40.1-5.3-3(i)	on max. duration of commitment 40.1-5.3-3(f)	discharge w/in 30 days 40.1-5.3-3(i)	unlikely that defendant will be competent prior to dismissal of charges 40.1-5.3-3(i)
S.C. Code Ann. (Law. Co-op. 1976)	superintendent of facility 44-23-460	or guardian 44-23-450	ct. on own motion, or prosecutor 44-23-450 44-23-460	44-23-450	fit to stand trial 44-23-460(3)	44-23-460(3)	OR 44-23-460(3)	release if unfit or if hospitalized for max. period of imprisonment for offense 44-23-460 (1), (2)	so much time elapsed that prosecution not in interest of justice 44-23-460(3)
S.D. Codified Laws Ann. (1979 & Supp. 1982)			competency presumed by failure to recommit civilly at prescribed time for review 23A-10A-12	presumption rebuttable 23A-10A-12	mentally competent to proceed 23A-10A-12	23A-10A-12			
TENN. Code Ann. (1977 & Supp. 1981)	superintendent 33-712 6-mo. status reports 33-708(c)		periodic 3-mo. examinations 33-714		restored to competence to stand trial 33-712			credit toward sentence for time hospitalized 33-713	

TABLE 12.2 RECOVERY OF COMPETENCY TO PROCEED WITH TRIAL—*Continued*

STATE	APPLICATION BY: Mental Health Official (1)	APPLICATION BY: Defendant (2)	APPLICATION BY: Other (3)	JUDICIAL HEARING (4)	CRITERIA (5)	DISPOSITION: Criminal Proceedings Resumed (6)	DISPOSITION: Dismissal of Charges (7)	DISPOSITION: Other (8)	CRITERIA FOR NOT RESUMING PROCEEDINGS (9)
TEX. Code Crim. Proc. (Vernon 1979 & Supp. 1982–83)	head of facility 46.02(5)(f)			if either party contests findings 46.02(5)(i)	competent to stand trial 46.02(5)(k)	46.02(5)(k)	if incompetent 46.02(7)	OR civil commitment 46.02(6)(a)	
UTAH Code Ann. (1978 & Supp. 1982)	clinical director of facility 77-15-7(1)	77-15-7(1)	ct. on own motion 77-15-7(2)	77-15-7	competent to proceed 77-15-7(1)	77-15-7			
VT. Stat. Ann. (1974 & Supp. 1983)				subsequent hearing by trial ct. 13, §4817(c)	competent to stand trial 13, §4817(c)	13, §4817(c)			
VA. Code (1983)	19.2-169.2 19.2-169.3			competency determination w/o hearing 19.2-169.3(A)					
WASH. Rev. Code. Ann. (1980 & Supp. 1983–84)				See table 12.1					
W. VA. Code (1980 & Supp. 1983)	periodic review by director 27-6A-5	27-6A-5	mandatory 6-mo. review of those civilly committed 27-6A-2(d)	27-6A-2(d) 27-6A-5	competent to stand trial 27-6A-2(d) 27-6A-5	27-6A-2(d) 27-6A-5		credit for time in involuntary confinement 27-6A-8(a)	
WIS. Stat. Ann. (West 1971 & Supp. 1983)	interim report by dep't 971.14(5)		re-examination every 6 mos. 971.14(5)	unless waived by both parties 971.14(5)	competent to proceed 971.14(5)	971.14(5)			
WYO. Stat. (1977 & Supp. 1983–84)	head of facility 7-11-303 (g)(ii) progress reports every 3 mos. 7-11-303(g)(ii)		discharge from civil commitment 7-11-303(g)(i)	if contested 7-11-303 (g)(ii)	fit to proceed 7-11-303 (g)(ii)	7-11-303 (g)(i), (ii)			inappropriate because of lapse of time since commitment 7-11-303(g)(i)

FOOTNOTES: TABLE 12.2

1. Md. Ann. Code art. 59, § 24 (Supp. 1981): "[I]n capital cases the court may not dismiss the charge until ten years have elapsed from the date of the finding of incompetency and in all other cases punishable by imprisonment . . . five years."

2. Nev. Rev. Stat. § 178.460(1) (1979): "(a) Knew the difference between right and wrong; (b) Understood the nature of the offense charged; and (c) Was of sufficient mentality to aid and assist counsel in defense of the offense charged, or to show cause why judgment should not be pronounced."

TABLE 12.3 SUSPENSION OF SENTENCE DUE TO INTERVENING INSANITY *fnn. 1, 2*

STATE	ISSUED RAISED By Whom (1)	ISSUED RAISED When (2)	ISSUED RAISED How (3)	CRITERIA (4)	APPROVAL BY (5)	ALTERNATIVE JURISDICTION (6)	PSYCHIATRIC EXAMINATION (7)	DISPOSITION ON BASIS OF EXAMINER'S REPORT (8)	HEARING (9)	ATTENDANCE (10)	JURY (11)	DISPOSITION If Under Sentence of Death (12)	DISPOSITION If Under Any Other Sentence (13)	DURATION (14)	REVIEW (15)	RESTORATION Automatic (16)	RESTORATION Application by (17)	RESTORATION Approval by (18)	RESTORATION Criteria (19)	RESTORATION Hearing (20)	RESTORATION Disposition (21)
ALA. Code (1975)		before execution of sentence 15-16-23	made to appear that convict insane 15-16-23	convict insane 15-16-23	trial ct. 15-16-23	none 15-16-23					if judge deems proper 15-16-23	execution suspended 15-16-23		fixed in order 15-16-23	barred 15-16-23	upon expiration of suspension 15-16-23		trial ct. 15-16-23	restored to sanity 15-16-23		execution of sentence 15-16-23
ARIZ. Rev. Stat. Ann. (1978)	superintendent of state prison 13-4021 (A)	after delivery to prison 13-4021 (A)	notice to county attorney; immediate petition 13-4021 (A)	insane 13-4021 (A)	superior ct. of county where prison located 13-4021 (A)				13-4021 (A)	county attorney 13-4022	13-4021 (A)	confined to state hospital 13-4023 13-4024 (B)		until restored 13-4023			superintendent of state hospital 13-4024 (C)	governor 13-4024 (C)	sane 13-4024 (C)		execution of judgment 13-4024 (C)
ARK. Stat. Ann. (1977)	circuit judge 43-1301	upon reason to believe that insane 43-1301		insane 43-1301	circuit ct.		43-1301		43-1303	prosecuting attorney & counsel for defendant 43-1301		postponement or not carrying out of any sentence 43-1303	postponement or not carrying out of any sentence 43-1303								
CAL. Penal Code (West 1983)	warden 3701	after delivery to warden 3701	notice to district attorney; immediate petition 3701	insane 3701	superior ct. of county where prison located 3701	governor 3700			3701	district attorney 3702	3701	confined to medical facility of dep't of corrections 3703 3704		until reason restored 3703			superintendent of medical facility 3704	superior ct. from which committed 3704	sane 3704	w/o jury 3704	execution of judgment 3704
COLO. Rev. Stat. (1978 & Supp. 1980)	superintendent 17-23-101 (1)	during imprisonment in correctional facility 17-23-101 (1)	certification by prison physician 17-23-101 (1)	mentally ill or retarded 17-23-101 (1)	executive director 17-23-101 (1)		17-23-101 (1)	17-23-101 (2)				placement in institution for care & treatment, if correctional facility inadequate 17-23-101 (2) 16-8-110 (1)	placement in institution for care & treatment, if correctional facility inadequate 17-23-101 (2) 16-8-110 (1)	until recovery 17-23-101 (2)			superintendent of facility 17-23-102	superintendent of correctional facility 17-23-102	no longer mentally ill or retarded 17-23-102		completion of sentence, if not expired 17-23-101 (2)
CONN. Gen. Stat. Ann. (West 1960 & Supp. 1980)	warden 54-101	awaiting execution of sentence 54-101	application 54-101	insane 54-101	superior ct. of Tolland 54-101 OR	if out of session, any superior ct. judge 54-101	54-101	54-101				transferred to state hospital for mentally ill 54-101		until recovered 54-101			state's attorney, upon report from superintendent 54-101	superior ct. 54-101	recovered 54-101		execution of sentence 54-101
DEL. Code Ann. (1979)	dep't of health & social services 11, §406 (a)	after conviction & sentence 11, §406 (a)		mentally ill 11, §406 (a)	superior ct. 11, §406 (a)		11, §406 (a)	11, §406 (a)					transfer to Del. State Hospital 11, §406 (a)	until discharged by ct. 11, §406 (b)				ct. 11, §406 (b)			
D.C. Code (1981)	director of dep't of corrections 24-302 ct. 24 U.S.C. §211	while serving sentence 24-302 during continuance of sentence 32-608	psychiatric certification 24-302 certification that insane 24 U.S.C. §211	mentally ill 24-302 insane 32-608	HEW secretary 24 U.S.C. §211		24-302	24-302					transfer to mental hospital 24-302 confined to St. Elizabeths Hospital 24 U.S.C. §211	until restored 24-303(b) 24 U.S.C. §211b			superintendent of hospital 24-303(b) 24 U.S.C. §211b	director of dep't of corrections 24-303(b) criminal ct. 24 U.S.C. §211b	restored to mental health 24-303(b) restored to sanity 24 U.S.C. §211b		delivery of prisoner to director 24-303(b) delivery to ct. 24 U.S.C. §211b

TABLE 12.3 SUSPENSION OF SENTENCE DUE TO INTERVENING INSANITY *fnn. 1, 2—Continued*

STATE	ISSUED RAISED By Whom (1)	When (2)	How (3)	CRITERIA (4)	APPROVAL BY (5)	ALTERNATIVE JURISDICTION (6)	PSYCHIATRIC EXAMINATION (7)	DISPOSITION ON BASIS OF EXAMINER'S REPORT (8)	HEARING (9)	ATTENDANCE (10)	JURY (11)	DISPOSITION If Under Sentence of Death (12)	If Under Any Other Sentence (13)	DURATION (14)	REVIEW (15)	RESTORATION Automatic (16)	Application by (17)	Approval by (18)	Criteria (19)	Hearing (20)	Disposition (21)
FLA. Stat. Ann. (West 1973 & Supp. 1981)		while serving sentence 394.461 (4)(a)(2)	by informing governor 922.07(1)	insane 922.07(1) in need of treatment for mental illness, dangerous to self or others, & a clear & present potential to escape 394.461 (4)(a)	governor 922.07 dep't of health & rehabilitative services 394.461 (4)(a)		922.07(1)	922.07 (2), (3)		convict's counsel & state attorney may attend examination 922.07(1)		commitment to state hospital for insane 922.07(3)	placement in a separate & secure facility 394.461 (4)(a)	until restored to sanity 922.07(4)			hospital official 922.07(4)	governor 922.07(4)	restored to sanity 922.07(4) 922.07(2)	psychiatric examination & report 922.07(4)	execution of sentence 922.07(2)
GA. Code Ann. (1978)		after conviction for capital offense 27-2602	upon satisfactory evidence offered to governor 27-2602	became insane after conviction 27-2602	governor 27-2602		discretionary 27-2602	27-2602				commitment to Milledgeville State Hospital (capital cases) 27-2602	commitment to Milledgeville State Hospital (capital cases) 27-2602	until sanity restored 27-2602			superintendent of hospital 27-2604	judge of ct. in which conviction occurred 27-2604	recovered & of sound mind 27-2604	by certificate, inquisition, or otherwise 27-2604	judge shall pass sentence 27-2604
IDAHO Code (1979)												"No person who . . . lacks capacity to [proceed] shall be tried, convicted, sentenced or punished . . . ." 18-210	"No person who . . . lacks capacity to [proceed] shall be tried, convicted, sentenced or punished . . . ." 18-210								
ILL. Ann. Stat. (Smith-Hurd 1973 & Supp. 1981–82)		after pronouncement of sentence 38, §1005 -2-3(b)	motion filed in sentencing ct. 38, §1005 -2-3(b)(1)	because of mental condition unable to understand nature & purpose of sentence 38, §1005 -2-3(a)	sentencing ct. 38, §1005 -2-3(b)(2)							remanded to custody of dep't of corrections 38, §1005 -2-3(b)(4)		until fit to be executed 38, §1005 -2-3(b)(4)							
KAN. Stat. Ann. (1974 & Supp. 1980)	director of correctional institution or sheriff having custody 22-4006 (1)	after sentencing 22-4006 (1)	notice 22-4006 (1)	insane 22-4006 (1), (2)	district judge in district where tried 22-4006 (1)		upon sufficient reason 22-4006 (1), (2)	if 3 members of examining commission find convict insane 22-4006 (3)				suspension of execution 22-4006 (3)		until further order 22-4006 (3)				district judge 22-4006 (4)	has become sane 22-4006 (4)	medical investigation 22-4006 (4)	day appointed for execution 22-4007
KY. Rev. Stat. Ann. (Michie 431.240 (1975 & Supp. 1980) 202A.190 (1977)	staff of penal or correctional institution 202A.190 (1)		report 202A.190 (1)	insane 431.240 (2) (1975) so mentally ill that can't be treated at facility 202A.190 (1)	secretary of dep't for human resources 202A.190 (2)		202A.190 (1)	202A.190 (2)				execution suspended; transfer to state forensic psychiatric facility 431.240 (2)	transfer to hospital or forensic psychiatric facility 202A.190 (2)	until restored to sanity *fn. 3* 431.240 (2) 202A.190 (2), (3)			staff of facility 202A.190 (2)	governor 431.240 (2) secretary 202A.190 (2)	restored to sanity 431.240 (2) so far improved that may be returned 202A.190 (2)		execution, unless stayed 431.240 (2) return to institution from which he came *fn. 1* 202A.190 (2), (3)

TABLE 12.3 SUSPENSION OF SENTENCE DUE TO INTERVENING INSANITY *fnn. 1, 2—Continued*

		ISSUED RAISED						DISPOSITION ON BASIS OF EXAMINER'S REPORT				DISPOSITION				RESTORATION					
STATE	By Whom (1)	When (2)	How (3)	CRITERIA (4)	APPROVAL BY (5)	ALTERNATIVE JURISDICTION (6)	PSYCHIATRIC EXAMINATION (7)	REPORT (8)	HEARING (9)	ATTENDANCE (10)	JURY (11)	If Under Sentence of Death (12)	If Under Any Other Sentence (13)	DURATION (14)	REVIEW (15)	Automatic (16)	Application by (17)	Approval by (18)	Criteria (19)	Hearing (20)	Disposition (21)
LA. Rev. Stat. Ann. (West) 28:59 (1975 & Supp. 1980); 15:830 (1981)	superin-tendent or sheriff 28:59(C) secretary of dep't of corrections 15:830(B)	while serving sentence 28:59(C)	recommen-dation of appropriate medical personnel 15:830(B)	becomes mentally ill 28:59(C) mentally ill or mentally retarded 15:830(A)	district ct. 28:59(c) dep't of health & human resources or other appropriate dep't 15:830(B)				judicial commit-ment 28:59(C) if civil commit-ment pro-ceedings initiated 15:830(B)	counsel 15:830(B)			commit-ment to proper institution 28:59(C) transfer to appropriate institution for diag-nosis & observation 15:830(B) civil com-mitment proceedings 15:830(B)	not to exceed length of sentence 15:830(B)			superin-tendent 28:59(C) administra-tor of in-stitution 15:830(C)	committing ct. 28:59(C) administra-tor of in-stitution 15:830(C)	recovered from con-dition which occasioned transfer 15:830(C)		period of commit-ment credited against sentence 28:59(C) returned to dep't, unless sentence expired 15:830(C)
ME. Rev. Stat. Ann. (1978 & Supp. 1981)	warden of state prison or superin-tendent of correction-al center 34, §136-A(1) inmate 34, §136-A(1)		emergency commit-ment *fn. 4* 34, §136-A(1) application for volun-tary hos-pitalization *fn. 5* 34, §136-A(1)		head of institution 34, §136-A(1) (to apply)								admission to state hospital for mentally ill 34, §136-A(1)			see table 4.3 *supra*					returned to appropriate officers of state prison or correc-tional cen-ter, if sen-tence not expired 34, §136-A(1)
MD. Ann. Code (1976)				insane 27, §75(c)	governor 27, §75(c)		27, §75(c)	27, §75(c)				warrant revoked; discretion-ary removal to state hospital for treat-ment 27, §75(c)		until recovered 27, §75(c)			superin-tendent of hospital 27, §75(c)	dep't of mental hygiene 27, §75(c)	no longer insane 27, §75(c)		sentence must be executed 27, §75(c)
MD. Ann. Code (1979)	division of correction or Patuxent Institution 59, §16		medical certification *fn. 6* 59, §16										admission to V.A. hospital or facility 59, §16 59, §12 (a)(1)	*fn. 6* 59, §16		see tables 4.3 & 4.5 *supra*					release to custody of division of correction or Patuxent Institution, if prior to expiration of sentence 59, §16
MASS. Ann. Laws (Michie/ Law. Co-op.) ch. 279 (1980) ch. 123 (1981)	person in charge of place of detention 123, §18 (a) (1981) person detained 123, §18 (b) (1981)	while under sen-tence of death 279, §48	examination by 2 psy-chiatrists designated by commis-sioner of mental health 279, §48 examina-tion by physicians designated by dep't 123, §18 (a) voluntary admission *fn. 7* 123, §18 (b)	insane 279, §48 in need of hospitali-zation by reason of mental illness 123, §18 (a)	governor & council 279, §48 district ct. w/juris-diction over place of deten-tion 123, §18 (a)		preliminary to applica-tion 279, §48 123, §18 (a)	279, §48	123, §18 (a)	person & counsel 123, §5		respite of execution; removal to hospital at Mass. Correctional Institution 279, §48 (1980)	commit-ment to facility or Bridgewater State Hospital 123, §18 (a) (1981)	for stated periods, until no longer insane 279, §48 (1980) initial commit-ment order good for 6 mos.; 1 yr. renewals thereafter 123, §18 (a) (1981)		examination 10 days prior to termination date 279, §48 (1980) see table 4.3 *supra*	certification by medical director of hospital 279, §48 (1980)	superin-tendent of state prison; ultimate review by governor & council 279, §48 (1980)	no longer insane 279, §48 (1980)		reconveyed to state prison pursuant to sentence; notice to governor 279, §48 (1980) return to place of detention, if sentence not expired 123, §18 (d)

TABLE 12.3 SUSPENSION OF SENTENCE DUE TO INTERVENING INSANITY *fnn. 1, 2—Continued*

	ISSUED RAISED							DISPOSITION ON BASIS OF EXAMINER'S REPORT				DISPOSITION				RESTORATION					
STATE	By Whom (1)	When (2)	How (3)	CRITERIA (4)	APPROVAL BY (5)	ALTERNATIVE JURISDICTION (6)	PSYCHIATRIC EXAMINATION (7)	REPORT (8)	HEARING (9)	ATTENDANCE (10)	JURY (11)	If Under Sentence of Death (12)	If Under Any Other Sentence (13)	DURATION (14)	REVIEW (15)	Automatic (16)	Application by (17)	Approval by (18)	Criteria (19)	Hearing (20)	Disposition (21)
MICH. Comp. Laws Ann. 791.265b (1968 & Supp. 1980) 330.2001 *et seq.* (1980)	director of bureau of penal institutions 791.265b (2) person confined 330.2002 a(2) any person 330.2002 a(3) 330.1424 (2)		by procedure promulgated by dep't of mental health 330.2002 a(2) judicial institutionalization *fn. 8* 330.2002 a(3)	mentally or physically disabled *fn. 9* 791.265b (1)(b), (2)			upon request of director 791.265b (3)						transfer to medical institution 791.265b (2) voluntary admission into state mental health facility 330.2002 a(2) involuntary admission to a state mental health facility 330.2002 a(3)	not to exceed term of sentence *fn. 10* 791.265b (2)							
MO. Ann. Stat. (1953 & Supp. 1985)	person in charge of correctional institution 552.050(1)		certification to division of classification & assignment, then transfer to state mental hospital 552.050(1)	reasonable cause to believe inmate needs mental care 552.050(1)		after detention not to exceed 96 hrs. voluntary admission or involuntary commitment if not suitable for return to correctional facility 552.050(1)							placement in state mental hospital; time spent there credited to sentence served 552.050 (1), (2)	initial 90 days; up to 1 additional yr. thereafter 552.050(1)			certification by superintendent of hospital 552.050(3)		when recovered 552.050(3)	certification in writing to prison's division of classification & assignment 552.050(3)	transfer back to correctional facility 552.050(3)
NEV. Rev. Stat. (1981)	trial ct. 178.405	when defendant brought up for judgment & sentencing 178.405	ct. to suspend pronouncement of judgment 178.405	if doubt arises as to defendant's competence 178.405			ct. to appoint 2 physicians 178.415		178.415				178.425								
PA. Stat. Ann. (Purdon 1969 & Supp. 1984)		while undergoing sentence 50, §7401 (a)		whenever prisoner is or becomes severely mentally disabled 50, §7401, (a)			proceedings instituted for examination & treatment under civil provisions of this act 50, §7401(a)		50, §7401 (a)												returned to authority entitled to have been in custody 50, §7401 (b)
S.C. Code Ann. (Law Co-op. 1985)	officer in charge of jail or prison 44-23-220	during confinement 44-23-220		mentally ill or mentally retarded 44-23-220			2 examiners designated by dep't of mental health or dep't of mental retardation 44-23-220	officer in charge of jail or prison to commence civil commitment proceedings if examiners' opinion so warrants 44-23-220	civil commitment proceedings 44-23-220												
TEX. Code Crim. P. (Vernon 1979 & Supp. 1985)	director of dep't of corrections 46.01 (1), (2) or county judge 46.01(3)	when sentence probated or suspended or person paroled 46.01(1) or during confinement 46.01 (2), (3)	on opinion of prison physician 46.01(2) or on certification of county health officer 46.01(3)	mentally ill & would benefit from treatment 46.01	head of hospital to advise whether facilities available 46.01 (2), (3)								hospitalized under civil procedures 46.01(1) transferred to mental hospital 46.01 (2), (3)				head of mental hospital 46.01(6)	notify director of dep't of corrections or county judge 46.01(6)	no longer requires or will not benefit from continued hospitalization 46.01(6)		back to prison or jail 46.01(6)

TABLE 12.3 SUSPENSION OF SENTENCE DUE TO INTERVENING INSANITY *fnn. 1, 2—Continued*

	ISSUED RAISED							DISPOSITION ON BASIS OF EXAMINER'S REPORT				DISPOSITION				RESTORATION					
STATE	By Whom (1)	When (2)	How (3)	CRITERIA (4)	APPROVAL BY (5)	ALTERNATIVE JURISDICTION (6)	PSYCHIATRIC EXAMINATION (7)	(8)	HEARING (9)	ATTENDANCE (10)	JURY (11)	If Under Sentence of Death (12)	If Under Any Other Sentence (13)	DURATION (14)	REVIEW (15)	Automatic (16)	Application by (17)	Approval by (18)	Criteria (19)	Hearing (20)	Disposition (21)
UTAH Code Ann. (1982)	defendant or convict himself, any person on his behalf, prosecuting attorney, or any person having custody or supervision 77-15-3 (2)	while serving prison sentence 77-15-3 (1)	petition alleging incom-petency 77-15-3 (1)	incom-petent 77-15-3(1)	ct. to enter order for hearing 77-15-5		ct. may order inpatient evaluation or exami-nation by 2 alienists 77-15-5 (2)(a), (b)		77-15-5(5)				committed to mental facility if incompetent 77-15-6	until competent 77-15-6			by committed person after 60 days; by clinical director or facility authorities or by ct. any time 77-15-7	notice to prosecuting attorney 77-15-6	competent 77-15-7	77-15-6, 7	

FOOTNOTES: TABLE 12.3

1. At least eight states have statutes generally providing that an incompetent person shall not be tried, convicted, sentenced, or punished so long as his incapacity endures, but no specific provisions or procedures for suspending the sentence or punishment (e.g., Minn. R. Crim. P. § 20.01(1) (West 1979 & Supp. 1985); N.C. Gen. Stat. § 15A-1001 (1983)). These general provisions are not charted in this table.

2. Other related provisions not tabulated here are those concerning incompetency to stand trial (which are in table 12.1) and recovery to proceed with trial (table 12.2) and those targeted specifically at suspending the death sentence of mentally incompetent persons (table 12.4). Also omitted as inappropriate to the focus of table 12.3 are statutes such as N.H. Stat. Ann. § 651:11 (1974 & Supp. 1983), which provides for the "transfer from jail" of "any insane person." Despite the reference to "any insane person," prior provisions (esp. § 651:8-a) make it clear that the transfer procedure is limited in application to persons who have pled not guilty by reason of insanity. Va. Code § 19.2-300 (1983) contains a provision authorizing the court to defer sentence and order a mental examination of a defendant convicted of a crime indicating sexual abnormality, but there are no suspension of sentence provisos for convicted persons with alleged or suspected mental abnormalities.

3. Ky. Rev. Stat. Ann. § 202A.190(2), (3) (Michie 1977):

> If the prisoner's sentence expires during his stay in the facility, and he is still mentally ill and presents an immediate danger or an immediate threat of danger to self or others, and he can reasonably benefit from treatment in a hospital, and hospitalization is the least restrictive alternative mode of treatment available, then the staff of the facility shall notify the court which sentenced the individual to the penal institution and petition . . . for involuntary comment.
>
> . . . .
>
> During the time of the prisoner's stay in a facility his legal status as a prisoner shall remain unchanged until the termination of his sentence. . . . The time the prisoner spends in the facility shall be counted as part of the prisoner's sentence."

4. See table 2.4 regarding emergency detention.

5. See table 3.1 regarding procedures for voluntary admission.

6. See table 2.14 regarding procedures for institutionalization by medical certification.

7. See table 3.1 concerning voluntary admission.

8. See tables 2.6, 2.7, 2.8, and 2.9 concerning judicial institutionalization.

9. Mich. Comp. Laws Ann. § 791.2656(1)(b) (1968 & Supp. 1980): "'Mentally or physically disabled prisoner' means a prisoner whose physical or mental health has deteriorated to a point which renders the prisoner a minimal threat to society."

10. *Id.* § 791.2656(2): "The transfer shall be effective for the duration of the prisoner's sentence, the duration of the existing medical condition causing the prisoner to be mentally or physically disabled, or for any other length of time considered necessary by the director, but shall not exceed the term of the sentence."

TABLE 12.4 STAY OF EXECUTION DUE TO INTERVENING INSANITY

	ISSUE RAISED										DISPOSITION				RESTORATION PROCEDURE					
STATE	By Whom (1)	How (2)	CRITERIA (3)	APPROVAL BY (4)	ALTERNATIVE JURISDICTION (5)	PSYCHIATRIC EXAMINATION (6)	DISPOSITION ON BASIS OF EXAMINER'S REPORT (7)	HEARING (8)	ATTENDANCE (9)	JURY (10)	Execution Stayed (11)	Placement (12)	Duration (13)	REVIEW (14)	Application By (15)	Approval By (16)	Criteria (17)	Hearing (18)	Alternative Procedure (19)	Disposition (20)
ALA. Code (1982)		made to appear that insane 15-16-23	made to appear that insane 15-16-23	trial ct. 15-16-23	none 15-16-23					if judge deems proper for guidance 15-16-23	15-16-23		fixed in order 15-16-23	barred 15-16-23		trial ct. 15-16-23	restored to sanity 15-16-23			execution of sentence 15-16-23
ARIZ. Rev. Stat. Ann. (1978 & Supp. 1982)	superin-tendent of state prison 13-4021(A)	notice to county attorney 13-4021(A)	insane 13-4021(A)	superior ct. of county where prison located 13-4021(A)				13-4021(A)	county attorney; may present witnesses 13-4022	13-4021(A)	13-4024(B)	state hospital 13-4024(B) 13-4023	until reason restored 13-4023		superin-tendent of state hospital 13-4024(c)	governor 13-4024(c)	sane 13-4024(c)			execution of judgment 13-4024(c)
ARK. Stat. Ann. (1977)	circuit judge 43-1301	upon reason to believe that insane 43-1301	upon reason to believe that insane 43-1301	judge of circuit ct. 43-1301		43-1301		43-1303	prosecuting attorney & counsel for defendant 43-1301		postpone-ment or not carrying out of any sentence 43-1303									
CAL. penal code (West 1983)	warden 3701	notice to district attorney 3701	insane 3701	superior ct. of county where prison located 3701	governor *fn. 1* 3700	automatic upon sentence *fn. 2* 3700.5		3701	district attorney may produce witnesses 3702	3701	3703	medical facilities of dep't of corrections 3703	until reason restored 3703		superin-tendent of medical facility 3704	superior ct. from which committed 3704	sane 3704	w/o jury 3704		execution of judgment 3704
COLO. Rev. Stat. (1978) *fn. 3*																				
CONN. Gen. Stat. Ann. (West 1960 & Supp. 1980)	warden 54-101	application 54-101	insane 54-101	superior ct. of Tolland 54-101 OR	if out of session any superior ct. judge 54-101	54-101	54-101				54-101	state hospital for men-tally ill 54-101	until recovered 54-101		state's attorney, upon report from super-intendent 54-101	superior ct. 54-101	recovered 54-101			execution of sentence 54-101
FLA. Stat. Ann. (West 1973)		by informing governor 922.07(1)	insane 922.07(1)	governor **922.07**		922.071(1)	922.07 (2), (3)		counsel & state attorney may attend examination 922.07(1)		922.07	state hospital for insane 922.07(3)	until restored to sanity 922.07(4)		proper official of hospital 922.07(4)	governor 922.07(4)	restored to to sanity *fn. 4* 922.07 (2), (4)		psychiatric examination & report 922.07(4)	execution of sentence 922.07(2)
GA. Code Ann. (1978)		by offering satisfactory evidence that insane 27-2602	insane 27-2602	governor 27-2602		discretionary 27-2602	27-2602				27-2602	Milledgeville State Hospital 27-2602	until sanity restored or determined by laws now in force 27-2602		superin-tendent of hospital 27-2604	judge of ct. in which conviction occurred 27-2604	recovered & of sound mind 27-2604	by certifi-cate, inqui-sition, or otherwise 27-2604	by certifi-cate, inqui-sition, or otherwise 27-2604	judge shall pass sen-tence & issue new warrant 27-2604
IDAHO Code (1979 & Supp. 1981) *fn. 5*																				
ILL. Ann. Stat. (Smith-Hurd 1980 & Supp. 1983)	*fn. 6* 38, §1005-2-3(b)	motion filed in sentenc-ing ct. 38, §1005-2-3(b)(1)	because of mental con-dition unable to under-stand nature & purpose of sentence 38, §1005-2-3(a)	sentenc-ing ct. 38, §1005-2-3(b)(2)	*fn. 6*						38, §1005-2-3(b)(4)	dep't of corrections 38, §1005-2-3(b)(4)	until fit to be executed 38, §1005-2-3(b)(4)				*fn. 6*			
KAN. Stat. Ann. (1981)	director of correctional institution or sheriff having custody 22-4006(1)	notice 22-4006(1)	insane 22-4006(1)	district judge in district where tried 22-4006(1)		upon sufficient reason 22-4006(2)	if 3 members of examining commission find convict insane 22-4006(3)				22-4006(3)		until further order 22-4006(3)			district judge 22-4006(4)	has become sane 22-4006(4)		another in-vestigation 22-4006(4)	day set for execution 22-4007

TABLE 12.4 STAY OF EXECUTION DUE TO INTERVENING INSANITY—*Continued*

STATE	ISSUE RAISED		CRITERIA (3)	APPROVAL BY (4)	ALTERNATIVE JURISDICTION (5)	PSYCHIATRIC EXAMINATION (6)	DISPOSITION ON BASIS OF EXAMINER'S REPORT (7)	HEARING (8)	ATTENDANCE (9)	JURY (10)	DISPOSITION			REVIEW (14)	RESTORATION PROCEDURE					
	By Whom (1)	How (2)									Execution Stayed (11)	Placement (12)	Duration (13)		Application By (15)	Approval By (16)	Criteria (17)	Hearing (18)	Alternative Procedure (19)	Disposition (20)
KY. Rev. Stat. Ann. (Michie 1975 & Supp. 1982)			insane 431.240(2)								431.240(2)	state forensic psychiatric facility 431.240(2)	until restored to sanity 431.240(2)			governor 431.240(2)	restored to sanity 431.240(2)			execution, unless stayed 431.240(2)
MD. Ann. Code (1982 & Supp. 1982)			insane 27, §75(c)	governor 27, §75(c)		27, §75(c)	27, §75(c)				27, §75(c)	discretionary removal to state hospital 27, §75(c)	until recovered 27, §75(c)		superin-tendent of hospital 27, §75(c)	mental hygiene adminis-tration 27, §75(c)	no longer insane 27, §75(c)			sentence executed 27, §75(c)
MASS. Ann. Laws. (Michie/ Law. Co-op. 1980 & Supp. 1982)		certification by 2 psychiatrists designated by commis-sioner of mental health 279, §62	insane 279, §62	governor & council 279, §62		preliminary to applica-tion 279, §62	279, §62				279, §62	hospital at Mass. Correctional Institution 279, §62	for stated periods, until no longer insane 279, §62		certification by medical director of hospital 279, §62	superin-tendent of state prison; ultimate & alternative review by governor & council 279, §62	no longer insane 279, §62			reconveyed to state prison pursuant to sentence; notice to governor 279, §62
MISS. Code Ann. (1972)	sheriff 99-19-57	summons an inquest 99-19-57	insane 99-19-57	concurrence of judge of circuit ct., chancellor, or president of board of super-visors 99-19-57		inquest 99-19-57	99-19-57	inquest 99-19-57		6 physicians if possible; otherwise; freeholders & electors of county 99-19-57	99-19-57	state insane asylum 99-19-57	until governor shall be satisfied of sanity 99-19-57		director of insane asylum 99-19-57	governor 99-19-57	sane 99-19-57			date appointed for execution 99-19-57
MO. Ann. Stat. (Vernon 1953 & Supp. 1981)	warden 552.060(2)	notification of governor, director of division of mental diseases, attorney general, circuit ct. & prosecuting attorney 552.060(2)	as result of mental disease or defect lacks capacity to understand nature & purpose of punishment 552.060(1)	circuit ct. of Cole County 552.060(3)	552.060(5)	upon request of any notified party 552.060(3)		inquiry 552.060(3)			552.060(4)	held in penal institution, subject to transfer to mental hospital 552.060(4) 552.050			director's certification 552.060(4)		free of mental disease or defect 552.060(4)			governor shall fix new date for execution 552.060(4)
MONT. Code Ann. (1981)		fn. 7									46-19-202 (2)	Warm Springs state hospital 46-19-202 (2)	for so long as lack of fitness endures 46-19-202 (2)		superin-tendent, prosecuting officer, defendant or counsel, or court on own motion 46-19-202 (3)	court 46-19-202 (3)	regained fitness to proceed 46-19-202 (3)	if requested 46-19-202 (3)		execution or discharge 46-19-202 (3)
NEB. Rev. Stat. (1979)	warden or sheriff having custody 29-2537	notice 29-2537	insane 29-2537	judge of district ct. of district where tried 29-2537		upon sufficient reason; by commission of super-intendents of state centers at Lincoln, Hastings, & Norfolk 29-2537	if 2 of commission find convict insane 29-2537				29-2537 29-1822		until recovery 29-1822		upon judge's own motion 29-2537	failure of commission to find convict insane 29-2537	has become sane 29-2537		investigation by sanity commission 29-2537	judge shall appoint day for execution 29-2538
NEV. Rev. Stat. (1979)	director of dep't of prisons 176.425(1)	petition, verified by physician 176.425(1)	insane 176.425	district judge of county in which prison located 176.415(3) 176.425(1)		176.425 (1)(b)		176.425 (1)(a)	attorney general or deputy, prosecuting attorney, & counsel 176.435(1)		176.455(1)	safe place of confinement 176.455(1)	until sane 176.455(1)		director 176.455(3)	judge of ct. staying execution 176.455(3)	sane 176.455(3)			order staying execution vacated 176.455(3)

TABLE 12.4 STAY OF EXECUTION DUE TO INTERVENING INSANITY—*Continued*

STATE	ISSUE RAISED		CRITERIA (3)	APPROVAL BY (4)	ALTERNATIVE JURISDICTION (5)	PSYCHIATRIC EXAMINATION (6)	DISPOSITION ON BASIS OF EXAMINER'S REPORT (7)	HEARING (8)	ATTENDANCE (9)	JURY (10)	DISPOSITION			REVIEW (14)	RESTORATION PROCEDURE					
	By Whom (1)	How (2)									Execution Stayed (11)	Placement (12)	Duration (13)		Application By (15)	Approval By (16)	Criteria (17)	Hearing (18)	Alternative Procedure (19)	Disposition (20)
N.M. Stat. Ann. (1978)	warden 31-14-4	notice to district attorney 31-14-4	insane 31-14-4	district ct. of county where state penitentiary located 31-14-4				31-14-4 31-14-5	district attorney 31-14-5		31-14-7	state hospital for insane 31-14-6	until reason restored 31-14-6		superin-tendent of hospital 31-14-7	governor 31-14-7	reason recovered 31-14-7		certification 31-14-7	execution of judgment 31-14-7
N.Y. Correct. Law (McKinney 1968 & Supp. 1983)		appointment of com-mission 655	insane 655	commission 655		fact-finding hearing/ examination 655	655	fact-finding hearing/ examination 655	district attorney, & counsel for defendant 655		656	state hospital for insane convicts (discre-tionary) 655	until restored to right mind 655	governor 655	director of hospital 655	justice of supreme ct. of district where hospital located 655	cured of insanity 655			returned to state institution to be dealt with accord-ing to law 655 execution, unless sentence commuted or pardoned 657
OHIO Rev. Code Ann. (Baldwin 1979)	warden or sheriff having custody 2949.28	notice 2949.28	insane 2949.28	judge of ct. of county pleas of county where confined 2949.28				2949.28	warden or sheriff, clerk of common pleas, & prosecuting attorney 2949.29	at judge's discretion 2949.28	2949.29		until restored 2949.29 2949.30		warden or sheriff having custody 2949.30	governor, if convinced finding of restoration correct 2949.30	restored 2949.30		submission to governor of copy of finding of restoration 2949.30	warrant issued for execution 2949.30
OKLA. Stat. Ann. (West 1958 & Supp. 1983)	warden 22, §1005	notice to county attorney 22, §1005	insane 22, §1005	district or superior ct. of county where prison located 22, §1005	none 22, §1004			22, §1005	county attorney & may produce witnesses 22, §1006	22, §1005	22, §1008	state hospital for insane 22, §1007	until reason restored 22, §1007		superin-tendent of hospital 22, §1008	governor 22, §1008	reason recovered 22, §1008		certification 22, §1008	execution of judgment 22, §1008
S.D. Codified Laws Ann. (1979)	warden 23A-27A-22	notice to governor 23A-27A-22	mentally incompetent to proceed 23A-27A-22	commission appointed by governor 23A-27A-24		commission 23A-27A-22 23A-27A-23	23A-27A-24	commission may call & examine witnesses 23A-27A-23	state's attorney or attorney general or assistant, & counsel 23A-27A-23		23A-27A-24	human services center, at governor's discretion 23A-27A-24	until no longer mentally ill 23A-27A-24	every 6 mos. 23A-27A-24	commission 23A-27A-25	chief justice of supreme ct. 23A-27A-25	no longer mentally incompetent to proceed 23A-27A-25		certification of commis-sion's report & submission to governor 23A-27A-25	execution, unless commuted or pardoned 23A-27A-26
UTAH Code Ann. (1982)	warden 77-19-13(1)	notice to ct., prosecuting attorney, & counsel 77-19-13(1)	incompetent to proceed 77-19-13 77-15-2	ct. in which sentence rendered 77-19-13(1)		77-19-13(2)	77-19-13(2)	77-15-5			77-19-13(1)	UTAH state hospital or another mental health facility 77-19-13(2) 77-15-6	until compe-tent to proceed 77-15-6		person committed, clinical director, or ct. on own motion 77-15-7 (1), (2)	ct. 77-15-7 (1), (2)	competent to proceed 77-15-7(2)	77-15-7		warrant issued for execution 77-19-13(2)
WYO. Stat. (1977 & Supp. 1982)	sheriff 7-13-901	notice to judge of district ct. 7-13-901	insane 7-13-901	jury 7-13-901				inquiry 7-13-902	judge, clerk, & district attorney 7-13-902	7-13-901	7-13-902		until warrant from governor ordering execution 7-13-902			governor 7-13-903	of sound mind 7-13-903			warrant appointing time for execution 7-13-903

FOOTNOTES: TABLE 12.4

1. Cal. Penal Code § 3602 (West 1983): "No judge, court, or officer, other than the Governor, can suspend the execution of a judgment of death, except the warden of the state prison to whom he is delivered for execution, . . . unless an appeal is taken."

2. Id. § 3700.5:

> It is the duty of the alienists so selected and appointed to examine such defendant and investigate his sanity, and to report their opinions and conclusions thereon, in writing, to the Governor, to the warden of the prison at which the execution is to take place at least 20 days prior to the day appointed for the execution . . . . The warden shall furnish a copy of the report to counsel for defendant upon his request.

3. Colo. Rev. Stat. § 16-8-110(1) (1978): "No person shall be tried, sentenced or executed if . . . incompetent to proceed." See Tables 12.1 and 12.2 for provisions and procedures concerning incompetency to proceed.

4. Fla. Stat. Ann. § 922.07(2) (West 1973): "has the mental capacity to understand the nature of the death penalty and the reasons why it was imposed upon him."

5. Idaho Code § 18-210 (1979): "No person who . . . lacks capacity to [proceed] shall be tried, convicted, sentenced or punished." See Tables 12.1 and 12.2 for provisions concerning incompetency to proceed.

6. Ill. Ann. Stat. ch. 38, § 1005-2-3(b) (Smith-Hurd 1973):

> The procedure for raising and deciding the question [of fitness to be executed] shall be the same as that provided for raising and deciding the question of fitness to stand trial subject to the following specific provisions:
>
> (1) the question shall be raised by motion filed in the sentencing court;
>
> (2) the question shall be decided by the court;
>
> (3) the burden of proving that the offender is unfit to be executed is on the offender;
>
> (4) if the offender is found unfit to be executed, he shall be remanded to the custody of the Department of Corrections until he becomes fit to be executed.

See Tables 12.1 and 12.2 for provisions concerning incompetency to proceed.

7. Mont. Code Ann. § 46-19-201 (1981): "If after judgment of death there is good reason to suppose that the defendant lacks mental fitness, the mental fitness of the defendant will be determined in accordance with the provisions of Chapter 14 of this title." See Table 12.1 for provisions concerning incompetency to proceed.

TABLE 12.5 THE INSANITY DEFENSE—PLEADING AND PROOF

					TEST OF INSANITY						STANDARD OF PROOF		
		TIME OF PLEADING							BURDEN OF PROOF				
STATE	FORM OR MODE OF PLEADING (1)	Arraignment (2)	Trial (3)	Other (4)	M'Naghten (right-wrong) (5)	And Irresistible Impulse (6)	ALI Model Penal Code (7)	Other (8)	On Prosecutor (9)	On Defendant (10)	Beyond Reasonable Doubt (11)	Preponderance of Evidence (12)	Other (13)
ALA. Code (1982)	special plea 15-16-1	15-16-1 OR		judge's order in capital cases 15-16-22(a)	*fn. 1, 2* annot. to 15-16-2 OR	*fn. 1, 2* annot. to 15-16-2 AND		product rule *fn. 1, 3* annot. to 15-16-2		15-16-2		*fn. 3* annot. to 15-16-2	reasonable satisfaction of jury 15-16-2
ALAS. Stat. (1980 & Supp. 1982)	affirmative defense 12.47.010(a)	12.47.010(b) OR		w/in 10 days thereafter 12.47.010(b)	nature & quality of act 12.47.010(a)		subsection (2) 12.47.010(c)		12.47.040(b)		NGRI 12.47.040(b)		
ARIZ. Rev. Stat. Ann. (1978 & Supp. 1982) R. Cr. P. (1973 & Supp. 1983)	affirmative defense R.15.2(b) & comment	R.15.2(b) OR		w/in 20 days thereafter R.15.2(b)	nature & quality of act 13-502					13-502(B), as amended by Laws 1983, ch. 198, §1			clear & convincing evidence 13-502(B), as amended by Laws 1983, ch. 198, §1
ARK. Stat. Ann. (1977 & Supp. 1983)	affirmative defense 41-601(1)			earliest practicable time 41-604(1)			criminality 41-601(1), (2)	omits "substantial" from MPC formulation		*fn. 4* annot. to 41-601		*fn. 4* annot. to 41-601	
CAL. Penal Code (West 1970 & Supp. 1982) CAL. Evid. Code §522 (West 1966)	special plea 1016(6)	1003	ct. may allow change in plea, for good cause, any time before trial 1016(6)				*fn. 5* annot. to 1026			522		522	
COLO. Rev. Stat. (1978 & Supp. 1982)	special plea 16-8-103(1)	16-8-103(1) OR	for good cause any time prior to trial 16-18-103(1)		16-8-101	16-8-101			16-8-105(2)		16-8-105(2)		
CONN. Gen. Stat. Ann. (West 1972 & Supp. 1982, as amended by P.A. 83-486)	affirmative defense 53a-13(a)						wrongfulness; "control" rather than "conform" conduct 53a-13	excludes defense where caused by voluntary ingestion of liquor or unpre-scribed drugs or manifested by compulsive gambling 53a-13		53a-12(b)		53a-12(b)	
DEL. Code Ann. (1979 & Supp. 1982)	affirmative defense 11, §401(a)		11, §304(a)		substantial capacity to appreciate wrongfulness 11, §401(a)		subsection (2) 11, §401(c)	excludes defense where caused by voluntary ingestion of liquor or unpre-scribed drugs *fn. 6* 11, §401(a)–(c)		11, §304(a)		11, §304(a)	
D.C. Code Ann. (1981 & Supp. 1983)	affirmative defense 24-301(j)	24-301(j) OR		w/in 15 days thereafter 24-301(j)			wrongfulness *fn. 7*			24-301(j)		24-301(j)	
FLA. R. Cr. P. (West 1975 & Supp. 1982)	written notice R.3.216	R.3.216(c) OR		15 days thereafter R.3.216 extensions for good cause R.3.216(f)	*fn. 8* annot. to R.3.217				*fn. 9* annot. to R.3.217		*fn. 9* annot. to R.3.217		

TABLE 12.5 THE INSANITY DEFENSE—PLEADING AND PROOF—*Continued*

STATE	FORM OR MODE OF PLEADING (1)	TIME OF PLEADING: Arraignment (2)	TIME OF PLEADING: Trial (3)	TIME OF PLEADING: Other (4)	TEST OF INSANITY: M'Naghten (right-wrong) (5)	TEST OF INSANITY: And Irresistible Impulse (6)	TEST OF INSANITY: ALI Model Penal Code (7)	TEST OF INSANITY: Other (8)	BURDEN OF PROOF: On Prosecutor (9)	BURDEN OF PROOF: On Defendant (10)	STANDARD OF PROOF: Beyond Reasonable Doubt (11)	STANDARD OF PROOF: Preponderance of Evidence (12)	STANDARD OF PROOF: Other (13)
GA. Code Ann. (1983 & Supp. 1983)	affirmative defense *fn. 10* annot. to 26-702				26-702	delusional compulsion 26-703	subsection (2) 27-1503(a)(1)			*fn. 10* annot, to 26-702		*fn. 10* annot. to 26-702	
HAWAII Rev. Stat. (1976 & Supp. 1982)	affirmative defense 704-402(1)						wrongfulness 704-400	language expanded to include physical or mental disease, disorder, or defect 704-400	*fn. 11*		*fn. 11*		
IDAHO Code (1979 & Supp. 1983)	not a defense 18-207							only mensrea considered 18-207(c)					
ILL. Ann. Stat. (Smith-Hurd 1972 & Supp. 1983–84)	affirmative defense 38, §115-3(b)						criminality *fn. 12* 38, §6-2 (a), (b) 38, §1005-1-11			38, §3-2(b)		38, §3-2(b)	
IND. Code Ann. (Burns 1979 & Supp. 1983–84)	notice 35-36-2-1			20 days before omnibus date, or, for good cause, any time before trial 35-36-2-1			wrongfulness 35-41-3-6			35-41-4-1(b)		35-41-4-1(b)	
IOWA Code Ann. (West 1979 & Supp. 1983) IOWA R. Cr. P. (West 1983)	pretrial motion R.10(11)(b)(1)			w/in 40 days after arraignment & 9 days before trial	701.4				*fn. 13*		*fn. 13*		
KAN. Stat. Ann. (1974 & Supp. 1982)	written notice 22-3219(1)			before trial & w/in 30 days after arraignment 22-3219(1)	*fn. 14* OR				*fn. 15*		*fn. 15*		
KY. Rev. Stat. Ann. (Michie 1975 & Supp. 1982)	written notice 504.070(1)		at least 20 days before trial 504.070(1) OR				criminality 504.020			*fn. 16* annot. to 504.020			
LA. Rev. Stat. Ann. §14:14 (West 1974 & Supp. 1983) LA. Code Crim. Proc. §§650, *et seq* (1981 & Supp. 1983)	combined plea 650	652(3)			14:14					652		652	
ME. Rev. Stat. Ann. (1983)	combined plea 17-A, §40(1)						wrongfulness 17-A, §39 (1), (2)			17-A, §39(1) 17-A, §40(4)		17-A, §39(1)	
MD. Ann. Code (1979 & Supp. 1983)	written notice 12-108						criminality 12-107	mental "disorder," rather than "disease" or "defect" 59, §25(a)	*fn. 17*		*fn. 17*		

TABLE 12.5 THE INSANITY DEFENSE—PLEADING AND PROOF—*Continued*

STATE	FORM OR MODE OF PLEADING (1)	TIME OF PLEADING: Arraignment (2)	TIME OF PLEADING: Trial (3)	TIME OF PLEADING: Other (4)	TEST OF INSANITY: M'Naghten (right-wrong) (5)	TEST OF INSANITY: And Irresistible Impulse (6)	TEST OF INSANITY: ALI Model Penal Code (7)	TEST OF INSANITY: Other (8)	BURDEN OF PROOF: On Prosecutor (9)	BURDEN OF PROOF: On Defendant (10)	STANDARD OF PROOF: Beyond Reasonable Doubt (11)	STANDARD OF PROOF: Preponderance of Evidence (12)	STANDARD OF PROOF: Other (13)
MASS. R. Cr. P. (Michie/Law. Co-op. 1979 & Supp. 1983)	written notice R.14(b)(2)(A)		not less than 5 days before R.13(d)(1)(A)(i) R.14(b)(2)(A) OR	at such later time as judge may allow R.14(b)(2)(A)			*fn. 18*		*fn. 18*		*fn. 18*		
MICH. Comp. Laws Ann. §768.20a *et. seq* (1982) MICH. Rev. Crim. Code §§705, 715 (1979)	written notice 768.20a(1)		at least 30 days before trial 768.20a(1) OR	at such other time as ct. directs 768.20a(1)			wrongfulness 768.21a(1) 705 mental "illness" & "retardation" instead of "disease" or "defect;" & excludes defense for voluntary ingestion of alcohol or controlled substances 705 768.21a(1), (2)		715 & committee commentary		715 & committee commentary		
MINN. Stat. Ann. (West 1964 & Supp. 1983); MINN. R. Cr. P. (West 1979 & 1983 Special Pamph.)	written notice of defenses R.9.02(3)(a); plea R.14.01(c)			before the omnibus (probable cause) hearing R.9.02(1)	*fn. 19* 611.026					20.2(6)(4)(b)		20.2(6)(4)(b)	
MISS. Code Ann. (1972 & Supp. 1982)					*fn. 20*				*fn. 21*		*fn. 21*		
MO. Ann. Stat. (Vernon 1973 & Supp. 1983)	plea or written notice 552.030(2)	552.030(2) OR		w/in 10 days thereafter, later for good cause 552.030(2)			nature, quality or wrongfulness 552.030(1) 552.010	alcoholism or drug abuse w/o psychosis excluded 552.010 omits the word "substantial" 552.030(1)		552.030(7)		552.030(7)	
MONT. Code Ann. (1983)	written notice 46-14-201(1)	46-14-201(1) OR		w/in 10 days thereafter; later for good cause 46-14-201(1)			no insanity defense, but evidence of mental disease or defect admissible when relevant to state of mind which is element of offense *fn. 22* 46-14-102	no insanity defense, but evidence of mental disease or defect admissible when relevant to state of mind which is element of offense *fn. 22* 46-14-102	no insanity defense, but evidence of mental disease or defect admissible when relevant to state of mind which is element of offense *fn. 22* 46-14-102	*fn. 23*			
NEB. Rev. Stat. (1979 & Supp. 1982)	written notice 29-2203		60 days before 29-2203		*fn. 24*				*fn. 25*		*fn. 25*		
NEV. Rev. Stat. (1981)	affirmative defense *fn. 26*				*fn. 27* 194.010					*fn. 26*		*fn. 26*	

TABLE 12.5 THE INSANITY DEFENSE—PLEADING AND PROOF—*Continued*

STATE	FORM OR MODE OF PLEADING (1)	TIME OF PLEADING			TEST OF INSANITY				BURDEN OF PROOF		STANDARD OF PROOF		
		Arraignment (2)	Trial (3)	Other (4)	M'Naghten (right-wrong) (5)	And Irresistible Impulse (6)	ALI Model Penal Code (7)	Other (8)	On Prosecutor (9)	On Defendant (10)	Beyond Reasonable Doubt (11)	Preponderance of Evidence (12)	Other (13)
N.H. Rev. Stat. Ann. (1974 & Supp. 1982)	628:2II			w/in 10 days after plea; later for good cause 628:2II				not criminally responsible *fn. 28* 628:2		*fn. 28* 628:2II		*fn. 28* 628:2II	
N.J. Stat Ann. (West (1982) N.J. R. Cr. Practice (West 1983)	affirmative defense 2C:4-1 written notice 2C:4-3(a) R.3:12	R.3:12 OR		w/in 30 days thereafter later for good cause R.3:12	2C:4-1					2C:4-1		2C:4-1	
N.M. R. Cr. P. for Dist. Ct. (1980 & Supp. 1983); N.M. Uniform Jury Instructions—Crim. (1978)	notice R.35(a)(1)	R.35(a)(1) OR		w/in 20 days thereafter; later for good cause R.35(a)(1)	UJI Crim. 41.01	UJI Crim. 41.01			UJI Crim. 41.00		UJI Crim. 41.00		
N.Y. Penal Law (McKinney 1975 & Supp. 1983–84)	defense 30.05(2)					*fn. 29*	30.05(1)		*fn. 30* annot. to 30.05		*fn. 30* annot. to 30.05		
N.C. Gen. Stat. (1983)	notice 15A-959(a)	15A-952(c) 15A-959(a) OR		later for good cause 15A-959(a)	*fn. 31*					*fn. 32*		to satisfaction of jury *fn. 32*	
N.D. Cent. Code (1976 & Supp. 1981) N.D. R. Cr. P. (1974 & Supp. 1981)	defense 12.1-04-03 notice R.12.2(a)	R.12(c) R.12.2(a) OR		as soon thereafter as practicable R.12(c); later as ct. may direct R.12.2(a)				*fn. 33* 12.1-04-03	"defense" 12.1-04-03 12.1-01-03(2) *compare* "affirmative defense" 12.1-01-03(3)		12.1-01-03(2)		
OHIO Rev. Code Ann. (Baldwin 1979 & Supp. 1982) OHIO R. Cr. P. (Baldwin 1981 & Supp. 1982)	written plea R.11(A)	R.11(H) OR	any time before trial for good cause R. 11(H)		*fn. 34*					*fn. 35* 2901.05(A)		*fn. 35* 2901.05(A)	
OKLA. Stat. Ann. (West 1958 & Supp. 1983)					*fn. 36* 21, §152(4)			morbid propensity no defense 21, §154	*fn. 37*		*fn. 37*		
OR. Rev. Stat. (1981)	affirmative defense 161.305 written notice 161.309(3)	161.309(3) OR	any time before trial for just cause 161.309(3) OR	after, if just cause for failure to file notice shown 161.309(3)			criminality 161.295			161.055(2) 161.305		166.055(2) 161.305	
PA. R. Cr. P. (West 1983)	written notice R.305(C)(1)(b)	R.307 OR		w/in 30 days thereafter unless extended by ct. for cause R.307	*fn. 38* 18, §314(d) 18, §315(b)					18, §315(a)		18, §315(b)	
R.I. Gen. Laws (1977 & Supp. 1982)							*fn. 39*			*fn. 40*		*fn. 40*	

TABLE 12.5 THE INSANITY DEFENSE—PLEADING AND PROOF—*Continued*

STATE	FORM OR MODE OF PLEADING (1)	TIME OF PLEADING: Arraignment (2)	TIME OF PLEADING: Trial (3)	TIME OF PLEADING: Other (4)	TEST OF INSANITY: M'Naghten (right-wrong) (5)	TEST OF INSANITY: And Irresistible Impulse (6)	TEST OF INSANITY: ALI Model Penal Code (7)	TEST OF INSANITY: Other (8)	BURDEN OF PROOF: On Prosecutor (9)	BURDEN OF PROOF: On Defendant (10)	STANDARD OF PROOF: Beyond Reasonable Doubt (11)	STANDARD OF PROOF: Preponderance of Evidence (12)	STANDARD OF PROOF: Other (13)
S.C. Code (1976 & Supp. 1982)					*fn. 41*					*fn. 42*		*fn. 42*	
S.D. Codified Laws Ann. (1979 & Supp. 1983)	special plea 23A-10-2 written notice 23A-10-3	23A-10-2 23-8-6 OR		as soon thereafter as practicable 23A-10-3	wrongfulness 22-1-2(22) 22-3-1(3)				*fn. 43*		*fn. 43*		
TENN. R. Cr. P. (1981)	written notice R.12.2(a)		before trial R.12.2(a) R.12(b) OR	at such later time as ct. may direct R.12.2(a)			wrongfulness *fn. 44*		*fn. 45*		*fn. 45*		
TEX. Code Crim. Proc. (Vernon 1966 & Supp. 1982–83) Penal Code Ann. §8.01 (Vernon 1974 & Supp. 1982–83)	not guilty plea 27.17 affirmative defense 8.01 written notice 46.03(2)(a)		10 days before 46.03(2)(a) OR	at pretrial hearing, if earlier; later only for good cause 46.03(2)(a)	*fn. 46* 8.01	*fn. 46* 8.01	substitutes knowledge for substantial capacity *fn. 46* 8.01			*fn. 47*		*fn. 47*	
UTAH. Code Ann. (1978 & & Supp. 1983)	written notice 77-14-3(1)	77-14-3(1) OR		as soon thereafter as practicable, but not less than 30 days before trial 77-14-3(1)			no insanity defense, but may show lack of requisite mental state as result of mental illness *fn. 48* 76-2-305	no insanity defense, but may show lack of requisite mental state as result of mental illness *fn. 48* 76-2-305	*fn. 49*		*fn. 49*		
VT. Stat. Ann. (1974 & Supp. 1983) VT. R. Cr. P. (1974 & Supp. 1982)	written notice R.12.1(a)	on date of status conference R.12.1(a) OR	10 days before trial whichever is sooner R.12.1(a)		expressly abolished 13, §4802		"adequate capacity" 13, §4801		*fn. 50*	13, §4801(b)	*fn. 50*	13, §4801(b)	
VA. Code (1983)	written notice 19.2-168		10 days before 19.2-168	right to continuance by state if psychiatric evidence presented w/o notice 19.2-168	*fn. 51*	*fn. 51*				*fn. 52*			to satisfaction of jury *fn. 52*
WASH. Rev. Code Ann. §§9A (1977 & Supp. 1983–84), 10 (1980 & Supp. 1983–84)	written notice 10.77.030(1)	10.77.030(1) OR		w/in 10 days thereafter; later for good cause 10.77.030(1)	*fn. 53* 9A.12.010(1)					9A.12.010(2) 10.77.030(2)		9A.12.010(2) 10.77.030(2)	
W. VA. Code (1980 & Supp. 1983)							"substantial" omitted *fn. 54*		*fn. 55*		*fn. 55*		
WIS. Stat. Ann. (West 1971 & Supp. 1983–84)	affirmative defense 971.15(3)						wrongfulness 971.15(1), (2)			971.15(3)		greater weight of the credible evidence 971.15(3)	
WYO. Stat. (1977)	plea 7-11-304(c)	7-11-304(c)		later for good cause shown 7-11-304(c)			wrongfulness 7-11-304 (a), (b)		7-11-305(b)	must overcome presumption of responsibility 7-11-305(b)	7-11-305(b)		

FOOTNOTES: TABLE 12.5

1. Hafley v. State, 342 So. 2d 408 (Ala. Crim. App. 1976), cert. denied, 342 So. 2d 412 (Ala. 1977). Annot. to Ala. Code § 15-16-2 (1982):

> Legal test for insanity as a defense requires showing that at the time of the commission of the crime the defendant was afflicted with a diseased mind to the extent that (1) she did not know right from wrong as applied to the particular act in question, or (2) if she did have such knowledge, she, nevertheless, by reason of the duress of such mental disease had so far lost the power to select the right and to avoid doing the act in question as that her free agency was at the time destroyed, and (3) that, at the same time, the crime was so connected with such mental disease, in the relation of cause and effect, as to have been the product of it solely.

2. The 1982 Alabama Legislature's "crime package," Acts 1982, Nos. 82-839 to 82-893, repealed inter alia Ala. Code §§ 15-16-1 & 15-16-24 (1982), and added a new section, Acts 1982, No. 82-888, abolishing the insanity defense. The Governor signed the bill, but the Alabama Court of Criminal Appeals, State v. Eley, Docket No. 82-98, cert. denied (Ala. Dec. 17, 1982), held a related provision, Acts 1982, No. 82-860 (appeal by the state in criminal cases from a pretrial decision), null and void for the executive's failure to file with the Secretary of State as required by Art. V, § 125 of the Alabama Constitution. Since all of the bills in the Third Special Session were signed as a package without the requisite filing, P.A. 888 appears similarly invalid.

3. See, e.g., Christian v. State, 351 So. 2d 623 (Ala. Crim. App. 1977), Annot. to Ala. Code § 15-16-2 (1982).

4. See, e.g., Campbell v. State, 265 Ark. 77, 576 S.W.2d 938 (1979), cited in annot. to Ark. Stat. Ann. § 41-601 (1977 & Supp. 1983).

5. The California Supreme Court, in People v. Drew, 22 Cal.3d 333, 583 P.2d 1318, 149 Cal. Rptr. 275 (1978), repudiated the M'Naghten rule in favor of the ALI formulation and upheld the constitutionality of Cal. Evid. Code § 522 (1966) requiring defendant to prove insanity by a preponderance of evidence. See Annot. to Cal. Penal Code §1026 (West 1970 and Supp. 1982).

6. Del. Code Ann. tit. 11, § 401 (1979 and Supp. 1982):

> (a) . . . [I]t is an affirmative defense that, at the time of the conduct charged, as a result of mental illness or defect, the accused lacked substantial capacity to appreciate the wrongfulness of his conduct. If the defendant prevails in establishing the affirmative defense . . . the trier of fact shall return a verdict of "not guilty by reason of insanity."
>
> (b) Where the trier of fact determines that, at the time of the conduct charged, a defendant suffered from a psychiatric disorder which substantially disturbed such person's thinking, feeling, or behavior and/or that such psychiatric disorder left such person with insufficient willpower to choose whether he would do the act or refrain from doing it, although physically capable, the trier of fact shall return a verdict of "guilty, but mentally ill."
>
> (c) . . . As used in this chapter, the terms 'insanity' and 'mental illness' do not include an abnormality manifested only by repeated criminal or other nonsocial conduct.

7. See generally United States v. Brawner, 471 F.2d 969 (D.C. Cir. 1972). See also Bethea v. United States, 365 A.2d 64 (D.C. App. 1976), cert. denied, 433 U.S. 911 (1977).

8. Florida has adhered to the M'Naghten rule since 1902, see Davis v. State, 44 Fla. 32, 32 So. 822 (1902), cited with approval in Anderson v. State, 276 So. 2d 17 (Fla. 1973); see also Bethel v. State, 305 So. 2d 251 (Fla. Dist. Ct. App. 1974), cited in annot. to Fla. R. Crim. P. 3.217 (West 1975 & Supp. 1982), and has expressly declined to adopt either the "irresistible impulse" doctrine, see Wheeler v. State, 344 So.2d 244 (Fla.) (per curiam) appealed after remand, 362 So. 2d 377, cert. denied, 440 U.S. 924 (1977), or the ALI Model Penal Code formulation. Id. See generally annot. to Fla. R. Crim. P. 3.217 (West 1975 & Supp. 1982).

9. See generally Holmes v. State, 374 So. 2d 944 (Fla. 1979), cert. denied, 446 U.S. 913, rehearing denied, 448 U.S. 910 (1980). See also annot. to Fla. R. Crim. P. 3.217 (West 1975 & Supp. 1982).

10. Grace v. Hopper, 566 F.2d 507 (5th Cir.), rev'g 425 F. Supp. 1355 (M.D. Ga. 1978), cited in annot. to Ga. Code Ann. §26-702 (1983), reviewed recent opinions by the Georgia Supreme Court, see e.g., Durham v. State, 239 Ga. 697, 238 S.E.2d 334 (1977), and concluded that although the state's criminal statutes do not specifically label insanity an affirmative defense, 566 F.2d 507, 509, citing Ga. Code Ann. §§26-702, 26-703, "It is now clear that under Georgia law, insanity is an affirmative defense that the accused must prove by a preponderance of the evidence." 566 F.2d at 510. See also Brown v. State, 250 Ga. 66, 295 S.E.2d 727 (1982).

11. See, e.g., State v. Moeller, 50 Hawaii 110, 433 P.2d 136 (1967). Accord, State v. Valentine, 1 Hawaii App. 1, 612 P.2d 117 (1980); State v. Nuetzel, 61 Hawaii 531, 606 P.2d 920 (1980).

12. In 1981 Illinois revised its provisions on criminal insanity to accommodate a verdict of "guilty, but mentally ill." See Ill. Ann. Stat. ch. 38, § 6-2 (Smith-Hurd 1972 & Supp. 1983-84). Subsection (d) provides that "'mentally ill' means a substantial disorder of thought, mood, or behavior afflicted a person at the time of the commission of the offense and which impaired that person's judgment, but not to the extent that he is unable to appreciate the wrongfulness of his behavior or is unable to conform his conduct to the requirements of law." Although § 6-2(a) defines legal insanity in terms of appreciating the "criminality" of behavior, and § 6-2(d) uses the word "wrongfulness,"

the two pleas (legal insanity and guilty, but mentally ill) are not intended to overlap. See, e.g., § 115-3(c). See also § 6-4:

> A defense based upon any of the provisions of Article 6 is an affirmative defense except that mental illness is not an affirmative defense, but an alternative plea or finding that may be accepted, under appropriate evidence, when the affirmative defense of insanity is raised or the plea of guilty but mentally ill is made.

13. See State v. Thomas, 219 N.W.2d 3 (Iowa 1974) (overruling prior practice of placing burden on defendant to show insanity by a preponderance of evidence).

14. The Kansas Supreme Court has repeatedly declined to adopt the ALI Model Penal Code formulation of the insanity defense, reaffirming instead the state's commitment to M'Naghten. See generally State v. Smith, 223 Kan. 203, 574 P.2d 548 (1977), and State v. Sanders, 587 P.2d. 893 (1978).

15. See, e.g., State v. Bates, 226 Kan. 277, 597 P.2d 646, 650 (1979); State v. Nemechek, 223 Kan. 766, 576 P.2d 682, 685 (1978).

16. "[T]he introduction of proof of insanity does not place a burden on the Commonwealth to prove [defendant] sane; rather, it entitles the defendant to an instruction to the jury that they may find him not guilty by reason of insanity." Edwards v. Commonwealth, 554 S.W.2d 380, 383 (Ky. 1977), cited in Wainscott v. Commonwealth, 562 S.W.2d 628, 630 (1978). See generally annot. to Ky. Rev. Stat. Ann. § 504.020 (Baldwin 1975 & Supp. 1980).

17. In Strawderman v. State, 4 Md. App. 689, 697-98, 244 A.2d 888, 893 (1968), the court of special appeals "filled in the statutory gaps" of Md. Ann. Code art. 59, § 25(b) by requiring that "when there has been offered proof of insanity . . . sufficient to overcome the initial presumption of sanity the state must prove sanity, as well as other elements of the offense, . . . beyond reasonable doubt."

18. The court in Commonwealth v. McHoul, 352 Mass. 544, 226 N.E.2d 556 (1967), reexamined the M'Naghten/irresistible-impulse test of insanity laid out by Chief Justice Shaw in Commonwealth v. Rogers, 48 Mass. 7 Met. 500 (1844), and held that, prospectively, the state should apply the ALI Model Penal Code formulation. See also Commonwealth v. Shelley, 409 N.E.2d 732 (Mass. 1980). The burden is on the commonwealth to prove beyond a reasonable doubt that defendant was criminally responsible, "although jury could reasonably presume that the great majority of men are sane and thus responsible." Commonwealth v. McAlister, 365 Mass. 454, 464, 313 N.E.2d 113, 119 (1974), cert. denied, 419 U.S. 1115 (1975).

19. Minn. Stat. Ann. § 611.026 (1964 & Supp. 1981) adopts M'Naghten. But the court in State v. Rawland, 294 Minn. 17, 199 N.W.2d 774 (1972), construed the statute to permit the jury to consider not only evidence relating to the defendant's cognition, that is, his knowledge of the nature of the act and its wrongfulness, but also the element of volition and his capacity to control his behavior. Thus the Minnesota statute has been judicially construed to permit a jury to consider the essential criteria contained in the ALI and irrestible=impulse tests.

20. In Hill v. State, 339 So. 2d 1382 (Miss. 1976), cert. denied, 430 U.S. 987 (1977), the Mississippi Supreme Court rejected arguments in favor of abandoning the M'Naghten rule of criminal responsibility and declined to accept the Model Penal Code formulation. Three of the nine judges concurred in the judgment but would have adopted the ALI test.

21. In McGarrh v. State, 249 Miss. 247, 257, 148 So. 2d 494, 497, cert. denied, 375 U.S. 816 (1963), the Mississippi Supreme Court ruled that: "At the moment that the proof warrants a reasonable doubt as to the ability of the accused at the time of the offense to distinguish right from wrong, it devolves upon the State . . . to remove it to the satisfaction of the jury beyond reasonable doubt." See also Herron v. State, 287 So. 2d 759 (Miss. 1974), cert. denied, 417 U.S. 972 (1974).

22. For the evolution of the Montana law in this area, see Mont. Code Ann. §§ 46-14-101 et seq. (1981) and Mont. Rev. Codes §§ 95-501 et seq. (1947); State v. Noble, 142 Mont. 284, 384 P.2d 504 (1963); Ex. rel. Krutzfeldt v. District Court of 13th Judicial Dist., 163 Mont. 164, 515 P.2d 1312 (1973).

23. The defendant must give notice of his intent to rely on a mental disease or defect and prove that he did not have the requisite state of mind for the offense.

24. State v. Myers, 205 Neb. 867, 871, 290 N.W.2d 660, 662 (1980).

> This jurisdiction has, since its very beginning, followed the rule in the M'Naghten case . . . [I]n the case of State v. Jacobs, 190 Neb. 4, 205 N.W.2d 662 (1973), this court was asked to abandon the M'Naghten rule and to replace it with either 'the irresistible impulse' rule . . . or the American Law Institute rule. We rejected both suggestions . . . We continue to adhere to [M'Naghten].

25. "A defendant in a criminal action is presumed sane until evidence of insanity is produced. The State then has the burden of proving beyond a reasonable doubt that the defendant was sane at the time the crime was committed." State v. Jacobs, 190 Neb. 4, 6, 205 N.W.2d 662, 663 (1973), cert. denied, 414 U.S. 860 (1973).

26. "It is well settled in Nevada that insanity is an affirmative defense and that the accused is presumed to be sane absent proof of insanity by a preponderance of the evidence." Clark v. State, 95 Nev. 25, 26, 588 P.2d 1027, 1028 (1979). See also Phillips v. State, 86 Nev. 720, 475 P.2d 671 (1970), cert. denied, 403 U.S. 940 (1970).

27. Although the statute is ambiguous, the case law clearly establishes M'Naghten as the test of criminal responsibility in Nevada. See, e.g., Williams v. State, 85 Nev. 169, 451 P.2d 848 (1969); Clark v. State, 588 P.2d 1027 (1979).

28. "A person who is insane at the time he acts is not criminally responsible for his conduct. Any distinction between a statutory and common law defense of insanity is hereby abolished and invocation of such defense waives no right an accused person would otherwise have." N.H. Rev. Stat. Ann. § 628:2(I) (1974).

29. N.Y. Penal Law § 30.05(1) (McKinney 1975):

> A person is not criminally responsible for conduct if at the time of such conduct, as a result of mental disease or defect, he lacks substantial capacity to know or appreciate either:
>
> (a) The nature and consequence of such conduct; or
>
> (b) That such conduct was wrong.

30. See, e.g., People v. Rivera, 78 A.D.2d 1002, 434 N.Y.S.2d 832 (1980); cf. People v. Woodworth, 47 A.D.2d 991, 366 N.Y.S.2d 707 (1975); annot. to N.Y. Penal Law § 30.05 (McKinney Supp. 1983-84).

31. The test of insanity that is recognized in North Carolina is whether the accused at the time of the alleged act was laboring under such defect of reason or from disease or defect of the mind as to be incapable of knowing the nature and quality of the act or if he does know it was by reason of such defect of reason, incapable of distinguishing between right & wrong in relation to such act. See State v. Barfield, 298 N.C. 306, 259 S.E.2d 510, 528 (1979). See also State v. Jones, 293 N.C. 413, 238 S.E.2d 482 (1977); State v. Hammonds, 290 N.C. 1, 244 S.E.2d 595 (1976); Comment, The Insanity Defense in North Carolina, 14 Wake Forest L. Rev. 1157 (1978).

32. See, e.g., State v. Wetmore, 298 N.C. 743, 259 S.E.2d 870, 872-73 (1979); State v. Barfield, 298 N.C. 306, 259 S.E.2d 510, 537 (1979); State v. Leonard, 296 N.C. 58, 64, 248 S.E.2d 853, 856 (1978); State v. Connley, 295 N.C. 327, 245 S.E.2d 663 (1978), vacated on other grounds and remanded, 441 U.S. 929 (1979).

33. N.D. Cent. Code § 12.1-04-03 (1976 & Supp. 1981), provides:

> A person is not responsible for the criminal conduct of, as a result of mental disease or defect existing at the time the conduct occurs, (1) he lacked substantial capacity to comprehend the harmful nature or consequences of his conduct, or (2) his conduct was the result of a loss or serious distortion of his capacity to recognize reality.

Prior to amendment in 1977 the code followed the ALI Model Penal Code test of criminal responsibility verbatim.

34. Although various state courts have cited State v. Jackson, 32 Ohio St. 2d 203, 291 N.E.2d 432, cert. denied, 411 U.S. 909 (1972), as adopting in substance the ALI standard (see, e.g., State v. Smith, 223 Kan. 203, 574 P.2d 548 (1977) (Prager, J., dissenting)), the inference is by no means clear from the language of the opinion:

> In order to establish the defense of insanity . . . the accused must establish by a preponderance of evidence that disease or other defect of his mind so impaired his reason that, at the time of the criminal act with which he is charged, either he did not know that such act was wrong or he did not have the ability to refrain from doing that act.

32 Ohio St. 2d at 203, 291 N.E.2d at 433.

35. Insanity is an affirmative defense within the meaning of § 2901.05. State v. Honze, 66 Ohio App.2d 41, 420 N.E.2d 131 (1979). See also State v. Humphries, 51 Ohio St. 2d 95, 99, 364 N.E.2d 1354, 1357 (1977): "The defense of insanity is clearly within the statutory definition since the defense is based on an excuse, of which the defendant has special knowledge for which he can produce evidence."

36. Suits v. State, 507 P.2d 1261, 1264 (Okla. Crim. App. 1973) ("[T]he M'Naghten rule is the present and exclusive test in this State to determine the question of sanity").

37. See, e.g., Garrett v. State, 586 P.2d 754 (Okla. Crim. App. 1978).

38. See, e.g., Commonwealth v. Green, 493 Pa. 409, 426 A.2d 614 (1981); Commonwealth v. Bruno, 466 Pa. 245, 352 A.2d 40 (1976); Commonwealth v. Demmitt, 456 Pa. 475, 321 A.2d 627 (1974).

39. In State v. Johnson, 121, R.I. 254, 399 A.2d 469 (1979), the Supreme Court of Rhode Island repudiated its long-standing adherence to the M'Naghten rule and formally adopted the ALI Model Penal Code test. See also State v. Arpin, 410 A.2d 1340 (R.I. 1980) (reaffirming prospective application).

40. See, e.g., State v. Page, 104 R.I. 323, 244 A.2d 258 (1968). For a rigorous defense of Rhode Island practice in light of recent U.S. Supreme Court decisions, e.g., In re Winship, 397 U.S. 358 (1970); Mullaney v. Wilbur, 421 U.S. 684 (1975); Patterson v. New York, 432 U.S. 197 (1977), see State v. Arpin, 410 A.2d 1340, (R.I. 1980).

41. See, e.g., State v. Valenti, 265 S.C. 380, 218 S.E.2d 726 (1975); State v. Cannon, 260 S.C. 537, 197 S.E.2d 678 (1973).

42. See, e.g., State v. Hinson, 253 S.C. 607, 172 S.E.2d 548 (1970).

43. See, e.g., State v. Standing Soldier, 299 N.W.2d 568 (S.D. 1980); State v. Kost, 290 N.W.2d 482 (S.D. 1980); State v. Viogett, 79 S.D. 292, 111 N.W.2d 598 (S.D. 1961).

44. After an extensive reconsideration of its century-long adherence to M'Naghten, the Tennessee Supreme Court, in Graham v. State, 547 S.W.2d 531 (Tenn. 1977), announced adoption of the ALI Model Penal Code standard. The court stated as its primary reason for departure from M'Naghten that "it is simpler to adopt a new rule in

harmony with the all but universal federal rule and with the rule being adopted by a significant number of state jurisdictions." Id. at 543.

45. See, e.g., State v. Voltz, 626 S.W.2d 291 (Tenn. 1981); State v. Patton, 593 S.W.2d 913 (Tenn. 1979); Graham v. State, 547 S.W.2d 531 (Tenn. 1977).

46. Tex. Penal Code § 8.01 (Vernon 1974):

(a) It is an affirmative defense to prosecution that, at the time of the conduct charged, the actor, as a result of mental disease or defect, either did not know that his conduct was wrong or was incapable of conforming his conduct to the requirements of the law he allegedly violated.

(b) The term "mental disease or defect" does not include an abnormality manifested only by repeated criminal or otherwise antisocial conduct.

47. See, e.g., Bonner v. State, 520 S.W.2d 901 (Tex. Crim. App. 1975); Fuller v. State, 423 S.W.2d 924 (Tex. Crim. App. 1968). See also Madrid v. State, 595 S.W.2d 106 (Tex Crim. App. 1980) (Clinton, J., dissenting).

48. Utah Code Ann. § 76-2-305 (Interim Supp. 1983):

(1) It is a defense to a prosecution under any statute or ordinance that the defendant, as a result of mental illness, lacked the mental state required as an element of the offense charged. Mental illness shall not otherwise constitute a defense.

(2) A person who is under the influence of voluntarily consumed or injected alcohol, controlled substances, or volatile substances at the time of the alleged offense shall not thereby be deemed to be excused from criminal responsibility.

49. See, e.g., State v. Holt, 449 P.2d 119 (Utah 1969).

50. See, e.g., State v. Smith, 136 Vt. 520, 396 A.2d 126 (1978); State v. Miner, 128 Vt. 55, 258 A.2d 815 (1969).

51. The irresistible impulse doctrine is applicable only to that class of cases where the accused is able to understand the nature and consequences of his act and knows it is wrong, but his mind has become so impaired by disease that he is totally deprived of the mental power to control or restrain his act.

Thompson v. Commonwealth, 193 Va. 704, 718, 70 S.E.2d 284, 292 (1952). Accord, Davis v. Commonwealth, 214 Va. 681, 204 S.E.2d 272 (1974).

52. See, e.g., Bloodgood v. Commonwealth, 212 Va. 253, 183 S.E.2d 737 (1971); Taylor v. Commonwealth, 208 Va. 316, 157 S.E.2d 185 (1967). See also Dillon v. Peylon, 288 F. Supp. 163, 164 (W.D. Va. 1968) (applying Virginia law).

53. Wash. Rev.Code Ann. § 9A.12.010 (1977):

To establish the defense of insanity, it must be shown that:

(1) At the time of the commission of the offense, as a result of mental disease or defect, the mind of the actor was affected to such an extent that:

(a) He was unable to receive the nature and quality of the act with which he is charged; or

(b) He was unable to tell right from wrong with reference to the particular act charged . . . .

54. See, e.g., State v. Hinckie, 286 S.E.2d 699 (W. Va. 1982); State v. Milam, 260 S.E.2d 295 (W. Va. 1979); Edwards v. Leverette, 258 S.E.2d 436 (W. Va. 1979).

55. State v. Myers, 222 S.E.2d 300, 305 (W. Va. 1976):

This Court, in State v. Grimm, 195 S.E.2d 637, 647 (W. Va. 1973), recommended for the evidence of trial courts . . . that they adopt an approach based on the Model Penal Code and suggested that the trial courts dispense with the more limited and archaic test of right and wrong under the M'Naghten Rule.

. . . .

This Court again announces its approval of ". . . an instruction to the effect that an accused is not responsible for his act if, at the time of the commissioin of the act, it was the result of a mental disease or defect causing the accused to lack the capacity either to appreciate the wrongfulness of the act, or to conform his act to the requirements of the law."

TABLE 12.6 THE INSANITY DEFENSE—EVALUATION AND VERDICT

	COURT-ORDERED EXAMINATION				RESTRICTIONS ON METHOD OF EXAMINATION	ACQUITTAL ON BASIS OF EXAMINATION	INDEPENDENT EXAMINATION BY PHYSICIAN OF DEFENDANT'S CHOICE PERMITTED	STATEMENTS BY DEFENDANT DURING EXAMINATION INADMISSIBLE EXCEPT WITH REGARD TO MENTAL STATE	PROVISIONS REGULATING PSYCHIATRIC TESTIMONY	FINDING BY		VERDICT		
STATE	By Whom (1)	Defendant's Physician Permitted to Attend (2)	Hospitalization Pending Examination (3)	Maximum Duration of Hospitalization (4)	(5)	(6)	(7)	(8)	(9)	Trial Jury or Judge (in Bench Trial) (10)	Separate Tribunal (11)	General Verdict of Not Guilty (12)	Not Guilty by Reason of Insanity (13)	Guilty but Mentally Ill (14)
ALA. Code (1982)	commission on lunacy (capital cases) 15-16-22(a)		15-16-22(b)	as long as necessary 15-16-22(b)		15-16-22(d)				15-16-2		if acquitted on any other ground 15-16-24	15-16-24	
ALAS. Stat. (1980 & Supp. 1982)	2 psychiatrists or forensic psychologists 12.47.070(a)	at ct.'s discretion 12.47.070(a)	12.47.070(a)	60 days; longer if necessary 12.47.070(a)	any accepted by medical profession 12.47.070(b)					12.47.040(b)			12.47.010(d) OR	12.47.030(a) or if not guilty by reason of insanity of greater offense but guilty of lesser offense 12.47.020(c)
ARIZ. Rev. Stat. Ann. (1978 & Supp. 1982); R. Cr. P. (1973 & Supp. 1982)	same number of medical doctors & psychologists as will testify for defense 13-3993(A)							13-3993(C) 13-4062(4)	inadmissible if defendant refuses state examination 13-3993(B)	R.25			R.23.2(b) 13-502(C), as amended by Laws 1983, ch. 198, §1	
ARK. Stat. Ann. (1977 & Supp. 1983)	1 or more psychiatrists 41-605(2)(a)		41-605(2)(d)	30 days; longer if necessary 41-605(2)(d)		41-609	41-610	41-615	41-611				41-601(3)	
CAL. Penal Code (West 1970 & Supp. 1982)	2 or 3 psychiatrists or psychologists 1027						1027(d)		1027		bifurcated process: sanity plea tried only after other pleas exhausted under conclusive presumption of sanity 1026(a)		1026(a)	
COLO. Rev. Stat. (1978 & Supp. 1982)	1 or more physicians who are specialists in nervous & mental diseases 16-8-106(1)		16-8-105(1) 16-8-106(1)		*fn. 1* 16-8-106(3)		16-8-106(1) 16-8-108(1)	privilege against self-incrimination 16-8-106(2)	no evidence acquired for the first time during the ct.-ordered exam admissible except as to mental condition 16-8-107(1)		separate trial & jury; sanity tried first 16-8-104		16-8-103(1)	

TABLE 12.6 THE INSANITY DEFENSE—EVALUATION AND VERDICT—*Continued*

	COURT-ORDERED EXAMINATION									FINDING BY		VERDICT		
STATE	By Whom (1)	Defendant's Physician Permitted to Attend (2)	Hospitalization Pending Examination (3)	Maximum Duration of Hospitalization (4)	RESTRICTIONS ON METHOD OF EXAMINATION (5)	ACQUITTAL ON BASIS OF EXAMINATION (6)	INDEPENDENT EXAMINATION BY PHYSICIAN OF DEFENDANT'S CHOICE PERMITTED (7)	STATEMENTS BY DEFENDANT DURING EXAMINATION INADMISSIBLE EXCEPT WITH REGARD TO MENTAL STATE (8)	PROVISIONS REGULATING PSYCHIATRIC TESTIMONY (9)	Trial Jury or Judge (in Bench Trial) (10)	Separate Tribunal (11)	General Verdict of Not Guilty (12)	Not Guilty by Reason of Insanity (13)	Guilty but Mentally Ill (14)
CONN. Gen. Stat. Ann. (West 1972 & Supp. 1982), as amended by P.A. 83-486													53a-47(a)(1)	
DEL. Code Ann. (1979 & Supp. 1982)		procedures prescribed by rules of ct. having jurisdiction over offense 11, §402(a)	procedures prescribed by rules of ct. having jurisdiction over offense 11, §402(a)	procedures prescribed by rules of ct. having jurisdiction over offense 11, §402(a)	procedures prescribed by rules of ct. having jurisdiction over offense 11, §402(a)	procedures prescribed by rules of ct. having jurisdiction over offense 11, §402(a)		11, §402(b)					11, §401(a)	OR 11, §401(b)
D.C. Code Ann. (1981 & Supp. 1983)										24-301(c)			24-301(c)	
FLA. R. Cr. P. (West 1975 & Supp. 1982); FLA. Stat. Ann. (West 1973 & Supp. 1982)	2 or 3 experts R.3.216(d) 916.11(1)	defendant's attorney R.3.216(d)								R.3.216(h)			R.3.217(a)	
GA. Code Ann. (1983 & Supp. 1983)										27-1503(c)			27-1503 (b)(3)	OR felony cases only 27-1503 (b)(4)
HAWAII Rev. Stat. (1976 & Supp. 1982)	3 qualified examiners *fn.* 2 704-404(2)	704-404(2)	704-404(2)	30 days; longer if necessary 704-404(2)	any accepted by medical profession 704-404(3)		704-409	or admission of guilt 704-416	704-410 (3), (4)	704-408			704-402(3)	
IDAHO Code (1979 & Supp. 1983)	1 psychiatrist or psychologist 19-2522				any accepted by medical profession 19-2522		19-2522							only affects sentencing 19-2523
ILL. Ann. Stat. (Smith-Hurd 1977 & Supp. 1983–84)	1 psychologist or psychiatrist, & if requested by state, 1 neurologist, psychologist, & electroencephalographer 38, §115-6							38, §115-6	38, §1005-2-5	jury trial 38, §115-4(j)			38, §115-3(b), 4(j)	38, §115-3(c)

TABLE 12.6 THE INSANITY DEFENSE—EVALUATION AND VERDICT—*Continued*

STATE	COURT-ORDERED EXAMINATION				RESTRICTIONS ON METHOD OF EXAMINATION (5)	ACQUITTAL ON BASIS OF EXAMINATION (6)	INDEPENDENT EXAMINATION BY PHYSICIAN OF DEFENDANT'S CHOICE PERMITTED (7)	STATEMENTS BY DEFENDANT DURING EXAMINATION INADMISSIBLE EXCEPT WITH REGARD TO MENTAL STATE (8)	PROVISIONS REGULATING PSYCHIATRIC TESTIMONY (9)	FINDING BY		VERDICT		
	By Whom (1)	Defendant's Physician Permitted to Attend (2)	Hospitalization Pending Examination (3)	Maximum Duration of Hospitalization (4)						Trial Jury or Judge (in Bench Trial) (10)	Separate Tribunal (11)	General Verdict of Not Guilty (12)	Not Guilty by Reason of Insanity (13)	Guilty but Mentally Ill (14)
IND. Code Ann. (Burns 1979 & Supp. 1983–84)	2 or 3 disinterested psychiatrists, clinical psychologists or physicians (1 of whom must be a psychiatrist) 35-36-2-2									35-36-2-3			35-36-2-3(3) OR	35-36-2-3(4)
IOWA R. Cr. P. (West 1983)	state-named expert R.10(11)(b)(2)									R.21(1), (8)			R.21(1), (8)	
KAN. Stat. Ann. (1974 & Supp. 1982)	physician or physicians 22-3219(2)						22-3219(2)			*fn.* 3 22-3428(6)			22-3428(1)	
KY. Rev. Stat. Ann. (Michie 1975 & Supp. 1982)	at least 1 psychiatrist 504.070(3)		504.080(1)	504.080(1)										504.130
LA. Code Cr. P. (1981 & Supp. 1983)	sanity commission of 2 or 3 physicians 650, 644(A)			30 days; longer at ct.'s discretion 645			646		653	805			650, 654, 805	
ME. Rev. Stat. Ann. (1983)	at least 1 psychiatrist or psychologist 15, §101		if necessary for complete examination 15, §101	60 days 15, §101						although defendant may elect to have trial in 2 stages 17-A, §40 (1), (3) *fn.* 4 17-A, §40 (5)	defendant may elect to have insanity issue tried by ct. w/o jury 17-A, §40 (3)	if acquitted in first stage 17-A, §40 (2)(A)	17-A, §40(4) 15, §103	
MD. Ann. Code (1979 & Supp. 1983)	dep't of health & mental hygiene 12-109		if appropriate for health & safety of defendant 12-109	60 days; longer for good cause 12-109						12-108(b)			special verdict 12-108(b)	
MASS. Ann. Laws (Michie/Law Co-op 1981 & Supp. 1983)	1 or more physicians 123, §15(a)		if further examination necessary 123, §15(b)	20 days; ct. may extend period by up to 20 days 123, §15(b)				233, §23B					123, §16(a)	

TABLE 12.6 THE INSANITY DEFENSE—EVALUATION AND VERDICT—*Continued*

STATE	COURT-ORDERED EXAMINATION				RESTRICTIONS ON METHOD OF EXAMINATION (5)	ACQUITTAL ON BASIS OF EXAMINATION (6)	INDEPENDENT EXAMINATION BY PHYSICIAN OF DEFENDANT'S CHOICE PERMITTED (7)	STATEMENTS BY DEFENDANT DURING EXAMINATION INADMISSIBLE EXCEPT WITH REGARD TO MENTAL STATE (8)	PROVISIONS REGULATING PSYCHIATRIC TESTIMONY (9)	FINDING BY		VERDICT		
	By Whom (1)	Defendant's Physician Permitted to Attend (2)	Hospitalization Pending Examination (3)	Maximum Duration of Hospitalization (4)						Trial Jury or Judge (in Bench Trial) (10)	Separate Tribunal (11)	General Verdict of Not Guilty (12)	Not Guilty by Reason of Insanity (13)	Guilty but Mentally Ill (14)
MICH. Comp. Laws Ann. (1968 & Supp. 1983–84)	personnel of the center for forensic psychiatry 768.20(a) (2)		if defendant fails to appear 768.20a (2)	30 days 768.20a (2)			768.20a (3)	768.20a (5)		768.29a (1)			768.29a (2) OR	768.29a (2)
MINN. Stat. Ann. (West 1971 & Supp. 1983); MINN. R. Cr. P. (West 1979 & Special Pamph. 1983)	at least 1 psychiatrist, psychologist or physician R.20.02(2)	R.20.02(2)	R.20.02(2) 253A.23(1)	60 days R.20.02(2)				if defendant elects bifurcated trial R.20.02 (6)(3)		although defendant may elect to have trial in 2 stages R.20.02 (6)(2)		if acquitted if first stage R.20.02 (6)(4)(b)	mental illness or defect R.14.01(c)	
MISS. Code Ann. (1972 & Supp. 1982	psychiatrist 99-13-11									99-13-7 OR	grand jury 99-13-5		99-13-7	
MO. Ann. Stat. (Vernon 1953 & Supp. 1981 & Supp. 1983)	at least 1 psychiatrist 552.030(4)			w/in 60 days, unless ct. for good cause orders otherwise 552.030(4)			552.030 (4)	552.030 (6)		552.030 (7)			552.030 (8)	
MONT. Code Ann. (1981)	at least 1 psychiatrist 46-14-202(1)	46-14-202(2)	46-14-202(2)	60 days; longer if ct. deems necessary 46-14-202(2)	any accepted by medical profession 46-14-202(3)		46-14-212		46-14-213	46-14-301(1)			verdict shall state if mental disease defense relied on 46-14-201(2)	
NEB. Rev. Stat. (1979 & Supp. 1982)	1 or more experts 29-2203												29-2203	
NEV. Rev. Stat. (1981)														
N.H. Rev. Stat. Ann. ch. 135 (1977 & Supp. 1982), ch. 651 (1974 & Supp. 1982)	psychiatrist 135:17		at N.H. hospital on outpatient basis; at local clinics on in- or outpatient basis 135:17	30 days 135:17						petit jury *fn.* 6 651:8 OR	grand jury *fn.* 6 651:8		651:8 *fn.* 6	
N.J. Stat. Ann. (West 1982); N.J. R. Cr. Practice (West 1983)								2C:4-10					2C:4-3(b) R.3:19-2	
N.M. R. Cr. P. for Dist. Cts. (1980 & Supp. 1983); N.M. Uniform Jury Instructions—Cr. (1978 & Supp. 1983)								sanity R.35(d)		special verdict R.35(a)(2)			UJI Cr. 50.11(2) R.35(a)	UJI Cr. 40.00 40.02
N.Y. Crim. Proc. Law (McKinney 1981 & Supp. 1983–84)								60.55(2)	60.55(1)				not responsible by reason of mental disease or defect 300.10(4)(d)	
N.C. Gen. Stat. (1983)						ct. may hold pretrial hearing w/o prejudice to right to rely on defense at trial 15A-959(c)	evidence of mental condition allowed if defendant files pretrial notice 15A-959(b)	no reference to or from pretrial hearing at trial 15A-959(c)		15A-1237(c)			15A-1237(c)	

TABLE 12.6 THE INSANITY DEFENSE—EVALUATION AND VERDICT—*Continued*

STATE	COURT-ORDERED EXAMINATION				RESTRICTIONS ON METHOD OF EXAMINATION (5)	ACQUITTAL ON BASIS OF EXAMINATION (6)	INDEPENDENT EXAMINATION BY PHYSICIAN OF DEFENDANT'S CHOICE PERMITTED (7)	STATEMENTS BY DEFENDANT DURING EXAMINATION INADMISSIBLE EXCEPT WITH REGARD TO MENTAL STATE (8)	PROVISIONS REGULATING PSYCHIATRIC TESTIMONY (9)	FINDING BY		VERDICT		
	By Whom (1)	Defendant's Physician Permitted to Attend (2)	Hospitalization Pending Examination (3)	Maximum Duration of Hospitalization (4)						Trial Jury or Judge (in Bench Trial) (10)	Separate Tribunal (11)	General Verdict of Not Guilty (12)	Not Guilty by Reason of Insanity (13)	Guilty but Mentally Ill (14)
N.D. Cent. Code (1976 & Supp. 1981); N.D. R. Cr. P. (1974 & Supp. 1981)	psychiatrist 12.1-04-06 R.12.2(c)		12.1-04-06	30 days; 30 more upon ct. order 12.1-04-06			counsel, family, & others necessary to assist in case 12.1-04-06	no statements admissible R.12.2(c)					12.1-04-10	
OHIO Rev. Code Ann. (Baldwin 1979 & Supp. 1982)	ct.-designated examiners 2945.39(A)		ct. may amend conditions of bail or recognizance if defendant refuses to submit 2945.39(B) transfer of pretrial detainees 2945.39(C)	20 days 2945.39(B) pretrial detainees: 30 days 2945.39(C)			2945.39(C)	no statements admissible on issue of guilt 2945.39(D)					2945.40(A)	
OKLA. Stat. Ann. (West 1958 & Supp. 1983)										22, §925			22, §§914, 925, 1161	
OR. Rev. Stat. (1981)	psychiatrist or psychologist; defendant may, for good cause, object to choice of examiner 161.315		161.315	30 days 161.315									not responsible due to mental disease or defect 161.319	
PA. Stat. Ann. (Purdon 1983)										bifurcated trial 50, §7404 pretrial 50, §7407				18, §314(a)
R.I. Gen. Laws (1977 & Supp. 1982)														
S.C. Code Ann. (Law. Co-op. 1976 & Supp. 1982)										44-23-610			44-23-610	

TABLE 12.6 THE INSANITY DEFENSE—EVALUATION AND VERDICT—*Continued*

STATE	COURT-ORDERED EXAMINATION				RESTRICTIONS ON METHOD OF EXAMINATION	ACQUITTAL ON BASIS OF EXAMINATION	INDEPENDENT EXAMINATION BY PHYSICIAN OF DEFENDANT'S CHOICE PERMITTED	STATEMENTS BY DEFENDANT DURING EXAMINATION INADMISSIBLE EXCEPT WITH REGARD TO MENTAL STATE	PROVISIONS REGULATING PSYCHIATRIC TESTIMONY	FINDING BY		VERDICT		
	By Whom (1)	Defendant's Physician Permitted to Attend (2)	Hospitalization Pending Examination (3)	Maximum Duration of Hospitalization (4)	(5)	(6)	(7)	(8)	(9)	Trial Jury or Judge (in Bench Trial) (10)	Separate Tribunal (11)	General Verdict of Not Guilty (12)	Not Guilty by Reason of Insanity (13)	Guilty but Mentally Ill (14)
S.D. Codified Laws Ann. (1979 & Supp. 1983)	psychiatrist 23A-10-4							inadmissible as to guilt except for impeaching defendant 23A-10-4		23A-26-12			23A-26-12	23A-26-14
TENN. Code Ann. (1977 & Supp. 1981); TENN. R. Cr. P. (1981)	psychiatrist R.12.2(c)						excluded unless defendant submits to state examiner R.12.2(c)	inadmissible on issue of guilt R.12.2(c)						
TEX. Code Crim. Proc. Ann. (Vernon 1978 & Supp. 1982–83)	disinterested experts 46.03(3)(a)		if defendant refuses to to submit 46.03(3)(b)	21 days 46.03(3)(b)			46.03(3)(f)			37.13 46.03(1)(b)			37.13 46.03(1)(b)	
UTAH Code Ann. (1978 & Supp. 1983)	2 examiners qualified in forensic mental health 77-14-4(1) suitable facility 77-35-21.5						barred unless defendant cooperates w/ct.-appointed examiners 77-14-4(2) considered as evidence 77-35-21.5			77-14-5(1)			77-14-5(1) 77-35-21	
VT. Stat. Ann. (1974 & Supp. 1983); VT. R. Cr. P. (1974 & Supp. 1982)	psychiatrist 13, §4814 (a)(1)(3); R.16.1(a)(1)(I)		13, §4815(b)	60 days; 15-day extensions if necessary 13, §4815 (b), (c)	any in accordance w/accepted standards of medical care & practice 13, §4815(e)			inadmissible as to proving commission of a crime or impeaching defendant's testimony 13, §4816(c)		13, §4819 or grand jury 13, §4818			13, §4819 or not indicted by reason of insanity 13, §4818	SB 28, passed while in press as Pub. Law 75 (1984)
VA. Code (1983)										19.2-181(1)			19.2-181(1)	

TABLE 12.6 THE INSANITY DEFENSE—EVALUATION AND VERDICT—*Continued*

STATE	COURT-ORDERED EXAMINATION				RESTRICTIONS ON METHOD OF EXAMINATION (5)	ACQUITTAL ON BASIS OF EXAMINATION (6)	INDEPENDENT EXAMINATION BY PHYSICIAN OF DEFENDANT'S CHOICE PERMITTED (7)	STATEMENTS BY DEFENDANT DURING EXAMINATION INADMISSIBLE EXCEPT WITH REGARD TO MENTAL STATE (8)	PROVISIONS REGULATING PSYCHIATRIC TESTIMONY (9)	FINDING BY		VERDICT		
	By Whom (1)	Defendant's Physician Permitted to Attend (2)	Hospitalization Pending Examination (3)	Maximum Duration of Hospitalization (4)						Trial Jury or Judge (in Bench Trial) (10)	Separate Tribunal (11)	General Verdict of Not Guilty (12)	Not Guilty by Reason of Insanity (13)	Guilty but Mentally Ill (14)
WASH. Rev. Code Ann. (1980 & Supp. 1983–84)	2 qualified experts 10.77.060(1)	may also have counsel present 10.77.020(4) 10.77.060(2)	10.77.060(1)	15 days 10.77.060(1)			10.77.020 (2) 10.77.070	defendant may refuse to answer any question on grounds of self-incrimination 10.77.020 (4)	10.77.100	10.77.040 OR	pretrial motion (w/prejudice to claim he did not commit act) 10.77.080		special verdict, including findings as to dangerousness & least restrictive means of treatment 10.77.040	
W. VA. Code §§62 (1977), 27 (1980 & Supp. 1983)	1 or more psychiatrist or a psychiatrist & psychologist 27-6A-1(a)		if further observation & examination necessary 27-6A-1(b)	20 days; 20 more upon written request of examining physician 27-6A-1(b)						27-6A-3 OR	grand jury 62-2-12		or not indicted by reason of insanity 62-2-12 27-6A-3	
WIS. Stat. Ann. (West 1971 & Supp. 1983–84)	1 to 3 physicians 971.16(1)						971.16(3)	971.18	971.16 (3), (4)	sequential order of proof as to guilt & mental responsibility before same jury in continuous trial 971.175			by reason of mental disease or defect 971.17(1) 971.175	
WYO. Stat. (1977 & Supp. 1982)	designated examiner 7-11-304(d) 7-11-303(b)		may include 7-11-303(b) 7-11-304(d)	30 days 7-11-303(b) 7-11-304(d)				7-11-304 (f)	7-11-305 (d), (e)	7-11-305 (a)			by reason of mental illness or deficiency 7-11-305(a)	

FOOTNOTES: TABLE 12.6

1. Colo. Rev. Stat. § 16-8-106(3) (1978):

> To aid in forming an opinion as to the mental condition of the defendant, it is permissible in the course of an examination . . . to use confessions and admissions of the defendant and any other evidence of the circumstances surrounding the commission of the offense, as well as the medical and social history of the defendant in questioning the defendant. It is also permissible to administer . . . sodium amytal, sodium pentothal, metrazol, and like drugs, and to subject the defendant to polygraph examination.

2. Hawaii Rev. Stat. § 704-404(2) (1976 & Supp. 1980):

> In each case the court shall appoint at least one psychiatrist and at least one certified clinical psychologist. The third member may be either a psychiatrist, certified clinical psychologist or qualified physician. One of the three shall be a psychiatrist or certified clinical psychologist designated by the director of health.

3. State v. Sanders, 223 Kan. 273, 574 P.2d 559, 565 (1977), reaffirmed the court's prior interpretation of Kan. Stat. Ann. § 22-3428 (1974); see State v. Lamb, 209 Kan. 453, 497 P.2d 275 (1972), cited in Annot. to Kan. Stat. Ann. § 22-3428 (1974 & Supp. 1980).

4. Me. Rev. Stat. Ann. tit. 17-A, § 40(5) (1981): "This section does not apply to cases tried before the court without a jury."

5. A bifurcated trial on the separate issues of guilt of the crime and insanity is not constitutionally mandated and may not be had in Maryland. See generally Langworthy v. State, 284 Md. 588, 399 A.2d 578 (1979), cited in Annot. to Md. Ann. Code art. 59, § 25 (1979 & Supp. 1981).

6. Kanteles v. Wheelock, 439 F. Supp. 505 (D.N.H. 1977), overruling State v. Novosel, 115 N.H. 302, 339 A.2d 16 (1975), held unconstitutional N.H. Rev. Stat. Ann. §§ 651:8, 651:9 insofar as grand jury's certification of insanity had same effect upon accused as a finding of not guilty by reason of insanity, in that it presupposed that accused committed the crime charged and attached the same loss of liberty and stigma of criminal commitment without being convicted of the crime. See generally Annot. to N.H. Rev. Stat. Ann. §§ 651:8, 651:9 (1974 & Supp. 1981).

TABLE 12.7 THE INSANITY DEFENSE—DISPOSITION AND RELEASE

STATE	DISPOSITION		APPLICATION FOR RELEASE BY			APPLICATION FOR RELEASE PROCEDURES						NATURE OF RELEASE				MAXIMUM PERIOD OF COMMITMENT (16)
	Civil Commitment Hearing (1)	Other (2)	Mental Health Official (3)	Court on Its Own Motion (4)	Committed Person (5)	Maximum Frequency of Application (6)	Criteria for Release (7)	Supporting Evidence (8)	Approval by (9)	Judicial Hearing (10)	Burden of Proof (11)	Unconditional (12)	Conditional (13)	Maximum Period of Conditions (14)	Mandatory Outpatient Treatment (15)	
ALA. Code (1982)		hearing held to determine if commitment necessary 15-16-41														
ALAS. Stat. (1980 & Supp. 1982)		commitment unless not dangerous to public peace 12.47.090(c) ordinary sentence if guilty but mentally ill 12.47.050 (a)	state 12.47.090 (g)		12.47.090 (e)	yearly 12.47.090 (e)	not suffering from mental disease or defect that makes him dangerous to public 12.47.090 (c)				upon defendant (clear & convincing evidence) 12.47.090 (c)					max. term for crime 12.47.090 (d) 12.47.050 (a)
ARIZ. Rev. Stat. Ann. (1978 & Supp. 1982); R. Cr. P. (1973 & Supp. 1982)	R.25 after evaluation period 13-3994, added by Laws 1983, ch. 198, §3	mandatory 120-day inpatient evaluation 13-3994, added by Laws 1983, ch. 198, §3			*see generally* table 4.5	*see generally* table 4.5										see table 2.7
ARK. Stat. Ann. (1977 & Supp. 1983)		ct. determination of risk of danger to self or others 41-612(1)	director of state hospital 41-613(1)		41-613(2)	1 application per yr. 41-613(2)	no longer affected by mental disease or defect, or not dangerous 41-613 (1), (2)	examination by 1 or more psychiatrists 41-613(3)	ct. 41-613(5)	if medical reports contested 41-613(4)		if no longer affected by mental disease or defect 41-613(5)	if still affected but not dangerous 41-613(5)	5 yrs. 41-614(2)	such conditions as ct. may deem appropriate 41-613(5)	max. sentence for offense 41-612.1 civil commitment thereafter 41-612.1, 612.2
CAL. Penal Code (West 1970 & Supp. 1982)		commitment or outpatient status unless fully recovered 1026(a)	medical director of facility 1026.2		1026.2	1 application per yr. 1026.2	sanity restored 1026.1(a)		ct. 1026.2	1026.2	upon applicant 1026.2	1026.5(a) (4) OR	1026.5(a) (4)			longest term of imprisonment, had he been sane 1026.5(a) (1) *fn. 1* 1026.5(b) (1)
COLO. Rev. Stat. (1978 & Supp. 1982)		mandatory commitment 16-8-105 (4)	chief officer of institution 16-8-116 (1)	or motion by prosecuting attorney 16-8-115 (1)	16-8-115 (1)	1 hearing per yr. 16-8-115 (1)	no dangerous, abnormal mental condition 16-8-120 (1)	ct.-ordered examination 16-8-115 (2)	ct. or jury 16-8-115 (2)	if report of chief officer of institution contested *fn. 2* 16-8-115 (2)	upon person contesting report (preponderance of evidence) 16-8-115 (2)	16-8-115 (3) OR	16-8-115 (3)		16-8-115 (3)(b)	until eligible for release 16-8-105 (4)
CONN. Gen. Stat. Ann. (West 1972 & Supp. 1982), as amended by P.A. 83-486	following 90-day examination period 53a-47(a) (1), (3), (4)(b)	release 53a-47(a) (1)	superintendent of hospital or institution 53a-47(c) (1)	at least once every 5 yrs. 53a-47(c) (3)			no longer dangerous 53a-47(c) (1)	right to call a psychiatrist to examine & testify 53a-47(e) (1)	ct. 53a-47(c) (1)	if requested by state prosecutor 53a-47(c) (2)	upon defendant (preponderance of evidence) 53a-47(c) (2)	53a-47(a) (1) OR	53a-47(a) (1) 53a-47(e) (2)		such conditions as ct. deems appropriate 53a-47(e) (2)	max. sentence for offense 53a-47(b) involuntary commitment proceedings thereafter if dangerous 53a-47(d)

TABLE 12.7 THE INSANITY DEFENSE—DISPOSITION AND RELEASE—*Continued*

	DISPOSITION		APPLICATION FOR RELEASE BY		
STATE	Civil Commitment Hearing (1)	Other (2)	Mental Health Official (3)	Court on Its Own Motion (4)	Committed Person (5)
DEL. Code Ann. (1979 & Supp. 1982)		commitment upon motion of attorney general 11, §403(a) ordinary sentence if guilty but mentally ill 11, §408(b)	state hospital 11, §403(b)	11, §403(b)	
D.C. Code Ann. (1981 & Supp. 1983) *fn. 3*		mandatory commitment 24-301(d) (1)	superin-tendent of hospital 24-301(e)	hearing w/in 50 days of confinement 24-301(d) (2)	24-301(k) (1)
FLA. R. Cr. P. (1975 & Supp. 1982); FLA. Stat. Ann. (West 1973 & Supp. 1982)	R.3.217(b)	outpatient treatment or discharge R.3.217(b) 916.15(1)(a)	administrator R.3.218 916.15(2)	hearing 6 mos. after confinement; yearly thereafter R.3.218 916.15(2)	
GA. Code Ann. (1983 & Supp. 1983)	following 30-day evaluation period 27-1503 (d), (e) ordinary sentence if guilty but mentally ill 27-1503(g)		superintend-ent of state hospital 27-1503(f)		27-1503(f)
HAWAII Rev. Stat. (1976 & Supp. 1982)		commitment if dangerous & not a proper subject for conditional release 704-411(1)	director of health 704-412(1)		704-412(2)
IDAHO Code (1979 & Supp. 1983)					
ILL. Stat. Ann. (Smith-Hurd 1977 & Supp. 1983—84)	38, §115-3 (b), (c)	to Dep't of M.H. & D.D. for evalua-tion; followed by ct. hearing 38, §1005-2-4	facility director 38, §1005-2-4(d)		defendant or any person on his behalf 38, §1005-2-4(e)
IND. Code Ann. (Burns 1979 & Supp. 1983–84)	35-36-2-4 *fn. 4*		*see generally* table 4.5		

	APPLICATION FOR RELEASE PROCEDURES					
STATE	Maximum Frequency of Application (6)	Criteria for Release (7)	Supporting Evidence (8)	Approval by (9)	Judicial Hearing (10)	Burden of Proof (11)
DEL. Code Ann. (1979 & Supp. 1982)		public safety not endan-gered by release 11, §403(b)		superior ct. 11, §403(b)		
D.C. Code Ann. (1981 & Supp. 1983) *fn. 3*	once every 6 mos. 24-301(k) (5)	entitled to release 24-301(d) (2) sane, not dangerous, & entitled to release 24-301(e)		ct. 23-301(d) (2) 24-301(k) (3) ct. 24-301(e)	24-301(d) (2) 24-301(k) (3) at ct.'s discretion 24-301(e)	upon person confined (preponder-ance of evidence) 24-301(d) (2)
FLA. R. Cr. P. (1975 & Supp. 1982); FLA. Stat. Ann. (West 1973 & Supp. 1982)			ct.-ordered examination R.3.218(b)	committing ct. R.3.218(a) 916.16	R.3.218(a) 916.15(3)	
GA. Code Ann. (1983 & Supp. 1983)	once per yr. 27-1503(f)	does not meet cri-teria for civil com-mitment 27-1503(f)		committing ct. 27-1503(f)		upon applicant 27-1503(f)
HAWAII Rev. Stat. (1976 & Supp. 1982)	once per yr. 704-412(2)	may be safely released on conditions applied for or discharged 704-415	examination by 3 qualified examiners 704-414	ct. 704-415	if ct. not satisfied by application & evidence 704-415	upon applicant 704-415
IDAHO Code (1979 & Supp. 1983)						
ILL. Stat. Ann. (Smith-Hurd 1977 & Supp. 1983—84)	no new petition for 60 days	no longer subject to involuntary commitment or in need of mental health services 38, §1005-2-4(d), (e)	facility director to give basis for recomm. 38, §1005-2-4(d)		38, §1005-2-4(d), (e)	upon state 38, §1005-2-4(g)
IND. Code Ann. (Burns 1979 & Supp. 1983–84)						

	NATURE OF RELEASE				MAXIMUM PERIOD OF COMMITMENT (16)
STATE	Unconditional (12)	Conditional (13)	Maximum Period of Conditions (14)	Mandatory Outpatient Treatment (15)	
DEL. Code Ann. (1979 & Supp. 1982)					
D.C. Code Ann. (1981 & Supp. 1983) *fn. 3*	24-301(d) (2), (k)(3) 24-301(e) OR	24-301(d) (2), (k)(3) OR 24-301(e)	subject to challenge 24-301(k) (1)	such condi-tions as ct. sees fit 24-301(e)	
FLA. R. Cr. P. (1975 & Supp. 1982); FLA. Stat. Ann. (West 1973 & Supp. 1982)	R.3.219(c) 916.17(3) OR	R.3.219(d) 916.17(1)	until no longer required R.3.219(c) 916.17(3)	R.3.219(a) 916.17(1)	
GA. Code Ann. (1983 & Supp. 1983)					*see* table 2.7
HAWAII Rev. Stat. (1976 & Supp. 1982)	704-415 OR	704-415	5 yrs. 704-413(2)	such condi-tions as ct. determines to be necessary 704-415	
IDAHO Code (1979 & Supp. 1983)					
ILL. Stat. Ann. (Smith-Hurd 1977 & Supp. 1983—84)	38, §1005-2-4(d), (e)	38, §1005-2-4(d), (e)	5 yrs. 38, §1005-2-4(h)	such condi-tions as ct. may impose 38, §1005-2-4(d)	not to ex-ceed max. sentence 38, §1005-2-4(b)
IND. Code Ann. (Burns 1979 & Supp. 1983–84)					*see* table 2.7

TABLE 12.7 THE INSANITY DEFENSE—DISPOSITION AND RELEASE—*Continued*

STATE	DISPOSITION		APPLICATION FOR RELEASE BY			APPLICATION FOR RELEASE PROCEDURES						NATURE OF RELEASE				MAXIMUM PERIOD OF COMMITMENT (16)
	Civil Commitment Hearing (1)	Other (2)	Mental Health Official (3)	Court on Its Own Motion (4)	Committed Person (5)	Maximum Frequency of Application (6)	Criteria for Release (7)	Supporting Evidence (8)	Approval by (9)	Judicial Hearing (10)	Burden of Proof (11)	Unconditional (12)	Conditional (13)	Maximum Period of Conditions (14)	Mandatory Outpatient Treatment (15)	
IOWA R. Cr. P. (West 1983)		hearing to determine whether dangerous to public peace or safety R.21(8)					good mental health & no longer dangerous to public peace or safety or self R.21(8)									
KAN. Stat. Ann. (1974 & Supp. 1982)		mandatory commitment 22-3428(1)	chief medical officer of state hospital 22-3428(2)		22-3428a(1)	annually 22-3428a (1)	not a danger to self or others or property of others 22-3428(3)	mental evaluation 22-3428(3) 22-3428a (1)	district ct. 22-3428(3) 22-3428a (1)	if requested by district or county attorney w/in 15 days of notice 22-3428(3) 22-3418a (1), (2)	upon patient (preponderance of evidence) 22-3428(3) 22-3428a (3)	22-3428 (3) 22-348a (3) OR	22-3428 (3), (4) 22-3428a (3)		22-3428(4)	
KY. Rev. Stat. Ann. (Michie 1975 & Supp. 1982)	following motion for examination by ct. or prosecuting attorney or its own motion fn. 5 504.030(1)															see table 2.7
LA. Code Cr. Proc. (1981 & Supp. 1983)		mandatory commitment in capital cases: hearing as to dangerousness in all others 654	superintendent of mental institution 655(A)		655(B)	yearly 655(B)	can be released w/o danger to self or others 657	ct. may order additional mental examinations 656	ct. which ordered commitment 655(A), 657	at ct.'s discretion 657	upon person committed 657	657 OR	probation 657, 658	indeterminate		
ME. Rev. Stat. Ann. (1983)		mandatory commitment 15, §103	yearly reports by head of institution 15, §104-A (1)	OR	spouse or next of kin, for outpatient release 15, §104-A (2)	every 6 mos. 15, §104-A (2)	not likely to cause injury to self or others due to mental disease or defect 15, §104-A (1), (2)	testimony of at least 1 psychiatrist 15, §104-A (1), (2)	superior ct. for county where hospitalized 15, §104-A (1), (2)	15, §104-A (1), (2)		15, §104-A(1)(B) OR	14, §104-A (1)(A) 15, §104-A (2)	subject to annual review 15, §104-A (1)(A)(3)	15, §104-A (1)(A)(1) 15, §104-A	not restricted by prohibition against indeterminate sentences fn. 6 Annot. to 15, §103
MD. Ann. Code (1979 & Supp. 1983)		examination by dep't of health & mental hygiene 12-110 discharge, conditional release, or commitment following hearing 12-112	dep't of mental health (to modify or allow conditional release) 12-114	state's attorney (to modify conditions of release) 12-114	12-114(a)	annually 12-114(d)	no longer has mental disorder & no longer a danger to self, others, or property 12-114(c)	evaluation by dep't of health, if administrative hearing sought 12-114(b)	ct. 12-114	judicial release provisions (w/jury) for involuntary commitment, or administrative hearing & judicial determination 12-114		12-113(d) OR	12-113(d)	5 yrs., unless modified by ct. order 12-115		

TABLE 12.7 THE INSANITY DEFENSE—DISPOSITION AND RELEASE—*Continued*

STATE	DISPOSITION		APPLICATION FOR RELEASE BY			APPLICATION FOR RELEASE PROCEDURES						NATURE OF RELEASE				MAXIMUM PERIOD OF COMMITMENT (16)
	Civil Commitment Hearing (1)	Other (2)	Mental Health Official (3)	Court on Its Own Motion (4)	Committed Person (5)	Maximum Frequency of Application (6)	Criteria for Release (7)	Supporting Evidence (8)	Approval by (9)	Judicial Hearing (10)	Burden of Proof (11)	Unconditional (12)	Conditional (13)	Maximum Period of Conditions (14)	Mandatory Outpatient Treatment (15)	
MASS. Ann. Laws (Michie/Law Co-op. 1981 & Supp. 1983)	ct. may order 40-day observational hospitalization 123, §16 (a), (b)				*see generally* table 4.5	*see generally* table 4.5										*see* table 2.7
MICH. Comp. Laws Ann. (1968 & Supp. 1983–84)																
MINN. Stat. Ann. (West 1971 & Supp. 1983); MINN. Rev. Cr. P. (West 1979 & 1983 Special Pamph.)	R.20.02(8)								notification R.20.02 (8)(4)	prosecuting attorney may participate in administrative hearings R.20.02 (8)(4)						
MISS. Code Ann. (1972 & Supp. 1982)		if certified by jury as still insane & dangerous 99-13-7			*see generally* table 4.5	*see generally* table 4.5										*see* table 2.7
MO. Ann. Stat. (Vernon 1953 & Supp. 1983)	552.040(1)	mandatory commitment 552.040(1)	superintendent 552.040(4)		552.040(4)	every 180 days 552.040(4)	does not have mental disease or defect rendering dangerous or unable to conform conduct to requirements of law 552.040(1)	any party may compel medical examination 552.040(4)	trial ct.; release automatic unless superintendent or state objects 552.040(4)	552.040(4)		552.040(4) OR	552.040(4)			
MONT. Code Ann. (1981)		hearing to determine appropriate disposition; commitment if dangerous to others 46-14-301	superintendent 46-14-302 (1)	w/in 180 days of confinement 46-14-301 (3)	46-14-303	yearly 46-14-303	may be released w/o danger to others 46-14-301 (3)	ct.-ordered examination, if application by superintendent or committed person 46-14-302 (2) 46-14-303	ct. which ordered commitment 46-14-301 (3) 46-14-302 (3)	if not satisfied by examiner's report 46-14-302 (4) 46-14-301 (3)	upon defendant (preponderance of evidence) 46-14-301 (3) 46-14-302 (4)	46-14-301 (4) 46-14-302 (3), (4) OR	46-14-301 (4) 46-14-302 (3), (4)	5 yrs. 46-14-304		
NEB. Rev. Stat. (1979 & Supp. 1982)	90-day commitment for evaluation if found dangerous at 29-3701(1) indeterminate commitment hearing thereafter 29-3702	hearing as to dangerousness 29-3701(1)		or motion by prosecutor 29-3703(1) & annually 29-3703(1)	29-3703(1)		not dangerous to self or others in foreseeable future 29-3703(2)		trial ct. 29-3703(1)	29-3703 (1), (2)		29-3703(2)				
NEV. Rev. Stat. (1981)		as if adjudged insane 175.521(1)														*see* table 2.7

TABLE 12.7 THE INSANITY DEFENSE—DISPOSITION AND RELEASE—*Continued*

	DISPOSITION		APPLICATION FOR RELEASE BY			APPLICATION FOR RELEASE PROCEDURES						NATURE OF RELEASE				MAXIMUM PERIOD OF COMMITMENT
STATE	Civil Commitment Hearing (1)	Other (2)	Mental Health Official (3)	Court on Its Own Motion (4)	Committed Person (5)	Maximum Frequency of Application (6)	Criteria for Release (7)	Supporting Evidence (8)	Approval by (9)	Judicial Hearing (10)	Burden of Proof (11)	Unconditional (12)	Conditional (13)	Maximum Period of Conditions (14)	Mandatory Outpatient Treatment (15)	(16)
N.H. Stat. Ann. ch. 135 (1977 & Supp. 1982), ch. 651 (1974 & Supp. 1982)		commitment for life, if dangerous, see fn. 6 of table 12.6 651:9 651:9-a	superintendent 135:28	justice of superior ct. 135:28	135:30		further detention unnecessary 135:28	ct. may supply independent medical examination if hearing requested & person indigent 135:30-a	superintendent or justice of superior ct. 135:38	if requested by presiding justice or counsel for state 135:28-a	*fn. 7*	135:28	parole		parole on such conditions as justice requires 135:29	2 yrs. subject to judicial hearing & renewal *fn. 7* 651:11-a
N.J. Stat. Ann. (West 1982); N.J. R. Cr. Practice (West 1983)	commitment if dangerous 2C:4-8(b)(3) R.3:19-2	discharge or conditional release 2C:4-8(b) (1), (2)	commissioner, designee, or superintendent 2C:4-9(a)		2C:4-9(c)		may be safely released or discharged 2C:4-9(a)	ct. may order examination by 2 psychiatrists 2C:4-9(a) (b)	committing ct. 2C:4-9(a)	if ct. not satisfied by examiners' report 2C:4-9(b)						
N.M. R. Cr. P. for Dist. Ct's. (1980 & Supp. 1983); N.M. Uniform Jury Instructions—Cr. (1978 & Supp. 1983)	R.35(a)(2)				*see generally* table 4.5	*see generally* table 4.5										*see* table 3.3 *supra*
N.Y. Cr. P. Law (McKinney 1971 & Supp. 1983)	psychiatric examination, if already confined or if necessary 330.20 (2), (3) civil commitment thereafter 330.20(6), (7)		commissioner, for a furlough order 330.20(10) or for release or discharge order 330.20(12), (13)	upon receipt of application by commissioner for retention or release order at expiration of period in commitment order 330.20(8), (9)	may obtain rehearing w/in 30 days of order 330.20(16)		does not have a dangerous mental disorder & is not mentally ill 330.20(8), (9), (12) furlough consistent w/public safety & welfare 330.20(10) both criteria for discharge 330.20(13)		committing ct., or superior ct. where facility located 330.20	330.20	upon state 330.20	discharge 330.20(13)	OR release 330.20(12), or furlough 330.20(10)		any conditions ct. deems reasonably necessary or appropriate (release) 330.20(12)	
N.C. Gen. Stat. (1983)	if judge determines reasonable grounds exist (judicial hearing if necessary) 15A-1321	temporary restraint pending proceedings if imminently dangerous 15A-1322					*fn. 8*									*see* table 2.7
N.D. Cent. Code (1976 & Supp. 1981)	12.1-04-10					*see* table 4.5										*see* table 2.7
OHIO Rev. Code Ann. (Baldwin 1979 & Supp. 1981)	2945.40		or custodian 2945.40 (E), (F)		2945.40(E) 5122.15(H) 5123.76(H)	*see* table 2.6			trial ct. 2945.40 (D)(4), (F)	if requested by ct. or prosecutor 2945.40 (D)(4), (F)	*see* table 2.6	2945.40(F)	OR 2945.40 (D), (F)	max. sentence person could have served if convicted 2945.40 (D)(6)	least restrictive alternative, including "any conditions . . . that insure . . . public safety" 2945.40 (D)(1)	*see* table 2.7

TABLE 12.7 THE INSANITY DEFENSE—DISPOSITION AND RELEASE—*Continued*

	DISPOSITION		APPLICATION FOR RELEASE BY			APPLICATION FOR RELEASE PROCEDURES						NATURE OF RELEASE				MAXIMUM PERIOD OF COMMITMENT
STATE	Civil Commitment Hearing (1)	Other (2)	Mental Health Official (3)	Court on Its Own Motion (4)	Committed Person (5)	Maximum Frequency of Application (6)	Criteria for Release (7)	Supporting Evidence (8)	Approval by (9)	Judicial Hearing (10)	Burden of Proof (11)	Unconditional (12)	Conditional (13)	Maximum Period of Conditions (14)	Mandatory Outpatient Treatment (15)	(16)
OKLA. Stat. Ann. (West 1958 & Supp. 1983–84)		to state hospital for examination; followed by ct. hearing 22, §1161				*see generally* table 4.5	*see generally* table 4.5	*see generally* table 4.5				*fn. 9*				*see* table 2.7
OR. Rev. Stat. (1981)		dispositional hearing *fn. 10* 161.325, 327, 329	person responsible for supervision or treatment 161.336 (7)(b) superintendent 161.341 (2)		by person under conditional release 161.336 (7)(a) 161.341 (4)	once every 6 mos. 161.336 (7)(a) 161.341 (5)	no longer affected by mental disease or defect, or not dangerous & not in need of supervision, medication, or treatment 161.336 (7)(a) or may be safely conditionally released 161.341 (4)		hearing before psychiatric security review board 161.336 (7)(a)	subject to petition for judicial review 161.385 (9)(b)	on applicant (preponderance of evidence) 161.336 (7)(a) 161.341 (5) 161.346 (10)	161.336 (10) 161.346 (1)(a)	OR 161.336 (10) 161.346 (1)(b) *fn. 11*	max. sentence had defendant been found responsible 161.336 (8) hearing at least every 5 yrs. 161.351 (3)	161.332 161.336 (4)(a)	max. sentence had defendant been responsible *fn. 12* 161.327(1) 161.341(1) 161.341(7)(b)
PA. Stat. Ann. (Purdon 1969 & Supp. 1980)		*fn. 13* *fn. 14*	*fn. 13* *fn. 14*													
R.I. Gen. Laws (1977 & Supp. 1982)		observational commitment to determine dangerousness 40.1-5.3-4 (b) commitment following hearing if dangerous 40.1-5.3-4 (e)	petition every 6 mos. for review by director of dep't or when patient meets criteria for release 40.1-5.3-4 (f)		40.1-5.3-4 (g)		no likelihood of serious harm from unsupervised presence in community 40.1-5.3-4 (h)	director's report 40.1-5.3-4 (f), (h)	trial ct. 40.1-5.3-4 (a)(1), (f)	40.1-5.3-4 (h)	upon state (clear & convincing evidence) 40.1-5.3-4 (h)	40.1-5.3-4 (h)				
S.C. Code Ann. (Law. Co-op. 1976 & Supp. 1982)	if ct. believes person requires hospitalization 44-23-610	release w/in 15 days if proceedings not initiated 44-23-610			*see generally* table 4.5	*see generally* table 4.5										*see* table 2.7
S.D. Codified Laws Ann. (1979 & Supp. 1983)	if in custody & discharge dangerous to public safety 23A-26-12				*see generally* table 2.12	*see generally* table 2.12					*see generally* table 2.13	*see generally* table 2.13				*see* table 2.13

TABLE 12.7 THE INSANITY DEFENSE—DISPOSITION AND RELEASE—*Continued*

	DISPOSITION		APPLICATION FOR RELEASE BY			APPLICATION FOR RELEASE PROCEDURES						NATURE OF RELEASE				MAXIMUM PERIOD OF COMMITMENT
STATE	Civil Commitment Hearing (1)	Other (2)	Mental Health Official (3)	Court on Its Own Motion (4)	Committed Person (5)	Maximum Frequency of Application (6)	Criteria for Release (7)	Supporting Evidence (8)	Approval by (9)	Judicial Hearing (10)	Burden of Proof (11)	Unconditional (12)	Conditional (13)	Maximum Period of Conditions (14)	Mandatory Outpatient Treatment (15)	(16)
TENN. Code Ann. (1977 & Supp. 1984)	if certified following diagnosis & evaluation 33-7-303	60-90 day detention for diagnosis & evaluation 33-709(a) ct. may order outpatient treatment if not committed 33-709(b)			*see generally* table 4.5	*see generally* table 4.5										*see* table 2.7
TEX. Code Crim. P. (Vernon 1978 & Supp. 1984)	when act did not involve serious bodily injury 46.03(4)(a)	automatic commitment when serious act or threat; hearing w/in 30 days 46.03(4)(d)	director of facility 46.03(5)	ct.'s own motion or of district or county attorney 46.03(5)		90 days after last hearing 46.03(5)	whether acquittee continues to meet criteria for involuntary commitment 46.03(5)			46.03(5)					ct. may order outpatient care 46.03 (4), (5)	not to exceed max. sentence 46.03(7)
UTAH Code Ann. (1978 & Supp. 1983)		mandatory commitment if ct. finds defendant mentally ill & dangerous to self or others 77-14-5(2)	certification by clinical director of state hospital 77-14-5(2)		77-14-5(2)	after 6 mos. & once per yr. 77-14-5(2)	recovery from mental illness & not dangerous 77-14-5(2)			77-14-5(2)	on applicant 77-14-5(2)					
VT. Stat. Ann. (1974 & Supp. 1983)	13, §4820 13, §4822 (a)				*see generally* table 4.5	*see generally* table 4.5			district ct., Waterbury circuit 13, §4822 (c)	at discretion of committing ct. in any case involving personal injury or threat of personal injury 13, §4822 (a)		13, §4822(e)				*see* table 2.7
VA. Code (1983)		examination & hearing; commitment if insane, feeble-minded, or dangerous 19.2-181 (1)	director of state hospital 19.2-181 (2)		19.2-181(4)	6 mos. after date of confinement & yearly thereafter 19.2-181 (4)	not insane or feeble-minded & may be discharged or released w/o danger to public or self *fn. 15* 19.2-181 (2), (7)	examination by 2 psychiatrists 19.2-181 (2)	committing ct. 19.2-181 (3), (5)	if ct. not satisfied by application & examiners' report 19.2-181 (3)	upon committed person 19.2-181 (3)	19.2-181 OR (3)	or conversion to civil commitment status 19.2-181 (3)			

TABLE 12.7 THE INSANITY DEFENSE—DISPOSITION AND RELEASE—*Continued*

	DISPOSITION		APPLICATION FOR RELEASE BY			APPLICATION FOR RELEASE PROCEDURES						NATURE OF RELEASE				MAXIMUM PERIOD OF COMMITMENT
STATE	Civil Commitment Hearing (1)	Other (2)	Mental Health Official (3)	Court on Its Own Motion (4)	Committed Person (5)	Maximum Frequency of Application (6)	Criteria for Release (7)	Supporting Evidence (8)	Approval by (9)	Judicial Hearing (10)	Burden of Proof (11)	Unconditional (12)	Conditional (13)	Maximum Period of Conditions (14)	Mandatory Outpatient Treatment (15)	(16)
WASH. Rev. Code Ann. (1980 & Supp. 1983–84)		commitment or less restrictive alternative if a substantial danger or in need of control 10.77.110	secretary of dep't *must* forward recommendations & patient's application for conditional release to ct. 10.77.150 (1) secretary *may* forward petition for discharge 10.77.200		to secretary of dep't 10.77.150 (1) 10.77.200 (1)	every 6 mos. 10.77.150 (3)	may be conditionally released or discharged without substantial danger to others 10.77.200 (2), (3)	state or patient may demand an examination 10.77.200 (2)	committing ct. 10.77.150 (2) 10.77.200 (2)	either party may demand jury at discharge hearing 10.77.200 (2) 10.77.120	ct. may disapprove conditional release only on the basis of substantial evidence 10.77.150 (2) upon petitioner at discharge hearing (preponderance of evidence) 10.77.200 (2)	10.77.200	10.77.150 (2)	ct. review 1 yr. after order & every 2 yrs. thereafter 10.77.180	10.77.160	max. sentence for any offense for which he was acquitted 10.77.200 (3)
W. Va. Code §§ 62 (1977), 27 (1980)	ct. may order 40 days observational hospitalization 27-6A-3 (a), (b)	ct. may order hospitalization or discharge if not indicted by reason of insanity 62-2-12														*see* table 2.7
WIS. Stat. Ann. (West 1971 & Supp. 1983–84)		placement in an appropriate institution for care, custody, & treatment 971.17(1)	for reexamination 971.17(2)		for reexamination 971.17(2)		may be safely discharged or released w/o danger to self or others 971.17(2)		committing ct. 971.17(2)			971.12(2) OR	971.17(2)	5 yrs. 971.17(3)	such conditions as ct. determines necessary 971.17(2)	max. sentence for conviction 971.17(2)
WYO. Stat. (1977 & Supp. 1982)		commitment if mentally ill, dangerous, & not a proper subject of release or supervision 7-11-306 (d)	head of facility 7-11-306(e)		7-11-306 (f)		not mentally ill or deficient, & no substantial risk of danger to self or others 7-11-306 (e), (g)	report of fact's supporting head of facility's opinion 7-11-306 (e) examination 7-11-306 (h)	committing ct. 7-11-306(e)	7-11-306 (g)	upon state to contest head of facility's report; otherwise on applicant (preponderance of evidence) 7-11-306 (e), (f)	7-11-306 OR (g)	7-11-306 (g)			

FOOTNOTES: TABLE 12.7

1. Upon petition and trial by jury, the court may order a patient recommitted for an additional period of two years beyond the date of termination of previous commitment, if patient had been committed for certain felonies, and if patient by reason of a mental disease, defect, or disorder presents a substantial danger of physical harm to others. See generally Cal. Penal Code § 1026.5(b) (West 1970 & Supp. 1982).

2. Colo.Rev. Stat. § 16-8-115(2) (1978 & Supp. 1982): "When none of [the examiners'] reports indicate the Defendant is eligible for release,defendant's request for release hearing may be denied by the court if the defendant is unable to show by way of an offer of proof any other evidence that would indicate that he is eligible for release."

3. Cf. United States v. Cohen, 674 F.2d 8 (D.C. Cir. 1982), where the court held unconstitutional on equal protection grounds the district's restoration provisions for persons found not guilty by reason of insanity. The court ruled that D.C. Code Ann. § 24-301(d), (k), prescribing automatic commitment upon acquittal and procedures for continued commitment thereafter, impermissibly disadvantaged persons charged with criminal violations of the United States Code who raised the defense of insanity in comparison with defendants elsewhere in the United States. Interestingly, the opinion appears only in the advance sheets; rehearing was granted, and the opinion was vacated en banc.

4. Persons found guilty but mentally ill are sentenced in the ordinary manner but evaluated for treatment within the prisons or transfer to mental health facilities. Also, they may later be required to accept treatment as a condition of probation. Ind. Code Ann. § 35-36-2-5- (Burns Supp. 1983).

5. A person found guilty but mentally ill is sentenced in the ordinary manner but shall be provided with treatment during imprisonment, probation, shock probation, conditional discharge, parole, or conditional release, unless he is no longer mentally ill. Ky. Rev. Stat. Ann. § 504.150 (Michie Supp. 1982).

6. Where defendant was found not guilty by reason of insanity, an authorized commitment to the commissioner of mental health and corrections is not deemed punishment and, therefore, is not restricted by the prohibition against indeterminate sentences. See State v. Fleming, 409 A.2d 220, (Me. 1979). See also Annot. to Me. Rev. Stat. Ann. tit. 15, § 103 (1980 & Supp. 1981).

7. State v. Gregoire, 118 N.H. 140, 384 A.2d 132 (1978), decided the same day as Novosel v. Helgemoe, 118 N.H. 115, 384 A.2d 124 (1978) (making insanity an affirmative defense to be established by the preponderance of evidence), held that insofar as N.H. Rev. Stat. Ann. § 651:11-a (1974 & Supp. 1975) "permits recommittal if a mere preponderance of the evidence indicates that a person still suffers from mental disease and that it would be dangerous for him to be at large, it is unconstitutional." 384 A.2d at 134. The court relied, in part, on its holding in Gibbs v. Helgemoe, 116 N.H. 825, 367 A.2d 1041 (1976), that New Hampshire Constitution pt. I, art. 15, commanded that "in a criminal recommitment hearing the State must prove beyond a reasonable doubt that a patient's present medical condition is such that it would be dangerous for him to be at large." 384 A.2d at 133. See generally Annot. to N.H. Rev. Stat. Ann. § 651:11-a (1974 & Supp. 1981). Compare State v. Hesse, 117 N.H. 329, 373 A.2d 345 (1977) (petitioner seeking release from hospital for the criminally insane, following commitment after plea of not guilty by reason of insanity, was the party asserting the affirmative issue and therefore was not unconstitutionally burdened by a requirement that he demonstrate nondangerousness by a preponderance of the evidence).

8. Senate Bill 75, An Act Regarding Involuntary Commitment of Persons Found Incapable of Proceeding or Not Guilty by Reason of Insanity, modified the existing statutes to protect against the release by mental hospitals of persons accused of violent crimes. Patients hospitalized following or pending determinations of their incompetency to proceed and persons hospitalized after being found not guilty by reason of insanity may only be released upon court approval if the charges against them concerned violent crimes. See 1983 N.C. Sess. Laws ch. 380.

9. Though the statute provides that the acquittee shall be "subject to discharge pursuant to the procedure set forth in the Mental Health Law," it simultaneously contains a section requiring the hospital superintendent to give notice to the court, the district attorney, and the patient's advocate 20 days prior to the acquittee's scheduled release and it provides for the possibility of a special judicial discharge hearing, upon motion by the district attorney. Okla. Stat. Ann. tit. 22, § 1161 (West 1958 & Supp. 1983-84).

10. Or. Rev. Stat. § 161.327(1), (3) (1981).

> [I]f the court finds that the person would have been guilty of a felony, or of a misdemeanor during a criminal episode in the course of which the person caused physical injury or risk of physical injury to another, and if the court finds by a preponderance of evidence that the person is affected by mental disease or defect and presents a substantial danger to others requiring commitment to a state mental hospital . . . or conditional release, the court shall order the person placed under the jurisdiction of the Psychiatric Security Review Board for care and treatment. . . .
>
> For purposes of this section, a person affected by a mental disease or defect in a state of remission is considered to have a mental disease or defect requiring supervision when the disease may, with reasonable medical probability, occasionally become active and, when active, render the person a danger to others.

If the criminal episode for which defendant would be responsible but for his insanity did not cause or risk physical injury to another, commitment must be by way of civil hospitalization procedures, except insofar as standard of proof is not preponderance of evidence and period of jurisdiction may be longer than the maximum sentence the defendant could have received had he been found responsible. Id. § 161.328.

If defendant is no longer affected by mental disease or defect, or no longer presents a substantial danger to others and is not in need of care, supervision or treatment, the court shall order the person discharged. Id. § 161.329.

11. Id. § 161.332 (1981): "[C]onditional release includes, but is not limited to, the monitoring of mental and physical health treatment."

12. Id. § 161.341(7)(b): "In no case shall a person be held pursuant to this section for a period exceeding two years without a hearing before the board to determine whether the person should be conditionally released or discharged."

13. Mental illness of a convicted person is taken into account in sentencing. Pa. Stat. Ann. tit. 50, § 7405 (Purdon Supp. 1983 N.84).

14. Persons found guilty but mentally ill shall be provided with treatment either in prison or in a mental facility, and treatment may be made a condition of probation, prerelease status, or parole. Id. tit. 42, § 9727.

15. Va. Code § 19.2-18(7) (1975 & Supp. 1981):

> In applying this section the term "feebleminded" shall be construed to mean a person who is adjudicated legally incompetent because of mental deficiency by a circuit court in which he is charged with crime and who is also found to lack the mental condition to enable him to be discharged without danger to the public peace and safety or to himself.

TABLE 12.8 SEXUAL PSYCHOPATH LAWS

		PROCEEDINGS INITIATED BY			TIME OF PROCEEDINGS			MEDICAL EXAMINATION					
STATE	APPLIES TO (1)	Prosecuting Attorney (2)	Court (3)	Defense Attorney or Accused (4)	Precon-viction (5)	Postcon-viction, Presentence (6)	Postcon-viction, After Sentence (7)	Psychiatrist (8)	Psychologist (9)	Other (10)	HEARING (11)	JURY (12)	RIGHT TO COUNSEL (13)
CAL. Welf. & Inst. Code §6301 (West 1972 & Supp. 1981)	6301												
CAL. Penal Code §1364 (West 1972 & Supp. 1981)	persons convicted of sex offense against person under 14 yrs. or accomplished against victim's will by force, violence, duress, menace, or fear of bodily injury		1364				1364				hospital treatment if offender consents to transfer to hospital after serving min. of 2 yrs. of criminal sentence		
COLO. Rev. Stat. (1978 & Supp. 1981)	sex offenders 16-13-201	district attorney 16-13-205	district ct. 16-13-203	16-13-205		w/in 20 days after conviction 16-13-205		*fn. 1* 16-13-207			16-13-210		16-13-206 (b)
CONN. Gen. Stat. Ann. (West 1975 & Supp. 1980)	convicted of violent or compulsive sex offenses or ones w/large age disparity 17-244(a)	state's attorney or assistant state's attorney 17-244(b)	17-244(a)	17-244(b)		initial diagnostic commitment 17-244(a) hearing on recommendation of commitment 17-245(b)				*fn. 2* 17-244(a)	hearing prior to diagnostic commitment 17-244(a) hearing on recommendation of confinement for custody, care, & treatment 17-245(b)		
D.C. Code Ann. (1981 & Supp. 1982)	sexual psychopath *fn. 3* 22-3503 22-3504(a)	U.S. attorney for D.C.; proceedings may be initiated though no criminal charge or conviction 22-3504(a), (b)	22-3504(c)		before trial 22-3504 (d)(1)	22-3504 (d)(2)	before completion of probation 22-3504 (d)(3)	two 22-3506(a)			required if psychiatric reports indicate sexual psychopathy, or are inconclusive due to patient's refusal to submit to exam 22-3507	if demanded 22-3508	22-3505
FLA. Stat. Ann. (West 1973 & Supp. 1981)	mentally disordered sex offenders *fn. 4* 917.012		*fn. 5* 917.012 (1)(a), (b)				917.012 (1)(a)			evaluation by dep't of corrections & by dep't of health & rehabilitative services; examiners not specified 917.012 (1)(c), (d)			
ILL. Ann. Stat. (Smith-Hurd 1966 & Supp. 1981)	sexually dangerous persons 38, §105-1.01	attorney general or state's attorney 38, §105-3			when any person charged w/criminal offense 38, §105-3			two 38, §105-4			38, §105-5	on demand 38, §105-5	38, §105-5
MASS. Ann. Laws (Michie/Law. Co-op. 1974 & Supp. 1982)	sexually dangerous person 123A, §1	district attorney 123A, §4	123A, §4			123A, §4	*fn. 8* 123A, §6	not less than 2 123A, §4			123A, §5		*fn. 9* 123A, §5
MINN. Stat. (West 1975 & Supp. 1981) *fn. 11*	psychopathic personality *fn. 12* 526.09 526.10	county attorney 526.10									526.10		
NEB. Rev. Stat. (1979)	mentally disordered sex offender 29-2911		29-2912			presentence evaluation, postsentence commitment 29-2912 29-2915		2 psychiatrists, or 1 psychiatrist & 1 clinical psychologist 29-2913					

COMMITMENT PERIOD			RELEASED WHEN			RELEASE INITIATED BY PATIENT PETITION	AUTHORITY FOR RELEASE		TYPE OF RELEASE		DISPOSITION OF ORIGINAL OFFENSE		
Indeterminate (14)	Specified Term (15)	No Longer Dangerous (16)	No Longer Necessary (17)	Sufficiently Recovered (18)	Other (19)	(20)	Administrator (21)	Court (22)	Absolute (23)	Probation or Parole (24)	Returned for Trial (25)	Returned for Sentence (26)	APPEAL (27)
	6316.1 6316.2	6325(a)			sentence served 1364		6325(a), (b)						
min.: 1 day; max.: natural life 16-13-203		would not constitute threat of bodily harm to public 16-13-216(5)			in best interests of that person & public 16-13-216(5)		state board of parole 16-13-216 (5)		16-13-216(5)	parole or reparole 16-13-216(4)			16-13-212
	ct. may sentence to custody, care, & treatment at state institute; however, no one may be confined there beyond max. period specified in sentence 17-245(c)			sufficiently improved 17-251(a)	consideration of benefit to patient & society 17-251(a)	request of defendant or attorney 17-251(a)	director has authority to transfer, grant leave of absence, or parole; also may discharge subject to notice to ct. & ct. order 17-251(a)	also gives order for release in administrative proceedings 17-251(a), (b)	17-251(a), (b)	leave of absence 17-251(a), (b)		ct. has option to return patient to custody of commissioner of corrections for further disposition if max. period of sentence has not run 17-251(b)	habeus corpus 17-256
22-3508		22-3509		22-3509			superintendent of St. Elizabeth's Hospital 22-3509		22-3509	22-3509	criminal proceeding stayed when psychopathy proceeding begun; upon discharge from hospital, criminal disposition resumes 22-3509 22-3510	22-3509 22-3510	22-3508
	fn. 6 917.012 (1)(e)						917.012 (1)(h)					those committed prior to July 1, 1979, returned to committing ct. for further disposition, including sentencing 917.011	
director of corrections acts as guardian & retains custody until "recovered and released" 38, §105-8		38, §§105-9			conditional release when ct. not certain patient no longer dangerous 38, §§105-9, 105-10	38, §105-9		38, §§105-9, 105-10	38, §105-9	conditional release 38, §§105-9, 105-10	*fn. 7* 38, §105-9		as provided by Civil Practice Act 38, §105-3.01
min.: 1 day *fn. 10* 123A, §5 max.: natural life 123A, §9		no longer sexually dangerous 123A, §9				or petition by parents, spouse, issue, next of kin, or any friend 123A, §9	parole board 123A, §9	123A, §9	123A, §9	parole or conditional release 123A, §9			
											psychopathic personality not defense to charge of crime 526.11		
	shall not exceed max. length of sentence 29-2915		has received max. benefit of treatment 29-2915		no longer mentally disordered 29-2915		ct. makes final decision based on sentencing review committee report 29-2915, 29-2918		defendant returned to sentencing ct. for further disposition 29-2919			defendant has already been sentenced; may be compelled to serve remainder of sentence in penal institution 29-2919	29-2915

TABLE 12.8 SEXUAL PSYCHOPATH LAWS—*Continued*

		PROCEEDINGS INITIATED BY			TIME OF PROCEEDINGS			MEDICAL EXAMINATION					
STATE	APPLIES TO (1)	Prosecuting Attorney (2)	Court (3)	Defense Attorney or Accused (4)	Precon-viction (5)	Postcon-viction, Presentence (6)	Postcon-viction, After Sentence (7)	Psychiatrist (8)	Psychologist (9)	Other (10)	HEARING (11)	JURY (12)	RIGHT TO COUNSEL (13)
N.H. Rev. Stat. Ann. (1978 & Supp. 1981)	dangerous sex of-fender *fn. 13* 173-A:2	county attorney files petition at urging of committing ct. 173-A:3(II)	convicting ct. orders evaluation 173-A:3(I)			173-A:3(I)		173-A:3(I)			173-A:4	no right to trial by jury 173-A:4(VI)	173-A:4(I)
N.J. Stat. Ann. (West 1972 & Supp. 1982)	*fn. 15* 2C:47-1		judge 2C:47-1			*fn. 16* 2C:47-3				referred to adult diagnostic & treatment center for phys-ical & psycho-logical exam 2C:47-1			
OR. Rev. Stat. (1981)	sexually dangerous persons 426.510		426.675(1)			426.675(1)				defendant committed to facility for evalua-tion & report 426.675(1)	defendant may waive hearing 426.675(2)		
TENN. Code Ann. (1980 & Supp. 1982)	sex offender 33-1301	*fn. 19* *fn. 20* 33-1303 33-1304 33-1305	*fn. 19* *fn. 20* 33-1303 33-1304 33-1305	*fn. 19* *fn. 20* 33-1303 33-1304 33-1305			examined after admittance to penal institution 33-1303	33-1303 33-1305	33-1303 33-1305				
UTAH Code Ann. (1978 & Supp. 1982)	persons convicted of certain sex crimes 77-16-1		77-16-1			77-16-1				alienist 77-16-2			
VA. Code (1980 & Supp. 1982) *fn. 22*	person con-victed of of-fense indicat-ing sexual ab-normality 19.2-300	19.2-300	19.2-300	or other person acting for defendant 19.2-300		19.2-300		19.2-301					
WASH. Rev. Code Ann. (1975 & Supp. 1981) *fn. 23*	sexual psychopath 71.06.010 71.06.020	71.06.020			71.06.020		*fn. 24* 71.06.020 71.06.030			2 duly licensed physicians 71.06.040	71.06.060	on demand of defendant 71.06.070	
WYO. Stat. (1977 & Supp. 1982)	persons con-victed of sex crimes involving children 7-13-601		7-13-601			7-13-601		*fn. 25* 7-13-602		*fn. 25* 7-13-602			

COMMITMENT PERIOD		RELEASED WHEN				RELEASE INITIATED BY PATIENT PETITION	AUTHORITY FOR RELEASE		TYPE OF RELEASE		DISPOSITION OF ORIGINAL OFFENSE		APPEAL
Indeterminate (14)	Specified Term (15)	No Longer Dangerous (16)	No Longer Necessary (17)	Sufficiently Recovered (18)	Other (19)	(20)	Administrator (21)	Court (22)	Absolute (23)	Probation or Parole (24)	Returned for Trial (25)	Returned for Sentence (26)	(27)
173-A:5		173-A:9(I)	not benefited by further treatment 173-A:9(I)	173-A:9(I)		petition by patient or attorney *fn. 14* 173-A:9(III)	director of mental health sets terms of parole release, subject to approval of committing ct. 173-A:6(III) director of mental health recommends release to committing ct., which may, after hearing, discharge 173-A:9(I), (III)		173-A:9(III)	173-A:6(III)		173-A:10	
	offender is sentenced to treatment center according to procedures in 2C:43 & 2C:44 2C:47-3		continued confinement not necessary 2C:47-4		capable of making acceptable social adjustment in community 2C:47-5		special classification review board *fn. 17* 2C:47-5 2C:47-4(c)	*fn. 17* 2C:47-4(c)	2C:47-4(c)	2C:47-5			
fn. 18 426.675(3) (a), (b)													
fn. 21 33-1305					*fn. 21* 33-1305	33-609	33-609	33-609	33-1305 33-609				
77-16-2				77-16-5			board of pardons 77-16-5		77-16-5	77-16-5		optional w/board of pardons 77-16-5	
71.06.091		safe to be at large 71.06.091	max. benefit from treatment or not amenable to treatment 71.06.091					71.06.091	71.06.091	conditional release 71.06.091		at ct.'s discretion 71.06.091	
	period of confinement, parole, or probation shall not exceed max. provided by law for that crime 7-13-609				capable of social adjustment 7-13-610			7-13-610		7-13-610 7-13-605		ct. may order commitment to state penitentiary 7-13-605	

FOOTNOTES: TABLE 12.8

1. Colo. Rev. Stat. § 16-13-207 (1978 & Supp. 1981). Defendant examined by two psychiatrists of the receiving institute if committed to state or university hospital. Defendant examined by two court appointed psychiatrists if committed to the county jail.

2. Conn. Gen. Stat. Ann. § 17-244(a) (West 1975 & Supp. 1981). An initial medical exam is conducted by "qualified personnel of the institute (Whiting Forensic Institute)." If the offender is committed for 60 days to the diagnostic unit of the institute, another exam is conducted by "the staff of the unit."

3. D.C. Code Ann. § 22-3504e (1981 & Supp. 1982). The sexual psychopath law does not apply to persons charged with or convicted of rape or assault with intent to rape.

4. Fla. Stat. Ann. § 917.012 (West 1973 & Supp. 1981). Florida's commitment procedure for sexual psychopaths is an administrative procedure handled by the department of corrections and the department of health and rehabilitative services.

5. Id. §§ 917.012(1)(a), (b). The sentenced sex offender is placed in the custody of the Department of Corrections, which determines further disposition.

6. Id. § 917.012(1)(e) "The Department of Health and Rehabilitative Services shall determine for each offender transferred . . . the manner and sequence of treatment based on his length of sentence and his presumptive parole eligibility date."

7. Ill. Ann. Stat. ch. 38, § 105-9 (Smith-Hurd 1966 & Supp. 1981). "Upon an order of discharge every outstanding information and indictment, the basis of which was the reason for the present detention, shall be quashed."

8. Mass. Ann. Laws ch. 123A, § 6 (Michie/Law. Co-op. 1974 & Supp. 1982). Special proceedings for hospitalization of prisoners under sentence in jail exist.

9. Id. ch. 123A, §5. Upon motion of [defendant] or upon its own motion the court shall, if necessary to protect the rights of such person, appoint counsel for him.

10. Id. ch. 123A, §9. Mandatory parole consideration during first year and every three years thereafter (provided such person is otherwise eligible). Also right to hearing for discharge every 12 months upon filing of petition.

11. Minn. Stat. Ann. § 526.10 (West 1975 & Supp. 1981). Statute does not specify a charge or conviction of a criminal offense as prerequisite to initiation of proceedings.

12. Id. The provisions of § 253A pertaining to persons mentally ill and dangerous to the public shall apply to those alleged to have a psychopathic personality.

13. N.H. Rev. Stat. Ann. § 173-A:2 (1978 & Supp. 1981). Any person "suffering from such conditions of emotional instability or impulsiveness of behavior, or lack of customary standards of good judgment, or failure to appreciate the consequences of his act, or any combination of any such conditions, as to render such person irresponsible with respect to sexual matters and thereby dangerous to himself or other persons."

14. Id. § 173-A:9 (II). Petition must be accompanied by affidavit of psychiatrist that defendant has improved.

15. N.J. Stat. Ann. 2C:47-1 (West 1972 & Supp. 1982). Applies to those convicted of the offense of aggravated sexual assault, sexual assault, or aggravated criminal sexual contact, or an attempt to commit any such crime.

16. Id. § 2C:47-3. The offender is "sentenced" to a treatment center.

17. id. § 2C:47-4(c). If, in the opinion of the commissioner, upon the written recommendation of the Special Classification Review Board continued confinement is not necessary, he shall move before the sentencing court for modification of the sentence originally imposed.

18. Or. Rev. Stat. 426.675(3):

"(a) The court may . . . place the defendant on probation on condition that the person participate in and successfully complete a treatment program for sexually dangerous persons.

"(b) The court may impose a sentence of imprisonment with the order that the defendant be assigned . . . to participate in a treatment program for sexually dangerous persons."

19. Tenn. Code §§ 33-1303 to -1305 (1980 & Supp. 1982). The convicted sex offender is examined and certified for treatment to be undergone during his sentence. If as a result of an exam prior to release it is determined that the prisoner is still mentally ill, dangerous, and in need of treatment, judicial commitment may be petitioned for. This commitment (§ 33-604) is the standard civil commitment—indeterminate with mandatory review provisions.

20. Id. § 33-1305. Any person convicted of a sex crime shall be examined within a year of release from a penal institution to determine whether that person is mentally ill and poses a likelihood of serious harm and is in need of care and treatment in a mental hospital. If such a determination is made, the director of the correctional institution may petition for judicial commitment to a hospital or treatment resource.

21. Id. Defendant is released after serving his sentence, or—if committed to an institution after serving his sentence—when no longer mentally ill, dangerous and in need of treatment.

22. Va. Code § 19.2-300 (1980 & Supp. 1982). Virginia does not have a separate hearing procedure; a psychiatrist's report simply affects the dispositional decision of the judge.

23. Wash. Rev. Code Ann. §§ 71.06.150-250 (1975 & Supp. 1981). Washington has separate proceedings for dealing with psychopathic delinquents.

24. Id. § 71.06.020, .030. Petition alleging defendant is a sexual psychopath must be filed and served on defendant ten days before trial of criminal charge. Court may proceed to hear criminal charge. If defendant is convicted or has previously pleaded guilty to charge, sentence is pronounced; court then proceeds to hear sexual psychopathy allegation. Acquittal does not suspend hearing on issue of psychopathy.

25. Wyo. Stat. § 7-13-602 (1977 & Supp. 1982): "Examination shall be conducted by two disinterested, reputable, and legally qualified physicians (or by one (1) such physician, if only one (1) is available). At least one of such physicians, if available, shall be expert in the field of psychiatry."

Table of Cases

"A" Family, *In re,* 602 P.2d 157 (Mont. 1979).
Aaron, *In re,* 434 So. 2d 624 (La. Ct. App. 1983).
Abrahamson v. Hershman, No. 80-2513-K, 5 MDLR 93 (D. Mass. Jan. 30, 1981).
A.B.V.C., 477 N.Y.S.2d 281 (App. Div. 1984).
Ackerman, *In re,* 409 N.E.2d 1211 (Ind. Ct. App. 1980).
Adams Central School District v. Deist, 334 N.W.2d 775 (Neb. 1983).
Adashunas v. Negley, 626 F.2d 600 (7th Cir. 1980).
Addington v. Texas, 441 U.S. 418 (1979).
Aden v. Younger, 57 Cal. App. 3d 662 (1976).
Adoption of Crane, *In re,* 417 N.Y.S.2d 629 (Putnam County Fam. Ct. 1979).
A.E. & R.R. v. Mitchell, No. C-78-466, 5 MDLR 154 (D. Utah June 16, 1980).
Ahlman v. Wolf, 413 So. 2d 787 (Fla. Dist. Ct. App. 1982).
Ake v. Oklahoma, 105 S. Ct. 1087 (1985).
Akers v. Bolton, 531 F. Supp. 300 (D. Kan. 1981).
A.L. v. G.R.H., 325 N.E.2d 501 (Ind. Ct. App. 1975).
Alcoholism Services of Erie County, Inc. v. Common Council, 453 N.Y.S.2d 390 (App. Div. 1982) (mem.).
Alexander v. Choate, 105 S. Ct. 712 (1985).
Alexander v. Minnesota Jewish Group Homes, Inc., No. 746834, 3 MDLR 36 (4th Jud. Dist. Ct. of Minn. July 26, 1978).
Alexieff's Will, *In re,* 94 N.Y.S.2d 32 (Sup. Ct. 1949), *aff'd,* 97 N.Y.S.2d 532 (1950).
Allard v. Helgemoe, 572 F.2d 1 (1st Cir. 1978).
Allen v. Heckler, 35 Fair Empl. Prac. Cas. (BNA) 281 (D.D.C. May 4, 1984).
Allen v. McDonough, No. 14948, 4 MDLR 402 (Mass. Sup. Ct. Aug. 19, 1980).
Alley v. Anne Arundel County Board of Education, No. K-79-2211, 4 MDLR 179 (D. Md. Apr. 29, 1980).
Alter v. Morris, 536 P.2d 630 (Wash. 1975).
Alyeska Pipeline Service Co. v. Wilderness Society, 421 U.S. 240 (1975).
American Academy of Pediatrics v. Heckler, 561 F. Supp. 395 (D.D.C. 1983).
Anderson v. Community Unit District No. 228, 449 N.E.2d 1018 (Ill. App. Ct. 1983).
Anderson v. Thompson, 495 F. Supp. 1256 (E.D. Wis. 1980), *aff'd on other grounds,* 658 F.2d 1205 (7th Cir. 1981).
Anderson v. Wolff, 468 F.2d 252 (8th Cir. 1972).
Application of Cicero, 421 N.Y.S.2d 965 (Sup. Ct. Spec. Term 1979).
Application of President and Directors of Georgetown College, Inc., 331 F.2d 1000 (D.C. Cir.), *cert. denied,* 377 U.S. 978 (1964).
Application of True, 645 P.2d 891 (Idaho 1982).
Aquino v. Harris, 516 F. Supp. 265 (E.D. Pa. 1981).
Area V Developmental Disabilities Board v. Brown, No. 543060-2, 5 MDLR 180 (Cal. Super. Ct. filed Feb. 27, 1981).
Argersinger v. Hamlin, 407 U.S. 25 (1972).
Armijo's Will, *In re,* 261 P.2d 833 (N.M. 1953).
Armstrong v. Kline, 476 F. Supp. 583 (E.D. Pa. 1979), *remanded sub nom.* Battle v. Pennsylvania, 629 F.2d 269 (3d Cir. 1980).
Arnett v. Kennedy, 416 U.S. 134 (1974).
Association for Retarded Citizens v. Department of Developmental Services, No. S.F. 24761, 9 MPDLR 199 (Cal. Sup. Ct. Mar. 21, 1985).
Association for Retarded Citizens in Colorado v. Frazier, 517 F. Supp. 105 (D. Colo. 1981).
Association for Retarded Citizens of North Dakota v. Olson, 713 F.2d 1384 (8th Cir. 1983).
Atascadero State Hospital v. Scanlon, No. 84-351 (U.S. Sup. Ct. June 28, 1985).
Attorney General v. Travelers Insurance Co., 463 N.E.2d 548 Mass. 1984).
Austin Independent School District, *In re,* No. 06791572, 4 MDLR 403 (OCR HEW Aug. 1980).
A.W., *In re,* 637 P.2d 366 (Colo. 1981).
Ayres v. Dempsey, No. 81-72047, 8 MPDLR 413 (E.D. Mich. Mar. 27, 1984).

"B," *In re,* 394 A.2d 419 (Pa. 1978).
Baber v. San Bernardino Superior Court, 170 Cal. Rptr. 353 (Ct. App. 1980).
Baker v. Butler Public School District, No. Civ. 79-629-W, 4 MDLR 265 (W.D. Okla. May 22, 1980).
Balanced Mental Health Laws, Inc. v. Ohio Department of Mental Retardation and Development Disabilities, No. 83 CV-04-233, 7 MDLR 241 (Ohio C.P. Franklin County filed Apr. 19, 1983).
Ballay, *In re,* 482 F.2d 648 (D.C. Cir. 1973).
Banos v. Crosland, No. 80-2677, 5 MDLR 35 (D.D.C. Dec. 11, 1980).
Barbee v. Kolb, 179 S.W. 2d 701 (1944).
Barber v. Superior Court of California, Los Angeles County, 195 Cal. Rptr. 484 (Ct. App. 1983).
Barber v. Time, Inc., 159 S.W.2d 291 (Mo. 1942).
Barefoot v. Estelle, 103 S. Ct. 3383 (1983).
Barker, *In re,* 2 Johns ch. 232 (N.Y. 1816).
Barker v. Barker, 440 P.2d 137 (Idaho 1968).
Barnard, *In re,* 455 F.2d 1370 (D.C. Cir. 1971).
Barnett v. Rodgers, 410 F.2d 995 (D.C. Cir. 1969).
Bartley v. Kremens, 402 F. Supp. 1039 (E.D. Pa. 1975).
Battle v. Cameron, 260 F. Supp. 804 (D.D.C. 1966).
Battle v. Pennsylvania, 629 F.2d 269 (3d Cir. 1980).
Baugh v. Woodard, 287 S.E.2d 412 (N.C. Ct. App. 1982).
Baxstrom v. Herold, 383 U.S. 107 (1966).
Becker v. Hobby Horse Ranch School, No. 79-303, 4 MDLR 112 (D. Ariz. Dec. 17, 1979).
Becker v. Schwartz, 386 N.E.2d 807 (N.Y. 1978).
Bell v. State, 385 So. 2d 78 (Ala. Crim. App. 1980).
Bell v. Burson, 402 U.S. 535 (1971).
Bell v. Wayne County General Hospital, 456 F.2d 1062 (6th Cir. 1972).
Bell v. Wayne County General Hospital, 384 F. Supp. 1085 (E.D. Mich. 1974).
Bell v. Wolfish, 441 U.S. 520 (1979).
Bellah v. Greenson, 146 Cal. Rptr. 535 (Ct. App. 1978).
Bellarmine Hills Association v. Residential Systems Co., No. CR24-78, 3 MDLR 187 (Mich. Sup. Ct. Feb. 7, 1979).
Bellavance v. State, 390 So. 2d 422 (Fla. Dist. Ct. App. 1980).
Benham v. Edwards, 678 F.2d 511 (5th Cir. 1982).
Benner v. Negley, 725 F.2d 446 (7th Cir. 1984).
Bennett, *In re,* 434 A.2d 1155 (N.J. 1981).
Bentivegna v. United States Department of Labor, 694 F.2d 619 (9th Cir. 1982).
Berger v. State, 364 A.2d 993 (N.J. 1976).
Berman v. Allan, 404 A.2d 8 (N.J. 1979).
Bernard B. v. Blue Cross and Blue Shield of Greater New York, 528 F. Supp. 125 (S.D.N.Y. 1981).

Berry v. Schweiker, 675 F.2d 464 (2d Cir. 1982).
Beverley's Case, 4 Coke 123b, 76 Eng. Rep. 1118 (K.B. 1603).
Bidstrup, *In re,* 285 S.E.2d 304 (N.C. Ct. App. 1982).
Bisgaard v. Duvall, 169 Iowa 711, 151 N.W. 1051 (1915).
Bishop v. United States, 350 U.S. 961 (1956).
Blackburn v. State, 23 Ohio 146 (1872).
Blalock v. Richardson, 483 F.2d 773 (4th Cir. 1972).
Blue Cross of Virginia v. Virginia, No. 800056, 4 MDLR 418 (Va. Sup. Ct. Aug. 28, 1980).
Blue Shield of Virginia v. McCready, 457 U.S. 465 (1982).
Blum v. Stenson, 104 S. Ct. 1541 (1984).
Bly v. Rhoads, 222 S.E.2d 783 (Va. 1976).
B.M. v. State, 649 P.2d 425 (Mont. 1982).
Board of Education v. Ambach, 436 N.Y.S.2d 564 (Sup. Ct. 1981).
Board of Education v. Ambach, 458 N.Y.S.2d 680 (App. Div. 1982).
Board of Education v. Rowley, 458 U.S. 176 (1982).
Boarding Home Advocacy Team v. O'Bannon, No. 81-2872 (3d Cir. filed Dec. 15, 1981).
Boedy v. Department of Professional Regulation, 44 So. 2d 503 (Fla. Dist. Ct. App. 1984).
Boesch v. Kick, 116 A. 796 (N.J. 1922).
Boldt v. Wisconsin, 297 N.W.2d 29 (Wis. Ct. App. 1980).
Bolick v. Cole, 271 S.E.2d 540 (N.C. Ct. App. 1980).
Bolling v. Sharpe, 347 U.S. 497 (1954).
Bolton v. Harris, 395 F.2d 642 (D.C. Cir. 1968).
Borgogna, *In re,* 175 Cal. Rptr. 588 (Ct. App. 1981).
Boutilier v. Immigration and Naturalization Service, 387 U.S. 118 (1967).
Bouvia v. County of Riverside, No. 159780, 8 MPDLR 377 (Cal. App. Dep't Super. Ct. Dec. 16, 1983).
Bowers v. DeVito, 686 F.2d 616 (7th Cir. 1982).
Bowring v. Godwin, 551 F.2d 44 (4th Cir. 1977).
Boxall v. Sequoia Union High School District, 464 F. Supp. 1104 (N.D. Cal. 1979).
Boyd, *In re,* 403 A.2d 744 (D.C. 1979).
Boyd v. Board of Registrars of Voters of Belchertown, 334 N.E. 2d 629 (Mass. 1975).
Boyd v. U.S. Postal Service, 32 Fair Empl. Prac. Cas. (BNA) 1217 (W.D. Wash. 1983).
Boyer, *In re,* 636 P.2d 1085 (Utah 1981).
Bradley Center, Inc. v. Wessner, 296 S.E.2d 693 (Ga. 1982).
Brady v. Hopper, 570 F. Supp. 1333 (D. Colo. 1983).
Brady v. Royal Manufacturing Company, 160 S.E.2d 424 (Ga. Ct. App. 1968).
Branzburg v. Hayes, 408 U.S. 665 (1972).
Bray, *In re,* Cir. Ct. No. 78-802-572 AV, 3 MDLR 33 (Wayne County Cir. Ct. Sept. 12, 1978).
Breed v. Jones, 421 U.S. 519 (1975).
Brelje v. Pates, 426 N.E.2d 275 (Ill. App. Ct. 1981).
Brendendick, *In re,* 393 N.E.2d 675 (Ill. App. Ct. 1979).
Brenem v. Harris, 621 F.2d 688 (5th Cir. 1980).
Brewer v. Valk, 167 S.E. 638 (N.C. 1933).
Brewster v. Dukakis, 520 F. Supp. 882 (D. Mass. 1981).
Brewster v. Dukakis, 544 F. Supp. 1069 (D. Mass. 1982).
Brewster v. Dukakis, 675 F.2d 1 (1st Cir. 1982).
Brewster v. Dukakis, 687 F.2d 495 (1st Cir. 1982).
Brice-Nash v. Brice-Nash, 615 P.2d 836 (Kan. Ct. App. 1980).
Briggs v. Arafeh, 411 U.S. 911 (1973).
Briggs v. Clinton County Bank and Trust Co., 452 N.E.2d 989 (Ind. Ct. App. 1983).
Brookhart v. Illinois State Board of Education, 697 F.2d 179 (7th Cir. 1983).
Brooks' Estate, *In re,* 205 N.E.2d 435 (Ill. 1965).
Brown v. Board of Education, 347 U.S. 483 (1954).
Brown v. Culpepper, 559 F.2d 274 (5th Cir. 1977).
Brown v. District of Columbia Board of Education, No. 78-1646, 3 Educ. for the Handicapped L. Rep. 552:152 (D. Minn. Jan. 21, 1980).
Brown v. Peyton, 437 F.2d 1228 (4th Cir. 1971).
Brown v. Sibley, 650 F.2d 760 (5th Cir. 1981).
Brown v. Warden, Great Meadow Correctional Facility, 682 F.2d 348 (2d Cir. 1982).
Browndale International Ltd. v. Board of Adjustments, 208 N.W.2d 121 (Wis. 1973).
Brownfield v. State, 407 N.E.2d 1365 (Ohio 1980).
Buck v. Bell, 274 U.S. 200 (1927).
Bullock v. Carter, 405 U.S. 134 (1972).
Bundy, *In re,* 186 P. 811 (Cal. Dist. Ct. App. 1919).
Burbanks, *In re,* 310 N.W.2d 138 (Neb. 1981).
Burchett v. Bower, 355 F. Supp. 1278 (D. Ariz. 1973).
Burgin v. Henderson, 536 F.2d 501 (2d Cir. 1976).
Burlington Mills Corporation v. Hagood, 13 S.E.2d 291 (Va. 1941).
Buttonow, *In re,* 244 N.E. 2d 677 (N.Y. 1968).

Caesar v. Mountanos, 542 F.2d 1064 (9th Cir. 1976).
Cafeteria Workers v. McElroy, 367 U.S. 886 (1961).
Cain v. Delaware Securities Investments, No. 7236, 7 MDLR 384 (Del. Ch. Ct. Aug. 11, 1983).
Cain v. Yukon Public Schools District 1-27, 556 F. Supp. 605 (W.D. Okla. 1983).
Cairl v. State, 323 N.W.2d 20 (Minn. 1982).
Calhoun v. Illinois State Board of Education, 550 F. Supp. 796 (N.D. Ill. 1982).
California Paralyzed Veterans Association v. F.C.C., 496 F. Supp. 125 (C.D. Cal. 1980).
Calkins, *In re,* 420 N.E.2d 861 (Ill. App. Ct. 1981).
Camenisch v. University of Texas, 616 F.2d 127 (5th Cir. 1980).
Campbell v. Campbell, 5 So. 2d 401 (Ala. 1941).
Campbell v. Grisett, No. 79-M-277, 5 MDLR 168 (N.D. Ala. Mar. 31, 1981).
Campbell v. Talledega County Board of Education, 518 F. Supp. 47 (N.D. Ala. 1981).
Campochiaro v. Califano, No. H-78-64, 2 MDLR 558 (D. Conn. May 18, 1978).
Cannon v. University of Chicago, 441 U.S. 677 (1979).
Canterbury v. Spence, 464 F.2d 772 (D.C. Cir. 1972).
Carey v. Population Services International, 431 U.S. 678 (1977).
Caritativo v. California, 357 U.S. 549 (1958).
Carmi v. Metropolitan St. Louis Sewer District, 620 F.2d 672 (8th Cir. 1980).
Carter v. General Motors Corporation, 106 N.W.2d 105 (Mich. 1960).
Carter v. Independent School District No. 6, 550 F. Supp. 172 (W.D. Okla. 1981).
Carter v. Orleans Parish Public Schools, 725 F.2d 261 (5th Cir. 1984).
Carter v. State, 611 S.W.2d 165 (Tex. Civ. App. 1981).
Casement v. Douglas County School District, No. 4935, 4 MDLR 38 (Colo. Dist. Ct. Douglas County Oct. 25, 1979).
Castillo, *In re,* 632 P.2d 855 (Utah 1981).
Castillo v. United States, 552 F.2d 1385 (10th Cir. 1977).
Caswell v. Secretary of United States Department of Health and Human Services, No. 77-0488-C-V-W-8, 7MDLR 221 (W.D. Mo. Feb. 8, 1983).
Cavitt, *In re,* 157 N.W.2d 171 (Neb. 1968), *rehearing,* 159 N.W.2d 566 (Neb. 1968), *prob. juris. noted,* 393 U.S. 1078 (1969), *appeal dismissed,* 396 U.S. 996 (1970).

C.D.M., *In re,* 627 P.2d 607 (Alaska 1981).
Central Data Center v. Commonwealth, Unemployment Compensation Board of Review, 458 A.2d 335 (Pa. Commw. Ct. 1983).
Chacko v. State, 630 S.W.2d 842 (Tex. Ct. App. 1982).
Chaplin v. Consolidated Edison Company of New York, 482 F. Supp. 1165 (S.D.N.Y. 1980).
Charles J. v. Johnson, No. 79-236 (D.S.C. 1979).
Chicago and North Western Railroad v. Labor and Industry Review Commission, 283 N.W.2d 603 (Wis. Ct. App. 1979).
Child Saving Institute v. Knobel, 37 S.W.2d 920 (Mo. 1931).
Child v. Pegelow, 321 F.2d 487 (4th Cir. 1963).
Christiansen v. Weston, 284 P. 149 (Ariz. 1930).
Christopher N. v. McDaniel, 569 F. Supp. 291 (N.D. Ga. 1983).
Christopher T. v. San Francisco Unified School District, 553 F. Supp. 1107 (N.D. Cal. 1982).
Chrysler Outboard Corporation v. Wisconsin Department of Industry, Labor and Human Relations, 14 Fair Empl. Prac. Cas. (BNA) 344 (Wis. Cir. Ct. 1976).
Ciampa v. Massachusetts Rehabilitation Commission, 718 F.2d 1 (1st Cir. 1983).
Cincinnati Association for the Blind v. NLRB, 672 F.2d 567 (6th Cir. 1982).
City of Cleburne v. Cleburne Living Center, Inc., No. 84-468 (U.S. Sup. Ct. July 1, 1985).
City of Livonia v. Department of Social Services, 333 N.W.2d 151 (Mich. Ct. App. 1983).
City of Los Angeles v. California Department of Health, 133 Cal. Rptr. 771 (Ct. App. 1976).
City of New York v. Heckler, 742 F.2d 729 (2d Cir. 1984).
City of San Francisco v. Superior Court of San Francisco, 231 P.2d 26 (Cal. 1951).
City of Santa Barbara v. Adamson, 610 P.2d 436 (Cal. 1980).
City of West Monroe v. Ouachita Association for Retarded Children, Inc., 402 So. 2d 259 (La. Ct. App. 1981).
City of White Plains v. Ferraioli, 313 N.E.3d 756 (N.Y. 1974).
Civil Service Employees Association v. Director, Manhattan Psychiatric Center, 420 N.Y.S.2d 909 (App. Div. 1979).
Civil Service Employees Association, Inc. v. Soper, 431 N.Y.S.2d 909 (Sup. Ct. 1980).
Civitans Care, Inc. v. Board of Adjustment, 437 So. 2d 540 (Ala. Civ. App. 1983).
Clark v. Clark, 372 So. 2d 814 (La. Ct. App. 1979).
Clark v. State, 266 S.E.2d 466 (Ga. 1980).
Clark v. State, 12 Ohio Rep. 483 (1843).
Clarke v. FELEC Services, Inc., 489 F. Supp. 165 (D. Alaska 1980).
Cleburne Living Center, Inc. v. City of Cleburne, 726 F.2d 191 (5th Cir. 1984).
Cleveland Board of Education v. La Fleur, 414 U.S. 632 (1974).
Clifford, *In re,* (Legal Services Corp. Region 2 filed Jan. 3, 1980).
Clites v. State, 322 N.W.2d 917 (Iowa Ct. App. 1982).
C.L.M., *In re,* 625 S.W.2d 613 (Mo. 1981).
Clonce v. Richardson, 379 F. Supp. 338 (W.D. Mo. 1974).
Cobbs v. Grant, 502 P.2d 1 (Cal. 1972).
Cochenour v. Psychiatric Security Review Board, 615 P.2d 1155 (Or. Ct. App. 1980).
Cohen v. Crumpacker, 586 S.W.2d 370 (Mo. Ct. App. 1979).
Cole v. Taylor, 301 N.W.2d 766 (Iowa 1981).
Coleman v. Casey County Board of Education, 510 F. Supp. 301 (W.D. Ky. 1980).
Coleman v. Darden, 595 F.2d 533 (10th Cir. 1979).
Coleman v. Noland Co., 21 Fair Empl. Prac. Cas. (BNA) 1248 (W.D. Va. 1980).
Colin K. v. Schmidt, 536 F. Supp. 1375 (D.R.I. 1982).
Coliseum House Hospital v. Bonis, 396 So. 2d 495 (La. Ct. App. 1981).
Coll v. Hyland, 411 F. Supp. 905 (D.N.J. 1976).
Collis v. Zoning Hearing Board, 465 A.2d 53 (Pa. Commw. Ct. 1983).
Colorado Developmental Disabilities Council v. Colorado Rural Legal Services, 5 MDLR 34 (Legal Services Corp. Region VIII filed Sept. 8, 1980).
Colyar v. Third Judicial District Court 469 F. Supp. 424 (D. Utah 1979).
Comiskey v. State, 418 N.Y.S.2d 233 (App. Div. 1979).
Commissioner of Social Services v. Patricia A., 432 N.Y.S.2d 137 (N.Y. County Fam. Ct. 1980).
Commitment of S.L., *In re,* No. A-47, 7 MDLR 378 (N.J. Sup. Ct. July 20, 1983).
Commonwealth v. Edward, 450 A.2d 15 (Pa. 1982).
Commonwealth v. Leate, 327 N.E.2d 866 (Mass. 1966).
Commonwealth v. Mosler, 4 Pa. 264 (1846).
Commonwealth v. Pear, 66 N.E. 719 (Mass. 1903), *aff'd sub nom.* Jacobson v. Massachusetts, 197 U.S. 11 (1905).
Commonwealth v. Rogers, 48 Mass. 500 (1844).
Commonwealth *ex rel.* Cummins v. Price, 218 A.2d 758 (Pa. 1966).
Commonwealth *ex rel.* Finken v. Roop, 339 A.2d 764 (Pa. Super. Ct. 1975), *cert. denied,* 424 U.S. 960 (1976).
Compensation of Gygi, *In re,* 639 P.2d 655 (Or. Ct. App. 1982).
Concerned Parents and Citizens for the Continuing Education at Malcolm X (PS 79) v. New York City Board of Education, 629 F.2d 751 (2d Cir. 1980).
Connecticut v. Heckler, No. 245 (2d Cir. Mar. 10, 1983).
Connecticut Association for Retarded Citizens v. State Board of Education, No. H-77-122, 3 MDLR 109 (D. Conn. 1978).
Connecticut Department of Income Maintenance v. Heckler, 105 S. Ct. 2210 (1985), *aff'g* 731 F.2d 1052 (2d Cir. 1984).
Connelly v. Gibbs, 445 N.E.2d 477 (Ill. App. Ct. 1983).
Conners v. New York State Association of Retarded Children, Inc., 370 N.Y.S.2d 474 (Sup. Ct. Spec. Term 1975).
Conservatorship of Bradlee, 415 A.2d 1144 (N.H. 1980).
Conservatorship of Early, 190 Cal. Rptr. 578 (Ct. App. 1983).
Consolidated Rail Corporation v. Darrone, 104 S. Ct. 1248 (1984).
Cooper, *In re,* 94 N.Y.S. 270 (App. Div. 1905).
Cooper v. Board of Medical Examiners, 123 Cal. Rptr. 563 (Ct. App. 1975).
Cooper v. Pate, 378 U.S. 546 (1964).
Corbit v. Smith, 7 Iowa 60 (D.C. Iowa 1858).
Cornell v. Creasy, 491 F. Supp. 124 (N.D. Ohio 1978).
Cornella v. Schweiker, 728 F.2d 978, 986 (8th Cir. 1984).
Corr v. Mattheis, 407 F. Supp. 847 (D.R.I. 1976).
Cosgrove v. Cosgrove, 217 N.E.2d 754 (Mass. 1966).
Costley v. Caromin House, Inc., 313 N.W.2d 21 (Minn. 1981).
Counts v. U.S. Postal Service, 17 Fair Empl. Prac. Cas. (BNA) 1161 (N.D. Fla. 1978).
Covenhoven, *In re,* 1 N.J. Eq. 19 (ch. 1830).
Covey v. Town of Somers, 351 U.S. 141 (1956).
Covington v. Harris, 419 F.2d 617 (D.C. Cir. 1969).
Cox v. Fouts, No. N13288, 4 MDLR 175 (Cal. Sup. Ct. San Diego County Jan. 8, 1980).
Cramer v. Shay, 156 Cal. Rptr. 303 (Ct. App. 1979).
Crane Neck Association, Inc. v. New York City/Long Island County Services Group, 460 N.Y.S.2d 69 (App. Div. 1983), *aff'd,* 460 N.E.2d 1336 (N.Y. 1984).
Crawford v. Brown, 151 N.E. 911 (Ill. 1926).
Crawford v. Pittman, 708 F.2d 1028 (5th Cir. 1983).
Cross, *In re,* 662 P.2d 828 (Wash. 1983).
Cross v. Harris, 418 F.2d 1095 (D.C. Cir. 1969).
Cruz v. Beto, 405 U.S. 319 (1972).
Cruz v. Ward, 558 F.2d 658 (2d Cir. 1977).
Curlender v. Bio-Science Laboratories, 165 Cal. Rptr. 477 (Ct. App. 1980).
Custody of a Minor, 434 N.E.2d 601 (Mass. 1982).

Cuyahoga County Association for Retarded Children and Adults v. Essex, 411 F. Supp. 46 (N.D. Ohio 1976).
C.V. v. State, 616 S.W.2d 441 (Tex. Civ. App. 1981).
C.W.M., *In re,* 407 A.2d 617 (D.C. 1979).
Cynthia B. v. New Rochelle Hospital Medical Center, 50 U.S.L.W. 2683 (N.Y. App. Div. May 1982).
Cypen v. Burton, No. 80-6183-Civ-ALH, 4 MDLR 417 (S.D. Fla. July 25, 1980).

Dale v. State, 355 N.Y.S. 484 (1974).
Daniels v. Kendrick, No. 16, 165-79-5, 3 MDLR 423 (Tex. Dist. Ct. Nacogdoches County May 24, 1979).
Darlene L. v. Illinois State Board of Education, 568 F. Supp. 1340 (N.D. Ill. 1983).
Dash v. Mitchell, 356 F. Supp. 1292 (D.D.C. 1972).
David B., *In re,* 5 Fam. L. Rep. (BNA) 2531 (Cal. 5th Dist. Ct. App. Mar. 28, 1979).
Davis, *In re,* 452 N.Y.S.2d 1007 (Fam. Ct. 1982).
Davis v. Balson, 461 F. Supp. 842 (N.D. Ohio 1978).
Davis v. Berry, 216 F. 413 (S.D. Iowa 1914), *rev'd for mootness,* 242 U.S. 468 (1916).
Davis v. Bucher, 451 F. Supp. 791 (E.D. Pa. 1978).
Davis v. District of Columbia Board of Education, 530 F. Supp. 1215 (D.D.C. 1982).
Davis v. Henderson, 535 F. Supp. 407 (E.D. Pa. 1982).
Davis v. Hubbard, 506 F. Supp. 915 (N.D. Ohio 1980).
Davis v. Hubbard, No. C-73-205, 4 MDLR 396 (W.D. Ohio Sept. 16, 1983).
Davis v. Page, No. 77-2731, 2 MDLR 386 (Fla. Cir. Ct. Leon County Jan. 4, 1978).
Davis v. United Air Lines, Inc., 25 Fair Empl. Prac. Cas. (BNA) 565 (E.D.N.Y 1980), *rev'd,* 662 F.2d 120 (2d Cir. 1981).
Davis v. United States, 160 U.S. 469 (1895).
Davis v. Watkins, 384 F. Supp. 487 (D. Minn. 1974).
Davis v. Watkins, 384 F. Supp. 1196 (N.D. Ohio 1974).
D.C. v. Surles, No. 78-91, 4 MDLR 169 (D. Vt. Dec. 21, 1979).
D.D., *In re,* 285 A.2d 283 (N.J. Super. Ct. App. Div. 1971).
De Marcos v. Overholser, 137 F.2d 698 (D.C. Cir. 1943).
Dean v. Jordan, 79 P.2d 331 (Wash. 1938).
Deckard v. Cerro Gordo County, No. 1C81-3014, 6 MDLR 374 (N.D. Iowa Sept. 8, 1982).
Delan v. Delan, 458 N.Y.S.2d 608 (App. Div. 1983).
Delta Airlines v. United States, 490 F. Supp. 907 (N.D. Ga. 1980).
Department of Health and Rehabilitative Services v. Davis, 616 F.2d 828 (5th Cir. 1980).
Department of Social Services v. Ryder, 425 N.Y.S.2d 944 (Rockland County Fam. Ct. 1980).
Derheim v. Hennepin County Bureau of Social Servs. 524 F. Supp. 1321 (D. Minn. 1981).
Developmental Disabilities Advocacy Center, Inc., v. Melton, 521 F. Supp. 365 (D.N.H. 1981).
Developmental Disabilities Advocacy Center, Inc. v. Melton, 689 F.2d 281 (1st Cir. 1982).
DeVito v. Murphy, No. 79 CH 2369, 3 MDLR 247 (Ill. Cook County Cir. Ct. May 1, 1979).
Dewalt v. Burkholder, No. 80-0014-A, 3 Educ. for Handicapped L. Rep. 551:550 (E.D. Va. Mar. 1980).
Dexter v. Hall, 82 U.S. (15 Wall.) 9 (1872).
Dibrin v. Superior Court, 231 P.2d 809 (Cal. 1951)
Director of Patuxent Institute v. Daniels, 221 A.2d 397 (Md.), *cert. denied,* 385 U.S. 940 (1966).
Ditler v. Workers' Compensation Appeals Board, 182 Cal. Rptr. 839 (Ct. App. 1982).
Dixon v. Attorney General, 325 F. Supp. 966 (M.D. Pa. 1971).
Dixon v. Weinberger, 405 F. Supp. 974 (D.D.C. 1975).
D.L.R., *In re,* 432 A.2d 196 (Pa. 1981).
Dockery v. Dockery, No. 51439, 1 MDLR 453 (3d Ch. Div. Pt. 2, Hamilton County, Tennessee Feb. 11, 1977).
Doe, *In re,* 649 P.2d 510 (N.M. Ct. App. 1982).
Doe, *In re,* 440 A.2d 712 (R.I. 1982).
Doe v. Beal, No. 76-1396, 2 MDLR 387 (E.D. Pa. Dec. 6, 1977).
Doe v. Board of Education, No. 135, 7 MDLR 83 (Md. Ct. App. Dec. 22, 1982).
Doe v. Brookline School Committee, 722 F.2d 910 (1st Cir. 1983).
Doe v. Doe, 385 N.E.2d 995 (Mass. 1979).
Doe v. Gallinot, 486 F. Supp. 983 (C.D. Cal. 1979).
Doe v. Koger, 480 F. Supp. 225 (N.D. Ind. 1979).
Doe v. National Transportation Safety Board, No. 79-7030, 5 MDLR 259 (9th Cir. Feb. 17, 1981).
Doe v. New York University, 442 F. Supp. 522 (S.D.N.Y. 1978).
Doe v. New York University, 666 F.2d 761 (2d Cir. 1981).
Doe v. Region 13 Mental Health-Mental Retardation Commission, 704 F.2d 1402 (5th Cir. 1983).
Doe v. Roe, 400 N.Y.S.2d 668 (1977).
Doe v. Syracuse School District, 508 F. Supp. 333 (N.D.N.Y. 1981).
Doe v. Younger, No. 4, Civ. 14407, 1 MDLR 119 (Cal. Ct. App. 4th Dist. Apr. 23, 1976).
Donaldson v. O'Connor, 493 F.2d 507, (5th Cir. 1974).
Donaldson v. O'Connor, 422 U.S. 563 (1975).
Donohue v. Copiague Union Free School District, 391 N.E.2d 1352 (N.Y. 1979).
Dooling v. Overholser, 243 F.2d 825 (D.C. Cir. 1957).
Doremus v. Farrell, 407 F. Supp. 509 (D. Neb. 1975).
Downs v. Department of Public Welfare, 368 F. Supp. 454 (E.D. Pa. 1973).
Doyle v. United States, 530 F. Supp. 1278 (C.D. Cal. 1982).
D.S.W. v. Fairbanks North Star Borough School District, 628 P.2d 554 (Alaska 1981).
Dubner v. Ambach, 426 N.Y.S.2d 164 (App. Div. 1980).
The Duchess of Kingston Trial, 20 How. St. Trials 355 (1776).
Duncan v. Louisiana, 391 U.S. 145 (1968).
Dunn v. Blumstein, 405 U.S. 330 (1972).
Duquette v. Dupuis, 582 F. Supp. 1365 (D.N.H. 1984).
Durflinger v. Artiles, 673 P.2d 86 (Kan. 1983).
Durham v. United States, 214 F.2d 862 (D.C. Cir. 1954).
Dusky v. United States, 362 U.S. 402 (1960).
Dyer v. Brooks, No. 93758, 1 MDLR 122 (Or. Cir. Ct. Marion County June 10, 1976).
Dyer v. Wall, 645 S.W.2d 317 (Tex. Ct. App. 1982).

Eberle v. Board of Public Education, 444 F. Supp. 41 (W.D. Pa. 1977).
Eckerhart v. Hensley, 475 F. Supp. 908 (W.D. Mo. 1979).
Edelman v. Jordan, 415 U.S. 651 (1974).
Edge v. Pierce, Jr., No. 82-51, 8 MPDLR 387 (D.N.J. May 22, 1984).
EE Black Ltd. v. Marshall, 23 Fair Empl. Prac. Cas. (BNA) 1253 (D. Hawaii 1980).
Eichner v. Dillon, 426 N.Y.S.2d 517 (App. Div. 1980).
Eisenstadt v. Baird, 405 U.S. 438 (1972).
Elam v. Henderson, 472 F.2d 582 (5th Cir. 1973), *cert. denied,* 414 U.S. 868 (1973).
Elliot v. Board of Education, 380 N.E.2d 1137 (Ill. App. Ct. 1978).
Ellis v. United States, 484 F. Supp. 4 (D.S.C. 1978).
Employees of the Department of Public Health and Welfare of Missouri v. Department of Public Health and Welfare, 411 U.S. 279 (1973).
Espino v. Besteiro, 520 F. Supp. 905 (S.D. Tex. 1981).

Espino v. Besteiro, 708 F.2d 1002 (5th Cir. 1983).
Estate of Bradshaw, *In re,* 606 P.2d 578 (Okla. 1980).
Estate of Davis v. Treharne, 177 Cal. Rptr. 369 (Ct. App. 1981).
Estate of Decker, *In re,* 422 N.Y.S.2d 293 Ulster County Sur. Ct. 1979).
Estate of DeKoekkoek, *In re,* 395 N.E.2d 113 (Ill. App. Ct. 1979).
Estate of Donnelly, *In re,* 445 N.E.2d 49 (Ill. App. Ct. 1983).
Estate of Fairbairn, *In re,* 392 N.Y.S.2d 152 (App. Div. 1977).
Estate of Galvin v. Galvin, 445 N.E.2d 1223 (Ill. App. Ct. 1983).
Estate of Glesenkamp, *In re,* 107 A.2d 731 (Pa. 1954).
Estate of Head, *In re,* 615 P.2d 271 (N.M. Ct. App. 1980).
Estate of Hinds v. State, 394 N.E.2d 943 (Ind. Ct. App. 1979).
Estate of Hymes, *In re,* 424 N.Y.S.2d 608 (N.Y. County Surr. Ct. 1979).
Estate of Lemley, *In re,* 653 S.W.2d 141 (Ark. Ct. App. 1983).
Estate of Roulet, 590 P.2d 1 (Cal. 1979).
Estate of Rumoro v. Leoni, 413 N.E.2d 70 (Ill. App. Ct. 1980).
Estate of Vicic, *In re,* 398 N.E.2d 420 (Ill. App. Ct. 1979).
Estate of Weber, *In re,* v. Hampshire, 401 N.E.2d 245 (Ill. App. Ct. 1980).
Estelle v. Gamble, 429 U.S. 97 (1976).
Estelle v. Smith, 451 U.S. 454 (1981).
Eubanks v. Clarke, 434 F. Supp. 1022 (E.D. Pa. 1977).
Evans v. Paderick, 443 F. Supp. 583 (E.D. Va. 1977).
Evans v. Washington, 459 F. Supp. 483 (D.D.C. 1978).
Everhardt v. City of New Orleans, 217 So. 2d 400 (1968), *appeal dismissed for want of jurisdiction,* 395 U.S. 212 (1969).
Expungement of Commitment Records of D.G., *In re,* Docket No. 2X-77, 3 MDLR 18 (N.J. Essex County Juv. & Dom. Rel. Ct. Aug. 1, 1977).
Expungement of Commitment Records of H., *In re,* Docket No. 1X-77, 2 MDLR 28 (N.J. Essex County Juv. & Dom. Rel. Ct. Mar. 8, 1977).

Fansler v. Fansler, 75 N.W.2d 1 (Mich. 1956).
Farrow, *In re,* 255 S.E.2d 777 (N.C. Ct. App. 1979).
Fast v. Ross, Civ. No. G-78-775, 3 MDLR 34 (W.D. Mich. Dec. 11, 1978).
Fasulo v. Arafeh, 378 A.2d 553 (Conn. 1977).
Fayne v. Fieldcrest Mills, Inc., 282 S.E.2d 539 (N.C. Ct. App. 1981).
Fazio v. Fazio, 378 N.E.2d 951 (Mass. 1978).
F.B., *In re,* 615 P.2d 867 (Mont. 1980).
Federal Energy Regulatory Commission v. Mississippi, 456 U.S. 742 (1982).
Fells v. Brooks, 522 F. Supp. 30 (D.D.C. 1981).
Ferry v. Powers, 433 N.E.2d 1250 (Mass. App. Ct. 1982).
Fhagen v. Miller, 278 N.E.2d 615 (Ct. App. N.Y. 1972), *cert. denied,* 409 U.S. 845 (1972).
FHD, *In re,* 80-042, No. HDY 2400-80, 5 MDLR 41 (N.J. Dep't of Human Servs. Oct. 10, 1980).
Fialkowski v. Shapp, 405 F. Supp. 946 (E.D. Pa. 1975).
Ficklin v. MacFarlan, 550 P.2d 1295 (Utah 1976).
Fidelity Financial Services, Inc. v. McCoy, 392 So. 2d 118 (La. Ct. App. 1980).
Field, *In re,* 412 A.2d 1032 (N.H. 1980).
Finney v. Arkansas Board of Correction, 505 F.2d 194 (8th Cir. 1974).
Finney v. Mabry, 534 F. Supp. 1026, 1037 (E.D. Ark. 1982).
Fireman's Fund Insurance Co. v. Industrial Commission, 579 P.2d 555 (Ariz. 1978).
Fisher, *In re,* 313 N.E.2d 851 (Ohio 1974).
Fitz v. Intermediate Unit No. 29, 403 A.2d 138 (Pa. Commw. Ct. 1979).
Flakes v. Percy, 511 F. Supp. 1325 (W.D. Wis. 1981).
Flavin v. Connecticut Board of Education, 553 F. Supp. 827 (D. Conn. 1982).
Fleuti v. Rosenberg, 302 F.2d 652 (9th Cir. 1969).
Flick v. Noot, No. 4-78 Civil 359, 3 MDLR 299 (D. Minn. July 6, 1979).
Florida Board of Bar Examiners Re: Applicant, 443 So. 2d 71 (1983).
Folliard v. Semler, 538 F.2d 121 (4th Cir. 1976), *cert. denied,* 429 U.S. 827 (1976).
Followill v. Emerson Electric Co., 674 P.2d 1050 (Kan. 1984).
Foody v. Manchester Memorial Hospital, 40 Conn. Supp. 127 (Super. Ct. 1984).
Forbis v. Forbis, 274 S.W.2d 800 (Mo. Ct. App. 1955).
Ford v. Second Judicial District Court, 635 P.2d 578 (Nev. 1981).
Forsyth v. Board of Commissioners, No. 83-4986, 6 MDLR 409 (Fla. Cir. Ct. Oct. 22, 1982).
Foster v. Tourtellotte, No. Civ. 81-5046-RMT (AAX), 6 MDLR 15 (C.D. Cal. Nov. 16, 1981).
Fowler v. United States, 633 F.2d 1258 (8th Cir. 1980).
Frazier v. Donelon, 381 F. Supp. 911 (E.D. La. 1974).
Frazier v. Levi, 440 S.W.2d 393 (Tex. Civ. App. 1969).
Frederick v. Mulcahy, No. 76-257, 4 MDLR 170 (D. Vt. filed Dec. 16, 1979).
Frederick L. v. Thomas, 419 F. Supp. 960 (E.D. Pa. 1976).
Freeman, *In re,* 636 P.2d 1334 (Colo. Ct. App. 1981).
Freeman v. Chaplic, 446 N.E.2d 1369 (Mass. 1983).
French v. Blackburn, 428 F. Supp. 1351 (M.D.N.C. 1977), *aff'd,* 443 U.S. 901 (1979).
Frendak v. United States, 408 A.2d 364 (D.C. 1979).
Frick, *In re,* 271 S.E.2d 84 (N.C. Ct. App. 1980).
Fujimoto, *In re,* 226 P. 505 (Wash. Sup. Ct. 1924).
Furr v. Spring Grove State Hospital, 454 A.2d 414 (Md. 1983).
Fussa, *In re,* No. 66110, 1 MDLR 332 (Minn. P. Ct. Hennepin County June 4, 1976).

G.A. v. Public Health Trust of Dade County, No. 80-2924, 5 MDLR 179 (S.D. Fla. filed Oct. 28, 1980).
Garrett v. McAnville, CA No. 79-1470 (D.S.C. 1979).
Gary B. v. Cronin, No. 79C5383, 4 MDLR 26 (N.D. Ill. 1980).
Gamble & Cummings, *In re,* 394 A.2d 308 (N.H. 1978).
Gandolfo, *In re,* 185 Cal. Rptr. 911 (Ct. App. 1982).
Gannon, *In re,* 301 A.2d 493 (N.J. Somerset County Ct. 1973).
Garcia v. San Antonio Metropolitan Transit Authority, 105 S. Ct. 1005 (1985).
Garcia v. Siffrin Residential Association, 407 N.E.2d 1369 (Ohio 1980).
Garcia v. State Department of Institutions, 97 P.2d 264 (Cal. Dist. Ct. App. 1939).
Gardner, *In re,* 459 N.E.2d 17 (Ill. App. Ct. 1984).
Garrett v. McAnville, CA No. 79-1470 (D.S.C. 1979).
Garrity v. Gallen, 522 F. Supp. 171 (D.N.H. 1981).
Gary B. v. Cronin, No. 79C5383, 4 MDLR 26 (N.D. Ill. June 10, 1980).
Gary W. v. Louisiana, 601 F.2d 240 (5th Cir. 1979).
G.A.S. v. S.I.S., 407 A.2d 253 (Del. Fam. Ct. 1978).
Gatson, *In re,* 593 P.2d 423 (Kan. Ct. App. 1979).
Gault, *In re,* 387 U.S. 1 (1967).
Geen v. Foschio, No. Civ. 82-83B(C), 4 MDLR 253 (W.D.N.Y. May 4, 1982).
Geitner v. Townsend, 312 S.E.2d 236 (N.C. Ct. App. 1984).
Georgia Association of Retarded Citizens v. McDaniel, 511 F. Supp. 1263, *aff'd,* 716 F.2d 1565 (11th Cir. 1983).
Gerrard v. Blackman, 401 F. Supp. 1189 (N.D. Ill. 1975).

G.H., *In re,* 218 N.W.2d 441 (N.D. 1974).
Gideon v. Wainwright, 372 U.S. 335 (1963).
Gilmore v. Utah, 429 U.S. 1012 (1976).
Gipson v. Gipson, 379 So. 2d 1171 (La. Ct. App. 1980).
Gladys J. and Laura J. v. Pearland Independent School District, 520 F. Supp. 869 (S.D. Tex. 1981).
Glenn v. Rich, 147 P.2d 849 (Utah 1944).
Goedecke v. State Department of Institutions, 603 P.2d 123 (Colo. 1979).
Goldberg v. Kelly, 397 U.S. 254 (1970).
Goldsby v. Carnes, 365 F. Supp. 395 (W.D. Mo. 1973).
Goldstein v. Coughlin, 83 F.R.D. 613 (1979).
Goldy v. Beal, 429 F. Supp. 640 (D.C. Pa. 1976).
Gomez v. Miller, 337 F. Supp. 386 (S.D.N.Y. 1971).
Good's Estate, *In re,* 274 S.W.2d 900 (Tex. Civ. App. 1955).
Goodwill Industries of Southern California v. Local Freight Drivers, 231 N.L.R.B. 49 (1977).
Goodwin v. Shapiro, 545 F. Supp. 826 (D.N.J. 1982).
Goss v. Lopez, 419 U.S. 565 (1975).
Gotkin v. Miller, 379 F. Supp. 859 (E.D.N.Y. 1974), *aff'd,* 514 F.2d 125 (2d Cir. 1975).
Grady, *In re,* 426 A.2d 467 (N.J. 1981).
Graham v. State, 566 S.W.2d 941 (Texas 1978).
Granville House, Inc. v. Department of Health and Human Services, 550 F. Supp. 628 (D. Minn. 1982).
Gray v. Sanders, 372 U.S. 368 (1963).
Green, *In re,* 417 A.2d 708 (Pa. Super. Ct. 1980).
Greenya v. George Washington University, 512 F.2d 556 (D.C. Cir., *cert. denied,* 423 U.S. 995 (1975).
Gregg v. Georgia, 428 U.S. 153 (1976).
Griswold v. Connecticut, 381 U.S. 479 (1965).
Gross v. Pomerleau, 465 F. Supp. 1167 (D. Md. 1979).
Grove City College v. Bell, 104 S. Ct. 1211 (1984).
Grymes v. Delaware Board of Education, No. 79-55, 5 MDLR 95 (D. Del. Jan. 7, 1981).
Grymes v. Madden, 672 F.2d 321 (3d Cir. 1982).
Guajardo v. Estelle, 580 F.2d 748 (5th Cir. 1978).
Guardianship and Estate of P.A.H., *In re,* 340 N.W.2d 577 (Wis. Ct. App. 1983).
Guardianship of Bassett, *In re,* 385 N.E.2d 1024 (Mass. App. Ct. 1975).
Guardianship of Becker, *In re,* No. 101981, 5 MDLR 326 (Cal. Santa Clara County Super. Ct. Aug. 7, 1981).
Guardianship of Corless, *In re,* 440 N.E.2d 1203 (Ohio Ct. App. 1982).
Guardianship of Daniel Aaron D., *In re,* 403 N.E.2d 451 (N.Y. 1980).
Guardianship of Eberhardy, *In re,* 307 N.W.2d 881 (Wis. 1981).
Guardianship of Frank, *In re,* 137 N.W.2d 218 (N.D. 1965).
Guardianship of Gallagher, *In re,* 441 N.E.2d 593 (Ohio Ct. App. 1981).
Guardianship of Hayes, *In re,* 608 P.2d 635 (Wash. 1980).
Guardianship of Howard, *In re,* 349 P.2d 547 (N.M. 1960).
Guardianship of Klisurich, *In re,* 296 N.W.2d 742 (Wis. 1980).
Guardianship of Lake, *In re,* 644 P.2d 1368 (Kan. Ct. App. 1982).
Guardianship of Nelson, *In re,* 296 N.W.2d 736 (Wis. 1980).
Guardianship of Nelson, *In re,* 663 P.2d 316 (Mont. 1983).
Guardianship of Pankey, *In re,* 38 Cal. App. 3d 919 (Dist. Ct. App. 1974).
Guardianship of Phillip B., *In re,* 188 Cal. Rptr. 781 (Ct. App. 1983).
Guardianship of Polin, *In re,* 675 P.2d 1013 (Okla. Sup. Ct. 1984).
Guardianship of Roe, *In re,* 421 N.E.2d 40 (Mass. 1981).
Guardianship of Tulley, *In re,* 146 Cal. Rptr. 266 (Ct. App. 1978).
Guardianship of Tyrrell, *In re,* 92 Ohio L. Abs. 253 (P. Ct.), *aff'd* (App. 1962), *appeal dismissed for lack of debatable constitutional question,* 190 N.E.2d 687 (1963).
Guardianship of Walters, 231 P.2d 473 (Cal. 1951).
Guertin v. Hackerman, 496 F. Supp. 593 (S.D. Tex. 1980).
Guess v. State, 157 Cal. Rptr. 618 (Ct. App. 1979).
Guffey, *In re,* 283 S.E.2d 534 (N.C. Ct. App. 1981).
Gundy v. Pauley, No. 80-CA-1737-MR, 5 MDLR 321 (Ky. Ct. App. Aug. 21, 1981).
Gurmankin v. Costanzo, 556 F.2d 184 (3d Cir. 1977).
Guzan, *In re,* 405 A.2d 1036 (Pa. 1979).

Hairston v. Drosick, 423 F. Supp. 180 (S.D.W. Va. 1976).
Halderman v. Pennhurst State School and Hospital, 446 F. Supp. 1295 (E.D. Pa. 1977), *aff'd in part, rev'd and remanded in part,* 612 F.2d 84 (3d Cir. 1979).
Halderman v. Pennhurst State School and Hospital, 612 F.2d 84 (3d Cir. 1979), *rev'd in part and remanded,* 451 U.S. 1 (1981).
Halderman v. Pennhurst State School and Hospital, 533 F. Supp. 661 (E.D. Pa. 1982).
Halderman v. Pennhurst State School and Hospital, 555 F. Supp. 1142 (E.D. Pa. 1982).
Halderman v. Pennhurst State School and Hospital, 673 F.2d 647 (3d Cir. 1982), *cert. granted,* 102 S. Ct. 2956 (1982).
Halderman v. Pennhurst State School and Hospital, 707 F.2d 702 (3d Cir. 1983).
Halderman v. Pennhurst State School and Hospital, No. 78-1490, 8 MPDLR 296 (3d Cir. filed Apr. 24, 1984).
Halderman v. Pennhurst State School and Hospital, No. 74-1345, 8 MPDLR 464 (E.D. Pa. filed July 23, 1984).
Hall's Estate, *In re,* 195 P.2d 612 (Kan. 1948).
Hamel v. Brooks, No. 78-115, 4 MDLR 97 (D. Or. Dec. 1979).
Hamilton v. Verdow, 414 A.2d 914 (Md. 1980).
Hammer v. Rosen, 165 N.E.2d 756 (N.Y. 1960).
Hanes v. Ambrose, 437 N.Y.S.2d 784 (App. Div. 1981).
Hanks v. McNeal Coal Corp., 168 P.2d 256 (Colo. 1946).
Hanrahan v. Hampton, 446 U.S. 754 (1980).
Hanson Buick, Inc. v. Chatham, 292 S.E.2d 428 (Ga. Ct. App. 1982).
Harbaugh v. Myron Harbaugh Motor, Inc., 597 P.2d 18 (Idaho 1979).
Harbeson v. Parke-Davis, Inc. 656 P.2d 483 (Wash. 1983).
Hark v. School District, 505 F. Supp. 727 (E.D. Pa. 1980).
Harkin v. Foods, Inc., No. CP 03-77-4339, 4 MDLR 260 (Iowa Civil Rights Comm'n May 15, 1980).
Harmon v. McNutt, 587 P.2d 537 (Wash. 1978)
Harper v. Virginia Board of Elections, 383 U.S. 663 (1966).
Harrell V. Wilson County Schools, 293 S.E.2d 687 (N.C. Ct. App. 1982).
Harris, *In re,* 617 P.2d 739 (Wash. 1980).
Harris v. Ballone, 681 F.2d 225 (4th Cir. 1982).
Harris v. Campbell, 472 F. Supp. 51 (E.D. Va. 1979).
Harris v. State, 615 S.W.2d 330 (Tex. Civ. App. 1981).
Hart v. County of Alameda, 485 F. Supp. 66 (N.D. Cal. 1979).
Hartogs v. Employers Mutual Insurance Company of Wisconsin, 391 N.Y.S.2d 962 (Sup. Ct. Spec. Term 1977).
Haskins, *In re,* 304 N.W.2d 125 (Wis. Ct. App. 1980).
Hatcher v. Wachtel, 269 S.E.2d 849 (W. Va. 1980).
Hathaway v. Worcester City Hospital, 475 F.2d 701 (1st Cir. 1973).
Haughton Elevator Division v. State, 367 So. 2d 1161 (La. 1979).
Hawaii v. Standard Oil Co., 405 U.S. 251 (1972).
Hawaii Department of Education v. Katherine D., 727 F.2d 809 (9th Cir. 1983).
Hawaii Housing Authority v. Midkiff, 104 S. Ct. 2321 (1984).
Hawaii Psychiatric Society v. Ariyoshi, 481 F. Supp. 1028 (D. Hawaii 1979).

Hawaii Psychiatric Society v. Ariyoshi, No. CV79-0113, 7 MDLR 229 (D. Hawaii Dec. 27, 1982).
Hawkins v. King County Department of Rehabilitative Services, 602 P.2d 361 (1979).
Hayes, *In re,* 608 P.2d 635 (Wash. 1980).
Haynes v. Lapeer Circuit Judge, 166 N.W. 938 (Mich. 1918).
Heckler v. Day, 104 S. Ct. 2249 (1984).
Heflin v. Sanford, 142 F.2d 798 (5th Cir. 1944).
Helms v. Independent School District No. 3, No. 82-C-752-C, 7 MDLR 397 (N.D. Okla. Aug. 29, 1983), *aff'd,* 750 F.2d 820 (10th Cir. 1984).
Helvey v. Rednour, 408 N.E.2d 17 (Ill. App. Ct. 1980).
Hemphill v. Smith, 91 So. 337 (Miss. 1922).
Henkin v. South Dakota Department of Social Services, 498 F. Supp. 659 (D.S.D. 1980).
Hensley v. Eckerhart, 461 U.S. 424 (1983).
Hernandez, *In re,* 264 S.E.2d 780 (N.C. Ct. App. 1980).
Herridge v. Richardson, 464 F.2d 198 (5th Cir. 1972).
Herron v. State, 287 So. 2d 759 (Miss. 1974), *cert. denied* 417 U.S. 972 (1974).
Heryford v. Parker, 396 F.2d 393 (10th Cir. 1968).
Hess v. Hess, No. 73-7139, 2 MDLR 26 (Ill. Cir. Ct. Winnebago County Feb. 4, 1977).
Hessler v. State Board of Education, 700 F.2d 134 (4th Cir. 1983).
Hessling v. City of Broomfield, 563 P.2d 12 (Colo. 1977).
Hiatt v. Soucek, 36 N.W.2d 432 (Iowa 1949).
Hicks v. United States, 511 F.2d 407 (D.C. Cir. 1975).
Hildebrand v. Smith, Civil Action No. 77-0399, 2 MDLR 182 (E.D. Mich. filed Feb. 18, 1977).
Hilden v. Evans, No. 80-511-RE, 5 MDLR 27 (D. Or. Nov. 5, 1980).
Hill v. District of Columbia Department of Employment Services, 467 A.2d 134 (D.C. 1983).
Hill v. Immigration and Naturalization Service, 52 U.S.L.W. 2165 (9th Cir. Sept. 7, 1983).
Hillsborough Association for Retarded Citizens, Inc. v. City of Temple Terrace, 332 So. 2d 610 (Fla. 1976).
Hinds v. State, 390 N.E.2d 172 (Ind. Ct. App. 1979).
Hines v. Pitt County Board of Education, 497 F. Supp. 403 (E.D.N.C. 1980).
H.L. v. Matheson, 450 U.S. 398 (1981).
Hodel v. Virginia Surface Mining & Reclamation Association, 452 U.S. 264 (1981).
Hoehn v. Hoehn, 418 N.E.2d 648 (Mass. App. Ct. 1981).
Hoffman v. Board of Education, 410 N.Y.S.2d 99 (App. Div. 1978).
Hoffman v. Board of Education, 400 N.E.2d 317 (N.Y. 1979).
Hoggro v. Pontesso, 456 F.2d 917 (10th Cir. 1972).
Holiway by Korriem v. Woods, 192 Cal. Rptr. 445 (Ct. App. 1983).
Holley, *In re,* 308 N.W.2d 341 (Neb. 1981).
Holloway v. United States, 148 F.2d 665, 666 (D.C. Cir. 1945).
Holmes, *In re,* 422 A.2d 969 (D.C. 1980).
Holmes v. Powers, 439 S.W.2d 579 (Ky. 1968).
Hoopes v. Equifax, Inc., 611 F.2d 134 (6th Cir. 1979).
Hop, *In re,* 623 P.2d 282 (Cal. 1981).
Hopkins v. Zoning Hearing Board, 423 A.2d 1082 (Pa. Commw. Ct. 1980).
Horacek v. Thone, 710 F.2d 496 (8th Cir. 1983).
Houchins v. KQED, Inc., 438 U.S. 1 (1978).
Horne v. Patton, 287 So. 2d 824 (Ala. 1973).
Hospital Services, Inc. v. Dumas, 297 N.W.2d 320 (N.D. 1980).
Howard v. Uniroyal, Inc., 719 F.2d 1552 (11th Cir. 1983).
Howard S. v. Friendswood Independent School District, 454 F. Supp. 634 (S.D. Tex. 1978).
Hruska's Guardianship, *In re,* 298 N.W. 664 (Iowa 1941).
Hudson v. Hudson, 373 So. 2d 310 (Ala. 1979).
Hughes v. Rowe, 449 U.S. 5 (1980).
Hughes v. Webster Parish Public Jury, 414 So. 2d 1353 (La. Ct. App. 1982).
Hull v. Louth, 10 N.E. 270 (Ind. 1887).
Humphrey v. Cady, 405 U.S. 504 (1972).
Hurry v. Jones, 560 F. Supp. 500 (D.R.I. 1983).
Hyman v. Jewish Chronic Disease Hospital, 206 N.E.2d 338 (N.Y. 1965).

Ibero-American Action League, Inc. v. Palma, 366 N.Y.S.2d 747 (1975).
Illinois v. Allen, 397 U.S. 337 (1970).
Indiana *ex rel.* Mental Health Commissioner v. Guardianship of Wiseman, 393 N.E.2d 235 (Ind. Ct. App. 1979).
Ingraham v. Wright, 430 U.S. 651 (1977).
Inhabitants of Winslow v. Inhabitants of Troy, 53 A. 1008 (Me. 1902).
Ipock v. Atlantic & N.C.R. Co., 74 S.E. 352 (N.C. 1912).
I.R., *In re,* No. A-3820-79, 5 MDLR 182 (N.J. Super. Ct. App. Div. Feb. 26, 1981).
Irving Independent School District v. Tatro, 104 S. Ct. 3371 (1984).

Jackson v. Foti, 670 F.2d 516 (5th Cir. 1982).
Jackson v. Godwin, 400 F.2d 529 (5th Cir. 1968).
Jackson v. Indiana, 406 U.S. 715 (1972).
Jackson v. Metropolitan Edison Co., 419 U.S. 345 (1974).
Jacobson v. Massachusetts, 197 U.S. 11 (1905).
James v. Brown, 629 S.W.2d 781 (Tex. Ct. App. 1981).
Jamison v. Farabee, No. C 780445 WHO, 7 MDLR 436 (N.D. Cal. Apr. 26, 1983).
Jankowski v. Milwaukee County, No. 79-1896, 6 MDLR 29 (Wis. Sup. Ct. Nov. 3, 1981).
Janovitz, *In re,* 403 N.E.2d 583 (Ill. App. Ct. 1980).
Jansen, *In re,* 405 So. 2d 1074 (Fla. Dist. Ct. App. 1981).
Januszko v. State, 391 N.E.2d 297 (N.Y. 1979).
J.C., *In re,* HDCC-8-76, 1 MDLR 264 (N.J. Hudson County Super. Ct. Nov. 16, 1976).
Jennings, *In re,* 453 A.2d 572 (N.J. Super. Ct. Ch. Div. 1981).
Jeralds v. Richardson, 445 F.2d 36 (7th Cir. 1971).
Jillson v. Caprio, 181 F.2d 523 (D.C. Cir. 1950).
J.L. v. Parham, 412 F. Supp. 112 (M.D. Ga. 1976).
Jobson v. Henne, 355 F.2d 129 (2d Cir. 1966).
John F. Kennedy Memorial Hospital v. Bludworth, 452 So. 2d 921 (Fla. Sup. Ct. 1984).
Johnpoll v. Elias, 513 F. Supp. 430 (E.D.N.Y. 1980).
Johnson v. Brelje, 525 F. Supp. 183 (N.D. Ill. 1981).
Johnson v. Solomon, 484 F. Supp. 278 (D. Md. 1979).
Johnson v. Zerbst, 304 U.S. 458 (1938).
Johnston v. Ciccone, 260 F. Supp. 553 (W.D. Mo. 1966).
Jones, *In re,* 612 P.2d 1211 (Kan. 1980).
Jones, *In re,* 401 N.E.2d 351 (Mass. 1980).
Jones v. Alabama, 439 So. 2d 1338 (Ala. Crim. App. 1983).
Jones v. Illinois Department of Rehabilitation Services, No. 81-1267, 6 MDLR 389 (7th Cir. Sept. 27, 1982).
Jones v. Metropolitan Atlanta Rapid Transit Authority, No. 81-7746, 6 MDLR 314 (11th Civ. Aug. 6, 1982).
Jones v. Minc, 462 P.2d 927 (Wash. 1969).
Jones v. State, 610 S.W.2d 535 (Tex. Civ. App. 1980).
Jones v. United States, 103 S. Ct. 3043 (1983).
Jones v. Wittenberg, 323 F. Supp. 793 (N.D. Ohio 1971), *aff'd sub nom.* Jones v. Metzger, 456 F.2d 854 (6th Cir. 1972).
Jorgensen v. Board of Adjustment, 336 N.W.2d 423 (Iowa 1983).
Joyner v. Dumpson, 533 F. Supp. 233 (S.D.N.Y. 1982).
J.T. Hobby & Son, Inc. v. Family Homes of Wake County, Inc., 274 S.E.2d 174 (N.C. 1981).
Junior Chamber of Commerce of Kansas City, Missouri v. Missouri

State Junior Chamber of Commerce, 508 F.2d 1031 (8th Cir. 1975).
Junior Chamber of Commerce of Rochester, Inc. v. United States Jaycees, Tulsa, Oklahoma, 495 F.2d 883 (10th Cir.), *cert. denied,* 419 U.S. 1026 (1974).
Jurek v. Texas, 428 U.S. 262 (1976).
Juvenile Case 1089, *In re,* 398 A.2d 65 (N.H. 1979).
J.W., *In re,* 130 A.2d 64 (N.J. Super. Ct. App. Div.), *cert. denied,* 132 A.2d 558 (1957).
J.W. v. City of Tacoma, 720 F.2d 1126 (9th Cir. 1983).

Kadota v. Hosogai, 608 P.2d 68 (Ariz. Ct. App. 1980).
Kaelin v. Grubbs, 682 F.2d 595 (6th Cir. 1982).
Kai v. Blum, 440 N.Y.S.2d 91 (App. Div. 1981).
Kaimowitz v. Department of Mental Health, No. 73-19434-AW, 1 MDLR 147 (Cir. Ct. of Wayne County, Mich. July 10, 1973), *reprinted in* A.D. Brooks, Law, Psychiatry, and the Mental Health System 902 (1974).
Kamp v. Kamp, No. 5514, 6 MDLR 171 (Wyo. Sup. Ct. Jan. 28, 1982).
Katic, *In re,* 439 A.2d 1235 (Pa. Super. Ct. 1982).
Katz v. Katz, 382 P.2d 331 (Kan. 1963).
Katz v. State, 258 N.Y.S.2d 912 (Ct. Cl. 1965).
K.B. v. Sprenger, No. 770292, 5 MDLR 182 (Minn. Dist. Ct. Hennepin County Sept. 10, 1980).
K.C.M. v. Alaska, No. 4764, 5 MDLR 232 (Alaska Apr. 24, 1981).
Keal v. Rhydderck, 148 N.E. 53 (Ill. 1925).
Keleher v. Putnam, 60 N.H. 30 (1880).
Kelsey v. Green, 37 A. 679 (Conn. 1897).
Kendall v. True, 391 F. Supp. 413 (W.D. Ky. 1975).
Kent v. United States, 383 U.S. 541 (1966).
Kentucky Association for Retarded Citizens v. Conn, No. C-77-0048, 1 MDLR 456 (W.D. Ky. filed June 2, 1977).
Kentucky Association for Retarded Citizens v. Conn, 510 F. Supp. 1233 (W.D. Ky. 1980), upheld in Sixth Circuit, No. 80-3560 (6th Cir. Apr. 6, 1982).
Kinner v. Florida, 382 So. 2d 756 (Fla. Dist. Ct. App. 1980).
K.K.B., *In re,* 609 P.2d 747 (Okla. 1980).
Klein v. Califano, 586 F.2d 250 (3d Cir. 1978).
Klostermann v. Cuomo, 463 N.E.2d 588 (N.Y. 1984).
Knecht v. Gillman, 488 F.2d 1136 (8th Cir. 1973).
Knight v. Radomski, 414 A.2d 1211 (Me. 1980).
Knight v. State, 297 N.W.2d 889 (Mich. 1980).
Knott v. Hughes, No. Y-80-2832, 4 MDLR 412 (D. Md. filed Oct. 27, 1980).
Kossow, *In re,* 393 A.2d 97 (D.C. Ct. App. Oct. 2, 1978).
Kramer v. Union Free School District, 395 U.S. 621 (1969).
Kremens v. Bartley, 431 U.S. 119 (1977).
Kruelle v. Biggs, 489 F. Supp. 169 (D. Del. 1980), *aff'd sub nom.*
Kruelle v. New Castle County School District, 642 F.2d 687 (3d Cir. 1981).
Kruse v. Campbell, 431 F. Supp. 180 (E.D. Va. 1977).
Kunz v. New York, 340 U.S. 290 (1951).
K.W. v. Kort, No. C-2030, Div. D, 3 MDLR 90 (Colo. Pueblo County Dist. Ct. Feb. 8, 1978).

Ladson v. Board of Education, 615 F.2d 1369 (D.C. Cir. 1980).
Lake v. Cameron, 364 F.2d 657 (D.C. Cir. 1966).
Lake v. Cameron, 267 F. Supp. 155 (D.D.C. 1967).
Lambert v. Powell, 24 So. 2d 773 (Miss. 1946).
Landman v. Royster, 333 F. Supp. 621 (E.D. Va. 1971).
Lane v. Candura, 376 N.E.2d 1232 (Mass. App. Ct. 1978).
Lang v. Braintree School Committee, 545 F. Supp. 1221 (D. Mass. 1982).
Lansing v. Commonwealth, Department of Public Welfare, 410 A.2d 982 (Pa. Commw. Ct. 1980).
Lape, *In re,* 437 N.Y.S.2d 509 (Fam. Ct. 1981).
Larry P. v. Riles, 495 F. Supp. 926 (N.D. Cal. 1979).
Larry P. v. Riles, No. 80-4027, 8 MPDLR 302 (9th Cir. Jan. 23, 1984).
Lassiter v. Department of Social Services, 452 U.S. 18 (1981).
Lassiter v. Northampton Election Board, 360 U.S. 45 (1959).
Laura A., *In re,* 419 N.Y.S.2d 40 (Fam. Ct. 1979).
Laura M. v. Special School District No. 1, 79 Civ. 123, 3 Educ. for Handicapped L. Rep. 552:152 (D. Minn. Jan. 21, 1980).
Laurent v. Brelji, 392 N.E.2d 929 (Ill. App. Ct. 1979).
Lausche v. Commissioner of Public Welfare, 225 N.W.2d 366 (Minn. 1974); *cert. denied,* 420 U.S. 993 (1975).
Le Strange v. Consolidated Rail Corporation, 687 F.2d 767 (3d Cir. 1982).
Leach v. Akron General Medical Center, 426 N.E.2d 809 (Ohio Ct. Com. Pl. 1980).
Leedy v. Hartnett, 510 F. Supp. 1125 (M.D. Pa. 1981).
Leland v. Oregon, 343 U.S. 790 (1952).
Lelsz v. Kavanagh, No. S. 74-95-CA, 7 MDLR 379 (E.D. Tex. July 21, 1983), *appeal dismissed,* 710 F.2d 1040 (5th Cir. 1983).
Leon R. v. Bulliard, Civ. No. H-76-327, 3 MDLR 27 (D. Conn. Sept. 20, 1978).
Lessard v. Schmidt, 349 F. Supp. 1078 (E.D. Wis. 1972), *vacated and remanded,* 414 U.S. 473 (1974), *on remand,* 379 F. Supp. 1376 (E.D. Wis. 1974), *vacated and remanded on appeal,* 421 U.S. 957 (1975).
Lessard v. Schmidt, 413 F. Supp. 1318 (E.D. Wis. 1976) (*reinstating* prior judgment of District Court, 349 F. Supp. 1078).
LeVier v. Woodson, 443 F.2d 360 (10th Cir. 1971).
Levine v. New Jersey Department of Institutions and Agencies, 418 A.2d 229 (N.J. 1980).
Levy v. City of New York, 345 N.E.2d 556 (N.Y. 1976).
Levy v. Commonwealth, Department of Education, 399 A.2d 159 (Pa. Commw. Ct. 1979).
Lewis, *In re,* 403 A.2d 1115 (Del. 1979).
Lewis v. Donahue, 437 F. Supp. 112 (W.D. Okla. 1977).
Lewis v. Ottaviano, Civ. Act. No. 76-0422-H, 2 MDLR 26 (S.D. W.Va. Mar. 1, 1977).
Lifschutz, *In re,* 467 P.2d 557 (Cal. 1970).
Linder, *In re,* 419 N.Y.S.2d 375 (Sup. Ct. App. Div. 1979).
Linder v. Wake County Board of Education, 273 S.E.2d 735 (N.C. Ct. App. 1981).
Lipari v. Sears Roebuck and Co., 497 F. Supp. 185 (D. Neb. 1980).
Lippmann v. Johnson, 429 N.E.2d 167 (Ohio Ct. App. 1980).
Little v. Little, 576 S.W.2d 493 (Tex. Civ. App. 1979).
Littreal v. Littreal, 253 S.W.2d 247 (Ky. 1952).
Lizotte v. Secretary of Health and Human Services, 654 F.2d 127 (1st Cir. 1981).
Lloyd v. Regional Transportation Authority, 548 F.2d 1277 (7th Cir. 1977).
Lockett v. Ohio, 438 U.S. 586 (1978).
Locklear v. Hultine, 528 F. Supp. 982 (D. Kan. 1981).
Logan v. Arafeh, 346 F. Supp. 1265 (D. Conn. 1972), *aff'd sub nom.* Briggs v. Arafeh, 411 U.S. 911 (1973).
Loh Lin v. Burroughs Corporation, 427 N.Y.S.2d 78 (App. Div. 1980).
Look v. Dean, 108 Mass. 116 (1871).
Lopucki v. Ford Motor Co., 311 N.W.2d 338 (Mich. Ct. App. 1981).
Lora v. Board of Education, 623 F.2d 248 (2d Cir. 1980).
Loughran v. Flanders, 470 F. Supp. 110 (D. Conn. 1979).
Louisiana v. Peters, 441 So. 2d 403 (La. Ct. App. 1983).
Lowry *ex rel.* Joyner v. Dumpson, 712 F.2d 770 (2d Cir. 1983).

L.R.C. v. Klein, 400 A.2d 496 (N.J. Super. Ct. App. Div. 1979).
Lynch v. Baxley, 386 F. Supp. 378 (M.D. Ala. 1974).
Lynch v. Baxley, 651 F.2d 387 (5th Cir. 1981).
Lynch v. Maher, 507 F. Supp. 1268 (D. Conn. 1981).
Lyon's Guardianship, *In re,* 299 N.W. 322 (Neb. 1941).

Mabry v. Mabry, 90 S.E.2d 221 (N.C. 1955).
McAuliffe v. Carlson, 386 F. Supp. 1245 (D. Conn. 1975).
McCoy v. Secretary of Health and Human Services, 532 F. Supp. 359 (S.D. Ohio 1981).
McDonald v. United States, 312 F.2d 847 (D.C. Cir. 1962).
McGarrah v. State Accident Insurance Fund Corporation, 675 P.2d 159 (Or. 1983).
McGill v. Alton, No. 74-1164, 1 MDLR 19 (W.D. Pa. Jan. 26, 1976).
McGrath v. Weinberger, 541 F.2d 249 (10th Cir. 1976).
McGrew v. Mutual Life Insurance Co., 64 P. 103 (Cal. 1901).
McGuffin v. State, 571 S.W.2d 56 (Tex. Civ. App. 1978).
McInnis v. Ogilvie, 394 U.S. 322 (1969).
McInnis v. Shapiro, 293 F. Supp. 327 (N.D. Ill. 1968), *aff'd sub nom.* McInnis v. Ogilvie, 394 U.S. 322 (1969).
McIntosh v. Milano, 403 A.2d 500 (N.J. 1979).
McKeiver v. Pennsylvania, 403 U.S. 528 (1971).
McKenzie v. Jefferson, 566 F. Supp. 404 (D.D.C. 1983).
McLaughlin, *In re,* 87 N.J. Eq. 138, 102 A. 439 (Ch. 1917).
McMahon v. Anaconda Co., 678 P.2d 661 (Mont. 1984).
M'Naghten's Case, 10 Clark & Fin. 200, 8 Eng. Rep. 718 (1843).
McNeil v. Director, Patuxent Institution, 407 U.S. 245 (1972).
McRae v. McRae, 250 N.Y.S.2d 778 (Sup. Ct. 1964).
Mackey v. Procunier, 477 F.2d 877 (9th Cir. 1973).
Maine v. Thiboutot, 448 U.S. 1 (1980).
Majors v. Housing Authority, 652 F.2d 454 (5th Cir. 1981).
Malloy v. Hogan, 378 U.S. 1 (1964).
Manchester Board of Education v. Connecticut Board of Education, 41 Conn. L.J. 35 (Conn. 1980).
Manecke v. School Board, 553 F. Supp. 787 (M.D. Fla. 1982).
Maness v. Meyers, 419 U.S. 466 (1975).
Mangeris v. Gordon, 580 P.2d 481 (Nev. 1978).
Manhattan State Citizens' Group, Inc. v. Bass, 524 F. Supp. 1270 (S.D.N.Y. 1981).
Marcia R., *In re,* No. C267-75 Rc, 4 MDLR 258 (Vt. Rutland County Super. Ct. June 11, 1980).
Markey v. Wachtel, 264 S.E.2d 437 (W. Va. Sup. Ct. App. 1979).
Maroon v. State Department of Mental Health, 411 N.E.2d 404 (Ind. Ct. App. 1980).
Marquardt, *In re,* 427 N.E.2d 411 (Ill. App. Ct. 1981).
Marriage of Higgason, *In re,* 516 P.2d 289 (Cal. 1973).
Marshall v. Kleinman, 438 A.2d 1199 (Conn. 1982).
Martin v. Commonwealth, Department of Labor and Industry, 461 A.2d 1351 (Pa. Commw. Ct. 1983).
Martinez v. Bynum, 461 U.S. 321 (1983).
Martinez v. California, 444 U.S. 277 (1980).
Marvin H. v. Austin Independent School District, 714 F.2d 1348 (5th Cir. 1983).
Maryland v. Wirtz, 392 U.S. 183 (1968).
Maryland Association for Retarded Citizens v. Maryland, No. 77676 (Baltimore County Cir. Ct. May 3, 1974).
Massey v. Moore, 348 U.S. 105 (1954).
Mathews v. Eldridge, 424 U.S. 319 (1975).
Mathews v. Oregon, 46 Or. App. 757, *cert. denied,* 49 U.S.L.W. 3743 (U.S. Apr. 6, 1981).
Matter of Josiah Oakes, 8 Law Rep. 123 (Mass. 1845).
Matthews v. Hardy, 420 F.2d 607 (D.C. Cir. 1969), *cert. denied,* 397 U.S. 1010 (1970).
Mattie T. v. Halloday, No. DC 75-31-S, 2 MDLR 177 (N.D. Miss. July 28, 1977).
Mattie T. v. Halloday, No. DC 75-31-S, 3 MDLR 98 (N.D. Miss. Jan. 26, 1979).
Mavroudis v. Superior Court of San Mateo County, 162 Cal. Rptr. 724 (Cal. Ct. App. 1980).
Maxwell v. Maxwell, 177 N.W. 541 (Iowa 1920).
Meachum v. Fano, 427 U.S. 215 (1976).
Medley v. Ginsberg, No. 78-2099 CH, 5 MDLR 393 (S.D.W. Va. Oct. 8, 1981).
Medley v. Ginsberg, 492 F. Supp. 1294 (S.D.W. Va. 1980).
Meier v. Ross General Hospital, 445 P.2d 519 (Cal. 1968).
Meisel v. Kremens, 405 F. Supp. 1253 (E.D. Pa. 1975).
Melville v. Sabbatino, 30 Conn. Supp. 320 (Super. Ct. 1973).
Meneses v. Secretary of Health, Education and Welfare, 442 F.2d 803 (D.C. Cir. 1971).
Mental Health Association of Minnesota v. Heckler, No. 83-1263, 7 MDLR 455 (8th Cir. Nov. 4, 1983).
Mental Health Association of Minnesota v. Schweiker, No. 4-82-Civ.-83, 7 MDLR 18 (D. Minn. Dec. 22, 1982).
Mental Health Association of Union County, Inc. v. City of Elizabeth, 434 A.2d 688 (N.J. Super. Ct. Law Div. 1981).
Merchants National Bank and Trust Co. of Fargo v. United States, 272 F. Supp. 409 (D.N.D. 1967).
Merriken v. Cressman, 364 F. Supp. 913 (E.D. Pa. 1973).
Metropolitan Life Insurance Co. v. Massachusetts, 105 S. Ct. 2380 (1985).
Meyer, *In re,* 438 N.E. 2d 639 (Ill. App. Ct. 1982).
Meyerson v. State of Arizona, 526 F. Supp. 129 (D. Ariz. 1981).
Michigan Ass'n for Retarded Citizens v. Wayne County Probate Judge, No. 77-535, 2 MDLR 364 (Mich. Ct. App. Nov. 9, 1977).
Michigan Department of Treasury v. Ivy, 46 U.S.L.W. 2205 (Mich. Oct. 6, 1977).
Mickle v. Henrichs, 262 F. 687 (D. Nev. 1918).
Middlesex County Sewerage Authority v. National Sea Clammers Association, 453 U.S. 1 (1981).
Miener v. Missouri, 673 F.2d 969 (8th Cir. 1982).
Millard v. Cameron, 373 F.2d 468 (D.C. Cir. 1966).
Millard v. Harris, 406 F.2d 964 (D.C. Cir. 1968).
Miller v. Abilene Christian University, 517 F. Supp. 437 (N.D. Tex. 1981).
Miller v. Woods, 196 Cal. Rptr. 69 (Ct. App. 1983).
Mills, *In re,* 27 N.W.2d 375 (Wis. 1947).
Mills v. Board of Education, 348 F. Supp. 866 (D.D.C. 1972).
Mills v. Board of Education, No. 1939-71, 4 MDLR 267 (D.D.C. June 18, 1980).
Mills v. Rogers, 457 U.S. 291 (1982).
Minnesota v. Andring, 342 N.W.2d 128 (Minn. 1983).
Minnesota *ex rel.* Pearson v. Probate Court, 309 U.S. 270 (1940).
Miranda v. Arizona, 384 U.S. 436 (1966).
Mitchell v. State, 176 So. 743 (Miss. 1937).
Mitchell v. United States, 316 F.2d 354 (D.C. Cir. 1963).
Mitchell C. v. Board of Education, 414 N.Y.S.2d 923 (App. Div. 1979).
M.K.R., *In re,* 515 S.W.2d 467 (Mo. 1974) (en banc).
Moe, *In re,* 432 N.E.2d 712 (Mass. 1982).
Monahan v. Nebraska, 645 F.2d 592 (8th Cir. 1981).
Monahan v. Nebraska, 687 F.2d 1164 (8th Cir. 1982).
Money v. Krall, 180 Cal. Rptr. 376 (Ct. App. 1982).
Mongony v. Bevilacqua, 432 A.2d 661 (R.I. 1981).
Monmouth Medical Center v. Harris, No. 78-3139, 4 MDLR 264 (D.N.J. May 16, 1980), *aff'd on appeal,* No. 80-2138, 5 MDLR 194 (3d Cir. Apr. 1, 1981).

Moore v. City of East Cleveland, 431 U.S. 494 (1977).
Moosa v. Abdalla, 178 So. 2d 273 (La. 1965).
Morales v. Turman, 535 F.2d 864 (5th Cir. 1976).
Morgan v. Potter, No. 25657, 3 MDLR 109 (Ohio C.P. May 11, 1978).
Morphis v. Dallas Housing Authority, No. CA3-80-0830-G, 4 MDLR 330 (N.D. Tex. July 2, 1980).
Morrissey v. Brewer, 408 U.S. 471 (1971).
Morrow v. State, 443 A.3d 108 (Md. 1982).
Mountain View-Los Altos Union High School District v. Sharron B.H., 709 F.2d 28 (9th Cir. 1983).
Moyer, *In re,* 263 So. 2d 286 (Fla. Dist. Ct. App. 1972).
M.R. v. Milwaukee Public Schools, 495 F. Supp. 864 (E.D. Wis. 1980).
Mrs. A.J. v. Special School District No. 1, 478 F. Supp. 418 (D. Minn. 1979).
Mullaney v. Wilbur, 421 U.S. 684 (1975).
Muller v. De Vries, 188 N.W. 885 (Iowa 1922).
Munden v. Munden, No. 1-279A56, 4 MDLR 107 (Ind. Ct. App. Dec. 26, 1979).

Nason v. Superintendent of Bridgewater State Hospital, 233 N.E.2d 908 (Mass. 1968).
Natanson v. Kline, 350 P.2d 1093 (Kan. 1960).
National League of Cities v. Marshall, 429 F. Supp. 703 (D.D.C. 1977) (declaratory judgment Mar. 9, 1977, amended May 25, 1977).
National League of Cities v. Usery, 426 U.S. 833 (1976), *rev'd and remanded sub nom.* Garcia v. San Antonio Metropolitan Transit Authority, 105 S. Ct. 1005 (1985).
Naughton v. Goodman, 363 A.2d 1345 (R.I. 1976).
Near v. Minnesota, 283 U.S. 697 (1931).
Nebbia v. New York, 291 U.S. 502 (1934).
Nebraska Methodist Hospital v. City of Omaha, No. 83-0-534, 8 MPDLR 35 (D. Neb. Oct. 7, 1983).
Nectow v. Cambridge, 277 U.S. 183 (1928).
Negron v. Ward, 74 Civ. 1480, 1 MDLR 191 (S.D.N.Y. July 13, 1976).
Nelson v. Sandritter, 351 F.2d 284 (9th Cir. 1965).
Nelson v. Tuscarora Intermediate Unit No. 11, 426 A.2d 1234 (Pa. Commw. Ct. 1981).
Nemser, *In re,* 273 N.Y.S.2d 624 (Sup. Ct. 1966).
New Hampshire v. Brosseau, No. 82-064, 8 MPDLR 128 (N.H. Sup. Ct. Dec. 1, 1983).
New Hampshire v. Pike, 49 N.H. 399 (1869).
New Hampshire v. Robert H., No. 78-090, 3 MDLR 22 (Merrimack County Prob. Ct. Oct. 30, 1978).
New Jersey Association for Retarded Citizens, Inc. v. New Jersey Department of Human Services, 445 A.2d 704 (N.J. Sup. Ct. 1982).
New Mexico Association for Retarded Citizens v. New Mexico, 495 F. Supp. 391 (D.N.M. 1980).
New Mexico Association for Retarded Citizens v. New Mexico, 678 F.2d 847 (10th Cir. 1982).
New Mexico Health and Social Services Department v. Smith, 600 P.2d 294 (N.M. Ct. App. 1979).
New York v. 11 Cornwell Company, 508 F. Supp. 273 (E.D.N.Y. 1981), *aff'd,* 695 F.2d 34 (2d Cir. 1982).
New York *ex rel.* Overton v. Director, Central New York Psychiatric Center, 418 N.Y.S.2d 254 (Sup. Ct. 1979).
New York Gaslight Club, Inc. v. Carey, 447 U.S. 54, 70 n.9 (1980).
New York State Association for Retarded Children, Inc. v. Carey, 393 F. Supp. 715 (E.D.N.Y. 1975).
New York State Association for Retarded Children, Inc. v. Carey, 456 F. Supp. 85 (E.D.N.Y. 1978).
New York State Association for Retarded Children, Inc. v. Carey, 706 F.2d 956 (2d Cir. 1983).
New York Times Co. v. United States, 403 U.S. 713 (1971).
Nobles v. Georgia, 168 U.S. 398 (1897).
Noot *ex rel.* Minnesota v. Heckler, 718 F.2d 852 (8th Cir. 1983).
North v. District of Columbia Board of Education, 471 F. Supp. 136 (D.D.C. 1979).
North Carolina Association for Retarded Children v. North Carolina, 420 F. Supp. 451 (M.D.N.C. 1976).
Northern California Psychiatric Society v. City of Berkeley, No. 566778-3 (Cal. Super. Ct. Sept. 14, 1983).
Novak v. Rathnam, 457 N.E.2d 158 (Ill App. Ct. 1983).

O'Brien v. Skinner, 414 U.S. 524 (1974).
O'Connor v. Donaldson, 422 U.S. 563 (1975).
Ochs v. Borrelli, 445 A.2d 883 (Conn. 1982).
Office of Federal Contract Compliance Programs v. Western Electric Company, NO. 80-OFCCP-29, 5 MDLR 171 (U.S. Dep't. of Labor Mar. 4, 1981).
Ohlinger v. Watson, 652 F.2d 775 (9th Cir. 1980).
Olmstead v. United States, 277 U.S. 438 (1928).
Ormond v. Garrett, 175 S.E.2d 371 (N.C. Ct. App. 1970).
Osborne, *In re,* 294 A.2d 372 (D.C. 1972).
O.S.D., *In re,* 672 P.2d 1304 (Alaska 1983).
Oswald, *In re,* 28 A.2d 299 (N.J. Ch. 1942).
Owen v. Owen, 376 So. 2d 26 (Fla. Dist. Ct. App. 1979).

Painter v. Horne Brothers, Inc., 710 F.2d 143 (4th Cir. 1983).
Palmigiano v. Travisono, 317 F. Supp. 776 (D.R.I. 1970).
Panitch v. Wisconsin, 371 F. Supp. 955 (E.D. Wis. 1977).
Papchristou v. City of Jacksonville, 405 U.S. 156 (1972).
Parental Rights of PP, *In re,* 648 P.2d 512 (Wyo. 1982).
Parents in Action on Special Education (PASE) v. Hannon, 506 F. Supp. 831 (N.D. Ill. 1980).
Parham v. J.R., 442 U.S. 584 (1979).
Paris Adult Theatre I v. Slaton, 413 U.S. 49 (1973).
Parker v. Barefoot, 300 S.E.2d 571 (N.C. Ct. App. 1983).
Parks v. Pavkovic, 557 F. Supp. 1280 (N.D. Ill. 1983).
Parsons v. Estate of Wambaugh, 442 N.E.2d 571 (Ill. App. Ct. 1982).
Parton v. Robinson, 574 S.W.2d 679 (Ky. Ct. App. 1978).
Pasbrig, *In re,* No. 22305, 3 MDLR 182 (Wis. Milwaukee County Cir. Ct. in Probate Dec. 19, 1978).
Pate v. Robinson, 383 U.S. 375 (1966).
Pathfinder Co. v. Industrial Comm'n, 343 N.E.2d 913 (Ill. 1976).
Patsel v. District of Columbia Board of Education, 530 F. Supp. 660 (D.D.C. 1982).
Patton v. Dumpson, 498 F. Supp. 933 (S.D.N.Y. 1980).
Paul P., *In re,* No. 114, 3 MDLR 187 (Pa. Sec'y of Educ. Spec. Educ. App. Sept. 26, 1978).
Paulson v. Idaho Forest Industries, Inc. 591 P.2d 143 (Idaho 1979).
Peck v. Califano, 454 F. Supp. 484 (D. Utah 1977).
Pegues v. United States, 415 A.2d 1374 (D.C. 1980).
Pehowski v. Blatnik, No. 78-0030-W(H), 4 MDLR 174 (N.D.W. Va. Apr. 14, 1980).
Pell v. Procunier, 417 U.S. 817 (1974).
Pennhurst State School and Hospital v. Halderman, 451 U.S. 1 (1981).
Pennhurst State School and Hospital v. Halderman, 104 S. Ct. 900 (1984).

Pennsylvania Association for Retarded Children v. Commonwealth, 343 F. Supp. 279 (E.D. Pa. 1972).
Pennsylvania *ex rel.* Platt v. Platt, 404 A.2d 410 (Super. Ct. 1979).
Penny N., *In re,* 414 A.2d 541 (N.H. 1980).
Penobscot Area Housing Development Corporation v. City of Brewer, 434 A.2d 14 (Me. 1981).
People v. Breese, 213 N.E.2d 500 (Ill. 1966).
People v. Burnick, 535 P.2d 352 (Cal. Sup. Ct. 1975).
People v. Collins, 429 N.E.2d 531 (Ill. App. Ct. 1981).
People v. Couvion, 211 N.E.2d 746 (Ill. 1965).
People v. Dalfonso, 321 N.E.2d 379 (Ill. App. Ct. 1974).
People v. De Anda, 170 Cal. Rptr. 830 (Ct. App. 1980).
People v. Freeman, 636 P.2d 1134 (Colo. Ct. App. 1981).
People v. Freshley, 451 N.Y.S.2d 73 (App. Div. 1982).
People v. Froom, 166 Cal. Rptr. 786 (Ct. App. 1980).
People v. Germich, 431 N.E.2d 1092 (Ill. App. Ct. 1981).
People v. Goedecke, 423 P.2d 777 (Cal. 1967).
People v. Gomez, 185 Cal. Rptr. 155 (Ct. App. 1982).
People v. Hays, 126 Cal. Rptr. 770 (Ct. App. 1976).
People v. Heral, 342 N.E.2d 34 (Ill. 1976).
People v. Hill, 391 N.E.2d 51 (Ill. App. Ct. 1979).
People v. McLeod, 258 N.W.2d 214 (Mich. Ct. App. 1979).
People v. McQuillan, 221 N.W.2d 569 (Mich. 1974).
People v. Nunn, 438 N.E.2d 1342 (Ill. App. Ct. 1982).
People v. Pembrock, 342 N.E.2d 28 (Ill. 1976).
People v. Phipps, 398 N.E.2d 650 (Ill. App. Ct. 1979).
People v. Prosenjit Poddar, 518 P.2d 342 (Cal. 1974).
People v. Reliford, 382 N.E.2d 72 (Ill. App. Ct. 1978).
People v. Renaissance Project, Inc., 324 N.E.2d 355 (N.Y. 1975).
People v. Rensing, 199 N.E.2d 489 (N.Y. 1964).
People v. Rizer, 409 N.E.2d 383 (Ill. App. Ct. 1980).
People v. Salas, 165 Cal. Rptr. 82 (Ct. App. 1980).
People v. Spencer, 457 N.E.2d 473 (Ill. App. Ct. 1983).
People v. Stanley, 217 N.E.2d 636 (N.Y. 1966).
People v. Superior Court of California for Humboldt County, 157 Cal. Rptr. 157 (Ct. App. 1979).
People v. Taylor, 618 P.2d 1127 (Colo. 1980).
People v. Wells, 202 P.2d 53 (Cal. 1949).
People v. Wolff, 394 P.2d 959, (Cal. 1964).
People *ex rel.* Anonymous No. 1 v. La Burt, 217 N.E. 2d 31 (N.Y. 1966).
People *ex rel.* Book v. Hooker, No. 77-2533, 2 MDLR 545 (Mich. Ct. App. May 22, 1978).
People *ex rel.* Nabstedt v. Barger, 121 N.E.2d 781 (Ill. 1954).
People *ex rel.* Wallace v. Labrenz, 104 N.E.2d 769, *cert. denied,* 344 U.S. 824 (1952).
Peret v. Purse, No. 79505, 7 MDLR 269 (Idaho Dist. Ct. 1982).
Ex parte Perry, 43 A.2d 885 (N.J. Eq. 1945).
Peter W. v. San Francisco Unified School District, 131 Cal. Rptr. 854 (Ct. App. 1976).
Petersen v. State, 671 P.2d 230 (Wash. 1983).
Petition of Longstaff, *In re,* No. 82-1218, 7 MDLR 458 (5th Cir. Sept. 28, 1983).
Philipp v. Carey, 517 F. Supp. 513 (N.D.N.Y. 1981).
Phillip B., *In re,* 156 Cal. Rptr. 48 (Ct. App. 1979).
Phillips v. United States, 508 F. Supp. 537 (D.S.C. 1980).
Phipps v. New Hanover County Board of Education, 551 F. Supp. 732 (E.D.N.C. 1982).
Pierce v. Society of Sisters, 268 U.S. 510 (1925).
Pinkerton v. Moye, 509 F. Supp. 107 (W.D.W. Va. 1981).
Planned Parenthood of Missouri v. Danforth 428 U.S. 52 (1976).
Plitt v. Madden, 413 A.2d 867 (Del. 1980).
Plummer v. Branstad, 731 F.2d 574 (8th Cir. 1984).
Plyler v. Doe, 457 U.S. 202 (1982).
Poe v. Califano, Civ. Act. No. 74-1800, 3 MDLR 10 (D.D.C. Sept. 25, 1978).
Poe v. Lynchburg Training School and Hospital, No. 80-0172 (L), 5 MDLR 33 (W.D. Va. filed Dec. 29, 1980).
Polaski v. Heckler, 751 F.2d 943 (8th Cir. 1984).
P-1 v. Shedd, No. 78-58, 3 MDLR 167 (D. Conn. Mar. 23, 1979).
Ponter v. Ponter, 342 A.2d 574 (N.J. Super. Ct. Ch. Div. 1975).
Porter v. Estelle, 709 F.2d 944, 949 (5th Cir. 1983).
Powell v. Alabama, 287 U.S. 45 (1932).
Powell v. Defore, 699 F.2d 1078 (11th Cir. 1983).
Powell v. Florida, 579 F.2d 324 (5th Cir. 1978).
Powell v. Texas, 392 U.S. 514 (1968).
Prewitt v. United States Postal Service, 662 F.2d 292 (5th Cir. 1981).
Price v. Price, 255 S.E.2d 652 (N.C. Ct. App. 1979).
Price v. Sheppard, 239 N.W.2d 95 (Minn. 1976).
Prince v. Massachusetts, 321 U.S. 158 (1944).
Procanik v. Cillo, 478 A.2d 755 (N.J. 1984).
Prochaska v. Brinegar, 102 N.W.2d 870 (Iowa 1960).
Proctor v. Harris, 413 F.2d 383 (D.C. Cir. 1969).
Procunier v. Martinez, 416 U.S. 396 (1974).
Proffitt v. Florida, 428 U.S. 242 (1976).
Project Release v. Prevost, 722 F.2d 960 (2d Cir. 1983).
Pugh v. Locke, 406 F. Supp. 318 (M.D. Ala. 1976).
Pushkin v. Regents of the University of Colorado, 658 F.2d 1372 (10th Cir. 1981).

Quada v. Quada, 396 S.W.2d 232 (Tex. Civ. App. 1965).
Quenot v. Iowa Department of Job Services, 339 N.W.2d 624 (Iowa Ct. App. 1983).
Quesnell v. State, 517 P.2d 568 (Wash. 1968).
Quinlan, *In re,* 137 N.J. Super. 227 (1975).
Quinlan, *In re,* 355 A.2d 647, *cert. denied, sub nom.* Garger v. New Jersey, 429 U.S. 922 (1976).
Quogue Union Free School District No. 3 v. County of Suffolk, 424 N.Y.S.2d 261 (App. Div. 1980).

R., *In re,* 641 P.2d 704 (Wash. 1982).
Rainey v. Tennessee Department of Education, No. A-3100, 1 MDLR 336 (Tenn. Ch. Ct. Davidson County Jan. 28, 1977).
R.A.J. v. Miller, No. C-A-3-74-394-H, 6 MDLR 373 (N.D. Tex. Apr. 22, 1982).
Raleigh Fitkin-Paul Morgan Memorial Hospital v. Anderson, 201 A.2d 537 (N.J. 1964), *cert. denied.,* 377 U.S. 985 (1964).
Ramos, *In re,* 445 N.Y.S.2d 891 (Sup. Ct. Bronx County 1981).
Reagon v. State, 251 N.E.2d 829 (Ind. 1969), *cert. denied,* 397 U.S. 1042 (1970).
Rees v. Peyton, 384 U.S. 312 (1966).
Region 10 Client Management, Inc. v. Town of Hampstead, 424 A.2d 207 (N.H. 1980).
Reigosa v. State, 362 So. 2d 714 (Fla. Dist. Ct. App. 1978).
Rennie v. Klein, 462 F. Supp. 1131 (D.N.J. 1978), *modified and remanded,* 653 F.2d 836 (3d Cir. 1981).
Rennie v. Klein, 476 F. Supp. 1294 (D.N.J. 1979).
Rennie v. Klein, 458 U.S. 1119 (1982).
Rennie v. Klein, 720 F.2d 266 (3d Cir. 1983).
Residents of Los Lunas Hospital and Training School, *In re,* No. 111-Misc., 2 MDLR 710 (N.M. Valencia County Dist. Ct. Feb. 13, 1978).
Rettig v. Kent City School District, 539 F. Supp. 768 (N.D. Ohio 1981).
Rettig v. Kent City School District, 720 F.2d 463 (6th Cir. 1983).
Reynolds v. Ross, 25 Fair Empl. Prac. Cas. (BNA) 462 (N.D.N.Y. 1981).
Reynolds v. Sims, 377 U.S. 533 (1964).

Richard, *In re,* 655 S.W.2d 110 (Mo. Ct. App. 1983)
Richard F., *In re,* No. 01-80-1047, 4 MDLR 337 (E.D.O.C.R. June 16, 1980).
Riggins v. Riggins, 294 P.2d 751 (Cal. Dist. Ct. App. 1956).
Riggs v. American Tract Society, 84 N.Y. 330 (1881).
Riley v. Ambach, 508 F. Supp. 1222 (E.D.N.Y. 1980), *rev'd,* 668 F.2d 635 (2d Cir. 1981).
Roanoke City Public Schools, *In re,* No. 03801083, 5 MDLR 241 (Va. E.D.O.C.R. Nov. 20, 1980).
Robak v. United States, 658 F.2d 471 (7th Cir. 1981).
Robert M. v. Benton, 622 F.2d 370 (8th Cir. 1980).
Roberts, *In re,* 4 MDLR 427 (E.E.O.C. Sept. 1980).
Roberts v. Louisiana, 428 U.S. 325 (1976).
Roberts v. Paine, 199 A. 112 (Conn. 1938).
Robinson v. California, 370 U.S. 660 (1962).
Rodriguez v. Miera, No. 78-194P, 2 MDLR 565 (D.N.M. Apr. 11, 1978) (consent judgment).
Roe v. Ingraham, 403 F. Supp. 931 (S.D.N.Y. 1975).
Roe v. Wade, 410 U.S. 113 (1973).
Roether v. Roether, 191 N.W. 576 (Wis. 1923).
Roger S., *In re,* Crim. 19558, 2 MDLR 7 (Cal. July 18, 1977).
Rogers v. Commissioner of Department of Mental Health, 458 N.E. 2d 308 (Mass. 1983).
Rogers v. Frito Lay, Inc., 611 F.2d 1074 (5th Cir. 1980), *cert. denied,* 449 U.S. 889 (1980).
Rogers v. Okin, 478 F. Supp. 1342 (D. Mass. 1979), *modified,* 634 F.2d 650 (1st Cir. 1980), *cert. granted,* 101 S. Ct. 1972 (1981).
Rolfe v. Psychiatric Security Review Board, 633 P.2d 846 (Or. Ct. App. 1981).
Roller v. Kurtz, 129 N.E.2d 693 (Ill. 1955).
Rollison v. Biggs, 567 F. Supp. 964 (D. Del. 1983).
Romero, *Ex parte,* 181 P.2d 811 (N.M. 1947).
Roncker v. Walter, 700 F.2d 1058 (6th Cir. 1983).
Rone v. Fireman, 473 F. Supp. 92 (N.D. Ohio 1979).
Ronstrom, *In re,* 436 So. 2d 588 (La. Ct. App. 1983).
Rose v. United States, 513 F.2d 1251 (8th Cir. 1975).
Rosenberg v. Fleuti, 374 U.S. 449 (1963).
Rossi, *In re,* 455 N.Y.S.2d 505 (Sup. Ct. Spec. Term 1982).
Rouse v. Cameron, 373 F.2d 451 (D.C. Cir. 1966) (as amended Apr. 4, 1967).
Rowley v. Board of Education, 483 F. Supp. 528 (S.D.N.Y. 1980), *aff'd,* 632 F.2d 945 (2d Cir. 1980), *rev'd and remanded,* 458 U.S. 176 (1982).
Royal State National Insurance Co. v. Labor and Industrial Relations Appeal Board, 487 P.2d 278 (Hawaii 1971).
Rubenstein v. Dr. Pepper Co., 228 F.2d 528 (8th Cir. 1955).
Ruby v. Massey, 452 F. Supp. 361 (D. Conn. 1978).
Rum River Lumber Co. v. State, 282 N.W.2d 882 (Minn. 1979).
Ryans v. New Jersey Commission for the Blind and Visually Impaired, 542 F. Supp. 841 (D.N.J. 1982).

Sabol v. Board of Education, 510 F. Supp. 892 (D.N.J. 1981).
Sacchi v. Blodig, 341 N.W.2d 326 (Neb. Sup. Ct. 1983).
Saia v. New York, 334 U.S. 558 (1948).
St. Louis Developmental Disabilities Treatment Center Parents Association v. Mallory, 591 F. Supp. 1416 (W.D. Mo. 1984).
Salgo v. Stanford University Board of Trustees, 317 P.2d 170 (Cal. Ct. App. 1957).
Salyer Land co. v. Tulare Lake Basin Water Storage District, 410 U.S. 719 (1973).
Salz, *In re,* 436 N.Y.S.2d 713 (App. Div. 1981).
Samson v. Southern Bell Telephone and Telegraph Co., 205 So. 2d 496 (La. Ct. App. 1967).
San Antonio Independent School District v. Rodriquez, 411 U.S. 1 (1973).
Sanchez v. State, 567 P.2d 270 (Wyo. 1977).
Santana v. Collazo, 533 F. Supp. 966 (D.P.R. 1982).
Santosky v. Kramer, 455 U.S. 745 (1982).
Sas v. Maryland, 295 F. Supp. 389 (D. Md. 1969), *aff'd sub nom.* Tippet v. Maryland, 436 F.2d 1153 (4th Cir. 1971), *cert. dismissed as improvidently granted sub nom.* Murel v. Baltimore City Criminal Court, 407 U.S. 355 (1972).
Saville v. Treadway, 404 F. Supp. 430 (M.D. Tenn. 1974).
Savka v. Commonwealth, Department of Education, 403 A.2d 142 (Pa. Commw. Ct. 1979).
Sawyer v. Pacific Indemnity Co., 233 S.E.2d 227 (Ga. Ct. App. 1977).
S.C., *In re,* 421 A.2d 853 (Pa. Super. Ct. 1980).
Scanlon v. Atascadero State Hospital, 677 F.2d 1271 (9th Cir. 1982).
Schaps v. Lehner, 55 N.W. 911 (Minn. 1893).
Scharlow v. Schweiker, 655 F.2d 645 (5th Cir. 1981).
S.C.E., *In re,* 378 A.2d 144 (Del. Ch. 1977).
Scherz v. Peoples National Bank, 218 S.W.2d 86 (Ark. 1949).
Scheuer v. Rhodes, 416 U.S. 232 (1974).
Schiller, *In re,* 372 A.2d 360 (N.J. Super. Ct. Ch. Div. 1977).
Schindenwolf v. Klein, No. L-41293-75 P.W., 5 MDLR 60 (N.J. Mercer County Super. Ct. Dec. 22, 1980).
Schisler v. Heckler, 574 F. Supp. 1538 (W.D.N.Y. 1983).
Schloendorff v. Society of New York Hospital, 105 N.E. 92 (N.Y. 1914).
Schmerber v. California, 384 U.S. 757 (1966).
Schmidt, *In re,* 429 A.2d 631 (Pa. 1981).
Schmidt v. Harris, 498 F. Supp. 1181 (W.D. Mo. 1980).
Schmidt v. Lessard, 349 F. Supp. 1078 (E.D. Wis. 1972), *vacated and remanded on other grounds,* 94 S. Ct. 713 (1974).
Schmidt v. Schubert, 422 F. Supp. 57 (E.D. Wis. 1976).
Schneider v. Vine Street Clinic, 397 N.E.2d 194 (Ill. 1979).
Schoeller v. Dunbar, 423 F.2d 1183 (9th Cir. 1970).
Schonnings v. People's Church Home, Inc., No. 7188, 2 MDLR 17 (Sup. Ct. Worcester Mass. Jan. 28, 1977).
School Committee of the Town of Burlington v. Department of Educ., No. 84-433, 9 MPDLR 203 (U.S. Sup. Ct. Apr. 29, 1985).
School District #1 v. Department of Industry, Labor and Human Relations, 215 N.W.2d 373 (Wis. 1974).
Schornstein v. New Jersey Division of Vocational Rehabilitation Services, 519 F. Supp. 773 (D.N.J. 1981), *aff'd,* 688 F.2d 824 3d Cir. 1982).
Schroeder v. Perkel, 432 A.2d 834 (N.J. 1981).
Schweiker v. Gray Panthers, 49 U.S.L.W. 4792 (U.S. June 25, 1981).
Scott v. Plante, 691 F.2d 634 (3d Cir. 1982).
Scurlock, *In re,* 455 N.Y.S.2d 131 (App. Div. 1982).
Seaton v. Clifford, 100 Cal. Rptr. 779 (Ct. App. 1972).
Secretary of Public Welfare v. Institutionalized Juveniles, 442 U.S. 640 (1979).
Seefeld, *In re,* No. 454-225, 2 MDLR 363 (Wis. Milwaukee County Cir. Ct. Oct. 31, 1977).
Sehr v. Lindemann, 54 S.W. 537 (Mo. 1899).
Seibert v. Wayne County Probate Court, No. 79-921-758 CZ, 4 MDLR 340 (Mich. Wayne County Cir. Ct. June 24, 1980).
Selelyo v. Drury, 508 F. Supp. 122 (S.D. Ohio 1980).
Selelyo v. Drury, No. C-3-78-369, 5 MDLR 241 (S.D. Ohio Apr. 30, 1981).
Semler v. Psychiatric Institute of Washington, D.C., 538 F.2d 121 (4th Cir. 1976).
Senn v. Old American Insurance Corporation, 120 F. Supp. 422 (E.D.S.C. 1954).

Sepe, *In re,* 421 So. 2d 27 (Fla. Dist. Ct. App. 1982).
Sessions v. Livingston Parish School Board, 501 F. Supp. 251 (M.D. La. 1980).
Severns v. Wilmington Medical Center, Inc., 421 A.2d 1334 (Del. 1980).
Shabazz v. Barnauskas, 598 F.2d 345 (5th Cir. 1979).
Shanberg v. Commonwealth, Secretary of Education, 426 A.2d 232 (Pa. Commw. Ct. 1981).
Shanklin v. Boyce, 204 S.W. 187 (Mo. 1918).
Shapiro v. Thompson, 394 U.S. 618 (1969).
Sharon R., *In re,* No. H-1205/80, 4 MDLR 329 (N.Y. Queens County Fam. Ct. July 14, 1980).
Shaw v. Delta Air Lines, Inc., 103 S. Ct. 2890 (1983).
Shelton v. Shelton, 74 S.E.2d 5 (Ga. 1953).
Shelton v. Tucker, 364 U.S. 479 (1960).
Sherer v. Waier, 457 F. Supp. 1039 (W.D. Mo. 1977).
Sherry v. New York State Education Department, 479 F. Supp. 1328 (W.D.N.Y. 1979).
Shirey v. Devine, 670 F.2d 1188 (D.C. Cir. 1982).
Shumway v. Shumway, 2 Vt. 339 (1829).
Sieling v. Eyman, 478 F.2d 211 (9th Cir. 1973).
Silver v. United States, 498 F. Supp. 610 (N.D. Ill. 1980).
Silverstein v. Sisters of Charity of Leavenworth Health Services Corporation, 614 P.2d 891 (Colo. Ct. App. 1979).
Simon v. St. Louis County, 497 F. Supp. 141 (E.D. Mo. 1980).
Simpson v. Reynolds Metals Co., 629 F.2d 1226 (7th Cir. 1980).
Sims v. Slovin, 207 A.2d 597 (Del. Ch. Ct. 1965), *aff'd,* 213 A.2d 903 (Del. 1965).
Sinclair v. State, 132 So. 581 (Miss. 1931).
Sisneros v. District Court, Tenth Judicial District, 606 P.2d 55 (Colo. 1980) (en banc).
Sitar v. Schweiker, 671 F.2d 19 (1st Cir. 1982).
Sites v. McKenzie, 423 F. Supp. 1190 (N.D.W. Va. 1976).
Skills Development Services, Inc. v. Donovan, 728 F.2d 294 (6th Cir. 1984).
Skinner v. Oklahoma *ex rel.* Williamson, 316 U.S. 535 (1942).
S. L., *In re,* No. A-1734-80T1, 5 MDLR 252 (N.J. Super. Ct. App. Div. appeal docketed Jan 6, 1981).
Smith v. Administrator of Veterans Affairs, 32 Fair Empl. Prac. Cas. (BNA) 986 (C.D. Cal. 1983).
Smith v. Alameda County Social Services Agency, 153 Cal. Rptr. 712 (Ct. App. 1979).
Smith v. Board of Examiners of Feeble-Minded, 88 A. 963 (N.J. 1913).
Smith v. Command, 204 N.W. 140 (Mich. 1925).
Smith v. Cumberland School Committee, 415 A.2d 168 (R.I. 1980).
Smith v. Cumberland School Committee, 703 F.2d 4 (1st Cir. 1983).
Smith v. Goguen, 415 U.S. 566 (1974).
Smith v. Robinson, 104 S. Ct. 3457 (1984).
Smith v. Superior Court, 173 Cal. Rptr. 145 (Ct. App. 1981).
Smith v. United States, 36 F.2d 548 (D.C. Cir. 1929).
Smith v. United States, 437 F. Supp. 1004 (E.D. Pa. 1977).
Smrcka v. Ambach, 555 F. Supp. 1227 (E.D.N.Y. 1983).
Society for Good Will to Retarded Children, Inc. v. Cuomo, 572 F. Supp. 1300 (E.D.N.Y. 1983), *vacated and remanded,* 737 F.2d 1239 (2d Cir. 1984).
Solesbee v. Balkcom, 339 U.S. 9 (1950).
Solloway v. Department of Professional Regulation, 421 So. 2d 573 (Fla. Dist. Ct. App. 1982).
S-1 v. Turlington, 635 F.2d 342 (5th Cir. 1981).
Souder v. Brennan, 367 F. Supp. 808 (D.D.C. 1973).
Souder v. Watson, Civ. Act. No. 74-279, 2 MDLR 388 (M.D. Pa. Dec. 20, 1977).
South Carolina Department of Mental Health v. Turbeville, 257 S.E.2d 493 (S.C. 1979).
South Carolina Department of Social Services v. McDow, 280 S.E.2d 208 (S.C. 1981).
Southeast Warren Community School District v. Department of Public Instruction, 285 N.W.2d 173 (Iowa 1979).
Southeastern Community College v. Davis, 442 U.S. 397 (1979).
Specht v. Patterson, 386 U.S. 605 (1967).
Speck v. Finegold, 268 Pa. Super. 342 (1979).
Speight v. Knight, 11 Alan 461 (1847).
Spring, *In re,* 405 N.E.2d 115 (Mass. 1980).
Springdale School District No. 50 v. Grace, 494 F. Supp. 266 (W.D. Ark. 1980), *aff'd,* 656 F.2d 300 (8th Cir. 1981).
Springdale School District No. 50 v. Grace, 693 F.2d 41 (8th Cir. 1982).
Stacey G. v. Padadena Independent School District, 547 F. Supp. 61 (S.D. Tex. 1982).
Stacey G. v. Pasadena Independent School District, 695 F.2d 949 (5th Cir. 1983).
Stafford v. Stafford, 1 Mart. 551 (La. Sup. Ct. 1823).
Stafford v. State, 455 N.E.2d 402 (Ind. Ct. App. 1983).
Stamus v. Leonhardt, 414 F. Supp. 439 (S.D. Iowa 1976).
Stanley v. Georgia, 394 U.S. 557 (1969).
Stanley v. Schweiker, 529 F. Supp. 236 (E.D.N.Y. 1981).
State v. Alto, 589 P.2d 402 (Alaska 1979).
State v. Aumann, 265 N.W.2d 316, 320 (Iowa 1978).
State v. Austad, 641 P.2d 1373 (Mont. 1982).
State v. Blythman, 302 N.W.2d 666 (Neb. 1981).
State v. Bridges, 468 P.2d 604 (Ariz. Ct. App. 1970).
State v. Civil Service Employees Association, Inc., 430 N.Y.S.2d 510 (Erie County Sup. Ct. 1980).
State v. Cole, 295 N.W.2d 29 (Iowa 1980).
State v. Elson, 208 N.W.2d 363 (Wis. 1973).
State v. Feilen, 126 P. 75 (Wash. 1912).
State v. Felter, 25 Iowa 67 (1868).
State v. Hamann, 285 N.W.2d 180 (Iowa 1979).
State v. Hampton, 218 So. 2d 311 (La. 1969).
State v. Heger, 326 N.W.2d 855 (N.D. 1982).
State v. Hudson, 425 A.2d 255 (N.H. 1981).
State v. Kee, 510 S.W.2d 477 (Mo. 1974).
State v. Khan, 417 A.2d 585 (N.J. Super. Ct. App. Div., 1980).
State v. Korell, 690 P.2d 992 (Mont. 1984).
State v. Krol, 344 A.2d 289 (N.J. 1975).
State v. Ladd, 433 A.2d 294 (Vt. 1981).
State v. Lange, 123 So. 639 (La. 1929).
State v. Lucas, 152 A.2d 50 (N.J. 1959).
State v. McClendon, 437 P.2d 421 (Ariz. 1968).
State v. Maryott, 492 P.2d 239 (Wash. Ct. App. 1971).
State v. O'Neill, 545 P.2d 97 (Or. 1976).
State v. Pike, 49 N.H. 399 (1869).
State v. Pugh, 283 A.2d 537 (N.J. Super. Ct. App. Div. 1971).
State v. Rima, 310 N.W.2d 138 (Neb. 1981).
State v. Shaw, 471 P.2d 715 (Ariz. 1970).
State v. Staten, 247 N.E.2d 293 (Ohio 1969).
State v. Strasburg, 110 P. 1020 (Wash. 1910).
State v. Taylor, 283 S.E.2d 761 (N.C. 1981).
State v. Troutman, 299 P. 668 (Idaho 1931).
State v. Tsavaris, 382 So. 2d 56 (Fla. Dist. Ct. App. 1980).
State Department of Social and Health Services v. Latta, 601 P.2d 520 (Wash. 1979).
State *ex rel.* Boyd v. Green, 355 So. 2d 789 (Fla. 1978).
State *ex rel.* Causey, 363 So. 2d 472 (La. 1978).
State *ex rel.* Doe v. Sister Mary Madonna, 295 N.W.2d (Minn. 1980).
State *ex rel.* E. and B. v. J.T., 578 P.2d 831 (Utah 1978).
State *ex rel.* Fuller v. Mullinax, 269 S.W.2d 72 (Mo. 1954).
State *ex rel.* Hawks v. Lazaro, 202 S.E.2d 109 (W.Va. 1974).

State *ex rel.* Kennedy v. District Court, 194 P.2d 256 (Mont. 1948).
State *ex. rel.* Krutzfeldt v. District Court of 13th Judicial District, 515 P.2d 1312 (Mont. 1973).
State *ex rel.* Martin v. Superior Court of King County, 172 P. 257 (Wash. 1918).
State *ex rel.* Memmel v. Mundy, 249 N.W.2d 573 (Wis. 1977).
State *ex rel.* Mental Health Commissioner v. Guardianship of Wiseman, 393 N.E.2d 235 (Ind. Ct. App. 1979).
State *In re* R.B.W., 342 A.2d 869 (N.J. Super. Ct. App. Div. 1975), *aff'd,* 358 A.2d 473 (N.J. 1976).
State *ex rel.* Smith v. Schaffer, 270 P. 604 (Kan. 1928)
State *ex rel.* Vandenberg v. Vandenberg, 617 P.2d 675 (Or. Ct. App. 1980).
Steinhiser, *In re,* 424 A.2d 1006 (Pa. Commw. Ct. 1981).
Stemple v. Board of Education, 464 F. Supp. 258 (D. Md. 1979).
Stemple v. Board of Education, 623 F.2d 893 (4th Cir. 1980).
Stewart *ex rel.* Stewart v. Salem School District 24J, 670 P.2d 1048 (Or. Ct. App. 1983).
Stock v. Massachusetts Hospital School, 467 N.E.2d 448 (Mass. 1984).
Storar, *In re,* 420 N.E. 2d 64 (N.Y. 1981).
Strain v. Rossman, 614 P.2d 102 (Or. Ct. App. 1980).
Strunk v. Strunk, 445 S.W.2d 145 (Ky. Ct. App. 1969).
Stuart v. Nappi, 443 F. Supp. 1235 (D. Conn. 1978).
Stubbs. v. Kline, 463 F. Supp. 110 (W.D. Pa. 1978).
Stump v. Sparkman, 435 U.S. 349 (1978).
Sullivan v. State, 352 So. 2d 1212 (Fla. Dist. Ct. App. 1977).
Superintendent of Belchertown State School v. Saikewicz, 370 N.E.2d 417 (Mass. 1977).
Superintendent of Worcester State Hospital v. Hagberg, 372 N.E.2d 242 (Mass. 1978).
Suzuki v. Quisenberry, 411 F. Supp. 113 (D. Hawaii 1976).
Suzuki v. Yuen, 617 F.2d 173 (9th Cir. 1980).
Suzuki v. Yuen, 507 F. Supp. 819 (D. Hawaii 1981).
Swanson v. Boschen, 120 A.2d 546 (Conn. 1956).
Sylvia M. and Alicia M., *In re,* 443 N.Y.S.2d 214 (App. Div. 1981).
Szymanski v. Halle's Department Store, 407 N.E.2d 502 (Ohio 1980).

Tant v. Heckler, 577 F. Supp. 448 (N.D. Ga. 1983).
Tarasoff v. Regents of the University of California, 529 P.2d 553 (Cal. 1974).
Tarasoff v. Regents of University of California, 551 P.2d 334 (Cal. 1976).
Tartaglia v. Commonwealth, 416 A.2d 608 (Pa. Commw. Ct. 1980).
Tatro v. Texas, 625 F.2d 557 (5th Cir. 1980).
Tatro v. Texas, 516 F. Supp. 968 (N.D. Tex. 1981).
Tatro v. Texas, 703 F.2d 823 (5th Cir. 1983).
Taylor v. Avi, 415 A.2d 894 (Pa. Super. Ct. 1979).
Taylor v. Gilmartin, 686 F.2d 1346 (10th Cir. 1982).
Taylor v. State, 199 So. 2d 694 (Ala. Ct. App. 1967).
Tedesco, *In re,* 421 N.E.2d 726 (Ind. Ct. App. 1981).
Tennessee Department of Human Services v. Ogle, 617 S.W.2d 652 (Tenn. Ct. App. 1981).
Tepen, *In re,* 599 S.W.2d 533 (Mo. Ct. App. 1980).
Teresa Diane P. v. Alief Independent School District, 744 F.2d 484 (5th Cir. 1984).
T.G. v. Board of Education, 576 F. Supp. 420 (D.N.J. 1983).
Theriault v. Blackwell, 437 F.2d 76 (5th Cir. 1971), *cert. denied,* 402 U.S. 953 (1971).
Thomas v. Commonwealth, Workmen's Compensation Appeal Board, 423 A.2d 784 (Pa. Commw. Ct. 1980).
Thomson, *In re,* 169 N.Y.S. 638 (Sup. Ct. 1918), *aff'd mem. sub nom.* Osborn v. Thomson, 171 N.Y.S. 1094 (App. Div. 1918).
Thompson v. County of Alameda, 614 P.2d 728 (Cal. 1980).
Thompson v. Lenoir Transfer Co., 268 S.E.2d 534 (N.C. Ct. App. 1980).
Thorn v. Superior Court of San Diego County, 464 P.2d 56 (Cal. 1970).
Thornock v. Evans, No. 78704, 7 MDLR 234 (Idaho Dist. Ct. Apr. 4, 1983).
Thorton v. Schweiker, 663 F.2d 1312 (5th Cir. 1981).
Tidwell v. Weinberger, Nos. 73-C-3104 & 74-C-183, 1 MDLR 192 (N.D. Ill. June 28, 1976).
Tierney, *In re,* 421 A.2d 610 (N.J. 1980).
Timms v. Metropolitan School District, 718 F.2d 212, *amended,* 722 F.2d 1310 (7th Cir. 1983) (reaching same result on partially different grounds).
Tina A. v. Shedd, No. H-80-462, 4 MDLR 403 (D. Conn. 1980).
Tinch v. Waters, 573 F. Supp. 346 (E.D. Tenn. 1983).
Tippett v. Maryland, 436 F.2d 1153 (4th Cir. 1971), *cert. dismissed as improvidently granted sub nom.* Murel v. Baltimore City Criminal Court, 407 U.S. 355 (1972).
Tolbert v. McGriff, 434 F. Supp. 682 (M.D. Ala. 1976).
Torsney, *In re,* 394 N.E.2d 262 (N.Y. 1979).
Town of Burlington v. Department of Education, 736 F.2d 773 (1st Cir. 1984).
Town of Hempstead v. Commissioner, New York Office of Mental Retardation and Developmental Disabilities, 453 N.Y.S.2d 32 (App. Div. 1982).
Townsend v. Clover Bottom Hospital and School, 560 S.W.2d 623 (Tenn. 1978).
Townsend v. Maine Bureau of Public Safety, 404 A.2d 1014 (Me. 1979).
Township of Washington v. Central Bergen Community Mental Health Center, Inc., 383 A.2d 1194 (N.J. Super Ct. Law Div. 1978).
Trageser v. Libbie Rehabilitation Center, 590 F.2d 87 (4th Cir. 1978).
Trapnell v. Smith, 205 S.E.2d 875 (Ga. Ct. App. 1974).
Trish v. Newell, 62 Ill. 196 (1871).
Trott, *In re,* 288 A.2d 303 (N.J. Super. Ct. Ch. Div. 1972).
Troy Ltd. v. Renna, 727 F.2d 287 (3d Cir. 1984).
Tubell v. Dade County Public Schools, 419 So. 2d 388 (Fla. Dist. Ct. App. 1982).
Turillo v. Tyson, 535 F. Supp. 577 (D.R.I. 1982).
Tuntland, *In re,* 390 N.E.2d 11 (Ill. App. Ct. 1979).
Turpin v. Sortini, 174 Cal. Rptr. 128 (Ct. App. 1981).
Two Minor Children, *In re,* 592 P.2d 166 (Nev. 1979).
Tyars v. Finner, 518 F. Supp. 502 (C.D. Cal. 1981).
Tyler v. Harris, 226 F. Supp. 852 (W.D. Mo. 1964).
Tytell v. Kaen, N.Y.L.J., June 11, 1979, at 12 col. 3, 3 MDLR 249 (Bronx County Sup. Ct. 1979).

Underwood v. United States, 356 F.2d 92 (5th Cir. 1966).
United States v. Alvarez, 519 F.2d 1036 (3d Cir. 1975).
United States v. Ashe, 427 F.2d 626 (D.C. Cir. 1970).
United States v. Baylor University Medical Center, 564 F. Supp. 1495 (N.D. Tex. 1983).
United States v. Bodey, 547 F.2d 1383 (9th Cir. 1977).
United States v. Brawner, 471 F.2d 969 (D.C. Cir. 1972).
United States v. Cabrini Medical Center, 639 F.2d 908 (2d Cir. 1981).
United States v. Chisolm, 149 F. 284 (S.D. Ala. 1906).
United States v. Dannon, 481 F. Supp. 152 (W.D. Okla. 1979).
United States v. David, 511 F.2d 355 (D.C. Cir. 1975).
United States v. DiGilio, 538 F.2d 972, 988 (3d Cir. 1978).

United States v. Driscoll, 399 F.2d 135 (2d Cir. 1968).
United States v. Ecker, 543 F.2d 178 (D.C. Cir. 1976).
United States v. Freeman, 357 F.2d 606 (2d Cir. 1966).
United States v. Hinckley, 525 F. Supp. 1342 (D.D.C. 1981).
United States v. Indiana, No. 1P84-411C, 8 MPDLR 320 (S.D. Ind. Apr. 6, 1984).
United States v. Lewellyn, 723 F.2d 615 (8th Cir. 1983).
United States v. Masthers, 539 F.2d 721 (D.C. Cir. 1976).
United States v. Nichelson, 550 F.2d 502 (8th Cir. 1977).
United States v. Odorn, 736 F.2d 104 (4th Cir. 1984).
United States v. Robertson, 430 F. Supp. 444 (D.D.C. 1977).
United States v. Sermon, 228 F. Supp. 972 (W.D. Mo. 1964).
United States v. Solomon, 419 F. Supp. 358 (D.C. Md. 1977).
United States v. Sullivan, 406 F.2d 180 (2d Cir. 1969).
United States v. Torniero, 570 F. Supp. 721 (D. Conn. 1983).
United States v. University Hospital, 575 F. Supp. 607 (E.D.N.Y. 1983), *aff'd*, 729 F.2d 144 (2d Cir. 1984).
United States v. Voice, 627 F.2d 138 (8th Cir. 1980).
United States *ex rel.* Mathew v. Nelson, 461 F. Supp. 707 (N.D. Ill. 1978).
United States *ex rel.* Schuster v. Herold, 410 F.2d 1071 (2d Cir. 1969), *cert. denied,* 396 U.S. 847 (1969).
United States *ex rel.* Smith v. Baldi, 344 U.S. 561 (1953).
United States *ex rel.* Souder v. Watson, 413 F. Supp. 711 (M.D. Pa. 1976).
United States *ex rel.* Stachulak v. Coughlin, 520 F.2d 931 (7th Cir. 1975).
United States *ex rel.* Wolfersdorf v. Johnston, 317 F. Supp. 66 (S.D. N.Y. 1970).
United States *ex rel.* Wulf v. Esperdy, 277 F.2d 537 (2d Cir. 1960).
United States Fidelity and Guaranty Co. v. Spring Brook Farm Dairy, Inc., 64 A.2d 39 (Conn. 1949).
United Transportation Union v. Long Island Railroad Co., 455 U.S. 678 (1982).

Valenti v. United States, No. 78C5198, 6 MDLR 386 (N.D. Ill. July 13, 1982).
Vanderzeil v. Hudspeth, Civ. Act. No. J76-262(R), 1 MDLR 450 (S.D. Miss. Feb. 11, 1977).
Vasquez v. Fleming, 617 F.2d 334 (1980).
Vecchione v. Wohlgemuth, 377 F. Supp. 1361 (E.D. Pa. 1974).
Vecchione v. Wohlgemuth, 426 F. Supp. 1297 (E.D. Pa. 1977).
Vecchione v. Wohlgemuth, 558 F.2d 150 (3d Cir. 1977).
Vecchione v. Wohlgemuth, 481 F. Supp. 776 (E.D. Pa. 1979).
Village of Belle Terre v. Boraas, 416 U.S. 1 (1974).
Village of Euclid v. Ambler Realty Co., 272 U.S. 365 (1926).
Village of Maywood v. Health, Inc., 433 N.E.2d 951 (Ill. App. Ct. 1982).
Village of Westbury v. Prevost, 467 N.Y.S.2d 70 (App. Div. 1983).
Virginia Academy of Clinical Psychologists v. Blue Shield of Virginia, 501 F. Supp. 1232 (E.D. Va. 1980), *cert. denied,* 49 U.S.L.W. 3617 (U.S. Feb. 23, 1981).
Vitek v. Jones, 445 U.S. 480 (1980).
Von Bulow, *In re,* 470 N.Y.S.2d 72 (1983).
Von Luce v. Rankin, 588 S.W.2d 445 (Ark. 1979).
Voshake's Guardianship, *In re,* 189 A. 753 (Pa. Super. Ct. 1937).

Wade v. Department of Mental Hygiene, 418 N.Y.S.2d 154 (App. Div. 1979).
Waggoner v. Atkins, 162 S.W.2d 55 (Ark. 1942).
Wagstaff, *In re,* 287 N.W.2d 339 (Mich. Ct. App. 1979).
Wais, *In re,* 464 N.Y.S.2d 634 (Sup. Ct. Albany County 1983).
Waite, *In re,* 180 N.W. 159 (Iowa 1920).
Walker v. Graves, 125 S.W.2d 154 (Tenn. 1939).
Walsh's Estate, *In re,* 223 P.2d 322 (Cal. Dist. Ct. App. 1950).
Ward v. Booth, 197 F.2d 963 (9th Cir. 1952).
Ware v. Schweicker, 651 F.2d 408 (5th Cir. 1981).
Warker v. Warker, 151 A. 274 (N.J. Eq. 1930).
Warren v. Harvey, 632 F.2d 925 (2d Cir. 1980).
Washburn *ex rel.* Baby Jane Doe v. Abrams, No. 83-CV1711, 8 MPDLR 113 (N.D.N.Y. Jan. 20, 1984).
Washington *ex rel.* Seattle Title Trust Co. v. Roberge, 278 U.S. 116 (1928).
Watson, *In re,* 154 Cal. Rptr. 151 (Ct. App. 1979).
Webb, *Ex parte,* 625 S.W.2d 372 (Tex. Civ. App. 1981).
Weber v. Stony Brook Hospital, 52 U.S.L.W. 2267 (N.Y. Ct. App. Oct. 28, 1983).
Weberlist, *In re,* 360 N.Y.S.2d 783 (N.Y. County Sup. Ct. 1974).
Weller v. Copeland, 120 N.E. 578 (Ill. 1918).
Wellman, *In re,* 45 P. 726 (Kan. 1896).
Welsch v. Commonwealth, Department of Education, 400 A.2d 234 (Pa. Commw. Ct. 1979).
Welsch v. Likins, 373 F. Supp. 487 (D. Minn. 1974), *aff'd,* 550 F.2d 1122 (8th Cir. 1977).
Welsch v. Noot, No. 4-72 Civ. 451, 5 MDLR 155 (D. Minn. Sept. 15, 1980).
Wentzel v. Montgomery General Hospital, 293 Md. 685 (1982).
West Virginia State Board of Education v. Barnette, 319 U.S. 624 (1943).
Westbrook v. Arizona, 384 U.S. 150 (1966).
Whalem v. United States, 346 F.2d 812 (D.C. Cir. 1965).
Whalen v. Roe, 429 U.S. 589 (1977).
Whitaker v. Board of Higher Education, 461 F. Supp. 99 (E.D.N.Y. 1978).
White v. White, 196 S.W. 508 (1917).
Whitree v. State, 290 N.Y.S.2d 486 (Ct. Cl. 1968).
Wieman v. Updegraff, 344 U.S. 183 (1952).
Wieter v. Settle, 193 F. Supp. 318 (W.D. Mo. 1961).
Wilhelm v. Continental Title Co. 720 F.2d 1173 (10th Cir. 1983).
Wilkinson v. Wilkinson, 585 P.2d 599 (Colo. Ct. App. 1978).
Will of Maynard, *In re,* 307 S.E.2d 416 (N.C. Ct. App. 1983).
William C. v. Board of Education, 390 N.E.2d 479 (Ill. App. Ct. 1979).
William M., *In re,* 3 MDLR 184 (Ohio Franklin County Ct. of C.P. Probate Div. Mar. 15, 1979).
William S. v. Gill, 572 F. Supp. 509 (N.D. Ill. 1983).
Williams, *In re,* No. 83-135, 8 MDLR 90 (D.C. Ct. App. Jan. 9, 1984).
Williams v. Hillsborough County School Board, 389 So. 2d 1218 (Fla. Dist. Ct. App. 1980).
Williams v. Mashburn, 602 P.2d 1036 (Okla. 1979).
Williams v. Smith, 131 N.E. 2 (Ind. 1921).
Williams v. Superintendent, 406 A.2d 1302 (Md. 1979).
Willie M. v. Hunt, No. C-C-79-294-M, 7 MDLR 308 (W.D.N.C. June 2, 1983).
Williford v. People of California, 217 F. Supp. 245 (N.D. Cal. 1963).
Wilmington Medical Center, Inc. v. Severns, 433 A.2d 1047 (Del. 1981).
Wilson v. United States, 391 F.2d 460 (D.C. Cir. 1968).
Winburn, *In re,* 145 N.W.2d 178 (Wis. 1966).
Winship, *In re,* 397 U.S. 358 (1970).
Winslow v. Troy, 53 A. 1008 (Me. 1902).
Winstead, *In re,* No. 9388, 4 MDLR 96 (Ohio Ct. App. 9th Dist. Jan. 9, 1980).
Winters v. Miller, 446 F.2d 65 (2d Cir. 1971), *cert. denied,* 404 U.S. 985 (1971).
Wisconsin v. Yoder, 406 U.S. 205 (1972).
Woe v. Cuomo, 729 F.2d 96 (2d Cir. 1984).

Wolfe v. Beal, 384 A.2d 1187 (Pa. 1978).
Wolfe v. Maricopa County General Hospital, 619 P.2d 1041 (Ariz. 1980).
Wolff v. McDonnell, 418 U.S. 539 (1974).
Wong v. Bucks County, No. 81-1331, 6 MDLR 89 (E.D. Pa. Feb. 8, 1982).
Wood v. Strickland, 420 U.S. 308 (1975).
Woodard v. Schweiker, 668 F.2d 370 (8th Cir. 1981).
Woods v. Idaho Department of Health and Welfare, No. 74139, 6 MDLR 46 (Idaho Ada County Dist. Ct. Oct. 27, 1980).
Woodson v. North Carolina, 428 U.S. 280 (1976).
Wuori v. Zitnay, Civ. No. 75-80-SD, 2 MDLR 693, 729 (D. Maine July 14, 1978).
Wyatt v. Aderholt, 368 F. Supp. 1383 (M.D. Ala. 1974).
Wyatt v. Aderhold, 503 F.2d 1305 (5th Cir. 1974).
Wyatt v. Hardin, No. 3195-N, 1 MDLR 55 (M.D. Ala. Feb. 28, 1975, *modified* July 1, 1975).
Wyatt v. Stickney, 325 F. Supp. 781 (M.D. Ala. 1971), 344 F. Supp. 373 (M.D. Ala. 1972), *aff'd sub nom.* Wyatt v. Aderholt, 503 F.2d 1305 (5th Cir. 1974).

X. (Bryant) v. Carlson, 363 F. Supp. 928 (E.D. Ill. 1973).

Yapalater v. Bates, 494 F. Supp. 1349 (S.D.N.Y. 1980), *aff'd,* 644 F.2d 131 (2d Cir. 1981).
Yick Wo v. Hopkins, 118 U.S. 356 (1886).
Young, *In re,* 600 P.2d 1312 (Wash. Ct. App. 1979).
Youngberg v. Romeo, 457 U.S. 307 (1982).
Youtsey v. United States, 97 F. 937 (6th Cir. 1899).

Zablocki v. Redhail, 434 U.S. 374 (1978).
Zeigler v. Coffin, 123 So. 22 (Ala. 1929).
Zerega v. Okin, 79-1895-Z, 3 MDLR 408 (D. Mass. filed Sept. 17, 1979).
Zipkin v. Freeman, 436 S.W.2d 753 (Mo. 1969).
Zorek v. Attleboro Area Human Services, Inc., No. 2450 (Mass. Sup. Ct. Nov. 1975).
Zorick v. Tynes, 372 So. 2d 133 (Fla. Dist. Ct. App. 1979).
Zvi D. v. Ambach, 694 F.2d 904 (2d Cir. 1982).

Select Bibliography

Allen, R.C., E.Z. Ferster, and J.G. Rubin, eds. *Readings in Law and Psychiatry*. Baltimore: Johns Hopkins University Press, 1975.

__________, E.Z. Ferster, and H. Weihofen. *Mental Impairment and Legal Incompetency*. Englewood Cliffs, N.J.: Prentice-Hall, 1968.

American Bar Association. Section of Real Property, Probate and Trust Law. "Limited Guardianship: Survey of Implementation Considerations." 15 *Real Property, Probate and Trust Journal* 544 (1980).

__________. Standing Committee on Association Standards for Criminal Justice. *Criminal Justice Mental Health Standards*. 1st Tentative Draft. Washington, D.C.: American Bar Association, 1983.

American Psychiatric Association, *Diagnostic and Statistical Manual of Mental Disorders*. 3d ed. Washington, D.C.: American Psychiatric Association, 1980.

__________. "Official Action: Model Law on Confidentiality of Health and Social Service Records." 136 *American Journal of Psychiatry* 137 (1979).

__________. "Statement on the Insanity Defense." 140 *American Journal of Psychiatry* 681 (1983).

__________. Task Force on Electroconvulsive Therapy. *Electroconvulsive Therapy: Report of the Task Force on Electroconvulsive Therapy*. Washington, D.C.: American Psychiatric Association, 1978.

__________. Task Force on the Role of Psychiatry in the Sentencing Process. *Report of the Task Force on the Role of Psychiatry in the Sentencing Process*. Washington, D.C.: American Psychiatric Association, 1984.

Andalman, E., and D.L. Chambers. "Effective Counsel for Persons Facing Civil Commitment: A Survey, a Polemic, and a Proposal," 45 *Mississippi Law Journal* 43 (1974).

Axilbund, M.T. *Substituted Judgment for the Disabled: Report of an Inquiry into Limited Guardianship, Public Guardianship and Adult Protective Services in Six States*. Washington, D.C.: American Bar Association, Commission on the Mentally Disabled, 1979.

Bachrach, L. *Deinstitutionalization: An Analytical Review and Sociological Perspective*. Rockville, Md.: National Institute of Mental Health, 1977.

Biegler, J. "Privacy and Confidentiality." In *Law and Ethics in the Practice of Psychiatry*, edited by C.K. Hofling. New York: Brunner-Mazel, 1980.

Beresford, H.R. "Professional Liability of Psychiatrists," 21 *Defense Law Journal* 123 (1972).

Biggs, J., Jr. *The Guilty Mind: Psychiatry and the Law of Homicide*. New York: Harcourt, Brace, 1955.

Birnbaum, M. "The Right to Treatment," 46 *American Bar Association Journal* 499 (1960).

Blackstone, W. *Commentaries on the Laws of England*. 9th ed. by R.I. Burn. Vol. 1. London: W. Strahan, T. Cadell & D. Prince, 1783.

Bloch, S., and P. Chodoff, eds. *Psychiatric Ethics*. Oxford: Oxford University Press, 1981.

Bonnie, R.J. "Morality, Equality, and Expertise: Renegotiating the Relationship Between Psychiatry and the Criminal Law," 12 *Bulletin of the American Academy of Psychiatry and Law* 5 (1984).

Brakel, S.J. "Legal Aid in Mental Hospitals." 1981 *American Bar Foundation Research Journal* 21.

Brooks, A.D. *Law, Psychiatry and the Mental Health System*. Boston: Little, Brown, 1974.

Burgdorf, R.L., Jr. *The Legal Rights of Handicapped Persons: Cases, Materials, and Texts*. Baltimore: Paul H. Brookes, 1980.

Burt, R.A., and N. Morris. "A Proposal for the Abolition of the Incompetency Plea." 40 *University of Chicago Law Review* 66 (1972).

Cohen, F. "The Function of the Attorney and the Commitment of the Mentally Ill," 44 *Texas Law Review* 424 (1966).

Deutsch, A. *The Mentally Ill in America: A History of Their Care and Treatment from Colonial Times*. 2d ed. New York: Columbia University Press, 1949.

"Duty to Warn," 2 *Behavioral Sciences and the Law* (No. 3, 1984).

Edwards, R.B. *Psychiatry and Ethics: Insanity, Rational Autonomy, and Mental Health Care*. Health Care and Medical Ethics Series. Buffalo, N.Y.: Prometheus Books, 1982

Effland, R.W. "Trusts and Estate Planning." In *Mentally Retarded Citizens and the Law*, edited by M. Kindred, J. Cohen, D. Penrod, and T. Schaeffer. New York: Free Press, 1976.

Eger, C.L. "Psychotherapists' Liability for Extrajudicial Breaches of Confidentiality." 18 *Arizona Law Review* 1061 (1976).

Ennis, B.J. *Prisoners of Psychiatry: Mental Patients, Psychiatrists, and the Law*. New York: Harcourt Brace Jovanovich, 1972.

Fingarette, H., and A.F. Hasse. Mental Disabilities and Criminal Responsibility. Berkeley: University of California Press, 1979.

Fleming, J.G., and B. Maximov. "The Patient or His Victim: The Therapist's Dilemma." 62 *California Law Review* 1025 (1974).

Freud, A., J. Goldstein, and A. Solnit. *Beyond the Best Interests of the Child*. New York: The Free Press, 1979.

Friedman, P.R., ed. *Legal Rights of Mentally Disabled Persons*. 3 vols. New York: Practising Law Institute, 1979.

__________. "The Mentally Handicapped Citizen and Institutional Labor," 87 *Harvard Law Review* 567 (1974).

Frolik, L.A. "Estate Planning for Parents of Mentally Disabled

Children." 40 *University of Pittsburgh Law Review* 305 (1979).

__________. "Plenary Guardianship: An Analysis, a Critique and a Proposal for Reform." 23 *Arizona Law Review* 599 (1981).

Goffman, E. *Asylums: Essays on the Social Situation of Mental Patients and Other Inmates.* Garden City, N.Y.: Doubleday, Anchor Books, 1961.

Goldman, H.H., N.H. Adams, and C.A. Taube. "Deinstitutionalization: The Data Demythologized." 34 *Hospital and Community Psychiatry* 129 (1983).

Group for the Advancement of Psychiatry. *Confidentiality and Privileged Communication in the Practice of Psychiatry.* Report No. 45, formulated by the Committee on Psychiatry and the Law. New York: Group for the Advancement of Psychiatry, 1960.

__________. *Misuse of Psychiatry in the Criminal Courts: Competency to Stand Trial.* Report No. 89. New York: Group for the Advancement of Psychiatry, 1974.

__________. *Psychiatry and Sex Psychopath Legislation: The 30s to the 80s.* Report No. 98. New York: Group for the Advancement of Psychiatry, 1977.

Gutheil, T.G., and P.S. Appelbaum. *Clinical Handbook of Psychiatry and the Law.* New York: McGraw-Hill, 1982.

Guttmacker, M.S. *The Role of Psychiatry in Law.* Springfield, Ill.: Charles C. Thomas, 1968.

__________, and H. Weihofen. *Psychiatry and the Law.* New York: W.W. Norton, 1952.

Herr, S.S. "The New Clients: Legal Services for Mentally Retarded Persons." 21 *Stanford Law Review* 553 (1979).

__________. *Rights and Advocacy for Retarded People.* Lexington, Mass.: D.C. Heath, Lexington Books, 1983.

Hoffling, C.K., ed. *Law and Ethics in the Practice of Psychiatry.* New York: Brunner-Mazel, 1981.

Holdsworth, W. *A History of English Law.* 7th ed. London: Methuen, 1956.

Humber, J.M., and R.F. Almeder. *Biomedical Ethics and the Law.* New York: Plenum Press, 1976.

Kaplan, H.I., A.M. Freedman, and B.J. Sadock, eds. *Comprehensive Textbook of Psychiatry.* 3d ed. Baltimore: Williams & Wilkins, 1980.

Kapp, M.B. "Residents of State Mental Institutions and Their Money (or the State Giveth and the State Taketh Away)." 6 *Journal of Psychiatry and Law* 287 (1978).

Kindred, M., J. Cohen, D. Penrod, and T. Schaeffer, eds. *The Mentally Retarded Citizen and the Law.* New York: Free Press, 1976.

Kittrie, N.N., H.L. Hirsch, and G. Wegner, eds. *Medicine, Law, and Public Policy.* New York: AMS Press, 1975.

Laing, R.D. *The Politics of Experience.* New York: Pantheon Books, 1967.

Legal Rights of Mentally Disabled Persons. Litigation and Administrative Practice Course Handbook Series. 3 vols. New York: Practising Law Institute, 1979.

Levine, M. *The History and Politics of Community Mental Health.* New York and Oxford: Oxford University Press, 1981.

Lidz, C.W., A. Meisel, E. Zeruvabel, M. Carter, R.M. Sestak, and L.H. Roth. *Informed Consent: A Study of Decision-making in Psychiatry.* Perspectives in Law and Behavior Series. New York: Guilford Press, 1984.

"Malpractice." 1 Behavioral Sciences and the Law (No. 1, 1983).

Mason, B.G., and F.J. Menolascino. "Mental Health: The Right to Treatment for Mentally Retarded Citizens: An Evolving Legal and Scientific Interface." 10 *Creighton Law Review* 124 (1976).

Matthews, A.R. *Mental Disability and the Criminal Law: A Field Study.* Chicago: American Bar Foundation, 1970.

McGarry, A.L. *Competency to Stand Trial and Mental Illness.* Crime and Delinquency Issues Series. Rockville, Md.: National Institute of Mental Health, 1973.

Menninger, K. *The Crime of Punishment.* New York: Viking Press, 1968.

"Mentally Retarded People and the Law: A Symposium." 31 *Stanford Law Review* 541 (1979).

Merton, V. "Confidentiality and the 'Dangerous' Patient: Implications of *Tarasoff* for Psychiatrists and Lawyers." 31 *Emory Law Journal* 263 (1982).

Mickenberg, I. "Competency to Stand Trial and the Mentally Retarded Defendant: The Need for a Multi-Disciplinary Solution to a Multi-Disciplinary Problem." 17 *California Western Law Review* 365 (1981).

__________. "The Silent Clients: Legal and Ethical Considerations in Representing Severely and Profoundly Retarded Individuals," 31 *Stanford Law Review* 625 (1979).

Miller, F.W., R.O. Dawson, G.E. Dix, and R.I. Parnas, eds. *The Mental Health Process.* Mineola, N.Y.: Foundation Press, 1976.

Monahan, J., and H.J. Steadman, eds. *Mentally Disordered Offenders: Perspectives from Law and Social Science.* Perspectives in Law and Psychology Series. New York: Plenum Press, 1983.

Morris, N. "Psychiatry and the Dangerous Criminal." 41 *Southern California Law Review* 514 (1968).

Packard, E.P.W. *Modern Persecution, or Insane Asylums Unveiled, as Demonstrated by the Report of the Investigating Committee of the Legislature of Illinois.* Mental Illness and Social Policy: The American Experience, series edited by G.N. Grob. Reprint ed. 1973 in one vol. of 1875 ed. 2 vols.

Pasewark, R.A. "Insanity Plea: A Review of the Research Literature." 9 *Journal of Psychiatry and Law* 357 (1981).

Perlin, M.L. "The Right to Voluntary, Compensated, Therapeutic Work as Part of the Right to Treatment: A New Theory in the Aftermath of *Souder*." 7 *Seton Hall Law Review* 298 (1976).

Pollock, F., and F.W. Maitland. *The History of English Law.* Vol. 2. 2d ed. London: Cambridge University Press, 1911.

President's Commission on Mental Health. *Task Panel Reports Submitted to the President's Commission on Mental Health.* Vol. 4. Appendix. Washington, D.C.: U.S. Government Printing Office, 1978.

Ray, I. *A Treatise on the Medical Jurisprudence of Insanity.* Reprint. New York: DaCapo Press, 1983. (original ed. Boston: C.C. Little & J. Brown, 1838).

Rhoden, N.K. "The Right to Refuse Psychotropic Drugs," 15 *Harvard Civil Rights–Civil Liberties Law Review* 363 (1980).

Robitscher, J. *The Powers of Psychiatry.* Boston: Houghton Mifflin, 1980.

Rock, R.S., with M.A. Jacobson, and R.M. Janopaul. *Hospitalization and Discharge of the Mentally Ill.* Chicago: University of Chicago Press, 1968.

Roesch, R., and S.L. Golding. *Competency to Stand Trial.* Urbana: University of Illinois Press, 1980.

Rogers, R., O.E. Wasyliw, and J.L. Cavanaugh, Jr. "Evaluating Insanity: A Study of Construct Validity." 8 *Law and Human Behavior* 293 (1984).

Rosoff, A.J. *Informed Consent: A Guide for Health Care Providers.* Rockville, Md.: Aspen Systems Corporation, 1981.

Sales, B.D., D.M. Powell, R. Van Duizend, and Associates. *Disabled Persons and the Law.* New York: Plenum Press, 1982.

Saltzburg, S.A. "Privileges and Professionals: Lawyers and Psychitrists." 66 *Virginia Law Review* 597 (1980).

Schoenfeld, B.N. "A Survey of Constitutional Rights of the Mentally Retarded." 32 *Southwestern Law Journal* 605 (1978).

Segal, S.P., and U. Aviram. *The Mentally Ill in Community-Based Sheltered Care: A Study of Community Care and Social Inte-*

gration. New York: John Wiley & Sons, 1978.

Sharfstein, S., S. Muszynski, and E. Myers. *Health Insurance and Psychiatric Care: Update and Appraisal.* Washington, D.C.: American Psychiatric Press, 1984.

Sherman, R.B. "Guardianship: Time for a Reassessment." 49 *Fordham Law Review* 350 (1980).

Shuman, D.W., and M.F. Weiner. "The Privilege Study: An Empirical Examination of the Psychotherapist-Patient Privilege." 60 *North Carolina Law Review* 893 (1982).

Slawson, P.F. "The Clinical Dimension of Psychiatric Malpractice." 14 *Psychiatric Annals* 358 (1984).

Slovenko, R. *Psychiatry and Law.* Boston: Little, Brown, 1973.

__________, and G.L. Usdin. *Psychotherapy, Confidentiality and Privileged Communication.* Springfield, Ill.: C.C. Thomas, 1966.

Spicker, S.F., H.T. Engelhardt, Jr., and J.M. Healey, Jr., eds. *The Law-Medicine Relation: A Philosophical Exploration.* Boston: D. Reidel, 1981.

Spitzer, R.L., and D.F. Klein. *Critical Issues in Psychiatric Diagnosis.* New York: Raven Press, 1978.

Steadman, H.J., and J.J. Cocozza. *Careers of the Criminally Insane: Excessive Social Control of Deviance.* Lexington, Mass.: D.C. Heath, Lexington Books, 1974.

Stone, A.A. *Mental Health and Law: A System in Transition.* Crime and Delinquency Series. Rockville, MD: National Institute of Mental Health, 1975.

Stromberg, C.D., and A.A. Stone. "A Model State Law on Civil Commitment of the Mentally Ill." 20 *Harvard Journal on Legislation* 275 (1983).

Symonds, E. "Mental Patients' Rights to Refuse Drugs: Involuntary Medication as Cruel and Unusual Punishment," 7 *Hastings Constitutional Law Quarterly* 701 (1980).

"A Symposium: The Right to Treatment." 57 *Georgetown Law Journal* 673 (1969).

Szasz, T. *Ideology and Insanity: Essays on the Psychiatric Dehumanization of Man.* Garden City, N.Y.: Doubleday, Anchor Books, 1970.

__________. *Law, Liberty, and Psychiatry: An Inquiry into the Social Uses of Mental Health Practices.* New York: Macmillan, 1963.

__________. *The Manufacture of Madness: A Comparative Study of the Inquisition and the Mental Health Movement.* New York: Harper & Row, 1970.

__________. *The Myth of Mental Illness: Foundations of a Theory of Personal Conduct.* Rev. ed. New York: Harper & Row, 1974.

Thornberry, T.P., and J.E. Jacoby. *The Criminally Insane: A Community Follow-up of Mentally Ill Offenders.* Chicago: University of Chicago Press, 1979.

Valenstein, E. *The Psychosurgery Debate.* San Francisco: W.H. Freeman, 1980.

Warren, C.A.B. *The Court of Last Resort: Mental Illness and the Law.* Chicago: University of Chicago Press, 1982.

Wexler, D.B. *Mental Health Law: Major Issues.* Perspectives in Law and Psychology Series. New York: Plenum Press, 1981.

Winick, B.J. "Psychotropic Medication and Competence to Stand Trial." 1977 *American Bar Foundation Research Journal* 769.

Wolfensberger, W., B. Nirje, S. Olshansky, R. Perske, and P. Roos. *The Principle of Normalization in Human Services.* Toronto: National Institute of Mental Retardation, 1972.

Wooton, B. *Crime and the Criminal Law.* London: Stevens & Sons, 1963.

Ziskin, J. *Coping with Psychiatric and Psychological Testimony.* 3d ed. Venice, Cal.: Law and Psychology Press, 1981.

Index

Page numbers in italics indicate tables. Authors and references cited in the footnotes are not included in this index. Only landmark cases in mental disability law and cases critical to the most recent interpretation of statutes or changes in the law are covered in this index. Readers may consult the Table of Cases for a complete listing.

WIDENER UNIVERSITY
WOLFGRAM
LIBRARY
CHESTER, PA.
DISCARD